D0206230

The Amartya Sen and Jean Drèze Omnibus

∞

comprising
Poverty and Famines
Hunger and Public Action
India: Economic Development and Social
Opportunity

OXFORD
UNIVERSITY PRESS

OXFORD

UNIVERSITY PRESS

YMCA Library Building, Jai Singh Road, New Delhi 110001

Oxford University Press is a department of the University of Oxford. It furthers the University's objective of excellence in research, scholarship, and education by publishing worldwide in

Oxford New York

Auckland Cape Town Dar es Salaam Hong Kong Karachi
Kuala Lumpur Madrid Melbourne Mexico City Nairobi
New Delhi Shanghai Taipei Toronto

With offices in

Argentina Austria Brazil Chile Czech Republic France Greece
Guatemala Hungary Italy Japan Poland Portugal Singapore
South Korea Switzerland Thailand Turkey Ukraine Vietnam

Published in India
by Oxford University Press, New Delhi

First published in India 1999
Eleventh impression 2008

ISBN-13: 978-0-19-564831-7
ISBN-10: 0-19-5644831-5

Printed at Rashtriya Printers, New Delhi 110 032
Published by Oxford University Press
YMCA Library Building, Jai Singh Road, New Delhi 110 001

PREFACE TO THE OMNIBUS EDITION

The individual prefaces of the three monographs in this collection are reproduced further on. Since both of us stand by what we wrote at that time, there is little to add here, except perhaps a few words about the relation between the three studies.

The first monograph, *Poverty and Famines,* was written by my esteemed colleague Amartya Sen. The main concern of this study was to present a broad framework for the analysis of poverty and famines, building in particular on the 'entitlement approach'. This approach focuses on the ability of a person to acquire food and other commodities within the prevailing economic, social and legal arrangements. It contrasts with various other lines of analysis, focusing for instance on aggregate food availability or individual 'purchasing power'.

Following on this approach, one particular point made in *Poverty and Famines* is that famines can occur even in the absence of any decline in aggregate food availability. This specific point has attracted considerable attention, and some of the case studies used to illustrate it even triggered minor controversies. It is important to note, however, that the scope of this study goes much beyond this specific point. This observation that famines can happen without food availability decline (which had already been made earlier, notably in the Famine Commission Reports of 19th century India) is only one useful corollary of the entitlement approach. The main interest of the first monograph is the exploration of that general approach, and of its implications in different contexts.

The second monograph in this collection, *Hunger and Public Action,* was written jointly by the two of us. Here the focus shifts from the *causation* of hunger and famines to their *prevention.* The central theme of this monograph is that public action has a crucial role to play in eradicating famines as well as endemic hunger. The term 'public action' refers both to the initiatives of the state as well as to the activities of the public at large—whether of a collaborative or adversarial type The central importance of public action in the modern world, and also in the specific context of eliminating hunger and famines, should be obvious to the candid observer. Yet it is often overlooked in the prevailing climate of faith in the market mechanism and suspicion of state intervention. To illustrate, it is easy to forget that in the 'market economies' of western Europe, public expenditure standardly accounts for 40 to 50 per cent of GNP, with about two-thirds of these public resources being spent on education, health and social security. These patterns are rarely mentioned when developing countries are urged to emulate the 'market economies'. Against this background, the central role of public action in many recent experiences of famine prevention and rapid elimination of undernutrition was perhaps worth documenting.

Since both of us have a long-standing interest in India's development, it was natural to extend this programme of research with a more in-depth study of the causes and prevention of endemic deprivation in that country. This is the object of the third monograph, *India: Economic Development and Social Opportunity*. To some extent, this study may be seen as a further exploration of the main themes of *Hunger and Public Action*, with a more detailed treatment of specific issues, such as the role of basic education in development. In addition, this third monograph highlights the *complementarities* between public action and the market mechanism. These have been seriously neglected in the ongoing debate on 'liberalization', which tends to be framed in terms of the pros and cons of the market mechanism *as opposed* to state intervention, overlooking the possibility of making a skilful use of both.

If we were to start all over again, would we write in the same way? By and large, the answer is yes, though both of us would want to catch up with one significant lacuna in the whole project. This concerns the link between hunger and famines on the one hand, and war and militarism on the other. Though this issue is occasionally discussed in this collection, it deserves deeper treatment than we have given it so far. Indeed, the recent history of famines is full of painful reminders of the link between armed conflict and starvation (Sudan and Iraq are the most recent examples). The elimination of endemic hunger, too, has been drastically slowed down by the disruptions of war and the large-scale diversion of scarce resources for military purposes. India itself has not escaped this pattern. In short, each of the three monographs that follow is a little short on the question of war and militarism. We hope to have a chance to make up for this at some stage.

Jean Drèze
Delhi, 4 December 1998

Poverty and Famines

&

An Essay on Entitlement and Deprivation

Preface

Much about poverty is obvious enough. One does not need elaborate criteria, cunning measurement, or probing analysis, to recognize raw poverty and to understand its antecedents. It would be natural to be impatient with long-winded academic studies on 'poor naked wretches' with 'houseless heads and unfed sides' and 'loop'd and windowed raggedness', to use King Lear's graphic description. And furthermore it may also be the case, as Lear told the blind Gloucester, that 'a man may see how this world goes with no eyes'. There is indeed much that is transparent about poverty and misery.

But not everything about poverty is quite so simple. Even the identification of the poor and the diagnosis of poverty may be far from obvious when we move away from extreme and raw poverty. Different approaches can be used (e.g. biological inadequacy, relative deprivation), and there are technical issues to be resolved within each approach. Furthermore, to construct an overall picture of poverty, it is necessary to go well beyond identifying the poor. To provide an aggregate profile based on the characteristics of those who are identified as poor, problems of aggregation have to be squarely faced. Finally—and most importantly—the *causation* of poverty raises questions that are not easily answered. While the 'immediate' antecedents of poverty may be too obvious to need much analysis, and the 'ultimate' causation too vague and open-ended a question to be settled fully, there are various intermediate levels of useful answers that are worth exploring. The problem is of particular relevance in the context of recent discussions on the causation of hunger and starvation.

This monograph is concerned with these questions. The main focus of this work is on the causation of starvation in general and of famines in particular. The basic approach, which involves analysing 'entitlement systems', is introduced in general terms in Chapter 1. This is done even before the concepts of poverty are examined in any detail, because that is where the thrust of this monograph lies. In Chapters 2 and 3 problems of conceptualization and measurement of poverty are examined. The specific problem of starvation is taken up in very general terms in Chapter 4, and the 'entitlement approach' is analysed in Chapter 5. This is followed by case studies of famines from different parts of the world: the Great Bengal Famine of 1943 (Chapter 6), the Ethiopian famines of 1973–75 (Chapter 7), famines in the Sahel region of Africa during the early 1970s (Chapter 8), and the Bangladesh famine of 1974 (Chapter 9). In Chapter 10 the entitlement approach is consolidated, taking up general issues of deprivation related to entitlement systems.

There are four technical appendices. Appendix A presents a formal analysis of the notion of exchange entitlement—an important aspect of entitlement systems. The relevance of failures of exchange entitlement for the development of famine situations is brought out in Appendix B in terms of some illustrative models. Appendix C provides an examination of the problem of poverty measurement, including a scrutiny of various measures that have been used or proposed. Finally, the pattern of famine mortality is discussed in Appendix D based on a case study of the Bengal famine of 1943.

This work has been prepared for the World Employment Programme of ILO. I am grateful for, among other things, their extraordinary patience; the work took a good deal longer than they—and for that matter I—imagined it would. I am also most grateful for helpful discussions with Felix Paukert and others involved in the Income Distribution and Employment Programme. I have also benefited greatly from detailed comments of Judith Heyer and Jocelyn Kynch on an earlier draft of this manuscript. For useful suggestions and advice, I am also grateful to Mohiuddin Alamgir, Sudhir Anand, Asit Bhattacharya, Robert Cassen, Dipankar Chatterjee, Pramit Chaudhuri, Amiya Dasgupta, Meghnad Desai, John Flemming, Madangopal Ghosh, David Glass, Ruth Glass, Terence Gorman, Keith Griffin, Carl Hamilton, Roger Hay, Julius Holt, Leif Johansen, J. Krishnamurti, Mukul Majumdar, Ashok Mitra, John Muellbauer, Suzy Paine, Debidas Ray, Debraj Ray, Samir Ray, Tapan Raychaudhuri, Carl Riskin, Joan Robinson, Suman Sarkar, John Seaman, Rehman Sobhan, K. Sundaram, Jaroslav Vanek and Henry Wan, among others.

I have drawn on my earlier writings, including articles

published in *Economic and Political Weekly* (1973, 1976), *Econometrica* (1976, 1977), *Review of Economic Studies* (1976), *Cambridge Journal of Economics* (1977), *Scandinavian Journal of Economics* (1979), *Journal of Economic Literature* (1979), *World Development* (1980), and *Quarterly Journal of Economics* (1981).

Finally, a remark on presentation. While some mathematical concepts and notation have been used in Appendices A–C, the text of the monograph is almost entirely informal. Someone concerned with the detailed structures would have to consult the Appendices, but there should be no difficulty in following the main lines of the argument (including the case studies) without reference to them. I have tried to make the book accessible to as wide an audience as possible, since the subject matter of this work is important. I am also immodest enough to believe that the analysis presented in this monograph has a certain amount of relevance to matters of practical concern.

A. K. S.

Contents

Chapter 1

Poverty and Entitlements

1.1 ENTITLEMENTS AND OWNERSHIP

Starvation is the characteristic of some people not *having* enough food to eat. It is not the characteristic of there *being* not enough food to eat. While the latter can be a cause of the former, it is but one of many *possible* causes. Whether and how starvation relates to food supply is a matter for factual investigation.

Food supply statements say things about a commodity (or a group of commodities) considered on its own. Starvation statements are about the *relationship* of persons to the commodity (or that commodity group).[1] Leaving out cases in which a person may deliberately starve, starvation statements translate readily into statements of ownership of food by persons. In order to understand starvation, it is, therefore, necessary to go into the structure of ownership.

Ownership relations are one kind of *entitlement* relations. It is necessary to understand the entitlement systems within which the problem of starvation is to be analysed.[2] This applies *more generally* to poverty as such, and *more specifically* to famines as well.

An entitlement relation applied to ownership connects one set of ownerships to another through certain rules of legitimacy. It is a recursive relation and the process of connecting can be repeated. Consider a private ownership market economy. I own this loaf of bread. Why is this ownership accepted? Because I got it by exchange through paying some money I owned. Why is my ownership of that money accepted? Because I got it by selling a bamboo umbrella owned by me. Why is my ownership of the bamboo umbrella accepted? Because I made it with my own

---

[1] The contrast between commodities on the one hand and the relationship of commodities to persons on the other is central also to many other economic exercises. The evaluation of real national income is an important example, and for a departure from the traditional approaches to national income to a relationship-based evaluation in the light of this distinction, see Sen (1976b, 1979a).

[2] The 'entitlement approach' to starvation analysis was presented in Sen (1976c, 1977b), and is developed and extended in Chapter 5 and Appendix A, and applied to case studies in Chapters 6–9 below.

labour using some bamboo from my land. Why is my ownership of the land accepted? Because I inherited it from my father. Why is his ownership of that land accepted? And so on. Each link in this chain of entitlement relations 'legitimizes' one set of ownership by reference to another, or to some basic entitlement in the form of enjoying the fruits of one's own labour.[3]

Entitlement relations accepted in a private ownership market economy typically include the following, among others:

(1) *trade-based entitlement*: one is entitled to own what one obtains by trading something one owns with a willing party (or, multilaterally, with a willing set of parties);

(2) *production-based entitlement*: one is entitled to own what one gets by arranging production using one's owned resources, or resources hired from willing parties meeting the agreed conditions of trade;

(3) *own-labour entitlement*: one is entitled to one's own labour power, and thus to the trade-based and production-based entitlements related to one's labour power;

(4) *inheritance and transfer entitlement*: one is entitled to own what is willingly given to one by another who legitimately owns it, possibly to take affect after the latter's death (if so specified by him).

These are some entitlement relations of more or less straightforward kind, but there are others, frequently a good deal more complex. For example, one may be entitled to enjoy the fruits of some property without being able to trade it for anything else. Or one may be able to inherit the property of a deceased relation who did not bequeath it to anyone, through some rule of kinship-based inheritance accepted in the country in question. Or one may have some entitlements related to unclaimed objects on the basis of discovery. Market entitlements may even be supplemented by rationing or coupon systems, even in private ownership market economies, such as in Britain during the last war.[4]

---

[3] The interpretation of entitlement relations here is descriptive rather than prescriptive. In contrast, Robert Nozick's (1974) well-known exploration of 'the entitlement theory' of justice is prescriptive, discussing private property rights and other rights in normative terms. The two exercises are thus differently motivated, and must not be confused with each other.

[4] This may or may not be combined with price 'control', and that in its turn may or may not be combined with a flourishing 'black market'; see Dasgupta (1950) for an illuminating analysis of black market prices.

The scope of ownership relations can vary greatly with economic systems. A socialist economy may not permit private ownership of 'means of production', thereby rendering 'production-based entitlements' inoperative except when it involves just one's own labour and some elementary tools and raw materials. A capitalist economy will not only *permit* the private ownership of means of production; that is indeed one of its main *foundations*. On the other hand, a capitalist economy—like a socialist one—will not permit ownership of one human being by another, as a slave economy will. A socialist economy may restrict the employment of one person by another for production purposes, i.e. constrain the possibility of private trading of labour power for productive use. A capitalist economy will not, of course, do this, but may impose restrictions on binding contracts involving labour-power obligations over long periods of time. This, however, is the standard system under some feudal practices involving bonded labour, and also in some cases of colonial plantations.

1.2 EXCHANGE ENTITLEMENT

In a market economy, a person can exchange what he owns for another collection of commodities. He can do this exchange either through trading, or through production, or through a combination of the two. The set of all the alternative bundles of commodities that he can acquire in exchange for what he owns may be called the 'exchange entitlement' of what he owns.

The 'exchange entitlement mapping' is the relation that specifies the set of exchange entitlements for each ownership bundle. This relation—E-mapping for brevity—defines the possibilities that would be open to him corresponding to each ownership situation. A person will be exposed to starvation if, for the ownership that he actually has, the exchange entitlement set does not contain any feasible bundle including enough food. Given the E-mapping, it is in this way possible to identify those ownership bundles—call them collectively the starvation set—that must, thus, lead to starvation in the absence of non-entitlement transfers (e.g. charity). E-mappings, starvation sets, and related concepts are discussed in Chapter 5 and are formally analysed in Appendix A, and here we are concerned only with the underlying ideas.

Among the influences that determine a person's exchange

entitlement, given his ownership bundle (including labour power), are the following:
(1) whether he can find an employment, and if so for how long and at what wage rate;
(2) what he can earn by selling his non-labour assets, and how much it costs him to buy whatever he may wish to buy;
(3) what he can produce with his own labour power and resources (or resource services) he can buy and manage;
(4) the cost of purchasing resources (or resource services) and the value of the products he can sell;
(5) the social security benefits he is entitled to and the taxes, etc., he must pay.

A person's ability to avoid starvation will depend both on his ownership and on the exchange entitlement mapping that he faces. A general decline in food supply may indeed cause him to be exposed to hunger through a rise in food prices with an unfavourable impact on his exchange entitlement. Even when his starvation is *caused* by food shortage in this way, his immediate reason for starvation will be the decline in his exchange entitlement.

More importantly, his exchange entitlement may worsen for reasons other than a general decline of food supply. For example, given the same total food supply, other groups' becoming richer and buying more food can lead to a rise in food prices, causing a worsening of exchange entitlement. Or some economic change may affect his employment possibilities, leading also to worse exchange entitlement. Similarly, his wages can fall behind prices. Or the price of necessary resources for the production he engages in can go up relatively. These diverse influences on exchange entitlements are as relevant as the overall volume of food supply *vis-à-vis* population.

1.3 MODES OF PRODUCTION

The exchange entitlements faced by a person depend, naturally, on his position in the economic class structure as well as the modes of production in the economy. What he owns will vary with his class, and even if exactly the same E-mapping were to hold for all, the actual exchange entitlements would differ with his ownership position.

But even with the same ownership position, the exchange

entitlements will be different depending on what economic prospects are open to him, and that will depend on the modes of production and his position in terms of production relations.[5] For example, while a peasant differs from a landless labourer in terms of ownership (since he owns land, which the labourer does not), the landless share-cropper differs from the landless labourer not in their respective ownerships, but in the way they can use the only resource they own, viz. labour power. The landless labourer will be employed in exchange for a wage, while the share-cropper will do the cultivation and own a part of the *product.*

This difference can lead not merely to contrasts of the levels of typical remuneration of the two, which may or may not be very divergent, but also to sharp differences in exchange entitlements in distress situations. For example, a cyclone reducing the labour requirement for cultivation by destroying a part of the crop in each farm may cause some casual agricultural labourers to be simply fired, leading to a collapse of their exchange entitlements, while others are retained. In contrast, in this case the share-croppers may all operate with a lower labour input and lower entitlement, but no one may become fully jobless and thus incomeless.

Similarly, if the output is food, e.g. rice or wheat, the share-cropper gets his return in a form such that he can directly eat it without going through the vagaries of the market. In contrast, the agricultural labourer paid in money terms will have to depend on the exchange entitlement of his money wage. When famines are accompanied by sharp changes in relative prices— and in particular a sharp rise in food prices—there is much comparative merit in being a share-cropper rather than an agricultural labourer, especially when the capital market is highly imperfect. The greater production risk of the share-cropper compared with the security of a fixed wage on the part of the agricultural labourer has been well analysed (see, for example, Stiglitz, 1974); but a fixed money wage may offer no security at all in a situation of sharply varying food prices (even when employment is guaranteed). In contrast, a share of the food output does have some security advantage in terms of exchange entitlement.

<hr/>

[5] See Marx (1857–8, 1867) for the classic treatment of modes of production and their relevance to production and distribution.

Similarly, those who sell services (e.g. barbers or rickshaw-pullers) or handicraft products (e.g. weavers or shoemakers) are—like wage labourers—more exposed, in this respect, to famines involving unexpected rises of food prices than are peasants or share-croppers producing food crops. This is the case even when the *typical* standard of living of the latter is no higher than that of the former.

In understanding general poverty, or regular starvation, or outbursts of famines, it is necessary to look at both ownership patterns and exchange entitlements, and at the forces that lie behind them. This requires careful consideration of the nature of modes of production and the structure of economic classes as well as their interrelations. Later in the monograph, when actual famines are analysed, these issues will emerge more concretely.

1.4 SOCIAL SECURITY AND EMPLOYMENT ENTITLEMENTS

The exchange entitlements depend not merely on market exchanges but also on those exchanges, if any, that the state provides as a part of its social security programme. Given a social security system, an unemployed person may get 'relief', an old person a pension, and the poor some specified 'benefits'. These affect the commodity bundles over which a person can have command. They are parts of a person's exchange entitlements, and are conditional on the absence of other exchanges that a person might undertake. For example, a person is not entitled to unemployment benefit if he exchanges his labour power for a wage, i.e. becomes employed. Similarly, exchanges that make a person go above the specified poverty norm will make him ineligible for receiving the appropriate relief. These social security provisions are essentially supplementations of the processes of market exchange and production, and the two types of opportunities together determine a person's exchange entitlements in a private ownership market economy with social security provisions.

The social security arrangements are particularly important in the context of starvation. The reason why there are no famines in the rich developed countries is not because people are generally rich on the average. Rich they certainly are when they have jobs and earn a proper wage; but for large numbers of people this condition fails to hold for long periods of time, and the exchange entitlements of their endowments in the absence of social security arrangements could provide very meagre commodity bundles indeed. With the proportion of unemployment as high as it is, say, in Britain or America today, but for the social security arrangements there would be widespread starvation and possibly a famine. What prevents that is not the high average income or wealth of the British or the general opulence of the Americans, but the guaranteed minimum values of exchange entitlements owing to the social security system.

Similarly, the elimination of starvation in socialist economies —for example in China—seems to have taken place even without a dramatic rise in food availability per head, and indeed, typically the former has *preceded* the latter. The end of starvation reflects a shift in the entitlement system, both in the form of social security and—more importantly—through systems of guaranteed employment at wages that provide exchange entitlement adequate to avoid starvation.

1.5 FOOD SUPPLY AND STARVATION

There has been a good deal of discussion recently about the prospect of food supply falling significantly behind the world population. There is, however, little empirical support for such a diagnosis of recent trends. Indeed, for most areas in the world—with the exception of parts of Africa—the increase in food supply has been comparable to, or faster than, the expansion of population.[6] But this does not indicate that starvation is being systematically eliminated, since starvation—as discussed—is a function of entitlements and not of food availability as such. Indeed, some of the worst famines have taken place with no significant decline in food availability per head (see Chapters 6, 7, and 9).

To say that starvation depends 'not merely' on food supply but also on its 'distribution' would be correct enough, though not remarkably helpful. The important question then would be: what determines distribution of food between different sections of the community? The entitlement approach directs one to questions dealing with ownership patterns and—less obviously

[6] See Aziz (1975), Sinha (1976a, 1976b, 1977), Sinha and Gordon Drabek (1978), Interfutures (1979), and also the FAO *Production Yearbooks* and FAO *Monthly Bulletins* (e.g., vol. 3, No. 4, 1980, pp. 15–16). See also chapters 5 and 10 below.

but no less importantly—to the various influences that affect exchange entitlement mappings (see Appendices A and B, and Chapters 5–10). In so far as food supply itself has any influence on the prevalence of starvation, that influence is seen as working *through* the entitlement relations. If one person in eight starves regularly in the world,[7] this is seen as the result of his inability to establish entitlement to enough food; the question of the physical availability of the food is not directly involved.

The approach of entitlements used in this work is very general and—I would argue—quite inescapable in analysing starvation and poverty. If, nevertheless, it appears odd and unusual, this can be because of the hold of the tradition of thinking in terms of what *exists* rather than in terms of who can *command* what. The mesmerizing simplicity of focusing on the ratio of food to population has persistently played an obscuring role over centuries, and continues to plague policy discussions today much as it has deranged anti-famine policies in the past.[8]

---

[7] See Aziz (1975), pp. 108 and 123.
[8] See Chapters 6, 7, 9 and 10.

Chapter 2

Concepts of Poverty

2.1 REQUIREMENTS OF A CONCEPT OF POVERTY

On his deathbed in Calcutta, J. B. S. Haldane wrote a poem called 'Cancer's a funny thing'.[1] Poverty is no less funny. Consider the following view of poverty:

> People must not be allowed to become so poor that they offend or are hurtful to society. It is not so much the misery and plight of the poor but the discomfort and cost to the community which is crucial to this view of poverty. We have a problem of poverty to the extent that low income creates problems for those who are not poor.[2]

To live in poverty may be sad, but to 'offend or [be] hurtful to society', creating 'problems for those who are not poor' is, it would appear, the real tragedy. It isn't easy to push much further the reduction of human beings into 'means'.

The first requirement of the concept of poverty is of a criterion as to *who* should be the focus of our concern. The specification of certain 'consumption norms', or of a 'poverty line', may do part of the job: 'the poor' are those people whose consumption standards fall short of the norms, or whose incomes lie below that line. But this leads to a further question: is the concept of poverty to be related to the interests of: (1) only the poor, (2) only the non-poor, or (3) both the poor and the non-poor?

It seems a bit grotesque to hold that the concept of poverty should be concerned only with the non-poor, and I take the liberty of dropping (2)—and the 'view' quoted in the first paragraph—without further ado. Alternative (3) might, however, appear to be appealing, since it is broad-based and unrestrictive. There is little doubt that the penury of the poor does, in fact, affect the well-being of the rich. The real question is whether such effects should enter into the concept of poverty as

---

[1] *Oxford Book of 20th Century English Verse*, ed. P. Larkin, Oxford, 1973, p. 271.

[2] Rein (1971), p. 46. I hasten to add that here Professor Rein is describing one of the *three* 'broad concepts' of poverty, viz. (1) 'subsistence', (2) 'inequality', and (3) 'externality'; the view quoted corresponds to 'externality'.

such, or whether they should figure under the possible *effects* of poverty. I believe a good case can be made for choosing the latter alternative, since in an obvious sense poverty must be a characteristic of the poor rather than of the non-poor. One can, for instance, argue that, if one considers a case of reduction of real income and increase in the suffering of all the poor, it *must* be described as an increase of poverty, no matter whether this change is accompanied by a reduction in the adverse effects on the rich (e.g. whether the rich are less 'offended' by the sight of penury).

This conception of poverty based on (1) does not, of course, imply any denial of the fact that the suffering of the poor themselves may depend on the condition of the non-poor. It merely asserts that the focus of the concept of poverty has to be on the well-being of the poor as such, no matter what influences affect their well-being. *Causation* of poverty and *effects* of poverty will be important issues to study in their own rights, and the conceptualization of poverty in terms of the conditions only of the poor does not affect the worthwhileness of studying these questions. Indeed, there will be much to say on these questions later on in the book.

It is perhaps worth mentioning in this context that in some discussions one is concerned not with the prevalence of poverty in a country in the form of the suffering of the *poor*, but with the relative opulence of the nation *as a whole*.[3] In those discussions it will, of course, be entirely legitimate to be concerned with the well-being of all the people in the nation, and the description of a nation as 'poor' must obviously relate to such a broader concept. These are *different* exercises, and so long as this fact is clearly recognized there need not be any confusion.

Even after we have identified the poor and specified that the concept of poverty is concerned with the conditions of the poor, much remains to be done. There is the problem of aggregation— often important—over the group of the poor, and this involves moving from the description of the poor to some over-all measure of 'poverty' as such. In some traditions, this is done very simply by just counting the number of the poor, and then expressing poverty as the ratio of the number of the poor to the total number of people in the community in question.

[3] See, for example, Paul Streeten, 'How Poor Are the Poor Countries and Why?' in Streeten (1972).

This 'head-count measure'—*H* for short—has at least two serious drawbacks. First, *H* takes no account of the *extent* of the short-fall of incomes of the poor from the 'poverty line': a reduction in the incomes of all the poor without affecting the incomes of the rich will leave this head count measure completely unchanged. Second, it is insensitive to the distribution of income among the poor; in particular, no transfer of income from a poor person to one who is richer can increase this head count measure. Both these defects make the measure *H*, which is by far the most widely used measure, quite unacceptable as an indicator of poverty, and the conception of poverty that lies implicit in it seems eminently questionable.

In this chapter I am not concerned with problems of measurement as such, which will be taken up in the next two chapters and in Appendix C. But behind each measure lies an analytical concept, and here I am concerned with the general ideas on the conception of poverty. If the preceding argument is right, then the requirements of a concept of poverty must include two distinct—but not unrelated—exercises, namely (1) a method of identifying a group of people as poor ('identification'); and (2) a method of aggregating the characteristics of the set of poor people into an over-all image of poverty ('aggregation'). Both these exercises will be performed in the next two chapters, but before that we need to study the kinds of considerations that may be used in choosing the operations (both identification and aggregation). The rest of the chapter will be concerned with these issues.

The underlying considerations come out most sharply in the alternative approaches to the concept of poverty that one can find in the literature. Some of these approaches have been subjected to severe attacks recently, while others have not been examined sufficiently critically. In attempting an evaluation of these approaches in the following sections, I shall try to assess the approaches as well as their respective critiques.

2.2 THE BIOLOGICAL APPROACH

In his famous study of poverty in York, Seebohm Rowntree (1901) defined families as being in 'primary poverty' if their 'total earnings are insufficient to obtain the minimum necessities for the maintenance of merely physical efficiency'. It is not surprising that biological considerations related to the requirements of survival or work efficiency have been often used in defining the poverty line. Starvation, clearly, is the most telling aspect of poverty.

The biological approach has come under rather intense fire recently.[4] There are indeed several problems with its use. First, there are significant variations related to physical features, climatic conditions and work habits.[5] In fact, even for a specific group in a specific region, nutritional requirements are difficult to define precisely. People have been known to survive with incredibly little nutrition, and there seems to be a cumulative improvement of life expectation as the dietary limits are raised. In fact, physical opulence seems to go on increasing with nutrition over a very wide range; Americans, Europeans and Japanese have been growing measurably in stature as their diets have continued to improve. There is difficulty in drawing a line somewhere, and the so-called 'minimum nutritional requirements' have an inherent arbitrariness that goes well beyond variations between groups and regions.

Second, the translation of minimum *nutritional* requirements into minimum *food* requirements depends on the choice of commodities. While it may be easy to solve the programming exercise of a 'diet problem', choosing a minimum cost diet for meeting specified nutritional requirements from food items sold at specified costs, the relevance of such a minimum cost diet is not clear. Typically, it turns out to be very low-cost indeed,[6] but monumentally boring, and people's food habits are not, in fact, determined by such a cost minimization exercise. The actual incomes at which specified nutritional requirements are met will depend greatly on the consumption habits of the people in question.

Third, for non-food items such minimum requirements are not easy to specify, and the problem is usually solved by assuming that a specified proportion of total income will be spent on food. With this assumption, the minimum food costs can be used to derive minimum income requirements. But the proportion spent on food varies not merely with habits and culture, but also with relative prices and availability of goods and services. It is not

---

[4] See, for example, Townsend (1971, 1974) and Rein (1971).

[5] See Rein (1971), Townsend (1974), Sukhatme (1977, 1978), and Srinivasan (1977a, 1979).

[6] See, for example, Stigler's (1945) astonishing estimates of 'the cost of subsistence'. See also Rajaraman (1974).

surprising that the assumptions made often turn out to be contradicted by actual experience; for example, Lord Beveridge's estimate of subsistence requirements of income during the Second World War proved to be far from correct, since the British were spending a much lower proportion of their income on food than was assumed (see Townsend, 1974, p. 17).

In view of these problems, one may well agree with Martin Rein's (1971) assertion that 'almost every procedure in the subsistence-level definition of poverty can be reasonably challenged' (p. 61). But the question that does remain is this: after we have challenged every one of the procedures used under the biological approach, what do we do *then*? Do we simply ignore that approach,[7] or do we examine whether something remains in it to be salvaged? I would argue that there does remain something.

First, while the concept of nutritional requirements is a rather loose one, there is no particular reason to suppose that the concept of poverty must itself be clear-cut and sharp. In fact, a certain amount of vagueness is implicit in both the concepts, and the really interesting question is the extent to which the areas of vagueness of the two notions, as commonly interpreted, tend to coincide. The issue, thus, is not whether nutritional standards are vague, but whether the vagueness is of the required kind.

Second, to check whether someone is getting a specified bundle of nutrition, one need not necessarily go through the procedure of examining whether that person has the income level that would generate that bundle. One can simply examine whether the person is, in fact, meeting that nutritional requirement or not. Even in poor countries, direct nutritional information of this type can be collected through sample surveys of consumption bundles and can be extensively analysed (see, for example, Srinivasan and Bardhan, 1974, especially the paper by Chatterjee, Sarkar and Paul, and Panikar *et al.*, 1975); and the 'identification' exercise under the nutritional approach need not go through the intermediary of income at all.

---

[7] Much depends on what the alternatives are. Rein (1971) himself recommends that 'other' conceptions 'deserve more attention and developments' (p. 62). Since 'subsistence' is one of his three 'broad concepts' of poverty, we are left with 'externality' and 'inequality'. Inequality—though related to poverty in terms of both causation and evaluation—is, however, a *distinct* issue from poverty, as will be presently argued (see Section 2.3). 'Externality', in terms of the effects of poverty on the *non-poor*, is an approach that we have already discussed (in Section 2.1), critically.

Third, even when we do go through the intermediary of income, the translation of a set of nutritional norms (or of alternative sets of such norms) into a 'poverty line' income (or poverty-line *incomes*) may be substantially simplified by the wide prevalence of particular patterns of consumption behaviour in the community in question. Proximity of *actual* habits and behaviour makes it possible to derive income levels at which the nutritional norms will be 'typically' met. (This question is discussed further in Chapter 3.)

Finally, while it can hardly be denied that malnutrition captures only one aspect of our idea of poverty, it is an important aspect, and one that is particularly important for many developing countries. It seems clear that malnutrition must have a central place in the conception of poverty. How exactly this place is to be specified remains to be explored, but the recent tendency to dismiss the whole approach seems to be a robust example of misplaced sophistication.

2.3 THE INEQUALITY APPROACH

The idea that the concept of poverty is essentially one of inequality has some immediate plausibility. After all, transfers from the rich to the poor can make a substantial dent on poverty in most societies. Even the poverty line to be used for identifying the poor has to be drawn with respect to contemporary standards in the community in question, so that poverty may look very like inequality between the poorest group and the rest of the community.

Arguments in favour of viewing poverty as inequality are presented powerfully by Miller and Roby, who conclude:

Casting the issues of poverty in terms of stratification leads to regarding poverty as an issue of inequality. In this approach, we move away from efforts to measure poverty lines with pseudo-scientific accuracy. Instead, we look at the nature and size of the differences between the bottom 20 or 10 per cent and the rest of the society. Our concern becomes one of narrowing the differences between those at the bottom and the better-off in each stratification dimension.[8]

There is clearly quite a bit to be said in favour of this approach. But one can argue that inequality is fundamentally a different

[8] Miller and Roby (1971, p. 143). Also Miller, Rein, Roby and Cross (1967). See Wedderburn (1974) for discussions of alternative approaches.

issue from poverty. To try to analyse poverty 'as an issue of inequality', or the other way round, would do little justice to either. Inequality and poverty are not, of course, unrelated. But neither concept subsumes the other. A transfer of income from a person in the top income group to one in the middle income range must *ceteris paribus* reduce inequality; but it may leave the perception of poverty quite unaffected. Similarly, a general decline in income that keeps the chosen measure of inequality unchanged may, in fact, lead to a sharp increase in starvation, malnutrition and obvious hardship; it will then be fantastic to claim that poverty is unchanged. To ignore such information as starvation and hunger is not, in fact, an abstinence from 'pseudo-scientific accuracy', but blindness to important parameters of the common understanding of poverty. Neither poverty nor inequality can really be included in the empire of the other.[9]

It is, of course, quite a different matter to recognize that inequality and poverty are *associated* with each other, and to note that a different distribution system may cure poverty even without an expansion of the country's productive capabilities. Recognizing the distinct nature of poverty as a concept permits one to treat it as a matter of interest and involvement in itself. The role of inequality in the prevalence of poverty can then figure in the analysis of poverty without making the two conceptually equivalent.

2.4 RELATIVE DEPRIVATION

The concept of 'relative deprivation' has been fruitfully used in the analysis of poverty,[10] especially in the sociological literature. Being poor has clearly much to do with being deprived, and it is natural that, for a social animal, the concept of deprivation will be a relative one. But within the uniformity of the term 'relative deprivation', there seem to exist some distinct and different notions.

One distinction concerns the contrast between *'feelings* of

[9] It is also worth noting that there are many measures of inequality, of which the gap 'between the bottom 20 or 10 per cent and the rest' is only one. See Atkinson (1970), Sen (1973a), Kolm (1976a, 1976b), and Blackorby and Donaldson (1978, 1980b). Also, inequality is not just a matter of the *size distribution* of income but one of investigating contrasts between different sections of the community from many different perspectives, e.g. in terms of *relations of production*, as done by Marx (1859, 1867).

[10] See Runciman (1966) and Townsend (1971), presenting two rather different approaches to the concept.

deprivation' and '*conditions* of deprivation'. Peter Townsend has argued that 'the latter would be a better usage'.[11] There is indeed much to be said for a set of criteria that can be based on concrete conditions, so that one could use 'relative deprivation' 'in an objective sense to describe situations where people possess less of some desired attribute, be it income, favourable employment conditions or power, than do others'.[12]

On the other hand, the choice of '*conditions* of deprivation' can not be independent of '*feelings* of deprivation'. Material objects cannot be evaluated in this context without reference to how people view them, and even if 'feelings' are not brought in explicitly, they must have an implicit role in the selection of 'attributes'. Townsend has rightly emphasized the importance of the 'endeavour to define the style of living which is generally shared or approved in each society and find whether there is . . . a point in the scale of the distribution of resources below which families find it increasingly difficult . . . to share in the customs, activities and diets comprising that style of living'.[13] One must, however, look also at the feelings of deprivation in deciding on the style and level of living the failure to share which is regarded as important. The dissociation of 'conditions' from 'feelings' is, therefore, not easy, and an objective diagnosis of 'conditions' requires an objective understanding of 'feelings'.

A second contrast concerns the choice of 'reference groups' for comparison. Again, one has to look at the groups with which the people in question actually compare themselves, and this can be one of the most difficult aspects of the study of poverty based on relative deprivation. The horizon of comparison is not, of course, independent of political activity in the community in question,[14] since one's sense of deprivation is closely related to one's expectations as well as one's view of what is fair and who has the right to enjoy what.

These different issues related to the general notion of relative deprivation have considerable bearing on the social analysis of

---

[11] Townsend (1974), pp. 25–6.
[12] Wedderburn (1974), p. 4.
[13] Townsend (1974), p. 36.
[14] For example, Richard Scase (1974) notes that Swedish workers tend to choose rather wider reference groups than British workers, and relates this contrast to the differences in the nature of the two trade union movements and of political organization generally.

poverty. It is, however, worth noting that the approach of relative deprivation—even including all its variants—cannot really be the *only* basis for the concept of poverty. A famine, for example, will be readily accepted as a case of acute poverty no matter what the relative pattern within the society happens to be. Indeed, there is an irreducible core of *absolute* deprivation in our idea of poverty, which translates reports of starvation, malnutrition and visible hardship into a diagnosis of poverty without having to ascertain first the relative picture. Thus the approach of relative deprivation supplements rather than supplants the analysis of poverty in terms of absolute dispossession.

2.5 A VALUE JUDGEMENT?

The view that 'poverty is a value judgement' has recently been presented forcefully by many authors. It seems natural to think of poverty as something that is disapproved of, the elimination of which is regarded as morally good. Going further, it has been argued by Mollie Orshansky, an outstanding authority in the field, that 'poverty, like beauty, lies in the eye of the beholder'.[15] The exercise would, then, seem to be primarily a subjective one: unleashing one's personal morals on the statistics of deprivation.

I would like to argue against this approach. It is important to distinguish between different ways in which the role of morals can be accommodated into the exercise of poverty measurement. There is a difference between saying that the exercise *is itself* a prescriptive one and saying that the exercise must *take note* of the prescriptions made by members of the community. To describe a prevailing prescription is an act of description, not prescription. It may indeed be the case that poverty, as Eric Hobsbawm (1968) puts it, 'is always defined according to the conventions of the society in which it occurs' (p. 398). But this does not make the exercise of poverty assessment in a given society a value judgement. Nor a subjective exercise of some kind or other. For the person studying and measuring poverty, the conventions of society are matters of fact (what *are* the contemporary standards?), and not issues of morality or of subjective search (what *should be* the contemporary standards? what *should be* my values? how do I *feel* about all this?).[16]

---

[15] Orshansky (1969), p. 37. For a critique of this position, see Townsend (1974).

[16] This does not, of course, in any way deny that one's values may implicitly affect one's

The point was brought out very clearly by Adam Smith more than two hundred years ago:

By necessaries I understand not only the commodities which are indispensably necessary for the support of life, but what ever the custom of the country renders it indecent for creditable people, even the lowest order, to be without. A linen shirt, for example, is, strictly speaking, not a necessary of life. The Greeks and Romans lived, I suppose, very comfortably though they had no linen. But in the present times, through the greater part of Europe, a creditable day-labourer would be ashamed to appear in public without a linen shirt, the want of which would be supposed to denote that disgraceful degree of poverty which, it is presumed, nobody can well fall into without extreme bad conduct. Custom, in the same manner, has rendered leather shoes a necessary of life in England. The poorest creditable person of either sex would be ashamed to appear in public without them.[17]

In a similar vein Karl Marx (1867) argued that, while 'a historical and moral element' enters the concept of subsistence, 'nevertheless, in a given country, at a given period, the average quantity of the means of subsistence necessary for the labourer is practically known' (p. 150).

It is possible that Smith or Marx may have overestimated the extent of uniformity of views that tends to exist in a community on the content of 'subsistence' or 'poverty'. Description of 'necessities' may be very far from ambiguous. But the presence of ambiguity in a description does not make it a prescriptive act— only one of ambiguous description. One may be forced to be arbitrary in eliminating the ambiguity, and if so that arbitrariness would be worth recording. Similarly, one may be forced to use more than one criteria because of non-uniformity of accepted standards, and to look at the *partial* ordering generated by the criteria taken together (reflecting 'dominance' in terms of all the criteria).[18] But the partial ordering would still reflect a descript-

---

assessment of facts, as indeed they very often do. The statement is about the *nature* of the exercise, viz. that it is concerned with assessment of facts, and not about the way it is typically performed and the psychology that lies behind that performance. (The doctor attached to the students' hostel in which I stayed in Calcutta would refuse to diagnose influenza on the powerful ground that 'flu shouldn't be a reason for staying in bed'.) The issue is, in some respects, comparable to that of one's interests influencing one's values; for an important historical analysis of various different aspects of that relationship, see Hirschman (1977).

[17] Smith (1776), pp. 351–2.
[18] Sen (1973a), Chapters 2 and 3.

ive statement rather than a prescriptive one. Indeed, the statement would be rather like saying, 'Nureyev may or may not be a better dancer than Nijinsky, but he dances better than this author, according to contemporary standards', a descriptive statement (and sadly non-controversial).

2.6 A POLICY DEFINITION?

A related issue is worth exploring in this context. The measurement of poverty may be based on certain given standards, but what kind of statements do these standards themselves make? Are they standards of public policy, reflecting either the objectives of actual policy *or* views on what the policy should be? There is little doubt that the standards must have a good deal to do with some broad notions of acceptability, but that is not the same thing as reflecting precise policy objectives—actual *or* recommended. On this subject too a certain amount of confusion seems to exist. For example, the United States President's Commission on Income Maintenance (1969) argued thus for such a 'policy definition' in its well-known report, *Poverty amid Plenty*:

If society believes that people should not be permitted to die of starvation or exposure, then it will define poverty as the lack of minimum food and shelter necessary to maintain life. If society feels some responsibility for providing to all persons an established measure of well-being beyond mere existence, for example, good physical health, then it will add to its list of necessities the resources required to prevent or cure sickness. At any given time a policy definition reflects a balancing of community capabilities and desires. In low income societies the community finds it impossible to worry much beyond physical survival. Other societies, more able to support their dependent citizens, begin to consider the effects that pauperism will have on the poor and non-poor alike.[19]

There are at least two difficulties with this 'policy definition'. First, practical policy-making depends on a number of influences, going beyond the prevalent notions of what should be done. Policy is a function of political organization, and depends on a variety of factors including the nature of the government; the sources of its power, and the forces exerted by other organizations. In the public policies pursued in many countries, it is, in fact, hard to detect a concern with the elimination of deprivation in any obvious sense. If interpreted in terms of actual

[19] US President's Commission on Income Maintenance (1969), p. 8.

policy, the 'policy definition' may fail to catch the political issues in policy-making.

Second, even if 'policy' is taken to stand not for actual public policy, but for policy recommendations widely held in the society in question, there are problems. There is clearly a difference between the notion of 'deprivation' and the idea of what should be eliminated by 'policy'. For one thing, policy recommendations must depend on an assessment of feasibilities ('ought implies can'[20]), but to concede that some deprivations cannot be immediately eliminated is not the same thing as conceding that they must not currently be seen as deprivations. (Contrast: 'Look here, old man, you aren't really poor even though you are starving, since it is impossible in the present economic circumstances to maintain the income of everyone above the level needed to eliminate starvation.') Adam Smith's notion of subsistence based on 'the commodities which are indispensably necessary for the support of life' and 'what ever the custom of the country renders it indecent' for someone 'to be without' is by no means identical with what is generally accepted as could and should be provided to all as a matter of policy. If in a country suddenly impoverished, say, by war it is agreed generally that the income maintenance programme must be cut down to a lower level of income, would it be right to say that the country does not have any greater poverty since a reduction of incomes has been *matched* by a reduction of the poverty line?

I would submit that the 'policy definiton' is based on a fundamental confusion. It is certainly true that with economic development there are changes in the notion of what counts as deprivation and poverty, and there are changes also in the ideas as to what should be done. But while these two types of changes are interdependent and also intertemporally correlated with each other, neither can be *defined* entirely in terms of the other. Oil-rich Kuwait may be 'more able to support their dependent citizens' with its new prosperity, but the notion of what is poverty may not go up immediately to the corresponding level. Similarly, the war-devastated Netherlands may keep up its standard of what counts as poverty and not scale it down to the level commensurate with its predicament.[21]

[20] Cf. Hare (1963), Chapter 4.
[21] For an account of that predicament, see Stein, Susser, Saenger, and Marolla (1975).

If this approach is accepted, then the measurement of poverty must be seen as an exercise of description assessing the predicament of people in terms of the prevailing standards of necessities. It is primarily a factual rather than an ethical exercise, and the facts relate to what is regarded as deprivation, and not directly to what policies are recommended. The deprivation in question has both absolute and relative aspects (as argued in Sections 2.2 and 2.4 above).

2.7 STANDARDS AND AGGREGATION

This still leaves two issues quite untouched. First, in comparing the poverty of two societies, how can a common standard of necessities be found, since such standards would vary from society to society? There are actually two quite distinct types of exercises in such inter-community comparisons. One is aimed at comparing the extent of deprivation in each community in relation to their respective standards of minimum necessities, and the other is concerned with comparing the predicament of the two communities in terms of some given minimum standard, e.g. that prevalent in one community. There is, indeed, nothing contradictory in asserting both of the following pair of statements:

(1) There is *less* deprivation in community A than in community B in terms of some *common* standard, e.g. the notions of minimum needs prevailing in community A.
(2) There is *more* deprivation in community A than in community B in terms of their *respective* standards of minimum needs, which are a good deal higher in A than in B.[22]

It is rather pointless to dispute which of these two senses is the 'correct' one, since it is quite clear that both types of questions are of interest. The important thing to note is that the two questions are quite distinct from each other.

Second, while the exercise of 'identification' of the poor can be based on a standard of minimum needs, that of 'aggregation' requires some method of combining deprivations of different people into some overall indicator. In the latter exercise some relative scaling of deprivations is necessary. The scope for

---

[22] There is also no necessary contradiction in asserting that community A has less deprivation in terms of one community's standards (e.g. A's itself), while community B is less deprived in terms of another community's standards (e.g. B's).

arbitrariness in this is much greater, since conventions on this are less firmly established and the constraints of acceptability would tend to leave one with a good deal of freedom. The problem is somewhat comparable with the criteria for making *aggregative descriptive statements* in such fields as, say, comparisons of sporting achievements of different groups. While it is clear that certain circumstances would permit one to make an aggregative statement like 'Africans are better at sprint than Indians' (e.g. the circumstance in which the former group keeps winning virtually all sprint events over the Indians), and other circumstances would force one to deny this, there are intermediate cases in which either of the two aggregative descriptive statements would be clearly disputable.

In this context of arbitrariness of 'aggregate description', it becomes particularly tempting to redefine the problem as an 'ethical' exercise, as has indeed been done in the measurement of economic inequality.[23] But the ethical exercises involve exactly similar ambiguities, and furthermore end up answering a different question from the descriptive one that was originally asked.[24] There is very little alternative to accepting the element of arbitrariness in the description of poverty, and making that element as clear as possible. Since the notion of the poverty of a nation has some inherent ambiguities, one should not have expected anything else.

2.8 CONCLUDING REMARKS

Poverty is, of course, a matter of deprivation. The recent shift in focus—especially in the sociological literature—from *absolute* to *relative* deprivation has provided a useful framework of analysis (Section 2.4). But relative deprivation is essentially incomplete as an approach to poverty, and supplements (but cannot supplant) the earlier approach of absolute dispossession. The much maligned biological approach, which deserves substantial re-formulation but not rejection, relates to this irreducible core of absolute deprivation, keeping issues of starvation and hunger at the centre of the concept of poverty (Sections 2.2 and 2.4).

To view poverty as an issue in inequality, as is often recommended, seems to do little justice to either concept.

---

[23] See Dalton (1920), Kolm (1969), and Atkinson (1970).
[24] See Bentzel (1970), Hansson (1977), and Sen (1978b).

Poverty and inequality relate closely to each other, but they are distinct concepts and neither subsumes the other (Section 2.3).

There is a good case for viewing the measurement of poverty not, as is often asserted, as an ethical exercise, but primarily as a descriptive one (Section 2.5). Furthermore, it can be argued that the frequently used 'policy definition' of poverty is fundamentally flawed (Section 2.6). The exercise of describing the predicament of the poor in terms of the prevailing standards of 'necessities' does, of course, involve ambiguities, which are inherent in the concept of poverty; but ambiguous description isn't the same thing as prescription.[25] Instead, the arbitrariness that is inescapable in choosing between permissible procedures and possible interpretations of prevailing standards requires recognition and appropriate treatment.

[25] The underlying methodological issues have been discussed in Sen (1980a).

Chapter 3

Poverty: Identification and Aggregation

3.1 COMMODITIES AND CHARACTERISTICS

It was argued in the last chapter that the measurement of poverty can be split into two distinct operations, viz. the *identification* of the poor, and the *aggregation* of their poverty characteristics into an over-all measure. The identification exercise is clearly prior to aggregation. The most common route to identification is through specifying a set of 'basic'—or 'minimum'—needs,[1] and regarding the inability to fulfil these needs as the test of poverty. It was claimed in the last chapter that considerations of relative deprivation are relevant in specifying the 'basic' needs, but attempts to make relative deprivation the *sole* basis of such specification is doomed to failure since there is an irreducible core of absolute deprivation in the concept of poverty. Within the general perspective that was presented in the last chapter, some detailed—and more technical—issues are taken up in this chapter before moving from identification to aggregation.

Are the basic needs involved in identifying poverty better specified in terms of commodities, or in terms of 'characteristics'? Wheat, rice, potatoes, etc., are commodities, while calories, protein, vitamins, etc., are characteristics of these commodities that the consumers seek.[2] If each characteristic could be obtained from only one commodity and no others, then it would be easy to translate the characteristics needs into commodity needs. But this is very often not the case, so that characteristics requirements do not specify commodity requirements. While calories are necessary for survival, neither wheat nor rice is.

[1] The literature on basic needs is vast. For some of the main issues involved, see ILO (1976a, 1976b), Haq (1976), Jolly (1976), Stewart and Streeten (1976), Beckerman (1977), Bhalla (1977), Ghai, Khan, Lee and Alfthan (1977), Streeten (1977), Balogh (1978), Griffin and Khan (1978), Perkins (1978), Rudra (1978), Singh (1978), and Streeten and Burki (1978). On related issues, see also Adelman and Morris (1973), Chenery, Ahluwalia, Bell, Duloy and Jolly (1974), Morawetz (1977), Reutlinger and Selowsky (1976), Drewnowski (1977), Grant (1978), Chichilnisky (1979), Morris (1979), and Fields (1980).

[2] For analyses of consumer theory in terms of characteristics, see Gorman (1956, 1976), and Lancaster (1966).

The characteristics needs are, in an obvious sense, prior to the needs for commodities, and translation of the former to the latter is possible only under special circumstances. Multiplicity of sources is, however, not uniform. Many commodities provide calories or proteins; rather few commodities provide shelter. Literacy comes almost entirely from elementary schooling, even though there are, in principle, other sources. In many cases, therefore, it is possible to move from characteristics requirements to commodity requirements—broadly defined—with rather little ambiguity. It is for this reason that 'basic' or 'minimum' needs are often specified in terms of a hybrid *vector*—e.g. amounts of calories, proteins, housing, schools, hospital beds—some of the components being pure characteristics while others are un-abashed commodities. While there is some evidence that such mongrelism disconcerts the purist, it is quite economic, and typically does little harm.

An interesting intermediate case arises when a certain charac-teristic can be obtained from several different commodities, but the tastes of the community in question guarantee that the characteristic is obtained from one commodity only. A com-munity may, for example, be wedded to rice, and may not treat the alternative sources of calories (or carbohydrates) as acceptable. A formal way of resolving the issue is to define the characteristic 'calories from rice' as the thing sought by the consumer in question, so that rice and rice alone can satisfy this. This is analytically adequate if a little underhand. But there are also other ways of handling the problem, e.g. the assumption that the group seeks calories as such but treats rice as its only *feasible* source. While these conceptual distinctions may not have much immediate practical importance, they tend to suggest rather different approaches to policy issues involving taste variations.

The role of knowledge accumulation in reforming ideas of feasible diets may in fact be an important part of nutritional planning. The knowledge in question includes both information about nutrition as such and experience of how things taste (once one breaks out of the barrier spotted by the old Guinness ad: 'I have never tasted it because I don't like it').

Dietary habits of a population are not, of course, immutable, but they have remarkable staying power. In making inter-community comparisons of poverty, the contrast between formulating needs in terms of characteristics and formulating needs in terms of commodities may turn out to be significant. For example, the ranking of rural living standards in different states in India changes significantly when the basis of comparison is shifted from command over commodities to command over characteristics such as calories and protein.[3] There is little doubt that ultimately characteristics provide the more relevant basis for specification of basic needs, but the relative inflexibility of taste factors makes the conversion of these basic needs into minimum cost diets a function not merely of prices but also of consumption habits.[4] Explicit account would have to be taken of this issue in completing the identification exercise. This last question is further discussed in the next section.

3.2 THE DIRECT METHOD VERSUS THE INCOME METHOD

In identifying the poor for a given set of 'basic needs', it is possible to use at least two alternative methods.[5] One is simply to check the set of people whose actual consumption baskets happen to leave some basic need unsatisfied. This we may call the 'direct method', and it does not involve the use of any income notion, in particular not that of a poverty-line income. In contrast, in what may be called the 'income method', the first step is to calculate the minimum income π at which all the specified minimum needs are satisfied. The next step is to identify those whose actual incomes fall below that poverty line.

In an obvious sense the direct method is superior to the income method, since the former is not based on particular assumptions of consumption behaviour which may or may not be accurate. Indeed, it could be argued that *only* in the absence of direct information regarding the satisfaction of the specified needs can there be a case for bringing in the intermediary of income, so that the income method is at most a second best.

There is much to be said for such a view, and the income method can indeed be seen as a way of approximating the results

---

[3] See Sen (1976d) on this general issue, and Rath (1973), Bhattacharya and Chatterjee (1974, 1977), and Sen (1976b), on the underlying empirical studies.

[4] While dietary habits are not easy to change, they do, of course, undergo radical transformation in a situation of extreme hunger, for example in famine conditions. In fact, one of the more common causes of death during a famine is diarrhoea caused by eating unfamiliar food—*and* non-food (see Appendix D below).

[5] The distinction relates closely to Seebohm Rowntree's (1901) contrast between 'primary' and 'secondary' poverty.

of the direct method. However, this is not all there is to the contrast of the two methods. The income method can also be seen as a way of taking note of individual idiosyncrasies without upsetting the notion of poverty based on deprivation. The ascetic who fasts on his expensive bed of nails will be registered as poor under the direct method, but the income method will offer a different judgement in recognition of his level of income, at which typical people in that community would have no difficulty in satisfying the basic nutritional requirements. The income of a person can be seen not merely to be a rough aid to predicting a person's actual consumption, but also as capturing a person's *ability* to meet his minimum needs (whether or not he, in fact, chooses to use that ability).[6]

There is a difficult line to draw here. If one were to look merely for the ability to meet minimum needs without being bothered by tastes, then one would, of course, set up a cost-minimizing programming problem and simply check whether someone's income falls short of that minimum cost solution. Such minimum cost diets are typically very inexpensive but exceedingly dull, and are very often regarded as unacceptable. (In Indira Rajaraman's (1974) pioneering work on poverty in Punjab, in an initial round of optimization, unsuspecting Punjabis were subjected to a deluge of Bengal grams.) Taste factors can be introduced through constraints (as Rajaraman did, and others do), but it is difficult to decide how pervasive and severe these constraints should be. In the extreme case the constraints determine the consumption pattern entirely.

But there is, I believe, a difference in principle between taste constraints that apply broadly to the entire community and those that essentially reflect individual idiosyncrasies. If the poverty-level income can be derived from typical behaviour norms of society, a person with a higher income who is choosing to fast on a bed of nails can, with some legitimacy, be declared to be non-poor. The income method does, therefore, have some merit of its own, aside from its role as a way of approximating what would have been yielded by the direct method had all the detailed consumption data been available.

The 'direct method' and the 'income method' are not, in fact,

---

[6] The income method has close ties with the welfare economics of real income comparisons; see Hicks (1958).

two alternative ways of measuring the same thing, but represent two alternative *conceptions* of poverty. The direct method identifies those whose actual consumption fails to meet the accepted conventions of minimum needs, while the income method is after spotting those who do not have the ability to meet these needs within the behavioural constraints typical in that community. Both concepts are of some interest on their own in diagnosing poverty in a community, and while the latter is a bit more remote in being dependent on the existence of some typical behaviour pattern in the community, it is also a bit more refined in going beyond the observed choices into the notion of ability. A poor person, on this approach, is one whose income is not adequate to meet the specified minimum needs in conformity with the conventional behaviour pattern.[7]

The income method has the advantage of providing a metric of numerical distances from the 'poverty line', in terms of income short-falls. This the 'direct method' does not provide, since it has to be content with pointing out the short-fall of each type of need. On the other hand, the income method is more restrictive in terms of preconditions necessary for the 'identification' exercise. First, if the pattern of consumption behaviour has no uniformity, there will be no specific level of income at which the 'typical' consumer meets his or her minimum needs. Second, if prices facing different groups of people differ, e.g. between social classes or income groups or localities, then the poverty line will be group-specific, even when uniform norms and uniform consumption habits are considered.[8] These are real difficulties and cannot be wished away. That the assumption of a uniform poverty line for a given society distorts reality seems reasonably certain. What is much less clear, however, is the *extent* to which reality is thus distorted, and the seriousness of the distortion for the purposes for which the poverty measures may be used.

3.3 FAMILY SIZE AND EQUIVALENT ADULTS

Another difficulty arises from the fact that the family rather than the individual is the natural unit as far as consumption behaviour

---

[7] The income method is based on *two* distinct sets of conventions, viz. (1) those used to identify the minimum needs, and (2) those used to specify behaviour and taste constraints.

[8] For evidence of sharp differences in income-group-specific price deflators in India, see Bardhan (1973), Vaidyanathan (1974) and Radhakrishna and Sarma (1975), among others. See also Osmani (1978).

is concerned. In calculating the income necessary for meeting the minimum needs of families of different size, some method of correspondence of family income with individual income is needed. While the simplest method of doing this is to divide the family income by the number of family members, this overlooks the economies of large scale that operate for many items of consumption, and also the fact that the children's needs may be quite different from those of adults. To cope with these issues, the common practice for both poverty estimation and social security operations is to convert each family into a certain number of 'equivalent adults' by the use of some 'equivalence scale', or, alternatively, to convert the families into 'equivalent households'.[9]

There tends to be a lot of arbitrariness in any such conversion. Much depends on the exact consumption pattern of the people involved, which varies from family to family and with age composition. Indeed, both the minimum needs of children as well as variations of consumption behaviour of families with variations of the number and age composition of children are complex fields for empirical investigation. The question of maldistribution *within* the family is also an important issue requiring a good deal more attention than it has received so far.

There are also different bases for deriving appropriate equivalence of needs.[10] One approach is to take the nutritional requirements for each age group separately and then to take the ratios of their costs, given established patterns of consumer behaviour. The acceptability of this approach depends not merely on the validity of the nutritional standards used, but also on the assumption that family behaviour displays the same concern for fulfilling the respective nutritional requirements of members of different age groups in the family.[11] It also ignores economies of scale in consumption which seem to exist even for such items as food.

A second approach is to examine how the people involved regard the equivalence question themselves, viz. how much extra

[9] See Orshansky (1965), Abel-Smith and Townsend (1965), and Atkinson (1969), among others. See also Fields (1980).

[10] For an illuminating account of these methods and their underlying logic, see Deaton and Muellbauer (1980).

[11] Another important variable is the work load, including that of the children, which too can be high in many poor economies; see Hansen (1969) and Hamilton (1975).

income they think is needed to make a larger family have the same standard of well-being as a smaller one. Empirical studies of these 'views' (e.g., Goedhart, Halberstadt, Kapteyn, and van Praag, 1977) have shown considerable regularities and consistency.

A third way is to examine the actual conšumption behaviour of families of different size and to treat some aspect of this behaviour as an indicator of welfare. For example, the fraction spent on food has been treated as an indicator of poverty: two families of different size are regarded as having 'equivalent' incomes when they spend the same proportion of their incomes on food.[12]

No matter how these equivalent scales are drawn up, there remains the further issue of the weighting of families of different size. Three alternative approaches may be considered: (1) put the same weight on each *household*, irrespective of size; (2) put the same weight on each *person*, irrespective of the size of the family to whom they belong; and (3) put a weight on each *family* equal to the number of equivalent adults in it.

The first method is clearly unsatisfactory since the poverty and suffering of a large family is, in an obvious sense, greater than that of a small family at a poverty level judged to be equivalent to that of the former. The third alternative might look like a nice compromise, but is, I believe, based on a confusion. The scale of 'equivalent adults' indicates conversion factors to be used to find out how well off members of that family are, but ultimately we are concerned with the sufferings of *everyone* in the family and not of a hypothetical equivalent number. If two can live as cheaply as one and a half and three as cheaply as two, these facts must be taken into account in comparing the relative well-beings of two-member and three-member families; but there is no reason why the suffering of two three-member families should receive any less weight than that of three two-member families at the same level of illfare. There is, thus, a good case for using procedure (2), after the level of well-being or poverty of each person has been ascertained by the use of equivalent scales taking note of the size and composition of the families to which they belong.

[12] See Muellbauer (1977b) and Deaton and Muellbauer (1980), Chapter 8. The method goes back to Engel (1895). On this approach and others addressed to the problem of comparing well-beings of households, see Friedman (1952), Brown (1954), Prais and Houthakker (1955), Barten (1964), Theil (1967), Nicholson (1976), Muellbauer (1977a), Deaton and Muellbauer (1980), Fields (1980), Kakwani (1980a), and Marris and Theil (1980).

3.4 POVERTY GAPS AND RELATIVE DEPRIVATION

The income short-fall of a person whose income is less than the poverty-line income can be called his 'income gap'. In the aggregate assessment of poverty, these income gaps must be taken into account. But does it make a difference whether or not a person's short-fall is unusually large compared with those of others? It seems reasonable to argue that any person's poverty cannot really be independent of how poor the others are.[13] Even with exactly the same absolute short-fall, a person may be thought to be 'poorer' if the other poor have short-falls smaller than his, in contrast with the case in which his short-fall is less than that of others. Quantification of poverty would, thus, seem to need the marrying of considerations of absolute and relative deprivation even *after* a set of minimum needs and a poverty line have been fixed.

The question of relative deprivation can be viewed also in the context of a possible transfer of a unit of income from a poor person—call him 1—to another—christened 2—who is richer but still below the poverty line and remains so even after the transfer. Such a transfer will increase the absolute short-fall of the first person by exactly the same amount by which the absolute short-fall of person 2 will be reduced. Can one then argue that the over-all poverty is unaffected by the transfer? One can dispute this, of course, by bringing in some notion of diminishing marginal utility of income, so that the utility loss of the first may be argued to be greater than the utility gain of the second. But such cardinal utility comparisons for different persons involves the use of a rather demanding informational structure with well-known difficulties. In the absence of cardinal comparisons of marginal utility gains and losses, is it then impossible to hold that the overall poverty of the community has increased? I would argue that this is not the case.

Person 1 is relatively deprived compared with 2 (and there may be others in between the two who are more deprived than 2 but less so than 1). When a unit of income is transferred from 1 to 2, it increases the absolute short-fall of a *more* deprived person and reduces that of someone *less* deprived, so that in a straightforward

[13] Cf. Scitovsky (1976) and Hirsch (1976). See also Hirschman and Rothschild (1973).

sense the over-all relative deprivation is increased.[14] And this is the case quite irrespective of whether absolute deprivation is measured by income short-falls, or—taking utility to be an increasing function of income—by utility short-falls, from the break-even poverty line. One does not, therefore, have to introduce an interpersonally comparable *cardinal* welfare scale to be able to say that the transfer specified will increase the extent of relative deprivation.

In the 'aggregation' exercise the magnitudes of absolute deprivation may have to be supplemented by considerations of relative deprivation. Before this exercise is studied, it will be useful to review the standard measures of poverty used in the literature and to examine their shortcomings.

3.5 CRITIQUE OF STANDARD MEASURES

The commonest measure of over-all poverty, already discussed in Chapter 2, is the head-count measure H, given by the proportion of the total population that happens to be identified as poor, e.g. as falling below the specified poverty-line income. If q is the number of people who are identified as being poor and n the total number of people in the community, then the head-count measure H is simply q/n.

This index has been widely used—explicitly or by implication—ever since quantitative study and measurement of poverty began (see Booth, 1889; Rowntree, 1901). It seems to be still the mainstay of poverty statistics on which poverty programmes are based (see Orshansky, 1965, 1966; Abel-Smith and Townsend, 1965). It has been extensively utilized recently both for intertemporal comparisons as well as for international contrasts.[15]

Another measure that has had a fair amount of currency is the

---

[14] A complex problem arises when the transfer makes person 2 cross the poverty line— a possibility that has been deliberately excluded in the postulated case. This case involves a reduction in one of the main parameters of poverty, viz. the identification of the poor, and while there is an arbitrariness in attaching a lot of importance to whether a person actually crosses the poverty line, this is an arbitrariness that is implicit in the concept of poverty itself based on the use of a break-even line. The question is investigated further in Section C. 3, pp. 192–4.

[15] See, for example, the lively debate on the time trend of Indian poverty: Ojha (1970), Dandekar and Rath (1971), Minhas (1970, 1971), Bardhan (1970, 1971, 1973), Mukherjee, Bhattacharya and Chatterjee (1972), Bhatty (1974), Kumar (1974), Vaidyanathan (1974), Lal (1976), Ahluwalia (1978), and Dutta (1978). For international comparisons, see Chenery, Ahluwalia, Bell, Duloy and Jolly (1974).

so-called 'poverty gap', which is the aggregate short-fall of income of all the poor from the specified poverty line.[16] The index can be normalized by being expressed as the percentage short-fall of the average income of the poor from the poverty line. This measure—denoted I—will be called the 'income-gap ratio'.

The income-gap ratio I is completely insensitive to transfers of income among the poor so long as nobody crosses the poverty line by such transfers. It also pays no attention whatever to the number or proportion of poor people below the poverty line, concentrating only on the aggregate short-fall, no matter how it is distributed and among how many. These are damaging limitations.[17]

The head-count measure H is, of course, not insensitive to the number below the poverty line; indeed, for a given society it is the only thing to which H is sensitive. But H pays no attention whatever to the extent of income short-fall of those who lie below the poverty line. It matters not at all whether someone is just below the line or very far from it, in acute misery and hunger.

Furthermore, a transfer of income from a poor person to one who is richer can never increase the poverty measure H—surely a perverse feature. The poor person from whom the transfer takes place is, in any case, counted in the value of H, and no reduction of his income will make him count any more than he does already. On the other hand, the person who *receives* the income transfer cannot, of course, move below the poverty line as a consequence of this. *Either* he was rich and stays so or was poor and stays so, in both of which cases the H measure remains unaffected; *or* he was below the line but is pulled above it by the transfer, and this makes the measure H fall rather than rise. So a transfer from a poor person to one who is richer can *never* increase poverty as represented by H.

There are, thus, good grounds for rejecting the standard poverty measures in terms of which most of the analyses and debates on poverty have traditionally taken place. The head-count measure in particular has commanded implicit support of a kind that is quite astonishing. Consider A. L. Bowley's (1923) famous assertion: 'There is, perhaps, no better test of the progress

---

[16] The poverty gap has been used by the US Social Security Administration; see Batchelder (1971). See also Kakwani (1978) and Beckerman (1979a, 1979b).

[17] The underlying issues have been discussed in Sen (1973b, 1976a). See also Fields (1980).

of the nation than that which shows what proportion are in poverty' (p. 214). The spirit of the remark is acceptable enough, but surely not the gratuitous identification of poverty with the head-count measure H.

What about a combination of these poverty measures? The head-count measure H ignores the extent of income short-falls, while the income-gap ratio I ignores the numbers involved: why not a combination of the two? This is, alas, still inadequate. If a unit of income is transferred from a person below the poverty line to someone who is richer but who still is (and remains) below the poverty line, then both the measures H and I will remain completely unaffected. Hence any 'combined' measure based only on these two must also show no response whatsoever to such a change, despite the obvious increase in aggregate poverty as a consequence of this transfer in terms of relative deprivation.

There is, however, a special case in which a combination of H and I might just about be adequate. Note that, while individually H is insensitive to the extent of income short-falls and I to the numbers involved, we could criticize the *combination* of the two only for their insensitivity to variations of distribution of income among the poor. If we were, then, to confine ourselves to cases in which all the poor have precisely the same income, it may be reasonable to expect that H and I together may do the job. Transfers of the kind that have been considered above to show the insensitivity of the combination of H and I will not then be in the domain of our discourse.

The interest of the special case in which all the poor have the same income does not arise from its being a very likely occurrence. Its value lies in clarifying the way absolute depriv-ation *vis-à-vis* the poverty line may be handled when there isn't the additional feature of relative deprivation *among* the poor.[18] It helps us to formulate a condition that the required poverty measure P should satisfy when the problem of distribution among the poor is assumed away by postulating equality. It provides *one* regularity condition to be satisfied among others.

[18]   As was discussed in Section 2.1, the question of relative deprivation *vis-à-vis* the rest of the community is involved also in the fixing of minimum needs on which the choice of the poverty line is based, so that the estimation of 'absolute' deprivation *vis-à-vis* the poverty line involves implicitly some considerations of *relative* deprivation as well. The reference in the text here is to issues of relative deprivation that remain even after the poverty line has been drawn, since there is the further question of one's deprivation compared with others who are also deprived.

3.6 AXIOMATIC DERIVATION OF A POVERTY MEASURE AND VARIANTS

We may require the poverty measure P to be a weighted sum of the short-falls of all people who are judged to be poor. This is done in a very general way with weights that can be functions of other variables. If we wished to base the poverty measure on some quantification of the sum-total loss of utility arising from the penury of the poor, then the weights should be derived from the familiar utilitarian considerations. If, additionally, it is assumed that the utility of each person depends only on his own income, then the weight on each person's income gap will depend only on the income of that person, and not also on the incomes of others. This will provide a 'separable' structure, each person's component of the overall poverty being derived without reference to the conditions of the others. But this use of the traditional utilitarian model will miss the idea of relative deprivation, which—as we have already argued—is rather central to the notion of poverty. Furthermore, there are difficulties with such cardinal comparisons of utility gains and losses, and even if these were ignored, it is no easy matter to secure agreement on using one particular utility function among so many that can be postulated, all satisfying the usual regularity conditions (such as diminishing marginal utility).

Instead, the concentration can be precisely on aspects of relative deprivation. Let $r(i)$ be the rank of person i in the ordering of all the poor in the decreasing order of income; e.g. $r(i) = 12$ if i is the twelfth worst off among the poor. If more than one person has the same income, they can be ranked in any arbitrary order: the poverty measure must be such that it should not matter which particular arbitrary order is chosen among those with the same income. Clearly, the poorest poor has the largest rank value q, when there are q people altogether on this side of the poverty line, while the least poor has the rank value of 1. The greater the rank value, the more the person is deprived in terms of relative deprivation with respect to others in the same category.[19] It is, thus, reasonable to argue that a poverty measure capturing this aspect of relative deprivation must make the weight on a person's income short-fall increase with his rank value $r(i)$.

[19] Cf. Runciman (1966) and Townsend (1971).

A rather distinguished and simple case of such a relationship is to make the weight on any person i's income gap equal the rank value $r(i)$. This makes the weights equidistanced, and the procedure is in the same spirit as Borda's (1781) famous argument for the rank-order method of voting, choosing equal distances in the absence of a convincing case for any alternative assumption. While this too is arbitrary, it captures the notion of relative deprivation in a simple way, and leads to a transparent procedure, making it quite clear what precisely is being assumed.[20]

This axiom of 'Ranked Relative Deprivation' (axiom R) focuses on the distribution of income among the poor, and may be combined with the kind of information that is presented by the head-count measure H and the income-gap ratio I in the special case in which everyone below the poverty line has the same income (so that there is no distribution problem among the poor). H presents the proportion of people who are deprived in relation to the poverty line, and I reflects the proportionate amount of absolute income deprivation *vis-a-vis* that line. It can be argued that H catches one aspect of overall deprivation, viz. how many (never mind how much), while I catches another aspect of it, viz. how much on the average (never mind suffered by how many). In the special case when all the poor have the same income, H and I together may give us a fairly good idea of the extent of poverty in terms of over-all deprivation. Since the problem of relative distribution among the poor does not arise in this special case, we may settle for a measure that boils down to some function of only H and I under these circumstances. A simple representation of this, leading to a convenient normalization, is the product HI. This may be called the axiom of 'Normalized Absolute Deprivation' (axiom A).[21]

If these two axioms are imposed on a quite general format of

[20] It is, in fact, possible to derive the characteristic of equidistance from other—more primitive—axioms (see Sen, 1973b, 1974).

[21] It should be remembered that in fixing the poverty line considerations of relative deprivation have already played a part, so that absolute deprivation *vis-à-vis* the poverty line is non-relative only in the limited context of the 'aggregation' exercise. As was discussed earlier, the concepts of absolute and relative deprivation are both relevant to *each* of the two exercises in the measurement of poverty, viz. identification and aggregation. Axioms A and R are each concerned exclusively with the aggregation exercise.

the poverty measure being a weighted sum of income gaps, then a precise measure of poverty emerges (as shown in Sen, 1973b, 1976a). When G is the Gini coefficient of the distribution of income among the poor, this measure is given by $P = H\{I + (1 - I)G\}$. The precise axiomatic derivation is discussed in Appendix C. When all the poor have the same income, then the Gini coefficient G of income distribution among the poor equals zero, and P equals HI. Given the same average poverty gap and the same proportion of poor population in total population, the poverty measure P increases with greater inequality of incomes below the poverty line, as measured by the Gini coefficient. Thus, the measure P is a function of H (reflecting the number of poor), I (reflecting the aggregate poverty gap), and G (reflecting the inequality of income distribution below the poverty line). The last captures the aspect of 'relative deprivation', and its inclusion is indeed a direct consequence of the axiom of Ranked Relative Deprivation.

Many interesting empirical applications of this approach to the measurement of poverty have been made,[22] and several variants of it have also been considered in the literature,[23] which will be discussed in Appendix C. While the measure P has certain unique advantages which its axiomatic derivation brings out, several of the variants are certainly permissible interpretations of the common conception of poverty. There is nothing defeatist or astonishing in the acceptance of this 'pluralism'. Indeed, as argued in Chapter 2, such pluralism is inherent in the nature of the exercise. But the important point to recognize is that the assessment of overall poverty has to take note of a variety of considerations capturing different features of absolute and relative deprivation. Such simplistic measures as the commonly used head-count ratio H, or the poverty-gap ratio I, fail to do justice to some of these features. It is necessary to use complex measures such as the index P to make the measurement of

[22] See, for example, Ahluwalia (1978), Alamgir (1976, 1978a), Anand (1977), Bhatty (1974), Clark, Hemming and Ulph (1979), Dutta (1978), Fields (1979), Ginneken (1980), Kakwani (1978, 1980), Osmani (1978), Pantulu (1980), Sastry (1977, 1980), Seastrand and Diwan (1975), Szal (1977), among others.

[23] See Anand (1977), Blackorby and Donaldson (1980a), Clark, Hemming and Ulph (1979), Hamada and Takayama (1978), Kakwani (1978, 1980), Osmani (1978), Pyatt (1980), Szal (1977), Takayama (1979), Thon (1979, 1980), Fields (1980), and Chakravarty (1980a, 1980b), among others.

poverty sensitive to the different features that are implicit in our ideas on poverty. In particular, the question of distribution remains relevant even when incomes *below* the poverty line are considered. It will be necessary to go into this question further in the context of analysing starvation and famines, as is done in the chapters that follow.[24]

---

[24] The relevance of this aspect of the distributional question is brought out in the empirical studies of starvation and famine (Chapters 6–9), and the general argument is assessed in that light (Chapter 10).

Chapter 4

Starvation and Famines

4.1 FAMINES

Famines imply starvation, but not vice versa. And starvation implies poverty, but not vice versa. The time has come for us to move from the general terrain of poverty to the disastrous phenomenon of famines.

Poverty, as was discussed in Chapter 2, can reflect relative deprivation as opposed to absolute dispossession. It is possible for poverty to exist, and be regarded as acute, even when no serious starvation occurs. Starvation, on the other hand, does imply poverty, since the absolute dispossession that characterizes starvation is more than sufficient to be diagnosed as poverty, no matter what story emerges from the view of *relative* deprivation.

Starvation is a normal feature in many parts of the world, but this phenomenon of 'regular' starvation has to be distinguished from violent outbursts of famines. It isn't just regular starvation that one sees in 436 BC, when thousands of starving Romans 'threw themselves into the Tiber'; or in Kashmir in AD 918, when 'one could scarcely see the water of Vitasta [Jhelum] entirely covered as the river was with corpses'; or in 1333–7 in China, when—we are told—four million people died in one region only; or in 1770 in India, when the best estimates point to ten million deaths; or in 1845–51 in Ireland, when the potato famine killed about one-fifth of the total Irish population and led to the emigration of a comparable number.[1] While there is quite a literature on how to 'define' famines,[2] one can very often

[1] For some absorbing accounts of the phenomenon of famines in different parts of the world and some comparative analysis, see Mallory (1926), Ghosh (1944), Woodham-Smith (1962), Masefield (1963), Stephens (1966), Bhatia (1967), Blix, Hofvander and Vahlquist (1971), Johnson (1973), Aykroyd (1974), Hussein (1976), Tudge (1977), and Alamgir (1978b, 1980), among a good many other studies. Early accounts of famines in the Indian subcontinent can be found in Kautilya (*circa* 320 BC) and Abul Fazl (1592), among other documents.

[2] A few of the many definitions: 'On balance it seems clear that any satisfactory definition of famine must provide that the food shortage is either widespread or extreme if not both, and that the degree of extremity is best measured by human mortality from starvation' (Masefield, 1963, pp. 3–4). 'An extreme and protracted shortage of food

diagnose it—like a flood or a fire—even without being armed with a precise definition.[3]

In distinguishing between starvation and famine, it is not my intention here to attribute a sense of deliberate harming to the first absent in the second, as intended by the Irish American Malone in Bernard Shaw's *Man and Superman*:

Malone: Me father died of starvation in the black 47. Maybe you've heard of it?
Violet: The Famine?
Malone: No, the starvation. When a country is full o food and exporting it, there can be no famine. Me father was starved dead; and I was starved out to America in me mother's arms.[4]

The history of famines as well as of regular hunger is full of blood-boiling tales of callousness and malevolence—and I shall have something to say on this—but the distinction between starvation and famine used in this work does not relate to this. Starvation is used here in the wider sense of people going without adequate food, while famine is a particularly virulent manifestation of its causing widespread death; that is, I intend to use the two words in their most common English sense.[5]

4.2 THE TIME CONTRAST

In analysing starvation in general, it is important to make clear distinctions between three different issues. (1) *lowness of the typical level* of food consumption; (2) *declining trend* of food consumption;

resulting in widespread and persistent hunger, evidenced by loss of body weight and emaciation and increase in the death rate caused either by starvation or disease resulting from the weakened condition of the population' (Johnson, 1973, p. 58). 'In statistical term, it can be defined as a severe shortage of food accompanied by a significant increase in the local or regional death rate' (Mayer, 1975). 'Famine is an economic and social phenomenon characterised by the widespread lack of food resources which, in the absence of outside aid, leads to death of those affected' (UNRISD, 1975). I hope the reader has got the point.

[3] The definitional exercise is more interesting in providing a pithy description of what happens in situations clearly diagnosed as one of famine than in helping us to do the diagnosis—the traditional function of a definition. For example, Gale Johnson's (1973) pointer to disease in addition to starvation directs our attention to an exceptionally important aspect of famines (see Chapter 8 and Appendix D below). See also Morris (1974).

[4] G. Bernard Shaw, *Man and Superman*, Penguin, Harmondsworth, 1946, p. 196.

[5] The meaning of 'starve' as 'to cause to die, to kill, destroy' is described by *The Shorter Oxford English Dictionary* as 'obsolete' (with its latest recorded use being placed in 1707), but—of course—the meaning 'to cause to perish of hunger' or 'to keep scantily supplied with food' survives, and—alas—has much descriptive usage in the modern world.

and (3) *sudden collapse* of the level of food consumption. Famine is chiefly a problem of the third kind, and while it can— obviously—be helped by the first two features, it often does not work that way.

For example, in dealing with the trend of foodgrains availability in India in this century, S. R. Sen (1971) notes the following dichotomy between the trend of the moving average and the level of the minimal values (pp. 2–3):

A study of these data shows that during the first 24 years of the century foodgrains production increased at an average annual rate of 0.81 per cent per annum on the average, the trough points showed a declining trend of 0.14 per cent per annum on the average and there was a growing divergence. Thus, while the foodgrains production showed a rising trend, the instability was also on the increase. . . . The next 24 years, however, presented a completely different picture. During this period, foodgrains production showed a declining trend of 0.02 per cent per annum on the average, in spite of the fact that droughts turned out to be relatively moderate and less frequent. In contrast with the previous period, while the peak points reached showed a declining trend of 0.04 per cent, the trough points recorded a rising trend of 0.10 per cent per annum on the average and the two were converging.

A similar contrast has been suggested for Japan in comparing food consumption in the Meiji period with that in the Tokugawa period by Nakamura (1966).[6] He argues:

In fact food consumption picture of the Tokugawa period (and earlier) is that of periodic food shortages and famine owing to the high incidence of natural calamities. In view of this, it is even possible that the Japanese *ate more regularly but consumed less food on the average* in the later Meiji era than they did in late Tokugawa before food imports became available to relieve shortages.[7]

There is, of course, nothing in the least bit surprising about a rising trend being accompanied by bigger fluctuations, or a falling trend going with greater stability.[8] Even more obvious is

[6] The underlying empirical generalisation about trends of food availability has been, however, the subject of some controversy. See also Ohkawa (1957) and Ohkawa and Rosovsky (1973).

[7] Nakamura (1966), p. 100; italics added. See also a similar contrast in Eric Hobsbawm's analysis of the British standard of living during 1790–1850 (Hobsbawm, 1957, especially p. 46).

[8] The empirical issue as to whether the quoted views of the Indian or Japanese economic history are correct is, of course, a different question.

the fact that a rising trend need not *eliminate* big fluctuations. Indeed, there are good reasons to think that the trend of food availability per head in recent years has been a rising one in most parts of the world,[9] but nevertheless acute starvation has occurred quite often, and there is some evidence of intensification of famine threats.[10] While this is partly a problem of distribution of food between different groups in a nation—an issue to which I shall turn presently—there is also the time contrast (in particular, the problem of sharp falls against a generally rising trend). Famines can strike even when regular starvation is on firm decline.

The food crisis of 1972 is a global example of this time contrast. Colin Tudge (1977) describes the development in dramatic terms:

The 1960s brought good harvests, augmented by the Third World's 'green revolution', based on American-developed dwarf strains of wheat and rice. The world's food problem was not shortage, apparently, but over-production, leading to low prices and agricultural depression. The US took land out of production, and in the early 1970s both the US and Canada ran down their grain stores. Then the bad weather of 1972 brought dismal harvests to the USSR, China, India, Australia and the Sahel countries south of Sahara. Russia bought massively in the world grain markets before others, including the US, realized what was happening. By mid-1974 there was only enough grain left in store to feed the world's population for three-and-a-half weeks; terrifying brinkmanship.[11]

In all this the focus has been on the *total* availability of food—for the nation as a whole, or even for the world as a whole. But exactly similar contrasts hold for food availability to a particular section of a given community. A sudden collapse of the command of a group over food can go against a rising trend (or against a typically high level of food consumption). Problems of (i) existence of much regular starvation, (ii) worsening trend of regular starvation, and (iii) sudden outbreak of acute starvation, are quite distinct. While they can accompany each other, they need not, and often do not, do so.

[9] See FAO (1979). See also Aziz (1975), p. 116, Table 2; and Sinha (1976a), p. 6, Table 1.
[10] See Blix, Hofvander and Vahlquist (1971); UNRISD (1975, 1978); Aziz (1975); and Tudge (1977)
[11] Tudge (1977), p. 2.

4.3 THE GROUP CONTRAST

While famines involve fairly widespread acute starvation, there is no reason to think that it will affect all groups in the famine-affected nation. Indeed, it is by no means clear that there has ever occurred a famine in which all groups in a country have suffered from starvation, since different groups typically do have very different commanding powers over food, and an over-all shortage brings out the contrasting powers in stark clarity.

There has been some speculation as to whether such a comprehensive famine was not observed in India in 1344–5 (see Walford 1878, and Alamgir 1980, p. 14). There is indeed some evidence for this famine being a very widespread one. In fact, the authoritative *Encyclopaedia Britannica* saw the famine as one in which even 'the Mogul emperor was unable to obtain the necessaries for his household' (Eleventh Edition, 1910–1, vol. X, p. 167). This is most unlikely since the Mogul empire was not established in India until 1526! But it is also doubtful that the Tughlak king then in power—Mohammad Bin Tughlak—was really unable to obtain his household necessities, since he had the resources to organize one of the most illustrous famine relief programmes, including remitting taxes, distributing cash, and opening relief centres for the distribution of cooked food (see Loveday, 1916). One has to be careful about anecdotal history, just as a companion volume of the same Encyclopaedia points out: 'the idea that Alfred, during his retreat at Athenley, was a helpless fugitive rests upon the foolish legend of the cakes'. This is, however, not to deny that some famines are much more widespread than others, and Alamgir is certainly right that the Dutch famine during 1944 was very widely shared by the Dutch population.[12]

The importance of inter-group distributional issues rests not merely in the fact that an over-all shortage may be very unequally shared by different groups,[13] but also in the recognition that some groups can suffer acute absolute deprivation

[12] See Aykroyd (1974), Chapter 10, and Stein, Susser, Saenger and Marolla (1975).
[13] One contrast that has received much professional attention recently is that between urban and rural population (see particularly Lipton, 1977). This contrast is indeed relevant to conflicts implicit in some famines (see for example Chapter 6 below), but there are other, more specialized, group conflicts which deserve more attention (some of these contrasts are taken up in Chapters 6, 7, 8, and 9).

even when there is no over-all shortage. There is no reason whatsoever to think that the food consumption of different groups must vary in the same *direction* (even if by different proportions and amounts), and in later chapters cases will be encountered in which different groups' fortunes moved sharply in opposite directions.

Chapter 5

The Entitlement Approach

5.1 ENDOWMENT AND EXCHANGE

The entitlement approach to starvation and famines concentrates on the ability of people to command food through the legal means available in the society, including the use of production possibilities, trade opportunities, entitlements *vis-à-vis* the state, and other methods of acquiring food. A person starves *either* because he does not have the ability to command enough food, *or* because he does not use this ability to avoid starvation. The entitlement approach concentrates on the former, ignoring the latter possibility. Furthermore, it concentrates on those means of commanding food that are legitimized by the legal system in operation in that society. While it is an approach of some generality, it makes no attempt to include all possible influences that can in principle cause starvation, for example illegal tranfers (e.g. looting), and choice failures (e.g. owing to inflexible food habits).

Ownership of food is one of the most primitive property rights, and in each society there are rules governing this right. The entitlement approach concentrates on each person's entitlements to commodity bundles including food, and views starvation as resulting from a failure to be entitled to a bundle with enough food.

In a fully directed economy, each person i may simply get a particular commodity bundle which is assigned to him. To a limited extent this happens in most economies, e.g. to residents of old people's homes or of mental hospitals. Typically, however, there is a menu—possibly wide—to choose from. E_i is the entitlement set of person i in a given society, in a given situation, and it consists of a set of alternative commodity bundles, any one of which the person can decide to have. In an economy with private ownership and exchange in the form of trade (exchange with others) and production (exchange with nature), E_i can be characterized as depending on two parameters, viz. the *endowment* of the person (the ownership bundle) and the *exchange entitlement mapping* (the function that specifies the set of alternative commodity bundles that the person can command respectively for each endowment bundle).[1] For example, a peasant has his land, labour power, and a few other resources, which together make up his endowment. Starting from that endowment he can produce a bundle of food that will be his. Or, by selling his labour power, he can get a wage and with that buy commodities, including food. Or he can grow some cash crops and sell them to buy food and other commodities. There are many other possibilities. The set of all such available commodity bundles in a given economic situation is the exchange entitlement of his endowment. The exchange entitlement *mapping* specifies the exchange entitlement set of alternative commodity bundles respectively for each endowment bundle. The formal relations are analysed in Appendix A.

The exchange entitlement mapping, or E-mapping for short, will depend on the legal, political, economic and social characteristics of the society in question and the person's position in it. Perhaps the simplest case in terms of traditional economic theory is one in which the endowment bundle can be exchanged in the market at fixed relative prices for any bundle costing no more, and here the exchange entitlement will be a traditional 'budget set'.

Bringing in production will make the E-mapping depend on production opportunities as well as trade possibilities of resources and products. It will also involve legal rights to apportioning the product, e.g. the capitalist rule of the 'entrepreneur' owning the produce. Sometimes the social conventions governing these rights can be very complex indeed—for example those governing the rights of migrant members of peasant families to a share of the peasant output (see Sen, 1975).

Social security provisions are also reflected in the E-mapping, such as the right to unemployment benefit if one fails to find a job, or the right to income supplementation if one's income would fall otherwise below a certain specified level. And so are employment guarantees when they exist—as they do in some socialist economies—giving one the option to sell one's labour power to the government at a minimum price. E-mappings will depend also on provisions of taxation.

[1] Formally, an exchange entitlement mapping $E_i(.)$ transforms an endowment vector of commodities x into a set of alternative availability vectors of commodities $E_i(x)$.

Let the set of commodity bundles, each of which satisfies person i's minimum food requirement, be F_i. Person i will be forced to starve because of unfavourable entitlement relations if and only if he is not entitled to any member of F_i given his endowment and his exchange entitlement mapping. The 'starvation set' S_i of endowments consists of those endowment bundles such that the exchange entitlement sets corresponding to them contain no bundles satisfying his minimum food requirements.[2]

5.2 STARVATION AND ENTITLEMENT FAILURES

Person i can be plunged into starvation if his endowment collapses into the starvation set S_i either through a fall in the endowment bundle, or through an unfavourable shift in the exchange entitlement mapping. The distinction is illustrated in Figure 5.1 in terms of the simple case of pure trade involving only two commodities, food and non-food. The exchange entitlement mapping is taken to assume the simple form of constant price exchange. With a price ratio p and a minimum food requirement OA, the starvation set S_i is given by the region OAB. If the endowment vector is $\mathbf{x}$, the person is in a position to avoid starvation. This ability can fail either (1) through a lower endowment vector, e.g. $\mathbf{x}^*$, or (2) through a less favourable exchange entitlement mapping, e.g. that given by p^*, which would make the starvation set OAC.

It is easy to see that starvation can develop for a certain group of people as its endowment vector collapses, and there are indeed many accounts of such endowment declines on the part of sections of the poor rural population in developing countries through alienation of land, sale of livestock, etc. (see, for example, Griffin, 1976, 1978; Feder, 1977; and Griffin and Khan, 1977).[3] Shifts in exchange entitlement mappings are rather less palpable, and more difficult to trace, but starvation can also develop with *unchanged* asset ownership through move-

[2] For formalities, see Appendix A. For applications see Chapters 6–10 and Appendix B. See also Sen (1976c, 1977b, 1979c); Griffin (1978); Hay (1978b); Ghosh (1979); Penny (1979); Shukla (1979); Seaman and Holt (1980); and Heyer (1980).

[3] Asset loss affects not merely the ability to exchange the asset directly with food, but also the ability to borrow against one's future earning power. Given the nature of the capital markets, substantial borrowing is typically impossible without tangible securities. The limitations of the capital markets often constitute an important aspect of famine conditions.

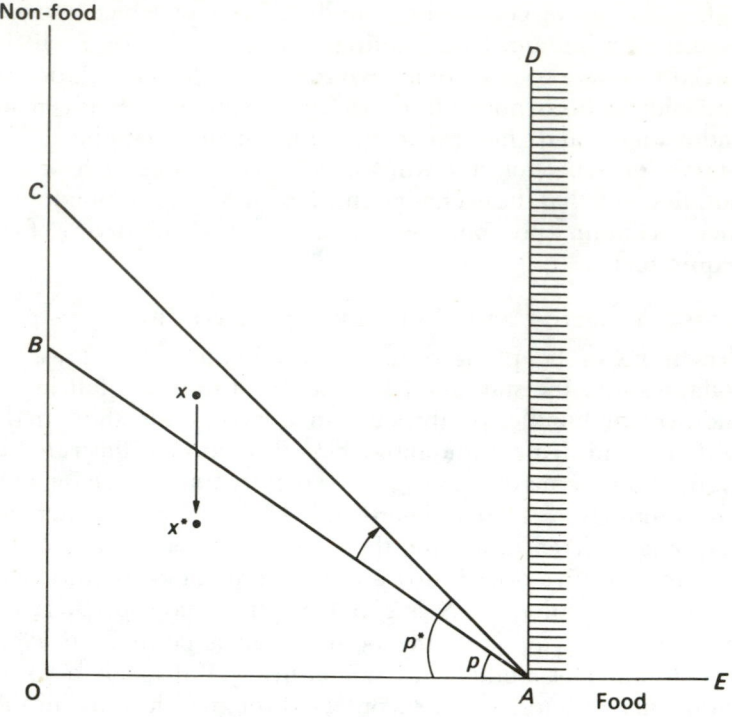

Fɪɢ. 5.1 Illustration of Endowment and Entitlement

ments of exchange entitlement mapping.[4] This would be impossible only if the endowment vector itself contained enough food, for example, in figure 5.1, if it belonged to the region DAE. The characteristics of commodities in most people's endowment bundles rule out this possibility.

5.3 LIMITATIONS OF THE ENTITLEMENT APPROACH

Before proceeding to the use of the entitlement approach, a few of the limitations may be briefly noted. First, there can be

---

[4] Shifts in E-mapping may arise from different sources, e.g. growth of unemployment, changes in relative prices and terms of trade, variations in social security (see Chapter 1 and Appendix A). For an insightful analysis of the role of terms of trade in economic development, see Mitra (1977).

ambiguities in the specification of entitlements. Even in capitalist market economies, entitlements may not be well defined in the absence of a market-clearing equilibrium,[5] and in pre-capitalist formations there can be a good deal of vagueness on property rights and related matters.[6] In many cases the appropriate characterization of entitlements may pose problems,[7] and in some cases it may well be best characterized in the form of 'fuzzy' sets and related structures— taking precise note of the vagueness involved.[8] In empirical studies of actual famines the question of precision is compromised by data problems as well, and the focus here will be not on characterizing entitlements with pretended exactitude, but on studying shifts in some of the main ingredients of entitlements. Big shifts in such ingredients can be decisive in causing entitlement failures, even when there is some 'fuzziness' in the entitlement relations.

Second, while entitlement relations concentrate on rights within the given legal structure in that society, some transfers involve violation of these rights, such as looting or brigandage. When such extra-entitlement transfers are important, the entitlement approach to famines will be defective. On the other hand, most recent famines seem to have taken place in societies with 'law and order', without anything 'illegal' about the processes leading to starvation. In fact, in guarding ownership rights against the demands of the hungry, the legal forces uphold entitlements; for example, in the Bengal famine of 1943 the people who died in front of well-stocked food shops protected by the state[9] were denied food because of *lack* of legal entitlement, and not because their entitlements were violated.[10]

[5] See Hicks (1939), Debreu (1959), and Arrow and Hahn (1971).

[6] There are also legal and economic ambiguities in an *open* 'black market' (see Dasgupta, 1950)

[7] There is also the critique by Ronald Dworkin (1977) of 'legal positivism', disputing the view of law as a set of 'rules', and emphasizing the role of 'principles, policies, and other sorts of standards' (p. 22), which are, of course, inherently more ambiguous.

[8] A similar problem arises from the ambiguity of values in economic planning, requiring 'range'—rather than 'point'—specification of shadow prices leading to partial orders (see Sen, 1975). Correspondingly here, the possible set of endowment vectors may be partitioned into three subsets, viz. definitely starvation set, definitely non-starvation set, and neither.

[9] See Ghosh (1944) and also Famine Inquiry Commission (1945a).

[10] Cf. 'A concept of law which allows the invalidity of law to be distinguished from its immorality, enables us to see the complexity and variety of these separate issues' (Hart, 1961, p. 207).

Third, people's actual food consumption may fall below their entitlements for a variety of other reasons, such as ignorance, fixed food habits, or apathy.[11] In concentrating on entitlements, something of the total reality is obviously neglected in our approach, and the question is: how important are these ignored elements and how much of a difference is made by this neglect?

Finally, the entitlement approach focuses on starvation, which has to be distinguished from famine mortality, since many of the famine deaths—in some cases *most* of them—are caused by epidemics, which have patterns of their own.[12] The epidemics are, of course, induced partly by starvation but also by other famine characteristics, e.g. population movement, breakdown of sanitary facilities.

5.4 DIRECT AND TRADE ENTITLEMENT FAILURES

Consider occupation group j, characterized as having only commodity j to sell or directly consume. Let q_j be the amount of commodity j each member of group j can sell or consume, and let the price of commodity j be p_j. The price of food per unit is p_f. The maximum food entitlement of group j is F_j, given by $q_j p_j / p_f$, or $q_j a_j$, where a_j is occupation j's *food exchange rate* (p_j/p_f).

Commodity j may or may not be a *produced* commodity. The commodity that a labourer has to sell is labour power. It is his means of survival, just as commodities in the shape of baskets and jute are the means of survival of the basket-maker and the jute-grower, respectively.[13]

A special case arises when the occupation consists of being a producer of food, say rice, which is also what members of that

---

[11] Also, people sometimes choose to starve rather than sell their productive assets (see Jodha, 1975, for some evidence of this in Indian famines), and this issue can be accommodated in the entitlement approach using a relatively long-run formulation (taking note of future entitlements). There is also some tendency for asset markets to collapse in famine situations, making the reward from asset sales rather puny.

[12] See Appendix D for a study of the pattern of mortality in the Great Bengal Famine. See also McAlpin (1976).

[13] In general, it may be necessary to associate several different commodities, rather than one, with the same occupation, but there is not much difficulty in redefining q_j and p_j appropriately.

[14] Given the selective nature of calamities such as floods and droughts, affecting one group but not another, it will be sometimes convenient to partition the occupation f into a number of subgroups (f, i) for famine analysis. With $q_{f,i}$ the food grown by subgroup (f, i), we have: $F_{f,i} = q_{f,i}$.

occupation live on. In this case $p_j = p_f$, and $a_f = 1$. Thus $F_f = q_f.$[14]

It is worth emphasizing that this drastically simple modelling of reality makes sense only in helping us to focus on some important parameters of famine analysis; it does not compete with the more general structure outlined earlier (and more formally in Appendix A). Furthermore, these simplifications will be grossly misleading in some contexts, for example in analysing entitlements in an industrialized economy, because of the importance of raw materials, intermediate products, asset holdings, etc. Even in applying this type of structure to analyse rural famines in developing countries, care is needed that the distortions are not too great.

For any group j to start starving *because of* an entitlement failure, F_j must decline, since it represents the *maximum* food entitlement. F_j can fall either because one has produced less food for own consumption, or because one can obtain less food through trade by exchanging one's commodity for food. The former will be called a 'direct entitlement failure', and the latter a 'trade entitlement failure'. The former can arise for food-producing groups, while the latter can occur for others (i.e. for those who sell their commodities to buy food), because of a fall in a_j, or a fall in q_j. Such a fall in q_j can occur either owing to an autonomous production decline (e.g. a cash crop being destroyed by a drought), or owing to insufficiency of demand (e.g. a labourer being involuntarily unemployed, or a basket-maker cutting down the output as the demand for baskets slackens).

It is, in fact, possible for a group to suffer both direct entitlement failure and trade entitlement failure, since the group may produce a commodity that is both directly consumed and exchanged for some other food. For example, the Ethiopian pastoral nomad both eats the animal products directly and also sells animals to buy foodgrains (thereby making a net gain in calories), on which he is habitually dependent.[15] Similarly, a Bengali fisherman does consume some fish, though for his survival he is dependent on grain-calories which he obtains at a favourable calorie exchange rate by selling fish—a luxury food for most Bengalis.[16]

[15] See Chapter 7.
[16] See Chapter 6.

Chapter 6
The Great Bengal Famine

6.1 A BRIEF OUTLINE

The official Famine Inquiry Commission reporting on the Bengal famine of 1943 put its death toll at 'about 1.5 million'.[1] W. R. Aykroyd, who as a member of the Commission was primarily responsible for the estimation, has said recently: 'I now think it was an under-estimate, especially in that it took little account of roadside deaths, but not as gross an under-estimate as some critics of the Commission's report, who preferred three to four million, declared it to be' (Aykroyd, 1974, p. 77). In fact, it can be shown that the Commission's own method of calculation does lead to a figure around three million deaths, and there will be an occasion to go into this demographic issue in Appendix D. But for the present purpose it does not really matter which of the estimates we accept. Our chief concern here is with the causation of the Bengal famine, and in particular with the role of food supply and that of exchange entitlements in the genesis of the famine.[2]

First, a bit of background. There are three rice crops in Bengal: (1) *aman*, sown in May and June, harvested in November and December (the winter crop); (2) *aus*, sown around April and harvested in August and September (the autumn crop); and (3) *boro*, planted in November and harvested in February and March (the spring crop). The winter crop is by far the most important, and the respective shares of the three crops during the five years 1939–43 were: 73, 24, and 3 per cent. In 1942 the autumn crop was a little less than normal (97 per cent of the preceding four years), and the winter crop quite a bit less (83 per cent of the preceding four years). This was largely the result of a cyclone in October, followed by torrential rain in some parts of Bengal and a subsequent fungus disease. Further, the Japanese occupation of Burma in 1942—Rangoon fell on 10 March 1942—cut off rice imports from there, which affected the

[1] Famine Inquiry Commission, India (1945a), pp. 109–10.
[2] This chapter relies heavily on an earlier paper, viz. Sen (1977b).

supply to Bengal. Since the famine hit Bengal in 1943, it is quite natural, in view of the cyclone, flooding, fungus diseases, the disruption of the war, and the loss of Burma rice, that its primary cause should be seen in 'the serious shortage in the total supply of rice available for consumption in Bengal as compared with the total supply normally available' (Famine Inquiry Commission, India, 1945a, p. 77). This thesis will be examined presently.

FIG. 6.1 Bengal, 1943

The wholesale price of rice, which had been between Rs. 13 and Rs. 14 per 'maund' (about 82.3 lbs.) on 11 December 1942, rose to Rs. 21 by 12 March 1943 and to above Rs. 30 by 21 May; by 20 August it had risen to Rs. 37 (see Table 6.1). Because of a government order fixing a maximum price, quotations for rice transactions are difficult to obtain from September 1943

TABLE 6.1

Wholesale Price of Rice in Calcutta, 1942 and 1943
(rupees per maund)

Date	Ballam no. 1 Price (Rs.)	Index	Kalma no. 1 Price (Rs.)	(mill-cleaned) Index
1941				
19 December	7.00–7.25	100	(not quoted)	
1942				
16 January	6.25–6.50	90	(not quoted)	
20 February	6.13–6.38	88	(not quoted)	
20 March	6.13–6.38	88	(not quoted)	
17 April	6.25	88	(not quoted)	
15 May	6.25–6.38	89	(not quoted)	
19 June	8.00	112	(not quoted)	
31 July	7.75–8.00	111	(not quoted)	
21 August	9.25	130	(not quoted)	
18 September	9.88–10.38	142	(not quoted)	
30 October	9.88–10.38	142	(not quoted)	
13 November	9.25–9.75	133	(not quoted)	
11 December	13.00–14.00	190	(not quoted)	
1943				
15 January	14.00–15.00	204	(not quoted)	
12 February	14.00–15.00	204	(not quoted)	
12 March	21.00	295	(not quoted)	
16 April	(not quoted)		22.00–23.00	306
21 May	30.00–31.00	428	31.00	428
18 June	(not quoted)		32.00–33.00	442
16 July	(not quoted)		32.00–33.00	442
20 August	(not quoted)		37.00	503

Notes

1 The price quotations are taken from the respective numbers of the *Indian Trade Journal*, a weekly publication, for 1942 and 1943.

2 Price data are given in the *Indian Trade Journal* typically either for Ballam no. 1 variety or for Kalma no. 1 variety, and very rarely for both. The index for Ballam no. 1 is constructed by setting the price on 19 December 1941 as 100. Since there is no quotation for Kalma no. 1 at that time, the index value of Kalma is equated to that of Ballam on 21 May 1943, when *both* prices are reported *for the first time* in the period covered. This provides the base for the Kalma index.

onwards, but there are non-official reports of further rises, especially in retail markets, such as in October that rice was being sold in Chittagong at Rs. 80 per maund (see *The Statesman*, 5 November 1943; Bhatia, 1967, p. 323), and in Dacca at Rs. 105 per maund (see Ghosh, 1944, p. 42).

The economic experience of Bengal leading to and during the famine can be split into three phases:

Phase I: from the beginning of 1942 to March 1943;

Phase II: from March 1943 to November 1943;

Phase III: From November 1943 through most of 1944.

The death rate reached its peak only in Phase III, but the most acute period of starvation had by then passed; epidemics were raging in a famine-devastated country. Phase II is when starvation death reached its peak. In contrast, what I am calling Phase I is usually taken to be a period when the famine had not yet begun. In a sense that view is correct, since starvation deaths were still relatively rare, but the economic distress that paved the way for the famine had already gripped a substantial part of the population.

The famine revealed itself first in the districts away from Calcutta, starting early in 1943. Its progress can be watched in the reports of the commissioners and district officers all over the province. Beginning with descriptions of 'hunger marches organized by communists' on 28 December 1942, a selection of the reports include: 'people having to go without food' (10 February); 'indications of distress among local people' (27 February); 'acute distress prevails' (26 March); 'crime -against property increasing and paddy looting cases have become frequent' (28 March); 'major economic catastrophe apprehended' (27 April); 'economic conditions approach a crisis' (13 May); 'bands of people moving about in search of rice' (12 June); 'deaths in streets' (12 June); 'town filled with thousands of beggars who are starving' (17 July); 'passing through the most acute stage of distress' (10 August); 'deaths still occurring' (9 September); 'disposal of dead bodies . . . a problem' (27 September); 'supplies arriving but no hope of saving those who are starving' (25 October).[3] Mortality reached its peak only in December 1943 and stayed up for quite a while longer, but this was mostly the result of famine-induced epidemics, e.g. of

[3] See Famine Inquiry Commission (1945a), Appendix VI.

cholera, malaria, and smallpox. Death directly from starvation and 'famine diarrhoea' had passed its peak in late summer and autumn of 1943.[4]

The experience was quite different in Calcutta. The official policy was based on the firm conviction that 'the maintenance of essential food supplies to the industrial area of Calcutta must be ranked on a very high priority among their [the government's] war time obligations', and as early as August 1942 the Bengal government had explained to the Bengal Chamber of Commerce that as far as Calcutta was concerned the government promised to do 'all in their power to create conditions under which essential supplies may be obtainable in adequate quantities and at reasonable prices'.[5] The 'Bengal Chamber of Commerce Foodstuffs Scheme', guaranteeing essential items of food to the grain shops of industrial concerns connected with the Chamber, came into existence with the government's help in August 1942; it covered 620,000 employees by December of that year. The other chambers of commerce developed similar schemes with government backing, covering another 170,000 employees. Public arrangements for provision of supplies to those employed by the central and provincial governments, the railways, the Port Trust, and the Calcutta Corporation covered another 300,000 employees. These schemes guaranteed freedom from starvation to more than a million employees and their dependants. In addition, 'controlled shops' were started in Calcutta in August and September 1942, supplemented in 1943 by a scheme of 'approved markets' by which government stocks were made available to selected private shops for sale to the public. The government helped to feed Calcutta through three successive schemes of procurement at controlled prices between December 1942 and March 1943, but since they did not prove to be very successful, free purchase at market prices was resumed in the districts from March 1943, leading to very sharp rises in the price of rice in the districts.[6]

---

[4] See Sen (1977b, 1980b). An illuminating and insightful account of the Bengal famine in the economic, social and cultural perspective of Bengal has recently been provided by Greenough (1979).

[5] Famine Inquiry Commission (1945a), p. 30.

[6] See *The Calcutta Gazette* Supplements over this period; also Famine Inquiry Commission (1945a), p. 40.

Calcutta saw the famine mainly in the form of masses of rural destitutes, who trekked from the districts into the city; by July 1943 the streets were full. To start with, relief was confined to personal charity and to kitchens organized by charitable organizations, but by August relief for destitutes in Calcutta was accepted as an official policy. While cautious parsimony prevailed—meals were given 'at the same time of day in all kitchens, to prevent destitutes from getting more than one meal'[7]—there is little doubt that a destitute who had found his way into Calcutta had a much better chance of survival than anywhere else in Bengal. Nevertheless, since the relief offered was quite inadequate, unattended dead bodies could be found everywhere in the city—3,363 had to be disposed of by relief organizations in October alone.[8]

The number of starving and sick destitutes in Calcutta was estimated to be 'at least 100,000' in October. A decision was taken by the end of the month to remove the destitutes from the city. The Bengal Destitute Persons (Repatriation and Relief) Ordinance, passed on 28 October, was a rather controversial piece of legislation, since it was alleged that 'repatriation' was rather more firmly achieved than 'relief' in the many 'destitute homes' and 'camps' set up outside Calcutta.[9] For Calcutta, however, the worst of the famine was over, and the death rate came down sharply.[10] In fact, the situation in the districts also eased as some relief reached there directly, and with the harvesting of a good autumn crop and an outstanding winter one. The continued increase in the death rates in the districts was largely the result of famine-induced epidemics (see Appendix D).

6.2 A FOOD SUPPLY CRISIS?

The most common approach to famines is to propose explanations in terms of *food availability decline* (FAD). This FAD approach has been extensively used to analyse and explain the Bengal famine. The Famine Inquiry Commission's view that the primary cause of the famine was 'a serious shortage in the total supply of rice available for consumption in Bengal' provides the

[7] Famine Inquiry Commission (1945a), p. 71.
[8] See Ghosh (1944), pp. 119–20.
[9] See Famine Inquiry Commission (1945a), p. 71–2.
[10] See Ghosh (1944), p. 121.

standard explanation of the famine. As Blyn notes in his authoritative account of 'agricultural trends in India' (1966), referring to the Report of the Famine Inquiry Commission and to the *Census of India 1951*:[11] 'In 1942–43 cyclones and floods reduced the Bengal rice crop by about a third; this, coupled with the absence of exports from Japanese-controlled Burma, and inadequate relief, led to famines, epidemics (malaria, cholera and smallpox), aggravated by widespread starvation' (p. 98).

But is this explanation really supported by the facts—even by data to be found in the body of the *Report* of the Famine Inquiry Commission itself? First, consider what the Commission calls the 'current supply' for a given year, obtained by adding the winter crop of the *preceding* year (harvested in December, and usually sold in the following three months) to the spring and autumn crops of the year in question, plus net imports. Calculated from data given in the *Report* of the Famine Inquiry Commission (1945a), these are presented in columns (2), (3), and (4) of Table 6.2 below. While 1943 was not a very good year in terms of crop availability, it was not by any means a disastrous year either. The current supply for 1943 was only about 5 per cent lower than the average of the preceding five years. It was, in fact, 13 per cent *higher* than in 1941, and there was, of course, no famine in 1941.

However, certain further calculations are needed before the FAD view can be rejected.

Correction 1: Adjustment of official production estimates

The official estimates of agricultural production in India have been criticized for a long time, e.g. by P. C. Mahalanobis. Among recent contributions, Blyn (1966) provides fairly comprehensive estimates of agricultural trends in India, though yield data are not given separately for Bengal, only for 'Greater Bengal', including Bengal, Bihar, and Orissa. But the picture of a better food production situation in 1943 compared with 1941 is confirmed (see his Appendices 3A and 4C). Even the rice yield *per acre*, which is given separately for the Bengal province (Appendix Table 7A), is shown to have been higher in the year 1942–3 than in 1940–1, despite the fact that the acreage in 1942–3 was known to be much higher than in 1940–1.

[11] *Census of India*, 1951, vol. 1, pp. 291–92. See also the *Census of Pakistan*, 1951, vol. 3; and Bhatia's well-known book on Indian famines (1967), pp. 231–4.

Some corrections to the official estimates were carried out by the Famine Inquiry Commission itself, on the lines suggested by Mahalanobis and others. These included corrections also to the trade data, to increase coverage of 'movements across the frontier by road or by country-boat'. The Commission's 'adjusted' figures from their Statement III (p. 215) are presented in columns (5) and (6) in Table 6.2 below. Once again, the 1943 figure for current supply is not exceptionally low, and is higher than that for 1941.

Correction 2: Changes in wheat imports

While rice is by far the dominant food in Bengal, wheat is also consumed in considerable amounts, so that foodgrains availability should reflect variations in both rice and wheat. Very little wheat is grown in Bengal, but a fair amount is imported. The net imports of wheat and wheat flour into Bengal by rail and river-borne trade for 1938 to 1943 are calculated from *Accounts Relating to the Inland (Rail and Riverborne) Trade of India*, a then-current monthly publication of the Department of Commercial Intelligence and Statistics, Government of India.[12] These statistics do not, however, include road-based trade. The Famine Inquiry Commission's (1945a) figure of net arrivals in Bengal in 1943 (p. 54) is 36 per cent higher than the rail and river net imports, and its statement that in the 'five years ending 1941–42, [Bengal] imported from outside the province an average of 21,000 tons a month' (p. 3) makes the total for this period 33 per cent higher than the total of the rail and river net imports. To cover the gaps in the trade statistics from the rail and river data, these amounts have been raised by 36 per cent to get the total net imports of wheat into Bengal. This is almost certainly an overestimate for 1941 *vis-à-vis* 1943, but this is an acceptable bias as it favours the thesis we are rejecting.

The rice and wheat current supply figures are given in column (7) together with indices based on 1941 = 100 in column (8) in Table 6.2 below. The supply in 1943 was 11 per cent higher than in 1941.

---

[12] The figures for Calcutta are given separately from Bengal in these *Accounts* and the net figures presented here are computed as 'imports into Bengal' plus 'imports into Calcutta', less 'exports out of Bengal' and 'exports out of Calcutta'. Note also that 'wheat' and 'wheat flour' are given separately and have to be added together for each month.

Correction 3: Per capita supply

Since population of Bengal was growing over this period, the availability figure must be scaled down correspondingly to arrive at an index of *per capita* availability. The annual rate of *natural increase* in population in West Bengal was calculated to be 0.46 per cent per year during 1941–50 in the *Census of India* 1951 (vol. VI, part 1B, p. 2). But this is an underestimate for our period since the decade average reflects the impact of the famine itself; also, the 1941 figure was acknowledged to have been overstated owing to excessive registration of both the Hindu and Muslim communities to exaggerate their respective strengths in pre-partition India. A figure of 1 per cent per year is, however, a reasonably safe overestimate, and it is chosen here with a bias *in favour* of the thesis to be rejected. In the last column of Table 6.2, the *per capita* indices of food availability (rice and wheat) are presented with an assumed population growth of 1 per cent per year, again with 1941 being taken as 100. The *per capita* availability index for 1943 is higher by about 9 per cent than that for 1941.

Correction 4: Late availability of imported food in 1943

It can be argued that the availability of foodgrains was particularly bad in the earlier part of 1943; imports of rice and wheat were rather lower then and rose sharply in the last quarter of 1943. While the death rate seems to have reached its peak only in December 1943, there is evidence that starvation was at its peak in the third quarter of 1943.

During the last quarter of 1943, Bengal imported 100 thousand tons of rice (as opposed to an average of 55 thousand tons per quarter earlier in the year), and 176 thousand tons of wheat (as opposed to an earlier average of 54 thousand tons).[13] To bias the figures as much as possible against 1943, the extra amounts of rice and wheat imports during the last quarter of 1943 over the averages for the three previous quarters may be simply deducted from the total 1943 figure. This yields a current supply of rice and wheat of 9.068 million tons in 1943, with an index value of 109 of foodgrains supply and of 107 of *per capita* food grains availability. The former is, thus, fully 9 per cent higher and the latter nearly 7

---

[13] See Famine Inquiry Commission, India (1945a), p. 54.

TABLE 6.2
Foodgrains Availability in Bengal, 1938–43

Period	Output of rice (official estimates)	Net imports of rice (official estimates)	Current supply of rice (official)	Adjusted output of rice	Adjusted current supply of rice	Rice and wheat: adjusted current supply	Index of total foodgrains supply	Index of per capita foodgrains availability
	(1)	(2)	(3)	(4)	(5)	(6)	(7)	(8)
I Annual data								
1938	8.474	0.033	8.507	9.848	9.981	10.217	123	127
1939	7.922	0.382	8.304	9.114	9.596	9.787	118	120
1940	8.223	0.258	8.481	9.524	9.882	10.196	122	123
1941	6.768	0.223	6.991	7.631	7.954	8.332	100	100
1942	9.296	−0.102	9.194	10.776	10.774	10.947	131	130
1943	7.628	0.264	7.892	8.632	8.896	9.235	111	109
II Moving averages: 2 years								
1938–39			8.406		9.789	10.002	120	123
1939–40			8.393		9.739	9.992	120	122
1940–41			7.736		8.918	9.264	111	112
1941–42			8.093		9.364	9.640	116	115
1942–43			8.543		9.835	10.091	121	119
III Moving averages: 3 years								
1938–40			8.431		9.820	10.067	121	123
1939–41			7.925		9.144	9.438	113	114
1940–42			8.222		9.537	9.825	118	118
1941–43			8.026		9.208	9.505	114	113

Note
Unit = 1 million tons for columns (1)–(6); 1941 value = 100 for columns (7) and (8).

per cent larger than the values for 1941, for which no deduction whatsoever for the last quarter is made.

Correction 5: The so-called 'carry-over' of old rice

The figures presented so far take no account of the 'carry-over' stock from before the December harvest of the previous year. The Famine Inquiry Commission (1945a) thought that one cause of the famine was 'a shortage in the stock of old rice carried forward from 1942 to 1943' (p. 77). Indeed, it argued that the 'carry-over' was substantially smaller than in 1941 (p. 15), and gave this an important role in precipitating the famine (p. 77). But it gave no data on this, and as Mr M. Afzal Hussain, a member of the Commission, noted in his 'Minute', 'absolutely no data are available regarding the stock position of rice (or any other food grain) from month to month, or year to year, in Bengal, or any other part of India' (p. 179). The Commission's majority view that 'the carry-over at the beginning of 1943 was probably sufficient for about six weeks' requirements' (p.15) is just as much a pure surmise as is Husain's view that 'a carry-over in the sense of surplus over consumption must have vanished years ago' (p. 182).[14]

A reasonable way of looking at the carry-over problem in the absence of direct information is to examine moving averages over two or three years ending in the year in question. This will indicate the build-up to the year under examination. Moving averages for two-year and three-year periods are given in rows under II and III for the main columns in Table 6.2. As it happens, the two-year average ending in 1943 is the *highest* in the series for total foodgrains availability—hardly the build-up for a famine. The three-year average ending in 1943 takes a dip from the preceding average, but it is still of the same order of magnitude as the average ending in 1941—indeed, it is just a bit higher. For *per capita* figures, even with our deliberately raised population growth assumption, the three-year average ending in 1943 is only just a shade lower than that ending in 1941, and the two-year average ending in 1943 is, in fact, quite a bit higher than that for 1941.

[14] Husain's scepticism regarding carry-over was directed towards arguing that the *absolute* shortage in 1943 was larger that the Commission thought. The scepticism, however, naturally extends to *relative* positions in 1943 *vis-à-vis* 1941.

It seems safe to conclude that the disastrous Bengal famine was not the reflection of a remarkable over-all shortage of foodgrains in Bengal.[15]

6.3 EXCHANGE ENTITLEMENTS

The Bengal famine was essentially a rural phenomenon. Urban areas, especially Calcutta, substantially insulated from rising food prices by subsidized distribution schemes, saw it mainly in the form of an influx of rural destitutes. Is the growth of rural destitution understandable in terms of shifting exchange entitlements? In what follows exchange entitlements will be

---

[15] This general conclusion, presented earlier in Sen (1977b), has been questioned by Alamgir (1980), pp. 81–3. His arguments seem to centre on three points: (1) *regional* distribution: 'many districts suffered more relative to others' (p. 81); (2) *temporal* distribution: 'between April and October of 1943, many parts of Bengal witnessed a drastic shortfall in foodgrain availability per capita, which is not entirely captured by the aggregate annual index of per capita foodgrain availability calculated by Sen' (p. 82); and (3) *redefinition* of availability: 'foodgrain availability' can be 'defined broadly' so as to 'subsume the contending hypotheses presented by Sen and others' (p. 83). These are all important issues, but I do not believe they affect my general conclusion and the rejection of FAD. First, so far as (1) is concerned, while there were inter-regional variations, the famine was a comprehensive one affecting every region of Bengal. Alamgir (1980) himself notes that 'all subdivisions of Bangladesh were affected with various intensities' (p. 92), and this is true of all regions of the rest of Bengal also, as is readily checked from Table D. 4 below (Appendix D). Of course, food moved out of rural Bengal into urban areas, notably Calcutta, but that is not a question of over-all availability but of the operation of market and political forces affecting 'entitlements' and they were analysed as such in Sen (1977b), and are further analysed below. Second, so far as (2) is concerned, the reported shortage during April to October, i. e., during the famine, is of course a picture of shortage for some but not for others, and that is indeed how entitlement forces operate. How regions like Calcutta with greater market command pulled foodgrains out of the rest of Bengal over this period is a part of the economic analysis of the famine. The over-all availability did, of course, also have some variations over the year. But the annual availability figures calculated and presented in Sen (1977b), and here, include the *aman* harvest of December-January 1942–43 and excludes that of December-January 1943–44 (as already explained) and thus the issue of 'late arrival' would not arise with production. So far as import of foodgrains from *outside* Bengal is concerned, there was indeed 'late arrival' of central supplies, but that has already been corrected under 'Correction 4' above, without changing the general conclusion. Finally, the general conclusion I have put forward here (and in Sen, 1977b) deals with 'availability' as conventionally defined (e.g., as used in Malthus's analyses), viz., total available supply, rather than with marketing and disposal of the over-all availability. Alamgir (1980) is certainly right in emphasizing such issues as 'panic hoarding by producers, consumers and traders', 'favourable treatment of Calcutta as opposed to the rest of Bengal', 'inefficiency of the administration in storage and distribution of foodgrains to districts', 'delayed action since there was emphasis on a "wait and see" policy', etc. (pp. 81–3), but it seems unhelpful to lump them all together in some redefined figure of 'food availability'. FAD is a specific hypothesis—much used in the literature—and deserves to be examined on its own terms, rather than being rescued by *redefinition*. On its own terms, FAD stands rejected.

viewed in terms of entitlement to rice—the main source (indeed, the overwhelmingly dominant source) of calories to the population of Bengal. (It can be checked that the entitlement trends would be substantially similar if the exchange entitlements were calculated for other cereals, e.g. wheat.)

Consider first the class of agricultural labourers. While agricultural wage data are not available on a regular basis over this period, in the Final Report of the Famine Inquiry Commission (1945b) some indices were given for 'the province generally' (p. 484–5). These are presented in Table 6.3 below along with indices of exchange rates of agricultural labour *vis-à-vis* foodgrains. The wages, however, are given for financial years (April–March), while food prices refer to calendar years. Since wages earned are typically spent subsequently, and the main peak period of earning is around December, the exchange rates have been calculated with the wage in each financial year (ending in March) being related to the price of the calendar year (ending in the following December)—except for 1943–4, where the wage of the first six months of the financial year (April–September) has been related to the price in that calendar year.

TABLE 6.3

Indices of Exchange Rates between Agricultural Labour and Foodgrains in Bengal, 1939–44

Year	Wage index	Foodgrains price index	Index of exchange rate
1939–40 (1940)	100	100	100
1940–1 (1941)	110	109	101
1941–2 (1942)	115	160	72
1942–3 (1943)	125	385	32
1st half of 1943–4 (1943)	130	385	34

Source: Based on the data presented in Appendix IV of Famine Inquiry Commission (1945b).

This is not satisfactory, but no other information on this is given by the Commission.

A dramatic decline in the exchange rate against labour emerges from Table 6.3. It is quite clear that agricultural labour did not share in the inflationary rise enjoyed by many other sections of the community in the war economy of Bengal. Table 6.3 is, however, somewhat inconclusive, since the level of aggregation involved and the difference in the periods covered make the exchange rate indices difficult to interpret. One would have preferred a monthly series with data on wages and prices contemporary to each other. This the Famine Inquiry Commission did not provide.

While the Agro-Economic Research Centre for East India (1960) gives wage data in Birbhum from January 1939 to December 1941, and again from January 1946, the data for the intermediate period are not presented. But the sources of the wage data—the log books of the Sriniketan Farm and the Sriniketan Dairy—are still available for certain parts of the period, and using these it has been possible to obtain the local daily wage rate for male unskilled labour from September 1942 to January 1944. Treating the figures of unskilled male wage and the price of rice (no. 2 quality) for December 1941 as 100 respectively, the indices of both prices and of the exchange rate for labour against rice are given in Table 6.4.

While in September 1942 the wage stood where it was in December 1941 and the price of rice stood only a bit higher, a wild upsurge in the rice price followed thereafter, without a matching movement of the wage rate. In fact, while the price index of rice rose to 221 by November, the wage rate actually fell in absolute terms—against the usual seasonal pattern—and the index of the exchange rate declined to 38. After a partial recovery during the harvest months and immediately thereafter, the exchange rate fell some more and stood at 24 in May 1943. By July the index of the exchange rate had been below 30 for three months in succession.

In understanding the significance of the wage price data in Table 6.4, it is also worth bearing in mind that agricultural labourers tend to earn a great part of their incomes in the peak seasons of planting and harvesting of the main crop; and even if

TABLE 6.4

Daily Wage of Agricultural, Male, Unskilled Labour and the Price of Rice and Indices of Exchange Rates: Birbhum District around Bolpur

Mid-month	Rice (no. 2): Rs. per seer	Rice: price index	Wage: Rs. per day	Wage index	Exchange rate index: labour vis-à-vis rice
1941					
December	0.14	100	0.37	100	100
1942					
September	0.16	114	0.37	100	88
October	0.25	179	0.37	100	56
November	0.31	221	0.31	84	38
December	0.25	179	0.44	119	66
1943					
January	0.27	193	0.50	135	70
February	0.25	179	0.50	135	75
March	0.38	271	0.44	119	44
April	0.52	371	0.50	135	36
May	0.78	557	0.50	135	24
June	0.72	514	0.50	135	26
July	0.73	521	0.53	143	27
August	0.75	536	0.62	168	31
September	0.50	357	0.50	135	38
October	0.56	400	0.56	151	38
November	0.44	314	0.56	151	48
December	0.33	236	0.69	186	79
1944					
January	0.36	257	0.62	168	65

Sources: (1) Log books of contemporary wage records in Sriniketan Dairy and Sriniketan Farm;

(2) Log books of contemporary retail prices kept at the Agro-Economic Research Centre for East India;

(3) Agro-Economic Research Centre for East India (1960); the rice price in August 1943 is, however, corrected using (2). See also Sen (1977b).

wages had kept pace with the current rice prices, there would have been distress owing to the failure of the peak wages to anticipate the rise of food prices following the peak. The system of wage payments in Bengal had been geared to the experience of largely stable prices over the preceding decades, and there was no reflection at all in the peak wage rate of December–January of the tripling of rice prices that was to follow before the next peak in May–June.

We have rather little direct information on employment. The counter-seasonal decline in money wages in November 1942 and the low level of real wages through the winter harvesting period and post-harvest months may reflect some decline in employment. This would have been natural given the partial destruction of the winter crop of 1942 from cyclone, floods, and fungus disease. However, the lack of solid data on employment makes this part of the analysis rather speculative, even though there is some direct evidence of a fall in employment compared with the normal pattern (see Mahalanobis, Mukherjea and Ghosh, 1946, pp. 33–4; and Das, 1949, pp. 65–6).

Turning now from agricultural labour to other occupations, the exchange rates *vis-à-vis* rice of a number of commodities are presented in Table 6.5 based on retail prices in Bolpur in the Birbhum district, obtained from contemporary records. While some items, e.g. wheat flour, cloth, and mustard oil, more or less kept pace with rice in terms of price movements in Phase I, fish and bamboo umbrellas fell behind, and milk and haircuts declined sharply in value *vis-à-vis* rice.[16] In Phase II, these declines became more dramatic; for example, by summer the value of a haircut in units of rice had dropped to less than a fifth of what it was in December 1941.

As far as fish is concerned, after an early decline it seems to recover in the middle of Phase I (June–September 1942), to slump again. The temporary recovery was due partly to seasonal factors in the catching of fish (see June–September prices for other years in Agro-Economic Research Centre for East India, 1960, p. 49 onwards), but it may have also been connected with the general rise in fish price in Bengal as a consequence of the 'boat denial' policy carried through for military reasons. By Orders issued in May boats capable of carrying more than ten passengers were removed from a vast area of river-based Bengal to 'deny' them to the possibly-arriving Japanese, and this interfered with both river transport and fishing (see Famine Inquiry Commission, 1945a, pp. 26–7).[17] Thus the distress of

[16] See also the relative prices of other commodities covered in Agro-Economic Research Centre for East India (1960), pp. 73–4.

[17] The 'boat denial' policy was coupled with a 'rice denial' policy initiated in May 1942, aimed also at the elusive Japanese; rice stocks were removed from certain coastal districts (viz. Bakarganj, Khulna, and Midnapore). While the amount involved was not very large—about 40,000 tons altogether—and the rice thus bought and removed was later sold mostly within Bengal (chiefly in Calcutta), it did contribute to local scarcities.

TABLE 6.5

Indices of Exchange Rates vis-à-vis *Rice at Retail Prices: Bolpur in Birbhum District*

Mid-Month	Wheat flour	Mustard oil	Cloth	Bamboo umbrellas	Milk	Fish (pona)	Haircut
1941							
December	100	100	100	100	100	100	100
1942							
January	121	93	108	114	108	95	108
February	112	93	108	127	108	95	108
March	121	100	108	152	108	95	108
April	109	88	113	145	88	88	88
May	91	74	142	134	74	74	74
June ·	98	89	169	160	88	132	88
July	92	82	165	150	83	124	83
August	83	94	165	129	74	110	74
September	130	125	197	145	88	132	88
October	99	80	126	92	56	84	56
November	79	71	102	69	45	68	45
December	125	95	134	85	66	84	56
1943							
January	116	88	132	85	61	65	52
February	168	95	142	98	66	70	56
March	111	74	94	69	44	46	37
April	108	59	68	60	32	34	27
May	72	51	46	43	21	27	18
June	78	50	49	48	23	39	19
July	77	49	49	47	23	38	19
August	75	64	47	44	22	37	19
September	112	95	76	66	33	56	28
October	100	85	68	57	30	50	25
November	95	118	86	73	47	80	32
December	75	145	118	90	62	106	42
1944							
January	64	127	111	91	57	97	58

Sources: As in Table 6.4, (2) and (3). Note that the cloth index is based on the price of rural handwoven towels (*gamcha*), the only cotton good for which data are available.

fishermen cannot be judged by looking only at the fish–rice exchange rate. However, even that exchange rate declined sharply afterwards. Since Bolpur is a rather small market for fish, the fish–rice exchange rates in Calcutta are presented in Table 6.6; here the decline took place a bit later and somewhat less severely than in Bolpur.

TABLE 6.6

Indices of Retail Prices of Rice and Fish and of Fish–Rice Exchange Rates: College Street Market in Calcutta

	Price of rice (dhekichata)	Price of fish: rohi (cut pieces)	Price of whole fish	Exchange rate index: rohi fish vis-à-vis rice	Exchange rate index: whole fish vis-à-vis rice
1941					
December	100	100	100	100	100
1942					
January	100	100	100	100	100
February	100	100	100	100	100
March	100	100	100	100	100
April	100	100	100	100	100
May	100	110	140	110	140
June	119	110	140	92	118
July	130	130	180	100	138
August	137	150	160	109	117
September	133	150	180	113	135
October	147	140	180	95	122
November	154	170	180	110	117
December	170	170	180	100	106
1943					
January	228	150	180	66	79
February	218	150	180	69	83
March	219	150	180	68	82
April	330	n.a	n.a		
May	435	210	180	48	41
June	435	220	240	51	55
July	435	300	280	69	64
August	491	280	320	57	65

Sources: Calculated from data collected from the weekly *Calcutta Municipal Gazette* during 1941–3. The data refer to the mid-range value for the last observation in each month. Rice prices are discontinued from September, when 'price control' made higher market quotations illegal.

One group that could not have suffered a deterioration of exchange entitlement *vis-à-vis* rice would have been the rice producers. This category would include large farmers as well as peasants. To some extent this would apply to share-croppers as well, since the share is fixed as a proportion of the output, which in this case is rice. There can, of course, be a decline in employment opportunities of share-croppers, but in terms of exchange rates their position would have been distinctly less vulnerable than that of wage labourers, especially since most wages were fixed in money terms. The exchange entitlement approach would, therefore, tend to predict a lower impact of the famine on peasants and share-croppers than on agricultural labourers and sellers of certain commodities and services (fishermen, craftsmen, barbers, etc., who suffered sharp deteriorations of exchange entitlements).

6.4 THE CLASS BASIS OF DESTITUTION

Who were the famine victims? From which occupation categories did the destitutes come?

Data about famines are never plentiful. However, there are at least three important surveys of famine victims conducted during and just ·after the Bengal famine. First, P. C. Mahalanobis, R. Mukherjea and A. Ghosh (1946) have published the results of a detailed sample survey conducted in collaboration with K. P. Chattopadhyaya during 1944–5 covering 20 per cent of the families in 386 villages in rural Bengal.[18] The subdivisions of Bengal were chosen for the survey with an eye to the 'intensity of incidence' of the famine (41 subdivisions out of a total of 86), and then the villages in each subdivision, and 20 per cent of the population in each village, were chosen on a random basis. The occupational status of the families were recorded for three points of time: in January 1939 (before the famine), January 1943 (immediately preceding the famine—in fact, in terms of our phase structure towards the end of Phase I of the famine), and in May 1944 (after the famine). Second, K. Mukerji (1965) studied the economic conditions of five villages in the Faridpur district immediately after the famine in early 1944, and the results of that survey are of relevance to that particular region of East Bengal much affected by the famine. Third, while these two studies were conducted after the famine was over, a study of the destitutes in Calcutta during the famine was carried out in September 1943 by T. Das (1949), with the help of others, covering 820 destitute family units.

Data from the study by Mahalanobis, Mukherjea and Ghosh (1946) can be used to construct transition matrices in the period immediately preceding the famine, including Phase I of it (January 1939–January 1943), as well as over the severe phase of

---

[18] See also Chattopadhyaya and Mukherjea (1946).

the famine (January 1943–May 1944), and these are presented in Tables 6.9 and 6.10 at the end of the chapter. It should be observed that there is a fairly close relation between the inter-occupational orderings of pauperization in the 'immediate pre-famine' and the 'famine' periods.[19] (The value of Spearman's rank correlation happens to be 0.75.) It seems possible to argue that the destitution that took place during the famine was similar to what had been happening in the immediate pre-famine period. The extent of the pauperization rose sharply during the famine, and every occupation category—other than paupers themselves—experienced greater destitution in the period than in the four years preceding it (see Table 6.7, columns marked A), but the ranking of occupations in terms of pauperization rates remained similar.

In the famine period, the worst affected groups seem to have been fishermen, transport workers, paddy huskers, agricultural labourers, those in 'other productive occupations', craftsmen,

TABLE 6.7

Transition to (A) Destitution and (B) Destitution or Husking Paddy for Different Occupations

| | Between January 1939 and January 1943 | | Between January 1943 and May 1944 | |
	A	B	A	B
	%	%	%	%
Peasant cultivation and share-cropping	0.7	0.9	1.3	1.5
Part peasant, part labour	0.9	1.1	1.4	2.0
Non-cultivating owners	0.7	1.3	1.6	2.4
Profession and services	1.4	1.9	2.1	2.6
Trade	1.1	1.5	2.2	2.6
Craft	3.0	3.1	3.8	4.3
Non-agricultural labour	1.8	1.8	3.7	4.5
Other productive occupations	1.9	2.2	4.6	4.6
Agricultural labour	1.7	2.5	4.6	6.1
Transport	2.4	30.6	6.0	6.9
Fishing	1.6	1.6	9.6	10.5
Husking paddy	3.6	–	4.7	–

Source: Calculated from the data presented in Mahalanobis, Mukherjea and Ghosh (1946).

[19] As explained earlier, these terms are somewhat deceptive since the 'immediate pre-famine period' includes much of Phase I of it.

and non-agricultural labourers, in that order. The least affected were peasant cultivators and share-croppers. They were also the least affected group in the pre-famine period (including what we have been calling Phase I of the famine).

One of the occupation categories,—'paddy husking'—displays certain interesting features. It happens to be one of those marginal occupations that many rural families pass through on the way to total destitution. It has rather easy entry, and it is a lowly paid occupation done almost exclusively by women.[20] While—the destitution rates in husking paddy are so high—3.6 and 4.7 per cent respectively in the pre-famine and famine periods—the proportion of rural families dependent on these activities *rose* substantially both in the immediate pre-famine period as well as during the famine. It is interesting, in this connection, to note that, on the basis of the detailed information on sex, family status, and personal history obtained from the survey, Chattopadhyaya and Mukherjea (1946) observed that, while 'many of these women husking paddy are unattached persons . . . who have been following this occupation for making a livelihood for themselves', others with 'children dependent on them have been reduced to rely entirely on this occupation through death of earners and finally brought to destitution' (p. 7). Despite a high rate of destitution during 1939–43 as well as 1943–4, the number of families dependent on husking paddy showed a net increase by a little over 66 per cent between January 1939 and May 1944.

Treating entry into paddy husking as typically a sign of distress, columns marked B in Table 6.7 present the proportions of each occupation group moving to destitution *or* to living on husking paddy, in the immediate pre-famine period and during the famine. Again, the rank-ordering of this redefined index of distress in the pre-famine period is quite close to that during the famine (e.g., Spearman's rank correlation coefficient of the two series works out at 0.78).

In terms of recruitment to economic distress (defined as destitution or husking paddy), 'fishing', 'transport' and

[20] See Chattopadhyaya and Mukherjea (1946), p. 7. Note also that in a period of rice shortage, paddy husking also becomes a more lucrative occupation (in relative terms), permitting entry of labour thrown out from other walks of life. The fact that husking can be carried out on an extremely small scale is also relevant to this phenomenon of easy entry.

'agricultural labour' have the highest frequencies among the occupations. It is a bit difficult to conclude anything firmly about transport workers since the sample size was rather small, and there is also some relation between the distress of the fishermen and that of rural transport workers, since river transport 'is largely looked after by members of the fishermen caste' (Chattopadhyaya and Mukherjea, 1946, p. 7). But there is little doubt about fishermen and agricultural labourers being among the hardest hit by the famine. Other hard-hit groups were 'other productive occupations', 'non-agricultural labour', and 'craft'.

In absolute numbers, by far the largest group of destitutes came from the category of agricultural labourers, according to the data presented by Mahalanobis, Mukherjea and Ghosh (1946). Similarly, in his survey of the destitutes who had trekked to Calcutta at the height of the famine, conducted in September 1943, it was found by T. Das (1949) that about 41 per cent of those destitutes—the largest group—were from families of agricultural labour. It is not, however, possible to calculate the proportionate incidence of destitution from Das's data.

Finally, in Mukherji's survey of Faridpur villages, the highest rate of proportionate destitution is observed among agricultural labourers (a destitution rate of 52 per cent compared with an over-all average destitution rate of 29 per cent). The proportion of families 'wiped off during 1943' is also the highest among the agricultural labourers (40 per cent compared with an over-all average of 15 per cent; indeed, 77 per cent of those agricultural labourers who were destituted by the famine got 'wiped off'). The relative rates for the different occupation categories are given in Table 6.8. Next tc agricultural labourers, the highest destitution rate is displayed in a category named 'unproductive', which is a bit decepetive since it includes people who traditionally live by beggary in these villages, and of course were easily destituted further. The next highest group is 'artisan' (35 per cent destitution and 10 per cent 'wiped off'). The peasant cultivators and share-croppers had a relatively lower famine incidence (18 per cent destitution and 6 per cent wiped off), higher only than office employees and landlords.

The picture that emerges from these data seems to be entirely in line with what one would expect from the use of the entitlement approach. The high incidence among agricultural

nanite.

TABLE 6.8
Destitution in Five Surveyed Villages in Faridpur

Occupation on 1/1/43	Total nos. of families on 1/1/43	Nos. of destitute families in each group on 1/1/43	Proportion of destitution (%)	Nos. of families in each group 'wiped off during 1943'	Proportion being 'wiped off during 1943' (%)
Peasant cultivation and share-cropping	266	49	18.4	17	6.4
Agricultural labour	124	65	52.4	50	40.3
Artisan	20	7	35.0	2	10.0
Petty trader	107	34	31.8	15	14.0
Crop-sharing landlord	16	1	6.3	0	0.0
Priest and petty employee	11	3	27.3	3	27.3
Office employee	20	2	10.0	0	0.0
Landlord	10	0	0.0	0	0.0
'Unproductive'	18	8	44.4	3	16.7
Total	592	169	28.5	90	15.2

Source: Based on Mukerji (1965), **Table** 63, p. **178**.

labourers *vis-à-vis* the low impact on peasants and share-croppers was to be expected. The food entitlements had, indeed, deteriorated sharply for the former, but not so much for the latter.[21] The relatively large effects on fishermen, non-agricultural labour, craftsmen, etc., are also consistent with the observed pattern of shifts in entitlement relations.

6.5 CAUSES OF THE SHARP MOVEMENTS OF EXCHANGE ENTITLEMENTS

What caused the exchange entitlements to move so violently? While data limitations rule out definitive discrimination between alternative causal hypotheses, some tentative diagnoses seem possible.

First, the increase in rice price in Phase I was essentially related to demand factors; supply was exceptionally high in 1942 (see Table 6.2). The price increase in the Phase I period, while not confined to Bengal, was much more acute in Bengal than elsewhere (see Singh, 1965, pp. 95–9; Palekar, 1962). This was, to a great extent, a result of general inflationary pressure in a war economy. Bengal saw military and civil construction at a totally unprecedented scale, and the war expenditures were financed to a great extent by printing notes. While a substantial part—indeed, more than half from 1941 to 1942—of the total war expenditure incurred by India was 'recoverable' as sterling balances owed by Britain, this did not reduce the immediate inflationary pressure, since the 'recovery' took place much later. Indeed, given the Indian monetary system, these sterling balances were treated as assets against which the Reserve Bank of India was 'entitled to print notes worth about two and a half times their total value', so that the recoverable war expenditure tended to have a *stronger* inflationary impact than expenditure on India's own account (see Gadgil and Sovani, 1943, pp. 12–14). The 1943 famine can indeed be described as a 'boom famine' related to powerful inflationary pressures initiated by public expenditure expansion.

[21] Indeed, peasants growing rice and living on exchanging rice for other commodities might be thought to have had an *improvement* in exchange entitlements in terms of other commodities. But the high retail price of food was often not correspondingly reflected in the price paid to the peasant. Furthermore, at the initial post-harvest high price many peasants sold off more rice than their surplus and had to repurchase some rice later at a very much higher price still.

Second, in Phase II the demand forces were reinforced by the 'indifferent' winter crop and by vigorous speculation and panic hoardings. The hoarding was financially profitable on the basis of even 'static expectations': rice prices had more than doubled in the preceding year, while the 'bazar bill rate' in Calcutta still stood around 7 per cent per year (the bank deposit rate was below 2 per cent per annum).[22] There was a abnormally higher withholding of rice stock by farmers and traders from the winter harvest of 1942–3; the normal release following the harvest did not take place.[23] A moderate short-fall in *production* had by then been translated into an exceptional short-fall in *market release*. The 'current supply' figures of the Famine Inquiry Commission no longer reflected supply to the market.

Third, speculative withdrawal and panic purchase of rice stocks was encouraged by administrative chaos,[24] especially the inept handling of three procurement schemes, tried and hurriedly abandoned between December and March, ending with the sudden abolition of price control in the wholesale market on 11 March.[25] But the expectation of a famine and further price rises were most forcefully fed by the sight of distress and hunger that had already developed by the end of Phase I and the beginning of Phase II.[26] Many of the groups had already suffered severe declines in exchange entitlements in Phase I itself (see Tables 6.3–6.5) and had helped to fill the distress reports of commissioners and district officers (discussed earlier). The speculative price increase in rice in Phase II led to further deterioration of exchange entitlements, covering additional occupation groups. The Bengal government's propaganda drive that 'the supply position did not justify the high prices prevailing' failed totally.[27]

[22] Gadgil and Sovani (1943), p. 24.

[23] See Ghosh (1944), pp. 33–48; Famine Inquiry Commission, India (1945a), pp. 33–4, 38–41 and 83–5; and Das (1949), p. 119.

[24] Including a change of ministry in Bengal. The old Bengal government under the premiership of Fazlul Haq fell on 31 March, and a new ministry under Khwaza Nazimmuddin was sworn in on 23 April.

[25] See Famine Inquiry Commission (1945a), pp. 36–50. Similarly, the scheme to requisition traders' stocks in Calcutta a few months earlier had yielded little except the belief that not much stock existed to be requisitioned.

[26] See Ghosh (1944), Das (1949), and Famine Inquiry Commission, India (1945a), Appendix VI.

[27] The ineptness of the propaganda drive was exceptional. On 18 May the Finance Minister, T. C. Goswami, offered the following remarkable explanation of events,

Fourth, the prohibition of export of cereals in general and of rice in particular from each province, which had come into operation during 1942 with the consent of the government of India, prevented the price spiral in Bengal being broken by imports from the other provinces.[28] After much fumbling with various all-India schemes of food distribution, the government of India eventually ordered free trade in the eastern region of the country towards the middle of May 1943. But this was abandoned in July since the prices in these neighbouring provinces soon reached the 'maximum' levels laid down by the provincial governments. A 'Basic Plan' of centralized inter-state grain movements eventually came into operation in late summer, improving the supply position in Bengal in the last quarter of 1943.

Fifth, an important aspect of the famine was its association with an uneven expansion in incomes and purchasing powers. Those involved in military and civil defence works, in the army, in industries and commerce stimulated by war activities, and almost the entire normal population of Calcutta covered by distribution arrangements at subsidized prices (see Section 6.1) could exercise strong demand pressures on food, while others excluded from this expansion or protection simply had to take the consequences of the rise in food prices. Agricultural labour did not in general share in the war-based expansion, except 'in certain areas . . . where military or civil defence works were in progress'.[29] The abundance of labour in the agricultural sector (see Mahalanobis, Mukherjea and Ghosh, 1946; and Chatopadhyaya and Mukherjea, 1946) made the economic position of the labourers in the agricultural sector weak. The weakness of their position is also reflected in the fact that, while the famine killed millions, with agricultural labourers forming by far the

---

backing up a cheerful prediction: 'Before long the price will come down. The speculators were in their last grasp [*sic*] and the reason why the prices were not coming down could be assigned to their last desperate attempt to keep prices up' (quoted in Ghosh, 1944, pp. 40–1). See also Famine Inquiry Commission, India (1945a), p. 55.

[28] The price difference between Bengal and its neighbouring provinces had already become substantial by the end of 1942. Compared with a mean harvest price of winter rice in Assam of Rs. 8.81, in Bihar of Rs. 8.00 and in Orissa of Rs. 6.19, the mean price of winter rice in Bengal was Rs. 14.00, and even the 1942 autumn harvest mean price had been Rs. 13.88 (see *Indian Agricultural Statistics 1939–40 to 1942–43*, Government of India, New Delhi, 1950, vol. 1, Table VII).

[29] Famine Inquiry Commission, India (1945b), p. 485.

largest group of those killed, Bengal was producing the largest rice crop in history in 1943. While I resist the temptation to propose a 'test' of the surplus labour hypothesis along Schultzian lines,[30] which rejected the surplus labour hypothesis on grounds of declines in agricultural output following the influenza epidemic of 1918, it is remarkable that agricultural operations could take place on such a gigantic scale despite deaths, debilitating diseases and migration in search of food, affecting a large part of the agricultural labour force.

Sixth, as far as occupation groups involving crafts, services, 'superior' foods (e.g. fish, milk) are concerned, Phase II could have created problems of its own. As distress developed generally in the rural economy of Bengal, the demand for these 'luxury' goods declined sharply—a phenomenon that has been observed in other famines as well.[31] This feedback helped to plunge additional groups of people into destitution.

Finally, it is perhaps significant that the Bengal famine stood exactly at the borderline of two historical price regimes. Prices had been more or less stationary for decades (the 1941 rice price was comparable to that in 1914), and the price rises (especially of food) that started off in 1942 were to become a part of life from then on. Institutional arrangements, including wage systems, were slow to adjust to the new reality.

6.6   THE ROLE OF THEORY IN POLICY FAILURES

The inadequacy of official policy in tackling the Bengal famine has been widely noted and criticized. The Famine Inquiry Commission (1945a) provided a detailed analysis of the policy failures both of the Bengal government as well as of the Indian government (see especially Chapters X and XI). The famine became a focal point of nationalist criticism of British imperial policy in India (for a classic work on this, see Ghosh, 1944), and official complacency came under particular attack. The refusal of the British government to permit more food imports into India through reallocation of shipping as an emergency measure to tackle the famine was severely criticized.[32] Lord Wavell, who

---

[30] See Schultz (1964); for a critique, see Sen (1967b), followed by Schultz's reply.

[31] See, for example, Wrigley (1969), p. 68, on the seventeenth-century famine in Mouy in France.

[32] For the international—especially American—reaction, see the interesting study of Venkataramani (1973).

became the new Viceroy at the last stage of the famine and who had to battle hard for increasing food imports into India, went on record in this context that he felt that 'the vital problems of India are being treated by His Majesty's Government with neglect, even sometimes with hostility and contempt'.[33]

Does our thesis that the Bengal famine did not arise from a drastic decline in food availability negate these criticisms? I don't believe it does, since no matter how a famine is *caused*, methods of *breaking* it call for a large supply of food in the public distribution system. This applies not only to organizing rationing and control, but also to undertaking work programmes and other methods of increasing purchasing power for those hit by shifts in exchange entitlements in a general inflationary situation. (One curious aspect of the Bengal famine was that it was never officially 'declared' as a famine, which would have brought in an obligation to organize work programmes and relief operations specified by the 'Famine Code', dating from 1883; Sir T. Rutherford, the Governor of Bengal, explained to the Viceroy: 'The Famine Code has not been applied as we simply have not the food to give the prescribed ration.')[34] A large food stock would have also helped in breaking the speculative spiral that ushered in the Phase II of the famine. Thus there is no reason to revise the criticisms made of the official failure to obtain more food in the public distribution system through greater procurement and larger imports from outside Bengal. Nor are there reasons to dispute the Famine Inquiry Commission's indictment of the Bengal government for administrative bungling and of the government of India for its failure to evolve an integrated food policy for India as a whole.

But the conspicuous failure of the Government to anticipate the famine and to recognise its emergence does appear in a new light. When the existence of the famine was eventually acknowledged officially in Parliament by the Secretary of State for India in a statement in October 1943, the influential Calcutta daily *The Statesman* wondered why 'the speech contained no direct admission of grave misjudgement on the higher authorities' part or even of error', overlooking 'previous official assertions in London and New Delhi that there existed virtually no food problem in

---

[33] Letter to Winston Churchill, dated 24 October 1944; quoted in Wavell (1973), p. 95.

[34] Document no. 158 in Mansergh (1973), p. 363.

India.'[35] In view of what we have discussed earlier (Section 6.2), one can argue that the Raj was, in fact, fairly right in its estimation of overall food availability, but disastrously wrong in its theory of famines.

The government's thinking on the nature of the food problem seems to have been persistently influenced by attempts to estimate the size of the 'real shortage' based on 'requirements' and 'availability'; it was a search in a dark room for a black cat which wasn't there. The approach provided no warning of the development of a gigantic famine arising from shifting exchange entitlements. The approach also contributed to some reluctance to accept the magnitude of the disaster even after the famine had in fact appeared.

Estimates of food shortages were periodically made by the Government of India. An estimate of 'shortage of rice' was made in December 1942, taking full note of 'loss of Burma rice, floods in Sind, cyclones in rice growing areas of Bengal and Orissa and an *indifferent* rice crop generally in Bengal'.[36] But the shortage seemed absorbable, and the Government of India used this 'rice shortage' estimate only to supplement its request to London for shipping allocation to meet the existing 'wheat shortage', viz., shipping facilities to import 'an additional 600,000 tons of wheat'.[37] In his 'memorandum' on this request, the Secretary of State for India observed:

No account is taken in it of the statistical shortage of 140,000 tons of rice and 650,000 tons of millets which is the background against which the Government of India have to view their wheat difficulties. *These shortages, serious as they are, would not from the statistical standpoint bear a catastrophic proportion of the Indian cereal crop of 60/70 million tons.*[38]

[35] "Seen from a distance", editorial, *The Statesman*, 14 October 1943; see also the editorial on 16 October following, entitled "The death-roll". *The Statesman*, a British-owned newspaper, had carried out a powerful campaign with news reports, photographs and editorial comments on the calamity – a role that would be praised later by the Famine Inquiry Commission. For the editor's account of the campaign and also for an interesting, anecdotal account of the Bengal famine, see Stephens (1966, chs. 13 and 14). Recognition of the reality of the famine seemed to decrease step by step in the move from the local administration via Calcutta and New Delhi to Whitehall.

[36] Document no. 265 in Mansergh (1971), p. 357; italics added. Note that the rice crop in Bengal was recognized to be 'indifferent' rather than exceptionally bad (cf. Section 6.2 above).

[37] Document no. 265 in Mansergh (1971), p. 358; see also Documents nos 282, 297, and 332 in the same volume.

[38] Document no. 330 in Mansergh (1971), p. 474; italics added.

While taking an essentially FAD approach, the Secretary's detailed memorandum went also into 'aggravating factors', particularly the problems of the urban population, who 'are dependent on the marketed part of the crop, who are the first to experience any shortage and . . . on whose labour the Indian munitions and supply industries depend'.[39] The distress of the rural population, especially of agricultural labour, arising from shifting exchange entitlements, which—as we have seen in Section 6.3—had already been quite substantial by then, was not noted. The reference to 'distribution' was only in the context of 'the strain put upon the railways by military and other loadings'.[40] (The tendency to view 'distribution' essentially as a transport problem rather than as one involving purchasing power and exchange was, incidentally, a persistent feature of official thinking on the subject.)[41]

As it happens, even the request for permission to import 600,000 tons of wheat was turned down in London on 16 January, only a small part of it being met.[42] This was received, it appears, with equanimity, since the government itself did not take its 'shortage' estimates too seriously in the context of over-all supply. The government immediately proceeded to decontrol the wholesale price of wheat, set up a government Purchasing Agency, and prohibit 'the export of foodgrains beyond Provincial and State boundaries on private account', and it issued a communiqué promising 'imports from abroad' and confiding that 'the Government of India believed that the food shortages were mainly due to hoarding'.[43]

On 26 January, the Viceroy wrote to the Secretary of State for India: 'Mindful of our difficulties about food I told him [the

[39] ibid. Even when the Bengal countryside was gripped by the famine and rural destitutes were pouring into relatively well-fed Calcutta, the government of India was concentrating chiefly on 'signs that difficulty is likely to arise in the non-rural and industrial districts' (see War Cabinet Paper WP (43) 345, dated 30 July 1943, Document no. 66 in Mansergh (1973), p. 134).

[40] Document no. 330 in Mansergh (1971), p. 476.

[41] See, for example, Document no. 102 in Mansergh (1973); see also Famine Inquiry Commission, India (1945a), pp. 59–62.

[42] See the Secretary of State's telegram to the Viceroy on 16 January 1943, Document no. 350 in Mansergh (1971), pp. 514–15. London continued to turn down requests by the government of India for shipping allocations throughout 1943; see Documents nos. 59, 71, 72, 74, 98, 139, 157, 207, and 219 in Mansergh (1973), and also Wavell (1973), Chapters 2 and 3).

[43] Mansergh (1971), p. 541.

Premier of Bengal] that he simply *must* produce some more rice out of Bengal for Ceylon even if Bengal itself went short! He was by no means unsympathetic, and it is possible that I may in the result screw a little out of them'.[44] The estimates of 'shortage' based on production figures (including that of the 'indifferent' winter crop) did not make such a suggestion look preposterous, even though—as we have seen—the forces leading to the famine were already in full swing.

Later in the spring, when the famine was about to reveal itself fully, the Viceroy sent, on 18 March, the cheerful news to the Secretary of State that 'the food situation in India generally is at present much improved'. While 'the situation in Bengal at present is disquieting', the food situation could be 'treated with guarded optimism, with special reference to the recent improvement of ths situation in India generally and the excellent prospects of the *rabi* harvest'.[45]

The severity of the famine when it did surface caused much official surprise; the Viceroy came to the conclusion that the 'chief factor' was 'morale'.[46] But the adherence to the FAD approach was not abandoned; the values of 'shortages' were recalculated specifically for Bengal for the period until the next crop. In a report transmitted to London by the Viceroy, the Governor of Bengal, Sir T. Rutherford, presented on 2 October 1943 a detailed account of the 'present food situation', including a lament about 'the dubiety of all available statistics and therefore lack of accurate knowledge of what the *real shortage* is',[47] without questioning the wisdom of the approach itself. 'Allowing 1 lb. a day' to those above fifteen years and '½ lb. a day to those below 15', and taking note of traders' stocks and estimates of 'carryover from 1941–42', it was now calculated that for the period until the next harvest 'the shortage was in the neighbourhood of 655,000 tons'.[48] This figure had to be revised upwards by the Viceroy within eight days, since an expert 'says my estimate of 655,000 tons as shortage is too low and suggests one million tons'.[49]

[44] Document no. 362 in Mansergh (1971), p. 544.
[45] Document no. 599 in Mansergh (1971), pp. 825–6.
[46] Wavell quoting Linlithgow, in Wavell (1973), p. 34.
[47] Document no. 158 in Mansergh (1973), p. 361; italics added.
[48] ibid., p. 362.
[49] Document no. 174 in Mansergh (1973), p. 390; the expert quoted was A.M.A.H. Ispahani, a businessman much involved in rice trading.

While practical considerations outside the FAD approach were often introduced in an *ad hoc* way in government notes on the food problem,[50] especially after the famine had broken out, the FAD view continued to occupy a pre-eminent position in the government's theory of the food crisis. By January 1944, the government appeared to have worked out a complicated FAD explanation of the famine: 'The experience of the past years has convinced the authorities in India that the loss of imports since 1942 has meant the consumption of the carry-over, and now, reserves having been consumed, is a major cause of shortage, and that, though the exhaustion of a concealed reserve has not been evident till now, its results will persist'.[51] As was noted earlier, not a single piece of serious statistics exists on the 'carry-over', and a study of the moving averages of availability taking note of production and net imports suggests no reason for presuming a sharp decline of carry-over (see Section 6.2).

Finally, when the time came to report on the famine and assess what had happened, the Famine Inquiry Commission also adopted FAD as its main approach—as we have already seen. The occurence of the famine was squared with production and trade figures by assuming a sharp decline of that mysterious— and unobserved—'carry-over from previous years'. Like the Phoenix, the FAD theory arose rejuvenated from the ashes, and it can be found today chirping in the current literature on the food crisis of the world, even making occasional references to the Bengal famine, 'when floods destroyed the rice crop, costing some 2 million to 4 million lives'.[52]

[50] See Mansergh (1971), Chapter 10, and Mansergh (1973), Chapter 4.

[51] Memorandum by the Secretary of State for India, War Cabinet Paper WP (44) 63, Document no. 347 in Mansergh (1973), p. 680.

[52] Brown and Eckholm (1974), p. 27. See also Masefield (1963), p. 14; quoted also in Aziz (1975), p. 27.

TABLE 6.9

Occupational Transition Matrix in Rural Bengal in the Pre-famine Period: January 1939–January 1943

1939	Peasant cultivation or sharecropping	Part-time agricultural labour	Agricultural labour	Non-cultivating owner	Fishing	Craft	Husking paddy	Transport	Trade	Profession and service	Non-agricultural labour	Other productive occupations	Destitute
	%	%	%	%	%	%	%	%	%	%	%	%	%
Peasant cultivation and share-cropping	91.8	3.3	1.9	0.9	0.0	0.2	0.2	0.1	0.4	0.3	0.1	0.1	0.7
Part-time agricultural labour	1.7	90.3	3.9	0.4	0.1	1.3	0.2	0.0	0.3	0.5	0.1	0.4	0.9
Agricultural labour	2.6	4.3	87.1	1.0	0.0	0.5	0.8	0.0	0.3	1.0	0.2	0.6	1.7
Non-cultivating owner	3.7	0.7	1.2	90.5	0.0	0.2	0.6	0.0	0.4	1.3	0.3	0.4	0.7
Fishing	3.8	2.8	1.3	0.3	68.3	21.0	0.0	0.0	0.3	0.0	0.3	0.3	1.6
Craft	8.0	0.7	1.6	2.7	0.0	81.1	0.1	0.1	0.6	1.0	0.3	0.7	3.0
Husking paddy	8.8	1.0	2.6	4.1	0.0	1.6	73.7	0.5	0.5	1.0	1.6	1.0	3.6
Transport	5.3	2.9	2.4	4.9	0.0	0.0	28.2	51.0	1.9	0.0	0.5	0.5	2.4
Trade	11.9	1.8	1.9	2.5	0.0	0.7	0.4	0.1	77.1	1.6	0.7	0.3	1.1
Profession and service	7.3	1.6	2.2	5.8	0.0	0.9	0.5	0.0	1.5	77.6	0.7	0.5	1.4
Non-agricultural labour	9.9	1.8	0.0	4.5	0.0	0.9	0.0	0.0	0.9	0.9	79.3	0.0	1.8
Other productive occupations	3.7	1.9	1.5	4.3	0.0	0.3	0.3	0.0	0.9	0.9	0.3	84.0	1.9
Destitute	0.4	0.0	2.2	0.0	0.0	0.4	2.2	0.0	2.9	1.8	1.5	1.1	87.6

TABLE 6.10
Occupational Transition Matrix in Rural Bengal in the Famine Period
January 1943–May 1944

1943	Peasant cultivation or share cropping	Part-time agricultural labour	Agricultural labour	Non-cultivating owner	Fishing	Craft	Husking paddy	Transport	Trade	Profession and services	Non-agricultural labour	Other productive occupations	Destitute
	%	%	%	%	%	%	%	%	%	%	%	%	%
Peasant cultivation or share-cropping	91.6	1.9	2.4	1.3	0.1	0.4	0.2	0.1	0.4	0.2	0.0	0.3	1.3
Part-time agricultural labour	2.6	86.9	6.8	0.5	0.0	0.2	0.6	0.1	0.3	0.3	0.2	0.2	1.4
Agricultural labour	0.9	1.5	88.2	0.0	0.1	0.5	1.5	0.2	0.3	1.2	0.2	0.8	4.6
Non-cultivating owner	0.6	0.1	0.8	92.6	0.0	1.1	0.8	0.1	0.5	1.2	0.2	0.5	1.6
Fishing	0.5	0.0	2.3	0.5	78.6	0.5	0.9	0.5	4.6	0.0	0.9	1.4	9.6
Craft	1.8	0.5	2.9	1.1	0.1	87.4	0.5	0.3	0.3	0.9	0.5	0.1	3.8
Husking paddy	0.0	0.4	0.8	0.0	0.4	0.8	90.6	0.4	0.8	0.0	0.4	0.8	4.7
Transport	0.9	1.7	7.8	0.0	0.0	3.5	0.9	78.5	0.0	0.9	0.0	0.0	6.0
Trade	1.8	0.6	2.8	1.1	0.1	0.6	0.4	17.5	69.6	2.0	0.5	0.8	2.2
Profession and services	1.4	0.4	0.9	1.2	0.0	0.6	0.5	0.5	0.9	91.5	0.1	0.1	2.1
Non-agricultural labour	3.7	2.2	5.2	0.0	0.0	0.0	0.8	0.0	0.0	0.0	82.8	1.5	3.7
Other productive occupations	0.6	1.8	1.5	0.6	0.0	0.6	0.0	0.3	0.3	1.5	0.0	88.4	4.6
Destitute	0.2	0.7	2.8	1.9	0.0	1.9	1.7	0.2	1.4	0.5	1.2	2.1	85.4

Chapter 7

The Ethiopian Famine

7.1 THE FAMINE 1972-4

The first recorded famine in Ethiopia goes back to the ninth century. Between 1540 and 1742 there were, apparently, more than ten major famines.[1] The so-called 'great Ethiopian famine' hit the country during 1888-92, killing off possibly a third of the total population,[2] and it is still remembered as *kifu qan* (evil days). In comparison with the great Ethiopian famine, the famine that Ethiopia experienced in 1972-4 might appear to be a moderate affair, with mortality estimates varying between 50,000 and 200,000, in a population of about 27 million.[3] But as Aykroyd (1974) puts it, 'a death toll of perhaps over 100,000' is 'inexcusable at this stage in the history of famine' (p. 203).

The province that was hit hardest by the famine was Wollo in the north-east of Ethiopia, but it also affected the province of Tigrai, further north, and some of the rest of the country, e.g. Harerghe.[4] For Wollo the famine reached its peak in 1973, and recovery was well under way by the end of that year. The same is true of Tigrai, the other northern province affected by the famine (though much less affected). But for Harerghe the famine came into its own only in 1974. In a sense, there were really two Ethiopian famines during this period: the first in 1972-3 with its focus on north-east, especially Wollo, and the second in 1973-4 affecting mainly some provinces further south, particularly

[1] Zewde (1976), p. 52. See also Pankhurst (1961).

[2] See Pankhurst (1966).

[3] The lower of the two limits, viz. 40,000, comes from the estimate of 'total deaths due to famine between 40,000 and 80,000', suggested by Miller and Holt (1975), p. 171, but refers primarily to the first phase of the famine. The higher of the two limits, viz. 200,000, represents mortality estimates presented in Shepherd (1975), which Gebre-Medhin and Vahlquist (1977) suggest 'is hardly an exaggeration' (p. 197). For the total period 1972-5, Rivers, Holt, Seaman, and Bowden (1976) estimate 'an excess of at least 100,000 deaths due to starvation and associated diseases' (p. 355).

[4] According to the figures given by the Ethiopian Relief and Rehabilitation Commission (1975), the proportion of 'affected' population in late 1973 was 41 per cent for Wollo, 17 per cent for Tigrai, 8 per cent for Harerghe, 2.6 per cent for Shewa, 0.8 per cent for Gemu Gofa, and negligible for the other provinces. See Hussein (1976), p. 45.

Harerghe. The biggest part of the mortality owing to starvation occurred in 1973, much of it in Wollo.

The 1971–2 rains were rather erratic, but the big drought that affected north-east Ethiopia, particularly Wollo, was largely the result of the failure of the main—*kremt*—rains in mid-1972, followed by the near-total failure of the spring—*belg*—rains in early 1973. The former had particularly disastrous effects on the lowlands, and the latter mainly on the highlands. The drought in Wollo and the north-east broke with the *kremt* rains in mid-1973, but a new drought situation developed further south.[5] Since the bulk of the crop is dependent on the main rains, the big decline in terms of food output in the north-east took place quite early, i.e. with the failure of the main rains of 1972 and the short-fall of the December 1972 harvest.

There is little doubt that by late 1972 there were many early signs of developing distress. In December 1972 the Ethiopian Red Cross was already trying to help over a thousand refugees from Wollo who had arrived outside Addis Ababa, the Ethiopian capital. By early 1973 crowds were lining parts of the north–south highway through Wollo, stopping buses and cars to ask for food (Holt and Seaman, 1976). A march by one and a half thousand agriculturists to Addis Ababa in March 1973 was apparently turned back by the police (Wiseberg, 1976). Official recognition of the developing famine came, however, very slowly, even though a study done by the Ministry of Agriculture in November 1972 had sounded a note of grim warning. In fact, the seriousness of the famine seems to have been systematically minimized by the government at the early stages. The international organizations were also rather slow in recognizing the situation as what it was—a severe famine—even though the local UNICEF area office and the Swedish-financed Ethiopian Nutrition Institute played an important part in the early stages of counter-famine initiatives.

The relief camps that were set up were, to start with, mainly the result of local initiative, often organized by local town committees, and relying heavily on the selfless efforts of a handful of local community development officers and public health workers. Reports of extraordinary overcrowding, sanitary

---

[5] See Hussein (1976), Seaman, Holt, and Rivers (1974) and Gebre-Medhin, Hay, Licke, and Maffi (1977).

failures, and grossly inadequate medical attention in the relief camps were rather horrifying, but not surprising given the limitation of the resources available in comparison with the gigantic size of the problem. When the starvation crisis was reaching its peak, in August 1973, 'over 60,000 people were crowded in relief camps which could not deal with a third of their number, and many more flooded into the towns'.[6] By the time foreign relief started arriving in a large scale two months later, the pēak of the starvation crisis was already over, and the camp population had dwindled to 15,000.

A major international rescue operation eventually went into action. While the famine in Wollo and Tigrai had by then ebbed, there were plenty of poor people seeking relief. And fresh destitutes were being created elsewhere in the country as the focus of drought moved south and further east, for example to the Ogaden region of Harerghe. The Relief and Rehabilitation Commission's estimate of 'affected populatiom' went on *increasing* well into 1975, but there is little doubt that the severity of the distress was never as great as in 1973. In fact, the worst period of the famine went virtually unnoticed by the international community and only half acknowledged by the Ethiopian government, and the relief activity peaked well after the famine had ebbed.[7]

Even in terms of regional distribution of food aid, there were some curious mismatching of aid with distress:

The contrast between the chronology of the famine and that of bulk of food aid is startling. Government statistics . . . indicate that up to November 1973 only 12,000 tonnes of grain were distributed to all areas by the government. . . . Some 6,500 tonnes only went to Wollo. . . . In contrast between November 1973 and December 1974 Ethiopia received foreign relief grain donations of 126,000 tonnes, together with 11,000 tonnes of 'rehabitable foods'. Wollo and Tigrai received 70 per cent of this, despite the fact that their problems were nearly over. Harerghe, where famine was at its height, received only 8 per cent.[8]

7.2 FOOD AVAILABILITY

Since the Ethiopian famine clearly was initiated by a drought, and since drought causes crop failures (and, indeed, did so in this

---

[6] Holt and Seaman (1976), p. 4.
[7] See Wiseberg (1976).
[8] Rivers, Holt, Seaman, and Bowden (1976), p. 352.

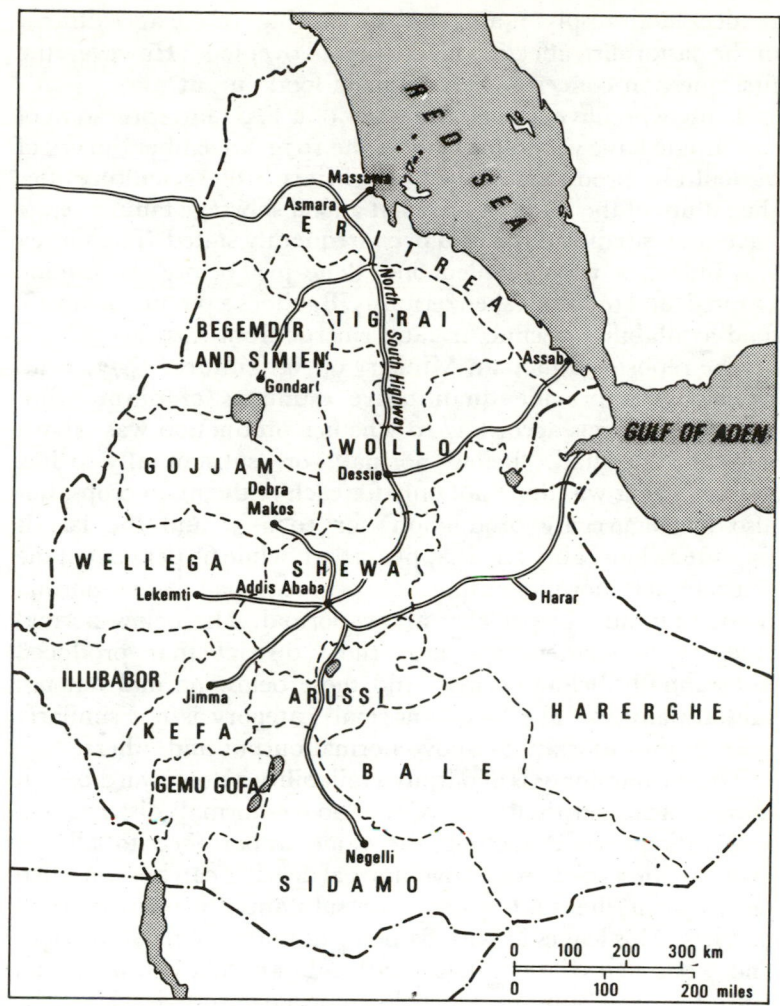

FIG. 7.1 Map of Ethiopia

case), it is easy to be predisposed towards accepting an explanation of the famine in terms of food availability decline (FAD). But a drought causing an agricultural or pastoral crisis not only reduces food supply; it also cuts the earnings of the agriculturist or the pastoralist, affecting his command over food. However, the first question concerns the volume of food output.

Those who have argued in favour of a FAD interpretation of the famine have very often quoted the 1972 November Survey of agricultural production done by the Ministry of Agriculture after the failure of the main rains. That a food shortage famine *should* have been predicted has also been frequently stated. The survey was indeed a very detailed one, done just before the famine erupted, and must be taken seriously. But does a picture of drastic food availability decline, in fact, emerge from this survey?

The report—Ethiopian Ministry of Agriculture (1973)—did not actually provide quantitative estimates of output, but classified districts according to whether production was 'above normal', 'normal', 'below normal', or 'substantially below normal'. This was done not only for each of the main crops, but also for 'aggregate production' for 1972–3, and the last is reproduced in Table 7.1. It appears that, while 65 per cent of the districts had normal output, 21 per cent had below-normal production and 14 per cent above-normal. The below-normal category is further split into those district that produced 'substantially below normal' and those below normal but not substantially so. The 'above-normal' category is not similarly split up into substantial above-normal output and others.

To give our analysis of output availability a downward bias, it may be assumed that none of the 'above-normal' districts was substantially so. Attaching the same importance to all the districts, the 14 per cent above-normal districts can be 'cancelled out' against the 14 per cent non-substantially below-normal districts. This leaves us with 65 per cent normal output districts, and 7 per cent of the districts with substantially below-normal output. Even if 'substantially below-normal output' is taken to be no output at all, which is clearly an underestimate, this indicates a displacement from normal output of 7 per cent. A 7 per cent decline in the output of food crops is hardly a devastating food availability decline (especially in an economy with primarily rain-dependent agriculture).

It is possible to use some other data, also provided by the same report, to arrive at an estimate of output decline. The report provides aggregates for each crop separately, noting which

TABLE 7.1
1972–3 Crop Production in Ethiopia: Provincial Evaluations

Region	Number of districts reporting	Percentage of districts in various categories				
		Normal	Above normal	Below normal	Net below normal	Substantially below normal
	(1)	(2)	(3)	(4)	(5) = (4) − (3)	(6), included in (4)
1. Wollo	21	10	0	90	90	52
2. Arussi	20	70	5	25	20	10
3. Harerghe	22	39	23	39	16	9
4. Eritrea	23	78	4	18	14	9
5. Shewa	72	54	17	29	12	8
6. Tigrai	42	84	6	10	4	8
7. Wellega	35	86	0	14	14	0
8. Gemu Gofa	17	82	6	12	6	0
9. Illubabor	14	64	22	14	−8	0
10. Gojjam	22	82	14	4	−10	0
11. Kefa	9	45	33	22	−11	0
12. Begemdir and Simien	29	72	21	7	−14	0
13. Sidamo	23	78	22	0	−22	0
14. Bale	11	9	82	9	−73	0
Total	360	65	14	21	7	7

Source: Based on data presented in Ethiopian Ministry of Agriculture (1973) and Hussein (1976), Table 10.

districts were below normal, which above normal, etc. These are presented in Table 7.2. The relative weights to be attached to different crops have been calculated from their respective importance in terms of physical weight in the pre-famine year 1971–2 (using data presented in Hussein, 1976, Appendix 5).

The weighted deficit works out as a decline corresponding to below-normal production in 5.74 districts in *net*. Again, biasing the estimate towards the FAD view, it may be assumed that in these 5.74 districts nothing at all was produced, which will amount to an over-all reduction of under 6 per cent compared with normal production.

There is, thus, very little evidence of a dramatic decline in food availability in Ethiopia coinciding with the famine. Indeed, a modest increase in agricultural output for Ethiopia as a whole is recorded by the National Bank of Ethiopia (1976) for the famine year *vis-à-vis* the preceding years (Table 21, p. 79). The food output estimate given by the Food and Agriculture Organization of the United Nations for 1973 seems to vary (contrast the figures for this year in the *FAO Production Yearbooks* for 1974, 1975, and 1976 respectively), but the calorie consumption estimate indicated no significant diminution and possibly a sizeable rise over the preceding years. Table 7.3 presents the per head calorie consumption figures for 1973 and 1974 compared with 1961–5, 1964–6, 1967–9, 1970, and 1972, obtained from the *FAO*

TABLE 7.2

1972–3 Crop Production in Ethiopia: Crop Evaluations

Crop	Percentage of districts in various categories Above normal	Below normal	Net below normal	Relative weight 1971–2	Weighted net below normal districts (%)
	(1)	(2)	(3) = (2) − (1)	(4)	(5) = (4) × (3)
Barley	21	15	−6	0.259	−1.55
Teff	18	25	7	0.228	1.60
Sorghum	16	33	17	0.182	3.09
Maize	17	28	11	0.160	1.76
Wheat	18	22	4	0.145	0.58
Others	14	24	10	0.026	0.26
Total				1.000	5.74

Source: Based on data presented in Ethiopian Ministry of Agriculture (1973) and Hussein (1976).

TABLE 7.3
Food Availability in Ethiopia: Calories per head, 1961–74

| Period | Calories | Index value of calories per capita with row period = 100 | |
		1973	*1974*
1961–5	2,092	99	91
1964–6	1,910	109	100
1967–9	1,950	107	98
1970	1,980	105	97
1972	2,152	97	89
1973	2,081	100	92
1974	1,912	109	100

Source: The data for 1961–5, 1972, 1973, and 1974 are taken from *FAO Production Yearbook 1976*, vol. 30; and for 1964–6, 1967–9, and 1970 from *FAO Production Yearbook 1971*, vol. 25. Information for 1971 could not be obtained, which reflects a remaining gap in the published FAO series which was discontinued for the Production Yearbooks for 1972–5. There is probably some difference between the 1971 and 1976 Yearbooks for the early 1960s data, since the averages for 1961–3 and 1964–6 given in the 1971 Yearbook are *both* lower than the average for 1961–5 given in the 1976 Yearbook, though obviously this is not *necessarily* inconsistent since the year 1966 does not figure in the last average.

Production Yearbook for 1971 and 1976. (The food consumption series had been discontinued in the Yearbooks for 1972 to 1975, and the remaining gap is that for the year 1971, since the 1976 Yearbook provides data from 1972 onwards.) It appears from this that, while the 1973 availability figure is just a bit lower than that in 1972, it is hardly lower than the 1961–5, average, and a good deal higher than the averages for 1964–6, 1967–9, and 1970. Indeed, no picture of a sharp fall in food consumption per head in the famine year 1973 emerges from any of these data. There is, however, more evidence of a fall in the following year, 1974.

7.3 WOLLO: TRANSPORT CONSTRAINT OR
     ENTITLEMENT CONSTRAINT?

While there was no noticeable food availability decline for Ethiopia as a whole in the famine year of 1973, there was clearly a shortage of food in the province of Wollo. This shortage could in principle be explained in at least two quite different ways. One is to take the entitlement approach, and argue that the fall in food output in Wollo resulted in a *direct entitlement failure* on the part of

Wollo farmers and a *trade entitlement failure* for other classes in Wollo, e.g. labourers and providers of services. There was not merely a decline in the food to which the Wollo population was directly entitled out of its own production, but also a collapse of income and purchasing power and of the ability of the Wollo population to attract food from elsewhere in Ethiopia. The alternative explanation is to attribute the food shortage in Wollo to transport difficulties in moving food to the province from elsewhere in Ethiopia. According to this view, while there was no food shortage in Ethiopia, food could not be moved into Wollo because of a transport bottleneck. Indeed, transport limitation has been much discussed in explaining the food shortage in Wollo.

Roads are indeed quite underdeveloped *within* Wollo, and problems of moving food deep into rural areas of Wollo must not be underestimated. Nevertheless, I would like to argue that the transport limitation explanation cannot explain the Wollo famine, and the explanation has to be sought in entitlement failures.

First, while roads are few and bad in much of Wollo, two highways run through it, and the main north–south Ethiopian highway linking Addis Ababa and Asmera runs right through the area most affected by the famine.[9] Indeed, much of the early information about the famine came from travellers being stopped on the highway and asked for food (see Holt and Seaman, 1976). Nearly all the relief camps that were eventually set up were located near the highway, not merely because of easy access for supplies coming in, but also because of the high intensity of destitution in that region.[10] Underdeveloped roads would not explain the starvation in these famine-affected regions.

Second, there were reports of movements of food *out of* Wollo through the famine period. Food from Wollo went to Addis Ababa and to Asmera.[11] This probably was not very large in volume, but it provides some support for the market entitlement view rather than the transport limitation view of food shortage in Wollo.

Third, despite the disastrous failure of food output, food prices

[9] See Holt and Seaman (1976) and Belete *et al.* (1977).
[10] See Belete *et al.* (1977).
[11] See Holt and Seaman (1976), p. 5.

did not go up very much and for long in Wollo. When in October 1973 Holt and Seaman started their collection of food prices in the hardest hit district of Raya and Kobo, which had more than a tenth of its population in relief camps by May–June 1974,[12] they found that food prices were within 15 per cent of the pre-drought levels.[13]

Food prices in Dessie—the main grain market in Wollo—are given in Table 7.4.[14] Taking the average prices of 1970–2 as the 'pre-famine' levels, prices in the famine year 1973 were, on the whole, remarkably close to pre-famine levels: somewhat higher

TABLE 7.4

Wholesale Prices of Food Crops in Dessie, Wollo Province: 1970–3

Food crop	1970	1971	1972	1973	Percentage excess of 1973 price over 1970–2 average
White wheat	36	34	27	28	−13
Milling wheat	22	30	23	25	0
White sorghum	27	28	23	26	0
Other sorghum and zengada	23	24	19	21	−5
White teff	37	35	33	36	+3
Seregenga teff	33	31	29	34	+10
Red and abolse teff	31	29	27	30	+3
White barley	28	27	19	24	−3
Other barley	24	23	15	20	−3
Maize	21	20	23	21	−2
Millet (*dagussa*)	20	21	24	22	+2
Mixed peas	21	24	17	21	+2
Niger seed	37	32	24	25	−19
Rape seed	26	31	22	26	−1
Lin seed	40	42	25	30	−16

Source: National Bank of Ethiopia (for 1970 and 1971 data) and Ethiopian Grain Agency (for 1972 and 1973 data). I am most grateful to Julius Holt for making these unpublished figures available to me.

Note
Unit = Ethiopian Birr per quintal.

12 Belete *et al.* (1977), Tables I and II.
13 Holt and Seaman (1976). There were, however, reports of an earlier short period rise; see Seaman and Holt (1980).
14 These prices collected by the Ethiopian Grain Agency relate to the Ethiopian calendar. So 1973 corresponds to September 1972–September 1973. While it begins a bit early (and no time breakdown could be obtained), it avoids the period of very late 1973 in which relief supplies started coming into Wollo in some volume. Also, the main crop failure was clear by September 1972, the *kremt* rains having already failed.

for some and somewhat lower for others. People starved to death without there being a substantial rise in food prices. In terms of the entitlement approach, there is, of course, no puzzle in this. Since the farmers' food entitlement is a direct entitlement (without going through the market), a collapse of it can operate without a rise in market prices. On the other hand, the transport limitation view would have suggested a substantial increase in prices because of the excess demand arising from supply limitation.

The transport limitation view is, therefore, not easy to defend. In so far as the starving people in Wollo could draw on food from the rest of Ethiopia *if* they had the market power to pull food into Wollo, the appropriate unit for a FAD analysis has to be Ethiopia rather than Wollo. Food didn't move into Wollo in sufficient amount (and some moved out), not so much because the roads didn't permit such movement, but because the Wollo residents lacked the market command.[15]

7.4 THE ECONOMIC BACKGROUND OF THE DESTITUTES

Who were the famine victims? What economic background did they come from? While no systematic survey of the occupational background of famine victims was undertaken,[16] there are several sources of information on this subject. Putting them together, something of a clear picture does emerge about the groups involved, even though the quantitative importance of different groups is difficult to establish.

It is quite clear that one group that was severely affected was the Afar community of nomadic pastoralists. They were among the group of refugees seeking help in Addis Ababa in December 1972, and they figured most prominently in the crowds lining in the north–south highway through Wollo in early 1973, stopping cars and buses asking for food. There is, in fact, overwhelming evidence that 'Afar pastoralists were amongst the first to face the acute problems after the rain failure of 1972'.[17]

In a study carried out in May–June 1974 of the inmates in the thirteen shelters in Wollo province, it was found that the different

[15] According to Ethiopian Grain Agency data, the Wollo grain prices in 1973 remained in the neighbourhood of—typically only a little higher than—those ruling in Addis Ababa, despite the starvation in Wollo.

[16] There is here a sharp contrast with the availability of occupational statistics for the Bengal famine of 1943, to a great extent because of the broad-based sample survey carried out by Mahalanobis, Mukherjea, and Ghosh (1946).

[17] Holt and Seaman (1976), p. 3.

regions of Wollo were remarkably differently represented in these relief camps. Table 7.5 presents the number of households from different *awrajas* (subregions) in Wollo, and it is clear that three of the *awrajas* stand out as having very much higher incidence of destitution: Raya and Kobo, Yeju, and Ambassel. Even in absolute numbers they provided more than three-quarters of all the destitutes in the relief camps. As it happens, all three of these subregions are mostly in the eastern lowlands of Wollo, and this is where the nomadic herdsmen primarily live. While community-specific incidence rates cannot be calculated from the data, it is quite clear that nomadic herdsmen were hit hard, and 'in the Wollo famine of 1973, the pastoral population hardest hit were the Afar'.[18]

But while the nomads may have been hit relatively hardest, in absolute numbers the destitutes were dominated by

TABLE 7.5
Subregional Variation of Relief Seeking in Wollo

Subregion (awraja)	Population (thousands)	Household numbers from the subregion in the relief camps	Number in relief camp per thousand from the subregion	Relative destitution index
(1)	(2)	(3)	(4)	(5)
1. Raya and Kobo	54	1,350	112.5	100
2. Yeju	159	1,994	56.4	50
3. Ambassel	261	1,639	28.3	25
4. Kalu	126	515	18.4	16
5. Awsa	73	184	11.3	10
6. Wag	142	169	5.4	5
7. Lasta	292	182	2.8	2
8. Dessie Zuria	179	110	2.8	2
9. Wadla Delanta	147	18	0.6	0.5
10. Wore Himenu	225	22	0.4	0.4
11. Borena	265	15	0.3	0.3
12. Were Ilu	137	0	0.0	0.0

Source: Columns (1), (2), and (3) are taken from Tables I and II in Belete *et al.* (1977). Column (4) is calculated from them, taking a household size of 4.5 persons, and agrees with the figures given in Table II of Belete *et al.* (1977) except for the elimination of what appears to be a computational slip there regarding the subregion Wag. Column (5) converts the figures in column (4) into a 0–100 linear index.

[18] Hussein (1976), p. 19.

agriculturists, since the latter is a very much larger group. In terms of numbers, the 'relief-centre populations were mainly made up of members of the farming peoples of principally low-land area which are many times more densely populated than the Afar region'.[19] In fact, even in the subregions of Raya and Kobo, Yeju, and Ambassel, the bulk of the destitutes came from the agricultural communities.

The agriculturists came to distress quite early as well. The 1,500 Wollo people who marched to Addis Ababa to beg for help in March 1973 were reported to be 'peasants'.[20] While it is always problematic to judge distress from protest movements, since it may reflect better organization and militancy rather than greater distress, there is little doubt that Wollo agriculturists were widely suffering from destitution very early in the 1973 famine.[21]

Among the population of the relief camps, the following groups seem to have predominated:

(1) women and children 'drawn from the surrounding agricultural land', who formed a majority of the relief camp population;

(2) a large number of men who had migrated to the more southerly camps, particularly in Dessie and Kombolcha 'from more northerly districts in search of work';

(3) people from roadside towns and their peripheries, consisting of 'professional beggars', 'male daily labourers who could no longer find sufficient work', and 'women in service occupations who were not wanted in these hard economic times: household servants of the less wealthy, water carriers whose work was taken over by members of clients' families, beer-sellers and prostitutes'.[22]

Interviews with the relief camp inhabitants also threw much light on the sequence of destitution in the settled farming communities.[23] With reduced crops and grazing as the crisis deepened, servants and dependants of farmers were evicted, and they were among the first to move to look for work elsewhere.

---

[19] Holt and Seaman (1976), p. 3.

[20] See Wiseberg (1976), p. 108, on contemporary records on this and other aspects of the early stages of the famine.

[21] See Hussein (1976) and Gebre-Medhin and Vahlquist (1977).

[22] Holt and Seaman (1976), pp. 3–5.

[23] See Gebre-Medhin et al. (1974); Holt and Seaman (1976); and Belete, Gebre-Medhin, Hailemariam, Maffi, Vahlquist, and Wolde-Gabriel (1977).

There followed a good deal of eviction of tenants from the land, and they too were set on the move. Both tenants as well as small-scale family-land (*rist*) holders were gradually led to sell livestock, in addition to losing a great many owing to the drought, and many seem to have run out of seeds when a second planting became necessary after a false start to the rains. While movement in search of work elsewhere is by no means uncommon in this part of Ethiopia, there was now an unusually large movement in search of employment for daily labour or harvest work. Among the places to which the migrants went were local towns within the Wollo region, the Setit-Humera cash cropping region near the border with Sudan, and the cotton plantations on the Awash River in the southern parts of the province. The wives and children of the migrating men either stayed with relatives, or came to town to beg for a living, or sought shelter in the relief camps.

There are also other sources of information on migration, including a study of ninety-two Muslim families from Koreb and Gayint, two villages near the border of Wollo and Begemdir-Simien (A. P. Wood, 1976). The vast majority of the migrants, in this case, earned their livelihood by cultivation. Other occupations mentioned were weaving, domestic service, and the sale of alcoholic drinks. In terms of propensity to move, it appears that neither those who owned much land nor the very poor moved easily, and 'those who moved were the wealthier tenants, and the small landowners' (p. 71). The explanation offered by Adrian Wood is as follows:

The poorer tenants had, as a result of seven years of drought, already exhausted their meagre resources and either left the area, become deeply indebted and hence tied to their benefactor, or died. The wealthier tenants, having more resources in terms of livestock and land under cultivation, had until this stage been able to survive independently but many were finding this increasingly difficult. Landowners, not having to pay rent, which most tenants appear to have paid throughout the drought, were less affected by the reduced yields. However, many of those with only small areas under cultivation and few livestock had exhausted their reserves after seven years of drought.[24]

Piecing together the available information, the destitution groups in the 1973–4 famine in Wollo would seem to include at

[24] A. P. Wood (1976), p. 71.

least the following occupation categories (and their dependants):
(1) pastoralists, particularly from the Afar community;
(2) evicted farm servants and dependants of farmers, and rural labourers;
(3) tenant cultivators, sometimes evicted, but often simply squeezed by economic circumstances;
(4) small land-owning cultivators;
(5) daily male labourers in urban areas;
(6) women in service occupations;
(7) weavers and other craftsmen;
(8) occupational beggars.

In contrast with the famine in Wollo and the north-east of Ethiopia, the later 'southern' famine was relatively small, in terms of both mortality and economic destitution. It affected principally Harerghe, the country's largest province, and to a lesser extent Bale and Sidamo. There is a good deal of mortality data from Harerghe,[25] and it would appear that the hardest-hit group were the pastoralists who were Ogaden Somalis and Issa Somalis. While a substantial majority of the population even of the Harerghe province are agriculturists, the famine victims were very largely the pastoralists from these nomadic groups. Because of the differences in normal nutritional levels of the different communities, this contrast is not easy to detect on the basis of the standard anthropometric measures, but descriptive accounts of the famine as well as survey of the relief camp inmates bring out the contrast sharply.[26] The differences are apparent also in the mortality statistics. This is especially clear from the data on mortality of children under five.[27] It appears, on the basis of a survey in 1974, that 'during the previous year this mortality rate of the under-five was virtually unchanged for agricultural peoples, but increased by about three-fold amongst pastoralists'.[28] Thus, in understanding the 'southern famine' in Harerghe, it is appropriate to concentrate on the pastoralists and

[25] See Seaman, Holt, and Rivers (1974; 1978) and Gebre-Medhin, Hay, Licke, and Maffi (1977).

[26] See Seaman, Holt, and Rivers (1974; 1978), Gebre-Medhin and Vahlquist (1977), p. 198; and Gebre-Medhin, Hay, Licke, and Maffi (1977), pp. 29–34.

[27] In Ethiopian famines a high mortality level of under-five children seems to be a common characteristic. In the 'north-eastern famine' also the children under five were especially affected. See Belete, Gebre-Medhin, Hailemariam, Maffi, Vahlquist, and Wolde-Gabriel (1977), pp. 18–19.

[28] Rivers, Holt, Seaman, and Bowden (1976), p. 352.

on the particular areas in which they lived, namely the northern and southern Ogaden regions and the Issa Desert.

7.5 AGRICULTURAL DESTITUTION AND ENTITLEMENTS

As was mentioned earlier, the biggest group of destitutes in the Wollo famine came from the agricultural background, and indeed were farmers—both tenants and small land-owning cultivators. The entitlement decline here took the form of *direct entitlement failure* (see Chapter 5) without involving the market in the immediate context. The output—typically of foodgrains— was severely reduced, and this led to starvation in a direct way. In so far as the Ethiopian farmer eats the food grown by the family without becoming involved in exchange to acquire food, the immediate influence affecting starvation is the decline of the food grown and owned by the family, rather than the fall in the total food output in the region as a whole.[29] The distinction is important, since the FAD approach would focus on the latter variable. The hunger of the Wollo peasant had a more direct origin.

But, of course, once his own crop had failed, the Wollo peasant would have tried to get hold of food through the market *in so far as* he could have exercised market command. But since the agricultural failure also amounts to a collapse of his *source* of market command (namely his income), he was not in a position to supplement his reduced food output by market purchase. As discussed in Section 7.3, the Wollo agriculturist could not provide much effective demand for food in the market, and despite widespread starvation the food prices in Dessie and elsewhere recorded very little increase.

The effective demand of the agriculturist was further restrained by three subsidiary factors in addition to the fall in agricultural output: (1) a fall in the market price of land,[30] (2) loss of livestock,[31] and (3) a fall in the market price of livestock.[32]

---

[29] So far as the *tenant* farmers are concerned, they also suffered from the inflexibility of rents and feudal dues, on which there was little relief (see Cliffe, 1974, and Hussein, 1976). There was also some rearrangement of rental agreements unfavourable to the tenants (see Hussein, 1976, and also Cohen and Weintraub, 1975).

[30] See A. P. Wood (1976) and Belete *et al.* (1977).

[31] See Miller and Holt (1975) and Hussein (1976).

[32] This was pointed out already in March 1973 by the Ethiopian Ministry of Agriculture (1973), while reporting on the November 1972 survey of crop losses: 'depressed prices for livestock in most deficient areas' were 'making losses high in

The decline in land and livestock prices is a common phenomenon in famine situations affecting agriculturists, since they represent assets that the agriculturist tries to sell to acquire food when all else fails; and the sudden increase in supply of these assets in the market causes a price decline. The livestock *quantity* declined largely as a result of the drought, and the interesting point is that, despite this quantity reduction, the *prices* of farm animals also fell. This too is a common combination in pastoral famines, and will be taken up for a fuller discussion in the next section.

Turning now to agricultural labour, the eviction of farm servants was very widespread in Wollo during the famine. This was a natural economy measure on the part of farmers faced with an economic crisis of gigantic proportion, and fits into the general pattern of 'derived destitution' also observed elsewhere (see Chapter 6 and Appendix B). The resource ownership of the farm servants is confined, for all practical purposes, to own labour-power, and as unemployment develops the exchange entitlement of the group collapses radically. Migration in search of work elsewhere may or may not provide any substantial remedy, and for those who died or ended up in relief camps it presumably did not. Even for those who were successful in finding employment elsewhere, the wives and children often died meanwhile, or had to live in camps, since the process typically involved travelling over distance and spending substantial amounts of time there to earn enough to save something and return. In the mean time, many of their dependants perished, especially children under five.[33] Also, a great many families became permanently split as a consequence of the prolonged separation.

The eviction of farmers' dependants reflected partly just hard-headedness in hard times, but also the fact that many dependants play a role not altogether dissimilar to servants—being given 'food and shelter in return for farm labour'.[34] They were turned away for much the same reasons as farm servants were, and once evicted they typically shared the same fate as the farm servants.

transactions involving livestock sales to supplement grain supplies' (pp. 8–9). See also A. P. Wood (1976), pp. 72–3.

[33] See Belete, Gebre-Medhin, Hailemariam, Maffi, Vahlquist, and Wolde-Gabriel (1977), pp. 18–9.

[34] Holt and Seaman (1976), p. 4.

Other occupational categories, e.g. weavers, craftsman, service sellers, urban labourers, and beggars, suffered mostly from straightforward 'derived destitution'. The economic decline of a large section of the community leads to a shrinkage of demand for commodities sold by other groups, in this case clothing, craft products, services, and even general labour power. Also, of course, living on charity is made that much more difficult. One decline leads to another, and so on, through the multiplier effect. Some of these occupations also became more competitive, with the influx of displaced rural men and women seeking work for survival, after migration into urban areas (see Hussein, 1976). These trade entitlement failures are the indirect results of agricultural decline in Wollo.

Two questions can be asked here. Since the destitution of the Wollo farmer was seen in terms of a *direct* entitlement failure, isn't there some inconsistency in assuming that the farmers cut down their demand for other products, since direct entitlements are calculated on the assumption of the whole of the own produce being used for consumption within the family (see Chapter 5)? The answer is no. While food entitlement reflects the *maximum* amount of food a person or a family can command, actual consumption can be less than that, and there is no inconsistency in taking a farmer (whose direct entitlement is calculated as his whole produce) to be selling a part of that produce to buy other goods and services. It might be quite natural in a famine situation to assume that the whole of the food entitlement will be consumed, but not so in non-famine situations. There is, thus, no inconsistency in assuming that the farmer in the famine year will *reduce* his consumption of non-food commodities and will consume more—perhaps all—of his food entitlement.

Second, this reduced demand for non-food commodities and the related reduced supply of food to the market can be seen as exerting an upward pressure on the prices of food. Isn't this inconsistent with the observed largely stationary prices of foodgrains at Dessie and elsewhere? The answer again is no. The reduced supply of foodgrains to the market will go hand in hand with a reduced demand for non-food commodities and a consequent reduced demand for food by the producers and sellers of these non-food commodities. The food demand will thus also go down with food supply in these markets, and it is not clear that food prices would have risen much in these markets even if they had been cut off from the foodgrains supply in the rest of Ethiopia. There is, of course, the additional fact that these markets were not thus cut off, and any big rise in food prices in Dessie would have led to an increased food movement into Dessie.

So far, little has been said about the destitution of the pastoralist. To this group I now turn.

7.6 PASTORAL ENTITLEMENTS AND THE NOMADIC HERDSMAN

As was noted earlier, in the 'north-eastern famine', especially in Wollo, the pastoralist—particularly of the Afar community—was hit very hard, and in the later 'southern famine' the most affected group in Hererghe were the pastoral nomads from the Ogaden Somali and the Issa Somali communities. It might appear that, while their sufferings were severe, the explanation would be simple enough: the drought killed animals and the nomads, not being able to eat animals, died of starvation. But the picture is a good deal more complex than this.

First, the pastoralists, particularly of the Afar community, were affected not merely by the drought in north-eastern Ethiopia, but also by the loss of grazing land owing to the expansion of commercial agriculture. About 50,000 hectares of good land in the Awash Valley were 'developed' during 1970–1 for growing commercial crops, particularly cotton and sugar, by a few big companies—mostly foreign-owned[35]—and this growth of commercial agriculture continued through the early 1970s. The land thus developed had been among the best of the grazing land available to the Afar pastoralist during the long dry season lasting from September to May, and this land alienation led to severe economic problems of its own for the Afar.[36] As Glynn Flood (1975) noted, 'if they are to be able to exploit the vast areas into which they move during the wet season, Afar pastoralists must have access to adequate dry season grazing near the river', and 'when a small area close to the river is made unavailable for dry season grazing, a much larger area away from the river is

[35] This development can be viewed, more generally, as part of the negative influence of international capitalist expansion. On that more general question, see the analyses of Baran (1962), Furtado (1964), Baran and Sweezy (1966), Magdoff (1968), Frank (1969), and Amin (1974), among other contributions.

[36] Bondestam (1974), Gebre-Medhin (1974), Flood (1975), and Hussein (1976).

rendered useless' (p. 65). The land that was 'developed' was particularly valuable to the Afar, being mostly in an area that 'flooded easily and took a long time to drain'—'land which gave good grazing during the hottest and driest part of the year from February to June' (p. 64).

It was in this situation that the drought of 1972–3 in north-eastern Ethiopia came. The wet season was late and short and not particularly wet, while the refuge of the dry weather had been already crucially curtailed by the alienation of land for commercial agriculture. Thus the impact of the drought was a great deal magnified by this structural change in the economy of the Awash Valley.[37]

· Second, the economic distress of the pastoralist during the Ethiopian famine was not confined only to the loss of animals, whether this was due to drought or to displacement from traditional grazing grounds. The exchange entitlement associated with any given stock of animals *vis-à-vis* grains also fell sharply. It is sometimes overlooked that a pastoralist does not live only by eating animals or consuming animal products like milk. He also exchanges animals for other means of sustenance, chiefly grains. Indeed, given the 'normal' market prices prevailing in Ethiopia, animal calories cost about twice as much as grain calories,[38] and therefore a pastoral family can survive on a much lower holding of animals if they sell animals to buy grains for eating. Indeed, the typical pastoralist in these regions tends to meet about half of his calorie requirements through agricultural rather than pastoral products.[39]

While in the north-eastern famine in Wollo and elsewhere the exchange rates between animals and grains did fall, in the southern famine in Harerghe they collapsed in a totally dramatic manner. From a detailed survey of market prices conducted by Seaman, Holt, and Rivers (1974) covering different regions of Harerghe in May–June 1974, contemporary prices are available as well as the recollection of previous year's prices and the level of

---

[37] The Afar mainly use the middle and lower Awash Valley. The development of commercial agriculture was not, however, confined only to these parts of the Awash Valley. The growth of commercial agriculture in the upper valley of Awash led to the displacement of Kerega Oromo communities to find new pastures and also to the displacement of some peasant cultivation (see Bondestam, 1974, p. 480, and Hussein 1976, pp. 19–20).

[38] See Seaman, Holt, and Rivers (1978), pp. 38–9; also Hay (1975).

[39] See Rivers, Holt, Seaman, and Bowden (1976), p. 354.

'normal' prices. While the recall method is somewhat defective, especially in the context of prices,[40] the exchange rates between animals and grains calculated from these data are nevertheless of interest. Table 7.6 presents these derived exchange rates.[41]

It is clear that the exchange rate declines for animals against grains are very substantial, especially in pastoral (rather than agricultural) areas. Nevertheless, they may in fact *understate* the unfavourable exchange position of the pastoralists during the famine, since the animal prices had relatively recovered when the observations were made. Those who conducted the survey noted that 'it was stated by respondents in pastoral areas that livestock prices, and especially cattle prices, had fluctuated considerably within the last year, and that they were remarkably low in many localities at the time six to nine months before this survey, when the effects of drought were most severe' (Seaman, Holt and Rivers, 1974, p. 64; see also Seaman, Holt and Rivers, 1978, p. 39).

This decline in the exchange position was coupled with the loss of animals during the drought. The two effects are put together in Table 7.7. The value weights on the different types of animals have been calculated from their relative shares in the 'normal' pre-drought market value of the estimated 'average' stock of animals owned by a pastoral family in each region. The 'normal' pre-drought prices are taken from Table XVII of Seaman, Holt, and Rivers (1974), p. 62, and are the same as given in Table 7.6 above. The average animal holdings in the pre-drought situation are calculated from the observed average in June 1974 (given by Table X of Seaman, Holt, and Rivers, 1974, p. 45), and the relation between this observed herd and 'last year's herd' as estimated by these authors from the ratios of sale and death of animals (1974, Tables XII and XIII, pp. 46–7). Percentage of animal lost by death, presented in the next row of our Table 7.7, are also obtained from Table XII of Seaman, Holt, and Rivers (1974). The percentage losses of grain entitlement owing to

[40] The notion of 'normal' prices is particularly problematic, and earlier reports give somewhat different figures. See Seaman, Holt, and Rivers (1974), pp. 66–73, dealing with price levels given by two unpublished reports prepared respectively by the Ministry of Water Resources and the Ministry of Agriculture of the Imperial Ethiopian Government. However, the dramatic decline of the exchange rates of animals for grains follow from these figures as well.

[41] See also Gebre-Medhin, Hay, Licke, and Maffi (1977).

TABLE 7.6
Animal–Grain Exchange Rates in Different Strata in Harerghe

	Southern Ogaden stratum (pastoral)			Northern Ogaden stratum (pastoral)			Issa stratum (pastoral)			Strata in Harerghe strata (agricultural)		
	'Normal'	1973	1974	'Normal'	1973	1974	'Normal'	1973	1974	'Normal'	1973	1974
A *Prices* (Ethiopian dollars per quintal)												
Sorghum	16	37	51	17	27	42	16	24	32	15	25	31
Maize	14	34	48	14	24	36	15	21	27	14	20	27
Cattle	86	83	77	87	85	61	132	74	101	87	109	125
Sheep and goats	18	16	19	21	18	18	24	14	18	15	19	25
Camels	222	216	223	238	219	193	234	151	166	158	147	159
B *Exchange rates* (Index)												
Sorghum–Cattle	100	42	28	100	62	28	100	37	38	100	75	70
Maize–cattle	100	40	26	100	57	27	100	40	43	100	88	74
Sorghum–sheep	100	38	33	100	54	35	100	39	38	100	76	81
Maize–sheep	100	37	31	100	50	33	100	42	42	100	89	86
Sorghum–camel	100	42	32	100	58	33	100	43	35	100	56	49
Maize–camel	100	40	29	100	54	32	100	46	39	100	65	52

Source: Calculated from Seaman, Holt, and Rivers (1974), Tables XVI and XVII.

TABLE 7.7
Grain Entitlement Loss due to Animal Loss and Exchange Rate Change

	Southern Ogaden stratum				Northern Ogaden stratum				Issa stratum			
	Cattle	Goats and sheep	Camels	Average stock	Cattle	Goats and sheep	Camels	Average stock	Cattle	Goats and sheep	Camels	Average stock
Value weights in pre-drought holdings	0.571	0.157	0.271	1.000	0.295	0.276	0.429	1.000	0.396	0.425	0.179	1.000
Percentage animal loss owing to death (q)	47	45	52	48	56	61	55	57	88	74	69	79
Percentage grain entitlement loss owing to exchange rate change (p)	72	67	68	70	72	65	67	68	62	62	65	62
Percentage total grain entitlement loss $(p + q - pq)$	85	82	85	84	88	86	85	86	95	90	89	92
Ratio of exchange rate loss to animal ownership loss (p/q)	1.53	1.49	1.31	1.46	1.29	1.07	1.22	1.19	0.70	0.84	0.94	0.78

Source: see text.

exchange rate change *vis-à-vis* the predrought 'normal' levels are simply taken from the calculations presented in Table 7.6 above, taking sorghum as the grain in question for the purpose of these calculations. The percentage losses of grain entitlement from animal holdings as a combined result of animal loss and exchange rate deterioration are given in the next row, and these could be seen to be astonishingly large for all the pastoral areas, viz., 84 per cent for southern Ogaden, 86 per cent for northern Ogaden, and as much as 92 per cent for Issa desert.[42]

Another remarkable feature of these results concerns the relative contribution of animal loss and exchange rate deterioration on the total loss of entitlement to grains of the average pastoralist. In both southern Ogaden and northern Ogaden the contribution of the exchange rate seems substantially larger than that of animal loss as such. This is not so only in the Issa Desert, which was estimated to contain less than a third of the Ogaden population.

In fact, the relative contribution of the exchange rate change must be recognized to be even larger, when it is taken into account that (1) taking maize rather than sorghum as the index grain would increase the force of the exchange rate revision, and (2) the effect of animal loss is very considerably exaggerated in these calculations because of ignoring normal mortality in animals, which even in the absence of the drought conditions are typically quite large.[43] If the figures are revised to reflect these corrections, the relative contribution of exchange rate deterioration *vis-à-vis* animal mortality in the loss of grain entitlement would be even larger in all the areas under study. The *total* loss of grain entitlement, however, would be reduced, because more than half the recorded mortality in southern and northern Ogaden could be then attributed to normal death balanced by births.[44]

The grain entitlements are worth calculating, not because the pastoralist is likely to sell all his animals and buy grains, but—as

[42] Data presented by Gebre-Medhin, Hay, Licke and Maffi (1977) suggest a further deterioration in the year following, but they also note some doubts about the animal holding figures (p. 32). See also Hay (1975).

[43] See Seaman, Holt, and Rivers (1978), pp. 48, 56–7.

[44] For the same reason one can dispute the method of estimating 'last year's herd' used by Seaman, Holt, and Rivers (1974), which provides the basis for the weights used in Table 7.7 here. Summing 'the observed herd plus the number of animals reported to have

noted before—the pastoralist can normally acquire calories a good deal more cheaply through exchanging animals for grains. The typical pastoralist does depend on this, and in a situation of economic difficulty arising from loss of herd he is pushed to be even more dependent on grains. This is one reason why a drought that reduces both the animal stock and the grain output[45] very often leads to a reduction in animal price compared with grains. The proportionate reduction of animal offered in the market is typically a good deal less than the proportionate reduction in animal holdings, and can easily be a lot less than the proportionate reduction in the grain offered in the market.

There are three features in this that are worth distinguishing. First, grains at normal prices are cheaper sources of nutrition, and in a situation of economic decline demand tends to shift in that direction. Animals are 'superior' goods, and suffer in times of income collapse. When animal prices fall *vis-à-vis* grain this situation may change, but the emaciation of the animals in a drought situation also tends to lower the break-even exchange rate.

Second, for the pastoralist savings for the future takes the form of storing animals 'on the hoof', and in times of difficulty he may have to 'dissave' out of that stock by selling animals. For the peasant the saving is partly in the form of livestock, which he may also have to fling, and partly in the form of land. An unusual increase in land offer in a situation of economic decline is common, often leading to a fall in the relative price of land. Saving in the form of grain-stock is much less common, because of storage cost and perishability and also because the stock has no concurrent use value. Thus animals for the pastoralist serve both as output (like grains for the agriculturist) and as stored savings (like land—and animals—for the agriculturist). This too puts a bigger burden of adjustment on animal supply to the market in

---

died plus the number of animals reported to have been sold in the past year' (p.46) ignores new births and thus overestimates last year's real stock. In using these figures for weighting it would have to be assumed that *relative* weights are not much changed by the exclusion of birth data.

[45] While the animal stock holding in the different strata in Harerghe fell between 20 and 50 per cent in terms of average stock between June 1973 and June 1974 (see Table 7.7 above), the foodgrains output of Harerghe fell by about 30 per cent between 1972 and 1973 including the respective December harvests supplying food for the following year (see Ethiopian Ministry of Agriculture, 1974, p. 321).

times of distress, to meet the herdsmen's grain demand as well as his other needs for cash.

Finally, the consumption profile of a grain-stock is much more adjustable and amenable to control than that of livestock. Grain is divisible in a way that animals are not. Furthermore, whatever can be got out of a grain-stock can be got out immediately, in a manner that is impossible for the flow of animal products like milk. Thus, in terms of adjustability of the time pattern of food supply, animals are worse than grains when flexibility of the time pattern of consumption is important. This puts a further premium on grains *vis-à-vis* animals in situations of emergency compared with their normal price ratios, and the break-even exchange rate in terms of over-all calorie-value becomes a deceptive basis of comparison. This is one reason why the demand for grains as a source of food stays up even when animal prices drop sharply and grains become relatively much dearer than in the pre-crisis situation.

7.7. CONCLUDING REMARKS

The famine of 1972–74 in Ethiopia had two rather distinct parts: one affecting the north-east—especially the Wollo province—in 1972–73, and the other happening in the more southern provinces—especially Hararghe—in 1973–74. Total famine mortality seems to have been much higher in the north-eastern famine, for which relief came much too late. While in the north-eastern famine the relative incidence of starvation was probably greatest for the pastoral people, a majority of the famine victims in absolute numbers seem to have come from the agricultural community. In the southern famine—especially in Hararghe—the pastoral population has been the main group to suffer from the famine.

The Ethiopian famine took place with no abnormal reduction in food output, and consumption of food per head at the height of the famine in 1973 was fairly normal for Ethiopia as a whole. While the food output in Wollo was substantially reduced in 1973, the inability of Wollo to command food from outside was the result of the low purchasing power in that province. A remarkable feature of the Wollo famine is that food prices in general rose very little, and people were dying of starvation even when food was selling at prices not very different from pre-drought levels. The phenomenon can be understood in terms of extensive entitlement failures of various sections of the Wollo population.

The pastoral population—severely affected in both the north-eastern and southern parts of the famine—belonged to nomadic and semi-nomadic groups. They were affected not merely by the drought but also by the growth of commercial agriculture, displacing some of these communities from their traditional dry-weather grazing land, thereby vastly heightening the impact of the drought. The effect of the loss of animal stock was also compounded by a severe worsening of terms of trade of animals for grain, disrupting the pastoralist's normal method of meeting his food requirements. The characteristics of exchange relations between the pastoral and the agricultural economies thus contributed to the starvation of the herdsmen by making price movements reinforce—rather than counteract—the decline in the livestock quantity. The pastoralist, hit by the drought, was decimated by the market mechanism.

Chapter 8

Drought and Famine in the Sahel

8.1 THE SAHEL, THE DROUGHT, AND THE FAMINE

The name Sahel is derived from an Arabic word meaning 'shore' or 'border'. The Sahel refers to the border of the world's largest tropical desert: the Sahara. It is, in fact, the fringe of the desert, lying between the desert and the tropical rain forests of Africa. But within this general conception of the Sahel, a great many alternative specifications of it can be found in the vast literature on the Sahel produced by geographers and climatologists. It is useful to begin by sorting out the different approaches, if only to avoid possible confusion later in the analysis of the Sahelian drought.

(1) *The ecological definitions* The Sahel can be defined as the 'dry zone', comprising the 'arid' zone (with average rainfall per year less than 100 mm, or 4 in.) and the 'semi-arid' zone (with rainfall between 100 and 500 mm, or between 4 and 20 in.), on the southern fringe of the Sahara, and this coincides with a 'tropical steppe vegetation belt'.[1] It runs across the broadest part of Africa from the Atlantic to the Red Sea. The Sahel is sometimes defined not as the entire dry zone immediately south of the Sahara, but as only the semi-arid zone there. While covering less than the whole dry zone in this part of the world, it too runs from the Atlantic to the Red Sea.[2]

(2) *The politico-ecological definitions* On this view, the Sahel is defined as the 'semi-arid vegetation belt' in six West African countries, viz. Mauritania, Senegal, Mali, Upper Volta, Niger, and Chad.[3] Alternatively, and more broadly, the Sahel could refer to the 'dry zone' in these six countries.

---

[1] Harrison Church (1973), p. 62; see also Harrison Church (1961).

[2] See Winstanley (1976), p. 189. Winstanley's specification of rainfall for the semi-arid region is also on the *higher* side, viz. 'between 200 and 600 mm', so that not merely the arid zone but also regions at the northern end of the semi-arid zone as defined by Harrison Church (1973) is excluded in this view of the Sahel.

[3] See Matlock and Cockrum (1976) and Swift (1977b). Sometimes Gambia and Cape Verde are added to this list of six countries.

(3) *The political definitions* The word Sahel could be used, as it has been by the international news media, simply to refer to these six *countries* in West Africa (Mauritania, Senegal, Mali, Upper Volta, Niger, and Chad), affected by the recent drought.[4]

There is no point in spilling blood over the choice of the definition that should be used, but one must be careful to distinguish between the different senses of the word Sahel to be found in the literature, since not a little confusion has arisen from vagueness owing to this plethora of definitions—sometimes used implicitly rather than explicitly.

In this work the Sahel in the purely political characterization will be called 'Sahelian countries', covering Mauritania, Senegal, Mali, Upper Volta, Niger, and Chad. The politico-ecological definition will be used in the form of calling the dry Sahel region in the Sahelian countries as 'the dry Sahel region'. Finally, the purely ecological definition applied to the whole of Africa (without noting political divisions) will be captured by the expression 'the Sahel belt of Africa'.

I turn now to the drought in question. The reference is to the period of low rainfall during 1968–73. There is some controversy as to whether 1968 or even 1969 were, in fact, years of drought. It has been argued that 'the 1968–69 rains were more or less normal; they only appeared low by comparison with the pluvian 1960s, which detracted attention from the cyclical nature of rainfall in that area'.[5] It appears that 'the Sahel and Sudan zones probably received more rain between 1956 and 1965 than at any time in this century', and, it has been argued, after that 'just less than average rainfall' appeared as 'drought'.[6] But there can be little doubt that the drought period involved a very considerable shift in the rainfall isohyets in a southerly direction, making an arid zone out of parts of semi-arid regions and turning non-dry regions into semi-arid ones. And this is so not only in contrast with the immediate pluvial past, but also compared with earlier record.[7] While it is certainly not correct to say that 'the Sahel has never had a drought like this one',[8] the shift in the rainfall pattern

---

[4] See the map of Sahel countries on p. 130.
[5] Wiseberg (1976), p. 122, quoting the views of an MIT group of climatologists.
[6] Matlock and Cockrum (1976), p. 238.
[7] See Winstanley (1976), Bradley (1977), Schove (1977).
[8] Brown and Anderson (1976), p. 162; it must, however, be said in fairness to the authors that the drought *was* very unusual in terms of its *impact*, though not as a drought as

was very substantial, and the contrast with the rainy 1960s was particularly sharp.

The problem applied not merely to the dry Sahel region in the Sahelian countries, but to the whole of the Sahel belt of Africa, covering also parts of Sudan and Ethiopia. Indeed, there were clear links in the drought pattern associated with the Ethiopian famine studied in the last chapter and the drought affecting the Sahelian countries.

It is also worth noting that the short-fall of rain compared with normal was more severe further north within the Sahelian region; i.e., areas that normally receive less rainfall anyway suffered a bigger relative short-fall as well.[9] This is not altogether unusual, since there is some evidence that as we move north in this part of Africa not only does the mean rainfall level fall, but the coefficient of variation rises substantially.[10]

The pastoral and agricultural economy of the Sahel region was severely affected by the drought.[11] While, as we shall presently see, there were factors other than the drought in the causation of the famine, it would be stupid to pretend that the drought was not seriously destructive. The peak year of suffering seems to have been 1973, and the drought waned only with the good rains of 1974. The animal loss altogether was estimated, according to some calculations, to be as high as 'some 40 percent to 60 percent',[12] but there is a good deal of disputation on these quantitative magnitudes, and much variation from region to region. There is, however, very little scope for doubting the severity of the suffering that accompanied the drought, and the famine conditions that developed during this period. Of the six countries, Mauritania, Mali, and Niger seem to have been hit harder than the other countries.

Already by 1969 there were reports of 'prolonged drought across West Africa'.[13] The situation got worse as the drought progressed, and by the spring of 1972 the United Nations World

such. On the comparative evidence from earlier periods, see the technical papers cited above, and also Dalby and Harrison Church (1973), pp. 13–16, 29–45.

[9] See Bradley (1977), p. 50, Figure 2.

[10] See Winstanley (1976), p. 197, Figure 8.6.

[11] See Shear and Stacy (1976), Winstanley (1976), and Matlock and Cockrum (1976). In Section 8.2 of this chapter the output situation is reviewed.

[12] El-Khawas (1976), p. 77. See also Winstanley (1976) and Matlock and Cockrum (1976).

[13] See Sheets and Morris (1976), p. 36.

Food Programme noted that drought in the Sahelian countries had become 'endemic', requiring that 'special treatment' be given to the region in providing emergency food aid. By September that year the FAO had identified a coming 'disaster', with 'an acute emergency situation developing in large areas due to exceptionally poor harvests in the Sahel'. The level of starvation was by then, it appears, much greater than in the preceding four years of drought, and 'children and the elderly had already begun to succumb'.[14]

The peak year of the famine in the Sahelian countries was 1973, the starvation having by then gathered momentum in a cumulative process of destitution and deprivation.[15] The number of famine deaths during that year was estimated to be around 100;000.[16] But there is a good deal of disputation about the mortality estimates,[17] and rather little direct evidence on which a firm estimate can be based. There is also much debate on the extent to which the famine unleashed the forces of epidemic in the Sahelian countries. The threat of epidemics was widely noted, and reports of flaring up of diseases like measles did come through, but it has been argued that the epidemics were rather mild and to a great extent were confined to the relief camps where infections could spread fast.[18] Certainly, the epidemic flare-up was nothing in comparison with what was observed in some earlier famines, e.g. the Bengal famine of 1943 (see Appendix D below).

The relief operations, though slow to start with, were on quite a massive scale, and the provision of food, medicine, and shelter was helped by a good deal of international co-operation. The efficiency of the relief operations remains a highly disputed topic. Some have seen in such operations the clue to 'how disaster was avoided',[19] and have assigned a good deal of credit to international efforts as well as to efforts within the countries

[14] Sheets and Morris (1976), p. 38. The authors provide a blow-by-blow account of the international recognition of the Sahelian disaster and a sharp critique of the delay in responding to it.

[15] See Newman (1975).

[16] Center for Disease Control (1973), and Kloth (1974). See also Imperato (1976).

[17] See Seaman, Holt, Rivers, and Murlis (1973), Imperato (1976), and Caldwell (1977), pp. 94–5.

[18] See Imperato (1976), pp. 295–7, Sheets and Morris (1976), pp. 61–3, and Seaman, Holt, Rivers, and Murlis (1973), p. 7.

[19] See Imperato (1976) and Caldwell (1977).

themselves. Others have emphasized the sluggishness, the chaos, and the discrimination between different communities of victims as evidence of unpardonable mismanagement.[20]

8.2 FAD VIS-À-VIS ENTITLEMENTS

Was the Sahelian famine caused by a decline in food availability? The *per capita* food output did go down quite substantially. The figures of food availability per head in the six Sahelian countries as presented by the FAO are given in Table 8.1. There is much less of a decline in the food consumption per head judging by the FAO figures on calorie and protein consumption per head, as presented in Table 8.2. But, apart from Senegal, the other countries had a decline in food consumption per head as well, so that the FAD hypothesis does not stand rejected on the basis of these data.

TABLE 8.1
Net Food Output per Head (Index)

	1961–5	*1968*	*1969*	*1970*	*1971*	*1972*	*1973*	*1974*	*1975*
Chad	100	90	87	84	84	69	63	69	71
Mali	100	93	99	97	90	73	61	65	80
Mauritania	100	98	100	98	92	80	67	68	68
Niger	100	92	99	88	88	81	57	65	60
Senegal	100	81	87	66	89	56	67	88	107
Upper Volta	100	106	103	102	93	85	76	84	90

Source: FAO Production Yearbook 1976, Table 6.

TABLE 8.2
Calorie Consumption per head in Sahel countries

	1961–5	*1972*	*1973*	*1974*
Chad	100	76	73	76
Mali	100	86	86	88
Mauritania	100	91	94	95
Niger	100	86	89	85
Senegal	100	93	104	107
Upper Volta	100	86	85	96

Source: Calculated from data given in Table 97 of *FAO Production Yearbook 1976*.

[20] See Sheets and Morris (1976), El-Khawas (1976) and Wiseberg (1976).

It is also worth emphasizing that the FAD view is not rejected even by the otherwise important observation that nearly all the Sahelian countries had enough food within their borders to prevent starvation had the food been divided equally, and that 'throughout the whole Sahel [the Sahelian countries] in every year from 1968 to 1972 the per caput supply [of cereals] exceeded this figure [FAO/WHO recommended food-intake per person] comfortably'.[21] It appears that an FAO survey 'documented that every Sahelian country, with the possible exception of mineral-rich Mauritania, actually produced enough grain to feed its total population even during the worst drought year'.[22] This is obviously relevant in emphasizing the importance of unequal distribution in starvation as well as giving us an insight into the type of information that FAO looked into in understanding the famine, but it does not, of course, have any bearing on the correctness of the FAD view of famines. The FAD approach is concerned primarily not with the *adequacy* of over-all food supply, but with its *decline* compared with past experience. In particular, the FAD claim is not that famines occur if and only if the average food supply per head is insufficient compared with some nutritional norm, but that famines occur if and only if there is a sharp *decline* in the average food availability per head. And, it could be argued, such a decline did take place for the Sahelian countries as a group during the drought of 1969–73. If the FAD approach to famines were to seek refuge in some comforting bosom, it probably couldn't do better in the modern world than choose the Sahelian famine: the food availability did go down, and—yes—there was a famine!

Despite this, I would argue that, even for the Sahelian famine, the FAD approach delivers rather little. First, in the peak year of famine, 1973, the decline in food availability per head was rather small even in comparison with the pluvial early 1960s for Mali, Mauritania, Niger, and Upper Volta (less than a 15 per cent decline of calorie availability per head), and none at all for Senegal. While the decline was much sharper for Chad (27 per cent), Chad was one of the less affected countries in the region,

[21] Marnham (1977), p. 17. See also Lappé and Collins (1977, 1978), and Lofchie (1975).

[22] Lappé and Collins (1977), p. 2, and footnote 6, quoting a letter from Dr. M. Ganzin, Director, Food Policy and Nutrition Division, FAO, Rome, a major authority on the Sahelian economy.

the famine having been most severe in Mauritania, Mali, and Niger, and possibly Upper Volta.[23] But none of these latter countries had a very sharp decline in food availability per head (Table 8.2). It could, however, be argued that in terms of food *output* per head (Table 8.1), Niger and Mali did have the biggest decline in the famine year of 1973, with the indices standing respectively at 57 and 61. But Senegal, which was less affected, had an index value of 56 for 1972, the lowest index value for any country for any year. As we move away from the gross factual statements to a bit more detailed information, the FAD analysis starts limping straightway.

Second, the rationale of the FAD approach, concentrating as it does on aggregate supply, rests in ignoring distributional changes. But there is clear evidence that dramatic shifts in the distribution of purchasing power were taking place in the drought years in the Sahelian countries, mainly between the dry Sahel regions in these countries and the rest of the regions. The drought affected the Sahel area rather than the savanna, in which the vast majority of the population of Sahelian countries live. The relief camps even in the south were full of people who had migrated from the Sahelian north into less dry areas in the south. The famine victims were almost exclusively the nomadic pastoral population from the Sahel region (including nomads, semi-nomads, and transhumants) and the sedentary population living in the Sahel region (agriculturists, fishermen, etc.).[24] Rather than looking at aggregate statistics like those of food availability per head, it would clearly make much more sense to look at the economic conditions of these groups of people in understanding the Sahelian famine.

Third, we indeed have direct evidence of the decline in income and purchasing power of pastoralists and agriculturists living in the Sahelian region. The destruction of crops and the death of animals in these parts of the Sahelian countries were very substantial.[25] While the crops affected were often of foodgrains and the animals do supply edible products, most sections of the Sahelian population rely also on trade for food.[26] The severe

[23] See Center for Disease Control (1973) and Kloth (1974).
[24] See Sheets and Morris (1976), Kloth (1974), Copans *et al.* (1975), Lofchie (1975), and Imperato (1976).
[25] See Winstanley (1976) and Matlock and Cockrum (1976).
[26] The role of the commercialization in heightening the impact of the drought on the

decline in agricultural and pastoral output in these particular regions thus meant a sharp reduction in the ability of the affected people to command food, whether from one's own output or through exchange. The situation is somewhat comparable to the picture we already found in Ethiopia during the drought and famine there (see Chapter 7 above), which could be seen as a related phenomenon in another part of the Sahel belt of Africa.

It is worth mentioning in this context that, from the point of view of the suffering of the individual agriculturist, it matters rather little whether the crop destroyed happens to be a food crop which is consumed directly, or a cash crop which is sold to buy food. In either case the person's entitlement to food collapses. It is this collapse that directly relates to his starvation (and that of his family) rather than some remote aggregate statistics about food supply per head. The same applies to the pastoralist who lives by selling animals and animal products; and, like the Afar or Somali pastoralists in Ethiopia, the Sahel pastoralists also rely substantially on trading animals and animal products for other goods, including grains, which provide cheaper calories.[27]

Thus, despite superficial plausibility, the FAD approach throws rather little light on the Sahelian famine. It is not my contention that the FAD *always* makes wrong predictions. (If it did, then the FAD approach could have provided a good basis of prediction, *applied in reverse!*) Predictions based on FAD may sometimes prove right (as in gross statements about the over-all Sahelian famine), sometimes wrong (as in the Bengal famine or in the Ethiopian famine). So the first point is that it isn't much of a predictor to rely on. But the more important point is that, even when its prediction happens to come out right about the existence of a famine in a broad area, it provides little guidance about the character of the famine—*who* died, *where*, and *why*?

8.3 DESTITUTION AND ENTITLEMENT

Of the total population of some 25 million in the Sahelian countries in 1974, about 10 per cent can be described as nomadic.[28] The definition includes semi-nomads and transhum-

---

Sahelian economy has been particularly emphasized by Comité Information Sahel (1974). See also Meillassoux (1974), Raynaut (1977), and Berry, Campbell and Emker (1977). Also Imperato (1976), pp. 285–6.

[27] See, among others, Seaman, Holt, Rivers, and Murlis (1973), and Haaland (1977).
[28] See Caldwell (1975).

ants in addition to pure nomads. At the time the drought hit, the population of the dry Sahel region in these countries was roughly 5 to 6 million.[29] So the nomads were no more than half the population of the dry Sahel region itself, and quite a small proportion of the total population of the Sahelian countries. But the share of the nomads in the mortality induced by the famine and in nutritional deficiency were both remarkably high,[30] and even among the victims of the famine there is some evidence of 'a shocking contrast between the nutritional state of sedentary victims of the drought and the deep starvation of the nomads'.[31]

The destitution of the nomadic pastoralist seems to have followed a process not dissimilar to the fate of the Ethiopian herdsmen of the Afar or Somali communities, studied in the last chapter. The animal loss in the dry Sahel area varied between 20 to 100 per cent depending on the region,[32] and this was compounded, as in Ethiopia, by the 'rapid destocking of animals in the Sahel' coinciding with 'a sharp drop in prices'.[33] The reasons for the fall in price seem to have been similar to those encountered in analysing the Ethiopian famine (see Chapter 7). A pastoralist depends on consuming cereals part of the year as a cheaper source of calories,[34] and may become more—and not less—dependent on exchanging animals for cereals in the straitened circumstances caused by the loss of animals.[35] The fixed money obligations arising from taxes, etc., that have to be met makes the pastoralist inclined to sell more rather than less, when the relative prices of animals fall.[36] The emaciation of animals would provide a more direct explanation of the sharp fall in prices. Whatever the cause, the statistics of the loss of animals understate the magnitude of the economic decline sustained by the pastoralist.

[29] See Imperato (1976), p. 285, and Marnham (1977), p. 7.
[30] See Kloth (1974), Sheets and Morris (1976), and Imperato (1976).
[31] Sheets and Morris (1976), p. 53.
[32] See Glantz (1976), pp. 77–8, 199–200, and FAO *Production Yearbook*, 1974, Tables 107–10.
[33] Club du Sahel (1977), p. 55.
[34] See Chapter 7 and also the references cited in note 27 in this chapter.
[35] The sale of 'an unusual proportion of their animals' was thus 'one of the pastoralists' means of defence' (Caldwell, 1977, p. 96).
[36] This notion leads naturally to the possibility of a backward-bending supply curve, which has been frequently mentioned. But since this is only one factor among many, such a backward bend may not occur in the *total* supply curve. The position also depends on the precise circumstances facing the pastoralist (see Haaland, 1977), and there is some empirical evidence against the backward bend (see Khalifa and Simpson, 1972).

The pastoralists migrated down south in quite large numbers during the Sahelian famine, and this movement of people and animals was one way of reducing the impact of the famine— indeed, according to one view was this group's 'chief defence'.[37] Better feeding conditions for the animals as well as opportunities for wage labour in the south permitted some relief, and the relief camps set up there also took a good many of the pastoralists from the north. There is some evidence, however, of discriminating treatment against the pastoral nomadic people in the relief camps, and a firm suggestion that the Sahelian governments were closely tied to (and more responsive to the needs of) the majority sedentary communities.[38]

Another group severely affected by the famine was the sedentary agriculturists from the dry Sahel region. While the position of the dry Sahel pastoralist was rather similar to that of the Afar and Somali nomads in the Ethiopian famine, that of the dry Sahel agriculturist could be compared with the predicament of the Wollo cultivator. His output was down, and whether he lived by eating his own product or by selling it in the market, his entitlement to food underwent a severe decline. For many cash crops, e.g. groundnuts, the impact of the drought seems to have been no less than on the total quantity of food output as such (see Table 8.3). The food output in the country in which he lived might have gone down by a moderate ratio, but his command over the food that was there slipped drastically. The extent of the decline varied depending on the precise region in question since the drought was far from uniform,[39] but for some of the dry Sahel agriculturists it was a case of straightforward ruin. The problem was made more difficult by the monetary obligations of taxation,[40] which had to be paid despite the drought, and by the loss of job opportunity arising from what we have been calling 'derived deprivation'.[41]

[37] Caldwell (1977), p. 96.
[38] See Sheets and Morris (1976).
[39] See Bradley (1977), pp. 39–40.
[40] It has been argued that the obligation to pay taxes in monetary terms has been an important reason for Sahelian farmers for moving from food crops to cash crops (see Berry, Campbell and Emker, 1977, p. 86). See also Comité Information Sahel (1974).
[41] See Chapters 1, 6, and 7. In the drought year the Sahelian labourer sought employment further away from home than normal. See, for example, Faulkingham (1977), Tables 17.7 and 17.8; there is a remarkable increase in the number of labourers from this Hausa village in Niger going to distant Kano (360 km), Lagos (910 km) and Abidjan (1,420 km) for wage employment in such occupations as being 'water career'.

TABLE 8.3
Food Output Compared with Output of Groundnuts in shell

	1966–8	1969	1970	1971	1972	1973	1974
Senegal							
Food	100	101	78	108	70	84	94
Groundnut	100	88	65	110	65	85	95
Niger							
Food	100	99	97	89	88	64	80
Groundnut	100	92	79	82	93	29	64
Mali							
Food	100	107	101	108	86	68	88
Groundnut	100	97	125	121	119	79	151
Chad							
Food	100	104	103	102	80	72	76
Groundnut	100	119	119	78	47	52	52

Source: Calculated from Tables 7 and 43 in *FAO Production Yearbook 1975*, changing the base of the index to the average for 1966, 1967, and 1968, with unchanged weights.

8.4 SOME POLICY ISSUES

Droughts may not be avoidable, but their effects can be. 'The weather and climate modification schemes proposed since 1900 for the regions in West and Central Africa surrounding and including the Sahara Desert'[42] are worthy fields of investigation. I expect some day one might indeed grow rice or catch fish in the Sahara. But while science marches on slowly, some means have to be found for freeing the Sahelian population from vulnerability to droughts and the prospect of famines. I end this chapter with brief comments on this issue.

One approach is to argue that the problem is not as bad as it might look from the perspective of the recent drought. One could say that droughts come and go, and they don't come all that frequently either: in this century the serious ones for the Sahel countries have been 1910–14, 1941–2, 1969–73. Is there a real need for special action? While smugness—like virtue—is its own reward, it is not a reward on which the Sahelian population can bank. Periodic famines may not be as bad as perpetual starvation, but one can scarcely find that situation acceptable.

Another approach is to argue that there is no real need to make the dry Sahel region economically non-vulnerable, since people

[42] Glantz and Parton (1976). See also Franke and Chasin (1979).

can emigrate. It has been argued that 'the inevitably limited funds available for development can be more effectively employed' in the moister area south of the dry Sahelian region, and that 'relevant governments should consider the feasibility of a strategic withdrawal from areas of very low and unreliable rainfall'.[43] This approach is further supported by the observation that many nomads interviewed in the south during and immediately after the drought years indicated a willingness to stay on in the south.

Depopulation as a solution to the problem of the Sahelian region overlooks a number of important factors. First, it seems that the bulk of the population from the Sahelian north who migrated south have, in fact, returned north again. Even if many had stayed on, that would have still left the Sahelian countries with the problem of what to do with the remaining dry Sahel population. It is not easy to change the way of life of a large community, nor is there any reason to suppose that the Sahelian northerner typically finds the economic opportunities in the south to be superior to those ruling in the north in the normal years. The problem is one of fluctuation of economic circumstances between wet and dry years rather than of a collapse of the economic potential of the north in general.

Second, it does seem economically most wasteful to give up the use of the resources available for agriculture, pastoralism, and fishing in the north and to crowd the southern savanna even more than it is already crowded. The southerner typically did not welcome the northern invasion, and there is good reason to think that large-scale permanent immigration would indeed worsen the economic conditions of the southern population.

Finally, the Sahelian countries do get many things from the economic production in the north, both of pastoral products as well as of cash crops. The Sahelian north is no 'basket case', and while a severe drought may make the northerner dependent on the southerner for his survival, the southerner normally gets various commodities and foreign exchange from the production taking place in the north.

It is necessary, therefore, to think of solutions of the Sahelian problem without choosing the drastic simplicity of depopulating

[43] This view is attributed to 'Professor Hodder of the School of Oriental and African Studies and others' by David Dalby in Dalby and Harrison Church (1973), p. 21.

the Sahel region. Since the source of the problem is variability rather than a secular decline, it is tempting to think in terms of insurance arrangements. The first question then is: what is to be insured? If FAD had been a good theory of famines and total food availability a good guide to starvation, then the thing to insure would have been the over-all supply of food in these countries. Some system of international insurance could be used to make resources available for import of food from abroad when domestic production of food fails and when the earnings of foreign exchange go down, making it difficult to import food by using currently earned exchange. While the Sahelian countries have had a declining trend of food output per head over the last decade or so, the trend rates have been much influenced by the sequence of drought years. Also, there have been some substantial shifts from food crops to cash crops, which reduce the food output per head but not necessarily the country's ability to buy food, since cash crops can be sold and exchanged for food in the international market. On the FAD approach, therefore, the problem may look simple enough: it is a case of occasional fall in food supply per head, which could be made good by an international insurance mechanism, so that enough food is available within the country.

But FAD isn't a very reliable guide. Despite its superficial plausibility in explaining the Sahelian famine, it delivers rather little even in this case, as we saw in the last section. There is need for concern not merely with how to get food into the country, but also with the way it could be commanded by the affected population. It is necessary to devise ways by which the population most affected by drought and economic difficulty can have the ability to obtain food through economic mechanisms. This contrast is particularly important in the context of recent developments such as growth of cash cropping, which have added to the country's over-all earning power but seem to have led to a decline of the exchange entitlement of particular sections of the population.

Thus, the insurance arrangements have to deal with command over food at the family level, and not merely at the national level. Private insurance of families of nomadic pastoralists and other groups in the dry Sahel region isn't an easy task, and indeed, such insurance rarely exists in any poor and backward country. Thus, the public sector would have to play a major role in the task of guaranteeing food to the vulnerable sections. Famine relief operations are, of course, insurance systems in some sense, but if a long-run solution to the problem of vulnerability has to be found, then clearly a less *ad hoc* system would have to be devised. Various alternative ways of doing this, varying from guaranteed social security benefits in the form of income supplementation to employment guarantee schemes, can be considered in this context.

But social security is not the only aspect of the problem. It is important to recognize the long-run changes in the Sahelian economy that have made the population of the dry Sahel region more vulnerable to droughts. One factor that has been noted is the increased vulnerability arising from the growing commericialization of the Sahelian economy.[44] As the Sahelian population has become more depenaent on cash crops, there has been an increased dependence on markets for meeting its food requirements, and this has tended to supplement the variability arising from climatic fluctuations.[45] In the light of the analysis of variation of entitlement relations with which this book has been much concerned (see Chapters 1, 5, 6, and 7), this point may not need very much elaboration here. Compared with the farmer or the pastoralist who lives on what he grows and is thus vulnerable only to variations of his own output (arising from climatic considerations and other influences), the grower of cash crops, or the pastoralist heavily dependent on selling animal products, is vulnerable both to output flucutations and to shifts in marketability of commodities and in exchange rates.[46] The worker employed in wage-based farms or other occupations is, of course, particularly vulnerable, since employment fluctuations owing to climatic shifts, or to other factors such as 'derived deprivation', can be very sharp indeed. While commercialization may have

[44] See Comité Information Sahel (1974).

[45] See Meillassoux (1974) and Comité Information Sahel (1974). See also Ball (1976) and Berry, Campbell, and Emker (1977).

[46] While price and quantity fluctuations can operate in opposite directions, thereby tempering the effects of each other, this is far from guaranteed. Indeed, as was seen in the last chapter and also in Section 8.3 above, the pastoralists often have to face a price decline along with a reduction in quantities. Similarly, a decline in agricultural output could lead to a reduction of wage employment, thereby leading to a collapse of the 'effective price' of labour power for those who are fired.

opened up new economic opportunities, it has also tended to increase the vulnerability of the Sahel population.

Commercialization has also had other worrying effects. The 'traditional symbiotic relationship between nomadic livestock and the crops' may have been disrupted in some regions by the growth of cash crops with a different seasonal rhythm (e.g., cotton being harvested later than the traditional food crops).[47] The livestock eating the post-harvest stubs from the agricultural fields, and in its turn fertilizing the fields by providing dung, may have fitted in nicely with traditional agriculture, but have often not co-ordinated at all well with cash crops. Furthermore, when traditional grazing land has been taken over for commercial farming, the pastoral population has, of course, directly suffered from a decline of resources.

Another long-run trend that seems to have been important is the partial breakdown of the traditional methods of insurance.[48] The political division of the dry Sahel region has put arbitrary constraints on pastoral movements, reducing the scope for anti-drought responses. The practice of storing animals on the hoof as insurance seems to have become more expensive because of taxes. 'Fall-back hunting' has become almost impossible because of reduction of wild animals in the region.[49] The collapse of the traditional methods of fighting economic problems arising from periodical droughts may have played an important part in making the dry Sahel region more vulnerable to draught in recent years than it need have been. On some of these changes corrective policy actions are worth considering, but many of these developments are difficult to reverse.

Additional vulnerability has also arisen from over-grazing and an increase in the size of livestock population in the dry Sahelian region. To some extent, this was the result of the pluvial 1960s, preceding the drought,[50] and the problem would be different for

[47] See Norton (1976), pp. 260–1. Also Swift (1977b), pp. 171–3.

[48] See Swift (1977a, 1977b). See also Copans *et al.* (1975), Haaland (1977), and Caldwell (1977).

[49] Another long-run factor working in the same direction is the decline of trading possibilities across the Sahara, especially the disruption of the traditional Tuareg caravan trade, first by French interference and then by competition from traders with motorized transport (Baier, 1974; cited by Berry, Campbell and Emker, 1977, pp. 87–8).

[50] See Norton (1976), p. 261.

quite some time after the drought. But the nature of the nomadic economy has built-in forces operating in that direction. Since the pastures are held communally and animals owned privately, there is a conflict of economic rationale in the package, which becomes relevant when pasture land gets short in supply. Having additional animals for grazing adds to families' incomes, and while this might lead to loss of grass cover and erosion, and thus to reduced productivity for the pastoralists as a group, the loss to the individual family from the latter may be a good deal less than its gain from having additional animals. Thus a conflict of the type of the so-called 'prisoners' dilemma'[51] is inherent in the situation.

The problem is further compounded by the fact that the animals, aside from adding to the family's usual income, also serve as insurance, as was noted before, so that the tendency to enlarge one's herd, causing over-grazing, tends to be stimulated as uncertainty grows. And the over-grazing, in its turn, adds to the uncertainty, by denuding the grass cover and helping desert formation.

Contrary to what is sometimes said, the tendency of the pastoralist to have a large stock, contributing to over-grazing, does not indicate anything in the least foolish or shortsighted from his personal point of view. Policy formulation can hardly be helped by the failure to recognize this important fact.

The complexity of the problem was recently suggested by an official from a major donor country who had interviewed a Fulani herder in northern Upper Volta in the spring of 1973. He reported that the farmer, asked how he had been affected by the recent drought, said he had 100 head of cattle and had lost 50. The farmer continued, 'Next time I will have 200,' implying that by starting with twice as many he would save the 100 cattle he wants. Yet the land's carrying capacity is such that he will still have only 50 cattle, but his loss will have been much greater.[52]

As a piece of economic reasoning, this is, of course, sheer rubbish, as the Fulani herder must have seen straightaway, unless mesmerized by respect for the 'major donor country'. If the Fulani herder had begun with 200 rather than 100 animals, he would not have ended up with the same 50, and in fact in large

[51] For the basic Prisoners' Dilemma model, see Luce and Raiffa (1958), and conflicts of this kind can be found in many economic situations (see Sen, 1967a).
[52] Glantz (1976), p. 7.

pastoral communities he would have a good chance of retaining the same proportion, viz. 50 per cent, thereby ending up with the planned 100. The proportion of herd loss does depend on the *total* stock of animals, given the availability of grazing land, but the influence of one herder's individual herd size on the total animal stock will be very small indeed. So it isn't that he himself loses by starting off with 200 rather than 100 head of cattle, but that he thus contributes a little bit to the general reduction of survival possibility of animals in the whole region, and if many herders do the same then the survival ratio will indeed come down significantly. But the individual herder can hardly undo this general problem by keeping his own herd small unilaterally. The herder is sensible enough within his sphere of control, which is his own stock, but the totality of these individually sensible actions produces a social crisis.

In tackling this aspect of the problem, several alternative approaches are possible, varying from incentive schemes using taxes and subsidies, or regulations governing the size of the herds, to the formation of pastoral co-operatives.[53] The problem arises from private entitlement being positively responsive to one's private ownership of animals while being negatively responsive to ownership by others, and from each herder having direct control only over his own stock. The object of institutional change will be to eliminate the conflicts that arise from this dichotomy.

The food problem of the population in the dry Sahel region depends crucially on this set of institutional factors affecting food entitlement through production and exchange, and there is scope for action here. As discussed earlier, there is also need for a mechanism for directly tackling the problem of vulnerability through public institutions guaranteeing food entitlement. The last category includes not merely distribution of food when the problem becomes acute, but also more permanent arrangements for entitlement through social security and employment protection. What is needed is not ensuring food availability, but guaranteeing food entitlement.

[53] Various institutional reforms have been discussed in recent years. See Comité Information Sahel (1974), Copans *et al.* (1975), Widstrand (1975), Dahl and Hjort (1976, 1979), Glantz (1976), Norton (1976), Rapp, Le Houérou, and Lundholm (1976), Swift (1977a, 1977b), and Toupet (1977), among many other important contributions.

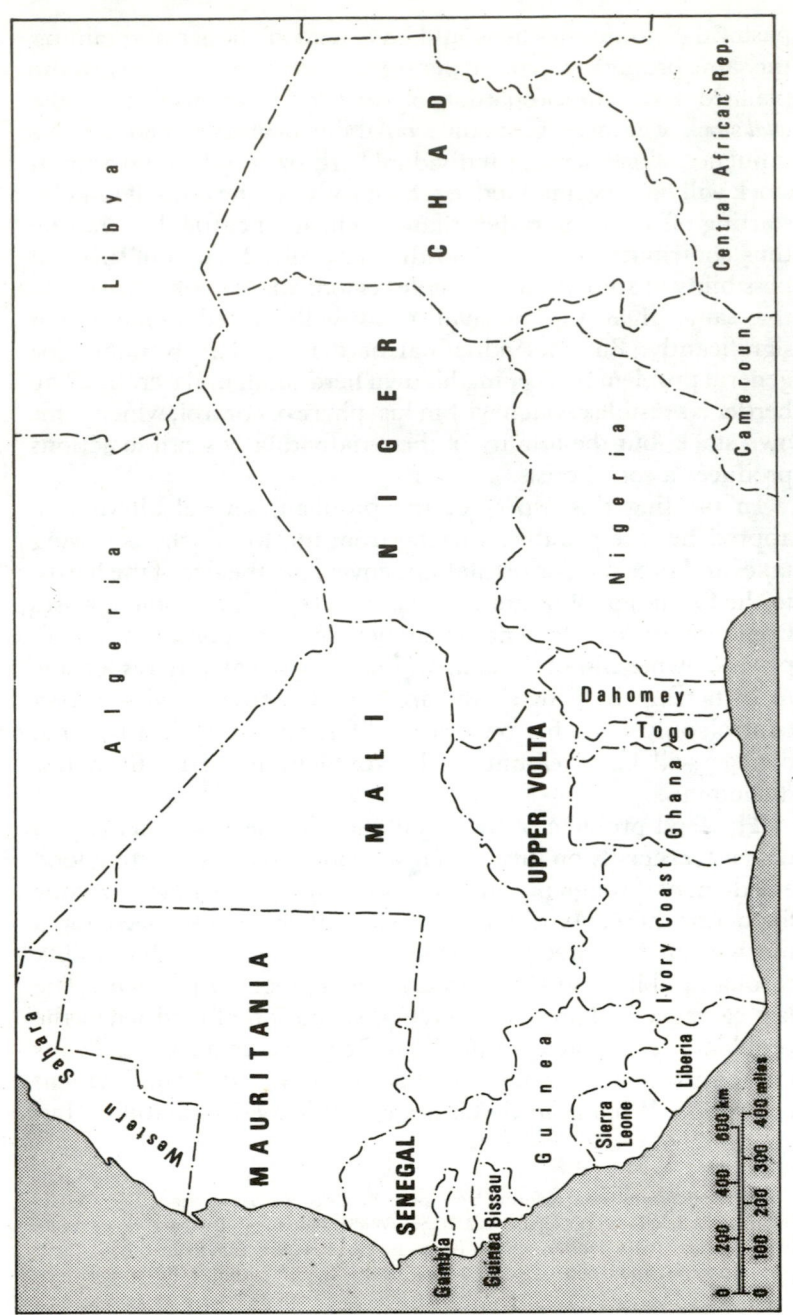

FIG. 8.1 Map of Sahel Countries

Chapter 9

Famine in Bangladesh

9.1 FLOODS AND FAMINE

First the floods; then the famine. So runs the capsule story of the Bangladesh famine of 1974. Gilbert Etienne describes the 1974 floods thus:

The floods of 1974 caused severe damage in the Northern districts. In normal years, the Brahmaputra encroaches on its Western bank by 30–60 m during peak floods. In 1974, over a distance of 100 km, it flooded land on a strip 300 m wide in areas having a density of 800 per sq. km. 24,000 people suffered heavy losses. Moreover alluvial deposits, while fertile in some areas, have such a high sand content in others that they are sterile. . . . Severe floods occurred at the end of June, taking away part of the *aus* [rice crop harvested in July–August]. A fortnight later the Brahmaputra again crossed the danger level just at the time of *aus* harvesting. After another fortnight the level of river rose again and seedlings of *aman* [rice crop transplanted in July–September and harvested in November–January] in their nurseries were in danger. Then, by the middle of August, floods reached their maximum for the year, affecting recently transplanted *aman*. It was not the end. At the begining of September the Brahmaputra again crossed the danger line, hitting once more what was left of paddy which has been transplanted after the previous floods.[1]

The price of rice rocketed during and immediately after the floods, as Table 9.1 shows. In some of the most affected districts, the rice price doubled in the three months between July and October. Reports of starvation could be heard immediately following the flood, and grew in severity. The government of Bangladesh officially declared famine in late September. Some *langarkhanas*, providing modest amounts of free cooked food to destitutes, were opened under private initiative early in September, and government-sponsored *langarkhanas* went into full operation in early October. At one stage nearly six thousand *langarkhanas* were providing cooked food relief to 4.35 million people—more than 6 per cent of the total population of the

[1] Etienne (1977a), pp. 113–4.

country. By November rice prices were begining to come down, and the need for relief seemed less intense. By the end of the month the *langarkhanas* were closed down.

TABLE 9.1

Rise in the Price of Rice in Bangladesh following the 1974 Floods

| Month in 1974 – | Bangladesh average | Index of retail price of coarse rice | | |
		Mymensingh	Rangpur	Sylhet
July	100	100	100	100
August	121	130	116	129
September	150	169	184	160
October	178	202	183	204
November	151	162	113	167
December	133	132	85	155

Source: Calculated from Table 3.3 of Alamgir *et al.* (1977), p. 58.

TABLE 9.2

*Number Obtaining Food Relief in Langarkhanas:
Bangladesh Famine, 1974*

District	Number of persons fed daily (thousands)	Number fed as proportion of total population (%)
Rangpur	935.6	17.18
Mymensingh	899.0	11.88
Dinajpur	221.0	8.60
Sylhet	362.7	7.62
Barisal	281.0	7.15
Khulna	245.7	6.91
Bogra	123.0	5.51
Noakhali	178.4	5.50
Patuakhali	65.8	4.39
Jessore	128.5	3.86
Faridpur	148.2	3.65
Comilla	205.1	3.52
Rajshahi	147.5	3.46
Kushtia	64.9	3.45
Tangail	70.5	3.39
Pabna	57.9	2.06
Dacca	155.7	2.05
Chittagong	54.7	1.27
Chittagong Hill Tracts	0	0

Source: Data provided by Alamgir (1979).

The severity of the famine varied from region to region. Table 9.2 presents the proportion of a district's population that

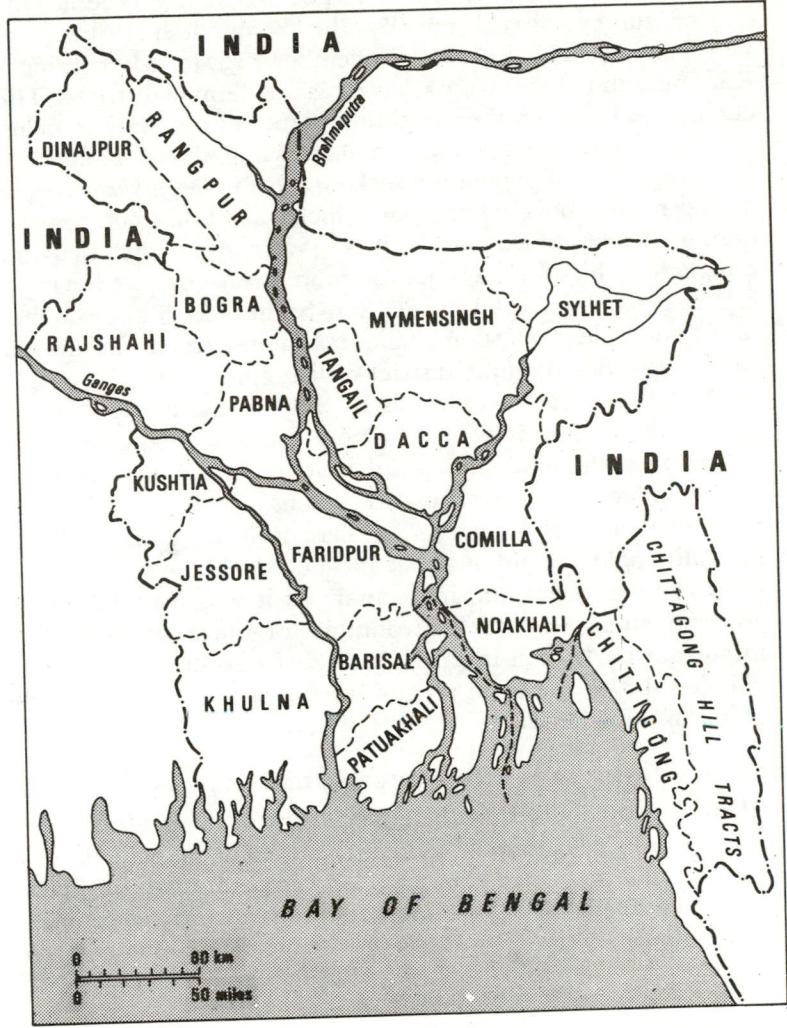

FIG. 9.1 Map of Bangladesh

obtained relief from the *langarkhanas*, varying from 17 per cent in Rangpur to none in Chittagong Hill Tracts. Judged by this criterion, the five most affected districts were Rangpur, Mymensingh, Dinajpur, Sylhet, and Barisal, in that order. In the famine survey carried out by the Bangladesh Institute of Development Studies[2] in November 1974, Mymensingh, Rangpur, and Sylhet were selected as the 'famine districts'. The choice was based on the 'maximum depth of inundation' being '6 feet and above in a period of 3 months and above', along with 'the proportion of population seeking relief in *langarkhanas* being 5 per cent and above'.[3] Dinajpur, which is some distance from the raging Brahmaputra and other rivers (see the map of Bangladesh, Fig. 8.1), did not figure in this list despite having a higher percentage seeking relief than Sylhet, but it appears that 'a considerable proportion of *langarkhana* inmates in this district came from the adjoining district of Rangpur.'

Mortality estimates vary widely. The official figure of death due to the famine is 26,000.[4] Other estimates indicate much higher mortality, including the estimation that in Rangpur district alone '80 to 100 thousand persons died of starvation and malnutrition in 2–3 months'.[5] There is little doubt that the mortality figure would have been a good deal higher but for the massive relief operation, inadequate as it was. In addition to government-sponsored relief, voluntary organizations played an important part, both in providing relief outside the distressed villages and in the form of movements of self-reliance within many of the villages.[6]

9.2 FOOD IMPORTS AND GOVERNMENT STOCKS

There is little doubt that the government of Bangladesh found itself severely constrained by the lack of an adequate food stock, and that this prevented running a larger operation at the height of the famine.[7] By 1974 Bangladesh was already chronically

[2] See Alamgir *et al.* (1977), and Alamgir (1980). As will be clear, this chapter draws heavily on the information provided by this survey, and on other data, analyses, and insights provided by Alamgir (1978a, 1980).

[3] Alamgir (1980).

[4] Alamgir (1978a, p. 2).

[5] Haque, Mehta, Rahman and Wignaraja (1975), p. 43. Alamgir (1980) suggests an excess-death figure around one million between August 1974 and January 1975, and a further half a million in the year following (pp. 142–3).

[6] See Rahman (1974a, 1974b).

[7] See N. Islam (1977).

dependent on import of food from abroad, and despite the famine conditions the government succeeded in importing less food-grains in 1974 than in 1973 (see Table 9.3). In fact, in the crucial months of September and October the imports fell to a trickle, and the amount of foodgrains imported during these two months, rather than being larger, was less than one-fifth of the imports in those months in the preceding year. In constraining the oper-ations of the Bangladesh government, the shortage of food stock clearly did play an important negative part.

TABLE 9.3

Import of Foodgrains into Bangladesh, 1973 and 1974

Month	1973	1974
January	228	38
February	194	90
March	467	99
April	212	147
May	179	224
June	126	135
July	83	291
August	159	225
September	263	29
October	287	76
November	59	190
December	83	149
Total	2,340	1,693

Source: Table 6.18 in Alamgir (1980).
Note
Unit = 1,000 tons

It is worth mentioning in this context that Bangladesh, like many other countries in the world, had been receiving regular food aid from the United States. But the US food aid came under severe threat precisely at this point of time, since the United States decided to seek stoppage of Bangladesh's trade with Cuba. This apparently came shortly after a desperately dollar-short Bangladesh government had to cancel two purchase orders from American grain companies for delivery in autumn.

The U.S. threatened to cut off food aid in September 1974. At that time the American ambassador called upon Dr. Nurul Islam, Chairman of Bangladesh's Planning Commission, under instructions from the State

Department, to formally request that Bangladesh cease exporting jute to Cuba. Under PL480, a recipient country cannot trade with blacklisted countries such as Cuba. Islam retorted by expressing surprise and shock that the United States would actually insist that a destitute Bangladesh should restrict its exports. The government of Bangladesh cancelled further exports of jute to Cuba at a time when competition from Indian jute and low world market prices had substantially eroded its foreign exchange earnings.[8]

Only after Bangladesh gave in and sacrificed its trade with Cuba was the flow of American food resumed. By then the autumn famine was largely over.[9]

The problem of import planning had been compounded by rise of international prices of grains and shortage of credit. The government's expectation of a much larger food output in 1974 also led to disappointment. It can be seen that the import of food in the early months of 1974 was also substantially short of the corresponding figures for the year before. Furthermore, internal procurement had been less successful than planned; and, with a total foodgrains production of 11.8 million tons in 1974, the government stock varied from month to month between 347 thousand and 130 thousand over the year.[10] This affected the scale of relief operations not merely in terms of the number that could be covered, but also—and more importantly—in terms of the amount of food that could be given to each destitute.[11]

That food availability served as a constraint in government relief operations is not in dispute. But this would establish nothing about the causation of the famine itself. Was the famine caused by a decline of food availability resulting from the floods? Was there a general shortage of food? Does the FAD explantaion hold? I take up these questions next.

---

[8] McHenry and Bird (1977), p. 82.

[9] For further details of this episode, see McHenry and Bird (1977); also Sobhan (1979). For more general discussions of negative features of food aid, see George (1976) and Lappé and Collins (1977, 1978).

[10] Table 6.2 of Alamgir (1980). However, Alamgir argues that even with the import problems the government was unduly conservative in its relief operations, with the disbursement of food in the crucial famine months being a small proportion of the government stock. See also Rahman (1974a, 1974b) for a critique of the scale and organization of government relief operations.

[11] See Table 5.15 of Alamgir (1979).

9.3 FOOD AVAILABILITY DECLINE?

As was mentioned in Chapter 6 when analysing the great Bengal famine of 1943, there are three main rice crops in Bengal: *aman*, *aus*, and *boro*. The relative importance of these crops in Bangladesh now as well as their exact timing, are not however quite the same as in Bengal 1943, partly because of the fact that Bangladesh does not cover the whole of undivided Bengal, but also because of changes in the types of seeds and cropping methods over the years since 1943. In Bangladesh for the period 1971–6, the relative shares were the following: *aman* (harvested in November–January), 56 per cent; *aus* (harvested in July–August), 25 per cent; and *boro* (harvested in April–June), 19 per cent.

Like the Bengal famine of 1943, the peak of the Bangladesh famine of 1974 coincided with the *aus* harvesting time and preceded the time of *aman* harvesting. It is thus best to define the production-based supply of 1974 by adding the *aman* crop of 1973–4 (November–January) to the *boro* and *aus* crops of 1974. Indeed, as in Chapter 6, that is how the production of a particular year will be defined, i.e. including the *aman* crop harvested during the *preceding* November to January of that year. Table 9.4 presents the yearly rice output from 1971 to 1975. It also presents the index of *per capita* rice output. It can be seen that 1974 was a local peak year in terms of both total output and *per capita* output of rice.[12]

TABLE 9.4
Rice Output of Bangladesh, 1971–5

Year	Production of rice (thousand tons)	Index of rice production	Per capita rice output (tons)	Index of per capita rice output
1971	10,445	100	0.133	100
1972	9,706	93	0.120	90
1973	10,459	100	0.126	95
1974	11,778	113	0.139	105
1975	11,480	110	0.132	99

Basis: Data taken from Table 6.4 of Alamgir (1980).

[12] It is, however, worth remarking that, as far as *per capita* output is concerned, this is a local peak, and the highest levels achieved in the 1960s were not quite matched in these

In moving from rice production to foodgrains availability, wheat output, though tiny, has to be added and international trade must be taken into account. This is done in Table 9.5. It is found, once again, that 1974 was a local peak.[13] If one went by over-all food availability, one would expect a famine less in 1974 than in *any* of the other years. And yet the famine did occur precisely in 1974.

TABLE 9.5

Foodgrains Availability in Bangladesh, 1971–5

Year	Total available foodgrains for consumption (million tons)	Population (millions)	Per capita availability (oz./day)	Index of per capita availability
1971	10.740	70.679	14.9	100
1972	11.271	72.535	15.3	103
1973	11.572	74.441	15.3	103
1974	12.355	76.398	15.9	107
1975	12.022	78.405	14.9	100

Source: Data taken from Table 6.23 of Alamgir (1980).

It is, however, necessary to consider the possibility that the decline in food availability was a regional one, and that it could not get sorted out within Bangladesh because of problems of food movement including the inter-district barriers imposed officially (mainly to help procurement). Was there an exceptional decline in the districts most affected by the famine?

Table 9.6 presents the amounts of rice produced in the different districts, and also the percentage change in output between 1973 and 1974. It appears from it that output declined only in two districts, whereas the famine was much more widespread. It also appears that the most famine-affected

years in the 1970s. Nevertheless, two-year and three-year moving averages also rise rather than dip as we take up periods ending in 1974 (following one method used, among others, in Chapter 6), and it is difficult to deny that the output picture improved rather than worsened as the 'famine year' 1974 came.

[13] One area of some uncertainty is the extent of smuggling of foodgrains into India from Bangladesh. Some accounts suggest that this would have been very small indeed (see Reddaway and Rahman, 1975), while others suggest the possibility of the figures being substantially higher. Whatever the truth about these absolute magnitudes, there is no reason to expect that the smuggling of rice out of Bangladesh would have *increased* in the famine year when the relative price of rice in Bangladesh *vis-à-vis* that in India rose sharply.

TABLE 9.6
Production of Rice in Bangladesh Districts, 1973 and 1974

District	1974	1973	Change from 1973 to 1974 (%)
Khulna	462	325	+42.2
Chittagong Hill Tracts	93	67	+38.8
Dinajpur	666	504	+32.1
Bogra	478	380	+25.8
Jessore	531	426	+24.6
Kushtia	221	180	+22.8
Mymensingh	1,065	871	+22.3
Tangail	322	264	+22.0
Faridpur	484	403	+20.1
Rangpur	1,122	958	+17.1
Chittagong	725	644	+12.6
Pabna	282	251	+12.4
Sylhet	1,068	968	+10.3
Dacca	675	625	+8.0
Noakhali	538	505	+6.5
Rajshahi	679	638	+6.4
Comilla	836	805	+3.9
Barisal	600	664	−9.6
Patuakhali	229	342	−33.0

Source: Data taken from Table 6.28 of Alamgir (1980); the percentage change figure for Dinajpur is corrected.

Note
Unit = 1,000 tons

districts, namely Mymensingh, Rangpur, Sylhet, had substantial *increases* in output (22, 17, and 10 per cent respectively). Looking instead at the three top-ranked districts in terms of lowness of output growth, we obtain Patuakhali, Barisal, and Comilla, which together account for only 12.7 per cent of the destitutes receiving relief in *langarkhanas*. In general, the ranking of inter-district indicators of famine intensity (Table 9.2) and the ranking of lowness of output growth (Table 9.6) hardly relate to each other, and the rank correlation coefficient between the two is *minus* .5.

The corresponding availability estimates of foodgrains *per capita* are presented in Table 9.7. The three so-called famine districts typically had comfortable *rises* in availability per head: 3 per cent in Sylhet, 10 per cent in Rangpur, and 11 per cent in Mymensingh. If, on the other hand, we look at the three top-

TABLE 9.7

Per capita Availability of Foodgrains in Bangladesh Districts,
1973 and 1974

(oz./day)

District	1974	1973	Change (%)
Dinajpur	25.1	20.4	+ 23.0
Mymensingh	22.8	20.6	+ 10.7
Sylhet	22.1	21.4	+ 3.3
Bogra	20.8	19.3	+ 7.8
Rangpur	20.1	18.3	+ 9.8
Chittagong	19.7	18.4	+ 7.1
Noakhali	16.7	17.8	− 6.2
Jessore	16.3	14.6	+ 11.6
Khulna	16.2	13.8	+ 17.4
Barisal	16.0	18.6	− 14.0
Rajshahi	15.8	15.6	+ 1.3
Patuakhali	15.7	24.1	− 34.9
Tangail	15.3	14.7	+ 4.1
Comilla	14.9	16.1	− 7.5
Chittagong Hill Tracts	14.4	14.8	− 2.7
Dacca	13.8	14.5	− 4.6
Faridpur	13.5	12.0	+ 12.5
Kushtia	12.8	12.0	+ 6.7
Pabna	10.8	10.4	+ 3.8

Source: Table 6.29, Alamgir (1980) based on figures of the Directorate of Procurement, Distribution, and Rationing of the Government of Bangladesh.

ranked districts in terms of lowness of availability change (Patuakhali, Barisal, and Comilla), this again would account for only about 13 per cent of the destitutes in the *langarkhanas*. The rank correlation coefficient between inter-district famine intensity and the lowness of availability change is *minus* .33, hardly an encouraging piece of statistics.

If, instead of looking at the *change* of availability, the districts are ranked according to the lowness of *absolute* availability *per capita*, again the explanation of famine conditions is not enhanced. The so-called famine districts come at the *other* end— the ranks of Rangpur, Sylhet, and Mymensingh being respectively 15, 17 and 18 out of nineteen states—each with relatively high availability of foodgrains per head.[14] The top-ranked low-availability districts (Pabna, Kushtia, and Faridpur) account for

[14] Even the estimates of July–October availability put these three states among the relatively better supplied; see Table 6.37 of Alamgir (1980).

only about 6 per cent of the *langarkhana* destitutes. Finally, the rank correlation coefficient of inter-district famine intensity and lowness of availability is *minus* .73, which does little in favour of the FAD view.

Undoubtedly, these high and significant negative rank correlations may be partly influenced by the fact that the famine-stricken districts received preferential treatment in the governmental allocation of foodgrains, but that would have hardly transformed shortages into relative opulence. Indeed, as was shown already, the output figures also give no comfort to the FAD view. The relief-oriented distributions were a relatively small part of total food consumption, and furthermore the amount of food given per destitute was—as noted before—*lower* in the more severely stricken districts.[15]

The food availability approach offers very little in the way of explanation of the Bangladesh famine of 1974. The total output, as well as availability figures for Bangladesh as a whole, point precisely in the opposite direction, as do the inter-district figures of production as well as availability. Whatever the Bangladesh famine of 1974 might have been, it wasn't a FAD famine.

9.4 OCCUPATIONAL DISTRIBUTION AND INTENSITY OF DESTITUTION

Who were the famine victims? Thanks to the survey of *langar-khana* inmates conducted by the Bangladesh Institute of Development Studies in November 1974, it is possible to give some kind of an answer to this question (even though the sample was not quite randomly chosen). Table 9.8 presents a broad occupational breakdown according to the major source of income. The largest group of destitutes in the *langarkhanas* were labourers (45 per cent), followed closely by farmers (39 per cent). If the labourers are split into agricultural and non-agricultural workers, the groups of farmers would appear to be the single largest category. This fact has been widely noted, and rightly so. On the other hand, it must not be forgotten that farmers as defined for the surveys were also the largest single group of rural households. To get an idea of the relative intensity of destitution, the

---

[15] See Table 5.15 of Alamgir (1980). The calorie equivalent of daily wheat ration in October 1974 varied between 452 in *langarkhanas* in the famine districts of Mymensingh and Rangpur to 2,069 in the non-famine district of Pabna.

TABLE 9.8

Occupational Distribution of Destitution in Bangladesh 1974

Occupation	Number of langarkhana inmates	Percentage of total langarkhana inmates
Labourers	351	44.5
of whom:		
(1) agricultural labourers	190	24.1
(2) other labourers	161	20.4
Farmers	305	38.7
Others	132	16.8
Total	788	100.0

Source: Table 5.3 of Alamgir (1980).

occupational distribution of destitutes has to be compared with the occupational distribution of the population from which the destitutes were drawn. This isn't easy to do since there is no survey that covers exactly the population from which the destitutes came. However, to get some idea it is possible to use Mia's (1976) study of the occupational distribution of rural heads of households and also the study by the Bangladesh Institute of occupational distribution of rural households by major sources of income. These are used in Table 9.9 to calculate two indices of intensity of destitution.

According to both indices, labourers do stand out as the most affected group by substantial margins. While it will be a mistake to attach too much importance.to the exact values of these indices, the relative ordering of labourers *vis-à-vis* others including farmers is clear enough.

A similar conclusion emerges from the estimates of occupation-specific death rates during the famine months as obtained by the survey of selected villages by the Bangladesh Institute. These are presented in Table 9.10. While the small group of transport workers had a higher mortality rate than general wage labourers, the latter came close to the top and exceeded considerably the mortality rate of other groups—including farmers.

The land ownership statistics of *langarkhana* inmates are also worth noting. Table 9.11 presents the available information on

TABLE 9.9
Intensity of Destitution by Occupation in Bangladesh, 1974

Occupation	Percentage of total langarkhana inmates	Percentage of heads of rural households in Bangladesh	Percentage of rural households by major sources of income in Bangladesh	Intensity index I	Intensity index II
	(1)	(2)	(3)	(4) = (1)/(2)	(5) = (1)/(3)
Labourers	44.5	27.9	23.4	1.59	1.90
Farmers	38.7	41.8	59.7	0.93	0.65
Others	16.8	30.3	17.0	0.55	0.99
All	100.0	100.0	100.0	1.00	1.00

Source: Column (1) from Table 9.8 above; Column (2) from Mia (1976) and Alamgir (1978a), Table XII; Column (3) from Alamgir (1980), Table 8.12.

TABLE 9.10

Occupation-specific Mortality Rates in
Selected Bangladeshi Villages during
August–October 1974

Occupation	Death rate per 1,000	Death rate among children 10 years and below per 1,000
Transport	100	286
Wage labour	88	128
Trade	53	80
Farming	38	64
'Others'	29	n.a.
Service	16	12
Total	47	74

Source: Table 5.5 of Alamgir (1980)

this from the *langarkhana* survey by the Bangladesh Institute. Of
the inmate households, 32 per cent owned no land at all. Perhaps
more importantly, 81 per cent owned less than half an acre of
land *if* they owned any land at all. This compares with 33 per
cent of rural households owning half an acre or less of land in the

TABLE 9.11

Land Ownership of Langarkhana Inmates, Bangladesh, 1974

Size group of land	Number of inmate households	Percentage of inmate households	Percentage of rural population households	Incidence of destitution
	(1)	(2)	(3)	(4) = (2)/(3)
Less than ½ acre	639	81.09	32.69	2.481
½ acre or more; less than 1 acre	57	7.23	13.13	0.551
1 acre or more; less than 2½ acres	81	10.28	28.80	0.357
2½ acres or more; less than 5 acres	10	1.27	16.74	0.076
5 acres or more	1	0.13	8.62	0.015
Total	788	100.0	100.0	1.000

Source: Calculated from Table 5.2 of Alamgir (1980), and Table 6.11 of Alamgir *et al.*
(1977). The 'rural population' refers to the households sampled in eight villages in
the latter work.

villages surveyed by the Bangladesh Institute. It is the landless end of the village spectrum that is caught firmly at the *langarkhanas*. The average chance of ending up in *langarkhanas* for those with less than half an acre of land was 4½ times that of those owning between half an acre and one acre of land, and 165 times that of those with five acres or more. This corroborates the picture based on occupational statistics, and asserts in addition that quite a few of the farmers who are distinguished from landless labourers among the *langarkhana* inmates are, in fact, very tiny farmers indeed.

9.5 EXCHANGE ENTITLEMENT OF LABOUR POWER

Since the typical destitutes had as their endowment only labour power with—at best—little bits of land, the most important part of the entitlement relation to look at is the entitlement based on labour power. In Table 9.12 the indices of rice-exchange for rural labour for each month in 1974 are presented with two alternative bases: (a) December 1973 as 100, and (b) the same month in 1973 as 100. The decline of the e_j indices in the months just preceding

TABLE 9.12

Indices of Rice-Exchange Rate e_j of Rural Labour during the Bangladesh Famine, 1974

Base: (*a*) December 1973 values; (*b*) Same month 1973 values

	Rural wage rate		Price of rice		Index value of rice-exchange rate e_j for 1974 month	
Month	1973	1974	1973	1974	(a)	(b)
January	4.78	6.22	72.37	92.11	86	102
February	4.91	6.36	76.68	98.93	82	100
March	5.14	7.17	83.84	117.33	78	100
April	5.35	8.22	96.49	136.98	77	108
May	5.47	8.72	96.29	135.68	82	113
June	5.83	8.26	91.11	139.04	76	93
July	6.02	8.61	87.06	141.78	78	88
August	5.81	8.82	85.92	171.25	66	76
September	5.72	8.80	89.47	212.80	53	65
October	5.85	8.64	94.11	251.78	44	55
November	6.00	8.39	89.65	213.73	50	59
December	6.32	8.70	80.90	188.98	59	59

Source: Calculations based on data compiled by the Bangladesh Institute of Development Studies, reported in Alamgir *et al.* (1977), Tables 3.3 and 4.3.

the famine and through the famine months is very sharp indeed. The fall is a bit less if we use the same-month–previous-year base, which does something to eliminate the seasonal drop, but even there the fall is large. At the peak of the famine the fall is 35 to 45 per cent compared with the same month in the previous year, for a group of people already close to subsistence.

The sharpest decline comes just after the floods started, and Table 9.13 presents the fall of the rice-exchange rate of rural labour from June to October. There was no such decline in the preceding year (see Table 9.12), and data for earlier years also show no substantial seasonal fall over these months.

Turning now to the inter-district picture, the three famine districts also turn out to be precisely the three top ranked districts in terms of decline in the rice-entitlement of wages (see Table

TABLE 9.13

Rice Entitlement of Wage Rate: Index Values for October 1974 with June 1974 as 100

	Wage rate index	Rice price index	Percentage decline of the exchange rate of wage labour with rice in rural Bangladesh
Bangladesh	104.6	181.1	42.2
Mymensingh	69.0	225.9	69.5
Rangpur	80.0	190.3	58.0
Sylhet	100.0	236.0	57.6
Noakhali	100.0	209.8	52.3
Barisal	87.0	177.3	50.9
Chittagong Hill Tracts	100.0	201.3	50.3
Tangail	106.3	211.4	49.7
Pabna	100.0	172.3	42.0
Chittagong	100.0	170.5	41.3
Patuakhali	100.0	167.9	40.4
Dacca	118.9	192.6	38.3
Khulna	96.2	153.9	37.5
Bogra	100.0	158.2	36.8
Dinajpur	114.3	179.1	36.2
Comilla	135.7	205.0	33.8
Jessore	108.3	155.0	30.1
Kushtia	112.0	151.4	26.0
Rajshahi	123.1	156.4	21.3
Faridpur	158.3	164.5	3.8

Source: Calculated from Tables 3.3 and 4.3 of Alamgir *et al.* (1977), pp. 57–8 and 92.

9.13). The entitlement ratio fell by 58 per cent in Rangpur and Sylhet and by 70 per cent in Mymensingh, and with that kind of decline in the entitlement to rice, labourers would be pushed firmly towards starvation and death. The over-all picture for *all* districts considered is a bit muddier, even though the rank correlation coefficient, while not high (.32), is positive and significant, and contrasts sharply with the significantly negative results we obtained with various versions of the FAD approach. The exchange entitlement approach—applied in the simple form of only looking at rice-entitlement of wages—already provides a good bit of the explanation of destitution, even though it leaves room for other factors to be brought in.[16].

Finally, the share of *langarkhana* destitutes accounted for by the three top-ranked states in terms of rice-entitlement decline is over 50 per cent. This contrasts with 6 to 13 per cent in the various versions of the food availability approach, as found in Section 9.3. The difference is partly a matter of district size, but also a matter of district identification. The percentages of destitution in the three 'worst affected' districts under the rice-entitlement approach are (18%, 12%, 8%) as opposed to (7%, 4%, 4%) and (4%, 3%, 2%) under different versions of the FAD approach.

The decline in terms of trade of labour power *vis-à-vis* rice was clearly reinforced by a decline in employment opportunities in the famine year.[17] Here the floods played a part. While the decline in the *aman* crop that got partly washed out in June–September 1974 did not reflect itself in the form of a lower output until after the famine, the decline in employment opportunities was immediate.[18] Table 9.14 presents the normal seasonal

[16] One such factor was the deterioration of the terms of trade of jute *vis-à-vis* rice, which has been commented on in other contexts, mainly the reduced incentive to grow raw jute (see Faaland and Parkinson, 1976, pp. 59–61, 135–6). In terms of entitlement rather than price incentive for production, this meant a drop in the rice-entitlement for jute growers, and would have added to the distress of the farmers producing raw jute. For famine conditions in neighbouring Assam in India in the same period, a sharp decline in the relative price of jute clearly played a major part (see Prabhakar, 1974, p. 1767). There was also a decline in acreage under jute during 1974 leading to some loss of employment (see Alamgir, 1980, p. 304, foqtnote 9).

[17] See Rahman (1974a, 1974b), Adnan and Rahman (1978), and Alamgir (1978a, 1980), among others.

[18] The 'derived destitution' in the form of reduced demand for rural services and crafts leading to reduction of exchange entitlements of the related occupations was also immediate.

TABLE 9.14
*Normal Seasonal Pattern of Employment in
Cultivation: Char Shamraj Village*
(days worked)

Month	Cultivation	Activity rank
Baisak (April–May)	1,872	9
Jaistha (May–June)	2,496	8
Ashar (June–July)	4,804	1
Sravan (July–August)	4,786	2
Bhadra (August–Sept.)	2,665	7
Aswin (Sept.–Oct.)	526	12
Kartik (Oct.–Nov.)	3,181	5
Agrahayan (Nov.–Dec.)	4,667	3
Poush (Dec.–Jan.)	3,239	4
Magh (Jan.–Feb.)	2,811	6
Falgoon (Feb.–March)	1,791	10
Chaitra (March–April)	1,243	11

Source: Fieldwork by Village Study Group in Char Samraj reported in Rushidan Islam (1977), p. 12.

rhythm of work, in terms of days worked, in cultivation in a Bengali village (in this case, Char Shamraj). It is seen that peak employment takes place in June–August, and this is of course precisely the time when the floods hit, drastically reducing the scope of employment in cultivation. The decline in the rice-entitlement of wage was thus compounded by the fall in the employment opportunity—a vital determinant of exchange entitlement of labour power.[19]

In understanding the causation of destitution, therefore, one has to go much beyond the statistics of food availability. The output and availability of foodgrains may have peaked in 1974, but the market forces determining the relative wage *vis-à-vis* rice was moving sharply against the former. While we haven't got the data that would permit a satisfactory causal analysis of the factors affecting the exchange rates, it is possible to make a few observations on its general nature.

First, even though the decline in the *aman* crop could not have affected the total amount of foodgrains in Bangladesh during the

[19] Recovery from the famine took place in November as the next season of busy activity began—mercifully free from natural calamities.

famine months (since that crop would not have been harvested until November–January *following* the famine), the expectation of the decline must have had some effect on the level of rice price.[20] In fact, the rumour of decline was rather stronger than the actual fall in *aman* output, but speculative withdrawals can feed comfortably on such rumours.

Second, the rise in rice price could not, however, have been the result of the flood only. Indeed, in the early months of 1974, long before the floods, rice prices were rising sharply—almost as fast as they did during the flood and immediately after. Table 9.15 presents the monthly rise in rice price through 1974, and it is seen that in Bangladesh as a whole, and specifically in the famine districts, there are sharp rises in the earlier part of the year, much before the floods hit. Thus the explanation of the rise in rice price must be sought partly in influences that have nothing to do with

TABLE 9.15
Rise in the Price of Rice in Bangladesh in 1974

| Month in 1974 | Bangladesh average | Percentage rise in the retail price of coarse rice in each month over the preceeding month | | |
		Mymensingh	Rangpur	Sylhet
January	+14	+14	+16	+6
February	+7	+11	+2	+22
March	+19	+27	+19	+15
April	+17	+16	+16	+19
May	−1	−16	+17	−17
June	+2	−2	0	−2
July	+2	+12	+4	+16
August	+21	+30	+16	+29
September	+24	+29	+58	+24
October	+18	+20	0	+28
November	−15	−20	−38	−18
December	−12	−19	−25	−7

Source: Calculated from Table 3.3 of Alamgir *et al.* (1977), pp. 57–8.

[20] If we replace the *aman* harvested in December 1973 by that harvested in December 1974 in the 1974 production figure in Table 9.4, the index value of 1974 falls from 103 to 97. Re-indexing all the years by replacing the preceding *aman* crop by the *aman* that comes at the end of the relevant year, the index values stand as follows: 1971, 100; 1972, 91; 1972, 107; 1973, 100; 1974, 99; 1975, 108. It has the effect of converting 1974 from a local peak to a local trough.

the floods. And this is where a macroeconomic study dealing with such factors as effective demand, money supply, etc., could contribute substantially.

Third, while the decline in the rice-entitlement of wage is to a great extent the result of the rise in rice price, there was also a decline in absolute money wage rate in a few districts, including the famine districts of Mymensingh and Rangpur, between June and October of 1974 (see Table 9.13). It is quite remarkable that, not merely did the money wage fail to stay in line with rice price; it actually fell in absolute terms in these districts. The weakening of the market strength of labour that this reflects may be partly traceable to the decline in employment opportunities as a result of the flood and related contraction of rural economic activities.

9.6 A QUESTION OF FOCUS

The enormity of economic problems facing Bangladesh has been widely observed. The fear of population running ahead of food production has been regularly voiced. It is not my intention to dismiss these problems and fears. But what emerges irresistably from the preceding analysis is the danger of concentrating only on the aggregative issues, overlooking the details of the entitlement system on which the survival of millions of Bangladeshi people crucially depends. The focus on population and food supply would have been innocuous but for what it does to hide the realities that determine who can command how much food.

Bangladesh remains a traditional rural economy in many significant respects. Nearly three-quarters of its population live on agriculture and about 90 per cent live in rural areas.[21] Yet the economic organization is not one of market-independent peasant agriculture. About a quarter of the rural population survive by exchanging labour at market wages and commanding food with what they earn. For them a variation of the exchange relationships can spell ruin. There is, in fact, some evidence that in recent years in Bangladesh the wage system itself has moved more towards money wages, away from payments in kind—chiefly food.[22] More modern, perhaps; more vulnerable, certainly.

The process of sale of land by small peasants cuts down not

[21] On the general nature of the Bangladesh economy and various aspects of its economic performance, see Faaland and Parkinson (1976); also Etienne (1977a).
[22] See Clay (1976).

only the peasant's normal income, but also the stability of his earnings—making him more vulnerable to exchange rate shifts. Table 9.16 presents this pattern of land sales in the villages studied by the Bangladesh Institute in the years leading up to the famine. One sees a clear bias towards land alienation on the part of the smaller landholders.[23] The development not merely generally impoverished the group of small peasants;[24] it also increased the ease with which members of the class could sink into starvation even in a year of relative plenty as a result of shifts of rice-entitlement of labour power.

TABLE 9.16

Proportion of Owned Land Sold According to Landholding of Sellers, 1972–4

Landholding group	Percentage of owned land sold		
	1972	*1973*	*1974*
Less that 1 acre	39	29	54
1 to less than 2 acres	19	17	24
2 to less than 5 acres	12	18	12
5 acres and above	10	10	11

Source: Table XXVII of Alamgir (1978a).

Other occupation groups also depend on being able to command food by exchanging things that they produce and sell. Boatmen and transport workers had a high mortality in the Bengal famine in 1943; they had again exceptionally high mortality in the famine of 1974. Village craftsmen, producers of services, petty traders, and a whole host of other occupations live by exchange—and from time to time perish by exchange.

There has been a welcome tendency recently to move away from figures of national income per head (and other such national aggregates) to income distribution, in particular to poverty. But even the group of the poor is too broad a category, and it is possible for the proportion of population below the poverty line to fall while those who are in poverty experience a deepening of

[23] See also Rahman (1974a, 1974b), Khan (1977), Abdullah (1976a, 1976b), Adnan and Rahman (1978), and Hartmann and Boyce (1979).
[24] For a global analysis of the relation between rural poverty and land concentration, see Griffin (1976).

their deprivation. This was one of the reasons why it was argued that distribution below the poverty line has to be taken into account in arriving at a fuller picture of poverty (see Chapter 3 and Appendix C).

It seems that an example of a divergent development of this kind can be found in the recent experience of Bangladesh. Some calculations done by Azizur Rahman Khan are presented in Table 9.17. It would appear from this that, while the proportion of people below the poverty line (defined as the level of income at which people meet 90 per cent of the recommended calorie intake) *fell*, or at least rose little, between late 1960s and mid-1970s, the proportion in 'extreme poverty'—defined as having levels of income less than adequate to meet 80 per cent of the recommended calorie intake—*rose* sharply.[25] Thus a general intensification of starvation may have gone hand in hand with a reduction of the head-count measure of poverty for the defined 'poverty line'. Shocking disasters can lie deeply hidden in comforting aggregate magnitudes.

The analysis of exchange entitlements and the study of the

TABLE 9.17

Percentage of Rural Population in Poverty and in Extreme Poverty

	Poor	Extremely poor	Change of the percentage of the poor since 1968–9	Change of the percentage of the extremely poor since 1968–9
1968–9	76.0	25.1		
1973–4	78.5	42.1	+3.3	+67.7
1975 (first quarter)	61.8	41.1	−18.7	+63.7

Basis: Table 48 of Khan (1977). 'Poor' people are those with incomes less than adequate for meeting 90 per cent of recommended calorie intake, and 'extremely poor' are those with less than adequate incomes to meet 80 per cent of the recommended calorie intake.

[25] See also Osmani (1978).

famine presented here can be extended in many ways by taking a more detailed view of the relationships that govern people's ability to command food and other essential goods. But even this simple analysis has been sufficient to demonstrate that the FAD view provides no explanation of the Bangladesh famine, and that a better understanding of the famine can be found through the entitlement approach.

Chapter 10

Entitlements and Deprivation

10.1 FOOD AND ENTITLEMENTS

The view that famines are caused by food availability decline—the FAD view—was questioned on grounds of cogency in the first chapter of this monograph. Empirical studies of some of the larger recent famines confirmed that famines could thrive even without a general decline in food availability (see Chapter 6, 7, and 9). Even in those cases in which a famine *is* accompanied by a reduction in the amount of food available per head, the causal mechanism precipitating starvation has to bring in many variables other than the general availability of food (see Chapter 8). The FAD approach gives little clue to the causal mechanism of starvation, since it does not go into the *relationship* of people to food. Whatever may be the oracular power of the FAD view, it is certainly Delphic in its reticence.

A food-centred view tells us rather little about starvation. It does not tell us how starvation can develop even without a decline in food availability. Nor does it tell us—even when starvation is accompanied by a fall in food supply—why some groups had to starve while others could feed themselves. The over-all food picture is too remote an economic variable to tell us much about starvation. On the other hand, if we look at the food going to *particular* groups, then of course we can say a good deal about starvation. But, then, one is not far from just describing the starvation itself, rather than explaining what happened. If some people had to starve, then clearly, they didn't have enough food, but the question is: *why* didn't they have food? What allows one group rather than another to get hold of the food that is there? These questions lead to the entitlement approach, which has been explored in this monograph, going from economic phenomena into social, political, and legal issues.

A person's ability to command food—indeed, to command any commodity he wishes to acquire or retain—depends on the entitlement relations that govern possession and use in that society. It depends on what he owns, what exchange possibilities are offered to him, what is given to him free, and what is taken away from him. For example, a barber owns his labour power and some specialized skill, neither of which he can eat, and he has to sell his hairdressing service to earn an income to buy food. His entitlement to food may collapse even without any change in food availability if for any reason the demand for hairdressing collapses and if he fails to find another job or any social security benefit. Similarly, a craftsman producing, say, sandals may have his food entitlement squashed if the demand for sandals falls sharply, or if the supply of leather becomes scarce, and starvation can occur with food availability in the economy unchanged. A general labourer has to earn his income by selling his labour power (or through social security benefit) before he can establish his command over food in a free-market economy; unemployment *without* public support will make him starve. A sharp change in the relative prices of sandals, or haircuts, or labour power (i.e. wages) *vis-à-vis* food can make the food entitlements of the respective group fall below the starvation level. It is the totality of entitlement relations that governs whether a person will have the ability to acquire enough food to avoid starvation, and food supply is only one influence among many affecting his entitlement relations.

It is sometimes said that starvation may be caused not by food shortage but by the shortage of income and purchasing power. This can be seen as a rudimentary way of trying to catch the essence of the entitlement approach, since income does give one entitlement to food in a market economy. While income may not always provide command in a fully planned economy, or in a 'shortage economy', in which a different system of entitlement might hold,[1] the income-centred view will be relevant in most circumstances in which famines have occurred.[2] But the inadequacy of the income-centred view arises from the fact that, even in those circumstances in which income does provide command, it offers only a partial picture of the entitlement pattern, and starting the story with the shortage of income is to

---

[1] See Kornai (1979a) for a far-reaching probe into economics of the 'shortage economy'. See also Kornai (1979b).

[2] A possible exception might conceivably be the Russian famines of 1932–4, but they have not been fully studied yet. See, however, Dalrymple (1964, 1965) and Brown and Anderson (1976, Chapter 6).

leave the tale half-told. People died because they didn't have the income to buy food, but how come they didn't have the income? What they can earn depends on what they can sell and at what price, and starting off with incomes leaves out that part of the entitlement picture. Futhermore, sometimes the income may be just 'notional', e.g. a peasant's possession of the foodgrains he has grown, and then the income-and-purchasing-power story is a bit oblique. To talk about his entitlement to the food he has grown is, of course, more direct. But the main advantage of the entitlement approach rests not in simplicity as such, but—as explained above—in providing a more comprehensive account of a person's ability to command commodities in general and food in particular.

10.2 THE POOR: A LEGITIMATE CATEGORY?

The entitlement approach requires the use of categories based on certain types of discrimination. A small peasant and a landless labourer may both be poor, but their fortunes are not tied together. In understanding the proneness to starvation of either we have to view them not as members of the huge army of 'the poor', but as members of particular classes, belonging to particular occupational groups, having different ownership endowments, and being governed by rather different entitlement relations. Classifying the population into the rich and the poor may serve some purpose in some context, but it is far too undiscriminating to be helpful in analysing starvation, famines, or even poverty.

The grossest category is, of course, the category of the entire population. It is on this that FAD concentrates, in checking food availability per head, and comes to grief (Chapters 6–9). The entitlement approach not merely rejects such grossness; it demands much greater refinement of categories to be able to characterize entitlements of different groups, with each group putting together different people who have similar endowments and entitlements. As a category for causal analysis, 'the poor' isn't a very helpful one, since different groups sharing the same predicament of poverty get there in widely different ways. The contrast between the performances of different occupation groups in famine situations, even between groups that are all typically poor, indicates the need for avoiding gross categories such as the poor and the rich.

So much for causal analysis. But it might be thought that, while the category of the poor isn't very helpful in such causal analysis, it is useful in the *evaluation* of the extent of poverty in the nation. Indeed, the poor are usually huddled together for a head count in quantifying poverty. There is clearly some legitimacy in the category of the poor in this evaluative context in so far as there is a clear break in our concern about people at the 'poverty line'. In Chapter 2 it was argued that the problem of poverty assessment is quite distinct from the issue of assessment of inequality and requires paying particular attention to the category of the poor. On the other hand, even for evaluative purposes there is need for discrimination *among* the poor according to the severity of deprivation. In the head-count measure, the starving wreck counts no more than the barely poor, and it is easy to get examples in which in an obvious sense there is an intensification of poverty while the head-count measures is unchanged or records a diminution (see Chapters 3, 5, 9, and Appendix C). Thus, while the category of the poor has some legitimacy in the evaluative context, it is still far too gross a category and requires to be broken down.

The category of the poor is not merely inadequate for evaluative exercises and a nuisance for causal analysis, it can also have distorting effects on policy matters. On the causal side, the lack of discrimination between different circumstances leading to poverty gives rise to a lack of focus in policy choice. Evaluative grossness can also distort. With the use of the head-count measure of poverty, the best rewards to poverty-removal policies are almost always obtained by concentrating on the people who are *just* below the poverty line rather than on those suffering from deep poverty. There is indeed a certain amount of empirical evidence that gross characterizations of poverty do lead to distortions of public policy.[3]

10.3 WORLD FOOD AVAILABILITY AND STARVATION

The FAD approach applied to the food availability for the population of an entire country is a gross approach, lacking in

[3] See Sen (1975, Appendix A; 1976d).

relevant discrimination. What is a good deal more gross is the FAD approach applied to the population of the world as a whole. The balancing of world supply and world population has nevertheless received a lot of attention recently. While a fall in food availability per head for the world as a whole is neither a necessary nor a sufficient condition for intensification of hunger in the world, it has typically been assumed that the two *are* rather well correlated with each other. The evidence in favour of that assumption is not abundant, but it may be reasonable to suppose that, if the food availability per head were to go on persistently declining, starvation would be sooner or later accentuated. Different institutions and authors have provided estimates of 'short-falls' for the 1980s and beyond, some more alarming than others.[4]

I have little to add to this exacting exercise, except to point out the sensitivity of the results to the assumptions chosen and the remarkable lack of uniformity in the methodologies that have been thought to be appropriate. As far as the present is concerned—rather than the future—there is no real evidence of food supply falling behind population growth for the world as a whole, even though this has been observed for a number of countries. There is no outstripping of food growth by population expansion even when we look at the global picture leaving out the United States, which has been such a large supplier of food to other countries. The 'balance' in the future will depend on a variety of economic and political conditions,[5] but there is as yet no indication that world population expansion has started gaining on the growth of world food supply.

But if the analysis presented in the earlier chapters of this monograph is correct, it is quite possible that severe famine conditions can develop for reasons that are not directly connected with food production at all. The entitlement approach places food production within a network of relationships, and shifts in some of these relations can precipitate gigantic famines even without receiving any impulse from food production.

[4] See, for example, Borgstrom (1969), Ehrlich and Ehrlich (1972), Brown and Eckholm (1974), and Aziz (1975).

[5] See, among others, D. G. Johnson (1967, 1975), Borgstrom (1973), Aziz (1977), Taylor (1975), Sinha (1976a, 1976b, 1977), Barraclough (1977), Buringh (1977), Etienne (1977b), Lappé and Collins (1977), Poleman (1977), Rado and Sinha (1977), Harle (1978), Hay (1978a, 1978b), Sinha and Gordon Drabek (1978), and Interfutures (1979).

It is not my purpose to deny the importance of food production, or of some of the well-analysed issues in international food policy. It *is* rewarding to consider international insurance arrangements to reduce the food supply vulnerability of particular countries.[6] It *is* relevant to know how international food aid affects domestic production and distribution, and the world food prices.[7] It *is* also useful to do food balance sheets and integrate them into social account procedures, and to go into more elaborate analysis of 'food systems'.[8] The focus that emerges from this monograph looks at a different direction, namely the need to view the food problem as a relation between people and food in terms of a network of entitlement relations.

Some of the relations are simple (e.g. the peasant's entitlement to the food grown by him), while others are more complex (e.g. the nomad's entitlement to grain through exchange of animals, leading to a net gain in calories—see Chapters 7 and 8). Some involve the use of the market mechanism (e.g. selling craft products to buy food—see Chapter 6), while others depend on public policy (e.g. unemployment benefits, or relief in *langar - khanas* and destitution camps—see Chapters 6–9). Some are affected by macroeconomic developments (e.g. demand-pull inflation—see Chapters 6 and 9), while others deal with local calamities (e.g. regional slump—see Chapter 7), or with microeconomic failures (e.g. denial of fishing rights to a particular community in a particular region[9]). Some are much influenced by speculative activities, while others are not.[10]

It is the set of these diverse influences seen from the perspective of entitlement relations that received attention in this

[6] See, D. G. Johnson (1975, 1976), Kaldor (1976), Taylor and Sarris (1976), Aziz (1977), Josling (1977), Weckstein (1977), Reutlinger (1978), Konandreas, Huddleston and Ramangkura (1979), among others.

[7] See Mann (1968), Rogers, Srivastava and Heady (1972), Isenman and Singer (1977), Lappé and Collins (1977), Taylor (1977), and Svedberg (1978, 1979).

[8] See Joy and Payne (1975), Pyatt and Thorbecke (1976), Lörstad (1976), UNRISD (1976), Dickson (1977), Manetsch (1977), Hay (1978a, 1980), de Haen (1978), Chichilnisky (1979), and others, for pointers to different approaches.

[9] See Rangasami (1975), dealing with a local famine in the Goalpara district of Assam in India. See also Rangasami (1974a, 1974b).

[10] In the Bengal famine of 1943 professional speculators played an important part in the *second* phase of the famine (see Chapter 6, and Sen, 1977b). Holt and Seaman (1979) have argued for analysing this phase in terms of a 'catastrophe' pattern, and in this rapid change speculation was clearly important. On catastrophe theory, see Thom (1975) and Zeeman (1977).

monograph, through the analysis of actual famines which have taken place in recent years. In considering food policy, what emerges from this work is the importance of this angle of vision.

10.4 MARKET AND FOOD MOVEMENTS

Whether markets serve well the remedial function of curing famines by food movements has been the subject of a good deal of debating over centuries. Adam Smith (1776) took the view that they did, and that point of view was eloquently defended by Robert Malthus (1800) among others (see Appendix B). These arguments in political economy were widely used by policy-makers, not least in the British Empire.[11]

When a famine was developing in Gujerat in 1812, the Governor of Bombay turned down a proposal for moving food into an affected areas by asserting the advisability of leaving such matters to the market mechanism, quoting 'the celebrated author of the *Wealth of Nations*'.[12] Warren Hastings, who had tackled a famine in Bengal in 1783-4 by using public channels for moving food into the region, was rapped on the knuckles by Colonel Baird-Smith for not having understood his Adam Smith, adding that Hastings could 'scarcely have been expected' to have absorbed Adam Smith so soon (1783) after the publication (1776) of the *Wealth of Nations*.[13] The basically non-intervention-ist famine policy in India lasted late into the nineteenth century, changing only around the last quarter of it.

Firm believers in the market mechanism were often disap-pointed by the failure of the market to deliver much. During the Orissa famine of 1865-6, Ravenshaw the Commissioner of Cuttack Division, expressed disappointment that private trade did not bring much food from outside which should have happened since 'under all ordinary rules of political economy the urgent demand for grain in the Cuttack division *ought to have created* a supply from other and more favoured parts'.[14]

Rashid (1979) has argued that even a non-monopolized group of traders can act together in a monopolistic way to hinder

[11] See Bhatia (1967), Ambirajan (1978) and Rashid (1980).
[12] Quoted in Ambirajan (1978), p. 71. See also Aykroyd (1974).
[13] Quoted in Ambirajan (1978), p. 75.
[14] See Ambirajan (1980), p. 76; italics added.

movement of grains to relieve excess demand.[15] This could be so, but in a slump famine starvation and hunger can go hand in hand with little market pull, and even competitive traders may have little incentive to bring in foodgrain from elsewhere. Adam Smith's proposition is, in fact, concerned with efficiency in meeting a market demand, but it says nothing on meeting a need that has not been translated into effective demand because of lack of market-based entitlement and shortage of purchasing power.

Indeed, in many famines complaints have been heard that, while famine was raging, food was being *exported* from the famine-stricken country or region. This was, in fact, found to be the case in a relatively small scale in Wollo in 1973 (Chapter 7), and also in Bangladesh in 1974 (Chapter 9). It was a major political issue in the Irish famine of 1840s: 'In the long and troubled history of England and Ireland no issue provoked so much anger or so embittered relations between the two countries as the indisputable fact that huge quantities of food were exported from Ireland to England throughout the period when the people of Ireland were dying of starvation.'[16] Such movements out of famine-stricken areas have been observed in Indian famines as well.[17] In China, British refusal to ban rice exports from famine-affected Hunan was one of the causes of an uprising in 1906, and latter a similar issue was involved in the famous Changsha rice riot of 1910.[18]

Viewed from the entitlement angle, there is nothing extraordinary in the market mechanism taking food away from famine-stricken areas to elsewhere. Market demands are not reflections of biological needs or psychological desires, but choices based on exchange entitlement relations. If one doesn't have much to exchange, one can't demand very much, and may thus lose out in competition with others whose needs may be a good deal less acute, but whose entitlements are stronger.[19] In

[15] It is also possible to show how easily speculation can be destabilizing (see Hart, 1977).

[16] Woodham-Smith (1975), p. 70.

[17] See Ghosh (1979). Also Bhatia (1967) and Rashid (1980).

[18] Esherick (1976). Food movement from Bangladesh into India during the Bangladesh famine was also a politically explosive issue.

[19] This is one of the reasons why it is misleading to characterize a famine arising from a crop failure as being due to a fall in food availability. With crop failure people's incomes also collapse—and their ability to attract food from elsewhere—and the situation is best seen as a failure of entitlement and not as just a drop in food availability.

fact, in a slump famine such a tendency will be quite common, unless other regions have a more severe depression. Thus, food being *exported* from famine-stricken areas may be a 'natural' characteristic of the market which respects entitlement rather than needs.

10.5 FAMINES AS FAILURES OF ENTITLEMENT

The entitlement approach views famines as economic disasters, not as just food crises. The empirical studies brought out several distinct ways in which famines can develop—defying the stereotyped uniformity of food availability decline (FAD). While famine victims share a common predicament, the economic forces leading to that predicament can be most diverse.

A comparative picture of some aspects of four famines studied in Chapters 6, 7, and 9 is presented in Table 10.1, though it misses out many other contrasts discussed in detail in those chapters. (The famines in the six Sahel countries analysed in Chapter 8 have not been included in the table because of some lack of uniformity between the experiences of the different Sahel countries, but the over-all picture is rather similar to that of the Ethiopian famines.)

That famines can take place without a substantial food availability decline is of interest mainly because of the hold that the food availability approach has in the usual famine analysis.[20] It has also led to disastrous policy failure in the past.[21] The entitlement approach concentrates instead on the ability of different sections of the population to establish command over food, using the entitlement relations operating in that society depending on its legal, economic, political, and social characteristics.

I end with four general observations about the entitlement approach to famines. First, the entitlement approach provides a general framework for analysing famines rather than one particular hypothesis about their causation. There is, of course, a

---

[20] In addition to explicit use of the FAD approach, very often it is implicitly employed in separating out the total food supply per head as the strategic variable to look at.

[21] The failure to *anticipate* the Bengal famine, which killed about three million people, and indeed the inability even to *recognise* it when it came, can be traced largely to the government's overriding concern with aggregate food availability statistics (see Chapter 6 above, and Sen, 1977b).

TABLE 10.1
Comparative Analysis of Four Famines

Which famine?	Was there a food availability collapse?	Which occupation group provided the largest number of famine victims?	Did that group suffer substantial endowment loss?	Did that group suffer exchange entitlement shifts?	Did that group suffer direct entitlement failure?	Did that group suffer trade entitlement failure?	What was the general economist climate
Bengal famine 1943	No	Rural labour	No	Yes	No	Yes	Boom
Ethiopian famine (Wollo) 1973	No	Farmer	A little, Yes	Yes	Yes	No	Slump
Ethiopian famine (Harerghe) 1974	Yes	Pastoralist	Yes	Yes	Yes	Yes	Slump
Bangladesh famine 1974	No	Rural labour	Earlier, yes	Yes	No	Yes	Mixed

very *general* hypothesis underlying the approach, which is subject to empirical testing. It will be violated if starvation in famines is shown to arise not from entitlement failures but either from choice characteristics (e.g. people refusing to eat unfamiliar food which they are in a position to buy,[22] or people refusing to work[23]), or from non-entitlement transfers (e.g. looting [24]). But the main interest in the approach does not, I think, lie in checking *whether* most famines are related to entitlement failures, which I suspect would be found to be the case, but in characterizing the nature and *causes* of the entitlement failures where such failures occur. The contrast between different types of entitlement failures is important in understanding the precise causation of famines and in devising famine policies: anticipation, relief, and prevention.

Second, it is of interest that famines can arise in over-all *boom* conditions (as in Bengal in 1943) as well as in *slump* conditions (as in Ethiopia in 1974). Slump famines may appear to be less contrary to the 'common sense' about famines, even though it is, in fact, quite possible for such a slump to involve contraction of

---

[22] However, anecdotal accounts of dietary inflexibilities can be less flexible than the dietary habits themselves, as judged by the following interesting statement by Dom Moraes, the distinguished poet: '. . . in India in the 1940's there was a famine in Bengal and millions of people died. During the famine, the British brought in a large amount of wheat. Now, the people of Bengal are traditionally rice eaters and they would not change their eating habits; they literally starved to death in front of shops and mobile units where wheat was available. Education must reach such people' (Moraes, 1975, p. 40). Education must, of course, reach all, but there is, in fact, little evidence of the hungry refusing any edible commodities during the Bengal famine (see Famine Inquiry Commission, 1945a; also Ghosh, 1944 and Das 1949). The explanation of people dying in front of shops has to be sought elsewhere, in particular in the shortage of purchasing power and the minuteness of free distribution compared with the size of the hungry population queuing up for any food whatsoever (see Chapter 6 above).

[23] Haile Selassie, the Emperor of Ethiopia, apparently provided the following remarkable analysis of the famine in his country in June 1973: 'Rich and poor have always existed and always will. Why? Because there are those that work...and those that prefer to do nothing....We have said wealth has to be gained through hard work. We have said those who don't work starve.' (Interview report by Oriana Fallaci; quoted by Wiseberg, 1976, p. 108.) They have indeed 'said' that for many centuries, in different lands.

[24] Such non-entitlement transfers have played a part in some famines of the past. As an example, see Walter Mallory's (1926) account of the 1925 famine in Szechwan: 'The Kweichow troops invaded southern Szechwan and after some fighting were driven out. When they left they took with them all available beasts of burden, loaded with grain. The Szechwan troops who replaced them brought very little in the way of supplies and forthwith appropriated the remainder of the food reserves of the district—leaving the population, who had no interests in either side, to starve' (pp. 78–9).

outputs *other than* those of food (e.g. of cash crops). Boom famines might seem particularly counter-intuitive; but, as discussed, famines can take place with increased output in general and of food in particular if the command system (e.g. market pull) shifts against some particular group. In this relative shift the process of the boom itself may play a major part if the boom takes the form of uneven expansion (for example favouring the urban population and leaving the rural labourers relatively behind). In the fight for market command over food, one group can suffer precisely from another group's prosperity, with the Devil taking the hindmost.[25]

Third, it is important to distinguish between decline of food *availability* and that of *direct entitlement* to food. The former is concerned with how much food there is in the economy in question, while the latter deals with each food-grower's output of food which he is entitled to consume directly. In a peasant economy a crop failure would reduce both availability and the direct entitlement to food of the peasants. But in so far as the peasant typically lives on his own-grown food and has little ability to sell and buy additional food from the market anyway, the immediate reason for his starvation would be his direct entitlement failure rather than a decline in food availability in the market. Indeed, if his own crop fails while those of others do not, the total supply may be large while he starves. Similarly, if his crop is large while that of others go down, he may still be able to do quite well despite the fall in total supply. The analytical contrast is important even though the two phenomena may happen simultaneously in a general crop failure. While such a crop failure may superficially look like just a crisis of food availability, something more than availability is involved. This is important to recognize also from the policy point of view, since just moving food into such an area will not help the affected population when what is required is the generation of food entitlement.

Finally, the focus on entitlement has the effect of emphasizing

---

[25] When the fast progressing groups are themselves poor, the development of the famine may be accompanied by a reduction in the number of people below some general 'poverty line', leading to a recorded reduction of poverty as it is conventionally measured, i.e. in terms of head-count ratio. The problem is less acute with distribution-sensitive measures of poverty. See Appendix C.

legal rights. Other relevant factors, for example market forces, can be seen as operating *through* a system of legal relations (ownership rights, contractual obligations, legal exchanges, etc.). The law stands between food availability and food entitlement. Starvation deaths can reflect legality with a vengeance.

Appendix A
Exchange Entitlement

X is the non-negative orthant of n-dimensional real space, representing the amounts of n commodities; it is the set of all non-negative vectors of all commodities. Y is the power-set of X, i.e., the set of all subsets of X. Let $\mathbf{x}$ be the vector of commodities (including 'labour power') that the person owns, and $\mathbf{p}$ is the n-vector of prices faced by him.

Given his ownership vector $\mathbf{x}$, his exchange entitlement set $E(\mathbf{x})$ is the set of vectors any one of which he can acquire by exchanging $\mathbf{x}$.

(A1) $$E(\mathbf{x}) = \{\mathbf{y}\,|\,\mathbf{y} \in X \,\&\, \mathbf{p}\,\mathbf{y} \leqslant \mathbf{p}\,\mathbf{x}\}.$$

The function $E(.)$ from X to Y is his 'exchange entitlement mapping', or E-mapping, for short.

Two explanatory points. First, clearly $\mathbf{x} \in E(\mathbf{x})$. Second, the exchanges covered by (A1) are not, of course, confined to selling all of $\mathbf{x}$, and a part of it can be retained (since this will not affect the exchange-possibility of the remainder, as given by (A1)).

Let the set of commodity vectors that satisfy the specified minimum food requirement be given by $F \subseteq X$. Starvation must occur, in the absence of non-entitlement transfers (such as looting), if $E(\mathbf{x}) \cap F = \varnothing$. The 'starvation set' S of ownership vectors consists of those vectors $\mathbf{x}$ in X such that the exchange entitlement set $E(\mathbf{x})$ contains no vector satisfying the minimum food requirements. Obviously, S depends on F and the E-mapping.

(A2) $$S = \{\mathbf{x}\,|\,\mathbf{x} \in X \,\&\, E(\mathbf{x}) \cap F = \varnothing\}.$$

To illustrate consider a simple two-commodity case with commodity 1 standing for food, and let OA in Figure A1 represent the minimum food requirement. The price ratio is given by p. The starvation set S is given by the region OAB.

More generally, when food is not one commodity but many and the 'food requirements' can be met in many different ways, let the minimum cost of meeting the food requirements, i.e. for attaining any vector in F, be $m(\mathbf{p}, F)$.

(A3) $$m(\mathbf{p}, F) = \min_{\mathbf{x}} \mathbf{p}\,\mathbf{x}\,|\,\mathbf{x} \in F.$$

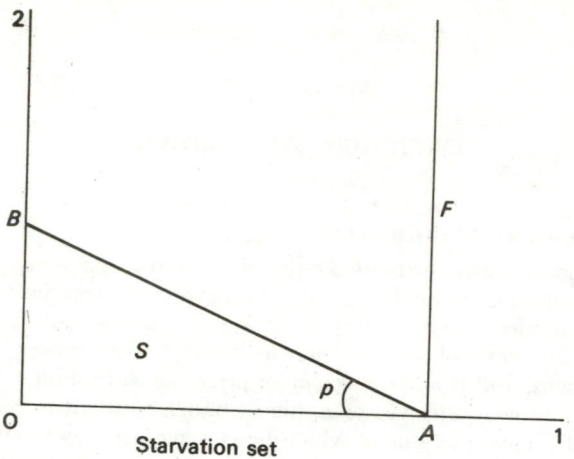

FIG. A1 Starvation set

The starvation set can be alternatively characterized for this case as:

(A4) $S = \{\mathbf{x} \mid \mathbf{x} \in X \;\&\; \mathbf{px} < m(\mathbf{p}, F)\}.$

Finally, it may be noted that it is possible to specify F taking into account taste constraints (see Chapter 2). In applying these concepts to the analysis of famines as opposed to regular poverty the taste constraints may, however, play a rather limited role. It is also possible to include essential non-food requirements in the specification of F.

A.2 VARIABLE PRICE EXCHANGES

If the person is not a price-taker, then the simple model outlined above will not work, in particular equations (A1), (A3), and (A4). In general, we can characterize the exchange possibilities in terms of a 'net cost function' $f(\mathbf{y}, \mathbf{z})$, representing the net cost of buying $\mathbf{y}$ and selling $\mathbf{z}$:

(A5) $f(\mathbf{y}, \mathbf{z})$ is a real-valued function, with $f(\mathbf{O}, \mathbf{O}) = O.$

The E-mapping can now be redefined as:

(A6) $E(\mathbf{x}) = \{(\mathbf{x} - \mathbf{z} + \mathbf{y}) \mid \mathbf{y}, \mathbf{z} \in X \;\&\; \mathbf{z} \leqslant \mathbf{x} \;\&\; f(\mathbf{y}, \mathbf{z}) \leqslant O\}.$

The interpretation of $\mathbf{z}$ is, of course, that of the vector of sales by this person, while $\mathbf{y}$ stands for his purchases. Obviously, $\mathbf{x} \in E(\mathbf{x}).$

The starvation set S is still given by (A2), but now coupled with (A5) and (A6).

A.3 DIRECT PRODUCTION AND TRADE

The person can use his ownership vector not only for trade, or for his own consumption, but also for production. The production possibilities open to him can be characterized by another mapping $Q(.)$ from X to Y, representing, for any vector of inputs $\mathbf{s}$, the set $Q(\mathbf{s})$ of output vectors, any of which he can produce.

(A7) $\qquad Q(.)$ mapping from X to Y

with $Q(\mathbf{O}) = \{\mathbf{O}\}$, unit set consisting of the null vector.

Consider, now, the person owning $\mathbf{x}$, buying $\mathbf{r}$ to be used as inputs, buying $\mathbf{y}$ to be used for consumption, selling $\mathbf{z}$ to meet the cost of purchases, and producing $\mathbf{q}$ by using a part $\mathbf{s}$ of $\mathbf{x}$ *plus* purchased inputs $\mathbf{r}$. The exchange entitlement mapping is now given by:

(A8) $\quad E(\mathbf{x}) = \{(\mathbf{x} - \mathbf{s} + \mathbf{q} - \mathbf{z} + \mathbf{y}) \,|\, \mathbf{r}, \mathbf{s}, \mathbf{y}, \mathbf{z} \in X \,\&\, (\mathbf{s} + \mathbf{z})$
$\leqslant (\mathbf{x} + \mathbf{q}) \,\&\, \mathbf{q} \in Q(\mathbf{s} + \mathbf{r}) \,\&\, f(\mathbf{r} + \mathbf{y}, \mathbf{z}) \leqslant O\}.$

The functions $f(.)$ and $Q(.)$ can be defined to take note of taxes, subsidies, social security benefits, etc.

The starvation set once again is given by (A2), combined with this.

A.4 SPECIAL CASES

We can now consider some special stipulations, taking (A2), (A5), (A7), and (A8) as the general structure.

Stipulation (i): $\mathbf{r} = \mathbf{O}$.
Stipulation (ii): $Q(\mathbf{s}) = \{\mathbf{s}\}$, unit set, keeping $\mathbf{s}$ unaffected.
Stipulation (iii): $f(\mathbf{y}, \mathbf{z}) = \mathbf{p}(\mathbf{y} - \mathbf{z})$, where $\mathbf{p}$ is a non-negative n-vector.

If we stipulate (i), (ii), and (iii), we are back to the case covered in Section A.1, with exchange entitlement mapping characterized by (A1) and the starvation set by (A4). If only (i) and (ii) are stipulated but not (iii), then we have the case without direct production, but also without fixed prices for exchange, essentially the same[1] as the one discussed in Section A.2. If only stipulation (i) is imposed, direct production is permitted with owned resources only, without the person being able to set himself up at all as an 'entrepreneur', purchasing inputs for productive use. Combined with (iii) this provides an

---

[1] The only difference is a purely formal one, viz., that production being 'undertaken' with $\mathbf{s}$ yielding just $\mathbf{s}$ is not really a 'production' at all, though $Q(\mathbf{s}) = \{\mathbf{s}\}$ makes it look like that, formally.

analogue to the usual simple characterization of production and competitive trade, as in figure A2, with OAB standing for $E(\mathbf{x})$, given the production frontier CD and the inter-good exchange rate given by angle ABO.

A.5 ECONOMIC STATUS AND MODES OF PRODUCTION

The landless labourer, having nothing to sell other than his 'labour power' and not in a position to undertake production on his own, is covered by stipulations (i) and (ii), i.e. the case discussed in Section A.2. If the wage rate is fixed and so are the commodity prices, then this reduces to the simpler case covered in Section A.1, with stipulation (iii) being imposed as well.

The small peasant farmer, undertaking production with his own resources, including his labour power, land, etc., corresponds to the case with stipulation (i). Since typically small peasants, even in the poor developing countries, buy some inputs from outside, and sometimes even labour power (especially at the time of harvesting), it is perhaps best to think of stipulation (i) as being a bit of an exaggeration, with the true situation being captured accurately only in some model within the general framework of Section A.3.

The share-cropper also falls in this category, since he undertakes production, gets some part of the return (and $Q(.)$ must now be seen as his return function and not the function of total production), and buys some inputs (though typically not all). If the owner provides all the resources other than the share-cropper's labour power, then the case is one in which stipulation (i) does hold, interpreting $Q(.)$ as a function of his own labour.

The large farmer will clearly violate all the stipulations in question. But if he is an absentee landlord, then there will be a new stipulation that $\mathbf{s}$ will not contain any of one's own labour. If the absentee landlord rents out his land at a fixed rent then it will again be a case as in Section A.1 or A.2, without production being directly involved in the landlord's exchange entitlement. If he leases it out to a share-cropper, then whether the production circumstances are directly involved or not will depend on whether he plays an active part in the production decisions. If he does, then the choices introduced by $Q(.)$ are open to him; if not, he is just selling the services of his land for a reward, which, though variable, is not within his control once contracted out.

Similar contrasts can be drawn outside agriculture as well, e.g. the industrial proletariat living on selling his labour power, the capitalist industrialist producing mainly with purchased inputs, and so on.

When a labourer fails to find employment, the entitlement question depends on what arrangements for social security there happens to be.

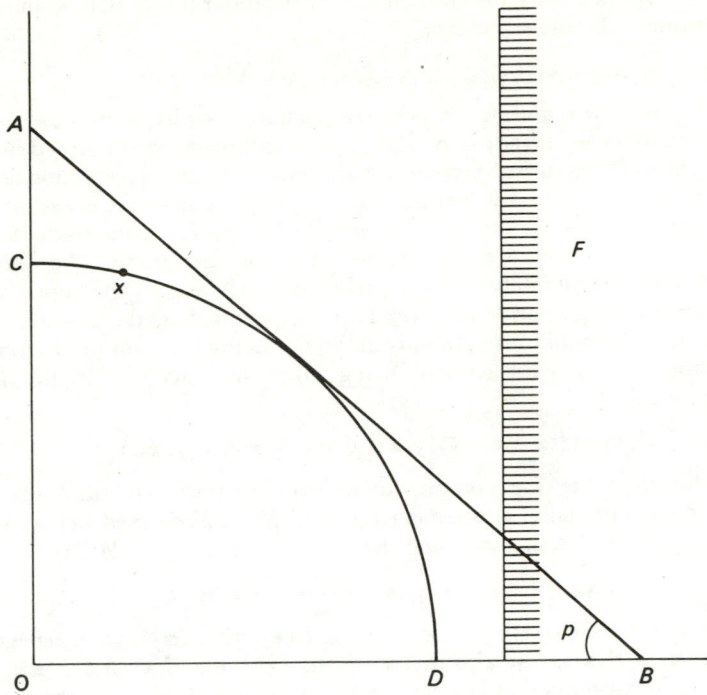

FIG. A2 Entitlement set with Own Production and Competitive Trade

If there are guaranteed unemployment benefits, then the entitlements arising therefrom can be characterized as a special case of entitlement related to labour power as such. This will require a dual set of prices for labour power, viz. a wage rate w if the person finds employment and a social insurance benefit b if he does not, with $w > b$. The entitlement is characterized not in terms of what he *expects*, but in terms of whether or not he can actually find employment. The focus is not on a person's subjective assessment, but on the real possibilities. This means that even in a given market situation there may be big differences between the positions of different workers in it, depending on whether the person's entitlement gets determined by his wage rate (or wage rates) or by social security benefits. In the absence of a social security system, the contrast is even sharper, since the entitlement of his labour power will be zero if he cannot obtain employment.[2]

A.6 OWN-PRODUCTION ENTITLEMENT

In Sections A.1 and A.2 a person's exchange entitlement was considered in terms of trade only. Later, production was incorporated into the general structure of exchange entitlement, treating production as a form of exchange (with 'nature'). But in some contexts, it is useful to distinguish between the entitlements arising purely from trade and those arising purely from production without any trade. The 'pure trade entitlement relation' $T(.)$ can be defined in exactly the same way as the exchange entitlement relation was defined in the absence of production possibilities—the only difference being that now production possibilities can exist without being taken into account in the T-mapping.

(A9). $\quad T(\mathbf{x}) = \{(\mathbf{x} - \mathbf{z} + \mathbf{y}) \,|\, \mathbf{y}, \mathbf{z} \in X \ \& \ \mathbf{z} \leqslant \mathbf{x} \ \& \ f(\mathbf{y}, \mathbf{z}) \leqslant \mathrm{O}\}.$

The other pure case is production without any trade, and this leads to the 'own-production entitlement relation' $P(.)$, as defined below. In Chapter 5 $P(.)$ was also called the 'direct entitlement relation'.

(A10) $\quad P(\mathbf{x}) = \{(\mathbf{x} - \mathbf{s} + \mathbf{q}) \,|\, \mathbf{s} \in X \ \& \ \mathbf{s} \leqslant \mathbf{x} \ \& \ \mathbf{q} \in Q(\mathbf{s})\}$

It is easily checked that $T(\mathbf{x}), P(\mathbf{x}) \subseteq E(\mathbf{x})$, but $E(\mathbf{x})$ is *not* in general $\subseteq T(\mathbf{x}) \cup P(\mathbf{x})$. Note also that $\mathbf{x}$ belongs to both $T(\mathbf{x})$ and $P(\mathbf{x})$.

The own-production entitlement relation gives an idea of what the person can secure independently of the working of the rest of the economy. If $P(\mathbf{x}) \cap F$ is non-empty, then the person can see to it that he does not starve, no matter how the rest of the economy operates. This consideration is of some importance when the trade relations are subject to sharp fluctuations owing to forces operating on the economy as a whole, as is frequently the case in times of famine. The case of $P(\mathbf{x}) \cap F \neq \emptyset$ will be called 'trade-independent security'.

In the literature of 'general equilibrium', it is typically assumed that every one has trade-independent security. As Tjalling Koopmans (1957) puts it, 'they assume that each consumer can, if necessary, survive on the basis of the resources he holds and the direct use of his own labor, without engaging in exchange, and still have something to spare of some type of labor which is sure to meet with a positive price in

---

[2] This is one reason why the concept of 'exchange entitlement' cannot be reduced to a derivative of '*terms* of trade', since the possibility of trade is itself a part of the picture captured by exchange entitlement, including non-trade (e.g. unemployment). Another reason is, of course, the fact that exchange entitlements include production possibilities as well.

any equilibrium' (p. 59).[3] But this is a very exacting assumption, and is violated by most of humanity in modern societies. While a peasant with his own land and other resources needed to grow food may indeed have trade-independent security,. an industrial worker with only his labour power to sell clearly does not. Nor would even the industrial capitalist, unless he happens to keep a large stock of food, since the strength of his position in terms of command over food arises from exchange and not from direct holding or of own-production entitlement.

Even within the rural economy, landless agricultural labourers have little chance of survival except through selling their labour power, and the position contrasts sharply with that of peasants. Indeed, the growth of a labouring class with nothing but labour power to sell (i.e., the emergence of labour power as a 'commodity' in the Marxian sense) has led to a very widespread absence of trade-independent security, and— as discussed in Chapter 5—the problem of vulnerability to famine situation has much to do with this development. The phase of economic development *after* the emergence of a large class of wage labourers but *before* the development of social security arrangements is potentially a deeply vulnerable one.[4]

Finally, even for landless rural population, the exchange entitlement can vary a great deal depending precisely on tenancy arrangements. Security of tenure gives an entitlement of a kind that, while formally involving trade, can be seen as something very like own-production entitlement. Even a share-cropper with security of tenure is, in this respect, in a much less vulnerable position than an agricultural labourer, who can be fired quite easily. Another advantage that the share-cropper has over agricultural labourer relates to the fact that his returns typically take the form of a part of the actual output. If the output happens to be foodgrains, this makes him a good deal less vulnerable to the vagaries of the market than the agricultural labourer employed at a monetary wage. This lower vulnerability can, of course, co-exist with vicious 'exploitation' of the share-cropper, viewed from a different perspective.

---

[3] See also Arrow and Hahn (1971), pp. 116–22.
[4] Some problems of this "pure exchange system transition"—PEST for short—are discussed in Sen (1980d).

Illustrative Models of Exchange Entitlement

B.1 INTRODUCTORY REMARKS

The determination of exchange entitlements in any real economy is a complex process, since a variety of influences—economic, social, *and* political—operate on the parameters in $f(.)$, $Q(.)$, etc., for each group. The process, as discussed in the text, will also vary substantially according to the precise institutional structure of the economy. While there is clearly little point in trying to develop a general theory of exchange entitlement determination (Appendix A was, of course, concerned exclusively with *characterization* rather than *determination* of exchange entitlements), there is perhaps some merit in illustrating the nature of the problem by considering some simple models. Two such models are presented in this Note, one based on Malthus's analysis in *An Investigation of the Cause of the Present High Price of Provisions* (1800), and the other trying to capture an important aspect of the causation of the Bengal famine in 1943, analysed in Chapter 6.

B.2 MALTHUS ON THE POOR LAWS AND THE PRICE OF CORN

There is little doubt that Malthus's analysis of food shortage in 1800 was a supplement to his theory of population presented two years earlier:

> To what then can we attribute the present inability in the country to support its inhabitants, but to the increase of population? I own that I cannot but consider the late severe pressures of distress on every deficiency in our crops, as a very strong exemplification of a principle which I endeavoured to explain in an essay published about two years ago, entitled, *An Essay on the Principle of Population, as it affects the future Improvement of Society*. It was considered by many who read it, merely as a specious argument, inapplicable to the present state of society; because it contradicted some preconceived opinions on these subjects. Two years' reflection have, however, served strongly to convince me of the truth of the principle there advanced, and of its being the real cause of the continued depression and poverty of the lower classes of society, of the total inadequacy of all the present establishments in their favour to relieve them, and of the periodical returns of such seasons of distress as we have of late experienced.[1]

But over and above claiming confirmation for his theory of food shortage arising from population expansion, Malthus also presented a theory linking food shortage to the behaviour of prices and

---

[1] Malthus (1880), p. 25.

distribution, and that theory was not essentially dependent on the *genesis* of the food shortage. It is that theory with which I am concerned in this Note, and not with Malthus's theory of population.

Malthus's analysis of adjustments of food prices had two notable features. First, prices had to rise to eliminate a sufficient number of demanders from the market to make the current supply last. The price rise was caused not by speculative activities but simply by the role of prices to adjust demand to supply.

It seems now to be universally agreed, that the stock of old corn remaining on hand at the beginning of the harvest this year was unusually small, notwithstanding that the harvest came on nearly a month sooner than could have been expected in the beginning of June. This is a clear, decided, and unanswerable proof that there had been no speculations in corn that were prejudicial to the country. All that the larger farmers and cornfactors had done, was to raise the corn to that price which excluded a sufficient number from their usual consumption, to enable the supply to last throughout the year.[2]

The second feature was the role attributed to the operation of the system of parish allowances in making it difficult to eliminate the demand for food by the poor, thereby leading to a much larger increase in prices.

This price, however, has been most essentially and powerfully affected by the ability that has been given to the labouring poor, by means of parish allowances, of continuing to purchase wheat notwithstanding its extraordinary rise.[3]

Malthus did not, of course, condemn the parish allowances for this reason, but regarded it as absurd that the poor should complain of the price rise.

I do not, however, by any means, intend to infer, from what I have said, that the parish allowances have been prejudicial to the state; or that, as far as the system has been hitherto pursued, or is likely to be pursued, in this country, that it is not one of the best modes of relief that the circumstances of the case will admit. The system of the poor laws, in general, I certainly do most heartily condemn, as I have expressed in another place, but I am inclined to think that their operation in the present scarcity has been advantageous to the country. The principal benefit which they have produced, is exactly that which is most bitterly complained of—the high price of all the necessaries of life. The poor cry out

---

[2] Malthus (1880), p. 16. It is worth remarking that Malthus's arguments in favour of the stabilizing role of speculation, on grounds that if the speculator 'be wrong in his speculation, he loses perhaps very considerably himself' (p. 15), is in line with the modern defence of speculation as a stabilizing activity. Indeed, Malthus anticipates by a good many years John Stuart Mill's similar argument, to which the ancestry of the defence of the stabilizing role of speculation is usually traced. (See Hart, 1977, for an illuminating analysis of the limitation of the argument.)

[3] Malthus (1880), p. 16.

loudly at this price; but, in so doing, they are very little aware of what they are about; for it has undoubtedly been owing to this price that a much greater number of them has not been starved.[4]

Indeed, in the system of parish allowances, Malthus saw a mechanism that would magnify the price rise owing to the food shortage in an almost unending price explosion.

The poor complained to the justices that their wages would not enable them to supply their families in the single article of bread. The justices very humanely, and I am far from saying improperly, listened to their complaints, inquired what was the smallest sum on which they could support their families, at the then price of wheat, and gave an order of relief on the parish accordingly. The poor were now enabled for a short time, to purchase nearly their usual quantity of flour; but the stock in the country was not sufficient, even with the prospect of importation, to allow of the usual distribution to all its members. The crop was consuming too fast. Every market day the demand exceeded the supply; and those whose business it was to judge on these subjects, felt convinced, that in a month or two the scarcity would be greater than it was at that time. Those who were able, therefore, kept back their corn. . . . The corn, therefore, naturally rose. The poor were again distressed. Fresh complaints were made to the justices, and a further relief granted; but, like the water from the mouth of Tantalus, the corn still slipped from the grasp of the poor; and rose again so as to disable them from purchasing a sufficiency to keep their families in health. The alarm now became still greater, and more general. . . . With further relief and additional command of money in the lower classes, and the consequent increased consumption, the number of purchasers at the then price would naturally exceed the supply. The corn would in consequence continue rising.[5]

Malthus was most critical of the proposal to insulate the poor against price rises by making the wages paid to the poor proportional to food prices. He saw in this the possibility of dragging the middle classes down to starvation also.

It has often been proposed, and more than once I believe, in the House of Commons, to proportion the price of labour exactly to the price of provisions. This, though it would be always a bad plan, might pass tolerably in years of moderate plenty, or in a country that was in the habit of considerable exportation of grain. But let us see what would be its operation in a real scarcity. We suppose, for the sake of the argument, that by law every kind of labour is to be paid accurately in proportion to the price of corn, and that the rich are to be assessed to the utmost to support those in the same manner who are thrown out of employment, and fall upon the parish. We allow the scarcity to be an irremediable deficiency of one-fourth of all the provisions of the country. . . . The middle classes of society would very soon be blended with the poor; and the largest fortunes could not long stand against the accumulated

---

4 Malthus (1800), pp. 18–19.
5 Malthus (1800), pp. 11–13.

pressure of the extraordinary price of provisions, on the one hand, and the still more extraordinary assessments for allowances to those who had no other means of support, on the other. The corn-factors and farmers would undoubtedly be the last that suffered, but, at the expiration of the three quarters of a year, what they received with one hand, they must give away with the other; and a most complete levelling of all property, would take place. All would have the same quantity of money. All the provisions of the country would be consumed; and all the people would starve together.[6]

Malthus hastened to reassure his readers, most of whom had—I take it—little to gain from 'a most complete levelling of all property' and from the food shortage being shared by all starving 'together', that 'there is no kind of fear, that any such tragic event should ever happen in any country' (p. 18).

Malthus's analysis can be captured in terms of a simple model, dealing both with the influence of poor laws on prices, and consequently on the exchange entitlement of the different classes, and with the 'tragic' possibility so feared by Malthus. Let the money incomes of the rich and poor be y_1 and y_2 per head respectively, and their respective numbers be n_1 and n_2. The income of the poor consists of their money earning w and receipt of transfer t from the rich arranged by the Poor Laws, while the income of the rich consists of their money earning u *minus* what they have to pay for the Poor Law transfers. The transfers are aimed at giving the poor the ability to buy a decent ration r of food grains at the prevailing price p, if that is possible. The 'tragic event' considered by Malthus refers to the hypothetical possibility that there are no limits to transfers as long as the rich are richer than the poor.

Considering the exchange entitlement of the rich and the poor only for the special case of command over corn, they are given respectively by e_1 and e_2:

(B1) $e_i = y_i/p$,   with $i = 1, 2$

(B2) $y_1 = u - (tn_2/n_1)$,   subject to $y_1 \geq y_2$.

(B3) $y_2 = w + t$.

If the proposed Poor Law transfer t is inadequate to provide the poor with adequate exchange entitlement for them to enjoy the decent ration r, then the transfer t is to be revised upwards, as long as the income of the rich y_1 remains higher than y_2. So there are two alternative conditions of equilibrium, viz.:

(B4)   either $e_2 = r$

         or $y_1 = y_2$.

<hr>

[6] Malthus (1800), pp. 17–18.

As long as $e_2 < r$, and $y_2 < y_1$, the value of the transfer t is to be raised upwards.

Finally, the model of price determination that Malthus considers in this case is simply one of the price being high enough to meet the money demand for a given supply of corn. Assuming that the poor spend all their income on corn, while the rich spend a proportion $c \leqslant 1$ of their income on corn, the total money demand is given by:

(B5) $$D = cy_1 n_1 + y_2 n_2.$$

The price of corn for the given supply q is, then,

(B6) $$p = D/q.$$

The exchange entitlement of the poor can be shown, by combining (B1), (B5), and (B6), to equal the following:

(B7) $$e_2 = (y_2 q)/(cy_1 n_1 + y_2 n_2).$$

If e_2 is large enough to meet the ration requirement r, then an equilibrium is well established at that point without the rich being levelled down to the level of the poor. This is one case that Malthus considers, and he comments on the effect of Poor Law transfers on raising the price of corn. It is easily checked that the price of corn is indeed positively related to the transfer value t, given $c < 1$:

(B8) $$p = \{ cun_1 + wn_2 + tn_2(1-c) \}/q$$

It is the recognition of this relationship that prompts Malthus to express his ire that the poor, in crying out 'loudly at this high price', are 'very little aware of what they are about; for it has undoubtedly been owing to this price that a much greater number of them has not been starved'. Malthus also spells out the process of equilibration in terms of a sequence of steps with the value of transfer t having to be raised to meet r, and then this rise in t causing the price of corn to rise, leading to the need for a fresh upward revision of the transfer value t. While the dynamic model is under-specified, it is easy to complete it, in more than one way.

The other case that Malthus considered is the 'tragic event' in which the equilibration takes place with $y_1 = y_2$: 'all would have the same quantity of money'. The stage is set for this by combining the plan of making the income of the poor proportional to 'the price of provisions' for them to be able to meet food requirements in full, while there is 'an irremediable deficiency of one-fourth of all the provisions of the country'. Forgetting the arbitrary figure of one-fourth, the point is that the food supply q is being taken to be less than what will be needed to entitle everyone to the norm of the food ration of r. This amounts to the following:

(B9) $$q < (n_1 + n_2)r.$$

Considering the inequality (B9) with the equation (B7), it is easily obtained:

(B10) $$e_2 < \{y_2(n_1 + n_2)r\}/(cy_1 n_1 + y_2 n_2).$$

Assuming that, as long as the rich have an income at least as large as that of the poor, i.e. $y_1 \geqslant y_2$, the expenditure on food by the rich must also be at least as large as that of the poor, i.e. $cy_1 \geqslant y_2$, it follows from (B10) that $e_2 < r$. Thus, assuming that c goes to 1 as y_1 approaches y_2, the only possible equilibrium emerges when $c = 1$ at $y_1 = y_2$, that 'tragic event' when 'all the people would starve together', rather than the rich starving less than the poor.

In this formulation of Malthus's model the effect of price rise on the income of grain sellers has not been explicitly brought in. This is, of course, easy enough to do—most simply by making u and w rise with price p—and it will not affect either of the two propositions under discussion. It will introduce a 'money-expenditure multiplier effect' of a rise in t, reinforcing its direct price-raising effect. And it will leave the reasoning about the only possible equilibrium being one of $e_2 = r$, or of $y_1 = y_2$, quite unaffected.

B.3 A MODEL OF INTER-CLASS DISTRIBUTION AND EXCHANGE ENTITLEMENT

Malthus's model is one of short-run price determination with supply of foodgrains being given. This feature of it is not inappropriate for analysing a famine situation developing when the foodgrains output has already been fixed by the preceding crop for quite a few months. In providing a simple model of interdependence to capture one aspect of the Bengal famine of 1943, I shall retain this feature. But the classification of the population has to be different from that of Malthus to bring in different classes with different economic roles. And the 'circularity' of exchange has to be studied.

In what follows, a five-class economy will be considered, denoted by the indices $1, \ldots, 5$ respectively as:

1 agricultural capitalists and landlords;
2 peasants;
3 urban and semi-urban workers (urban industrial labour force, military construction workers, urban casual labourers, etc.);
4 rural workers (agricultural labourers);

5 rural household producers (rural service providers, craftsmen etc.).[7]

This is, of course, quite a drastic simplification (contrast the class structure considered in Chapter 6), but it is adequate for the purpose of bringing out some of the more important contrasting movements of exchange entitlement.

The number of people in each group is denoted by n_i, with $i = 1, \ldots,$ 5, respectively. The foodgrains output in peasant farms is given by q_2 per peasant, and in non-peasant farms by q_1 per person of the landed class. The money wage rates of protected and unprotected workers are given respectively by w_3 and w_4. The money income of the rural household producers is denoted by v per person; the physical units of output is taken to be one unit per person (thus the price of the product per unit is also v).

The price of foodgrains is determined by the money demand D^f for the marketed supply of foodgrains and that supply is determined by proportions m_1 and m_2 marketed out of the non-peasant and peasant farming outputs respectively.

(B11)
$$p = D^f / (n_1 m_1 q_1 + n_2 m_2 q_2).$$

The money demand for the marketed supply of foodgrains comes from urban and semi-urban workers, rural workers and rural household producers, with the respective money demands being represented by D^f_i, with $i = 3, 4, 5$.

(B12)
$$D^f = \sum_{i=3}^{5} D^f_i.$$

The price of household products of group 5 are determined also by the money demand for it, D^v, and its supply, which is given by n_5, since the physical output is one per person. D^v is made up of demands from the various groups.

(B13)
$$v = D^v / n_5.$$

(B14)
$$D^v = \sum_{i=1}^{5} D^v_i.$$

Now the demand relations. Agricultural capitalists and landlords, and peasants, respectively spend proportions h_1 and h_2 of their money

[7] In this model, the industrial capitalists have not been explicitly considered. They are, of course, implicitly present in the determination of employment and wage rates to the urban and semi-urban labour force, and in the political economy underlying rationing of foodgrains. But as far as their own demands are concerned it is assumed that industrial capitalists' demand for foodgrains and rural household products is a negligible part of the total demand in the two respective markets.

incomes on rural household products. Urban and semi-urban workers are taken here to be protected by a wage policy—or rationing at controlled prices with government subsidizing real income by food subsidy (see Chapter 6)—in such a way that each of them can obtain r amount of foodgrains. They do not demand any rural household services or goods. Rural workers spend a proportions c_4 and h_4 on foodgrains and rural household products; respectively, and $c_4 + h_4 = 1$. Rural household producers spend proportions c_5 and h_5 on foodgrains and rural household products, respectively, and $c_5 + h_5 = 1$. (It is assumed that rural household producers also demand products of their sector in the market; this is to take note of the fact that there are many types of such products in reality.)

(B15) $D_i^v = q_i n_i m_i p h_i,$ with $i = 1, 2$.

(B16) $D_3^f = n_3 r p.$

(B17) $D_4^f = n_4 w_4 c_4.$

(B18) $D_4^v = n_4 w_4 h_4.$

(B19) $D_5^f = n_5 v c_5.$

(B20) $D_5^v = n_5 v h_5.$

(B21) $D_1^f = D_2^f = D_3^v = 0.$

Piecing together (B13), (B14), (B15), (B18), (B20), and (B21), the price v of rural household products is seen to be given by the following:

(B22) $v = [p(n_1 m_1 q_1 h_1 + n_2 m_2 q_2 h_2) + n_4 w_4 h_4]/n_5(1 - h_5)$

Using (B11), (B12), (B16), (B17), (B19), (B21), and (B22), and noting that $c_i + h_i = 1$ for $i = 4, 5$, it can be shown that the price of foodgrains is given by the following:

(B23) $p = n_4 w_4 /[n_1 m_1 q_1 (1 - h_1) + n_2 m_2 q_2 (1 - h_2) - n_3 r].$

In this short-run model the following parameters are taken as fixed: the outputs q_i, the shares marketed m_i, the numbers involved n_i, and the consumption ratios h_i and c_i. The money wage w_4 of the rural workers is also taken as fixed, the payments being seasonal and having been made. The difference that is being considered arises from an expansion of the urban and semi-urban activities owing to military expenditure, defence-related industries, and construction, and related economic activities. The simplest characterization of that is in terms of a raising of r, the real ration guaranteed in the urban sector. (Much of the change in 1943 Bengal, which this model tries to imitate in general terms, took the form of drawing labour from ill-paid occupations or the pool of nemployment to a rather buoyant wage sector. The industrial labour force and the general residents of Calcutta were also guaranteed fairly substantial food rations through the state policy of procurement and subsidization of the retail price; see Chapter 6.)

It is easily checked, from (B22) and (B23), that

$$(B24) \qquad \frac{dp}{dr} > 0, \text{ and} \frac{dv}{dr} > 0.$$

This is straightforward enough, but the more interesting question concerns the effect of a higher r on the exchange entitlement of each class of people considered. While exchange entitlement $E(\mathbf{x})$ specifies a *set* of commodity vectors, any of which can be commanded by the person in question by using his ownership vector $\mathbf{x}$ (see Appendix A), I shall in this particular exercise confine the analysis to the total amount of foodgrains e_i that could be commanded by a typical member of each class i.

The entitlement per head e_3 of the protected urban labour force is, of course, given by r, and that of the peasants e_2 is simply given by the food produced per head in peasant farms. The entitlement e_4 of rural workers is given by the amount of food that the wage rate w_4 will buy, and the corresponding figure for rural household producers e_5 equals the food that v will buy. And the entitlement of agricultural capitalists and landed classes is determined by the output q_1 *minus* the amount of food that has to be sold to meet the wage bill per person in class 1, i.e. the wages of (n_4/n_1) rural workers.

(B25.1) $\quad e_1 = q_1 - (n_4 w_4 / n_1 p) = q_1 - e_4 (n_4 / n_1).$

(B25.2) $\quad e_2 = q_2.$

(B25.3) $\quad e_3 = r.$

(B25.4) $\quad e_4 = (w_4 / p)$

(B25.5) $\quad e_5 = (v/p) = [n_1 m_1 q_1 h_1 + n_2 m_2 q_2 h_2 + n_4 h_4 (w_4 / p)]/n_5 (1 - h_5).$

It follows from (B24) and (B25) that the effect of a higher value of r is to:

(1) *increase* the exchange entitlement e_1 of *agricultural capitalists*, etc.:
(2) keep *unaffected* the exchange entitlement e_2 of *peasants*;
(3) *increase* the exchange entitlement e_3 of the *protected urban labour force*;
(4) *reduce* the exchange entitlement e_4 of the *rural labour force*;
(5) *reduce* the exchange entitlement e_5 of the *rural household producers*.

In so far as this simple model catches an aspect of the Bengal famine of 1943, this is more obviously so for Phase I than for Phase II of the famine (see Chapter 6). Phase II of the famine was much dominated by speculative activities which have not been brought in at all in the model presented above.

A speculative reduction of the proportion of foodgrains marketed, i.e. lower values of m_1 and m_2, will have the consequence of *reinforcing* the effects noted above (see B25.1–B25.5). Such a reduction, compared with normal years, was observed in Phase I as well (see Chapter 6). But in Phase II the speculative activities of professional traders as well as the market movements reflecting a terrible panic would require the analysis presented above to be supplemented in a more radical way.

I end this Appendix with five remarks. First, in so far as the 1943 output (including the December 1942 harvest) was somewhat—though not severely—lower than average, the position of the peasants too would have been worse in 1943 compared with that in a typical year. The analysis presented above assumes everything else the same, and while it does capture the fact that the famine affected most the agricultural labour force and the providers of rural services and crafts, it does not bring out that other groups also suffered a certain amount. In the case of the peasants, there is also the further fact, which has been noted, that some peasants sold off their grains supply too early, egged on by traders dangling before them higher prices than usual, and then had to buy back grains later for their own consumption at a much higher price. This type of dynamic process must be an important feature of a more complete model, especially of Phase II.

Second, the distress of the rural labour force has been captured in the model presented here only in terms of a declining command over food given by the wages,[8] but another feature was a reduction of employment, on which there are few firm data but much informal evidence. This, of course, would have led to a dramatic decline of exchange entitlement for those thrown out of employment.

Third, while the urban labour force is characterized here as being fully cushioned against food price rise, this was not so for the whole period or for all the urban labour force. Again, the model· has exaggerated a true feature into an over-simplified generalization. Perhaps it is also worth remarking that the protection enjoyed by the urban labour force in the Bengal famine· of 1943 was also rather unusual, and in considering the relevance of the model presented here for other famines, the economic operations of the different classes will have to be differently delineated.

Fourth, the model presented here is one of single-period interdependence. It is possible to investigate the same interdependences in a multi-period context; and even to consider a cumulative buildup of these· effects.

[8] In the model the money wages w_4 of agricultural workers have been taken to be given, but in reality w_4 typically went up with food prices but much less than proportionately (see Chapter 6).

Finally, in the model presented above the decline of the rural household producers is traceable ultimately to the distress of others, viz. the rural labourers. This interdependence could be heightened by incorporating the fact that destitution of rural labourers would also lead to their incomes being largely spent all on foodgrains, involving a dramatically lower h_4—the *proportion* of income spent on non-food household products—and thus even greater distress for rural household producers. The characterization of this interdependence presented in the model is, of course, an over-simplification; but—as discussed in Chapters 5–10—the general phenomenon of 'derived destitution' is one of the features of famines that requires a good deal more attention than it tends to get. This feature is among the consequences of interdependence analysed in this section.

Appendix C
Measurement of Poverty

C.I. POVERTY GAPS AND HEAD COUNTS

S is the set of people in a community of n people. Person i's income is y_i, and those whose incomes are no higher than π (the poverty line) are poor, making up the set $T \subseteq S$. The poor, q in number, are ranked according to income, and person i in T has the rank $r(i)$, being $r(i)$th richest among the poor. Equi-incomed persons are ranked in any arbitrary order, but once the ranking has been done, $r(i)$ is, in fact, a strict ordering.

The poverty gap of person i in T is g_i, given by:

$$(\text{C1}) \qquad g_i = \pi - y_i.$$

The total poverty gap of the poor is denoted g, and is given by:

$$(\text{C2}) \qquad g = \sum_{i \in T} g_i.$$

The two standard measures of poverty are the head-count ratio H and the income-gap ratio I, given respectively by:

$$(\text{C3}) \qquad H = q/n$$
$$(\text{C4}) \qquad I = g/q\pi.$$

Denote the mean income of the poor as y^* and their mean poverty gap as g^*:

$$(\text{C5}) \qquad y^* = \sum_{i \in T} y_i/q$$
$$(\text{C6}) \qquad g^* = \pi - y^* = g/q.$$

The income-gap ratio can also be expressed as:

$$(\text{C4*}) \qquad I = g^*/\pi.$$

Consider now the following axioms of legitimacy of poverty measures. Take $\mathbf{x}$ and $\mathbf{y}$ as two n-vectors of income with x_i and y_i the incomes of person i in the two cases, respectively, and let the poverty measures be such that $\mathbf{x}$ and $\mathbf{y}$ yield values $P(\mathbf{x})$ and $P(\mathbf{y})$ respectively (given π and S). In all the axioms proposed in this section the set S of people and π the poverty-line income are assumed to be given. $T(\mathbf{x})$ and $T(\mathbf{y})$ are the poor in S respectively for $\mathbf{x}$ and $\mathbf{y}$.

Monotonicity Axiom If for some $j \in T(\mathbf{x}) \cap T(\mathbf{y})$: $x_j > y_j$, and for all $i \in S$ such that $i \neq j$: $x_i = y_i$, then $P(\mathbf{x}) < P(\mathbf{y})$.

Weak Transfer Axiom If for some $j \in [\{T(\mathbf{x}) \cap T(\mathbf{y})\} \cup \{(S - T(\mathbf{x})) \cap (S - T(\mathbf{y}))\}]$ and $k \in T(\mathbf{x}) \cap T(\mathbf{y})$: $[(x_j > y_j \geqslant y_k > x_k)$ & $(x_j - y_j = y_k - x_k)]$, and for all $i \in S$ such that $i \neq j, k$: $x_i = y_i$, then $P(\mathbf{x}) > \mathbf{P}(\mathbf{y})$.

The monotonicity axiom says that, given other things, a reduction in income of someone below the poverty line must increase the poverty measure. The weak transfer axiom says that a pure transfer of income to a poor person below the poverty line from a richer person, without making either cross the poverty line, must reduce the poverty measure.[1]

It is easily checked that the head-count measures H violates both the monotonicity axiom and the weak transfer axiom. H is invariant with respect to both the fall of the income of a poor person, and to transfers of the kind envisaged in the weak transfer axiom.[2] In fact, a *reverse* transfer, i.e. from the poor to someone richer, will either leave H unchanged or make it go down, but will *never* make it go up. The income-gap ratio I satisfies the monotonicity axiom, but violates the weak transfer axiom when j is below the poverty line throughout, i.e. when $j \in T(\mathbf{x})$. It follows immediately that no function of H and I, $\psi(H, I)$, can satisfy the weak transfer axiom. Indeed, both H and I are blind to distribution among the poor.

However, both H and I satisfy one of the possible qualities of a poverty measure that was discussed in Chapter 2, to wit, independence of the income levels of those who are *above* the poverty line. One consequence of this is that no fall in the income of the poor can be *outweighed* by any rise—no matter how large—in the incomes of the rich.

Focus Axiom If $x_i = y_i$ for all $i \in T(\mathbf{x}) \cup T(\mathbf{y})$, then $P(\mathbf{x}) = P(\mathbf{y})$.

The focus axiom is motivated by the view that the poverty measure is a characteristic of the poor, and not of the general poverty of the nation. It does not, however, try to reflect the *relative* burden of poverty, viz. what proportion of income of the rich would be needed to wipe out the poverty gaps of the poor,[3] since that is clearly eased by the rich being

---

[1] In Sen (1976a) the 'transfer axiom' was more demanding in that the poverty measure was required to record a decline even if the transfer made the richer person fall below the poverty line, thus swelling the number of the poor. That version makes poverty measurement, in an important way, independent of the number below the poverty line, which raises other problems (see Section C.3 below).

[2] Contrast: 'Its [the new Poor Law's] only effect was that whereas previously three to four million half paupers had existed, a million total paupers now appeared, and the rest, still half paupers, merely went without relief. The poverty of agricultural districts has increased every year' (Engels, 1892, p. 288).

[3] See Anand (1977) and Beckerman (1979a, 1979b) for the relevance of that perspective for policy discussion.

richer, even when all the poor remain just as poor and miserable.

C.2 AXIOMATIC DERIVATION OF MEASURE P

The approach used in the derivation of measure P, which was informally discussed in Chapter 3, can be justified either by bringing in the notion of personal welfare conceived in ordinal terms (or—redundantly—in more demanding cardinal terms), or by directly axiomatizing on income distributions. In earlier contributions (Sen, 1973b, 1976a), the former, welfare-based, notion was used, but here the simpler and directly income-based format will be employed.

Poverty can be conceived of as a weighted sum of the poverty gaps of the poor:

$$(\text{C7}) \qquad P = A(n, q, \pi) \sum_{i \in T} v_i g_i$$

where v_i is the weight on the poverty gap g_i of person i, and $A(n,q,\pi)$ is a normalizing parameter dependent on the total number of people n, the number of poor people q, and the poverty line π. Note that it has *not* been specified that v_i must depend only on the size of person i's poverty gap g_i or income level y_i, so that—despite the superficially additive form—no separability requirement has been imposed by (C7).

In the light of the perspective of relative deprivation (see Chapter 3), it may be reasonable to think of the weight v_i of the poverty gap of i to be dependent on i's relative position *vis-à-vis* others in the same reference group. If the reference group is the group of the poor, this makes $r(i)$, i.e. the rank of the poor person i among the poor, a relevant determinant of v_i. Going one step further, v_i can be made an increasing function of $r(i)$, so that the weight depends on where i stands in the ranking *vis-à-vis* other poor people. The simplest case of such as increasing function is the identity mapping $m = f(m)$.

Ranked Relative Deprivation (Axiom R) Poverty is measured as in (C7) with the weight v_i on person i's poverty gap equalling i's income rank among the poor:

$$(\text{C8}) \qquad v_i = r(i).$$

The rule, as discussed in Chapter 3, is in the same spirit as Borda's (1781) use of rank-order weighting.[4]

The other axiom used at this stage is based on the idea that the inadequacy of the head-count ratio and the income-gap measure taken together arises from their inability to be sensitive to the distribution of

---

See Sen (1976b) for the use of a similar axiom in making distribution-sensitive comparisons of real income. On that general problem, see also Graaff (1977), Hammond 1978), Osmani (1978), Sen (1979a), Marris (1980), and Broder and Morris (1980).

income among the poor, and when that distributional problem is eliminated, a combination of H and I should suffice. Thus, in dealing with alternative cases in *each* of which all the poor persons have the same income, H and I should be informationally adequate. One of the simplest ways of combining H and I in a function $\psi(H, I)$ is to take their product, which provides a convenient normalization.

Normalized Absolute Deprivation (Axiom A) If for all $i \in T$: $y_i = y^*$, then:

(C9) $$P = HI.$$

THEOREM C1 For large numbers of the poor, the only poverty measure satisfying Axioms R and A is given by:

(C10) $$P = H\{I + (1 - I)G\}$$

when G is the Gini coefficient of income distribution among the poor.
  Proof. In (C7), putting $g^* = g_i$ for all i, we get:

(C11) $$P = \tfrac{1}{2}\{A(n,q,\pi)\, g^*\, q(q+1)\}.$$

This, combined with (C3), (C4*), and (C9), yields:

(C12) $$A(n,q,\pi) = 2/(q+1)n\pi.$$

Combining (C7), (C8), and (C12), we obtain:

(C13) $$P = \frac{2}{(q+1)n\pi} \sum_{r(i)=1}^{q} (\pi - y_i)\, r(i).$$

Noting that the Gini coefficient for any q-membered population with mean income y^* and income ranks $r(i) = 1, \ldots, q$ can be easily written as (see Sen, 1973a, p. 31):

(C14) $$G = 1 + \frac{1}{q} - \frac{2}{q^2 y^*} \sum_{r(i)=1}^{q} y_i r(i)$$

a little simplification yields:

(C15) $$P = H[1 - (1 - I)\{1 - Gq/(q+1)\}].$$

For large q, (C15) reduces to (C10), thereby establishing the theorem.[5]
  An alternative expression of P can be obtained by eliminating I and

---

[5] This proof is essentially the same as in Sen (1976a), except for the somewhat remoter axiomatization used there, involving personal welfare levels. In fact, in Sen (1976a), the axioms are first used to translate the welfare-based requirements into corresponding income requirements, and then the proof goes through on the income space, in the same way as above. See also Osmani (1978).

replacing it by its equivalent $1 - (y^*/\pi)$, as seen from $(C4^*)$ and $(C6)$. This procedure, discussed by Anand (1977), yields:

$$(C16) \qquad P = H\{1 - y^*(1 - G)/\pi\}.$$

Note also that the measure P satisfies the monotonicity axiom, the weak transfer axiom, and the focus axiom.

C.3 ALTERNATIVES AND VARIATIONS

In this section some variations of the poverty measure P are considered. Axioms R and A can be varied in certain ways, yielding measures that differ from P in some specific respects. The concept of poverty has enough ambiguity to permit such alternative interpretations (see Chapters 2 and 3). But all these variations share with measure P a sensitivity to distributional considerations among the poor, in addition to the aspects of poverty captured by H and I.

One idea is to modify the income-gap element I in the measure of deprivation by taking the mean poverty gap not as a percentage of the poverty level income π but as a percentage of the mean income of the community, where μ is the mean income of the entire community.

$$(C17) \qquad I^* = g^*/\mu.$$

HI^* clearly equals the ratio of the aggregate poverty gap to total national income or GDP:[6]

$$(C18) \qquad HI^* = g/n\mu.$$

Alternative Normalized Absolute Deprivation (Axiom A^*) If for all $i \in T$: $y_i = y^*$, then:

$$(C19) \qquad P = HI^*.$$

It is easily checked that Axioms A^* and R lead to a modified poverty measure P_1, which has been proposed and extensively explored by Sudhir Anand (1977), and which differs from P by a multiplicative constant reflecting normalization per unit of national mean income rather than the poverty line income:

$$(C20) \qquad P_1 = P\pi/\mu.$$

P_1 has the feature of being sensitive to the income of the non-poor as well. A rise in the income of a non-poor person, given other things, will reduce I^* and obviously will also reduce the modified poverty measure P_1. If a rise in the income of *anyone* can be taken to be a reduction of the poverty of the nation, then P_1 is to be preferred over P, since P is

---

[6] Beckerman (1979a, 1979b) puts this measure to good use as an indicator of the relative burden of poverty, but also warns against reading too much into this ratio.

insensitive to income rises of the rich. It may also be noted that HI^* expresses the percentage of national income that would have to be devoted to transfers if poverty were to be wiped out by redistribution, and in this sense HI^* reflects the *relative* burden of poverty of the nation compared with its aggregate income.

On the other hand, it can be argued that the relative burden of poverty is really a different exercise from the description of poverty in terms of prevailing notions of deprivation. More importantly, P_1 has the characteristic that some increase in the income shortfall of the poor may be compensated by a sufficently high rise in the income of the non-poor. And this can be objected to on the ground that poverty is a characteristic of the poor, and a reduction of the incomes of the poor must increase the measure of poverty, no matter how much the incomes of the non-poor go up at the same time (see Chapter 2). P satisfies this condition, formalized as the focus axiom, but P_1 does not.

The choice of the index must ultimately depend on the purpose for which such a measure is sought. For descriptive excercises on 'the state of the poor' (to quote the title of the famous treatise of F. M. Eden (1797)), P would have an obvious advantage over P_1. But if, on the other hand, the intention is to check the country's *potential* ability to meet the challenge of poverty, P_1 has a clear advantage. The two versions, therefore, are concerned with two rather different things.

Variants of Axiom R may also be considered. Nanak Kakwani (1980a) has provided various alternatives to Axiom R yielding some measures closely related to the measure P. An especially interesting one—we may call it P_2—makes the weight v_i on the short-fall of person i depend not on the number of people among the poor *vis-à-vis* whom i is relatively deprived, but on the aggregate income of these people. P_2 has the merit of making i's extent of deprivation sensitive to the actual incomes enjoyed by those who are richer than him though lying below the poverty line. On the other hand, P_2 takes no note of how the aggregate income of these people is divided among them, and, more importantly, no note even of the number of persons among whom this aggregate income is divided. The sense of relative deprivation is made to depend on the sum-total of income of those who, while poor, are better off then the person in question, and no other information is used regarding the disposition of that sum-total.

In a different contribution, Kakwani (1980b) modifies Axiom R to provide a more general structure. Essentially, Kakwani's axiom makes the weight v_i the kth power of the income rank of person i among the poor.

Axiom R*   Poverty is measured as in (C7) with the weights v_i given by:

(C21) $$v_i = [r(i)]^k.$$

For the poverty measure, call it P_3, derived from this, the sensitivity of between-poor income distribution will depend on the value of k. The poverty measure P obviously corresponding to $k = 1$, making it, as Kakwani (1980b) puts it, 'equally sensitive to a transfer of income at all positions'. The generalization involved in P_3 permits various alternative assumptions about transfer sensitivity, e.g. giving greater weight to transfers of income at the lower end of the distribution of income.

A different generalization based on a reinterpretation of the poverty index P has been proposed by Blackorby and Donaldson (1980a). They note that the measure P can be seen as the product of the head-count ratio H and the proportionate gap between the poverty-line income π and the Atkinson–Kolm 'equally distributed equivalent income' (e^g) of the incomes of the poor when the evaluation is done with the Gini social evaluation function.[7]

(C22) $P = H (\pi - e^g)/\pi, \quad \text{with } e^g = y^* (1 - G).$

If the social evaluation function is changed, a new poverty measure would emerge correspondingly, with the equally distributed equivalent income defined according to *that* social evaluation function.[8]

(C23) $P_4 = H(\pi - e)/\pi.$

Blackorby and Donaldson chose an ethical interpretation of the poverty measures. The value of e reflects that level of income which, if shared by all the poor, would be judged by the social evaluation function to be exactly as good as the actual distribution of income among the poor. But it is easily seen that the format permits a descriptive interpretation as well, viz. e standing for that level of income which, if shared by all the poor, will be regarded as displaying as much over-all poverty as the actual distribution of income among the poor. The issues involved in the choice between descriptive and ethical interpretations of poverty have been discussed in Chapters 2 and 3 and will not be pursued further.[9] The poverty measures can be mathematically interpreted in either way, and the real question is one of relevance

---

[7] For the concept of equally distributed equivalent income, see Kolm (1969) and Atkinson (1970). For the relation of the poverty measure P to the Gini evaluation function, see Sen (1973b, 1976a), and related matters in Sen (1974, 1976b). See also Graaff (1946), Gastwirth (1972, 1975), Sen (1973a), Pyatt (1976, 1980), Sastry (1977, 1980), Osmani (1978), Dorfman (1979), Kakwani (1980a), Yitzhaki (1979), Fields (1980), Donaldson and Weymark (1980a, 1980b), Radhakrishna and Sarma (1980), and Sastry and Suryanarayana (1980).

[8] Blackorby and Donaldson (1980a) point out the need for some assumptions about the general characteristics of such a social evaluation function, especially its homotheticity, and strict separability of a kind that permits one to rank the distribution of income among the poor independently of the incomes of those who are richer.

[9] See also Sen (1978b).

of the excercise to the motivation that leads to the search for a measure of poverty.

A particular descriptive characteristic of the poverty measure P has been the subject of some detailed investigation. While it is clear that the measure P of poverty must record a rise when there is a transfer of income from a poorer person to one who is richer provided that does not make the richer person cross the poverty line, exactly the opposite *can* happen—depending on the exact values—when such a crossing does take place (see Sen, 1977a, p. 77). It is arguable whether a poverty measure should not show increased poverty *whenever* some income is transferred from a poorer to a richer person, no matter whether this makes the richer person cease to be regarded as poor because of his crossing the poverty line. Thon (1979, 1980) has explored the analytical relations involved in such monotonic transfer sensitivity, and has proposed a variation of P that would ensure that the poverty measure records an increase whenever there is a transfer of income from a person who is poor to one who is richer. He modifies Axiom R to make the weight v_i on the poor i's income gap g_i equal his income rank $R(i)$ among *all* the people in the community, and not merely among the poor (as under Axiom R).

Axiom R** Poverty is measured as in (C7) with the weights v_i given by:

$$(C24) \qquad\qquad v_i = R(i).$$

Combined with the original structure with slight modifications, Axiom R** precipitates Thon's variant—we may call it P_5—of the poverty measure satisfying this monotonic property.[10]

There remains, of course, the substantial issue as to whether a poverty measure *should* always register an increase whenever there is such a transfer, even when the transfer actually reduces the number of the poor.[11] In so far as the index of poverty is interpreted to represent the condition of the poor—how many and each precisely how poor—a good case can perhaps be made for permitting the possibility that a

[10]
$$P_5 = \{2/(n+1)n\pi\} \sum_{r(i)=1}^{q} (\pi - y_i) R(i).$$

This can be easily compared with the poverty measure P as expressed in (C13).

[11] The 'transfer axiom' considered (but not used in the derivation of P) in Sen (1976a) demanded: 'Given other things, a pure transfer of income from a person below the poverty line to anyone who is richer must increase the poverty measure' (p. 219). In Sen (1977a) this was modified to the less demanding requirement, corresponding to the weak transfer axiom considered here: 'Given other things, a pure transfer of income from a person below the poverty line to anyone richer must strictly increase the poverty measure unless the number below the poverty line is strictly reduced by the transfer' (p. 77) This contrast is the central one between P and P_5.

reduction of the prevalence of the poor might under some circumstances compensate a rise in the extent of penury of those who remain below the poverty line. The old measure P includes this possibility, while Thon's P_5 does not. If, however, the focus is on inequality or living standard and not specifically on the predicament of people in falling below the poverty line, then the unqualified transfer axiom would make a good deal of sense, since the poverty-alleviating role of crossing the poverty line would be then rendered less crucial.[12] Again, the variation proposed has merits that are conditional on the purpose for which the poverty measure is being sought.

Another interesting variant of the poverty measure P has been proposed by Takayama (1979), related to an approach that has been extensively explored by Hamada and Takayama (1978). From the actual income distribution a 'censured' income distribution is obtained by replacing the incomes that exceed the poverty line by incomes exactly equalling the poverty line (π). Takayama (1979) then takes the Gini coefficient G_c of the censured income distribution as the measure of poverty—we may call it P_6. Other measures of inequality are also applied to the censured distribution to derive corresponding measures of poverty in Hamada and Takayama (1978).

The approach has some clear merits. The Gini coefficient of the censured distribution is a much neater—and closer—translation of the Gini measure of inequality into a poverty measure. It doctors the income distribution itself by ignoring the information on the actual incomes of the people who are not poor, but counts them in with poverty line incomes. Takayama (1979) has also provided an interest-

---

[12] The unqualified 'transfer axiom' is, of course, essentially the same as the 'Pigou-Dalton condition' used in the measurement of inequality (see Atkinson, 1970), and of the living standard of a community (see Sen, 1976b, 1979a). The measurement of poverty is, however, quite a different type of exercise for which note must be taken of the 'poverty line', and the unqualified transfer axiom takes no note of this at all. An important result recently established by Kundu and Smith (1981) throws further light on this question. They show that no uniformly continuous poverty measurement function can satisfy simultaneously the unqualified 'transfer axiom' and 'population monotonicity axioms' demanding that an addition to the poor population (respectively, non-poor population), other things given, must increase (respectively, decrease) the poverty value. While Kundu and Smith's 'population monotonicity axioms' are really very demanding in this particular form, the conflict that they pinpoint is a more general one. The tension arises from the fact that the unqualified 'transfer axiom' takes no note whatever of the poverty line, whereas the 'population monotonicity axioms' treat that line as the great divider. Sensitivity to the poverty line is indeed an appropriate characteristic of axioms for poverty measurement, and this can be incorporated in many different ways. The 'week transfer axiom' used here (and in Sen, 1977a) takes note of the poverty line in the way already specified. It is this modified axiom—and not the unqualified 'transfer axiom'—that the measure P satisfies (see Sen, 1977a, p. 77), determining precise trade-offs through axioms R and A.

ing axiomatization of his measure of poverty G_c, and Hamada and Takayama (1978) have suggested derivations for similar poverty measures based on other inequality indexes applied to the censured distribution.

The main drawback of this approach lies in its robust violation of the monotonicity axiom, viz. that a reduction of income of anyone below the poverty line, given everything else, must increase the poverty measures. A person below the poverty line may still be among the relatively richer in the censured distribution of income with an income above the mean and the median of that distribution. A reduction of his income will in an obvious sense reduce the extent of inequality in the censured distribution, but in an equally obvious sense the community must now be having *more*—not less—poverty. So the simplicity of the formulae used by Takayama (1979) and Hamada and Takayama (1978) is achieved at some real cost—to wit, dropping the monotonic relation between the poverty measure and vector-dominance of deprivation of the poor.

While P has certain unique advantages, which its axiomatization brings out, several of the variants are certainly permissible interpretations of the common conception of poverty.[13] There. is nothing defeatist or astonishing in the acceptance of this 'pluralism'. Indeed, as argued earlier (Chapters 2 and 3), such pluralism is inherent in the nature of the exercise. The variants are all in the same tradition as measure P, being concerned not merely with H and I, but also with the distribution among the poor.

[13] Osmani (1978) has also analysed several different poverty indicators, and has taken explicit note of multi-commodity issues.

Appendix D

Famine Mortality: A Case Study

In this Appendix[1] the size and pattern of mortality in the great Bengal famine of 1943 are studied. Mortality in the Bengal famine was a hotly debated issue during and just after the famine, and has, in fact, remained so. The pattern of mortality is worth studying also for the light it throws on the nature of the famine. The general features of the famine and its possible causation were studied in Chapter 6.

D.1. HOW MANY PER WEEK: 1,000, 2,000, 26,000, 38,000?

'The Secretary of State for India', wrote *The Statesman*, the Calcutta newspaper, on 16 October 1943,

seems to be a strangely misinformed man. Unless the cables are unfair to him, he told Parliament on Thursday that he understood that the weekly death-roll (presumably from starvation) in Bengal including Calcutta was about 1000, but that 'it might be higher'. All the publicly available data indicate that it is very much higher; and his great office ought to afford him ample means of discovery.[2]

Sir T. Rutherford, the Governor of Bengal, wrote to the Secretary of State for India on 18 October 1943, two days after *The Statesman* editorial:

Your statement in the House about the number of deaths, which was presumably based on my communications to the Viceroy, has been severely criticised in some of the papers. My information was based on what information the Secretariat could then give me after allowing for the fact that the death-roll in Calcutta would be higher owing to the kind of people trekking into the city and exposure to inclement weather. . . . The full effects of the shortage are now being felt, and I would put the death-roll now at no less than 2000 a week.[3]

Was this higher figure of 2,000 close to the mark?

The Famine Inquiry Commission (1945a) noted that 'from July to December 1943, 1,304,323 deaths were recorded as against an average of 626,048 in the previous quinquennium', and the difference attributed

---

[1] This Appendix draws heavily on Sen (1980b), written in memory of Daniel Thorner.

[2] 'The Death-Roll', editorial, *The Statesman*, 16 October 1943. See also Stephens (1966). Ian Stephens was the editor of *The Statesman*, a British-owned paper, which distinguished itself in its extensive reporting of the famine and its crusading editorials.

[3] Letter to Mr. L. S. Amery, no. L/E/8/3311; document no. 180 in Mansergh, (1973), vol. IV, pp. 397–8. The earlier communication referred to by Rutherford is document no. 158 in the same volume.

to the famine comes to a bit over 678,000.[4] This would make the average weekly death-roll in excess of 26,000 rather than 2,000.

The Famine Inquiry Commission went on to note that 'all public health statistics in India are inaccurate', and 'even in normal times deaths are not fully recorded'. In rural Bengal deaths were reported by the village *chowkidar* (village watchman), in addition to his other duties, and he was 'usually illiterate, and paid about Rs. 6 or Rs. 7 a month'. During the famine period, 'in certain places the salaries of *chowkidars* were not paid and they deserted their posts to obtain work on military projects and aerodromes', while 'some of them died'.

The replacement of dead and vanished *chowkidars* was no easy matter and several weeks and months might elapse before successors could be found, during which deaths presumably went unrecorded. Further, in the height of the famine thousands of people left their homes and wandered across the countryside in search of food. Many died by the roadside—witness the skulls and bones which were to be seen there in the months following the famine. Deaths occuring in such circumstances would certainly not be recorded in the statistics of the Director of Public Health.[5]

Taking note of all this, the Commission arrived at the conclusion that 'the number of deaths in excess of the average in 1943 was of the order of one million'—nearly all of it in the second half of the year.[6] On this estimate the death-roll in the second half of 1943 would seem to have been around 38,000 *per week.*

D.2 HOW MANY IN FACT?

No reason was given by the Commission for choosing the particular correction ratio that was used, except the thoroughly respectable one that it was arrived at 'after due consideration of the available facts' (1945a, p. 109). To this figure of one million deaths attributed to the famine of 1943, the Commission added the number of registered deaths in the first half of 1944 in excess of the previous quinquennial average without any correction. The reason for this asymmetry stemmed from the Commission's belief that there was 'an unquestionable improvement in the collection of mortality statistics' at the end of 1943 owing to efforts made by civil and military medical authorities (p. 109). The excess death registration for the first half of 1944 amounts to 422,371. Adding this to the estimate of one million for 1943, the Commission rounded off the mortality toll of the famine thus:

---

[4] Famine Inquiry Commission (1945a), p. 108. For the year as a whole the difference came to 688, 846.

[5] Famine Inquiry Commission (1945a), p. 109. See also *Census of India 1951*, vol. VI, part IB, pp. 1–2.

[6] Famine Inquiry Commission (1945a), pp. 108–9.

'about 1.5 million deaths occurred as a direct result of the famine and the epidemics which followed in its train' (p. 110).

Dr Aykroyd, a distinguished nutrition expert, who was a member of the Commission and who in fact made the Commission's estimates of mortality, has recently stated (as was quoted in Chapter 6) that he now thinks 'it was an under-estimate, especially in that it took too little account of roadside deaths, but not as gross an under-estimate as some critics of the Commission's report, who preferred 3 to 4 million, declared it to be' (Aykroyd, 1974, pp. 77). Who were these critics and how did they arrive at their figures?

The most quoted estimate—from the Anthropology Department of the Calcutta University—was based on a sample survey. The following estimates were released on 21 February 1944—much before the Famine Inquiry Commission had even been appointed:

The Anthropology Department of the University of Calcutta has carried out a sample survey of ten of the famine-affected districts of Bengal. The statistics for eight districts have so far been tabulated. They cover eight hundred sixteen-family units with a total membership of three thousand eight hundred and eighty. The total deaths in these groups during June–July 1943 and November–December 1943, has been three hundred eighty-six or ten per cent during six months (i.e. 100 per thousand). As the death rate for Bengal does not exceed thirty per thousand per annum, i.e., fifteen per thousand for six months, the excess mortality (100–15) of eighty-five per thousand, that is, eight and a half percent, has to be ascribed to famine and the pestilence that followed in its wake. As some areas in North Bengal were much less affected than Western or Central Bengal or the deficit areas of Eastern Bengal, some reduction has to be made to estimate the total mortality figures for Bengal. It will probably be an under-estimate of the famine to say that two-thirds of the total population were affected more or less by it. On this basis the probable total number of deaths above the normal comes to well over three and a half millions.[7]

The applicability of an excess mortality rate of $8\frac{1}{2}$ per cent to two-thirds of the population of Bengal is, in fact, a piece of *pure* guesswork—and an illegitimate one at that, since the sample that was surveyed was chosen from the worst affected areas in Bengal. Later the leader of the group, Professor K. P. Chattopadhyaya, himself pointed out limitations of this estimate, and proposed a figure of 2.2 million for excess deaths in 1943. Adding the half a million excess deaths taken by the Famine Inquiry Commission for 1944, Chattopadhyaya came to a 'minimum' estimate of 'total excess mortality' equalling 2.7 million.[8]

Between Chattopadhyaya's figure of 2.7 million and the Famine Inquiry Commission's 1.5 million (not to mention the minute estimates

---

[7] Reprinted in Ghosh (1944), Appendix G.
[8] Chattopadhyaya and Mukherjea (1946), p. 5.

in contemporary official statements in London and New Delhi[9]), there remains a wide gap. The lack of evidence on the representative nature of Chattopadhyaya's sample renders it dubious and the arbitrariness of Commission's correction factor makes it difficult to evaluate their estimate also.[10] But a more fundamental question concerns the time coverage of the mortality estimates. Both these figures cover up to June 1944. The acute starvation associated with the famine had ended around December 1943, even though 'the death rate remained high throughout the greater part of 1944' (Famine Inquiry Commission, 1945a, p. 1). When did the death rate, in fact, return to 'normal'? The Famine Inquiry Commission did not answer this question.

It could not have. At the time the Report was submitted in 1945, the death rate had not *yet* returned to normal. When did it do so? This is clearly one of the first things to ascertain, since the forces of post-famine epidemics to which the Commission refers in incorporating the excess deaths in the first half of 1944 in its total mortality estimate, went on raging for years.

For this, and indeed for any other year-to-year study, we have to rely on death registration data with suitable corrections. It is argued in the *Census of India 1951*, in its report on the 'Vital Statistics of West Bengal: 1941–50', that, while there are errors in registration, 'under-registrations are fairly uniform and do not take sudden leaps and bounds from year to year' (vol. VI, Part 1B, pp. 1–2).[11] While it seems most likely that the registration ratio did decline in 1943 and improved again in 1944, there seems to be little reason for assuming a radically different proportion of post-1944 registration compared with pre-1943 ratios.

For West Bengal, Jain's use of the reverse survival method yields an under-registration of deaths of 33.9 per cent in 1941–50. This makes the actual mortality 51 per cent higher on the average than registered

---

[9] There is something puzzling about the official statements on the minute size of mortality. Lord Wavell records in his 'journal' on 19 October 1943, when he became the new viceroy, that the outgoing viceroy, Lord Linlithgow, confessed to him that 'in July he expected that deaths in Bengal might be up to 1,000,000 or 1½ million, and that we looked like getting off better than he had thought possible' (Wavell, 1973, p. 34). Presumably the government had meanwhile persuaded themselves that the situation was *incomparably* better than had been 'thought possible'!

[10] Aykroyd (1974) is candid in acknowledging the arbitrariness of his estimate: 'at all events, the figure of 1.5 million deaths is in the history books, and whenever I come across it I remember the process by which it was reached' (p. 77).

[11] It is perhaps also worth remarking that, for India as a whole, the ratio of registered deaths to the estimated number of deaths obtained by using the 'reverse survival method' for 1941–50 by S. P. Jain (1954) is 0.73, while the same method had yielded a ratio of 0.74 for 1931–40. See Jain (1954), p. 44. The estimates for earlier decades are of Kingsley Davis: 0.74 for 1931–40, 0.72 for 1921–30, and 0.70 for 1911–20.

mortality. I shall use this ratio of correction uniformly, though it should be noted that this would tend to *underestimate* famine mortality, since registration was especially bad in 1943—the year of the famine and of peak death even in terms of registration data. There is, thus, a *downward* bias in our estimation of famine deaths.[12]

In Table D1 numbers of the registered deaths for each year from 1941 to 1950 are given for West Bengal. The time pattern is one of *monotonic* decline except for the one severe jump upwards in 1943. In fact, despite falling each year after 1943, annual mortality did not return to the 1942 level even by the end of the decade. Since the number of deaths had tended to fall each year, the Famine Inquiry Commission's procedure of taking the average mortality in the previous *quinquennium* as the 'normal' mortality may understate excess mortality for the famine years. Instead, I have made two sets of estimates: estimate A, with the 'normal' being taken to be the average of the deaths in 1941 and 1942, and estimate B, with the 1942 death rate being taken as the 'normal'. Estimate B yields, naturally, a higher series of 'excess deaths', which are presented for 1943–50 in Table D1 and Figure D1. However, even estimate B can be thought to be understating the magnitude of excess mortality, since the relevant comparison is not with the level in the *pre-famine* year, but with the level to which the expected death rates *would*

TABLE D1
Recorded Deaths in West Bengal, 1941–50

		Excess deaths	
	Deaths	A	B
1941	384,220		
1942	347,886		
1941–2 Average	*366,053*		
1943	624,266	258,213	276,380
1944	577,375	211,322	229,489
1945	448,600	82,547	100,714
1946	414,687	48,634	66,801
1947	387,165	21,112	39,279
1948	385,278	19,225	37,392
1949	372,559	6,506	24,673
1950	356,843	−9,210	8,957

Source: Based on death statistics from *Census of India 1951* vol. VI, part 1B, Table 6.

[12] A substantial *net* migration from East to West Bengal during the late 1940s would also tend to underestimate the actual death rate during 1941–50, and thus underestimate the under-registration of deaths, thereby underestimating famine mortality.

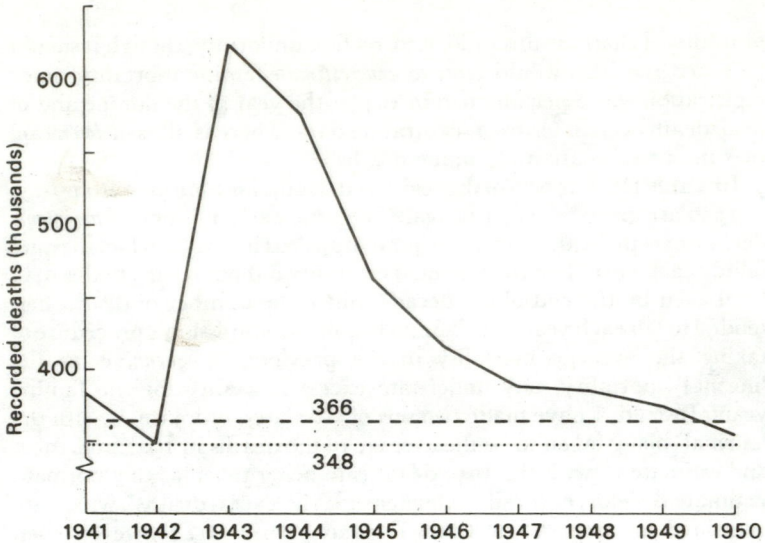

FIG. D1   Recorded Deaths during 1941–50 in West Bengal

have fallen in the post-famine years *but for* the intervention of the famine.[13]

The numbers of excess deaths under assumptions A and B respectively for each year are given in Table D1. The 'excess' becomes negative for A from 1950 onwards and for B—it can be checked from later data—from 1951 onwards; this is so with a stationary *total* death norm, which—as discussed above—*understates* the levels of excess mortality.

Adding up until the excess mortality is eliminated yields a total of excess mortality owing to the famine of 648,000 for Assumption A and 784,000 for assumption B. If the turmoil of the partition of Bengal in 1947 and the displacement resulting from it make us reluctant to read the impact of the famine in the excess mortality figures beyond 1946, we

[13] Note that the *absolute* number of deaths went on falling through the decades, despite the increase in the size of the population, which failed to increase only during the immediate famine years; see *Census of India 1951*, vol. VI, part IB, pp. 2–4.

can be conservative and count the excess figures only during 1943–6.[14] This yields a total registration excess mortality of 601,000 under assumption A and 673,000 under B.

If Jain's (1954) estimate of under-registration in West Bengal during 1941–50 is applied uniformly, then these excess registration figures would have to be raised by 51 per cent to arrive at the actual excess mortality.[15] This yields 908 thousand and 1.016 million respectively under A and B.

All of this relates to West Bengal only. The famine was at least as serious in East Bengal—later East Pakistan, now Bangladesh.[16] Unfortunately, there is no 'reverse survival' estimate of under-registration for East Bengal comparable with Jain's calculation for the West of Bengal. I have not, therefore, tried to make an independent estimate of famine mortality in East Bengal. However, the Census of Pakistan 1951 reports an estimate, viz. a figure of 1.714 million, 'worked out from official statements, which as explained are largely estimates in the absence of reliable reports'.[17] Added to my estimates for West Bengal, this yields 2.622 million and 2.730 million respectively, under assumptions A and B. Note that the East Bengal figures given in the Pakistan Census take account of deaths only up to 1944 and not up to 1946, as in our West Bengal estimates. Taking note of the facts that (1) the population of what became West Bengal was almost exactly a third of the population of undivided Bengal in 1941; (2) the registered number of deaths in West Bengal tended to be around a third of the total number of deaths in Bengal before 1943; and (3) in the famine year the number of registered deaths in West Bengal was again almost exactly a third of that in Bengal as a whole,[18] if we feel bold enough to treat

[14] Note, however, that the strictly monotonic decline of the number of deaths continued right through 1947 (see Table D1). The *death rate per thousand* also underwent a strictly monotonic decline, since a declining number of deaths with an increasing population size implies a strictly monotonic fall of the death rate. Excess mortality figures beyond 1946 have, however, been ignored to avoid overestimating famine mortality, by biassing the procedures in the opposite direction.

[15] This may be compared with the Famine Inquiry Commission's correction of recorded excess mortality in 1943 of 688,846 to one million, which amounts to a correction factor of 45 per cent. (For some inexplicable reason the Commission notes the correction ratio to be 'some 40 per cent'—p. 109.) For 1944, however no correction was made by the Commission. A 'pilot survey' conducted by government of Bengal in 1948 found the correction factor to be 46.4 per cent (see Chaudhuri, 1952, p. 9).

[16] See Famine Inquiry Commission (1945a, pp. 114–15).

[17] *Census of Pakistan 1951*, Chapter III, p. 30. The arbitrary nature of this estimate is emphasized, and reference is also made to the fact that, 'according to popular belief, however, the deaths from famine in East Bengal were between two and two and a half million'.

[18] The number of registered deaths in 1943 was 624,266 for West Bengal and 1,873,749 for Bengal as a whole (see Famine Inquiry Commission, 1945a, p. 108, and *Census of India, 1951*, vol. VI, part IB, p. 21).

famine excess mortality in West Bengal to be a third of that in undivided Bengal, then the total Bengal famine mortality works out as 2.724 million and 3.048 million respectively under assumptions A and B.

These figures are put together in Table D2. Since the Famine Inquiry Commission and K. P. Chattopadhyaya both gave excess mortality figures separately for the famine year 1943, the results of our calculation with blow-up for Bengal are shown separately for 1943 also. It is interesting that Chattopadhyaya's over-all estimate comes fairly close to those presented here, but the coincidence is accidental, since his figure refers to mortality in 1943 and in the first half of 1944 only. In fact, for 1943 as such the estimates given here are quite close to those of the Famine Inquiry Commission. The bulk of the difference in our respective total estimates arise from (1) the longer time coverage in my estimates (using, however, the same logic as employed by the Commission itself in attributing high post-famine mortality to the famine), and (2) continued correction for under-registration of deaths even beyond 1943 (using results of corrections through the 'reverse survival' method).

TABLE D2
Estimates of Bengal Famine Mortality

	Excess mortality in 1943 (millions)	Total excess mortality due to the famine (millions)
Famine Inquiry Commission	1.00	1.50
K. P. Chattopadhyaya	2.20	2.70
Assumption A + Pakistan Census		2.62
Assumption B + Pakistan Census		2.73
Assumption A blown up for all Bengal	1.17	2.72
Assumption B blown up for all Bengal	1.25	3.05

Since there were several downward biases—as explained—built into the estimates presented here, we may be inclined to pick a figure around 3 million as the death toll of the Bengal famine. (It has also the merit of being a 'round' number—that arbitrary preference shown by our ten-fingered species captivated by the decimal system.) But what emerges most powerfully from our analysis is not so much the largeness of the size of total mortality, but its time pattern—lasting for years after the famine. This was largely due to the epidemics associated with the famine, and to this issue I now turn.

D.3 HOW DID THEY DIE?

In December 1943, Bengal reaped a harvest larger than any in the past. Curiously enough, it was also the month in which the death rate in Bengal reached its peak in this century. The famine in the form of starvation had by then come largely to an end—starvation deaths seemed to have peaked around September and October that year. Cholera mortality reached its maximum in October and November. Malaria peaked in December, and continued in its elevated position through the next year and later. Smallpox reached its height in March and April 1944, and a greater height still one year later. The starvation phase of the famine had given way to the epidemic phase.

Table D3 presents the yearly time series of registered deaths from some of the principal causes. The sharp jump upwards in 1943 of cholera, malaria, fever, dysentery, diarrhoea, etc., can be easily seen. For seasonal reasons the impact of smallpox was not felt until the following year since it hits primarily in early spring. Taking the average mortality in 1941 and 1942 as the 'normal' mortality for each disease respectively, 'excess mortality' from each disease has been calculated for the period 1943-6. The last row presents the inter-disease breakdown of excess mortality.

Before discussing the inter-disease pattern of excess mortality, it is worth commenting on the absence of starvation as a major reported cause of death during that great famine. One reason for this peculiarity is that starvation was not typically used as a separate category in reporting deaths. This was due partly to the habit of using traditional categories in reporting causes of death, but also to the fact that typical starvation deaths show other identifiable symptoms at the final stages, and these *proximate* 'causes' tend to fit well into the traditional categories. For example, it is common to die of starvation through diarrhoea (indeed, 'famine diarrhoea' is a well-known phenomenon) as well as dysentery—partly as a result of eating uneatable objects. Clearly, many of the deaths reported under 'dysentery, diarrhoea and enteric group of fevers' were, in fact, starvation deaths. The same holds for several other categories, including the general category of deaths owing to 'fever'.[19]

Excluding 'fever', which is a diverse basket of diseases varying from influenza and measles to cerebro-spinal fever and Kala-azar, the ranking of the main diseases in terms of their contributions to excess mortality were (in decreasing order): malaria, cholera, 'dysentery, diarrhoea and enteric group of fevers', and smallpox. The nature of these ailments as well as direct accounts suggest that the explosive

[19] Compare the problem of interpreting the large number of deaths from lethal scurvy during the Irish famine of 1845-6.

TABLE D3
Diseases and Deaths in West Bengal, 1941–6 Registrations

	Dysentery, diarrhoea, and enteric group of fevers	Cholera	Malaria	'Fever' (excl. malaria)	Smallpox	TB	Respiratory diseases other than TB	Total
1941	25,321	15,612	85,505	109,912	9,286	7,989	34,345	384,220
1942	23,234	11,427	85,078	97,764	1,023	6,734	32,847	347,886
1941–2 Average	*24,278*	*13,519*	*85,291*	*104,838*	*5,155*	*7,362*	*33,596*	*366,053*
1943	41,067	58,230	168,592	159,398	2,261	6,830	35,140	624,266
1944	36,040	20,128	166,897	176,824	19,198	7,318	37,052	577,375
1945	24,463	8,315	123,834	122,549	23,974	6,951	33,839	448,600
1946	25,651	9,774	102,339	121,391	4,971	7,227	31,926	414,687
Excess:								
1943–6	*30,109*	*42,371*	*220,498*	*164,810*	*29,784*	*−1,122*	*3,623*	*600,716*
Share of total excess (%)	5.0	7.1	36.7	27.4	5.0	−0.2	0.6	100.0

Source: Based on current registration data, reported in *Census of India 1951*, vol. VI, part 1B. Note that the 'enteric group of fevers' figure both under 'fever' and under 'dysentery, diarrhoea, and enteric group of fevers', but the overlap is quantitatively rather tiny.

outbursts of epidemics during and immediately following the famine were affected not merely by starvation and malnutrition, but also by other factors, e.g. the impact of the famine on sanitary arrangements, water supply, and other civic amenities, exposure to vectors through movements in search of food, as well as inability to receive medical attention owing to destitution and a breakdown of public health facilities.[20] In addition, infectious deseases can spread directly to people who may not have been affected otherwise by the famine. Epidemics do, of course, also have a rhythm of their own.[21] Once an epidemic occurs, its echo effects may last for quite a few years.

The diseases unleashed by the Bengal famine had the dual characteristics of being both (1) epidemic diseases associated with previous famines, and (2) endemic diseases in the region. Malaria had been associated with Indian famines at least from the nineteenth century,[22] and epidemics of cholera and smallpox had been observed in many previous famines, including the Bengal famine of 1770. Dysentery and diarrhoea are, of course, 'peculiarly famine diseases'—as the Famine Inquiry Commission described them. The same applies to the mixed bundle called 'fever' other then malaria. But all these diseases were also endemic in the region. Malaria and fevers, which are sometimes difficult to distinguish,[23] were the biggest killers in the pre-famine days, followed at quite some distance by 'dysentery, diarrhoea and enteric groups of fevers', cholera, and smallpox in that order. In the sharing of famine mortality, the relative positions are not very different, with malaria and fever being followed at a substantial distance by cholera, 'dysentery, etc.,' and smallpox, in that order.

Perhaps the most interesting case is that of the dog that did not bark, viz. respiratory diseases including TB. These diseases killed many more in the pre-famine period than any of the other group of diseases, with the exception of malaria and other fevers. But, remarkably, mortality from TB and from other respiratory diseases seem to have been hardly influenced by the Bengal famine (see Table D3). This experience is *not* unusual in the context of other Indian famines, in which TB and other respiratory diseases have not typically played a

[20] See Famine Inquiry Commission (1945a) on these disruptive consequences of the famine and on the large-scale trekking of destitutes in search of food. See also Ghosh (1944) and Das (1949).

[21] See Bailey (1957). In fact, because of the spread effects of epidemics, the Bengal famine may also have contributed to deaths outside Bengal, especially in Orissa and Bihar. See Famine Inquiry Commission (1945a), pp. 104–5. See also *Census of India 1951*, vol. XI, part I, p. 41.

[22] See the Reports of the Indian Famine Commissions of 1898 and 1901. Also the findings of S. R. Christophers regarding the nineteenth-century famines, quoted in Famine Inquiry Commission (1945a), p. 122.

[23] On this see the Report of Indian Famine Commission of 1898.

prominent part, but there is something of a puzzle in this in a more general context. The linkage of TB and other respiratory diseases with malnutrition is well established (see Keys, 1950), and seems to be conceded even by those who dispute the influence of starvation as such on other diseases spread through infectious contagion (see, for example, Chambers, 1972, pp. 82–6).

Tuberculosis is, of course, slow to develop and is influenced more by chronic undernourishment than by a short period of severe starvation; this might suggest that the spread of tuberculosis would not be much enhanced by a famine. But famine-induced movements and sanitary breakdowns may help in the expansion of the infection. More importantly, since tuberculosis and other respiratory diseases were already widespread in Bengal, it would be natural to expect that starvation during the famine would convert morbidity into mortality on a substantial scale. That this was not reported as having happened during and immediately after the Bengal famine thus does leave one with an interesting and important problem. Attributing this counter-intuitive phenomenon comfortably to an assumed error of reporting is tempting, but this explanation would be convincing only with empirical evidence of the existence of such a bias in a large enough scale. Also, since TB and other respiratory diseases typically had rather undistinguished records in previous Indian famines *as well*, an *ad hoc* explanation for the Bengal famine of 1943 as such is not what is needed.

The Bengal famine killed mostly by magnifying the forces of death normally present in the pre-famine period—a magnifying role that other famines had played in the past. The universality of this endemic-to-epidemic relationship is, however, seriously affected by the apparent inertness of TB and other respiratory disease. This inertness also seems to contrast quite sharply with the view taken of these diseases in the international literature on famine-induced epidemics (see for example Keys, 1950, Foege, 1971, Chambers, 1972).

D.4 WHAT REGIONAL DISTRIBUTION?

Excess mortality can be estimated separately for each district in West Bengal on the basis of the registration data presented in the *Census of India 1951* (vol. VI, part IB). These are presented in Table D4, with the 'normal' level of mortality being taken to be the average of the figures for 1941 and 1942. The percentage excesses for the famine year 1943 and for the period 1943–6 are presented separately, and the ranks in the two orderings of excesses are also given. The inter-district variations are quite remarkable, even though for every district the excess is positive both for 1943 and for the period 1943–6.

There are some differences between the two rankings. Malda, which ends up as the most affected district over-all, was one of the less affected

Excess Mortality in West Bengal: Breakdown by District

District	Average mortality, 1941-2 ('normal')	Excess mortality, 1943	Excess mortality, 1943-6	Percentage excess, 1943	Percentage excess, 1943-6 (annual)	Excess rank, 1943	Excess rank 1943-6	Intensity class according to Bengal Govt Revenue Dept	Intensity class according to Bengal Govt Dept of Industries
Malda	8,237	+3,080	+45,512	+37.4	+129.0	9	1	Slight	Slight
Howrah	18,842	+15,832	+52,444	+84.0	+69.6	3	2	Moderate	Slight
Murshidabad	32,382	+32,691	+87,869	+101.0	+67.8	2	3	Slight	Slight
Birbhum	23,007	+17,482	+51,369	+76.0	+55.8	5	4	Slight	Slight
Calcutta	30,385	+21,883	+61,588	+72.0	+50.7	6	5		
Midnapur	52,489	+72,250	+104,747	+137.6	+49.9	1	6	Severe	Severe
West Dinajpur	10,858	+1,600	+20,281	+14.7	+46.7	13	7	Slight	Slight
Nadia	21,819	+17,021	+31,914	+78.0	+36.6	4	8	Slight	Slight
24-Parganas	54,062	+37,151	+65,501	+68.7	+30.3	7	9	Severe	Severe
Jalpaiguri	20,171	+6,633	+21,062	+32.9	+26.1	11	10	Slight	Moderate
Hoogly	21,688	+5,808	+18,299	+26.8	+21.1	12	11	Moderate	Slight
Burdwan	35,401	+12,057	+26,382	+34.1	+18.6	10	12	Moderate	Slight
Bankura	26,212	+13,958	+15,953	+53.5	+15.2	8	13	Moderate	Slight
Darjeeling	10,495	+763	+1,779	+7.3	+4.2	14	14	Slight	Moderate

Source: Based on *Census of India* 1951, vol, VI, part IB.

districts in the famine year itself. Similarly, Midnapur, which was most affected in the famine year, ends up in a somewhat moderate position for the whole period. The pattern of the epidemics that followed the famine re-ordered the districts in terms of mortality. However, the two rankings are not unrelated, and the value of Spearman's rank correlation coefficient is 0.60, which offers no problem in rejecting the null hypothesis that the two rankings are independent.

What is perhaps of greater interest is the fact that the Bengal government's diagnoses of the relative severity of the famines in the different districts differed quite substantially from the excess mortality rankings for 1943–6 as well as for 1943 itself. A five-category classification of the subdivisions was issued by the Revenue Department in 1944, and a four-category classification by the Department of Industries in the same year.[24] Putting together the classification of the subdivisions within each district, I have presented a broad three-class partitioning in Table D4 reflecting the two official views of 'degree of incidence of famines'. Both put Malda—ultimately the most affected district—in the lowest category of incidence. The two did the same to Murshidabad and Birbhum, but in fact both the districts had a high incidence of excess mortality in 1943 as well as in the period 1943–6. On the other hand, 24-Parganas, which neighbours Calcutta, and from where many destitutes trekked into Calcutta at the height of the famine,[25] was put in the highest category of incidence in both the official lists, despite being only moderately placed in the excess mortality rankings for the famine year as well as the post-famine period.[26] Since relief operations were strongly influenced by these diagnoses, the discrepancies are of a certain amount of practical interest.

Finally, a remark on the excess mortality in Calcutta is worth making. Most people who died in Calcutta from starvation and from related diseases in the famine year were destitutes who had moved into Calcutta in search of food; the regular residents of Calcutta were protected by various public and semi-public schemes of food distri-

---

[24] Quoted in Mahalanobis, Mukherjea and Ghosh (1946), pp. 11–14.

[25] A sample survey of the destitutes in Calcutta conducted in September 1943 revealed that nearly 82 per cent of the destitutes surveyed came from this one district (see Das, 1949, p. 58).

[26] Deaths occurring in Calcutta of people normally residing in 24-Parganas should, in fact, be attributed to the 24-Parganas itself. This correction would tend to raise somewhat the excess mortality rates of the 24-Parganas. The required corrections are difficult to estimate because of lack of precise data on 'normal residence' of those dying in Calcutta during the famine and post-famine years. But rough breakdowns would seem to indicate that the relative position of the 24-Parganas would not change drastically, especially for the period 1943–6. The contrast between the reality and the official perception will still hold; and the importance of being close to Calcutta in having one's distress officially observed will not disappear.

bution (see Famine Inquiry Commission, 1945a). Based on this observation, it has been frequently stated that the residents of Calcutta escaped the famine.[27] This is largely true as far as starvation is concerned, but in the epidemics that were induced by the famine, Calcutta had its own share of casualties, reflected by the excess mortality figures after 1943, i.e. after virtually all the famine destitutes from elsewhere had left or been repatriated.

D.5 WHICH OCCUPATION CATEGORY?

The death registration figures do not specify occupational backgrounds. We can, however, surmise something about probable death rates by examining the rates of destitution of different income groups. These were computed on the basis of a sample survey conducted by Mahalanobis, Mukherjea and Ghosh (1946), already used in Chapter 6 above, and are presented in Table D5 (taken from Table 6.7 above). In the second column the destitution rates are added up with the transition to the occupation of 'paddy husking' – a typical destitution syndrome for rural women with children. On this basis it would appear that the

TABLE D5

Destitution Rates of Different Occupation Categories in Bengal:
January 1943–May 1944

	proportion of destitution	*Proportion of destitution and transition to paddy husking*
Peasant cultivation and share-cropping	1.3	1.5
Part-time agricultural labour	1.4	2.0
Agricultural labour	4.6	6.1
Non-cultivating owners	1.6	2.4
Fishing	9.6	10.5
Craft	3.8	4.3
Husking paddy	4.7	–
Transport	6.0	6.9
Trade	2.2	2.6
Profession and services	2.1	2.6
Non-agricultural labour	3.7	4.5
Other productive occupations	4.6	4.6

Source: See Table 6.7 above.

[27] E.g., 'In the end not a single man died of starvation from the population of Greater Calcutta, while millions in rural areas starved and suffered' (Sir Manilal Nanavati's note, Famine Inquiry Commission, 1945a, p. 102).

most affected groups were fishermen, transport workers, and agricultural labourers. In terms of absolute numbers, agricultural labourers as an occupation group were dominant.

One of the few direct surveys of the occupational basis of famine mortality was presented by Mukerji (1965) for five villages in the Faridpur district in East Bengal; the survey was conducted in 1944. The results are presented in Table D6. In these villages the highest mortality category is agricultural labour. The importance of agricultural labour among the famine victims is brought out also by the survey of destitutes in Calcutta conducted in 1943 by T. Das (1949).

Our information on this crucial aspect of famine mortality is limited and somewhat haphazard. And we have virtually no information at all on the occupational composition of post-famine mortality in the epidemics.

TABLE D6
Destitution in Five Surveyed Villages in Faridpur

Occupation on 1/1/43	Proportion of destitution (%)	Proportion being 'wiped off' during 1943 (%)
Peasant cultivation and share-cropping	18.4	6.4
Agricultural labour	52.4	40.3
Artisan	35.0	10.0
Petty trader	31.8	14.0
Crop-sharing landlord	6.3	0.0
Priest and petty employee	27.3	27.3
Office employee	10.0	0.0
Landlord	0.0	0.0
'Unproductive'	44.4	16.7
Total	28.5	15.2

Source: See Table 6.8 above.

D.6 FAMINE MORTALITY AS MAGNIFIED NORMAL MORTALITY

Peculiarities in the pattern of famine mortality compared with normal mortality have been a subject of discussion for a long time. A supposedly lower impact of famines on women is one of the 'regularities' that has received some attention in India. Sir Charles Elliot, Famine Commissioner of Mysore in 1876 and Census Commissioner of India for the 1881 Census, summarized the general belief regarding nineteenth-century Indian famines: 'all the authorities seem agreed that women succumb to famine less easily than men'.[28]

Was this the case with the Bengal famine? Das (1949) found, in his survey of destitutes in Calcutta in September 1943, that 'for every dead woman there were nearly two dead men' (p. 93). In its Report the Famine Inquiry Commission referred to Das's findings—then available in unpublished form—and also noted that there was a higher proportionate increase in male deaths compared with female deaths in 1943.[29] The Commission referred to the contrary result from Mahalanobis's survey of 2,622 families which found a higher percentage of mortality among women, but went on to comment on the 'considerable irregularity' in the various subdivisions covered in the survey.

The sex breakdown of pre-famine 'normal' mortality given by the average of 1941 and 1942 as well as that of the excess mortality in 1943 and in the period 1943–6 are all presented in Table D7, based on registration data. The ratios seem remarkably stable through the famine. While the proportion of men in excess mortality in 1943 is a bit higher than in the pre-famine average, the difference is small, and over the larger period of famine mortality the proportionate breakdown of the excess is just the same as for the pre-famine average.[30]

There may, of course, be biases in the registration system, but this should apply to registrations both before and during the famine. In fact, it is more likely that there was a serious bias in Das's sample-survey of destitutes in Calcutta which contained a large proportion of families that had 'lost their male earning members', and this bias would be reflected in the results of the survey, which asked respondents to recall which members of the family had died.[31] To what extent this type of observation bias was present also in the accounts of the nineteenth-century famines, I do not know, but certainly as far as the 1943 famine is concerned there is little need for going into the rather contrived explanations[32] that have been proposed to explain the supposed contrast of sex ratios.

[28] For this and other observations, see *Census of India 1911*, vol. I, part I, appendix to Chapter VI; and also Das (1949), pp. 93–6.

[29] Famine Inquiry Commission (1945a, pp. 110–11). The Department of Anthropology had noticed the same, and referred to it as 'a very sinister and significant feature' of the Bengal famine (see Ghosh, 1944, Appendix G, p. 183).

[30] The male population exceeded the female population in Bengal, and the recorded death rate per unit of population was higher for women in every year during the decade 1941–50 through the famine (see *Census of India 1951*, vol. VI, part IB, Tables 7 and 8, pp. 29–30).

[31] Das (1949), p. 93.

[32] My favourites are some of those proposed by Mr. W. C. Bennet, C. S.: 'Women find employment as maid-servants in the houses of rich men when men have no work to look

TABLE D7

Excess Mortality of Men, Women, Children, and the Old: West Bengal

	Average mortality, 1941–2		Excess mortality, 1943		Excess mortality, 1943–6	
	Numbers	Percentages of total	Numbers	Percentages of total	Numbers	Percentages of total
Men	191,943	52	140,439	54	315,282	52
Women	174,310	48	117,774	46	285,434	48
Children below 5	106,080	29	74,838	29	174,058	29
Old people above 60	57,044	16	40,212	16	93,600	16

Source: Based on current registration data, reported in *Census of India 1951*, vol. VI, part IB. Note that 'men' and 'women' include figures for all ages, and 'children below 5' and 'old people above 60' include those for both sexes.

Das (1949) also noted a much higher proportion of deaths among children, and opined that 'this will certainly cripple the next generation of the Bengalees'.[33] The Anthropology Department of Calcutta University had reported a similar bias in its press statement in 1944.[34]

Is this borne out by the registration data? The answer seems to be no. The data are given in Table D7. The proportion of children below five in average mortality in the immediate pre-famine period was 29 per cent, and that is also the percentage of children in excess mortality in the famine year (1943) as well as in the four-year period of famine mortality (1943–6).[35] The extraordinarily high level of mortality of children is, of course, an excruciating problem, but that is a characteristic not only of famine mortality but also of normal mortality in the absence of famine in this part of the world.

Table D7 also presents the mortality figures for the old people, those above sixty. Once again the proportions of famine mortality mirror the pattern of normal mortality.

I end this section with a final observation dealing with the monthly pattern of death at the height of the famine. Table D8 presents the monthly death registrations during June–July of 1943–4, when mortality was at its highest, and also the average monthly registrations in the preceding quinquennium.[36] The similarity between the two monthly patterns is striking.[37] This is brought out clearly by figure D2 as well. (For the benefit of the blind, I note that regressing monthly mortality y in the famine period on normal pre-famine monthly mortality x, by least-squares, yields a very high value of r^2. The estimated regression function, in fact, is $y = 3,175x - 122,535$, with r^2 having the convincing value of .95.) The famine seems to have worked by magnifying the forces of mortality each month, heightening the peak mortality relatively more.

---

for'; 'women possess ornaments of value which they may dispose for their own benefit whenever necessary'; 'the woman in a Hindu family always keeps the household stores, and has no scruple in availing herself of the advantage it gives her' (see *Census of India 1911*, vol. I, part I, appendix to Chapter VI, pp. 220–2).

[33] Das (1949), pp. 91–2.

[34] See Appendix G in Ghosh (1944).

[35] The Famine Inquiry Commission (1945a) noted a decrease in the number of deaths for infants under one month, but attributed this to a decrease in the number of births as well as to a reporting bias (p. 109). Adjustments for this group would not affect the total proportions of children in excess mortality by very much.

[36] The data come from Famine Inquiry Commission (1945a), p. 213.

[37] Cf. Jutikkala and Kauppinen's (1971) observation regarding 'catastrophic' and 'normal' mortality in pre-industrial Finland (1749–1850): 'The figures suggest that the seasonal distribution of deaths did not differ significantly between "catastrophic" and "normal" years' (p. 284).

TABLE D8
Mortality by Months during July 1943–June 1944 compared with Previous Quinquennial Average

	Deaths during 1943–4	Quinquennial average deaths: 1938–42
July	126,437	78,816
August	151,126	83,968
September	171,755	85,253
October	236,754	105,529
November	289,723	128,454
December	328,708	142,033
January	228,128	112,263
February	170,955	89,594
March	162,933	98,428
April	167,368	98,615
May	145,812	85,176
June	106,032	74,774

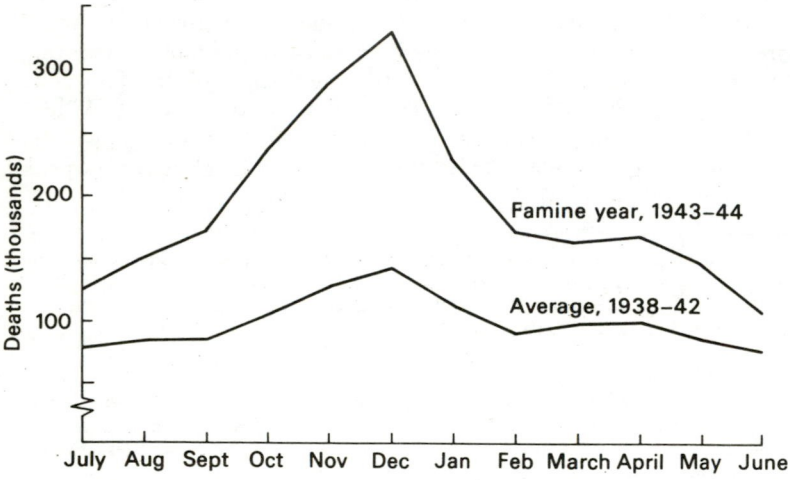

Fig. D2 Monthly Pattern of Recorded Mortality before and during the Famine

D.7 CONCLUDING REMARKS

While it is not possible to say at all precisely how many people were killed by the Bengal famine of 1943, there is evidence that an estimate of around 3 million would be closer to the mark than the figure of 1.5 million arrived at by the official Famine Inquiry Commission (and widely quoted in later works). The difference is largely due to:

1) continued high 'excess mortality' for several years after the famine, caused by famine-induced epidemics the impact of which the Commission considered only for 1943 and the first half of 1944;

(2) underestimation by the Commission of the actual extent of under-registration of deaths in official records.

Both these contrasts largely reflect differences between the data available to the Commission and those available now. Apropos(1), the Commission, working in late 1944 and early 1945, could hardly have gone beyond the first half of 1944 in its mortality coverage. Apropos (2), the Commission chose to use an arbitrary correction for under-registration, not having any way of estimating it directly or indirectly. In contrast, we can use the results of 'reverse survival' exercises based on Census data of 1951 *vis-à-vis* those of 1941 and the results of a direct sample survey held in 1948. There is thus no quarrel, only a very substantial difference in the respective estimates based on *current* information (see Section D.2).

While the gigantic size of excess mortality attributable to the famine is of a certain amount of interest, the *time pattern* of mortality is of possibly greater relevance. Very substantially more than half the deaths attributable to the famine of 1943 took place *after* 1943. The size of mortality did not return to the pre-famine situation for many years after the famine, and the epidemics of malaria and other fevers, cholera, smallpox, dysentery, and diarrhoea that sprung up during and immediately after the famine went on raging for a long time (see Tables D1 and D3 and Figure D1). This has obvious implications for health policy.

Regarding the regional pattern of famine mortality, the relative importance of different districts changed quite a bit between the starvation phase and the later epidemic phase (see Table D4). What is perhaps of greater interest is that the official diagnoses of the relative severity of the famine in the different districts differed substantially from the pattern emerging from the 'excess mortality' calculations, both for the starvation phase and for the later epidemic phase (see Section D.4). Since government relief and rehabilitation work was based on these official diagnoses, the contrasts were of practical import.

Information on the occupational pattern of mortality is very limited, but some general impressions emerge from a broadly based 1944 survey covering the occupational pattern of destitution, and two local 1943 surveys directly going into deaths related to occupations (see Section D5). In absolute terms, the most severe incidence of famine mortality during the famine itself fell almost certainly on the class of agricultural labourers. Their *relative incidence* was high too, but that applies also to other groups like fisherman, transport workers and non-agricultural labourers in rural areas. In Chapter 6 the nature and causation of the observed occupational pattern of destitution were analysed, relating them to the positions of the different groups in the structure of production and exchange in the economy.

Regarding the diseases that took most of the toll, they had the dual characteristics of being both (1) endemic diseases in the region, and (2) epidemic diseases in past famines (see Section D.3). Gigantic as the famine was, it killed mostly by adding fuel to the fire of disease and mortality normally present in the region. This possibly explains why the seasonal pattern of famine deaths even during the actual famine and its immediate aftermath was essentially the normal seasonal pattern—just linearly displaced severely upwards (see Table D 8 and Figure D2). The sex and age patterns of famine mortality also seem to show remarkable similarity with the normal pattern of mortality in pre-famine Bengal (see Table D7).

Bibliography

AALL, C. and HELSING, E. (1976), 'The Sahelian Drought', *Journal of Tropical Pediatrics and Environmental Child Health*, 22.

ABDEL-FADIL, M. (1975), *Development, Income Distribution and Social Change in Rural Eygpt (1952–1970)*, Cambridge: University Press.

ABDULLAH, A. A. (1976a), 'Land Reform and Agrarian Change in Bangladesh', *Bangladesh Development Studies*, 4.

ABDULLAH, A. A. (1976b), 'Agrarian Development and IRDP in Bangladesh', *Bangladesh Development Studies*, 4.

ABEL-SMITH, B. and TOWNSEND, P. (1965), *The Poor and the Poorest*, London: Bell.

ABUL FAZL (1592), *Ain-i-Akbari*, Agra. Translated by Blachmann and Jarrett, *Ain-i-Akbari*, 2nd edn. Calcutta, 1949.

ADELMAN, I. and MORRIS, C. T. (1971), 'The Anatomy of the Pattern of Income Distribution in Developing Countries', *American Economic Review*, 61.

ADELMAN, I. and MORRIS, C. T. (1973), *Economic Growth and Social Equity in Developing Countries*, Stanford: University Press.

ADELMAN, I. and ROBINSON, S. (1978), *Income Distribution Policy in Developing Countries: A Case Study of Korea*, Oxford: University Press.

ADNAN, S., KAMAL, A., KHAN, A. M. and MUQTADA, M. (1977), 'Differentiation and Class Structure in Char Shamraj', Working Paper no. 8, Village Study Group, Dacca University.

ADNAN, S. and RAHMAN, H. Z. (1978), 'Peasant Classes and Land Mobility: Structural Reproduction and Change in Rural Bangladesh', Working Paper no. 9, Village Study Group, Dacca University.

ADY, P. (1944), 'Inflation in India', *Bulletin of the Oxford Institute of Statistics*, 6.

Agro-Economic Research Centre for East India (1960), *Consumer Price Index and Wages for Agricultural Labourer in the Western Region of West Bengal*, Santiniketan: Visva-Bharati.

AHLUWALIA, M. (1976), 'Inequality, Poverty and Development', *Journal of Development Economics*, 3.

AHLUWALIA, M. (1978), 'Rural Poverty and Agricultural Performance in India', *Journal of Development Studies*, 14.

AHLUWALIA, M. (1979), 'Growth and Poverty in Developing Countries', World Bank Staff Working Paper no. 309.

AHMED, IFTIKHAR (1975a), 'The Green Revolution, Mechanisation and Employment', ILO Working Paper WEP 2–22/WP 12.

AHMED, IFTIKHAR (1975b), 'The Green Revolution in Bangladesh: Adoption, Diffusion and Distribution Questions', ILO Working Paper WEP 2–22/WP 16.

AHMED, IQBAL (1978), 'Unemployment and Underemployment in Bangladesh Agriculture', *World Development*, 6.

AHMED, RAISUDDIN (1979), *Foodgrain Supply, Distribution and Consumption Policies within a Dual Price Mechanism: A Case Study of Bangladesh*, Research Report no. 8, Washington DC: International Food Policy Research Institute.

ALAMGIR, M. (1976), 'Poverty, Inequality and Development Strategy in the Third World', mimeographed, Bangladesh Institute of Development Studies.

ALAMGIR, M. (1978a), *Bangladesh: A Case of Below Poverty Level Equilibrium Trap*, Dacca: Bangladesh Institute of Development Studies.

ALAMGIR, M. (1978b), 'Towards a Theory of Famine', Seminar Paper no. 103, Institute for International Economic Studies, University of Stockholm.

ALAMGIR, M. (1980), *Famine in South Asia—Political Economy of Mass Starvation in Bangladesh*, manuscript, Bangladesh Institute of Development Studies. Cambridge, Mass., Oelgeschlager, Gunn and Hain.

ALAMGIR, M., *et al.* (1977), *Famine 1974: Political Economy of Mass Starvation in Bangladesh, A Statistical Annex*. Dacca: Bangladesh Institute of Development Studies.

ALAVI, HAMZA (1973), 'Peasant Classes and Primordial Loyalties', *Journal of Development Studies*, 1.

AMBIRAJAN, S. (1978), *Classical Political Economy and British Policy in India*, Cambridge: University Press.

AMIN, SAMIR (1974), *Neo Colonialism in West Africa*, New York: Monthly Review Press.

AMIN, SAMIR (ed.) (1975), *L'Agriculture africaine et le capitalisme*, Paris: Anthropos-Idep.

AMIN, SAMIR (1977), *Unequal Development*, New York: Monthly Review Press.

AMIN, SAMIR and VERGOPOULOS, K. (1974), *La Question paysanne et le capitalisme*, Paris: Anthropos-Idep.

ANAND, S. (1977), 'Aspects of Poverty in Malaysia', *Review of Income and Wealth*, 23.

ANAND, S. (1978), *Inequality and Poverty in Malaysia: Measurement and Decomposition*, St Catherine's College, Oxford; to be published.

ARROW, K. and HAHN, F. (1971), *General Competitive Analysis*, Edinburgh: Oliver and Boyd.

ATKINSON, A. B. (1969), *Poverty in Britain and the Reform of Social Security*, Cambridge: University Press.

ATKINSON, A. B. (1970), 'On the Measurement of Inequality', *Journal of Economic Theory*, 2.

ATKINSON, A. B. (1975), *The Economics of Inequality*, Oxford: Clarendon Press.

AYKROYD, W. R. (1974), *The Conquest of Famine*, London: Chatto and Windus.

AZIZ, SARTAJ (ed.) (1975), *Hunger, Politics and Markets: The Real Issues in the Food Crisis*, New York: University Press.

AZIZ, SARTAJ (1977), 'The World Food Situation and Collective Self-Reliance', *World Development*, 5.

AZIZ, SARTAJ (1978), *Rural Development: Learning from China*, London: Macmillan.

BAIER, S. (1974), 'African Merchants in the Colonial Period: A History of Commerce in Damagaram (Central Niger) 1880– 968', PhD dissertation, University of Wisconsin.

BAILEY, N. T. J. (1957), *The Mathematical Theory of Epidemics*, New York.

BAISHYA, P. (1975), 'Assam: Man-Made Famine', *Economic and Political Weekly*, 10, 24 May.

BALL, N. (1976), 'Understanding the Causes of African Famine', *Journal of Modern African Studies*. 14.

BALOGH, T. (1966), *The Economics of Poverty*, London: Weidenfeld and Nicolson (2nd edn. 1974).

BALOGH, T. (1978), 'Failures in the Strategy against Poverty', *World Development*, 6.

BARAN, P. A. (1962), *Political Economy of Growth*, New York: Monthly Review Press.

BARAN, P. A., and SWEEZY, P. M. (1966), *Monopoly Capital*, New York: Monthly Review Press.

BARDHAN, P. K. (1970), 'On the Minimum Level of Living and the Rural Poor', *Indian Economic Review*, 6.

BARDHAN, P. K. (1971), 'On the Minimum Level of Living and the Rural Poor: A Further Note', *Indian Economic Review*, 6.

BARDHAN, P. K. (1973), 'On the Incidence of Poverty in Rural India', *Economic and Political Weekly*, February 1973; reprinted in Srinivasan and Bardhan (1974).

BARDHAN, P. K. (1974), 'The Pattern of Income Distribution in India: A Review', in Srinivasan and Bardhan (1974).

BARRACLOUGH, S. (1977), 'Agricultural Production Prospects in Latin America', *World Development*, 5.

220 Bibliography

BARTEN, A. P. (1964), 'Family Composition, Prices and Expenditure Pattern', in Hart and Mills (1964).

BATCHELDER, A. B. (1971), *The Economics of Poverty*, New York: John Wiley.

BAUER, P. T. (1971), *Dissent on Development*, London: Weidenfeld and Nicolson.

BECKERMAN, W. (1977), 'Some Reflections on "Redistribution with Growth",' *World Development*, 5.

BECKERMAN, W. (1978), 'Estimates of Poverty in Italy in 1975', ILO World Employment Programme Working Paper, WEP 2–23/WP 70.

BECKERMAN, W. (1979a), *The Impact of Income Maintenance Programmes on Poverty in Four Developed Countries*, Geneva: ILO.

BECKERMAN, W. (1979b), 'The Impact of Income Maintenance Payments on Poverty in Britain, 1975', *Economic Journal*, 89.

BELETE, S., GEBRE-MEDHIN, M., HAILEMARIAM, B., MAFFI, M., VAHLQUIST, B. and WOLDE-GABRIEL, Z. (1977), 'Study of Shelter Population in the Wollo Region', *Journal of Tropical Pediatrics and Environmental Child Health*, 23; republished from *Courrier*, (1976), 26.

BENGTSSON, B. (1979), *Rural Development Research: The Role of Power Relations*, SAREC Report, Stockholm: SIDA.

BENTZEL, R. (1970), 'The Social Significance of Income Distribution Statistics', *Review of Income and Wealth*, 16.

BERG, A. (1973), *The Nutrition Factor*, Washington, DC: Brookings Institution.

BERRY, L., CAMPBELL, D. J. and EMKER, I. (1977), 'Trends in Man–Land Interaction in West African Sahel'; in Dalby, Harrison Church and Bezzaz (1977).

BESHAH, T. W. and HARBISON, J. W. (1978), 'Afar Pastoralists in Transition and Ethiopian Revolution', *Journal of African Studies*, 5.

BHALLA, AJIT (1977), 'Technologies Appropriate for a Basic Needs Strategy', mimeographed, Geneva: ILO.

BHALLA, SHEILA (1979), 'Real Wage Rates of Agricultural Labourers in Punjab, 1961–77: A Preliminary Analysis', *Economic and Poltical Weekly*, 14, 30 June.

BHATIA, B. M. (1967), *Famines in India 1860–1965*, 2nd edn, Bombay: Asia.

BHATTACHARJEE, J. P. (1977), 'External Assistance and Agricultural Development in the Third World', *World Development*, 5.

BHATTACHARYA, N. and CHATTERJEE, G. S. (1974), 'Between-States Variation in Consumer Prices and Per Capita Household Consumption in Rural India', *Sankhyā*, 36.

BHATTACHARYA, N. and CHATTERJEE, G. S. (1977), 'A Further Note on

Between-States Variation in Level of Living in Rural India', Technical Report no. ERU/4/77, Indian Statistical Institute, Calcutta.

BHATTY, I. Z. (1974), 'Inequality and Poverty in Rural India', in Srinivasan and Bardhan (1974).

BLACKORBY, C. and DONALDSON, D. (1977), 'Utility vs. Equity: Some Plausible Quasi-orderings', *Journal of Public Economics*, 7.

BLACKORBY, C. and DONALDSON, D. (1978), 'Measures of Relative Equity and Their Meaning in Terms of Social Welfare', *Journal of Economic Theory*, 18.

BLACKORBY, C. and DONALDSON, D. (1980a), 'Ethical Indices for the Measurement of Poverty', *Econometrica*, 48.

BLACKORBY, C. and DONALDSON, D. (1980b), 'A Theoretical Treatment of Indices of Absolute Inequality', *International Economic Review*, 21.

BLIX, G., HOFVANDER, Y. and VAHLQUIST, B. (1971), *Famine: A Symposium Dealing with Nutrition and Relief Operations in Times of Disaster*, Uppsala: Swedish Nutrition Foundation.

BLYN, G. (1966), *Agricultural Trends in India 1891–1947: Output, Availability and Production*, Philadelphia: University of Pennsylvania Press.

BONDESTAM, L. (1974), 'People and Capitalism in the North-East Lowlands of Ethiopia', *Journal of Modern African Studies*, 12.

BOOTH, A., CHAUDHRI, D. P. and SUNDRUM, R. M. (1979), 'Income Distribution and the Structure of Production', mimeographed, Australian National University, Canberra.

BOOTH, C. (1889), *Life and Labour of the People in London*, London.

BORDA, J. C. (1781), 'Mémoire sur les élections au scrutin', in *Mémoires de l'Académie Royale des Sciences*.

BORGSTROM, G. (1969), *Too Many: An Ecological Overview of Earth's Limitations*, New York: Collier.

BORGSTROM, G. (1973), *World Food Resources*, New York: Intext Publishers.

BORKAR, V. V. and NADKARNI, M. V. (1975), *The Impact of Drought on Rural Life*, Bombay: Popular Prakashan.

BOURNE, G. H. (1943), *Starvation in Europe*, London: Allen and Unwin.

BOWLEY, A. L. (1923), *The Nature and Purpose of the Measurement of Social Phenomena*, London: P. S. King.

BRADLEY, P. N. (1977), 'Vegetation and Environmental Change in West African Sahel', in O'Keefe and Wisner (1977).

BRODER, I. E., and MÓRRIS, C. T. (1980), 'Socially Weighted Real Income Comparisons: An Application to India', mimeographed, American University.

BROWN, J. A. C. (1954), 'The Consumption of Food in Relation to Household Composition and Income', *Econometrica*, 22.

Brown, L. R. and Eckholm, E. P. (1974), *By Bread Alone*, Oxford: Pergamon Press.

Brown, W. R. and Anderson, N. D. (1976), *Historical Catastrophes: Famines*, Reading, Mass: Addison-Wesley.

Bruton, H. J. (1965), *Principles of Development Economics*, Englewood Cliffs, N J: Prentice-Hall.

Burger, G. C. E., et al. (1948), *Malnutrition and Starvation in Western Netherlands, September 1944–July 1945*, The Hague.

Buringh, P. (1977), 'Food Production Potential of the World', *World Development*, 5.

Butts, R. E., and Hintikka, J. (eds) (1977), *Foundational Problems in the Special Sciences*, Dordrecht: Reidel.

Caldwell, J. C. (1975), *The Sahelian Drought and its Demographic Implications*, Washington, DC.

Caldwell, J. C. (1977), 'Demographic Aspects of Drought: An Examination of the African Drought of 1970–74', in Dalby, Harrison Church and Bezzaz (1977).

Cannon, T. G. (1978), 'The Role of Environmental Influence and "Natural" Disasters', mimeographed, Thames Polytechnic, London.

Cassen, R. H. (1978), *India: Population, Economy, Society*, London: Macmillan.

Centre for Development Studies, Trivandrum (1975), *Poverty, Unemployment and Development Policy: A Case Study of Selected Issues with Reference to Kerala*, New York: United Nations.

Center for Disease Control (1973), *Nutritional Surveillance in Drought Affected Areas of West Africa (Mali, Mauritania, Niger, Upper Volta)*, Austin, Texas: US Public Health Service.

Chakravarty, Satya (1980a), 'New Indices for the Measurement of Poverty', mimeographed, Indian Statistical Institute, Calcutta.

Chakravarty, Satya (1980b), 'Some Further Results on the Measurement of Poverty', mimeographed, Indian Statistical Institute, Calcutta.

Chakravarty, S. and Pal, M. (1978), 'Some Results on Measurement of Inequality', Technical Report no. ERU/3/78, Indian Statistical Institute, Calcutta.

Chakravarty, Sukhomoy and Rosenstein-Rodan, P. N. (1965), *The Linking of Food Aid with Other Aid*, Rome: FAO.

Chambers, J. D. (1972), *Population, Economy and Society in Pre-industrial England*, London: Oxford University Press.

Chatterjee, G.S. and Bhattacharya, N. (1974), 'On Disparities in Per Capita Household Consumption in India', *Sankhya: The Indian*

Journal of Statistics, 36, Series C; reprinted in Srinivasan and Bardhan (1974).

CHATTOPADHYAYA, K. P. and MUKHERJEA, R. (1946), 'A Plan for Rehabilitation', in Mahalanabis *et al.* (1946).

CHAUDHURI, D.G. (1952), *Vital Statistics Special Report on Pilot Survey: Incompleteness of the Birth and Death Registration in Urban and Rural Areas in the Province of West Bengal during 1948 with Recommendations for its Improvement*, Calcutta: Government of West Bengal.

CHAUDHURI, PRAMIT (1978), *The Indian Economy: Poverty and Development*, London: Crosby Lockwood Staples.

CHENERY, H., AHLUWALIA, M. S., BELL, C. L. G., DULOY, J. H. and JOLLY, R. (1974). *Redistribution with Growth*, London: Oxford University Press.

CHICHILNISKY, GRACIELA (1979), 'Basic Needs and Global Models: Resources, Trade and Distribution', mimeographed, Essex University.

CLARK, S., HEMMING, R. and ULPH, D. (1979), 'On Indices for the Measurement of Poverty', mimeographed, Institute for Fiscal Studies, London.

CLARKE, T. (1978). *The Last Caravan*, New York: G. P. Tutnam's Sons.

CLAY, E. J. (1976), 'Institutional Change and Agricultural Wages in Bangladesh', *Bangladesh Development Studies*, 4.

CLIFFE, L. (1974), 'Feudalism, Capitalism and Famine in Ethiopia', *Review of African Political Economy*, 1.

CLINE, W. R. (1973), 'Interrelationship between Agricultural Strategy and Rural Income Distribution', *Food Research Institute Studies*, 12.

CLINE, W.R. (1975), 'Distribution and Development: A Survey of the Literature', *Journal of Development Economics*, 2.

Club du Sahel (1977), *Strategy and Programme for Drought Control and Development in the Sahel*, Paris: OECD.

COHEN, J. M. and WEINTRAUB, D. (1975), *Land and Peasants in Imperial Ethiopia: The Social Background to a Revolution*, Assen: Van Goreum.

COLE, J. (1976), *The Poor of the Earth*, London: Macmillan.

COLLIER, P. (1980), 'Poverty and Growth in Kenya', World Bank Staff Working Paper 389.

Comité Information Sahel (1974), *Qui se nourrit de la famine en Afrique?* Paris: Maspéro.

COPANS, J. *et al.* (1975), *Sécheresses et famines du Sahel*, Paris: Maspéro.

CURREY, B. (1978), 'The Famine Syndrome: Its Definition for Preparedness and Prevention in Bangladesh', *Ecology of Food and Nutrition*, 7.

DAHL, G., and HJORT, A (1976), *Having Herds: Pastoral Herd Growth and*

Household Economy, Stockholm: University of Stockholm.

DAHL, G. and HJORT, A. (1979), *Pastoral Change and the Role of Drought*, Stockholm: SAREC.

DALBY, D. and HARRISON CHURCH, R. J. (1973), *Drought in Africa*, London: International African Institute.

DALBY, D., HARRISON CHURCH, R. J. and BEZZAZ, F. (1977), *Drought in Africa 2*, London: International African Institute.

DALTON, H. (1920), 'The Measurement of the Inequality of Incomes', *Economic Journal*, 30.

DALRYMPLE, D. (1964), 'The Soviet Famine of 1932–1934', *Soviet Studies*, 15.

DALRYMPLE, D. (1965), 'The Soviet Famine of 1932–1934, Some Further References', *Soviet Studies*, 16.

DANDEKAR, V. M. and RATH, N. (1971), *Poverty in India*, Poona: Indian School of Political Economy.

DAS, T. (1949), *Bengal Famine (1943)*, Calcutta: University of Calcutta.

DASGUPTA, A. K. (1950), 'The Theory of Black Market Prices', *Economic Weekly*, 2, reprinted in Dasgupta (1965).

DASGUPTA, A. K. (1965), *Planning and Economic Growth*, London: Allen and Unwin.

DASGUPTA, BIPLAB (1977a), *Village Society and Labour Use*, Delhi: Oxford University Press.

DASGUPTA, BIPLAB (1977b), *Agrarian Change and the New Technology in India*, Geneva: UNRISD.

DASGUPTA, P., SEN, A. and STARRETT, D. (1973), 'Notes on the Measurement of Inequality', *Journal of Economic Theory*, 6.

DEATON, A., and MUELLBAUER, J. (1980), *Economics and Consumer Behaviour*, Cambridge: University Press.

DEBREU, G. (1959), *The Theory of Value*, New York: John Wiley.

DE HAEN, H. (1978), 'Analysing the World Food Problem', *Options: A IIASA News Report*, Winter.

DHARM, NARAIN (1976), *Growth of Productivity in Indian Agriculture*, Occasional Paper no. 93, Cornell University.

DICKSON, H. (1977), 'Agricultural Policy in the World Market', Working Paper, Nationalekonomiska Institutionen, Göteborgs Universitet.

DODGE, C. P. and WIEBE, P. D. (1979), 'Famine Relief and Development in Rural Bangladesh', *Economic and Political Weekly*, 11, 29 May.

DONALDSON, D. and WEYMARK, J. A. (1980a), 'A Single-Parameter Generalization of the Gini Indices of Inequality', *Journal of Economic Theory*, 22.

DONALDSON, D. and WEYMARK, J. A. (1980b), 'Ethically Flexible Gini Indices for Income Distribution in the Continuum', Discussion Paper no. 8020, CORE, Louvain.

DORFMAN, R. (1979), 'A Formula for the Gini Coefficient', *Review of Economics and Statistics*, 61.

DREWNOWSKI, J. (1977), 'Poverty: Its Meaning and Measurement', *Development and Change*, 8.

DUTT, R. C. (1900), *Famines and Land Assessment in India*, London.

DUTT, R. C. (1901), *Indian Famines: Their Causes and Prevention*, London.

DUTTA, BHASKAR (1978), 'On the Measurement of Poverty in Rural India', *Indian Economic Review*, 13.

DUTTA, BHASKAR (1979), 'Intersectoral Disparities and Income Distribution in India: 1960-61 to 1973-74', Working Paper no. 209, Delhi School of Economics.

DWORKIN, RONALD (1977), *Taking Rights Seriously*, London: Duckworth (2nd edn. 1978).

EDEN, F. M. (1797), *The State of the Poor*, London.

EDQUIST, C. and EDQVIST, O. (1979), *Social Carriers of Techniques of Development*, Stockholm: SIDA.

EHRLICH, P. R. and EHRLICH, A. H. (1972), *Population Resource Environment: Issues in Human Ecology*, San Francisco: Freeman.

EL KHAWAS, M. (1976), 'A Reassessment of International Relief Programs', in Glantz (1976).

EMMANUEL, A. (1972), *Unequal Exchange*, New York: Monthly Review Press.

ENGEL, E. (1895), 'Die Lebenskosten belgischer Arbeiter-Familien früher und jetzt', *International Statistical Institute Bulletin*, no. 9.

ENGELS, F. (1892), *The Condition of the Working-Class in England in 1844*, London: Allen and Unwin.

ESHERICK, J. (1972), 'Harvard on China: The Apologetics of Imperialism', *Bulletin of Concerned Asian Scholars*, 4.

ESHERICK, J. (1976), *Reform and Revolution in China*, Berkeley: University of California Press.

Ethiopian Ministry of Agriculture (1973), *Final Report of the Crop Condition Survey for 1972-73 Harvest*, Addis Ababa: Imperial Ethiopian Government.

Ethiopian Ministry of Agriculture (1974), *A Photogrammatic Assessment of 1966 E. C. Harvest Conditions in Eritrea, Tigra, Wollo, Northern Shea and Harerghe*, Addis Ababa: Imperial Ethiopian Government.

Ethiopian Relief and Rehabilitation Commission (1975), [Report on the first] 1½ *years: May Starvation Cease-'Ethiopia Tikdem'*, Addis Ababa: Imperial Ethiopian Government.

ETIENNE, G. (1968), *Studies in Indian Agriculture: The Art of the Possible*, Berkeley: University of California Press.

ETIENNE, G. (1977a), *Bangladesh: Development in Perspective*, Geneva: Graduate Institute of International Studies.

ETIENNE, G. (1977b). 'Foodgrain Production and Population in Asia: China, India and Bangladesh', *World Development*, 5.

FAALAND, J. and PARKINSON, J. R. (1976), *Bangladesh: The Test Case for Development*, London: Hurst.

Famine Inquiry Commission, India (1945a), *Report on Bengal*, New Delhi: Government of India.

Famine Inquiry Commission, India (1945b), *Final Report*, Madras: Government of India.

FAROUK, and ALI, M. (1977), *The Hardworking Poor (A survey of how people use their time in Bangladesh)*, Dacca: Bureau of Economic Research, University of Dacca.

FAULKINGHAM, R. H. (1977), 'Ecological Constraints and Subsistence Strategies: The Impact of Drought in a Hausa Village, A Case Study from Niger', in Dalby, Harrison Church and Bezzaz (1977).

FEDER, E. (1977), 'Agribusiness and the Elimination of Latin America's Rural Proletariat', *World Development*, 5.

FIELDS, G. S. (1976), 'A Welfare Economic Approach to Growth and Distribution in a Dual Economy', Discussion Paper no. 255, Economic Growth Centre, Yale University.

FIELDS, G. S. (1980), *Poverty, Inequality and Development*, Cambridge: University Press.

FIELDS, G. S. and FEI, J. C. H. (1978), 'On Inequality Comparisons', *Econometrica*, 46.

FISHLOW, A. (1972), 'Brazilian Size Distribution of Income', *American Economic Review*, 62.

FLERI, L. F. (1979), *Bangladesh Health Conditions*, mimeographed, UNADPI.

FLOOD, G. (1975), 'Nomadism and its Future: The Afar', *Royal Anthropological Institute News (RAIN)*, 6; reprinted in Hussein (1976).

FOEGE, H. W. (1971), 'Famine, Infections and Epidemics', in Blix, Hofvandor and Vahlquist (1971).

FRANK, A. G. (1969), *Capitalism and Underdevelopment in Latin America*, New York: Monthly Review Press.

FRANKE, R. W., and CHASIN, B. H. (1979), *The Political Economy of Ecological Destruction: Development in the West African Sahel*, Montclair, NJ: Allanheld.

FRIEDMAN, M. (1952), 'A Method of Comparing Incomes of Families Differing in Composition', *Studies in Income and Wealth*, 15.

FURTADO, C. (1964), *Development and Underdevelopment*, Berkeley: University of California Press.

GADGIL, D. R. and SOVANI, N. V. (1943), *War and Indian Economic Policy*, Poona: Gokhale Institute.

GASTWIRTH, J. L. (1972), 'The Estimation of Lorenz Curve and Gini Index', *Review of Economics and Statistics*, 54.

GASTWIRTH, J. L. (1975), 'The Estimation of a Family of Measures of Economic Inequality', *Journal of Econometrics*, 3.

GEBRE-MEDHIN, M. (1974), 'Famine in Ethiopia', *Ethiopian Medical Journal*, 12.

GEBRE-MEDHIN, M., *et al.* (1974), *Profile of Wollo under Famine*, Addis Ababa: Ethiopian Nutrition Institute, 24/74.

GEBRE-MEDHIN, M., HAY, R., LICKE, Y. and MAFFI, M. (1977), 'Initial Experience of a Consolidated Food and Nutrition Information System. Analysis of Data from the Ogaden Area', *Journal of Tropical Pediatrics and Environmental Child Health*, 23.

GEBRE-MEDHIN, M. and VAHLQUIST, B. (1976), 'Famine in Ethiopia: A Brief Review', *American Journal of Clinical Nutrition*, 29.

GEBRE-MEDHIN, M. and VAHLQUIST, B. (1977), 'Famine in Ethiopia— The Period 1973–75', *Nutrition Reviews*, 35.

GEERTZ, CLIFFORD (1963), *Agricultural Innovation: the Process of Ecological Change in Indonesia*, Berkeley: University of California Press.

GEORGE, P. S. (1979), *Public Distribution of Foodgrains in Kerala—Income Distribution Implications and Effectiveness*, Washington, DC: International Food Policy Research Institute.

GEORGE, Susan (1976), *How the Other Half Dies: The Real Reasons for World Hunger*, Harmondsworth: Penguin.

GHAI, D., KHAN, A. R., LEE, E. and ALFTHAN, T. A. (1977), *The Basic-Needs Approach to Development*, Geneva: ILO.

GHAI, D., KHAN, A. R., LEE, E. and RADWAN, S., eds. (1979), *Agrarian Systems and Rural Development*, London: Macmillan.

GHAI, D., LEE, E. and RADWAN, S. (1979), 'Rural Poverty in the Third World: Trend, Causes and Policy Reorientations', ILO Working Paper, WEP 10-6/WP 23, Geneva.

GHAI, Y. P. (1976), 'Notes towards a Theory of Law of Ideology: Tanzanian Perspectives', *African Law Studies*, no. 13.

GHOSH, AJIT (1979), 'Short-term Changes in Income Distribution in Poor Agrarian Economies: A Study of Famines with Reference to Indian Sub-Continent', ILO Working Paper, WEP 10-6/WP 28, Geneva.

GHOSH, ARUN (1977), 'Prices and Fluctuations in Economic Activity in India 1861–1967', mimeographed, New Delhi.

GHOSH, K. C. (1944), *Famines in Bengal 1770–1943*, Calcutta: Indian Associated Publishing.

GINNEKEN, W. VAN (1976), *Rural and Urban Income Inequalities in Indonesia, Mexico, Pakistan, Tanzania and Tunisia*, Geneva: ILO.

GINNEKEN, W. VAN (1980), 'Some Methods of Poverty Analysis: An Application to Iranian Data, 1975–1976', *World Development*, 8.

GINNEKEN, W. VAN (1979a), 'Income Distribution in LDCs—A Survey of Current Research' mimeographed, Geneva: ILO.

GINNEKEN, W. VAN (1979b), 'Basic Needs in Mexico: Analysis and Policies', ILO Working Paper, WEP 2–23/WP 76.

GLANTZ, M. H. (ed.) (1976), *The Politics of Natural Disaster: The Case of the Sahel Drought*, New York: Praeger.

GLANTZ, M. H. and PARTON, W. (1976), 'Weather and Climate Modification and the Future of the Sahel', in Glantz (1976).

GOEDHART, T., HALBERSTADT, V., KAPTEYN, A. and VAN PRAAG, B. (1977), 'The Poverty Line: Concept and Measurement', *Journal of Human Resources*, 4.

GORMAN, W. M. (1956), 'The Demand for Related Goods', *Journal Paper J3129*, Iowa Experimental Station, Ames, Iowa.

GORMAN, W. M. (1976), 'Tricks with Utility Function', in M. J. ARTIS and A. R. NOBAY (eds), *Essays in Economic Analysis*, Cambridge: University Press.

GRAAFF, J. DE V. (1946), 'Fluctuations in Income Concentration', *South African Journal of Economics*, 14.

GRAAFF, J. DE V. (1977), 'Equity and Efficiency as Components of the General Welfare', *South African Journal of Economics*, 45.

GRANT, J. P. (1978), *Disparity Reduction Rates in Social Indicators*, Washington, DC: Overseas Development Council.

GRAY, M. (1979), *Man against Disease: Preventive Medicine*, Oxford: University Press.

GREENOUGH, P. R. (1979), 'Prosperity and Misery in Modern India: The Bengal Famine 1943–44', mimeographed, Department of History, University of Iowa; to be published.

GRIFFIN, K. (1976), *Land Concentration and Rural Poverty*, London: Macmillan.

GRIFFIN, K. (1978), *International Inequality and National Poverty*, London: Macmillan.

GRIFFIN, K. (1979), *The Political Economy of Agrarian Change*, 2nd edn, London: Macmillan.

GRIFFIN, K. and GHOSE, A. (1979), 'Growth and Impoverishment in the Rural Areas of Asia', *World Development*, 7.

GRIFFIN, K. and JAMES, J. (1979), 'Problems of Transition to Egalitarian Development', *Manchester School*, 47.

GRIFFIN, K. and KHAN, A. R. (eds.) (1977), *Poverty and Landlessness in Rural Asia*, Geneva: ILO.

GRIFFIN, K. and KHAN, A. R. (1978), 'Poverty in the Third World: Ugly Facts and Fancy Models', *World Development*, 6.

GULATI, I. S. and KRISHNAN, T. N. (1975), 'Public Distribution and Procurement of Foodgrains: A Proposal', *Economic and Political Weekly*, 10, 24 May.

GULATI, I. S. and KRISHNAN, T. N. (1976), 'Public Distribution and Procurement of Foodgrains: A Correction and Some Elucidations and Observations', *Economic and Political Weekly*, 11, 21 February.

GUPTA, A. P. (1977), *Fiscal Policy for Employment Generation in India*, Delhi: Tata McGraw-Hill.

HAALAND, G. (1977), 'Pastoral Systems of Production: the Sociocultural Context and Some Economic and Ecological Implications', in O'Keefe and Wisner (1977).

HABIB, IRFAN (1963), *Agrarian Systems of Mughal India*, London: Asia Publishing House.

HAMADA, K. and TAKAYAMA, N. (1978), 'Censored Income Distribution and the Measurement of Poverty', *Bulletin of International Statistical Institute*, 47.

HAMILTON, C. (1975), 'Increased Child Labour—An External Diseconomy of Rural Employment Creation for Adults', *Asian Economies*, December.

HAMMOND, P. J. (1977), 'Dual Interpersonal Comparisons of Utility and the Welfare Economics and Income Distribution', *Journal of Public Economics*, 6.

HAMMOND, P. J. (1978), 'Economic Welfare with Rank Order Price Weighting', *Review of Economic Studies*, 45.

HANSEN, B. (1969), 'Employment and Wages in Rural Egypt', *American Economic Review*, 59.

HANSSON, B. (1977), 'The Measurement of Social Inequality', in Butts and Hintikka (1977).

HAQ, MAHBUBUL (1976), *The Poverty Curtain: Choices for the Third World*, New York: Columbia University Press.

HAQUE, W., MEHTA, N., RAHMAN, A. and WIGNARAJA, P. (1975), *Towards a Theory of Rural Development*, Bangkok: UN Asian Development Institute.

HARDIN, C. M. (ed.) (1969), *Overcoming World Hunger*, Englewood Cliffs, NJ: Prentice-Hall.

HARE, R. M. (1963), *Freedom and Reason*, Oxford: Clarendon Press.

HARLE, V. (ed.) (1978), *The Political Economy of Food*, Westmead: Saxon House.

HARRISON CHURCH, R. J. (1961), 'Problems and Development of the Dry Zone of Wes Africa', *Geographical Journal*, 127.

HARRISON CHURCH, R. J. (1973), 'The Development of the Water Resources of the Dry Zone of West Africa', in Dalby and Harrison Church (1973).

HART, HERBERT (1961), *The Concept of Law*, Oxford: Clarendon Press.

HART, OLIVER (1977), 'On the Profitability of Speculation', *Quarterly Journal of Economics*, 91.

230 Bibliography

HART, P. and MILLS, G. (1964), *Econometric Analysis for National Economic Planning*, London: Butterworth.

HARTMANN, B., and BOYCE, J. (1979), *Needless Hunger: Voices from a Bangladesh Village*, San Francisco: Institute for Food and Development Policy.

HARTWELL, R. M. (1972), *The Long Debate on Poverty*, London: Institute of Economic Affairs.

HAY, R. W. (1975), 'Analysis of Data from Ogaden—Hararghe Province', Consolidated Food and Nutrition Information System, Ethiopian Food and Nutrition Surveillance Programme, Addis Ababa.

HAY, R. W. (1978a), 'The Concept of Food Supply System—with Special Reference to Management of Famine', *Ecology of Food and Nutrition*, 7.

HAY, R. W. (1978b), 'The Statistics of Hunger', *Food Policy*, November.

HAY, R. W. (1980), 'The Food Accounting Matrix: An Analytical Device for Food Planning', mimeographed, Queen Elizabeth House, Oxford.

HAZLEWOOD, A. (1976), 'Kenya: Income Distribution and Poverty: An Unfashionable View', *Journal of Modern African Studies*, 16.

HELLEINER, G. K. (1966), *Peasant Agriculture, Government and Economic Growth in Nigeria*, Homewood, Ill.: Irwin.

HELWEG-LARSEN, P. *et al.* (1952), 'Famine Diseases in German Concentration Camps', *Acta Medica Scandinavia*, suppl. 274, Stockholm.

HEYER, JUDITH (1980), 'The Impact of Smallholder Rural Development Programme on Poverty in Tropical Africa', mimeographed, Queen Elizabeth House, Oxford.

HEYER, J., ROBERTS, P. and WILLIAMS, G. (eds) (1980), *Rural Development in Tropical Africa*, London: Macmillan.

HICKS, J. R. (1939), *Value and Capital*, Oxford: Clarendon Press.

HICKS, J. R. (1958), 'The Measurement of Real Income', *Oxford Economic Papers*, 10.

HICKS, J. R. (1979), *Causality in Economics*, Oxford: Basil Blackwell.

HIRSCH, F. (1976), *Social Limits to Growth*, Cambridge, Mass.: Harvard University Press.

HIRSCHMAN, A. O. (1977), *The Passions and the Interests*, Princeton, NJ: University Press.

HIRSCHMAN, A. O. and ROTHSCHILD, M. (1973), 'The Changing Tolerance for Income Inequality in the Course of Economic Development', *Quarterly Journal of Economics*, 87.

HOBSBAWM, E. J. (1957), 'The British Standard of Living, 1790–1850', *Economic History Review*, 10.

HOBSBAWM, E. J. (1968), 'Poverty', in *International Encyclopaedia of the Social Sciences*, New York.

HOBSBAWM, E. J., MITRA, A., RAJ, K. N., SACHS, I. and THORNER, A.(eds) (1980), *Peasants in History: Essays in Memory of Daniel Thorner*, Calcutta: Oxford University Press.

HOLT, J. and SEAMAN, J. (1976), 'The Scope of the Drought', in Hussein (1976).

HOLT, J. and SEAMAN, J. (1979), 'The Causes and Nature of Famine: A General Theory', mimeographed, International Disaster Institute, London.

HOLT, J., SEAMAN, J. and RIVERS, J. P. W. (1975), 'The Ethiopian Famine of 1973–74: 2. Harerghe Province', *Proceedings of the Nutritional Society*, 24.

HOPECRAFT, A. (1968), *Born to Hunger*, London: Pan Books.

HSIA, R. and CHAU, L. (1978), *Industrialisation, Employment and Income Distribution*, London: Croom Helm.

HUECKEL, G. (1973), 'War and the British Economy, 1815–1973: A General Equilibrium Analysis', *Explorations in Economic History*, 10.

HUQ, A. (ed.) (1976), *Exploitation and the Rural Poor*, Comilla: Bangladesh Academy of Rural Development.

HUSSEIN, A. M. (ed.) (1976), *Rehab: Drought and Famine in Ethiopia*, London: International African Institute.

HUTCHINSON, J. (1972), *Farming and Food Supply*, Cambridge: University Press.

ILO (1976a), *Employment, Growth and Basic Needs: A One-World Problem*, Geneva: ILO.

ILO (1976b), *Basic Needs and National Employment Strategies*, Background Papers, vol. I, Tripartite World Conference on Employment, Income Distribution and Social Progress and the International Division of Labour, Geneva, ILO.

IMPERATO, P. J. (1976), 'Health Care Systems in the Sahel before and after the Drought', in Glantz (1976).

Institute for Food and Development Policy (1979), 'The Aid Debate', Working Paper no. 1, San Francisco.

Interfutures (1979), *Facing the Future: Mastering the Probable and Managing the Unpredictable*, Paris: OECD.

ISENMAN, P. J. and SINGER, H. W. (1977), 'Food Aid: Disincentive Effects and Their Policy Implications', *Economic Development and Cultural Change*, 25.

ISHIKAWA, S. (1977), 'China's Food and Agriculture', *Food Policy*, May.

ISHIKAWA, S., KHAN, A. R., AHMED, I., NASEEM, S. M., WICKRAMASEKARA, P., LEE, E. and VAIDYANATHAN, A. (1980),

Employment Expansion in Asian Agriculture, Asian Employment Programme, Bangkok: ILO/ARTEP.

ISLAM, NURUL (1977), *Development Planning in Bangladesh: A Study in Political Economy*, London: Hurst.

ISLAM, RUSHIDAN (1977), 'Approaches to the Problem of Rural Development', Working Paper no. 10, Village Study Group, Dacca University.

JACKSON, D. (1972), *Poverty*, London: Macmillan.

JAIN, S. P. (1954), 'Computed Birth and Death Rates in India during 1941–1950', Annexure II, *Estimation of Birth and Death Rates in India during 1941–50*, 1951 Census of India, Paper no. 6, New Delhi, Government of India.

JODHA, N. S. (1975), 'Famine and Famine Policies: Some Empirical Evidence', *Economic and Political Weekly*, 10, October 11.

JOHNSON, B. L. C. (1975), *Bangladesh*, London: Heinemann.

JOHNSON, D. GALE (1967), *The Struggle against World Hunger*, New York: Foreign Policy Association.

JOHNSON, D. GALE (1973). 'Famine', in *Encyclopaedia Britannica*, 1973 edn.

JOHNSON, D. GALE (1975), *World Food Problems and Prospects*, Washington, DC: American Enterprises Institute for Public Policy Research.

JOHNSON, D. GALE (1976), 'Increased Stability of Grain Supplies in Developing Countries: Optimal Carryovers and Insurance', *World Development*, 4.

JOLLY, R. (1976), 'The World Employment Conference: The Enthronement of Basic Needs', *Overseas Development Institute Review*, no. 2.

JOSHI, NANDINI (1978), *The Challenge of Poverty: The Developing Countries in the New International Order*, Delhi: Vazirani and Arnold-Heinemann.

JOSLING, T. (1977), 'Grain Reserves and Government Agricultural Policies', *World Development*, 5.

JOY, L. and PAYNE, P. (1975), *Food and Nutrition Planning*, Nutrition Consultants Reports Series, no. 35; ESN: CRS/75/34, Rome: FAO.

JUTIKKALA, E. and KAUPPINEN, M. (1971), 'The Structure of Mortality during Catastrophic Year in Pre-Industrial Society', *Population Studies*, 25.

KAKWANI, N. (1977), 'Measurement of Poverty and Negative Income Tax', *Australian Economic Papers*, 16.

KAKWANI, N. (1980a), *Income Inequality and Poverty*, New York: Oxford University Press.

KAKWANI, N. (1979), 'Issues in Measurement of Poverty', Discussion Paper no. 330, Institute of Economic Research, Queen's University, Kingston, Ontario.

KAKWANI, N. (1980b), 'On a Class of Poverty Measures', *Econometrica*, 48.

KALDOR, NICHOLAS (1976), 'Inflation and Recession in the World Economy', *Economic Journal*, 86.

KAUTILYA (*circa* 320 BC), *Arthasastra*, Pataliputra (Patna); translated by R. SHAMASASTRY, *Kautiliya Arthasastra*, Mysore, 1909; 2nd edn, 1919; Bangalore, 1915; 2nd edn, 1923.

KEYS, A. (1950), *The Biology of Human Starvation*, Minneapolis.

KHALIFA, A. and SIMPSON, M. (1972), 'Perverse Supply in Nomadic Conditions', *Oxford Agrarian Studies*, 1.

KHAN, A. R. (1972), *The Economy of Bangladesh*, London: Macmillan.

KHAN, A. R. (1977), 'Poverty and Inequality in Rural Bangladesh', in Griffin and Khan (1977).

KHAN, A. R. (1979), 'The Comilla Model and the Integrat·d Rural Development Programme in Bangladesh: An Experiment in Cooperative Capitalism', *World Development*, 7.

KLOTH, T. I. (1974), *Sahel Nutrition Survey 1974*, Atlanta: US Public Health Service.

KLOTH, T. I. *et al.* (1976), 'Sahel Nutrition Survey: 1974', *American Journal of Epidemiology*, 103.

KNIGHT, C. G. and NEWMAN, J. L. (1976), *Contemporary Africa: Geography and Change*, Englewood Cliffs, NJ: Prentice-Hall.

KNUDSON, O. and SCANDIZZO, P. L. (1979), 'Nutrition and Food Needs in Developing Countries', World Bank, Staff Working Paper no. 328.

KOLM, S. Ch. (1969), 'The Optimal Production of Social Justice', in Margolis and Guitton (1969).

KOLM, S. Ch. (1976a), 'Unequal Inequalities: I', *Journal of Economic Theory*, 12.

KOLM, S. Ch. (1976b), 'Unequal Inequalities: II', *Journal of Economic Theory*, 13.

KONANDREAS, P., HUDDLESTON, B. and RAMANGKURA, V. (1979), *Food Security: An Insurance Approval*, Washington, DC: International Food Policy Research Institute.

KOOPMANS, T. C. (1957), *Three Essays on the State of the Economic Science*, New York: McGraw-Hill.

KORNAI, JÁNOS (1979a), *The Economics of Shortage*, mimeographed; to be published.

KORNAI, J. (1979b), 'Resource-constrained versus Demand-constrained Systems', *Econometrica*, 47.

KRELLE, W. and SHORROCKS, A. F. (1978), *Personal Income Distribution*, Amsterdam: North-Holland.

KRISHNAJI, N. (1976), 'Public Distribution and Procurement of Foodgrains: A Comment', *Economic and Political Weekly*, 11, 21 February.

KUMAR, DHARMA (1974), 'Changes in Income Distribution and Poverty in India: A Review of the Literature', *World Development*, 2.

KUMAR, S. K. (1979), *Impact of Subsidised Rice on Food Consumption in Kerala*, Washington, DC: International Food Policy Research Institute.

KUNDU, A., and SMITH, T. E. (1981), "On the Possibility of Poverty Indices", Working Paper 43, Regional Science and Transportation, University of Pennsylvania.

KUZNETS, S. (1966), *Modern Economic Growth*, New York: Norton.

LADEJINSKY, W. (1976), 'Food Shortage in West Bengal: Crisis or Chronic?', *World Development*, 4.

LAL, DEEPAK (1976), 'Agricultural Growth, Real Wages and the Rural Poor in India', *Economic and Political Weekly*, 11.

LANCASTER, K. J. (1966), 'A New Approach to Consumer Theory', *Journal of Political Economy*, 74.

LAPPÉ, F. M., and COLLINS, J. (1977), *Food First: Beyond the Myth of Scarcity*, New York: Houghton Mifflin (republished New York: Ballantine Books, 1979).

LAPPÉ, F. M. and COLLINS, J. (1978), *World Hunger: Ten Myths*, San Francisco: Institute for Food and Development Policy.

LARDY, N. R. (1978), *Economic Growth and Distribution in China*, Cambridge: University Press.

LEVINSON, F. J. (1974), *Morinda: An Economic Analysis of Malnutrition among Young Children in Rural India*, Cambridge, Mass.: Cornell–MIT International Nutrition Policy Series.

LIFSCHULTZ, L. (1975), 'The Crisis Has Not Passed', *Far Eastern Economic Review*, 5 December.

LIPTON, MICHAEL (1977), *Why Poor People Stay Poor: A Study of Urban Bias in World Development*, London: Temple Smith.

LIVINGSTONE, I. (1977), 'Economic Irrationality among Pastoral Peoples—Myth or Reality', *Development and Change*, 8.

LLOYD, E. M. H. (1956), *Food and Inflation in Middle East 1944–45*, Stanford: University Press.

LOFCHIE, M. F. (1975), 'Political and Economic Origins of African Hunger', *Journal of Modern African Studies*, 14.

LÖRSTAD, M. H. (1976), 'Nutrition Planning through Gaming', *Food and Nutrition*, 3.

LOVEDAY, A. (1916), *The History and Economics of Indian Famines*, London: G. Bell.

LUCE, R. D. and RAIFFA, H. (1958), *Games and Decisions*, New York: John Wiley.

LUNDHOLM, B. (1976), 'Domestic Animals in Arid Ecosystems', in Rapp, Le Houérou and Lundholm (1976).

MADISON, ANGUS (1970), 'The Historical Origins of Indian Poverty', *Banca Nazionale del Lavoro*, no. 92.

MAGDOFF, H. (1968), 'The Age of Imperialism', *Monthly Review*, 20.

MAHALANOBIS, P. C., MUKHERJE, R., and GHOSH, A. (1946), 'A Sample Survey of After-effects of the Bengal Famine of 1943', *Sankhya*, 7.

MAHALANOBIS, P. C., *et al.* (1946), *Famine and Rehabilitation in Bengal*, Calcutta: Statistical Publishing Society.

MALLORY, W. H. (1926), *China: Land of Famine*, New York: American Geographical Society.

MALTHUS, T. R. (1798), *Essay on the Principle of Population as It Affects the Future Improvement of Society*, London.

MALTHUS, T. R. (1800), *An Investigation of the Cause of the Present High Price of Provisions*, London.

MANETSCH, J. (1977), 'On the Role of Systems Analysis in Aiding Countries Facing Acute Shortages', *Man and Cybernetics*, 7 April.

MANN, H. H. (1955), *Rainfall and Famine*, Bombay: Indian Society of Agricultural Economics.

MANN, J. S. (1968), 'The Impact of Public Law 480 Imports on Prices and Domestic Supply of Cereals in India', *American Journal of Farm Economics*, 49.

MANSERGH, N. (ed.) (1971), *The Transfer of Power 1942–7*, vol. III, London: HMSO.

MANSERGH, N. (ed.) (1973), *The Transfer of Power 1942–7*, vol. IV, London: HMSO.

MARGLIN, S. A. (1974–5), 'What Do Bosses Do?' *Review of Radical Political Economics*, Part I, 6; Part II, 7.

MARGOLIS, J. and GUITTON, H. (eds) (1969), *Public Economics*, London: Macmillan.

MARNHAM, P. (1977), *Nomads of the Sahel*, London: Minority Rights Group.

MARRIS, R. and THEIL, H. 'International Comparisons of Economic Welfare', presented to A. E. A., Denver (1980), 'Towards a World Utility Function', mimeographed, Department of Economics, University of Maryland.

MARX, KARL (1857–8), *Grundrisse der Kritik der Politischen Okonomie*. Moscow: Marx-Engels-Lenin Institute, 1939 and 1941; English translation by M. Nicolaus (1973), *Grundisse: Foundations of the Critique of Political Economy*, Harmondsworth: Penguin; also part translation with supplementary texts of Marx and Engels, and with an Introduction by Eric Hobsbawm (1964), *Pre-Capitalist Economic Formations*, London: Lawrence and Wishart.

MARX, KARL (1859), *Zur Kritik der Politischen Ökonomie*, Berlin: Deitz Verlag, 1964; English translation by S. W. Ryazanskaya, with an Introduction by Maurice Dobb (1971), *A Contribution to the Critique of Political Economy*, London: Lawrence and Wishart.

MARX, KARL (1867), *Das Kapital*, vol. I; English translation by S. Moore and E. Aveling, edited by F. Engels (1887), *Capital: A Critical Analysis of Capitalist Production*, vol. I, London: Sonnenschein; republished by Allen and Unwin, 1938.

MASEFIELD, G. B. (1963), *Famine: Its Prevention and Relief*, Oxford: University Press.

MATHIAS, PETER (1972), 'Adam's Burden: Diagnoses of Poverty in Post-Medieval Europe and the Third World Now', Gildersleeve Lecture, Barnard College, Columbia University.

MATLOCK, W. G. and COCKRUM, E. L. (1976), 'Agricultural Production Systems in the Sahel', in Glantz (1976).

MAYER, JEAN (1975), 'Management of Famine Relief', *Science*, 5, 9 May.

McALPIN, MICHELLE (1976), 'The Demographic Effects of Famine in Bombay Presidency, 1871–1931: Some Preliminary Findings', mimeographed, Economics Department, Tufts University.

McHENRY, D. F. and BIRD, K. (1977), 'Food Bungle in Bangladesh', *Foreign Policy*, no. 27, Summer.

McLAREN, D. S. (1974), 'The Great Protein Fiasco', *Lancet*, 13 July.

MEADOWS, D. H., MEADOWS, D. L., RANDERS, J. and BEHRENS III, W. W. (1972), *The Limits to Growth*, Washington, DC: Potomac Associates.

MEILLASSOUX, C. (1972), 'From Reproduction to Production', *Economy and Society*, 1.

MEILLASSOUX, C. (1974), 'Development or Exploitation: Is the Sahel Famine Good for Business?' *Review of African Political Economy*, 1.

MEILLASSOUX, C. (1975), *Femme, greniers, et capitaux*, Paris: Maspéro.

MELLOR, J. W. (1976), *The New Economics of Growth: A Strategy for India and the Developing World*, Ithaca, NY: Cornell University Press.

MELLOR, J. W. (1978a), 'Food Price Policy and Income Distribution in Low-Income Countries', *Economic Development and Cultural Change*, 27.

MELLOR, J. W. (1978b), *Three Issues of Development Strategy: Food, Population, Trade*, Washington, DC: IFPRI.

MENCHER, J. P. (1978), 'Why Grow More Food?: An Analysis of Some Contradictions in the "Green Revolution" in Kerala', *Economic and Political Weekly*, 13.

MIA, AHMADULLAH (1976), *Problems of Rural Development: Some Household Level Indicators*, Dacca Integrated Rural Development Programme.

MILLER, D. S., and HOLT, J. F. J. (1975), 'The Ethiopian Famine', *Proceedings of the Nutritional Society*, 34.

MILLER, H. P. (1971), *Rich Man, Poor Man*, New York: Cromwell.

MILLER, S. M., REIN, M., ROBY, P. and CROSS, B. (1967), 'Poverty, Inequality and Conflict', *Annals of the American Academy of Political Science*.

MILLER, S. M. and ROBY, P. (1971), 'Poverty: Changing Social Stratification', in Townsend (1971).

MINHAS, B. S. (1970), 'Rural Poverty, Land Distribution and Development', *Indian Economic Review*, 5.

MINHAS, B. S. (1971), 'Rural Poverty and Minimum Level of Living', *Indian Economic Review*, 6.

MINHAS, B. S. (1974), 'Rural Poverty, Land Distribution and Development Strategy: Facts', in Srinivasan and Bardhan (1974).

MITRA, ASHOK (1977), *Terms of Trade and Class Relations: An Essay in Political Economy*, London: Frank Cass.

MONOD, T. (ed.) (1975), *Pastoralism and Development in Africa*, London: Oxford University Press.

MORAES, DOM (1974), *A Matter of People*, London: Deutsch.

MORAES, DOM (1975), 'The Dimensions of the Problem: Comment', in Aziz (1975).

MORAWETZ, D. (1977), *Twenty-five Years of Economic Development 1950 to 1975*, Baltimore: Johns Hopkins University Press.

MORRIS, M. D. (1974), 'What is Famine?', *Economic and Political Weekly*, 9. 2 November.

MORRIS, M. D. (1975), 'Needed—A New Famine Policy', *Economic and Political Weekly*, Annual Number, 10.

MORRIS, M. D. (1979), *Measuring the Condition of the World's Poor: The Physical Quality of Life Index*, Oxford: Pergamon Press.

MUELLBAUER, JOHN (1974a), 'Recent UK Experience of Prices and Inequality: An Application of True Cost of Living and Real Income Indices', *Economic Journal*, 84.

MUELLBAUER, JOHN (1974b), 'Household Composition, Engel Curves and Welfare Comparison between Households: A Duality Approach', *European Economic Review*, 5.

MUELLBAUER, JOHN (1974c), 'Inequality Measures, Prices and Household Composition', *Review of Economic Studies*, 41.

MUELLBAUER, JOHN (1975), 'Aggregation, Income Distribution and

Consumer Demand', *Review of Economic Studies*, 42.

MUELLBAUER, JOHN (1976), 'Community Preferences and the Representative Consumer', *Econometrica*, 44.

MUELLBAUER, JOHN (1977a), 'Cost of Living', in *Social Science Research*, London: HMSO.

MUELLBAUER, JOHN (1977b), 'Testing the Barten Model of Household Composition Effects and the Cost of Children', *Economic Journal*, 87.

MUELLBAUER, JOHN (1978), 'Distributional Aspects of Price Comparisons', in Stone and Peterson (1978).

MUELLBAUER, JOHN (1980), 'The Estimation of the Prais-Houthakker Model of Equivalent Scales', *Econometrica*, 48.

MUKERJI, K. (1952), *Socio-Economic Survey of 49 Villages*, Calcutta: Chatterjee and Co.

MUKERJI, K. (1957), *The Problems of Land Transfer*, Santiniketan: Visva-Bharati.

MUKERJI, K. (1965), *Agriculture, Famine and Rehabilitation in South Asia*, Santiniketan: Visva-Bharati.

MUKHERJEE, M., BHATTACHARYA, N. and CHATTERJEE, G. S. (1972), 'Poverty in India: Measurement and Amelioration', *Commerce* (Calcutta), 125.

MUNDLAK, Y. (1979), *Intersectoral Factor Mobility and Agricultural Growth*, Washington, DC: International Food Policy Research Institute.

MYINT, H. (1973), *The Economics of Developing Countries*, 4th edn, London: Hutchinson.

MYRDAL, GUNNAR (1957), *Economic Theory and Underdeveloped Regions*, London: Duckworth.

MYRDAL, GUNNAR (1968), *Asian Drama*, New York: Pantheon.

NAKAMURA, J. I. (1966), *Agricultural Production and the Economic Development of Japan 1873–1922*, Princeton, NJ: University Press.

NASH, V. (1900), *The Great Famine and Its Causes*, London: Longmans.

National Bank of Ethiopia (1976), *Eleventh Annual Report 1974/5*, Addis Ababa: Government of Ethiopia.

NEWMAN, J. L. (1975), *Drought, Famine and Population Movements in Africa*, Syracuse, NY: University Press.

NEWMAN, PETER (1977), 'Malaria and Mortality', *Journal of American Statistical Association*, 72.

NICHOLSON, J. L. (1976), 'Appraisal of Different Methods of Estimating Equivalent Scales and Their Results', *Review of Income and Wealth*, 22.

NOLAN, LIAM (1974), *The Forgotten Famine*, Dublin: Mercier Press.

NORTON, B. E. (1976), 'The Management of Desert Grazing Systems', in Glantz (1976).

NOZICK, ROBERT (1974), *Anarchy, State and Utopia*, Oxford: Basil Blackwell.

OECD Development Centre (1979), *Food Aid for Development*, Paris: OECD.

OHKAWA, K. and ROSOVSKY, H. (1960), 'The Role of Agriculture in Modern Japanese Economic Development', *Economic Development and Cultural Change*, 9.

OHKAWA, K. and ROSOVSKY, H. (1973), *Japanese Economic Growth*, Stanford: University Press.

OHKAWA, K., et al. (1957), *The Growth Rate of the Japanese Economy since 1878*, Tokyo: Kinokuniya Bookstore.

OJHA, P. D. (1970), 'A Configuration of Indian Poverty', *Reserve Bank of India Bulletin*, 24.

O'KEEFE, P. and WISNER, B. (1975), 'African Drought—The State of the Game', *African Environmental Special Report No. 1: Problems and Perspectives*. London: International African Institute.

O'KEEFE, P. and WISNER, B. (eds) (1977), *Landuse and Development*, London: International African Institute.

ORSHANSKY, M. (1965), 'Counting the Poor: Another Look at the Poverty Profile', *Social Security Bulletin*, 28.

ORSHANSKY, M. (1966), 'Recounting the Poor: A Five Year Review', *Social Security Bulletin*, 29.

ORSHANSKY, M. (1969), 'How Poverty is Measured', *Monthly Labor Review*.

OSMANI, S. R. (1978), 'Economic Inequality and Group Welfare: Theory and Application to Bangladesh'; to be published by Oxford University Press.

OXBY, C. (1975), *Pastoral Nomads and Development*, London: International African Institute.

PADDOCK, W. and PADDOCK, P. (1967), *Famine—1975!*, Boston: Little, Brown.

PALEKAR, S. A. (1962), *Real Wages in India 1939–1950*, Bombay: International Book House.

PALMER, INGRID (1972), *Food and New Agricultural Technology*, Geneva: UNRISD, United Nations.

PANIKAR, P. G. K., et al (1975), *Poverty, Unemployment and Development Policy*, New York: United Nations, ST/ESA/29.

PANKHURST, R. (1961), *An Introduction to the Economic History of Ethiopia from Early Times to 1800*, London: Lalibela House.

PANKHURST, R. (1966), 'The Great Ethiopian Famine of 1888–1892: A New Assessment', *Journal of the History of Medicine and Allied Sciences*, 21.

PANTULU, Y. V. (1980), 'On Sen's Measure of Poverty', mimeographed, Sardar Patel Institute of Economic and Social Research.

PATNAIK, P., RAO, S. K. and SANYAL, A. (1976), 'The Inflationary

Process: Some Theoretical Comments', *Economic and Political Weekly*, 11, 23 October.

PAUKERT, FELIX (1973), 'Income Distribution at Different Levels of Development: A Survey of Evidence', *International Labour Review*, 108.

PEN, J. (1976), *Income Distribution*, Harmondsworth: Penguin.

PENNY, D. H. (1966), 'The Economics of Peasant Agriculture: The Indonesian Case', *Bulletin of Indonesian Economic Studies*, no. 5, October.

PENNY, D. H. (1979), 'The Economics of Peasant Starvation', presented at the 1979 Conference of the Australian Agricultural Economics Society.

PERKINS, D. H. (1969), *Agricultural Development in China 1368–1968*, Chicago: Aldine.

PERKINS, D. H. (1978), 'Meeting Basic Needs in the People's Republic of China', *World Development*, 6.

PINSTRUP-ANDERSON, P., RAIZ DE LONDONA, N. and HOOVER, E. (1976), 'The Impact of Increasing Food Supply on Human Nutrition: Implications for Commodity Priorities in Agricultural Research and Policy', *American Journal of Agricultural Economics*, 58.

POLEMAN, T. T. (1977), 'World Food: Myth and Reality', *World Development*, 5.

POWER, J., and HOLENSTEIN, A. (1976), *World of Hunger*, London: Temple Smith.

PRABHAKAR, M. S. (1974), 'The Famine: A Report from Dhubri', *Economic and Political Weekly*, 9.

PRAIS, S. J. and HOUTHAKKER, H. S. (1955), *The Analysis of Family Budgets*, Cambridge: University Press (2nd edn 1971).

PYATT, GRAHAM (1976), 'On the Interpretation and Disaggregation of Gini Coefficients', *Economic Journal*, 86.

PYATT, GRAHAM (1980), 'Poverty and Welfare Measures Based on the Lorenz Curve', mimeographed, Development Research Center, World Bank, Washington, DC.

PYATT, G. and THORBECKE, E. (1976), *Planning for a Better Future*, Geneva: ILO.

RADHAKRISHNA, R. and SARMA, A. (1975), 'Distributional Effects of the Current Inflation', *Social Scientist*, 30–1.

RADHAKRISHNA, R. and SARMA, A. (1980), 'Intertemporal Welfare Comparisons of India', mimeographed, Sardar Patel Institute of Economic and Social Research.

RADO, E. and SINHA, R. (1977), 'Africa: A Continent in Transition', *World Development*, 5.

RAHMAN, ANISUR (1974a), 'Relief Tour of Shahbajpur, Brahmanbaria:

Daily Diary', mimeographed, Dacca University.

RAHMAN, ANISUR (1974b), 'Famine', mimeographed, Dacca University.

RAJARAMAN, INDIRA (1974), 'Constructing the Poverty Line: Rural Punjab, 1960–61', Discussion Paper no. 43, Research Program in Economic Development, Princeton University.

RAMACHANDRAN, L. (1977), *India's Food Problem: A New Approach*, New Delhi: Allied Publishers.

RANGASAMI, AMRITA (1974a), 'West Bengal: A Generation is Being Wiped Out', *Economic and Political Weekly*, 9, 30 November.

RANGASAMI, AMRITA (1974b), 'The Uses of "Drought" ', *Economic and Political Weekly*, 9, 14 December.

RANGASAMI, AMRITA (1975), 'The Paupers of Kholisabhita Hindupara: Report on a Famine', *Economic and Political Weekly*, Annual Number, 10.

RAPP, A., LE HOUÉROU, H. N. and LUNDHOLM, R. (eds) (1976), *Can Desert Encroachment Be Stopped?*, Ecological Bulletins, no. 24. Stockholm.

RASHID, S. (1980), 'The Policy of Laissez-faire during Scarcities', *Economic Journal*, 90.

RATH, N. (1973), 'Regional Variation in Level and Cost of Living in Rural India', *Artha Vijnana*, 15.

RATUIM, A. M. A. (1974), 'An Analysis of Smuggling in Bangladesh', *Bangladesh Bank Bulletin*, 14.

RAWSKI, T. G. (1979), *Economic Growth and Employment in China*, Oxford: University Press.

RAYNAUT, C. (1977), 'Lessons of a Crisis', in Dalby, Harrison Church and Bezzaz (1977).

REDDAWAY, W. B. and RAHMAN, M. (1975), 'The Scale of Smuggling Out of Bangladesh', Research Report no. 21, Bangladesh Institute of Development Studies, Dacca.

REES, J. D. (1901), *Famines: Facts and Fallacies*, London.

REIN, M. (1971), 'Problems in the Definition and Measurement of Poverty', in Townsend (1971).

Relief and Rehabilitation Commission, Ethiopia (1976), 'Relief and Rehabilitation for Famine Victims in Ethiopia', in Hussein (1976).

RETZLAFF, R. H. (1978), 'Structural Change: An Approach to Poverty in Asian Rural Development', *Economic and Political Weekly*, 13, 22–30 December.

REUTLINGER, S. (1977), 'Malnutrition: A Poverty or a Food Problem', *World Development*, 5.

REUTLINGER, S. (1978), 'Food Insecurity: Magnitude and Remedies', *World Development*, 6.

REUTLINGER, S. and SELOWSKY, M. (1976), *Malnutrition and Poverty:*

Magnitude and Policy Options, Baltimore: Johns Hopkins University Press.

RICARDO, DAVID (1822), Text of speech in Parliament on 10 July: published in P. Sraffa (ed.), *The Works and Correspondence of David Ricardo*, vol. V, 'Speeches and Evidence', Cambridge: University Press.

RISKIN, CARL, (1975), 'Incentives for Industrial Workers', in Joint Economic Committee, *People's Republic of China: A Reassessment of the Economy*, Washington, DC: US Government Printing Office.

RIVERS, J. P. W., HOLT, J. F. J., SEAMAN, J. A. and BOWDEN, M. H. (1976), 'Lessons for Epidemiology from the Ethiopian Famines', *Annales Société belge de Médecine Tropicale*, 56.

RODGERS, G. B. (1976), 'A Conceptualisation of Poverty in Rural India', *World Development*, 4.

ROGERS, K. D., SRIVASTAVA, U. K. and HEADY, E. O. (1972), 'Modified Price, Production and Income Impacts of Food Aid under Market Differentiated Distribution', *American Journal of Farm Economics*, 54.

ROTHSCHILD, M. and STIGLITZ, J. E. (1973), 'Some Further Results on the Measurement of Inequality', *Journal of Economic Theory*, 6.

ROWNTREE, S. (1901), *Poverty: A Study of Town Life*, London: Macmillan.

RUDRA, ASHOK (1978), *The Basic Needs Concept and Its Implementation in Indian Development Planning*, Bangkok: ILO/ARTEP.

RUNCIMAN, W. G. (1966), *Relative Deprivation and Social Justice*, London: Routledge & Kegan Paul.

SARMA, J. S. (1978), 'India—A Drive toward Self-Sufficiency in Food Grains', *American Journal of Agricultural Economics*, 60.

SARMA, J. S., ROY, S. and GEORGE, P. S. (1979), *Two Analyses of Indian Foodgrains Production and Consumption Data*, Washington, DC: International Food Policy Research Institute.

SARRIS, A. H., ABBOTT, P. C. and TAYLOR, L. (1977), *Grain Reserves, Emergency Relief and Food Aid*, Washington, DC: Overseas Development Council.

SASTRY, S. A. R. (1977), 'Poverty, Inequality and Development: A Study of Rural Andhra Pradesh', *Anvesak*, 7.

SASTRY, S. A. R. (1980), "Poverty: Concepts and Measurement," *Indian Journal of Economics*, 61.

SASTRY, S. A. R. and SURYANARAYANA, T. (1980), 'Optimum Diet and Poverty Lines', National Seminar on Employment, Levels of Living on Public Policy, Sardar Patel, Institute of Economics and Social Research, Ahmedabad.

SCASE, R. (1974), 'Relative Deprivation: A Comparison of English and Swedish Manual Workers', in Wedderburn (1974).

SCHOVE, D. J. (1977), 'African Droughts and the Spectrum of Time', in Dalby, Harrison Church and Bezzaz (1977).

SCHULTZ, T. W. (1960), 'Value of U.S. Farm Surpluses to Underdeveloped Countries', *Journal of Farm Economics*, 42.

SCHULTZ, T. W. (1964), *Transforming Traditional Agriculture*, New Haven: Yale University Press.

SCITOVSKY, TIBOR (1976), *The Joyless Economy*, New York: Oxford University Press.

SEAMAN, J., and HOLT, J. (1980), 'Markets and Famines in the Third World', *Disasters*, 4.

SEAMAN, J., HOLT, J., RIVERS, J. and MURLIS, J. (1973), 'An Inquiry into the Drought Situation in Upper Volta', *The Lancet*, 6 October.

SEAMAN, J., HOLT, J. and RIVERS, J. (1974), *Harerghe under Drought*, Addis Ababa, Ethiopian Relief and Rehabilitation Commission.

SEAMAN, J., HOLT, J. and RIVERS, J. (1978), 'The Effects of Drought on Human Nutrition in an Ethiopian Province', *International Journal of Epidemiology*, 7.

SEASTRAND, F., and DIWAN, R. (1975), 'Measurement and Comparison of Poverty and Inequality in the United States', presented at the Third World Econometric Congress, Toronto.

SELOWSKY, M. and TAYLOR, L. (1973), 'The Economics of Malnourished Children: An Example of Disinvestment in Human Capital', *Economic Development and Cultural Change*, 22.

SEN, A. K. (1960), *Choice of Techniques*, Oxford: Basil Blackwell (3rd edn 1968).

SEN, A. K. (1966) 'Peasants and Dualism with or without Surplus Labour'; *Journal of Political Economy*, 74.

SEN, A. K. (1967a), 'Isolation, Assurance and the Social Rate of Discount', *Quarterly Journal of Economics*, 81.

SEN, A. K. (1967b), 'Surplus Labour in India: A Critique of Schultz's Statistical Test', *Economic Journal*, 77.

SEN, A. K. (1970), *Collective Choice and Social Welfare*, Edinburgh: Oliver and Boyd; reprinted by North-Holland, Amsterdam.

SEN, A. K. (1973a), *On Economic Inequality*, Oxford: Clarendon Press.

SEN, A. K. (1973b), 'Poverty, Inequality and Unemployment: Some Conceptual Issues in Measurement', *Economic and Political Weekly*, 8, Special Number.

SEN, A. K. (1974), 'Informational Bases of Alternative Welfare

Approaches: Aggregation and Income Distribution', *Journal of Public Economics*, 4.

SEN, A. K. (1975), *Employment, Technology and Development*, Oxford: Clarendon Press.

SEN, A. K. (1976a), 'Poverty: An Ordinal Approach to Measurement', *Econometrica*, 44.

SEN, A. K. (1976b), 'Real National Income', *Review of Economic Studies*, 43.

SEN, A. K. (1976c), 'Famines as Failures of Exchange Entitlements', *Economic and Political Weekly*, 11, Special Number.

SEN, A. K. (1976d), *Poverty and Economic Development*, Second Vikram Sarabhai Memorial Lecture, Ahmedabad, Vikram A. Sarabhai AMA Memorial Trust.

SEN, A. K. (1977a), 'Social Choice Theory: A Re-examination', *Econometrica*, 45.

SEN, A. K. (1977b), 'Starvation and Exchange Entitlements: A General Approach and Its Application to the Great Bengal Famine', *Cambridge Journal of Economics*, 1.

SEN, A. K. (1977c), 'On Weights and Measures: Informational Constraints in Social Welfare Analysis', *Econometrica*, 45.

SEN, A. K. (1978a), 'On the Labour Theory of Value: Some Methodological Issues', *Cambridge Journal of Economics*, 2.

SEN, A. K. (1978b), 'Ethical Measurement of Inequality: Some Difficulties', in Krelle and Shorrocks (1978).

SEN, A. K. (1979a), 'The Welfare Basis of Real Income Comparisons: A Survey', *Journal of Economic Literature*, 17.

SEN, A. K. (1979b), 'Issues in the Measurement of Poverty', *Scandinavian Journal of Economics*, 81.

SEN, A. K. (1980a), 'Description as Choice', *Oxford Economic Papers*, 32.

SEN, A. K. (1980b), 'Famine Mortality: A study of the Bengal Famine of 1943', in Hobsbawm *et al.* (1980).

SEN, A. K. (1980c), 'Famines', *World Development*, 8.

SEN, A. K. (1980d), 'Economic Development: Objectives and Obstacles', in R. F. Dernberger, ed., *China's Development Experience in Comparative Perspective*, Cambridge, Mass.: Harvard University Press.

SEN, A. K. (1981), 'Ingredients of Famine Analysis: Availability and Entitlements', *Quarterly Journal of Economics*, 95.

SEN, S. R. (1971), *Growth and Instability in Indian Agriculture*, Calcutta: Firma K. L. Mukhopadhyay.

SEN, SUNIL (1979), *Agrarian Relations in India 1793–1947*, New Delhi: People's Publishing House.

SHANIN, T. (1972), *The Awkward Class*, Oxford: Clarendon Press.

SHEAR, D. and STACY, R. (1976), 'Can the Sahel Survive? Prospects for Long-term Planning and Development', in Glantz (1976).

SHEARS, P. (1976), 'Drought in South-Eastern Ethiopia', in Hussein (1976).

SHEETS, H. and MORRIS, R. (1976), 'Disaster in the Desert', in Glantz (1976).

SHEPHERD, J. (1975), *The Politics of Starvation*, New York: Carnegie Endowment for International Peace.

SHUKLA, ROHIT (1977), 'Employment Behaviour in Labour Surplus Economy in a Famine Situation: A Study of Gujarat', *Anvesak*, 7.

SHUKLA, ROHIT (1979), *Public Works Policy during Droughts and Famines and Its Lessons for an Employment Policy*, Ahmedabad: Sardar Patel Institute of Economic and Social Research.

SINGER, H., and ANSARI, J. (1977), *Rich and Poor Countries*, London: Allen and Unwin.

SINGH, A. (1965), *Sectional Price Movements in India*, Benares: Benares Hindu University.

SINGH, AJIT (1978), 'The "Basic Needs" Approach to Development vs. the New International Economic Order: The Significance of Third World Industrialization', mimeographed, Department of Applied Economics, Cambridge University.

SINGH, INDERJIT (1979), 'Small Farmers and the Landless in South Asia', World Bank Staff Working Paper no. 320.

SINGH, K. SURESH (1975), *The Indian Famine 1967: A Study in Crisis and Change*, New Delhi: People's Publishing House.

SINHA, RADHA (1976a), *Food and Poverty: The Political Economy of Confrontation*, London: Croom Helm.

SINHA, RADHA (1976b), 'The World Food Security', *Journal of Agricultural Economics*, 26.

SINHA, RADHA (1977), 'The World Food Problem: Consensus and Conflict', *World Development*, 5.

SINHA, R., and GORDON DRABEK, A. (1978), *The World Food Problem: Consensus and Conflict*, Oxford: Pergamon.

SINHA, R., PEARSON, P., KADEKODI, G. and GREGORY, M. (1979), *Income Distribution, Growth and Basic Needs in India*, London: Croom Helm.

SMITH, ADAM (1776), *An Inquiry into the Nature and Causes of the Wealth of Nations*.

SOBHAN, REHMAN (1979), 'Politics of Food and Famine in Bangladesh', *Economic and Political Weekly*, 14.

SRINIVASAN, T. N. (1977a), 'Poverty: Some Measurement Problems', in *Conference Proceedings*, 41st Seminar of the International Statistical Institute, held at New Delhi.

SRINIVASAN, T. N. (1977b), 'Development, Poverty and Basic Human Needs: Some Issues', *Food Research Institute Studies*, 16.

SRINIVASAN, T. N. (1979), 'Malnutrition: Some Measurement and Policy Issues', mimeographed, World Bank, Washington, D.C.

SRINIVASAN, T. N. and BARDHAN, P. K. (1974), *Poverty and Income Distribution in India*, Calcutta: Statistical Publishing Society.

SRIVASTAVA, H. S. (1968), *The History of Indian Famines 1858–1918*, Agra: Sri Ram Mehra.

STEIN, Z., SUSSER, M., SAENGER, G. and MAROLLA, F. (1975), *Famine and Human Development: The Dutch Hunger Winter of 1944–1945*, London: Oxford University Press.

STEPHENS, I. (1966), *Monsoon Morning*, London: Ernest Benn.

STEPHENS, I. (1977), *Unmade Journey*, London: Stacey International.

STEWART, F. and STREETEN, P. (1976), 'New Strategies for Development: Poverty, Income Distribution and Growth', *Oxford Economic Papers*, 28.

STIGLER, G. J. (1945), 'The Cost of Subsistence', *Journal of Farm Economics*, 27.

STIGLITZ, J. E. (1974), 'Incentives and Risk Sharing in Share Cropping', *Review of Economic Studies*, 41.

STONE, R. (1970), *Mathematical Models of the Economy and Other Essays*, London: Chapman and Hall.

STONE, R., and PETERSON, W. (eds) (1978), *Econometric Contributions to Public Policy*, New York: Macmillan.

STREETEN, PAUL (1972), *The Frontiers of Development Studies*, London: Macmillan.

STREETEN, PAUL (1977), 'The Constructive Features of a Basic Needs Approach to Development', mimeographed, World Bank, Washington, DC.

STREETEN, P. and BURKI, S. J. (1978), 'Basic Needs: Some Issues', *World Development*, 6.

SUKHATME, P. V. (1977), *Nutrition and Poverty*, New Delhi: Indian Agricultural Research Institute.

SUKHATME, P. V. (1978), 'Assessment of Adequacy of Diets at Different Income Levels', *Economic and Political Weekly*, 13, Special Number.

SUMMERS, R. S. (1978), 'Two Types of Substantive Reasons: The Core of a Theory of Common-Law Justification', *Cornell Law Review*, 63.

SVEDBERG, PETER (1978), 'World Food Sufficiency and Meat Consumption', *American Journal of Agricultural Economics*, 60.

SVEDBERG, PETER (1979), 'The Price Disincentive Effect of Food Aid Revisited: A Comment', *Economic Development and Cultural Change*, 28.

SUBRAMANIAN, V. (1975), *Parched Earth: The Maharashtra Drought 1970–73*, New Delhi: Orient Longmans.

SWIFT, J. (1977a), 'Sahelian Pastoralists—Underdevelopment, Desertification, and Famine', *Annual Review of Anthropology*, 6.

SWIFT, J. (1977b), 'Desertification and Man in the Sahel', in O'Keefe and Wisner (1977).

SZAL, R. J. (1977), 'Poverty: Measurement and Analysis', ILO Working Paper, WEP 2–23/WP60.

TADESSE, K. (1976), 'Health Problems Resulting from Famine', in Hussein (1976).

TAKAYAMA, N. (1979), 'Poverty, Income Inequality and Their Measures: Professor Sen's Approach Reconsidered', *Econometrica*, 47.

TAYLOR, LANCE (1975), 'The Misconstrued Crisis: Lester Brown and World Food', *World Development*, 3.

TAYLOR, LANCE (1977), 'Research Directions in Income Distribution, Nutrition, and the Economics of Food', *Food Research Institute Studies*, 16.

TAYLOR, L. and SARRIS, A. (1976), 'Cereal Stocks, Food Aid and Food Security for the Poor', *World Development*, 4.

THEIL, H. (1967), *Economics and Information Theory*, Amsterdam: North-Holland.

THEIL, H. (1976), *Theory and Measurement of Consumer Demand*, 2 vols., Amsterdam: North-Holland, volume I (1975), and volume II (1976).

THOM, R. (1975), *Structural Stability and Morphogenesis: An Outline of a General Theory of Models*, Reading: Benjamin.

THON, D. (1979), 'On Measuring Poverty', *Review of Income and Wealth*, 25.

THON, D. (1980), "A Contribution to the Axiomatic Approach to the Measurement of Income Inequality and Poverty", Ph.D. thesis, Toronto University.

TOUPET, C. (1977), 'La Grande Sécheresse en Mauritanie', in Dalby, Harrison Church and Bezzaz (1977).

TOWNSEND, PETER (1954), 'The Meaning of Poverty', *British Journal of Sociology*, 5.

TOWNSEND, PETER (1971), *The Concept of Poverty*, London: Heinemann.

TOWNSEND, PETER (1974), 'Poverty as Relative Deprivation: Resources and Styles of Living', in Wedderburn (1974).

TOWNSEND, PETER (1979), *Poverty in the United Kingdom*, Harmondsworth: Penguin.

TUDGE, COLIN (1977), *The Famine Business*, London: Faber and Faber.

TYDINGS, J. D. (1970), *Born to Starve*, New York: William Morrow.

UNRISD (1975), 'Famine Risk in the Modern World', mimeographed, United Nations, Geneva.

UNRISD (1976), 'Famine Risk and Famine Prevention in the Modern World: Studies in Food Systems under Conditions of Recurrent Scarcity', mimeographed, United Nations, Geneva.

US President's Commission on Income Maintenance (1969), *Poverty amid Plenty*, Washington, DC: US Government Printing Office.

VAIDYANATHAN, A. (1974), 'Some Aspects of Inequalities of Living Standards in Rural India', in Srinivasan and Bardhan (1974).

VENKATARAMANI, M. S. (1973), *Bengal Famine of 1943: The American Response*, Delhi: Vikas.

WAGSTAFF, HOWARD (1976), *World Food: A Political Task*, London: Fabian Society.

WALFORD, C. (1878), 'On the Famines of the World: Past and Present', *Journal of Statistical Society*, 41.

WALLACE, R. (1900), *Lectures on Famines in India*, Edinburgh.

WAVELL, ARCHIBALD, 1st Earl (1973), *The Viceroy's Journal*, ed. P. Moon, Oxford: University Press.

WECKSTEIN, R. S. (1977), 'Food Security: Storage vs. Exchange', *World Development*, 5.

WEDDERBURN, DOROTHY (ed.) (1974), *Poverty, Inequality and Class Structure*, Cambridge: University Press.

WEDDERBURN, D. and CRAIG, C. (1974), 'Relative Deprivation in Work', in Wedderburn (1974).

WEISBROD, B. A. (ed.) (1965), *The Economics of Poverty*, Englewood Cliffs, NJ: Prentice-Hall.

WIDSTRAND, C. G. (1975), 'The Rationale of the Nomad Economy', *Ambio*, 1.

WILES, P. (1974), *Distribution of Income: East and West*, Amsterdam: North-Holland.

WILKINSON, R. G. (1973), *Poverty and Progress*, London: Methuen.

WINSTANLEY, D. (1976), 'Climatic Changes and the Future of the Sahel', in Glantz (1976).

WISEBERG, L. (1976), 'An International Perspective on the African Famines', in Glantz (1976).

WOOD, A. P. (1976), 'Farmers' Responses to Drought in Ethiopia', in Hussein (1976).

WOOD, G. D. (1976), 'Class Differentiation and Power in Bangladesh', in Huq (1976).

WOODHAM-SMITH, CECIL (1962), *The Great Hunger: Ireland 1845–9* London: Hamish Hamilton (republished in new edition, London New English Library, 1975).

World Bank (1975), *Ethiopia—Grain Storage and Marketing*, Washington DC: World Bank.

World Bank (1980), *The World Development Report 1980*, Washington, DC: World Bank.

WRIGLEY, E. A. (1969), *Population and History,* London: Weidenfeld and Nicolson.

YITZHAKI, S. (1979), 'Relative Deprivation: A New Approach to the Social Welfare Function', *Quarterly Journal of Economics*, 93.

ZEEMAN, E. C. (1977), *Catastrophe Theory: Selected Papers 1972–77*, Reading, Mass.: Addison-Wesley.

ZEWDE, B. (1976), 'A Historical Outline of Famine in Ethiopia', in Hussein (1976).

ZIA BARANI (1291), *Tarikh-i-Firozshāhī*, Delhi.

Subject Index

Name index*

*The index refers also to the bibliography which includes—*inter alia*—contributions relevant to this work but not specifically cited in the text.

Hunger and Public Action

WIDER

Studies in Development Economics embody the output of the research programmes of the World Institute for Development Economics Research (WIDER), which was established by the United Nations University as its first research and training centre in 1984 and started work in Helsinki in 1985. The principal purpose of the Institute is to help identify and meet the need for policy-oriented socio-economic research on pressing global and development problems, as well as common domestic problems and their inter-relationships.

FOREWORD

No social or economic problem facing the world today is more urgent than that of hunger. While this distressing state of affairs is not new, its persistence in spite of the remarkable technological and productive advances of the twentieth century is nothing short of scandalous.

The subject of world hunger therefore has the highest priority in WIDER's research programme. Since its creation in 1985, WIDER has consistently sought to promote research on contemporary development problems with a practical orientation. The focus of this book by Jean Drèze and Amartya Sen, one of the first fruits of this effort, is on action—action to banish both the threat of famine and the reality of chronic hunger affecting many parts of the world.

There is no instant remedy to the scourge of persistent world hunger. The impulse to rush ahead and do something practical to relieve suffering is laudable and necessary. But good motives do not by themselves guarantee effective action. While the task of eradicating hunger in the world is too serious to be left entirely to politicians and too immediate to be left entirely to academics, it is also too complex to be left entirely to the compassionate instincts of human-kind. Action has to be based on clear thinking as well as on firm dedication.

This book, I believe, represents an important step towards a better under-standing of the issues involved. There is, for instance, much to learn from its appraisal of the possible roles that can be respectively played by government intervention, market mechanisms and the activism of the public at large in encountering the problem of world hunger. As the authors show, the import-ance of these influences is well illustrated in a number of recent experiences of famine prevention. The response of the market to the demands generated by income support programmes, the involvement of the state in food distribution to prevent collusive practices on the part of private traders, and the impact of public pressure on the timing and nature of government action, can all be crucial ingredients of an effective programme of famine prevention. Similarly, in their analysis of strategies to deal with chronic hunger and deprivation, the authors stress the interlinked contributions which participative economic growth and direct public support can make to the improvement of living conditions in poor countries.

Besides clearer thinking, it is my hope that Drèze and Sen's work will lead to greater awareness and motivation, particularly by bringing out the social and political ramifications of the problem of world hunger. As the authors argue, to confront this problem involves not only being alive to opportunities for cooperative action but also addressing the multiple conflicts (e.g. of class and gender) that pervade social living.

The subject of hunger and poverty continues to occupy a major place in WIDER's research programme. This book will be followed shortly by three volumes of papers, written by international experts (and edited by Drèze and Sen), on 'the political economy of hunger'.

As the Director of WIDER, I am happy to be able to present this book as one of the first results of our programme of 'research for action'.

Lal Jayawardena
Director, WIDER
31 July 1989

PREFACE

This is a book about hunger. Not just about the extent of it, or about the havoc it causes—debilitating and killing people, enfeebling and devastating societies. While there are important issues of assessment and evaluation in this grisly field (and we do address many of these questions in this study), nevertheless the primary focus of the book is on action, rather than on measurement.

By public action we mean not merely the activities of the state, but also social actions taken by members of the public—both 'collaborative' (through civic cooperation) and 'adversarial' (through social criticism and political opposition). The state does, of course, have a major role to play in eradicating famines and in eliminating persistent deprivation, and the various aspects of this role we have tried to discuss fairly extensively in the light of general reasoning and empirical evidence. But the reach of public action goes well beyond the doings of the state, and involves what is done *by* the public—not merely *for* the public. We also argue that the nature and effectiveness of the activities of the state can deteriorate very easily in the absence of public vigilance and activism.

In the first four chapters, constituting Part I of the book, we have presented some general analyses of the economic, social, political and medical background to the problems of starvation and undernutrition in the contemporary world. Chapters 5 to 8, constituting Part II of the book, are concerned with analysing the major strategic and tactical issues in famine prevention. The diverse problems of persistent undernutrition and endemic deprivation are examined in Part III (Chapters 9 to 12).

In the fourth and final part, consisting only of one chapter (Chapter 13), the diverse roles of public action in removing hunger are considered together, with specific comments on some of the more debatable issues. It is not meant as a 'summary' of the main points of the book, but there is an attempt to provide an overall view of the general approach we have adopted and used. We have particularly highlighted the features of our approach that may appear to be controversial. We have tried to take full note of other points of view. But a practical treatise on the role of public action has to be, ultimately, rather assertive, and it is fair to say that we have not been afflicted by excessive shyness regarding what we recommend and why.

On stylistic issues, we should make two brief comments. First, we have tried to make the discussion as non-technical and accessible as possible. On occasion we have had to settle for formulations that are somewhat less rigorous than would have been possible had we chosen a different—more formal—style.

Second, the issue of gender is of special significance in our study, and it is perhaps particularly important for us to avoid the implicit 'sexism' of the standard language (e.g., referring to women as well as men generally as 'he'). On the other hand, the practice of 'inverting' the usage (e.g., by referring to all as 'she') is somewhat open to the same charge of sexism—in reverse—aside from looking rather self-consciously contrary. Also, the compound expression 'he or she', while fine in many cases, is a bit of a mouthful if used everywhere. The appropriate non-sexist practice may be to de-escalate the issue, and in particular to use 'he', 'she' and 'he or she' entirely interchangeably. That, at any rate, is what we have done.

This study is an outgrowth of our work for the project on 'Hunger and Poverty' of the World Institute for Development Economics Research (WIDER). At every stage of our research and the writing of this book, we have received good advice, encouragement and help from Lal Jayawardena, the Director of WIDER. Others too, at WIDER, have given us all the help we could have asked for. We are most grateful for that.

A part of WIDER's research in the area of 'Hunger and Poverty' is currently in the press in the form of a three-volume book, edited by us, entitled *The Political Economy of Hunger*, to be published by Clarendon Press, Oxford. The first versions of most of these papers were written during 1985–6 and were presented at a conference on 'food strategies' in July 1986. The papers have been extensively revised since, and some new papers have been added. Aside from us, the contributors to these volumes are: Sudhir Anand, Kaushik Basu, Partha Dasgupta, Meghnad Desai, Christopher Harris, Barbara Harriss, Judith Heyer, Francis Idachaba, Ravi Kanbur, Gopu Kumar, Siddiq Osmani, Kirit Parikh, Jean-Philippe Platteau, N. Ram, Martin Ravallion, Debraj Ray, Carl Riskin, Ignacy Sachs, Rehman Sobhan, Peter Svedberg, Samuel Wangwe, and Ann Whitehead. We have greatly benefited from their collaboration.

While undertaking the research, we had the efficient assistance of Robin Burgess, Peter Lanjouw, Shailendra Mehta, Shantanu Mitra, Sanjay Reddy, Sangeeta Sethi and Madhura Swaminathan, and we are most grateful to them. We are greatly in debt to Jacky Jennings who has looked after the secretarial and administrative side of the entire project with outstanding skill. We have also been very fortunate in having the superb assistance of Anna-Marie Svedrofsky.

We have benefited much from communications and discussions with several voluntary organizations, including OXFAM, Save the Children Fund, and Shramjivi Samaj, among others. In the course of our analysis we have had to be, at times, somewhat critical of particular aspects of the work of voluntary agencies, but we have in general nothing but admiration for their contributions, within their chosen spheres of action. As a small token of appreciation, the royalties from this book will go to these agencies.

We have profited greatly from suggestions and criticisms made by those who have taken an interest in this study. For detailed and enormously helpful comments on earlier drafts and notes, we are extremely grateful to Sudhir Anand, Philippe Autier, Robin Burgess, Lincoln Chen, Marty Chen, Stephen Coate, Monica Das Gupta, Mrinal Datta Chaudhuri, Meghnad Desai, Carl Eicher, Susan George, Keith Griffin, Judith Heyer, Allan Hill, Roger Hay, Athar Hussain, Nurul Islam, Jong-il You, Robert Kates, Jocelyn Kynch, Michael Lipton, John Mellor, Siddiq Osmani, Dwight Perkins, V. K. Ramachandran, Martin Ravallion, Shlomo Reutlinger, Carl Riskin, Frances Stewart, John Shaw, Paul Streeten, Per Pinstrup-Andersen, and Joachim von Braun.

We have also received very useful counsel and suggestions on general analyses and on case-studies from Brian Abel-Smith, Frédérique Apffel-Marglin, Harold Alderman, Alice Amsden, José Pablo Arellano, Surjit Bhalla, Bela Bhatia, Lars-Erik Birgegard, John Borton, L. Burgess, Diana Callear, David Campbell, Monique Chastanet, Robert Chambers, Robert Collins, Jane Corbett, George Cumper, Partha Dasgupta, Rob Davies, Angus Deaton, Stephen Devereux, Thomas Downing, Tim Dyson, Ricardo Ffrench-Davis, John Field, Alvaro Garcia, Catherine Gibb, Nancy Godfrey, Hugh Goyder, Jim Gordon, T. F. Grannell, Peter Greaves, S. Guhan, Charles Harvey, Akiko Hashimoto, Cynthia Hewitt de Alcántara, Abraham Horwitz, Solomon Inquai, Richard Jolly, Nanak Kakwani, David Keen, Qaisar Khan, Byung Whan Kim, Arthur Kleinman, Jane Knight, Gopu Kumar, Keon Lee, François-Regis Mahieu, Stephen Marglin, Robert McAdam, Wendy McLean, Carmelo Mesa-Lago, S. T. Mhiribidi, Siddharta Mitter, Richard Morgan, Jon Moris, Christopher Murray, Philip Payne, Pauline Peters, Jean-Philippe Platteau, Samuel Preston, Dagmar Raczynski, Sanjay Reddy, Norman Reynolds, Lenin Saenz, David Sanders, Chris Scott, John Seaman, Sunil Sengupta, Hans Singer, K. Subbarao, Luc Spyckerelle, Nicholas Stern, Jeremy Swift, J. Tagwireyi, William Torry, R. van der Hoeven, Megan Vaughan, Tony Vaux, Isabel Vial, Peter Walker, Daniel Weiner, Helen Young, and Richard Zeckhauser.

It may seem somewhat incredible that two people can have reasons to be grateful to such a large number of commentators ('never', to alter Churchill, 'has so much been owed by so few to so many'). But this has been an exacting work and we have tried to consider and take note of as much criticism as we could manage to secure. If the work is still very imperfect, it is not for the lack of good advice.

Helsinki J.D.
25 July 1989 A.S.

CONTENTS

Part IV
Hunger and Public Action

LIST OF FIGURES

LIST OF TABLES

PART I

Hunger in the Modern World

1

Introduction

1.1 Past and Present

Hunger is not a new affliction. Recurrent famines as well as endemic under-nourishment have been persistent features of history. Life has been short and hard in much of the world, most of the time. Deprivation of food and other necessities of living has consistently been among the causal antecedents of the brutishness and brevity of human life.

Megasthenes, the envoy of Seleukos Nikator to the court of the Indian emperor Chandragupta Maurya in the fourth century BC, wrote—perhaps to impress his gullible Greek readers—that famine was completely unknown in Maurya India.[1] But Kautilya, the Indian political economist, who was an official adviser to Chandragupta, wrote extensively on how to deal with famines (on which more presently).[2] Ancient chronicles not only in India, but also in Egypt, Western Asia, China, Greece, Rome, North-east Africa, and elsewhere tell us about famines that ravaged ancient civilizations in different parts of the world.[3] Even when literary accounts are scarce or do not exist, archaeological data and other historical evidence tell stories of sudden depopulation and frantic migration, in addition to providing information concerning nutritional debilitation and significant stunting.[4] Hunger is not a modern malady.

Hunger is, however, intolerable in the modern world in a way it could not have been in the past. This is not so much because it is more intense, but because widespread hunger is so unnecessary and unwarranted in the modern world. The enormous expansion of productive power that has taken place over the last few centuries has made it, perhaps for the first time, possible to guarantee adequate food for all, and it is in this context that the persistence of

[1] See the translation by McCrindle (1877: 32). See also Dutt (1900, 1904).

[2] See Kautilya's *Arthaśāstra*, especially the 4th Book, particularly the section on 'Remedies against National Calamities'. There are various translations, e.g. Shama Sastry (1967).

[3] For interesting accounts of the history of famines in different parts of the world, see Walford (1878), Wright (1882), Dutt (1900, 1901), Loveday (1914), Mallory (1926), Ghosh (1944), Swann (1950), Cépède and Lengellé (1953), Pankhurst (1961), Masefield (1963), Bhatia (1967), Aykroyd (1974), Hussein (1976), Iliffe (1987), Alamgir (1980), Dando (1980), Will (1980), Cahill (1982), McAlpin (1983a), Rotberg and Rabb (1983), Bose (1987), Vaughan (1987), D'Souza (1988), Garnsey (1988), Newman *et al.* (forthcoming), among others. See also the bibliographies provided by Currey, Ali and Kohman (1981) and Golkin (1987).

[4] Old burial remains often provide tell-tale evidence of chronic stunting. The size of clothing, equipment, etc. also provides indirect data. It is not only that, say, the Roman soldiers and heroes, judging by such evidence, were astonishingly short (especially compared with Charlton Heston), but also that cases of clinically recognizable stunting are quite frequent. There is, of course, an interpretational issue as to whether stunting typically implies any significant impairment of human ability to function. This question and related nutritional disputes are taken up in Chapter 3.

chronic hunger and the recurrence of virulent famines must be seen as being morally outrageous and politically unacceptable. If politics is 'the art of the possible', then conquering world hunger has become a political issue in a way it could not have been in the past.

Aside from this political and ethical issue distinguishing modern hunger from past hunger, there are also a number of other important contrasts.

First, for a substantial part of humanity, the health problems connected with food consumption have ceased being the result of having too little and stem instead from having too much. While one part of humanity desperately searches for more food to eat, another part counts the calories and looks for new ways of slimming. Inequalities in the distribution of food are not a new phenomenon by any means, but while in the past affluence may have been confined to a small section of society, in the modern world the bulk of the population in many countries is now in the affluent category as far as food is concerned.

It is, of course, true that substantial pockets of hunger do survive in Europe and North America, and certainly call for serious attention in public policy.[5] We shall have some things to say on that problem of resilient undernourishment. But the fact that the *typical* person in Europe or North America tries to reduce—rather than increase—calorie intake makes the persistence of widespread nutritional deficiency and hunger in the rest of the world a particularly contrary phenomenon. This adds to the force of seeing world hunger as an international political issue in a way it has never been in the past.

Second, the persistence of hunger in many countries in the contemporary world is related not merely to a general lack of affluence, but also to substantial —often extreme—inequalities within the society. The issue of inequality in the genesis of hunger and famines is not in itself new. In his famous treatise on politics, diplomacy, and political economy called *Arthaśāstra* (roughly translated as 'instructions on material prosperity'), Kautilya, the ancient Indian political theorist and economist to whom we have already referred, included among his famine relief policies the possibility of raiding the provisions of the rich. In fact, he wrote with some eloquence on 'the policy of thinning the rich by exacting excess revenue [*karśanam*], or causing them to vomit their accumulated wealth [*vamanam*]'.[6]

The general issue of inequality has always been important in famine analysis. But with the development of modern economic relations and of extensive interdependences even between distant parts of the economy, there are many new ways in which different sections of the population can see their economic position and their command φver food shift violently and suddenly. For example, aside from the more traditional 'slump famines', in which starvation develops along with a general economic decline (e.g. a crop failure leading to

---

[5] See e.g. the reports on hunger in the United States produced by the Harvard School of Public Health (1985, 1987).

[6] *Arthaśāstra*, 4th Book. In the translation by Shama Sastry (1967), see pp. 237–8.

impoverishment), famines can and have taken place in recent years even in boom situations. In a 'boom famine', many occupation groups may improve their economic position substantially, thereby commanding a bigger share of the available food, which can lead to a decline—even an absolute decline—of food command on the part of those less favourably placed in the uneven expansion of money incomes. For instance, the Bengal famine of 1943 (in which, it is estimated, 3 million people died) had many characteristics of being such a 'boom famine'.[7]

Third, the dependence of one group's ability to command food on its relative position and comparative economic power *vis-à-vis* other groups can be especially important in a market economy. The institution of markets is, of course, an old one, but the reach and role of market transactions has substantially expanded in recent times. On the one hand, this has added new economic opportunities and new ways of achieving prosperity through specialization and exchange, and the development of extensive markets has been a major force behind the enhancement of the wealth of nations, as Adam Smith rightly foresaw.[8] But, on the other hand, the expansion of markets has also added a new source of vulnerability for some groups. For example, pastoralist nomads can be reduced to starvation if the relative price of animal products falls in relation to that of staple food, since their subsistence depends on their ability to sell animals and animal products (including meat) to buy enough calories from *cheaper* food materials such as grain. Similarly, fishermen may go hungry if the price of fish fails to keep up with that of, say, rice.[9]

Fourth, the importance of the institution of wage labour is a particular aspect of this general problem. People who possess no means of production excepting their own labour power, which they try to sell for a wage in order to earn an adequate income to buy enough food, are particularly vulnerable to changes in labour market conditions. A decline in wages *vis-à-vis* food prices, or an increase in unemployment, can spell disaster for this class. While hiring labour has existed for a long time, its relative importance—especially in the form of wage labour—has dramatically increased with the spread of capitalism, even in developing countries. The class of landless wage labourers has indeed recurrently produced famine victims in modern times. For example, in

[7] On this see Sen (1977a, 1981a). See also Alamgir (1980) and Greenough (1982). Ravallion (1987a) provides an extensive and far-reaching analysis of the general economic relationships between markets and famines.

[8] Smith (1776). Smith was, however, fully aware—in a way some of his followers evidently were not—that the market may also help to spread deprivation and famines, e.g. through employment loss in a general economic crisis. Smith's analysis of famines is discussed in Sen (1986a).

[9] Of course, meat and fish are both food themselves, but the poor pastoralist or fisherman often survives by selling these 'luxury' foods and buying cheaper calories; the meat and the fish themselves may not provide enough calories to the population dependent on herding animals or catching fish for the market. On this see Sen (1981a: chapters 6–8), and Desai (1988a). See also Hay (1975), Rivers *et al.* (1976), and Seaman, Holt and Rivers (1978) on the relative costs of animal calories and grain calories and the conditions of exchange faced by Ethiopian pastoralists. On the equilibrium of pastoral survival, including exchange, see Swift (1982), McCann (1987) and Horowitz and Little (1987), among others.

the Indian subcontinent, the majority of famine victims in this century and the last has come from this group.[10]

The acute vulnerability of wage labourers in a market economy is a problem which applies, in fact, also to the richer countries (including those of Western Europe and North America), since even there wage labourers have little ability to survive on their own when unemployment develops as dramatically as it did, say, in the early 1980s. People in this predicament have been spared the necessity of starvation because of the supplementation of the market mechanism by institutionalized social security, and in particular by unemployment insurance, in the absence of which there would have been, it is easy to see, acute and widespread hunger in many of these countries.

The importance of the vulnerability of wage labourers to famines can be particularly acute in that *intermediate* phase in which the class of wage labourers has become large (unlike in precapitalist formations), but a system of social security has not yet developed (unlike in the more advanced economies). This is not to say that traditional means of social security in pre-wage economies are typically adequate. Indeed, as we shall see later, they are often altogether insufficient and meagre. But the wage system has added a particular source of vulnerability which has to be specifically addressed.

Fifth, recent times have witnessed not only a rapid expansion of market exchange, but also significant developments in the conditions of 'exchange with nature', i.e. production. On the one hand, advances in agricultural technology have increased the potential for improving living conditions in rural areas. On the other hand, in many countries environmental degradation (in the form of deforestation, desertification, etc.) poses a grave threat to the livelihood of the rural population. While these processes are, once again, not new, their pace and reach are often greater than ever. So is the scope for public action to influence and reshape them.

Sixth, the state has an important role to play in combating world hunger, and in this book we shall, in fact, go into many of the policy issues that are involved in playing this role effectively. At the same time, it would be a mistake to overlook the fact that many famines in the world have actually arisen from and been sustained by inflexible government policies undermining the power of particular sections of the population to command food. The Soviet famines of the 1930s and the Kampuchean famines of the late 1970s are obvious examples of systematic undermining of the economic power of a large part of the population through state policy. It is easy to cite other terrible cases in which political dogma and the use of authoritarian political power have led to disastrous government policies, making it impossible for millions of people to earn a living.

In a sense this feature is not really new, since kings and rulers in the past have also often imposed extraordinary sacrifices on sections of the population, not

---

[10] See Drèze (1988*a*).

least due to invasions and wars. But with the growth of modern politics, the importance of ideology has grown dramatically. That can, of course, be a creative force in providing political commitment for combating world hunger, and we shall have quite a bit to say on the positive role of determined state policy. But ideological state action can also include dogmatic pursuit of policies that force large sections of the population into penury and deprivation. Strongly ideological politics has become—both positively and negatively—an inescapable part of the economics of food and starvation, and this too is a feature that has to be kept in view in analysing the challenge of hunger in the modern world.

There are many other, subtler differences between hunger in the past and that in the modern world. Hunger is a common predicament, but this does not indicate the existence of one shared cause. People can fail in their ability to command food and other necessities in many different ways, and the genesis of these failures can vary greatly with the nature of the economy and the society. In this book we must pay particular attention to the special features of hunger in the modern world, in addition to investigating more traditional aspects of poverty and starvation.

1.2 Famine and Chronic Undernourishment

There are many different ways of seeing hunger. The dictionary meaning of the term, e.g. 'discomfort or painful sensation caused by want of food', takes us in a particular and extremely narrow direction. In the demand for 'ending hunger' the concern is not merely with making it possible to avoid that discomfort or pain (even though the suffering involved is often underestimated by people who have never really experienced this pain), but also to conquer food deprivation in general—seen in terms of its manifold consequences. These consequences include undernourishment, debilitation, fatigue, morbidity, and possibly mortality, with obvious effects on human well-being and productivity.

In trying to come to grips with the problem of hunger in the modern world, it is necessary to get a clear understanding of the different issues that constitute it. The distinction between the problem of chronic hunger (involving sustained nutritional deprivation on a persistent basis) and that of famine (involving acute starvation and a sharp increase of mortality) is particularly important. In this book we shall encounter several important contrasts in the strategic choices that arise in facing these respective problems. To take one example, in the context of famine prevention the crucial need for speedy intervention and the scarcity of resources often call for a calculated reliance on existing distributional mechanisms (e.g. the operation of private trade stimulated by cash support to famine victims) to supplement the logistic capability of relief agencies. In the context of combating chronic hunger, on the other hand, there is much greater scope for slower but none the less powerful avenues of action such as institution building, legal reforms, asset redistribution, or provisioning in kind.

The importance of the contrast between chronic hunger and acute starvation is also reflected in the experiences of different countries. There are countries in which famines in the form of acute starvation leading to large-scale mortality have not taken place in recent years, but where chronic hunger is quite widespread. An example is India since its independence in 1947. The last major famine in India took place before independence, viz. the Bengal famine of 1943, in which about 3 million people died. Since then there have been a number of threats of severe famine (e.g. in Bihar in 1967, in Maharashtra in 1973, in West Bengal in 1979, in Gujarat in 1987), but they did not materialize, largely due to public intervention. There is, however, a great deal of regular hunger and endemic undernourishment in India, especially in rural areas. The frequency of undernutrition-related diseases also remains distressingly high.[11]

On the other hand, it is possible for a country to deal effectively with chronic hunger as an endemic feature, and at the same time to fall prey to substantial famine as a transient phenomenon. That seems to have been the experience of China, in which the problem of regular hunger has been tackled with much success—considerably more effectively than in India—but where a famine on a gigantic scale took place during 1958–61, with an excess mortality that has to be counted in terms of tens of millions.[12] The contrast between India and China is really rather striking, especially since India's success in famine prevention seems to have done little to help it combat chronic hunger, and China's remarkable achievement in improving the nutritional well-being of its people in normal times (and in expanding the longevity of the Chinese to the high sixties) has not been accompanied by an absence of famine in the post-revolutionary period. The complex economic and political causation of this contrasting pattern—and other important features of the experience of these two giant countries—will be examined later on in this volume (Chapter 11). But, for the moment, we shall leave this issue here, using it only to illustrate the importance of the distinction between chronic hunger, on the one hand, and acute starvation involved in a famine, on the other.

As a matter of fact, famine is a much more confined phenomenon in the modern world than endemic undernutrition and persistent deprivation. Most famines in recent decades have occurred in sub-Saharan Africa, with a few exceptions such as the Bangladesh famine of 1974 and the Kampuchean famine of 1979–80. In sub-Saharan Africa famines have afflicted a great many countries, and we shall be paying particular attention to that region in Part II of

---

[11] See Banerji (1982), Rao (1982), Gopalan (1987b), Nutrition Foundation of India (1988), Srinivasan and Bardhan (1988), and Subbarao (1989). On the role of public intervention in preventing famines in India since independence, see Drèze (1988a).

[12] On the basis of the recently available Chinese demographic statistics, Ashton et al. (1984) estimate the number of excess deaths in that famine to be 29.5 million, while Peng's (1987) estimate is 23 million. On China's success in addressing the challenge of chronic hunger, see Riskin (1986), and also Chapter 11 below.

this volume (Chapters 5–8), concerned with analysing the causation and prevention of famines.

While famines have been rare outside Africa in recent decades, the problem of endemic hunger is serious—indeed often colossal—in many other parts of the world as well, particularly South Asia. Even in Latin America, which is very much richer in terms of GNP per head than Africa or South Asia, particular sections of the population—related to class and location—are significantly affected by the persistence of hunger (see Kanbur 1986b).

Furthermore, as we shall argue presently (Chapter 3), the problem of chronic undernutrition is closely related not only to deficiency of food intake, but also to deprivations of other kinds, particularly those of education, health care, basic facilities, and social environment (including water supply, sanitary provisions, etc.). The effects of these deficiencies can be seen in such elementary failures as low longevity and high morbidity, in addition to clinical undernutrition. While life expectancy at birth is more than 75 years in many of the prosperous countries of the world, the corresponding figure is estimated to be below 60 years in most poor countries, below 50 for a great many, and even below 40 years for some. When we address problems of endemic undernutrition and deprivation in Part III of this book (Chapters 9–12), we shall have to take a broad view of poverty and indigence, and also take note of the wide geographical coverage of rudimentary deprivation.

1.3 Some Elementary Concepts

In the analysis to be presented in this book a number of elementary concepts will be frequently used, and it may be convenient to say a few words on the underlying ideas in this introductory chapter. There is nothing particularly complex, nor anything alarmingly novel, about these concepts. But the presentation of the arguments may be helped by some initial clarification.

Entitlements

What we can eat depends on what food we are able to acquire. The mere presence of food in the economy, or in the market, does not entitle a person to consume it. In each social structure, given the prevailing legal, political, and economic arrangements, a person can establish command over some alternative commodity bundles (any one bundle of which he or she can choose to consume). These bundles could be extensive, or very limited, and what a person can consume will be directly dependent on what these bundles are. The set of alternative bundles of commodities over which a person can establish such command will be referred to as this person's 'entitlements'.[13]

---

[13] Entitlement is being defined here in terms of ownership rights. There are other types of rights of *use* that do not involve ownership as such, but which have the effect of guaranteeing use nevertheless. For a more comprehensive characterization of entitlements, see Sen (1981a). Some of these additional features will also be discussed later on in this book.

To illustrate, a peasant who grows his own food is entitled to what he has grown, adjusted for any obligations he may have (e.g. to money-lenders). He can sell, if he wants, a part of the product for cash to buy other goods and services, and all the alternative commodity bundles he can acquire through these means lie within his entitlement set. Similarly, a wage labourer's entitlement is given by what he can buy with his wages, if he does in fact manage to find employment.[14]

Endowment and Exchange

A person's entitlements depend both on what she owns initially, and what she can acquire through exchange. For example, a wage labourer owns her labour power, and by exchanging that for a wage (the exchange takes the form of employment), she acquires some money, which she can then exchange for some commodity bundle or other. Similarly, a landlord who owns some land and leases out that land for rent can use the proceeds to purchase different commodity bundles. The 'endowment' of a person is given by the initial ownership (e.g. the labourer's labour power, the landlord's holding of land), and these endowments can be used to establish entitlements in the form of holdings of alternative commodity bundles through trade (e.g. a labourer taking up employment and purchasing commodities with the wage, a landlord renting out land and purchasing commodities with the rent).

The exchange can also be with 'nature', and this is one way of seeing production, as opposed to trade. For example, a peasant farmer can exchange the use of his land and his labour power (along with a few other inputs such as seeds) for a crop. This exchange with nature in the form of production may, of course, be followed by trade in the form of selling a part (or indeed the whole) of the output and buying other commodities with the proceeds. The alternative bundles of commodities a person can acquire through exchange (i.e. production and trade) for each particular endowment are the person's 'exchange entitlement' for that level of endowment.

Extended Entitlements

While the concept of entitlement focuses on a person's *legal* rights of ownership, there are some social relations that take the broader form of accepted *legitimacy* rather than legal rights enforceable in a court. For example, if, by a well-established convention, the male head of a household receives more favourable treatment in the division of the family's total consumption (e.g. having the first claim on, say, the meat or the fish in the family's diet, or receiving greater medical attention in case of illness), that person can be seen as having a claim the legitimacy of which is accepted and is thus effective, even though it is not a claim that can be upheld in a court or enforced by the power of the state.

---

[14] The 'budget set' of elementary consumer theory is a simple example of an entitlement set.

Despite their legally weaker form, such socially sanctioned rights may be extremely important in determining the amount of food or health care or other commodities that different members of a family get, and this too will play a part in our analysis of hunger. 'Extended entitlements' is the concept of entitlements extended to include the results of more informal types of rights sanctioned by accepted notions of legitimacy. This notion is particularly relevant in analysing intrafamily divisions, but it has other uses in social analysis as well.

Cooperative Conflicts

In the social relations that *inter alia* determine the entitlements enjoyed by different people, there tends to be a coexistence of conflict *and* congruence of interests. There are, in most situations, clear advantages to be gained by different people through cooperation with each other, and yet there are also elements of conflict reflecting the partly divergent interests of the same people. 'Cooperative conflicts' refer to this coexistence of congruence and conflict of interests, providing grounds for cooperation as well as for disputes and battles.

Cooperative conflicts may be illustrated from many different fields of social relations. Consider the relation between workers and industrialists in a particular industry. If production is disrupted, both the industrialists and the workers may lose, so that it is in the interest of both to cooperate with each other in the process of production. But the division of benefits obtained from production may also involve an extensive tussle between the industrialists and the workers. It may be in the interest of the capitalists to get a larger share of the output produced, and in the interest of the workers to obtain higher wages and better working conditions and resist 'exploitation'. In the context of productive activities of other kinds, the relations between, say, a share-cropper and a landlord, or between the members of a production team, or between the different parties in a cartel, also involve obvious situations of cooperative conflict.

To take another example, it is typically in the interest of all the members of a family to cooperate in living together. But at the same time there is also the issue of *intra*family division, and it may be in the interest of, say, the husband to secure a higher share of benefits and a lower share of household chores *vis-à-vis* his wife. The conflicts involved in gender division may, thus, arise against a background of generally cooperative behaviour. Indeed, given the importance of cooperation in family living, the elements of conflict may be kept very well hidden, so that a serious awareness of the elements of conflict may be suppressed by the use of conventional norms. The questioning of these norms may even appear to be aberrant and deviant behaviour. The issue of perception can, thus, be a very important aspect of the problem of gender-based inequality.[15]

[15] The role of cooperative conflicts in gender relations and in intrafamily divisions, and the part played in all this by perception problems, are discussed in Sen (1985c, 1987c).

Analysing cooperative conflicts is particularly important for a better understanding of the causes and remedies of hunger. In addition to the problems involved in production relations and in intrafamily divisions, even at the more aggregative level there tends to be coexistence of a good deal of congruence and conflict of interests. For example, there may be great gains for everyone in cooperation for the preservation of the environment, for the prevention of droughts, for improving agricultural technology and infrastructure, for reducing industrial wastage, or for eliminating epidemics. And yet there may also be extensive battles between different groups for, say, a bigger share of the total food available in the economy. Sometimes even a famine may be principally associated with one group losing out in a 'food battle' of this kind.

Capability and Living Standards

In any economic analysis it is important to distinguish between the ends and the means. At the very beginning of his *Nicomachean Ethics*, Aristotle had noted, while discussing the role of economics, the need to be aware that 'wealth is evidently not the good we are seeking; for it is merely useful and for the sake of something else'.[16] Aristotle saw 'the good of human beings' in terms of the richness of 'life in the sense of activity', and thus argued for taking human functionings as the objects of value.[17]

In a similar line of reasoning, with more specific concentration on the quality of life, the object of public action can be seen to be the enhancement of the capability of people to undertake valuable and valued 'doings and beings'.[18] This can extend from such elementary capabilities as the ability to avoid undernourishment and related morbidity and mortality, to more sophisticated social capabilities such as taking part in the life of the community and achieving self-respect.

Capability is a broad concept, and it incorporates the concerns that are associated with what is often called the 'standard of living', but goes beyond it. Living standards relate specifically to the richness of the person's own life, whereas a person may value his or her capability also to be socially useful and influential (going well beyond the pursuit of his or her own living standards). The distinction between the broader notion of capability and the narrower concept of living standard can be relevant in many contexts.[19] Concern with

[16] Aristotle, *The Nicomachean Ethics*, Book I, section 5; in the translation by Ross (1980: 7).

[17] Book I, section 7; Ross (1980: 12–15). Marx followed this line of reasoning and argued for a reorientation of economic preoccupations: 'It will be seen how in place of the wealth and poverty of political economy come the rich human being and rich human need. The rich human being is simultaneously in need of a totality of human life-activities' (Marx, 1844).

[18] There are interesting and important problems in the characterization and analysis of capabilities, on which see Sen (1985a, 1985b). Formally, a person's capability is a set of functioning bundles, representing the various alternative 'beings and doings' that a person can achieve with his or her economic, social, and personal characteristics.

[19] For an analysis of this and related distinctions, see Sen (1977b, 1987a, 1987b). On related matters see Hart (1987), Hawthorn (1987), Kanbur (1987), Muellbauer (1987), B. Williams (1987), Griffin and Knight (1988, 1989).

the lives of others is clearly a crucial ingredient of public action. Without acknowledging this basic human motivation, it would be impossible to understand the part that political parties, social leaders, journalists, relief agencies and grass-roots activists can play in encountering famines and chronic deprivation. However, in the context of defining the *objectives* to be pursued in the battle against hunger, the finer distinction between capability and living standard may not be of central importance. The important thing at this stage (and in much of this book) is to note the general concern with 'doings' and 'beings' and the corresponding capabilities, rather than just with incomes or wealth or utilities.

The focus on capability helps to clarify the purpose of public action in different fields, including that of combating hunger. The object, in this view, is not so much to provide a particular amount of food for each. Indeed, the relationship between food intake and nutritional achievement can vary greatly depending not only on features such as age, sex, pregnancy, metabolic rates, climatic conditions, and activities, but also on access to complementary inputs such as health care, drinking water and so on. A more reasoned goal would be to make it possible for all to have the capability to avoid undernourishment and escape deprivations associated with hunger. The focus here is on human life as it can be led, rather than on commodities as such, which are means to human life, and are contingently related to need fulfilment rather than being valued for themselves.[20] The focus on entitlements, which is concerned with the command over *commodities*, has to be seen as only instrumentally important, and the concentration has to be, ultimately, on basic human capabilities.[21]

The implications of focusing on capabilities in the analysis of public action in combating hunger will become clearer as we go along. One particular consequence relates to the need to broaden our attention from the command over food to other influences, including the command over other commodities that have a substantial impact on nutrition and health. A person's capability to avoid undernourishment may depend not merely on his or her intake of food, but also on the person's access to health care, medical facilities, elementary education, drinking water, and sanitary facilities. Similarly, the prevalence of epidemics and disease in a particular region may also be a factor influencing the extent of undernutrition. In so far as we concentrate on entitlements, the case

---

[20] Marx (1887) discussed the problems associated with what he called 'commodity fetishism' (ch. 1). There is a good case for defining 'basic needs' in terms of capabilities as such rather than in terms of commodities, as they are usually defined. On this, see Sen (1984a), Streeten (1984), and F. Stewart (1988). See also Streeten *et al*. (1981).

[21] While the *entitlement* of a person is a set of alternative *commodity* bundles, the *capability* of a person is a set of alternative *functioning* bundles. Larger entitlements contribute to wider capabilities, but the relationship is not the same for different persons. For example, a pregnant woman has greater nutritional requirements and also special needs for medical attention, and hence having the same command over food and health care as another—non-pregnant—person may not give her the same capability to be well nourished and healthy. Public action has to be based on an adequately discriminating analysis, and this calls for causal investigations of capabilities and of variations in the relation between entitlements and capabilities.

for broadening the coverage from food as such to all the commodities relevant to nutritional capabilities and good health is strong. This has a direct and far-reaching bearing on the nature of public action for combating hunger and deprivation.

Undernourishment and Undernutrition

A capability is 'nutrition-related' if and only if it can be enhanced by greater or better food intake. Two clarifications are due. First, while many capabilities are 'nutrition-related' in this sense, some (e.g. the ability to survive) are clearly more important than others (e.g. fitness to hop, skip and jump). Our primary concern is with those nutrition-related capabilities that are crucial to human well-being. Second, while the boundaries of the concept of 'nutrition-related capability' are defined with reference to the relevance or otherwise of improved food intake, most capabilities of this kind also depend on many other factors. The importance of epidemiological protection, health care, basic education, sanitation, etc., for nutritional well-being will be one of the recurrent themes of this book.

A distinction is sometimes made—typically implicitly—between 'under-nutrition' and 'undernourishment'. The former is usually seen in terms of *a shortage of food intake*, while the latter is taken to be an *unsatisfactory state of being*. In this contrast, undernutrition is connected with *commodities* (specifi-cally food—someone having less food, or less variety of food, than some specified nutritional standard would demand), while undernourishment is connected with the state of *human beings* (specifically, a person being somehow inadequate in energy or strength or some other feature associated with nutritional sufficiency).

While there is a distinction here, it is arguable that it is not perhaps as much of a dividing line as might first appear. This is the case *if* 'undernutrition' is defined taking full note of personal characteristics. That is, undernutrition has to be seen in terms of a person not getting as much as he or she would need for reaching some specified nutritional standards. What those standards should be is, of course, a subject of considerable interest as well as great controversy (as we shall see in Chapter 3), but at this stage all that is immediately relevant is that the standards in question are related to the nutritional states of *people*, rather than being defined in terms of *given* amounts of food or nutrients, specified *irrespective* of personal characteristics (such as body size, metabolic rate, sex, pregnancy, age, etc.). A sensible identification of 'undernutrition' already brings in the *state of the person's being*—specifically the person being in some sense 'undernourished'. Given that connection between 'undernutrition' and 'undernourishment', the two must be seen as tied concepts.

Deprivation and Poverty

There are different ways of seeing the deprivations in human life with which public action has to be concerned. From what has been said already it should be clear that deprivation may be fruitfully seen in terms of the failure of certain human capabilities that are important to a person's well-being. If a person does not have the capability of avoiding preventable mortality, unnecessary morbidity, or escapable undernourishment, then it would almost certainly be agreed that the person is deprived in a significant way. There may be other—more subtle—types of deprivation on which too there could be general agreement, such as the inability to appear in public without shame because of one's evident penury.[22]

It is, in fact, possible to see 'poverty' itself as a severe failure of basic capabilities. That approach has much to commend, since it relates poverty to the failure of the ability to achieve precisely those things that are ultimately important.[23] On the other hand, the more common definition of poverty is in terms of inadequacy of incomes (e.g. a person's income level falling below the 'poverty line'). It is perhaps fruitless to spend much time arguing about which definition of poverty is superior. Undoubtedly, the failure of basic capabilities must ultimately be the central concern in the context of this analysis. Also, we have to take note of the fact that capabilities are influenced not merely by personal incomes but also by social facilities (such as public health). Whether poverty is seen as the failure of basic capabilities itself (e.g. 'a person is poor if she has to lead a very deprived life'), or as a causal antecedent of that failure (e.g. 'a person is poor if she has too low an income'), may not really make much difference *provided* we gear our analysis, ultimately, to matters of intrinsic concern and examine all causal influences on those matters. It is the need to avoid deprivation of basic capabilities on which we have to concentrate in the analysis of public action. This priority holds no matter whether 'poverty' is identified with that deprivation itself, or defined as the lack of economic means to escape that deprivation.

Social Security

Hunger is a many-headed monster. The undernutrition that haunts a large part of humanity relates to a wide range of deprivations. The connections between different types of deprivation are not only biological (e.g. between illness and undernutrition) but also economic and social (e.g. between unemployment and illness).

The idea of 'social security' is that of using social means to prevent deprivation and vulnerability. Social means can be of various types. Perhaps the most immediate is to provide direct support to the ability of the vulnerable to acquire the means to basic capabilities. Providing free food or cash to potential famine victims is an obvious example of this. On a more regular basis,

---

[22] The last is, in fact, a capability failure on which Adam Smith had a good deal to say; see Smith (1776), vol. I, Book V, Section II, in the edition by Campbell and Skinner (1976: 869–72).

[23] For a discussion of the rationale underlying this view of poverty, see Sen (1980, 1983b). See also Townsend (1985), Sen (1985d) and Seidl (1988).

providing unemployment insurance, free health services and basic education, etc., are other examples of such direct support.

The social means could also be indirect. For example, creating the social conditions of economic growth may make a substantial—and lasting— contribution to eliminating deprivation, if growth involves widespread parti- cipation of the population in the process of economic expansion. Later on in this book we shall study the different social means that may be used to reduce or eliminate failures of basic capabilities. We shall also have to study the interconnections between alternative approaches to social security.

We should stress that 'social security' as we see it here is a much broader and far-reaching notion than the technical sense in which the term is sometimes used in the professional literature on social administration in the richer countries. Debates on social security issues in the more prosperous countries have tended, perhaps for good logistic reasons, to focus on a number of specific forms of intervention such as unemployment benefits, medical insurance or old age pensions. Often the very definition of 'social security' is associated with these specific programmes (see e.g. the publications of the International Social Security Association). There is some debate as to the part that these program- mes can play in removing deprivation in developing countries.[24] But no matter what position we take on this issue, there is some obvious advantage in considering all the relevant forms of intervention in a common framework. We see 'social security' essentially as an *objective* pursued through *public means* rather than as a narrowly defined set of particular strategies, and it is important to take a broad view of the public means that are relevant to the attainment of this objective.[25]

It is useful to distinguish between two different aspects of social security, viz *protection* and *promotion*. The former is concerned with the task of preventing a decline in living standards as might occur in, say, an economic recession, or—more drastically—in a famine. The latter refers to the enhancement of general living standards and to the expansion of basic capabilities of the population, and will have to be seen primarily as a long-run challenge. In this book we shall be concerned with both aspects of social security.

It must be emphasized that while the terms 'promotion' and 'protection' both have a somewhat paternalistic ring, these terms refer to the objectives of the exercise rather than to the agency that may pursue these objectives. As we shall argue in the next section, public action for social security is neither just a matter of state activity, nor an issue of charity, nor even one of kindly

---

[24] On this see Mouton (1975), Gilbert (1976, 1981), Mesa-Lago (1978, 1983a, 1985c, 1986), Cockburn (1980), Mallet (1980), Guhan (1981, 1988), International Social Security Association (1982), Midgley (1984a, 1984b), Abel-Smith (1986), Atkinson and Hills (1988), and various contributions in Ahmad, Drèze, Hills and Sen (forthcoming).

[25] The social security measures that have been historically associated with the pursuit of social security objectives in the richer countries, and which are now formalized in the conventional usage of the term (e.g. in ILO publications), are best seen as contingently relevant for social security in the broader sense.

redistribution. The activism of the public, the unity and solidarity of the concerned population, and the participation of all those who are involved are important features of public action for social security.

1.4 Public Action for Social Security

It would be hard to deny that there is a straightforward public-interest issue involved in the elimination of starvation and of nutritional deprivation. The challenge of confronting in an effective manner the scourge that chastises and haunts a substantial part of humanity inescapably calls for diverse forms of public action. The provision of social security cannot exclusively rely either on the operation of market forces, or on some paternalistic initiative on the part of the state, or on some other social institution such as the family.

The *need* for public action does not, however, in itself point to the *nature* of the action to be undertaken. There are different areas of action, different strategies to pursue, different agents for undertaking action. The decision problems implicit in the choices involved are both complex and momentous. The issues include political and social phenomena as well as economic ones. The strategy of public action can be as difficult as it is urgent.

The various facets of the challenge of public action for the elimination of famines and endemic hunger will receive close attention in different parts of this book, but a few elementary considerations deserve immediate mention. First, the orientation of public action must clearly depend on the feasibilities of different courses of action. These feasibilities relate not merely to the causal factors that lead to deprivation and hunger, but also to the nature and power of the agencies involved. In particular, the character of the state, and the nature of the government undertaking state actions, can be crucial. The questions raised include not merely the administrative capabilities of governments, but also the political commitments and loyalties as well as the power bases of the holders of political power.

The countries with which we shall be concerned in this book have enormously divergent political systems and social balances of power, and the forms that public action can take will undoubtedly depend on these political and social parameters. For example, whether the Chinese success in subduing chronic hunger can be repeated, say, in India, or whether Indian achievements in the elimination of famines can be emulated in sub-Saharan Africa, or whether the sub-Saharan African record of lower gender inequalities in nutritional well-being can be duplicated in India or China or the Middle East, are all important and complex questions that call for careful scrutiny of the backgrounds against which these experiences have taken place.

Second, the public is not a homogeneous entity, and there are divisions related to class, ownership, occupation, and also gender, community and culture. While public action for social security is in some sense beneficial for all groups, the division of the benefits involved cannot escape differential pulls coming from divergent interest groups. The art of public action has to take note of these cooperative conflicts. To think of public action as action for the benefit of a homogeneous public is to miss a crucial aspect of the challenge.

Third, state action for the elimination of hunger can take enormously divergent forms. It need not involve only food production or food distribution. It can take the form of income or employment creation on a regular basis to combat endemic undernourishment. It can also involve famine relief operations in the form of employment for wages in cash or in kind to regenerate the purchasing power of hard-hit occupation groups. It can include the provision of health care and epidemic control, which may be important not merely as basic ingredients of the general well-being of the population, but also in preventing undernourishment, which is often associated with parasitic ailments and other forms of morbidity. State action can also take the form of enhancing economic development, in general, and the growth of incomes and other means of subsistence, in particular, through the expansion of productive activities. The discipline of public action may be widely different in these various fields, and the strategy of public action for social security has to be alive to the respective issues involved. The complementarities and tradeoffs between different avenues of action also have to be firmly faced in developing an overall effective public programme for eliminating hunger in all its forms.

Fourth, some public institutions, in particular the market, have often been seen as being an alternative to state action. To some extent this is right, since market mechanisms determine certain allocations and distributions, and state actions can alter or even take over many of these functions. While the conflicts between the reliance on markets and that on state action have to be fully acknowledged, it is also important not to see these two avenues as being in constant combat with each other. A purist philosophy can be awfully short of logistic means.[26]

The need to consider a plurality of levers and a heterogeneity of mechanisms is hard to escape in the strategy of public action for social security. The internal diversities involved in an effective public action programme can be quite extensive. For example, several countries have achieved some success in preventing famines by combining cash transfers to vulnerable groups in the form of wages for public employment with reliance on the private sector for moving food to affected regions, along with public participation in food distribution to prevent the emergence of collusive manipulations by private traders. These combined strategies illustrate the fruitfulness of taking an integrated and pluralist view of public action.

Fifth, public action should not be confused with state action only. Various

---

[26] The either-this-or-that 'exclusive' view often attributed to leaders of classical political economy was by no means universally endorsed. The effectiveness of the market mechanism in achieving certain types of efficiency was clearly seen by that great critic of capitalism, Karl Marx, and the fact that 'want, famine and mortality' can arise from unemployment in a market economy was explicitly noted by that great defender of the efficiency of markets, Adam Smith.

social and political organizations have typically played a part in actions that go beyond atomistic individual initiatives, and the domain of public action does include many non-state activities. Indeed, in many traditional societies, individual security has tended to depend greatly on support from groups such as the extended family or the community.[27] The active role of the state in the modern world should not be seen as replacement of what these non-governmental groups and institutions can achieve.

Finally, even as far as state action is concerned, there is a close relationship between public understanding and awareness, on the one hand, and the nature, forms and vigour of state action in pursuit of public goals, on the other. Political pressure plays a major part in determining actions undertaken by governments, and even fairly authoritarian political leaders have, to a great extent, to accept the discipline of public criticism and social opposition. Public enlightenment may, thus, have the role both of drawing attention to problems that may otherwise be neglected, and of precipitating remedial action on the part of governments faced with critical pressure. For example, the role of newspapers and public discussions, which can be extremely crucial in identifying famine threats (an energetic press may be the best 'early warning system' for famine that a country can devise), can also help to keep the government on its toes so that famine relief and preventive measures take place rapidly and effectively.

The question of public enlightenment and awareness involves both institutional features and the nature of social and political movements in the country. Since these are not immutable factors, the role of public action must be examined not merely in terms of consolidation of past achievements, but also with a view to possible departures in new directions. It is important to see the public as an agent and not merely as a passive patient.

---

[27] The profound concern of traditional societies for social security, and the variety of institutions they have evolved in pursuit of that objective, have been explored by Jean-Philippe Platteau (1988b). See also Chapter 5.

2

Entitlement and Deprivation[1]

2.1 Deprivation and the Law

When millions of people die in a famine, it is hard to avoid the thought that something terribly criminal is going on. The law, which defines and protects our rights as citizens, must somehow be compromised by these dreadful events. Unfortunately, the gap between law and ethics can be a big one. The economic system that yields a famine may be foul and the political system that tolerates it perfectly revolting, but nevertheless there may be no violation of our lawfully recognized rights in the failure of large sections of the population to acquire enough food to survive.

The point is not so much that there is no law against dying of hunger. That is, of course, true and obvious. It is more that the legally guaranteed rights of ownership, exchange and transaction delineate economic systems that can go hand in hand with some people failing to acquire enough food for survival. In a private ownership economy, command over food can be established by either growing food oneself and having property rights over what is grown, or selling other commodities and buying food with the proceeds. There is no guarantee that either process would yield enough for the survival of any particular person or a family in a particular social and economic situation. The third alternative, other than relying on private charity, is to receive free food or supplementary income from the state. These transfers rarely have the status of legal rights, and furthermore they are also, as things stand now, rather rare and limited.

For a large part of humanity, about the only substantial asset that a person owns is his or her ability to work, i.e. labour power. If a person fails to secure employment, then that means of acquiring food (e.g. by getting a job, earning a wage, and buying food with this income) fails. If, in addition to that, the laws of the land do not provide any social security arrangements, e.g. unemployment insurance, the person will, under these circumstances, fail to secure the means of subsistence.[2] And that can result in serious deprivation—possibly even starvation death. In seeking a remedy to this problem of terrible vulnerability, it is natural to turn towards a reform of the legal system, so that rights of social security can be made to stand as guarantees of minimal protection and survival.

---

[1] This chapter draws substantially on *Poverty and Famines* (Sen 1981a), and those familiar with the arguments presented there may wish to shun it.

[2] It is, of course, still possible for the person to survive on the basis of charity, but this is not a matter of right. If those who own more than they need are not willing to help this person adequately, the person will have to starve and perish.

We shall indeed explore this line of reasoning in this book, but at this stage we are primarily concerned with diagnostics rather than with cure.

It should also be added that even a person who is engaged in growing food and who succeeds in growing more (even, much more) than enough food for survival may not necessarily survive on this basis, and may not even have the legal right to do so. As we discussed in the last chapter, in many famines the majority of the victims come from the class of agricultural labourers. They are often primarily engaged in growing food. However, the legal nature of their contract, which is often informal, basically involves a wage payment in exchange for employment. The contract typically includes no right to the output grown by the person's own labour—no entitlement to the food output which could be the basis of survival for that person and his or her dependents.

Even if a person is lucky enough to find employment and is paid a certain sum of money for it as a wage, he or she has to convert that into food by purchase in the market. How much that wage commands would, of course, depend on the price of food. If food prices rise very rapidly, without money wages rising correspondingly, the labourers who have grown the food themselves may fail to acquire the food they need to survive.[3] The food grown belongs to the employer (typically the owner of the land), and the wage payment is the end of the grower's right to the produce, even if that wage does not yield enough to survive.

Similarly, a person who acquires food by producing some other commodity and selling it in the market has to depend on the actual ability to sell that product and also on the relative price of that product *vis-à-vis* food. If either the sale fails to materialize, or the relative price of that product falls sharply *vis-à-vis* food, the person may again have no option but to starve.

It is also important to realize that uncertainty and vulnerability can be features of subsistence production (involving 'exchange with nature') as well as of market exchange. This precariousness is particularly visible in African famines, where a substantial proportion of the victims often come from the ranks of small farmers who are hit *inter alia* by a collapse of their 'direct entitlement' to the food they normally grow. It would be a misleading simplification to regard self-provisioning as synonymous with security. The peasant farmer, like the landless labourer, has no guaranteed entitlement to the necessities of life.

It is, of course, also the case that laws may be disrupted during a famine. But there is no necessity for that to happen in order for a famine to occur. Indeed, as it happens, quite a few famines have taken place without much violation of law and order. Even in the disastrous Irish famines of the 1840s (in which about an

---

[3] The exchange rate between labour and food (i.e. the ratio of money wage and food prices) may dramatically fall as a result of economic changes brought about by factors beyond the control of the labourer. On some examples of dramatic changes in labour–food exchange rates in the Bengal famine of 1943 and the Bangladesh famine of 1974, see Alamgir (1980), Sen (1981a), and Ravallion (1987a).

eighth of the population died, and which led to the emigration of a comparable number to North America), the law and order situation was, in many respects, apparently 'excellent'. In fact, even as the higher purchasing power of the English consumers attracted food away, through the market mechanism, from famine-stricken Ireland to rich England, with ship after ship sailing down the river Shannon laden with various types of food, there were few violent attempts to interfere with that contrary—and grisly—process. In many famines people starve and die in front of food shops, without attempting to seize law and order by the collar. It would be, particularly, a mistake to relate the *causation* of famines to violations of legality.

There have, of course, been well-known cases of protest and rebellion associated with food crises, and 'the food riot as a form of political conflict' has considerable historical significance.[4] Despite this important causal link, the exact period of a severe famine is often not one of effective rebellion. Indeed, the debilitation and general helplessness brought about by a famine situation is not typically conducive to immediate revolt and rebellion. This is not to deny that looting, raiding and other forms of unorganized crime can be quite frequent in famine situations. But the millions that die in a famine typically die in an astonishingly 'legal' and 'orderly' way.

2.2   Entitlement Failures and Economic Analysis

If a group of people fail to establish their entitlement over an adequate amount of food, they have to go hungry. If that deprivation is large enough, the resulting starvation can lead to death. There is nothing particularly novel in the recognition that starvation is best seen as a result of 'entitlement failure'. Since the aggregate food supply is not divided among the population through some distributive formula (such as equal division), each family has to establish command over its own food. Even though this fact is elementary enough, it is remarkable that food analysis is often conducted just in terms of production and total availability rather than taking note of the processes through which people establish their entitlements to food.[5]

The notion of entitlement in this context must not be confused with

---

[4] See Louise Tilly (1971, 1983) and Charles Tilly (1975, 1978). See also Walter and Wrightson (1976), Dirks (1980), Li (1982a) and Kynch (1988). The subject also relates to Sorokin's (1942, 1975) influential historical analysis, and to Hobsbawm's (1954) pioneering work on 'primitive rebellion'.

[5] The view of famines as entitlement failures (on which see Sen, 1976a, 1977a, 1981a) attempts to combine in one common framework various interrelated ideas that have been used to analyse specific cases of hunger and starvation for many centuries. Even though the lessons of these ideas have often been overlooked, it is possible to profit greatly from studying analyses of food command in the writings of various classical authors including Adam Smith (1776), Thomas Malthus (1800), David Ricardo (1822: 234–5), and Karl Marx (1857–8, 1887); on these links see Sen (1981a: Chapter 1 and Appendix B; 1986a).

normative ideas as to who might be 'morally entitled' to what. The reference instead is to what the law guarantees and supports.

The legal system that precedes and survives through the famine may not, in itself, be a particularly cruel one. The standardly accepted rights of ownership and exchange are not the authoritarian extravaganzas of a heartless Nero or some brutal Genghis Khan. They are, rather, parts of the standard legal rules of ownership and exchange that govern people's lives in much of the world. But when they are not supplemented by other rights (e.g. social security, unemployment insurance, public health provisions), these standard rights may operate in a way that offers no chance of survival to potential famine victims. On the contrary, these legal rights, backed by the state power that upholds them, may ensure that the 'have-nots' do not grab food from the 'haves', and the law can stand solidly between needs and fulfilment.

As was discussed in Chapter 1, the 'entitlement' of a person stands for the set of alternative commodity bundles that can be acquired through the use of the various legal channels of acquirement open to that person. In a private ownership market economy, the entitlement set of a person is determined by his original ownership bundle (what is called 'endowment') and the various alternative bundles that the person can acquire, starting with each initial endowment, through the use of trade and production (what is called his 'exchange entitlement').[6] A person has to starve if his entitlement set does not include any commodity bundle with an adequate amount of food.

A person can be reduced to starvation if some economic change makes it no longer possible for her to acquire any commodity bundle with enough food to survive. This 'entitlement failure' can happen either because of a fall in her endowment (e.g. alienation of land, or loss of labour power due to ill health), or because of an unfavourable shift in her exchange entitlement (e.g. loss of employment, fall in wages, rise in food prices, drop in the price of goods or services she sells, decline in self-employed production). Entitlement analysis has been used in recent years to study various famines, e.g. the Bengal famine of 1943, the Sahel famines of the 1970s, the Bangladesh famine of 1974, the Ethiopian famines of 1973–85, the Malawi (in fact, Nyasaland, as it was then

---

[6] Exchange entitlement is, mathematically, a 'mapping', specifying for each endowment bundle a set of alternative commodity bundles any one of which a person can choose to acquire. The formal structure of entitlement analysis (including definitions of endowments, exchange entitlement mappings, etc.) and the empirical relevance of this analysis are discussed in Sen (1981a). An interpretational error to guard against, which seems to have occurred in a number of contributions examining this approach, is to see the analysis exclusively in terms of exchange entitlements rather than in the more general terms of entitlements as such—influenced by endowments *as well as* exchange entitlements. While some famines have clearly resulted specifically from shifts in 'exchange entitlements' (e.g. the Bengal famine of 1943, analysed in Sen 1977a, 1981a), in general the 'entitlement approach' demands that attention be paid to both endowments and exchange entitlements.

called) famine of 1949–50, and also a number of historical and recent cases of widespread starvation.[7]

Entitlements need not, of course, consist only of rights of full ownership. The legal system of a country may—and typically does—include provisions for the right to *use* some commodities without owning them outright. This is often the case with durable goods for shared use such as public parks and roads. Free distribution of state-owned food for the purpose of public consumption might be construed as falling in the category of use without ownership. But given the single-use nature of food, it is perhaps more helpful to see a change of ownership as and when the public distribution takes place. These processes too are, in fact, matters of shifting entitlements (in this case, through public policy). However, the exact formal characterization of all this is far less important than the powerful empirical fact that such free-distribution arrangements—no matter how characterized—are rare even in socialist economies.

Just as there have been major famines in private ownership economies without state guarantee of basic subsistence rights, there have also been famines in socialist countries with their own systems of legality (e.g. in Ukraine in the early 1930s, in China during 1958–61, in Kampuchea in the late 1970s). The entitlements guaranteed by the law have, on those occasions, failed to provide the means of survival and subsistence to a great many people. In some cases, e.g. in the Ukrainian famines, state policy was in fact positively geared to undermining the entitlements of a large section of the population.[8]

In analysing the causation of famines and in seeking social changes that eliminate them, the nature of entitlement systems and their workings have to be understood and assessed. The same applies to the problem of regular hunger and endemic undernourishment. If people go hungry on a regular basis all the time, or seasonally, the explanations of that have to be sought in the way the entitlement system in operation fails to give the persons involved adequate means of securing enough food. Seeing hunger as entitlement failure points to possible remedies as well as helping us to understand the forces that generate hunger and sustain it. In particular, this approach compels us to take a broad view of the ways in which access to food can be protected or promoted, including reforms of the legal framework within which economic relations take place.

Since food problems have often been discussed in terms of the availability of food without going into the question of entitlement (there is a substantial tradition of concentrating only on food output per head, going back at least to Malthus's famous *Essay on Population* of 1798), it is particularly important to

---

[7] See Sen (1976a, 1977a, 1981a), Ghose (1982), Oughton (1982), Tilly (1983), Khan (1985), Snowdon (1985), Ratnavale (1986), Bose (1987), Griffin (1987), Ravallion (1987a), Vaughan (1987), Devereux and Hay (1988), Desai (1988b) D'Souza (1988), Garnsey (1988), Osmani (1988b), and various contributions to Drèze and Sen (forthcoming), among others.

[8] On the Soviet famines of the early 1930s, and their relation to Stalin's ruthless policies, see Dalrymple (1964), Hadzewycz et al. (1983), Bernstein (1984), Conquest (1986), Serbyn and Krawchenko (1986).

understand the relevance of seeing hunger as entitlement failures. Such failures can occur even when food availability is not reduced, and even when the ratio of food to population (on which Malthus concentrated) goes up rather than down.[9] Indeed, the relentless persistence of famines and the enormous reach of world hunger, despite the steady and substantial increase in food availability per head, makes it particularly imperative for us to reorientate our approach away from food availability to entitlements.

This can be done without losing sight of the elementary fact that food availability must be *among* the factors that determine the entitlements of different groups of people, and that food production is one of the important determinants of entitlements. But that is only part of the story (though an important part), and must not be seen as all of it. We examine this question further in the next section, since there has been considerable misunderstanding regarding what entitlement analysis does or does not assert.

2.3 Availability, Command and Occupations

The dissonance between the causal analysis of famines in terms of availability and that in terms of entitlement does not lie in the fact that availability and entitlements are unrelated to each other. In fact, the relations involved can be very important indeed. The links are worth pointing out, particularly to avoid the temptation—to which it seems easy to succumb—to replace the old error of concentrating *only* on food output and availability by a new error of ignoring altogether the influence of output and availability on the entitlements of different sections of the population.[10]

[9] In another contribution entitled *An Investigation of the Cause of the Present High Price of Provisions* (Malthus, 1800), published two years after the *Essay on Population*, Malthus did discuss illuminatingly the process of acquirement of food and the part that the market mechanism plays in it. In terms of *economic* analysis, that contribution contrasts sharply with the *Essay on Population*, even though Malthus himself tended to see the later analysis as a supplement to it (and the *motivational* links are indeed clear). On the two types of contributions by Malthus, see Sen (1981a: Appendix B).

[10] In the presentation of the so-called entitlement approach in Sen (1981a), care was taken to note the obvious fact that output and availability are *among* the several influences that determine entitlements, and that even though hunger is ultimately caused by entitlement failure, nevertheless changes in food output and availability can play significant parts in the causal processes yielding or sustaining hunger (see pp. 7–8, 157–9, 179–81). In some of the later contributions in which this work has been cited (in support or in dissent), the thesis of the *inadequacy* of the availability perspective seems to have been somewhat confused with an imagined thesis of the *irrelevance* of food availability for famine analysis. It is also important to avoid the simplistic idea of seeing entitlement and availability as 'two sides' of the food story, with entitlement representing the demand side and availability the supply side and a 'synthesis' being worked out between the two. In fact, entitlement is influenced by both demand and supply factors, and food availability is one of the influences on it. These and several related issues have figured in a number of critiques of the entitlement approach to famines; see Muqtada (1981), D. R. Basu (1984, 1986), Rangasami (1985), Bowbrick (1986, 1987), Baulch (1987), Devereux (1988), Eicher (1988a), Kula (1988, 1989), Swift (1989). While some of the points raised have been based on misinterpreting the content of the entitlement approach, a number of interesting supplementary issues have *inter alia* emerged from these contributions. For further discussion of some of the underlying questions, see Sen (1981a, 1986a, 1986b, 1987d, 1987e).

The links between food availability and entitlements are indeed numerous and often important. First, for some people, the output of food grown by themselves is also their basic entitlement to food. For example, for peasants engaged mainly in growing food crops, the output, availability, and entitlement of food for the family can be much the same. This is a matter of what may be called 'direct entitlement'.[11] Second, one of the major influences on the ability of anyone to purchase food is clearly the price of food, and that price is, of course, influenced by the production and availability of food in the economy. Third, food production can also be a major source of employment, and a reduction in food production (due to, say, a drought or a flood) would reduce employment and wage income through the same process that leads to a decline in the output and availability of food. Fourth, if and when a famine develops, having a stock of food available in the public distribution system is clearly a major instrument in the hands of the authorities to combat starvation. This can be done either by distributing food directly (in cooked or uncooked form), or by adding to the supply of food in the market, thereby exerting a downward pressure or a moderating influence on possibly rocketing prices.

For these and other reasons, food entitlements have close links with food availability and output. It would be amazing if such links were absent, since the physical presence of food cannot but be an influence on the possibility of acquiring food through direct ownership or exchange. The dissonance does not arise from a denial of these obvious and important links. When questions of economic policy and political action are taken up in the later chapters of this volume, these links will be further investigated.

The conflict between the availability view and the entitlement view of food deprivation has to be seized along with making sure that the basic links have been recognized. The dissonance arises from the fact that the links do not establish a tight connection between availability and entitlement in such a way that the food commands of different sections of the population move up and down together, in the same way as the total availability of food in the economy. If food were to be distributed over the population on some egalitarian principles operated by some central authority, that assumption might have been sensible. However, as was discussed earlier, the actual command over food that different sections of the population can exercise depends on a set of legal and economic factors, including those governing ownership, production, and exchange. The overall availability of food is thus a very poor guide to the fortunes of different socio-economic groups.

The inadequacy of the availability view is particularly important to note in the context of the making of economic policy. Indeed, an undue reliance —often implicit—on the availability view has frequently contributed to the development or continuation of a famine, by making the relevant authorities

---

[11] On the distinction between 'direct' and 'trade-based' entitlement, see Sen (1981a: 50–1). The policy implications of failure of entitlements of distinct kinds can be quite different.

Table 2.1 The Bangladesh famine 1974:
overall availability of food grains

Year	Per head availability (oz./day)	Index
1967	15.0	100
1968	15.7	105
1969	16.6	111
1970	17.1	114
1971	14.9	99
1972	15.3	102
1973	15.3	102
1974	15.9	106 (Famine!)
1975	14.9	99
1976	14.8	99

Source: Alamgir (1980), Table 6.23; see also Sen (1981a), Table 9.5.

smug about the food situation.[12] For instance, there have been famines, e.g. in Bengal in 1943 and in Ethiopia in 1973, when the absence of a substantial food availability decline has contributed to official smugness.[13]

The possibly contrary nature of the availability view and the entitlement view can be illustrated by considering the food availability picture during the Bangladesh famine of 1974. In Table 2.1, the availability of food per head (including food production and net imports) for the Bangladesh population as a whole is given for ten years during 1967–76. Treating the availability in 1967 as the base of the index (100), the availability in 1974—the year of the famine

[12] The 'role of theory in policy failures' (particularly in the making of policy relying heavily on an availability theory of famines) was discussed in the context of the 1943 Bengal famine in Sen (1981a), chapter 6. Just as the famine in Bengal was beginning to develop, the Viceroy of India could write to the Secretary of State for India in London that he had told the Premier of Bengal (in charge of the provincial government) that 'he simply must produce some more rice out of Bengal for Ceylon even if Bengal itself went short', and the Viceroy could report the cheerful possibility that he 'may in the result screw a little out of them' (Mansergh 1971: 544). Despite the possibility of viceregal callousness and low cunning, this apparently cruel remark can be understood only by recognizing the actual assessment of the food situation on the part of the Viceroy's advisers that the shortage in Bengal could not really be very great, given the fact that the food output and availability there were fairly normal. Indeed, as the famine was gathering momentum in late March, the Secretary of State for India received 'the comforting message' from the Viceroy that 'the food situation in India generally is at present much improved', that 'the situation in Bengal at present is disquieting', but that nevertheless the problem could be 'treated with guarded optimism, with special reference to the recent improvement of the situation in India generally and the excellent prospects of the rabi harvest' (Mansergh 1971: 825–6). Even in October 1943, when the famine had already peaked, the Governor of Bengal was still presenting calculations of 'the real shortage' based on comparing estimates of food availability with requirements of food per person, as if the distribution of food was determined by some kind of a rationing device, even though no such rationing existed in Bengal, except in Calcutta (see Sen 1981a: 82).

[13] See Sen (1981a), chapters 6–10. See also Cutler (1984a, 1985b), Snowdon (1985) and Kumar (1986) on recent Ethiopian famines.

Table 2.2 The Bangladesh famine 1974: famine districts *vis-à-vis* other districts

District	Rank of famine intensity among 19 districts[a]	Rank of per-head food availability among 19 districts[b]	Rank of per cent change in food availability per head *vis-à-vis* previous year among 19 districts[c]
Rangpur	1 (17%)	5 (126)	6 (*up* 10%)
Mymensingh	2 (12%)	2 (143)	5 (*up* 11%)
Dinajpur	3 (9%)	1 (158)	1 (*up* 23%)
Sylhet	4 (8%)	3 (139)	12 (*up* 3%)

[a] Based on the share of the total population in the district seeking relief (shares given in brackets).
[b] Index values *vis-à-vis* Bangladesh average in brackets.
[c] Proportionate change in brackets.

Source: Sen (1981*a*), Tables 9.2 and 9.7; see also Alamgir (1980), from which the data are obtained, and which explains the primary sources.

—was 106. In fact, the availability of food that year was higher than in any other year during 1971–6. And yet the famine hit Bangladesh exactly in that year of peak food availability! The families of rural labourers and other occupation groups who died because of their inability to command food were affected by a variety of influences (including loss of employment, the rise in food prices, etc.), and this occurred despite the fact that the actual availability of food in the economy of Bangladesh was at a peak.

The failure of the availability view of famine can be further brought out by comparing different districts of Bangladesh in terms of their food availability in 1974 *vis-à-vis* their experience of famine. In Table 2.2 the so-called 'famine districts', which were most affected by the famine, are compared with other districts in terms of food availability.

It turns out that among the nineteen districts of Bangladesh, one of the famine districts (Dinajpur) had the *highest* availability of food in the entire country, and indeed all four of the famine districts were among the top five in terms of food availability per head. Even in terms of change in food availability per head over the preceding year, *all* the famine districts without exception had a substantial increase, and three of the four were among the top six in terms of food availability increase among all the nineteen districts.

The entitlement failure of the famine victims in Bangladesh related to a variety of factors, over and above output and availability of food.[14] The floods that afflicted Bangladesh (particularly the famine districts) caused some havoc during June to August of 1974. The availability of food in the economy, however, remained high since the primary crop of Bangladesh (the *aman* crop, which tended to contribute substantially more than half of the total food output

[14] These factors have been studied by Alamgir (1980), Sen (1981*a*), Montgomery (1985), Osmani (1986), and Ravallion (1987*a*), among others.

of the country) is harvested during November to January, and this had been high in the *preceding* year (i.e. harvested in November 1973 to January 1974). The floods that hit Bangladesh did, of course, reduce the harvest in late 1974, including the primary *aman* crop. The famine, however, developed and peaked much before those reduced harvests arrived, and indeed by the time the primary crop (*aman*) was harvested, the famine was over and gone. During the famine months, the physical availability of food per head in Bangladesh thus remained high. And this was especially so for the famine districts, since they happened to have had rather good crops earlier, boosting the 1974 availability, even though the floods would eventually affect the availability of food in these districts in the *following* year (1975).

Among the influences that led to the collapse of entitlements of a large section of the population of Bangladesh in 1974 was the loss of employment as a result of the floods, which affected the planting and particularly the transplanting of rice, traditionally carried out in the period following the one in which the floods occurred. This would reduce the food output later, but its impact on employment was immediate and vicious.

The disruption of the economy of Bangladesh as a result of the floods was not, however, confined only to the decline of employment. The effect of the floods on the future output and availability of food and therefore on the expectation of food prices also played a major part. Indeed, as Ravallion's (1987a) careful analysis of the rice market of Bangladesh during the 1974 famine indicates, the expectation of high food prices in Bangladesh went far ahead of what would actually emerge in the future (i.e. the later *realized* future prices). The poor and chaotic functioning of rice markets, fed by alarmist anticipations, led to price explosions following the floods, resulting in a collapse of food entitlements for those who found the already low purchasing power of their earnings further undermined.

The failure of the government to institute a suitable stabilizing response also contributed to the unstable behaviour of the rice market.[15] Rural labourers found a sharply diminished ratio of food command per unit of employment, and on top of that many had, in fact, lost employment as a result of floods, especially in the famine districts.

There is, therefore, no paradox in the fact that the Bangladesh famine of 1974 occurred at a time when the physical availability of food in the economy was at a local peak. It is the failure of large sections of the population, particularly of the labouring families, to command food in the market that has to be examined in order to understand the causation of that major catastrophe.

The terrible story of the Bangladesh famine of 1974 brings out the folly of concentrating only on the physical availability of food in the economy, and points to the necessity of investigating the movements of food entitlements of the vulnerable occupation groups and the causal influences (including market

---

[15] On this see Alamgir (1980), Osmani (1986), and Ravallion (1987a).

operations) that affect these movements. Similar lessons can be drawn from other famines as well.

One of the central differences between the availability approach and the entitlement approach is the necessarily disaggregative nature of the latter, in contrast with the inherently aggregative perspective presented by the former. While it is possible to calculate how much food a country can command, and while such aggregative calculations of 'total food entitlement' for the economy as a whole may have some analytical value as one of the constituent elements in understanding the food situation affecting a particular economy,[16] the idea of entitlements applies ultimately to particular individuals and families.

When many individuals and families are in a similar situation (e.g. as a result of belonging to the same occupation group and having similar economic circumstances), it is possible and useful to study the entitlement relations of that group as a whole, to get some idea as to how typical members of the group may be faring. It is obvious that a totally disaggregative analysis would be quite impossible to pursue for a sizeable economy, since there may be many millions of people involved. But at the same time, the 'total food availability' for the economy as a whole is unduly aggregative as a concept, and for reasons that we have already discussed, an appropriate economic disaggregation would certainly be necessary.

The logic of the entitlement approach indicates that the analysis must *inter alia* concentrate on occupation groups. This is, of course, a tradition that goes back to classical political economy, and especially to the analyses presented by Adam Smith, David Ricardo, and Karl Marx. Marx in particular perhaps did more than any other author to emphasize the importance of analysing economic movements through disaggregation according to classes. The contrast between the economic positions of the proletariat, peasants, traders, capitalists, etc. formed the backbone of his analysis, which was fleshed out with details that fitted into that overall structure. That general perspective is of central importance in understanding the nature of entitlements, and the genesis of famines and starvation.

However, the extent of the aggregation that has to be sought depends on the nature of the exercise, and in analysing famines and hunger, it is often important to take a more disaggregative view of the economy than one might get from standard class analyses.[17] Sometimes, the entitlements of different families belonging broadly to the same class may move in divergent directions, depending on the particular economic influences that respectively operate on them. These influences can vary between different occupation groups. They can also lead to divergent experiences for different members of the *same* occupation group. For example, if there is a particular disease affecting one

---

[16] See e.g. Kanbur (1986a)

[17] There is, in fact, more to learn in this particular respect from Marx's highly disaggregated analysis presented in *The Eighteenth Brumaire of Louis Bonaparte* (1852) than from the broad political platform presented in the 'Communist Manifesto' (1848).

type of animal rather than another, a section of the pastoralists may be hit, but not another. Similarly, the collapse of regional fishing rights may affect one group of fishermen, leaving another group unaffected. Distinctions based on output structure, regional location, etc. have to be brought in to supplement the occupational picture.

Since the particular reference of entitlement analysis is to families and persons, any aggregation in analysing movements of entitlements has to be based on identifying similarities of circumstances that make such aggregation viable and useful. The usefulness involved in such aggregation may, of course, be very great indeed, since different people in the same occupation group in the same region are often affected by very similar economic and political forces. The skill of entitlement analysis would lie in being able to make use of these advantages of aggregation in understanding in a tractable way the influences affecting the fortunes of persons and families, without losing sight of the fact that it is the families and their members to whom entitlement analysis must ultimately relate.

2.4 The 'Food Crisis' in Sub-Saharan Africa

Alarm has often been expressed at the possibility of a decline in the amount of food available per person in the modern world. Indeed, there is a good deal of discussion centering on prospects of disaster, based on modern variants of Malthusian fears. As a matter of fact, however, there has not been any declining trend in food availability per head for the world as a whole in recent decades (nor, of course, any such trend since Malthus's own days).

On the other hand, there has been quite a flood of models—mostly fairly theoretical—predicting the onset of Malthusian decline in the 'near future'.[18] But the shrill announcements of impending disaster and doom have not, in fact, been based on a great deal of rigorous economic reasoning. The assumptions underlying the pessimistic models are rather arbitrary and often extreme. Since the results happen to be quite sensitive to the precise assumptions chosen, it is not obvious what faith can be put in these alarming predictions. Indeed, the more recent studies have not tended to confirm this pessimism. The underlying methodology has varied from model to model, but these studies have typically found less reason for general gloom, and also much more room for policy response.[19] Obviously, any such future gazing is hard to do,

[18] See e.g. Forrester (1971), Meadows et al. (1972), Mesarovic and Pestel (1974), among others. Various intellectual institutions of great standing and influence, such as the Club of Rome, seem to have been able to lend their support to these—at best tentative—studies.

[19] See particularly the 'United Nations World Model' (Leontief et al. 1977), the so-called 'Latin American World Model' (Herrera et al. 1976), the extensive study presented by 'Interfutures' under the leadership of Jacques Lesourne (Interfutures 1979), the IIASA study of world food systems (Parikh and Rabar 1981), the 'Global 2000 Report' commissioned by President Carter (Council on Environmental Quality and the Department of State 1982), and even the later study done for the Club of Rome—an original sponsor of the doom view—called the *Model of International Relations in Agriculture* (Linnemann 1981). See also Berry and Kates (1980) and Mellor and Johnston (1984).

Table 2.3 World trends in food output per head

Region	The last half decade: 1986–8 average over 1981–3 average	The last decade: 1986–8 average over 1976–8 average
All developed economies	up 2%	up 3%
All developing economies	up 5%	up 11%
Europe	up 5%	up 13%
USA	down 7%	up 7%
Africa	down 2%	down 8%
South America	unchanged	up 2%
Asia	up 8%	up 17%

Source: Calculated from data obtained from *FAO Production Yearbook 1988*, Table 4, and *FAO Quarterly Bulletin of Statistics*, vol. i, pt. 4, 1988.

but it seems unlikely that the real dangers in the near future can lie in the prospect of food output falling short of the growth of population.

Table 2.3 presents the trends in food output per head over the last half decade and the last decade (i.e. from 1981–3 to 1986–8, and from 1976–8 to 1986–8) for some of the major regions in the world. It would appear that for all *developed* economies taken together, food output per head went up by 2 per cent during the last half decade and by 3 per cent over the last decade. The corresponding increases for the *developing* economies taken together are, in fact, considerably higher, viz. 5 per cent and 11 per cent respectively.[20]

The fact that the trend of food output per head is so sharply upward for developing economies in particular is, naturally, a source of comfort. But it could be false comfort. In fact, different developing economies have done very differently over the last few decades. Specifically, in the last decade, when food output per head for all developing economies taken together went up by 11 per cent, that for Asia went up by 17 per cent and for South America by 2 per cent, while that for Africa came *down* by 8 per cent. Indeed, Africa has been plagued by production problems—in addition to other problems—over nearly two decades now. The aggregate picture for the developing economies put together is, thus, quite misleading.

Africa also has had—and continues to have—the fastest growth rate of population among the major regions of the world. However, it is easy to see that the contrasting trends of food output per head in Africa and other regions reflect differences in output performance at least as strongly as differences in

[20] There are certain weighting problems in these average figures. In fact, the same sources of information from which Table 2.3 has been derived give figures of increases of aggregate world food availability per head that are hard to tally with the separate figures for developed and developing countries. This contrariness arises from weighting problems, but also indicates that any such statistics must be taken with a pinch of salt, given the arbitrariness involved in such weighting exercises.

population growth rates (even with the assumption that the output growth rate in Africa is independent of the growth rate of population and labour supply).

This having been said, we must, however, resist the oversimplified suggestion that Africa's recent problems of hunger arise simply from declines in food output and supply. While food production and availability are undoubtedly among the more important influences in the determination of food entitlements, the connections are complex and there are also other matters involved (such as the performance of industries and non-food agriculture, and the general role of employment and economic participation).

It must be borne in mind that food production is not only a source of food supply, it is also a major source of income and livelihood for vast sections of the African population. As a result, any reduction in food output per head in Africa also tends to be associated with a reduction in overall income for many occupation groups. However, the observed decline in food output per head in Africa need not have resulted in a collapse of food entitlements, if that decline had been compensated by an expansion of alternative incomes usable to acquire food from other sources, e.g. through imports from abroad. The point can be illustrated by comparing the experiences of many of the sub-Saharan economies which have experienced declines in food output per head and have

Table 2.4 Declines in food production per head: intercountry comparisons

	1984–6 *vis-à-vis* 1979–81	1984–6 *vis-à-vis* 1974–6
Sub-Saharan Africa		
Sudan	down 4%	down 3%
Ethiopia	down 14%	down 10%
Somalia	down 10%	down 21%
Zimbabwe	down 7%	down 23%
Zambia	down 6%	down 24%
Mozambique	down 15%	down 30%
Senegal	down 1%	down 33%
Kenya	down 10%	down 33%
Botswana	down 20%	down 44%
Elsewhere		
Israel	up 2%	down 12%
Venezuela	down 11%	down 14%
Portugal	unchanged	down 15%
Costa Rica	down 11%	down 17%
Singapore	down 3%	down 19%
Hong Kong	up 15%	down 36%
Trinidad & Tobago	down 13%	down 40%

Source: Calculated from data presented in *FAO Production Yearbook 1986*, Table 4, and *FAO Monthly Bulletin of Statistics*, November 1987, Table 1.

also experienced food problems, with those of economies elsewhere which have also experienced declines in food output per head, but *without* experiencing famines or widespread undernourishment.

Table 2.4 compares the experiences over the decade 1974–6 to 1984–6 of nine sub-Saharan African economies with seven economies from elsewhere (Israel, Venezuela, Portugal, Costa Rica, Singapore, Hong Kong, and Trinidad and Tobago). Some of the sub-Saharan economies have indeed experienced famine in the middle eighties, and they did also have considerable declines in food output per head, e.g., Sudan (3 per cent), Ethiopia (10 per cent), Somalia (21 per cent), and Mozambique (30 per cent). On the other hand, several economies elsewhere have experienced comparable or even greater declines in food output per head (in some cases as large as 30 or 40 per cent), without having any problems of the kind which have afflicted these African countries.[21] This is so both because food production is a less important source of income and entitlement in these other economies, and also because they have achieved a more than compensating expansion of *non-food* production (with favourable effects on incomes and entitlements). What may superficially appear to be a problem of food production and supply in Africa has to be seen in the more general terms of entitlement determination.[22]

One important implication of this perspective is that even though current problems of hunger and famines in sub-Saharan Africa are undoubtedly connected *inter alia* with the decline of food production, remedial action need not necessarily take the form of attempting to reverse that historical trend. Other avenues of action, such as the diversification of economic activities and the expansion of public support, deserve attention as well. This general point will be further scrutinized in Chapter 9. We shall also have occasion, in Chapters 5–8, to discuss how a number of countries—including several African ones—have already achieved impressive success in preventing major (short-term or long-term) declines in food production or availability from causing famines or widespread deterioration in nutritional well-being.

---

[21] Table 2.4 also presents the figures of production change in the half-decade preceding 1984–6 (i.e. during 1979–81 to 1984–6), to confirm that the emerging picture of food output declines is not just a matter of the choice of base period.

[22] Among the adverse circumstances to consider here is the crippling burden of international debt on many economies of sub-Saharan Africa.

3

Nutrition and Capability

3.1 World Hunger: How Much?

The question is often asked, and we might as well face it. How many hungry people are there in the world? It is not easy to answer this question. This is not so much because we lack the data to do the estimation (though data limitations certainly exist), but primarily because there are great conceptual difficulties underlying the measurement exercise. While it is obviously not hard to recognize starving or acutely deprived people, it is much harder to find an agreed criterion in case of less severe food deprivation.

There is not much difficulty in agreeing that some estimates of the number of the hungry are obviously wrong, in terms of any reasonable criterion. For example, Lord John Boyd-Orr's well-known statement that 'a lifetime of malnutrition and actual hunger is the lot of at least two-thirds of mankind' would be hard to defend literally.[1] While not many estimators have reached the proportion specified by Boyd-Orr, it is by no means uncommon to encounter casual estimates of unbelievably many people suffering from crippling undernourishment.[2]

Moving away from casual figures to systematic and detailed estimation, a recent World Bank Policy Study, entitled *Poverty and Hunger*, calculates that the number of people suffering from nutritional deprivation (in the sense of not having an adequate calorie intake to prevent stunted growth and serious health risks) was 340 million in 1980, representing about 16 per cent of the population of the developing countries as a whole (about 23 per cent of the population in the 'low income countries'). The same study suggests that 730 million people in the developing world suffer from undernourishment in terms of having 'not enough calories for an active working life'. This amounts to 34 per cent of the population of developing countries as a whole (51 per cent in 'low income countries').[3]

These calculations are based on two particular methodological elements. One is to relate hunger to the low incomes of particular groups of people, rather

[1] Boyd-Orr (1950: 11). It should be mentioned that despite such exaggerated pronouncements, Lord Boyd-Orr did in fact play a very important and productive part in putting world hunger on the international agenda, and also in preparing the ground for scientific and systematic work in this difficult area. Whether the tendency to dramatize the extent of deprivation involved contributed to or detracted from the task that Boyd-Orr undertook is an interesting issue which we shall not address here.

[2] Poleman (1981) cites and critically discusses various examples of such high estimates.

[3] World Bank (1986: 17). For a succinct summary of some of the main findings and recommendations, see Reutlinger (1985).

than to food availability as such. In this respect the study involves the use of a more causal insight into the antecedence of hunger than would have been provided by the more traditional food-centred calculations.[4] The other element involves the use of particular 'calorie requirement' norms, and takes the form of relating income deficiency to alleged dietary deficiency, based on specified calorie norms.[5] The use of such norms has come under rather severe attack in recent years from critics who have stressed the importance of interpersonal variations as well as adaptive adjustments influencing the relation between food intakes and achieved nutritional levels. It has been suggested that many of those identified as falling below the calorie norms may, in fact, not be nutritionally deprived in any significant sense.[6]

It should be mentioned in this context that the report does not take the commonly used FAO–WHO 'requirement' figure, but only 80 per cent of that, to specify the calorie intake needed 'to prevent stunted growth and serious health risks', and 90 per cent of the FAO–WHO figure for identifying what amounts to 'not enough calories for an active working life'. Thus, a downward correction is introduced in the estimates of the number of the undernourished compared with what would have been obtained on the basis of the FAO–WHO norms. But the general methodological doubts still remain.

Other studies based on related methodologies have indicated figures of deprivation no less alarming than those derived in *Poverty and Hunger*, the World Bank study. For example, one estimate suggests that 'more than 500 million women, children and men are reported to suffer from chronic malnutrition or famine', and 'each year some 40 million people die from hunger and hunger-related diseases'.[7] To drive home the dimension of the problem, the same report presents the picture graphically by pointing out that this figure is 'equivalent to more than 300 jumbo jet crashes per day with no survivors, almost half of the passengers being children'.

---

[4] One of the major authors of the report *Poverty and Hunger*, viz. Shlomo Reutlinger, has been among the pioneers in shifting attention from food-supply-based analysis of hunger to an income-centred view. See particularly Reutlinger and Selowsky (1976), Reutlinger and Alderman (1980) and Reutlinger (1984). See also the contributions of Aziz (1975), Taylor (1975), Haq (1976), Griffin and Khan (1977) and Alamgir (1978).

[5] In fact, calorie is only one of the nutrients, and deprivation can also arise from the deficiency of proteins and other nutrients. There was a major controversy some years ago on the independent role that protein deficiency can play, and Sukhatme (1961, 1969, 1973, 1977) and Sukhatme and Margen (1978) have been enormously influential in showing the rather limited frequency of purely protein deficiency in the absence of calorie shortfall. As a matter of fact, for certain dietary patterns, meeting the calorie requirements automatically fulfils the protein norms given the proportions of these nutrients in these diets (see Osmani 1982). However, it must be noted that the problem of protein deficiency for children can be serious even when it is not so for the average adult. There are also interregional variations of dietary patterns. In concentrating only on calorie deficiency and in taking no note of protein deficiency in the absence of calorie shortfall, the report *Poverty and Hunger* introduces, if anything, a downward bias (in this particular respect) in the estimation of the number of the nutritionally deprived.

[6] See Sukhatme (1977, 1982*a*), Srinivasan (1981), Lipton (1983), and Payne (1987*a*).

[7] Nordic Conference on Environment and Development (1987: 1).

As was already mentioned, these estimates of the size of the population suffering from undernourishment are limited not only by the uncertainties of the data used but also by deep conceptual problems. Pertinent questions have been raised about the reliability of such estimates of undernourishment and hunger, based on fixed requirement norms, given the observed fact of (1) interpersonal variations of nutritional requirements, (2) the possibility of intertemporal variations of intake for a given person, and (3) the possibility of adjustment and perhaps even 'adaptation' to a long-run decline of nutritional intake.[8] The nature and force of these criticisms and the underlying methodological problems will be considered in the next section. But before we turn to that, it is worth asking whether this is an important issue at all. What difference can these figures make?

In one sense not a lot depends on the exactness of the figures. For example, even if the number of deaths from hunger and hunger-related diseases happened to be equivalent not to 300 jumbo jet crashes a day with no survivors, but only to 100 such crashes per day, the extraordinary nature of nutritional deprivation across the world would still be hard to dispute. The alarm that we ought to feel at these findings and the determination to work for a change may not be particularly sensitive to variations over a wide range of disastrous possibilities.

There is, however, an important policy aspect implicit in these measurement issues. A limited commitment of resources often forces certain choices as to whether economic or nutritional intervention should be aimed at a relatively small group of severely deprived people, or spread more broadly over a larger category of generally deprived population. To face these choices, the nutritional implications of deprivation have to be better understood. If a person falls a little below the nutritional norms, particularly the calorie requirement figures, what harm will come to such a person?

If the category of general deprivation is exaggerated, then there might possibly be a costly deflection of resources to tackle that problem, with comparative neglect of the less numerous but more urgent cases of extreme deprivation. Exaggeration can be, thus, counterproductive even for the cause of anti-hunger policy. On the other hand, underestimating the size of the affected population can lead to a neglect of the problem and underallocation of resources to anti-hunger programmes and policies altogether. There are hard choices to make, and the advantages of accurate evaluation cannot be summarily dismissed.

3.2   Food Deprivation and Undernourishment

How does the traditional nutritional analysis exactly work? Nutritional deprivation, in that approach, is judged by comparing a person's actual food intake

---

[8] Variations in nutritional needs can also lead to corresponding adjustments in food intakes. It can be hard to disentangle whether low nutritional intake in a particular case reflects deprivation or signifies an unusually low requirement level. See Osmani (1987a).

with some specific levels of 'requirements' for particular nutrients. Since different food items share common nutritional characteristics, the approach works through specifying the requirements not of particular foods, but of the nutritional characteristics themselves, e.g. calories or proteins. In practice, it is calorie norms which have been most widely used to identify the under-nourished. If a person's actual intake of nutrients, in particular calories, falls short of the 'requirement', the person is taken to be 'undernourished'.

This approach to the nutritional problem has come under rather severe fire in recent years.[9] It has been pointed out that there are, first of all, significant *inter*individual variations in the conversion of nutrients into nutritional achievements, so that 'requirement' figures cannot be specified in an individual-independent way. Basal metabolic rates vary from person to person, and there can be substantial differences in the nutritional needs of different people. This makes it particularly problematic to identify under-nourished individuals, though it need not rule out probabilistic arguments being used to estimate likely proportions of undernourished population, based on information on statistical patterns of interindividual variations of metabolic rates and other relevant factors.

Second, it has been argued that there can also be enormous '*intra*individual' variations over time and that a person can maintain a balanced equilibrium by compensating the lower intakes in some periods by higher intakes in others. Thus, a person who is observed to consume fewer calories than his or her own average 'requirements' are estimated to be (when such estimates are possible) may not, in fact, be in nutritional distress at all, but only in a low phase of his or her intake pattern. For this reason, the identification of all those falling below a calorie norm as being undernourished could quite possibly exaggerate the number of people with real nutritional deficiency, especially since intake data tend to be based on short-period samples.

Third, there may exist multiple equilibria, with the same person possibly achieving different states of balance at different average levels of nutritional intake. The scope for adjustment is widely accepted. The real issue concerns its forms, implications, and effects. Ultimately, the question is whether there is scope for much harmless adjustment—without detrimental effects on the person's well-being and productivity. The fact that a person being placed in a different nutritional regime would tend to adjust accordingly is plausible enough, and there is clear empirical evidence to suggest such responses. The question is whether the modification will be such that different levels of nutritional intake would produce essentially the same nutritional achieve-ments judged in terms of the person's well-being and productive ability. Would the modification related to lower intakes be, in the relevant sense, curative?

[9] See particularly Sukhatme (1977, 1982a, 1982b), Srinivasan (1981), Seckler (1982, 1984), Sukhatme and Margen (1982), Lipton (1983), Blaxter and Waterlow (1985), Kakwani (1986), Payne (1985, 1987a), Payne and Lipton (1988).

Two types of curative adjustment have been suggested. The first works through body size, with 'small but healthy' people living on relatively low nutritional intakes without experiencing, in any real sense, a diminished quality of life or functioning ability.[10] The other is 'adaptation' of nutritional requirements to variations in nutritional intakes for a given body size and permitting unchanged levels of activity.[11] Both adjustments work in the direction of compensating nutritional deprivation, and if they are effective, low levels of food intake—in terms of nutrients consumed per person—may not amount to undernutrition in any consequential sense. The obvious questions are: how effective are these adjustments? In what way and to what extent do they affect the important functionings of a person? In terms of the nature of the life that a person can lead, how restrictive are the adjusted states? In short, what are the feasibilities and costs of adjustment?

The 'small but healthy' hypothesis has been strongly disputed from several distinct perspectives.[12] It is, of course, true that not every kind of activity requires a large body size. Indeed, for many functionings, such as making intellectual contributions, body size may be irrelevant. Further, it is not hard to think of some occupations in which smallness might indeed be an advantage (for a jockey, or a 'cat burglar'). On the other hand, there are clearly many other activities for which the largeness of body size *is* important, e.g., various types of physical activities requiring carrying capacity or strengths of particular types. Even if being small is no bar to being healthy, a small stature can indeed be a limitation to productivity and earning power, in particular economic or social circumstances.

As far as the basic issue of smallness and health is concerned, many complex medical and social questions arise in examining the implications of small body size, in general, and stunting, in particular. But considerable evidence does exist linking, for given communities, height to morbidity and mortality. On these grounds height has, in fact, been plausibly used—within certain limits —as an indicator of general physical well-being.[13] The precise relationship between nutritional intake, height, weight, productivity, morbidity, and the quality of life certainly calls for much more extensive scrutiny. But as knowledge stands at the moment, to dismiss smallness as entirely costless would seem to be a dubious and premature position to take in the context of nutritional deprivation across the world. Indeed, given (1) the medical information on the observed relation between height, weight, morbidity, and learning (especially among children, and particularly for cases of severe stunting), (2) the economic information on the relevance of height for employment

[10] See Seckler (1982, 1984) and Sukhatme (1982*a*).
[11] See Sukhatme (1977, 1982*a*, 1982*b*), Srinivasan (1981), Lipton (1983), and Payne (1985).
[12] See particularly Gopalan (1983*a*, 1987*a*, 1987*b*). See also Beaton (1987*a*) and Osmani (1987*a*, 1987*b*).
[13] See the historical studies based on anthropometric measures of Floud and Wachter (1982), Fogel, Engerman and Trussell (1982), Fogel *et al.* (1983), Floud (1987), and Fogel (1987). See also Vaidyanathan (1985).

in some occupations and strength in others, (3) the social information on the relevance of height in moving up or down in the social ladder, and (4) the cultural information on people's own view of their height, weight, and strength, it would be difficult to view smallness of body size as being, in general, inconsequential and unproblematic.

The alternative avenue of costless adjustment would lie in the claimed possibility of nutritional adaptation for the same physical features and work abilities. That adaptations of this kind do take place has been forcefully argued by Sukhatme and others.[14] In this case the adjustment will not take the form of any change of stature or external appearance, nor of any variation in the actual ability to work—only a change in the efficiency with which the body converts nutritional intakes into results.[15]

The empirical support for extensive nutritional adaptation in a costless way is not very clear. It has been pointed out that the available clinical evidence cannot sustain the thesis of the presence of extensive and widespread costless adaptation mechanisms, or even the existence of such mechanisms in any significant sense.[16] Even if adaptation does take place in some cases, neither the ubiquity nor the quantitative reach of adaptation has been established in any way that can be taken to be scientifically definitive. In fact, from the point of view of nutritional planning and public health it may well be dangerous to proceed as if nutritional shortfall were typically costless over a wide range.

Scepticism about relying on curative adjustment mechanisms (whether the 'costless adaptation' version or the 'small but healthy' version) must not, however, be confused with defending the use of a set of fixed nutritional requirements to determine the number of the undernourished. The way in which calorie norms have been used in some of the policy literature does indeed leave room for considerable doubt. The motivation for specifying recommended energy intakes underlying the various studies produced by WHO, FAO, UNU and others was actually not so much to treat these as yardsticks for identifying *individuals* as being nutritionally deprived, but primarily to use them in aggregative contexts for rough estimations of the food needs of *communities*. If these norms are used for classifying individuals as being nutritionally deprived or otherwise, significant errors will be made both because of *inter*personal variations in basal metabolic rates and other factors, and because of *intra*personal variations of food intakes over time within normal intake profiles. These errors will be present even if no curative adjustment mechanism were to exist at all, since the prevalence of interindividual variations and intertemporal unevenness is hard to deny. It is, thus, important to

---

[14] See also Srinivasan (1981, 1987), Lipton (1983), and Payne (1985, 1987a).

[15] Biological adaptation relates to the reduction of nutritional requirements even for the same levels of activities. In addition, adaptation can be 'behavioural', and nutritional requirements may be reduced by varying the pattern of activities. See Payne and Lipton et al. (1988).

[16] See particularly Dasgupta and Ray (1986a) and the clinical literature analysed there. See also Gopalan (1983b, 1987b), Blaxter and Waterlow (1985), Osmani (1987a, 1987b), Scrimshaw (1987), and Hossain (1989).

recognize that the inappropriateness of the mechanical use of calorie norms in individual nutritional monitoring (as opposed to group monitoring) transcends the heated controversies surrounding the specific theses on 'costless adaptation' or being 'small but healthy'.

The question remains, however, as to whether the calorie norms can be used to provide some kind of statistical guidance regarding the extent of undernourishment and nutritional deprivation in particular communities. Indeed, a probabilistic argument can be easily constructed. While it is possible for a person to fall frequently below the calorie norm and still remain well nourished (maintaining 'homeostasis' of nutritional balance), nevertheless the probability of being undernourished in the sense of being nutritionally deprived in some clinical way can be related to levels of calorie intakes *vis-à-vis* the standard norms. There is, thus, a stochastic argument in favour of using these norms to construct a probabilistic picture of nutritional deprivation based on intake figures.[17]

There is, however, no reason whatsoever why nutritional monitoring should be confined to intake figures excluding other indicators. For one thing, calorie information can be usefully supplemented by other data regarding incomes, employment, assets, etc., so that the shortfall of nutritional intakes compared with norms can be interpreted in a way which helps to discriminate between involuntary deficiencies of calories and other nutrients, on the one hand, and variations in intake patterns maintaining overall nutritional balance, on the other. Furthermore, even when nutritional shortfalls are clearly caused by factors beyond one's control, such as the seasonality of earnings, the clinical question as to whether this would have disastrous consequences can be interpreted only by probing more deeply into the economic and social circumstances leading to these shortfalls and their frequency and duration. In general, nutritional assessment will require a great deal more than food intake information.[18]

Within the field of nutritional statistics itself, it is not clear at all why information should be confined to intake figures alone. There are other ways of judging nutritional successes or failures (e.g. from anthropometric measures, or morbidity information), and these data—directly related to nutritional status—can be systematically used, rather than confining attention to food intakes. It is only when they are supplemented by these other nutritional data as well as economic and social statistics that analyses of nutrient intakes can be best used as one important basis for nutritional judgement.

The complexity of the relationship between nutrient intakes and nutritional

---

[17] Such analysis must take into account the possibility, discussed earlier, that the observed intake figures may include *inter alia* the adjustment of food consumption to variations in nutritional requirements. The probabilistic analysis has to be based on the *joint* distribution of intakes and requirements. See Anand and Harris (1987).

[18] For interesting models and their applications, see Lipton (1983, 1988a), Anand and Harris (1986, 1987).

achievement should not, however, make us lose sight of the fact that the magnitude of uncontroversial deprivation is enormously large in this hungry world. The subtler issues of nutritional intervention and support cannot, of course, be settled without expanding the information base and they do ultimately have policy relevance, but nevertheless there are many urgent and uncontroversially important matters that can—indeed must—receive attention without waiting for the informational base and the diagnostics to be fully refined. While this may be somewhat of a consolation from a 'scientific' point of view, it does, of course, only reflect the terrible state of the world in which we live. In order to show how terrible it is and how much needs to be urgently done, we do not have to construct precise estimates of the total number of nutritionally deprived people in the world.

3.3   Poverty and Basic Capabilities

Aside from the biological and related controversies discussed in the previous section, the assessment of nutritional deprivation has to address some broader conceptual problems arising in the evaluation of human deprivation in general. Some of the issues involved have been extensively examined in the literature on 'poverty'.[19] Perhaps the most elementary issue relates to the nature of the variables of ultimate interest when dealing with human deprivation, for example, whether a 'poverty line' should be drawn in terms of an income level (below which people count as poor), or in terms of some failure of basic functionings including nutritional performance.

In the first chapter of this book we argued that deprivation is best seen in terms of the failure of certain basic 'functionings' (such as being physically fit), rather than in terms of variables such as income or calorie intake which should be seen as means and not as ends in themselves. We have also suggested that once this substantive issue is resolved, the terminological question as to whether the expression 'poverty' should be used to refer to deprivation in this general sense, or to the low level of income or commodity command contributing to that deprivation, is of secondary importance.

Functioning failures can themselves be assessed either in terms of *achievement* or in terms of the *freedom to achieve*. The notion of 'capability' was introduced in Chapter 1 to refer to the extent of the freedom that people have in pursuing valuable activities or funtionings.[20] The distinction between achieved functionings and the capability to function is of particular importance in the context of those functionings in which individual choices and behaviour

---

[19] See the surveys and critiques of Atkinson (1983, 1987a), Foster (1984), Seidl (1988). See also Wedderburn (1974), Sen (1976b, 1985d), and Townsend (1979a).

[20] Freedom to achieve has obvious instrumental importance in achievement, but in addition it can be seen as having intrinsic value. The intrinsic importance of freedom has figured prominently in many ethical frameworks, including those of Marx (1844) and Mill (1859). These issues are discussed in Sen (1985b, 1988a).

patterns vary greatly (especially 'social' ones, such as 'taking part in the life of the community'). The occurrence of voluntary fasting brings out the fact that even in the context of food and eating there is a potentially important basis of distinction here.

In general the dichotomy between the ability to avoid hunger and the actual choice of that option may be relatively unimportant, given that the alternative of avoiding undernourishment is usually chosen when it is available.[21] But the distinction between capability and achieved functioning can be important even in the field of nutrition, for example, due to the influence of food habits, which can have a major influence on the choice of diet and thus on the use actually made of the capability to meet nutritional needs. Even if taste constraints are not entirely inflexible, with completely binding effects within particular cultures, they are not removable at will. Nor can we ignore the valuable and valued aspects of non-nutritional uses of food in social living.[22]

The use of the 'capability approach' can focus either on functionings or on the capability to function, or both.[23] While that is a fairly general approach to the assessment of well-being and advantage, its relevance for nutritional concerns as such is not negligible.

First, given the interpersonal and intrapersonal variations in the relation between nutritional intakes and human functionings (discussed earlier in this chapter), the distinction between income and commodities, on the one hand, and functionings and capabilities, on the other, can be very substantial indeed. In matters of nutrition and health, the need for being clear about the nature of the ultimate value-objects is especially strong. In particular, as we have already discussed, the removal of nutritional deprivation cannot be seen merely in terms of achieving certain specific levels of income or calorie intake. The distinction between opulence and income level, on the one hand, and the capability of being well nourished and healthy on the other, will be seen to be of pervasive importance in analysing endemic deprivation and in characterizing the needed remedial policies (see Chapters 9 to 12).

Second, the distinction between commodity command and functioning ability can be particularly important when dealing with groups that have systematic disadvantages for biological or social reasons. For example, the old

---

[21] Some recent empirical studies indicate that calorie consumption may not increase much with income, even when the calorie intake is low; see Behrman and Deolalikar (1987, 1988b). The generality of these findings, however, remains to be fully investigated. There are also important interpretational questions, including the particular role of calories in nutritional well-being. On these and related issues, see L.C. Chen (1986b), Bhargava (1988), Bouis and Haddad (1988), Ravallion (1988), Schiff and Valdés (1988), and Alderman (forthcoming).

[22] On the non-nutritional uses of food and in general the need to consider the social role of goods, see particularly Douglas and Isherwood (1979), Vatuk (1979), Douglas (1984), Khare and Rao (1986), and Marglin (1986).

[23] There are several empirical studies related to each perspective. See particularly Sen (1982b, 1984b, and 1985a), Kynch and Sen (1983), Kynch (1985), Brannen and Wilson (1987), Kumar (1987), Ringen (1987), A. Williams (1987), Wilson (1987a, 1987b), Griffin and Knight (1988), I. Hossain (1988), and Koohi-Kamali (1988).

and the infirm are not only handicapped in *earning* an income, they also have greater difficulty in *converting* incomes into functionings in the form of disease-free living, enjoying adequate mobility, and so on.

Women too have, in most societies, special disadvantages in achieving particular functionings. The roots of these problems can be social as well as physical, and the remedies sought have to take note of the nature of the constraints involved and the extent to which they can be removed. For example, the enhanced deprivation associated with pregnancy may arise partly from social factors (e.g. difficulty in maintaining employment) and partly from physical ones (e.g. greater need for food). While the physical factors cannot be altered in the same way as the social roots of deprivation can be, the depriving effects of the physical factors can be eradicated through public policy aimed at maintaining capability (e.g. through dietary supplementation, health care, and the creation of economic and social opportunities).

Third, the capability approach draws attention to the general need to consider inputs other than food as determinants of nutritional functioning and capability. Nutritional achievements may be strongly influenced by the provision of and command over certain crucial non-food inputs such as health care, basic education, clean drinking water, or sanitary facilities. It would, therefore, be a mistake to relate nutritional status to food inputs only. Undernourishment is often precipitated or enhanced by debilitating diseases and parasitic infections, and recent experiences of nutritional intervention, such as those of the UNICEF, have seized the importance of marshalling the delivery of vital non-food inputs in addition to monitoring food consumption.[24]

Even in famines the vast majority of people who die are killed by various diseases, and not directly by starvation as such.[25] This process takes the form

[24] On some of the medical issues involved in dealing with diseases that interfere with nutrition and survival, see UNICEF (1987a, 1988, 1989). On the interaction between undernourishment and infection, see Scrimshaw, Taylor and Gopalan (1968), Pacey and Payne (1985), Dasgupta and Ray (1986a), Leslie (1987), Osmani (1987a).

[25] This emerges clearly from a large number of empirical studies of famine mortality, including those of Foege (1971), Stein *et al.* (1975), Chen and Chowdhury (1977), Sen (1981a), Lardinois (1982), Maksudov (1986), de Waal (1988a, 1989a), Dyson (1988), and O'Grada (1988a), among others. On related matters, see also Sorokin (1942), Rotberg and Rabb (1983) and Hugo (1984). In spite of the role of epidemics in famines, the impact of excess mortality is usually far from neutral between different occupation groups (see e.g. Klein 1973, Sen 1981a, and Drèze 1988a on the 'class' nature of famine mortality patterns in a number of past Indian famines). Mortality patterns do not, however, always follow simple class lines. In a major study of famine mortality in Sudan in 1985, Alex de Waal (1989a) observes that mortality differentials between socio-economic groups within particular localities are far less striking than differentials between localities, the latter being related mainly to factors such as population displacements and water contamination. The author concludes that 'mortality can be explained simply by a changed disease environment during the famine', and that this change is completely unrelated to economic destitution or 'entitlements' (p. 24). But population displacements and water contamination are not just 'natural' events. There is a close link between destitution and displacement, which has been observed in numerous famines, in Africa as well as elsewhere. The roots of water contamination also include social elements, influenced by economic destitution, distress migration, and upheavals in living conditions.

of food deprivation, debilitation, enhanced morbidity, and increased mortality, and this sequence is supplemented by the encouragement that famines give to other influences in spreading disease (e.g. population movements and the spread of vectors of infection). The consumption and use of food fit into a complex process with biological and social links. The analysis of the relation between food deprivation, on the one hand, and undernourishment, morbidity, mortality, productivity and well-being, on the other, has to take note of the influence of the social environment, in addition to the variations of personal features emphasized in the literature on nutritional biology.

The widespread failure of basic capabilities relates to a diverse set of entitlement inadequacies. Even if we concentrate specifically on the capability failures related to nourishment, the parameters of policy have to be concerned with a much wider field of action than command over food. The domain of entitlement analysis has to be correspondingly broad.

4

Society, Class and Gender

4.1 Are Famines Natural Phenomena?

A distinction is sometimes drawn between 'man-made' famines and famines caused by nature. The purpose is, perhaps, to distinguish between those famines in which some kind of a natural event (e.g. a flood or a drought) causes the disaster, as opposed to a famine in which people die despite there being no such act of nature. Certainly, a distinction can indeed be made between famines in which the proximate initiator is some physical phenomenon and those in which social changes of one kind or other act as the prime mover. For example, the Bengal famine of 1943, which has often been described as being 'man-made',[1] had more to do with the uneven nature of the war boom and the oddities of public policy than with any great natural disaster,[2] whereas the 1972–3 drought in the Wollo province of Ethiopia had an important initiating role in the Wollo famine of 1973.

However, recognizing the varying role of physical nature in the development of a famine is not quite the same thing as classifying famines into 'man-made' and 'nature-made' types. That classification can, in fact, be deeply misleading. Famine is, by its very nature, a social phenomenon (it involves the inability of large groups of people to establish command over food in the society in which they live), but the forces influencing such occurrences may well include, *inter alia*, developments in physical nature (such as climate and weather) in addition to social processes. The idea that the causation of famines can be neatly split into 'natural' and 'man-made' ones would seem to be a bit of a non-starter.

No less importantly, it has to be recognized that even when the prime mover in a famine is a natural occurrence such as a flood or a drought, what its impact will be on the population would depend on how society is organized.[3] For example, a country with an extensive irrigation network is much less influenced by a drought than one without it (a distinction that has *some* bearing on the differential experience of India and sub-Saharan Africa, even though the

---

[1] See Ghosh (1944) and Uppal (1984).

[2] There was, in fact, a cyclone in a few parts of Bengal in October 1942 preceding the 1943 famine, but its impact on output and employment was fairly moderate, and its effect was mainly to supplement in a relatively minor way the forces of the famine that had their origin in the redistribution of purchasing power in the war economy of Bengal (see Sen 1977a, 1981a; see also Alamgir 1980, Chattopadhyay 1981). The view that the role of the cyclone was in fact crucial, argued by Peter Bowbrick (1986, 1987), is contradicted by output information, and also by the time pattern of price increases (see Sen 1986b, 1987d).

[3] The crucial role that social arrangements can play in the development of famines has been illuminatingly discussed in historical terms by Louise Tilly (1983).

main contrasts, as we shall argue in Part II, lie elsewhere).[4] Also, even when agricultural output goes down, or normal sources of incomes are hit, as a result of a drought or a flood, whether or not this would lead to a famine would depend on what arrangements society makes for protecting vulnerable groups from these adverse shocks, e.g. through public provision of employment or the public distribution of food.

Furthermore, even the occurrence of droughts, floods, and so on is not independent of social and economic policies. Many deserts have been created by reckless human action, and the distinction between natural and social causation is substantially blurred by the impact that society can have on the physical environment. For example, the problems of hunger and famine in sub-Saharan Africa are often seen, not entirely without reason, as being related to changes in climatic factors, particularly persistent drought conditions. But to see in those changes *the* causal explanation of African hunger makes the double error of (1) treating climatic change as independent of society, and (2) overlooking the role of economic, social, and political factors in determining the impact of a drought (or any other climatic change) on what people can produce or consume.

Blaming nature can, of course, be very consoling and comforting. It can be of great use especially to those in positions of power and responsibility. Comfortable inaction is, however, typically purchased at a very heavy price—a price that is paid by others, often with their lives. If the subject had not been such a terribly practical one, it would have been fine to discuss in leisurely peace whether in some intellectually defensible sense a class of famines can be seen as primarily caused by nature while others may not be so describable. Undoubtedly the direct or indirect role of nature may be quite a bit greater in some cases than in others. But these may not be the most useful distinctions on which to concentrate in planning urgent public action.

The points of overriding importance are: that there is no real evidence to doubt that all famines in the modern world are preventable by human action; that many countries—even some very poor ones—manage consistently to prevent them; that when people die of starvation there is almost invariably some massive social failure (whether or not a natural phenomenon had an initiating role in the causal process); and that the responsibilities for that failure deserve explicit attention and analysis, not evasion. There is, of course, much more to be said, but we have to say the first things first.

4.2 Society and Cooperative Conflicts

Given the crucial role of social conditions in the genesis of hunger and deprivation, it is important to have some understanding of certain basic

---

[4] Economic and social arrangements that make countries less prone to natural disasters can be an important part of development planning. On this see Berry and Kates (1980) and Glantz (1987a). See also Cannon (1978).

features of social relations in this field. One general characteristic that is, in some sense, quite obvious and that tends, nevertheless, to be neglected often enough is the coexistence of conflicts as well as congruence of interests in most forms of human interaction. There *are* many advantages to be gained by different people from cooperation and collaboration, and yet there are also elements of clash and divergence of interests. Such coexistence of cooperation and conflict is endemic in social relations (this general issue was discussed in Chapter 1).

The cooperative elements are often strongly emphasized in the context of describing the social challenge involved in confronting hunger and famines. That can be exactly right, and there are indeed great gains to be made for most people, possibly even all, through such matters as protecting the environment, preventing droughts, or eliminating epidemics. But at the same time, serious mistakes can be made in the analysis of deprivation in general, and of hunger in particular, if we do not pay attention to the pervasive elements of conflict that are among the constitutive features of any society.

Conflicts of class interests have received, rightly, a good deal of attention, partly in connection with Marxian analysis. These conflicts are relevant in an obvious and elementary way in matters of hunger and famine, and the broad categorization of classes can be fruitfully extended by seeking further divisions related to occupation groups.[5] Famines are always divisive phenomena. The victims typically come from the bottom layers of society—landless agricultural labourers, poor peasants and share-croppers, pastoralist nomads, urban destitutes, and so on. Contrary to statements that are sometimes made, there does not seem to have been a famine in which victims came from all classes of the society.[6]

Sometimes there is extensive competition and combat between different classes or occupation groups in trying to secure a larger share of a given supply of food that is fixed in the short run. For example, in the Bengal famine of 1943, the rural agricultural labourers who had to buy food with their wages were hit by the rise in food prices related, at least partly, to the increase in the purchasing power of the urban population in the war economy of Bengal. When there is a limited amount of food, with the market dividing it among the

[5] See Chapter 2. The diverse positions of different occupation groups have been discussed in the context of specific famines in various empirical studies, e.g. Sen (1981a), Oughton (1982), Snowdon (1985), Kumar (1986), Osmani (1986), Ratnavale (1986), Sobhan (1986), Mahieu and Nour (1987), Ravallion (1987a, 1987b), Drèze (1988a), Desai (1988a, 1986b), D'Souza (1988).

[6] There are folklores about 'kings going begging' in some famines, but little hard evidence in that direction. One allegedly true example of this, according to the prestigious *Encyclopaedia Britannica*, was the Indian famine of 1344–5, in which it is claimed that even 'the Moghul emperor was unable to obtain the necessaries for his household' (*Encyclopaedia Britannica*, 11th ed., vol. x, London 1910–11: 167). However, that engrossing story cannot be exactly accurate, not just because the Moghul empire was not established in India until 1526, but also because the Tughlak king in power in 1344–5 had in fact managed to organize one of the most ambitious programmes of famine relief, including distributing food and cash, and remitting taxes (on this see Loveday 1914, Chapters 1 and 4; also Sen 1981a: 43).

population according to their respective purchasing powers and market pulls, a worsening of the relative position of some groups in the scale of money incomes can lead to an absolute decline in their ability to command food. In 'food battles', the Devil takes the hindmost.

There are conflicts of interests of various kinds that operate in the economy, and the importance of cooperative elements in social relations should not make us lose sight of the extensive and vital role that interest conflicts can play in worsening the predicament of some groups as it improves the position of others. Indeed, 'cooperative conflict' (i.e. the presence of strong elements of conflict embedded in a situation in which there are mutual gains to be made by cooperation) is a pervasive feature of social living, and to take note of this 'mixed' structure is as important in the analysis of hunger and famines as it is in any other substantive social investigation.

The outcomes of cooperative conflicts depend on a variety of factors and can be analysed in different ways.[7] Generally, it seems reasonable to predict that one of the important factors is the 'breakdown position' in case cooperation fails.[8] The more a party has to fear from such a breakdown, the less able it will be to secure a favourable outcome in the choice over alternative cooperative solutions. The workers with no ownership of means of production are, of course, particularly vulnerable to the breakdown of employment arrangements, and this contributes to the bad terms of employment that workers tend to get—an issue that has been extensively discussed by Marx, among others. In the context of hunger analysis, it is important to note both (1) the vulnerable 'breakdown position' of those owning few productive assets other than their labour power (they are often the first to starve when the normal operation of the economy is disrupted), and (2) the influence of this vulnerability on the deals that such people tend to get, for instance in exploitative rural employment.

The other side of the same coin can be seen in the enhanced bargaining power of labour in private employment when alternative earning opportunities improve. For example, there is some evidence that the security provided by the Employment Guarantee Scheme in the state of Maharashtra in India has had a significant impact on the terms of employment in the rural economy, and

---

[7] What J. F. Nash (1950) called 'the bargaining problem' is a particular type of 'cooperative conflict', with certain specific features, e.g. the interests of each are representable by the respective cardinal utilities, perception problems about interest and contributions are not directly involved in the characterization of the game, ideas of acceptable distribution have to depend only on utility information, the solution must satisfy certain specific characteristics of symmetry and consistency (see Sen, 1970). Formal models of bargaining for intrafamily divisions have been presented by Clemhout and Wan (1977), Manser and Brown (1980), McElroy and Horney (1981), among others. See also Brown and Chuang (1980), Rochford (1981), Pollak (1983), Folbre (1986).

[8] This was one of the important insights provided by the original Nash (1950) model of bargaining, which made the predicted solution sensitive to the outcome that would emerge in the absence of cooperation (sometimes called, perhaps a little misleadingly, the 'status quo position'). This feature has been retained in some form in most of the later models of bargaining; see Schelling (1960), Kalai and Smordinsky (1975), Harsanyi (1976), Kaneko and Nakamura (1979), Roth (1985), Binmore (1987), Binmore and Dasgupta (1987).

generally on the economic and social positions of agricultural labourers.[9] The benefits received from the Employment Guarantee Scheme by vulnerable groups in Maharashtra may thus go well beyond the additional earnings from public employment. In assessing various forms of public intervention (e.g. land reforms, literacy campaigns, or employment programmes), importance has to be *inter alia* attached to their impact on the breakdown position of vulnerable groups and through that on the deal that these people receive in the economy and the society.

There are other determinants of outcomes of 'cooperative conflicts' than the breakdown position of the various parties involved, e.g. perceptions of contributions to joint prosperity, threats that the parties can respectively employ. The relevance of different influences will depend crucially on the nature of the congruent interests and the understanding of conflicts faced by the different parties. Here too, public action, e.g. in the form of education and politics, can have a far-reaching impact on the deal that vulnerable groups receive in the society.

Cooperative conflict takes a particularly important but complex form in matters of gender relations, such as the distribution of joint benefits between men and women in the family.[10] In that context, as we shall argue presently, the nature of the perception of each person's contribution to the joint benefits can play a particularly important part (for example, whether women are seen as 'contributing' much to the family's economic prosperity can become a crucial variable even in the division of food and health care).[11] But the need to take note of the nature of cooperative conflicts in the analysis of hunger and deprivation is a more general requirement that has pervasive relevance because of the extensive coexistence of congruent and conflicting interests in the social relations that govern people's ability to establish entitlement over food and related necessities.

4.3   Female Deprivation and Gender Bias

One of the difficult fields of 'food battle' is that of intrafamily divisions. While economic models are often constructed on the assumption that the distribution of commodities among different members of the family is done on the basis of

---

[9] On this see Deshpande (1982, 1984), Dandekar (1983), Walker *et al.* (1986), Acharya and Panwalkar (1988*a*, 1988*b*), Mencher (1988).

[10] This is analysed in Sen (1985*c*, 1987*c*) in terms of the notion of 'extended entitlement' discussed in Chapter 1 of this book, which broadens the focus of entitlement analysis from legal rights to a framework in which accepted social notions of 'legitimacy' can be influential. See also Kynch and Sen (1983), Bryceson (1985), Jain and Banerjee (1985), Whitehead (1985), Agarwal (1986, 1988), Boserup (1986), Tilly (1986), Vaughan (1987), Wilson (1987*a*, 1987*b*).

[11] The issue of perception has some relevance also in the analysis of class relations. Indeed, it was in that context that the Marxian analysis of 'false consciousness' was first used, and it can make a difference as to how people view and understand the nature of society and how it produces as well as distributes the jointly generated goods.

equalizing well-being or need-fulfilment, there is considerable evidence that intrafamily divisions often involve very unequal treatments. The systematic deprivation of women *vis-à-vis* men in many societies (particularly that of girls *vis-à-vis* boys) has attracted a good deal of attention recently, and there is a fair amount of evidence in that direction from many parts of the world, including South Asia, West Asia, North Africa, and China.

It is not, of course, easy to observe directly who is eating how much from a shared kitchen.[12] Claims regarding unequal treatment in the division of food are typically based on indirect information.[13] A natural direction in which to go is that of examining direct evidence of various nutritional and related functionings, such as clinical signs of undernourishment, morbidity rates, or comparative mortality patterns.[14] This also has the merit of establishing comparisons in terms of those things that ultimately matter (what kind of life a person can lead), rather than trying to observe just commodity intakes, which are means to achievements rather than being important in themselves. Our ultimate concern, as was argued in the last chapter, is not with the size of nutritional intakes, but with the extent of nutritional well-being and with the capability to achieve that well-being.

Since there can be substantial interpersonal and intrapersonal variations in the relation between nutritional intakes and health achievements or functioning ability (as was discussed in the last chapter), comparisons of inputs can be a defective basis for the assessment of relative treatments. If, on the other hand, it is found that women are more frequently undernourished than men, or that the ratio of female to male mortality rates is higher than what can be expected when there is no serious sex bias in the division of food or health care, there would indeed be a good ground for questioning the thesis of equal treatment.

Such evidence of inequality does exist in many developing economies. Even the elementary statistics of the ratio of female to male population bring out a picture of remarkable variations. To illustrate, Table 4.1 presents values of female–male ratio—FMR for short—for different regions of the world. For the more developed economies in Europe or North America the FMR tends to average around 1.05, mainly reflecting certain survival advantages that women seem to have over men in the absence of serious anti-female bias in the division

---

[12] For some interesting attempts in this direction and discussion of the problems involved, see Chen, Huq and D'Souza (1981), Chimwaza (1982) and Chaudhury (1987, 1988). See also Wheeler (1984), Harriss (1986), and Wheeler and Abdullah (1988).

[13] The usual techniques of 'equivalent scales' for the analysis of household consumption and welfare (see Deaton and Muellbauer 1980) are not easy to apply for intrahousehold divisions, since the purchase data do not discriminate between different users. But some deductions can be made on the basis of different regularities of consumption patterns among households with different demographic and social characteristics. On this see Muellbauer (1987) and Deaton (1987, 1988); on related matters see also Deaton and Case (1987) and Blackorby and Donaldson (1988).

[14] See Bardhan (1974, 1984, 1987), Mitra (1980), Chen, Huq and D'Souza (1981), Miller (1981), Kynch and Sen (1983), Sen (1984b, 1985a), Kynch (1985), Harriss (1986, 1988a), Harriss and Watson (1987), Lipton (1987b), Momsen and Townsend (1987), among many other contributions.

Table 4.1 Female–male ratio (FMR) and 'missing women', 1986

Region	FMR	Missing women in relation to sub-Saharan African FMR	
		Number (millions)	Proportion (%)
Europe	1.050		
Northern America	1.047		
Sub-Saharan Africa	1.022		
South-east Asia	1.010	2.4	1.2
Latin America	1.000	4.4	2.2
North Africa	0.984	2.4	3.9
West Asia	0.948	4.3	7.8
Iran	0.942	1.4	8.5
China	0.941	44.0	8.6
Bangladesh	0.940	3.7	8.7
India	0.933	36.9	9.5
Pakistan	0.905	5.2	12.9

Notes: (i) The *number* of 'missing women' for a particular country is calculated as the difference between (1) the number of women the country would have if its FMR was the same as that of sub-Saharan Africa (i.e. 1.022), given its actual male population, and (2) the number of women it actually has. The *proportion* of 'missing women' is the ratio of missing women to the actual number of women in a particular coun⁻ry. (ii) 'Sub-Saharan Africa' here includes all of Africa except North Africa and South Africa.

Source: Calculated from data on male and female populations provided in *UN Demographic Yearbook 1986*, Tables 2 and 3. This publication does not give separate male and female population figures for India. The Indian figures are therefore based on the female–male ratio of the 1981 census and the 1986 population total, respectively provided in *ILO Yearbook of Labo.ir Statistics 1988*, Table 1, and *World Development Report 1988*, Table 27.

of such things as food and health care. In contrast, the FMR in South Asia, China, West Asia, and North Africa averages only around 0.93 or 0.94.[15] In India, not only is the mortality differential remarkably sharp among children (that is, mortality rates are much higher for girls than for boys), the higher mortality rate of females *vis-à-vis* males applies to all age groups until the late thirties.

However, not all poor regions of the world have very low female–male ratios. In fact, both South-east Asia and sub-Saharan Africa have female–male ratios higher than unity (though not as high as Europe or North America). We shall have to address the question as to why these differences are observed (on this

[15] For some comparative information on this, see Kynch and Sen (1983), Sen (1984a, 1985a, 1988c), Kynch (1985), Harriss and Watson (1987), Dyson (1988). The sex ratios observed in de/eloped countries are not, of course, in any sense 'natural'. They reflect a complex interaction of biological, environmental and social differences affecting the lives of men and women. However, the fact that, on balance, biological factors work in the direction of general survival advantages for females relative to males (especially in infancy) is not in doubt. These and related issues are insightfully discussed by several contributors in Lopez and Ruzicka (1983), especially Lopez (1983), Ruzicka and Lopez (1983) and Waldron (1983).

see section 4.5). It is also interesting to probe these differences to throw light on the magnitude of the problem of shortfall of women in the total population—primarily reflecting excess female mortality at present and in the recent past of the concerned region.[16] It may, for example, be asked how many more women there would be in India or China (given the number of men in each) if they had the female–male ratio that obtains in sub-Saharan Africa. The number of 'missing women', calculated in this way, works out as 37 million in India and 44 million in China. Table 4.1 presents the estimates for a number of regions.

The number of 'missing women' reflects an aspect of a complex and terrible problem. The shortfall of women arises from a higher sex differential in mortality rates in India and China than obtains in the sub-Saharan African economies, and reveals in quiet statistics a gruesome story of anti-female bias in social divisions. It is also interesting to note that while sub-Saharan Africa is taken to be, in some respects, the 'problem region' of the world, when it comes to sex bias, the more problematic countries are elsewhere.

The number of 'missing women' as we have calculated it is highest in China, but proportionate to the population it is even higher in Southern Asia. Pakistan has, in fact, the highest proportion of 'missing women'—as high as 13 per cent. There are significant numbers of 'missing women' also elsewhere, including in West Asia, North Africa, and even Latin America. The numbers would have been larger if we had used, for comparison, not the sub-Saharan African female-male ratio, but that of, say, Europe or North America.

It should be mentioned that the differential mortality rates need not be wholly or even primarily connected with unequal treatments in the division of *food* as such, and the divergence can arise from other inequalities, such as those of access to health care.[17] As was argued earlier (in Chapter 3), it is a mistake to concentrate exclusively on the delivery of food and to ignore the tremendous interdependence and complementarity that obtain between the use of food and other resources (such as health care). Here as elsewhere, entitlement comparisons have to go beyond the limited focus of food entitlements to the more comprehensive concern for entitlements to the different goods and services which influence our nutritional opportunities and achievements.

---

[16] The female–male ratio is also, of course, affected by the relative numbers of female and male births. It is easily shown that the *differences* in the interregional birth ratios, in so far as they exist, are much too tiny to explain any significant part of the FMR differences *between the regions*. It has sometimes been suggested that the low FMR in India is due to a particularly high ratio of males in Indian births. That hypothesis can be rejected on the basis of demographic analysis; on this see Visaria (1961).

[17] There is indeed some direct evidence of the disadvantaged access of women to medical care, and also of enhanced morbidity rates. See Chen, Huq and D'Souza (1981), Miller (1981), Bhatia (1983), Kynch and Sen (1983), Sen (1984a, 1985a), Leela Visaria (1985), Basu (1987, 1988), Chaudhury (1987, 1988), Das Gupta (1987, 1989a, 1989b), Ramalingaswami (1987), Harriss (1988a). See also Wyon and Gordon (1971), Levinson (1972), Dyson and Moore (1983), Kielman *et al.* (1983). In an extensive review of the literature on the intrafamily allocation of food in South Asia, Barbara Harriss (1986) finds no conclusive evidence that women are discriminated against in the division of food as such. However, there is strong evidence of discrimination in health care and in parental attention.

The sharp contrast between South Asia and sub-Saharan Africa which emerges from the evidence on female–male ratios is of considerable significance, and has several interesting features. First, many studies of food intake, nutritional status and survival chances confirm the pattern of gender differentials indicated by a demographic examination of female–male ratios. Anti-female discrimination in health and nutrition is endemic in South Asia, but much less noticeable (perhaps even absent) in the case of sub-Saharan Africa.[18]

Second, there are many possible reasons for this interregional contrast. A full explanation would have to take into account the profound cultural, economic and social differences between South Asia and sub-Saharan Africa. It is worth noting, however, that the lower incidence of anti-female bias in the latter region fits well with the view that the vulnerability of the respective parties is one important influence on the outcome of cooperative conflicts (including those involved in gender divisions). There is indeed a good deal of anthropological and statistical evidence on the greater autonomy of African women (in terms of land rights, access to gainful employment, control over property, freedom of movement, etc.) in comparison with the general position of South Asian women.[19] This point is further discussed in section 4.5, particularly in relation to the role of 'gainful' employment.

Third, the extent of sex discrimination in health and nutrition is not an immutable feature of any society, and important changes have taken place over time in both regions. It has been argued that sex differentials in mortality are slowly narrowing in South Asia, while they seem to be widening in at least some countries of sub-Saharan Africa.[20] The latter phenomenon, if confirmed, may relate in part to the decline of agriculture in these countries, and the greater reliance on non-agricultural activities to which men have a privileged access.

Finally, the relative absence of sex discrimination in health and nutrition in sub-Saharan Africa does not imply, by any means, that sex discrimination *in general* is of little importance in African societies. Indeed, even in the rich countries of West Europe and North America, where nutrition and survival are no longer areas of intense discrimination between the sexes, women remain disadvantaged in numerous ways. Similarly, there is considerable evidence that the general status of women in African societies involves significant and pervasive inequities.[21]

[18] For references to studies on South Asia, see the preceding footnote. On the absence of systematic anti-female bias in health and nutrition in sub-Saharan Africa, see e.g. the demographic studies of Ohadike (1983), Caldwell and Caldwell (1987a), and Gbenyon and Locoh (1987), the nutrition surveys of Nash (1986), Brett (1987), and von Braun (1988), and the review of the evidence by Svedberg (1986, 1988).

[19] On these issues, see Boserup (1970), Hill (1975), Buvinic (1976), Whitehead (1986), Caldwell and Caldwell (1987b), and the literature cited in these studies. Kandiyoti (1988) contrasts the bargains faced by women in the very different 'patriarchal systems' of South Asia and sub-Saharan Africa. The interlinkages between cultural and economic relations involved in these interregional contrasts are discussed in Basu (1988) and Sen (1989a).

[20] See e.g. Dyson (1987) on South Asia, and Gbenyon and Locoh (1987) on sub-Saharan Africa.

[21] See Whitehead (1986) and the literature cited there. See also Boserup (1970), Rogers (1980) and Stichter and Parpart (1988).

4.4 Famine Mortality and Gender Divisions

There is considerable dispute as to whether the intensity of female deprivation increases in famine situations. It is, in fact, possible that two divergent tendencies come into play in this context. First, as was discussed earlier, women appear to have certain biological advantages over men in survival, and there is some evidence that these general advantages enhance the relative ability of women to cope with temporary distress situations vis-à-vis men.[22] Second, the factors that govern the distribution of food, health care and general attention among men and women may undergo changes in famine situations. This influence can act in the opposite direction to the previous one, if it takes the form of greater discrimination against women.

These divergent tendencies can result in a rather complex pattern of sex differentials in the experience of famine. On the one hand, there is considerable evidence that the proportionate increase of mortality is typically lower for women than for men in famine situations. This was, in fact, the observed pattern in most of the famines for which relevant demographic data are available.[23]

On the other hand, a number of studies also bring out the fact that, in many societies, the priorities of the family are often pro-male in distress situations.[24] In so far as greater physical distress coexists with a smaller increase in mortality for females vis-à-vis males, the explanation may have to be sought, at least partly, in terms of greater female ability to survive nutritional stress.

The empirical evidence on this entire subject remains to be fully investigated. The two—possibly opposite—tendencies noted earlier can lead to different patterns of sex differentials in food intake, anthropometric status, mortality rates and socio-economic indicators of stress. There can also be important interregional differences in the connections (1) between economic distress and patterns of sex-and-age specific deprivation of food and other commodities, (2) between the distribution of deprivation in intake and that of undernourishment, and (3) between the distribution of undernourishment and that of mortality.

The overriding fact that is altogether difficult to escape is the remarkable relative deprivation of women in many parts of the world in normal (non-famine) situations; the nature of sex bias in famine situations has to be assessed

[22] See Shettles (1958), Widdowson (1976), Rivers (1982), Payne and Lipton (1988).

[23] See e.g. Boyle and O'Grada (1986), O'Grada (1988a) and Voglaire (1988) on the Irish famines of the 1840s, Lardinois (1982) and Kynch (1987b) on 19th-century famines in India, Maksudov (1986) on the Ukrainian famines of 1927–38, Valaoras (1946) on the Greek famine of 1941–2, Greenough (1982) on the Bengal famine of 1943, Hill (1988) on the Chinese famines of 1958–61, and de Waal (1987) on the Sudan famine of 1985. It is, however, sometimes the case that in particular age groups the increase of female mortality is more pronounced than that of male mortality, even when the overall increase of mortality may affect men more; see e.g. Greenough (1982) and Agarwal (1988).

[24] See Chen et al. (1981), Greenough (1982), Rivers (1982), Kynch and Sen (1983), Sen (1984a), Fernandes and Menon (1987), Vaughan (1985, 1987), Agarwal (1988), Arnold (1988), Kabeer (1989).

in that light. The observation of widespread female disadvantage in nutritional conditions is of direct interest in the analysis of hunger and deprivation in a substantial part of the world, and cannot but be a matter of great concern in the making of economic and social policy in such regions as South Asia, West Asia, North Africa, and China. The issue of comparative position of women during famines is perhaps of less general interest if only because famines, with a few exceptions, have been confined in recent decades to sub-Saharan Africa, which is, on the whole, a part of the world in which there is little evidence of systematic anti-female bias in nutrition and survival.[25]

This is not to say that issues of sex discrimination in famine situations are altogether inconsequential in sub-Saharan Africa. Indeed, even for that region, a number of surveys have brought out the sharp social and economic disadvantages that women can face in coping with a subsistence crisis.[26] These problems deserve serious attention. However, as far as the question of famine mortality and nutritional damage is concerned, it appears that sex discrimination at worst only supplements in a relatively small way the enormous destructive forces that come into play in African famines.

4.5 Gender and Cooperative Conflicts

The part that the coexistence of congruent and conflicting interests plays in social relations was discussed earlier, and its bearing on the problem of hunger and related deprivations was explored. The presence of substantial anti-female bias in well-being and survival in many parts of the world can be seen to have clear connections with the way problems of cooperative conflicts in gender relations are tackled.[27]

It can be argued that the 'deal' that women get in the division of joint benefits in the family is unfavourably affected by the more precarious position of the female in the event of 'breakdown' (e.g. the separation of spouses or their cohabitation in a state of permanent strife). The greater vulnerability of women may be only partly due to biological differences (connected with reproduction, differences in physical strength, etc.), and is, in fact, often socially generated. Nevertheless this greater precariousness is typically influential in determining the relative shares on which women and men can respectively lay claims in the division of family resources.

---

[25] See section 4.3. Comparisons of nutritional status based on either calorie intake or anthropometric evidence for children do not reveal any general bias against girls vis-à-vis boys in sub-Saharan Africa, even in distress situations (see Nash 1986, Brett 1987, Deaton 1988, von Braun 1988, Svedberg 1988, Wheeler and Abdullah 1988; Médecins Sans Frontières Belgium, personal communication).

[26] See Campbell and Trechter (1982), Rivers (1982), Vaughan (1985, 1987), Matiza et al. (1988). Examples of anti-female discrimination observed in some African famines are the greater frequency of fasting for women and the abandonment of women by their husbands.

[27] The analysis that follows is more extensively developed in Sen (1985c, 1987c).

The greater vulnerability of women is closely connected with lesser opportunities for getting outside work and paid employment. The extent of so-called 'gainful activities' can also be a factor of influence on its own (in addition to acting through its impact on the 'breakdown' situations). In determining how the family benefits should be divided, importance seems to be attached, as many studies bring out, to who is 'contributing' how much to the joint prosperity of the family.[28] Even though the ability to do outside work on the part of some members of the family may depend crucially on the willingness of the other members to do housework, nevertheless in the accounting of respective 'contributions', paid employment and outside 'gainful' activities seem to loom particularly large. In so far as 'perceived contributions' are an influence of importance in determining who 'ought' to get how much in intrafamily divisions, the traditional structure of work division inside and outside the home may particularly disfavour women vis-à-vis men. In general, various perception problems enter into this complex issue of cooperative conflict, and many of these perceptions have close links with the traditions of work division between males and females.[29]

While considerations of cooperative conflicts (including the relevance of breakdown positions, perception biases, etc.) take us in one direction of analysis, those of economic calculations by household heads take us along another track. In recent years there have been a number of interesting attempts to relate the neglect of female children in South Asia to the greater 'investment value' of the survival of boys in comparison with girls.[30] This line of argument too brings in the greater earning power of men, related to the way society is organized in most parts of the world. However, it sees this information not as a determinant of cooperative conflict affecting the status and deal that women get, but as a part of the investment accounting of the household head. While the cooperative conflict approach concentrates on women and men, and sees the position of girls vis-à-vis boys as being related to the same basic influences that colour the way women's contributions and deserts are viewed, the investment approach sees the child-rearing problem in terms of relative returns to investment and does not directly address the issue of relative deprivation of adult women.

It is not easy to assess precisely what part hard-headed investment calculations play in the treatment of children, and there has been a certain amount of understandable questioning as to whether this is getting the social anthropology of child rearing right. Also, whether there is any wilful neglect of female children—compared with the attention that boys get—has also itself been

[28] See Sen (1985c) and the empirical studies reviewed there.
[29] See Boserup (1970, 1986), Chen and Ghuznavi (1976), Loutfi (1980), Kynch and Sen (1983), P. Bardhan (1984, 1987), K. Bardhan (1985), Sen (1985c, 1987c), M. Chen (1986a, 1986b), Das Gupta (1987), Joekes (1987), Papanek (1987, 1989), Wilson (1987a, 1987b), Agarwal (1988), Aslanbeigui and Summerfield (1989).
[30] See particularly Rosenzweig and Schultz (1982), Behrman and Deolalikar (1987), Behrman (1988a, 1988b).

questioned, especially in India.[31] There is scope for argument on this, but the evidence of preference for having male children is well documented in South Asia,[32] and it is hard to rule out the possibility that for poor families such hard-headed calculations may play some part in determining intrafamily divisions. However, it is also difficult to ignore the influence of the *perception* of greater male 'contribution'—related to the traditional patterns of work division—in determining views of relative deserts of the different family members. The general picture of anti-female bias in intrafamily divisions would seem to call for something more than just the accounting of relative values of 'returns to investment in child survival'. The whole issue may involve a much greater mixing of economic, social, and cultural influences than the narrow economic models may admit.

Be that as it may, there is considerable evidence that greater involvement with outside work and paid employment does tend to go with less anti-female bias in intrafamily distribution.[33] This has important policy implications no matter whether the influence is due to the impact of female 'economic activity' on the breakdown position of women, *or* to its influence on the perception of 'contributions' made by women, *or* to its effect on the accounting of returns to investment, *or* to some other chain of social or economic causation.

Table 4.2   Activity-rate ratios and life expectancy ratios, 1980

Regions	Activity-rate ratios (female–male)		Life expectancy ratios (female–male)	
	Values	Ranks	Values	Ranks
Non-Northern Africa	0.645	1	1.071	1
Eastern & South Eastern Asia	0.610	2	1.066	2
Western Asia	0.373	3	1.052	3
Southern Asia	0.336	4	0.989	5
Northern Africa	0.158	5	1.050	4

Source: Sen (1987c, 1988c), calculated from country data given in ILO (1986) and the United Nations tapes on 'Estimates and Projections of Population' (1985). The activity rate ratios represent the proportions of total population of each sex engaged in so-called 'economic' (or 'gainful') activities.

[31] See e.g. Alaka Basu (1987, 1988).

[32] See Miller (1981). The preference for male children appears to be especially strong after the birth of one or more daughters; see Das Gupta (1987, 1989a, 1989b) and Amin (1988).

[33] Various micro-economic studies have also brought out the importance of outside work for women's status and for their power within the family. On this see Boserup (1970, 1986), Standing and Sheehan (1978), Auerbach (1979), Cain et al. (1979), Croll (1978), Lloyd and Niemi (1979), Amsden (1980), Bhatty (1980), Loutfi (1980), Banerjee (1982, 1985), Beneria (1982), Deere and de Leal (1982), Dixon (1982, 1983), ILO (1982a, 1982b), Mies (1982), Phongpaichit (1982), Dandekar (1983), Sen (1984a), Jain and Banerjee (1985), Mahmud and Mahmud (1985), Agarwal (1986, 1988), Adnan (1988), Basu (1988), Blumberg (1988). See also an examination of the empirical literature in Sen (1985c).

It may be useful to examine whether the differential involvement of women in outside work in different regions of Asia and Africa provides any clues as to the possible causation of greater anti-female bias in Asia than in Africa, in North Africa than in sub-Saharan Africa, and so on. Given the broad cultural contrasts involved, the focus of comparison has to be correspondingly wide (rather than being based on political boundaries of state and province). We present and compare in Table 4.2 the ratios of 'economic activity rates' (roughly pertaining to outside work, including paid employment) of women *vis-à-vis* men, and the ratios of female life expectancy to male life expectancy.[34]

It turns out that the ranking of the different regions in terms of life expectancy ratios is almost the same as that in terms of activity-rate ratios.[35] In particular, the higher female participation in 'gainful' activities in sub-Saharan Africa dominates all the other regions, just as its female–male life expectancy ratio does. That dominance includes not merely an Asia–Africa divergence, but also a sharp dichotomy within Africa, between North Africa and sub-Saharan Africa.[36]

A simple finding of this kind does not, of course, establish any firm connections, but it is interesting that the relations that are expected on the basis of general economic and social analyses are on the whole confirmed rather than contradicted by these data.[37] When we come to policy, it would be hard to leave out the possible importance of female participation in 'gainful' economic activities as a material factor in combating the special deprivation of women in many parts of the world.

[34] On some conceptual and empirical issues related to this analysis, see Sen (1987c). Life expectancy figures tell us more about *current* mortality rates, whereas the female–male ratios reflect the effects of past mortality rates as well. Since the *activity-rate ratios* are current figures, it makes more sense to relate them to the *life expectancy ratios*.

[35] There is only one variation, with the relative position of Southern Asia and Northern Africa being reversed as we move from one ranking to the other—the fourth becomes fifth and vice versa. Note also that China has not been included in this table. The Chinese case has a number of special features, including problems of accounting as well as some particular policy variations such as the rule of 'one-child family' (on this see Chapter 11), but it is on the whole an exception to the picture revealed by the table, since China has a high activity-rate ratio but a relatively lower-ranked life expectancy ratio.

[36] There is a similar contrast within India between the North and the South, with the Southern states having both higher female participation and less gender bias in female survival. See Boserup (1970), Miller (1981), Bardhan (1987), Harriss (1988a). See also Caldwell and Caldwell (1987a).

[37] Krishnaji (1987) notes that the female–male ratio is higher in families of labourers and small peasants than in those of bigger farmers in rural India. This is also in line with the same relations, since the extent of female participation in economic activities is much higher in households of labourers and small peasants than in those of larger farmers (on this and related issues, see Gulati 1975, Jain 1980, ILO 1981, Mukhopadhyay 1981, Chatterji 1984, Reddy 1985, Chakravarty 1986, Nayyar 1987, Nagaraj 1989). But there can be other influences as well, as Krishnaji notes. He also comments, not without reason, on the tendency to calculate 'the economic value of women', by 'economists who do not distinguish human beings from commodities' (p. 897). In this respect, the 'cooperative conflict' model is quite different from the 'investment return' model, since the former sees the influence of outside earning on the status and clout of women (and views the treatment of girls in that light), rather than seeing it just as an influence on the relative 'returns' of investment 'in' girls and boys. The economic factors merge with social and cultural issues in this broader approach.

4.6 *Protection, Promotion and Social Security*

This book is concerned primarily with action. Even though we have been spending a good bit of time sorting out the diagnostics (this is necessary to analyse the strategies needed for action), our primary concern is with the role of public action in the provision of social security on a wide basis. The elimination of famines and endemic undernourishment fits into that general approach.

We have distinguished earlier (in Chapter 1) between two different—though not unrelated—aspects of social security, viz. *protection* and *promotion*. The former is concerned with preventing a decline in living conditions in general and with averting starvation in particular. The problem of protection is paramount in the context of famine prevention, which is the subject matter of Part II (Chapters 5–8) of this book. The other objective of social security is enhancing normal living conditions, including the elimination of persistent deprivation and endemic undernutrition. Part III (Chapters 9–12) is primarily concerned with this issue.

It is perhaps useful to make a few clarificatory remarks about the dual objectives of protection and promotion. First, while the objectives of protection and promotion are distinct, they are not independent of each other. Success with the promotional objective may make protection easier. For example, if the normal level of prosperity is socially enhanced across the board, the task of protection becomes less intensely crucial for survival, since there is then more of a margin to fall back on, and also since the family's own insurance arrangements may become more feasible in those circumstances.

Similarly, successful protection from famines and other crises can help to preserve the family's capital stock and make promotional objectives that much easier to pursue. Indeed, one of the side effects of famines typically is the demolition of the poor rural family's assets, and preventing that from happening helps to maintain and enhance the normal—'non-crisis'—capabilities and levels of living.

Second, the contrast between protection and promotion will arise in the specification of means as well as ends. While we have outlined the distinction here as a categorization of objectives, a similar differentiation can be made in the category of means as well. For example, it is often useful to distinguish between the instrumental role of protection of incomes (preventing sharp declines) and that of promotion of incomes (raising persistently low incomes). There is also an important difference between entitlement protection and entitlement promotion. The protection–promotion distinction has to be integrated with other contrasts used in policy analysis.

Third, while both the terms 'protection' and 'promotion' might be thought to have a somewhat 'statist' presumption, their use in this context is to clarify the distinction between different types of social objectives rather than to see the state as a great promoter and a heroic protector. As we argue throughout this book, public action is neither just a matter of state activity, nor an issue of acting from some 'privileged ground'.

Public action includes not just what is done *for* the public by the state, but also what is done *by* the public for itself. The latter includes not merely the directly beneficial contributions of social institutions, but also the actions of pressure groups and political activists. Indeed, even in the determination of what the government itself will do, the role of public pressure may be an important one. There is, for example, considerable evidence that timely governmental action in preventing famines has often been precipitated by powerful newspaper reports on early cases of starvation and by the pressure of political and social organizations demanding action.[38] Similarly, the combating of gender inequality relates, as was discussed earlier in this chapter, to the economic and social roles of women (e.g. female involvement in so-called 'gainful' activities), and also to the political awareness of existing economic, social and legal inequities and of the possibilities of radical change.[39]

Public action against hunger and deprivation involves the agency of the public as well as its role as the beneficiary. While the activities of the state fit into this general picture and can play an important—even crucial—role, it would be a mistake to see it as the only, or even the primary, part of that picture. Ultimately, public action will be determined by what the public is ready to do, what sacrifices it is ready to make, what things it is determined to demand, and what it refuses to tolerate. The vehicles of public action are immensely varied. We must not impoverish the richness of the set of possibilities by choosing—explicitly or by implication—a narrow conception of public action. The terrible problems of resilient hunger in the modern world call for a more adequate challenge.

---

[38] See Sen (1981a, 1983a), Ram (1986), Drèze (1988a, 1989), Reddy (1988). See also Chapters 5, 8 and 11.

[39] On the latter, and its connections with general political movements in the Third World, see Sobhan (1978), Omvedt (1980), Mazumdar (1985), Jayawardena (1986), Afshar (1987), Papanek (1989) and Tinker (forthcoming), among other contributions.

PART II

Famines

5

Famines and Social Response

5.1 Famine Prevention and Entitlement Protection

Faith in the ability of public intervention to avert famines is a relatively new phenomenon. Even as confident a utilitarian as James Mill felt compelled to use the most fatalistic language to tell his friend David Ricardo about the likely effects of a spell of adverse weather in England:

> Does not this weather frighten you? . . . There must now be of necessity a very deficient crop, and very high prices—and these with an unexampled scarcity of work will produce a degree of misery, the thought of which makes the flesh creep on one's bones—one third of the people must die—it would be a blessing to take them into the streets and high ways, and cut their throats as we do with pigs.[1]

Ricardo had full sympathy for Mill's feelings, and assured him that he was 'sorry to see a disposition to inflame the minds of the lower orders by persuading them that legislation can afford them any relief'.[2]

Echoes of Mill's and Ricardo's pessimism can be found in abundance even today.[3] But an enormous amount of evidence now bears testimony to the potential effectiveness of public action for famine prevention. This part of the book examines the role of public intervention in the elimination of famines.

We discussed in Chapter 2 how famines develop from entitlement failures suffered by a large section of the population. Those who cannot establish command over an adequate amount of food have to perish from starvation. Famine prevention is essentially concerned, therefore, with the *protection of entitlements*. That much might be obvious enough, but a few interpretational issues should be addressed straightaway to avoid misunderstanding the content of that superficially simple message.

First, while famines involve—and are typically initiated by—starvation, many of the people who die from a famine die in fact not from starvation as such, but from various epidemic diseases unleashed by the famine. This happens primarily through the spread of infectious diseases helped by debilitation, attempts to eat whatever looks eatable, breakdown of sanitary arrangements, and massive population movements in search of food.[4] Famine

---

[1] Letter of Mill to Ricardo, August 14, 1816. Quoted in Jacquemin (1985), 'Annexe historique', p. 18.

[2] See Jacquemin (1985), 'Annexe historique', p. 18.

[3] The cult of the 'lifeboat ethics' (as well as the 'case against helping the poor' and the 'toughlove solution' advocated by Garrett Hardin 1974, 1981), discussing who to 'sacrifice' to let others survive, builds on a peculiarly heightened version of that pessimism.

[4] See Chapter 3, section 3.3, where the relation of these findings to the entitlement approach is also discussed.

prevention is, in fact, intimately connected with the avoidance of epidemics, even though the first and basic culprit may be the failure of food entitlements.

Thus, when acute deprivation has been allowed to develop, the task of containing famine mortality may require substantial attention to health care and epidemiological control. This consideration links with the general importance, discussed in Chapter 3, of seeing hunger and deprivation in terms of entitlement failures in a broader perspective than that of food entitlements only. At the same time, it is important to bear in mind that in the case of famines the collapse of food entitlements is the initiating failure in which epidemics themselves originate, and that the protection of food entitlements at an early stage is often a more effective form of action than medical intervention at a later stage.[5]

Second, while the entitlement approach asserts the inadequacy of aggregate food availability as a focus for the analysis of famines, it does not assert its irrelevance. Aggregate food availability remains important, but its influence has to be seen only as an element of a more complex entitlement process. This general point was discussed in Chapter 2 in the context of analysing the causation of famines, but it also has to be borne in mind when the attention is turned to the prevention of famines. In particular it is important to see that (1) the improvement of food availability can play a helpful or even crucial role in preventing the development of a famine, whether or not the threat of famine is accompanied by a decline in food availability, and (2) at the same time, many other influences are at work, and a broad view should be taken of possible options for action—including that of protecting the food entitlements of vulnerable groups even when it is not possible to bring aggregate food availability to a particular level.

Third, the protection of entitlements in the short run has to be contrasted with the general promotion of entitlements in the long run. In the short run, famine prevention is essentially a question of encountering an immediate threat of entitlement failure for vulnerable groups. In the long term, of course, much more is involved, and a durable elimination of vulnerability requires promotional policies, such as the expansion of general prosperity, the reduction of insecurity through economic diversification, and the creation of secure earning arrangements.

However, even within a long-term perspective, the task of building up reliable entitlement protection systems remains quite crucial. Indeed, in most cases it would be rather naïve to expect that efforts at eliminating vulnerability could be so successful as to allow a country to dispense with distinct and

---

[5] Many past experiences of famine prevention show the dramatic effectiveness that simple intervention measures can have on famine mortality. These measures have primarily taken the form of early protection of food entitlements, supplemented if possible with the provision of drinking water and basic health care (especially vaccination). For some examples (historical as well as contemporary), see Valaoras (1946), Ramalingaswami *et al.* (1971), Berg (1973), Krishnamachari *et al.* (1974), Binns (1976), Smout (1978), Will (1980), Kiljunen (1984), Otten (1986), de Waal (1987), and Drèze (1988*a*, 1989), among others.

specialized entitlement protection mechanisms. While famine prevention is not exclusively concerned with the protection of entitlements, much of the discussion in this part of the book will concentrate on this elementary and urgent aspect of the problem.

Fourth, the task of entitlement protection also has to be distinguished from the popular notion of 'famine relief' which conjures up the picture of a battle already half lost and focuses the attention on emergency operations narrowly aimed at containing large-scale mortality. Devising planned, coherent, effective and durable entitlement protection mechanisms is a much broader task. Entitlement crises have many repercussions on the rural economy and on the well-being of affected populations, and a comprehensive strategy for dealing with the scourge of famine must seek to ensure that human beings have both secure lives and secure livelihoods.

This is not just a question of immediate well-being, but also one of development prospects. Consider, for instance, the so-called 'food crisis in Africa'.[6] The current débâcle of agricultural production in much of sub-Saharan Africa has, not without reason, been held partly responsible for this region's continued vulnerability to famine. But it is legitimate to wonder how farmers who are condemned every so often to use up their productive capital in a desperate struggle for survival can possibly be expected to save, innovate, and prosper. There is indeed considerable evidence of the lasting adverse effects of famine on productive potential as well as on the distribution of assets.[7] It is reasonable to think that improved entitlement protection systems in Africa would not only save lives, but also contribute to preserving and rejuvenating the rural economy. The alleged dilemma between 'relief' and 'development' is a much exaggerated one, and greater attention has to be paid to the positive links between famine prevention and development prospects.

Finally, seeing famine prevention as an entitlement protection problem draws our attention to the plurality of strategies available for dealing with it. Just as entitlements can be threatened in a number of different ways, there are also typically a number of feasible routes for restoring them. Importing food and handing it over to the destitutes is one of the more obvious options. The overwhelming preoccupation of the journalistic and institutional literature on African famine relief has been with the logistics of food aid and distribution, reflecting the resilient popularity of this approach. But there is a good case for

[6] For valuable analyses of the problems involved, see Lofchie and Commins (1982), Berry (1984), Labonne (1984a, 1984b), IDS Bulletin (1985), Rose (1985), Society for International Development (1985), Eicher (1986a, 1988a), FAO (1986), Idachaba (1986), Lawrence (1986), Lofchie (1987), Mellor, Delgado and Blackie (1987), Platteau (1988a), Rukuni and Eicher (1987). See also Chapters 2 and 9.

[7] See e.g. Swanberg and Hogan (1981), Chastanet (1983), de Waal (1987), Glantz (1987b), McCann (1987), and Hay (1988). Numerous reports on the 1983–5 famines in sub-Saharan Africa also emphasize the acute problems caused (*inter alia*) by shortages of seeds, oxen, or human labour during the recovery period, often resulting in a shrinkage in sown area and other forms of production losses.

taking a broader view of the possible forms of intervention, and this part of our book will be much concerned with exploring other—often more effective —alternatives.

5.2 African Challenge and International Perception

It seems to be widely believed that most African countries lack the political framework (perhaps even the commitment) for successful pursuit of comprehensive strategies of entitlement protection. There may be truth in this in some cases. The inaction and confusion of some governments in the face of crises have been striking. The role of war in exacerbating food crises in Africa also needs persistent emphasis. Nevertheless, an excessive concentration on failure stories has given a vastly exaggerated and undiscriminating impression of the apathy, incompetence, and corruption of African governments in the context of famine prevention. In fact, contrary to popular belief, there is some evidence that the willingness and ability of many African countries to respond to crises have been improving over time, in some cases to a very considerable extent.[8]

Furthermore, as we shall argue later, state action is not immune to the influence of political ideology, public pressure, and popular protest, and there is nothing immutable in the nature of contemporary African politics. It is, of course, true that the development of a workable system of famine prevention calls for political as well as economic restructuring, but political changes—no less than economic transformations—are responsive to determined action and popular movements.

While examining experiences of success and failure in famine prevention, it has to be recognized that international perceptions of these past experiences are often seriously distorted. In particular, for reasons of journalistic motivation (which has its positive side as well, on which more presently), the media tend to overconcentrate on stories of failure and disaster. To the extent that successes do get reported, the balance of credit is heavily tilted in favour of international relief agencies, who enjoy—and need—the sympathy of a large section of the public.

This phenomenon is well illustrated by an episode of successful famine prevention in the state of Maharashtra in India in 1972–3. The impressive success achieved at the time by the government of Maharashtra in preventing a severe drought from developing into a famine by organizing massive public works programmes (at one point providing employment to as many as 5 million men and women) is described in Chapter 8. This event, however, caused very

---

[8] See e.g. Borton and Clay (1986), CILSS (1986), Caldwell and Caldwell (1987c), Hill (1987), Wood, Baron and Brown (1986), and World Food Programme (1986a). The last, for instance, reported on the basis of field missions in Burkina Faso, Chad, Mali and Niger after the crisis of 1983–5 that 'in all the countries visited, governments had made tremendous efforts to organise relief activities effectively' (p. 3). As we shall see, very impressive capabilities to respond are now clearly visible in such diverse countries as Botswana, Cape Verde, Kenya and Zimbabwe (see Chapter 8).

few ripples in the Western press, and received extraordinarily little attention from social scientists outside India.[9]

While the government of Maharashtra was employing millions of people on relief works, various international agencies were involved in feeding programmes on a relatively tiny scale—often importing modest amounts of wheat, biscuits, and milk powder from the other side of the globe. However, the role of the latter appeared to be oddly exaggerated. One of the relief organizations —indeed one that has altogether distinguished itself for many years by its far-sighted initiatives and actions—had no hesitation in reporting in its bulletin how a poor peasant sighed that the drought 'may be too big a problem for God; but perhaps OXFAM can do something'. There are other self-congratulatory snippets in the same vein about OXFAM's heroic deeds in Maharashtra and other drought-affected parts of India at that time:

'I suddenly realised that, driving 20 miles out of Ajmer on the road to Udaipur, all the scattered green patches I saw in the brown desert were in some way or another due to OXFAM.'

'In spite of the feeding programme the children have not gained weight. Stina at first thought her scale was wrong, but she discovered that the children now get almost nothing to eat at home. One shudders to think what would have happened to them without the feeding scheme. What's happening in other villages, where we aren't feeding?'[10]

The donor's exaggerated perception of its achievements is coupled with a comparatively patchy account of what the government was doing on an enormously larger scale. As late as December 1972, by which time the government-led relief programme was in full swing, the same bulletin reports 'we have no information as yet of the extent of the Indian Government's programme'. The fact that an organization with as remarkable a record of helpful action and leadership as OXFAM could fall into this trap of making mountains out of molehills and molehills out of mountains shows the difficulties of objective perception and reporting on the part of an institution directly involved in the act of relief and dependent on the preservation of a heroic public image.

The highly selective focus of public discussions on famine is also evident in the case of Africa. For instance, until recently Botswana's remarkable record of famine prevention had received very little recognition, to the point that a

---

[9] The first in-depth analysis of the Maharashtra drought published in an international professional journal outside India is that of Oughton (1982). On the role of public policy in averting a possible famine and the lessons to be drawn from this experience, see McAlpin (1987) and Drèze (1988a). See also Chapter 8.

[10] These citations are from OXFAM (1972, 1973) and Hall (1973). It must be emphasized that it is not the intention here to blame OXFAM in particular for sharing in a form of disaster reporting that seems to be, in fact, common to the publications of many relief agencies when these are addressed to the wider public. The point is simply to illustrate certain biases which an institution of this kind seems to find hard to resist.

Table 5.1 Food and agricultural production in sub-Saharan Africa, 1983–1984

Country	Per capita food production 1983–4		Per capita agricultural production 1983–4	Growth rate of agricultural production per capita 1970–84
	(1979–81 = 100) (1)	(1976–78 = 100) (2)	(1979–81 = 100) (3)	(% per year) (4)
Cape Verde	62	n/a	n/a	n/a
Zimbabwe	73	68	82	−1.4
Niger	83	78	83	0.7
Botswana	83	n/a	84	−3.8
Kenya	87	82	93	−1.3
Senegal	88	70	89	−2.1
Mozambique	88	75	87	−4.3
Ethiopia	88	94	88	−0.6
Sudan	89	72	93	−0.5
Togo	90	93	90	−1.1
Zambia	92	89	93	−1.1
Angola	93	81	91	−5.6
Guinea	93	92	94	−1.0
Malawi	93	100	96	0.1
Tanzania	95	91	93	−0.6
Burundi	95	87	95	0.5
Côte d'Ivoire	95	111	90	0.5
Cameroon	96	83	95	−0.8
Burkina Faso	98	90	99	−0.2
Uganda	98	96	100	−1.7
Ghana	98	80	98	−3.9
Nigeria	98	88	98	−1.0
Zaire	101	97	102	−0.6
Liberia	102	100	99	−1.4
Benin	103	85	104	−0.3
Sierra Leone	104	84	101	−0.5
Mali	106	90	105	0.8
Guinea-Bissau	114	92	114	−0.9

Note: The countries included in this table are all those for which data are available from each of the three sources; Cape Verde has been added using van Binsbergen (1986), Table 3. Figures for 1983–4 have been calculated as an unweighted average of 1983 and 1984.

Sources: (1) and (3): Calculated from FAO, *Monthly Bulletin of Statistics*, Nov. 1987. (2): Figures given by the United States Department of Agriculture, reproduced in J. Downing *et al.* (1987), Table 1.1. (4): Food and Agriculture Organization (1986), Annex I, Table 1.2.

leading expert on Africa described it as 'Africa's best kept secret'.[11] Examples of worthwhile but underreported successes in famine prevention in Africa, most of them involving large-scale government intervention, can also be found *inter alia* in countries as varied as Burkina Faso, Cape Verde, Kenya, Lesotho, Mali, Mauritania, Niger, Tanzania, Uganda, Zimbabwe, and even to some extent Chad and Ethiopia.[12]

It is arguable that popular interpretations of the 'African famine' of 1983–5 have themselves involved important misperceptions. Though drought threatened a large number of African countries at that time, only some of them—notably war-torn ones—actually experienced large-scale famine. There was no uniform disaster of the kind that has often been suggested. In fact, a probing interpretation of the mounting evidence on this tragedy could well uncover many more reasons for hope than for despair.[13]

It is, moreover, far from clear that those countries in which large-scale famine did occur were the ones most affected by drought. Such an impression is certainly *not* borne out by available food and agricultural production indices (see Table 5.1).[14] We shall argue, in fact, that the sharp contrasts which can be observed in the relationship between drought and famine in different countries have a lot to do with the contrasting quality of public action in various parts of Africa. In particular, a number of countries where drought was extremely severe in 1983–4 (indeed often more severe than in the much-discussed cases of Ethiopia or Sudan, in terms of declines in food and agricultural production indices) met with notable success in averting large-scale famine. Powerful illustrations are found in the experiences of Botswana, Cape Verde, Kenya and Zimbabwe (see Table 5.2, and also Chapter 8). There is as much to learn from these 'quiet successes' as from the attention-catching failures that can also be observed in Africa.

5.3 *Informal Security Systems and Concerted Action*

Rural communities faced with a precarious environment often develop sophisticated institutions and strategies to reduce or cope with the insecurity of their lives. A few examples of this phenomenon are the diversification of crops and herds, the exploitation of geographical complementarities in the eco-system, the pursuit of 'symbiotic exchanges' between different communities,

[11] Eicher (1986*b*: 5). The experience of this country will be further discussed in Chapter 8.
[12] See e.g. Kelly (1987) on Burkina Faso; Freeman *et al.* (1978) and van Binsbergen (1986) on Cape Verde; Borton and Clay (1986), Cohen and Lewis (1987) and Downing *et al.* (forthcoming) on Kenya; Bryson (1986) on Lesotho; Steele (1985) on Mali; UNDRO (1986) on Mauritania; de Ville de Goyet (1978), CILSS (1986) and World Food Programme (1986*e*) on Niger; Mwaluko (1962) on Tanzania; Brennan *et al.* (1984) and Dodge and Alnwick (1986) on Uganda; Bratton (1986) on Zimbabwe; Holt (1983), Nelson (1983), Firebrace and Holland (1984), Peberdy (1985), Grannell (1986) and World Food Programme (1986*a*) on Ethiopia (including Tigray and Eritrea); and Autier and d'Altilia (1985), Brown *et al.* (1986) and World Food Programme (1986*b*) on Chad.
[13] A large number of the references cited in the preceding footnote deal with the 1983–5 crisis.
[14] Nor is this impression confirmed by meteorological evidence (see J. Downing *et al.* 1987).

Table 5.2 Drought and famine in Africa, 1983–1984: contrasting experiences

Country	Percentage decline of production since 1979–81		Growth rate of per capita total gross agricultural production (1970–1984)	Outcome
	Food	Agriculture		
Cape Verde	38.5	n/a	n/a	Mortality *decline*. Nutritional *improvement*.
Zimbabwe	37.5	18.5	−1.4	Mortality *decline*. No sustained nutritional deterioration.
Botswana	17.0	16.5	−3.8	Normal nutritional situation. No starvation deaths.
Kenya	13.5	7.5	−1.3	No starvation deaths reported. Possibility of nutritional deterioration.
Ethiopia	12.5	12.5	−0.6	Large-scale famine.
Sudan	11.0	7.0	−0.5	Large-scale famine.

Sources: The figures on food and agricultural production performance are from the same sources as Table 5.1. On the assessment of 'outcome' in Botswana, Cape Verde, Kenya, and Zimbabwe, see Chapter 8. For estimates of excess mortality in Sudan and Ethiopia during the 1983–5 famines, see e.g. Otten (1986), de Waal (1987), Jansson *et al.* (1987) and Seaman (1987).

the development of patronage or reciprocal gift-giving, the recourse to complex dietary adjustments, and the storage of food or body fat.

It has been pointed out that informal security systems of this type have, *inter alia*, the great merit of not leaving the rural community at the mercy of undependable sources of external assistance. Appreciaton for these and other virtues of traditional responses to the threat of famine has, in fact, not infrequently resulted in an expression of considerable alarm at the prospect that traditional abilities to cope with the threat of famine might be dangerously weakened or even undermined by the interference of externally provided forms of entitlement protection.[15] This claim has to be taken seriously, and its

[15] For some variations around this theme, see Morris (1974, 1975), Colson (1979), Torry (1979), Wohlt *et al.* (1982), Cuny (1983), Turton and Turton (1984), Campbell (1986, 1987), Downing (1986), Zinyama *et al.* (1988), Devereux and Hay (1988), and Eldredge and Rydjeski (1988).

assessment must be based on a careful appreciation of how informal security systems function in practice.

Some of the coping strategies that have been referred to in the literature on informal security systems essentially consist of dealing with the risk of entitlement failure through some form of *individual precaution* at the household level. An important example is that of food storage, e.g. storing foodgrains, keeping animals, developing body fat. It is easy to see, however, that taking extensive precautions individually, without any pooling of risks, can be a difficult and costly business, and it can entail large losses of *average* entitlements compared to a situation where more efficient forms of insurance opportunities are available. For instance, storage has a high opportunity cost in the form of foregone investment in productive activities. Given their costs, therefore, it is hardly surprising that the scope for using precautionary measures can be rather limited for poor households. This way of tackling vulnerability may be nowhere near adequate.

Further opportunities for pursuing security arise from *mutual insurance*, and the attempt to obtain a better distribution of risks *across* households, rather than coping with them individually. A simple example may help to bring out the potentialities and limitations of mutual insurance. Consider a fishing community consisting of fishermen and their families, where fishermen go out every day to fish but their daily individual fortunes are not related to each other. If, every day, 'lucky' fishermen feel a social obligation to give some fish to the less fortunate ones, a measure of insurance against poor catches will exist.[16] In fact, if a well-developed system of mutual credit or reciprocal gift-giving operates, individual fluctuations in catches will not 'matter' at all: for each family the daily consumption of fish need bear no relation to the individual daily catch of the family. In this example, fishermen can costlessly insure against the entitlement risks arising from individual variations and fluctuations in catches, in the sense that—if the system works well—they have the opportunity to even out the consumption stream without lowering its average level.[17]

There are good reasons why, in practice, opportunities for costless insurance are often difficult to exploit. In fact, sometimes such opportunities can be altogether absent. In the last example, the possibility of costless insurance depended crucially on the fact that the fortunes of different individuals were

[16] The phenomenon of 'reciprocal gift-giving' has sometimes been interpreted by anthropologists as a mechanism of mutual insurance. For discussions of the anthropological literature on informal security systems, see Torry (1979, 1987), Posner (1980), Cashdan (1985), Dirks (1980), and Platteau (1988b). The last author investigates an instructive example of the operation of reciprocal gift-giving as a mutual insurance mechanism in an Indian fishing community. For economic analyses of gift exchange, see Lundahl (1983), Akerlof (1984), Platteau (1988b).

[17] The partners in a contract of mutual insurance need not, in general, make symmetric contributions to the reduction of risk as in this example. On the subtler distinctions between risk-sharing, risk-pooling, risk-shifting, etc., see Newbery and Stiglitz (1981) and Newbery (1987a).

not related to each other. Clearly, a system of reciprocal giving would be useless in dealing with collective risks. For instance, in the event of an adverse fluctuation in the total catch of the community (with the catches of individual fishermen going down together) there will be little scope for the 'unlucky' families to rely on the 'lucky' ones. Similarly, if fishermen rely on the exchange of fish for rice to survive, and if the price of fish in terms of rice collapses, the scope for evening out misfortunes within the fishing community will clearly be very limited. This is no small spanner in the wheel, since collective risks applying to large sections of a population are often precisely what we are most concerned with in the context of famine vulnerability.

Informal arrangements for mutual insurance are, therefore, deeply problematic when it comes to dealing with collective risks. Their failure in circumstances of widespread calamity is in fact well documented: in times of famine, the ordinary rules of patronage, credit, charity, reciprocity, and even family support tend to undergo severe strain and can hardly be relied upon to ensure the survival of vulnerable groups.[18] Nor is this failure a new phenomenon: during the famines of ancient Egypt several thousand years ago it was already found that 'each man has become a thief to his neighbour', and the story of biblical famines is similarly replete with tales of introversion, conflict, and even cannibalism on the part of famine victims.[19]

Quite aside from the problem of collective risks, there are many reasons why, in practice, the design and enforcement of insurance contracts tend to involve considerable difficulties.[20] The difficulties present (particularly those related to the revelation of information) are, in some respects, less acute in small face-to-face communities, but the fact remains that generally insurance opportunities are neither 'costless' nor even particularly attractive for poor households. The miserable employment conditions which permanent farm servants are often willing to accept in exchange for some security of employment are a telling example of the sacrifices that may be involved in insuring against the worst eventuality.[21]

[18] The so-called 'breakdown of the moral economy' in times of severe collective crisis, in the past as well as in the present, is one of the best documented aspects of social responses to food crises. Dirks (1980) provides a good discussion of this phenomenon, and a survey of the literature. For some relevant empirical studies, see Colson (1979), Greenough (1982), Jodha and Mascarenhas (1985), de Waal (1987), Vaughan (1987), Chen (1988), and Rahmato (1988), among others. It should be mentioned that the breakdown of social ties is a common feature of the *advanced* stages of famines, and that in the early stages *greater* sociality may well be observed.

[19] The citation is from an ancient inscription, mentioned in Aykroyd (1974: 25). On biblical famines, see Dando (1983). See also Garnsey (1988).

[20] These difficulties include the 'incentive' problems arising from the need for some parties to elicit information which other parties may have little interest in revealing (see Newbery 1987a, for an excellent discussion). These problems are particularly acute in large and anonymous societies, but some of them are also important even in small, face-to-face communities. See Cashdan (1985), Torry (1987), Rosenzweig et al. (1988), and Platteau (1988b).

[21] An extreme example is that of 'bonded labour'. There are, of course, many other aspects to the causation of this phenomenon than the quest for security on the part of dispossessed labourers. But this part of the story is, in some cases, clearly an important one. See Breman (1974), Deshpande (1982), and Ramachandran (1986), among other contributions.

These limitations of informal security systems have to be borne in mind—no less than the potentialities mentioned earlier—when assessing their place in a programme of public action for famine prevention. It has been argued by many that, in order to be effective, famine prevention strategies should strengthen rather than undermine traditional security systems. There is no doubt an element of wisdom in this, and there are several important examples of such strengthening. At the same time, it has to be recognized that there may be nothing embarrassing in famine prevention policies having a partial 'displacement' effect on informal security systems, as long as this displacement effect reflects the greater effectiveness of public intervention. While careful account always needs to be taken of the possible adverse effects of public intervention on informal security systems, it would be a poor principle of action to attempt to preserve the latter at all cost.

Consider, for instance, the case of private storage at the household level mentioned earlier. It is to be expected that, if they feel more secure (possibly as a result of successful public intervention), individual households will store less and devote their resources to other—perhaps more productive—purposes.[22] If this is really why the reduction of storage takes place, such a development may be welcome. An instinctive conservationism regarding traditional institutions may easily take the form of nostalgic hopes rather than contributing to a pragmatic integration of formal and informal security systems.

The revival or strengthening of informal security systems, important as it often is, cannot be an adequate response to the challenge of famine. The effective protection of vulnerable groups requires redistributive mechanisms going well beyond what individual precaution or traditional systems of mutual insurance can deliver. The need to devise famine prevention systems that do not leave the rural community to its own fragile devices is inescapable.

5.4 Aspects of Traditional Response

An effective programme of public action for famine prevention must be responsive to the empirical features of informal security systems. As a prelude to further discussion of the forms which concerted action for famine prevention might take, this section briefly recalls some relevant findings from the literature on traditional responses to the threat of famine.[23] The discussion will

---

[22] This is indeed a plausible interpretation of the considerable decline of on-farm storage in India since the last century (Drèze 1988*a*). The decline of private storage against a background of *decreasing* famine vulnerability in Kenya is also noted in Downing (1986).

[23] The empirical studies on which this section draws include Firth (1959), Morris (1974, 1975), Jodha (1975, 1978, 1981), Lallemand (1975), Jackson (1976), Bernus (1977*a*, 1977*b*, 1986), Faulkingham (1977), Gallais *et al.* (1977), Scott (1976), Colson (1979), Popkin (1979), Prindle (1979), Bertlin (1980), O'Leary (1980), Campbell and Trechter (1982), Greenough (1982), Schware (1982), Chastanet (1983, 1988), Watts (1983, 1984), Campbell (1984, 1986, 1987), Cutler (1984*a*, 1985*b*, 1986), Turton and Turton (1984), Cashdan (1985), Jodha and Mascarenhas (1985), Negus (1985), Pankhurst (1985, 1986), Lombard (1985), Swift (1985), Tobert (1985), Caldwell *et al.* (1986), Downing (1986), Fleuret (1986), de Waal (1987), Akong'a and Downing (1987),

footnote continued overleaf

focus mainly on sub-Saharan Africa, and our remarks will concentrate on a few strategic elements of informal security systems, viz. (1) diversification and exchange, (2) dietary adjustments, (3) migration and employment, and (4) intrahousehold redistribution.

Diversification and Exchange

One of the earliest and most robust findings of anthropological studies in uncertain environments is that diversification is among the chief strategies adopted by vulnerable communities to reduce the precariousness of their lives. People learn not to put all their eggs in the same unreliable basket. The diversification motive is a pervasive aspect of economic decisions in uncertain environments, including those on cropping patterns, livestock management, occupational choices, and migration routes.

Opportunities for diversification can, of course, be greatly helped by the institution of exchange. While complete autarky may often be an admired achievement, it tends to be, in fact, a poor basis for security. Numerous historical and anthropological studies confirm that over the world vulnerable communities have consistently seen exchange as an opportunity for enhancing the security of their existence.[24]

Exchange itself can assume a multiplicity of forms, and the cash economy accommodates only one of them. Nevertheless, the acquirement of cash (especially through wage employment, but also through the sale of livestock, charcoal, craft work, assets, and even 'superior' foods) has now become one of the foremost responses to the threat of entitlement failure in sub-Saharan Africa.[25] The development of market exchange offers both new opportunities

---

footnote continued.
McCorkle (1987), Mamadou (1987a, 1987b), Sperling (1987a, 1987b), Vaughan (1987), Zinyama et al. (1988), M. Chen (1988, 1989), Dupré and Guillaud (1988), Matiza et al. (1988), Platteau (1988b), Pottier (1988), Rahmato (1988), Wheeler and Abdullah (1988), Brown (forthcoming), Kamau et al. (forthcoming), von Braun (forthcoming). Valuable discussions of informal security systems in more general terms can also be found in Torry (1979, 1986a, 1986b, 1987), Dirks (1980), Wynne (1980), den Hartog (1981), van Appeldoorn (1981), Lundahl (1983), Toulmin (1983), Scott (1984), Jiggins (1986), Longhurst (1986), Agarwal (1988), Corbett (1988), de Garine and Harrison (1988), Platteau (1988b), Chambers (1989).

[24] See Pankhurst (1985, 1986) for an illuminating discussion of this issue. The author insists, inter alia, on the importance of 'extensive pre-capitalist regional systems of exchange' in both East Africa and the Sahel, and on the role of market exchange as a 'safeguard against the vulnerability of subsistence economies to environmental risk' in pre-colonial African societies (Pankhurst, 1985: 42–3). The historical role of exchange in enhancing security is confirmed by examples of famines occurring as a result of the disruption of traditional exchange channels in some parts of Africa during colonial times. For some interesting examples, see Lugan (1976) and Herlehy (1984), among others. On the historical importance of market exchange in Africa, see also Gray and Birmingham (1970a, 1970b), Jones (1980), Eicher and Baker (1982), Hill (1986), and the literature cited in these studies.

[25] This observation is reflected in numerous recent studies of famine responses, including those of Faulkingham (1977), Bertlin (1980), O'Leary (1980), Campbell and Trechter (1982), Chastanet (1983), Watts (1983), Cutler (1985b), Swift (1985), Downing (1986), Fleuret (1986), Hale (1986), Pankhurst (1986), Akong'a and Downing (1987), de Waal (1987), Holland (1987), Bush (1988), Matiza et al. (1988), Pottier (1988).

and new threats. It is natural to expect that potential famine victims would attempt to use the market to overcome their problems, whether or not the problems themselves have been partly generated by a greater exposure to market fluctuations. When we turn to strategic issues of famine prevention in the next three chapters, we shall have to investigate the part that market operations can play both in undermining and in helping to protect the entitlements of vulnerable groups.

Dietary Adjustments

An important characteristic of dietary habits in vulnerable communities is their flexibility.[26] There is, of course, nothing particularly encouraging in the observation that, in times of crisis, affected groups resort to many ingenious forms of dietary adjustments. Indeed some of these strategies (such as programmed fasting or the gathering of wild foods) can be extremely painstaking and even dangerous. Of greater interest, however, are the general findings that (1) the reduction of food consumption tends to be an *early* response to the threat of entitlement failure, apparently motivated, at least partly, by the preservation of productive assets, and (2) substantial adjustments of consumption patterns are observed in times of economic adversity even in the behaviour of richer people who are not immediately at great risk of starvation.[27]

As we shall see in the next chapter, these findings are of far-reaching relevance for entitlement protection strategies. For example, they suggest that, in the event of a moderate but unpreventable decline in the availability of food, there is some scope for inducing a reduction of food consumption on the part of the relatively richer and not-so-vulnerable households. This adjustment can help to support the consumption of the most affected population. For instance, income support measures for the destitute population can, by putting an upward pressure on food prices, bring down the consumption levels of the more privileged groups, thus releasing food to meet the newly generated demands of the income-supported destitutes. The tightening of belts can be shared more easily given the priority that seems to be attached by rural households to preserving assets through adjusting consumption.

Migration and Employment

Two general points of crucial importance for public policy seem to have emerged from studies of migration patterns during subsistence crises in

---

[26] On this see Bernus (1977*b*), Fleuret and Fleuret (1980), den Hartog (1981), Campbell and Trechter (1982), Watts (1983), Fleuret (1986), Longhurst (1986), Downing (1988*a*, 1988*b*), and Drèze (1988*a*), among others. See also Chapter 8 below.

[27] The evidence from India, reviewed in Drèze (1988*a*) and recently supplemented by Pinstrup-Andersen and Jaramillo (1986) and M. Chen (1989), is fairly conclusive on this point. Few quantitative studies are available for Africa, but qualitative studies suggest a strikingly similar pattern—see Colson (1979), Watts (1983), de Waal (1987), Corbett (1988), Rahmato (1988), and Kamau *et al.* (forthcoming). See also the literature on survival during the period of 'soudure' in different parts of Africa, including Campbell and Trechter (1982), Dupré and Guillaud (1984), Lombard (1985), and the earlier studies reviewed in Mondot-Bernard (1982).

sub-Saharan Africa. First, among sedentary communities the migration of entire families is generally a last resort option.[28] The reasons for this are not difficult to understand. On the one hand, for a family used to a sedentary life, leaving a home can mean a severe social and psychological stress, extreme hardship for those too weak to travel, and selling off one's possessions or exposing them to theft.[29] On the other hand, when everything else has failed, migration does provide a hope, however faint, of access to new opportunities: the hospitality of relatives, the charity of city dwellers, or the presence of public relief camps.

Second, the migration of single adults in search of work appears, by contrast, to be an early response to the threat of entitlement failures in sub-Saharan Africa.[30] These movements mainly involve adult males, moving either to cities or to more prosperous rural areas. It is not immediately clear, of course, how this particular strategy can be expected to affect different household members. In principle, the departure of adult males can reflect the pursuit of three distinct objectives: (1) the *supplementation* of household resources through remittances (typically earned as wages); (2) the *release* of the migrant's share of joint household resources for the benefit of those who stay behind; and (3) the *abandonment* of other family members by the migrant.

Empirical examples can be found illustrating the operation of each of these three motives. But there is much evidence that the first motive is often the dominant one, and that remittances from absent adult males during periods of stress now represent a crucial form of entitlement support for vulnerable households in most African countries.[31] Particularly interesting in this respect are several recent studies showing a clearly positive association between food security and the migration of adult members in different households.[32]

There can, of course, be a problem of intrahousehold inequality in a process

---

[28] See Corbett (1988) for a review of the evidence on this point. The same observation has often been made in South Asia, where one turn-of-the-century commentator went so far as to assert that 'the dislike of the people to leave their homes was so strong that they would rather starve in their village' (Government of India 1898: 77, citing the Famine Commissioner of Madras). On the phenomenon of distress migration in South Asia, see Chakravarty (1986), Agarwal (1988), and the literature cited in these works.

[29] See Negus (1985: 15), Schware (1982: 215), and Hale (1986) for some examples of these anxieties.

[30] See e.g. Mwaluko (1962), Lallemand (1975), Caldwell (1977), Smale (1980), Watts (1983), Autier and d'Altilia (1985), Cutler (1985b), Swift (1985), Downing (1986), Hay (1986), McLean (1986), Akong'a and Downing (1987), de Waal (1987), Holland (1987), Government of Mali (1987), Dupré and Guillaud (1988), Brown (forthcoming).

[31] On the supportive role of cash remittances in the context of subsistence crises, and their close connections with wage labour, see Faulkingham and Thorbahn (1975) for Niger, Leys (1986) and Bratton (1987a) for Zimbabwe, Bush (1988) for Sudan, Akong'a and Downing (1987), Downing *et al.* (forthcoming) for Kenya, Dupré and Guillaud (1984) for Burkina Faso, Government of Mali (1987) for Mali, Hay (1988) for Botswana, Lombard (1985) and Chastanet (1988) for Senegal, Smale (1980) for Mauritania, van Binsbergen (1986) and Freeman *et al.* (1978) for Cape Verde.

[32] On this question, see particularly Lombard (1985: 38–40). Similar findings are reported for diverse sub-Saharan countries in the empirical studies of Dupré and Guillaud (1984: 31), Leys (1986), Akong'a and Downing (1987), and Vaughan (1987: 47), among others. See also Chapter 8.

which leaves the survival of women and children thoroughly dependent on the earnings and remittances of male migrants.[33] This intrahousehold consideration has to be kept in view when assessing the contribution of labour migration to the survival of different household members.

Intrahousehold Redistribution

The issue of intrahousehold divisions during famines has an important bearing on the strategy of public action for famine prevention. For instance, whether entitlement protection should be aimed at households or at individuals would depend quite importantly on the pattern and intensity of intrahousehold inequalities. We have already commented, in the previous chapter, on the question of gender discrimination during famines. A complementary aspect of the problem of intrahousehold divisions is that of the fate of children vis-à-vis adults.[34]

The history of famines over the world is full of gruesome stories of neglect, abandonment, sale, or even murder of children.[35] It is not really surprising that family ties can be significantly undermined by severe famines and crises. Whether the family also provides inadequate protection to children in subsistence crises of moderate intensity is a more open question. In fact, on this point empirical findings are much less clear-cut. If anything, the limited evidence available suggests the strong possibility that in early stages of a famine young children are *protected* at the expense of other family members.

There are three types of findings in that direction. First, a number of anthropological studies have found that, when food is short at the household level, young children tend to get priority in feeding. In their study of hunger and poverty in the state of Orissa in India, for instance, Fernandes and Menon report that 'during scarcity, children get first priority, then come men and then only women'.[36] Very similar observations regarding the preferential treatment of children in food allocation during crises have been reported in different parts of sub-Saharan Africa.[37]

---

[33] On the question of gender conflicts in African famines and particularly in the context of male migration, see Vaughan (1987). Vaughan's insightful analysis underlines the conflicts involved in the phenomenon of male migration during the famine of 1949 in Malawi (including the possible abandonment of women by their husbands). But it also brings out the positive overall contribution which male migration made to the survival chances of both men and women. Husbands who were reluctant to migrate in search of work or food appeared to be cursed by their wives in sarcastic songs (p. 32).

[34] Another problem of great social importance concerns the fate of the elderly. There is considerable evidence from anthropological studies that the old fare particularly badly during famines (see Dirks 1980, Greenough 1982, Vaughan 1987, de Waal 1988a, Rahmato 1988). This remains, however, an understudied problem, and its implications for public policy in particular need to be pursued much more extensively.

[35] For a detailed review, see Dirks (1980). The secret murder of starving children by their desperate mothers during the 1949 famine in Malawi is discussed by Vaughan (1987: 36).

[36] Fernandes and Menon (1987: 109).

[37] See e.g. Hale (1986), Rahmato (1988) and Wheeler and Abdullah (1988). See also Jelliffe and Jelliffe (1971).

Second, several quantitative studies of anthropometric status and nutritional intake during famines confirm that the burden of nutritional adjustment often falls disproportionately on adults. For instance, the very careful nutrition surveys carried out by Médecins Sans Frontières during the 1983–5 crisis in the Sahel found a pro-children bias in intrafamily distribution compared to ordinary times.[38]

The third type of evidence, which is harder to interpret, relates to age patterns of mortality during famines. Given the greater biological vulnerability of young children to nutritional stress, one might expect that in spite of special protection they would often suffer disproportionately, from excess mortality during crises. In fact, the evidence does not seem to support this generalization.

Of course, the *absolute* mortality rates are almost invariably highest among young children during famines. But this is true in ordinary times as well, and there is no evidence that the *increase* in mortality is usually most pronounced for the lower age groups. In fact, among the few studies presenting reasonably accurate estimates of mortality by age groups both before and during a subsistence crisis, a surprisingly large proportion indicate a lower (or at least no higher) percentage increase in mortality for young children compared to other age groups.[39]

The fact that intrahousehold divisions in famine situations appear to operate often in favour of rather than against young children does not imply, of course, that this group requires no special attention. Given the high fragility of their lives, young children almost invariably account for a major share of famine mortality even when the percentage increase in mortality is no higher for them than for other age groups. The fact that systematic intrahousehold discrimination does not seem to be the clue to high infant and child mortality during famines has important implications, however, for the choice of remedial action. In particular, the case for striving to influence the intrahousehold distribution of food in favour of young children during crises (e.g. through direct feeding) would seem to lose some force to the extent that a bias in that

---

[38] See Autier and d'Altilia (1985) and Autier (1988). See also Binns (1976) on dietary change among the Yana of Papua New Guinea during the 1972–3 food crisis, Biellik and Henderson (1981) on the Karamoja famine of 1980, and Wheeler and Abdullah (1988) and Chaudhury (1988) on the intrafamily distribution of nutritional stress during the lean seasons in Bangladesh and Malawi.

[39] See e.g. Valaoras (1946) on the Greek famine of 1941–2, Sen (1981a: 210–4) and Greenough (1982: 238) on the Bengal famine of 1943, O'Grada (1988a: 9) on the Irish famines of the 1840s, Chen and Chowdhury (1977: Table 2) on the famines of 1971 and 1974 in Bangladesh, Maksudov (1986) on the Ukrainian famines of 1927–38, Hill (1988) on the Chinese famines of 1958–61, Meegama (1985: 324) on the food crisis of 1974 in Sri Lanka, and the work of Dyson (1989) on the demography of South Asian famines. In the case of *infants*, these findings have often been attributed to the protective value of breast-feeding; but the studies mentioned here found relatively low proportionate increases in mortality for non-infant young children as well. There are, of course, exceptions to this pattern; see e.g. de Waal (1988a, 1989a) on the 1985 famine in Darfur (Sudan).

direction often exists already within the family in such situations. We shall return to this issue in Chapter 7. From the analysis and evidence presented in this chapter and in Chapter 4, some typical patterns do seem to emerge. It appears that, during the early stages of subsistence crises: (1) the elderly are frequently neglected; (2) adult women often bear a disproportionate share of the burden of adjustment in comparison with adult men, but do not typically experience higher increases in mortality; (3) young children seem to be comparatively protected, at least initially, *vis-à-vis* other age groups; (4) in sub-Saharan Africa, there is no evidence of widespread discrimination against girls in comparison with boys, in the field of nutrition.

5.5   Early Warning and Early Action

Historical as well as contemporary documents on the subject of famine prevention repeatedly stress the advantages of *early intervention*—in pre-empting the disruption of population displacements, in containing the outbreak of epidemics, in preserving family solidarity, and in preventing the emergence of famine expectations. These considerations are all the more important if one accepts the view of famine prevention as being concerned not just with containing mortality but also with preserving a certain normality of life and preventing the loss of productive assets.

Arguing in favour of early intervention may sound like pushing against an open door, since nobody, presumably, is in favour of 'belated intervention'.[40] The sluggishness of action in the event of subsistence crises has indeed a lot more to do with the politics of famine situations than with doubts about the advantages of early intervention. But what bears emphasis is that the objective of early intervention sometimes has distinct implications for the choice of intervention method, and also that its attainment may require making concessions on other fronts. For instance, while feeding centres and relief camps may have a role to play in emergency operations, they clearly have little place in early intervention strategies since (as we have seen) most people are not eager to join relief camps until they have reached an advanced stage of destitution. And, generally, the ambition of remedying intrafamily inequalities in famine situations by *individual* intervention may have to be moderated in favour of coarser but swifter intervention mechanisms operating at the level of *household* entitlements.

This being said, the really important issues raised by the need for early intervention are concerned not so much with detailed strategic considerations as with the tougher problem of ensuring that resolute and early action will, in

[40] However, in some instances early intervention strategies *have* been criticized for involving the risk of 'overreacting' in the form of intervening in a situation where in fact people are quite capable of 'coping' (by which is usually meant surviving) on their own. See e.g. Morris (1974, 1975) and Waddell (1974), and the responses by Jodha (1975) and Binns (1976) respectively.

fact, be forthcoming in the event of a crisis. This is the context within which the related questions of preparedness, warning and response have to be seen.

The blame for delayed action is often put on inadequate information about the existence, or the exact character, of a crisis. There has, indeed, recently been a phenomenal surge of interest and involvement in so-called 'early warning systems'.[41] However, as we shall discuss in Chapter 8, it would be hard to see formal early warning techniques as having played a central role in recent experiences of successfully averted famine, whether in Botswana, Cape Verde, Kenya, Zimbabwe, or indeed India.

One frequently cited reason for the apparent redundancy of formal warning systems is their technical deficiency. There is certainly scope for refining existing approaches by moving away from mechanical analyses of the causation of entitlement failures. It is intriguing to note, for instance, that the Food and Agriculture Organization's Global Information and Early Warning System (this was, during the famine threats of 1983–5, the main source of regular information on potential food crises available to the member governments of the FAO) persists in concentrating on 'food balances' at the national level as the main variable of interest:

The Global Information and Early Warning System of the Food and Agriculture Organization (FAO) has three main functions. First, it monitors the *global food supply* position . . . Second, it monitors the food supply position at the national level and alerts governments to emerging *food supply problems* . . . Third, assistance is provided to strengthen national early warning capacities in developing countries . . . These national and regional projects aim at providing a low-cost system of monitoring which brings together all the indicators on the *food supply* position and prospects which are available in the country.[42]

This focus is perhaps not unnatural for an agency whose main concern is to assist various countries with food supply management. But it can clearly not form the basis of a reliable anticipation of threatening famines.[43]

---

[41] One study finds the current situation of duplication, heterogeneity and even inconsistency of independent efforts to be quite 'surrealistic' (CILSS 1986: 67). That study, which is not meant to be exhaustive, identifies no fewer than 39 different early warning systems in the Sahel alone, of which 14 are engaged in primary data collection and 25 'recycle' information collected by 'more or less competing agencies' (p. 69).

[42] Newhouse (1987: 6), italics added (on the GIEWS, see also FAO 1987a). Admittedly, the same document emphasizes that national early warning systems include the analysis of various 'socio-economic variables' of greater interest, such as 'cereal prices, cereal stocks, market arrivals, population movements, cattle prices and slaughter rates, length of queues at food shops, nutritional indicators, etc.' (p. 22). However, the role of these variables is seen as one of providing 'direct clues to emerging food supply problems', and the exercise therefore seems to remain instrumental to the ultimate purpose of gauging food supplies. It should be mentioned that many of the current problems of early warning systems are better understood when due recognition is given to the fact that, in practice, the purpose of these techniques is often more to *establish a credible claim for food aid* than to galvanize the domestic government into action.

[43] For a telling critique of the shortcomings of the 'food balances approach' with reference to the African crisis of 1983–5, see Torry (1988a). In the case of many African countries, the problem of misleading focus is compounded by that of atrocious production statistics, as a number of

Nor is the solution simply to shift the focus from food supply to another single variable (e.g. crop failures, changes in food prices, etc.), leaving out the rest of the system. The 'crop failures' approach, for instance, has been found quite useful in countries where the growing of crops (food *or* non-food) is, directly or indirectly, a major source of livelihood for vulnerable groups. But it can by no means be relied upon mechanically, and its predictive power has in some cases failed quite miserably.

A similar remark applies to early warning techniques based on food prices. Close association has been found between famine vulnerability and the level of food prices in a number of recent studies.[44] Indeed it is hard to think of a variable which exerts a comparable influence on the entitlements of large numbers of people. But it is also easy to see how starvation can hit particular occupational groups without being accompanied by a sharp increase in food prices. Again, historical experiences clearly point to the need for a more discerning assessment of the entitlement process.[45]

It is sometimes thought that a handy shortcut through this problem is to monitor nutritional status directly. This 'nutrition surveillance' approach has its uses, but for purposes of early warning it is now widely thought to be of limited value. The main reason is that, given the time needed for visible signs of increasing deprivation to develop, nutrition surveillance gives practically no advance indication of an impending crisis.[46]

There is no escape, then, from giving a solid place to economic and social analysis in attempts to predict future crises. Food balances, crop estimates, cereal prices, wage levels, population movements, and indeed many other variables are all useful clues, but the real challenge is to put them together to arrive at a coherent picture of the entitlement process. A number of recent

---

authors have emphasized; see e.g. Berry (1984), Lele and Candler (1984), Eicher and Mangwiro (1986), CILSS (1986), Hill (1986) and Lipton (1986). Some authors have gone so far as to question whether the alleged decline in food production in Africa during recent decades has been adequately ascertained; see e.g. Berry (1984), Hay (1986) and Hill (1986).

[44] See particularly the works of Peter Cutler on Ethiopia (Cutler 1985b) and Martin Ravallion on Bangladesh (Ravallion 1987a), as well as the historical studies of Meuvret (1946) and Lardinois (1982, 1985). See also Seaman and Holt (1980) and von Braun (forthcoming).

[45] In India, the Famine Commission of 1880 ended its pronouncement on the existence of a fairly systematic association between food price increases and famine with a strong word of caution: 'It is a well-ascertained fact that prices which would be regarded as indicating famine in one part of the country are quite compatible with undisturbed prosperity in another' (Government of India 1880, para. 78). The Ganjam famine of 1888–9 later revealed that 'food prices were no criteria of severity in a famine' (Srivastava 1968), and the Famine Commission of 1898 expressed an even more sceptical view on this general question (see e.g. Government of India 1898: 18, 44, 158). For similar observations in contemporary Ethiopia and Sudan, see Sen (1981a: Chapter 7) and de Waal (1988a).

[46] See e.g. Rivers et al. (1976), Mason et al. (1984), Autier and d'Altilia (1985), Borton and York (1987). Nutrition surveillance can, of course, have functions other than just early warning. It has, for instance, been used with good effect to monitor health conditions in non-crisis as well as crisis situations (see e.g., Morgan 1985 on its use in Botswana).

contributions to the development of early warning techniques have considerably advanced in that direction, and this progress deserves to be welcomed.[47]

It would, however, be a mistake to regard early warning only as a question of generating information for governmental policy making. As we have already discussed, the informational exercise has to be seen in the wider context of the need to trigger early action. In this process, the diffusion of information, and its use as a basis for public pressure, are no less important than the task of data gathering and analysis.

In that task, the media can play a crucial role, both as conveyors of information and as organs of public criticism and advocacy. Other important influences are the activities of political parties, of voluntary agencies, and indeed of the wider public. In Chapters 8 and 11 of this book, we shall encounter several instructive examples of the importance of adversarial politics in forcing an early response from governments in power in the event of a crisis. It will also be apparent how the interest that a political opposition typically has to find out, disseminate and use information about an impending food crisis can make a crucial difference, if the opposition is allowed to function.

Official tolerance of political pluralism and public pressure in many African countries is, at the moment, quite limited. The opposition is often muzzled. Newspapers are rarely independent or free. The armed forces frequently suppress popular protest. Further, to claim that there are clear signs of change in the direction of participatory politics and open journalism in Africa as a whole would be undoubtedly premature. However, there is now perhaps a greater awareness of the problem and of the need for change. The long-term value of creative dissatisfaction should not be underestimated.[48]

---

[47] See, for instance, the pioneering work of Médecins Sans Frontières in Chad (Autier 1988), the bulletins of the Système d'Alerte Précoce in Mali, the work of Jeremy Swift on Turkana in Kenya (Swift, forthcoming), and the econometric modelling by Meghnad Desai (1986). For a survey of the literature on early warning, see Walker (1988).

[48] A distinguishing feature of many of the African countries which have been relatively successful in responding adequately to the threat of famine in recent years is the greater accountability of their governments. This question is further discussed in Chapter 8 below. On the role of the press in the context of African famines, and the emerging signs of positive change in some countries, see Hoffer (1980), Yao and Kone (1986), Mitter (1988), Reddy (1988). On the general role of 'enfranchisement' in influencing entitlements of different groups, see Appadurai (1984).

6

Famines, Markets and Intervention

6.1   The Strategy of Direct Delivery

Famine prevention is primarily concerned with the protection of food entitlements where they are in danger of collapsing. The way of doing this that taxes the imagination least is to transport food into the affected area (possibly from abroad) and to feed the vulnerable population (distributing cooked food or food to be cooked). This is indeed how famine relief is very often instinctively conceived. As a USAID report on famine relief in Ethiopia put it, 'the number one priority was supplying food and getting to the people who needed it'.[1]

This particular strategy, which may be called the strategy of 'direct delivery', remains the most popular one today, and accordingly the key to the future prevention of famines is often seen primarily in terms of increased food aid, more trucks, better roads, more precise 'targeting' of food distribution, and the like. But the strategy of direct delivery is not always the most effective approach to the protection of entitlements. In fact, as we shall see in Chapter 8, it has played at best a secondary role in some of the most effective famine prevention systems in the world, not only in India but also in other regions including Africa. And the historical experience of famine prevention in different parts of the world actually includes a rather impressive variety of unevenly successful approaches to the protection of food entitlements: feeding, food distribution, public works, cash doles, price control, tax relief, crop insurance, the support of livestock prices, and many others.

The case for scrutinizing alternative entitlement protection strategies is all the more important because, apart from not being particularly ingenious, the strategy of direct delivery is intrinsically vulnerable to severe administrative and logistic failures. The requirement of transport makes the provision of relief dangerously contingent upon the successful and timely movement of food, sometimes all the way from the other end of the world to the very mouths of the starving, and often in painfully adverse conditions. The disruption of relief efforts as a result of the failed or delayed arrival of food is one of the most widely observed (and predictable) defects of the strategy of direct delivery, even in countries such as India and Botswana where management and logistic capabilities are comparatively good.

The difficulties arising in the process of distribution are no less important. If food is distributed through centralized feeding or distribution centres, intervention is inevitably confined to an advanced stage of distress (with all the

---

[1]   Office of Foreign Disasters Assistance (1985: 27).

attendant disadvantages mentioned earlier). Indeed, the attendance at feeding centres requires the displacement of families, and, as we discussed in the previous chapter, sedentary populations typically resist—with good reason —the decision of abandoning their homes until they are completely hopeless and their hardship has become very acute indeed.[2]

The distribution of food need not, of course, take place in large feeding or distribution centres, and many countries have a growing experience with decentralized distribution systems. But here the scope for concentrating public support on the most vulnerable is usually much more limited, because the close monitoring of food distribution at the local level requires administrative resources far exceeding those of most famine-prone countries. One is, therefore, constrained to rely on rather indiscriminate allocation mechanisms, such as public distribution with universal eligibility, or distribution mediated by local institutions. Given the limited resources that are typically obtainable for famine prevention efforts, a serious consequence of indiscriminate distribution is that it may become impossible to provide enough support to the most vulnerable people to protect them from starvation.

The defects of the strategy of direct delivery are visible in the experience of relief operations during the crisis of 1983–5 in Africa. In spite of commendable experiments with innovative approaches to famine relief in a number of places, direct delivery was the main plank of entitlement protection in this event. A number of adverse but predictable consequences of this strategic priority are discernible in the evaluation reports dealing with this experience. First, logistic failures have been the most persistent drag on the progress of relief operations.[3] Second, while Africa benefited from a massive amount of food aid (about 5 million tonnes in 1984, enough to feed more than 25 million people throughout the year), much of it was given away in indiscriminate, inequitable or simply unascertained ways, with the consequence that in many places the most vulnerable groups did not get enough support to survive through the crisis.[4] Third, while the delivery of food through feeding centres, where it applied, obviously was not entirely indiscriminate, it did little to prevent

[2] Nomadic populations are, naturally, more mobile. But many of them have been found to be strongly reluctant to join the regimented life of relief camps except under the most extreme hardship.

[3] On this, see the various periodical publications of the World Food Programme, the Office for Emergency Operations in Africa, the Office of the United Nations Disaster Relief Coordinator, the United Nations High Commissioner for Refugees, and the numerous evaluations of these emergency operations, including especially World Food Programme (1986a, 1986b).

[4] See e.g. Ray (1984), Tobert (1985), Hale (1986), Holthe (1986), Pearson (1986), World Food Programme (1986a, 1986b, 1986c), Keen (1988), and also The Economist, 20 July 1985 and 30 Nov. 1985. The World Food Programme, under whose auspices the bulk of emergency relief was provided, recognized in a refreshingly frank evaluation that 'the well known difficulties that relief authorities face in selecting the beneficiaries of emergency assistance . . . led [them] to effect general distributions to entire populations of drought-stricken areas' (World Food Programme 1986a: 3), and that 'in most cases, neither WFP nor bilateral food could be properly traced to the beneficiaries' (World Food Programme 1986b: 13). For an even more critical account, see Torry (1988a).

population displacements, with which the development of famine situations was chiefly associated.[5] Fourth, in several countries a large part of the food aid intended for famine relief in 1984 in fact arrived after the bumper harvest of 1985, aggravating the glut of local markets.[6]

The real question, of course, is whether more effective alternatives really exist to a strategy of direct delivery. One way of seeing the unnecessarily restrictive nature of this strategy is to recognize that the protection of entitlements through direct delivery essentially conflates two distinct forms of intervention in the single act of food distribution: first, an injection of food in the system; and second, selective generation of income, i.e. of the means to acquire food. Greater effectiveness in the provision of relief can often be achieved by 'separating' the two—for instance, by selling food in the market and separately providing some form of income support to the needy.

The case for concentrating on direct delivery relies implicitly on the combination of two assumptions: (1) that no effective entitlement protection is possible without a commensurate and simultaneous increase in food availability, and (2) that no reliable channel for increasing food availability exists other than the famine relief system itself.[7] Much of our concern in this chapter will be to reconsider these assumptions carefully.

6.2 Availability, Prices and Entitlements

As we have stressed in the first part of this book, it would be a gross mistake to conclude from the entitlement approach that food availability is unimportant or unhelpful in protecting food entitlements. A greater abundance of food, if nothing else, usually means cheaper food, and lower food prices improve the entitlements of those who are on the demand side of the market—the side to which vulnerable groups typically belong. The advantages of a greater abundance of food will tend to apply irrespective of the process through which the entitlements of these groups are threatened in the first place, and in particular irrespective of whether or not the threat of famine is accompanied by any decline in the availability of food.

An improvement in food availability in regions threatened by famine can, of course, be achieved in a number of different ways. Food aid is an obvious possibility, which tends to capture a lot of attention. An alternative comes from

---

[5] See World Food Programme (1986b).

[6] See CILSS (1986), Pearson (1986) World Food Programme (1986a, Annex IV), and McLean (1987, 1988). Great care is, however, needed in assessing the precise impact of plummeting post-harvest grain prices on different occupation groups. For a helpful analysis of this problem in the case of Sudan, see de Waal (1987).

[7] Strictly speaking, while direct delivery of food by the state or a relief agency tends to add to the supply of food in the area, the *net* increase may be quite different from the gross amount directly delivered since there can be a 'displacement effect' on the normal—usually private—operations in the food market. Usually the displacement effect would be negative (since the price reduction consequent on direct delivery will reduce the incentive of private traders to bring in food), though in situations of manipulative speculation direct delivery may also have the effect of countering strategic hoarding.

commercial imports on government account, and during the 1983–5 food crisis in Africa many countries did indeed make use of this opportunity.[8] The depletion of public stocks, when these exist, is another option. Food can also be moved into the affected region through the channel of private trade, which again has played a prominent role not only in India but also, quite often, in Africa as well. Finally, in some instances the availability of food can be substantially improved by greater local production, including foraging, gathering wild foods, growing root crops, and slaughtering livestock. In planning public policy, it is important to recognize both the instrumental role that improved food availability can play in protecting entitlements, and the plurality of mechanisms that can be brought to bear on the supply of food.

Closely related to the question of food availability is that of food prices. The level of food prices is, in fact, one of the crucial variables mediating the relationship between aggregate food availability and individual entitlements.[9] As was noted in the previous chapter, sharp increases in food prices are a common, though not universal, feature of famines. It is also easy to see that the successful containment of increases in food prices would generally be helpful in protecting the entitlements of vulnerable groups.

One natural thought in dealing with high prices of provisions is that of imposing direct control on food prices. This has obvious attractions.[10] There are, however, serious difficulties in making good use of this strategy in a largely market-based economy without rationing. For one thing, effective enforcement is very hard, and the cases of successful reduction of prices through direct control have been quite rare. There is the further problem that even if prices are successfully kept low through control, this in itself does not guarantee that the available food will be equitably distributed. If prices are lowered below the level at which total demand is met by supply, the people failing to make a purchase might quite possibly be among those who were most vulnerable and deprived in the first place. An additional requirement will then be that of providing a minimal amount of food for all, or at least for the more deprived, through some form of direct rationing.

With adequate preparation, rationing can certainly make a big difference to the distribution of scarce food.[11] But the administrative and logistic requirements involved in successful controls on food prices along with extensive rationing can be extremely exacting. Moreover, the operation of rationing need not be conditional on directly controlling free market prices *as well*, and there can be dual markets with the coexistence of a limited 'ration' of food for all and,

---

[8] See Borton and Clay (1986).

[9] This is one of the major themes of Martin Ravallion's important and far-reaching study, *Markets and Famines* (1987a).

[10] See e.g. Jean Mayer (1975), who argues that 'price control is an essential measure in any famine situation', and that 'it has to be vigorously enforced' (p. 81).

[11] For example, in Britain, war-time rationing in the 1940s certainly played a major part in maintaining—indeed in some ways improving—nutritional levels despite the strain on food supplies. On this see Chapter 10, and also Titmuss (1950) and Hammond (1951).

along with that, ordinary market operations. There are good examples of effective entitlement protection through food rationing without resorting simultaneously to comprehensive price control.[12]

There are also other ways of influencing food prices than the imposition of direct controls, for example through the importation of food, the participation of the public sector in food distribution, or various forms of regulation of the activities of private traders. The merits of some of these forms of intervention in different contexts will be discussed in later sections of this chapter.

It would be a mistake, however, to see the moderation of food prices as the overriding objective of famine relief policies. Indeed, in some cases an increase in food prices can emerge as an acceptable side effect of entitlement protection policies themselves. For instance, it is often sensible to protect entitlements by generating cash incomes for vulnerable groups, and some increase in food prices may then result from their greater purchasing power. Price increases will, in this case, play a positive part in shifting food in the direction of the poor. This will take place partly through the reduction of consumption on the part of other—less vulnerable—groups, and partly through increased flows of food from other regions, greater depletion of stocks, and perhaps some increase in the production of food even in the reasonably short run.

Price increases of this kind obviously have an altogether different significance from the price increases that would result, say, from the manipulative activities of colluding traders. Conversely, it is easy to think of examples where the moderation of prices would be achieved at the expense of a deterioration in the entitlements of vulnerable groups. When evaluating alternative forms of intervention, the focus has to be on the entitlement process as a whole, rather than simply on the level of prices as such.

6.3 Private Trade and Famine Vulnerability

The possible influence of private trade in alleviating or exacerbating distress during famines is a theme that is not always approached dispassionately. For some, the business of trafficking in food amidst raging starvation is a particularly objectionable form of anti-social profiteering. For others, faith in the positive contribution of private trade is part and parcel of reliance on the logic of the price system. Correspondingly, government policies towards private trade during famines have often varied between the dangerous extremes of indiscriminate liberalism and paralysing control. Famine victims have sometimes been sacrificed at the altar of economic ideology even when a willingness to rescue them apparently existed.

There is, in fact, abundant empirical evidence from various famines of both negative and positive influence of private trade. At times it has been responsible for manipulative operations on the part of professional speculators.

---

[12] Effective use of this means can be related, for instance, to the nutritional achievements of Kerala and Sri Lanka (see Chapters 11 and 12). The role of public distribution, both in protecting entitlements and in effectively promoting them, will receive further attention later on in this book.

Large-scale exports of food from famine-affected areas have also been commonly observed. But in other cases private trade has performed a more positive function, typically by moving food towards famine-affected areas and containing the increase of prices in those regions. And the disastrous consequences of deliberate paralysing of private trade by governments have been a notable feature of several modern famines. These empirical observations suggest the need for discrimination in appraising the role of private trade in entitlement protection.

Private traders tend to move food from low-price to high-price areas. This is indeed how they make profits.[13] Such food movements normally lead to a moderation of food prices in high-price importing areas and an increase in low-price exporting areas. As a result, price disparities between different regions should tend to get reduced.[14]

This process will typically alleviate the intensity of famine if two conditions are satisfied. First, in a given locality a moderation of food prices should improve the food entitlements of vulnerable groups. This is quite a plausible assumption, since vulnerable groups are rarely on the selling side of the food market. The second condition is that, across different localities, there should be a positive association between the intensity of distress and the level of prices. If, in contrast, the worst-affected areas are in fact low-price areas, the movement of food towards high-price areas will exacerbate—rather than reduce—the intensity of famine.

As we saw in the previous chapter, the fulfilment of this second condition is by no means universal. The history of famines in fact contains abundant examples of *export* of food through private trade *from* famine-affected regions to elsewhere. The Famine Commission of 1880 in India, for instance, recognized with embarrassment but also resolute apathy the persistence (and in fact expansion) of large-scale exports of grain from the country all the way through the preceding years of famine:

Unluckily for the Indian consumer, there have been several bad harvests in England, and this and the exchange have stimulated a great export of grain for the last few years. This gain of the producing class and its adjunct, the bunyah [trader], has been so far the loss of the consuming class. This seems inevitable.[15]

Other well-documented examples, such as that of the Irish famine of 1845–8, inescapably confirm the genuine possibility of food 'counter-movements' during famines.[16] This contrary phenomenon was not absent during the recent

[13] Private traders also make profits by speculating over time. This raises separate issues which will be considered in the next section.
[14] There are exceptions to this process, to be discussed later on in this section.
[15] Government of India (1880, Appendix I: 112).
[16] Substantial amounts of food were shipped from famine-affected Ireland in the 1840s to more prosperous England, where the ability to pay a high price for superior food was much greater than in Ireland. A moving account of the distressing experience of witnessing these counter-movements can be found in Woodham-Smith (1962). For analyses of food counter-movements, see Sen (1981a) and Chichilnisky (1983).

famines in Africa. There have, for instance, been consistent reports of large-scale food exports from famine-affected Chad towards countries such as Cameroon and Nigeria where food prices were more rewarding.[17]

While the possibility of such food counter-movements must be kept firmly in view, it would be a mistake to ignore the positive function that market-based transactions can play in relieving the distress of famines. As was discussed in the last chapter, within a country famine-affected areas are also quite often areas of relatively high food prices. In such cases the operation of private trade may reasonably be expected to have the effect of driving down food prices in hard-hit regions and thereby alleviating the intensity of the famine. It would, of course, be silly to insist on the generalization that the overall impact of private trade will invariably contribute to reducing aggregate mortality. But there is nevertheless some sense in seeing the sharing of distress over a wider area as essentially a good thing, when the configuration of prices is such that private trade does move food in the 'right' direction.[18]

An illustration, discussed in greater detail in Chapter 8 below, may help to explain the issue. This illustration relates to the behaviour of food prices in Botswana and Kenya during the droughts of 1982–7 and 1984 respectively.[19] In Botswana, food moves freely throughout the country, and the food market is fairly active and competitive (the government also participates in food trade and distribution). In this country, food prices have been found to remain strikingly close to each other in different regions during the drought. The increase in prices, aside from being quite uniform, was also fairly moderate (see Table 8.13 in Chapter 8). In Kenya, by contrast, food trade between different districts was severely controlled during the drought of 1984. While in some districts food prices were *falling* during the drought as a result of the inability of private traders to export surpluses to other parts of the country, in drought-affected areas food prices were rising very sharply in spite of government attempts to rush in food bought on the international market. The result was the emergence of extremely large price differentials between different regions, with food prices being, at one point, as much as ten times higher in some regions than in others. It would be hard to sustain the thesis that the sharp intensification of food price increases in drought-affected regions of Kenya in 1984, evidently associated with the restrictions imposed on interregional trade, was in any way helpful to vulnerable groups. It is easy to find

---

[17] See e.g. Hoeffel (1986) and Diesler (1986). There have been other recent cases of reported food counter-movements during famines, such as in the Wollo famine of 1973, the Bangladesh famine of 1974 and the famine of 1979–80 in parts of Kenya (see Hussein 1976, Holt and Seaman 1976, Belete *et al*. 1977, Alamgir 1980, Sen 1981*a*, Herlehy 1984).

[18] Ravallion (1987*a*) investigates the process through which a reduction of price differentials can lead to a moderation of overall famine mortality.

[19] See Chapter 8 for a more detailed account of the recent experiences of drought and famine prevention in these two countries, as well as of their respective marketing and distribution policies.

further illustrations from other countries pointing clearly in the same direction.[20]

There are, however, several important qualifications to the foregoing argument. First, the assumption of a positive association between the level of prices and the intensity of distress, while frequently justified, is not invariably so. If the famine region or country happens to be particularly deprived of purchasing power (because of low income and few assets), food prices can be lower there along with starvation. In these circumstances, free movement of food can worsen the situation by exporting food away from the most affected regions. On the other hand, an effective solution of this problem involves not only providing the distressed population with the ability to purchase food, but also making it possible for food supply to respond to the newly created purchasing power. This can be brought about by a combination of income support in the affected region along with permitting the movement of food in response to the demand generated by that income. On this more presently.

Second, private trade can take a direct role in reducing price differentials only as long as these differentials exceed transport costs. Where transport costs are high, as in many parts of Africa, the operation of private trade may allow quite alarming price differentials between regions to persist. This observation does not, of course, provide an argument for introducing *further* restrictions on private trade, but it is relevant for correctly gauging the extent of its influence on price differentials. A very similar remark applies to other limitations restricting the operation of private trade, such as credit constraints, poor information, or insufficient communications.

Finally, collusive behaviour by traders can interfere with the expected movement of food from low-price to high-price localities. The collective interest of traders is often to 'segment' markets and, in this instance, they may wish to prevent the moderation of prices in famine-affected areas by restricting their trade. This possibility must be taken seriously, and its empirical relevance has to be assessed in specific context. Cases of gross manipulation of the market by traders have certainly been noted, and public policy-making in this field should not fall into the trap of simply assuming this possibility away.[21] On the other hand, it must also be remembered that in most countries of Africa and Asia the 'traders' are not all portly merchants sitting on heaps of grain, but also include millions of poor buyers and sellers (many of them women) who are

---

[20] See e.g. the comparison between the drought of 1966–7 in the state of Bihar and the drought of 1970–3 in the state of Maharashtra (both in India) in Drèze (1988a), and the comparison between the droughts of 1910–15 and 1968–74 in the Sahel in Kates (1981). The emergence of enormous price differentials between adjacent regions of Ethiopia during droughts has also been attributed partly to the suppression of private trade in that country, inadequately compensated by positive state involvement in food distribution (see e.g. Cutler 1985b, Griffin and Hay 1985, and Griffin 1987).

[21] See e.g. Pearson (1986) and Bush (1988) on the Darfur famine of 1985 in Sudan.

willing to travel long distances, on foot if necessary, in order to transact food at more advantageous prices.[22]

In those cases in which the collusive and restrictive practices of traders may worsen the sufferings involved, there is also a serious issue in deciding on the best means of dealing with this threat. Legal restrictions on private food movements rarely prove helpful in counteracting collusive practices (sometimes quite the contrary), and the paralysis of private trade without a compensating state involvement in food trade can be a particularly dangerous policy. A more constructive way of preventing the emergence or persistence of such practices is often to ensure a measure of government participation in food trade—we shall return to this point in the next section. In this field, as in many others, the government's ability to help through positive action is both more promising and more often overlooked than the martial art of doing good through slapping down negative restrictions.

As far as traders are concerned, their contribution—positive and negative—is much too diverse to be summarizable in the form of some simple favourable or critical slogan. There is, of course, some wisdom in Bertolt Brecht's aphorism that 'famines do not occur, they are organised by the grain trade', but as a piece of causal explanation of famines it has some obvious shortcomings. The same qualification applies to Malthus's belief that famines are never exacerbated by trade, only ameliorated by it. That too is poetry rather than prose. The choice of public action in countering famines has to make use of the wisdom that prompted these remarks, without being blinded by their misleading claim to generality.

6.4 Speculation, Hoarding and Public Distribution

Many of the considerations applying to interregional trade are also relevant to the phenomenon of intertemporal transactions. To some extent, similar influences will be operating in determining the activities of private trade and their consequences on a famine-threatened economy. There are private gains to be made by successful intertemporal arbitrage, and one of the effects of this activity will often be to reduce the fluctuation of prices over time. Qualifications similar to those examined in the preceding section have to be considered in accepting the presumed outcomes of such arbitrage.

But the analogy between the temporal and the spatial is imperfect, and the evaluation of the role of intertemporal arbitrage cannot be based simply on mirroring the evaluation of interregional trade. There is a real asymmetry of

---

[22] Peter Cutler has noted that, during the early stages of the Ethiopian famine in 1984: 'There was grain available at normal prices some 60 km away from the drought zone. Indeed, peasants were walking this distance in order to purchase food and bring it home again—a very cumbersome load of some 50 kg being carried over a weary journey' (Cutler 1985b: 61). Similar findings have been reported from Mali (J. Downing et al. 1987: 234), Chad (Pol Barbier, personal communication), Malawi (Vaughan 1987: 123), and Zambia (Pottier 1988).

knowledge (in addition to that of operations) that applies between two time periods, and which does not have a clear counterpart in the case of two regions.[23] In particular, the role played by *expectations* about the unknown future in the process of speculation over time brings in a crucial complication.

Consider, for instance, a situation in which the general public is hoarding food at a ferocious rate in anticipation of a severe price rise, while the government happens to have reliable information about the arrival of a substantial amount of food from abroad in the near future. Even if the government publicizes the information it has, the public may still have good reasons (perhaps based on past experience) to be sceptical of the veracity of governmental statements. The immediate price rise caused by misguided speculation may lead to great hardship and even starvation on the part of the more vulnerable, and the government under these circumstances may well have good reasons to interfere severely with private markets to prevent that outcome. One can think of similar cases with a different scenario in which the government has a role in supplementing and supplanting private trade to deal with the adverse effects of misguided speculation. This type of problem of general failure of public knowledge about the future can be a serious reason for seeing a more crucial role for public action in the field of intertemporal transactions than in interregional trade.[24]

Professional speculators may, of course, be typically quite well informed, unlike the general public. The point has also been variously made, by Malthus, Mill, Friedman and others, that the unsuccessful speculators get eliminated by the market mechanism, and that the activities of surviving speculators can be expected to be stabilizing rather than the contrary. This argument is flawed for a variety of reasons, chiefly its inability to take an adequately detailed view of the different channels through which the actions of speculators affect the market.[25] Speculation *can* be destabilizing.

The real issue concerns what the government can do, faced with the possibly damaging effects of misguided or mischievous speculation. The administrative problems involved in imposing direct and effective controls on the holding of stocks by the public and by professional speculators can be enormous

---

[23] These asymmetries have different aspects. If food can be moved from region A to region B, it typically can also be moved from B to A. On the other hand, while passing on food from the present to the future can frequently be easily achieved (through stocking), there is no corresponding ease in moving food backwards in time. No less importantly, the future is unknown to people living now in a way that the present may not be unknown to the historians in future. There would tend to be, typically, more symmetry between regions in terms of their knowledge of prices and other information relating to the other regions.

[24] See Ravallion (1987a) for a study of the contribution of misguided private speculation (and inadequate public involvement) to the development of the Bangladesh famine of 1974.

[25] Even under favourable assumptions about the competitiveness of markets, the accuracy of traders' foresight, and risk-neutrality of individual behaviour, speculation can be 'destabilizing' (see Hart 1977, Hart and Kreps 1986, Newbery 1987b, and the discussion of this in relation to famines in Ravallion 1987d). *Additional* difficulties can arise from (1) the lack of competitiveness of markets, (2) inaccurate foresight, and (3) risk aversion on the part of speculators.

(especially when, as in much of sub-Saharan Africa, food stocks are mainly held by small farmers). Also, the atmosphere of emergency created by forced requisition may aggravate rather than appease the apprehensions of the public.

One of the alternatives to consider is the possibility of influencing expectations, and the behaviour of traders and speculators generally, by vigorous government *participation* in food trade and storage. The existence of public stocks, for instance, can go a long way towards reducing fears of future scarcity and also defeating the manipulative practices of private traders.

There is considerable empirical evidence of the potential effectiveness of this strategy. For instance, in his instructive analysis of the prevention of famine in Bangladesh in 1979, Siddiq Osmani persuasively argues that the public distribution system played a major role in inspiring public confidence in the stability of prices.[26] Similarly, in his account of the 1984–5 famine in Sudan, Roger Pearson describes how even marginal participation in food distribution and transport on the part of relief agencies could have dramatic effects on local prices: 'When it was heard that the first batch of food aid was to arrive in El Obeid in November 1984 the price of a 90 kg sack of sorghum declined from 135 to 75 Sudanese pounds'.[27] Strikingly similar observations have also been reported in a number of other countries.[28]

In food policy, there is no panacea. The dangers of leaving matters entirely to private trade are obvious enough. At the same time, it is hard to escape the recognition that in famine situations many African governments have missed the opportunity of supplementing their own logistic resources by a skilful use of what market trade can offer. Making room for private trade must not be confused with giving it an unrestrained and commanding influence on market operations, even when that influence has damaging effects on vulnerable people. It is possible to utilize the advantages—direct and indirect—of public distribution systems without taking on the Herculean task of managing all transactions through bureaucratic controls.

6.5   Cash Support

In section 6.1 we suggested that one of the important factors accounting for the frequently belated and insufficiently effective nature of famine prevention

---

[26]   See Osmani (1986), and also Clay (1985b), Crow (1987) and Ravallion (1987a).

[27]   Pearson (1986: 52). The author also argues that food aid had the immediate effect of breaking a traders' cartel in Sudan, which was 'perhaps the most important effect that the emergency operation has had on the lives of the majority of the poor in Sudan' (p. 87). On this question, see also Bush (1988).

[28]   A report from the FAO in Chad, for instance, notes how the maintenance of a small public food stock provides 'psychological pressure on prices' and ensures that 'traders will not hold precautionary stocks' (FAO 1987b: 7). In Kampuchea, rice prices have been reported to fall by 80% within two weeks of the introduction of free public distribution (Mason and Brown 1983: 82).

efforts in Africa is the dependence of the chosen entitlement protection measures on the timely arrival of food aid, and generally on the complicated logistics associated with the direct delivery of food. The question, however, is whether and how this situation can be remedied. Greater use of cash support is an obvious option.

Cash relief is not a new idea. It is mentioned in the Bible, and has a rich history covering many parts of the world.[29] But the suggestion that it has a contribution to make to famine prevention strategies in Africa today is often met with resilient suspicion. This suspicion cannot reasonably arise from the belief that the conversion of cash into food might prove impossible in a famine situation. Indeed, as we discussed in Chapter 5, the earning of cash is now one of the most vital survival strategies of famine victims in African countries.

But there is a deeper problem. Even if it is accepted that having cash can almost always help an individual to acquire food and avoid starvation, it is less obvious that cash support can help a *community* taken together. After all, one person's ability to command food through cash support may adversely affect other people's entitlements, e.g. by exerting an upward pressure on prices. As we have seen in Chapter 4, 'food battles' can be intense, and the competition for market command is one of the forms which such conflicts can take. The merits of cash support therefore need to be scrutinized with considerable care.[30]

The debate about the merits and limitations of cash support has, in fact, involved two distinct issues which should not be confused. The first issue concerns the relative merits of food and cash as the *medium* of entitlement protection. Is it better (1) to provide people directly with food, or (2) to give them an equivalent transfer in cash with the corresponding amount of food sold in the local market? In considering this question in its pure form, the amount of resources (food *and* cash) used by the relief system is held constant by hypothesis. The second issue concerns the wisdom of giving cash income to the potential victims *without* adding a corresponding amount of food to the system. Here the comparison is between (1) taking direct action using cash, and (2) waiting for an improvement in food availability (e.g. through food aid) before extending support to vulnerable groups. This is really where the question of potential conflicts in access to food comes in. For convenience we shall refer to

---

[29] On the former, see Dando (1983), Sider (1980), and The Bible, Acts 11: 27–30. Cash relief has a long history both in India (Loveday 1914; Drèze 1988a) and in China (Mallory 1926; Will 1980; Li 1987), and has also been an important feature of famine prevention in a number of African countries more recently, including Botswana (Hay et al. 1986), Cape Verde (van Binsbergen 1986), colonial Tanganyika (Mwaluko 1962), colonial Zimbabwe (Holland 1987), and contemporary Ethiopia (Bjoerck 1984; Hilsum 1984; RRC/UNICEF 1984, 1985; Kumar 1985; Padmini 1985; von Kohl 1988).

[30] For a lucid examination of some of the important issues involved, following a line of analysis rather different from the one used here, see Coate (1986, 1989).

these two distinct issues as the 'cash medium issue' and the 'cash injection issue', respectively.[31]

Regarding the cash medium issue, it seems plausible that in the specific context of famine prevention, the choice of support medium (cash or kind) would be unlikely to have a major influence on the effectiveness of entitlement protection strategies. One reason why the medium of entitlement protection is not completely irrelevant is that households often treat income acquired in the form of cash differently from income acquired in the form of food. A number of recent studies strongly suggest that, in ordinary times at least, using food as a medium of support tends to influence the consumption of families in the direction of greater food intake.[32] But it is not unreasonable to expect that the contrast applies with much less force in the case of famine victims, for whom food intake becomes an overriding concern and absorbs the bulk of the resources they may succeed in acquiring.[33] The choice between providing food and providing cash may still matter to some extent, but it is hardly likely to have momentous implications for the survival chances of famine victims.

The more important part of the debate about cash relief relates to the cash injection issue. To come to grips with it, consider a scheme of cash-based entitlement support to vulnerable populations, such as a cash-for-work programme or a scheme of cash hand-outs. This policy will have the immediate effect of exerting an upward pressure on food prices, since the effective demand for food increases. But, as we have already noted, this inflationary pressure may be functional: in this instance the increase of prices has its origin in the greater purchasing power of the needy and is part of the process of improving (rather than undermining) their command over food. In order to assess the precise impact of an income generation strategy of this kind on the allocation of food in the economy, one must examine carefully the effects it is likely to have, via the price mechanism, on (1) the total availability of food in the affected region (through changes in production, storage, and trade), and

---

[31] In the formulation of the 'cash medium issue', we are assuming that, when cash rather than food is given to the victims, the corresponding amount of food is additionally supplied in the *local* market. A further question is whether it is, in fact, important that the relief system itself should deliver the food all the way to the local market. In terms of standard 'general equilibrium' theory, if cash payments to the victims include the relevant transport costs, the location of food sale would not matter. However, that analysis takes little note of some specific problems which may be important in practice, e.g. the relative speed and efficiency of public delivery *vis-à-vis* private trade, the possible importance of preventing the destruction of the normal infrastructure of trade and commerce, and so on. Some of these issues are investigated in Kumar (1985), Coate (1986, 1989), Sen (1986*a*) and Johnson and Zeckhauser (1989).

[32] On this question, see the empirical studies of George (1979), Kumar (1979), Harbert and Scandizzo (1982), Senauer and Young (1986), Edirisinghe (1987), and especially Garcia and Pins'rup-Andersen (1987).

[33] This conjecture is particularly plausible if the different treatment of cash and food income in ordinary times is due to a form of 'illusion' on the part of recipients (rather than, say, to different treatments of intrahousehold conflicts depending on whether outside help is received by the family in the form of food *or* cash).

(2) the distribution of the food available between different sections of the population.[34]

To start with, higher prices can have the effect of stimulating the *production* of food. It is tempting to think that in a famine situation the production of food is not responsive to price changes, but there are in fact good reasons to be sceptical of this belief. The literature on informal security systems discussed in the previous chapter abundantly shows that repeated sowing, growing alternative crops, reducing livestock feeding, and gathering wild foods are all very common responses to food crises, and all these activities are—up to a point—rendered more attractive by increases in food prices. It has been widely observed, for instance, that wild foods ordinarily eaten only by the poorest households become prized objects of consumption *and* market transactions during famines.[35] Interestingly, one of the observed effects of a cash-for-work programme implemented in Ethiopia in 1984 was that peasants in the area 'began . . . growing more' in response to an increased demand for food.[36]

The likely effects of price increases on *storage* decisions during famines in Africa are not easy to assess. The discussion of the previous section points to serious difficulties in forming prior judgements on this question, and the empirical evidence is also very limited. Some researchers have argued that, in famine situations, an initial perturbation in the level of prices could escalate and spread, as farmers and traders withdraw their supplies from the market.[37] But others have come to much less pessimistic conclusions. The timely depletion of stocks during the 1973 famine in the Sahel, for instance, is reported by Caldwell:

> Even in 1973 some areas received close to their seasonal rainfall and grew adequate crops. The market encouraged the fortunate populations to tighten their belts and to sell food that they could spare either from the current harvest or from stored stocks. Indeed, it was the very high prices induced by the drought that led some farmers to sell stored stocks just at a time when the outsider might at first assume that he was storing most desperately.[38]

This judgement is not isolated, and further indications pointing in the same direction can be found elsewhere.[39] Great caution is of course required in

---

[34] There are other, potentially important price-sensitive aspects of food allocation which will not be investigated here, e.g. animal feeding, wastage and diet composition. For some relevant empirical findings in the context of subsistence crises, many of which strengthen the case for greater use of cash support in famine situations, see e.g. Faulkingham (1977), Tobert (1985), McLean (1986), Fleuret (1986), McCorkle (1987), and O'Grada (1988a).

[35] See Bernus (1977b), Dando (1982), Tobert (1985), Fleuret (1986), Longhurst (1986), McLean (1986), de Waal (1987) and M. Chen (1988).

[36] *Africa Emergency Report*, Apr./May 1986, p. 6.

[37] See particularly Seaman and Holt (1980).

[38] Caldwell (1981a: 8).

[39] The evaluation of the UNICEF cash relief project in Ethiopia in 1984 to which we have already referred, for instance, 'discovered that as demand for food grew within the area, peasants with small food surpluses began introducing them to local markets' (*Africa Emergency Report*, Apr./May 1986, p. 6). In his review of food security issues in the Sudano-Sahel, Brandt even comes

drawing conclusions from specific information of this kind, but there is certainly no strong evidence to support the view that the price increases that might accompany cash relief programmes would systematically encourage damaging speculative activities in sub-Saharan Africa (especially if public policy is intelligently used to counter manipulative practices).

Increases in food prices can also stimulate private *trade* and cause enlarged flows of food towards the famine affected area (or a reduction of food exports, if ·these are taking place). Reliance on this mechanism has indeed been one of the central planks of famine prevention in India for a long time.[40] India's circumstances are perhaps somewhat favourable to the smooth functioning of this mechanism, since crop failures in one part of the country are often compensated—at least partly—by good crops elsewhere, communications are well developed, and private trade is fairly alert. But the contrast between Indian and African conditions in these respects, while very real, is perhaps not as sharp as is often asserted.

In the common international perception, connected largely with the nature of media reports, African famines are often seen in terms of acute and more or less uniform 'shortages' of food everywhere in the affected country or countries. This is, however, little more than a myth, and in fact the scope for interregional food movements to alleviate the intensity of distress is often considerable. Large variations in food output between different regions are common in Africa, and a marketable surplus usually remains in or near the famine-affected territory.[41] This is most clearly the case when dealing with 'food crises' of a localized nature, as recurrently occur in different parts of Africa.[42] But even during the African famines of 1973 and 1984, both of which were rather extreme in terms of the extent and spread of the crop failures that accompanied them, a considerable potential for interregional food movements certainly existed in many places. John Caldwell, for instance, has argued that large regional variations existed in the severity of crop failures during the Sahel

---

to the conclusion that 'semi-commercial storage by farmers is already making a tremendous contribution towards the elimination of seasonal fluctuations of supply in the internal markets of the Sahel countries' (Brandt 1984: viii). A commentator on the famine situation in Africa in 1983–5 noted that 'in the Sahel, when the cereal crops (millet, sorghum) fail, other farmers who produce tubers (cassava, yam) rush to sell their surplus to the cereal farmers' (*The Economist*, 20 July 1985, p. 21).

[40] See Chapter 8 and also Drèze (1988*a*). The same strategy of trade stimulation through income generation played a crucial role in the famine relief system of 18th-century China under the Qing dynasty, on which see the major work of Étienne Will (1980). At one point the usual practice was to provide food relief and cash relief in identical proportions (Will 1980: Chapter 3).

[41] For examples of the sharp contrasts that are typically found in Africa in the extent of crop failures, not only between different regions, but also between different villages and even fields, see Caldwell (1975, 1977), Lallemand (1975), Rivers *et al.* (1976), Faulkingham (1977), Relief and Development Institute (1985), CILSS (1986), Fleuret (1986), Green (1986*a*, 1986*b*), Morgan (1986), Bratton (1987*a*), Vaughan (1987), Koponen (1988), von Braun (1988).

[42] The references cited in the preceding footnote provide many examples of localized entitlement crises in Africa. The persistence of famine in various parts of Africa in 1985, despite record harvests in most countries, has also been widely noted.

famine of 1973, and that sizeable movements of food were taking place within as well as towards famine-affected countries.[43] It would be a mistake to disregard the opportunity of reducing the forces of famine through encouraging food movements between different areas.

A further aspect of the problem, however, is whether private trade can be expected to provide adequate food movement when interregional movements of food *are* potentially helpful. The answer to this question cannot but be contingent on many specific considerations. In several parts of Africa (including much of the Sahel), there is a strong tradition of private food trade, sometimes over long distances. The dynamism of this tradition has been observed in several places during recent famines *in spite* of official discouragement.[44] Generally, there is considerable evidence that private trade in Africa is alive to economic opportunities when it is allowed to operate without bureaucratic restrictions.[45] Of course, sharp contrasts exist between different African countries, and it may well be that in some places a major reliance on the operation of private food trade to respond to the demands generated by cash support would be problematic. There are, however, no serious grounds for general pessimism in this respect.

Despite the possibly important effects of cash support on the total supply of food in the market through stimulating production, de-stocking, and trade, it is very likely that the increase in food availability will fall short of the increase in the consumption of those receiving cash support. Indeed, the same price rise which has an expanding effect on supply will also have a contracting effect on the demand for food of those who do not receive cash support but now face

---

[43] See Caldwell (1975, 1977). Similar observations have been made in the context of the 1983–5 crisis for different parts of Africa (World Food Programme 1986b: 14), and even for Ethiopia (see *Africa Emergency Report*, Apr./May 1985, p. 6, and Government of Ethiopia 1986). On the important contribution that interregional food movements seem to have made in alleviating a number of recent African famines, see also Caldwell (1977, 1984), Kates (1981), Hill (1987), Iliffe (1987).

[44] For instance, private trade (often clandestine) is reported to have flooded Burkina Faso in 1984 with Ghanaian maize and cereals imported from distant Abidjan and Lomé (Hesse 1985); imported 150,000 tonnes of cereals into drought-affected Mali in 1985 (Steele 1985); ensured 'a remarkable uniformity of grain prices throughout Nigerian Hausaland' during the 1973 famine (Iliffe 1987: 257); reached 'every day' a Sudanese town which was said by UN agencies to be hopelessly cut off by road mining (Garden and Musa 1986); and, less happily, *exported* large quantities of food from Chad in 1984–5 towards countries such as Cameroon and Nigeria (as noted earlier). The active role of private trade is also evident in many accounts of African famines during the colonial period. See e.g. Mwaluko (1962), Lugan (1976), O'Leary (1980), Herlehy (1984), Holland (1987), and de Waal (1989b).

[45] On the characteristics and functioning of food markets in Africa, see Bauer (1954), Club du Sahel (1977), Eicher and Baker (1982), Harriss (1982), and Berg (1986), among others. Of course, food markets in most African countries are far from completely 'integrated', but it is hard to separate out the extent to which this is due to bureaucratic regulation and control as opposed to the underdevelopment of trade.

higher prices. To that extent, a redistribution of consumption towards the protected groups will take place.[46]

The prospect of dealing with the threat of famine partly by inducing a redistribution process operating *within* affected areas strikes terror in the heart of many observers. They see this as a failure to respond to the 'real problem' of 'shortage' and as an attempt 'to transfer food from one victim to another'. It must be remembered, however, that large inequalities are a pervasive feature of most famine-prone societies. As was discussed in the previous chapter, the readiness of populations (poor and less poor) to alter their consumption patterns under the pressure of price and income changes in times of famine also seems to be much greater than is often imagined. The scope for redistribution from the relatively privileged to the most vulnerable may therefore be far from negligible. When direct delivery of food through the public relief system is hampered or slowed down by administrative and logistic difficulties, cash support may be a useful option, especially compared with leaving the problem unaddressed.

The feasibility of the redistributive mechanism is clearly illustrated by the experience of famine prevention in Maharashtra during the 1972–3 drought, to which we have already referred in the previous chapter. In this event, the government resorted to large-scale cash relief (in the form of cash-for-work programmes), and *separately* organized the supply of food through the public distribution system. The latter efforts, however, were hampered by logistic difficulties, and left a large gap between the availability of food in the state of Maharashtra as a whole and the normal level of aggregate consumption. To a considerable extent, this gap was reduced by the operation of private trade, which moved large amounts of food into Maharashtra (where public employment programmes generated a considerable expansion of purchasing power).[47] In spite of these additional food movements, a substantial decline in food availability occurred in the state during the drought, but the effect of targeted income generation measures was precisely to ensure that the reduction of average consumption was remarkably evenly distributed between different socio-economic groups, rather than the burden of reduction being entirely borne by the most vulnerable.

The success of the redistributive strategy, however, depends to a great extent on the ability of the relief system to provide preferential support to the entire vulnerable population. If substantial numbers of vulnerable people are excluded from entitlement protection measures but have to take the conse-

---

[46] It is conceivable that, in some rather special circumstances, cash transfers could lead (through 'general equilibrium' effects) to a *deterioration* of food entitlements for the recipient groups. But the empirical relevance of this 'transfer paradox' is rather limited in the context of cash support for famine victims.

[47] Interestingly enough, the drought occurred at a time when there were severe official restrictions on private interstate movements of foodgrains, so that the helpful movements of food were, in fact, 'illegal', even though the authorities evidently turned a blind eye on such movements.

quences of price increases, the overall vulnerability of the population could conceivably be exacerbated rather than diminished by the relief system.[48] An important question therefore concerns the need to cover all the major vulnerable groups, while continuing to exclude the more privileged in order to preserve the redistributive bias on which the success of the strategy of cash support depends. These and related questions are further discussed in the next chapter.

6.6 An Adequate Plurality

This chapter has explored the part that markets can play in precipitating or relieving a famine. We have also examined the possibility of making deliberate use of the market mechanism in public policy for famine prevention, in particular by providing large-scale cash support to famine victims. This investigation has focused on the substantial scope for effective use of cash support in famine situations.

We should, however, also warn against a possible misinterpretation of this conclusion. To recommend greater use of cash support is not to suggest that importing food into famine affected countries or areas is undesirable or unnecessary. Cash support and food supply management are not, by any means, mutually exclusive activities. Often, in addition to a strong case for the use of cash support, there is also a good argument for increasing the availability of food (e.g. by accepting food aid). Our contention is not that cash support should *replace* efforts to improve food availability, but only that in many circumstances there is no need to make entitlement protection conditional on the direct delivery of food.[49]

A related observation of some importance is that taking full advantage of the scope for cash support may require a careful integration of income generation programmes with other aspects of famine prevention policies. For instance, the case for imposing bureaucratic controls on food movements seems much weaker when the incomes of the poor are protected through public policy. In fact, an adequate market response to the demands newly generated by a strategy of cash support will often call for a relaxation of such controls. In turn, the threat of manipulative activities on the part of private traders may be much reduced by a substantial measure of public involvement in food distribution.

---

[48] It should, however, be mentioned that some of the excluded groups could gain from *derived benefits* obtained from the income support provided to other groups. For instance, a reduction of distress livestock sales on the part of those who receive support could substantially benefit vulnerable livestock owners outside the relief system by arresting an impending collapse of livestock prices. As was discussed in Chapter 2, the deterioration of livestock–grain exchange rates is indeed a causal antecedent of many famines. Another example of potentially important 'derived effects' is the 'multiplier effect' of the increase in the purchasing power of those who do receive support, i.e. their additional purchases will add to the incomes of the sellers, and so on.

[49] From the point of view of the affected country, the financial implications of combining cash support with food imports and the sale of food in the market need not be more taxing than those of a strategy of 'direct delivery'.

In so far as cash support emerges as an effective form of intervention in famine situations, it appeals to a combination of public action and private participation that may be worth emphasizing. Cash support, such as public works with cash wages, is quintessentially a 'public' activity, but its success is dependent on an adequate response from the market in the form of meeting the demands generated. In this sense, the success of a strategy of this kind is neither a question of pure governmental action, nor one of leaving matters to private initiative.

The tradition of thinking of famine relief in pure and rather extreme terms can be very misleading. To think only in terms of either direct delivery and feeding by the state, or in terms of leaving matters to the mercy of the market mechanism, cannot begin to be an appropriate approach to the threat of famine in the modern world. There is need to go beyond the bounds of that tradition, and to consider major departures in the relief practices of some of the most famine prone countries in the world. The penalty of purism can be high.

7

Strategies of Entitlement Protection

7.1 Non-exclusion, Targeting and Selection

The minimal ambition of a sound famine prevention system should be to protect (directly or indirectly) the entitlements of *all* those who are vulnerable to starvation. This typically requires the adoption of a suitable range of support strategies which, taken together, reach all the vulnerable individuals. We shall refer to this as the *non-exclusion* objective.

The safest and most obvious way of guaranteeing the universal protection of entitlements is to provide direct and unconditional support to everyone without distinction. The method of *universal support* is obviously a rather coarse one, but it does have the advantage of altogether bypassing the various difficulties which any form of selectivity in the provision of relief is bound to entail. There is something simple, practical and ethically appealing in the notion that everyone should be regarded as having an inalienable and unconditional right to the provision of a subsistence food ration—a notion that is actually widely supported when it comes to different types of basic necessities, such as education or health care. Universal support can be a simple expression of the much discussed 'right to food', and there was a time when, in European countries, the proposal of free bread for all was indeed considered seriously. More recently, universal suport has formed the basis of several highly impressive entitlement support schemes of a permanent nature, such as the early versions of the food subsidy systems of Sri Lanka (introduced in 1942) and Egypt.[1]

When it comes to famine prevention, however, the strategy of universal support would have several obvious disadvantages. To start with, it involves an administrative and logistic burden which can turn out to be quite exacting. More importantly, if it is to provide effective protection to those who depend entirely on public relief for their survival, universal support may require a commitment of resources that can be hard to obtain. We have to accept the fact that when limited resources are spread uniformly and indiscriminately over the whole population in a famine situation, lives are bound to be lost. Even in the event where adequate resources are available, one may still wish to impart a redistributive element to the entitlement protection process by restricting or 'targeting' support to selected groups. We shall refer to these redistributive considerations as the *targeting* objective.[2]

---

[1] The Sri Lankan experience is further examined in Chapter 12 of this book. For an excellent analysis of food subsidies in Egypt, see Alderman and von Braun (1984).

[2] While the principle underlying the notion of 'targeting' is simple enough, the operational notion of targeting-based protection is far from uncomplicated. Indeed, given the interdepend-

There can, in principle, be two different kinds of motivations underlying the targeting objective. One of them is to ensure the greatest *economy of resources* by *withholding* public support from less vulnerable groups. The other one is to make use of available resources to the greatest advantage of the most deprived groups, or in other words to promote the *redistribution of resources* by *concentrating* public support exclusively on these groups. In practice, it can of course be difficult to tell how the possibilities for improved targeting will be used —whether for reducing the resources devoted to entitlement protection, or for increasing the support given to vulnerable groups. The latter opportunity can be an important allocation issue for famine prevention, but it must be firmly distinguished from the fiscal temptations of the former.

There are, it must be said, good arguments for questioning the case for elaborate targeting even on distributional grounds. The ability of the poor to have access to public services, and the political support that the provision of these services can command, may depend crucially on the participation of a large part of the population in the benefits of public provisioning. For instance, the rapid expansion of public services in Britain during the Second World War, particularly impressive in contrast with the shocking apathy of the state in the 1930s, seems to have had much to do with factors of this kind:

That all were engaged in war whereas only some were affected with poverty and disease . . . had much to do with the less constraining, less discriminating scope and quality of the war-time social services . . . It was the universal character of these welfare policies which ensured their acceptance and success. They were free of social discrimination and the indignities of the poor law.[3]

We shall have more to say on this when we come to public action to deal with endemic deprivation, but there are good reasons to believe that in the context of famine prevention the case for targeting is fairly strong. Famines are typically situations where time is short and resources are limited, and the penalties of failing to come to the rescue of the most vulnerable by priority can be enormously high.

The potential importance of targeting for famine prevention can be illustrated by considering the experience of famine relief in Sudan in 1985.[4] As we saw in Chapter 5, there is little indication that the crisis of food and agricultural production which preceded famine in Sudan in that year was at all exceptional by the standards of what was happening elsewhere in Africa at the same time.

---

ences between different parts of the economy (including the so-called 'general equilibrium effects'), it must be recognized that in addition to direct beneficiaries any project will tend to influence—positively or negatively—the lives of many others.

[3] Titmuss (1950: 506, 514). The expansion of public services during and immediately after the Second World War in Britain, and the apparently dramatic impact of this expansion on the well-being of the population, are further discussed in Chapter 10.

[4] The following account draws on Chambers *et al.* (1986), Hale (1986), Pearson (1986), de Waal (1987, 1988a), Walker (1987), Bush (1988), Keen (1988), Maxwell (1988), Torry (1988b), and Borton and Shoham (1989b), as well as on personal communications from David Keen, Jeremy Swift, William Torry, Joachim von Braun and Peter Walker.

In fact, it has been argued that the extent of this crisis had initially been deliberately exaggerated for various political and tactical reasons.[5] Be that as it may, the country received massive amounts of food aid in 1984–5, and had the famine relief system succeeded in concentrating support on the most deprived, a famine could almost certainly have been averted.

Unfortunately it seems that the allocation of the bulk of food aid was far from redistributive. A careful study of this problem has put the situation thus:

> In general, it appears that wealthier people, and more politically influential groups, got more food aid than poorer and less influential groups. Broadly, the bigger towns got more than the smaller towns, townspeople got more than villagers, residents got more than migrants, and settled people got more than nomads . . . Areas designated as 'worst affected' received only a very small proportion of the grain distributed before the harvest . . . Within villages . . . richer households got more than poorer households.[6]

Sometimes the recipients of food aid were found to spend as much as 50 per cent of it on non-food items—a consumption pattern hardly compatible with extreme destitution. Even in feeding camps, it has been alleged that as few as 10 or 20 per cent of selected children were actually undernourished. The disquieting aspect of the story is not that too many people were helped, but rather that many were starving while relatively better-off groups were fattened by public support. In areas such as Darfur, the overall death rate in 1985 was estimated at three times the normal level.[7]

The simultaneous, and to some extent conflicting, objectives of 'non-exclusion' and 'targeting' can be pursued with varying emphasis, depending on the *selection* procedure adopted to determine the eligibility of different groups of people to public support. Common examples of alternative selection procedures are the reliance on village communities to allocate relief, the use of anthropometric measures of nutritional status as a criterion of eligibility for feeding, and the provision of support in exchange for work (leading to self-selection). Each of these approaches has many diverse implications aside from its ability to further the non-exclusion and targeting objectives, and it would be wrong to consider them solely from the point of view of selection issues. On the other hand, given the difficulty and importance of successfully implementing satisfactory selection mechanisms, it is natural to pay special attention to these issues in an examination of alternative strategies of entitlement protection.[8]

---

[5] On this question, see particularly Pearson (1986).

[6] Keen (1988: 3–4). This study relates to the region of Darfur. For similar findings elsewhere in Sudan, see Alfred (1986) and Hale (1986). According to a personal communication from David Keen, 'targeting began to improve in late 1985–6 as agency control over food increased'.

[7] De Waal (1988a: 83). The same author estimates famine mortality in Darfur in 1985 as 85,000 excess deaths.

[8] The evaluation reports of relief agencies are replete with indications of the anxieties arising from the dilemmas involved in choosing between alternative selection procedures. For various discussions of these problems, see e.g. Seaman and Holt (1980), Gooch and MacDonald (1981a),

7.2 Alternative Selection Mechanisms

The extent of economic distress experienced by different individuals is, to a great extent, a matter of common knowledge within a given rural community. An apparent solution to the selection problem would take the form of making the selection process rely on local institutions to allocate public support according to individual needs.

Would this method work in practice? The leaders of a village community undoubtedly have a lot of information relevant for appropriate selection. But in addition to the informational issue, there is also the question as to whether the community leaders have strong enough motivation—or incentives—to give adequately preferential treatment to vulnerable groups. Much will undoubtedly depend on the nature and functioning of political institutions at the local level, and in particular on the power that the poor and the deprived have in the rural community.[9] Where the poor are also powerless—as is frequently the case—the reliance on local institutions to allocate relief is problematic, and can end up being at best indiscriminate and at worst blatantly inequitous, as numerous observers have noted in diverse countries.[10]

In Africa, the intermediation of local communities in the distribution of food has been observed in a large number of cases to result simply in uniform household rations or, at best, rations related to household size. For instance, a careful study of food distribution in the Red Sea Province of Sudan in 1985 noted that the local leaders (or 'responsible men') in charge of food distribution did have a very clear and accurate perception of the needs of different families, but that the allocation process made no discriminating use of this informational advantage: 'Every family had to have a share. No responsible man felt able to

Mason and Brown (1983), Tabor (1983), Autier and d'Altilia (1985), Hay et al. (1986), Pearson (1986), Wood et al. (1986), McLean (1987), and Borton and Shoham (1989a) among many others. The distinction between the non-exclusion and targeting objectives is an old one (already prominent in discussions of famine policy in 18th-century China and 19th-century India), and has been recently considered by different authors under various labels such as 'vertical targeting efficiency and horizontal targeting efficiency' (Weisbrod 1969), 'E-mistakes and F-mistakes' (Cornia et al. 1987, Kumar and Stewart 1987), or 'specificity and sensitivity' (Alderman 1988a).

[9] For example, the change in the balance of power in the rural society of West Bengal in favour of the poorer sections of the population, largely as a result of left-wing activist movements, has certainly resulted in a much greater participation of the poor in poverty alleviation programmes. The contrast is particularly sharp with other states in Northern India such as Uttar Pradesh (see Drèze 1988b). The crucial difference that local institutions and the balance of power within a rural community can make to the success of public support measures is also clearly illustrated by the positive role attributed to participative village institutions in the context of recent famine prevention efforts in Tigray and Eritrea (Nelson 1983, English et al. 1984, Firebrace and Holland 1984, CAFOD 1986a, 1986b), and in independent Zimbabwe (see Chapter 8). In Ethiopia, the Peasant Associations are also widely reported to have greatly facilitated the equitable distribution of food and employment at the local level (McKerrow 1979, Holt 1983, Relief and Development Institute 1985, World Food Programme 1986d).

[10] For a few examples among many, see e.g. Bernus (1977a, 1977b), Gooch and MacDonald (1981a), van Appeldoorn (1981), Hartmann and Boyce (1983), Mason and Brown (1983), Watts (1983), Tobert (1985), York (1985), Bryson (1986), Hale (1986), Pearson (1986), and Bratton (1987a).

exclude any family on grounds of wealth. On the contrary, sheikhs, who usually had the largest herds, often got extra food.'[11] These findings are more or less echoed in a number of recent studies of famine prevention in sub-Saharan Africa.[12]

However, in sub-Saharan Africa it is sometimes the case that during a famine all sections of a particular village community experience acute deprivation and suffer from nutritional inadequacy. When intravillage inequalities are particularly less perspicuous than intervillage differences, *and* an effective procedure can be devised to identify the more vulnerable villages or areas, the rule of uniform distribution *within* the village community can be a commendable expedient.[13] While it may not be able to achieve the fine tuning that a full response to the non-extreme inequalities within the village would ideally call for, the non-divisive and participatory involvement of the entire village community in the exercise of public support can be seen to have distinct advantages. The reality and extent of these advantages in different social and cultural environments calls for cautious assessment.

Three ranges of alternative selection mechanisms suggest themselves: (1) using administrative criteria based on observable indicators of deprivation or need, such as anthropometric status, asset ownership, demographic characteristics, or geographical location; (2) intervening impersonally at the level of the market (e.g. by subsidizing food prices or supporting livestock prices), and letting the share of different groups in public support be determined by their market situation; and (3) relying on 'self-acting tests', such as the requirement of work in exchange for relief, in order to discourage privileged groups. We shall refer to these three ranges of options as *administrative selection, market selection* and *self-selection* respectively.

While these conceptual distinctions are helpful, it must be realized that most forms of intervention involve some explicit or implicit combination of these three elements. For instance, administrative selection methods almost invariably imply an element of self-selection as well, since the recipients usually have to present themselves and take some unpleasant or stigmatizing initiative to get

[11] Hale (1986: 36).

[12] See e.g. Ray (1984), Tobert (1985), Alfred (1986), World Food Programme (1986*d*), Keen (1988), Borton and Shoham (1989*a*, 1989*b*). See also Chapter 8. Another very common (and disquieting) observation is that the intermediation of local communites in food distribution tends to discriminate against displaced people, towards whom the administration or leadership of host communities often feel little responsibility (see Kelemen 1985, Relief and Development Institute 1985, Tobert 1985, Pearson 1986, McLean 1987, Keen 1988, Borton and Shoham 1989*b*).

[13] Daniel *et al.* (1984), for instance, argue that 'there are relatively few cases in SSA [sub-Saharan Africa] where inequality (and landlessness) within a low-income area makes it impossible to consider the people of the area as the target group, in the sense that households share similar levels of nutrition and income . . .' (p. 9). The apparent contrast in intrarural inequality between South Asia and sub-Saharan Africa is not surprising: economic inequality in South Asia is to a great extent derived from inequality in land ownership, which is typically less acute in sub-Saharan Africa, given the relative abundance of land. This contrast, while fairly uncontroversial, should not be exaggerated, and a number of authors have emphasized the existence of large inequalities in various African societies—see e.g. Watts (1983) and Hill (1986).

help based on the use of these indicators. Similarly, self-acting tests usually apply only to population groups possessing certain characteristics, such as being able-bodied enough for manual work in the case of the labour test. And most forms of intervention have important repercussions through the market, e.g. by influencing wages or food prices. Market selection mechanisms themselves are also usually of a mixed nature. For instance, the incidence of commodity subsidies depends on the regional focus of the subsidy (possibly involving administrative selection based on specific indicators), as well as on the individual behaviour patterns (e.g. dietary choices) of potential recipients.

Market responses are of pervasive relevance for famine prevention policies. It is always important to take them into account when evaluating alternative forms of intervention.[14] On the other hand, in most situations an exclusive reliance on market selection mechanisms to protect the entitlements of vulnerable groups would be a very doubtful approach. It is not only that market selection tends to be a blunt and inadequately discriminating mechanism for reaching the most vulnerable. In fact, market selection often has the effect of ending up discriminating against, rather than in favour of, the poor.

A good example of the perversely discriminating effects that market selection can have is provided by public policies of livestock price support. There are now several examples of famine relief schemes based on the idea that supporting livestock prices through public purchases would help pastoralists to survive droughts.[15] It is certainly the case that schemes of this kind do enhance the purchasing power of pastoralists *vis-à-vis* other occupation groups. On the other hand, it must be recognized that livestock price support helps pastoralists proportionately to the size of their herds, with large owners gaining much more than smaller ones.[16] Generally, what we have called 'market selection' is an undependable answer to the possibly crucial need of providing preferential support to the most vulnerable groups in famine situations.

7.3 Feeding and Family

When a food crisis has reached an advanced stage and extensive signs of enhanced deprivation or undernourishment have developed, it becomes possible even for outsiders to observe deprivation directly. The allocation of relief on the basis of observed nutritional status is one of the most widely used selection mechanisms, and the attractiveness of this method is easy to understand. Conflicting claims have been made, however, as to the real merits of this approach.

[14] For a careful analysis of market responses in relation to public policy for the prevention of famines and chronic hunger, see Ravallion (1987b).

[15] For examples of such schemes, see e.g. T. Downing et al. (forthcoming).

[16] Of course, it is possible to restrict public livestock purchases to particular sections of the pastoralist population. This would amount to supplementing the 'market selection' mechanism with some form of administrative selection or self-selection.

To start with, two important limitations of selection by nutritional status must be clearly recognized. First, contrary to popular belief the assessment of nutritional status is a skilled and complex task.[17] It is unfortunately often the case that nutritional assessment in famine situations is left—sometimes inevitably—to inexperienced and overworked staff. The risk of poor identification of vulnerable individuals and their nutritional problems as a result of this practice have been graphically brought out in several studies relating to recent African famines.[18] The requirements of competent nutritional assessment should therefore not be underestimated.

Second, there could conceivably be very important *incentive* problems associated with using individual nutritional status as a criterion of selection for support. One of the most common targeting techniques consists of providing support to households (e.g. in the form of take-home food rations) conditionally on the presence, in the recipient household, of at least one undernourished child.[19] It does not take a great deal of reflection to see the potential dangers of such a system in the form of disincentives against child care. Particularly in a famine situation it must be all too tempting for a household to 'ensure' that at least one child remains undernourished in order to retain eligibility for support. The operation of these adverse incentives can, of course, be extremely hard to observe, but there is a certain amount of anecdotal evidence confirming one's worst fears. It is worrying, for instance, to hear of the following response to feeding schemes in Ethiopia during the recent famine:

Undoubtedly, to some mothers, a malnourished child was seen as a 'meal ticket' for her and the family . . . Who would blame a mother who kept a child sufficiently undernourished to remain on the intensive feeding programme?[20]

[17] Some of the problems involved relate to the complexities of nutritional assessment discussed in Chapter 3.

[18] See e.g. W. Taylor (1983), Teuscher (1985), Chambers et al. (1986), Gibb (1986), Pearson (1986), and Soeters (1986). The last author describes how two independent survey teams from Médecins Sans Frontières and the League of Red Cross and Red Crescent Societies assessed the nutritional status of the same group of children on the same day using the same methods, and arrived at sharply different results (e.g. they respectively concluded that 24 per cent and 48 per cent of the children were below 80 per cent of a *common* weight-for-height standard). See also Borton and Shoham (1989a) on some disenchantment among relief agencies regarding the use of anthropometric measures of nutritional status for targeting purposes.

[19] This method is astonishingly widespread—it was, for instance, used in most of the feeding schemes run by OXFAM during the 1985–6 famine in Ethiopia (Helen Young, personal communication; see also Young 1987). Further examples can be found in many guidelines and evaluation studies of food distribution programmes. See, for instance, Gooch and MacDonald (1981a), Morgan (1986), Pearson (1986), OXFAM/UNICEF (1986), Garcia and Pinstrup-Andersen (1987), Brown and Mason (1988), Pinstrup-Andersen and Alderman (1988), Borton and Shoham (1989b) and Neumann et al. (forthcoming).

[20] Nash (1986). Other evaluations of recent supplementary feeding programmes in famine-stricken Ethiopia have also noted the problem of 'deliberate starving of children to obtain programme access' (Borton and Shoham 1989b, Case Study 12, p. 3). Personal communications from several relief agencies confirm that terrible events of this kind are unfortunately not isolated, though understandably enough they are not the object of much publicity.

Incentive problems of this specific kind do not arise when nutritional status is used as a criterion for helping undernourished *individuals*, rather than the households to which they belong. But there is an incentive problem in this case too. If a child is being looked after by a feeding scheme, that is so much less pressure on household resources. Thus, individual feeding still operates partly like an improvement in household entitlements and there remains an incentive for the household to do whatever is necessary to get one or more of its children selected for feeding. The temptation of neglect will, moreover, be no less if parents have genuine concern for the child's well-being. Indeed, the child's own interest may well be to undergo temporary undernourishment so as to become eligible for feeding. The widespread practices of 'discharging' children when their nutritional status improves, or of relating the amount of food provided to the extent of observed undernutrition, can create further disincentives against family care.

These important limitations being noted, it must be asked whether using nutritional status as a basis for selection has compensating advantages. Perhaps the greatest advantage of nutritional criteria is that, when carefully applied, they allow the identification of vulnerable individuals rather than households. An attempt can, thus, be made to help individuals directly, and to influence the distribution of food within households. This is how direct feeding schemes, especially, are thought to operate.

The desirability and importance of influencing intrahousehold distribution in this particular way raises many complex issues. For one thing, as was discussed in Chapters 4 and 5, the empirical evidence on the extent and typical patterns of intrahousehold discrimination during famines is not entirely clear. There is in particular a distinct possibility that, during the early stages of food crises at least, intrahousehold discrimination operates in favour, rather than against, young children (the main targets of feeding schemes). For another, there remains in any case a difficult ethical and practical question as to whether a relief worker is really better placed than a mother or a father to decide who should get food within a family.

But the feasibility of influencing intrahousehold allocation in the desired direction should also not be taken for granted. Indeed, it is not obvious why a household should treat the feeding of one of its members very differently from an improvement in household entitlements, if that member's share of the family food can be adjusted accordingly. There is considerable evidence from supplementary feeding programmes operating in ordinary times that this so-called 'leakage' problem is very real, although usually a certain degree of influence on intrahousehold allocation is in fact retained.[21] When food is badly short at the household level, as in a famine situation, the temptation to

[21] See particularly Beaton and Ghasseimi (1982), who discuss the leakage problem at length and conclude, after reviewing a large number of supplementary feeding schemes: 'Overall, the net increase in intake by the target recipient was 45 to 70% of the food collected' (p. 909). The more recent reviews of Kennedy and Knudsen (1985), Godfrey (1986a, 1986b) and Norgan (1988) arrive at broadly similar conclusions.

reduce the share of household food going to members who benefit from supplementary feeding could be particularly strong.

Many evaluations of feeding programmes have indeed insisted on the ineffectiveness of providing selective 'supplementary' feeding when 'basic rations' are themselves badly inadequate at the household level.[22] In the worst cases, supplementary feeding of this kind has been found to be not only ineffective but even counter-productive. This can happen, for instance, if the individual recipients of cooked food are no longer fed at home on the erroneous assumption that they have already been adequately fed.[23] While there is no reason to believe that disasters of this kind are a pervasive feature of feeding programmes, the general dangers of households overestimating the amount of nourishment received by the beneficiaries of feeding cannot be overlooked.

These problems can be avoided if a child is fed more than he or she would receive in the household in the absence of a feeding scheme. In this case, the child may well stop being fed at home, but there can be no 'leakage' beyond that, and in the end the child *is* better nourished. However, when the responsibility for the nutritional well-being of a child is entirely 'taken over' by a relief agency in this way, some of the incentive problems discussed earlier (e.g. the temptation of keeping a child famished for it to qualify for assistance) survive in a strong form. Moreover, it is well known that the resources required (in terms of personnel, logistics and administration) to spoon-feed every child individually and on a continuous basis make this type of intervention unsuitable for large-scale relief operations.

It seems, then, that providing direct support to vulnerable individuals when household entitlements are inadequate is a rather flawed procedure in many circumstances. The priority has to be to ensure adequate 'basic rations' to households, and direct feeding of individuals is best regarded as a possible supplementary measure.[24] Further, as we have stressed, it would generally be

---

[22] See e.g. Capone (1980), Autier and d'Altilia (1985), Lowgren (1985), Dick (1986), Godfrey (1986a, 1986b), Chambers et al. (1986), League of Red Cross and Red Crescent Societies (1986) and Borton and Shoham (1989a).

[23] In this event, the beneficiaries of selective feeding sometimes literally *lose* weight. For examples of such cases, and of other hazards associated with poorly designed or executed feeding schemes in famine situations, see Hall (1973), Barnabas et al. (1982), Kielman et al. (1982), Teuscher (1985), Wallstam (1985), Gibb (1986), Hay et al. (1986), Morris-Peel (1986) and Pearson (1986).

[24] This general conclusion is, in fact, in line with a number of recent evaluations of supplementary feeding programmes in famine situations. See e.g. Lowgren (1985), Dick (1986), Gibb (1986), Godfrey (1986a, 1986b), League of Red Cross and Red Crescent Societies (1986), Appleton (1987) and Borton and Shoham (1989a). There are, of course, important exceptions to the rule that household entitlements should be regarded as the priority. One of them arises when food *quality* strongly matters, as can be the case when undernutrition has reached an advanced stage. When an important objective of feeding is to influence the composition of the diet of vulnerable individuals (e.g. to give them a particular vitamin), the simplest procedure is to provide direct supplementation to these individuals (i.e. to give them the vitamins). Selective feeding can therefore be of special value when there is a concern for *both* quality and intrahousehold distribution. 'Therapeutic' feeding, addressed to severely malnourished children, is an example. The appropriateness of this type of intervention has to be assessed in the light of the qualifications discussed earlier.

very dangerous to use the nutritional status of children as a criterion of eligibility for support at the household level. A different selection procedure is needed.

The fact that nutritional status does not appear to perform very promisingly as a basic selection criterion does not mean that feeding schemes themselves have no role to play in famine prevention, since they can (1) operate on the basis of different selection criteria such as age, sex, or location; (2) complement rather than replace a strategy of household entitlement support. A successful use of individual feeding, however, would seem to depend on the existence of a reliable system of entitlement protection aimed at vulnerable households.

7.4 Employment and Entitlement

The provision of employment as a device for generating compensating income has been an important part of the entitlement protection systems of a number of countries in the past. One of the great advantages of this strategy is to make it possible to carry out large transfers to vulnerable households, while at the same time imparting a strong redistributive bias to the entitlement protection process. The employment mechanism involves a comparatively exacting selection procedure, but once the recipients are selected, they obtain what are, relatively speaking, fairly substantial payments in food or in cash. There is rarely a possibility of making transfers of a similar magnitude per head on a non-selective basis, since the total resources needed would be very much larger.

The strategy of employment provision has another important advantage which deserves special mention. Employment provision can go with either payments in kind or wages in cash. When the latter mode of payment is used, the employment approach to the protection of entitlements becomes a particular way of providing cash support. The advantages of cash support, as was discussed in the previous chapter, can be quite substantial in many contexts. Those advantages hold inter alia for cash-based employment programmes. In fact, the only effective and politically acceptable method of providing large-scale cash support is often that of employment provision with cash wages.

In addition to these two basic advantages, the strategy of employment provision has a number of further features (most of these will apply irrespective of whether the wages are paid in cash or in kind), the merits of which should be clear from the discussion in the two preceding chapters. These include: (1) being compatible with intervention at an early stage of a subsistence crisis (when affected people are looking hard for alternative sources of income but do not yet suffer from severe nutritional deprivation); (2) obviating the necessity of movements of entire families to feeding camps; (3) at the same time, obviating the necessity of taking food to every village (as in a system of decentralized distribution), to the extent that the work-seeking adult population is mobile; (4) preserving family ties, particularly when employment can be offered near homes (without families having to be huddled together with thousands of others into relief camps); (5) inducing positive market responses in the form of an upward pressure on local wages; (6) allowing reliance on 'self-selection'.

The last in particular is important in so far as it reduces the dependence on administrative selection. Apart from their high organizational burden, most forms of administrative selection involve greater risks of errors in coverage than a system where the initiative of joining the relief system rests with the affected people themselves.[25]

Employment provision has been extensively used as a tool of entitlement protection in India for many centuries (see Chapter 8). Even in the recent drought of 1987, which could have led to a very substantial famine given the disruption of the livelihood of hundreds of millions of people, employment provision in the form of large-scale public works programmes played a major part in averting that threat. In suggesting a greater use of this approach in Africa, we have to encounter the possible criticism (one which has been aired in response to some earlier presentations) that this is based on a hasty imitation of the 'Indian model'. This would be an undeserved accusation.

First, India is by no means the only country to have made extensive and effective use of employment provision for the prevention of famines.[26] In Africa itself, employment provision has already been a positive part of famine prevention efforts in a number of countries, including especially Botswana and Cape Verde.[27]

Second, as we have seen in Chapter 5, searching for employment has become one of the cornerstones of informal security systems in many African countries. Public provision of employment would seem to be a natural way of helping this effort. The common prescription, discussed at some length in section 5.3, that entitlement protection measures should seek to strengthen rather than undermine traditional security systems, would seem to point to employment provision as a commendable form of intervention.

Third, it is arguable that in some important respects the strategy of employment provision would in fact be *easier* to adopt in many parts of Africa than it has proved to be in India. Several of the problems which have limited the strategy of employment provision in India in the recent past would indeed

---

[25] For evidence of the high involvement of vulnerable groups in public works programmes, see e.g. Desai et al. (1979), Dandekar (1983), Chowdhury (1983), Osmani and Chowdhury (1983), and Drèze (1988a).

[26] Public works were, for instance, a major plank of famine prevention in China during the 1920s. On this see Edwards (1932), Nathan (1965), Li (1987), and various contributions to the *Chinese Recorder*, vol. 23 (1932).

[27] On these two countries, see Chapter 8. Positive experiences with the use of public works for famine prevention in Africa in recent years have also been reported in countries as diverse as Ethiopia (Holt 1983, Admassie and Gebre 1985, Grannell 1986, World Food Programme 1986d), Burkina Faso (Kelly 1987), Lesotho (Bryson 1986), Chad (Autier and d'Altilia 1985), and Uganda (Dodge and Alnwick 1986). On the contemporary African experience with public works in non-famine situations, see Thomas (1986).

seem to apply with less force in sub-Saharan Africa. For instance, public works programmes in India have been restrained by the scarcity of publicly owned land, and the attendant problems of property rights involved in finding suitable worksites. In this important respect, many African countries, with their relative abundance of land, would appear to be at considerable advantage compared to India in making good use of the employment strategy.

This being said, a number of difficulties associated with the employment strategy must also be considered.[28] Most of these difficulties are in no way specific to Africa, but their relevance for Africa deserves special attention.

One of the shortcomings of the employment approach is that it has the contrary feature of *increasing* calorie requirements precisely at a time when thère is a strong case for reducing activity levels. This can no doubt be a serious problem, and it must be remembered in particular that the strategy of employment provision has been found quite impractical, indeed sometimes damaging, in situations of advanced distress when people are too enfeebled to provide the required effort. The strategy of employment provision must be seen, intrinsically, as a strategy of *early* intervention. It is primarily preventive rather than curative as an anti-famine strategy.

The criticism of enhanced calorie requirements, however, overlooks the crucial fact that, while raising the calorie requirements of the labourers, public works often more than commensurately increase their entitlements by preventing relatively privileged groups from taking advantage of the public support system. In fact, it can be shown that the resources needed to cover the 'requirements' of vulnerable groups would typically be much smaller when relief is provided in the form of employment (even after taking note of the additional calorie requirements of work) rather than in the form of indiscriminate distribution.

The question of increased calorie requirements is closely related to another objection that has often been raised against the provision of employment in situations of famine vulnerability, and which is concerned with the excessively 'punitive' nature of this approach. The fact that a person has to *work* to receive support may be thought to be a denial of what is owed to him or her by the society. However, the vulnerable population can gain greatly from the discrimination that can be achieved through the insistence on work requirement which would prevent the available resources from being squandered on the privileged. Also, it must be remembered that potential famine victims tend to look positively for employment in order to deal with their deprivation, and providing that employment can scarcely be described as being 'punitive'. In fact, famine victims often prefer the status of being employed rather than being mere receivers of charity. Perhaps most importantly, while public works are often accused of creating 'dependency' and doing little to improve the situation

---

[28] For a critique of employment provision as a strategy of famine prevention, see Mayer (1975). Arguments in different directions are also discussed in Maxwell (1978a), Shukla (1979), Jackson and Eade (1982), Klein (1984), Reynolds (1984), Clay (1986) and Hay (1986), among others.

and prospects of the poor in the rural economy and society, in some instances they have been found, on the contrary, to be instrumental in enhancing the economic and social position of vulnerable groups (e.g. by boosting local wages, strengthening the bargaining power of the poor, and providing them with an opportunity to organize around common interests).[29]

Another possible criticism of the strategy of employment provision is that it can only succeed in protecting entitlements at the *household* level, and obviously provides very little scope for directly redressing intrahousehold inequalities where these are large. It is quite possible that in some situations this shortcoming would be an important one, and might militate against this approach (and in favour of a strategy of individual support, e.g. direct feeding). As was discussed earlier, however, in the case of sub-Saharan Africa there is little evidence of sharp intrafamily discrimination against the most vulnerable family members (e.g. young children) in the early stages of food crises.

As far as discrimination against adult women is concerned, not only is there little evidence of systematic anti-female bias in nutrition and survival in sub-Saharan Africa, the strategy of employment provision could be seen as being particularly beneficial to women in so far as they often form a large part of the labour force on public works programmes.[30] Even when this is not the case as things stand, female participation can be promoted as a policy decision when women are ready to work for a wage. Indeed in some cases the promotion of female employment has been an important and effective part of entitlement protection policies.[31] The issue of intrafamily inequality always deserves careful attention, but there is no general presumption that this would necessarily undermine the case for a strategy of employment provision.

[29] See Drèze (1988b) for further discussion of this point with reference to India; also Mencher (1988). The positive contribution of employment provision to the enfranchisement of the rural poor is, for instance, quite clear from the experience of the Employment Guarantee Scheme (EGS) in Maharashtra. As a pamphlet issued by a social action group in rural Maharashtra explains, 'the Employment Guarantee Scheme is an important instrument for those who have been involved in organizing the poor, oppressed, and exploited classes in rural areas over the years' (Deshpande 1984: 5; our translation). On this and other aspects of the Employment Guarantee Scheme, see also Government of India (1980), Desphande (1982, 1984), Dandekar (1983), D'Silva (1983), Herring and Edwards (1983), Lieberman (1984, 1985), Ezekiel (1986), and Acharya and Panwalkar (1988a, 1988b).

[30] In most countries, female participation rates tend to be quite high in public works. The proportion of women among labourers employed on public works has been estimated at 80% in Botswana (Tabor 1983), about 50% in Cape Verde (Spyckerelle 1987), 52% in Chile (Cheyre and Ogrodnick 1982), between 27 and 65% in Ethiopia (Admassie and Gebre 1985), 64% in Jamaica (Girling and Keith 1977), 95% in Lesotho (Reynolds 1984), and more than half in Maharashtra (Dandekar 1983). Involvement in public works not only increases women's earning power, it also enhances their 'bargaining position' within the household (see Chapter 4). As a poor woman in drought-stricken Mauritania put it, 'if a woman earns her salary, the man can no longer command the woman' (cited in Abeille 1979). On the general importance of the 'breakdown position' of women in famine situations, see Agarwal (1988).

[31] This has been the case in Bangladesh (Marty Chen, personal communication). On the far-reaching impact which the expansion of female employment seems to have had on the status of women in Bangladesh in recent years, see Adnan (1988).

Another objection that has been raised is based on questioning the productive value of public works programmes. This can scarcely be a serious route of attack on the strategy of employment provision, if the alternatives take the form of giving something away for nothing (as in feeding or food distribution schemes). Considerations of productivity are, in any case, clearly of secondary importance in the short run in a situation of famine vulnerability.[32]

A more solid objection related to productivity considerations is that public works are liable to divert labour from other activities, including the growing of food. Again, this is a consideration which may well be important in particular cases, but as a general argument against the strategy of employment provision it is hardly persuasive. In many cases, vulnerable groups will have very little access to alternative employment, and in fact alternative opportunities may even be *enhanced* by greater security. When the diversion of labour from productive activities is important, the positive influences of this displacement (e.g. an upward pressure on local wages) must be evaluated along with the negative ones (e.g. a loss of agricultural output).

Finally, it is often asserted that the administrative and logistic requirements of organizing public works programmes must be much more demanding than those of direct distribution or feeding schemes. In some ways, there may be an element of truth in this assertion, especially if public works programmes suddenly have to be improvised from nowhere by bureaucrats unused to such a system. A sound strategy of entitlement protection through employment provision cannot dispense with the need for careful contingency planning —any more than other reliable systems of famine prevention.[33]

There is very little evidence, however, that with appropriate contingency planning, the administrative and logistic requirements of large-scale employment provision are more demanding than those of direct food distribution. A rigorous comparison would in fact not be easy to make, and in particular it must be remembered that a proper comparison should take into account not only the numbers of people helped with a given amount of resources under each alternative, but also the extent of relief provided per recipient, as well as the composition of the protected population. This qualification is important since, as we have seen, employment provision typically provides a unique

---

[32] It is worth noting, however, that little empirical evidence supports the view that public works programmes are *generally* 'unproductive'. Some evaluations have come to quite different conclusions. See e.g. Frances Stewart's review of evaluation studies (Stewart 1987), and also Thomas *et al.* (1976), Grannell (1986), Hay *et al.* (1986), van Binsbergen (1986), World Food Programme (1986*d*), and Gaude *et al.* (1987).

[33] It should be mentioned that the administrative and logistic burden involved in organizing public works on a large scale can depend significantly on the importance that is attached to providing work at short distances from the homes of affected people. Given that labour migration is a common—and early—household response to the threat of famine in many countries of sub-Saharan Africa (see section 5.4), even somewhat centralized public works schemes would often provide very substantial protection to vulnerable populations in times of crisis. This option is important to bear in mind when organizational capabilities are severely limited.

opportunity for implementing large, redistributive transfers to the most affected groups.

Furthermore, it must be noted that the strategy of employment provision with *cash* wages provides an excellent—indeed perhaps unique—opportunity to take advantage of the administrative economies of using the market mechanism in the movement and distribution of food. That the advantages can be quite considerable was discussed in the last chapter. In a situation where the bureaucratic structure of governmental operations is already overstrained, the merits of sharing the logistic tasks with private trade cannot be neglected. When doubts are raised about the administrative capability of particular governments to protect the entitlements of potential famine victims through employment schemes, it is often overlooked that a particular form of the employment strategy (viz. that of cash-for-work) permits a reduction in the tasks to be performed by the government. In comparison with what the government has to do if the entire charge of taking the food from one place to another and distributing it to the recipients were to fall on its slender shoulders, the task of the government with cash-for-work programmes is much more limited.

7.5 A Concluding Remark

Effective famine prevention calls for much more than simply rushing food to the victims when they have started dying of starvation. It involves a network of decisions relating to diverse policy areas such as the generation of incomes, the delivery of health care, the stabilization of food prices, the provision of drinking water, and the rehabilitation of the rural economy. The general problem of 'entitlement protection' has many different facets.

Further, as should be clear from the preceding chapters, the occupational characteristics of the affected population, the pattern of intrafamily divisions, the structure of markets, the nature of cooperative village institutions, the mobility of vulnerable groups, are only some examples of the numerous considerations that are relevant to the choice of a strategy of entitlement protection when a famine threatens. There are significant heterogeneities within Africa in all these respects, and any serious programme of public intervention to prevent famines must come to grips with these diversities.

We have chosen to discuss the pros and cons of entitlement protection through employment provision in some detail because of the potential importance of much greater use of this method in preventing famines in the future, especially in Africa. We have seen that this strategy has some notable advantages, which can in many circumstances be consolidated by combining the provision of employment with the payment of cash wages. The use of this technique in sub-Saharan Africa has been, so far, rather limited, but there are good economic and social grounds for going much further in this direction.

The employment strategy can be especially effective if it is adopted at an early stage of a famine threat, and its success will be that much easier if it is incorporated in a general system of relief that is in a state of preparedness to be invoked without undue delay. Sometimes, the value of having such a system seems to be overlooked. An illustration comes from the experience of Ethiopia during the famine of 1984.

Until that year, the government of Ethiopia had been relatively successful in using food aid to run extensive public works programmes, and these played an important part in averting large-scale famine in 1982 and 1983.[34] However, when fears of a big famine developed in 1984, the famine relief agencies (including international organizations) decided that the priority was no longer 'development' but 'relief', and that food aid should be diverted from public works to emergency programmes of food distribution and feeding. As a result, hundreds of thousands of people either lost employment or, even worse, continued working while arrears in wage payments were mounting. The improvisation of feeding programmes, on the other hand, rapidly ran into considerable logistic difficulties.[35] One has to wonder whether the crisis could not have been much more effectively dealt with by expanding existing employment programmes on a larger scale rather than winding up one system of entitlement protection to be replaced by a hastily built—and by no means flawless—alternative device.

In highlighting the advantages of employment provision, we are not suggesting that exclusive reliance could in any way be placed on this one method of entitlement protection. Provision must clearly be made for supporting those who are unable to work themselves and who do not have able-bodied relatives on whom they can rely for support. The proportion of such people may or may not be large (depending *inter alia* on the demographic characteristics of affected groups and the nature of family ties), but a comprehensive system of entitlement protection must pay adequate attention to their needs. This is especially

[34] See e.g. Holt (1983) and Relief and Development Institute (1985). Food-for-work programmes in Ethiopia are also discussed in Admassie and Gebre (1985), Grannell (1986), World Food Programme (1986*d*), and Government of Ethiopia (1987). During the two years preceding mid-1984, more than 130,000 tonnes of wheat were distributed through WFP-assisted employment programmes, mainly in the most vulnerable areas (World Food Programme 1986*d*, Annex II). This corresponds to something like 200 million person-days of nourishment.

[35] These events are briefly described and discussed in Admassie and Gebre (1985), Gill (1986), Grannell (1986), Jansson *et al.* (1987), Goyder and Goyder (1988), and particularly World Food Programme (1986*d*). We are grateful to Hugh Goyder (Oxfam), John Shaw (World Food Programme), and Thomas Grannell (World Food Programme) for very helpful personal communications on this issue. The disruption of supplies to Food-For-Work programmes in Ethiopia in 1984 seems to have been the combined result of (1) deliberate restraint in shipments as a result of an overestimation of the stocks available in Ethiopia at the end of 1983; (2) unsettled quarrels between international agencies and the Government of Ethiopia concerning the modalities of food aid; and (3) massive diversion of supplies for 'emergency' programmes (see World Food Programme 1986*d*, and Grannell 1986). Ironically, as a result of the disruption of public works programmes many wage earners lost their employment and had to become recipients of 'emergency assistance' (World Food Programme 1986*b*, 1986*d*).

Table 7.1 'Gratuitous relief' in three villages of Bhiloda Taluka (Gujarat), 1987

Name	Sex	Age	Marital status	Relatives living in the same household	Number of grown-up sons	Ability to work	Land owned	Other productive assets	Remarks
Chanchiben	F	old	Widow	None	None	n/a	None	None	
Valiben	F	old	Widow	None	None	No	None	None	
Manabhai	M	old	Widower	Daughter	None	No	None	None	Daughter on relief works
Koshiben	F	≈50	Widow	None	None	No	None	None	Begging
Danabhai	M	n/a	Widower	Young son	One	n/a	None	None	Blind
Dhuliben	F	≈50	Widow	None	None	No	None	None	
Paliben	F	old	Widow	None	None	No	None	None	
Ratanben	F	old	Widow	None	None	No	None	None	
Phoolaben	F	old	Widow	None	None	n/a	None	None	Stopped attending relief works
Ramabhai	M	≈50	Married	Wife	None	No	None	n/a	Some self-employment (craft)
Jamnaben	F	≈50	Married	Husband	None	No	None	n/a	Wife of Ramabhai (above)
Uniashankar	M	≈50	Unmarried	None	None	No	None	n/a	Mental illness
Shankarbhai	M	≈50	Married	Wife	None	No	None	None	Husband of Buriben (below)
Buriben	F	≈50	Married	Husband	None	No	None	None	Wife of Shankarbhai (above)
Manjiben	F	≈70	Widow	None	None	No	None	None	
Natiben	F	n/a	Widow	Santokben	None	n/a	None	None	
Santokben	F	n/a	Widow	Natiben	None	n/a	None	None	
Hiraben	F	old	Widow	None	None	No	None	None	Begging
Divaben	F	≈60	Widow	None	None	n/a	None	n/a	Husband of Urmilaben (below)
Vekandas	M	old	Married	Wife	None	No	None	n/a	Wife of Vekandas (above)
Urmilaben	F	old	Married	Husband	None	No	None	n/a	
Galbabhai	M	≈70	Widower	None	None	No	None	None	
Kalabhai	M	≈50	Unmarried	None	None	No	None	n/a	Disabled
Manguben	F	≈60	Widow	None	None	No	None	None	
Shantaben	F	≈60	Widow	None	None	No	None	None	
Hansaba	F	≈30	Widow	Father and brothers	n/a	Yes	n/a	n/a	Father seems quite affluent

Source: Drèze (1988*b*), Table 21.
n/a = not available

important in view of the extremely high vulnerability of the elderly in famine situations which we noted earlier.

However, the inability to work is a relatively easily *observable* condition, and quite often this criterion can form a realistic basis for unconditional relief using what was called earlier 'administrative selection'.[36] To illustrate this point, Table 7.1 presents the characteristics of all the households who benefited from 'gratuitous relief' in three villages of Gujarat (India) during the 1987 drought.

It is remarkable that only one case out of the twenty-six (the last one in the table) can possibly be described as fraudulent in any sense. All the other recipients clearly belong to the intended target group of assetless households without able-bodied members. This success in identifying the most vulnerable is all the more impressive given that, in the same area, large-scale fraud can be observed in a number of other schemes of 'poverty alleviation' based on administrative selection with less easily observable criteria of eligibility such as 'having a low income'.[37]

Entitlement protection will almost always call for mixed systems, involving the use of different instruments to provide direct or indirect support to all vulnerable groups. The provision of employment—perhaps with cash wages —combined with unconditional relief for the 'unemployable' is likely to be one of the more effective options in many circumstances.

[36] This is especially the case when the able-bodied are already covered by employment provision. The able-bodied are not tempted to compete with the 'unemployable' in seeking unconditional relief, since the rewards from employment tend to be substantially higher (for obvious reasons).

[37] See Drèze (1988b) for details. This illustration of the feasibility of effecting direct transfers to the unemployable should not be taken to imply that the Indian system provides adequate support to households without fit adult members. In the area where the data presented in Table 7.1 were collected, only about half of all villages were actually covered by unconditional relief.

8

Experiences and Lessons

8.1 The Indian Experience

How has India avoided major famines since independence in 1947? It is tempting to attribute her success in this area to a steady improvement in food production. A close look at the facts, however, quickly reveals the inadequacy of this explanation. Indeed, the period during which the frequency of famines started to decline in India (the first half of this century) was actually one of steadily *declining* food production per head. Since independence, total food output has grown at a substantial rate, but per-head food production levels have not increased dramatically. They seem to remain, in fact, lower than late nineteenth-century levels, and also lower than per-capita food output levels in many countries affected by famines today. Moreover, the increase in per-capita production has resulted partly in the reduction of imports (and also to some extent the accumulation of large stocks), so that the net aggregate *consumption* of food per head has remained remarkably constant for the last forty years. Finally, almost every year large and heavily populated parts of India suffer from devastating droughts or floods which, through the disruption of rural livelihoods, remain quite capable of causing large-scale starvation.[1]

Nor is it possible to attribute India's success in preventing famines to a significant improvement in the general prosperity of the rural population. The removal of poverty in rural India since independence has, in fact, been shamefully slow.[2]

The prevention of famines in India cannot be understood without reference to the extensive entitlement protection efforts that have come into play on numerous occasions to sustain the rural population through a crisis. At the risk of oversimplification, it may be said that entitlement protection in India relies on the operation of two complementary forces, viz. (1) an administrative system that is intelligently aimed at recreating lost entitlements (caused by droughts, floods, economic slumps, or whatever), and (2) a political system that acts as the prime mover in getting the administrative system to work as and when required. We shall concentrate first on the administrative aspects, but we

---

[1] For an examination of the evidence supporting this assessment of post-independence trends in India, see Drèze (1988a).

[2] This question is further discussed in Chapter 11. On recent trends in the incidence of poverty in rural India, see e.g. Dandekar and Rath (1971), Bhatty (1974), Minhas (1974), Srinivasan and Bardhan (1974, 1988), Ahluwalia (1978), Dutta (1978), Gaiha and Kazmi (1981), Sundaram and Tendulkar (1981), Bardhan (1984), Gaiha (1987, 1988), Minhas et al. (1987), Sagar (1988), Sanyal (1988), and Subbarao (1989).

shall argue later that the administrative structure can be non-operational and ineffective in the absence of a political triggering mechanism.

The administrative aspects of the system can be traced to ideas championed —and to a limited extent used—in Indian history.[3] Kautilya, in the fourth century BC, spoke of employment creation and redistribution to the poor as parts of a sound administrative system to defeat famines. Various Indian rulers (such as Mohammad bin Tughlak in the fourteenth century) made extensive use of work projects and income creation for rebuilding lost entitlements.

As far as systematic exploration and exposition are concerned, the administrative analysis goes back, in many respects, to the detailed recommendations of the Famine Commission of 1880. The policy of governmental inaction that dominated British imperial administration in the early and middle nineteenth century gradually gave way to selective intervention concentrating mainly on the regeneration of cash incomes.

Among the more important of these recommendations of the Famine Commission of 1880 were (1) the framing of region-specific 'Famine Codes' embodying 'authoritative guidelines' to the local administration on the measures needed to anticipate and deal with the threat of famine, and (2) a strategy of entitlement protection based on the combination of guaranteed employment at a subsistence wage and unconditional relief (so-called 'gratuitous relief') for the unemployable. The reasoning behind this strategy is explained with great clarity in the Famine Commission Report, which is worth quoting at some length:

. . . we have to consider the manner in which the proper recipients of the public charity can be most effectually ascertained. The problem to be solved is how to avoid the risk of indiscriminate and demoralising profusion on the one hand, and of insufficient and niggardly assistance on the other—how to relieve all who really need relief, and to waste as little public money as possible in the process . . . where limited numbers have to be dealt with, and there is a numerous and efficient staff of officials, it may be possible to ascertain by personal inquiry the circumstances of every applicant for relief sufficiently for the purpose of admitting or rejecting his claim. But in an Indian famine the Government has to deal not with limited numbers, but with millions of people, and the official machinery at its command, however strengthened for the occasion, will inevitably be inadequate to the task of accurately testing the individual necessities of so great a multitude. Nor again is it possible to entrust the administration of public charity to a subordinate agency without providing sufficient checks against dishonesty and neglect on the part of its members. Some safeguards then are essential in the interests of the destitute people no less than of the public treasury, and they are best found in laying down certain broad self-acting tests by which necessity may be proved, and which may, irrespective of any other rule of selection, entitle to relief the person who submits to them . . . The chief of these tests, and the only one which in our opinion it is ordinarily

---

[3] On the history of famines and famine prevention in India, see Dutt (1900, 1901), Loveday (1914), Bhatia (1967), Srivastava (1968), Ambirajan (1978), Jaiswal (1978), McAlpin (1983a, 1983b), Brennan (1984), Klein (1984), and Drèze (1988a), among others.

desirable to enforce, is the demand of labour commensurate in each case with the labourer's powers, in return for a wage sufficient for the purposes of maintenance but not more. This system is applicable of course only to those from whom labour can reasonably be required . . . The great bulk of the applicants for relief being thus provided for, we believe that it will be possible for an efficient staff of officers to control with success the grant of relief, on the basis of personal inquiry and knowledge of the individual circumstances of each applicant, among the comparatively small numbers of destitute persons to whom the test of labour cannot be applied.[4]

Employment in public works was typically remunerated with cash wages. The expectation was that the demands generated by these wage payments would be met by the operation of private trade.

These broad principles are still relevant to the conception of India's entitlement protection system today. In particular the continued power of the strategy of employment generation supplemented by 'gratuitous relief' for the unemployable has been apparent in a number of experiences of successful famine prevention since independence.[5] At the same time, it would be a mistake to regard this system as a mere legacy of the British Administration. In fact, important advances have been made in famine prevention strategies since independence, even if we confine our attention to the administrative part of the story. One of the most important post-independence changes relates to the public distribution system.

The British Indian administration considered governmental involvement in food trade or distribution as sacrilegious. This position was grounded on a particular understanding of the teachings of classical economists (especially Adam Smith, John Stuart Mill, and Thomas Malthus), which were sometimes referred to as the 'Infallible Laws of the Great Masters of Economic Science'.[6] Suspicion of government interference with private trade extended also to any kind of public *participation* in food distribution.

While the government of independent India has, by and large, refrained from directly interfering with the activities of private traders, its own involvement in food trade and distribution has been extensive and important. In order

---

[4] Government of India (1880 36). In practice the British Administration did not, in fact, resist the temptation of providing 'niggardly assistance'. For instance, the failure of the relief system to prevent dramatic increases in mortality during the two famines which occurred in India at the very end of the 19th century has been partly attributed by several authors to the inadequate nature of relief measures (Bhatia 1967; Klein 1984; Guz 1987; Drèze 1988a). The stinginess of public provisions declined markedly after independence, though one may question how far the government of independent India has really departed from the earlier colonial view that 'while the duty of Government is to save life, it is not bound to maintain the labouring community at its normal level of comfort' (circular of the Government of India No. 44F, 9th June 1883), however low that 'level of comfort' is in the first place.

[5] See Singh (1975), Subramaniam (1975), Desai *et al.* (1979), McAlpin (1987), Drèze (1988a), and Chen (1989) for some case studies. It must be emphasized that the nature and effectiveness of the famine prevention system vary considerably between different regions of India. Some of these interregional contrasts are studied in Rangasami (1974) and Drèze (1988a).

[6] Etheridge (1868: 3). On the influence exercised by the teachings of classical economists on many prominent administrators in British India, see Ambirajan (1971, 1978) and Rashid (1980).

to assess correctly the contribution of India's public distribution system to famine prevention, we need to distinguish between its functions of *price stabilization* and *income generation*.

The stability of food prices in India today is quite remarkable (especially in comparison with the pre-independence period). For instance, during the most recent drought (that of 1987–8), which led to a considerable decline in food production, foodgrain prices increased by less than 10 per cent.[7] This was largely due to large-scale sales of food through the public distribution system, which held very large stocks at the beginning of the drought.[8] Clearly, the contribution of price stabilization measures to the protection of entitlements during crises in India today is a major one.

On the other hand, the income generation aspect of the public distribution of food has often been exaggerated. In per-capita terms, the subsidies involved in food sales to the rural population in so-called 'fair price shops' are very small indeed, even at times of drought.[9] In fact, in most states of India subsidized sales of food have a very limited coverage in rural areas. The really important vehicle of income generation in India during crises is that of large-scale public works, most frequently for cash wages. The irreplaceable role played by public works in sustaining the purchasing power of the rural poor is illustrated by the case-study of the Maharashtra drought of 1970–3 in the next section.

The distinction between the price stabilization role and the income generation role of the public distribution system has some bearing on the relevance of the Indian experience for other countries. The possible relevance of this experience for African countries, in particular, has often been dismissed on the grounds that (1) subsidized food sales to the rural population are the cornerstone of entitlement protection in India, and (2) most African countries lack a comparable infrastructure. This assessment is quite misleading. The generation of income through public works is not dependent on subsidized food sales. Adding to the incomes of the victims helps to prevent destitution, even without distributing cheap food. Furthermore, the price stabilization objective of the public distribution system can be pursued with substantial effect through *wholesale* food operations, and need not be dependent on the public network of 'fair price shops'.

---

[7] On this see Kumar (1988). According to the author, the prices of wheat, rice and 'all cereals' increased respectively by 7.3 per cent, 7.4 per cent and 7 per cent between 1986–7 and 1987–8 (p. 26). The decline in per-capita production of foodgrains during the 1987–8 agricultural year was of the order of 13 per cent compared to the 1984–6 average (calculated from Government of India 1989, Table 1.16). A little more than one century earlier, the Famine Commission of 1880 had boldly pronounced that 'in time of very great scarcity, prices of food grain rise to three times their ordinary amount, (Government of India 1880: 27).

[8] Public food stocks amounted to 23.6 million tonnes in January 1987, and declined to 10 million tonnes during the drought period (Kumar 1988: 13).

[9] Also, in spite of the considerable expertise which India has acquired in the field of food logistics and distribution, the public distribution system routinely falls way below target in its supply of food to the rural population during droughts. See e.g. Bhatia (1988), Drèze (1988a), and Harriss (1988b).

While developments in the administrative aspects of entitlement protection policies since independence have been important, the really crucial changes have taken place in the domain of politics. The *existence* of the Famine Codes did not, after all, ensure their *application*, let alone their early and energetic application. The Famine Codes did include very specific instructions on how to recognize and 'declare' a famine, and the duty they imposed on the administrative structure made it harder to ignore a threatening crisis. However, this 'early warning system' existed *within* the Famine Codes, and could not guarantee their use in practice. Indeed, the problem of triggering remained an important one, since the Famine Codes did not impose any legal obligation to 'declare' a famine. During the Bengal famine of 1943, for instance, the Famine Codes were never invoked and were deliberately ignored, and this fact may well have been responsible for a large part of the extraordinary excess mortality associated with that famine.[10]

After independence, the political incentives to recognize emergencies, and to take action against the threat of famine, had to assume a new form. The vigour of political opposition has now made it impossible for the government to remain passive without major political risks, and the fear of losing elections reinforces the general sensitivity to political embarrassment in the state assembly and in the central parliament. In the process of making the facts known and forcing the hands of the respective state and central governments, the press too plays a leading role. The affected populations themselves have a much greater ability than in the past to make their demands felt and to galvanize the authorities in .o action (especially in view of the importance of winning the rural vote). This is one of the positive aspects of Indian democracy. We shall return to this question for fuller assessment in Chapter 11, when we reconsider the respective achievements of India and China in recent decades in combating hunger and famines.[11]

8.2   A Case-Study: The Maharashtra Drought of 1970–1973[12]

The state of Maharashtra in Western India, which in the early 1970s had a population of a little over 50 million, is one of the more 'developed' among Indian states by a number of conventional *aggregate* indicators (including

---

[10] See Sen (1981a), Greenough (1982) and Brennan (1988) for further discussion of the non-declaration of famine in that event.

[11] For further discussion of the role of public pressure in famine prevention in India, see also Sen (1982b, 1982c, 1983a), Ram (1986) and Drèze (1988a).

[12] This section is largely based on Drèze (1988a). The interested reader is referred to that paper for further discussion, as well as for a more detailed examination of the empirical evidence presented here. On the Maharashtra drought of 1970–3, see also Ladejinski (1973), Government of Maharashtra (1973), Krishnamachari *et al.* (1974), Kulkarni (1974), Mundle (1974), Borkar and Nadkarni (1975), Jodha (1975), Mathur and Bhattacharya (1975), Subramaniam (1975), Oughton (1982), Brahme (1983), and various contributions to the *Economic and Political Weekly* from 1971 to 1974.

literacy, urbanization, life expectancy, and average income). However, the divide between urban and rural areas in Maharashtra is very sharp, and the proportion of the rural population below the 'poverty line' in this state is among the highest in India.[13] Even within the rural sector, there are enormous

Table 8.1 District-wise cereal production in Maharashtra, 1967–1973

District	Index of Cereal Production (1967–8 = 100)				Cereal production per capita, 1972–3 (kg./year)
	1969–70	1970–1	1971–2	1972–3	
Greater Bombay	77	81	54	31	
Thana	88	110	97	42	46
Kolaba	78	101	81	67	131
Ratnagiri	99	117	103	86	85
Nasik	81	107	55	26	32
Dhulia	106	119	74	49	54
Jalgaon	89	74	59	70	72
Ahmednagar	109	80	59	33	47
Poona	90	70	73	43	38
Satara	98	103	91	41	45
Sangli	90	86	90	18	20
Sholapur	92	51	63	18	27
Kolhapur	93	110	115	65	53
Aurangabad	89	74	48	20	31
Parbhani	76	54	42	41	66
Bhir	120	97	54	17	27
Nanded	77	36	48	29	51
Osmanabad	108	54	58	45	61
Buldhana	122	68	82	63	86
Akola	132	55	89	61	64
Amravati	103	61	68	79	62
Yeotmal	131	65	104	85	86
Wardha	97	59	73	68	80
Nagpur	96	71	76	67	49
Bhandara	121	139	114	58	92
Chandrapur	129	109	105	71	118
MAHARASHTRA	99	83	74	47	51

Source: Calculated from the *Annual Season and Crop Reports* (Government of Maharashtra) of the corresponding years. Per-capita production figures for 1972–3 (last column) are based on district-wise population estimates (for 1973) obtained by assuming identical 1973/1971 population ratios for each District; the all-Maharashtra 1973/1971 population ratio is taken from the *Bulletin on Food Statistics*, 1982–4. District-wise population estimates for 1971 are from the Census (as given in Brahme 1983: 13–14.)

[13] See e.g. Vaidyanathan (1987).

128   FAMINES

regional inequalities in living standards, and in the semi-arid parts of the state the precariousness of life is particularly acute.

At the time of the onset of the terrible drought of 1970–3, rural Maharashtra was facing an alarming problem of environmental degradation, agricultural decline and threatened rural livelihoods, in many ways similar to the crisis faced by a number of African countries today. The sustained downward trend in per-capita agricultural and food production, which went back at least to the early 1960s, turned into a disastrous crash in the early 1970s, when the larger part of the state was affected by a drought of exceptional intensity for three years in succession. The statistics of food production for that period show a decline which, in terms of rapidity and magnitude, finds few equivalents in the recent history of droughts and famines elsewhere (see Table 8.1, Figure 8.1, and also Table 5.1 in Chapter 5 for an instructive comparison). During the peak year of the drought in 1972–3, the per-capita production of cereals in the state was as low as 51 kg.—less than one-third of the average level (itself very low) of per-capita consumption for India as a whole.

This acute crisis of food and agricultural production, and of the rural economy in general (with a virtual collapse of private employment and incomes for large sections of the population for a prolonged period), represented a considerable threat of large-scale entitlement failures. In spite of this, there are good indications that the sufferings caused by the drought, while far from negligible, were remarkably confined. There is, indeed, very little evidence that any of the usual signs of famine developed to a significant extent in this

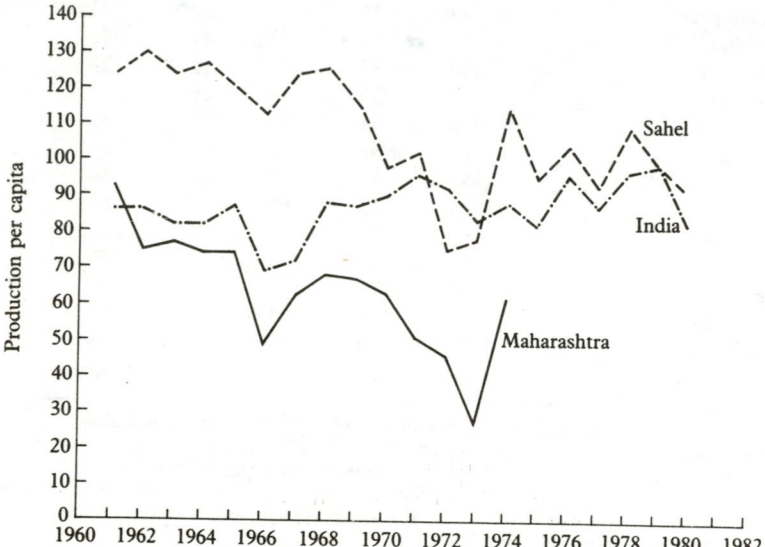

Source: Drèze (1988a), Figure 2.1. Unit: 100 = ½ kg. per day per capita.

Fig. 8.1 Production of cereals per capita, 1961–80: India, Maharashtra and Sahel

Table 8.2 Earnings from relief works and total income in seventy drought-affected villages, Maharashtra, 1972–1973

Percentage contribution of earnings on relief works to total income	Number of villages
0.0–20.0	7
20.1–40.0	8
40.1–50.0	9
50.1–60.0	10
60.1–70.0	14
70.1–80.0	15
80.1–90.0	6
90.1–100.0	1
TOTAL	70

Source: Brahme (1983: 59). The villages were located in the districts of Poona, Ahmednagar, Sholapur, Aurangabad, Bhir, and Osmanabad (all severely drought-affected).

event—whether 'starvation deaths', increases in mortality rates, nutritional deterioration, land sales, or migration to other states.[14]

How was famine averted? While it would be difficult to give a complete answer to this question, a major part of the story undoubtedly relates to public policies of entitlement protection. The cornerstone of these policies was the generation of employment for cash wages on a large scale, supplemented by 'gratuitous relief' for those unable to work and without able-bodied relatives. At the peak of the crisis, nearly 5 million labourers were employed on public works throughout the state. During the twelve months preceding July 1973 (the peak year of drought), relief works generated nearly one *billion* person-days of employment.[15] In the more severely drought-affected districts, the contribution of wage income from employment on public works to total income was well above 50 per cent for most villages (see Table 8.2).

One of the effects of this massive programme of income generation in drought-affected areas was to attract food from other parts of the country into Maharashtra through the channel of private trade. In theory, the drought period was one when severe restrictions were imposed on inter-state movements of food within India. But large amounts of foodgrains were imported into Maharashtra from neighbouring states in spite of these restrictions. This was an essential part of the mechanism of famine prevention, since the efforts made directly by the government to restore normal levels of food availability in

---

[14] See Drèze (1988a) for further discussion. The evidence on mortality rates is discussed in greater detail in the final version of that paper (to appear in Drèze and Sen, forthcoming), without major changes in the conclusions.

[15] Calculated from official figures given by Subramaniam (1975), Table II.3 (viii), based on attendance on the last day of each month.

Maharashtra (through public sales) fell far short of expectations.[16] In fact, had the trade restrictions been effectively enforced with an unchanged amount of food imported through the public distribution system, the aggregate consumption of foodgrains in the state would have been reduced by as much as 40 per cent. It would have been difficult to prevent a decline in *average* consumption

Table 8.3 Cereal consumption in Maharashtra: 1972–1973 compared to 'normal' years

Household class	Cereal consumption per capita (kg./month)	Percentage distribution of households by monthly per capita consumption class (kg./month)			
		<12	12–15	>15	Total
Large cultivators					
1967–8	15.6	25.5	28.7	45.8	100.0
1972–3	12.8	44.7	30.0	25.3	100.0
1973–4	15.3	n/a	n/a	n/a	100.0
Small cultivators					
1967–8	13.4	53.0	19.0	28.0	100.0
1972–3	11.1	61.2	25.2	13.6	100.0
1973–4	12.9	n/a	n/a	n/a	100.0
Farm labourers					
1967–8	14.5	41.4	19.9	38.6	100.0
1972–3	11.5	60.9	25.3	13.8	100.0
1973–4	13.7	n/a	n/a	n/a	100.0
Industrial workers					
1967–8	13.2	42.8	21.7	35.5	100.0
1972–3	12.0	65.3	27.1	7.6	100.0
1973–4	13.3	n/a	n/a	n/a	100.0
Others					
1967–8	12.4	n/a	n/a	n/a	100.0
1972–3	10.8	n/a	n/a	n/a	100.0
1973–4	12.1	n/a	n/a	n/a	100.0
All households					
1967–8	14.0	38.5	22.5	39.0	100.0
1972–3	11.7	59.9	25.2	15.9	100.0
1973–4	13.9	37.2	26.7	36.1	100.0

Source: Drèze (1988a), Tables 3.7 and 3.8. 1967–8 and 1973–4 were years of fairly normal harvest, and were the nearest (to 1972–3) 'normal' years for which data are available. The data cover the rural areas of ten drought-affected districts.

[16] The fact that the purchasing power generated by employment programmes had a dramatic impact on private food movements, and stimulated them in the right direction, does not imply that the public distribution itself played no important role in this episode of averted famine (or that it played a role that could have been easily supplanted by private trade). This should be clear from our earlier discussion of the interaction between private trade and public distribution (Chapter 6).

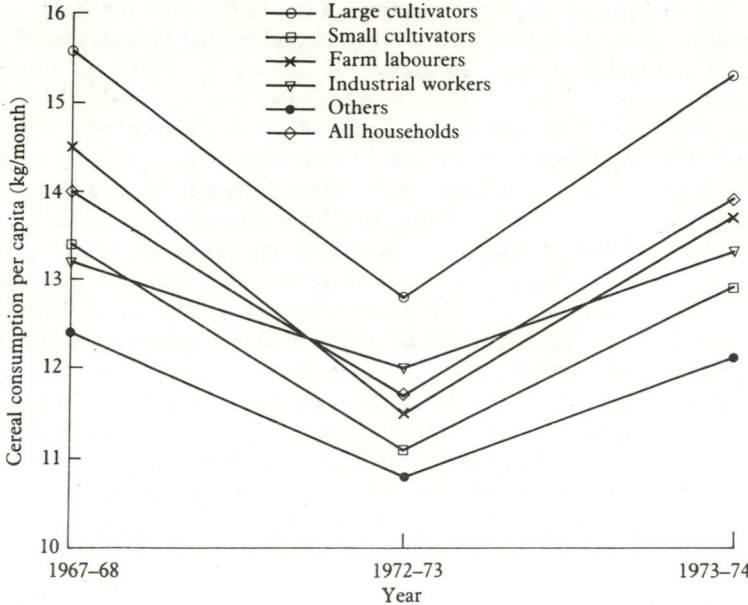

Source: Table 8.3.

Fig. 8.2 Cereal consumption in Maharashtra: drought year (1972–3) compared with normal years, by household class

of this magnitude (for a population as large as that of Maharashtra) from developing into a famine of major proportions.

In spite of large imports of food on both public and private accounts, a noticeable decline in average food consumption took place in Maharashtra in 1972–3. A striking feature of consumption patterns during that year, however, is that the reduction of aggregate consumption compared to ordinary years was distributed remarkably evenly among different socio-economic groups (see Table 8.3 and Figure 8.2). This phenomenon reflects the sustained purchasing power of vulnerable groups resulting from large-scale employment provision, and their ability to battle for their normal share of the available food in spite of the general penury. Correspondingly, the reduction of consumption on the part of relatively privileged groups resulted from the reduction of private money incomes, the increase of food prices, the desire of many asset owners to preserve their productive capital, and their reluctance to join relief works.[17]

[17] A decline in average consumption, along with a strikingly even reduction of intake for different socio-economic groups, is also observed by Marty Chen in her study of the impact of the 1987–8 drought on a village of Gujarat (Chen 1989). In fact, in that study the occupational group which experienced by far the *smallest* percentage decline in food consumption during the drought is found to be that of 'labourers' (Table 39). A completely different pattern has been found in the case of less well handled crises, such as the Bihar 'near-famine' of 1967, when the brunt of hardship was overwhelmingly borne by landless labourers (see Drèze 1988a).

As was discussed in the previous chapter, a crucial condition for the success of a redistributive strategy of this type is that preferential support should be given to vulnerable groups. An indication (among others) of the success achieved by the strategy of employment provision in reaching vulnerable groups and areas in this event can be obtained from considering the allocation of relief between different districts within Maharashtra. As can be seen from Figure 8.3, in 1972–3 a striking positive association was observable across districts between the intensity of the drought (as measured by the extent of crop failures) and the extensiveness of entitlement protection measures (as indicated by the proportion of the rural population employed on public works). This association is quite impressive considering the well-known difficulties that entitlement protection efforts often encounter in reaching the right people in famine situations.[18]

The success of a strategy based on large-scale cash support also depends, as discussed in Chapter 6, on the ability of the relief system to avoid the danger of large sections of the vulnerable population being left out of the purview of public support and at the same time remaining exposed to the price increases caused by the enhanced purchasing power of the others. This is where the

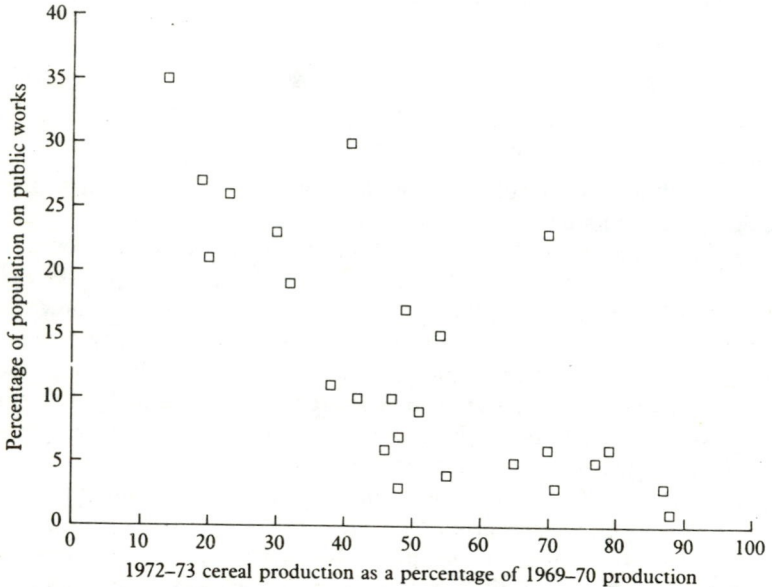

Source: Drèze (1988a), Figure 3.1. Each point in the figure represents one district of Maharashtra.

Fig. 8.3 Drought intensity and public relief in rural Maharashtra (1972–3), by district

---

[18] The difficulties and dilemmas involved in the 'selection problem' and the advantages of 'self-selection' were discussed in Chapter 7.

principle of *guaranteed* employment—imperfectly but usefully applied—played a crucial role.

The political factors involved in the response of the government, discussed in general terms in the previous section, are well illustrated by this particular event. The drought situation was the subject of 696 questions in the Maharashtra Legislative Assembly and Council in 1973 alone, and of numerous (often sharply critical) newspaper reports.[19] Much of the credit for galvanizing the government into action also belongs to the affected populations themselves, which pressed their demands in numerous ways—including marches, pickets and rallies. As one labourer aptly put it, 'they would let us die if they thought we would not make a noise about it'.[20]

8.3 Some African Successes[21]

In Chapter 5 of this book, we argued that African successes in famine prevention have failed to receive the attention they deserve. Of course, ultimately our concern has to be also with identifying mistakes and failures rather than taking idle comfort in past successes. However, there *is* a great deal to learn from the way in which various countries have successfully coped with the threat of entitlement failures. While the Indian experience is rich in general lessons, a number of recent successes with famine prevention in Africa are themselves of great interest. This section is devoted to a brief description and analysis of some of these successes. Their implications and lessons will be further discussed in the concluding section to this chapter.

Cape Verde

In his distinguished history of the Cape Verde Islands, Antonio Carreira wrote that 'everything in these islands combines to impose on man a hard, difficult and wretched way of life'.[22] A prominent aspect of the harshness of life in Cape Verde is the recurrence of devastating droughts, which have regularly affected the islands ever since their 'discovery' in 1460 by the Portuguese. Many of these droughts were associated with large-scale famine.[23]

[19] A useful guide to some of the newspaper reports on the drought can be found in Luthra and Srinivas (1976).

[20] Cited in Mody (1972: 2483). Many vivid accounts of popular protests during the drought can be found in the columns of *Economic and Political Weekly* (see e.g. Mody 1972, Anon. 1973, and Patil 1973). The demands involved often went beyond the mere provision of employment. For instance, in May 1973, a strike by 1.5 million labourers working on relief sites forced the government to grant them an increase in wages.

[21] We are extremely grateful to John Borton, Diana Callear, Jane Corbett, Rob Davies, Thomas Downing, Carl Eicher, Charles Harvey, Roger Hay, Judith Heyer, Francis Idachaba, Renée Loewenson, Siddhartha Mitter, S. T. W. Mhiribidi, Richard Morgan, Christopher Murray, David Sanders, Luc Spyckerelle, Samuel Wangwe, and Daniel Weiner for helpful comments, suggestions, and personal communications relating to the case-studies appearing in this section.

[22] Carreira (1982: 15). According to several analysts the climate of Cape Verde is even harsher and the droughts visiting it more frequent and severe than those of other Sahelian countries. See e.g. Meintel (1984: 56).

[23] For a chronology of droughts and famines in Cape Verde, see Freeman *et al.* (1978). For further discussion of famines in the history of Cape Verde, see Cabral (1980), Carreira (1982), Moran (1982), Meintel (1983, 1984), and Legal (1984).

Table 8.4   History of famine mortality in Cape
Verde, 1750–1950

	Mortality attributed to famine (percentage of total population)
1773–6	44
1830–3	42
1863–6	40
1900–3	15
1920–2	16
1940–3	15
1946–8	18

Source: Moran (1982), Table 1. The famines indicated here are only those for which an estimate of famine mortality is provided in that table. For the same period, the author mentions 22 further large-scale famines for which no mortality estimates are available.

In fact, it is hard to think of many famines in history that have taken a toll in human life proportionately as high as those which have periodically decimated Cape Verde in the last few centuries. Some of these famines are believed to have killed nearly half of the population (see Table 8.4). Even after assuming some exaggeration in these figures, there are very few parallels of such wholesale mortality in the long and terrible history of famines in the world.

These historical famines went almost entirely unrelieved. When one of the very few exceptions to this pattern occurred in 1825, the governor of the islands was sacked for using Crown taxes to feed the people.[24] Left to its own devices, the population had little other refuge than the attempt to emigrate—often encouraged by the colonial authorities. Cape Verde's history of persistent migration is indeed intimately connected with the succession of famines on the islands. However, for most people this option remained a severely limited one, and as recently as the 1940s large-scale mortality was a predictable feature of prolonged drought.

In recent years, Cape Verde may well have been the worst drought-affected of all African countries. Indeed, uninterrupted drought crippled the country's economy for almost twenty years between 1968 and 1986—leading to a virtual extinction of domestic food supplies and a near standstill of rural activity.[25]

[24] Freeman *et al.* (1978: 18). A strikingly similar incident occurred during the famine of the early 1940s (Cabral 1980: 150–1). A significant attempt at providing relief was however made during the famine of 1862–5, when employment was provided (with cash wage payments) on road-building works (see Meintel 1984).

[25] In 1970, 70% of agricultural products consumed in Cape Verde were produced in the country (CILSS 1976: 8). This ratio had fallen to 1.5% by 1973 (CILSS 1976:8), and only rose marginally thereafter (van Binsbergen 1986). According to one study, 'during the drought over 70% of the agricultural labour force has been unemployed' (Economist Intelligence Unit 1984: 38). It is not clear, however, how this calculation treats labour employed on public works programmes (on which more below).

Half-way through this prolonged drought in the middle 1970s, the event was already described as 'the longest and most severe [drought] on record' for the country.[26] In this case, however, not only was famine averted but, even more strikingly, significant *improvements* in living conditions took place during the drought period. The causation of these improvements is the centre of our interest here.

Famine prevention measures greatly gained in motivation and execution after the independence of Cape Verde in 1975. But even in the first period of the drought preceding independence (1968–75), the Portuguese rulers did make considerable efforts to provide famine relief (in contrast with the experiences earlier on in the colonial period).[27] Relief was provided almost exclusively in the form of employment for cash wages in makeshift work (the adequacy of food supplies being ensured separately by food imports). According to one study, as much as 84 per cent of total employment was provided by drought relief programmes in 1970 (this, however, still left 55.5 per cent of the labour force unemployed).[28]

These preventive measures succeeded to a great extent in averting a severe famine. There were no reports of large-scale starvation deaths, and the overall increase in mortality seems to have been moderate. The estimated infant mortality rate, for instance, which had shot up to more than 500 per thousand during the famine of 1947–8, was only a little above the 1962–7 average of 93.5 per thousand in the period 1968–75 (Table 8.5). On the other hand, a significant intensification of undernutrition during the same period has been reported in several studies.[29]

Since independence in 1975, Cape Verde has been ruled by a single party with a socialist orientation, viz. the Partido Africano da Independencia da Cabo Verde (PAICV).[30] This party, described by the current Prime Minister as 'reformist, progressist and nationalist',[31] is flanked by the Popular National Assembly, which is elected every five years by popular ballot (within a single party system). The government of independent Cape Verde has been consistently credited with progressive social reforms and development programmes. Notable areas of improvement have been those of education and health. Drought relief has been among the top political priorities.

Cape Verde's entitlement protection system since independence has

---

[26] Freeman *et al.* (1978: 98).

[27] Several commentators have argued that, in this case, action was motivated by the concern of the Portuguese government for its international image. See e.g. Meintel (1984: 68), CILSS (1976: 4), Davidson (1977: 394), and Cabral (1980: 134).

[28] Calculated from CILSS (1976: 3–4). This was the policy of *Apoio* or 'support', which was later criticized by the government of independent Cape Verde for the unproductive nature of the works undertaken (see CILSS 1976, Legal 1984, and Meintel 1983, 1984).

[29] See e.g. Meintel (1984: 68–9), CILSS (1976: 14), and Freeman *et al.* (1978: 149, 203).

[30] In fact, until 1981, Guinea-Bissau and Cape Verde were jointly ruled by the binational Partido Africano da Independencia da Guine e Cabo Verde, which had earlier led the independence struggle against the Portuguese rulers.

[31] *Courier* (1988: 27).

Table 8.5 Infant mortality in Cape Verde, 1912–1986

Year	Estimated infant mortality rate (deaths per 1000)	
	(1)	(2)
1912	220.6	
1913	174.2	
1915	117.9	
1920	155.0	
1927	217.6	
1931	206.7	
1937	223.4	
1943	317.9	
1946	268.7	
1947[a]	542.9	
1948[a]	428.6	
1949	203.9	
1950	130.7	
1962	106.1	
1963	109.7	
1964	85.3	
1965	76.7	
1966	83.6	
1967	99.9	
1968	91.7	
1969	123.1	
1970	95.0	
1971	130.9	
1972	90.9	
1973	110.6	
1974	78.9	
1975	103.9	104.9
1980–5		77.0
1985		70.0
1986		65.0

[a] Famine years.

Source: For the period 1912–75 (column 1), Freeman *et al.* (1978), Table V.26 (very close estimates are also reported for the 1969–74 period in CILSS 1976, Table VI). For 1975–86 (column 2), *World Health Statistics Annual 1985* and UNICEF (1987a, 1988).

consisted of three integrated components.[32] First, a competent and planned use of food aid has ensured an adequate and predictable food supply in spite of the nearly total collapse of domestic production. Food aid is legally bound to be *sold* wholesale in the open market, and the proceeds accrue to the National Development Fund.[33]

Second, the resources of the National Development Fund are used for labour-intensive public works programmes with a 'development' orientation. In 1983, 29.2 per cent of the labour force was employed in such programmes.[34] The works undertaken include afforestation, soil conservation, irrigation, and road building, and according to a recent evaluation 'the results of these projects are positive, even on the basis of high standards'.[35]

Third, unconditional relief is provided to selected and particularly vulnerable groups such as pregnant women, undernourished children, the elderly, and the invalid. This part of the entitlement protection system includes both nutritional intervention (such as school feeding) and cash transfers, and is integrated with related aspects of formal social security measures. In 1983, direct food assistance covered 14 per cent of the population (see van Binsbergen 1986: 10).

The effectiveness of this fairly comprehensive and well-integrated entitlement protection system is visible from the impact of the drought after 1975.[36] Indeed, the adverse effects of the drought on the living conditions of human beings seem to have been remarkably small.[37] In addition to the successful prevention of famine, there are indications that the post-1975 part of the drought period has witnessed: (1) a rapid *decline* in the infant mortality rate (see Table 8.5); (2) a significant *increase* in per-head food intake;[38] and (3) a significant *improvement* in the nutritional status of children (see Table 8.6).[39] By any criterion, the success achieved by the government of independent Cape

[32] For further details, see CILSS (1976), Davidson (1977), Freeman *et al.* (1978), USAID (1982), Meintel (1983), Legal (1984), Lesourd (1986), and particularly van Binsbergen (1986).

[33] This rule does not apply when the sale of food aid violates the conditions of delivery, e.g. in the case of the comparatively small quantities of food donated to Cape Verde under the World Food Programme. These are used for supplementary feeding.

[34] Economist Intelligence Unit (1984: 38).

[35] See van Binsbergen (1986: 9). See also *Courier* (1988).

[36] Both in the pre-independence and the post-independence periods, remittances from abroad also played an important role in mitigating the effects of the drought.

[37] There is a revealing contrast between this observation and the fact of huge livestock losses, which provide another measure of the intensity of the drought and of the threat of famine. The decline in livestock between 1968 and 1980 has been estimated at 12% for goats, 30% for pigs, 50% for sheep, and 72% for cows (calculated from Economist Intelligence Unit 1983: 43).

[38] On this, see Legal (1984: 12–16), who notes large increases in the consumption of maize, wheat, and rice in the post-independence period compared to the pre-drought period. The average consumption of calories, which 'for the vast majority of the population did not exceed 1500 calories per day' at the time of independence (CILSS 1976: 8; our translation), is now believed to have 'moved closer to the required level of 2800 calories per day' (van Binsbergen 1986: 3).

[39] A USAID study dated 1982 also mentions, without explicitly providing supporting figures, that 'by providing employment, the Government of Cape Verde's rural work program has had an acknowledged major effect on improving nutritional status' (USAID 1982: 15).

Table 8.6 Child undernutrition in Cape Verde, 1977 and 1984

District	Percentage of school children suffering from undernutrition (moderate to serious)	
	1977[a]	1984[b]
Boa Vista	41.8	7.8
Porto Novo	49.2	9.2
Ribeira Grande	54.3	5.8
São Vicente	38.1	10.7
Tarrafal	n/a	7.8
TOTAL	46.4	8.8

[a] Children aged 7–15 years.
[b] Children aged 6–18 years.

Source: van Binsbergen (1986), Table 2. According to the author, the two studies on which this table is based are 'reasonably comparable', and 'although the methodologies used by the different studies were not identical, it is safe to conclude that the nutritional status of school age children has significantly improved since 1977' (van Binsbergen 1986: 3–4). An independent study carried out in 1973 estimated that 38% of children aged 7–14 suffered from 'moderate protein-calorie malnutrition' (Freeman *et al.* 1978, Table V.24).

Verde in protecting the population from the adverse effects of a drought of unprecedented magnitude must be seen as exemplary.

Kenya

The history of Kenya, like that of Cape Verde, has been repeatedly marked by grim episodes of drought and famine.[40] As recently as 1980–1, famine struck substantial parts of the population in the wake of a drought of moderate intensity. The government of Kenya has been widely praised, however, for preventing a much more widespread and intense drought from developing into a famine in 1984. This event has been extensively studied elsewhere.[41] We shall only recall here the main features of this successful response, and comment briefly on some of its neglected aspects.

Like Cape Verde, Kenya has a single party system and an elected parliament. Since independence in 1963, the country has enjoyed a degree of political stability which compares favourably with many other parts of Africa. The freedom of the national media is limited, but nevertheless more extensive than in most African countries. The country also has a high degree of visibility in the international press.

More than 80 per cent of Kenya's population (around 19 million in 1984) is

---

[40] See e.g. Wisner (1977), O'Leary (1980), Herlehy (1984) and Ambler (1988).
[41] For in-depth analyses of the 1984 drought and the government's response, see Ray (1984), Deloitte *et al.* (1986), Cohen and Lewis (1987), Corbett (1987), J. Downing *et al.* (1987), and T. Downing *et al.* (forthcoming). A particularly useful and well-documented account of this event can be found in Borton (1988, forthcoming).

rural, and derives its livelihood largely from agriculture and livestock. Compared to most other parts of Africa, the rural economy is quite diversified, and has experienced relatively rapid growth since the early 1960s. Despite these favourable factors, large parts of the country remain vulnerable to climatic and economic instability, particularly in the largely semi-arid areas of the Eastern and North-eastern Provinces.

The strategies adopted by rural households in Kenya to cope with drought or the threat of famine appear to be increasingly geared to the acquisition of food in the market and the diversification of economic activities (partly through wage employment).[42] The importance of off-farm activities in the rural household economy can be seen from the fact that, according to a survey carried out in six districts of the Central and Eastern Provinces in 1985, more than half of smallholder households had at least one member in long-term wage employment (see Table 8.7 below).

The 1984 crisis followed a massive failure of the 'long rains' in March and April 1984. According to Cohen and Lewis:

It was the worst shortage of rains in the last 100 years. Production of maize, the nation's principal food crop, was approximately 50% below that normally expected for the main rains of March–May. Wheat, the second most important grain, was nearly 70% below normal. Potato production was down by more than 70%. Pastoralists reported losing up to 70% of their stock. The situation had the potential for a famine of major proportions.[43]

Regional disparities compound the problems reflected in these aggregate statistics. In the Central and Eastern Provinces, maize production for the agricultural year 1984–5 was estimated by the FAO at 14 per cent and 26 per cent (respectively) of the average for the previous six years. In districts such as Kitui and Machakos, maize production was virtually nil both in 1983 and in 1984.[44]

While in specific areas the drought of 1984 meant the second or even third consecutive crop failure, for most areas the crisis was one of limited duration. The 'short rains' of October to December 1984 were above average. However, in terms of intensity and geographical coverage the drought of 1984 was certainly an exceptional one, and distress continued until the harvest of mid-1985.

The use of formal early warning techniques apparently played little role in precipitating action. The need for action seems to have been detected partly from the visible failure of rains in early 1984 (followed by evident crop failures), and partly from the unusual increase in food purchases from the

[42] On coping strategies in Kenya, see Wisner (1977), Bertlin (1980), Campbell (1984), Swift (1985), Downing (1988b), Akong'a and Downing (1987), Sperling (1987a, 1987b), Anyango et al. (forthcoming) and Kamau et al. (forthcoming).

[43] Cohen and Lewis (1987: 274). The existence of a serious threat of large-scale famine in this event is also argued in detail in Corbett (1987). For statistical information on rainfall patterns and crop production during the drought, see Downing et al. (forthcoming).

[44] See Borton (1988), Table 3, and Maganda (forthcoming), Table 9.4.

National Cereals and Produce Board later in the year.[45] While Cohen and Lewis stress the role of 'political commitment' in ensuring an early and adequate response, others comment that 'the government felt the need to forestall political instability that would result in the event of a widespread famine'.[46] The threat of political unrest seems to have been exacerbated by the fact that, somewhat unusually, the drought of 1984 strongly affected a number of politically important and influential areas of the Central and Eastern Provinces, as well as Nairobi.

Active public response to the crisis began in April 1984.[47] The first step taken by the government to deal with the threat of famine was to import large amounts of food on a commercial basis. The initial availability of substantial food stocks ensured that the lags involved in the importation of food did not have disastrous consequences. Food aid pledges were also obtained, but with a few minor exceptions their fulfilment occurred only in 1985, several months after the arrival of commercial food imports. The ability of the government to buy large amounts of food on the international market was greatly helped by the availability of foreign exchange reserves and the peak in export earnings resulting largely from high world prices for tea and coffee.

Entitlement protection measures took two different forms. First, the government used food imports to ensure the continued availability of food at reasonable prices through normal commercial channels. In ordinary times, interdistrict food movements are exclusively organized by the National Cereals and Produce Board, which subcontracts the transport and distribution of food to licensed private traders. This arrangement was preserved and intensified during the drought, and most of the imported food was sold through the intermediation of private traders at 'gazetted' prices fixed by the government.

Second, direct support was provided to vulnerable households in affected areas. Initially, the government intended to provide such support mainly in the form of employment for cash wages.[48] In practice, however, the generation of employment fell far short of target, due to a lack of preparedness and supervisory capacity. On the other hand, the provision of unconditional relief in the form of free food rations (mainly from food aid) assumed considerable importance. In August 1984, nearly 1.4 million people, or 7 per cent of the total

[45] Cohen and Lewis describe the symptoms of an impending crisis as follows: 'By April 1984, the situation was obvious. The sun was shining beautifully, when it should have been raining; no early warning system was required' (Cohen and Lewis 1987: 276). Other authors, however, have also stressed the role of rapidly increasing purchases from the National Cereals and Produce Board in arousing concern for the possibility of a crisis (see e.g. Corbett 1987, and Borton forthcoming).

[46] J. Downing et al. (1987: 266). It appears that the drought enjoyed only limited coverage in the local media, but attracted considerable international attention and concern (Downing 1988a).

[47] For detailed and documented accounts of the famine prevention measures, see Cohen and Lewis (1987), J. Downing et al. (1987), Borton (1988, forthcoming) and T. Downing et al. (forthcoming). This case study concentrates mainly on the government response, which represents the greater part of these measures, though the involvement of non-government agencies was not insignificant.

[48] The two slogans propounded by the government early on during the crisis were 'planning, not panic' and 'food imports and employment generation' (Ray 1984).

population, were estimated to be in receipt of free food distribution, and in January 1985 a very similar estimate was reported.[49] In drought-affected areas, the proportion of the population receiving food rations was much larger, and the survey of smallholders in Central and Eastern Kenya mentioned earlier found that over the same period the proportion of households receiving food assistance in the surveyed districts was as high as 45 per cent (see Table 8.7). The size of the rations distributed, however, appears to have been very small prior to the large-scale arrival of food aid in 1985.[50]

The allocation of relief to the needy was the responsibility of the provincial administration, which itself relied on local famine relief committees and 'chiefs' to identify those in need of support. The precise way in which this system actually worked is far from clear. According to some, the local chiefs 'knew the needs of their people, and by most reports did an effective, equitable job of distributing the government-supplied grain'.[51] Another account, however, states that 'moving in the path of least resistance, the GOK [Government of Kenya] would seem to rather divide the available food equally among recipients at the distributions thus defusing potentially uncomfortable situations'.[52]

It is not implausible that the allocation of food within specific communities was largely indiscriminate, and that 'targeting' operated mainly between different villages or regions (the impact of the drought varied greatly between different areas). On the other hand, an important factor facilitating the fair allocation of free food was the fact that most of it consisted of *yellow* maize, which is generally considered as an 'inferior' commodity in Kenya. The element of 'self-selection' involved in distributing yellow maize has been said by a number of commentators to have contributed to an allocation more geared to the most desperate.

Table 8.7 presents some indicators of the impact of the drought on the rural population in different ecological zones of Central and Eastern Kenya, arranged in increasing order of drought-proneness. The table brings out, *inter alia*, (1) the role played by wage employment and remittances in sustaining affected households, (2) the responsiveness of consumption patterns to price and income changes (the composition of food consumption changed for most households even in the less affected areas), and (3) the extensive nature of the

[49] Deloitte *et al.* (1986: 12). In 1985, the numbers in receipt of unconditional relief gradually decreased, though the amount of food distributed increased with the enlarged flow of food aid.

[50] The same survey reveals that, between July and December 1984, the median food ration per recipient household varied between 197 and 633 calories per day in different regions (Downing 1988a, Table 5.16; see also Downing 1988b, Table 4.19). For the same period, Anyango *et al.* (1987) estimate that 'the food relief averaged 5–10 per cent of individual requirements' for the recipients (see also Kamau *et al.* forthcoming). In 1985, the size of food rations was much larger, and did not in fact differ very much on average from the 'target' of 10 kg. of maize per person per month (Borton 1988, forthcoming).

[51] Cohen and Lewis (1987: 281).

[52] Ray (1984: 2). Communications from two persons who were involved in the 1984 relief efforts confirm that food distribution centres typically did not discriminate between different groups of people, and provided identical rations to all recipients.

Table 8.7 The 1984 drought and smallholder households in Central and Eastern Kenya

Characteristic	Percentage of households with the specified characteristic, by ecological zone					
	1	2	3	4	5	All zones
Household member moved during 1984	23	7	21	26	38	25
Has a member in permanent employment	58	47	61	54	54	56
Received cash remittances from relatives or friends during drought	34	28	40	57	46	43
Major food changed during 1984	84	78	76	67	67	73
Received famine relief (from govt or NGOs)	14	35	25	67	77	45
Slaughtered, sold, lost or consumed cattle[a]	41 (26)	45 (35)	33 (29)	44 (46)	32 (51)	38 (58)

[a] In brackets, the percentage decrease in cattle holding, averaged over all households surveyed in the respective zone.

Source: Anyango *et al.* (forthcoming), Tables 13.6 and 13.9. Based on survey data collected in January 1985 by the Central Bureau of Statistics on behalf of the National Environment Secretariat. In Kenya, a smallholder is 'typically defined as a rural landowner with less than 22 hectares' (Akong'a and Downing 1987: 92). Ecological zones appear in increasing order of drought-proneness, based on rainfall data.

coverage of food distribution in these districts at that time.[53] The large cattle losses also confirm the exceptional severity of the drought.[54]

The overall effect of the drought on the well-being of the affected populations has not been fully ascertained. Most commentators consider that 'famine was averted'. The apparent absence of confirmed reports of 'starvation deaths', as well as of distress migration on the part of entire families, lends some support to this view. On the other hand, there is clear evidence of widespread hunger as well as rising undernutrition in 1984.[55]

[53] The general significance for famine prevention policies of the phenomena related to the first two observations was discussed in Chapters 5 and 7.

[54] For further details of livestock losses, see Borton (1988), Downing *et al.* (forthcoming), Chapter 1, Kamau *et al.* (forthcoming), Anyango *et al.* (forthcoming) and Mwendwa (forthcoming). The picture presented in other surveys is, if anything, grimmer than that offered by Table 8.7. According to Borton (1988), the drought of 1984 may have depleted the *national* cattle herd by as much as 50 per cent (p. vii).

[55] See the surveys of Anyango *et al.* (forthcoming), Neumann *et al.* (forthcoming) and Kamau *et al.* (forthcoming). The relative absence of distress migration is discussed in Anyango *et al.* (forthcoming). Unfortunately, the available data do not permit us to estimate the extent of excess mortality during the drought.

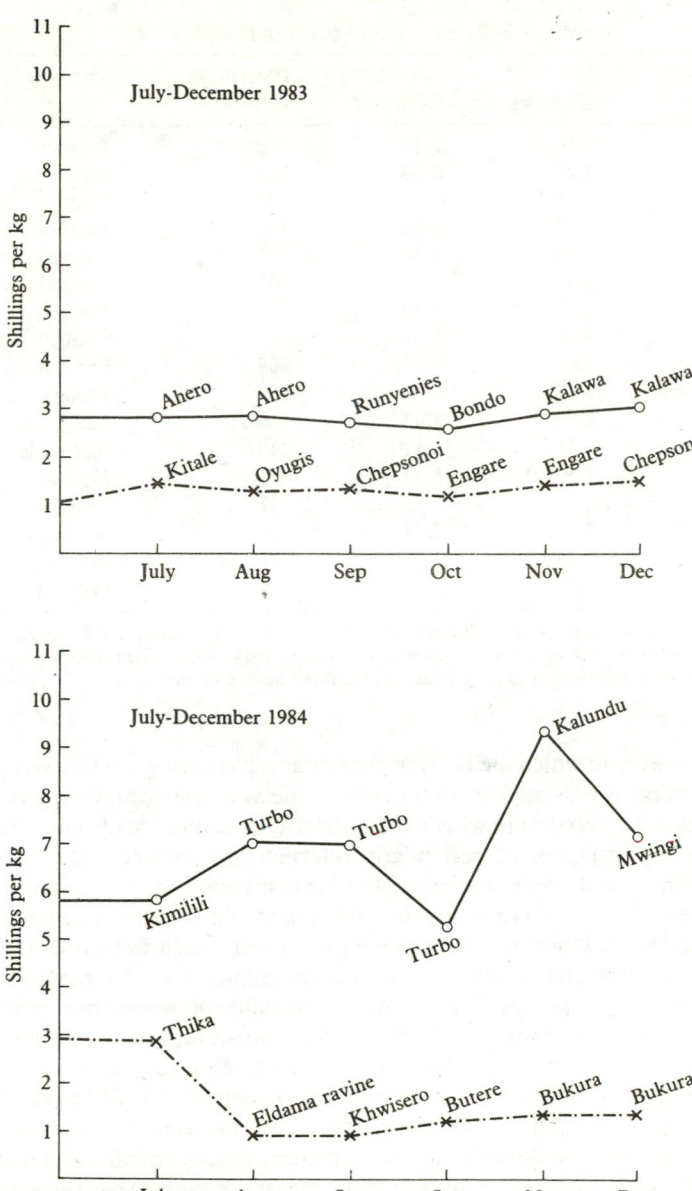

Source: As in Table 8.8. The upper line indicates the retail price of maize in the market where it was the highest in the corresponding month. The lower line indicates the retail price where it was the lowest.

Fig. 8.4 Minimum and maximum retail price of maize in Kenya, 1983 and 1984

Table 8.8 Retail prices of maize in Kenya, 1984

Market	Jan. 1984 (Kshs/kg.)	Nov. 1984 (Kshs/kg.)	Percentage increase	Province
Kalundu	2.50	9.31	272	Eastern
Mwingi	2.50	9.00	260	Eastern
Kiambu	2.14	5.30	148	Central
Machakos	2.40	5.76	140	Eastern
Iciara	2.53	5.94	135	Eastern
Limuru	2.02	4.19	107	Central
Runyenjes	2.57	4.70	83	Eastern
Thika	2.86	4.91	72	Central
Kandara	2.84	4.76	68	Central
Embu Town	2.92	4.89	67	Eastern
Eldoret	2.00	2.92	46	Rift Valley
Kitale	1.51	2.11	40	Rift Valley
Bondo	2.50	3.33	33	Nyanza
Ahero	2.51	3.19	27	Nyanza
Sondu	2.31	2.73	18	Nyanza
Mumias	2.35	2.69	14	Western
Luanda	2.71	2.57	−5	Western

Source: Republic of Kenya, Central Bureau of Statistics, Ministry of Finance and Planning, *Market Information Bulletin* (Jan.–June 1984 and July–Dec. 1984 issues). The markets in the table are all those for which data are provided in the Bulletin for both months.

While the credit which the Kenyan government has been given for averting a severe famine in 1984 appears to be largely deserved, an important query can nevertheless be raised as to whether the strategy it adopted made good use of available opportunities. A particularly relevant issue concerns the balance between income support and price stabilization measures. Considering the small size of food distribution to vulnerable households in per-capita terms (at least until 1985), it appears that famine prevention measures were geared to work mainly through the level of food *prices* rather than through the generation of compensating incomes.[56] In turn, the stability of prices was pursued through a policy of commercial imports from abroad into the worst affected districts. At the same time, however, government regulations prevented private traders from moving food from surplus to deficit areas within Kenya.

As was mentioned earlier, interdistrict food movements in Kenya are tightly regulated by the National Cereals and Produce Board, which subcontracts food transport to licensed private traders. Several studies have shown that these restrictions on interregional movements have the effect of exacerbating the intensity of local shortages and the disparity of retail food prices between

---

[56] According to Borton (1988), free distribution of food accounted for only 15 per cent of the cereals imported between September 1984 and June 1985 (p. 19).

regions.[57] This phenomenon was clearly visible during the drought year itself: while food prices were sharply rising in drought-affected districts, they were only sluggishly increasing or even *falling* in many others (see Figure 8.4 and Table 8.8). Maize prices in different markets varied, at one point, by a factor of nearly *ten*.[58] Even between adjacent districts, price disparities seem to have been exceptionally large (see Table 8.9).

The detrimental effects of this policy of trade restrictions on the entitlements of vulnerable groups in drought-affected areas are not difficult to guess. For instance, after stressing the role of food shortages and high prices in undermining the entitlements of poor households in the Samburu District of Northern Kenya, Louise Sperling comments:

[The] problem of local distribution was sufficiently severe to result in the convening of a district-level meeting as early as 14th June 1984. The District Commissioner called together the eleven or twelve wholesalers to discuss 'the erratic supply of commodities'. Maize prices are strictly controlled by the state, and the local traders claimed they were losing money on maize sales. The allowed mark-up could not cover the costs of transport and loading to these more remote areas. Even considerable government pressure to encourage traders to keep their shelves full did not result in an increase in the local availability of maize . . . Again, the poor disproportionately suffered from these shortages. They could not afford to buy grain in bulk when it did arrive. Equally, they did not have the means to purchase alternative, more costly foodstuffs.[59]

Table 8.9 Maize prices in Central and Eastern Kenya, 1984

Zone	Price of white maize (Kshs/kg.)		Percentage Increase (Jan.–Dec.)
	Jan.–Mar.	Oct.–Dec.	
1	3.98	5.94	49
2	3.25	5.50	69
3	2.80	6.20	121
4	2.94	7.22	146
5	3.49	10.24	193

Note: The ecological zones are the same as in Table 8.7.

Source: Anyango *et al.* (forthcoming), Table 13.10.

[57] On this, see particularly Olsen (1984). See also Akong'a and Downing (1987) and Sperling (1987a). Note that the volatility of *retail* prices is compatible with the control of 'gazetted prices' mentioned earlier.

[58] For details of food price patterns during the drought, see the Government of Kenya's *Market Information Bulletin*, and also Maganda (forthcoming). Careful econometric analysis of time-series data on food prices in Kenya confirms that the interregional disparity of prices sharply increased in 1984 (Jane Corbett, Food Studies Group, QEH, Oxford, personal communication).

[59] Sperling (1987a: 269).

To conclude, while the efforts made by the Government of Kenya in 1984 to import food into drought-affected areas well ahead of large-scale famine were no doubt remarkable, it may be that certain aspects of the relief programme are yet to receive adequately critical scrutiny. To some extent, the acute need to rush food from abroad into the worst affected regions was a result of the parallel efforts that were made, partly for political reasons, to prevent food exports from surplus areas, or to direct such exports towards Nairobi. It appears that, in some respects, government intervention during the drought was undoing with one hand the harm it had done with the other.

Zimbabwe

The so-called 'Zimbabwean miracle' in food production has received wide attention recently. By contrast, the impressive and largely successful pro-grammes of direct entitlement protection pursued by the Zimbabwean govern-ment to prevent the prolonged drought of 1982–4 from precipitating a major famine seem to have been relatively neglected.[60] While it is tempting to think that a country with growing food supplies cannot possibly know the threat of famine, the experience of famines all over the world shows how misleading and dangerous this assumption can be. In the case of Zimbabwe too, a closer examination of the facts reveals that the prevention of a famine in 1982–4 must be attributed as much to far-reaching measures of public support in favour of affected populations as to the growth of food supplies.

The political system in Zimbabwe is that of a limited multi-party democ-racy. Since independence in 1980, the country has been ruled by the elected and re-elected ZANU (Zimbabwe African National Union) party led by Robert Mugabe. A notable feature of ZANU is its very wide and largely rural support base, inherited from the independence struggle. Political debate is intense in Zimbabwe. The press is relatively unconstrained and one of the most active in Africa. The press played, in fact, a conspicuous role in keeping the government on its toes throughout the drought period.[61]

In spite of the socialist aims of the government, the economy has retained private ownership and market incentives. On the other hand, the government of independent Zimbabwe has carried out a major revolution in the area of

---

[60] To the best of our knowledge an in-depth analysis of these events has not been published to this day. However, see Government of Zimbabwe (1986a, 1986b), Gaidzanwa (1986), Leys (1986), Bratton (1987a), Davies and Sanders (1987a, 1987b), Loewenson (1986), Loewenson and Sanders (1988), Mitter (1988), Tagwireyi (1988), and Weiner (1988), for many valuable insights.

[61] On the extensive coverage of the drought in the Zimbabwean press, see the accounts of Leys (1986), Bratton (1987a), and Mitter (1988). Some of the more widely circulated newspapers, such as the *Herald*, did not always take a sharply adversarial stance given their generally supportive attitude vis-à-vis the ZANU government. However, even they played a role in maintaining a strong sense of urgency by constantly reporting on the prevalence of undernutrition and hardship in the countryside, echoing parliamentary debates on the subject of drought, calling for action against profiteering, and exposing the 'scandal' of rural women driven to prostitution by hunger (on this see *Herald* 1983).

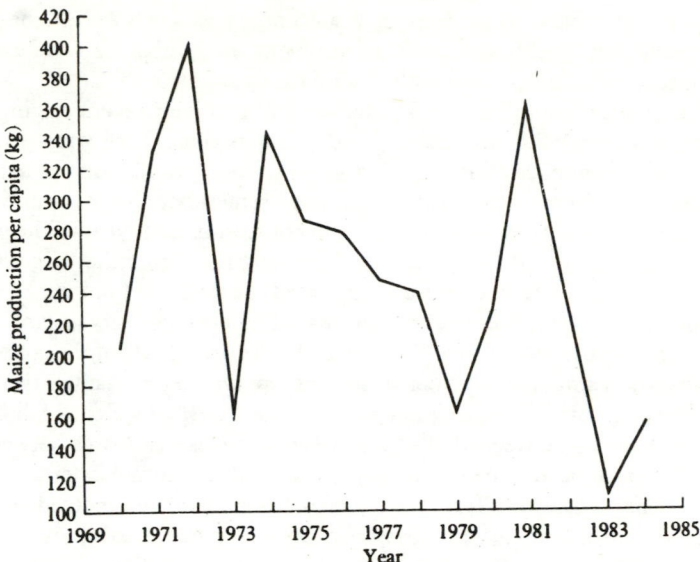

Source: Calculated from production figures provided in Rohrbach (1988), Figure 1, and from population data given in UNICEF (1988), Tables 1 and 5.

Fig. 8.5   Annual Maize production per capita in Zimbabwe, 1970–84

social services. The great strides made since 1980 in the areas of health and nutrition have, in particular, received wide recognition.[62]

In comparison with most other African countries, Zimbabwe's economy (including the agricultural sector) is relatively prosperous and diversified. However, the heritage of the colonial period also includes massive economic and social inequalities. The agricultural sector is highly dualistic, the larger part of the more fertile land being cultivated by a small number of commercial farms while peasant production remains the dominant feature of 'communal areas'. Even within the communal areas, sharp regional contrasts exist both in productive potential and in access to infrastructural support.[63] Further divisions exist between racial and class groups as well as between rural and urban areas. As a result, large sections of the population live in acute poverty in

[62] See e.g. Donelan (1983), Government of Zimbabwe (1984), Waterson and Sanders (1984), Mandaza (1986), Davies and Sanders (1987a, 1987b), Loewenson and Sanders (1988), and Tagwireyi (1988). To mention only two important areas of rapid advance, the percentage of children fully immunized in Zimbabwe increased from 27 per cent in 1982 to 85 per cent in 1988 (Tagwireyi 1988: 8), and school enrolment increased at an annual rate of 20 per cent between 1979 and 1985 (Davies and Sanders 1987b: 297).

[63] This point is stressed in Weiner (1987) and Weiner and Moyo (1988). For further discussion of production relations in Zimbabwe's rural economy and their implications for living standards and famine vulnerability, see Bratton (1987a, 1987b), Rukini and Eicher (1987), Rukuni (1988) and Weiner (1988).

spite of the relative prosperity of the economy as a whole. At the time of independence, health and nutrition problems in Zimbabwe were extremely serious, even in comparison with other African countries.[64]

The 'production miracle' in Zimbabwe is of relatively recent origin. In fact, from the early 1970s until after the drought period, there was—to say the least—little evidence of any upward trend in food production per capita (see Figure 8.5). On the other hand, it must be remembered that, over the same period, Zimbabwe remained a net *exporter* of food in most years. The plentiful harvest which immediately preceded the drought ensured that large stocks of maize were available when the country faced the threat of famine.[65]

The drought lasted three years, and was of highest intensity in agro-climatic terms during the second year (i.e. 1983). In the drier parts of the country, the maize crop (Zimbabwe's principal staple crop) was 'a total failure throughout the drought years'.[66] Maize sales to the Grain Marketing Board fell by more than two-thirds between 1980–1 and 1982–3. Livestock losses between 1978 and 1983 have been estimated at 36 per cent of the communal herd.[67]

For many rural dwellers, remittances from relatives involved in regular employment or migrant labour were a crucial source of support during the drought. As in the Sahel and in Kenya (discussed earlier), it was found in Zimbabwe that 'the households most engaged in selling labour to the wider economy . . . are the least susceptible to drought'.[68] Many households, however, did not have access to this broader source of sustenance, and for them government relief was often the main or even the only source of food.

The drought relief programme of the government was an ambitious and far-reaching one. Famine prevention measures were taken early in 1982, and given a high political and financial priority throughout the drought. The main entitlement protection measures were large-scale food distribution to the adult

[64] See e.g. Sanders (1982), World Bank (1983b), Loewenson (1984), and Government of Zimbabwe (1984). These studies give a clear picture of the connections between this poor record and the massive inequalities in economic opportunities and access to public services of the colonial period. In the early 1970s, for instance, the life expectancy of a European female was more than *twenty* years longer than that of an African female (Agere 1986: 359).

[65] It is worth noting that while the Zimbabwean 'miracle' has often been attributed to the astonishing power of price incentives (see e.g. *The Economist* 1985, and Park and Jackson 1985), the expansion of the rural economy since independence has in fact involved a great deal more than a simple 'price fix'. On the extensive and fruitful involvement of the government of independent Zimbabwe in infrastructural support, agricultural extension, credit provision, support of cooperatives, etc., see Bratton (1986, 1987a), Eicher and Staatz (1986), Eicher (1988a), Rohrbach (1988) and Weiner (1988).

[66] Bratton (1987a: 224). This statement refers, in fact, to the two least fertile among Zimbabwe's five agro-ecological regions. These two regions account for 64% of Zimbabwe's land, 74% of the 'communal lands', and about two-thirds of the communal area population.

[67] Bratton (1987a: 223–5). Weiner (1988) reports declines in draught stock during the drought period of 47% and 21% respectively in the two agro-ecological regions mentioned in the last footnote.

[68] Leys (1986: 262). On the importance of wage labour and remittances for the rural economy in general, and for mitigating the impact of the drought on the rural population in particular, see also Bratton (1987a), Weiner (1987) and Weiner and Moyo (1988).

Table 8.10 Drought and drought relief in Chibi district, Zimbabwe, 1983–1984

Village	Number of households	Percentage of cattle which died in previous twelve months	Percentage of population receiving food rations[a]
A	52	28	62
B	36	34	64
C	44	32	68
D	39	47	54

[a] Per capita rations of 20 kg. per month.

Source: Constructed from Leys (1986). According to the author, Chibi District was one of the worst affected districts.

population, and supplementary feeding for children under five. Commenting on the importance of free food distribution for the survival of the poor, one study of drought relief in Southern Zimbabwe comments that 'for those without access to cash and other entitlements it was their only food intake'.[69]

It is not easy to assess how large a part of the population benefited from free food distribution. Estimates of 2 to 3 million people being fed in rural areas at the peak of the programme, as against a total rural population of 5.7 million in 1982, have been cited in various studies.[70] A survey of 464 households carried out in four communal areas selected for their environmental diversity found that more than 50 per cent of the surveyed households were receiving free maize in 1982–3 and 1983–4.[71] Another study, focusing on four villages in one of the most affected districts, reveals a proportion of population in receipt of free food rations ranging from 54 to 68 per cent (see Table 8.10). Very similar findings are reported in a number of further household surveys.[72] While the precise extent of food distribution is difficult to ascertain, its scale was undoubtedly impressive. The size of individual food rations—officially 20 kg. of maize per head per month—was also astonishingly large.

Of course, the task of organizing food distribution on such a gigantic scale was by no means an easy one. While the implementation of relief measures,

[69] Leys (1986: 270). Similarly, Weiner (1988) states that 'during the 1982–4 period the government drought relief programme became the primary means of survival for about 2.5 million people' (p. 71). While the present discussion focuses largely on the food distribution component of the drought relief programme, it is worth noting that (1) policy developments during the drought included an increasingly marked preference for public works programmes (supplemented by unconditional relief for the destitute) as opposed to large-scale distribution of free food, and (2) the drought relief programme had a number of other important components, such as water supply schemes, cattle protection measures, and inputs provision. On both points, see Government of Zimbabwe (1986a).

[70] See e.g. Government of Zimbabwe (1983: 21), Bratton (1987a: 237), Mitter (1988: 4). The official version seems to be that 'at the height of the drought about 2.1 million people had to be fed every month' (Government of Zimbabwe 1986a).

[71] Bratton (1987a), Table 10.8(b).

[72] See especially Weiner (1988), Table 6.4, and Matiza et al. (1988).

much helped by the popular mobilization and political stability associated with the post-independence reconstruction efforts, has attracted favourable comments from many observers, frequent complaints on the part of recipients about the delays, uncertainties, and frauds involved in food distribution have also been reported.[73] In relieving logistic constraints, the subcontracting of food delivery to the private sector played a major role. In fact, disruptions in food deliveries seem to have intensified after the attempt was made (in September 1983) to substitute government transport for private transport.[74]

The free distribution of food raised its own problems. The population eligible for food rations seems to have been confined in practice to households without a member in regular employment.[75] How fairly this criterion was applied in practice is not easy to ascertain, and conflicting views have been expressed on this question. For instance, one author reports on the basis of extensive field work in Southern Zimbabwe that 'as far as I could assess, these criteria were applied fairly and, at the sub-district level, were felt to be fair', and the evidence presented from four village studies in one of the worst-affected districts broadly supports this assessment.[76] But another author suggests the possibility that 'in practice, the distribution pattern was indiscriminate; those who were ineligible received relief food, while those who were truly needy may have gone short'.[77]

The politicization of food distribution during the drought was also apparent in a number of ways—with both negative and positive implications. First, party cadres have played a major role in many places in implementing the distribution of food, and this seems to have led to some favouritism along party lines.[78] Second, the coverage of the drought relief programme in Matabeleland, the stronghold of political dissidents, has been described as 'exceedingly patchy'.[79] Third, food distribution was restricted to rural areas—a highly interesting feature of the relief programme given the frequent bias of public distribution systems in favour of urban classes. It is tempting to interpret this

[73] See e.g. USAID (1983), Leys (1986), Bratton (1987a), Davies and Sanders (1987b), and Mitter (1988).

[74] Leys (1986: 270).

[75] Bratton (1987a) describes the eligible population as 'the "needy" . . . , defined as those with insufficient grain in the home granary and without a close family member working for a wage' (p. 238). Leys (1986), on the other hand, states that free food distribution was intended for 'the members of households in which the head of the household earned an income under the statutory minimum wage' (p. 269), but later adds that this involved 'distinguishing between those households where the head of household held a formal sector job' and others (p. 270). In practice it is likely that the two sets of criteria described by these authors did not diverge substantially.

[76] Leys (1986: 270). Another author gives credit to the ZANU government for 'the smooth running of the relief committees' (Mitter 1988: 5).

[77] Bratton (1987a: 238). The viewpoint expressed by Bratton is based on a personal communication from a colleague at the University of Zimbabwe and could have been less robustly founded than that of Leys.

[78] Daniel Weiner (University of Toledo), personal communication. See also Leys (1986).

[79] Leys (1986: 271). The government put the blame on dissidents for disrupting relief efforts, and at one stage even held them 'responsible for the drought' (see Mitter 1988, for further discussion).

Table 8.11 Nutritional status of children in Zimbabwe, 1981–2 and 1983

| Area | Percentage of children (aged 0 to 5) suffering from second or third degree malnutrition | | | |
| | Weight for age | | Weight for height | |
	1981–2	1983	1981–2	1983
Commercial farming area	42	14, 20[a]	16	8, 7[a]
Communal area[b]	20	11	13	3
Mine area	22	9	6	4
Urban area	6	4	6	2

[a] These figures refer respectively to (1) farms benefiting from a health project initiated in 1981–2, and (2) farms excluded from the health project.
[b] Resurvey area adjacent to that of baseline survey.

Source: Loewenson (1986), Table 3. Based on a sample survey of nearly 2,000 children in Mashonaland Central. For further details and discussion, see also Loewenson (1984).

'rural bias' as a reflection of the politics of ZANU and the predominantly rural character of its support base.

In spite of these reservations, the overall effectiveness of entitlement protection measures during the drought is beyond question. It is not only that 'starvation deaths' have been largely and perhaps even entirely prevented.[80] The striking effect of the government's far-reaching relief programme, in combination with the general expansion of health and education facilities since independence, has been a noticeable *improvement* in the health status of the population of rural Zimbabwe in spite of the severe drought. The most striking aspect of this improvement has been the apparent *decline* in infant mortality throughout the drought period.[81] A significant decline in child morbidity, at least in relation to immunizable diseases, has also been reported, and related to the government's vigorous immunization campaigns.[82]

The evidence on the nutritional status of the population during the drought is mixed. Concern about sharply rising levels of undernutrition in the *early* phases of the drought has been expressed in many informal reports.[83] There is, however, some evidence of declining undernutrition after the relief programme expanded on a large scale in 1983 (see Table 8.11).[84] Taking the drought period as a whole, the available evidence suggests the absence of

[80] According to Bratton, 'it is safe to say that no person in Zimbabwe died as a direct result of starvation' (Bratton 1987a: 225). According to Leys, 'one consequence of the drought for some of the rural African population was hunger, and on occasion and specific places, deaths from starvation' (Leys 1986: 258).
[81] For detailed discussions of mortality decline in Zimbabwe since independence, see Davies and Sanders (1987a, 1987b), Loewenson and Sanders (1988) and Sanders and Davies (1988). It has been claimed that the extent of infant mortality reduction in Zimbabwe between 1980 and 1985 has been as large as 50% (*The Times* 1985; Bratton 1987a : 238).
[82] See Loewenson and Sanders (1988).
[83] See e.g. Bratton (1987a: 224), Mitter (1988: 3–4), Moto (1983).
[84] See Loewenson (1984, 1986) for further discussion of these findings.

, marked change in the nutritional status of the Zimbabwean population.[85] This is remarkable enough, given the severity of the initial threat.

Botswana

As a land-locked, sparsely populated, and drought-prone country experiencing rapid population growth, massive ecological deterioration, and shrinking food production, Botswana possesses many of the features that are thought to make the Sahelian countries highly vulnerable to famine. There are, of course, also important contrasts between the two regions. One of them arises from the highly democratic nature of Botswana's political regime, and—relatedly perhaps—the comparative efficiency of its administration. Also, while many Sahelian countries have suffered from declining or stagnating per-capita incomes in recent decades, Botswana has enjoyed a growth rate which is estimated as one of the highest in the world.

Economic growth in Botswana has, however, followed a highly uneven pattern. In fact, much of this rapid growth has to do with the recent expansion of diamond mining, a productive sector of little direct relevance to the rural poor. Against a background of booming earnings in industry, there is some evidence of increasing rural unemployment and falling rural incomes since the early 1970s. One study goes as far as suggesting that rural incomes in Botswana (inclusive of transfers and remittances) *declined* in real terms at the rate of 5 per cent per year during the period 1974–81.[86] The year 1981–2 marked the beginning of a prolonged and severe drought which lasted until 1986–7, and would certainly have been accompanied by an even sharper deterioration of income and employment opportunities in the absence of vigorous public support measures. Fast overall economic growth is no guarantee of protection against famine.

The rural economy, mostly based on livestock, crop production, and derived activities, suffered a predictable recession during the drought. The output of food crops fell to very low levels (Table 8.12). Cattle mortality increased substantially, and the decline of employment opportunities further aggravated the deterioration of rural livelihoods.[87] In a socio-economic survey

[85] See Davies and Sanders (1987a, 1987b), Loewenson and Sanders (1988) and Sanders and Davies (1988) for detailed reviews of the evidence. See also the results of regular surveys (carried out by the government of Zimbabwe) presented in Tagwireyi (1988).

[86] See the study of Hay et al. (1986), especially Table 2. A published summary of the main results of this major study of drought relief in Botswana can be found in Hay (1988). On the rural economy of Botswana, see Chernichovsky et al. (1985).

[87] For details, see Hay et al. (1986) and Quinn et al. (1987). It should be mentioned that while livestock losses during the drought were perhaps not dramatic in *aggregate* terms (according to Morgan 1986, the size of the national cattle herd declined by 22 per cent between 1982 and 1986), it has been frequently noted that these losses disproportionately hit small herds. Cattle deaths for small herds have been estimated at 'more than 40 per cent for several years' (Diana Callear, National Food Strategy Coordinator, personal communication). Also, poor households in rural Botswana derive a greater than average part of their total incomes from crops (even harder hit by the drought than livestock). The threat which the drought represented to the entitlements of vulnerable groups was therefore much more serious than aggregate figures about livestock mortality, and about the importance of livestock in the rural economy, would tend to suggest.

Table 8.12 Food crop performance in Botswana, 1968–1984

Year	Area planted (000 hectares)	Yield (kg./hect.)	Output (000 tonnes)
1968	200	180	36
1969	240	258	62
1970	202	69	14
1971	246	293	72
1972	251	343	86
1973	139	101	14
1974	255	290	74
1975	250	284	71
1976	261	295	77
1977	255	290	74
1978	260	192	50
1979	160	62	10
1980	268	172	46
1981	274	201	55
1982	193	89	17
1983	226	63	14
1984	197	36	7

Source: Hay *et al.* (1986), Tables 5 and 6.

of 284 rural households carried out in 1984, more than half of the respondents reported 'having no cash income' (other than relief income).[88]

By 1981–2, however, Botswana had set up an entitlement protection system exemplary in its scope and integration. This system was, in fact, the outcome of a long process of experimentation, evaluation and learning. Moderately successful but instructive experiments with famine relief in the 1960s and early 1970s were later followed by a series of evaluations and debates which provided the crucial foundation of Botswana's remarkable relief system.[89] The drought of 1979–80 played a particularly important role in this respect.

Famine relief during the 1979–80 drought was essentially an experiment in what we have called the 'strategy of direct delivery'.[90] The operation was considerably hampered by logistic difficulties connected with the transportation and distribution of food, though a noticeable improvement occurred after

[88] Hay *et al.* (1986: 85).

[89] The Sandford Report (Sandford 1977) provided a useful background investigation of drought in Botswana. The Symposium on Drought in Botswana (Botswana Society 1979) which was convened, quite remarkably, in spite of the then prosperity of agriculture and the economy, was an invaluable forum of discussion on numerous aspects of the problem. Gooch and MacDonald (1981*a*, 1981*b*) provided an illuminating evaluation of relief efforts during the 1979–80 drought and far-reaching recommendations for improvement. For an excellent analysis of the development of Botswana's entitlement protection system, see Borton (1984, 1986).

[90] The following details are based on Morgan (1985), Relief and Development Institute (1985), and especially Gooch and MacDonald (1981*a*, 1981*b*).

the adoption of extensive subcontracting to private truckers. Food deliveries in different parts of the country matched poorly with the extent of distress. The allocation of food within the rural population was largely indiscriminate, partly because the selective distribution of food was found to be 'socially divisive'.[91] While a large-scale famine was averted, the relief operations did not succeed in preventing increased malnutrition, excess mortality, or even starvation deaths.[92]

The lessons of this experiment were not lost, however. In fact, the detailed evaluation carried out by Gooch and MacDonald made a crucial contribution to the design of Botswana's entitlement protection system as it exists today. Their recommendations included (1) the issue of a Relief Manual providing clear and coherent advance guidelines to the administration about the provision of drought relief, and (2) the adoption of a famine prevention strategy based on the unlimited provision of employment (for a subsistence wage paid in cash) to the able-bodied supplemented by unconditional relief for vulnerable groups. These recommendations, while not literally implemented to this day, have provided the basis for a sustained improvement in famine prevention measures.

Careful planning (and buoyant government revenue) would not have gone far enough in the absence of a strong motivation on the part of the government to respond to the threat of famine. Drought relief, however, has consistently been a high political priority in Botswana, and an object of rival promises and actions on the part of competing parties. It is also interesting that, when drought struck the country again in 1981–2, early action was forthcoming in spite of the absence of a formal early warning system.[93] As in India, the politics of famine prevention in Botswana are intimately linked with the accountability of the ruling party to the electorate, the activism of opposition parties, the vigilance of the press, and—last but not least—the strong demands for public support on the part of the affected populations.[94]

The drought of 1982–7 provided a severe test of the country's growing ability to prevent famines. The entitlement protection measures invoked in this event involved three major areas of action: (1) the restoration of adequate food availability, (2) the large-scale provision of employment for cash wages, and (3) direct food distribution to selected groups.[95]

[91] Gooch and MacDonald (1981b: 11). In other cases, the distribution of food was vulnerable to frank abuses.

[92] On this, see Gooch and MacDonald (1981b: 12–13).

[93] Botswana does have a well developed 'nutrition surveillance' system, but this is used mainly for the purposes of monitoring and targeting rather than as a warning device. The decision to launch a major relief operation in 1982 was taken much *before* the system detected a significant increase in undernutrition (see Borton and York 1987). Nor do other components of Botswana's evolving early warning system seem to have played a major role in triggering the government's response (see e.g. Relief and Development Institute 1985).

[94] For a clear discussion of this issue, and of the 'political value of drought relief' in Botswana, see Holm and Morgan (1985) and Holm and Cohen (1988).

[95] It should be mentioned that the drought relief programme as a whole went much beyond

Table 8.13 Price of maize meal at selected centres, Botswana 1980–1983

Region	Price in August 1980 (Pula/bag)	Price in April 1983 (Pula/bag)	Percentage increase
Gaborone	3.39	4.51	33
Francistown	3.56	4.41	24
Lobatse	3.34	4.48	34
Selibe-Pikwe	3.33	4.71	41
Palapye	3.36	4.54	35
Mahalapye	3.48	4.86	40
Mochudi	3.41	4.55	33
Kanye	3.41	4.58	34
Serowe	3.56	4.80	35
Molepolole	3.70	4.81	30
Maun	4.22	5.38	27
Mmadinare	3.73	4.70	26
Tonota	3.59	4.68	30
Shoshong	3.38	4.82	43
Moshupa	3.38	5.02	49
Thamaga	3.35	4.97	48
Ramotswa	3.84	4.73	23
All regions, unweighted average	3.53	4.74	34

Source: Tabor (1983), Table 4.5.

Unlike in 1979–80, the restoration of food adequacy in 1982–7 relied on a more varied and discerning strategy than that of direct delivery. While Botswana did receive large amounts of food aid during the drought, the support of incomes through employment generation (financed out of general government revenue) was not tied to the receipt of food aid. Moreover, food aid was substantially complemented by private imports of food from abroad, and it is not implausible that had food aid been interrupted or delayed this alternative source of food supply would have enabled the relief system to operate with no major loss of effectiveness.[96]

Trade and distribution within the country has been largely ensured by

---

these measures of short-term entitlement protection. Public intervention was also very significant in areas such as the provision of water and the promotion of agricultural recovery. For comprehensive analyses of the drought relief programme, see Tabor (1983), Borton (1984, 1986), Holm and Morgan (1985), Relief and Development Institute (1985), Morgan (1985, 1986, 1988), Hay et al. (1986), Quinn et al. (1987), Hay (1988), Holm and Cohen (1988) and Moremi (1988). See also Government of Botswana (1980, 1985a, 1985b, 1987, 1988).

[96] Botswana belongs to the South African Customs Union (SACU), which *inter alia* allows the free movement of food between Botswana, South Africa, Lesotho and Swaziland. As a result, domestic variations in agricultural output have little effect on the availability and price of food in Botswana. For an econometric analysis of the effect of SACU membership on food prices and food security in Botswana, see Cathie and Herrmann (1988).

Botswana's 'widespread and highly competitive retail network operating in all but the remoter areas'.[97] The effectiveness of this system, and of the process of spatial arbitrage, is visible from the remarkable degree of uniformity in the level of food prices in different parts of the country during the drought (Table 8.13). The contrast with our earlier findings on Kenya is striking.

Another important contrast between drought relief in 1982–7 and in 1979–80 has been the much greater reliance, in the former case, on cash-based employment generation as a vehicle of income generation. The provision of employment has, in fact, fallen short of the vision of 'employment guarantee' contemplated by Gooch and MacDonald, and it has been repeatedly observed that the demand for employment has exceeded the number of jobs available.[98] Nevertheless, the extent of income support provided to vulnerable households by 'Labour-Based Relief Programmes' has been considerable. In 1985–6 they provided around 3 million person-days of employment to 74,000 labourers. It has also been estimated that Labour-Based Relief Programmes 'replaced' almost one-third of rural incomes lost from crop failures between 1983 and 1985.[99] Informal evaluations of the productive value of the works undertaken suggest that the contribution of these programmes to national investment has been far from negligible.[100]

Along with this strategy of employment generation, free food has been distributed on a large scale, mainly in the form of 'take-home' rations. The eligibility conditions for food distribution in various forms in rural areas are very broad, and include not only the destitutes but also other categories such as all pre-school children, all children in primary school, children aged 6–10 not attending school, and all pregnant or lactating women. As a result, the proportion of the total population in receipt of free food rations was as high as two-thirds in 1985.[101]

The experience of drought relief in Botswana in 1982–7 amply demonstrates the effectiveness of a famine prevention system based on the combination of adequate political incentives and insightful administrative guidelines. While the drought of 1982–7 was far more prolonged and severe than that of 1979–80, and led to a much greater disruption of the rural economy, the extent of human suffering was comparatively small. There is no significant evidence

---

[97] Morgan (1985: 49).

[98] See e.g. Hay et al. (1986) and Quinn et al. (1987). This finding must be interpreted bearing in mind that the level of wages paid is 'roughly equivalent to the salary earned by maids and security guards in urban areas and considerably more than cattle herders earned on cattle-posts' (Quinn et al. 1987: 18).

[99] Quinn et al. (1987: 18, 21). The population of Botswana was a little over one million at the time.

[100] See Hay et al. (1986) for a detailed discussion.

[101] Calculated from Hay et al. (1986), Tables 10 and 11. According to the same source the average size of rations amounted to nearly 60 kg. of food (mainly cereals) per recipient per year. For a helpful account of the various components of Botswana's food distribution programme, see Hay (1988).

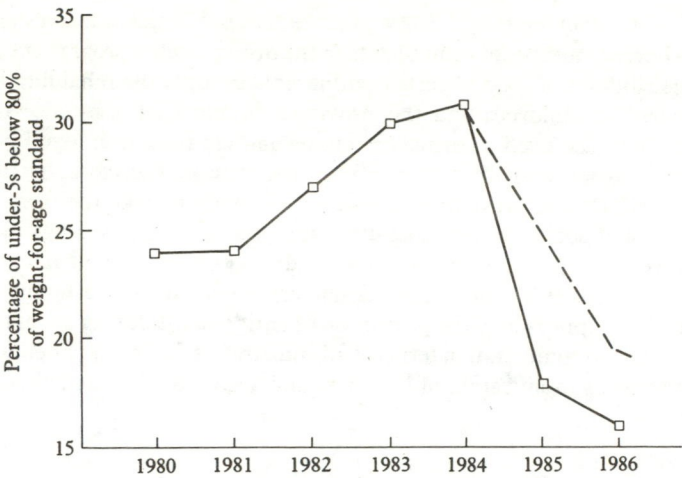

Source: Morgan (1988), Figure 5.

Note: The broken line shows the estimated incidence of undernutrition taking into account changes in the recording system in 1985. The figures are derived from Botswana's Nutrition Surveillance System, which covered about 60% of all under-fives in Botswana in 1984 (Morgan 1985: 45). The increase in observed undernutrition in the early years of the drought may partly reflect the large increase in the coverage of the surveillance system that took place during those years (Hay 1988: 1125).

Fig. 8.6 Incidence of child undernutrition in Botswana, 1980–6

of starvation deaths, or of distress migration on any significant scale.[102] The nutritional status of children only deteriorated marginally and temporarily (see Figure 8.6). One study also reports that 'those who have experienced previous droughts say that the decline in suffering among the disadvantaged is dramatic'.[103] Last but not least, drought relief measures in Botswana seem to have met with an impressive measure of success not only in preventing human suffering but also in preserving the productive potential of the rural economy.[104]

---

[102] According to Morgan (1988), 'starvation, even among extremely isolated communities, was entirely averted' (p. 33).

[103] Holm and Morgan (1985: 469). None of the studies cited in this section provide estimates of excess mortality during the drought. According to Borton, 'mortality estimates are poor in Botswana so it is not possible to estimate whether there has been a significant increase in the death rate' (Borton 1984: 92). Against the initial increase in undernutrition among children, it must be noted that (1) the incidence of *severe* undernutrition has been very small (Hay *et al*. 1986; Holm and Morgan 1985), and (2) seasonal fluctuations in nutritional status have virtually disappeared during the drought (Government of Botswana 1985: Table 5).

[104] On this, see Morgan (1986). The preservation of the productive potential of the rural economy is related partly to the entitlement protection measures discussed here, but also to a wide array of explicit rehabilitation and recovery programmes. Though they are not the focus of our attention in this chapter, the importance of these programmes must not be underestimated.

There is another aspect of Botswana's experience which deserves special mention here. A number of components of the drought relief programme, such as the distribution of food to certain vulnerable groups, the rehabilitation of undernourished children, and the provision of financial assistance to the destitute, have acquired a permanent status and are now an integral part of Botswana's social security system.[105] In the future, therefore, it can be expected that famine prevention measures will perhaps take the form of an *intensification* of social security measures applying in ordinary times. Such a policy development would be a natural extension of the current reliance on existing infrastructural and institutional arrangements for drought relief purposes. This approach to the protection of entitlements during crises has, in general, much to commend, in terms of administrative flexibility, likelihood of early response, simplification of logistics, and ability to elicit broad political support.

8.4 Lessons from African Successes

The African experiences analysed in the previous section illustrate the rich variety of political, social and economic problems involved in the protection of entitlements in a crisis situation. It would be stupid to attempt to derive from these case studies a mechanical blueprint for famine prevention in Africa. However, a number of commonalities involved in the recent experiences of famine prevention in Botswana, Cape Verde, Kenya and Zimbabwe provide, along with the general analyses of previous chapters, the basis of some useful lessons.

The Importance of Entitlement Protection Systems

There is a tendency, once the dust of an emergency has settled down, to seek the reduction of famine vulnerability primarily in enhanced economic growth, or the revival of the rural economy, or the diversification of economic activities. The potential contribution of greater prosperity, if it involves vulnerable groups, cannot be denied. At the same time, it is important to recognize that, no matter how fast they grow, countries where a large part of the population derive their livelihood from uncertain sources cannot hope to avert famines without specialized entitlement protection mechanisms involving direct public intervention. Rapid growth of the economy in Botswana, or of the agricultural sector in Kenya, or of food production in Zimbabwe, explain at best only a small part of their success in averting recurrent threats of famine. The real achievements of these countries (as well as of Cape Verde) lie in having provided direct public support to their populations in times of crisis.

[105] See Morgan (1986) and Holm and Cohen (1988) for further discussion of the interplay between drought relief and social security measures during the last few decades in Botswana.

Initiative and Agency

An important feature of recent famine prevention efforts in the four countries studied in the previous section is that, in each case, the initiative and responsibility of entitlement protection efforts rested squarely with the government of the affected country. This is not to say that international agencies played no positive part in such efforts. In fact, their contribution and partnership has, in each case, been helpful. But the essential tasks of coordination and leadership belonged primarily to the government and administration of the affected countries.

The general 'comparative advantage' that the governments of affected countries have in managing relief operations can indeed be important. This comparative advantage mainly takes the form of being able to draw at short notice on extensive networks of information, administration, communication, transport and storage. In a long term perspective, a sustainable and efficient system of famine prevention can hardly dispense with the close involvement and leadership of the governments of the concerned countries themselves. This makes it particularly important to see the current contribution of international agencies as cooperation with, rather than replacement of, the efforts of the respective governments.

Early Warning and Early Response

Formal 'early warning' techniques have played only a minor role in the famine prevention experiences studied in the preceding section. Early response has been much more a matter of political incentives and motivation than one of informational or predictive wizardry.

As was mentioned earlier, the political systems of the four countries concerned are, in comparison with most other African countries, relatively open and pluralist (e.g. they all have an elected parliament). All except possibly Cape Verde also have an active and largely uncensored press. The role of political opposition, parliamentary debate, public criticism and investigative journalism in galvanizing the national government into action has been central in Botswana as well as in Zimbabwe, and, to a lesser extent, in Kenya.

This does not mean that only countries with highly developed participatory institutions can consistently avert the threat of famine. Even fairly repressive governments are often wary of the prospects of popular discontent in the event of a famine. Political ideology—if it takes the form of a commitment to the more deprived sections of the population—can be another creative force in motivating response. In Cape Verde and Zimbabwe, this influence seems to have been important. As was pointed out in Chapter 5, the attitude of African governments to the threat of famine is not in general one of apathy and callousness.

Food Supply Management

In each of the four countries studied in the previous section, the government took necessary steps to ensure an adequate availability of food. But the exact nature of these steps varied a great deal, and appealed to different strategic elements such as government purchases on international markets, private trade, food aid and the depletion of public stocks.

This strategic diversity contrasts with the common belief that food aid is the only appropriate channel to enhance food availability in a famine-affected country. It is true that three of these four countries (namely, Botswana, Cape Verde and Kenya) have *made use* of substantial quantities of food aid in their efforts to avert famine, but in no case have their entitlement protection measures been significantly *contingent* on the timely arrival of food aid. In fact, entitlement protection policies have typically *preceded* the arrival of food aid pledged in response to the threat of famine. In this respect, entitlement protection measures in these countries have markedly departed from the strategy of 'direct delivery' discussed in Chapter 6.

A particularly significant departure from the strategy of direct delivery is the use of cash support to protect the entitlements of vulnerable groups. The general merits of this approach were discussed at some length in Chapter 6. It is worth noting that reliance on cash support, which is sometimes thought to be highly unsuitable in the context of African famines, has been used with excellent effect in two of the four countries concerned (Botswana and Cape Verde).

Private Trade and Public Distribution

Each of the four African countries discussed earlier have induced private trade to supplement the efforts of the public sector in moving food towards vulnerable areas. In Botswana and Cape Verde, this has taken the form of providing cash support to vulnerable groups on a large scale and leaving a substantial part of the task of food delivery to the market mechanism. In Kenya and Zimbabwe, it has taken the form of subcontracting to private traders the transport of food to specific destinations. In each case, private trade could be confidently expected to move food in the right direction, i.e. towards (rather than out of) affected areas.

At the same time, the direct involvement of the public sector in food supply management has also been substantial in each country. The benefits of this involvement were visible not only in terms of its direct effects on the flow of food, but also in the noticeable absence of collusive practices or panic hoarding in the private sector itself. The sharp contrast between the behaviour of food prices in Kenya and Botswana during recent droughts, discussed in sections 6.3 and 8.3, strongly suggests that the positive involvement of the public sector in food supply management is often a far more creative form of intervention than the imposition of negative restrictions on the operation of private trade.

Diversification and Employment

As a final observation, we should note the prominent role played by the diversification of economic activities (notably through wage employment), and the acquisition of food on the market, in the survival strategies of vulnerable groups in the countries studied in the previous section. As was discussed in Chapter 5, this observation is in line with a general assessment of survival strategies in Africa. Two of its implications are worth emphasizing.

First, while current problems of famine vulnerability in Africa clearly originate in part from the stagnation or decline of food production in that continent (leading to major losses of income and employment for the rural population), it does not follow that the remedy of this vulnerability must necessarily take the form of reversing that historical trend against all odds. Diversification and exchange have been an important part of the economic opportunities of rural populations in Africa for a long time, and open up alternative avenues of action that also need to be considered.

Second, there are strong reasons to think that the potential of employment provision as a tool of entitlement protection (e.g. in the form of public works programmes) is substantial in large parts of Africa. The general advantages of the strategy of employment provision (notably making possible the use of self-selection, and also the provision of cash support) were discussed in Chapter 7. The fact that affected populations positively look for work in crisis situations, and do this long before reaching an advanced stage of destitution, strengthens the case for seeing this strategy as a natural avenue of entitlement protection. In many circumstances, the spade is a more powerful tool of famine prevention than the spoon.

PART III

Undernutrition and Deprivation

9

Production, Entitlements and Nutrition

9.1 Introduction

This part of the book is primarily concerned with public action to combat persistent undernutrition and endemic deprivation (as opposed to transient famines and crises). In this chapter, we shall deal with questions related to the role of food production in this context. Other aspects of the problem of 'social security' will receive scrutiny in subsequent chapters.

Let us begin by distinguishing four different questions about a country's achievements in relation to ensuring adequate nutrition for all. Each points to a particular focus of attention:

1. Is the country *self-sufficient* in food?
2. Does the country have an adequate *food availability*?
3. Do the people in the country have sufficient *food entitlement*?
4. Do the people have adequate *nutritional capability*?

Substantial parts of this chapter will be concerned with discussing the far-reaching implications of distinguishing between these different questions.

There are causal links between the respective points of attention in these questions. For example, achieving food *self-sufficiency* can be one way for a country to ensure *adequate food availability*. Having an adequate supply of food will generally help, to a varying extent, the guaranteeing of sufficient *food entitlements* for all. And securing an adequate entitlement to food must contribute to a person's *nutritional capability*. But there are also complexities —indeed gaps—in such causal relationships. Public action to combat hunger has to take note both of the causal links and of the gaps in those links.

Reasoned decision in this field is hampered not merely by the difficulty of causal analysis, but also by the fact that certain canons of wise policy have acquired such intellectual standing and such widespread acceptance that they are not subjected to adequately critical scrutiny. These canons do, of course, have their rationale, and some of them can serve the purpose of drawing our attention forcefully to the causal links in a simple form. While there is a clear gain in this, there is also the danger of taking too simple a view of these links. A half-truth can be a dangerous source of wisdom.

9.2 Food Self-Sufficiency?

Few objectives of economic policy seem to be as widely valued as that of national self-sufficiency in food. Both India and China, for instance, have placed enormous emphasis on this objective, and they get a great deal of credit and acclaim for that achievement, even though both countries have also met with some failures in their attempt to eliminate hunger and famines.[1] The objective of food self-sufficiency has been forcefully stressed for Africa in the famous Lagos Plan of Action, which set the year 2000 as the target date for its fulfilment. Most African governments seem to take the need for food self-sufficiency as axiomatic, and even proclaim the attainment of this objective as imminent. The endorsement of self-sufficiency as a major goal also surfaces regularly in the publications of influential international organizations such as the Food and Agriculture Organization, the Club du Sahel, and even the World Bank.[2]

It has been argued, with some justice, that the dependence of a country on importing food from abroad for the survival of its own population can be a major source of vulnerability for that country. This is particularly so in, say, war situations. At a very elementary level, the desire to be less dependent on outsiders for the most basic necessity of life is easy to sympathize with.[3]

This does not, however, imply that a country less dependent on importing food from abroad would necessarily be better off in terms of food consumption or nutritional levels than another which is more dependent in this respect. The issue of self-sufficiency is, obviously, quite a distinct one from that of the adequacy of food supply, and nothing is gained by confounding the two concepts. Countries like Japan, Switzerland, or the United Kingdom depend a great deal on importing food from abroad, but their populations do not, to say the least, suffer from food inadequacy, compared with, say, the people of self-sufficient Burma, Uganda, or—for that matter—India. And even within Africa, we have seen in Chapter 8 that some countries (such as Botswana and Cape Verde) have succeeded in considerably enhancing the nutritional security of their population in spite of a poor record in terms of food self-sufficiency. Given the possibility of relying on the international market to acquire food,

---

[1] The comparative experiences of India and China are discussed in Chapter 11. It will be seen that their successes as well as their failures are related to administrative, economic, and political strategies that go well beyond food self-sufficiency.

[2] See e.g. Ross (1983), Please and Amoako (1984), and Food and Agriculture Organization (1986).

[3] Arguments for food self-sufficiency have sometimes sought added strength from the historical observation that many dependent economies lost their food self-sufficiency in the age of imperialism. Lappé and Collins, for instance, have argued: 'Food dependency originated with imperialism . . . Food self-reliance is the cornerstone of genuine self-determination and it is possible for every country in the world' (Lappé and Collins 1980: 139, 145). This historical observation certainly does apply to many countries, and the *possibility* of universal food self-sufficiency given adequate concentration of resources also seems plausible. The question is whether this policy serves the interest of the deprived and hungry population best. Lappé and Collins suggest some reasons why this might be the case. There are arguments on the other side as well, and the decision has to depend on the relative force of these conflicting arguments as they apply to the contemporary world, no matter what the historical explanation for the loss of food self-sufficiency of the pre-imperial world might be.

the issue of self-sufficiency and that of adequacy can and must be firmly distinguished.

One factor that has been responsible for the confounding of the two different ideas of food self-sufficiency and food adequacy is the observed fact that many economies that have become increasingly dependent on food imports from abroad have also developed problems of food inadequacy and hunger within the economy. Sub-Saharan Africa is, of course, an area in which many countries fit this description. Indeed, as was mentioned in Chapter 2, Africa is the only major region in the world in which food output per head has gone down substantially during recent decades. In many African countries the problem of hunger is thought to have greatly intensified in the last decade or two, and food imports have also had to be quite dramatically increased.

This relationship is not, of course, surprising. Indeed, it is easy to see the causal links that operated in the process through which Africa became both more dependent on food supply from abroad, and more prone to persistent hunger as well as recurring famines. If the food production of a country fails to keep pace with domestic demand, its imports from abroad will tend to increase. If, in addition, the failure of food production to keep up with demand is caused by a production crisis, with less output and perhaps less employment, then it will be natural to expect that there will be economic hardship too. If, furthermore, in the country in question substantial sections of the population derive their incomes and entitlements primarily from the production of food, then the proportion of the population affected by this economic hardship would be large. And, if those who are thus affected happen to be normally quite poor, with relatively little economic reserve to fall back on, then the result of that large-scale hardship may well be quite a major increase in hunger and deprivation. Finally, if no social security system of any sort is in operation, then that hunger and deprivation may remain unrelieved.

As it happens, all these conditions are, unfortunately, met for many of the sub-Saharan African countries, and there is, therefore, nothing particularly surprising in the association over time that we observe in Africa between the intensification of the problem of hunger at home and the increased dependence on food imports from abroad. But that temporal relationship is not a reflection of causal inevitability. There are sources of incomes and entitlements other than food production, and an increase in food imports would have gone with no intensification of hunger had these countries been able to expand non-food production and provide the population with enough income to buy imported food. Indeed, this has happened in many countries elsewhere, as was discussed in Chapter 2.

In seeking a remedy for Africa's current problems we have to examine *all* the real prospects—and *only* those—that exist now, rather than trying just to undo the changes that have been associated with its past decline. The extensive debate about 'Africa's food crisis' has often fallen prey to the fallacy involved in the assertion that since Africa's ills are caused by a crisis in food production, the remedy of this situation must lie exactly in countering that historical change. It could, of course, emerge on the basis of an unbiassed assessment of current prospects that giving priority to food production—perhaps even seeking food self-sufficiency—is the right policy to pursue for many African countries. But if that proves to be so, the ground for that conclusion will not be provided just by the observation of the simple historical fact that in these countries food output has declined or food imports have increased. Policy decisions have to be based on assessing the present circumstances and anticipated future ones rather than taking the simplistic form of trying to recreate the past.

9.3 Food Production and Diversification

As we have stressed in Chapter 2, it is important to distinguish clearly between (1) food production as a source of income and entitlement, and (2) food production as a source of supply of the commodity food. While it is certainly true that in terms of observed changes over time there may well be noticeable associations between variations in incomes and entitlements and changes in food production and imports from abroad, a better understanding of the former variations can be found by looking directly at the sources of entitlements and at the changes in the factors that govern them. In that more comprehensive picture, food production and trade will undoubtedly have a role. But given the possibility of earning incomes from activities other than food production, and given the complex relationship between production and distribution, one could not by any means simplify the lesson of all this in the form of a general slogan in favour of giving total priority to food production, irrespective of economic and social circumstances.

In so far as the crisis of food production in Africa relates, at least partly, to climatic uncertainties and to environmental deterioriation, that itself may be a good ground for considering other avenues of productive expansion. The ecological problems must, of course, themselves be encountered, and further the adverse impact of weather variations on economic activity must be reduced (through irrigation or other means). Perhaps there is a good chance that in the long run a much more favourable environment for agricultural expansion in general and increased food production in particular will materialize in Africa. But economic policies should not be determined on the basis of imagining that such a change has already taken place. If it turns out that given the actual climatic uncertainties and ecological problems, food production will remain very vulnerable to fluctuations in the near future, then it will be a mistake to rely too much on that uncertain source of income and entitlements, putting all one's eggs in the same fragile basket. This is an argument for making use of opportunities offered by other types of production, from which benefits may be derivable with greater certainty for the population in question.

Of course, an issue that has to be examined in considering the case for economic diversification is the nature of international markets. The level and variability of rewards associated with economic diversification away from food production will obviously depend *inter alia* on the stability and mode of operation of international markets for food as well as for the products to be exported by the country in question (the proceeds of which would provide the means to buy food from abroad). The experience of fluctuating commodity prices suggests caution, and points to the need to supplement the calculation of average returns by taking note of the variability in those returns.[4] However, the risks involved in self-provisioning (e.g. greater vulnerability to crop failures) have to be given due recognition as well. The important thing, in assessing the merits of alternative intersectoral balances, is to consider carefully the opportunities and uncertainties associated both with self-provisioning as well as with international trade.

The need for diversification has often not been adequately stressed in outlining possible solutions to the problem of hunger in Africa. As a matter of fact, diversification has been a part of the African tradition for a long time (see Chapter 5). In the anxiety to deal with the severe problems encountered in Africa in expanding and sustaining the production of food, we must not lose sight of the benefits that diversification has offered in the past and of the tremendous opportunities it can bring in the future.

As far as the current situation is concerned, it may be pointed out that the role already played by economic diversification in rural Africa tends to be severely underestimated. A considerable variety of economic activities can indeed be found in most African economies in the form of (1) diversification within the agricultural sector (e.g. between food crops and cash crops, or between crops and livestock), (2) combination of agricultural and non-agricultural activities (e.g. crafts and trade) within the rural sector, and (3) use of the extensive links between different rural regions as well as between rural and urban areas (especially through wage employment and remittances). As a study of the economy of rural Sudan notes:

So-called subsistence cultivators should not be seen as consuming only what they produce nor producing only for their own consumption. Even the most humble family participates and anticipates participating in the market place. Peasants expect to sell their labor, gather and sell firewood, make charcoal, migrate seasonally for work, produce cash crops, sell excess livestock and otherwise supplement their incomes.[5]

---

[4] These issues have received a good deal of attention in recent years. The imperfections and manipulations to which international food markets lend themselves have been emphasized by Susan George (1976, 1988) in particular; see also Lappé and Collins (1979, 1980). Others have stressed the potential gains of making use of the possibilities offered by international trade in food. See e.g. the discussions in Reutlinger and Bigman (1981), Valdés (1981), Donaldson (1984), Huddleston (1984), Bigman (1986), Mann and Huddleston (1986), World Bank (1986).

[5] Eldredge and Rydjeski (1988: 3). On the pervasive importance of economic activities other than food and agricultural production in rural Africa, see Heyer (1986), Hill (1986), Kilby and Liedholm (1988), Weber *et al.* (1988), von Braun (1988), and Liedholm and Kilby (1989), among other contributions.

As was discussed in Chapters 5–8, there is also considerable evidence that the rural population in Africa attaches enormous importance to these prospects for diversification. The picture of the typical African rural poor as a self-sufficient peasant exclusively engaged in food production is, for most African countries, little more than a misleading cliché.

These are elementary points, and they are worth mentioning only because the debates on this subject have often been so confusing. Specifically, so far as Africa is concerned, the case for giving an adequate place to the diversification of production in economic analysis and policy is undoubtedly strong, especially in view of the exposure of many parts of that continent to a variety of environmental uncertainties. Simple alleged solutions of the problem of African hunger based on putting all the resources in food or agricultural production, or on raising food prices to boost production incentives,[6] may deliver substantially less than they seem to promise. There is no substitute for a careful assessment of the gains and losses, including the respective uncertainties associated with alternative intersectoral balances.

9.4 Industrialization and the Long Run

The recognition that anti-hunger policies in Africa may profit greatly from diversification and from giving a very solid place to the expansion of non-food production raises the question as to whether industrial production may have an important role to play in that diversified strategy. There is a noticeable reluctance to consider the promise of industrialization in contemplating the future of Africa. Sometimes this reluctance arises from being unduly impressed by the favourable land–population ratio of most African countries compared with, say, Asia. But the choice between industry and agriculture has to be influenced by many considerations of advantages and costs, in addition to the availability of land.

On the positive side, the opportunity for economic growth that is provided by branching out into industries has been well demonstrated by the historical experience of many countries in different parts of the world, and Africa cannot ignore these long-run opportunities. An important consideration is the contribution that industrialization makes to skill formation and to the modernization of the economy and the society. The indirect influence of that technological transformation on agricultural productivity itself cannot, by any means, be ignored.

As it happens, most of the successful and highly productive agricultural economies in the world also happen to be industrialized, and this fact is not a

---

[6] Grand solutions of this kind, especially through price incentives for agricultural expansion, are a favourite theme of several recent World Bank reports. That case is well presented in the *World Development Report 1986*. Despite raising many interesting and diverse policy issues concerning African economic problems, it nevertheless comes down sharply in favour of solving Africa's food problems by 'getting prices right'. On this, see also the exchange between Michael Lipton (1987a, 1988b) and Anandarup Ray (1988a, 1988b).

mere accident. Skill is as important an input for agricultural production as land, and diversification of production helps the formation of skill. The favourable nature of the land–population ratio has, rightly, not been seen as a good ground for eschewing industrial production in Australia, Canada, or the United States. Dismissing that economic alternative for Africa on the grounds of its high land–population ratio would reflect, at the very least, some economic short-sightedness.

That is not to deny that industrialization is a long-run process, and that in the immediate future no great radical transformation can be brought about in Africa through the pursuit of industries. But the process of industrialization, if it is to be pursued, has to be started at some stage, for it to yield fruit in the future. Also, as the experience of many developing countries (e.g., the fast-growing economies of East Asia but also many others) has shown, rapid progress can be made by new entrants in some branches of industry, yielding benefits without much delay. The fact that some unassessed and badly planned efforts in the industrial direction have come to grief in Africa is not in itself an argument for closing the books in that field. The issue of industrialization has to be squarely faced sooner or later.[7]

To recognize the need for diversification is not, of course, to deny the importance of expanding food production. Expansion of agriculture in general and of food production in particular will undoubtedly be a major instrument in combating hunger in sub-Saharan Africa. Various strategic aspects of enhancing food production in sub-Saharan Africa have received expert attention and scrutiny in recent years, and there are many lessons to be learned from economic reasoning as well as from the empirical observation of actual experiences.[8] Given the number of people who derive their entitlements from food production in Africa, and given the limited speed at which this dependence can be reduced, enhancing food production in Africa has to be one of the principal strategies to combat hunger in that continent.

If we are attaching special importance to the case for considering production other than that of food, and emphasizing the need for diversification, the reason for that does not lie in any belief that African food production is unimportant in that diversified approach. Quite the contrary. It is rather that the needs of expanding food production in Africa are more easily—and more often—acknowledged than some of the other components of anti-hunger strategy. It is a question of trying to get the right balance of emphases and of making sure that less obvious but important issues are not ignored in an undue concentration on a partial picture.

[7] On the case for less pessimism on the prospects for industrialization in Africa and some relevant empirical studies, see Riddell et al. (1989) and the literature cited there.

[8] See e.g. Eicher (1986b, 1988a), Food and Agriculture Organisation (1986), and Mellor, Delgado and Blackie (1987). See also World Bank (1981, 1984b, 1986), Berry (1984), Eicher and Staatz (1984), Rose (1985), IDS Bulletin (1985), Commins, Lofchie and Payne (1986), Berg and Whitaker (1986), Idachaba (1986), Swaminathan (1986), Wangwe (1986), Lipton (1987a), Platteau (1988a) and the December 1984 issue of *African Studies Review*.

9.5   Cash Crops: Problems and Opportunities

There are many ways in which diversification can be achieved. Diversification within the rural economy, which itself can take many forms, is particularly important to consider. The part that can be played in this process by the so-called 'cash crops' deserves special examination if only because of the controversies that have surrounded this subject.[9]

Since cash crops are agricultural crops, they are, of course, exposed to climatic uncertainties similar to those affecting food crops. They also involve —as has often been stressed—additional vulnerability arising from greater dependence on markets. Cash crops have to be sold and the proceeds then used in buying food, and the food entitlements thus generated can be vulnerable to fluctuations in the markets for food as well as those for cash crops. But it is also true that cash crops are often highly remunerative in comparison with food crops, and if the income thus generated can be marshalled to support and secure the livelihood of the rural population, there need be no general reason to fear their expansion.

The promotion of cash crops in developing countries has, however, come under severe attack in recent years, and it has even been held responsible for a great deal of hunger in the modern world.[10] It is easy to see the need for caution regarding excessive reliance on cash crops. However, the evidence does not always support an unqualified censure of extensive use of cash crops. For instance, cash crop growers have often—though not invariably—been found to fare significantly better than subsistence farmers during famines.[11] And a number of countries have met with commendable success in using the economic opportunities provided by the cultivation of cash crops to enhance the nutritional status of the population.[12] A balanced assessment of the economic impact of cash crops has to account for these experiences as well as for the darker side of this complex picture.

---

[9] The notion of 'cash crops' is, in fact, rather complex, and can be confusing. This notion has been variously used to designate a number of distinct categories such as (1) crops which are exported instead of being consumed in the country where they are grown; (2) crops which are exchanged for cash by the people who grow them, instead of being consumed directly; (3) non-food crops as opposed to food crops. These alternative definitions overlap but do not coincide, and they would clearly lead to different crop classifications. Crops like potatoes or rice, for instance, are mainly subsistence crops in some countries, objects of local exchange in others, export crops in still others, and in many countries they are in fact a combination of all of these. We need not sort out these definitional problems here, but the potential difficulties of making precise sense of the notion of cash crops as an economic category is useful to bear in mind, especially in the context of blanket arguments for their condemnation or promotion.

[10] It is interesting that pastoralism, which from an economic point of view can be regarded as having much the same features as growing cash crops (including the use of land to produce something that is later exchanged for food), has not been viewed with nearly the same suspicion as 'cash crops'.

[11] For some examples of this in India and in Africa, see Oughton (1982), Derrick (1984), Herlehy (1984), Schmidt-Wulffen (1985), and de Waal (1987).

[12] Costa Rica, Cuba, Malaysia, Mauritius, and the state of Kerala in India are a few among many examples. The experiences of some of these economies will be discussed in later chapters.

A common argument implicitly or explicitly underlying the thesis that cash crops are responsible for exacerbating hunger in the modern world is that cash crops displace food crops and therefore lead to a reduction in the availability of food. This apparently appealing argument has in fact gained enormous popularity, and there is admittedly something contrary in the suggestion that a country in which masses of people are hungry could reasonably divert a large part of its productive agricultural resources away from growing food. However, as we have already seen, such simple availability-centred arguments can be misleading in analysing the problem of food entitlement. If cash crops provide greater means of acquiring food, then there is no reason why that avenue should be rejected in favour of sticking to growing only food crops even when the latter option provides comparatively meagre (or riskier) entitlements to food. To take for granted that increasing the production of cash crops could not bring in more food for the households is to beg the central question.

A more discerning case against cash crops would have to be based on the argument that their expansion undermines the entitlements of vulnerable groups, directly or indirectly.[13] But, we have to ask, why should people choose to produce cash crops rather than food crops if the expansion of cash crops makes them more vulnerable to hunger? Broadly speaking, the answer to this question can take four different forms: (1) Households are driven to adopt cash crops against their own interests, through coercion or delusion. (2) Economic and social changes, of which expansion of cash crops is an integral part, lead to impoverishment and vulnerability, even though in these reduced circumstances an individual household may gain from growing cash crops. (3) Some household members adopt cash crops to the detriment of *other members* of the household. (4) The adoption of cash crops by some households makes them rich at the cost of undermining the entitlements of *other households*. We examine each of these possibilities in turn.

It has been pointed out that peasants are often forced or persuaded to grow cash crops against their real interest, say by multinationals or predatory governments. In particular, agri-business interests have been accused of driving poor peasants off the land and reducing them to the status of wage labourers. Such things undoubtedly occur, but it is hard to explain the widespread adoption of cash crops primarily in these terms.[14] While the need to resist abuse and malpractice is by no means negligible (and not just in the context of cash crops), the reason for concern about cash crops goes much beyond these gross transgressions.

---

[13] For insightful analyses of various arguments along these lines, see Jalée (1965), Amin (1974, 1975), Meillassoux (1974), Raynaut (1977), Fleuret and Fleuret (1980), Franke and Chasin (1980), George (1984), Twose (1984), Bennett (1987), among others.

[14] On the variety of motivations and consequences linked to the expansion of cash crops in different parts of the world, see De Wilde (1984), Pinstrup-Andersen (1985a), von Braun and Kennedy (1986, 1987), Kennedy and Cogill (1987), Maxwell and Fernando (1987), Longhurst (1988), von Braun et al. (1989), and the special issue of *IDS Bulletin* on 'Cash Crops in Developing Countries' (Volume 19, Number 2, 1988).

In the second line of argument, the greater vulnerability of many sections of the rural African population in recent decades has been attributed—at least partly—to a shift in the pattern of economic production and activity towards greater 'commoditization', of which the expansion of cash crops is an integral part. This has involved, it has been argued, greater reliance on the sale of marketable commodities and the purchase of food on the market, with greater exposure to the uncertainties of exchange, sharper economic inequalities, and also important changes in the nature of social bonds within the rural community.[15]

These are important issues, and more can be said on each side. But the complex economic and social relationships involved in the economic changes with which the expansion of cash crops is associated must not be reduced to a simple question of shifts only in cropping patterns. The right variables to look at in this context are the relations of production and the nature of exchange, rather than the type of crop as such.

When commercialization of agriculture in the form of expanding cash crops goes hand in hand with more market-based uncertainty and exacerbates inequalities in the ownership of the means of production, the argument that cash crops are on the average and in total more remunerative than food crops can be seriously undermined. But the possible dangers of this process also have to be assessed against the sometimes enormous potential gains that can be made from a widening of economic opportunities through greater access to market exchange.

There is a certain amount of political interest in all this, since opposition to changes involving cash crops has sometimes come from Marxian analysts. It may be noted in this context that among the countries that have made good use of the opportunities provided by cash crop cultivation to promote the entitlements of vulnerable groups are several socialist ones, including Cuba and Nicaragua.[16]

Ultimately it is a matter of seeing the economic process as a whole, of which the growth of cash crops may be a part. If the development of cash crop production is associated with growing concentration of land, more unequal income distribution, uncertainty of wage employment, and insecurity of earnings, then that is indeed an unfavourable change, but it is not the fact of cash crop production as such that makes it so. The same cash crops can be

[15] See particularly Amin (1974, 1975), Comité Information Sahel (1974), Meillassoux (1974), Copans et al. (1975), Dalby et al. (1977), Raynaut (1977), Watts (1983, 1984), and Bryceson (1984).

[16] Marx, who was aware of the potentialities of market exchange (as well as of the related dangers), rightly saw economic exploitation as arising primarily from inequalities in ownership rather than from exchange per se, and cautioned against the mistake of focusing unduly on the latter: 'The relation of capitalist and wage labourer . . . has its foundation in the social character of production, not in the mode of exchange . . . It is, however, quite in keeping with the bourgeois horizon, everyone being engrossed in the transaction of shady business, not to see in the character of the mode of production the basis of the mode of exchange corresponding to it, but vice versa' (Marx 1893: 120). For an analysis of Lenin's views on these and related matters, see Desai (1976).

associated with a more favourable development of earnings and entitlements in a different overall economic situation without the dispossession and vulnerability associated with the first case. The role of cash crops has to be assessed in the fuller economic context.

The third problem in the list of four mentioned earlier relates to intrafamily divisions. Cash crops, it has been argued, are typically grown by men, and benefit men to the relative or even absolute detriment of women. Sometimes this view has taken the form of asserting that cash crops are 'male' crops whereas food crops are 'female' crops, but there is not much empirical evidence to support this overpowerful generalization.[17] On the other hand, it is plausible enough that the adoption or expansion of cash crops can in many circumstances intensify conflicts of interest within households. These could take the form of men having a privileged access to the new opportunities provided by cash crops (e.g. because of their greater mobility), or enjoying a greater control over household resources as a result of the enhanced role of cash in the household economy.

These considerations can be important, but it must be recognized that the complex changes in gender relations taking place along with a process of expansion in economic opportunities cannot be reduced to the simple format of a dilemma between food crops and cash crops. We have to look at the nature of labour markets, the access of women and men to employment opportunities, the gender features in land ownership, and the social traditions in the intrafamily division of consumption and work.

As Megan Vaughan emphasizes in her study of gender and famine in Malawi, 'the mere existence of a cash-cropping economy . . . does not define the economic role and status of women, and needs to be seen as acting together with a number of other variables, the most crucial being the availability of land and the degree of control over it exercised by women'.[18] Once again, policy decisions call for attention being paid to specific empirical features of the choices involved, and to the economic and social circumstances that condition the influence of cash crops on the entitlements of different groups.

The fourth issue mentioned earlier involves the potential conflict of interest between cash crop growers and non-growers. It is easy to see that the large-scale adoption of cash crops by some households can, in some circumstances, pose an important threat to the entitlements of other—possibly more

---

[17] It is easy to find examples of rural economies in Africa where the reverse pattern corresponds more closely to the truth, with women being more involved in cash crop cultivation than men. For some illustrations, involving countries as diverse as Senegal, Zambia, and Sierra Leone, see e.g. Chastanet (1983), World Health Organization (1986: 47), and Richards (1986: 105). For a general discussion of the ambiguities and pitfalls involved in discriminating between cash crops and food crops along gender lines, see Whitehead (1986).

[18] Vaughan (1987: 144). It is possible to find examples of socio-economic settings in which the expansion of cash crops appears to have *improved* rather than undermined the bargaining position of women. In her anthropological study of cocoa-farming in Ghana, for instance, Polly Hill argues that, for women, 'cocoa-farming ownership was a new and most welcome form of insurance against poverty arising from divorce' (Hill 1975: 131).

vulnerable—groups. For instance, in economies where many or most of the poor are landless labourers, an increase in food prices resulting from a switch towards cash crops on the part of farmers could clearly lead to a deterioration of the entitlements of the most vulnerable groups. Other possible forms of conflicts have been pointed out, such as conflicts arising from the damaging environmental effects of some cash crops,[19] or conflicts between pastoralists and cash crop growers who put under cultivation fallow land previously available for grazing animals.[20]

At the same time, it is important to recognize that the influence of cash crops on the entitlements of those who are not growing them can be positive as well as negative. Many cash crops, for instance, are enormously more labour-intensive than most food crops, and in an economy where many of the poor are wage labourers this factor could count heavily in favour of promoting cash crops.[21] Once again, there is no escape from analysing the entitlement process as a whole rather than relying on instant wisdom from simple slogans in favour of or against cash crops.

It is hardly surprising that there can be no invariant answer to the question as to whether cash crops help or hinder the battle against hunger. Indeed, in seeking straightforward and rigid links between the capabilities enjoyed by people (e.g. nutritional capabilities) and the production of particular commodities in the economy (specifically food crops), there is a danger of falling prey to a particular version of 'commodity fetishism' (discussed in the first part of this book).

In many contexts, the production of cash crops is likely to deserve an important place within a diversified strategy for the promotion of food entitlements in Africa. This recognition, which relates particularly to the distinction between food production and food entitlement and which connects up with the economic case for diversification, does not in any way overlook the possibility that, in some circumstances, the growing of cash crops can have an adverse effect on the ability of many people to establish entitlements over food.[22]

---

[19] In Western India, the rapid expansion of sugarcane cultivation by large farmers owning irrigated land, and encouraged by wealthy 'sugar barons', has been an object of considerable and often justified criticism (see e.g. Anon. 1985). The expansion of eucalyptus cultivation in India has also been repeatedly denounced as a clear case of anti-social private gains. On the damaging environmental effects of cash crops in the Sahel, see Franke and Chasin (1980).

[20] For examples of this type of conflict and their contribution to the vulnerability of pastoralists in Ethiopia and the Sudan, see Sen (1981a: Chapters 7 and 8), and the literature cited there.

[21] It has been estimated that in Kenya, where wage labour is a very important source of livelihood for the poor, a crop such as tea requires more than four times as much labour per hectare as maize, and more than eight times as much as wheat (Mwangi, 1986). A switch from cash crops (in this case jute) to less labour-intensive food crops as a result of price changes is alleged to have caused starvation among agricultural labourers in some parts of Assam in India in 1975 (Prabhakar 1975).

[22] To dispute that cash crops must be vigorously and systematically discouraged is not to deny that, in many countries, they may have been *excessively encouraged*, especially during the colonial period.

9.6 From Food Entitlements to Nutritional Capabilities

So far in this chapter we have discussed the related issues of self-sufficiency, food production and economic diversification in terms of the ability of alternative policy options to improve food entitlements. At this stage it is important to link up the question of entitlement guarantees with the import-ance of non-food items in ensuring the capability to be nourished, as well as other capabilities closely associated with nourishment, e.g. avoiding escapable morbidity and mortality. As we argued earlier (in Chapters 1 and 3), it is a mistake to view hunger in terms of food deprivation only. This is not merely because there are significant interindividual and intraindividual variations in food requirements for nutritional achievement. But also, the capability to be nourished depends crucially on other characteristics of a person that are influenced by such non-food factors as medical attention, health services, basic education, sanitary arrangements, provision of clean water, eradication of infectious epidemics, and so on. If we compare different countries, or different regions within a country, we may find considerable dissonance between the ranking of food intakes and the ranking of nutritional achievements.

The recognition of this point does not, of course, imply that we must not attach any importance to the deficiency of food intakes as such, and concen-trate only on the achieved qualities of nourishment. Eating is a major aspect of living, and the physical and psychological aspects of hunger (related directly to food intake) must command our attention.[23] Avoiding hunger, in the most elementary sense of the term, is certainly one part of the bigger programme of combating hunger in the broader sense.

The importance of food is obviously crucial in the prevention of hunger in the narrow sense, but the fact remains that the prevention of hunger in the broader sense, including nutritional deprivation, depends substantially also on an adequate access to vital non-food items. For example, in seeking an explanation of the contrast between the Sri Lankan life expectancy figure of 70 years at birth and the South African average of 55 years, we would get little help from comparing the calorie consumption levels in Sri Lanka and South Africa, viz. 2,385 calories and 2,979 calories respectively (in 1985).[24] Even if the inequalities in the respective distributions of calories were taken into account, the contrast would remain. The difference lies to a great extent in the fact that the health services, education and other features of the social environment of

---

[23] See Chapter 3. We also do know that, in personal consumption behaviour, a strong emphasis is placed on the maintenance of food intake and expenditure, in spite of possible short-run fluctuations in total income or total expenditure. See particularly Anand and Harris (1986, 1987). By showing the relative stability of food expenditure (in comparison with income and total consumption expenditure), and by placing the analysis of consumer behaviour in that perspective, Anand and Harris have argued for the use of food expenditure, even in the short run, as a better guide to long-run opulence than the more traditional variables used for this purpose, such as current income or expenditure.

[24] World Development Report 1987, Tables 1 and 30.

Sri Lanka are far more broadly distributed and equitable than those of South Africa.[25]

It is in the uneven delivery of crucial non-food items that the causation of some of the sharpest contrasts in the qualities of life of different countries and communities lie. The divergence, for example, between Sri Lanka with 93 per cent of the population having access to health services and Bhutan with a corresponding figure of 19 per cent, can make an extraordinary difference to the nature of the life that people can lead. One aspect of that is reflected in the widely different levels of life expectation at birth in the two countries, viz. 70 years for Sri Lanka and 44 years for Bhutan (contrasting with calorie consumption figures of 2,385 and 2,572 respectively).[26]

This broadening of our concern from food entitlements to more general entitlements (including crucial non-food items as well as food) has many significant consequences. One of them, which is of central importance in policy-making, relates to the fact that while food is typically purchased in a market (even when influenced by subsidies, rationing, etc.), provisions for medical, educational, and related facilities are more often—for good reasons —made directly by public institutions. In such matters as the operation of general health services, the provision of clean water, the elimination of infectious epidemics, and so on, the role of the state is typically even more direct and immediate. Entitlement guarantees in the context of these non-food items have to be seen mainly in terms of public planning rather than just the enhancement of purchasing power in the market. These issues will be taken up further in the analysis to follow.

In this chapter we have argued for broadening our attention respectively (1) from food self-sufficiency to food adequacy, (2) from food adequacy to food entitlements, and (3) from food entitlements to nutritional and related capabilities (involving *inter alia* entitlements to crucial non-food items). There are important links between these variables, but the links depend significantly on other variables of which note has to be taken. When we study the strategy of public action against endemic undernourishment and deprivation, we shall have to come to grips with the plurality of influences affecting nutritional capabilities and achievements.

---

[25] On Sri Lanka's record in public health, educational expansion and related matters, see Chapter 12 below. On South Africa, see Wilson and Ramphele (1989).

[26] *World Development Report 1987*, Tables 1 and 30, and UNICEF (1987*a*), Table 3.

10

Economic Growth and Public Support

10.1 Incomes and Achievements

The mistake involved in analysing hunger just in terms of food output and availability has been discussed extensively in earlier chapters of this book. The main issue concerns the power of vulnerable groups to command food and other essentials, rather than just the physical availability of commodities. While focusing on entitlements rather than on what is available has many complex implications (we have tried to analyse some of them and to draw lessons for policy), the basic contrast between command and availability is fairly straightforward.

Sometimes the position that hunger is essentially due to a *command* failure not necessarily caused by an output failure is summarized in the form of the simple slogan 'hunger is caused by a lack of income, not of food supply'. Extending this line of straightforward analysis, it is often argued that the real problem lies in the shortage of purchasing power, rather than of anything else.

That conclusion has some obvious sense, but as a causal theory it is rather misleading. This is so not merely because income is itself a derived variable which depends on ownership and exchange and therefore provides a rather poor focal point for the analysis of entitlement failures. But no less importantly, it is also the case that many essential commodities are not bought and sold in the market in the usual way, and conventional estimates of real income may not give us a good idea of the command over a number of inputs which, as we have seen, can play a crucial role in the removal of hunger, such as educational services, health care, clean water, or protection from infectious epidemics. The importance of these non-food commodities and facilities for nutrition and health was discussed earlier (in Chapters 3 and 9). Since their use may have a major impact on the nutritional status and health of a population, and since they are often provided directly through public delivery, the lacuna involved in concentrating on purchasing power is quite limiting. Income is a rather dubious indicator of the opportunity of being well nourished and having nutrition-related capabilities.

This is one reason, among others, why the association between Gross National Product per capita, on the one hand, and health, nutrition, morbidity, and mortality, on the other, is far from simple. In Table 10.1, we present some relevant figures for five selected countries to illustrate the point. South Africa, with nearly six times the GNP per head of China and Sri Lanka, has a

Table 10.1 Average opulence and survival achievement: selected intercountry comparisons, 1985

Country	GNP per head (dollars)	Infant mortality rate (per 1,000)	Expectation of life at birth (years)
China	310	35	69
Sri Lanka	380	36	70
Brazil	1,640	67	65
South Africa	2,010	78	55
Oman	6,730	109	54

Source: World Development Report 1987, Tables 1 and 29.

life expectancy of only 55 years, compared with 69 and 70 years respectively for the two poorer countries.[1] Similarly Brazil, with many times the income per head of China and Sri Lanka, has nevertheless lower life expectancy than the latter. Oman, with about 20 times the GNP per head of China or Sri Lanka, offers a life expectancy of only 54 years at birth.

The contrast of infant mortality rates brings out the same dissonance between GNP per head and the capability to survive premature death. Brazil, Oman, and South Africa, despite their much greater opulence, have enormously higher infant mortality rates than China and Sri Lanka.

There are, in fact, two distinct—and in principle separable—causes underlying the dissonance between GNP and achievements of quality of life. First, the GNP gives a measure of the aggregate opulence of the economy, and the translation of this into the pattern of individual prosperity would depend also on the distribution of income over the population.[2] Second, as we have seen, the capabilities enjoyed by people depend on many factors other than the command over commodities which can be purchased in the market. Among such factors, public provisions made by the state for health, education, sanitation, etc., are especially important.

While we must recognize this dissonance, there is no reason to dismiss GNP altogether.[3] There are, in fact, good grounds for expecting a positive general

[1] The figure of 69 years for China appearing in the World Development Reports may be a bit of an overestimate. On this see Chapter 11. There have been abrupt and unexplained upward revisions of the reported life expectancy for South Africa in the later World Development Reports.

[2] It is worth noting that just as we may be concerned with the distribution of GNP in addition to its mean value per capita, similarly also in the case of such indicators as life expectancy, there is the need to distinguish between their mean values and their patterns of distribution over the population.

[3] Cf. Robert Kennedy's remark: GNP 'measures everything, in short, except that which makes life worthwhile.' (Statement made by Robert Kennedy at the University of Kansas during his presidential campaign in 1968; cited in Dowd 1987.)

association between GNP and nutrition-related capabilities. This is partly because the increased incomes associated with greater general affluence do indeed offer the opportunity to buy a number of commodities that are *inter alia* crucially important for nutrition-related capabilities, the most notable of which is, of course, food itself. But, in addition, a higher GNP per capita enlarges the material base for public support in areas such as health care and education, and generally facilitates the provision of social security to the more vulnerable sections of the community.

The governments of some of the oil-rich countries, for example, have been able to use their unusual and relatively recent opulence to make widespread public provisions for their citizens, and this is one of the reasons why life expectancy at birth and similar indicators have, in recent decades, moved to comparatively high figures in countries such as Kuwait and United Arab Emirates (e.g. life expectancies above 70 years). The examples of these countries are admittedly rather exceptional, but the general principle that an expanded basis for public support *can be* one of the fruits of economic growth applies to other countries too. There are also many cases where average opulence has reached a high level, but public support has been comprehensively neglected, with correspondingly low levels of nutritional and related achievements.

At the risk of oversimplifying the problem, it can be argued that a high level of GNP per head provides an *opportunity* for improving nutrition and other basic capabilities, but that opportunity may or may not be seized. In the process of transforming this opportunity into a tangible achievement, public support in various forms (and influencing both the distribution of income and the relationship between income and basic capabilities) often plays a crucial role.

Improvements in the quality of life are sometimes seen simply as the result of increases in overall affluence *per se*, when in fact the expansion of public support may have been the crucial intermediator. Common perceptions of the historical experience of Western countries in enhancing life expectancy often involve this misleading belief in the power of simple opulence *per se* (e.g. high GNP per head). In fact, the idea that the rich countries have achieved high levels of basic capabilities simply because they are rich is, to say the least, an oversimplification. A good illustration of this point is provided by the history of longevity expansion in Britain during this century.

Table 10.2 presents the *increase* in life expectancy at birth in England and Wales in each of the first six decades of this century (starting with a life expectancy figure no higher than that of most developing countries today). Note that while the increase in life expectancy has been between one to four years in each decade, there were two decades in which the increase was remarkably greater (around seven years approximately). These were the decades of the two world wars, with dramatic increases in many forms of public support including public employment, food rationing and health care

Table 10.2 Longevity expansion in England and Wales

Decade	Increase in life expectancy per decade (years)	
	Male	Female
1901–11	4.1	4.0
1911–21	6.6	6.5
1921–31	2.3	2.4
1931–40	1.2	1.5
1940–51	6.5	7.0
1951–60	2.4	3.2

Source: Based on data presented in Preston, Keyfitz, and Schoen (1972: 240–71). See also Winter (1986) and Sen (1987e).

provisions.[4] The decade of the 1940s, which recorded the highest increase in British life expectancy during the century, witnessed an enormous expansion of public employment, extensive and equitable food rationing, and the birth of the National Health Service (introduced just after the war).

The nature of these experiences illustrates both the importance of the distinction between commodity availability and functioning achievement (discussed earlier), and the role that social intervention and public support played in the expansion of a very basic capability in the history of the first industrial nation.[5]

---

[4] See Winter (1986) for an illuminating analysis of the effects of the First World War on public distribution and public involvement, and their impact on living conditions in Britain. The experience of the Second World War is discussed in great detail by Titmuss (1950: Chapter 25), who examines the evidence indicating a strong relationship between the surprisingly good health conditions of the British population during the war (including a rapid improvement of the health status of children) and the extensive reach of public support measures in that period. As Titmuss put it, 'by the end of the Second World War the Government had, through the agency of newly established or existing services, assumed and developed a measure of direct concern for the health and well-being of the population which, by contrast with the role of Government in the nineteen-thirties, was little short of remarkable' (p. 506). According to Titmuss, the most influential part of social policy during the war related to employment provision and food rationing. This conclusion is strongly corroborated by Hammond's detailed study of the 'revolution in the attitude of the British State towards the feeding of its citizens' which took place after 1941 (Hammond 1951). On these issues, see also Marrack (1947), McKeown and Lowe (1966: 131–4), McNeill (1976: 286–7), Szreter (1988).

[5] It is of some interest to note that in the case of Japan, too, the rate of expansion of longevity was substantially higher during the period covering the Second World War and immediately after (see the figures presented in Preston *et al.* 1972, as well as the further discussion in Drèze and Sen 1988). This was also a period of rapid expansion of public support, and it is plausible that, as in the case of Britain, this expansion was a crucial factor in the reduction of mortality rates especially after the war. We are grateful to Akiko Hashimoto for helpful discussions on the empirical evidence related to this observation. See also Taeuber (1958), Shigematsu and Yanagawa (1985) and Morio and Takahashi (1986).

10.2 Alternative Strategies: Growth-Mediated Security and Support-Led Security

Given the distinct, though interconnected, roles played by overall opulence and public activism in enhancing capabilities, it is possible in principle to distinguish two contrasting approaches to the removal of precarious living conditions. One approach is to promote economic growth and take the best possible advantage of the potentialities released by greater general affluence, including not only an expansion of private incomes but also an improved basis for public support. This may be called the strategy of 'growth-mediated security'. Another alternative is to resort *directly* to wide-ranging public support in domains such as employment provision, income redistribution, health care, education, and social assistance in order to remove destitution without waiting for a transformation in the level of general affluence. Here success may have to be based on a discriminating use of national resources, the efficiency of public services, a redistributive bias in their delivery. This may be called the strategy of 'support-led security'.

The possibility of success through either approach is credible enough in principle. The real question is whether in practice they can be utilized in the way we might expect in theory. There have been, in fact, serious detractors questioning the viability of each of these two strategies. Some have questioned the soundness of a strategy which gives precedence to public support over growth on grounds of the allegedly extravagant nature of generous public provisions for a poor economy. They have argued that deflecting resources to social services from investment reduces economic growth and adversely affects future opportunities.[6] State provisioning as such has also been regarded, at times, with considerable suspicion, and it has in fact become a target of relentless criticism in the contemporary intellectual atmosphere of great faith in 'the market'.

Others have questioned the soundness of a strategy of growth-mediated security on the grounds that high growth is often accompanied by increased inequality in the distribution of incomes, so that the people in greatest need of capability enhancement may end up benefiting least (if at all) from the general process of economic expansion. It has also been argued that the potential opportunity for expanded public provisioning may not be typically seized by a growth-oriented government, because of its preoccupation with the expansion of material opulence rather than with the basic quality of human life. It is the slowness or absence of the so-called 'trickle down' (in itself not an electrifying prospect) that makes growth an unreliable means of general advance of a community.

---

[6] This line of reasoning has also been influential in bringing about drastic reductions in social services as part of 'adjustment programmes' in developing countries faced with mounting debts and trade imbalances. On the adverse social impact of such cut-backs, see Jolly and Cornia (1984), Cornia *et al.* (1987) Bell and Reich (1988), and the WIDER studies by Nora Lustig and others in Jayawardena (forthcoming).

Table 10.3 Proportionate reduction in U5MR (1960–1985): the top ten countries[a]

Country	Percentage reduction in U5MR	Percentage growth rate of GNP/capita		GNP per head (US dollars)	Level of U5MR
	(1960–85)	(1960–82)[b]	(1965–85)	(1985)	(1985)
Hong Kong	83	7.0	6.1	6,230	11
Chile	82	0.6	−0.2	1,430	26
UAE	82	−0.7	n/a	19,270	43
Costa Rica	81	2.8	1.4	1,300	23
Kuwait	80	−0.1	−0.3	14,480	25
Cuba	78	n/a	n/a	n/a	19
Singapore	76	7.4	7.6	7,420	12
China	75	5.0	4.8	310	50
Jamaica	72	0.7	−0.7	940	25
South Korea	71	6.6	6.6	2,150	35

[a] Excluded from the comparison are the countries of Eastern and Western Europe, Japan, New Zealand, Australia, USA, USSR, and Canada.

[b] In this column, figures in italics are for a period not exactly corresponding to 1960–82, due to non-availability of data for the early 1960s (see *World Development Report 1984*, Table 1).

Source: UNICEF (1987a), Table 1; *World Development Report* (1984, 1987), Table 1.

What have the actual experiences been in different countries of the world? While intercountry comparisons of performance are often quite unreliable and misleading, they sometimes do provide at least a tentative basis for noting certain elementary relationships and possibilities. We shall examine here in some detail one particular set of intercountry comparisons of performance, based on the observed reduction in infant and child mortality between 1960 and 1985 in different parts of the world. Of course, infant and child mortality can by no means be interpreted as a summary index of the quality of life as a whole, or even of the nutritional status of the population, and the performance of various countries in areas related to nutrition will call for further investigation later on in this book. However, as a starting-point for our enquiry the incidence of mortality among infants and children in different countries is a useful indicator to examine.

An internationally comparable set of estimates of the 'under-5 mortality rate' (hereafter U5MR) has been constructed recently by UNICEF, and provides a useful basis for a comparative assessment of performance.[7] From the information provided about under-5 mortality rates in 1960 and 1985, it is possible to calculate the percentage reduction of the U5MR in different countries over these 25 years. The ten best performers according to this

[7] The nature of the U5MR index is explained in UNICEF (1987a: 126). The information on U5MR for 130 countries, on which our analysis is based, appears in Table 1 of the same publication. In the remainder of this chapter, the term 'developing countries' will be used to refer to the hundred countries left in that table after excluding the countries of Western and Eastern Europe, North America, Japan, New Zealand, Australia and the USSR.

criterion, among the developing countries, are the following (in decreasing order of performance): Hong Kong, Chile, United Arab Emirates, Costa Rica, Kuwait, Cuba, Singapore, China, Jamaica, and South Korea.[8] The actual figures are presented in Table 10.3.[9]

On the basis of the information contained in Table 10.3, and of what is known about the experiences of the countries involved, it is possible to divide these ten countries into two distinct groups. Growth-mediated security has clearly been an important part of the experiences of Hong Kong, Singapore, and South Korea. In fact, it is interesting to note that these three countries were among the five *fastest* growing economies in the world during the period under consideration, in terms of the growth rate of real GNP per capita.[10] The United Arab Emirates and Kuwait can also be put broadly in the same group, even though in this period their growth rates of GNP per capita, as it is standardly measured, are not high. The phenomenal increase in the incomes of these two countries that has in fact taken place as a result of changes in international prices (in this case involving oil) fails to be captured by the growth rate of the real *quantity-index* of GNP per capita.[11] The fact is that both these countries have become very rich over this period, and their remarkable

---

[8] In fact, North Korea was also in our preliminary list of countries selected for highest reduction in U5MR. However, it was removed from the list because it turns out that the figures of U5MR for North Korea published by UNICEF were not obtained independently but were simply *assumed* to be the same as those applying to South Korea. Note also that the recorded reduction in U5MR for the period 1960–85 in China would be completely misleading if the base-level mortality rate actually corresponded to 1960, when famine was raging and mortality had shot up sharply (see Chapter 11). However, the 1960 figure given in UNICEF (1987a) is clearly *not* one based on the famine years, and rather appears to be based on an extrapolation from pre-famine figures (see the infant mortality data in Piazza 1986, and Jamison and Piazza 1987).

[9] It could be argued that a given percentage reduction in U5MR between 1960 and 1985 provides different indications about a country's 'performance' in mortality reduction depending on the *initial* level of U5MR in 1960. However, when percentage reductions in U5MR over this period are examined after 'controlling' for these initial levels (this is done by looking at the residuals of a regression of the 1985 U5MR levels on the 1960 levels, both in logarithmic form), the identification of the best performers is not substantially affected. In fact, by this alternative criterion *all* the 'top ten' countries appearing in Table 10.3 still outperform *all* other developing countries except three (viz. Jordan, Saudi Arabia, and Syria).

[10] See *World Development Report 1987*, Table 1. This statement refers to the period 1965–85 (rather than 1960–85), the only one for which the figures are presented in that report. For the period 1960–82, however, these three countries are also among the five fastest growing economies in the world (see *World Development Report 1984*, Table 1).

[11] This problem is explicitly mentioned in the Technical Notes accompanying the *World Development Reports*, with special reference to oil-producing countries (see e.g. *World Development Report 1984*, p. 275). In the case of these countries, the use of, say, a Consumer Price Index to deflate nominal GDP figures (instead of the GDP deflator applied in the *World Development Report* figures) gives a much fairer idea of the massive increase in purchasing power experienced by their populations in recent decades. For instance, using the Consumer Price Index published in the *Annual Statistical Abstract of Kuwait* as a deflator, the annual growth rate of real GDP in Kuwait after 1973 (the starting year of this price index series) is of the order of 11% until the early 1980s (after which it decelerates due to a sharp reduction in oil prices). The annual growth rate of real consumption expenditure (public and private) over the 1973–81 period is even higher, of the order of 14% (all figures have been calculated from the 1970, 1982, and 1987 issues of the *Annual Statistical Abstract of Kuwait*).

success in reducing under-5 mortality rates has been much helped by their —relatively new—opulence. Thus, a half of the ten highest performers in terms of percentage reduction of under-5 mortality rate seem to have resorted to a strategy of growth-mediated security, of one sort or another.

On the other hand, the other five countries (viz. Chile, Costa Rica, Cuba, China, Jamaica) have had quite different experiences. Their growth rates have been comparatively low. Moreover, as we shall discuss later in this chapter, these countries stand out sharply in having achieved far lower mortality rates than most other countries at a comparable income level. The basis of their success does not seem to rest primarily in rapid income growth, and suggests the possibility of support-led security.[12]

Before we move on, two points must be stressed. First, the outstanding record of these five countries can by no means be dismissed as a statistical artefact. The demographic and health records of *each* of these countries have, in fact, attracted widespread attention on their own, and the statistical evidence establishing their record has been extensively scrutinized in each case.[13] As will be discussed later, there is also strong independent evidence (e.g. in the form of anthropometric data and morbidity indicators) of very rapid nutritional improvement in these five countries, in addition to the observed trends in infant and child mortality rates.

Second, the prominent role of public support in bringing about these successes is also well established. All the five countries under consideration have repeatedly attracted attention for their active public involvement in various forms of social support, including the direct provision of vital commodities and social services. We shall return to this at greater length in

[12] The Chinese growth rate appearing in Table 10.3 is quite impressive, and might be seen as suggesting that the basis of China's success may well lie as much in economic growth as in direct public support. This question is further discussed in the next chapter, where it is argued that (1) China's growth rate during the period of interest has been much exaggerated, and (2) economic growth has followed rather than preceded the wide-ranging measures of public support which must be seen as the main source of China's success.

[13] There tend to be many gaps in international statistics of life expectancy and related indicators (on this see Murray 1987). However, the reliability of such statistics is much greater for these five countries. The abundance and quality of demographic and health statistics in Costa Rica and Chile since the 1950s are rather exceptional, and the impressive records of these two countries in the areas of health and nutrition have attracted very wide attention—the experiences of these two countries are further discussed in Chapter 12. Cuban statistics have to be used with great care, but health and demographic statistics are among the more reliable ones (see the thorough discussions in Mesa-Lago 1969, 1979, Diaz-Briquets 1983, and Santana 1987: Appendix), and Cuba's achievements in the area of health and nutrition are well established—see Brundenius (1981, 1984), Handelman (1982), Diaz-Briquets (1983), Valdes-Brito and Henriquez (1983), Werner (1983), Muniz *et al.* (1984), Meegama (1985), Eckstein (1986), and Santana (1987). The literature on China's experience of rapid health and nutritional improvement (further discussed in the next chapter) is enormous. Some useful references, which also carefully discuss the statistical evidence, include Jamison and Trowbridge (1984), World Bank (1983a, 1984a, 1985), Jamison *et al.* (1984), Jamison (1985), Xu Su-en (1985), Piazza (1986), Riskin (1986), Banister (1987), Jamison and Piazza (1987), Hussain (1987), and Hussain and Feuchtwang (1988). On the Jamaican experience, which too will be commented on (Chapter 12), see Jameson (1981), Cumper (1983), Gunatilleke (1984), Boyd (1987), Samuels (1987), Moran *et al.* (1988), and Mesa-Lago (1988a).

Chapters 11 and 12, but at this point it must already be noted that the evidence in favour of the feasibility of support-led security is quite substantial.

10.3 Economic Growth and Public Support: Interconnections and Contrasts

The distinction made in the previous section between growth-mediated security and support-led security reflects an important strategic aspect of public action, but many interconnections are also involved, which have to be noted to avoid a false, total dichotomy. The precise nature of the contrast should become clearer as we re-examine the experiences of growth-mediated security in different countries later on in this chapter, but a few preliminary clarifications and general disclaimers might be helpful here.

First, the distinction involved is definitely not a question of activism versus disengagement on the part of the state. The governments of some of the countries which have pursued growth-mediated security have, in fact, often been active in widely disseminating the fruits of growth. In these distributive efforts, the constructive role of the state has not been confined only to the domain of public provisioning. This role has also been geared to facilitating wide participation of the population in the process of economic growth. This has been done particularly through widespread promotion of skills and education, and the maintenance of full employment. In addition, state policies have in many cases been crucial in promoting growth itself.

Second, the contrast we have pursued is also not a simple one of market versus state provisioning. The masses can gain a share in general opulence not only through the increase of private incomes, but also through wide-ranging public provisioning. A striking example is that of Kuwait, where enhanced opulence has provided the material basis for what is clearly one of the most comprehensive welfare states in the world.[14] But in fact all the countries which we have identified as pursuing the strategy of growth-mediated security have taken considerable advantage of the enhanced opportunities for public support provided by rapid economic growth. Other countries with high economic growth but little effort to combine it with social provisioning (e.g. Brazil or Oman) have done much worse in terms of the index of mortality decline, as we have already noted earlier in this chapter.

Third, the distinction made in the last section has little to do with the dilemma that has sometimes been construed between the pursuit of 'growth' and the satisfaction of 'basic needs'. A strategy of 'growth-mediated' *security* is not at all the same thing as the pursuit of economic growth *tout court* (an issue further pursued in the next section). The former need not conflict with the satisfaction of basic needs—indeed it is an *approach* to their satisfaction. Conversely, support-led security does not imply surrendering the goal of

---

[14] See section 10.5 below. It is important to note that welfare provisions in Kuwait, while generally extensive, also discriminate sharply in favour of Kuwaiti citizens as opposed to other residents.

economic growth. In fact, often improvements in the quality of human life (e.g. through better health and education) also substantially enhance the productivity of the labour force. And economic growth can be crucial to the sustainability of a strategy based on generous public support. The interconnections and contrasts between the two strategies are both more extensive and more complex than would be portrayed by a simplistic dichotomy between growth and basic needs.

The real source of the contrast lies in the fact that the countries which have been identified as having made substantial use of the strategy of support-led security have not *waited* to grow rich before providing large-scale public support to guarantee certain basic capabilities. The contrast is a real one, but it should not obscure the complementarities that exist between economic growth and public support—and in particular, the prominent role played by public support in the strategies of growth-mediated as well as support-led security.

Despite these complementarities, dilemmas can arise in seeking a balance between the two strategies. Both growth-oriented measures and support-oriented measures make substantial claims on public resources as well as on public administrative capabilities. There are choices to be made in public policy-making, and we have to face the conflicts involved.

The strategy of growth-mediated security and the strategy of support-led security are basically distinct, but they are not unconnected. It is just as important to recognize that much can be done to improve living standards even when growth has not yet led to a high level of GNP per head, as it is to see that economic growth can be used to provide the basis for raising the quality of life.

10.4   Growth-Mediated Security and Unaimed Opulence

The strategy of growth-mediated security is of somewhat deceptive simplicity, and it is important to realize how widely it actually differs from the indiscriminate pursuit of economic expansion or what might be called a strategy of 'unaimed opulence'. A particularly crude version of the latter approach, which is in fact not uncommon, consists of attempting to *maximize* economic growth without paying any direct attention to the transformation of greater opulence into better living conditions. Unaimed opulence, in general, is a roundabout, undependable, and wasteful way of improving the living standards of the poor. In countries like Brazil where the poorest quintile of the population have to get by with as little as 2 per cent of national income, exclusively relying on the enhancement of general opulence would amount to accepting the need for generating 50 units of income for *one* unit that would go to the poor.[15] In addition, opportunities for the conversion of private incomes into basic

---

[15] Even this is conditional on the assumption that the distribution of income remains unchanged; in fact, inequalities may well increase with the single-minded pursuit of economic growth. The income distribution figures are from *World Development Report 1987*, Table 26.

capabilities might be expected to be particularly poor in a country where public services are persistently sacrificed at the altar of economic growth.

There are remarkable heterogeneities in what has been achieved by different countries through economic expansion and enhanced opulence. At the simplest level, the effect of increased affluence on the quality of life can be expected to depend strongly on the *distribution* of income. The twenty-five developing countries for which income distribution data are available in the *World Development Report 1987* include Hong Kong and South Korea from the group of five growth-mediated successes; both have among the least inegalitarian distributions in the entire list of twenty-five countries. In contrast, Brazil emerges as the country where the share of the richest quintile is highest, and the share of the poorest quintile second lowest. It is hardly surprising, then, that rapidly increasing general opulence in Brazil seems to have yielded so little in terms of improvements in basic aspects of the quality of life.[16] It would not be difficult to find other examples to illustrate how a strategy of unaimed opulence can lead to a tremendous waste of the opportunities provided by rapid economic growth. For example, as was discussed earlier the living-standard records of countries such as South Africa and Oman (also highly inegalitarian, with the poor left mostly to their own devices) are quite dismal, despite their relative opulence.

In many cases, an important part of the difference between unaimed opulence and growth-mediated security relates to the expansion of employment opportunities. Each of the five countries with successful pursuit of growth-mediated security has in fact experienced extraordinarily low rates of unemployment by the standards of developing economies, and several of them have in fact been large importers of labour power.[17] The role of the state in promoting full employment in these countries has also been quite conspicuous.

Note that the actual means employed to promote or guarantee full employment have themselves displayed a great variety in different countries. In South Korea, for instance, employment promotion has been based on (1) the encouragement of labour-intensive export industries, (2) the maintenance of comparative advantage in labour-intensive manufacturing through the ruthless preservation of highly competitive labour markets, (3) an active policy of education, skills diffusion and training, and (4) supplementary public works

[16] In 1985, Brazil had exactly the same U5MR as Burma, even though the latter had just about one-tenth of Brazil's GNP per capita. In fact, Burma had started off with a 43% higher U5MR in 1960, and grew at about only a quarter of the rate of Brazil, and still caught up with Brazil in terms of U5MR by 1985. Among all developing countries, Brazil had the tenth fastest growing economy between 1960 and 1982 (with an estimated annual growth rate of GNP per capita of 4.8%), but only occupies the 56th position in terms of percentage reduction in U5MR (1960–85). See UNICEF (1987a), Table 1, and *World Development Report 1984*, Table 1. For an informative analysis of Brazil's experience, see Sachs (1986).

[17] For further evidence and discussion of the outstanding employment records of these five countries, see al-Sabah (1980), Ismael (1982), Koo (1984), Sherbiny (1984), Hajjar (1985), Nijim (1985), Government of Hong Kong (1986), Krause (1988), Richardson and Kim (1986), and Hahn (1989).

programmes.[18] In Kuwait, on the other hand, the munificence of the welfare state has extended to nothing short of guaranteeing a job in the public sector to every Kuwaiti not employed in the private sector.[19] Here too, one finds a plurality of strategic options for public action. But the instrumental role of the expansion of employment opportunities to share the benefits of affluence must generally be seen as a crucial one.

10.5 Opulence and Public Provisioning

We should recall that a strategy of growth-mediated security does not necessarily make private incomes an exclusive vehicle for spreading the fruits of growth. Direct provisioning by the state can, as we have emphasized, assume an important role even when security is mediated by general economic growth. This fact is clearly illustrated by the experience of several of the countries which we have identified as having pursued the strategy of growth-mediated security. One obvious case is that of Kuwait.[20]

The genesis of Kuwait's present affluence goes back to 1946, when the country started exporting oil. Since then, earnings in the oil sector have grown to remarkable heights, and in 1980 they accounted for two-thirds of Kuwait's Gross Domestic Product.[21] Until 1975, when the Kuwait Oil Company (KOC) was fully acquired by the Government of Kuwait, oil earnings accrued mainly in the form of taxes and royalties levied on the foreign-owned KOC. At the time of nationalization, oil and gas exploitation provided employment only to a tiny fraction of the labour force. The same pattern continued after 1975, though the KOC was from then run by the government, which therefore appropriated its entire profits.

The livelihood of the bulk of Kuwait's population depends directly or indirectly on the use of these huge oil earnings through government activities and transfers. The percolation of oil revenues from the KOC to the masses has of course not assumed a particularly egalitarian character. A sizeable chunk, for instance, goes straightaway to various members of the ruling family in the form of permanent salaries, which allow this privileged élite to live in the material abundance that has often made the headlines in the Western press. Nevertheless, the greater part of oil revenues has been allocated to a massive programme of development activities, public sector employment, social services provision, and direct transfers.

A very large proportion of domestic government expenditure is accounted

[18] See section 10.6 of this chapter.

[19] See e.g. Ismael (1982). We should stress that the guarantee of employment applies only to Kuwaiti *nationals*. With respect to non-Kuwaiti residents (a large part of the population), full employment seems to be ensured through the no-nonsense method of stipulating that 'a non-Kuwaiti must leave the country once unemployed' (Ismael 1982: 119).

[20] The factual basis of the following account is derived from al-Sabah (1980), Ismael (1982), Harrison (1985), Nijim (1985), Public Institution for Social Security (1985), Hammoud (1986, 1987), and Nagi (1986), aside from official statistical sources.

[21] *Annual Statistical Abstract of Kuwait 1987*, pp. 266–7. As noted earlier, the contribution of oil revenues to Kuwait's economy declined after 1980 due to the fall in oil prices.

Table 10.4 Kuwait, 1960–1985: selected indicators

	1960	1965	1970	1975	1980	1985
Population (000s)	322[a]	467	739	995	1,357	1,697
Government oil revenue (million KD)	159	216	289	2,440	5,187	2,295
Public health expenditure (million KD)	n/a	6	16	39	105	193
Public education expenditure (million KD)	n/a	15	32	81	172	275
Number of teachers in government schools	2,133	4,625	8,652	14,842	22,219	26,463
Number of students in government schools (000)	43	85	134	192	294	361
Number of physicians in government hospitals	n/a	451	540	932	1,921	2,528
Rate of illiteracy (percentage of population aged 10 and above)	n/a	46	39	36	29	16

[a]. For the year 1961.

Source: Government of Kuwait, Ministry of Planning, Central Statistical Office, *Annual Statistical Abstract* (1970, 1974, 1978, 1980, 1982, 1984, 1987).

for by wages and salaries, and the magnitude of public sector employment has indeed assumed staggering proportions. As we have already noted, every Kuwaiti citizen not otherwise employed is guaranteed a job in the public sector. The army of government employees has primarily busied itself with implementing the multitudinous activities of the welfare state, and in 1975 as much as 69 per cent of the Kuwaiti labour force was employed in the 'social services' sector.[22] As Ismael (1982) puts it, Kuwait is a 'total service society with almost every human need from the cradle to the grave serviced by institutional arrangements'.[23]

The availability of public services in Kuwait has indeed expanded in record time from one typical of low-income countries to one typical of rich, industrialized economies; on this see Table 10.4. The stick of compulsory school attendance (first brandished in 1965), combined with the carrot of free education, free books, free meals, free transport, and even free clothes, has lured the younger generation to school in spite of some conservative resistance (particularly regarding girls). In 1977, government subsidies on education exceeded $600 per student.[24] The male secondary-school enrolment ratio of 86 per cent in Kuwait in 1982–4 is bettered only by South Korea and a handful of industrialized market economies (interestingly enough, the Kuwaiti ratio is

[22] *Annual Statistical Abstract of Kuwait 1987*, p. 136.
[23] Ismael (1982: 105).   [24] al-Sabah (1980: 58).

higher than those of France and the United Kingdom). The female secondary-school enrolment ratio of 79 per cent is a little lower but is still extremely impressive, especially by the standards of developing economies. This ratio of 79 per cent compares, for instance, with 19 per cent in Oman and 36 per cent in Brazil.[25]

Sophisticated medical services are provided free of charge to the entire population, Kuwaiti and non-Kuwaiti. Far-reaching public provisions are also made in areas such as housing, water supply (a precious commodity in Kuwait), electricity, transport and communications, and the subsidization of basic commodities. In addition, Kuwait has a system of large-scale direct transfers and financial help to low-income families which is by any standards one of the most generous in the world.[26] If socialism were reduced simply to state ownership of the means of production and generous provision of 'social wages', Kuwait would appear to be one of the most obviously socialist countries in the world!

The case of Kuwait is admittedly a special one in many respects, but the general notion that growth can facilitate public support applies more generally. In fact, it is rather striking how extensively the governments of the five 'growth-mediated security' countries have been driven (under the influence of a variety of political pressures and motivations) to use wide-ranging public provisioning in order to transform the material fruits of growth into secure minimal living standards for the greater part of the population. This applies even to governments which have a fierce reputation of non-interventionism in the private enterprise economy, of which Hong Kong is a classic example.

It is true that the government of Hong Kong, in sharp contrast with that of Kuwait, commands a relatively small proportion of the national income. However, within total government expenditure social services are the main item, with a share as large as 38 per cent in 1986.[27] This has permitted not only substantial improvements in the provision of educational facilities and health care but also the development of a sophisticated system of social assistance, including means-tested income support along similar lines to the Supplementary Benefits in the UK. It also includes huge housing subsidies which, in terms of generosity and coverage, count among the most substantial income support schemes in the world.[28] The results of economic growth as well as

[25] UNICEF (1987a), Table 4.

[26] According to al-Sabah, the percentage of Kuwaiti families benefiting from direct financial aid from the government is the highest in the world (about 25 per cent), and the government of Kuwait is strongly committed to the 'lower-income Kuwaitis', the latter being defined as those 'whose *monthly* income does not exceed $550' (al-Sabah 1980: 57, 158; emphasis added).

[27] Government of Hong Kong (1987), Appendix 8a.

[28] The strides that have been made in Hong Kong during the last few decades in the areas of health care, education, social assistance, and housing are discussed in Heppell (1973, 1974), Chow (1981), Drakakis-Smith (1981), King and Lee (1981), Lee (1983), Yeh (1984), and Government of Hong Kong (1987). The role played by welfare provisions in the development experience of the 'four little tigers' (Hong Kong, South Korea, Singapore, and Taiwan) is also investigated in Midgley (1986).

public support founded on it include a remarkably high life expectancy (viz. 76 years, which is comparable with the expectation of life in the most advanced industrial economies).

The opportunity for enlarged public provisioning provided by rapid growth has also been seized to various degrees by the other three of the five countries identified earlier as cases of 'growth-mediated security'. The experience of the United Arab Emirates bears some resemblance to that of Kuwait.[29] In Singapore, the government has an impressive record of extensive activism in both economic and social matters, which has been seen as a major factor behind the rapid improvement of living conditions in that country in the last few decades.[30] The experience of South Korea is discussed at greater length in the next section.

10.6 Growth-mediated Security: The Case of South Korea

A good illustration of the subtleties involved in a strategy of growth-mediated security, and of the role played at different levels by public action, is provided by South Korea. As we have seen, the growth rate of GNP per capita in that country over the last few decades has by any standards been a highly impressive one. Nor can it be denied that in this case rapid growth has provided the basis for very tangible improvements in basic components of the quality of life. We have already noted South Korea's outstanding reduction in infant and child mortality rates. There are many other, direct and indirect, indications of rapid advances in living standards. Indeed, there is solid evidence that during the period under consideration (viz. 1960 to 1985), the nutritional status of children has markedly improved; morbidity rates for communicable diseases have shrunk very fast; the incidence of absolute poverty (as standardly measured) has rapidly decreased, both in rural and in urban areas; the unemployment rate has stabilized at a remarkably low value (around 4 per cent); general educational standards have reached exceptionally high levels; and real wage rates have consistently increased, both in agriculture and in manufacturing. Some relevant indicators are presented in Table 10.5.[31]

The extent of government involvement in income redistribution and social welfare programmes has been, until recently, rather small by international standards. To take only one example, before 1976, South Korea had no public

[29] See e.g. Taryam (1987), especially Chapter 7.

[30] On this see the in-depth analysis of Ng Shui Meng (1986b). The pervasive influence of the government on economic and social life in Singapore (which ranges from housing 81% of the population in 1986 to 'discouraging long hair and corrupting music and dance') is also discussed in detail by Krause (1988).

[31] See also Suh (1984) on nutrition and morbidity; Richardson and Kim (1986) on employment; and McGinn et al. (1980) on education. According to UNICEF (1987a), Table 4, in 1985 South Korea had the fourth highest male literacy among all developing countries. Its secondary-school enrolment rate was the highest among developing countries for males (92%), and second highest for females (86%). In the latter respect South Korea surpassed a large number of developed, industrialized countries.

Table 10.5 South Korea, 1960–1985: selected indicators

Year	Infant mortality rate (per 1,000)	Height of children aged 6 (cm.)		Incidence of poverty (%)	Gini index of income inequality	Unemployment rate (%)	Index of real wages in industry (1970 = 100)	Secondary school enrolment (%)
		Male	Female					
	(1)	(2a)	(2b)	(3)	(4)	(5)	(6)	(7)
1960	85	111.1[a]	110.4[a]	n/a	0.448	n/a	n/a	n/a
1965	n/a	111.7	110.8	41	0.344	7.4	58	54
1970	53	112.7	111.7	23	0.332	4.5	100	66
1975	41	113.3	112.3	15[b]	0.391	4.1	127	77
1980	37	115.0	113.7	10	0.389	4.5	219	96
1985	27	116.5	115.4	7	0.363	4.0	286	99

[a] Figure relating to 1962.
[b] Figure relating to 1976.

Sources: (1) Suh (1984: 162) and UNICEF (1987a), Table 1. (2) Government of the Republic of Korea (1963, 1965, 1970, 1987). (3)–(5) Hahn (1989), Figures 5, 7, and 13b. (6) Calculated from Hasan and Rao (1979), Table D.38, and Hahn (1989), Figure 22. (7) Hahn (1989), Figure 28. We are extremely grateful to Byung Whan Kim (London School of Economics) for guidance to South Korean statistics.

health care system worth the name, and no form of broad-based medical assistance or medical insurance scheme. Health care was predominantly in the hands of private professionals, especially pharmacists.[32] Many other aspects of social welfare have also been rather neglected until recently, and the South Korean government has consistently rejected the option of developing into a 'welfare state'.[33] Nor has it expressed much direct concern about income redistribution.[34]

One could be led by all this to conclude that in South Korea private enterprise has been the driving force not only of economic growth in the narrow sense (as is widely recognized), but also of wider improvements in the quality of life. It is perhaps not without reason, then, that South Korea has been variously seen as an archetype of the fecundity of capitalism, a 'free enterprise model' for other developing countries, an illustration of the redundancy of planning, and, generally, a brilliant product of what some have called the 'market order'.[35]

There is clearly an element of truth in these characterizations. However, there are also serious qualifications to be made from several different perspectives.

First, it must be pointed out that the South Korean economy in the late 1940s offered a rather unusual base for equitable growth. A particularly important factor was the relatively equal distribution of assets (including skills, education and land), in the creation of which the government played a major role.[36] Equitable growth was reinforced by the labour-intensive orientation of industry (we have already noted South Korea's remarkable wage and employment figures), and this orientation took place within a structure of incentives and inducements carefully planned by the government. It is impossible to understand South Korea's experience without reference to the major role which the government has played in enabling the population at large to *participate* fruitfully in the process of economic growth.

Second, as has been widely noted, the hands which signalled South Korea's economic expansion have been much less 'invisible' than would appear at first sight. It is true that South Korean economic policy and planning has mainly taken the form of creating an environment conducive to private enterprise of

[32] South Korea's health care system is discussed in detail in Park and Yeon (1981) and Yeon (1982, 1986). See also Golladay and King (1979), Suh (1984), Yoon and Park (1985a), and Bahl *et al*. (1986). The year 1976 marked a turning-point in the development of health care policy in Korea, with the introduction of the medical assistance and medical insurance programmes. In recent years increasing efforts have also been made to develop the public health care system.

[33] See the references cited above, and also Republic of Korea (1979). It is worth noting that important changes have taken place in South Korea in the area of social welfare policy since the mid-1970s—see e.g. Suh (1984), Government of Korea (1986), Midgley (1986), and Suh and Williamson (1987).

[34] See e.g. Kim and Yun (1988).

[35] On these various characterizations and important analyses related to these perspectives, see Bauer (1972, 1981, 1984), Little (1982), Lal (1983) and Balassa (1988).

[36] See e.g. Suh (1984), Bahl *et al*. (1986), Michell (1988).

the favoured kind. However, the role of government policy in planning the nature of economic growth and in intervening to shape the direction of investment and expansion has been both pervasive and enormously effective.[37]

Government involvement in this field has taken a wide variety of forms, including extensive credit controls and incentives, import substitution measures, infrastructural investments, the dissemination of information, a sophisticated tax administration system, and the promotion of an active and competitive labour market.[38] As far as the alleged 'redundancy of planning' is concerned, South Korea has, in fact, had regular Five-Year Plans since 1962 and also the rare distinction of implementing them successfully.[39] The various instruments of state policy for shaping the South Korean economy are systematically put together in this exercise of integrated planning.

Third, a further question concerns the precise involvement of the South Korean government in measures of direct public support. The record in this respect has been highly uneven between different areas of intervention, and is therefore difficult to assess. For instance, while public provisions for health care were rather meagre until the late 1970s (as noted earlier), the state has been extremely active in the area of education for a long time.[40] And while it is true that the South Korean government has, at least until recently, eschewed the idea of large-scale welfare programmes, it has, on the other hand, had a long-standing and (in some ways) pioneering concern for the prevention of acute destitution.[41]

Moreover, there have been important policy developments within the period under consideration (viz. 1960 to 1985). Specifically, the commitment of the government to social policies has rapidly increased in the second half of this period. In the area of health care, for instance, ambitious programmes of medical assistance and medical insurance initiated in the late 1970s have marked a reorientation of earlier policies.[42] Government expenditure on health, education, housing, and social security has grown

---

[37] Numerous writers have stressed and documented this point. See, for instance, Datta Chaudhuri (1979), Hasan and Rao (1979), Sen (1981b), Wade (1983), Evans and Alizadeh (1984), Koo (1984), Bahl et al. (1986), Hamilton (1986), Midgley (1986), Richardson and Kim (1986), Bagchi (1987), Toye (1987), Amsden (1989), Kim and Yun (1988), Kuznets (1988), Michell (1988), Qi (1988), White (1988), and Alam (1989).

[38] On the last point, see e.g. Richardson and Kim (1986). It must be noted in particular that the South Korean government's anxiety to maintain competitive labour market conditions has had a counterpart in very energetic and effective policies aimed at upgrading skills through education and training.

[39] See Suh (1984) and Kuznets (1988).

[40] See McGinn et al. (1980) and Amsden (1989).

[41] This concern has been visible, for instance, in the promotion of a 'Work-conditioned Assistance Programme' (initiated in 1964) and in the provisions associated with the Livelihood Protection Act of 1961. For further discussion of these and related social security measures, see Yoon and Park (1985a, 1985b).

[42] On this, see e.g. Park and Yeon (1981) and Yeon (1986).

very fast since then—as fast as 33 per cent per year during the period 1978–82.[43]

The important role played by direct measures of public support in supplementing the normal operation of the economy in South Korea has been particularly clear during the recession of the early 1980s. It has been observed that, in this event, direct measures of public support (such as public works programmes and direct transfers to the needy) emerged as crucial policy instruments for the protection of vulnerable groups.[44]

The Korean experience is thus far from one of *laissez-faire*, and in fact richly illustrates the diverse roles that state planning and action can play in influencing—directly and indirectly—the expansion of basic capabilities within a strategy of growth-mediated security. The active nature of state policy in South Korea within the structure of promoting security through participatory growth would be hard to deny.

The positive involvement of the state in promoting participatory growth may seem surprising given the repressive nature of the Korean government over this period. The possible contribution of—open or latent—political opposition in influencing the state in the direction of promoting living standards should not, however, be underestimated. The government has had to cope with vocal political dissent (especially from the student community) and frequent outbursts of public protest, which have also been widely reported abroad.[45] The precise role of adversarial public action in affecting the direction of state policy is an aspect of the South Korean experience that merits further attention.

10.7 Support-Led Security and Equivalent Growth

In the preceding sections we have discussed the experiences of some of the countries that have successfully pursued what we have called 'growth-mediated security'. In Chapters 11 and 12, we will examine selected cases of 'support-led security'. In this last section of the present chapter, we discuss some general issues related to assessing the effectiveness of the strategy of support-led security.

To start with, it is of some interest to consider briefly how the levels of under-5 mortality in the countries which we have identified as having pursued a strategy of support-led security compare today with the levels observed in

[43] Suh (1984), Table XII.3. As Yeon observes: 'In recent years government policy in the Republic of Korea has recognised the fact that rapid economic growth is a necessary but not sufficient condition for improving the income and standard of living of the population' (Yeon 1986: 153). This concern is indeed evident in recent planning documents (e.g. Government of Korea 1986).

[44] For a detailed analysis of this issue, see Suh and Williamson (1987), as well as Cornia *et al.* (1987), vol. i.

[45] See Steinberg (1988) on adversarial politics in South Korea and their relation to economic policies. See also McGinn *et al.* (1980).

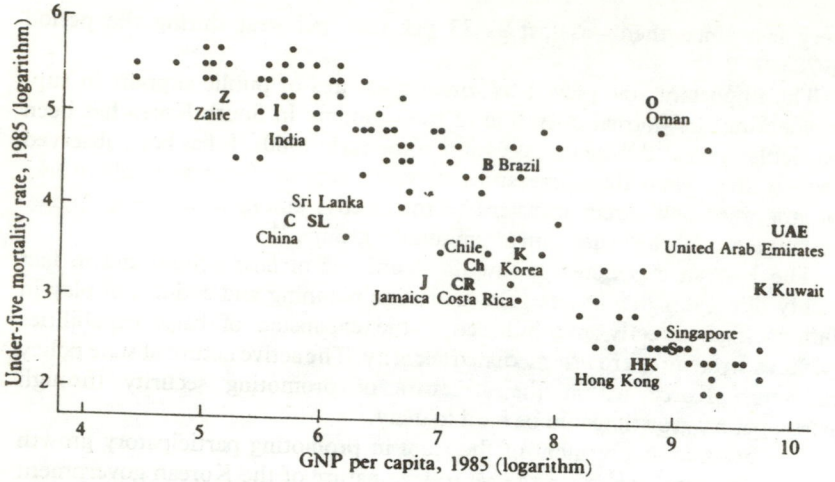

Source: Based on data for 120 countries provided in UNICEF (1987*a*) (nine observations represent two countries each due to 'superimposition'). Data on GNP are not available for Cuba.

Fig. 10.1 GNP per capita and under-5 mortality (1985): international comparison

other countries with a similar level of GNP per capita. This can be appreciated from a simple scatter diagram showing the levels of GNP per capita and U5MR (in 1985) for different countries—see Figure 10.1 and also Table 10.6.[46]

The interpretation of the position of different countries requires some caution. For instance, it would not make much sense to presume that any country with a low U5MR relative to other countries at a comparable income level must be particularly exemplary (as is sometimes assumed in analysing 'basic needs performance'). This is so not only because one simple way to reach that position is to do it, as it were, the Zaire way, to wit, by producing *negative* growth![47] As income goes down, the U5MR looks better in comparative terms. But more importantly, this way of identifying successful countries would hide the success of countries that have achieved a low U5MR *through* a growth-mediated strategy.

The goal of development is to improve the quality of life, not to improve the

[46] Note that Figure 10.1 is drawn on the basis of logarithmic scales. This means that, each time we move one unit up the vertical axis, U5MR is multiplied by a little less than *three* (and correspondingly for GNP per capita along the horizontal axis). Table 10.6 is based on a log-linear, ordinary-least-squares regression of U5MR (1985) on per-capita GNP (1985) for 120 countries. The over-all results reported in this section are quite robust to alternative specifications of the set of countries considered in the analysis (e.g. including or excluding developed economies, or oil-exporting countries).

[47] Zaire had an annual growth rate of –2.1% in 1965–85 (*World Development Report 1987*, Table1). It has also experienced a steady deterioration of its living standards in recent years.

Tabel 10.6 Actual value of U5MR (1985) as percentage of value predicted on the basis of GNP per capita

	Ratio (%)	Growth rate of GNP per head (1965–85)
Ten developing countries with lowest ratio		
China	32	4.8
Jamaica	33	−0.7
Sri Lanka	35	2.9
Guyana	36	−0.2
Costa Rica	37	1.4
Burma	42	2.4
Chile	45	−0.2
Mauritius	46	2.7
Hong Kong	50	6.1
Madagascar	52	−1.9
Other (selected) countries		
Singapore	61	7.6
Zaire	73	−2.1
South Korea	79	6.6
Brazil	172	4.3
Kuwait	216	−0.3
Oman	819	5.7

Note: Calculated from the same sources as Table 10.3. The 'predicted value' of U5MR is obtained from OLS regression of U5MR on GNP per capita (both in logarithmic form). The regression involves 120 countries for which data were available on both variables. (For 10 countries including Cuba, U5MR estimates existed but not GNP estimates.)

quality of life *relative* to income. In pursuing the former goal, the growth of income can, as we have already seen, play an important role. The achievement of a low level of under-5 mortality relative to income (through, say, extensive public provisioning) would give little grounds for congratulation if the expenses involved had the effect of slowing down the growth of incomes to the extent that the *absolute* value of U5MR ended up being higher than it would have been with less public support and more growth.

In spite of these reservations, the information provided by Figure 10.1 and Table 10.6 is instructive in giving us a part—an important part—of the picture. It can, in fact, assist our understanding of the gains that can be obtained through public support for a given level of opulence. The figures indicate the extent to which the success of the five countries which we have identified as having made effective use of a support-led strategy (viz. Chile, China, Costa Rica, Cuba, Jamaica) has indeed relied on their ability to deviate from the 'standard' relationship between GNP and mortality. Their record in breaking the shackles of low income and poverty is indeed impressive, with (for instance) China achieving a level of under-5 mortality rate (U5MR) less than a *third* of that predicted on the basis of its income level alone. Similarly striking advantages are enjoyed by the other countries in this group.[48]

This exercise is also helpful in identifying other countries which have achieved great success in reducing mortality despite low incomes, but did not appear in our initial group of 'top ten' performers because the period of rapid improvement in their case failed to overlap substantially with the time period used in this classification (viz. 1960–85). On the basis of Figure 10.1 and Table 10.6, the most obvious candidate for this diagnosis is Sri Lanka. It can be seen that Sri Lanka, like China, has a level of U5MR about a third of what one would expect (on the basis of international comparisons) given its level of GNP per capita. But the period of spectacular advance in Sri Lanka did not lie primarily in the last two or three decades, and for the 1960–85 period specifically Sri Lanka has not been an outstanding performer. Accelerated breakthrough in mortality reduction occurred earlier, during the 1940s and 1950s. These were, in fact, also the decades of rapid growth of public support in the form of free or subsidized distribution of rice (introduced in 1942) and intensive expansion of public health services (beginning in the forties, partly related to a campaign to conquer malaria). Though it has a different time pattern from the other countries discussed in this chapter, Sri Lanka's pioneering experience is of great general interest, and will be further investigated in Chapter 12.[49]

A careful examination of the levels of per-capita GNP and under-5 mortality can also help us to assess the relative gains that different countries might expect to obtain from alternative strategies. We could, for instance, examine questions of the following sort. If a country like, say, China had resorted to a 'standard' amount of public support instead of an exceptional one, how much *faster* would it have had to grow over a specified period in order to reach the level of U5MR it is observed to have in 1985? Clearly, only rather speculative —and at best approximate—answers to this question can be arrived at. Simple examinations of the current relationship between U5MR and per-capita GNP in different countries can, however, assist our intuition about the plausibility of different answers.

An elementary but nevertheless useful answer to the question posed can, for instance, be obtained in the following manner. First, we estimate the level of

[48] For Cuba, however, the relevant data (particularly GNP estimates) needed for inclusion in Table 10.6 are not available.

[49] The case of Mauritius (also appearing in Table 10.6) bears some resemblance to that of Sri Lanka. Indeed, the links between public policy and social achievements in Mauritius in the 1940s and 1950s have attracted considerable attention. On this and related aspects of Mauritius's development experience, see Meade *et al.* (1968), Titmuss and Abel-Smith (1968), Tabutin (1975), Mehta (1981), Minogue (1983), Tabutin and Sombo (1983), Selwyn (1983), Joynathsingh (1987).

per-capita GNP which an 'average' country appears to need in order to experience China's current level of infant and child mortality.[50] Second, we calculate the extra growth of income that China would have been required to achieve over a specified period to reach that level of GNP per capita.[51] The results of such a calculation, taking 1960–85 as the reference period, are presented in the first column of Table 10.7. They suggest that, to reach the observed level of U5MR in 1985 in the absence of outstanding public support measures, China would have had to raise its annual growth rate over the whole period by 7 to 10 per cent of the GNP per capita (e.g., if the actual growth rate experienced was 4 per cent, it would have had to raise it to somewhere between 11 and 14 per cent per year).

It may be argued that this calculation can be somewhat misleading in that it attributes the whole of China's deviation from the average relationship between GNP and U5MR to its outstanding measures of public support. What if China's outstanding record is due, say, to favourable ecological circumstances, or some other advantage applying to China as a country? There is no obvious reason to believe that such advantages—ecological or otherwise—are enjoyed by China. Nevertheless, Table 10.7 also presents (in the last three columns) alternative estimates assuming different levels of 'country advantage', where the latter is defined as the proportion of China's deviation from the average relationship between GNP and U5MR that can be attributed to favourable circumstances unrelated to public support.[52] For reasonable values of country advantage, *additional* growth requirements over the 1960–85 period in the absence of outstanding public support measures remain very high—5 per cent of GNP per capita each year under the set of assumptions most favourable to the growth scenario.[53]

---

[50] This estimated level of income, say y^*, is inferred from the regression relating U5MR (1985) to per-capita GNP (1985), mentioned earlier.

[51] It is easy to show that, if y is China's actual per-capita GNP in 1985, and t the length of the specified period, then this 'extra growth requirement', say g, is simply $(\ln y^* - \ln y)/t$. Note that this formula does *not* require us to know China's *actual* growth rate at any time. This is fortunate since, as we shall see in the next chapter, China's past growth rates are extremely hard to ascertain.

[52] Formally, the 'country advantage' is the proportion of China's 'residual' in the earlier regression that is considered attributable to favourable circumstances rather than to public support. It can be shown that, if the assumed value of the country advantage is α, then the 'extra growth requirement' is simply $(1-\alpha).g$, where g is calculated as before.

[53] The highest value of 'country advantage' for China used in Table 10.7 is 30 per cent. This upper bound is obtained by treating country advantage analogously to a 'fixed effect', and attributing *all* of China's favourable deviation from the international regression line around 1960 to its country advantage. Note that this is likely to be a substantial *overestimate* of China's 'country advantage' since by that time China already had an outstanding history of public support. Of course, whether there is *any* 'country advantage' at all for China is far from clear, and our use of this 'scaling down' of the achievements of support-led strategy is motivated by making as conservative an estimate as possible.

Table 10.7 Extra annual growth of per-capita GNP required by China between 1960 and 1985 in order to reach its observed level of U5MR in 1985 in the absence of outstanding public support measures (%)

Additional growth requirement for alternative assumed values of 'country advantage' (CA)			
CA = 0	CA = 0.10	CA = 0.20	CA = 0.30
7.1	6.4	5.7	5.0
(9.9)	(8.9)	(7.9)	(6.9)

Source: See text. 'The numbers without brackets are based on a regression involving all countries for which the relevant data are available in UNICEF (1987a, 1988). The numbers within brackets are based on a regression involving only developing countries.

In spite of their illustrative nature, the calculations we have presented bring out that the 'economic growth equivalent' of well-planned public support is very large indeed.[54] That is, the results that countries such as China have achieved through direct public support could only have been obtained through extremely fast economic growth if they had followed a 'path' similar to that typical of other developing countries.[55]

Whether immediate and extensive measures of public support in a poor country *lead to* slower economic growth is, of course, an extremely complex question, and we shall not pursue it here. As was mentioned earlier, the interactions between public support and economic growth include not only dilemmas and trade-offs (e.g. the allocation of resources between immediate consumption and investment), but also many positive links (e.g. the effects of improved health and nutrition on productivity). What is worth nothing here is that, given the very large 'growth equivalent' of public support, only the existence of some remarkably powerful (and negative) trade-off between public support and economic growth would seriously undermine the case for extensive involvement in public support at an early stage of development.

[54] An alternative approach to the analysis of the 'growth equivalent' of public support, leading to a similar general conclusion, was presented in Sen (1981b). For a critical examination of the possible interconnections, see Birdsall (1988, 1989).

[55] It must be emphasized that this 'standard' path as it exists today is *not* the same as what we have called 'growth-mediated security'. In fact, it is interesting that *all* the countries identified earlier as having followed that strategy have large negative residuals in regressions of U5MR (1985) on GNP (1985) and U5MR (1960). This confirms that their experiences have involved a great deal more than a vague reliance on economic growth, as with 'unaimed opulence'.

In the next two chapters, we shall discuss in some detail the experiences of selected countries in the pursuit of support-led security. Some of the general issues and dilemmas arising from a programme of public action for social security will be reconsidered in the concluding part of this book.

11

China and India

11.1   Is China Ahead?

When development planning began in China after the revolution (1949) and in India after its independence (1947), both countries were starting from a very low base of economic and social achievement. The gross national product per head in each country was among the lowest in the world, hunger was widespread, the level of illiteracy remarkably high, and life expectancy at birth not far from 40 years. There were many differences between them, but the similarities were quite striking. Since then things have happened in both countries, but the two have moved along quite different routes. A comparison between the achievements of China and India is not easy, but certain contrasts do stand out sharply.

Perhaps the most striking is the contrast in matters of life and death. Life expectancy at birth in China appears to be firmly in the middle to upper 60s (close to 70 years according to some estimates),[1] while that in India seems to be around the middle to upper 50s.[2] The under-5 mortality rate, according to UNICEF statistics, is 47 per thousand in China, and more than three times as much in India, viz. 154.[3] The percentage of infants with low birth weight in 1982–3 is reported to be about 6 in China, and five times as much in India.[4] Analyses of anthropometric data and morbidity patterns confirm that China has achieved a remarkable transition in health and nutrition.[5] No comparable transformation has occurred in India.

Things have diverged radically in the two countries also in the field of elementary education. The percentage of adult literacy is about 43 in India, and around 69 in China.[6] If China and India looked similar in these

---

[1] The *World Development Report 1988* puts the Chinese life expectancy at birth in 1986 at 69 years. The Chinese official statistics based on the 1982 census place it at 68 years in 1981. Judith Banister (1987) gives a lower estimate based on corrections for incomplete reporting, viz. 65 years, for the same year.

[2] The *World Development Report 1988* gives the figure of 57 years as life expectancy at birth in India in 1986. The last reliable estimate based on sample registration survey for 1976–80 puts the figure at 52.3 years, but later estimates also exist suggesting a life expectancy in the mid-50s.

[3] See UNICEF (1988), Table 1.

[4] UNICEF (1988), Table 2. Serious doubts have, however, been expressed about the reliability of these figures of birth weights, for purposes of international comparison, especially since there are some variations in the criteria used.

[5] See World Bank (1983a, 1984a, 1985), Piazza (1986), Hussain (1987), Jamison and Piazza (1987), and Hussain and Feuchtwang (1988).

[6] UNICEF (1988), Table 4. The male and female adult literacy rates given by UNICEF for each country are respectively 82 and 56 in China and 57 and 29 in India. The total population averages have been obtained from these data by weighting the female and male figures by the ratio of females to males in the two countries.

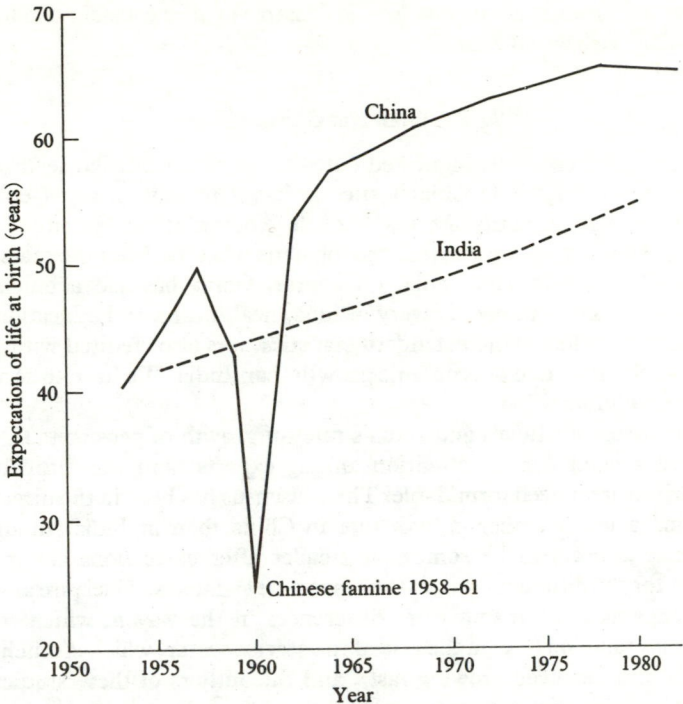

Sources: J. Banister, 'An Analysis of Recent Data on the Population of China', *Population and Development Review*, 10 (1984); S. Preston and P. N. Mari Bhat, 'New Evidence on Fertility and Mortality Trends in India', *Population and Development Review*, 10 (1984), for 1966–81 based on 'the low variant' procedure; *Statistical Pocket Book of India 1984* (New Delhi, 1985), for 1955 (as the 1951–61 decade average).

Fig. 11.1   Life expectancy at birth in China and India

matters at the middle of this century, they certainly do not do so now.[7]

The comparison is not, however, entirely one-sided. There are skeletons in China's cupboard—millions of them from the disastrous famine of 1958–61. India, in contrast, has not had any large-scale famine since independence in 1947. We shall take up the question of comparative famine experience later on (in section 11.3), and also a few other problems in China's success story (sections 11.4 and 11.5), but there is little doubt that as far as morbidity, mortality and longevity are concerned, China has a large and decisive lead over India.[8]

[7] The picture is more diverse if *intra*country differences are also considered. In particular, the public intervention programmes in the state of Kerala in India seem to have made the achievements of that state comparable to China's. The mixed nature of these contrasts also points towards some policy lessons. The issue is taken up in the last section of this chapter.

[8] China's lead in the field of literacy is also clear enough, though India has a much more extensive tertiary education sector with a much higher percentage of the relevant age-cohort going to the universities.

What has brought about that lead is a matter of very considerable interest, and to that issue we now turn.

11.2   What Put China Ahead?

In the last chapter we distinguished between 'growth-mediated security' and 'support-led security'. Is China's success based mainly on rapid economic growth, or is it primarily the result of developing a vast system of public support? It might not be immediately obvious what has been the main factor behind China's lead over India. Of course, China has had a much more extensive system of public delivery of food, health care, and education. But, according to widely quoted standard statistics, it is also credited with having had a much faster rate of economic growth than India. We have to scrutinize both sets of information.

Comparison of China's and India's rates of growth of per-capita GNP has attracted a good deal of attention among experts, and the difficulties of comparison are indeed formidable. The consensus has been in the direction of accepting a much higher growth rate in China than in India, though the difference appears to be somewhat smaller after corrections are made to account for the different bases of the respective estimates. There are also some non-comparabilities arising from differences in the way in which the two economies function (e.g. in the role of the service sector, which is much larger in India and has been growing fast), and the authors of these studies have warned us to be careful in interpreting the comparative estimates.[9]

World Development Report 1988 gives the growth rate of GNP per head during 1965–86 as 1.8 per cent in India and 5.1 per cent—nearly three times as large—in China. If the comparative growth picture is really something like that, it would be natural to assume that the Chinese achievement in matters of life and death must have been substantially 'growth-mediated'. Growing at 5.1 per cent per year over decades would, for one thing, make a country's per-capita income a great deal higher than what would result from hastening slowly at 1.8 per cent, and that—as the arguments of the last chapter indicated—could make a lot of resources potentially available for public support in addition to enhancing average personal affluence.

These comparative growth figures do not, however, bear any scrutiny. Indeed, the same *World Development Report 1988* gives the Chinese per-capita GNP in 1986 as $300 and that of India as $290. If the figures of GNP level and GNP growth are put together, it would appear that in 1965 India had about twice the per-capita GNP of China (about $200 for India and $106 for China at 1986 prices). That is, in order for the Chinese GNP per head to have grown at

---

[9] Wilfred Malenbaum (1956, 1959, 1982) has provided careful and illuminating comparisons of economic growth in the two countries over the decades. See also Swamy (1986a), and the previous literature cited there and in Malenbaum (1982). See also Perkins (1983, 1988) on methodological problems and substantive results in assessing China's growth performance.

5.1 per cent while India's grew at 1.8 per cent, and for the two to have ended up with their respective 1986 GNP figures, the Chinese per-capita GNP in the middle 1960s would have had to be only a little over a half that of India.[10]

That inference would be contrary to all available estimates of Chinese and Indian GNP for the 1960s. It would have also made China then a great deal poorer than the *poorest* country in the contemporary world.[11] In fact, Simon Kuznets's estimates indicated a similar GNP per head in 1958 for China and India, with 'product per head' about 20 per cent *higher* in China.[12] The story of the Chinese GNP per head growing about three times as fast as the Indian simply does not bear empirical scrutiny.

In fact, the World Bank's own *World Tables 1987* puts the GNP per head in the mid-1960s, specifically 1966, at $110 for China and $90 for India, i.e. 22 per cent *higher* in China. *World Tables 1987* also gives the 1986 GNP per head of China and India as $300 and $270 respectively. Putting their 1966 and 1986 figures together indicates implicit growth rates that are very similar for the two countries (5.1 per cent per year for China and 5.6 per cent in India). That is a very different picture from that of China's growth rate of 5.1 per cent per year being nearly three times as high as India's 1.8 per cent, as given by the more widely used publication of the same World Bank—the *World Development Report*. The picture is confused and confounded, to say the least.

One should not make heavy weather of these inconsistencies. We do know that international comparisons of GNP are plagued by the usual complications of exchange-rate variations and changes in relative prices.[13] But the complete lack of relation between GNP levels and growth rates in *World Development Report*'s account of China's and India's respective performance makes it hard to put much reliance on the respective growth statistics.[14] In particular, the

[10] These results are not particularly sensitive to the exact years chosen for the backward extrapolation based on World Bank data. Putting together the GNP figures for 1982 and the growth rates for 1960–82, as given in *World Development Report 1984*, yields 1960 per-head GNP figures of $106 for China and $196 for India, i.e. a Chinese GNP per head 46% *lower* than India's (on this see Sen 1985a: 78–80 and Table A.2).

[11] The poorest country covered in the *World Development Report 1988* is Ethiopia with a GNP per head of $120 in 1986 (see Table 1, p. 222). This figure is much higher than the attributed GNP per head in China of $106 in 1965 (at 1986 prices). [12] Kuznets (1966: 36).

[13] *World Development Report 1988* itself shows the limitations of its estimates and draws attention to the assumptions on the basis of which the figures are arrived at (see pp. 290–1). The issue here is not one of accusing the World Bank of deception or perfidy, but to see the case for rejecting the comparative numbers that are presented in some of these widely used tables and which are in fact quoted again and again in discussions relating to China and India.

[14] On the rapid revisions of China's GNP figures made by the World Bank, see Malenbaum (1982): 'As noted, Bank data for China's GNP per capita were of the order of $400 for 1976 and 1977 (current US prices). Comparable figures for India were $150, some 37.5% of the Chinese levels. In 1980, the respective figures for 1978 were listed as $230 and $180 (1978 US prices); the ratio was 78.5%. The levels for 1979 are now shown as $260 and $190. A comparative development history that pictured China with a long-period growth advantage of about 150% per capita over India by the late 1970s now shows an advantage only one-quarter as large, some 30%–35%, over the same period. No structural explanation is offered for this radical revision' (pp. 81–2). To continue the story where Malenbaum left off, the World Bank made the figures converge for all practical purposes by 1986, with (as mentioned in the text) a GNP per head of $300 for China and

footnote continued overleaf

story of a growth rate in China very much higher than that of India (5.1 per cent against India's 1.8 per cent) is difficult to firm up. It is hard to see the Chinese attainment in health and nutrition as primarily a 'growth-mediated' success.

In fact, it seems fairly clear that the Chinese growth rate was not radically higher than that of India before the economic reforms of 1979, by which time the tremendous surge ahead in health and longevity had already taken place.[15] In the pre-reform period, agricultural expansion in particular was sluggish in China, as it was in India, and the dramatic reduction in hunger and under-nourishment and expansion of life expectancy in China were not ushered in by any spectacular rise in rural incomes or of food availability per head. As Judith Banister notes: 'It also appears that the quantity of food produced per capita and the quality of the Chinese diet did not improve between 1957 and the late 1970's. . . . annual per capita grain production through 1977 was about the same as in the late 1950's: it averaged 301 kilograms in 1955–57 and 305 kilograms in 1975–77.'[16]

This is indeed the crucial point. The Chinese level of average opulence judged in terms of GNP per head, or total consumption per capita, or food consumption per person, did not radically increase during the period in which China managed to take a gigantic step forward in matters of life and death, moving from a life expectancy at birth in the low 40s (like the poorest countries today) to one in the high 60s (getting within hitting distance of Europe and North America).

Since the far-reaching economic and social reforms introduced in 1979 (with much greater use of market-based incentives), the Chinese growth rate has been fast—very much faster than earlier. But this has not been a period of further reduction in mortality. In fact, quite the contrary. The death rate in China reached, according to official statistics, its lowest level in 1978, just *before* the reforms, and went *up* in the period following the reforms, precisely when the growth of output and income accelerated impressively. On the lessons of the post-reform period in China, we shall have to say more (see section 11.4).

At the moment we only note the fact that the great increase in longevity and reduction in mortality took place in China before the reforms, during a period of fairly moderate economic growth, whereas the post-reform period of rapid growth has witnessed no further rise and possibly some deterioration in survival chances. China's remarkable achievements in matters of life and death

---

footnote continued
$290 for India. While the GNP figures for China were made to come down closer to India's GNP per head, the figures for GNP growth rates of China were kept sharply higher than those of India. What we are looking at here is not an account with just some little inconsistency somewhere, but one that is altogether contrary within its own internal structure.

[15] See Riskin (1986, 1987).

[16] See Banister (1987: 354). See also Carl Riskin's (1986) paper on the strategy of 'feeding China', and the empirical studies cited there.

cannot in any way be ascribed simply to a strategy of 'growth-mediated' security.

As far as support-led security is concerned, the Chinese efforts have been quite spectacular. The network of health services introduced in post-revolutionary China in a radical departure from the past—involving cooperative medical systems, commune clinics, barefoot doctors, and widespread public health measures—has been remarkably extensive.[17] The contrast with India in this respect is striking enough. It is not only that China has more than twice as many doctors and nearly three times as many nurses per unit of population as India has.[18] But also these and other medical resources are distributed more evenly across the country (even between urban and rural areas), with greater popular access to them than India has been able to organize.[19]

Similar contrasts hold in the distribution of food through public channels and rationing systems, which have had an extensive coverage in China (except in periods of economic and political chaos, as during the famine of 1958–61, on which more presently). In India public distribution of food to the people, when it exists, is confined to the urban sector (except in a few areas such as the state of Kerala where the rural population also benefits from it, on which, too, more presently). Food distribution is, in fact, a part of a far-reaching programme of social security that distinguishes China from India.[20] The impact of these programmes on protecting and promoting entitlements to food and basic necessities, including medical care, is reflected in the relatively low mortality and morbidity rates in China.

The contrast between China and India in public distribution systems and in social security programmes is certainly very striking, and it is plausible to see China's success story as one of support-led security. The growth-mediated interpretation would be much harder to defend, especially since there are so many uncertainties about what GNP growth rates China did, in fact, achieve. We shall come back to the growth question again in section 11.4 when we review the impact of the recent experience of high economic growth in China

[17] See World Bank (1983a, 1985), Jamison et al. (1984), Perkins and Yusuf (1984), L. C. Chen (1988), and Shao (1988), among many other contributions.

[18] World Development Report 1988, Table 29, p. 278. Population per physician is reported to be 3,700 in India and 1,730 for China in 1981. The corresponding figures for population per nursing person are 4,670 in India and 1,670 in China. It is often claimed, with some justice, that the medical training programmes in India are typically more exacting than the Chinese programmes have been (at least until recently). But the big difference in having *some* medical services available across the country (even in the remotest parts) makes the Chinese overall situation altogether distinct from that in India, and in this achievement the logistic advantages of having many more doctors and nurses per unit of population have been quite crucial.

[19] For some interesting comparisons between China and India in the domain of health, see A. Bhalla (1987); see also Chen (1987). The Chinese arrangements, especially for the rural areas, provide a major contrast with the lack of penetration of health services in rural India, especially among vulnerable groups (see Bose and Tyagi 1983, and Murthy et al. 1988).

[20] On the nature and reach of the social security system and public services in China, see Riskin (1986, 1987), Ahmad and Hussain (1988) and Hussain et al. (1989), and the literature cited there.

since the reforms. But before that we examine the big blot in China's past record, viz. the famine of 1958–61.

11.3　The Chinese Famine and the Indian Contrast

The Chinese famine of 1958–61 followed the débâcle of the so-called Great Leap Forward that was tried out from late 1957 onwards.[21] While the failure of the Great Leap Forward came to be widely recognized after the initial euphoria, the existence of the famine oddly escaped open scrutiny and even public recognition, until very recently.[22] This is particularly interesting given the monumental scale of the famine—arguably the largest in terms of total excess mortality in recorded history.

Comparing actual mortality with pre-famine mortality yields remarkably high figures of extra deaths in this famine. Estimates of extra mortality vary from 16.5 million to 29.5 million.[23] These figures are extraordinarily large. For example, the excess mortality in the last Indian famine, viz. the so-called Great Bengal famine of 1943 (occurring four years before independence), is estimated to be about 3 million.[24] In the scale of 'extra deaths' the Chinese famine was, thus, about five to ten times as large as the largest famine in India in this century.[25]

Many things are still uncertain about the causation of the famine, but it is clear that there was an enormous collapse of agricultural output and income. Food availability decline certainly played an important part in the genesis of hunger that gripped China for three years. Taking the average national grain output per capita of 308 kg. in 1956 and 1957 as the point of reference, the 1959 output was 17 per cent below this and by 1960 the per-capita grain output was as much as 30 per cent down. Even in 1961, the shortfall vis-à-vis the 1956–7

---

[21] Various regions of China also suffered from adverse weather conditions during 1959–61, involving drought and flooding in different parts of the country. These conditions certainly contributed to the production problems, but it is hard to escape the conclusion that the bulk of the problem was caused by the failure of the policy changes initiated by the Great Leap Forward. In fact, the adverse climatic conditions were particularly important in making it harder to identify precisely how fully the 'Leap' had failed.

[22] On this see Sen (1982c, 1983a), Bernstein (1983), Riskin (1986, 1987).

[23] See Coale (1981), Aird (1982), Ashton et al. (1984), Peng (1987). The largest estimate of 29.5 million (Ashton et al. 1984) attempts to take full note of unreported deaths. Peng's (1987) estimation based on provincial demographic data suggests a figure of 23 million.

[24] That figure was obtained also by using the same method of comparing actual mortality with pre-famine mortality, and making allowances for unreported deaths (Sen 1981a, Appendix D). The official estimate of excess mortality was 1.5 million, but that involved an undercounting due to incomplete temporal coverage.

[25] It must, however, be remembered that since the Chinese mortality rates had come down sharply already prior to the famine, the 'extra death' estimates based on pre-famine mortality rates are in comparison with a pre-famine death rate lower than that of most poor countries in the world. But even if considerably higher pre-famine mortality rates are used, the excess mortality in China still amounts to astonishingly high figures.

average was 28 per cent, and the pre-famine figure was not reattained until the latter half of the 1960s.[26]

Further, some regions suffered particularly serious declines and the sharp differences between food availability in the different regions continued through the period of distress.[27] For example, in 1960, while the provinces of Heilongjiang and Yunnan had respectively 229 and 209 kg. of grains per head for their rural population, the corresponding figures for Henan, Sichuan, and Hebei were respectively 143, 137, and 122 kg. The contrast between the rural and urban areas was also striking (for example, between 288 kg. in urban Hebei as against 122 in the rural areas of that province).[28]

Public distribution at the local level was comprehensively disrupted. The problem for the rural areas was made much worse by the sharp increase in state procurement of foodgrains, and the rural communes were in many cases desperately short of food. In addition to that, there were also remarkable inequalities in the distribution of whatever food was available. This applied not only between the regions and between urban and rural areas, but even within a given rural region. Some provinces evidently suffered from much sharper *intra*regional inequalities than others did, with correspondingly higher mortality. For instance, rural Sichuan and Henan suffered from much greater death rates than rural Hebei which did not have, on the average, any more food. Particularly, there was a great deal of wastage and excess consumption in particular 'commune mess halls'.[29]

The Chinese famine of 1958–61 was closely linked with policy failures —first in the débâcle of the Great Leap Forward, then in the delay in rectifying the harm done, and along with that in accentuating distributional inequalities through enhanced procurement and uneven sharing. The remarkable aspect of the famine is its continuation over a number of years without an adequate recognition of the nature of the crisis (and without leading to the necessary changes in public policy).

This is one respect in which India's record since independence must be seen to be very much superior. The fact that there has been no large-scale famine in India since independence is a positive contrast with the Chinese experience. The contrast is particularly interesting when account is taken of the fact that there have been several alarming dips in food output and availability in India over the same period (the latest being in the drought of 1987), and that on many occasions the entitlements of large parts of the population have been severely threatened both directly and indirectly (particularly through employment declines associated with droughts or floods).

[26] See Peng (1987: 653–5, esp. Table 3).
[27] See Riskin (1986, 1987) and Peng (1987).
[28] The data are taken from Peng (1987).
[29] On this see Peng (1987). 'Ironically,' notes Peng, 'almost all the provinces that were praised by a *People's Daily* article for their "good performance" in establishing rural mess halls experienced severe excess mortality' (p. 664).

The Indian system of famine prevention was discussed in Chapter 8 of this book. There are, as was argued, two different features involved in the system. One is a worked-out procedure for entitlement protection through employment creation (usually paying the wages in cash), supplemented by direct transfers to the 'unemployable'. The origins of this procedure go back to the 1880s and the Famine Codes of the late nineteenth century, though a number of important developments (including the use of the public distribution system to stabilize food prices) have taken place since independence. The other part is a political 'triggering mechanism' which brings the protection system into play and indeed which keeps the public support system in a state of preparedness. It was this triggering mechanism that was lacking in the famine prevention system of British India after the Famine Codes were set up. In the Bengal famine of 1943, not only were the Famine Codes not invoked, that was indeed a deliberate decision of the government.[30]

On the other hand, given the political system of post-independence India, it is extremely hard for any government in office—whether at the state level or at the centre—to get away with neglecting prompt and extensive anti-famine measures at the first signs of a famine. And these signs are themselves more easily transmitted given India's relatively free media and newspapers, and the active and investigative role that journalists as well as opposition politicians can and do play in this field. The adversarial participation of newspapers and opposition leaders is, as we have discussed earlier, an important part of the Indian famine prevention system. It yields a rapid triggering mechanism and encourages preparedness for entitlement protection.

The contrast with China is striking primarily in the second respect. Given its system of public distribution, China did not lack a delivery and redistribution mechanism to deal with food shortages as the famine threatened in 1958 and later. Despite the size of the decline of food output and the loss of entitlement of large sections of the population, China could have done a much better job of protecting the vulnerable by sharing the shortage in a bearable way.

What was lacking when the famine threatened China was a political system of adversarial journalism and opposition.[31] The Chinese famine raged on for three years without it being even admitted in public that such a thing was occurring, and without there being an adequate policy response to the threat. Not only was the world ignorant of the terrible state of affairs in China, even the population itself did not know about the extent of the national calamity and the extensive nature of the problems being faced in different parts of the country.

Indeed, the lack of adversarial journalism and politics hit even the govern-

---

[30] The Governor of Bengal, Sir T. Rutherford, wrote to the Viceroy of India explaining that a famine had not been declared to avoid the obligation to undertake the relief measures mandated by the Famine Codes. See Mansergh (1973, 363, Document No. 158).

[31] The reasons for this diagnosis and the empirical evidence for this view are discussed in Sen (1982c, 1983a).

ment, reinforcing the ignorance of local conditions because of politically motivated exaggeration of the crop size during the Great Leap Forward and the fear of local leaders about communicating their own problems. The pretence that everything was going all right in Chinese agriculture and rural economy to a great extent fooled the national leaders themselves. 'Leaders believed in 1959–60', as Bernstein puts it, 'that they had 100 MMT more grain than they actually did.'[32] This misconception was crucial in keeping down Chinese imports of foodgrains, which fell to virtually nothing in 1959 (about two thousand tons compared with 223 thousand tons in 1958), and stayed incredibly low in 1961 (66 thousand tons), before jumping to 5.8 million tons in 1961 as the fact of the famine and the agricultural débâcle became at long last clear. Chinese exports of foodgrains, similarly, peaked in 1959, and stayed high in 1960, before beginning to come down in 1961. The Chinese net exports of cereals rose from 1.9 million tons in 1957, to 2.7 in 1958, 4.2 in 1959, and 2.7 in 1960—as the famine devastated the lives of tens of millions of people across the country.[33]

The misinformation and misreading also led to a sharp *increase* in the extent of food procurement from the rural areas. The percentage net procurement out of total output went up from 15 to 17 per cent in 1956 and 1957 to 21 per cent in 1958 and 28 per cent in 1959.[34] The rural Chinese—hit by a production decline—were hit again by having to part with a larger proportion of the reduced output as procurement by the state.

The misinformation also contributed to the non-revision of production and distribution policies and to the absence of any emergency entitlement-protection programme.[35] Aside from the government's informational inadequacy, which made its own assessment of the situation disastrously wrong, the absence of an adversarial system of politics and journalism also meant that there was little political pressure on the government from any opposition group and from informed public opinion to take adequate anti-famine measures rapidly.

We end this section with three interpretative remarks. First, as was dis-

---

[32] Bernstein (1984: 13).

[33] The figures are from the *Statistical Yearbook of China 1981*. See also Riskin (1986, 1987) and Jowett (1988).

[34] Riskin (1987), Table 6.5. See also Bernstein (1984) and Peng (1987).

[35] In 1962, shortly after the famine, when the recent experiences were being reviewed, Mao Zedong noted the problem of informational failure for planning in the absence of local democracy: 'If there is no democracy and ideas are not coming from the masses, it is impossible to establish a good line, good general and specific policies and methods . . . Without democracy you have no understanding of what is happening down below; the situation will be unclear; you will be unable to collect sufficient opinions from all sides; there can be no communication between top and bottom; top-level organs of leadership will depend on one-sided and incorrect material to decide issues, thus you will find it difficult to avoid being subjectivist; it will be impossible to achieve unity of understanding and unity of action, and impossible to achieve true centralism' (Mao Zedong 1974: 164). On this pronouncement and its context and relevance, see Sen (1983a, 1984a)

cussed in Chapter 8, famine prevention is an important achievement of India, and there is something to learn from that experience in this famine-ridden world. The fact that even post-revolutionary China, with its outstanding record of entitlement promotion and enhancement of living conditions, could fall prey to a gigantic famine indicates that the lesson may be far from negligible. In fact, the precise feature of absence of adversarial politics and open journalism that may have contributed to the occurrence, magnitude and duration of the Chinese famines of 1958–61 are also present in most sub-Saharan African countries today. While the political systems are quite different, this feature of absence of political opposition and free journalism in African politics is a cause of famine vulnerability in Africa as it was in China at the time it had its own disaster. Also, greater tolerance of criticism and more open journalism in China would have a positive effect on helping to make China secure against the kind of political and economic crisis that ushered in the famines of 1958–61. But unfortunately political democratization in China has not really kept pace with the speed of economic liberalization (on which more presently).

Second, as India's experience shows, open journalism and adversarial politics provide much less protection against endemic undernutrition than they do against a dramatic famine. Starvation deaths and extreme deprivation are newsworthy in a way the quiet persistence of regular hunger and non-extreme deprivation are not. Endemic hunger may increase the morbidity rate and add to the mortality rate (in these respects India's performance continues to be quite awful), but that is primarily a statistical picture rather than being immediately palpable and—no less importantly—being 'big news'. To bring endemic deprivation into the fold of news reporting and to make it a major focus of political confrontation are inherently more difficult tasks, and seem to have been largely beyond the normal activities of journalists and politicians in India.[36] That situation could change (there are some signs of that already), and this is clearly a field in which there is scope for the public to play a very creative role in India. But as things stand, the Chinese political commitment—not unrelated to the ideological predispositions of the Chinese political system —seems to have served the country well for combating endemic deprivation, despite its failure as a defence against famines.

Finally, it is important to note that despite the gigantic size of excess mortality in the Chinese famine, the extra mortality in India from regular deprivation in normal times vastly overshadows the former. Comparing India's death rate of 12 per thousand with China's of 7 per thousand, and applying that difference to the Indian population of 781 million in 1986, we get an estimate of excess normal mortality in India of 3.9 million per year. This implies that every eight years or so more people die in India because of its higher regular death rate than died in China in the gigantic famine of

---

[36] On this see Sen (1982c, 1983a, 1984a) and Ram (1986).

Table 11.1 China since the 1979 reforms

	Gross value of output (index)		Death rate (index)		Female–male ratio (value)
	Industry	Agriculture	National	Rural	
1979	100	100	100	100	94.3
1980	109	104	102	101	94.4
1981	113	111	102	102	94.2
1982	122	123	106	110	94.1
1983	135	135	114	120	93.9
1984	154	159	108	105	93.7
1985	181	181	106	104	93.5
1986	197	201	108	105	93.6

Source: People's Republic of China, *Statistical Yearbook of China 1986* (in English); *1987* (in Chinese).

1958–61.[37] India seems to manage to fill its cupboard with more skeletons every eight years than China put there in its years of shame.

11.4   Chinese Economic Reforms: Opulence and Support

The economic reforms introduced in China in 1979 have now gone through nearly a decade of practice, and it is possible to begin assessing some of their impacts. On the side of commodity production, there is little doubt that the Chinese economy has surged ahead in response to market incentives, and the agricultural sector has really had—at long last—a proper 'leap forward'. As Table 11.1 indicates, the gross value of agricultural output doubled between 1979 and 1986 (a growth rate of more than 10 per cent per year). Growth in the agricultural sector has also kept pace with industrial expansion, which is in fact quite remarkable in itself, particularly since industrial expansion has been very fast as well. There may be some questions about the exact figures (there might have been incentives to understate output prior to the reforms), and it is not easy to be certain of the exact growth rates achieved. There has also been a slow-down after the initial leap, as well as some worry that the production of food crops has not kept up with the expansion of other types of production. Nevertheless, taking everything into account, there can be little doubt that the economic reforms have been quite remarkable in expanding the supply of nutrients in China as well as agricultural outputs and incomes in general.[38]

The economic reforms can be and have been questioned from many points of view. The fact that the reforms have led to an inflationary situation with price

[37] This is so with the highest of the estimated mortality figures, viz. 29.5 million (due to Ashton *et al.* 1984). If instead we take, say, Peng's figure of 23 million, then every *six* years there is more extra mortality in India than in the Chinese famine of 1958–61.

[38] See Riskin (1986, 1987), Johnson (1988) and Perkins (1988). On the incentive problems of collective agriculture, see Putterman (1986), and also Nee (1986).

rises destabilizing the consumers' equilibrium has been widely acknowledged, and this has caused some rethinking on how far and how fast to go on the path of economic change. There have also been fears that the price mechanism, while successful in raising total outputs and incomes, may increase inequalities in the distribution of incomes. But, again, even after taking note of these qualifications, it is quite clear that the average opulence of the Chinese population, especially the rural population, has expanded greatly since the reforms.

Even in the reduction of poverty, calculated in terms of personal incomes, a great deal has been recently achieved. It appears that the number of rural Chinese below the poverty line of 200 yuan in 1986 prices has fallen from 200 million in 1979 to 70 million in 1986.[39] That is a striking decline of which there are few parallels. If 'growth-mediated security' were the chief means of promotion of longevity in China, this post-reform experience should have provided an excellent basis for further enhancement of life expectancy at a rapid rate.

In fact, however, this has not occurred, as we noted earlier. The death rate in China, rather than declining rapidly, seems to have gone *up* after the reforms, as Table 11.1 indicates. Indeed, in no year since 1979 has the death rate—as given in Chinese official statistics—been lower than that achieved by 1978 and 1979, viz. 6.2 per thousand. The death rate, as reported in the *Statistical Yearbook of China*, went up to 7.1 by 1983, and even after coming down, it has hovered around 6.6 and 6.7 in 1985 and 1986.

There is much room for doubt about the correctness of the official Chinese mortality data. It must be particularly noted that an increase in the coverage of mortality statistics may have the effect of raising the reported death rate. It is quite possible that at least some part of the apparent increase in mortality rates after 1979 is connected with better coverage of death data. Also, we have to take note of the changing age composition of the Chinese population when interpreting overall death rates.[40] But even after note has been taken of these factors, there is evidence of an increase in forces of mortality since the reforms compared with what had been achieved before them.[41] The downward trend in mortality which made China reach truly unusual levels of longevity (given its low per-capita income) has been at least halted, and possibly reversed.

The effect of the changing age composition can be eliminated by looking not at the crude death rate, which is in effect a simple average, but at the life expectancy figures. Life expectancy is estimated by using 'endogenous weights' (in the sense that the population in different age groups is estimated

[39] See Riskin (1988: 21).

[40] See Banister (1987) and Hussain and Stern (1988).

[41] Hussain and Stern (1988) argue that 'the year to year fluctuations [in death rates] are likely to be largely the result of changing data sources and methods', but confirm a broad pattern of 'a reduction [in the death rate] to the end of 1970s followed by an increase of around 7% in the death rate from 1979–86' (p. 18).

Table 11.2 Life and death in China, 1978–1984

Year	Crude death rate (per thousand): Banister's adjusted estimates	Life expectancy at birth (years): Banister's estimates	Infant mortality rate (per thousand)	
			Banister's adjusted estimates	Yang and Dowdle indirect estimates
1978	7.5	65.1	37.2	40
1979	7.6	65.0	39.4	41
1980	7.7	64.9	41.6	44
1981	7.7	64.8	43.7	53
1982	7.9	64.7	45.9	61
1983	8.0	64.6	48.0	—
1984	8.0	64.6	50.1	—

Source: Banister (1987) Table 4.18 and Yang and Dowdle (1985).

by using the mortality rates in the previous age groups), and does not depend on the actual age structure of the existing population. Thus, concentrating on life expectancy gives us a good idea of what we are looking for.

Judith Banister's estimates of life expectancy at birth are given in Table 11.2. These suggest a steady decline in life expectancy since 1978 (up to and including 1984, which is the last year in Banister's series). The fall is moderate, though firm and consistent, but it has to be judged particularly as a contrast with steadily declining mortality rates and expansion of life expectancy up to the late 1970s (with the exception, of course, of the period of the famine of 1958–61, discussed earlier). The real issue is the slowing down of social progress just when overall economic growth has quickened.

While the reduction of life expectancy is fairly moderate, the rise of infant mortality according to some estimates appears to be sharp (see Table 11.2). This is so according to both Banister's estimates and also the indirect estimates made by Yang and Dowdle (1985) on the basis of a fertility survey questionnaire. The extent to which this is connected with China's enforced population policy introduced also in 1979—especially the insistence on a one-child limit in many parts of the country and a two-child limit elsewhere—is not crystal clear, but there is strong circumstantial evidence in that direction.[42] One of the sinister signs is a decline in the reported birth ratio of females to males, and this can reflect infanticide, or at least death due to severe neglect, of female children, with their births as well as deaths remaining unregistered.[43] The recent

[42] See Banister (1987: Chapter 7). 'Many couples, determined to have a son, have killed their infant daughters, either outright or by severe neglect, so that they could try again for a son' (Banister 1987: 40).
[43] See Hull (1988) on this general question, and also on the results of a 1 per cent survey of the population carried out by the State Statistical Bureau in 1987.

Table 11.3 Gender differential in mortality in China, 1978–1984

Year	Life expectancy at birth (years)			Infant mortality per thousand		
	Females	Males	Female advantage	Females	Males	Female advantage
1978	66.0	64.1	1.9	37.7	36.8	−0.9
1979	65.7	64.3	1.4	42.7	36.3	−6.4
1980	65.3	64.4	0.9	47.7	35.8	−11.9
1981	65.0	64.5	0.5	52.6	35.3	−17.3
1982	64.7	64.7	0.0	57.5	34.9	−22.6
1983	64.4	64.8	−0.4	62.4	34.4	−28.0
1984	64.1	64.9	−0.8	67.2	33.9	−33.3

Source: Banister (1987), Table 4.12.

relaxation of the one-child limit when the first child is a girl may have been the result of recognizing the prevalence of this problem.

No matter what role the population policy may have played in this, there is considerable evidence that the mortality picture has possibly darkened for girls in comparison with boys in recent years. In fact, Banister's estimations suggest that in the post-reform period while male infant mortality has continued to fall (though only quite slowly), it is female infant mortality that has apparently had an *upward* jump (see Table 11.3). Similarly and correspondingly, male life expectancy at birth has continued to rise (again, very moderately since the reforms), but female life expectancy reached a peak in the pre-reform year of 1978 and has fallen apparently since then. These estimates are speculative and must not be taken too seriously, but altogether there is much evidence of (1) a slow down or a halt in the steadily improving survival chances of both men and women, and specifically children, and (2) on top of that, an evident increase in gender bias, specifically affecting female children.

The increase in gender bias, if confirmed, would no doubt relate (at least partly) to recent population policies. However, enforced limitation of population size, since it is in principle 'gender neutral', can have a devastating effect on female children *only* when there is already a strong parental preference for male children, and ultimately we have to be concerned also with the causal roots of that preference.

Such male-preference is not, of course, a new thing in China, but it is arguable that the responsibility system may itself have contributed a little to the undermining of the position of women. As was argued in Chapter 4, there is considerable evidence that the involvement of women in so-called 'gainful employment' tends to reduce gender bias against females. In this respect, the communal form of agriculture used in pre-reform China provided much easier scope for female 'gainful' involvement, and the proportion of women in such employment had risen quite radically in the 1960s and 1970s. However, with the new responsibility system, Chinese agricultural production has become more family-based, with the usual division of labour that tends to place women in activities of the typical 'household' kind.[44]

This can indeed be an influence towards worsening the position of women in 'cooperative conflicts', and through a general regression of women's economic position and social status, can also strengthen the anti-female bias in the caring of children. It is not obvious that this type of effect, which—if important—is most likely to be so only in the long run, could have had any role already in the Chinese rural society. But no matter what view is taken of that question (and more generally of any strengthening of anti-female bias in the Chinese society), the pre-existing level of anti-female bias would, in any case, tend to make any restrictive policy fall disproportionately on the female child.

The restrictive developments of the post-reform period include not merely the enforced control of family size, but also a considerable reduction in the general medical care and health services available in rural China. The 'support-led security' on the basis of which China had achieved so much prior to the reforms has been weakened rather than strengthened in some important ways by the reforms affecting the economy and the society.[45] In fact, despite the increase in outputs and incomes, the support system that the Chinese had built up with such success has been under severe strain. There is a clear weakening of commitment to public support measures, which may be partly ideological, related to the recent passion for economic liberalism.[46] But it is also connected with the undermining of the financial and institutional basis of public support measures at the local level in rural areas, as a result of the abandonment of previous communal arrangements and their replacement by the 'responsibility system', which we discussed earlier.[47]

The rural production brigades used to offer a widespread cooperative medical system of health insurance, but the proportion offering this support has declined from 90 per cent in 1977 to about 34 per cent by 1985.[48] It appears that the earlier cooperative health insurance survives only in 5 per cent of the villages, according to the Ministry of Public Health.[49] The number of village-level medical workers has fallen from 3.3 million in 1975 to 1.2 million by 1984. The number of 'barefoot doctors' working in Chinese villages and brigade

---

[44] On this see Aslanbeigui and Summerfield (1989). On the comparison with the pre-reform situation, see also Croll (1983), Hemmel and Sindbjerg (1984), Nee (1986), Wolf (1987) and Kelkar (1989).

[45] It is, in fact, also possible that the breakdown of social support provisions regarding old age security may have added to the existing 'pro-male-child' bias, given the association of male-preference with the motive of insuring support in old age. On related matters, see Hussain et al. (1989).

[46] Riskin (1988) notes that the style is a hybrid one involving 'a strange mixture of residual socialist rhetoric and Chicago School values'. But the socialist rhetoric has been distinctly in retreat in recent years.

[47] On this see Banister (1986, 1987), Nee (1986), Panikar (1986), Bhalla (1987), Ahmad and Hussain (1988), Johnson (1988), Shao (1988), and Hussain et al. (1989).

[48] See Banister (1986: 2–3).

[49] See Shao (1988).

clinics went down from 1.8 million in 1977 to 1.3 million by 1984, and is known to have fallen greatly since. The number of female barefoot doctors fell even more sharply. By now, that entire system of medically imperfect but socially useful service is in complete decline, and the number of barefoot doctors is no longer reported in the *Statistical Yearbook*.[50]

Further, the balance between urban and rural areas in terms of medical services—less unequal in China than in most developing countries—has also been disrupted by the changes accompanying the reforms. By 1983 the three-quarters of China's total population who happen to live in rural areas had to make do with the services of only half the practising doctors, i.e. a third of what the urban areas had in per capita terms.[51]

The impact of these declines in rural health services must have been significant in general and particularly detrimental to vulnerable groups, and its role in halting the rapidly declining trend of Chinese mortality would have been substantial. Also, the burden of decreased health services seems to have been unequally shared between boys and girls, and given the pre-existing anti-female bias (whether strengthened or not in the post-reform period), the gender inequalities can be expected to be most consequential in periods of general contraction.[52]

Despite these disruptions of communal health facilities, China does, of course, remain considerably ahead of India in terms of its widespread public health provisions and related social security facilities. The Chinese also remain firmly in the lead in the fields of longevity, nutrition and health. But the recent economic reforms, with their negative effects on public support (especially at the local level in the rural areas), have moved China a little bit in the direction of India, and that—in this context—is not a particularly helpful development. The weakening of the support-led system has not been outweighed by a growth-mediated new development.

It is too early to judge what kind of a new equilibrium China will achieve. At the moment it is clear that there is a pause and perhaps even some regress in the expansion of longevity and in the reduction of morbidity, despite the progress in incomes and opulence. The authoritarian nature of Chinese politics has permitted an abrupt reduction in the social security provisions that had contributed so much to China's earlier successes.

It is not our purpose to prognosticate what will happen in China in the long run. From the point of view of public action against hunger and deprivation, what is especially important is an understanding of the policy issues raised by China's varied experience. A particularly important one concerns the role of public support, especially the universality of the coverage of public support. The contribution that universal (or near-universal) support-led security can

---

[50] From 1986 the *Statistical Yearbooks* discontinued giving the numbers of barefoot doctors, and the last year of report is 1984. See also World Bank (1984a) and Banister (1986).

[51] See Banister (1986: 2).

[52] On the general issue of gender bias and intrahousehold distribution, see Chapter 4.

make to living conditions is exemplified both by (1) China's progress in expanding some of the most basic capabilities up to the late 1970s despite little increase in per-capita GNP and food consumption, and (2) her comparative regress in these vital fields in the post-reform period despite rapidly rising outputs and incomes.

11.5 China, India and Kerala

India offers within its own boundaries quite a variety of experiences. There are great interstate differences, and one state in particular, viz. Kerala, deserves special attention in terms of public action against hunger and deprivation. Kerala is one of the poorer Indian states.[53] Yet it has achieved a remarkably high level of life expectancy—by a long margin higher than any other Indian state, including the richest states of Punjab and Haryana.

The last rigorous estimate of life expectancy at birth in India available at the time of writing this monograph is for the period 1976–80. The figures for the next half-decade 1981–5 have not yet been published. The all-India average figure in 1976–80 was 52 years, but that for Kerala was as high as 66 years (68 for females and 64 for males), which is not materially different from China's achievement.[54] Early estimates indicate considerable increases in life expectancy in India as a whole, but Kerala's overwhelming lead has been maintained.

Doubts have been raised as to whether Kerala's outstanding longevity indicators are reflective of a comparable breakthrough in general health and nutritional well-being.[55] These doubts have arisen mainly from the additional evidence provided by (1) low calorie intakes, and (2) high self-reported morbidity rates. The significance of these indicators is, however, open to serious question. As was discussed at some length in Chapter 3, calorie intake offers a poor basis of assessment of nutritional status, and when it comes to more direct measures of nutritional well-being (especially the avoidance of severe undernourishment), it appears that Kerala remains firmly ahead of other Indian states.[56] As far as high morbidity rates are concerned, these are

[53] The standard comparative data can be found in Agrawal, Verma and Gupta (1987). For a probing analysis of the comparative real incomes of the different Indian states (taking note of distributional differences), see Bhattacharya, Chatterjee and Pal (1988). See also Sanyal (1988) on Kerala's comparative poverty in terms of landholding.

[54] This figure of 65.5 years is, in fact, a little higher than Judith Banister's estimate of life expectancy for China even before the reforms (65.1), and a fortiori so afterwards (64.6 in 1984 according to Banister's estimate). It must, of course, be mentioned that there is a lot of regional diversity within China (on this see Prescott and Jamison 1985), and the life expectancies in the more advanced regions are higher than that in Kerala.

[55] See e.g. Panikar and Soman (1984) and B. G. Kumar (1987).

[56] See e.g. the anthropometric evidence presented in B. G. Kumar (1987), Table 6.7, and Subbarao (1989), Table 6 (both based on survey data collected by the National Nutrition Monitoring Bureau). The very low incidence of 'severe undernutrition' in Kerala is particularly striking—a matter of particular importance for health, well-being and survival (on this see Lipton 1983, and also Chapter 3 above). The percentage of 'severe undernutrition' for children between 1 and 5 years of age in 1982 was 6.1 for India as a whole and only 1.5 for Kerala (Kumar 1987, Table 6.7).

Table 11.4 China, India and Kerala: selected comparisons

	Adult literacy rate (per cent)		Life expectancy at birth (years)		Female–male ratio
	Female	Male	Female	Male	
China[a]	56	82	64.1	64.9	0.935
India[b]	26	55	52.1	52.5	0.934
Kerala[b]	71	86	67.6	63.5	1.032

[a] 1984 and 1985
[b] 1981

Notes and sources: Adult literacy rates for China for 1985 are taken from UNICEF, *The State of the World's Children 1988*, and for India and Kerala, they are calculated from the data presented in the *Census of India 1981*. Life expectancy figures for China are taken from Banister (1987), Table 4.18, and relate to 1984. The official *Statistical Yearbook of China 1986* gives figures of 69.3 years for females and 66.4 years for males for 1982. The life expectancy figures for India and Kerala relate to the period 1976–80, and are taken from *SRS Based Abridged Life-Tables 1976–80* (Occasional Paper No. 1, 1985), published by the Registrar General of India. The female–male ratio for China in 1985 is obtained from *Statistical Yearbook of China 1986*, and that for India and Kerala for 1981 from the *Census of India 1981*.

based on *self-reported* illnesses, and it is not easy to determine the extent to which they reflect a greater level of articulation of a population that is enormously more literate and health-conscious than people anywhere else in India. It has been argued, in fact, that self-reported morbidity indicators as they exist today are extremely misleading in the context of interpersonal comparisons of well-being.[57] While there is some scope for disputation as to the precise relationship between longevity and other aspects of nutrition or health in Kerala, the overall picture of success is hard to deny.

The role of public support in Kerala's achievement has attracted justified attention.[58] ṭhis has partly taken the form of extensive medical coverage of the population through public health services, helped by the determination of the population—much more educated than elsewhere in India—to seek medical attention.[59] Kerala is also the only Indian state in which the public distribution

[57] For the evidential basis of this claim, see Murray and Chen (1989). As shown by these authors, many contrary findings arise from assessments of well-being based on self-reported morbidity data. For instance, while self-reported morbidity rates in India are highest in Kerala (and lowest in Uttar Pradesh, where the expectation of life is about 25 years *shorter* than in Kerala), they are even higher in the United States, and within the United States they are highest in the higher income groups. Such findings do not imply, of course, that self-reported morbidity data are entirely useless. Self-perception of morbidity as well as articulate reporting are of obvious interest in the social analysis of *perception* and *communication*.

[58] See Centre for Development Studies (1975), S. K. Kumar (1979), Gwatkin (1979), Gwatkin et al. (1980), Jose (1984), Panikar and Soman (1984), Halstead et al. (1985), Krishnan (1985, 1989), Stewart (1985), Caldwell (1986), B. G. Kumar (1987), Osmani (1988a).

[59] It is arguable that the higher incidence of reported morbidity can be seen as a positively contributory factor in Kerala's success in dealing with diseases and in expanding longevity. Treatment can begin only when attention is paid to the disease from which one is suffering. A large proportion of the Indian rural population die from undiagnosed—often ignored—diseases.

of food goes well beyond the limits of urban areas and provides significant support to the rural population.

The high literacy level of Kerala is also a major asset, especially in making people more eager and more skilled in seeking modern remedies for treatable ailments. It may also have a role in facilitating public participation in social change and in generating public demand for social security.[60] The innovative programmes in the distribution of health care and food in Kerala have frequently followed articulated social and political demands.[61] The same is true of a range of institutional changes, notably wage legislation and land reforms.

In contrast with the all-India adult literacy rate of 41 per cent (age 15 or over) in 1981, Kerala's literacy rate is 78 per cent. That ratio is also substantially higher than China's 70 per cent for 1985. There is also a particularly important feature in Kerala's pattern of literacy. It shows relatively less gender bias. The percentage of adult literacy in Kerala in 1981 was 71 for women and 86 for men, compared with 26 and 55 respectively for India as a whole. The gender bias in literacy is also substantially less in Kerala than in China, as Table 11.4 indicates. The female literacy rate of 71 per cent in Kerala compares well with the corresponding rate of 56 per cent in China.

In fact, the history of literacy expansion through public action goes back a long time in Kerala. The state of Kerala was formed at the time of independence by amalgamating, on grounds of linguistic uniformity and cultural unity, two so-called 'native Indian states' (viz. Travancore and Cochin) with a part of the old Madras Presidency in British India (viz. Malabar). As it happens, public policy in both the native Indian states put much greater emphasis on general education and literacy than was the case in the rest of India, and the emphasis on female education was particularly exceptional. In fact, as early as 1817, the ruler of Travancore, Rani (Queen) Gouri Parvathi Bai, had issued a rescript commanding that 'the State should defray the entire cost of the education of its people in order that there might be no backwardness in the spread of enlightenment among them, that by diffusion of education they might become better subjects and public servants and that the reputation of the State might be advanced thereby'.[62] The Rani was probably right, and the wide educational base in Kerala seems to have had a major impact on other public policies in that state (including medical care and food policy), in addition to encouraging intelligent health practice at the family level.

Gender bias is a topic of some interest in the context of both China and India. As was noted in Chapter 4, both China and India have an exceptionally low female–male ratio (FMR) in the population, and the issue of female survival is

---

[60] See Halstead et al. (1985) and Caldwell (1986). See also Mencher (1980).

[61] The radicalism of Kerala's politics found some expression in 1957 in its being the first Indian state to elect a communist government. Since then different political coalitions have ruled the state, and the parties in office have been typically kept on a short leash.

[62] Quoted in Census of India, 1931, vol. xxviii (Trivandrum, 1932), p. 301.

an important one in both countries. Life expectancy at birth has been lower for females than for males in India until very recently and the cross-over—bringing India in line with much of the rest of the world—is supposed to have occurred only in this decade.[63] In China, the move in recent years has been in the opposite direction, and the female life expectancy, which used to be higher than the male, has now become lower (see Table 11.3 and the discussion in the last section). In both countries the female–male ratio remains dismally low —around 93 females per 100 males. It contrasts with the ratio of 1.05 or higher observed in those countries (e.g. in Europe or North America) in which there is little gender bias in health care and food distribution (though there may be much sexism in other areas), and it is much lower (as discussed in Chapter 4) than the sub-Saharan African ratio of 1.02.

In contrast with both China and the rest of India, the female–male ratio in Kerala was higher than 1.03 in the last census, and is taken to have risen further since then. This is a higher female–male ratio than that for every region of the developing world for which we examined aggregated data in Chapter 4 (including sub-Saharan Africa, which was the basis for our calculation of 'missing women').

To what extent the relative absence of gender bias in Kerala relates to its radical public policy (discussed earlier) is hard to say. It would be surprising if a greater level of female education—and less gender inequality in the sharing of education—had not contributed to better prospects of a plausible life for women, both through raising the status of women and through increasing female economic power and independence in 'cooperative conflicts' (discussed in Chapter 4).

But there are also other factors to be considered here, including the partially matrilineal system of inheritance in parts of Kerala and the relatively long history of its left-wing activist politics. It would be well beyond the scope of the present inquiry to go into this important but difficult question, and the sorting out of different but interrelated causal influences can be a particularly hard exercise. But it is worth noting, as a preliminary observation for closer scrutiny, that the one state in India that has made extensive use of support-led security has also been able to avoid some of the disastrous implications of gender bias that   gues so many parts of the world. The possibility of support-led systems making a contribution to gender equality is something that would deserve further investigation.[64]

---

[63] See Dyson (1987).

[64] It should be mentioned here that the female–male ratio being greater than unity has been a feature of Kerala since before this century. In the *Census of India* for 1881, it was remarked: 'In Travancore, as in other southern populations, the proportions of the sexes approach more nearly to European standards than is the case in the northern states and Provinces' (*Report on the Census of British India*, vol. i (London: HMSO 1883), p. 70). This fact should not be seen as automatically turning the table against the importance of support-led security for reducing gender bias, since the active promotion of primary education, especially female education, in Kerala (in particular in

The success of Kerala in achieving support-led security adds force to the plausibility of following this route even when the economy is very poor. The fact that Kerala has achieved such success through careful and wide-coverage public support shows how much can be achieved even at a low level of income, if public action is aimed at promoting people's basic entitlements and capabilities.

People's capability to conquer preventable illness and to escape premature mortality depends crucially on their command over basic necessities and their ability to use these with skill. Public support of education, health, employment, etc. can contribute both to that command and to the necessary abilities. The varying experiences of China and India, and the internal diversity of those experiences (both over time and over regions), bring out the importance of these roles in varying contexts.

Travancore and Cochin) goes back to early in the last century. *Both* the features of higher FMR and higher involvement in basic education (especially for girls) go back to the 19th century in the case of Kerala.

12

Experiences of Direct Support

12.1 Introduction

In this chapter, we examine the strategy of support-led security as it is reflected in the experiences of some selected countries, in particular Sri Lanka, Chile, and Costa Rica. The distinction between 'growth-mediated security' and 'support-led security' has already been discussed in some detail in the two preceding chapters. It was explained, in particular, that the distinction between the two does not lie in the use of public support in one case and not in the other. Even the cases of growth-mediated security (e.g. in South Korea and Kuwait) studied in Chapter 10 involved crucial use of public support provisions utilizing the resources generated by economic growth, and indeed in this respect the contrast between growth-mediated security and 'unaimed opulence' can be both striking and important.

The strategy of support-led security is distinguished by the use of public support without waiting for the country in question to get rich as a result of sustained economic growth. The rationale of this approach consists of using public support directly for raising the standard of living, rather than waiting for economic growth to do this (by increasing private incomes *and* providing resources for public support at a later stage). It is the direct use of public support in expanding the capabilities of people, not qualified by achieved growth, that characterizes the distinct nature of this strategy.

The countries that are studied in this chapter are all relatively poor in terms of GNP per head. Even for the two richer ones, viz. Costa Rica and Chile, the levels of GNP per capita (respectively $1,480 and $1,320 in 1986) are substantially lower than that of, say, South Korea ($2,370), in spite of superior achievements in some aspects of quality of life (e.g. expectations of life of 74 and 71 years respectively, as against 69 years for South Korea). The contrast is much sharper in the case of Sri Lanka, with its GNP per capita of only $400 and a life expectancy of 70 years.[1] In this respect, Sri Lanka's position is somewhat similar to that of China and Kerala, discussed in the last chapter.

Before we turn to the country experiences, one general point is perhaps worth mentioning. It may be wondered whether a poor country—especially one as poor as, say, Sri Lanka—can at all 'afford' to have programmes of public support in any way comparable with those of countries many times richer. That worry is a legitimate one, but in considering feasibilities one must not fall into the trap of assuming exactly similar real costs in different countries. In

---

[1] These figures are taken from *World Development Report 1988*, Table 1.

particular, in a poor country not only are the GNP and the public budget quite restricted, the labour costs involved in providing, say, education and health care are also low (because of tinier wages).[2] Indeed, even the cost of support of public employment is lower in these economies for the same reason. This does not make the resource problem disappear for the poorer economies (health services in particular tend to have substantial non-labour costs as well), but the apparent enormity of the gap between what the richer and the poorer countries can afford has to be scaled down considerably to take note of this fact. The ambitious public support programmes in the low income countries to be studied in this chapter would have been probably unaffordable had this not been the case.

12.2 Sri Lanka

The case of Sri Lanka was singled out earlier as one of remarkable achievement despite its low GNP. Judged in terms of life expectancy, child mortality, literacy rates, and similar criteria, Sri Lanka does indeed stand out among the poor countries in the world.[3]

Sri Lanka's experience is particularly worth studying not only for the exceptional nature of its achievement, but also for its timing. Large-scale expansion of basic public services began early in Sri Lanka. The active promotion of primary education goes back to the early decades of this century.[4] The sharp increase in public health measures took place later, but still as early as the middle 1940s. The radically innovative scheme of providing free or heavily subsidized rice to all was introduced in 1942. The fruits of this expansion were also reaped early, and by the end of the 1950s, Sri Lanka was altogether exceptional in having an astonishingly higher life expectancy at birth than any other country among the low-income developing countries.[5]

The issue of timing is of some importance in assessing Sri Lanka's experience. Given the much wider availability of internationally comparable data in later periods, such as 1960 onwards, it is tempting to compare the changes in Sri Lanka's achievement in the post-1960 world with those of other countries.

---

[2] This applies even in terms of market wages, but the contrast may be sharper in terms of social cost of labour, because of underemployment and surplus labour. On this issue, see Dobb (1960), Sen (1960, 1984a), Chakravarty (1969), Marglin (1976), and Drèze and Stern (1987).

[3] In view of the domestic problems that Sri Lanka has had in recent years, involving political violence and social strife, it is easy to think of Sri Lanka as a much troubled country. That it certainly is, even though it is also the country with the highest life expectancy among all the low income countries of the world. There are, *inter alia*, considerable disparities between the different communities, and the appreciation of Sri Lanka's achievements has to be qualified by an adequate recognition of these—and other—inequalities.

[4] There is a similarity in this respect with the expansion of literacy in the Indian state of Kerala. Kerala too, as was discussed in Chapter 11, reaped the rewards of early expansion in literacy.

[5] Nutrition indicators based on anthropometric measurements as well as on dietary intakes confirm that the post-war period in Sri Lanka was one of rapid improvements in living conditions. On this see Gray (1974) and the literature cited there.

Table 12.1 Sri Lanka: intervention and achievement

Year	Public distribution of food	Number of medical personnel	Death rate per thousand
1940	No (introduced 1942)	271	20.6
1950	Yes	357	12.6
1960	Yes	557	8.6
1970	Yes (reduced 1972, 1979)	693	7.5
1980	Yes	664	6.1

Source: Sen (1988d), Table 7.

This does not bring out the nature of Sri Lanka's achievement, since it managed a radical transformation in life expectancy *earlier* than 1960, and the absence of further radical expansion later on was partly due to the high level of longevity accomplished already. The right period for examining Sri Lanka's transformation is the one *preceding* 1960, rather than following it.

Indeed, judged in terms of further reduction of under-5 mortality rate during 1960–85, Sri Lanka is only a moderately good performer—not an exceptional one—even though in terms of absolute levels its current record remains better than that of any other low-income developing country. The same applies to life expectancy and other related indicators. The neglect of the timing of Sri Lanka's public intervention programme can lead to the spurious conclusion that its achievements are not exceptional, or that public intervention achieved little in that country. This is worth mentioning since that interpretational error has often been made, and since the alleged debunking of the role of public support in Sri Lanka has received wide attention.[6]

The temporal relation between the expansion of public support and the reduction of mortality rates in Sri Lanka is brought out by Table 12.1. Between 1940 and 1960 the death rate fell from 20.6 per thousand to 8.6 per thousand —a level not far from that of Europe and North America. This occurred along with the radical expansion of health services brought in with great vigour in the middle 1940s and with the bold introduction of free rice distribution in 1942.[7]

It should also be noted that the vigour of public intervention slackens a good

[6] On this see Bhalla and Glewwe (1986) and Bhalla (1988), and also Bhagwati (1987). On some technical problems in the Bhalla–Glewwe analysis, in addition to the issue of the misleading choice of time period, see Anand and Kanbur (1987), Glewwe and Bhalla (1987), Isenman (1987), Pyatt (1987), and Ravallion (1987c). See also Sen (1988f).

[7] The eradication of malaria was one of the first targets of public health care measures, and this campaign was remarkably successful. However, this success only accounts for a part of total mortality reduction during this period. For an excellent discussion of this question, and a review of earlier contributions, see Gray (1974). The author concludes on the basis of careful statistical analysis that the control of malaria altogether accounted for 23 per cent of the decline in average crude death rates in Sri Lanka in the post-war period. Somewhat higher estimates, with a 'preferred value' of 44 per cent, were obtained by Peter Newman (1970, 1977).

deal in the later decades, particularly in the 1970s, with a decrease (rather than an increase) in the number of medical personnel and a sharp reduction in the subsidized distribution of food. Given these disengagements, the slowing down of Sri Lanka's expansion of life expectancy in the later decades would not be any kind of 'proof' against the effectiveness of public support as a policy—quite the contrary.[8]

The temporal connection between the expansion of public support in Sri Lanka and the corresponding achievements is easy to see.[9] To move from time-relations to asserting causal connections is, of course, always problematic, and this can be done only with careful attention being paid to the evidence on the causal links that can explain the observed relations. The causal role of health services and public distribution of food has been the subject of a good deal of empirical analysis recently, and there is much evidence of the causal connections proceeding the way that time-relations suggest.[10]

Sri Lanka's experience in support-led security is particularly interesting not merely because it was one of the first developing countries to go that way (preceding even the spectacular case of China), but also because it was then—and still is—a good deal poorer than many other countries that have traversed the path of security through direct support (e.g. Costa Rica, Chile, or Jamaica). Sri Lanka's strategic experience as a pioneer in overcoming the major penalties of low income remains one of great significance for understanding the prospects for support-led security in poor countries.

12.3 Chile

Is there a natural affinity between the strategy of support-led security and particular political regimes? An association of this kind is not implausible, since the attempt to remove hunger through direct public support rather than through the intermediation of growth naturally involves a strong bias in favour of the more deprived sections of the population. Not unexpectedly, regimes where political power is particularly concentrated in the hands of the rich have a tendency to favour development models which give greater prominence to economic growth—whether as an element of a strategy of growth-mediated security, or in the form of unaimed opulence (or indeed in the form of opulence aimed at the privileged classes!).

An examination of the political systems of the six countries (China, Costa

---

[8] This is quite aside from the fact that by 1960 Sri Lanka's achievements in longevity and low mortality were already high. This made further improvements in absolute terms that much harder to achieve compared with countries having still a long distance to go.

[9] There is also some indication of a possible temporal relation between the reduction of public support from the late 1970s and the increase in morbidity and mortality of the affected groups. On this see Edirisinghe (1987), Jayawardena *et al.* (1987), Sahn (1987), UNICEF (1987*b*), Sahn and Edirisinghe (forthcoming). See also Anand and Kanbur (1987).

[10] See Newman (1970, 1977), Jayawardena (1974), Gwatkin (1979), Fields (1980), Isenman (1980), Alailima (1985), Basu (1986), Anand and Kanbur (1987), Samarasinghe (1988), among others.

Rica, Cuba, Chile, Jamaica, and Sri Lanka) identified earlier as illustrations of the strategy of support-led security reveals an interesting pattern. The only country in the list which can be described as being ruled by a right-wing dictatorship is Chile. The others have either communist governments (China and Cuba), or are multi-party democracies (Costa Rica, Sri Lanka and Jamaica).[11] Chile was democratic until 1973 when Allende was overthrown and replaced by General Pinochet.

There is something intriguing in the fact that continued improvements in basic aspects of the quality of life should have taken place in Chile during the grim period of its contemporary history following the coup of 1973—a period marked not only by enormous economic instability but also by the rapid deterioration of many social services, ruthless political repression, and systematic violation of basic human rights. And yet there is, as we shall see, fairly incontrovertible evidence that, in the area of nutrition and particularly child health, the very rapid progress that was already taking place in the 1960s has continued and consolidated throughout the 1970s.[12] Since General Pinochet does not have a reputation of being a soft-hearted do-gooder, the unusual record of the post-1973 period stands in need of some explanation.

Chile's experience must be seen in historical perspective. Particularly relevant here is the very long tradition of public action for the improvement of living standards, especially in the areas of health care, education, nutrition intervention, and social insurance. This tradition, which goes back to the social reforms of the 1920s, has been intimately linked with the trade union movement and other forms of political activism. Social provisions have been a sensitive political issue, and an area of intense competition among political parties—many pieces of social legislation were indeed enacted in the context of electoral tactics or promises.[13]

Initially, social services were importantly biased towards the more vocal constituencies of the various parties, and especially towards urban dwellers and the organized sections of the working classes. But the reach of public intervention spread systematically over the years, and by the 1960s Chile had not only the most comprehensive social insurance system in Latin America but also a unified National Health Service (with nearly universal coverage), large-scale nutrition intervention programmes, and virtually free education at

---

[11] The state of Kerala in India was also separated out as having a distinguished record of support-led security (see Chapter 11). Kerala has, of course, a multi-party system, as in the rest of India. It has also had substantial periods of communist government within that system.

[12] During the early 1980s, progress continued but apparently at a slower pace.

[13] This applies, right from the start, to the Social Security Act of 1924, which inscribed itself in a broad range of social and constitutional reforms, represented Chile's pioneering introduction of social insurance in the American continent and also marked the beginning of supplementary feeding in Chile (Mesa-Lago 1985b, Vial et al. 1987). On the history of social services in Chile, and its intimate connection with adversarial politics until 1973, see Arellano (1985a, 1985b). See also Hakim and Solimano (1978), who provide a particularly instructive account of the development and politics of milk distribution programmes.

all levels.[14] Since then, there have been further advances in primary health care (including birth attendance and vaccination), female education, family planning, nutrition intervention, sanitation, and related areas. Today, Chile is probably the only country in the world where public health services ensure not only the monitoring of nearly all young children in the country, but also the provision of food supplements, primary care, and, when identifiably necessary, direct nutritional rehabilitation.[15]

After the abandonment of Allende's socialist experiment in 1973 following a military coup intended to 'rescue the country from the clutches of Marxism–Leninism' (Pinochet 1976), the new government adopted orthodox monetarist policies which put heavy emphasis on 'liberalizing' the economy, drastically reducing the scope of government intervention in the economic sphere, and restoring macro-economic balance through fiscal restraint, greater competition, outward orientation, devaluation, and other tenets of the 'Chicago school'. This so-called 'monetarist experiment', which lasted until 1982 in its pure form, has been the object of much controversy, but few have claimed it to be a success.[16] The failure of the monetarist experiment to lead to a sustained and broad-based increase in economic prosperity is apparent from the macro-economic indicators presented in Table 12.2 (see also Figure 12.1). The most conspicuous feature of the post-1973 period is that of considerable instability, with two sharp recessions (in 1975–6 and again in 1983–5) and no firm and consistent upward trend (to say the least) in the conventional indicators of economic prosperity.

The question of whether or not the disengagement of the state in the economic sphere during this period has also taken the form of a decline in the provision of social services has been a matter of some disputation. The government has claimed a sustained and in some ways even increased involvement in this area. This claim, however, has been forcefully challenged by a number of critics, who have emphasized the disengagement of the state and the deterioration of many social services since 1973.[17]

---

[14] On these and other aspects of social services in contemporary Chile, see e.g. Hakim and Solimano (1978), Foxley et al. (1979), Harbert and Scandizzo (1982), Gonzalez et al. (1983), Monckeberg (1983), Wallich (1983), Arellano (1985a, 1985b), Mesa-Lago (1985b, 1985d), Valiente et al. (1985), Ffrench-Davis and Raczynski (1988), and Vial et al. (1987). The redistributive effects of social services in Chile, and particularly of public health and nutrition programmes, have been clearly brought out in a number of studies—see e.g. Foxley et al. (1979), Grossi (1985), and Torche (1985).

[15] It is important to note that while the National Health Service (through which the most important nutrition and health programmes are implemented) does not quite provide universal coverage of infants and young children, there is no indication that the excluded population consists primarily of disadvantaged groups. In fact, the reverse may often be nearer the truth. On this see Torche (1985), Valiente et al. (1985), and Vial et al. (1987).

[16] For various evaluations of this experiment, see Harberger (1982), Ffrench-Davis (1983), Foxley (1983), Sigmund (1984), Corbo (1985), Edwards (1985), and Moran (1989), among others.

[17] See e.g. Ruiz (1980), Foxley and Raczynski (1984), Solimano and Haignere (1984), Scarpaci (1985), Raczynski (1987), Scheetz (1987), Arellano (1988), and Ffrench-Davis and Raczynski (1988), among others.

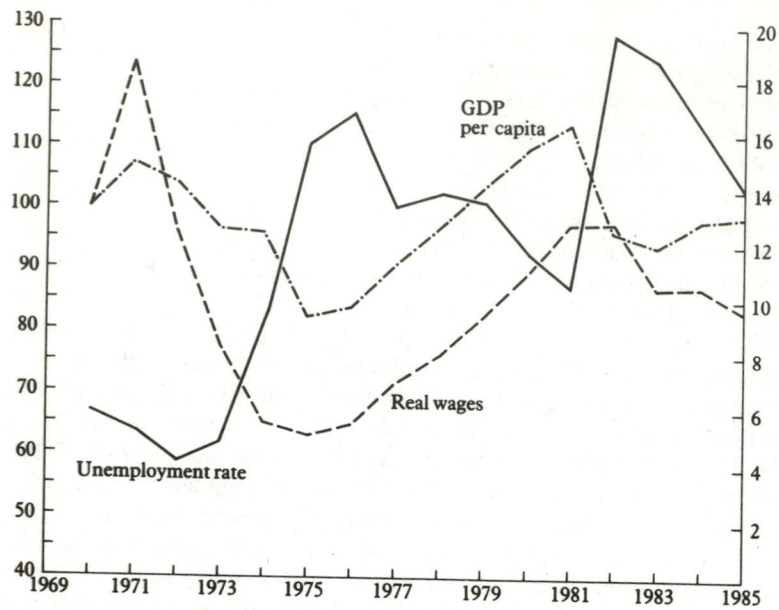

Source: Table 12.2. The right-hand vertical axis indicates the unemployment rate. The left-hand vertical axis provides the relevant scale for the indices of per-capita GDP and real wages (1970 = 100).

Fig. 12.1 Chile, 1970–85: selected economic indicators

Some relevant indicators (constructed from official statistics) appear in Table 12.3, and they do seem to confirm the latter view. At the same time, it is arguable that the observed reduction of social expenditure since 1973 has perhaps been surprisingly *smaller* in aggregate terms than one might have expected given the ideological predilections of the Pinochet regime. Though total social expenditure per capita was considerably reduced during the recession of the mid-70s, it was, on average, only 4% below the 1970 level during the 1981–5 period.[18]

More striking, however, is the noticeable shift in the *composition* of social expenditures since 1973. This point deserves some elaboration. Right through the monetarist experiment, the official policy of the government has been to 'target' social expenditures much more sharply than in the past towards the

[18] As shown in Cabezas (1988), alternative studies and sources lead to very similar conclusions regarding broad post-1973 trends in aggregate 'public social expenditure' (shown in the second column of Table 12.3). The concept of public social expenditure has to be distinguished from the narrower notion of 'fiscal social expenditure', which has been used as a basis of the official claim that social expenditures have risen in per-capita terms under the Pinochet regime (see Scheetz 1987, and Arellano 1988).

Table 12.2 Chile, 1960–1985: selected economic indicators

Year	GDP per capita (1970 = 100)	Private consumption per capita (1970 = 100)	Index of real wages and salaries (1970 = 100)	Index of wage earnings per capita[a] (1970 = 100)	Unemployment rate (percentage)
	(1)	(2)	(3)	(4)	(5)
1960–4	86.4	90.9			
1965–70	96.4	97.4	90.9[b]		
1970	100.0	100.0	100.0	100.0	5.9
1971	107.0	111.1	122.7	124.1	5.2
1972	103.8	117.6	96.1	96.5	4.1
1973	96.4	108.0	77.6[c]	75.2[c]	4.8
1974	95.8	86.8	65.0	61.9	9.1
1975	82.1	75.7	62.9	54.2	15.6
1976	83.7	74.7	64.7	54.8	16.7
1977	90.6	85.5	71.4	62.8	13.3
1978	96.7	90.6	76.0	69.7	13.8
1979	103.2	95.1	82.2	75.8	13.5
1980	109.5	100.0	89.3	83.8	11.7
1981	113.7	108.9	97.3	94.4	10.4
1982	96.0	94.1	97.6	81.8	19.6
1983	93.7	89.4	86.9	69.5	18.7
1984	98.0	89.0	87.1	76.3	16.3
1985	98.7	86.5	83.2	76.1	14.1

[a] Calculated as the ratio of total wage earnings (real wage index multiplied by employment) to population.
[b] This value refers specifically to 1969.
[c] This value is for the last trimester of the year.

Sources: (1)–(3) Arellano (1988), Tables 1 and 3. (4) Calculated from Arellano (1988), Table 3, and Ffrench-Davis and Raczynski (1988), Tables 7 and A27. (5) Ffrench-Davis and Raczynski (1988), Table 7.

poorest groups, and to put greater reliance on the private sector for general provisioning. This strategy is reiterated in a large number of official documents.[19] It has been accompanied by an important reorientation in the pattern of public support, including (1) the large-scale 'privatization' of social insurance, (2) the freezing or reduction of mass provisions in the areas of health, housing, and education (in particular a dramatic decline of *investment* in

[19] For statements of the official view of social policy in Chile since 1973, and of the general philosophy of the government in economic and social matters, see Government of Chile (1974), Pinochet (1976), Mendez (1979, 1980), Banco Central de Chile (1984), and particularly Government of Chile (1988). The last document describes the 'new objectives' of the 'social reforms in Chile since 1973' as (1) the eradication of extreme poverty, and (2) the promotion of true equality of opportunities (p. 6). The former objective is explicitly distinguished from, and contrasted with, a policy of income redistribution. The second objective alludes essentially to the virtues of privatization.

Table 12.3 Chile, 1970–1985: social policies

Year	Public social expenditure per capita (1970 = 100)						Public investment in social sectors (1970 = 100)		Percentage of labour force on emergency programmes	Quantity of milk distributed through PNAC (000 tons)
	Total	Education	Health	Social insurance and social assistance	Housing	Other	Total	Health		
	(1)	(2)	(3)	(4)	(5)	(6)	(7)	(8)	(9)	(10)
1970	100.0	100.0	100.0	100.0	100.0	100.0	100.0	100.0	0.0	17.1
1971	n/a	n/a	n/a	n/a	n/a	n/a	n/a	n/a	0.0	19.0
1972	n/a	n/a	n/a	n/a	n/a	n/a	n/a	n/a	0.0	19.3
1973	n/a	n/a	n/a	n/a	n/a	n/a	n/a	n/a	0.0	20.3
1974	75.9	79.9	86.6	59.6	129.8	127.3	148.7	124.9	0.0	20.8
1975	63.4	63.2	67.1	60.6	74.1	39.2	80.3	55.4	0.0	23.6
1976	61.9	67.6	62.7	59.9	54.8	101.7	55.0	37.4	2.0	24.5
1977	71.0	78.9	67.8	68.6	61.4	195.4	69.6	18.1	5.2	28.7
1978	79.3	83.0	75.0	82.0	57.4	171.6	46.1	23.1	5.6	29.8
1979	87.6	90.8	73.8	91.6	71.7	209.1	57.2	30.4	4.2	28.7
1980	90.1	88.7	82.4	95.3	71.2	211.4	55.3	20.6	3.8	29.2
1981	97.5	92.1	74.8	110.7	70.5	174.5	39.2	32.1	5.3	29.8
1982	104.4	93.0	78.4	127.6	49.4	135.4	28.3	30.6	4.7	30.3
1983	93.6	78.8	62.4	118.4	40.9	205.6	n/a	n/a	6.5	22.0
1984	93.7	76.2	65.9	117.9	47.8	180.1	n/a	n/a	12.6	27.8
1985	90.0	75.6	63.6	108.0	65.6	172.9	n/a	n/a	8.4	30.3

Note: PNAC stands for the National Programme of Supplementary Feeding. The contributions of different sectors to total public social expenditure in 1970 were as follows: education (25%), health (13%), social insurance and social assistance (51%), housing (10%), other (1%).

Source: (1)–(6): Calculated from Cabezas (1988), Table 11. (7)–(8): Calculated from Foxley and Raczynski (1984), Table V.5. (9): Calculated from Ffrench-Davis and Raczynski (1988), Table 7. (10): Vial *et al* (1987), Tables 1 and 2; Ffrench-Davis and Raczynski (1988), Table A. 19.

these sectors), (3) the maintenance, and in some cases an expansion, of nutrition programmes, along with a reorientation towards the most vulnerable groups, and (4) a very large expansion of emergency employment programmes in years of high unemployment (see Table 12.3).

Against this background, there is unambiguous evidence of rapid improvement in infant and child mortality as well as in anthropometric measures of the nutritional status of children during the post-1973 period. Health statistics in Chile have a long history and a reputation of high reliability, and from 1975 annual statistics on the nutritional status of children have been produced on the basis of very large samples. The indications provided by these statistics are striking: between 1973 and 1985, the infant mortality rate plunged from 66 to 19 per thousand live births, while between 1975 and 1985 the assessed percentage of undernourished children below 5 years of age declined from 15.5 to 8.7 (see Table 12.4). It is important to note that critics of government policies have mostly focused on the interpretation of these figures rather than on their validity.[20]

Conflicts of interpretation have taken place around the question of whether or not the advances we have just noted can be taken as reflective of broader improvements in living standards. Critics have argued that, on the contrary, the decline in infant and child mortality has taken place against a background of steady deterioration in living standards as a whole, and they have attributed this apparent paradox to the effects of specific intervention in the domains of child health and nutrition.[21]

The question of whether or not general living standards have indeed deteriorated since 1973 is, again, a controversial one. Some have claimed a sharp reduction in 'extreme poverty' as a result of government policies, and even an improvement in income distribution.[22] But many others have documented sharp declines in real wages and wage income, rapidly increasing inequality of incomes, rising incidence of certain diseases, deterioration of housing conditions, falling primary school enrolment ratios, and other indications of adverse changes in living standards.[23]

Given the turbulence of the period, and the opposite directions in which different variables may move, it is not easy to find one's way through these apparently conflicting indications and claims. Among the contrary evidential

[20] See in particular Ruiz (1980), Foxley and Raczynski (1984), Solimano and Haignere (1984), Ffrench-Davis and Raczynski (1988), Raczynski (1987), and Arellano (1988). Solimano and Haignere, for instance, acknowledge in spite of their severe criticisms of recent government policies that 'Chile, fortunately, has had a highly competent system for collecting health statistics since the early 1950s, and there is evidence that the reliability of mortality data has not deteriorated significantly' (p. 5), and note in connection with trends in the incidence of child malnutrition that 'there is no reason to believe that the overall decline is unreal' (p. 9).

[21] This view has been expressed by a large number of authors, including those cited in the preceding footnote.

[22] See e.g. Haindl and Weber (1986), Mujica and Rojas (1986), Rojas (1986), and Government of Chile (1988). For rejoinders see Arellano (1988) and Ffrench-Davis and Raczynski (1988).

[23] See the critiques of government policies cited earlier.

Table 12.4 Chile, 1960–1985: child health and nutrition

Year	Infant mortality rate (per 1,000) (1)	Prevalence of undernourishment among children aged 0–5 (%)				Percentage of low birthweights (6)	Percentage of under-5s under nutrition surveillance (7)
		Total (2)	Mild (3)	Moderate (4)	Severe (5)		
1960	119.5						
1965	97.3						
1970	82.2						
1971	73.9						
1972	72.7						
1973	65.8						
1974	65.2						
1975	57.6	15.5	12.1	2.7	0.7	11.4	72
1976	56.6	15.9	12.1	3.0	0.8	11.4	74
1977	50.1	14.9	11.9	2.5	0.5	10.9	75
1978	40.1	13.0	10.8	1.8	0.3	9.1	72
1979	37.9	12.2	10.4	1.6	0.2	9.0	69
1980	33.0	11.5	10.0	1.4	0.1	8.6	70
1981	27.0	9.9	8.7	1.1	0.1	7.8	70
1982	23.6	8.8	7.8	0.9	0.1	6.9	75
1983	21.9	9.8	8.7	1.0	0.1	6.5	76
1984	19.6	8.4	7.5	0.8	0.1	6.5	77
1985	19.5	8.7	7.8	0.8	0.1	n/a	78

Source: (1) Banco Central de Chile, *Boletín Mensual*; no. 725 (1988), 2055. (2)–(7) República de Chile, Instituto Nacional de Estadísticas, *Anuario de Recursos y Atenciones*, various issues (1975 to 1985). The prevalence of undernourishment is based on weight-for-age measurements.

Table 12.5 Life expectancy in Chile

Year	Infant mortality rate (per 1,000)	Life expectancy at age 1 (years)	Life expectancy at birth (years)
1960	119.5	64.4	57.6
1965	97.3	66.0	60.5
1970	82.2	68.9	64.2
1971	73.9	68.6	64.5
1972	72.7	68.8	64.8
1973	65.8	68.6	65.1
1974	65.2	68.9	65.4
1975	57.6	68.7	65.6
1976	56.6	68.9	65.9
1977	50.1	68.7	66.2
1978	40.1	68.2	66.5
1979	37.9	68.4	66.7
1980	33.0	68.3	67.0
1981	27.0	68.1	67.3
1982	23.6	68.1	67.5
1983	21.9	68.3	67.8
1984	19.6	68.4	68.0
1985	19.5	68.6	68.3

Source: Banco Central de Chile, *Boletín Mensual*, no. 725 (1988), 2055 (original source: Instituto Naçional de Estadísticas).

directions is the combination of a stagnating life expectancy at age 1 with an increase in life expectancy at birth (reflecting a strong reduction in infant mortality). The relevant figures are given in Table 12.5, and would seem to provide some support for the view that favourable infant mortality trends in Chile since 1973 have not been reflective of a corresponding general improvement in living conditions.[24]

It also seems possible that a distinction would have to be made between the living standards of the poorer sections as a whole (particularly of the working class as a class), and the incidence of extreme poverty among particular groups.

[24] After pointing out that infant mortality and life expectancy in Chile are strongly correlated, and stating that 'life expectancy is a very general indicator of quality of life' (p. 9), Hojman (1988) argues against the 'widely held preconception that infant mortality has been artificially reduced with purposes of propaganda, by means which have no relation whatsoever to wider quality of life indicators' (p. 19). Note, however, that *by construction* life expectancy at birth is very sensitively related to infant mortality. This does not apply to the expectation of life *at age one*, and when this indicator is compared with infant mortality, the strong (inverse) correlation on which Hojman's claim is based seems to disappear (see Table 12.5).

Given the explicit and consistent policy of concentrating public support on the poorest, the hypothesis of a decline in extreme poverty is not obviously incompatible with the picture of falling living standards for the poorer groups as a whole.[25]

These methodological issues are not without importance. They bring out, in particular, the limitations involved in concentrating exclusively on health and nutrition indicators for children and infants for the purpose of assessing changes in basic living conditions (even when the primary concern is confined to nutrition and related capabilities). It is certainly sometimes the case that movements in these indicators *can* be taken as reflective of general trends in health, nutrition and related capabilities. But this is not always true, and the case of Chile illustrates the possible difficulties arising from divergent trends coexisting with each other.

As far as the question of the effectiveness of public support is concerned, however, there is little disagreement as to what caused the observed improvements in the area of child health and nutrition. There have, as discussed earlier, been important debates regarding the relation of these improvements to general trends in the quality of life in Chile since 1973, and also regarding overall changes in the government's commitment to public support. But the role and effectiveness of public support in the specific domain of child health and nutrition is not in dispute.

There is, moreover, nothing really surprising in the fact that targeted intervention programmes (including income support) should have been responsible for a large part of the observed improvements.[26] In fact, it would be hard to attribute the impressively steady decline in infant mortality during the last three decades (despite several major economic recessions and political upheavals) to anything *else* than the maintenance of extensive public support measures, and in particular the remarkable consistency of child health and nutrition programmes. Moreover, the noticeable impact of nutrition and health programmes in Chile has been convincingly brought out in a large number of studies (including several econometric investigations), and it is natural to expect that this impact would continue and be consolidated as these programmes were more vigorously extended to disadvantaged groups.[27]

---

[25] The role of public works programmes in this context is particularly noteworthy. At their peak in 1983, emergency employment programmes employed as much as 13% of the labour force, and their importance for poor households is easily seen (e.g. Cheyre and Ogrodnik 1982, Raczynski and Serrano 1985, and Raczynski 1987).

[26] Of course, other factors have also played a role, notably the continued expansion of female education and the reduction in fertility (according to Valiente *et al.* 1985, the contribution of the latter to the decline of infant mortality has been estimated at about 20% by two different studies). These factors are themselves closely linked with various forms of public action, e.g. in the domains of education and family planning.

[27] For studies and discussions of the impact of health and nutrition intervention in Chile, both before and after 1973, see Hakim and Solimano (1978), Harbert and Scandizzo (1982), Medina and Kaempffer (1982), Castaneda (1984, 1985), Torche (1985), Valiente *et al.* (1985), and various contributions in Underwood (1983) as well as the review by Vial *et al.* (1987).

This account leaves open the intriguing question why a government which had no hesitation in resorting to the most brutal political repression in order to protect the privileges of the dominant classes was so interested in looking after child health and extreme poverty. As far as *non-withdrawal* is concerned, an obvious explanation lies in the political difficulties of withdrawing what different sections of the population had come to regard as their legitimate claim to state support in various forms.[28] This is perhaps most visible in the domain of health, and in the preservation of the National Health Service along with a dramatic reduction of investment in this sector.[29]

In some respects, however, there has been an *expansion* of public support, notably in the area of public works and nutrition programmes. It is tempting to interpret this as a strategy for checking popular discontent at a time of political repression, economic instability, and diminished general social provisions. It has been persuasively argued, for instance, that the expansion of emergency employment programmes was largely a response to the shifting political threats represented respectively by unionized and unemployed workers as a result of mounting unemployment and massive clampdown on trade unions.[30] The expansion of targeted nutrition and health programmes also has an obviously populist ring in a country where popular expectations of public provisioning are very high, and the Chilean government has indeed consistently endeavoured to build political capital from its achievements in the area of child nutrition.[31]

In recognizing Chile's achievements, we have to see the role of public intervention in selected aspects of the quality of life, but also we cannot but observe the part that political pressure and a search for a popular mandate may play even in a country with an authoritarian political atmosphere. Chile does, of course, have a long tradition of democratic and pluralist politics. But the general lesson about the power of adversarial politics even under authoritarian systems may have a wider relevance.

---

[28] An official document on social policy states that Chile's 'long history of State intervention in social matters' has 'both positive and negative aspects . . . On the negative side, it is difficult to modify already existing social programs and to adapt them to the ever changing reality of poverty' (Government of Chile 1988: 33).

[29] This 'concealed disengagement', and a number of other aspects of social policy under Pinochet (e.g. the emphasis on 'targeting' and 'privatisation'), bear interesting analogies with recent experiences of liberalization in a number of other countries, including Sri Lanka since 1977 (Sahn and Edirisinghe, forthcoming) and Britain in the 1980s (Atkinson et al. 1987 and Welfare State Programme, forthcoming).

[30] On this, see particularly Arellano et al. (1987, 1988). The authors claim, inter alia, that 'whereas in 1973 there were almost 10 times more unionized than unemployed workers or "pobladores", by 1983 the number of unemployed ("pobladores") was more than three times that of unionized workers' (Arellano et al. 1987: 16).

[31] Official documents and public speeches since 1973 are full of self-congratulatory references to the rapid progress achieved in the area of child health and nutrition, and to this day 'the pro-Pinochet press regularly runs stories noting that Chilean newborns are among the fattest in the hemisphere' (Contrera 1988: 24).

12.4   Costa Rica

If 'development' is to be recognized by the expansion of basic capabilities, there is little doubt that Costa Rica is one of the most outstanding success stories of the last few decades. In areas related to health and nutrition, the record of this country is particularly clear from the convergent indications of many direct and indirect pieces of evidence (see Tables 12.6 and 12.7). Infant mortality, which had already declined to the respectable level of 76 per thousand live births in 1960, further plunged to 19 over the next 20 years.[32] During the same period, life expectancy at birth leapt by an entire decade to reach 73 years, a figure comparable to those of most European countries. The percentage of women (aged 20–34) having completed primary education increased from 27 to 66. Severe undernourishment as a phenomenon virtually disappeared, and nutritional standards attained levels comparable to those of rich countries. The marital fertility rate (which had been rising steadily before 1960) declined from 7.3 to 3.7. The incidence of a wide range of parasitic and infectious diseases retreated dramatically, and morbidity patterns approached those typical of affluent countries. The extent of poverty as measured by conventional income criteria also declined.[33]

Table 12.6   Costa Rica, 1960–1980: selected well-being indicators

Year	GNP per capita (1960 = 100)	Infant mortality rate (per 1,000)	Life expectancy (years)	Percentage of women aged 20–34 with completed primary education	Total marital fertility rate	Percentage of newborns below 2.5 kg.
1960	100	76	62.6	27	7.3	12.5
1965	115	75	62.9	31	6.5	
1970	138	63	65.4	43	4.9	9.1
1975	164	38	69.6	55	3.8	
1980	185	19	72.6	66	3.7	7.0

Source: Mata (1985), Table 7; Mata and Rosero (1988), Tables 4.1, 2.25, and 2.26.

[32] As in the case of Chile, the pace of improvement in living conditions seems to have decelerated in the 1980s under the impact of world recession—see Peek and Raabe (1984), Mesa-Lago (1985a) and Mata and Rosero (1988). The general issues of world recession, adjustment policies and human well-being are discussed in Jolly and Cornia (1984), Cornia *et al.* (1987), Taylor (1988a), Jayawardena (forthcoming). It must be stressed that the economic difficulties of Costa Rica in the 1980s are overwhelmingly attributable to world-wide fluctuations in economic activity as well as commodity prices, and in this respect Costa Rica shares the common predicament of most Latin American countries.

[33] These trends have been established and discussed in a large number of studies, and the statistical evidence establishing them is robust enough. See e.g. Haines and Avery (1982), Saenz

Table 12.7 Costa Rica, 1960–1980: selected indicators of public support

Year	Percentage of the population covered by 'Social Insurance' and 'Social Assistance'	Per capita real public expenditure on education (1970 US $)	Percentage of births taking place in hospital	Percentage of rural population with water supply connection
1960	15.4	19.3	50	n/a
1965	30.6	23.8		34[a]
1970	38.2	35.4	71	39
1975	54.7	49.3		58[a]
1980	85.1	63.6	91	62

[a] These figures are in fact for the proximate years, respectively 1966 and 1974.

Source: Mesa-Lago (1985a), Table 2; Mata (1985), Tables 7 and 8; Mata and Rosero (1988), Table 4.1.

Two factors have accounted for these impressive trends. First, the fairly healthy growth of the economy during these two decades, led by a rapid expansion in the export of 'cash crops' (such as coffee), and resulting in this case in a broad-based improvement of private incomes. Second, the exceptionally rapid expansion of the 'welfare state', and in particular extensive public efforts in the domains of health, education, social insurance and income support.

The expansion of the welfare state in Costa Rica must in turn be understood against a unique political background. Located in the heart of a region where social and political repressions are rife, Costa Rica is widely regarded as a leading exception. In fact, since independence in 1821, Costa Rica has had a long history of active democracy, minimal violence and progressive social legislation.[34] Slavery was abolished as early as 1813, and capital punishment in 1882. The abolition of the army (sic!) itself took place in 1949. A high value has consistently been placed on education, and secondary schooling has been free and compulsory since 1869. Elections take place every four years under the supervision of the autonomous Supreme Electoral Tribunal, and Costa Rica

---

(1982, 1985), Jaramillo (1983), Mohs (1983a, 1983b), Rosero (1984, 1985a, 1985b), Peek and Raabe (1984), Halstead et al. (1985), Mata (1985), and the meticulous review by Mata and Rosero (1988). The last authors present, inter alia, clear evidence of nutritional improvement as indicated by anthropometric measurements.

[34] For an excellent account of the nature of Costa Rican democracy, see Ameringer (1982). For background details on the economy and society of Costa Rica we have also drawn on Rosemberg (1979, 1983), Seligson (1980), Castillo et al. (1983), Mesa-Lago and Diaz-Briquets (1988), Peek and Raabe (1984), Wesson (1984a), Gonzalez-Vega (1985), Mesa-Lago (1985a), Fields (1988), and Mata and Rosero (1988).

has been said to enjoy 'the freest and fairest electoral machinery of any country in the world'.[35] Turn-out at the polls is very high (about 80 per cent), and quite often the opposition wins. Most of the police force are replaced at the time of election.[36]

Costa Rica's achievements have sometimes been seen as a reflection of an egalitarian society and economy. This thesis, while not entirely dismissible, is somewhat misleading. Although inequalities were non-extreme in the early colonial days, the relatively egalitarian land tenure pattern did not survive the emergence of large coffee and banana estates in the nineteenth century.[37] Today the distribution of land in Costa Rica is highly unequal even in comparison with other Latin American countries, and approximately two-thirds of the agricultural labour force consists of landless wage earners.[38] It is true that the distribution of *income* is much less unequal, and that income inequality in Costa Rica is relatively small by Latin American standards. But these standards are hardly exacting, and it is very hard to see a great contrast between Costa Rica and other developing countries in terms of income distribution.[39] The fact is that Costa Rica's economic system is a fundamentally inegalitarian one, and falls far short of guaranteeing adequate entitlements to all—as widespread hunger during the depression of the 1930s had dramatically illustrated. However, cooperative social and political traditions have recently found a new expression in the welfare state, whose far-reaching activities have provided an increasingly important source of security for the poor.

The foundations of the modern welfare state in Costa Rica were firmly laid down by the social reforms of the 1940s. During the first forty years of this century, the Costa Rican state, dominated by a small and conservative oligarchy, had maintained essentially non-interventionist policies. However, changes occurred in the early 1940s under the presidency of Calderón Guardia, an enterprising pediatrician turned politician who, among other things, promoted innovative legislation in the area of social insurance, and proposed the introduction of wide-ranging 'social guarantees' to protect the interests of workers. The constitution of 1949 not only consolidated the advances made under Guardia, but also institutionalized the process of social reforms and

---

[35] Ameringer (1982: 33).

[36] It would be an exaggeration, of course, to describe Costa Ricans as 'non-violent', as has often been done. The homicide rate in Costa Rica, for instance, is much smaller than in neighbouring Latin American countries, but it is not negligible, and some concern has recently been expressed at the fact that homicides increasingly take more violent forms than 'the traditional straight killing', partly as a result of rising alcoholism (Mata and Rosero 1988). Another important social problem in Costa Rica is the disadvantaged position of ethnic minorities.

[37] See Seligson (1980), who discusses the importance of Costa Rica's colonial history, including the evolution of land tenure and the relatively homogeneous ethnic composition of the population.

[38] Peek and Raabe (1984: 12).

[39] See e.g. the tables on income distribution in recent issues of *World Development Report*. For a careful study of land and income distribution in Costa Rica, see Peek and Raabe (1984).

government intervention in economic and social matters by creating a large number of 'autonomous institutions' responsible for the pursuit of various forms of supportive government activity—including *inter alia* educational and health programmes, social insurance, assistance to the needy, land reforms, and public works. These legal foundations, and the pressures generated by the democratic process, have ensured the continued vitality of the welfare state.[40]

Two closely related and interconnected areas of active intervention deserve special attention here: 'fiscal social security measures' and the public health care system.[41] The system of fiscal social security measures, which includes contributory and non-contributory pensions, health insurance, various social welfare programmes and direct financial assistance to needy families, is of a markedly different nature from similar systems in other countries of Latin America. In most of these countries, the fiscal social security system has evolved into a regressive form of large-scale government support to the more influential groups, especially the urban élites.[42] In Costa Rica, this criticism does not seem to apply today. A constitutional amendment was passed in 1961 calling for 'universalization' of social security within a decade, and since then the drive in that direction has been very strong. According to Mesa-Lago, 'in 1980 practically all the population was covered, between two-thirds and three-fourths by social insurance and the rest through social assistance and public health programmes'.[43]

Fiscal social security measures cover a part of the system of public health[44] (e.g. in the form of health insurance). But the latter also includes community health and primary health care programmes implemented directly under the Ministry of Health. These programmes underwent a leap forward in the 1970s with the formulation of a National Health Plan in 1971, and the subsequent

[40] On the role of democratic politics in shaping social policy in Costa Rica, see e.g. Ameringer (1982), Rosemberg (1983), and Mesa-Lago (1985c).

[41] By 'fiscal social security measures' we understand social security in the narrower and more conventional sense than the broader idea of 'social security' used in this book (discussed in section 1.3). This conventional notion is perhaps best reflected by the legislative concerns of the ILO covering 'social insurance' and 'social assistance'. On fiscal social security measures in Costa Rica, see e.g. Green (1977), Rosemberg (1979, 1983), Briceño and Méndez (1982), Mesa-Lago (1985a, 1985c), and Rodriguez (1986).

[42] This verdict is extensively defended and documented in numerous writings by Carmelo Mesa-Lago—see e.g. Mesa-Lago (1978, 1985b, 1985c, 1986, 1988b). It is worth noting that the three countries which Mesa-Lago singles out as departing from this pattern happen to be Chile, Costa Rica, and Cuba (see Mesa-Lago 1985d). These three countries distinguish themselves by having unified fiscal social security systems with universal (or nearly universal) coverage.

[43] Mesa-Lago (1985b: 45; our translation).

[44] The literature on public health in Costa Rica is enormous. Some useful references include Mata (1978, 1985), Haines and Avery (1982), Jaramillo (1983), Mohs (1983a, 1983b), Tomic (1983), Asociación Demográfica Costarricense (1984), Mesa-Lago (1985a), Rosero (1985a, 1985b), Caldwell (1986), and various contributions in Halstead et al. (1985). For a particularly useful and up-to-date account, which also summarizes neatly the existing evidence on the relation between health intervention and health and nutritional improvement, see Mata and Rosero (1988).

implementation of vigorous health campaigns, including especially the Rural Health Programme (started in 1973) and the Community Health Programme (started in 1976). There is considerable evidence that these programmes have made a major contribution to rapid health and nutritional improvement in Costa Rica since their inception.[45]

The links between public support and the improvement of living conditions in Costa Rica are particularly well reflected in the decline of infant and child mortality. The decline of infant mortality over the period 1960–85 in Costa Rica has been overwhelmingly concentrated in the decade of the 1970s. Indeed, the 70 per cent decline in infant mortality over that single decade (from 63 to 19 per thousand live births) may well be an all-time record—all the more impressive because the base mortality level was itself already quite low. Not surprisingly, many factors seem to have accounted for this achievement. The moderate but broad-based growth of private incomes must have exercised its influence.[46] The expansion of female education, which is known to exercise a strong influence on infant mortality, almost certainly played a role as well. The decline of fertility (itself partly the result of declining infant and child mortality) made a further contribution, which has indeed been quantitatively estimated.[47]

Interestingly enough, one factor that does *not* seem to have played a significant role in mortality reduction is the quantitative increase of nutritional intakes. Indeed, nutritional intakes do not seem to have increased much (if at all) over the period under consideration (see Table 12.8). This confirms once again the need to relate nourishment and health not to food entitlements as such but to a broader notion of entitlements including command over crucial non-food items.[48]

The relative unimportance of quantitative increases in nutritional intake in Costa Rica's success contrasts with the crucial role that has been widely ascribed to the vigorous health programmes initiated in the 1970s. Careful statistical studies confirm that, in addition to the positive factors mentioned

[45] The evidence on this point is discussed in many of the contributions cited in the preceding footnote.

[46] The rate of decline of infant mortality in Costa Rica since 1911 seems to have been more rapid during periods of economic prosperity than through recessions. See Rosero (1985b) and Mata and Rosero (1988). Note, however, that the growth of income per capita in Costa Rica does not seem to have been more rapid in the 1970s than in the 1960s. According to the *World Development Report 1984*, the growth rate of GDP per capita in Costa Rica was 3.2% over the 1960–70 period, and only 2.0% between 1970 and 1982 (calculated from Tables 2 and 19).

[47] According to Rosero, the decline of fertility is estimated to have been responsible for 24% of the observed reduction in infant mortality in Costa Rica between 1960 and 1977 (Rosero 1985a: 131). Note that the decline of fertility is itself closely related to social policy, including education and family planning programmes—see Stycos (1982) for a detailed analysis. In 1981, two-thirds of those using contraception utilized state-provided services—the proportion rising to 90% among agricultural labourers (Rosero 1985a: 131).

[48] Of course, it must be remembered that Costa Rica is more prosperous than most countries of Africa or South Asia, and it is not clear that substantial improvements in nutritional status could be easily achieved in much poorer countries without *inter alia* an increase in calorie intake.

Table 12.8 Nutritional status and nutritional intake in Costa Rica, 1966–1982

Year	Percentage of stunted children	Percentage of wasted children	Average calorie intake (Kcal./cap.)		Average protein intake (g./cap.)	
			Rural	Urban	Rural	Urban
1966	16.9	13.5	1,894	2,330	53.6	67.3
1975	7.2	12.5				
1978	7.6	8.6	2,020	1,947	54.0	58.2
1982	n/a	4.1				

Source: Mata and Rosero (1988), Tables 2.10 and 2.13, summarizing a number of surveys conducted by the Ministry of Health.

earlier, these programmes have indeed had a strong independent effect on mortality decline. The evidence presented is of two kinds. First, it is observed that while until 1970 the infant mortality rate in Costa Rica could be reasonably accurately 'predicted' from its general social and economic indicators on the basis of the relationships (between these indicators and infant mortality) observed elsewhere in Latin America, during the 1970s infant mortality in Costa Rica deviated markedly downward from its predicted value. Second (and more importantly), by utilizing the rich data available at the canton level in Costa Rica, it has been possible to carry out statistical tests to ascertain whether mortality decline was more rapid in regions where the coverage of rural health programmes was more comprehensive, controlling for the effect of regional differences in incomes, education levels, fertility, sanitation, and so on. Detailed investigations of this type have tended to demonstrate that the influence of health care programmes in the 1970s was indeed extremely important.[49]

Table 12.9 gives a very elementary illustration of the results obtained. It is clear from this table that the rural health programmes of the 1970s were targeted to the cantons with higher initial infant mortality rates (this was indeed a conscious and declared policy). It can be seen that the annual declines of infant mortality, which were relatively slow in these cantons in the 1960s, sharply accelerated in the 1970s. Indeed the ranking of mortality reduction rates in different cantons got largely reversed as a result of these programmes. Basically the same conclusion is retained when the exercise is extended by 'controlling' for factors such as education, fertility and economic development.[50]

[49] On both types of evidence, see the detailed review of evidence in Mata and Rosero (1988). Rosero (1985a) estimates that 41% of the infant mortality decline between 1972 and 1980 is attributable to the expansion of primary health care, and another 32% to secondary health care (mainly out-patient consultations at hospitals). See also Haines and Avery (1982) on the importance of maternal and child health programmes during the period 1968–73.

[50] See Mata and Rosero (1988) for details.

Table 12.9 Rural health programmes and mortality reduction in cantons in Costa Rica, 1968–1980

Ranges of coverage of population in community and rural health programmes in different cantons	Percentage of all births in Costa Rica taking place in the cantons within the respective ranges of coverage	Health indicators in the corresponding cantons			
		Infant Mortality Rate (per 1,000)		Annual Decline in IMR (%)	
		1968–9	1979–80	1965–72	1973–80
0–9	(15)	49	21	8	7
10–24	(25)	49	19	8	7
25–49	(13)	64	23	3	14
50–74	(37)	76	22	4	15
75–100	(10)	80	17	5	16
All cantons	(100)	64	21	5	12

Source: Mata and Rosero (1988), Table 4.10. All 79 cantons of Costa Rica are included in the table.

There is, of course, nothing contrary in these results. Many of the studies mentioned earlier have noted that the decline of infant mortality in Costa Rica over the last few decades has been associated with an impressive retreat of infectious and parasitic diseases. It would be rather odd if carefully managed programmes of primary health care concentrating on enterprises such as immunization, deworming, environmental improvements, oral rehydration and prenatal care did not succeed in substantially accelerating this process and making a dent in the undernutrition-infection complex. Costa Rica went directly at the problem and has reaped as it sowed.

12.5   Concluding Remarks

In this chapter and the previous one, we have examined selected country experiences of direct support. We have paid special attention to China, Costa Rica, Chile, Sri Lanka and the Indian state of Kerala. All these experiences suggest a close connection between the expansion of public support measures and the improvement of living conditions. Public support can take various forms, such as public health services, educational facilities, food subsidies, employment programmes, land redistribution, income supplementation, and social assistance, and the country experiences that were examined have involved various combinations of these measures.

While there are significant contrasts in the relative importance of these different forms of public support in the different country experiences, the basic commonality of instruments is quite striking (especially in view of the great diversity of the political and economic regimes). Underlying all this is something of a shared approach, involving a public commitment to provide direct support to raise the quality of life, especially of the deprived sections of the respective populations.

The causal links between public efforts and social achievements in these as well as other countries have received a good deal of attention in the recent development literature. The investigations have taken different forms. One group of studies have been concerned with examining similarities in the nature of public support efforts in *different countries* (each with good records in mortality reduction and other achievements), and the commonalities involved in their respective efforts have been assessed, especially in contrast with the experience of other countries.[51] A second group of studies have been concerned with *interregional comparisons within single countries*, comparing the achievements of regions with greater or lesser involvement in public support.[52] A third set of studies have presented *intertemporal comparisons within single countries* of public efforts and social achievements.[53] A fourth set of studies have examined the direct impact of public support measures, such as health and nutrition programmes, at the *micro* level.[54] The causal links between public support provisions and social achievements have been clearly brought out in different ways in these diverse empirical investigations.

In this chapter and the preceding one, our focus has been concentrated on five specific 'case-studies'. Three of the five cases studied (viz. China, Chile and Costa Rica) were among the five countries identified in Chapter 10 as being the top performers in the 'support-led' category in reducing child mortality during the period 1960–85.[55] The other two countries in this identified list were Jamaica and Cuba. These countries are harder to study for a variety of reasons, including data limitation. Nevertheless, we may make a few brief remarks on particular aspects of the experiences of these two countries.

Regarding Jamaica, the data on infant and child mortality rates, already examined in Chapter 10, suggest a rapid improvement in basic living

---

[51] See e.g. Sen (1981*b*), Flegg (1982), Halstead *et al.* (1985), Stewart (1985), Caldwell (1986).

[52] See e.g. Patel (1980), Castaneda (1984, 1985), Jain (1985), Nag (1985), Prescott and Jamison (1985), Morrison and Waxler (1986), Kumar (1987), Mata and Rosero (1988).

[53] See e.g. Castaneda (1984, 1985) on Chile, Anand and Kanbur (1987) on Sri Lanka, and Mata and Rosero (1988) on Costa Rica.

[54] See e.g. Gwatkin *et al.* (1980), Harbert and Scandizzo (1982), Garcia and Pinstrup-Andersen (1987), Berg (1987*a*), Mata and Rosero (1988), and the studies of health and nutrition programmes cited earlier in this chapter in connection with specific country studies.

[55] The two other cases studied did not qualify in the 'top performer' list in Chapter 10 for rather special reasons. In the case of Sri Lanka the programme of support-led security began substantially earlier (and gathered particular momentum in the 1940s) and by 1960 Sri Lanka already had a very low level of child mortality, leaving less scope for exceptional performance in the period 1960–85 on which the international comparison in Chapter 10 concentrated (see section 12.2). In the case of Kerala as well, the interventionist history pre-dates 1960 but, more importantly, it did not even 'qualify' to be included in the international comparisons in Chapter 10 since Kerala is not a country but only a state within India.

conditions during the last few decades. This is indeed confirmed by other relevant indicators. By 1985, the expectation of life at birth in Jamaica was 74 years, a level as high as that of Britain or West Germany. Adult literacy was virtually universal for both men and women. And morbidity patterns had undergone a radical transformation, including a considerable retreat of infectious and parasitic diseases.[56]

As far as programmes of public support are concerned, Jamaica has an impressively activist record. This includes 'a distinguished history of accomplishments in public health care since early in the twentieth century'.[57] The record of public involvement in the provision of basic education is equally strong, with the bulk of Jamaica's outstanding literacy record being attributable to public, rather than private, educational institutions. The supportive role of the state, kept alive by a highly assertive electorate, has extended to many other fields of action including those of housing, sanitation, public employment, food subsidies, nutritional intervention, social insurance and social assistance.[58]

It is plausible enough that, as with the other countries studied in this chapter, a strong link exists between public support and social achievements in this case. This view is all the more convincing given that, during the period under consideration (1960–85), the rate of economic growth in Jamaica has been dismally low—in fact *negative* (see Table 10.3 in Chapter 10).

There is a further and rather striking aspect of Jamaica's experience which deserves mention here. The negative growth rate of GNP per capita for the 1960–85 period is mainly due to the record of the economy between 1973 and 1980, when Jamaica had the unique distinction of a negative growth rate *every year*.[59] This was also a period of socialist government, when the People's National Party (PNP, elected in 1972 and re-elected in 1976) was in office. It is possible that the PNP's policy of retaining an essentially capitalistic economy, while simultaneously cracking down in many ways on private initiative, reinforced the negative external factors to produce the economic morass of this period. But the socialist programme of the PNP government also included many positive and ambitious initiatives in domains such as health care, education, housing, food subsidies and public employment. Under the circumstances, if it were to turn out that the 1970s were also a decade of particularly rapid improvements in health and nutrition, Jamaica's experience

---

[56] See UNICEF (1987a), Cumper (1983) and Moran *et al.* (1988).

[57] Moran *et al.* (1988: 13). For a detailed investigation of these accomplishments, and of their economic and political basis, see Cumper (1983).

[58] On various aspects of public support in Jamaica today, see G. Cumper (1972), Gobin (1977), Girling and Keith (1977, 1980), Jameson (1981), G. E. Cumper (1983), Gunatilleke (1984), Samuels (1987), Mesa-Lago (1988a, 1988c), and Moran *et al.* (1988). The prominent role of public assertiveness and participatory politics in Jamaica's experience of support-led security is evident from several of these contributions. On this see also Duncan (1984).

[59] See e.g. the data presented in Boyd (1987), Table 5.1. In the 1960s, the economy had enjoyed a period of positive and fairly substantial economic growth.

would provide strong confirmation of the powerful influence that public support measures can have in removing hunger and deprivation even in the face of highly adverse macroeconomic circumstances.[60]

The available demographic evidence supports this hypothesis, with, *inter alia*, a decline of infant mortality of the order of 50 per cent during the decade of the 1970s.[61] Nutrition surveys provide some further evidence in the same direction. For instance, the incidence of rural undernutrition among children aged 5 and below appears to have declined from 12.1 per cent to 8.3 per cent between 1970 and 1978.[62] There is, thus, a strong possibility that indicators of economic opulence and nutritional well-being were moving in sharply contrasting directions during the 1970s.

This interpretation of Jamaica's experience calls for fuller investigation. The potential adverse effects of rapidly declining incomes on living conditions, with a decline in average real incomes of as much as 25 per cent or so between 1973 and 1980, should not be taken lightly. The combined evidence from independent nutrition surveys must be handled with some caution. Even mortality data are much less reliable for Jamaica than for the other countries studied in this chapter.[63] A closer examination of the available evidence (from anthropometric data, morbidity surveys, demographics statistics, etc.) would be needed to confirm the apparent achievements of the 1970s. As things stand, however, the period of socialist government in Jamaica does appear to be one of substantial success in support-led security.

In the case of Cuba, there is—as with Jamaica—a clear temporal association between expansion of public support on the one hand and improvements in health and nutrition on the other. Indeed, the sharp decline in infant and child mortality since 1960 (observed in Chapter 10) coincides with the post-

---

[60] The People's National Party was beaten in the 1980 election by the rival Jamaica Labour Party, which immediately adopted extensive measures of economic liberalization and 'adjustment', including very severe cuts in social programmes and public support. In spite of some economic recovery, the 1980–5 period seems to have been one of stagnation and possibly even deterioration in living standards. On this, see Boyd (1987), Melville *et al.* (1988a, 1988b), Mesa-Lago (1988c) and Moran *et al.* (1988).

[61] See Government of Jamaica (1985), Annex 6, Table A3, Moran *et al.* (1988), Table A1, and FAO (1988), Table 2.6. The precise magnitude of the decline is hard to ascertain, and substantially different estimates are provided by different studies.

[62] Samuels (1987), Table 4.11, based on weight-for-age measurements (the incidence of stunting also decreased considerably). Striking improvements during the 1970s have also been observed in the studies of Alderman *et al.* (1978) and Marchione (1977, 1984), which cover specific 'Parishes'. The data presented by Marchione (1984) apparently indicate some setback between 1975 and 1978–80 in the parish studied, but the 1978–80 figures—as Marchione explains—are not comparable with the earlier ones. Comparable figures for 1973 and 1975 indicate a decline of about 40% in the incidence of undernutrition for children below age 3 (calculated from his Table 3 first column). For evaluations of recent nutrition surveys in Jamaica, see Omawale and McLeod (1984), Davis and Witter (1986), Landman and Walker (1987), and Melville *et al.* (1988a, 1988b).

[63] There is, in fact, a possibility that the UNICEF estimates used in Chapter 10 give a slightly exaggerated picture of Jamaica's recent achievements, due to some decline in the quality of death reporting (George Cumper, London School of Hygiene and Tropical Medicine, personal communication).

revolutionary period, which has witnessed not only a radical land reform and a great deal of income redistribution, but also ambitious initiatives in the domains of health care, fiscal social security measures, nutrition programmes, basic education and food rationing. To cite only a few relevant facts, between the years immediately preceding the revolution of 1959 and the mid-1970s, the share of the poorest 20 per cent of the population in national income appears to have roughly quadrupled, secondary school enrolment ratios increased more than eightfold, the rate of open unemployment dropped by around 75 per cent, and the number of nurses per inhabitant more than tripled.[64]

The successes of China and Cuba in removing endemic undernutrition and deprivation are of some relevance in assessing the development experience of post-revolutionary socialist countries. The economic performances of these countries have been the object of a good deal of criticism—both internal and external—in recent years. The reprimands have often been well deserved, and the inefficiencies of bureaucratic planning have emerged powerfully enough. But the criteria of appraisal have often been rather limited, e.g. focusing on the size of commodity production rather than on the achievements in nutrition, health, education, morbidity, longevity and other basic aspects of the quality of life. As was discussed earlier (Chapter 1) and illustrated with empirical experiences (Chapters 10 and 11), aggregate economic opulence can be a very misleading indicator of achievements in developing basic human capabilities. The growth of GNP is no more than one important *means* to deeper ends, and as the variations in the intertemporal experiences of China show, the growth of commodity production can have quite a contrary pattern to that of life expectancy and related indicators (see Chapter 11).

The impressive records of Cuba and pre-reform China in the fields of health, education, nutrition and life expectancy have to be incorporated in a fuller and fairer assessment of the performance of these socialist economies. Of course, in this broader assessment other aspects of the quality of life must also be brought in, including the political freedoms enjoyed or denied. Sometimes the lack of these freedoms may not only vitiate the quality of life directly, it could indirectly also affect adversely health and longevity themselves. We have discussed, for example, the role of political suppression in the genesis of the Chinese famines of 1958–61 (see Chapter 11). But these complex considerations contribute to (rather than detract from) the need to broaden the criteria of success from the narrow concentration—currently fashionable—on the growth of commodity production and GNP. In that broadened evaluation, the successes of the socialist economies of China and Cuba in nutrition and health

[64] The figures are based on Brundenius (1982), Tables 8.1, 8.4, 8.5, 8.6. On the transformation of living conditions in Cuba since 1959, and the role of public support in bringing about this transformation, see Brundenius (1981, 1982, 1984), Eckstein (1980, 1982, 1986), Aldereguia (1983), Diaz-Briquets (1983), Muniz *et al.* (1984), Halebsky and Kirk (1985), Santana (1987), Ghai *et al.* (1988), among others. For interesting comparisons of the experience of Cuba with those of Costa Rica, Jamaica, Sri Lanka, and Chile, see Jameson (1981), Monckeberg (1983), Meegama (1985), Mesa-Lago and Diaz-Briquets (1988).

must figure prominently, along with other relevant assessments (many of which would be much less favourable). A proper reassessment of the experiences of socialist countries cannot be carried out in the narrow format that has come to be used so widely.

Before concluding the empirical investigations of this part of the book, something should be said about the resource requirements (and affordability) of the kind of public support measures that we have found crucial to the strategy of support-led security. Scepticism regarding the feasibility of large-scale public provisioning in a poor country often arises precisely from the belief that these measures are inordinately 'expensive'. The experiences studied in this chapter and the previous one (particularly those that have succeeded in spite of a low GNP per capita, e.g. China, Sri Lanka and Kerala) suggest that this diagnosis is, at least to some extent, misleading.

Indeed, the costs of many of the social security programmes in the countries we have studied have been in general astonishingly small. This applies, in particular, to public provisioning of health care and education. It has been estimated, for instance, that in China the percentage of GDP allocated to public expenditures on health has been only around 2 per cent. Moreover, only about 5 per cent of total health expenditure has tended to go to preventive health care, which has been one of the major influences behind the fast retreat of infectious and parasitic diseases.[65] There are similarly striking figures for the other experiences of support-led success we have studied.[66]

As was discussed in the first section of this chapter, the relatively inexpensive nature of public provisions in the domains of health and education is not, in fact, so surprising given the low level of wages in many developing countries.[67] The distinction of China or Kerala or Sri Lanka does not lie in the size of financial allocations to particular public provisions. Their real success

---

[65] Baumgartner (1989). On this general question, see also World Bank (1984a) and Jamison (1985).

[66] The percentage of GDP allocated to public expenditures on health in Sri Lanka in 1981 was barely 1% (Perera 1985: Table 8). The corresponding figure for Cuba was around 2.7% (Muniz *et al*. 1984: Tables VI.1 and VI.6). In Kerala, per-capita government expenditure on health is not much greater than in the rest of India (Nag 1985: Table 16). In Costa Rica, overall government expenditure on health is relatively high, but the public health programmes described in the preceding section accounted for only 2% of the total (Saenz 1985: 143). For further evidence and discussion of the scope for low-cost public provisions in the domain of health, with special reference to China, Costa Rica, Kerala and Sri Lanka, see various contributions in Halstead *et al*. (1985), and also Caldwell (1986).

[67] There are also other considerations that would lead to a reduction of the real resource burden of public support in developing countries. First, financial costs are not always a good reflection of social costs, and in particular a good case can often be made for regarding the social cost of labour in labour-surplus economies as being lower than the market wage. Second, the opportunities for raising revenue are not independent of the existence of a social security system. For instance, the scope for resorting to exacting indirect taxation may be much larger when vulnerable groups are protected from possibly severe deprivation. Third, there is an element of investment in public provisioning (e.g. through the relation between health, nutrition, education and productivity). This reduces the diversion from investment opportunities that is apparently involved in a programme of public support.

seems to be based on creating the political, social and economic conditions under which ambitious programmes of public support are undertaken with determination and effectiveness, and can be oriented towards the deprived sections of the population.

We should close this part of the book with a few general remarks about the empirical experiences of 'support-led security' examined in this chapter and the preceding one. The connection between programmes of public support and achievements in the quality of life has obvious relevance for policy making, and that is why we have attempted to study various aspects of these experiences in some detail. But the existence of such a connection is not in itself particularly remarkable. It is, in fact, not enormously surprising that efforts in providing extensive public support are rewarded by sustained results, and that public sowing facilitates social reaping.[68]

Perhaps what is more remarkable is the fact that the connections studied here are so frequently overlooked in drawing up blueprints for economic development. The temptation to see the improvement of the quality of life simply as a consequence of the increase in GNP per head is evidently quite strong, and the influence of that point of view has been quite pervasive in policy making and policy advising in recent years. It is in the specific context of that simple growth-centred view that the empirical connections between public support measures and the quality of life deserve particular emphasis.

Indeed, the simple growth-centred view is misleading not only because of the importance of public support in the successful implementation of 'support-led security' (with which this chapter and the last one have been concerned), but also because of the role that public support clearly plays even in the successful experiences of what we have been calling 'growth-mediated security'. As was discussed earlier (in Chapter 10), the contrast between a strategy of 'growth-mediated security' and the tactics of 'unaimed opulence' can be very significant indeed, and there are plenty of examples of countries with high growth rates of GNP, real incomes, food output, etc., with extremely sluggish improvement of the quality of life. A shared feature of support-led security and growth-mediated security is that they *both* involve crucial use of public support. Neither strategy hands over the job of raising life expectancy, reducing undernutrition, morbidity, illiteracy, etc. to an unaimed process of GNP growth.

What the particular studies of support-led security—on which we have concentrated in this chapter and the last—bring out is the force with which public support programmes can work even when a country is quite poor in

[68] Hunger and deprivation are, to a large extent, social conditions that cannot be seen only in isolated individual terms. There are strong interdependences and so-called 'externalities' involved in health (e.g. through the spread of diseases), education (e.g. through influencing each other), and nutrition (e.g. through food habits being dependent on social customs). The importance of social intervention in ensuring adequate entitlements to 'public goods', and in dealing with externalities generally, has been well recognized for a long time in economics (see Samuelson 1955, and Arrow 1963).

terms of GNP per head. This makes it possible to do something immediately about conquering deprivation and raising the quality of life without having to wait quite some time before ploughing back the fruits of economic growth into improved health and longevity. That immediacy is an important aspect of the promise of support-led security, and it can substitute for a good deal of fast economic growth (on which see section 10.7 of Chapter 10). Given that most countries are in situations such that they cannot hope to grow as fast as Kuwait or South Korea or Hong Kong have done over the last few decades, immediacy is a distinct advantage of the strategy of support-led security over that of growth-mediated security.

This recognition should not, however, be seen as establishing any general superiority of 'support-led security' over 'growth-mediated security'. Indeed, it is arguable that the latter strategy has its own advantages too. In particular, it makes it possible to establish the material basis of *further* progress in the future—even in the fields of health and longevity—going well beyond the elementary task of eradication of undernutrition and acute deprivation on which we have concentrated in this book.

Moreover, an assessment of the respective advantages of each strategy ultimately has to go beyond the concerns that have been the focus of this book. High incomes and extensive public support are both important to many other basic capabilities than those of being well nourished and healthy. High incomes provide individual access to commodities (such as better housing and more elaborate forms of entertainment) which can be used to lead a more varied life. Public support, on the other hand, can be an effective route to enhancing capabilities in domains where social interdependences are particularly strong, e.g. higher education.

Both growth-mediated security and support-led security have much to offer. Their advantages are partly congruent and partly divergent. In this chapter and the preceding one, the empirical analyses have pointed *inter alia* to the merits of support-led security and the process through which these merits are realized. The possibility of immediacy in encountering hunger and acute deprivation is certainly a serious virtue in that context. But this and related virtues of support-led security have to be assessed in the light of more comprehensive considerations relevant to this evaluation, including those brought out by the empirical and evaluative analyses in the *earlier* chapters of this book.

PART IV

Hunger and Public Action

13

The Economy, the State and the Public

13.1   Against the Current?

This is a book about what public action can do to eradicate hunger in the modern world. A question that would occur to many people is this. Is this not a hopeless time to write in defence of public action? The world has, in recent years, moved decisively towards unhesitating admiration of private enterprise and towards eulogizing and advocating reliance on the market mechanism. Socialist economies—from China to the USSR and East Europe—are busy de-socializing. Capitalist economies with a tradition of 'welfare state' policies —from the UK and the USA to Australia—have been absorbed in 'rolling back the frontiers of the state', with a good bit of privatization of public enterprise. The 'heroes' at this moment are the private ownership economies with high growth rates—not only old successes such as Japan, but also the new 'trail blazers'—South Korea, Hong Kong, Singapore. What chance is there of getting much of a hearing at this time for an argument in favour of *more* public action? And, more importantly, how can we possibly *defend* such a case, given the empirical regularities that are taken to have emerged in the recent decades?

There is indeed some sense in seeing the developments in the modern world in these terms. But there is also a good deal of nonsense mixed with that sense. We have had the occasion, in earlier parts of this book, to discuss fairly extensively the enormously positive role of public action in the success stories in the modern world. This applies *inter alia* to the outstanding and decisive contribution made by constructive public action in eradicating famines (see Part II), as well as in eliminating endemic undernutrition and deprivation (see Part III).

In the field of famine prevention, the decisive role of public action is illustrated not only by the elimination of famines in India since independence, but also by the unsung and underappreciated achievements of many African countries (see Chapters 5 and 8). These experiences firmly demonstrate how easy it is to exterminate famines if public support (e.g., in the form of employment creation) is well planned on a regular basis to protect the entitlements of vulnerable groups. Ensuring that the concerned governments take early and effective steps to prevent a threatening famine is itself a matter of public action. It is also clear that the eradication of famines need not *await* a major breakthrough in raising the per-capita availability of food, or in radically reducing its variance (even though these goals are important in themelves and can be—and must be—promoted in the long run by well-organized public policy). Public action can decisively eliminate famines *now*, without waiting for some distant future.

Regarding the elimination of regular, persistent deprivation (as opposed to the eradication of intermittent famines), the analysis presented here has indicated the positive contribution that can be made by public provisioning (especially of education and health services) and more generally by public support (including such different policies as epidemiological control, employment generation and income support for the vulnerable). Expectations based on general reasoning are, in fact, confirmed by the empirical experiences of different countries.

Public support in these different forms has played a major part in combating endemic deprivation not only in economies that are commonly seen as 'interventionist' (e.g., China, Costa Rica, Jamaica, Sri Lanka), but also in the market-oriented economies with high growth (e.g., Hong Kong, Singapore, South Korea); on this see Chapters 10–12. Indeed, the contrast between what was called 'growth-mediated security' (as in, say, South Korea) and 'unaimed opulence' (as in, say, Brazil) relates closely to the extensive and well-planned use of public support in the former cases, in contrast with the latter (see Chapter 10). When it comes to enhancing basic human capabilities and, in particular, beating persistent hunger and deprivation, the role played by public support—including public delivery of health care and basic education —is hard to replace.

The crucial role of public support in diverse economic environments is well illustrated by the intertemporal variations in the experience of China. The radical transformation in the health and nutritional status of the Chinese population (visible *inter alia* in a sharp increase in life expectancy, a dramatic decline of infectious and parasitic diseases, and improved anthropometric indicators) took place *before* the reforms of 1979, at a time of relatively moderate growth of GNP but enormously effective public involvement in the promotion of living conditions. The post-reform period has seen an impressive acceleration in the growth of GNP and private incomes, but also a crisis of public provisioning (especially of health services), and an *increase* in mortality. Much more is involved in increasing human capabilities—and in preventing their decline—than the stimulation of economic growth through revamping private incentives and market profits.

We have also discussed how the crucial role of public support in removing endemic deprivation is visible not only in the achievements and failures of developing countries today, but also in the historical experiences of the rich and industrialized countries. This is well illustrated by the sharp increases in longevity in Britain during the decades of the world wars, which were periods of rapid expansion of public support in the form of public food distribution, employment generation and health care provisioning (not unconnected with the war efforts).[1] There is nothing particularly *ad hoc* in the findings regarding the contribution of public support to human lives in the developing countries today.

Public action is not, of course, just a question of public delivery and state initiative. It is also, in a very big way, a matter of participation by the public in the process of social change. As we have discussed, public participation can have powerful positive roles in both 'collaborative' and 'adversarial' ways *vis-à-vis* governmental policy. The collaboration of the public is an indispensable ingredient of public health campaigns, literacy drives, land reforms, famine relief operations, and other endeavours that call for cooperative efforts for their successful completion. On the other hand, for the initiation of these endeavours and for the government to act appropriately, adversarial pressures from the public *demanding* such action can be quite crucial. For this adversarial function, major contributions can be made by political activism, journalistic pressures and informed public criticism. Both types of public participation —collaborative and adversarial—are important for the conquest of famines and endemic deprivation.

To emphasize the vital role of public action in eliminating hunger in the modern world must not be taken as a general denial of the importance of incentives, nor indeed of the particular role played by the specific incentives provided by the market mechanism. Incentives are, in fact, central to the logic of public action. But the incentives that must be considered are not only those that offer profits in the market, but also those that motivate governments to implement well-planned public policies, induce families to reject intrahousehold discrimination, encourage political parties and the news media to make reasoned demands, and inspire the public at large to cooperate, criticize and coordinate.[2] This complex set of social incentives can hardly be reduced to the narrow—though often important—role of markets and profits.[3]

This *is* indeed a good time to keep in view the crucial role that public action—in various forms—can play in eradicating hunger in the modern world. The empirical experiences of different countries point to certain systematic connections, and it is important not to lose sight of them in the scramble to be more 'private'—more exclusively 'market-based'—than the next country. We have to recognize the functions of public action and the rewards they can bring. The cost of overlooking them can be very high—in terms of unnecessary misery, morbidity and mortality.

---

[1] On this and related experiences, see Chapter 10. Some contemporary developments point to similar lessons to these historical experiences. For instance, the resilient persistence of hunger and deprivation in some sections of the population even in the richest countries of the world (e.g., the USA) seems to have a clear connection with the neglect of public support (see Harvard School of Public Health 1985, 1987). This is an important issue for further exploration in analysing the survival of undernutrition and preventable morbidity (and the persistence of inequalities in health and longevity between different classes and regions) within the rich countries of North America and Europe (see, e.g., Townsend and Davidson 1982).

[2] See Chapters 4, 5–8, 10–12.

[3] We have also discussed the importance of combining and connecting state action and market response in strategies to combat hunger (see particularly Chapters 6 and 7).

13.2 Famines and Undernutrition

The two forms of calamity related to hunger with which this book is concerned are (1) famines, and (2) endemic undernutrition and deprivation. The distinction between the intermittent and explosive occurrence of famines and the quieter and persistent phenomenon of regular undernutrition is important both from the point of view of diagnosis (they have different features and often quite dissimilar causal antecedents) and that of action (they call for substantially distinctive policies and activities).

In the earlier chapters we have had the occasion to discuss the shared conceptual background and interconnected causal circumstances of the two phenomena (Part I: Chapters 1–4). We have also examined and assessed the specific demands on strategies and actions imposed respectively by famines (Part II: Chapters 5–8) and by endemic deprivation (Part III: Chapters 9–12). The distinction relates closely to the different demands of what we have respectively called 'entitlement *protection*' and 'entitlement *promotion*'.[4] The task of entitlement protection is largely a matter of making sure that vulnerable groups do not face a collapse of their ability to command food and related necessities. Possible threats can arise not only from production failures—of non-food commodities as well as food—but also from worsening opportunities of acquiring the basic necessities (e.g. through unemployment, collapse of real wages, worsening of terms of trade). The concentration here has to be on preventing sharp declines in the economic circumstances of those who live close to the borderline of starvation. In contrast with the largely conservative task of entitlement protection, the exercise of entitlement *promotion* is, in many respects, more radical. In this case the concentration has to be on expanding the general command that people—particularly the more deprived sections of the population—have over basic necessities.

Of the two phenomena, famine clearly is much more visible and easier to diagnose. It is also a good deal easier to eradicate than regular undernutrition. Indeed, it is remarkable that famines continue to occur in the modern world despite the relative ease with which they can be totally eliminated through public action. The possibility of such termination has been amply illustrated by the experiences of many countries that have successfully achieved the transition.[5]

To make the eradication of famines more universal, some of the common tactics of anti-famine policy would have to be replaced by strategies that take fuller account of the economic and social realities in the famine-prone coun-

---

[4] See Chapter 1 on the respective definitions and ⬤cterizations, including that of the notion of 'entitlements' itself. In this concluding chapter, as in the earlier ones, several specific concepts and categories are freely used without redefinition, since they have been explicitly discussed and explained in the first chapter of this book.

[5] As was mentioned earlier, this applies not only to the often-discussed case of India, but also to many success stories from sub-Saharan Africa, e.g., in Botswana, Cape Verde, Zimbabwe (on these and other experiences, see Chapter 8).

tries. We have tried to clarify the nature of these required strategies (Part II), and we shall make a few further remarks on them in the next section.

Endemic undernutrition is a less obvious—less 'loud'—phenomenon than famine. Though it kills many more people in the long run than famines do, it does not get the kind of dramatic media attention that famines generate. But even in terms of sheer mortality, many times more people are killed slowly by regular undernourishment and deprivation than by the rarer and more confined occurrence of famine. Endemic deprivation is also a more complex social condition, involving deep-rooted economic and social deficiencies. Eliminating it is a much more difficult task than preventing famines. But it has been achieved to varying extents by many different developing countries, and there are lessons in these experiences.

The objectives of public action against endemic hunger have to go well beyond the enhancement of food intake. Human well-being relates to the lives that people can live—their 'capabilities'—rather than only to the commodities they can command. In the context of hunger, we are concerned with the ability that people have to lead a life without undernourishment, and not with the quantities of their food intake as such (on this see Chapter 3).

Even as far as *entitlements* are concerned (i.e. the command over commodities that people have), the relevant characterization must take note of all the commodities that can significantly influence a person's ability to lead a life without undernourishment. This would typically include not only food, but also health care and medical attention, since parasitic and other diseases contribute substantially to undernourishment as well as ill health. The list of important commodities must also include such items as clean water, living space and sanitation.

In fact, capabilities depend not only on the commodities consumed, but also on their *utilization*, as was discussed in Chapter 1. Variations in utilization (i.e. in the conversion of commodities into capabilities) can arise from the biological and social characteristics of persons, e.g., a pregnant woman may need more nutrients to achieve the same level of nourishment as another person. These variations can be important for policy planning, and entitlement analysis —focused as it always is on commodities as opposed to capabilities—cannot be a fully adequate basis for assessment of public action. Even when the utilization rates are not much influencible by policy, the fact of varying utilization rates has to be taken into account, particularly for assessing distributions of commodity entitlements (e.g. between women and men).[6]

But quite often rates of utilization may well be influencible by public action and policy. For example, if lack of information and knowledge about nutrition and health, or blind acceptance of injurious practices and traditions, reduces the capabilities that a person can get from a given entitlement to food and health care, then an expansion of education can—quite possibly—much

---

[6] On this see Sen (1984a, 1985a, 1987c).

enhance the person's nutritional capabilities. In this case, the entitlement to—and the actual use of—educational opportunities must also be included among the relevant focal points for policy. Education is not only of direct importance to living (e.g., in broadening a person's horizon of perception and thought), it can also influence the conversion of other entitlements into human abilities (e.g., the conversion of incomes into nutritional capabilities).

In fact, the expansion of basic education in general, and of female education in particular, can have several distinct roles in reducing endemic undernourishment.[7] Some of the influences of educational expansion may operate *through* affecting the person's entitlement to food and health care, e.g., by making the person more employable (and thus raising her income), or by making her more influential in demanding public provisioning of these basic essentials (through informed criticism of public policy and more articulate demands). The influence of education may also work through increasing the person's ability to *use* the available opportunities and entitlements (including the public services offered, e.g., through more extensive and better informed utilization of health services).[8] Finally, educational expansion can also lead to a less prejudiced intrahousehold distribution of food and health care. For example, greater female literacy tends to increase the bargaining power of women within the household and can reduce anti-female bias in nutritional division.[9]

In assessing the policies and programmes that have been used in different countries to promote entitlements and to expand basic capabilities of the people, we identified some common elements in the effective strategies, but also noted some genuine plurality of possible approaches (see Part III). We shall comment briefly on the similarities and pluralities in section 13.4 of this chapter.

13.3　*Famine Prevention*

In Chapters 5 to 8 of this book we have examined various aspects of anti-famine strategies. While there is much to learn from the informal security systems that have existed for a long time in famine-prone countries, it is also clear that an adequate system of famine prevention has to go well beyond strengthening these traditional security systems. For example, sometimes informal insurance arrangements based on community-centred mutual support can be of great use

---

[7] The positive connection between female education and the elimination of undernutrition has been investigated in a number of recent studies; see, e.g., Caldwell (1979), Behrman and Wolfe (1984, 1987), Cornia (1984), Ware (1984), Jain (1985), Mosley (1985a), Cleland and van Ginneken (1987), Levine (1988), Senauer and Garcia (1988), Thomas *et al.* (1988a, 1988b).

[8] For example, there is considerable evidence that the high level of basic education, especially female literacy, in Kerala leads to a better search for and exploitation of available medical services compared with the rest of India (see Nag 1985, 1989, and Caldwell 1986). This reinforces Kerala's advantage in having more public health services on offer. On Kerala's experience, see Chapter 11.

[9] On this issue, see Chapter 4, and also Chapter 11.

(as has indeed been found on different occasions in the past), but in other cases such arrangements can help very little since the economic viability of the entire community may be simultaneously undermined leaving little room for mutual support. The entitlements of the vulnerable groups may be threatened in many different ways, and the preventive system has to cover all the likely sources.

In the recent literature on famine prevention, much attention has been paid to formal systems of 'early warning' of famine threats. The advantages of getting such warnings are clear enough, but nevertheless we have not found the refinement of formal 'early warning systems' to be a crucial requirement of an effective anti-famine strategy. Countries that have been remarkably successful in preventing famines through timely public action typically have not made much use of such formal systems. This applies to countries as diverse as India, Botswana, Cape Verde and Zimbabwe.

Indeed, most often the warnings of imminent dangers have tended to come from general reports of floods or droughts or economic dislocations and from newspaper coverage of early hardship and visible hunger. In countries with relatively pluralist political systems, open channels of protest have also helped to direct forcefully the attention of the authorities to the need for preventive action without delay. Varieties of administrative, journalistic and political communications have served the 'early warning' role in the absence of elaborate systems of famine prediction or of formal procedures of 'early warning'.

Of course, informal ways of anticipating famine threats can sometimes mislead. But so can formal systems of 'early warning', which are often based on some rather simple model (explicitly invoked or implicitly presumed), paying attention to a few variables and ignoring many others. There is undoubtedly scope for improving famine warning systems based on economic analysis.[10] But there is little chance that a formal model can be developed that would be practically usable (with all the necessary data inputs being marshallable with the required speed) and that would take adequate note of all the variables that may possibly be relevant in the wide variety of cases that can, in fact, arise. The supplementation of formal economic models by more informal systems of communication and analysis is, to a great extent, inescapable.

In fact, most cases of neglected famine threats reflect not so much a lack of knowledge that could have been remedied only with formal systems of prediction, but negligence or smugness or callousness on the part of the non-responding authorities. In this context it is important to note that such informal systems of warning as newspaper reports and public protests carry not only information that the authorities *can* use, but also elements of pressure that may make it politically compelling to respond to these danger signals and do something about them urgently. It is, we have argued, no accident that the

---

[10] On different lines of possible improvement, see e.g. Cutler (1985*b*), Desai (1986), Borton and York (1987), Autier (1988), Walker (1988), Autier *et al.* (1989), Swift (forthcoming).

countries that have been most successful in famine prevention in the recent past have typically had rather pluralistic politics with open channels of communication and criticism. A relatively free newspaper system may be the most effective 'early warning' system a famine-prone country can rely on.

The issue of early warning is closely linked to that of preparedness. There is great advantage in being able to rely on ongoing famine prevention systems that do not have to be devised as and when a particular threat arises. Contingency plans indicating what to do and when to do it can make the exercise of famine prevention a great deal more reliable. Aside from avoiding the confusions that are typical of suddenly devised *ad hoc* response, a general system of this kind also has the advantage of integrating different programmes of action in which many agents may be involved but which do call for coordination at the national level.

As far as policies for entitlement protection are concerned, in Chapters 6 to 8 we had the opportunity to assess various methods that have been tried. Since most of the particular findings were put together in the concluding sections of these chapters, we need not cover that specific ground again. However, it is perhaps worth mentioning that we have argued in favour of strategies of entitlement protection based on employment creation, particularly in the form of public works programmes. This strategy is an efficient counter-measure to the loss of entitlements resulting from one of many possible changes (such as loss of employment or income or output due to droughts or floods) which may induce starvation of the affected group of people. This policy is also in line with the fact that, in most sub-Saharan African countries, seeking wage labour has become, these days, one of the chief survival strategies for vulnerable populations in times of crisis. Further, public employment is also a particularly effective solution to the 'selection problem', i.e., identifying *whom* to assist (discussed in Chapter 7).

The other major advantage of a strategy of employment provision (discussed in Chapter 6) is that it offers the possibility of greater reliance on 'cash support' (as opposed to the direct provision of food, cooked or uncooked). Indeed the payment of cash wages in exchange for labour may be the only practicable form of large-scale cash support in famine situations. Given the urgency of relief in a situation of famine threat, the advantages of being able to avoid the delays involved in moving and distributing food through bureaucratic channels can be quite crucial. By combining (1) public intervention (through cash wage payments—rather than leaving potential famine victims unaided), and (2) selective use of markets (in allowing food to be moved by the normal channels of trade—in response to the newly generated demand), it is possible to avoid both the inefficiency of bureaucratic food distribution and the unreliability of depending only on market-generated entitlements. It is the combination of different institutional arrangements that seems to provide, in many cases, the most reliable means of preventing famines effectively.

The possibility of using the market mechanism to supplement public intervention should not, however, be interpreted to imply that there is, then, no need for a substantial public stock of food grains. Public holding of food stocks can be crucial, even when the main burden of entitlement protection is carried by income generation programmes, and even when food movements and trade are largely left in private hands.

As was discussed in Chapter 6, public food stocks can help famine prevention in a variety of ways. First, they may be important to prevent collusive actions by traders in response to the enhanced demand for food resulting from income generation programmes. The 'threat' of breaking artificially generated price increases through releasing public stocks of food in the market can be very effective in preventing traders' collusion. Second, public food stocks can also prevent price rises due to panic and overestimation of future increases in food prices. This can be important even if there is no collusion on the part of traders.[11] Third, while we have argued that entitlement protection measures need not necessarily *await* an improvement of food availability through the public distribution system, the process of famine prevention can, of course, be very substantially helped by the release of food in the market—exercising a downward pressure on rising prices. Public stocks of food can be particularly important for market stabilization given the delays that are typically involved in importing food.

Famine prevention strategies are often designed on the assumption that it is crucial to achieve a strong influence on the intra-family distribution of food (e.g., in favour of young or undernourished children). We have argued that, in practice, the information and control needed for such discrimination are typically hard to obtain. There may, in fact, be good grounds for seeking the cooperation of the family unit in situations of famine vulnerability, rather than threatening its cohesiveness through divisive distribution practices.[12] This view relates partly to the incentive problems associated with attempts to influence the distribution of food within the family (see Chapter 7), and partly

---

[11] See Ravallion (1987*a*) on the process through which a market can 'overshoot' in anticipating price increases even without much collusion by traders. See also his analysis of the overreaction of food markets in the Bangladesh famine of 1974. Those food markets undoubtedly suffered from the general knowledge that there was relatively little food in public stock held by the government in Bangladesh. The suspension of US food aid to Bangladesh in the crucial period also added to the helplessness of the government to break the price rise through its own stock. The US government resumed its food aid only after Bangladesh accepted its demand that it should stop exporting jute to Cuba—by which time the famine was nearly over (on this see Rothschild 1976, McHenry and Bird 1977, Sobhan 1979, 1986). The lessons of that experience certainly underline further the advantages of holding a sizeable public stock of food grains as a general precautionary strategy.

[12] This point refers specifically to famine situations, and is not meant to indicate any general scepticism regarding the merits of nutritional intervention through individual feeding. In fact, rather different issues are raised in assessing such intervention in the context of chronic hunger and endemic undernutrition. See Chapters 3 and 6, and also Berg (1973, 1981, 1987*a*, 1987*b*), Gwatkin *et al*. (1980), Austin and Zeitlin (1981), Beaton and Ghasseimi (1982), Underwood (1983), Sen and Sengupta (1983), Pinstrup-Andersen and Biswas (1985), Godfrey (1986*a*, 1986*b*), Field (1987), Kumar and Stewart (1987), Norgan (1988), among others.

to the evidence of preferential treatment of young children in the early stages of a famine in many societies (Chapter 5).

As far as gender discrimination is concerned, we have found ample evidence of the enormity of the problem of chronic female disadvantage in nutrition and health in many parts of the world (Chapter 4). This problem is, however, distinctly less acute in sub-Saharan Africa—where most famines tend to take place these days—than in, say, South Asia or China or West Asia. Also, there is little evidence that gender discrimination plays a major additional role in the causation of *famine mortality* in particular, despite its importance in the determination of mortality in general (see section 4.4). The need to counter gender inequality—important in general—would not, therefore, seem to undermine, in the specific context of famines, the case for greater reliance on prevention strategies which concentrate on the regeneration of *household* incomes (e.g., through employment provision) rather than on *individual* support (e.g., through feeding). In fact, given the very high rates of female participation in public works programmes observed in most parts of the developing world, and the importance of female employment for the reduction of intra-family inequalities, gender considerations would seem to add strength to the case for employment-based famine prevention strategies.

The provision of employment cannot, of course, be an answer to all the different aspects of the famine prevention problem. For one thing, the choice of selection mechanism requires enough versatility to take note of the diversity of potential famine victims. In particular, additional provision must always be made for those (usually in relatively small numbers) who can neither work nor rely on the support of able-bodied relatives. However, the inability to work is a relatively easily observable condition, which can form the basis of administrative selection for 'unconditional relief'. Direct distribution of cash or food on the basis of fairly unambiguous selection criteria has indeed been found eminently practicable in many countries (see the case studies of Chapter 8).

It must also be remembered that the strategy of employment provision operates mainly through private incomes. While a good case can be made for regarding income generation as the most urgent and basic task in a situation of famine vulnerability, the survival of vulnerable groups also depends substantially on adequate access to a number of crucial public goods and services, including especially clean water, health care and sanitation. A comprehensive strategy of entitlement protection requires paying adequate attention to these public provisions.

13.4   Eliminating Endemic Deprivation

As was mentioned earlier, the elimination of regular hunger and undernutrition is a much harder task than the eradication of famines. The phenomenon of endemic deprivation is more pervasive; it affects many times the number of people who are threatened by famines. It is also more resistant to change, since it requires widespread promotion—on a long-term basis—of entitlements beyond well-established levels, and not just protecting established entitlements from short-term declines (as in the case of famine prevention).

Nevertheless, it is not hard to see what is needed for the elimination of endemic undernutrition and deprivation. People earn their means of living through employment and production, and they use these means to achieve certain functionings which make up their living. Entitlements and the corresponding capabilities can be promoted by the expansion of private incomes on a widespread basis, including all the deprived sections of the population. They can also be promoted by extensive public provisioning of the basic essentials for good living such as health care, education and food. Indeed, participatory growth and public provisioning are among the chief architects of the elimination of endemic deprivation—illustrated amply by historical experiences across the world. The basic challenge of 'social security' (in the broad sense in which we have used this term) is to combine these instruments of action to guarantee adequate living standards to all.

The problem of undernutrition cannot be divorced from that of morbidity and ill health—both because undernourishment makes one prone to illness and also because a good deal of the observed undernourishment in the world is due to the effect of parasitic and other diseases which make the absorption and retention of nourishment that much more difficult. Thus—as was discussed earlier—the entitlements that have to be promoted for eliminating persistent undernutrition are not merely of food, but also of health care, medical attention and epidemiological environment (just as the entitlements to be promoted for eliminating preventable morbidity include food as well as medical care).

Further, as we discussed earlier, basic education too has a major role in the eradication of both undernourishment and preventable morbidity. This is not merely because education helps in the use of one's personal means to buy food and medicine in a more informed way, but also because widespread elementary education leads to greater utilization of public health services. It can also generate more effective political demand that such services be provided. Furthermore, an educated public can more easily participate in national economic growth—partly through the expansion of remunerative employment—making the fruits of growth more widely shared. All this is in addition to the part that education directly plays in making human lives more worthwhile through broadening one's horizon of thought and experience.

The essential entitlements to be promoted for eliminating endemic deprivation and undernutrition, thus, include basic health care and elementary education in addition to food as such. They also include other necessities such as clean water, living space and basic sanitation. Many countries have achieved great success over the last few decades in widespread promotion of these essential entitlements and the corresponding capabilities to function. In terms of a simple criterion of the promotion of elementary capabilities (specifically, the reduction of infant and child mortality), ten countries were identified in Chapter 10 as having produced the fastest transformation since 1960. All of them have impressive records of gearing public policy towards guaranteeing widespread access to these basic ingredients of living.

However, there are also interesting diversities in their experiences. We have distinguished between two broad strategies for promoting basic social security for all. One strategy—called 'growth-mediated security'—has taken the form of fast growth of real national income per head and the use of the fruits of this growth to enhance the living conditions on a wide basis. Countries in this category among the identified ten include both newly industrializing countries such as South Korea, Hong Kong and Singapore, and also countries that have benefited from the rise in oil prices, in particular Kuwait and United Arab Emirates. All these countries have not only achieved much higher real income per head, they have used the fruits of that growth to expand the basic entitlements to food, health care and elementary education for all (see Chapter 10). Indeed, despite the role of private enterprise in these economies, in all cases the state has played a major part in promoting social security by bringing the basic ingredients of living within the reach of all the citizens—either through direct provisioning or through ensuring a participatory form of economic growth.

The other strategy, which has been called 'support-led security', has taken the form of promoting—through direct public support—entitlements to education, health care and food, without waiting for the national income per head to rise to a high level through general economic growth. Countries in this category among the ten include not only China and Cuba, but also Costa Rica, Chile and Jamaica.[13] The experiences of these countries (on which see Chapters 11 and 12) bring out the possibility of avoiding a longish 'wait' in the elimination of hunger and acute deprivation by immediate use of extensive public support.

In seeing the range of possibilities that are open to different developing countries, it is important to examine both the common elements and the contrasting features of the experiences of successful countries. The strategies of support-led security and growth-mediated security have the common feature of marshalling public action to involve diverse sections of the population in the process of social and economic transformation. In particular, countries in both groups have made extensive use of public provisioning

---

[13] One country that has achieved no less than any of these five in terms of support-led security is Sri Lanka. But in its case the main expansion took place *prior to* 1960, and it is thus not included in the list of top performers in the 1960–85 comparison. On this and on the assessment of Sri Lanka's policies, see Chapter 12. Another interesting experience is that of the state of Kerala in India which has also achieved extraordinary success in support-led security. Kerala is not included in the list of top performing countries since it is not a country but only a state in a federal country (even though in population size it is much larger than several of the countries actually included in the list, such as Hong Kong, Singapore, Kuwait and United Arab Emirates). For an analysis of Kerala's experience, see Chapter 11.

(especially in health care, basic education and food distribution) to enhance living conditions.

The experience of each group here contrasts with that of countries which have grown fast—in terms of GNP or real income per head—without using the fruits of growth to bring the essential ingredients of living within the reach of most people. In this respect the contrast between, say, Kuwait or South Korea or Singapore, on the one hand, and Brazil or Oman, on the other, is very sharp indeed. While the latter countries too have experienced fast economic growth, they have failed to ensure widespread public participation in the process of expansion of private incomes, and have not used extensive public support programmes to guarantee basic entitlements to the vulnerable sections of the population. For example, the fruits of growth have been used for public provisioning of education and health care in Kuwait, South Korea and Singapore in a way that simply has not happened in, say, Brazil or Oman.

The experiences of what we called 'unaimed opulence', of which Brazil provides a good illustration, show that growth as such is not a dependable strategy for enhancing elementary well-being and capability. If it is to serve as a solid basis for promoting living conditions, growth must take a participatory form (e.g., with widespread creation of remunerative employment), *and* a substantial part of the resources made available by economic growth has to be devoted to the expansion of public provisioning. Since the participatory nature of the growth process, particularly in the form of widespread access to remunerative employment, is itself dependent on certain preconditions that can be influenced by public provisioning (e.g., of elementary education), the role of public provisioning in distinguishing between 'unaimed opulence' and 'growth-mediated security' is quite central.

The use of public support in general—and of public provisioning in particular—is, thus, a common element in the experiences of growth-mediated security and support-led security, and the main difference is one of timing and sequencing. In the case of China or Cuba or Sri Lanka or Costa Rica, the countries concerned have not waited to get rich before embarking on ambitious programmes of public support. In the case of Kuwait, opulence has come first, but the gains from wealth have been transformed into better living conditions mainly through generous public provisioning. In South Korea, the expansion of private incomes played a relatively larger part, but public support—especially in the promotion of education, skills and employment —was crucial in ensuring participatory growth.[14] There are clearly different

---

[14] Another major factor in this success story of private enterprise has been Korea's fairly comprehensive land reforms, which took place early and contributed greatly to the sharing of the fruits of economic growth. Further, the role of the state in that country's planned economic expansion based on guided private enterprise is also important to study (e.g., the part played by state planning in industrial expansion, in a way not altogether dissimilar to what had happened in Japan earlier). As was discussed in Chapter 10, the Korean 'miracle' must not be seen in terms of an imaginary policy of *laissez faire*, since that has not been a feature of that country's route to success.

time patterns of social and economic change in the two broad strategies identified here, but also a commonality of the use of state involvement and public action in particular fields that are directly relevant for enhancing the basic capabilities of the population.

In promoting the elementary capabilities of living without undernourishment, escapable morbidity and preventable mortality, major contributions are made by the entitlements that people enjoy to food, health services, medical attention, good epidemiological environment and basic education. In the promotion of guaranteed entitlements to these essentials, public provisioning can play an important part. In fact, in most countries in the world, public provisioning is—for good economic and social reasons—a standard part of the delivery system of many of these vital ingredients of basic living. This applies even to the richer—more industrialized—countries in the world, and, as was discussed in Chapter 10, the history of longevity expansion in these countries has commonly involved crucial contributions of direct public provisioning. What the experiences of the countries with 'support-led security' bring out is the possibility of making these vital ingredients of quality of life widely available even when the country is still quite poor.

We have discussed earlier (in Chapter 12) the apparently perplexing question as to how this type of public provisioning could possibly be affordable by poor countries. One simple point to note is that some of the epidemiological transformations in health care, e.g., the elimination of infectious vectors, are remarkably economic in terms of resource use, and a great deal can be achieved in reducing preventable morbidity and premature mortality through fairly simple and inexpensive public policy. The same applies to the promotion of literacy and basic education.

A more complex aspect of this issue is the relevance of relative prices in the determination of real costs. Both elementary education and health care are extremely labour-intensive in their provisioning, and one of the characteristics of a poor economy is the cheapness of labour—and of training labour for elementary education and basic medical services. Thus, the poorer economies not only have less money to spend on providing these services, they also *need* less money for making these provisions. The handicap of national poverty is, therefore, to some extent reduced through the cheapness of labour costs as far as these public services are concerned, provided the country orientates its public policy to generate enough training of the appropriate kind. The bite of the financial constraints can also be substantially reduced by giving priority to basic services and to the needs of the most deprived people.[15]

13.5   Food Production, Distribution and Prices

The recognition of the role of direct public support in enhancing capabilities does not, of course, deny the importance of aggregate production. Indeed,

[15] See Chapters 11 and 12.

public provisioning should not be seen simply as a distributive device, even though it may be aimed at bringing basic ingredients of living within the reach of all. When elementary education or basic health services are provided more widely, the total production of these commodities is also expanded, so that the process is one of enlargement of production as well as of equitable distribution. It is not so much that the same bundle of commodities is more equally distributed as a result of this process, but that larger aggregate outputs of education and health services are produced, and it is from this enhanced production that the new recipients get their own share.[16]

This is not to deny that there can be, in particular cases, a conflict between aggregative and distributive considerations in policy making. A number of such conflicts were discussed earlier on in this book in the context of specific policies. In the particular context of food policy as such a conflict that has received some attention recently is that between the productive influences of high food prices *vis-à-vis* their possibly regressive distributional effects.[17] That low food prices tend to depress production incentives is certainly correct, and it has been argued with some force that this has been one of the factors behind the food production crisis in sub-Saharan Africa. While there are clearly many other aspects of the African food production problem (as was discussed in Chapters 2 and 9), low food prices can be seen as being among the contributory factors.

There is not much difficulty in accepting fairly readily that higher food prices can lead to a larger volume of food output being produced, but it would be a mistake to assume that, whenever that is the case, good public policy would require a considerable raising of food prices. We have to be concerned not only with the total volume of food produced, but also—indeed primarily —with the food consumption of the different sections of the population. Higher food prices, even as they increase the total food output, may reduce drastically the ability of the poor to buy food, and thus a larger volume of aggregate food output might actually go with a reduced consumption of the most vulnerable people. There is a real issue of conflict involved between the positive production incentives and the reduced affordability associated with

---

[16] Indeed, even the greater *use* of available health services as a result of the expanded education of the population (discussed earlier) must be seen as an enhancement of actual *production* of these services, since more of these services are then produced and used. Unfortunately, the usual estimations of the 'output' of public health services often does not record this basic fact. One reason for this is the tendency to measure the output generated by public provisioning in some mechanical way, e.g., in terms of the volume of public expenditure itself, or in units of theoretically available capacities rather than the actual volume of services used by the public.

[17] It is a common belief that the problem of regressive distributional effects of high food prices does not apply in much of sub-Saharan Africa, where most of the poor are thought to be peasant farmers who would *benefit* from an increase in the ordinary level of food prices. Recent empirical studies, however, suggest that in many African countries the number of poor who depend on market purchases of food for their survival is in fact large (and rapidly growing). On this see, among other contributions, Iliffe (1987), von Braun (1988), Weber *et al.* (1988), Liedholm and Kilby (1989).

high food prices. Which way the balance of advantages would lie is not just a matter of being either a hard-nosed 'productionist' or a soft-hearted 'distributionist', but also of knowing precisely how the different groups of consumers would be affected by the new equilibrium with higher food prices.[18]

In this book we have not tried to argue in general for 'high' or 'low' food prices. These are instrumental issues and can be resolved only in terms of the relevant features of each case, taking into account the production effects as well as distributional impact.[19] That itself amounts to a denial of such often-advocated policies as total reliance on 'getting prices right'. This is not only because the 'rightness' of prices depends ultimately on our overall objectives (including the assessment of social welfare) and must not be seen simply as a matter of what the market mechanism would have determined, but also because there is so much more to a sound food strategy than just fiddling with food prices.[20] Other issues include policy matters (e.g., technology, environmental improvement) related to the production of food and also of crucial non-food commodities (e.g., other outputs that generate income, or the supply of commodities such as health and education). The solution of the food problem requires a great deal more than getting food prices 'right'.

We have also emphasized the links between the economic and the political aspects of the food problem. Even in the context of the general diagnosis that the food production crisis in, say, sub-Saharan Africa arises partly from having unduly low food prices, the question can be asked as to why this is the direction in which food prices tend to 'err' in so many different countries. It would be amazing if the answer had nothing to do with the relative political powers enjoyed by the different classes and groups, e.g., the contrasting interests of food-growing peasants and the food-buying urban élite. Whether we see this in terms of the hold of a handful of administrators with interests of their own, or in line with what has been called a general 'urban bias' in development policies, or in terms of some other political analysis, it would be naïve to concentrate on 'getting prices right' without also addressing the underlying political factors that lead to these price biases.[21]

---

[18] Dharm Narain (1988) in particular has clarified a number of issues involved in this conflict. On his contributions and their general bearing on economic policy, see also Mellor and Desai (1985). On different aspects of 'food price dilemmas' in developing countries, see Timmer (1984, 1986), Pinstrup-Andersen (1985*b*), Ghai and Smith (1986), Kanbur (1986*a*), Lipton (1987*a*), Streeten (1987), Besley and Kanbur (1988), Mellor and Ahmed (1988), Ray (1988*a*, 1988*b*), among others.

[19] These effects would, of course, depend *inter alia* on the particular way in which it is proposed to influence food prices (e.g. through devaluation, imports, indirect taxes, food price subsidies).

[20] For analyses of the relationship between general development problems and food strategies, see Valdés (1981), K. Basu (1984), Swaminathan (1986), Boyce (1987), Gittinger *et al.* (1987), Mellor *et al.* (1987), Pinstrup-Andersen (1987, 1988*b*), Rukini and Eicher (1987), Eicher (1988*a*), Lipton (1988*a*). Many of the underlying issues have been investigated by various authors in the papers included in Drèze and Sen (forthcoming).

[21] On various political aspects of these economic relations, see among others Bauer (1954), Lipton (1977), Mitra (1977), Byres (1979), Bates (1981, 1983, 1986), Sobhan (1986), Hopkins (1988), Streeten (1989).

Discussion of food problems in Africa and elsewhere has often suffered from a systematic narrowing of vision to a few variables, overlooking the reach and relevance of many other factors. This can be seriously misleading for public policy. We have discussed earlier on in this book how the nature of the problem of hunger—both famines and endemic deprivation—calls for a broader political economic analysis taking note of the variety of influences that have a bearing on the commodity commands and basic capabilities that people enjoy. The case for such a broader focus—rejecting a cramped analysis—should not be interpreted as being something equally simplistic, though on the 'opposite' side, e.g., being 'anti-price-policy' or 'anti-production'. Production and prices belong to the analysis, but do so along with other concerns.

13.6   International Cooperation and Conflict

The agents of change in conquering hunger can come from inside or outside the country in question. It may be thought that the focus of this book has been primarily on forces that operate from *inside*. This would be fair comment. We have indeed mainly concentrated on what can be done through public action *within* the country to eradicate hunger. This should not be taken to imply that we believe that international help cannot be of any great use in combating hunger. We do believe that both famine prevention and the eradication of endemic undernutrition call for leadership and coordination coming from inside rather than outside the country, but that does not imply that international help cannot supplement these efforts effectively.[22] Nor that international conflicts of interest do not hinder an adequate solution of the problem of hunger in the modern world.[23]

Some of the policies we have discussed will undoubtedly call for international reform and coordination. Environmental protection is an obvious example. This type of international effort will be increasingly important in the future. There is also a good case for making sure that the countries battered by famines or undernutrition do not have to face severely restricted world markets, e.g., markets in the rich countries from which their goods are systematically excluded. The need for confronting and eliminating collusion and manipulation in food markets can also be important. Further, there is need for international cooperation in dealing with the excessive burden of debt that is borne by some of the poorest countries, especially in sub-Saharan Africa.[24]

---

[22] We have discussed in the context of famine prevention the helpful part that international agencies can play in strengthening and supplementing national efforts. But we have also discussed the advantages of the leadership of famine prevention being in the hands of national governments, with public participation (see Chapters 6–8).

[23] Various aspects of the bearing of international interest conflicts on the problem of hunger have been investigated by George (1976, 1984, 1988), Lappé and Collins (1979, 1980), Byron (1982), Twose (1984), Parikh (1986), among others.

[24] On the scope for 'cooperative debt relief', with special reference to Africa, see Jacques Drèze *et al.* (1989).

These and many other areas of possible international cooperation are of obvious importance.

There has recently been a great deal of debate about the pros and cons of aid in general and of food aid in particular. This is not the occasion to attempt a general assessment of that complex and tangled problem.[25] There is indeed a need to 'de-escalate' the issue. It is not hard to find cases in which aid will help, e.g., by providing timely relief, by permitting a larger investment for the benefit of living standards. Nor is it difficult to find other cases in which much harm does follow from aid, e.g., through economic or political dependency, or through the spread of corruption. It is hard to believe that aid can emerge as being just generally good or generally bad. Like all other policies and institutions, aid too has to be assessed by balancing its positive and negative consequences in the respective contexts.

It may, however, be worth commenting briefly on a particular argument that has often been used to argue generally against food aid as such. It has been pointed out that food aid tends to depress food prices and thus reduces the incentive to produce more food. There is some truth in this way of looking at the problem, but it can scarcely be seen as a decisive rebuttal of the case for food aid. First, production is, as was discussed earlier, only one part of the overall picture of entitlement determination, and has to be supplemented by distributive considerations, which can be especially important when the use of food aid is geared to giving relief to the needy. Second, food production is only one part of total production, and the ability of people to command food will depend also on the effects on the production of *other* goods which generate employment and income; it is quite inadequate to look only at the incentive effects on food output. Third, what the impact of food aid will be on food prices is not a fact of nature but a matter of policy. It is not particularly complex to make sure, if it is so desired, that food aid does not lower the food prices that producers receive. Indeed, the element of income-gain involved in receiving food aid makes it also possible to have a consumer subsidy that makes the prices that producers receive exceed the prices the consumers have to pay. In general the effects of food aid on prices will depend on what is done with it. The tendency to believe that it must—of necessity—adversely affect incentives is far from correct.

While aid is often seen as the central 'international' aspect of the problem of world hunger, it is possible to argue that an international issue that is no less important is that of war and peace. The problem of hunger is made much worse by the war-torn nature of the world. Many of the great famines in the world have been associated with actual wars—varying from armed conflicts in Biafra and Eritrea to the 'killing fields' of Kampuchea. Wars increase a country's

---

[25] For a general analysis of the contribution of aid, see Cassen *et al.* (1986). For a strong defence of food aid, see Dawson (1985), Singer *et al.* (1987); see also Clay and Singer (1985). On the other side, see Jackson and Eade (1982), Bauer (1984), Griffin (1987).

vulnerability to famines in many different ways: (1) through the destruction of crops, (2) by destroying resources including land and the environment, (3) by deflecting resources from economic development and welfare programmes to military expenditure, (4) by disrupting trade, commerce and economic activity, (5) by making the provision of organized relief for the hungry much harder, (6) by causing population displacements and generating masses of destitute refugees, and (7) through the suppression of the freedom of the press and civil rights, and by making the country less tolerant of protest and pluralism.

Sub-Saharan Africa in particular has been especially torn by strife and warfare, with terrible consequences on hunger and deprivation. Angola, Chad, Ethiopia, Mozambique, Somalia, Sudan, and many other countries have been transformed to a greater or lesser extent into veritable battlefields. Quite a few of these wars have been directly or indirectly associated with global conflicts and the cold war, with the African governments falling in line with one international side or another. The big powers have also been remarkably tolerant of regimes on their respective sides despite persistent violations of the very principles of democracy and socialism on behalf of which the big powers allegedly wage their respective battles. It is a story in which there is little honour—either locally, or in the distant capitals from which many international conflicts have been pursued with such vigour and lethal arms pushed with such energetic cunning. It is arguable that one of the biggest contributions that the big powers can make to the solution of the problem of world hunger is to refrain from exacerbating armed conflicts in the 'third world'.

The disastrous effects of wars (and war preparations) on the problem of human well-being and hunger sharply contrast with the success that some of the poorer countries have achieved by giving low priority to military expenditure. Costa Rica which abolished its army in 1949 is the most obvious example. The saving of resources involved has certainly helped to channel economic efforts to the improvement of living standards.

The international aspects of world hunger are indeed extensive. In addition to the much-debated issues of aid, trade and debt, they include problems of international coordination involved in environmental protection and—less palpably but most surely—the problems of war and peace, which can have such a crucial influence on the successes and failures of different countries in eradicating famines and endemic hunger. Once again the need is to take an adequately broad view of the causal antecedents of starvation and undernutrition. That general theme has, of course, been a recurrent one in this book.

13.7 Public Action and the Public

The persistence of widespread hunger is one of the most appalling features of the modern world. The fact that so many people continue to die each year from famines, and that many millions more go on perishing from persistent deprivation on a regular basis, is a calamity to which the world has, somewhat incredibly, got coolly accustomed. It does not seem to engender the kind of shock and disquiet that might be reasonable to expect given the enormity of the tragedy. Indeed, the subject often generates either cynicism ('not a lot can be done about it'), or complacent irresponsibility ('don't blame me—it is not a problem for which I am answerable').

Perhaps this is what one should expect with a resilient and continuing calamity of this kind. But it is not at all easy to see why we do not owe each other even the minimal amounts of positive sympathy and solidarity that would make it hard for us to cultivate irresponsible complacency.[26] While we shall not wait for an answer to that ethical question, we must address the issue of cynical pessimism (i.e., the belief that 'not a lot can be done'). There is, in fact, little reason for presuming that the terrible problems of hunger and starvation in the world cannot be changed by human action. Much of this book has been concerned with exploring and clarifying what can be done and how.

As we have discussed, the eradication of famines is a fairly straightforward task, and there is not much difficulty in achieving it given systematic prepared-ness and the will to act quickly to protect or recreate threatened entitlements (Part II). Indeed, the successes achieved in different Asian and African countries in eliminating famines seem eminently repeatable in others. While the problem of endemic undernutrition and deprivation is harder to deal with, here too the possible lines of policy are clear enough and well illustrated by particular strategies that have already been used in one form or another (Part III). There is little room for cynical pessimism or for paralysing scepticism.

The types of public action needed in different contexts have been discussed earlier on in the book, and there is no need here—in this final section—to go once again into these questions. But it is worth emphasizing that throughout this book, we have seen public action as something involving a great deal more than activities of the state. This is partly because the public can do a great deal for itself even without governmental assistance, but also because the nature of government policy can depend very extensively on the nature of public activism, including articulated demands and criticisms. The connections are easy to identify in many contexts, e.g., the role of adversarial politics and of an active press in forcing the hands of the government to act rapidly enough to abort threatening famines (see Chapter 5). In other contexts, the precise part played by public activism may be harder to identify exactly, even though the influence may be understood to be generally quite strong. For example, the social impact of women's political movements and economic organizations —and more generally of informed discussion and criticism of women's relative deprivation—can be recognized to be quite substantial even when it is

---

[26] This book is not directly concerned with exploring ethical issues as such, and we shall resist going into the question as to what we owe each other as human beings. On the ethical issues raised by the hunger and suffering of people at a distance from us, see Onora O'Neill's (1987) powerful and far-reaching analysis. See also Sen (1982*d*, 1985*a*, 1988*e*).

hard to specify the exact details of the process of influence (see Chapters 4 and 11).

It is also worth noting, in general, that effective action is not only a matter of informed analysis, but also one of determination and will. The idea of the 'political will' has often been invoked in social analysis. That concept, however, is hard to make very precise, and the tendency to treat it as a 'black box' for 'completing' incomplete explanations has been viewed—rightly —with some suspicion. There are, in fact, many problems in trying to specify the exact process through which a 'political will' is supposed to operate, and there are certainly many connections here that are hard to observe. But, at the same time, it would be a mistake to leave no room whatever in our social analysis for the general influence of firm commitment, uncompromising resolve and dedicated action by the political leadership, and to take no account of the way in which an inspired leadership can generate effective social response.

Indeed, without bringing in the class of concepts that are associated with the general idea of political will and determination, it is difficult to provide an adequate analysis of the process through which, say, a country like China achieved a remarkably rapid improvement in longevity and general health even without a massive increase in GNP per head or in aggregate economic opulence. This success was based on a politically inspired and forcefully led transformation of the access to basic ingredients of living enjoyed by the Chinese population, and we have discussed some of the ways in which that transformation took a concrete shape (see Chapter 11). While there are technical issues here concerning institutional structure, financing arrangements and relative costs, underlying all this was the force provided by a politically committed leadership determined to achieve a radical transformation.

However, it must also be acknowledged that dogmatic commitment and inflexible resolve on the part of the leadership can sometimes be associated with a negative—rather than a constructive—role in combating hunger and deprivation. For example, the same China that achieved so much success through determined public action in transforming health conditions, also carried out—with misplaced confidence—a disastrous set of public policies leading to the largest famine in this century in 1958–61 in the wake of the so-called Great Leap Forward (see Chapter 11). Despite their destructive consequences, these wrong-headed policies could not be modified by the pressure of public criticism both because the leadership was uncompromising and overconfident and because the system did not encourage—or indeed allow—such criticism.[27]

[27] Similarly, the reduction of communal health services in rural China and the imposition of the 'one child' policy and related measures of compulsory birth control, which accompanied the reforms of 1979, were carried out with remarkably little public discussion and opportunity of social criticism, despite the dangers of serious adverse effects on mortality rates (especially on infant mortality).

Aside from this issue of political commitment, we have had several occasions to note the positive role that political *pluralism* can play in the eradication of hunger and deprivation. The contribution of political pluralism relates to the importance of adversarial politics and social criticism in influencing state action in the direction of greater sensitivity to the well-being of the population. The power of public pressure is not, of course, confined to pluralist political systems, and indeed we have discussed how even fairly authoritarian political regimes may have strong incentive to respond to popular demands (as in South Korea or Chile). But it is clear that the scope for effective public influence on the activities of the state tends to be greater in political systems that make room for opposition and criticism. We have discussed, for instance, how the accountability of the Indian government to the electorate (combined with a relatively free press) has made the prevention of famines a political compulsion, in a way that has not applied in China (or in sub-Saharan Africa). We have also noted the crucial role played by participatory politics in the development of public support systems in countries such as Costa Rica, Sri Lanka and Jamaica.

This is not to say that the political systems of these countries are in any way 'exemplary' as far as pluralism and participation are concerned. The demands of different classes typically do not receive equal attention because of the strong links between economic inequality and the distribution of political power. Ultimately, genuine political participation involves a great deal more than the elementary political rights that are recognised in these countries. Also, formal political rights may fall far short of providing a sound basis for political participation when large sections of the public are deprived of the means of effectively exercising these rights and of articulating their demands. We have noted, for instance, how the extraordinary persistence of mass illiteracy in India has contributed to the neglect of many social problems, and has tended to prevent chronic deprivation from becoming a politically sensitive issue in the way that famine has become.[28] But these qualifications, however real and important, do not detract from the general connection that can be observed between the scope for pluralist politics and the role of public activism.

The distinction between the 'collaborative' and 'adversarial' roles of the public has some relevance to this dichotomy between the advantages of political commitment *vis-à-vis* those of political pluralism. While a leadership committed to radical social change can often inspire more public collaboration, having a committed leadership is not adequate for—and may even be hostile to—the exercise of the adversarial role of the public. Since both the roles have value in combating deprivation, it is natural to look for the possibility of combining the advantages of committed leadership with those of pluralist tolerance. Whether such combinations are possible, especially in the circum-

---

[28] The Indian state of Kerala is an exception to this pattern, and we have discussed how the longstanding achievements of this state in the field of education have borne fruit in the form of a more effective and broad-based system of public support than exists in the rest of India.

stances that rule in most developing countries, remains a challenging question.[29] There is no reason, in principle, why a political system that allows, encourages and helps the public to be active (both adversarially as well as collaboratively) cannot also lead to governments that provide bold initiatives and inspiring leadership. But it is obvious that in practice the actual possibilities are much constrained by social, political and economic circumstances, and the 'ideal combinations' are hard to realize, as the history of the world has shown again and again.

In these concluding comments, we have taken the liberty of raising some very broad questions, drawing on—but going beyond—the analyses presented earlier in the book. Some of these questions are easier to raise than they are to answer. But it is nevertheless important to ask these bigger questions even when the answers are far from clear. While much of this book has been concerned with issues of diagnosis and policy that admit of relatively clear-cut answers (and these we have tried to present sharply enough), it would be misleading not to point to the broader—and 'grander'—questions that lie close to the fields of our inquiry and which can profoundly influence the nature of these fields.

It is important, in this concluding section, to re-emphasize our focus on public participation—collaborative and adversarial—in eradicating famines, undernutrition and deprivation. It is, as we have tried to argue and illustrate, essential to see the public not merely as 'the patient' whose well-being commands attention, but also as 'the agent' whose actions can transform society. Taking note of that dual role is central to understanding the challenge of public action against hunger.

---

[29] This is a question that has come even more to the forefront with the recent demands for democratic rights in China and Eastern Europe.

REFERENCES

ABEILLE, B. (1979), 'A Study of Female Life in Mauritania', mimeo, Office of Women in Development, US Agency for International Development, Washington, DC.

ABEL-SMITH, B. (1986), 'Funding Health for All: Is Insurance the Answer?', *World Health Forum*, 7.

ABELSON, P. H. (ed.) (1975), *Food, Politics, Economics, Nutrition and Research* (Washington, DC: American Association for the Advancement of Science).

ABRAHAM, A. (1980), 'Maharashtra's Employment Guarantee Scheme', *Economic and Political Weekly*, 15.

ACHARYA, S., and PANWALKAR, V. G. (1988a), 'The Maharashtra Employment Guarantee Scheme: Impacts on Male and Female Labour', Regional Re: earch Paper (South and South East Asia), The Population Council, Bangkok.

—— —— (1988b), 'Labour Force Participation in Rural Maharashtra: A Temporal, Regional and Gender Analysis', Studies on Women Workers No. 2, Asian Employment Programme, International Labour Organization, New Delhi.

ADAMS, M. E. (1986), 'Merging Relief and Development: The Case of Turkana', *Development Policy Review*, 4.

ADMASSIE, Y., and GEBRE, S. (1985), *Food-for-Work in Ethiopia: A Socio-economic Survey* (Addis Ababa: Institute of Development Research, Addis-Ababa University).

ADNAN, S. (1988), 'Birds in a Cage: Institutional Change and Women's Position in Bangladesh', paper presented at a IUSSP Conference on Women's Position and Demographic Change held in Asker (Norway), June 1988.

AFSHAR, H. (ed.) (1987), *Women, State and Ideology: Studies from Africa and Asia* (London: Macmillan).

AGARWAL, B. (1986), 'Women, Poverty and Agricultural Growth in India', *Journal of Peasant Studies*, 13.

—— (1988), 'Social Security and the Family', paper presented at a Workshop on Social Security in Developing Countries held at the London School of Economics, 4–5 July 1988; to be published in Ahmad, S. E., *et al.* (eds.) (forthcoming), *Social Security in Developing Countries*.

—— (ed.) (1989), *Structures of Patriarchy* (London: Zed).

AGERE, S. T. (1986), 'Progress and Problems in the Health Care Delivery System', in Mandaza, I. (ed.) (1986), *Zimbabwe: The Political Economy of Transition 1980–1986*.

AGRAWAL, A. N., VERMA, H. O., and GUPTA, R. C. (1987), *Economic Information Yearbook 1987–88* (New Delhi: National Publishing House).

AHLUWALIA, M. S. (1978), 'Rural Poverty and Agricultural Performance in India', *Journal of Development Studies*, 14.

AHMAD, Q. K. (1985), 'Food Shortages and Food Entitlements in Bangladesh: An Indepth Enquiry in Respect of Selected Years', mimeo, Food and Agriculture Organization, Rome.

AHMAD, S. E., and HUSSAIN, A. (1988), 'Social Security in China: A Historical Perspective', paper presented at a Workshop on Social Security in Developing Countries held at the London School of Economics, 4–5 July 1988; to be published in Ahmad, S. E., *et al.* (eds.) (forthcoming), *Social Security in Developing Countries*.

—— DRÈZE, J. P., HILLS, J., and SEN, A. K. (eds.) (forthcoming), *Social Security in Developing Countries* (Oxford: Oxford University Press).

AIRD, J. (1982), 'Population Studies and Population Policy in China', *Population and Development Review*, 8.

AKERLOF, G. A. (1984), *An Economic Theorist's Book of Tales* (Cambridge: Cambridge University Press).

AKONG'A, J. (1982), *Famine, Famine Relief and Public Policy in Kitui District* (Nairobi: Institute for Development Studies).

—— and DOWNING, T. (1987), 'Smallholder Vulnerability and Response to Drought', in Akong'a, J., *et al.* (1987), 'The Effects of Climatic Variations on Agriculture in Central and Eastern Kenya'.

—— —— KONIJN, N. T., MUNGAI, D. N., MUTURI, H. R., and POTTER, H. L. (1987), 'The Effects of Climatic Variations on Agriculture in Central and Eastern Kenya', mimeo, IIASA, Laxenburg; preprinted from Parry, M. L., *et al.* (eds.) (forthcoming), *The Impact of Climatic Variations on Agriculture* (Dordrecht: Reidel).

ALAILIMA, P. (1985), 'Evolution of Government Policies and Expenditure on Social Welfare in Sri Lanka During the 20th Century', mimeo, Colombo.

ALAM, M. S. (1989), 'The South Korean "Miracle": Examining the Mix of Government and Markets', *Journal of Developing Areas*, 23.

ALAMGIR, M. (1978), *Bangladesh: A Case of Below Poverty Level Equilibrium Trap* (Dhaka: Bangladesh Institute of Development Studies).

—— (1980), *Famine in South Asia* (Cambridge, MA: Oelgeschlager, Gunn and Hain).

ALDEREGUIA, J. (1983), 'The Health Status of the Cuban Population', *International Journal of Health Services*, 13.

ALDERMAN, H. (1986), *The Effects of Food Price and Income Changes on the Acquisition of Food by Low-Income Households* (Washington, DC: International Food Policy Research Institute).

—— (1987), 'Allocation of Goods Through Non-Price Mechanisms: Evidence on Distribution by Willingness to Wait', *Journal of Development Economics*, 23.

—— (1988a), 'Do Food Subsidies Reach the Poor?', mimeo, International Food Policy Research Institute, Washington, DC.

—— (1988b), 'Food Subsidies and State Policies in Egypt', in Richards, A. (ed.) (1988), *Food, States and Peasants: Analysis of the Agrarian Question in the Middle East* (Boulder: Westview Press).

—— (forthcoming), 'Poverty and Undernutrition: How Strongly Linked?', mimeo, International Food Policy Research Institute, Washington, DC.

—— and VON BRAUN, J. (1984), 'The Effects of the Egyptian Food Rationing and Subsidy System on Income Distribution and Consumption', Research Report No. 45, International Food Policy Research Institute, Washington, DC.

ALDERMAN, M. H., WISE, P. H., FERGUSON, R. P., LAVERDE, H. T., and D'SOUZA, A. J. (1978), 'Reduction of Young Child Malnutrition and Mortality in Rural Jamaica', *Journal of Tropical Pediatrics*, 24.

ALFRED, C. (1986), 'Famine and Food Aid Among the Beja', mimeo, OXFAM, Oxford.

ALLEN, G. (1986), 'Famines: The Bowbrick–Sen Dispute and Some Related Issues', *Food Policy*, 11.

ALLISON, C., and GREEN, R. (eds.) (1985), 'Sub-Saharan Africa: Getting the Facts Straight', special issue of *IDS Bulletin*.

AL-SABAH, Y. S. F. (1980), *The Oil Economy of Kuwait* (London: Kegan Paul).

AMBIRAJAN, S. (1971), 'Political Economy of Indian Famines', *South Asia*, 1.

—— (1978), *Classical Political Economy and British Policy in India* (Cambridge: Cambridge University Press).

AMBLER, C. H. (1988), *Kenyan Communities in the Age of Imperialism: The Central Region in the Late Nineteenth Century* (New Haven: Yale University Press).

AMERINGER, C. D. (1982), *Democracy in Costa Rica* (Stanford: Praeger).

AMIN, S. (1988), 'The Effect of Women's Status on Sex Differentials in Infant and Child Mortality in South Asia', mimeo, Office of Population Research, Princeton University.

AMIN, SAMIR (1974), *Neo-colonialism in West Africa* (New York: Monthly Review Press).

—— (ed.) (1975), *L'Agriculture africaine et le capitalisme* (Paris: Anthropo-Idep).

AMSDEN, A. H. (ed.) (1980), *The Economics of Women and Work* (Harmondsworth: Penguin).

—— (1989), *Asia's Next Giant: Late Industrialization in South Korea* (Oxford: Oxford University Press).

ANAND, S., and HARRIS, C. (1986), 'Food and Standard of Living: An Analysis Based on Sri Lankan Data', paper presented at a Conference on Food Strategies held at WIDER, Helsinki, 21–5 July 1986; to be published in Drèze, J. P., and Sen, A. K. (eds.) (forthcoming), *The Political Economy of Hunger*.

—— —— (1987), 'Issues in the Measurement of Undernutrition', paper presented at a Conference on Poverty, Undernutrition and Living Standards held at WIDER, 27–30 July 1987; to be published in Osmani, S. R. (ed.) (forthcoming), *Nutrition and Poverty*.

—— and KANBUR, S. M. R. (RAVI) (1987), 'Public Policy and Basic Needs Provision: Intervention and Achievement in Sri Lanka', mimeo, to be published in Drèze, J. P., and Sen, A. K. (eds.) (forthcoming), *The Political Economy of Hunger*.

ANDREU, J. (1984), 'Health Sector Development Issues', mimeo, World Bank, Washington, DC.

Anon. (1973), 'Food Riots: Hungry Stomachs Must Hunger On', *Economic and Political Weekly*, 28 Apr.

Anon. (1984), 'Cape Verde: Drought as a Way of Life', *West Africa*, 6 Feb.

Anon. (1985), 'Fighting Famine', *Economic and Political Weekly*, 2 Nov.

Anon. (1988), 'Cash for Food in Ethiopia', *UNICEF/INTERCOM*, 47.

ANYANGO, G. J., et al. (forthcoming), 'Drought Vulnerability in Central and Eastern Kenya', in Downing, T. E., et al. (eds.) (forthcoming), *Coping with Drought in Kenya: National and Local Strategies*.

APPADURAI, A. (1984), 'How Moral is South Asia's Economy? A Review Article', *Journal of Asian Studies*, 43.

APPLETON, J. (1987), *Drought Relief in Ethiopia: Planning and Management of Feeding Programmes* (London: Save the Children Fund).

—— (1988), 'Nutritional Status Monitoring in Wollo, Ethiopia, 1982–1984: An Early Warning System', mimeo, Save the Children Fund, UK.

ARELLANO, J. P. (1985a), 'Social Policies in Chile: An Historical Review', *Journal of Latin American Studies*, 17.

—— (1985b), Políticas sociales y desarrollo, Chile 1924–1984 (Santiago: CIEPLAN).

—— (1988), 'La situación social en Chile', Notas técnicas No. 94, CIEPLAN, Santiago.

—— CORTÁZAR, R., and SOLIMANO, A. (1987), 'Chile', Country Study No. 10, Stabilization and Adjustment Policies and Programmes, WIDER, Helsinki.

—— —— —— (1988), 'Medium-Term Development: Some Issues Relevant for Chile', paper prepared for a Conference on Medium Term Development Strategy, WIDER, Aug. 1988.

ARNOLD, D. (1988), Famine: Social Crisis and Historical Change (Oxford: Blackwell).

ARROW, K. (1963), 'Uncertainty and the Welfare Economics of Health Care', American Economic Review, 53.

ASHTON, B., HILL, K., PIAZZA, A., and ZEITZ, R. (1984), 'Famine in China, 1958–61', Population and Development Review, 10.

ASLANBEIGUI, N., and SUMMERFIELD, G. (1989), 'Impact of the Responsibility System on Women in Rural China: An Application of Sen's Theory of Entitlements', World Development, 17.

Asociación Demográfica Costarricense (1984), Mortalidad y fecundidad en Costa Rica (San José: ADC).

ATKINSON, A. B. (1983), Social Justice and Public Policy (Brighton: Wheatsheaf and Cambridge, MA: MIT Press).

—— (1987a), 'On the Measurement of Poverty', Econometrica, 55.

—— (1987b) 'Income Maintenance and Social Insurance: A Survey', in Auerbach, A., and Feldstein, M. (eds.) (1987), Handbook of Public Economics (Amsterdam and New York: North-Holland).

—— and HILLS, J. (1988), 'Social Security in Developed Countries: Are There Lessons for Developing Countries?', paper presented at a Workshop on Social Security in Developing Countries held at the London School of Economics, 4–5 July 1988; to be published in Ahmad, S. E., et al. (eds.) (forthcoming), Social Security in Developing Countries.

—— —— and LEGRAND, J. (1987), 'The Welfare State', in Dornbusch, R., and Layard, R. (eds.) (1987), The Performance of the British Economy (Oxford: Oxford University Press).

AUDETTE, R. and GROLLEAUD, M. (1984), Le Stockage non-étatique des grains dans les pays sahéliens: bibliographie générale, inventaire, analyse et recommandations (Paris: Club du Sahel).

AUERBACH, L. S. (1979), 'Women's Jobs Means Women's Money: The Social Ramifications of the Increased Participation of Women in the Work Structure of a Tunisian Town', paper presented at the annual meeting of the American Anthropological Association.

AUSTIN, J. E., and ZEITLIN, M. F. (1981), Nutrition Intervention in Developing Countries: An Overview (Cambridge, MA: Oelgeschlager, Gunn and Hain).

AUTIER, P. (1988), 'Nutrition Assessment Through the Use of a Nutritional Scoring System', Disasters, 12.

—— and D'ALTILIA, J. P. (1985), 'Bilan de 6 mois d'activité des équipes mobiles médico-nutritionnelles de Médecins Sans Frontières', mimeo, Médecins Sans Frontières, Brussels.

—— —— DELAMALLE, J. P., and VERCRUYSSE, V. (1989), 'The Food and Nutrition

Surveillance System of Chad and Mali: The "SAP" after Two Years', mimeo, European Association for Health and Development, Brussels.

AYKROYD, W. (1974), *The Conquest of Famine* (London: Chatto and Windus).

AZBITE, M. (1981), 'A Famine Relief Operation at Qorem, Ethiopia in 1966', *Disasters*, 5.

AZIZ, S. (ed.) (1975), *Hunger, Politics and Markets* (New York: New York University Press).

BAGCHEE, S. (1984), 'Employment Guarantee Scheme in Maharashtra', *Economic and Political Weekly*, 19.

BAGCHI, A. (1987), *Public Intervention and Industrial Restructuring in China, India and Republic of Korea* (New Delhi: ILO).

BAHL, R., KIM, C. K., and PARK, C. K. (1986), *Public Finances During the Korean Modernization Process* (Cambridge, MA: Harvard University Press).

BALASSA, B. (1984), 'Política económica en Chile: 1973–83', Estudios Públicos, No. 14, Centro de Estudios Públicos, Santiago.

—— (1985), 'The National Economic Policies of Chile', in Altman, E., and Walker, I. (eds.) (1985), *Contemporary Studies in Economic and Financial Analysis*, No. 51, Graduate School of Business Administration, New York University, New York.

—— (1988), 'The Lessons of East Asian Development: An Overview', *Economic Development and Cultural Change*, 36.

BALL, N. (1981), *World Hunger: A Guide to the Economic and Political Dimensions* (Santa Barbara, California and Oxford: ABC-Clio Press).

Banco Central de Chile (1984), *Economic Report of Chile 1983* (Santiago: Central Bank of Chile).

BANERJEE, N. (1982), *Unorganised Women Workers: The Calcutta Experience* (Calcutta: Centre for Studies in Social Sciences).

—— (1985), 'Women's Work and Discrimination', in Jain, D., and Banerjee, N. (eds.) (1985), *Tyranny of the Household: Investigative Essays in Women's Work*.

BANERJI, D. (1982), *Poverty, Class and Health Culture in India* (New Delhi: Prachi Prakashan).

BANG, F. B. (1981), 'The Role of Disease in the Ecology of Famine', in Robson, J. R. K. (ed.) (1981), *Famine*.

BANISTER, J. (1984a), 'An Analysis of Recent Data on the Population of China', *Population and Development Review*, 10.

—— (1984b), 'Population Policy and Trends in China 1978–83', *China Quarterly*, 100.

—— (1986), 'China: Recent Trends in Health and Mortality', Paper No. 23, Center for International Research, Washington, DC.

—— (1987), *China's Changing Population* (Stanford: Stanford University Press).

BARDHAN, K. (1985), 'Women's Work, Welfare and Status', *Economic and Political Weekly*, 20.

BARDHAN, P. K. (1974), 'On Life and Death Questions', *Economic and Political Weekly*, 9, Special Number.

—— (1984), *Land, Labor and Rural Poverty* (New York: Columbia University Press).

—— (1987), 'On the Economic Geography of Sex Disparity in Child Survival in India: A Note', paper presented at the BAMANEH/SSRC Workshop on Differential Female Mortality and Health Care in South Asia, Dhaka.

BARNABAS, G., LOVEL, H. J., and MORLEY, D. C. (1982), 'Supplementary Food for the Few in a Refugee Camp', *Lancet*, July 3.

BASTA, S. S. (1977), 'Nutrition and Health in Low Income Urban Areas in the Third World', *Ecology of Food and Nutrition*, 6.

BASU, A. (1987), 'Is Discrimination in Food Really Necessary for Explaining Sex Differentials in Childhood Mortality?', mimeo, National Council of Applied Economic Research, New Delhi.

—— (1988), *Culture, Status of Women and Demographic Behaviour* (New Delhi: National Council of Applied Economic Research).

BASU, D. R. (1984), 'Food Policy and the Analysis of Famines', *Indian Journal of Economics*, 64.

—— (1986), 'Discussion: Sen's Analysis of Famine: A Critique', *Journal of Development Studies*, 22.

BASU, K. (1981), 'Food for Work Programmes: Beyond Roads that Get Washed Away', *Economic and Political Weekly*, 16.

—— (1984), *The Less Developed Economy* (Oxford: Basil Blackwell).

—— (1986), 'The Elimination of Endemic Hunger in South Asia: Some Policy Options', paper presented at a Conference on Food Strategies held at WIDER, Helsinki, 21–5 July 1986; to be published in Drèze, J. P., and Sen, A. K. (eds.) (forthcoming), *The Political Economy of Hunger*.

BATES, R. H. (1981), *Markets and States in Tropical Africa: The Political Basis of Agricultural Policies* (Berkeley: University of California Press).

—— (1983), *Essays on the Political Economy of Rural Africa* (Berkeley: University of California Press).

—— (1986), 'The Political Framework for Price Policy Decisions' in Mann, C. K., and Huddleston, B. (eds.) (1986), *Food Policy: Frameworks for Analysis and Action*.

—— and LOFCHIE, M. F. (eds.) (1980), *Agricultural Development in Africa: Issues of Public Policy* (New York: Praeger).

BAUER, P. T. (1954), *West African Trade: A Study of Competition, Oligopoly and Monopoly in a Changing Economy* (London: Cambridge University Press).

—— (1972), *Dissent on Development* (London: Weidenfeld).

—— (1981), *Equality, the Third World and Economic Delusion* (London: Weidenfeld).

—— (1984), *Reality and Rhetoric: Studies in the Economics of Development* (London: Weidenfeld and Nicholson).

BAULCH, B. (1987), 'Entitlements and the Wollo Famine 1982–1985', *Disasters*, 11.

BAUMGARTNER, R. (1989), 'China: Long-Term Issues in Options for the Health Sector', mimeo, World Bank, Washington, DC.

BEATON, G. (1983), 'Adaptation to an Accommodation of Long-Term Low Energy Intake', in Pollitt, E., and Amante, P. (eds.) (1983), *Current Topics in Nutrition and Disease: Energy Intake and Activity* (New York: Alan R. Liss/UNU).

—— (1987a), ' "Small but Healthy?": Are We Asking the Right Question?', paper presented at the 86th Annual Meeting of the American Anthropological Association, Chicago, Nov. 1987.

—— (1987b), 'Energy in Human Nutrition: A Reconsideration of the Relationship between Intake and Functional Consequences', in Gittinger, J. P., *et al.* (eds.) (1987), *Food Policy*.

—— and GHASSEIMI, G. (1982), 'Supplementary Feeding Programs for Young Children in Developing Countries', *American Journal of Clinical Nutrition*, 34 (Suppl.).

BEHM, H. (1982), 'Determinantes socioeconómicos de la mortalidad en América Latina', *Boletín de población de las Naciones Unidas*, 13.

BEHRMAN, J. R. (1987), 'Intrahousehold Allocation of Nutrients and Gender Effects', paper presented at a Conference on Poverty, Undernutrition and Living Standards held at WIDER, 27–30 July 1987; to be published in Osmani, S. R. (ed.) (forthcoming), *Nutrition and Poverty*.

—— (1988*a*), 'Nutrition, Health, Birth Order and Seasonality: Intrahousehold Allocation in Rural India', *Journal of Development Economics*, 28.

—— (1988*b*), 'The Impact of Economic Adjustment Programs', in Bell, D. E., and Reich, M. R. (eds.) (1988), *Health, Nutrition and Economic Crises*.

—— and DEOLALIKAR, A. B. (1987), 'Will Developing Country Nutrition Improve with Incomes? A Case Study for Rural South India', *Journal of Political Economy*, 95.

—— —— (1988*a*), 'How Do Food Prices and Income Affect Individual Nutritional and Health Status? A Latent Variable Fixed-Effects Analysis', mimeo, University of Pennsylvania.

—— —— (1988*b*), 'Health and Nutrition', in Chenery, H., and Srinivasan, T. N. (eds.) (1988), *Handbook of Development Economics*.

—— —— (1988*c*), 'The Intrahousehold Demand for Nutrients in Rural South India: Individual Estimates, Fixed Effects and Permanent Income', mimeo, University of Pennsylvania.

—— and Wolfe, B. L. (1984), 'More Evidence on Nutrition Demand: Income Seems Overrated and Women's Schooling Underemphasized', *Journal of Development Economics*, 14.

—— —— (1987), 'How Does Mother's Schooling Affect Family Health, Nutrition, Medical Care Usage, and Household Sanitation?', *Journal of Econometrics*, 36.

BELETE, S., GEBRE-MEDHIN, M., HAILEMARIAM, B., MAFFI, M., VAHLQUIST, B., and WOLDE-GABRIEL, Z. (1977), 'Study of Shelter Population in the Wollo Region', *Journal of Tropical Pediatrics and Environmental Child Health*, 23.

BELL, D. E., and REICH, M. R. (eds.) (1988), *Health, Nutrition and Economic Crises* (Dover, MA: Auburn House).

BENERIA, L. (ed.) (1982), *Women and Development: The Sexual Division of Labour in Rural Societies* (New York: Praeger).

BENNETT, J. (1983), 'The Tigray Drought', mimeo, Relief Society of Tigray, London.

—— (1987), *The Hunger Machine: The Politics of Food* (Cambridge, England: Polity Press).

BERG, A. (1973), *The Nutrition Factor* (Brookings Institution).

—— (1981), *Malnourished People: A Policy View* (Washington, DC: The World Bank).

—— (1987*a*), *Malnutrition: What Can be Done?* (Baltimore: Johns Hopkins).

—— (1987*b*), 'Rejoinder: Nutrition Planning is Alive and Well, Thank You', *Food Policy*, 12.

BERG, E. (1986), 'La Réforme de la politique céréalière dans le Sahel', SAHEL D(86) 294, Club du Sahel.

BERG, R. J., and WHITAKER, J. S. (eds.) (1986), *Strategies for African Development* (Berkeley: University of California Press).

BERNSTEIN, T. P. (1983), 'Starving to Death in China', *New York Review of Books*, 30.

—— (1984): 'Stalinism, Famine, and Chinese Peasants', *Theory and Society*, 13.

BERNUS, E. (1977*a*), 'Les Éleveurs face à la sécheresse en Afrique sahélienne: exemples nigériens', in Dalby, D., *et al.* (eds.) (1977), *Drought in Africa 2*.

—— (1977*b*), 'Famines et sécheresses chez les Touaregs sahéliens', in Dalby, D. *et al.* (eds.) (1977), *Drought in Africa 2*.

—— (1986), 'Mobilité et flexibilité pastorales face à la sécheresse', *Bulletin de Liaison*, No. 8, ORSTOM, Paris.

BERRY, L., and KATES, R. (1980), *Making the Most of the Least* (New York: Holmes and Meier).

BERRY, S. S. (1984), 'The Food Crisis and Agrarian Change in Africa: A Review Essay', *African Studies Review*, 27.

BERTLIN, J. (1980), 'Adaptation and Response to Drought: Traditional Systems and the Impact of Change', a special study submitted in part fulfilment of the requirements for the M.Sc. in Agricultural Economics, Wye College, University of London.

BESLEY, T. (1989), 'Ex Ante Evaluation of Health Status and the Provision for Ill-Health', *Economic Journal*, 99.

—— and KANBUR, S. M. R. (RAVI) (1988), 'Food Subsidies and Poverty Alleviation', *Economic Journal*, 98.

BHAGWATI, J. (1988), 'Poverty and Public Policy', *World Development*, 16.

BHALLA, A. (1987), 'Access to Health Services in China and India', mimeo, Geneva.

BHALLA, S. (1988), 'Is Sri Lanka an Exception? A Comparative Study in Living Standards', in Srinivasan, T. N., and Bardhan, P. K. (eds.) (1988), *Rural Poverty in South Asia*.

—— and BANDYOPADHYAY, S. (1988), 'The Politics and Economics of Drought in India', paper presented at a Conference on Development Economics and Policy held at the Delhi School of Economics, 18–21 Dec. 1988.

—— and GLEWWE, P. (1986), 'Growth and Equity in Developing Countries: A Reinterpretation of Sri Lankan Experience', *World Bank Economic Review*, 1.

BHARGAVA, A. (1988), 'Estimating Short and Long Run Income Elasticities of Food and Nutrients for Rural South India', mimeo, Department of Economics, University of Pennsylvania.

BHATIA, B. M. (1967), *Famines in India: A Study in Some Aspects of the Economic History of India 1860–1965* (Bombay: Asia Publishing House).

BHATIA, BELA (1988), 'Official Drought Relief Measures: A Case Study of Gujarat', *Social Action*, 38.

BHATIA, S. (1983), 'Traditional Practices Affecting Female Health and Survival', in Lopez, A. D., and Ruzicka, L. T. (eds.) (1983), *Sex Differentials in Mortality: Trends, Determinants and Consequences*.

BHATTACHARYA, N., CHATTERJEE, G. S., and PAL, P. (1988), 'Variations in Level of Living across Regions and Social Groups in Rural India, 1963/64 and 1973/74', in Srinivasan, T. N., and Bardhan, P. K. (eds.) (1988), *Rural Poverty in South Asia*.

BHATTY, I. (1974), 'Inequality and Poverty in Rural India', in Srinivasan, T. N., and Bardhan, P. K. (eds.) (1974), *Poverty and Income Distribution in India*.

BHATTY, Z. (1980), 'Economic Role and Status of Women: A Case Study of Women in the Beedi Industry in Allahabad', ILO Working Paper.

BIELLIK, R. J., and HENDERSON, P. L. (1981), 'Mortality, Nutritional Status, and Diet During the Famine in Karamoja, Uganda, 1980', *Lancet*, 12 Dec.

BIENEN, H., and GERSOVITZ, M. (1986), 'Consumer Subsidy Cuts, Violence and Political Stability', *Comparative Politics*, 19.

BIGMAN, D. (1986), *Food Policies and Food Security under Instability* (Lexington, MA.: Lexington Books).

—— and REUTLINGER, S. (1979), 'Food Price and Supply Stabilization: National Buffer Stocks and Trade Policies', *American Journal of Agricultural Economics*, Nov.

BINMORE, K. (1987), 'Nash Bargaining Theory', in Binmore, K., and Dasgupta, P. (eds.) (1987), *The Economics of Bargaining*.

—— and DASGUPTA, P. (eds.) (1987), *The Economics of Bargaining* (Oxford and New York: Basil Blackwell).

BINNS, C. W. (1976), 'Famine and the Diet of the Enga', *Papua New Guinea Medical Journal*, 19.

BINSWANGER, H. P., DOHERTY, V. S., BALARAMAIAH, T., BHENDE, M. J., KSHIRSAGAR, K. G., RAO, V. B., and RAJU, P. S. S. (1984), 'Common Features and Contrasts in Labor Relations in the Semiarid Tropics of India', in Binswanger, H. P., and Rosenzweig, M. R. (eds.) (1984), *Contractual Arrangements, Employment, and Wages in Rural Labor Markets in Asia* (New Haven: Yale University Press).

BIRDSALL, N. (1988), 'Thoughts on Good Health and Good Government', paper presented at a Colloquium on Development, Cambridge, MA, May 19–20.

—— (1989), 'Pragmatism, Robin Hood, and Other Themes: Good Government and Social Well-Being in Developing Countries', mimeo, World Bank, Washington, DC.

—— and GRIFFIN, C. C. (1988), 'Fertility and Poverty in Developing Countries', *Journal of Policy Modelling*, 10.

BJOERCK, W. A. (1984), 'An Overview of Local Purchase of Food Commodities (LPFC)', mimeo, UNICEF.

BLACKORBY, C., and DONALDSON, D. (1988), 'Adult Equivalence Scales and the Economic Implementation of Interpersonal Comparisons of Well-Being', mimeo, University of British Columbia.

BLAXTER, K. (1985), 'Energy Intake and Expenditure', in Blaxter, K., and Waterlow, J. C. (eds.) (1985), *Nutritional Adaptation in Man*.

—— and WATERLOW, J. C. (eds.) (1985), *Nutritional Adaptation in Man* (London: John Libbey).

BLIX, G., HOFVANDER, Y., and VAHLQUIST, B. (eds.) (1971), *Famine: Nutrition and Relief Operations in Times of Disaster* (Uppsala, Sweden: Swedish Nutrition Foundation).

BLUMBERG, R. L. (1988), 'Income under Female and Male Control: Hypotheses from a Theory of Gender Stratification and Data from the Third World', *Journal of Family Issues*, 9.

BONGAARTS, J., and CAIN, M. (1982), 'Demographic Responses to Famine', in Cahill, K. M. (ed.) (1982), *Famine*.

BORKAR, V. V., and NADKARNI, M. V. (1975), *Impact of Drought on Rural Life* (Bombay: Popular Prakashan).

BORTON, J. (1984), 'Disaster Preparedness in Botswana', report prepared for the Ford Foundation, Relief and Development Institute, London.

—— (1986), 'Botswana Food Aid Management', paper presented at the WFP/ADB Conference on Food Aid for Development Abidjan, Sept. 1986.

—— (1988), 'The 1984/85 Drought Relief Programme in Kenya: A Provisional Review', Discussion Paper No. 2, Relief and Development Institute, London.

—— (forthcoming), 'Overview of the 1984/85 National Drought Relief Program', in Downing, T., *et al.* (eds.) (forthcoming), *Coping with Drought in Kenya: National and Local Strategies*.

—— and Clay, E. (1986), 'The African Food Crisis of 1982–86', *Disasters*, 10.

—— and Shoham, J. (1989a), 'Experiences of Non-governmental Organisations in the

Targeting of Emergency Food Aid', report on a workshop held at the London School of Hygiene and Tropical Medicine, Jan. 1989.

—— —— (1989*b*), 'Emergency Food Aid Targeting: Case Studies', collection of background papers prepared for a workshop held at the London School of Hygiene and Tropical Medicine, Jan. 1989.

—— STEPHENSON, R. S., and MORRIS, C. (1988), 'ODA Emergency Aid to Africa 1983–86', Evaluation Report EV 425, Overseas Development Administration, UK.

—— and YORK, S. (1987), 'Experiences of the Collection and Use of Micro-level Data in Disaster Preparedness and Managing Emergency Operations', *Disasters*, 11.

BOSE, A., and TYAGI, R. P. (1983), 'Rural Health Services: Present Status', in Goyel, R. P., *et al.* (eds.) (1983), *Studies in Social Dynamics of Primary Health Care* (Delhi: Hindustan Publishing).

BOSE, S. (1987), 'Starvation Amidst Plenty: The Making of Famine in Bengal, Honan and Tonkin, 1942–45', paper presented at the India–China Seminar, Fairbank Center, Harvard University, Dec. 1987.

BOSERUP, E. (1970), *Women's Role in Economic Development* (London: Allen and Unwin).

—— (1980), 'The Position of Women in Economic Production and in the Household, with Special Reference to Africa', in Presvelan, C., and Spijkers-Zwart, S. (eds.) (1980), *The Household, Women and Agricultural Development*.

—— (1983), 'The Impact of Scarcity and Plenty on Development', in Rotberg, R. S., and Rabb, T. K. (eds.) (1983), *Hunger and History*.

—— (1986), 'Economic Change and the Role of Women', mimeo.

Botswana Society (1979), *Symposium on Drought in Botswana* (Gaborone: Botswana Society).

BOUIS, H. E., and HADDAD, L. J. (1988), 'Comparing Calorie–Income Elasticities Using Calories Derived from Reported Food Purchases and a Twenty-four Hour Recall of Food Intakes: An Application Using Philippine Data', Discussion Paper No. 88, Development Economics Research Centre, University of Warwick.

BOWBRICK, P. (1986), 'The Causes of Famine: A Refutation of Professor Sen's Theory', *Food Policy*, 11.

—— (1987), 'Rejoinder: An Untenable Hypothesis on the Cause of Famine', *Food Policy*, 12.

BOYCE, J. K. (1987), *Agrarian Impasse in Bengal* (New York: Oxford University Press).

BOYD, D. (1987), 'The Impact of Adjustment Policies on Vulnerable Groups: The Case of Jamaica, 1973–1985', in Cornia, G., *et al.* (eds.) (1987), *Adjustment With a Human Face*.

BOYD-ORR, J. (1950), 'The Food and People Dilemma', *Scientific American*, 183.

BOYLE, P. P., and O'GRADA, C. (1986), 'Fertility Trends, Excess Mortality, and the Great Irish Famine', *Demography*, 23.

BRAHME, S. (1983), *Drought in Maharashtra 1972*, Gokhale Institute Series No. 68, Pune, India.

BRANDT, H. (1984), *Food Security Programmes in the Sudano-Sahel* (Berlin: German Development Institute).

BRANNEN, J., and WILSON, G. (eds.) (1987), *Give and Take in Families* (London: Allen and Unwin).

BRASS, P. R. (1986), 'The Political Uses of Crisis: The Bihar Famine of 1966–1967', *Journal of Asian Studies*, 45.

BRATTON, M. (1986), 'Farmer Organizations and Food Production in Zimbabwe', *World Development*, 14.

—— (1987a), 'Drought, Food and the Social Organization of Small Farmers in Zimbabwe', in Glantz, M. (ed.) (1987a), *Drought and Hunger in Africa*.

—— (1987b), 'The Comrades and the Countryside: The Politics of Agricultural Policy in Zimbabwe', *World Politics*, 29.

BREMAN, J. (1974), *Patronage and Exploitation: Changing Agrarian Structure in South Gujarat, India* (Berkeley: University of California Press).

BRENNAN, L. (1984), 'The Development of the Indian Famine Codes: Personalities, Politics and Policies', in Currey, B., and Hugo, G. (eds.) (1984), *Famine as a Geographical Phenomenon*.

—— (1988), 'Government Famine Relief in Bengal, 1943', *Journal of Asian Studies*, 47.

—— HEATHCOTE, R. L., and LUCAS, A. E. (1984), 'The Role of the Individual Administrator in Famine Relief: Three Case Studies', *Disasters*, 8.

BRETT, A. (1987), 'Nutrition Survey, Basic Needs Assessment Survey Cycle 3, December 1986–January 1987, Dawi Rahmedo Wareda and Delanta Wareda', mimeo, OXFAM.

BRICEÑO, A., and MÉNDEZ, E. A. (1982), 'Salud pública y distribución del ingreso en Costa Rica', *Revista ciencias económicas*, 1.

BROWN, E. P. (forthcoming), 'Sex and Starvation', to be published in Downs, R. E., Kerner, D. O., and Reyna, S. P. (eds.) (forthcoming), *The Political Economy of African Hunger*.

BROWN, L. R. and ECKHOLM, E. P. (1974), *By Bread Alone* (Oxford: Pergamon).

—— (1987), 'Food Growth Slowdown: Danger Signal for the Future', in Gittinger, J. P., *et al.* (eds.) (1987), *Food Policy*.

BROWN, M., and CHUANG, C. F. (1980), 'Intrahousehold Power and Demand for Shared Goods', mimeo, SUNY, Buffalo, NY.

BROWN, R., and MASON, L. (1988), 'Fire Blown by Wind: Famine in the Sudan', mimeo.

BROWN, V. W., BROWN, E. P., ECKERSON, D., GILMORE, J., and SWARTZENDURBER, H. D. (1986), 'Evaluation of the African Emergency Food Assistance Program 1984–1985: Chad', report submitted to USAID, Washington, DC.

BRUNDENIUS, C. (1981), *Economic Growth, Basic Needs and Income Distribution in Revolutionary Cuba* (Lund, Sweden: Research Policy Institute, University of Lund).

—— (1982), 'Development Strategies and Basic Needs in Revolutionary Cuba', in Brundenius, C., and Lundhal, M. (eds.) (1982), *Development Strategies and Basic Needs in Latin America: Challenges for the 1980s*.

—— (1984), *Revolutionary Cuba: The Challenge of Economic Growth with Equity* (Boulder: Westview).

—— and LUNDAHL, M. (eds.) (1982), *Development Strategies and Basic Needs in Latin America: Challenges for the 1980s* (Boulder: Westview).

BRYCESON, D. (1981a), 'Colonial Famine Responses: The Bagamoyo District of Tanganyika, 1920–61', *Food Policy*, 6.

—— (1981b), 'Changes in Peasant Food Production and Food Supply in Relation to the Historical Development of Commodity Production in Pre-colonial and Colonial Tanganyika', *Journal of Peasant Studies*, 7.

—— (1984), 'Nutrition and the Commoditization of Food Systems in sub-Saharan Africa', paper presented at a Conference on Political Economy of Health and Disease in Africa and Latin America sponsored by the Social Science Research Council, UK.

—— (1985), *Women and Technology in Developing Countries* (Santo Domingo: United Nations).

BRYSON, J. C. (1986), 'Case Study: The Lesotho Food for Work Programme of Catholic Relief Services', paper presented at the WFP/ADB Conference on Food Aid for Development, Abijan, Sept. 1986.

BUCKLEY, R. (1988), 'Food Targeting in Darfur: Save the Children Fund's Programme in 1986', *Disasters*, 12.

BURGESS, R., and Stern, N. H., (forthcoming), 'Social Security in Developing Countries: What, Why, Who and How?', in Ahmad *et al.* (forthcoming), *Social Security in Developing Countries*.

BUSH, R. (1987), 'Explaining Africa's Famine', *Social Studies Review*, 2.

—— (1988), 'Hunger in Sudan: The Case of Darfur', *African Affairs*, 87.

BUVINIC, M. (1976), *Women and World Development: An Annotated Bibliography* (Washington, DC: Overseas Development Council).

—— LYCETTE, M., and McGREEVEY, W. P. (eds.) (1983), *Women and Poverty in the Third World* (Baltimore: Johns Hopkins).

BYRES, T. J. (1979), 'Of Neo-populist Pipe Dreams: Daedalus in the Third World and the Myth of Urban Bias', *Journal of Peasant Studies*, 6.

BYRON, W. (ed.) (1982) *The Causes of World Hunger* (New York: Paulist Press).

CABEZAS, M. (1988), 'Revisión metodológica y estadística del gasto social en Chile: 1970–86', Notas Técnicas No. 114, CIEPLAN, Santiago, Chile.

CABRAL, N. E. (1980), *Le Moulin et le pilon: les Îles du Cap Vert* (Paris: L'Harmattan).

CAFOD (1986a), 'Emergency Relief Programmes in Eritrea 1985: A Report by CAFOD on Food, Medical and Transportation Programmes Implemented by the Eritrean Relief Association', mimeo, Catholic Fund for Overseas Development, London.

—— (1986b), 'Report on CAFOD Assistance to the Relief Society of Tigray (REST) in 1985', mimeo, Catholic Fund for Overseas Development, London.

CAHILL, K. M. (ed.) (1982), *Famine* (New York: Orbis Books).

CAIN, M. (1978), 'The Household Lifecycle and Economic Mobility in Bangladesh', Center for Policy Studies Working Paper, Population Council, New York.

CAIN, M., KHONAM, S. K., and NAHAR, S. (1979), 'Class, Patriarchy and the Structure of Women's Work in Rural Bangladesh', Center for Policy Studies Working Paper, Population Council, New York.

CALDWELL, J. C. (1975), 'The Sahelian Drought and Its Demographic Implications', Overseas Liaison Committee Paper No. 8, American Council of Education, Washington, DC.

—— (1977), 'Demographic Aspects of Drought: An Examination of the African Drought of 1970–74', in Dalby, D., *et al.* (eds.) (1977), *Drought in Africa 2*.

—— (1979), 'Education as a Factor in Mortality Decline: An Examination of Nigerian Data', *Population Studies*, 33.

—— (1981a), 'Food Production and Crisis in the West African Savannah', Occasional Paper No. 25, Development Studies Centre, Australian National University.

—— (1981b), 'Maternal Education as a Factor in Child Mortality', *World Health Forum*, 2.

—— (1984), 'Desertification: Demographic Evidence, 1973–1983', Occasional Paper No. 37, Development Studies Centre, Australian National University.

—— (1986), 'Routes to Low Mortality in Poor Countries', *Population and Development Review*, 12.

—— and CALDWELL, P. (1985), 'Education and Literacy as Factors in Health', in Halstead, S. B., *et al.* (eds.) (1985), *Good Health at Low Cost*.

—— REDDY, P. H., and CALDWELL, P. (1986), 'Periodic High Risk as a Cause of Fertility Decline in a Changing Rural Environment: Survival Strategies in the 1980–1983 South Indian Drought', *Economic Development and Cultural Change*, 34.

CALDWELL, P., and CALDWELL, J. C. (1987a), 'Where There is a Narrower Gap Between Female and Male Situations', mimeo, Australian National University.

—— —— (1987b), 'The Cultural Context of High Fertility in Sub-Saharan Africa', *Population and Development Review*, 13.

—— —— (1987c), 'Famine in Africa', paper presented at a IUSSP Seminar on Mortality and Society in sub-Saharan Africa, Iford, Yaoundé, Cameroon, Oct. 1987.

CAMPBELL, D. J. (1984), 'Response to Drought Among Farmers and Herders in Southern Kajiado District, Kenya', *Human Ecology*, 12.

—— (1986), 'Coping Strategies as Indicators of Food Shortage in African Villages', paper presented at the Annual Meeting of the American Anthropological Association, Philadelphia, Dec. 1986.

—— (1987), 'Strategies for Coping with Severe Food Deficits in Northeast Africa', *Northeast African Studies*, 9.

—— and TRECHTER, D. D. (1982), 'Strategies for Coping with Food Consumption Shortage in the Mandara Mountains Region of North Cameroon', *Social Science and Medicine*, 16.

CAMPBELL, R. H., and SKINNER, A. S. (eds.) (1976), *Adam Smith: An Inquiry into the Nature and Causes of the Wealth of Nations* (Oxford: Clarendon Press).

CANNON, T. G. (1978): 'The Role of Environmental Influence and "Natural" Disasters', mimeo, Thames Polytechnic.

CAPONE, C. (1980), 'A Review of an Experience with Food-Aided Nutrition Programs', *Nutrition Planning*, 3.

—— JACOB, F., and O'LAUGHLIN, A. (1978), 'Catholic Relief Services: Nutrition Intervention Programme for the Drought Areas of Kenya (1975–1976)', *Disasters*, 2.

CARLSON, D. G. (1982), 'Famine in History: With a Comparison of Two Modern Ethiopian Disasters', in Cahill, K. (ed.) (1982), *Famine*.

CARREIRA, A. (1982), *The People of the Cape Verde Islands: Exploitation and Emigration* (London: Hurst & Co).

CASHDAN, E. (1985), 'Coping with Risk: Reciprocity Among the Basarwa of Northern Botswana', *Man*, 20.

CASSEN, R., and associates (1986), *Does Aid Work?* (Oxford: Clarendon).

CASTANEDA, T. (1984), 'Contexto socioeconómico y causas del descenso de la mortalidad infantil en Chile', Documento de Trabajo No. 28, Centro de Estudios Públicos, Santiago, Chile.

—— (1985), 'Determinantes del descenso de la mortalidad infantil en Chile 1975–1983', *Cuadernos de economía*, 22.

—— and RACZYNSKI, D. (1984), 'Contexto socioeconómico del descenso de la mortalidad infantil en Chile', *Estudios públicos*, No. 16, Santiago.

CASTILLO, G., FIGUEROA, E., GUTIÉRREZ, J. M., *et al.* (1983), *Costa Rica: Disarmed Democracy* (San José: Imprenta Nacional).

CATHIE, J. and HERRMANN, R. (1988), 'The Southern African Customs Union, Cereal

Price Policy in South Africa, and Food Security in Botswana', *Journal of Development Studies*, 24.

Centre for Development Studies (1975), *Poverty, Unemployment and Development Policy: A Case Study of Selected Issues with Reference to Kerala* (New York: United Nations).

CÉPÈDE, M., and LENGELLÉ, M. (1953), *Economie alimentaire du globe* (Paris: Librairie de Médicis).

CESPEDES, V. H., and GONZALEZ-VEGA, C. (1985), *Growth and Equity: Changes in Income Distribution in Costa Rica, 1960–1980* (New York: DIESA, United Nations).

CHAKRAVARTY, L. (1986), 'Poverty Studies in the Context of Agricultural Growth and Demographic Pressure (Case of Post-Independence India)', mimeo, Indraprastha College, Delhi.

CHAKRAVARTY, S. (1969), *Capital and Development Planning* (Cambridge, MA.: MIT Press).

CHAMBERS, R. (1983), *Rural Development: Putting the Last First* (New York: Longman).

—— (ed.) (1989), *Vulnerability: How the Poor Cope*, special issue of *IDS Bulletin*.

—— LONGHURST, R., and PACEY, A. (eds.) (1981), *Seasonal Dimensions to Rural Poverty* (London: Frances Pinter).

—— *et al.* (1986), 'An Independent Review and Evaluation of the Africa Drought Relief Operations 1984–86 of the League of Red Cross and Red Crescent Societies', IDS, Report No. 1, mimeo.

CHASTANET, M. (1983), 'Les Crises de subsistances dans les villages Soninke du Cercle de Bakel de 1858 à 1945', *Cahiers d'études africaines*, 89–90/23.

—— (1988), 'Survival Strategies of a Sahelian Society: The Case of the Soninke in Senegal from the Middle of the XIXth Century to Nowadays', paper presented at a Conference on Afro-Asian Studies on Social Systems and Food Crises, New Delhi, Mar. 1988; to be published in Floud, J., and Rangasami, A. (eds.) (forthcoming), *Essays on Famine and Society* (New Delhi).

CHATTERJI, R. (1984), 'Marginalisation and the Induction of Women into Wage Labour: The Case of Indian Agriculture', WEP Working Paper No. 32, ILO.

CHATTOPADHYAY, B. (1981), 'Notes Towards an Understanding of the Bengal Famine of 1943', *CRESSIDA Transactions*, 1.

CHAUDHURY, R. H. (1987), 'Dietary Adequacy and Sex Bias', *Social Action*, 37.

—— (1988), 'Adequacy of Child Dietary Intake Relative to That of Other Family Members', *Food and Nutrition Bulletin*, 10.

CHAZAN, N., and SHAW, T. M. (eds.) (1988), *Coping with Africa's Food Crisis* (Boulder: Lynne Rienner).

CHEN, L. C. (1986a), 'Primary Health Care in Developing Countries: Overcoming Operational, Technical, and Social Barriers', *Lancet*, 29 Nov.

—— (1986b), 'Explorations of Food Consumption and Nutritional Status: Bangladesh', in Mann, C. K., and Huddleston, B. (eds.) (1986), *Food Policy: Frameworks for Analysis and Action*.

—— (1987), 'Coping with Economic Crisis: Policy Developments in China and India', *Health Policy and Planning*, 2.

—— (1988), 'Health Policy Responses: An Approach Derived from the China and India Experiences', in Bell, D. E., and Reich, M. R. (eds.) (1988), *Health, Nutrition and Economic Crises*.

—— and CHOWDHURY, A. K. M. (1977), 'The Dynamics of Contemporary Famine', paper presented at the International Population Conference of the International Union for the Scientific Study of Population, Mexico.

—— HUQ, E., and D'SOUZA, S. (1981), 'Sex-Bias in the Family Allocation of Food and Health Care in Rural Bangladesh', *Population and Development Review*, 7.

—— *et al.* (1980), 'Anthropometric Assessment of Energy Protein Malnutrition and Subsequent Risk of Mortality Among Pre-school Age Children', *American Journal of Clinical Nutrition*, 33.

CHEN, M. (1986*a*), *A Quiet Revolution: Women in Transition in Rural Bangladesh* (Dhaka: BRAC).

—— (1986*b*), 'Poverty, Gender, and Work in Bangladesh', *Economic and Political Weekly*, 21.

—— (1988), 'The Drought Situation in Devdholera Village', mimeo, Harvard Institute for International Development.

—— (1989), 'Coping with Seasonality and Drought: The Study of a Village in a Semi-arid Region of India', mimeo, Harvard Institute for International Development; to be published as a monograph.

—— and GHUZNAVI, R. (1976), *Women in Food-for-Work: The Bangladesh Experience* (Rome: World Food Programme).

CHENERY, H., *et al.* (eds.) (1974), *Redistribution with Growth* (London: Oxford University Press).

CHENERY, H., and SRINIVASAN, T. N. (eds.) (1988), *Handbook of Development Economics* (Amsterdam: North-Holland).

CHERNICHOVSKY, D., LUCAS, R. E. B., and MUELLER, E. (1985), 'The Household Economy of Rural Botswana: An African Case', World Bank Staff Working Paper No. 715, World Bank, Washington, DC.

CHEYRE, H., and OGRODNICK, E. (1982), 'El programa de empleo mínimo: análisis de una encuesta', *Revista de economía*, Nov.

CHICHILNISKY, G. (1983), 'North–South Trade with Export Enclaves: Food Consumption and Food Exports', mimeo, Columbia University.

CHIMWAZA, B. M. (1982), 'Food and Nutrition in Malawi', unpublished Ph.D. thesis, London University.

CHOW, N. W. S. (1981), 'Social Security Provision in Singapore and Hong Kong', *Journal of Social Policy*, 10.

CHOWDHURY, A. K. M. (1988), 'Child Mortality in Bangladesh: Food versus Health Care', *Food and Nutrition Bulletin*, 10.

CHOWDHURY, O. H. (1983), 'Profile of Workers in the Food for Work Programme in Bangladesh', *Bangladesh Development Studies*, 11.

CILSS (1976), 'Aperçu sur la situation aux Îles du Cap Vert du fait de la continuation de la sécheresse', DPP/5-10-1976, Comité Permanent Interétats de Lutte Contre la Sécheresse dans le Sahel, Paris.

——(1986), *La prévision des situations alimentaires critiques dans les pays du Sahel: systémes et moyens d' alerte précoce* (Paris: OECD).

CLAY, E. (1985*a*), 'Organizing Food Security: Lessons from South Asia', mimeo, Institute of Development Studies, University of Sussex.

—— (1985*b*), 'The 1974 and 1984 Floods in Bangladesh: From Famine to Food Crisis Management', *Food Policy*, 10.

—— (1986), 'Rural Public Works and Food-for-Work: A Survey', *World Development*, 14.

—— and HARRISS, B. (1988), 'Emergency Measures for Food Security: How Relevant to Africa is the South Asian Model?', in Curtis, D., *et al.* (eds.) (1988), *Preventing Famines.*

—— and SHAW, J. (eds.) (1987), *Poverty, Development and Food* (London: Macmillan).

—— and SINGER, H. W. (1985), 'Food Aid and Development: Issues and Evidence', Occasional Paper No. 3, World Food Programme, Rome.

CLELAND, J., and VAN GINNEKEN, J. (1987), 'The Effect of Maternal Schooling on Childhood Mortality: The Search for an Explanation', paper presented at a Conference on Health Intervention and Mortality Change in Developing Countries, University of Sheffield, Sept. 1987.

CLEMHOUT, S., and WAN, Jr., H. Y. (1977), 'Symmetric Marriage, Household Decision Making and Impact on Fertility', Working Paper No. 152, Department of Economics, Cornell University.

Club du Sahel (1977), *Marketing, Price Policy and Storage of Food Grains in the Sahel: A Survey* (University of Michigan: Center for Research on Economic Development).

COALE, A. (1981), 'Population Trends, Population_Policy and Population Studies in China', *Population and Development Review*, 7.

—— (1984), *Rapid Population Change in China 1952–82* (Washington, DC: National Academy Press).

COATE, S. (1986), 'Should Food Aid Be Given Away or Sold During a Famine?', Discussion Paper No. 701, Center for Mathematical Studies in Economics and Management Science, Northwestern University, Evanston.

—— (1989), 'Cash Versus Direct Food Relief', forthcoming in *Journal of Development Economics.*

COCKBURN, C. (1980), 'The Role of Social Security in Development', *International Social Security Review*, 33.

COHEN, J., and LEWIS, D. (1987), 'Role of Government in Combatting Food Shortages: Lessons from Kenya 1984–85', in Glantz, M. (ed.) (1987*a*), *Drought and Hunger in Africa.*

COHEN, J. M., and ISAKSSON, N. I. (1988), 'Food Production Strategy Debates in Revolutionary Ethiopia', *World Development*, 16.

COHEN, M. M. (1977), *The Food Crisis in Prehistory: Overpopulation and the Origins of Famine* (New Haven: Yale University Press).

COLLINS, J., and LAPPÉ, F. M. (1980), 'Food Self-Reliance', in Galtung, J., *et al.* (eds.) (1980), *Self-Reliance: A Strategy for Development.*

COLSON, E. (1979), 'In Good Years and in Bad: Food Strategies of Self-Reliant Societies', *Journal of Anthropological Research*, 35.

Comité Information Sahel (1974), *Qui se nourrit de la famine en Afrique?* (Paris: Maspéro).

COMMINS, S., LOFCHIE, M., and PAYNE, R. (1986), *Africa's Agrarian Crisis* (Boulder: Lynne Rienner).

CONQUEST, R. (1986), *The Harvest of Sorrow: Soviet Collectivization and the Terror-Famine* (London: Hutchinson).

CONTRERA, J. (1988), 'Glow of Prosperity: Most of Chile is Riding High on an Economic Boom', *Newsweek*, 22 Aug.

COPANS, J., *et al.* (1975), *Sécheresses et famines du Sahel* (Paris: Maspéro).

CORBETT, J. (1987), 'Drought and the Threat of Famine in Kenya in 1984', mimeo, Food Studies Group, Oxford.

—— (1988), 'Famine and Household Coping Strategies', *World Development*, 16.

CORBO, V. (1985), 'Reforms and Macroeconomic Adjustments in Chile During 1974–84', *World Development*, 13.

CORNIA, G. (1984), 'A Survey of Cross-Sectional and Time-Series Literature on Factors Affecting Child Welfare', in Jolly, R., and Cornia, G. (eds.) (1984), *The Impact of World Recession on Children*.

—— (1987), 'Adjustment at the Household Level: Potentials and Limitations of Survival Strategies', in Cornia, G., *et al.* (eds.) (1987), *Adjustment with a Human Face*.

—— JOLLY, R., and STEWART, F. (1987), *Adjustment with a Human Face* (Oxford: Clarendon).

CORTAZAR, R. (1980), 'Distribución del ingreso, empleo y remuneraciones reales en Chile, 1970–78', Colección Estudios CEIPLAN, No. 3., Santiago, Chile.

Council on Environmental Quality and the Department of State (1982), *The Global 2000 Report to the President: Entering the Twenty First Century* (New York: Penguin).

Courier (1988), 'Country Report: Cape Verde', *Courier*, No. 107.

CROLL, E. (1978), *Feminism and Socialism in China* (London: Routledge and Kegan Paul).

—— (1983), *Chinese Women Since Mao* (New York: Zed).

CROW, B. (1987), 'US Policies in Bangladesh: The Making and the Breaking of Famine?', Development Policy and Practice Working Paper No. 4, The Open University, UK.

CULLEN, L. M., and SMOUT, T. C. (eds.) (1978), *Comparative Aspects of Scottish and Irish Economic and Social History, 1600–1900* (Edinburgh: Donald).

CUMPER, G. (1984), *Determinants of Health Levels in Developing Countries* (Letchworth, UK: Research Studies Press).

CUMPER, G. E. (1983), 'Jamaica: A Case Study in Health Development', *Social Science and Medicine*, 17.

CUMPER, GLORIA (1972), *Survey of Social Legislation in Jamaica* (Mona: University of West Indies Institute for Social and Economic Research).

CUNY, F. C. (1983), *Disasters and Development* (Oxford: Oxford University Press for Oxfam-America).

CURREY, B., ALI, M., and KOHMAN, N. (1981), *Famine: A First Bibliography* (Washington, DC: Agency for International Development).

—— and HUGO, G. (eds.) (1984), *Famine as a Geographical Phenomenon* (Dordrecht, Holland: Reidel).

CURTIS, D., HUBBARD, M., and SHEPHERD, A. (1988), *Preventing Famine: Policies and Prospects for Africa* (London and New York: Routledge).

CUTLER, P. (1984*a*), 'Famine Forecasting: Prices and Peasant Behaviour in Northern Ethiopia', *Disasters*, 8.

—— (1984*b*), 'Food Crisis Detection: Going Beyond the Balance Sheet', *Food Policy*, 9.

—— (1985*a*), 'Detecting Food Emergencies: Lessons from the 1979 Bangladesh Crisis', *Food Policy*, 10.

—— (1985*b*), 'The Use of Economic and Social Information in Famine Prediction and Response', report prepared for the Overseas Development Administration, London.

—— (1986), 'The Response to Drought of Beja Famine Refugees in Sudan', *Disasters*, 19.

DALBY, D., HARRISON CHURCH, R. J., and BEZZAZ, F. (eds.) (1977), *Drought in Africa 2* (London: International Africa Institute).

DALRYMPLE, D. (1964), 'The Soviet Famine of 1932–34', *Soviet Studies*, 15.

DANDEKAR, K. (1983), *Employment Guarantee Scheme: An Employment Opportunity for Women* (Pune: Orient Longman).

—— and SATHE, M. (1980), 'Employment Guarantee Scheme and Food for Work Programme', *Economic and Political Weekly*, 15.

DANDEKAR, V. M. and RATH, N. (1971), *Poverty in India* (Poona: Indian School of Political Economy).

DANDO, W. A. (1980), *The Geography of Famine* (London: Edward Arnold).

—— (1983), 'Biblical Famines, 1850 B.C.–A.D.46: Insights for Modern Mankind', *Ecology of Food and Nutrition*, 13.

DANIEL, P., GREEN, R., and LIPTON, M. (1984), 'Towards a Strategy for the Rural Poor in Sub-Saharan Africa', Discussion Paper No. 193, Institute of Development Studies, University of Sussex.

DAS, T. (1949), *The Bengal Famine (1943)* (Calcutta: University of Calcutta).

DAS, V., and NICHOLAS, R. (1981), 'Welfare and "Well-Being" in South Asian Societies', ACLS–SSRC Joint Committee on South Asia (New York: SSRC).

DAS GUPTA, M. (1987), 'Selective Discrimination Against Female Children in Rural Punjab', *Population and Development Review*, 13.

—— (1989a), 'Death Clustering, Maternal Education and the Determinants of Child Mortality in Rural Punjab, India', mimeo, Center for Population Studies, Harvard University.

—— (1989b), 'The Effects of Discrimination on Health and Mortality', mimeo, Center for Population Studies, Harvard University.

DASGUPTA, P., and RAY, D. (1986a), 'Adapting to Undernourishment: The Biological Evidence and Its Implications', paper presented at a Conference on Food Strategies held at WIDER, Helsinki, 21–5 July 1986; Economic Theory Discussion Paper No. 106, Department of Applied Economics, University of Cambridge, 1987; to be published in Drèze, J. P. and Sen, A. K. (eds.) (forthcoming), *The Political Economy of Hunger*.

—— —— (1986b), 'Inequality as a Determinant of Malnutrition and Unemployment: Theory', *Economic Journal*, 96.

—— —— (1987), 'Inequality as a Determinant of Malnutrition and Unemployment: Policy', *Economic Journal*, 97.

DATTA CHAUDHURI, M. K. (1979), 'Industrialization and Foreign Trade: An Analysis Based on the Development Experience of the Republic of Korea and the Philippines', Working Paper II-4, Asian Employment Programme, ARTEP, ILO, Bangkok.

DAVIDSON, B. (1977), 'Mass Mobilization for National Reconstruction in the Cape Verde Islands', *Economic Geography*, 53.

DAVIES, R., and SANDERS, D. (1987a), 'Stabilisation Policies and the Effects on Child Health in Zimbabwe', *Review of African Political Economy*, 38.

—— —— (1987b), 'Adjustment Policies and the Welfare of Children: Zimbabwe, 1980–1985', in Cornia, G., *et al.* (eds.) (1987), *Adjustment With a Human Face*.

DAVIS, O., and WITTER, M. (1986), *Issues in Food Security in Jamaica* (Kingston: Caribbean Food and Nutrition Institute).

DAWSON, A. (1985), 'In Defence of Food Aid: Some Answers to its Critics', *International Labour Bulletin*, 124.

DEACON, B. (1983), *Social Policy and Socialism: The Struggle for Socialist Relations of Welfare* (London: Pluto Press).

DEATON, A. (1987), 'The Allocation of Goods Within the Household: Adults, Children and Gender', mimeo, Princeton University.

—— (1988), 'Household Behavior in Developing Countries', Occasional Paper No. 1, The Economic Growth Center, Yale University.

—— and CASE, A. (1987), 'Analysis of Household Expenditure', Working Paper No. 28, Living Standards Measurement Study, World Bank, Washington, DC.

—— and MUELLBAUER, J. (1980), *Economics and Consumer Behaviour* (Cambridge and New York: Cambridge University Press).

DEERE, C. D., and DE LEAL, M. L. (1982), *Women in Andean Agriculture* (Geneva: ILO).

DE GARINE, I., and HARRISON, G. A. (eds.) (1988), *Coping with Uncertainty in Food Supply* (Oxford: Clarendon).

Deloitte, Haskins and Sells Management Co. (1986), 'Final Monitoring Report on the Drought Emergency Relief Program for USAID Mission to Kenya', report prepared for USAID.

DEMENY, P. (1986), 'Population and the Invisible Hand', Working Paper No. 123, Center for Policy Studies, Population Council, New York.

DEN HARTOG, A. (1981), 'Adjustment of Food Behaviour During Famine', in Robson, J. (ed.) (1981), *Famine: Its Causes, Effects, and Management*.

DERRICK, J. (1984), 'West Africa's Worst Year of Famine', *African Affairs*, 83.

DESAI, G. M., SINGH, G., and SAH, D. C. (1979), 'Impact of Scarcity on Farm Economy and Significance of Relief Operations', CMA Monograph No. 84, Indian Institute of Management, Ahmedabad.

DESAI, M. (1976), 'The Role of Exchange and Market Relationships in the Economics of the Transition Period: Lenin on the Tax in Kind', *Indian Economic Review*, 11.

—— (1986), 'Modelling an Early Warning System for Famines', paper presented at a Conference on Food Strategies held at WIDER, Helsinki, 21–5 July 1986; to be published in Drèze, J. P., and Sen, A. K. (eds.) (forthcoming), *The Political Economy of Hunger*.

—— (1988a), 'Rice and Fish', Discussion Paper No. 14, Development Economics Research Programme, London School of Economics.

—— (1988b), 'The Economics of Famine', in Harrison, G. A. (ed.) (1988), *Famines*.

—— (ed.) (1989), *Lenin's Economic Writings* (London: Lawrence and Wishart).

—— and SHAH, A. (1988), 'An Econometric Approach to the Measurement of Poverty', *Oxford Economic Papers*, 40.

DESHPANDE, V. D. (1982), *Employment Guarantee Scheme* (Pune: Tilak Maharashtra Vidyapeeth).

—— (1984), *Rojgar Hami* (Pune: Gramayan Prakashan).

DEVEREUX, S. (1988), 'Entitlements, Availability and Famine: A Revisionist View of Wollo, 1972–1974', *Food Policy*, 13.

—— and HAY, R. (1988), 'Origins of Famine: Theories and Management', mimeo, Food Studies Group, Oxford.

Devres, Inc. (1986), *Evaluation of the African Emergency Food Assistance Pro-*

gram 1984–1985: Synthesis Report (Washington DC: US Agency for International Development).

DE VILLE DE GOYET, C. (1978), 'Disaster Relief in the Sahel: Letter to the Editor', *Disasters*, 2.

—— SEAMAN, J., and GEIJER, U. (1978), *The Management of Nutritional Emergencies in Large Populations* (Geneva: WHO).

DE WAAL, A. (1987), 'Famine That Kills: Darfur 1984–85', mimeo, Save the Children Fund UK, London; to be published by Clarendon Press, Oxford.

—— (1988a), 'Famine Early Warning Systems and the Use of Socio-Economic Data', *Disasters*, 12.

—— (1988b), 'A Re-assessment of Entitlement Theory in the Light of Recent Famines in Africa', Ld'A-QEH Development Studies Working Paper No. 4, Queen Elizabeth House, Oxford.

—— (1989a), 'Famine Mortality: A Case Study of Darfur, Sudan 1984–5', *Population Studies*, 43.

—— (1989b), 'The Sudan Famine Code of 1920: Successes and Failures of the Indian Model of Famine Relief in Colonial Sudan', mimeo, Nuffield College, Oxford.

—— and EL AMIN, M. M. (1986), 'Survival in Northern Darfur 1985–1986: Report of the SCF Survey Team', mimeo, Save the Children Fund, London.

DE WILDE, J. (1984), *Agricultural Marketing and Pricing in Sub-Saharan Africa* (Los Angeles: University of California African Studies Centre and African Studies Association).

DHAGAMWAR, V. (1987), 'The Disadvantaged and the Law', paper presented at a Workshop on Poverty in India held at Queen Elizabeth House, Oxford, Oct. 1987.

DIAZ-AMADOR, C. (1982), 'Situación nutricional de la población Costarricense', in Saenz, L. (ed.) (1982), *Análisis de la situación alimentaria-nutricional en Costa Rica*.

DIAZ-BRIQUETS (1983), *The Health Revolution in Cuba* (Austin: University of Texas Press).

DICK, B. (1986), 'Supplementary Feeding for Refugees and Other Displaced Communites: Questioning Current Orthodoxy', *Disasters*, 10.

DIESLER, E. (1986), 'Rapport analytique sur les operations de la ligue au Tchad (1984–1986)', internal report, League of Red Cross and Red Crescent Societies, Geneva.

DIRKS, R. (1980), 'Social Responses During Severe Food Shortages and Famine', *Current Anthropology*, 21.

DIXON, J. (ed.) (1987), *Social Welfare in the Middle East* (London: Croom Helm).

DIXON, R. (1982), 'Mobilizing Women for Rural Employment in South Asia: Issues of Class, Caste, and Patronage', *Economic Development and Cultural Change*, 30.

—— (1983), 'Land, Labour and the Sex Composition of the Agricultural Labour Force: An International Comparison', *Development and Change*, 14.

DOBB, M. (1960), *An Essay on Economic Growth and Planning* (London: Routledge).

DODGE, C. P., and ALNWICK, D. (1986), 'Karamoja: A Catastrophe Contained', *Disasters*, 10.

DOMES, J. (1982), 'New Policies in the Communes: Notes on Rural Societal Structures in China, 1976–1981', *Journal of Asian Studies*, 41.

DONALDSON, G. (1984), 'Food Security and the Role of the Grain Trade', *American Journal of Agricultural Economics*, 66.

DONELAN, A. (1983), 'Zimbabwe: A Study of the New Nation's Attempts to Progress

Since Independence, with Particular Reference to Health and Nutrition', report submitted to the University of London in partial fulfilment of the requirements for the Diploma in Food Resources related to Community Development.

DOUGLAS, M. (1984), 'Fundamental Issues in Food Problems', *Current Anthropology, 25*.

——and ISHERWOOD, B. (1979), *The World of Goods* (New York: Basic Books).

DOWD, M. (1987), 'Discreet Use of Flattery Hurts Biden', *International Herald Tribune*, 17 Sept.

DOWNING, J., BERRY, L., DOWNING, L., DOWNING, T., and FORD, R. (1987), 'Drought and Famine in Africa, 1981–1986: The U.S. Response', report prepared for USAID, Settlement and Resources Systems Analysis, Clark University/Institute for Development Anthropology.

DOWNING, T. (1986), 'Smallholder Drought Coping Strategies in Central and Eastern Kenya', paper presented at the Annual Meeting of the Association of American Geographers, Minneapolis, 3–7 May 1986.

—— (1988a), 'Coping with Drought in Kenya: National and Household Strategies, 1984–1985', transcript of a presentation made at a Workshop on Famine and Famine Policy, Tufts University, 24 Sept. 1987.

—— (1988b), 'Climatic Variability and Food Security Among Smallholder Agriculturalists in Six Districts of Central and Eastern Kenya', unpublished Ph.D. dissertation, Clark University, Worcester, MA.

—— AKONG'A, J., MUNGAI, D. N., MUTURI, H. R., and POTTER, J. L. (1987), 'Introduction to the Kenya Case Study', in Akong'a et al. (1987), 'The Effects of Climatic Variations on Agriculture in Central and Eastern Kenya'.

—— GITU, K., and KAMAU, C. (eds.) (forthcoming), *Coping with Drought in Kenya: National and Local Strategies* (Boulder: Lynne Rienner).

DOWNS, R. R., KERNER, D. O., and REYNA, S. C. (eds.) (forthcoming), *The Political Economy of African Hunger: The Class and Gender Bias of Hunger* (New York: Gordon and Breach).

DRAKAKIS-SMITH, D. (1981), *Urbanization, Housing and the Development Process* (London: Croom Helm).

DRÈZE, J. H., KERVYN DE LETTENHOVE, A., PLATTEAU, J. P., and REDING, P. (1989), 'A Proposal for "Cooperative Relief of Debt in Africa" (CORDA)', Working Paper No. 60, WIDER, Helsinki.

DRÈZE, J. P. (1988a), 'Famine Prevention in India', Discussion Paper No. 3, Development Economics Research Programme, London School of Economics; to be published in Drèze, J. P., and Sen, A. K. (eds.) (forthcoming), *The Political Economy of Hunger*.

—— (1988b), 'Social Insecurity in India', paper presented at a Workshop on Social Security in Developing Countries held at the London School of Economics, 4–5 July 1988; Discussion Paper, Development Economics Research Programme, London School of Economics.

—— (1989), 'Famine Prevention in Africa', Discussion Paper No. 17, Development Economics Research Programme, London School of Economics; to be published in Drèze, J. P., and Sen, A. K. (eds.) (forthcoming), *The Political Economy of Hunger*.

—— and SEN, A. K. (1988), 'Public Action for Social Security', paper presented at a Workshop on Social Security in Developing Countries held at the London School of Economics, 4–5 July 1988; to be published in Ahmad, S. E., et al. (eds.) (forthcoming), *Social Security in Developing Countries*.

—— —— (eds.) (forthcoming), *The Political Economy of Hunger* (Oxford: Clarendon Press).

—— and STERN, N. H. (1987), 'The Theory of Cost-Benefit Analysis', in Auerbach, A., and Feldstein, M. (eds.) (1987), *Handbook of Public Economics* (Amsterdam and New York: North-Holland).

D'SILVA, E. (1983), 'The Effectiveness of Rural Works Programs in Labor-Surplus Economies: The Case of the Maharashtra Employment Guarantee Scheme', Cornell International Agriculture Mimeo No. 97, Cornell University, Ithaca, NY.

D'SOUZA, F. (1988), 'Famine: Social Security and an Analysis of Vulnerability', in Harrison, G. A. (ed.) (1988), *Famines*.

DUNCAN, W. R. (1984), 'Jamaica: Alternative Approaches', in Wesson, R. (ed.) (1984), *Politics, Policies and Economic Development in Latin America*.

DUPRÉ, G., and GUILLAUD, D. (1984), 'Rapport préliminaire sur la situation alimentaire dans le pays d'Aribinda', mimeo, ORSTOM, Ouagadougou.

—— —— (1988), 'L'Agriculture de l'Aribinda (Burkina Faso) de 1875 à 1983', *Cahiers sciences humaines*, 24.

DUTT, R. C. (1900), *Famines and Land Assessment in India* (London).

—— (1904), *The Economic History of India* (London: Kegan Paul Trench, Trubner; repr. 1969, New York: A. M. Kelley).

DUTTA, B. (1978), 'On the Measurement of Poverty in Rural India', *Indian Economic Review*, 15.

DYSON, T. (1987), 'Excess Female Mortality in India: Uncertain Evidence on a Narrowing Differential', to be published in Srinivasan, K., and Mukerji, S. (eds.) (forthcoming), *Dynamics of Population and Family Welfare* (Bombay: Himalaya).

—— (1988), 'The Population History of Berar Since 1881 and its Potential Wider Significance', mimeo, Department of Population Studies, London School of Economics.

—— (1989), 'On the Demography of South Asian Famines', mimeo, London School of Economics.

—— and CROOK, N. (eds.) (1984), *Indian Demography* (New Delhi: South Asia Publishers).

—— and MOORE, M. (1983), 'On Kinship Structure, Female Autonomy, and Demographic Behavior in India', *Population and Development Review*, 9.

EASTERLIN, R. A. (ed.) (1980), *Population and Economic Change in Developing Countries* (Chicago: University of Chicago Press).

ECKSTEIN, S. (1980), 'Income Distribution and Consumption in Post Revolutionary Cuba', *Cuban Studies*, 10.

—— (1982), 'The Impact of Revolution on Social Welfare in Latin America', *Theory and Society*, 11.

—— (1986), 'The Impact of the Cuban Revolution: A Comparative Perspective', *Comparative Studies in Society and History*, 28.

The Economist (1985), 'Where Africans Feed Themselves', *The Economist*, 12 Jan. 1985.

Economist Intelligence Unit (1983), 'Quarterly Economic Review of Angola, Guinea Bissau, Cape Verde, São Tomé, Príncipe: Annual Supplement 1983'.

—— (1984), 'Quarterly Economic Review of Angola, Guinea Bissau, Cape Verde, São Tomé, Príncipe: Annual Supplement 1984'.

EDIRISINGHE, N. (1987), 'The Food Stamp Scheme in Sri Lanka: Costs, Benefits, and

Options for Modification', Research Report No. 58, International Food Policy Research Institute, Washington, DC.

EDWARDS, D. W. (1932), 'The Missionary and Famine Relief', *Chinese Recorder*, 63.

EDWARDS, S. (1985), 'Stabilization with Liberalization: An Evaluation of Ten Years of Chile's Experiment with Free Market Policies: 1973–83', *Economic Development and Cultural Change*, 33.

EICHER, C. K. (1985), 'Famine Prevention in Africa: The Long View', in *Food for the Future: Proceedings of the Bicentennial Forum* (Philadelphia: Philadelphia Society for Promoting Agriculture).

—— (1986a), 'Transforming African Agriculture', The Hunger Project Papers, No. 4, The Hunger Project, San Francisco.

—— (1986b), 'Food Security Research Priorities in Sub-Saharan Africa', keynote address presented at the OAU/STRC/SAFGRAD International Drought Symposium held at the Kenyatta International Center, Nairobi, May 1986.

—— (1988a), 'Food Security Battles in Sub-Saharan Africa', paper presented at the 7th World Congress for Rural Sociology, Bologna, 25 June–2 July 1988.

—— (1988b), 'An Economic Perspective on the Sasakawa–Global 2000 Initiative to Increase Food Production in Sub-Saharan Africa', mimeo, Department of Agricultural Economics, Michigan State University, East Lansing.

—— and BAKER, D. C. (1982), 'Research on Agricultural Development in Sub-Saharan Africa: A Critical Survey', International Development Paper No. 1, Michigan State University, East Lansing.

—— and MANGWIRO, F. (1986), 'A Critical Assessment of the FAO Report on SADCC Agriculture and Agricultural Sector Studies', mimeo, Department of Agricultural Economics and Extension, University of Zimbabwe, Harare.

—— and STAATZ, J. M. (eds.) (1984), *Agricultural Development in the Third World* (Baltimore: Johns Hopkins).

—— —— (1986), 'Food Security Policy in Sub-Saharan Africa', in Maunder, A., and Renborg, U. (eds.) (1986), *Agriculture in a Turbulent World Economy* (London: Gower).

ELDREDGE, E., and RYDJESKI, D. (1988), 'Food Crises, Crises Response and Emergency Preparedness: The Sudan Case', *Disasters*, 12.

ENGLISH, J., BENNETT, J., and DICK, B. (1984), 'Tigray 1984: An Investigation', mimeo, OXFAM, Oxford.

ETHERIDGE, A. T. (1868), *Report on the Past Famines in the Bombay Presidency* (Bombay: Education Society's Press).

ETTEMA, WM., and MSUKVA L. (1985), *Food Production and Malnutrition in Malawi* (Zomba: Centre for Social Research, University of Malawi).

EVANS, D., and ALIZADEH, P. (1984), 'Trade, Industrialization and the Visible Hand', *Journal of Development Studies*, 21.

EZEKIEL, H. (1986), 'A Rural Employment Guarantee Scheme as an Early Warning System', mimeo, International Food Policy Research Institute.

FAI-MING WONG (1981), 'Effects of the Employment of Mothers on Marital Role and Power Differentiation in Hong Kong', in King, A. Y. C., and Lee, R. P. L. (eds.) (1981), *Social Life and Development in Hong Kong*.

FAULKINGHAM, R. H. (1977), 'Ecologic Constraints and Subsistence Strategies: The Impact of Drought in a Hausa Village, A Case Study from Niger', in Dalby, D. *et al.* (eds.) (1977), *Drought in Africa 2*.

—— and THORBAHN, P. F. (1975), 'Population Dynamics and Drought: A Village in Niger', *Population Studies*, 29.

FENELON, K. (1976), *The UAE: An Economic and Social Survey* (London: Longman).

FERNANDES, D. F. S. (1985), 'Health Statistics in Sri Lanka, 1921–80', in Halstead, S. B., *et al.* (eds.) (1985), *Good Health at Low Cost*.

FERNANDES, W., and MENON, G. (1987), *Tribal Women and Forest Economy: Deforestation, Exploitation and Status Change* (New Delhi: Indian Social Institute).

FEUCHTWANG, S., HUSSAIN, A., and PAIRAULT, T. (eds.) (1988), *Transforming China's Economy in the Eighties* (London: Zed).

FFRENCH-DAVIS, R. (1983), 'The Monetarist Experiment in Chile: A Critical Survey', *World Development*, 11.

—— and RACZYNSKI, D. (1988), 'The Impact of Global Recession on Living Standards: Chile, 1973–87', Notas Técnicas No. 97 (2nd edn., updated), CIEPLAN, Santiago.

FIELD, J. O. (1987), 'Multisectoral Nutrition Planning: A Post-Mortem', *Food Policy*, 12.

FIELDS, G. S. (1980), *Poverty, Inequality and Development* (Cambridge: Cambridge University Press).

—— (1988), 'Employment and Economic Growth in Costa Rica', *World Development*, 16.

FIREBRACE, J., and HOLLAND, S. (1984), *Never Kneel Down—Drought, Development and Liberation in Eritrea* (London: Spokesman).

FIRTH, R. (1959), *Social Change in Tikopia* (London: Allen and Unwin).

FLEGG, A. T. (1982), 'Inequality of Income, Illiteracy and Medical Care as Determinants of Infant Mortality in Underdeveloped Countries', *Population Studies*, 36.

FLEURET, A. (1986), 'Indigenous Responses to Drought in Sub-Saharan Africa', *Disasters*, 10.

FLEURET, P., and FLEURET, A. (1980), 'Nutrition, Consumption, and Agricultural Change', *Human Organization*, 39.

FLOUD, R. C. (1987), 'Anthropometric Measures of Nutritional Status in Industrial Societies: Europe and North America Since 1750', paper presented at a Conference on Poverty, Undernutrition and Living Standards held at WIDER, 27–30 July 1987; to be published in Osmani, S. R. (ed.) (forthcoming), *Nutrition and Poverty*.

—— and WACHTER, K. W. (1982), 'Poverty and Physical Stature: Evidence on the Standard of Living of London Boys 1770–1870', *Social Science History*, 6.

FOEGE, W. H. (1971), 'Famine, Infections and Epidemics', in Blix, G., *et al.* (eds.) (1971), *Famine: Nutrition and Relief Operations in Times of Disaster*.

FOGEL, R. W. (1987), 'Second Thoughts on the European Escape from Hunger: Crop Yields, Price Elasticities, Entitlements, and Mortality Rates', paper presented at a Conference on Poverty, Undernutrition and Living Standards held at WIDER, 27–30 July 1987; to be published in Osmani, S. R. (ed.) (forthcoming), *Nutrition and Poverty*.

—— ENGERMAN, S. L., and TRUSSELL, J. (1982), 'Exploring the Use of Data on Height: The Analysis of Long-Term Trends in Nutrition, Labour Welfare and Labour Productivity', *Social Science History*, 6.

—— *et al.* (1983), 'Secular Changes in American and British Stature and Nutrition', in Rotberg, R. I., and Rabb, T. K. (eds.) (1983), *Hunger and History*.

FOLBRE, N. (1986), 'Cleaning House: New Perspectives on Household and Economic Development', *Journal of Development Economics*, 22.

Food and Agriculture Organization (1984), *Assessment of the Agriculture, Food Supply and Livestock Situation: Kenya* (Rome: Office for Special Relief Operations, FAO).

—— (1985), 'Guidelines for Use by FAO Crop Assessment Missions to Africa', W/R6323, FAO Global Information and Early Warning System on ,Food and Agriculture, FAO, Rome.

—— (1986), *African Agriculture: The Next 25 Years* (Rome: FAO).

—— (1987a), 'Methodology for the Assessment of the Food Supply Situation and Requirements for Exceptional Assistance Arising from Crop Failure or Unusual Crop Surplus', FAO Global Information and Early Warning System on Food and Agriculture, FAO, Rome.

—— (1987b), 'Approche d'une politique céréalière: quelques idées forces tirées de l'expérience vécue sur le terrain', mimeo, Food and Agriculture Organization, N'Djaména, Chad.

—— (1988), *Potentials for Agricultural and Rural Development in Latin America and the Caribbean, Annex II: Rural Development* (Rome: FAO).

FORBES, J. D. (1985), *Jamaica: Managing Political and Economic Change* (Washington and London: American Enterprise Institute for Public Policy Research).

FORRESTER, J. W. (1971), *World Dynamics* (Cambridge, MA: Wright-Allen).

FORSTER, N., and HANDELMAN, H. (1985), 'Food Production and Distribution in Cuba: The Impact of the Revolution', in Super, J. C., and Wright, T. C. (eds.) (1985), *Food, Politics and Society in Latin America*.

FOSTER, J. (1984), 'On Economic Poverty: A Survey of Aggregate Measures', *Advances in Econometrics*, 3.

FOXLEY, A. (1983), *Latin American Experiments in Neo-conservative Economics* (Berkeley: University of California Press).

—— ANINAT, E., and ARELLANO, J. P. (1979), *Redistributive Effects of Government Programmes* (Oxford: Pergamon).

—— and RACZYNSKI, D. (1984), 'Vulnerable Groups in Recessionary Situations: The Case of Children and the Young in Chile', in Jolly, R., and Cornia, G. A. (eds.) (1984), *The Impact of World Recession on Children*.

FRANKE, R., and CHASIN, B. H. (1980), *Seeds of Famine: Ecological Destruction and the Development Dilemma in the West African Sahel* (Montclair: Allanheld and Osmun).

FREEMAN, P. H., GREEN, V. E., HICKOK, R. B., MORAN, E. F., and WHITAKER, M. D. (1978), 'Cape Verde: Assessment of the Agricultural Sector', Report CR-A-219A submitted to USAID, General Research Corporation, McLean, VA.

GAIDZANWA, R. (1986), 'Drought and the Food Crisis in Zimbabwe', in Lawrence, P. (ed.) (1986), *World Recession and the Food Crisis in Africa*.

GAIHA, R. (1987), 'Micro Data on Rural Poverty', paper presented at a Workshop on Poverty in India held at Queen Elizabeth House, Oxford, Oct. 1987.

—— (1988), 'On Measuring the Risk of Rural Poverty in India', in Srinivasan, T. N., and Bardhan, P. K. (eds.) (1988), *Rural Poverty in Asia*.

—— and KAZMI, N. P. (1981), 'Aspects of Rural Poverty in India', *Economics of Planning*, 17.

GALLAIS, J., et al. (1977), *Stratégies pastorales et agricoles des Sahéliens durant la sécheresse 1969–1974* (Bordeaux: Centre d'Études de Géographie Tropicale).

GALTUNG, J., O'BRIEN, P., and PREISWERK, R. (eds.) (1980), *Self-Reliance: A Strategy for Development* (London: Bogle-L'Ouverture Publications).

GANGRADE, K. D., and DHADDA, S. (1973), *Challenge and Response: A Study of Famines in India* (Delhi: Rachana Publications).

GARCIA, M., and PINSTRUP-ANDERSEN, P. (1987), 'The Pilot Food Price Subsidy Scheme in the Philippines: Its Impact on Income, Food Consumption, and Nutritional Status', Research Report No. 61, International Food Policy Research Institute, Washington, DC.

GARCIA, R. (ed.) (1985), *Chile: 1973–1984* (Stockholm: Institute of Latin American Studies).

GARCIA, R. V. (1981), *Drought and Man: The 1972 Case History*, i: *Nature Pleads not Guilty* (Oxford: Pergamon).

—— and ESCUDERO, J. C. (1982), *Drought and Man: The 1972 Case History*, ii: *Constant Catastrophe: Malnutrition, Famines and Drought* (Oxford: Pergamon).

—— and SPITZ, P. (1986), *Drought and Man: The 1972 Case History*, iii: *The Roots of Catastrophe* (Oxford: Pergamon).

GARDEN, B., and MUSA, K. (1986), 'Deterioration, Improvement Mark Crisis in Sudan', *Africa Emergency Report*, Apr./May 1986.

GARNSEY, P. (1988), *Famine and Food Supply in the Graeco-Roman World: Responses to Risk and Crises* (Cambridge: Cambridge University Press).

GAUDE, J., GUICHAOUA, A., MARTENS, B., and MILLER, S. (1987): 'Rural Development and Labour-Intensive Schemes: Impact Studies of Some Pilot Programmes', *International Labour Review*, 126.

GAVAN, J., and CHANDRASEKERA, I. (1979), 'The Impact of Public Foodgrain Distribution on Food Consumption and Welfare in Sri Lanka', Research Report No. 13, International Food Policy Research Institute, Washington, DC.

GBENYON, K., and LOCOH, T. (1987), 'Différences de mortalité selon le sexe dans l'enfance en Afrique au sud du Sahara', paper presented at the Séminaire sur Mortalité et Société en Afrique Sud du Sahara, Yaoundé, Cameroon, Oct. 1987.

GENDELL, M. (1985), 'Stalls in the Fertility Decline in Costa Rica, Korea and Sri Lanka', World Bank Staff Working Paper No. 693, World Bank, Washington, DC.

GEORGE, F. S. (1979), 'Public Distribution of Foodgrains in Kerala: Income Distribution Implications and Effectiveness', Research Report No. 7, International Food Policy Research Institute, Washington, DC.

GEORGE, S. (1976), *How the Other Half Dies* (Harmondsworth: Penguin).

—— (1984), *Ill Fares the Land* (Washington, DC: Institute for Policy Studies).

—— (1987), 'Food Strategies for Tomorrow', The Hunger Project Papers, No. 6, The Hunger Project, San Francisco.

—— (1988), *A Fate Worse Than Debt* (London: Penguin).

GHAI, D., KAY, C., and PEEK, P. (1988), *Labour and Development in Rural Cuba* (Basingstoke: Macmillan).

—— and SMITH, L. D. (1986), *Agricultural Prices, Policy, and Equity in Sub-Saharan Africa* (Boulder: Lynne Rienner).

GHOSE, A. K. (1982), 'Food Supply and Starvation: A Study of Famines with Reference to the Indian Subcontinent', *Oxford Economic Papers*, 34.

GHOSH, K. C. (1944), *Famines in Bengal, 1770–1945* (Calcutta: Indian Associated Publishing Co.).

GIBB, C. (1986), 'A Review of Feeding Programmes in Refugee Reception Centres in Eastern Sudan', *Disasters*, 10.

GILBERT, N. (1976), 'Alternative Forms of Social Protection for Developing Countries', *Social Services Review*, 50.

—— (1981), 'Social Security in Developing Countries', in Wallace, H. M., and Ebrahim, G. (eds.) (1981), *Maternal and Child Health Around the World*.

GILL, P. (1986), *A Year in the Death of Africa: Politics, Bureaucracy and the Famine* (London: Paladin).

GIRLING, R., and KEITH, S. (1977), 'Jamaica's Employment Crisis: A Political Economic Evaluation of the Jamaican Special Employment Program', World Employment Programme Research Working Paper 8, ILO, Geneva.

—— —— (1980), 'The Planning and Management of Jamaica's Special Employment Programme: Lessons and Limitations', *Social and Economic Studies*, 29.

GITTINGER, J. P., LESLIE, J., and HOISINGTON, C. (eds.) (1987), *Food Policy: Integrating Supply, Distribution and Consumption* (Baltimore: Johns Hopkins).

GLANTZ, M. (ed.) (1976), *The Politics of Natural Disaster: The Case of the Sahel Drought* (New York: Praeger).

—— (ed.) (1987a), *Drought and Hunger in Africa: Denying Famine a Future* (Cambridge: Cambridge University Press).

—— (1987b), 'Drought and Economic Development in Sub-Saharan Africa', in Glantz, M. (ed.) (1987), *Drought and Hunger in Africa*.

GLEWWE, P., and BHALLA, S. (1987), 'Response', *World Bank Economic Review*, 1.

GOBIN, M. (1977), 'The Role of Social Security in the Development of the Caribbean Territories', *International Social Security Review*, 30.

GODFREY, N. (1986a), 'Supplementary Feeding in Refugee Populations: Comprehensive or Selective Feeding Programmes', *Health Policy and Planning*, 1.

—— (1986b), 'Supplementary Feeding in Refugee Populations: A Review and Selected Annotated Bibliography', Evaluation and Planning Centre Paper No. 11, London School of Hygiene and Tropical Medicine.

GOLKIN, A. (1987), *Famine: A Heritage of Hunger* (Claremont, Calif.: Regina Books).

GOLLADAY, F., and KING, T. (1979), 'Social Development', in Hasan, P., and Rao, C. C. (eds.) (1979), *Korea: Policy Issues for Long-Term Development*.

GONZALEZ, N., INFANTE, A., SCHLESSINGER, C., and MONCKEBERG, F. (1983), 'Effectiveness of Supplementary Feeding Programs in Chile', in Underwood, B. (ed.) (1983), *Nutrition Intervention Strategies in National Development*.

GONZALEZ-VEGA, C. (1985), 'Health Improvements in Costa Rica: The Socioeconomic Background', in Halstead, S. B., *et al.* (eds.) (1985), *Good Health at Low Cost*.

GOOCH, T., and MACDONALD, J. (1981a), *Evaluation of 1979/80 Drought Relief Programme* (Republic of Botswana: Ministry of Finance and Development Planning).

—— (1981b), *Evaluation of 1979/80 Drought Relief Programme: Synopsis* (Republic of Botswana: Ministry of Finance and Development Planning).

GOODY, J. (1987), 'Futures of the Family in Rural Africa', paper presented at the Expert Consultation on Population and Agricultural and Rural Development, FAO, Rome, June–July 1987.

GOPALAN, C. (1983a), ' "Small is Healthy"? For the Poor not for the Rich!', *Bulletin of the Nutrition Foundation of India*, Oct.; also reprinted in *Future*, Autumn, 1983.

—— (1983b), 'Measurement of Undernutrition: Biological Considerations', *Economic and Political Weekly*, 18.

—— (1987a), 'Undernutrition: Concepts, Measurement and Implications', paper presented at a Conference on Poverty, Undernutrition and Living Standards held at WIDER, 27–30 July 1987; to be published in Osmani, S. R. (ed.) (forthcoming), *Nutrition and Poverty*.

—— (ed.) (1987b), *Combating Undernutrition* (New Delhi: Nutrition Foundation of India).

GORDON, A. M., Jun. (1983), 'The Nutriture of Cubans: Historical Perspective and Nutritional Analysis', *Cuban Studies*, 13.

Government of Botswana (1980), *A Human Drought Relief Programme for Botswana* (Gaborone: Ministry of Local Government and Lands).

—— (1985a), *The Drought Situation in Botswana* (Gaborone: Ministry of Finance and Development Planning).

—— (1985b), *Report on the National Food Strategy* (Gaborone: Ministry of Finance and Development Planning).

—— (1987), 'The Drought Situation in Botswana, March 1987, and Estimated Requirements for Relief and Recovery Measures', *aide-mémoire*, Ministry of Finance and Development Planning, Gaborone.

—— (1988), 'The Drought Recovery Situation in Botswana, March 1988, and Estimated Requirements for Relief and Recovery Measures', *aide-mémoire*, Ministry of Finance and Development Planning, Gaborone.

Government of Chad (1986), 'Système d'alerte précoce', various monthly bulletins (Ministère de la Sécurité Alimentaire et des Populations Sinistrées, N'Djaména).

Government of Chile (1974), 'Declaration of Principles of the Chilean Government', reprinted in Mendez, J. C. (ed.) (1979), *Chilean Economic Policy*.

—— (1988), *Social Reforms in Chile Since 1973 (An Experience in Infant Nutrition)* (Santiago: Secretaria de Desarrollo y Asistencia Social, Government of Chile).

Government of Ethiopia (1986), '1985 Meher (Main) Crop Season Synoptic and 1986 Food Supply Prospect—Final Report', Early Warning and Planning Services, Relief and Rehabilitation Commission, Addis Ababa.

—— (1987), *Workshop on Food-for-Work in Ethiopia, Proceedings of the Workshop Held in Addis-Ababa in July 1986* (Addis Ababa: Office of the National Committee for Central Planning).

Government of Hong Kong (1986), *Hong Kong Annual Digest of Statistics 1986* (Hong Kong: Census and Statistics Department).

—— (1987), *Hong Kong 1986* (Hong Kong: Government Information Services).

Government of India (1880), *Report of the Indian Famine Commission 1880* (London: HMSO).

—— (1898), *Report of the Indian Famine Commission 1898* (Simla).

—— (1901), *Report of the Indian Famine Commission 1901* (Calcutta).

—— (1945), *Famine Inquiry Commission, Report on Bengal* (New Delhi: Manager of Publications).

—— (1980), 'Joint Evaluation Report on Employment Guarantee Scheme of Maharashtra', Planning Commission and Directorate of Economics and Statistics, New Delhi.

—— (1989), *Economic Survey 1988–89* (New Delhi: Ministry of Finance).

Government of Jamaica (1985), Economic and Social Survey of Jamaica 1984 (Kingston: Planning Institute of Jamaica).

Government of Kenya (1985), 'CBS/NES Survey of Drought Responses: Preliminary Findings', mimeo, National Environment Secretariat, Nairobi.

Government of Maharashtra (1973), Report of the Fact Finding Committee for Survey of Scarcity Areas of Maharashtra State (Bombay).

Government of Mali (1987), 'Projet système d'alerte précoce', various bulletins (Bamako: Comité National d'Aide aux Victimes de la Sécheresse).

Government of the Republic of Korea (1963), Annual Survey of Education (Seoul: Ministry of Education).

—— (1965), Annual Survey of Education (Seoul: Ministry of Education).

—— (1970), Statistic Yearbook of Education (Seoul: Ministry of Education).

—— (1986), The Sixth Five-Year Economic and Social Development Plan (Seoul: Government of Korea).

—— (1987), Social Indicators in Korea (Seoul: Economic Planning Board).

Government of Sri Lanka (1984), Nutritional Status and Its Determinants and Intervention Programmes (Colombo: Ministry of Plan Implementation).

Government of Zimbabwe (1983), 'Development Policies and Programmes for Food and Nutrition in Zimbabwe', Ministry of Finance, Economic Planning and Development, Harare.

—— (1984), 'Planning for Equity in Health: A Sectoral Review and Policy Statement', Ministry of Health, Harare.

—— (1986a), 'Zimbabwe's Experience in Dealing with Drought 1982 to 1984', mimeo, Ministry of Labour, Manpower Planning and Social Welfare, Harare.

—— (1986b), 'Memorandum on Drought Relief 1986', mimeo, Ministry of Labour, Manpower Planning and Social Welfare, Harare.

GOYDER, C., and GOYDER, H. (1988), 'Famine in Ethiopia', in Curtis, D., Hubbard, M., and Shepherd, A. (eds.) (1988), Preventing Famine: Policies and Prospects for Africa.

GRANDIN, N. E., and LEMBUYE, P. (1987), 'The 1984 Drought: A Case Study from a Maasai Group Ranch in South-Eastern Kajiado District', Pastoral Network Paper No. 23e, Overseas Development Institute, London.

GRANNELL, T. F. (1986), 'Ethiopia: Food-for-Work for the Rehabilitation of Forest, Grazing and Agricultural Lands in Ethiopia', paper presented at the WFP/ADB Conference on Food Aid for Development, Abijan, Sept. 1986.

GRANT, J. P. (1978), Disparity Reduction Rates in Social Indicators (Washington, DC: Overseas Development Council).

—— (1985), 'Famine Today—Hope for Tomorrow', Working Paper No. 1, The Alan Shawn Feinstein World Hunger Program, Brown University, Providence.

GRAY, R. H. (1974), 'The Decline of Mortality in Ceylon and the Demographic Effects of Malaria Control', Population Studies, 28.

GRAY, R., and BIRMINGHAM, D. (eds.) (1970a), Pre-colonial African Trade (Oxford: Oxford University Press).

—— (1970b), 'Some Economic and Political Consequences of Trade in Central and Eastern Africa in the Pre-colonial Period', in Gray, R. and Birmingham, D. (eds.) (1970a), Pre-colonial African Trade.

GREEN, D. W. (1977), 'Some Effects of Social Security Programs on the Distribution of Income in Costa Rica', unpublished Ph.D. dissertation, University of Pittsburgh.

GREEN, R. H. (1986a), 'Food Policy, Food Production and Hunger in Sub-Saharan Africa: Retrospect and Prospect', *International Journal*, 41.

—— (1986b), 'Hunger, Poverty and Food Aid in Sub-Saharan Africa: Retrospect and Potential', paper presented at the WFP/ADB Conference on Food Aid for Development, Abijan, Sept. 1986.

GREENOUGH, P. R. (1982), *Prosperity and Misery in Modern Bengal: The Famine of 1943–1944* (Oxford: Oxford University Press).

GRIFFIN, K. (1976), *Land Concentration and Rural Poverty* (London: Macmillan).

—— (1978), *International Inequality and National Poverty* (London: Macmillan).

—— (1987), *World Hunger and the World Economy* (London: Macmillan).

—— (1988), *Alternative Strategies for Economic Development* (London: Macmillan).

—— and HAY, R. (1985), 'Problems of Agricultural Development in Socialist Ethiopia: An Overview and a Suggested Survey', *Journal of Peasant Studies*, 13.

—— and JAMES, J. (1981), *The Transition to Egalitarian Development* (London: Macmillan).

—— and KHAN, A. R. (1977): *Poverty and Landlessness in Rural Asia* (Geneva: ILO).

—— and KNIGHT, J. (1988), 'Human Development in the 1980s and Beyond', report for the United Nations Committee for Development Planning.

—— —— (eds.) (1989), *Human Development in the 1980s and Beyond*, special issue of *Journal of Development Planning*, No. 19; to be published as a book.

GROSSI, J. R. (1985), 'El acceso a la salud, la eficacia hospitalaria y la distribución de los beneficios de la salud pública', *Cuadernos de economía*, 22.

Grupo de Investigaciones Agrarias (1984), 'Coyuntura agraria 1984: el costo de la reactivación', mimeo, GIA, Academia de Humanismo Cristiano, Santiago, Chile.

GUHA, S. (1981), 'Income Redistribution Through Labour-Intensive Rural Public Works: Some Policy Issues', *International Labour Review*, 120.

GUHAN, S. (1981), 'Social Security: Lessons and Possibilities from the Tamil Nadu Experience', *Madras Institute of Development Studies Bulletin*, 11.

—— (1988), 'Social Security and Insurance: Looking One Step Ahead', keynote address, Annual Conference, Insurance Institute of India, Madras.

GULATI, L. (1975), 'Female Work Participation: A Study of Inter-state Differences', *Economic and Political Weekly*, 10.

GUNATILLEKE, G. (ed.) (1984), *Intersectoral Linkages and Health Development*, Offset Publication No. 83, World Health Organization, Geneva.

—— (1985), 'Health and Development in Sri Lanka: An Overview', in Halstead, S. B., et al. (eds.) (1985), *Good Health at Low Cost*.

GUPTA, A. K. (1987), 'The Role of Women in Risk Adjustment in Drought Prone Regions', Working Paper No. 704, Indian Institute of Management, Ahmedabad.

GUZ, D. (1987), 'Population Dynamics of Famine in 19th Century Punjab, 1896–7 and 1899–1900', mimeo, London School of Economics.

GWATKIN, D. R. (1979), 'Food Policy, Nutrition Planning and Survival: The Case of Kerala and Sri Lanka', *Food Policy*, 4.

—— WILCOX, J. R., and WRAY, J. D. (1980), *Can Health and Nutrition Interventions Make a Difference?* (Washington, DC: Overseas Development Council).

HADZEWYCZ, R., ZARYCKY, C., and KOLOMAYETS, M. (eds.) (1983), *The Great Famine in Ukraine: The Unknown Holocaust* (Jersey City, NJ: The Ukrainian National Association for the National Committee to Commemorate Genocide Victims in Ukraine 1932–33).

HAHN, S. (1989), 'The Effects of an Export-Led Strategy of Growth on Income Distribution: South Korea, 1963–1985', unpublished undergraduate thesis, Harvard University.

HAIFENG, C., and CHAO, Z. (eds.) (1984), *Modern Chinese Medicine* (Lancaster: MTP Press).

HAIGNERE, C. S. (1983), 'The Application of the Free-Market Economic Model in Chile and the Effects on its Population's Health Status', *International Journal of Health Services*, 13.

HAINDL, E., and WEBER, C. (1986), 'Impacto redistributivo del gasto social', Series de Investigación, Departamento de Económica, Universidad de Chile.

HAINES, M., and AVERY, R. (1982), 'Differential Infant and Child Mortality in Costa Rica: 1968–1973', *Population Studies*, 36.

HAJJAR, S. G. (ed.) (1985), *The Middle East:From Transition to Development* (Leiden: E. J. Brill).

HAKIM, P., and SOLIMANO, G. (1978), *Development, Reform, and Malnutrition in Chile* (Cambridge, MA: MIT Press).

HALE, S. (1986), 'The OXFAM Food Targeting and Monitoring Programme in the Red Sea Province, Sudan', mimeo, OXFAM, Oxford.

HALEBSKY, S., and KIRK, J. M. (eds.) (1985), *Cuba: Twenty-Five Years of Revolution 1959 to 1984* (New York: Praeger).

HALL, E. (1973), 'One Shudders to Think What Would Have Happened to the Children Without the Feeding Scheme', *Oxfam News*, July.

HALSTEAD, S. B., WALSH, J. A., and WARREN, K. S. (1985), *Good Health at Low Cost* (New York: Rockefeller Foundation).

HAMILTON, C. (1986), *Capitalist Industrialization in Korea* (Boulder: Westview).

HAMILTON, S., POPKIN, B., and SPICER, D. (1984), *Women and Nutrition in Third World Countries* (South Hadley, MA: Bergin and Garvey Publishers).

HAMMOND, R. J. (1951), *History of the Second World War: Food* (London: HMSO).

HAMMOUD, H. R. (1986), 'The Impact of Technology on Social Welfare in Kuwait', *Social Service Review*, 60.

—— (1987), 'Kuwait', in Dixon, J. (ed.) (1987), *Social Welfare in the Middle East*.

HANCOCK, G. (1985), *Ethiopia: The Challenge of Hunger* (London: Gollancz).

HANDELMAN, H. (1982), 'Cuban Food Policy and Popular Nutritional Levels', *Cuban Studies*, 11 and 12.

HANSEN, A., and MCMILLAN, D. E. (eds.) (1986), *Food in Sub-Saharan Africa* (Boulder, CO: Lynne Rienner).

HAQ, M. (1976), *The Poverty Curtain* (New York: Columbia University Press).

HARBERGER, A. (1982), 'The Chilean Economy in the 1970s: Crisis, Stabilization, Liberalization, Reform', in Brunner, K., and Meltzer, A. (eds.) (1982), *Economic Policy in a World of Change*, Carnegie-Rochester Conference Series on Public Policy, Vol. 17.

HARBERT, L., and SCANDIZZO, P. (1982), 'Food Distribution and Nutrition Intervention: The Case of Chile', World Bank Staff Working Paper No. 512, World Bank, Washington, DC.

HARDEE-CLEAVELAND, K., and BANISTER, J. (1988), 'Fertility Policy and Implementation in China 1986–88', *Population and Development Review*, 14.

HARDIN, G. (1974), 'Lifeboat Ethics: The Case Against Helping the Poor', *Psychology Today*, 8.

—— (1981), 'The Toughlove Solution', *Newsweek*, 26 Oct.

HARREL-BOND, B. (1986), *Imposing Aid: Emergency Assistance to Refugees* (Oxford: Oxford University Press).

HARRIS, N. (1983), *Of Bread and Guns* (Harmondsworth: Penguin).

HARRISON. A. (1985), 'Les Services de santé du Koweit et leurs usagers', *Forum mondial de la santé*, 6.

HARRISON, G. A. (ed.) (1988), *Famines* (Oxford: Oxford University Press).

HARRISS, B. (1982), 'The Marketing of Foodgrains in the West African Sudano-Sahelian States', Progress Report 31, Economics Program, ICRISAT, Hyderabad.

—— (1983), 'Markets and Rural Undernutrition', mimeo, London School of Hygiene and Tropical Medicine, London.

—— (1986), 'The Intrafamily Distribution of Hunger in South Asia', paper presented at a Conference on Food Strategies held at WIDER, Helsinki, 21–5 July 1986; to be published in Drèze, J. P., and Sen, A. K. (eds.) (forthcoming), *The Political Economy of Hunger*.

—— (1988a), 'Differential Female Mortality and Health Care in South Asia', mimeo, Queen Elizabeth House, Oxford; forthcoming in *Journal of Social Studies*.

—— (1988b), 'Policy is What it Does: State Trading in Rural South India', *Public Administration and Development*, 8.

—— (1988c), 'Limitations of the "Lessons from India"', in Curtis, D., Hubbard, M., and Shepherd, A. (eds.) (1988), *Preventing Famine: Policies and Prospects for Africa*.

—— and WATSON, E. (1987), 'The Sex Ratio in South Asia', in Momsen, J. H., and Townsend, J. (eds.) (1987), *Geography of Gender in the Third World*.

HARSANYI, J. (1976), *Rational Behaviour and Bargaining Equilibrium in Games and Social Situations* (Cambridge: Cambridge University Press).

HART, K. (1987), 'Commoditisation and the Standard of Living', in Sen, A. K. (1987a), *The Standard of Living*.

HART, O. D. (1977), 'On the Profitability of Speculation', *Quarterly Journal of Economics*, 91.

—— and KREPS, D. M. (1986), 'Price Destabilizing Speculation', *Journal of Political Economy*, 94.

HARTMANN, B., and BOYCE, J. (1983), *A Quiet Violence: View from a Bangladesh Village* (London: Zed Press).

Harvard School of Public Health (1985), *Hunger in America: The Growing Epidemic* (Cambridge, MA: Harvard University).

—— (1987), *Hunger Reaches Blue Collar America* (Cambridge, MA: Harvard University).

HASAN, P., and RAO, D. C. (eds.) (1979), *Korea: Policy Issues for Long-Term Development* (Baltimore: Johns Hopkins).

HAWTHORN, G. (1987), 'Introduction', in Sen, A. K. (1987a), *The Standard of Living*.

HAY, R. W. (1975), 'Analysis of Data from Ogaden-Hararghe Province' (Addis Ababa: Consolidated Food and Nutrition Information System, Ethiopian Food and Nutrition Surveillance Programme).

—— (1986), 'Food Aid and Relief-Development Strategies', *Disasters*, 10.

—— (1988), 'Famine Incomes and Employment: Has Botswana Anything to Teach Africa?', *World Development*, 16.

—— BURKE, S., and DAKO, D. Y. (1986), 'A Socio-economic Assessment of Drought

Relief in Botswana', report prepared by UNICEF/UNDP/WHO for the Inter-ministerial Drought Committee, Government of Botswana, Gabrone.

—— and CLAY, E. J. (1986), 'Food Aid and the Development of Human Resources', paper presentd at a WFP/ADB Conference on Food Aid for Development, Abidjan, Sept. 1986.

—— and RUKUNI, M. (1988), 'SADCC Food Security Strategies: Evolution and Role', *World Development*, 16.

HEBERT, J. R. (1987), 'The Social Ecology of Famine in British India: Lessons for Africa in the 1980s?', *Ecology of Food and Nutrition*, 20.

HEMMEL, V., and SINDBJERG, P. (1984), *Women in Rural China: Policy Towards Women Before and After the Cultural Revolution* (Copenhagen: Humanities Press).

HENDERSON, P. L., and BIELLIK, R. J. (1983), 'Comparative Nutrition and Health Services for Victims of Drought and Hostilities in the Ogaden: Somalia and Ethiopia, 1980–1981' *International Journal of Health Services*, 13.

HEPPELL, T. S. (1973), 'Social Security and Social Welfare: A "New Look" from Hong Kong', *Journal of Social Policy*, 2.

—— (1974), 'Social Security and Social Welfare: A "New Look" from Hong Kong', *Journal of Social Policy*, 3.

Herald (1983), 'Hungry Buhera Women Search for Husbands', *Herald*, 16 Mar. 1983.

HERLEHY, T. J. (1984), 'Historical Dimensions of the Food Crisis in Africa: Surviving Famines along the Kenya Coast 1880–1980', Working Paper No. 87, African Studies Center, Boston University.

HERRERA, A. O., et al. (1976), *Catastrophe or New Society? A Latin American World Model* (Ottawa: IDRC).

HERRING, R. J. (1987), 'Openness and Democracy in the Rise and Decline of Economic Interventionism: Liberalization in Sri Lanka', paper presented at the Annual Meeting of the American Political Science Association, Sept. 1987.

—— and EDWARDS, R. M. (1983), 'Guaranteeing Employment to the Rural Poor: Social Functions and Class Interests in the Employment Guarantee Scheme in Western India', *World Development*, 11.

HESSE, C. (1985), 'An Evaluation of the 1984–1985 Food Situation in Burkina Faso', *Disasters*, 9.

—— (1988), 'Famine Early Warning Systems as a Famine Prevention Tool', mimeo, OXFAM, Oxford.

HEWITT, K. (ed.) (1983), *Interpretation of Calamity From the View Point of Human Ecology* (Winchester, MA: Allen and Unwin).

HEYER, J. (1986), 'Poverty and Food Deprivation in Kenya's Smallholder Agricultural Areas', paper presented at a Conference on Food Strategies held at WIDER, Helsinki, 21–5 July 1986; to be published in Drèze, J. P., and Sen, A. K. (eds.) (forthcoming), *The Political Economy of Hunger*.

HILL, A. (ed.) (1985), *Population, Health and Nutrition in the Sahel* (London: Routledge and Kegan Paul).

—— (1987), 'Demographic Responses to Food Shortages in the Sahel', paper presented at the Expert Consultation on Population and Agricultural and Rural Development, FAO, Rome, June–July 1987.

HILL, K. (1988), 'Demographic Trends in China from 1950 to 1982', Discussion Paper No. 22, World Bank, Washington, DC.

HILL, P. (1970), *Studies in Rural Capitalism in West Africa* (Cambridge: Cambridge University Press).

—— (1975), 'The West African Farming Household', in Goody, J. (ed.) (1975), *Changing Social Structure in Ghana* (London: International Africa Institute).

—— (1986), *Development Economics on Trial: The Anthropological Case for a Prosecution* (Cambridge: Cambridge University Press).

HILSUM, L. (1984), 'Ethiopia: Coping with Drought: Cash Instead of Food', *Ideas Forum*, 18 (UNICEF).

HOBSBAWM, E. J. (1954), *Primitive Rebels* (Manchester: Manchester University Press).

HOEFFEL, P. H. (1986), 'Famine, Harvests Co-exist in Sahel', *Africa Emergency Report*, Feb.–Mar.: 3.

HOFFER, W. (ed.) (1980), *Formation des journalistes en Afrique: l'esquisse d'une vue d'ensemble* (Bonn: Fondation Friedrich Naumann).

HOJMAN, D. E. (1988), 'Infant Mortality in Chile: Issues in Employment, Welfare, Nutrition and Care from Import Substitution to the Neo-liberal Period', mimeo, Department of Economics, University of Liverpool; to be published in Abel, C., and Lewis, C. M. (eds.) (forthcoming), *Welfare, Equity and Development in Latin America* (London: Macmillan).

—— (1989), 'Neoliberal Economic Policies and Infant and Child Mortality: Simulation Analysis of a Chilean Paradox', *World Development*, 17.

HOLLAND, P. (1987), 'Famine Responses in Colonial Zimbabwe: 1912–1947', mimeo, London School of Economics.

HOLM, J. D., and COHEN, M. S. (1988), 'Enhancing Equity in the Midst of Drought: The Botswana Approach', *Journal of Social Development in Africa*, 3.

—— and MORGAN, R. (1985), 'Coping with Drought in Botswana: An African Success', *Journal of Modern African Studies*, 23.

HOLT, J. (1983), 'Ethiopia: Food for Work or Food for Relief', *Food Policy*, 8.

—— and SEAMAN, J. (1976), 'The Scope of the Drought', in Hussein, A. M. (ed.) (1976), *Rehab: Drought and Famine in Ethiopia*.

HOLTHE, K. (1986), 'Final Report', internal report, League of Red Cross and Red Crescent Societies, Khartoum.

HOPKINS, R. (1988), 'Political Considerations in Subsidizing Food', in Pinstrup-Andersen, P. (ed.) (1988), *Consumer-Oriented Food Subsidies: Costs, Benefits, and Policy Options for Developing Countries*.

—— and PUCHALA, D. J. (1978), *The Global Political Economy of Food* (Madison: University of Wisconsin Press).

HOROWITZ, M. M., and LITTLE, P. O. (1987), 'African Pastoralism and Poverty: Some Implications for Drought and Famine', in Glantz, M. (ed.) (1987), *Drought and Hunger in Africa*.

HOSKEN, F. P. (1981), 'Female Genital Mutilation in the World Today: A Global Review', *International Journal of Health Services*, 11.

HOSSAIN, I. (1988), 'Poverty as Capability Failure', mimeo, WIDER, Helsinki.

—— (1989), 'Measuring Undernourishment: Some Empirical Difficulties', mimeo, University of Stockholm.

HUDDLESTON, B. (1984), *Closing the Cereals Gap with Trade and Food Aid*, Research Report No. 43, International Food Policy Research Institute, Washington, DC.

HUGO, G. J. (1984), 'The Demographic Impact of Famine: A Review', in Currey, B., and Hugo, G. (eds.) (1984), *Famine as a Geographical Phenomenon*.

HULL, T. H. (1988), 'Implications of Rising Sex Ratios in China', mimeo, Australian National University.

HUSSAIN, A. (1987), 'Nutrition and Nutritional Insurance in China 1949–84', mimeo, London School of Economics.

—— and FEUCHTWANG, S. (1988), 'The People's Livelihood and the Incidence of Poverty', in Feuchtwang, S., et al. (eds.) (1988), Transforming China's Economy in the Eighties.

—— LIU, H., and LIU, X. (1989), 'Compendium of Literature on the Chinese Social Security System', Discussion Paper, Development Economics Research Programme, London School of Economics.

—— and STERN, N. H. (1988), 'On the Recent Increase in Death Rates in China', mimeo, London School of Economics.

HUSSEIN, A. M. (ed.) (1976), Rehab: Drought and Famine in Ethiopia (London: International Africa Institute).

IDACHABA, F. S. (1986), 'Policy Options for African Agriculture', paper presented at a Conference on Food Strategies held at WIDER, Helsinki, 21–5 July 1986; to be published in Drèze, J. P., and Sen, A. K. (eds.) (forthcoming), The Political Economy of Hunger.

—— (1987), 'Sustainability Issues in Agricultural Development', invited symposium lecture presented at the Seventh Agriculture Symposium, Agriculture and Rural Development, World Bank, Washington, DC.

IDS Bulletin (1985), Sub-Saharan Africa: Getting the Facts Straight, Vol. 16, No. 3.

ILIFFE, J. (1987), The African Poor: A History (Cambridge: Cambridge University Press).

ILLANES, J. P. (1984), 'Desarrollo social e indicadores de salud', Documento de Trabajo No. 27, Centro de Estudios Públicos, Santiago, Chile.

ILO (1981), Women in the Indian Labour Force (Bangkok: ILO-ARTEP).

—— (1982a), Rural Development and Women in Asia (Geneva: ILO).

—— (1982b), Rural Women Workers in Asia (Geneva: ILO).

—— (1986), Economically Active Population Estimates and Projections, 1950–2025 (Geneva: ILO).

Independent Commission on International Humanitarian Issues (1985), Famine: A Man-Made Disaster? (London: Pan).

Institute of Social Studies (1979), Impact on Women Workers: Maharashtra Employment Guarantee Scheme—A Study (New Delhi: Institute of Social Studies).

Interfutures (1979), Facing the Future (Paris: OECD).

International Institute for Environment and Development (1986), Report on the African Emergency Relief Operation 1984–1986 (London: IIED).

International Social Security Association (1982), Medical Care under Social Security in Developing Countries (Geneva: ISSA).

ISENMAN, P. (1980), 'Basic Needs: The Case of Sri Lanka', World Development, 8.

—— (1987), 'A Comment on "Growth and Equity in Developing Countries: A Reinterpretation of the Sri Lankan Experience" by Bhalla and Glewwe', World Bank Economic Review, 1.

ISMAEL, J. S. (1982), Kuwait: Social Change in Historical Perspective (Syracuse, NY: Syracuse University Press).

JACKSON, A. J. K. (1976), 'The Family Entity and Famine Among the 19th Century

Akamba of Kenya: Social Responses to Environment Stress', *Journal of Family History*, 2.

JACKSON, T., and EADE, D. (1982), *Against the Grain: The Dilemma of Project Food Aid* (Oxford: OXFAM).

JACQUEMIN, J. C. (1985), 'Politiques de stabilisation par les investissements publics', unpublished Ph.D. thesis, Facultés des Sciences Economiques et Sociales, University of Namur, Belgium.

JAIN, A. K. (1985), 'Determinants of Regional Variations in Infant Mortality in Rural India', *Population Studies*, 39.

JAIN, D. (1980), *Women's Quest for Power* (Ghaziabad: Vikas).

—— and BANERJEE, N. (eds.) (1985), *Tyranny of the Household: Investigative Essays in Women's Work* (New Delhi: Vikas).

JAISWAL, N. K. (1978), *Droughts and Famines in India* (Hyderabad: National Institute of Rural Development).

JALÉE, P. (1965), *Le Pillage du Tiers-Monde* (Paris: Maspéro).

JAMESON, K. P. (1981), 'Socialist Cuba and the Intermediate Regimes of Jamaica and Guyana', *World Development*, 9.

—— and WILBER, C. K. (1981), 'Socialism and Development: Editors' Introduction', *World Development*, 9.

JAMISON, D. (1985), 'China's Health Care System: Policies, Organization, Inputs and Finance', in Halstead, S. B., *et al.* (eds.) (1985), *Good Health at Low Cost*.

—— and PIAZZA, A. (1987), 'China's Food and Nutrition Planning', in Gittinger, J. P., *et al.* (eds.) (1987), *Food Policy: Integrating Supply, Distribution and Consumption*.

—— and TROWBRIDGE, F. L. (1984), 'The Nutritional Status of Children in China: A Review of the Anthropometric Evidence', Population, Health and Nutrition Department Technical Note GEN 17, World Bank, Washington, DC.

—— EVANS, J., KING, T., PORTER, I., PRESCOTT, N., and PROST, A. (1984), *China: The Health Sector* (Washington, DC: World Bank).

JANSSON, K., HARRIS, M., and PENROSE, A. (1987), *The Ethiopian Famine* (London: Zed).

JARAMILLO, J. (1983), *Los problemas de la salud en Costa Rica* (San José, Costa Rica: Litografía Ambar).

JAYAWARDENA, K. (1986), *Feminism and Nationalism in the Third World* (London: Zed Press).

JAYAWARDENA, L. (1974), 'Sri Lanka', in Chenery, H., *et al.* (eds.) (1974), *Redistribution with Growth*.

—— (ed.) (forthcoming), *The Impact of the Global Recession on Living Standards*.

—— MAASLAND, A., and RADHAKRISHNAN, P. N. (1987), 'Sri Lanka', Country Study No. 15, WIDER Series on Stabilization and Adjustment Policies and Programmes, WIDER, Helsinki.

JAYNE, T. S., and WEBER, M. T. (1988), 'Market Reform and Food Security in Sub-Saharan Africa: A Review of Recent Experience', MSU International Development Working Paper, Department of Agricultural Economics, Michigan State University, East Lansing.

JELLIFFE, D. B., and JELLIFFE, E. F. P. (1971), 'The Effects of Starvation on the Function of the Family and of Society', in Blix, G., *et al.* (eds.) (1971), *Famine: Nutrition and Relief Operations in Times of Disaster*.

JIGGINS, J. (1986), 'Women and Seasonality: Coping with Crisis and Calamity', *IDS Bulletin*, 17.

JODHA, N. S. (1975), 'Famine and Famine Policies: Some Empirical Evidence', *Economic and Political Weekly*, 10.

—— (1978), 'Effectiveness of Farmers' Adjustment to Risk', *Economic and Political Weekly*, 13.

—— (1981), 'Role of Credit in Farmers' Adjustment Against Risk in Arid and Semi-arid Tropical Areas of India', *Economic and Political Weekly*, 16.

—— and MASCARENHAS, A. C. (1985), 'Adjustment in Self-Provisioning Societies', in Kates, R. W., Ausubel, J. H., and BERBERIAN, M. (eds.) (1985), *Climate Impact Assessment* (John Wiley and Sons).

JOEKES, S. (1987), *Women in the World Economy: An INSTRAW Study* (New York: Oxford University Press).

JOHNSON, D. G. (1988), 'Economic Reforms in the People's Republic of China', *Economic Development and Cultural Change*, 36.

JOHNSON, D. H., and ANDERSON, D. M. (eds.) (1988), *The Ecology of Survival: Case Studies from Northeast African History* (Boulder: Westview).

JOHNSON, S., and ZECKHAUSER, R. (1989), 'Robin Hooding Rents: A New Case for In-Kind Redistribution', mimeo, Kennedy School of Government, Harvard University.

JOLLY, R. (1985), *Adjustment with a Human Face*, Barbara Ward Lecture (New York: UNICEF).

—— and CORNIA, G. A. (eds.) (1984), *The Impact of World Recession on Children* (Oxford: Pergamon).

JONES, L. P., and SAKONG, I. (1980), *Government, Business and Entrepreneurship in Economic Development: The Korean Case* (Cambridge, MA: Harvard University Press).

JONES, W. O. (1988), 'Agricultural Trade within Tropical Africa: Historical Background', in Bates and Lofchie (1980), *Agricultural Development in Africa*.

JORGENSON, D. W., and SLESNICK, D. T. (1987), 'Redistributional Policy and the Measurement of Poverty', paper presented at a Conference on Poverty, Undernutrition and Living Standards held at WIDER, Helsinki, July 1987.

JOSE, A. J. (1984), 'Poverty and Inequality: The Case of Kerala', in Khan, A. R., and Lee, E. (eds.) (1984), *Poverty in Rural Asia*.

JOWETT, A. J. (1988), 'Famine in the People's Republic of China', Occasional Paper No. 21, Geography Department, Glasgow University.

JOYNATHSINGH, M. (1987), 'Mauritius', in Dixon, J. (ed.) (1987), *Social Welfare in Africa* (London: Croom Helm).

KABEER, N. (1989), 'Monitoring Poverty as if Gender Mattered: A Methodology for Rural Bangladesh', Discussion Paper No. 255, Institute of Development Studies, University of Sussex.

KADYAMPAKENI, J. (1988), 'Pricing Policies in Africa with Special Reference to Agricultural Development in-Malawi', *World Development*, 16.

Kakwani, N. (1985), *Income Inequality and Poverty* (New York: Oxford University Press).

——(1986), 'On Measuring Undernutrition', Working Paper No. 8, WIDER, Helsinki.

—— (1988), 'Economic Crisis in the 1980s and Living Standards in Eighty Developing Countries', mimeo, WIDER, Helsinki.

KALAI, E., and SMORDINSKY, M. (1975), 'Other Solutions to Nash's Bargaining Problem', *Econometrica*, 43.

KAMAU, C. M., GITAU, M., WAINAINA, M., ANYANGO, G. J., and DOWNING, T. E. (forthcoming), 'Case Studies of Drought Impacts and Responses in Central and Eastern Kenya', to be published in Downing, T. E., *et al.* (eds.) (forthcoming), *Coping with Drought in Kenya: National and Local Strategies.*

KANBUR, S. M. R. (RAVI) (1986a), 'Global Food Balances and Individual Hunger: Three Themes in an Entitlements Based Approach', paper presented at a Conference on Food Strategies held at WIDER, Helsinki, 21–5 July 1986; to be published in Drèze, J. P., and Sen, A. K. (eds.) (forthcoming), *The Political Economy of Hunger.*

—— (1986b), 'Malnutrition and Poverty in Latin America', mimeo, WIDER, Helsinki; to be published in Drèzè, J. P., and Sen, A. K. (eds.) (forthcoming), *The Political Economy of Hunger.*

—— (1987), 'The Standard of Living: Uncertainty, Inequality and Opportunity', in Sen, A. K. (1987a), *The Standard of Living.*

KANDIYOTI, D. (1988), 'Bargaining With Patriarchy', *Gender and Society*, 1.

KANEKO, M., and NAKAMURA, K. (1979), 'The Nash Social Welfare Function', *Econometrica*, 47.

KAPLAN, R. (1988), *Surrender or Starve: The Wars Behind the Famine* (Boulder: Westview).

Kasongo Project Team (1983), 'Anthropometric Assessment of Young Children's Nutritional Status as an Indicator of the Subsequent Risk of Dying', *Journal of Tropical Pediatrics*, 29.

KATES, R. (1980), 'Disaster Reduction: Links Between Disaster and Development', in Berry, L., and Kates, R. (eds.) (1980), *Making the Most of the Least.*

—— (1981), 'Drought Impact in the Sahelian–Sudanic Zone of West Africa: A Comparative Analysis of 1910–1915 and 1968–1974', Environment and Development Background Paper No. 2, Center for Technology IDS, Clark University.

—— CHEN, R. S., DOWNING, T. E., KASPERSON, J. X., MESSER, E., and MILLMAN, S. R. (1988), 'The Hunger Report 1988', The Alan Shawn Feinstein World Hunger Program, Brown University, Providence.

KEEN, D. (1988), 'Some Problems with Targeting Emergency Grain in Western Sudan, 1985', paper presented at a Workshop on Food Security in the Sudan held at the Institute of Development Studies, University of Sussex, Oct. 1988 (revised version).

KELEMEN, P. (1985), 'The Politics of the Famine in Ethiopia and Eritrea', Occasional Paper No. 17, Department of Sociology, University of Manchester.

KELKAR, G. (1989), '. . . Two Steps Back? New Agricultural Policies in Rural China and the Woman Question', in Agarwal, B. (ed.) (1989), *Structures of Patriarchy.*

KELLMAN, M. H. (1987), *World Hunger: A Neo-Malthusian Perspective* (New York: Praeger).

KELLY, C. (1987), 'The Situation in Burkina Faso', *Disasters*, 11.

KENNEDY, E., and ALDERMAN, H. (1987), *Comparative Analysis of Nutritional Effectiveness of Food Subsidies and Other Food Related Interventions* (Washington, DC: IFPRI, and New York: UNICEF).

—— and COGILL, B. (1987), 'Income and Nutritional Effects of the Commercialization of Agriculture in South-Western Kenya', Research Report No. 63, International Food Policy Research Institute, Washington, DC.

—— and KNUDSEN, O. (1985), 'A Review of Supplementary Feeding Programmes and Recommendations on their Design', in Pinstrup-Andersen, P., and Biswas, M. (eds.) (1985), *Nutrition and Development*.

KHAN, A. R. (1977), 'Poverty and Inequality in Rural Bangladesh', in Griffin, K., and Khan, A. R. (1977), *Poverty and Landlessness in Rural Asia* (Geneva: ILO).

KHAN, Q. M. (1985), 'A Model of Endowment Constrained Demand for Food in Agricultural Economy with Empirical Applications to Bangladesh', *World Development*, 13.

KHARE, R. S. (1986), 'The Indian Meal: Aspects of Cultural Economy and Food Use', in Khare, R. S., and Rao, M. S. A. (eds.) (1986), *Food, Society and Culture*.

—— and RAO, M. S. A. (eds.) (1986), *Food, Society and Culture* (Durham, NC: Carolina Academic Press).

KIELMAN, A. A., AJELLO, C. A., and KIELMAN, N. S. (1982), 'Nutrition Intervention: An Evaluation of Six Studies', *Studies in Family Planning*, 13.

—— et al. (eds.) (1983), *Child and Maternal Health Services in Rural India: The Narangwal Experiment*, i (Baltimore: Johns Hopkins).

KILBY, P., and LIEDHOLM, C. (1988), 'The Role of Nonfarm Activities in the Rural Economy', in Rukuni, M., and Bernsten, R. H. (eds.) (1988), *Southern Africa: Food Security Policy Options*.

KILJUNEN, K. (ed.) (1984), *Kampuchea: Decade of the Genocide* (London: Zed).

KIM, W. S., and YUN, K. Y. (1988), 'Fiscal Policy and Development in Korea', *World Development*, 16.

KING, A. Y. C., and LEE, R. P. L. (eds.) (1981), *Social Life and Development in Hong Kong* (Hong Kong: The Chinese University Press).

KLEIN, I. (1973), 'Death in India, 1871–1921', *Journal of Asian Studies*, 32.

—— (1984), 'When the Rains Failed: Famine, Relief and Mortality in British India', *Indian Economic and Social History Review*, 21.

KOO, H. (1984), 'The Political Economy of Income Distribution in South Korea: The Impact of the State's Industrialization Policies', *World Development*, 12.

KOOHI-KAMALI, F. (1988), 'The Pattern of Female Mortality in Iran and Some of its Causes', Applied Economics Discussion Paper No. 62, Institute of Economics and Statistics, Oxford.

KOPONEN, J. (1988), 'War, Famine, and Pestilence in Late Precolonial Tanzania: A Case for Heightened Mortality', *International Journal of African Historical Studies*, 21.

KOSO-THOMAS, O. (1987), *The Circumcision of Women: A Strategy for Eradication* (London: Zed).

KRAUSE, L. B. (1988), 'Hong Kong and Singapore: Twins or Kissing Cousins?', *Economic Development and Cultural Change*, 36.

KRISHNA, RAJ (1963), 'Farm Supply Response in India-Pakistan: A Case Study of the Punjab Region', *Economic Journal*, 73.

KRISHNAJI, N. (1987), 'Poverty and Sex Ratio: Some Data and Speculations', *Economic and Political Weekly*, 22.

KRISHNAMACHARI, K. A. V. R., RAO, N. P., and RAO, K. V. (1974), 'Food and

Nutritional Situation in the Drought Affected Areas of Maharashtra: A Survey and Recommendations', *Indian Journal of Nutrition and Dietetics*, 11.

KRISHNAN, T. N. (1985), 'Health Statistics in Kerala State, India', in Halstead, S. B., et al. (eds.) (1985), *Good Health at Low Cost*.

—— (1989), 'Kerala's Health Transition: Facts and Factors', mimeo, Center for Population Studies, Harvard University.

KULA, E. (1988), 'The Inadequacy of the Entitlement Approach to Explain and Remedy Famines', *Journal of Development Studies*, 25.

—— (1989), 'Politics, Economics, Agriculture and Famines', *Food Policy*, 14.

KULKARNI, S. N. (1974), *Survey of Famine Affected Sinnar Taluka* (Pune: Gokhale Institute of Politics and Economics).

KUMAR, B. G. (1985), 'The Ethiopian Famine and Relief Measures: An Analysis and Evaluation', mimeo, UNICEF.

—— (1986), 'Ethiopian Famines 1973–1985: A Case Study', paper presented at a Conference on Food Strategies held at WIDER, Helsinki, 21–5 July 1986; Working Paper No. 26, WIDER, 1987; to be published in Drèze, J. P., and Sen, A. K. (eds.) (forthcoming), *The Political Economy of Hunger*.

—— (1987), 'Poverty and Public Policy: Government Intervention and Levels of Living in Kerala, India', unpublished Ph.D. thesis, University of Oxford.

—— (1988), 'Consumption Disparities, Food Surpluses and Effective Demand Failures: Reflections on the Macroeconomics of Drought Vulnerability', Working Paper No. 229, Centre for Development Studies, Trivandrum.

—— and STEWART, F. (1987), 'Tackling Malnutrition: What Can Targeted Nutritional Intervention Achieve?', paper presented at a Conference on Poverty in India, Queen Elizabeth House, Oxford, Oct. 1987.

KUMAR, S. K. (1979), 'Impact of Subsidised Rice on Food Consumption and Nutrition in Kerala', Research Report No. 5, International Food Policy Research Institute, Washington, DC.

—— and LIPTON, M. (1988), 'Editors' Introduction', *World Development*, 16.

KUZNETS, P. W. (1988), 'An East Asian Model of Economic Development: Japan, Taiwan, and South Korea', *Economic Development and Cultural Change*, 36.

KUZNETS, S. (1966), *Modern Economic Growth* (New Haven: Yale University Press).

KYNCH, J. (1985), 'How Many Women are Enough? Sex Ratios and the Right to Life', in *Third World Affairs 1985* (London: Third World Foundation).

—— (1987a), 'Food Scarcity and Jail Population in British India', mimeo, Institute of Economics and Statistics, Oxford.

—— (1987b), 'Some State Responses to Male and Female Need in British India', in Afshar, H. (ed.) (1987), *Women, State and Ideology: Studies from Africa and Asia*.

—— (1988), 'Scarcities, Distress and Crime in British India', paper presented at the 7th World Congress of Rural Sociology, Bologna, July 1988.

—— and SEN, A. K. (1983), 'Indian Women: Well-Being and Survival', *Cambridge Journal of Economics*, 7.

LABONNE, M. (1984a), *Sur la question alimentaire en Afrique* (Paris: Institut National de la Recherche Agronomique).

—— (1984b), *Origines et perspectives de la crise alimentaire dans les pays du Sahel* (Paris: Institut National de la Recherche Agronomique).

LADEJINSKI, W. (1973), 'Drought in Maharashtra: Not in a Hundred Years', *Economic and Political Weekly*, 17 Feb.

LAL, D. (1983), *The Poverty of 'Development Economics'* (London: Institute of Economic Affairs).

LALLEMAND, S. (1975), 'La Sécheresse dans un village Mossi de Haute-Volta', in Copans, J., *et al.* (1975), *Sécheresses et famines du Sahel.*

LANDMAN, J., and WALKER, S. (1987), 'Towards Food and Nutrition Security in Jamaica: The Nutrition Perspective', in Leslie, K. A., and Rankine, L. B. (eds.) (1987), *Papers and Recommendations of the Workshop on Food and Nutrition Security in Jamaica in the 1980s and Beyond.*

LANGFORD, C. (1984), 'Sex Differentials in Mortality in Sri Lanka: Changes since the 1920s', *Journal of Bio-social Science*, 16.

—— (1988), 'Sex Differentials in Sri Lanka: Past Trends and the Situation Recently', mimeo, London School of Economics.

LANGSTEN, R., and CHOWDHURY, S. A. (1984), 'The Demographic Effects of Famine in Contemporary Bangladesh', mimeo, Carolina Population Center, University of North Carolina.

LAPPÉ, F. M., and COLLINS, J. (1979), *World Hunger: Ten Myths* (London: IFDP).

—— —— (1980), *Food First: The Myth of Scarcity* (London: Souvenir Press).

LARDINOIS, R. (1982), 'Une conjoncture de crise démographique en Inde du Sud au XIXe siècle: la famine de 1876–1878', *Population*, 37.

—— (1985), 'Famine, Epidemics and Mortality in South India', *Economic and Political Weekly*, 20.

—— (1987), 'Population, famines et marché dans l'historiographie indienne', *Annales économies, sociétés, civilisations*, 3.

LAWRENCE, P. (ed.) (1986), *World Recession and the Food Crisis in Africa* (London: James Currey).

League of Red Cross and Red Crescent Societies (1986), 'The Red Cross Policy on the Nutritional Aspects of Relief Operations', Resolution passed at the XXVth International Conference of the Red Cross, Geneva, Oct. 1986.

LEE, R. D., ARTHUR, W. B., KELLEY, A. C., RODGERS, G., and SRINIVASAN, T. N. (eds.) (1988), *Population, Food and Rural Development* (Oxford: Clarendon Press).

LEE, R. P. L. (1982), 'Comparative Studies of Health Care Systems', *Social Science and Medicine*, 16.

—— (1983), 'Problems of Primary Health Care in a Newly Developing Society: Reflections on the Hong Kong Experience', *Social Science and Medicine*, 17.

LEFTWICH, A., and HARVIE, D. (1986), 'The Political Economy of Famine', Discussion Paper No. 116, Institute for Research in the Social Sciences, University of York.

LEGAL, P. Y. (1984), 'Alimentation et énergie dans le développement rural en Cabo Verde', Série Énergie, Alimentation et Développement, No. 2, Centre International de Recherche sur l'Environnement et le Développement, École des Hautes Études en Sciences Sociales, Paris.

LEGRAIN, C. (1980), 'Nutrition et santé des enfants aux Îles du Cap Vert', *Environnement africain*, Nos. 14, 15, 16, ENDA, Dakar.

LEITINGER, I. A. (1985), 'Women's Legal Status and Role Choices in Six Latin American Countries: A Cross-Cultural Longitudinal Analysis (1950–70) and a Single-Case Update (1980)', Working Paper No. 91, Office of Women in International Development, Michigan State University.

LELE, U., and CANDLER, W. (1984), 'Food Security in Developing Countries: National Issues', in Eicher, C. K., and Staatz, J. M. (eds.) (1984), *Agricultural Development in the Third World*.

LEONTIEF, W., *et al.* (1977), *The Future of the World Economy* (New York: Oxford University Press).

LESLIE, J. (1987), 'Interactions of Malnutrition and Diarrhoea: A Review of Research', in Gittinger, J. P., *et al.* (eds.) (1987), *Food Policy*.

—— (1988), 'Women's Work and Child Nutrition in the Third World', *World Development*, 16.

LESLIE, K. A., and RANKINE, L. B. (eds.) (1987), *Papers and Recommendations of the Workshop on Food and Nutrition Security in Jamaica in the 1980s and Beyond* (Kingston: Caribbean Food and Nutrition Institute).

LESOURD, M. (1986), 'Sécheresse et émigration aux Îles du Cap Vert', paper presented at a conference on 'Comparaison des sécheresses dans le Nordeste brésilien et le Sahel africain', IHEAL, Paris, Jan. 1986.

LEVINE, R. A. (1988), 'Women's Schooling and Patterns of Fertility and Child Survival', mimeo, forthcoming in *Educational Research*.

LEVINSON, F. J. (1972), *Morinda: An Economic Analysis of Malnutrition Among Young Children in Rural India* (Cambridge, MA and Ithaca, NY: MIT/Cornell University Press).

LEYS, R. (1986), 'Drought and Drought Relief in Southern Zimbabwe', in Lawrence, P. (ed.) (1986), *World Recession and the Food Crisis in Africa*.

LI, L. (1982a), 'Food, Famine and the Chinese State', *Journal of Asian Studies*, 41.

—— (1982b), 'Feeding China's One Billion: Perspectives from History' in Cahill, K. (ed.) (1982), *Famine*.

—— (1987), 'Famine and Famine Relief: Viewing Africa in the 1980s from China in the 1920s', in Glantz, M. (ed.) (1987a), *Drought and Hunger in Africa*.

LIEBERMAN, S. S. (1984), 'An Organisational Reconnaissance of the Employment Guarantee Scheme', *Indian Journal of Public Administration*, 30.

—— (1985), 'Field-Level Perspectives on Maharashtra's Employment Guarantee Scheme', *Public Administration and Development*, 5.

LIEDHOLM, C., and KILBY, P. (1989), 'The Role of Non-Farm Activities in the Rural Economy', in Williamson, J. G., and Panchamukhi, V. R. (eds.) (1989), *Balance Between Industry and Agriculture in Economic Development*, ii: *Sector Proportions* (London: Macmillan).

LIN, T. B., LEE, R. P. L., and SIMONIS, U. (eds.) (1979), *Hong Kong: Economic, Social and Political Studies in Development* (New York: M. E. Sharpe).

LINNEMANN, H. (1981), *MOIRA: A Model of International Relations in Agriculture* (Amsterdam: North Holland).

LIPTON, M. (1977), *Why Poor People Stay Poor: Urban Bias in World Development* (London: Temple Smith).

—— (1983), 'Poverty, Undernutrition and Hunger', World Bank Staff Working Paper No. 597, World Bank, Washington, DC.

—— (1986), 'Food Production Data: Does Anyone Care?', paper presented at a Workshop on Statistics in Support of African Food Policies and Strategies, Brussels, May 1986.

—— (1987a), 'Limits of Price Policy for Agriculture: Which Way for the World Bank?', *Development Policy Review*, 5.

—— (1987*b*), 'Variable Access to Food', in Gittinger, J. P., *et al.* (eds.) (1987), *Food Policy*.

—— (1988*a*), 'The Poor and the Poorest: Some Interim Findings', World Bank Discussion Paper No. 25, World Bank, Washington, DC.

—— (1988*b*), 'A Rejoinder to Ray', *Development Policy Review*, 6.

—— (1988*c*), 'The Place of Agricultural Research in the Development of Sub-Saharan Africa', *World Development*, 16.

LITTLE, I. (1982), *Economic Development* (New York: Basic Books).

LITTLE, P. O., and HOROWITZ, M. M. (1987), 'Subsistence Crops *Are* Cash Crops: Some Comments with Reference to Eastern Africa', *Human Organization*, 46.

LLOYD, C. B., and NIEMI, B. T. (1979), *The Economics of Sex Differentials* (New York: Columbia University Press).

LOEWENSON, R. (1984), 'The Health Status of Labour Communities in Zimbabwe: An Argument for Equity', dissertation presented for the M.Sc. Degree in Community Health in Developing Countries, University of London.

—— (1986), 'Farm Labour in Zimbabwe: A Comparative Study in Health Status', *Health Policy and Planning*, 1.

—— and SANDERS, D. (1988), 'The Political Economy of Health and Nutrition', in Stoneman, C. (ed.) (1988), *Zimbabwe's Prospects: Issues of Race, Class, State and Capital in Southern Africa*.

LOFCHIE, M. F. (1975), 'The Political and Economic Origin of African Hunger', *Journal of Modern African Studies*, 13.

—— (1987), 'The Decline of African Agriculture: An Internationalist Perspective', in Glantz, M. (ed.) (1987*a*), *Drought and Hunger in Africa*.

—— and COMMINS, S. E. (1982), 'Food Deficits and Agricultural Policies in Tropical Africa', *Journal of Modern African Studies*, 20.

LOMBARD, J. (1985), *Disponibilités alimentaires en céréales et stratégies de survie en pays Serer* (Dakar: ORSTOM).

LONGHURST, R. (1986), 'Household Food Strategies in Response to Seasonality and Famine', *IDS Bulletin*, 17.

—— (1987), 'Famines, Food and Nutrition: Issues and Opportunities for Policy and Research', *Food and Nutrition Bulletin*, 9.

—— (1988), 'Cash Crops, Household Food Security and Nutrition', *IDS Bulletin*, 19.

LOPEZ, A. D. (1983), 'The Sex Mortality Differentials in Developed Countries', in Lopez, A. D., and Ruzicka, L. T. (eds.) (1983), *Sex Differentials in Mortality: Trends, Determinants and Consequences*.

—— and RUZICKA, L. T. (eds.) (1983), *Sex Differentials in Mortality: Trends, Determinants and Consequences* (Canberra: Australian National University).

LOUTFI, M. F. (1980), *Rural Women: Unequal Partners in Development* (Geneva: ILO).

LOVEDAY, A. (1914), *The History and Economics of Indian Famines* (London: A. G. Bell and Sons; reprinted by Usha Publications, New Delhi, 1985).

LOWGREN, M. (1985), 'A Nutritional Sejour to Africa', mimeo, League of Red Cross and Red Crescent Societies.

LUGAN, B. (1976), 'Causes et effets de la famine "Ramanura" au Rwanda, 1916–18', *Canadian Journal of African Studies*, 10.

LUNDAHL, M. (1983), 'Insuring Against Risk in Primitive Economies: The Role of Prestige Goods', in Söderström, L. (ed.) (1983), *Social Insurance*.

LUTHRA, S., and SRINIVAS, S. (1976), 'Famine in India: A Select Bibliography', mimeo, Social Science Documentation Centre, New Delhi.

MCALPIN, M. (1983a), *Subject to Famine: Food Crises and Economic Change in Western India, 1860–1920* (Princeton: Princeton University Press).

—— (1983b), 'Famine, Epidemics, and Population Growth: The Case of India', in Rotberg, R. I., and Rabb, T. K. (eds.) (1983), *Hunger and History*.

—— (1987): 'Famine Relief Policy in India: Six Lessons for Africa', in Glantz, M., (ed.) (1987a), *Drought and Hunger in Africa*.

MCCANN, J. (1987), 'The Social Impact of Drought in Ethiopia: Oxen, Households, and Some Implications for Rehabilitation', in Glantz, M. (ed.) (1987a), *Drought and Hunger in Africa*.

MCCORKLE, C. (1987), 'Foodgrain Disposals as Early Warning Famine Signals: A Case From Burkina Faso', *Disasters*, 11.

MCCRINDLE, J. W. (1877), translation of *Ancient India* by Megasthenes.

—— (1901): *Ancient India as Described in Classical Literature* (Westminster: Constable and Co. Ltd.).

MCELROY, M. B., and HORNEY, M. J. (1981), 'Nash Bargained Household Decisions: Toward a Generalization of Theory of Demand', *International Economic Review*, 22.

MCGINN, N. F., SNODGRASS, D. R., KIM, Y. B., KOM, S. B., and QUEE-YOUNG (1980), *Education and Development in Korea* (Cambridge, MA: Harvard University Press).

MCHENRY, D. F., and BIRD, K. (1977), 'Food Bungle in Bangladesh', *Foreign Policy*, 27.

MCKEOWN, T. (1976), *The Modern Rise of Population* (London: Edward Arnold).

—— and LOWE, C. R. (1966), *An Introduction to Social Medicine* (Oxford: Blackwell).

MCKERROW, R. J. (1979), 'Drought in Ethiopia 1977/1979', *Disasters*, 3.

MACKINTOSH, M. (1985), 'Economic Tactics: Commercial Policy and the Socialization of African Agriculture', *World Development*, 13.

MCLEAN, W. (1986), 'A Profile of Mali with Focus on Current Food Shortages', mimeo, London School of Hygiene and Tropical Medicine.

—— (1987), 'Assessment of the Food Emergency in Mali 1983–85', paper presented at the 5th IDS Food Aid Seminar on The Use of Information in Emergencies, Apr. 1987.

—— (1988), 'Intervention Systems in Food Crises: The Role of International Agencies', paper presented at the Seventh International Congress for Rural Sociology, Bologna, Italy, June 1988.

MCNEILL, W. H. (1976), *Plagues and People* (Garden City, NY: Anchor Press).

MAGANDA, B. F. (forthcoming), 'Surveys and Activities of the Central Bureau of Statistics Related to Food Monitoring', to be published in Downing, T., *et al.* (eds.) (forthcoming), *Coping With Drought in Kenya: National and Local Strategies*.

MAHIEU, F. R., and NOUR, M. M. (1987), 'The Entitlement Approach to Famines and the Sahelian Case: A Survey of the Available Literature', mimeo, WIDER, Helsinki.

MAHMUD, W., and MAHMUD, S. (1985), 'Age–Sex Aspects of the Food and Nutrition Problems in Rural Bangladesh', ILO Working Paper, WEP10-6/WP74, Geneva.

MAKSUDOV, M. (1986), 'Ukraine's Demographic Losses 1927–1938', in Serbyn, R., and Krawchenko, B. (eds.) (1986), *Famine in Ukraine*.

MALENBAUM, W. (1956), 'India and China: Development Contrasts', *Journal of Political Economy*, 64.

—— (1959), 'India and China: Contrasts in Development Performance', *American Economic Review*, 49.

—— (1982), 'Modern Economic Growth in India and China: The Comparison Revisited, 1950–1980', *Economic Development and Cultural Change*, 31.

MALLET, A. (1980), 'Social Protection of the Rural Population', *International Social Security Review*, 33.

MALLORY, W. H. (1926), *China: Land of Famine* (New York: American Geographical Publishing Society).

MALTHUS, T. R. (1798), *Essay on the Principle of Population as it Affects the Future Improvement of Society* (London: J. Johnson).

—— (1800), *An Investigation of the Cause of the Present High Price of Provisions* (London).

MAMADOU, P. T. (1987*a*), 'Dans quelles mesures la place des individus détermine leur droit à la nourriture: example du pays Senoufo (nord Côte d'Ivoire)', mimeo, Université Nationale de Côte d'Ivoire, Abidjan.

—— (1987*b*), 'La Notion des droits, de la privation, de la pauvreté et de la famine chez les Natara Rouges—Senoufo du nord de la Côte d'Ivoire', mimeo, Université Nationale de Côte d'Ivoire, Abidjan.

MANDAZA, I. (ed.) (1986), *Zimbabwe: The Political Economy of Transition 1980–1986* (Dakar: CODESRIA).

MANN, C. K., and HUDDLESTON, B. (eds.) (1986), *Food Policy: Frameworks for Analysis and Action* (Bloomington: Indiana University Press).

MANSER, M., and BROWN, M. (1980), 'Marriage and Household Decision Making: A Bargaining Analysis', *International Economic Review*, 21.

MANSERGH, N. (ed.) (1971), *The Transfer of Power 1942–7*, iii (London: HMSO).

—— (ed.) (1973), *The Transfer of Power 1942–7*, iv (London: HMSO).

MAO ZEDONG (TSE-TUNG) (1974), *Mao Tse-tung Unrehearsed, Talks and Letters: 1956–71* (London: Penguin Books).

MARCHIONE, T. J. (1977), 'Food and Nutrition in Self-Reliant National Development: The Impact on Child Nutrition of Jamaica Government Policy', *Medical Anthropology*, 1.

—— (1984), 'Evaluating Primary Health Care and Nutrition Programmes in the Context of National Development', *Social Science and Medicine*, 19.

MARGLIN, F. (1986), 'An Anthropological View on Food, Hunger and Poverty', paper presented at a conference on Food Strategies held at WIDER, Helsinki, July 1986.

MARGLIN, S. (1976), *Value and Price in the Labour-Surplus Economy* (Oxford: Clarendon).

MARI BHAT, P. N. (forthcoming), 'Mortality and Fertility in India, 1881–1961', to be published in Dyson, T. (ed.) (forthcoming), *India's Historical Demography: Studies in Famine, Disease and Society* (London: Curzon Press).

MARRACK, J. R. (1947), 'Investigations of Human Nutrition in the United Kingdom During the War', *Proceedings of the Nutrition Society*, 5.

MARTORELL, R. (1987), 'Body Size, Adaptation, and Function', paper presented at the 86th Annual Meeting of the American Anthropological Association, Nov. 1987, Chicago.

—— and SHARMA, R. (1985), 'Trends in Nutrition, Food Supply and Mortality Rates', in Halstead, S. B., *et al.* (eds.) (1985), *Good Health at Low Cost*.

MARX, K. (1844), *The Economic and Philosophic Manuscript of 1844*, English translation (London: Lawrence and Wishart).

—— (1852), *The 18th Brumaire of Louis Bonaparte* (2nd ed. 1869).

—— (1857–8), *Grundrisse der Kritik der politischen Okonomie*; 1939 and 1941 (Moscow: Marx-Engels-Lenin Institute); English trans. by M. Nicolaus (1973): *Grundrisse: Foundations of the Critique of Political Economy* (Harmondsworth: Penguin); also part trans. with supplementary texts of Marx and Engels, and with an Introduction by Eric Hobsbawm (1964), *Pre-Capitalist Economic Formations* (London: Lawrence and Wishart).

—— (1875), *Critique of the Gotha Programme*, English trans. (New York: International Publishers).

—— (1887), *Capital: A Critical Analysis of Capitalist Production*; English trans. by S. Moore and E. Aveling; edited by F. Engels (London: Sonnenschein; republished by Allen and Unwin, 1938).

MASEFIELD, G. B. (1963), *Famine: Its Prevention and Relief* (Oxford: Oxford University Press).

MASON, J. B., HABICHT, J. P., TABATABAI, H., and VALVERDE, V. (1984), *Nutritional Surveillance* (Geneva: World Health Organization).

—— HAAGA, J. G., MARKS, G., QUINN, V., TEST, K., and MARIBE, T. (1985), 'Using Agricultural Data for Timely Warning to Prevent the Effects of Drought on Child Nutrition: An Analysis of Historical Data from Botswana', mimeo, Cornell University Agricultural Experiment Station.

MASON, L., and BROWN, R. (1983), *Rice, Rivalry and Politics* (Notre Dame: University of Notre Dame Press).

MATA, L. (1978), *The Children of Santa Maria Cauque: A Prospective Field Study of Health and Growth* (Cambridge, MA: MIT Press).

—— (1985), 'The Fight Against Diarrhoeal Diseases: The Case of Costa Rica', in Vallin, J., and Lopez, A. D. (eds.) (1985), *Health Policy, Social Policy and Mortality Prospects*.

—— and ROSERO, L. (1988), 'National Health and Social Development in Costa Rica: A Case Study of Intersectoral Action', Technical Paper No. 13, Pan American Health Organization, Washington, DC.

MATHUR, K., and BHATTACHARYA, M. (1975), *Administrative Response to Emergency: A Study of Scarcity Administration in Maharashtra* (New Delhi: Concept).

MATIZA, T., ZINYAMA, L. M., and CAMPBELL, D. J. (1988), 'Household Strategies for Coping with Food Insecurity in Low Rainfall Areas of Zimbabwe', paper presented at the Fourth Annual Conference on Food Security Research in Southern Africa, Oct.–Nov. 1988, Harare, Zimbabwe.

MATTHEWS, A. (1988), 'Growth and Employment Considerations in the Food vs. Export Crops Debate', *IDS Bulletin*, 19.

MAXWELL, S. (1978a), 'Food Aid, Food For Work and Public Works', Discussion Paper No. 127, Institute of Development Studies, University of Sussex.

—— (1978b), 'Food Aid for Supplementary Feeding Programs: An Analysis', *Food Policy*, 4.

—— (1988), 'Editorial', *IDS Bulletin*, 19.

—— and Fernando, A. (1987), 'Cash Crops in Developing Countries: The Issues, the Facts, the Policies', paper presented at a Workshop on Cash Crops held at the Institute of Development Studies, University of Sussex, 5–6 Jan. 1987.

MAYER, J. (1974), 'Coping with Famine', *Foreign Affairs*, 53.
—— (1975), 'Management of Famine Relief', in Abelson, P. H. (ed.) (1975), *Food: Politics, Economics, Nutrition and Research*.
MAYOUX, L. (1988), 'Income Generation for Women in West Bengal', mimeo, University of Cambridge.
MAZUMDAR, V. (1985), *Emergence of Women's Questions in India and the Role of Women's Studies* (New Delhi: Centre for Women's Development Studies).
MBITHI, P., and WISNER, B. (1972), *Drought and Famine in Kenya: Magnitude and Attempted Solutions* (Nairobi: Institute for Development Studies).
MEADE, J. E., *et al.* (1968), *The Economic and Social Structure of Mauritius* (London: Frank Cass).
MEADOWS, D. N., *et al.* (1972), *The Limits to Growth* (Washington, DC: Potomac).
MEDINA, E., and KAEMPFFER, A. (1982), 'La salud en Chile durante la década del setenta', *Revista Médica de Chile*, 110.
MEEGAMA, S. A. (1985), 'The Mortality Decline in the "Fast-Declining" Countries', in *International Population Conference, Florence, 1985*, ii (Liège: International Union for the Scientific Study of Population).
MEHTA, S. R. (1981), *Social Development in Mauritius* (New Delhi: Wiley).
MEIER, G., and STEEL, W. F. (eds.) (1987), *Industrial Adjustment in Sub-Saharan Africa* (Washington, DC: Economic Development Institute, World Bank).
MEILLASSOUX, C. (1974), 'Development or Exploitation: Is the Sahel Famine Good Business?', *Review of African Political Economy*, 1.
—— (1976), *Femmes, greniers et capitaux* (Paris: Maspéro).
MEINTEL, D. (1983), 'Cape Verde: Survival Without Self-Sufficiency', in Cohen, R. (ed.) (1983), *African Islands and Enclaves* (Beverley Hills: Sage).
—— (1984), *Race, Culture and Portuguese Colonialism in Cape Verde*, Foreign and Comparative Studies, African Series 41, Maxwell School of Citizenship and Public Affairs, Syracuse University.
MELLOR, J. W., and AHMED, R. (eds.) (1988), *Agricultural Price Policy for Developing Countries* (Baltimore: Johns Hopkins).
—— DELGADO, C. L., and BLACKIE, C. L. (eds.) (1987), *Accelerating Food Production in Sub-Saharan Africa* (Baltimore: Johns Hopkins).
—— and DESAI, G. (eds.) (1985), *Agricultural Change and Rural Poverty: Variations on a Theme by Dharam Narain* (Baltimore: Johns Hopkins).
—— and JOHNSTON, B. (1984), 'The World Food Equation: Interrelationships Among Development, Employment and Food Consumption', *Journal of Economic Literature*, 22.
MELVILLE, B., LAWRENCE, O., WILLIAMS, M., FRANCIS, V., COLLINS, L., and ARCHER, E. (1988), 'Childhood Malnutrition in Three Ecological Zones in Western Jamaica', *Ecology of Food and Nutrition*, 20.
—— WILLIAMS, M., FRANCIS, V., LAWRENCE, O., and COLLINS, L. (1988), 'Determinants of Childhood Malnutrition in Jamaica', *Food and Nutrition Bulletin*, 10.
MENCHER, J. (1980), 'The Lessons and Non-lessons of Kerala: Agricultural Labourers and Poverty', *Economic and Political Weekly*, 15.
—— (1988), 'Peasants and Agricultural Labourers: An Analytical Assessment of Issues Involved in Their Organizing', in Srinivasan, T. N., and Bardhan, P. K. (eds.) (1988), *Rural Poverty in South Asia*.

MENDEZ, J. C. (ed.) (1979), *Chilean Economic Policy* (Santiago: Budget Directorate, Government of Chile).

—— (1980), *Chilean Socio Economic Overview* (Santiago: Budget Directorate, Government of Chile).

MESA-LAGO, C. (1969), 'Availability and Reliability of Statistics in Socialist Cuba', *Latin American Research Review*, 4.

—— (1971), 'Cuba: teoría y práctica de los incentives', Occasional Paper No. 7, Center for Latin American Studies, University of Pittsburgh.

—— (1978), *Social Security in Latin America* (Pittsburgh: University of Pittsburgh Press).

—— (1979), 'Cuban Statistics Revisited', *Cuban Studies*, 9.

—— (1983a), 'Social Security and Extreme Poverty in Latin America', *Journal of Development Economics*, 12.

—— (1983b), *La economía en Cuba socialista: una evaluacíon de dos décadas* (New Mexico: University of New Mexico Press).

—— (1985a), 'Health Care in Costa Rica: Boom and Crisis', *Social Science and Medicine*, 21.

—— (1985b), *El desarrollo de la seguridad social en América Latina*, Estudios e Informes de la CEPAL, Naciones Unidos, Santiago, Chile.

—— (ed.) (1985c), *The Crisis of Social Security and Health Care*, Latin American Monograph and Document Series, No. 9, Center for Latin American Studies, University of Pittsburgh.

—— (1985d), 'Alternative Strategies to the Social Security Crisis: Socialist, Market and Mixed Approaches', in Mesa-Lago, C. (ed.) (1985c), *The Crisis of Social Security and Health Care*.

—— (1986), 'Comparative Study of the Development of Social Security in Latin America', *International Social Security Review*, 2.

—— (1988a), 'Social Insurance: The Experience of Three Countries in the English-Speaking Caribbean', *International Labour Review*, 127.

—— (1988b), 'Social Security in Latin America and the Caribbean', paper presented at a Workshop on Social Security in Developing Countries held at the London School of Economics, 4–5 July 1988; to be published in Ahmad, S. E., *et al.* (eds.) (forthcoming), *Social Security in Developing Countries*.

—— (1988c), 'Jamaica', unpublished report prepared for the International Labour Organization, Geneva.

—— and DIAZ-BRIQUETS (1988), 'Costa Rica y Cuba', *Annuario de estudios centro americano*, 14.

—— and PEREZ-LOPEZ, J. (1985), 'A Study of Cuba's Material Product System, Its Conversion to the System of National Accounts, and Estimation of Gross Domestic Product per Capita and Growth Rates', World Bank Staff Working Paper No. 770, World Bank, Washington, DC.

MESAROVIC, M. D., and PESTEL, E. (1974), *Mankind at Turning Point* (New York: Dutton).

MEUVRET, J. (1946), 'Les Crises de subsistance et la démographie de la France d'ancien régime', *Population*, 1.

MICHELL, T. (1988), *From a Developing to a Newly Industrialised Country: The Republic of Korea, 1961–82* (Geneva: ILO).

MIDGLEY, J. (1984a), *Social Security, Inequality and the Third World* (Chichester: Wiley).

—— (1984b), 'Social Assistance: An Alternative Form of Social Protection in Developing Countries', *International Social Security Review*, 3/84.

—— (1986), 'Industrialization and Welfare: The Case of the Four Little Tigers', *Social Policy and Administration*, 20.

MIES, M. (1982), *The Lace Makers of Narsapur: Indian Housewives Produce for the World Market* (London: Zed Press).

MILL, J. S. (1859), *On Liberty* (repr. Harmondsworth: Penguin, 1974).

MILLER, B. (1981), *The Endangered Sex: Neglect of Female Children in Rural North India* (Ithaca, NY: Cornell University Press).

MINHAS, B. (1974), *Planning and the Poor* (New Delhi: Chand & Co.).

—— JAIN, L. R., KANSAL, S. M., and SALUJA, M. R. (1987), 'On the Choice of Appropriate Consumer Price Indices and Data Sets for Estimating the Incidence of Poverty in India', *Indian Economic Review*, 22.

MINOGUE, M. (1983), 'Mauritius: Political, Economic and Social Development in a Small Island', *Manchester Papers on Development*, 8.

MITRA, ASHOK (1977), *Terms of Trade and Class Relations: An Essay in Political Economy* (London: Frank Cass).

MITRA, ASOKE (1980), *Implications of Declining Sex Ratios in India's Population* (Bombay: Allied Publishers).

MITTER, S. (1988), 'Managing the Drought Crisis: The Zimbabwe Experience, 1982–83', undergraduate essay, Harvard University.

MODY, N. (1972), 'To Some, a God-Send', *Economic and Political Weekly*, 23 Dec.

MOHS, E. (1983a), 'Infectious Diseases and Health in Costa Rica: The Development of a New Paradigm', *Pediatric Infectious Diseases*, 1.

—— (1983b), *La salud en Costa Rica* (San José: Editorial Universidad Estatal a Distancia).

MOKYR, J. (1985), *Why Ireland Starved* (London: Allen and Unwin).

MOLYNEUX, M. (1981), 'Women's Emancipation Under Socialism: A Model for the Third World?', *World Development*, 9.

MOMSEN, J. H., and TOWNSEND, J. (eds.) (1987), *Geography of Gender in the Third World* (London: Butler and Tanner).

MONCKEBERG, F. (1983), 'Socioeconomic Development and Nutritional Status: Efficiency of Intervention Programs', in Underwood, B. (ed.) (1983), *Nutrition Intervention Strategies in National Development*.

—— MARDONES, R., and VALIENTE, S. (1984), 'Evolución de la desnutrición y mortalidad infantil en Chile en los últimos años', *Creces*, 10.

MONDOT-BERNARD, J. (1982), 'Les Études en nutrition et alimentations dans les pays du Sahel: bibliographie analytique', mimeo, Club du Sahel, OECD, Paris.

MONTGOMERY, R. (1985), 'The Bangladesh Floods of 1984 in Historical Context', *Disasters*, 9.

MORALES, E., and ROJAS, S. (1986), 'Relocalización Socio-espacial de la pobreza: políticas estatal y presión popular, 1979–85', Documento de Trabajo No. 280, FLACSO, Santiago.

MORAN, C. (1989), 'Economic Stabilisation and Structural Transformation: Lessons from the Chilean Experience', *World Development*, 17.

MORAN, E. (1982), 'The Evolution of Cape Verde's Agriculture', *African Economic History*, 11.

MORAN, R., *et al.* (1988), 'Jamaica: Summary Review of the Social Well-Being Program', Report No. 7227-JM, World Bank, Washington, DC.

MOREMI, T. C. (1988), 'Transition from Emergency to Development Assistance: Botswana Experience', paper presented at a Conference on Nutrition in Times of Disasters, World Health Organization, Geneva, 27–30 Sept. 1988.

MORGAN, R. (1985), 'The Development and Applications of a Drought Early Warning System in Botswana', *Disasters*, 9.

—— (1986), 'From Drought Relief to Post-Disaster Recovery: The Case of Botswana', *Disasters*, 10.

—— (1988), 'Social Welfare Policies and Programmes and the Reduction of Household Vulnerability in the Post-Independence SADCC States of Southern Africa', paper presented at a Workshop on Social Security in Developing Countries held at the London School of Economics, 4–5 July 1988; to be published in Ahmad, S. E., *et al.* (eds.) (forthcoming), *Social Security in Developing Countries*.

MORIO, S., and TAKAHASHI, S. (1986), 'Socio-economic Correlates of Mortality in Japan', in Ng Shui Meng (ed.) (1986), *Socio-economic Correlates of Mortality in Japan and ASEAN*.

MORIS, J. (1988), 'Failing to Cope with Drought: The Plight of Africa's Ex-pastoralists', *Development Policy Review*, 6.

MORLEY, D., ROHDE, J., and WILLIAMS, G. (eds.) (1983), *Practising Health for All* (Oxford: Oxford University Press).

MORRIS, M. D. (1974), 'What is a Famine?', *Economic and Political Weekly*, 9.

—— (1975), 'Needed—A New Famine Policy', *Economic and Political Weekly*, Annual Number.

—— (1979), *Measuring the Conditions of the World's Poor: The Physical Quality of Life Index* (Oxford: Pergamon).

MORRISON, B., and WAXLER, N. (1986), 'Three Patterns of Basic Needs Distribution within Sri Lanka: 1971–73', *World Development*, 14.

MORRIS-PEEL, S. (1986), 'A Review of the Health and Nutritional Aspects of the League's Drought Relief Operations in Chad, Mali and the Sudan 1984–86', mimeo, Institute of Development Studies, University of Sussex.

MOSLEY, W. H. (1985a), 'Will Primary Health Care Reduce Infant and Child Mortality? A Critique of Some Current Strategies with Special Reference to Africa and Asia', in Vallin, J., and Lopez, A. (eds.) (1985), *Health Policy, Social Policy and Mortality Prospects*.

—— (1985b), 'Remarks', in Halstead, S. B., *et al.* (eds.) (1985), *Good Health at Low Cost*.

—— and CHEN, L. C. (eds.) (1984), *Child Survival: Strategies for Research* (New York: Population Council).

Moto (1983), 'Facing the Drought', *Moto Magazine*, Harare.

MOUTON, P. (1975), *Social Security in Africa: Trends, Problems and Prospects* (Geneva: ILO).

MUELLBAUER, J. (1987), 'Professor Sen on the Standard of Living', in Sen, A. K. (1987a), *The Standard of Living*.

MUJICA, R., and ROJAS, A. (1986), 'Mapa de la extrema pobreza en Chile: 1982',

Documento de Trabajo, Instituto de Economía, Pontificia Universidad Católica de Chile, Santiago.

MUKHOPADHYAY, S. (1981), 'Women Workers in India: A Case of Market Segmentation', mimeo, ILO-ARTEP.

—— (ed.) (1985a), *The Poor in Asia: Productivity-Raising Programmes and Strategies* (Kuala Lumpur: Asia and Pacific Development Centre).

—— (ed.) (1985b), *Case Studies on Poverty Programmes in Asia* (Kuala Lumpur: Asia and Pacific Development Centre).

MUNDLE, S. (1974), 'Relief Planning in Maharashtra', *Indian Journal of Public Administration*, 20.

MUNIZ, J. G., FABIAN, J. C., and MAURIQUEZ, J. C. (1984), 'The Recent Worldwide Economic Crisis and the Welfare of Children: The Case of Cuba', *World Development*, 12.

MUQTADA, M. (1981), 'Poverty and Famines in Bangladesh', *Bangladesh Development Studies*, 9.

MURAGE, F. G. (forthcoming), 'Agricultural Yields, Production and Monitoring Methods of the National Cereals and Produce Board', to be published in Downing, T., *et al.* (eds.) (forthcoming), *Coping with Drought in Kenya*.

MURDOCH, W. W. (1980), *The Poverty of Nations: The Political Economy of Hunger and Population* (Baltimore: Johns Hopkins).

MURRAY, C. J. L. (1987), 'A Critical Review of International Mortality Data', *Social Science and Medicine*, 25.

—— and CHEN, L. C. (1989), 'Patterns of the Health Transition', mimeo, Center for Population Studies, Harvard University; to be published in Chen, L. C., *et al.* (eds.) (forthcoming), *Social Change and Health*.

MURTHY, N., HIRWAY, I., PANCHAMUKHI, P. R, and SATIA, J. K. (1988), 'Social Services Design, Delivery and Impact in Relation to the Poor', mimeo, Indian Institute of Management, Ahmedabad.

MWALUKO, E. P. (1962), 'Famine Relief in the Central Province of Tanganyika, 1961', *Tropical Agriculture*, 39.

MWANGI, W. M. (1986), 'Alternatives for Improving Production, Employment and Income Distribution in Kenyan Agriculture', mimeo, Institute of Development Studies, University of Sussex.

MWENDWA, H. (forthcoming), 'Agricultural and Livestock Monitoring Using Aerial Photography', in Downing, T., *et al.* (eds.) (forthcoming), *Coping with Drought in Kenya: National and Local Strategies*.

NADARAJAH, T. (1983), 'The Transition from Higher Female Mortality to Higher Male Mortality in Sri Lanka', *Population and Development Review*, 9.

NAG, M. (1985), 'The Impact of Social and Economic Development on Mortality: Comparative Study of Kerala and West Bengal', in Halstead, S. B., *et al.* (eds.) (1985), *Good Health at Low Cost*.

—— (1988), 'The Kerala Formula', *World Health Forum*, 9.

—— (1989), 'Political Awareness as a Factor in Accessibility of Health Services: A Case Study of Rural Kerala and West Bengal', *Economic and Political Weekly*, 25 Feb.

NAGARAJ, K. (1986), 'Infant Mortality in Tamil Nadu', mimeo, Madras Institute of Development Studies.

—— (1989), 'Female Workers in Rural Tamil Nadu—A Preliminary Study', mimeo, Madras.

NAGI, M. H. (1986), 'The Welfare State in Kuwait: Policy Issues and Impact', *Sociology and Social Welfare*.

NARAIN, DHARM (1965), *The Impact of Price Movements on Areas Under Selected Crops in India, 1900–1939* (Cambridge: Cambridge University Press).

—— (1988), *Studies on Indian Agriculture*, ed. K. N. Raj *et al.* (Delhi: Oxford University Press).

NASH, J. F. (1950), 'The Bargaining Problem', *Econometrica*, 18.

NASH, T. (1986), 'Report on Activities of the Child Feeding Centre in Korem', mimeo, Save the Children Fund, London.

NATHAN, A. J. (1965), *A History of the China International Famine Relief Commission* (Cambridge, MA: East Asian Research Center).

NAYYAR, R. (1987), 'Female Participation Rates in Rural India', *Economic and Political Weekly*, 22.

NEE, V. (1986), 'The Peasant Household Economy and Decollectivization in China', *Journal of Asian and African Studies*, 21.

NEGUS, D. (1985), 'Aid with Dignity: Helping Malian Nomads to Survive Drought in 1984', *Disasters*, 9.

NELSON, H. (1983), 'Report on the Situation in Tigray: December 1983', mimeo, Manchester University.

NEUMANN, C. G., BWIBO, N. O., CARTER, E., WEINBERG, S., JANSEN, A. A., CATTLE, D., NGARE, D., BAKSH, M., PAOLISSO, M., and COULSON, A. H. (forthcoming), 'Impact of the 1984 Drought on Food Intake, Nutritional Status and Household Response in Embu District', to be published in Downing, T. E., *et al.* (eds.) (forthcoming), *Coping with Drought in Kenya: National and Local Strategies*.

NEWBERY, D. (1987a), 'Agrarian Institutions for Insurance and Stabilization', mimeo, Churchill College, Cambridge; Published in Bardhan, P. K. (ed.) (1989), *The Economic Theory of Agrarian Institutions* (Oxford: Oxford University Press).

—— (1987b), 'When Do Futures Destabilize Spot Prices?', *International Economic Review*, 28.

—— and STIGLITZ, J. (1981), *The Theory of Commodity Price Stabilization: A Study in the Economics of Risk* (Oxford: Clarendon).

NEWHOUSE, P. (1987), 'Monitoring Food Supplies', *UNDRO News*, Jan./Feb. 1987.

NEWMAN, L. F., CROSSGROVE, W., KATES, R. W., MATTHEWS, R., and MILLMAN, S. (eds.) (forthcoming), *Hunger and History: Food Shortage, Poverty and Deprivation* (Oxford: Blackwell).

NEWMAN, P. (1970), 'Malaria Control and Population Growth', *Journal of Development Studies*, 6.

—— (1977), 'Malaria and Mortality', *Journal of American Statistical Association*, 72.

NG SHUI MENG (ed.) (1986a), *Socio-economic Correlates of Mortality in Japan and ASEAN* (National Institute for Research Advancement, Japan, and Institute of Southeast Asian Studies, Singapore).

—— (1986b), 'Socio-economic Correlates of Mortality in Singapore', in Ng Shui Meng (ed.) (1986a), *Socio-economic Correlates of Mortality in Japan and ASEAN*.

NIJIM, B. K. (1985), 'Spatial Aspects of Demographic Change in the Arab World', in Hajjar, S. G. (ed.) (1985), *The Middle East: From Transition to Development*.

Nordic Conference on Environment and Development (1987), background papers, mimeographed.

NORGAN, N. G. (1988), 'Chronic Energy Deficiency and the Effects of Energy

Supplementation', in Schürch, B., and Scrimshaw, N. (eds.) (1988), *Chronic Energy Deficiency: Consequences and Related Issues* (Lausanne: IDECG Secretariat).

NUSSBAUM, M., and SEN, A. K. (eds.) (forthcoming), *Quality of Life* (Oxford: Clarendon).

Nutrition Foundation of India (1988), *Profiles of Undernutrition and Underdevelopment: Studies of Poor Communities in Seven Regions of the Country* (New Delhi: Nutrition Foundation of India).

Office of Foreign Disasters Assistance (1985), *OFDA Annual Report, FY 1985* (Washington, DC: USAID).

O'GRADA, C. (1988a), 'For Irishmen to Forget?—Recent Research on the Great Irish Famine', Working Paper No. WP88/7, Centre for Economic Research, University College, Dublin.

—— (1988b), *Ireland Before and After the Famine: Explorations in Economic History 1800–1930* (Manchester: Manchester University Press).

—— (forthcoming), *The Great Famine in Irish History* (London: Macmillan).

OHADIKE, P.O. (1983), 'Evolving Indications of Mortality Differentials by Sex in Africa', in Lopez, A., and Ruzicka, L. T. (eds.) (1983), *Sex Differentials in Mortality: Trends, Determinants and Consequences.*

O'LEARY, M. (1980), 'Response to Drought in Kitui District, Kenya', *Disasters*, 4.

OLSEN, W. (1984), 'Kenya's Dual Grain Market: The Effects of State Intervention', mimeo, Food Studies Group, Oxford.

OMAWALE and McLEOD, J. (1984), 'Food Consumption and Poverty in Rural Jamaica', *Ecology of Food and Nutrition*, 14.

OMVEDT, G. (1980), *We Will Smash This Prison! Indian Women in Struggle* (London: Zed).

O'NEILL, O. (1987), *Faces of Hunger* (London: Allen and Unwin).

OSMANI, S. R. (1982), *Economic Inequality and Group Welfare* (Oxford: Clarendon).

—— (1986), 'The Food Problems of Bangladesh', paper presented at a Conference on Food Strategies held at WIDER, Helsinki, 21–5 July 1986; Working Paper No. 29, WIDER, 1987; to be published in Drèze, J. P., and Sen, A. K. (eds.) (forthcoming), *The Political Economy of Hunger.*

—— (1987a), 'Nutrition and the Economics of Food: Implications of Some Recent Controversies', Working Paper No. 16, WIDER; to be published in Drèze, J. P., and Sen, A. K. (eds.) (forthcoming), *The Political Economy of Hunger.*

—— (1987b), 'On Some Recent Controversies in the Measurement of Undernutrition', paper presented at a Conference on Poverty, Undernutrition and Living Standards held at WIDER, Helsinki, 27–30 July 1987; to be published in Osmani, S. R. (ed.) (forthcoming), *Nutrition and Poverty.*

—— (1988a), 'Social Security in South Asia', paper presented at a Workshop on Social Security in Developing Countries held at the London School of Economics, 4–5 July 1988; to be published in Ahmad, S. E., et al. (eds.) (forthcoming), *Social Security in Developing Countries.*

—— (1988b), 'Food and the History of India: An "Entitlement" Approach', Working Paper No. 50, WIDER, Helsinki.

—— (ed.) (forthcoming), *Nutrition and Poverty* (Oxford: Clarendon).

—— and CHOWDHURY, O. H. (1983), 'Short Run Impacts of Food for Work Programme in Bangladesh', *Bangladesh Development Studies*, 11.

O'SULLIVAN, G., EBRAHIM, S., O'SULLIVAN, J., and TATTS, C. (1980), 'Nutritional

Status of Laotian Refugee Children in Uban Camp, Thailand', *Journal of Epidemiology and Community Health*, 34.

OTTEN, M. W. (1986), 'Nutritional and Mortality Aspects of the 1985 Famine in North Central Ethiopia', mimeo, Centre for Disease Control, Atlanta, USA.

OUGHTON, E. (1982), 'The Maharashtra Droughts of 1970–73: An Analysis of Scarcity', *Oxford Bulletin of Economics and Statistics*, 44.

OXFAM (1972, 1973), unpublished field reports.

OXFAM/UNICEF (1986), 'Nutritional Surveillance and Drought Monitoring Project, Darfur, Report of March/April Survey 1986', mimeo.

PACEY, A., and PAYNE, P. (eds.) (1985), *Agricultural Development and Nutrition* (London: Hutchinson).

PADMINI, R. (1985), 'The Local Purchase of Food Commodities: "Cash for Food" Project', mimeo, UNICEF, Addis Ababa.

PANIKAR, P. G. K. (1985), 'Health Care System in Kerala and Its Impact on Infant Mortality', in Halstead, S. B., *et al.* (eds.) (1985), *Good Health at Low Cost*.

—— (1986), 'Financing Health Care in China', *Economic and Political Weekly*, 21.

—— and SOMAN, C. R. (1984), *Health Status of Kerala* (Trivandrum: Centre for Development Studies).

—— —— (1985), 'Recent Trends in the Health Status of Indian Children: A Reappraisal', Working Paper No. 209, Centre for Development Studies, Trivandrum.

PANKHURST, A. (1985), 'Social Consequences of Drought and Famine: An Anthropological Approach to Selected African Case Studies', unpublished MA dissertation, Department of Social Anthropology, University of Manchester.

—— (1986), 'Social Dimensions of Famine in Ethiopia: Exchange, Migration and Integration', paper presented to the 9th International Conference of Ethiopian Studies, Moscow.

PANKHURST, R. (1961), *An Introduction to the Economic History of Ethiopia from Early Times to 1800* (London: Lalibela House).

PAPANEK, H. (1987), 'The World Is Not Like Us: Limits or Feminist Imagination', paper, presented at the 82nd Annual Meeting of the American Sociological Association.

—— (1989), 'Socialization for Inequality: Entitlements, the Value of Women, and Domestic Hierarchies', mimeo, Center for Asian Development Studies, Boston University.

PARIKH, K. (1986), 'Chronic Hunger in the World: Impact of International Policies', paper presented at a Conference on Food Strategies held at WIDER, Helsinki, 21–5 July 1986; to be published in Drèze, J. P., and Sen, A. K. (eds.) (forthcoming), *The Political Economy of Hunger*.

—— and RABAR, F. (eds.) (1981), *Food for All in a Sustainable World* (Laxenburg: IIASA).

PARK, C. K., and YEON, H. C. (1981), 'Recent Developments in the Health Care System of Korea', *International Social Security Review*, 2/81.

PARK, P., and JACKSON, T. (1985), 'Lands of Plenty, Lands of Scarcity: Agricultural Policy and Peasant Farmers in Zimbabwe and Tanzania', OXFAM, Oxford.

PASSMORE, R. (1951), 'Famine in India: An Historical Survey', *Lancet*, 303.

—— (1974), *Handbook on Human Nutritional Requirements* (Rome: FAO).

PATEL, M. (1980), 'Effects of the Health Service and Environmental Factors on Infant

Mortality: The Case of Sri Lanka', *Journal of Epidemiology and Community Health*, 34.

PATIL, S. (1973), 'Famine Conditions in Maharashtra: A Survey of Sakri Taluka', *Economic and Political Weekly*, 28 July.

PAYNE, P. R. (1985), 'Nutritional Adaptation in Man: Social Adjustment and their Nutritional Implications', in Blaxter, K., and Waterlow, J. C. (eds.) (1985), *Nutritional Adaptation in Man*.

—— (1987a), 'Undernutrition: Measurement and Implications', paper presented at a Conference on Poverty, Undernutrition and Living Standards held at WIDER, 27–30 July 1987; to be published in Osmani, S. R. (ed.) (forthcoming), *Nutrition and Poverty*.

—— (1987b), 'Malnutrition and Human Capital: Problems of Theory and Practice', in Clay, E., and Shaw, J. (eds.) (1987), *Poverty, Development and Food*.

—— and LIPTON, M., with LONGHURST, R., NORTH, J., and TREAGUST, S. (1988), 'How Third World Rural Households Adapt to Dietary Energy Stress', mimeo, International Food Policy Research Institute, Washington, DC.

PEARSON, R. (1986); 'Lessons from Famine in Sudan (1984–1986)', mimeo, UNICEF, Khartoum.

PEBERDY, M. (1985), *Tigray: Ethiopia's Untold Story* (London: Relief Society of Tigray UK Support Committee).

PEEK, P., and RAABE, C. (1984), 'Rural Equity in Costa Rica: Myth or Reality?', Working Paper No. 67, Rural Employment Policy Research Programme, ILO, Geneva.

PENG, X. (1987), 'Demographic Consequences of the Great Leap Forward in China's Provinces', *Population and Development Review*, 13.

PERERA, P. D. A. (1985), 'Health Care Systems of Sri Lanka', in Halstead, S. B., *et al.* (eds.) (1985), *Good Health at Low Cost*.

PERKINS, D. H. (1983), 'Research on the Economy of the People's Republic of China: A Survey of the Field', *Journal of Asian Studies*, 42.

—— (1988), 'Reforming China's Economic System', *Journal of Economic Literature*, 26.

—— and YUSUF, S. (1984), *Rural Development in China* (Baltimore: Johns Hopkins).

PHILLIPS, M. A., FEACHEM, R. G., and MILLS, A. (1987), 'Options for Diarrhoea Control', EPC Publication No. 13, Evaluation and Planning Centre for Health Care, London School of Hygiene and Tropical Medicine.

PHONGPAICHIT, P. (1982), *From Peasant Girls to Bangkok Masseuses* (Geneva: ILO).

PIAZZA, A. (1986), *Food Consumption and Nutritional Status in the People's Republic of China* (Boulder: Westview).

PINOCHET, Augusto (1976), 'We Are Truly Independent Thanks to the Efforts of All Chileans', public presidential address, reprinted in Mendez, J. C. (ed.) (1979), *Chilean Economic Policy*.

PINSTRUP-ANDERSEN, P. (1985a), 'The Impact of Export Crop Production on Human Nutrition', in Pinstrup-Andersen, P., and Biswas, M. (eds.) (1985), *Nutrition and Development*.

—— (1985b), 'Food Prices and the Poor in Developing Countries', *European Review of Agricultural Economics*, 12.

—— (1987), 'Nutrition Interventions', in Cornia, G., et al. (eds.) (1987), *Adjustment With a Human Face*.

—— (ed.) (1988a), *Consumer-Oriented Food Subsidies: Costs, Benefits and Policy Options for Developing Countries* (Baltimore: Johns Hopkins).

—— (1988b), 'Assuring Food Security and Adequate Nutrition for the Poor', in Bell, D. E., and Reich, M. R. (eds.) (1988), *Health, Nutrition and Economic Crisis*.

—— (ed.) (forthcoming), *The Political Economy of Food and Nutrition*.

—— and ALDERMAN, H. (1988), 'The Effectiveness of Consumer-Oriented Food Subsidies in Reaching Rationing and Income Transfer Goals', in Pinstrup-Andersen, P. (ed.) (1988a), *Consumer-Oriented Food Subsidies: Costs, Benefits and Policy Options for Developing Countries*.

—— and BISWAS, M. (eds.) (1985), *Nutrition and Development* (Oxford: Oxford University Press).

—— and JARAMILLO, M. (1986), 'The Impact of Technological Change in Rice Production on Food Consumption and Nutrition in North Arcot, India', mimeo, International Food Policy Research Institute, Washington, DC.

PLATTEAU, J. P. (1988a), 'The Food Crisis in Africa: A Comparative Structural Analysis', Working Paper No. 44, WIDER; to be published in Drèze, J. P., and Sen, A. K. (eds.) (forthcoming), *The Political Economy of Hunger*.

—— (1988b), 'Traditional Systems of Social Security and Hunger Insurance, paper presented at a Workshop on Social Security in Developing Countries held at the London School of Economics, 4–5 July 1988; to be published in Ahmad, S. E., *et al.* (eds.) (forthcoming), *Social Security in Developing Countries*.

PLEASE, S., and AMOAKO, K. (1984), 'The World Bank's Report on Accelerated Development in Sub-Saharan Africa: A Critique of Some of the Criticisms', *African Studies Review*, 27.

POLEMAN, T. T. (1981), 'Quantifying the Nutrition Situation in Developing Countries', *Food Research Institute Studies*, 18.

POLLAK, R. A. (1983), 'A Transaction Cost Approach to Families and Households', mimeo, University of Pennsylvania.

POPKIN, S. L. (1979), *The Rational Peasant: The Political Economy of Rural Society in Vietnam* (Berkeley: University of California Press).

POSNER, R. (1980), 'A Theory of Primitive Society, With Special Reference to Law', *Journal of Law and Economics*, 23.

POTTIER, J. (1988), *Migrants no More: Settlement and Survival in Mambwe Villages, Zambia* (Manchester: Manchester University Press).

PRABHAKAR, M. S. (1975), 'Death in Barpeta', *Economic and Political Weekly*, 10.

PRESCOTT, N., and JAMISON, D. (1985), 'The Distribution and Impact of Health Resource Availability in China', *International Journal of Health Planning and Management*, 1.

PRESTON, S. (1975), 'The Changing Relation Between Mortality and Level of Economic Development', *Population Studies*, 29.

—— (1980), 'Causes and Consequences of Mortality Declines in Less Developed Countries During the Twentieth Century', in Easterlin, R. A. (ed.) (1980), *Population and Economic Change in Developing Countries*.

—— KEYFITZ, N., and SCHOEN, R. (1972), *Causes of Death: Life Tables for National Populations* (New York: Seminar Press).

PRESVELAN, C., and SPIJKERS-ZWART, S. (eds.) (1980), *The Household, Women and Agricultural Development* (Wageningen: Veenman and Zonen).

PRINDLE, P. H. (1979), 'Peasant Society and Famines: A Nepalese Example', *Ethnology*, 1.

PROSTERMAN, R. L. (1984), 'The Decline of Hunger-Related Deaths', The Hunger Project Papers, No. 1, The Hunger Project, San Francisco.

Public Institution for Social Security (1985), 'Recent Developments in the Social Security System in Kuwait', *Asian News Sheet*, 15.

PUTTERMAN, L. (1986), *Peasants, Collectives and Choice* (Greenwich, Conn.: JAI Press).

—— (1988), 'Ration Subsidies and Incentives in the Pre-reform Chinese Commune', *Economica*, 55.

PYATT, G. (1987), 'A Comment on "Growth and Equity in Developing Countries: A Reinterpretation of the Sri Lankan Experience" by Bhalla and Glewwe', *World Bank Economic Review*, 1.

QI, W. (1988), 'South Korea and Taiwan: A Comparative Analysis of Economic Development', Discussion Paper No. 252, Institute of Development Studies, University of Sussex.

QUINN, V. (1986), 'Malawi: Agricultural Development and Malnutrition', paper presented at the SOEC/WFC Workshop on Statistics in Support of African Food Strategies and Policies, Brussels, 13–16 May 1986.

—— COHEN, M., MASON, J., and KGOSIDINTSI, B. N. (1987), 'Crisis-Proofing the Economy: The Response of Botswana to Economic Recession and Drought', in Cornia, G., *et al.* (eds.) (1987), *Adjustment with a Human Face*.

RACZYNSKI, D. (1987), 'Social Policy, Poverty, and Vulnerable Groups: Children in Chile', in Cornia, G., *et al.* (eds.) (1987), *Adjustment with a Human Face*.

—— and OYARZO, C. (1981), 'Por qué cae la tasa de mortalidad infantil en Chile?', Colección Estudios CIEPLAN 6, Estudio No. 55, Santiago, Chile.

—— and SERRANO, C. (1985), *Vivir en la pobreza: testimonios de mujeres* (Santiago: CIEPLAN-PISPAL).

RAHMATO, D. (1987), *Famine and Survival Strategies: A Case Study From Northeast Ethiopia* (Geneva: International Institute for Relief and Development).

—— (1988), 'Peasant Survival Strategies', mimeo, Institute of Development Research, Addis Ababa University.

RAJARAMAN, I. (1974), 'Constructing the Poverty Line: Rural Punjab, 1960–61', Discussion Paper No. 43, Research Program in Economic Development, Princeton University.

RAM, N. (1986), 'An Independent Press and Anti-hunger Strategies: The Indian Experience', paper presented at a Conference on Food Strategies held at WIDER, Helsinki, 21–5 July 1986; to be published in Drèze, J. P., and Sen, A. K. (eds.) (forthcoming), *The Political Economy of Hunger*.

RAMACHANDRAN, V. K. (1986), 'Socioeconomic Characteristics of Agricultural Labourers in a Vanguard Agrarian Region: A Case Study of Gokilapuram Village, Madurai District', unpublished Ph.D. thesis, University of Madras.

RAMALINGASWAMI, P. (1987), 'Women's Access to Health Care', *Economic and Political Weekly*, 22.

RAMALINGASWAMI, V., DEO, M. G., GULERIA, J. S., MALHOTRA, K. K., SOOD, S. K., OM PRAKASH, and SINHA, R. V. N. (1971), 'Studies of the Bihar Famine of 1966–67', in Blix, G., *et al.* (eds.) (1971), *Famine: Nutrition and Relief Operations in Times of Disaster*.

RANGASAMI, A. (1974), 'A Generation Being Wiped Out', *Economic and Political Weekly*, 30 Nov.

—— (1985), '"Failure of Exchange Entitlements" Theory of Famine: A Response', *Economic and Political Weekly*, 20.

RAO, V. K. R. V. (1982), *Food, Nutrition and Poverty in India* (Brighton: Harvester Press).

RASHID, S. (1980), 'The Policy of Laissez-Faire during Scarcities', *Economic Journal*, 90.

RATCLIFFE, J. (1983), 'Social Justice and the Demographic Transition: Lessons from India's Kerala', in Morley, D., *et al.* (eds.) (1983), *Practising Health for All.*

RATNAVALE, A. (1986), 'Famine in the Sahel: The Situation from 1979 to 1984', mémoire présenté en vue de l'obtention du Diplôme, Institut Universitaire de Hautes Études Internationales, Geneva, Switzerland.

RAVALLION, M. (1984), 'How Much is a Transfer Payment Worth to a Rural Worker?', *Oxford Economic Papers*, 36.

—— (1987a), *Markets and Famines* (Oxford: Clarendon).

—— (1987b), 'Market Responses to Anti-Hunger Policies: Effects on Wages, Prices and Employment', Working paper No. 26, WIDER; to be published in Drèze, J. P., and Sen, A. K. (eds.) (forthcoming), *The Political Economy of Hunger.*

—— (1987c), 'Growth and Equity in Sri Lanka: A Comment', mimeo, World Bank, Washington, DC.

—— (1987d), 'The Economics of Famine: An Overview of Recent Research', Working Papers in Trade and Development, No. 87/13, The Australian National University Research School of Pacific Studies; to be published in Pearce, D. W., and Rau, N. J. (eds.) (forthcoming), *Economic Perspectives: An Annual Survey of Economics* (New York: Harwood).

—— (1988), 'Income Effects on Calorie Undernutrition', mimeo, Australian National University.

RAVENHILL, J. (ed.) (1986), *Africa in Economic Crisis* (New York: Columbia University Press).

RAY, A. (1988a), 'A Response to Lipton's (June 1987) Review of "World Development Report 1986"', *Development Policy Review*, 6.

—— (1988b), 'Postscript', *Development Policy Review*, 6.

RAY, T. (1984), 'Drought Assessment: Kenya', mimeo, USAID/Kenya, Nairobi.

RAYNAUT, C. (1977), 'Lessons of a Crisis', in Dalby, D., *et al.* (eds.) (1977), *Drought in Africa 2.*

REARDON, T., MATLON, P., and DELGADO, C. L. (1989), 'Coping with Food Insecurity at the Household Level in Drought-Affected Areas of Burkina Faso', *World Development*, 17.

REDDY, C. R. (1985), 'Rural Labour Market in Varhad: A Case Study of Agricultural Labourers in Rain-Fed Agriculture', WEP Working Paper No. 75, ILO, Geneva.

REDDY, S. (1988), 'An Independent Press Working Against Famine: The Nigerian Experience', *Journal of Modern African Studies*, 26.

REICH, M. (1989), 'Another Look at Political Will and Good Government in the Health Transition', Health Transition Seminar, mimeo, Harvard University.

Relief and Development Institute (1985), 'Strengthening Disaster Preparedness in Six African Countries', report prepared for the Ford Foundation, Relief and Development Institute, London.

Relief Society of Tigray (1983), 'The Drought and its Effects', mimeo, REST, Khartoum.

REPETTO, R. C. (1981), *Economic Development, Population Policy and Demographic Transition in the Republic of Korea* (Cambridge, MA: Harvard University Press).

Republic of Korea, Bureau of Social Welfare, Ministry of Health and Social Affairs (1979), 'Changing Family Patterns and Social Security Protection: The Case of the Republic of Korea', *International Social Security Review*, 1.

REUTLINGER, S. (1977), 'Malnutrition: A Poverty or Food Problem', *World Development*, 5.

—— (1984), 'Policy Implications of Research on Energy Intake and Activity Levels with Reference to the Debate on the Energy Adequacy of Existing Diets in Developing Countries', in *Energy Intake and Activity* (New York: Alan Liss).

—— (1985), 'Food Security and Poverty in LDCs', *Finance and Development*, 22.

—— and ALDERMAN, H. (1980), 'The Prevalence of Calorie-Deficient Diets in Developing Countries', *World Development*, 8.

—— and BIGMAN, D. (1981), 'Feasibility, Effectiveness and Costs of Food Security Alternatives in Developing Countries', in Valdés, A. (ed.) (1981), *Food Security for Developing Countries*.

—— and SELOWSKY, M. (1976), *Malnutrition and Poverty: Magnitude and Policy Options* (Baltimore: Johns Hopkins).

Review of African Political Economy (1979), 'The Roots of Famine', special double issue.

—— (1985), *War and Famine*, special issue.

REYNOLDS, N. (1984), 'Citizens, the State and Employment: Public Works as the Core of a Rural Development Strategy', Carnegie Conference Paper No. 234, Southern African Foundation for Economic Research, Harare.

RICARDO, D. (1822), draft text of speech for delivery in Parliament, included in Sraffa, P. (ed.) (1971), *The Works and Correspondence of David Ricardo*, v (Cambridge: Cambridge University Press).

RICHARDS, P. (1986), *Coping with Hunger* (London: Allen and Unwin).

RICHARDSON, J. H. (1956), 'Social Security Problems, with Special Reference to the British West Indies', *Social and Economic Studies*, 5.

RICHARDSON, R., and KIM, B. W. (1986), 'Adjustments to Policy Changes: The Case of Korea, 1960–1985', Report No. DRD 239, Labor Markets Division, Development Research Department, World Bank, Washington, DC.

RIDDELL, R. C., and associates (1989), 'Manufacturing Africa: Performance and Prospects of Seven Countries in Sub-Saharan Africa', mimeo, Overseas Development Institute, London.

RINGEN, S. (1987), *The Possibility of Politics: A Study of the Economy of the Welfare State* (Oxford: Clarendon).

RISKIN, C. (1986), 'Feeding China: The Experience Since 1949', paper presented at a Conference on Food Strategies held at WIDER, Helsinki, 21–5 July 1986; Working Paper No. 27, WIDER, 1987; to be published in Drèze, J. P., and Sen, A. K. (eds.) (forthcoming), *The Political Economy of Hunger*.

—— (1987), *China's Political Economy: The Quest for Development since 1949* (Oxford: Oxford University Press).

—— (1988), 'Reform: Where is China Going?', mimeo, Columbia University.

—— (forthcoming), 'Hunger and Poverty in China since 1949', to be published in Newman, L. F., *et al*. (eds.) (forthcoming), *Hunger and History*.

RIVERS, J. P. W. (1982), 'Women and Children Last: An Essay on Sex Discrimination in Disasters', *Disasters*, 6.

—— (1988), 'Nutritional Biology of Famines', in Harrison, G. A. (ed.) (1988), *Famines*.

—— HOLT, J., SEAMAN, J., and BOWDEN, M. (1976), 'Lessons for Epidemiology from the Ethiopian Famine', *Annales de la Société Belge de Médicine Tropicale*, 56.

ROBSON, J. R. K. (ed.) (1981), *Famine: Its Causes, Effects and Management* (New York: Gordon and Breach).

ROCH, J., HUBERT, B., NGYRIE, E., and RICHARD, P. (1975), 'Selective Bibliography on the Famines and the Drought in the Sahel', *African Environment*, 1.

ROCHFORD, S. C. (1981), 'Nash-Bargained Household Decision-Making in a Peasant Economy', mimeo.

RODRIGUEZ, A. V. (1986), 'El gasto público en programas de seguridad social: estudio de su efecto redistributivo en 1982', Instituto de Investigaciones en Ciencias Económicas, Universidad de Costa Rica, San José.

ROGERS, B. (1980), *The Domestication of Women* (London: Tavistock).

ROHDE, J. (1983), 'Health for All in China: Principles and Relevance for Other Countries', in Morley, D., *et al*. (eds.) (1983), *Practising Health for All*.

ROHRBACH, D. D. (1988), 'The Growth of Smallholder Maize Production in Zimbabwe (1979–1985): Implications for Food Security', in Rukuni, M., and Bernsten, R. H. (eds.) (1988), *Southern Africa: Food Security Policy Options*.

ROJAS, A. (1986), 'Extrema pobreza: concepto cuantificación y caracterización', *Estudios públicos*, 24.

ROSE, T. (1985), *Crisis and Recovery in Sub-Saharan Africa* (Paris: OECD).

ROSEMBERG, M. B. (1979), 'Social Security Policy Making in Costa Rica: A Research Report', *Latin American Research Review*, 14.

—— (1983), *Las luchas por el seguro social en Costa Rica* (San José: Editorial Costa Rica).

ROSENZWEIG, M. R. and SCHULTZ, T. P. (1982), 'Market Opportunities, Genetic Endowments, and Intrafamily Resource Distribution', *American Economic Review*, 72.

—— BINSWANGER, H. P., and McINTIRE, J. (1988), 'From Land Abundance to Land Scarcity: The Effects of Population Growth on Production Relations in Agrarian Economies', in Lee, R. D., *et al*. (eds.) (1988), *Population, Food and Rural Development*.

ROSERO, L. (1984), 'Las políticas socio-economicas y su efecto en el descenso de la mortalidad', in Asociación Demográfica Costarricense (1984), *Mortalidad y fecundidad en Costa Rica*.

—— (1985*a*), 'Infant Mortality Decline in Costa Rica', in Halstead, S. B., *et al*. (eds.) (1985), *Good Health at Low Cost*.

—— (1985*b*), 'The Case of Costa Rica', in Vallin, J., and Lopez, A. (eds.) (1985), *Health Policy, Social Policy and Mortality Prospects*.

ROSS, C. G. (1983), 'A Program for Food Grain Self-Sufficiency in the Sahel', paper presented at the Fifth Conference of the Club du Sahel, Brussels, 26–8 Oct. 1983.

ROSS, D. (ed.) (1980), *Aristotle: The Nicomachean Ethics* (Oxford: Oxford University Press).

ROTBERG, R. I., and RABB, T. K. (eds.) (1983), *Hunger and History: The Impact of Changing Food Production and Consumption Patterns on Society* (Cambridge: Cambridge University Press).

ROTH, A. E. (1985), *Axiomatic Models of Bargaining* (Berlin: Springer Verlag).

ROTHSCHILD, E. (1976), 'Food Politics', *Foreign Affairs*, 54.

—— (1977), 'The Economics of Starvation' and 'The Rats Don't Starve', *New York Times*, 10 and 11 Jan.

RRC–UNICEF (1984), 'Local Purchase of Food Commodities Project, Ethiopia 1984: Evaluation Report', mimeo, RRC–UNICEF, Addis Ababa.

—— (1985), 'Evaluation Report on Cash for Food Project in Dodota Wereda (Chilalo, Arsi, Ethiopia)', mimeo, RRC–UNICEF, Addis Ababa.

RUBINSTEIN, A. (1987), 'Perfect Equilibrium in a Bargaining Model', in Binmore, K., and Dasgupta, P. (eds.) (1987), *The Economics of Bargaining*.

RUIZ, O. (1980), 'Economic Politics and the Nutritional State of the Urban Poor in Chile 1968–1976', in Solimano, G., and Taylor, L. (eds.) (1980), *Food Price Policies and Nutrition in Latin America* (Tokyo: United Nations University).

RUKUNI, M. (1988), 'The Evolution of Smallholder Irrigation Policy in Zimbabwe: 1982–1986', *Irrigation and Drainage Systems*, 2.

—— and BERNSTEN, R. H. (eds.) (1988), *Southern Africa: Food Security Policy Options*, Proceedings of the Third Annual Conference on Food Security Research in Southern Africa, 1–5 Nov. 1987 (University of Zimbabwe–Michigan State University Food Security Research Project, Department of Agricultural Economics and Extension, Harare).

—— and EICHER, C. K. (eds.) (1987), *Food Security for Southern Africa* (Harare, UZ–MSU Food Security Project, University of Zimbabwe).

RUZICKA, L. T. (1984), 'Mortality in India', in Dyson, T., and Crook, N. (eds.) (1984), *Indian Demography*.

—— and Lopez, A. D. (1983), 'Conclusions and Prospects', in Lopez, A. D., and Ruzicka, L. T. (eds.) (1983), *Sex Differentials in Mortality*.

SACHS, I. (1986), 'Growth and Poverty: Some Lessons from Brazil', paper presented at a Conference on Food Strategies held at WIDER, Helsinki, 21–5 July 1986; to be published in Drèze, J. P., and Sen, A. K. (eds.) (forthcoming), *The Political Economy of Hunger*.

SAENZ, L. (ed.) (1982), *Análisis de la situación alimentaria-nutricional en Costa Rica* (San José, Costa Rica: Ministerio de Salud).

—— (1985), 'Health Changes During a Decade: The Costa Rican Case', in Halstead, S. B., *et al.* (eds.) (1985), *Good Health at Low Cost*.

SAGAR, D. (1988), 'Rural Poverty in India: An Evaluation of the Integrated Rural Development Programme in Uttar Pradesh and Bihar', unpublished M.Phil. thesis, Department of Land Economy, University of Cambridge.

SAHN, D. E. (1986), *Food Consumption Patterns and Parameters in Sri Lanka: Causes and Control of Malnutrition* (Washington, DC: International Food Policy Research Institute).

—— (1987), 'Changes in Living Standards of the Poor in Sri Lanka During a Period of Macroeconomic Restructuring', *World Development*, 15.

—— and EDIRISINGHE, N. (forthcoming), 'The Politics of Food Policy in Sri Lanka: From Basic Human Needs to an Increased Market Orientation', to be published in Pinstrup-Andersen, P. (ed.) (forthcoming), *The Political Economy of Food and Nutrition*.

SAITH, A. (ed.) (1987), *The Reemergence of the Chinese Peasantry* (London: Croom Helm).

SAMARASINGHE, S. W. R. de A. (1988), 'Sri Lanka, A Case Study from the Third World', in Bell, D. E., and Reich, M. R. (eds.) (1988), *Health, Nutrition and Economic Crisis.*

SAMUELS, A. (1987), 'Health Sector Review: 1987', report prepared for the Ministry of Health, Government of Jamaica, Kingston.

SAMUELSON, P. A. (1955), 'Diagrammatic Exposition of a Theory of Public Expenditure', *Review of Economics and Statistics*, 37.

SANDERS, D. (1982), 'Nutrition and the Use of Food as a Weapon in Zimbabwe and Southern Africa', *International Journal of Health Services*, 12.

—— and DAVIES, R. (1988), 'Economic Adjustment and Current Trends in Child Survival: The Case of Zimbabwe', *Health Policy and Planning*, 3.

SANDFORD, S. (1977), 'Dealing with Drought and Livestock in Botswana', Report to the Government of Botswana, Gaborone.

SANTANA, S. M. (1987), 'The Cuban Health Care System: Responsiveness to Changing Population Needs and Demands', *World Development*, 15.

SANYAL, S. K. (1988), 'Trends in Landholding and Poverty in Rural India', in Srinivasan, T. N., and Bardhan, P. K. (eds.) (1988), *Rural Poverty in South Asia.*

SARMA, J. S. (1983), *Contingency Planning for Famines and Other Acute Food Shortages: A Brief Review* (Washington, DC: International Food Policy Research Institute).

SCARPACI, J. L. (1985), 'Restructuring Health Care Financing in Chile', *Social Science and Medicine*, 21.

SCHEETZ, T. (1987), 'Public Sector Expenditures and Financial Crisis in Chile', *World Development*, 15.

SCHELLING, T. C. (1960), *The Strategy of Conflict* (Cambridge, MA: Harvard University Press).

SCHEPER-HUGHES, N. (ed.) (1987), *Child Survival: Anthropological Perspectives on the Treatment and Maltreatment of Children* (Dordrecht: Reidel).

SCHIFF, M., and VALDÉS, A. (1988), 'Nutrition: Alternative Definitions and Policy Implications', mimeo, International Food Policy Research Institute; forthcoming in *Economic Development and Cultural Change.*

SCHMIDT-WULFFEN, W. (1985), 'Dürre- und Hungerkatastrophen in Schwarzafrika —das Fallbeispiel Mali', *Geographische Zeitschrift*, 73.

SCHWARE, R. (1982), 'Official and Folk Flood Warning Systems: An Assessment', *Environmental Management*, 6.

SCITOVSKY, T. (1985), 'Economic Development in Taiwan and South Korea, 1965–81', *Stanford Food Research Institute Studies*, 19.

SCOTT, E. (ed.) (1984), *Life Before the Drought* (Boston: Allen and Unwin).

SCOTT, J. (1976), *The Moral Economy of the Peasant* (New Haven: Yale University Press).

SCRIMSHAW, N. (1987*a*), 'Biological Adaptation in the Maintenance of Nutrition and Health', paper presented at the 86th Annual Meeting of the American Anthropological Association, Nov. 1987, Chicago.

—— (1987*b*), 'The Phenomenon of Famine', *Annual Review of Nutrition*, 7.

—— TAYLOR, C. E., and GOPALAN, J. E. (1968), *Interactions of Nutrition and Infection*, WHO Monograph No. 57, World Health Organization, Geneva.

SEAMAN, J. (1987), 'Famine Mortality in Ethiopia and Sudan', paper presented at a IUSSP seminar on Mortality and Society in Sub-Saharan Africa, Yaoundé, Cameroon, Oct. 1987.

—— HOLT, J., and RIVERS, J. (1978), 'The Effects of Drought on Human Nutrition in an Ethiopian Province', *International Journal of Epidemiology*, 7.

—— —— (1980), 'Markets and Famines in the Third World', *Disasters*, 4.

—— RIVERS, J., HOLT, J., and MURLIS, J. (1973), 'An Inquiry into the Drought Situation in Upper Volta', *Lancet*, No. 7832.

SEAVOY, R. E. (1986), *Famine in Peasant Societies* (Connecticut: Greenwood Press).

SECKLER, D. (1982), 'Small but Healthy?: A Basic Hypothesis in the Theory, Measurement and Policy of Malnutrition', in Sukhatme, P. V. (ed.) (1982a), *Newer Concepts in Nutrition and Their Implications for Policy*.

—— (1984), 'The "Small but Healthy?" Hypothesis: A Reply to Critics', *Economic and Political Weekly*, 19.

SEELEY, J. A. (1986a), *Famine in Africa: A Guide to Bibliographies and Resource Centres* (Cambridge: African Studies Centre).

—— (1986b), *Famine in Sub-Saharan Africa: A Select Bibliography* (Cambridge: African Studies Centre).

SEIDL, C. (1988), 'Poverty Measurement: A Survey', in Bos, D., Rose, M., and Seidl, C. (eds.) (1988), *Welfare and Efficiency in Public Economics* (Berlin: Springer-Verlag).

SELIGSON, M. A. (1980), *Peasants of Costa Rica and the Development of Agrarian Capitalism* (Madison: University of Wisconsin Press).

SELWYN, P. (1983), 'Mauritius: The Meade Report Twenty Years After', in Cohen, R. (ed.) (1983), *African Islands and Enclaves* (Beverley Hills: Sage).

SEN, A. K. (1960), *Choice of Techniques* (Oxford: Blackwell).

—— (1970), *Collective Choice and Social Welfare* (San Francisco: Holden-Day; republished, Amsterdam: North-Holland, 1979).

—— (1976a), 'Famines as Failures of Exchange Entitlements', *Economic and Political Weekly*, 11.

—— (1976b), 'Poverty: An Ordinal Approach to Measurement', *Econometrica*, 44.

—— (1976c), 'Real National Income', *Review of Economic Studies*, 43.

—— (1977a), 'Starvation and Exchange Entitlements: A General Approach and Its Application to the Great Bengal Famine', *Cambridge Journal of Economics*, 1.

—— (1977b), 'Rational Fools: A Critique of the Behavioural Foundations of Economic Theory', *Philosophy and Public Affairs*, 6; repr. in Sen, A. K. (1982a), *Choice, Welfare and Measurement*.

—— (1980), 'Equality of What?', in McMurrin, S. (ed.) (1980), *Tanner Lectures on Human Values* (Cambridge: Cambridge University Press); repr. in Sen, A. K. (1984a), *Resources, Values and Development* and also in Rawls, J., *et al.* (eds.) (1987), *Liberty, Equality and Law* (Cambridge: Cambridge University Press).

—— (1981a), *Poverty and Famines* (Oxford: Clarendon).

—— (1981b), 'Public Action and the Quality of Life in Developing Countries', *Oxford Bulletin of Economics and Statistics*, 43.

—— (1982a), *Choice, Welfare and Measurement* (Oxford: Basil Blackwell).

—— (1982b), 'Food Battles: Conflicts in Access to Food', Coromandel Lectures, New Delhi; repr. in *Food and Nutrition*, 10 (1984).

—— (1982c), 'How is India Doing?', *New York Review of Books*, 29.

—— (1982*d*), 'The Right Not To Be Hungry', in Floistad, G. (ed.) (1982), *Contemporary Philosophy*, vol. ii (The Hague: Martinus Nijhoff).

—— (1983*a*), 'Development: Which Way Now?', *Economic Journal*, 93.

—— (1983*b*), 'Poor, Relatively Speaking', *Oxford Economic Papers*, 35; repr. in Sen, A. K. (1984*a*) *Resources, Values and Development*.

—— (1984*a*), *Resources, Values and Development* (Oxford: Basil Blackwell).

—— (1984*b*), 'Family and Food: Sex Bias in Poverty', in Sen, A. K. (1984*a*), *Resources, Values and Development*.

—— (1985*a*), *Commodities and Capabilities* (Amsterdam: North-Holland).

—— (1985*b*), 'Well-Being, Agency and Freedom: The Dewey Lectures 1984', *Journal of Philosophy*, 82.

—— (1985*c*), 'Women, Technology and Sexual Divisions', *Trade and Development (UNCTAD)*, 6.

—— (1985*d*), 'A Sociological Approach to the Measurement of Poverty: A Reply to Professor Townsend', *Oxford Economic Papers*, 37.

—— (1986*a*), 'Food, Economics and Entitlements', *Lloyds Bank Review*, 160; to be repr. in Drèze, J. P., and Sen, A. K. (eds.) (forthcoming), *The Political Economy of Hunger*.

—— (1986*b*), 'The Causes of Famine: A Reply', *Food Policy*, 11.

—— (1987*a*), *The Standard of Living*, Tanner Lectures with discussion by J. Muellbauer and others, ed. G. Hawthorn (Cambridge: Cambridge University Press).

—— (1987*b*), *On Ethics and Economics* (Oxford: Blackwell).

—— (1987*c*), 'Gender and Cooperative Conflicts', Working Paper No. 18, WIDER, Helsinki; to be published in Tinker, I. (ed.) (forthcoming), *Persistent Inequalities*.

—— (1987*d*), 'Reply: Famines and Mr. Bowbrick', *Food Policy*, 12.

—— (1987*e*), *Hunger and Entitlements* (Helsinki: WIDER).

—— (1988*a*), 'Freedom of Choice: Concept and Content', *European Economic Review*, 32.

—— (1988*b*), 'Capability and Well-Being', paper presented at a Conference on The Quality of Life held at WIDER, Helsinki, July 1988; to be published in Nussbaum, M., and Sen, A. K. (eds.) (forthcoming), *Quality of Life*.

—— (1988*c*), 'Africa and India: What Do We Have to Learn From Each Other?', in Arrow, K. J. (ed.) (1988), *The Balance Between Industry and Agriculture in Economic Development*, i: *Basic Issues* (London: Macmillan).

—— (1988*d*), 'Food and Freedom', Sir John Crawford Memorial Lecture, to be published in *World Development*.

—— (1988*e*), 'Property and Hunger', *Economic Philosophy*, 4.

—— (1988*f*), 'Sri Lanka's Achievements: How and When', in Srinivasan, T. N., and Bardhan, P. K. (eds.) (1988), *Rural Poverty in South Asia*.

—— (1989*a*), 'Women's Survival as a Development Problem', *Bulletin of the American Academy of Arts and Sciences*, 43, 2.

—— (1989*b*). 'Indian Development: Lessons and Non-lessons', *Daedalus*, 118.

—— and SENGUPTA, S. (1983), 'Malnutrition of Rural Children and the Sex Bias', *Economic and Political Weekly*, 19 (annual number).

SENAUER, B., and GARCIA, M. (1988), 'The Determinants of Food Consumption and Nutritional Status Among Preschool Children: Evidence from the Rural Philippines', Staff Paper Series, No. P88-33, Department of Agricultural and Applied Economics, University of Minnesota.

—— and YOUNG, N. (1986), 'Impact of Food Stamps on Food Expenditures', *American Journal of Agricultural Economics*, 68.

SERBYN, R., and KRAWCHENKO, B. (eds.) (1986), *Famine in Ukraine* (Edmonton: University of Alberta Press).

SHAH, C. H. (1982), 'The Demand for Higher-Status Food and Nutrition in Rural India: The Experience of Matar Taluka', *Food and Nutrition Bulletin*, 8.

SHAMA SASTRY, R. (1967), *Kautilya's Arthasastra* (Mysore: Mysore Publishing House).

SHAO, Y. (1988), *Health Care in China* (London: Office of Health Economics).

SHAWCROSS, W. (1984), *The Quality of Mercy: Cambodia, Holocaust and Modern Conscience* (New York: Simon and Schuster).

SHEETS, H., and MORRIS, R. (1974), *Disaster in the Desert: Failure of International Relief in West African Drought* (Washington: Carnegie Endowment for International Peace).

SHERBINY, N. A. (1984), 'Expatriate Labor Flows to the Arab Oil Countries in the 1980s', *Middle East Journal*, 38.

SHETTLES, L. B. (1958), 'Biological Sex Differences with Special Reference to Disease, Resistance and Longevity', *Journal of Obstetrics and Gynaecology of the British Empire*, 65.

SHIGEMATSU, I., and YANAGAWA, H. (1985), 'The Case of Japan', in Vallin, J., and Lopez, A. (eds.) (1985), *Health Policy, Social Policy and Mortality Prospects*.

SHUKLA, R. (1979), *Public Works during Drought and Famines and Its Lessons for an Employment Policy* (Ahmedabad: Sardar Patel Institute of Economic and Social Research).

SIDER, R. J. (1980), *Cry Justice: The Bible on Hunger and Poverty* (New York: Paulist Press).

SIGMUND, P. E. (1984), 'Chile: Free-Market Authoritarianism', in Wesson, R. (ed.) (1984), *Politics, Policies and Economic Development in Latin America*.

SINGER, H., and MAXWELL, S. (1979), 'Food Aid to the Developing Countries: A Survey', *World Development*, 7.

—— WOOD, J., and JENNINGS, T. (1987), *Food Aid: The Challenge and the Opportunity* (Oxford: Clarendon).

SINGH, I. (1988), 'Land and Labor in South Asia', World Bank Discussion Paper No. 33, World Bank, Washington, DC.

SINGH, S. K. (1975), *The Indian Famine, 1967* (New Delhi: People's Publishing House).

SMALE, M. (1980), 'Women in Mauritania: The Effects of Drought and Migration on Their Economic Status and Implications for Development Programs', report prepared for the Office of Women in Development, US Agency for International Development, Washington, DC.

SMITH, A. (1776), *An Inquiry into the Nature and Causes of the Wealth of Nations*; republished in Campbell and Skinner (1976).

SMITH, R. (1987), *Unemployment and Health* (Oxford: Oxford University Press).

SMOUT, T. C. (1978), 'Famine and Famine-Relief in Scotland', in Cullen, L. M., and SMOUT, T. C. (eds.) (1978), *Comparative Aspects of Scottish and Irish Economic History 1600–1900*.

SNOWDON, B. (1985), 'The Political Economy of the Ethiopian Famine', *National Westminster Bank Quarterly Review*, November.

SOBHAN, R. (1979), 'Politics of Food and Famine in Bangladesh', *Economic and Political Weekly*, 14.

—— (1986), 'Politics of Hunger and Entitlements', paper presented at a Conference on Food Strategies held at WIDER, Helsinki, 21–5 July 1986; to be published in Drèze, J. P., and Sen, A. K. (eds.) (forthcoming), *The Political Economy of Hunger*.

SOBHAN, S. (1978), *Legal Status of Women in Bangladesh* (Dhaka: Bangladesh Institute of Law and International Affairs).

Society for International Development (1985), *Report of the North–South Roundtable on the Crisis in Africa* (Islamabad: NSRT).

SÖDERSTRÖM, L. (ed.) (1983), *Social Insurance* (Amsterdam: North-Holland).

SOETERS, R. (1986), 'Pitfalls with Weight for Height Measurements in Surveys of Acute Malnutrition', *Tropical Doctor*, 16.

SOLIMANO, G., and HAIGNERE, C. (1984), 'Free-Market Politics and Nutrition in Chile: A Grim Future after a Short-Lived Success', Working Paper No. 7, Center for Population and Family Health, Faculty of Medicine, Columbia University.

SOROKIN, P. A. (1942), *Man and Society in Calamity: The Effects of War, Revolution, Famine and Pestilence Upon Human Mind, Behaviour, Social Organization and Cultural Life* (New York: E. P. Dutton and Co.).

—— (1975), *Hunger as a Factor in Human Affairs* (Gainsville: University of Florida Press).

SPERLING, L. (1987a), 'Food Acquisition During the African Drought of 1983–84: A Study of Kenyan Herders', *Disasters*, 11.

—— (1987b), 'Wage Employment Among Samburu Pastoralists of Northcentral Kenya', *Research in Economic Anthropology*, 9.

SPITZ, P. (1978), 'Silent Violence: Famine and Inequality', *International Social Sciences Journal*, 30.

—— (1980), *Drought and Self-Provisioning* (Geneva: UNRISD).

SPRING, A. (1986), 'Women Farmers and Food in Africa', in Hansen, A., and McMillan, E. E. (eds.) (1986) , *Food in Sub-Saharan Africa*.

SPYCKERELLE, L. (1987), 'Integrated Natural Resources Management in Cape Verde', term paper, Institute of Development Studies, University of Sussex.

SRINIVASAN, T. N. (1981), 'Malnutrition: Some Measurement and Policy Issues', *Journal of Development Economics*, 8.

—— (1983), 'Malnutrition in Developing Countries: The State of Knowledge of the Extent of Its Prevalence, Its Causes and Its Consequences', background paper prepared for FAO's Fifth World Food Survey.

—— (1987), 'Undernutrition: Concepts, Measurement and Policy Implications', paper presented at a Conference on Poverty, Undernutrition and Living Standards held at WIDER, 27–30 July 1987; to be published in Osmani, S. R. (ed.) (forthcoming), *Nutrition and Poverty*.

—— and BARDHAN, P. K. (eds.) (1974), *Poverty and Income Distribution in India* (Calcutta: Statistical Publishing Society).

—— —— (eds.) (1988), *Rural Poverty in South Asia* (New York: Columbia University Press).

SRIVASTAVA, H. S. (1968), *History of Indian Famines and Development of Famine Policy 1858–1918* (Agra: Sri Ram Mehra and Co.).

STANDING, G., and SHEEHAN, G. (eds.) (1978), *Labour Force Participation in Low Income Countries* (Geneva: ILO).

STAVIS, B. (1982), 'Ending Famines in China', in Garcia, R., and Escudero, J. (eds.) (1982), *Drought and Man*, ii.

STEELE, I. (1985), 'Mali Battles Drought', *Africa Emergency Report*, Apr.–May 1985.

STEIN, Z., SUSSER, M., SAERGER, G., and MAROLLA, F. (1975), *Famine and Human Development: The Dutch Hunger Winter of 1944/45* (New York: Oxford University Press).

STEINBERG, D. I. (1988), 'Sociopolitical Factors and Korea's Future Economic Policies', *World Development*, 16.

STEWART, F. (1985), *Planning to Meet Basic Needs* (London: Macmillan).

—— (1987), 'Supporting Productive Employment Among Vulnerable Groups', in Cornia, G., *et al.* (eds.) (1987), *Adjustment with a Human Face*.

—— (1988), 'Basic Needs Strategies, Human Rights and the Right to Development', Ld'A-QEH Development Studies Working Paper No. 2, Queen Elizabeth House, Oxford.

STEWART, P. J. (1988), 'The Ecology of Famine', in Harrison, G. A. (ed.) (1988), *Famines*.

STICHTER, S., and PARPART, J. (1988), *Patriarchy and Class: African Women in the Home and Workforce* (Boulder: Westview).

STIGLER, J. G. (1945), 'The Cost of Subsistence', *Journal of Farm Economics*, 27.

STONEMAN, C. (ed.) (1988), *Zimbabwe's Prospects: Issues of Race, Class, State and Capital in Southern Africa* (London: Macmillan).

STREETEN, P. (1984), 'Basic Needs: Some Unsettled Questions', *World Development*, 12.

—— (1987), *What Price Food?* (London: Macmillan).

—— (1989), 'The Politics of Food Prices', in Islam, N. (ed.) (1989), *Balance between Industry and Agriculture in Economic Development*, vol. v (London: Macmillan).

STREETEN, P., with BURKI, S. J., MAHBUB UL HAQ, HICKS, N. and STEWART (1981), *First Things First: Meeting Basic Needs in Developing Countries* (New York: Oxford University Press).

STYCOS, J. M. (1982), 'The Decline of Fertility in Costa Rica: Literacy, Modernization and Family Planning', *Population Studies*, 36.

SUBBARAO, K. (1989), 'Improving Nutrition in India: Policies, Programs and Impact', Discussion Paper No. 49, World Bank, Washington, DC.

SUBRAMANIAM, V. (1975), *Parched Earth: The Maharashtra Drought 1970–73* (Bombay: Orient Longmans).

SUH, S. M. (1984), 'Effects of the Current World Recession on the Welfare of Children: The Case of Korea', in Jolly, R.; and Cornia, G. (eds.) (1984), *The Impact of World Recession on Children*.

—— and WILLIAMSON, D. (1987), 'The Impact of Adjustment and Stabilization Policies on Social Welfare: The South Korean Experiences During 1978–1985', in Cornia, G., *et al.* (eds.) (1987), *Adjustment with a Human Face*.

SUKHATME, P. V. (1961), 'The World's Hunger and Future Needs in Food Supplies', *Journal of Royal Statistical Society*, Ser. A, Vol. 124.

—— (1969), 'The Incidence of Protein Deficiency in India', *Indian Journal of Medical Research*, 57.

—— (1973), 'The Protein Problem', *Everyman's Science*, 8.

—— (1977), *Nutrition and Poverty* (New Delhi: Indian Agricultural Research Institute).

—— (ed.) (1982a), *Newer Concepts in Nutrition and Their Implications for Policy* (Pune: Maharashtra Association for the Cultivation of Science).

—— (1982*b*), 'Measurement of Undernutrition', *Economic and Political Weekly*, 16.

—— and MARGEN, S. (1978), 'Models of Protein Deficiency', *American Journal of Clinical Nutrition*, 31.

—— —— (1982), 'Autoregulatory Homeostatic Nature of Energy Balance', *American Journal of Clinical Nutrition*, 35; also repr. in Sukahtme, P. V. (ed.) (1982*a*), *Newer Concepts in Nutrition and Their Implications for Policy*.

SUNDARAM, K., and TENDULKAR, S. D. (1981), 'Poverty Reduction in the 6th Plan', Working Paper No. 233, Delhi School of Economics.

SUPER, J. C. and WRIGHT, T. C. (eds.) (1985), *Food, Politics and Society in Latin America* (Lincoln and London: University of Nebraska Press).

SVEDBERG, P. (1986), 'Undernutrition in Sub-Saharan Africa: A Critical Assessment of the Evidence', Working Paper No. 15, WIDER; to be published in Drèze, J. P., and Sen, A. K. (eds.) (forthcoming), *The Political Economy of Hunger*.

—— (1988), 'Undernutrition in Sub-Saharan Africa: Is There a Sex Bias?', Working Paper No. 47, WIDER, Helsinki.

SWAMINATHAN, MADHURA (1988), 'Inequality and Economic Mobility: An Analysis of Panel Data from a South India Village', D.Phil. dissertation, Oxford University.

SWAMINATHAN, M. C., RAO, K. V., and RAO, D. H. (1969), 'Food and Nutrition Situation in the Drought-Affected Areas of Bihar', *Journal of Nutrition and Dietetics*, 6.

SWAMINATHAN, M. S. (1986), *Sustainable Nutrition Security for Africa: Lessons from India* (San Francisco: The Hunger Project).

SWAMY, S. (1986*a*), 'A Comparative Perspective of the Economic Growth of China and India: 1870–1985', mimeo, Harvard University; to be published as a monograph.

—— (1986*b*), 'Efficiency, Productivity and Income Distribution in China and India: 1952–84', mimeo, Harvard University.

SWANBERG, K. G., and HOGAN, E. (1981), 'Implications of the Drought Syndrome for Agricultural Planning in East Africa: The Case of Tanzania', Discussion Paper 120: 1–49, Harvard Institute for International Development.

SWANN, N. L. (trans.) (1950), *Food and Money in Ancient China*, an annotated translation of Pan Ku's *Han Shu 24*, with related texts (Princeton: Princeton University Press).

SWIFT, J. (1977), 'Sahelian Pastoralists—Underdevelopment, Desertification, and Famine', *Annual Review of Anthropology*, 6.

—— (1982), 'The Future of African Hunter-Gatherer and Pastoral Peoples', *Development and Change*, 13.

—— (1985), 'Planning Against Drought and Famine in Turkana, Northern Kenya', mimeo, Institute of Development Studies, University of Sussex.

—— (1989), 'Why Are Rural People Vulnerable to Famine?', in Chambers, R. (ed.) (1989), *Vulnerability: How the Poor Cope*.

—— (forthcoming), 'Planning Against Drought and Famine in Turkana: A District Contingency Plan', to be published in Downing, T. E., *et al.* (eds.) (forthcoming), *Coping with Drought in Kenya: National and Local Strategies*.

SZRETER, S. (1986), 'The Importance of Social Intervention in Britain's Mortality Decline c. 1850–1914: A Re-interpretation', *Social History of Medicine*, 1.

TABOR, S. (1983), 'Drought Relief and Information Management: Coping Intelligently with Disaster', Family Health Division, Ministry of Health, Government of Botswana.

TABUTIN, D. (1975), 'Origines, composantes et conséquences de l'évolution démographique à Maurice', Working Paper No. 19, Département de Démographie, Université Catholique de Louvain, Belgium.

—— and SOMBO, N. (1983), 'Tendances et causes de la mortalité à Maurice depuis 1940', Working Paper No. 115, Département de Démographie, Université Catholique de Louvain, Belgium.

TAEUBER, I. B. (1958), *The Population of Japan* (Princeton: Princeton University Press).

TAGWIREYI, J. (1988), 'Experiences in Increasing Food Access and Nutrition in Zimbabwe', paper presented at the Fourth Annual Conference on Food Security Research in Southern Africa, Oct.–Nov., Harare, Zimbabwe.

TALBOT, R. B., HAWLEY, J., and POORMAN, J. (1985), *Selected Bibliography on World Food Politics and Policies* (Ames: Iowa State University Press).

TARYAM, A. O. (1987), *The Establishment of the United Arab Emirates 1950–85* (London: Croom Helm).

TAYLOR, C. E. (1983), 'Synergy Among Mass Infections, Famines, and Poverty', in Rotberg, R. I., and Rabb, T. K. (eds.) (1983), *Hunger and History*.

TAYLOR, L. (1975), 'The Misconstrued Crisis: Lester Brown and World Food', *World Development*, 3.

—— (1988a), *Varieties of Stabilization Experiences: Towards Sensible Macroeconomics in the Third World* (Oxford: Clarendon).

—— (1988b), 'Macro Effects of Myriad Shocks: Developing Countries in the World Economy', in Bell, D. E., and Reich, M. R. (eds.) (1988), *Health, Nutrition and Economic Crises*.

TAYLOR, W. (1983), 'An Evaluation of Supplementary Feeding in Somali Refugee Camps', *International Journal of Epidemiology*, 12.

TEUSCHER, T. (1985), 'Report on Nutritional Aspects of the Ongoing LRCS Food-Aid Program', internal report, League of Red Cross and Red Crescent Societies, Geneva.

THOMAS, D., STRAUSS, J., and HENRIQUES, M. H. (1988a), 'How Does Mother's Education Affect Child Height?', Discussion Paper No. 89, Development Economics Research Centre, University of Warwick.

—— —— —— (1988b), 'Child Survival, Height for Age and Household Characteristics in Brazil', Discussion Paper No. 90, Development Economics Research Centre, University of Warwick.

THOMAS, J. W., BURKI, S. J., DAVIES, D. G., and HOOK, R. H. (1976), 'Public Works Programs in Developing Countries: A Comparative Analysis', World Bank Staff Working Paper No. 224, World Bank, Washington, DC.

—— (1986), 'Food for Work: An Analysis of Current Experience and Recommendations for Future Performance', Discussion Paper No. 213, Harvard Institute for International Development, Cambridge, MA.

TILLY, C. (1975), 'Food Supply and Public Order in Modern Europe', in Tilly, C. (ed.) (1975), *The Formation of National States in Europe* (Princeton: Princeton University Press).

—— (1978), *From Mobilization to Revolution* (Reading, MA: Addison-Wesley).

TILLY, L. A. (1971), 'The Food Riot as a Form of Political Conflict in France', *Journal of Interdisciplinary History*, 2.

—— (1983), 'Food Entitlement, Famine, and Conflict', in Rotberg, R. I., and Rabb, T. K. (eds.) (1983), *Hunger and History*.

350 REFERENCES

—— (1986), 'Sex and Occupation in Comparative Perspective', mimeo, New School for Social Research, New York.

The Times (1985), 'Harare Health Drive Cuts Infant Mortality', *The Times*, 4 Nov. 1985.

TIMMER, C. P. (1984), *Private Decisions and Public Policy: The Food Price Dilemma in Developing Countries* (Cambridge, MA: Harvard Business School).

—— (1986), *Getting Prices Right: The Scope and Limits of Agricultural Price Policy* (Ithaca: Cornell University Press).

—— (1988), 'Food Policy and Economic Adjustment', in Bell, D. E., and Reich, M. R. (eds.) (1988), *Health, Nutrition and Economic Crises*.

—— FALCON, W., and PEARSON, S. (1983), *Food Policy Analysis* (Baltimore: Johns Hopkins).

TINKER, I. (ed.) (forthcoming), *Persistent Inequalities* (New York: Oxford University Press).

TITMUSS, R. M. (1950), *History of the Second World War: Problems of Social Policy* (London: HMSO).

—— and ABEL-SMITH, B. (1968), *Social Policies and Population Growth in Mauritius* (London: Frank Cass).

TOBERT, N. (1985), 'The Effect of Drought Among the Zaghawa in Northern Darfur', *Disasters*, 9.

TOMIC, B. (1983), 'Descentralización y participación popular: la salud rural en Costa Rica', Monografias Sobre Empleo No. 34, Institute of Social Studies, PREALC, International Labour Office.

TORCHE, A. (1985), 'Una evaluación económica del programa nacional de alimentación complementaria (PNAC)', *Cuadernos de economía*, 22.

TORDOFF, W. (1988), 'Local Administration in Botswana', *Public Administration and Development*, 8.

TORRY, W. I. (1979), 'Anthropological Studies in Hazardous Environments: Past Trends and New Horizons', *Current Anthropology*, 20.

—— (1984), 'Social Science Research on Famine: A Critical Evaluation', *Human Ecology*, 12.

—— (1986a), 'Drought and the Government–Village Emergency Food Distribution System in India', *Human Organization*, 45.

—— (1986b), 'Morality and Harm: Hindu Peasant Adjustments to Famines', *Social Science Information*, 25.

—— (1987), 'Evolution of Food Rationing Systems with Reference to African Group Farms in the Context of Drought', in Glantz, M. (ed.) (1987a), *Drought and Hunger in Africa*.

—— (1988a), 'Famine Early Warning Systems: The Need for an Anthropological Dimension', *Human Organization*, 47.

—— (1988b), 'Information for Food: Community Famine Surveillance in Sudan', mimeo, Department of Sociology/Anthropology, West Virginia University.

TOULMIN, C. (1983), 'Economic Behaviour Among Livestock-Keeping Peoples: A Review of the Literature on the Economics of Pastoral Production in Semi-arid Zones of Africa', Occasional Paper No. 25, School of Development Studies, University of East Anglia.

TOWNSEND, P. (1979a), *Poverty in the United Kingdom* (Harmondsworth: Penguin).

—— (1979b), 'The Development of Research on Poverty', in Department of Health and Social Security, *Social Science Research: The Definition and Measurement of Poverty* (London: HMSO).

—— (1985), 'A Sociological Approach to the Measurement of Poverty: A Rejoinder to Professor Amartya Sen', *Oxford Economic Papers*, 37.

—— and DAVIDSON, N. (eds.) (1982), *Inequalities in Health* (Harmondsworth: Penguin).

TOYE, J. (1987), *Dilemmas of Development* (Oxford: Basil Blackwell).

TURTON, D. (1977), 'Response to Drought: The Mursi of Southwestern Ethiopia', *Disasters*, 1.

—— (1985), 'Mursi Response to Drought: Some Lessons for Relief and Rehabilitation', *African Affairs*, 84.

—— and TURTON, P. (1984), 'Spontaneous Resettlement After Drought: An Ethiopian Example', *Disasters*, 8.

TWOSE, N. (1984), *Cultivating Hunger* (Oxford: OXFAM).

UNDERWOOD, B. (ed.) (1983), *Nutrition Intervention Strategies in National Development* (New York: Academic Press).

UNDRO (1984), 'Sécheresse en Mauritanie', internal report, Office of the United Nations Disaster Relief Coordinator, Geneva.

—— (1986), *UNDRO in Africa 1984–85* (Geneva: Office of the United Nations Disaster Relief Coordinator).

UNICEF (1987a), *The State of the World's Children 1987* (Oxford: Oxford University Press).

—— (1987b), 'Sri Lanka: The Social Impact of Economic Policies During the Last Decade', in Cornia, G., *et al.* (eds.) (1987), *Adjustment with a Human Face*.

—— (1988), *The State of the World's Children 1988* (Oxford: Oxford University Press).

—— (1989), *The State of the World's Children 1989* (Oxford: Oxford University Press).

United Nations (1987), *First Report on the World Nutrition Situation*, Administrative Committee on Coordination, Subcommittee on Nutrition, United Nations.

—— (1988), 'Mortality of Children Under Age 5: World Estimates and Projections, 1950–2025', Population Studies No. 105, Department of International Economic and Social Affairs, United Nations, New York.

United Nations Office for Emergency Operations in Africa (1985a), *Status Report on the Emergency Situation in Africa* (New York: OEOA).

—— (1985b), *Supplement to the Status Report on the Emergency Situation in Africa* (New York: OEOA).

United States Department of Agriculture (1986), 'Sub-Saharan Africa: Situation and Outlook Report', Economic Research Services, United States Department of Agriculture.

UPPAL, J. N. (1984), *Bengal Famine of 1943: A Man-Made Tragedy* (Delhi: Atma Ram).

USAID (1982), 'Cape Verde: Food for Development Program (PL480 Title II, Section 206)', mimeo, USAID, Washington, DC.

—— (1983), 'U.S. Aid to Zimbabwe: An Evaluation', AID Program Evaluation Report No. 9, US Agency for International Development, Washington, DC.

VAIDYANATHAN, A. (1985), 'Food Consumption and Size of People: Some Indian Evidence', *Economic and Political Weekly*, 20.

—— (1987), 'Poverty and Economy: The Regional Dimension', paper presented at a Workshop on Poverty in India, Queen Elizabeth House, Oxford, Oct. 1987.

VALAORAS, V. G. (1946), 'Some Effects of Famine on the Population of Greece', *Milbank Memorial Fund Quarterly Bulletin*, 24.

VALDÉS, A. (ed.) (1981), *Food Security for Developing Countries* (Boulder: Westview).

VALDES-BRITO, J. A., and HENRIQUES, J. A. (1983), 'Health Status of the Cuban Population', *International Journal of Health Services*, 13.

VALIENTE, S., MONCKEBERG, F., and GONZALEZ, N. (1985), 'The Political Economy of Nutrition in Chile', paper presented at a IFPRI/UNU workshop on the Political Economy of Nutritional Improvements, Berkeley Springs, W. Va.

VALLIN, J., and LOPEZ, A. D. (eds.) (1985), *Health Policy, Social Policy and Mortality Prospects* (Liège: International Union for the Scientific Study of Population).

VAN APPELDOORN, G. J. (1981), *Perspectives on Drought and Famine in Nigeria* (London: Allen and Unwin).

VAN BINSBERGEN, A. (1986), 'Cape Verde: Food Aid Resource Planning in Support of the National Food Strategy', paper presented at a WFP–ADB Seminar on Food Aid in sub-Saharan Africa, Abijan, Sept. 1986.

VATUK, S. (1979), 'The Sharing and Giving of Food in South Asian Society', draft paper prepared for the Social Science Research Council Committee on South Asia.

VAUGHAN, M. (1985), 'Famine Analysis and Family Relations: 1949 in Nyasaland', *Past and Present*, 108.

—— (1987), *The Story of an African Famine: Hunger, Gender and Politics in Malawi* (Cambridge: Cambridge University Press).

VIAL, I., MUCHNIK, E., and KAIN, J. (1987), 'Chile's Main Nutrition Intervention Programs: A Synthesis', mimeo, Institute of Nutrition and Food Technology, Santiago.

—— —— —— (1988), 'Evolution of Chile's Main Nutrition Intervention Programs', mimeo, University of Chile and Catholic University, Santiago.

VISARIA, L. (1985), 'Infant Mortality in India', *Economic and Political Weekly*, 20.

VISARIA, P. (1961), *The Sex Ratio of the Population of India*, Monograph 10, Census of India 1961 (New Delhi: Office of the Registrar General).

VIVEROS-LONG, A. (1986), 'Changes in Health Financing: The Chilean Experience', *Social Science and Medicine*, 22.

VOGLAIRE, A. (1988), 'La Théorie économique à l'épreuve des faits: le cas de la grande famine irlandaise de 1845–1849', unpublished M.Sc. thesis, Facultés Universitaires Notre-Dame de la Paix, Namur, Belgium.

VON BRAUN, J. (1988), 'Households' Responses to Severe Food Shortages in Two Very Different African Settings: Rwanda and The Gambia', transcript of a presentation made at a Workshop on Famine and Famine Policy held at Tufts University, 25 Mar. 1988.

—— (forthcoming), 'Social Security in Sub-Saharan Africa: Reflections on Policy Challenges', mimeo, International Food Policy Research Institute; to be published in Ahmad, S. E., et al. (eds.) (forthcoming), *Social Security in Developing Countries*.

—— and KENNEDY, E. (1986), 'Commercialization of Subsistence Agriculture: Income and Nutritional Effects in Developing Countries', Working Papers on Commercialization of Agriculture and Nutrition, No. 1, IFPRI, Washington, DC.

—— —— (1987), 'Cash Crops Versus Subsistence Crops: Income and Nutritional Effects in Developing Countries', in Gittinger, J. P., et al. (eds.) (1987), *Food Policy*.

—— —— and BOUIS, H. (1989), 'Comparative Analysis of the Effects of Increased Commercialization of Subsistence Agriculture on Production, Consumption, and

Nutrition', mimeo, International Food Policy Research Institute, Washington, DC.

VON KOHL, M. A. (1988), 'Cash for Food in Ethiopia', INTERCOM–UNICEF, No. 47.

WADDELL, E. (1974), 'Frost over Ningini: A Retrospect on Bungled Relief', *New Guinea*, 8.

WADE, R. (1983), 'South Korea's Agricultural Development: The Myth of the Passive State', *Pacific Viewpoint*, 24.

—— (1988), 'State Intervention in "Outward-Looking" Development: Neo-classical Theory and Taiwanese Practice', in White, G. (ed.) (1988), *Developmental States in East Asia*.

WALDRON, I. (1983), 'The Role of Genetic and Biological Factors in Sex Differences in Mortality', in Lopez, A. D., and Ruzicka, L. T. (eds.) (1983), *Sex Differentials in Mortality: Trends, Determinants and Consequences*.

WALFORD, C. (1978), 'On the Famines of the World: Past and Present', *Journal of Statistical Society*, 41.

WALKER, G. A., *et al.* (1986), 'Maternal Mortality in Jamaica', *Lancet*, 1.

—— ASHLEY, D. E. C., McCAW, A. M., and BERNARD, G. W. (1987), 'Maternal Deaths in Jamaica', *World Health Forum*, 8.

WALKER, P. (1987), 'Food for Recovery: Food Monitoring and Targeting in Red Sea Province, Sudan 1985–87', mimeo, OXFAM, Oxford.

—— (1988), 'Famine and Rapid Onset Disaster Warning Systems: A Report by the International Institute for Environment and Development for the Red Cross', mimeo, International Institute for Environment and Development, London.

WALKER, T. S., SINGH, R. P., and ASOKAN, M. (1986), 'Risk Benefits, Crop Insurance, and Dryland Agriculture', *Economic and Political Weekly*, 21.

WALLACE, H. M., and EBRAHIM, G. J. (eds.) (1981), *Maternal and Child Health Around the World* (London: Macmillan).

WALLICH, C. (1983), 'Savings Mobilization through Social Security: The Experience of Chile during 1916–17', World Bank Staff Working Paper No. 553, World Bank, Washington, DC.

WALLSTAM, E. (1985), 'A Nutritional Perspective on LORCS' Drought Relief Operations in Eastern and Southern Africa', internal report, League of Red Cross and Red Crescent Societies, Geneva.

WALTER, J., and WRIGHTSON, K. (1976), 'Dearth and Social Order in Early Modern England', *Past and Present*, 71.

WALTON, G. M. (ed.) (1985), *National Economic Policies of Chile* (Greenwich, Conn.: JAI Press).

WANGWE, S. (1986), 'The Contribution of Industry to Solving the Food Problem in Africa', paper presented at a Conference on Food Strategies held at WIDER, Helsinki, 21–5 July 1986; to be published in Drèze, J. P., and Sen, A. K. (eds.) (forthcoming), *The Political Economy of Hunger*.

WARE, H. (1984), 'Effects of Maternal Education, Women's Roles, and Child Care on Child Mortality', in Mosley, W. H., and Chen, L. C. (eds.) (1984), *Child Survival: Strategies for Research*.

WATERSON, T., and SANDERS, D. (1984), 'Zimbabwe: Health Care Since Independence', *Lancet*, 18 Feb.

WATKINS, S., and MENKEN, J. (1985), 'Famines in Historical Perspective', *Population and Development Review*, 11.

WATTS, M. J. (1983), *Silent Violence: Food, Famine and Peasantry in Northern Nigeria* (Berkeley: University of California Press).

—— (1984), 'The Demise of the Moral Economy: Food and Famine in a Sudano-Sahelian Region in Historical Perspective', in Scott, E. (ed.) (1984), *Life Before the Drought*.

WEBER, M. T., STAATZ, J. M., HOLTZMAN, J. S., CRAWFORD, E. W., and BERNSTEN, R. H. (1988), 'Informing Food Security Decisions in Africa: Empirical Analysis and Policy Dialogue', Staff Paper No. 88–58, Michigan State University, East Lansing.

WEDDERBURN, D. (ed.) (1974), *Poverty, Inequality and Class Structure* (Cambridge: Cambridge University Press).

WEINER, D. (1987), 'Agricultural Transformation in Zimbabwe: Lessons for a Liberated South Africa', paper presented at the Annual Meeting of the Association of American Geographers, Portland, Oregon, 23–6 Apr. 1987.

—— (1988), 'Land and Agricultural Development', in Stoneman, C. (ed.) (1988), *Zimbabwe's Prospects*.

—— and MOYO, S. (1988), 'Wage Labor, Environment and Peasant Agriculture', mimeo, Zimbabwe Institute of Development Studies, Harare; forthcoming in *Journal of African Studies*.

WEISBROD, A. (1969), 'Collective Action and the Distribution of Income: A Conceptual Approach', in Joint Economic Committee, *The Analysis and Evaluation of Public Expenditure* (Washington, DC: US Government Printing Office).

Welfare State Programme (forthcoming), *The Welfare Audit: The Extent and Effectiveness of the Welfare State since 1974* (Oxford: Oxford University Press).

WERNER, D. (1983), 'Health Care in Cuba: A Model Service or a means of Social Control—or Both?', in Morley, D., *et al.* (eds.) (1983), *Practising Health for All*.

WERTHEIM, J. (1979), 'Cuba: Economic Change and Education Reform, 1955–1974', World Bank Staff Working Paper No. 317, World Bank, Washington, DC.

WESSON, R. (1984*a*), 'Costa Rica, Problems of Social Democracy', in Wesson, R. (ed.) (1984), *Politics, Policies and Economic Development in Latin America*.

—— (eds.) (1984*b*), *Politics, Policies and Economic Development in Latin America* (Stanford: Hoover Institution Press).

WESTERGAARD, K. (1986), *People's Participation, Local Government and Rural Development: The Case of West Bengal, India* (Copenhagen: Centre for Development Research).

WHEELER, E. F. (1984), 'Intrahousehold Food Allocation: A Review of Evidence', mimeo, London School of Hygiene and Tropical Medicine.

—— and ABDULLAH, M. (1988), 'Food Allocation Within the Family: Response to Fluctuating Food Supply and Food Needs', in de Garine, I., and Harrison, G. A. (eds.) (1988), *Coping with Uncertainty in Food Supply*.

WHITE, G. (ed.) (1988), *Developmental States in East Asia* (Basingstoke: Macmillan).

WHITEHEAD, A. (1985), 'Gender and Famine in West Africa', mimeo, University of Sussex.

—— (1986), 'Rural Women and Food Production in Sub-Saharan Africa', paper presented at a Conference on Food Strategies held at WIDER, Helsinki, 21–5 July 1986; to be published in Drèze, J. P., and Sen, A. K. (eds.) (forthcoming), *The Political Economy of Hunger*.

WIDDOWSON, E. M. (1976), 'The Response of the Sexes to Nutritional Stress', *Proceedings of the Nutrition Society*, 35.

WIGLEY, T. M., INGRAM, M. G., and FARMER, G. (eds.) (1981), *Climate and History* (Cambridge: Cambridge University Press).

WILL, P. E. (1980), *Bureaucratie et famine en Chine au 18e siècle* (Paris: Mouton).

WILLIAMS, A. (1987), 'What is Health and Who Creates It?', mimeo, University of York.

WILLIAMS, B. (1987), 'The Standard of Living: Interests and Capabilities', in Sen, A. K. (1987a), *The Standard of Living*.

WILLIAMSON, J. (ed.) (1988), *Balance Between Industry and Agriculture in Economic Development* (London: Macmillan).

WILSON, F., and RAMPHELE, M. (1989), *Uprooting Poverty: The South African Challenge* (Cape Town: W. W. Norton & Co.).

WILSON, G. (1987a), *Money in the Family—Financial Organisation and Women's Responsibility* (Aldershot: Avebury Publishers).

—— (1987b), 'Patterns of Responsibility and Irresponsibility in Marriage', in Brannen, J., and Wilson, G. (eds.) (1987), *Give and Take in Families*.

WINTER, J. M. (1986), *The Great War and the British People* (London: Macmillan).

WISNER, B. G. (1977), 'The Human Ecology of Drought in Eastern Kenya', unpublished Ph.D. Dissertation, Clark University, Worcester.

WOHLT, P., ALLEN, B. J., GOIE, A., and HARVEY, P. W. (1982), 'An Investigation of Food Shortages in Papua New Guinea', mimeo, Institute of Applied Social and Economic Research, Boroko, Papua New Guinea.

WOLF, M. (1987), *Revolution Postponed: Women in Contemporary China* (Stanford: Stanford University Press).

WOOD, D. H., BARON, A., and BROWN, V. W. (1986), *An Evaluation of the Emergency Food Assistance Program: Synthesis Report* (Washington, DC: USAID).

WOODHAM-SMITH, C. (1962), *The Great Hunger* (United Kingdom: Hamish Hamilton).

World Bank (1980), *Poverty and Human Development* (Washington, DC: World Bank).

—— (1981), *Accelerated Development in Sub-Saharan Africa: An Agenda for Action* (Washington, DC: World Bank).

—— (1983a), *China: Socialist Economic Development* (3 vols.) (Washington, DC: World Bank).

—— (1983b), *Zimbabwe: Population, Health and Nutrition Sector Review* (Washington, DC: World Bank).

—— (1984a), *China, The Health Sector*, World Bank Country Study (Washington, DC: World Bank).

—— (1984b), *Towards Sustained Development in Sub-Saharan Africa: A Joint Program of Action* (Washington, DC: World Bank).

—— (1985), *China: Long-Term Development Issues and Options* (Baltimore: Johns Hopkins).

—— (1986), *Poverty and Hunger: Issues and Options for Food Security in Developing Countries* (Washington, DC: World Bank).

—— (1988a), *The World Bank's Support for the Alleviation of Poverty* (Washington, DC: World Bank).

—— (1988b), *The Challenge of Hunger: A Call to Action* (Washington, DC: World Bank).

World Food Programme (1986a), 'Lessons Learned from the African Food Crisis: Evaluation of the WFP Emergency Response (note by the Executive Director)', WFP/CFA: 22/7, World Food Programme, Rome.

—— (1986b), 'Lessons Learned from the African Food Crisis: Summary Evaluation Report on the WFP Emergency Response', WFP/CFA: 22/7, Add. 1, World Food Programme, Rome.

—— (1986c), 'Recent Developments in Regard to the Main Aspects Covered by the Evaluation', WFP/CFA: 22/7, Add. 2, World Food Programme, Rome.

—— (1986d), 'Interim Evaluation Summary Report on Project Ethiopia 2488', WFP/CFA: 21/14-A (WPME) Add. 1, World Food Programme, Rome.

—— (1986e), 'Aide alimentaire d'urgence fournie à la suite de la sécheresse 1984–85 au Niger', mimeo, World Food Programme, Niamey.

World Health Organization (1983), *Primary Health Care: The Chinese Experience* (Geneva: WHO).

—— (1984), 'Nutrition Surveillance: Morbidity and Mortality from the 1983 Famine', *Weekly Epidemiological Record*, 59.

—— (1986), 'Intersectoral Action for Health', background document prepared for the 39th World Assembly of the World Health Organization, Geneva, May 1986.

—— (1988), 'Nutrition: Sex Bias of Nutritional Status of Children 0–4 Years', *Weekly Epidemiological Record*, 20 May.

WRIGHT, K. (1983), *Famine in Tigray: Eye Witness Report* (London: Relief Society for Tigray).

WRIGHT, W. (1882), *The Chronicle of Joshua the Stylite* (Cambridge: Cambridge University Press).

WRIGLEY, C. (1976), 'Changes in East African Society', in Low, D. A., and SMITH, A. (eds.) (1976), *History of East Africa* (Oxford: Clarendon).

WRIGLEY, E. A. (1969), *Population and History* (London: Weidenfel and Nicholson).

WYNNE, E. A. (1980), *Social Security: A Reciprocity System Under Pressure* (Boulder: Westview).

WYON, J. B., and GORDON, J. E. (1971), *The Khanna Study* (Cambridge, MA: Harvard University Press).

XU SU-EN (1985), 'Health Statistics of the People's Republic of China', in Halstead, S. B., et al. (eds.) (1985), *Good Health at Low Cost*.

YANG, SHUZHANG, and DOWDLE, N. (1985), 'Trends and Levels of Mortality in China', paper presented at an International Symposium on China's National Sample Fertility Survey, Beijing.

YAO, F. K., and KONE, H. (1986), 'The African Drought Reported by Six West African Newspapers', Discussion Paper No. 14, African Studies Center, Boston University.

YEH, R. (1984), 'Urban Low Income Housing in South East Asia', in Richards, P. J., and Thomson, A. M. (eds.) (1984), *Basic Needs and the Urban Poor* (London: Croom Helm).

YEON, H. C. (1982), 'Medical Insurance Programme and Its Future Development in Korea', *International Social Security Review*, 30.

—— (1986), 'Social Welfare Policies in the Republic of Korea', *International Social Security Review*, 34.

YOON, S. B., and PARK, T. K. (1985a), 'Strategies and Programmes for Raising the Productivity of the Poor and the Eradication of Poverty in Korea', in Mukhopadhyay, S. (ed.) (1985a), *The Poor in Asia: Productivity-Raising Programmes and Strategies*.

—— —— (1985b), 'An In-Depth Follow-Up Study of a Poor Rural Village of

Jukchon', in Mukhopadhyay, S. (ed.) (1985*b*), *Case Studies on Poverty Programmes in Asia*.

YORK, S. (1985), 'Report on a Pilot Project to Set Up a Drought Information Network in Conjunction with the Red Crescent Society in Darfur', *Disasters*, 9.

YOUNG, H. (1987), 'Selective Feeding Programmes in Ethiopia and East Sudan, 1985/1986', *Disasters*, 11.

YOUNG, K., WOLKOWITZ, C., and McCULLAGH, R. (1981), *Of Marriage and the Market: Women's Subordination in International Perspective* (London: CSE Books).

ZAHLAN, R. S. (1978), *The Origins of the United Arab Emirates* (London: Macmillan).

ZENG YI (1988), 'Changing Demographic Characteristics and the Family Status of Chinese Women', *Population Studies*, 42.

ZINYAMA, L. M., CAMPBELL, D. J., and MATIZA, T. (1988), 'Traditional Household Strategies to Cope with Food Insecurity in the SADCC Region', in Rukuni, M., and Bernsten, R. H. (eds.) (1988), *Southern Africa: Food Security Policy Options*.

NAME INDEX

Abdullah, M. 51 n., 56 n., 76 n., 79 n., 80 n.
Abeille, B. 116 n.
Abel-Smith, B. ix, 16 n., 200 n.
Acharaya, S. 50 n., 116 n.
Admassie, Y. 114 n., 116 n., 119 n.
Adnan, S. 58 n., 116 n.
Afshar, H. 61 n.
Agarwal, B. 50 n., 55 n., 57 n., 76 n., 78 n., 116 n.
Agere, S. T. 148 n.
Agrawal, A. N. 221 n.
Ahluwalia, M. S. 122 n.
Ahmad, S. E. 16 n., 209 n., 219 n.
Ahmed, R. 272 n.
Aird, J. 210 n.
Akerlof, G. A. 73 n.
Akong'a, J. 75 n., 76 n., 78 n., 139 n., 142, 145 n.
Alailima, P. 229 n.
Alam, M. S. 196 n.
Alamgir, M. 3 n., 5 n., 21 n., 27, 28 n., 29 n., 36 n., 46 n., 91 n.
Aldereguia, J. 250 n.
Alderman, H. ix, 36 n., 43 n., 107 n., 110 n., 249 n.
Alfred, C. 106 n., 108 n.
Ali, M. 3 n.
Alizadeh, P. 196 n.
Alnwick, D. 71 n., 114 n.
al-Sabah, Y. S. F. 189 n., 190 n., 191 n., 192 n.
Ambirajan, S. 122 n., 124 n.
Ambler, C. H. 138 n.
Ameringer, C. D. 241 n., 242 n., 243 n.
Amin, S. 58 n.
Amin, Samir 173 n., 174 n.
Amoako, K. 166 n.
Amsden, A. H. ix, 58 n., 196 n.
Anand, S. viii, ix, 41 n., 177 n., 228 n., 229 n., 247 n.
Anyango, G. J. 139 n., 141 n., 142 n., 145.
Appadurai, A. 84
Appleton, J. 112 n.
Arellano, J. P. ix, 230 n., 231 n., 232 n., 233, 235 n., 239 n.
Aristotle 12
Arnold, D. 55
Arrow, K. 252 n.
Ashton, B. 8 n., 211 n., 215 n.
Aslanbeigui, N. 57 n., 218 n.
Atkinson, A. B. 16 n., 42 n., 239 n.
Auerbach, L. S. 58 n.
Austin, J. E. 265 n.

Autier, P. ix, 71 n., 78 n., 80 n., 83 n., 84 n., 107 n., 112 n., 114 n., 263 n.
Avery, R. 241 n., 243 n., 245 n.
Aykroyd, W. 3 n., 74 n.
Aziz, S. 36 n.

Bagchi, A. 196 n.
Bahl, R. 195 n., 196 n.
Baker, D. C. 76 n., 100 n.
Balassa, B. 195 n.
Banerjee, N. 50 n., 58 n.
Banerji, D. 8 n.
Banister, J. 186 n., 204 n., 208, 216–18, 219 n., 220 n., 221 n., 222
Barbier, P. 93 n.
Bardhan, K. 57 n.
Bardhan, P. K. 8 n., 51 n., 57 n., 59 n., 122 n.
Barnabas, G. 112 n.
Baron, A. 68 n.
Basu, A. 53 n., 54 n., 58 n.
Basu, D. R. 25 n.
Basu, K. viii, 229 n., 272 n.
Bates, R. 272 n.
Bauer, P. T. 100 n., 195 n., 272 n., 274 n.
Baulch, B. 25 n.
Baumgartner, R. 251 n.
Beaton, G. 39 n., 111 n., 265 n.
Behrman, J. R. 43 n., 57 n., 262 n.
Belete, S. 91 n.
Bell, D. 183 n.
Beneria, L. 58 n.
Bennett, J. 173 n.
Berg, A. 66 n., 247 n., 265 n.
Berg, E. 100 n.
Berg, R. J. 171 n.
Bernstein, T. P. 24 n., 210 n., 213 n.
Bernus, E. 75 n., 77 n., 98 n., 107 n.
Berry, L. 31 n., 47 n.
Berry, S. S. 67 n., 83 n., 171 n.
Bertlin, J. 75 n., 76 n., 139 n.
Besley, T. 272 n.
Bhagwati, J. 228 n.
Bhalla, S. ix, 209 n., 219 n., 228 n.
Bhargava, A. 43 n.
Bhatia, Bela ix, 125 n.
Bhatia, B. M. 3 n., 123 n., 124 n.
Bhatia, K. 53 n.
Bhattacharaya, M. 126 n., 221 n.
Bhatty, I. 122 n.
Bhatty, Z. 58 n.
Biellik, R. J. 80 n.
Bigman, D. 169 n.

Binmore, K. 49 n.
Binns, C. W. 66 n., 80 n., 81 n.
Bird, K. 265 n.
Birdsall, N. 202
Birgegard, L. E. ix
Birmingham, D. 76 n.
Biswas, M. 265
Bjoerck, W. A. 96 n.
Blackie, C. L. 67 n., 171 n.
Blackorby, C. 51 n.
Blaxter, K. 38 n., 40 n.
Blumberg, R. L. 58 n.
Borkar, V. V. 126 n.
Borton, J. ix, 68 n., 71 n., 83 n., 88 n.,
    105 n., 107 n., 108 n., 110 n., 112 n., 133,
    138 n., 139 n., 140 n., 141 n., 142 n.,
    144 n., 153 n., 154 n., 155 n., 157 n., 263 n.
Bose, A. 209 n.
Bose, S. 3 n., 24 n.
Boserup, E. 50 n., 54 n., 57 n., 58 n., 59 n.
Bouis, H. E. 43 n.
Bowbrick, P. 25 n., 46 n.
Boyce, J. 107 n., 272 n.
Boyd, D. 186 n., 248 n., 249 n.
Boyd-Orr, John, Lord 35
Boyle, P. P. 55 n.
Brahme, S. 126 n., 127, 129
Brandt, H. 98–9 n.
Brannen, J. 43 n.
Bratton, M. 71 n, 78 n., 99 n., 107 n., 146 n.,
    147 n., 148 n., 149 n., 150 n., 151 n.
Breman, J. 74 n.
Brennan, L. 71 n., 123 n., 126 n.
Brett, A. 54 n., 56 n.
Briceño, A. 243 n.
Brown, E. P. 76 n., 78 n.
Brown, M. 49 n.
Brown, R. 95 n., 107 n., 110 n.
Brown, V. W. 68 n., 71 n.
Brundenius, C. 186 n., 250 n.
Bryceson, D. 50 n., 174 n.
Bryson, J. C. 71 n., 107 n., 114 n.
Burgess, L. ix
Burgess, R. viii, ix
Bush, R. 76 n., 78 n., 92 n., 95 n., 105 n.
Buvinic, M. 54 n.
Byres, T. J. 272 n.
Byron, W. 273 n.

Cabezas, M. 232 n., 234
Cabral, N. E. 133 n., 134 n., 135 n.
Cahill, K. M. 3 n.
Cain, M. 58 n.
Caldwell, J. C. 54 n., 59 n., 68 n., 75 n.,
    98 n., 99–100, 222 n., 223 n., 243 n.,
    247 n., 251 n., 262 n.
Caldwell, P. 54 n., 59 n., 68 n.
Callear, D. ix, 133, 152 n.

Campbell, D. J. ix, 56 n., 72 n., 75 n., 76 n.,
    77 n., 139 n.
Campbell, R. H. 15 n.
Candler, W. 83 n.
Cannon, T. G. 47 n.
Capone, C. 112 n.
Carreira, A. 133
Carter, J. 31 n.
Case, A. 51 n.
Cashdan, E. 73 n., 74 n., 75 n.
Cassen, R. 274 n.
Castaneda, T. 239 n., 247 n.
Castillo, G. 241 n.
Cathie, J. 155 n.
Cépède, M. 3 n.
Chakravarty, L. 59 n., 78 n.
Chakravarty, S. 227
Chambers, R. ix, 76 n., 105 n., 110 n., 112 n.
Chasin, B. H. 173 n., 176 n.
Chastanet, M. ix, 67 n., 75 n., 76 n., 78 n.,
    175 n.
Chatterjee, G. S. 221 n.
Chatterji, R. 59 n.
Chattopadhyay, B. 46 n.
Chaudhury, R. H. 51 n., 53 n., 80 n.
Chen, L. C. ix, 43 n., 44 n., 51 n., 53 n.,
    55 n., 74 n., 209 n., 222 n.
Chen, M. ix, 57 n., 76 n., 77 n., 98 n.,
    116 n., 124 n., 131 n.
Chernichovsky, D. 152 n.
Cheyre, H. 116 n., 238 n.
Chichilnisky, G. 90 n.
Chimwaza, B. M. 51 n.
Chow, N. W. S. 192 n.
Chowdhury, A. K. M. 44 n., 80 n., 114 n.
Chuang, C. F. 49 n.
Clay, E. 68 n., 71 n., 88 n., 95, 115 n.,
    274 n.
Cleland, J. 262 n.
Clemhout, S. 49 n.
Coale, A. 210 n.
Coate, S. ix, 96 n., 97 n.
Cockburn, C. 16 n.
Cogill, B. 173 n.
Cohen, J. 71 n., 138 n., 139–40, 141 n.
Cohen, M. S. 154 n., 155 n., 158 n.
Collins, J. 166 n., 169 n., 273 n.
Collins, R. ix
Colson, E. 72 n., 74 n., 75 n., 77 n.
Commins, S. E. 67 n., 171 n.
Conquest, R. 24 n.
Contrera, J. 239 n.
Copans, J. 174 n.
Corbett, J. ix, 76 n., 77 n., 78 n., 133, 138 n.,
    139 n., 145 n.
Corbo, V. 231 n.
Cornia, G. 107 n., 183 n., 197 n., 240 n.,
    262 n.

SUBJECT INDEX

India
Economic Development and
Social Opportunity

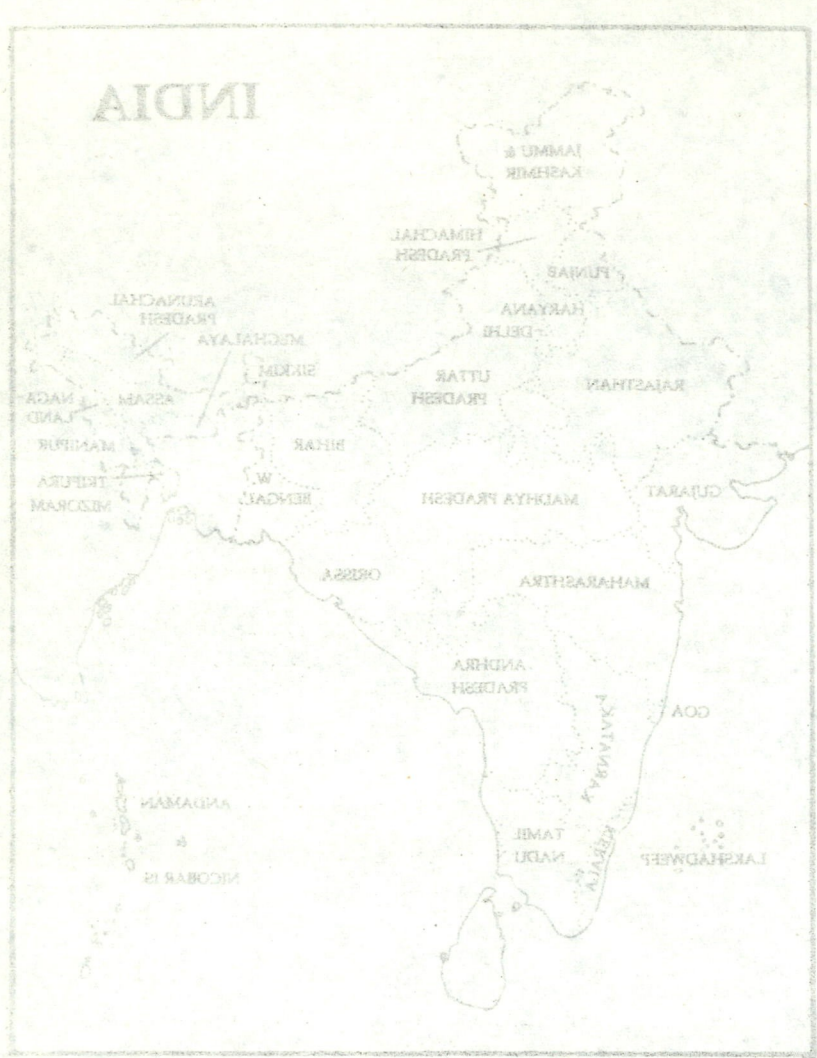

PREFACE

We have tried, in this monograph, to analyse the task of economic development in India in a broad perspective, in which social as well as economic opportunities have central roles. We consider, therefore, not only the facilities offered—important as they are—by well-functioning markets and beneficial exchanges, but also the fundamental role of human capabilities, and their dependence on basic education, health services, ownership patterns, social stratification, gender relations, and the opportunity of social cooperation as well as political protest and opposition. Variations in social opportunities not only lead to diverse achievements in the quality of life, but also influence economic performance, and in particular, the extent to which the facilities offered by functioning markets can be used by the citizens in general.

This general approach is explored fairly extensively, drawing on empirical findings from different parts of India, and also on international comparisons. We outline in particular what can be learned from the experiences of other countries—successful as well as unsuccessful ones—and also from the varieties of experiences *within* India. Special attention is paid to the role of basic education in social transformation as well as economic expansion. The importance of women's agency in bringing about major changes is another central area of investigation in this work. There is also considerable discussion of the role of political and social movements, particularly in confronting deep-seated inequalities.

At the end of the monograph we present a substantial Statistical Appendix, partly as a supplement to the empirical arguments presented here, but also as general information which might be of interest to the reader. Since we do discuss in reasonable detail the nature of the economic challenge faced in India at this time, there is some possibility of treating this book also as an introduction to aspects of the Indian economy (usable even by those readers—those dreadful ones!—who are uninterested in the main theses of this monograph).

The broad perspective presented here, we believe, has some relevance in understanding the obstacles to economic development in India and the basic failure of public policies to remove them. Even though the expansion of social opportunities was very much the central theme in the vision that the leaders of the Indian independence movement had presented to the country at the time the British left, rather little attempt has, in fact, been made to turn that vision into any kind of reality. An opportunity for a break from the past, in this respect, could have been seized when economic reforms were initiated in 1991, but the focus of attention in that programme has been almost exclusively on the opening up of the Indian economy and on broadening the reach of the markets. Those are certainly worthy goals, and the need for reform had been strong for a long time in the over-regulated Indian economy, but the lack of any initiative towards a radical change in social policies, including those in basic education and elementary health care, is a major failure, with deeply negative implications on the prospects of improving living conditions and even on the chances of success of the market reforms themselves. While this book is not primarily a commentary or a critique of contemporary economic policies in India, that subject receives some attention in the general context of diagnosing the roots of India's economic and social backwardness.

The study draws on comparisons of India's achievements with those of other countries, including the ones that have skilfully used market opportunities and international economic integration, such as South Korea and other economies of east Asia and south-east Asia, and more recently post-reform China. In terms of social opportunities, each of these countries had done much more *already* at the time when they were initiating their major economic changes than India has achieved even by *now* (for example, each of them had a much higher level of literacy, already then, than India—still half illiterate—has now). India is in some danger of emulating the divisive pattern of economic growth experienced in countries such as Brazil, with much social inequality, rather than the more participatory development seen in, say, South Korea.[1]

---

[1] The contrast between 'participatory' and 'non-participatory' economic growth was discussed in our previous book, *Hunger and Public Action* (1989).

Expansions of basic human capabilities, including such freedoms as the ability to live long, to read and write, to escape preventable illnesses, to work outside the family irrespective of gender, and to participate in collaborative as well as adversarial politics, not only influence the quality of life that the Indian people can enjoy, but also affect the real opportunities they have to participate in economic expansion. An illustration of the compartmentalized nature of official Indian thinking on this subject is provided by the statement made on behalf of the Government of India to the 'Group of 77' in its meeting at the United Nations in New York last September, asserting that 'the concepts of sustainable human development and of human security' involve a 'conceptual derailment of our basic purpose of development cooperation'. The statement was made precisely at a time when the mini-epidemic of plague in India was frightening foreign tourists and businessmen away from India, and the consequences of neglecting 'sustainable human development and human security' were painfully apparent not only in living conditions in India but also in its impact on India's putative attempt at integration with the world economy.

The policy limitations relate not only to governmental decisions, but also to the nature of public discussion, particularly the potential for criticizing these decisions. So much energy and wrath have been spent on attacking or defending liberalization and deregulation that the monumental neglect of social inequalities and deprivations in public policy has received astonishingly little attention in these debates. The issues underlying liberalization are not, of course, trivial, but engagement on these matters—in opposition or in defence—cannot justify the conformist tranquillity on the neglected provisions of public education, health care, and other direct means of promoting basic human capabilities. In fact, sometimes contentious regulational matters seem to get astonishing priority in political discussions over more foundational concerns related directly to the well-being and freedom of the mass of Indian citizens. Debates on such questions as the details of tax concessions to be given to multinationals, or whether Indians should drink Coca Cola, or whether the private sector should be allowed to operate city buses, tend to 'crowd out' the time that is left to discuss the abysmal situation of basic education and elementary health care, or the persistence of debilitating social inequalities, or other issues that have a crucial bearing on the well-being and freedom of the population. In a multi-party democracy, there is scope for influencing the agenda of the government through systematic opposition, and the need to examine the priorities of public criticism is as strong as is the necessity that the government should scrutinize its own relative weights and concerns.

The interstate comparisons presented in this monograph draw on more comprehensive studies of the Indian development experience, focusing in particular on three Indian states (Kerala, West Bengal, and Uttar Pradesh), presented in a companion volume, edited by us, and prepared for the World Institute for Development Economics Research.[2] The Kerala study has been prepared by V.K. Ramachandran, the West Bengal study by Sunil Sengupta and Haris Gazdar, and the Uttar Pradesh study by Jean Drèze and Haris Gazdar. We are extremely grateful to Ramachandran, Sengupta, and Gazdar for their contributions. Parts of Chapter 7 of this book also draw on recent research undertaken by Jean Drèze in collaboration with Mamta Murthi and Anne-Catherine Guio.

The work for the present monograph was done at the Delhi School of Economics, at STICERD (London School of Economics), and at Harvard University (particularly the Center for Population and Development Studies), and we would like to acknowledge the facilities offered by these institutions. We would also like to thank the International Development Research Centre (IDRC, Canada) for supporting our collaborative work.

For commenting on parts of the manuscript and for extensive discussions, we are most grateful to Sudhir Anand, Robin Burgess, Robert Cassen, Bhaskar Dutta, Haris Gazdar, Athar Hussain, A.K. Shiva Kumar, Peter Lanjouw, Mamta Murthi, Jenny Olson Lanjouw, V.K. Ramachandran, Carl Riskin, Meera Samson, Sunil Sengupta, Amrit Singh, and Limin Wang. We have been greatly helped by the information and analyses provided to us by the Registrar General, Amulya Nanda, and his colleagues Madan Mohan Jha and K.S. Natarajan. We have also benefited from helpful discussions with Bina Agarwal, Satish Agnihotri, Sanjay Ambatkar, David Archer, Roli Asthana, R.V. Vaidyanatha Ayyar, Amiya Bagchi, Kaushik Basu, Bela Bhatia, Bipul Chattopadhyay, Lincoln Chen, Marty Chen, Ansley Coale, Max Corden, Monica Das Gupta, Gaurav Datt, Angus Deaton, S. Mahendra Dev, Tim Dyson, Fang Jianqun, Michel Garenne, Arun

[2] Jean Drèze and Amartya Sen, eds., *Indian Development: Selected Regional Perspectives*, to be published by Oxford University Press, in its series, WIDER Studies in Development Economics.

Ghosh, Debasish Ghosh, Anne-Catherine Guio, Stephen Howes, Praveen Jha, Shikha Jha, Inge Kaul, Stuti Khemani, Sunita Kishor, Stephan Klasen, Atul Kohli, John Kurian, Chris Langford, James Manor, George Matthew, S.S. Meenakshisundaram, Nidhi Mehrotra, Aditi Mehta, Ajay Mehta, Sumati Mehta, Kaivan Munshi, Nirmala Murthy, Sarmistha Pal, S.S. Parmar, Xizhe Peng, Ritu Priya, Ajit Ranade, Sharad Ranjan, Nina Rao, Jon Rohde, Paul Romer, Emma Rothschild, Denzil Saldanha, Sudipta Sarangi, S.K. Shetty, Amarjeet Sinha, E. Somanathan, Rohini Somanathan, P.V. Srinivasan, T.N. Srinivasan, K. Sundaram, Suresh Tendulkar, Sarojini Thakur, J.B.G. Tilak, and John Williamson. For research assistance at different stages of this work, we are indebted to Jason Furman, Jackie Loh, Pia Malaney, Shanti Rabindran, and Snigdha Srivastava. We would also like to thank Meera Samson and Anomita Goswami for invaluable editorial advice. Jackie Jennings kept track of the organizational tasks at the London School of Economics, as did Anna Marie Svedrofsky at Harvard, and to both of them we are most grateful.

J.D.
A.K.S.

CONTENTS

FIGURES

TABLES

1

INTRODUCTION

1.1. *India since Independence*

It is nearly half a century now since India achieved independence. On the eve of the departure of the British, on 14 August 1947, Jawaharlal Nehru declared: 'Long years ago we made a tryst with destiny, and now the time comes when we shall redeem our pledge.' 'The achievement we celebrate today,' Nehru went on, 'is but a step, an opening of opportunity, to the great triumphs and achievements that await us.' He reminded the country that the task ahead included 'the ending of poverty and ignorance and disease and inequality of opportunity.'[1] It is with that task that this book is concerned.

It is not hard to notice that the task that Nehru had identified remains, alas, largely unaccomplished. This is not to deny that progress has certainly been made in particular fields. One example is the elimination of substantial famines that continued to wreck the country right up to independence (the last major famine was the Bengal famine in 1943 which killed between 2 and 3 million people). That achievement is far from negligible since many other countries in Asia and Africa have had large famines over this period. Famine has been, for example, a continuing curse in sub-Saharan African countries (Sudan, Somalia, Ethiopia, Nigeria, Mozambique, and others), and even China suffered from a major famine during 1959–61, in which around 23 to 30 million people died. There are also other achievements to which one can point, varying from successful functioning of a multiparty democratic system to the emergence of a

---

[1] Jawaharlal Nehru's speech at the Constituent Assembly, New Delhi, on 14 August 1947; reprinted in Gopal (1983), pp. 76–7.

large scientific community. There are, indeed, many areas of economic and social development in which India's achievements have been quite creditable.

However, the overall success in the task, identified by Nehru, of 'ending of *poverty* and *ignorance* and *disease* and *inequality of opportunity*' has been quite limited. The intensities of many of the deprivations of which Nehru spoke have been considerably reduced, but there is nevertheless a very long way to go before Nehru's objectives can be seen as anywhere near being achieved. For example, while there have been substantial declines in age-specific mortality rates, and the expectation of life at birth in India today (just about 60 years) is certainly a lot higher than at the time of independence in 1947 (around 30 years), many other developing countries that were in a comparable position to India not long ago have meanwhile surged ahead—with life expectancies around or above 70 years in many cases. Similar remarks can be made about other aspects of living conditions, dealing with elementary education, nutritional characteristics, protection from illness, social security, and consumption levels. India's progress over the decades, while far from the worst, has been substantially and systematically outclassed by many other developing countries.

One important point to note here is that these more successful countries, which have left India behind, have pursued very diverse economic policies, from market-oriented capitalism (South Korea, Taiwan, Thailand) to communist-party-led socialism (Cuba, Vietnam, pre-reform China), and also various mixed systems (Costa Rica, Jamaica, Sri Lanka). As far as economic growth is concerned, their records have been extremely diverse, and yet all of them have been able to achieve a radical reduction in human deprivation and insecurity. Despite substantial differences in economic policy, these economically diverse countries have had much in common in terms of social policies, particularly those relating to the expansion of basic education and health care, and India contrasts with all of them in this fundamental respect. There is much to learn from these diverse countries and the commonality of their achievements, even when we might have good reason to shun emulating them in other respects. We shall have more to say on this general contrast in this monograph.

There is one field in which India clearly has done worse than *even* the average of the poorest countries in the world, and that is elementary education. The rate of adult literacy for India has reached only about 50 per cent, which is low not only in comparison with China's 78 per cent, but even compared with the average figure of 55 per cent for all 'low-income economies' excluding China as well as India.[2] India has been left way behind in the field of basic education even by countries which have not done better than India in many other developmental achievements, such as Ghana, Indonesia, Kenya, Myanmar (Burma), Philippines, Zimbabwe, and Zambia.

The comparative perspectives are important in assessing India's performance. The more effective performances (of, say, China, Sri Lanka, Thailand, or South Korea) indicate what has or has not been feasible elsewhere and provide some guidance about the yardstick on the basis of which India's record might be scrutinized. The point is not that there has been no progress in India, nor that other countries are all doing better, but specifically that India's success in removing 'poverty, ignorance, disease, and inequality of opportunity' has been markedly less substantial than that of many other countries. And in one particular field—that of elementary education—India stands considerably behind even the average of the poorest countries in the world. This particular failure will receive considerable attention in this monograph, both because literacy is an important social achievement, and also because it has an important instrumental role in facilitating other achievements.

This monograph is an attempt to understand what has been done and what policy priorities might be helpful in attempting a more rapid elimination of the deprivations identified by Nehru at the time of independence. Just as the yardstick of achievement calls for an international perspective, so does any discussion of policy priorities, since there is so much to be learned from the experience of successes and failures elsewhere.

Another important issue concerns learning from India *itself.* One of the most interesting aspects of India's development record is its remarkable regional diversity in the elimination of basic deprivations. For example, while India's life expectancy figure of around 60 years compares quite unfavourably with China's 69 years, Kerala's life expectancy—about 72 years—appears on the other side of China's achievement. Similarly, the infant mortality rate of 79 per thousand

---

[2] *World Development Report 1994*, Table 1, p. 162. We have updated the Chinese figure (reported as 73 per cent in *World Development Report 1994*) in the light of the latest census results; see the Statistical Appendix of this book for details.

live births in India is very high indeed in comparison with China's 31, but Kerala's rate of 17 is much better than China's. Again, while India's literacy rate is much lower than that of China, Kerala's is substantially higher than China's. In fact, Kerala's female literacy rate is higher than that of *every individual province* in China (see chapter 4). On the other side, some of the Indian states (for example, Uttar Pradesh, Rajasthan, Madhya Pradesh, Bihar) have much lower achievements than even the low Indian average.

These contrasts *within* India are important to study for their own interest. But there is also much to be learned, we argue, from the light that is thrown by these comparative experiences on what can or cannot be achieved elsewhere in the country. This applies to learning from high achievements in some fields (as in Kerala) as well as from low ones in those very fields (as in Uttar Pradesh), and also from the rather mixed cases (as in West Bengal). One of the main themes of this work is the importance of the lessons to be learned *by* India *from* India, and this can be just as important as learning from the achievements of other countries.[3]

1.2. *On Learning from Others*

International comparisons have been much used recently to motivate and defend a programme of economic reforms (involving liberalization of trade, deregulation of some governmental restrictions, encouragement of private enterprise, and so on), citing the achievements of South Korea, Hong Kong, Singapore, Thailand, and other countries that have made splendid use of market-based economic opportunities. Such comparisons are indeed illuminating, but the exercise cannot be sensibly confined only to a few preselected aspects of policies there, related only to one type of institutional reform. Note has to be taken of what the better performing countries did in the fields of education, health services, social security, land reform, gender relations, and generally in the various areas of public action that bear on the identified social goals. The contrast between these countries and India in terms of what has been done in these fields is no

---

[3] The study of the diverse experiences within India is crucial to understanding the role of public action in creating social opportunities. A companion volume of essays, Drèze and Sen (1996), includes case studies of three Indian states: Kerala (by V.K. Ramachandran), Uttar Pradesh (by Jean Drèze and Haris Gazdar), and West Bengal (by Sunil Sengupta and Haris Gazdar).

less striking than the contrasts relating to economic growth and market institutions.

These international comparisons also raise an important general question about the complementarity between the opening up of economic opportunities and the social conditions that facilitate the use of those opportunities (e.g. widespread literacy). There is, in fact, some empirical evidence suggesting that the returns to educational expansion tend to increase with the expansion of market opportunities, and such a complementarity is natural to expect on the basis of general economic reasoning. Education has done much for the quality of life in, say, Sri Lanka, without doing quite so much for economic growth as such.

Similarly, Kerala's poor growth performance despite high educational and social achievements indicates that something more than just education and other social inputs may be needed to accomplish rapid growth of the kind that countries such as South Korea or Thailand (and now China as well) have been experiencing. Kerala's human resources have found plentiful markets outside India, seizing remunerative work in the Gulf and in other countries abroad. The scope for using these human resources at home can certainly be increased to a great extent by expanding economic opportunities within the borders of India.

However, there is also the other side of the complementarity between economic opportunities and social conditions. The effectiveness of the opening up of new economic opportunities and of expanding the possibility of good use of labour and skill may depend greatly on basic educational facilities and related circumstances. This is where a fuller reading of the experiences of the rapidly-growing countries in Asia is badly needed. As will be presently discussed (in chapter 3), India's current level of literacy is not only enormously lower than that of South Korea or China, India's literacy achievements *today* are also very much lower than what South Korea, Thailand, and the other newly industrializing Asian countries had already achieved *by 1960*, when they moved ahead with their rapid economic growth. Since broad-based economic growth in these countries involved using a range of modern industries, and made considerable demand on widely-shared skills and education, the instrumental role of basic education in these development experiences can hardly be overlooked. A similar point can be made about China's recent experience of market-based rapid economic growth, since China too was starting, at the time of its economic reforms, from a much higher base of elementary education than India has achieved so far (see chapter 4). To understand what happened in these countries, it is necessary to take a fairly comprehensive view of their economic and social conditions, rather than just proposing to imitate a specific aspect of their performance, namely, their use of market-based incentives. *Learning* from an integrated experience has to be distinguished from simply *copying* some particular features of it.

1.3. *Social Opportunity and Public Policy*

Nehru's visionary statement on the elimination of deprivation had identified 'inequality of opportunity' as one of the principal deficiencies that needed to be addressed. The approach used in this study is much concerned with the opportunities that people have to improve the quality of their lives, and with the failures that relate both to the low average level and the high inequality of opportunities that citizens enjoy.[4] The word 'social' in the expression 'social opportunity', which figures even in the title of this book, is mainly a reminder not to view individuals and their opportunities in isolated terms. The options that a person has depend greatly on relations with others and on what the state and other institutions do. We shall be particularly concerned with those opportunities that are strongly influenced by social circumstances and public policy.

The use of the term 'social' is not intended as a contrast with 'economic'. Indeed, it will be argued that various economic arrangements (including the market mechanism) are of central importance to the presence or absence of 'social opportunities', and there is, thus, a deep-seated complementarity here. On the one hand, the opportunities offered by a well-functioning market may be difficult to use when a person is handicapped by, say, illiteracy or ill-health. On the other hand, a person with some education and fine health may still be unable to use his or her abilities because of the limitation of economic opportunities, related to the absence of markets, or overzealous bureaucratic control, or the lack of access to finance, or some other restraint that limits economic initiatives. Social opportunities are, thus, influenced by a variety of factors—among other things, the state of educational and health services (and public policies

---

[4] On different aspects of this approach, see Sen (1987) and Drèze and Sen (1989, 1990).

that deal with them), the nature and availability of finance (and policies that affect them), the presence or absence of markets (and policies that promote or restrict them), and the form and reach of bureaucratic control in general (including the barriers to enterprise imposed by such control). It is right to rail against bureaucratic controls and other barriers that stifle economic activity and individual initiative, but that line of reasoning, which has been—rightly—aired a great deal in India recently has to be seen as one part of a much bigger story about the determination of social opportunities that individuals enjoy. In focusing on social opportunities, we propose a perspective that is substantially *broader* than the narrow view that concentrates simply on promoting markets and competition, as well as the similarly narrow 'contrary' view that just wants to debunk liberalization.

Economic development can, in fact, be seen in terms of expansion of opportunities that the individuals in the society enjoy, and this approach will be briefly discussed in the next chapter. That will also be the occasion to distinguish between (1) the *intrinsic importance* of opportunities (one of the main objectives of economic development is to expand the effective freedom that different individuals enjoy), and (2) the extensive *instrumental role* of individual opportunities in the promotion of other objectives. Opportunities, thus, have both direct and indirect significance.

While Nehru's pointer to the ultimate objectives remains relevant and momentous, we cannot see the challenge *only* in terms of these ultimate goals. Much of economic development consists in bringing these achievements within the realm of possibility, and that requires more instrumental reasoning. We have to pay particular attention to accomplishing those intermediate tasks that would bring the more basic destinations within India's reach. While we can scarcely do better than starting off from where Nehru wanted India to go (to wit, 'the ending of poverty and ignorance and disease and inequality of opportunity'), we are not required—nor particularly well advised—to follow exactly the strategic path that Nehru himself chose. That path has led to some successes but also substantial failures, though the sources of those failures are often misidentified.

The blame for independent India's past failures is often put on the insufficient development of market incentives. We shall argue that while there is considerable truth in that diagnosis, it is quite inadequate as an analysis of what has gone wrong in this country.

There are many failures, particularly in the development of public educational facilities, health care provisions, social security arrangements, local democracy, environmental protection, and so on, and the stifling of market incentives is only one part of that larger picture. The failures can, thus, be scarcely seen simply as the result of an 'overactive' government. What can be justifiably seen as overactivity in some fields has been inseparably accompanied by thoroughgoing *underactivity* in others.

It is not a simple question, we argue, of 'more' or 'less' government. Rather, it is a question of the *type* of governance to have, and of seeing the role of public policies in promoting as well as repressing social opportunities. Indeed, the interrelations between the state, the public, and the market have to be seen in a larger framework, with influences operating in different directions. The recognition of that broader framework does not lend itself to the derivation of simple formulae used by different sides in the contemporary debates (selling liberalization over all else, or rubbishing it forcefully). But that loss of simplicity is a gain as well.

In so far as a general lesson emerges from the diverse investigations undertaken in this book, it may well be the necessity to get the debates on contemporary India's political economy *beyond* the familiar battle-lines around the issues of economic reform, liberalization, and deregulation. There are, of course, things to be discussed there and pros and cons to be assessed, but the main problem with focusing on that question is the resulting neglect of other public policy matters, dealing in particular with education, health, and social security. Both the vigorous defences of economic reforms and the spirited attacks on it contribute to hiding other—basic and urgent—issues.

If the central challenge of economic development in India is understood in terms of the need to expand social opportunities, then liberalization must be seen as occupying only one part of that large stage. By spotlighting that one part, the rest of the stage is left obscure. The limitations of the Indian experience in planning lie as much in omissional errors in the dark part of the stage as it does in the commissioning mistakes in the spotlit section. That uneven concentration extracts a heavy price. The first step is to bring the darker part of the stage more into consideration. The attention needed, as the book argues, is not just from the government, but also from the public at large.

2

ECONOMIC DEVELOPMENT AND SOCIAL OPPORTUNITY

2.1. *Development, Freedom and Opportunities*

When the subject of development economics emerged as a distinct field of study, shortly after the second world war, it appeared to be something of a bastard child of growth economics. Some influence other than growth economics was clearly involved in the origin of development economics, but it was not altogether clear what form this influence had taken. In one respect at least, the offspring did not differ from what could be expected from a genuine 'son of growth economics', namely an overarching preoccupation with the growth of real income per head.

Ian Little reflected this understanding very well in his depiction of 'development economics' (in *The Fontana Dictionary of Modern Thought*) as a field that 'in a broad sense comprises all work on *the growth of incomes per head*, including that of the classical economic theorists from Smith to Mill.'[1] The focus of development economics here is uncompromisingly on the growth of incomes. However, while the two classical authors cited by Little, namely Smith and Mill, did indeed write a great deal on the growth of real income per head, they saw income as one of several different means to important ends, and they discussed extensively the nature of these ends—very different as they are from income.

These classical authors were deeply concerned with the recognition that we have reasons to value many things other than income and

---

[1] Little (1977), p. 222. See, however, Little's much broader treatment of development economics in his own major treatise on development economics: Little (1982).

wealth, which relate to the real opportunities to lead the kind of life we would value living. In the writings of Smith, Mill, and other classical political economists, there is much interest in the foundational importance of our ability to do the things we value, so that they saw the freedom to lead valuable lives as intrinsically important—not merely instrumentally so. They did comment fairly extensively on the connection between these matters, on the one hand, and income, wealth, and other economic circumstances, on the other, and they had much to say on economic policies that promote the more basic ends.[2] Neither Smith nor Mill would have had any quarrel with taking a much broader view of the changes that are involved in the process we now call economic development—even with putting into that category Nehru's list of things to do.

In recent years, the profession of development economics has also moved increasingly in that direction, taking a much more inclusive view of the nature of economic development.[3] One way of seeing development is in terms of the expansion of the real freedoms that the citizens enjoy to pursue the objectives they have reason to value, and in this sense the expansion of human capability can be, broadly, seen as the central feature of the process of development.[4]

The 'capability' of a person is a concept that has distinctly Aristotelian roots.[5] The life of a person can be seen as a sequence of things the person does, or states of being he or she achieves, and these constitute a collection of 'functionings'—doings and beings the person achieves. 'Capability' refers to the alternative combinations of functionings from which a person can choose. Thus, the notion

---

[2] In the case of Smith, see both *The Wealth of Nations* and *The Theory of Moral Sentiments* (Smith, 1776, 1790), and in the case of Mill, *Principles of Political Economy, Utilitarianism, On Liberty*, and also *The Subjection of Women* (Mill, 1848, 1859, 1861, 1869).

[3] See, for example, Adelman and Morris (1973), Sen (1973, 1984), Grant (1978), Morris (1979), Streeten et al. (1981), Stewart (1985), Chenery and Srinivasan (1988), Desai (1991), Dasgupta (1993), Anand and Ravallion (1993), Kakwani (1993), Toye (1993), Thirlwall (1994); also the *Human Development Reports*, published by UNDP from 1990 onwards.

[4] See Sen (1980, 1985a, 1985b), Desai (1989, 1993b), Drèze and Sen (1989, 1990), Griffin and Knight (1990), UNDP (1990, 1994), Crocker (1991, 1992), Nussbaum (1992, 1993), Anand and Ravallion (1993), Gasper (1993), Lane (1994), Atkinson (1995).

[5] Discussed by Aristotle in *The Nicomachean Ethics* in particular, but also in his *Politics*. On this and on the connection between the Aristotelian focus and the recent analyses of capabilities, see Nussbaum (1993) and the other articles included in Nussbaum and Sen (1993).

of capability is essentially one of freedom—the range of options a person has in deciding what kind of a life to lead. Poverty of a life, in this view, lies not merely in the impoverished state in which . the person actually lives, but also in the lack of real opportunity—given by social constraints as well as personal circumstances—to choose other types of living. Even the relevance of low incomes, meagre possessions, and other aspects of what are standardly seen as economic poverty relates ultimately to their role in curtailing capabilities (that is, their role in severely restricting the choices people have to lead valuable and valued lives). Poverty is, thus, ultimately a matter of 'capability deprivation', and note has to be taken of that basic connection not just at the conceptual level, but also in economic investigations and in social or political analyses.[6] This broader and more foundational view of poverty has to be kept in view while concentrating, as we often would in this monograph, on the deprivation of such basic capabilities as the freedom to lead normal spans of life (undiminished by premature mortality), or the freedom to read or write (without being constrained by illiteracy). While the term 'poverty' will typically not be explicitly invoked in such contexts, the underlying concern is one of deprivation and impoverished lives. Even when we focus on economic poverty in the more conventional sense (in the form of insufficient incomes), the basic motivation will be its relevance as a substantial influence on capability deprivation.

The basic objective of development as the expansion of human capabilities was never completely overlooked in the modern development literature, but the focus has been mainly on the generation of economic growth, in the sense of expanding gross national product

[6] On this see Sen (1984, 1985a, 1992a). There is an enormous literature on 'poverty in India', which addresses many of the issues taken up in this book, although the general orientation of that literature has been somewhat different, with a more concentrated focus on the specific problem of low income or expenditure. Important contributions to this literature include Dandekar and Rath (1971), Srinivasan and Bardhan (1974), Ahluwalia (1978, 1990), Bardhan (1984a), Ghate (1984), Agarwal (1986), Das (1987), Jain et al. (1988), Srinivasan and Bardhan (1988), Kurian (1989), Kakwani and Subbarao (1990), Krishnaswamy (1990), Saith (1990), I. Singh (1990), Minhas et al. (1991), Nayyar (1991), Osmani (1991), Datt and Ravallion (1992, 1994), Krishnaji (1992), Harriss, Guhan, and Cassen (1992), Mahendra Dev et al. (1992), Ravallion and Subbarao (1992), EPW Research Foundation (1993), Gaiha (1993, 1994b), Parikh and Sudarshan (1993), Roy Choudhury (1993), Tendulkar et al. (1993), Vyas et al. (1993), Beck (1994), Dutta (1994), Dutta et al. (1994), Government of India (1994d), Lipton and Ravallion (1994), Ninán (1994), among others.

and related variables.[7] The expansion of human capabilities can clearly be enhanced by economic growth (even in the limited sense of growth of real income per head), but (1) there are many influences other than economic growth that work in that direction, and (2) the impact of economic growth on human capabilities can be extremely variable, depending on the nature of that growth (for example, how employment-intensive it is, and whether the economic gains from growth are channelled into remedying the deprivations of the most needy).

What is crucial in all this is the need to judge the different policies, ultimately, by their impact on the enhancement of the capabilities that the citizens enjoy (whether or not this comes about through the growth of real incomes). This differs sharply from the more standard practice of judging economic policies by their contribution to the growth of real incomes—seen as a merit in itself. To dispute that practice must not be seen as an invitation to ignore the important instrumental role of economic growth in enhancing basic objectives such as human capabilities; it is mainly a matter of being clear about ends and means.[8]

The recent attempts, in India and elsewhere, to open up market opportunities without being thwarted by bureaucratic barriers has been justified primarily in terms of the expected impact of this change on economic expansion, enhancing outputs and incomes in the economy. To quote the semi-official and distinctly authoritative report by Bhagwati and Srinivasan (1993), 'these structural reforms were necessary because we had evidently failed to generate adequate rates of growth of income and of per capita income' (p. 2). This is indeed a significant direction of causal analysis.[9] On the other side, the

[7] W.A. Lewis, one of the pioneers of development economics, emphasized that the appropriate objective of development is increasing 'the range of human choice', but nevertheless he decided to concentrate specifically on 'the growth of output per head', since that 'gives man greater control over his environment and thereby increases his freedom' (Lewis, 1955, pp. 9–10, 420–1).

[8] On this see Drèze and Sen (1989), and Anand and Ravallion (1993).

[9] For other evaluations of the performance of the Indian economy, and analyses of different approaches to economic policy in India, see Singh (1964), Bhagwati and Desai (1970), Chaudhuri (1971, 1974), Bhagwati and Srinivasan (1975), Nayyar (1976), Cassen (1978), Jha (1980), Bagchi (1982), Alagh (1986), Ahluwalia (1985, 1991, 1992), Chakravarty (1987), Lal (1988), Marathe (1989), Dhar (1990), Guha (1990), Kelkar et al. (1990), Jalan (1991, 1992), Byres (1994), Lewis (1995), Osmani (forthcoming), among others.

justification for focusing on outputs and incomes lies ultimately in the impact that their augmentation may have on the freedoms that people actually enjoy to lead the kind of lives they have reason to value. The analysis of economic development must take note of both the causal connections, and also of other policies and institutional changes that contribute to the enhancement of human capabilities. The success of development programmes cannot be judged merely in terms of their effects on incomes and outputs, and must, at a basic level, focus on the lives that people can lead. This applies as much to the assessment of economic reforms and current economic policies in India today as it does to evaluations of development programmes anywhere else in the world.

2.2. *On Education and Health*

Importance has to be attached to the distinct influences that promote or constrain the freedoms that individuals have, including their ability to make use of economic opportunities. As was discussed in the last chapter, education and health can be important 'promoting' factors. The role of these so-called 'social' variables in the fostering of economic progress has recently received much attention in the development literature. But, of course, the subject is of some antiquity, and classical political economists such as Smith or Turgot or Condorcet or Mill or Marx would have seen the recognition of this role as quite non-controversial.[10]

The remarkable neglect of elementary education in India is all the more striking given the widespread recognition, in the contemporary world, of the importance of basic education for economic development. Somehow the educational aspects of economic development have continued to be out of the main focus, and this relative neglect has persisted despite the recent radical changes in economic policy. Similar remarks apply to health care. Even Bhagwati and Srinivasan's (1993) lucid discussion of the challenge of economic reforms is entirely silent on the subject of education and health, and their possible roles in promoting the use of the economic opportunities that may be created by the reforms. Their discussion

---

[10] Theodore Schultz (1962, 1963, 1971, 1980) has made outstanding contributions in clarifying and emphasizing the importance of the connection between education and economic progress. See also T. Paul Schultz (1988), who provides an excellent account and critique of the relatively recent literature on the subject.

of the problem of 'infrastructure'—fine enough as far as it goes—is confined effectively to transport and power generation (pp. 52–4). An opportunity is missed here to question an old imbalance in Indian planning efforts. The issue relates to the tendency, which was discussed in the last chapter, to see the economic reforms as standing on their own,[11] without linking the case for reform *inter alia* to the failures in social policies (demanding radical changes in social programmes, particularly basic education, *along with* more narrowly economic changes).

Education and health can be seen to be valuable to the freedom of a person in *at least* five distinct ways.

(1) *Intrinsic importance*: Being educated and healthy are valuable achievements in themselves, and the opportunity to have them can be of *direct* importance to a person's effective freedom.

(2) *Instrumental personal roles*: A person's education and health can help him or her to do many things—*other* than just being educated and healthy—that are also valuable. They can, for instance, be important for getting a job and more generally for making use of economic opportunities. The resulting expansion in incomes and economic means can, in turn, add to a person's freedom to achieve functionings that he or she values.

(3) *Instrumental social roles*: Greater literacy and basic education can facilitate public discussion of social needs and encourage informed collective demands (e.g. for health care and social security); these in turn can help expand the facilities that the public enjoys, and contribute to the better utilization of the available services.

(4) *Instrumental process roles*: The process of schooling can have benefits even aside from its explicitly aimed objectives, namely formal education. For example, the incidence of child labour is intimately connected with non-schooling of children, and the expansion of schooling can reduce the distressing phenomenon of child labour so prevalent in India.[12] Schooling also brings young people in touch

[11] Cf. 'Prime Minister Nehru's vision of a strong, independent India, with a sound economy generating rapid growth and reduction of the poverty afflicting many among us, is within our grasp if only the economic reforms are sustained and intensified' (Bhagwati and Srinivasan, 1993, p. 1).

[12] This issue has been extensively discussed by Myron Weiner (1991). On child labour in India, see also Rosenzweig and Evenson (1977), Government of India (1979), Khatu et al. (1983), Naidu and Kapadia (1985), Burra (1986, 1988, forthcoming), A.N. Singh (1990), Kanbargi (1991), Pati (1991).

with others and thereby broadens their horizons, and this can be particularly important for young girls.[13]

(5) *Empowerment and distributive roles*: Greater literacy and educational achievements of disadvantaged groups can increase their ability to resist oppression, to organize politically, and to get a fairer deal. The redistributive effects can be important not only between different social groups or households, but also *within* the family, since there is evidence that better education (particularly female education) contributes to the reduction of gender-based inequalities (see chapter 7 below).

These influences need not work only for the person who receives education or health care. There are also interpersonal effects. For example, one person's educational ability can be of use to another (e.g. to get a pamphlet read, or to have a public announcement explained).[14] The interpersonal connections can be of political significance as well; for example, a community may benefit generally from the civic attention it receives through the educated activism of a particular group within that community. Also, the use of economic opportunity by one person can, in many circumstances, open up further opportunities for others, through backward and forward linkages in supply and demand.[15] It is hard to evaluate the contributions of education except through a broad 'social choice' approach.[16] There are similar interconnections in matters of health because of the obvious importance of externalities in morbidity, preventive care, and curative treatment.[17] Expansion of health and education can have influences that go much beyond the immediate personal effects.

Through these various interconnections, education and health can be variables of great strategic importance in the process of economic development.[18] India's failure to have an adequate public policy in

---

[13] See e.g. Karuna Chanana (1988b).

[14] There are typically significant 'externalities' in the contribution of education to the adoption of innovation, as for example in agriculture, so that one family can benefit from the knowledge and experiences of neighbouring families; on this and related issues, see Chaudhri (1979).

[15] See Hirschman (1958, 1970) on this and related issues.

[16] On the social-choice perspectives in education, see Tapas Majumdar (1983).

[17] This characteristic affects, in many different ways, the nature of 'the health economy' (see Fuchs, 1986).

[18] On various aspects of the relationship between education, health, and economic development, see Behrman and Deolalikar (1988), Psacharopoulos (1988, 1993),

educational and health matters can be, thus, of profound significance in assessing the limited success of Indian development efforts over the last half a century. A policy reform that concentrates just on liberalization and deregulation cannot deal with this part of the failure of past planning.

The removal of counterproductive government controls may indeed expand social opportunities for many people. However, to change the circumstances (such as illiteracy and ill health) that severely constrain the actual social opportunities of a large part of the population, these permissive reforms have to be supplemented by a radical shift in public policy in education and health. If we see economic development in the perspective of social opportunities in general, both for their intrinsic importance and for their instrumental value, we cannot afford to miss this crucial linkage.

2.3. *The Government, the State and the Market*

The competing virtues of the market mechanism and governmental action have been much discussed in the literature. But the comparative merits of the two forms of economic decision are so thoroughly context–dependent that it makes little sense to espouse a *general* 'pro state' or 'pro market' view. To illustrate the point at the most obvious level, we could note the simple fact that what a government can do, and will in fact do, must depend on the *nature* of that government. Unfortunately, the history of the modern world is no less full of tales of tyrannies and tortures than the medieval chronicles of the barbarity of those times. The terrifying success that the Khmer Rouge had in Cambodia in quickly disposing off a million people on extraordinary ideological grounds is an obvious example. Idi Amin's Uganda provides an illustration of brutality of another kind—less ideological but not much less vicious. That this is not a simple 'third world' phenomenon is easily illustrated by the enormity of the Nazi atrocities and genocide in twentieth-century Germany. The implicit belief, expressed in some writings, that government interventions are, by and large, guided by the demands of social progress is surely a gigantic folly.

Even when the government's objectives are not as vicious as

Osmani (1990, 1992), Summers (1992), Colclough (1993), Dasgupta (1993), among others, and the literature cited in these studies. See also Robert Lane's (1994) discussion of governmental responsibility in developing 'qualities of persons'.

they were in Pol Pot's Cambodia, or in Amin's Uganda, or in Nazi Germany, there is still a question as to who is trying to achieve what through the mechanism of governmental activities. The implicit faith in the goodness and the good sense of the government that underlies much reasoning in favour of government-led economic development cannot, frequently, stand up to scrutiny.

The distinction between the state and the government may be of some significance in this context. The state is, in many ways, a broader concept, which includes the government, but also the legislature that votes on public rules, the political system that regulates elections, the role that is given to opposition parties, and the basic political rights that are upheld by the judiciary. A democratic state makes it that much harder for the ruling government to be unresponsive to the needs and values of the population at large. The nastiness of the Khmer Rouge's governance was sustainable because Pol Pot did not have to face elections or cater to opposition parties, and it is the militarist, undemocratic state that made the genocidal policy of the Khmer Rouge politically feasible. So we have to ask questions not merely about the nature of the actual government in office, but, going beyond that, also about the nature of the state of which the ruling government is only one part.

There is a similar question about the context-dependence of the role of the market mechanism as well.[19] What kinds of markets are we talking about? Most of the theory of efficiency or effectiveness of the market mechanism relates to competitive markets in equilibrium. It is not unreasonable to assume that small violations of those competitive conditions need not alter the results violently (some kind of Leibnizian belief in the 'continuity of nature' is clearly involved in this implicit faith), but actual markets can take very different forms indeed. For example, the cornering by a few operators of goods in short supply—leading to a massive accentuation of shortage and suffering—has happened too often to be dismissed as imaginary nightmares. The recent history of Asia and Africa provides plentiful examples of market exchanges being used to make profits out of the miseries of millions.

There are also cases where the market manages to misjudge the extent of a shortage quite badly, and causes suffering—even chaos—as

---

[19] The market mechanism also has social influences in the formation of attitudes and ideas, which too can be critically evaluated from alternative perspectives; see e.g. Hirschman (1992), and also Lane (1991).

a result, without this being the result of much wilful manipulation. This happened, for example, in the Bangladesh famine of 1974, when misguided speculation on the part of traders contributed to an enormous hiking of rice prices, followed later by a sharp fall towards pre-hike prices (meanwhile the famine had taken its toll).[20] To take a general 'pro market' view without conditions attached is no less problematic than taking a general 'pro government' view.

The contrast between market-based and government-based economic decisions, thus, requires a clearer understanding of the nature of the markets and the governments involved. These are not, of course, all-or-none questions. There are variations in market forms, in the extent of competition, in the openness of entry, in the actual scope for manipulability, and so on. And there are diversities in the nature of governments, depending on the political system underlying the state, the legal system that sustains political freedom, the power of ruling political groups, the treatment of opposition and dissent, and so on. The assessment of the respective merits of market-based decisions and governmental policies cannot but be thoroughly dependent on the reading of the markets and of the governments involved.

2.4. *Interdependence between Markets and Governance*

In assessing the relative merits of the market and the government, note has to be taken of their thoroughgoing interdependence. In particular, the operation and successes of the market mechanism can be deeply influenced by the nature of government actions that go with it. This is so for various reasons—some more obvious than others.

First, it is fairly straightforward to recognize that markets can hardly function in the absence of legal backing of contracts and particular rights. While some of these obligations are carried out automatically (and business ethics can play an important part in the fulfilment of contractual market exchanges), the possibility of legal action in the absence of such compliance is an important background condition for the smooth operation of systems of exchange and production. It is not surprising that the development of the market mechanism

---

[20] See particularly Ravallion (1987) for an econometric study of this process; see also Alamgir (1980). Coles and Hammond (1995) have discussed the operation of markets in the development of famines in general.

during the industrial revolution in Europe closely followed the establishment of law and order that could provide security to business and economic operations. To take a different type of example, it is impossible to understand why the market mechanism is so weak in, say, contemporary Somalia without seeing it in the context of the breakdown of law and order—the form that the 'comeuppance' of the militarist regime has taken in that country. Indeed, the Somalian famine of 1992 was, to a great extent, the result of the breakdown of the market mechanism which in turn had resulted from the breakdown of governance.

Second, the government may have a major role in initiating and facilitating market-reliant economic growth. This has been studied a great deal in the history of such successful capitalist countries as Germany and Japan. More recently, the role of the government has received much attention in interpreting the so-called 'East Asian miracle'—the tremendous success of the newly industrializing countries in east Asia (in particular South Korea, Taiwan, Hong Kong, Singapore, and more recently China and Thailand).[21] This role is easy to understand in the light of economic theory—particularly related to difficulties of initiation, connected with such factors as difficulties of 'tatonnement' (pre-exchange negotiations about market prices, leading to simultaneous production decisions), economies of large scale, importance of technological externalities, and the integral nature of skill formation. The nurturing of an early market mechanism by an active state does not, of course, preclude a more self-sufficient role of the market *later on*.

Third, even the formal theory of achievements of the market mechanism is, implicitly, much dependent on governmental action. Consider the so-called fundamental theorems of welfare economics.[22]

---

[21] Recent studies of the so-called 'East Asian miracle' include Amsden (1989), Wade (1990), Birdsall and Sabot (1993a), Corden (1993), Johansen (1993), Lucas (1993), World Bank (1993c), Fallows (1994), Rodrik (1994a), among others. In this and related contexts, see also Cole and Lyman (1971), Corden (1974), Bhagwati and Krueger (1975), Frank, Kim, and Westphal (1975), Hong and Krueger (1975), Kim (1977), Adelman and Robinson (1978), Westphal (1978), Datta Chaudhuri (1979, 1990), Krueger (1979), Scott (1979), Little (1982, 1994), Chenery et al. (1986), Blomstrom (1989), Wade (1989), Balassa (1991), Dollar (1992), Chowdhury and Islam (1993), Christensen et al. (1993), Fields (1993), Findlay (1993), Findlay and Wallisz (1993), Pack (1993), Stiglitz (1993), Fishlow et al. (1994), Little (1994), Muscat (1994).

[22] See Arrow (1951), Debreu (1959), McKenzie (1959), Arrow and Hahn (1971). For a helpful non-technical introduction, see Koopmans (1957).

The first theorem, which shows that—given some standard conditions—any competitive equilibrium is Pareto efficient, is thought to be less interesting than the second, since a Pareto efficient allocation can be terribly unequal and thoroughly revolting. The second theorem, on the other hand, shows that under some—rather more stringent—assumptions (including the absence of significant economies of large scale), any Pareto efficient allocation is a competitive equilibrium for some set of prices and some initial distribution of resources. If Pareto efficiency is regarded as a necessary condition for overall social optimality, this entails that a socially optimum allocation can be—given the assumed framework—sustained through a competitive equilibrium, provided the initial distribution of resources is appropriately fixed.

The question is: *who* would fix the initial distribution of resources in this way? Here again, the agency of the government would generally be required. Thus, the significance of the so-called 'fundamental theorem of welfare economics' is deeply dependent on governmental action. There may be good reasons for scepticism regarding the political scope, in many societies, for redistributing initial endowments in this way—certainly to the extent that would be needed for social optimality with an equity-sensitive social welfare function. But what can be made achievable by the market in the direction of equity (via the second theorem) would be conditional on appropriate governmental activism.

The interdependence between market and government works, in fact, in the other direction also. It is hard to think of a government achieving anything like an acceptable social arrangement if citizens are prohibited from exchanging commodities, or producing goods and services, on their own initiative. These activities—involving transactions and compacts—form integral parts of the market mechanism, no ·matter how rudimentary that mechanism might be.

The recent developments in economic theory that have stressed the importance of economies of large scale, and of endogenous growth, have done much to clarify the role of markets and trade.[23] Indeed, as Adam Smith (1776) had argued, markets provide great opportunities

---

[23] See particularly Paul Romer (1986, 1987a, 1987b, 1990, 1993). On related issues, in the context of international trade, see also Krugman (1979, 1986, 1987), Lucas (1988, 1993), Grossman and Helpman (1990, 1991a, 1991b), Helpman and Krugman (1990), Helpman and Razin (1991), Krugman and Smith (1994), and the collection of contributions in Buchanan and Yoon (1994).

for acquiring benefits from trade based on specialization and division of labour, and the recent departures in growth theory and trade theory have involved what Buchanan and Yoon (1994) have aptly called 'the return to increasing returns'.

This line of analysis has also brought out the extent to which the pattern of international division of labour is not given simply by natural blessings and comparative advantages, but is also substantially influenced by the actual history of past experiences and specializations. Thus public policy can have a lasting role in the way the markets are used. The issue of interdependence is, indeed, of even greater significance than a history-free analysis might suggest. While markets must be, in this analysis, an essential vehicle of realizing economic potentials, the long-run influence of active public policy, for example, in initiating particular industries and in providing a wide base of public education (as occurred, say, in Japan or South Korea) can be more easily interpreted and understood in this light.

The wider interdependences discussed here call for a clearer understanding of the relation between government policy and market operations. In particular, it is quite important to distinguish between market-excluding and market-complementary government interventions.

2.5. *Market-excluding and Market-complementary Interventions*

The contributions and failures of any social arrangement involve both commission (what it does) and omission (what it fails to do).[24] The markets do certain things, and abstain from doing others. A 'failure' can arise from *either* positively doing something that would have harmful consequences, *or* from not doing something that would have to be done for good results. To illustrate from a different field of ethical judgement, murdering would be an example of harmful commission, whereas failing to stop a preventable murder would be a case of omission.[25]

The market, like other institutions, does certain things, and abstains from doing others. There is a real asymmetry here which is hidden by unclear contrasts between the market mechanism and 'non-market'

---

[24] The relevance of the distinction in assessing the achievements and failures of the market mechanism has been discussed in Sen (1993a, 1993b).

[25] There are, however, plenty of philosophical difficulties with pressing this distinction very far.

systems. An economic arrangement can be 'non-market' in the sense that markets are not allowed to operate freely or even to operate at all. This can be called a 'market-excluding' arrangement. Or it can be 'non-market' in the sense that many things are done, say, by the state, that the market would not do. Such supplementary operations do not have to prohibit markets and exchanges. This can be called a 'market-complementary' arrangement.

Obviously, it is possible for a system to have a mixture of market-excluding and market-complementary interventions. The respective implications of the two types of 'non-market' arrangements may be very different indeed. The nature of the issue can be usefully illustrated with concrete examples from a particular area of contemporary concern, namely the terrible phenomenon of famine, which continues to plague the modern world. Famines have, of course, occurred in non-market socialist economies as well as in market-based systems. But looking for the moment at famines in market economies, we can ask: why has the market system not been able to avoid them?

It has often been argued that the markets can and do distort food trade. Certainly, examples of markets being manipulated by organized traders are not hard to find. These manipulations have sometimes heightened the suffering and misery associated with famines. On the other hand, it is hard to find evidence to suggest that active trade distortion has been a *primary* cause of famines in market economies. The most obvious failure of the market mechanism lies, in this context, in the things that the market leaves *undone*. If some groups lose their purchasing power and their entitlement to food, say, due to employment loss as a result of a drought or a flood, the market may not do much to regenerate incomes or to recreate their lost command over food. That is an error of *omission*, which has to be distinguished from the positively bad things that the market might do. The remedy in this case need not be sought in 'market-excluding' interventions.

It is not being argued here that *all* the problems associated with the market mechanism in the context of a famine are invariably of the 'omission' type, that is, the result of what the markets do *not* do, rather than of their active presence. The working of the market can positively worsen the situation of particular groups of people, by making things worse through its operation. An example is the role of the market in the decimation of pastoralists when the price of animals and animal products fall in relation to the cost of cheaper staple food, as is common in many famines (for reasons which have been discussed elsewhere; see Sen, 1981, chapters 7 and 8). Pastoralists suffer in this way because their economic existence has come to depend on the way the market functions, due to commercialization. Similarly, the decline in the ratio of wages to food prices that occurs when the demand for labour falls (due to a drought or a flood that affects agricultural activities) can certainly worsen the position of the labourer in an active way, and this vulnerability is related to dependence on market exchange.

Even when there is a problem of market-driven commission, however, the threat of famine cannot be eliminated by outlawing the market, that is, by adopting any *general* 'market-excluding' intervention.[26] Indeed, what is happening in these cases is that the benefits the individuals receive from participating in the market (e.g. by selling labour-power and buying food with one's wage, or by selling animal products and buying cheap food) can suddenly be severely compromised by changed economic circumstances. The process, thus, works through a *reduction of the advantages* of market transaction—advantages that may be vital for survival, and on which people may have come to rely. The process of destitution is sustained by the failure of the market mechanism to provide security of these exchange arrangements and terms of trade.

Lack of clarity about the distinction between market-excluding and market-complementary interventions has been responsible for some misanalysis and misinterpretation. For example, Adam Smith's (1776) defence of private trade in foodgrains and criticism of prohibitory restrictions by the state have often been interpreted as a proposition that state interference can only make a famine worse. But Smith's defence of private trade took the form of disputing the belief that food trades produce serious errors of *commission*. That disputation does not deny in any way the need for state action,

---

[26] In some specific cases, stopping the market from functioning can possibly be useful, for example in preventing 'food countermovements' occurring in certain types of famine situations (see Sen, 1981, Chichilnisky, 1983). Sometimes food can move out from famine-stricken areas to more prosperous regions where people have greater ability to pay for food (for example, from famished Ireland to relatively opulent England during the Irish famines of the 1840s). In such situations, selective restrictions on the market can be useful (in the case of food countermovement, by preventing price increases in the famine-affected food-exporting country or region). But such cases are, on the whole, rather rare.

in tackling a threatening famine, to supplement the operations of the market by creating incomes (e.g. through work programmes) because the market *omits* to do this. Smith's is a rejection of market-excluding systems, but not of public intervention for market-complementary arrangements.

Indeed, Smith's famine analysis is consistent with arguing for a discriminatingly activist government that would create incomes and purchasing power for the disentitled population, and then leave the supply of food to respond to the newly created demand through private trade. There is evidence—both from south Asia and from sub-Saharan Africa—that this combination of (1) undertaking state action to generate incomes and purchasing power of the potential famine victims, and (2) letting private markets respond then to those incomes and demands, often works remarkably well in preventing famines.[27] That combination was explicitly discussed by Smith's friend Condorcet, and Smith's own analysis is entirely consistent with taking that route.[28]

Smith did provide a strong defence of the commissioning aspects of the market mechanism. His famous statement about gains from trade between the butcher, the brewer, and the baker, on the one hand, and the consumer, on the other, points to the advantages that the market positively produces for all the parties involved in the exchange. It does not deny that if we lack the *means* to buy meat, beer, or bread, the butcher, the brewer, and the baker won't do much for us. Stifling that trade would, he argued, be an active mistake, but waiting with hopeful passivity for incomes to be generated that would set the baker et al. to supply the needy can also be a costly error.

The distinction between omission and commission is important in understanding the division between the respective roles of the market and of non-market institutions in modern economies. In fact, it is possible to argue at the same time both (1) for *more* market institutions, and (2) for going *more beyond* the market. Indeed, in the context of the challenges of Indian planning, such a combination may be exactly what is needed. The fact that the form of the Indian political debates has tended to be quite traditional ('pro' or 'against'

---

[27] On the circumstantial and strategic aspects of this combined policy, see Drèze (1990a, 1990b) and Drèze and Sen (1989).

[28] See Rothschild (1992a, 1992b).

the market) has certainly contributed to confounding the nature of the issues. The need for more active use of the market in, say, industrial production and trade does not do away with the need for more state activity in raising India's abysmal level of basic education, health care, and social security. Similarly, on the other side, the recognition of the latter need does nothing to reduce the importance of reforming the over-bureaucratized Indian economy.

The market-complementary arrangements needed to eliminate famines have, on the whole, worked quite well in post-independent India.[29] However, the problem of omission remains a central one in the context of the contemporary Indian economy—not in terms of vulnerability to famine, but in the form of regular undernourishment, widespread illiteracy, and high rates of morbidity and mortality. These are denials of basic freedoms that human beings have reasons to value. Furthermore, these deprivations can also be instrumentally significant by severely constraining the opportunity to participate in the process of economic expansion and social change. In trying to guarantee these freedoms, combining the functionings of markets and those of governments can be critically important. In these circumstances, market-complementary interventions can have favourable effects in a way that neither market-excluding intervention, nor non-intervention, can achieve.

2.6. *A Positive Focus*

The literature on freedom in political philosophy is full of discussions that turn on the distinction between 'negative' and 'positive' liberties. That distinction can be interpreted in many different ways, but one way of seeing the contrast is to identify 'negative' liberty with *not being prevented* from doing certain things, while 'positive' liberty also includes those *supportive influences* which actually help a person to do the things that she wants to do.[30] While libertarians have been inclined to stress negative liberty, advocates of public support have tended to concentrate on positive versions of it.

A similar—though not identical—distinction can be made about

[29] See Drèze and Sen (1989), chapter 8, Drèze (1990a), and the literature cited there.

[30] For different ways of characterizing the distinction between positive and negative liberty, see Berlin (1969), Nozick (1974), Dworkin (1978, 1981), Sen (1980, 1985b), Roemer (1982), Hamlin and Pettit (1989), Raz (1986), Arneson (1989), Cohen (1990, 1993), Dasgupta (1993), among other contributions.

the readings of the government's 'duties' *vis-à-vis* the citizens. The *negative* roles consist in preventing what are taken to be bad developments (for example, outlawing monopolistic arrangements), whereas *positive* roles concern supporting constructively the efforts of the citizens to help themselves (for example, by arranging public education, by redistributing land, by protecting the legal rights of disadvantaged groups). Leaving out extremist advocacies, most political theories tend to provide room for both positive and negative roles of the government, but the relative importance that is given to the respective spheres can vary greatly.

Much of the debate on liberalization and deregulation is concerned with removing what is diagnosed to be the counterproductive nature of negative operations of the government. This position has been forcefully presented by the central government and the supporters of the new policies. On the other hand, opposition to these types of reforms tends to come from those who see beneficial consequences of these negative governmental functions. The debate on current policy in India has been preoccupied with this battle.

There are certainly issues to be sorted out in this 'negative' sphere, but what the debate neglects altogether is the importance of positive functions, such as provision of public education, health services, and arrangements for social security. There is scope for debate in this field as well (for example, on how, and how much, and how soon), but nothing is sorted out in these matters by concentrating almost completely on the pros and cons of negative roles of the government (and the corresponding advantages and disadvantages of liberalization and deregulation). What is needed most of all at this time is a broadening of focus.

3

INDIA IN
COMPARATIVE PERSPECTIVE

3.1. *India and the World*

In historical terms, the improvement of living conditions that has taken place in the developing world during the last few decades has been quite remarkable. To illustrate, it is estimated that, between 1960 and 1992, life expectancy at birth in developing countries has expanded from 46 to 63 years, infant mortality has declined by more than 50 per cent, and real per-capita income has almost trebled.[1] These global *trends* are quite at variance with the gloomy predictions of famine and chaos that have been regularly made over the same period, even if absolute levels of deprivation remain intolerably high in large parts of the world.[2]

The pace of improvement has, of course, been quite uneven between different countries and regions, and recent decades have also seen the emergence of striking diversities within the developing world. In fact, the leading countries in the developing world are now, in many ways, much closer to industrialized market economies than to the poorer developing countries. It is not just that real

---

[1] UNDP, *Human Development Report 1994*, p. 207.

[2] For examples of these predictions, see Ehrlich (1968), Paddock and Paddock (1968), Brown and Eckholm (1974), Ehrlich and Ehrlich (1990), Hardin (1993), and Kaplan (1994). India has held centre-stage in many of the gloomy prophecies in question, particularly during the 1960s. To illustrate: 'In thirteen years India is going to add two hundred million more people to their population. In my opinion, as an old India hand, I don't see how they can possibly feed two hundred million more people by 1980. They could if they had the time, say until year 2000. Maybe they could even do it by 1990, but they can't do it by 1980' (Dr Raymond Ewell, in Ehrlich, 1968, pp. 39–40).

per-capita income is now as high in Hong Kong as in France or Sweden, and quite similar in Saudi Arabia and Ireland. Even countries such as Venezuela and South Korea seem to have more in common with Greece or Portugal, which have comparable levels of real per-capita income, than with Tanzania or Bhutan, where real per-capita income is about 15 times as low. Similarly, the adult literacy rate is a little higher in Jamaica (98 per cent) than in Spain (95 per cent), and quite similar in Uruguay and Italy (about 96 per cent each), but only 18 per cent in Burkina Faso and 26 per cent in Nepal. And the expectation of life at birth is no different in Costa Rica or Cuba (76 years each) from what it is in Germany or Belgium (also 76 years each), while a person born in Afghanistan or Sierra Leone or Uganda can only expect to live for a little over 40 years.[3] While the common division of the world between 'North' and 'South' may have political interest and historical relevance, it is quite misleading in terms of many of the central features of development.

An important aspect of this diverse picture is that elementary deprivation is now heavily concentrated in two particular regions of the world: south Asia and sub-Saharan Africa. Consider, for instance, the set of all countries where the expectation of life at birth is below 60 years. According to recent estimates, there are 52 such countries, with a combined population of 1,685 million.[4] Only 6 of these countries (Afghanistan, Cambodia, Haiti, Laos, Papua New Guinea, and Yemen) are outside south Asia and sub-Saharan Africa; their combined population is only 59 million, or 3.5 per cent of the total population of this set of countries. The remaining 46 countries

---

[3] The figures mentioned in this paragraph are taken from *World Development Report 1994*, Tables 1, 1a, and 30 (the 'real per-capita income' comparisons are based on purchasing-power-parity estimates of GNP per capita). Some of the figures presented in that report, as well as in *Human Development Report 1994* (also used in this chapter), involve substantial margins of error. This has to be borne in mind when comparing India's reasonably firm estimates with the corresponding—often less reliable—figures for other developing countries. The comparisons presented in this section give a rough idea of where India stands *vis-à-vis* the rest of the developing world, but the detailed inter-country comparisons would, in many cases, call for more scrutiny. For further discussion of the data sources used in this book, see the Statistical Appendix.

[4] The figures cited in this paragraph are calculated from *World Development Report 1994*, Tables 1 and 1a (the reference year is 1992). For India, this report gives a life expectancy estimate of 61 years, but more recent calculations for 1991 by the Office of the Registrar General put life expectancy at birth in India a little below 60 years (59.0 for males and 59.4 years for females). See Statistical Appendix for details.

consist of the whole of south Asia except Sri Lanka (i.e. India, Pakistan, Bangladesh, Nepal, and Bhutan, with a combined population of 1,139 million), and the whole of sub-Saharan Africa except South Africa, Zimbabwe, Lesotho, Botswana, and a collection of tiny islands (e.g. Mauritius and the Seychelles). Of course, even in countries where life expectancy at birth is above 60 on the *average*, it can be well below that figure for particular sections of the population (just as life expectancy can be much above 60 for the more privileged sections of the population in the below-60 countries). But it is clear that there are few regions where elementary deprivation is as endemic as in south Asia and sub-Saharan Africa.

India alone accounts for more than half of the combined population of these 52 deprived countries. It is not the worst performer by any means (in fact, life expectancy in India is very close to 60 years), but this observation has to be interpreted bearing in mind that there are large regional variations in living conditions *within* India. While India is doing significantly better than, say, Ethiopia or Zaire in terms of most development indicators, there are large areas within India where living conditions are not very different from those prevailing in these countries.

To illustrate this point, Table 3.1 compares the levels of infant mortality and adult literacy in the least developed regions of sub-Saharan Africa and India. For each of these two indicators, the table presents 1991 estimates not only for India and sub-Saharan Africa as a whole (first and last rows), but also for the three worst-performing countries of sub-Saharan Africa, the three worst-performing Indian states, and the worst-performing districts of each of these three states. It turns out that there is no country in sub-Saharan Africa—or indeed in the world—where estimated infant mortality rates are as high as in the district of Ganjam in Orissa, or where the adult female literacy rate is as low as in the district of Barmer in Rajasthan. Each of these two districts, incidentally, has a larger population than Botswana or Namibia, and their combined population is larger than that of Sierra Leone, Nicaragua, or Ireland. Even entire states such as Uttar Pradesh (which has a population as large as that of Brazil or Russia) are not doing much better than the least developed among sub-Saharan countries in terms of basic indicators of the kind presented in Table 3.1.[5]

---

[5] Shiva Kumar's (1991) estimates of UNDP's 'human development index' (HDI) for

TABLE 3.1. *India and Sub-Saharan Africa: Selected Comparisons (1991)*

	Infant mortality rate comparisons			Adult literacy rate comparisons		
	Region	Population (millions)	Infant mortality rate (per 1,000 live births)	Region	Population (millions)	Adult literacy rate[a] (female/male)
INDIA	India	846.3	80	India	846.3	39/64
'Worst' three Indian states	Orissa	31.7	124	Rajasthan	44.0	20/55
	Madhya Pradesh	66.2	117	Bihar	86.4	23/52
	Uttar Pradesh	139.1	97	Uttar Pradesh	139.1	25/56
'Worst' district of each of the 'worst' Indian states	Ganjam (Orissa)	3.2	164	Barmer (Rajasthan)	1.4	8/37
	Tikamgarh (Madhya Pradesh)	0.9	152	Kishanganj (Bihar)	1.0	10/33
	Hardoi (Uttar Pradesh)	2.7	129	Bahraich (Uttar Pradesh)	2.8	11/36
'Worst' three countries of sub-Saharan Africa	Mali	8.7	161	Burkina Faso	9.2	10/31
	Mozambique	16.1	149	Sierra Leone	4.3	12/35
	Guinea-Bissau	1.0	148	Benin	4.8	17/35
SUB-SAHARAN AFRICA	Sub-Saharan Africa	488.9	104	Sub-Saharan Africa	488.9	40/63

Note. [a] The age cut-off is 15 years for African figures, and 7 years for Indian figures. Note that, in India, the 7+ literacy rate is usually a little higher than the 15+ literacy rate (e.g. the all-India 7+ literacy rate in 1981 was 43.6%, compared with 40.8% for the 15+ literacy rate).

Sources. *World Development Report 1993,* Tables 1 and 28, and *Human·Development Report 1994,* Table 5, for sub-Saharan Africa. Nanda (1992), Tables 2 and 7, *Sample Registration Bulletin,* January 1994 (Table 8), Tyagi (1993), pp. 24–40 and Government of India (1988), for India (as discussed in the Statistical Appendix, the all-India figures from these sources are broadly consistent with the corresponding figures reported in *World Development Report 1993* and *Human Development Report 1994*). The district-level infant mortality rates (IMR) for India are based on the assumption that, within each state, the ratios of district IMR to state IMR were the same in 1991 as in 1981 (district-level IMR estimates are not available for more recent years than 1981); these figures should be considered as illustrative. All figures relate to 1991, except the African literacy figures, which relate to 1992.

Considering the figures for India and sub-Saharan Africa as a whole, we find that the two regions are not very different in terms of either adult literacy or infant mortality. This is not to say that both regions are generally in the same boat as far as development performance is concerned. As was mentioned already, the expectation of life in India is now around 60 years, while it is still much below that figure in sub-Saharan Africa (averaging about 52 years).[6] Also, since independence, India has been relatively free of the problems of famine and internal armed conflict that periodically ravage a large number of African countries. And many countries of sub-Saharan Africa have had a specific problem of economic *decline* — partly related to these calamities—which makes it particularly hard to improve living standards. On the other side, economic and social inequalities are, in some respects at least, more acute in India. These inequalities, aside from being social failures on their own, also imply much lower levels of well-being for disadvantaged sections of the population than the country or regional aggregates suggest. Gender inequalities, for instance, tend to be larger in India than in sub-Saharan Africa, and are responsible for extremely high levels of female deprivation in India.[7] A comparative assessment of the achievements and failures of the two regions would have to take note of these and other aspects of their respective development experiences.

It is interesting, however, that one problem which India and sub-Saharan Africa have in common is the persistence of endemic illiteracy (a feature which, like low life expectancy, sets south Asia and sub-Saharan Africa apart from most of the rest of the world).

Indian states put Uttar Pradesh near the bottom of the international scale, between Ethiopia and Zaire. Uttar Pradesh's performance is even worse in terms of some indicators not included in that HDI index (which is essentially a weighted average of life expectancy, adult literacy, and real income indicators). For instance, it appears that there is no country in the world where the female–male ratio in the population—a useful indicator of basic gender inequality—is as low as in Uttar Pradesh (if one excludes oil-exporting countries such as Kuwait, United Arab Emirates, and Bahrain, where massive male immigration has produced exceptionally low female–male ratios). On this and related issues, see the case study of Uttar Pradesh by Drèze and Gazdar (1996) in the companion volume (Drèze and Sen, 1996).

[6] This figure of 52 years as the weighted average for sub-Saharan Africa is given by *World Development Report 1994* (Table 1, p. 163).

[7] On gender gaps in survival, literacy, and related indicators, see e.g. the data presented in the *Human Development Reports*. For further discussion of this particular contrast between India and sub-Saharan Africa, see Sen (1988).

As Table 3.1 indicates, literacy rates are very similar in the two regions. In India, as in sub-Saharan Africa, every other adult is illiterate.

It is rather striking that India turns out to be doing no better than sub-Saharan Africa in this respect.[8] Unlike many countries of sub-Saharan Africa, India has been relatively protected from the calamities of political instability, military rules, divisive wars, and recurring famines for a period of almost fifty years, but it has failed to take advantage of these favourable circumstances to achieve a breakthrough in the field of basic education. This failure, which stands in sharp contrast with a relatively good record in higher education and scientific research, is one of the most deplorable aspects of India's contemporary development experience.

3.2. *Lessons from Other Countries*

The cases of successful economic development in other developing countries are often cited in Indian policy debates. It is, in general, appropriate to do this: many countries have achieved much more than India has been able to do, and it is natural to learn from the accomplishments of these countries. The countries frequently selected for comparison (such as South Korea and the other three of the so-called 'four tigers', and also Thailand and post-reform China) are indeed among the countries from which India can expect to learn greatly, since they have, in different ways, done so very well. To claim that 'India is unique' would be true enough in itself but thoroughly misleading as an alleged ground for refusing to try to learn from other countries.

However, in learning from the experiences of others, we have to be careful to avoid taking an over-simple view of what it is that the 'others' have done, or identifying the relevant 'others' from an over-narrow perspective. First, it would be a great mistake to

---

[8] In fact, if anything, India comes out worse in the comparison, after taking into account differences in age cut-offs. The 1991 census figures for literacy in the 15+ age group in India have not been released at the time of writing, but figures for the 7+ age group are available, and we have used those in Table 3.1 for comparison with the adult literacy figures for sub-Saharan Africa, which relate to the standard 15+ age group. As mentioned in Table 3.1, the use of an age cut-off of 7 years for India—instead of the standard 15 years—has the effect of *raising* the Indian adult literacy rates by a few percentage points. The estimates of 15+ literacy rates in India presented in *World Development Report 1994* (Table 1) and *Human Development Report 1994* (Table 2) are a little lower than the corresponding estimates for sub-Saharan Africa.

assume—as is often done—that all that these successful experiences of, say, the four so-called 'tigers' (South Korea, Hong Kong, Singapore, Taiwan) teach us is the importance of 'freeing' the markets. Much else happened in these countries other than freeing the markets, such as educational expansion, reasonable health care, extensive land reforms, determined governmental leadership in promoting economic growth, and so on.[9] These countries—and also post-reform China— have all been well ahead of India in many 'social' respects that have made it much easier for them to make use of the economic opportunities offered by the expansion of markets, and they have, in fact, been in that 'better prepared' position even at the inception of their market-based leap forward. To overlook these differences on some imagined ground of separating out alleged 'essentials' from other 'ancillary' features would be both mistaken and quite counter-productive in learning from these experiences. We shall examine these issues in the next section.

Second, the 'others' to learn from are not just the countries that have experienced high economic growth (such as the four 'tigers', or Thailand, or post-reform China), but also those that have managed to raise the quality of life through other means (even in the absence of fast economic growth), such as public support for general health care and basic education. It is worth remembering that despite high growth performance, Thailand and even South Korea still have rather lower life expectancy at birth than, say, Sri Lanka or Jamaica, and even Singapore has not yet overtaken Costa Rica in life expectancy, despite large income differences in the opposite direction. China's remarkable success in transforming many aspects of the quality of life during the pre-reform period, at a time of relatively slow economic growth, is also relevant here (we shall have more to say on this, as well as on some of China's failures, in the next chapter). These and other experiences of rapid improvement in living conditions despite slow economic growth are full of important lessons—about the feasibility of achieving radical social progress at an early stage of economic development, about the powerful effects of well-devised

---

[9] Some of these countries—South Korea in particular—have also benefited from low levels of antecedent economic inequality, which helped to make the process of economic expansion more participatory, and also reduced the political pressure for redistribution, with its efficiency costs. Alesina and Rodrik (1994) have investigated the contribution of lesser inequality to economic growth and development; see also Persson and Tabellini (1991), Fishlow et al. (1994), and Rodrik (1994a).

public programmes in the fields of health and education, about the relatively inexpensive nature of labour-intensive public provisions such as primary education in a low-wage economy, about the collaborative and adversarial roles of public action, and so on.[10] It is just as important to identify these lessons as to learn from countries that have achieved rapid economic growth, and succeeded in using rapid growth as a basis for improving the quality of life.

Third, it must be remembered that not all countries with high growth rates have succeeded in translating an expanded command over material resources into a corresponding transformation of living conditions for broad sections of the population. In fact, the development experiences of some fast-growing countries during the last few decades has resembled one of 'unaimed opulence', combining high rates of economic growth with the persistence of widespread poverty, illiteracy, ill health, child labour, criminal violence, and related social failures.[11] Brazil is one widely-discussed example. In many cases (including Brazil itself), the roots of this failure to use economic growth as a basis for transforming the quality of life include high levels of economic and social inequality as well as a lack of public involvement in the protection of basic entitlements. The dangers of unaimed opulence, which may be particularly real for India, form an integral part of the lessons to be learnt from discriminating analyses of the experiences of fast-growing countries.

Fourth, as was argued earlier, given the heterogeneity of India, the question of learning from India itself has to be integrated with learning from others. We cannot, for example, altogether ignore the fact that Kerala, despite its low income level and poor record in generating economic growth, has a higher life expectancy at birth (about 72 years) than what can be found in some of the more economically successful countries further east, such as Indonesia (60 years), or Thailand (69 years), or even South Korea (71), despite per-capita income being a great many times larger in these other countries than in Kerala. We have to learn from the experiences *within* India itself, and this applies to failures as well as successes.

---

[10] We have tried to discuss some of these lessons in Drèze and Sen (1989). For insightful studies of specific country experiences, see also Castaneda (1984, 1985), Alailima (1985), Halstead et al. (1985), Caldwell (1986), Riskin (1987, 1990), Mata and Rosero (1988), Anand and Kanbur (1990), Bruton et al. (1993), among others.

[11] On this phenomenon of unaimed opulence, see Drèze and Sen (1989), chapter 10. On the specific case of Brazil, see Sachs (1990) and Birdsall and Sabot (1993b).

The relevant failures include not only the continued social backwardness of many states (such as Uttar Pradesh), but also the failure of Kerala to achieve reasonable economic growth, despite a remarkably high performance in terms of many aspects of the quality of life.

In an earlier study, we found that, among ten developing countries that had achieved the largest reductions in infant and child mortality rates between 1960 and 1985, five were cases of what we called 'growth-mediated' success, while the other five succeeded in reducing mortality on the basis of organized programmes of public support for health, education, and social security, without fast economic growth and without achieving much increase in average real income.[12] The latter approach—what we called 'support-led' success—proved to be feasible largely because the costs of elementary health care and education tend to be comparatively low in low-wage economies (because of the labour-intensive nature of these activities), so that a poorer economy is not as disadvantaged in providing these services as might be imagined on the basis of considering only their lower ability to pay. In drawing lessons for India from recent development experiences elsewhere in the world, it is important to pay attention to both types of progress, based respectively on economic growth and public support. It is also important to be aware of the possibility of 'unaimed opulence', and to take note of the fact that India could go the way of Brazil rather than of South Korea. We have to discriminate, rather than assume some 'stylized model' of liberalization.

3.3. *East Asia and Growth-mediated Progress*

In learning from the experiences of other countries, it is also essential to integrate our 'theory' of what is causing what with an understanding of the facts of the case. The importance of markets and trades in generating economic expansion has been a part of mainstream economic principles for a very long time. Even Adam Smith's (1776) classic analysis of the 'causes' of the wealth of nations dealt precisely with this question, among others. The recent revival of growth-oriented trade theory has done much to bring out the importance of two issues on which Adam Smith himself had much to say, to wit, (1) the importance of economies of large scale, and (2) the

---

[12] Drèze and Sen (1989), chapter 10.

influence of skill formation and human qualities in causing prosperity.[13] The shift in emphasis from seeing the gains from trade primarily in terms of given comparative advantages (the traditional 'Ricardian' focus) is important in interpreting 'the East Asian miracle' and its relevance to India and other countries.

The growing recognition of the role and importance of economies of large scale has also changed one of the intellectual bases of closed-economy planning that was so fashionable—in India as well as else-where—from the nineteen-sixties onwards.[14] Underlying that acceptance of economic autarchy was a sense of export pessimism that made planners in India and elsewhere look for more inter-nally-oriented economic development, aimed at producing within the borders whatever the country needed. The concentration, then common, on 'comparative advantage' as the real source of gainful trade (dependent on differences of factor ratios, natural endowments, etc.) did not persuade those analysts who tended to be sceptical of the possibility of trade expansion, and who underestimated the real gains from trade. Autarchy was, often enough, not so much a policy of jubilant rejection of trade, but the result of a pessimistic perception that the opportunities of trade were severely limited.[15]

With the shifting focus in trade theory, from Ricardo's comparative advantage to Adam Smith's economies of scale, the limits of trade expansion have been substantially reformulated and the grounds for export pessimism have been largely debunked. The limits of trade

[13] See Krugman (1979, 1986, 1987), Romer (1986, 1987b, 1990), Lucas (1988, 1993), Grossman and Helpman (1990, 1991a, 1991b). On different aspects of the lessons to be learned from recent experiences of rapid growth and trade expansion, see also Lucas (1988), Stokey (1988), Helpman and Krugman (1990), Helpman and Razin (1991), Helleiner (1992), Ethier, Helpman, and Neary (1993), Findlay (1993), Krugman and Smith (1994), among other contributions.

[14] For a fine account of the rationale behind planning approaches used in India, see Chakravarty (1987). See also Jalan (1992).

[15] One of the authors of this monograph was, in fact, involved in constructing a model, jointly with K.N. Raj, explicitly assuming this pessimism, entitled 'Alternative Patterns of Growth under Conditions of Stagnant Export Earnings' (Raj and Sen, 1961). While the main interest in that analysis had nothing to do with trade, but with the relations between different sectors in a growth model with constant returns to scale (on this see Atkinson, 1969, and Cooper, 1983), it was the sense—mistaken as it happens—of export pessimism that made models of this kind look at all relevant to Indian planning. Even when export pessimism was not explicitly assumed, it tended to colour the growth scenarios that were explored in development models in that period (see, for example, Chakravarty, 1969).

are not to be seen as being constrained simply by differences in factor ratios and endowments, and what a country loses from autarchy includes the efficiency advantages of a division of labour that uses, *inter alia*, scale advantages and gains from specialization. The need for a radical departure in this respect in Indian economic planning is brought out both by reasoning based on modern growth theory, and by the actual experience of the economies—such as those in east Asia—that have made such excellent use of trade-using patterns of economic growth.

Recent work on economic growth has also brought out sharply the role of labour and the so-called 'human capital'. The economic roles of school education, learning by doing, technical progress, and even economies of large scale can all be seen as contributing—in different ways—to the centrality of direct human agency in generating economic expansion. In terms of economic theory, this shift in emphasis has provided one way of filling the large 'residual' that was identified in the basic neo-classical model of economic growth of Solow (1956), and recent growth theory has done much to bring out the function of direct human agency in economic growth, over and above the contribution made through the accumulation of physical capital.[16] Our attempt to learn from the experiences of 'the East Asian miracle' and other cases of growth-mediated progress cannot ignore the wealth of insights that these analyses have provided.[17]

The crucial role of human capital makes it all the more essential to pay attention to the close relation between sensible public action and economic progress, since public policy has much to contribute to the expansion of education and the promotion of skill formation. The role of widespread basic education in these countries with successful growth-mediated progress cannot be overemphasized.[18] The

[16] There is a vast literature in this field, beginning with Solow's own works that followed his 1956 model (see particularly Solow, 1957). For aspects of the recent revival of the subject, involving 'new' growth theory as well as further exploration of older neo-classical models, see Romer (1986, 1987a, 1987b), Krugman (1987), Barro (1990b), Matsuyama (1991), Stokey (1991a), Young (1992), Mankiw, Romer, and Weil (1992), Barro and Lee (1993a, 1993b), Lucas (1993), among other contributions.

[17] See Rodrik (1994a) for a different reading of 'the East Asian miracle', with more focus on the investment boom in South Korea and Taiwan; see also Fishlow et al. (1994).

[18] On different aspects and interpretations of this role, see Behrman (1987), Behrman and Schneider (1992), Stevenson and Stigler (1992), Barro and Lee (1993a, 1993b), Birdsall and Sabot (1993a), Easterly, Kremer, Pritchett, and Summers (1993), World Bank (1993c), among many other contributions.

modern industries in which these countries have particularly excelled demand many basic skills for which elementary education is essential and secondary education most helpful. While some studies have emphasized the productivity contribution of learning by doing and on-the-job training, rather than the direct impact of formal education, the ability to achieve such training and learning is certainly helped greatly by basic education in schools prior to taking up jobs.[19]

The development of basic education was very much more advanced in all these countries with successful growth-mediated progress at the time of their economic breakthrough compared with India today. Table 3.2 presents some comparative information on this subject. The point to notice is not so much that India's literacy rate *is* far lower than in these countries *today,* nor that India *was* much more backward than these countries in basic education at the time when these countries jumped forward economically, but that India *today* is far behind where these countries *were* when they initiated their rapid economic expansion. The really instructive comparison is between India now and South Korea in 1960 or China in 1980. Despite the passage of time, India's literacy rate now is much below what these countries had achieved many years ago when they began their market-based economic transformation.

In the educational expansion of the high-performing Asian economies, the state has played a major part in every case. An essential

TABLE 3.2. *Adult Literacy Rates in Selected Asian Countries*

	1960	1980	1992
India	28	36	50
South Korea	71	93	97
Hong Kong	70	90	≈ 100
Thailand	68	86	94
China	n/a	69	80

Sources. World Development Report 1980, Table 23, for 1960; *World Development Report 1983,* Table 1, for 1980; *Human Development Report 1994,* Table 2, pp. 132–3, for 1992 (see also the Statistical Appendix of this book).

[19] The World Bank (1993c) study of 'the East Asian miracle', which draws on a wide range of empirical works, has particularly emphasized the importance of this linkage: 'We have shown that the broad base of human capital was critically important to rapid growth in the HPAEs [high-performing Asian economies]. Because the HPAEs attained universal primary education early, literacy was high and cognitive skill levels were substantially above those in other developing economies. Firms therefore had an easier time upgrading the skills of their workers and mastering new technology' (World Bank, 1993c, p. 349).

goal of public policy has been to ensure that the bulk of the young population had the capability to read, write, communicate, and interact in a way that is quite essential for modern industrial production. In India, by contrast, there has been a remarkable apathy towards expanding elementary and secondary education, and certainly 'too little' government action—rather than 'too much'—is the basic failure of Indian planning in this field.[20]

India does, of course, have a large body of people with higher education, and there is certainly an opportunity to use their proficiency to develop skill-centred industries, as has begun to happen to a considerable extent (for example, in and around Bangalore, involving computer software and related industries). These achievements are important and are certainly good signs for the Indian economy. But the abysmal inequalities in India's education system represent a real barrier against widely sharing the fruits of economic progress, in general, and of industrialization, in particular, in the way it has happened in economies like South Korea and China—economies which have succeeded in flooding the world market with goods the making of which requires no great university training, but is helped by widespread basic education that enables people to follow precise guidelines and maintain standards of quality. In contrast, even if India were to take over the bulk of the world's computer software industry, this would still leave its poor, illiterate masses largely un-touched. It may be much less glamorous to make simple pocket knives and reliable alarm clocks than to design state-of-the-art com-puter programmes, but the former gives the Chinese poor a source of income that the latter does not provide—at least not directly—to the Indian poor. It is in the making of these unglamorous products, the market for which is very large across the world, that a high level of basic education is a major asset for China—and for many other high-growth economies of east and south-east Asia.

Despite 'local booms' in a particular range of high-skill industries, the overall growth rate of the Indian economy and that for the industrial sector *as a whole* are still rather low. In fact, taking industrial production as a whole, there has been rather little growth since 1990–1 (Government of India, 1995, p.2). This is not to deny that

---

[20] As argued in chapter 6, this failure reflects not only the low priority given by the state to educational expansion, but also a serious lack of concern for basic education in social and political movements.

India can quite possibly achieve higher rates of growth of GNP or GDP even with present levels of massive illiteracy. But the low coverage and poor quality of basic education in India make it harder to move from the dynamism of a limited range of industries (the expansion of which has been so eulogized in specialist financial journals abroad) to a really broad-based economic advance of a sweeping, shared, and participatory kind that has happened further east. It is a question of the strength and the nature of the economic expansion that can occur in India today, and the extent to which the growth in question can be widely participatory. For reasons presented earlier on in this monograph, the social opportunities offered by market-based economic growth are severely limited in a society in which very large numbers (even majorities in large parts of the country) cannot read or write or count, cannot follow printed or hand-written instructions, cannot operate comfortably in a modern industry, and so on.[21] Inequality in basic education thus translates into inefficiency as well as further inequality in the use of new economic opportunities. The *distributive* failure supplements the effect of educational backwardness in restricting the *overall* scale of expansion of skill-related modern production.

The relationship between education and inequality applies also to gender-based disparities. Again, the high-performing Asian economies have been able to reduce the gender gap in basic education much more rapidly than happened elsewhere, and this achievement has certainly played an important part in reducing the relative disadvantage of women in social opportunities, including economic participation. The growth-mediated success of the east Asian economies has drawn particularly on the expansion of employment options and other opportunities for women. The contrast with India is extremely sharp. In fact, in this respect, south Asia—including India—lags behind every other substantial region of the developing world (including Latin America and Africa, in addition to east Asia).[22]

While the contrast in the field of education is perhaps the most radical difference between India and the high-growth countries in east Asia, there are also other areas in which supportive public policies in social fields have helped these successful Asian economies in a

[21] As noted in chapter 1, there is also considerable evidence that the rate of return to basic education tends to be higher in countries that are more 'open', with less restriction on trade. On this and related issues, see Birdsall and Sabot (1993a).

[22] See World Bank (1993c), pp. 46–7.

way that has not happened in India. These countries have typically had much better levels of health conditions even before their period of rapid economic growth. Greater provision of medical facilities in the east Asian countries, particularly in terms of preventive health care, is an important factor in explaining this contrast. In the case of China, the expansion of rural health care has been one of the most remarkable achievements of the *pre-reform* period.[23] It has proved to be an asset of great value in the economic reforms. This is an important issue not only for the quality of life, but also for economic performance, since morbidity and undernourishment can be serious barriers to productive work and economic performance.[24]

Another area in which many of the great practitioners of growth-mediated progress have done much better than India is that of *land reform*. Land reforms were carried out most extensively in many of the east Asian countries, including Japan, South Korea, Taiwan, and of course China. The advantages of the abolition of landlordism from the point of view of equity are obvious enough, but it also has much to contribute to the general incentive to expand production, and to making it easier for agricultural producers to respond to the opportunities offered by a freer market.[25] Significantly enough, one of the least successful growth performers among the east Asian economies, namely the Philippines, is also an example of an extensive failure to carry out adequate land reforms.[26] The Indian record is even worse than the general situation in the Philippines; some success

[23] On this see Drèze and Sen (1989), chapter 11, and the studies cited there; also chapter 4 of this book.

[24] See Bliss and Stern (1978), Sahn and Alderman (1988), Dasgupta and Ray (1986, 1987, 1990), Osmani (1990, 1992), Dasgupta (1993), among other contributions. The east Asian achievements in this field are reviewed in World Bank (1993c).

[25] It has been argued that sharecropping need not be inefficient when certain conditions are met, for example, when the relative shares can be fully varied and freely negotiated (see, for example, Cheung, 1969). But the assumptions needed are quite strong and seem to be in some conflict with the actual observation of 'lumpiness' in relative shares. On the historical experiences of land reform in some of these east Asian countries, such as Taiwan and South Korea (and their extensive consequences), see Galenson (1979), Kuo (1983), Kim and Leipziger (1993), World Bank (1993c). On the theory of resource allocation under share tenancy, see, among other contributions, Johnson (1950), Cheung (1969), Stiglitz (1974), Newbery (1977), Berry and Cline (1979), Bardhan (1989), and the literature surveys in Bliss and Stern (1982), Binswanger and Rosenzweig (1984), Quibria and Rashid (1984), Otsuka and Hayami (1988), Otsuka et al. (1992).

[26] See World Bank (1993c), p. 169.

in land reforms has been achieved in West Bengal and Kerala, but the overall achievements in most Indian states are quite dismal.

The lessons of successful growth-mediated progress in east Asia include the importance of various areas of state action, including basic education, general—particularly preventive—health care, and land reform. In understanding and interpreting the 'economic miracle' in east Asia, these roles of public action have to be viewed along with the part played by governments in directly promoting industrial expansion and export orientation and in guiding the pattern of industrialization. These directly interventionist functions have been brought out sharply by some—so-called 'revisionist'—studies of the east Asian miracle, which have interpreted the achievements as integrally related to productive public intervention.[27] While other studies have had somewhat different emphases,[28] there is much evidence that the government did play a significant role in directly promoting industrialization in the east Asian success stories, *inter alia* through systematic intervention (for example, through variable financial terms) in advancing particular industries, and in giving priority to chosen directions of international trade (in particular, selective export promotion). The special contributions of governmental initiative in educational expansion, general health care, land reforms, etc., can be seen as important examples of this general state activism. It would be quite bizarre to read the east Asian success stories as simple results of liberalization and of the 'freeing' of markets.

3.4. Human Capital and More Basic Values

While we have been occasionally using the language of 'human capital' in this book, to conform to general practice, that term is somewhat misleading in general, and particularly so in the context of one of the issues on which we want to put some emphasis. This concerns the intrinsic importance of the quality of human life—not seeing it *just* as an instrument for promoting economic growth and success. There is a real asymmetry between what is called 'human capital' (such as education, skill, good health, etc.) and physical capital,

---

[27] See particularly Amsden (1989), Wade (1990), Kim and Leipziger (1993). See also Westphal et al. (1985) and Datta Chaudhuri (1990).

[28] See World Bank (1993c) and the large literature, cited there, on which it has drawn. See also the critical reviews of Amsden (1994) and Rodrik (1994a), and other contributions to the special section of *World Development*, 22 (4), edited by Alice Amsden.

in that the items covered by the former can have importance of their own (aside from being instrumentally important in production) in a way that does not apply to a piece of machinery. To put it another way, if a machinery did nothing to raise production, it would be quite eccentric to value its existence nevertheless, whereas being educated or being in good health could be valued *even if* it were to do nothing to increase the production of commodities. The constituents of human capital, which are parts of human lives, can be valued for their own sake—above and beyond their instrumental importance as factors of production. Indeed, being a 'component of human capital' cannot be the most fulfilling achievement to which a human being can aspire.

While the distinction between the intrinsic and instrumental importance of human capabilities is of some significance for clarity about means and ends, which is central to rational resource allocation, we should not make heavy weather of this dichotomy. It is important to bear in mind: (1) that health, education, and other features of a good quality of life are of importance on their own (and not just as 'human capital', geared to commodity production), (2) they can also be, in many circumstances, extremely good for promoting commodity production, and (3) they can also have other important personal and social roles (as discussed in chapter 2). There is no particular difficulty in using the language of 'human capital' if it is also recognized that there are other—more direct—rewards of human health, knowledge, and skill.

While human capabilities have both intrinsic and instrumental value, growth of GNP per head must be seen as having only instrumental importance. As discussed in chapter 2, success in economic growth must ultimately be judged by what it does to our lives—the quality of life we can enjoy, and the liberties we can exercise. In general, economic success cannot be dissociated from the 'end' of promoting human capabilities and of enhancing well-being and freedom. The tradition of judging success by the growth of GNP per head, or by some distribution-corrected value of GNP per head, is quite well established in economics. There is no great harm in this so long as the purely instrumental nature of the role of real incomes and commodities is borne in mind—not confusing instrumental effectiveness with intrinsic importance. In this connection, it has been noted that variations in real income per head have considerable explanatory power in accounting for differences in life expectancy, child mortality, literacy, and related indicators of well-being. For example, Anand and Ravallion (1993) find, in regressing proportionate shortfalls of life expectancy from the postulated maximum of 80 years against the logarithm of per-capita GNP, that nearly half the variations in life expectancy can be attributed to differences in GNP per head.[29]

There can be little doubt about the value of higher real income in opening up possibilities of living worthwhile lives that are not available at lower levels of income. On the other hand, it is also interesting to note that the main impact of higher GNP per head on life expectancy seems to work via factors in which public policies play a significant part. Anand and Ravallion (1993) also report that when they relate life expectancy to public health spending per person, the proportion of people below the poverty line (defined in terms of per-capita expenditure), and GNP per head, the significantly positive relationship between GNP and life expectancy entirely vanishes.[30] This need not entail that GNP does not contribute to the raising of longevity. Rather, it would appear that in so far as GNP does contribute to expanding life expectancy, it does this largely through making it possible to have higher public spending (particularly on health care) and through reducing the proportion of people in poverty. The Anand–Ravallion findings are not a denial of the effectiveness of 'growth-mediated' progress, but an argument for seeing the role of growth-mediation through its connection with public services and poverty removal.

This is one illustration of the important interrelations between economic growth, sensible governmental action, and the enhancement of social and economic opportunities for the individuals in the society. These interrelations are particularly crucial in the task of transforming the Indian economy.

3.5. *Internal Diversities*

As was mentioned in chapter 1, the relevant comparative lessons for Indian economic development come not only from abroad, but

---

[29] On related matters, see also Anand (1993) and Anand and Kanbur (1993).

[30] Anand and Ravallion's (1993) analysis is based on all the developing countries for which they could find reasonably reliable data on these variables—22 countries in all. Obviously, all such studies need more corroboration and scrutiny, but these results seem to be broadly in line with economic arguments that have been presented elsewhere (see Drèze and Sen, 1989).

also from within the country. Indeed, India is characterized by enormous variations in regional experiences and achievements. Even in terms of the standard economic indicators, these diversities are quite remarkable. Some states, such as Punjab and Haryana, have become much richer than others based on a far better growth performance. Compared with India's gross domestic product per capita of Rs 5,583 in 1991–2, Punjab's figure is Rs 9,643 and Haryana's is Rs 8,690 (Government of India, 1994a). Correspondingly, the proportion of the rural population below the poverty line is only 21 per cent in Punjab and 23 per cent in Haryana, about half the corresponding figure for India as a whole (45 per cent), and one-third of the figure for Bihar and Orissa (66 per cent each).[31]

The contrasts are even sharper in some fields of social development. There are, for example, striking contrasts in literacy levels between different states of India, with the female literacy rate varying from 20 per cent in Rajasthan to 86 per cent in Kerala. These inter-regional contrasts are only one aspect of the internal diversities that characterize India's literacy achievements. A detailed analysis of the literacy situation would have to take note of other types of disparities, e.g. related to gender and caste. While 94 per cent of males in Kerala are literate, for instance, the literacy rate is *well below 10 per cent* among scheduled-caste women in Bihar or Rajasthan.[32]

Remarkable internal diversities can also be seen in other indicators of living conditions, relating to health, nutrition, morbidity, gender inequality, etc. These other indicators tend to be less easy to obtain at a disaggregated level than literacy rates (the latter have nice 'decomposition' properties, in the sense that aggregate literacy rates can be seen as a simple population-weighted average of group-specific literacy rates). But some elementary comparisons of living conditions in different regions are possible, using the relevant state-level indicators.

These state-level indicators remain highly aggregative. The internal diversities within, say, Uttar Pradesh (which had a population of 139 million in 1991) are of much interest in themselves, and cannot

---

[31] See Statistical Appendix, Table A.3 (the figures are based on National Sample Survey data). The reference year is 1987–8, the latest year for which state-specific estimates of the head-count ratio are available.

[32] Tyagi (1993), pp. 26–8, based on the 1991 census. The literacy rates cited here refer to the age group of 7 years and above. For further evidence and discussion of social disparities in educational achievements, see chapter 6.

be fully captured in these broad inter-state comparisons.[33] It must also be remembered that the states in question have very different sizes (even if we restrict ourselves, as we shall do in this section, to states with a population of at least 5 million in 1991), and therefore very different 'weights' in the national indicators. Nevertheless, state-level indicators are of interest in so far as the state is a crucial political and administrative unit. A wide range of relevant fields of action (including health and education) are constitutionally defined as 'state subjects', to be handled at the level of individual states rather than of the central government, or as 'concurrent subjects', involving both state and central governments. This provides a strong motivation for the examination of state-level indicators.

Table 3.3 presents a sample of the available indicators.[34] As this table illustrates, striking contrasts can be observed between the achievements of different states in terms of various indicators of well-being. Female life expectancy at birth varies from 54 years to 74 years between different states; rural female literacy rates in the 10–14 age group range from 22 to 98 per cent; the child death rate is more than ten times as high in Madhya Pradesh as in Kerala; the proportion of the rural population below the poverty line is as high as 66 per cent in Orissa and Bihar, but only 21 per cent in Punjab; the number of women per 1,000 men varies from 865 in Haryana (a level lower than that of any country in the world) to 1,036 in Kerala (a level typical of advanced industrial economies);[35] and so on. There is almost as much diversity within India, in terms of these indicators, as in the rest of the developing world.

While Kerala is an exceptional case of extraordinary achievement in the social field, which broadens the range of regional contrasts within India, it would be a mistake to think that the rest of the country —after taking out Kerala—is mainly homogeneous. The variations

[33] Some of these internal diversities within Uttar Pradesh are discussed in the chapter on this state's experience, authored by Drèze and Gazdar (1996), in the companion volume (Drèze and Sen, 1996).

[34] More detailed information can be found in the Statistical Appendix to this book (particularly Table A.3). For an informative analysis of levels and trends in well-being indicators in different states of India, see Dutta et al. (1994).

[35] The female–male ratio is, in fact, even lower than 865 in a few oil-exporting countries (e.g. Kuwait, United Arab Emirates, Bahrain), but this is mainly due to large-scale immigration of male labourers from abroad; the same explanation would not apply to Haryana or Uttar Pradesh (see e.g. Agnihotri, 1994). On the significance of the female–male ratio as an indicator of basic gender inequality, see chapter 7.

TABLE 3.3. *Selected Indicators for Major Indian States*

State	Population, 1991 (million)	Life expectancy at birth, 1990–2 Female	Life expectancy at birth, 1990–2 Male	Death rate for 0–4 age group, 1991	Total fertility rate, 1991	Female–male ratio, 1991	Literacy rate in 7+ age group, 1991 Female	Literacy rate in 7+ age group, 1991 Male	Rural literacy rate in 10–14 age group, 1987–8 Female	Rural literacy rate in 10–14 age group, 1987–8 Male	Incidence of poverty, 1987–8 (head-count ratio) Rural	Incidence of poverty, 1987–8 (head-count ratio) Urban
Kerala	29.1	74.4	68.8	4.3	1.8	1,036	86	94	98	98	44.0	44.5
Himachal Pradesh	5.2	n/a	n/a	19.3	3.1	976	52	75	81	95	24.8	3.3
Maharashtra	78.9	64.7	63.1	16.3	3.0	934	52	77	68	86	54.2	35.6
Tamil Nadu	55.9	63.2	61.0	16.1	2.2	974	51	74	71	85	51.3	39.2
Punjab	20.3	67.5	65.4	17.0	3.1	882	50	66	69	76	21.0	11.2
Gujarat	41.3	61.3	59.1	23.3	3.1	934	49	73	61	78	41.6	38.8
West Bengal	68.1	62.0	60.5	20.6	3.2	917	47	68	61	69	57.2	30.6
Karnataka	45.0	63.6	60.0	23.6	3.1	960	44	67	56	74	42.3	45.0
Assam	22.4	n/a	n/a	32.4	3.5	923	43	62	78	83	53.1	11.4
Haryana	16.5	63.6	62.2	23.0	4.0	865	41	69	63	87	23.2	18.3
Orissa	31.7	54.8	55.9	39.0	3.3	971	35	63	51	70	65.6	44.5
Andhra Pradesh	66.5	61.5	59.0	21.3	3.0	972	33	55	42	66	31.6	40.0
Madhya Pradesh	66.2	53.5	54.1	44.5	4.6	931	29	58	40	68	49.8	46.0
Uttar Pradesh	139.1	54.6	56.8	35.6	5.1	879	25	56	39	68	47.7	41.9
Bihar	86.4	58.3	n/a	22.8	4.4	911	23	52	34	59	66.3	56.7
Rajasthan	44.0	57.8	57.6	30.9	4.6	910	20	55	22	72	41.9	41.5
INDIA	846.3	59.4	59.0	26.5	3.6	927	39	64	52	73	44.9	36.5

Sources. See Statistical Appendix, which also presents more detailed information on different aspects of living conditions in Indian states. This table includes all states with a population of at least 5 million in 1991, except Jammu and Kashmir (where the 1991 census, on which many of these figures are based, was not conducted). The states have been ranked in descending order of female literacy.

within India are enormous whether or not Kerala is included in these comparisons. For example, while Kerala's fertility rate of 1.8 in 1991 contrasts very powerfully with the rate of 5.1 for Uttar Pradesh, the contrast between Uttar Pradesh and Tamil Nadu is also sharp enough, since the latter's fertility rate of 2.2, though higher than Kerala's 1.8, is much less than half the figure of 5.1 for Uttar Pradesh. To look at these numbers in another way, the fertility rate of Tamil Nadu (2.2) is of a similar order of magnitude as that for the United States and Sweden (2.1), and lower than the rate for *every* 'low income country' in the world, with the exception of China (2.0), whereas the fertility rate of 5.1 in Uttar Pradesh is significantly higher than the average for all 'low income countries' (3.4) and much in excess of the rates for such countries as Sri Lanka (2.5) and Indonesia (2.9), and even Bangladesh (4.0) and Myanmar or Burma (4.2).[36] When we include Kerala in the inter-state comparisons, the contrasts are made sharper, but the divergences are not lost even when Kerala is excluded. Even though we shall often concentrate specifically on Kerala, since there is so much to learn from this very powerful illustration of internal diversity within India, we must nevertheless resist the temptation to see it all as 'Kerala versus the rest'.

In interpreting the picture of internal diversities within India, it is also important to remember that human deprivation has different aspects, involving failures of different kinds of capabilities (see chapter 2). Further, different indicators of deprivation need not be closely correlated with each other, as Table 3.3 brings out clearly enough with respect to the different regions within India. Thus, the relative intensity of deprivation in different parts of the country depends on which aspect or indicator of deprivation we are concerned with. The incidence of rural poverty as measured by the conventional head-count ratio, for instance, is clearly highest in the eastern states, especially Bihar and Orissa, and to a lesser extent West Bengal.[37]

[36] These figures for different countries are taken from the *World Development Report 1994*, Table 26 (see World Bank, 1994b). 'Low income countries' are defined here, as in that report, as countries with GNP per capita below $675 in 1992. The figures for the Indian states come from Government of India (1993b).

[37] Independent information on the incidence of hunger seems to conform to this regional pattern. The proportion of rural persons who report that they do not get two square meals a day throughout the year is below 20 per cent in all major Indian states except Orissa, Bihar, and West Bengal, where it is as high as 36.8 per cent, 37.3 per

But child death rates follow quite a different regional pattern, with the central and north-western states of Uttar Pradesh, Madhya Pradesh, and Rajasthan doing considerably worse than West Bengal or Bihar, while Orissa combines a high incidence of poverty with high levels of child mortality. And the female–male ratio figures suggest that gender inequalities are most acute in the north-west, including the relatively prosperous states of Punjab and Haryana—a finding on which there is a good deal of independent evidence.[38] There is, thus, no single 'problem region' within India, and public policy has to be alive to the different kinds of challenges that arise in different parts of the country. In so far as any broad pattern can be identified, it is mainly one of deprivation being endemic in most of north India (except in Punjab and Haryana, where there is a specific problem of gender inequality despite other indicators being relatively favourable), with the south Indian states doing significantly better in most respects, especially in matters of mortality, fertility, literacy, and gender equity.

A related issue is that well-being indicators in different states are poorly correlated with income or expenditure indicators. To illustrate, Figure 3.1 plots the child mortality rate against the incidence of poverty (as measured by the head–count ratio) in different states, for 1987–8. The association between the two is rather weak, to say the least. Some aspects of this weakness of association are indeed rather striking; for instance, child mortality is more than six times as high in Uttar Pradesh as in Kerala even though the head-count measures of poverty are very similar—and quite close to the all-India average— in the two states.[39] This need not be taken to imply that income or

---

cent, and 39.6 per cent, respectively (Minhas, 1991, p. 28). The robustness of this information requires examination, given the ambiguities that may be attached to the notion of 'getting two square meals a day', but there is some congruence of diagnosis in that the results of this inquiry point in the same direction as those of consumer expenditure surveys so far as the deficiency of purchasing power in eastern India is concerned.

[38] See chapter 7, and the references cited there.

[39] Estimates of the head–count ratio in Kerala in the 1980s seem to be somewhat sensitive to the choice of price indices used to adjust for differences in prices between different states and time periods. The estimates used in Figure 3.1, which suggest that the head–count ratio in Kerala (44.1) is close to the all-India average (42.7), are based on the expert study by Minhas et al. (1991); see also Tendulkar et al. (1993). It may be worth noting that, according to all available studies, the head–count ratio in Kerala was a good deal higher than in India as a whole until the late 1970s (see EPW Research Foundation, 1993). It is clear that Kerala's lead in health, education, and related fields

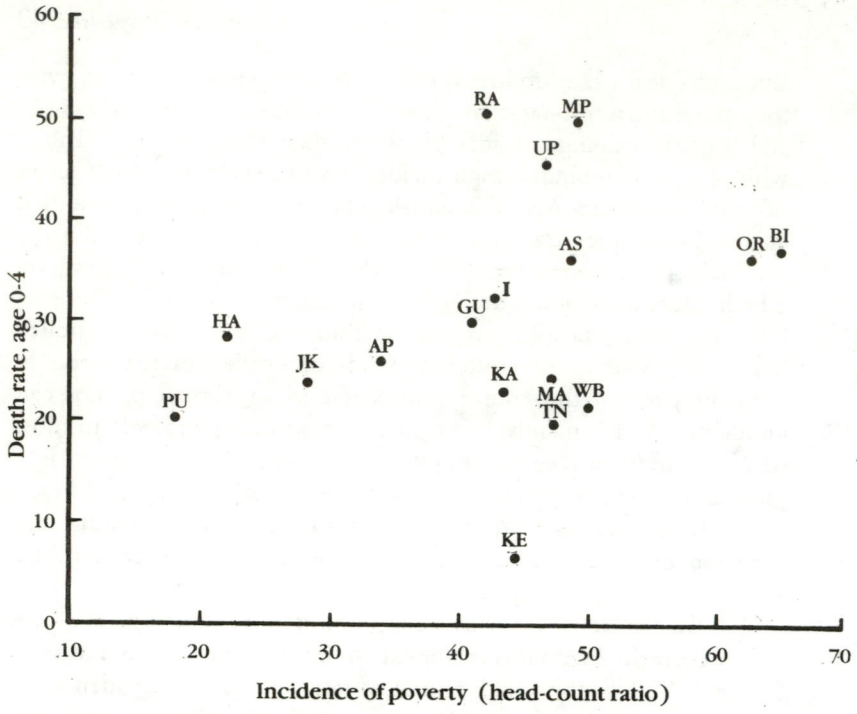

FIG. 3.1. *Indian States : Poverty and Child Mortality, 1987– 8*

Source. Minhas et al. (1991); *Sample Registration System 1988,* Statement 39 (p. 48).

I = India

AP = Andhra Pradesh	AS = Assam
BI = Bihar	HA = Haryana
GU = Gujarat	JK = Jammu & Kashmir
KA = Karnataka	KE = Kerala
MA = Maharashtra	MP = Madhya Pradesh
OR = Orissa	PU = Punjab
RA = Rajasthan	TN = Tamil Nadu
UP = Uttar Pradesh	WB = West Bengal

expenditure have no effect on child mortality and related indicators of health or well-being. There is plenty of evidence, in India and in other countries, that health achievements do improve with higher incomes (it is the fast growth of incomes, for instance, that has clearly been the driving force behind the expansion of life expectancy in Punjab). The point is that many *other* factors are involved, which tend to weaken the simple correlation between income and health (or other aspects of well-being), when these other factors are not themselves well correlated with income.

Among the factors (other than private income) that have a strong influence on living conditions, important roles are played by particular kinds of public actions, e.g. those geared to the provision of social services, the removal of traditional inequalities, the promotion of widespread literacy. The contrast between Kerala and Uttar Pradesh, pursued in the next section, provides a useful illustration of this point.

3.6. *Studying Indian States*

As discussed earlier, there is much to learn from the diversity of development experiences among different Indian states. In a companion volume of essays (Drèze and Sen, 1996), some of the lessons to be drawn are pursued, based on case studies of Kerala (by V.K. Ramachandran), Uttar Pradesh (by Jean Drèze and Haris Gazdar), and West Bengal (by Sunil Sengupta and Haris Gazdar). In subsequent chapters of this book, we shall make frequent use of the insights arising from these case studies.[40]

The contrast between Kerala and Uttar Pradesh is of particular interest, and we shall have the occasion to refer to that contrast in various contexts. These two states are poles apart in the scales of many indicators of well-being, without being very different—as noted in the preceding section—in terms of conventional measures of the incidence of poverty. As V.K. Ramachandran's case study of Kerala documents in some detail, Kerala's success can be traced to the role of public action in promoting a range of social opportunities relating *inter alia* to elementary education, land reform, the role of women in society, and the widespread and equitable provision of health

---

was achieved at a time when the incidence of poverty, as measured by the head-count ratio, was no lower in Kerala than in India as a whole.

[40] This section itself draws extensively on these case studies.

care and other public services.[41] Interestingly, Uttar Pradesh's *failures* can be plausibly attributed to the public *neglect* of the very same opportunities.[42] The fact that both case studies identify much the same factors of success (in Kerala) and failure (in Uttar Pradesh) is of considerable significance in understanding the diversity of social achievements in different parts of India. Among the identified determinants of social achievements, the following deserve strong emphasis.[43]

First, the role of literacy (and particularly of female literacy) in promoting basic capabilities emerges forcefully in both case studies. One of the distinguishing features of Kerala's development experience is the early promotion of literacy, and this feature has led to important social achievements later on, based on the diverse social and personal roles of literacy (discussed in chapter 2). In Uttar Pradesh, by contrast, the adult female literacy rate is still as low as 25 per cent, and two-thirds of all adolescent girls in rural areas have *never* been to school. This educational backwardness has wide-ranging penalties, including very high mortality and fertility rates.[44]

Second, another element in social success that clearly emerges from both experiences is the agency of women. Uttar Pradesh has a long history of oppressive gender relations, and even now inequalities between men and women in that part of the country are extraordinarily sharp (as we noted earlier, for instance, very few countries in the world have as low a female–male ratio as Uttar Pradesh). As with

---

[41] On these and related aspects of Kerala's development experience, see also Krishnan (1976, 1991, 1994, forthcoming), Mencher (1980), Nair (1981), Nag (1983, 1989), Raj and Tharakan (1983), Panikar and Soman (1984, 1985), Robin Jeffrey (1987, 1992), Franke and Chasin (1989), Mari Bhat and Rajan (1990, 1992), Kannan et al. (1991), Kabir and Krishnan (1992), Sibbons (1992), Kannan (1993), Mahendra Dev (1993c), Oommen (1993a), Prakash (1994), Zachariah et al. (1994), among others, and also the extensive collection of papers summarized in AKG Centre for Research and Studies (1994).

[42] See the case study of Uttar Pradesh by Drèze and Gazdar (1996) in the companion volume.

[43] There are, of course, close interconnections between these different social influences. For instance, the expansion of literacy in Kerala has been both an *outcome* of extensive state involvement in the provision of basic services and a *determinant* of further expansion of social provisions. Public provisioning and widespread literacy have developed together.

[44] On the role of literacy (especially female literacy) in reducing mortality and fertility rates, see chapter 7.

illiteracy, the suppression of women's active and liberated participation in the economy and the society has been a cause of much social backwardness in Uttar Pradesh. In Kerala, by contrast, the position of women in society has been relatively favourable for a long time, and the informed agency of women has played a crucial role in a wide range of social achievements.[45] The expansion of literacy itself owes a great deal to that agency, reflected even in the fact that almost two-thirds of primary-school teachers in Kerala are women (compared with 18 per cent in Uttar Pradesh).

TABLE 3.4. *India, Uttar Pradesh and Kerala: Contrasts in Access to Public Services*

	India	Uttar Pradesh	Kerala
Percentage of rural children aged 12–14 who have never been enrolled in a school, 1986–7			
Female	51	68	1.8
Male	26	27	0.4
Proportion of children aged 12–23 months who have not received any vaccination, 1992–3 (%)	30	43	11
Percentage of recent births preceded by an antenatal check-up, 1992–3	49	30	97
Proportion of births taking place in medical institutions, 1991 (%)	24	4	92
Number of hospital beds per million persons, 1991	732	340	2,418
Proportion of villages with medical facilities, 1981 (%)	14	10	96
Proportion of the population receiving subsidized cereals from the public distribution system, 1986–7 (%)	29	3	87

Sources. See Statistical Appendix, and the Explanatory Note in that appendix. Although the contrasts presented here relate primarily to the provision and utilization of *public* services, they may also reflect some differences in the functioning of private services. For further discussion of public services in Uttar Pradesh and Kerala, see Drèze and Gazdar (1996) and Ramachandran (1996) in the companion volume, and the literature cited there.

[45] On this, see particularly Robin Jeffrey (1992).

Third, the contrast between Uttar Pradesh and Kerala brings out the essential role of well-functioning public services in improving living conditions. As we noted earlier in this chapter, the widely divergent levels of well-being in the two states cannot be explained in terms of higher incomes and lower levels of poverty in Kerala (since Uttar Pradesh and Kerala are, in fact, not very different in these respects). If entitlements to basic commodities and services differ so sharply between the two states, it is because of a marked difference in the scope and quality of a wide range of public services such as schooling facilities, basic health care, child immunization, social security arrangements, and public food distribution. In Uttar Pradesh, these public services are comprehensively neglected, sometimes even non-existent, especially in rural areas (Table 3.4 presents some illustrative indications of this particular contrast between Uttar Pradesh and Kerala).

Fourth, both case studies highlight the social influence of public action in a wide sense, going beyond the initiative of the state and involving the public at large. The early promotion of literacy in Kerala has enabled the public to play an active role in state politics and social affairs in a way that has not happened in Uttar Pradesh. Public action in Kerala has been particularly important in orienting the priorities of the state in the direction of a strong commitment to the promotion of social opportunities. Even the expansion of public services has often taken place in response to the organized demands of a well-educated public. The vigilance of the public has also been essential to ensure the adequate *functioning* of public services such as health centres and primary schools in Kerala.[46]

Finally, Uttar Pradesh and Kerala point to the special importance of a particular type of public action—the political organization of deprived sections of the society. In Kerala, informed political activism—building partly on the achievement of mass literacy—has played a crucial role in the reduction of social inequalities based on caste, gender, and (to some extent) class.[47] Political organization has also been important in enabling disadvantaged groups to take an active

---

[46] On this issue, see Mencher (1980), Nag (1989), and Majumdar (1993), and chapter 6 of this book.

[47] The reduction of social and economic inequalities in Kerala is extensively discussed by V.K. Ramachandran (1996) in the companion volume. In tackling class inequalities, land reforms and social security arrangements have played an important part. On the relationship between social security and inequality, see section 5.4.

part in the general processes of economic development, public action, and social change. In Uttar Pradesh, traditional inequalities and social divisions remain extremely powerful, and their persistence hinders many social endeavours.[48] It is still possible, for instance, to find villages in Uttar Pradesh where a powerful landlord has deliberately obstructed the creation of a village school by the government (see section 5.5). More generally, the concentration of political power in the hands of privileged sections of the society has contributed, perhaps more than anything else, to a severe neglect of the basic needs of disadvantaged groups in state and local politics.

Underlying many of these contrasts is the general importance of politics in the development process. Kerala does, of course, possess some special cultural and historical characteristics which may have helped its social transformation. But the political process itself has played an extremely important role in Kerala's development experience, supplementing or supplanting these inherited characteristics.[49] This issue has a strong bearing on the 'replicability' of Kerala's success. Given the role of political movements, there is no reason why Uttar Pradesh—and other states of India where basic deprivations remain endemic—should not be able to emulate many of Kerala's achievements, based on determined and reasoned political activism.

A good illustration of the feasibility of political transformation comes from West Bengal.[50] This is a state where political organization of disadvantaged classes has succeeded in ushering in a significant change in the balance of political power. A concrete expression of this change occurred in 1977, when the Left Front coalition came to office at the state level. The main electoral base of the Left Front, which has retained office since then through successive elections, consists of landless labourers, sharecroppers, slum dwellers, and other disadvantaged groups. This change in the balance of power has made it possible to implement a number of far-reaching social programmes that are often considered 'politically infeasible' in many

---

[48] On inequality as an obstacle to social progress, see chapter 5.

[49] One important indication of this comes from the comparative experiences of Kerala's three different regions—Travancore, Cochin, and Malabar. We will return to this in the concluding chapter (section 8.6).

[50] For further discussion, see the case study of West Bengal by Sunil Sengupta and Haris Gazdar (1996) in the companion volume.

other states. Two notable examples are land reform and the revitalization of democratic institutions at the village level.[51]

The government of West Bengal has been notably less active in promoting some other types of social opportunities. While issues such as land reform have received high priority in the programme of the Left Front coalition (partly because of the importance of these issues in the political battles that led this coalition to power), public policies concerned with health, education, and related matters have been comparatively neglected. Correspondingly, the improvement of living conditions in West Bengal in recent years has remained relatively slow. An important opportunity has been missed here, since the skills of popular mobilization of the West Bengal government (amply demonstrated in other fields) could have been used with good effect to achieve a real transformation in the fields of education and health.[52] These are serious failures of the West Bengal experience, but they do not detract from the importance of the positive achievements, nor from the general value of that experience as an example of the possibility of radical political change in India today.

---

[51] See Sengupta and Gazdar (1996), and the literature cited in that study. A number of other public programmes also appear to have been more successful in West Bengal than in most other states, due to the political commitments of the government and the improved scope for collective action at the local level. Examples include public programmes relating to poverty alleviation (see Drèze, 1990d, and Swaminathan, 1990), rural infrastructure (Saha and Swaminathan, 1994, Sengupta and Gazdar, 1996), and paticipatory management of environmental resources (Shah, 1987, Malhotra and Poffenberger, 1989, S.B. Roy, 1992, Gadgil and Guha, 1993).

[52] There have been some important initiatives in that direction during the last few years, e.g. in the context of the Total Literacy Campaign (see C. Sengupta, 1992, S. Banerjee, 1994, Ghosh et al., 1994, and Sengupta and Gazdar, 1996).

4

INDIA AND CHINA

4.1. *Perceptions of China*

'An' the dawn comes up like thunder outer China 'crost the Bay!' This isn't politics, but Kipling on nature, on the road to Mandalay. However, following the establishment of the People's Republic of China in 1949, the *political* perceptions of many activists in India began to match this arresting description of the coming dawn from China. Comparison with China and the lessons to be learned from its experience became staple concerns in Indian politics.

Indeed, it is natural to judge Indian successes and failures in comparative terms with China. Some of these comparisons have been academic and scholarly, even distant.[1] Others have been used to precipitate particular political debates in India, with considerable practical impact—in some cases linked to specific revolutionary causes (particularly in giving shape to Maoist political parties). Even non-revolutionary parties of the 'left', which are well integrated in India's parliamentary system of governance, have paid sustained attention to the perceived economic and social achievements of China—looking for lessons and guidance on how to make things move faster in India.

Since the economic reforms introduced around 1979, China's example has been increasingly quoted by quite a different group of political commentators and advocates, to wit, those keen on promoting liberalization—and integration of India into the world economy. China's successful liberalization programmes and its massive entry

---

[1] Fine examples of academic attempts at comparison can be found in Malenbaum (1956, 1959, 1982), S.J. Patel (1985), Bhalla (1992), Howes (1992), Matson and Selden (1992), Rosen (1992), and Srinivasan (1994), among others.

into international trade has been increasingly projected as a great model for India to act on. The pro-market new 'dawn' may be quite a different event from what the Naxalites dreamed about in their grim struggle, but it too looked to many 'like thunder outer China 'crost the Bay!'

The People's Republic of China was established in October 1949, just a few months before the constitution of the federal Republic of India came into force in January 1950. The Indian leadership—at that stage on good terms with China—tended to underplay the competing importance of China's example, treating the respective efforts at economic development and political emancipation as similar in spirit. As Jawaharlal Nehru put it in a speech in 1954, 'these new and revolutionary changes in China and India, even though they differ in content, symbolize the new spirit of Asia and new vitality which is finding expression in the countries in Asia.'[2]

The sense that there is much to learn from China's experience was immediate and powerful. The radicalism of Chinese politics seemed to many to be deeply relevant to India, given the enormity of its poverty and economic misery. China was the only country in the world comparable with India in terms of population size, and it had similar levels of impoverishment and distress. The fact that as a solution China sought a revolutionary transformation of society had a profound impact on political perceptions in the subcontinent. Similarly, later on, China's choice of market-oriented reform and of a policy of integration with the world economy has given those policies a much wider hearing in India than they could have conceivably had on the basis of what had happened in countries that are much smaller and perceived to be quite dissimilar to India: Hong Kong, Taiwan, Singapore, even South Korea. From revolutionary inspiration to reformist passion, China has got India's ear again and again.

We shall presently argue that there is indeed a great deal to learn from China. For that to happen, however, it is crucial to have a clear view of the roots of Chinese triumphs and successes, and also of the sources of its troubles and failures. It is, of course, first of all necessary to distinguish between—and contrast—the different phases of the Chinese experience, in particular, *before* and *after* the economic reforms initiated in 1979. But going beyond that, it is

---

[2] Speech made on 23 October 1954, reproduced in Gopal (1983), pp. 371–3.

also important to take note of the *interdependence* between the achievements in the different periods. We argue, in particular, that the accomplishments relating to education, health care, land reforms, and social change in the pre-reform period made significantly positive contributions to the achievements of the post-reform period. This is so in terms of their role not only in sustaining high life expectancy and related achievements, but also in providing firm support for economic expansion based on market reforms.

It may have been very far from Mao's own intentions to develop literacy and basic health care in ways that would help to promote market-based, internationally-oriented enterprises (though that dialectical contrariness must have some interest for a Marxist theorist). But these structural achievements in the pre-reform period have certainly served as direct and valuable inputs in fostering economic performance in post-reform China. In drawing lessons from China, these apparently contrary interconnections can be particularly important.

This chapter is much concerned with understanding Chinese political and economic developments (both before and after the reforms of 1979), the interdependence between them, and the lessons that India might draw from what China has or has not done. But we should begin with taking stock of the relative positions of China and India as they are now.

4.2. *Conditions of Life and Death*

Living conditions in China at the time of the political transformation in 1949 were probably not radically different from those in India at that time. Both countries were among the poorest in the world and had high levels of mortality, undernutrition, and illiteracy. While generalizations about living standards in India or China of those times are subject to wide margins of error, the available evidence makes it hard to support the idea that a large gap between the two countries already existed in the late forties.[3]

---

[3] *Human Development Report 1994*, Table 4, gives the following estimates for 1960: real GDP per capita: India 617, China 723; life expectancy at birth: India 44, China 47; infant mortality rate: India 165, China 150. These are, of course, just estimates, rather than hard information, but there is also other evidence to suggest that the sharp contrasts in development indicators between the two countries are of relatively recent origin; see Drèze and Sen (1989), chapter 11, and the literature cited there.

TABLE 4.1. India, China and Kerala: Selected Comparisons

	India	China	Kerala
Real GNP per capita, based on purchasing power parities, 1992 (USA = 100)	5.2	9.1[a]	4.6[a]
Annual growth rate of per-capita GNP, 1980–92 (%)	3.1	7.6	0.3[b]
Life expectancy at birth, 1992 (years)	59	69	72
Infant mortality rate, 1992 (per 1,000 live births)	79	31	17
Total fertility rate, 1992	3.7	2.0	1.8
Proportion of low-birthweight babies, 1985–90 (%)	33	9	n/a
Adult literacy rate, 1990–1[c]			
Female	39	68	86
Male	64	87	94

Notes. [a] Subject to a wide margin of error (see text and Statistical Appendix).
[b] Annual growth rate of per-capita 'state domestic product' (at constant prices), 1980–90.
[c] Age 15+ for China; 7+ for India and Kerala. It should be noted that 7+ literacy rates in India are usually a little *higher* than 15+ literacy rates.

Sources. The figures for India and China, other than literacy and life expectancy, are compiled from *World Development Report 1994*, Tables 1, 26, 27, and 30; on the literacy and life expectancy figures, see Statistical Appendix. The sources used for the figures relating to Kerala are given in the Statistical Appendix.

Since then, however, a striking contrast has emerged between the two countries. This applies even to per-capita real income. The standard figures of GNP per capita are hard to use for international comparison because of differences in price levels, but recent estimates of gross domestic product per head take note of purchasing power parities and are partly aimed at making such comparisons possible. These estimates suggest that China's GNP per head is about twice as high as India's (see Table 4.1).[4] If China and India were comparably poor in the late forties, they now stand quite far apart.

---

[4] The Chinese figures relating to per-capita GNP are subject to a wide margin of error. The figures given in *Human Development Report 1994* suggest an even larger gap, with China's GDP per capita more than two and a half times as large as India's. Some figures

The contrasting achievements of India and China can be seen no less forcefully in terms of direct indicators of living standards. Particular aspects of this contrast are summarized in Table 4.1 (Kerala is also included for later reference). While life expectancy at birth in India is still as low as 59 years, the Chinese figure is a decade more (69 years), not very far behind life expectancies in much richer South Korea or in the more advanced countries in Latin America. Infant mortality is two and half times as high in India (79 per thousand live births in comparison with China's 31), and the proportion of low birthweight babies is three and a half times as high (33 per cent in India compared with China's 9). Further evidence based on child anthropometry, disease patterns, and related information support the notion that China is well ahead of India as far as the elimination of health deprivation is concerned.[5]

Another important area in which the contrast is extremely sharp is basic education and literacy. In the next section China and India are compared in this field.

4.3. *Contrasts in Basic Education*

As Table 4.1 shows, literacy rates are a good deal higher in China than in India. This particular contrast can be examined more closely, using recent census-based information. Both China and India conducted careful censuses in the early eighties and nineties—in 1981 and 1991 in the case of India, and 1982 and 1990 in the case of China. Each of these four censuses includes detailed information on literacy, which provides a useful basis of comparison.

Table 4.2 presents some relevant figures, derived from these censuses. For convenience, we shall take the reference year '1981–2' to mean 1981 for India and 1982 for China, and '1990–1' to stand for 1991 for India and 1990 for China. In Figures 4.1 and 4.2,

---

published by the World Bank (eg. in *World Development Report 1994*, Table 30, in terms of 'current international dollars') suggest a somewhat smaller gap, with China's GNP per head roughly 50 per cent above India's. There is some uncertainty as to the exact magnitude of the gap in real income per head between the two countries, but what is not in doubt is that China is now well ahead of India in this respect.

[5] See Bumgarner (1992), *World Development Report 1993* (particularly on morbidity), *Human Development Report 1994*, and also the literature cited in Drèze and Sen (1989), chapter 11.

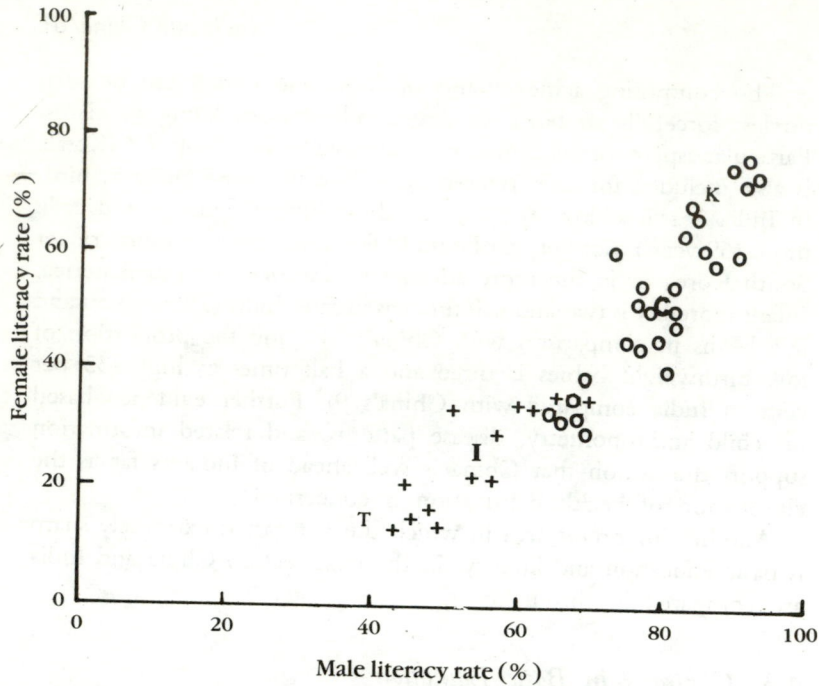

FIG. 4.1. *Adult Literacy Rates in Indian States and Chinese Provinces (1981–2)*

Source. Loh (1993) and Drèze and Loh (1995), based on census data. The literacy rates on which this graph is based apply to persons aged 15 and above.

C - All China   **I - All India**

O = Chinese province   + = Indian state

T = Tibet   K = Kerala

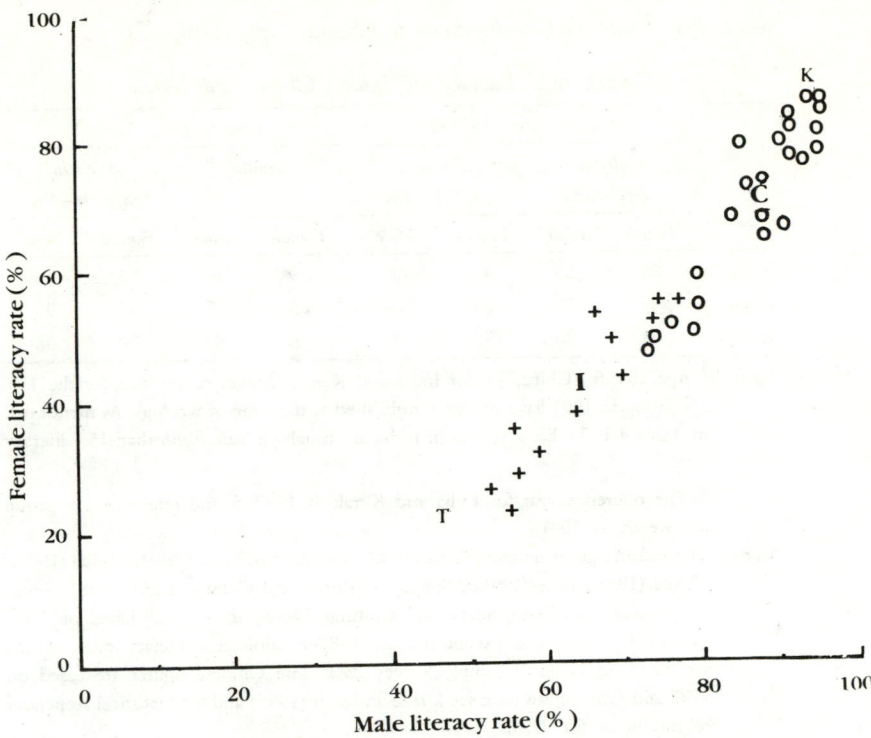

FIG. 4.2. *Adult Literacy Rates in Indian States and Chinese Provinces (1990 – 1)*

Source. Loh (1993) and Drèze and Loh (1995), based on census data. Indian literacy rates apply to persons aged 7 and above; Chinese literacy rates apply to persons aged 15 and above. In India, the 7+ literacy rates are usually a little *higher* than the corresponding 15+ literacy rates.

C - All China	**I - All India**
O = Chinese province	**+** = Indian state
T = Tibet	K = Kerala

TABLE 4.2. *Literacy in India, China and Kerala*

	Literacy rates, 1981–2				Literacy rates, 1990–1			
	Adults (age 15+)		Adolescents (age 15–19)		Adults[a]		Adolescents[b] (age 15–19)	
	Female	Male	Female	Male	Female	Male	Female	Male
India	26	55	43	66	39	64	52	74
China	51	79	85	96	68	87	92	97
Kerala	71	86	92	95	86	94	98	98

Notes. [a] Age 15+ for China, 7+ for India and Kerala (Indian census data for the 15+ age group in 1991 have not been published at the time of writing). As mentioned in Table 4.1, 7+ literacy rates in India are usually a little *higher* than 15+ literacy rates.

[b] The reference year for India and Kerala is 1987–8; the reference age group for Kerala is 10–14.

Sources. The Indian figures are compiled from Government of India (1991), Nanda (1992), Verma (1988), Bose (1991a), Sengupta (1991), and Census of India 1981, Series 10 (Kerala), Part IV-A, Social and Cultural Tables; they are all based on 1981 and 1991 census data, except for the 1987–8 adolescent literacy rates, which are based on National Sample Survey data. The Chinese figures are based on 1982 and 1990 census data; see Drèze and Loh (1995) and the Statistical Appendix of this book for details.

we plot male and female literacy rates in 1981–2 and 1990–1 for each province of China and each state of India.[6] The following observations emerge from these basic comparisons.[7]

First, census data unambiguously show that India is well behind China in the field of basic education. Adult literacy rates in India were as low as 39 per cent for women and 64 per cent for men in 1990–1, compared with 68 per cent for Chinese women and 87 per cent for Chinese men.[8]

[6] The literacy figures used in Table 4.2 and Figures 4.1–4.2 are directly compiled from census publications. As explained in the Statistical Appendix, these figures are more reliable than those presented in, say, *World Development Report 1994*; the latter are based on projections made *before* detailed results from the 1990–1 Chinese and Indian censuses were made available (see e.g. *World Development Report 1994*, p. 232). In any case, the two sets of figures are fairly consistent with each other.

[7] For a more detailed discussion, see Drèze and Loh (1995).

[8] As mentioned in Table 4.2, the Indian figures cited here relate to persons aged 7 and above, because 1991 census data for the 15+ age group have not been released at the time of writing. The literacy gap between India and China would look a little *larger* if one were to use the same age cut-off of 15 years for both countries.

Second, age-specific literacy rates bring out a crucial feature of the Chinese advantage. In 1987–8, 26 per cent of adolescent boys in India, and 48 per cent of adolescent girls, were found to be *illiterate*. The corresponding figures for China in 1990 are only 3 per cent for boys and 8 per cent for girls (Table 4.2). In other words, China is now quite close to universal literacy in the younger age groups. In India, by contrast, there is still a massive problem of illiteracy among young boys and—especially—girls.

Third, the 1981–2 census data show that China's lead over India was achieved *before* China embarked on a wide-ranging programme of economic reforms at the end of the seventies. During the eighties, there has been progress in both countries, with no major change in their comparative positions. The Chinese relative advantage over India is, thus, a product of its pre-reform groundwork, rather than its post-reform redirection.

Fourth, female literacy rates are well below male literacy rates in both countries. The gender gap is particularly large in India, where only a little more than half of all adolescent girls are able to read and write. In China, the gender gap in literacy is narrowing quite rapidly, due to near-universal literacy in the younger age groups.

Fifth, there are wide inter-regional disparities in literacy rates in both countries. The regional contrasts are, to a large extent, driven by differences in female literacy. The persistence of high levels of female illiteracy in particular states or provinces is a matter of concern in both countries, but especially so in India.

Sixth, in spite of sharp regional contrasts within each country, most Chinese provinces have much higher literacy rates than every Indian state except Kerala. The state of Kerala in India stands in sharp contrast to the general pattern of Indian disadvantage. With an adult literacy rate of 90 per cent in 1991, and near-universal literacy among adolescent males *and* females, Kerala is not only well ahead of all other Indian states but also in the same league as the most advanced Chinese provinces. In fact, Kerala has a higher female literacy rate than any Chinese province (Figure 4.2), and also a higher male literacy rate for rural areas than every Chinese province (Drèze and Saran, 1995). Furthermore, in Kerala there is no gender bias in literacy rates in the younger age groups, and in that respect too, Kerala does better than all Chinese provinces. As documented in the case study of Kerala by V.K. Ramachandran (1996) in the companion volume, Kerala's remarkable record in the field of literacy is the outcome of more than a hundred years of public action, involving activities of the general public as well as of the state, in the widespread provision of elementary education.

Finally, a prominent exception to the general lead of Chinese provinces over Indian states is Tibet. Literacy rates in Tibet are not only abysmally low (even lower than in the educationally backward states of north India), they also show little sign of significant improvement over time. While the interpretation of census data for Tibet requires further scrutiny, there is a strong possibility of comprehensive neglect of Tibet in the promotion of elementary education.[9] There is an issue here of some importance in linking political freedom with economic and social achievements (see section 4.7).

4.4. *Pre-reform Achievements*

If we look at relative rates of growth of GNP per head in pre-reform China and in India over the same period, we do not get any definitive evidence that the Chinese rate of growth was substantially faster than India's. That situation has, of course, changed since the reforms of 1979, which have ushered in a remarkable period of sustained rapid expansion of the Chinese economy. We shall comment on the post-reform experience in the next section, but as far as the pre-reform period is concerned, it is hard to claim that China was really marching ahead in terms of GNP per head, or the related measures of real national income or gross domestic product.

To be sure, the Chinese official statistics claimed high rates of GNP growth over the pre-reform period as well, and organizations such as the World Bank—not to mention the United Nations—went on faithfully reflecting these claims in the statistics distributed in such documents as *World Development Reports*. For example, in the tables included in the Annexe in *World Development Report 1979*, an annual growth rate of 5.1 per cent in GNP per head is attributed to China over 1960–77, compared with India's 1.3 per cent over the same period. But these claims do not square with other statistics that are also available, some of which are, in fact, presented in the

---

[9] It should be mentioned that the Chinese censuses count persons who are able to read and write in *any* local language or script as literate (Dr Peng Xizhe, Institute of Population Research, Shanghai, personal communication). This suggests that census evidence on high levels of illiteracy in Tibet cannot be dismissed as an artificial result of misdefining literacy as command over Chinese.

same documents (on this, see Drèze and Sen, 1989, chapter 11). There is much evidence that if the per-capita growth rate of GNP in China was higher than that in India in the period up to the reforms of 1979, the gap was not especially large.[10]

China's real achievement in this period lies in what it managed to do *despite* poor economic growth, rather than in what it could do *through* high economic growth. For example, the remarkable reduction in chronic undernourishment took place despite the fact that there had been relatively little increase in food availability per person; as Judith Banister (1987) notes, 'annual per capita grain production through 1977 was about the same as in the late 1950's: it averaged 301 kilograms in 1955–57 and 305 kilograms in 1975–77' (p. 354). The causal processes through which the reduction of undernutrition was achieved involved extensive state action including redistributive policies, nutritional support, and of course health care (since undernourishment is frequently caused by parasitic diseases and other illnesses).[11]

China's achievements in the field of health during the pre-reform period include a dramatic reduction of infant and child mortality and a remarkable expansion of longevity. By 1981, the expectation of life at birth was estimated to be already as high as 68 years (compared with 54 years in India), and infant mortality as low as 37 deaths per 1,000 live births (compared with 110 in India).[12] Progress in health and longevity during the eighties has been in the nature of a continuation of these earlier trends, rather than a new departure.

As was noted earlier, China's breakthrough in the field of elementary education had also taken place before the process of economic reform was initiated at the end of the seventies. Census data indicate, for instance, that literacy rates in 1982 for the 15–19 age group were already as high as 96 per cent for males and 85 per cent for females (the corresponding figures for India at that time were 66 per cent

---

[10] An independent study published by the World Bank (1983), which does not rely on official statistics, estimates that the growth rate of real per-capita GNP in China was 2.7 in 1959–79, compared with 1.4 for India. This is consistent with the available evidence from other independent studies (see Perkins, 1983, 1988, for a review).

[11] On this see Riskin (1987, 1990). On the connection between disease and undernutrition, see also Drèze and Sen (1989, 1990), Tomkins and Watson (1989), Dasgupta and Ray (1990), Osmani (1990).

[12] The figures are from Coale (1993), Tables 1 and 2, and Government of India (1994a), p. 147; see Table 4.3 in the next section.

and 43 per cent—see Table 4.2). The eighties continued that progress and consolidated China's lead, but the relative standings had been decisively established *before* the Chinese reforms.

4.5. Post-reform Records

The developments that have taken place in China since the reforms of 1979 have been quite remarkable. The rates of economic growth have been outstandingly high. Between 1980 and 1992, the GNP per capita in China seems to have grown at an astonishing 7.6 per cent per year (Table 4.1). Industrial production has grown at more than 11 per cent per year, and even agricultural production—traditionally much more sluggish than industry—has experienced an annual growth rate of 5.4 per cent.[13]

The high rates of growth of output and real income have permitted the use of economic means to reduce poverty and to improve living conditions. The scope for removing poverty is obviously much greater in an economy where per-capita income *doubles every ten years,* as the annual growth rate of 7.6 per cent implies, than in a country where it limps along at 2 or 3 per cent per year, as has been the case in India for much of the last five decades. For China, it is estimated that the proportion of the rural population below the poverty line has fallen from 33 per cent in 1978 to 11 per cent in 1990 (World Bank, 1992). This is a very rapid decline. While India too has achieved a significant reduction of rural poverty in this period, the magnitude of the reduction has been much more modest: a fall from 55 per cent in 1977–8 to 42 per cent in 1988–9.[14] There can be little doubt that China has done much better than India in this particular respect,[15] and in explaining this difference, the much higher growth rate of the Chinese economy must receive

---

[13] *World Development Report 1994*, Table 2. On these and other aspects of economic reform in China, see also Perkins (1988), Hussain (1989), Byrd and Lin (1990), Bhalla (1992), Chen et al. (1992), Lin (1992), Rosen (1992), Riskin (1993), among others.

[14] Tendulkar et al. (1993), Table 4.2.1. The estimates of B.S. Minhas and colleagues, and of the recent report of the Planning Commission's Expert Group on Poverty Estimation, all presented in EPW Research Foundation (1993), suggest a similar pace of decline during the 1980s. See also Statistical Appendix.

[15] The poverty lines used in China and India are not the same, so that what is being compared here are the relative *declines* in poverty during the 1980s, rather than the absolute poverty levels.

the bulk of the credit. Indeed, the post-reform period in China has not been one of substantial redistributive efforts, and the available evidence indicates that income inequality has probably increased rather than decreased since the reforms were initiated.[16] It is participatory growth, rather than radical redistribution, that accounts for the rapid decline of poverty in China in the eighties. In India, the eighties have witnessed some acceleration of economic growth, with little change in economic inequality, and these trends have coincided with the emergence of a marked decline in the head-count index, but the decline of poverty has remained comparatively modest.

This way of evaluating poverty relies on what has been called the head-count index, defined as the proportion of the population with per-capita income (or expenditure) below a specified 'poverty line'. It is based on the notion of poverty as insufficient income or expenditure, and this can be quite inadequate since deprivations can take many different forms—various inadequacies of basic capabilities that relate to many different causal factors (such as public health services and social insurance systems) in addition to private incomes.[17] Further, even within that income-centred perspective, the head-count measure is insensitive to the levels and inequalities of incomes below the poverty line, and a more distribution-sensitive evaluation of poverty may be necessary for a fuller understanding of even income deprivation.[18]

Trends in the head-count ratio do, of course, have obvious informational value, even when we adopt a broader approach to poverty.[19]

---

[16] See A.R. Khan et al. (1992), Bramall and Jones (1993), Griffin and Zhao Renwei (1993), Howes (1993), Knight and Song (1993b), Riskin (1993), Howes and Hussain (1994).

[17] On this, see Sen (1984, 1992a), and chapter 2 of this book. The approach of poverty as capability inadequacy relates to Adam Smith's (1776) treatment of 'necessities', and it treats the lowness of income (such as income levels being below a specified 'poverty line') as being only instrumentally and contingently relevant (with the appropriate poverty line varying between different societies and with diverse individual and social conditions).

[18] See Sen (1976b), Blackorby and Donaldson (1980), Foster, Greer, and Thorbecke (1980), Foster (1984), Kakwani (1986), Atkinson (1989), and Ravallion (1994).

[19] In the literature on poverty in India, the head-count measure has been far more used than any other indicator of poverty, and the rationale for this arises not from any intrinsic importance of this indicator, but rather from the likelihood of its correlation with other—more significant—characterizations of deprivation. On the relationship between different indicators of poverty in the Indian economy, see Tendulkar, Sundaram, and Jain (1993), and Dutta et al. (1994).

The reduction in income poverty in China in the post-reform period is an achievement of great importance, given that lack of income often drastically constrains the lives that people can lead. But this finding needs to be supplemented with further information about what has been happening in matters of living conditions, e.g. mortality rates and related indicators. In fact, while the improvements of living conditions during the pre-reform period, including the expansion of life expectancy and the reduction of infant mortality and illiteracy, have been consolidated and extended in the post-reform period, the rate of progress in these fields since 1979 has been, in some important respects, rather moderate in comparison with (1) the radical transformations of the *pre-reform* period, (2) what has been achieved during the post-reform period in terms of raising *income levels* and reducing head-count measures of poverty, (3) what many *other countries* at a comparable stage of development have achieved since the late seventies.

This statement is illustrated in Table 4.3 with reference to life expectancy and infant mortality. It can be seen that while China achieved an outstanding transformation during the sixties and seventies (starting with levels of infant mortality and life expectancy similar to India's, but catching up with Kerala, Sri Lanka, and South Korea within two decades), the pace of improvement during the post-reform period has been less remarkable.[20] In fact, in comparative international terms, China has not fared particularly well during this period. Life expectancy, for instance, has expanded by only 1.6 years between 1981 and 1991 in China, compared with about 2 years in Sri Lanka, 4 years in South Korea, 4.6 years in Kerala, and 5.3 years in India as a whole.

The comparison with Kerala is especially instructive. At the end of the seventies, China and Kerala had much the same level of infant mortality, and China was a little ahead of Kerala in terms of life expectancy. During the eighties, infant mortality in Kerala further declined from 37 per 1,000 live births to 16.5, and life expectancy increased by another 4.6 years; in China, by contrast, infant mortality only declined from 37 to 31, and life expectancy

---

[20] Some official mortality statistics series even suggest a recorded *increase* in mortality rates in the immediate post-reform years (as discussed in Drèze and Sen, 1989, pp. 215–18). But there are reasons to doubt the accuracy of these statistics. In Table 4.3, we have used the more reliable life tables recently derived from 1982 and 1990 census data (Coale, 1993).

TABLE 4.3 *Mortality Decline in China and Selected Economies*

	Infant mortality rate (per 1,000 live births)				Life expectancy at birth (years)			
	1960	*1981*	*1991*[a]	*Percentage decline between 1981 and 1991*[a]	*1960*	*1981*	*1991*[a]	*Expansion between 1981 and 1991*[a] *(years)*
China	150	37	31	16	47.1	67.7	69.3	1.6
India	165	110	80	27	44.0	53.9[b]	59.2	5.3
Kerala	93[c]	37	16	57	50.3[c]	66.9[b]	71.5	4.6
South Korea	85	33	23	30	53.9	66	70	4
Sri Lanka	71	43	26	40	62.0	69	71	2

Notes. [a] 1990, in the case of China.
[b] Unweighted average of SRS-based estimates for 1976–80 and 1981–5.
[c] Unweighted average of census-based estimates for 1951–60 and 1961–70.

Sources. Infant mortality rate and life expectancy, 1960 (except Kerala): *Human Development Report 1994*, Table 4 (pp. 136–7). Infant mortality rate and life expectancy, 1981, Sri Lanka and South Korea: *World Development Report 1983*, pp. 148–9 and 192–3. Infant mortality rate and life expectancy, China, 1981 and 1990: Coale (1993), Tables 1–4. Infant mortality rate and life expectancy, 1991, Sri Lanka and South Korea: *World Development Report 1993*, pp. 238–9 and 292–3. Infant mortality rate, 1981 and 1991, India: *Sample Registration Bulletin*, January 1994, Table 1, p. 5. Life expectancy, 1981, India: calculated from Statement 1, *Sample Registration System Abridged Life Table 1986–90* (Office of the Registrar-General, New Delhi). Life expectancy, 1991, India and Kerala: unpublished estimates based on Sample Registration System data, obtained from the Office of the Registrar-General, New Delhi. Infant mortality rate, 1991, Kerala: *Sample Registration Bulletin*, January 1994, Table 8, p. 19. Life expectancy and infant mortality, 1960 and 1981, Kerala: calculated from Ramachandran (1996), based on census and Sample Registration System data. For further comments on the different sources, see the Explanatory Note in the Statistical Appendix of this book.

increased by less than 2 years.[21] This contrast is all the more striking if we remember that China has experienced extraordinary growth of commodity production during the eighties, whereas Kerala's economy has shown remarkable sluggishness.[22]

The preceding observations point to the fact that economic growth is far more effective in expanding some aspects of living standards than in improving others. The difficult areas for post-reform China have been precisely those for which income expansion alone is not a solid basis of rapid progress. While the eighties have witnessed a dramatic expansion of private incomes in China, there seems to have been less success in the further development of public services, particularly in the poorer rural areas. There have been several reasons for this.[23] First, the post-reform period has seen a transition from a system where the collective had the first claim on the products of economic activity (as in the pre-reform commune system) to one where local public services have to be financed by taxing private incomes (a method which raises standard problems of incentives and administrative barriers). This has eroded the financial basis of local public services in some areas, particularly those which have experienced relatively slow economic growth. Second, the rapid expansion of the private economy has tended to drain human resources away from the public sector, where income-earning opportunities (e.g. for teachers and doctors) are far less attractive. Third, there is also some evidence of a reduced state commitment to the widespread and equitable provision of public services. One symptom of this

---

[21] It is plausible that the slowing down of infant mortality decline in China during the 1980s is partly a reflection of the effects of the 'one-child policy' (see section 4.8). But the same explanation cannot be invoked for the slowing down of mortality decline in other age groups. Even if infant mortality had declined as fast in China as in Kerala during the 1980s, the expansion of life expectancy in China would have been only around 3 years (taking as given the pace of mortality decline in the *other* age groups), compared with 4.6 years in Kerala.

[22] In fact, Kerala's real per-capita 'state domestic product' has remained virtually constant during the 1980s (A.N. Agrawal et al., 1992, p. 49; see also Statistical Appendix). It is right to note that, in Kerala, remittances from abroad are an important source of income, in addition to domestic production. However, recent estimates indicate that the share of remittances in total consumption is below 20 per cent, and has not grown much, if at all, during the 1980s (Krishnan, 1994; see also Ramachandran, 1996).

[23] For further discussion of these diverse developments, see Drèze and Sen (1989), World Bank (1992a), Yu Dezhi (1992), De Geyndt et al. (1992), Bloom (1994), Wong (1994), Drèze and Saran (1995), and the literature cited in these studies.

is the extension of the 'enterprise responsibility' model of public-sector management to social services, leading to widespread introduction of user fees as a means of ensuring cost recovery.

For these and other reasons, public services in large parts of rural China have come under some strain during the post-reform period. Village health services, for instance, have been comprehensively privatized. Whatever adverse effects these developments have had in the post-reform period have clearly been, on balance, outweighed by the favourable impact of rapid growth of private incomes, and the overall progress of living conditions has continued. But the result of this tension has been to moderate China's rate of progress in some social achievements, just when it has done so very well in stimulating economic growth.

This line of reasoning does not dispute the importance of what has been achieved in China in the post-reform period, but it suggests that China's progress on the income front has been diluted in the social field by its changed approach to public services, which could have got more from the expanded resources made available by rapid economic growth. These observations also guard us against 'rubbishing' what China had already done before the reforms. That general conclusion receives further support from the need to consider and scrutinize the factors underlying China's rapid economic growth in the post-reform period.

4.6. *Pre-reform and Post-reform Performances*

The spread of basic education across the country is particularly relevant in interpreting the nature of the Chinese economic expansion in the post-reform period. The role of mass education in facilitating fast and widely-shared growth has been much analysed in the recent development literature, particularly in the context of the performance of east Asian economies.[24] In China, the big step in that direction was taken in the pre-reform period. The fact, already noted, that by 1982 literacy rates in China were already as high as 96 per cent for males in the 15–19 age group, and 85 per cent even for females in that age group, made participatory economic expansion possible in a way it would not have been in India *then*—and is very difficult in India even *now*.

---

[24] See chapters 2 and 3 above, and also the works cited there.

Another area in which the post-reform expansions benefited from pre-reform achievements is that of land reforms, which has been identified as an important factor of economic development in east Asia in general.[25] In China, things went, of course, much further than land reforms, and the development of communal agriculture certainly was a considerable handicap for agricultural expansion in the pre-reform period, and indeed had a direct role in precipitating the great famines of 1958–61 (on which more presently). But that process of collectivization had also, *inter alia*, abolished landlordism in China (through a process that had often been quite brutal). When the Chinese government opted for the 'responsibility system' in the late seventies, the country had a land-tenure pattern that could readily support individual farming without the social problems and economic inefficiencies of highly unequal land ownership, in sharp contrast with India.

It is interesting that the institutional developments that have favoured participatory economic growth throughout east Asia (in particular, the spread of basic education and health care, and the abolition of landlordism) had come to different countries in the region in quite different ways. In some cases, even foreign occupation had helped, for example, in the land reforms of Taiwan and South Korea. In the case of China, the pre-reform regime, with its own goals and commitments, carried out some changes that turned out to be immensely useful in the market-based economic expansion of the post-reform period. That connection is extremely important to note for an adequately informed interpretation of the Chinese successes of recent years. If India has to emulate China in market success, it is not adequate just to liberalize economic controls in the way the Chinese have done, without creating the social opportunities that post-reform China inherited from the pre-reform transformation. The 'magic' of China's market rests on the solid foundations of social changes that had occurred earlier, and India cannot simply hope for that magic, without making the enabling social changes—in education, health care, land reforms, etc.—that help make the market function in the way it has in China.

---

[25] See, for example, Amsden (1989) and Wade (1990), and also World Bank (1993c) and the literature cited there.

4.7. *Authoritarianism, Famines and Vulnerability*

In learning from China, it is not enough to look only at positive lessons—what can be fruitfully emulated; it is important to examine the 'non-lessons' as well—what may be best avoided. An obvious instance is the Chinese experience of famine compared with India's better record in that field. The famines of 1958–61 killed, it appears, between 23 and 30 million people.[26] India's performance in famine prevention since independence has been much more successful, and even when a natural calamity like a drought has led to a potential famine situation, the occurrence of an actual famine has been averted through timely government action.[27]

The causation of the Chinese famines can be analysed from different perspectives. First, the disastrous experience of the Great Leap Forward and the related programme of rapid collectivization of agriculture are important elements in this story. The incentive system crashed badly and the organizational base of the Chinese agricultural economy collapsed.

Second, the problem was made worse by the arbitrary nature of some of the distributional policies, including features of communal feeding.[28] There was also an important question of distribution between town and country. The proportion of procurement for the urban areas actually went up precisely when the food output had plummeted.[29]

Third, the Chinese government did not wake up to the nature and magnitude of the calamity for quite a long time, and the disastrous policies were not substantially revised for three years, while the famine raged on. The informational failure was linked to a controlled press, which duped the public in suppressing information about the famine, but in the process deluded the government as well. The local leaders competed with each other to send rosy reports of their alleged success,

[26] Peng's (1987) estimate is 23 million extra deaths, whereas that of Ashton et al. (1984) is close to 30 million.

[27] See Drèze and Sen (1989) and Drèze (1990a). For case studies of famine prevention in post-independence India, see also Ramalingaswami et al. (1971), Choudhary and Bapat (1975), Mathur and Bhattacharya (1975), K.S. Singh (1975), Subramaniam (1975), Desai et al. (1979), Hubbard (1988), Government of India (1989b), Chen (1991), among others.

[28] On this see Peng (1987), who argues that communal kitchens led to over-consumption in some areas while starvation was widespread in others.

[29] See Riskin (1987, 1990).

outdoing their regional rivals, and at one stage the Chinese government was convinced that it had a 100 million more metric tons of foodgrains than it actually had.[30]

Fourth, the government was immune to public pressure, because no opposition party or political dissent was tolerated. There was, thus, no organized demand for the government to resign despite sights of starvation and mortality, and the political leaders could hang on to the disastrous policies for an incredibly long time. This particular aspect of the Chinese famine—its linkage with the lack of democracy in China—fits into a more general pattern of association between democracy and successful prevention of famines, or—seen the other way—between the absence of democracy and the lack of any guarantee that serious attempts to avert famines will be undertaken.[31]

Indeed, it is a remarkable fact that no substantial famine has ever occurred in a democratic country where the government tolerates opposition, accepts the electoral process, and can be publicly criticized. A government which has to deal with opposition parties, to answer unfriendly questions in the parliament, to face condemnation from the public media, and to go to the polls on a regular basis, simply cannot afford *not* to take prompt action to avert a threatening famine. But a non-democratic country has no such guarantee against famines.

In some ways, even the *other* causal factors in the above story of the Chinese famine relate ultimately to the lack of democracy. A policy as disruptive and drastic as the Great Leap Forward could not have been initiated in a pluralist democracy without its being debated extensively. Similarly, government decisions relating to food distribution—between individuals and between town and country— could not have been placed above criticism and public scrutiny. And of course the controlling of news and information would not have been possible in a multiparty democracy in the way it happened routinely in China when it experienced that gigantic famine. In the multi-faceted causal account of the great famine in China, the absence of democracy must be seen as being quite central, with influences on the other elements in the string of causation.

India's democratic system has many flaws, but it certainly is radically more suited to deal with famines. Underlying that specialized point

---

[30] See Bernstein (1984) and Riskin (1987).

[31] On this see Sen (1982, 1983a) and Drèze and Sen (1989).

about famines and famine prevention, there is a more general issue which is worth considering in this context. The successes of the Chinese economic and social policies have depended crucially on the concerns and commitments of the leadership. Because of its radical commitment to the elimination of poverty and to improving living conditions—a commitment in which Maoist as well as Marxist ideas and ideals played an important part—China did achieve many things that the Indian leadership failed to press for and pursue with any vigour. The elimination of widespread hunger, illiteracy, and ill health falls solidly in this category. When state action operates in the right direction, the results can be quite remarkable, as is illustrated by the social achievements of the pre-reform period.

The fragility of this way of doing things turns on the extreme dependence of the process on the values and politics of the leadership. If and when there is no commitment on the part of the leadership to pursue some particular cause, that cause can be very badly neglected. Also, whenever the leadership is deluded into getting the causal relations wrong, the whole system might still operate as if those mistaken presumptions were exactly right and in no need of exacting scrutiny. When the political leaders, for one reason or another, fail to address a problem, or refuse even to recognize it, there is little scope for public pressure to challenge their inertia or to expose their mistakes. The famines of 1958–61 represent a clear example of this pattern, but there are many others, including the acceptance of endemic illiteracy in Tibet (see section 4.3), the imposition of a draconian one-child policy (discussed in the next section), the excesses of the Cultural Revolution, and the frequent violation of basic human rights. Authoritarianism is an unreliable route to social progress.

4.8. *Coercion, Population and Fertility*

One particular field in which the operation of the authoritarianism of contemporary China can be seen in a very clear form is that of population policy, and it is often suggested, particularly in activist international circles, that India should emulate China in this important area. China has adopted fairly draconian measures to force the birth rate down, and its success in this respect has been widely studied and admired, given the alarmist views of the 'world population problem' that are currently shared by many international leaders.

The fear of an impending crisis makes many policy advocates seek forceful measures in the third world for coercing people to have fewer children, and despite criticism from diverse quarters including women's groups, China's attempts in that direction have received much attention and praise.

How alarming the 'population crisis' actually is in a country such as China (or for that matter India) is a debatable question. The case for concern about rapid population has, in fact, involved a combination of excellent arguments with rather misleading interpretations of the nature of the problem. One of these misinterpretations relates to the relationship between population growth and economic growth. It is sometimes thought that restraining population growth is an essential means of raising the rate of growth of per-capita GNP (or of preventing its decline). In fact, however, for countries such as India and China, population policies—important as they may in general be—are likely to make relatively little difference to the rate of per-capita economic growth.

TABLE 4.4. *India and China:*
Economic Growth and Population Growth

Country	Growth rate of population (1980–92)	Growth rate of GDP (1980–92)	Growth rate of GDP per capita, assuming the population growth rate of:[a]	
			India	China
India	2.1	5.2	3.1	3.8
China	1.4	9.1	7.0	7.7

Note. [a] Calculated by subtracting the population growth rate of the country mentioned in the column heading from the GDP growth rate of the country mentioned in the row heading.

Source. Calculated from *World Development Report 1994*, Tables 2 and 25.

This point is illustrated in Table 4.4. If China had a population growth rate similar to India's (i.e. 2.1 per cent instead of 1.4 per cent), its growth rate of per-capita GDP—assuming no change in the growth rate of *total* GDP—would only decline from 7.7 per cent per year to 7.0 per cent.[32] Similarly, should India succeed in

[32] The decline would be even smaller under the alternative assumption that a higher rate of population growth raises the growth rate of total GDP. This alternative assumption is rather more plausible than the assumption of unchanged growth of total GDP, which implies that the additional population is totally unproductive.

cutting down the rate of population growth to 1.4 per cent (as in China), its growth rate of per-capita GDP would only increase from 3.1 to 3.8 per cent. The contrast in growth rates of per-capita income between India and China are primarily due to China's much faster growth rate of total income, with differences in population growth rates playing relatively little role in that contrast.

This remark is not intended to dismiss the need for concern about rapid population growth. There are good reasons for such concern, based, for example, on environmental considerations (particularly the impact of population pressure on the local environment),[33] and on the quality of life of women burdened by frequent pregnancies. The point is to recognize that the force and characteristics of the problem are quite different from what are usually stressed in the much-publicized fears about 'the population problem' as a cause of low economic growth.

Coercive methods such as the 'one-child policy' have been tried in large parts of China since the reforms of 1979. Also, the government often refuses to offer housing and related benefits to families with several children—thus penalizing the children as well as the unconforming adults. By 1992 the Chinese birth rate had fallen sharply to 19 per thousand, compared with 29 per thousand in India, and 37 per thousand for the average of poor countries other than China and India. China's total fertility rate (a measure of the average number of children born per woman) is now 2.0, just below the 'replacement level' of around 2.1, and much below India's 3.7 or the weighted average of 4.9 for low-income countries other than China and India.[34] This has been seen—understandably—as a story of much success.

The difficulties with this 'solution' of the population problem arise from different sides.[35] First, the lack of freedom associated with this approach is a major social loss in itself. Human rights groups and women's organizations in particular have been especially concerned with the lack of reproductive freedom involved in any coercive system.[36]

Second, apart from the fundamental issue of individual freedom,

---

[33] See Dasgupta (1993).

[34] The figures cited here are from *World Development Report 1994*, Table 26.

[35] On coercive and collaborative approaches to family planning, see Sen (1994a, 1994b).

[36] On the general subject of reproductive freedom and its relation to the population problem, see Sen, Germain, and Chen (1994). This issue is also discussed in chapter 7 of this book, with reference to India.

there are specific consequences to consider in evaluating compulsory birth control. Coercion works by making people do things they would not freely choose to do. The social consequences of such compulsion, including the ways in which an unwilling population tends to react when it is coerced, can be appalling. For example, the demands of a 'one-child family' can lead to the neglect—or worse—of infants, thereby increasing the infant mortality rate. Also, in a country with a strong preference for male children—a characteristic shared by China with India and many other countries in Asia and north Africa—a policy of allowing only one child per family can easily be particularly detrimental for girls, e.g. in the form of fatal neglect of female children. This, it appears, is exactly what has happened on a fairly large scale in China.[37]

Third, it is not at all clear how much additional reduction in the birth rate has actually been achieved through these coercive methods. Many of China's longstanding social and economic programmes have been valuable in reducing fertility, including those that have expanded education (for women as well as men), made health care more generally available, provided more job opportunities for women, and stimulated rapid economic growth. These factors would themselves have reduced the birth rate, and it is not clear how much 'extra lowering' of fertility rates has been achieved in China through compulsion. For example, we can check how many countries in the world which match (or outmatch) China in life expectancy achievements, female literacy rates, and female participation in the labour force, actually have a *higher* fertility rate than China does. Of all the countries in the world for which data are given in the *World Development Report 1994*, there are only three such countries: Jamaica (2.7), Thailand (2.2), and Sweden (2.1)—and the fertility rates of two of these are close enough to China's (2.0). It is, thus, by no means clear what the *extra* contribution of coercion is in reducing fertility in China.

[37] These and other consequences of the one-child policy in China (such as the sharp decline in the female–male ratio at birth, primarily reflecting widespread abortion of female foetuses) have been discussed by Hull (1990), Johansson and Nygren (1991), Banister (1992), Greenhalgh et al. (1993), Zeng Yi et al. (1993), among others. Between 1981 and 1990, male infant mortality in China declined by 10 percentage points (from 38.4 to 28.4 deaths per 1,000 live births), but female infant mortality only declined by 3.5 percentage points, from 36.3 to 32.8 (Coale, 1993). Had infant female mortality declined by 10 percentage points, like male infant mortality, the number of female infant deaths in China would now be below what it actually is by about 78,000 deaths *per year*.

Despite all these problems, many commentators point out that China has nevertheless achieved something in its birth control programme that India has not been able to do. This is indeed the case, and in terms of national averages, it is easy to see that China with its low fertility rate of 2.0 has got population growth under control in a way that India, with its average fertility rate of 3.7, simply has not achieved. However, what is far from clear is the extent to which this contrast can be attributed to the effectiveness of the coercive policies used in China, since we would expect the fertility rate to be much lower in China given its higher level of female literacy (almost twice as high as India's), higher life expectancy (about 10 years more), larger female involvement in gainful employment (fifty per cent higher, in terms of share of the total labour force), and so on.

In order to sort out this issue, it is useful to look at those parts of India which have relatively high literacy rates, and other social features that are associated with voluntary reduction of fertility rates. The state of Kerala does provide an interesting comparison with China, since it too enjoys high levels of basic education, health care, and so on. Kerala's birth rate of 18 per thousand is actually lower than China's 19 per thousand, and this has been achieved without any compulsion by the state. Kerala's fertility rate is 1.8 for 1991, compared with China's 2.0 for 1992. This is in line with what we could expect through progress in factors that help voluntary reduction in birth rates. Kerala has a higher adult female literacy rate—86 per cent—than China (68 per cent). In fact, as was mentioned earlier, the female literacy rate is higher in Kerala than in every single province in China. Also, as was mentioned, in comparison with male and female life expectancies at birth in China of 68 and 71 years, the 1991 figures for Kerala's life expectancy are 69 and 74 years, respectively. Further, women have played an important role in Kerala's economic and political life, and to some extent in property relations and educational movements.[38]

Kerala's success in reducing the birth rate, based on these and other positive achievements, disputes the necessity of coercion for cutting down fertility in poor economies. And since this low fertility has been achieved voluntarily, there is no sign of the adverse effects

---

[38] See Robin Jeffrey (1992), and also V.K. Ramachandran's paper on Kerala in Drèze and Sen (1996).

that were noted in the case of China, e.g. heightened female infant mortality and widespread abortion of female foetuses. As was discussed earlier, Kerala's infant mortality rate (16.5) is now much lower than China's (31), even though both regions had the same infant mortality rate around the time of the introduction of the one-child policy in China. Further, while in China the infant mortality rate is much lower for males (28) than for females (33), in Kerala the opposite is the case, with female infant mortality (16) a little below the male figure (17).[39]

It is sometimes argued that what makes compulsory birth control important and necessary is the speed with which birth rates can be cut down through coercive means, in a way that cannot happen with voluntary processes. However, Kerala's birth rate has fallen from 44 per thousand in the fifties to 18 by 1991—a decline no less fast than that in China. It could, of course, be argued that looking at this very long period does not do justice to the effectiveness of one-child family and other coercive policies that were introduced in 1979, and that we ought really to compare what has happened between 1979 and now.

Table 4.5 presents the comparative picture of fertility rates in China and Kerala in 1979 (when the 'one-child policy' was introduced) and now (to be exact in 1991). The figures for Tamil Nadu are also presented here, since Tamil Nadu has had an active family planning programme (see Antony, 1992), one of the highest literacy rates among the major Indian states, and also relatively high female

TABLE 4.5. *Fertility Rates in China, Kerala and Tamil Nadu*

	1979	1991
China	2.8	2.0
Kerala	3.0	1.8
Tamil Nadu	3.5	2.2

Sources. For China, Peng (1991), Li Chengrui (1992), and *World Development Report 1994*. For India, *Sample Registration System 1979–80* and *Sample Registration System 1991*.

[39] The Chinese figures are taken from Coale (1993); the figures from Kerala are derived from India's *Sample Registration System* (Government of India, 1993b, p. 31). It is worth noting that the survival disadvantage of infant females *vis-à-vis* males in China apparently did not exist in the 1970s (before the introduction of the one-child policy). In fact, infant mortality rate estimates for 1981 suggest some female *advantage* at that time (see Coale, 1993, Tables 1 and 2).

participation in gainful employment and low infant mortality (third among major states in both respects), all of which have contributed to a steady reduction of fertility. It appears that both Kerala and Tamil Nadu have achieved much bigger declines in fertility than China has since 1979. Kerala in particular began with a *higher* fertility rate than China in 1979 and ended in 1991 with a fertility rate as much *below* China's as it had been above it in 1979. Despite the added 'advantage' of the one-child policy and other coercive measures, the Chinese fertility rate seems to have fallen much less sharply.

Contrasts between the records of Indian states offer some further insights on this subject. While Kerala, and to a smaller extent Tamil Nadu, have radically reduced fertility rates, other states in the so-called 'northern heartland' (such as Uttar Pradesh, Bihar, Madhya Pradesh, Rajasthan) have much lower levels of education, especially female education, and of general health care. These states all have high fertility rates—between 4.4 and 5.1. This is in spite of a persistent tendency to use heavy-handed methods of family planning in those states (see sections 5.4 and 7.4), in contrast with the more 'collaborative' approach used in Kerala and Tamil Nadu. The regional contrasts within India strongly argue for collaboration (based *inter alia* on the active and educated participation of women), as opposed to coercion.

India has much to learn from China, but the need for coercion and for the violation of democracy is not one of them. India's democracy is faulty in many ways, but the faults are not reduced by making the system *less* democratic. It is possible to admire China's various achievements and to learn from them discriminatingly, *without* emulating its non-democratic features.

4.9. *The Real Lessons for India from China*

The 'dawn' may or may not come up 'like thunder outer China', but there are really many things to learn from China's experience, if we take a discriminating approach. Perhaps the first and the most obvious lesson arises from the demonstration of the possibility of making excellent use of the market system in a poor economy without losing the political commitment to economic development and the elimination of mass deprivation. People moved by the intensity of poverty in India often remain sceptical of what the market mechanism can do. To some extent that scepticism is justified, and indeed we have argued that the market mechanism *on its own* may not take us very far in eliminating deprivation in India, if liberalization goes hand in hand with a continued neglect of other conditions of social progress. But the Chinese experience convincingly demonstrates that, properly supplemented, a thriving market economy can help a great deal to lift the masses out of poverty and transform their living conditions. People who have admired China for its other achievements over the decades cannot sensibly shut their eyes to this rather large message.

Second, China's experience also brings out the complementarity between two essential bases of expansion of social opportunities, namely (1) *supportive public intervention*, especially in fields such as education, health care, social security, and land reforms, and (2) *the market mechanism*—an effective basis of trade and production arrangements. We discussed how the achievements of the pre-reform period in the former area have helped China to sustain and promote the market-based opportunities in the post-reform period. .

Third, China's liberalization programme has certain pragmatic features that distinguish it from some other attempts at surging towards a market economy. The market mechanism has been used in China to create additional channels of social and economic opportunities, without any attempt to rely on the market itself as a surrogate social system on its own. There has been no breathless attempt at privatization of state enterprises, and no abdication of governance; instead the focus has been on opening up new possibilities for the private sector together with reforming management practices in collectively-owned enterprises. While the privatization attempts in the former Soviet Union and eastern Europe could not but threaten a large section of the established labour force with deep insecurity, the operative mode of the Chinese reforms has been based on a more positive combination of public-sector reform with expansion of private enterprises. There is a great deal to learn from the non-purist pragmatism of the Chinese planners.

Fourth, the pragmatism of the Chinese economic policies has included combining the pursuit of economic growth with continuation of a basic social security system.[40] In urban areas, social security

---

[40] On China's social security system, see Hussain and Liu (1989), Ahmad and Hussain (1991), Hussain (1993, 1994), and the literature cited there.

is based on guaranteed employment, and the continuing social responsibilities of the enterprise.[41] In carrying out the rural reforms (based on a new stress on 'household responsibility'), land has been kept under collective ownership, with each adult person in a village—male or female—being entitled to cultivate a given amount of land. The land-based social security arrangements have largely prevented the emergence of a class of dispossessed landless households, and have provided some protection against extreme destitution.[42] This combination of collective ownership and individual use rights has been a special feature of Chinese economic reforms.[43]

Fifth, even with that pragmatism, China's market-oriented reforms have been much more successful in raising income levels and in reducing income poverty than in expanding social services (notably in the field of health care) and the social opportunities that depend on these services. While real incomes have galloped forward, life expectancies have moved upwards rather slowly. Oddly enough, China's lead over India in life expectancy has narrowed rather than widened since the reforms began, and despite its massively faster economic growth, China has actually fallen behind Kerala in this field exactly over this period of economic dynamism.

Finally, while India has much to learn from China in the field of economic and social policy, the lessons do not include any overwhelming merit of its more authoritarian system. This is not to deny that the larger success of the Chinese efforts at social progress has been, to a great extent, the result of the stronger political commitment

---

[41] This 'dual' function of enterprises in urban China (as employers in an economy where markets and competition are increasingly important, and as providers of social security) raises some important issues of enterprise reform, on which see Hussain (1990, 1992, 1993, 1994), Wood (1991), and Hussain and Stern (1992), among others. It should also be mentioned that the 'floating population' of unofficial migrants to urban areas does not enjoy the social protection measures that are available to registered urban residents; the growth of this floating population, too, raises important issues of economic policy (see e.g. World Bank, 1992a).

[42] Additional social security measures in rural areas include (i) collective insistence on support of the elderly by the younger generation, and (ii) unrequited transfers (the *wu bao* or 'five guarantee' system) for those who are deprived of family support and unable to work.

[43] The combination of collective ownership with enterprise responsibility is also a feature of the spectacularly successful 'township and village enterprises' (TVEs). For a good discussion of this aspect of China's TVEs, see Weitzman and Chenggang Xu (1993). See also Byrd and Lin (1990), and the literature cited there.

of its leadership to eliminating poverty and deprivation. But the less challenged powers of the leaders have also left the Chinese economy and society more vulnerable to the kind of crises and disasters of which the famine of 1958–61 is an extreme example. The general problem of lack of democratic control remains, and has manifested itself in different forms. It has also had implications on such subjects as coercive family planning and the loss of reproductive and political freedoms. The fact that India's record is terrible in some related fields does not provide a good reason to be tempted by the political authoritarianism to be found in China.

In learning from China what is needed is neither *piecemeal emulation* (involving liberalization without the supportive social policies), nor indeed *wholesale emulation* (including the loss of democratic features). There is much to learn from causal analyses relating Chinese policies in different periods to the corresponding achievements. The relationships between the accomplishments in China before and after the economic reforms are particularly important to study. There is much for India to learn from China on a *discriminating* basis.

5

PUBLIC ACTION
AND SOCIAL INEQUALITY

5.1. The Public and Its Role

'Beware the fury of the patient man,' John Dryden had warned three hundred years ago. Unfortunately, the ruling authorities often have excellent reason to ignore that piece of ancient wisdom. The patient man—or woman—may be much too patient to come into the reckoning of those who are in charge of the levers of control. Successive governments in India have had reason enough to rely on the unending patience of the neglected and deprived millions in India, who have not risen in fury about illiteracy, hunger, illness, or economic insecurity. The stubborn persistence of these deprivations has much to do with that lack of fury.

What the government ends up doing can be deeply influenced by pressures that are put on the government by the public. But much depends on what issues are politicized and which deprivations become widely discussed and electorally momentous. The fact, discussed in the preceding chapter, that major famines have never taken place in a democratic country with a relatively free press and tolerance of opposition parties, indicates the power of public criticism and also the political salience of mass starvation, which receives instant attention in multiparty, electoral politics.[1] A government that has to face criticism from opposition parties and free newspapers, and that has to seek reelection cannot afford to neglect famines, since famines are conspicuous miseries which can be easily brought into

---

[1] See Sen (1982, 1984), Reddy (1988), Drèze and Sen (1989), Drèze (1990a, 1990b), Ram (1990).

the arena of public discussion by newspapers, opposition parties, and active Parliamentarians. India's success in escaping major famines since the Bengal famine of 1943 (four years *before* independence) has not been unrelated to this feature of public action in the Indian democratic polity.[2]

However, the reach of public criticism can be less effective when the deprivations are less extreme, more complex to analyse, and less easy to remedy, as in the case of regular—but non-extreme—undernourishment and economic insecurity, and of lack of medical care for endemic diseases. Similarly, lack of school facilities or clean water may or may not receive crucially critical attention, depending on the particular nature of politics and journalism in the regions involved. While any responsible editor of a newspaper cannot but write about a famine as and when it begins to emerge, and while the subject of mass starvation is easy to write about politically (even a simple picture of an emaciated mother holding a shrivelled baby speaks volumes as a political statement), journalistic attention on less immediate, less catastrophic deprivations depend much on the skill and political commitment of the practising journalists.[3] Also, what is or is not politicized depends, to a great extent, on the visions and preoccupations of opposition parties. For deprivations less dramatic than famines or catastrophic epidemics, a crucial variable, thus, is the activism of public participation. This depends on a variety of factors, including the nature of the political parties and their leadership, the skill and traditions of investigative journalism, and also the level of literacy and education in the region.[4]

---

[2] Similar successes in famine prevention have been observed in those sub-Saharan African countries that managed to remain democratic even when democracies were largely wiped out in that broad region. In the 1980s, democratic Zimbabwe and Botswana prevented famines with appropriate and timely public policies despite facing food crises no less severe than those that precipitated famines in dictatorial Ethiopia, Somalia, Sudan, and many other countries there (see Drèze and Sen, 1989, chapter 5).

[3] On this see N. Ram's (1990) analysis of the reach and limitations of the Indian press as it has evolved. A similar point can be made, in the field of health care, about the contrast between the government's swift response to sensational epidemics and its passive acceptance of endemic morbidity. The outbreak of plague in India in September 1994 immediately became a major political issue, lending itself to thundering editorials, and was brought under control within a few days. During the same period, enormous numbers of people died of tuberculosis, hepatitis, tetanus, malaria, diarrhoea, and other endemic diseases, without their plight eliciting anything like the same public response.

[4] See Drèze and Sen (1989), Ram (1990), and Robin Jeffrey (1992).

Public action, in this broad sense, can play a central role in economic development and in bringing social opportunities within the reach of the people as a whole. Sometimes public action is characterized in the economic literature as action by the government, not as action by the public itself. As we have discussed in Drèze and Sen (1989), this interpretation can be seriously misleading, as it draws attention away from the influence that the public can have in determining the direction of governmental action. As we tried to illustrate, actions of the public can be of profound significance to the successes and failures of economic and social change in general, and to development efforts in particular.

The role of public activism in influencing government policy can be particularly important in promoting the positive functions of the government, discussed in the concluding section of chapter 2. These positive functions include the provision of basic public services such as health care, child immunization, primary education, social security, environmental protection, and rural infrastructure. The vigilance and involvement of the public can be quite crucial not only in ensuring an adequate expansion of these essential services, but also in monitoring their functioning. Indeed, the actual reach and effective quality of the services that are meant to be, in principle, available often depends a great deal on the information that the local community gathers and the extent to which it can get its voice heard. The shirking and absenteeism of village teachers, for example, are much more easily observed by the villagers themselves than by government inspectors, and the search for redress can be more effectively achieved with local activism. Similar arguments apply to the diversion of ration supplies from publicly subsidized shops, the misuse of public funds and facilities in rural health centres, the disposal of village trees by local leaders for personal gain, or the stealing of electric wires by enterprising embezzlers. Also, schools, hospitals, etc. can be made more sensitive to public needs if there is local pressure in that direction, in a way that general instructions from high above might not be able to achieve.

Public action can also affect outcomes without having to work through swaying government policy. Public discussions can influence social behaviour, and sometimes even personal behaviour. For example, enlightened public discussion in Kerala clearly has had a considerable role in creating a cultural atmosphere that has acted against the gender bias in the family, and it also seems to have played an important part in spreading the use of birth control in Kerala and thus in the decline in the fertility rate that has been so dramatic there in recent years.[5] Similarly, public action and social movements can do a great deal to challenge social inequalities without necessarily involving the agency of the government. In understanding the process of economic development in India and the barriers that are faced, attention must be paid to the diverse roles and potentially extensive reach of public action.

As far as the influence of public action on governmental decision-making is concerned, attention has to be paid not only to the positive influences that may be exerted on the process of development, but also to negative impacts that particular types of public action might have. Active pressure groups, which too are (in a broad sense) part of the public, can make economic policy severely constrained by extracting concessions for sectarian interests that may divert resources from broad development objectives to narrow pursuit of sectional advantages.[6]

Even the neglect of primary education in governmental planning in India—discussed earlier—has a clear relation with the biased impact of political activism and pressures.[7] On the one hand, the lack of political pressure in favour of elementary education—a deprivation that affects the least powerful sections of the Indian society—has resulted in this need having only a very weak influence on the actual making of public policy. On the other hand, pressure groups in favour of higher education—a subject that directly interests people who are much more dominant in the society—have constituted a powerful force in the direction of giving priority to tertiary education. The neglect of literacy and elementary education relates, to a considerable extent, to the extraordinary priority that has actually been given to expanding higher education.

This is, in fact, an integral component of general *inequality* in India, and it relates to the well-being as well as the agency of the different groups involved. The sections of the population that are most affected by the absence of literacy are typically much worse off than the groups that benefit from higher education. In terms

---

[5] See T.N. Krishnan (1976, 1991, 1994), Mari Bhat and Rajan (1990, 1992), and Robin Jeffrey (1992).

[6] On this see Myrdal (1968), Olson (1982, 1993), Bardhan (1984b), Datta Chaudhuri (1990), among others.

[7] On this see Sen (1970) and Weiner (1991).

of *consequences*, the bias in educational priorities has tended to reinforce existing inequalities, and has been least kind to the most deprived. But moving from consequences to the *origins*, these iniquitous policies reflect, to a great extent, the pre-existent inequalities in Indian society. The more privileged groups, who clamour for further expansion of higher education, are politically much more powerful and better organized in pressing for what they want.[8] There is, thus, something of a self-sustaining circle here.

To counter this resilient stratification, what is needed is more activism in the political organization of the disadvantaged sections of Indian society.[9] This can be a challenging task, but recent history provides many examples of positive achievements in this field. The immensely impressive expansion of basic education in Kerala, for instance, has been much influenced by the contribution of political organizations working in the direction of more literacy and elementary education.[10] To some extent the lower-caste movements in south and western India, in general, have had this reforming feature.[11] Recently, in other regions as well, the disadvantaged groups (including 'scheduled' and 'backward' castes, and to a lesser extent scheduled tribes) have begun to show their ability to organize and act in a politically decisive manner. There is a great opportunity here for channelling that political activism in the direction of forcefully demanding expansion of basic education for those who are left out of the system, and in asking for greater attention to health care, social

[8] On this feature of Indian education, see Sen (1970), Naik (1975c, 1982), Weiner (1991, 1994), Tilak (1993), among others. The traditionally elitist tendencies of the ruling cultural and religious traditions in India may have added to this political problem. Both Hinduism and Islam have, in different ways, had considerable inclination towards religious elitism, with reliance respectively on Brahmin priests and powerful Mullahs, and while there have been many protest movements against each (the medieval poet Kabir fought against both simultaneously), the elitist hold is quite strong in both these religions. This contrasts with the more egalitarian and populist traditions of, say, Buddhism. Indeed, most Buddhist countries have typically had much higher levels of basic literacy than societies dominated by Hinduism or Islam. Thailand, Sri Lanka, and Myanmar (Burma) are good examples.

[9] For different analyses of the political situation in India, and of the prospects for change, see Rudolph and Rudolph (1972, 1987), Frankel (1978), Bardhan (1984b), Dhagamwar (1987), Kohli (1987, 1988, 1990), Frankel and Rao (1989), Vanaik (1991), Brass (1992), Kurrien (1992), Omvedt (1993), among others.

[10] See the chapter on Kerala by V.K. Ramachandran (1996) in the companion volume.

[11] See e.g. Irschick (1969), Rudolph and Rudolph (1972, 1987), Barnett (1976), O'Hanlon (1985), Omvedt (1994).

security, and related forms of public support. The direction of rural politics in India will be particularly important in turning this political evolution into a major force for economic development and the creation of social opportunities. Much would depend on whether the nature of such sectional politics stays confined to narrow issues (such as securing the privilege of guaranteed governmental jobs for a few members of the disadvantaged castes), or whether it can take on broader concerns that affect most people in the deprived categories (such as expansion of education, health care, social security, land reform, and so on). There is a real challenge here for the political parties and movements that claim to represent the underdogs of Indian society.

5.2. *The Reach of Inequalities*

India's record in reducing social and economic inequalities since independence has been very disappointing. Despite a virtual consensus about some kind of 'socialism' being a fundamental goal of economic policy, few practical steps have been taken to remove the pervasive inequalities that divide Indian society.

The relevant inequalities take different forms, relating not only to large disparities of income and wealth but also to other bases of advantage such as caste, gender, and education. In so far as it has been concerned with inequality at all, public policy has largely concentrated on the standard economic inequalities (e.g. those relating to income and land ownership), perhaps because these inequalities are particularly conspicuous, and lend themselves to convenient measurement. To a limited extent, there is sense in this, given the extreme nature of these inequalities, which leave some to struggle for their next meal while others lead opulent lives.

It is sometimes argued that the persistence of economic inequality does not matter very much, so long as poverty diminishes.[12] This view might have some plausibility if individual well-being were just a question of income. When, however, well-being is seen in terms

---

[12] This argument is sometimes used to legitimize the current bias of economic policy-making in favour of the so-called 'middle class'. This nebulous entity, most commonly defined as including everyone *above* a certain level of income (there is, it appears, no room for an 'upper class' in India's 'socialist' society), is increasingly regarded as the great engine of future growth in India's economy, with the reduction of poverty being a convenient by-product of a consumerism-driven process of economic expansion.

of basic capabilities, private income must be regarded as one among several relevant means that can be used to enhance well-being. Even if poverty remains unchanged, high levels of economic inequality directly curtail some of the relevant capabilities for the disadvantaged groups; examples of these capabilities include self-esteem, protection from violence, and the ability to participate in society and politics. People have reason to value these equality-related capabilities, even if they are poor and hungry.

Aside from this direct link between inequality and well-being, high levels of economic inequality can also indirectly undermine the ability of a society to promote valued capabilities. Economic disparities affect the character of social life, the nature of the political process, and the priorities of the state. Inequality, for instance, can be a source of social tension and even violence; this may help to explain why levels of violence are so high in, say, Brazil, South Africa, the United States, and the state of Bihar in India (all of which are plagued by persistent inequalities). And, as was discussed in the preceding section, the positive role of the government in expanding social opportunities can be severely undermined by political pressure from privileged groups geared to the protection of sectional interests. On the positive side, low levels of inequality often facilitate cooperative action and the pursuit of collective goals, such as the provision of public services. Even at the village level, it has often been observed that the outcomes of collective action and social provisions are greatly influenced by the nature of economic and social divisions.[13]

In so far as anything has been done to reduce economic inequalities in India, the chosen measures have often consisted of interfering with market transactions that are perceived to generate these inequalities. Examples of such measures include legal controls on share-cropping and moneylending, minimum-wage provisions, restrictions on the scale of private enterprises, rent-control laws, and prohibitions on land sales by tribal people. Some of these measures could be, if appropriately devised, helpful means of reducing inequality. There are persuasive redistributive arguments, for instance, in favour of legislation raising the minimum wage above the market level, and of some forms of positive discrimination in employment policies.

[13] On these issues, see Doherty and Jodha (1979), Wade (1988a, 1988b), Chambers et al. (1989), Platteau (1991), Swamy (1991), Bardhan (1993a), Putnam et al. (1993), Drèze and Gazdar (1996), among others; see also Bardhan (1995), and the empirical and theoretical studies cited there.

At the same time, it must be recognized that interference with market exchange has severe limitations as a redistributive device. The roots of economic inequality in private-ownership market economies lie not in market exchange *per se,* but market exchange based on unequal ownership. Economic or legislative measures that interfere with market exchange without altering the distribution of resources, and without creating an alternative—and more equitable—allocation mechanism, can be quite ineffective and counterproductive. First, such measures sometimes have high efficiency costs, which are borne partly by disadvantaged groups. It is well known, for instance, that extreme rent-control laws supposedly geared to the protection of tenants have often crippled the housing market in urban India, ultimately hurting the interests not only of landlords but also of potential tenants.[14] Second, even the distributive effects of these measures can be quite disappointing. While minimum-wage legislation can be a useful redistributive tool (especially in situations of monopsony), excessive wage demands can lead to labour-saving technological investment and widespread unemployment. The large-scale shift from labour-intensive cultivation to plantations in rural Kerala, where unemployment is now exceptionally high, is often cited as an example of this possibility. Third, it must be borne in mind that market exchange is sometimes a factor of liberation for disadvantaged sections of the population. It is by taking advantage of new opportunities for selling their labour, for instance, that many agricultural labourers in India have managed to free themselves from traditional bonds and feudal oppression.[15] Distributive policies have to take note of these liberating aspects of market exchange, as well as of its potentially exploitative features. Finally, the bureaucratic controls involved in widespread interference with market exchange are often themselves a major source of inequality, and may end

---

[14] See K. Basu (1994) for a discussion of this point. Instances of this phenomenon can also be found in rural areas. Kapadia (1992), for instance, documents how misguided tenancy legislation has paralysed the lease market, and led to large-scale eviction of landless tenants, in parts of Tamil Nadu.

[15] For reviews of the evidence, see Pal (1994) and Platteau and Baland (1994). For some case studies, see Breman (1974), Ramachandran (1990), and the literature cited in Drèze and Mukherjee (1989). That the market mechanism may serve as an instrument of liberation from traditional inequities was discussed by Karl Marx (1857–8), among others.

up compounding rather than reducing the disparities they are meant to address.

Given these limitations of redistributive measures based on interference with market exchange, it is important to consider alternative (or complementary) means of reducing economic inequalities. An obvious possibility is redistribution of ownership, e.g. through land redistribution. One advantage of ownership-focused redistributive measures is that their adverse effects on efficiency are often less serious than those of exchange-focused redistributive measures. In fact, in the former case, the efficiency effects can even be positive; the high. efficiency of small-farm owner-cultivation, for instance, often provides a strong argument for land redistribution on efficiency grounds alone.[16]

Redistributive measures such as land reform, of course, tend to be politically demanding, since privileged classes have a strong interest in resisting them. But the experiences of West Bengal and Kerala, discussed in the papers by V.K. Ramachandran, Sunil Sengupta and Haris Gazdar in the companion volume (Drèze and Sen, 1996), show that a political situation where land reforms are seriously implemented is not impossible to achieve. The reforms that have been implemented in these two states are relatively modest, in terms of total area distributed, but they have succeeded in guaranteeing minimum land entitlements to millions of people, and their benefits in terms of increased economic security, greater self-respect, and improved bargaining power are far from negligible. There is no reason to think that the political conditions that have led to these achievements are impossible to replicate elsewhere in India.

While land is perhaps the most obvious asset to redistribute, it has to be borne in mind that economic opportunities in India depend on a much wider range of endowments. Even in rural areas, land is no longer the overwhelming determinant of economic inequality. The distribution of formal-sector employment, of environmental resources, of educational facilities, and of affordable credit arrangements are examples of other influential factors. Opportunities for redistribution relating to these diverse endowments have to be considered, along with the scope for land redistribution.

No matter how far it will prove possible to go in these directions,

---

[16] See e.g. Bauer (1948), Chayanov (1966), Rao (1966), Berry and Cline (1979), Dasgupta (1993), among many others.

it is important to remember that the standard view of economic inequality (which focuses on income distribution and related issues) only captures a small part of the social inequalities with which we ought to be concerned. The relevant dimensions of inequality include not only income (or expenditure) but also health achievements, literacy rates, self-esteem, and other aspects of well-being. And the social divisions to be considered include not only different income groups but also other divisions, based on caste, gender, age, occupation, education levels, and related attributes. Many of the relevant inequalities are less conspicuous than disparities of purchasing power, but no less perverse.

It is in terms of these broader egalitarian concerns that India's record has been most disappointing, and that the scope for action may be particularly extensive.[17] The reduction of income inequality is a difficult challenge in India as elsewhere, partly due to the incentive problems that tend to arise when there is no strong link between productivity and reward, and partly because of the resistance of privileged classes. But there is no reason to tolerate widespread gender discrimination, the continued oppression of disadvantaged castes, the persistent divide between the literates and the illiterates, the exploitation of child labourers, and other destructive social inequalities. The dilemmas that arise in reducing economic inequality (e.g. the possible conflict between efficiency and equity) often have little force in addressing these inequalities. In fact, in many circumstances, distributional concerns are *congruent* with other social objectives, including economic efficiency. Reduced gender discrimination, for instance, expands the scope of women's agency, which is an important factor of social change and economic success (see chapter 7).

The congruence between distributional concerns and other social objectives is also striking in the context of basic education. As we noted in the preceding section, large disparities of educational achievements are a major form—and cause—of social inequality in India. While higher education is remarkably well developed, a large proportion of the population is still illiterate. Further, these disparities of educational achievements tend to perpetuate and reinforce other kinds of social inequality. The link between caste and literacy, for instance, clearly emerges from a wide range of empirical investigations, including

[17] On the role of India's 'new social movements' in challenging diverse types of social inequalities, see Omvedt (1993).

the case studies presented in the companion volume (Drèze and Sen, 1996). Surveys carried out in Uttar Pradesh and West Bengal show how, in the same village, some privileged castes can ' e found to have enjoyed near-universal adult literacy for several decades, while literacy rates are still close to zero among disadvantaged castes, particularly for females.[18] Eradicating illiteracy in India would, there-fore, not only promote greater equality in educational achievements, but also contribute to the elimination of social inequalities based on caste, gender, and related personal attributes. Widespread literacy would also serve a wide range of other economic and social objectives, given the diverse personal and social roles of education.[19] The com-patibility between egalitarian concerns and other social objectives makes the expansion of basic education a particularly important step towards the reduction of inequality in India.

5.3. *Social Inequality and Economic Reform*

The preceding discussion has some bearing on the issue of social inequality and economic reform. Opposition to greater reliance on market allocation in India is often based on the fear that such a policy might intensify existing inequalities. This argument deserves serious examination. As we noted earlier, there is a case for considering inequality as a social failure on its own, even when rising inequality goes hand in hand with a decline in poverty. It is right to be concerned about the prospect of further intensification of economic and social inequalities that are already extremely large.

Having said this, apprehensions of rising inequality may be mis-guided or exaggerated in several distinct ways. First, it is difficult to be sure about the effects of market-oriented reforms on economic inequality. Market allocation can certainly have some unequalizing influences, but so do bureaucratic controls, public-sector inefficiency, and trade restrictions. Some of the effects of reform can certainly be expected to be positive. Trade liberalization, for instance, tilts economic activity towards the production of exportable commodities, which tend to be labour-intensive, and this can be expected to have, often enough, an inequality-reducing influence. These positive

[18] See Sengupta and Gazdar (1996) and Drèze and Gazdar (1996).

[19] See chapter 2.

aspects have to be considered along with the unequalizing features of liberalization.

Second, the relationship between market-oriented reforms and social inequality is not just a question of their impact on the distribution of income or expenditure. Their consequences for other kinds of social divisions and inequalities are equally relevant. Here again, some important positive effects can be expected. Many studies have documented, for instance, how the expansion and diversification of employment prospects can undermine the traditional caste hierarchy based on a rigid occupation structure.[20] Similarly, a greater emphasis on economic achievement rather than inherited and immutably ascribed characteristics as a basis of social status can be expected to lead to some dissolution of traditional hierarchies. Women, too, may have much to gain from labour-intensive economic growth, given the positive effects of expanded opportunities for gainful female employment on gender relations and intra-household equity (see chapter 7). These positive links between economic reform and social equality have to be considered together with the equally real fact that privileged social groups are often in a stronger position to take advantage of new economic opportunities.

Third, the impact of market-oriented reforms on social inequality depends a great deal on the precise content of these reforms; and it is also strongly influenced by *other* aspects of social and economic policy. If the reforms in question take the form of simply removing controls, and leaving things to the market, it is difficult to predict in which direction the distributional effects will go. On the other hand, if economic policy involves a strong emphasis on promoting labour-intensive economic activity, on enabling disadvantaged groups to participate in the process of economic growth, on making use of growing resources to expand public services, and on developing social security arrangements, the reform process may provide a real opportunity to achieve greater equity *as well* as to reduce poverty.

In short, there is no predetermined link between economic reform and social inequality. A conscious choice has to be made between participatory growth and unaimed liberalization.

---

[20] For some relevant studies, see Ramachandran (1990), Kapadia (1992), Wadley and Derr (1989). Da Corta (1993), Drèze, Lanjouw, and Sharma (forthcoming), among others.

5.4. *Basic Equality, Social Security and Health Care*

One part of the task of reducing social and economic inequalities in India involves the expansion of social security provisions, broadly understood as social arrangements to protect all members of society from extreme deprivation and insecurity.[21] It is, indeed, difficult for persons who live in a condition of acute insecurity and dependence to challenge the inequalities of which they are victims. The availability of independent means of subsistence based on social support makes it that much easier for agricultural labourers to resist exploitative employment relations, for the oppressed castes to rise beyond humiliating occupations, and for women to challenge patriarchal institutions. Also, widespread acceptance of the notion of basic social equality can be much enhanced when some essential entitlements are guaranteed to all citizens as a matter of right. It is difficult to claim that all human beings have equal rights in any substantial sense while the streets are full of unemployed labourers, hungry children, destitute beggars, abandoned widows, and forsaken victims of dreadful diseases. Social security is an essential requirement of social justice.[22]

The case for expanded social security arrangements arises partly from these ethical considerations of basic equality, and partly from the more direct contributions they can make to the well-being of the persons who benefit from them. In devising these arrangements, it is important to take a broad view of the relevant means of intervention. With the help of ample budgetary and administrative resources, many industralized countries have been able to design effective social security systems based on particular programmes such as unemployment benefits, health insurance, and old-age pensions. In a country such as India, these particular means of intervention raise important problems of financing, administration, and incentives, which severely constrain their effectiveness as tools of social security.

However, alternative means are often available to address the same needs. For instance, even if unemployment insurance is not a feasible

---

[21] On the strategy of social security in developing countries, see Drèze and Sen (1991), and other contributions in Ahmad et al. (1991). Guhan (1981, 1990, 1992, 1993a, 1993b) has presented pioneering analyses of social security issues in India, and discussed a number of feasible policy initiatives in this field. The large literature on land reform, anti-poverty programmes, famine prevention, employment schemes, food distribution, health care, etc., is also relevant.

[22] See Rawls (1971, 1993), Sen (1980, 1992a), Dworkin (1981), Cohen (1989), van Parijs (1990, 1991), Patnaik (1991).

way of dealing with rural unemployment in India, labour-intensive public works programmes themselves can play a helpful role in addressing that problem. These programmes have less exacting financial requirements than unemployment insurance schemes, have limited disincentive effects, and are comparatively easy to administer (partly because they are based on a simple 'self-selection' mechanism). Public provisions relating to land entitlements, health care, public distribution, water supply, supportive credit, and school meals are other examples of relevant means of intervention in the Indian context.

One particular aspect of social security in which India has been quite successful since independence, as discussed earlier, is that of famine prevention. This achievement reflects, first and foremost, the political compulsion to respond to crisis situations in a democratic society: accountability to the electorate makes it very difficult for the government in office to ignore clamours for action when a famine threatens to develop, or electoral debacles that may follow an unprevented famine. But the successful prevention of famine in India has also involved a well-devised system of public intervention to protect the entitlements of vulnerable groups, chiefly based on large-scale employment programmes. The implementation of these programmes is sometimes quite chaotic, but they have nevertheless been effective, on numerous occasions since independence, in preventing the outbreak of a major famine. This experience illustrates the feasibility of certain kinds of social security arrangements, even in a poor country, when the government has adequate incentives to take action.

Putting in place social security arrangements to deal with chronic deprivation is undoubtedly a more demanding challenge, partly because the political pressures that are easy to mobilize in famine situations are often less immediate in other contexts, and partly because the problem to be addressed is intrinsically more complex. Here too, public employment programmes can be an important means of action, as the experience of Maharashtra's Employment Guarantee Scheme illustrates.[23] But other initiatives of different kinds have also proved helpful in several states. As mentioned earlier, for instance, the land reforms implemented in West Bengal and Kerala can be seen as fulfilling important social security objectives as well as some basic

---

[23] There is a large literature on Maharashtra's Employment Guarantee Scheme; see Acharya (1990), Bhende et al. (1992), Mahendra Dev (1992, 1993a, 1993b), Ravallion et al. (1993), Mahendra Dev and Ranade (1995), among recent contributions.

egalitarian goals. In recent years, Tamil Nadu has also taken some far-reaching initiatives in the field of social security, involving school meal programmes, innovative pension schemes, improved health care provisions, and related measures.[24] These and other pioneering experiences are highly relevant for other states. Grameen Bank and BRAC in Bangladesh, and SEWA in Gujarat, also provide excellent examples of how imaginative credit arrangements can be used to reduce insecurity.

Among the different forms of intervention that can contribute to the provision of social security, the role of health care deserves forceful emphasis. Illness is, obviously enough, one of the most widespread causes of human deprivation and economic insecurity in India. It affects not only the actual patients and those who depend on them for their subsistence, but also other members of the society, in so far as the *threat* of disease arising from widespread morbidity reduces the quality of life. Further, the limitations of private provision in the domain of health care are well known. A well-developed system of public health is an essential contribution to the fulfilment of social security objectives.

This is one field where there is an overwhelming need for bold initiatives and comprehensive reform. Compared with many other developing countries, India has poor health achievements despite spending a comparatively large part of its GNP on health (if one adds up public and private spending).[25] Much of this mismatch between resources and achievements is due to the poor functioning of the public health care system, especially in rural areas. In some states, this system is little more than a collection of deserted primary health centres, filthy dispensaries, unmotivated doctors, and chaotic hospitals.[26]

There have, in recent years, been some important initiatives geared to better public health provisions. The recent expansion of child

---

[24] For some studies of these different programmes, see Babu and Hallam (1989), Guhan (1990, 1993b), Harriss (1991), Rajivan (1991), Mina Swaminathan (1991), Antony (1992), Mahendra Dev (1993c), Visaria and Visaria (1995), among others.

[25] See e.g. Berman (1992).

[26] On this, see particularly the studies of health care in north India carried out by the Operations Research Group (including Khan and Prasad, 1983, Khan et al., 1980, 1983, 1986, 1987, 1988, 1989) and the Public Systems Group (Indian Institute of Management, 1985, Shah, 1989, Murthy, 1992); also Priya (1987), Budakoti (1988), Prakasamma (1989), Indian Council of Medical Research (1989), among others, for case studies.

immunization programmes, for instance, is certainly a positive (and long-overdue) development, and may have made a significant contribution to the comparatively rapid decline of child death rates during the last few years.[27] But there have also been alarming signs of neglect and deterioration in the basic framework of public health care. One of these signs is the massive displacement of health care activities by family planning programmes (mainly based on female sterilization).

As many field-based investigations have noted, the rural health care system in many states gives overwhelming priority to family planning, to the detriment of other health care services. A recent review of health care policy, for instance, observes that 'the whole rural primary health care system is geared towards family planning work' (Priya, 1990, p. 1820). Similarly, a field study in rural Rajasthan concludes that '[family planning] targets have now become the hallmark of all government activity in the name of health' (Gupta et al., 1992, p. 2330); a survey of 'auxiliary nurse midwives' in rural Maharashtra finds that two-thirds of the respondents regard family planning 'as the top priority work' (Jesani, 1990, p. 1103); a case study of health care in Uttar Pradesh states that 'during the main months for family planning campaigns (usually December to March) virtually all the energies of maternal and child health staff may be directed towards those ends' (Jeffery et al., 1989, p. 216); another study of health and family welfare services in rural Uttar Pradesh reports that 'the sterilization target achievement has the highest priority or rather the single priority' (Maurya, 1989, p. 167); yet another study in Uttar Pradesh found that 'the rampages of the family planning programme are particularly devastating... [the] preoccupation with attaining of the given family planning targets has had devastating effects on the other health activities' (Budakoti, 1988, pp. 153–4); an enquiry made in Andhra Pradesh reveals that 'family planning was taken as the priority function at all levels of health organization and ANMs [Auxiliary Nurse Midwives] would even leave attending delivery for a [sterilization] case' (Raghunandan et al., 1987); a survey

[27] For up-to-date information on immunization in India, see International Institute for Population Sciences (1994). Despite some recent progress, the level of child immunization remains very low in many Indian states. As recently as 1992–3, 30 per cent of all Indian children aged 12–23 months had not received *any* vaccine; in states such as Uttar Pradesh, Bihar, and Rajasthan, the corresponding proportion ranged between 43 and 54 per cent; see Statistical Appendix for further details.

of four north Indian states concludes that 'as from the highest level to the lowest everybody is asking regarding sterilization targets... health workers under the pretext of work of motivating sterilization cases neglect other work' (M.H. Shah, 1989, p. 120); a field report from rural Gujarat notes that 'the primary health care machinery, village, taluka and district level machinery including teachers, officials, non-officials, etc., were geared to work for achieving the [family planning] targets' (Iyengar and Bhargava, 1987, p. 1087); and a World Bank assessment of health care policy mentions that 'more than half of all health worker activities are directly associated with family planning' (World Bank, 1989, p. 142).[28] These are highly disturbing findings, which call for a major reassessment of health policy in India.

The record of public involvement in the provision of health care and social security is not similarly poor in all the states of India. Kerala, in fact, has a distinguished record in this respect, which has made a major contribution to the rapid expansion of life expectancy in that state (now around 72 years). But other states have also taken important initiatives in recent years. Nutrition programmes in Tamil Nadu, employment schemes in Maharashtra and Gujarat, primary education in Himachal Pradesh, public distribution in Andhra Pradesh, and land reform in West Bengal are some examples. In contrast, in the large north Indian states (notably Uttar Pradesh, Bihar, Rajasthan, and Madhya Pradesh), where the need for action is in many respects particularly urgent, apathy towards the need to develop social security programmes seems to be most resilient.

In this connection, it is interesting to note that most of the initiatives observed in the more active states have been taken in the context of electoral politics. In some cases, as with school meals in Tamil Nadu, land reforms in West Bengal, and public distribution in Andhra Pradesh, they have even been at the forefront of electoral debates. In the large north Indian states, by contrast, social security and related issues have little place in party programmes and electoral debates;

---

[28] For further reports along the same lines, see Khan, Prasad, and Qaiser (1983), Priya (1987), D. Banerji (1989), Roger Jeffery (1988), pp. 269–73, Prakasamma (1989), Sundari (1993), p. 32, Qadeer and Priya (1992), Rose (1992), p. 246. An important observation made in many of these studies is that family planning targets set by the centre, and the general priority given to family planning in the central government's health policy, are major reasons for this widespread displacement of other health care activities.

there, electoral politics seem to give more room to tactical factionalism, with alliances being made and broken depending on personalities and power bases, and little time being 'wasted' on real issues such as undernutrition, illiteracy, unemployment, or ill health.[29]

There is a plausible connection between this low visibility of basic social issues in north Indian politics and the persistence of widespread illiteracy. Literacy is not a requirement of effective participation in the political process (West Bengal's experience, briefly discussed in chapter 3, is a significant illustration of this point), but it is certainly a useful tool of active involvement. In the more literate states, disadvantaged sections of the population have been relatively successful in putting their needs on the political agenda. The best example is Kerala, where high levels of literacy achieved early on have helped to empower the public to demand extensive state involvement in the provision of health care, public distribution, social security, and, of course, education itself. But the same phenomenon is increasingly important in several other states, particularly in south India.

In the educationally backward states of north India, by contrast, the political agenda is overwhelmingly dominated by the concerns of privileged classes and castes. At the time of elections, the illiterate masses have a reasonable chance to make their voice heard, an opportunity which they have seized with striking sagacity on several occasions (for example in 1977, when the ruling party was massively defeated following the excesses of the Emergency). Between elections, however, the vocal demands of the upper castes, the large farmers, and the urban middle-class receive immensely greater attention than the needs of disadvantaged groups.[30]

These observations bring us back to some general points already raised earlier in this chapter and in chapter 3, including (1) the central role of politics in the development process (of which the expansion of social security arrangements is a crucial aspect), (2) the need for more effective political organization of deprived groups,

---

[29] An interesting symptom of this feature of the political agenda in north India is that even the grants made available by the central government for expanding public services are not fully utilized in some states (see section 6.8).

[30] A related issue is the widely-noted 'criminalization of politics' in many north Indian states. In Uttar Pradesh, for instance, almost half of the 425 Members of Legislative Assembly (MLAs) are known to have a criminal record (T.N. Seshan, Chief Election Commissioner, quoted in *Hindustan Times*, 16 October 1994). This feature of north Indian politics also hinders broad-based participation in the democratic process.

and (3) the importance of basic education as a means of successful participation in political activity.

5.5. *Local Governance and Social Reform*

Many of the public provisions that have to be made in order to promote basic equality and ensure minimal social security involve *local* public services. A primary school, for instance, is a public facility available to the local community. The same can be said of primary health care centres, fair price shops, labour-intensive public works schemes, and a whole range of other relevant provisions.

The effective management of these local public services depends crucially on the existence of credible institutions for local governance. To illustrate, it is difficult to see how the endemic problem of teacher absenteeism and shirking in rural India (on which more in the next chapter) can be successfully tackled without involving the proximate and informed agency of village communities. Shirking cannot be easily detected by distant outsiders, and the system of centralized school inspection has proved quite ineffective in much of rural India. It is much easier for the concerned parents, and other local residents, to monitor the behaviour of school teachers; but translating their specific knowledge into remedial action involves a challenging problem of local governance. As things stand, there is no mechanism to ensure any kind of accountability of village teachers to the local community in large parts of India, and this is an important factor in the persistence of endemic dereliction of duty.

Local democracy is a highly neglected institutional base of political participation in India. The case study of Uttar Pradesh by Drèze and Gazdar (1996) in the companion volume brings out how many villages in that state still function in much the same way as in the colonial period, with a single 'headman' acting as an all-purpose intermediary between the local community and the state. An important development, of course, is that the headman is now elected, rather than being selected by the government. In the absence of effective political organization of disadvantaged groups, however, the coveted position of headman is usually seized by some member of the local elite, who often uses his position to further his personal interests much more than to pursue any social goal.[31] This weakness of local

---

[31] One recent survey in eastern Uttar Pradesh, for instance, finds that as many as

democracy, rooted in centralized political institutions and deep social inequalities, has played a major role in the comprehensive breakdown of local public services in Uttar Pradesh. And that failure, in turn, is a chief cause of economic and social backwardness in that state.[32]

The importance of local democracy is not confined, of course, to this issue of public services, or other instrumental roles of participatory politics. Participation also has intrinsic value for the quality of life. Indeed, being able to do something not only for oneself but also for other members of the society is one of the elementary freedoms which people have reason to value. The popular appeal of many social movements in India confirms that this basic capability is highly valued even among people who lead very deprived lives in material terms.

The inadequacies of local governance in rural India have several roots, which call for distinct responses. First, the weakness of democratic institutions at the village level reflects a long tradition of centralized governance. The historical roots of this go back to the colonial period, when hierarchical centralization was crucial in making it possible for a handful of foreigners to administer a large and potentially rebellious population (see e.g. Guha, 1982, 1983, and Guha and Spivak, 1988). But it has been consistently perpetuated by the successive governments of independent India.

Second, the flourishing of local participatory politics has been greatly slowed down by low levels of literacy and basic education. Literacy obviously helps people to understand the functioning of the system, to deal with the government bureaucracy, to be aware of their rights, to understand and tackle new problems, and to achieve other abilities that are important for an effective role in local politics. Also, the possibility of decentralizing particular functions of the government (such as some aspects of school management) depends on adequate expertise being available at the local level. Just as more widespread education has enhanced the quality of *state-level* politics in the more

---

two-thirds of the headmen in 82 surveyed villages belonged to the Thakur caste—the traditional landowning upper caste in that region, notorious for oppressive subjugation of the lower castes. See H.N. Singh (1993).

[32] See Drèze and Gazdar (1996) for further discussion. There is also much evidence that the poor functioning of local public services elsewhere in India relates to the centralized, hierarchical, and non-participatory nature of their management. See, for instance, Robert Wade's (1992) insightful contrast of canal irrigation in India and South Korea, and Somanathan's (1991) analysis of environmental protection in the Himalayan region.

literate states, most notably Kerala, it has also led to more vigorous practice of *local* democracy in those states.

Last but not least, local democracy has often been undermined by acute social inequalities.[33] The low involvement of women in local representative institutions such as village panchayats is a clear illustration of this problem. In large parts of the country, local governance is in the hands of upper-caste men from privileged classes, who are only weakly accountable to the community and often end up using local public services as instruments of patronage. In some cases, the rural elite has been known not only to be indifferent to the general promotion of local public services but even to *obstruct* their expansion, to prevent the empowerment of disadvantaged groups. In Uttar Pradesh, for instance, it is still possible to find villages where a powerful landlord has actively opposed the creation of a village school.[34]

The first of these three reasons for the fragile nature of local democracy in India has recently been addressed in the form of the 73rd and 74th constitutional amendments (the 'Panchayati Raj' amendments), which require all the state governments to introduce certain legislative measures geared to the revitalization of local representative institutions. The measures in question include mandatory elections at regular intervals, reservation of seats in village panchayats for women and members of scheduled castes or tribes, and some devolution of government responsibilities to local authorities. These legislative reforms certainly provide an *opportunity* for correcting the current failures of local governance in rural India. Nevertheless, it would be naive to expect too much from them unless the *other* causes of this problem are also addressed.

Recent experiences in different parts of India bring out these

[33] In this connection, it is worth noting that tribal societies in India, which tend to be relatively egalitarian, have a long tradition of participatory local democracy. In some states, notably Nagaland, this tradition has formed a good basis for participatory programmes of economic development and social change. The relatively cohesive nature of many tribal societies in India has also been conducive to diverse types of collective action, ranging from environmental protection to resistance against forced displacement. For some relevant studies, see K.S. Singh (1983, 1985), Deliège (1985), Hardiman (1987), Gokhale (1988), Elwin (1989), Swamy (1991), Baviskar (1992), Brass (1992), Maithani and Rizwana (1992), Drèze, Samson, and Singh (forthcoming), among others.

[34] For an example, see Drèze and Gazdar (1996). This phenomenon of landlord resistance to the spread of elementary education has also been noted elsewhere in north India; see e.g. Wadley and Derr (1989), p. 111, and Banerjee (1994).

opportunities and limitations related to legislative reform. On the positive side, the relatively successful experience of West Bengal discussed by Sengupta and Gazdar (1996) in the companion volume illustrates the scope for radical improvement in local democracy. The formation of all-women panchayats in parts of rural Maharashtra (Omvedt, 1990) is another interesting example of transformation of village politics based on a combination of legislative reform and political organization. On the other side, several empirical studies have underlined the limitations of decentralization in the context of continued inequalities of political power.[35]

The recent legislative reforms hold much promise, but their actual success depends a great deal on other types of public action. If these reforms are not supplemented with a more active programme of social change, they stand in some danger of leading to a proliferation of bureaucracy without any real improvement in local democracy. On the other side, if they go hand in hand with an expansion of public initiatives and social movements aimed at more widespread literacy, a stronger political organization of disadvantaged groups, and a more vigorous challenge to social inequalities, they would represent a real opportunity to transform village politics in rural India.

---

[35] Based on an in-depth study of Karnataka, for instance, Crook and Manor (1994) conclude that, despite many positive achievements, decentralization initiatives in that state have failed to enhance the effectiveness of redistributive poverty alleviation programmes, due to the absence of any commitment to these programmes on the part of the local elites. For a general discussion of the limitations of decentralization in the absence of social change, see Bardhan (1992).

6

BASIC EDUCATION
AS A POLITICAL ISSUE

6.1. *Education and Social Change*

The diverse personal and social roles of education were discussed in general terms in chapter 2 of this book. In connection with the issue of social inequality examined in the preceding chapter, the empowerment and redistributive role of education may be worth further exploration. Literacy is a basic tool of self-defence in a society where social interaction often involves the written media. An illiterate person is that much less equipped to defend herself in court, to obtain a bank loan, to enforce her inheritance rights, to take advantage of new technology, to compete for secure employment, to get on the right bus, to take part in political activity, in short, to participate successfully in the modern economy and society. Similar things can be said about numeracy and other skills acquired in the process of basic education.

Basic education is also a catalyst of social change. The contrasts between different states of India, on which we have already commented in chapter 3, provide ample illustration of this elementary fact. For instance, the historical analysis of Kerala's experience presented by V.K. Ramachandran (1996) in the companion volume powerfully brings out the dialectical relationship between educational progress and social change: the spread of education helps to overcome the traditional inequalities of caste, class, and gender, just as the removal of these inequalities contributes to the spread of education. Kerala made an early start down that road, in the nineteenth century, leading to wide-ranging social achievements later on. At the other extreme, the educationally backward states of north India (discussed by Drèze and Gazdar, 1996, in the same volume, with special reference to Uttar Pradesh) have made comparatively little progress in eradicating traditional inequalities, particularly those of caste and gender.

The value of basic education as a tool of social affirmation has not been lost on the Indian people. In fact, a common finding of village studies and household surveys is that education is widely perceived by members of socially or economically disadvantaged groups as the most promising chance of upward mobility for their children.[1] The relationship between education and social change was also well understood by many social leaders during the independence movement. Gokhale, for instance, was a strong advocate of the promotion of basic education, and, as soon as the Indian Councils Act of 1909 made it possible for Indians to propose legislative reforms, he formulated a pioneering Elementary Education Bill (later rejected by the British administration) which would have empowered local authorities to introduce compulsory education. Dr Ambedkar, whose own scholarship helped him to overcome the stigma of low caste (indeed 'untouchability'), saw education as a cornerstone of his strategy for the liberation of oppressed castes—a strategy which has been put to good effect in some parts of India. Education was also of paramount concern to Rammohan Roy, Maharshi Karve, Pandita Ramabai, Swami Vivekananda, Jotirao Phule, Rabindranath Tagore, Mahatma Gandhi, Abdul Ghaffar Khan, Jayaprakash Narayan, and numerous other social reformers and political figures of the pre-independence period.

The empowerment value of basic education is so obvious that there is something puzzling in the fact that the promotion of education has received so little attention from social and political leaders in the post-independence period. One aspect of this neglect is the flagrant inadequacy of government policy in the field of elementary education; we will return to that in section 6.3. But lack of attention to education has not been confined to government circles. It has also been a common attitude of political parties, trade unions, revolutionary organizations, and other social movements.[2]

---

[1] For some relevant empirical studies, see Vlassoff (1980, 1993), Nair et al. (1984), J.C. Caldwell et al. (1985), Bara et al. (1991), Chanana (1988b, 1993), Drèze and Saran (1995), among others. On the relationship between education and social change, see also Nair (1981), Aparna Basu (1988), Karlekar (1988), Nag (1989), Nautiyal (1989), Verma (1989), Raza (1990), Robin Jeffrey (1992), Sengupta (1992), Lieten (1993), Majumdar (1992), Ghosh et al. (1994), and the case studies presented in Drèze and Sen (1996).

[2] This feature of social movements in India stands in sharp contrast with the Latin

Several ideological convictions have contributed to this neglect, including: (1) the conservative upper-caste notion that knowledge is not important or appropriate for the lower castes;[3] (2) a distorted understanding of Gandhi's view that 'literacy in itself is no education';[4] and (3) the belief, held in some radical quarters, that the present educational system is a tool of subjugation of the lower classes or a vestige of the colonial period. It is hard to overstate the need for unequivocal rejection of these and other sceptical views of the value of education. A firm commitment to the widespread and equitable provision of basic education is the first requirement of rapid progress in eradicating educational deprivation in India.

6.2. The State of School Education

The limited reach of basic education in India has been mentioned on several occasions earlier in this book. Before examining some reasons for these low educational achievements, it may be helpful to recapitulate some essential features of the educational situation in India.

Table 6.1 presents a set of relevant indicators. Aside from reporting the figures for India as a whole, we have added the corresponding figures for Uttar Pradesh and Kerala. This is partly to give an idea of the extent of regional contrasts within India, and partly because the specific contrast between Uttar Pradesh and Kerala receives some attention in this book and the companion volume.[5] The figures

---

American experience, where basic education has often been a cornerstone of popular mobilization and a major focus of radical politics; see e.g. Archer and Costello (1990).

[3] The influence exercised by this traditional view over a long period is evident in a large number of historical documents, from the second-century *Manusmriti* (which forbids the reading of the Vedas to the lower castes) to the writings of the eleventh century Arab traveller Alberuni (who commented on 'those castes who are not allowed to occupy themselves with science'). There are similar traditional attitudes towards the education of women (see e.g. Chanana, 1988b), including 'the prevalent view [in the early nineteenth century] that widowhood would result if women were educated' (Karlekar, 1988, p. 136).

[4] Mahatma Gandhi, cited in Kurrien (1983), p. 45. Gandhi's main concern was that education should go *beyond* literacy, but his emphasis on productive handicraft as the foremost school activity, and the related insistence on the financial self-sufficiency of individual schools, have contributed to some confusion in educational policy in the post-independence period, as Kurrien aptly argues.

[5] See particularly section 3.6 of this book, and Drèze and Sen (1996).

TABLE 6.1. *Basic Education in India: Achievements and Diversities*

	India	Uttar Pradesh	Kerala
Literacy rates (age 7+) for selected groups, 1991			
Total population:			
Female	39	25	86
Male	64	56	94
Rural scheduled castes:			
Female	19	8	73
Male	46	39	85
Literacy rates among children aged 10–14, 1987–8			
Rural: Female	52	39	98
Male	73	68	98
Urban: Female	82	69	98
Male	88	76	97
Proportion of rural children attending school, 1987–8 (%)			
Age 5–9: Female	40	28	83
Male	52	45	87
Age 10–14: Female	42	31	91
Male	66	64	93
Percentage of never-enrolled children in the 12–14 age group, 1986–7			
Rural: Female	51	68	1.8
Male	26	27	0.4
Urban: Female	19	39	0.6
Male	11	19	0.0
Percentage of persons aged 15 and above who have completed primary education, 1981[a]			
Female	21	11	56
Male	44	37	68

Note. [a] The corresponding census figures for 1991 have not been released at the time of writing.

Sources. Calculated from census and National Sample Survey data presented in P. Visaria et al. (1993), pp. 31–3, 53, Sengupta (1991), pp. 15, 28, Nanda (1992), p. 57, Nanda (1993), pp. 22–31, and Census of India 1981, Series-C, Social and Cultural Tables, Table C-2. See also Statistical Appendix.

presented in Table 6.1 are based on two independent and reasonably reliable sources—the census and the National Sample Survey (NSS). We should mention that Table 6.1 makes no use of official data on 'school enrolment', and related statistics released by the Department of Education. Official school enrolment figures are known to be grossly inflated, partly due to the incentives that government employees at different levels have to report exaggerated figures.[6] According to these figures, for instance, the gross enrolment ratio for boys at the primary level (number of boys enrolled in a primary school as a proportion of the relevant age group) is *above 100 per cent* in all major states except Haryana and Kerala. Even for girls, the gross enrolment ratio is as high as 93 per cent.[7] These cheerful enrolment figures are impossible to reconcile with the survey-based evidence (see Table 6.1). In contrast, the broad consistency between NSS data and independent census data gives additional reason to accept these sources as more authoritative, and to reject the official enrolment figures.[8]

The highly misleading 'official' figures are often reported in international publications that depend on government sources, such as the *Human Development Reports* and *World Development Reports*. According to *Human Development Report .1994*, for instance, India had a gross enrolment ratio of 99 per cent in 1990.[9] Statistics of this kind can easily lead to over-optimistic assessments of India's record in the field of basic education. In their insightful and otherwise illuminating analysis of the Indian economy, for instance, Joshi and Little (1994) give India some credit for the fact that 'school enrolment has risen to 99 per cent' during the eighties (p.17). This statement

[6] For further discussion of this issue, see Sen (1970), Prasad (1987), and Drèze and Gazdar (1996).

[7] The figures are from Tyagi (1993), p. 102, and the reference year is 1992–3. It is possible, in principle, for the gross enrolment ratio to exceed 100 per cent, due to the enrolment in primary classes of girls or boys outside the standard age group. But this can hardly explain the enormous discrepancy between official enrolment figures and survey-based data on school enrolment and attendance. Nor can it explain other anomalies of the official enrolment figures, such as the fact that *Kerala* (which has the highest school enrolment rates in the country according to survey data) is one of the only two states with a gross enrolment ratio of boys below 100 per cent.

[8] On the consistency between census and NSS data relating to education, see Sengupta (1991) and P. Visaria et al. (1993).

[9] *Human Development Report 1994*, Table 14, p. 157; *World Development Report 1994* gives a figure of 98 per cent for 1991 (Table 28, p. 216).

corresponds only to the official figures, which do not tally with census and National Sample Survey data.

Coming back to Table 6.1, important features of educational achievements in India include the following. First, average literacy rates are low—64 per cent for males and 39 per cent for females in India as a whole.[10] We have already commented on this on several occasions. We have noted, for instance, how literacy rates in India are much lower than in China (chapter 4), lower than literacy rates in many east and south-east Asian countries 30 years ago (section 3.3), lower than the average literacy rates for 'low-income countries' other than China and India (section 1.1), and also no higher than estimated literacy rates in sub-Saharan Africa (section 3.1).

Second, the problem of low average literacy rates is exacerbated by enormous *inequalities* in educational achievements. One aspect of these inequalities, already mentioned in chapter 3, concerns the existence of large disparities in educational achievements between different states. The female literacy rate, for instance, varies from 20 per cent in Rajasthan and 25 per cent in Uttar Pradesh to 86 per cent in Kerala. This reflects the fact that efforts to expand basic education in different states have enormously varied in strength and effectiveness. As discussed earlier (see particularly chapter 3), there is much to learn from these regional contrasts about the causes of success and failure in the promotion of basic education.

Third, there are also large inequalities in educational achievements between males and females, between urban and rural areas, and between different social groups. These diverse inequalities, combined with low average literacy rates, are responsible for the persistence of extremely low levels of education for disadvantaged sections of the population. To illustrate, the rural female literacy rate is only 19 per cent among scheduled castes (which represent 16 per cent of the Indian population); 16 per cent among scheduled tribes (representing 8 per cent of the population); and below 10 per cent, for *all* females aged 7 and above, in many educationally backward districts of Bihar, Madhya Pradesh, Orissa, Rajasthan, and Uttar Pradesh. When different sources of disadvantage are combined (e.g. the handicap of being female is added to that of belonging to a

---

[10] Unless stated otherwise, all the literacy rates mentioned in this section refer to the age group of 7 years and above, and are based on 1991 census data presented in Tyagi (1993), pp. 24–40. For further information on literacy rates and related indicators of educational achievements, see also the Statistical Appendix of this book.

scheduled caste and living in a backward region), the literacy rates for the most disadvantaged groups come down to minuscule figures. For instance, in 1981 the crude literacy rate among rural scheduled-caste women was below 2.5 per cent in a majority of districts of Uttar Pradesh and Rajasthan (and even below 1 per cent in many districts of those states).[11]

Fourth, illiteracy is widespread not only in the older age groups (as would apply even in, say, China), but also among young boys and girls, particularly in rural areas. For instance, half of all rural females in the 10–14 age group in India (almost two-thirds in Uttar Pradesh) are illiterate. The persistence of endemic illiteracy in the younger age groups is the most distressing aspect of the educational situation in contemporary India.

Fifth, that failure can also be identified using survey-based school enrolment and attendance data. The proportion of rural females aged 12–14 who have never been enrolled in any school is above one-half in India as a whole, above two–thirds in Uttar Pradesh, Madhya Pradesh, and Bihar, and as high as 82 per cent in Rajasthan.[12] Similarly, only 42 per cent of rural females in the 10–14 age group (and 40 per cent in the 5–9 age group) are reported to be attending school. It might be added that these school attendance figures refer to the 'usual' status of a boy or girl at the time of the survey.[13] School attendance figures based on a 'time-rate' notion of school attendance (e.g. the proportion of rural children attending school on an average *day*) would be much lower, given that even children who are reported as usually attending school spend a large proportion of days out of school.[14]

Sixth, an important reason for these low school-attendance figures is a very high drop-out rate. Available information suggests that only half of all children enrolled in Class 1 are still at school four

[11] For the last set of figures, we have taken 1981 as the reference year because the corresponding figures for 1991 are still to be published. The figures are from Nuna (1990), pp. 113–14, and based on the 1981 census.

[12] See Statistical Appendix, Table A.3. These four states account for about 40 per cent of the total population of India.

[13] The 1981 census, for instance, has only *one* question on school attendance, which asks whether the person is attending school or not. There is no scope for the investigator to record, say, the number of days of actual attendance during the month or week preceding the survey.

[14] See e.g. Prasad (1987), and Drèze and Gazdar (1996) in the companion volume.

years later.[15] Low levels of basic education in India reflect *both* (1) the low duration of schooling for children who are enrolled at some stage, and (2) the fact that a large proportion of children are *never* enrolled at all.

Seventh, the low enrolment and retention rates imply that the proportion of persons who complete the primary cycle of five classes is extremely low.[16] In 1981, for instance, the proportion of Indian adults who had completed primary education was below one-third (the corresponding figures from the 1991 census are still to be released). In the same year, only one out of nine adult women in Uttar Pradesh had completed the primary cycle.

International comparisons corroborate the diagnosis of low schooling levels in India. We have already discussed this in the context of literacy rates. Further evidence comes from international data on other indicators of educational achievements, such as 'mean years of schooling'. The average number of years of schooling for persons aged 25 and above is only 2.4 in India (1.2 for females and 3.5 for males), compared with 5.0 in China, 7.2 in Sri Lanka, and 9.3 in South Korea.[17] The state of school education in India is indeed dismal.

6.3. Biases and Confounded Strategies

Education policy in India since independence has suffered from a good deal of inconsistency and confusion.[18] One of the directive

[15] Tyagi (1993), p. 100. It should be said that these estimates are based on official enrolment figures (the 'retention rate' is calculated as the ratio of Class-5 enrolment to Class-1 enrolment four years earlier), and it is not clear how the reporting biases mentioned earlier affect these estimates. Interestingly, the available estimates suggest very little difference in retention rates between males and females at the primary level (at higher levels, retention rates are much lower for girls than for boys).

[16] Literacy alone is not, of course, the only educational achievement of importance (even though it has great personal and social significance). With competent teaching, a child can learn to read and write in a few weeks, in most Indian languages. The five years of schooling involved in the full primary cycle provide opportunities for learning many other useful skills.

[17] *Human Development Report 1994*, Table 5, pp. 138–9.

[18] This major problem has been noted in a number of distinguished analyses of educational policy in India, including Naik (1975a, 1975b, 1975c, 1982), Kurrien (1983), K. Kumar (1991), Weiner (1991, 1994), Tilak (1993). On the evolution of educational policy in India, see also Biswas and Agrawal (1986), Agrawal and Aggarwal (1992), Singha (1992), among others.

principles of the Constitution (Article 45) urges the state to provide free and compulsory education up to the age of 14 by 1960. This was an ambitious goal, and the practical measures that were taken to implement it have fallen far short of what was required. To this day, compulsory education has not been actually implemented anywhere in India, even though state governments and even local authorities are empowered to make primary education compulsory. And the provision of educational facilities remains completely out of line with the stated goal of universal school education until the age of 14. There are, for instance, as many as 58 children in the 6–10 age group for each teacher at the primary level (Table 6.2).[19] Even under the unrealistic assumption that teachers are evenly distributed all over the country, in proportion to the number of children in that age group, this overall child–teacher ratio is clearly in conflict with the requirements of universal education in classes of reasonable size up to the age of 10—let alone 14.

Similar inconsistencies of ends and means can be found in a series of commission reports and policy statements that have appeared since 1947. The elusive goal of providing free and compulsory education until the age of 14 within a few years has been regularly reiterated, without any effective steps being taken to reach it. As recently as 1986–7, less than half of all enrolled children managed to complete the initial cycle of 5 years of primary education; barely one-third completed the 8 years corresponding to the stated goal of compulsory and free education; and nearly half of all rural children in the 6–11 age group had never been enrolled in any school.[20] This did not prevent the National Policy on Education of 1986 from declaring with blind optimism that 'by 1995 all children will be provided free and compulsory education up to 14 years of age' (Singha, 1992, p. 12), without giving any sense of the revolutionary policy changes that would be needed to achieve this goal. Not surprisingly, the cheerful expectations of instant success did not materialize. In fact, official figures on retention rates show no improvement after 1986 (see Tyagi, 1993, p. 100).

The revised National Policy on Education, 1992, is in line with

---

[19] The calculations in Table 6.2 *underestimate* the effective child–teacher ratio, since they ignore the fact that some children have to repeat one or more classes.

[20] Tyagi (1993), p. 100, and P. Visaria et al. (1993), p. 53.

TABLE 6.2. *The Child–Teacher Ratio in India, 1991*

Number of children		
Total population, 1991 (thousands)	846,303	(A)
Proportion of population in 6–10 age group, 1981 (%)	14.6	
Estimated proportion of population in 6–10 age group, 1991[a] (%)	13.3	(B)
Estimated number of children in 6–10 age group, 1991 (A x B) (thousands)	112,558	(C)
Number of teachers		
Number of primary-school teachers, 1991 (thousands)	1,637	(D)
Estimated number of teachers in upper-primary and secondary schools who teach primary classes, 1991[b] (thousands)	312	(E)
Estimated total number of teachers in primary sections, 1991 (D+E)	1,949	(F)
Number of children in 6–10 age group per primary-section teacher, 1991 (C/F)	58	

Notes. [a] Based on assuming that the rate of decline of the proportion of the population in the 6–10 age group between 1981 and 1991 is the same as the rate of decline of the proportion of the population in the 5–9 age group (for the latter group, year-wise estimates are available from *Sample Registration System*).

[b] Based on the assumption that the proportion of primary-section teachers to primary sections in these schools is the same as in primary schools. The precise assumption used here does not make much difference, since the proportion of primary sections located in upper-primary and secondary schools is small (16 per cent in 1986).

Sources. Calculated from Nanda (1992), p. 86; Tyagi (1993), p. 82; National Council of Educational Research and Training (1992), p. 34; Census of India 1981, Series 1 (India), Part IV-A, Social and Cultural Tables, Tables C-4 and C-5; *Sample Registration System 1982*, p. 61; *Sample Registration System 1991*, p. 59.

the earlier tradition.[21] Despite stressing that it was 'imperative for the Government to formulate and implement a new Education Policy for the country' (p. 4), the Policy did little more than to repeat the old credo with a different time frame: 'it shall be ensured that free and compulsory education of satisfactory quality is provided to all children up to 14 years of age before we enter the twenty-first century' (p. 20). Once again, the Policy gave no hint of the practical steps that would make this so-called 'resolve' a reality, and did not go much beyond a remarkable collection of platitudes such as 'all

---

[21] All the quotes in this paragraph are from Government of India (1992c). This document spells out the policy of the central government, and leaves room for wide differences in state-level policies, which have indeed varied a great deal in content and effectiveness.

teachers should teach and all students should study' (p. 34), 'the New Education Policy... will adopt an array of meticulously formulated strategies based on micro-planning to ensure children's retention at school' (p. 20), and 'a warm, welcoming and encouraging approach, in which all concerned share a solicitude for the needs of the child, is the best motivation for the child to attend school and learn' (p. 18).[22] Nevertheless, the authors felt able to conclude on an upbeat note:

The future shape of education in India is too complex to envision with precision. Yet, given our tradition which has almost always put high premium on intellectual and spiritual attainment, we are bound to succeed in achieving our objectives.

The main task is to strengthen the base of the pyramid, which might come close to a billion people at the turn of the century. Equally, it is important to ensure that those at the top of the pyramid are among the best in the world. Our cultural well springs had taken good care of both ends in the past; the skew set in with foreign domination and influence. It should now be possible to further intensify the nation-wide effort in Human Resource Development, with Education playing its multifaceted role.[23]

One implication of these vague pieties is that they have opened the door to further inconsistencies between stated goals and actual policy. Since everyone knows that free and compulsory education up to the age of 14 is not going to be achieved by the end of this century (and possibly for long after that), this stated goal provides no concrete guidance. This has made it possible, in particular, to combine the highly egalitarian slogan of free and universal education with extreme inequality in practice. One symptom of this elitism, already noted in the preceding chapter, is the bias against elementary schooling within the educational system. Child labour is considered perfectly acceptable for the boys and girls of poor families, while

---

[22] In a companion document (Government of India, 1992d), an eminent group of educationists and other experts have made a valuable attempt to translate the feeble exhortations of the National Policy on Education into concrete policy guidelines. This 'programme of action', however, only has the status of a set of expert recommendations, and these have, so far, made rather little impact on actual policies at the state level, especially in the educationally backward states. For instance, so far the only states that have implemented the recommendation of framing their own, state-level programme of action are Kerala, Maharashtra, and Tamil Nadu—three of the most advanced states as far as basic education is concerned. (We are grateful to Dr Vaidyanatha Ayyar, Joint Secretary, Department of Education, for a helpful discussion on this.)

[23] Government of India (1992c), p. 50.

the privileged classes enjoy a massively subsidized system of higher education.[24]

In short, the lamentable history of post-independence education policy has suffered from diverse kinds of inconsistencies and con-tradictions, including (1) a confusion of objectives, (2) inconsistencies between stated goals and actual policy, and (3) a specific contradiction between stated goals and resource allocation. The formulation of a more effective policy must begin with the elementary tasks of setting clear goals that are adequately ambitious yet realizable, devising practical measures to meet them, and providing the resources required to implement these measures. This should really go without saying, but, given the failures of earlier policies, there is a case for saying it nevertheless.

6.4. *The Role of Expenditure*

The last ten years have seen a growing awareness of India's failures in the field of basic education, and of the inadequacy of existing provisions. The response, as far as the central government is concerned, has mainly taken the form of increasing expenditure on education without really introducing major policy changes.[25]

The expansion of government expenditure on education is certainly a welcome development. Indeed, inadequate public expenditure is one important reason for India's poor educational achievements. Among one hundred and sixteen countries for which the relevant data are available, India ranks as low as eighty-second in terms of

[24] Even *within* the field of elementary education, there is a good deal of elitism in educational policy. In particular, the current thrust of official policy for dealing with the non-participation of disadvantaged groups in the elementary education system is mainly to encourage the creation of second-track 'non-formal education' facilities, rather than to affirm an uncompromising commitment to their inclusion in the formal schooling system (see e.g. Government of India, 1992d, chapter 7). Some of these alternative channels of schooling are certainly useful in the short term, but a complacent reliance on this two-track formula as a basis for universalizing elementary education carries the real danger of institutionalizing rather than eliminating the elitist features of Indian education.

[25] There has been a diversity of responses at the level of state governments (which have the primary responsibility for providing education), ranging from bold initiatives in states such as Kerala, Tamil Nadu, and Himachal Pradesh to continued apathy in states such as Uttar Pradesh. Some state-level responses are discussed in the companion volume (Drèze and Sen, 1996).

the proportion of public expenditure on education to GNP.[26] From 1968 onwards, successive versions of the National Policy on Education have 'resolved' to raise this proportion to 6 per cent, but this target has not been approached to this day.[27]

The problem of inadequate aggregate resources is compounded by severe imbalances in allocation. Because education expenditure is borne primarily by individual states, rather than by the central government, there are large inter-state variations in per-capita expenditure on education; and states with lower educational achievements, where the need for public investment is most acute, tend to be those where financial resources are particularly scarce.[28] Another form of imbalance, mentioned earlier, is the relatively low share of elementary education in total education expenditure. This share is not only low (currently less than 50 per cent) in terms of the stated objective of universalizing elementary education, it has also declined significantly from the first Five-Year Plan until the mid-eighties, and, despite some improvement during the last ten years, it remains lower now than in the fifties (Tilak, 1993, pp. 51–9).

If public expenditure on education in India remains low by international standards, recent trends have at least been in the right direction. After stagnating for 25 years, the proportion of public expenditure on education to GNP started increasing noticeably around the mid-eighties, and there has also been some improvement in

[26] *Human Development Report 1994*, Tables 15, 36, and 49 (the reference year is 1990). India's position is even lower (68th from the top among 89 countries for which data are given) in terms of the proportion of education expenditure in total public spending. The expenditure figures used here include outlays of the state governments as well as those of the central government. For a comprehensive analysis of education expenditure in India, see Tilak (1989, 1990, 1993, 1994a, 1994b); also Ghosh (1992).

[27] This does not prevent Government of India (1994a) from making the apparently triumphant statement that public expenditure on education as a proportion of GNP is 'well over 3 per cent now', just after noting that the 6 per cent target has been 'reiterated time and again by committees and experts and also by the Prime Minister' (p. 152). This is another example of the inconsistencies discussed earlier.

[28] Per-capita public expenditure on education in a particular state can be seen as the product of (1) per-capita income in that state, (2) the ratio of government expenditure to state income, and (3) the proportion of state government expenditure allocated to education. By and large, each of these parameters tends to be low in states with high levels of illiteracy. The third one reflects the priority attached by the relevant state government to education (e.g. it is about twice as large in Kerala as in Haryana), but the other two are important constraints on education expenditure in the disadvantaged states.

TABLE 6.3. *Aspects of Government Expenditure on Elementary Education*

Period	Growth rates of selected variables relating to elementary schools (% per year)			
	Recurring expenditure, at 1970–1 prices [a]	Number of teachers	Recurring expenditure per teacher [b]	Teacher–population ratio
1950–1 to 1960–1	8.5	5.6	3.0	3.6
1960–1 to 1970–1	5.8	4.5	1.3	2.3
1970–1 to 1980–1	2.8	2.7	0.2	0.5
1980–1 to 1984–5	11.1	2.1	9.0	0.0
1984–5 to 1989–90	10.8	1.6	9.2	–0.5

Notes. [a] Recurring expenditure on elementary education accounts for 98 per cent of total government expenditure on elementary education; salaries account for 96 per cent of recurring expenditure; teachers' salaries account for 97 per cent of all salaries (1983–4 figures from Tilak, 1993, p. 60).
[b] This can be taken as a rough index of teachers' real salaries, given that these salaries account for 93 per cent of recurring expenditure.
Sources. Calculated from Tilak (1993), p. 57, Tyagi (1993), p. 82, Agrawal et al. (1992), p. 234, and Bose (1991a), p. 48. The wholesale price index (all commodities) has been used to deflate nominal expenditure figures. Elementary schools refer to primary and 'upper primary' schools (classes 1 to 8 in most states).

the share of elementary education (Tilak, 1993), together with some reduction of inter-state disparities (Tyagi, 1993, p. 122).

But where is this extra money going? Table 6.3 provides a clue on this, for elementary education.[29] The table presents figures on the growth rates of government expenditure at 1970–1 prices, of the number of teachers, and of government expenditure per teacher; the latter can be taken as a rough index of teachers' real salaries, given that these salaries absorb well over 90 per cent of recurring expenditure. It can be seen that while the growth rate of expenditure in the eighties has been higher than at any other time since independence (above 10 per cent per year), the increase of expenditure over that period is almost entirely accounted for by sharp increases

---

[29] The term 'elementary education' officially covers both primary schools (classes 1–5 in most states) and upper primary or 'middle' schools (classes 6–8 in a majority of states).

in teachers' emoluments; these have grown at an extraordinary rate of 9 per cent per year in real terms. The number of teachers, on the other hand, has never grown more slowly. In fact, for the first time, the number of teachers has grown less fast than the population, and much more slowly than the number of children attending primary and upper-primary schools. As a result, there has been a sharp increase in the pupil–teacher ratio during the eighties.[30]

The available evidence indicates no substantial improvement in patterns of education expenditure in the nineties. On the contrary, the growth of education expenditure has slowed down after structural adjustment measures were introduced in 1991, and education expenditure has even declined in real terms in many states (see Gupta and Sarkar, 1994, Jalan and Subbarao, 1995, and table A.4 in the Statistical Appendix of this book). One symptom of these adverse developments is a *decline* in the *absolute number* of teachers in primary and upper-primary schools between 1991–2 and 1992–3 (the latest year for which the relevant data are available).[31] There could hardly be a more inappropriate response to the current failures of basic education in India.

Education expenditure in India needs to be increased, especially at the primary level and in the educationally backward states. At the same time, it would be naive to think that India's educational achievements can be transformed simply by spending more, and especially by spending more on the same—or a smaller number of—teachers. Achieving a real change in the situation of primary education in India is a much more demanding task.

6.5. *Priorities and Challenges*

Recent innovations of the central government in the field of education policy have largely consisted of introducing ad hoc 'schemes' to

---

[30] Pupil–teacher ratios have risen in most states over this period (Tyagi, 1993, p. 84), but the increase seems to have been particularly sharp in the educationally backward states. While Kerala has succeeded in preventing any increase in the pupil–teacher ratio during the eighties, Uttar Pradesh has allowed it to increase by *fifty per cent* between 1981–2 and 1992–3.

[31] Tyagi (1993), p. 82. Interestingly, the decline has not been impartial between male and female teachers. In fact, the number of male teachers in primary and upper-primary schools remained virtually unchanged between these two years, while nearly 14,000 female teaching jobs were lost.

address specific problems that happen to come to the attention of policy-makers. In its 350-page annual report for 1993–4 (Government of India, 1994f), the Department of Education provides details of dozens of such schemes, from the sinking 'Operation Blackboard' to the new 'District Primary Education Programme'. By contrast, the same report devotes only one or two pages each to 'universalization of elementary education', 'education of scheduled castes and scheduled tribes' and 'female education'.

Many of the schemes in question are aimed at creating second-track educational facilities such as *shramik vidyapeeths, mahila shikshan kendras, jan shiksha kendras, mahila samakhya, shiksha karmis,* and numerous types of 'non-formal education' centres. Some of these initiatives are undoubtedly useful. Impressive achievements, for instance, have been reported for the recently-launched Total Literacy Campaign, in districts where the local administration and popular organizations have actively seized this opportunity for mass mobilization on the issue of literacy.[32] But as useful as these programmes might be in localized contexts, the basic problem of endemic illiteracy in the younger age groups cannot be solved through such ad hoc schemes and campaigns, many of which represent an over-simple response to a particular—often rather narrow—aspect of the problem of educational backwardness. The priority should be to ensure that every village in the country has a free, functioning, well-staffed, and well-attended regular primary school.

One requirement of this basic objective is the provision of adequate educational facilities within the basic framework of village schools (the issue of child attendance will be taken up further on in this chapter). In this respect, there are no signs of rapid improvement or bold initiatives. In fact, as was discussed earlier, the number of teachers at the elementary level is now growing more slowly than the population, and considerably more slowly than the school-going population at that level. Nor is there much evidence of a sustained improvement in the performance of school teachers. In fact, the problem of teacher absenteeism and shirking seems to be growing rather than declining in some states.

---

[32] On this, see particularly the recent evaluation by Arun Ghosh et al. (1994), who argue that 'for all its deficiencies... [the Total Literacy Campaign] has been among the best things promoted by the government since independence' (p. 37). On the Total Literacy Campaign, see also Ghosh (1991), S. Banerjee (1992), Sengupta (1992), Rao (1993), Rokadiya et al. (1993), Government of India (1994b), Saldanha (1994), among others.

In connection with the last point, some telling findings emerge from a recent field investigation in rural Uttar Pradesh, which covered 15 village schools in four different districts.[33] As a matter of fact, very little teaching activity was observed in the sample schools. Teacher absenteeism was endemic (*two-thirds* of the teachers employed in the sample schools were absent at the time of the investigators' unannounced visits), and the acting teachers did little more than keep a semblance of order among the pupils. In effect, the schools visited were little more than child-minding centres, when they were open at all. Further, it was a virtually unanimous view among residents of the sample villages that the problems of teacher absenteeism and shirking had consistently increased over time.

These field observations are not exceptional. For instance, the main findings of Prasad's (1987) investigation of the functioning of village schools in backward areas of Andhra Pradesh bear striking resemblance with those reported for Uttar Pradesh by Drèze and Gazdar (1996) in the companion volume.[34] Other studies and first-hand reports have also highlighted the pervasive problem of non-functioning or poor functioning of village schools in many parts of the country, especially the large north Indian states.[35] The record of the schooling system is not uniformly poor (some states have done much better than others in this respect), but the deplorable quality of schooling facilities in large parts of rural India is certainly a major issue.

It is tempting to look for increased reliance on private schools as an easy remedy for the inadequacies of the public sector. There is certainly no reason to decry the expansion of private schooling,

[33] See the case study of Uttar Pradesh by Drèze and Gazdar (1996) in the companion volume. The districts included in this field investigation are Moradabad (western UP), Rae Bareli (central UP), Pratapgarh (eastern UP), and Banda (southern UP).

[34] Among the similarities of interest is the widespread prevalence, in both Andhra Pradesh and Uttar Pradesh, of a system of implicit sub-contracting of teaching duties by government teachers to private teachers. See Drèze and Gazdar (1996) for further discussion.

[35] See e.g. Narain (1972) and Ghose (1993) on Rajasthan, Shankari (1993) on Andhra Pradesh, Middleton et al. (1993) on Uttar Pradesh, and Sainath (1993) on Bihar. Anil Bordia, former Education Secretary, takes the view that 'a large proportion of schools do not function in most parts of the country' (Bordia, 1993, p. 8). Even the Government of India (1993d) acknowledges 'the chronic problem of teacher absenteeism' (p. 31) in states such as Rajasthan. See Weiner (1991), chapter 4 for some further testimonies, including that of a senior Education Department official who candidly stated: 'The teachers aren't any good. Often they don't even appear at the school... our schools are trash!'

where such an expansion takes place. Indeed, private schools already make a significant contribution to the availability of schooling facilities in India, even in rural areas. But the private sector has already shown its limitations, as far as basic education in rural areas is concerned, and the reasons are not hard to follow, given the poverty of the potential students. In fact, private schooling facilities are overwhelmingly biased in favour of secondary or tertiary education, urban areas, and male children.[36]

There is, in short, no escape from the need for a major improvement of public schooling facilities in rural India. Two essential steps in that direction are to increase the number of teachers, and to ensure that they teach. While the first step is primarily a matter of financial commitment, the second one raises more difficult organizational issues. Given that school teachers have permanent posts, and a good deal of bureaucratic protection, the basic incentive structure is very weak.

A substantial increase in the number of teachers, by itself, could be expected to lead to better teaching performance of individual teachers. Indeed, field studies suggest that teaching standards tend to be higher in schools with more teachers.[37] As many observers have noted, teaching standards are particularly low in single-teacher schools, which accounted for almost *one-third* of all primary schools in 1986.[38] Work motivation cannot be expected to be very high for a single teacher who acts as his or her own supervisor, and has a guaranteed job irrespective—in practice—of performance. Also, motivation would

[36] For further discussion of these issues, see Drèze and Gazdar (1996); also Tilak (1993, 1994a). On the bias of private schooling facilities in favour of higher education levels and urban areas, see the Fifth All-India Education Survey (National Council of Educational Research and Training, 1992), pp. 384–5. According to this survey, the private sector ('aided' and 'unaided' combined) accounted for 54 per cent of all secondary schools in 1986, but only 7 per cent of all primary schools, and barely 3 per cent of primary schools in rural areas. Even after allowing for some underestimation of the number of primary schools in the private sector (given the difficulty of identifying small informal schools in rural areas), the contribution of the private sector to primary schooling appears to be very limited, especially in comparison with its contribution to secondary schooling.

[37] See Drèze and Gazdar (1996). Possible reasons for the positive relationship between teaching standards and the number of teachers include peer monitoring effects, competition between teachers, and greater scope for supervision. Larger schools also tend to be more visible, making it harder to shelter them from public scrutiny.

[38] National Council of Educational Research and Training (1992), p. 895. Here again, there are striking regional variations, with the proportion of single-teacher schools being below 1 per cent in Kerala but well above 50 per cent in Rajasthan.

not be enough: teaching five different grades simultaneously also demands extraordinary skill. Even in two-teacher schools, teaching practices are likely to be poor, if only because frequent absenteeism transforms these schools into single-teacher schools for a large part of the year.[39] In 1986, the proportion of primary schools with only one or two teachers was above 60 per cent in India as a whole.[40] Better staffing of schools is one important means of improving teaching standards.

Other means of improving work incentives and teaching performance require discriminating assessment. The best hope may well be the vigilance of parents. Unlike government inspectors, who seem to prosper by extorting bribes from shirking teachers, parents have a strong personal interest in an improved performance of school teachers.[41] The problem is that, as things stand, they have no easy means of taking action. In most states, teachers are accountable to the Education Department, not to the village community. Official complaints have to go through complicated bureaucratic channels, and are particularly difficult to make for parents who are themselves illiterate. Reforming the chain of accountability, and bringing the levers of control closer to the village community, are important means of improving teaching standards. In fact, this route has already been used with good effect in some parts of the country. In Karnataka, for instance, it is reported that 'after the panchayati raj system was implemented... attendance of primary school teachers and health workers went up by 91 per cent'.[42] In Tamil Nadu, too, it has

[39] According to Middleton et al. (1993), school teachers in Uttar Pradesh 'frequently take turns in attending' (p. 11). The same observation is made in the survey of village schools in Uttar Pradesh by Drèze and Gazdar (1996), mentioned earlier.

[40] Tyagi (1993), p. 88. The corresponding figure for Kerala is 1 per cent. In fact, in Kerala, 94 per cent of primary schools have four teachers or more. The figures cited in this paragraph relate to 1986 because more recent figures are not available. Given the slow rate of growth of the number of primary-school teachers in recent years (see section 6.4), it is unlikely that a major improvement in teacher–school ratios has taken place since then.

[41] For a good case study of the ineffectiveness of official school inspection procedures, see Prasad (1987), pp. 75–81.

[42] L.C. Jain, cited in Ford Foundation (1992), and based on the recent Krishnaswamy Report. A more recent study (Crook and Manor, 1994) also finds that the recent decentralization experiment in Karnataka has considerably reduced absenteeism and shirking among teachers, health workers, and other government employees in rural areas. As the authors put it, 'all manner of government employees were now made to work because they were for the first time under the supervision of the questioning public mind' (Crook and Manor, 1994, p. 37). For similar observations, see also Gadgil and

been observed that 'close monitoring by a politically conscious parent community' has been an essential factor in the success of pre-school education and school meal programmes (Swaminathan, 1991, p. 2989). Community institutions and the building up of public accountability have also played a crucial role in the history of Kerala's educational expansion (Krishnan, 1994, Santha, 1994, Ramachandran, 1996).

The recent Panchayati Raj legislation offers new opportunities for extending these experiments elsewhere in India. Given the highly unequal character of the rural society, and the frequent connections between government teachers and local leaders, it would be unwise to expect an automatic transformation of the quality of schooling facilities as a result of the decentralization measures involved in this legislation.[43] But the initiatives that will be taken by different state governments within that framework are worth careful monitoring and evaluation. There may also be much to learn from the experiences of states that have already been relatively successful in improving the performance of village teachers. The first step is to recognize that the poor quality of schooling facilities in rural India is a major social issue, which calls for urgent investigation and action.

6.6. *Provision, Utilization and Compulsion*

An expansion of the quantity and quality of schooling facilities in India can be expected to lead, on its own, to a large increase in school attendance and educational achievements. Indeed, empirical studies suggest that popular demand for basic education in India is strong—at least strong enough to induce most parents to send their young children to school in situations where a free and well-functioning school is available close to their homes.[44] One symptom

---

Guha (1993), p. 79, Vyasulu (1993), Aziz (1994), p. 26, Seetharamu (1994), p. 45.

[43] In fact, the results so far have been rather disappointing in most states (this is one of the major conclusions of a recent Seminar on Management of Education under Panchayati Raj held at the National Institute of Educational Planning and Administration; see also NIEPA, 1994). This outcome partly reflects the fact that there has been far more promise than action, as far as decentralization is concerned. It also relates to the point, discussed in section 5.5, that legislative reform alone is not an adequate basis for the promotion of local democracy.

[44] For some empirical studies pointing in this direction, see J.C. Caldwell et al. (1985), Prasad (1987), Nautiyal (1989), Alderman et al. (1993), Drèze and Saran (1995), and the case study of Uttar Pradesh by Drèze and Gazdar (1996) in the companion volume. The specific problem of low parental motivation for female education will be discussed in

of this strong demand for basic education is the fact that, when the local school functions poorly, parents often send their children (especially boys) to study in other villages with better schools, or in private schools where fees have to be paid. While the blame for low attendance levels is often put on reluctant parents, the inadequacy of the schooling establishment may well be the more basic failure.

A good example of what can be achieved on the basis of a sustained expansion of the quantity and quality of schooling facilities is provided by Himachal Pradesh. As recently as 1961, crude literacy rates in Himachal Pradesh (21 per cent for males and 9 per cent for females) were below the corresponding all-India averages.[45] By 1987–8, literacy rates in the 10–14 age group in Himachal Pradesh were as high as 95 per cent for males and 81 per cent for females in rural areas, and even higher in urban areas (96 per cent for males and 97 per cent for females); in that respect, Himachal Pradesh was second to Kerala among the major states.[46] In the same year, 93 per cent of boys aged 10–14 in Himachal Pradesh were attending school—the same figure as in Kerala. For girls in the same age group, Himachal Pradesh did a little better than Kerala in urban areas (95 per cent attendance, compared with 94 per cent in Kerala), but not so in rural areas (91 per cent attendance in Kerala but only 73 per cent in Himachal Pradesh). Even for female attendance in rural areas, Himachal Pradesh was well ahead of all states other than Kerala.[47] The strong commitment of the state government and community institutions to a rapid expansion and improvement of schooling facilities has played a major part in this success.[48]

Aside from this scope for expanding educational achievements by improving the availability and quality of schooling facilities, public

section 6.7.

[45] Karkal (1991), Table 5, based on census data.

[46] Sengupta (1991); see also Statistical Appendix.

[47] The school attendance figures are from P. Visaria et al. (1993), based on NSS data; see Statistical Appendix for further details.

[48] On this, see e.g. Goyal and Mehrotra (1995). One symptom of this commitment is a high level of public expenditure on education. Per-capita government expenditure on education in Himachal Pradesh is about twice as high as the all-India average (Tyagi, 1993, p. 122). The teacher–population ratio is also twice as high as the national average, and a good deal higher than in any of the other major states (calculated from Government of India, 1994f, p. 289).

policy must also seek to promote the *utilization* of existing facilities. The most common reasons for non-attendance or non-enrolment reported in household surveys are, in order of frequency, (1) the high opportunity cost of children's time (in terms of forgone earnings in wage labour, forgone production in household activities, forgone help with minding younger children, etc.), and (2) 'lack of interest in education'.[49] These answers, of course, have to be interpreted in the light of the current functioning of the schooling system in different regions of the country. 'Interest in education', for instance, is likely to be a function of the quality of teaching. Bearing in mind the low standards of teaching in large parts of the country, it is no surprise that many children quickly lose interest in going to school.[50] But these responses also tell us that insufficient valuation of education (relative to child labour, leisure, or other activities) on the part of young children or—more plausibly—their parents may contribute to low attendance levels.

That issue may be particularly relevant in the case of social groups for whom education has traditionally been considered unimportant. We have referred earlier, for instance, to the old notion that education is not important for members of the 'lower' castes. Whatever survives of this notion cannot but affect (1) the educational aspirations of children from these castes, (2) the parental and social support which they receive in pursuit of these aspirations, and (3) the strength of public commitment to the promotion of education among these disadvantaged groups. There is, indeed, some evidence that school attendance levels are particularly low among disadvantaged castes even after controlling for other relevant variables such as household income and educational facilities.[51]

As far as public policy is concerned, there are several ways of addressing the possible problem of inadequate parental motivation and high opportunity cost of schooling. In some parts of India,

---

[49] See e.g. J.C. Caldwell et al. (1985), Prasad (1987), Minhas (1992), P. Visaria et al. (1993), and *Sarvekshana*, January–March 1991; also the earlier literature cited in Patil (1984).

[50] The surveys mentioned here (in particular, the National Sample Survey) make no room for responses such as 'teacher absenteeism', 'lack of learning activities in the school', etc., as possible reasons for non-enrolment.

[51] See the case studies by Drèze and Gazdar (1996) and Sengupta and Gazdar (1996) in the companion volume. Similar considerations apply to female education (on which more in the next section).

notably Tamil Nadu and Kerala, school meals and related incentives have been used with good effect to boost school attendance rates.[52] Popular attitudes to education can also be decisively influenced by active public campaigns; that, indeed, is one of the chief lessons of the recent Total Literacy Campaign.[53] More extensive use can be made of these and other means of promoting school attendance.[54]

Compulsory education is another frequently-advocated means of intervention. On this issue, the inconsistencies of official policy have been particularly flagrant. As was mentioned earlier, official pronouncements urging a rapid introduction of compulsory education until the age of 14 have been made at regular intervals. In contrast to this appearance of official commitment to compulsory education, most policy-makers are of the view that compulsory education is a bad idea, or that it will take many years before compulsory education is feasible or desirable.[55]

It is time to address these inconsistencies, and to initiate a reasoned debate on compulsory education and the forms it might take. The issues involved are quite complex and call for detailed analysis as well as empirical investigation. There is a need to go beyond all-or-nothing positions which fail to do justice to the range of feasible options. For instance, to suggest that compulsory education can be effectively introduced at once in the whole of India and for all children in the 6–14 age group is as counterproductive as the argument that compulsory education is not an issue at all. A concrete proposal has to take into account the inadequacies of the schooling system, the danger of harassment of child labourers, the economic dependence of particular groups (such as young widows) on child labour, and so on. It must also take note of the possibility of perversion of

[52] See e.g. Babu and Hallam (1989), Swaminathan (1991), R. Singh (1994), and Mehrotra (1995). For wide-ranging suggestions of means to improve school attendance in India, see Patil (1984).

[53] See particularly Ghosh et al. (1994), who report that 'tremendous enhancement of demand for primary education and enrolment of children in primary schools have been noticed in many literacy campaign districts' (p. 23).

[54] The feeble nature of earlier campaigns to influence popular perceptions of the value of education contrasts with the extraordinary propaganda efforts that have been made in the field of family planning. These efforts may have contributed to the relatively wide acceptance of a 'small family' norm: according to a recent survey, only 30 per cent of Indian women with two children (and 15 per cent of women with three children) want to have another child (International Institute for Population Sciences, 1994, Table 14).

[55] For a wide range of relevant testimonies, see Weiner (1991).

standards that may result from nominal compliance to overexacting bureaucratic demands.[56] In practice, the desirability and feasibility of introducing compulsory education must depend quite crucially on the proposed time frame, the precise age limits, the enforcement mechanism to be used, the social security arrangements that can be introduced to obviate the need for child labour, and other relevant parameters.

It is also worth remembering that much clarity can be gained on some of these issues on the basis of a *gradual* introduction of compulsory education. Since state governments and local authorities are empowered to introduce compulsory education in the areas under their jurisdiction, there is no need to think only in terms of an all-India policy. The way ahead may well be to begin with compulsory education for the 6–10 age group (corresponding to the primary stage) in the more advanced states, and to expand the scope of compulsory education on the basis of the experiences gained there. Of course, a gradual approach involves some danger of slowing down the whole process. But the process is even slower when it takes the form of setting lofty goals that cannot proceed beyond the stage of pious statements.

Finally, compulsory education *on its own* is obviously not an adequate programme of public action for the promotion of basic education. It can be an important *part* of such a programme, but the more exacting issue is the need for a substantial improvement of the schooling system. Making it legally compulsory for children to attend schools that cannot receive them would not be a great gift.

6.7. On Female Education

The recognition of female education as a social issue is very recent in India. The dominant Brahminical tradition reserves the study of the Vedas to men of the twice-born castes, and tends to consider female education as a threat to the social order. Female scholars and writers make occasional appearances in Indian history (and there

---

[56] For an example of this phenomenon, see Prasad's (1987) case study of education in Andhra Pradesh, where government pressure to increase enrolment figures at all cost has proved rather counterproductive in a number of ways, aside from failing to lead to a genuine increase in actual attendance: 'the actual attendance during the day(s) of my investigation was between 20–30 per cent of the impressive number of children found in the school records in most of the villages' (Prasad, 1987, p. 76).

are also many examples of remarkable female intellectuals, such as Maitreyi and Gargee, in the ancient scriptures), but widespread female literacy is a twentieth-century phenomenon.[57] In fact, at the end of the nineteenth century, the female literacy rate was still below *one* per cent in every province of British India and every 'native state', with a few exceptions such as Coorg, the Andaman and Nicobar Islands, and the native states of Travancore and Cochin in what is now Kerala.[58] Even in Travancore and Cochin, the female literacy rate was below one per cent as late as 1875, and remained as low as 3 per cent in 1901.[59]

Against this historical background, the expansion of female literacy in the twentieth century (and particularly after independence) is a positive development. In comparative international terms, however, India's record in this respect remains dismal. For instance, as we saw in chapter 3, the available estimates suggest that adult female literacy is higher even in sub-Saharan Africa than in India. A comparison with China (let alone south-east Asia) is even more sobering: in India, half of all females in the 15–19 age group are illiterate, compared with less than 10 per cent in China (see chapter 4).

The poor functioning of India's schooling system, discussed earlier, is one reason for the persistence of endemic female illiteracy. In this connection, it is important to stress that the failure of government primary schools in large parts of the country in not gender-neutral, especially in rural areas. As discussed in the case study of Uttar Pradesh in the companion volume (see Drèze and Gazdar, 1996), a common response of parents to the poor functioning or non-functioning of a government-run village school is to send their sons to study in other villages, or in private schools. But the same response is far less common in the case of girls, because parents are often reluctant to allow their daughters to wander outside the village, or to pay the fees that would be necessary to secure their admission in a private school. The breakdown of a government village school typically affects female children more than male children.[60]

---

[57] A useful anthology of women's writings in Indian history can be found in Tharu and Lalita (1991).

[58] Census of India, 1901. The female literacy rate was also above 1 per cent in what is now Myanmar (Burma), where it was around 4 per cent.

[59] Census figures on literacy rates in Kerala are presented in the chapter by V.K. Ramachandran (1996) in the companion volume.

[60] Another aspect of the poor quality of the schooling system which may also discourage

This is not say that low levels of female education in India are exclusively due to the poor functioning of the schooling system. Indeed, field investigations indicate that, even when local teaching standards are relatively good, male participation in education is usually much higher than female participation.[61] The problem of low parental motivation for female education needs attention on its own, in addition to the issue of poor functioning of the schooling system.

The low value attached to female education in much of India links with some deep-rooted features of gender relations. Three of these links have been widely observed.[62]

First, the gender division of labour (combined with patrilineal property rights) tends to reduce the perceived benefits of female education. In rural India, a large majority of girls are expected to spend most of their adult life in domestic work and child-rearing (and possibly some family labour in agriculture). It is in the light of these social expectations about the adult life of women that female education appears to many parents to be somewhat 'pointless'. Of course, female education can bring immense benefits even within the limited field of domestic work and child-rearing, but these benefits do not always receive adequate recognition.[63]

Second, the norms of patrilocal residence and village exogamy (requiring a woman to settle in her husband's village at the time of marriage, in effect forcing her to sever most links with her own family), prevalent in large parts of India, have the effect of further undermining the economic incentives which parents might have to

---

female education more than male education is the low number of female teachers in many states. While the proportion of female teachers among primary-school teachers is as high as 63 per cent in Kerala, the corresponding figure is only 29 per cent for India as a whole, 18 per cent in Uttar Pradesh, and 13 per cent in rural Uttar Pradesh (Government of India, 1992b, p. 307). Further, there is considerable evidence that, in north India in particular, daughters are often withdrawn from school due to the absence of female teachers or of separate schools for girls (see Patil, 1984). According to Gupta et al. (1993), p. 55, 'reluctance to have daughters taught by male teachers may begin as early as 7 to 8 years of age'.

[61] See e.g. J.C. Caldwell et al. (1985).

[62] For further discussion, see Drèze and Saran (1995). The focus of the present discussion is primarily on rural areas.

[63] This lack of recognition derives partly from an observational bias (the benefits of female education in household-based activities are less easy to identify than, say, differences in salaries between educated and uneducated men), and partly from the general undervaluation of female activities in a patriarchal society.

send their daughters to school. Since 'an Indian girl is but a sojourner in her own family', as Sudhir Kakar (1979) aptly puts it, the investments that parents make in the education of a daughter primarily 'benefit' other, often distant households. This can strongly reduce the perceived value of female education, at least from the point of view of parental self-interest. The perception is neatly summed up in such popular sayings as 'bringing up a daughter is like watering a plant in another's courtyard'.[64]

Third, the practice of dowry and the ideology of hypergamous marriage (it being thought best that a woman should marry 'up' in the social scale), also influential in large parts of India, can turn female education into a liability. If an educated girl can only marry a *more* educated boy, and if dowry payments increase with the education of the groom, then, given other things, an educated girl is likely to be more expensive to marry off. There is some evidence that this preoccupation is quite real for many parents.[65]

Given these and other links between female education and gender relations, it is not surprising that the twentieth-century progress of female education has been particularly slow in areas of India (such as the large north Indian states) where the gender division of labour, patrilineal inheritance, patrilocal residence, village exogamy, hypergamous marriage, and related patriarchal norms tend to be particularly influential.[66] The positive side of the same coin is that the expansion of female literacy has been comparatively rapid in areas where gender

[64] Quoted by Leela Dube (1988), p. 168. Interestingly, this is a Telugu proverb, confirming the notion that the social influence of patrilocal residence norms is not confined to north India (as Dube herself observes), even though it may be stronger there. For a fine empirical investigation of the relationship between patrilocal residence, village exogamy, and the relative neglect of female children, see Kishor (1993).

[65] The problem has been noted, for instance, in Committee on the Status of Women in India (1974), p. 74, Almeida (1978), p. 264, Seetharamu and Ushadevi (1985), van Bastelaer (1986), p. 61, and Khan (1993). Here again the problem is not confined to north India, even though dowry is more widely practised in that region. In rural Karnataka, for instance, some parents are reported to be worried that education 'would make daughters unmarriageable', because a woman 'must be married to a male with at least as much education' (J.C. Caldwell et al., 1985, pp. 39, 41).

[66] Punjab and Haryana might seem like exceptions to this pattern. But in fact, the record of these two states in the field of female literacy is quite poor, if one controls for their high income levels. While Punjab and Haryana come first and second in the income scale, they only come fifth and tenth, respectively, in the scale of female literacy (see Table 3.3 in chapter 3). Punjab, however, provides a good example of how attitudes to female education can, in some circumstances, change quite rapidly.

relations are less patriarchal. Kerala is the most obvious example, but the same observation applies to much of south India, and also to parts of the Himalayan region in north and north-east India, including Manipur, Meghalaya, and Himachal Pradesh.[67]

Another important corollary of the preceding observations is that the considerations involved in educational decisions are radically different for boys and girls. In the case of male education, the economic incentives are strong, because improved education enhances employment prospects, and parents have a strong stake in the economic advancement of their sons (including—but not exclusively—for reasons of improved old-age security). The influence of these economic motives in educational decisions relating to male children emerges quite clearly in household surveys.[68] Economic returns and parental self-interest, on the other hand, provide very weak incentives for female education, given the prevailing gender division of labour, marriage practices, and property rights. Parental concern for the well-being of a daughter in her own right, and recognition of the contribution which education can make to the quality of her life (and that of others), are more important motivations.

This contrast has strong implications for public policy. As far as male education is concerned, parental motivation is generally high, and can be expected to reinforce any efforts that are made to improve the schooling system. In the case of female education, however, it is particularly important to address the conservatism of social attitudes and parental inertia. As it happens, there is some evidence that the value attached to female education in India can change very substantially over a relatively short period of time under the impact of economic change, public action, and social movements.[69] Even in states such as Rajasthan, where

---

[67] These three states have the highest female literacy rates in the country after Kerala, for the younger age groups (see Sengupta, 1991, pp. 27–8). Several studies have noted the relatively egalitarian character of gender relations in parts of the Himalayan region (Berreman, 1962, 1993, Sopher, 1980a, Miller, 1981, Agnihotri, 1995), some symptoms of which include high female–male ratios in the population, high female labour force participation rates, and a female advantage in child survival (see Nuna, 1990, for some evidence). For Manipur, Meghalaya, and Himachal Pradesh, these features are quite well documented (see e.g. B. Agarwal, 1989, A.K. Shiva Kumar, 1992, Sharma, 1980).

[68] For some relevant studies, see J.C. Caldwell et al. (1985), Raza and Ramachandran (1990), Alderman et al. (1993), Drèze and Saran (1995).

[69] This has been noted in several field studies, including J.C. Caldwell et al. (1985), Chanana (1993), and Vlassoff (1993). The experience of the recent Total Literacy Campaign is particularly instructive in this regard. On the high involvement of women

gender bias in education and related gender inequalities are extremely large, there have been some encouraging cases of rapid change in attitudes to female education, driven by well-planned campaigns.[70] There is a need for more activism in that direction, if the expansion of female education is not to trail well behind that of male education in the future, as in the past.

6.8. *Education and Political Action*

In this chapter, we have had occasion to present brief comments on a number of shortcomings of government activity in the field of basic education, including the inconsistencies of official statistics (section 6.2), the confusion of educational policy (section 6.3), the inadequacy and poor use of education expenditure (section 6.4), the mismanagement and lack of accountability of the schooling establishment in rural areas (section 6.5), the absence of a serious debate on compulsory education (section 6.6), the neglect of female education (section 6.7), among others. We have also argued that a deep lack of real commitment to the widespread and equitable provision of basic education lies at the root of these diverse failures (section 6.1).

What is perhaps most striking of all is that the failures of government policy over an extended period have provoked so little political challenge. Had the government shown similar apathy and inconsistency in dealing with, say, the demands of the urban population for basic amenities, or of farmers' organizations for adequately high crop prices, or of the military establishment for modern hardware, or of the World Bank for structural adjustment measures, it is safe to predict that a major political battle would have followed. The fact that the government was able to get away with so much neglect in the field of primary education relates to the lack of political clout of the illiterate masses (we have commented on this issue in section 5.1). It also reflects the fact, discussed at the beginning of this chapter, that the social value of basic education has been neglected not only by government authorities but also in social and political movements.

Much the same remarks also apply at the local level. The case

---

in this campaign (both as learners and as instructors), and the diverse achievements linked with this positive response, see Ghosh et al. (1994); also Sengupta (1992), Agnihotri and Sivaswamy (1993), Saldanha (1994).

[70] See e.g. Ghosh (1991), Rokadiya et al. (1993), Ghosh et al. (1994), and evaluation reports on the Mahila Samakhya programme in different states.

study of Uttar Pradesh by Drèze and Gazdar (1996) in the companion volume, for instance, shows how it is quite possible for a village school to be non-functional for as long as ten years (due to teacher absenteeism and shirking) without any action being taken and any collective protest being organized.[71] There is a crucial contrast to be found here between Uttar Pradesh and Kerala, where a comparable state of affairs would not be passively tolerated.[72] It is, of course, also the case that public expenditure on education is higher in Kerala than in Uttar Pradesh, and this factor is undoubtedly important in Kerala's higher educational achievements. But this difference in expenditure levels is much less striking than the difference relating to the politics of education. In fact, Uttar Pradesh is notorious for having considerably *underutilized* the large grants that have been made available to that state in recent years (by the central government as well as international agencies) for primary education.[73] Similarly, in Uttar Pradesh, very little interest has been taken in the recent Total Literacy Campaign, and, as a result, almost nothing has been gained from it (in contrast with the positive achievements observed in several other states, including Kerala where this campaign was initially launched).[74] The main constraint on educational expansion in Uttar Pradesh is not basically a financial one—it is the low importance attached to basic education in public policy.[75] The responsibility

[71] Similar observations have been made for other states of north India. Narain (1972), for instance, notes that in Rajasthan 'all the villagers may be dissatisfied with a school teacher, yet if he is in the good books of the *sarpanch* and *pradhan* he is not transferred' (p. 152).

[72] The same point has been made with reference to health services; see, for example, Mencher (1980), Nag (1989), and Ramachandran (1996). Mencher, in particular, stresses the role of 'political awareness' in ensuring the effective functioning of health services in Kerala: 'In Kerala, if a PHC was unmanned for a few days, there would be a massive demonstration at the nearest collectorate led by local leftists, who would demand to be given what they knew they were entitled to. This had the effect of making health care much more readily available for the poor in Kerala' (p. 1782). This account is in sharp contrast with the corresponding state of affairs in Uttar Pradesh, where widespread absenteeism of government doctors is passively accepted as a normal state of affairs (see e.g. Khan et al., 1986).

[73] We are grateful to Dr Vaidyanatha Ayyar (Joint Secretary, Department of Education, New Delhi) for drawing our attention to this fact.

[74] See Ghosh et al. (1994), who attribute this poor response in Uttar Pradesh to a 'low political commitment to the eradication of illiteracy' in that state (p. 39).

[75] In the very same state of Uttar Pradesh, students enrolled for higher education are a significant political force. The fact that the first decision taken by the newly-elected

for this failure lies not only with the government, but also with the political movements in this part of India.

Ultimately, the expansion of basic education in India depends a great deal on these political factors. There is no question that, even in a country as poor as India, means can be found to ensure universal attainment of literacy and other basic educational achievements, at least in the younger age groups. There are important strategic questions to consider in implementing that social commitment, but the primary challenge is to make it a more compelling political issue.

---

government of Uttar Pradesh in December 1993 was to repeal the Anti-Copying Act (sic) is a symptomatic example of their influence. Incidentally, the Anti-Copying Act should not be mistaken for copyright legislation. It is what it says—an act outlawing the practice of copying in higher-education examinations; this restriction has now been largely revoked.

7

GENDER INEQUALITY AND WOMEN'S AGENCY

7.1. *Female Deprivation and Missing Women*

Inequality between men and women is one of the most crucial disparities in many societies, and this is particularly so in India. Differences in female and male literacy rates, discussed in the last chapter, are one aspect of this broader phenomenon of gender-based inequality in India. In much of the country, women tend in general to fare quite badly in relative terms compared with men, even within the same families. This is reflected not only in such matters as education and opportunity to develop talents, but also in the more elementary fields of nutrition, health, and survival. Indeed, the mortality rates of females tend to exceed those of males until the late twenties, and even the late thirties in some states, and this—as we know from the experiences of other countries—is very much in contrast with what tends to happen when men and women receive similar nutritional and health care.[1] One result is a remarkably low ratio of females to males in the Indian population compared with the corresponding ratio not only in Europe and North America, but also in sub-Saharan Africa. The problem is not, of course, unique to India, but it is particularly serious in this country, and certainly deserves public attention as a matter of major priority.

There are, in fact, striking variations in the ratio of females to males in the population (hereafter 'female–male ratio', or FMR for short) in different regions of the world. While there are important

---

[1] See Sen (1992c), and the literature cited there; see also Kynch (1985).

social and cultural influences on survival rates,[2] there is fairly strong medical evidence to the effect that—given similar care—women tend to have lower age-specific mortality rates than men (indeed, even female foetuses are relatively less prone to miscarriage than their male counterparts). Even though males outnumber females at birth (and even more at conception), women tend to outnumber men substantially in Europe and North America, with an average ratio around 1.05. While that includes some remnant effects of greater male mortality in past wars, the ratio would still be considerably above unity after adjusting for that. In contrast, many parts of the Third World have female–male ratios substantially below unity, for example, 0.96 in North Africa, 0.94 in China, Bangladesh, and West Asia. The average FMR in India is around 0.93—one of the lowest in the world (it is no consolation that Pakistan's ratio of 0.91 is even lower).[3] There is much direct evidence, in India and in the other countries with a sharp 'deficit' of women, of relative neglect of the health and well-being of women (particularly young girls including female infants), leading to survival disadvantage of females *vis-à-vis* males over long periods.

It is easily calculated that no matter what female–male ratio we use as a benchmark for comparison (whether the FMR in contemporary Europe, or in sub-Saharan Africa, or one based on the historical experience of parts of Europe), we would find that there are many millions of 'missing women' in India. The sub-Saharan African ratio had yielded the colossal number of 37 million missing women in India in 1986 (Drèze and Sen, 1989, Table 4.1, p. 52).[4] Klasen's history-based calculation suggests figures closer to 35 million. These are gigantic figures—and again there is no consolation here in the

---

[2] On this see particularly Johansson (1991) and Alaka Basu (1992). See also Sopher (1980b) and Dyson and Moore (1983).

[3] On this see Bardhan (1974, 1984a, 1988), Mitra (1979), Miller (1981), Kynch and Sen (1982), Kynch (1985), Sen (1984, 1985c, 1989, 1992c), Mazumdar (1985), Drèze and Sen (1989), Coale (1992), and Klasen (1994).

[4] It was on the basis of the sub-Saharan African FMR that the figure of 'more than a hundred million missing women' was presented for Asia and north Africa as a whole in Drèze and Sen (1989) and Sen (1989). Coale (1991) suggested a number closer to 60 million, on the basis of the historical experience of Europe, whereas Klasen (1994) arrives at around 90 million missing women on a different reading of the European experience. While refinements of the exact numbers can certainly continue, it is important to emphasize that no matter which standard FMR we use, we do get incredibly large numbers of missing women.

fact that the absolute number of missing women (though not its ratio to the population) in China is estimated to be even higher—between 38 and 40 million. We do have a problem of basic inequality here of extraordinary proportions.

7.2. On the Female–Male Ratio

We have noted in the preceding section that India has an exceptionally low female–male ratio. This problem is not, of course, equally acute in every region of India. As noted in chapter 3, there are large variations in the female–male ratio between different states. The female–male ratio is particularly low in large parts of north India, especially the north-western states (e.g. 0.87 in Haryana, 0.88 in Punjab and Uttar Pradesh, 0.91 in Rajasthan), and comparatively high in the south (e.g. 0.97 in Tamil Nadu and Andhra Pradesh, 0.96 in Karnataka). In Kerala, the female–male ratio is well above unity; in fact, it is as high as 1.04, a figure comparable to that of Europe and North America.[5]

These regional patterns of female–male ratios are consistent with what is known of the character of gender relations in different parts of the country. The north-western states, for instance, are notorious for highly unequal gender relations, some symptoms of which include the continued practice of female seclusion, very low female labour-force participation rates, a large gender gap in literacy rates, extremely restricted female property rights, strong boy preference in fertility decisions, widespread neglect of female children, and drastic separation of a married woman from her natal family. In all these respects, the social standing of women is somewhat better in south India.[6] And Kerala, of course, has a distinguished history of a more liberated position of women in society.[7] Important aspects of this history include a major success in the expansion of female literacy (see chapter 4), considerable prominence of women in influential social and political

[5] Kerala's high female–male ratio is partly due to high levels of male outmigration, but even the migration-adjusted female–male ratio is well above unity (see e.g. Agnihotri, 1994).

[6] On these regional contrasts in gender relations, see Karve (1965), Bardhan (1974, 1984), Sopher (1980a, 1980b), Miller (1981), Dyson and Moore (1983), Kolenda (1984), Jain and Banerjee (1985), Caldwell and Caldwell (1987), Mandelbaum (1988), Alaka Basu (1992), Gupta, Basu, and Asthana (1993), Agarwal (1994), Agnihotri (1995), among others.

[7] See e.g. Robin Jeffrey (1992).

activities, and a tradition of matrilineal inheritance for an important section of the population.[8]

These regional contrasts, and also changes in the female–male ratio over time, provide a useful means of investigating different aspects of the problem of low female–male ratios in India. This investigation will be pursued a little further in this section and the next one. The motivation for focusing on the female–male ratio is partly that this indicator of gender inequality is important in its own right, and partly that it sheds some interesting light on other aspects of gender relations.

Two misconceptions

To begin with, we should deal with two misunderstandings that arise from time to time in popular discussions of the issue of low female–male ratios in India.

First, it is sometimes thought that the main cause of the problem is some phenomenon of hidden female infanticide, not captured in reported death statistics. In fact, census figures on female–male ratios are quite consistent with what one would predict based on (1) a standard female–male ratio at birth of about 0.95, and (2) independently recorded age- and sex-specific mortality rates. To illustrate, the predicted female–male ratio at age 5 in India in 1981, using information on age-specific mortality rates from the Sample Registration System, is 0.921.[9] The *actual* female–male ratio at age 5 for that year, obtained from the 1981 census, is 0.920—very close to the predicted value.

It is possible, of course, that recorded child deaths include some female infant deaths due to infanticide, which are reported by the parents as due to some other cause. But the anthropological evidence suggests that female infanticide, when it does occur, takes place very

---

[8] Property has traditionally been inherited through the female line for a powerful community in Kerala—the Nairs. While the Nairs constitute about 20 per cent of the total population, and the practice has changed a good deal in recent years, nevertheless the social and political importance of a long tradition of this kind, which goes against the conventional Indian norms, must not be underestimated.

[9] This predicted female–male ratio at age 5 is calculated using the simple formula $FMR = (0.95) (1-q^f_5) / (1-q^m_5)$, where q^f_5 and q^m_5 are, respectively, the female and male probability of dying before the fifth birthday. The SRS-based estimates of q^f_5 and q^m_5 for 1976–80 are taken from Government of India (1988a), p. 3.

soon after birth.[10] The bulk of excess female mortality in childhood, on the other hand, occurs after the age of one, with a less unequal pattern in the first year. In 1981, for instance, 113 out of 1,000 male children born alive died before the age of one, compared with 115 out of 1,000 for female children; in contrast, of the surviving children, another 68 males died before the age of five, compared with as many as 91 females.[11]

The force of excess female mortality, therefore, lies in mortality rates in age groups beyond that of female infanticide. The female disadvantage in these age groups is itself due to a well-documented practice of preferential treatment of boys and neglect of female children in intra-household allocation. There is, indeed, considerable direct evidence of neglect of female children in terms of health care, nutrition, and related needs, particularly in north India.[12]

It may be argued that the deliberate neglect of female children ought to come under the label of infanticide. There might be a case for this, but the point to recognize is that the social practices that lead to excess female mortality are far more subtle and widespread than the graphic stories of infant drowning, poisoning, or asphyxiation that periodically make headlines in the newspapers.[13] This is not to deny that female infanticide, strictly defined, does indeed occur in India today and has done so in the past.[14]

The second misinterpretation concerns some alleged 'Muslim influence'. The reasoning, in so far as there is any, is that female–male

---

[10] See e.g. Panigrahi (1972), Miller (1981), George et al. (1992), and Venkatachalam and Srinivasan (1993).

[11] Calculated from Sample Registration System data presented in Government of India (1988a), p. 3. This pattern of concentration of excess female child mortality in the 1–5 age group is even more pronounced in the states where the problem of excess female mortality in childhood is particularly acute (e.g. Uttar Pradesh, Punjab, Haryana).

[12] See e.g. Chen, Huq, and D'souza (1981), Miller (1981), Kynch and Sen (1983), Sen and Sengupta (1983), Das Gupta (1987, 1994b), Alaka Basu (1989, 1992), M.E. Khan et al. (1989), Chatterjee (1990), Harriss (1990), B. Agarwal (1991), Deolalikar and Vashishta (1992), among many other studies. For a recent review, see Kishor (1994).

[13] A similar point might apply to the tendency to assume too readily that low female–male ratios in the younger age groups in China reflect explicit female infanticide on a large scale.

[14] Female infanticide has a long history in north India, and remains quite common in particular areas or communities; see e.g. Panigrahi (1972) and Miller (1981). See also George et al. (1992) and Venkatachalam and Srinivasan (1993) on the current practice of female infanticide in parts of south India.

ratios in India tend to be particularly low in the north-west of the country, which is geographically close to Islamic countries, has been under Muslim influence for a long time and, even now, has a large Muslim population.[15] But a glance at the figures immediately exposes the fragility of this hypothesis. The state of Kerala, which has the highest female–male ratio among Indian states (1.04 in 1991), comes second in terms of the proportion of Muslims in the population. The state with the lowest proportion of Muslims in the population (1 per cent in 1981) is Punjab, which has had the lowest female–male ratio among all Indian states until it was overtaken by Haryana in 1981. Haryana itself has an extremely small Muslim population (4 per cent of the total population).

We can take a closer look at this whole issue by examining the extent of gender bias in child mortality rates among Hindus and Muslims in different parts of India. The evidence is summarized in Figure 7.1. This diagram shows the ratio of female child mortality to male child mortality in different states, both for the Hindu population (on the horizontal axis) and for the Muslim population (on the vertical axis). The point representing a particular state lies to the right of the point marked '1' on the horizontal axis if and only if female mortality is higher than male mortality among Hindus, and above the point marked '1' on the vertical axis if the same statement applies for Muslims. Further, a state lies above the diagonal if and only if the ratio of female to male child mortality (which can be interpreted as a measure of anti-female bias in child survival) is *higher* among Muslims than among Hindus.[16]

This figure highlights two points. First, *regional* contrasts in the extent of gender bias in child survival are far more striking than the contrast relating to *religious identity*. Specifically, the relative survival chances of girls are low in large parts of north India (including Punjab, Haryana, Uttar Pradesh, Rajasthan, and Bihar), and this applies

---

[15] The political value of this kind of argument has not been lost on either side of the north-western border, judging from a recent report of the Pakistan Institute of Development Economics on the condition of women in Pakistan (Shah, 1986). In its analysis of the 'roots of the Pakistani woman's status' (pp. 19–21), this report primarily blames the historical influence of the 'traditions of the Hindu majority in undivided India' for the deprived condition of women in contemporary Pakistan.

[16] The mortality estimates on which Figure 7.1 is based are indirect estimates grounded on census information, and the individual numbers are subject to some margin of error. The purpose of Figure 7.1 is to highlight a broad pattern, rather than to convey precise estimates for particular states.

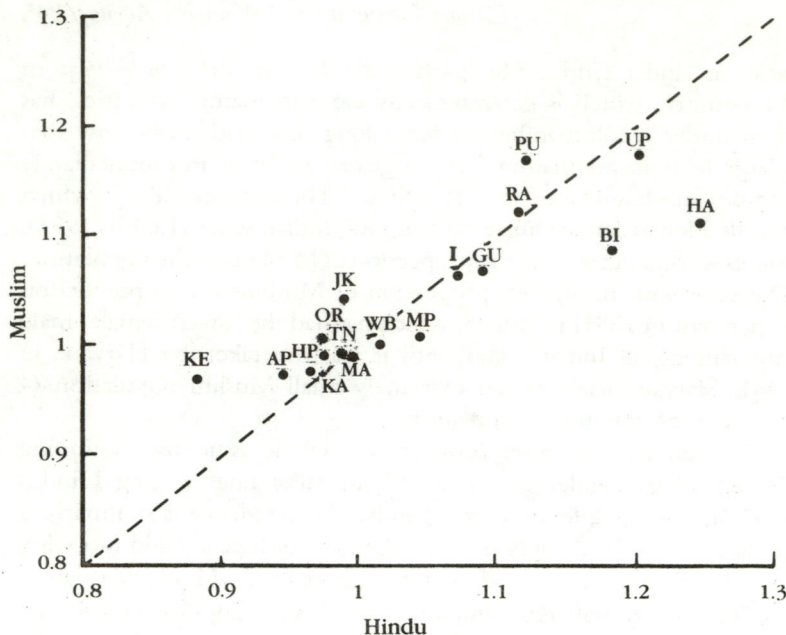

Fig. 7.1. *Ratio of Female to Male Child Mortality Among Hindus and Muslims in Different States, 1981*

Note. The horizontal axis indicates the ratio of female child mortality to male child mortality among Hindus in different states; similarly with Muslims on the vertical axis. The child mortality measure used here is 'q_5', the probability of dying before age 5.

Source. Calculated from Government of India (1988a).

I = India

AP = Andhra Pradesh	HP = Himachal Pradesh
BI = Bihar	HA = Haryana
GU = Gujarat	JK = Jammu & Kashmir
KA = Karnataka	KE = Kerala
MA = Maharashtra	MP = Madhya Pradesh
OR = Orissa	PU = Punjab
RA = Rajasthan	TN = Tamil Nadu
UP = Uttar Pradesh	WB = West Bengal

whether they are Hindus or Muslims. Second, there is no evidence of any overall tendency for the female disadvantage to be particularly large among Muslims.

Time trends

It is well known that the female–male ratio in India has steadily declined since the beginning of this century. In fact, there has been an almost monotonic decline from 1901 to 1991, when the female–male ratio in India reached its lowest-ever recorded value (927 females per 1,000 males).[17]

The same pattern does not apply at the state level, where a good deal of diversity can be found: since 1901, the female–male ratio has steadily declined in some states (e.g. Bihar, Uttar Pradesh, Orissa), steadily increased in others (e.g. Kerala, Himachal Pradesh), and fluctuated or stagnated in quite a few cases (e.g. West Bengal, Maharashtra).[18]

The root causes of the all-India decline are far from obvious.[19] The fall cannot be explained by sex-selective migration, enumeration biases, or a change in the sex ratio at birth.[20] Nor can it be attributed

---

[17] The decline of the female–male ratio from 1901 onwards was preceded by a slight rise between 1891 and 1901 (from 963 to 972). This may reflect the demographic effect of the famines of 1896–7 and 1899–1900. Indeed, male mortality typically rises more than female mortality in famine situations (Drèze and Sen, 1989, chapter 4), and this pattern applies in particular to late-nineteenth century famines in India (Maharatna, 1992). Further, the increase of India's female–male ratio between 1891 and 1901 was overwhelmingly concentrated in the districts that now make up the states of Madhya Pradesh, Maharashtra, Orissa, and Rajasthan, and each of these regions was severely affected by the famines of 1896–7 and 1899–1900 (see Bhatia, 1967).

[18] For the latest figures on state-specific female–male ratios since 1901, see Nanda (1992), pp. 102–3. Note that these state-specific female–male ratios, to be used further in this chapter, consistently refer to the 1991 state boundaries.

[19] Important contributions on this subject include P. Visaria (1961, 1967), Mitra (1979), Miller (1981, 1989), Bardhan (1984a, 1988), Dyson (1988), Kanitkar (1991), Kishor (1993), and Agnihotri (1994). It should be mentioned that the focus of this section is primarily on the long-term decline of the female–male ratio since 1901, rather than on the latest developments, which are quite complex and controversial. On the latter, see I. Sen (1986), Karkal (1987), Dyson (1988), Miller (1989), Kundu and Sahu (1991), Rajan et al. (1991, 1992), Srinivas (1991), Nanda (1992), Raju and Premi (1992), among others.

[20] See P. Visaria (1961) and Nanda (1992), pp. 9–14. The female–male ratio at birth has been declining in recent years, possibly due to sex-selective abortion. But this is a

to a change in the age distribution of the population (e.g. due to fertility decline). Indeed, if we combine 1981 age-specific female–male ratios with the 1901 age distribution of the population (available in S.B. Mukherjee, 1976), we obtain an overall female–male ratio of 936, very close to the actual female–male ratio of 934 in 1981. And similarly, combining the 1901 age-specific female–male ratios with the 1981 age distribution of the population, we find an overall female–male ratio of 976, very close to the actual 1901 female–male ratio of 972. The decline of India's female–male ratio over time is overwhelmingly due to the decline of age-specific female–male ratios, rather than to changes in the age distribution of the population.

Another possibility is that states with low initial female–male ratios have tended to experience faster population growth than others, pulling down the all-India average. This has indeed happened to some extent, but it only explains a very small part of the observed decline. In fact, had the 1901 state-specific female–male ratios remained unchanged to 1991, we would now observe an all-India female–male ratio of 970 per thousand (taking as given the current interstate distribution of the population), only 2 points down from the female–male ratio of 972 in 1901.[21]

The contribution of different states to the decline of the female–male ratio at the all-India level is examined in Table 7.1, where we decompose the all-India decline between 1901 and 1991 into: (a) a population-weighted sum of state-specific changes in female–male ratios; (b) a 'differential growth rate effect', which captures the fact that states with different initial female–male ratios grow at different rates (roughly speaking, this term tells us how the all-India female–male ratio would have changed, due to different state-specific population growth rates, had state-specific female–male ratios remained unchanged); and (c) a residual (or 'second-order term') which measures the difference between the actual FMR decline and the linear approximation to this decline obtained by adding up (a) and (b). In this table, the different states are arranged in descending order of female–male ratio in 1901 (except for the residual category of 'other

---

relatively new phenomenon, which cannot explain the sustained decline of the female–male ratio since 1901. In fact, a large-scale survey carried out in the nineteen-fifties in health institutions found a female–male ratio at birth of 942 (Nanda, 1992, p. 11), which is quite standard.

[21] The calculations are based on population figures for 1901 and 1991 presented in Nanda (1992), pp. 86–113.

TABLE 7.1. *Decomposition of the Decline of India's Female–Male Ratio, 1901–91*

	Share of India's male population		Female–male ratio			Effect of change in state-specific FMR on Indian FMR[a]
	1901 (s^0)	1991 (s^1)	1901 (f^0)	1991 (f^1)	Change $(f^1 - f^0)$	
INDIA	1.000	1.000	972	927	−45	−
Bihar	0.111	0.104	1,054	911	−143	−15.87
Tamil Nadu	0.079	0.065	1,044	974	−70	−5.50
Orissa	0.042	0.037	1,037	971	−66	−2.79
Kerala	0.027	0.033	1,004	1,036	+32	+0.85
Madhya Pradesh	0.071	0.079	990	931	−59	−4.17
Andhra Pradesh	0.080	0.078	985	972	−13	−1.04
Karnataka	0.055	0.053	983	960	−23	−1.26
Maharashtra	0.081	0.094	978	934	−44	−3.60
Gujarat	0.039	0.049	954	934	−20	−0.78
West Bengal	0.073	0.082	945	917	−28	−2.04
Uttar Pradesh	0.210	0.170	937	879	−58	−12.15
Assam	0.014	0.027	919	923	+4	+0.06
Rajasthan	0.045	0.053	905	910	+5	+0.23
Himachal Pradesh	0.009	0.006	884	976	+92	+0.78
Haryana	0.021	0.020	867	865	−2	−0.04
Punjab	0.034	0.025	832	882	+50	+1.72
Other states/UTs	0.009	0.025	943	887	−56	−0.50

Decomposition of the all-India change in FMR		
	(a) Total effect of changes in state-specific FMRs (column total)	−46.1
	(b) 'Differential growth rate effect': $f^0 \star (s^1 - s^0)$	−2.3
	(c) Second-order term: $(f^1 - f^0) \star (s^1 - s^0)$	3.4
	Change in female–male ratio (a+b+c)	−45.0

Notes. [a] Change in state-specific FMR, multiplied by initial share of the male population

UT = Union Territory $\star$ denotes vector product

Sources. Calculated from Nanda (1992), pp. 86–105. All figures exclude Jammu and Kashmir (not covered by the 1991 census).

states/UTs'). It can be seen that the broad regional patterns of female–male ratios that are observed today, and that have been much discussed in the literature, already existed at the beginning of this century. In particular, the north-western region (including Punjab, Haryana, Rajasthan, and Uttar Pradesh) has had the lowest female–male ratios all along, and, similarly, the states of the southern region (Kerala, Andhra Pradesh, Karnataka, and Tamil Nadu) already had above-average female–male ratios in 1901. But there have also been some significant changes in regional patterns. In particular, the relative position of the eastern states (Bihar, Orissa and, to a lesser extent, West Bengal) in the scale of female–male ratios has considerably declined.

Changes in state-specific female–male ratios between 1901 and 1991 have partly taken the form of a 'convergence' effect, with most of the states starting off with a high female–male ratio experiencing a particularly large decline over that period, and some increase taking place in the states with the lowest initial female–male ratios. The main exceptions to this pattern are Kerala (where the female–male ratio increased from a high initial value) and Uttar Pradesh (where there was a large decline despite a low base value). In addition to this convergence pattern, however, there has been a fairly widespread decline of the female–male ratio, not confined to any specific region. The largest absolute declines in female–male ratios have taken place in Bihar, Orissa, Tamil Nadu, Madhya Pradesh, Maharashtra, and Uttar Pradesh. As can be seen from the decomposition in the last column of the table, these six states (which combine large declines in FMR with large populations) account for an overwhelming proportion of the all-India decline in the female–male ratio. Bihar and Uttar Pradesh alone account for about half of the all-India decline.

Figure 7.2 shows the evolution of the female–male ratio in India between 1901 and 1981 (the last census for which age-specific population totals are available), distinguishing between two different age groups: 0–29 and 30+. As this figure suggests, the decline in the overall female–male ratio seems to be driven by a sustained decline in the ratio of women to men in the second age group (this group accounted for about one-third of the population in 1981). The same pattern is observed for each of India's broad geographical regions.[22]

---

[22] The last statement is based on age-specific population totals for the western, northern, southern, central, and eastern 'zones' presented in S.B. Mukherjee (1976). In each of these zones, there has been a sharp and sustained decline in the female–male ratio for

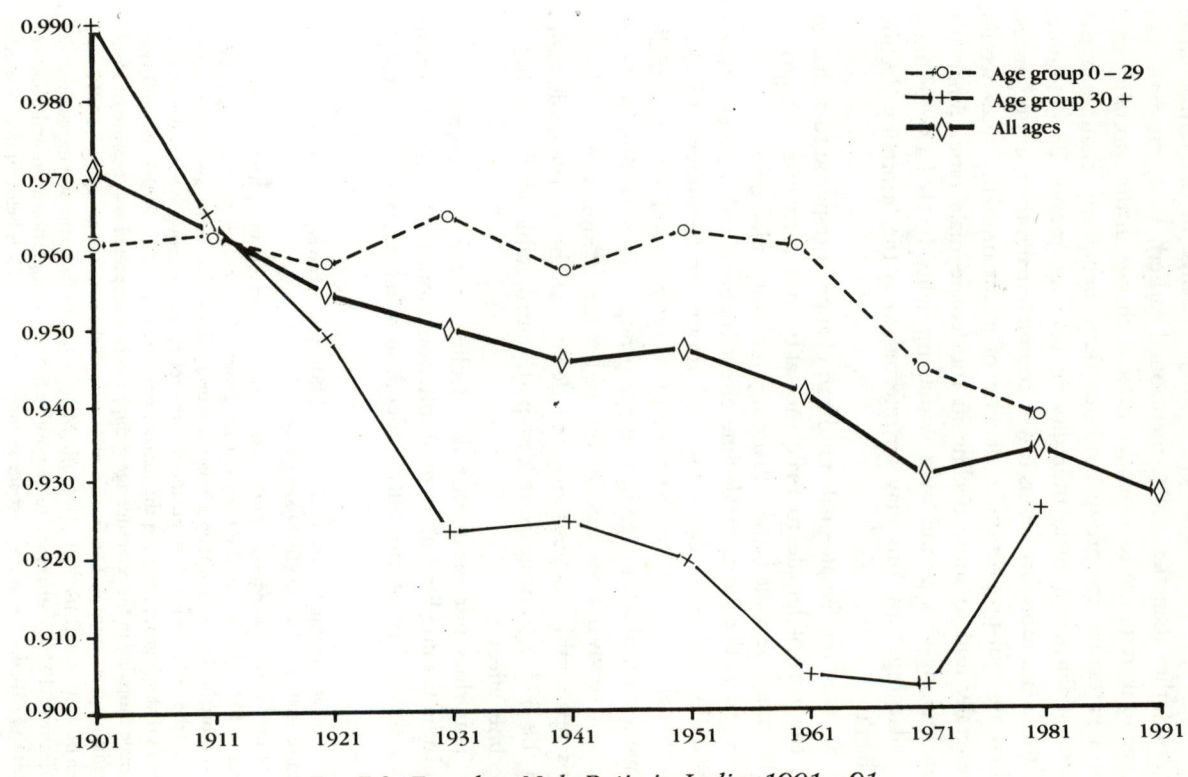

FIG. 7.2. *Female – Male Ratio in India, 1901– 91*

In order to understand this pattern, it is useful to distinguish between two possible causes of major change in the female–male ratio (other than the effects mentioned earlier). First, the ratio can change in response to a gender-neutral change in the mortality *level* in a particular age group, without there being any change in the *ratio* of female to male mortality in that age group. For instance, if the infant mortality rate is lower among females than among males, then an equi-proportionate decline of infant mortality rates would generally lead to some decline in the female–male ratio. Since we are looking at a period over which mortality levels have declined in all age groups, this may be referred to as the 'mortality decline effect'.

Second, the female–male ratio can change in response to a change in the *ratio* of female to male mortality in a particular age group. This may be called the 'changing mortality bias effect'.

As far as the mortality decline effect is concerned, gender-neutral mortality decline in a particular age group can be shown to reduce the female–male ratio in the subsequent age groups if women initially have a survival advantage in that age group.[23] Since women typically have a survival advantage in the older age groups, even in India, this relationship suggests that the decline of the female–male ratio in the 30+ age group is at least partly attributable to the mortality decline effect.

This does not mean that the decline in the female–male ratio in India is some kind of 'natural' phenomenon, reflecting little more than the decline of mortality. Indeed, in other regions of the world,

---

the 30+ age group between 1901 and 1981, and relatively little change in the female–male ratio for the 0–29 age group.

[23] More precisely, an equi-proportionate decline of mortality in a particular age group leads to FMR decline in all subsequent age groups if and only if the ratio of female to male mortality in that age group is lower than unity. To see this, let M_0 and F_0 respectively denote the male and female populations in the reference age group, q the male mortality rate in that age group, and k.q the female mortality rate, where k (the ratio of female to male mortality in the reference age group) can be interpreted as a measure of female disadvantage in survival. The female–male ratio in the next age group (say, FMR_1) can then be written as $FMR_1 = [F_0.(1-k.q)]/[M_0.(1-q)]$. The last expresson implies that the derivative of FMR_1 with respect to q is positive (i.e. equi-proportionate mortality decline leads to FMR decline in the next age group) if and only if k is below unity. A similar reasoning can be used to show that, if k is below unity, then equi-proportionate mortality decline leads to FMR decline in all subsequent age groups.

the decline of mortality in the twentieth century has usually gone hand in hand with an *increase* in the female–male ratio, reflecting a sustained improvement in the survival chances of females relative to males.[24] Even in Kerala and Sri Lanka, recent demographic trends have followed this typical pattern.[25] The all-India FMR decline seems to reflect a combination of the 'mortality decline effect' in the older age groups with a *failure to remove* the anti-female bias in the younger age groups. As Figure 7.2 shows, the female–male ratio in the 0–29 age group has stagnated around 0.96 until 1961; this figure is very close to the typical female–male ratio at birth, indicating roughly equal male and female mortality in that age group.[26] As was mentioned earlier, in countries where young males and females receive similar treatment in terms of food, health care, and related necessities, females have substantial survival advantages. India's female–male ratio of 0.96 in the 0–29 age group suggests some considerable anti-female discrimination, which—in contrast with many other countries—has not gone away with the decline of mortality.[27]

In fact, after 1961, the female–male ratio has declined even in the 0–29 age group, and this cannot be explained in terms of the 'mortality decline effect'. By 1971, female mortality rates were *higher* than male mortality rates throughout that age group (except immediately after birth), and that is still the case today.[28] This development

[24] See e.g. Preston (1976), chapter 6, and Lopez and Ruzicka (1983).

[25] As noted earlier, the female–male ratio in Kerala has steadily increased since 1901 (see also Table 7.1). Similarly, mortality decline in Sri Lanka has gone hand in hand with a major improvement in the relative survival chances of females *vis-à-vis* males; see Nadarajah (1983), Langford (1984, 1988), and Langford and Storey (1993).

[26] This statement does not apply to each age group within the 0–29 age group. In fact, female–male ratios for more narrowly-defined age groups (e.g. 0–4, 5–9, etc.) have followed rather complex patterns over time, which call for more detailed analysis than can be presented in this chapter.

[27] The female–male ratio for the 0–29 age group in, say, Western Europe is also around 0.96 (United Nations, 1993, p. 40), but this is because mortality rates for the younger age groups in that region are very low, so that the female–male ratio in the 0–29 age group remains relatively close to the female–male ratio at birth (around 0.95 in Western Europe). A more relevant comparison may be with sub-Saharan Africa, which has high mortality rates (like India) but relatively little female disadvantage in survival (unlike India). In that region, the female–male ratio for the 0–29 age group was just above unity in 1985 (United Nations, 1993, p. 68).

[28] See e.g the Sample Registration System (SRS) data presented in Karkal (1987), and in the annual SRS publications. It should be mentioned that, since 1971, there has been a consolidation of female survival advantage in the older age groups, and the age at which

is in sharp contrast with the typical pattern of reduced female disadvantage in the younger age groups as mortality declines.

The preceding discussion does not rule out the possibility that, even in the older age groups, the decline in the female–male ratio reflects some adverse change in the relative survival chances of women *vis-à-vis* men. Since 1971, the trend has been in the direction of an increase in female survival advantage in these age groups, but this does not rule out a contrary trend earlier on. The FMR decline, in fact, is most pronounced in the pre-1971 period (Figure 7.2), and for that period there is no reliable evidence of the direction of change in the relative survival rates of adult men and women.

If it is the case that the relative survival rates of men and women in the older age groups were changing in favour of men at one stage, contrary to the usual pattern in a phase of longevity expansion, the main explanation may simply be that adult men disproportionately benefited from improvements in living conditions and medical care. Such a phenomenon is quite plausible, given the tendency of economic development to affect men more rapidly than women: the current lifestyle of women in, say, rural Bihar or Uttar Pradesh is probably much closer to what it was at the beginning of this century than in the case of men. The fact that professional attendance at birth remains so rare in these states, while modern medical treatment is very often used to cure diseases that are not specific to women, is a good illustration of this point.[29]

A further possibility is that, aside from men benefiting more than women from medical advances and related improvements, there has also been a more basic change in gender relations, leading to a shift in the distribution of resources in favour of men. An example of this possibility is considered presently.

---

this advantage begins has also come down (see e.g. Karkal, 1987, Dyson, 1988, and Rajan et al., 1992). As a result, female life expectancy has overtaken male life expectancy. These developments will get reflected, in due course, in the female–male ratio, which may start rising as a result (unless other developments, such as the spread of sex-selective abortion, work in the other direction).

[29] In 1991, the proportion of all births taking place in medical institutions was as low as 4 per cent in Uttar Pradesh and 12 per cent in Bihar, compared with 92 per cent in Kerala (see Statistical Appendix, Table A.3). Maternal health, in general, remains one of the most neglected areas of health policy in India; see Karkal (1985), M.E. Khan et al. (1986), Bang et al. (1989), Sundari (1993, 1994), Das Gupta (1994b), Germain (1994), Jejeebhoy and Rama Rao (1994), and Mari Bhat et al. (1994).

Gender and caste

The decline of the female–male ratio in India has not been at all even between different castes and religious communities. Specifically, the decline appears to have been significantly more pronounced among disadvantaged castes.[30]

Many census reports of the pre-independence period have noted that the female–male ratio tends to be considerably higher among the 'lower' castes than in the population as a whole.[31] This is no longer the case: in 1991, the female–male ratio among scheduled castes was 922 per thousand, compared with 927 in the population as a whole.[32] As far as the female–male ratio is concerned, the scheduled castes are now much like the rest of the population, in contrast with the earlier pattern.

A detailed examination of this development is complicated by the fact that pre-independence and post-independence census reports use different caste classifications. Pre-independence census reports give caste-specific population totals (for males and females), but post-independence reports do not provide a caste breakdown, except among the scheduled castes. A further difficulty is that the names under which particular castes are recorded often change over time.

In order to keep things reasonably simple, we shall restrict our discussion of the relationship between female–male ratios and caste to the state of Uttar Pradesh (as we saw earlier, Uttar Pradesh accounts for a large part of the all-India decline in the female–male ratio since 1901). For this state, the 1981 census lists 66 'scheduled castes', of which 47 can be readily identified in the 1901 census volumes. Assuming that these 47 castes are more or less representative of the whole group of scheduled castes, we can reconstruct the 1901 female–male ratio for this group. The results are presented in Table 7.2.

As the table indicates, castes that are now classified as scheduled castes (previously often referred to simply as 'untouchables') had

---

[30] For a pioneering discussion of this issue with reference to the post-independence period, see Agnihotri (1994).

[31] See e.g. Census of India, 1931, United Provinces of Agra and Oudh, vol. XVIII, part I, p. 278.

[32] Nanda (1993), p. 12, based on 1991 census data. The female–male ratio remains higher among scheduled tribes (972 per thousand in 1991) than in the population as a whole, but that gap too is slowly narrowing over time (Agnihotri, 1994).

TABLE 7.2. *Female–Male Ratio and Caste in Uttar Pradesh, 1901 and 1981*

	Total population, 1901 (thousands)	Female– male ratio, 1901	Female– male ratio, 1981[a]
(i) Scheduled castes (SC)			
Chamar	5,891	986	880
All SCs[b]	9,821	970	892
(ii) Kshatriya, Rajput, Thakur	3,354	887	878[c]
(iii) Other Hindu	27,517	929	
Hindu (i + ii + iii)	40,692	935	881
Muslim	6,731	957	903
Other	269	783	884
Total	47,692	937	885

Note. [a] The corresponding 1991 figures are still to be published.

[b] Only 47 of the 66 castes listed as 'scheduled castes' in the 1981 census could be confidently identified in the 1901 census; the 1901 figures in this row apply to these 47 castes. The 1981 figures include a tiny proportion (about 1 per cent) of scheduled-caste persons who were not counted as 'Hindus' in that census.

[c] Female–male ratio for all Hindus not belonging to a scheduled caste (post-independence censuses provide no information on the caste composition of the population outside the scheduled castes).

Sources. Calculated from Census of India 1901, North-West Provinces and Oudh (Allahabad, 1902), volume 16A; Census of India 1981, Series 22, Uttar Pradesh, Parts IX-i and IX-vii; Census of India 1981, Series 22, Uttar Pradesh, Paper 1 of 1985. The list of scheduled castes is from Census of India 1981, Series 22, Uttar Pradesh, Paper 2 of 1982.

much above average female–male ratios in 1901. The Chamars, for instance, who are by far the largest scheduled caste in Uttar Pradesh, had a female–male ratio of 986 in 1901, compared with 937 for the state population as a whole. By 1981, however, the female–male ratio among scheduled castes (including the Chamars) was very close to the UP average. This is one indication that, as far as gender relations are concerned, the scheduled castes in Uttar Pradesh are now more like the 'higher' castes than they used to be.[33]

---

[33] The female–male ratio among Muslims in Uttar Pradesh has also declined a good deal since the beginning of the century (from 957 in 1901 to 903 in 1981), but remains higher than the female–male ratio for the Hindu population in that state.

The contrast between the scheduled castes and the martial castes (Kshatriya et al.) is particularly interesting. The martial castes, which have a high rank in the caste hierarchy, and an important place in the history and culture of large parts of north India (including Uttar Pradesh), have a long tradition of fierce patriarchy. In fact, the martial castes in north India have played a leading role in the history of female infanticide, child marriage, seclusion, dowry, *sati, johar*, levirate, polygamy, and related patriarchal practices.[34] Among these castes, in Uttar Pradesh, the female–male ratio was already very low at the beginning of the period under consideration (887 in 1901). Further, it has changed little over the years, at least during the pre-independence period (the relevant caste-specific figures are not available for the post-independence period). This is an important indication, suggesting that whatever factors led to a decline in the female–male ratio among other castes did not operate among the martial castes over this period—or had already operated earlier.

This pattern is consistent with the hypothesis, widely discussed in the literature on social anthropology, that the patriarchal norms of the higher castes are gradually spreading to other castes. The most common interpretation of this phenomenon is that it reflects a process of emulation of the higher castes by the lower castes, with the lifestyle of women playing a central role in this process as a symbol of social status.[35] This process is likely to be particularly strong when the disadvantaged castes experience upward economic mobility. That the norms of the martial castes should often have been taken as the 'model' in Uttar Pradesh is not surprising, given the dominant position which these castes have occupied in that region for a long time.[36]

[34] See e.g. Tod (1929), Altekar (1956), Karve (1965), Panigrahi (1972), Hitchcock (1975), Bahadur (1978), Miller (1981), Kolenda (1984), Singh (1988).

[35] The notion of 'Sanskritization' was developed by M.N. Srinivas (1962, 1965, 1967, 1989); see also Berreman (1993), and the more recent studies cited there. Increased resistance to widow remarriage among upwardly-mobile castes (the prohibition of widow remarriage being widely perceived as an upper-caste norm) is a well-documented example of how restrictions on the lifestyle of women often play an important role in the Sanskritization process. On this, see Kolenda (1983), Drèze (1990c), Chen and Drèze (1994), Chen (forthcoming, a), and the literature cited there.

[36] On the long-standing dominance of martial castes in rural Uttar Pradesh, see Drèze and Gazdar (1996), and the literature cited there. It should be mentioned that the dominant position of these castes in the rural society of Uttar Pradesh derives less from their martial activities as such (which are now largely confined to local feuds and fist

The observed convergence of female–male ratios among scheduled castes and higher castes may have causes other than this process of emulation. It has often been suggested, for instance, that gender inequality in India tends to be relatively low among poorer households.[37] In the cross-section analysis of district female–male ratios discussed further in this chapter, it is also found that higher levels of poverty tend to go with higher female–male ratios, for a *given* composition of the population in terms of the proportion of scheduled castes and scheduled tribes. It is, in fact, plausible that the partnership aspect of gender relations is stronger in poorer households, where survival depends on effective cooperation, than among privileged households, where women tend to have a more dependent and symbolic position. And this feature of gender relations within the household, in turn, may affect the general status of women in different classes. If there is a causal association of this kind between poverty and gender inequality, then economic growth and poverty reduction may, in some respects at least, be a source of intensified female disadvantage. The sharp decline of female–male ratios among scheduled castes may be a manifestation of this economic process, rather than being directly related to caste as such.

What is not in doubt is that the convergence effect has taken place (not only in Uttar Pradesh but also in India as a whole), and that it has made some contribution to the overall decline of the female–male ratio in India since 1901.[38] The time pattern of this convergence is also interesting. Specifically, the decline of the female–male ratio among scheduled castes seems to have been particularly dramatic after 1961. In Uttar Pradesh, for instance, the female–male ratio in 1961 was not yet terribly low for the scheduled castes—941 to be exact, compared with 909 for the population as a whole. Thirty years later, the corresponding values were 877 and

---

fights) than from their temporal power as traditional landowners.

[37] For some relevant studies, see Miller (1981, 1993a), Das Gupta (1987), Krishnaji (1987), Alaka Basu (1992), Dasgupta (1993), Rogaly (1994), Murthi, Guio, and Drèze (1995).

[38] The FMR decline among scheduled castes, on its own, must have made a relatively modest contribution to the overall FMR decline in India, given the small share of this group in the total population (about 16 per cent in 1991). But the process of diffusion of the patriarchal culture of the higher castes, and related causal antecedents of the convergence effect, may have affected a broader section of the population. The widespread transition from bride-price to dowry among large parts of the population in south India illustrates this possibility.

879, indicating a massive decline of the female–male ratio among scheduled castes after 1961.[39] A similar pattern applies in India as a whole, with the female–male ratio among scheduled castes falling from 957 in 1961 (compared with 941 for the population as a whole) to 922 in 1991 (compared with 927 for the whole population). It is quite possible that the post-1961 decline of the female–male ratio in the 0–29 age group at the all-India level, noted earlier in this section, relates at least partly to the convergence effects we have just discussed.

All this is a useful reminder of the fact that economic progress on its own does not necessarily do very much to reduce gender inequalities. In fact, in so far as the convergent decline of the female–male ratio among scheduled castes is due to some process of emulation linked with their upward economic mobility, or to some other causal process related to the expansion of the economy, this seems to be a case where economic growth leads to some *intensification* of gender bias. The fact that higher levels of poverty are associated with higher female–male ratios in cross-section analysis reinforces these observations based on time trends. Clearly, the removal of gender inequalities cannot be based on some presumption that the problem will resolve itself on its own in the process of economic expansion. Punjab and Haryana are good illustrations of this point: both states have experienced rapid economic growth since independence, and are now far ahead of all other Indian states in terms of per-capita income, but they still have lower female–male ratios than any other state except Uttar Pradesh. Achieving greater gender equality involves a process of active social change which has no obvious link with economic growth.

7.3. Women's Agency and Child Survival

A number of empirical studies indicate that the extent of anti-female bias in survival is substantially reduced by various influences that give women more voice and agency within the family. One of these influences is female education, and this consideration adds to those already presented in earlier chapters on the crucial role of basic education in general and female education in particular. Another

---

[39] See Agnihotri (1994), who also presents an excellent analysis of the phenomenon of accelerated FMR decline, after 1961, among the scheduled castes in many Indian states.

factor of importance is women's ability to earn an independent income through paid employment.[40] This opportunity tends to enhance the social standing of a woman in the household and the society. Her contribution to the prosperity of the family is, then, more visible, and she also has more voice, because of being less dependent on others. Further, outside employment often has useful 'educational' effects, in terms of exposure to the world outside the family. These positive links between gainful female employment and the status of women are also relevant to the female child, in so far as they affect the importance that is attached to her development and well-being.[41]

It is worth examining more closely how these and other aspects of female agency influence male and female mortality rates, and the extent of gender bias in survival. The age patterns of male and female mortality are complex (Kynch and Sen, 1983), and the discussion in this section will be confined to mortality in the 0–4 age group—hereafter 'under-five mortality'. Countries with basic gender inequality—including India, Pakistan, Bangladesh, China, West Asia, and so on—tend to have a high ratio of female to male mortality even in this age group, in contrast with the situation in Europe or America or sub-Saharan Africa, where female children typically have a substantial survival advantage. In India itself, male and female death rates in the 0–4 age group are now quite close to each other in terms of averages for the country as a whole, but a strong female disadvantage persists in regions where gender inequality is particularly pronounced, including most states of north India.[42]

---

[40] A higher participation rate of women in so-called 'gainful' activities in sub-Saharan Africa seems to play a major role in placing women there at a less disadvantaged position compared with their counterparts in north Africa and Asia. On this see Boserup (1970), Kynch and Sen (1983), Bardhan (1984a, 1988), Sen (1984, 1989). Within India, high rates of female labour-force participation among tribal communities, and in the Himalayan region, also help to explain the comparatively favourable status of women (and relatively high female–male ratio) in these societies.

[41] See Miller (1981), Rosenzweig and Schultz (1982), Kynch and Sen (1983), Sen (1985c, 1990), Alaka Basu (1992), Guio (1994), Murthi, Guio, and Drèze (1995); also Kishor (1993, 1994), and the literature cited there. The strength of these relations, however, depends on the nature of the female employment, its social standing, and economic rewards. For further discussion of this issue, see Ursula Sharma (1980, 1986), Kalpana Bardhan (1985), Bina Agarwal (1986), Desai and Jain (1992), among others, and also Nirmala Banerjee's (1982) illuminating study of the condition of 'unorganised women workers' in Calcutta.

[42] In 1991, the death rate in the 0–4 age group (per thousand) was 25.6 for males and 27.5 for females at the all-India level. The female mortality rate in that age group was

In a recent study, Murthi, Guio, and Drèze (1995) present an analysis of variations in under-five mortality rates between different districts of India in 1981 (the latest year for which adequately detailed data are available). One aspect of this analysis is an examination of the relationship between an index of female disadvantage in child survival (reflecting the *ratio* of female to male mortality in the 0–4 age group at the district level) and a number of other district-level variables such as the female literacy rate, female labour-force participation, the incidence of poverty, the level of urbanization, the availability of medical facilities, and the proportion of scheduled castes and scheduled tribes in the population. The basic results are presented in the first column of Table 7.3.[43]

As discussed in Murthi, Guio, and Drèze (1995), what is rather striking is that the variables directly relating to women's agency (in particular, the female labour-force participation rate and the female literacy rate) have strong effects on the extent of female disadvantage in child survival, and go in the expected direction, i.e. higher levels of female literacy and labour-force participation are associated with lower levels of female disadvantage in child survival. By contrast, variables that relate to the *general* level of development and modernization either turn out to have no statistically significant effect, or suggest that modernization, if anything, *amplifies* the gender bias in child survival. This applies *inter alia* to urbanization, male literacy, the availability of medical facilities, and the level of poverty (with lower levels of poverty being associated with a *larger* female disadvantage). These results, based on cross-section evidence, reinforce an observation made earlier in connection with the decline of the female–male ratio over time: on their own, the forces of development and modernization do not necessarily lead to a rapid reduction in gender inequalities. In so far as a positive connection does exist in India between the level of development and reduced gender bias in survival,

---

lower than the male mortality rate in Andhra Pradesh, Assam, Himachal Pradesh, Kerala, and Tamil Nadu, but higher in all other major states. The female disadvantage was most pronounced in Bihar, Haryana, Madhya Pradesh, Punjab, Rajasthan, and Uttar Pradesh. See the Statistical Appendix for further details.

[43] For a detailed discussion of these results, see Drèze, Guio, and Murthi (1995) and Murthi, Guio, and Drèze (1995). Some of the findings presented there have much in common with those of an independent study carried out earlier by Sunita Kishor (1993). For related analyses based on Indian district data, see also Rosenzweig and Schultz (1982), Gulati (1992), and Khemani (1994).

TABLE 7.3. Basic Results of a Cross-section Analysis of the Determinants of Child Mortality, Fertility and Gender Bias in Indian Districts (1981)

Independent variable	Dependent variable		
	Female disadvantage in child survival (FD)	Under-five mortality rate, male and female combined (Q5)	Total fertility rate (TFR)
Constant	0.86 (3.00)*	205.82 (14.37)*	6.594 (23.10)*
Female labour-force participation (proportion of 'main workers' in the female population)	−0.02 (−3.85)*	0.44 (1.82)	−0.017 (−3.57)*
Female literacy rate (proportion of literate women in the female population)	−0.04 (−4.46)*	−0.87 (−2.45)*	−0.031 (−4.28)*
Male literacy rate (proportion of literate men in the male population)	0.015 (1.97)*	−0.49 (−1.40)	−0.005 (−0.70)
Level of urbanization (proportion of the population living in urban areas)	0.005 (1.73)	−0.31 (−2.40)*	−0.0004 (−0.15)
Availability of medical facilities (proportion of villages with some medical facilities)	0.005 (1.84)	−0.25 (−2.23)*	−0.002 (−1.04)
Level of rural poverty ('Sen index')	−0.02 (−3.13)*	0.54 (1.76)	0.007 (1.14)
Scheduled castes (proportion of scheduled-caste persons in the population)	−0.01 (−1.13)	0.55 (1.89)	−0.007 (−1.23)
Scheduled tribes (proportion of scheduled-tribe persons in the population)	−0.01 (−3.96)*	−0.60 (−3.57)*	−0.011 (−3.40)*
Dummy variables for different regions[a]			
South	−0.82 (−4.91)*	−41.50 (−3.85)*	−0.548 (2.60)*
East	0.154 (0.81)	−38.08 (−2.91)*	−0.254 (−0.99)
West	−0.15 (−0.87)	−12.35 (−1.32)	−0.379 (−2.06)*

Notes. [a] The different regions are defined as follows: South = Andhra Pradesh, Karnataka, Kerala, and Tamil Nadu; East = Bihar, Orissa, and West Bengal; West = Gujarat and Maharashtra. The 'control region', for which no dummy variable is included, consists of the northern and central states of Haryana, Madhya Pradesh, Punjab, Rajasthan, and Uttar Pradesh.

[*] Significant at 5% level (asymptotic t-ratios in brackets).

Source. Drèze, Guio, and Murthi (1995).

Explanatory Note. The observations on which these regressions are based consist of 296 districts for which the relevant data are available. All the variables relate to 1981, and are based on the 1981 census, except for the 'poverty' indicator. The poverty indicator used for each district is the Sen index of rural poverty in 1972–3 for the National Sample Survey 'region' in which the district in question is situated (the 296 districts are located in 51 different NSS regions). The regressions are based on maximum-likelihood estimation, in a model which takes into account spatial correlation in the error terms. These regressions can be interpreted as the 'reduced form' of a system of simultaneous equations which determines three endogenous variables: the total fertility rate (TFR), the level of child mortality for both sexes combined (Q5), and the extent of female disadvantage in child survival (FD), as measured by the proportionate difference between female and male child mortality (or, more precisely, by $FD = [Q5_f - Q5_m]/Q5_f$, where $Q5_f$ and $Q5_m$ are the levels of female and male child mortality, respectively). For further details on definitions, sources, estimation, diagnostics, and related issues, and a detailed discussion of the results, see Murthi, Guio, and Drèze (1995).

it seems to work *through* variables that are directly related to women's agency, such as female literacy and female labour-force participation.[44] The analysis also includes dummy variables for different regions, and it turns out that at least some of these regional dummies (particularly the 'South India' dummy) are statistically significant even after the other variables are included. In other words, the sharp contrasts that are observed between different regions of India, in terms of the relative survival chances of male and female children, are only partly explained by differences in female literacy, female labour-force participation, and other variables included in this analysis. This suggests that other variables, which may be hard to quantify, also have an important influence. Women's property rights, cultural or ideological

---

[44] There is also some evidence, from the same study, of high fertility rates being associated with low survival chances of female children *vis-à-vis* male children. This is consistent with the fact that the survival disadvantages of female children progressively worsen as we consider children of higher 'parity', that is, the second girl in a family tends to do worse than the first, and so on. On this, see particularly Das Gupta's (1987) pioneering work on rural Punjab; also M.E. Khan et al. (1989) on rural Uttar Pradesh

influences, and some aspects of the kinship system (e.g. the rules of exogamy and patrilocality) are plausible examples of such variables.[45]

A similar analysis can be used to examine the effects of different variables on the *level* of under-five mortality for males and females combined. We have already noted that higher female labour-force participation improves the *relative* survival chances of girls *vis-à-vis* boys. But this does not tell us how female labour-force participation affects the absolute levels of under-five mortality. It is, in fact, difficult to predict whether the effect of higher female labour-force participation on child survival is positive or negative.[46] There are at least two important effects to consider, working in opposite directions. First, as was discussed earlier, involvement in gainful employment has many positive effects on a woman's agency roles, which often include child-care. Second, the 'double burden' of household work and outside employment can impair women's ability to ensure the good health of their children, if only by reducing the time available for child-care activities (since men typically show great reluctance to share the domestic chores).[47] In the case of girls, a third consideration is that higher levels of female labour-force participation in the society may enhance the importance attached to the survival of a female child. The net result of these different effects is a matter of empirical investigation. The analysis of district-level data summarized in Table 7.3 (second column) suggests a positive association between female

[45] On these different influences, see the studies cited in Drèze and Sen (1989), D.B. Gupta et al. (1993), and Dasgupta (1993); also Das Gupta (1990, 1994b), Alaka Basu (1992), Sunita Kishor (1993), Bina Agarwal (1994), and Satish Agnihotri (1994, 1995), among other recent contributions. The persistence of regional influences on relative survival chances, even after controlling for a wide range of district characteristics on which quantitative data are available, has been noted earlier by Kishor (1993).

[46] The variable used to measure female labour-force participation is the ratio of female 'main workers' (women engaged in 'economically productive work' for at least 183 days in the year) to the total female population. The instructions to census investigators make it clear that unpaid 'household duties' are not to be counted as economically productive work (Government of India, 1981, pp. 106–7). The census definition of 'economically productive work' is questionable, but it serves our purpose, since we are interested in the relationship between child survival and women's independent income-earning opportunities (rather than their economic contribution generally—whether or not rewarded).

[47] For useful empirical analyses of this 'maternal dilemma' in the Indian context, see Alaka Basu (1992) and Gillespie and McNeill (1992). On the related issue of the relationship between maternal labour-force participation and child nutrition, see Leslie (1988), Leslie and Paolisso (1989), and the literature cited there.

labour-force participation and under-five mortality, but this association is not statistically significant.[48]

Female literacy, on the other hand, is unambiguously found to have a negative and statistically significant impact on under-five mortality, even after controlling for male literacy. This is consistent with growing evidence of a close relationship between female literacy and child survival in many countries, including India.[49] Further, the authors find that female literacy has a larger effect on female under-five mortality than on male under-five mortality; this is why the *ratio* of female to male mortality is lower at higher levels of female literacy, even though mortality rates fall for both male and female children as female literacy increases.

It is worth adding that, in quantitative terms, the effect of female literacy on child mortality is quite large. This point is illustrated in Table 7.4, which shows how the predicted values of the 'dependent variables' in this analysis (the extent of female disadvantage in child survival, the level of under-five mortality, and the total fertility rate) respond to changes in female literacy when the *other* exogenous variables are kept at their mean value, and similarly with male literacy and poverty. For instance, keeping other variables constant, an increase in the crude female literacy rate from, say, 22 per cent (the actual 1981 figure) to 75 per cent reduces the predicted value of under-five mortality for males and females combined from 156 per thousand (again, the actual 1981 figure) to 110 per thousand. The powerful effect of female literacy contrasts with the comparatively ineffective roles of, say, male literacy or general poverty reduction as instruments of child mortality reduction. An increase in male literacy over the same range (from 22 to 75 per cent) only reduces under-five mortality from 167 per thousand to 141 per thousand. And a 50 per cent

---

[48] As discussed in Murthi, Guio, and Drèze (1995), there is a real possibility of this association being, in fact, negative after controlling more carefully for the economic and social disadvantages that often motivate Indian women to seek paid employment. That possibility is consistent with international evidence on the relationship between female employment and child nutrition. Based on a review of 50 relevant studies, for instance, Joanne Leslie (1988) concludes that 'overall there is little evidence of a negative effect of maternal employment on child nutrition' (p. 1341).

[49] On this, see J.C. Caldwell (1979, 1986), Behrman and Wolfe (1984, 1987), Ware (1984), A.K. Jain (1985), Cleland and van Ginneken (1987, 1988), Nag (1989), Beenstock and Sturdy (1990), Cleland (1990), Das Gupta (1990), Bhuiya and Streatfield (1991), Bourne and Walker (1991), Thomas et al. (1991), Alaka Basu (1992), Barro and Lee (1993a, 1993b), D.B. Gupta et al. (1993), Subbarao and Raney (1994), among others.

TABLE 7.4. *Effects of Selected Independent Variables (Female Literacy, Male Literacy and Poverty) on Child Mortality (Q5), Female Disadvantage (FD) and Fertility (TFR)*

Assumed level of the independent variable (%)	Predicted values of Q5, FD and TFR when the female literacy rate takes the value indicated in the first column			Predicted values of Q5, FD and TFR when the male literacy rate takes the value indicated in the first column			Predicted values of Q5, FD and TFR when the proportion of the population below the poverty line takes the value indicated in the first column[a]		
	Q5	FD	TFR	Q5	FD	TFR	Q5	FD	TFR
10	166.4	10.7	5.38	172.9	−2.0	5.18	151.5	9.8	4.79
20	157.7	5.9	5.07	168.0	−0.1	5.13	152.7	8.5	4.85
30	149.0	1.1	4.76	163.1	1.8	5.08	153.8	7.1	4.91
40	140.2	−3.3	4.45	158.2	3.9	5.03	154.9	5.8	4.97
50	131.5	−7.1	4.15	153.3	5.9	4.98	156.0	4.4	5.03
60	122.8	−10.3	3.84	148.4	8.0	4.93	157.2	3.1	5.09
70	114.0	−12.8	3.53	143.5	10.1	4.88	158.3	1.8	5.15
80	105.3	−14.8	3.22	138.7	12.2	4.83	159.5	0.5	5.21

Note. [a] For convenience of interpretation, the 'Sen index' of poverty has been replaced, in this table, by the 'head–count ratio' (i.e. the proportion of the population below the poverty line). The figures presented in the last three columns are based on the same regressions as in Table 7.3, with the Sen index replaced by the head–count ratio.

Source. Drèze, Guio, and Murthi (1995), based on the regressions presented in Table 7.3. The variables Q5, FD, and TFR are defined as in that table.

reduction in the incidence of poverty (from the actual 1981 level) only reduces the predicted value of under-five mortality from 156 per thousand to 153 per thousand.

Here again, the message seems to be that some variables relating to women's agency (in this case, female literacy) often play a much more important role in promoting social well-being (in particular, child survival) than variables relating to the general level of opulence in the society. These findings have important practical implications, given that both types of variables can be influenced through public action, but require very different forms of intervention.

7.4. *Fertility and Women's Emancipation*

It is not surprising that the agency of women is also particularly important for achievements in population policy. The serious adverse effects of high birth rates include their impact on the lives women can lead, and the drudgery of continuous child bearing and rearing, which is routinely imposed on many Asian and African women. There is, as a result, a close connection between women's *well-being* and women's *agency* in bringing about a change in the fertility pattern. Women in India have to face the lack of freedom to do other things that goes with a high frequency of births, not to mention the dangers of repeated pregnancy and high maternal mortality. It is, thus, understandable that reductions in birth rates have often been associated with enhancement of women's status and voice.

These connections are indeed reflected in inter-district variations of the total fertility rate, as Tables 7.3 and 7.4 indicate. In fact, among all the variables included in the analysis, other than regional dummies and ethnic composition, the only ones that have a statistically significant effect on fertility are female literacy and female labour-force participation. Once again, the importance of women's agency emerges forcefully from this analysis, especially in comparison with the weaker effects of variables relating to general economic progress.

The link between female literacy and fertility is particularly clear. This connection has been widely observed in other countries, and it is not surprising that it should emerge in India too.[50] The un-

---

[50] For recent empirical analyses of this connection at the international level, see Barro and Lee (1993a, 1993b), Cassen (1994), and Subbarao and Raney (1994). On the connection between fertility and female education in India, see Vlassoff (1980), Jain and Nag (1985, 1986), J.C. Caldwell et al. (1989), Satia and Jejeebhoy (1991), Alaka Basu

willingness of educated women to be shackled to continuous child-rearing clearly plays a role in bringing about this change. Education also makes the horizon of vision wider, and, at a more mundane level, helps to disseminate the knowledge of family planning.

As we discussed in chapter 4, Kerala's particular experience of fertility reduction based on women's agency is quite remarkable, and has extremely important lessons for the rest of India. While the total fertility rate for India as a whole is still as high as 3.7, that rate in Kerala has now fallen below the 'replacement level' of 2.1 to 1.8. Kerala's high level of female education has been particularly influential in bringing about this decline in the birth rate.[51]

There is also some demographic evidence to indicate that birth rates tend to go down following the decline of death rates. This is partly because the need for having many children to ensure some survivors goes down with lower mortality rates, but also because of the complementarity between the respective means of birth control and death control (giving people access to contraception can be effectively combined with delivery of medical attention and health care). In Kerala, the sharp reduction of death rates has been followed by a rapid decline of fertility, with the birth rate falling from 44 per thousand in 1951–61 to 18 by 1991. Since female agency and literacy are important in the reduction of mortality rates (as was discussed in the last section), this is another—more indirect—route through which women's agency, in general, and female literacy, in particular, can reduce birth rates (in addition to the direct impacts mentioned earlier).

Recently, there has been a good deal of discussion of the imperative need to reduce birth rates in the world, and those in India in particular. China's achievement in cutting down birth rates over a short period through rather draconian measures has suggested to many the need for India to emulate China in this respect. As was discussed in chapter 4, however, the coercive methods do involve many social costs, including the direct one of the loss of the effective freedom of people—in particular, women—to decide themselves on matters that are clearly rather personal. That aspect of the problem is often dismissed, especially in the West, on the grounds that cultural differences between

(1992, 1993), Das Gupta (1994a), Egerö et al. (1994), Parikh (1995), Visaria and Visaria (1994); also Alaka Basu and Roger Jeffery (forthcoming) and the literature cited there.

[51] On these issues, see also Krishnan (1976, 1991, 1994), Kabir and Krishnan (1992), Mari Bhat and Rajan (1990, 1992), Zachariah et al. (1994).

Asia and the West make such policies acceptable in the Third World in a way they would not be in the West.[52] Cultural relativism is a tricky terrain, and while it is easy enough to refer to despotic Oriental traditions, that line of reasoning would be no more convincing than making judgements on what to do in the Western societies today on the basis of the history of Spanish inquisitions or Nazi concentration camps.

It is not clear how the acceptability of coercion can be tested except through democratic confrontation. While that testing has not occurred in China, it was indeed attempted in India during the Emergency period in the seventies when compulsory birth control was tried by Mrs Gandhi's government, along with suspending various legal rights and civil liberties. The policy of coercion in general—including that in birth control—was overwhelmingly defeated in the general elections that followed. Furthermore, family-planning experts have noted how voluntary birth-control programmes received a severe set-back from that brief programme of compulsory sterilization, as people had become deeply suspicious of the entire movement. The coercive measures of the Emergency period, in fact, aside from having little immediate impact on fertility rates, were followed by a long period of *stagnation* in the birth rate, which only ended in 1985.[53]

There is evidence that some forms of compulsion or forceful pressure to accept birth control (especially sterilization) continue to be used in some Indian states, particularly in the north, where fertility rates tend to be high. Even when coercion is not part of official policy, the government's firm insistence on 'meeting the family-planning targets' often leads administrators and health-care personnel at different levels to resort to all kinds of pressure tactics that come close to compulsion.[54] Examples of such tactics include verbal threats, making sterilization a condition of eligibility for anti-poverty programmes,

---

[52] See, for example, Hardin (1993).

[53] See Bose (1991a), pp. 67–8. The Emergency period also caused a substantial *decline* in medical attendance at birth, and a large *increase* in neo-natal mortality rates, and it took five years for the pre-Emergency levels of these variables to be restored; on this, see Tulasidhar and Sarma (1993).

[54] This phenomenon is mentioned in many field-based studies recently carried out in north India; see e.g. Iyengar and Bhargava (1987), p. 1087, D. Banerji (1989), p. 1477, P. Jeffery et al. (1989), p. 216, H.N. Singh (1993), p. 35, Gidwani (1994), p. 40, Drèze, Lanjouw, and Sharma (forthcoming). It is no consolation that family-planning targets are apparently being replaced, in official parlance, by 'expected levels of achievement' (see Visaria and Visaria, 1994).

depriving mothers of more than two children from maternity benefits, reserving certain kinds of health care services to persons who have been sterilized, and forbidding persons who have more than two children from contesting panchayat elections.[55] The long-run consequences of these practices can be quite disastrous both for health care and for the consensual emergence of social norms favouring smaller families.

What also has to be borne in mind is the fact, discussed in chapter 4, that compulsion has not produced a lower birth rate in China compared with what Kerala has already achieved entirely through voluntary channels, relying on the educated agency of women. In fact, it is not at all clear (for reasons discussed earlier) exactly how much of *extra* reduction in birth rate China has been able to achieve by resorting to coercive methods. What must be taken into account in trying to assess the contribution of compulsion is that China has had many social and economic attainments that are favourable to fertility reduction, including expansion of education in general and female education in particular, augmentation of health care, enhancement of employment opportunities for women, and, recently, rapid economic development. These factors would themselves have reduced the birth rates (well below that of the Indian average, for example). While China seems to get too much credit for its authoritarian measures, it gets far too little credit for other—supportive—policies that have helped to cut down the birth rate.

Kerala's low birth rate—lower than China's—also suggests that these supportive influences may be effective enough to render compulsion quite redundant, even if it were acceptable otherwise. As has been noted before, Kerala not only has a much higher level of female literacy (86 per cent) than India as a whole (39 per cent), it is also well ahead of China's female literacy rate (68 per cent).[56] The fact that the ranking of female literacy is exactly the same as that

[55] It is quite extraordinary that the last measure (recently introduced in Rajasthan and Haryana) has been widely praised, even though it involves a strong violation not only of personal liberty but also of basic democratic values. Even the government's draft National Population Policy, despite placing emphasis on the need to reject coercive methods, gives full support to this measure as one means of meeting the overriding goal of bringing the total fertility rate down to 2.1 by the year 2010 (Government of India, 1994c, p. 40). At the time of writing, there is a strong possibility of the proposed measure being adopted at the all-India level, and extended to diverse forms of political participation other than the contesting of panchayat elections.

[56] See Table 4.2 in chapter 4.

of birth rates is in line with other evidence for the close connection between the two. It might also be mentioned here, in passing, that the increasing popularity of sex-selective abortion of female foetuses in China, as well as parts of India, contrasts sharply with the absence of such a practice in Kerala. While the solution of this problem has been sought in India through banning sex-selective abortion—a ban that may well be evaded easily enough—the real resolution of the problem must lie ultimately in a shift in family preference away from the rejection of female children.

As we saw in chapter 4, Kerala is not alone in having achieved a rapid reduction of the birth rate without compulsion. A similar—if not equally rapid—success has also occurred in Tamil Nadu, where the total fertility rate (2.2 in 1991) is now very close to the replacement level. A significant acceleration of fertility decline has also occurred during the eighties in a number of other states.[57] Further, what is rather striking is that the states where fertility decline remains extremely slow (including Uttar Pradesh, Bihar, Rajasthan, and Madhya Pradesh) are precisely those where coercive methods, by all available accounts, have been most extensively used.

These diverse experiences reinforce the general arguments presented earlier in favour of a collaborative approach to fertility reduction, based on due recognition of the agency of women in bringing down fertility and mortality rates. An unequivocal rejection of all coercive and heavy-handed methods (including those that are currently being used) is essential from many points of view, including those of fertility reduction, mortality reduction, women's well-being, and elementary freedom.[58]

---

[57] See Visaria and Visaria (1994).

[58] Aside from the imperative need to reject coercive methods, it is also important to promote the *quality* and diversity of non-coercive means of family planning. As things stand, family planning in India is overwhelmingly dominated by female sterilization, even in the southern states. To illustrate, while nearly 40 per cent of currently-married women aged 13–49 in south India are sterilized, only 14 per cent of women in that group have *ever* used a non-terminal, modern contraception method. Even the *knowledge* of modern methods of family planning other than sterilization is extraordinarily limited in India. Only half of rural married women aged 13–49, for instance, seem to know what a condom or IUD is. On these matters, see International Institute for Population Sciences (1994), and also Table A.3 in the Statistical Appendix of this book.

7.5. Widowhood and Gender Relations

One consequence of the low participation of Indian women in public life and political activity is that many social issues relating to women and gender relations receive far too little attention. In recent years, there has been improved awareness of some specific aspects of gender inequality and female deprivation, such as the problem of low female–male ratios and the anti-female bias in child survival. But many other issues continue to get low social recognition; they apparently haven't yet caught the attention of the male-dominated society. Examples include the problem of reproductive health and maternal mortality (severely neglected in health research and policy), the widespread violation of women's legal property rights (aside from the persistence of continued anti-female bias in the law itself), and the general acceptance of endemic violence against women.

Another striking example of the low social visibility of some important aspects of the condition of women concerns the well-being of widows.[59] There are about 33 million widows in India, representing 8 per cent of the female population—a proportion similar to that of agricultural labourers in the male population.[60] Further, there is a good deal of evidence of the deprived condition of many widows in India. A recent demographic study, for instance, concludes that mortality rates are, on average, 86 per cent higher among elderly widows than among married women of the same age.[61] Similarly, economic surveys indicate that the loss of one's husband often leads to a sharp decline of household income. Anthropological studies have also highlighted the fact that many widows suffer from social marginalization and psychological hardship, in addition to being particularly vulnerable to poverty.

It should be added that the *prospect* of widowhood reduces the quality of life of most Indian women, even if only a minority of

---

[59] On this, see Drèze (1990c), Chen and Drèze (1994, 1995) Chen (forthcoming, a), and the literature cited there. This section draws extensively on these studies. It should be mentioned that, while widows represent the vast majority of single adult women in India, other single women (e.g. those who are divorced or separated) also tend to experience major social disadvantages. For some relevant studies, see Krishnakumari (1987) and Dandavate et al. (1989).

[60] See Government of India (1993b), p. 71, and Nanda (1992), pp. 115, 155. The reference year is 1991.

[61] See Mari Bhat (1994). These results corroborate earlier findings for Bangladesh (see Rahman et al., 1992).

them are actually widowed at any particular point in time. The proportion of widows in the female population rises sharply with age, reaching 63 per cent among women aged 60 and above, and close to 80 per cent among women aged 70 and above. In other words, an Indian woman who survives to old age is most likely to become a widow. The prospect of losing their husband at some stage cannot but affect the lives of Indian women even before that event. For instance, there is a close relationship between widowhood, old-age insecurity, and fertility decisions in the early stages of married life.

In spite of their magnitude and significance, the deprivations of widows rarely feature in public debates, in the media, or even in social science research, except when—in a small number of cases—they take a sensational form, such as *sati*. This fact relates to the general point, made in section 5.1, that endemic but quiet deprivations are often much harder to bring to public attention than sensational events such as a famine or natural disaster. A similar point can be made in relation to other aspects of women's deprivation. The frequent media focus on rape, for instance, contrasts with the quiet acceptance of widespread domestic violence against women.

If widowhood is such a neglected social issue, it is partly because the experience of losing one's spouse is, overwhelmingly, a woman's experience. Only 2.5 per cent of all Indian men are widowed, compared with 8.1 per cent of women.[62] Further, the consequences of losing one's spouse are very different for men and women. A widower not only has greater freedom to remarry than his female counterpart, he also has more extensive property rights, wider opportunities for remunerative employment, and a more authoritative claim on economic support from his children. Had the living conditions of widowers been as precarious as those of widows, it is likely that widowed persons would have attracted far more attention.

The circumstances of widows vary a great deal between different regions, communities, classes, and age groups. Nevertheless, it is possible to identify some basic factors of disadvantage and insecurity experienced by many Indian widows. The following considerations emerge with particular force from recent surveys carried out in north India.[63]

[62] Government of India (1993b), p. 71. This large gender gap primarily reflects a high incidence of remarriage among widowers.

[63] For the evidence, and further discussion, see Drèze (1990c) and Chen and Drèze (1994, 1995).

First, a strong tradition of patrilineal ownership, which modern legislation has only begun to challenge, makes it hard for many widows to defend their legal inheritance rights. Formally, according to contemporary Indian law, a widow has an unequivocal right to a share of her husband's property, including his land.[64] This is in addition to the legal rights she has—irrespective of her marital status—to a share of her parents' property. Field studies, however, indicate that these legal rights are comprehensively violated, and that a large majority of widows have very limited and insecure property rights. This deprivation of property rights not only represents the loss of a potential source of independent income, but also diminishes the bargaining power of a widow *vis-à-vis* her in-laws, sons, and other potential supporters.

Second, the norms of patrilocal residence are an important cause of social isolation. In north India, widows are expected to remain in their husband's village, and most of them do so. At the same time, they are unlikely to receive much support from their in-laws. On the contrary, the relationship between a widow and her in-laws is typically quite tense (property rights being one of the most common sources of tension). Widows are thus denied both the freedom to leave their husband's village, and the support they need to live there happily.

Third, widows have a limited freedom to remarry. In some communities, particularly in north-west India, ascriptive leviratic unions (e.g. between a widow and her brother-in-law) remain quite common. Elsewhere, the standard pattern is that most childless widows remarry, but only a small proportion of widowed mothers do so.

Fourth, the gender division of labour severely restricts employment opportunities for widows. Census data indicate that age-specific labour-force participation rates are a little higher for widows than for married women. But the low involvement of north Indian women in gainful employment—irrespective of marital status—is the basic problem. Further, because widows tend to be concentrated in the older age groups, their average labour-force participation rate is lower than that of married women.

Fifth, most widows can expect little economic support from their

---

[64] According to the Hindu Succession Act of 1956, for instance, a widow is entitled to the same share of her husband's land as other 'Class 1' heirs (these also include the deceased person's children and widowed mother, if alive). On the general issue of women's land rights in India, see Bina Agarwal (1988, 1994).

family or community, except possibly in the form of co-residence with one of their adult sons. In particular, the notion that the joint family provides economic security to widows in rural India is little more than a myth. Most surveys find that co-residence of a widow with her in-laws is rare in north India (except in cases of leviratic unions), and that the relationship between a widow and her deceased husband's family is often far from harmonious. An overwhelming majority of widows live on their own, with their unmarried children, or as a dependent in the household of one of their adult sons.

As these observations illustrate, there are close links between the position of widows in society and a whole range of patriarchal institutions such as patrilineal inheritance, patrilocal residence, remarriage norms, and the gender division of labour. In that sense, the cause of widows must be seen as an integral part of the larger battle against gender inequalities.

Taking effective action (e.g. aimed at expanding women's land rights) requires a combination of public pressure and state response. The first task is to bring the issue closer to the centre of public attention. The agency of the women's movement is central to this challenge, and so is that of widows themselves.[65]

7.6. *Gender Equality and Social Progress*

Earlier in this chapter, we have had several occasions to note the role of women's agency in social progress. In particular, we have discussed the connections between women's agency and child survival, and also between women's agency and fertility, based on an analysis of inter-district variations in under-five mortality. These connections also show up in more aggregative comparisons of different regions in India. In fact, it is rather striking that the demographically 'backward' regions of India (where mortality, and also fertility, are particularly

---

[65] Many Indian widows—and other single women—have shown that they are not just victims of the existing social order, but also spirited agents of change; see e.g. Bhatia (forthcoming), Chen (forthcoming, b), and Omvedt (1989a). The last author, in a very enlightening account of collective action by single women in Sangli district (Maharashtra), emphasizes 'the militancy of these women, who tend to provide the vanguard of toiling women's struggles everywhere' (p. 911). It is, in fact, not surprising that single women have often been found at the forefront of social and political movements. Indeed, freedom from conjugal control and the need to earn an independent living often lead single women to adopt a more autonomous and assertive lifestyle than their married sisters.

high) tend to be those where gender relations are highly unequal. This applies particularly to the large north Indian states (Uttar Pradesh, Bihar, Madhya Pradesh, and Rajasthan). Even in Punjab and Haryana, mortality and fertility rates are not much lower than the all-India averages (in fact, the fertility rate in Haryana is higher than the Indian average), despite very high levels of per-capita income in comparison with other Indian states, and this may have something to do with the comprehensive subordination of women in these two states.

Conversely, states which have experienced rapid progress in improving health and reducing mortality and fertility are often those where women play an important social or economic role. Two striking examples are Kerala and Manipur.[66] The empowerment of women has had a different basis in each case: the early promotion of female literacy (and, perhaps, the influence of matrilineal communities) has played a crucial role in Kerala, while other sources of female emancipation (including the economic roles of women) appear to have been more central in the case of Manipur. But the common feature is that, in both cases, women have ended up with a far more equal and active role in the society than their sisters in, say, the large north Indian states. And, correspondingly, there has been far more progress in the fields of health and mortality reduction, not just in terms of reducing the female disadvantage in survival, but also in improving survival chances for *everyone*.

There is a sense in which this connection is quite obvious. Given the gender division of labour that prevails in most of India, nutrition, child health, and related matters typically depend primarily on women's decisions and actions. It is hardly surprising that social achievements in this domain are more impressive where women are better educated, more resourceful, more valued, more influential, and generally more equal agents within the household and in society.

The importance of women's agency, of course, is not confined to the field of demographic change. When the creative abilities and personal contributions of one half of the society are stifled by constant subjugation, in addition to the drudgery of constant domestic work and child-bearing, social opportunities are suppressed in a wide range of domains. Even the level of economic production is likely to

---

[66] On Kerala, see the case study by V.K. Ramachandran (1996) in the companion volume, and the literature cited there. The case of Manipur, where birth and death rates are comparable to those of Kerala, is examined in A.K. Shiva Kumar (1992, 1994).

be higher, other things being equal, in a society where women are able to engage in a diverse range of activities compared with that in a society where their life is confined to domestic work. The realms of politics and social reform can also be considerably enriched by the active participation of women.

This general connection, too, emerges from broad inter-regional comparisons. Kerala not only has much lower levels of mortality and fertility than, say, Uttar Pradesh or Rajasthan, it has also made far more progress in removing traditional social inequalities, in using public services as a basis for enhancing the quality of life, and in evolving a vigorous civil society. By comparison, the large north Indian states are notorious for the persistence of feudal agrarian relations, for the continued oppression of disadvantaged castes, for chaotic public services, and for the comprehensive corruption of political institutions. Even in comparison with south India as a whole (not just Kerala), these north Indian states present a picture of resilient social backwardness. If one were to look for the deep historical roots of these inter-regional contrasts in the nature of society and politics, the position of women in society is certainly one of the influences that would command attention.

What is also striking is how the gender factor can overpower many other influences that often receive more attention, such as religious identity and national boundaries. We have already seen that the extent of anti-female bias in child survival does not vary much, if at all, between Hindus and Muslims in north India. Nor does it vary much between north India and Pakistan. The entire northern region is one where the agency of women has been comprehensively repressed, among Hindus as much as among Muslims or Sikhs, leading not only to a severe female disadvantage in child survival but also to the persistence of very high levels of mortality and fertility. Similarly, it is remarkable that Kerala and Sri Lanka have so much in common in terms of social achievements, cutting across the religious, cultural, and national boundaries. Here again, the common heritage of less unequal gender relations (which includes less patriarchal kinship systems, less male-dominated property rights, and a greater prominence of women in influential economic, social, and political activities) appears to be a causal factor of major importance.

By way of conclusion, we would like to focus on four elementary points. First, the persistence of extraordinarily high levels of gender inequality and female deprivation are among India's most serious social failures. Few other regions in the world have achieved so little in promoting gender justice.

Second, gender inequality does not decline automatically with the process of economic growth. In fact, we have seen that some important forces operate in the reverse direction (e.g. the tendency of upwardly-mobile castes to restrict the lifestyle of women in order to achieve a higher social status). Even where economic growth has a positive influence on the status of women, e.g. by expanding female employment opportunities or literacy rates, this influence tends to be slow and indirect. It is important to aim at more radical and rapid social change based on public action.

Third, gender inequality is not only a social failure in itself, it also leads to other social failures. We have illustrated this link in some detail with particular reference to child mortality and general fertility, but have also pointed to similar links that apply in other fields where the agency of women is important.

Finally, the agency of women as a force for change is one of the most neglected aspects of the development literature, and this neglect applies as forcefully—or more—in India as anywhere else. There has, happily, been a growing awareness in recent years of the disadvantaged predicament of women in Indian society. That understanding of the victimization of women has to be supplemented by a recognition of women as agents of social change. It is not merely that more justice must be received by women, but also that social justice can be achieved only through the active agency of women. The suppression of women from participation in social, political, and economic life hurts the people as a whole, not just women. Those regions in India, such as Kerala, which have moved in the direction of more gender equality have received more for all from that move. The emancipation of women is an integral part of social progress, not just a 'women's issue'.

8

WELL BEYOND LIBERALIZATION

8.1 *What is the Cage?*

A tiger in a cage adorned the cover of the informative survey of the Indian economy that *The Economist* published on 4 May 1991.[1] The Indian economy was then in deep trouble, and the special report began with a crisp diagnosis: 'The future of India looks more threatened than for many years'. The analysis put much of the blame for India's economic predicament on its 'ever-proliferating bureaucracy' and its 'licence raj', and expressed the dialectic hope that with the election then due, 'the new government will immediately face a fiscal crisis' and as a consequence it 'might—just might—start a reappraisal of the economic role of government that is so long overdue'. The events that ushered in the economic reforms after the new elections did not depart very far from that scenario.

The analogy of the caged tiger was an appropriate one in many ways (even if *The Economist* might have been over-kind in referring to 'India's boundless potential'). India does have a long history of commerce, trade, and sophisticated industrial production; even at the time of the industrial revolution, Lancashire had to resort to rather wily tactics to compete with India's unpowered but refined cotton textile industry. It has had a labour force of talent which has shown the ability to adapt to new technical challenges given the opportunity to do so. And Indian entrepreneurs and professionals have been remarkably successful in a variety of economic operations outside India, varying from running neighbourhood grocery stores

---

[1] 'A Survey of India', *The Economist*, 4 May 1991. The report was prepared by Clive Crook.

(outdoing, for example, 'the nation of shopkeepers' in efficient shop-keeping) to making industrial and trading fortunes (taking an ell whenever they have been given an inch). There certainly is some animal in the cage.

The reforms that were introduced by the end of 1991 have indeed concentrated on removing the 'licence raj' and the 'ever-proliferating bureaucracy'. While the reforms have not moved as fast as was anticipated, there have been serious attempts in that general direction, and a promise of furtherance as and when circumstances permit. The liberalization that has occurred has led to a considerable expansion of exports in some sectors and a substantial improvement in the foreign exchange balance. It also has already led to a remarkable international response—involving a buoyant investment interest and high financial rating of the new economic policies. The appreciation has not been confined only to financial commentators with a long-standing interest in the Indian economy (such as *The Economist*), but has also included the normally more aloof American business interest groups, with the redoubtable *Forbes* magazine picturing India on the cover (23 May 1994), with the note: 'India may be the best emerging market of all'.

Yet the development performance of the Indian economy remains quite moderate. Even in terms of just the growth of GNP, GDP, and industrial production, the annual rates of expansion during 1991–4 (since the reforms) are all significantly *lower* than those achieved in the previous decade.[2] While the growth rate of GDP has risen over time from the first year of reform (a point that is often repeated by the government), it has not so far caught up with the pre-reform average growth of the eighties. The 'uncaging of the tiger' has not—at least not yet—led to any dynamic animal springing out and sprinting ahead.

The central issue, however, is not the moderate performance in overall economic growth. Rather, it is a question of the preparedness of the country for large-scale *participatory* growth, an issue to which we shall return presently. The year-to-year growth of GNP and GDP can, quite possibly, move up rapidly (as it is already doing to some extent), but the country remains handicapped economically and socially by its overwhelming illiteracy, backwardness in health

---

[2] See the Government of India's (1995) latest *Economic Survey* (p. 2 and Appendix); also Table A.4 in the Statistical Appendix of this book.

care, and other crucial deprivations. The hesitancy of the overall growth rate may well be cured soon enough, but these limitations would still continue to restrain the participatory possibilities of the growth process. As was argued earlier, the cage that keeps the Indian economy well tamed is not only that of bureaucracy and governmental overactivity, but also that of illiteracy, undernourishment, ill health, and social inequalities, and their causal antecedents: governmental neglect and public apathy.[3]

This recognition does not entail a dismissal of the diagnosis of bureaucratic overactivity, or a disputation of the need for basic economic reforms. In this monograph we have tried to argue for a broader view of economic development, which has to be seen in terms of expanding social opportunities.[4] While the removal of barriers to using markets can significantly enhance such opportunities, the practical usability of these opportunities requires the sharing of certain basic capabilities—including those associated particularly with literacy and education (and also those connected with basic health, social security, gender equality, land rights, local democracy). The rapid expansion of these capabilities depends crucially on public action of a kind that has been severely neglected in India—both before and after the recent reforms. The real issue in 'uncaging' the tiger is the need to go *well beyond* liberalization.

In principle, the social role of the government seems to be widely accepted by all. In particular, the rhetoric of every Indian government—without exception—has included handsome tribute to the importance of basic education. The real issue is not rhetorical acceptability, but the willingness to put actual—not imagined—emphasis on this particular requirement for the transformation of the Indian economy. This simply has not happened. While India has a highly developed—if overextended—higher education sector (sending nearly six times as many people to the universities and institutions of higher learning as China does, compared with its population), it remains one of the most backward countries in the world in terms of elementary education.[5] Its literacy rates are low in the Asian

---

[3] See chapters 3–6.

[4] See chapters 1–3.

[5] This was already beginning to be the case in 1970 when one of the authors of this monograph gave the Lal Bahadur Shastri Memorial Lecture on this subject, under the title 'The Crisis in Indian Education' (Sen, 1970), but all the criticisms then made are even more true today—25 years further on.

context (though higher in comparison with its like-minded neighbours, Pakistan and Bangladesh), and they are well behind the achievements of the more forward-looking countries in sub-Saharan Africa.[6]

With nearly half the people—and close to two-thirds of the women—illiterate, the transformation of the Indian economy is no easy task.[7] Even an efficient utilization of the world market requires production to specification, needs quality control, and depends on an informed consciousness of the economic tasks involved. The success of the east Asian 'tigers', and more recently of China, has been based on a much higher level of literacy and basic education than India has. This is one layer of the 'cage' that incarcerates the Indian economy and society.

This diagnosis is not concerned primarily with the overall rate of growth of GNP per head, even though it is hard to assume that illiteracy and ill health are not barriers to achieving high economic performance. India has had comparatively high rates of growth of per capita GNP in the eighties (before the reforms), and can achieve that again—and much more—in the future. The overall growth rate can be pushed up by rapid expansion of some favourably placed sectors. It is also quite possible, as many commentators have argued, that the slowness of the economic reforms is holding things up, and that a quickening of essential reforms would speed up the average growth rate of the Indian economy. Some sectors of the economy, especially those that rely on high skills of the kind that India already has plentifully (such as basic computer proficiency), have already been growing fast and can expand a lot faster. But, to have an impact on India's widespread poverty, what is needed is an expansion on a much wider basis (as has happened in, say, South Korea or China), and this would be extremely difficult to achieve without a much more inclusive base of basic education.[8]

The central issue, as was already stated, is not just the overall growth rate, and the reasons for concern go much beyond the current 'growth frustration', which could well change in the near future. We have particularly emphasized the need for *participatory* economic expansion, which is not the same thing as high achievement in

---

[6] Chapters 3 and 6.

[7] *The Economist* in its 'caged tiger' report had also, in fact, noted the need for public programmes of elementary education.

[8] See chapters 3 and 4.

some particular sectors (oriented to more specialized—and more middle-class—skills), nor just the same as a high rate of growth of aggregate GNP per head.[9] For example, in the sixties and seventies, the Brazilian economy grew very fast but achieved rather little reduction of poverty, particularly in terms of social backwardness and sectional deprivation. The lack of participatory nature of that growth was extremely important in that outcome. Comparing Brazil's problems with patterns of more inclusive growth processes in east Asia tends to bring out the big difference made by a process of widely-shared, participatory growth, and the specific role of widespread basic education in fostering growth of this kind.[10] There is something quite important in this choice.[11] India stands in some danger of going Brazil's way, rather than South Korea's.

This does not affect in any way the diagnosis that India offers great investment opportunities in particular sectors even without any further expansion of basic education and health care. The *Forbes* magazine could well be exactly right in identifying India as 'the best emerging market of all' (India's middle class is probably larger than that of any other country), and yet this does not entail—and *Forbes* had not suggested it would—that this is a big force in eliminating poverty and deprivation of the Indian masses. The lessons from east Asia and China are not just about growth, but about widely-shared growth, assisted by careful social support.

8.2. People as Ends and as Means

We began this monograph by quoting Nehru's speech at the eve of independence, when he identified the 'tasks ahead' as 'the ending of poverty and ignorance and disease and inequality of opportunity'. The elimination of ignorance, of illiteracy, of remediable poverty, of preventable disease, and of needless inequalities in opportunities

[9] On this see also Drèze and Sen (1989), Part iii, and particularly the analysis of what was called 'unaimed opulence'.

[10] See particularly Birdsall and Sabot (1993a, 1993b). On aspects of the Brazilian experience, see also Sachs (1990). On aspects of Korean economic development, see also Amsden (1989), Wade (1990), and the earlier studies of Hong and Krueger (1975), Adelman and Robinson (1978), Datta Chaudhuri (1979), and Westphal et al. (1988).

[11] On the contrast between growth in Brazil and South Korea, and more generally between Latin American and east Asian patterns of economic expansion, see also McGuire (1994).

were to be seen as objectives that are valued for their own sake. They expand our freedom to lead the lives we have reason to value, and these elementary capabilities are of importance on their own.[12]

These capabilities can and do also contribute much to economic growth and to making the growth process participatory (as was discussed in the earlier chapters of this book), and human capabilities are among the chief means of economic success. But this excellence as means should not overshadow the *intrinsic* importance of human capabilities and effective freedom as the ends of social and political organization. We must not make the mistake—common in some circles—of taking the growth rate of GNP to be the ultimate test of success, and of treating the removal of illiteracy, ill health, etc., as—at best—possible means to that hallowed end. The first and the most important aspect of Nehru's listing of what we have to do is to make clear that the elimination of illiteracy, ill health and other avoidable deprivations are valuable for their own sake—they are 'the tasks' that we face.

In this sense, it is perhaps a mistake to see the development of education, health care, and other basic achievements *only* or *primarily* as expansions of 'human resources'—the accumulation of 'human capital'—as if people were just the *means* of production and not its ultimate *end*. The bettering of human life does not have to be justified by showing that a person with a better life is also a better producer. As Kant had noted, there is a categorical need to 'treat humanity, whether in their own person or in that of any other, in every case as an end withal, never as means only'. In arguing for a view of economic development that focuses on human capabilities, we are not just arguing for giving importance to so-called 'human capital'.

However, after noting this basic point, and getting our ends and means sorted out, we have every reason to pay full attention to the importance of human capabilities *also as instruments* for economic and social performance. A quality that is of intrinsic importance can, in addition, also be instrumentally momentous, without compromising its intrinsic value. Basic education, good health, and other human attainments are not only directly valuable as constituent elements of our basic capabilities, these capabilities can also help in

---

[12] See chapter 2 and the literature cited there.

generating economic success of a more standard kind, which in turn can contribute to enhancing the quality of human life in other ways.

The instrumental analysis has to be integrated with the intrinsic importance of human capabilities and effective freedoms. There are, thus, two distinct elements in this view of economic development: (1) the intrinsic and inalienable eminence of basic capabilities and the quality of life, and (2) the contingent but significant practical importance of many of these capabilities (especially those related to education, health, and elementary freedoms) in promoting participatory economic growth and, through it, further advancing the quality of life that people can enjoy. It is this dual concern that has largely motivated the approach we have tried to present in this work—a 'people-centred' approach, which puts human agency (rather than organizations such as markets or governments) at the centre of the stage.

8.3. *Radical Needs and Moderate Reforms*

The concentration on participatory growth calls for an integrated view of the process of economic expansion—focusing on the significance of economic growth, on the one hand, and on the importance of the participatory character of that growth, on the other. The crucial role of wide participation is central to this approach, and in so far as this requirement is missed out in policy discussions, that omission calls for rectification. At the same time, we must not confound that requirement with a rejection of the importance of economic growth itself. There has to be growth for it to be participatory.

While the neglect of social opportunities through the lack of adequate progress in basic education, health care, social security, land reforms, and similar fields has been detrimental to economic and social development in India, so has been the neglect of the appropriate incentives for economic efficiency and expansion. In pointing to the part of the 'cage' that the reformers often tend to ignore, we have no intention of dismissing the other part of the 'cage' that does motivate them. We are arguing for a more complete view of the difficulties that the Indian economy faces, not for shifting our diagnosis from one lopsided view to another. The fact that the boat of Indian officialdom has managed, in the past, to crash on both Scylla and Charybdis at the same time (a feat unknown to Ulysses) does not tell us to avoid only one of these dangers, overlooking the other.

There is scope for serious debate about many aspects of the economic reforms that are currently being introduced in India, and specific arguments have been presented in different directions.[13] Both the exact content of the reforms, and the policy approach in which they are embedded, call for much scrutiny. But these questions do not undermine the general necessity and desirability of removing counterproductive regulations and restrictions, nor of allowing greater use of the opportunities of international exchange. India has paid a heavy price for its overregulated and dysfunctional rules of economic governance, and there is a clear case for removing that handicap.

The counterproductive effects of many governmental restrictions, controls, and regulations in India have been clear for a long time, and have indeed been denounced by scholars and observers of many different persuasions. This problem has not been confined to India only, and has been a general feature of a number of developing countries, including India's neighbours in south Asia.[14] But the limitations have been particularly strong and resilient in India, and have survived many other changes of economic policies. The rhetoric of 'equity' has often been invoked to justify governmental interventions without any scrutinized political assessment of how those powers will be exercised and what actual effects they will have. In practice, these ill-directed regulations have not only interfered often enough with the efficiency of economic operations (especially of modern industries), they have also failed fairly comprehensively to promote any kind of real equity in distributional matters. Typically, the bureaucracy's rewards from being able to control economic operations,

---

[13] For some important contributions to this debate, on different sides, see Rudra (1991), Srinivasan (1991a, 1991b, 1993), Ahluwalia (1992), Desai (1992, 1993a), Parikh (1992, 1995), Patel (1992), Ravallion and Subbarao (1992), Kaushik Basu (1993, 1994), Bhagwati (1993), Bhagwati and Srinivasan (1993), Bhattacharya and Mitra (1993), Chandrasekhar and Ghosh (1993), Harriss (1993), Joshi and Little (1993, 1994), A. Mukherjee (1993), Mundle (1993), Oommen (1993), Parikh and Sudarshan (1993), A. Singh (1993), Toye (1993), Bagchi (1994), EPW Research Foundation (1994), Eswaran and Kotwal (1994), Gaiha (1994a), Ghosh (1994), Indira Gandhi Institute of Development Research (1994), Krishnaswamy (1994), Nayyar (1994), Patnaik (1994), S.L. Rao (1994), Sau (1994), S. Sen (1994), Cassen and Joshi (1995), among others.

[14] For an early analysis of the negative role of counterproductive regulations in a number of developing countries, see Little, Scitovsky, and Scott (1970). See also Corden (1974), Krueger (1974), and Bhagwati and Srinivasan (1975), among other contributions.

distribute favours, or cause (or threaten to cause) obstructions, have been exploited by those who were already in privileged positions. While a lot of all this was done in the name of the Indian poor, that hapless creature has got very little from it.

Similar remarks apply to the need for making better use of the opportunities offered by international trade. Many countries have made excellent use of these opportunities, and India too can reap much more fully the benefits of economies of scale and efficient division of labour.[15] While greater involvement in trade is sometimes seen as something that compromises the country's economic independence, or that jeopardizes India's sovereignty, there is little objective basis for such fears. Given the diversity of trading partners, the worry that India would be an economic prisoner in the international world of open exchange is quite unfounded. This does not deny the importance of getting the terms and conditions of trade right, including having fair regulations from GATT (or its successor) and other international institutions, which have often been far from evenhanded. But in general there is little reason for fearfully abstaining from the benefits offered by international trade and exchange. In fact, it is worth recalling that India's share of international trade used to be about four times as high, forty years ago, as it is now, so that an expansion of India's involvement in international trade, far from putting the country in a new and uncertain position, would merely help to restore its position prior to decades of spiralling decline in the world economy.[16] On this whole issue, India has much to learn from China, which has boldly seized the opportunities of international trade in recent years, with remarkable results in terms of broad-based expansion of living standards, and without much sign of its economic or political sovereignty being compromised.[17]

While much energy has been spent on sorting out these issues, too little attention has been paid to what is *lacking* in the current

---

[15] See chapter 3. The dynamic role of trade as an aspect of economic change applies to national as well as international trade; on this see Bauer and Yamey (1957) and Bauer (1972, 1991). The restrictions imposed by interstate fiscal barriers in India (e.g. through the 'octroi') have recently led to protests by lorry drivers because of the harassment and delays involved, but there is here a more general economic issue as well.

[16] On 'India's regression in the world economy', see S.J. Patel (1985, 1994).

[17] The 'open door' policy of the Chinese government involved eschewing one of the most cherished principles of the Mao era, i.e. that of self- sufficiency. This is another illustration of the pragmatism of economic policy in China, discussed in chapter 4.

orientation of economic policy in India. The removal of counter-productive regulations on domestic production and international trade can form a helpful *part* of a programme of participatory and wide-ly-shared growth, but it may achieve relatively little in the absence of more active public policy aimed at removing the other social handicaps that shackle the Indian economy and reduce the well-being of the population. The absence of real reform in the field of basic education is a telling illustration of the government's neglect of that part of the agenda. There has been much talk, in recent years, about the importance of basic education and the need to give it a 'high priority'. Many official pronouncements in this direction have been made, many new 'schemes' have been launched, and many glossy publications extolling the virtues of these initiatives have been produced. But, as we saw in chapter 6, this rhetoric has gone hand in hand with a remarkably slow actual expansion of basic schooling facilities, and even falling teaching inputs in per capita terms. We have also discussed how the dismal functioning of the schooling system, and related failures of education policy, contribute to the persistence of widespread illiteracy in much of the country, especially north India. To illustrate, the fact that, according to a recent survey of 15 primary schools in rural Uttar Pradesh, two-thirds of the village teachers were absent from the school at the time of the investigators' unannounced visit is another remarkable example of the gap between rhetoric and reality in the field of basic education.

In the field of health care, too, there is little sign of any determination to address the tragic limitations of current policy. As we noted in chapter 5, health care facilities in many parts of rural India have been extensively diverted to forceful programmes of family planning (mainly based on female sterilization), compounding the problem of persistently high levels of morbidity and mortality. Similarly, a recent survey of family health in India reveals that 30 per cent of all children aged 12–23 months have never received *any* vaccination, that only half of all pregnant women go through some kind of antenatal check-up, and that only a tiny minority of married women have convenient access to non-terminal methods of modern con-traception (with much worse figures in rural areas, among disad-vantaged social groups, and in states where health policy has been particularly neglected).[18] These failures in a crucially important field

[18] These figures are derived from the National Family Health Survey, as reported in

of government action receive extraordinarily little attention in current debates. Similar things can be said of recent trends in many other areas of social and economic policy.

The absence of any real commitment to social reform fits into that general pattern. We have discussed, in chapter 7, how the persistence of extraordinary gender inequalities in India is a major obstacle to social progress. There has been no decisive attempt on the part of the government, before or after the reforms, to challenge these inequalities. The general attitude of the administration, the courts, the police, and other government institutions has rather been to endorse and enforce the traditional view of Indian women as subordinate members of society. Similarly, there has been little real challenge to caste-based inequalities, and the somewhat checkered introduction of reservation policies for disadvantaged castes has gone hand in hand with a tacit acceptance of a caste hierarchy in the Indian society. As we saw in chapter 5, these and other traditional inequalities are resilient factors of economic and social backwardness in India, particularly in rural areas.

In earlier chapters of this book, we have discussed how policy developments in India, including those since the 'reforms', have continued the tradition of neglecting the fundamental importance of basic capabilities in economic development, and of the positive role of the state in promoting these capabilities.[19] Judged in that perspective, the current reorientation of economic policy is much less of a radical departure from the past than it is often considered to be, and it leaves unaddressed some of the most debilitating biases of earlier regimes. Correcting these biases—not just in political rhetoric but in practical action—calls for a major shift of emphasis in policy-making. There is also an acute need to pay more attention to these issues in public debates and social and political movements, involving the opposition as well as the government.

8.4. *Governance and Public Action*

The positive roles of the state in economic development span a

International Institute for Population Sciences (1994); some further results of this survey are given in the Statistical Appendix of this book. The inter-state contrasts suggest a clear relation between health achievements and public initiatives in this field. Here again, the large north Indian states stand out with a particularly poor record in both respects.

[19] See particularly chapters 2 and 5–7.

wide range of activities. In this book, we have paid particular attention to specific activities that demand priority attention at this stage, such as the expansion of basic education. But there are many other relevant fields of action, including not only those which we have had occasion to discuss (e.g. health care, social security, population policy, land reform, local democracy, women's rights), but also others which are less closely related to the central concerns of this book (e.g. the need for sound environmental policies, for improved rural infrastructure, or for a credible legal system). The key issue is that many of the basic entitlements that people need in order to improve their lives (e.g. to primary education, child vaccination, safe contraception, clean water, social security, environmental resources, legal protection) depend to varying extents on some form of positive government activity. The positive role of the state is, thus, potentially quite extensive.

At the same time, the standards of government activity in many of these fields are, as things stand, absymally low (and, in some cases, deteriorating). The task of making the positive role of the state more effective in India is, therefore, extremely challenging.

The quality of governance ultimately relates, to a considerable extent, to the practice of domestic politics and to 'public action' in the broad sense of action *by* the public (rather than just *for* the public, by the government).[20] Even though many of the weighty decisions that have to be taken are ultimately settled by the government in office (in New Delhi or in the respective state capitals), they are, to varying extents, influenced by the actions and demands of the public. Thus, political parties and public activists have an important role in the emergence and survival of particular policies and economic strategies. The democratic framework of the Indian polity permits this exercise in ways that are not open in many other developing economies.

The role of the public is not confined to influencing or challenging the decisions of the government. The agency of the public is also directly important in many fields of economic and social activity. There are, indeed, many different types of community-based action where public activism can be very rewarding.[21] The monitoring of

[20] See chapters 5–7; also Drèze and Sen (1989).

[21] Robert Putnam (1993) has brought out the importance of 'civic traditions' and non-governmental public action for successful political, economic, and social life, in the specific context of Italy, with important general lessons for other countries as well.

school education, including the prevention of large-scale absenteeism on the part of rural teachers (common in many parts of India), is a good illustration (this was discussed in chapter 5). To cite another example, recent experiences in different parts of India have also shown that community management can, in some circumstances, provide an excellent institutional basis for the protection of local environmental resources.[22]

The agency of the public can also play an essential part in the task of reducing social inequalities. As discussed in chapter 5, there are many good reasons to be concerned about the persistence of extraordinary inequalities in Indian society. We have argued for taking a broad view of inequality, which pays attention not only to the standard economic inequalities but also to other relevant social divisions based on gender, caste, literacy, and other characteristics. In combating these diverse inequalities, social movements and collective action have a crucial role to play.[23]

Whether the involvement of the public at large takes the form of pressing for particular forms of government action, or of working for social change outside the sphere of government activity, the results can depend a great deal on effective political organization of disadvantaged groups. India's democratic institutions provide many potential bases of public action (including not only the electoral process but also the news media, the legal system, village panchayats, etc.), but an important organizational task is involved in seizing these opportunities. The extent to which this process of political organization of disadvantaged groups has occurred has varied a great deal between different parts of India. Kerala stands out as a case of early success, but there have also been commendable achievements elsewhere. In West Bengal, for instance, effective organization of disadvantaged groups under the leadership of the 'left front' parties has led to a significant change in the balance of political power, and this, in turn, has provided the basis for important social achievements, notably land reform.[24] In some states of south and western

---

[22] See e.g. Agarwal and Narain (1989), Gadgil and Guha (1993), and the literature cited there.

[23] V.K. Ramachandran's chapter in the companion volume (Drèze and Sen, 1996) extensively discusses the role of social movements in breaking the old inequalities of class, caste, and gender in Kerala. Other examples, elsewhere in India, are discussed by Fernandes (1985), Shah (1990), and Omvedt (1993); see also the literature cited there.

[24] See chapter 3, and also the case study of West Bengal by Sunil Sengupta and Haris

India, the ability of disadvantaged groups to organize and participate in the political process has also significantly improved in recent years. Consolidating these achievements (and extending them to states where government institutions and the political process are still comprehensively dominated by privileged groups) is one of the major challenges ahead.

Both the state and the public have central roles to play in economic development. While different schools of thought tend to place different emphasis on their respective roles, it is hard to avoid seeing them as thoroughly interdependent. Just as the nature of state activities depends a great deal on public demands and pressures, the actions of the public—both collaborative and adversarial—are all the more effective when the state plays its part in helping to empower the citizens by guaranteeing basic democratic freedoms, ensuring widespread literacy, protecting the legal rights of disadvantaged groups, and providing some security against extreme destitution. There is, in this sense, a deeply complementary relationship between state action and public action.

This dialectical feature of the relationship between state action and public action makes it possible for a society to be caught in a vicious circle of (1) government apathy towards the needs of the citizens, and (2) public inability to challenge that apathy, as has happened in states such as Uttar Pradesh.[25] On the positive side, it also means that the rewards of efforts aimed at breaking that vicious circle (e.g. based on the political organization of disadvantaged groups, or on the promotion of widespread literacy) can be very large, as Kerala's experience illustrates. This is one reason why the promotion of literacy—to which both state action and public action have much to contribute—is so central to the transformation of Indian politics. Among the many adverse effects of illiteracy and educational backwardness in India are their role in muting public pressure for social change and governmental responsibility. The rewards of

Gazdar (1996) in the companion volume. As discussed in that study, political developments in West Bengal have provided an improved basis for many social reforms, but there has been uneven success in actually using this opportunity. In particular, while issues of land reform and local democracy have been addressed with relatively good effect, public policies dealing with health, education, and related matters have been—so far—largely neglected.

[25]On this reading of Uttar Pradesh's development experience, see Drèze and Gazdar (1996) in the companion volume.

expanding basic education include its impact on the nature and force of public action. In arguing for greater attention to the role of social opportunities in economic development, we have tried to emphasize not only the use of these opportunities to generate higher earnings and better lives for the individuals directly involved, but also the social use of these freedoms to influence the government and the society at large.

8.5. *Women's Agency and Social Change*

In the course of different arguments in this monograph, we have had the occasion to comment on the importance of women's agency for social progress.[26] The focus on women's agency has to be distinguished from the more usual concentration on women's well-being. There are good reasons to pay particular attention to each in examining the requirements of economic development and social change in India. The persistence of sharp gender inequalities in many different forms is one of the most striking aspects of the Indian economy, and it yields disparities in well-being as well as differences in power and decision-making authority.

Perhaps the most telling expression of gender inequality of well-being is to be found in the low female–male ratio in India, and the high proportion of 'missing women' whose absence can be attributed to differential care, including medical attention.[27] Unequal sharing of the rewards of family life is one of the prominent features of gender relations in India. In remedying these inequalities, the activities of women's organizations and other forms of agency can be of crucial importance, and in several different contexts, the effectiveness of such activities has already been well demonstrated.[28]

The first reason for the importance of women's agency is, thus, the persistence of gender-based inequalities of well-being, and the relevance of women's actions and movements in bringing about a change in this field. The need for women's own agency in securing gender justice arises partly from the fact that gender inequality does

---

[26] See chapters 3–7.

[27] See chapter 7.

[28] See Omvedt (1980, 1989a, 1993), K. Bardhan (1985), Poitevin and Rairkar (1985), Desai (1988), Duvvury (1989), Stree Shakti Sanghatana (1989), Kishwar and Vanita (1991), Dietrich (1992), Rose (1992), D.K.S. Roy (1992), Chaudhuri (1993), among others.

not decline automatically with the process of economic growth. In fact, as we saw in chapter 7, in some respects economic progress can even lead to an actual deterioration in the position of women in society. In so far as economic expansion does reduce gender inequality, this happens mainly *through* other variables that relate more closely to women's agency, such as female labour-force participation and female literacy. Economic growth, for instance, can positively influence the status of women through expanding opportunities for remunerative female employment, which often results in an improvement in the 'deal' that a woman receives within the family. But even these influences, though fairly extensive in some cases, can be slow, and in great need of supplementation by more direct public action in pursuit of gender equity, focusing for instance on educational transformation, women's ownership rights, and political activism.

Second, women's empowerment can positively influence the lives not only of women themselves but also of men, and of course those of children. There is much evidence, for instance, that women's education tends to reduce child mortality rates, for both boys and girls. In fact, there is good reason to relate the remarkably high life-expectancy levels in Kerala to its educational achievements, particularly of women, and on the other side, to relate the low life expectancies of some of the northern states to backwardness in female education.[29] The subordination of women in Indian society tends to impair their effectiveness in reducing deprivation in general, and it is not only the well-being of female children or adult women which is improved by the enhanced agency of women.

Third, as we have also seen (chapter 7), women's emancipation, in the form of basic education and economic independence, tends

[29] See section 7.3, and the studies cited there. It is worth emphasizing that the positive link between female education and child survival is likely to relate not only to the agency of women *within* the family, but also to their role in politics and public life. In particular, a more active and informed public role of women in society tends to be associated with greater pressure in the direction of expanding health care and related public services, and with an improved use of these services. After noting that 'women have invariably been the large majority of the participants' (p. 22) in the Total Literacy Campaign, for instance, Ghosh et al. (1994) observe that the campaign has led to 'greater and more vociferous demand for [education and] other services to meet [the participants'] basic needs in regard to employment, housing, health, etc.' (p. 38). Similarly, according to a recent study of the renowned Self-Employed Women's Association based in Ahmedabad, 'SEWA found that health care was the most urgent need after economic issues that the women wanted to organize around' (Rose, 1992, p. 249).

to have quite a strong impact on fertility rates. This linkage has been widely obser¬ed in international comparisons, but it is consistent also with Kerala's remarkable reduction of fertility rates, and to some extent, with Tamil Nadu's recent success in that direction.[30] On the other side, the low position of women in the 'northern heartland' clearly does contribute not a little to the high fertility rates that are found in such states as Uttar Pradesh, Madhya Pradesh, Rajasthan, and Bihar. Through this connection with demographic change, the role of women's agency extends well beyond the interests of today's women, and even beyond the interests of all living people today, and has a significant impact on the lives of future generations.

Fourth, aside from specialized roles, women's agency is important as a part of the agency of all people. Women's decisions and actions can have a profound impact on the policies that the government decides to pursue and the lives that people can lead. Women have often been very active in demanding and working for basic social change, and the discussion in the last section on the importance of actions of the public applies particularly to women. In much of India, women tend to remain rather homebound and politically unassertive, and given the critical importance of political action and pressure, a real difference can be made by women taking an active role in these activities.[31] The effectiveness of public action and the expansion of social opportunities depend a great deal on the effective freedom of women to exercise their reasoned agency.

8.6. *Comparative Perspectives*

International comparisons have been used fairly extensively in this book, in a variety of contexts. We have invoked them, for instance, in discussing the intrinsic as well as instrumental roles of human capabilities in economic development, the respective contributions of economic growth and public support in expanding social opportunities, the role of markets in fostering economic growth, and the enormity of India's failures in areas such as basic education and gender inequality.[32]

---

[30] See chapter 7, and also Sen (1994b).

[31] See, for example, Robin Jeffrey (1987, 1992), including his account of 'how women made Kerala literate'.

[32] See particularly chapters 3, 4, and 7.

We have paid special attention to the contrast between India and China, not only because of the obvious relevance of the Chinese experience for India, but also because of the sustained influence of that particular comparison in Indian political debates (see section 4.1). In interpreting China's experience (particularly involving a much more radical elimination of endemic deprivations than India has been able to achieve so far), we have emphasized the complementarities between the *pre-reform* achievements and the *post-reform* success in promoting rapid economic expansion on a widespread basis.[33] When China adopted its programme of market-oriented economic reforms in the late seventies, it had already gone a long way towards achieving the conditions that facilitate broad-based involvement of people in the process of economic expansion. The relevant achievements include (1) land reform, (2) near-universal literacy in the younger age groups, (3) a radical reduction of endemic morbidity and undernutrition, (4) the foundations of a social security system, (5) a functioning system of local governance, and (6) a major expansion of the basis of high participation of women in the labour force. India is nowhere near achieving these solid foundations of broad-based economic expansion, and the challenges of economic and social reform in India have to be seen in that light.

At the same time, we have also guarded against the temptation of advocating imitative emulation of the Chinese experience. China's experience of expanding social opportunities, while most impressive in many respects, has included some failures of monumental proportions. As was discussed in chapter 4, many of these failures reflect China's authoritarian system of governance, which keeps government policies outside the reach of public scrutiny and popular challenge. The famines of 1958–61, the excesses of the Cultural Revolution, the widespread and continuing violation of elementary freedoms, and the devastating human consequences of coercive population policies, are telling illustrations of that pattern. Just as China's positive achievements provide a powerful illustration of the scope for positive government activity in economic development, its failures clearly point to the dangers of authoritarian governance—and that, too, is a lesson of major importance for India.

These basic lessons from China's experience are, to a great extent, reinforced by a consideration of regional diversities within India.

---

[33] See chapter 4.

As we have discussed on several occasions, India has much to learn not only from China and other countries but also from its own experience. This is particularly so given that India is a most diverse country, and that the records of different regions and states are extremely disparate. The diversity of experiences within India relates especially to the varieties of public policies pursued in the respective states, and, in particular, to the dissimilar use of public action to enhance the quality of life and to expand basic human capabilities.[34]

Kerala's experience is particularly instructive in that respect, and has received sustained attention in this book. There is, indeed, much evidence of the extensive links between Kerala's outstanding social achievements (including a life expectancy of 72 years, a fertility rate below the replacement level, near-universal literacy in the younger age groups, a virtual absence of child labour, and relatively low levels of gender inequality) and its rich history of public action (involving early state initiatives and social movements for the promotion of literacy, the implementation of land reforms, the elimination of traditional inequalities, the provision of wide-ranging public services, and related goals).[35] Kerala's experience of early promotion of social opportunities based on public action is of far-reaching significance for other Indian states, and indeed for other countries also.

Kerala's record includes some failures as well, and we have noted in particular how Kerala's performance in generating economic growth has been very moderate indeed. In fact, there has been virtually no growth of the domestic economy in Kerala during the eighties (see Statistical Appendix). While the social opportunities of living long, healthy, and literate lives have been radically enhanced in an exemplary manner, the opportunities that depend on economic success have been more stagnant.

This contrast raises interesting issues concerning the causal antecedents of participatory growth. Kerala has been very successful in developing the social opportunities (related to widespread education, health care, land reforms, social security, etc.) that constitute the centrally important *social* conditions for having participatory economic growth. And yet Kerala has had, in fact, little participatory economic growth at home. The failure in this case has arisen not from any

---

[34] See particularly chapter 3.

[35] See the study by V.K. Ramachandran (1996) in the companion volume, and also the literature cited there and in section 3.6 of this book.

lack of participation but from the low growth of Kerala's domestic economy; as we have argued earlier, there has to be growth for it to be participatory. The roots of this failure include the continuation of overregulated economic governance that has blighted the prospects of economic expansion all over India for many decades, the removal of which has met more resistance in Kerala than in most other Indian states.

The radical commitments of left-leaning governments, on the one hand, and of activist general politics, on the other, have done much in Kerala to guarantee widespread social opportunities in many crucial fields. But that political climate has also tended to encourage economic policies that are extremely hostile to the market mechanism, even in areas where this hostility—and the excessive reliance on government regulation that goes with it—is quite counterproductive. This has made it harder to change the overregulated economy of Kerala, even in comparison with the situation in other Indian states. As was argued earlier, programmes of positive public action need not be combined with a general rejection of the economic advantages of the market. Kerala's experience illustrates the need for a discriminating choice of public intervention, which is one of the central themes of this monograph.

The contrast between (1) the advantages of Kerala's radical social preparedness, and (2) the handicaps of its essentially conservative economic policies (often clinging forcefully to old-fashioned bureaucratic regulations), has tended to produce an odd mismatch. As a result, the people of Kerala have been much more inclined to make use of economic opportunities outside the state than at home. While Kerala's domestic economy has continued to stagnate over the decades, its 'outside incomes' (including remittances) have been very large over that same period, reflecting extensive use by the people of Kerala of economic opportunities elsewhere, often in other countries.[36]

Kerala, it would appear, has to learn as well as teach. But while Kerala's *learning* can be easily integrated into the contemporary reformist focus on incentives, economic growth, and deregulation, what it has to *teach* takes us well beyond these concerns. As far as these positive lessons are concerned, however, there is a tendency to dismiss

---

[36] On the role of migration and remittances in Kerala's economy, see Krishnan (1994, forthcoming).

the exemplary force of Kerala's achievements as those of 'merely a state, not a country'. Since intercountry comparisons for policy analysis typically focus on nations as a whole, Kerala's experience tends not to receive the international attention that is given to the achievements of particular countries—from Sri Lanka and Costa Rica to South Korea and Hong Kong. This is not a sensible neglect for several distinct reasons.

First, with its 29 million people, Kerala has a larger population than most countries in the world (even Canada), including many from which comparative lessons are often drawn, such as Sri Lanka (17.4 million) and Costa Rica (3.2 million), and, of course, the primarily city states of Hong Kong (5.8 million) and Singapore (2.8 million). Even South Korea, which receives a great deal of attention in the development literature and is often seen as a development 'model', had about the same population size in the early sixties (when its rapid transformation began) as Kerala has now. To achieve as much as Kerala has done for a population of its size is no mean record in world history.

Second, given the political federalism of the Indian union, each state has considerable autonomy in such fields as school education and health care. To be sure, an initiative of the central government can be extremely powerful in its impact on state policies, partly through fiscal linkages (a large proportion of each state's resources comes from allocation of central revenue such as income tax collections), but also through political connections and party contacts that operate between the centre and the states. But this does not prevent a state from taking a bold initiative in matters of education and health care, and to go well forward on its own if it so chooses. This is what Kerala has done with remarkable canniness and determination.

There is a different kind of objection that could be a more legitimate reason for doubting that Kerala's experience can be emulated. Kerala has been fortunate with its past. For one thing, the bulk of what is now Kerala consisted of two 'native states'—Travancore and Cochin —formally outside British India. They were not subjected to the general shortage of official interest of Whitehall in Indian elementary education (as opposed to higher education). When Rani Gouri Parvathi Bai, the young queen of Travancore, made her pioneering statement in 1817 on the importance of basic education, there was no need to bring that policy initiative in line with what was happening in the rest of India, under the Raj.[37]

Kerala has also been fortunate in having strong social movements that concentrated on educational advancement—along with general emancipation—of the lower castes, and this has been a special feature of left-wing and radical political movements in Kerala. It has also profited from a tradition of openness to the world, which has included welcoming early Christians (at least from the fourth century), Jews (from shortly after the fall of Jerusalem), and Muslims (from the days of Arab trading, as settlers rather than as conquerors). Into this rather open and receptive environment, the extensive educational efforts of Christian missionaries in the nineteenth century fitted comfortably. Kerala has also benefited from the matrilineal tradition of property inheritance for an important part of the community (the Nairs), which has contributed to giving women in Kerala a better social position, even in the past.

Having good luck in one's history is not, however, a policy parameter that one can adjust. Those who see a unique and unrepeatable pattern in Kerala's remarkable record in educational expansion can point to the very special nature of its past, and suggest that other states can learn rather little from it. This, however, would be quite the wrong conclusion to draw from Kerala's heterogeneous history. When the state of Kerala was created in independent India, it was made up, on linguistic grounds, of the erstwhile native states of Travancore and Cochin, and the region of Malabar from the old province of Madras in British India (later Tamil Nadu). The Malabar region, transferred from the Raj, was very much behind Travancore and Cochin in terms of literacy, life expectancy, and other achievements that make Kerala so special. But by the eighties, Malabar had 'caught up' to such an extent with the rest of Kerala that it could no longer be seen in divergent terms.[38] The initiatives

---

[37] The independence from general British Indian policy applied not only to the princely rulers of these states, but also to the British 'Residents' in Trivandrum. The Residents could consider independent initiatives, and indeed in the big move in Travancore in the direction of elementary education in the early nineteenth century, the Resident Mr Munro played an extremely supportive—and possibly even catalytic—role. There is some evidence that he drafted Rani Parvathi Bai's 1817 statement, whether or not the initiative was also his (on this, see Ramachandran, 1996).

[38] On this see Kabir and Krishnan (1992), George (1994), Krishnan (1994), and Ramachandran (1996).

that the state governments of Kerala took, under different 'manage-ments' (led by the Communist Party as well as by the Congress), succeeded in bringing Malabar rather at par with the rest of Kerala over a short period of time. So there is a lesson here that is not imprisoned in the fixity of history. Other parts of India can indeed learn a lot from Kerala's experience on what can be done here and now through determined public action.

It is also worth noting that while Kerala was already very advanced compared with British India at the time of independence, much of the great achievements of Kerala that are so admired now are the results of post-independence public policies. In fact, in the fifties Kerala's adult literacy rate was around 50 per cent compared with 90 now, its life expectancy at birth was 44 years *vis-à-vis* 72 now, and its birth rate was 32 as opposed to 18.5 now.[39] Kerala did have a good start, but the policies that have made its achievements so extraordinary are the products of more recent political initiatives and public action. In fact, as we showed in chapter 4, it is only over the last decade or so that Kerala has actually overtaken China with considerable rapidity in raising life expectancy, reducing infant mortality, cutting down fertility rates, and so on.

As was discussed earlier, there are also other states in India which indicate that substantial rewards can be obtained from serious public efforts in raising human capabilities. West Bengal provides a good example of the possibility and rewards of land reform programmes (enhancing equity as well as the efficiency of local agriculture).[40] Tamil Nadu shows how the fertility rate can be quite dramatically reduced through well-coordinated family planning programmes, making good use of its base of comparatively favourable social back-ground (being among the top three major states in primary education, in female participation in outside employment, and in low infant mortality, along with having a traditionally higher age at marriage).[41] Himachal Pradesh provides a helpful example of rapid reduction of illiteracy among children, partly based on a relatively bold schooling programme. Punjab illustrates the possibility of encouraging economic growth through infrastructural development (though its economic

---

[39] On these figures and the general history that they represent, see Ramachandran (1996).

[40] See chapter 3, and the paper by Sunil Sengupta and Haris Gazdar (1996) in the companion volume.

[41] See chapters 4 and 7, and the Statistical Appendix.

success has been hit hard recently by conflict and violence). There are other examples of this kind, from which lessons can be drawn and used. While Kerala stands out as the leader in social developments, it does not stand alone.

On the other side, the penalties of governmental neglect and public inertia are well illustrated by a number of other states, such as Uttar Pradesh, where basic deprivations remain endemic. In fact, as we saw in chapter 3, there is an interesting complementarity between the lessons emerging from positive and negative experiences. Just as Kerala's achievements richly illustrate the positive influences of widespread literacy, public services, women's agency, adversarial politics, collective organization, and related factors of social progress, the failures of Uttar Pradesh illustrate the tremendous stifling of social opportunities that often results from neglecting these positive influences.

8.7. A Concluding Remark

Economic policies in India have undergone much change over the last few years, and more changes are in the process of being implemented. The debate surrounding these reforms has mobilized enormous attention and energy, and the arguments presented on each side have been quite forceful and firm, even acrimonious.

In this monograph, we have emphasized the need to take the debates on economic policy well *beyond* the issue of economic reforms in their present form. This is not because we see particularly great merit in avoiding acrimonious debates (a bit of healthy mud-slinging might indeed have something to commend in making people take an interest in complex and apparently dull problems), but because we believe that the concentration on attacking or defending economic reforms as the central policy issue distracts attention from a broader view of social opportunities of which the use of the market can be *an important yet quite incomplete* part. The economic reforms do constitute an important departure, but there are many other issues of great importance which have been thoroughly overshadowed by the focus on arguments—both *for* and *against*—the reforms. This has also led to summary assessments—both championing and dismissal—of economic policies that cannot really be judged adequately without placing them in a much broader context.

We have argued for the necessity of asking—and addressing—a

very different set of questions, rather than confining the analysis to examining different answers to the old familiar questions. The central issue, we have argued, is to expand the social opportunities open to the people. In so far as these opportunities are compromised—directly or indirectly—by counterproductive regulations and controls, by restrictions on economic initiatives, by the stifling of competition and its efficiency-generating advantages, and so on, the removal of these hindrances must be seen as extremely important. But we have also discussed why the creation and use of social opportunities for all require much more than the 'freeing' of markets. While the case for economic reforms may take good note of the diagnosis that India has too much government interference in some fields, it ignores the fact that India also has insufficient and ineffective government activity in many other fields, including basic education, health care, social security, land reform, and the promotion of social change. This inertia, too, contributes to the persistence of widespread deprivation, economic stagnation, and social inequality.

What needs curing is not just 'too little market' or 'too much market'. The expansion of markets is *among* the instruments that can help to promote human capabilities, and, given the imperative need for rapid elimination of endemic deprivation in India, it would be irresponsible to ignore that opportunity. But much more is involved in freeing the Indian economy from the cage in which it has been confined, and many of the relevant tasks call for more—not less—government activity and public action.

The distinction between market-complementary and market-excluding governmental activities—discussed in chapter 2—is central to this proposition. Many of the traditional government interventions in India have tended to take a market-excluding form: for example, regulations and controls that stifle economic initiatives in certain areas, the prohibition of trade that shuts out economic options in particular fields, and so on. And at the same time, some types of supportive—as opposed to negative and restrictive—government activities (such as a comprehensive policy of basic education for all, an adequately widespread programme of health care, and so on) have been systematically neglected. It is possible to go more beyond the market in rectifying the latter neglect, while giving greater scope to the market in curing the former transgression.

Policy debates in India have to be taken away from the narrow concentration on issues of liberalization. The nostalgia of the old debates 'Are you *pro* or *anti* market?', or 'Are you *in favour* or *against* state activities?' seems to have an odd 'hold' on all sides, so that we concentrate only on some issues and ignore many—often more important—ones. The focus of government policy at this time seems to be overwhelmingly concerned with the need to remove counterproductive regulations, while continuing the traditional neglect of positive activities. We have also argued that there is a strong case for reorienting public discussion and criticism from the merits and demerits of liberalization towards taking adequate note of the tremendous social and economic deprivations that blight living conditions in India and limit the actual prospects of participatory economic expansion. The terms of the debate need radical change.

STATISTICAL APPENDIX

EXPLANATORY NOTE

This Appendix presents statistical information on aspects of Indian economic and social development. Table A.1 focuses on international comparisons of development indicators for selected Asian countries. Table A.2 attempts to integrate some of these comparisons with internal contrasts within India. The Indian states appearing in Table A.2 are those for which case studies are presented in the companion volume (Drèze and Sen, 1996). Table A.3 gives a more detailed picture of economic development and social opportunity in different Indian states. This table presents information on: per-capita income and related indicators; mortality and fertility; literacy and related educational achievements; school attendance and enrolment; gender-related indicators; maternal health and related matters; and social infrastructure. Table A.4 provides some information relating to trends over time.

1. Sources

In constructing the tables included in this Appendix as well as in the text, we have tried to concentrate on indicators for which the informational basis is relatively reliable. Even for these indicators, there are occasional difficulties, including minor discrepancies between different statistical sources. For the purpose of international comparisons (such as those presented in Table A.1), we have typically used *World Development Report 1994* (and earlier issues of that Report, when applicable). When the relevant indicator is not available in that publication, we have used *Human Development Report 1994*. The main exceptions to this procedure concern (1) literacy figures, and (2) longevity indicators for India and China. These exceptions are discussed in the next section.

For state-specific indicators within India, we have relied, in each case, on the most appropriate national statistical source, e.g. the 1991 census for literacy rates, the National Sample Survey for per-capita expenditure, the Sample Registration System for mortality and fertility rates, and so on. In some tables (e.g. Table A.3), we have also made use of the all-India figure from the same source. It is worth mentioning that, in most cases, these all-India figures from national statistical sources are very close to the corresponding figures given in *World Development Report 1994,* which are used here for the purposes of international comparisons.

Some figures are quite sensitive to the choice of reference year. Generally, we have used the most recent year for which the relevant information is available as the reference year, unless there were specific reasons to use some other year. There are also cases where different issues of an annual statistical publication give different figures for the same indicator and the same reference year. In these cases, we have used the most recent issue of the publication in question, on the assumption that these changes reflect a refinement rather than a deterioration of the estimation methods used to produce these figures.

2. Comments on Specific Indicators

Literacy rates in India and China

The literacy rates for India and China used in chapter 4, and in this Appendix, are taken directly from the relevant census volumes, rather than from international publications such as *World Development Report.* The results of the most recent censuses in India and China, it appears, are yet to be incorporated in these international publications. For instance, the adult literacy rate figures presented in *World Development Report 1994,* Table 1, are based on 'projections prepared in 1989 by UNESCO' (p. 232), and these figures are obviously out of date compared with the more recent figures made available by the 1990 census in China and the 1991 census in India. We have, therefore, preferred to use the census figures, and, for consistency, we have also used census figures from direct sources for earlier years.[1]

---

[1] For a more detailed discussion of the different sources, and of the methodological issues arising in comparisons of literacy rates in India and China, see Drèze and Loh (1995). The literacy figures derived from India's 1991 census can be found in Nanda (1992). The 1990 census figures for China can be found in State Statistical Bureau of

At the time of writing, the only age groups for which literacy figures are available from the 1991 census in India are those of 'all ages combined' and '7 years and above'. The latter age group has frequently been used in this book for comparison with 'adult literacy rates' in other countries, which usually refer to the age group of 15 years and above (see, for example, Tables 3.1, 4.1, and 4.2). This is not particularly misleading, since 7+ literacy rates in India tend to be very close to (though usually a little *higher* than) the 15+ literacy rates.

Literacy rates in other countries

As mentioned above, the literacy figures given in *World Development Report 1994* (with 1990 as reference year) are rather out of date. The same literacy figures are given in *Human Development Report 1993*, but *Human Development Report 1994* presents an updated series, with 1992 as the reference year. This updated series is also based on UNESCO projections, but it appears to incorporate more recent information. For instance, the literacy figures given for China in this new series are much closer to the 1990 census figures than those given in the old series.[2] Since the literacy figures given in *Human Development Report 1994* seem to be more up to date, we have used these figures, rather than those given in *World Development Report 1994*, for purposes of international comparison (e.g. in Table A.1, for countries other than India and China).

Life expectancy in India and China

World Development Report 1994 and *Human Development Report 1994* give figures for life expectancy at birth in India (1992) of 61 years and 60 years, respectively. These figures appear to be projections based on published estimates of the Office of the Registrar General, which relate to 1986–90, and place life expectancy for that period at 57.7 years for males and 58.1 years for females. In this book, we have used more recent, unpublished estimates of life expectancy calculated by the Office of the Registrar General from Sample Registration System data. According to these estimates, life expectancy at

---

the People's Republic of China (1992, 1993a, 1993b).

[2] A personal communication from the UNDP office confirms that the Chinese literacy figures reported in *Human Development Report 1994* incorporate some information based on the 1990 census. We are grateful to Inge Kaul for this clarification.

birth in India in 1990–2 (with 1991 as the mid-point of the reference period) was 59.0 for males and 59.4 for females. These recent estimates are not very different from the projected figures presented in *World Development Report 1994* and *Human Development Report 1994*.

For life expectancy in China, the estimates presented in *World Development Report 1994* are consistent with those calculated by Ansley Coale (1993) based on the 1990 census. Both sources suggest that life expectancy in China was around 69 years in 1992. We have used this estimate, rather than the somewhat higher figure (71 years) given in *Human Development Report 1994*. We have also used Ansley Coale's census-based estimates for life expectancy in China in 1981 (see e.g. Table 4.3 in chapter 4).

Estimates of purchasing-power-parity income in Indian states

Table A.2 presents some tentative estimates of real per-capita income in three Indian states (Kerala, Uttar Pradesh, and West Bengal), relative to the United States. These estimates attempt to measure the state-level equivalent of the familiar 'PPP–GNP' indicator (a measure of real Gross National Product based on 'purchasing-power-parity') used in international comparisons. The estimate for each state is calculated by multiplying the all-India figure (namely 5.2, with USA = 100), obtained from *World Development Report 1994*, by a state-specific coefficient c defined as $c = SDP/(p. GDP)$, where SDP denotes per-capita 'state domestic product' at current prices, GDP is all-India gross domestic product per capita at current prices, and p is an index of state-level prices relative to all-India prices.[3]

To ensure internal consistency of the calculations, the all-India per-capita GDP figure was calculated as a population-weighted average of the state-specific per-capita SDP figures. The latter are given in *Economic Survey 1994–95* (Government of India, 1995), Appendix, Table 1.8. The reference year for these figures is 1991–2.

Minhas et al. (1991) give estimates of the index p for 1970–1, 1983, and 1987–8.[4] These estimates suggest that this index is fairly

---

[3] In the case of Kerala, we have multiplied the estimate so obtained by 1.2, to account for remittances from outside the state (the total value of these remittances is estimated at roughly 20 per cent of Kerala's domestic product; see Krishnan, 1994).

[4] See Minhas et al. (1991), Table 1. The authors give separate indices for rural and urban areas. We have calculated the state price index p as an average of the rural and urban indices.

stable over time, at least for the states we are concerned with in this table (Kerala, Uttar Pradesh, and West Bengal). In order to calculate the 1991–2 value of the coefficient c, we have assumed that p remained constant between 1987–8 and 1991–2.

Obviously, a substantial margin of error is involved in these calculations, given the difficulties involved in estimating state domestic products as well as relative price levels. The resulting estimates presented in Table A.2 should be considered as tentative.

3. *Poverty Estimates for India*

The estimates of poverty indices in India (and in different Indian states) presented earlier in this book, and in Tables A.3 and A.4 of this Appendix, are based on a study by Tendulkar, Sundaram, and Jain (1993), which covers the period 1970–1 to 1988–9. In Table A.4, we also present another series of estimates, based on recent work by Gaurav Datt (1995), who has calculated estimates of different poverty indices for the entire 1951–91 period. Although there are methodological differences between the two studies, their results are broadly consistent. In addition to the 'head-count ratio' indices calculated by Tendulkar, Sundaram, and Jain (1993), we present two alternative poverty indices: the 'Sen index' (from Tendulkar et al., 1993) and the 'squared poverty gap' index (from Datt, 1995).[5] All these poverty estimates are based on National Sample Survey data.

Preliminary results from the 48th round of the National Sample Survey suggest that the incidence of poverty in India in 1992–3 (in terms of the head-count ratio) was somewhat higher than at the end of the eighties.[6] Although this phenomenon partly reflects short-run factors of a transient kind (particularly the sharp increase in foodgrain prices in that year), it also reinforces the considerations presented earlier in this book on the overarching need for economic growth to be participatory and widely-shared, in a way that the

[5] The head-count ratio simply indicates the proportion of the population below the poverty line. The other two indices, unlike the head-count ratio, are sensitive to the distribution of consumer expenditure below the poverty line. The Sen index also takes note of *relative* deprivations below the poverty line (since the weights given to different households reflect their *rank* in the scale of per-capita expenditure). On the definitions and properties of these different poverty indices, see Sen (1976b, 1983b), Foster (1984), Foster and Shorrocks (1991), Ravallion (1994).

[6] Suresh Tendulkar, Delhi School of Economics, personal communication.

experience of Indian economic expansion has not been, *either* before *or* after the reforms.

4. *Sources Used in Table A.3*

For convenience, the sources used in Table A.3 (which provides state-specific information on a range of social and economic indicators), along with brief explanatory remarks, are listed in a chart at the end of this appendix.

TABLE A.1. *Economic and Social Indicators in India and Selected Asian Countries*

	India	Bangladesh	Nepal	Pakistan	Sri Lanka	China	South Korea	Indonesia	Thailand
POPULATION, mid-1992 (millions)	883.6	114.4	19.9	119.3	17.4	1,162.2	43.7	184.3	58.0
PER-CAPITA INCOME AND RELATED INDICATORS									
GNP per capita, 1992 (US$)	310	220	170	420	540	470	6,790	670	1,840
PPP estimates of GNP per capita, 1992 (1992 international dollars)	1,210	1,230	1,100	2,130	2,810	1,910[a]	8,950	2,970	5,890
PPP estimates of GNP per capita, 1992 (USA = 100)	5.2	5.3	4.8	9.2	12.2	9.1[a]	38.7	12.8	25.5
Average annual growth rate of per-capita GNP, 1980–92 (%)	3.1	1.8	2	3.1	2.6	7.6	8.5	4	6
LONGEVITY, MORTALITY AND FERTILITY									
Life expectancy at birth, 1992[b] (years)									
Female	59	56	53	59	74	71	75	62	72
Male	59	55	54	59	70	68	67	59	67
Persons	59	55	54	59	72	69	71	60	69
Crude death rate, 1992 (per 1,000)	10	11	13	10	6	8	6	10	6
Infant mortality rate, 1992 (per 1,000 live births)	79	91	99[a]	95	18	31	13	66	26
Proportion of low-birthweight babies, 1990 (%)	33	50	n/a	25	25	9	9	14	13
Crude birth rate, 1992 (per 1,000)	29	31	38	40	21	19	16	25	20
Total fertility rate, 1992	3.7	4.0	5.5[a]	5.6	2.5	2.0	1.8	2.9	2.2[a]
LITERACY AND EDUCATION									
Adult literacy rate (age 15+)[c], 1992 (%)									
Female	39	23	14	22	85	68	95	77	92
Male	64	49	39	49	94	87	99	91	96
Persons	52	37	27	36	89	78	97	84	94

Table A.1 (contd.)

	India	Bangladesh	Nepal	Pakistan	Sri Lanka	China	South Korea	Indonesia	Thailand
Mean years of schooling (age 25+), 1992	2.4	2	2.1	1.9	7.2	5	9.3	4.1	3.9
Proportion of first-grade entrants who complete the primary cycle of school education (%)	62	47	n/a	48	97	85	99	77	87
OTHER GENDER-RELATED INDICATORS									
Female–male ratio (ratio of females to males in the population), 1992 (%)	93	94	95	92	99	94	100	101	99
Female share of the labour force, 1990–2 (%)	29	41	34	14	33	43	40	40	47
SAVINGS, INVESTMENT AND TRADE									
Gross domestic savings as proportion of GDP, 1992[d] (%)	22	6	12	14	15	43	37	37	35
Gross domestic investment as proportion of GDP, 1992[d] (%)	23	12	22	21	23	39	37	35	40
Exports of goods and non-factor services as proportion of GDP, 1992[d] (%)	10	10	19	17	32	18	32	29	36
Average annual growth rate of exports, 1980–92 (%)	5.9	7.6	9.7	11.1	6.5	11.9	11.9	5.6	14.7
Net present value of total external debt as proportion of GNP, 1992 (%)	26	29	29	37	41	13	14	62	35
Total debt service as proportion of exports, 1992 (%)	25	17	12	24	14	10	7	32	14

Notes.   [a] Subject to more than the usual margin or error.   [b] 1991 for India, 1990 for China.   [c] Age 7+, in the case of India (see Explanatory Note).   [d] 1990 for China and South Korea.

Sources.   *World Development Report 1994*, Tables 1, 9, 13, 23, 26–30 (pp. 162–221), *World Development Report 1992*, Table 9, and *Human Development Report 1994*, Tables 5, 9, 14, 15, 18, 21 (pp. 130–83). On the literacy and life expectancy figures for India and China, see the Explanatory Note in this Appendix.

TABLE A.2. India in Comparative Perspective

Country/ state	Population, 1992 (millions)	Estimated PPP per-capita GNP, 1992 (USA=100)	Growth rate of per-capita GDP, 1980–92 (% per year)	Adult literacy rate, 1992 (%)		Life expectancy at birth, 1992 (years)		Crude death rate, 1992 (per 1,000)	Infant mortality rate, 1992 (per 1,000 live births)	Total fertility rate, 1992	Female–male ratio, 1992
				Female	Male	Female	Male				
Bangladesh	114	5.3	1.9	23	49	56	55	11	91	4.0	94
Pakistan	119	9.2	3.0	22	49	59	59	10	95	5.6	92
Sri Lanka	17	12.2	2.6	85	94	74	70	6	18	2.5	99
Kerala[a]	29	4.6[b]	0.3[c]	86	94	74	69	6	17	1.8	104
West Bengal[a]	68	5.1[b]	2.5[c]	47	68	62	61	8	66	3.2	92
Uttar Pradesh[a]	139	4.1[b]	2.2[c]	25	56	55	57	12	98	5.1	88
INDIA	884	5.2	3.1	39	64	59	59	10	79	3.7	93
China	1,162	9.1	7.7	68	87	71	68	8	31	2.0	94
South Korea	44	38.7	8.3	95	99	75	67	6	13	1.8	100
Thailand	58	25.5	6.4	92	96	72	67	6	26	2.2	99

Notes. [a] In the case of Indian states, figures mentioned in the column heading as applying to 1992 apply, in fact, to 1991, or (in the case of IMR and CDR) to 1990–2.
[b] Tentative estimates (see Explanatory Note).
[c] 1980–90.

Sources. For countries: see Table A.1 (also *World Development Report 1994*, Table 2, for growth rate of per-capita GDP). For Indian states: see Table A.3 and the Explanatory Note.

Table A.3. Selected Indicators for Indian States

PART 1. Per-capita income and related indicators

State	Population, 1991 (millions)	Per-capita net state domestic product at current prices, 1991-2 (Rs/year)	Growth rate of per-capita SDP, 1980-90 (% per year)	Average per-capita consumer expenditure, 1987-8 (Rs/month at 1970-1 prices)		Measures of poverty, 1987-8				Gini coefficient of per-capita consumer expenditure, 1987-8	
						Head-count ratio (%)		Sen index			
				Rural	Urban	Rural	Urban	Rural	Urban	Rural	Urban
Andhra Pradesh	67	5,570	1.7	44.7	57.9	31.6	40.0	9.5	14.2	0.31	0.36
Assam	22	4,230	2.9	41.7	73.9	53.1	11.4	16.0	2.3	0.23	0.31
Bihar	86	2,904	1.8	37.2	47.4	66.3	56.7	25.0	20.0	0.26	0.31
Gujarat	41	6,425	2.2	40.8	57.4	41.6	38.8	11.4	12.1	0.26	0.28
Haryana	16	8,690	3.2	56.8	65.3	23.2	18.3	6.7	5.2	0.29	0.28
Himachal Pradesh	5	5,355	2.0	54.2	96.1	24.8	3.3	6.7	3.3	0.28	0.28
Jammu & Kashmir	8[a]	4,051	-0.1	47.6	63.0	33.1	11.0	8.9	2.3	0.30	0.28
Karnataka	45	5,555	3.0	39.9	53.2	42.3	45.0	15.3	17.0	0.30	0.34
Kerala	29	4,618	0.3	52.2	64.4	44.0	44.5	15.4	16.9	0.32	0.36
Madhya Pradesh	66	4,077	3.1	37.2	57.3	49.8	46.0	17.9	17.4	0.29	0.33
Maharashtra	79	8,180	2.8	42.6	66.5	54.2	35.6	19.9	14.1	0.32	0.34
Orissa	32	4,068	2.7	33.4	58.1	65.6	44.5	26.8	17.4	0.27	0.31
Punjab	20	9,643	3.2	63.1	73.3	21.0	11.2	4.9	2.6	0.30	0.28
Rajasthan	44	4,361	2.4	40.7	57.6	41.9	41.5	17.1	14.0	0.32	0.35
Tamil Nadu	56	5,078	2.5	38.7	55.5	51.3	39.2	20.2	14.5	0.33	0.36
Uttar Pradesh	139	4,012	2.2	37.7	55.1	47.7	41.9	16.2	14.8	0.29	0.33
West Bengal	68	5,383	2.5	40.5	65.1	57.2	30.6	20.1	9.1	0.26	0.35
INDIA	846[b]	5,583[c]	3.1	41.2	61.2	44.9	36.5	15.5	12.8	n/a	n/a

Notes.
[a] Projection from earlier censuses.
[b] Including the estimated population of Jammu and Kashmir.
[c] Per-capita net national product at current prices.

Table A.3 (contd.)

State	Life expectancy at birth, 1990–2 (years)		Infant mortality rate, 1990–2 (per 1,000 live births)	Death rate, age 0–4, 1991 (per 1,000)		Estimated maternal mortality rate, 1982–6 (per 100,000 live births)	Death rate, 1990–2 (per 1,000)	Birth rate, 1990–2 (per 1,000)	Total fertility rate, 1991
	Female	Male		Female	Male				
Andhra Pradesh	61.5	59.0	71	20.2	22.3	402	9.3	25.5	3.0
Assam	n/a	n/a	76	30.4	34.4	1,028	10.8	30.4	3.5
Bihar	58.3	n/a	72	24.8	20.9	813	10.4	31.9	4.4
Gujarat	61.3	59.1	69	23.5	23.1	355	8.8	28.3	3.1
Haryana	63.6	62.2	71	23.8	22.3	435	8.4	32.3	4.0
Himachal Pradesh	n/a	n/a	70	18.0	20.4	n/a	8.7	27.9	3.1
Jammu & Kashmir	n/a	n/a	69[a]	n/a	n/a	n/a	8.0[a]	31.5[a]	3.3[a]
Karnataka	63.6	60.0	73	23.9	23.4	415	8.5	27.0	3.1
Kerala	74.4	68.8	17	4.1	4.5	234	6.1	18.5	1.8
Madhya Pradesh	53.5	54.1	111	46.6	42.4	535	13.0	35.7	4.6
Maharashtra	64.7	63.1	59	16.7	15.9	393	7.8	26.3	3.0
Orissa	54.8	55.9	120	39.2	38.8	778	12.1	28.9	3.3
Punjab	67.5	65.4	57	18.4	15.6	n/a	7.9	27.5	3.1
Rajasthan	57.8	57.6	84	33.8	28.4	938	10.1	34.4	4.6
Tamil Nadu	63.2	61.0	58	15.3	16.9	319	8.6	21.0	2.2
Uttar Pradesh	54.6	56.8	98	38.4	33.2	931	12.1	35.8	5.1
West Bengal	62.0	60.5	66	20.8	20.4	551	8.3	26.6	3.2
INDIA	59.4	59.0	80	27.5	25.6	555	9.8	29.5	3.6

Note.   [a] 1989 (or 1988–90, for three-year averages).

Table A.3 (contd.)

State	Literacy rate, age 7+, 1991 (%)		Literacy rate, age 10–14, 1987–8 (%)				Proportion of persons aged 6 and above who have completed primary education, 1992–3 (%)	
			Rural		Urban			
	Female	Male	Female	Male	Female	Male	Female	Male
Andhra Pradesh	32.7	55.1	42.3	65.7	80.0	87.7	26.4	45.3
Assam	43.0	61.9	78.1	82.5	86.8	92.9	28.5	41.2
Bihar	22.9	52.5	34.1	59.5	71.0	80.5	17.4	42.9
Gujarat	48.6	73.1	60.9	78.2	83.3	87.5	33.5	53.6
Haryana	40.5	69.1	63.5	87.3	88.6	93.4	30.9	53.5
Himachal Pradesh	52.1	75.4	80.7	95.1	97.2	96.0	39.2	56.8
Jammu & Kashmir	n/a	n/a	49.7	78.7	79.5	83.6	37.7[a]	56.3[a]
Karnataka	44.3	67.3	55.8	74.2	85.9	86.8	30.4	46.8
Kerala	86.2	93.6	98.2	98.1	97.8	97.3	60.5	65.8
Madhya Pradesh	28.9	58.4	40.0	67.8	85.5	92.3	21.0	44.6
Maharashtra	52.3	76.6	68.2	86.3	90.7	94.7	35.9	55.1
Orissa	34.7	63.1	51.4	70.0	79.4	89.6	23.0	42.8
Punjab	50.4	65.7	68.8	76.5	87.3	89.5	41.0	51.6
Rajasthan	20.4	55.0	22.2	71.6	62.5	89.1	15.6	41.8
Tamil Nadu	51.3	73.8	70.8	85.1	85.6	91.7	40.1	58.7
Uttar Pradesh	25.3	55.7	39.0	68.0	68.8	76.0	21.4	47.3
West Bengal	46.6	67.8	60.7	69.0	82.2	87.4	29.2	47.4
INDIA	39.3	64.1	51.7	72.9	81.6	87.9	28.1	48.6

Note. [a] Jammu region only.

PART 4. School Attendance and Enrolment

State	Proportion of rural children attending school, 1987–8 (%)				Proportion of never-enrolled children in 12–14 age group, 1986–7 (%)			
	age 5–9		age 10–14		Rural		Urban	
	Female	Male	Female	Male	Female	Male	Female	Male
Andhra Pradesh	45.2	63.3	30.9	57.0	59.7	32.7	18.9	9.4
Assam	47.8	48.6	70.9	76.1	28.5	22.9	18.0	5.1
Bihar	19.7	33.0	28.7	54.6	67.3	41.9	38.0	19.5
Gujarat	52.1	63.1	52.2	76.5	38.7	22.5	17.7	10.2
Haryana	53.8	60.2	51.6	81.8	42.4	12.9	14.6	6.2
Himachal Pradesh	63.3	73.6	73.0	92.5	n/a	n/a	n/a	n/a
Jammu & Kashmir	40.3	53.4	45.8	77.5	47.6	21.5	29.3	18.9
Karnataka	50.6	57.0	45.5	65.0	46.5	26.0	17.4	11.7
Kerala	82.8	86.9	91.2	93.3	1.8	0.4	0.6	0.1
Madhya Pradesh	26.3	43.9	29.9	61.6	66.4	30.6	18.1	6.6
Maharashtra	54.4	64.0	59.3	72.1	27.7	12.6	12.4	4.6
Orissa	44.9	55.4	19.2	69.6	54.7	34.0	20.3	20.2
Punjab	59.1	66.3	59.3	72.1	33.3	22.6	7.9	7.9
Rajasthan	25.5	47.8	19.2	69.6	81.7	26.1	36.0	12.5
Tamil Nadu	77.7	84.9	48.7	70.7	26.3	11.5	5.6	3.7
Uttar Pradesh	28.2	45.4	30.7	63.8	68.0	27.2	38.8	19.2
West Bengal	40.9	44.8	52.8	64.3	45.9	34.6	15.2	13.0
INDIA	40.4	52.5	41.9	66.1	50.7	26.4	19.3	10.9

Table A.3 (contd.)

State	Female–male ratio, 1991	Ratio of female death rate to male death rate, age 0–4, 1991 (%)	Married women as percentage of all women in 15–19 age group, 1981	Female labour-force participation rate, 1991 (%)	Female employment as percentage of total public-sector employment, 1989
Andhra Pradesh	972	90.6	56	30.1	10.2
Assam	923	88.4	n/a	12.6	n/a
Bihar	911	118.7	64	10.0	6.8
Gujarat	934	101.7	27	13.7	14.4
Haryana	865	106.7	48	6.0	13.4
Himachal Pradesh	976	88.2	32	19.4	11.1
Jammu & Kashmir	n/a	n/a	28	n/a	9.5
Karnataka	960	102.1	36	22.7	14.8
Kerala	1036	91.1	14	12.8	29.5
Madhya Pradesh	931	109.9	62	22.8	9.5
Maharashtra	934	105.0	38	26.5	13.1
Orissa	971	101.0	31	12.1	7.4
Punjab	882	117.9	13	2.8	14.8
Rajasthan	910	119.0	64	13.0	10.9
Tamil Nadu	974	90.5	23	25.1	19.0
Uttar Pradesh	879	115.7	61	7.5	7.7
West Bengal	917	102.0	38	8.0	9.9
INDIA	927	107.4	46	16.0	n/a

Table A.3 (contd.)

State	Percentage of currently-married women aged 13–49 who are aware of, have ever used, are currently using any modern non-terminal method of contraception, 1992–3			Proportion of currently-married women below 49 who are sterilized, 1992–3 (%)	Percentage of recent births preceded by different kinds of maternal care, 1992–3		Proportion of births taking place in medical institutions, 1991 (%)	Proportion of children aged 12–23 months who have not received any vaccination, 1992–3 (%)
	aware of	ever used	currently using		tetanus vaccine	antenatal check-up		
Andhra Pradesh	61	6	2	38	81	66	38	18
Assam	82	18	5	12	44	47	18	44
Bihar	68	6	3	17	37	27	12	54
Gujarat	77	14	6	38	70	50	24	19
Haryana	91	23	10	30	70	67	20	18
Himachal Pradesh	88	25	9	33	71	74	22	9
Jammu & Kashmir	89[a]	24[a]	10[a]	25[a]	78[a]	79[a]	15[b]	16[a]
Karnataka	84	14	5	41	77	65	41	15
Kerala	97	27	6	42	94	97	92	11
Madhya Pradesh	57	12	4	26	51	35	13	34
Maharashtra	77	16	6	40	82	70	34	8
Orissa	61	8	3	28	63	39	10	28
Punjab	94	32	17	32	87	86	7	18
Rajasthan	59	7	3	25	35	23	5	49
Tamil Nadu	86	16	6	38	94	78	57	3
Uttar Pradesh	80	11	6	12	44	30	4	43
West Bengal	91	23	7	26	78	69	31	22
INDIA	76	14	5.5	27	61	49	24	30

Notes. [a] Jammu region only. [b] 1989.

Table A.3 (contd.)

State	Proportion of villages with medical facilities, 1981 (%)	Per-capita supply of foodgrains through the public distribution system, 1986–7 (kg/year)	Proportion of the population receiving subsidized food-grains from the public distribution system, 1986–7		Proportion of households having access to safe drinking water, 1991 (%)		Number of hospital beds per million persons, 1991		Proportion of households with electricity connection, 1991	
			Rural	Urban	Rural	Urban	Rural	Urban	Rural	Urban
Andhra Pradesh	23.0	22.8	59.7	51.4	57.4	87.1	76	1,827	37.5	73.3
Assam	n/a	30.5	24.6	43.0	60.9	88.2	175	4,414	12.4	63.2
Bihar	13.8	6.5	1.7	7.1	62.4	85.5	31	2,276	5.6	58.8
Gujarat	26.2	24.5	44.5	32.0	67.0	93.1	185	2,904	56.4	83.0
Haryana	57.1	6.2	3.1	7.1	68.3	95.5	44	1,593	63.2	89.1
Himachal Pradesh	13.4	25.0	28.2	25.3	76.7	94.2	102	1,871	85.9	96.2
Jammu & Kashmir	17.9	34.6	23.3	78.6	n/a	n/a	77	4,215	n/a	n/a
Karnataka	10.8	19.9	61.9	62.7	73.2	90.3	81	2,297	41.8	76.3
Kerala	96.3	60.2	87.7	87.0	71.2	85.1	1,768	4,230	42.0	67.7
Madhya Pradesh	5.6	7.4	9.1	17.4	54.4	87.0	39	1,313	34.5	72.5
Maharashtra	17.6	22.4	47.7	43.8	62.0	95.2	250	3,251	58.5	86.1
Orissa	10.6	7.1	1.7	13.8	46.8	81.2	107	2,610	17.5	62.1
Punjab	24.3	4.7	0.1	4.6	94.3	98.0	196	2,040	77.0	94.6
Rajasthan	13.2	17.4	8.8	5.6	53.0	91.2	38	2,039	22.4	76.7
Tamil Nadu	23.4	25.4	53.5	55.4	67.7	87.7	115	2,336	44.5	76.8
Uttar Pradesh	9.6	2.9	2.1	7.0	60.1	90.7	23	1,619	11.0	67.8
West Bengal	13.2	26.1	26.9	59.8	84.1	94.8	154	2,479	17.8	70.2
INDIA	14.0	18.1	26.8[a]	35.5[a]	63.6	90.7	152	2,409	30.5	75.8

Note. [a] Calculated as a weighted average of the state-specific figures.

Table A.4. *Time Trends for Selected Indicators (India)*

	1950–1	1960–1	1970–1	1973–4	1977–8	1980–1	1983–4	1987–8	1990–1	1991–2	1992–3	1993–4	Index of annual rate of change, 1970–1 to 1990–1[a] (%)
Per-capita net national product at constant prices[b] (1950–1 = 100)	100	120	135	132	145	145	159	169	197	193	198	203[c]	1.8
Index of agricultural production[b] (1950–1 = 100)	100	148	191	192	228	231	266	259	328	319	335[c]	342[c]	2.5
Index of industrial production[b] (1950–1 = 100)	100	198	357	396	533	546	658	909	1,162	1,161	1,195	1,244[c]	5.8
Gross domestic capital formation (as % of GDP)	10.2	15.7	16.6	19.1	19.5	22.7	20.1	22.9	27.1	23.6	22.0	20.4[c]	2.0
'Volume index' of foreign trade (1978–9 = 100)													
Exports	–	–	59.0	69.5	93.2	108.1	113.0	140.0	194.1	208.6	222.9	272.4	5.5
Imports	–	–	67.2	87.2	100.0	137.9	185.4	204.8	237.7	228.0	282.0	329.1	6.5
Employment in organized private sector[d] (thousand persons)	–	5,040	6,742	6,794	7,043	7,395	7,346	7,392	7,677	7,846	–	–	0.6
Employment in the public sector (thousand persons)	–	7,050	10,731	12,486	14,200	15,484	16,869	18,320	19,058	19,210	–	–	2.8

Table A.4. (contd.)

	1950–1	1960–1	1970–1	1973–4	1977–8	1980–1	1983–4	1987–8	1990–1	1991–2	1992–3	1993–4	Index of annual rate of change, 1970–1 to 1990–1[a] (%)
Per-capita earnings of public-sector employees (Rs/year at 1960 prices)	–	–	–	2,229	3,101	3,551	3,939	4,421	5,171	5,237	5,484	5,672	4.6
Real wages of agricultural labourers (Rs/day at 1960 prices)	–	–	1.52	1.37	1.74	1.65	1.71	2.36	2.57	2.44	–	–	2.9
Per-capita net availability of cereals and pulses (grams/day)	395	469	469	451	468	455	480	449	510	469[c]	464[c]	474[c]	0.3
Head-count index of poverty (%)													
Rural	–	–	57.3	56.2	54.5	–	49.0	44.9	–	–	–	–	–1.4
Urban	–	–	45.9	49.2	43.0	–	38.3	36.5	–	–	–	–	–1.7
'Sen index' of poverty													
Rural	–	–	23.6	22.4	22.3	–	18.8	15.5	–	–	–	–	–2.3
Urban	–	–	18.0	18.6	16.5	–	13.6	12.8	–	–	–	–	–2.3
'Squared poverty gap' index of poverty													
Rural	7.5	5.5	6.8	7.1	6.1	–	4.8	3.4	2.9	–	–	–	–4.6
Urban	4.8	5.8	5.4	5.2	4.5	–	3.6	3.3	3.1	–	–	–	–2.9

Table A.4. (contd.)

	1950–1	1960–1	1970–1	1973–4	1977–8	1980–1	1983–4	1987–8	1990–1	1991–2	1992–3	1993–4	Index of annual rate of change, 1970–1 to 1990–1[a] (%)
Gini coefficient of per-capita consumer expenditure													
Rural	33.7	32.5	28.8	28.5	30.9	–	30.1	30.1	27.7	–	–	–	0.0
Urban	40.0	35.6	34.7	30.8	34.7	–	34.1	35.6	34.0	–	–	–	0.2
Literacy rate[e] (%)													
Female	9	15	22	–	–	30	–	–	39	–	–	–	2.9
Male	27	40	46	–	–	56	–	–	64	–	–	–	1.7
Birth rate[f] (per 1,000)	39.9	41.7	36.9	34.5	33.3	33.9	33.9	31.5	29.5	29.2	28.7	–	–0.9
Life expectancy at birth[g] (years)	32.1	41.3	45.6	–	–	50.4	–	–	59.2	–	–	–	1.3
Government expenditure on education, health, and defence[h] (Rs per person per year, at constant 1981–2 prices)													
Education	10.2	29.2	47.6	46.3	56.0	57.1	68.2	97.4	115.4	109.5	111.9	112.5	4.6
Health	4.8	11.9	18.5	18.8	25.5	28.9	37.9	47.6	49.0	47.2	47.4	46.6	5.5
Defence and police	n/a	45.8	80.8	76.0	82.6	78.1	94.6	136.9	137.7	128.8	125.8	123.0	3.1

Notes. [a] Annual growth rate, calculated by OLS regression of the logarithm of the relevant variable on time, based on the available observations for the 1970–91 period.

[b] The original figures are based on different 'base years' (1980–1, in the case of per-capita net national product and industrial production, and 'triennium ending 1969–70', in the case of agricultural production), and have been normalized by simple division of the original figure for each year by the original 1950–1 figure.

[c] Provisional estimates, from Government of India (1995).

[d] Non-agricultural establishments employing 10 persons or more.

[e] Age 7 and above for 1981 and 1991, 5 and above for other years.

[f] Data for 1950–1 and 1960–1 relate to the decades 1941–50 and 1951–60, respectively (census estimates).

[g] Data for 1950–1, 1960–1, 1970–1, and 1980–1 relate to the decades 1941–50, 1951–60, 1961–70, and 1971–80, respectively (census estimates).

[h] Central and state governments combined.

Sources. Government of India, *Economic Survey 1980–81* (pp. 69, 98, 99), *Economic Survey 1984–85* (pp. 94, 166–7), *Economic Survey 1987–88* (p. S-79), *Economic Survey 1990–91* (p. S-38), *Economic Survey 1991–92* (p. S-91), *Economic Survey 1993–94*, (pp. 2, S-1, S-2, S-9, S-13, S-24, S-39, S-53 to S-55, S-98), *Economic Survey 1994–95*, (pp. S-3, S-7, S-13, S-24, S-39, S-54, S-55, S-56, S-99, S-100). The following sources have also been used: Tendulkar, Sundaram, and Jain (1993) and Datt (1995) for estimates of poverty indices and Gini coefficients; *Sample Registration Bulletin*, July 1993, Table 1 (p. 5), for birth rates from 1970–1 to 1990–1; Chandhok (1990), p. 1072; unpublished estimates from the Office of the Registrar-General, for birth rates in 1992 and 1993, and life expectancy in 1991. The index of real wages for (male) agricultural labourers was calculated by Bipul Chattopadhyay (Institute of Economic Growth, New Delhi), from data published in various issues of *Agricultural Wages in India*, based on the method described in Acharya (1989). The figures on government expenditure (last row) are calculated from Centre for Monitoring the Indian Economy (1994a), *Basic Statistics Relating to the Indian Economy*, Tables 2.3, 2.8, 17.2, 22.2 (we have used the Wholesale Price Index to deflate expenditure figures at current prices). In cases where the original source gives figures for *calendar* years, we have placed the figure for a particular year in the column corresponding to the pair of years *ending* in that year (e.g. the 1991 literacy rate estimate appears in the 1990–1 column, etc.).

Sources Used in Table A.3

Indicator	Source and Remarks
Population, 1991	Census of India 1991, 'final population totals', as reported in Nanda (1992), pp. 86–95.
Per-capita state domestic product, 1991–2	*Economic Survey 1993–94* (Government of India, 1994a), Tables 1.1 and 1.8, pp. S-3 and S-12.
Growth rate of per-capita SDP, 1980–90	Calculated (by OLS regression of the logarithm of per-capita SDP at constant prices on time) from Central Statistical Organisation (1991a, 1991b).
Average per-capita consumer expenditure, 1987–8	Tendulkar et al. (1993), Table A.5, based on the 43rd round of the National Sample Survey, 1987–8.
Measures of poverty	Tendulkar et al. (1993), Table A.5, based on the 43rd round of the National Sample Survey, 1987–8. Some of these estimates are also presented in Minhas et al. (1991).
Gini coefficient of per-capita consumer expenditure, 1987–8	National Sample Survey, 43rd round, 1987–8, special tabulation by Dr P.V. Srinivasan, Indira Gandhi Institute of Development Research, Bombay.
Life expectancy at birth, 1991	Unpublished estimates based on Sample Registration System data, supplied by the Office of the Registrar-General, New Delhi.
Infant mortality rate, 1990–2	Three-year average based on Sample Registration System, presented in *Sample Registration Bulletin*, January 1994, Tables 14 and 17 (pp. 46–53 and 62–4).
Death rate, age 0–4, 1991	*Sample Registration System: Fertility and Mortality Indicators 1991* (Government of India, 1993b), Table 7, pp. 152–74.
Estimated maternal mortality rate	Mari Bhat et al. (1992), Table 4.
Death rate, 1990–2	Three-year average based on Sample Registration System, presented in *Sample Registration Bulletin*, January 1994, pp. 22–9 and 58–61.
Birth rate, 1990–2	Three-year average based on Sample Registration System, presented in *Sample Registration Bulletin*, January 1994, pp. 22–9 and 54–7.
Total fertility rate, 1991	*Sample Registration System: Fertility and Mortality Indicators 1991* (Government of India, 1993b), pp. 94–105.
Literacy rates, age 7 and above, 1991	Census of India 1991, 'final population totals', as reported in Nanda (1992), pp. 210–17.
Literacy rates, age 10–14, 1987–8	Sengupta (1991), Statements 2.3, 3.5, and 3.6 (pp. 17 and 28), based on National Sample Survey data.

Indicator	Source and Remarks
Proportion of persons aged 6 and above who have completed primary education, 1992–3	International Institute for Population Sciences (1994), Tables 6 and 7. The IIPS survey (1992–3) was not aimed at collecting data on education, but the broad consistency between the literacy figures derived from this survey and those obtained from the 1991 census suggests that the IIPS figures on completion of primary education, too, are reasonably accurate.
School attendance, 1987–8	Visaria et al. (1993), Tables 5 and 6 (pp. 31–4), based on National Sample Survey data.
School enrolment, 1986–7	Visaria et al. (1993), Table 15, p.53, based on National Sample Survey data.
Female–male ratio, 1991	Census of India (1991), 'final population totals', as reported in Nanda (1992), Tables 5.3 and 6 (pp. 206–17).
Ratio of female to male death rate, age 0–4, 1991	Calculated from *Sample Registration System: Fertility and Mortality Indicators 1991* (Government of India, 1993b), Table 7, pp. 152–74.
Proportion of married women in the 15–19 age group, 1981	Nuna (1990), p. 98, based on 1981 census data.
Female labour-force participation rate, 1991	Nanda (1992), Table 3.1, pp. 115–23, based on 1991 census data.
Female employment in the public sector, 1989	Nuna (1990), p. 99.
Awareness and use of contraception, 1992–3	International Institute for Population Sciences (1994), Tables 15, 17, and 18.
Incidence of female sterilization, 1992–3	International Institute for Population Sciences (1994), Table 18.
Antenatal care, 1992–3	International Institute for Population Sciences (1994), Table 24.
Birth attendance, 1991	*Sample Registration System: Fertility and Mortality Indicators 1991* (Government of India, 1993b), Statement 25, p. 27.
Child vaccination, 1992–3	International Institute for Population Sciences (1994), Table 28.
Medical facilities in rural areas, 1981	Calculated from district-level data on medical facilities available in the *District Census Handbooks* of the 1981 census.
Supply of foodgrains through the public distribution system, 1986–7	Jha (1994), based on special tabulations of the 42nd round of the National Sample Survey.
Coverage of public distribution system, 1986–7	Parikh (1994), based on special tabulations of the 42nd round of the National Sample Survey.

Indicator	Source and Remarks
Access to safe drinking water, 1991	Sundaram and Tendulkar (1994), based on 1991 census data.
Availability of hospital beds, 1991	Calculated from Government of India (1992e), Table 8.01, p. 117.
Electrification, 1991	Government of India (1993e), Table 3.3, based on 1991 census data.

Note. Some of the demographic statistics for 'India' (last row in Table A.3) exclude Jammu and Kashmir, where the 1991 census was not conducted, and where the Sample Registration System (SRS) has also been inoperative in recent years. In Table A.3, SRS-based data for Jammu and Kashmir relate to the latest year for which information is available (as specified in the tables), and are taken from the relevant issues of *Sample Registration System* and *Sample Registration Bulletin*.

REFERENCES

Acharya, Sarthi (1989), 'Agricultural Wages in India: A Disaggregated Analysis', *Indian Journal of Agricultural Economics*, 44.

—— (1990), *Maharashtra Employment Guarantee Scheme: A Study of Labour Market Intervention* (Delhi: ILO-ARTEP).

Adelman, Irma, and Morris, Cynthia T. (1973), *Economic Growth and Social Equity in Developing Countries* (Stanford: Stanford University Press).

Adelman, Irma, and Robinson, Sherman (1978), *Income Distribution Policy in Developing Countries: A Case Study of Korea* (Oxford: Clarendon Press).

Agarwal, Anil, and Narain, Sunita (1989), *Towards Green Villages* (New Delhi: Centre for Science and Environment).

Agarwal, Bina (1986), 'Women, Poverty and Agricultural Growth in India', *Journal of Peasant Studies*, 13.

—— (1988), 'Who Sows? Who Reaps? Women and Land Rights in India', *Journal of Peasant Studies*, 15.

—— (1989), 'Tribal Matriliny in Transition: The Garos, Khasis and Lalungs of North-East India', mimeo, Institute of Economic Growth, New Delhi.

—— (1991), 'Social Security and the Family: Coping with Seasonality and Calamity in Rural India', in Ahmad et al. (1991).

—— (1994), *A Field of One's Own: Gender and Land Rights in South Asia* (Cambridge: Cambridge University Press).

Agnihotri, Anita, and Sivaswamy, G. (1993), *Total Literacy Campaign in the Sundergarh District of Orissa* (New Delhi: Directorate of Adult Education).

Agnihotri, Satish (1994), 'Missing Females: A Disaggregated Analysis', mimeo, University of East Anglia; forthcoming in *Economic and Political Weekly*.

—— (1995), 'Sex Ratio Variations in India: What Do Languages Tell Us?', mimeo, University of East Anglia.

Agrawal, A.N., Varma, H.O., and Gupta, R.C. (1992), *India: Economic Information Yearbook 1991–92* (New Delhi: National Publishing House).

Agrawal, S.P., and Aggarwal, J.C. (1992), *Women's Education in India* (New Delhi: Concept).

Ahluwalia, Isher Judge (1985), *Industrial Growth in India* (New Delhi: Oxford University Press).

Ahluwalia, Isher Judge (1991), *Productivity and Growth in Indian Manufacturing* (New Delhi: Oxford University Press).

—— (1992), *Trade Policy and Industrialisation in India* (Bombay: Export-Import Bank of India).

Ahluwalia, Montek S. (1978), 'Rural Poverty and Agricultural Performance in India', *Journal of Development Studies*, 14.

—— (1990), 'Policies for Poverty Alleviation', *Asian Development Review*, 8.

Ahmad, E., Drèze, J.P., Hills, J., and Sen, A.K. (eds.) (1991), *Social Security in Developing Countries* (Oxford: Oxford University Press).

Ahmad, E., and Hussain, A. (1991), 'Social Security in China: A Historical Perspective', in Ahmad et al. (1991).

AKG Centre for Research and Studies (1994), *International Congress on Kerala Studies: Abstracts*, 5 volumes (Thiruvananthapuram: AKG Centre for Research and Studies).

Alagh, Yoginder K. (1986), *Some Aspects of Planning Policies in India* (Allahabad: Vohra Publishers).

Alailima, Patricia (1985), 'Evolution of Government Policies and Expenditure on Social Welfare in Sri Lanka during the 20th Century', mimeo, Colombo.

Alamgir, Mohiuddin (1980), *Famine in South Asia* (Boston: Oelgeschlager, Gunn and Hain).

Alderman, H., Behrman, J.R., Khan, S., Ross, D.R., and Sabot, R. (1993), 'Public School Expenditures in Rural Pakistan: Efficiently Targeting Girls in a Lagging Region', mimeo, World Bank, Washington, DC.

Alesina, Alberto, and Rodrik, Dani (1994), 'Distributive Politics and Economic Growth', *Quarterly Journal of Economics*, 109.

Almeida, A. (1978), 'The Gift of a Bride: Sociological Implications of the Dowry System in Goa', mimeo, Université Catholique de Louvain, Louvain-la-Neuve, Belgium.

Altekar, A.S. (1956), *The Position of Women in Hindu Civilization* (Delhi: Motilal Banarsidass).

Amsden, Alice H. (1989), *Asia's Next Giant: Late Industrialization in South Korea* (Oxford: Clarendon Press).

—— (1994), 'Why Isn't the Whole World Experimenting with the East Asian Model to Develop?', *World Development*, 22.

Anand, Sudhir (1993), 'Inequality between and within Nations', mimeo, Center for Population and Development Studies, Harvard University.

Anand, Sudhir, and Kanbur, S.M. Ravi (1990), 'Public Policy and Basic Needs Provision: Intervention and Achievement in Sri Lanka', in Drèze and Sen (1990), vol. III.

—— (1993), 'Inequality and Development: A Critique', *Journal of Development Economics*, 40.

Anand, Sudhir, and Ravallion, Martin (1993), 'Human Development in Poor Countries: On the Role of Private Incomes and Public Services', *Journal of Economic Perspectives,* 7 (Winter).

Anand, Sudhir, and Sen, Amartya (1994), 'Sustainable Human Development', UNDP Working Paper; forthcoming in *World Development.*

Antony, T.V. (1992), 'The Family Planning Programme: Lessons from Tamil Nadu's Experience', *The Indian Journal of Social Science,* 5(3).

Archer, David, and Costello, Patrick (1990), *Literacy and Power: The Latin American Battleground* (London: Earthscan Publications).

Arneson, R. (1989), 'Equality and Equality of Opportunity for Welfare', *Philosophical Studies,* 56.

—— (1990), 'Liberalism, Distributive Subjectivism, and Equal Opportunity for Welfare', *Philosophy and Public Affairs,* 19.

Arrow, Kenneth J. (1951), 'An Extension of the Basic Theorems of Classical Welfare Economics', in J. Neyman (ed.), *Proceedings of the Second Berkeley Symposium on Mathematical Economics* (Berkeley, CA: University of California Press).

Arrow, Kenneth J., and Hahn, Frank (1971), *General Competitive Analysis* (San Francisco: Holden-Day).

Ashton, B., Hill, K., Piazza, A., and Zeitz, R. (1984), 'Famine in China, 1958–61', *Population and Development Review,* 10.

Atkinson, A.B. (1969), 'Import Strategy and Growth under Conditions of Stagnant Export Earnings', *Oxford Economic Papers,* 21.

—— (1989), *Poverty and Social Security* (New York: Harvester and Wheatsheaf).

—— (1995), 'Capabilities, Exclusion, and the Supply of Goods', in Basu et al. (1995).

Aziz, Abdul (1994), 'History of Panchayat Reforms in Karnataka', paper presented at a Seminar on Management of Education under Panchayati Raj held at the National Institute of Educational Planning and Administration, 27–8 October, 1994.

Babu, S.C., and Hallam, J.A. (1989), 'Socioeconomic Impacts of School Feeding Programmes: Empirical Evidence from a South Indian Village', *Food Policy,* 14.

Bagchi, Amiya K. (1982), *The Political Economy of Underdevelopment* (Cambridge: Cambridge University Press).

—— (1994), 'Making Sense of Government's Macroeconomic Stabilization Strategy', *Economic and Political Weekly,* April 30.

Bahadur, K.P. (1978), *History, Caste and Culture of the Rajputs* (Delhi: Ess Publications).

Balassa, Bela (1991), *Economic Policies in the Pacific Area Developing Countries* (New York: New York University Press).

Bandyopadhyay, R.(1991), 'Education for an Enlightened Society: A Review', *Economic and Political Weekly*, February 16.

Banerjee, Nirmala (1982), *Unorganised Women Workers: The Calcutta Experience* (Calcutta: Centre for Studies in Social Sciences).

—— (1985), 'Women's Work and Discrimination', in Jain and Banerjee (1985).

Banerjee, Sumanta (1992), ' "Uses of Literacy": Total Literacy Campaign in Three West Bengal Districts', *Economic and Political Weekly*, February 29.

—— (1994), 'Obstacles to Change', *Economic and Political Weekly*, March 26.

Banerji, Debabar (1985), *Health and Family Planning Services in India* (New Delhi: Lok Paksh).

—— (1989), 'Rural Social Transformation and Change in Health Behaviour', *Economic and Political Weekly*, July 1.

Bang, R.A., et al. (1989), 'High Prevalence of Gynaecological Diseases in Rural Indian Women', *The Lancet*, January 14.

Banister, Judith (1992), 'Demographic Aspects of Poverty in China', background paper prepared for the World Bank (1992) report *China: Strategies for Reducing Poverty in the 1990s* (Washington, DC: World Bank).

Bara, D., Bhengra, R., and Minz, B. (1991), 'Tribal Female Literacy: Factors in Differentiation among Munda Religious Communities', *Social Action*, 41.

Bardhan, Kalpana (1985), 'Womens' Work, Welfare and Status', *Economic and Political Weekly*, 20 (50–52).

Bardhan, Pranab (1974), 'On Life and Death Questions', *Economic and Political Weekly*, 9 (Special Number).

—— (1984a), *Land, Labor and Rural Poverty* (New York: Columbia University Press).

—— (1984b), *The Political Economy of Development in India* (Oxford: Blackwell).

—— (1988), 'Sex Disparity in Child Survival in Rural India', in Srinivasan and Bardhan (1988).

—— (1992), 'The State Against Society: The Great Divide in Indian Social Science Discourse', paper presented at a workshop on 'Production Units in Micro and Macrostructural Perspectives' held at the School of Oriental and African Studies, London, 12–18 July 1992.

—— (1993a), 'Symposium on Management of Local Commons', *Journal of Economic Perspectives*, 7 (4).

—— (1993b), 'Economics of Development and the Development of Economics', *Journal of Economic Perspectives*, 7 (Spring).

—— (1995), 'Rational Fools and Cooperation in a Poor Hydraulic Economy', in Basu et al. (1995).

Bardhan, Pranab (ed.) (1989), *The Economic Theory of Agrarian Institutions* (Oxford: Clarendon Press).

Barnett, Marguerite Ross (1976), *The Politics of Cultural Nationalism in South India* (Princeton: Princeton University Press).

Barro, Robert J. (1990a), 'Government Spending in a Simple Model of Endogenous Growth', *Journal of Political Economy*, 98.

—— (1990b), 'Economic Growth in a Cross Section of Countries', *Quarterly Journal of Economics*, 105.

Barro, Robert J., and Lee, Jong-Wha (1993a), 'Losers and Winners in Economic Growth', Working Paper 4341, National Bureau of Economic Research.

—— (1993b), 'International Comparisons of Educational Attainment', paper presented at a conference on 'How Do National Policies Affect Long-Run Growth?', World Bank, Washington, DC.

Basu, Alaka Malwade (1989), 'Is Discrimination in Food Really Necessary for Explaining Sex Differentials in Childhood Mortality?', *Population Studies*, 43 (2).

—— (1991), 'Demand and its Sociocultural Context', in Satia and Jejeebhoy (1991).

—— (1992), *Culture, the Status of Women and Demographic Behaviour* (Oxford: Clarendon Press).

—— (1993), 'Fertility Decline and Increasing Gender Imbalances in India: Including the South Indian Turnaround', mimeo, Institute of Economic Growth, Delhi University.

Basu, Alaka M., and Jeffery, Roger (eds.) (forthcoming), *Girls' Schooling, Women's Autonomy and Fertility Change in South Asia* (New Delhi: Sage).

Basu, Aparna (1988), 'A Century's Journey: Women's Education in Western India, 1820–1920', in Chanana (1988b).

Basu, Kaushik (1993), 'Structural Reform in India, 1991–93: Experience and Agenda', *Economic and Political Weekly*, November 27.

—— (1994), 'Where There is no Economist: Some Institutional and Legal Prerequisites of Economic Reforms in India', Working Paper No. 6, Centre for Development Economics, Delhi School of Economics.

Basu, K., Pattanaik, P., and Suzumura, K. (eds.) (1995), *Choice, Welfare, and Development* (Oxford: Clarendon).

Bauer, Peter (1948), *The Rubber Industry* (London: Longmans).

—— (1972), *Dissent on Development* (London: Weidenfeld).

—— (1991), *The Development Frontier* (Cambridge, MA: Harvard University Press).

Bauer, Peter, and Yamey, Basil (1957), *The Economics of Underdeveloped Countries* (Cambridge: Cambridge University Press).

Baviskar, Amita (1992), 'Development, Nature and Resistance: The Case of Bhilala Tribals in the Narmada Valley', unpublished Ph.D. thesis, Cornell University.

Beck, Tony (1994), *The Experience of Poverty: Fighting for Respect and Resources in Village India* (London: Intermediate Technology Publications).

Beenstock, M., and Sturdy, P. (1990), 'The Determinants of Infant Mortality in Regional India', *World Development*, 18.

Behrman, Jere R. (1987), 'Schooling in Developing Countries: Which Countries Are the Under- and Over-Achievers and What Is the Schooling Impact?', *Economics of Education Review*, 6.

Behrman, Jere R., and Deolalikar, Anil B. (1988), 'Health and Nutrition', in Chenery and Srinivasan (1988).

Behrman, Jere R., and Schneider, Ryan (1992), 'An International Perspective on Schooling Investment in the Last Quarter Century in Some Fast-Growing Eastern and Southeastern Countries', mimeo, World Bank, Washington, DC.

Behrman, Jere R., and Srinivasan, T.N. (eds.) (1994), *Handbook of Development Economics*, vol. III (Amsterdam: North-Holland).

Behrman, J.R., and Wolfe, B.L. (1984), 'More Evidence on Nutrition Demand: Income Seems Overrated and Women's Schooling Underemphasized', *Journal of Development Economics*, 14.

―― (1987), 'How Does Mother's Schooling Affect Family Health, Nutrition, Medical Care Usage, and Household Sanitation?', *Journal of Econometrics*, 36.

Berlin, I. (1969), *Four Essays on Liberty*, 2nd edition (Oxford: Oxford University Press).

Berman, Peter (1992), 'Health Care Expenditure in India', paper presented at a workshop on 'Health and Development in India', 2–4 January, 1992; to be published in M. Das Gupta et al. (forthcoming).

Berman, Peter, and Khan, M.E. (eds.) (1993), *Paying for India's Health Care* (New Delhi: Sage).

Bernstein, T.P. (1984), 'Stalinism, Famine, and Chinese Peasants', *Theory and Society*, 13.

Berreman, Gerald D. (1962), 'Village Exogamy in Northernmost India', *Southwestern Journal of Anthropology*, 18.

―― (1993), 'Sanskritization as Female Oppression in India', in Miller (1993b).

Berry, R. Albert, and Cline, William (1979), *Agrarian Structure and Productivity in Developing Countries* (Baltimore, MD: Johns Hopkins University Press).

Bhagwati, Jagdish (1993), *India in Transition* (Oxford: Clarendon Press).

Bhagwati, Jagdish, and Desai, Padma (1970), *India: Planning for Industrialization* (Oxford: Oxford University Press).

Bhagwati, Jagdish, and Krueger, Anne O. (eds.) (1975), *Trade Strategies for Economic Development* (New York: National Bureau of Economic Research).

Bhagwati, Jagdish, and Srinivasan, T.N. (1975), *Foreign Trade Regimes and Economic Development: India* (New York: National Bureau of Economic Research).

―― (1993), *India's Economic Reforms*, with a 'Preface' by the Finance Minister, Manmohan Singh (New Delhi: Ministry of Finance, Government of India).

Bhalla, A.S. (1992), *Uneven Development in the Third World: A Study of India and China* (London: Macmillan).

Bhatia, Bela (forthcoming), 'Social Action with Rural Widows in Gujarat', in Chen (forthcoming, b).

Bhatia, B.M. (1967), *Famines in India* (Bombay: Asia Publishing House).

Bhattacharya, B.B., and Mitra, Arup (1993), 'Employment and Structural Adjustment', *Economic and Political Weekly*, September 18.

Bhende, M.J., Walker, T.S., Lieberman, S.S., and Venkataram, J.V. (1992), 'EGS and the Poor: Evidence from Longitudinal Village Studies', *Economic and Political Weekly*, March 28.

Bhuiya, A., and Streatfield, K.(1991), 'Mothers' Education and Survival of Female Children in a Rural Area of Bangladesh', *Population Studies*, 45.

Binswanger, Hans, and Rosenzweig, Mark (1984), *Contractual Arrangements, Employment and Wages in Rural Labor Markets in Asia* (New Haven: Yale University Press).

Birdsall, Nancy (1993), 'Social Development Is Economic Development', Policy Research Working Paper 1123, World Bank, Washington, DC.

Birdsall, Nancy, and Sabot, Richard H. (1993a), 'Virtuous Circles: Human Capital, Growth and Equity in East Asia', mimeo, World Bank, Washington, DC.

Birdsall, Nancy, and Sabot, Richard H. (eds.) (1993b), *Opportunity Forgone: Education, Growth and Inequality in Brazil* (Washington, DC: World Bank).

Biswas, A., and Agrawal, S.P. (1986), *Development of Education in India: A Historical Survey of Educational Documents Before and After Independence* (New Delhi: Concept).

Blackorby, Charles, and Donaldson, David (1980), 'Ethical Indices for the Measurement of Poverty', *Econometrica*, 48.

Bliss, Christopher, and Stern, Nicholas (1978), 'Productivity, Wages and Nutrition', *Journal of Development Economics*, 5.

—— (1982), *Palanpur: The Economy of an Indian Village* (Oxford: Oxford University Press).

Blomstrom, Magnus (1989), *Foreign Investments and Spillovers* (London: Routledge).

Bloom, Gerald (1994), 'Financing Rural Health Services: Lessons from China', mimeo, Institute of Development Studies, University of Sussex.

Bordia, Anil (1993), 'Universalization of Primary Education in India: Is Compulsion the Answer?', mimeo, New Delhi.

Bose, Ashish (1991a), *Demographic Diversity of India* (Delhi: B.R. Publishing).

—— (1991b), *Population of India: 1991 Census Results and Methodology* (Delhi: B.R. Publishing).

Boserup, Ester (1970), *Women's Role in Economic Development* (New York: St Martin's).

Bourne, K., and Walker, G.M.(1991), 'The Differential Effect of Mothers' Education on Mortality of Boys and Girls in India', *Population Studies*, 45.

Bramall, Chris, and Jones, Marion (1993), 'Rural Income Inequality in China since 1978', *Journal of Peasant Studies*, 21(1).

Brass, Paul R. (1992), *The Political Economy of India since Independence*, first corrected Indian edition (New Delhi: Cambridge University Press).

Breman, Jan (1974), *Patronage and Exploitation* (Berkeley, CA: University of California Press).

Brown, Lester R., and Eckholm, Erik P. (1974), *By Bread Alone* (Oxford: Pergamon).

Bruton, Henry, with Abeyesekara, G., Sanderatne, N., and Yusof, Z.A. (1993), *The Political Economy of Poverty, Equity, and Growth: Sri Lanka and Malaysia* (New York: Oxford University Press).

Buchanan, James M., and Yoon, Yong J. (1994), *The Return to Increasing Returns* (Ann Arbor: University of Michigan Press).

Budakoti, D.K. (1988), 'Study of the Community and Community Health Work in Two Primary Health Centres in Chamoli District of Uttar Pradesh', M.Phil. dissertation, Centre for Social Medicine and Community Health, Jawaharlal Nehru University, New Delhi.

Bumgarner, R. (1992), 'China: Long-Term Issues in Options for the Health Transition', World Bank Country Study, World Bank, Washington, DC.

Burra, Neera (1986), 'Child Labour in India: Poverty, Exploitation and Vested Interests', *Social Action*, 36.

—— (1988), *Child Labour Health Hazards* (New Delhi: Seminar Publications).

—— (forthcoming), *Born to Work: Child Labour in India* (Delhi: Oxford University Press).

Byrd, W., and Lin, Q. (eds.) (1990), *China's Rural Industry: Structure, Development, and Reform* (Oxford: Oxford University Press).

Byres, T. (ed.) (1994), *The State and Development Planning in India* (Oxford: Oxford University Press).

Cain, Mead (1981), 'Risk and Insurance: Perspectives on Fertility and Agrarian Change in India and Bangladesh', *Population and Development Review*, 7.

Caldwell, J.C. (1979), 'Education as a Factor in Mortality Decline: An Examination of Nigerian Data', *Population Studies*, 33.

—— (1986), 'Routes to Low Mortality in Poor Countries', *Population and Development Review*, 12.

Caldwell, J.C., Reddy, P.H., and Caldwell, P. (1985), 'Educational Transition in Rural South India', *Population and Development Review*, 11 (1).

—— (1989), *The Causes of Demographic Change* (Madison: University of Wisconsin Press).

Caldwell, Pat, and Caldwell, John (1987), 'Where There is a Narrower Gap between Female and Male Situations: Lessons from South India and Sri Lanka', paper presented at a workshop on 'Differentials in Mortality and Health Care', BAMANEH/SSRC, Dhaka.

Cassen, Robert (1978), *India: Population, Economy, Society* (London: Macmillan).

Cassen, Robert, with contributors (1994), *Population and Development: Old Debates, New Conclusions* (Washington, DC: Transaction Books for Overseas Development Council).

Cassen, Robert, and Joshi, Vijay (eds.) (1995), *India: The Future of Economic Reform* (Delhi: Oxford University Press).

Castaneda, T. (1984), 'Contexto Socioeconómico y Causas del Descenso de la Mortalidad Infantil en Chile', Documento de Trabajo No. 28, Centro de Estudios Públicos, Santiago, Chile.

—— (1985), 'Determinantes del Descenso de la Mortalidad Infantil en Chile 1975–1983', *Cuadernos de Economía*, 22.

Central Statistical Organisation (1991a), *Estimates of State Domestic Product and Gross Fixed Capital Formation* (New Delhi: CSO).

—— (1991b), *National Accounts Statistics* (New Delhi: CSO).

—— (1994), *National Accounts Statistics* (New Delhi: CSO).

Centre for Monitoring the Indian Economy (1994a), *Basic Statistics Relating to the Indian Economy* (Bombay: CMIE).

—— (1994b), *Basic Statistics Relating to States of India* (Bombay: CMIE).

Chaitanya, K. (1991), 'Bihar: Government's Discrimination against Women Teachers', *Economic and Political Weekly*, December 21.

Chakravarty, Sukhamoy (1969), *Capital and Development Planning* (Cambridge, MA: MIT Press).

—— (1987), *Development Planning: The Indian Experience* (Oxford: Oxford University Press).

Chambers, Robert, Saxena, N.C., and Shah, Tushaar (1989), *To the Hands of the Poor: Water and Trees* (New Delhi: Oxford and IBH).

Chanana, Karuna (1988a), 'Social Change or Social Reform: The Education of Women in Pre-Independence India', in Chanana (1988b).

—— (1993), 'Educational Attainment, Status Reproduction and Female Autonomy: Case Studies of Punjabi Women', paper presented at a workshop on 'Female Education, Autonomy and Fertility Change in South Asia', New Delhi, 8–10 April 1993.

Chanana, Karuna (ed.) (1988b), *Socialisation, Education and Women: Explorations in Gender Identity* (New Delhi: Orient Longman).

Chandhok, H.L. (1990), *Indian Database*, vol. II (New Delhi: The Policy Group).

Chandrasekhar, C.P., and Ghosh, Jayati (1993), 'Economic Discipline and External Vulnerability: A Comment on Fiscal and Adjustment Strategies', *Economic and Political Weekly*, April 10.

Chatterjee, Meera (1990), 'Indian Women: Their Health and Productivity', Discussion Paper No. 109, World Bank, Washington, DC.

Chaudhri, D.P. (1979), *Education, Innovations, and Agricultural Development* (London: Croom Helm).

Chaudhuri, M. (1993), *Indian Women's Movement* (New Delhi: Radiant).

Chaudhuri, Pramit (1974), *The Indian Economy* (London: Crosby, Lockwood and Staples).

Chaudhuri, Pramit (ed.) (1971), *Aspects of Indian Economic Development* (London: Allen & Unwin).

Chayanov, A.V. (1966), *The Theory of the Peasant Economy*, English translation, edited by D. Thorner, B. Kerblay, and R.E.F. Smith (Homewood, IL: Irwin).

Chen, Kang, Jefferson, Gary H., and Singh, Inderjit (1992), 'Lessons from China's Economic Reform', *Journal of Comparative Economics*, 16.

Chen, Lincoln, Huq, E., and D'Souza, S. (1981), 'Sex Bias in the Family Allocation of Food and Health Care in Rural Bangladesh', *Population and Development Review*, 7.

Chen, Marty (1991), *Coping with Seasonality and Drought* (London: Sage).

Chen, Marty (forthcoming, a), *The Lives of Widows in Rural India*, to be published as a monograph.

Chen, Marty (ed.) (forthcoming, b), Proceedings of a conference on 'Widows in India' held in Bangalore, March 1994, to be published as a monograph.

Chen, Marty, and Drèze, Jean (1994), 'Widowhood and Well-being in Rural North India', in M. Das Gupta et al. (1994).

—— (1995), 'Recent Research on Widows in India: A Workshop and Conference Report', mimeo, Delhi School of Economics; forthcoming in *Economic and Political Weekly*.

Chenery, Hollis, Robinson, Sherman, and Syrquin, Moshe (eds.) (1986), *Industrialization and Growth: A Comparative Study* (New York: Oxford University Press).

Chenery, Hollis, and Srinivasan, T.N. (eds.) (1988), *Handbook of Development Economics*, vol. I (Amsterdam: North-Holland).

Cheung, S.N.S. (1969), *The Theory of Share Tenancy* (Chicago: University of Chicago Press).

Chichilnisky, Graciela (1983), 'North–South Trade with Export Enclaves: Food Consumption and Food Exports', mimeo, Columbia University.

Chinese Academy of Social Sciences (1987), *Almanac of China's Population 1986* (Beijing: Population Research Centre).

Choudhary, K.M., and Bapat, M.T. (1975), 'A Study of Impact of Famine and Relief Measures in Gujarat and Rajasthan', mimeo, Agricultural Economics Research Centre, Sardar Patel University.

Chowdhury, Anis, and Islam, Iyanatul (1993), *The Newly-Industrialising Economies of East Asia* (London and New York: Routledge).

Christensen, Scott, Dollar, David, and Siamwalla, Ammar (1993), 'Thailand: The Institutional and Political Underpinnings of Growth', mimeo, World Bank, Washington, DC.

Cleland, J. (1990), 'Maternal Education and Child Survival: Further Evidence and Explanations', in J. Caldwell et al. (eds.), *What We Know About Health Transition: The Cultural, Social and Behavioural Determinants of Health* (Canberra: Health Transition Centre, Australian National University).

Cleland, J., and van Ginneken, J. (1987), 'The Effect of Maternal Schooling on Childhood Mortality: The Search for an Explanation', paper presented at a conference on 'Health Intervention and Mortality Change in Developing Countries', University of Sheffield, September 1987.

—— (1988), 'Maternal Education and Child Survival in Developing Countries: The Search for Pathways of Influence', *Social Science and Medicine*, 27 (12).

Coale, Ansley J. (1991), 'Excess Female Mortality and the Balance of the Sexes: An Estimate of the Number of "Missing Females"', *Population and Development Review*, 17.

—— (1993), 'Mortality Schedules in China Derived from Data in the 1982 and 1990 Censuses', Working Paper No. 93–7, Office of Population Research, Princeton University.

Cohen, G.A. (1989), 'On the Currency of Egalitarian Justice', *Ethics*, 99.

—— (1990), 'Equality of What? On Welfare, Goods and Capabilities', *Recherches Economiques de Louvain*, 56.

—— (1993), 'Equality of What? On Welfare, Resources and Capabilities', in Nussbaum and Sen (1993).

Colclough, Christopher, with Lewin, Keith (1993), *Educating All the Children* (Oxford: Oxford University Press).

Cole, D.C., and Lyman, P.N. (1971), *Korean Development: The Interplay of Politics and Economics* (Cambridge, MA: Harvard University Press).

Coles, J.L., and Hammond, P.J. (1995), 'Walrasian Equilibrium without Survival: Existence, Efficiency, and Remedial Policy', in Basu et al. (1995).

Committee on the Status of Women in India (1974), *Towards Equality* (New Delhi: Ministry of Education and Social Welfare).

Cooper, Charles (1983), 'Extensions of the Raj–Sen Model of Economic Growth', *Oxford Economic Papers*, 35.

Corden, W. Max (1974), *Trade Policy and Economic Welfare* (Oxford: Clarendon Press).

—— (1993), 'Seven Asian Miracle Economies: Overview of Macroeconomic Policies', mimeo, World Bank, Washington, DC.

Crocker, D.A. (1991), 'Toward Development Ethics', *World Development*, 19.

—— (1992), 'Functioning and Capability: The Foundations of Sen's and Nussbaum's Development Ethics', *Political Theory*, 20.

Crook, R.C., and Manor, J. (1994), 'Enhancing Participation and Institutional Performance: Democratic Decentralisation in South Asia and West Africa', report to the Overseas Development Administration, January 1994.

Da Corta, Lucia (1993), 'Inequality, Household Mobility and Class Differentiation in South Indian Villages: A Study in Method', unpublished D.Phil. thesis, University of Oxford.

Dandavate, P., Kumari, R., and Verghese, J. (eds.) (1989), *Widows, Abandoned and Destitute Women in India* (New Delhi: Radiant Publishers).

Dandekar, V.M., and Rath, N. (1971), *Poverty in India* (Bombay: Sameeksha Trust).

Das, Arvind (1987), 'Changel: Three Centuries of an Indian Village', *Journal of Peasant Studies,* 15 (1).

—— (1995), 'One from the Wild Heart', *The Telegraph,* March 27.

Das Gupta, Monica (1987), 'Selective Discrimination against Female Children in Rural Punjab', *Population and Development Review,* 13.

—— (1990), 'Death Clustering, Mother's Education and the Determinants of Child Mortality in Rural Punjab, India', *Population Studies,* 44.

—— (1993), 'Fertility Decline in Punjab, India: Parallels with Historical Europe', mimeo, Center for Population and Development Studies, Harvard University.

—— (1994a), 'What Motivates Fertility Decline? Lessons from a Case Study of Punjab, India', mimeo, Center for Population and Development Studies, Harvard University.

—— (1994b), 'Life Course Perspectives on Women's Autonomy and Health Outcomes', paper presented at a meeting of the Population Association of America, Miami, May 1994.

Das Gupta, Monica, Krishnan, T.N., and Chen, Lincoln (eds.) (1994), *Women's Health in India: Risk and Vulnerability* (Bombay: Oxford University Press).

—— (forthcoming) *Health, Poverty and Development in India* (Bombay: Oxford University Press).

Dasgupta, Partha (1993), *An Inquiry into Well-being and Destitution* (Oxford: Clarendon Press).

Dasgupta, Partha, and Ray, Debraj (1986), 'Inequality as a Determinant of Malnutrition and Unemployment: Theory', *Economic Journal,* 96.

—— (1987), 'Inequality as a Determinant of Malnutrition and Unemployment: Policy', *Economic Journal,* 97.

—— (1990), 'Adapting to Undernourishment: The Biological Evidence and Its Implications', in Drèze and Sen (1990), vol. I.

Datt, Gaurav (1995), 'Poverty in India: 1951–1991', mimeo, World Bank, Washington, DC.

Datt, Gaurav, and Ravallion, Martin (1992), 'Regional Disparities, Targetting, and Poverty in India', in M. Lipton and J. van der Gaag (eds.), *Including the Poor* (Washington, DC: World Bank).

—— (1994), 'Growth and Poverty in Rural India', mimeo, World Bank.

Datta Chaudhuri, Mrinal K. (1979), *Industrialization and Foreign Trade: An Analysis*

Based on the Development Experience of the Republic of Korea and the Philippines, ILO Working Paper II-4 (Bangkok: ARTEP, ILO).

Datta Chaudhuri, Mrinal K. (1990), 'Market Failure and Government Failure', Journal of Economic Perspectives, 4.

Debreu, Gérard (1959), Theory of Value (New York: Wiley).

De Geyndt, W., Zhao Xiyan, and Liu Shunli (1992), 'From Barefoot Doctor to Village Doctor in Rural China', World Bank Technical Paper No. 187, Asia Technical Department Series, World Bank, Washington, DC.

Deliège, Robert (1985), The Bhils of Western India (New Delhi: National Publishing House).

Deolalikar, Anil, and Vashishtha, Prem (1992), 'The Utilization of Government and Private Health Services in India', mimeo, National Council of Applied Economic Research, New Delhi.

Desai, G.M., Singh, G., and Sah, D.C. (1979), 'Impact of Scarcity on Farm Economy and Significance of Relief Operations', CMA Monograph No. 84, Indian Institute of Management, Ahmedabad.

Desai, Meghnad (1989), 'Poverty and Capability: Towards an Empirically Implementable Measure', in F. Bracho (ed.), Towards a New Way to Measure Development (Caracao: Office of the High Commission, Venezuela, 1989).

—— (1991) 'Human Development: Concepts and Measurement', European Economic Review, 35.

—— (1992), 'Is There Life After Mahalanobis? The Political Economy of India's New Economic Policy', Indian Economic Review, special number in memory of Sukhamoy Chakravarty.

—— (1993a), Capitalism, Socialism and the Indian Economy (Bombay: Export–Import Bank of India).

—— (1993b), 'The Measurement Problem in Economics', Invited Lecture at the Annual Conference of the Scottish Economics Association; forthcoming in the Scottish Journal of Political Economy.

Desai, Neera (ed.) (1988), A Decade of Women's Movement in India (Bombay: Himalaya Publishing House).

Desai, Sonalde, and Jain, Devaki (1992), 'Maternal Employment and Changes in Family Dynamics: The Social Context of Women's Work in Rural South India', Working Paper No. 39, The Population Council, New York.

Deshpande, L.K., and Rodgers, G. (eds.) (1992), 'The Indian Labour Market in the Face of Structural Economic Change', special issue of the Indian Journal of Labour Economics.

Dhagamwar, Vasudha (1987), 'The Disadvantaged and the Law', paper presented at a workshop on 'Poverty in India', Queen Elizabeth House, Oxford, October 1–6, 1987.

Dhar, P.N. (1990), Constraints on Growth: Reflections on the Indian Experience (Delhi: Oxford University Press).

Dietrich, Gabriele (1992), *Reflections on the Women's Movement in India: Religion, Ecology, Development* (New Delhi: Horizon India Books).

Dixit, Avinash K., and Norman, Victor (1980), *Theory of International Trade* (Cambridge: Cambridge University Press).

Doherty, V.S., and Jodha, N.S. (1979), 'Conditions for Group Action among Farmers', in J. Wong (ed.), *Group Farming in Asia*, (Singapore: Singapore University Press).

Dollar, David (1992), 'Outward-Oriented Developing Economies Really Do Grow More Rapidly: Evidence from 95 LDCs, 1976–1985', *Economic Development and Cultural Change*, 40.

Drèze, Jean (1990a), 'Famine Prevention in India', in Drèze and Sen (1990), vol. II.

—— (1990b), 'Famine Prevention in Africa', in Drèze and Sen (1990), vol. II.

—— (1990c), 'Widows in Rural India', Discussion Paper No. 26, Development Economics Research Programme, STICERD, London School of Economics.

—— (1990d), 'Poverty in India and the IRDP Delusion', *Economic and Political Weekly*, September 29.

Drèze, Jean, and Gazdar, Haris (1996), 'Uttar Pradesh: The Burden of Inertia', in Drèze and Sen (1996).

Drèze, Jean, Guio, Anne-Catherine, and Murthi, Mamta (1995), 'Demographic Outcomes, Economic Development and Women's Agency', Working Paper No. 28, Centre for Development Economics, Delhi School of Economics.

Drèze, Jean, Lanjouw, Peter, and Sharma, Naresh (forthcoming), 'Economic Development in Palanpur, 1957–94', to be published in P. Lanjouw and N. Stern (eds.), *A Kind of Growth: Palanpur 1957–94* (Oxford: Clarendon Press).

Drèze, Jean, and Loh, Jackie (1995), 'Literacy in India and China', Working Paper No. 29, Centre for Development Economics, Delhi School of Economics.

Drèze, Jean, and Mukherjee, Anindita (1989), 'Labour Contracts in Rural India: Theories and Evidence', in S. Chakravarty (ed.), *The Balance between Industry and Agriculture in Economic Development*, vol. III (London: Macmillan).

Drèze, Jean, Samson, Meera, and Singh, Satyajit (eds.) (forthcoming), *Displacement and Resettlement in the Narmada Valley* (New Delhi: Sage).

Drèze, Jean, and Saran, Mrinalini (1995), 'Primary Education and Economic Development in China and India: Overview and Two Case Studies', in Basu et al. (1995).

Drèze, Jean, and Sen, Amartya (1989), *Hunger and Public Action* (Oxford: Clarendon Press).

—— (1991), 'Public Action for Social Security', in Ahmad et al. (1991).

Drèze, Jean, and Sen, Amartya (eds.) (1990), *The Political Economy of Hunger*, 3 volumes (Oxford: Clarendon Press).

Drèze, Jean, and Sen, Amartya (eds.) (1996), *Indian Development: Selected Regional Perspectives* (Oxford and Delhi: Oxford University Press).

Dube, Leela (1988), 'On the Construction of Gender: Hindu Girls in Patrilineal India', in Chanana (1988b).

Dutta, Bhaskar (1994), 'Poverty in India: Trends, Determinants and Policy Issues', Discussion Paper No. 94–16, Indian Statistical Institute, New Delhi.

Dutta, B., Panda, M., and Wadhwa, W. (1994), 'Human Development in India: An Inter-state Analysis', mimeo, Indian Statistical Institute, New Delhi.

Duvvury, Nata (1989), 'Women in Agriculture: A Review of the Indian Literature', *Economic and Political Weekly*, October 28.

Dworkin, Ronald (1978), *Taking Rights Seriously*, second edition (London: Duckworth).

—— (1981), 'What is Equality? Part 1: Equality of Welfare', and 'What is Equality? Part 2: Equality of Resources', *Philosophy and Public Affairs,* 10.

Dyson, Tim (1979), 'A Working Paper on Fertility and Mortality Estimates for the States of India', mimeo; partly published in *World Health Statistics Quarterly,* 37 (2), (1984).

—— (1987), 'Excess Female Mortality in India: Uncertain Evidence on a Narrowing Differential', in K. Srinivasan and S. Mukerji (eds.), *Dynamics of Population and Family Welfare* (Bombay: Himalaya).

Dyson, Tim, and Moore, Mick (1983), 'On Kinship Structure, Female Autonomy, and Demographic Behavior in India', *Population and Development Review,* 9.

Easterly, William, Kremer, Michael, Pritchett, Lant, and Summers, Lawrence (1993), 'Good Policy or Good Luck? Country Growth Performance and Temporary Shocks', mimeo, World Bank, Washington, DC.

Egerö, Bertil, and Hammarskjöld, Mikael (eds.) (1994), *Understanding Reproductive Change: Kenya, Tamil Nadu, Punjab, Costa Rica* (Cambridge, MA: Harvard Series on Population and International Health).

Ehrlich, Paul (1968), *The Population Bomb* (New York: Ballantine Books).

Ehrlich, P., and Ehrlich, A. (1990), *The Population Explosion* (New York: Simon and Schuster).

Elwin, Verrier (1989), *The Tribal World of Verrier Elwin: An Autobiography* (Delhi: Oxford University Press).

EPW Research Foundation (1993), 'Poverty Levels in India: Norms, Estimates and Trends', *Economic and Political Weekly*, August 21.

—— (1994), 'What Has Gone Wrong with Economic Reforms?', *Economic and Political Weekly*, April 30.

Eswaran, Mukesh, and Kotwal, Ashok (1994), *Why Poverty Persists in India* (Delhi: Oxford University Press).

Ethier, Wilfred, Helpman, Elhanan, and Neary, Peter (1993), *Theory, Policy,* and *Dynamics in International Trade: Essays in Honor of Ronald W. Jones* (New York: Cambridge University Press).

Fallows, James (1994), *Looking at the Sun: The Rise of the New East Asian Economic and Political System* (New York: Pantheon).

Fernandes, Walter (ed.) (1985), *Social Activists and People's Movements* (New Delhi: Indian Social Institute).

Fields, Gary S. (1980), *Poverty, Inequality and Development* (Cambridge: Cambridge University Press).

—— (1993), 'Changing Labor Market Conditions and Economic Development in Hong Kong, Korea, Singapore and Taiwan', mimeo, World Bank, Washington, DC.

Findlay, Ronald (1993), *Trade, Development, and Political Economy: Selected Essays of Ronald Findlay* (Brookfield, VT: Aldershot, Hants).

Findlay, Ronald, and Wallisz, Stanislaw (eds.) (1993), *The Political Economy of Poverty, Equity, and Growth* (New York: Oxford University Press).

Fishlow, A., Gwin, C., Haggarad, S., Rodrik, D., and Wade, R. (1994), *Miracle or Design? Lessons from the East Asian Experience* (Washington, DC: Overseas Development Council).

Ford Foundation (1992), *Perspectives on India's Development in the 1990s: Symposium Review* (New Delhi: Ford Foundation).

Foster, James (1984), 'On Economic Poverty: A Survey of Aggregate Measures', *Advances in Econometrics*, 3.

Foster, J., Greer, J., and Thorbecke, E. (1984), 'A Class of Decomposable Poverty Measures', *Econometrica*, 52.

Foster, J., and Shorrocks, A.F. (1991), 'Subgroup Consistent Poverty Indices', *Econometrica*, 59.

Frank, C.R., Kim, K.S., and Westphal, L. (1975), *Foreign Trade Regimes and Economic Development* (New York: National Bureau of Economic Research).

Franke, Richard, and Chasin, Barbara (1989), *Kerala: Radical Reform as Development in an Indian State* (San Francisco: Institute for Food and Development Policy).

Frankel, Francine (1978), *India's Political Economy 1947–1977* (Princeton: Princeton University Press).

Frankel, Francine, and Rao, M.S.A. (eds.) (1989), *Dominance and State Power in Modern India* (Delhi: Oxford University Press).

Fuchs, Victor (1986), *The Health Economy* (Cambridge: Harvard University Press).

Furer-Haimendorf, C. von (1982), *Tribes of India: The Struggle for Survival* (Delhi: Oxford University Press).

Gadgil, M., and Guha, R. (1993), 'Ecology and Equity: Steps Towards an Economy of Permanence', mimeo, Delhi School of Economics; to be published as a monograph.

Gaiha, Raghav (1993), *Design of Poverty Alleviation Strategy in Rural Areas* (Rome: Food and Agriculture Organization).

Gaiha, Raghav (1994a), 'Structural Adjustment in India: Rationale and Content', mimeo, Faculty of Management Studies, University of Delhi.

—— (1994b), 'Structural Adjustment, Rural Institutions and the Poor in India: A Comparative Analysis of Andhra Pradesh, Maharashtra and Karnataka', mimeo, Faculty of Management Studies, University of Delhi.

Galenson, Walter (ed.) (1979), *Economic Growth and Structural Change in Taiwan* (Ithaca: Cornell University Press).

Gandhi, Geeta (1994), 'An Economic Evaluation of School Management-Types in Urban India: A Case Study of Uttar Pradesh', unpublished Ph.D. thesis, Faculty of Social Studies, University of Oxford.

Gasper, Des (1993), 'Entitlements Analysis: Relating Concepts and Contexts', *Development and Change*, 24.

George, P.S. (1994), 'Management of Education in Kerala', paper presented at a seminar on 'Management of Education under Panchayati Raj' held at the National Institute of Educational Planning and Administration, 27–8 October, 1994.

George, S., Abel, R., and Miller, B.D. (1992), 'Female Infanticide in Rural South India', *Economic and Political Weekly*, May 30.

Germain, Adrienne (1994), 'Gender and Health: From Research to Action', in M. Das Gupta et al. (1994).

Ghate, Prabhu (1984), *Direct Attacks on Rural Poverty* (New Delhi: Concept).

Ghose, Sanjoy (1993), 'Tryst with Textbooks', *Indian Express*, March 24.

Ghosh, A. (1991), 'Annals of the Literacy Programme: A Scenario from Rajasthan', *Economic and Political Weekly*, October 19.

—— (1992), 'Education for All: The Financing Problem', *Economic and Political Weekly*, April 4.

—— (1994), 'Structural Adjustment and Industrial and Environmental Concerns', *Economic and Political Weekly*, February 19.

Ghosh, A., Ananthamurthy, U.R., Béteille, A., Kansal, S.M., Mazumdar, V., and Vanaik, A. (1994), 'Evaluation of Literacy Campaigns in India', report of an independent Expert Group appointed by the Ministry of Human Resource Development (New Delhi: Ministry of Human Resource Development).

Ghurye, G.S. (1969), *Caste and Race in India*, fifth edition (Bombay: Popular Prakashan).

Gidwani, D. (1994), 'What Population Problem? Sterilisation Targets Achieved with Nepali Help', *India Today*, March 31.

Gillespie, S.R., and McNeill, G. (1992), *Food, Health and Survival in India and Developing Countries* (Delhi: Oxford University Press).

Gokhale, A.M. (1988), 'Panchayati Raj in Nagaland', mimeo, Department of Rural Development, Ministry of Agriculture, New Delhi.

Goodburn, E., Ebrahim, G.J., and Senapati, Sishir (1990), 'Strategies Educated

Mothers Use to Ensure the Health of Their Children', *Journal of Tropical Pediatrics*, 36.

Gopal, Sarvepalli (ed.) (1983), *Jawaharlal Nehru: An Anthology* (Oxford and Delhi: Oxford University Press).

Government of India (1979), *Report of the Committee on Child Labour* (New Delhi: Ministry of Labour).

—— (1981), *Census of India 1981: Series I (India), Part II-A(i), General Population Tables, Tables A-1 to A-3* (New Delhi: Office of the Registrar-General).

—— (1982), *Sample Registration System 1979–80*, (New Delhi: Office of the Registrar General).

—— (1988a), 'Child Mortality Estimates of India', Occasional Paper No.5 of 1988, Demography Division, Office of the Registrar General, Ministry of Home Affairs, New Delhi.

—— (1988b), 'Fertility in India: An Analysis of 1981 Census Data', Occasional Paper No.13 of 1988, Demography Division, Office of the Registrar General, Ministry of Home Affairs, New Delhi.

—— (1989a), 'Child Mortality, Age at Marriage and Fertility in India', Occasional Paper No.2 of 1989, Demography Division, Office of the Registrar General, Ministry of Home Affairs, New Delhi.

—— (1989b), *The Drought of 1989: Response and Management* (New Delhi: Ministry of Agriculture).

—— (1991), *Family Welfare Programme in India: Yearbook 1989–90* (New Delhi: Ministry of Health and Family Welfare).

—— (1992a), *Sample Registration System 1989* (New Delhi: Office of the Registrar General).

—— (1992b), *Annual Report 1991–92 (Part I) of the Department of Education* (New Delhi: Ministry of Human Resource Development).

—— (1992c), *National Policy on Education 1986 (With Modifications Undertaken in 1992)* (New Delhi: Ministry of Human Resource Development).

—— (1992d), *National Policy on Education 1986: Programme of Action 1992* (New Delhi: Ministry of Human Resource Development).

—— (1992e), *Health Information of India: 1991* (New Delhi: Central Bureau of Health Intelligence, Ministry of Health and Family Welfare).

—— (1993a), *Sample Registration System: Fertility and Mortality Indicators 1990* (New Delhi: Office of the Registrar General).

—— (1993b), *Sample Registration System: Fertility and Mortality Indicators 1991* (New Delhi: Office of the Registrar General).

—— (1993c), *Education for All: The Indian Scene* (New Delhi: Ministry of Human Resource Development).

—— (1993d), *Education for All, The Indian Scene: Widening Horizons* (New Delhi: Ministry of Human Resource Development).

—— (1993e), 'Housing and Amenities: A Brief Analysis of the Housing

Tables of 1991 Census', Census of India 1991, Paper 2 of 1993, Office of the Registrar General, New Delhi.

Government of India (1994a), *Economic Survey 1993–94* (New Delhi: Ministry of Finance).

——— (1994b), *Status Report of Literacy and Post Literacy Campaigns* (New Delhi: Directorate of Adult Education).

——— (1994c), 'National Population Policy', draft report of the 'Committee on Population' appointed by the National Development Council.

——— (1994d), *Poverty Eradication through Growth, Employment and Social Development*. (New Delhi: Planning Commission).

——— (1994e), *Learning without Burden: Report of the National Advisory Committee Appointed by the Ministry of Human Resource Development* (New Delhi: Ministry of Human Resource Development).

——— (1994f), *Annual Report 1993–94 (Part I) of the Department of Education* (New Delhi: Ministry of Human Resource Development).

——— (1995), *Economic Survey 1994–95* (New Delhi: Ministry of Finance).

Government of Karnataka (1989), *Report of the Zilla Parishad and Mandal Panchayat Evaluation Committee* (Bangalore: Government of Karnataka).

Goyal, Sangeeta, and Mehrotra, Nidhi (1995), 'Primary Schooling in Rural India: A Field Report', mimeo, Centre for Development Economics, Delhi School of Economics.

Grant, James P. (1978), *Disparity Reduction Rates in Social Indicators* (Washington, DC: Overseas Development Council).

Greenhalgh, S., Zhu Chuzhu, and Li Nan (1993), 'Restraining Population Growth in Three Chinese Villages: 1988–93', Working Paper No. 55, Population Council, New York.

Gribble, James, and Preston, Samuel (1993), *The Epidemiological Transition: Policy and Planning Implications for Developing Countries* (Washintgon, DC: National Academic Press).

Griffin, Keith, and Knight, John (eds.) (1990), *Human Development and the International Development Strategy for the 1990s* (London: Macmillan).

Griffin, Keith, and Zhao Renwei (eds.) (1993), *The Distribution of Income in China* (London: Macmillan).

Grossman, Gene M., and Helpman, Elhanan (1990), 'Comparative Advantage and Long-run Growth', *American Economic Review*, 80.

——— (1991a), 'Quality Ladders and Product Cycles', *Quarterly Journal of Economics*, 106.

——— (1991b), *Innovation and Growth in the Global Economy* (Cambridge, MA: MIT Press).

Guha, Ashok (ed.) (1990), *Economic Liberalization, Industrial Structure and Growth in India* (New Delhi: Oxford University Press).

Guha Ranajit (1983), *Elementary Aspects of Peasant Insurgency in Colonial India* (Delhi: Oxford University Press).

Guha, Ranajit (ed.) (1982), *Subaltern Studies, vol. I: Writings on South Asian History and Society* (Delhi: Oxford University Press).

—— (1986), *Subaltern Studies*, vol. I (Delhi: Oxford University Press).

Guha, R., and Spivak, G. (eds.) (1988), *Selected Subaltern Studies* (New York: Oxford University Press).

Guhan, S. (1981), 'Social Security: Lessons and Possibilities from the Tamil Nadu Experience', Bulletin, Madras Development Seminar Series, 11 (1).

—— (1990), 'Social Security Initiatives in Tamil Nadu 1989', Working Paper No. 96, Madras Institute of Development Studies.

—— (1992), 'Social Security in India: Looking One Step Ahead', in Harriss et al. (1992).

—— (1993a), 'Social Security Options for Developing Countries', paper presented at a symposium on 'Poverty: New Approaches to Analysis and Policy', International Institute of Labour Studies, Geneva, November 1993.

—— (1993b), 'Social Security for the Unorganised Poor: A Feasible Blueprint for India', mimeo, Madras Institute of Development Studies.

Guio, Anne-Catherine (1994), 'Aspects du Sex Ratio en Inde', unpublished M.Sc. thesis, Université de Namur, Belgium.

Gulati, S.C. (1992), 'Developmental Determinants of Demographic Variables in India: A District Level Analysis', *Journal of Quantitative Economics*, 8 (1).

Gupta, D.B., Basu, A., and Asthana, R. (1993), 'Population Change, Women's Role and Status, and Development in India: A Review', mimeo, Institute of Economic Growth, Delhi University.

Gupta, N., Pal, P., Bhargava, M., and Daga, M. (1992), 'Health of Women and Children in Rajasthan', *Economic and Political Weekly,* October 17.

Gupta, S.P., and Sarkar, A.K. (1994), 'Fiscal Correction and Human Resource Development: Expenditure at Central and State Levels', *Economic and Political Weekly*, March 26.

Halstead, S.B., Walsh, J., and Warren, K. (1985), *Good Health at Low Cost* (New York: Rockefeller Foundation).

Hamlin, A., and Pettit, P. (eds.) (1989), *The Good Polity: Normative Analysis of the State* (Oxford: Blackwell).

Hardiman, David (1987), *The Coming of the Devi: Adivasi Assertion in Western India* (Delhi: Oxford University Press).

Hardin, Garrett (1993), *Living Within Limits* (New York: Oxford University Press).

Harriss, Barbara (1990), 'The Intrafamily Distribution of Hunger in South Asia', in Drèze and Sen (1990), vol. I.

—— (1991), *Child Nutrition and Poverty in South India* (New Delhi: Concept).

Harriss, Barbara (1993), 'Economic Reforms and Social Welfare in India', mimeo, Queen Elizabeth House, Oxford.

Harriss, B., Guhan, S., and Cassen, R. (eds.) (1992), *Poverty in India: Research and Policy* (Delhi: Oxford University Press).

Hasan, Zoya (1989), 'Power and Mobilization: Patterns of Resilience and Change in Uttar Pradesh Politics', in Frankel and Rao (1989).

Helleiner, G.K. (ed.) (1992), *Trade Policy, Industrialization, and Development* (Oxford: Clarendon).

Helpman, Elhanan, and Krugman, Paul R. (1990), *Market Structure and Foreign Trade* (Cambridge, MA: MIT Press).

Helpman, Elhanan, and Razin, Assad (eds.) (1991), *International Trade and Trade Policy* (Cambridge, MA: MIT Press).

Heyer, Judith (1992), 'The Role of Dowries and Daughters' Marriages in the Accumulation and Distribution of Capital in a South Indian Community', *Journal of International Development*, 4 (4).

Hirschman, Albert O. (1958), *The Strategy of Economic Development* (New Haven, CT: Yale University Press).

—— (1970), *Exit, Voice and Loyalty* (Cambridge, MA: Harvard University Press).

—— (1992), *Rival Views of Market Society and Other Recent Essays* (Cambridge, MA: Harvard University Press).

Hitchcock, John T. (1975), 'The Idea of the Martial Rajput', in M. Singer (ed.), *Traditional India: Structure and Change* (Jaipur: Rawat Publications).

Hong, W., and Krueger, Anne O. (eds.) (1975), *Trade and Development in Korea* (Seoul: Korea Development Institute).

Howes, Stephen (1992), 'Purchasing Power, Infant Mortality and Literacy in China and India: An Inter-provincial Analysis', Discussion Paper No. 19, Research Programme on the Chinese Economy, STICERD, London School of Economics.

—— (1993), 'Income Inequality in Urban China in the 1980s: Levels, Trends and Determinants', Discussion Paper No. 3, Series on 'Economic Transformation and Public Finance', STICERD, London School of Economics.

Howes, Stephen, and Hussain, Athar (1994), 'Regional Growth and Inequality in Rural China', Discussion Paper No. 11, Series on 'Economic Transformation and Public Finance', STICERD, London School of Economics.

Hubbard, Michael (1988), 'Drought Relief and Drought-Proofing in the State of Gujarat, India', in D. Curtis, M. Hubbard, and A. Shepherd (eds.), *Preventing Famine: Policies and Prospects for Africa* (New York and London: Routledge).

Hull, Terence (1990), 'Recent Trends in Sex Ratios at Birth in China', *Population and Development Review*, 16 (1).

Hussain, Athar (1990), 'The Chinese Enterprise Reform', Discussion Paper No.

5, Research Programme on the Chinese Economy, STICERD, London School of Economics.

Hussain, Athar (1992), 'The Chinese Economic Reforms in Retrospect and Prospect', Discussion Paper No. 24, Research Programme on the Chinese Economy, STICERD, London School of Economics.

—— (1993), 'Reform of the Chinese Social Security System', Discussion Paper No. 24, Research Programme on the Chinese Economy, STICERD, London School of Economics.

—— (1994), 'Social Security in Present-Day China and Its Reform', *American Economic Review*, 84.

Hussain, Athar (ed.) (1989), *China and the World Economy* (London: Suntory-Toyota International Centre for Economics and Related Disciplines).

Hussain, A., and Liu, H. (1989), 'Compendium of Literature on the Chinese Social Security System', Discussion Paper No. 3, Research Programme on the Chinese Economy, STICERD, London School of Economics

Hussain, Athar, and Stern, Nicholas (1992), 'Economic Reforms and Public Finance in China', Discussion Paper No. 23, Research Programme on the Chinese Economy, STICERD, London School of Economics.

Indian Council of Medical Research (1989), *Evaluation of Quality of Maternal and Child Health and Family Planning Services* (New Delhi: ICMR).

Indian Institute of Management (1985), *Study of Facility Utilization and Programme Management in Family Welfare* (Ahmedabad: Public Systems Group, Indian Institute of Management).

Indira Gandhi Institute of Development Research (1994), 'Mid Year Review 1994–95', mimeo, IGIDR, Bombay.

International Institute for Population Sciences (1994), *National Family Health Survey: India 1992–93* (Bombay: IIPS).

Irschick, Eugene (1969), *Politics and Social Conflict in South India: The Non-Brahman Movement and Tamil Separatism 1916–1929* (Berkeley: University of California Press).

Iyengar, Sudarshan, and Bhargava, Ashok (1987), 'Primary Health Care and Family Welfare Programme in Rural Gujarat', *Economic and Political Weekly*, July 4.

Jain, A.K. (1985), 'Determinants of Regional Variations in Infant Mortality in Rural India', *Population Studies*, 39.

Jain, A.K., and Nag, M. (1985), 'Female Primary Education and Fertility Reduction in India', Working Paper No.114, Center for Policy Studies, Population Council, New York.

—— (1986), 'Importance of Female Primary Education for Fertility Reduction in India', *Economic and Political Weekly*, September 6.

Jain, A.K., and Visaria, P. (eds.) (1988), *Infant Mortality in India: Differentials and Determinants* (New Delhi: Sage).

Jain, Devaki, and Banerjee, Nirmala (eds.) (1985), *Tyranny of the Household: Investigative Essays in Women's Work* (New Delhi: Vikas).

Jain, L.R., Sundaram, K., and Tendulkar, S.D. (1988), 'Dimensions of Rural Poverty: An Inter-Regional Profile', *Economic and Political Weekly*, November (special issue); reprinted in Krishnaswamy (1990).

Jalan, Bimal (1991), *India's Economic Crisis* (Delhi: Oxford University Press).

Jalan, Bimal (ed.) (1992), *The Indian Economy: Problems and Prospects* (New Delhi: Viking).

Jalan, J., and Subbarao, K. (1995), 'Adjustment and Social Sectors in India', in Cassen and Joshi (1995).

Jeffery, P., Jeffery, R., and Lyon, P. (1989), *Labour Pains and Labour Power: Women and Child-bearing in India* (London: Zed).

Jeffery, Roger (1988), *The Politics of Health in India* (Berkeley: University of California Press).

Jeffrey, Robin (1987), 'Culture and Governments: How Women Made Kerala Literate', *Pacific Affairs*, 60 (4).

―――― (1992), *Politics, Women and Well-Being: How Kerala Became 'A Model'* (Cambridge: Cambridge University Press).

Jejeeboy, Shireen, and Rama Rao, S. (1994), 'Unsafe Motherhood: A Review of Reproductive Health', in M. Das Gupta et al. (1994).

Jena, B., and Pati, R.N. (eds.) (1989), *Health and Family Welfare Services in India* (New Delhi: Ashish).

Jesani, Amar (1990), 'Limits of Empowerment: Women in Rural Health Care', *Economic and Political Weekly*, May 19.

Jha, Prem Shankar (1980), *India: A Political Economy of Stagnation* (Bombay: Oxford Univesity Press).

Jha, Shikha (1994), 'Foodgrains Price and Distribution Policies in India: Performance, Problems and Prospects', Reprint No. 134–1994, Indira Gandhi Institute of Development Research, Bombay; forthcoming in *Asia-Pacific Development Journal*.

Johansen, Frida (1993), 'Poverty Reduction in East Asia: The Silent Revolution', Discussion Paper No. 203, East Asia and Pacific Region Series, World Bank, Washington, DC.

Johansson, Sheila R. (1991), 'Welfare, Mortality and Gender: Continuity and Change in Explanations for Male/Female Mortality Differences over Three Centuries', *Continuity and Change*, 6.

Johansson, S., and Nygren, O. (1991), 'The Missing Girls of China: A New Demographic Account', *Population and Development Review*, 17 (1).

Johnson, D. Gale (1950), 'Resource Allocation under Share Constraints', *Journal of Political Economy*, 58.

Jones, Ronald W., and Kenen, Peter B. (eds.) (1985), *Handbook of International Economics* (Amsterdam: North Holland).

Joshi, Vijay, and Little, Ian (1993), 'Macro-Economic Stabilization in India, 1991–93 and Beyond', *Economic and Political Weekly*, December 4.

——— (1994), *India: Macroeconomics and Political Economy 1964–91* (Washington, DC: World Bank).

Kabir, M., and Krishnan, T.N. (1992), 'Social Intermediation and Health Transition: Lessons from Kerala', paper presented at a workshop on 'Health and Development in India', 2–4 January, 1992; to be published in M. Das Gupta et al. (forthcoming).

Kakar, Sudhir (1979), 'Childhood in India', *International Social Science Journal*, 31.

——— (1981), *The Inner World: A Psycho-analytic Study of Childhood and Society in India* (Delhi: Oxford University Press).

Kakwani, Nanak (1986), *Analyzing Redistribution Policies* (Cambridge: Cambridge University Press).

——— (1993), 'Peformance in Living Standards: An International Comparison', *Journal of Development Economics*, 41.

Kakwani, Nanak, and Subbarao, K. (1990), 'Rural Poverty and Its Alleviation in India', *Economic and Political Weekly*, June 3.

Kanbargi, R. (ed.) (1991), *Child Labour in the Indian Subcontinent* (New Delhi: Sage).

Kanitkar, T. (1991), 'The Sex Ratio in India: A Topic of Speculation and Research', *Journal of Family Welfare*, 37 (3).

Kannan, K.P. (1993), 'Public Intervention and Poverty Alleviation: A Study of the Declining Incidence of Poverty in Kerala', paper presented at a workshop on 'Poverty Alleviation in India' held at the Institute of Development Studies, Jaipur, February 1993.

Kannan, K.P., Thankappan, K.R., Raman Kutty, V., and Aravindan, K.P. (1991), *Health and Development in Rural Kerala* (Trivandrum: Kerala Sastra Sahitya Parishad).

Kapadia, Karin (1992), 'Pauperizing the Rural Poor: Landless Labour in Tamil Nadu', mimeo, London School of Economics.

Kapadia, K.M. (1966), *Marriage and the Family in India,* third edition (Bombay: Oxford University Press).

Kaplan, Robert D. (1994), 'The Coming Anarchy', *Atlantic Monthly*, 273 (February 2).

Karkal, Malini (1985), 'Health of Mother and Child Survival', in K. Srinivasan and S. Mukerji (eds.), *Dynamics of Population and Family Welfare 1985* (Bombay: Himalaya).

——— (1987), 'Diifferentials in Mortality by Sex', *Economic and Political Weekly*, August 8.

——— (1991), 'Progress in Literacy in India: A Statistical Analysis', *Indian Journal of Social Work,* 52 (2).

Karlekar, Malavika (1988), 'Woman's Nature and the Access to Education', in Chanana (1988b).

Karve, Irawati (1965), *Kinship Organisation in India* (Bombay: Asia Publishing House).

Kelkar, Vijay, Kumar, Rajiv, and Nangia, Rita (1990), *India's Industrial Economy: Policies, Performance and Reforms* (Manila: Asian Development Bank).

Khan, A.R., Griffin, K., Riskin, C., and Zhao Renwei (1992), 'Household Income and its Distribution in China', *The China Quarterly*, 132.

Khan, M.E. (1988), 'Infant Mortality in Uttar Pradesh: A Micro-level Study', in A.K. Jain and P. Visaria (eds.), *Infant Mortality in India: Differentials and Determinants* (New Delhi: Sage).

Khan, M.E., Anker, R., Ghosh Dastidar, S.K., and Bairathi, S. (1989), 'Inequalities between Men and Women in Nutrition and Family Welfare Services: An In-depth Enquiry in an Indian Village', in J.C. Caldwell and G. Santow (eds.), *Selected Readings in the Cultural, Social and Behavioral Determinants of Health*, Health Transition Series No.1 (Canberra: Health Transition Centre, Australian National University).

Khan, M.E., Ghosh Dastidar, S.K., and Singh, R. (1986), 'Nutrition and Health Practices among the Rural Women: A Case Study of Uttar Pradesh', *Journal of Family Welfare*, 33 (2).

Khan, M.E., Gupta, R.B., Prasad, C.V.S., and Ghosh Dastidar, S.K. (1988), *Performance of Health and Family Welfare Programmes in India* (Bombay: Himalaya Publishing House).

Khan, M.E., and Prasad, C.V.S. (1983), *Under-Utilization of Health Services in Rural India: A Comparative Study of Bihar, Gujarat and Karnataka* (Baroda: Operations Research Group).

Khan, M.E., Prasad, C.V.S., and Majumdar, A. (1980), *People's Perceptions about Family Planning in India* (New Delhi: Concept).

Khan, M.E., Prasad, C.V.S., and Qaiser, N. (1983), 'Reasons for Under-utilization of Health Services: Case Study of a PHC in a Tribal Area of Bihar', paper presented at the ICMR/Ford Foundation workshop on 'Child Health, Nutrition and Family Planning'.

Khan, M.E., Gupta, R.B., Prasad, C.V.S., and Ghosh Dastidar, S.K. (eds.) (1987), *Performance of Family Planning in India: Observations from Bihar, Uttar Pradesh, Rajasthan and Madhya Pradesh* (New Delhi: Himalaya Publishing House).

Khan, Sharukh R. (1993), 'South Asia', in King and Hill (1993).

Khatu, K.K., Tamang, A.K., and Rao, C.R. (1983), *Working Children in India* (Baroda: Operations Research Group).

Khemani, Stuti (1994), 'Neoclassical vs. Nash-bargained Model of Household Fertility: Evidence from Rural India', undergraduate thesis, Department of Economics, Mount Holyoke College, USA.

Kim, C.K. (ed.) (1977), *Industrial and Social Development Issues* (Seoul: Korea Development Institute).

Kim, Kiwan, and Leipziger, Danny (1993), 'Korea: A Case of Government-Led Development', mimeo, World Bank, Washington, DC.

King, Elizabeth, and Hill, Anne (eds.) (1993), *Women's Education in Developing Countries: Barriers, Benefits and Policy* (Baltimore: Johns Hopkins University Press).

Kishor, Sunita (1993), ' "May God Give Sons to All": Gender and Child Mortality in India', *American Sociological Review*, 58.

—— (1994), 'Gender Differentials in Child Mortality: A Review of the Evidence', in M. Das Gupta et al. (1994).

Kishwar, Madhu, and Vanita, Ruth (eds.) (1991), *In Search of Answers*, second revised edition (New Delhi: Horizon India).

Klasen, Stephan (1994), ' "Missing Women" Reconsidered', *World Development*, 22.

Knight, John, and Song, Lina (1993a), 'The Length of Life and the Standard of Living: Economic Influences on Premature Death in China', *Journal of Development Studies*, 30 (1).

—— (1993b), 'The Spatial Contribution to Income Inequality in Rural China', *Cambridge Journal of Economics*, 17 (2).

Kohli, Atul (1987), *The State and Poverty in India: The Politics of Reform* (Cambridge: Cambridge University Press).

—— (1988), *India's Democracy: An Analysis of Changing State–Society Relations* (Princeton, NJ: Princeton University Press).

Kohli, Atul (ed.) (1990), *Democracy and Discontent* (Cambridge: Cambridge University Press).

Kolenda, Pauline (1983), 'Widowhood among "Untouchable" Chuhras', in A. Ostor, L. Fruzzetti, and S. Barnett (eds.), *Concepts of Person: Kinship, Caste and Marriage in India* (Delhi: Oxford University Press).

—— (1984), 'Woman as Tribute, Woman as Flower: Images of "Woman" in Weddings in North and South India', *American Ethnologist*, 11.

Koopmans, T. (1957), *Three Essays on the State of Economic Science* (New Haven: Yale University Press).

Krishnaji, N. (1987), 'Poverty and Sex Ratio: Some Data and Speculations', *Economic and Political Weekly*, June 6.

—— (1992), *Pauperising Agriculture: Studies in Agrarian Change and Demographic Structure* (Delhi: Oxford University Press).

Krishnakumari, N.S. (1987), *Status of Single Women in India* (Delhi: Uppal).

Krishnan, T.N. (1976), 'Demographic Transition in Kerala: Facts and Factors', *Economic and Political Weekly*, 11 (31–33), special number.

—— (1991), 'Kerala's Health Transition: Facts and Factors', Center for Population and Development Studies, Harvard University.

Krishnan, T.N. (1994), 'Social Intermediation and Human Development: Kerala State, India', a study prepared for the World Summit on Social Development; mimeo, Centre for Development Studies, Thiruvananthapuram.

—— (forthcoming), *Society, State and Economy in Kerala*; to be published.

Krishnaswamy, K.S. (1994), 'Agricultural Development under the New Economic Regime', *Economic and Political Weekly*, June 25.

Krishnaswamy, K.S. (ed.) (1990), *Poverty and Income Distribution* (Delhi: Oxford University Press).

Krueger, Anne O. (1974), 'The Political Economy of the Rent-Seeking Society', *American Economic Review*, 64 (June).

—— (1979), *The Development Role of Foreign Sector and Aid* (Cambridge, MA: Harvard University Press).

—— (1985), 'Trade Policies in Developing Countries', in Jones and Kenen (1985).

Krugman, Paul R. (1979), 'Increasing Returns, Monopolistic Competition, and International Trade', *Journal of International Economics*, 9.

—— (1986), *Strategic Trade Policy and the New International Economics* (Cambridge, MA: MIT Press).

—— (1987), 'The Narrow Moving Band, the Dutch Disease, and the Consequences of Mrs. Thatcher: Notes on Trade in the Presence of Scale Economies', *Journal of Development Economics*, 27.

Krugman, Paul R., and Smith, Alisdair (eds.) (1994), *Empirical Studies of Strategic Trade Policy* (Chicago: University of Chicago Press).

Kulkarni, M.N. (1992), 'Universal Immunisation Programme in India: Issues of Sustainability', *Economic and Political Weekly*, July 4.

Kumar, A.K. Shiva (1991), 'UNDP's Human Development Index: A Computation for Indian States', *Economic and Political Weekly*, October 12.

—— (1992), 'Maternal Capabilities and Child Survival in Low Income Regions: An Economic Analysis of Infant Mortality in India', unpublished Ph.D. thesis, Harvard University.

—— (1994), 'Women's Capabilities and Infant Mortality: Lessons from Manipur', in M. Das Gupta et al. (1994).

Kumar, K. (1991), *The Political Agenda of Education* (New Delhi: Sage).

Kundu, Amitabh, and Sahu, Mahesh (1991), 'Variation in Sex Ratio: Development Implications', *Economic and Political Weekly*, October 12.

Kuo, S. (1983), *The Taiwan Economy in Transition* (Boulder, CO: Westview).

Kurian, N.J. (1989), 'Anti-Poverty Programmes: A Reappraisal', *Economic and Political Weekly*, March 25.

Kurrien, John (1983), *Elementary Education in India: Myth, Reality, Alternative* (New Delhi: Vikas).

Kynch, Jocelyn (1985), 'How Many Women Are Enough?', in *Third World Affairs 1985* (London: Third World Foundation).

Kynch, Jocelyn, and Sen, Amartya (1983), 'Indian Women: Well-being and Survival', *Cambridge Journal of Economics*, 7.

Lakshmamma, T. (1989), 'Underutilization of MCH and Family Planning Services: A Case Study of Andhra Pradesh', in Jena and Pati (1989).

Lal, Deepak (1988), *The Hindu Equilibrium* (Oxford: Clarendon Press).

Lane, Robert E. (1991), *The Market Experience* (Cambridge: Cambridge University Press).

—— (1994), 'Quality of Life and Quality of Persons: A New Role for Government', *Political Theory*, 22.

Langford, Christopher (1984), 'Sex Differentials in Mortality in Sri Lanka: Changes since the 1920s', *Journal of Bio-social Science*, 16.

—— (1988), 'Sex Differentials in Sri Lanka: Past Trends and the Situation Recently', mimeo, London School of Economics.

Langford, Christopher, and Storey, Pamela (1993), 'Sex Differentials in Mortality Early in the Twentieth Century: Sri Lanka and India Compared', *Population and Development Review*, 19.

Leslie, Joanne (1988), 'Women's Work and Child Nutrition in the Third World', *World Development*, 16.

Leslie, J., and Paolisso, M. (eds.) (1989), *Women, Work and Child Welfare in the Third World* (Boulder, CO: Westview).

Lewis, John (1995), *India's Political Economy: Governance and Reform* (Delhi: Oxford University Press).

Lewis, W. Arthur (1955), *The Theory of Economic Growth* (London: Allen & Unwin).

Li Chengrui (1992), *A Study of China's Population* (Beijing: Foreign Languages Press).

Lieten, G.K. (1993), *Continuity and Change in Rural West Bengal* (London: Sage).

Lin, Justin Yifu (1992), 'Rural Reforms and Agricultural Growth in China', *American Economic Review*, 82.

Lipton, Michael, and Ravallion, Martin (1994), 'Poverty and Policy', in Behrman and Srinivasan (1994).

Little, Ian M.D. (1977), 'Development Economics', in Alan Bullock, Oliver Stallybrass, and Stephen Trombley (eds.), *The Fontana Dictionary of Modern Thought* (London: Fontana Press, 2nd edition).

—— (1982), *Economic Development* (New York: Basic Books).

—— (1994), 'Trade and Industrialization Revisited', Iqbal Memorial Lecture, Pakistan Institute of Development Economics, April 2.

Little, Ian M.D., Scitovsky, Tibor, and Scott, Maurice Fg. (1970), *Industry and Trade in Some Developing Countries* (Oxford: Clarendon Press).

Lopez, Alan D., and Ruzicka, Lado T. (eds.) (1983), *Sex Differentials in Mortality: Trends, Determinants and Consequences*, Miscellaneous Series No. 4, Department of Demography, Australian National University, Canberra.

Lucas, Robert E. (1988), 'On the Mechanics of Economic Development', *Journal of Monetary Economics*, 22.

―― (1993), 'Making a Miracle', *Econometrica*, 61.

McGuire, James W. (1994), 'Development Policy and its Determinants in East Asia and Latin America', forthcoming in *Journal of Public Policy*.

McKenzie, Lionel (1959), 'On the Existence of General Equilibrium for a Competitive Market', *Econometrica*, 27.

Maharatna, Arup (1992), 'The Demography of Indian Famines: A Historical Perspective', Ph.D. thesis, London School of Economics; to be published by Oxford University Press, New Delhi, 1996.

Mahendra Dev, S. (1992), 'Poverty Alleviation Programmes: A Case Study of Maharashtra with Emphasis on Employment Guarantee Scheme', Discussion Paper No.77, Indira Gandhi Institute of Development Research, Bombay.

―― (1993a), 'India's (Maharashtra) Employment Guarantee Scheme: Lessons from Long Experience', paper presented at a workshop on 'Employment for Poverty Alleviation and Food Security', October 11–14, 1993, Virginia, coordinated by the International Food Policy Research Institute, Washington, DC.

―― (1993b), 'In Defence of Maharashtra's EGS', mimeo, Indira Gandhi Institute of Development Research, Bombay.

―― (1993c), 'Social Security in the Unorganized Sector: Lessons from the Experiences of Kerala and Tamil Nadu', mimeo, Indira Gandhi Institute of Development Research, Bombay.

Mahendra Dev, S., and Ranade, Ajit (1995), 'Secondary Benefits of Rural Works Programmes', mimeo, Indira Gandhi Institute of Development Research, Bombay.

Mahendra Dev, S., Suryanarayana, M.H., and Parikh, K. S. (1992), 'Rural Poverty in India: Incidence, Issues and Policies', *Asian Development Review*, 10.

Maithani, B.P., and Rizwana, A. (1992), 'Nagaland's Village Development Board Programme', *Journal of Rural Development*, 11.

Majumdar, Tapas (1983), *Investment in Education and Social Choice* (Cambridge: Cambridge University Press).

―― (1992), 'Educational Attainments and Social Security Provisions in the States of India', mimeo, WIDER, Helsinki.

―― (1993), 'The Relation between Educational Attainment and Ability to Obtain Social Security in the States of India', research paper, WIDER, Helsinki.

Malenbaum, W. (1956), 'India and China: Development Contrasts', *Journal of Political Economy*, 64.

―― (1959), 'India and China: Contrasts in Development Performance', *American Economic Review*, 49.

Malenbaum, W. (1982), 'Modern Economic Growth in India and China: The Comparison Revisited, 1950–1980', *Economic Development and Cultural Change*, 30.

Malhotra, K.C., and Poffenberger, M. (eds.) (1989), *Forest Regeneration through Community Protection: The West Bengal Experience*, Proceedings of the Working Group Meeting on Forest Protection Committees, Calcutta, June 21–2, 1989.

—— (1988), *Women's Seclusion and Men's Honor: Sex Roles in North India, Bangladesh and Pakistan* (Tucson: University of Arizona Press).

Mankiw, N. Gregory, Romer, David, and Weil, David (1992), 'A Contribution to the Empirics of Economic Growth', *Quarterly Journal of Economics*, 107.

Marathe, Sharad S. (1989), *Regulation and Development: India's Policy Experience of Controls over Industry* (New Delhi: Sage Publications).

Mari Bhat, P.N. (1994), 'Widows and Widowhood Mortality in India', paper presented at a conference on 'Widows in India', Bangalore, March 1994; to be published in Chen (forthcoming, b).

Mari Bhat, P.N., Navaneetham, K., and Rajan, S.I. (1992), 'Maternal Mortality in India', paper presented at a workshop on 'Health and Development in India', India International Centre, 2–4 January 1992.

—— (1994), 'Maternal Mortality: Model Estimates of Levels, Trends and State Differentials', in M. Das Gupta et al. (1994).

Mari Bhat, P.N. and Rajan, S.I. (1990), 'Demographic Transition in Kerala Revisited', *Economic and Political Weekly*, September 1–8.

—— (1992), 'Demographic Transition in Kerala: A Reply', *Economic and Political Weekly*, June 6.

Marx, Karl (1857–8), *Grundrisse: Foundations of the Critique of Political Economy*, English translation, M. Nicolaus (Harmondsworth: Penguin Books, 1973).

—— (1867), *Capital*, vol. I (London: Allen and Unwin).

Mata, L., and Rosero, L. (1988), 'National Health and Social Development in Costa Rica: A Case Study of Intersectoral Action', Technical Paper No. 13, Pan American Health Organization, Washington, DC.

Mathur, K., and Bhattacharya, M. (1975), *Administrative Response to Emergency: A Study of Scarcity Administration in Maharashtra* (New Delhi: Concept).

Matson, Jim, and Selden, Mark (1992), 'Poverty and Inequality in China and India', *Economic and Political Weekly*, April 4.

Matsuyama, Kiminori (1991), 'Increasing Returns, Industrialization and Indeterminacy of Equilibrium', *Quarterly Journal of Economics*, 106.

Maurya, K.N. (1989), 'An Analysis of Causative Factors Responsible for Low Utilisation of Health and Family Welfare Services', in Jena and Pati (1989).

Mazumdar, Vina (1985), *Emergence of Women's Questions in India and the Role of Women's Studies* (New Delhi: Centre for Women's Development Studies).

Mencher, Joan (1980), 'The Lessons and Non-Lessons from Kerala', *Economic and Political Weekly*, Special Number, 1781–1802.

Mendis, P. (1992), 'The Debate on Size and Productivity in Developed and Developing Countries', *Journal of Contemporary Asia*, 22.

Mehrotra, Nidhi (1995), 'Primary Schooling in Rural India: Determinants of Demand', paper presented at a workshop on 'Applied Development Economics' held at the Delhi School of Economics, January 1995; forthcoming as a Ph.D. thesis, University of Chicago.

Middleton, John, et al. (1993), 'Uttar Pradesh Basic Education Project: Staff Appraisal Report', report No. 11746-IN, Population and Human Resources Operations Division, World Bank, Washington, DC.

Mill, John Stuart (1848), *Principles of Political Economy* (London: Parker; republished Fairfield: Augustus Kelley, 1976).

—— (1859), *On Liberty* (republished, Harmondsworth: Penguin, 1954).

—— (1861), *Utilitarianism* (republished, London: Dent, 1929).

—— (1869), *The Subjection of Women*, (London); republished in S. Alice Rossi (ed.), *Essays on Sex Equality* (Chicago: University of Chicago Press, 1970).

Miller, Barbara (1981), *The Endangered Sex* (Ithaca: Cornell University Press).

—— (1989), 'Changing Patterns of Juvenile Sex Ratios in Rural India, 1961 to 1971', *Economic and Political Weekly*, June 3.

—— (1993a), 'On Poverty, Child Survival and Gender: Models and Misperceptions', *Third World Planning Review*, 15.

Miller, Barbara (ed.) (1993b), *Sex and Gender Hierarchies* (Cambridge: Cambridge University Press).

Minhas, B. (1991), 'On Estimating the Inadequacy of Energy Intakes: Revealed Food Consumption Behaviour versus Nutritional Norms', *Journal of Development Studies*, 28(1).

—— (1992), 'Educational Deprivation and its Role as a Spoiler of Access to Better Life in India', in A. Dutta and M.M. Agrawal (eds.), *The Quality of Life* (Delhi: B.R. Publishing).

Minhas, B.S., Jain, L.R., and Tendulkar, S.D. (1991), 'Declining Incidence of Poverty in India in the 1980s', *Economic and Political Weekly*, July 6–13.

Mitra, A. (1979), *Implications of Declining Sex Ratio in India's Population* (Bombay: Allied Publishers).

Mookherjee, Dilip (1992), 'Indian Economy at the Crossroads', *Economic and Political Weekly*, April 11–18.

Morris, Morris D. (1979), *Measuring the Condition of the World's Poor* (Oxford: Pergamon Press).

Mukherjee, Amitava (1993), 'Structural Adjustment Programme and the Common Man', mimeo, Lal Bahadur Shastri National Academy of Administration, Mussoorie.

Mukherjee, Sudhansu Bhusan (1976), *The Age Distribution of the Indian Population:*

A Reconstruction for the States and Territories, 1881–1961 (Honolulu: East–West Centre).

Mundle, Sudipto (1993), 'Unemployment and the Financing of Relief Employment in a Period of Stabilisation: India 1992–94', mimeo, National Institute of Public Finance and Policy, New Delhi.

Murthi, Mamta, Guio, Anne-Catherine, and Drèze, Jean (1995), 'Mortality, Fertility and Gender Bias in India', Discussion Paper No. 61, Development Economics Research Programme, STICERD, London School of Economics.

Murthy, Nirmala (forthcoming), 'Issues in Health Policies and Management in India', paper presented at a workshop on 'Health and Development in India', 2–4 January 1992; to be published in M. Das Gupta et al. (forthcoming).

Muscat, Robert (1994), *The Fifth Tiger: A Study of Thai Development Policy* (Tokyo: United Nations University Press).

Myrdal, Gunnar (1968), *Asian Drama* (New York: Pantheon).

Nadarajah, T. (1983), 'The Transition from Higher Female to Higher Male Mortality in Sri Lanka', *Population and Development Review*, 9.

Nag, Moni (1983), 'Impact of Social Development and Economic Development on Mortality: Comparative Study of Kerala and West Bengal', *Economic and Political Weekly*, 28 (annual number, May).

—— (1989), 'Political Awareness as a Factor in Accessibility of Health Services: A Case Study of Rural Kerala and West Bengal', *Economic and Political Weekly*, February 25.

Naidu, U.S., and Kapadia, K.R. (eds.) (1985), *Child Labour and Health: Problems and Prospects* (Bombay: Tata Institute of Social Sciences).

Naik, J.P. (1975a), *Elementary Education in India: A Promise to Keep* (Bombay: Allied).

—— (1975b), *Policy and Performance in Indian Education, 1947–74* (New Delhi: Dr K.G. Saiyidain Memorial Trust).

—— (1975c), *Equity, Quality and Quantity: The Elusive Triangle in India* (Bombay: Allied).

—— (1982), *The Education Commission and After* (New Delhi: Allied).

Nair, K.N., Sivanandan, P., and Retnam, V.C.V. (1984), 'Education, Employment and Landholding Pattern in a Tamil Village', *Economic and Political Weekly*, June 16–23.

Nair, P.R.G. (1981), *Primary Education, Population Growth and Socio-Economic Change: A Comparative Study with Particular Reference to Kerala* (New Delhi: Allied).

Nanda, Amulya Ratna (1992), 'Final Population Totals: Brief Analysis of Primary Census Abstract', Census of India 1991, Series-1, Paper-2 of 1992, Office of the Registrar-General, New Delhi.

—— (1993), 'Union Primary Census Abstract for Scheduled Castes and Scheduled Tribes', Census of India 1991, Series-1, Paper-1 of 1993, Office of the Registrar-General, New Delhi.

Narain, I. (1972), 'Rural Local Politics and Primary School Management', in Rudolph and Rudolph (1972).

National Council of Educational Research and Training (1992), *Fifth All-India Educational Survey*, 2 volumes (New Delhi: NCERT).

National Institute of Public Cooperation and Child Development (1992), *Statistics on Children in India: Pocket Book 1992* (New Delhi: NIPCCD).

Nautiyal, K.C. (1989), *Education and Rural Poor* (New Delhi: Commonwealth Publishers).

Nayyar, Deepak (1976), *India's Exports and Export Policies in the 1960s* (Cambridge: Cambridge University Press).

Nayyar, Deepak (ed.) (1994), *Industrial Growth and Stagnation: The Debate in India* (Oxford: Oxford University Press).

Nayyar, Rohini (1991), *Rural Poverty in India: An Analysis of Inter-state Differences* (New York: Oxford University Press).

Newbery, D.M.G. (1977), 'Risksharing, Sharecropping and Uncertain Labour Markets', *Review of Economic Studies*, 44.

NIEPA (1994), 'Management of Education under Panchayati Raj: A Review of Literature', report prepared for a seminar on 'Management of Education under Panchayati Raj' held at the National Institute of Educational Planning and Administration, New Delhi, 27–8 October 1994.

Ninan, K. (1994), 'Poverty and Income Distribution in India', *Economic and Political Weekly*, June 18.

North, D.C. (1981), *Structure and Change in Economic History* (New York: Norton).

Nozick, Robert (1974), *Anarchy, State and Utopia* (Oxford: Blackwell).

Nuna, Sheel C. (1990), *Women and Development* (New Delhi: National Institute of Educational Planning and Administration).

Nussbaum, Martha (1992), 'Human Functioning and Social Justice', *Political Theory*, 20.

——— (1993), 'Non-relative Virtues: An Aristotelian Approach', in Nussbaum and Sen (1993).

Nussbaum, Martha, and Sen, Amartya (eds.) (1993), *The Quality of Life* (Oxford: Clarendon Press).

O'Hanlon, Rosalind (1985), *Caste, Conflict, and Ideology: Mahatma Jotirao Phule and Low Caste Protest in Nineteenth-century Western India* (Cambridge: Cambridge University Press).

Olson, Mancur (1965), *The Logic of Collective Action* (Cambridge, MA: Harvard University Press.

——— (1982), *The Rise and Decline of Nations* (New Haven: Yale University Press).

——— (1993), 'Dictatorship, Democracy and Development', *American Political Science Review*, 87 (3).

Omvedt, Gail (1980), *We Will Smash This Prison! Indian Women in Struggle* (London: Zed).

—— (1989a), 'Rural Women Fight for Independence', *Economic and Political Weekly*, April 29.

—— (1989b), 'India's Movements for Democracy: Peasants, "Greens", Women and People's Power', *Race and Class*, 31.

—— (1990), 'Women, Zilla Parishads and Panchayati Raj: Chandwad to Vitner', *Economic and Political Weekly*, August 4.

—— (1993), *Reinventing Revolution: New Social Movements and the Socialist Tradition in India* (London: M.E. Sharpe).

—— (1994), *Dalits and the Democratic Revolution: Dr. Ambedkar and the Dalit Movement in Colonial India* (New Delhi: Sage).

Oommen, M.A. (1993a), *The Kerala Economy* (New Delhi: Oxford & IBH).

—— (1993b), 'Bhagwati–Srinivasan Report on Economic Reforms', *Economic and Political Weekly*, October 2.

Osmani, Siddiq R. (1990), 'Nutrition and the Economics of Food: Implications of Some Recent Controversies', in Drèze and Sen (1990), vol. I.

—— (1991), 'Social Security in South Asia', in Ahmad et al. (1991).

—— (1995), 'The Entitlement Approach to Famine: An Assessment', in Basu et al. (1995).

—— (forthcoming), *Growth and Poverty in South Asia* (Oxford: Clarendon Press).

Osmani, Siddiq R. (ed.) (1992), *Nutrition and Poverty* (Oxford: Clarendon Press).

Otsuka, K., and Hayami, Y. (1988), 'Theories of Share Tenancy: A Critical Survey', *Economic Development and Cultural Change*, 36.

Otsuka, K., et al. (1992), 'Land and Labor Contracts in Agrarian Economies: Theories and Facts', *Journal of Economic Literature*, 30.

Pack, Howard (1993), 'Industrial and Trade Policies in the High-Performing Asian Economies', mimeo, World Bank, Washington, DC.

Paddock, William, and Paddock, Paul (1968), *Famine—1975!*(London: Weidenfeld and Nicolson).

Pal, Sarmistha (1994), 'Choice of Casual and Regular Labour Contracts in Indian Agriculture: A Theoretical and Empirical Analysis', Ph.D. thesis, London School of Economics.

Panigrahi, Lalita (1972), *British Social Policy and Female Infanticide in India* (New Delhi: Munshiram Manoharlal).

Panikar, P.G.K., and Soman, C.R. (1984), *Health Status of Kerala: The Paradox of Economic Backwardness and Health Development* (Trivandrum: Centre for Development Studies).

—— (1985), *Status of Women and Children in Kerala* (Trivandrum: Centre for Development Studies).

Parikh, Kirit (1992), 'Privatisation and Deregulation: Irrelevant Hypotheses', *Economic and Political Weekly*, February 29.

―― (1994), 'Who Gets How Much from PDS: How Effectively Does It Reach the Poor?', mimeo, Indira Gandhi Institute of Development Research, Bombay.

―― (1995), 'The Lost Decades, 1971–91: Population, Development and Poverty', mimeo, Indira Gandhi Institute of Development Research, Bombay.

Parikh, Kirit, and Sudarshan, R. (eds.) (1993), *Human Development and Structural Adjustment* (Madras: Macmillan).

Parkin, Robert (1992), *The Mundas of Central India: An Account of their Social Organization* (Delhi: Oxford University Press).

Patel, I.G. (1992), 'New Economic Policies: A Historical Perspective', *Economic and Political Weekly*, January 4–11.

Patel, Surendra J. (1985), 'India's Regression in the World Economy', *Economic and Political Weekly*, September 28.

―― (1994), *Indian Economy Towards the 21st Century* (Bombay: Orient Longman).

Pati, R.N. (1991), *Rehabilitation of Child Labourers in India* (New Delhi: Ashish Publishing).

Patil, B.R. (1984), *Problem of School Drop-outs in India: An Annotated Bibliography* (New Delhi: Council for Social Development).

Patnaik, Prabhat (1991), *Economics and Egalitarianism* (Oxford: Oxford University Press).

―― (1994), 'International Capital and National Economic Policy: A Critique of India's Economic Reforms', *Economic and Political Weekly*, March 19.

Peng, Xizhe (1987), 'Demographic Consequences of the Great Leap Forward in China's Provinces', *Population and Development Review*, 13.

―― (1991), *Demographic Transition in China: Fertility Trends since the 1950s* (Oxford: Clarendon Press).

―― (1994), 'Recent Trends in China's Population and Their Implications', Discussion Paper No. 30, Research Programme on the Chinese Economy, STICERD, London School of Economics.

Perkins, Dwight (1983), 'Research on the Economy of the People's Republic of China: A Survey of the Field', *Journal of Asian Studies*, 42.

―― (1988), 'Reforming China's Economic System', *Journal of Economic Literature*, 26.

Persson, Torsten, and Tabellini, Guido (1991), 'Is Inequality Harmful to Growth? Theory and Evidence', mimeo.

Platteau, Jean-Philippe (1991), 'Traditional Systems of Social Security and Hunger Insurance', in Ahmad et al. (1991).

Platteau, Jean-Philippe, and Baland, Jean-Marie (1994), 'A Broad Framework for Analysis of Evolving Patron–Client Ties in Agrarian Economies', mimeo, Faculté des Sciences Economiques, Université de Namur, Belgium.

Poitevin, Guy, and Rairkar, Hema (1985), *Inde: Village au Féminin* (Paris: Harmattan).

Prakasamma, M. (1989), 'Analysis of Factors Influencing Performance of Auxiliary Nurse Midwives in Nizamabad District', Ph.D. thesis, Centre for Social Medicine and Community Health, Jawaharlal Nehru University, New Delhi.

Prakash, B.A. (1994), *Kerala's Economy: Performance, Problems and Prospects* (New Delhi: Sage).

Prasad, K.V. Eswara (1987), *Wastage, Stagnation and Inequality of Opportunity in Rural Primary Education: A Case Study of Andhra Pradesh* (New Delhi: Ministry of Human Resource Development).

Preston, Samuel H. (1976), *Mortality Patterns in National Populations* (New York: Academic Press).

Priya, Ritu (1987), 'Family Planning and Health Care: A Case Study from Rajasthan', paper presented at the 12th Annual Meeting of Medico Friends Circle.

—— (1990), 'Dubious Package Deal: Health Care in Eighth Plan', *Economic and Political Weekly*, August 18.

Psacharopoulos, G. (1985), 'Returns to Education: A Further International Update and Implications', *Journal of Human Resources,* 20.

—— (1988), 'Education and Development: A Review', *The World Bank Research Observer*, 3 (1).

—— (1993), 'Returns to Investment in Education: A Global Update', Working Paper, World Bank, Washington, DC.

Putnam, Robert D., with Leonardi, Robert and Nanetti, Raffaella Y. (1993), *Making Democracy Work: Civic Traditions in Modern Italy* (Princeton, NJ: Princeton University Press).

Qadeer, I., and Priya, R. (1992), 'Planning for Health in Independent India', paper presented at a seminar on 'Understanding Independent India', Jawaharlal Nehru University, March 1992.

Quibria, M.G., and Rashid, S. (1984), 'The Puzzle of Sharecropping: A Survey of Theories', *World Development*, 12.

Quibria, M.G. (ed.) (1994), *Rural Poverty in Asia: Priority Issues and Policy Options* (Oxford: Oxford University Press).

Rahman, Omar, Foster, Andrew, and Menken, Jane (1992) 'Older Widow Mortality in Rural Bangladesh', *Social Science and Medicine*, 34.

Raghunandan, D., Baru, Rama, Lakshmi, G., and Sengupta, A. (1987), 'Health Seeking Behaviour and the Primary Health Care System: Case Study of a Backward Village in Andhra Pradesh', report submitted to the United Nations University, Tokyo; mimeo, Society for Economic and Social Studies, New Delhi.

Raj, K.N., and Sen, A.K. (1961), 'Alternative Patterns of Growth under Conditions of Stagnant Export Earnings', *Oxford Economic Papers*, 13.

Raj, K.N., and Tharakan, M. (1983), 'Agrarian Reform in Kerala and Its Impact on the Rural Economy', in A. Ghose (ed.) *Agrarian Reform in Contemporary Developing Countries* (London: Croom Helm).

Rajan, S.I., Mishra, U.S., and Navaneetham, K. (1991), 'Decline in Sex Ratio: An Alternative Explanation?', *Economic and Political Weekly*, December 21.

—— (1992), 'Decline in Sex Ratio: Alternative Explanation Revisited', *Economic and Political Weekly*, November 14.

Rajivan, Anuradha K. (1991), 'Weight Variations among Preschoolers: An Analysis of Evidence from Rural Tamil Nadu', unpublished Ph.D. thesis, University of Southern California.

Raju, S., and Premi, M.K. (1992), 'Decline in Sex Ratio: Alternative Explanation Re-examined', *Economic and Political Weekly*, April 25.

Rakshit, Mihir (1992), 'Issues in Structural Adjustment of the Indian Economy', paper presented at the Tenth World Congress of the International Economic Association, Moscow.

Ram, N. (1990), 'An Independent Press and Anti-Hunger Strategies: The Indian Experience', in Drèze and Sen (1990), vol. I.

Ramachandran, V.K. (1990), *Wage Labour and Unfreedom in Agriculture: An Indian Case Study* (Oxford: Clarendon Press).

—— (1996), 'Kerala's Development Achievements', in Drèze and Sen (1996).

Ramalingaswami, V., Deo, M.G., Guleria, J.S., Malhotra, K.K., Sood, S.K., Om, P., and Sinha, R.V.N. (1971), 'Studies of the Bihar Famine of 1966–1967', in G. Blix et al. (eds.), *Famine: Nutrition and Relief Operations in Times of Disaster* (Uppsala: Swedish Nutrition Foundation).

Rao, C.H.H. (1966), 'Alternative Explanations of the Inverse Relationship Between Farm Size and Output Per Acre in India', *Indian Economic Review*, 1.

Rao, Nitya (1993), 'Total Literacy Campaigns: A Field Report', *Economic and Political Weekly*, May 8.

Rao, S.L. (1994), 'Labour Adjustment as Part of Industrial Restructuring', *Economic and Political Weekly*, February 5.

Ravallion, Martin (1987), *Markets and Famines* (Oxford: Clarendon Press).

—— (1994), *Poverty Comparisons* (Chur, Switzerland: Harwood Academic Press).

Ravallion, Martin, and Datt, Gaurav (1995), 'Growth and Poverty in Rural India', Policy Research Working Paper 1405, World Bank, Washington, DC.

Ravallion, M., Datt, G., and Chaudhuri, S. (1993), 'Does Maharashtra's Employment Guarantee Scheme Guarantee Employment? Effects of the 1988 Wage Increase', *Economic Development and Cultural Change*, 41 (2).

Ravallion, M., and Subbarao, K. (1992), 'Adjustment and Human Development in India', *Journal of the Indian School of Political Economy*, January–March.

Rawls, J. (1971), *A Theory of Justice* (Cambridge, MA: Harvard University Press).

—— (1993), *Political Liberalism* (New York: University of Columbia Press).

Raz, J. (1986), *The Morality of Freedom* (Oxford: Clarendon Press).

Raza, M. (1990), *Education, Development and Society* (New Delhi: Vikas Publishing House).

Raza, M., and Ramachandaran, H. (1990), 'Responsiveness to Educational Inputs: A Study of Rural Households', *Indian Journal of Social Science*, 3 (1).

Reddy, Sanjay (1988), 'An Independent Press Working Against Famine: The Nigerian Experience', *Journal of Modern African Studies*, 26.

Riskin, Carl (1987), *China's Political Economy: The Quest for Development since 1949* (Oxford: Oxford University Press).

—— (1990), 'Feeding China', in Drèze and Sen (1990), vol. III.

—— (1993), 'Income Distribution and Poverty in Rural China', in Griffin and Zhao Renwei (1993).

Rodrik, Dani (1992), 'The Limits of Trade Policy Reform in Developing Countries', *Journal of Economic Perspectives*, 6.

—— (1994a), 'King Kong Meets Godzilla: The World Bank and *The East Asian Miracle*', Discussion Paper No. 944, Centre for Economic Policy Research, London.

—— (1994b), 'Trade and Industrial Policy Reform in Developing Countries: A Review of Recent Theory and Evidence', in Behrman and Srinivasan (1994).

Roemer, John (1982), *A General Theory of Exploitation and Class* (Cambridge, MA: Harvard University Press).

Rogaly, Ben (1994), 'Rural Labour Arrangements in West Bengal, India', unpublished Ph.D. thesis, University of Oxford.

Rokadiya, B.C., Mehta, C.S., Jain, A.K., and Tripathi, V. (1993), 'The Final Evaluation of the Total Literacy Campaign of Ajmer District', mimeo, National Institute of Adult Education, New Delhi.

Romer, Paul M. (1986), 'Increasing Returns and Long-Run Growth', *Journal of Political Economy*, 94.

—— (1987a), 'Growth Based on Increasing Returns Due to Specialization', *American Economic Review*, 77.

—— (1987b), 'Two Strategies for Economic Development: Using Ideas and Producing Ideas', in World Bank, *Proceedings of the World Bank Annual Conference on Development Economics 1992* (Washington, DC: World Bank).

—— (1990), 'Endogenous Technical Change', *Journal of Political Economy*, 98.

—— (1993), 'Idea Gaps and Object Gaps in Economic Development', *Journal of Monetary Economics*, 32.

Rose, Kalima (1992), *Where Women are Leaders: The SEWA Movement in India* (London: Zed Books).

Rosen, George (1992), *Contrasting Styles of Industrial Reform: China and India in the 1980s* (Chicago: University of Chicago Press).

Rosenzweig, Mark R., and Evenson, R. (1977), 'Fertility, Schooling, and the Economic Contribution of Children in Rural India: An Econometric Analysis', *Econometrica*, 45 (5).

Rosenzweig, Mark R., and Schultz, T. Paul (1982), 'Market Opportunities, Genetic Endowments, and Intrafamily Resource Distribution: Child Survival in Rural India', *American Economic Review*, 72.

Rothschild, Emma (1992a), 'Adam Smith and Conservative Economics', *The Economic History Review*, 45 (February).

—— (1992b), 'Commerce and the State: Turgot, Condorcet and Smith', *Economic Journal*, 102.

Rowley, Charles, Tollison, R., and Tullock, Gordon (eds.) (1988), *The Political Economy of Rent-Seeking* (Boston: Kluwer).

Roy, D.K.S. (1992), *Women in Peasant Movements: Tebhaga, Naxalite and After* (New Delhi: Manohar Publications).

Roy, S.B. (1992), 'Forest Protection Committees in West Bengal', *Economic and Political Weekly*, July 18.

Roy Choudhury, Uma Datta (1993), 'Inter-state and Intra-state Variations in Economic Development and Standards of Living', *Journal of the Indian School of Political Economy*, 5 (1).

Rudolph, S.H., and Rudolph, L.I. (1987), *In Pursuit of Lakshmi: The Political Economy of the Indian State* (Chicago: University of Chicago Press).

Rudolph, S.H., and Rudolph, L.I. (eds.) (1972), *Education and Politics in India: Studies in Organization, Society, and Policy* (Cambridge, MA: Harvard University Press).

Rudra, Ashok (1991), 'Privatisation and Deregulation', *Economic and Political Weekly*, December 21.

Sachau, E.C. (ed.) (1992), *Alberuni's India*, originally published in 1910 (New Delhi: Munshiram Manoharlal Publishers).

Sachs, Ignacy (1990), 'Growth and Poverty: Some Lessons from Brazil', in Drèze and Sen (1990), vol. III.

Saha, Anamitra, and Swaminathan, Madhura (1994), 'Agricultural Growth in West Bengal in the Eighties', *Economic and Political Weekly*, March 26.

Sahn, David, and Alderman, Harold (1988), 'The Effects of Human Capital on Wages, and the Determinants of Labor Supply in a Developing Country', *Journal of Development Economics*, 29.

Sainath, P. (1993), 'A Teacher Too Many, A Student Too Few', *The Times of India*, 28 October.

Saith, Ashwani (1990), 'Development Strategies and the Rural Poor', *Journal of Development Studies*, 17.

Saldanha, Denzil (1994), 'Literacy Campaigns in Maharashtra and Goa: Issues, Trends and Policy Implications', mimeo, Tata Institute of Social Sciences, Bombay.

Santha, E.K. (1994), 'Local Self-Government in Malabar (1800-1960)', Occasional Paper No. 12, Institute of Social Sciences, New Delhi.

Satia, J.K., and Jejeebhoy, S.J.(eds.) (1991), *The Demographic Challenge: A Study of Four Large Indian States* (Delhi: Oxford University Press).

Sau, Ranjit (1994), 'World Capitalism and Globalisation', *Economic and Political Weekly*, October 8.

Schultz, T. Paul (1988), 'Education Investments and Returns', in Chenery and Srinivasan (1988).

Schultz, Theodore W. (1962), 'Reflections on Investment in Man', *Journal of Political Economy*, 70.

—— (1963), *The Economic Value of Education* (New York: Columbia University Press).

—— (1971), *Investment in Human Capital* (New York: Free Press and Macmillan).

—— (1980), *Investing in People* (San Francisco: University of California Press).

Scott, Maurice Fg. (1979), 'Trade', in Galenson (1979).

Seetharamu, A.S. (1994), 'Structure and Management of Education in Karnataka State', paper presented at a seminar on 'Management of Education under Panchayati Raj' held at the National Institute of Educational Planning and Administration, New Delhi, 27–8 October, 1994.

Seetharamu, A.S., and Ushadevi, M.D. (1985), *Education in Rural Areas: Constraints and Prospects* (New Delhi: Ashish).

Sen, Amartya (1970), 'Aspects of Indian Education', Lal Bahadur Shastri Memorial Lecture at the Institute of Public Enterprises, Hyderabad; reprinted in S.C. Malik (ed.), *Management and Organization of Indian Universities* (Simla: Institute of Advanced Study, 1970), and partly reprinted in P. Chaudhuri (1971).

—— (1973), 'On the Development of Basic Income Indicators to Supplement GNP Measures', *Economic Bulletin for Asia and the Far East*, United Nations, 24.

—— (1976a), 'Real National Income', *Review of Economic Studies*, 43.

—— (1976b), 'Poverty: An Ordinal Approach to Measurement', *Econometrica*, 44.

—— (1980), 'Equality of What?', in S. McMurrin (ed.), *Tanner Lectures on Human Values*, vol. I (Cambridge: Cambridge University Press); reprinted in Amartya Sen, *Choice, Welfare and Measurement* (Oxford: Blackwell, and Cambridge, MA: MIT Press, 1982).

—— (1981), *Poverty and Famines* (Oxford: Clarendon Press).

Sen, Amartya (1982), 'How Is India Doing?', *New York Review of Books*.

——— (1983a), 'Development: Which Way Now?', *Economic Journal*, 93.

——— (1983b), 'Poor, Relatively Speaking', *Oxford Economic Papers*, 35.

——— (1984), *Resources, Values and Development* (Oxford: Blackwell, and Cambridge, MA: Harvard University Press).

——— (1985a), *Commodities and Capabilities* (Amsterdam: North-Holland).

——— (1985b), 'Well-being, Agency and Freedom: The Dewey Lectures 1984', *Journal of Philosophy*, 82.

——— (1985c), 'Women, Technology and Sexual Divisions', *Trade and Development* (UNCTAD), 6.

——— (1987), *The Standard of Living*, Tanner Lectures with discussion by J. Muellbauer and others, ed. G. Hawthorn (Cambridge: Cambridge University Press).

——— (1988), 'India and Africa: What Do We Have to Learn from Each Other?', in K.I. Arrow (ed.), *The Balance between Industry and Agriculture in Economic Development*, vol. I (London: Macmillan).

——— (1989), 'Women's Survival as a Development Problem', *Bulletin of the American Academy of Arts and Sciences*, 43; shortened version published in *The New York Review of Books*, Christmas number, 1993.

——— (1990), 'Gender and Cooperative Conflict', in Tinker (1990).

——— (1992a), *Inequality Reexamined* (Oxford: Clarendon Press, and Cambridge, MA: Harvard University Press).

——— (1992b), 'Life and Death in China: A Reply', *World Development*, 20.

——— (1992c), 'Missing Women', *British Medical Journal*, 304 (March).

——— (1993a), 'Markets and Freedoms', *Oxford Economic Papers*, 45.

——— (1993b), 'Markets and the Freedom to Choose', paper presented at the Kiel Institute of World Economics; published in a volume on 'The Ethical Foundations of the Market Economy'.

——— (1993c), 'Positional Objectivity', *Philosophy and Public Affairs*, 22.

——— (1994a), 'Population and Reasoned Agency', in K. Lindahl-Kiessling and H. Landberg (eds.), *Population, Economic Development, and the Environment* (Oxford: Oxford University Press).

——— (1994b), 'Population: Delusion and Reality', *New York Review of Books*, September 22.

Sen, Amartya, and Sengupta, Sunil (1983), 'Malnutrition of Rural Children and the Sex Bias', *Economic and Political Weekly*, 19 (annual number).

Sen, Geeta, Germain, Adrienne, and Chen, Lincoln (eds.) (1994), *Population Policies Reconsidered: Health, Empowerment, and Rights* (Harvard Series on Population and International Health).

Sen, Ilina (1986), 'Geography of Secular Change in Sex Ratio in 1981: How Much Room for Optimism?', *Economic and Political Weekly*, March 22.

Sen, Sunanda (1994), 'Dimensions of India's External Economic Crisis', *Economic and Political Weekly*, April 2.

Sengupta, Chandan (1992), 'Sociological Impact of Total Literacy Campaign: The Case of Midnapore', unpublished report, Tata Institute of Social Sciences, Bombay.

Sengupta, S. (1991), 'Progress of Literacy in India during 1983 to 1988', *Sarvekshana*, April–June.

Sengupta, Sunil (1981), 'West Bengal Land Reforms and the Agrarian Scene', *Economic and Political Weekly*, Review of Agriculture, 16 (25–6).

Sengupta, Sunil, and Gazdar, Haris (1996), 'Agrarian Politics and Rural Development in West Bengal', in Drèze and Sen (1996).

Shah, Ghanshyam (1990), *Social Movements in India: A Review of the Literature* (New Delhi: Sage).

Shah, M.H. (1989), 'Factors Responsible for Low Performance of Family Welfare Programme', in Jena and Pati (1989).

Shah, Nasra M. (ed.) (1986), *Pakistani Women: A Socioeconomic and Demographic Profile* (Islamabad: Pakistan Institute of Development Economics).

Shah, Tushaar (1987), 'Gains from Social Forestry: Lessons from West Bengal', mimeo, Institute of Rural Management, Anand.

Shankari, Uma (1993), 'A Story from the Field', *Lokayan Bulletin*, 10.

Sharma, Ursula (1980), *Women, Work and Property in North-West India* (London: Tavistock).

———— (1986), *Women's Work, Class, and the Urban Household: A Study of Shimla, North India* (New York, Tavistock).

Sibbons, Maureen (1992), 'Health for All by the Year 2000: The Good Example of Kerala?', Papers in International Development, No. 5, University of Wales, Swansea.

Singh, A.K. (1993), 'Social Consequences of New Economic Policies with Particular Reference to Levels of Living of Working Class Population', *Economic and Political Weekly*, February 13.

Singh, A.N. (1990), *Child Labour in India: A Socioeconomic Perspective* (New Delhi: Shipra Publications).

Singh, H.N. (1993), 'Social Background and Role Performance of Village Pradhans', Occasional Paper Series, No. 10, Institute of Social Sciences, New Delhi.

Singh, Inderjit (1990), *The Great Ascent: The Rural Poor in South Asia* (Baltimore: Johns Hopkins).

Singh, K.B.K. (1988), *Marriage and Family System of Rajputs* (New Delhi: Wisdom Press).

Singh, K.S. (1975), *The Indian Famine, 1967* (New Delhi: People's Publishing House).

———— (1985), *Tribal Society in India* (New Delhi: Manohar).

Singh, K.S. (1993), *The Scheduled Castes* (Delhi: Oxford University Press).

Singh, K.S. (ed.) (1983), *Tribal Movements in India,* 2 volumes (New Delhi: Manohar).

Singh, Manmohan (1964), *India's Export Trends and Prospects for Self-Contained Growth* (Oxford: Clarendon Press).

Singh, R.R. (1994), 'Impact of Nutritive Meal Programme on Enrolment and Health of Girls in Tamil Nadu Primary Schools', mimeo.

Singha, H.S. (1992), *School Education In India: Contemporary Issues and Trends* (New Delhi: Sterling Publishers).

Smith, Adam (1776), *An Inquiry into the Nature and Causes of The Wealth of Nations;* republished in R.H. Campbell and A.S. Skinner (eds.), *Adam Smith: An Inquiry into the Nature and Causes of The Wealth of Nations* (Oxford: Clarendon, 1976).

—— (1790), *The Theory of Moral Sentiments,* revised edition (republished, Oxford: Clarendon Press, 1975).

Solow, Robert M. (1956), 'A Contribution to the Theory of Economic Growth', *Quarterly Journal of Economics,* 70.

—— (1957), 'Technical Change and Aggregate Production Function', *Review of Economics and Statistics,* 39.

Somanathan, E. (1991), 'Deforestation, Property Rights and Incentives in Central Himalaya', *Economic and Political Weekly,* January 26.

Sopher, David (1980a), 'The Geographical Patterning of Culture in India', in Sopher (1980b).

Sopher, David (ed) (1980b), *An Exploration of India: Geographical Perspectives on Society and Culture* (Ithaca, NY: Cornell University Press).

Srinivas, K. (1991), 'The Demographic Scenario Revealed by the 1991 Census Figures', *Journal of Family Welfare,* 37 (3).

Srinivas, M.N. (1962), *Caste in Modern India and Other Essays* (Bombay: Allied).

—— (1965), *Religion and Society among the Coorgs of South India* (Bombay: Asia Publishing House).

—— (1967), 'The Cohesive Role of Sanskritization', in P. Mason (ed.), *India and Ceylon: Unity and Diversity* (London: Oxford University Press).

—— (1989), *The Cohesive Role of Sanskritization and Other Essays* (Delhi: Oxford University Press).

Srinivasan, T.N. (1991a), 'Reform of Industrial and Trade Policies', *Economic and Political Weekly,* September 14.

—— (1991b), 'Indian Development Strategy: An Exchange of Views', *Economic and Political Weekly,* August 3–10.

—— (1993), 'Indian Economic Reforms: Background, Rationale and Next Steps', mimeo, Economic Growth Center, Yale University.

Srinivasan, T.N. (ed.) (1994), *Agriculture and Foreign Trade in China and India since 1950* (San Francisco: International Center for Economic Growth).

Srinivasan, T.N., and Bardhan, Pranab (eds.) (1974), *Poverty and Income Distribution in India* (Calcutta: Statistical Publishing Society).

Srinivasan, T.N., and Bardhan, Pranab (eds.) (1988), *Rural Poverty in South Asia* (New York: Columbia University Press).

State Statistical Bureau of the People's Republic of China (1985), *1982 Population Census of China*, Chinese edition (Beijing: Population Census Office).

—— (1992), *China Population Statistics Yearbook 1992* (Beijing: Population Census Office).

—— (1993a), *Tabulation of the 1990 Census of the People's Republic of China*, vol. II, Chinese edition (Beijing: Population Census Office).

—— (1993b), *China Statistical Yearbook 1993* (Beijing: China Statistical Information and Consultancy Service Center).

Stevenson, H., and Stigler, J. (1992), *The Learning Gap* (New York: Summit).

Stewart, Frances (1985), *Basic Needs in Developing Countries* (Baltimore: Johns Hopkins).

Stiglitz, Joseph (1974), 'Incentives and Risk Sharing in Share-cropping', *Review of Economic Studies*, 61.

—— (1993), 'Some Lessons from the Asian Miracle', mimeo, World Bank, Washington, DC.

Stockholm International Peace Research Institute (1994), *SIPRI Yearbook 1994* (Oxford: Oxford University Press).

Stokey, Nancy L. (1988), 'Learning by Doing and the Introduction of New Goods', *Journal of Political Economy*, 96.

—— (1991a), 'Human Capital, Product Quality and Growth', *Quarterly Journal of Economics*, 106.

—— (1991b), 'The Volume and Composition of Trade between Rich and Poor Countries', *Review of Economic Studies*, 58.

Stree Shakti Sanghatana (1989), *'We Were Making History': Women and the Telangana Uprising* (London: Zed Books).

Streeten, Paul, with Burki, S.J., Mahbub ul Haq, Hicks, N., and Stewart, F. (1981), *First Things First: Meeting Basic Needs in Developing Countries* (New York: Oxford University Press).

Subbarao, K., and Raney, L. (1994), 'Social Gains from Female Education: A Cross-National Study', Discussion Paper No. 194, World Bank, Washington, DC.

Subramaniam, V. (1975), *Parched Earth: The Maharashtra Drought 1970–73* (Bombay: Orient Longman).

Summers, Lawrence H. (1992), 'Investing in *All* the People: Educating Women in Developing Countries', Working Paper, World Bank, Washington, DC.

Sundaram, K., and Tendulkar, S.D. (1994), 'On Measuring Shelter Deprivation in India', Discussion Paper No. 23, Centre for Development Economics, Delhi School of Economics.

Sundari, T.K. (1993), 'Women and the Politics of Development in India', *Reproductive Health Matters*, 1.

——— (1994), 'Women's Health in a Rural Poor Population in Tamil Nadu', in M. Das Gupta et al. (1994).

Swaminathan, Madhura (1990), 'Village Level Implementation of IRDP: Comparison of West Bengal and Tamil Nadu', *Economic and Political Weekly*, March 31.

Swaminathan, Mina (1991), 'Child Care Services in Tamil Nadu', *Economic and Political Weekly*, December 28.

Swamy, G.V. (1991), 'Common Property Resources and Tribal Economy', paper presented at the Ninth Annual Conference of the Andhra Pradesh Economic Association, Vijaywada; published in the proceedings of the conference.

Swamy, V.S., and Sinha, S.K. (1994), 'A Note on Disaggregation of Data Below State Level from Sample Registration System', *Sample Registration Bulletin*, 28 (1).

Taylor, Lance (ed.) (1993), *The Rocky Road to Reform: Adjustment, Income Distribution, and Growth in the Developing World* (Cambridge, MA: MIT Press).

Tendulkar, S.D., Sundaram, K., and Jain, L.R. (1993), 'Poverty in India, 1970–71 to 1988–89', Working Paper, ILO-ARTEP, New Delhi.

Tharu, S., and Lalita., K. (eds.) (1991), *Women Writing in India*, 2 volumes (Delhi: Oxford University Press).

Thirlwall, A.P. (1994), *Growth and Development*, fifth edition (London: Macmillan).

Thomas, D., Strauss, J., and Henriques, M.H. (1991), 'How Does Mother's Education Affect Child Height?', *Journal of Human Resources*, 26.

Tilak, Jandhyala B.G. (1989), 'Centre–State Relations in Financing Education in India', *Comparative Education Review*, 33.

——— (1990), 'Expenditure on Education in India: A Comment', *Journal of Education and Social Change*, 4 (2).

——— (1993), 'Costs and Financing of Education in India: A Review of Issues, Problems and Prospects', mimeo, National Institute of Educational Planning and Administration, New Delhi; forthcoming as a Discussion Paper of the Centre for Development Studies, Trivandrum.

——— (1994a), 'South Asian Perspectives', *International Journal of Educational Research*, 21.

——— (1994b), 'Elementary Education in India in the 1990s: Problems and Perspectives', mimeo, National Institute of Educational Planning and Administration, New Delhi.

Tinker, Irene (ed.) (1990), *Persistent Inequalities* (New York: Oxford University Press).

Tod, James (1929), *Annals and Antiquities of Rajasthan*, 2 volumes, reprinted 1972 (London: Routledge and Kegan Paul).

Tomkins, Andrew, and Watson, Fiona (1989), *Malnutrition and Infection: A Review* (London: London School of Hygiene and Tropical Medicine).

Toye, John (1993), *Dilemmas of Development*, second edition (Oxford: Blackwell).

Tulasidhar, V.B. (1993), 'Expenditure Compression and Health Sector Outlays', *Economic and Political Weekly*, November 6.

Tulasidhar, V.B., and Sarma, J.V.M. (1993), 'Public Expenditure, Medical Care at Birth and Infant Mortality: A Comparative Study of States in India', in Berman and Khan (1993).

Tyagi, P.N. (1991), *Education for All: A Graphic Presentation*, first edition (New Delhi: National Institute of Educational Planning and Administration).

—— (1993), *Education for All: A Graphic Presentation*, second edition (New Delhi: National Institute of Educational Planning and Administration).

Uberoi, P. (ed.) (1993), *Family, Kinship and Marriage in India* (Delhi: Oxford University Press).

United Nations (1993), *The Sex and Age Distribution of the World Populations: The 1992 Revision* (New York: Department of Economic and Social Development, United Nations).

UNDP (1990), *Human Development Report 1990* (Oxford: Oxford University Press).

—— (1993), *Human Development Report 1993* (Oxford: Oxford University Press).

—— (1994), *Human Development Report 1994* (Oxford: Oxford University Press).

UNICEF (1994), *The State of the World's Children 1994* (New York: UNICEF).

van Bastelaer, T. (1986), 'Essai d'Analyse des Systèmes de Paiements de Mariage: Le Cas de l'Inde', unpublished M.Sc. thesis, Faculté des Sciences Economiques et Sociales, Université de Namur, Belgium.

van Parijs, P. (1990), 'Equal Endowments as Undominated Diversity', *Recherches Economiques de Louvain*, 56.

—— (1991), 'Why Surfers Should be Fed: The Liberal Case for an Unconditional Basic Income', *Philosophy and Public Affairs*, 20.

Vanaik, Achin (1991), *The Painful Transition: Bourgeois Democracy in India* (London: Verso).

Venkatachalam, R., and Srinivasan, V. (1993), *Female Infanticide* (New Delhi: Har-Anand).

Verma, Jyoti (1989), 'Women Education: A Media of Social Change', *Social Change*, 19.

Verma, V.S. (1988), *A Handbook of Population Statistics* (New Delhi: Office of the Registrar General).

Visaria, Leela, and Visaria, Pravin (1995), 'Acceleration of Fertility Decline in Tamil Nadu since 1981: Some Hypotheses', Working Paper, Gujarat Institute of Development Research, Ahmedabad.

Visaria, Pravin (1961), *The Sex Ratio of the Population of India*, Monograph No. 10, Census of India 1961, Office of the Registrar General, New Delhi.

—— (1967), 'The Sex Ratio of the Population of India and Pakistan and Regional Variations during 1901–1960', in A. Bose (ed.), *Pattern of Population Change in India 1951–1961* (Bombay: Allied Publishers).

—— (1993), 'Demographic Aspects of Development: The Indian Experience', *Indian Journal of Social Science*, 6 (3).

Visaria, P., Gumber, A., and Visaria, L. (1993), 'Literacy and Primary Education in India, 1980–81 to 1991', *Journal of Educational Planning and Administration*, 7 (1).

Visaria, Pravin, and Visaria, Leela (1994), 'Demographic Transition: Accelerating Fertility Decline in 1980s', *Economic and Political Weekly*, December 17–24.

Vlassoff, Carol (1980), 'Unmarried Adolescent Females in Rural India: A Study of the Social Impact of Education', *Journal of Marriage and the Family*, 42 (2).

—— (1993), 'Against the Odds: The Changing Impact of Education on Female Autonomy and Fertility in an Indian Village', paper presented at a workshop on 'Female Education, Autonomy and Fertility Change in South Asia', New Delhi, 8–10 April 1993.

Vyas, V.S., Sagar, V., and Bhargava, P. (1993), 'Nature and Direction of Poverty Alleviation Efforts in India: An Overview', mimeo, Institute of Development Studies, Jaipur.

Vyasulu, Vinod (1993), 'Management of Poverty Alleviation Programmes in Karnataka: An Overview', paper presented at a workshop on 'Poverty Alleviation in India' held at the Institute of Development Studies, Jaipur, February.

Wade, Robert (1989), 'What Can Economies Learn from East Asian Success?', *Annals of the American Academy of Political Science*, 505.

—— (1988a), *Village Republics: Economic Conditions for Collective Action in South India* (Cambridge: Cambridge University Press).

—— (1988b), 'Why Some Indian Villages Co-operate', *Economic and Political Weekly*, April 16.

—— (1990), *Governing the Market: Economic Theory and the Role of the Government in East Asian Industrialization* (Princeton: Princeton University Press).

—— (1992), 'How to Make "Street Level" Bureaucracies Work Better: India and Korea', *IDS Bulletin*, 23 (4).

Wadley, S., and Derr, B. (1989), 'Karimpur 1925–1984: Understanding Rural India Through Restudies', in P.K. Bardhan (ed.), *Conversations between Economists and Anthropologists* (Delhi: Oxford University Press).

Ware, H. (1984), 'Effects of Maternal Education, Women's Roles, and Child Care on Child Mortality', in W.H. Mosley and L.C. Chen (eds.), *Child Survival: Strategies for Research* (New York: Population Council).

Weiner, Myron (1991), *The Child and the State in India: Child Labor and Education Policy in Comparative Perspective* (Princeton: Princeton University Press).

Weiner, Myron (1994), 'Compulsory Education and Child Labour', lecture delivered at the Rajiv Gandhi Foundation, New Delhi, 8 January 1994; mimeo, Massachussetts Institute of Technology.

Weitzmann, Martin L., and Chenggang Xu (1993), 'Chinese Township and Village Enterprises as Vaguely Defined Cooperatives', Discussion Paper No. 26, Research Programme on the Chinese Economy, STICERD, London School of Economics.

Westphal, Larry E. (1978), 'The Republic of Korea's Experience of Export Led Development', *World Development*, 6.

Westphal, L.E., Kim, L., and Dahlman, C. (1985), 'Reflections on Korea's Acquisition of Technological Capability', in N. Rosenberg et al. (eds.), *International Technology Transfer: Concepts, Measures and Comparisons* (New York: Praeger).

Westphal, Larry E., Rhee, Yung Whee, and Pursell, Garry (1988), *Korean Industrial Competence: Where It Came From* (Washington, DC: World Bank).

Wong, L. (1994), 'Privatization of Social Welfare in Post-Mao China', *Asian Survey*, 34.

Wood, A. (1991), 'China's Economic System: A Brief Description, with Some Suggestions for Further Reform', Discussion Paper No. 29, Research Programme on the Chinese Economy, STICERD, London School of Economics.

World Bank (1983), *China: Socialist Economic Development* (Washington, DC: World Bank).

—— (1989), *India: Poverty, Employment, and Social Services* (Washington, DC: World Bank).

—— (1992a), *China: Strategies for Reducing Poverty in the 1990s* (Washington, DC: World Bank).

—— (1992b), 'India: Health Sector Financing', Report No. 10859-IN, World Bank, Washington, DC.

—— (1993a), *The World Food Outlook* (Washington, DC: World Bank).

—— (1993b), *World Development Report 1993* (New York: Oxford University Press).

—— (1993c), *The East Asian Miracle* (New York: Oxford University Press).

—— (1994a), 'India: Policy and Finance Strategies for Strengthening Primary Health Care Services', mimeo, World Bank, Washington, DC.

—— (1994b), *World Development Report 1994* (New York: Oxford University Press).

Young, Alwyn (1991), 'Learning by Doing and the Dynamic Effects of International Trade', *Quarterly Journal of Economics*, 106.

—— (1992), 'A Tale of Two Cities: Factor Accumulation and Technical Change in Hong Kong and Singapore', NBER *Macroeconomics Annual 1992*.

Yu Dezhi (1992), 'Changes in Health Care Financing and Health Status: The

Case of China in the 1980s', Innocenti Occasional Papers, Economic Policy Series, No. 34, International Child Development Centre, Florence.

Zachariah, K.C., Rajan, S.I., Sarma, P.S., Navaneetham, K., Nair, P.S.G., and Mishra, U.S. (1994), *Demographic Transition in Kerala in the 1980s* (Trivandrum: Centre for Development Studies).

Zeng Yi, Tu Ping, Gu Baochang, Xu Yi, Li Bohua, and Li Yongping (1993), 'Causes and Implications of the Recent Increase in the Reported Sex Ratio at Birth in China', *Population and Development Review*, 19 (2).

NAME INDEX

Acharya, Sarthi 100n, 226
Adelman, Irma 10n, 19n, 183n
Agarwal, Anil 191n
Agarwal, Bina viii, 11n, 136n, 142n, 144n, 160n, 164n, 174n
Aggarwal, J.C. 116n
Agnihotri, Anita 137n
Agnihotri, Satish viii, 46n, 136n, 142n, 147n, 155n, 159n, 164n
Agrawal, A.N. 72n, 122
Agrawal, S.P. 116n
Ahluwalia, Isher Judge 186n
Ahluwalia, Montek S. 11n
Ahmad, S.E. 84n, 99n
Alagh, Yoginder K. 12n
Alailima, Patricia 34n
Alamgir, Mohiuddin 18n
Alberuni 111n
Alderman, Harold 41n, 128n, 136n
Alesina, Alberto 33n
Almeida, A. 135n
Altekar, A.S. 157n
Ambatkar, Sanjay viii
Ambedkar, B.R. 110
Amsden, Alice H. 19n, 42n, 74n, 183n
Anand, Sudhir viii, 10n, 12n, 34n, 44, 44n
Antony, T.V. 101n
Archer, David viii, 111n
Aristotle 10n
Arneson, R. 25n
Arrow, Kenneth J. 19n
Ashton, B. 75n
Asthana, Roli viii, 142n
Atkinson, A.B. 10n, 36n, 69n
Ayyar, Vaidyanatha R.V. 119n, 138n
Aziz, Abdul 128n

Babu, S.C. 101n, 131n

Bagchi, Amiya K. viii, 12n, 186n
Bahadur, K.P. 157n
Baland, Jean-Marie 94n
Balassa, Bela 19n
Bangladesh Rural Advancement Committee (BRAC) 101
Banerjee, Nirmala 142n, 160n
Banerjee, Sumanta 56n, 107n, 124n
Banerji, Debabar 103n, 169n
Bang, R.A. 154n
Banister, Judith 67, 80n
Bapat, M.T. 75n
Bara, D. 110n
Bardhan, Kalpana 160n, 193n
Bardhan, Pranab 11n, 41n, 90n, 91n, 93n, 108n, 141n, 142n, 147n, 160n
Barnett, Marguerite Ross 91n
Barro, Robert J. 37n, 165n, 167n
Basu, Alaka Malwade 141n, 142n, 144n, 158n, 160n, 164n, 165n, 167n, 168n
Basu, Aparna 110n
Basu, Kaushik viii, 94n, 186n
Bauer, Peter 95n, 187n
Baviskar, Amita 107n
Beck, Tony 11n
Beenstock, M. 165n
Behrman, Jere R. 15n, 37n, 165n
Berlin, I. 25n
Berman, Peter 101n
Bernstein, T.P. 76n
Berreman, Gerald D. 136n, 157n
Berry, R. Albert 41n, 95n
Bhagwati, Jagdish 12, 12n, 13, 14n, 19n, 186n
Bhalla, A.S. 57n, 68n
Bhargava, Ashok 103, 169n
Bhatia, Bela viii, 175n
Bhatia, B.M. 147n

SUBJECT INDEX

AIP Conference Proceedings
Series Editor: Hugh C. Wolfe
Number 85
Particles and Fields Subseries No. 26

Proton-Antiproton
Collider Physics—1981
(Madison, Wisconsin)

Editors
V. Barger, D. Cline, F. Halzen
University of Wisconsin

American Institute of Physics
New York   1982

L.C. Catalog Card No. 82-072141
ISBN 0–88318–184–3
DOE CONF- 811231

Preface

The purpose of this book is twofold: (i) To review our physics prospects for the new energy range in particle physics opened up by the proton-antiproton collider projects (ii) To have a first glance at proton-antiproton interactions observed in the CERN-SPS collider. We thought it would be useful to collect reviews on related experiments in this volume, e.g. proton-antiproton experiments at the CERN ISR and cosmic ray experiments in the new energy range covered by the CERN SPS collider.

We thank the University of Wisconsin, the Department of Energy and the National Science Foundation for their encouragement and generous financial support for the organization of a workshop in Madison, Wisconsin (December 10-12, 1981) from which the material in this volume emerged.

The Editors.

TABLE OF CONTENTS

ISR Physics

Summary

*No Manuscript Available

RECENT RESULTS ON THE HADRONIC PRODUCTION OF CHARM

S. L. Olsen
University of Rochester, Rochester, NY 14627

ABSTRACT

Various recent measurements of the charm production cross sections are discussed. A large energy variation between Fermilab/SPS energies and the ISR is observed. Comparisons of Fermilab data with the intrinsic charm model fail to give the expected level of intrinsic charm in the proton. A discrepancy between the ISR charm production cross sections and limits deduced from the measured direct electron yield is noted.

I. INTRODUCTION

The production of charmed particles in hadronic collisions has been the subject of a considerable amount of theoretical and experimental effort. This is motivated by a number of reasons, among them:

1) Checks of QCD

Since the charmed quark is heavy, $1/M_c \sim .1$ fermi, perturbative QCD calculations are expected to be valid. Thus this is one of the few hadronic processes where QCD can be tested. Since similar calculations are used to estimate Z^0 and $W^\pm$ production at the CERN and Fermilab colliders, tests of these theories have considerable practical significance.

Perturbative QCD estimates have been made by Halzen[1]. They correspond to the two types of diagrams shown in Fig. 1. Fig. 1a shows typical single gluon contributions. These are similar to the Drell-Yan diagrams for lepton pair production, with the virtual photon replaced by a gluon. These diagrams give a charm cross section of about 0.1 µb at Fermilab energies, increasing to about 1 µb at the ISR. The two gluon processes shown in Fig. 1b are apparently more important. These graphs provide a cross section of 3 to 4 µb at Fermilab and 20 µb at the ISR. Figure 2 shows the cross section estimates as a function of p_{Lab} for both types of diagrams. Also included in Fig. 2 are estimates for b quark production. Note that for c quark production, the 2 gluon processes are expected to dominate.

In this picture we expect the following production characteristics:
  i) $\sigma \sim 4$ µb at Fermilab energies $\rightarrow \sim 20$ µb at ISR
  ii)   Central production
  iii) Since these are constituent interactions we expect $\sigma \sim A^{1.0}$
  iv)   Since 2 gluon processes dominate we do not expect to be
        sensitive to the valence quark makeup. Thus we expect pp,
        πp and p̄p to be similar.

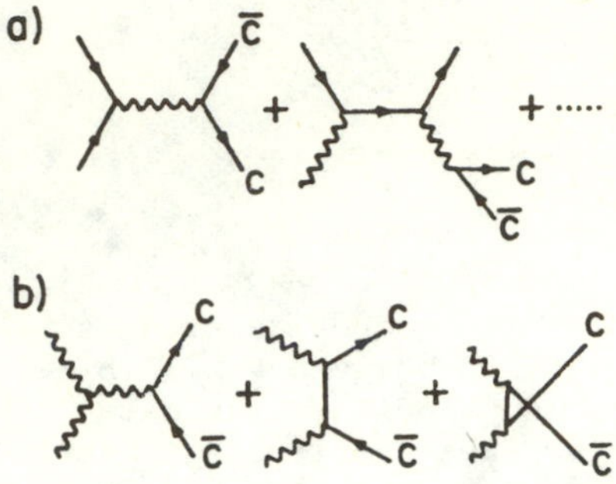

2

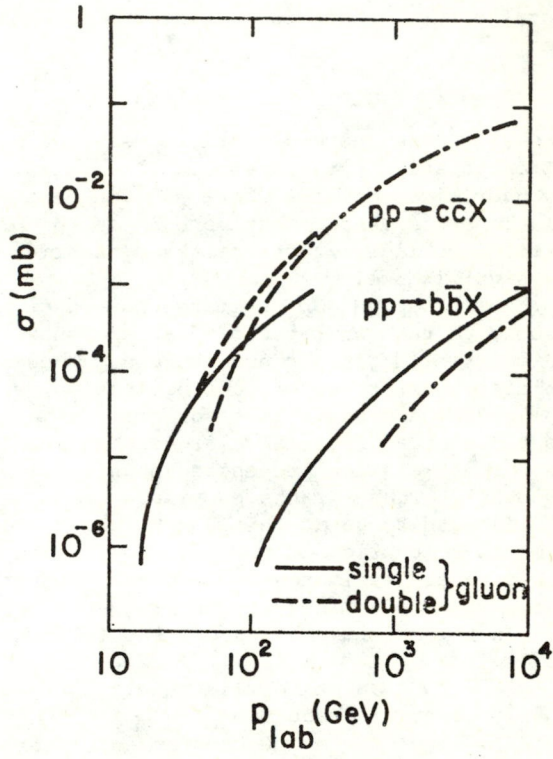

Fig. 1. QCD diagrams for hadronic production of charm a) single gluon processes b) double gluon processes.

Fig. 2. QCD predictions for charm production cross sections (see ref. 1).

2) Possible intrinsic charm in hadrons

Brodsky, Hoyer, Peterson and Sakai[2] have pointed out that the proton ground state may include a considerable amount of 5 quark configurations as shown in Fig. 3. The ground state wave function of the proton thus looks like

$$a_0|uud> + a_1|uudu\bar{u}> + a_2|uudd\bar{d}> + a_3|uuds\bar{s}> + a_4|uudc\bar{c}> \tag{1}$$
$$+ a_5|uudb\bar{b}> + \dots \quad .$$

In the MIT bag model specific estimates of the relative probabilities of the various configurations can be made. For example, Donoghue and Golowich[3] find

$$P(|uudu\bar{u}>): P(|uudd\bar{d}>): P(|uuds\bar{s}>): P(|uudc\bar{c}>)$$
$$= 0.20 : 0.15 : 0.09 : 0.01 \quad . \tag{2}$$

Thus 1% of the time it is expected that the proton has a $c\bar{c}$ quark pair inside it. So, at high energies, when threshold effects are not important, this picture predicts that about 1% of diffractive processes will produce charmed particle final states. Since the total diffractive cross section is about 15 mb (including elastic scattering) we can estimate $\sigma_{diff}(c\bar{c}) \sim 150$ µb. The production process looks like Fig. 4a, so we expect to see forward charmed baryons accompanied by forward <u>anti</u> charmed mesons. No significant forward production of charmed mesons or <u>anti</u> charmed baryons is expected.

The above arguments can be applied to strange particles and we would estimate a diffractive strange particle cross section which is ~9% of the total diffractive cross section or ~ 1.5 mb. We also would expect forward $\Lambda°$ production but central $\bar{\Lambda}°$ production. Results from the CZF group[4] which demonstrate this behavior are shown in Fig. 4b. Included in this figure are their results on charmed baryon (Λ_c^+) production. This cross section shows a remarkable similarity to $\Lambda°$ production.

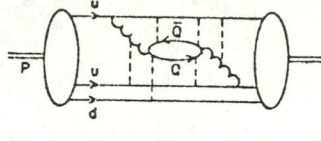

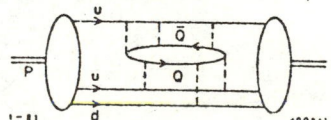

To compare results from Fermilab energies with those at the ISR it is necessary to make some estimate of the energy dependence of diffractive production from intrinsic charmed states. I have made estimates for this in two ways:

Fig. 3. Diagrams which give rise to the intrinsic heavy quarks ($Q\bar{Q}$) within the proton. Curly and dashed lines represent transverse and longitudinal-scalar (instantaneous) gluons, respectively.

i) If one looks at data for the reaction

$$p + p \rightarrow p X \tag{3)}$$

4

Fig. 4a. Quark line diagrams for diffractive charm production.

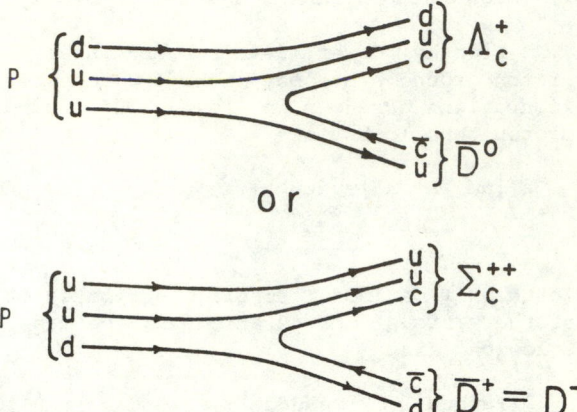

o r

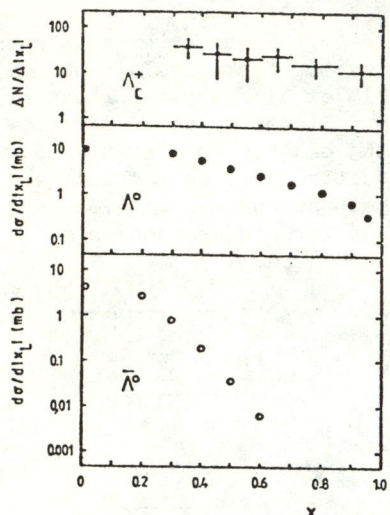

Fig. 4b. a) Λ_c^+ , b) Λ° , and c) Λ° production vs x_L at ISR energies (see Ref. 4).

as a function of M_x , the mass of the excited system, one finds a cross section, $d\sigma/dM_x^2$, which falls as $1/M_x^2$

$$\frac{d\sigma}{dM_x^2} \sim \frac{c}{M_x^2} \tag{4}$$

(see Fig. 5). If we integrate this cross section from some threshold mass up to $M_x^2 = s/2$ we find

$$\sigma = \int_{M_{th}^2}^{s/2} \frac{c}{M_x^2} \, dM_s^2 = c \, \ell n \, \frac{s}{2M_{th}^2} \tag{5}$$

Fig. 5. Differential cross sections versus M_x^2 for t = 0.035 and 0.05 for p_{lab} = 275 GeV/c. Data for M_x^2 < 4 GeV^2 are from Ref. 5.

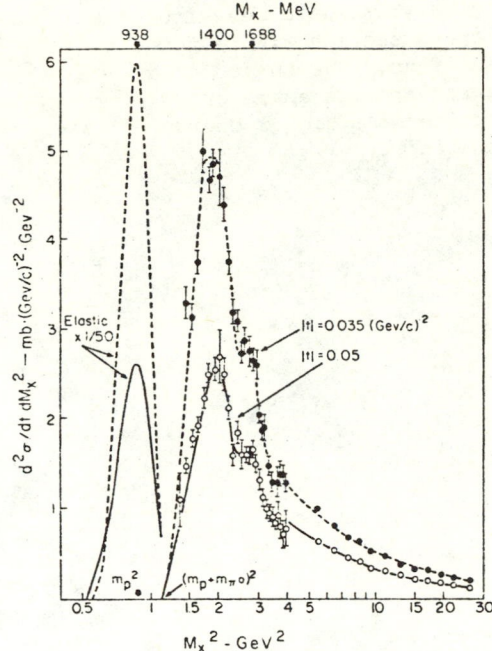

Thus comparing Fermilab energies (s ~ 750 GeV) to the ISR (s ~ 3800 GeV^2), we find, for M_{th}^2 = 25 GeV^2/c^4,

$$\frac{\sigma_{ISR}}{\sigma_{FNAL}} \simeq 1.5. \qquad \qquad (6)$$

ii) Another way to estimate the energy dependence is to note that for high mass diffractive processes

$$\frac{d\sigma}{dt} \sim c\, e^{-bt} \qquad (t \gg t_{min}) \qquad . \qquad (7)$$

Here $t_{min} = \left(\dfrac{M_x^2 - M_p^2}{2 p_{lab}} \right)^2$ corresponds to the threshold t value needed to produce a state with mass M_x. By this picture the excitation doesn't depend so much on the energy in the collision, but rather on what fraction of the momentum transfers are able to excite the final state. In Fig. 6 I have sketched what $d\sigma/dt$ might look like for 2 different energies (note that it must go to 0 as $t \to t_{min}$). The difference in cross section is then just the extra area between the two curves. We can estimate this by saying the intregal is approximated by

6

Fig. 6. Threshold behaviour for a cross section with a fixed t behaviour. The shaded area represents the extra cross section at a higher energy (smaller t_{min}).

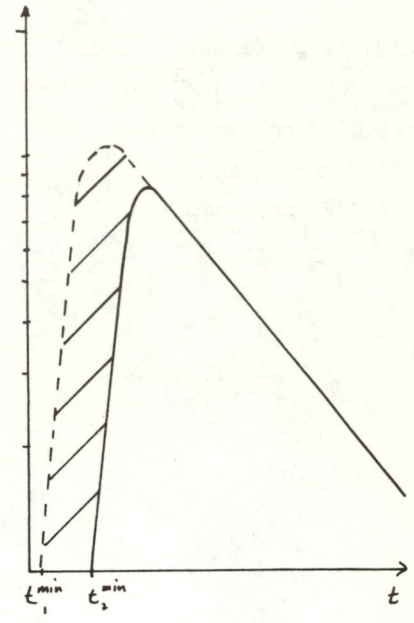

$$\sigma \sim \int_{k \cdot t_{min}}^{\infty} \frac{d\sigma}{dt} \cdot dt = c \, e^{-k t_{min}} \qquad (k > 1) \qquad (8)$$

Thus

$$\frac{\sigma(p_1)}{\sigma(p_2)} = e^{-k(t_{min}^{(1)} - t_{min}^{(2)})}$$

$$= \exp\left[-\frac{k}{2} M_x^4 \left(\frac{1}{p_1^2} - \frac{1}{p_2^2}\right)\right] \qquad (9)$$

We can compare both approaches to results for Λ° production, which has been measured at a variety of energies[6]. To do this we use a threshold mass of 2 GeV and get the results shown in Fig. 7. The linear curve is the $\ell n s$ dependence predicted by approach i) and the curve which flattens out is the results of approach ii). Either approach appears to accommodate the data reasonably well. (The high point at $s = 3800$ GeV^2 only misses either curve by 30 or 40% at most.) Note that when applied to charm, approach i) pre-picts an increase in cross sections of about a factor of $\lesssim 2$, while approach ii) predicts a M_x^4/p^2 dependence thus the region of rapid change should occur at p_{lab} (or s) a fac-tor $(M_{th}^C(\text{Charm})/M_{th}(\text{Strange}))^2 \simeq 6$ higher. Thus the action

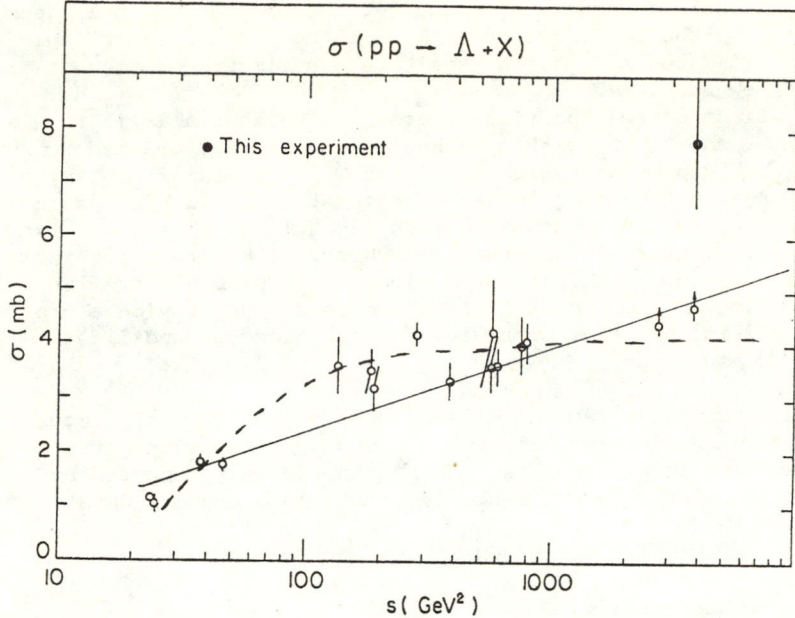

Fig. 7. The energy dependence for Λ° production takes from Ref. 6.
The solid curve is the ℓns energy behaviour predicted by model i).
The dashed curve reflects the behaviour of model ii).

that takes place between s = 50 and 100 GeV^2 for Λ° production (in Fig. 7) should occur between s = 300 and 600 GeV^2
for charmed particle production, i.e. below the Fermilab
energy region. Thus in either approach we don't expect a
considerable variation in cross section from Fermilab energies
to those of the ISR, i.e. about a factor of ∼ 2 at most.

Summarizing the prediction for the intrinsic charm model we
have
  i)   σ ∼ 150 μb .
  ii) Diffractive like forward production of charmed baryons
       and anti-charmed mesons.
  iii) Since these are coherent diffractive processes we
       expect σ ∼ A$^{2/3}$.
  iv) Energy variations between Fermilab and ISR of a factor
       of 2 or less.

3)   Further Motivation

  i) Since heavy quarks produce prompt leptons via their semileptonic decays, these produce backgrounds for detection signals for W's, Z°'s etc. at the high energy colliders. Thus their production at high energies must be reliably estimated in order to evaluate experiments at these new machines.

ii) Since charmed particles decay semileptonically in to X e ν_e and X μ ν_μ with apparently equal rates, charmed mesons could provide a rich source of ν_e's for experimentation. Again, the design of an experiment crucially depends upon the production cross section.[7]

iii) Since charm is apparently produced with large cross sections in hadronic reactions ($\sigma \sim 20$ μb at Fermilab and $\sigma > 200$ μb at ISR), these reactions provide a prolific source of particles for spectroscopy and lifetime measurements.

In the following remarks I'll comment on the current status of our knowledge of charm production cross sections with particular emphasis on recent results at Fermilab energies reported by the Cal Tech-Chicago-Fermilab-Rochester-Stanford group (CCFRS).

II.   EXPERIMENTAL RESULTS

A)   Types of Experiments

There are two general types of experiments which purport to measure charm production in hadronic processes. These rely either on inclusive lepton measurements, i.e. neutrinos or leptons from semileptonic decays, or bump hunts where enhancements at appropriate masses are seen in effective mass histograms of various multiparticle configurations.

B)   Beam Dump Experiments

Inclusive lepton measurements have been done in ν beam dump experiments both at Fermilab and at the CERN SPS. These experiments differ from normal ν experiments in that the drift space which allows π's and k's to decay is eliminated. Thus the fraction of ν's and $\bar{\nu}$'s from promptly decaying charmed particles is enhanced. (See Fig. 8). Resulting ν and $\bar{\nu}$ events can be used to infer charm production cross sections. Results from these experiments will be reviewed at this meeting by Prof. Reeder so I'll just summarize the results reported from the CERN SPS beam dump run.

TABLE I   Results from CERN/SPS Beam Dump Expt.

Group	$\sigma(c\bar{c})$	$\nu/\bar{\nu}$
CHARM[8]	18 ± 6 μb	~ 1
BEBC[9]	17 ± 4 μb	~ 1
CDHS[10]	14 ± 4 μb	~ 2.3

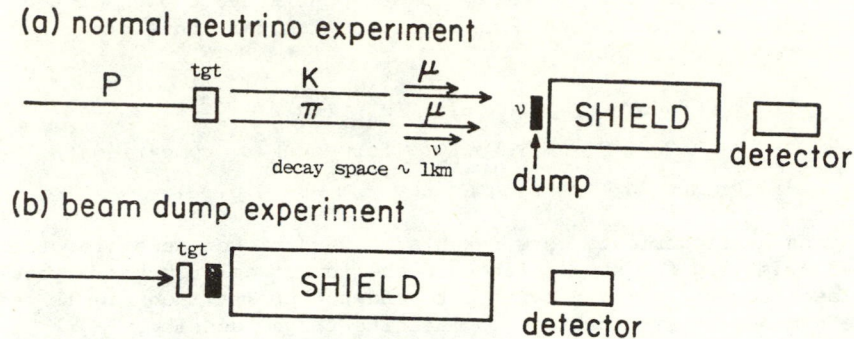

(a) normal neutrino experiment

(b) beam dump experiment

Fig. 8. a) Schematic representation of a normal ν experiment, b) a ν beam dump experiment, where the decay space is eliminated.

To evaluate these cross-sections a production distribution of $E \, d\sigma/d^3p \sim (1-x)^4 \, e^{-2P_T}$ was used, with an assumption of an $A^{1.0}$ dependence on atomic numbers of the target. Assuming a flatter x dependence would give smaller cross-sections. An $A^{2/3}$ behaviour would result in an increase of $\sigma(c\bar{c})$ by about a factor of 4. A branching ratio for $D \to X \, \ell \, \nu$ of 8% has been used.

In the CCFRS[11] beam dump experiment at Fermilab an opposite approach was used. In this experiment 350 GeV protons and 278 GeV π^-'s were sent into a calorimeter/target which was situated in front of the CFNRR neutrino detector in Lab E (See Fig. 9).

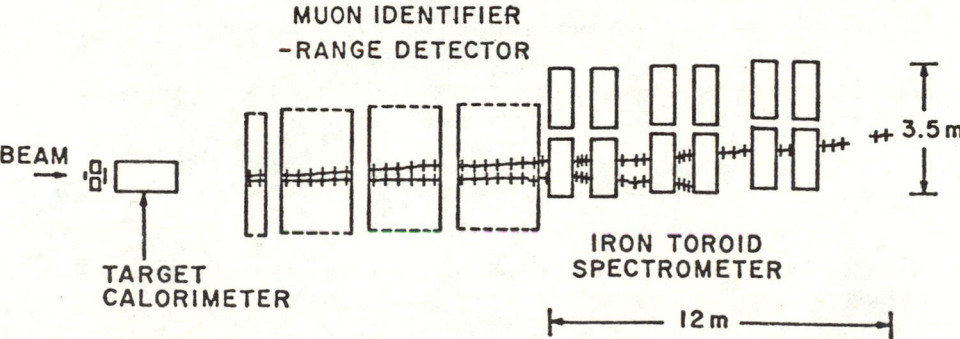

**MUON IDENTIFIER
-RANGE DETECTOR**

BEAM

3.5 m

**TARGET
CALORIMETER**

**IRON TOROID
SPECTROMETER**

12 m

Fig. 9. Plan view of the CCFRS apparatus.

The calorimeter target identified interactions and measured the total electromagnetic and hadronic energy ($\Delta E/E \sim 4\%$); the neutrino detector identified muons and measured their energy by range and by curvature in magnetized iron toroids. Data were taken with a variety of triggers including a trigger on any interaction which produced a muon with momentum above 8 GeV/c and another trigger (used at higher beam intensities) which required a muon to traverse the entire apparatus, i.e. $p_\mu > 20$ GeV. Note that only those muons with p > 15 GeV penetrated enough of the toroids to enable a sign determination. So far, this group has reported results from:

1) p_μ > 8 GeV   p-Fe only ($\sigma_{tot}(c\bar{c})$)

2) p_μ > 20 GeV   p-Fe only (forward μ^+/μ^- comparison)

3) Prompt 2μ + missing energy (π-Fe & p-Fe)

For each trigger data were taken at 3 mean target densities (arranged by moving the steel plates in the target/calorimeter either closer together or further apart) and the prompt muon signal was determined by extrapolated to infinite target density.

The p_μ > 8 GeV   p-Fe data is characterized by a rather complete acceptance for μ's from D mesons which are produced in the forward hemisphere (see Fig. 10). Thus the extrapolation of a total cross section for $c\bar{c}$ production is quite insensitive to the shape of the differential production cross section. The results of extrapolating the single μ and double μ rates to infinite target density are shown in Fig. 11. The intercept corresponds to a total prompt μ rate of 3.30 ± .45 x 10^{-4} per primary proton interaction.[11] As can be seen in Fig. 11, many of these come from dimuon events. Subtracting the dimuon contribution from this gives a rate for prompt single muons of 1.1 x 10^{-4} per primary proton interaction. To extract a $c\bar{c}$ cross section we correct for acceptance (40%), use 8% for the D $\to$ X μ ν Branching Fraction and extrapolate from our Fe target to a proton target using the assumption that $\sigma(c\bar{c}) \propto A^{1.0}$. This results in a cross section[12] of

$$\sigma(c\bar{c}) = 22 \pm 9 \quad \mu b/nucleon \tag{10}$$

Note that the prompt muon rate of 3.3 x 10^{-4} per primary interaction translates to a prompt μ/π ratio of

$$\frac{\mu^+ + \mu^-}{\pi^+ + \pi^-} = .93 \pm .13 \times 10^{-4} \quad \text{(single } \mu\text{'s + dimuons)} \tag{11}$$

averaged over the forward hemisphere. The corresponding μ/π ratio for prompt single μ's is

$$\frac{\mu^+ + \mu^-}{\pi^+ + \pi^-} = .31 \times 10^{-4} \quad \text{single } \mu\text{'s only} \tag{12}$$

A few comments should be mentioned in association with these results:

1) The cross section thus determined is insensitive to the details of the production. A diffractive like production (E dσ/d^{3}p ~ flat in x) or a central production (E dσ/d^{3}p ~ $(1-x)^n$) both give the same answer within the quoted error.

Fig. 10. The acceptance for the $p_\mu > 8$ GeV/c trigger. A calculated spectrum for pions produced in 350 GeV p-Fe interactions with $p_\pi > 8$ GeV/c is shown.

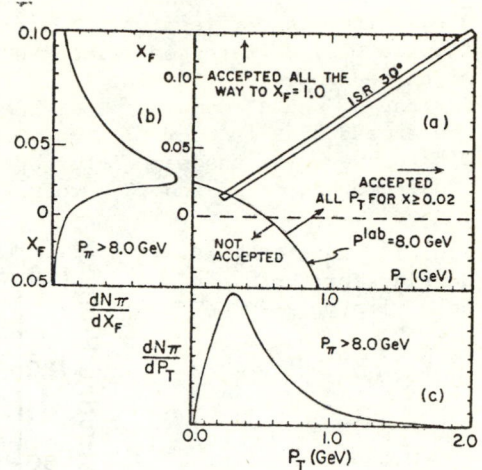

Fig. 11. The extrapolation of the $p_\mu > 8$ GeV/c data to infinite density. Curve a is for single muon events and curve b is for dimuons.

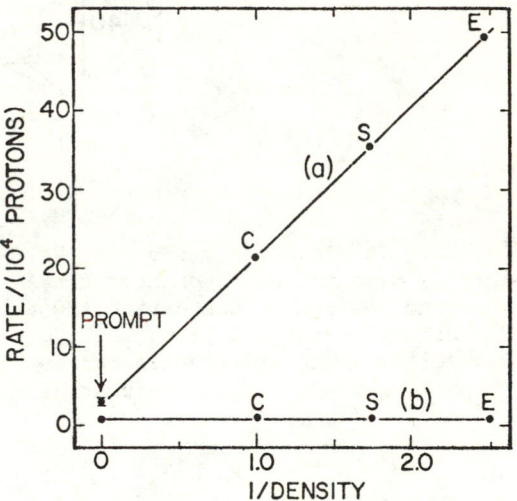

2) Extrapolating the pFe cross section to a nucleon cross section using $\sigma \propto A^{2/3}$ would increase the cross section above the quoted value by a factor of 3.8. Note that recent results for the A dependence for ψ production in π Nucleus[13] give $\sigma(\psi) \propto A^{0.94\pm.02}$.

3) A single μ/π ratio of $.3 \times 10^{-4}$ averaged over the forward hemisphere corresponds to ~ 20 μb of charm production.

CCFRS also reports results on prompt μ production in p-Fe interaction with $p_\mu > 20$ GeV/c.[14] In these data the μ's have traversed the toroid system and thus the sign of their charge is measured. In the charm picture μ^+'s come from Λ_c^+ and D's while μ^- come from

12

$\bar{D}$'s. Since in diffractive production we expect forward $\bar{D}$'s but not forward D's, differences between μ^+ production and μ^- production might be expected. In Fig. 12, I show the density extrapolation for the μ^+ and μ^- sample. The steeper slope for the μ^+'s reflects the excess of π^+'s over π^-'s in the forward direction. Note that both curves give the same intercept at $1/\rho = 0$, corresponding to equal amounts of μ^+ and μ^- production.

Fig. 12. Event rates vs density for the μ^+ and μ^- data with $p_\mu > 20$ GeV/c.

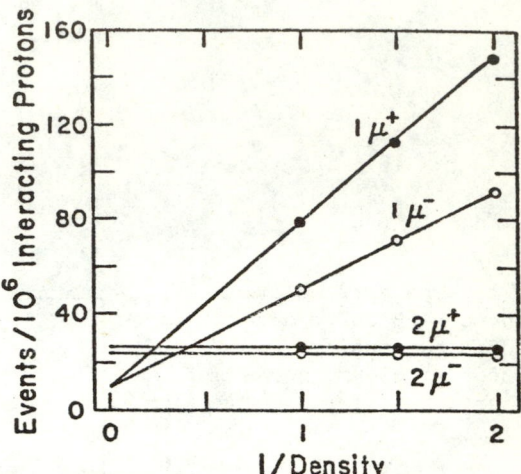

Shown in Fig. 13 a and b are the results of these extrapolations done for each momentum bin. The curves in each figure correspond to fits to the data using a central production model and a diffractive model using the x distributions suggested by Bodsky et al. The diffractive curves are fit only to those points with $p_\mu > 50$ GeV/c. From the central model, using

$$E \frac{d^3\sigma}{dp^3} \propto (1-x_D)^\alpha e^{-\beta P_T} \tag{13}$$

with $\alpha = 4.7 \pm 1.0$, $\beta = 2.5$ (fixed), $B_\mu = .08$ and $A^{1.0}$ behaviour we get

$$\sigma_{D\bar{D}} = 16 \pm 4 \ \mu b/nucleon \ . \tag{14}$$

In the diffractive model, using and $A^{2/3}$ dependence we get

$$\sigma \cdot BR(\Lambda_c \to \mu^+ + \ldots) = .27 \pm .08 \ \mu b/nucleon \ ,$$

$$\sigma \cdot BR(\bar{D} \to \mu^- + \ldots) = .23 \pm .08 \ \mu b/nucleon \ .$$

Using only the μ^- result coupled with the $BR(D \to X\mu\nu) = 8\%$ gives

$$\sigma_{\Lambda\bar{D}_{diffractive}} = 3 \pm 1 \ \mu b/nucleon \tag{15}$$

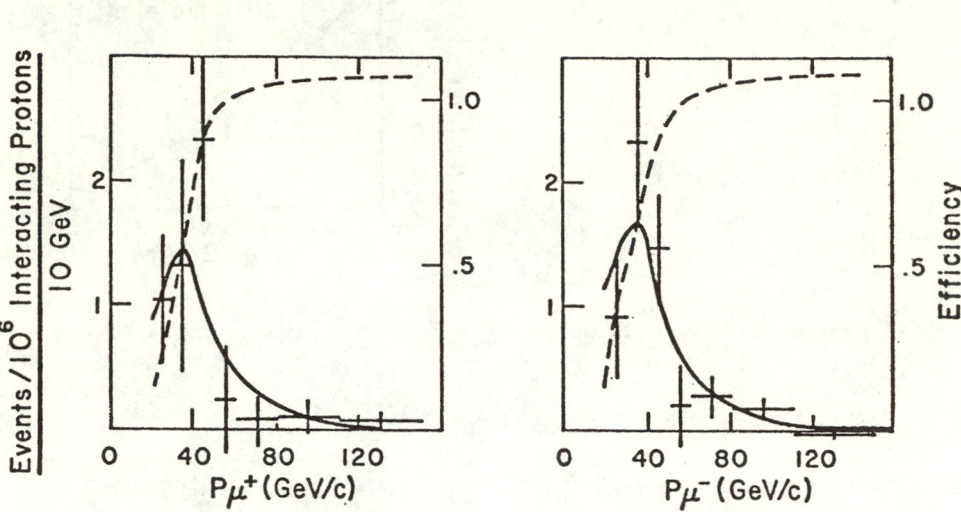

Fig. 13. Prompt single muon rates versus momentum for μ^+ (a) and μ^- (b). The rates are not corrected for trigger efficiency. The dashed line is the efficiency. It can be greater 1.0 because it includes resolution smearing effects. The solid line is from the central $D\bar{D}$ production model.

Comments:

1) Using an $A^{1.0}$ dependence here would <u>reduce</u> the quoted cross section by a factor of 3.8.
2) This rate for diffractive production translates into a probability for intrinsic charm in the proton of about 0.02%. This should be contrasted to the 1% predicted by the proponents of this model.

In Fig. 14 we show the integral p_μ spectrum for the $p_\mu > 20$ GeV/c data together with the result for the $p_\mu > 8$ GeV/c data. The curve is what would be expected for the central production model described in equation 13. Note the good agreement between the two measurements and also with the central production picture.

Another result from the same group comes from the analysis of events which have 2 high momentum muons and a significant amount of "missing" energy.[15] The total measured energy corresponds to the energies of the 2 muons E_{μ^+} and E_{μ^-}, inferred from the magnetic measurements plus the total hadronic energy E_{had}, as determined by the target calorimeter. The missing energy, i.e.

14

Fig. 14. Total prompt single
μ rates (μ⁺ + μ⁻) with p
greater than p_{min}.

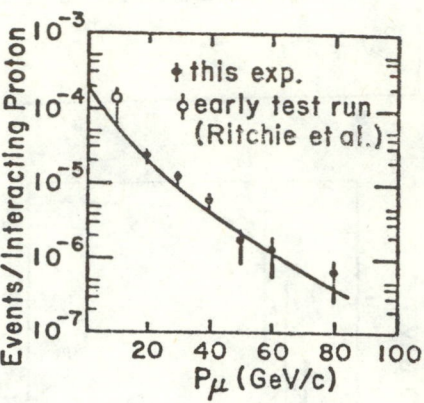

that presumably carried away by ν's in double semileptonic decays
is then

$$E_{missing} \ (=E_\nu + E_{\bar{\nu}}) = E_{beam} - E_{\mu^+} - E_{\mu^-} - E_{had}$$

Results for E_{TOT} (= E_{μ^+} + E_{μ^-} + E_{had}) are shown as histograms in
Fig 15a for 350 Gev/c incident protons and Fig. 15b for 278 GeV/c
incident π⁻'s. The solid points correspond to E_{TOT} measurements
made using randomly triggered interactions. Note an excess of
events in each sample for dimuon events on the low side of the
curve. These events are interpreted as coming from charm-anti
charm production where both the charmed and anti charmed particle
subsequently undergo semileptonic decays. The energy deficiency
corresponds to energy of the neutrinos. The gaussian shape (no
significant non-gaussian tails) of the curve corresponding to unbiased triggers and the lack of an excess of events with E_{TOT} >
E_{beam} provides confidence to this interpretation.

Dimuon events with $E_{missing}$ > 45 GeV for the proton sample
and > 40 GeV for the π⁻ sample were selected as candidates for
double charm decay. This corresponded to 59 μ⁺μ⁻ events for the
proton sample and 154 events for the π⁻ sample. These numbers
were corrected for possible backgrounds from π and K decay,
Drell-Yan production of τ⁺τ⁻ pairs followed by two leptonic decays
and leakage from ordinary dimuon events. These corrections
corresponded to total of about 10% in each data sample. (The
number of same sign dimuons satisfying the same cuts were 0 ± 1
for the protons sample and 3 ± 1.7 for the π⁻ sample.)

The acceptance for central $D\bar{D}$ production is small (~ 1%).
On the other hand, for charm production via diffractive processes
ala the intrinsic charm model of Brodsky et al. it is quite good.
In this model the x distributions of the Λ_c and $\bar{D}$ (with incident
protons) and D and $\bar{D}$ (with incident π⁻'s) peak near x = ½. Here
we find the acceptance of our cuts to be about 16%. Thus these

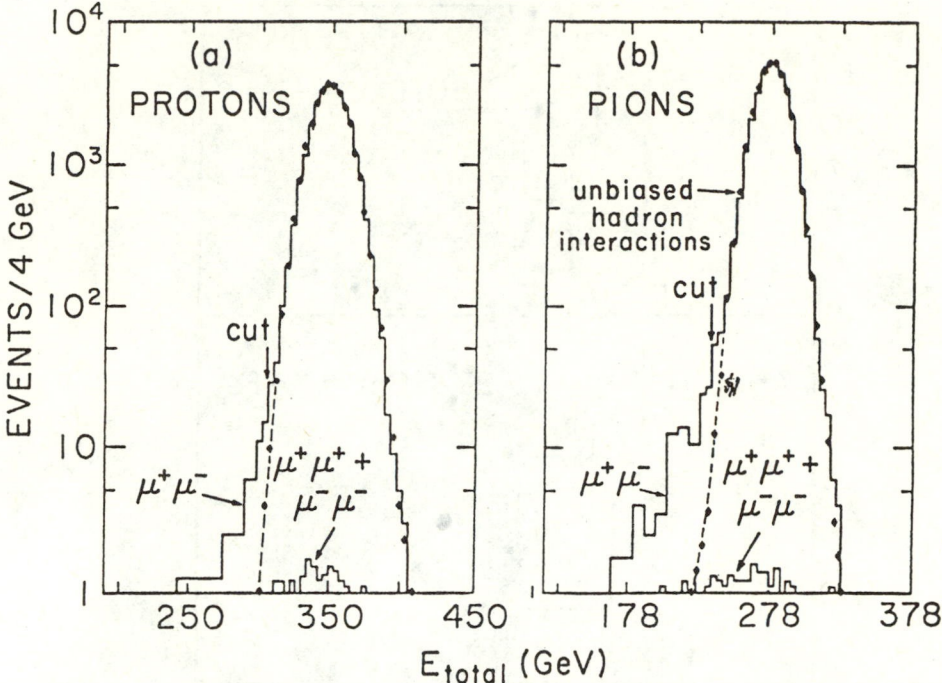

Fig. 15. Total energy distributions for accepted opposite sign
and same sign dimuon events. The solid circles correspond to the
observed energy distributions for unbiased hadron interactions
taken simultaneously with the dimuon data; a) proton data, b) pion
data.

data are quite sensitive to diffractive like production but are
poorer than the $p_\mu > 8$ Gev/c data for determining $\sigma(c\bar{c})$ in the
case of central production.

Fig. 16a (b) shows the distribution of events for the proton
(π^-) sample vs $E_{lep}(=E_{\mu^+} + E_{\mu^-} + E_{miss} = E_{beam} - E_{had})$. The
dashed curve shows the result of normalizing the Brodsky model to
all of the data and the solid curve shows the results of normalizing only to 3 points with $E_{lep} > 160$ GeV. Neither curve fits
the data very well indicating that perhaps a combination of
diffractive and central production is happening. From these data
we can estimate diffraction cross sections to be 2.5 μb for pN
and 1.9 μb for πN using an $A^{2/3}$ dependence. This corresponds to
an intrinsic charm content of the proton or pion of ~ .02%. Note
that an $A^{1.0}$ behaviour would result in diffractive cross sections
which are a factor of 3.8 smaller.

16

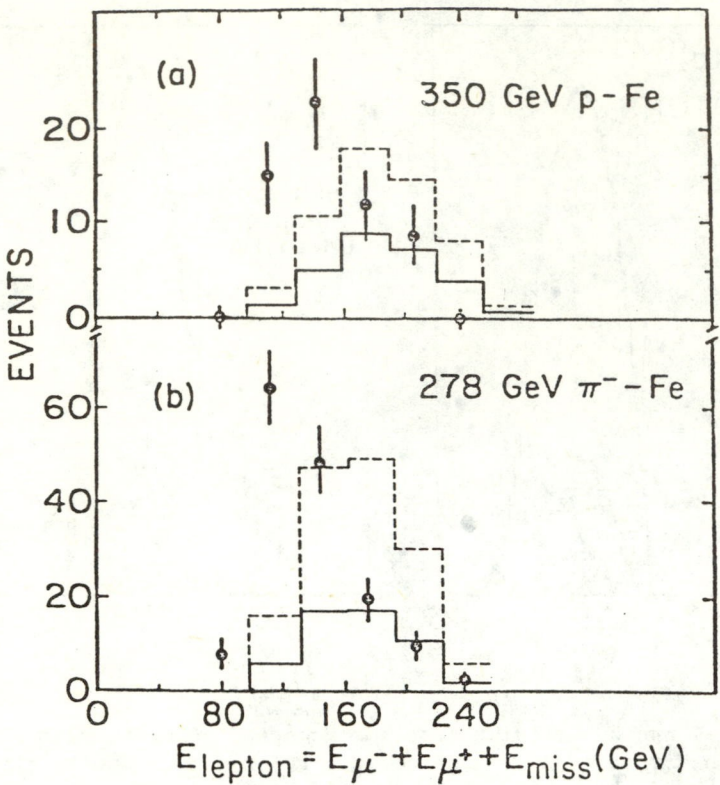

Fig. 16. The $E_{lep} = E_{\mu^+} + E_{\mu^-} + E_{miss} = E_{beam} - E_{had}$ distribution for a) proton, b) pion events with missing energy. The lines are the predictions of the intrinsic charm model. The dashed line is normalized to the data, the solid curve is normalized to the data with $E_{lep} > 160$ GeV.

C) Bump Hunts

Most of the results on bump hunt type experiments come from the ISR, where surprisingly large cross-sections have been observed. Since these results will be summarized at this meeting by Dr. DiBitonto, I will not discuss them in detail.

A number of lower energy results have been recently reported. For example the CYCLOPS experiment[16] at Fermilab reports observations of D meson final states in reaction such as

$$
\begin{aligned}
\pi^- p &\rightarrow P\ M_x \\
&\quad\ \ \rightarrow D\bar{D} + x \\
&\qquad\qquad\ \rightarrow \mu + x \\
&\qquad\quad\ \rightarrow K\pi,\ K\pi\pi
\end{aligned}
\tag{16}
$$

In this experiment diffractive production is required by the trigger in that the recoiling proton in reaction 17 was required to be in an energy region which corresponded to diffraction. This experiment reports D signals in the $K^{\mp}\pi^{\pm}\pi^{\pm}$ channel (49 ± 13 ev), the $K_s^{\circ}\ \pi^{\pm}$ channel (13 ± 5 ev) and the $K_s^{\circ}\ \pi^+\ \pi^-$ channel (26 ± 8 ev). With these signals they expect to see a 25 ± 12 ev signal in the $K^{\pm}\ \pi^{\mp}$ channel but they see none. Since the experiment requires a prompt μ in the trigger, and the semileptonic BR is apparently different for charged and neutral D's, their resulting cross section depends upon the relative amounts of $D^{\circ}\bar{D}^{\circ}$ vs D^+D^- production. The resulting cross section estimates are shown in Fig. 17. Note that for $D^{\circ}\bar{D}^{\circ}/D^+D^- = 1$, they find a cross section (which is diffraction-like) of about 40 μb. Thus there is a clear discrepancy between this experiment and the CCFRS results.

Fig. 17. The CYCLOPS cross section vs the ratio of $D^{\circ}\bar{D}^{\circ}$ to D^+ D^- cross section. The double shaded curve corresponds to $D^{ch}\to\mu$ = 22% $D^{\circ}\to\mu$ = 0%. The single shaded corresponds to $D^{ch}\to\mu$ = 18% and $D^{\circ}\to\mu$ = 47.

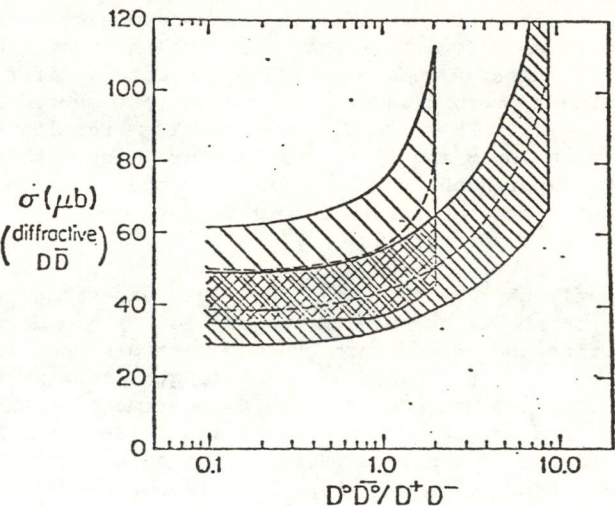

Another spectrometer experiment, the ABCCMR experiment[17] at the CERN SPS sees D's produced in π^-Be reactions via the reaction

$$\pi^-\ Be \to D^{\circ}\ \bar{D}^{\circ}\ +\ x$$
$$\hookrightarrow e + x \tag{17}$$
$$\longrightarrow K\pi$$

and also in the reaction

$$\pi^-\ Be \to D^{\circ*}\ \bar{D}^{\circ}\ +\ x$$
$$\hookrightarrow e + x \tag{18}$$
$$\longrightarrow \pi\ D^{\circ}$$
$$\longrightarrow K\pi$$

Using an uncorrelated central production model they estimate a charm cross section of

$$\sigma(c\bar{c}) \simeq 5 \pm 2 \ \mu b \qquad . \qquad\qquad (19)$$

In a short run with protons this group reports a rather strong signal for the reaction

$$p \ Be \rightarrow \Lambda_c^+ \ \bar{D} + x$$
$$\hookrightarrow e + x$$
$$\hookrightarrow K^- p \pi^+$$

where the Λ_c^+ seems to be produced via cascade decays from a Λ_c^{++} at 2.44 GeV. For this reaction they find, using a diffractive type production

$$\sigma(\Lambda_c^+ \ \bar{D}) \simeq 75 \pm 50 \ \mu b \qquad . \qquad\qquad (20)$$

This last result is also in apparent disagreement with the CCFRS limits on diffractive charm production. Note that also that while the results of this experiment indicate a diffractive component for incident protons which is close to that quoted for incident π^-'s by the CYCLOPS group. The experiment's results for incident π^-'s is much lower and in fact in disagreement with the CYCLOPS result. This experiment, which has rather good acceptance and particle identification will take more data in the future and hopefully clarify the situation.

Another experiment, rather unique in nature, is the LEBC-EHS experiment[18] at the CERN SPS. This experiment uses a high reso-lution bubble chamber in conjunction with a downstream detector to find and reconstruct charmed particle decays. Events are selected on the basis of track lengths seen in the bubble chamber. An interesting feature of this experiment is the large probability for finding both charmed particles in an event (out of 20 charmed particles 14 occur as pairs in the same event), enabling a direct measurement of the correlations in the production. This is demon-strated in Fig. 18 which shows a strong correlation in rapidity for produced charmed pairs. Another interesting feature is the lifetime measurement. Aside from its intrinsic interest, the inter-nal consistency of the lifetime measurement should provide a strin-gent check on the experimentors knowledge of their acceptance.

In a sample of $\pi^- p$ data this experiment reports a cross section for $D^\pm$ production of

$$\sigma_{TOT}(D^\pm) = 11 \pm 5 \ \mu b \qquad .$$

(Their lifetime determination are $\tau(D^\pm) = 8.0 \ {}^{+ \ 4.9}_{- \ 2.4} \times 10^{-13}$ sec. and $\tau(D^\circ) = 3.2 \ {}^{+ \ 2.2}_{- \ 1.0} \times 10^{-13}$ sec.) From the data they find evidence for central production with $E \dfrac{d^3\sigma}{dp^3}$ favoring $(1-x)^3$. No evidence for diffraction-like production is seen.

Finally, the FPS group at Fermilab[19] report an observation of charm production via the reaction

$$\pi^- \, \text{Be} \rightarrow D^{\pm *} + x$$
$$\quad \rightarrow D^\circ \, \pi^\pm \qquad\qquad (21)$$
$$\qquad \rightarrow K\pi$$

Using a central production model, they find a cross section (per nucleon) for this reaction of 4 ± 1 μb.

Results from the fixed target experiments reviewed here are summarized in Table II. Note that this is not a comprehensive list of all experiments, I have concentrated on recent results and have left out those experiments with only 3 or 4 events.

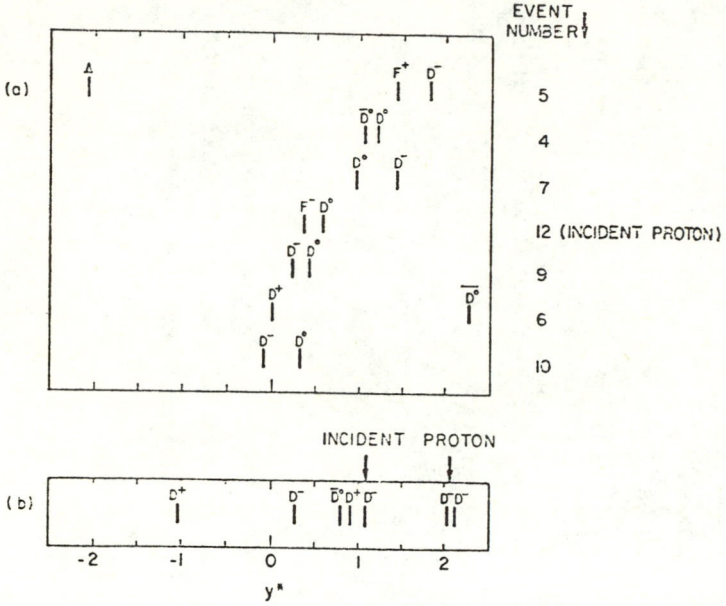

Fig. 18. Center of mass rapidity for pair events a) and single events b). Note that the geometrical acceptance is close to zero for $y \leq 0.0$ and high for $y > 0.0$.

Results from the ISR are shown in Table III. Here very large cross sections are seen in all of the experiments (except for the CZF (ref. 20) electron — muon coincidence measurement). These cross sections, which are typically of order 1 mb should be contrasted with the ~20 μb seen at fixed target energies. Neither the QCD model nor the diffractive model can easily accommodate such a large increase in cross section over this energy difference. (Recall that the Fermilab/SPS energies are already well above charm threshold.) I am uneasy about these large cross sections for another reason. A number of groups[27] have measured the e/π ratio at around $P_T = 1$ GeV/c

TABLE II. Summary of Fixed Target Results

Experiment type	Group	P_{lab}	Model	$\sigma(\mu b)$
ν beam dump	BEBC[9]	400 pN	$(1-x)^4$	17 ± 4
ν beam dump	CHARM[8]	400 pN	$(1-x)^4$	18 ± 6
ν beam dump	CDHS[10]	400 pN	$(1-x)^4$	14 ± 4
μ beam dump	CCFRS[11]	350 pN	$\sim$independent	22 ± 9
Bump Hunts	CYCLOPS[16]	225 πN	diffractive	~ 40
Bump Hunt	ABCCMR[17]	200 πN	$(D^*\to D\pi)(1-x)^3$	5 ± 2
		150 pBe	diffractive	70 ± 50
Bump Hunt	FPS[19]	200 πN	$(D^*\to D\pi)(1-x)^3$	4 ± 1
High resolution Hybrid B.C.	LEBC[18]	360 πp	$(1-x)^3$	11 ± 5

Cross section results from the ISR vary considerably depending upon what production model is assumed. Thus in summarizing the ISR results in Table III, I have explicitly listed each model used and the resulting cross section.

TABLE III. Summary of ISR Results for Charm Production

Model 1 and Model 2 refer to the production mechanism assumed for the detected particles and the particle whose semileptonic decay provides the lepton trigger respectively (when appropriate). Note that σ is given in mb.

Experiment type	Group	Channel	Model 1	Model 2	σ(mb)
e μ correlation	CZF[20]		$e^{-\alpha y^2}$	$e^{-\alpha y^2}$	.022
e triggered bump hunt	LSM[21]	$\Lambda_c^+ \to K^- p \pi^+$	flat x	flat x	1.2 ± .5
			flat y	flat y	1.7 ± .5
			$(1-x)^3$	$(1-x)^3$	2.4 ± 1
e triggered bump hunt (in SFM)	CBF[22]	$D^\circ \to K^- \pi^+$	flat x	flat x	> 5.0
			flat y	flat y	1.3
			$(1-x)^3$	$(1-x)^3$	0.6
			flat x	$(1-x)^3$	1.0
			$(1-x)^3$	flat x	3.6
e triggered bump hunt (in SFM)	CBF[23]	$\Lambda_c^+ \to K^- p \pi^+$	flat x	flat x	1.1
			flat y	flat y	0.8
			$(1-x)^3$	$(1-x)^3$	4.2
			flat x	$(1-x)^3$	0.2
e triggered bump hunt	CCHK[24]	$D^+ \to \overline{K^*} \pi^+$	flat x		.16
			flat y		.32
			$(1-x)^3$		.80
e triggered bump hunt	ACCDHW[25]	$\Lambda_c \to \Delta^{++} k^-$ $\to \overline{K^{\circ *}} p$	flat y		~ 2.0
			flat x		~ 1.0
Bump Hunt (no lepton trigger)	LAS[26]	$\Lambda_c \to \Lambda^\circ \pi^+ \pi^+ \pi^-$ $\to K^- \pi^+ p$	flat x		~ 1.0

at the ISR to be about 1.5×10^{-4}. Even if all of the direct electrons came from charm decays this would translate into a total cross section for charm production of about 100 μb. (Recall that in the CCFRS expt. an e/π ratio of 0.3×10^{-4} translates to a charm section of ~ 20 μb. Scaling this to e/π = 1.5×10^{-4} gives 100 μb. More detailed calculations[28] have been made with results very similar to this estimate.) Note that the ISR results give σ ~ 1 mb in both the $\Lambda_c^+ \bar{D}$ channel as well as the $D\bar{D}$ channel. Thus there is a discrepancy of about an order of magnitude between the quoted ISR cross-sections and the upper limit allowed by the e/π ratio. The understanding of this discrepancy perhaps the most important question in this subject at this time.

III SUMMARY

The various data discussed in this summary, and listed in Tables II and III are shown in Fig. 19. In this figure the allowed range for each experiment is indicated (this is usually larger than the quoted statistical errors). The sharp contrast between the ISR and the Fermilab/SPS results is apparent. Also shown in the figure is the upper limit of 100 μb expected if e/π = 1.5×10^{-4} and all of the prompt e's come from charm. My conclusion is that lots of work has yet to be done before the hadronic production of charm can be quantitatively understood.

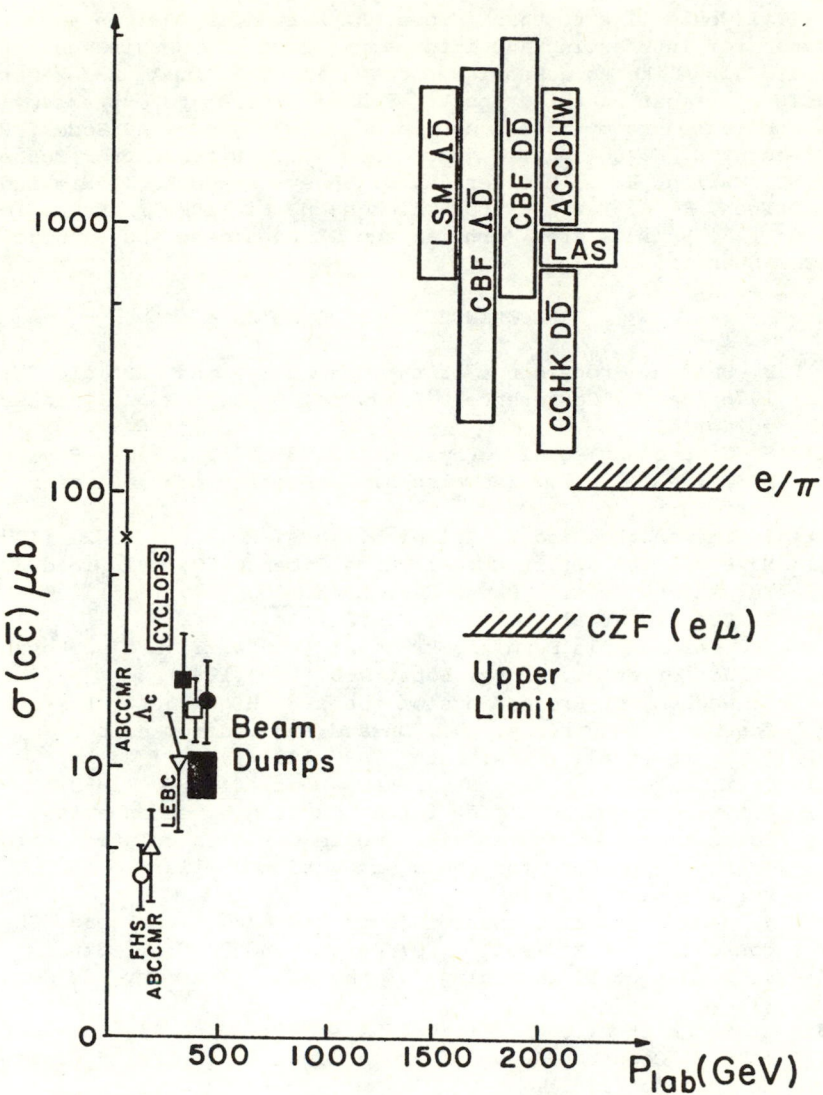

Fig. 19. Summary of the data listed in Tables II and III. Also
shown is the upper limit of 100 μb expected from an e/π ratio
of 1.5 x 10^-4.

IV ACKNOWLEDGMENTS

I would like to thank Profs. A. Kernan, F. Halzen and M. Jacob for interesting and informative remarks on this subject. I would also like to acknowledge the help of Prof. A. Bodek for his help in preparing this report. Finally I wish to express my appreciation to my colleagues in the CCFRS group, A. Bodek, R. Breedon, R. N. Coleman, W. Marsh and J. L. Ritchie from Rochester, B. C. Barish, R. L. Messner, M. H. Shaevitz and E. J. Siskind from Cal Tech, F. S. Merritt from Chicago, H. E. Fisk, Y. Fukushima and P. A. Rapidis from Fermilab and G. Donaldson and S. Wojcicki from Stanford.

- REFERENCES AND FOOTNOTES -

1) F. Halzen, Proceedings of the Cosmic Ray and Particle Physics 1978 (Bartol Conference), Delaware, p. 261, R. K. Gaisser, editor.
2) S. J. Brodsky et al., Phys. Lett. 93B, 451 (1980); Phys. Rev. D23, 2745 (1981). See also S. J. Brodsky proceedings of this conference.
3) J. F. Donoghue and E. Golowich, Phys. Rev. D15, 3421 (1977).
4) M. Basile et al., Lett. al Nuovo Cimento 30, 481; ibid 30, 487.
5) Yu. Akimov et al., Phys. Rev. Lett. 35, 763 (1975).
6) D. Drijard et al., CERN/EP 81-121.
7) See for example Fermilab Proposal #625 W. Y. Lee spokesman.
8) M. Jonker et al., Phys. Lett. 96B, 435 (1981).
9) H. Wachsmuth, Proceedings of the 1980 High Energy Physics Conference at Madison p. 591, Durand and Pondrom editors.
10) T. Hause et al., Phys. Lett. 74B, 139 (1978).
11) J. L. Ritchie et al., Phys. Rev. Lett. 44, 230 (1980).
12) A 10% correction is made for production by secondaries. This correction is computed via a monte carlo calculation using an energy dependence for charm production similar to that observed for J/ψ production.
13) J. Badier et al., Proceedings of the 1980 High Energy Physics Conference at Madison p. 207 Durand and Pondrom editors.
14) J. L. Ritchie, Proceedings of the XVIth Rencontre de Moriond (1981).
15) A. Bodek et al., UR report #804 submitted to Physics Letters B.
16) John W. Cooper UPR-0057E, Proceedings ot the XVIth Rencontre de Moriond (1981).
17) C. Daam et al., papers submitted to the International Conference on High Energy Physics, Lisbon, Portugal, July 1981.
18) M. Aguilar-Benitez et al., CERN/EP 81-131 (1981), presented at the International Conference on High Energy Physics, Lisbon, Portugal, July 1981.
19) V. L. Fitch et al., Phys. Rev. Lett. 46, 761 (1981).
20) A. Chilingarov et al., Phys. Lett. 83B, 136 (1979).
21) J. Irion et al., Phys. Lett. 99B, 495 (1981).
22) M. Basile et al., CERN-EP/81-73 (Submitted to Nuovo Cimento).

23) M. Basile et al., Nuovo Cimento A, 63, 230 (1981).

24) D. Drijard et al., Phys. Lett. 81B, 250 (1979).

25) D. Drijard et al., Phys. Lett. 85B, 452 (1979).

26) W. Lockman et al., Phys. Lett. 85B, 443 (1979).

27) See for example M. Basile et al., CERN-EP/81-92 and references cited therein.

28) F. Halzen et al., DAMTP 81/121 or MAD/PH/10 (1981). Note that in this calculation the authors only consider positrons from Λ_c^+ decays. Decays of associated $\bar{D}$'s and D's from $D\bar{D}$ production reduce their cross section estimates considerably.

DATA ON CHARM AND BEAUTY PRODUCTION AT THE CERN ISR

D. DiBitonto
CERN, 1211 Geneva, Switzerland

ABSTRACT

This paper will present data on the latest ISR results on charm and beauty production, in an effort towards a more global synthesis of previous ISR data. The total charmed hadron cross-section of 1 mb implied by these new results will be discussed. Expectations for new heavy flavor production at the CERN $p\bar{p}$ Collider will finally be discussed, based on what we have learned thus far at the ISR.

INTRODUCTION

During the last three years the CERN ISR has experienced literally a revolution in new flavor production in hadronic interactions, firstly with the observation of D^+ production, closely followed by the obervation of charmed baryon production and most recently by the first claim of beauty baryon production. While much of what we already know about charmed hadron production in hadronic interactions has already been summarized in many excellent review talks[1], I will instead concentrate on the latest ISR results on charmed hadron production, in particular the implication on previous data of the new kinematic information recently available on Λ_c^+ and D production.

One worrisome feature of earlier ISR data is its obvious model dependence of the partial cross-sections, although as will be seen, the sum total of the many ISR experiments involved cover a wide kinematic range in Feynman x. (The center of mass energy $\sqrt{s}$ is nearly constant for all data discussed, taken at fixed values of 53 GeV and 62 GeV.) With the recent kinematic information on charmed hadrons, the production mechanism possibilities are obviously restricted, although the precise mechanisms are still not yet clearly understood. Λ_c^+ production is most probably associated production $(\Lambda_c^+, \bar{D})$, while information on the accompanying anti-charmed hadron is available only in the semi-leptonic decay channel; D meson production (charm = +1) appears to be central, and while the pair production hypothesis $(D\bar{D})$ is certainly plausible, associated production with an accompanying $\bar{\Lambda}_c$ is by no means excluded. The interpretation here, however, is less clear. This last possibility is important in light of the reported observation of $\bar{\Lambda}_c$ production at the ISR, although statistically much less significant than for Λ_c^+.

Beauty production will next be discussed, and a comparison will be made of the reported total cross-sections with the charmed hadron cross-sections derived in the previous section. Due to the rather controversial nature of these data, reconfirmation of these effects from other experiments is needed before any definitive statement can be made regarding beauty production.

CHARMED HADRON PRODUCTION

Work done on charmed hadron production at the ISR comes from four major experimental groups, involving the combined effort of over 100 physicists. A brief review of these experiments will follow, summarizing the reactions studied and charmed hadrons observed. All of these experiments reported large forward production of charmed particles, identified by their invariant mass spectra.

LSM (Aachen, CERN, Harvard, Munich, Northwestern, Riverside)

This experiment studied two reactions: a) the single diffraction dissociation of an excited high mass state M into a charmed baryon and $\bar{D}$ pair, and b) charmed baryon production in association with an electron trigger from the semi-leptonic decay of the accompanying anti-charmed hadron.

a) Single Diffraction Dissociation[2]

The reaction here was:

$$p_1 + p_2 \rightarrow p_1' + M$$
$$\hookrightarrow \Lambda_c^+ + \bar{D} + X \qquad (1)$$
$$\hookrightarrow K^-p\pi^+, \ \Lambda^0\pi^+\pi^-\pi^+$$

p_1' is a quasi elastic proton recoiling against the excited high mass state M. This experiment reported Λ_c^+ production and decay in two channels, $K^-p\pi^+$ and $\Lambda^0\pi^+\pi^-\pi^+$. The $\sqrt{s}$ energy was 62 GeV.

b) Associated Leptonic Production[3]

In a later phase of the experiment, an electron trigger was used to search for charmed baryons:

$$p + p \rightarrow e^- + X$$
$$\hookrightarrow \Lambda_c^+ + x \qquad (2)$$
$$\hookrightarrow K^-p\pi^+$$

$$(\rightarrow e^+ + X$$
$$\hookrightarrow \bar{\Lambda}_c + X \qquad (3)$$
$$\hookrightarrow K^+\bar{p}\pi^-)$$

While the Λ_c^+ (and $\bar{\Lambda}_c$) were produced forward, no other particle except for the triggering lepton was tagged. Thus in addition to process a) shown in Fig. 1, the production mechanism may also include a "pick-up" reaction involving the second proton (Fig. 2).

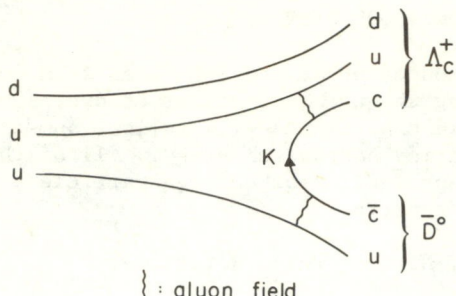

{ : gluon field

Fig. 1 Diffractive dissociation of the state M into a charmed c = +1 baryon and a charmed c = -1 meson

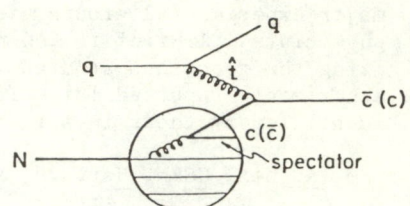

Fig. 2 Pick-up reaction involving both protons

CCHK (CERN, Collège de France, Heidelberg, Karlsruhe)

This experiment was performed at the CERN Split Field Magnet (SFM) and reported D^+ production[4] at $\sqrt{s} = 53$ GeV in the forward region $|x| > 0.5$:

$$
\begin{aligned}
p + p &\rightarrow X \\
&\quad\hookrightarrow D^+ + x \\
&\qquad\quad\hookrightarrow (K^{0*})\pi^+ \\
&\qquad\qquad\quad\hookrightarrow (K^-\pi^+)
\end{aligned}
\tag{4}
$$

The cross-sections reported for D^+ production are highly model dependent, spanning over an order of magnitude between forward and central production (see Table I).

Table I D^+ total cross-sections

Model	σ_T	Production mechanism
$\dfrac{d\sigma}{dx} = $ const.	150 µb	$B_c \rightarrow D^+N + x$
$E\,\dfrac{d\sigma}{dx} \propto (1-x)^3$	2 mb	$D\bar{D}$

As will be shown, charmed baryons are produced in the forward direction, with a rather flat x dependence. In the first model, D^+ mesons are produced from the strong decay of excited charmed baryon states. A later analysis[5] of the data from the above mentioned experiment has shown evidence also for the process

$$p + p \rightarrow X$$
$$\hookrightarrow \Lambda_c^+ + x \qquad (5)$$
$$\hookrightarrow K^{0*}(890)p, \; K^- \Delta^{++}(1236) \; .$$

ACCDHW (Annecy, CERN, Collège de France, Dortmund, Heidelberg, Warsaw)

In this later SFM experiment (R416) the production of charmed baryons and mesons was studied at $\sqrt{s}$ = 62 GeV in reactions triggered by a prompt lepton.
The reactions investigated were:

$$p + p \rightarrow e^- + X$$
$$\hookrightarrow \Lambda_c^+ + x \qquad (6)$$
$$\hookrightarrow K^- p \pi^+$$

$$(\rightarrow e^+ + X$$
$$\hookrightarrow \bar{\Lambda}_c + x \qquad (7)$$
$$\hookrightarrow K^+ \bar{p} \pi^-)$$

$$p + p \rightarrow e^- + X$$
$$\hookrightarrow D^0 + x \qquad (8)$$
$$\hookrightarrow K^- \pi^+$$

A Λ_c^+ signal[5] was observed in a rather central region ($|x| \leq 0.3$), to-gether with $\bar{\Lambda}_c$ and D^0 signals[6] of smaller statistical significance. In the last reaction, the D^0 mesons were observed in the central region near $x = 0$.

UCLA (UCLA, Saclay)

This experiment reported inclusive charmed baryon production[7] in two decay channels, $K^- p \pi^+$ and $\Lambda^0 \pi^+ \pi^- \pi^+$ at $\sqrt{s}$ = 53 GeV and 62 GeV:

$$p + p \rightarrow X$$
$$\hookrightarrow \Lambda_c^+ + x \qquad (9)$$
$$\hookrightarrow K^- p \pi^+, \; \Lambda^0 \pi^+ \pi^- \pi^+$$

BCF (Bologna, CERN, Frascati)

This is another SFM experiment (R415), which reported charmed baryon[8] and charmed meson[9a,b,c] production at $\sqrt{s}$ = 62 GeV, studied in the following reactions:

$$p + p \rightarrow e^- + X$$
$$\hookrightarrow \Lambda_c^+ + x \qquad\qquad (10)$$
$$\hookrightarrow pK^-\pi^+$$

$$p + p \rightarrow e^- + X$$
$$\hookrightarrow D^+ + x \qquad\qquad (11)$$
$$\hookrightarrow K^-\pi^-\pi^+$$

$$p + p \rightarrow e^- + X$$
$$\hookrightarrow D^0 + x \qquad\qquad (12)$$
$$\hookrightarrow K^-\pi^+,\ K^-\pi^+\pi^+\pi^-$$

$$p + p \rightarrow e^+ + X$$
$$\hookrightarrow D^- + x \qquad\qquad (13)$$
$$\hookrightarrow K^+\pi^-\pi^-$$

$$p + p \rightarrow e^+ + X$$
$$\hookrightarrow \bar{D}^0 + x \qquad\qquad (14)$$
$$\phantom{p + p \rightarrow e^+ + \hookrightarrow \bar{D}^0}\hookrightarrow K^+\pi^-\pi^-\pi^+$$

$$p + p \rightarrow e^+ + X$$
$$\hookrightarrow \bar{\Lambda}_c + x \qquad\qquad (15)$$
$$\phantom{p + p \rightarrow e^+ + \hookrightarrow \bar{\Lambda}_c}\hookrightarrow \bar{p}K^+\pi^-$$

The results from this experiment also provided new kinematic information on the x and p_T dependence of the Λ_c^+ and D charmed hadrons produced according to reactions (10), (11) and (12).

The case for Λ_c^+ production at the ISR

Most of what we know about charm production at the ISR lies in
the $K^-p\pi^+$ decay channel of the Λ_c^+. This is due principally to the
following reasons: i) the high statistics available on the subject,
as demonstrated by the previous reactions; ii) the known branching
ratio in this channel, $B(\Lambda_c^+ \rightarrow K^-p\pi^+) = (2.2 \pm 1.0)\%$ from SPEAR[10];
iii) the strong evidence for associated production in reactions trig-
gered by a prompt electron arising from the semi-leptonic decay of
the $\bar{D}$, and iv) the recently available data on the kinematic properties
of the Λ_c^+. Note that the decay channel $\Lambda_c^+ \rightarrow \Lambda^0\pi^+\pi^-\pi^+$ has also been
observed (Ref. 10), however the branching ratio in this channel is

still unknown. The current world average for the Λ_c^+ mass[10] is (2273 ± 6) MeV/c^2. The LSM and previous SFM groups quote values near 2260 MeV/c^2, while the BCF group quotes 2330 MeV/c^2, 55 MeV/c^2 higher than the world average (believed by the authors to be due to local systematic effects in chamber alignment). Some representative invariant mass spectra from ISR data are shown in Figs. 3, 4[11] and 5.

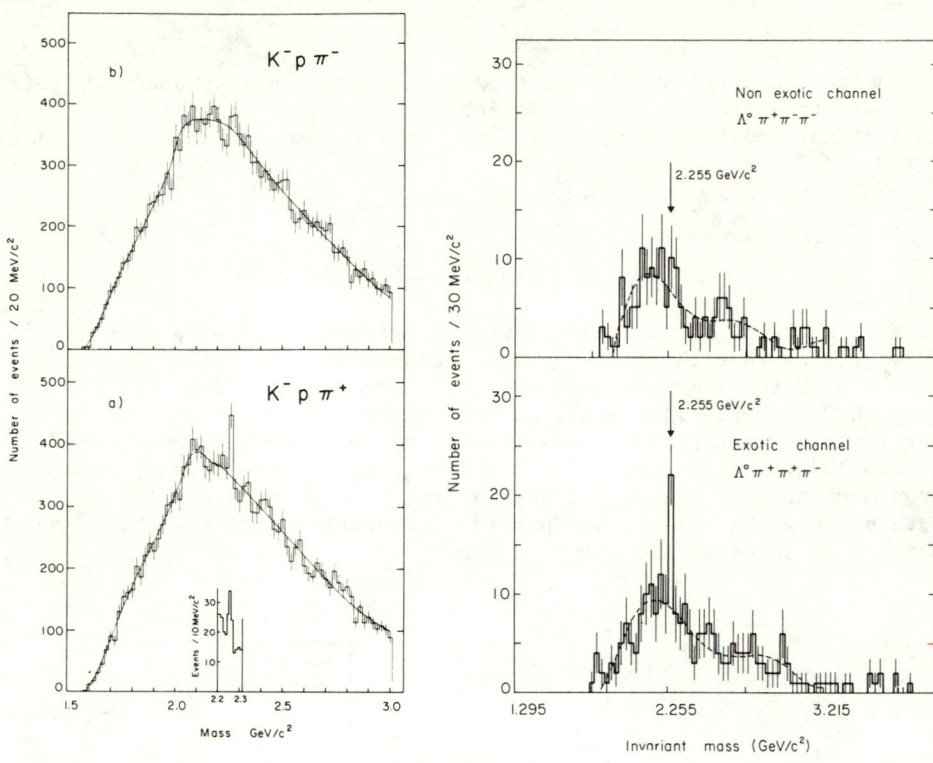

Fig. 3 LSM data, $\Lambda_c^+ \to K^- p \pi^+$ Fig. 4 LSM data, $\Lambda_c^+ \to \Lambda^0 \pi^+ \pi^- \pi^+$

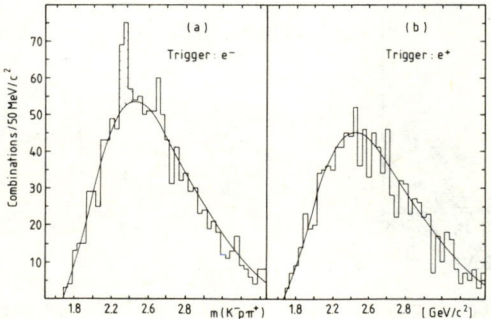

Fig. 5 BCF data, e$^-$ trigger

32

Cross-sections

The most likely production mechanism for charmed baryons is associated production. This model will be the working assumption in determining the partial and total cross-sections:

$$p + p \to \Lambda_c^+ + (\bar{D} + X)$$
$$\hookrightarrow (e^- + x)$$

(16)

Inclusive reactions absorb the $\bar{D}$ production mechanism. However, for leptonic triggers certain assumptions must be made about the $\bar{D}$ production. Following Wojcicki[1], we shall assume the following model:

$$\bar{D} : E \frac{d\sigma}{dx} \propto (1-x)^3$$

$$\Lambda_c^+ : \frac{d\sigma}{dx} = \text{const.} \; \underline{\text{within } \Delta x}$$

(17)

As will be seen, there is ample strong evidence that Λ_c^+ production is forward, and that the differential cross-section is rather flat, following much the same x dependence of Λ^0 production. Up until the Madison Conference last year, no experimental evidence existed supporting a central production mechanism for $\bar{D}$; the only evidence presently available comes from the BCF group[8] in the triggering electron momentum spectrum. The dashed line in Fig. 6 is a fit to the data based on Eq. (17). The partial differential cross-sections summarized by Wojcicki are shown in Fig. 7.

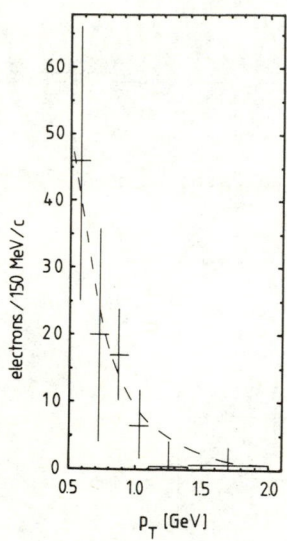

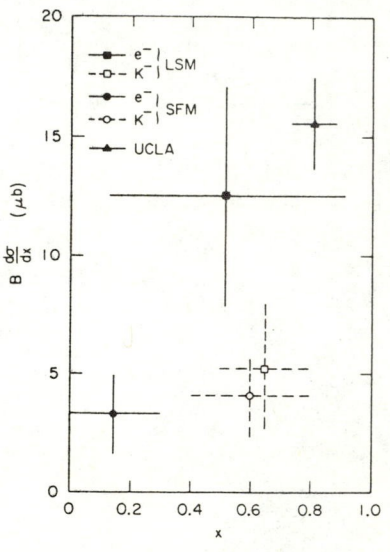

Fig. 6 BCF data for triggering e⁻ spectrum in events with an identified Λ_c^+

Fig. 7 ISR data for Λ_c^+ production, $K^- p \pi^+$ decay channel (S. Wojcicki, Madison Conference)

BCF results (Λ_c^+)

The experimental results here cover a wide kinematic range in x: for the proton, $|x_L| > 0.3$. The kinematic information on the longitudinal[12] and transverse momentum[13] distribution of the Λ_c^+ are summarized below (see Figs. 8-11):

$$\frac{dN}{dx} \propto (1-x)^\alpha \, , \quad \alpha = 0.4 \pm 0.25$$

$$\frac{dN}{dp_T} \propto p_T \, e^{-bp_T} \, , \quad b = 2.5 \pm 0.4 \, . \tag{18}$$

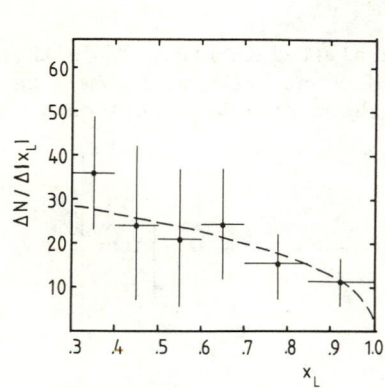

Fig. 8 Λ_c^+ x_L distribution

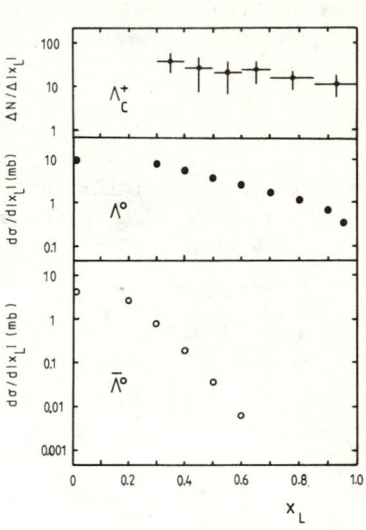

Fig. 9 $d\sigma/dx$ for Λ_c^+, Λ^0 and $\bar{\Lambda}^0$

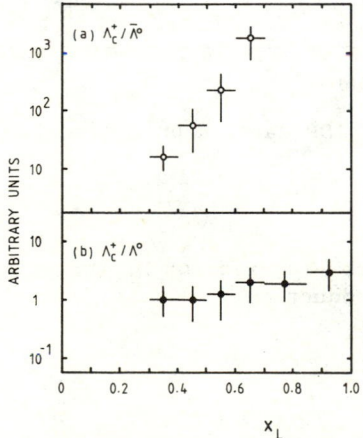

Fig. 10 Normalized $d\sigma/dx$ (Λ_c^+)

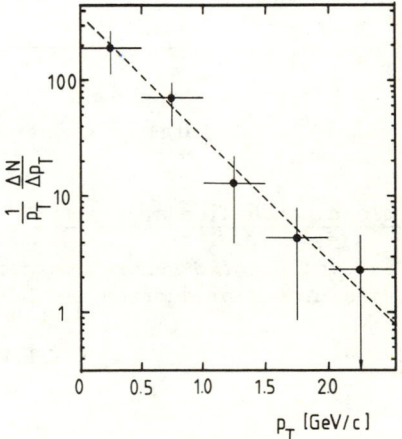

Fig. 11 dN/dp_T for Λ_c^+

34

The suppression near $x = 1$ of the Λ_c^+ x_L distribution (Fig. 8) can be understood on purely kinematic grounds, due to the large $\bar{D}$ mass accompanying the Λ_c^+. Note that while the x_L distributions for the Λ_c^+ and Λ^0 are both flat (Fig. 9), the corresponding $\bar{\Lambda}^0$ distribution is strikingly different, peaking strongly near $x = 0$ more in a central-like fashion. The total $\bar{\Lambda}^0$ cross-section implied by Fig. 9 is smaller by at least an order of magnitude with respect to Λ^0 production.

$\sigma_T(\Lambda_c^+)$

Given the partial differential cross-sections for Λ_c^+ in Fig. 7, the known branching ratio in $K^- p \pi^+$ and now the available kinematic information in Eq. (18), we may now ask what we expect for the total Λ_c^+ cross-section

$$\sigma_T = \frac{1}{B} \int_{-1}^{1} \left(B \cdot \frac{d\sigma}{dx} \right) dx \ . \tag{19}$$

The results for all ISR data are shown plotted in Fig. 12. With the exception of the UCLA point and one LSM point, all data show a remarkable clustering near 400 μb. (Errors shown exclude errors on B and α.)

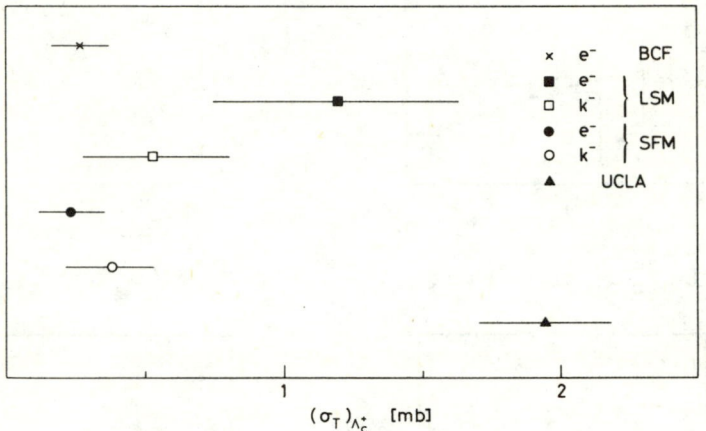

Fig. 12 Total Λ_c^+ cross-section, ISR data, $K^- p \pi^+$ channel

D meson production at the ISR

Consider two general mechanisms most favored for D production: a) associated production and b) pair production.

a)
$$p + p \rightarrow B_c + \bar{D} + X$$

$$\uparrow$$

$$\sim \text{flat } x \tag{20}$$

Given the substantially large Λ_c^+ cross-section observed at the ISR, we would expect to see a correspondingly large $\bar{D}$ production of the same value. However, only preliminary experimental evidence[9c] exists for $\bar{D}$ final states of definite strangeness s = +1, e.g. involving K^+ mesons. Recall that K_s^0 is a state of mixed strangeness[11]. There are certain considerations for this negative result, namely that most K searches at the ISR are done in the forward region where K^+ separation from protons is more difficult than for K^-, and also that searches in the forward region are unfavorable for central, or central-like processes, $\propto (1-x)^3$. Note, however, that in the high x region, $D^{0,+}$ production may more likely be <u>flat</u>, if arising from the strong decay of an excited c = +1 charmed baryon B_c^* (see Table I), in direct analogy with what has been observed for $\bar{\Delta}$, Λ^* and Σ^* resonances.

As seen in reactions (3), (7), and (15), $\bar{\Lambda}_c$ production has also been observed at the ISR. $D^{0,+}$ production within the framework of associated production is certainly plausible, though much less unlikely. As shown in Fig. 9, $\bar{\Lambda}^0$ (and presumably $\bar{\Lambda}_c$) production is suppressed with respect to Λ^0 (Λ_c^+) production, and the surprisingly large and comparable total cross-sections derived for D production would tend to rule out associated production for D mesons. Unfortunately, as in the case for the $\bar{D}$, sufficient experimental evidence is still lacking to be able to make definite conclusions. And in the case of leptonically triggered reactions, the leptonic branching ratio of the Λ_c^+ is also not yet known.

b) $$p + p \rightarrow D\bar{D} + X \qquad\qquad (21)$$

Pair production processes are expected to be central, obeying a $(1-x)^3$ dependence, or otherwise stated, having once determined the kinematic dependence of one charmed meson, the same dependence is expected to hold for the other. One important prediction of process (21) is that both mesons are expected to be produced with equal probability and the same kinematic dependence.

Results

All SFM groups have observed D meson production, and with one exception[4], all searches here triggered on the semi-leptonic decay of the D. From the BCF group[9a,b] D^0 and D^+ meson production was reported (Figs. 13 and 14), in addition to presenting new kinematic information on these mesons (Figs. 15 and 16). The longitudinal[14] and transverse momentum[15] dependence of the D mesons by this group is summarized below:

$$E \frac{d\sigma}{dx} \propto (1-x)^3$$

$$\frac{dN}{dp_T} \propto p_T \, e^{-bp_T} , \qquad b = 2.35 \pm 0.47 . \qquad (22)$$

In Fig. 15 the dashed line fits correspond to central production, $(1-x)^3$ (Model I), flat y (Model II) and flat x (Model III). For the

36

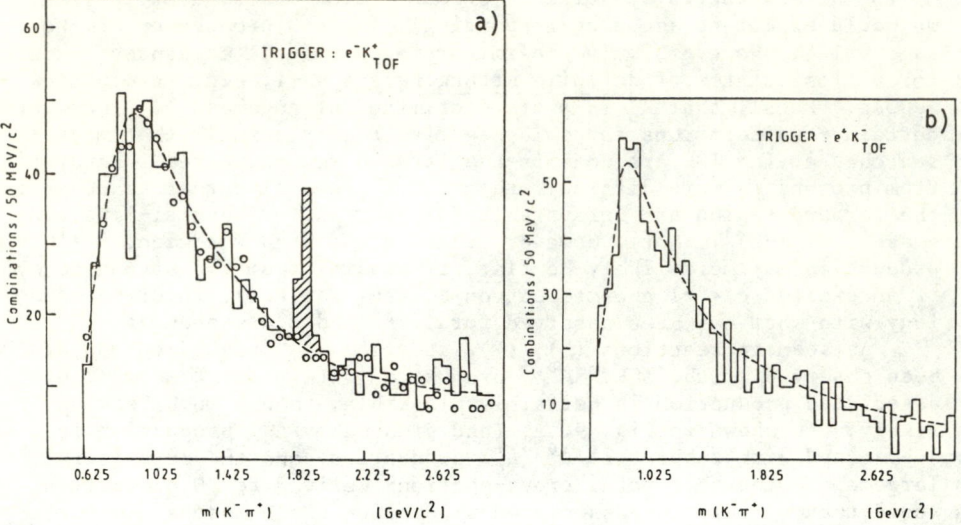

Fig. 13 $(K^-\pi^+)$ invariant mass, $p_T(K^-\pi^+) > 0.7$ GeV/c

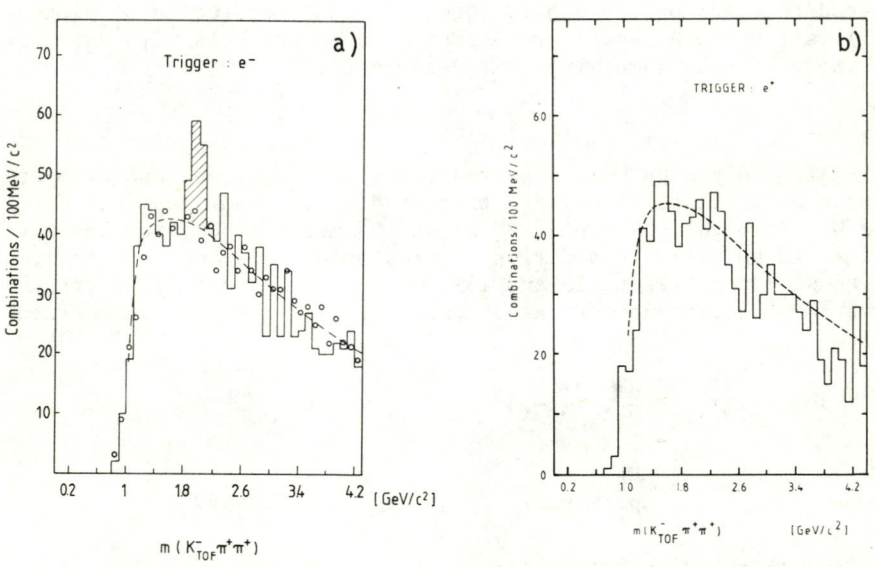

Fig. 14 $(K^-\pi^+\pi^+)$ invariant mass, $p_T(K^-\pi^+\pi^+) > 0.7$ GeV/c

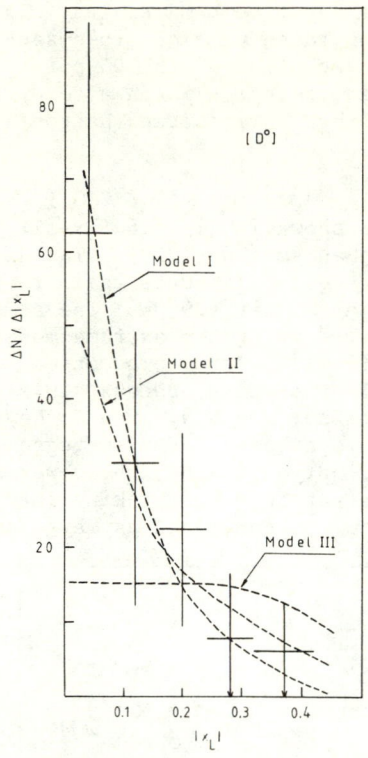

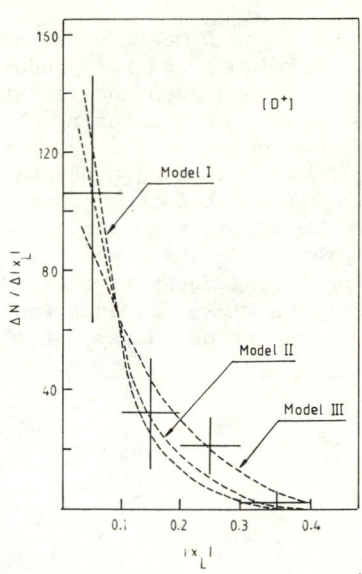

Fig. 15 x_L distribution, D^0 Fig. 16 x_L distribution, D^+

D^0, central production is clearly favored, although for the D^+, the case is less clear. The mean p_T for these mesons is $\sim$ 900 MeV/c.

Cross-sections

The partial differential cross-sections for D meson production at the ISR, corrected for the known branching ratios, are shown in Fig. 17 for all SFM data, excluding the BCF results[1]. The hatched

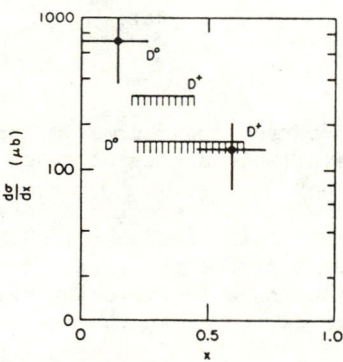

Fig. 17 D meson partial cross-sections, ISR data (S. Wojcicki)

38

regions correspond to upper limits from negative LSM results. The production mechanism used in calculating these partial cross-sections is pair production, with the important exception of the D^+ point for $x > 0.5$. This point is from an inclusive reaction which already absorbs the production mechanism of the other anti-charmed hadron.

$\sigma_T(D)$

The total D meson cross-section is shown in Fig. 18 for all ISR data, based on a central production mechanism (Eq. (22)). The data of Fig. 17 have been analyzed following Eq. (19). Once again there appears a strong clustering of all the data near 400 μb. The same SFM point (open circles) has been analyzed using two extreme models, $(1-x)^{0.4}$ following Λ_c^+ production, and $(1-x)^3$ central production. Although all other data support a central production process, this one point, observed in an inclusive reaction for $x > 0.5$, expands beyond the 1 mb region when a central process is assumed. For the case involving strong decay of excited charmed baryon states, the power dependence in $(1-x)^\alpha$ is expected to be larger than 0.4, taking into account the strong decay into D^+, although clearly not as large as 3.

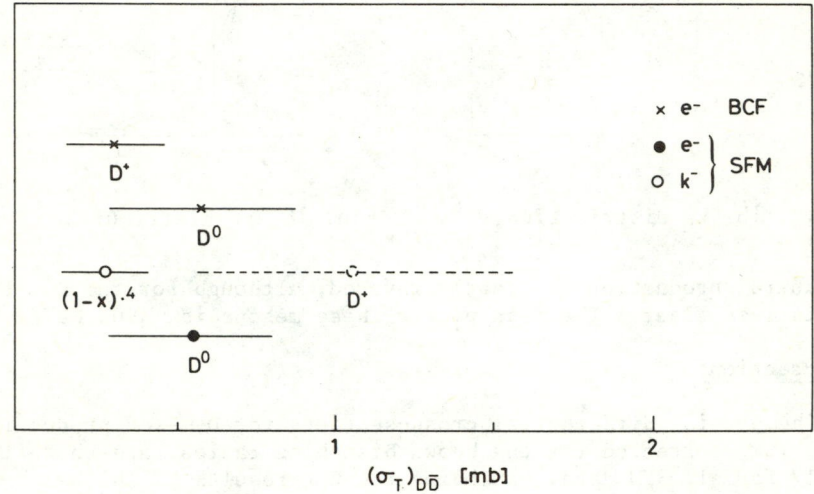

Fig. 18 Total D cross-section for all ISR data

Charm summary

Table II summarizes the total charmed baryon and charmed meson cross-sections observed at the ISR. The available center of mass energies for these data are 53 GeV and 62 GeV.

On the basis of Table II, the total charm cross-section observed at the ISR (baryons and mesons) is therefore of the order of 1 mb. This is indeed a surprising result, considering that the total cross-section at these energies is 40 mb. Comments on a possible interpretation and implication of these cross-sections are given in the Appendix.

Table II Total charm cross-sections at the ISR

Hadron	σ_T	Production characteristics
Λ_c^+	(200–400) μb	$\frac{d\sigma}{dx} \propto (1-x)^{0.4}$ (forward)
$D^0 + D^+$	(800–900) μb	$E \frac{d\sigma}{dx} \propto (1-x)^3$ (central)

BEAUTY PRODUCTION AT THE ISR

Hidden beauty

The $\Upsilon(9460)$ provides the best evidence for hidden beauty production[10], the interpretation here being a bound state $(b\bar{b})$ pair. One example of hidden new flavor production at the ISR is experiment R209, dimuon production in high mass states at $\sqrt{s} = 62$ GeV:

$$p + p \rightarrow \mu^+\mu^- + X \tag{23}$$

Table III summarizes the reported cross-sections for Ψ/J and Υ production[16].

Table III Ψ/J and Υ cross-sections

Channel	$\left.\frac{d\sigma}{dx}\right|_{x=0.2}$	σ
Ψ/J	(0.51 ± 0.16) μb	(0.14 ± 0.04) μb
$\Upsilon + \Upsilon' + \Upsilon''$	——	(0.66 ± 0.16) nb

One obvious remark is that the Ψ/J production mechanism is obviously quite different from charmed hadron production, the total cross-section being nearly four orders of magnitude smaller than the total charm cross-section derived in the previous section. (The cross-section for the Υ and its excited states are quoted together due to the mass resolution $\Delta m/m = 11\%$.)

Bare beauty

As in the case of charm, we expect to see a new hadron spectroscopy, e.g. $(b\bar{d})^0$, $(b\bar{u})^-$, $(bud)^0$, etc. (for $q_b = -1/3$). The masses for these lowest lying ground state hadrons can be inferred from the $\Upsilon(10.55)$ state seen in e^+e^- collisions[17]. The broad width of this state is consistent with the interpretation of a dominant strong

40

decay into $B\bar{B}$ mesons, in direct analogy to the decay $\Psi/J(3700) \rightarrow D\bar{D}$. The implied B meson mass is 5.3 GeV/c^2.

But what are the couplings of the b quarks to the other quarks, if any? At the ISR two recent SFM experiments, R415 and R416, reported results on beauty baryon production (bud)^0 in a search for the Cabibbo favored sequential weak decay process[18]

$$b \rightarrow c \rightarrow s \tag{24}$$

by triggering on a prompt e^+ from the semi-leptonic decay of the associated $\bar{B}$ hadron. The reaction studied was:

$$
\begin{array}{l}
p + p \rightarrow \Lambda_b^0 + \bar{B} + X \\
\qquad\quad\; \rightarrow e^+ + x \\
\qquad\quad\; \rightarrow pD^0\pi^- \\
\qquad\qquad\qquad \rightarrow K^-\pi^+
\end{array}
\tag{25}
$$

The idea here was to search for beauty baryon production in the forward region, as in the case for Λ_c^+ production. An additional requirement was made on the triggering positron $(p_T)^e > 0.8$ GeV/c in order to suppress positrons originating from charm decay.

The "leading" baryon condition was demanded on a set of four particles: i) $|x_F| \geq 0.32$ for the proton; ii) $|y|_{pK^-\pi^+\pi^-} \geq 1.4$; and iii) $(n_{ch.}) \geq 4$, with at least one track opposite to the e^+. Thus the total number of tracks demanded per event was at least nine. Both experiments applied the same cuts to their respective data.

BCF (R415)

This data[19] is shown in Figs. 19-26. The analysis begins with events satisfying the conditions defined above; events are then selected with a $(K^-\pi^+)$ invariant mass pair lying in the D^0 mass range (1.7-2.0) GeV/c^2 (Fig. 19), and the resulting $\{p(K^-\pi^+)_{D^0}\pi^-\}$ invariant mass plot is shown in Fig. 20. The same plot without the offline D^0

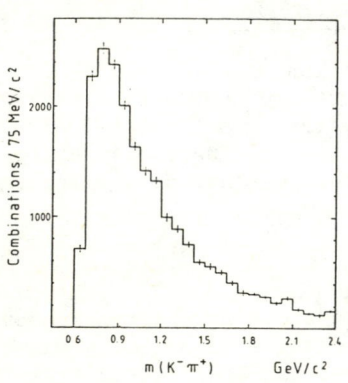

Fig. 19 $(K^-\pi^+)$ mass with leading condition

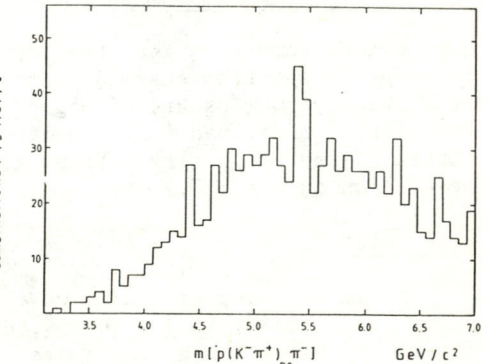

Fig. 20 $\{p(K^-\pi^+)_{D^0}\pi^-\}$ mass plot with offline D^0 trigger

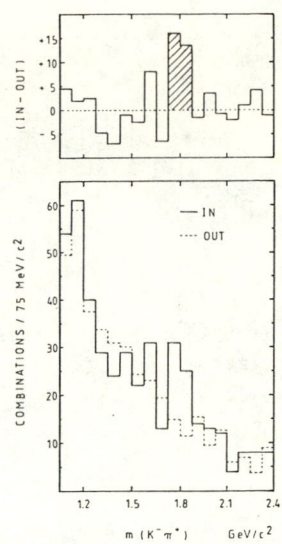

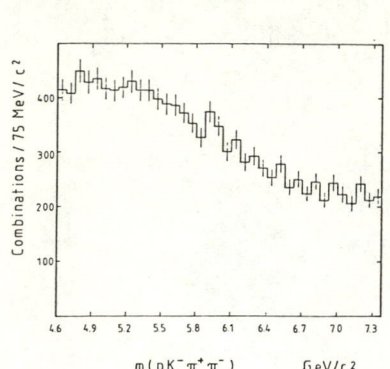

Fig. 21 (pK⁻π⁺π⁻) mass plot, no D⁰ trigger

Fig. 22 m(K⁻π⁺) in Λ_b^0 region

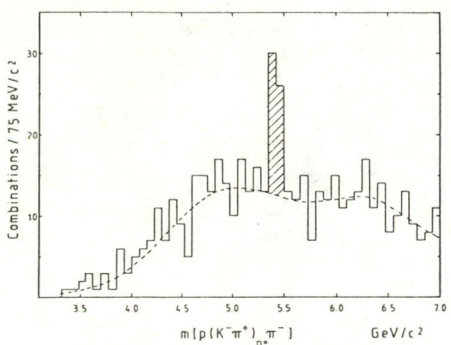

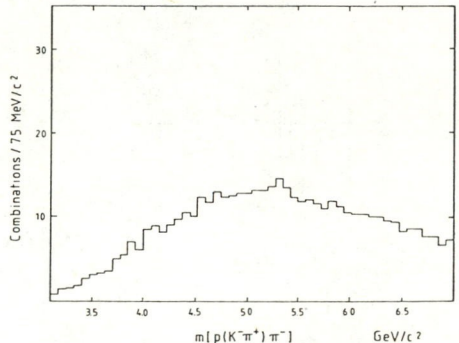

Fig. 23 $\{p(K^-\pi^+)_{D^0}\pi^-\}$ mass plot with tight D⁰ trigger

Fig. 24 $\{p(K^-\pi^+)_{D^0}\pi^-\}$ mass, event mixing

trigger is shown in Fig. 21 with no apparent structure evident. By selecting, from the events without D⁰ trigger, those events where a $p(K^-\pi^+)\pi^-$ combination falls in the peak region (5.35-5.5) GeV/c² of Fig. 20, the $(K^-\pi^+)$ invariant mass spectrum shown in Fig. 22 is obtained, in which an enhancement in the D⁰ mass range (1.725-1.875) GeV/c² is now observed. Despite the systematic 60 MeV/c² offset of the D⁰ mass, the authors replot the $\{p(K^-\pi^+)_{D^0}\pi^-\}$ invariant mass, but this time by narrowing their D⁰ trigger about the D⁰ enhancement appearing at 5.425 GeV/c². The corresponding background mass spectra are shown for event mixing (Fig. 24), a hadron trigger (Fig. 25) and

42

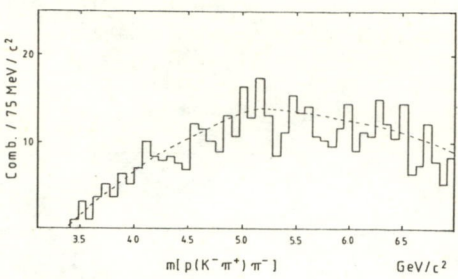

Fig. 25 $\{p(K^-\pi^+)_{D^0}\pi^-\}$ mass, hadron trigger

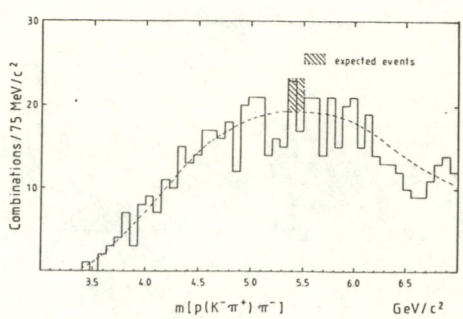

Fig. 26 $\{p(K^-\pi)_{D^0}\pi^-\}$ mass, electron trigger

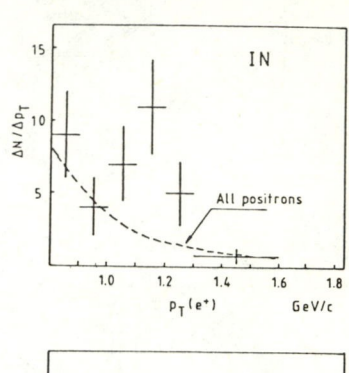

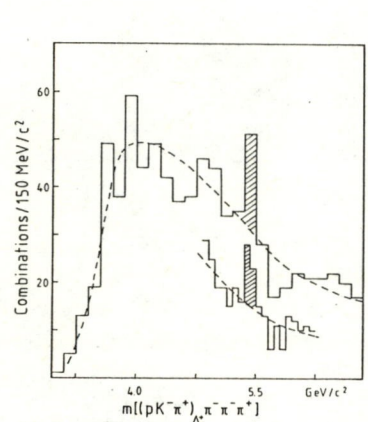

Fig. 27 $m\{(pK^-\pi^+)_{\Lambda_c^+}\pi^-\pi^-\pi^+\}$

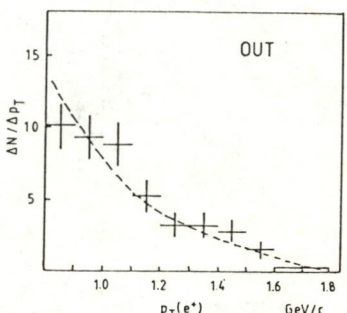

Fig. 28 $p_T(e^+)$ for events in Λ_b^0 mass

an electron trigger (Fig. 26). The $\{(pK^-\pi^+)\pi^-\pi^-\pi^+\}$ invariant mass spectrum is shown in Fig. 27, with the $(pK^-\pi^+)$ mass $\pm$ 100 MeV/c^2 around the Λ_c^+ mass[20]. The enhancement indicated appears at 5.42 GeV/c^2 and would be an indication for the decay channel $\Lambda_b^0 \rightarrow \Lambda_c^+\pi^-\pi^-\pi^+$.

The corresponding positron trigger spectrum[20] in the pp c.m. system is shown for events in and out of the Λ_b^0 region of Fig. 23, in Fig. 28. The enhancement visible at $\sim$ 1.1 GeV/c should be compared with the electron momentum spectrum from $B\bar{B}$ in e^+e^- collisions[17], where the momentum spectrum peaks near 1.5 GeV/c, taking into account that in pp reactions the $B\bar{B}$ pair is not produced at rest as in e^+e^- collisions (Fig. 29).

Finally, the longitudinal momentum distribution[21] of the Λ_b^0 enhancement is shown in Fig. 30, and the corresponding comparisons with Λ_c^+, Λ^0 and $\bar{\Lambda}^0$ x_L distributions are shown in Fig. 31.

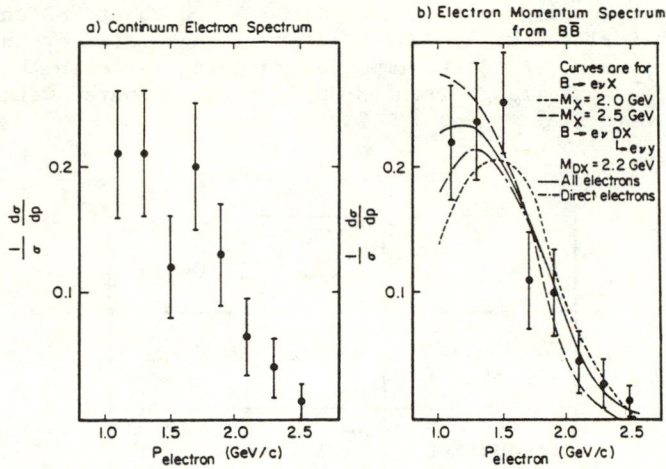

Fig. 29 $p_T(e^-)$ from $e^+e^- \to B\bar{B}$ (CLEO)

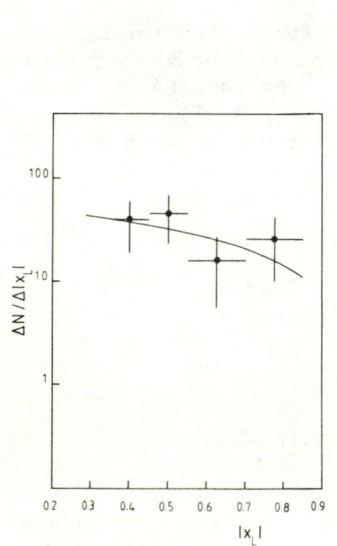

Fig. 30 x_L distribution, events with identified Λ_b^0

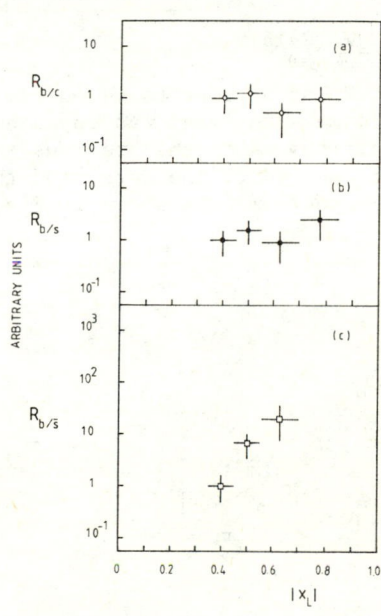

Fig. 31 Normalized x_L(b) for x_L(c), x_L(s) and $x_L(\bar{s})$

44

Λ_b^0 summary (BCF)

Table IV summarizes data on beauty baryon production, as reported by the R415 group. Despite the expected mass value and forward production characteristic of the Λ_b^0 claim, the cross-sections quoted, in this author's opinion, are unusually high. In a perturbative QCD model where the total heavy flavor cross-section is proportional to m_q^{-2}, then for a total charm cross-section on the order of 1 mb, the implied total beauty cross-section $\sigma_T(b) \sim 100$ μb at ISR energies. Assuming that all of this cross-section is associated production, producing always a Λ_b^0, then the implied branching ratio in the decay channel $pD^0\pi^-$ would range from (3-30)%, to be compared with the branching ratio $B(\Lambda_c^+ \to K^- p\pi^+) \sim 2\%$.

Table IV Λ_b^0 summary

Mass	$5.425 \begin{array}{c} + 175 \\ - 75 \end{array}$ GeV/c^2
$\sigma_T \cdot B$ $(\Lambda_b^0 \to pD^0\pi^-)$	(2.7-27) μb
Production Character	$\dfrac{d\sigma}{dx} \propto (1-x)^\alpha$ $\alpha = (0.87 \pm 1.26)$

ACCDHW (R416)

In an attempt to reconfirm the new results from the BCF group, the same experiment was repeated under similar, though not identical conditions as in the previous experiment. The same R415 analysis cuts were applied to the data, and the resulting $\{p(K^-\pi^+)_{D^0}\pi^-\}$ invariant mass spectrum[22] is shown in Fig. 32 (to be compared with Fig. 23).

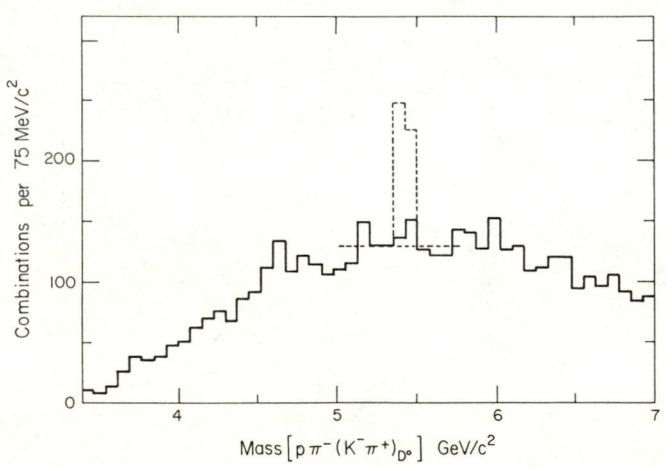

Fig. 32 ACCDHW data, $m\{p(K^-\pi^+)_{D^0}\pi^-\}$ with same cuts as in BCF analysis

No statistically significant structure was observed by this group; only the background level increased nearly ten times, although the actual exposure of both experiments was nearly the same. The dashed peak (213 combinations) is the signal expected by this group, based on scaling the signal/background level of the BCF results to their own observed background and taking into account the estimated R416 background on the triggering e^+.

Discussion

The existing controversy between the BCF and ACCDHW groups is by no means resolved, and settling this issue requires intimate knowledge of both experiments, which this author does not pretend to have. However, a closer look into the specific quantities involved is appropriate for a better understanding of this problem. An important difference in these experiments was the use of electromagnetic shower detectors (EMSD) in the trigger of R415, providing a higher yield of prompt positrons. Table V presents a run summary of both experiments. It should be noticed, however, that the BCF group does not agree[23] with the ACCDHW e^+ background estimate in the R416 e^+ sample. Using particles identified as hadrons in the EMSD the BCF group has measured the rejection power against charged hadrons of the C counters which have been used by both experiments. The corresponding contamination in the R416 trigger and the fraction of prompt e^+ in the R416 event sample are reported in brackets in Table V.

Table V R415/R416 run summary

	R415 (BCF)	R416 (ACCDHW)
$\sqrt{s}$	62 GeV	
$\int$ Ldt	4.4×10^{36} cm^{-2}	3.6×10^{36} cm^{-2}
e^+ ident.	$\check{C}$ + EMSD	$\check{C}$
% prompt e^+	45%	32% (16%)
charged hadron contam. in trigger	< 2%	36% (68%)

Another important difference in both experiments was the track reconstruction program used by each group, owing to an improved MWPC set-up for protons in R416 and an overall improvement in program reconstruction efficiency. The ACCDHW group has assumed that the different background level of the two experiments represent their overall different Λ_b^0 detection efficiency. The BCF group has estimated the relative Λ_b^0 detection efficiency of the two experiments on the basis of the single track detection efficiency estimated by each group via Monte Carlo simulations and the study of various physical processes. These efficiencies[23] are summarized in Table VI.

The expected signal in R416, on the basis of the exposure and percentage of prompt positrons in Table V and the efficiencies as determined by R415, should then be:

$$S = S_0 \cdot R_p \cdot R_{K^-\pi^+\pi^-} \cdot R_{lead} \cdot R_{(n_{ch})} \cdot (F) \cdot \frac{\int Ldt(416)}{\int Ldt(415)} \qquad (26)$$

$$= (25-49) \text{ combinations}$$

Table VI Track reconstruction efficiencies

$\dfrac{\varepsilon(416 : \text{protons})}{\varepsilon(415 : \text{protons})}$	1.53 R_p
$\dfrac{\varepsilon(416 : K^-\pi^+\pi^-)}{\varepsilon(415 : K^-\pi^+\pi^-)}$	1.33 $R_{K^-\pi^+\pi^-}$
$\dfrac{\varepsilon(416 : (n_{ch}) \geq 4)}{\varepsilon(415 : (n_{ch}) \geq 4)}$	1.10 $R_{(n_{ch})}$
$\dfrac{\varepsilon(416 : \text{protons from } \Lambda_b^0, \ |x_L| > 0.32)}{\varepsilon(415 : \text{protons from } \Lambda_b^0, \ |x_L| > 0.32)}$	1.26 $R_{lead.}$

where $S_0 = 30$ combinations observed by R415 (in two bins of 75 MeV/c^2), and the fraction F appearing in Eq. (22) is the correction for the percentage of prompt positrons. The expected signal-to-background ratio is then:

$$\frac{S}{B} = \frac{(13-25) \text{ comb.}/75 \text{ MeV/c}^2 \text{ bin}}{130 \text{ comb. background}} \qquad (27)$$

corresponding to a (1.1-2.1) σ effect at the 95% confidence level, the upper limit value normally quoted for negative results.

Conclusion

In light of the current unresolved controversy on this subject, the best conclusion here is that these results should be reconfirmed with more data.

COLLIDER EXPECTATIONS

The CERN $p\bar{p}$ Collider opens new physics frontiers in new heavy flavor production with the highest available c.m. energy, $\sqrt{s} = 540$ GeV; searches for the top quark are immediately accessible for masses much in excess of 18 GeV/c^2 (the current upper limit from PETRA), given the rather high production rates and luminosities.

In this energy region, where the quark mass $m_q \ll \sqrt{s}$ (even up to quark masses of 50 GeV/c^2), the heavy flavor cross-section is expected to obey the dependence $\sigma_q \propto m_q^{-2}$, based on perturbative QCD calculations[24]. Recall that in hadronic interactions, the K/π ratio is a canonical number $\sim$ 20%, spanning a wide energy range; given now the total charm cross-section of $\sim$ 1 mb observed at the ISR, we would expect an analogous canonical value for charm:

$$\frac{c}{\pi} \sim \frac{1}{40} . \tag{28}$$

At the Collider the corresponding t/π ratio for m_t = 18 GeV/c^2 is:

$$\frac{t}{\pi} \sim \frac{1}{5760} \tag{29}$$

with an expected total top cross-section for the same mass of:

$$\sigma_T(t) \sim 10 \ \mu b . \tag{30}$$

At modest luminosities of 10^{28} cm^{-2} sec^{-1}, the implied total number of top hadrons produced is $\sim$ 360 events per hour (or equivalently $\sim$ 40 events per hour for m_t = 50 GeV/c^2).

Based on what has been observed at the ISR, the ground state heavy flavor baryons $\Lambda_{s,b,c}$ are produced in the forward region, while the production mechanism for the respective heavy mesons is central. Reactions similar to those of Eqs. (10) and (12) are therefore expected for top hadron production. A method to observe the production of open top baryonic states at the CERN p$\bar{p}$ Collider has been presented by the BCF group[25]. It is based on the "leading" production mechanism[8,12,21] extended to the heaviest flavored baryon and antibaryon states, and on the charge asymmetry of the leptons originated from their semi-leptonic decays to be searched for in a phase space region where the contributions from the other various lepton sources are suppressed. Another interesting possibility to search for top quarks has recently been suggested by Horgan and Jacob (Ref. 26). As in previous heavy flavor searches at the ISR, the basic idea is to search in the semi-leptonic decay mode of the accompanying (anti-) top hadron, but by triggering on very high p$_T$ prompt leptons. The distinguishing feature of the top quark is its presumably high mass, already at least four times heavier than the beauty quark mass. Thus for m_t = 18 GeV/c^2, the mean p$_T$ of the lepton is $\sim m_q/4$, or $\sim$ 5 GeV/c. The expected p$_T$ background in this kinematic region such as the Drell-Yan mechanism is strongly suppressed, and while charm and beauty production are more abundant, their contribution at this high p$_T$ is also suppressed by the mass differences.

Acknowledgement

This work was made possible by the University of Wisconsin, and I am most grateful to Professor David Cline. I wish also to thank Professor Antonino Zichichi for his comments on the text, and Dr. Daniel Drijard for useful discussions.

REFERENCES

1. S. Wojcicki, Proc. Int. Conf. on High Energy Physics, Madison, 1430 (1980), eds. L. Durand and L.G. Pondrom (Am. Inst. Phys., New York, 1981).
D. Treille, CERN-EP/81-133 (1981), and references therein.
2. K. Giboni et al., Phys. Lett. 85B, 437 (1979).
3. J. Irion et al., Phys. Lett. 99B, 495 (1981).
4. D. Drijard et al., Phys. Lett. 81B, 250 (1979).
5. D. Drijard et al., Phys. Lett. 85B, 452 (1979).
6. G. Sajot, Proc. Int. Conf. on High Energy Physics, Madison, 192 (1980).
7. W. Lockman et al., Phys. Lett. 85B, 443 (1979).
8. M. Basile et al., Nuovo Cimento 63A, 230 (1981).
9. a. M. Basile et al., Nuovo Cimento 65A, 457 (1981).
   b. M. Basile et al., CERN-EP/81-125 (1981).
   c. M. Basile et al., CERN EP Internal report 81-02 (1981) and A. Contin, Charm Production at the CERN Intersecting Storage Rings Split Field Magnet, EPS Int. Conf. on High Energy Physics, Lisbon, 9-15 July 1981, to appear in the Proceedings.
10. Review of Particle Properties, reprinted from Reviews of Modern Physics 52, No. 2 (1980).
11. D. DiBitonto, Ph.D. thesis, Harvard University, October 1979.
12. M. Basile et al., Nuovo Cimento Lett. 30, 487 (1981).
13. M. Basile et al., Nuovo Cimento Lett. 30, 481 (1981).
14. M. Basile et al., CERN-EP/81-126.
15. M. Basile et al., CERN-EP/81-127.
16. D. Antreasyan et al., Phys. Rev. Lett. 45, 863 (1980).
17. Contribution to the 1981 International Symposium on Lepton and Photon Physics at High Energies, the CLEO Collaboration, Bonn, W. Germany (1981).
18. H. Fritzsch and P. Minkowski, Physics Reports 73, 67 (1981).
19. M. Basile et al., Nuovo Cimento Lett. 31, 97 (1981).
20. P. Giusti, Beauty Production at the CERN Intersecting Storage Rings Split-Field Magnet, EPS Int. Conf. on High Energy Physics, Lisbon, 9-15 July 1981, to appear in the Proceedings.
21. M. Basile et al., Nuovo Cimento 65A, 408 (1981).
22. D. Drijard et al., CERN-EP/81-96 (1981).
23. M. Basile et al., CERN-EP/81-150 (1981).
24. S.J. Brodsky et al., SLAC PUB 2660 (1981).
25. M. Basile et al., CERN-EP/81-151.
26. R. Horgan and M. Jacob, Phys. Lett. 107B, 395 (1981).

APPENDIX

Charmed baryons

Based on what has been observed for high mass excited strange
and non-strange baryon decays, such as for the Δ, Λ^* and Σ^* resonances,
one would also expect to produce excited charmed baryon states, which
would then decay strongly into ground state Λ_c^+ + mesons, and into
D + nucleon + mesons. This is particularly true in diffractive excitation processes (Fig. 1). The relative strong branching ratios into
Λ_c^+ and DN are not known, although owing to the relatively large and
comparable mass of the Λ_c^+ and D, a rough but reasonable estimate is
that they are nearly equal:

$$
\begin{aligned}
B_c &\to \Lambda_c^+ + X \qquad &\sim 50\% \\
&\hookrightarrow N + D + X \qquad &\sim 50\% \\
&\qquad \hookrightarrow D^+, D^0 \sim 50\% : 50\%
\end{aligned}
\tag{A1}
$$

(The F^+ contribution is suppressed by the ratio $K/\pi \sim 20\%$.) The implied total charmed baryon cross-section is $\sigma_T(B_c) \sim 2 \times \sigma_T(\Lambda_c^+)$, or
roughly 1 mb. For the case of forward D^+ production (see Table I),
the implied $\sigma_T(B_c)$ is $\sim 4 \times \sigma_T(D^+)$, or also 1 mb. These results
should be compared with the total D meson cross-section (0.8-0.9) mb,
the implication here being that for charmed hadrons, associated production is as large as pair production, both of the order of 1 mb.

PROMPT PRODUCTION OF NEUTRINOS BY 400 GEV PROTONS ON TUNGSTEN: FIRST RESULTS FROM FERMILAB E613[1]

Don D. Reeder

Physics Department, University of Wisconsin

Madison, Wisconsin 53706 USA

Abstract

Preliminary results from a measurement of the prompt ν_μ and $\bar{\nu}_\mu$ fluxes obtained in a beam dump experiment at Fermilab indicate that $D\bar{D}$ charmed particles are produced centrally with a cross section of ~ 20 μb per nucleon. The measured value of the flux of $\bar{\nu}_\mu$ is non zero and approximately equal to the ν_μ flux.

The measurement of the flux of prompt neutrinos can provide insight into mechanisms which produce short lived hadrons. For example, the question of whether charmed particles are produced diffractively or from the quark sea is still open. This preliminary report of the results of experiment E-613 concerns measurement of the flux of muon neutrinos[1]. When completed E-613 will also measure the ν_e flux and the dependence of these fluxes on atomic number.

As shown in Figure 1 the 400 GeV proton beam is incident on a tungsten target of either full density or one-third density. A 150 ton calorimeter-spectrometer is located 60 m from the target and is shielded by a beam dump of 11 m of magnetized iron followed by 11 m of passive iron.

The detector, shown schematically in Figure 2, is made in 30 modules, each containing 12 teflon coated lead plates. A module has 14.4 radiation lengths and 0.5 hadron absorption lengths (106 gm/cm^2). Light produced in the liquid scintillator surrounding the plates is detected by 300 photomultiplier tubes (10 per module). Interspersed between modules are two planes of proportional wire chambers which have both horizontal and vertical wires on 2.5 cm centers. These are operated in proportional mode with analog readout of pulse height. The calorimeter is followed by a muon spectrometer with drift chambers and solid iron magnets.

A "typical" ν_μ charged current event is shown in Figure 3. The length of a line within the calorimeter represents the pulse height. In this event the energy of the neutrino was 168 GeV.

To form a trigger the signals from the modules are summed in twenty-four overlapping groups - eight modules longitudinally and two vertically. The requirement that the summed pulse heights exceed a minimum together with the attenuation of light within the module results in an energy threshold for triggering which varies with position. This variation of efficiency of triggering with position is shown in Figure 4. For energies greater than 10 GeV, 100% triggering efficiency is found.

The extension of the beam line strikes the detector 0.75 m from one side horizontally and is centered vertically. The distribution of event vertices is shown in Figure 5. This horizontal assymmetry makes it possible to record neutrinos whose production angle varies from 0 to 40 mr.

In the run during Spring 1982, 1.87×10^{17} protons on target were obtained. The useful flux corrected for live time, bad spills, etc. was about half this value. Because of the long (1 sec) spill and the absence of an effective veto, about one-third of the 30 triggers per pulse were caused by cosmic rays. The remaining beam related triggers were largely due to muon interactions in the floor and in the concrete shield above the apparatus.

However, muon neutrino charged current events are unambiguous and nearly background free. The raw numbers of ν_μ and $\bar{\nu}_\mu$ events found are presented in Table I together with the numbers within a fiducial volume.

Table I
Raw Numbers of Muon Neutrino Charged Current Events

	Full density tungsten	One-third density tungsten
Protons on target (in live time)	0.53×10^{17}	0.15×10^{17}
N_μ total	637	302
$N_\mu-$	397	188
$N_\mu+$	134	68
$N_\mu-$ (in Fid. Vol)	363	173
$N_\mu+$ (in Fid. Vol)	119	56

The events must be corrected for the effects of the trigger threshold and the acceptance of the muon spectrometer which distort the scaling x and y distributions. As shown in Figures 6 and 7 the data are reasonably well described by calculation of the distortion. In Figure 8 the energy distribution for diffractive production would be nearly energy independent, so apparently only a rather small fraction of the events appear to be diffractively produced.

Some of the neutrino events are due to neutrinos from pions and kaons which decay before absorption in the target. The true prompt rate can be determined using the two targets of different density and extrapolating to infinite density as shown in Figure 9. In a prompt neutrino experiment control of upstream background is essential. We continually monitored upstream scraping by a series of monitors around the beam pipe. These were calibrated by introducing known amounts of materials into the beam. The background estimated from these monitors was less than 1% of the non-prompt signal inherent in our high density tungsten target. Material just upstream of the target (SWICS, SEM, etc) introduced a larger but calculable background of 8.3% of the non-prompt high density tungsten rate. A correction averaging about 15% was introduced by hadrons punching through the targets into the essentially infinite iron and copper absorber in back of the target. The net effect of these corrections to the extra-polation is to reduce the effective density ratio of the two targets from 3 to about 2.5. In Figure 9 these corrections are omitted in extrapolation A and included in extrapolation B.

In order to determine the prompt cross section as a function of energy and angle, we have divided the events into bins of energy and angle and have extrapolated bin-by-bin correcting for backgrounds which vary with energy. If we assume that the major production mode is $D\bar{D}$ and that the cross section is proportional to A, we can go further. We use the mean $D°-D^+$ semi-leptonic branching ratio as obtained from e^+e^- interactions i.e. 16.4 ± 2.4%, and we parameterize the cross section in the conventional manner as

$$E \frac{d^3\sigma}{dp^3} \, \alpha \, (1 - 1x1)^n \, e^{-ap_T}$$

where x is the scaling x and P_T is transverse momentum. We must further assume that the protons cascade in the target with an average elasticity E = 0.6 and that the cross section for charm production varies as s^k. We note the the BEBC group at CERN used k = 0.5, however J. Leveille[2] suggests k = 1.3 is a more appropriate value. The results of this calculation are shown in Table II.

Table II Cross Section for $D\bar{D}$ Production

n	a	ε	k	σ (μb)	stat. error	syst. error
				$D\bar{D}$		
3	2	.67	.5	15.6	± 3.1	± 3.1 (BEBC model)
3	2	.67	1.3	17.2	± 3.4	± 3.4
4	2	.67	1.3	21.4	± 4.3	± 4.3
3	1.6	.67	1.3	18.6	± 3.7	± 3.7
3	2	.3	1.3	24.4	± 4.9	± 4.9

The BEBC group has obtained a value of $\sigma_{D\bar{D}}$ (n=3, a=2, k=0.5) of 30±10μb from $\nu_\mu + \bar{\nu}_\mu$ and 17±10μb from $\nu_e + \bar{\nu}_e$ events.[3] The CHARM group reported (n=4, a=2, no cascading) 19±6 μb.[4].

The E-613 data were separated into μ^+ and μ^- events. From the relative event rates the ratio R of $\bar{\nu}_\mu/\nu_\mu$ fluxes was derived. We find that for $E_\nu > 25$ GeV, R=0.8±0.35. The ν flux is 2.9σ from zero. The ratio R is expected to be one if the flux is dominated by neutrinos from $D\bar{D}$ production while DY_c production should give R<1.

This is to be compared to the value obtained by the CDHS collaboration of 0.114 ± 0.3 (extrapolation) or $0.09^{+0.45}_{-0.09}$.[5]

In summary, the preliminary results of the E-613 beam dump experiment indicate that the prompt ν_μ flux arises from a $D\bar{D}$ production cross section of about 20 μb, that central production is predominate, and that the $\bar{\nu}_\mu$ flux is non-zero and comparable in magnitude to the ν_μ flux.

Various problems remain in the interpretation of the cross section measurement. At this stage of the analysis the amount and character of the production of charm by the hadronic cascade in the dump is estimated to contribute to the cross section value, an amount $\sim$ 70%. The unknown A dependence of the charm production cross section could change the value by $\sim$ 50%. Also the yet unmeasured separation into central and diffractive production parts makes the comparison to other results at higher energies difficult to interpret.

As a final cautionary note, the smallest mass diffractive charmed state produced by a proton is $\Lambda_c^+ \bar{D}^\circ$. At 400 GeV the cross section for larger mass states is suppressed. Since the semi-leptonic branching ratios for both $D^\circ/\bar{D}^\circ$ and Λ_c^+ are $\lesssim$ a few percent, the detection efficiency for this lowest mass state by its semi leptonic decay is abnormally small. Thus the measurement of charm diffraction production near threshold might be a factor $\sim$ 3 to 6 less sensitive than for $D\bar{D}$ central production.

REFERENCES AND FOOTNOTES

1)   Members of the E-613 Collaboration are:

R.C. Ball[b], S. Childress[d], C.T. Coffin[b], G. Conforto[a,b],

M.B. Crisler[c], M.E. Duffy[e], G.K. Fanourakis[e], H.R. Gustafson[b],

J.S. Hoftun[c], L.W. Jones[b], T.Y. Ling[c], M.J. Longo[b], R.J. Loveless[e],

D.D. Reeder[e], T.J. Roberts[b], B.P. Roe[b], T.A. Romanowski[c],

D.L. Schumann[e], E.S. Smith[e], J.T. Volk[c] and E. Wang[b]

a)   Istituto Nazionale di Fisica Nucleare, Firenze 50125, Italy

b)   Department of Physics, University of Michigan, Ann Arbor, MI
     48109 U.S.A.

c)   Department of Physics, Ohio State University, Columbus, OH
     43210 U.S.A.

d)   Department of Physics, University of Washington, Seattle, WA
     98195 U.S.A.

e)   Department of Physics, University of Wisconsin, Madison, WI
     53706 U.S.A.

2)   J. Leveille, private communication.

3)   P. Fritze et al. Phys. Lett 96B (1980).

4)   M. Jonker et al. Phys. Lett. 96B, 435 (1980).

5)   G. Conforto, Proceedings of the European Physical Society
     Study Conference on: The Search for Charm, Beauty and Truth
     at High Energies, Erice, Italy (to be published).

E 613 EXPERIMENT - OVERALL PLAN VIEW

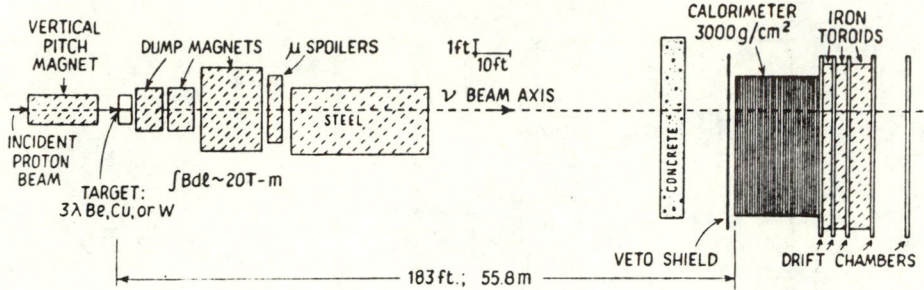

Fig. 1 Plan view of the overall experimental arrangement

E 613 DETECTOR - PLAN VIEW

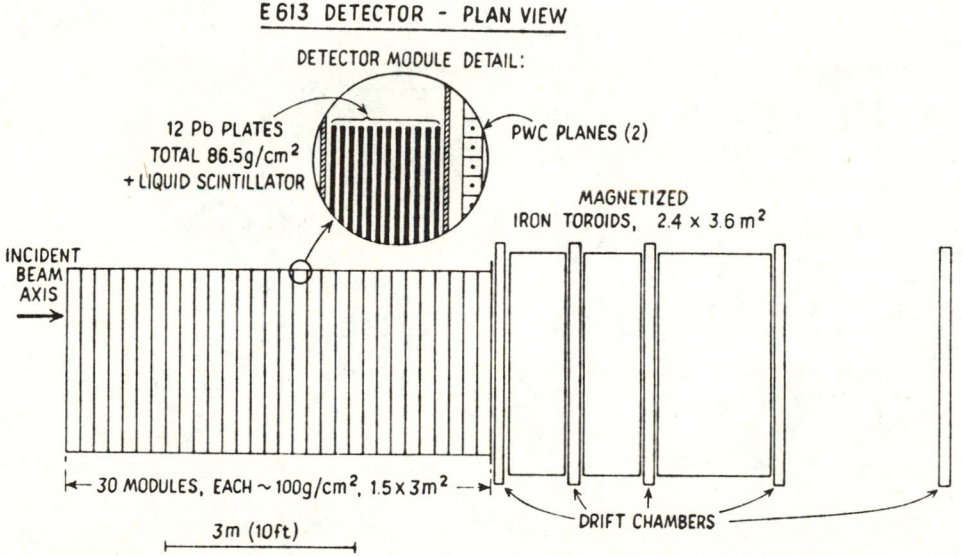

Fig. 2 Plan view of the detector - Calorimeter and μ Spectrometer

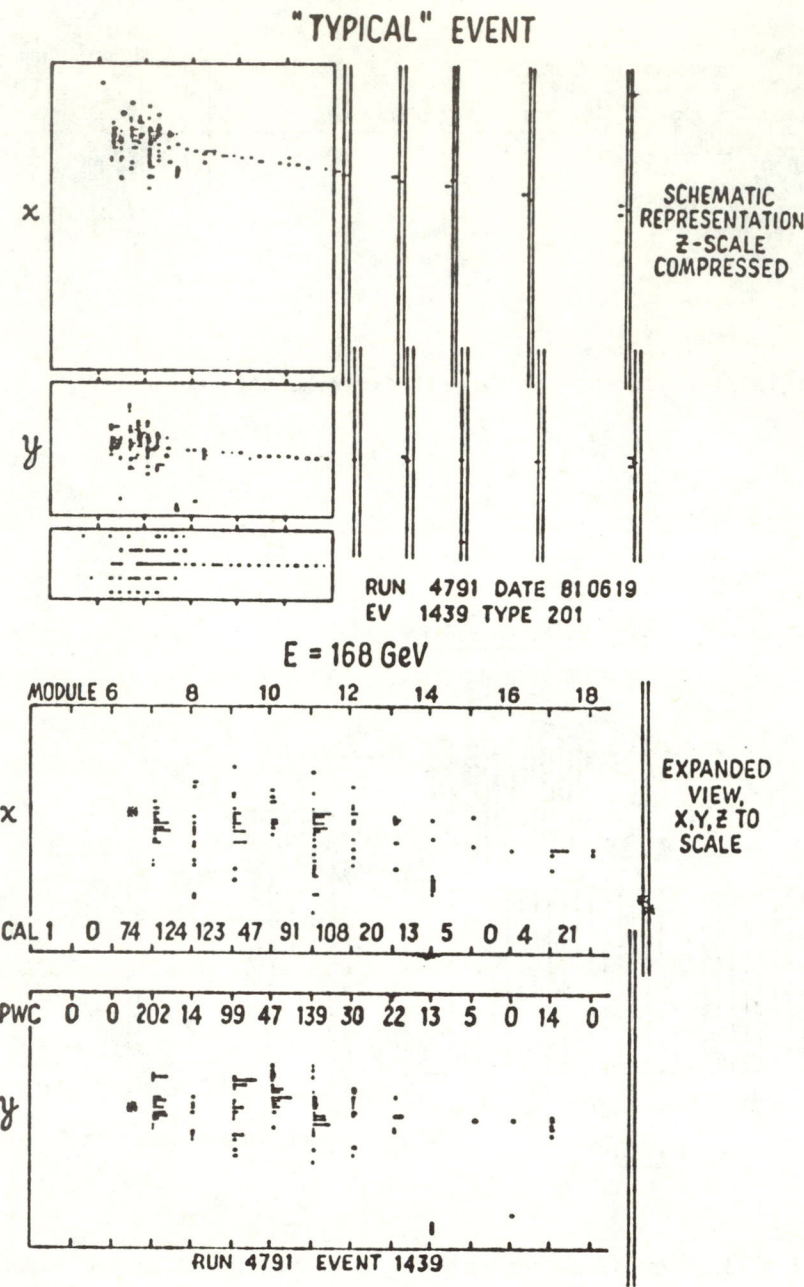

"TYPICAL" EVENT

SCHEMATIC
REPRESENTATION
Z-SCALE
COMPRESSED

RUN 4791 DATE 81 06 19
EV 1439 TYPE 201

E = 168 GeV

MODULE 6   8   10   12   14   16   18

EXPANDED
VIEW,
X,Y,Z TO
SCALE

CAL 1   0 74 124 123 47 91 108 20 13 5 0 4 21

PWC 0 0 202 14 99 47 139 30 22 13 5 0 14 0

RUN 4791 EVENT 1439

Fig. 3 A computer reconstruction of a typical event.

The length of a small line is proportional to the
energy deposition in that tube.
Pairs of vertical lines denote drift chambers.

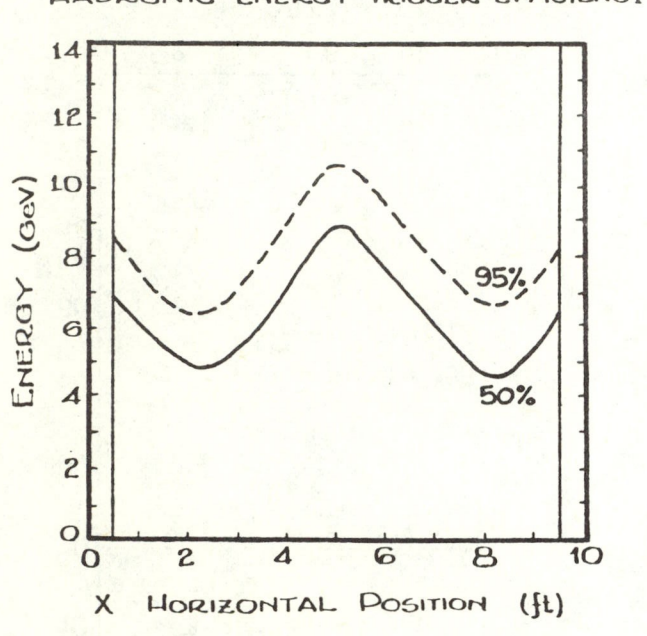

Fig. 4 Variation of the trigger efficiency (50% or 95%) with hydronic energy and horizontal position.

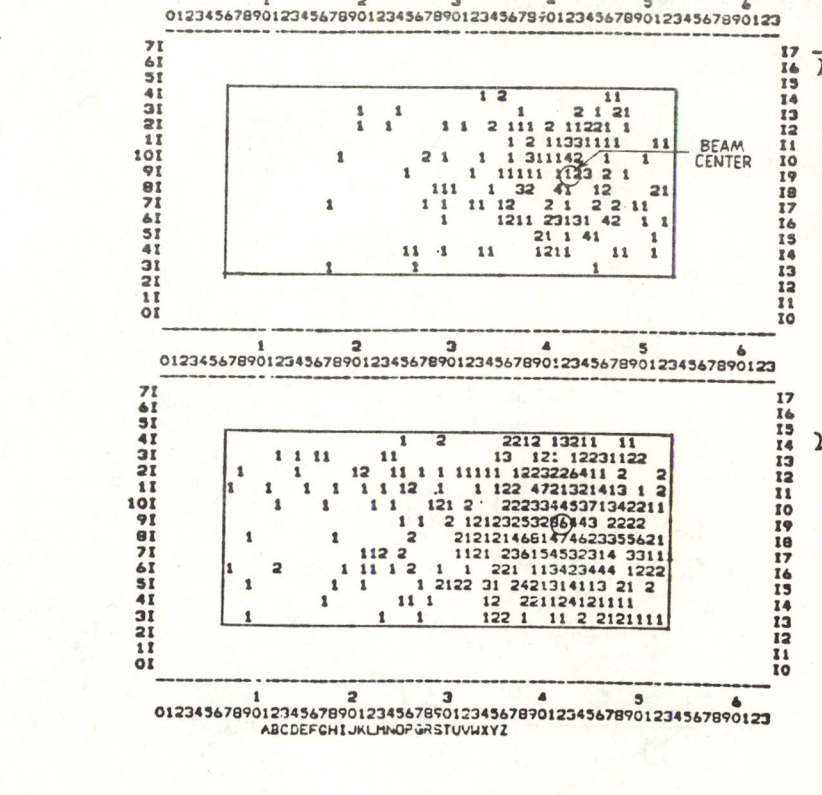

Fig. 5 Scatter plot of event vertices for ν and $\overline{\nu}$ events.

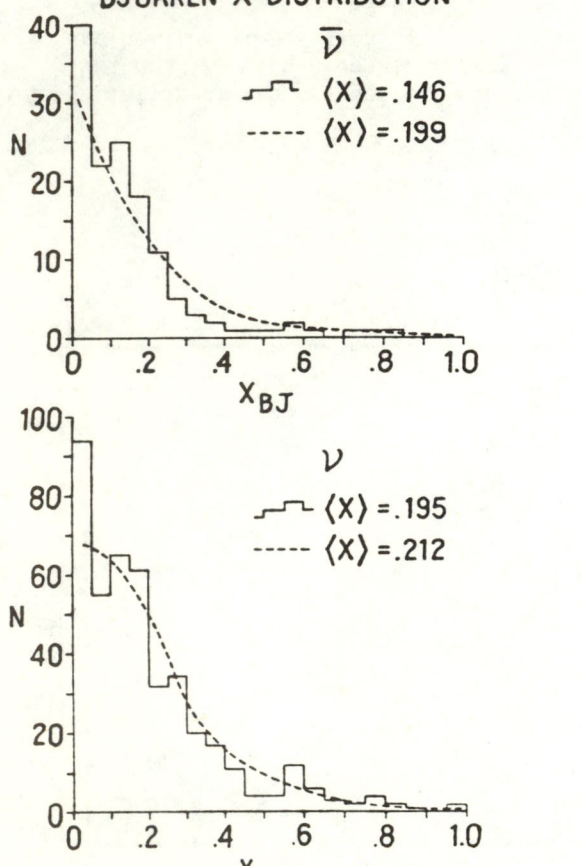

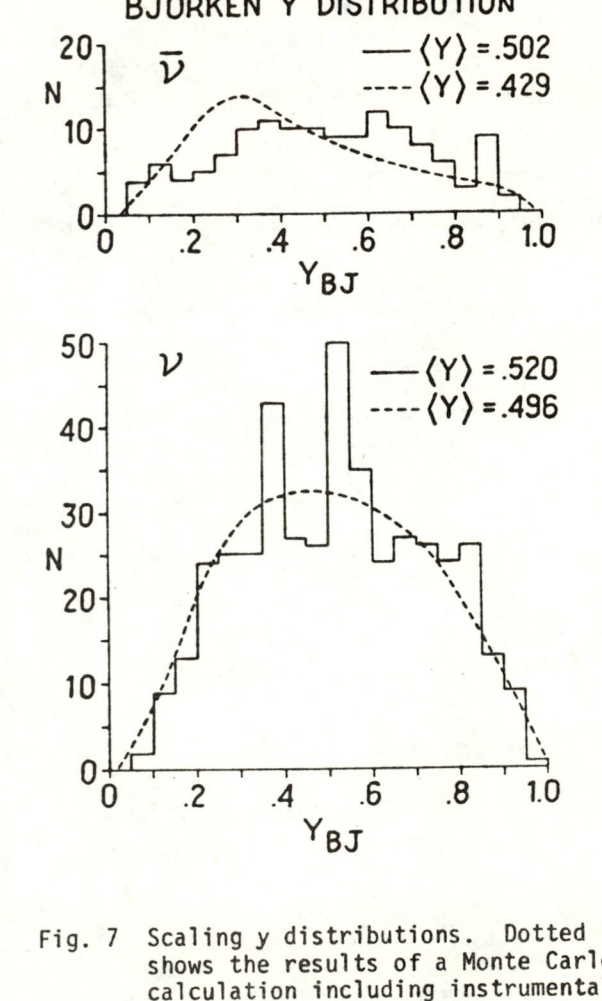

Fig. 6 Scaling x distributions. Dotted lines shows the results of a Monte Carlo calculation including instrumental effects.

Fig. 7 Scaling y distributions. Dotted lines shows the results of a Monte Carlo calculation including instrumental effects.

63

NEUTRINO ENERGY DISTRIBUTION

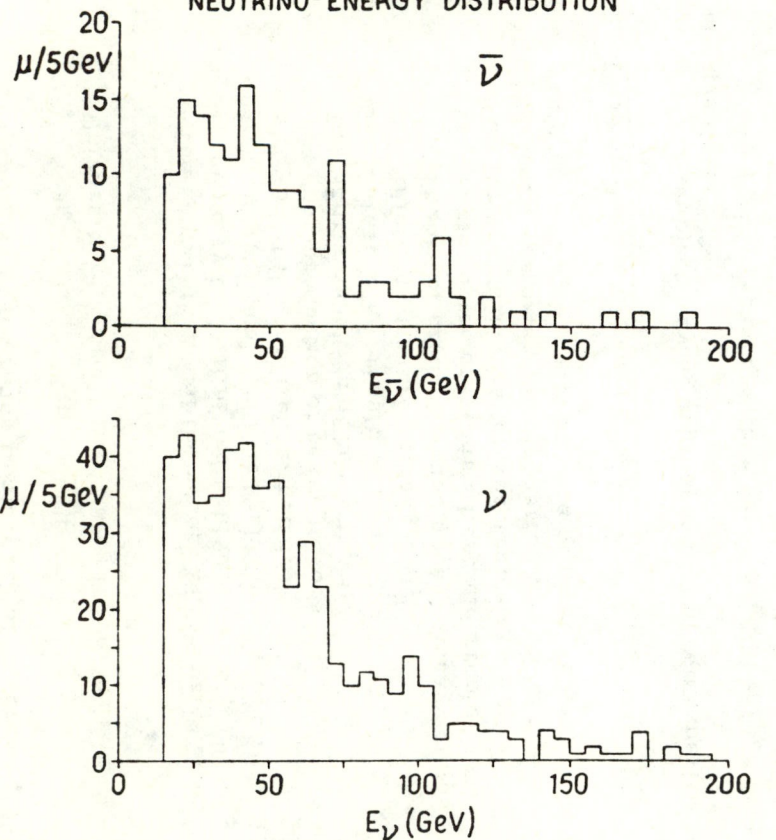

Fig. 8 Distributions in neutrino energy for both ν_μ and $\bar{\nu}_\mu$ events.

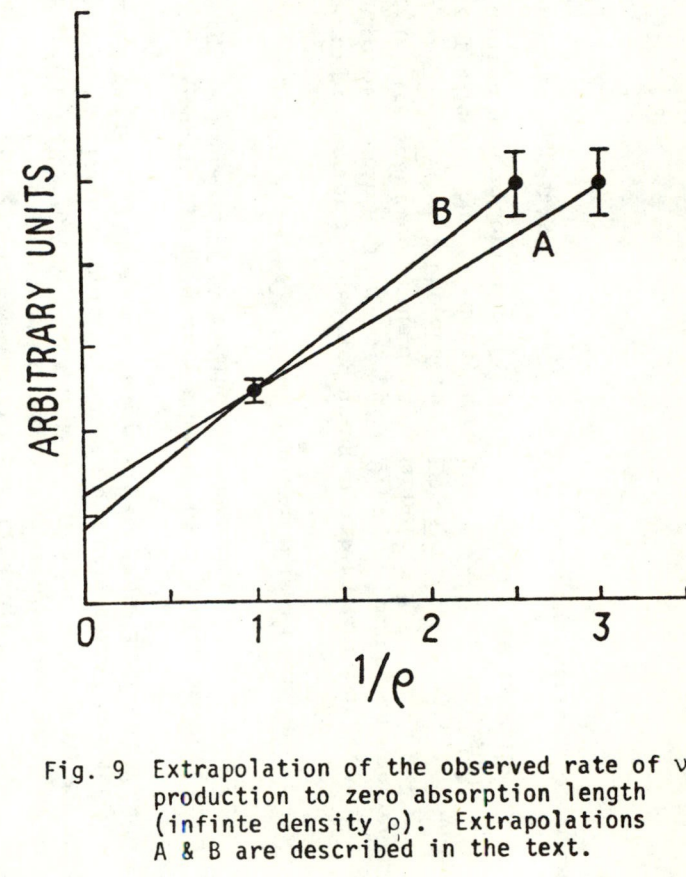

Fig. 9 Extrapolation of the observed rate of ν production to zero absorption length (infinte density ρ). Extrapolations A & B are described in the text.

Highlights of the Erice Conference of November 1981

R. Ruchti

University of Notre Dame, Notre Dame, Indiana 46556

The central theme of the recent Europhysics Study Conference organized by G. Bellini and held at Erice was "The Search for Charm, Beauty, and Truth at High Energies." A list of specific topics covered at the conference includes

I. Photoproduction of heavy flavors
II. Hadroproduction of heavy flavors
III. Latest e^+e^- results
IV. Lifetime measurements
V. Theory of production and decay of heavy states
VI. Vertex detectors - visual and electronic
VII. Trigger schemes for spectrometers

Although there was extensive discussion of each of these topics at the conference, I will report on each of these subjects briefly.[1]

I. Photoproduction of heavy flavors

This subject may be approached from two experimental perspectives:

(1) real γ - using either broad band or tagged photon beams;

or (2) virtual γ - using lepton (specifically muon) beams and extrapolating to $Q^2 = 0$.

Several recent experiments involving the real γ approach are: Fermilab E400[2] (broad band γ), E516[3] (tagged γ), and CERN WA4[4] (tagged γ). E516 is in initial phases of analysis and has not yet quoted results. There is a wealth of data from E400 and WA4.

Experiment E400 uses a broad-band photon beam of mean energy $< E > \sim 150$ GeV to study the reaction:

$$\gamma + \text{tgt} \rightarrow C_1 + \overline{C}_2 + x \qquad \text{(the target is a scintillator)}$$

Charm production is observed using an interaction trigger with a total cross section of $\sigma_{c\bar{c}} \sim 1 \, \mu b \pm 0.25 \, \mu b$. Strong enhancements ($\sim 6 \, \sigma$) are observed in the decay channels $\Lambda_c, \overline{\Lambda}_c \rightarrow pK_s^o, \overline{p}K_s^o$ and $D^{*\pm} \rightarrow K^\mp \pi^\pm \pi^\pm$. The observed $D^o, \overline{D}^o \rightarrow K^\mp \pi^\pm$ signal is weak ($\sim 2 \, \sigma$ effect). No $F^\pm$ decays are observed. In addition the measured production ratio $D^{*+}/D^{*-} = 1 \pm 0.3$ is indicative of charm pair production (rather than associative production). In fact the pair production of D^* is directly observed:

$$\frac{\gamma + tgt \rightarrow D^{*+} + D^{*-} + x}{\gamma + tgt \rightarrow D^{*+} + x} = 0.45 \pm 0.25.$$

Finally, the group sets a limit on D^0, $\overline{D}^0$ mixing of $< 11\%$ (95% CL).

Experiment WA4 is an experiment at lower energy, with tagged γ of energy $< E > \sim 50$ GeV/c. Experimental targets were hydrogen and emulsion. This group reports a large charm cross section $\sigma_{c\bar{c}} \simeq 1$ μb for this energy regime. In addition they see the $\overline{D}^0$ but not the D^0, and observe a considerable number of $F^\pm$ meson decays in several channels:

channel	events
$F^\pm \rightarrow \phi\rho^\pm$	33 ± 10
$\eta\pi$	27 ± 7
$\eta 3\pi$	20 ± 8
$\eta' 3\pi$	60 ± 15

Clearly WA4 and E400 are in conflict in terms of the observed particle production. In Fig. 1 is displayed $\sigma_{c\bar{c}}$ for the two photoproduction experiments. The figure also includes the extrapolated cross sections obtained from two muon experiments (BFP[5] at Fermilab and EMC[6] at CERN). The photon-gluon fusion model adequately describes the trend of the data.

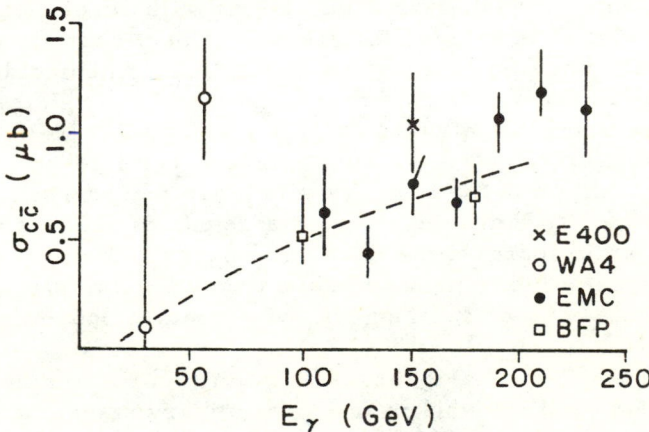

Fig. 1   Charm photoproduction total cross sections. Dashed curve is trend of γ-gluon fusion model.

II. Hadroproduction of heavy flavors

Charm hadroproduction experiments have already been covered in Steve Olsen's review talk at this conference. Essentially the same ground was covered at Erice, with one additional experiment reported, Fermilab E515[7].

E515 is studying charm production in 200 GeV/c π^- nucleon interactions via the process:

$$\pi^- + Be \rightarrow C_1 + \overline{C}_2 + x$$

with the decays $\rightarrow e^-, \mu^-, K^+\pi^- \ldots$ and $\rightarrow \mu^+$.

The experimental strategy is to trigger on a prompt muon from the semi-leptonic decay of one of the charm particles and to examine the decay of the associated state with open geometry and minimum bias.

The detector (Fig. 2) is a two-arm spectrometer. Trigger muons are selected and identified in the upward arm ($\theta_{vert} \geq 40$ mr) consisting of tungsten, iron, polarized iron and instrumented with chambers and counters. Using a beam which is strongly-focused vertically (full width 2 mm), and positioned within 1 mm of the absorber arm - the available decay length is held to ~20 cm. The forward arm of the detector is a conventional magnetic spectrometer consisting of wire chambers, π/K Čerenkov-detection, and a highly segmented liquid argon calorimeter (with resolution $\sigma(E)/E \simeq 20\%$). The trigger for the experiment consists of an incident beam particle (unaccompanied by halo) in coincidence with at least one detected particle which penetrates through the length of the muon arm (BEAM · $\overline{HALO}$ · M1 · M2 · M3 · M4). The observed trigger rate is ~ 4 x 10^{-5} triggers per interacting beam pion. The fraction of the triggers which are from prompt muons was determined by removing various amounts of absorber from the muon arm to increase the decay component. Using the measured rates to extrapolate to zero decay length, it was observed that ~ 20% of the triggers are from prompt muons.

Roughly 2 x 10^6 triggers have been recorded using the spectrometer, and analysis is in a preliminary stage. A simple and definitive topology to examine for charm production is the process:

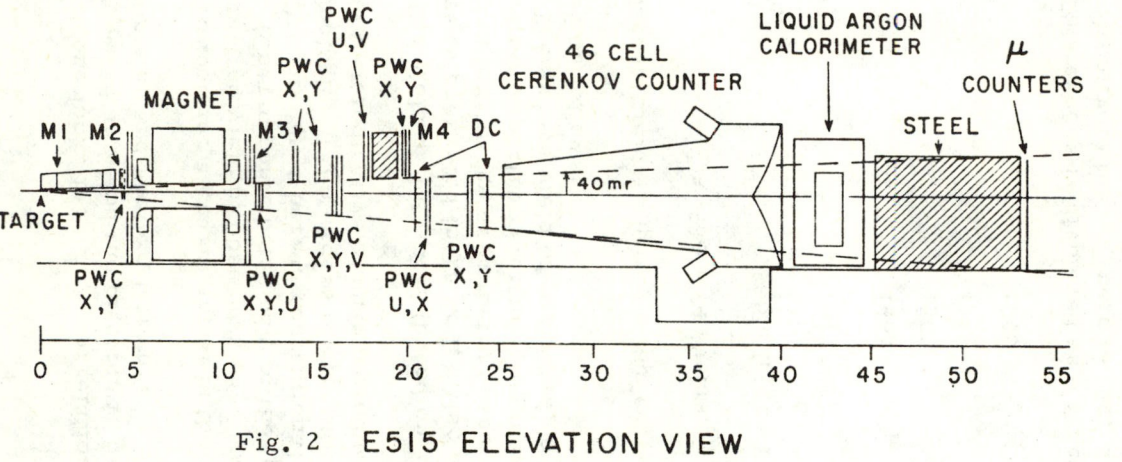

Fig. 2   E515 ELEVATION VIEW

$$\pi^- + N \rightarrow C_1 + \overline{C}_2 + x$$

$$\quad \Big\downarrow \quad \Big\downarrow_{\rightarrow e^-, \mu^-}$$

$$\quad \Big\downarrow_{\rightarrow \mu^+, e^+}$$

in which one looks for $\mu^{\pm}e^{\mp}$ correlations. The muon is detected in the upward arm and the electron is detected in the forward-arm spectrometer and shower detector.

To look for a charm signal in the μe event sample, one compares the yield of observed $\mu^{\pm}e^{\mp}$ pairs to the yield of $\mu^{\pm}e^{\pm}$ pairs. (Charm contributes only to the $\mu^{\pm}e^{\mp}$ yield in the absence of $D^o\overline{D}^o$ mixing, whereas conventional backgrounds contribute to both topologies.) An excess of opposite-sign pairs over like-sign pairs is then indicative of charm production.

The yield of μe pairs (based on a raw data sample of $\sim 450\,K$ triggers is presented in Table I. Also shown are the μe yields corrected for charge asymmetry observed in the events due in part to beam/spectrometer misalignment and detection inefficiencies. The excess yield of corrected, opposite-sign pairs is obtained as follows:

$$\text{Excess Yield} = N(\mu^+e^-) + N(\mu^-e^+) - N(\mu^+e^+) - N(\mu^-e^-)$$

$$= 534 \pm 74 \text{ events.}$$

Table I: μe Yields

Topology	Yield (raw)	Yield (corrected)
μ^+e^-	1483	1498
μ^-e^+	1303	1511
μ^+e^+	1251	1251
μ^-e^-	1045	1224

This excess is displayed as a function of the momentum of the electron from the μe pair in Fig. 3. The lack of events below 5 GeV/c is due to the acceptance cutoff of the shower detector.

For electron momenta below 10 GeV/c the Čerenkov counter

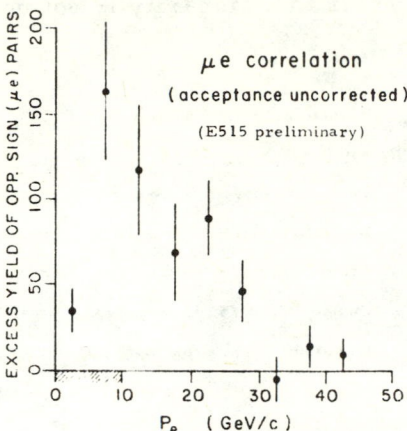

Fig. 3 Excess yields of $\mu^\pm e^\mp$ pairs as a function of the momentum of the electron of the μe pair. Acceptance for electrons deteriorates below 5 GeV/c. Cross hatched region indicates momentum range where Cerenkov constraints applies. (See text)

was used as an additional constraint in the electron identification. Since the Čerenkov radiator was N_2 gas at atmospheric pressure, π/e separation could be performed unambiguously below ~ 6 GeV/c and on a statistical basis up to 10 GeV/c. This analysis indicated that 50% of electrons identified in the shower detector were due to hadron "feedthrough." Since the energy resolution of the shower detector improves as the electron energy increases, the 50% "feedthrough" factor should be considered as an upperbound over the extended momentum range of 0-40 GeV/c. Thus the yield of opposite sign μe pairs is:

$$267 \pm 52 \text{ events} \leq \text{excess yield} < 534 \pm 74 \text{ events}$$

which translates into a production cross section of

$$16 \ \mu b \leq \sigma_{c\bar{c}} < 32 \ \mu b/\text{nucleon.}$$

Although a detailed model calculation has not yet been performed, the μe data are strongly suggestive of central production for charm.

A summary of the results on hadronic charm production presented at Erice is shown in Table II. The fixed target experiments ($\sqrt{s} \simeq 20$) tend to observe small charm cross sections in marked contrast to the large cross sections observed at ISR ($\sqrt{s} \simeq 60$). The reason for this disparity is not understood.

Table II

Hadronic Charm Production

Experiment	Experiment Type/Beam/Energy	Results
CHARM[8]	Dump / prompt ν	$\sigma_{D\bar{D}} = 18 \pm 6 \, \mu b$
BEBC[8]	Dump / prompt ν	$\sigma_{D\bar{D}} = 17 \pm 4 \, \mu b$
CDHS[8]	Dump / prompt ν	$\sigma_{D\bar{D}} \sim 10 \, \mu b$
E613[9]	Dump/400 GeV/c p/prompt ν	$\sigma = 16.1 \pm 3.9 \pm 3.2 \, \mu b$
E595[10]	Dump/350 GeV/c p/prompt μ, $\mu\mu$	$\sigma = 16 \, \mu b$ linear A $(1-x)^3$
NA-11[11]	electron trigger/200 GeV/c π^- or p	$\sigma_{c\bar{c}} = 5 - 6.5 \, \mu b$ $(1-x)^3$ $\sigma_{\Lambda_c} = 75 \pm 50 \, \mu b$
NA16[12]	LEBC/EHS/360 GeV/c π^- or p	$\sigma(D^{\pm}) = 11 \pm 5 \, \mu b$ $x_F > 0$ $(1-x)^{3.2}$
E515	prompt μ trigger/200 GeV/c π^-	$\sigma_{c\bar{c}} \simeq 16 - 32 \, \mu b$ central production indicated
ISR[13] (en masse)	pp / $\sqrt{s} \simeq 60$	$10 - 30 \, \mu b \le \sigma \le 1 \, mb$

III. Recent e^+e^- results

Here I will make only the briefest of comments. First concerning charm, I found the recent DELCO (SPEAR) result [14] for the relative branching ratios of $D^0 \to e$, $D^{\pm} \to e$ to be most interesting. The preferred values of electronic branching ratio are $Br(D^0 \to e) < 4\%$ and $Br(D^{\pm} \to e) \simeq 22\%$. This result bears directly on the lifetimes of the charged and neutral D mesons, and suggests that $\tau_{D^0} < \tau_{D^{\pm}}$.

The Crystal Ball group at SPEAR reported the observation of η_c, η_c' mesons through the decays: $\Psi' \to \eta_c \gamma$ and $\Psi' \to \eta_c' \gamma$. Mass values for the pseudoscalars are $m_\eta = 2984 \pm 2 \pm 4$, $m_\eta' = 3592 \pm 5 \, MeV/c^2$.

Recent results from CESR on B decays now place the mass of the lowest lying B-meson in the range $5.17 \le M_B \le 5.28 \, GeV/c^2$, the range based on the Υ'', Υ''' mass values. Another very important result is the observed difference in mean charge-particle multiplicity in semileptonic B decay versus B decay into hadrons:

$$< n_c > = 6.3 \qquad B \rightarrow \text{hadrons}$$

$$< n_c > = 3.5 \qquad B \text{ semileptonic decay.}$$

The measured semi-muonic branching ratio for B decay is

$$\frac{(B \rightarrow \mu + x)}{(B \rightarrow \text{all})} = 8\% \pm 2.7\% \pm 2\%.$$

Finally a recent result from JADE (DESY) places an upper limit on the B lifetime of: $\tau_B < 5 \times 10^{-12}$ sec.

IV. Lifetime measurements

Lifetime measurements for charm states have been studied using several different beams and vertex detection techniques. Among the experiments reported, the most notable were:
1) E531[15] - uses a ν beam, emulsion target, and forward magnetic spectrometer
2) WA58[16] - uses a γ beam, emulsion target, and omega spectrometer
3) NA16 - uses π^-/p beams (360 GeV/c), LEBC and the European Hybrid Spectrometer
4) FRAMM[17] - uses a γ beam, multilayered silicon wafer target, and forward spectrometer
5) SLAC/HBC[18] - uses backscattered laser beam, rapid-cycling bubble chamber and forward spectrometer.

The newest results are from FRAMM and SLAC/HBC groups; the E531 results have been available in the literature for some time. The lifetime measurements are summarized in Table III[19]. With the exception of the SLAC/HBC result, $\tau_{D^{\pm}} > \tau_{D^0}$ seems to be the general trend.

Table III
Charm Particle Lifetimes
(multiply all listed values x 10^{-13} sec)

Particle type	E531	WA58	LEBC	FRAMM	SLAC/HBC
$D^0, \bar{D}^0$	$3.2^{+1.1}_{-0.7}$ (18)[+]	$1.34^{+.56}_{-.34}$ (8)	$3.2^{+2.2}_{-1.0}$ (6)		$9.4^{+13}_{-3.4}$ (20)
$D^\pm$	$10.3^{+10}_{-4.2}$ (6)	$6^{+6}_{-2.5}$ (2)	$8.0^{+4.9}_{-2.4}$ (7)	$8.2^{+2.9}_{-1.7}$ (78)[*]	$6.1^{+4.0}_{-2.0}$
$F^\pm$	$2.0^{+1.8}_{-0.8}$ (3)	$3.8^{+4}_{-2.1}$ (2)			
Λ_c^+	$2.3^{+1.1}_{-0.7}$ (8)	$2.5^{+2}_{-1.1}$			

[+] Numbers encircled indicate the number of observed decays.

[*] The FRAMM data are uncorrected for a 20% admixture of D^0 decays. If one performs this correction, one obtains $\tau_{D^\pm} = 9.5 \times 10^{-13}$ sec.

V. Theory of heavy particle production and decay

At Erice the theory of heavy particle production was discussed at length by Professors Brodsky and Odorico. Since they presented similar papers at this conference, I refer the interested reader to their articles elsewhere in these proceedings. A review of recent theoretical study by the Rome group on heavy particle decay was presented by Altarelli. Starting from the most simplistic assumption that charm particle decay is identical to free charm quark decay - in which the semileptonic decay branching ratios for D^0 and $D^\pm$ are equal, he then applied further corrections due to QCD (color corrected/disconnected diagrams), spectator quark effects (exchange diagrams), mass effects (finite mass for the strange quark), and annihilation diagrams. Table IV indicates the impact of successive theoretical assumptions on the semi-leptonic branching ratios in the Altarelli analysis.

Table IV
Semi-leptonic branching ratios for charm mesons under different theoretical assumptions

Assumptions	$B_{SL}(D^0)$	$B_{SL}(D^\pm)$
(1) Free Quark Decay	20%	20%
(2) QCD effects + (1)	8 – 13%	8 – 13%
(3) Spectator Quarks + (1, 2)	8 – 13%	11 – 16%
(4) Mass Effects + (1, 2, 3)	10 – 15%	13 – 18%
(5) Annihilation + (1, 2, 3, 4)	4 – 5%	12 – 17%

The end result (5) yields a theoretical ratio:

$$B_{SL}(D^{\pm}) \Big/ B_{SL}(D^o) \simeq 3 - 4.$$

This result is consistent with the DELCO measurement indicated in section III and with the lifetime measurements indicated in section IV above. Further refinements in the understanding of charm decay await high statistics lifetime measurements. Important ingredients are a refined lifetime ratio for $D^{\pm}/D^o$ and substantive observation of Λ_c^+ and $F^{\pm}$ decays.

VI. Vertex detectors - visual and electronic

A. Visual Techniques:

Presently, the most successful visual detectors for observing charm particle decay have been emulsions and small bubble chambers. Emulsions provide superb spatial accuracy at the expense of low event rate capability. Small bubble chambers have lower quality spatial resolution but allow one to record substantially more events. Neither of the devices is triggerable and hence the experiment runs using an interaction trigger. Improvements can be expected in bubble chamber resolution with the implementation of holographic techniques.

A less well known detection technique is the scintillation camera[20], which records photographically the scintillation light produced in a NaI crystal which is used as the experimental target. Light produced in the scintillator is imaged through a lens system onto a multi-stage intensifier (see Fig. 4). An intermediate stage is

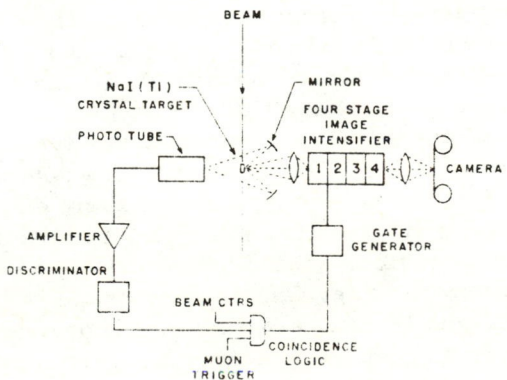

Fig. 4   SCINTILLATION CAMERA SCHEMATIC

quiescently off until receipt of an appropriate trigger pulse gates it on. The stored image is then transferred to film. Sample photographs of this technique are shown in Fig. 5. The target is fast and triggerable, the dot size is small and the spatial resolution is good ($\gtrsim 5\ \mu$). Two drawbacks of this device are: very small depth of field, and substantial radiation length.

A comparison of visual detection techniques is presented in Table V.

Table V

Visual Vertex Detectors

Technique	Track Element Size	Density of Hits	Track Length in View	Lifetime Sensitivity	Remarks
Emulsion	0.5 - 1 μ	20-30/100 μ	100-300 μ	$\geq 10^{-14}$	low rate
BC	20 - 45 μ	60-150/cm	few cm	$\geq 10^{-13}$	
BC + holography	10 μ	200 / cm	few cm	$\geq 0.5 \times 10^{-13}$	
Scintillation Camera (NaI)	30 - 40 μ	3 - 8/mm	few cm	$\geq 10^{-3}$	high rate triggerable

B. Electronic Techniques

Electronic detectors for vertex localization involve two basic types: layered silicon wafer detectors, and silicon strip detectors with numerous fine strip electrodes appended to the surface.

1) Layered wafer structures: this technique has already been used successfully by the FRAMM[17] group in a charm photoproduction experiment at SPS. The detectors are typically $\sim 300\ \mu$ thick and separated from each other by $\sim 50\ \mu$. One detects charm decays by looking for a charge change of two units in successive layers indicating a particle decay. This method works beautifully in photon interactions where charged particle multiplicity is low.

2) Strip Detectors[21] are currently under test in the NA11 experiment at CERN. These devices are operable with $10\ \mu$ - $40\ \mu$ pitch (the spacing between strip electrodes) and have reasonable lifetime in high intensity beams. These multielectrode devices should prove especially useful for high resolution tracking. One obvious usage is in linking outgoing charged tracks back into visual vertex detectors such as emulsions where scanning for vertices is tedious.

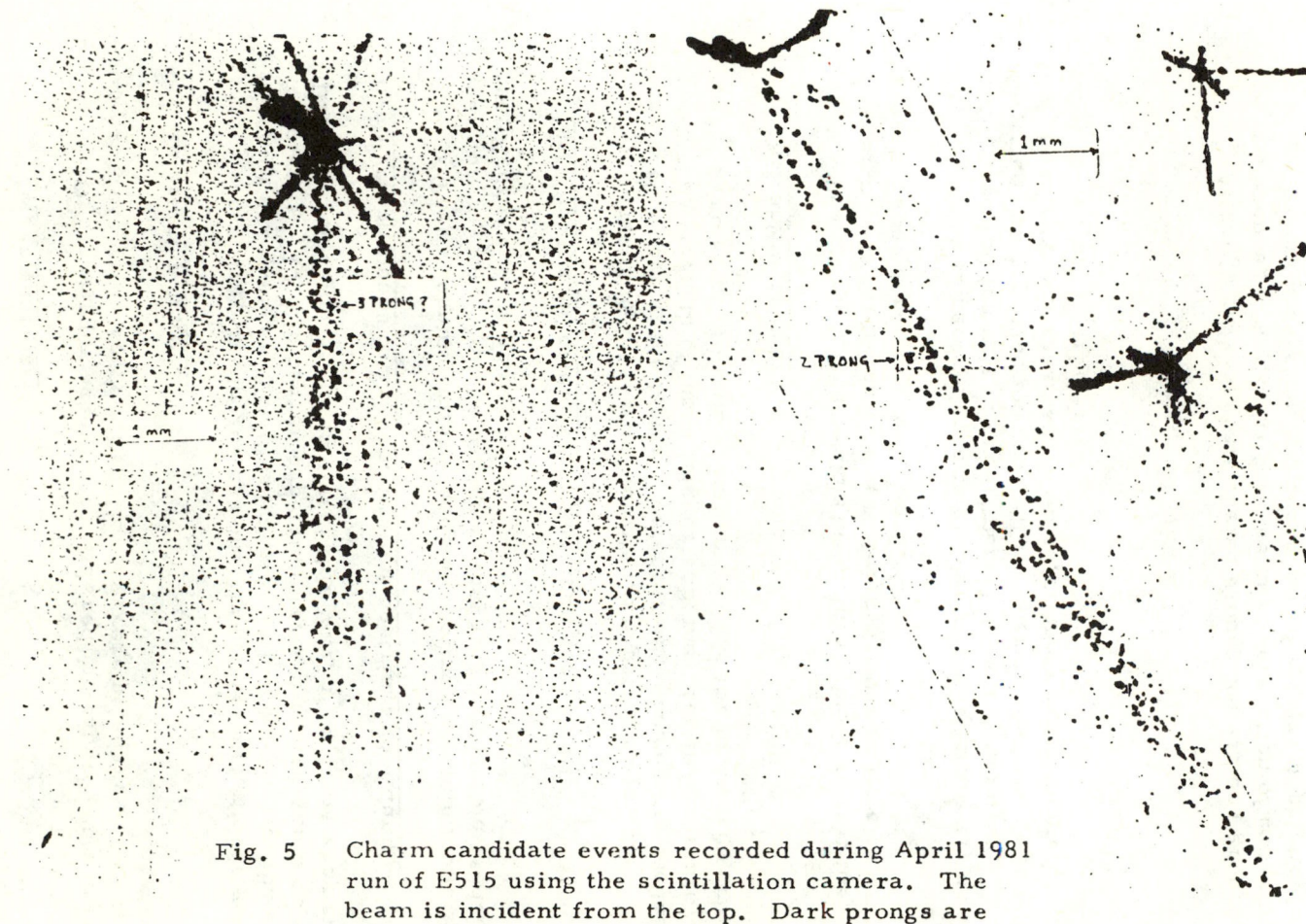

Fig. 5   Charm candidate events recorded during April 1981
run of E515 using the scintillation camera. The
beam is incident from the top. Dark prongs are
nuclear breakup. Sight in the plane of the paper to
see topology better. (This fourth generation reproduction of the originals does not do justice to the
data film.)

VII. Trigger schemes

Of the trigger schemes considered for experiments currently in progress or proposed, the following were popular:

A. Interaction trigger:

This trigger imposes essentially no bias and affords good detector acceptance. The disadvantage is that for charm, the signal to noise is $\sim 10^{-3}$ in hadron experiments, and beauty would be difficult if not impossible to detect this way, if $\sigma_{B\bar{B}}$ is very small.

B. Prompt muons in a dump, prompt neutrinos in a dump:

These schemes afford large acceptance and minimum trigger bias for $x_F > 0$. A disadvantage is that it is impossible to identify the parent particle or particles.

C. Prompt muons or electrons and open geometry:

Triggering biases are inevitable depending upon the kinematic range of the lepton. Detector acceptances are modest to good. The strength of these trigger schemes lies in the improved signal to noise in hadronic reactions ($\sim 10^{-1}$ for muon triggering).

D. Diffractive triggers:

The strength (and weakness) of this scheme is that the trigger bias is forced on events to select forward particles. Detector acceptance is usually good.

Which trigger scheme to employ depends intimately on the beam used and the type of experimental detection exployed. Neutrino, photoproduction and LEBC experiments have usually used the A trigger whereas hadron beam/counter experiments have used B, C, or D triggers.

SUMMARY

Although physics goals varied among the various groups at the conference, it was clear that the next generation of experiments to study beauty production and decay would require sophisticated spectrometry and precision vertex detection capable of detecting lifetimes in the range $10^{-14} \leq \tau \leq 10^{-13}$ sec.

REFERENCES

1. Definitive references on the reported results may be found in the conference proceedings: Europhysics Study Conference, The Search for Charm, Beauty and Truth at High Energies, Erice, Sicily, Italy, 15-22 November 1981, G. Bellini, ed., to be published by PLENUM.

2. E-400 is the Columbia-Illinois-Fermilab Collaboration at Fermilab. Results were reviewed by J. Appel in Reference 1. The author wishes to thank J. Butler for further discussion of the experimental results.

3. E-516 is the Tagged-Photon Spectrometer Collaboration at Fermilab.

4. WA4 is the BCEGLMOPPRS Collaboration at CERN. Specific references may be found under D. Aston et al., Phys. Lett. 94B, 113 (1980) and D. Aston et al., Phys. Lett. 100B, 9 (1981).

5. BFP is the Berkeley-Fermilab-Princeton Collaboration at Fermilab. See A.R. Clark et al., Phys. Rev. Lett. 45, 698 (1980).

6. EMC is the European Muon Collaboration. See for example W. Bacino et al., Phys. Rev. Lett. 45, 329 (1980). Further results were presented by V. Korbel under Reference 1.

7. E515 is the Northwestern-Carnegie Mellon-Notre Dame-Fermilab-Rutgers Collaboration. Results were presented by R. Ruchti under Reference 1.

8. For CHARM, BEBC, and CDHS results, see D. Treille's review under Reference 1, or S. Olsen's review in these proceedings.

9. E-613 - Fermilab-Michigan-Ohio State-Washington-Wisconsin Collaboration at Fermilab. Results were presented by B. Roe under Reference 1.

10. E-595 - CCFRS Collaboration at Fermilab. See S. Olsen's review in these proceedings, or R. Coleman's paper under Reference 1.

11. NA11 is the ABCCMR Collaboration which uses an electron trigger. See D. Treille's review under Reference 1.

12. NA16 is the LEBC/European Hybrid Spectrometer Collaboration. See M. Aguilar-Benitez et al., CERN/EP 81-131 (1981).

13. ISR cross sections vary widely depending upon experimental group and model assumptions. The smallest cross section values were reported by the CSZ group, A. Chilingarov et al. Phys. Lett. 83B, 136 (1979). Larger cross section values were reported recently by M. Basile et al., CERN/EP 81-73,

M. Basile et al., CERN/EP 81-75, and M. D'Ali's paper presented under Reference 1.

14. W. Bacino et al., Phys. Rev. Lett. 45, 329 (1980).
15. N. Ushida et al., Phys. Rev. Lett. 45, 1049 (1980), N. Ushida et al., Phys. Rev. Lett. 45, 1053 (1980) and N. Reay's paper under Reference 1.
16. WA58 is the BCFGMPSV Collaboration at CERN.
17. FRAMM - Implementation of Si wafer target into the NA1 detector at CERN. See paper presented by G. Bellini under Reference 1.
18. SLAC/HBC - See paper by I. Kitagaki under Reference 1.
19. Table III was derived from the review talk of G. Diambrini-Palazzi under Reference 1.
20. See D. Potter's paper under Reference 1.
21. See H. Hejne's review under Reference 1.

HEAVY QUARKS IN HADRONIC COLLISIONS[*]

Stanley J. Brodsky
Institute for Advanced Study
Princeton, New Jersey 08540

and

Stanford Linear Accelerator Center
Stanford University, Stanford, California 94305

and

Carsten Peterson[†]
Stanford Linear Accelerator Center
Stanford University, Stanford, California 94305

ABSTRACT

It is suggested that the presence of $c\bar{c}$-pairs on the 1-2% level in the hadron Fock state decomposition (intrinsic charm) gives a natural description of the ISR data for charm hadron production. The theoretical foundations of the intrinsic charm hypothesis together with its consequences for lepton- and hadron-induced reactions are discussed in some detail. There is no contradiction with the EMC data on F_2^c provided the appropriate threshold dependence is taken into account.

1. INTRODUCTION

Charmed hadron production as observed at the ISR has several remarkable features:

(1) The total cross section for open charm production in pp-collisions at $\sqrt{s}$ = 63 GeV is at the 1 mb level.[1]

(2) Charmed hadrons are abundantly produced in the forward region of phase space. The pp $\rightarrow \Lambda_c X$ distribution is roughly flat in x_L;[2]

---

[*] Work supported in part by the Department of Energy contract DE-AC03-76SF00515 and by the Swedish Natural Science Research Council under contract F-PD8207-101.

[†] On leave of absence from NORDITA, Copenhagen, Denmark.

(Presented also at the Europhysics Study Conference: Search for Charm, Beauty and Truth at High Energies, Erice, Italy, Nov. 15-22, 1981)

$$\frac{d\sigma}{dx_L} (pp \to \Lambda_c X) \sim (1 - x_L)^{0.4} \tag{1}$$

Also D^0 and D^+ (which carry no valence quarks in common with the proton) are produced with a flat rapidity distribution; the $pp \to D^0 X$ x_L-distribution[3] is consistent with $\sim (1 - x_L)^3$. The corresponding strange hadron cross section[4] $d\sigma/dx_L$ ($pp \to K^- X$) falls much steeper, $(1 - x_L)^{6 \pm 1}$.

(3) The Λ_c can be produced with a diffractive trigger, $pp \to p\Lambda_c X$ with a cross section of the order of 240 ± 120 µb.[5]

In contrast, standard models for charm production based on hard scattering, gluon fusion,[6] predicts smaller cross sections and much more steeply falling longitudinal momentum distributions than observed (the final charm distribution are steeper than the incoming gluons by a factor $(1 - x)$ in perturbative calculations). The gluon fusion model is, however, successful in explaining hidden heavy flavor production, $pp \to XX \to \psi\gamma X$, etc.[7,8]

There is, however, another mechanism for heavy quark production, which occurs naturally in QCD. The proton wavefunction at equal time* can be decomposed in terms of Fock state components

$$|uud\rangle, \ |uudg\rangle, \ |uudq\bar{q}\rangle, \ \dots \tag{2}$$

including a small contribution for $|uudc\bar{c}\rangle$. The Fock states containing heavy flavors first appear in perturbative theory via vacuum polarization insertions in the gluons exchanged between valence quarks. We will refer to these preexisting Fock components as intrinsic charm states,[9] since they are present in the hadron without regard to external reactions. Since all the intrinsic quarks of a bound state tend to have the same velocity, the charm quarks carry most of the hadron momentum in the Fock state where they are present; i.e., the intrinsic charm quark x-distribution can be as hard as those of the standard valence quarks. A Bag model calculation of the cc-probability in fact gives $P(|uudc\bar{c}\rangle) \approx 1\%$. Thus, qualitatively the intrinsic charm mechanism can yield cross sections of correct shape and the magnitude observed at the ISR (2% of $\sigma_{tot}(pp)$). Furthermore, it is natural with such states to have large cross sections for the diffractive excitation of preexisting hadron components of the proton (at high energies where kinematic and t_{min} effects are negligible).

There are several reasons why it is important to understand charm production in detail:

(1) If $d\sigma \sim 1/M_Q^2$ (as suggested by the perturbative QCD-vacuum polarization for intrinsic charm), then one expects an appreciable production of b-quarks at the ISR and a non-negligible production of t-quarks at the SPS and Tevatron colliders. The use of a diffractive trigger and the possibility of production at large x will reduce the combinatorial background in the search for t-quark hadrons.

---

*In practice the decomposition is made at equal $\tau = t + z$ on the light cone in $A_0 + A_3 = 0$ gauge.

(2) In general, heavy quark production will be useful as a probe of hadron dynamics: in particular, for understanding the basic mechanisms for large x hadron production. The distinctive role of the intrinsic (preexisting) and extrinsic (created by the collision) mechanisms highlights two complementary aspects of QCD. Each contribution has its distinguishing nuclear A-dependence ($A^{2/3}$ versus A), s-dependence and x_L-dependence.

(3) In the case of the intrinsic charm component there are fundamental questions regarding the importance of non-perturbative confining forces on the heavy quark distributions.[10] From the point of view of perturbative theory or operator product expansion, the leading $1/M_c^2$-contribution can be calculated using free quark propagation with up to four interactions in the heavy quark loop.

(4) Because of the heavy mass one expects strong kinematical scale breaking effects in the measured charm distribution.

(5) The presence of intrinsic charm at large x in the nucleon with strong threshold dependence has serious implications for the scale breaking parameterization of perturbative QCD, since the onset of charm masks the effects of QCD-evolution in deep inelastic structure functions.[11]

(6) For the unexpectedly high rate of observed same sign dimuons in ν-reactions[12] the 1% intrinsic charm contributes in the right direction but probably not in sufficient magnitude.

This talk is organized as follows: We first (Sec. 2) review the theoretical expectations for heavy quark production starting with estimates for "soft" production mechanisms and then elaborating more on what is expected from perturbative QCD with regard to open heavy flavor production. Comparisons with experimental data on $c\bar{c}$ are found in Sec. 3. In Sec. 4 a general discussion of higher Fock state decomposition of hadronic states is given and in Sec. 5 we argue for the existence of $|uudc\bar{c}\rangle$ of the 1% level and construct a model for the c(x) distributions. Hadronic production of charm is discussed in Sec. 6. In Sec. 7 our model for c(x) is confronted with data from leptoproduction experiments.

2. "CONVENTIONAL" THEORETICAL EXPECTATIONS FOR HEAVY QUARK PRODUCTION

The production of heavy quarks in hadronic collisions from soft mechanisms is normally expected to be very suppressed. As an example, when considering hadronic production of particles as a tunneling phenomena one finds the probability to produce a qq-pair[13]

$$P(q\bar{q}) \sim \exp\left(-\frac{\pi}{\kappa} m_\perp^2\right) \qquad (3)$$

where $m_\perp = \sqrt{p_\perp^2 + m_q^2}$ and κ is the string constant ≈ 0.2 GeV^2. Using $m_u = m_d \approx 0$ MeV, $m_s = 100$ MeV, $m_c = 1500$ MeV and $\langle p_\perp \rangle = 350$ MeV one gets from Eq. (3)

82

$$u:d:s:c = 1:1:\frac{1}{3}:10^{-10} \tag{4}$$

The reason for the strong suppression of c-quark production is that it is very difficult to localize the energy of a substantial part of a string. Also, in other pictures one obtains a strong suppression. For example, in the statistical model[13] approach the probability for D-meson production is given by

$$P \sim \exp(-2m_D/160 \text{ MeV}) \tag{5}$$

which gives the ratio $\pi:K:D = 1:0.13:3.10^{-5}$.

However, since large masses are involved one expects calculations based on perturbative QCD to be valid. Perturbative QCD gives contributions of order $1/M^2$ in contrast to the $\exp(-\beta M^2)$-behavior for the soft tunneling processes discussed above.

Hadronic production of hidden heavy quark pairs, e.g., ψ, are well described by the hard scattering processes (see Refs 7,8). In the case of open $Q\bar{Q}$ production the following hard scattering processes contribute[6] (see Fig. 1a,b)

$$q\bar{q} \rightarrow Q\bar{Q} \tag{6a}$$

$$gg \rightarrow Q\bar{Q} \tag{6b}$$

together with the flavor excitation processes[14] (Fig. 1c)

$$qQ(\bar{Q}) \rightarrow qQ(\bar{Q}) \tag{7}$$

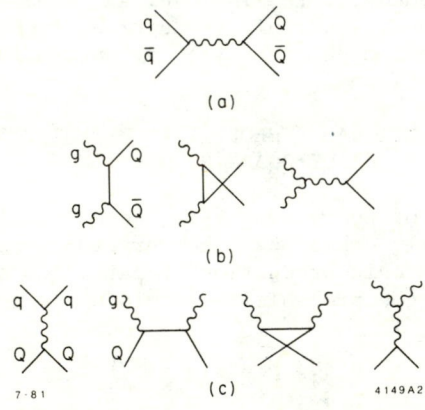

(a)

(b)

(c)

Fig. 1. Lowest order QCD subprocesses for hadron + hadron → $Q\bar{Q}$ + X.

Predictions from the latter ones depend in detail on the understanding of the charm quark distribution in the proton.

The gluon amalgamation process (6b) is expected to be dominant at very high energies due to the abundance of low-x gluons. The cross section is given by convolution of distribution functions and the sub-process cross section ($\hat{\sigma}$)

$$\sigma(h + h \rightarrow Q\bar{Q}X) = \iint_{x_1 x_2 \, > \, s_{min}/s} dx_1 dx_2 \, G(x_1) \, G(x_2) \, \hat{\sigma}(x_1, \, x_2, s)$$

There are several theoretical uncertainties entering Eq. (8).

i) The lower limit of Eq. (8). The true kinematical threshold $\sqrt{s_{min}}$ is $2m_D$ but $2m_c$ is presumably more relevant since the charmed hadrons are formed in a fragmentation/recombination process, thereby gaining energy.

ii) The value of m_c. Most authors use m_c = 1.6 GeV. A lower value like m_c = 1.2 GeV, as obtained from potential calculations, would increase the cross section by a factor 4.

iii) Higher order graphs are not yet included.

iv) Higher twist contributions. These are unknown and could be important at such small masses as m_c = 1.6 GeV.

v) Initial state corrections could alter the result by a large factor.[15]

The cross section for $c\bar{c}$ and $b\bar{b}$-production in the FNAL/SPS-ISR energy range from Eq. (8) is given by (see Fig. 2)

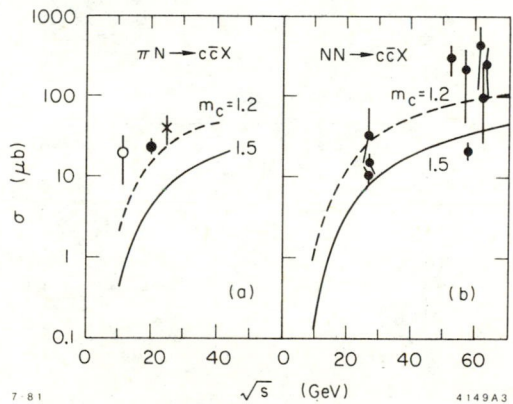

Fig. 2. (a) $\sigma(\pi N \rightarrow c\bar{c}X)$ as a function of c.m.s. energy, from Ref. 16.
(b) $\sigma(NN \rightarrow c\bar{c}X)$ as a function of c.m.s. energy, from Ref. 16.

84

$$\sigma(c\bar{c}) = 1\text{--}50 \ \mu b$$

$$\sigma(b\bar{b}) = 0.1\text{--}100 \ nb \tag{9}$$

The energy dependence is logarithmic which is due to the 1/x-behavior of the gluon distributions. The single particle spectrum for the observed charmed hadrons is expected to be soft, reflecting the incoming gluon distribution.

3. COMPARISON WITH EXPERIMENTAL RESULTS ON OPEN CHARM PRODUCTION

The experimental results on charm production are reviewed in detail in Ref. 1. Here we only briefly mention the most important results. They are:

i) At ISR one observes a large cross section (0.1-0.5 mb) for the reaction $pp \to \Lambda_c^+ X$ (see Fig. 2b). The cross sections for the other channels $pp \to D^+ X$, $pp \to D^o X$ are in similar range.

ii) Moreover, the Λ_c^+ seems to be produced diffractively in the forward region of phase space (see Fig. 3a,b). At least one of the experiments has an explicit diffractive trigger.[5] The x_L-distributions of $pp \to D^o X$ is $\sim (1-x)^3$ much more forward than the corresponding strange meson distributions for $pp \to K^- X$ indicating that the charm quark carry a significant fraction of the proton momentum.

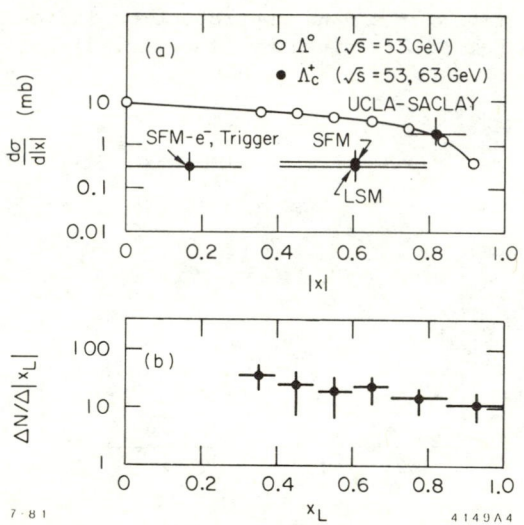

Fig. 3. (a) $d\sigma/d|x|$ for Λ_c^+ at 53 and 63 GeV.[1] The smooth curve is a fit to the Λ^o data points. (b) Unnormalized x_L-distribution for Λ_c^+ from Ref. 2.

iii) The situation for SPS/FNAL experiments is not so clear. One experiment with a diffractive trigger,[17] $\pi^- p \to D\bar{D}X$, observes a forwardly oriented single particle spectrum.

iv) A signal for forwardly produced Λ_b at ISR has also been reported.[18]

The important discrepancy with the hard scattering approach is the x_L-spectrum of Λ_c^+ (see Fig. 3); on general grounds one would expect the Λ_c^+ wave function to favor configurations where the c-quarks have the most momentum (see Fig. 4). On the other hand, the c-quarks produced in a hard scattering process have small x. Hence such c-quarks would most unlikely end up in a fast Λ_c^+. The way to produce fast Λ_c^+ is to have hard c(c̄)-quarks initially present in the proton, i.e., $|uudc\bar{c}\rangle$ states.[9] In fact, the similarity between $pp \to D^0(c\bar{u})X$ and $pp \to K^+(u\bar{s})X$ momentum distributions suggests that the c- and u-quark distributions are quite similar. We will discuss this intrinsic charm hypothesis in some detail below. Before doing so we briefly mention some recent attempts[19,20] to "improve" on the hard scattering approach.

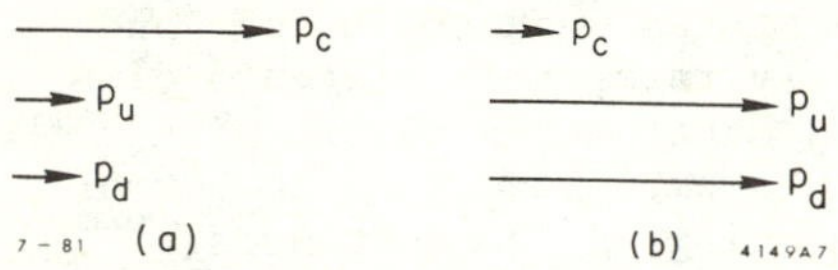

Fig. 4. (a) Typical quark momentum configuration in a Λ_c^+. (b) Typical quark momentum configuration after a hard scattering with a slow c-quark and two fast valence quarks.

i) In Ref. 19 it is hypothesized that a hard c(x)-distribution may arise from a mechanism where the c-quarks gain momentum after the scattering process. We regard such a mechanism as highly unlikely.

ii) In Ref. 20 a diquark process is discussed for producing fast Λ_c^+. This mechanism would, however, not explain the abundant production of fast D^0 (which contain no proton valence quarks). This model can be consistent only if the D^0 are decay products of charmed baryon resonances. The production of $\bar{\Lambda}_c$ at large x_L in pp-collisions would be decisive.

4. HADRONIC FOCK STATE DECOMPOSITIONS

As mentioned in the introduction, the proton has a general decomposition in terms of color singlet eigenstates of the free Hamiltonian. The existence of higher proton Fock states such as $|uudg\rangle$ has support from hadron spectroscopy: The p-Δ mass splitting (ΔE), which is believed to originate from the one gluon exchange graph, is by cutting the diagram in Fig. 5 related to the probability of having extra gluon states, (P($|uudg\rangle$)), through the relation

$$\Delta E = \sum_{\substack{\text{gluon} \\ \text{modes}}} P(|uudg\rangle) (E_{uud} - E_{uudg}) \qquad (10)$$

86

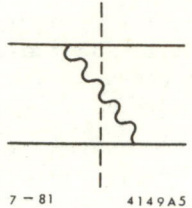

7 – 81   4149A5

Fig. 5. One gluon exchange diagram responsible for spin-spin splitting of masses and the existence of higher Fock states containing an extra gluon.

The presence of higher Fock states is implicitly present in Ref. 21, where it is shown that rigorous constraints from $\pi \to \mu\nu$ and $\pi \to \gamma\gamma$ decays give a probability <0.25 for having a pion in a pure $q\bar{q}$-state at equal time on the light cone with $A_+ = 0$ gauge for a large class of wavefunctions.

In the next section we explore the consequences of heavy quark pairs $Q\bar{Q}$ in the Fock state decomposition of the bound state wavefunction of ordinary mesons and baryons. Although proton states such as $|uudc\bar{c}\rangle$ and $|uudb\bar{b}\rangle$ are surely rare, the existence of hidden charm and other heavy quarks within the proton bound state will lead to a number of striking phenomenological consequences.

It is important to distinguish two types of contributions to the hadron quark and gluon distributions: Extrinsic and intrinsic. Extrinsic quarks and gluons are generated on a short time scale in association with a large transverse momentum reaction; their distributions can be derived from QCD bremsstrahlung and pair production processes and lead to standard QCD evolution. The intrinsic quarks and gluons exist over a time scale independent of any probe momentum, and are associated with the bound state hadron dynamics. In particular, we expect the presence of intrinsic heavy quarks, $c\bar{c}$, $b\bar{b}$, etc., within the proton state by virtue of gluon exchange and vacuum polarization graphs as illustrated in Fig. 6.

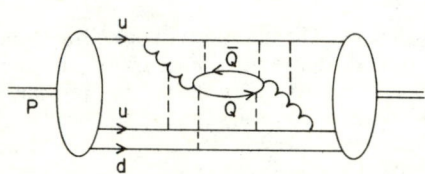

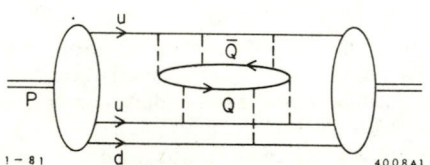

1 – 81   4008A1

Fig 6. Diagrams which give rise to the intrinsic heavy quarks ($Q\bar{Q}$) within the proton. Curly and dashed lines represent transverse and longitudinal-scalar (instantaneous) gluons, respectively.

The "extrinsic" quarks and gluons correspond to the standard bremsstrahlung and $q\bar{q}$ pair production processes of perturbative QCD. These perturbative contributions yield wavefunctions with minimal power-law fall-off

$$|\psi(k_{\perp i}, x_i)|^2 \sim \frac{1}{k_{\perp i}^2} \qquad (11)$$

and lead to the logarithmic evolution of the structure functions. In contrast, the intrinsic contributions to the quark distribution are associated with the bound state dynamics and necessarily have a faster fall-off in $k_{\perp i}$ ($\psi \sim 1/k_\perp^2$ or faster).[22] The intrinsic states thus contribute to the initial

quark and gluon distributions. A simple illustration of extrinsic
and intrinsic $|uudq\bar{q}\rangle$ contributions to the deep inelastic structure
functions is shown in Fig. 7a and b. We see that the existence of
gluon exchange graphs plus vacuum polarization insertions automati-
cally yield an intrinsic $|uudq\bar{q}\rangle$ Fock state.

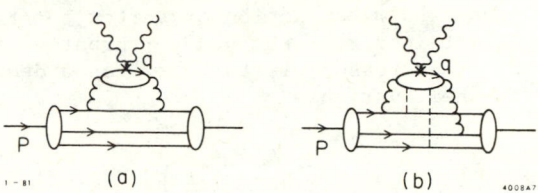

Fig. 7. (a) Example with contribution to
the deep inelastic structure functions
from an _extrinsic_ quark q. (b) Example
with contribution to the deep inelastic
structure functions from an _intrinsic_
quark q.

A complete calculation must take into account the binding of the
gluon and $q\bar{q}$ constituents inside the hadron (see Fig. 6) so that the
analysis is presumably non-perturbative.

We also note that the normalization of the $|uudq\bar{q}\rangle$ state is not
necessarily tied to the normalization of the $|uudg\rangle$ components since
the latter only refer to transversely polarized gluons; Fig. 7 shows
that $q\bar{q}$-pairs also arise from the longitudinal-scalar (instantaneous)
part of the vector potential.

5. INTRINSIC HEAVY QUARK STATES

The intrinsic heavy quark states exist on a long time scale.
Hence, an estimate of the mixing probability should be possible in
the static bag model. Such a study was done by Donoghue and
Golowich[23] in the rest frame of the proton. Summing over the lowest
states the authors of Ref. 15 obtain the result

$$P(|uudu\bar{u}\rangle):P(|uudd\bar{d}\rangle):P(|uuds\bar{s}\rangle):P(|uudc\bar{c}\rangle)$$

$$= 0.20:0.15:0.09:0:0.01$$

(12)

which, as far as charm is concerned, is in agreement with the order
of magnitude of the charm cross section observed at the ISR. It
should also be remarked that the results of Eq. (12) are still consistent with previous bag calculations for the static quantities like
magnetic moments and average square radii. (For our purposes it would
be desirable to have the calculation of the intrinsic charm content
of the proton performed in the infinite momentum frame.
We now proceed to discuss the c-quark momentum distribution in a
$|uudc\bar{c}\rangle$ state. The general form of a Fock state wavefunction is

$$\psi(k_{\perp i}, x_i) = \frac{\Gamma(k_{\perp i}, x_i)}{M^2 - \sum_{i=1}^{n} \left(\frac{m^2 + k_\perp^2}{x}\right)_i} \qquad (13)$$

where Γ is the truncated wavefunction or vertex function. The actual form of Γ must be obtained from the non-perturbative theory, but following Ref. 21 it is reasonable to take Γ as a decreasing function of the off-energy-shell variable

$$\mathscr{E} = M^2 - \sum_{i=1}^{n} \left(\frac{m^2 + k_\perp^2}{x}\right)_i . \qquad (14)$$

Independent of the form $\Gamma(\mathscr{E})$, we can read off some general features of the quark distributions:

(1) In the limit of zero binding energy ψ becomes singular and the fractional momentum distributions peak at the values $x_i = m_i/M$. More generally, $\mathscr{E}$ is minimal and the longitudinal momentum distributions are maximal when the constituents with the largest transverse mass $m_\perp = \sqrt{m^2 + k_\perp^2}$ have the largest light-cone fraction x_i. This is equivalent to the statement that constituents in a moving bound state tend to have the same rapidity.

(2) If one considers the proton as a state with virtual fluctuations of $\pi^+ n$, $K^+ \Lambda$, $D \Lambda_c$, etc., the most probable configurations are those closest to the energy shell, i.e., $\mathscr{E} \sim 0$. In the case of virtual hidden charm states, the dominant configurations thus have maximal x_c and $x_{\bar{c}}$.

(3) The intrinsic transverse momentum of each quark in a Fock state generally increases with the quark mass. In the case of power law wavefunction $\psi \sim (\mathscr{E})^{-\beta}$ we have $\langle k_\perp^2 \rangle \propto m_Q^2$; for an exponential wavefunction $\psi \sim e^{-\beta \mathscr{E}^{1/2}}$, the dependence is $\langle k_\perp^2 \rangle \propto m_Q$.

In the limit of large $k_\perp$ one can use the operator product expansion near the light cone (or equivalently gluon exchange diagrams) to prove that, modulo logarithms, the Fock state wavefunctions fall off as inverse powers of $k_\perp^2$.[22] For our purpose, which is to illustrate the characteristic shape of the Fock states containing heavy quarks, we will choose a simple power-law form for the Fock state longitudinal momentum distributions

$$P_{(n)}(x_1 \cdots x_n) = N_n \frac{\delta\left(1 - \sum_{i=1}^{n} x_i\right)}{\left(M^2 - \sum_{i=1}^{n} \frac{\hat{m}_i^2}{x_i}\right)^2} \qquad (15)$$

where the $\hat{m}_i^2$ are identified now as effective transverse masses $\hat{m}_i^2 = m_i^2 + \langle k_\perp^2 \rangle_i$ and the $\langle k_\perp^2 \rangle_i$ are average transverse momenta. With this choice, single-quark distributions have power law fall-offs $(1-x)^2$ and $(1-x)^3$ for mesons and baryons, respectively. (This is the most simple model for the hadronic wavefunction.)

For a $|uudc\bar{c}\rangle$ proton Fock state the momentum distribution is given by

$$P(x_1, \ldots, x_5) = N_5 \frac{\delta\left(1 - \sum_{i=1}^{5} x_i\right)}{\left(m_p^2 - \sum_{i=1}^{5} \frac{\hat{m}_i^2}{x_i}\right)^2} \tag{16}$$

In the limit of heavy quarks $\hat{m}_4^2 = \hat{m}_5^2 = \hat{m}_6^2 \gg m_p^2, \hat{m}_i^2$ ($i = 1,2,3$) we get

$$P(x_1, \ldots, x_5) = N_5 \frac{x_4^2 x_5^2}{(x_4 + x_5)^2} \delta\left(1 - \sum_{i=1}^{5} x_i\right) \tag{17}$$

where $N_5 = 3600$, P_5 is determined from $\int dx_1 \ldots dx_5 P(x_1, \ldots, x_5) = P_5$, where P_5 is the $|uudc\bar{c}\rangle$ Fock state probability. Integrating over the light quarks (x_1, x_2 and x_3) we get the charmed quark distributions

$$P(x_4, x_5) = \frac{1}{2} N_5 \frac{x_4^2 x_5^2}{(x_4 + x_5)^2} (1 - x_4 - x_5)^2 \tag{18}$$

By performing one more integration we obtain the charmed quark distribution

$$P(x_5) = \frac{1}{2} N_5 x_5^2 \left[\frac{1}{3} (1 - x_5)\left(1 + 10 x_5 + x_5^2\right) - 2x_5(1 - x_5) \log \frac{1}{x_5}\right] \tag{19}$$

which has average $\langle x_5 \rangle = 2/7$ and is shown in Fig. 8. This is to be contrasted with the corresponding light quark distribution derived from Eq. (17) and shown in Fig. 9

$$P(x_1) = 6(1 - x_1)^2 P_5 \tag{20}$$

A more proper calculation of $c(x)$ can be done by integrating Eq. (16) over 11 variables using, e.g., exponential behavior for Γ. This was done in Ref. 24 using Monte Carlo techniques and the resulting $c(x)$ was found to be somewhat smoother than that of Eq. (19).

90

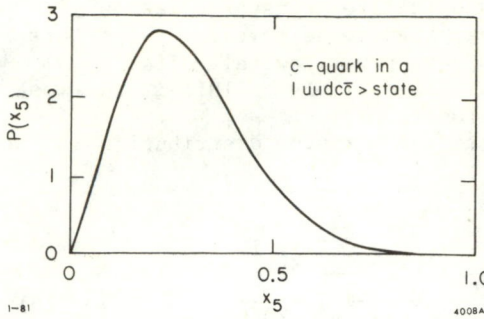

Fig. 8. The x distribution of the charmed quark in a $|uudc\bar{c}\rangle$ state.

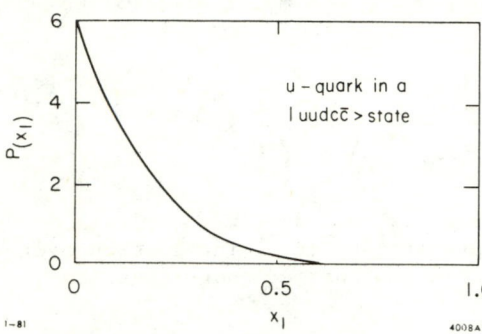

Fig. 9. The x distribution of a light quark in a $|uudcc\rangle$ state.

A more detailed calculation of the perturbative diagrams in Fig. 6 yields an extra power $(1 - x_4 - x_5)$. The controlling factor in the distribution for large x is the energy denominator.

The corresponding c- and u-quark distributions in a $|udc\bar{c}\rangle$ are obtained in the same way. In order to see the contribution of the intrinsic $c\bar{c}$-pairs to the proton structure function, we use the value for $P_5 = 0.01$ from the bag model calculations discussed above. The magnitude of the charm cross section at ISR $(0.1-0.5 \text{ mb})[1]$ gives for P_5:

$$P_5 = \frac{\sigma_{\Lambda_c}}{2\sigma_{inel}} \approx \frac{250 \ \mu b}{2.30 \ mb} = 0.004$$

(21)

If the production mechanism is <u>inelastic</u> and

$$P_5 = \frac{\sigma_{\Lambda_c}}{2\sigma_{diff}} \approx \frac{250 \ \mu b}{2.10 \ mb} = 0.01$$

(22)

if it is <u>diffractive</u>. These two possibilities will be discussed in the next section. We conclude that the charm cross section at ISR is compatible with $P_5 = 0.01$.

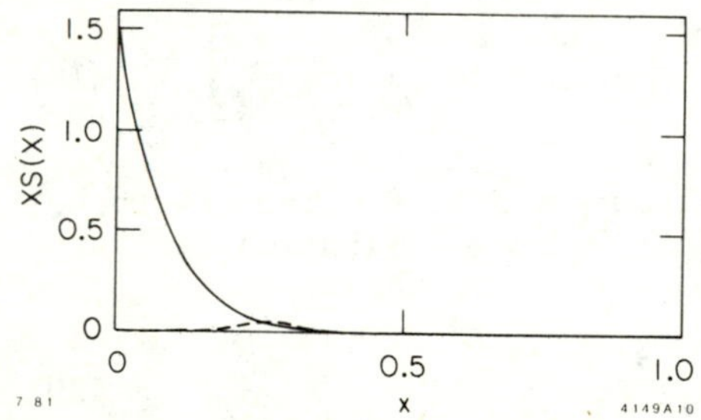

The charmed quark distribution $c(x) = P(x_5)$ should be measurable in lepto-production for high enough Q^2 and $W^2 > W^2_{th} = 25 \text{ GeV}^2$. Hence to measure $c(x)$ at, e.g., $x = 0.5$ requires $Q^2 = 25 \text{ GeV}^2$ ($x = Q^2/(Q^2 + W^2)$). We emphasize that the intrinsic charm sea $c(x)$ is "rare" but not "wee" as is clear from Fig. 10. A discussion on comparing $c(x)$ with lepto-production data is found in Sec. 6. In order to obtain intrinsic u, d and s- distributions ($|uuduu\rangle$ states, etc.) the wavefunction in Eq. 15 needs a minor modification.

Fig. 10. Comparison of the intrinsic charm sea $xc(x)$ (dashed line) with the total sea at $Q^2 = 5 \text{ GeV}^2$ as parameterized by Ref. 25.

6. HADRONIC PRODUCTION OF CHARM

Hadronic production of multiparticle final states occurs in two different ways, diffractive disassociation and nondiffractive inelastic production. Although at least one experiment of Λ_c^+-production has an explicit diffractive trigger,[5] the situation for charm production is far from settled. We will discuss the two production mechanisms below in the light of intrinsic charm.

i) Diffractive production of high M^2-states can be interpreted as a phenomenon of short distance where the ideas for perturbative QCD could be applied. Thus perturbative QCD should be applicable to some extent. This idea was first considered in Ref. 26 in the context of charm production. Recently these questions have been studied in more detail for high mass diffraction in general in terms of so-called "transparent states."[27-30] The idea is simple and appealing: When the valence quarks of a hadron are close together the net color extension is almost zero and the hadron does not interact with other hadrons. Hence the absorptive cross section is small and the hadron scatters diffractively off the target which then appears to be transparent. This situation is, as pointed out by Ref. 28, very similar to an analogous process in QED: When e^+e^--pairs are produced in very high energy emulsion experiments, they can only be separated by distances smaller than atomic sizes. The e^+e^- has net charge zero — it is not "seen" by surrounding atoms and hence it does not ionize and give rise to visible tracks. In Ref. 30 the knowledge of the pion wavefunction in QCD at short distances is used to derive results for the pion-induced jets emerging from the "transparent" target.

As was discussed in connection with Eq. (13) one expects intrinsic heavy quark states to have large $\langle k_\perp \rangle$ and consequently small transverse dimension. It is therefore tempting to assume that the intrinsic heavy quark states scatter diffractively. With this assumption one obtains in the case of 1% intrinsic charm on a nuclear target[30]

$$\sigma_{charm}^{diff} = 0.01 \cdot \sigma_{el} \approx 0.5 \text{ mb} \cdot A^{2/3} \quad . \tag{23}$$

This high value is encouraging as far as production of b- and t-quarks are concerned. A diffractive production mechanism of heavy quarks is also very favorable as far as the combinatorial background is concerned.

For the charm case the Λ_c and D-spectra can be calculated in principle from the strong overlap between the 5-quark and the charmed-hadron state wavefunctions, allowing for decays of excited state, etc. For the purpose of obtaining the x_F-distribution we use a very simple recombination mechanism for the quarks involved in the states. Neglecting its binding energy, the Λ_c spectrum is given by combining the u, d and c-quark in $|uudc\bar{c}\rangle$ to obtain

$$P(x_{\Lambda_c}) = N_5 \int_0^1 \prod_{i=1}^{5} dx_i \delta(x_{\Lambda_c} - x_2 - x_3 - x_5) \left(\frac{x_4 x_5}{x_4 + x_5} \right)^2 \delta\left(1 - \sum_{i=1}^{5} x_i\right)$$

$$\tag{24}$$

92

(see Fig. 11) with $\langle x_{\Lambda_c}\rangle = 1/7 + 1/7 + 2/7 = 4/7$. The ISR data for $d\sigma/dx$ ($pp \to \Lambda_c x$) is consistent with the prediction that $\langle x_{\Lambda_c}\rangle \approx 0.5$ although the data is even flatter than predicted by Eq. (24). We expect that the low x region for charm production will be filled in by both perturbative and higher Fock state intrinsic contributions. Assume that a hadron interacts strongly only when one of its constituents is very peripheral, $k^2 - m^2 \sim 0$. Since $k^2 - m^2 = x\mathscr{E}$ this implies that the important interacting Fock states have one constituent with $x \simeq 0$.[31] Consequently, the spectator system carry more momentum than in Eq. (24). This effect improves our agreement with the data. The corresponding distribution for $D^-(\bar{c}d)$ is given by

$$P(x_{D^-})=N_5 \int_0^1 \prod_{i=1}^5 dx_i \, \delta(x_D - x_3 - x_5) \left(\frac{x_4 x_5}{x_4 + x_5}\right)^2 \delta\left(1 - \sum_{i=1}^5 x_i\right) \qquad (25)$$

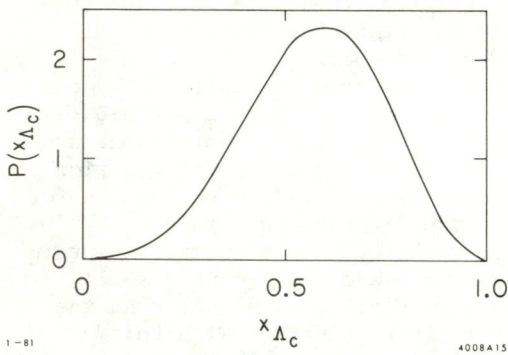

Fig. 11. The x distribution of the Λ_c^+ from the intrinsic charm component of the proton.

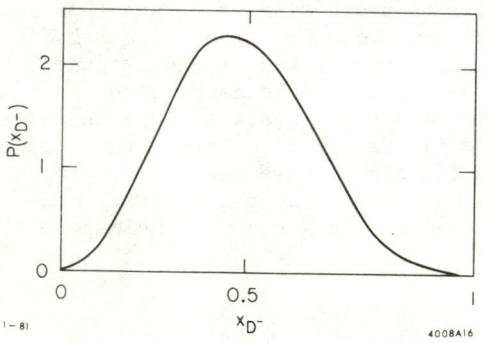

Fig. 12. The x distribution of the D^- from the intrinsic charm component of the proton.

with $\langle x_{D^-}\rangle = 1.7 + 2/7 = 3/7$, and is shown in Fig. 12. The $D^+(c\bar{d})$ distribution would, in principle, be obtained from the $|uudc\bar{c}d\bar{d}\rangle$ Fock state of the proton, where the $d\bar{d}$ could be extrinsic or intrinsic. Assuming that the $\bar{d}$ momentum is small, the D^+ distribution should be close to that of the c-quark shown in Fig. 8. These predictions apply for forward production ($x_F \gtrsim 0.1$), where perturbative contributions and higher Fock state contributions can be neglected. Spectra for pion induced reactions are obtained in the same way.

In addition to charmed mesons and baryons, the J/ψ may also be produced diffractively from the intrinsic charm component of the proton. Compared to the charm production cross section at FNAL energies

$$\sigma(\pi N \to DX) \simeq 20 \ \mu b \quad , \quad (26)$$

J/ψ production data around 200 GeV give[32]

$$\sigma(\pi N \to \psi X) \simeq 100 \ nb$$

Further, the observed x_F-distribution appears to be more strongly peaked near $x \simeq 0$ compared to what would be expected from the intrinsic charm distribution. Evidently most of the ψ production comes from other central production mechanisms such as gluon and $q\bar{q}$ fusion. In order for the intrinsic charm model to be consistent, there must be a large suppression factor for the ψ production from the intrinsic charm compared to the D production

$$\left.\frac{\sigma(\pi N \to \psi X)}{\sigma(\pi N \to DX)}\right|_{\text{intrinsic charm}} \lesssim 5 \times 10^{-5} \quad . \tag{27}$$

As was shown in Ref. 9, such a suppression factor is obtained using the intrinsic charm wavefunction and taking flavor and color suppression into account.

ii) A simple mechanism for _inelastic_ charm _production_ is gluon exitation of preexisting c-quarks (see Fig. 1c). This process is discussed in Ref. 33.

To study the energy dependence of the "diffraction" mechanism with "intrinsic" heavy quarks we will use the empirical formula for high mass diffraction[34]

$$\frac{d\sigma}{dM^2} = \sigma_0 \frac{1}{M^2} \tag{28}$$

valid for $M^2 \gtrsim 2$ GeV^2. The integrated charm cross section is given by

$$\sigma = \sigma_0^c \int_{M_0^2}^{M_1^2} \frac{dM^2}{M^2} = \sigma_0^c \log \frac{(1-x_1)s}{\left(M_{\Lambda_c}+M_D\right)^2} \quad , \tag{29}$$

where in this case M_0^2 is the threshold value for associated production of a pair of hadrons containing charmed quarks. The upper limit M_1^2 is determined from the kinematical relation $M_1^2 = s(1-x_1)$ where x_1 is the lower fractional momentum cut on the recoiling proton. In the ISR $pp \to p_1 \Lambda_c X$ experiment[5] one triggers on events with $x_1 \geq 0.8$. If we assume that essentially all the charm cross section $\sigma_c \sim 300$ µb is due to diffractive production, then we can determine $\sigma_0 = 77$ µb. From this we predict that at SPS and FNAL energies ($s \cong 400$–600 GeV^2), the total $pp \to$ charm cross section should be of the order of 150 µb. Clearly this prediction is larger than present experimental data at SPS/FNAL with both pion and proton beams.[35] The energy dependence thus seems to be stronger than what is implied by Eq. (29).

Concerning production of heavy quarks on nuclear targets one expects an $A^{2/3}$-dependence from the intrinsic charm model. This is in contrast to the perturbative hard scattering cross section, which should be proportional to A.

As far as the production of b- and t-quarks are concerned, one can argue on general grounds that the probability of a hadron to contain an intrinsic heavy quark pair should fall as

$$P_{Q\bar{Q}} \propto \frac{\alpha_s^2(R^{-2})}{R^2 m_Q^2} \tag{30}$$

where R is a hadron size parameter. Assuming $\sigma_c \simeq 300$ b, $m_c = 1.5$ GeV, $m_b = 5$ GeV, and $m_t = 20$ GeV and using Eq. (29), one obtains the cross sections for b- and t-quark production as shown in Table I.

Table I. Cross section for b- and t-production at ISR and Tevatron energies from Eqs. (29) and (30). The numbers in parentheses are the conventional perturbative QCD-predictions.

	ISR ($\sqrt{s}$ = 63 GeV)	Tevatron ($\sqrt{s}$ = 2000 GeV)
b	15 µb (0.5)	70 µb (2)
t (m_t = 20 GeV)	0	3 µb (0.1)

7. THE INTRINSIC CHARM AND LEPTOPRODUCTION EXPERIMENTS

An important test of the intrinsic charm content of the proton is the direct measurement of the charm quark distribution in deep inelastic scattering:

$$F_2^c(x,Q^2) = \frac{4}{9} x \left[c(x,Q^2) + \bar{c}(x,Q^2) \right] \tag{31}$$

As is clear from Fig. 10, the intrinsic charm sea is very small compared to the total sea. However, it should be visible in experiments explicitly looking for leptoproduction of charm. This is the case in dimuon production (Fig. 13a)

$$\mu^{\pm}N \rightarrow \mu^{\pm}\mu^{\pm}X \tag{32}$$

where one of the final state muons originates from charm decay.

There are, however, a number of complications:

a) The model dependence of the charm fragmentation function and the associated experimental acceptance corrections.[36]

b) A strong scale-breaking effect associated with a high mass threshold:

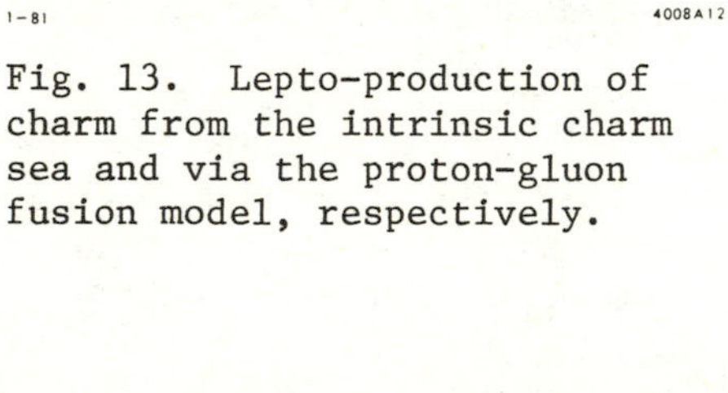

1-81   4008A12

Fig. 13. Lepto-production of charm from the intrinsic charm sea and via the proton-gluon fusion model, respectively.

$$W^2 = (p + q)^2 > W_{th}^2 = (m_D + m_{\Lambda_c})^2 \simeq 17 \text{ GeV}^2 \tag{33}$$

The W^2-threshold enters explicitly in the Bjorken condition. Let x_i^+ be the light cone momentum fractions $x_i^+ = (k_i^0 + k_i^3)/(P^0 + P^3)$ of the hadronic constituents with $\Sigma x_i^+ = 1$ and $\Sigma k_{\perp i} = 0$. The Bjorken condition for putting the final state on shell (p^--conservation) is then

$$\frac{2M_P \nu}{Q^2} = \frac{1}{x_{Bj}} = \frac{1}{x_c} + \frac{1}{Q^2} \left[\frac{m_{c_\perp}^2}{x_c} + \frac{m_{\bar c_\perp}^2}{x_{\bar c}} + \sum_{i=u,u,d} \frac{m_{i_\perp}^2}{x_i} - M_P^2 \right] \tag{34}$$

$$\geq \frac{1}{x_c} + \frac{W_{th}^2 - M_P^2}{Q^2}$$

Thus, in general, the light cone momentum fraction of the charmed quark is larger than the Bjorken value x_{Bj} with the excess controlled by W_{th}^2/Q^2. Since $c(x,Q^2)$ falls with x, this means that $F_2^c(x_{Bj},Q^2)$ increases with Q^2 for fixed x_{Bj} unless $Q^2 \gg 17 \text{ GeV}^2$. The usual rescaling variable

$$\zeta = x_{Bj} + \frac{m_c^2}{Q^2} \tag{35}$$

is incorrect since it ignores the heavy mass of the spectator system.

The EMC-[37] and BFP-data[38] which are binned at fixed x_{Bj} do show significant rise with Q^2. This kinematic effect has to be extrapolated to $Q^2 \gg W_{th}^2$ before accurate comparisons with the intrinsic charm distribution can be made. Threshold factors of the form $(1 - (W_{th}/W)^2)^n$ may be useful for the parameterization of the data.

c) The $c(x)$-distribution as measured in deep inelastic scattering at large Q^2 differs from that determined in low momentum transfer hadron-production because of standard QCD-evolution. This tends to further suppress $F_2^c(x,Q^2)$ at large x and Q^2 (see Fig. 14).

The comparison of the intrinsic charm production (see Eq. (19)) with data was done in Ref. 39. The limits on intrinsic charm is $\lesssim 0.5\%$. However, the comparison does not include the threshold suppression from Eq. (34), so that the net result is not inconsistent with the predicted form and 1% normalization of intrinsic charm. A definitive comparison requires a detailed analysis of the scale breaking effects.

A very interesting implication of intrinsic charm for νN and $\bar\nu N$ charge current reactions is the production of beauty quarks ($\bar\nu c \to \mu^+ b$ and $\nu \bar c \to \mu^- \bar b$)[12] The subsequent leptonic decay of the b and $\bar b$ then leads to same-sign muon pairs (see Fig. 15). The experimentally observed rate of same-sign muon pairs is unexpectedly high, although the different experiments do not all agree. The $c \to b$ process works in the right direction, but with present limits on the standard left-handed c-b coupling the theoretical prediction from intrinsic charm

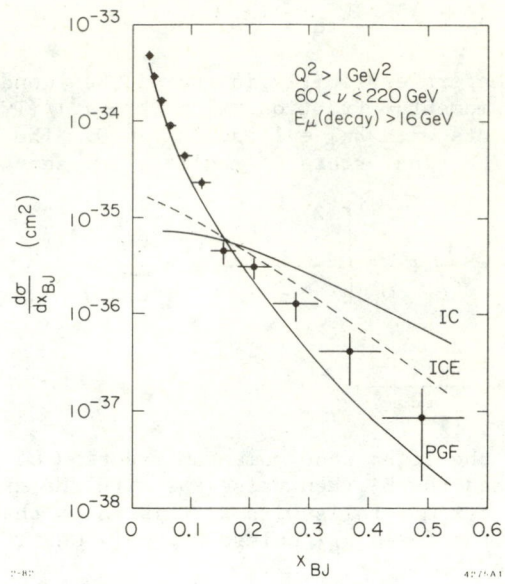

Fig. 14.   Variation of $d\sigma/dx_{Bj}$ with x_{Bj}
for dimuons in the range $Q^2 > 1$ GeV^2,
$60 < \nu < 220$ GeV, decay muon energy
>16 GeV. The horizontal bars represent
the bin widths. The figure is taken
from Ref. 39. The curves are:
　　PGF: photon-gluon fusion model,
　　 IC: intrinsic charm model,
　　ICE: intrinsic charm model with
　　　　maximum Q^2 evolution.

is below some experimental data. However, in the context of topless
models, right-handed couplings, $(c,b)_R$, have been suggested[40] which
increases the same sign dimuon production from the intrinsic charm.

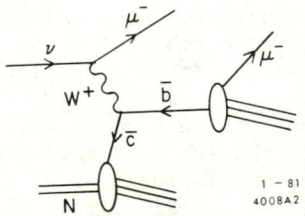

Fig. 15.   Same sign dimuon
pair production from the
intrinsic charm component
of nucleons.

8. CONCLUSIONS

There are a number of theoretical and phenomenological issues related to intrinsic charm:

i) Do the Fock states containing heavy quarks have a small transverse dimension? Note that the structure of the energy denominator in Eq. (15) implies that all the quarks in the $|uudc\bar{c}\rangle$ state have larger $k_\perp$ than in the $|uud\rangle$ state.

ii) How much of the strange sea can be attributed to the intrinsic $|uuds\bar{s}\rangle$-Fock state rather than standard evolution? A phenomenological analysis given by R. Phillips[24] gives $P(|uuds\bar{s}\rangle) \approx 0.031$.

iii) What is the correct mechanism for the high energy excitation of the charm component? Note that, in general, gluon (or Pomeron) interactions occur coherently with all the quarks of the nucleon Fock state. In time ordered perturbation theory the charm production can occur before, during, or after the hadronic interaction.

iv) A more detailed calculation on the intrinsic charm wavefunction may be possible in Bag models, lattice calculations or more directly from the QCD equations of motion.[41] The magnitude of the p-Δ hyperfine splitting can give a bound on the intrinsic gluon and $q\bar{q}$ Fock state components. Much more experimental information is needed to unravel the role of the **different** QCD contribution

a) The x_L-dependence of Σ_c, $\Lambda_{\bar{c}}$, D^0 and D^+. The $\Lambda_{\bar{c}}$ distribution is particularly important since it determines the $\bar{c}(x)$ without complications from valence quark recombination or resonance decays.

b) The physics of intrinsic charm can depend in detail on the nature of the incoming hadron; K, π, p and γ.

c) The threshold dependence, $(1 - s_{th}/s)^n$, of heavy quark production must reflect the nature of the production mechanism.

d) The nuclear A-dependence separates the intrinsic and hard scattering contributions. The A^α-behavior is a function of x; at large x we expect $\alpha = 2/3$.

e) Hidden charm states, χ, ψ, ..., should be seen at some level at large x from the intrinsic charm.

In conclusion, a valence-like charm quark distribution c(x) in the nucleon at the 1% level accounts qualitatively for hadron induced charm production in magnitude, shape and diffractive features at ISR energies. There is no contradiction with the EMC-data on $F_2^c(x)$ provided the appropriate threshold dependence is taken into account.

In any event, determination of the charm quark distribution is important for understanding the Fock state structure of the hadronic wavefunctions and as a probe of hadron dynamics in the non-perturbative domain.

REFERENCES

[1] For a review see, e.g., C. Heusch, Lectures given at the 1981 SLAC Summer Institute on Particle Physics, SLAC-PUB-2876.

[2] M. Basile et al., Nuovo Cimento Lett. 30, 481 (1981); ibid 30, 487 (1981).

[3] M. Basile et al., CERN EP/81-125.

[4] S. Singh et al., Nucl. Phys. B 140, 189 (1978).

[5] K. L. Giboni et al., Phys. Lett. 85B, 437 (1979) and A. Kernan, private communication.

[6] H. Fritzsch, Phys. Lett. 67B, 217 (1977). F. Halzen, Phys. Lett. 96B, 105 (1977). L. M. Jones and H. W. Wyld, Phys. Rev. D 17, 759, 1782, 2332 (1978). M. L. Gluck and E. Reya, Phys. Lett. 79B, 453 (1978); 83B, 98 (1979). M. Gluck, J. F. Owens, and E. Reya, Phys. Rev. D 17, 2324 (1978). J. Babcock, D. Sivers and S. Wolfram, Phys. Rev. D 18, 162 (1978). C. E. Carlson and R. Suaya, Phys. Rev. D 18, 760 (1978); Phys. Lett. 81B, 329 (1979). H. Georgi et al., Ann. Phys. 114, 273 (1978). K. Hagiwara and T. Yoshino, Phys. Lett. 80B, 282 (1979). J. H. Kuhn, Phys. Lett. 89B, 385 (1980). J. H. Kuhn and R. Ruckl, MPI-PAE/pTH 7/80. V. Barger, W. Y. Keung and R.J.N. Phillips, Phys. Lett. 91B, 253; 92B, 179 (1980); Z. Phys. C6, 169 (1980). Y. Afek, C. Leroy and B. Margolis, Phys. Rev. D 22, 86, 93 (1980).

[7] C. Peterson, Proc. of XII International Conference on Multiparticle Dynamics, University of Notre Dame, Indiana, June 22-26, 1981.

[8] R. Raja, Proc. of XII International Conference on Multiparticle Dynamics, University of Notre Dame, Indiana, June 22-26, 1981.

[9] S. J. Brodsky, P. Hoyer, C. Peterson, and N. Sakai, Phys. Lett. 93B, 451 (1980); P. Hoyer, in High Energy Physics - 1980, Proceedings of the XX International Conference, Madison, Wisconsin, edited by L. Durant and L. G. Pondrom (AIP, New York), 1981. S. J. Brodsky, C. Peterson and N. Sakai, Phys. Rev. D 23, 2745 (1981).

[10] See, e.g., the discussion of A. H. Mueller, in Proceedings of International Symposium on Lepton and Photon Interactions at High Energy, Bonn, West Germany, August 24-29, 1981.

[11] D. P. Roy, Phys. Rev. Lett. 47, 213 (1981).

[12] See, e.g., T. Y. Ling, Proceedings of ν'81 International Conference on Neutrino Physics and Astro Physics.

[13] For a more detailed discussion, see C. Peterson, Proceedings of the Topical Workshop on Forward Production at High-Mass Flavors at Collider Energies, College de France, Paris (1979).

[14] B. L. Combridge, Nucl. Phys. B 151, 429 (1979).

[15] G. T. Bodwin, S. J. Brodsky, G. P. Lepage, Phys. Rev. Lett. 47, 1799 (1981); SLAC-PUB-2860.

[16] R. Phillips, in High Energy Physics - 1980, Proceedings of the XX International Conference on High Energy Physics, Madison, Wisconsin, edited by L. Durand and L. G. Pondrom (AIP, New York), 1981.

[17] L. J. Koester, in High Energy Physics - 1980, Proceedings of the XX International Conference on High Energy Physics, Madison, Wisconsin, edited by L. Durand and L. G. Pondrom (AIP, New York, 1981); D. E. Bender, Ph.D. thesis, 2980, University of Illinois (unpublished); J. Cooper, Proceedings of the XV Recontre de Moriond, 1981 (unpublished).

[18] M. Basile et al., Nuovo Cimento Lett. 31, 97 (1981).

[19] V. Barger and F. Halzen, Phys. Rev. D $\underline{4}$, 1428 (1981).

[20] R. Horgan and M. Jacob, Phys. Lett. $\underline{107B}$, 395 (1981).

[21] S. J. Brodsky, T. Huang and G. P. Lepage, SLAC-PUB-2540; T. Huang, in High Energy Physics - 1980, Proceedings of the XX International Conference on High Energy Physics, Madison, Wisconsin, edited by L. Durand and L. G. Pondrom (AIP, New York), 1981.

[22] S. J. Brodsky and G. P. Lepage, Phys. Rev. D $\underline{22}$, 2157 (1980) and S. J. Brodsky, Y. Frishman, G. P. Lepage, and C. Sachrajda, Phys. Lett. $\underline{91B}$, 239 (1980), and references therein.

[23] J. F. Donoghue and E. Golowich, Phys. Rev. D $\underline{15}$, 3421 (1977).

[24] R.J.N. Phillips, Rutherford Laboratory Preprint RL-82-004.

[25] A. J. Buras and K.J.F. Gaemers, Nucl. Phys. B $\underline{132}$, 249 (1978).

[26] G. Gustafson and C. Peterson, Phys. Lett. $\underline{67B}$, 81 (1977).

[27] J. F. Gunion and D. E. Soper, Phys. Rev. D $\underline{15}$, 2617 (1977).

[28] J. Pumplin and E. Lehman, Zeitschrift für Physik $\underline{C9}$, 25 (1981).

[29] G. Gustafson, LUTP 81-1, talk given at the "IX International Winter Meeting on Fundamental Physics," Siguenza, Spain, February 1981.

[30] G. Bertsch, S. J. Brodsky, A. S. Goldhaber and J. F. Gunion, Phys. Rev. Lett. $\underline{47}$, 297 (1981).

[31] C. Peterson, in preparation.

[32] J. Badier et al., Proc. Lepton-Photon Conf. at Fermilab, 1979, p. 161; CERN/EP 79-61.

[33] R. Odorico, Phys. Lett $\underline{107B}$, 231 (1981).

[34] M. G. Albrow et al., Nucl. Phys. B $\underline{108}$, 1 (1976).

[35] R. C. Ruchti, Proc. of XII International Conference on Multiparticle Dynamics, University of Notre Dame, Indiana, June 22-26, 1981.

[36] R. V. Gavai and D. P. Roy, Zeit. Phys. $\underline{C10}$, 333 (1981).

[37] H. Best, Proc. of XVI Recontre de Moriond, 1981.

[38] M. Strovink, Proc. of 10th Int. Symp. on Lepton and Photon Interactions at High Energy, Bonn, West Germany, August 24-29, 1981.

[39] J. J. Aubert et al., CERN-EP/81-161 (1981).

[40] V. Barger, W. Y. Keung and R.J.N. Phillips, Phys. Rev. D $\underline{24}$, 244 (1981).

[41] See, e.g., S. J. Brodsky, T. Huang and G. P. Lepage, SLAC-PUB-2868.

HADRONIC PRODUCTION OF OPEN CHARM

R. Odorico

Istituto di Fisica dell'Università and I.N.F.N., Bologna

ABSTRACT

It is shown that existing difficulties in the perturbative QCD approach to the data for hadronic production of charm are eliminated once the flavour excitation contribution is duly taken into account. A stable calculation of this contribution is presented whose main ingredients are: i) a QCD Monte Carlo calculation of the evolution of the charm sea, with constraints from the existing F_2(charm) data; ii) use of p_T data for charmed mesons to fix the t_{min} cutoff which regulates the $t \simeq 0$ divergence in the diagrams. Diffractive production of Λ_c is shown to be naturally understood with a simple recombination model. Qualitative predictions for bottom production are also discussed.

INTRODUCTION

Recent experimental surveys of this field can be found in the rapporteur talks of Wojcicki [1] at the Madison Conference (1980) and of Treille [2] at the Bonn Symposium (1981). The theoretical understanding of the data has been reviewed by Phillips [3] at the Madison Conference. His main conclusions about the conventional treatment of charm hadroproduction in terms of fusion diagrams (Fig. 1) alone were:

i) production of hidden charm is adequately reproduced;

FUSION

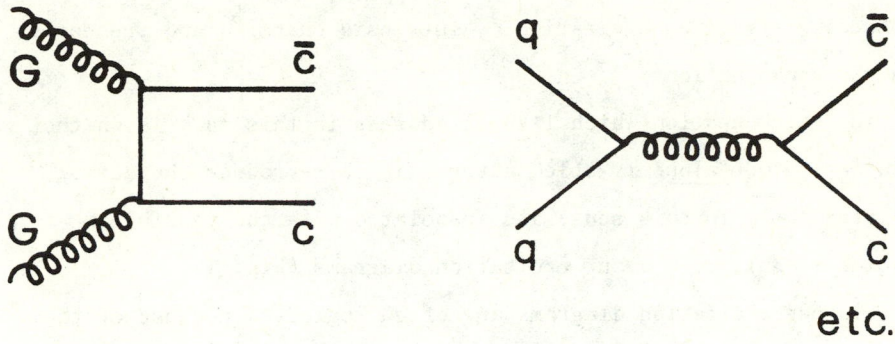

EXCITATION

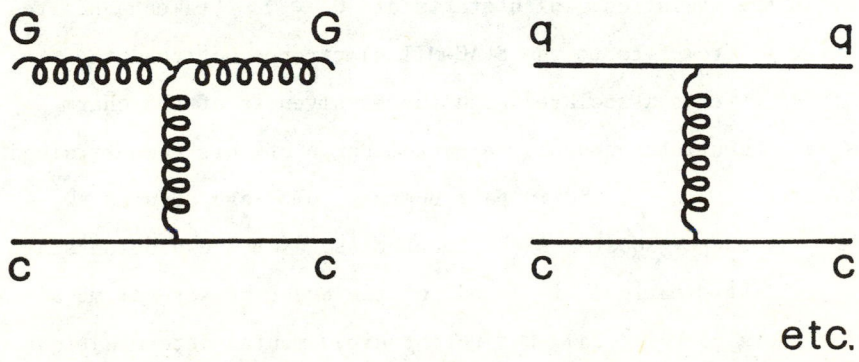

Fig. 1. Typical fusion and flavour excitation diagrams contributing to heavy flavour production.

ii) cross sections for open charm are too low when compared to data;

iii) calculated longitudinal spectra of charmed hadrons are too soft and insufficient to explain diffractive production of Λ_c.

A number of alternatives to perturbative QCD models have been proposed: diffraction excitation [4], intrinsic charm [5] and ,recently, diquark recombination [6].

The main question which I shall address in this talk is whether perturbative QCD alone is able, after all, to reproduce the data. Surviving hopes in this sense are associated with the possible (crucial ?) role of flavour excitation diagrams (Fig. 1).

Flavour excitation diagrams are often neglected because of the poor knowledge of the charm sea distribution, $c(x,Q^2)$, which is required in their calculation. Combridge [7] has been the first to give serious consideration to them. To estimate their contribution he took $c(x,Q^2)$ as given by the Buras and Gaemers [8] parametrization. In [8] $c(x,Q^2)$ is evoluted as normal (light) sea apart from a delay in the evolution, which starts at $Q^2 = Q_o^2$ (taken equal to $1.8 \ (GeV/c)^2$ from fits to the SLAC-MIT electroproduction data). No phase-space effects associated with the massiveness of the charm quarks are taken into account. In part because of this unconstrained evolution of $c(x,Q^2)$, and in part because Combridge assumes $Q^2 = \hat{s}$, the c.m. energy square in the subprocess, as the evolution scale a huge $\sigma_{c\bar{c}}(\text{excitation})$ is found, of the order of several mb at collider energies (Fig. 2a). But recent experimental determinations [9,10] of the charm structure function, $F_2(\text{charm})$, show that the Buras and Gaemers parametrization is not able to account, even qualitatively, for the experimental behaviour of $F_2(\text{charm})$.

With a paper appeared this summer Barger, Halzen and Keung [11] (BHK) have revived interest in these diagrams. They assume that a

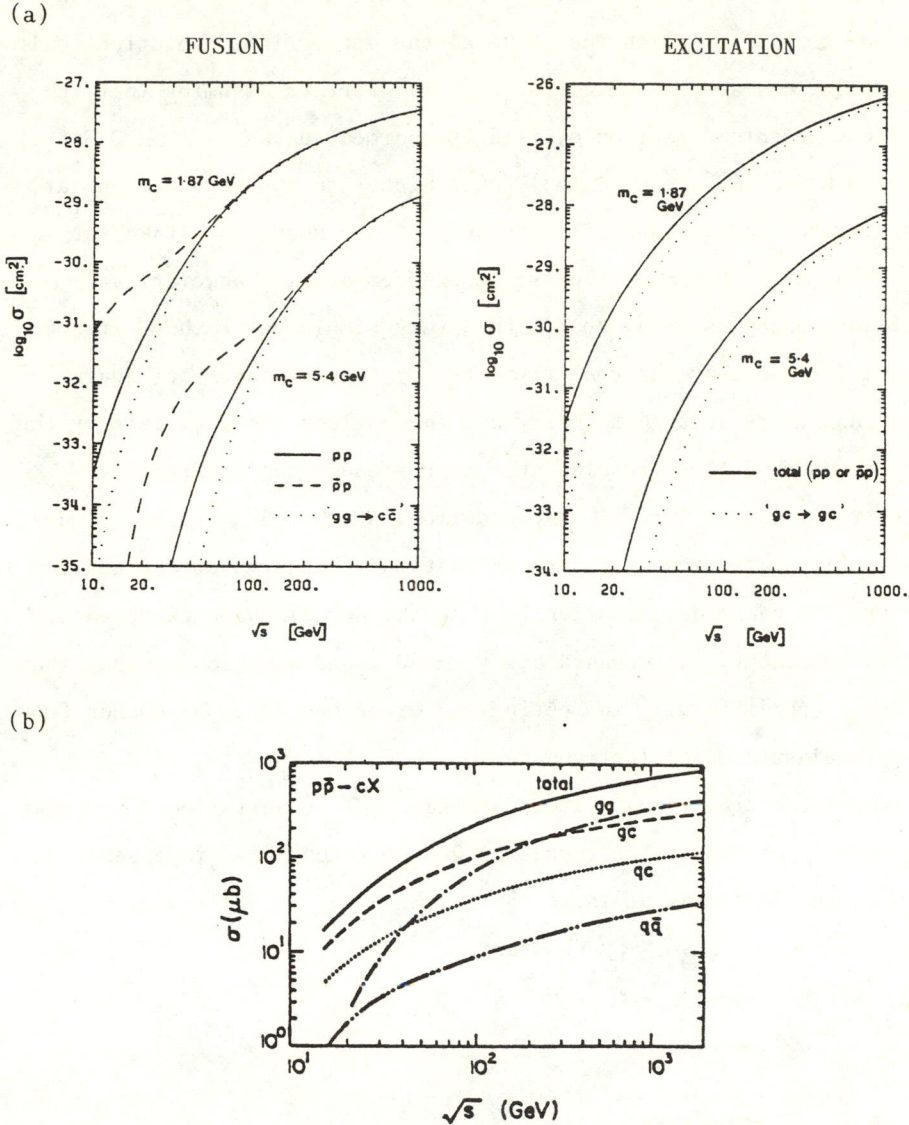

Fig. 2. Charm cross sections as calculated by Combridge [7] (a), and Barger et al. [11] (b).

properly QCD evoluted $c(x,Q^2)$ should have a shape $\sim x^{m-1}(1-x)^m$ at $Q^2 \simeq 4 m_c^2$, which they take as the appropriate evolution scale (calculations are presented for $m = 1$). Further assuming that the nucleon momentum fraction carried by charmed quarks is $\simeq 0.5\%$, they find a $\sigma_{c\bar{c}}$(excitation) much higher than $\sigma_{c\bar{c}}$(fusion) at accelerator and ISR energies. Because of the shape they take for $c(x,Q^2)$ near $x \simeq 0$ the two become comparable, however, at collider energies (Fig. 2b). With a very simple but rather extreme model for the charm hadron originated by the spectator c quark (the hadron is assumed to carry <u>all</u> the nucleon momentum left by the active quark), they are also able to reproduce the diffractive spectrum observed for Λ_c production. At the Q^2 typical of deep inelastic scattering it is argued that the ordinary QCD degradation brings the charm distribution back to the normal shape expected for a sea component, i.e. peaked at $x \simeq 0$, and a as consequence that there is no difficulty in meeting the experimental upper bounds from deep inelastic multi-lepton data.

These estimates make it clear that $\sigma_{c\bar{c}}$(excitation) can play a central role in the perturbative QCD approach. That is essentially due to the fact that at large $\hat{s}$:

$$\hat{\sigma}(Gc \to Gc) \propto \text{constant}$$
$$\hat{\sigma}(qc \to qc) \propto \text{constant}$$
$$\hat{\sigma}(GG \to c\bar{c}) \propto \frac{1}{\hat{s}} \log \hat{s} \qquad (1)$$
$$\hat{\sigma}(q\bar{q} \to c\bar{c}) \propto 1/\hat{s}$$

and to the $d\hat{\sigma}/d\hat{t} \propto 1/\hat{t}^2$ behaviour exhibited by the excitation contribution. If the non-perturbative cutoff, $\hat{t}_{min}$, is sufficiently small, $\sigma_{c\bar{c}}$(excitation) can turn out to be very large. A proper calculation of these diagrams, however, requires:

i) a correct procedure to fix $\hat{t}_{min}$ (BHK take $-\hat{t}_{min} \sim m_c^2$, where

$m_c = 1.5$ GeV is the charm quark mass, but they recognize that an ambiguity by a factor $2 \div 4$ remains; Combridge simply assumes $-\hat{t}_{min} = Q_o^2 = 1.8 \ (\text{GeV/c})^2$);

ii) a reliable perturbative QCD calculation of the evoluted $c(x,Q^2)$ and, to discuss hadron distributions, of the spectator charm quark distribution.

In order to comply with ii) one must absolutely use a calculational framework in which phase-space constraints associated with the massiveness of charm quarks are duly taken into account. This rules out the inclusive treatment offered by the conventional QCD evolution equations and calls necessarily for an <u>exclusive</u> treatment. (This becomes even more necessary if one wants to calculate the spectator charm distribution). At present the only known way to do that is a QCD Monte Carlo.

CHARM SEA EVOLUTION BY QCD MONTE CARLO

The QCD Monte Carlo technique has been originally developed for parton jet calculation in electron-positron annihilation [12]. More recently it has been extended to calculate the evolution of structure functions in the LLA [13,14]. By appropriate modifications of splitting probability functions one can include in the calculation also next-to-leading order corrections [15]. There are no limitations in the precision attainable with the technique. Fig. 3 shows a comparison of next-to-leading-order corrections to the QCD evolution of non-singlet structure function moments as calculated by the Monte Carlo with the corresponding analytic results [15]. Of course the QCD Monte Carlo gives much more information than an analytic calculation can ever provide, since it calculates the full final state, including

106

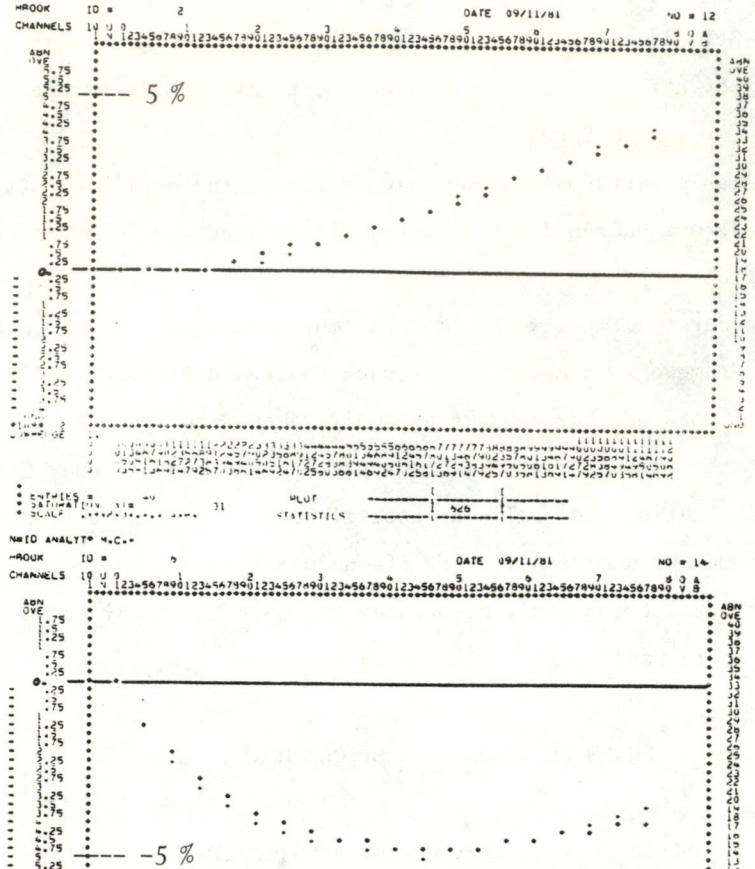

Fig. 3. $(M_n^{NXT} - M_n^{LLA})/M_n^{LLA}$ versus $\log(\log(Q^2/\Lambda^2)/$ $/\log(Q_0^2/\Lambda^2))$, where M_n^{LLA} and M_n^{NXT} are the nth moments of the non-singlet structure function calculated in the LLA and including next-to-leading corrections, respectively (Λ = 0.3 GeV , Q_0^2 = 1 $(GeV/c)^2$, Q_{MAX}^2 = 200 $(GeV/c)^2$). Stars: analytic calculation. Crosses: Monte Carlo results. n = 2 above, n = 6 below. [15]

longitudinal and transverse distributions and all conceivable parton correlations. For instance it is easy to calculate with it the LLA evolution of the transverse momentum distribution of Drell-Yan pairs including also non-abelian effects [16] (see also [17]), which is practically impossible to do analytically. FORTRAN programs for the simulation of parton jets in electron-positron annihilation [18] and for the QCD evolution of structure functions, including heavy quark effects [19], are available.

The only dynamical input in this mathematical technique is the elementary emission probability:

$$d\,P_E = \frac{\alpha_s(K^2)}{2\pi}\,\frac{d\,K^2}{K^2}\int_{\mathcal{E}_1(K^2)}^{1-\mathcal{E}_2(K^2)} P(z)\,dz \tag{2}$$

where $P(z)$ is one of the appropriate splitting probability functions $(q \to qG\,,\ G \to GG\,,\ G \to q\bar{q})$. $\mathcal{E}_1(K^2)$ and $\mathcal{E}_2(K^2)$ embody phase-space bounds. For a $G \to c + \bar{c}$ branching in a space-like evolution the bounds can be derived from the positivity condition on the transverse momentum square K_T^2 generated in the branching [20]:

$$K_T^2 = z(1-z)\,(K^2 - \frac{K_{act}^2}{z} - \frac{K_{spect}^2}{1-z}) \geqslant 0 \tag{3}$$

where $K^2\ (<0)$, K_{act}^2 and K_{spect}^2 are the 4-momentum squares of the parent, the spacelike secondary and the timelike secondary, respectively, and z is the fraction of the momentum of the parent carried by the spacelike secondary. Since $K_{spect}^2 \geqslant m_c^2$, where m_c is the mass of the c quark, and $K_{act}^2 \geqslant -Q^2$, where Q^2 (>0) is the evolution scale $(|K_{act}^2| \gg |K^2|$ for the LLA to be valid), one obtains immediately after the branching [20]:

$$x_{spect} \geqslant x_{act}\frac{m_c^2}{Q^2} \tag{4}$$

For $Q^2 \gg m_c^2$ (e.g. the deep inelastic scattering regime) the condition is ineffective. But for $Q^2 \simeq m_c^2$ it clearly favours the flow of momentum to the timelike quark. For gluon initiated cascades with $x_G \equiv 1$, one obtains the results of Fig. 4 for small Q^2 ($Q^2 = m_c^2/4$, $m_c = 1.5$ GeV , and K^2 replaced by $K^2 + 1.5\, m_c^2$ in eq. 2, see below). At smaller Q^2 the $x \simeq 0$ peak in the spectator distribution disappears completely, while at larger Q^2 it is the $x \simeq 1$ peak which gradually goes away. In an actual calculation these distributions are to be convoluted with the initial gluon distribution to obtain the final answer. The result of Fig. 4 is of course of crucial importance when discussing diffractive production of charm. It simply follows from taking kinematics thoroughly into account, which is something that LLA analytic calculations are not able to do.

One should be aware that the calculation depends on the treatment of the $K^2 \simeq 0$ divergence present in eq. 2. It is clear that it is beyond the possibilities of perturbative QCD to cure it, and that (in lack of a non-perturbative calculational technique) one must adopt an effective procedure using experimental and/or phenomenological input. For this sake one can use the recent experimental measurements [9,10] of F_2(charm). In photon-gluon fusion model calculations covering these data one obtains satisfactory fits by assuming [3] $\alpha_S = \alpha_S(Q^2 + m(c\bar{c})^2)$, where $m(c\bar{c})$ is the invariant mass of the $c\bar{c}$ system. Mimicking this successful recipe we replace $K^2 \to K^2 + a\, m_c^2$ in eq. 2, where a is a free parameter to be fixed by a best fit to the data. For $a = 1.5$ one obtains the curves of Fig. 4 which provide a fit of the same quality as that of the photon-gluon fusion model (data compilation from [21]; $x\, G(x) = 0.5 (1 + \eta)(1-x)^{\eta}$ with $\eta = 5$ has been assumed for the initial

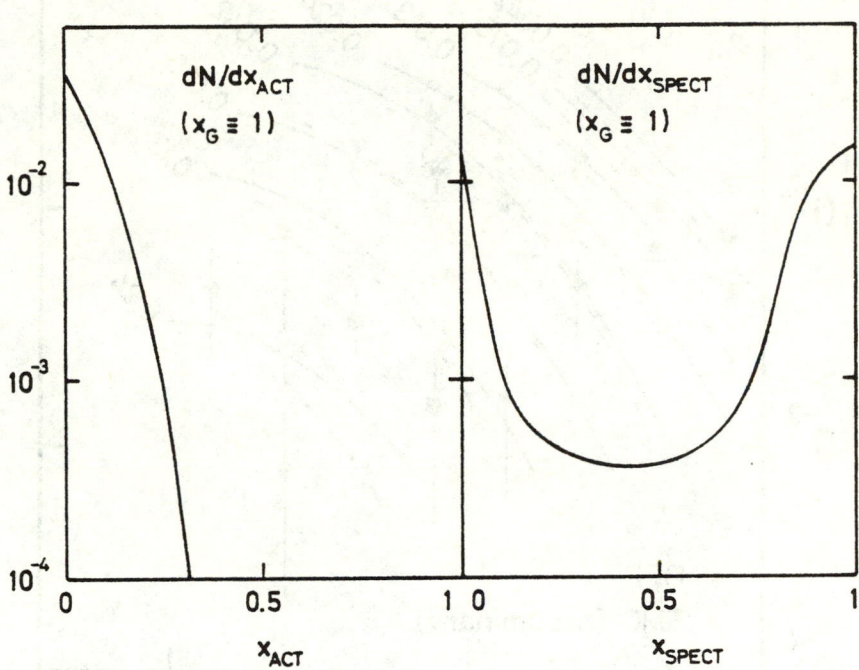

Fig. 4. x distributions of active (spacelike) and spectator (timelike) charm quarks resulting from gluon initiated QCD cascades as calculated by the QCD Monte Carlo ($x_G \equiv 1$ for the initial gluon, $\alpha_s = \alpha_s(Q^2 + 1.5\ m_c^2)$, $m_c = 1.5$ GeV, $Q^2_{evol} = 0.25\ m_c^2$).

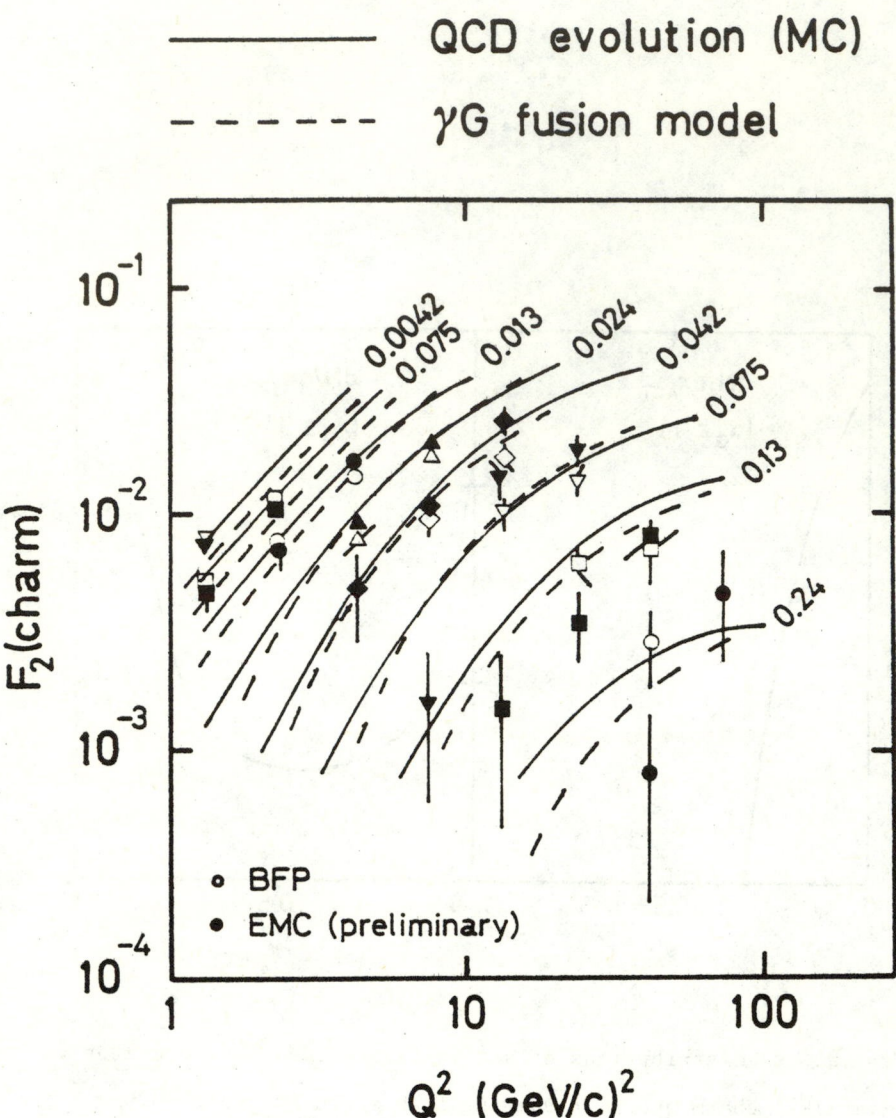

Fig. 5. Comparison of F_2(charm) calculated by the QCD Monte Carlo ($\alpha_S = \alpha_S(Q^2 + 1.5\ m_c^2)$) with experimental data [9,10,21]. Dashed lines represent the photon-gluon fusion model results [21].

gluon distribution; initial quarks give a contribution $\lesssim 1/10$ of the total).

CALCULATION OF FLAVOUR EXCITATION

The basic formula for the charm cross section is

$$\sigma_{c\bar{c}} = \iint_{\hat{s}_{th}/s} dx_1 dx_2 \, f_1(x_1,Q^2) \, f_2(x_2,Q^2) \, \hat{\sigma}(\hat{s}) \qquad (5)$$

where $\hat{\sigma}$ is the cross section for the parton subprocess, f_1 and f_2 are the appropriate parton density functions, s and $\hat{s}$ are the c.m. energy squares of the hadron and parton processes, respectively, $\hat{s}_{th}$ defines the threshold of the subprocess. When s increases, smaller x's become accessible. Because of the $1/x$ behaviour of the parton densities this gives an extra $\log^2 s$ factor besides the energy dependence implied by $\hat{\sigma}(\hat{s})$. The calculation of the cross section results from the combination of an essentially small factor, the charm sea, and a large one, the excitation cross section (see Fig. 6). The calculation is therefore potentially unstable, and special care is required when fixing the intervening parameters.

$\hat{\sigma}(\hat{s})$ for excitation is dominated by the $d\hat{\sigma}/d\hat{t} \propto 1/\hat{t}^2$ singularity, which must be regularized. Adopting an obvious analogy with deep inelastic scattering, the virtual "hard" gluon replacing the virtual photon, it appears sensible to take $Q^2_{evol} = -\hat{t}$, where Q^2_{evol} is the scale up to which the charm sea is evoluted. Since events accumulate at $\hat{t} \simeq \hat{t}_{min}$, to avoid inessential complications in the calculation one can simply take $Q^2_{evol} = -\hat{t}_{min}$. Thus increasing Q^2_{evol} the charm sea is increased, but $\hat{\sigma}$ is reduced. One

FLAVOUR EXCITATION

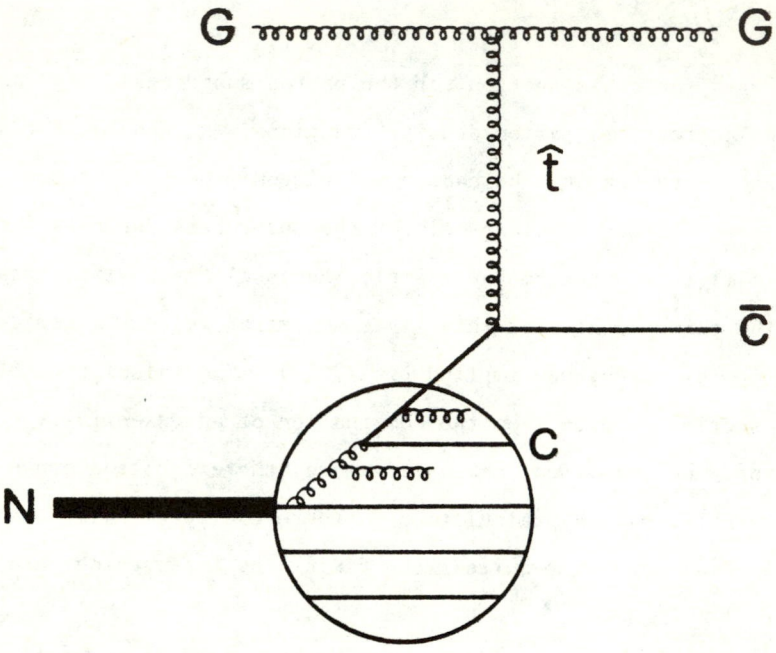

Fig. 6. Basic scheme of the flavour excitation calculation.

expects $Q^2_{evol} \approx m^2_c$, but the resulting cross section $\sigma_{c\bar{c}}$ varies considerably for Q^2_{evol} moving around this value (Fig. 7).

In practice, what is left undefined because of the divergence is the radius of the interaction. In the calculation that I am going to present this radius has been fixed using existing data on the p_T distributions of charm hadrons. Experimentally at ISR [22] $d N / d p^2_T$ $\propto \exp(-b\ p_T)$ with $b = 2.5 \pm 0.4$ $(GeV/c)^{-1}$ for Λ_c , and $b = 2.35 \pm 0.47$ $(GeV/c)^{-1}$ for D^0 and D^+, which corresponds to $\langle p_T \rangle \simeq 0.8$ GeV/c. The transverse momentum of the spectator charm quark is originated in the evolution process. I calculate it with the QCD Monte Carlo, assuming an intrinsic transverse momentum for the initiating gluon $\langle K^2_T \rangle_{intrinsic} = 0.4$ $(GeV/c)^2$ obtained from an LLA analysis [16] of Drell-Yan data (only a fraction $\sim x^2_c$ of it goes to the charm quark). The resulting p_T grows fast with Q^2_{evol} (Fig. 8). The struck charm quark gets its transverse momentum also from the collision process. For near collinear kinematics: $(p^2_T)_{interaction} \simeq -\hat{t}$. Taking into account that some extra transverse momentum is generated in the hadronization process one thus obtains approximately Q^2_{evol} , $-\hat{t}_{min} \lesssim m^2_c/4$, with $m_c = 1.5$ GeV. For the present calculation we have used $Q^2_{evol} = -\hat{t}_{min} = 0.25\ m^2_c$ obtained by fits to the p_T data and assuming a recombination model for the hadronization (see below). Results, however, negligibly depend on the hadronization picture used. The fact that the effective scale $\sim m^2_c/4$ obtained with this procedure is only a fraction of what a priori one would consider as the natural scale for the process should be compared with results obtained in QCD calculations for large p_T processes. There one observes that the reabsorption of higher order corrections into a redefinition of the scale appearing in α_s leads to a reduction of the "natural" scale by a substan-

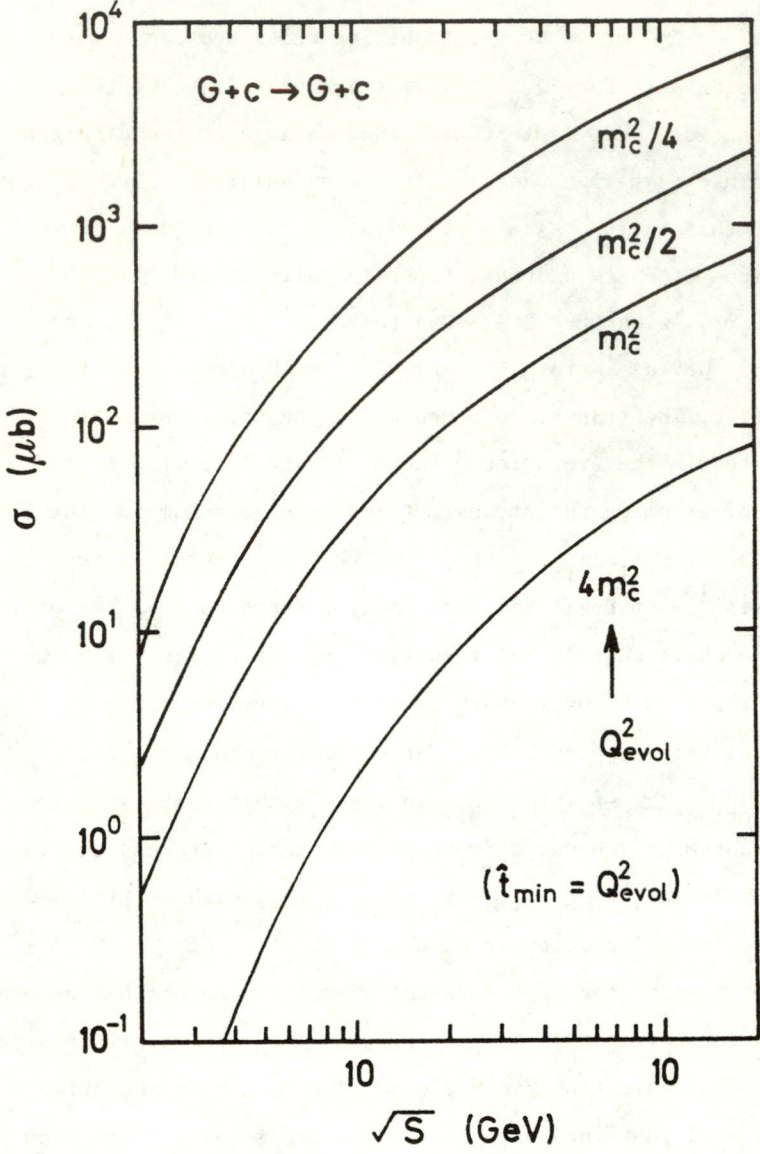

Fig. 7. Dependence of the G+c $\longrightarrow$ G+c contribution to σ(charm) on Q^2_{evol}.

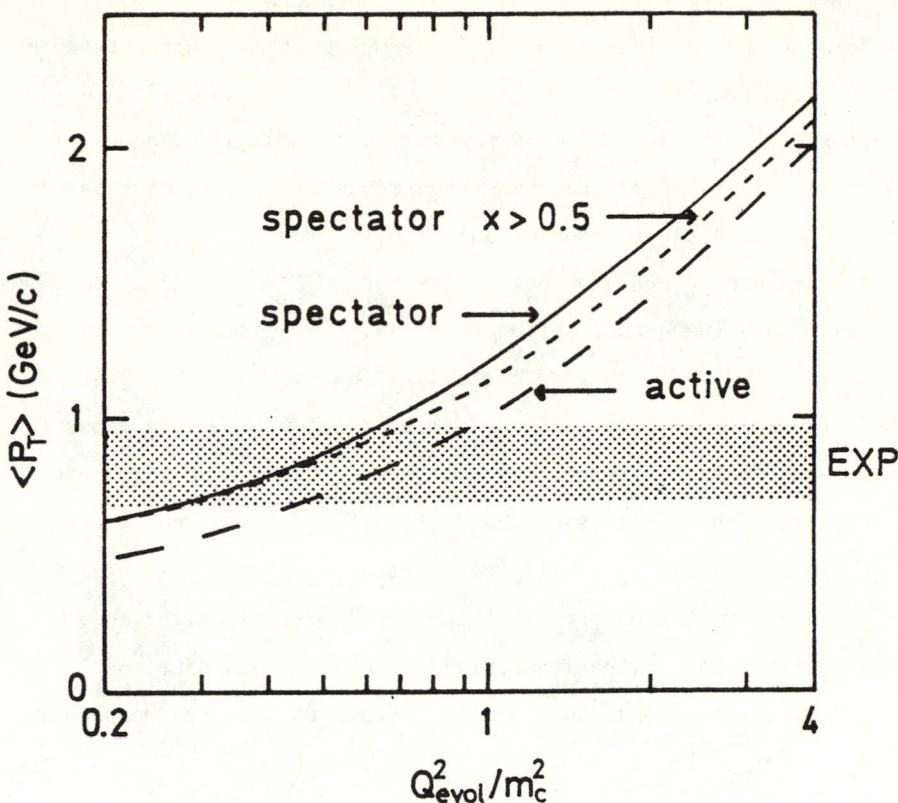

Fig. 8. Dependence of $\langle p_T \rangle$ for the spectator and active charm quarks, immediately after the evolution, on the evolution scale. The dotted region corresponds to the $\langle p_T \rangle$ measurement for charmed hadrons of the BCF experiment [22].

tial factor ($\sim$ 1/7) [23].

Other less important sources of ambiguity in the calculation are associated with the choice of the argument of α_s and the off-shellness of the initial (spacelike) charm leg. The results presented here are obtained for $\alpha_s = \alpha_s(-t_{min})$ (Λ = 0.5 GeV), and neglecting the off-shell mass of the initial charm quark. However, full account is taken of the transverse momentum of colliding partons when dealing with the threshold condition.

Figs. 9 and 10 contain the results for $\sigma_{c\bar{c}}(s)$ and a comparison with data (data compilation from [2]). $\sigma_{c\bar{c}}$(excitation) turns out to be considerably larger than $\sigma_{c\bar{c}}$(fusion) and the relative ratio increases with energy. The experimental level for the cross section and the fast rise between accelerator and ISR energies are correctly reproduced, and thus the difficulty met when considering fusion diagrams alone is finally eliminated.

The huge excitation cross section found does not alter the already satisfactory situation for hidden charm cross sections [3], since $\sigma_{c\bar{c}}$(excitation) does not contribute to the $c\bar{c}$ mass interval of interest (Fig. 11).

Not plotted in Fig. 10 is the result from the balloon flown emulsion experiments reported by Niu [24]. From these data one estimates a charm production rate of 1 $\sim$ 5 % at 10 $\leq p_{LAB} \leq$ 30 TeV (corresponding to $\sqrt{s} \simeq$ 200 GeV) and an even higher percentage in the 100 TeV range. Within the uncertainties (which include those associated with the atomic number dependence) these results are consistent with our calculation.

Consistency with the $e/\pi \simeq 10^{-4}$ ratio measured at ISR at 90° is hard to check because of the poor knowledge of the D meson distribution in this angular region [2,25].

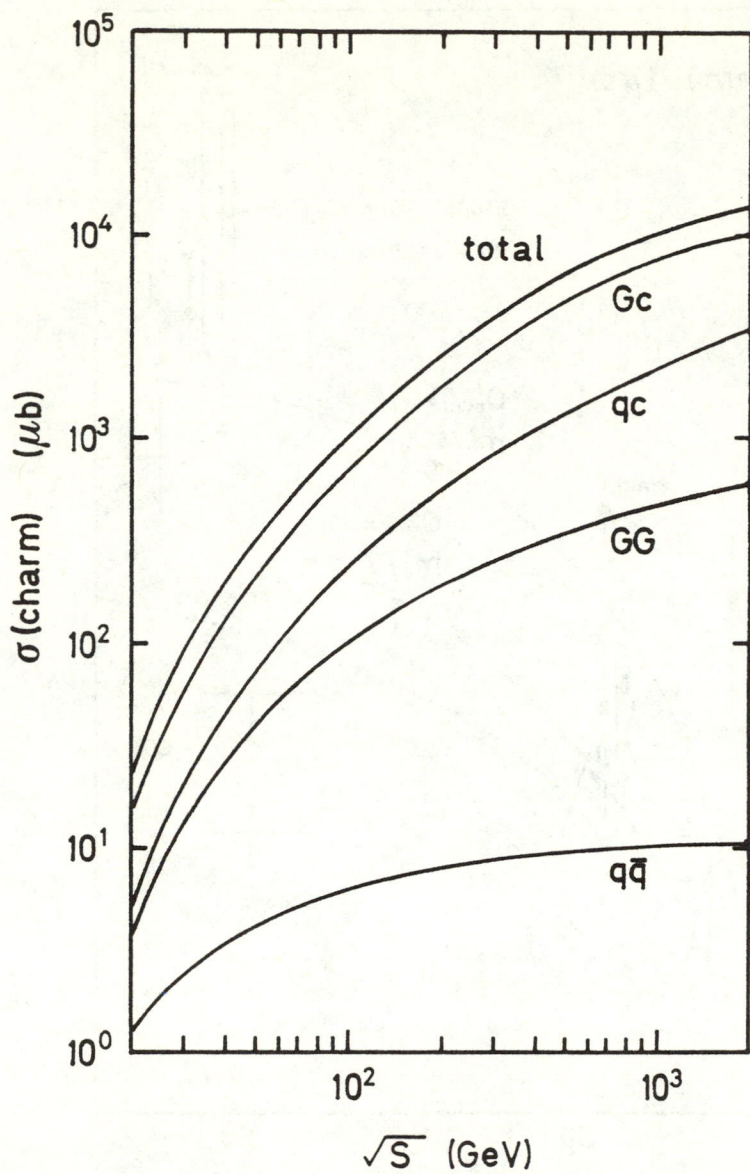

Fig. 9. Calculated charm cross sections for p̄p collisions.

118

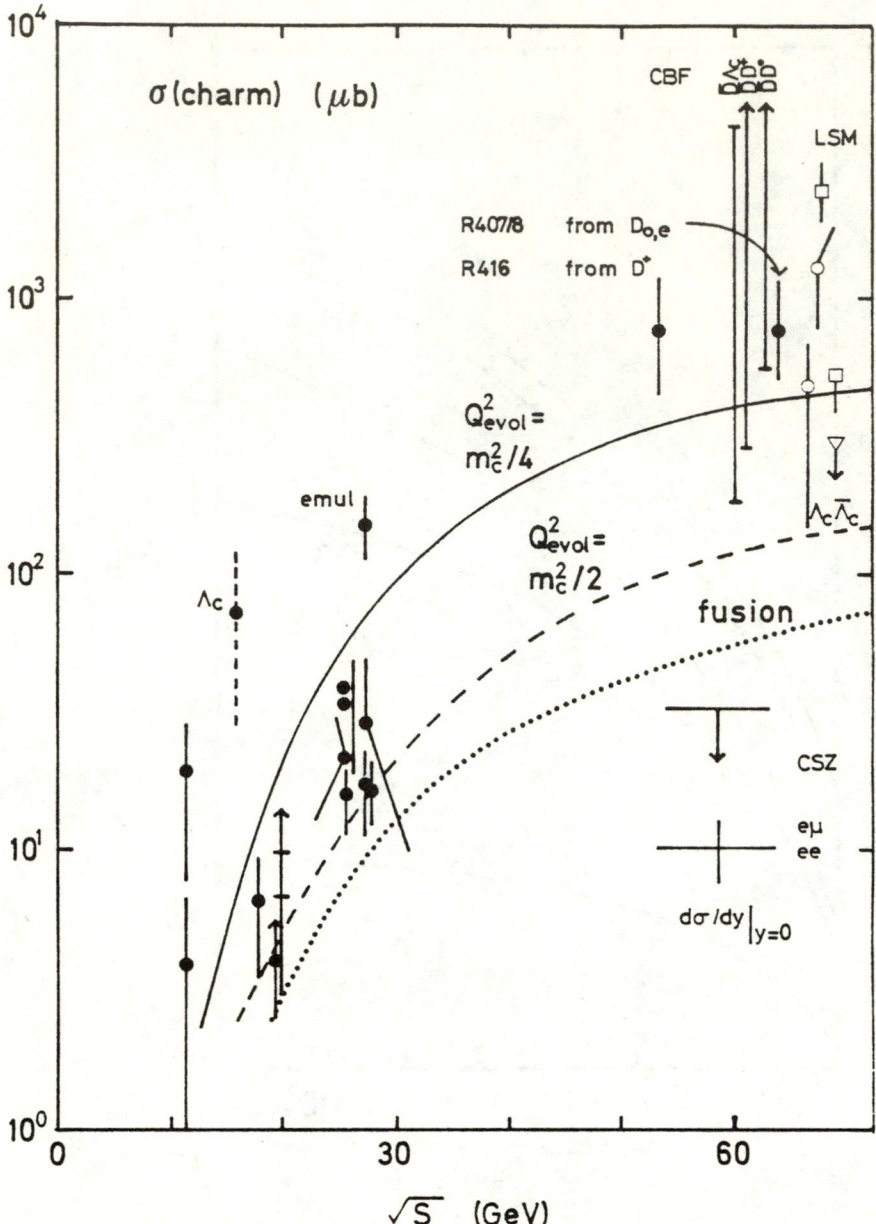

Fig. 10. Comparison of the calculated charm cross section with experimental data (data compilation from [2]).

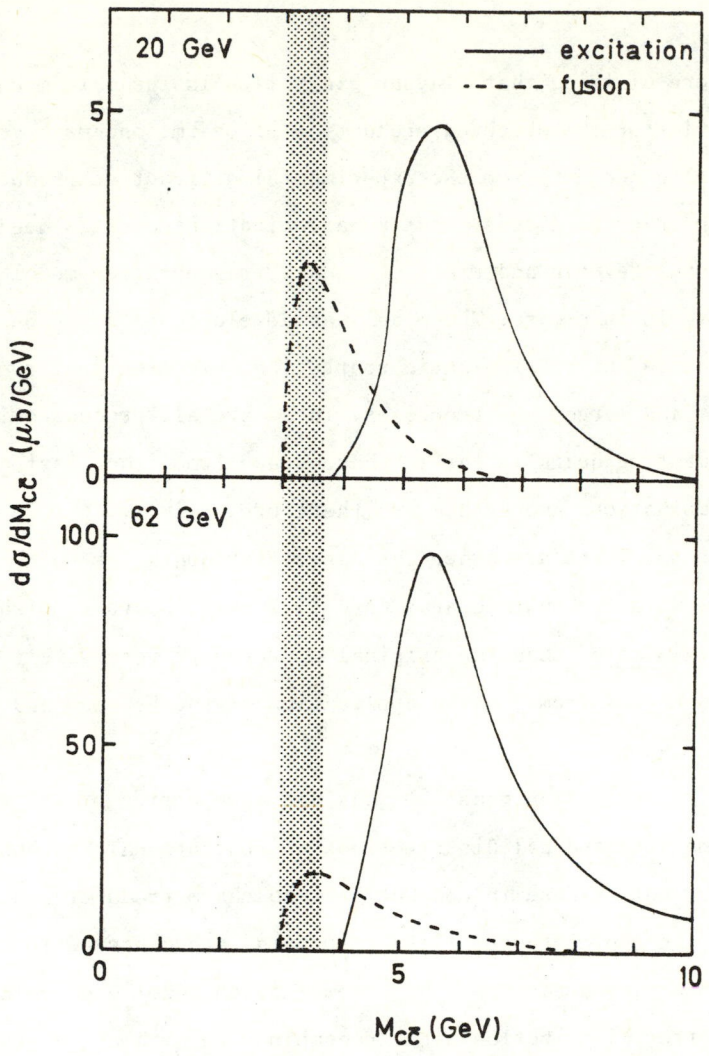

Fig. 11. Invariant c c̄ mass distribution resulting
from fusion and excitation contributions. The dotted
region corresponds to the mass interval attributed
to hidden charm production.

CHARM HADRON DISTRIBUTIONS

Before claiming that flavour excitation is the main mechanism responsible for the observed production of charm, one must verify that it also accounts for the experimental diffractive production of Λ_c. In order to discuss that a hadronization model is needed. The conventional Feynman and Field[26] quark fragmentation model looks inadequate in this case. The model was developed to describe quark fragmentation in deep inelastic scattering, electron-positron anni-hilation, and large p_T processes. These are all processes in which the fragmenting quark is far in phase space from other fast quarks and recombinations among them are therefore unlikely. But in our case it is not so. There are other fast spectator quarks around which may recombine with the charm quarks into (low mass) hadrons which as a result move <u>faster</u> than the original charm quark (oppositely to what one would expect from a naïve application of the Feynman and Field model).

The recombination model[27] has had some degree of success in explaining longitudinal distributions of conventional hadrons. Cri-ticism against its use in connection with charm production has been raised[3] in two respects: i) fast D^+ ($c\bar{d}$) are observed in pp collisions[28], whereas from the recombination model one would expect a much softer distribution since recombination with a sea quark is involved; ii) by Bjorken's argument[29] (requiring closeness in rapi-dity for the recombining partons) the c quark should be fast in order to have a fast charmed hadron, and thus the momentum contri-bution of the uncharmed quarks should not affect anyway the hadron spectrum sizeably.

With a Monte Carlo calculation one can easily verify whether

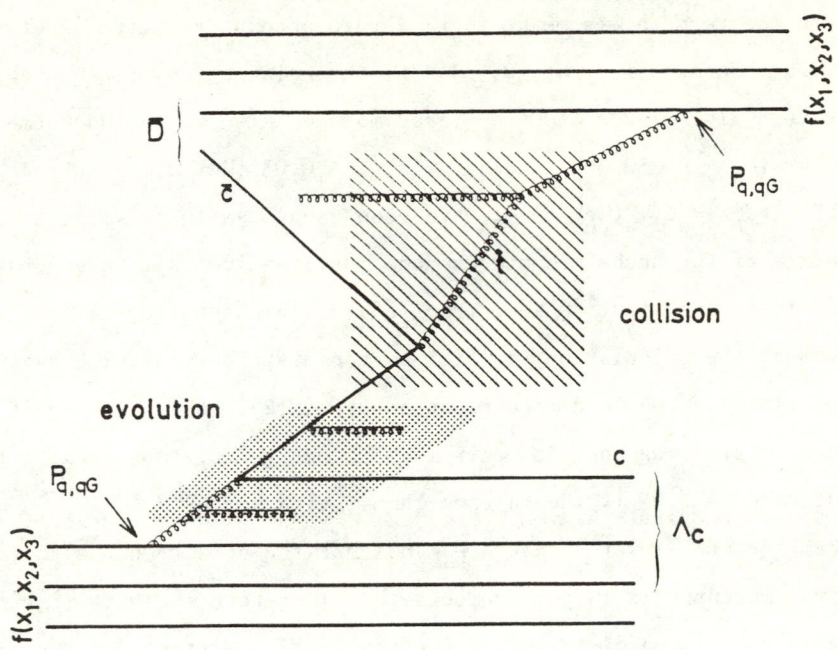

Fig. 12. Basic scheme of the calculation involving the recombination process.

the second type of criticism has reason to exist. Indeed one can directly impose a $\underline{\text{mass cut}}$ on the invariant mass of the recombining quarks as the condition to have a hadron recombination:

$$m_c \leq m_{\text{recombination}} \leq m_{\text{hadron}} + h \qquad (6)$$

where the term h is meant to take into account the effects of soft interaction dynamics ($h = 0.5$ GeV in the calculation). To use eq. 6 one must give masses and transverse momenta also to the uncharmed quarks ($m_q = 0.350$ GeV and $<K_T^2>_q = 0.05$ $(\text{GeV}/c)^2$, so that $<K_T^2>_\pi = 0.1$ $(\text{GeV}/c)^2$, have been used). As to the longitudinal momenta of the uncharmed quarks, one must realize that in generating them it is important to keep track of the momentum flow in all the steps of the calculation: initial parton distributions, QCD evolution, interaction, and recombination (Fig. 12). For instance, if the gluon originating the $\bar{c}c$ pair is more energetic, thus leading to a faster $c_{\text{spectator}}$, the valence quarks with which $c_{\text{spectator}}$ will recombine are slower on average, and thus the effect on the charm hadron momentum is in part compensated. Therefore one must start from a correlated distribution for the initial partons and then go on. It is clear that in order to keep the calculation within manageable proportions only few-parton configurations can be treated. But according to the recombination model these are just the ones mainly responsible for the production of $\underline{\text{fast}}$ hadrons ($x_F \gtrsim 0.5$).

Let us assume a correlated valence quark distribution[30]:

$$f(x_1, x_2, x_3) \propto x_1 x_2 x_3 \, \delta(1 - x_1 - x_2 - x_3) \qquad (7)$$

which complies with the counting rule result[31]:

$$f_q(x_1) = \iint dx_2 \, dx_3 \, x_1 x_2 x_3 \, \delta(1 - x_1 - x_2 - x_3) =$$
$$= \frac{1}{6} x_1 (1 - x_1)^3 \qquad (8)$$

The vanishing at $x_1 \simeq 0$ is of course due to the neglect of multi-parton configurations, and therefore is not physical.

Let us further assume that gluons are generated off valence quarks with a distribution $dN = P_{q,Gq}(z) \, dz \propto dz/z$, where z is the momentum fraction of the parent valence quark taken by the gluon. The resulting gluon distribution is $f_G(x) = (5-4(1-x))(1-x)^4/x$.

To treat recombinations of the spectator charm quark (into fast hadrons) one must: i) generate the momentum fractions of the valence quarks and of the gluon in the charm originating nucleon; ii) evolute the gluon; iii) look for recombinations of the charm spectator with the three valence quarks after the interaction has occurred.

For recombinations of the struck charm quark one can adopt a similar procedure. Indeed one finds that fast struck c quarks (present only at small and moderate c.m. energies, Fig. 13) all move in the direction opposite to that of the charm-originating nucleon. Therefore they will recombine with the quarks of the nucleon, and in order for them to be fast the other colliding parton must be energetic. For recombinations of the struck c quark one can thus generate the parton configuration of the other nucleon in the same way as above.

Results for nucleon-nucleon collisions at the energies of the CERN $p\bar{p}$ collider ($\sqrt{s} = 540$ GeV) and ISR (62 GeV) are shown in Figs. 14 – 17. Although results are reported for the full range of x_F , it is understood that they apply only to the large x_F region, $x_F \gtrsim 0.5$.

At collider energies one observes for baryon recombinations (3 quarks) a clear leading particle effect which is absent in meson recombinations (quark-antiquark). The difference is simply due to the fact that for baryons one adds up 3 quark momenta, whereas for mesons only 2. An interesting (theoretical) feature is that fast ba-

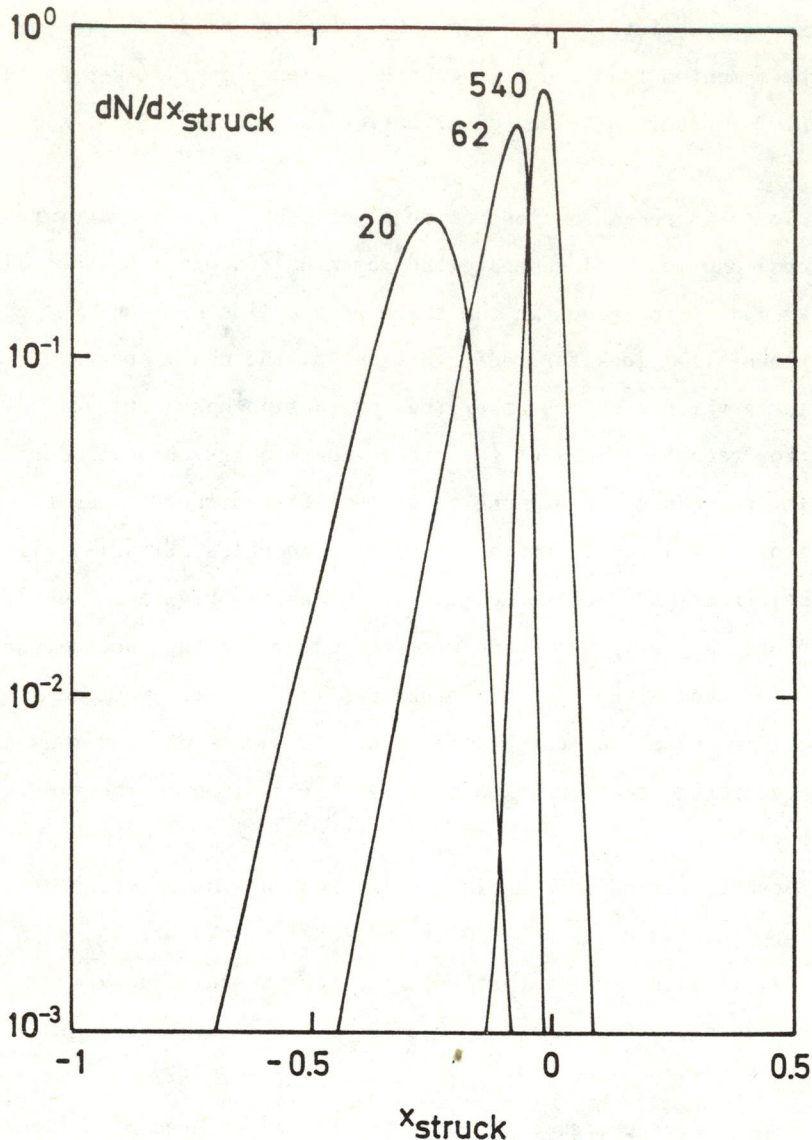

Fig. 13. x distributions of the struck charm quark after interaction at $\sqrt{s}$ = 20, 62 and 540 GeV.

ryons are almost exclusively generated by the charm spectator, in agreement with the suggestion of [11]. This is less true for fast mesons.

At ISR energies the overall results remain the same, but the theoretical picture behind them appears distorted with respect to the simple situation observed at higher energies. Now the effects of the threshold condition become more severe, and in order to pass it the momentum fraction of c_{active} must be favoured at the expenses of $c_{spectator}$. For the same reason the other colliding parton is more energetic on average, which results in a harder spectrum for c_{struck}. As a consequence the role of $c_{spectator}$ in fast hadron recombinations is reduced and that of c_{struck} increased. The theoretical curve for baryons nicely agrees with the Λ_c data of the BCF experiment [32] (the relative normalization is free). A similar comparison is not possible for D mesons, since existing data do not cover the $x_F \gtrsim 0.5$ region.

Figs. 18 and 19 show a comparison of calculated p_T distributions with the BCF data [22] for Λ_c and D^0. The mean p_T of these data has been used to fix Q^2_{evol}.

It is interesting to look at the x distribution of spectator c quarks entering baryon recombinations (Fig. 20). One learns that once all effects are quantitatively taken into account (including transverse momenta, and thus the m_T fluctuations which alter rapidities) $c_{spectator}$ must not be necessarily very fast, but just moderately fast, in order to recombine with valence quarks.

The results of Figs. 14 - 17 for the spectator recombinations can be qualitatively reproduced with a simple, although approximate analytic treatment. If we introduce a recombination probability $R = (x_c/x_{hadron})^n$, which penalizes recombinations of slow charm

126

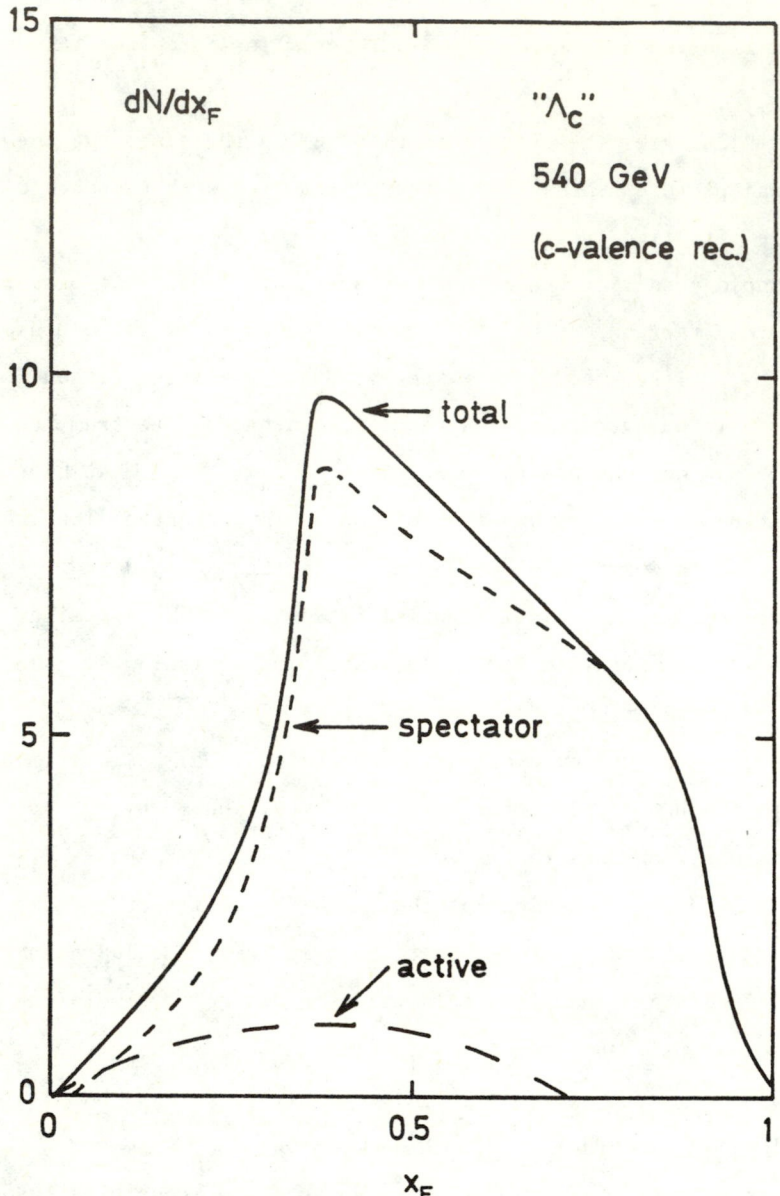

Fig. 14. Calculated x_F distribution for fast charmed baryons at $\sqrt{s}$ = 540 GeV.

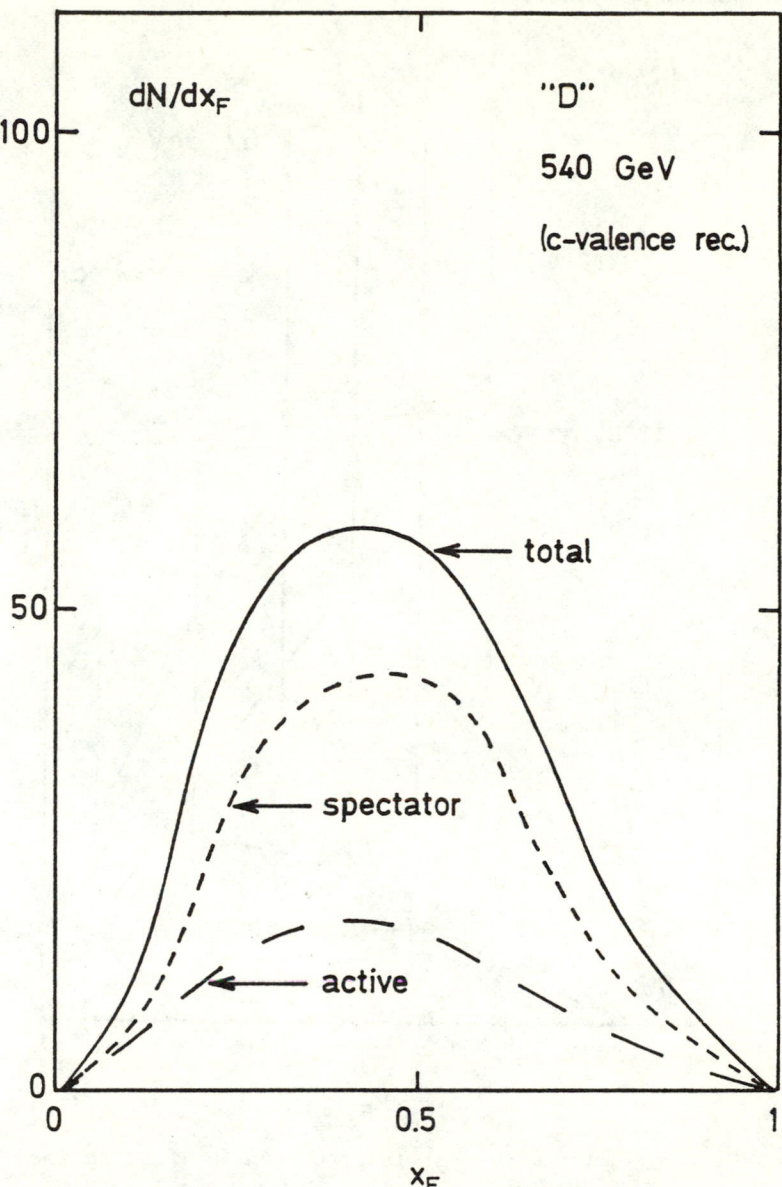

Fig. 15. Calculated x_F distribution for fast charmed mesons at $\sqrt{s}$ = 540 GeV.

128

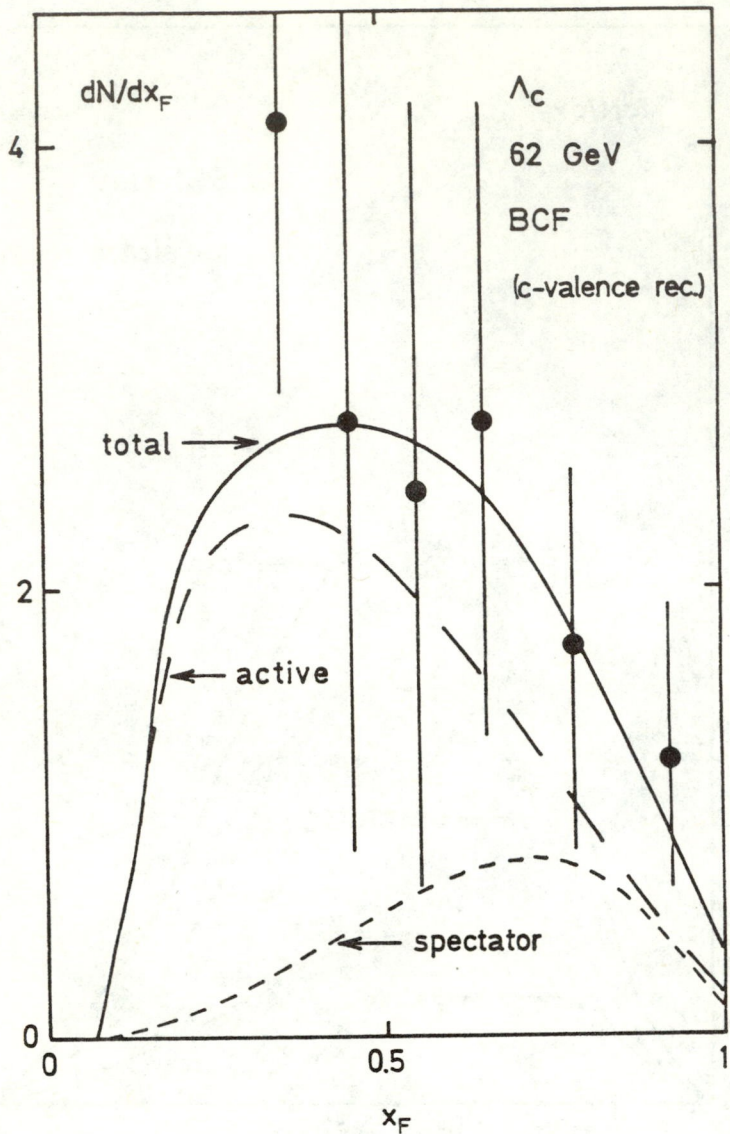

Fig. 16. Calculated x_F distribution for fast charmed baryons at $\sqrt{s}$ = 62 GeV compared with BCF data [32] for Λ_c (the relative normalization is free).

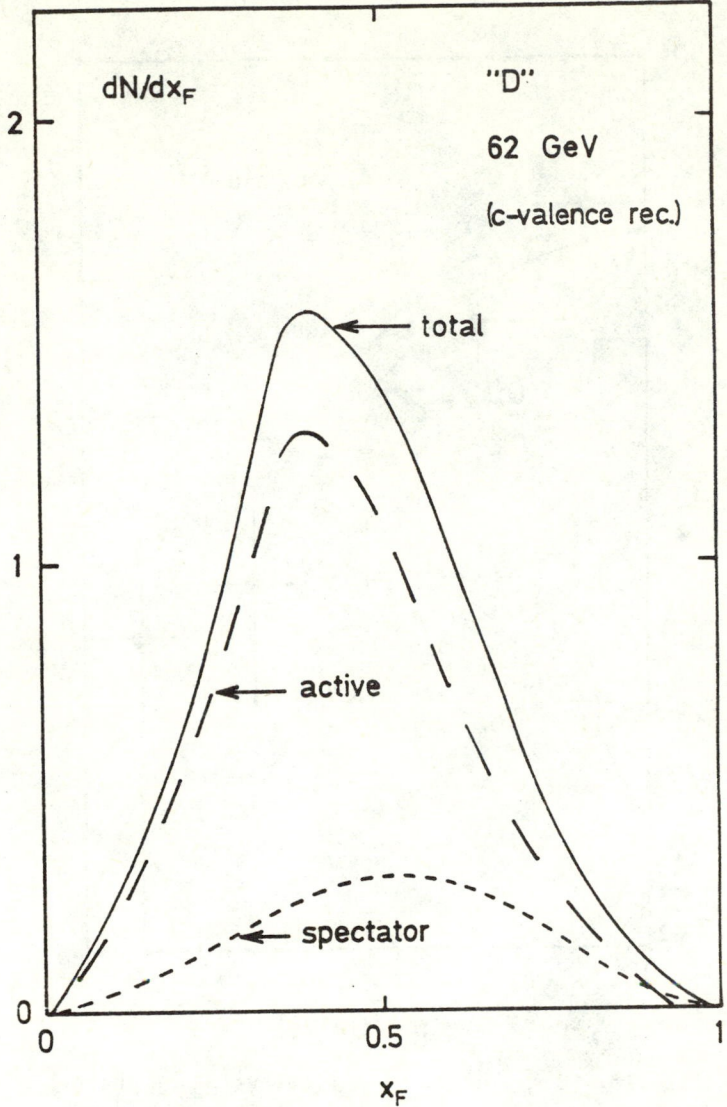

Fig. 17. Calculated x_F distribution for fast charmed mesons at $\sqrt{s}$ = 62 GeV.

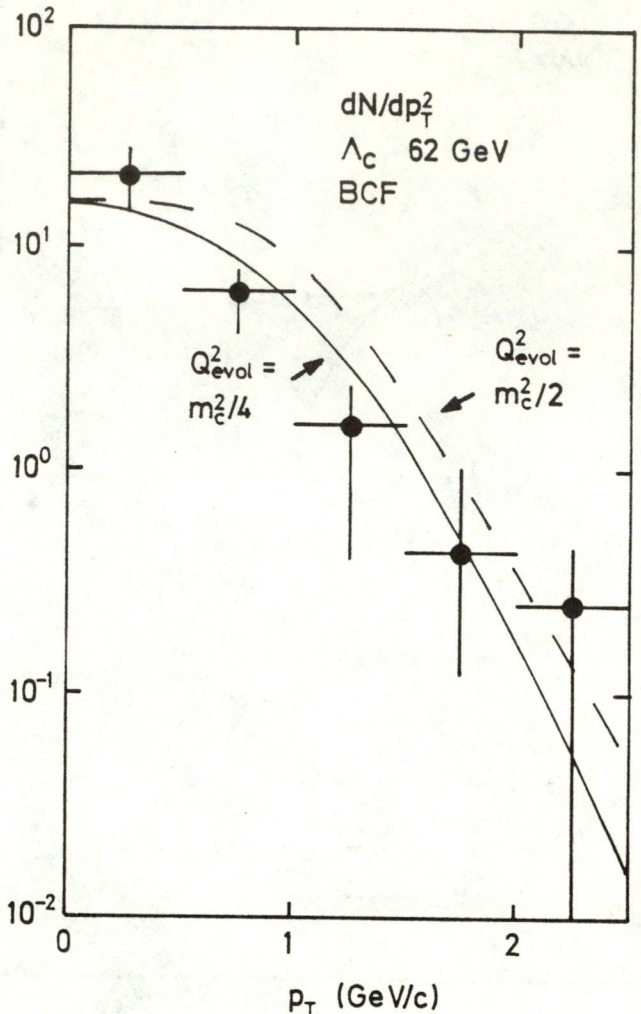

Fig. 18. Calculated p_T distribution of charmed baryons at $\sqrt{s} = 62$ GeV compared with Λ_c data [22] (the relative normalization is free).

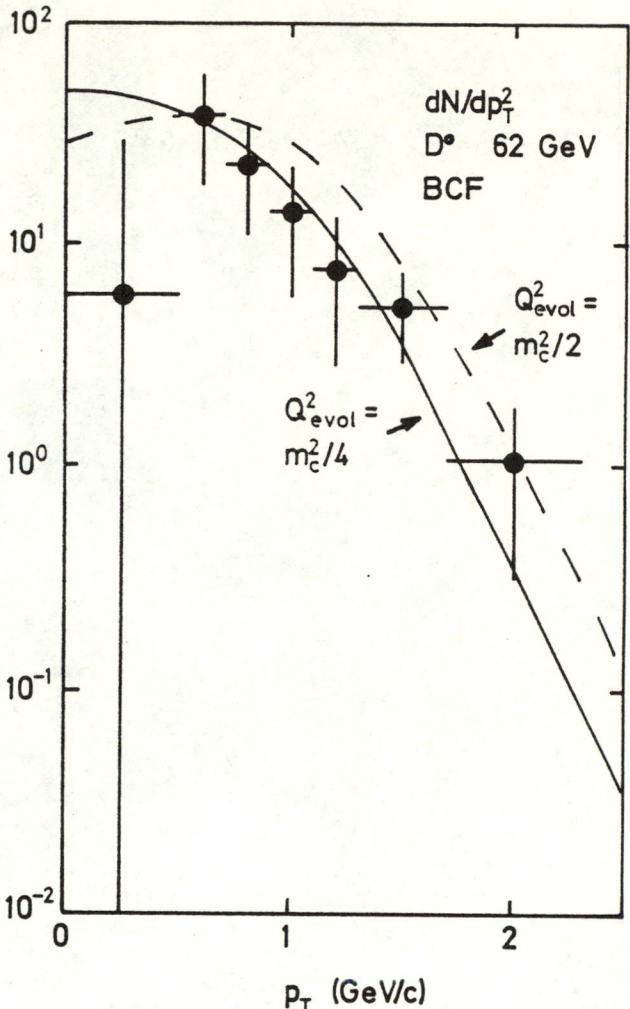

Fig. 19. Calculated p_T distribution of charmed mesons at $\sqrt{s} = 62$ GeV compared with D^o data[22] (the relative normalization is free).

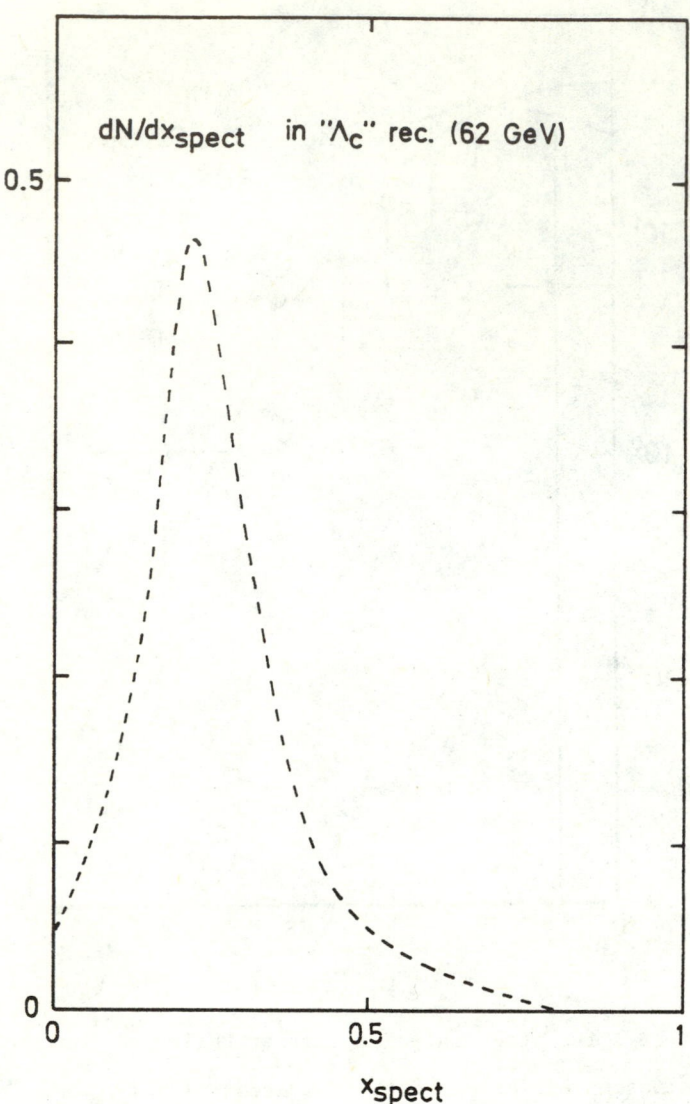

Fig. 20. x distribution of spectator charm quarks entering baryon recombinations with valence quarks ($\sqrt{s}$ = 62 GeV).

quarks, and we further approximate $x_c \simeq x_G$, where x_G is the momentum fraction of the gluon initiating the evolution cascade, by making simple analytic integrals one obtains at large x ($n = 1$):
$f_{baryon}(x) \propto (1+24(1-x))$ and $f_{meson}(x) \propto (1-x)^2$, in qualitative agreement with the Monte Carlo results.

The meson distributions which have been obtained are of course meant for charm mesons resulting from recombinations with valence quarks. If a recombination with a sea quark is involved one expects a much softer spectrum. This appears in contrast with the observation of fast D^+ ($c\bar{d}$) in pp collisions. I believe, though, that this does not disprove the direct recombination model, but rather clarifies its limitations. In fact, one may first have a recombination into a high mass excited baryon, e.g. Λ_c^*, which subsequently decays, e.g. $\Lambda_c^* \longrightarrow D^+ + n$. If Λ_c^* is produced with a $\sim (1-x)$ distribution, two body kinematics for the decay gives $\sim (1-x)^2$ for the D^+. In other words, if a channel appears depleted for direct recombinations, it may be easily contaminated or even refilled by multistep processes. Therefore care must be used in interpreting the predictions of the model in such cases.

BOTTOM AND TOP PRODUCTION

The stability of the calculation for the charm excitation cross section has largely depended on the use of experimental input to fix the evolution of the charm sea (F_2(charm) data) and of the interaction radius (p_T distribution of charmed hadrons). For higher flavours crucial information for the heavy sea is missing at present. Fig. 21 shows results for bottom production obtained by keeping the same values for the relevant parameters as in the case of charm

134

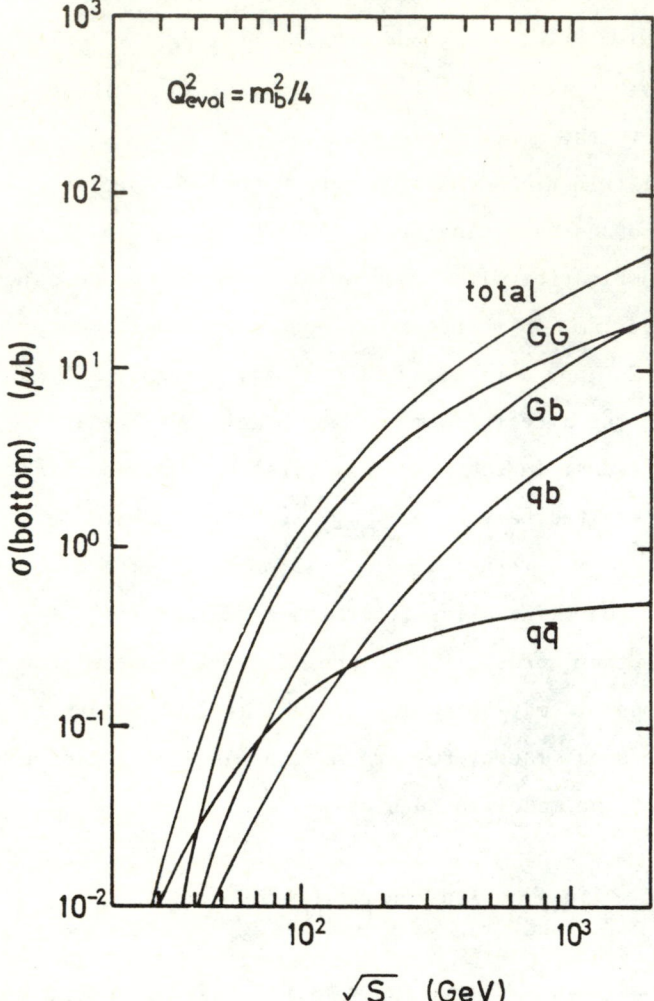

Fig. 21. Cross sections for bottom production
calculated using the same parameters for bottom
sea evolution as determined for charm production
($\alpha_S = \alpha_S(Q^2 + 1.5 \, m_b^2)$, $Q^2_{evol} = -\hat{t}_{min} = m_b^2/4$,
$m_b = 4.7$ GeV).

production and varying only the quark mass ($\alpha_s = \alpha_s(Q^2 + 1.5\, m_b^2)$,
$Q^2_{evol} = 0.25\, m_b^2$, $m_b = 4.7$ GeV). The excitation cross section
appears to be less important than that of fusion at the energies of
current interest. In particular, according to this naïve calculation
one is not able to bridge the gap which separates the fusion contribution from the observed level of the Λ_b signal reported at ISR
by the BCF experiment [33]. This numerology, however, should not hide
the basic fact that there is no sound input in the calculation for
the amount of bottom sea at the Q^2 of interest.

The same considerations apply of course to top production.

CONCLUSIONS

The difficulties met by perturbative QCD models in explaining
the data for hadroproduction of open charm appear to go away after
a proper determination of the flavour excitation contribution. The
calculation presented here for the charm cross section does not
suffer from the ambiguities encountered in previous attempts because:
i) an appropriate technique, taking into account phase-space bounds,
is used to calculate the evolution of the charm sea; ii) the remaining uncertainty for the charm sea is eliminated using the recent
F_2(charm) data; iii) the radius of the interaction, left theoretically undefined because of the perturbative $\sim 1/t^2$ divergence,
is fixed using recent measurements of the p_T distribution of charmed hadrons. As a result, the level and the energy behaviour observed for the charm cross section are correctly reproduced.

The leading particle effect observed in Λ_c production has
been shown to be naturally understood with a simple recombination
model.

Unfortunately, predictions for higher flavours are unreliable at present because of lack of the necessary experimental input to stabilize the calculation.

More details about this work can be found in [34].

The collaboration of S. Wada at the early stages of this work, especially in connection with the recombination model calculations, is gratefully acknowledged.

REFERENCES

1. S. Wojcicki, Proc. Int. Conf. on High-Energy Physics, Madison (1980), p. 1430.

2. D. Treille, Proc. Int. Symp. on Lepton and Photon Interactions at High Energies, Bonn (1981), CERN-EP/81-133 (1981).

3. R. J. N. Phillips, Proc. Int. Conf. on High-Energy Physics, Madison (1980), p. 1470.

4. G. Gustafson and C. Peterson, Phys. Lett. $\underline{67\ B}$, 81 (1977); C. Peterson, Talk at the Topical Workshop on Forward Production of High-Mass Flavours at Collider Energies, Paris (1979), Nordita preprint 80-2 (1980).

5. S. J. Brodsky, P. Hoyer, C. Peterson and N. Sakai, Phys. Lett. $\underline{93\ B}$, 451 (1980); S. J. Brodsky, C. Peterson and N. Sakai, Phys. Rev. $\underline{D\ 23}$, 2745 (1981); D. P. Roy, Phys. Rev. Lett. $\underline{47}$, 213 (1981); R. V. Gavai and D. P. Roy, Tata preprint, TIFR/TH/81-7 (1981).

6. R.Horgan and M. Jacob, CERN-TH 2824 (1981).

7. B. L. Combridge, Nucl. Phys. $\underline{B\ 151}$, 429 (1979).

8. A. J. Buras and K. J. F. Gaemers, Nucl. Phys. B 132, 249 (1978).

9. A. R. Clark et al. (BFP Collaboration), Phys. Rev. Lett. 45, 1465 (1980).

10. C. H. Best (EMC Collaboration), Talk at the XVI Rencontre de Moriond, Les Arcs (1981), Rutherford preprint RL–81–044 (1981); G. Coignet (EMC Collaboration), Talk at the EPS Int. Conf., Lisbon (1981).

11. V. Barger, F. Halzen and W. Y. Keung, Madison preprint DOE–ER/ 00881–215 (1981).

12. R. Odorico, Nucl. Phys. B 172, 157 (1980); P. Mazzanti and R. Odorico, Phys. Lett. 95 B, 133 (1980); Z. Physik C 7, 61 (1980); R. Odorico, Phys. Lett. 103 B, 465 (1981); P. Mazzanti, R. Odorico and V. Roberto, Nucl. Phys. B 193, 541 (1981); G. C. Fox and S. Wolfram, Nucl. Phys. B 168, 285 (1980); S. Wolfram, Talk at the XIV Rencontre de Moriond, Les Arcs (1980); R. D. Field, Talk at the Conference on Perturbative QCD, Tallahassee (1981).

13. R. Odorico, Phys. Lett. 102 B, 341 (1981).

14. R. Odorico, "HEVOL: a Monte Carlo program to calculate the evolution of structure functions with the inclusion of heavy quark effects (long write up)", Bologna preprint IFUB 81/9 (1981), in course of publication in Computer Physics Communications.

15. A. Sansoni, Thesis, University of Bologna (1981).

16. R. Odorico, "A QCD calculation of the transverse momentum distribution of Drell-Yan pairs including soft emission and non-abelian effects", Bologna preprint IFUB 81/21 (1981), in

138

course of publication in Nuclear Physics B.

17. G. C. Fox, Lectures at the SLAC Summer Institute (1981).

18. R. Odorico,"A Monte Carlo program for QCD event simulation in electron-positron annihilation at LEP energies (long write up)", Computer Physics Communications $\underline{24}$, 73 (1981).

19. See [14].

20. R. Odorico, Phys. Lett. $\underline{107\ B}$, 231 (1981).

21. M. Strovink, Proc. Int. Symp. on Lepton and Photon Interactions at High Energies, Bonn (1981), LBL-13478 (1981).

22. M. Basile, CERN-EP/81-23, 127 (1981), submitted to Lettere al Nuovo Cimento.

23. R. K. Ellis, M. A. Furman, H. E. Haber and I. Hinchliffe, Nucl. Phys. $\underline{B\ 173}$, 397 (1980);

W. Furmanski and W. Slominski, Cracow preprint, TPJU-11/81 (1981);

W. Celmaster and D. Sivers, Argonne preprint, ANL-HEP-PR-80-61; J. F. Owens, Talk at the XIII Int. Symp. on Multiparticle Dynamics, Notre Dame (1981).

24. K. Niu, Proc. Conf. on Cosmic Rays and Particle Physics, Bartol (1979), (AIP Conf. Proc. No. 49), p. 181.

25. F. Halzen, A. D. Martin and D. M. Scott, Cambridge preprint DAMTP 81/21 (1981).

26. R. P. Feynman and R. D. Field, Nucl. Phys. $\underline{B\ 136}$, 1 (1978).

27. K. P. Das and R. Hwa, Phys. lett. $\underline{68\ B}$, 459 (1977); L. Van Hove, CERN-TH 2628 (1979).

28. D. Drijard et al., Phys. Lett. $\underline{81\ B}$, 250 (1979); $\underline{85\ B}$, 452 (1979).

29. J. D. Bjorken, Phys. Rev. $\underline{D\ 17}$, 171 (1978).

30. J. F. Gunion, Phys. Rev. $\underline{D\ 12}$, 3469 (1975);

S. J. Brodsky and P. Lepage, SLAC-PUB-2478 (1980);

J. F. Gunion, Talk at the XI Int. Symp. on Multiparticle Dynamics, Bruges (1980), SLAC–PUB–2607 (1980).

31. S. J. Brodsky and G. R. Farrar, Phys. Rev. Lett. <u>31</u>, 1153 (1973).

32. M. Basile et al., CERN–EP/81–22 (1981), submitted to Lettere al Nuovo Cimento.

33. M. Basile et al., CERN–EP/81–38 (1981), submitted to Lettere al Nuovo Cimento.

34. R. Odorico, in preparation.

STRANGE AND CHARM QUARKS IN HADRONS

Rudolph C. Hwa
Institute of Theoretical Science and Department of Physics
University of Oregon, Eugene, Oregon 97403

ABSTRACT

Hadron productions in hard and soft processes are reviewed in the framework of partons, valons and the recombination model. Kaon structure is examined by analyzing the $K^+p \rightarrow K^n X$ data; strange and non-strange quark distributions in a kaon are determined. Charm production is then discussed. It is shown that data on Λ_c^+ and D production in hadronic collisions can be understood in the valon model for low-p_T reactions.

INTRODUCTION

I have at times been asked the question: "How is the recombination model doing?" My answer has been something to the effect that the issue is not so much the recombination mechanism which is as good as it has always been, but rather what the distributions are for the partons that are to recombine. Indeed, the main effort on hadronization in the past several years has been to determine the momentum distributions of the recombining partons either in hard processes for which perturbative QCD can be used, or in soft processes for which the valon model has been suggested. The parton distributions are therefore the main ingredients for hadronization on the exit end, but they also contain key information about the nature of the incident particles on the entry side. It is in this connection that we have advanced the view that soft-hadronic processes are well suited for the determination of hadron structure.[1]

In order that the discussion in this paper be intelligible, it is necessary to give here a brief summary of the valon model. For a review of the subject the reader is referred to my Erice lectures in Ref. 1. The valon model is a way of unifying the bound-state and scattering properties of a hadron. In the static problem a proton is known to be a bound-state of three constituent quarks, but in deep inelastic scattering it is described in terms of current quarks and gluons. The two pictures can coexist if we regard each of the three valence quarks as carrying its own cloud of sea quarks and gluons generated through QCD virtual processes. A valence quark together with its own sea quarks and gluons is, for brevity's sake, referred to as a valon.[2] Thus a proton is made up of three valons which carry all the momentum of the proton except for that associated with the soft gluons which effect the binding. Static properties of the composite system are consequences of the long-range (hadron-size) character of the interaction between valons, so they are insensitive to the internal structure of the valons. That is why the naive quark model in which the valons are regarded as point-like quark is adequate to describe hadron spectroscopy. However, dynamical properties of a hadron as revealed under probing by deep inelastic scattering reflect the short-distance behaviors of the partons. For that the structure of the valons becomes highly relevant.

In term of Fock states the proton wave function in a particular sector may be written as $<uud\bar{q}q...g...|p>$. Inserting a complete set of valon states we have

$$\int \prod_i \frac{dy_i}{y_i} <uudq\bar{q}...g...|UUD><UUD|p>$$

where y_i are the momentum fractions of the three valons. The valon model assumes factorizability of the first scalar product in the form

$$<uudq\bar{q}...g...|UUD> = <uq\bar{q}...g...|U>$$
$$\cdot <uq\bar{q}...g...|U> \qquad (1.1)$$
$$\cdot <dq\bar{q}...g...|D>$$

Thus the probability for a parton to have momentum fraction x can be expressed as a convolution

$$q_i(x) = \sum_v \int \frac{dy}{y} G_v^p(y) P_i^v(x/y) \qquad (1.2)$$

where

$$G_{v_1}^p(y_1) = \int dy_2 dy_3 |<v_1(y_1)v_2(y_2)v_3(y_3)|p>|^2 \qquad (1.3)$$

$$P_i^v(z) = \int dz_2...dz_n |<q(z)\bar{q}(z_2)...|v>|^2 \qquad (1.4)$$

Clearly, $<UUD|p>$ is the wave function of the proton and is known only as a result of solving the confinement problem, unattainable at present. $G_v^p(y)$ is the probability of finding the valon v at y. $P_i^v(z)$ is the momentum distribution of quark i in valon v. It is dependent on Q^2 in a known way at high Q^2.

Since neither G_v^p nor P_i^v can at present be calculated from first principles, they have been determined phenomeno logically. There are two ways that have been used to determine G_v^p: one is by deep inelastic scattering[3] (DIS) and the other form factor[4] (FF). The former makes use of leading log approximation and extrapolates to low Q_o^2; hence, it gives an effective distribution that is not strictly the true distribution at Q_o^2 but nevertheless is useful for evolving back up again to high Q^2 in the same leading log approximation. The second method determines directly the valon

142

distribution at low Q^2 (<1 GeV^2) and is therefore more reliable but cannot be used as a starting input for evolution to high Q^2 since there exists no accurate evolution function from low Q^2. The two sets of distributions therefore complement each other. They have the form [3,4]

$$G_U^p(x) = [B(a+1,3)]^{-1} \, x^a(1-x)^2 \tag{1.5a}$$

$$G_D^p(x) = [B(2-a,2a+2)]^{-1} \, x^{1-a}(1-x)^{2a+1} \tag{1.5b}$$

where $a = 0.65$ for DIS and $a = 0.9$ for FF. It is comforting that the distributions obtained from such diverse phenomenological inputs are so close to each other.

There is a striking confirmation of a prediction by the valon model. It is the ratio $R_1 = F_2^{\nu p}/F_2^{\mu p}$. Parameterization of the quark distributions determined in the valon model[3] can be used to calculate the quantity R_1.[5] The result agrees perfectly with the data.[6] This is shown in Fig. 1. It is a fit with no adjustable parameters.

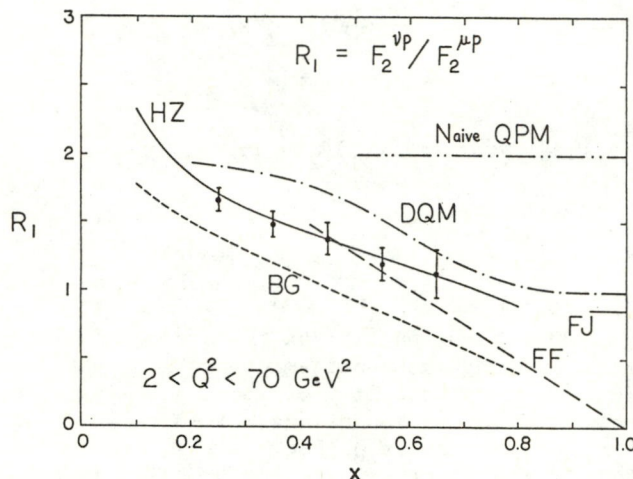

Fig. 1. Data are from Ref. 6. Solid curve is the prediction using the parameters determined in Ref. 3. Other predictions are based on parameters given in Field-Feynman (FF, dashed line), Buras-Gaemers (BG, dotted line), diquark model (DQM, dash-dot line), and Farrar-Jackson (FJ). References for those works are given in Ref. 5.

FRAGMENTATION OF WOUNDED HADRON

In deep inelastic scattering or lepton-pair production a current quark is removed from a hadron which subsequently fragments. The distribution of the decay products should depend on the probe (i.e. the type of quark removed), the momentum x_{bj} of the quark, and Q^2 of the process. It therefore reveals in a very sensitive way the detail nature of the hadronization process. Accurate data that exhibit the dependences on x_{bj} and Q^2 are most effective in selecting the correct model on hadronization.

There exists a naive view on the subject in which the wounded hadron is regarded as a diquark whose fragmentation is treated as that of a color anti-triplet. This view is an oversimplification of a very complicated process because a proton does not consist of just three quarks, but three valons. Each valon contains partons that can contribute to the formation of a final hadron, including the struck valon. The latter has only one of its constituents participating in the hard process, e.g. its valence quark interacting with the virtual photon. Not only are there sea quarks and gluons in the same valon that must hadronize in the target fragmentation region, there are others created by the hard process that must also hadronize. It is known in perturbative QCD that gluons emitted by the quark that is eventually struck by the high-Q^2 virtual photon become increasingly more off-mass-shell the closer the emission vertex is to the photon interaction vertex. Those virtual gluons must degrade in their off-shell-ness before hadronization can occur. It is therefore necessary to evolve up and down to account for their contributions. These complications make the problem far more complex than the usual low-p_T problem since it is a mixture of hard and soft processes.[1]

The valon model supplemented by perturbative QCD is just the right framework to treat this problem. There are no free parameters. The only complications are to keep track of all possible diagrams that contribute to the hadron production under consideration and in computing. The investigation of this problem is near completion, but at this point I have no quantitative result to report.

KAON STRUCTURE

Since unstable particles cannot be used as target for DIS, low-p_T reactions offer the best means of probing their structures. Kaon is a case in point. We use the reaction $K^+p \to K^oX$ as experimental input from which the kaon structure is extracted. In the valon model there are two parts: one is the valon wave function in the kaon which is involved in both the incident and outgoing channels; the other is the quark distributions in the valons. It is the fast quarks which traverse the interaction region without significant attenuation, not the fast valons.[1] A valon contains wee partons and therefore interacts strongly with the target with σ_{vp} roughly equal to $\sigma_{pp}/3$. The problem with kaon is made more complicated by the fact that the strange valon is more massive than the non-strange one. Their momentum distributions are therefore not symmetrical. Moreover, the strange and non-strange quark distributions in valons are no longer universal in the sense of being independent of the flavor of the valon. These are the quantities that we must determine.

We start with the general form for the valon distribution in a kaon [7]

$$G_{U\bar{S}}^{K}(y_1, y_2) = [B(c+1, d+1)]^{-1} \, y_1^{\ c} \, y_2^{\ d} \, \delta(y_1 + y_2 - 1) \qquad (3.1)$$

From this double distribution we can calculate the average momenta of the U and $\bar{S}$ valons, obtaining

$$\bar{y}_U = (c+1)/(c+d+2), \qquad \bar{y}_{\bar{S}} = (d+1)/(c+d+2) \qquad (3.2)$$

Since the average momentum of a valon should be proportional to its mass in any reasonable model, we demand that $\bar{y}_{\bar{S}}/\bar{y}_U = m_S/m_U$ which we take to be 3/2. We thus have one constraint on c and d

$$\frac{d+1}{c+1} = \frac{3}{2} \qquad (3.3)$$

leaving one free parameter to be determined by data.

For the cluster distribution in U the valence and sea parts, denoted by $K_{NS}(z)$ and $L(z)$ respectively, have been determined from $p \to \pi$ fragmentation.[8,9] They are

$$K_{NS}(z) = 0.36 \, \sqrt{z} \, (1-z)^{-0.4} \qquad (3.4)$$

$$L(z) = 0.33 \, (1-z)^{2.7} \qquad (3.5)$$

where the normalization of the sea has been "saturated", i.e. adjusted so that the sea quarks carry all the momentum of the valon except for the momentum of the valence quark. The total number of flavor has assumed to be 3. For the S valon the quark distributions would be different since the strange quark (current and constituent) is more massive than the non-strange counterpart so the proportion of momentum carried is different. Moreover, while the Regge intercept $\alpha_\rho(0) \sim \frac{1}{2}$ controls the small z behavior of $K_{NS}(z)$, that for $K_{NS}^{s}(z)$ for the strange valon would be $\alpha_\phi(0) \sim 0$. We therefore set

$$K_{NS}^{s}(z) = [B(1, b'+1)]^{-1} z(1-z)^{b'} \qquad (3.6)$$

while the sea quark distribution in S is assumed to be the same as L(z) (due to universality in the QCD virtual processes), but with normalization altered to accommodate (3.6), i.e.

$$L^s(z) = \frac{3.7}{6}(1-\bar{z}^s)(1-z)^{2.7} , \quad \bar{z}^s = \int_o^1 dz\ K_{NS}^s(z) \qquad (3.7)$$

Thus there are two adjustable parameters c and b' to be determined by fitting the $K^+ \to K^n$ (i.e. K^O or $\bar{K}^O$) data in accordance to the valon model for low-p_T reactions.[7]

We have used the K^+p data at 70 GeV/c[10] as shown in Fig. 2.

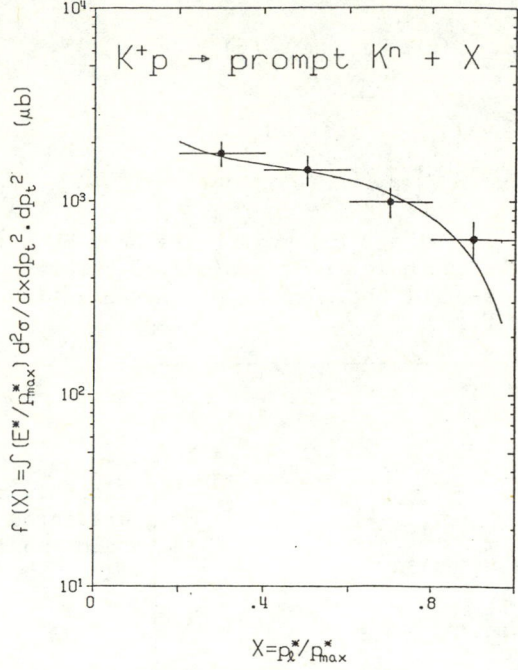

Fig. 2. Data on $K^+p \to K^n + X$ at 70 GeV/c are from Ref. 10. Solid curve is a fit of the data based on the valon model, Ref. 9.

The fact that the inclusive cross section falls gently with x means that the strange quark has a high probability in carrying a large fraction of the momentum of K^+. This is reflected in the result of our fit[11]

$$c = 0 \qquad \text{and} \qquad b' = -0.6 \qquad (3.8)$$

for which the theoretical distribution is shown by the solid curve

146

in Fig. 2. On account of (3.3) we have d=½. To test the validity of (3.3) we calculated the same for d=0 and failed to get a good fit, the χ^2 being ten times greater than that for the d=½ case. Thus we have phenomenologically verified (3.3) as a realistic constraint.

Note that both K_{NS} and K_{NS}^S are peaked at z=1. It means that in soft hadronic reactions the virtual QCD processes that dress up a valence quark do not take away too much of its momentum. This corresponds to the fact that there is no large Q^2 variable in the problem.

The quark distributions in a kaon can now be calculated according to

$$xu_{val}(x) = \int_x^1 dy \ G_U^K(y) \ K_{NS}(x/y) \tag{3.9}$$

$$xs_{val}(x) = \int_x^1 dy \ G_S^K K_{NS}^S(x/y) \tag{3.10}$$

$$x\bar{q}_{sea}(x) = \int_x^1 dy \ [G_U^K(y)L(\tfrac{x}{y})+G_S^K(y)L^S(\tfrac{x}{y})] \tag{3.11}$$

The normalization of $\bar{q}_{sea}(x)$ must be reduced by a factor of 5 in order to describe the quiescient sea[7] (i.e. before enhancement to the "saturated" sea for the purpose of hadronization). The results are shown in Fig. 3.

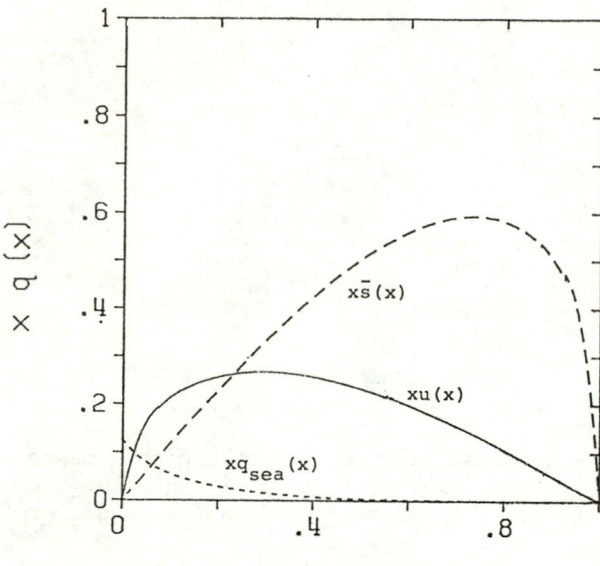

Fig. 3. Valence and sea quark distributions in a kaon as predicted in the valon model.

The strange quark dominates the large-x region because the strange valon is more massive than the non-strange valon. The distributions in Fig. 3. describe the structure of kaon as extracted from low-p_T reaction; as such they correspond to some low Q^2 values, roughly 1-2 GeV^2.[8] For application to hard processes such as lepton-pair production in kaon-initiated reactions, one would need to evole those distributions to higher Q^2. The procedure discussed here demonstrates the feasibility of learning about the structure of unstable hadrons from soft hadronic processes.

CHARM QUARKS IN HADRONS

The surprisingly large cross section in producing fast Λ_c^+ in pp collisions [11,12] raises questions about the charm content of proton and illustrates how low-p_T reactions "probe" the structure of hadrons. Various mechanisms have been suggested to explain the observed level of charm production.[13] Barger et al.[14] consider $c\bar{c}$ pair production in perturbative QCD, while Brodsky et al[15] postulate the existence of an intrinsic Fock state $|uudc\bar{c}>$ in the proton. We outline here a simple argument which shows that recent data on Λ_c^+ and D-meson productions can all be naturally understood in the framework of the valon model.[16]

Let me first assert that the available data on charm production are all consistent with the charm-quark distribution in proton being

$$x \, c(x) \sim (1-x)^3 \tag{4.1}$$

provided that recombination is the mechanism for hadronization. Since the x dependence in (4.1) is the same as that for the u quark in proton, we expect that the spectrum for Λ_c^+ production in pp collision to be similar to the proton spectrum. This is substantiated by the data as shown in Fig. 4. Experience with the recombination model has led us to the recognition that the hadron distribution is not sensitive to the precise form of the recombination function, but is very sensitively dependent on the distributions of the recombining quarks in the initial hadron. Thus although the wave functions for proton and Λ_c^+ are undoubtedly different (and therefore their recombination functions also), the essential equivalence of uud and cud distributions in a proton (except for normalization) would lead to the result exhibited in Fig. 4. Both p and Λ_c^+ inclusive cross sections are rather flat, reflecting the characteristics associated with the recombination of three quarks whose momenta add up to the baryon momentum, with each component distributed in the valence or valence-like manner.

148

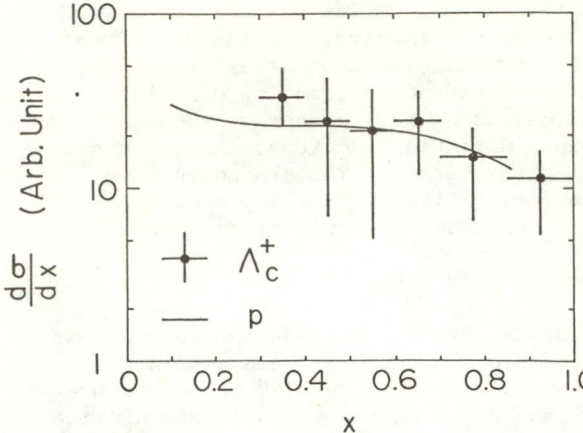

Fig. 4. Inclusive distribution of Λ_c^+ in pp collision is taken from Ref. 12. The solid curve is proton distribution averaged over p_T=0.5 and 0.75 GeV/c according to data given in F.E. Taylor et al., Phys. Rev. D14, 1217 (1976).

For D^o and D^+ production for the recombining quarks are $c\bar{u}$ and $c\bar{d}$, respectively. Since the antiquarks are peaked at small x, the sums of their momenta with that of the c quark would not deviate very much from the latter alone. Thus the distributions of D^o and D^+ production in pp collisions are expected to be $(1-x)^3$, which is just what has been observed.

For $\bar{D}^o$ and D^-, on the other hand, the recombining quarks are $\bar{c}$, u, and d, all of which behave as $(1-x)^3$ (the d quark being only slightly steeper). Thus we expect their inclusive cross sections to be broader than those of D^o and D^+, but not as flat as those of p and Λ_c^+. A distribution of roughly $(1-x)^2$ would therefore be reasonable. No data now exist to verify or contradict this prediction.

Having shown that (4.1) is sufficient to explain the observed characteristics of charm production, it is now our task to explain how (4.1) can arise in the valon model. Without attempting to explain the normalization of the charm distribution, the task is simple. In the valon model all sea quarks, including charm pairs, belong to one of the three valons in the proton. Thus from (1.2) we see that

$$c(x) = \sum_v \int_x^1 \frac{dy}{y} \, G_v^p(y) \, P_c^v(x/y) \qquad (4.2)$$

where $G_v^p(y)$ behaves as $(1-y)^2$ at large y, in accordance to (1.5). We only need to know the distribution $P_c^v(z)$ at large z in order to conclude about c(x) at large x. Now, a charm pair $c\bar{c}$ has mass ~3 GeV whereas a non-strange valon has a mass of about 0.3 GeV. Thus $c\bar{c}$ is a highly virtual, and tightly bound state in a valon, much more so than $u\bar{D}$ valons are in a pion. By the uncertainty principle tightly bound states are localized in coordinate space, but spread-out in momentum space. For that reason the valon wave function in a pion is constant.[1,7] So similarly the $c\bar{c}$ wave function in a valon should also be a constant, i.e.

$$P_c^v(z) = a \qquad (4.3)$$

where a is a small number, signifying the low probability of finding a $c\bar{c}$ pair in a valon.

Since perturbative QCD is not reliable in bound-state problems it is meaningless to discuss the lifetime of the $c\bar{c}$ pair in a valon on the grounds of perturbative arguments. We regard the value of a in (4.3) to have incorporated the unlikelihood of a highly virtual $c\bar{c}$ pair to live long enough to hadronize into a charm particle by recombination. Substituting (4.3) into (4.2) then yields $c(x) \sim (1-x)^3$ at large x; the result is equivalent to (4.1) for the level of accuracy that is being considered here. Hence, we have the desired charm·quark distribution and consequently also the correct charm particle inclusive cross section apart from normalization. Using the observed rate as an input, one can conclude that $a \sim 0.01 - 0.02$.

Knowing $P_c^v(z)$ enables us to predict about the charm content in a pion. Since the valon distribution in a pion is constant, we have

$$xc^\pi(x) \propto 1-x \qquad (4.4)$$

It then follows that in the π^+ fragmentation region π^o, D^o and D^- should all have essentially the same distributions, whereas D^o, D^+ and Λ_c^+ are more likely to be similar.

Our estimates in this section are crude, but are adequate for the quality of data on charm production now available. Careful calculations in the valon model can be worked out, but the problem will require some computation that has not yet been performed.

ACKNOWLEDGMENTS

I am grateful to L. Gatignon, R.T. Van de Walle, and M.S. Zahir for collaboration on different parts of the work discussed here. The research is supported in part by U.S. Department of Energy under Contract No. DE-ATOG-76ER70004.

REFERENCES

1. R.C. Hwa, Erice lectures in "Partons in Soft-Hadronic Process-es" Ch. IV, ed. R.T. Van de Walle (World Scientific, Singapore, 1981).
2. R.C. Hwa, Phys. Rev. D22, 759 (1980).
3. R.C. Hwa and M.S. Zahir, Phys. Rev. D23, 2539 (1981).
4. R.C. Hwa and C.S. Lam, Phys. Rev. D (to be published).
5. R.C. Hwa and M.S. Zahir, OITS-180 (1981).
6. P. Allen et al., Phys Lett. 103B, 71 (1981).
7. R.C. Hwa, Phys. Rev. D22, 1593 (1980).
8. M. Barth et al., Nijmegen preprint HEN-208, 1981.
9. L. Gatignon, R.C. Hwa, and R.T. Van de Walle, HEN-214 and OITS-170, to be published in the Proc. for EPS Conference on High Energy Physics, Lisbon, 1981.
10. M. Barth et al., Nijmegen preprint HEN-202, 1981.
11. D. Drijard et al., Phys. Lett. 81B, 250 (1979); K.L. Giboni et al., Phys. Lett. 85B, 437 (1979); W. Lockman et al., Phys. Lett. 85B, 443 (1979).
12. M. Basile et al., CERN-EP/81-22, to be published in Lett. Nuovo Cim.
13. R.J.N. Phillips, AIP Conf. Proc. No. 68, ed. L. Durand and L.G. Pondrom (AIP, 1981), p. 1470.
14. V. Barger, F. Halzen and W.Y. Keung, Phys. Rev. D24, 1428 (1981); D25, 112 (1982).
15. S.J. Brodsky, C. Peterson, and N. Sakai, Phys. Rev. D23, 2745 (1981).
16. R.C. Hwa, OITS-182 (1982).

GETTING TO THE TOP

D.M. Scott
Department of Applied Mathematics and Theoretical Physics,
University of Cambridge, England

ABSTRACT

We review estimates for bound and naked top decay modes, cross
sections, signatures and backgrounds at hadron collider energies.

1. INTRODUCTION

The top quark t, expected in the standard $SU(2) \times U(1)$ electroweak model, remains inaccessible to the highest available energy in
e^+e^- annihilation, implying $m_t \gtrsim 19$ GeV. The next, and for some time
the only, opportunity for discovering the top flavour will be provided
by the CERN $\bar{p}p$ collider, operating at a centre of mass energy $\sqrt{s} =$
540 GeV. Here we assess[1] the possibility of discovering t at the
collider if 20 GeV $\lesssim m_t \lesssim$ 60 GeV. Calculations of cross sections[1-6]
and decay rates[1,7-12] for states with hidden and naked t[13] are carried
out using the standard electroweak model, perturbative QCD, and a
little magic (in the form of phenomenological scaling laws). The
results will be somewhat inconclusive in that rates are low or backgrounds high for the most obvious signatures of dileptons from the
leptonic decay of toponium, $V(t\bar{t}) \rightarrow \ell^+\ell^-$, and single leptons from the
semileptonic decay of a meson with naked t, $M(t\bar{q}) \rightarrow \ell^+ + X$ (throughout
ℓ = lepton; q = u,d,s; Q = c,b; g = gluon). But with sufficiently
good experimental resolution the former, and with sufficiently large
diffraction-like component of the t cross section (which has its own
troubles) the latter signature may work. Finally we list more complicated signatures involving multileptons or the jet of hadrons in the
semileptonic decay of M(t$\bar{q}$). All calculations will be done for $\bar{p}p$
interactions at centre of mass energy $\sqrt{s}$ = 540 GeV.

2. TOPONIUM

The traditional way of discovering a new flavour Q in hadron
interactions is through the leptonic decay of the vector onium state
with hidden flavour[14]. To see whether it is possible to discover
toponium this way we need to estimate its decay and production
characteristics. This information will be combined with luminosity
and resolution expectations for the CERN $\bar{p}p$ collider - the discovery
of toponium depends crucially on these parameters.

2.1 DECAY CHARACTERISTICS

The expected decays of toponium have been studied in detail in, for example, refs. 1, 7-12. A thorough description is given by Leveille[11]. Here we mention only three important decays, shown in Figure 1, omitting those expected to be small and those involving the Higgs boson. The calculation proceeds in the rest frame by treating toponium as a free $t\bar{t}$ system, and the rate for annihilation

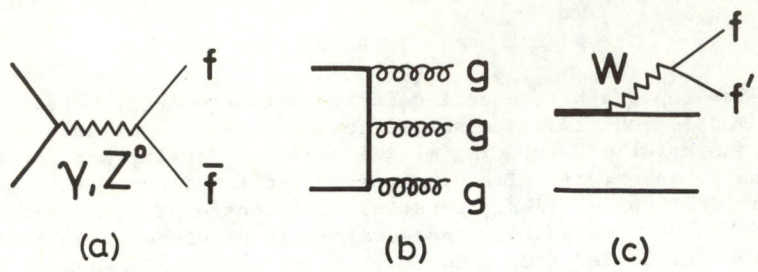

$$(a) \qquad (b) \qquad (c)$$

Fig. 1. Toponium decays.

decays is normalised to the $t\bar{t}$ wavefunction at the origin, or the toponium$-t-\bar{t}$ vertex in a completely relativistic treatment[15]. Attempts have been made to estimate the high mass toponium wave function at the origin in potential models[9,10,12], but instead we will use a phenomenological scaling law relating to the quantity $\Gamma(V(t\bar{t}) \rightarrow \gamma^* \rightarrow e^+e^-)/e_t^2$, where e_t is the charge of the t quark (2/3). For the $\rho,\omega,\phi,\psi,\Upsilon$ the corresponding quantities are all approximately equal to $\Gamma_o = 10$ KeV, and we assume that the same is true for toponium $V(t\bar{t})$. Annihilation decays can now be normalised relative to this.

For the decays shown in Figure 1:

(a) The width by annihilation through γ^* or Z^o into fermion-anti-fermion $f\bar{f}$ is

$$\Gamma(f\bar{f}) = \{ e_f^2 e_t^2 + \frac{(1+v_f^2)\, v_t^2}{K^2} \frac{\eta_Z^2}{(1-\eta_Z)^2 + \gamma_Z}$$

$$- \frac{2e_f e_t v_f v_t}{K} \frac{(1-\eta_Z)\eta_Z}{(1-\eta_Z)^2 + \gamma_Z} \} \, \Gamma_o , \tag{1}$$

where $x = \sin^2\theta_w$ (=0.23), $v_f = 2(T_f - 2e_f x)$ with T weak isospin, e is electric charge, $K = 16 \sin^2\theta_w \cos^2\theta_w$, $\gamma_Z = \Gamma_Z^2/m_Z^2$, $\eta_Z = m_V^2/m_Z^2$, and quark-antiquark final states need a factor 3 for colour. Note that we have ignored annihilation through the W in the t-channel.

(b) The width by annihilation into three gluons is[16]

$$\Gamma(ggg) = \frac{10(\pi^2 - 9)\,\alpha_s^3}{81\,\pi\,\alpha^2}\,\Gamma_o\,, \tag{2}$$

where the strong coupling

$$\alpha_s = \frac{12\pi}{23\ln(m^2/\Lambda_{\overline{MS}}^2)} - \frac{4176\pi\,\ln\ln(m^2/\Lambda_{\overline{MS}}^2)}{12167\,\ln^2(m^2/\Lambda_{\overline{MS}}^2)}\,, \tag{3}$$

with $m = 0.47m_V$, $\Lambda_{\overline{MS}} = 0.1$, incorporates next-to-leading order effects[16]

(c) The "free" decay of the t-quark, with $\bar{t}$ a spectator, is the analogue of μ decay. As the width is proportional to m_t^5, this decay becomes important for high toponium masses. When $m_V > 2m_W$, real W's can be produced this way. In the rest frame of the t-quark, the differential decay rate for $t \to b\,e^+\nu_e$ is

$$\frac{d\Gamma}{dX} = \frac{G^2 m_t^5}{192\pi^3}\,\frac{2(x^2-4r)^{\frac{1}{2}}\{3x(1+r)^{\frac{1}{2}} - 2x^2 - 4r\}}{(1+xq-p-q)^2 + \Gamma_W^2/m_W^2} \tag{4}$$

where $x = 2E_b/m_t$, $p = m_b^2/m_W^2$, $q = m_t^2/m_W^2$, $r = m_b^2/m_t^2$ and $2m_b/m_t \le x \le 1 + m_t^2$. If we let $m_W \to \infty$ and $m_b \to 0$, we find the familiar

$$\Gamma = \frac{G^2 m_t^5}{192\pi^3} \tag{5}$$

Counting all allowed final states, and remembering that the $\bar{t}$ can decay instead, one finds a factor $\simeq 18$ multiplying this rate.

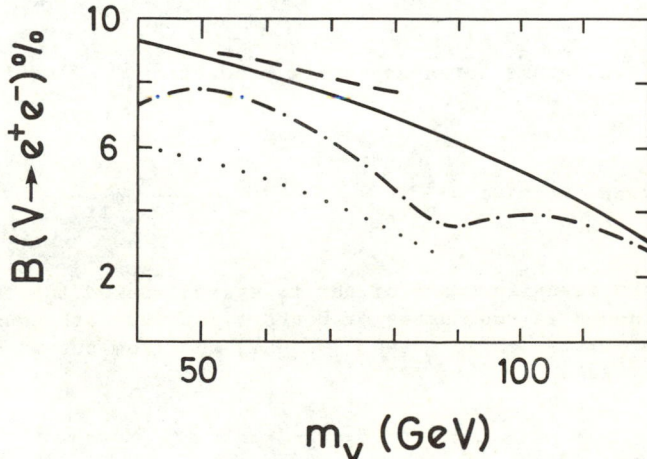

Fig. 2. Calculations of the e^+e^- branching ratio of toponium (——— Pakvasa et al.[1]; - - - - Bigi and Kraseman[10]; .... Leveille[11]; -·-·- Rizzo[12]).

154

In Figure 2 we show the results of four calculations[1,10,11,12] for the leptonic branching ratio of toponium $B(V(t\bar{t}) \to e^+e^-)$ as a function of its mass. The answers are different because of different approximations, different choices of $t\bar{t}$ wave function at the origin, and different $\sin^2\theta_w$. In what follows we choose $B(V(t\bar{t}) \to e^+e^-) = 0.05$ for simplicity.

2.2 PRODUCTION

We consider three possible production mechanisms for toponium:
(a) By $q\bar{q} \to \gamma^*, Z^o \to V(t\bar{t})$, that is the inverse of the decay into $q\bar{q}$. The subprocess cross section, averaged over initial spin and colour is

$$\sigma(q\bar{q} \to \gamma^*, Z^o \to V(t\bar{t})) = \frac{4\pi^2\Gamma_o}{m_V} \{ \} \delta(s - m_V^2) \qquad (6)$$

where $\{ \}$ represents the same curly bracket as in Equation (1).
(b) In photon, lepton and hadron initiated interactions, ψ and Υ production have been successfully described by the QCD "semilocal duality" model[17,18], and we will use this for toponium. First calculate the production of $t + \bar{t}$ from the $O(\alpha_s^2)$ QCD diagrams shown in Figure 3. The cross section for bound $t\bar{t}$ states is supposed to be that part of the $t + \bar{t}$ cross section with the invariant mass of the $t + \bar{t}$ system below naked top threshold, and the cross section for the toponium ground state is a particular fraction of this bound $t\bar{t}$ cross section. This fraction is estimated from the number of bound $t\bar{t}$

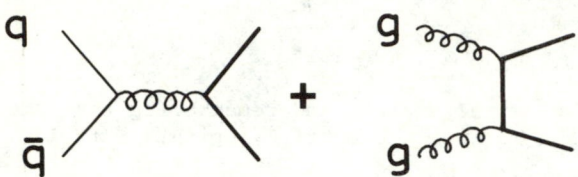

Fig. 3. $O(\alpha_s^2)$ diagrams for heavy quark production.

states. So

$$\sigma(\bar{p}p \to V(t\bar{t})X) = \frac{1}{n} \int_{2m_t}^{2m_t+\delta} \frac{d\sigma(\bar{p}p \to t\bar{t}X)}{dm_{t\bar{t}}} dm_{t\bar{t}} \ . \qquad (7)$$

Here $m_{t\bar{t}}$ is the invariant mass of the $t\bar{t}$ system, naked top threshold is at $2m_t+\delta$, and n is the number of bound $t\bar{t}$ states with masses below $2m_t+\delta$. In our estimates we guess $\delta = 1$ GeV, and from potential model calculations[19] take

$$n = 10(m_t/m_c)^{\frac{1}{2}} \ . \qquad (8)$$

The resulting cross sections depend quite strongly on the choice of gluon density. In calculations, we will take a hard gluon density $xG(x) = 3(1-x)^5$. Parametrisations which include QCD scaling violations lead typically to softer gluon densities, and lower cross sections for high masses.

(c) A scaling law was proposed by Gaisser, Halzen and Paschos[20] for the production of heavy vector states V :

$$\sigma(pp \to VX) = \frac{\Gamma_{hadronic}}{m_V^3} \, F(m_V/\sqrt{s}) \, , \tag{9}$$

where F is a universal function, and $\Gamma_{hadronic}$ is the direct decay into hadrons, interpreted as the decay into three gluons in perturbative QCD. Evidence for the validity of this scaling law is shown in Figure 4a which contains data[21] for ϕ, ψ, ψ', Υ, Υ' production. For

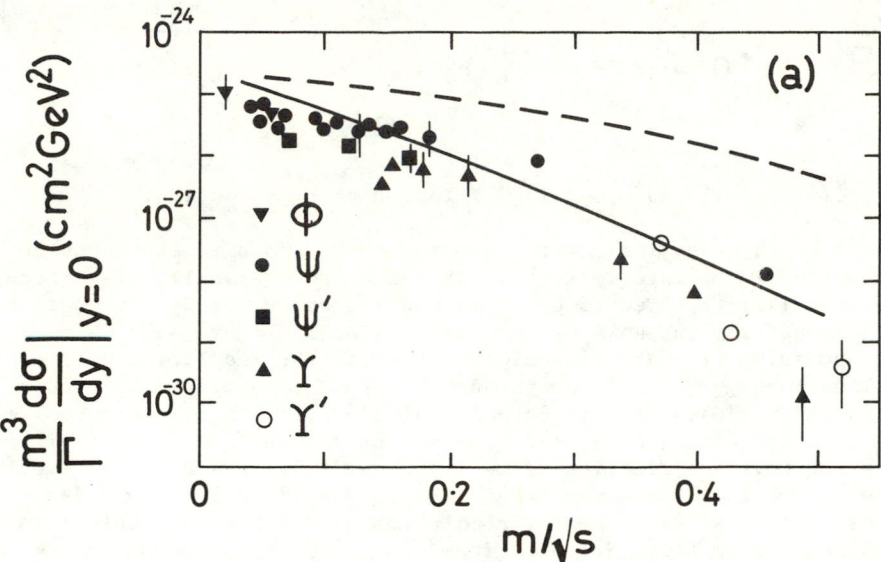

Fig. 4(a)   Gaisser-Halzen-Paschos[20] scaling of vector meson production.

comparison we show in Figure 4b the familiar Drell-Yan scaling[22] of high mass lepton pair cross sections[21]. The two sets of data can be described by curves of the same shape, as shown. Then to describe the normalisation as well we take[6,21]

$$\frac{d\sigma}{dy} (pp \to VX) = (1.5 \times 10^7) \, \Gamma(V \to ggg) \, \frac{d\sigma^{th}}{dmdy} (pp \to e^+e^-X) \, , \tag{10}$$

where σ^{th} is the theoretical Drell-Yan cross section (we use Owens-

156

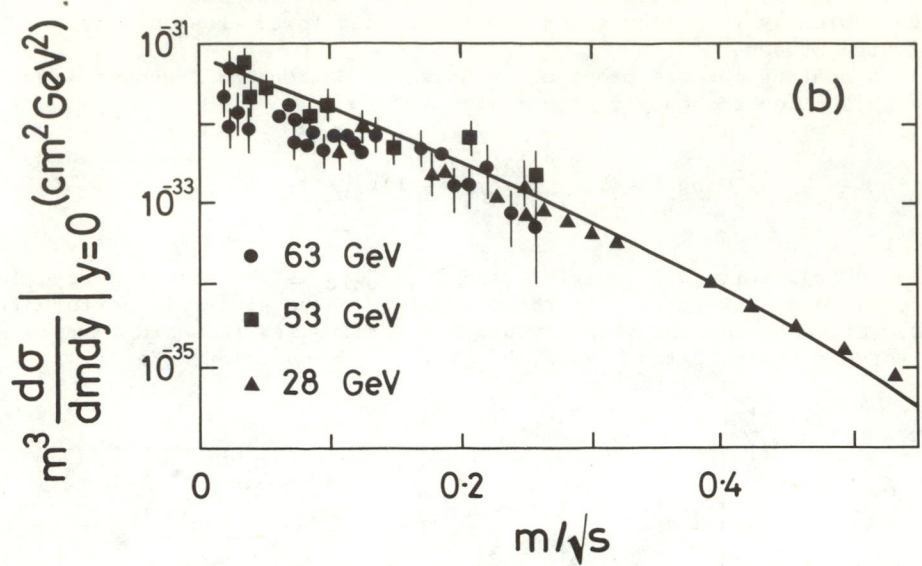

Fig. 4(b) Drell-Yan[22] scaling of lepton pair production.

Reya[23] quark densities), with no K factor[24]. To estimate toponium
production in $\bar{p}p$ interactions we will use the GHP scaling law through
Equation (19), applied to $\bar{p}p$. The scaling curve for $\bar{p}p$ interactions
at ISR energies is shown by the dashed line in Figure 4a. As m_V
approaches m_Z, we have to decide whether to use the lepton pair cross
section through just γ^*, or through γ^* and Z^O, on the right hand side
of Equation (10). We will actually display results for both choices.

The calculated cross sections for $\bar{p}p \rightarrow (V(t\bar{t}) \rightarrow e^+e^-) + X$ at
$\sqrt{s} = 540$ GeV as a function of m_V are shown in Figure 5a. The event
rate per year at a luminosity of $10^{29}/cm^2/sec$ is also shown. We
choose a typical experimental resolution $\Delta m = 0.01m$, and calculate
background from Drell-Yan e^+e^- from

$$\sigma_{background} = \int_{m-\frac{1}{2}\Delta}^{m+\frac{1}{2}\Delta} \frac{d\sigma(\bar{p}p \rightarrow e^+e^-)}{dm'} dm' . \qquad (11)$$

We show the "theoretical" background, calculated with no K factor. In
practice the background may be larger than we show by an uncomfortable
factor K = 2-3. Related information is displayed in Figure 5b. We
have taken the most optimistic toponium cross section from Figure 5a,
and show the height of the peak above theoretical Drell-Yan background,
assuming a Gaussian resolution. Multiplying the background by a K
factor 2-3 would have a sad effect on the height of the peak above it.

It is clear that good experimental resolution is crucial. But
even 1% resolution may not be enough if dileptons from production and

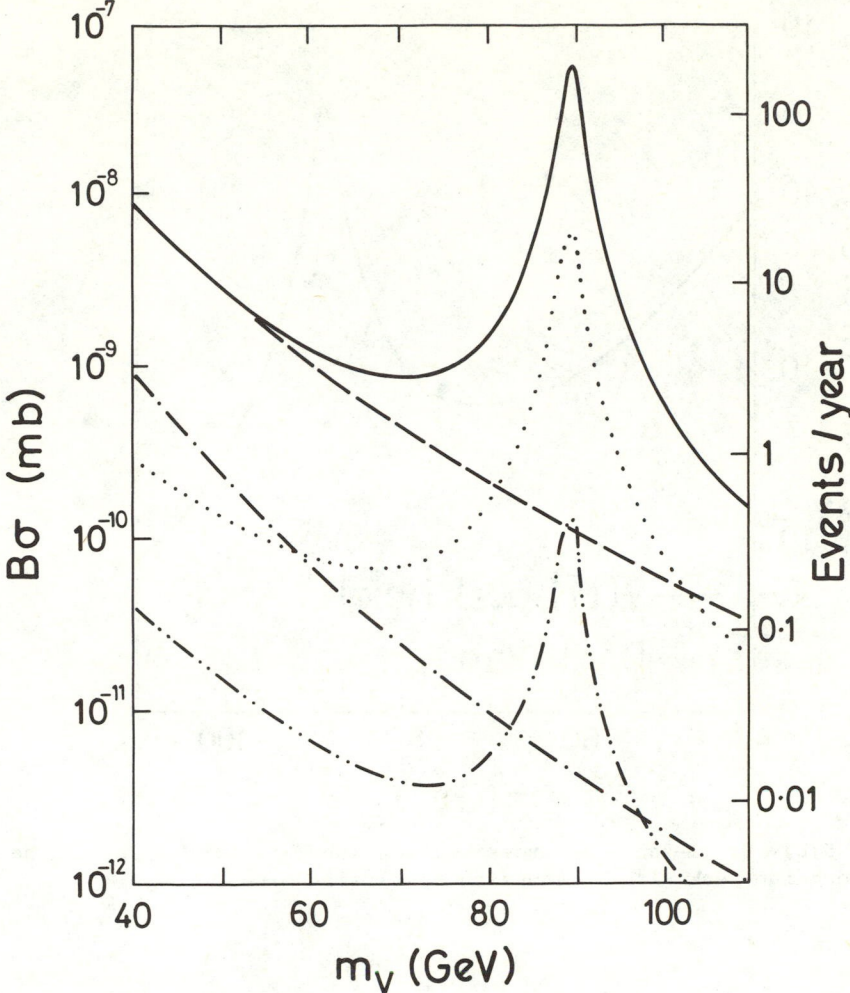

Fig. 5(a) Cross section for $\bar{p}p \to (V(t\bar{t}) \to e^+e^-) + X$: ———(————) GHP scaling with (without) Z^0; -·-· semilocal duality; -··- direct through γ^* and Z^0; .... Drell-Yan background (no K factor). Events/year are calculated with $L = 10^{29}/cm^2/sec$.

semileptonic decay of heavy quarks c,b cannot be removed; such dileptons dominate those from Drell-Yan out to high masses $\simeq 80$ GeV[1,6]. The production will be described in detail in the next section, but here we point out that such leptons will be accompanied by a hadronic shower, which may be sufficient to distinguish them.

Finally, the calculated cross sections may be enhanced if more than one vector state falls within the resolution, and if there is important cascading from $\chi(t\bar{t})$, $V'(t\bar{t})$ states.

158

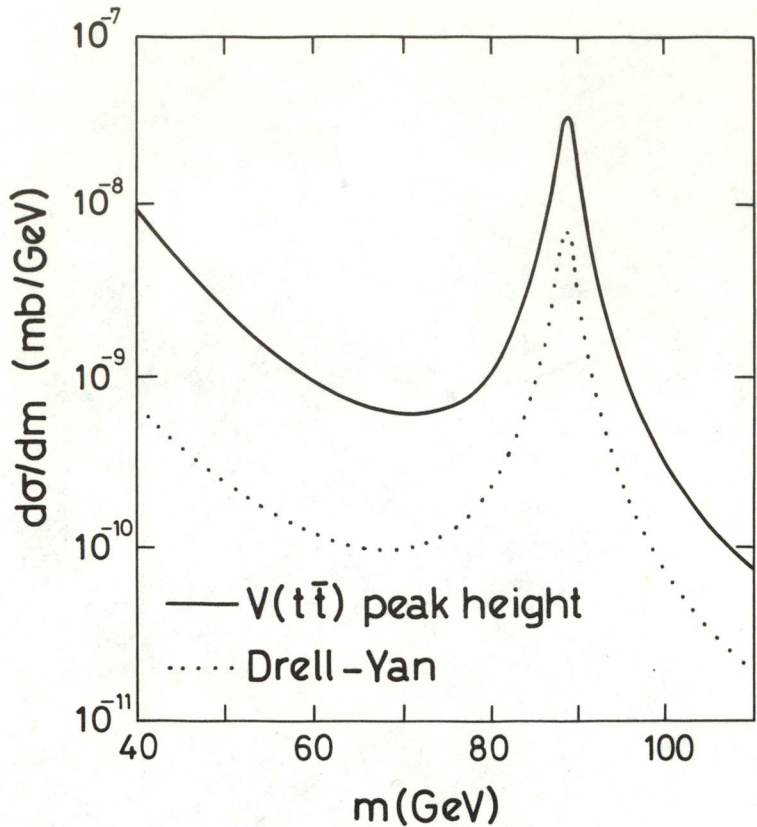

Fig. 5(b) Drell-Yan e^+e^- cross section (no K factor) ...., and height of toponium peak with 1% gaussian resolution —— .

3. NAKED TOPS

The cross section for naked top production is calculated[2] in $O(\alpha_s^2)$ QCD from the diagrams of Figure 3, and is shown in Figure 6 for $\bar{p}p$ collisions at $\sqrt{s}$ = 540 GeV. We use Owens-Reya[23] quarks, and the two solid curves come from choosing their $G(x)$ (which is scale violating) or $xG(x) = 3(1-x)^5$. We are interested in a top signal in the high transverse momentum (p_T) single lepton cross section, and so we must decide how the t fragments into a meson $M(t\bar{q})$ with naked top and how the meson undergoes semileptonic decay, Figure 7. After calculating the signal, we estimate backgrounds which come mainly from c,b production and semileptonic decay. We also discuss an enhancement[5] coming from possible diffraction-like production of the top with large cross section. Finally, we briefly discuss multilepton and lepton-hadron correlation signatures.

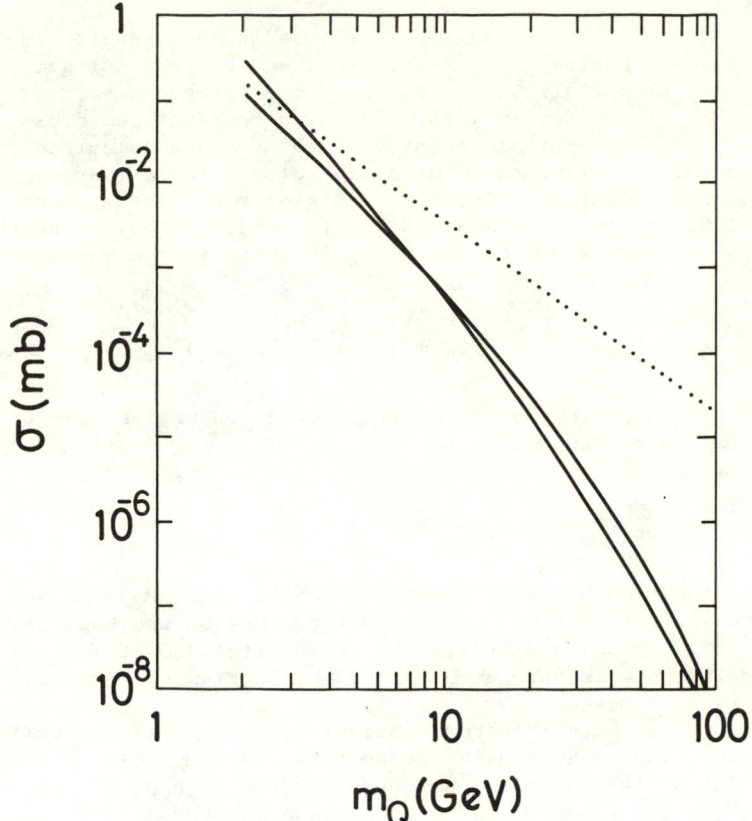

Fig. 6. Heavy quark production in $\bar{p}p$ at $\sqrt{s}$ = 540 GeV through the $O(\alpha_s^2)$ diagrams of Fig.3 (———), and through the diffraction-like cross section of Eq.(18) (....).

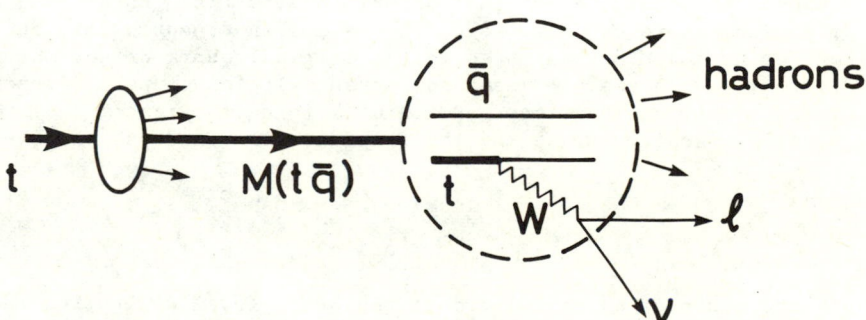

Fig. 7. A t-quark fragments into a t-meson which decays semi-leptonically.

3.1 LEPTON SPECTRUM

The arguments of refs. 25 suggest that when a heavy quark fragments into a meson containing the heavy quark and a light antiquark,
the meson carries almost all the momentum of the parent quark. If
this is true, the cross section for $M(t\bar{q})$ is the same as the cross
section for t. The semileptonic decay of $M(t\bar{q})$ is then calculated[26]
at the quark level, treating the $\bar{q}$ as a spectator. While there may
be problems in doing this for D's, the spectator model is expected
to become much better for real heavies[27]. The charged lepton energy
E_ℓ spectrum in the rest frame of the $M(t\bar{q})$ is given in the spectator
model to be[26]

$$\frac{dN}{dE_\ell} \propto E_\ell^2 (m_t^2 - m_r^2 - 2E_\ell m_t)^2 / (m_t^2 - 2E_\ell m_t) \tag{12}$$

where m_r is the mass of the recoil quark, and lepton masses have been
neglected. Putting $m_r = 0$ gives

$$\frac{dN}{dE_\ell} = 96B (m_t - 2E_\ell) E_\ell^2 / m_t^4 , \tag{13}$$

which is normalised to the semileptonic branching ratio B. The semi-
leptonic branching ratio at the quark level depends on the Kobayashi-
Maskawa angles[28], but for simplicity we take $B(M(t\bar{q}) \to e^+X) = 0.1$.
The resulting lepton spectrum[1] at 90° is shown in Figure 8, for a
selection of t-quark masses.

Single leptons at high transverse momentum can come from a variety
of other sources[1], for example pair production from high mass, low p_T
or low mass, high p_T (almost real) photons, or from high p_T ψ. But the
dominant source is the production at high p_T and subsequent semi-leptonic
decay of c,b. Such leptons are annoying backgrounds not only in the
single lepton spectrum, but also in the dilepton cross section when both
Q and $\bar{Q}$ undergod semileptonic decay. These leptons can also provide
important backgrounds to weak boson signatures[1,6,29].

The calculation of the lepton cross section from c,b production
anddecay isthe same as we just described from t's. But in the high
p_T region, where $p_T \gg m_Q$, we can use a collinear approximation[1],
neglecting momenta transverse to the original quark direction, see
Figure 7. Both quark → meson and meson → lepton steps are described
by fragmentation functions. Defining z to be the fraction of the
parent's momentum carried by the fragmentation product, we have

$$D_{Q \to M}(z) = \begin{cases} 1 & , \quad c , \\ \delta(1-z) & , \quad b , \end{cases} \tag{14}$$

and the meson decay calculated at the quark level neglecting the
recoil quark mass gives[1,26,30] (for charged leptons)

$$D_{M \to \ell}(z) = \begin{cases} 2(1-z)^2(1+2z)B & , \quad c , \\ \frac{1}{3}(1-z)(5+5z-4z^2)B & , \quad b , \end{cases} \tag{15}$$

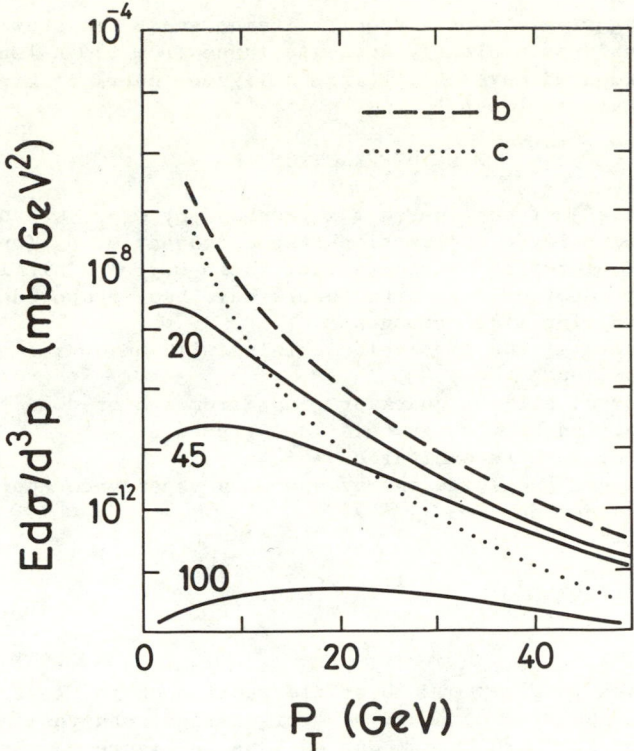

Fig. 8. Single lepton cross section at 90° in $\bar{p}p$ at $\sqrt{s}$ = 540 GeV.
Leptons from the W have been omitted (for those see Martin[29]). The
t mass in GeV is indicated.

where $B \simeq 0.1$ is the semileptonic branching ratio. The difference
between the two distributions in Equation (14) is because the c is not
a real heavy; the difference in Equation (15) is because e^+ is an
antifermion while e^- is a fermion. Note that both Equations (14)
and (15) favour b over c, and so at high p_T where masses are unimportant,
leptons from b dominate those from c. Fragmentation functions in
series are combined by

$$D_{Q \to \ell}(z) = \int_z^1 \frac{dy}{y} \, D_{Q \to M}(z/y) \, D_{M \to \ell}(y) \qquad (16)$$

and the lepton cross section is derived from the quark cross section by

$$E_\ell \, \frac{d\sigma^\ell}{d^3 p_\ell}(p_T, \theta) = \int_1^{p_T^{max}/p_T} D\left(\frac{1}{\alpha}\right) E_Q \, \frac{d\sigma^Q}{d^3 p_Q}(\alpha p_T, \theta) \, d\alpha \,. \qquad (17)$$

162

The resulting single lepton spectra from c and b are shown in Figure 8. Leptons from b clearly dominate those from t. A lepton at high p_T can be produced more easily from a lighter quark at high p_T than a heavier quark at low p_T.

3.2 DIFFRACTION

So far we have just considered t's produced by $O(\alpha_s^2)$ QCD diagrams. The observation of a large diffraction-like component of Λ_c (and Λ_b) production at ISR energies[31] suggests that there may be a similar component to Λ_t production. Several models have been proposed to explain the diffraction-like component:

(a) Intrinsic charm at the 1% level combining with ud quarks in the proton's wave function[3].

(b) A QCD scatter of a light quark or gluon from a c or $\bar{c}$ in the proton's wave function $qc \to qc$, $gc \to gc$[4]; see Figure 9.

(c) Charm quark-diquark recombination[6,32].

For simplicity we can guess the energy and mass dependence appropriate to diffractive production:

$$\sigma_{diff} \simeq \frac{0.1}{m_Q^2} \ln \frac{\sqrt{s}}{m_Q} \ mb. \ , \tag{18}$$

which is normalised to give $\simeq 0.2$ mb of diffractive charm at $\sqrt{s} = 63$ GeV, $m_Q = m_c = 1.5$ GeV (which could be a significant underestimate[31]). This cross section is shown by the dotted line in Figure 6. We emphasize that this is just a guess, and indeed the model of Barger, Halzen and Keung[4], where the energy and mass dependence can be calculated, gives a cross section in disagreement with Equation (18). At $\sqrt{s} = 540$ GeV the model gives similar cross sections to Equation (18) for c,b but is an order of magnitude smaller for $m_Q \simeq 20$ GeV.

We see from Figure 6 that the t cross section could be much larger than that given by $O(\alpha_s^2)$ perturbative QCD. Horgan and Jacob[5] have argued that such a large cross section could give a prominent top signature in the single lepton spectrum: raising the spectrum of leptons from t decays by a factor ~100 in Figure 8 certainly lends support to this idea. We can easily calculate the lepton spectrum from diffractive t's by assuming that they are produced with $p_T = 0$, and by guessing a momentum dependence[5]

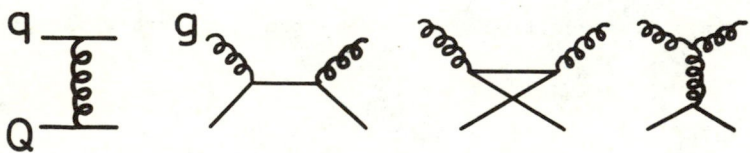

Fig. 9. Excitation of a single heavy quark[2,4].

$$\frac{d\sigma^t}{dx} = \frac{f+1}{2} \sigma_{diff}(1-x)^f \tag{19}$$

where $x = 2p_L/\sqrt{s}$ is Feynman x. The cross section of the decay lepton is then given by[5]

$$E_\ell \frac{d\sigma^\ell}{d^3p_\ell}(y_\ell, p_T) = \frac{1}{4\pi} \int_{p_T}^{\frac{1}{2}m_t} \frac{dE}{E^2(1-p_T^2/E^2)^{\frac{1}{2}}} \frac{d\sigma^t}{dy_t} \frac{dN}{dE}, \tag{20}$$

where we must sum over the two possibilities $y_t = y_\ell \mp \frac{1}{2}\ell n((1+c)/(1-c))$, $c = (1-p_T^2/E^2)^{\frac{1}{2}}$, and y is centre of mass rapidity. The resulting single lepton spectrum is shown in Figure 10, for $m_t = 20$ GeV. We

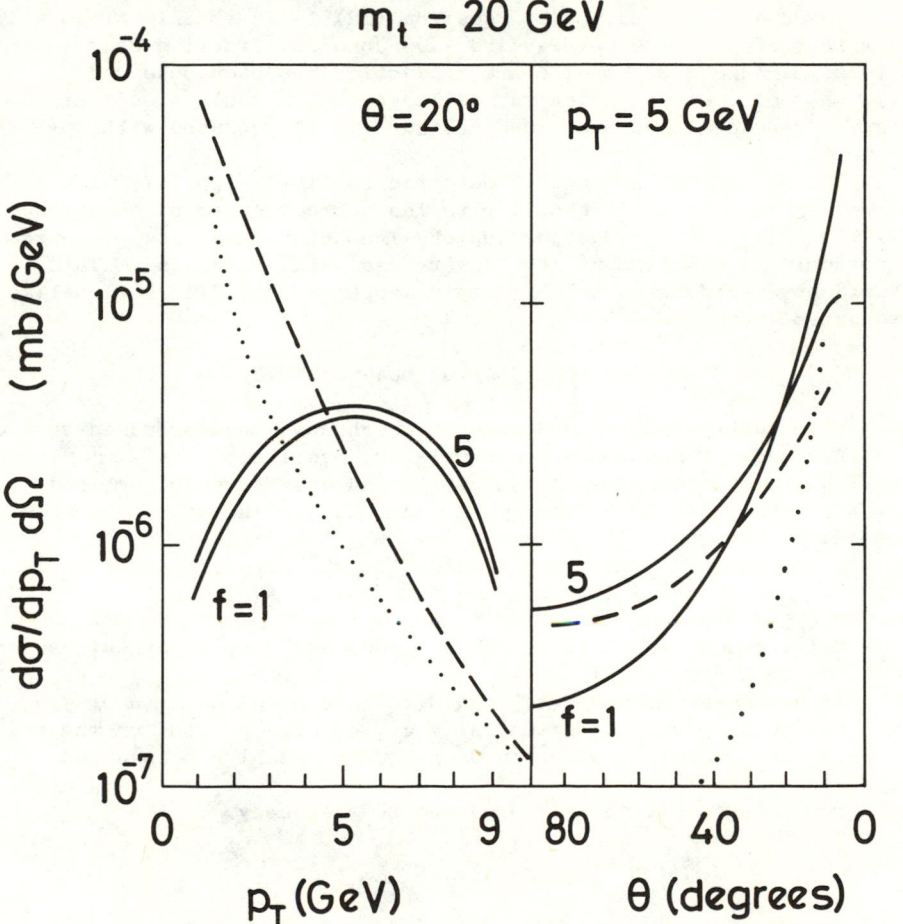

Fig. 10. Single lepton cross section from diffractive t in $\bar{p}p$ at $\sqrt{s} = 540$ GeV with cross section given by Eq.(18) (——), and backgrounds from semileptonic decay of b produced through $O(\alpha_s^2)$ QCD, and through single b excitation in the model of ref. 4 (---- and ....).

164

also show an estimate of background from b production and semileptonic decay, calculated using the collinear approximation described earlier. Shown separately are leptons from b's produced through the $O(\alpha_s^2)$ QCD diagrams of Figure 3, and through the qb $\to$ qb, gb $\to$ gb diagrams[4] calculated at face value (that is, with no scaling violations). We remark:

(a) The diffractive cross sections for b and t are really no more than guesses; and also the BHK model[4] gives a diffractive t cross section about an order of magnitude smaller than Equation (18). In fact the diffractive cross section in Equation (18) may already be in trouble at $\sqrt{s}$ = 63 GeV where it gives $\simeq$10 µb for b production. The measured prompt lepton cross section $\ell/\pi \simeq 10^{-4}$ gives a bound[33] $\sigma_{diffractive}(b) \lesssim$ 2-5 µb. Note that if we underestimated the magnitude of Equation (18) by normalising to too small a charm cross section, the violation of the bound is even more serious. Further, the slow energy dependence in Equation (18) is in trouble at Fermilab energies: at p_L = 300 GeV we find $\simeq$100 µb of diffractive charm, while a total of around 20 µb of charm production has been observed[34].

(b) $<p_T>$ of the production may be large, which would smear out the signal (remember that W,Z are expected[29] to be produced with $<p_T> \simeq$ 10 GeV).

(c) For $p_T \simeq$ 5 GeV and $m_b \simeq$ 5 GeV, the collinear approximation is surely wrong (though it should give the correct order of magnitude).

(d) For $O(\alpha_s^2)$ QCD production leptons from high mass, low p_T quarks were dominated by leptons from lower mass, high p_T quarks. This should be a warning as to what could happen if the diffraction-like mechanism were indeed QCD.

3.3 CORRELATION MEASUREMENTS

Some multiparticle measurements which have been proposed to aid the search for naked top are now briefly described:

(a) Same sign leptons with associated hadrons[30], whose combined invariant mass is approximately m_W, may contain the decay products of a t-quark through

$$W^+ \to (t \to \ell^+ + X) + (\bar{b} \to \ell^+ + X) \ . \tag{21}$$

(b) Multilepton final states can be produced[35]: up to 5 leptons can be found in the decay of $M(t\bar{q})$.

(c) If high mass mesons $M(t\bar{q})$ and $M(\bar{t}q)$ are produced with $p_T \simeq$ 0, they can both decay semileptonically giving high p_T $e^\pm\mu^+$ on the same side[1]. The production of $b\bar{b}$ in $O(\alpha_s^2)$ QCD gives high p_T $e^\pm\mu^+$ on opposite sides.

(d) The charged dileptons[36] produced in the decay

$$\begin{aligned} t &\to b + \ell^+ + \nu \\ & \hookrightarrow q + \ell^- + \bar{\nu} \end{aligned} \tag{22}$$

have invariant mass up to m_t, while those from b decay have invariant mass less than m_b.

(e) In the semileptonic decay of a heavy quark, the charged lepton is produced in association with a jet of hadrons, and the system of leptons and hadrons carries information about the mass of the parent quark[6]. The invariant mass of the system can be as large as m_t, and the lepton's momentum transverse to the parent quark direction (which apart from the missing ν is the direction of the sum of the lepton and hadron momentum) can be as great as $m_t/2$.

4. CONCLUSIONS

(1) The predicted toponium cross section varies a great deal between the different models for the production mechanism. Taking the most optimistic estimate, the event rate at $L = 10^{29}/cm^2/sec$ for $\bar{p}p \rightarrow (V(t\bar{t}) \rightarrow e^+e^-) + X$ at $\sqrt{s} = 540$ GeV is above 10 events per year for $m_V \lesssim 50$ GeV, and around Z^0. It is crucial to have good experimental resolution and further to remove background lepton pairs from the semileptonic decay of heavy quarks. Such lepton pairs dominate those from Drell-Yan up to $m = 60-70$ GeV.
(2) When the heavy quark cross section is calculated in $O(\alpha_s^2)$ QCD, single leptons from t's are masked by those from b's. A large diffraction-like t cross section may enable the t to be seen in the single lepton spectrum. However (i) it is difficult to estimate both signal and background, and (ii) the energy and mass dependences of the cross section in Equation (18) may already be in conflict with data.
(3) There is a variety of suggestions of more complication correlation measurements to disentangle the t from the large number of particles $<n> \simeq 30$ with which it will be produced.

ACKNOWLEDGEMENTS

I thank M. Dechantsreiter, F. Halzen, P. McIntyre, A. Martin and S. Pakvasa for enjoyable collaborations, R. Horgan and J. Léveillé for helpful discussions, and the SERC for financial support.

REFERENCES

1.   S. Pakvasa, M. Dechantsreiter, F. Halzen and D.M. Scott, Phys. Rev. D20, 2862 (1979); D.M. Scott; Proceedings of Workshop on the Production of New Particles in Super High Energy Collisions, Madison, 1979; F. Halzen and D.M. Scott, Proceedings of XX International Conference on High Energy Physics, Madison, 1980; M. Dechantsreiter, F. Halzen, P. McIntyre and D.M. Scott, Madison report DOE-ER/00881-202, Phys. Rev. D. to appear.

2.   See B. Combridge, Nucl. Phys. B151, 429 (1979).

3.   S. Brodsky et al., Phys. Lett. 93B, 451 (1980); SLAC-PUB-2660 (1981).

4.   V. Barger, F. Halzen and W.-Y. Keung, Madison reports DOE-ER/00881-211, -215.

5.   R.R. Horgan and M. Jacob, Phys. Lett. 107B, 395 (1981).

6.   F. Paige, Brookhaven report BNL 30154; talk at this Conference.

7.   K.Fujikawa, Prog. Theor. Phys. 61, 1186 (1979).

8.   J. Ellis et al., Phys. Lett. 83B, 339 (1979).

9.   J. Kuhn, preprint MPI-PAE/PTh 37/80.

10. I. Bigi and H. Kraseman, Z. Phys. C7, 127 (1981).

11. J. Léveillé, talk at Cornell Z^0 Workshop 1981, preprint UM HE 81-11.

12. T.G. Rizzo, Phys. Rev. D23, 1987 (1981).

13. We discuss top. Those in search of truth may like to consult John Walker & Sons Ltd., Kilmarnock, Scotland.

14. J.J. Aubert et al., Phys. Rev. Lett. 33, 1404 (1974); S.W. Herb et al., Phys. Rev. Lett. 39, 252 (1977).

15. A. Donnachie, R.R. Horgan and P.V. Landshoff, Z. Phys. C10, 71 (1981).

16. P.B. Mackenzie and G.P. Lepage, Phys. Rev. Lett. 47, 1244 (1981).

17. H. Fritzsch, Phys. Lett. 67B, 217 (1977); F. Halzen, Phys. Lett. 69B, 105 (1977).

18. For detailed analyses see J. Léveillé, Proceedings of Workshop on the Production of New Particles in Super High Energy Collisions, Madison, 1979, and R.J.N. Phillips, Proceedings of XX International Conference on High Energy Physics, Madison, 1980.

19. C. Quigg and J.L. Rosner, Fermilab-Pub 79/22-THY, and references therein.

20. T. Gaisser, F. Halzen and E. Paschos, Phys. Rev. D15, 2572 (1977).

21. Data analysis by C. Kourkoumelis et al., Phys. Lett. 91B, 481 (1980).

22. S.D. Drell and T.-M. Yan, Ann. Phys. 66, 578 (1971).

23. J.F. Owens and E. Reya, Phys. Rev. D17, 3003 (1978).

24. See R.K. Ellis, Proceedings of Moriond Workshop on Lepton Pair Production, Les Arcs, 1981.

25. J.D. Bjorken, Phys. Rev. D17, 171 (1978); M. Suzuki, Phys. Lett. 68B, 164 (1977); D.M. Scott, Phys. Rev. D18, 210 (1978).

26. V. Barger and R.J.N. Phillips, Phys. Rev. D14, 80 (1976).

27. For a review and references see V. Barger, J.P. Léveillé and P.M. Stevenson, Proceedings of XXth International Conference on High Energy Physics, Madison, 1980.

28. M. Kobayashi and K. Maskawa, Prog. Theor. Phys. 49, 652 (1973).

29. A.D. Martin, talk at this Conference.

30. M. Abud, R. Gatto and C.A. Savoy, Phys. Lett. <u>79B</u>, 435 (1978).

31. See S. Wojcicki, Proceedings of XXth International Conference on High Energy Physics, Madison, 1980; D. Dibitonto, talk at this Conference.

32. A. Donnachie, Z. Phys. <u>C4</u>, 161 (1980); and quoted in P.V. Landshoff, Proceedings of International Conference on High Energy Physics, Lisbon, 1981.

33. F. Halzen, A.D. Martin and D.M. Scott, preprint DAMTP 81/21, to appear in Z. Phys. C.

34. See talks by S. Olsen, D. Reeder, K.-W. Lai at this Conference.

35. N. Cabibbo and L. Maiani, Phys. Lett. <u>87B</u>, 366 (1979).

36. L.-L. Chau, W.-Y. Keung and S.C.C. Ting, Phys. Rev. <u>D24</u>, 2862 (1981).

MONTE CARLO SIMULATION OF HEAVY QUARK PRODUCTION IN pp AND p̄p REACTIONS.

Frank E. Paige
Brookhaven National Laboratory, Upton, NY 11973

ABSTRACT

Monte Carlo results are reported on the leptons arising from semileptonic decays of heavy quarks, and on a D* tag for heavy quark jets.

I. INTRODUCTION

Serban Protopopescu and I have for some time been working on a Monte Carlo program called ISAJET[1] to simulate pp and p̄p interactions at ISABELLE energies. The program is by no means complete, but it is sufficiently developed that some (hopefully) useful physics can be extracted. In this talk I will report on several results related to heavy quark production in hadronic reactions.

We have studied the production of single leptons and lepton pairs arising from semileptonic decays of heavy quarks produced by the standard perturbative QCD mechanisms. In agreement with previous work[2] we find that the $\ell^+\ell^-$ cross sections from this source dominates the Drell-Yan cross section for masses up to nearly the Z^0 mass. However, the structure of the events is quite different: leptons from heavy quarks are contained in jets of hadrons, while Drell-Yan leptons have no particular correlation with hadrons. We find that this difference provides a rather clean separation between the two processes. The leptons from quarks also tend to be at smaller angles, so the forward direction is a good place to look for them.

We have also investigated a purely hadronic signature for charm, namely the decay sequence

$$D^{*+} \rightarrow D^0 \pi^+$$
$$\phantom{D^{*+} \rightarrow D^0} \downarrow K^- \pi^+$$

The small Q value for the first π^+ leads to a very small ΔQ, greatly suppressing the combinatorial background. This fact has been exploited in several recent experiments[3]. Assuming a detector performance which seems plausible, at least over a limited solid angle, we find that heavy quark jets can be separated from the much more numerous light quark and gluon ones with a signal-to-background ration of about 1 : 1.

II. LEPTONS FROM HEAVY QUARKS

Heavy quarks are produced strongly by the perturbative QCD processes $g + g \rightarrow Q + \bar{Q}$ and $q + \bar{q} \rightarrow Q + \bar{Q}$, where $Q = c,b,t$ and $q = u,d,s$. Also, the semileptonic branching ratios of heavy quarks are quite large. The background of leptons from heavy quarks to the Drell-Yan process $q + \bar{q} \rightarrow \gamma, Z^0 \rightarrow \ell^+ + \ell^-$ was first calculated by Pakvasa, et al[2]. They found that the $\ell^+ \ell^-$ pairs from heavy quarks dominate the Drell-Yan ones for masses up to almost the Z^0 mass. We have confirmed this result. Also, since ISAJET generates complete events, we have been able to study the associated hadrons.

For the production of heavy quarks we include only the perturbative QCD process $g + g \rightarrow Q + \bar{Q}$ and $q + \bar{q}, Q + \bar{Q}$. We ignore any heavy quarks in the incoming protons, and hence processes like $q + Q \rightarrow q + Q$. These could be significant for the single lepton distribution, but they should be insignificant for high-mass $\ell^+ \ell^-$ pairs. We also ignore any diffractive production of heavy quarks, such as has been observed by several ISR experiments[4]. Presumably diffraction is important only at extremely small angles and the perturbative processes dominate over most of the solid angle.

In fragmenting the jets into hadrons we take into account the leading-log QCD scaling violations but not the closely related spread in transverse momentum about the jet axis. This means that our jets have about the right longitudinal momentum distribution but are too narrow. More specifically, the probability $G_{i/k}$ of finding a parton i in a parton k with momentum fraction x and

$$\xi = \frac{1}{4\pi b_0} \ \ell n \ \frac{\alpha_s(Q_0^2)}{\alpha_s(Q^2)}$$

$$\alpha_s(Q^2) = \frac{1}{b_0 \ \ell n \ (Q^2/\Lambda^2)} \ , \qquad b_0 = \frac{33 - 2n_f}{12\pi}$$

is given by the Altarelli-Parisi equations[5]

$$\frac{1}{2} \frac{\partial}{\partial \xi} \ G_{i/k}(x,\xi) = \sum_j \int_x^1 \frac{dy}{y} \ P_{ij}\left(\frac{x}{y}\right) G_{j/k}(y,\xi)$$

We carry out a Monte Carlo evolution in ξ according to these equations to produce an ensemble of collinear quarks and gluons. Then we fragment each of these into hadrons using the Field-Feynman ansatz[6].

In the full QCD jet evolution[7], which will be incorporated in the next version of ISAJET, the partons can be emitted at large angles, but configurations with fairly small angles are dominant. We will define our jets to include all hadrons in a fairly large cone ($\Delta y = \pm 1$, $\Delta\phi = \pm 45°$) so the more realistic algorithm should not give very different results.

We take the t mass to be 20 GeV and use quark decays plus the same jet algorithm for b and t decays. Note that this assumes there is no light charged Higgs, since otherwise $t \to bH^+$ would dominate.

Finally we add beam jets to the events. The limited evidence available[8] suggests that the beam jets in high $p_\perp$ events are rather similar to those in minimum bias events except for the absence of a diffractive peak at $x = 1$. We assume this and use a simple modification of the Field-Feynman algorithm adusted to fit the ISR minimum bias average multiplicity[9]. This model has only short range correlations, so it underestimates the fluctuations.

For the Drell-Yan processes $p + p \to W + X$, where W stands for any of γ, W^+, W^-, or Z^0, we felt it essential to include the transverse momentum q of the W. For large $q_\perp$, $q_\perp > m_W$, QCD perturbation theory is applicable. For small $q_\perp$ perturbation theory gives a series in $\alpha_s(q_\perp^2) \ln^2 (m_W^2/q_\perp^2)$, which obviously is not convergent. This series was first studied by Dokshitser, Dyakanov, and Troyan[10], and their results were extended by Parisi and Petronzio[11]. The essential idea is that the probability of emitting no gluons with more than a fixed $k_\perp$ is exponentially small (c.f radiative corrections in QED). This means that some gluons are always emitted, and they wash out the primordial transverse momentum. Hence the cross section is calculable even for $q_\perp = 0$. Parisi and Petronzio find for $m_W \to \infty$

$$\frac{d\sigma}{dq_\perp^2}\bigg|_{q_\perp=0} \sim \left(\frac{m_W^2}{\Lambda^2}\right)^{-0.6} , \quad \frac{\partial}{\partial q_\perp^2}\left(\ln \frac{d\sigma}{dq_\perp^2}\right)\bigg|_{q_\perp=0} \sim \left(\frac{m_W^2}{\Lambda^2}\right)^{-0.31}$$

This is a remarkable result which should be tested.

To generate events at any $q_\perp$ we have adopted a very simple ansatz. We start with the perturbative cross sections $g + q \to W + q$ and $q + \bar{q} \to W + g$ applicable for high $q_\perp$. These are singular as $q_\perp \to 0$; we mutilate them in such a way as to agree roughly with the results of Parisi and Petronzio. Then the integral over $q_\perp$ agrees roughly with the Drell-Yan formula, although this is not guaranteed by the ansatz.

We can now describe our results. We have generated a total of 56000 events $p + p \rightarrow Q + \bar{Q} + X$ in 14 $p_\perp$ ranges at $\sqrt{s} = 800$ GeV. We used the Baier, et al.[12], structure functions, which generally fit the existing data quite well. We also chose $\Lambda = 0.1$ GeV; small values of Λ are favored by recent determinations[13]. The older Owens - Reya[14] structure functions have a softer gluon distribution and so give fewer heavy quarks. Increasing Λ also decreases the cross section: the increased scaling violations outweigh the increased coupling constant. We have not repeated the calculation for pp scattering, but we would not expect the results to be very different.

The single lepton distribution vs. $p_\perp$ is shown in Fig. 1 summed over e^+, e^-, μ^+ and μ^- to improve the statistics. Divide by 4 to obtain any one channel. The μ^+ distribution from

$$p + p \rightarrow W^+ + X$$
$$\qquad\qquad \hookrightarrow \mu^+ + \nu$$

is shown in Fig. 2; its high $p_\perp$ tail comes from high $q_\perp$ W production as discussed above. Evidently the single lepton distribution from heavy quarks is well below the W^+ peak and remains below its high-$p_\perp$ tail. However, it is substantially larger than the other backgrounds discussed previously[15].

The $\ell^+\ell^-$ spectrum summed over e^+e^-, $e^+\mu^-$, μ^+e^-, and $\mu^+\mu^-$ is shown in Fig. 3. This cross section, again divided by 4, is to be compared with the $\mu^+\mu^-$ Drell-Yan cross section in Fig. 4. The heavy quark process dominates for $M\ell\bar{\ell} < 60$ GeV. The precise relative normalization is sensitive to poorly known input assumptions, including the gluon distribution and the fragmentation functions for heavy quarks. Nevertheless, it is clear that heavy quarks constitute a very large background for the measurement of the Drell-Yan cross section at masses below the Z^0.

The same-sign $\ell^\pm\ell^\pm$ cross section summed over e^+e^+, $e^+\mu^+$, μ^+e^+, and $\mu^+\mu^+$ is shown in Fig. 5. It is typically $\sim 20\%$ of the $\ell^+\ell^-$ cross section.

All of these results are substantially similar to those of Pakvasa et al.[2] The advantages of the Monte Carlo program is that it can also be used to study the associated hadrons. Thus we can make quantitative the statement that the leptons from heavy quarks are contained in jets. Specifically, we define $H_\perp$ to be the total transverse momentum of all particles except neutrinos in a cone of rapidity $\Delta y = \pm 1$ and azimuthal angle $\Delta\phi = \pm \pi/4$ about the lepton:

$$H_\perp = \left| \sum_h \vec{p}_{h_\perp} \right|, \quad |y_h - y_\ell| < 1, \quad |\phi_h - \phi_\ell| < \pi/4.$$

The $H_\perp$ distribution for leptons from quarks with $20 < p_{\ell_\perp} < 50$ GeV is shown in Fig. 6. The $H_\perp$ distribution for Drell-Yan events depends only weakly on the mass; it is shown in Fig. 7 for $20 < M_{\ell\bar{\ell}} < 50$ GeV. From these distributions we can extract the efficiencies ε for various types of events as a function of the H cut:

Table I

H	$\varepsilon_{\text{Drell-Yan}}$	$\varepsilon_{Q \to \ell}$	$\varepsilon_{Q \to \ell}$
(GeV)	(20<M<50 GeV)	(10<$p_{\ell_\perp}$<20 GeV)	(20<$p_{\ell_\perp}$<50 GeV)
0.5	44%	3.1%	1.7%
1.0	73%	6.6%	3.3%
1.5	87%	9.8%	5.1%
2.0	93%	13.1%	6.6%

The relative efficiency is typically a factor of 10, or a factor of 100 for dilepton events. The efficiencies given for the Drell-Yan events are probably high, since we have only one recoil jet and we do not have enough fluctuations in our beam jets. With them, however, one could measure the Drell-Yan cross section down to M ~ 20 GeV.

The $q_\perp$ distribution for $\ell^+\ell^-$ pairs from heavy quarks is shown in Fig. 8. One might expect this distribution to be rather broad because the leptons carry varying fractions of the jet momenta. In fact it is if anything narrower than the Drell-Yan distribution, Fig. 9. This reflects a trigger bias favoring leptons carrying most of the jet momentum. The same trigger bias accounts for the events with very low $H_\perp$.

III. D* TAG FOR HEAVY QUARK JETS

A prompt lepton is the most obvious tag for a heavy quark jet, but it is always accompanied by a missing neutrino. The best hope for a purely hadronic tag seems to be to exploit the small Q value of the decay

$$D^{*+} \to D^0 \pi^+$$
$$\hookrightarrow K^- \pi^+$$

A small Q leads to a very small error ΔQ and so greatly reduces the combinatorial background. Using this method an AGS experiment set an upper limit of 80 nb for D* production, and an FNAL experiment observed a signal of 1.6 ± 0.5 μb.[3] Of course, a D* could also tag a heavier quark decaying via $t \to b \to c$.

We have used ISAJET to investigate whether a D* tag could separate heavy quark jets from the much more numerous light quark and gluon ones. We generated samples of light and heavy quark jets in two $p_\perp$ ranges, $20 < p_\perp < 40$ GeV and $50 < p_\perp < 70$ GeV. We also required $\left| y_{jet} \right| < 1$, which is hardly in the spirit of this workshop but improves the signal/background somewhat. In reality, since we require both good resolution and particle identification, a suitable detector probably must have limited solid angle. Then it may be better to work at smaller angles so as to cover a larger rapidity range.

For the heavy quarks we forced the $D \to K\pi$ decay and multiplied by the branching ratio afterwards. We also imposed the experimental cuts

$p_\pi > 0.2$ GeV for $D^* \to D\pi$
$p_K > 2$ GeV, $p_\pi > 1.25$ GeV for $D \to K\pi$.

For the light quarks we found all $K\pi\pi$ combinations with $M_{K\pi} = m_D \pm 50$ MeV and $Q < 25$ MeV. Then we multiplied by the 2σ bin sizes assuming a resolution of $\Delta M_{K\pi} = \pm 5$ MeV, $\Delta Q = \pm .25$ MeV, a factor of two better than the MPS experiment using magnetostrictive spark chambers.

Our results are summarized in the following:

Table II

Jets	$p_\perp$	σ	ε	$\varepsilon\sigma$
c,b,t	20–40 GeV	31 nb	5.9×10^{-3}	0.18 nb
g,u,d,s	20–40 GeV	5.0 μb	1.4×10^{-5}	0.07 nb
c,b,t	50–70 GeV	.80 nb	6.9×10^{-3}	5.5 pb
g,u,d,s	50–70 GeV	.11 μb	6.4×10^{-5}	7.0 pb

Evidently with these resolutions we obtain a signal-to-background ratio of about 1:1, albeit with dismal efficiency. At least in principle one could improve the efficiency by including more D^0 decay modes.

The D^0 momentum distribution is shown in Fig. 10. Because of the $t \to b \to c$ cascade the t quarks produce more D mesons with lower momenta.

We have not addressed at all the problem of triggering on jets. It is clear that a transverse energy trigger does not work[16]. This is not unexpected: the standard picture[17] of multiparticle production clearly predicts large fluctuations in the multiplicity of low $p_\perp$ particles. What is needed is a trigger which selects genuinely hard interactions without introducting too much bias towards jet-like events. One possibility might be a restricted transverse energy

$$E'_\perp = \sum_{E_{i\perp} > E_0} E_{i\perp}$$

summing over only particles with significantly more than the average transverse momentum. This would not force jet-like events if E_0 were much smaller than $E'_\perp$.

Even assuming that the problem of triggering on jets can be solved, much more work must be done to decide if a D* tag might be useful. It seems, however, that the required detector would be quite different from the usual ones and so might be worth some thought.

ACKNOWLEDGMENT

This work supported by Department of Energy Contract DE-AC02-76CH00016.

REFERENCES

1. F.E. Paige and S.D. Protopopescu, BNL-29777 (1981).
2. S. Pakvasa, M. Dechantsreiter, F. Halzen, and D.M. Scott, Phys. Rev. D20, 2862 (1979).
3. V.L. Fitch, et al., Phys. Rev. Letts. 46, 761 (1981); S.U. Chung, et al., BNL-30437 (1981).
4. For a review see S. Olsen, these proceedings.
5. G. Altarelli and G. Parisi, Nucl. Phys. B126, 298 (1977).
6. R.D. Field and R.P. Feynman, Nucl. Phys. B136, 1 (1978).
7. G.C. Fox and S. Wolfram, Nucl. Phys. B168, 285 (1980); R.D. Field, Proc. of the 1981 ISABELLE Summer Study, BNL-51443, pp. 11, (1981).
8. British-French-Scandanavian Collaboration, Physics Scripta 19, 99 (1979); C. Bromberg, et al., Phys. Rev. Letts. 45, 769 (1980).
9. W. Thome, et al., Nucl. Phys. B129, 365 (1977).
10. Yu. L. Dokshitser, D.I. Dyakanov and S.I. Troyan, SLAC-Trans-183 (1978), Phys. Repts. 58C, 269 (1980).

11. G. Parisi and R. Petronzio, Nucl. Phys. B154, 427 (1979).
12. R. Baier, J. Engels, and B. Petersson, Z. Physik C2, 265 (1979).
13. P.B. MacKenzie and G.P. LePage, CLNS 81/498 (1981).
14. J.F. Owens and E. Reya, Phys. Rev. D17, 3003 (1978).
15. R.F. Peierls, T.L. Trueman, and L.L. Wang, Phys. Rev. D16, 1397 (1977); C. Quigg, Rev. Mod. Phys. 49, 297 (1977); F.E. Paige, in Proc. of the Topical Workshop on the Production of New Particles in Super High Energy Collisions, (Madison, WI, 1979).
16. For a review see K. Pretzl, these proceedings.
17. V.A. Abramovskii, O.V. Kancheli, and V.N. Gribov, Proc. of the XVI International Conf. on High Energy Physics, (Fermilab, 1972), Vol. 1, p. 389.

176

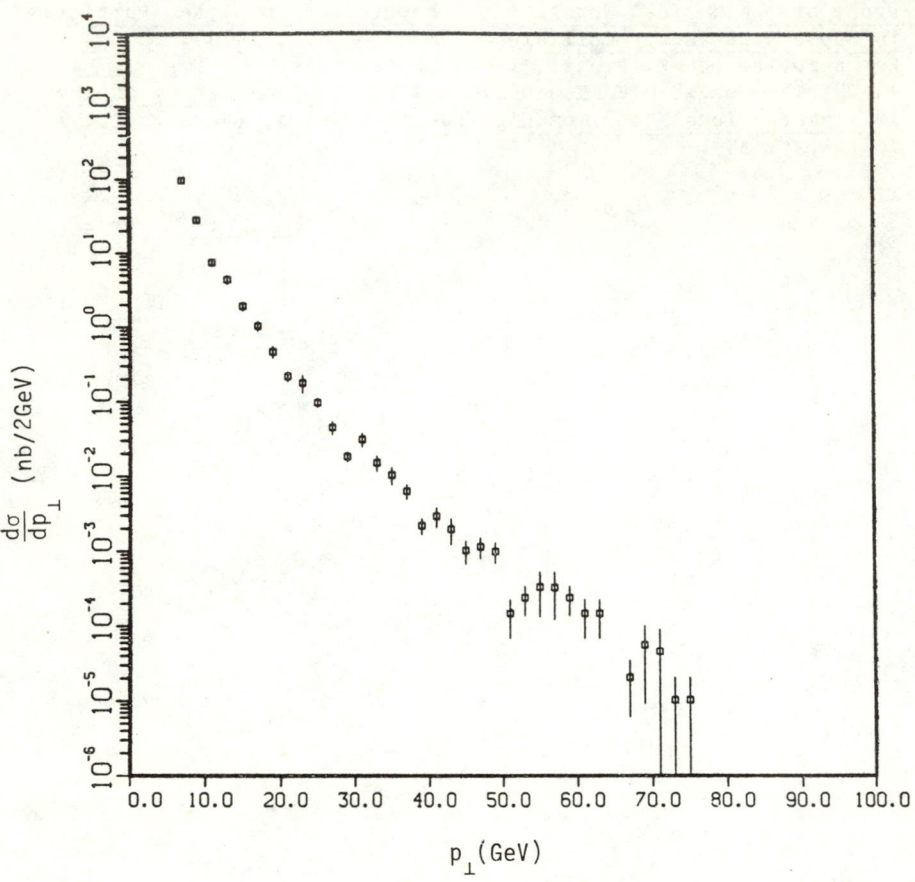

$p_\perp$ (GeV)

Fig. 1: Cross section vs $p_\perp$ of e^+, e^-, μ^+, and μ^- leptons from heavy quarks. Divide by 4 to compare with Fig. 2. All histograms are for pp scattering at $\sqrt{s}$ = 800 GeV.

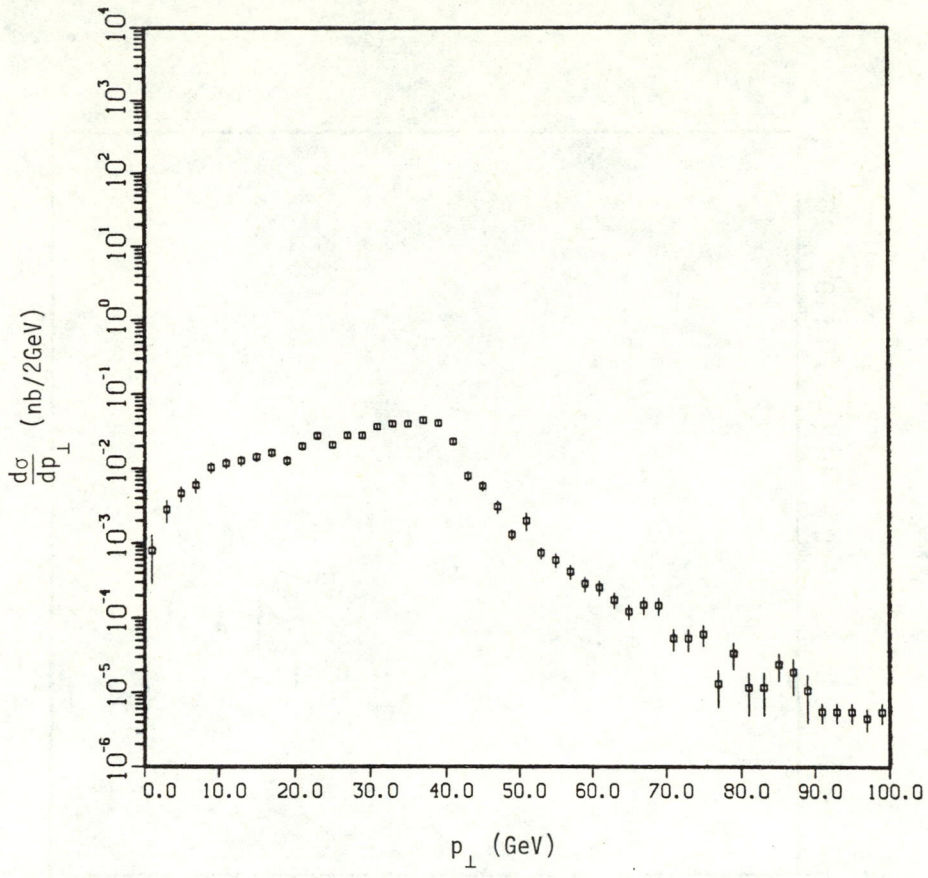

Fig 2: Cross section vs $p_\perp$ of μ^+ from W^+

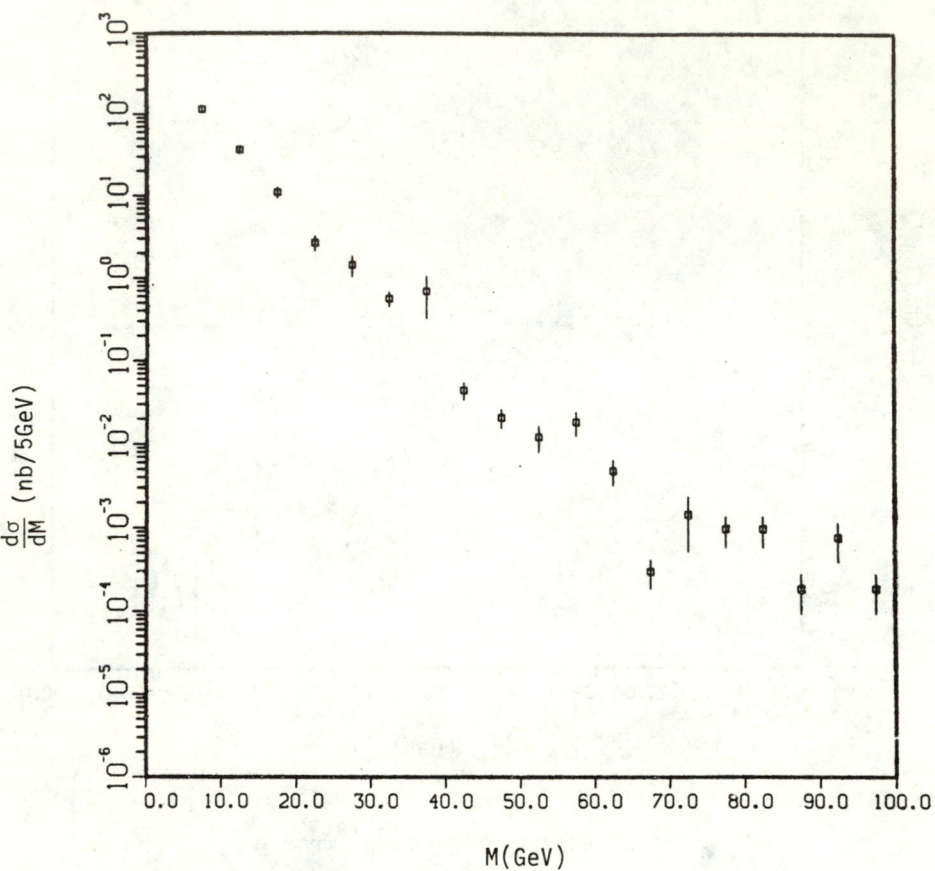

$\frac{d\sigma}{dM}$ (nb/5GeV)

M(GeV)

Fig. 3: Cross section vs mass of e^+e^-, $e^+\mu^-$, μ^+e^-, and $\mu^+\mu^-$ pairs from heavy quarks. Divide by 4 to compare with Fig. 4.

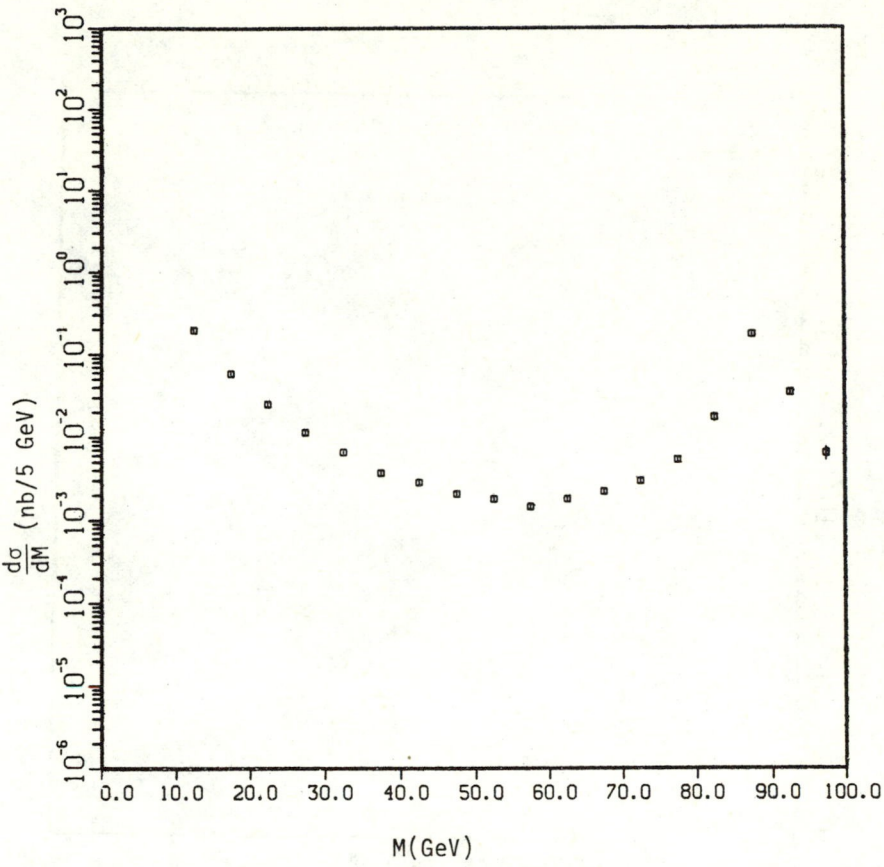

Fig. 4: Cross section vs mass of $\mu^+\mu^-$ pairs from γ and Z^0.

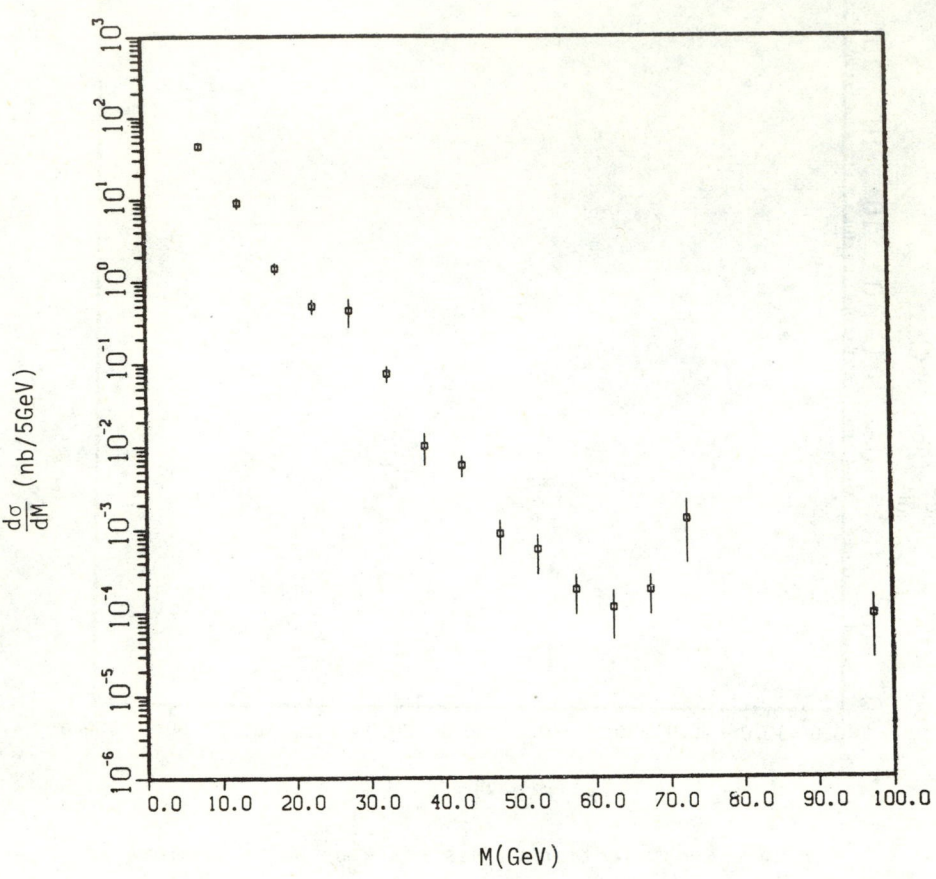

Fig. 5: Cross section vs mass of all same-sign lepton
pairs from heavy quarks.

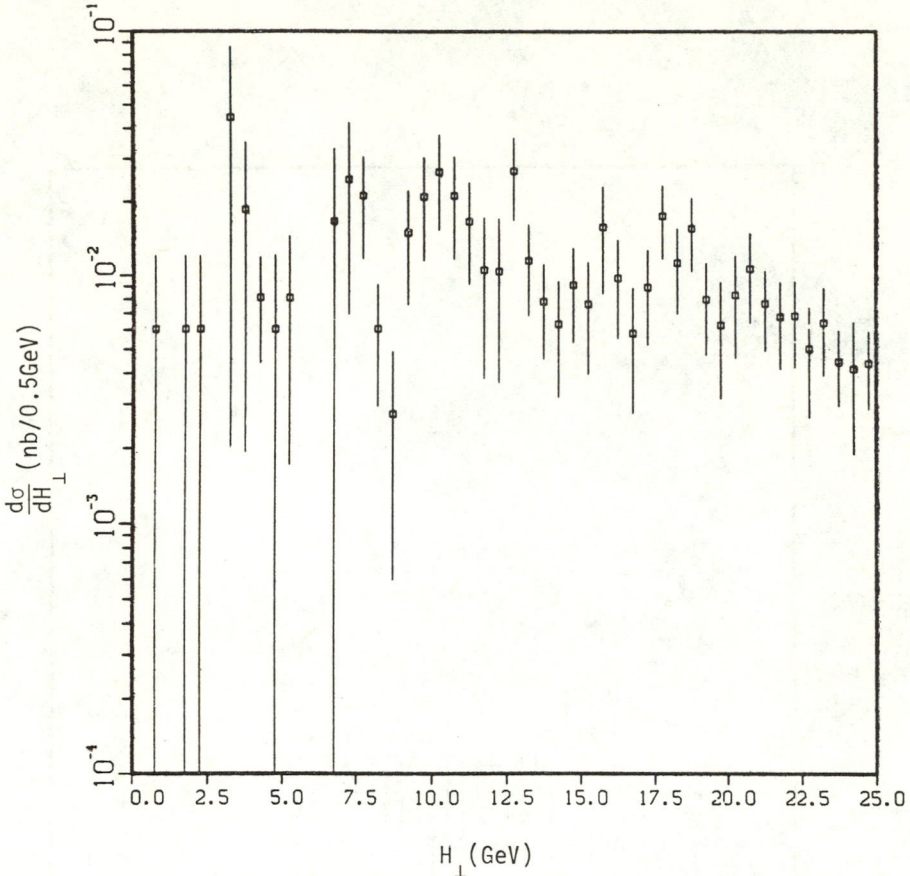

Fig. 6: Distribution of associated hadronic momentum $H_\perp$ for e^+, e^-, μ^+, and μ^- from heavy quarks with $20 < p_{\ell\perp} < 50$ GeV.

182

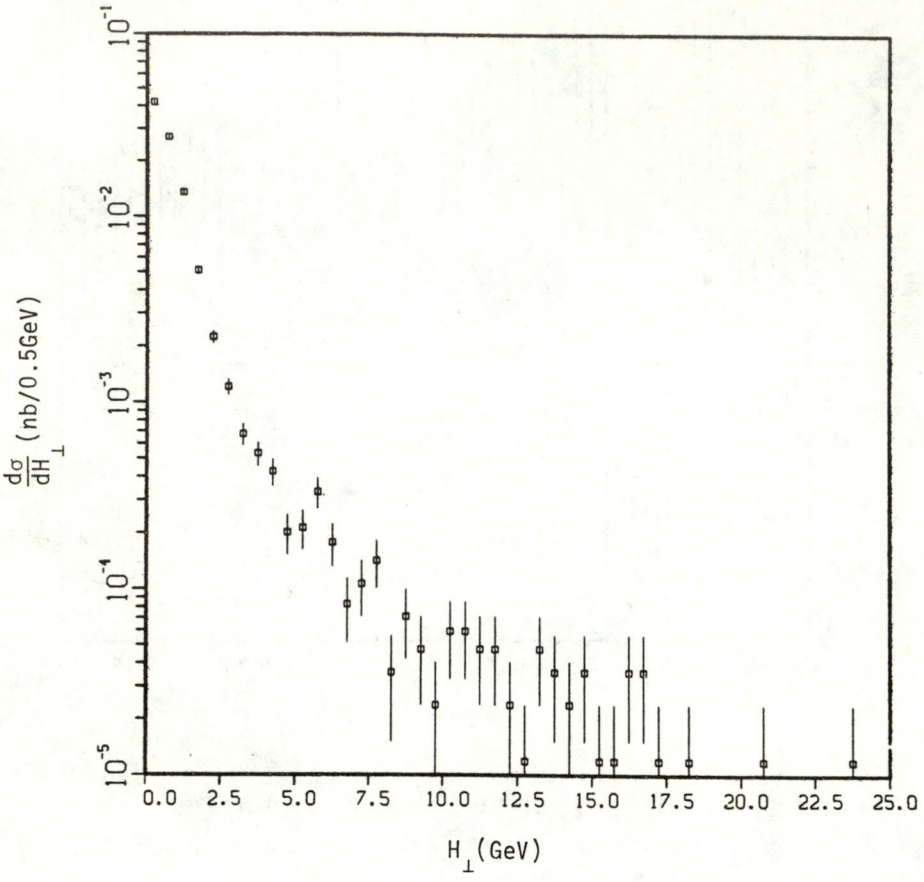

Fig. 7: Distribution of associated hadronic momentum $H_\perp$ for μ^+ and μ^- from γ and Z^0 with 20<m<50GeV.

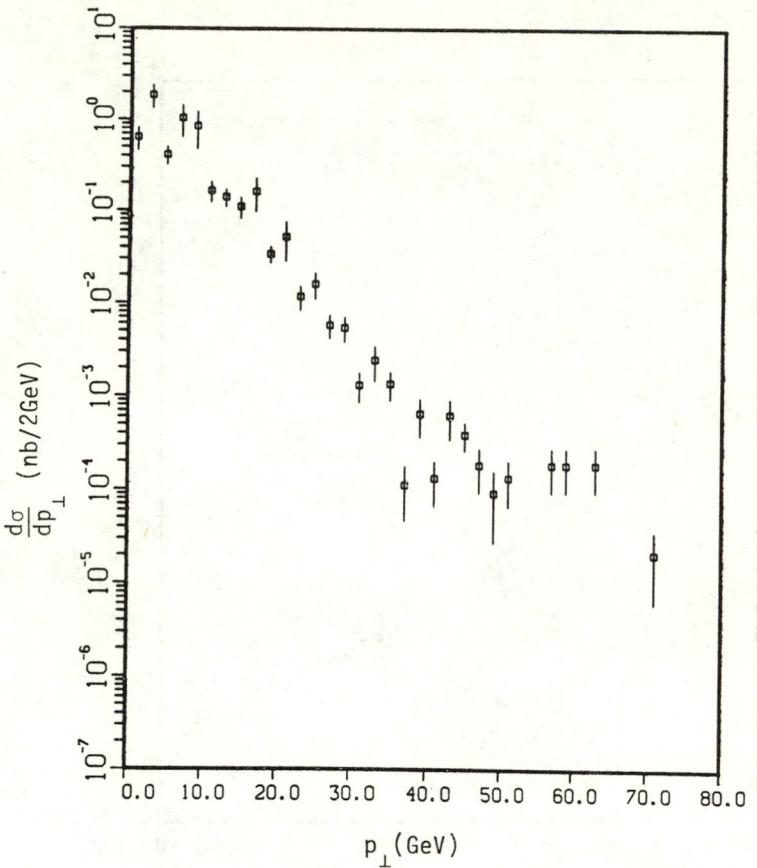

Fig. 8: Cross section vs $p_\perp$ of e^+e^-, $e^+\mu^-$, μ^+e^- and $\mu^+\mu^-$ pairs from heavy quarks, 20<M<50GeV. Divide by 4 to compare with Fig. 9.

184

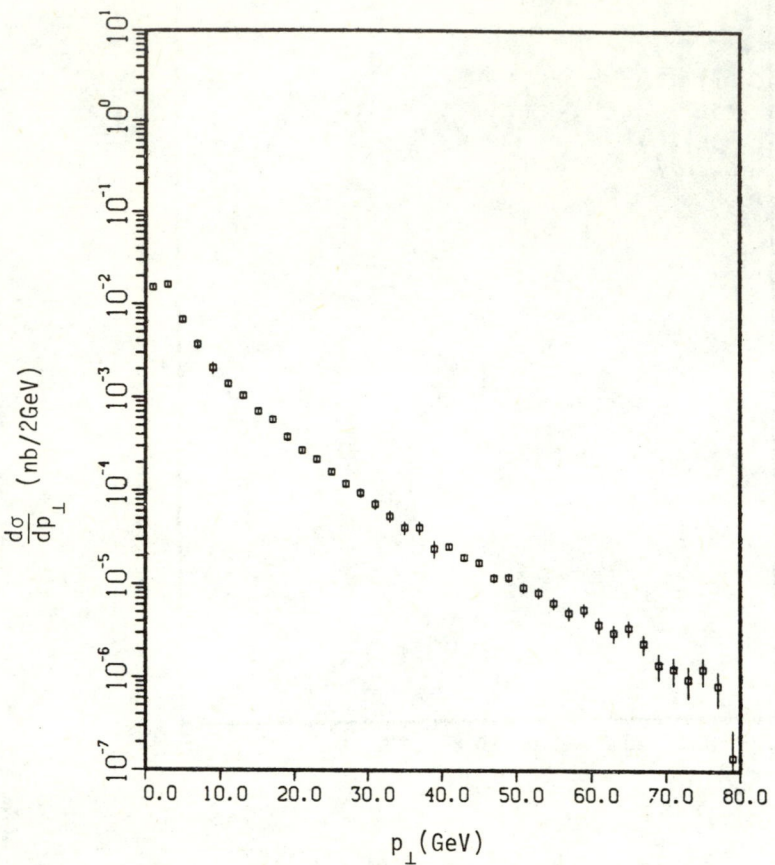

$$\frac{d\sigma}{dp_\perp} \ (nb/2GeV)$$

$p_\perp (GeV)$

Fig. 9: Cross section vs $p_\perp$ of $\mu^+\mu^-$ pairs from γ and Z^0, 20<M<50GeV.

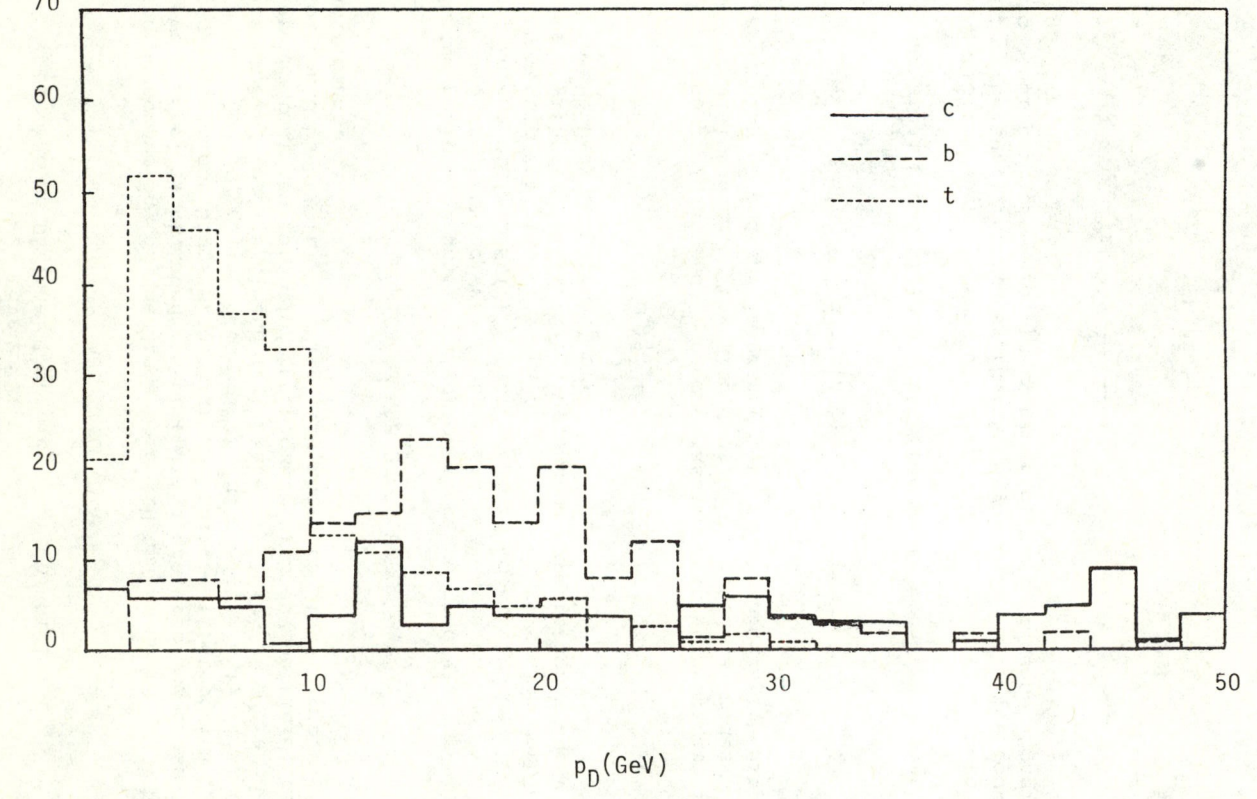

Fig. 10: D^0 momentum spectrum for heavy quark jets with $50 < p_\perp < 70$GeV.

186

HIGGS HUNTING

Wai-Yee Keung*
Physics Department
Brookhaven National Laboratory, Upton, NY 11973

ABSTRACT

The phenomenology of the Higgs boson in the standard SU(2) × U(1) electroweak model is reviewed. We compare signatures and cross sections for various Higgs production mechanisms: (i) toponium radiative decay ($\zeta \to H^0 \gamma$); (ii) gluon gluon fusion ($gg \to H^0$); (iii) Compton-like process ($gc \to H^0 c$) and (iv) bremsstrahlungs at Z^0 resonance. It is argued that new detection techniques for heavy particle identification could be helpful in triggering the rare Higgs signals from the backgrounds.

I. BASICS OF THE HIGGS BOSON

In the picture of unified electroweak gauge theory[1], the vacuum acts as a medium carrying weak isospin and weak hypercharge. This is achieved in the minimal SU(2) × U(1) standard model through the non-vanishing vacuum expectation value of an elementary scalar doublet $\Phi = (\phi^+, \phi^0)$ with $<\Phi> = (0, v/\sqrt{2})$. The vacuum expectation value v is related to the weak coupling G_F by

$$v = (\sqrt{2}\, G_F)^{-\frac{1}{2}} \simeq 246 \text{ GeV} . \tag{1}$$

The gauge field $W^\pm$ and Z^0 become massive as they propagate in this non-trivial vacuum. They also develop longitudinal modes, $W_L^\pm$ and Z_L^0, by absorbing $\phi^\pm$ and the imaginary part of ϕ^0 through the Higgs mechanism

$$(\phi^+, \phi^0) \longrightarrow \left(\cdots, \frac{v + H^0 + \cdots}{\sqrt{2}} \right) . \tag{2}$$

Only one physical Higgs field H^0 is left over from the real part of ϕ^0.

To establish such a scenerio, it is a high priority task to search for the surviving trademark: the Higgs boson H^0. The couplings of H^0 to other particles are simply given by their masses. Consider the Higgs-fermion coupling:

$$g\phi^0 \bar{f}f \to g\, \frac{v + H^0}{\sqrt{2}}\, \bar{f}f,$$

$$\mathcal{L}_{f\bar{f}H^0} = m_f \bar{f}f + (m_f/v) \bar{f}f H^\circ \tag{3}$$

*This work was supported in part by the U.S. Department of Energy under Contract No. DE-AC02-76CH00016.

where the coefficient of the bilinear term is identified as the mass. Correspondingly, the couplings of H^0 to gauge fields are:

$$(D\Phi)^+ (D\Phi) \rightarrow W^+W^-(v + H^0)^2 + \cdots$$

$$\mathcal{L}_{W^+W^-H^0} = M_W^2 \, W^+W^-(1 + 2H^0/v + H^0H^0/v^2) , \tag{4}$$

and also

$$\mathcal{L}_{ZZH^0} = \frac{1}{2} M_Z^2 \, Z^2(1 + 2H^0/v + H^0H^0/v^2) . \tag{5}$$

We list various Feynman amplitudes below with a combinatorial factor 2 already given to the ZZH^0 vertex:

$$\text{vertex} \quad ; \quad \bar{f}fH^0 \qquad W^+W^-H^0 \qquad ZZH^0$$

$$\text{amplitude}; \quad m_f/v \qquad 2M_W^2/v \qquad 2M_Z^2/v$$

We learn that the Higgs boson prefers to couple to the fermions and gauge bosons with an intrinsic strength proportional to their masses. The couplings[2,3] involving photons ($\gamma\gamma \leftrightarrow H^0$) or gluons ($gg \leftrightarrow H^0$) are non-zero only in higher orders in α or α_s.

All couplings of the Higgs boson are known in the standard SU(2) × U(1) electroweak model. By contrast, the mass m_H of the Higgs boson is an unknown parameter. The value of m_H can fall into a range[4] from 300 MeV to 1 TeV without endangering the theory or contradicting present experimental limits. There is an interesting possibility that m_H is generated from radiative corrections through the Coleman-Weinberg mechanism[5] which predicts that

$$m_H^2 = (3/8)\alpha^2 v^2 [2\csc^4\theta_w + \cot^4\theta_w - 0(m_f/m_H)^4 + O(\alpha)]. \tag{6}$$

Thus, for the present value of the Weinberg angle $\sin\theta_w \simeq 0.2$, Eq. (6) gives

$$m_H \simeq 10 \text{ GeV.} \tag{7}$$

For this value of m_H, the physics in the high energy e^+e^- and hadron collider is exciting. We will stress this possibility.

II. HIGGS DECAYS

Figure 1 illustrates the updated branching fractions[2] of the Higgs boson into the following different channels:

$$t\bar{t}, \ b\bar{b}, \ c\bar{c}, \ s\bar{s}, \ gg, \ \mu\bar{\mu} \text{ and } \gamma\gamma .$$

The magnitudes are arranged approximately in decending order starting from the channel which is kinematically available.

188

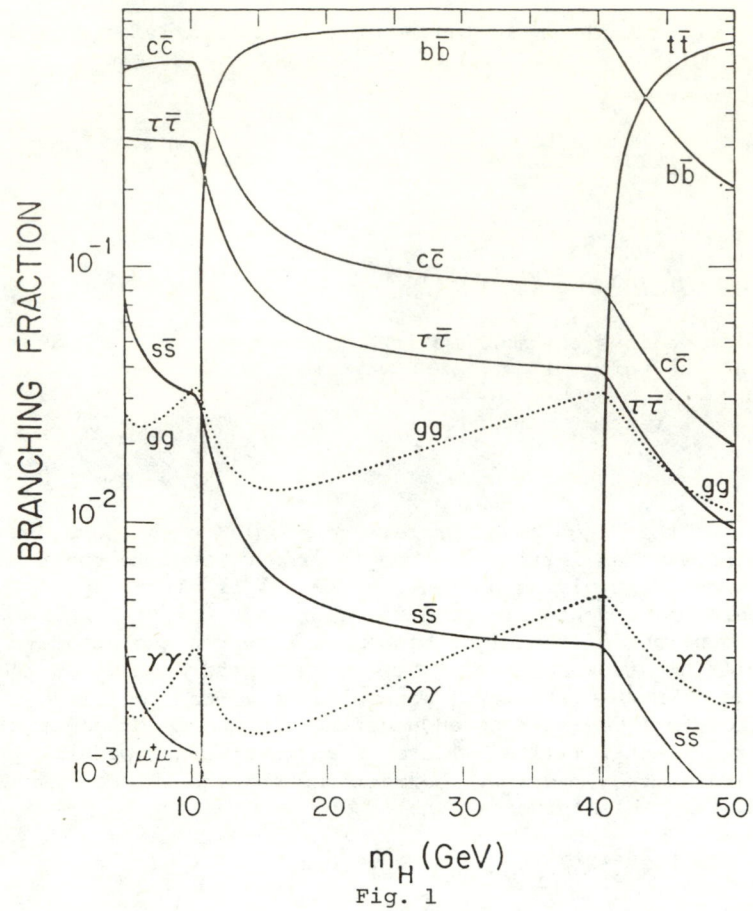

$$m_H (GeV)$$

Fig. 1

The conventional methods to identifying a new state by tagging the decay products $\mu\bar{\mu}$, $\gamma\gamma$ or $e\bar{e}$ fail in the search for the Higgs boson because of their tiny branching fractrons. Instead, the preferential modes for H^0 decay are $\tau\bar{\tau}$, $c\bar{c}$, $b\bar{b}$ or $t\bar{t}$. These final products travel a short distance before subsequently decaying and leave a pair of narrow gaps, (or kinks) which, if observable in the future well designed detectors, could serve as an excellent identifier for the Higgs particle.

III. PRODUCTION OF THE HIGGS BOSON

(i) Toponium ζ radiative decay (Wilzcek mechanism[3])

The decay rate for $\zeta \rightarrow H^0\gamma$ can be calculated in the non-relativistic approximation,

$$\frac{\Gamma(\zeta \rightarrow H^0\gamma)}{\Gamma(\zeta \rightarrow \mu\mu)} = \frac{G_F m_\zeta^2}{4\sqrt{2}\pi\alpha} \left(1 - \frac{m_H^2}{m_\zeta^2}\right) . \qquad (8)$$

The branching fraction $\Gamma(\zeta \to H^0\gamma)/\Gamma(\zeta \to \text{all})$ is estimated to be about 1% for $m_\zeta = 40$ GeV and $m_H = 10$ GeV. In the e^+e^- collider, with $\sqrt{s}$ at the toponium resonance, the monochromatic energy of the emitted photon provides a unique signature for Higgs hunting if the toponium is present. In the hadron collider, the photon has a high transverse momentum, but is no longer monochromatic. The event rate is estimated to be

$$\sigma(\bar{p}p \to H^0\gamma) \simeq 0.5 \text{ pb} \tag{9}$$

for $\sqrt{s} = 540$ GeV, $m_\zeta = 40$ GeV and $m_H = 10$ GeV. Comparable backgrounds from ordinary prompt photon production easily cover up the signal unless the Higgs boson can be identified through the decay gaps (or kinks) from $H^0 \to b\bar{b}$, $c\bar{c}$ or $\tau\bar{\tau}$. Even then, it is still a difficult task as probably only 10 events would be recorded with an integrated luminosity of 20×10^{36} cm^{-2}.

(ii) Gluon gluon fusion[6]

The vertex $gg \to H^0$ is induced through the heavy quark loop in the Feynman diagrams in the lowest order in α_s. The suppression of α_s^2 in the cross section is compensated for by the rich gluon content in the incident hadrons. In contrast, the cross section due to quark anti-quark fusion is much less because of the small current quark masses. In our calculations, we use a scaling gluon distribution of form

$$xG(x) = 3(1 - x)^5 \tag{10}$$

for the proton. The gluon gluon fusion gives a sizable cross section among all other Higgs production mechanisms. For $m_H = 10$ GeV, gluon gluon fusion cross sections are listed below:

$$\sqrt{s}\,(\text{GeV}) \qquad 540 \quad 800 \quad 2000 \tag{11}$$

$$\sigma(p\overset{(-)}{p} \to H^0 X) \text{ (pb)} \qquad 40 \quad 70 \quad 100$$

The only way to identify this process is through the detection of the heavy leptons or heavy quarks from the Higgs decays. Unfortunately, even if such a detection technique is achieved, the Higgs signal in the $c\bar{c}$ mode is completely masked by a large background from the sub-process $q\bar{q} \to c\bar{c}$ and $gg \to c\bar{c}$ and the $H \to \tau\tau$ signal is below the $q\bar{q} \to \gamma^* \to \tau\bar{\tau}$ background. Figure 2 illustrates the $p\bar{p}$ or pp fusion cross section for Higgs boson production [via $gg \to H^0 \to c\bar{c}$ or $\tau\bar{\tau}$ with $B(H \to c\bar{c}) = B(H \to \tau\bar{\tau}) = 0.5$, and backgrounds due to $q\bar{q} \to \gamma^* \to \tau\bar{\tau}$ and $gg \to c\bar{c}$, $q\bar{q} \to c\bar{c}$ for an invariant mass resolution of 1 GeV.

190

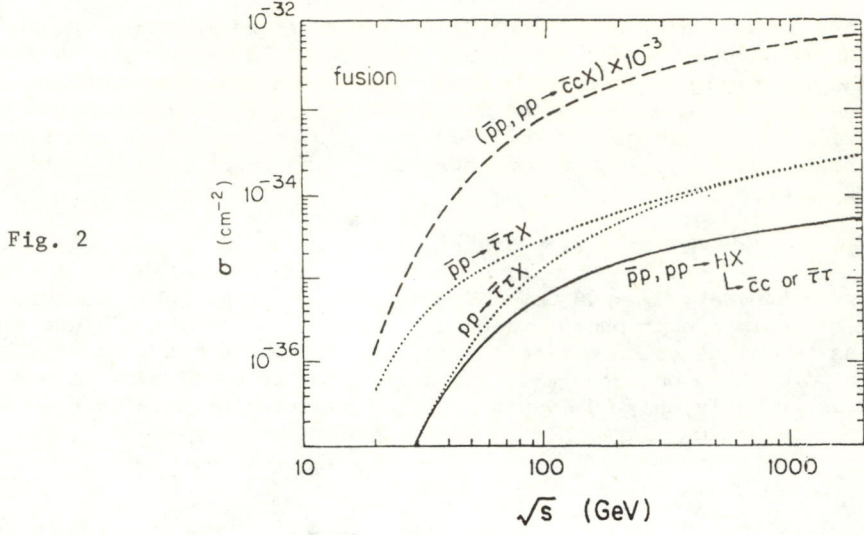

Fig. 2

(iii) Compton-like process[7]

This is an ignored process that may be used in the search for Higgs bosons in hadronic collisions: Compton scattering $gc \to Hc$ of gluons in one nuclon from charmed quarks in the other nucleon. This suggestion is prompted by recent interpretations[8-10] of diffractive Λ_c^+ production[11] in terms of charm quarks in the nucleon. With a charm distribution that accounts for Λ_c^+ data, we estimate a $pp \to HX$ cross section of order 10^{-36} cm^2. The longitudinal scaling distribution of the Higgs bosons produced by the Compton process is characteristically diffractive, in contrast to the central production of the Higgs boson in gluon gluon fusion. Although this mechanism has a rather low yield, the signature is dramatic and identification of a Higgs boson should be possible with just a few events. The signal is a fast $\bar{c}$ (or c) spectator quark, fast $\bar{c}c$ or $\bar{\tau}\tau$ decay products of the Higgs boson, and a relatively slow interacting c (or $\bar{c}$) quark. The background from the electromagnetic pair production process is well below the signal. The charm or τ particles can be identified with detectors that can resolve decay gaps or by detection of charm jets.

The cross section for the Compton scattering subprocess $gc \to Hc$ is given by

$$\frac{d\hat{\sigma}}{d\hat{t}} (gc \to Hc) = \frac{G_F m_c^2 \alpha_s}{12\sqrt{2}(\hat{s}-m_c^2)^2} \left\{ \left[\frac{\hat{s}-m_c^2}{\hat{u}-m_c^2} + \frac{\hat{u}-m_c^2}{\hat{s}-m_c^2} \right] \left[\frac{2m_c^2(m_H^2-\hat{t})}{(\hat{s}-m_c^2)(\hat{u}-m_c^2)} - 1 \right] \right.$$

$$- \frac{2(\hat{u}+m_c^2-m_H^2)(\hat{s}+m_c^2-m_H^2)}{(\hat{s}-m_c^2)(\hat{u}-m_c^2)} - \frac{2m_c(2m_c^2-\hat{t})(m_H^2-\hat{t})^2}{(\hat{s}-m_c^2)^2(\hat{u}-m_c^2)^2}$$

$$\left. -4m_c^2 \left[\frac{1}{(\hat{s}-m_c^2)^2} + \frac{1}{(\hat{u}-m_c^2)^2} \right] \right\}$$

(12)

where $\hat{s}$, $\hat{t}$, $\hat{u}$ are the Mandelstam variables of the subprocess. The background to the gc → Hc process is due to gc → γ*c with the virtual photon converting to a $\bar{\tau}\tau$ or $\bar{c}c$ pair. Denoting the invariant mass of this pair by μ, the cross section for the gc → $\bar{\tau}\tau$c electromagnetic subprocess is given by

$$\frac{d\hat{\sigma}}{d\mu d\hat{t}} = \frac{8\alpha_s \alpha^2}{81\mu(s-m_c^2)^2} \left(1 + \frac{2m_\tau^2}{\mu^2}\right) \left(1 - \frac{4m_\tau^2}{\mu^2}\right)^{\frac{1}{2}} \left\{ \frac{\hat{s}-m_c^2}{m_c^2-\hat{u}} + \frac{\hat{u}-m_c^2}{m_c^2-\hat{s}} \right.$$

$$\left. + 2(\mu^2 + 2m_c^2) \left[m_c^2 \left(\frac{1}{\hat{s}-m_c^2} + \frac{1}{\hat{u}-m_c^2}\right)^2 - \frac{\hat{t}}{(m_c^2-\hat{s})(m_c^2-\hat{u})} \right] \right\}. \tag{13}$$

In our calculations, we use a charm distributuion of the form

$$xc(x) = 0.03x(1 - x) , \tag{14}$$

based on the description of the diffractive $\Lambda_c^{\pm}$ data given in Ref. 9. We also examine an alternate choice for c(x) based on a symmetric SU(4) sea at $Q^2 = m_H^2$ for the light-quark sea distribution of Ref. 12. In our calculations we take m_H = 10 GeV.

Figure 3 shows the Higgs cross section versus $\sqrt{s}$ from the Compton process in $\bar{p}p$ or pp interactions. The Higgs cross section is of order 1 picobarn for the diffractive charm distribution of Eq. (14). With the SU(4) symmetric charm sea the cross section is more than an order of magnitude higher at large $\sqrt{s}$.

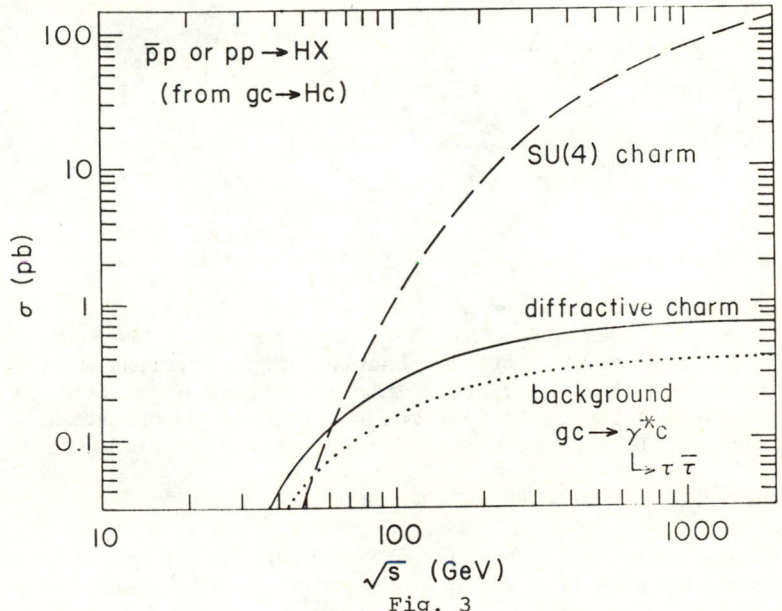

Fig. 3

192

The Higgs decay branching fractions into $\bar{\tau}\tau$, $\bar{c}c$, and $\bar{s}s$ for $m_c = 1.5$ GeV and $m_s = 0.3$ GeV are expected to be approximately 30%, 63% and 3%. The background due to $gc \to \gamma^*c$ with $\gamma^* \to \bar{\tau}\tau$ is also shown in Fig. 3 for an experimental $\bar{\tau}\tau$ mass resolution of 1 GeV. The Higgs signal is well above this $\bar{\tau}\tau$ background. The background in the $\bar{c}c\bar{c}c$ channel would be due to the higher order QCD process $gc \to g^*c$ with $g^* \to \bar{c}c$. Also note that when the Higgs decay products are detected through kinks (or gaps), the $\bar{\tau}\tau$ signal is cleaner, since no fragmentation is involved.

The differential distributions in pp scattering at $\sqrt{s} = 43$ GeV with respect to the longitudinal scaling variable $x_L = 2p_L/\sqrt{s}$ are shown in Fig. 4 for the Compton mechanism. The x_L distributions of the Higgs boson and the spectator charm quark are both diffractive in character. In this mechanism the Higgs boson is produced with mean p_T of about 2 GeV.

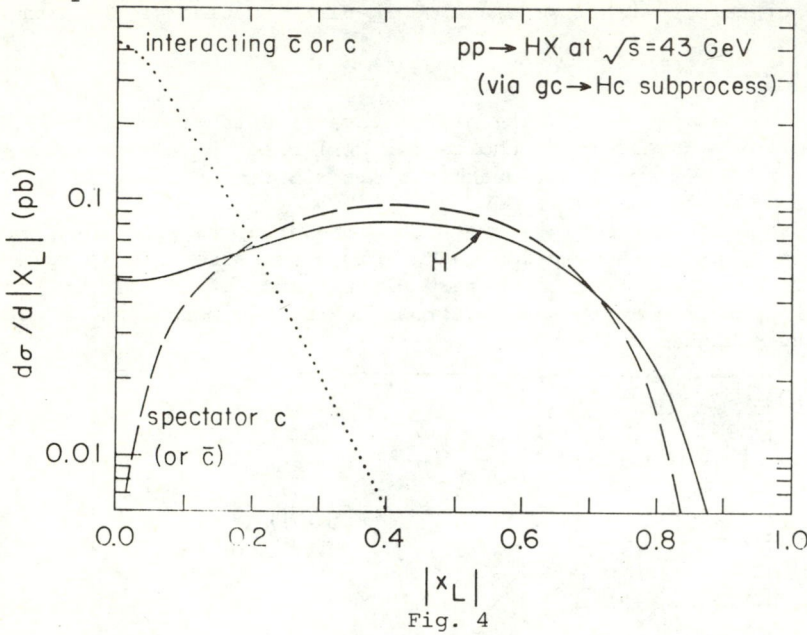

Fig. 4

At present energies ($\sqrt{s} = 30 \sim 60$ GeV) observation of a few of these $\bar{c}c\bar{c}c$ or $\bar{c}c\bar{\tau}\tau$ events from Higgs production should be possible in dedicated experiments with streamer chamber, rapid cycling mini-bubble chamber, or microvertex detectors. In a 1000 hours experiment, a mini-bubble chamber taking 10^7 particles per second could reach a sensitivity level of 10^{-2} pb assuming 100% detection efficiency.

(iv) BREMSSTRAHLUNGS AT Z RESONANCES (Z → Hff)

The Higgs boson can either be radiated from the Z boson line[13], (Z-bremsstrahlung), or from the heavy fermion line[14], (f-bremsstrahlung), at the Z resonance. The total rate[15] for Higgs production followed by H → $\bar{c}c$ or $\bar{\tau}\tau$ decay.

$$\frac{\Gamma(Z \rightarrow H; \; H \rightarrow \bar{c}c, \bar{\tau}\tau)}{\Gamma(Z \rightarrow \mu^+ \mu^-)} \simeq 3\% \; . \tag{15}$$

This substantial rate results from the fact that the cross section is dominated by Higgs from Z-bremsstrahlung, and is therefore inclusive in the type of fermion f. In 53% of these events the fermions from the decay of the virtual Z are long-lived (s, b, c, t or τ). Therefore[15] about half of the Higgs production events contain four long-lived particles, two having invariant mass m_H. These events have no significant competing background and have a spectacular signature. A few of them are sufficient to establish the Higgs signal when some heavy particle trigger is employed in the experiment. At the SLAC linear collider it should be possible to trigger on c and τ by observing their decay path. It is larger than the size of the interaction region, which is of the order of several microns.

The total branching fraction $Z \rightarrow Hf\bar{f}$ relative to $Z \rightarrow \mu^+\mu^-$ is shown in Fig. 5 as a function of the Higgs mass for each fermion type f, based on $m_t = 20$ GeV and $\sin^2\theta_w = 0.23$.

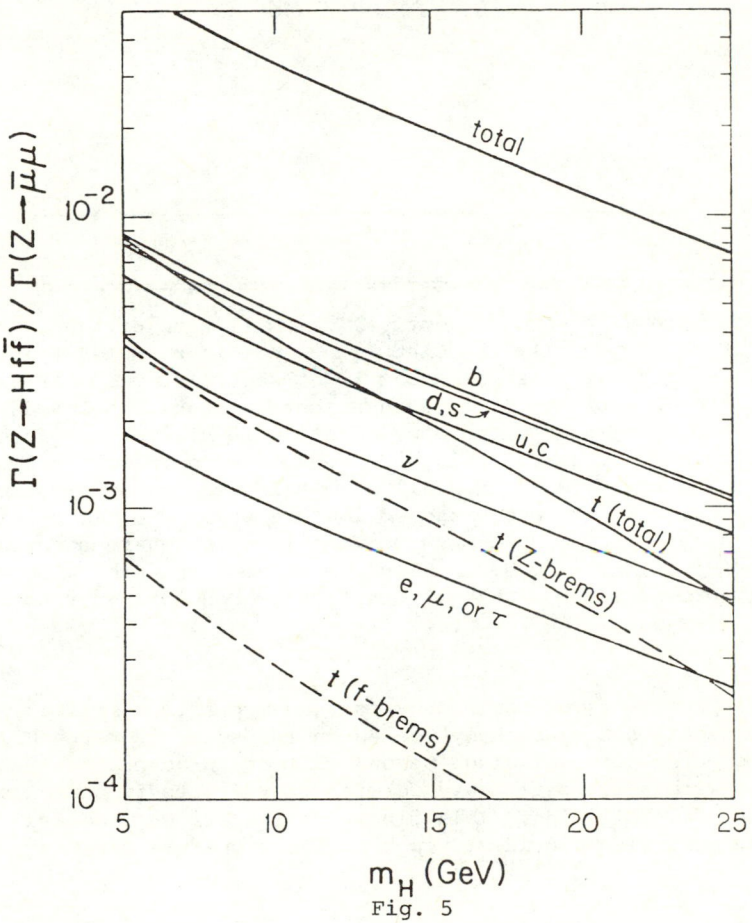

Fig. 5

194

The results are summarized in the table below for $m_H = 10$ GeV. We include all contributions from the diagrams of Z-bremsstrahlung and f-bremsstrahlung. The latter and the interference contributions are significant only for the t-quark.

fermion f	$\dfrac{\Gamma(Z \to H f \bar{f})}{\Gamma(Z \to \mu \bar{\mu})}$
ν	$3 \times (2 \times 10^{-3})$
e or μ	$2 \times (1 \times 10^{-3})$
τ	10^{-3}
u	3.4×10^{-3}
d or s	$2 \times (4.4 \times 10^{-3})$
c	3.4×10^{-3}
b	4.7×10^{-3}
t	3.9×10^{-3}
Total	3.3×10^{-2} (total)

We conclude with some comments. The small size of the beams of e^+e^- colliders, especially the SLAC linear collider, makes triggering on particles with lifetimes of order 10^{-12} sec relatively easier. Moreover, over 50% of the Higgs events contain four long-lived particles. This trigger deserves consideration in view of the fact that the alternative[16] of establishing a 10 GeV missing mass by triggering on $Z \to \mu^+\mu^-$ is not an easy task. The rate is over an order of magnitude smaller than the one proposed in this paper and the requirements on the accuracy of the muon momenta lead to severe constraints on the magnet. It should be finally pointed out that the process $e^+e^- \to H\nu\nu$ provides a possible alternative method for neutrino counting.

IV. CONCLUSION

Developments of new techniques for heavy particle ($\tau\bar{\tau}$, $c\bar{c}$, $b\bar{b}$ or $t\bar{t}$) identification are urgently needed in the search for the Higgs boson. We point out that Higgs bosons that are produced are usually associated with additional heavy fermion pairs, both in hadron collision and e^+e^- collision. This final configuration of several heavy long lived particles provides a spectacular signature for Higgs hunting.

ACKNOWLEDGMENT

This work is borne out of the collaboration with V. Barger and F. Halzen, to whom the author gives many thanks.

REFERENCES

1. S. Weinberg, Phys. Rev. Lett. $\underline{19}$, 1264 (1967), and Phys. Rev. $\underline{D5}$, 1412 (1972); A. Salam, in Elementary Particle Theory: Relativistic Groups and Analyticity, Nobel Symposium No. 8, ed. by N. Svartholm (Almqvist and Wiksel, Stockholm, 1968), p. 367; S.L. Glashow, Nucl. Phys. $\underline{22}$, 579 (1961); S.L. Glashow, J. Iliopoulos and L. Maiani, Phys. Rev. $\underline{D2}$, 1285 (1970).
2. J. Ellis, M.K. Gaillard and D.V. Nanopoulos, Nucl. Phys. $\underline{B106}$, 292 (1976).
3. F. Wilczek, Phys. Rev. Lett. $\underline{39}$, 1304 (1977).
4. B.W. Lee et al., Phys. Rev. Lett. $\underline{38}$, 883 (1977); M. Veltman, Phys. Lett. $\underline{70B}$, 253 (1977); A.D. Lande, JETP Lett. $\underline{19}$, 183 (1974) and JETP Lett. $\underline{23}$, 64 (1976); S. Weinberg, Phys. Rev. Lett. $\underline{36}$, 294 (1976); P. Frampton, Phys. Rev. Lett. $\underline{37}$, 1378 (1976).
5. S. Coleman and E. Weinberg, Phys. Rev. $\underline{D7}$, 1888 (1973); B. Gildener and S. Weinberg, Phys. Rev. $\underline{D13}$, 3333 (1976).
6. H. Georgi et al., Phys. Rev. Lett. $\underline{40}$, 692 (1978).
7. V. Barger, W.Y. Keung and F. Halzen, Wisconsin Preprint MAD/PH/9 (1981).
8. S.J. Brodsky et al., Phys. Lett. $\underline{93B}$, 451 (1980); Phys. Rev. $\underline{D23}$, 2745 (1981).
9. V. Barger, F. Halzen and W.Y. Keung, Phys. Rev. $\underline{D24}$, 1428 (1981); ibid. $\underline{D25}$, 112 (1982).
10. R. Odorico, Phys. Lett. $\underline{107B}$, 231 (1981).
11. M. Basile et al., Lett. Nuovo Cimento $\underline{30}$, 481 (1981); Earlier data on charm production are summarized by S. Wojciciki, in AIP Conf. Proc. $\underline{68}$, 1430 (1981).
12. J.F. Owens and E. Reya, Phys. Rev. $\underline{D17}$, 3003 (1978).
13. B.L. Ioffe and V.A. Khoze, Leningrad report 274 (1976); J.D. Bjorken, Proceedings of SLAC Summer Institute, SLAC-198 (1976); S.L. Glashow, D.V. Nanopoulos and A. Wildiz, Phys. Rev. $\underline{D18}$, 1724 (1978).
14. K.J.F. Gaemers and G.J. Gounaris, Phys. Lett. $\underline{77B}$, 379 (1978).
15. V. Barger, F. Halzen and W.Y. Keung, Wisconsin Preprint MAD/PH/27 (1981).
16. E. Ma and J. Okada, Phys. Rev. $\underline{D20}$, 1052 (1979).

Experimental Constraints on Supersymmetric Theories

J.P. Leveille
Randall Lab of Physics, University of Michigan, Ann Arbor, MI 48109

ABSTRACT

We extend the analyses of Fayet, and Fayet and Farrar, of experimental searches for gluinos, the supersymmetric partners of gluons. Because of their large production cross sections, present data appears to exclude gluino masses below 3.5-6 GeV/c^2 and may be more restrictive. Since gluinos remain very light in many models, they will either be detected soon or many supersymmetric theories will be excluded.

INTRODUCTION

In this talk we would like to address the question: Is supersymmetry a symmetry of nature? We will conclude that present experimental data places very strong constraints on possible supersymmetric models. To obtain these constraints we restrict ourselves to the study of gluinos, the supersymmetric partners of the gluons. For clarity, a brief introduction to supersymmetry and a user's guide to the plethora of supersymmetric particles is first given. After explaining why the gluinos are a sensitive probe of supersymmetry, the results will be presented. The last part of the talk will explain how these results are arrived at, by studying the properties of gluinos and the constraints from present data, and data soon to be obtained.

The details of the analysis are contained in a paper by G.L. Kane and the author, ["Experimental Constraints on Gluino Masses and Supersymmetric Theories", Michigan preprint UM HE 81-68] from which large sections of this write up are plagiarized. We refer the interested reader to that paper for more details and the necessary references.

SUPERSYMMETRY

Supersymmetry (SS) is a symmetry between bosons and fermions. Recall what we mean by isospin: the proton and the neutron are different isospin states, related by isospin generators T, i.e. $T^+|neutron\rangle = |proton\rangle$.

In SS, there are fermionic generators Q_α, which connect fermion states with boson states: $Q_\alpha|boson\rangle = |fermion\rangle$. These fermionic generators also commute with the Hamiltonian, $[H,Q_\alpha] = 0$. Consequently, there must be a degeneracy in the mass spectrum of boson and fermions if SS is a symmetry of the world! This is clearly not the case: there are no scalars degenerate in mass with the electron or the muon for example. Rather than throw out the whole concept, today's theoretical prejudices lead us to believe that <u>supersymmetry could be a broken symmetry of nature.</u> Since it necessarily must be broken, one may well ask what is the use of SS? There are great hopes that gravity could be incorporated more easily into a supersymmetric theory. However in our days of unified theories, the real appeal of supersymmetric models is that they would: (a) naturally incorporate scalars (bosons) into the theory, (b) because the bosons and the fermions are connected by the supersymmetry keeping the fermions massless would also lead to massless bosons. This latter point is crucial. The model one envisages is a GUT model together with a supersymmetry SS. The supersymmetry commutes with the grand unified group. When the grand unified group breaks, at M_{GUT}, the supersymmetry remains unbroken, e.g. SS × GUT → SS × SU(3) × SU(2) × U(1). Because the broken theory is still supersymmetric we can now keep the fermions and hence the Higgs bosons associated with them massless in a natural way, for example, using a chiral symmetry. When the supersymmetry finally breaks at $\Lambda_{SS} \sim M_W$, the ordinary Higgs mechanism gives masses to bosons $\sim M_W$. So although this model of the world would not explain why $M_{GUT} \gg M_W$, at least the introduction of SS makes the theory natural: we do not force the scalar masses to vanish, a symmetry does it!

The models of supersymmetry which exist nowadays, always have a large number of particles. To orient the reader we now give a guide to the particles likely to exist in a model such as the one outlined above. First of all each conventional particle has a supersymmetric partner differing in spin by half a unit. All the internal quantum numbers of the supersymmetric partner are the same as those of the conventional particle. In the list below we only include the electric charge Q, but the same is true for color, isospin etc...

CONVENTIONAL	SPIN	Q	SS PARTNER		SPIN
Leptons: $e, \mu, \tau \ldots$	1/2	-1	Scalar leptons:	$\phi_e, \phi_\mu, \phi_\tau \ldots$	0
Quarks: $\begin{cases} u, c \ldots \\ d, s, b \ldots \end{cases}$	1/2 1/2	2/3 -1/3	Scalar quarks:	$\begin{cases} \phi_u, \phi_c \\ \phi_d, \phi_s, \phi_b \ldots \end{cases}$	0 0
gluons: g	1	0	gluinos	$\tilde{g}$	1/2
Photon: γ	1	0	photino	$\tilde{\gamma}$	1/2
$\vdots$					
Z	1	0	Zino	$\tilde{Z}$	1/2
NONE		0	GOLDSTINO	G	1/2

Note that there is one particle the goldstino, G, which does not have a conventional partner. This particle is a Goldstone fermion, which appears when a global SS is spontaneously broken. It has the same quantum numbers as the vacuum, but has spin 1/2.

If the SS was a local symmetry, then the goldstino would become part of a spin 3/2 particle, in much the same way as Goldstone bosons become the zero helicity states of the gauge bosons in the standard model of weak interactions.

We will now explain why gluinos are interesting and can potentially constrain SS models. Indeed it turns out that in the simplest SS models of strong, weak and electromagnetic interactions which can be unified, it is very difficult to give the gluinos a large mass. If we consider the collection of existing models which are not ruled out by other diseases, we find very conservatively that the gluino mass $\tilde{m}$ is always bounded above by 2 GeV: $\tilde{m} \lesssim 2$ GeV. Why? Well, first there are no bare mass terms because of the supersymmetry. Otherwise gluons would have a mass term. When one breaks the SS, one does not want to break color, so no mass term can be generated for the gluinos (it would require a VEV for a colored scalar, which would break color). Hence the gluino masses must be generated radiatively. One loop diagrams actually vanish because of a spurious (accidental) symmetry, called R-invariance, which crept up in the original Lagrangian without one wanting to put it there. So the masses only arise at two loop level, hence their smallness.

So we expect the gluinos to be "light" colored fermions, which will therefore be produced copiously at hadron machines. Failure to detect them constrains the models. Detecting them also constrains the models (amongst other things).

The results of our analysis are presented in Figure 1. There we

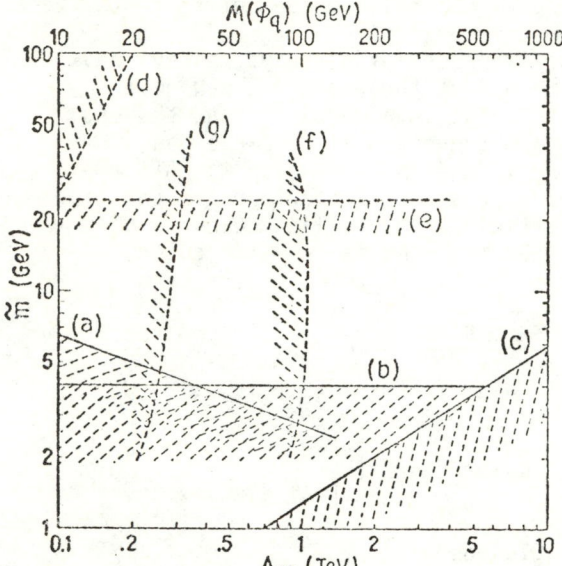

Fig. 1. Excluded region in the $\tilde{m}$-Λ_{SS} plane. Solid curves are from present data. Dashed curves are attainable limits from future experiments. (a) Valid if $\tilde{g}gG$ vertex is present. (b) From $\tilde{g} \to q\bar{q}\tilde{\gamma}$ with subsequent $\tilde{\gamma}$ interactions in a beam dump detector. This curve is always present. We have assumed $M_{\phi_q} = M_W/2$. (c) Gives upper limit on Λ_{SS} (lower scale) or M_{ϕ_q} (upper scale) from the require-ment that $\tilde{g}$ lifetime not be too long. (d) Upper limit on $\tilde{m}$ from double goldstino production at Isabelle. (e) The region below this line would be excluded by a failure to detect gluino production by an SPS detector with $\mathcal{L}=10^{29}/cm^2$. (f) The region to the left is excluded if 100 events of G+$\tilde{g}$ production are not detected at ISABELLE. (g) Same as (f) for FNAL collider.

show the regions of the gluino mass $\tilde{m}$ - scale of supersymmetry breaking Λ_{SS} plane excluded by present data (shaded regions below solid curves) and accessible to future experiments (shaded regions below dashed curves). Note that present experiments already rule out gluinos lighter than 4 GeV. This alone signals the demise of existing models.

RESULTS

We now indicate how the results of Fig. 1 are arrived at. The basic strategy will be to calculate the production cross-sections for gluinos as a function of their mass $\tilde{m}$. After specifying their decay modes, experiments will set lower limits on their masses.

(1) <u>Gluino couplings</u>: Since gluinos are the partners of gluons they will have the interactions shown in Fig. 2.a. The coupling at each vertex is the standard QCD coupling g. In addition, for a broken SS a coupling to the goldstino is introduced, as in Fig. 2b. Gauge invariance requires a magnetic type coupling, $h\bar{u}_G \sigma^{\mu\nu} u_{\tilde{g}}^a F_{\mu\nu}^a$ where u_G and $u_{\tilde{g}}^a$ are spinors for a goldstino and gluino of color a, respectively, and $F_{\mu\nu}^a$ the gluon field strength. The coupling strength h is fixed by supercurrent algebra. Indeed taking the matrix element of the supercurrent S_μ between a gluino and a gluon, including the goldstino pole term and requiring zero divergence, yields $h = \tilde{m}/2\Lambda_{SS}^2$ where $\tilde{m}$ is the gluino current algebra mass and Λ_{SS} sets the scale of SS breaking, defined by $\langle 0|S_\mu|G\rangle = \Lambda_{SS}^2 \gamma_\mu u_G$.

Some of our results only require the interactions of Fig. 2a, for production of gluinos via gluons. They hold in any theory

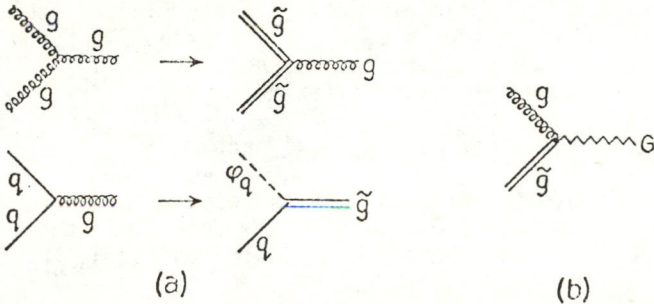

(a)   (b)

Fig. 2. Gluino couplings in supersymmetric theories. We represent gluons by g, gluinos by $\tilde{g}$, goldstinos by G, quarks by q, scalar partners of quarks by ϕ_q, and the photino by $\tilde{\gamma}$. The vertices of (a) will be present in every supersymmetric theory when gluinos carry color. The vertex of (b) is present in global supersymmetric theories.

where the gluinos are color octets. In local SS the Goldstino may become the helicity 1/2 part of a spin 3/2 state so our results involving Goldstinos may not directly hold. However, since the gluinos will have to decay (see below), essentially equivalent results will be valid.

(2) <u>Gluino Lifetimes and Interactions</u>: In a spontaneously broken global SS, the decay of the gluino proceeds dominantly via the vertex in Fig. 2b. We obtain the lifetime

$$\tilde{\tau}_G = \frac{.33\times10^{-15}}{h^2 \Lambda_{SS}^4} \; (\frac{\Lambda_{SS}}{M_Z})^4 \; (\frac{1 \text{ GeV}}{\tilde{m}})^3 \text{ sec.} \qquad (1)$$

Since current algebra arguments yield $h \simeq \tilde{m}/2\Lambda_{SS}^2$, this becomes

$$\tilde{\tau}_G \simeq 1.1\times10^{-15} \; (\frac{\Lambda_{SS}}{M_Z})^4 \; (\frac{1 \text{ GeV}}{\tilde{m}})^5 \text{ (sec)} \qquad (2)$$

If observations imply $\tilde{m} > 3$ GeV, and $\Lambda_{SS} < 1$ TeV for the cases of interest, then $\tilde{\tau} < .7\times10^{-13}$ sec. If $\tilde{g}$ is produced with $\gamma=20$, it will travel typically .4 mm. On the other hand, if $\tilde{m} \simeq 1$ GeV, and $\Lambda_{SS}=1$ TeV, it goes 3^6 times further, typically 0.30 meters with, of course, some going over a meter. Note that Eq. (2) provides an interesting upper limit on Λ_{SS} for a given $\tilde{m}$ (See Fig. 4). If data excludes production of a gluino which travels more than about 10 cm. (see below), then any theory must satisfy $\Lambda_{SS}/\tilde{m}^{1.5} \lesssim 1000$, with Λ_{SS} and $\tilde{m}$ in GeV units.

If the $\tilde{g}gG$ vertex is suppressed or absent as perhaps could occur in a local SS, the gluino will decay via a virtual scalar quark to a quark-antiquark pair and a photino ($\tilde{\gamma}$) (provided that the gluino is heavier than the photino).

For the mode $\tilde{g} \rightarrow qq\tilde{\gamma}$, the lifetime is

$$\tilde{\tau}_{\tilde{\gamma}} = 0.8\times10^{-6} \; (m_\mu/\tilde{m})^5 \; (M_\phi/M_W)^4 \text{ sec.}$$

M_ϕ is the lightest scalar quark mass associated with quarks lighter than the gluino. By comparison, the $\tilde{\gamma}$ mode dominates if $M_\phi < 0.09 \Lambda_{SS}$; if $M_\phi = M_W/2$, the photino mode dominates for $\Lambda_{SS} \gtrsim 400$ GeV (see Fig. 1).

Thus we expect that experiments sensitive to neutral hadrons that can travel centimeters or meters will give a lower limit on the gluino mass. When a gluino is produced it will be shielded to make a color singlet hadron. Most probably the gluino will bind with a gluon, because of the octet binding forces, though sometimes the gluino could attach to a color octet $q\bar{q}$ pair. The electrically neutral, color singlet, hadron will interact like a normal hadron, with a total interaction probability like that of a kaon or a D°, with $\sigma_{TOT} \sim$ few mb. As observed by Fayet and Farrar, and as we will reaffirm below, any objects produced with several µb cross sections, and having such lifetimes and interactions, would probably have been observed.

(3) <u>Gluino and Goldstino Production</u>:

Once the small mass range $\tilde{m} \lesssim 1$ GeV is excluded by the absence of long-lived, electrically neutral, strongly interacting hadrons, we can reliably use perturbative QCD to calculate (lower limits on) the production cross sections, and these are very large for color octet gluinos. Further, in any theory where there is a $\tilde{g}gG$ coupling, the double or single direct goldstino production cross (Fig. 3b-c) sections increase with $\tilde{m}$ and the absence

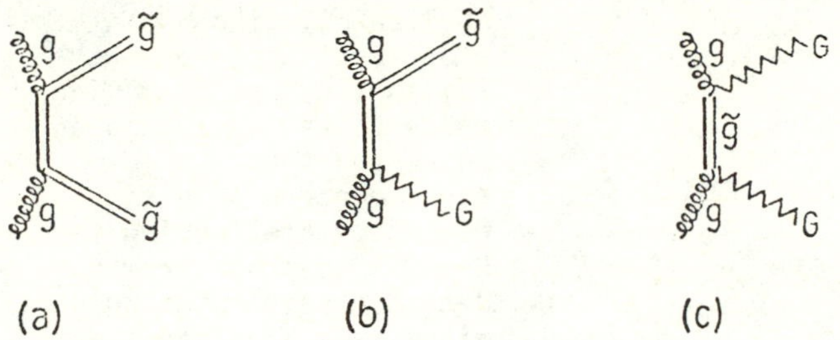

(a)   (b)   (c)

Fig. 3. Production mechanism for gluinos and goldstinos. (a) is present in any theory where gluinos carry color. It gives the cross sections of Fig. 4 for color octet gluinos. (b) and (c) are present in globally supersymmetric theories and give upper limits of Fig. 1.

of experimental detection of such events will give an upper limit on $\tilde{m}$.

We show the gluino pair-production mechanisms for pp and p$\bar{\text{p}}$ collisions in Fig. 3. Figure 4 shows the production cross sections vs. the gluino mass $\tilde{m}$ for a number of beam energies. Since the curves fall rapidly, a small error in estimating the cross section limit has little effect on the associated mass limit. Once again these are expected to be conservative lower limits since production of $c\bar{c}$ and $b\bar{b}$ is larger than the perturbative prediction.

It should be emphasized that the cross sections are quite large. The actual calculation includes not only the diagram of Fig. 3a, but the crossed graph, the direct gluon pole term, and the production via quarks, $q\bar{q} \rightarrow g \rightarrow \tilde{g}\tilde{g}$. In the region of interest the subprocess shown is the largest one in the Feynman gauge, and to understand the size of the cross section we can compare it to $q\bar{q}$ production. With generators F^a in the octet representation and $\lambda^a/2$ in the fundamental representation, we have for equal kinematics, and infinite energy,

$$\frac{\sigma(gg\rightarrow\tilde{g}\tilde{g})}{\sigma(gg\rightarrow q\bar{q})} \approx \frac{\text{Tr}F^aF^aF^bF^b}{\text{Tr}\lambda^a\lambda^a\lambda^b\lambda^b/16} = 13.5.$$

202

For the actual calculation the gluino pair cross section varies from 16-20 times the cross section for production of a pair of quarks of the same mass.

(4) Retroactive Analysis of Data: It is obviously difficult to analyze existing experiments to see what limits they put on gluino masses. It has even been suggested that experimenters only find what they are looking for. We will abstract from past data some estimates on what might have been seen; our results are summarized in Fig. 1. We want to emphasize that they are only estimates, and should not be taken as firm limits until experimenters have analyzed their own data with a full knowledge of backgrounds, cuts, etc. Experiments in progress can set significantly better limits than we obtain if they are analyzed with gluino (or goldstino) detection in mind, and experiments at SPS, ISABELLE or FNAL can go to very high masses.

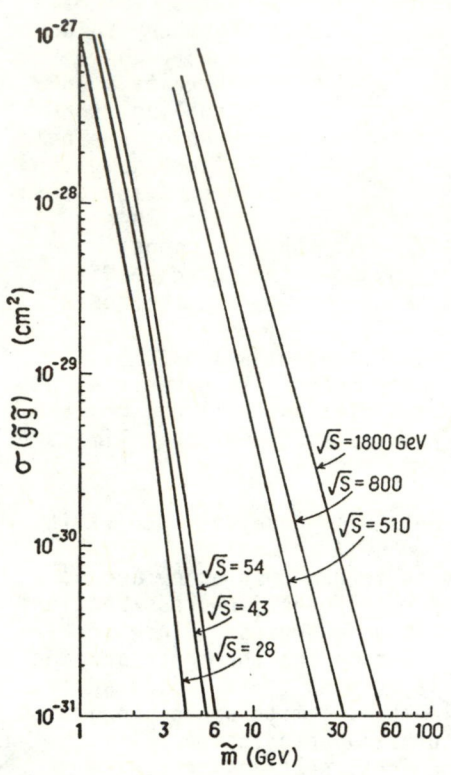

Fig. 4. Gluino production cross sections computed from Fig. 3a, including scaling violations, as parameterized by Baier et al. for several values of $\sqrt{s}$ (in GeV).

(a) Small Gluino Masses and Longer Lifetimes: As discussed above, if $\tilde{m}$ is of the order of 1 GeV the lifetime is fairly long. Fayet and Farrar have already argued that this is not allowed by data, and we agree. The case can be made very strong. For small $\tilde{m}$, while perturbative calculations are not reliable, the production cross section will not be smaller than that of Fig. 4, so $\sigma \gtrsim 1$ mb. Produced gluinos will be shielded by gluons or $q\bar{q}$ octet pairs, so an electrically neutral hadron will be produced, travel a distance from millimeters to meters, and decay into an even number of charged hadrons (often four or more hadrons) which do not point back to the production vertex. There is missing energy because of the Goldstino (or photino) but no charged leptons. The shielded gluino will interact with a total cross section in the mb range. The experiment of Gustafson et al can put limits of order 10^{-32} cm^2 on any neutral object produced in appropriate regions of p_T and X_F which goes several meters and then interacts with a millibarn cross section. Experiments in hyperon beams may be able to put limits of order 10^{-3}-10^{-4} times the Λ cross section on objects which go a few meters and decay into an even number of charged prongs which do not point back to the production vertex. In hydrogen bubble chambers there are strong restrictions on events which would give a visible gap and an even number of prongs (neutrons give a recoil proton and an odd number of prongs). Altogether, we think it is convincing that objects with the properties of light gluinos are not produced with cross sections of even a few μb, so $\tilde{m} \gtrsim$ 2-3 GeV. If $\sigma < 1/2$ μb, then $m \gtrsim$ 3.5 GeV. We assume fixed target pp collisions with $\sqrt{s}$ $\simeq$ 28 Gev for these numbers; they vary a little for other energies or beams.

(b) Beam Dump Experiments: Once the mass is as large as established in (a) above, most gluinos decay within a few cm, and either beam dump or missing energy detectors will be most restrictive. In beam dump experiments the goldstino will interact in the detector, giving no charged lepton and thus candidate neutral current (NC) events. Recent experiments looking for axions quote an upper limit (2σ) • $\sigma_{int} < 2 \times 10^{-67}$ cm^4 where σ is the production cross-section for the gluino in our case and σ_{int} the interaction cross-section for the goldstino. Assuming that the goldstino interaction is like a charged current neutrino interaction, and an average energy of 60 GeV for the goldstino (a typical ν energy in such an experiment), we find again that $\sigma \lesssim 1/2$ μb or equivalently $\tilde{m} \gtrsim$ 3.5 GeV.

For some ranges of $\tilde{m}$ and Λ_{SS} this result can be considerably strengthened by further data analysis. First, in any theory with a $\tilde{g}gG$ vertex the goldstino interaction will be much larger than the ν charged cross-section. Indeed the Goldstino can interact with protons in the detector by fusing with a constituent gluon. Using 60 GeV for a mean goldstino energy and Λ_{SS} = 300 GeV, we find that the goldstino interaction cross section σ_G is larger than σ_ν in the range 1 GeV $\lesssim \tilde{m} \lesssim$ 6 GeV and the Goldstino interaction cross-section is increased by a factor of 4-6 over the contributions considered previously. This strengthens the previous limits and pushes $\tilde{m}$ to about 4.5 GeV. Second, a ν NC event has large missing p_T for the hadrons, and a spectrum of visible hadron energy (E_{vis}) which peaks at low E_{vis} and does not have a long tail. A goldstino induced event, on the other hand, will have considerably larger E_{vis} (thus it could not account for any extra events at small E_{vis}) and much smaller $(p_T/p_L)_{had}$. Cuts on these variables could eliminate most ν NC candidates and allow a small goldstino signal to be found, or give a limit well below 1 μb.

The photino interaction cross section is dominated by the process $\tilde{\gamma}+q \rightarrow q+\tilde{g}$, with a scalar quark exchanged, as discussed by Fayet. This gives a cross section

$$\sigma_{int}=1.2\times10^{-38} \; E(M_W/M_\phi)^4 \sum_q \int_{\tilde{m}^2/s}^1 x \; q(x) \; (1-m^2/xs)^3 dx \; e_q^2 \; (cm^2)$$

with E in GeV. We assume that the lightest scalar quark has $M_\phi = M_W/2$. Then combining this with the beam dump limit gives curve (b) of Fig. 1, drawn for fixed M_ϕ and Λ_{SS} (in a particular theory, M_ϕ may depend on Λ_{SS}). Even if the goldstino is not present the photino decay together with the beam dump data already provides a stringent lower limit on m.

(c) Missing Energy and p_T Experiments: The most powerful limits will come from experiments, at Tevatron and collider energies, which constrain missing energy and momentum as well as possible. Again, we emphasize SS theories with a $\tilde{g}gG$ vertex, but our remarks apply also to theories without such a vertex so far as a lower limit on $\tilde{m}$ is concerned. The upper limit on $\tilde{m}$ depends crucially on such a vertex.

Consider an experiment at the ISR pp collider with a typical integrated luminosity of $10^{37}/cm^2$. Then if $\sigma > 10^{-33}$ cm^2 it had 10^4 gluino pairs produced. This corresponds to $\tilde{m} \gtrsim 10$ GeV if gluinos were not found. Similarly, consider $\int \pounds dt = 10^{35}/cm^2$ at the SPS collider. Then 10^4 events correspond to $\sigma=10^{-31}$ cm^2, or $m \gtrsim 24$ GeV!

Could such events have been seen already? Their signature is fairly dramatic. The gluinos are produced in the central region, and decay, say, via $\tilde{g} \rightarrow gG$. The gluon gives a hadronic jet, so there is a pair of acoplanar jets, plus a lot of missing transverse energy and momentum, and no prompt charged leptons. Typically, about 25% of the energy will go into the central collision, so 10-15% of the total energy and about half of the central energy will be missing. Certainly 10^4 such events could be found in ISR or SPS experiments specifically looking for them in the near future.

(d) Upper Limits: Since the cross sections for double goldstino production grow as $\tilde{m}$, they give upper limits on $\tilde{m}$ or lower limits on Λ_{SS} if a signal is not found. The signature for goldstino pair production is an event with an interaction and beam jets but essentially no central region energy. The goldstino-gluino production is easier to see as $\tilde{g} \rightarrow gG$ giving one jet (or $\tilde{g} \rightarrow q\bar{q}\tilde{\gamma}$), with no particles detected in the opposite direction. Neither type of event has prompt charged leptons. These give the future curves d,f,g of Fig. 1.

Conclusions

Since gluinos tend to be lighter than other supersymmetric partners, and are produced with large cross sections, they should be considered as the prime hope in deciding experimentally whether nature is supersymmetric. We think, conservatively, that gluinos would probably have been detected if their masses were in the excluded region of Fig. 1; basically, m > 4 GeV. Analysis of existing data by experimenters, and experiments in progress, can strengthen these limits considerably if gluinos are not detected. Since gluino properties depend on the scale of SS breaking and on scalar quark masses, interesting upper/lower limits on all of these are implied by upper limits on lifetimes of long-lived neutral hadrons and on production cross sections.

ACKNOWLEDGMENTS

Many thanks to Alice and Gordy for letting me go skiing while they completed this manuscript. This work supported in part by the U.S. Department of Energy.

NON-STANDARD ELECTROWEAK GAUGE MODELS

V. Barger

Department of Physics and Astronomy, University of Hawaii at Manoa
Honolulu, HI   96822
and
Department of Physics, University of Wisconsin-Madison
Madison, WI   53706

ABSTRACT

Weak boson mass spectra of gauge model alternatives to the standard model are examined. In extended gauge models $SU(2)_L \times U(1) \times G$ with fermion assignments of the standard model and simple Higgs, a Z-boson exists with mass between 65 and 115 GeV. In left-right electroweak models the lightest Z is less than 5-10 GeV below the standard model Z-mass. In models with strong gauge couplings, weak bosons of high mass and broad width are realized. Decays of weak bosons to doubly-charged Higgs scalars $(W^+ \to \chi^{++}\chi^-,\ Z \to \chi^{++}\chi^{--})$ occur in models that give Majorana masses to neutrinos through spontaneous breakdown of lepton number conservation; spectacular signatures can result from $\chi^{++} \to \mu^+\mu^+,\ \mu^+e^+,\ e^+e^+$ leptonic decays.

INTRODUCTION

The standard $SU(2)_L \times U(1)$ electroweak gauge model[1] predicts a simple mass spectrum for the $W^\pm$ and Z vector bosons. Including radiative corrections at the one-loop level,[2-4] the predicted masses are[2]

$$M_W = 83 \pm 3 \text{ GeV}$$

$$M_Z = 94 \pm 2 \text{ GeV} .$$

The expected widths are $\Gamma_W \simeq \Gamma_Z \simeq 2.9$ GeV. A richer weak boson mass spectrum and/or broader widths may be realized in non-standard gauge models. A basic requirement of any viable alternative model is that it reproduce the highly successful phenomenology of the standard model at low momentum transfer. Four classes of gauge model alternatives that satisfy this criteria are discussed below.

EXTENDED ELECTROWEAK GAUGE MODELS

This class of alternative models is based on the extended gauge group $SU(2)_L \times U(1) \times G$ with G not necessarily simple. The known fermions are neutral under G and transform under $SU(2)_L \times U(1)$ as in the standard model. Spontaneous symmetry breakdown occurs via the Higgs doublet of the standard model and additional Higgs

0094-243X/82/850206-10$3.00 Copyright 1982 American Institute of Physics

that link $SU(2)_L$ or $U(1)$ to G. The charge operator is a linear combination of all diagonal generators.

According to the Georgi-Weinberg theorem,[5] if the additional Higgs multiplets <u>link only U(1) and G</u>, then neutrino interactions at low momentum transfers are exactly the same as in the standard model. Further, at least <u>one Z is lighter than the standard model Z</u> and one W is at the standard model mass. Under more general conditions,[6] allowing a Higgs link between $SU(2)_L$ and G, there exists no upper bound on the mass of the lightest Z.

The effective Hamiltonian for charged fermion interactions at low energies also duplicates the standard model result, except that there is an additional piece proportional to the square of the electromagnetic current Q

$$\mathcal{H}_{eff} = \frac{G_F}{\sqrt{2}} [j^+ j^- + (j^3 - \sin^2\theta_W Q)^2 + CQ^2] .$$

The extra neutral current term does not contribute to parity violation and is masked by the photon contribution at low q^2. This form for $\mathcal{H}_{eff}$ is derived in models[7-9] with $G = SU(2)^N$ or $G = U(1)^N$ and with doublet and quartet Higgs multiplets. The $I = 1/2$ properties of the Higgs yield a ratio of neutral-to-charged current effective coupling strengths which is naturally the same as the standard model (i.e., without adjustment of parameters); from experiment $\rho = NC/CC = 1.00 \pm 0.02$. The expressions found for $\sin^2\theta_W$ in terms of the gauge couplings and Higgs vacuum expectation values turn out to give $0 < \sin^2\theta_W < 1$.

Several minimal extensions of the standard model (including the usual <u>Higgs</u> doublet) are described below.

$S\widehat{U}(2)_L \times \widehat{U}(1) \times U(1)'$. The additional Higgs is a singlet linking $U(1)$ and $\overline{U(1)'}$. [DGS model[7]] The masses of the two Z-bosons straddle the standard model mass, $M_{Z_1} < M_Z < M_{Z_2}$, and

$$C = (\cos\theta_W)^4 \ r \sim 0.6r \text{ where } r \equiv (M_{Z_1}^{-2} - M_Z^{-2})(M_Z^{-2} - M_{Z_2}^{-2})M_{Z_1}^2 \ M_{Z_2}^2 .$$

$S\widehat{U}(2)_L \times U(1) \times S\widehat{U}(2)'$. A Higgs quartet links $S\widehat{U}(2)_L$ and $SU(2)'$. [BKM model[8]] The premises of the Georgi-Weinberg theorem are not satisfied, yet still $M_{Z_1} < M_Z < M_{Z_2}$. The C-parameter is much <u>smaller than</u> that of the DGS model; $C^2 = (\sin\theta_W)^4 \ r \sim 0.05r$.

$S\widehat{U}(2)_L \times \widehat{U}(1) \times S\widehat{U}(2)'$. An extra Higgs doublet links $U(1)$ and $SU(2)'$ and a quartet links $SU(2)_L$ and $SU(2)'$. [BMW model[9]] <u>This model allows all weak bosons to be above the standard Z and W masses.</u> The lore based on the Georgi-Weinberg theorem that one Z is always lighter than the standard model Z must therefore be disregarded. A constraint on the maximum value of the Z_1 mass in the BMW model is obtained from experimental bounds on the C-parameter. The limits from Mark J and Jade experiments[10] of $e^+ e^-$ cross sections from QED predictions restrict C as follows:

208

$$C < 0.027 \qquad e^+ e^- \to \mu^+ \mu^-$$

$$C < 0.016 \qquad e^+ e^- \to \text{hadrons} .$$

The corresponding upper bound on M_{Z_1} is[9]

$$M_{Z_1} < 115 \text{ GeV} .$$

This numerical value allows for radiative corrections to the Z_1 mass of about 4 GeV. More generally, in the BMW one Z (not necessarily the lighter one) must lie in the mass interval 65 GeV to 115 GeV. The BMW can be further extended to SU(2) × U(1) × SU(2)' × SU(2)" × SU(2)" × ... . In this generalization the upper bound on M_{Z_1} is not appreciably raised.

Based on these natural extensions of the standard model, we conclude that <u>the Z_1 can be below, at, or up to 20 GeV above the standard Z mass</u>. Typical results for the $\overline{p}p \to \mu^+\mu^- X$ cross section $d\sigma/dm$ and integrated asymmetry A at $\sqrt{s} = 2$ TeV in the BMW model are illustrated in Fig. 1 (solid curves) along with standard model expectations (dashed curves).

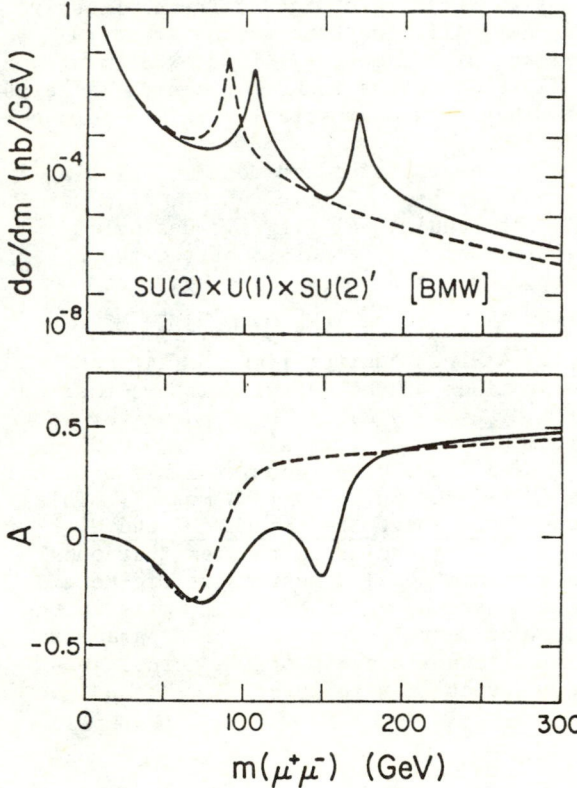

Fig. 1. Typical results of the BMW model for the $\overline{p}p \to \mu^+\mu^- X$ cross section $d\sigma/dm$ at $\sqrt{s} = 2$ TeV versus $m(\mu^+\mu^-)$ and the integrated $\mu^+\mu^-$ asymmetry A.

A special case of the BMW model provides a possible explanation of why the C-parameter is observed to be small. Heavy fermions are assigned to U(1) × SU(2)' and an equality of SU(2) and SU(2)' gauge couplings is assumed [BKW model][11]. A hierarchy v << u,w of the vacuum expectation values (vev) is motivated by the high mass of the new fermions. Two weak angles θ_W and θ_W', with $1 < \sin^2\theta_W'/\sin^2\theta_W < 2$ completely specify the model. The C-parameter is constrained to values C < 0.007. See Fig. 2, which gives the relation of C and the weak boson masses to $\sin\theta_W'/\sin\theta_W$. Allowing for radiative corrections, the Z-masses in the model satisfy

$$M_{Z_1} < 104 \text{ GeV} \qquad M_{Z_2} > 215 \text{ GeV} .$$

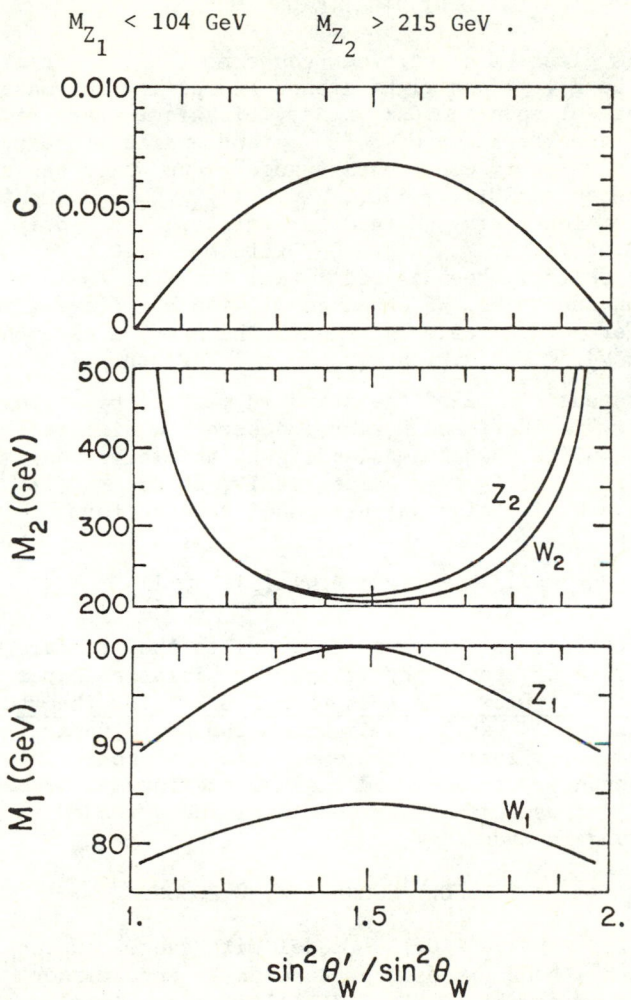

Fig. 2. Predictions of the BKW model for the strength C of the Q^2 effective interaction term and for the weak boson masses versus the ratio $\sin^2\theta_W'/\sin^2\theta_W$.

210

In another variant[12] of the BMW model, based on $U(1) \times SU(2) \times SU(2)' \times SU(2)''$, each fermion generation is assigned to transform under a different $SU(2)$. A hierarchy of vev's is employed to reproduce the mass scales of the three fermion generations and to obtain approximate e-μ universality. An interesting consequence is a longer τ-lifetime than the standard model predicts, due to smaller than G_F charged-current coupling of the third generation. Another consequence is a small but non-negligible $b \to s\ell^+\ell^-$ flavor-changing neutral current.

LEFT-RIGHT GAUGE MODELS

In this class of electroweak gauge models[13-15] fermions transform under both left and right groups and parity nonconservation is a consequence of spontaneous symmetry breaking. Left-right models result from the breakdown of $SO(10)$ grand unified theory.

The "left-right" electroweak gauge group which has usually been considered is $SU(2)_L \times SU(2)_R \times U(1)_{B-L}$. Experimental constraints from low energy charged currents require[16] only that $M_{W_L}/M_{W_R} < 0.36$ (e.g., $M_{W_R} > 220$ GeV with $M_{W_L} = 80$ GeV). However, it has been recently been argued[17] that the $K_L - K_S$ mass difference contribution due to W_L, W_R exchanges in the box diagram requires $M_{W_R} > 1.6$ TeV. In a left-right model the heavy Z is expected[14] to have a mass $M_{Z_2} \gtrsim M_{W_R}$. With M_{W_R} above 1 TeV, the light W and Z will be located[14,15] below the standard masses, by at most 5-10 GeV.

Recently Robinett and Rosner proposed[18] a different final stage of the $SO(10)$ breakdown leading to an electroweak gauge group $SU(2)_L \times U(1)_R \times U(1)_{B-L}$ [or alternately, $SU(2)_L \times U(1)_Y \times U(1)_\chi$]. The effective Hamiltonian of this model has the form

$$\mathcal{H}_{eff} = \frac{4G_F}{\sqrt{2}} [j_L^+ j_L^- + (j_L^3 - x_L Q)^2] + \frac{4G_F'}{\sqrt{2}} [j_R^3 - x_R Q]^2 .$$

Neutrino interactions are thus identical to the standard model. The constraints of atomic physics parity violation experiments require that <u>the lighter Z be less than 2 GeV below the standard Z mass</u>. The second Z can be as light as 250 GeV. Polarized beam or final lepton polarization measurements in e^+e^- collisions at the lower Z resonance, or polarized e^-e^- scattering measurements, could distinguish[19] these left-right models or the extended gauge models from the standard model.

STRONGLY COUPLED W, Z BOSONS

An $SU(2)_L \times U(1)_Y \times U(1)_{Y'}$ model with gauge couplings $g, g_B \gg e$ and $g_{B'} \approx e$ has been proposed by Berezinsky and Smirnov[20] [the BS model]. The vector boson B' of $U(1)_{Y'}$ is approximately the electromagnetic field. The charge operator is $Q = T_3 + 1/2(Y+Y')$. The fermions have $Y = Y'$ and the usual $SU(2)_L$ assignments. The Higgs structure is complicated and includes a multiplet with large T, Y and Y'. The parameters G_F, ρ, $\sin^2\theta_W$, and C of the effective low-energy Hamiltonian are essentially determined by the vev's and the vev's are almost uniquely determined by data. The gauge couplings g, g_B remain as parameters. The masses of the W, Z scale with (g,g_B) and the widths scale as $(g,g_B)^3$. The strong couplings $g,g_B \sim 1$ give high W, Z masses and broad decay widths. Figure 3 illustrates the $\overline{p}p$ pair production cross section and asymmetry that could result in such a model.

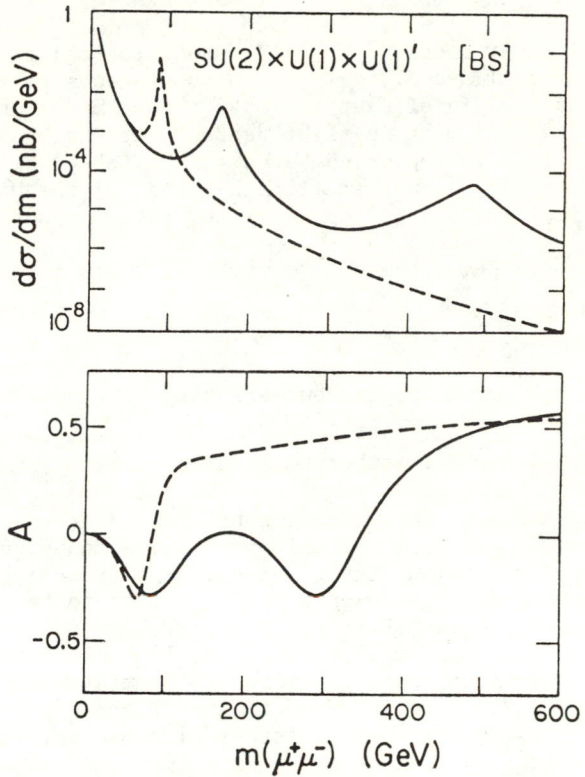

Fig. 3. Representative results of the BS model for $\overline{p}p \to \mu^+\mu^-X$ at $\sqrt{s}$ = 2 TeV.

Strong coupling $SU(2)_L \times U(1)$ models with substructure of leptons, quarks and weak bosons have been suggested.[21,22] In the Abbott-Farhi model[21] the left-handed fermions are composites of elementary fermions and elementary scalars, and the weak bosons and a scalar field are bound states of the elementary scalars. There is no spontaneous symmetry breaking in the model. Because of a global SU(2) symmetry in the model, the W^+, W^-,W^0 bosons are degenerate in mass. Since the $SU(2)_L$ gauge coupling g is of order unity, the W-bosons are heavier and broader than in the standard model. The J^3Q cross term in the effective neutral current interaction appears as a consequence of the composite structure of fermions. This is analogous to the non-gauge models of Bjorken[23] and Hung-Sakurai.[24] A possible difficulty is that a ≈ 100 GeV scale of fermion form factors is needed to reproduce the J^3Q cross term, whereas the limit on bound state structure is $\gtrsim 600$ GeV from measurements of the muon anamolous magnetic moment.

WEAK BOSON DECAYS TO SCALARS

Additional decay modes of W and Z bosons to scalars occur in the Gelmini-Roncadelli model,[25] in which spontaneously broken lepton number is the origin of neutrino mass. This model enlarges the standard $SU(2)_L \times U(1)$ with no right-handed neutrino by introduction of a Higgs triplet with lepton number $L = 2$. The vev of the neutral member of the triplet is much smaller than that of the Higgs doublet. The physical scalars in the model and their masses are

χ^{++} $M > 15$ GeV (from e^+e^- experimental limits)

χ^+ $M/\sqrt{2}$

χ^o $m < 100$ keV

M^o $m = 0$ (from spontaneous breaking of global B-L symmetry)

H^o usual doublet member with unknown mass

The extra decay modes of the gauge bosons[26] are $W^+ \to \chi^{++}\chi^-$, $\chi^+\chi^o$, χ^+M^o and $Z \to \chi^{++}\chi^{--}$, $\chi^+\chi^-$, $M^o\chi^o$. Figure 4 gives the predicted branching fractions[27] versus the χ^{++} mass. The branching fractions to the doubly-charged Higgs boson are high enough to be interesting, especially if $M < 25$ GeV in which case $B(W^+ \to \chi^{++}\chi^-) > 4\%$ and $B(Z \to \chi^{++}\chi^{--}) > 2\%$. Sequential $\chi^{++} \to \ell_1^+ \ell_2^+$ leptonic decays could provide spectacular signatures. Figure 5 illustrates combined muon and electron leptonic branching fractions[27] of the χ^{++}, for choices of the couplings $g_{\ell\ell}$, that are consistent with present limits from other processes.[26-29] Detection of a signal of this origin would constitute dramatic evidence of lepton number nonconservation.

ACKNOWLEDGMENTS

I thank K. Whisnant for valuable assistance in the preparation of this report. I also thank H. Baer, W. Y. Keung, E. Ma, S. Pakvasa, R.J.N. Phillips and K. Whisnant for collaboration and for helpful comments regarding the contents of this report.

This research was supported in part by the University of Wisconsin Research Committee and in part by the Department of Energy under contracts DE-AC02-76ER00881 and DE-AM03-76SF00235.

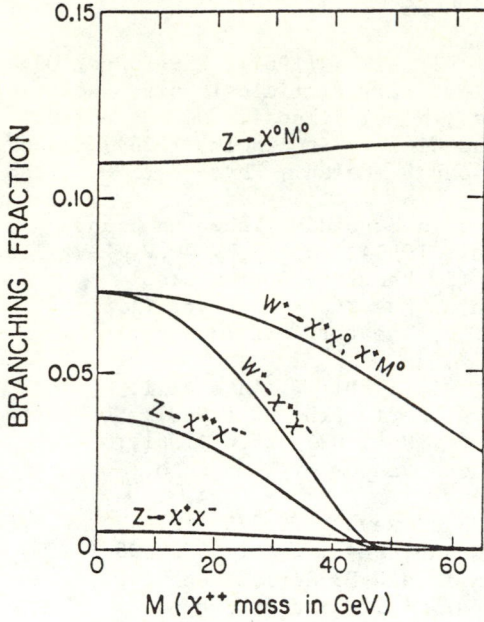

Fig. 4. Predicted branching fractions of W, Z bosons into scalars in the GR model.

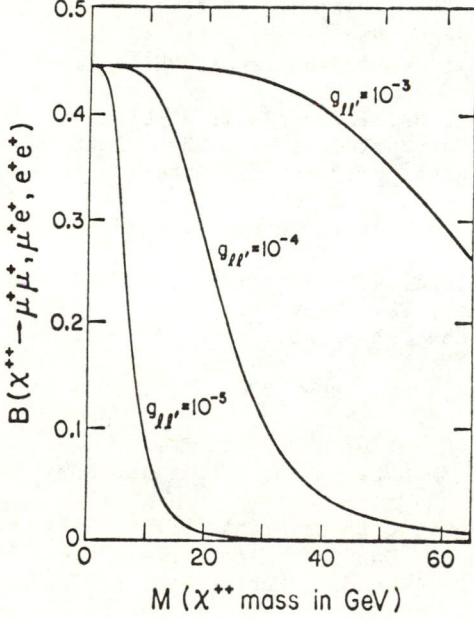

Fig. 5. Branching fraction into electrons or muons of the doubly-charged Higgs boson of the GR model for allowed values of the χ^{++} coupling $g_{\ell\ell'}$ to leptons ℓ and ℓ'.

REFERENCES

1. S. Weinberg, Phys. Rev. Lett. 19, 1264 (1967); Phys. Rev. D5, 1412 (1972); A. Salam, in Elementary Particle Theory: Relativistic Groups and Analyticity, Nobel Symposium No. 8, edited by N. Svartholm (Almqvist and Wiksel, Stockholm, 1968), p. 367; S. L. Glashow, J. Ilipoulos and L. Maiani, Phys. Rev. D2, 1285 (1970).
2. W. J. Marciano and A. Sirlin, in Second Workshop on Grand Unification (Ann Arbor, Mich., 1981), edited by J. P. Leveille, L. R. Sulak and D. G. Unger (Birkhauser, Boston-Basel-Stuttgart, 1981), p. 151; Phys. Rev. Lett. 46, 163 (1981).
3. C. H. Llewellyn-Smith and J. F. Wheater, Oxford preprint (1981).
4. M. Veltman, Phys. Lett. 91B, 95 (1980); F. Antonelli, M. Consoli and G. Corbo, Phys. Lett. 91B, 90 (1980); S. Dawson, J. S. Hagdin and L. Hall, Phys. Rev. D23, 2666 (1981); D. Yu. Bardin, D. Ch. Christova and O. M. Fedorenko, Nucl. Phys. B175, 435 (1980).
5. H. Georgi and S. Weinberg, Phys. Rev. D17, 275 (1978).
6. V. Barger, E. Ma and K. Whisnant, Phys. Lett. 107B, 95 (1981).
7. E. H. De Groot, G. J. Gournaris and D. Schildknecht, Phys. Lett. 85B, 399 (1979); 90B, 427 (1980); Zeit. Phys. C5, 127 (1980) [The DGS model]; E. H. De Groot and D. Schildknecht, Phys. Lett. 95B, 128 (1980).
8. V. Barger, W. Y. Keung and E. Ma, Phys. Rev. Lett. 44, 1169 (1980); Phys. Rev. D22, 727 (1980) [The BKM model]; V. Barger, W. Y. Keung and E. Ma, Phys. Lett. 94B, 377 (1980).
9. V. Barger, E. Ma and K. Whisnant, Phys. Rev. Lett. 46, 1501 (1981); Phys. Rev. (in press); UW-Madison report PH/11 [The BMW model].
10. B. H. Wiik, in AIP Conf. Proc. 68, 1379 (1981); P. Dittman and V. Hepp, DESY Report 81/030; W. Bartel et al., Phys. Lett. 101B, 361 (1981); H. Rykaczewski, private communication of Mark J data.
11. V. Barger, W. Y. Keung and K. Whisnant, Phys. Rev. D25, 291 (1982) [The BKW model].
12. X. Li and E. Ma, Phys. Rev. Lett. 47, 1788 (1981).
13. R. N. Mohapatra and J. C. Pati, Phys. Rev. D11, 566 (1975); R. N. Mohapatra and D. P. Sidhu, Phys. Rev. Lett. 38, 667 (1977).
14. T. G. Rizzo and G. Senjanovic, Phys. Rev. D24, 704 (1981) and BNL preprint 29716.
15. X. Li and R. E. Marshak, VPI preprint HEP 81/5.
16. M. A. Beg, R. V. Budny, R. N. Mohapatra and A. Sirlin, Phys. Rev. Lett. 38, 1252 (1977).
17. G. Beall, M. Bander and A. Soni, UCLA preprint TEP29 (1981).
18. R. W. Robinett and J. L. Rosner, Unov. of Minn. preprint 430 (1981); N. G. Deshpande and D. Iskander, Nucl. Phys. B167, 223 (1980); Phys. Lett. 87B, 3831 (1979).

19. W. Hollik, Z. Phys. C8, 149 (1981); H. A. Olsen and P. Asland, Harvard preprint (1981); T. G. Rizzo, Ames Report J-666-1981; M. J. Puhala, T. G. Rizzo and B.-L. Young, Ames Report J-693-1981.

20. V. S. Berezinsky and A. Yu. Smirnov, Phys. Lett. 94B, 505 (1980); Yad. Fiz. 31, 1551 (1980).

21. L. F. Abbott and E. Farhi, Phys. Lett. 101B, 69 (1981) and Nucl. Phys. B189, 547 (1981).

22. H. Fritzsch and G. Mandelbaum, Phys. Lett. 102B, 319 (1981).

23. J. D. Bjorken, Phys. Rev. D19, 335 (1979).

24. P. Q. Hung and J. J. Sakurai, Nucl. Phys. B143, 81 (1978); E. H. De Groot and D. Schildknecht, Z. Phys. C10, 55 (1981); N. Wright, UCLA Report 81/TEP/14.

25. G. B. Gelmini and M. Roncadelli, Phys. Lett. 99B, 411 (1980).

26. H. Georgi, S. Glashow and S. Nussinov, Nucl. Phys. B293, 297 (1981).

27. V. Barger, H. Baer, W. Y. Keung and R.J.N. Phillips, UW-Madison Report PH/37.

28. V. Barger, W. Y. Keung and S. Pakvasa, Phys. Rev. in press, MAD/PH/15.

29. G. B. Gelmini, S. Nussinov and M. Roncadelli, Max-Planck Institute preprint PAE/PTh 59/81.

PRODUCTION OF Z AND W BOSONS AT THE $\bar{p}p$ COLLIDERS

A.D. Martin

Department of Physics, University of Durham, U.K.

ABSTRACT

We study the leptonic signatures of W and Z bosons at the $\bar{p}p$ colliders. A central topic is the transverse momentum distribution of the produced weak boson; for the Z this is an ideal testing ground for QCD, for the W it is a necessary ingredient in determining the shape of the Jacobian peak in the transverse momentum distribution of the decay lepton. We display predictions for the Jacobian peak and for the angular distributions of lepton arising from the process $\bar{p}p \to WX \to \ell X$. We discuss background leptons arising from heavy quark production.

INTRODUCTION

It is widely believed[1-14] that the best signatures for the production of Z and W bosons at $\bar{p}p$ colliders are through their leptonic decay modes

$$\bar{p}p \to ZX \qquad\qquad \bar{p}p \to WX.$$
$$\hookrightarrow \ell^+\ell^- \qquad\qquad\qquad \hookrightarrow \ell\nu$$

In the standard model (with 3 generations) the boson branching ratios to each leptonic channel are predicted to be

$$\text{B.R. } (Z \to \ell^+\ell^-) \simeq 0.03$$
$$\text{B.R. } (W \to \ell\nu) \simeq 0.08,$$

and their masses are, to lowest order, given by

$$M_W = \frac{37.7}{\sin\theta_W} \simeq 80 \text{ GeV}, \qquad M_Z = \frac{M_W}{\cos\theta_W} \simeq 91 \text{ GeV},$$

taking $\sin^2\theta_W = 0.22$. Both the mass formulae and the relation between $\sin^2\theta_W$ and experiment are subject to electro-weak radiative corrections. These corrections have recently been the subject of detailed investigations[15,16] and are found to shift the masses upwards by about 4 GeV. Thus provided the boson masses can be measured with an accuracy better than this shift, a test of the electro-weak gauge structure is possible.

Here we discuss the detection and the determination of the masses of the weak bosons. For $Z \to \ell^+\ell^-$ this is an experimental problem, but for an accurate measurement of the mass of $W \to \ell\nu$ a theoretical knowledge of the momentum distribution of the observed decay lepton is required. A crucial intermediate step in this determination is the computation of the transverse momentum (Q_T) distribution of the parent W, produced in $\bar{p}p \to WX$ at small Q_T. We therefore focus attention on

QCD techniques for evaluating weak boson production in the vital small Q_T region.

DETECTION OF THE Z BOSON

The Z should be identifiable as a peak in the observed $\ell^+\ell^-$ invariant mass spectrum. The main problem is the expected event rate. To estimate the cross section we assume that the Z is produced by the Drell-Yan process. Using quark structure functions obtained from deep inelastic scattering we find, for each lepton flavour,

$$\sigma(\bar{p}p \rightarrow ZX \rightarrow \ell^+\ell^- X) \simeq 2 \times 10^{-33} \text{ cm}^2 .$$

For a luminosity of 10^{30} cm^{-2} sec^{-1}, this is equivalent to the production of about 5 events/day.

Gluon corrections will modify this estimate. First we should use structure functions $q(x,Q^2)$ evolved in Q^2 up to M_Z^2. For CERN collider energies, $\sqrt{s} \simeq 500$ GeV, $x \simeq M_Z/\sqrt{s}$ is typically 0.2 and the structure functions approximately scale, so no enhancement of the cross section is expected. However at $\sqrt{s} \simeq 2000$ GeV we see $x \simeq 0.05$ and scaling violations should produce a useful enhancement in the event rate. For example, using the Owens-Reya[17] parametrization of the structure functions we have a four-fold increase, although such estimates should be treated with caution as we are extrapolating a long way in Q^2. A second enhancement is expected from the K factor (K$\approx$2.3) associated with Drell-Yan processes.

In figure 1 we compare the Z signal and background. We show the lepton-pair production cross section from $\bar{q}q \rightarrow \gamma^*$ or Z, together with that arising from the production and subsequent semi-leptonic decays of a pair of heavy quark states $\bar{Q} + Q$ (with Q=b,c). The expected Z signal is sitting well above the background.

DETECTION OF W BOSONS

Since we cannot observe the ν from the $W \rightarrow \ell\nu$ decay, the best signature of the W is a Jacobian peak in the transverse momentum (p_T) distribution of the observed lepton[1-14]. The idea is sketched in figure 2. If the W is produced at rest in the $\bar{p}p$ centre-of-mass frame (fig.2a) then it is easy to show that the lepton distribution is

$$\frac{d\sigma}{dp_T^2} \propto (\tfrac{1}{4}M_W^2 - p_T^2)^{-\frac{1}{2}} \qquad \text{for } p_T < \frac{M_W}{2}$$

$$= 0 \qquad \text{for } p_T > \frac{M_W}{2} ,$$

giving a Jacobian peak at $p_T = \tfrac{1}{2}M_W$. The distribution sketched in figure 2b allows for the effects of the longitudinal motion of the

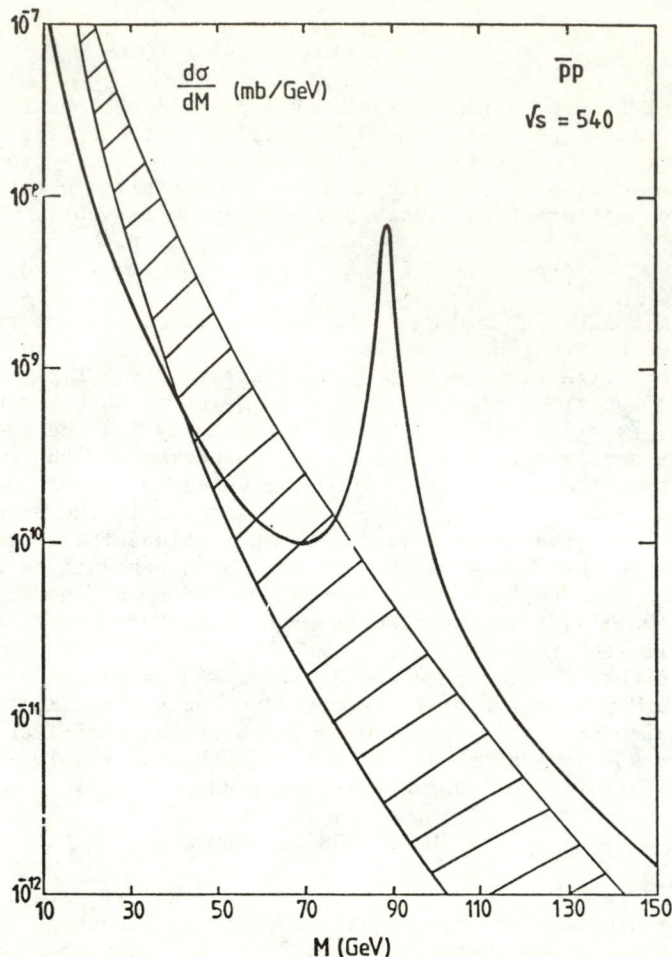

Fig.1 The lepton-pair production cross sections arising from
$\bar{q}q \rightarrow \gamma^*$ or Z, and from $\bar{q}q$, gg $\rightarrow \bar{b}b$ or $\bar{c}c$, calculated using the
parton densities of Owens and Reya[17]. The band for the $\bar{Q}Q$
background shows the variation between using the Owens-Reya
gluon density and taking simply x G(x) = $3(1-x)^5$. No K factor
is included.

parent W and its finite width (which according to the standard model is Γ_W = 2.5 GeV). However the main uncertainty in this lepton signal for the W arises from the transverse momentum, Q_T, of the parent W itself. This we now discuss.

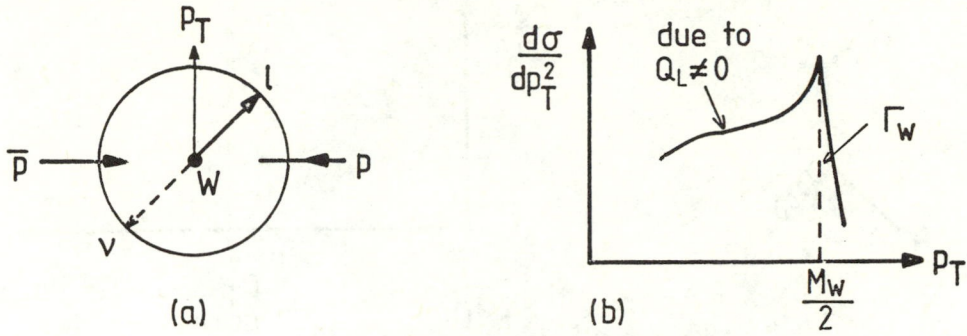

Fig. 2   (a) The process $\bar{p}p \to WX \to \ell\nu X$ assuming the W momentum $\vec{Q}$=0.

(b) The transverse momentum spectrum of the observed lepton assuming Q_T=0. The longitudinal motion of the W is responsible for the shoulder in the distribution.

TRANSVERSE MOMENTUM OF THE W

A great deal of attention has been paid to the transverse momentum (Q_T) distribution of W's (and of massive photons, γ^*'s) produced in high energy hadronic collisions. In particular the confrontation between perturbative QCD and Drell-Yan $\gamma^* \to \ell^+\ell^-$ data is an interesting and ongoing saga[19]. A major problem is that QCD predictions are most reliable in kinematic regions that are not easily accessible to experiment. The situation for weak boson production appears to be more favourable.

There are two distinct regions in which the Q_T distribution can be calculated using QCD : (a) $Q_T \sim M_W$ and   (b) $Q_T^2 \ll M_W^2$.

(a) $\underline{Q_T \sim M_W}$

Here there is only one large mass scale and the usual QCD perturbation series is obtained. In the $0(\alpha_s)$ approximation we have contributions from subprocesses $\bar{q}q \to Wg$, $gq \to Wq$, $g\bar{q} \to W\bar{q}$, where a single hard gluon (or quark) recoils against the emitted W (see figure 3a). The p_T distribution of the observed lepton from $W \to \ell\nu$ decay has been predicted[9,12] using the $0(\alpha_s)$ approximation to the Q_T distribution of the W. However the $0(\alpha_s)$ approximation diverges as $Q_T \to 0$ and is only justified for $Q_T \sim M_W$. This means an $0(\alpha_s)$ calculation can only reliably predict the lepton p_T distribution in an experimentally remote

220

region of phase space (see figure 3b).

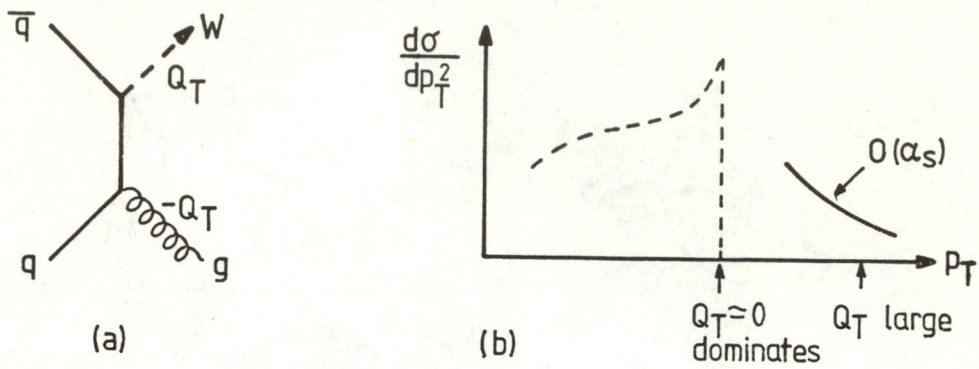

(a)

(b)

Fig.3 (a) An $O(\alpha_s)$ subprocess for W production.
(b) The region of validity of an $O(\alpha_s)$ calculation of the transverse momentum distribution of the decay lepton.

(b) $\underline{Q_T^2 \ll M_W^2}$

Now we have a second large mass scale and order-by-order the leading contributions have the form $[\alpha_s \ln^2(M_W^2/Q_T^2)]^N$. Resummation is therefore required to obtain a meaningful result. This was first studied in the pioneering work by DDT[20], although their original result was slightly wrong in detail (the correct answer is given in refs.21-23). As it will be relevant, we sketch the derivation below. A more complete discussion is given, for example, in refs. 23,24.

Leading Double Logarithm Summation :

We begin by noting that the leading logarithm approximation (LLA) to the $O(\alpha_s)$ result for the Q_T distribution is

$$\frac{1}{\sigma_o} \frac{d\sigma^1}{dQ_T^2}\bigg|_{LLA} = \frac{4\alpha_s}{3\pi Q_T^2} \log \frac{M_W^2}{Q_T^2} , \qquad (1)$$

which arises from the single gluon emission process (figure 3a) and manifests the $Q_T=0$ divergence. σ_o is the Drell-Yan Q_T-integrated cross section for $\bar{q}q \to W$, and the superscript 1 on σ indicates the $O(\alpha_s)$ cross section.

Proceeding now to the cross section for W production accompanied by 2-gluon emission, $\bar{q} + q \rightarrow W(Q_T) + g(k_{T1}) + g(k_{T2})$, we find

$$\frac{1}{\sigma_o} \left. \frac{d\sigma^2}{dQ_T^2} \right|_{LLA} = \frac{1}{2\pi} \int \frac{d^2 k_{T1}}{k_{T1}^2} \int \frac{d^2 k_{T2}}{k_{T2}^2} \left(\frac{4\alpha_s}{3\pi} \right)^2 \ell n \left(\frac{M_W^2}{k_{T1}^2} \right) \ell n \left(\frac{M_W^2}{k_{T2}^2} \right) \delta^{(2)} (\vec{k}_{T1} + \vec{k}_{T2} + \vec{Q}_T) .$$

$$(2)$$

Following the leading logarithm approach, we note that the dominant regions of integration are

$$k_{T1,2}^2 << k_{T2,1}^2 \sim Q_T^2 . \tag{3}$$

With this approximation the δ function disappears, and the expression factorizes corresponding to independent gluon emission, and so eq.(2) becomes

$$\frac{1}{\sigma_o} \left. \frac{d\sigma^2}{dQ_T^2} \right|_{LLA} = \frac{4\alpha_s}{3\pi Q_T^2} \ell n \left(\frac{M_W^2}{Q_T^2} \right) \left[\int^{Q_T^2} \frac{dk_T^2}{k_T^2} \frac{4\alpha_s}{3\pi} \ell n \left(\frac{M_W^2}{k_T^2} \right) \right.$$

$$\left. \underbrace{} - \frac{2\alpha_s}{3\pi} \ell n^2 \left(\frac{M_W^2}{Q_T^2} \right) \right] . \tag{4}$$

The apparent divergence at the lower limit of the k_T^2 integration is cancelled by the contributions from the $O(\alpha_s^2)$ virtual diagrams.

Similarly for three or more gluons emitted the leading logarithms comes from regions of integration where the k_{Ti}'s are strong-ordered (cf.(3)) and so again the integrals factorize. Moreover these leading double logarithms can be summed to give the following Q_T distribution of the W

$$\frac{1}{\sigma_o} \left. \frac{d\sigma}{dQ_T^2} \right|_{LLA} = \frac{4\alpha_s}{3\pi Q_T^2} \ell n \left(\frac{M_W^2}{Q_T^2} \right) \exp \left[- \frac{2\alpha_s}{3\pi} \ell n^2 \left(\frac{M_W^2}{Q_T^2} \right) \right] . \tag{5}$$

222

The extra exponential factor (cf.(1)), which arises as a result of the incomplete cancellation between the real and virtual multi-gluon contributions, can be regarded as the form factor of the quark. We note that it corresponds to the probability of multi-gluon emission with each $k_{Ti} < Q_T$, and that it leads to a vanishing cross section as $Q_T \to 0$. However this last result must be treated with suspicion because approximation (3) is no longer valid as $Q_T \to 0$. To study the $Q_T \to 0$ behaviour we need to circumvent this approximation.

Impact Parameter Summation :

Parisi and Petronzio[21] noted that by going to impact parameter space, both the factorization of the k_{Ti} integrals and exact transverse momentum conservation can be achieved. The procedure is to write the transverse momentum δ-function in the form

$$\delta^{(2)}(\vec{k}_{T1}+..+\vec{k}_{Tn}+\vec{Q}_T) = \frac{1}{(2\pi)^2} \int d^2b \; e^{i(\vec{k}_{T1}+...+\vec{k}_{Tn}+\vec{Q}_T)\cdot\vec{b}} \quad . \tag{6}$$

Each multigluon contribution (for example (2)) is then a completely factorized product of k_{Ti} integrals, every one of which is given by

$$\Delta(b) = \frac{1}{\pi} \int d^2k_T \left[\frac{1}{\sigma_o}\frac{d\sigma^1}{dk_T^2}\right]_{LLA} (e^{i\vec{k}_T\cdot\vec{b}} - 1)$$

$$= \int^{M_W^2} dk_T^2 \left[\frac{1}{\sigma_o}\frac{d\sigma^1}{dk_T^2}\right]_{LLA} (J_o(k_T b) - 1) \tag{7}$$

where the $O(\alpha_s)$ distribution in square brackets is given by eq.(1). The -1 arises from the virtual gluon diagrams which regularize the infrared ($k_T \to 0$) divergences. The Q_T distribution arising from these multi-gluon emissions is thus a power series in Δ, which is found to sum to an exponential

$$\frac{1}{\sigma_o}\frac{d\sigma}{dQ_T^2} = \frac{1}{4\pi} \int d^2b \; e^{i\vec{Q}_T\cdot\vec{b}} \; e^{\Delta(b)} \quad . \tag{8}$$

The inverse Fourier transform is

$$e^{\Delta(b)} = \frac{1}{\pi} \int d^2Q_T \left(\frac{1}{\sigma_o} \frac{d\sigma}{dQ_T^2}\right) e^{-i\vec{Q}_T \cdot \vec{b}} . \tag{9}$$

Unlike the leading double logarithm approximation (LLA), distribution (8) peaks at $Q_T = 0$, as we shall see from the explicit calculations shown below. The peak arises from (non-leading) contributions in which two or more gluons with large k_T's add vectorally to give $Q_T \sim 0$, whereas in the LLA one gluon is required to have $k_T \sim Q_T$ and the others to have smaller transverse momenta. Taking a running coupling constant

$$\alpha_s(k_T^2) = \frac{16}{33-2N_f} \frac{1}{\ln(k_T^2/\Lambda^2)} \tag{10}$$

in eq.(7) (cf.eq.(1)), the important region of integration satisfies[24] $\Lambda^2 \ll k_T^2 \ll M_W^2$ ensuring that the impact resummation makes sense.

Q_T DISTRIBUTION OF THE Z AS A TEST OF QCD

Although the above QCD predictions apply equally well to either W or Z production, we present results for the Z since its Q_T distribution can be directly measured.

To gain insight into the Q_T distribution obtained by impact parameter summation we note three properties[18] which follow directly from eqs.(7-9).

$$\text{(i)} \quad \int \frac{d\sigma}{dQ_T^2} dQ_T^2 = \sigma_o e^{\Delta(o)} = \sigma_o . \tag{11}$$

$$\text{(ii)} \quad \langle Q_T^2 \rangle \equiv \int Q_T^2 \left(\frac{1}{\sigma_o} \frac{d\sigma}{dQ_T^2}\right) dQ_T^2$$

$$= \left[-\frac{\partial}{\partial b_\mu} \frac{\partial}{\partial b^\mu} e^{\Delta(b)}\right]_{b=0}$$

$$= \int Q_T^2 \left(\frac{1}{\sigma_o} \frac{d\sigma^1}{dQ_T^2}\right) dQ_T^2$$

$$= \langle Q_T^2 \rangle_1 . \tag{12}$$

In other words, although multigluon emission ($n \geqslant 2$) regularizes and alters the shape of the $O(\alpha_s)$ distribution it does not change the average value of Q_T^2.

(iii) We can readily investigate the effects of the intrinsic transverse momentum distribution of the incident quarks.[21] For example we can insert a smearing function $\exp(-b^2 <Q_T^2>_i/4)$ into eq.(8) which corresponds to a parton instrinsic momentum distribution $\exp(-Q_T^2/<Q_T^2>_i)$. Eq.(12) is then modified to

$$<Q_T^2> \; = \; <Q_T^2>_1 \; + \; <Q_T^2>_i . \qquad\qquad (13)$$

Typically we expect $<Q_T^2>_i \sim 0.5$ GeV^2, which for Z (or W) production at $\bar{p}p$ collider energies gives a negligible effect.

Figure 4a shows the transverse momentum distribution of the Z produced in $\bar{p}p$ collisions calculated from eqs.(8) and (7). For comparison the dotted curve gives the $O(\alpha_s)$ distribution, eq.(1), that is input in the calculation. We notice that the resummation regularises the $O(\alpha_s)$ divergence to a finite peak at $Q_T = 0$. Further we see that the 'output' and 'input' distributions are approximately equal at high Q_T; in fact the curves must cross to ensure the equality of the Q_T^2 moments of the two distributions, cf. eq.(12).

We note that the above results, together with previous calculations[13,14] and theoretical studies,[21,23-29] are based on the validity of the leading logarithm approximation (LLA), eq.(1), to $O(\alpha_s)$. It is in this approximation that the multi-gluon contributions factorize and allow summation. Furthermore, analytic estimates of the integrals can readily be obtained[21,24,30]. There are, however, two unpleasant features of the resulting Q_T distributions. At high Q_T we expect the 'output' distribution to approximate the exact $O(\alpha_s)$ result. This does not happen. The reason can be traced to the fact that the LLA, eq.(1), considerably exceeds the exact $O(\alpha_s)$ result at moderate and high Q_T. Secondly, contrary to our QCD beliefs, the Q_T distribution does not depend on the $\bar{p}p$ centre-of-mass energy, $\sqrt{s}$, or on the rapidity, y, of the produced Z. Note that the k_T^2 integration is cut-off at M^2, see eq.(7).

To overcome these diseases, it has been advocated[21,18] that we substitute for σ^1 in eq.(7) the exact $O(\alpha_s)$ cross section, including the non-logarithmic terms as well as the contributions from $gq \rightarrow Zq$ and $g\bar{q} \rightarrow Z\bar{q}$. This has the advantage that the resultant cross section approximates the exact $O(\alpha_s)$ cross section in the high Q_T region, see figure 4b. Moreover taking the maximum allowed k_T^2 to be the upper limit of the k_T^2 integration, rather than M_Z^2, leads to the expected energy and rapidity dependence of the Q_T distribution of the Z. The sample distribution of figure 4b is for $\sqrt{s} = 540$ GeV and y = 0; the distribution is broadened with increasing $\sqrt{s}$ and narrowed as y approaches the kinematic limits.

Figure 4c compares the two output Q_T distributions discussed above; one using the LLA and the other the exact $O(\alpha_s)$ as input. Although factorization is only proven in the LLA, it is argued[21,18] that

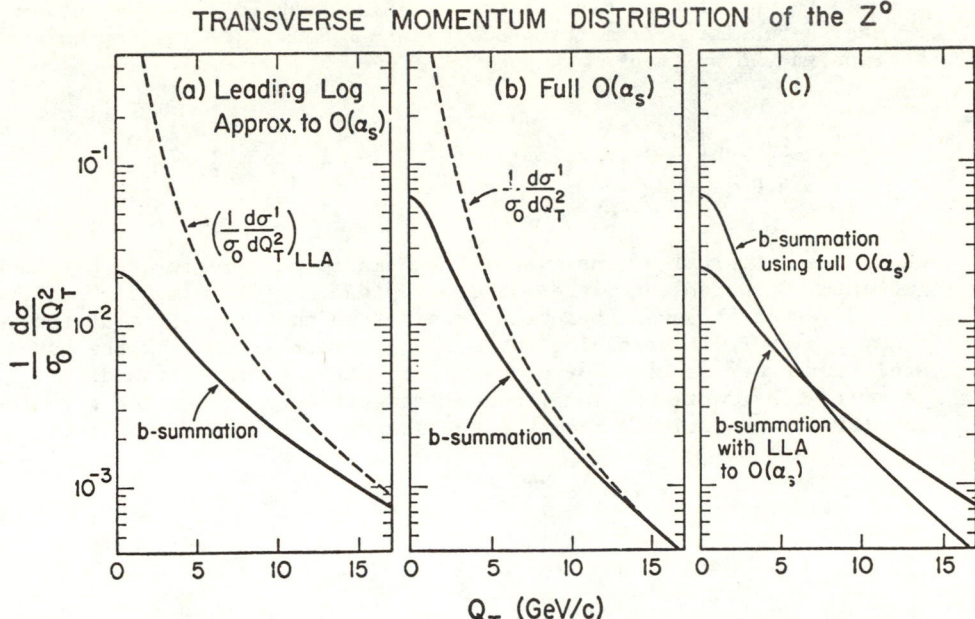

Fig.4 The Q_T distribution of the Z produced in the process
$\bar{p}p \to ZX$ at $\sqrt{s}$ = 540 GeV. The continuous curves come
from the impact parameter summation, eq.(8), using
(a) the LLA, eq.(1), and (b) the exact $O(\alpha_s)$. The two
distributions are compared in (c). The dotted curves
show the input $O(\alpha_s)$ distributions. The figure is taken
from ref.18.

exponentiation of the exact $O(\alpha_s)$ subprocess cross section should give
the more reliable prediction, because it gives the correct factorizing
result at low k_T and gives back the $O(\alpha_s)$ cross section at high Q_T, and
moreover leads to the expected energy dependence of $<Q_T^2>$. More
theoretical work remains to be done to check the phenomenological
validity of this prescription. It is relevant to refer to the ambitious
programme of Collins and Soper[31-33], in which they are studying non-
leading terms in the impact parameter formalism; see also ref. 34. It
should be clear from this discussion that a measurement of the Q_T
distribution of the Z will be very informative from a QCD standpoint.
The QCD predictions require $Q_T^2 \ll M^2$ and in this regime $Z \to \ell^+\ell^-$ data
appear more accessible than those for the Drell-Yan $\gamma^* \to \ell^+\ell^-$ process
(cf. figure 1).

JACOBIAN PEAK

To be specific we discuss the Jacobian peak in the p_T spectrum of the ℓ^+ resulting from the process $\bar{p}p \to W^+X \to \ell^+X$. The lepton cross section may be written

$$p_o \frac{d\sigma}{d^3p} = \int \frac{d^3Q}{Q_o} \left[F(x_1,x_2) \frac{1}{\sigma_o} \frac{d\sigma}{dQ_T^2} \right] \left[\frac{B_\ell}{2\pi} \delta(Q \cdot p - \tfrac{1}{2} M_W^2) \right] \qquad (14)$$

where the integration runs over all kinematic configurations of the W (momentum Q) which can yield a decay lepton of given momentum p. The second factor in square brackets arises from the kinematics of the decay $W \to \ell\nu$ (with branching ratio B_ℓ). $F(x_1,x_2)$ contains the usual Drell-Yan cross section for producing a W from annihilation of a $\bar{q}q$ pair with fractional longitudinal momenta x_1,x_2, together with the angular factors arising from the V-A structure of the W couplings

$$F(x_1,x_2) = \frac{\pi\alpha}{4M_W^2 \sin^2\theta_W} \left[d(x_1)u(x_2) (1+\cos\hat\theta)^2 + \right.$$

$$\left. + s(x_1)s(x_2) \left\{ \tfrac{1}{2}N_f (1-\cos\hat\theta)^2 + (\tfrac{1}{2}N_f - 1)(1+\cos\hat\theta)^2 \right\} \right], \qquad (15)$$

where the quark structure functions are required at $Q^2 = M_W^2$. Here u,d include valence and sea u,d contributions, and the sea quark distributions are assumed to be the same for all N_f flavours of quark. We show results for $N_f = 6$. The angle $\hat\theta$ specifies the lepton direction with respect to the incident $\bar{p}$ direction in the rest frame of the W; here we neglect the effect of the transverse momentum of the produced W. See ref.14 for the relation between $\hat\theta$ and the angle θ at which the decay lepton is produced in the $\bar{p}p$ frame.

The width of the Jacobian peak reflects the underlying Q_T distribution of the W. For example in figure 5 we compare the p_T distributions at 90° obtained from eq.(14) with $d\sigma/dQ_T^2$ evaluated in the impact parameter approach using respectively the exact $O(\alpha_s)$ and the LLA for $d\sigma^I/dk_T^2$ (cf.eq.(7) and figure 4c). We argued above that the use of the exact $O(\alpha_s)$ input leading to the narrow Jacobian peak, is expected to be the more reliable QCD prediction; the results presented below correspond to this choice of Q_T distribution. Of course, eventually, the appropriate input Q_T distribution of the W will be dictated by the measured distribution for Z production. We emphasize that an exact knowledge of the shape of the Jacobian peak is essential for a precise measurement of the W mass.

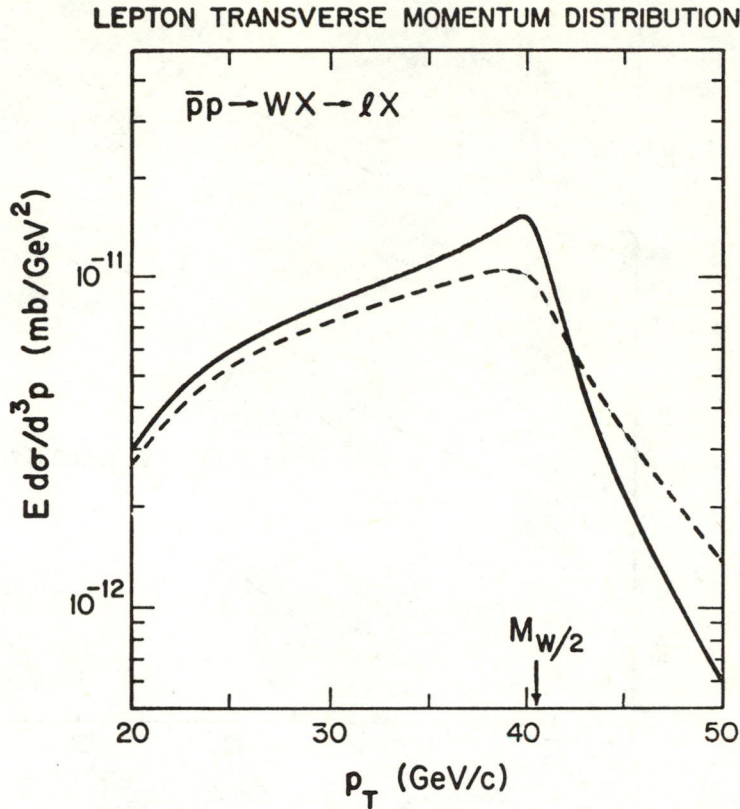

LEPTON TRANSVERSE MOMENTUM DISTRIBUTION

$\bar{p}p \rightarrow WX \rightarrow \ell X$

$E\,d\sigma/d^3p$ (mb/GeV^2)

$M_W/2$

p_T (GeV/c)

Fig.5: The Jacobian peak in the p_T spectrum of the decay lepton calculated using two different Q_T distributions of the parent W (cf. figure 4c). The finite width of the W is neglected. The figure is taken from ref.18.

In figure 6 we show the Jacobian peaks at $\theta=90^\circ$ predicted at CERN and FNAL $\bar{p}p$ collider energies, together with the single lepton p_T distribution expected from Z production and decay. Smaller x values are sampled at $\sqrt{s} = 2000$ GeV and the scaling violations of the quark structure functions lead to a larger cross section than at $\sqrt{s} = 540$ GeV. Figure 7 shows the ℓ^+ lepton p_T distribution expected at other centre-of-mass angles with respect to the incident $\bar{p}$ direction.

228

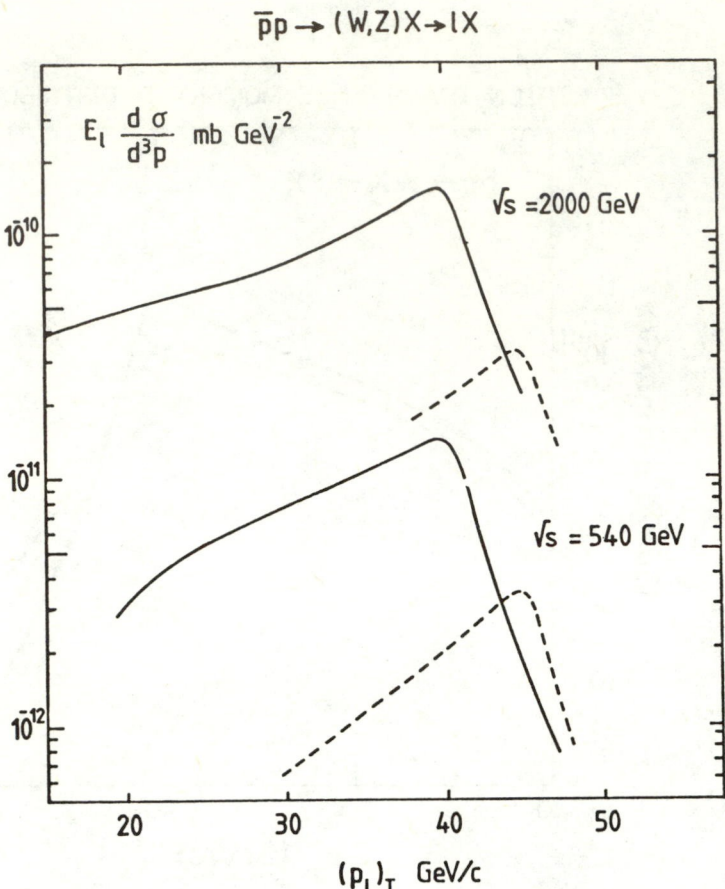

$$\bar{p}p \rightarrow (W,Z)X \rightarrow lX$$

Fig.6: The Jacobian peaks at $\theta=90°$ arising from W and Z production and decay at CERN and FNAL $\bar{p}p$ collider energies. The dashed curves correspond to the Z.

LEPTON ASYMMETRY AND BACKGROUND

In this section we discuss the dependence of the lepton signal on the centre-of-mass angle, θ, at which the lepton ℓ^+ is detected in $\bar{p}p$ collisions. Figures 8 and 9 exhibit the predicted values of

$$\frac{d\sigma}{dp_T d\Omega} = \frac{p_T}{\sin^2\theta} (p_0 \frac{d\sigma}{d^3p}) \tag{16}$$

for the process $\bar{p}p \rightarrow W^+X \rightarrow \ell^+X$ at CERN and FNAL $\bar{p}p$ collider energies

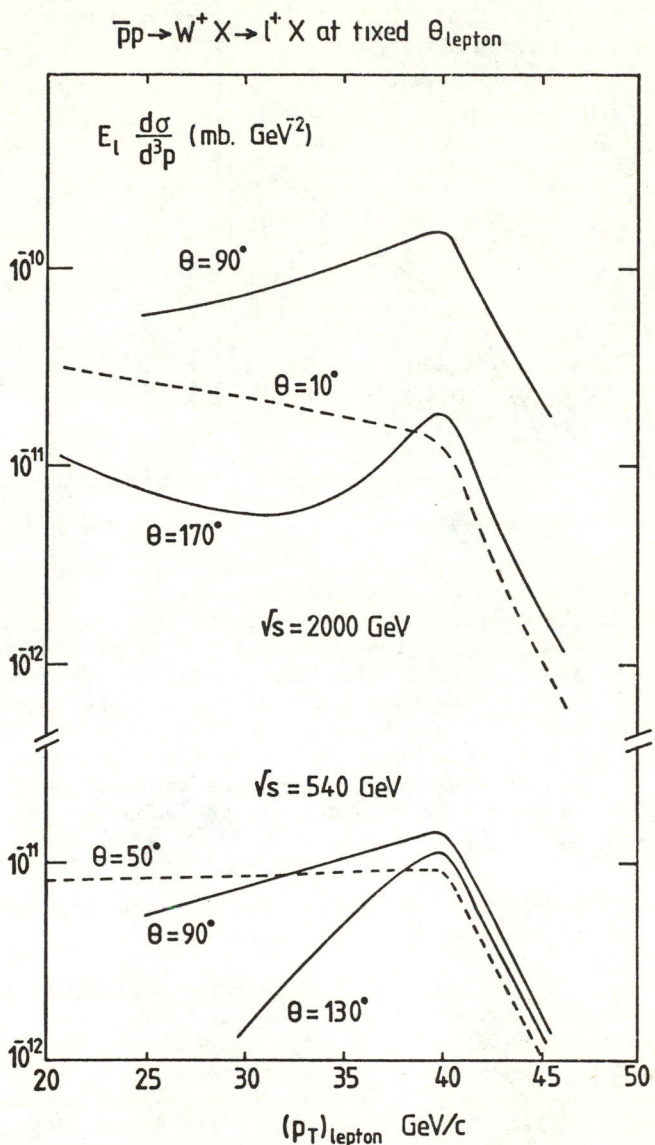

Fig.7: The predicted transverse momentum (p_T) distribution of the observed lepton from the process $\bar{p}p \to W^+X \to \ell^+X$ at various c.m. angles with respect to the incident $\bar{p}$ direction.

230

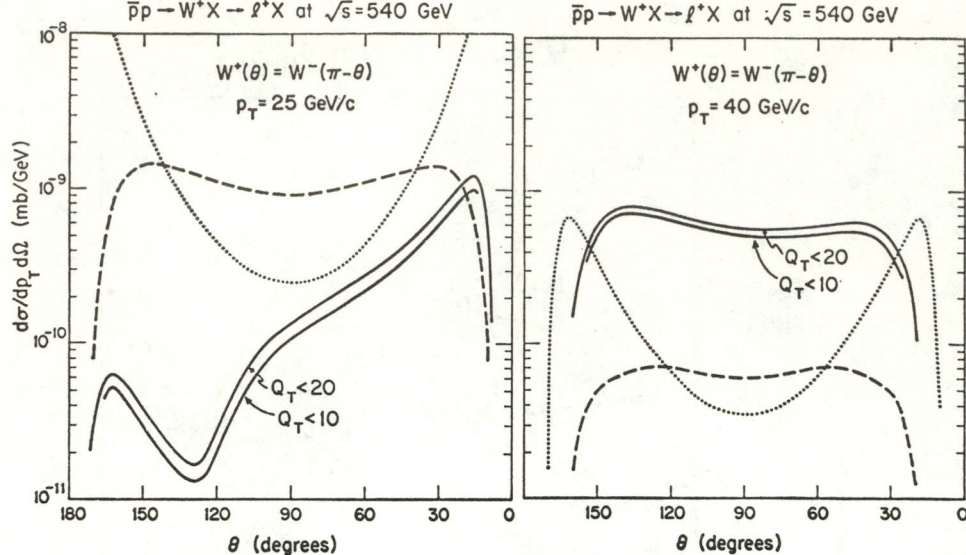

Fig.8: The continuous curves are the angular distributions of the decay lepton arising from the process $\bar{p}p \to W^+X \to \ell^+X$ at $\sqrt{s}$ = 540 GeV for (a) p_T = 25 GeV/c and (b) p_T = 40 GeV/c. The parent W's momentum is restricted to Q_T < 20 GeV/c, though in fact the dominant contribution comes from Q_T < 10 GeV/c. The dashed (dotted) curves are the backgrounds arising from the semi-leptonic decays of heavy quarks produced via the subprocesses $gg, \bar{q}q \to \bar{Q}Q$ ($gQ \to gQ$, $qQ \to qQ$).

respectively. The angular distributions of the lepton are plotted for two different values of the lepton transverse momentum, namely p_T = 25 and 40 GeV/c.

At p_T = 25 GeV/c we see, particularly at CERN $\bar{p}p$ energies, a strong forward-backward asymmetry which reflects the V-A structure of the W couplings. The resulting helicity structure (cf.eq.(15)) is such that the ℓ^+ from W^+ decay is emitted preferentially in the direction of the incoming $\bar{p}$, whereas the ℓ^- from W^- decay follows the incident proton direction. In fact for $\bar{p}p \to W^{\pm}X \to \ell^{\pm}X$ the lepton angular distributions satisfy

$$W^+(\theta) = W^-(\pi-\theta). \tag{17}$$

The small peak in $W^+(\theta)$ in the backward direction arises from the $(1-\cos\hat{\theta})^2$ form of the sea quark-antiquark annihilations, see eq.(15).

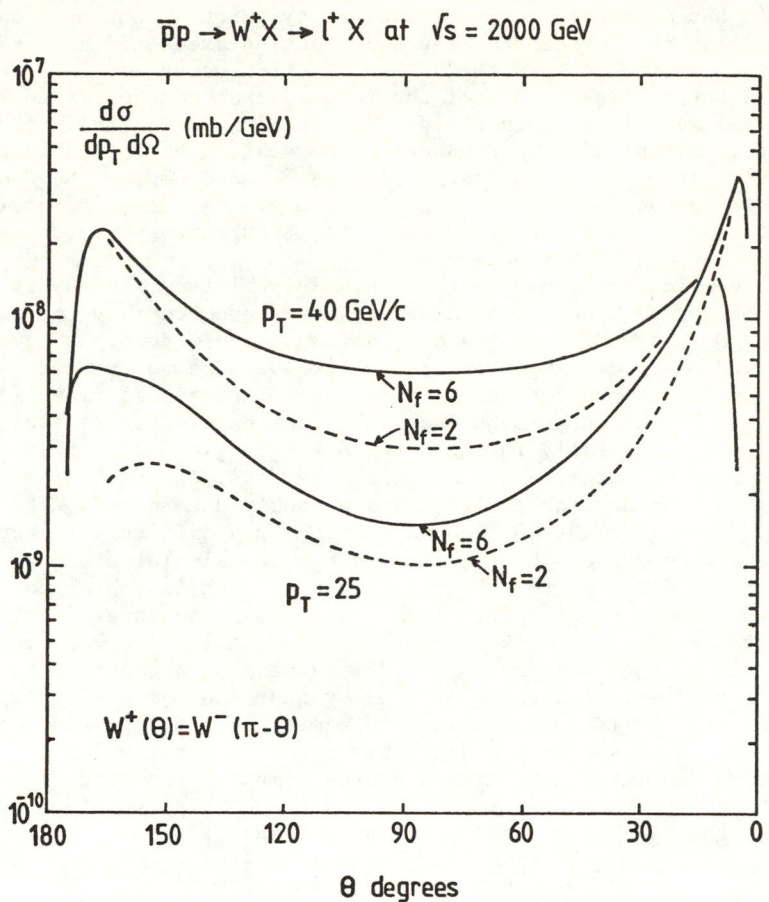

Fig.9: Angular distributions of ℓ^+ produced by $\bar{p}p \to W^+X \to \ell^+X$ at $\sqrt{s}$ = 2000 GeV.

The distinctive $(1\pm\cos\hat{\theta})^2$ distributions in the W rest frame can, however, be masked by the longitudinal motion of the produced W. Indeed as p_T approaches $M_W/2$ the asymmetry disappears and, to a considerable extent, the distribution reflects the Q_L distribution of the W. The longitudinal motion is also one reason why the predicted asymmetry at p_T = 25 GeV/c is weaker at the higher c.m. energy (figure 9).

   In figure 8 the results are shown using two different ranges of the parent W's transverse momentum, $Q_T < 10$ and 20 GeV/c. We see that the dominant contribution comes from Q_T < 10 GeV/c. The dependence of the results on the degree of excitation of heavy quark flavours can be seen in figure 9, where the results are shown for N_f=2, as well as N_f=6.

As has been previously emphasized by Paige[11], an important observation is the forward lepton production predicted at FNAL energies. For example, the peak in the ℓ^+ distribution occurs at θ=5° for p_T = 25 GeV/c. The origin of the forward peak can be traced to valence-sea quark annihilation in the du contribution of eq.(15). The precise magnitude is therefore dependent on the scaling violation assumed for the quark structure functions. Figures 8 and 9 employ the Owens-Reya[17] parametrization. Note that figure 9 can give a false impression of the event rate in the forward peak; for this purpose it is useful to re-draw the distribution versus $\cos\theta$.

The main background to the lepton signal from W decay is due to the semi-leptonic decays of heavy quarks[35] produced via the subprocesses $gg, \bar{q}q \rightarrow \bar{Q}Q$ and $gQ \rightarrow gQ$, $qQ \rightarrow qQ$. Here g,q and Q denote a gluon, light quark and heavy quark (Q=c,b) respectively. The background distributions shown on figure 8 are taken from the calculations described in ref.36. Estimates of the background should be considered less reliable than the signal, especially in the forward and backward directions since, as has been discussed at this conference[36,37], the mechanisms[38-40] for heavy quark production at large x are poorly understood. The background arising from $gQ \rightarrow gQ$, $qQ \rightarrow qQ$ is particularly difficult to estimate reliably; the curves shown in figure 8 were calculated using the diffractive model of ref.39 at face value. The lepton signal arising from this model should probably be regarded as an upper limit.

We see that the backgrounds mask the distinctive weak interaction asymmetry that occurs for p_T < $M_W/2$. However, in contrast to the W signal, the leptons arising from heavy quark decays are accompanied by hadrons. It is thus possible to remove such background leptons by observing the associated hadron shower, or alternatively, by measuring the large missing transverse momentum from the ν in the $W \rightarrow \ell\nu$ decay. Experiments underway at the CERN $\bar{p}p$ collider plan to enhance the signal-to-background in this way.[41]

SUMMARY AND CONCLUSIONS

The best way of detecting weak bosons at the $\bar{p}p$ colliders is through their leptonic decay channels

$$\bar{p}p \rightarrow ZX \rightarrow \ell^+\ell^- X$$
$$\bar{p}p \rightarrow W^\pm X \rightarrow \ell^\pm \nu X.$$

The Z peak in the lepton-pair invariant mass spectrum is predicted to sit well above background. The presence of the decay ν means the detection of the W cannot be so direct. The signature is a Jacobian peak in the transverse momentum distribution of the charged lepton just below p_T = $M_W/2$.

The structure of the Jacobian peak is controlled by the transverse momentum (Q_T) distribution of the parent W at small Q_T, namely Q_T < 10 GeV/c. In the small Q_T region $O(\alpha_s)$ QCD predictions are clearly not applicable. However, following the approach of DDT, Parisi and Petronzio exposed a remarkable feature of perturbative QCD. They showed that multi-gluon emissions can be resummed so that the Q_T distribution can be predicted in the relevant small Q_T region, $Q_T^2 \ll M_W^2$. We noted some difficulties in the phenomenological application of these ideas. To ensure the impact parameter resummation approximates the $O(\alpha_s)$ prediction at high Q_T, it is essential to base the calculation on exponentiation of the exact $O(\alpha_s)$ cross section, rather than the leading log approximation (LLA) to it. On the other hand resummation is based on independent gluon emission, which in turn is only proven in the LLA. Further theoretical study is required, but we argued on physical grounds that the appropriate phenomenological prescription is the exponentiation of the exact $O(\alpha_s)$ cross section. This prescription yields a reasonably sharp Jacobian peak just below $p_T = M_W/2$, which augurs well for a precise determination of the W mass, and for the tests of electro-weak gauge theory based on the weak boson masses.

From a QCD standpoint the measurement of the transverse momentum (Q_T) spectrum of the Z will be particularly informative. It is experimentally accessible via $\bar{p}p \to ZX \to \ell^+\ell^-X$, and provides an ideal testing ground for QCD resummation techniques at $\bar{p}p$ collider energies. The requirement $M^2 \gg Q_T^2$ is well satisfied and the effects of intrinsic parton k_T are negligible. Moreover such measurements tell us the Q_T distribution of the W. Knowledge of this distribution will be essential for a precise determination of the W mass from the Jacobian peak.

A distinctive feature of the process $\bar{p}p \to WX \to \ell\nu X$ is the asymmetry in the angular distribution of the observable lepton, for lepton transverse momenta p_T < $M_W/2$. This asymmetry is somewhat more pronounced at CERN, than at FNAL, collider energies, and disappears for $p_T \sim M_W/2$. At FNAL collider energies the angular distribution is peaked in the forward direction. To be precise the ℓ^+ and ℓ^- from $W^\pm \to \ell^\pm\nu$ are produced about the direction of the incident $\bar{p}$ and p respectively. For example at p_T = 25 GeV/c (40 GeV/c) the ℓ^+ distribution peaks at $\theta \approx 5^o$ ($\theta \approx 12^o$).

The background leptons to the W signal come predominantly from the semi-leptonic decays of heavy quarks (Q=b,c) via subprocesses such as $\bar{q}q \to \bar{b}b$. Sizeable contributions from subprocesses $gQ \to gQ$, $qQ \to qQ$ have been invoked to account for the unexpectedly large cross section for forward charm production, and the mechanisms for large x heavy quark production is, at present, a subject of much controversy. This gives considerable uncertainty in the background lepton contribution at forward and backward angles.

Unless the leptons from heavy quark production are vetoed, they pose a serious background at $p_T \simeq$ 25 GeV/c, masking the distinctive weak interaction asymmetry. At $p_T \sim M_W/2$ the W signal appears well above background. A veto is possible because the background leptons, unlike the W signal, are accompanied by hadrons. They can therefore be identified by observing the associated hadron shower. Another

234

valuable way to enhance the W signal is to record the large missing transverse momentum due to the ν in the $W \rightarrow \ell\nu$ decay.

Finally we come to the luminosity of the $\bar{p}p$ colliders. This is crucial for the detection and study of W and Z bosons. The estimates of cross sections indicate an exciting experimental challenge is underway. It is clear that much will be learnt from these pioneering and exacting experiments, not only about electro-weak gauge theory, but also concerning QCD.

ACKNOWLEDGEMENTS

I thank Francis Halzen, Mike Pennington and David Scott for numerous, stimulating and valuable discussions. Also I thank the organizers for their efforts in arranging such a successful meeting on $\bar{p}p$ collider physics. Finally I acknowledge the support of the U.K. Science and Engineering Research Council.

REFERENCES

1. F. Halzen, Phys. Rev. D15, 1929 (1977).
2. I. Hinchliffe and C.H. Llewellyn-Smith, Nucl. Phys. B128, 93 (1977).
3. J. Kogut and J. Shigemitsu, Nucl. Phys. B129, 461 (1977).
4. L.B. Okun and M.B. Voloshin, Nucl. Phys. B120, 459 (1977).
5. C. Rubbia, P. McIntyre and D. Cline, Proceedings of the Aachen Neutrino Conference (1977).
6. R.F. Peierls, T.L. Trueman and L.L. Wang, Phys. Rev. D16, 1397 (1977).
7. C. Quigg, Rev. Mod. Phys. 49, 297 (1977).
8. H.E. Haber and G.L. Kane, Nucl. Phys. B146, 109 (1978).
9. F. Halzen and D.M. Scott, Phys. Letts. 78B, 318 (1978).
10. F.E. Paige, T.L. Trueman and T.N. Tudron, Phys. Rev. D19, 935 (1979).
11. F.E. Paige, Proceedings of the Topical Conference on the Production of New Particles in Super High Energy Collisions eds. V. Barger and F. Halzen (1979).
12. P. Aurenche and J. Lindfors, Nucl. Phys. B185, 301 (1981).
13. F. Halzen, A.D. Martin, D.M. Scott and M. Dechantsreiter, Phys. Lett. 106B, 147 (1981).
14. F. Halzen, A.D. Martin and D.M. Scott, Phys. Rev. D, to appear.
15. W.J. Marciano and A. Sirlin, Phys. Rev. D22, 2695 (1980).
16. C.H. Llewellyn-Smith and J.F. Wheater, Oxford preprint (1981).
17. J.F. Owens and E. Reya, Phys. Rev. D17, 3003 (1978).
18. F. Halzen, A.D. Martin and D.M. Scott, Madison preprint MAD/PH/31 (1981).
19. See, for example, Proc. of Workshop on Lepton Pair Production, Les Arcs, 1981 ed. J.J. Tran Thanh Van.
20. Yu. L. Dokshitser, D.I.D'Yakonov and S.I. Troyan, Phys. Lett. 78B, 290 (1978); 79B, 269 (1978); Phys. Reports 58, 269 (1980).
21. G. Parisi and R. Petronzio, Nucl. Phys. B154, 427 (1979).
22. C.Y. Lo and J.D. Sullivan, Phys. Lett. 86B, 827 (1979).

23. S.D. Ellis and W.J. Stirling, Phys. Rev. D23, 214 (1980).
24. P.E.L. Rakow and B.R. Webber, Nucl. Phys. B187, 254 (1981).
25. G. Curci, M. Greco and Y. Srivastava, Nucl. Phys. B159, 451 (1979).
26. G. Gurci and M. Greco, Phys. Lett. 92B, 175 (1980).
27. S.D. Ellis, N. Fleishon and W.J. Stirling, Phys. Rev. D24, 1386 (1981).
28. S.D. Ellis, Proc. of Tallahassee Conf. on Perturbative QCD, AIP Conf. Proc. 74, 1 (1981).
29. R. Odorico, Bologna preprint IFUB 81-21 (1981).
30. H. Jones and J. Wyndham, Nucl. Phys. B176, 446 (1980).
31. J.C. Collins and D.E. Soper, Nucl. Phys. B193, 381 (1981).
32. J.C. Collins and D.E. Soper, in ref.19.
33. J.C. Collins, Proc. of Tallahassee Conf. on Perturbative QCD, AIP Conf. Proc. 74, 41 (1981).
34. M.R. Pennington, Durham preprint (1982).
    A. Sen, Phys. Rev. D24, 3281 (1981).
35. S. Pakvasa, M. Dechantsreiter, F. Halzen and D.M. Scott, Phys. Rev. D20, 2862 (1979).
36. D.M. Scott, these proceedings.
37. S.J. Brodsky, F. Paige, R. Odorico, these proceedings.
38. S.J. Brodsky, P. Hoyer, C. Peterson and N. Sakai, Phys. Lett. 93B, 451 (1980); Phys. Rev. D23, 2745 (1981).
39. V. Barger, F. Halzen and W.Y. Keung, Phys. Rev. D25, 112 (1982).
40. C. Peterson, Proc. of XIIth Int. Conf. on Multiparticle Dynamics, Indiana,1981.
41. C. Rubbia, these proceedings.

CROSS-SECTIONS OF W's, W PAIRS AND THE HIGGS BOSON FOR THE UA1 EXPERIMENT AT CERN

R. Kinnunen

CERN, Geneva, Switzerland

ABSTRACT

The leptonic decay rates of $W^{\pm}$ and Z^0 are calculated for the UA1 experiment at CERN. The production characteristics of $W^{\pm}$ and Z^0 are studied. Pair production of W's and the production of the Higgs boson at the energy of the CERN $\bar{p}p$ collider are also briefly discussed.

1. INTRODUCTION

The CERN antiproton-proton collider has started its operation and for the first time provides sufficient centre-of-mass energies for the production of intermediate vector bosons. The cross-sections at the collider energies for the leptonic channels of W and Z^0 are of the order of 10^{-37} cm^2 and are thus expected to be found in the near future in antiproton-proton collisions. Finding these particles and studying their properties and the underlying gauge theory is one of the principal aims of the UA1 experiment.

The minimal theory of weak and electromagnetic interactions is the $SU(2) \times U(1)$ gauge theory, which has been made a gauge symmetry by introducing three gauge mesons, A_{μ}^i, associated with SU(2) and a fourth, B_{μ}, associated with a U(1) subgroup. The gauge mesons are massless in order to preserve local gauge symmetry.

In the Weinberg-Salam model the gauge mesons become the intermediate vector bosons and the masses are generated through the Higgs mechanism[1]. There are two interesting points about the theory. Firstly, there are interactions among the vector bosons themselves, which implies that the investigation of the pair production of intermediate vector bosons can provide direct evidence for gauge theories. Secondly, with the Higgs mechanism one ends up with one heavy scalar meson. The coupling of the Higgs meson is fully specified, but its mass remains a free parameter in the theory.

In this paper we first introduce in Section 2 the necessary formulae for the calculation of W and Z^0 cross-sections. The theoretical background follows the works of Aurenche and Lindfors[2,3] for the hadronic production of W's. In Section 3 we discuss the production characteristics of W and Z^0 bosons and the effects of QCD corrections on their production. Section 4 deals with the leptonic decay rates and the signatures of weak bosons for the UA1 experiment. The production of W pairs and especially the production of $W\gamma$ pairs in $\bar{p}p$ collisions will be briefly discussed in Section 5. This subject has been extensively studied by Brown and Mikaelian[4], Brown, Sahdev and Mikaelian[5] and Mikaelian, Samuel and Sahdev[6]. Finally in Section 6 we very briefly discuss the prospects for finding the Higgs boson at the collider through its associated production with Z^0 [7,8].

2. W and Z^0 CROSS-SECTIONS

The basic Drell-Yan diagram for the annihilation of a quark and an antiquark to leptons is shown in Fig. 1. The intermediate vector

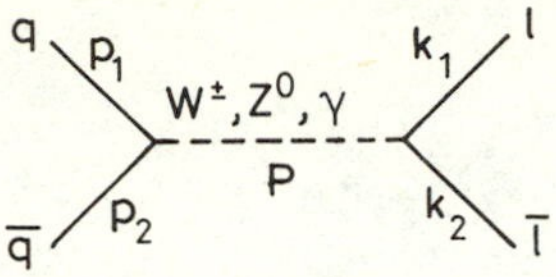

Fig. 1 The Feynman diagram for the Drell-Yan process $q\bar{q} \to \ell\bar{\ell}$.

meson is either $W^\pm$, Z^0, or γ. The amplitude can be written in the following general form

$$\mathcal{M} = C\bar{v}(p_2)\gamma_\mu(a^q + b^q\gamma_5)u(p_1) \frac{g^{\mu\nu} - P^\mu P^\nu/M^2}{P^2 - M^2 + i\Gamma M}$$

$$\times \bar{u}(k_1)\gamma_\nu(a^\ell + b^\ell\gamma_5)v(k_2) , \qquad (1)$$

where M is the mass and Γ the width of $W^\pm$ or Z^0. The vector and axial parts of the couplings are given for $W^\pm$ by

$$a^q = a^\ell = 1 , \quad b^q = b^\ell = -1 , \quad C = \frac{e}{2\sqrt{2}\sin\theta_W} , \qquad (2)$$

for Z^0 by

$$\begin{aligned} a^u &= \tfrac{1}{4} - \tfrac{2}{3}\sin^2\theta_W , & b^u &= -\tfrac{1}{4} , \\ a^d &= -\tfrac{1}{4} + \tfrac{1}{3}\sin^2\theta_W , & b^d &= \tfrac{1}{4} , \\ a^\nu &= \tfrac{1}{4} , & b^\nu &= -\tfrac{1}{4} , \\ a^\ell &= -\tfrac{1}{4} + \sin^2\theta_W , & b^\ell &= \tfrac{1}{4} , \end{aligned} \qquad (3)$$

$$C = \frac{e}{\sin\theta_W \cos\theta_W}$$

and for γ by

$$a^q = a^\ell = 1 , \quad b^q = b^\ell = 0 , \quad C = eQ_q . \qquad (4)$$

Using the Weinberg angle $\sin^2\theta_W = 0.23$ the mass and width become

$$M_W = \left(\frac{\pi\alpha}{G_F\sqrt{2}}\right)^{\frac{1}{2}} \frac{1}{\sin^2\theta_W} = 77.8 \text{ GeV} \qquad (5)$$

$$\Gamma_W = \frac{M_W}{\cos^2\theta_W} = 88.7 \text{ GeV}$$

$$\Gamma_W = \frac{\alpha M_W}{24\sin^2\theta_W}(3n_q + n_\ell) = 2.47 \text{ GeV} \qquad (6)$$

$$\Gamma_Z = \tfrac{1}{3}\frac{M_Z}{\sin^2\theta_W}\left\{3\sum_q\left[(a^q)^2 + (b^q)^2\right] + \sum_\ell\left[(a^\ell)^2 + (b^\ell)^2\right]\right\} = 2.49 \text{ GeV}$$

with $n_q = n_\ell = 6$.

For the single lepton coming from $W^{\pm}$ the differential cross-section in the centre of mass of $\bar{p}p$ is given by

$$\frac{d\sigma}{dk_T\,d\Omega} = \frac{k_T}{\sin^2\theta_W}\,k_0\,\frac{d\sigma}{d^3k}$$

$$= \frac{k_T}{\sin^2\theta_W}\sum_{j,k}\int_0^1 d\xi_1 f^j(\xi_1,k_T^2)\int_0^1 d\xi_2\,f^k(\xi_2,k_T^2)\,k_0\,\frac{d\hat{\sigma}^{j,k}}{d^3k}\,, \qquad (7)$$

where ξ_1 and ξ_2 are the longitudinal momentum fractions of the partons. For the quark distribution functions $f^j(\xi,Q^2)$ we use the parametrizations of Owens and Reya[9], choosing k_T^2 for the large scale in the process. The factor $k_0(d\hat{\sigma}^{j,k}/d^3k)$ is the cross-section for the parton level process $q_j + \bar{q}_k \rightarrow W^{\pm} + X$.

For Z^0 the best signature is obtained in the invariant mass of the decay leptons and is given by the following formula

$$\frac{d\sigma}{dM^2} = \frac{4\pi\alpha^2}{3M^2}\frac{1}{3}\frac{1}{s}\sum_{j,k}\int_0^1\frac{d\xi}{\xi}\,f^j(\xi,M^2)\,f^k(\xi,M^2)\,N(M^2) \qquad (8)$$

with

$$N(M^2) = Q_q^2 + \frac{(a_\ell^2 + b_\ell^2)(a_q^2 + b_q^2)}{\sin^4\theta_W\cos^4\theta_W}\frac{M^4}{(M^2 - M_Z^2)^2 + (\Gamma_Z M_Z)^2}$$

$$- 2Q_q\frac{a^\ell a^q}{\sin^2\theta_W\cos^2\theta_W}\frac{M^2(M^2 - M_Z^2)}{(M^2 - M_Z^2)^2 + (\Gamma_Z M_Z)^2}$$

3. PRODUCTION CHARACTERISTICS OF W AND Z^0

Figure 2 shows the transverse momentum distribution for the antilepton from W^+ for different values of $\cos\theta$. The positive z-axis is chosen in the direction of the antiproton. As $\cos\theta$ decreases, only the high p_T (Jacobian) peak at $M_W/2$ is left in the spectrum. The same effect is also visible in Fig. 3, which presents the angular distribution of the antilepton for different values of p_T. At low p_T values the forward direction is strongly enhanced, whereas at high p_T the distribution is flat. This effect is a consequence of the helicity conservation which forces the antilepton to move in the direction of the antiproton. The peak is further enhanced by the Jacobian $p_T/\sin^2\theta$ near $\cos\theta = 1$. However, when the transverse momentum of the lepton reaches the value $M_W/2$ the lepton can no longer have longitudinal momentum in the rest frame of W and then reflects the longitudinal motion of the parent particle in the centre of mass of the incident hadrons.

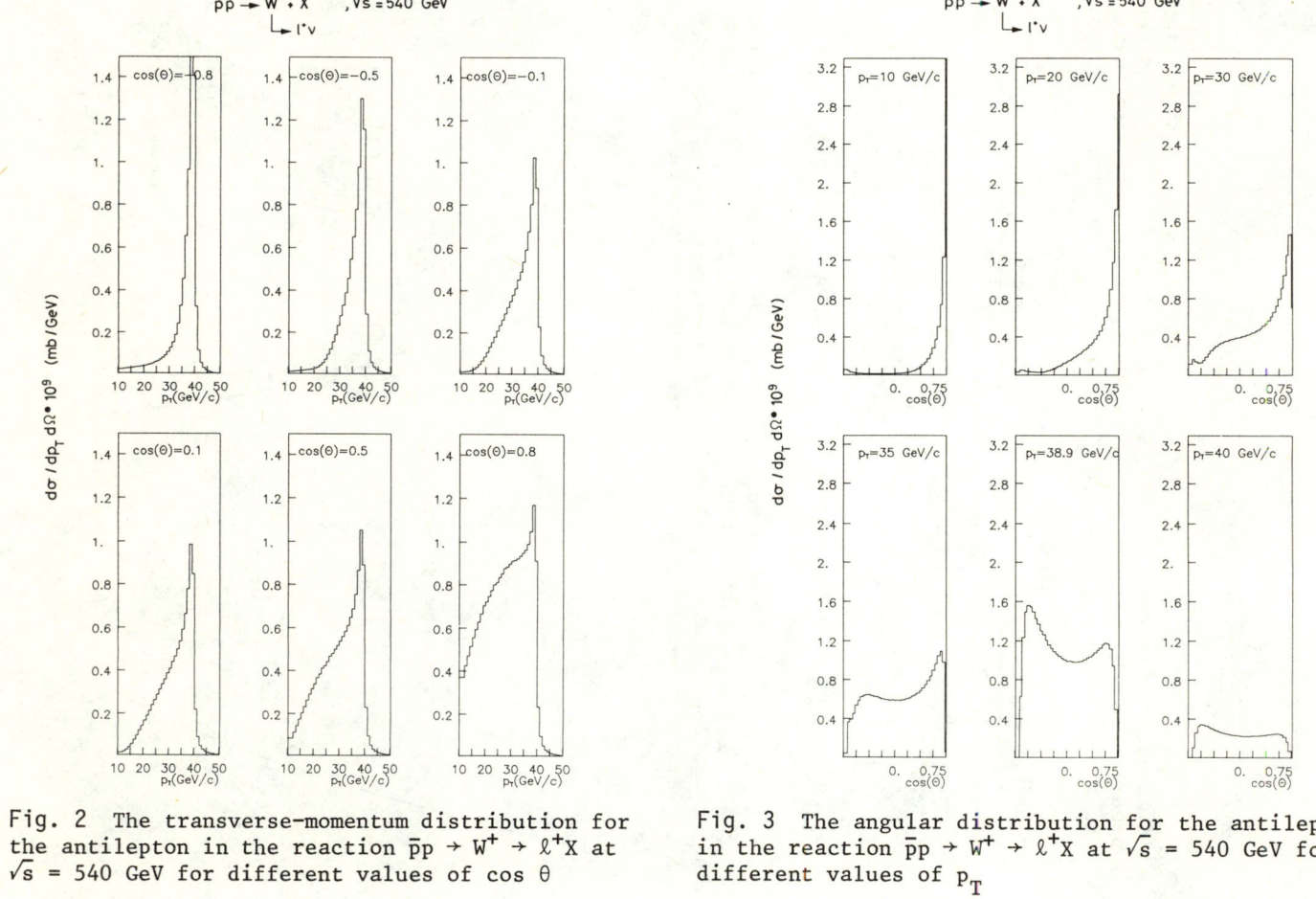

Fig. 2 The transverse-momentum distribution for the antilepton in the reaction $\bar{p}p \to W^+ \to \ell^+X$ at $\sqrt{s} = 540$ GeV for different values of cos θ

Fig. 3 The angular distribution for the antilepton in the reaction $\bar{p}p \to W^+ \to \ell^+X$ at $\sqrt{s} = 540$ GeV for different values of p_T

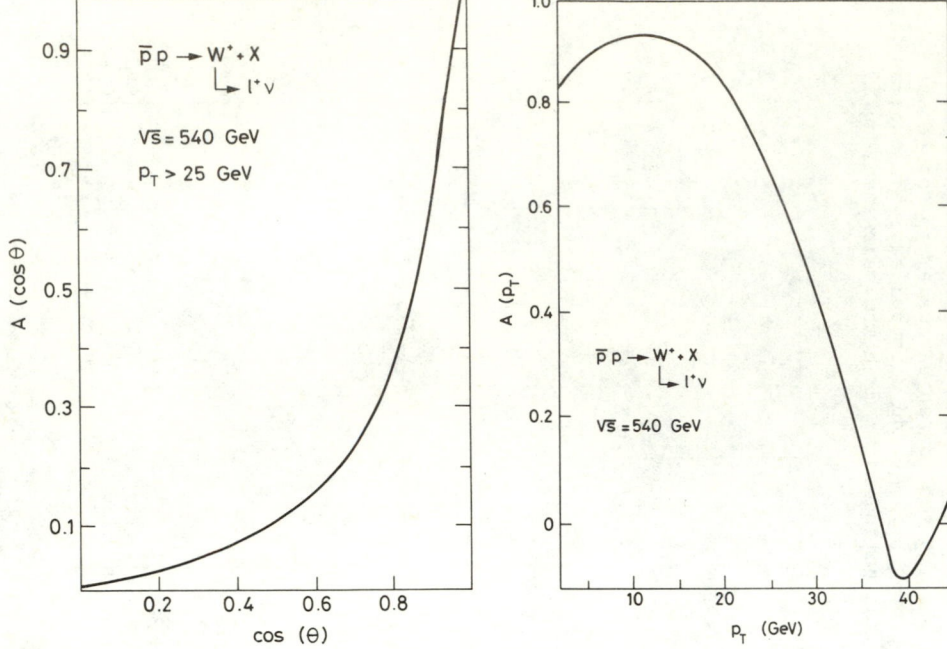

Fig. 4 The forward-backward asymmetry for the antilepton in the reaction $\bar{p}p \to W^+ \to \ell^+X$ as a function of $\cos \theta$ and for $p_T > 25$ GeV.

Fig. 5 The forward-backward asymmetry for the antilepton in the reaction $\bar{p}p \to W^+ \to \ell^+X$ as a function of p_T.

Figure 4 shows the forward-backward asymmetry, defined by

$$A(\cos \theta) = \frac{\int\limits_{25}^{\infty} dp_T \left.\frac{d\sigma}{dp_T\, d\cos\theta}\right|_{\cos\theta=+1} - \int\limits_{25}^{\infty} dp_T \left.\frac{d\sigma}{dp_T\, d\cos\theta}\right|_{\cos\theta=-1}}{\int\limits_{25}^{\infty} dp_T \left.\frac{d\sigma}{dp_T\, d\cos\theta}\right|_{\cos\theta=+1} + \int\limits_{25}^{\infty} dp_T \left.\frac{d\sigma}{dp_T\, d\cos\theta}\right|_{\cos\theta=-1}}$$

for the antilepton from W^+ for $p_T > 25$ GeV. The asymmetry is significant especially at small angles. In Fig. 5 we show the forward-backward asymmetry as a function of lepton transverse momentum p_T, defined by

$$A(p_T) = \frac{\int\limits_{0}^{1} d\cos\theta \frac{d\sigma}{dp_T\, d\cos\theta} - \int\limits_{-1}^{0} d\cos\theta \frac{d\sigma}{dp_T\, d\cos\theta}}{\int\limits_{0}^{1} d\cos\theta \frac{d\sigma}{dp_T\, d\cos\theta} + \int\limits_{-1}^{0} d\cos\theta \frac{d\sigma}{dp_T\, d\cos\theta}}$$

The asymmetry is large but drops to zero at the Jacobian peak owing to the flat distribution at large transverse momenta.

Figure 6 shows the invariant mass distribution for the lepton pair in the process $\bar{p}p \to X + Z^0(Z^0 \to \ell^+\ell^-) + \gamma(\gamma \to \ell^+\ell^-)$ at $\cos \theta = 0$. The Z^0 peak shows up clearly over the Drell-Yan background. In Fig. 7 we show the angular distribution for the antilepton in the rest frame of the lepton pair at $M = M_Z$. The distribution shows a symmetric behaviour because for $\cos \theta_W = 0.23$ the parity-violating axial part ($\propto \cos \theta$) for the Z^0 cross-section is small compared with the vector part ($\propto 1 + \cos^2 \theta$).

How are the results changed by the QCD corrections? So far only the leading logarithmic QCD corrections are included in our calculations by using the QCD corrected (non-scaling) quark distribution functions[9]. These corrections arise from the diagrams of Fig. 8a and they give a positive correction over the whole p_T range.

The first-order QCD corrections have been calculated by Aurenche and Lindfors[2]. They are given by the emission or absorption of a gluon, and the corresponding diagrams are shown in Fig. 8b. The first-order QCD corrections turn out to be important at the Jacobian peak and above it, as can be seen from Fig. 9 which compares the QCD-corrected p_T distribution for the antilepton from W^+ (from Ref. 3) with our result. The Jacobian peak becomes somewhat smeared and the

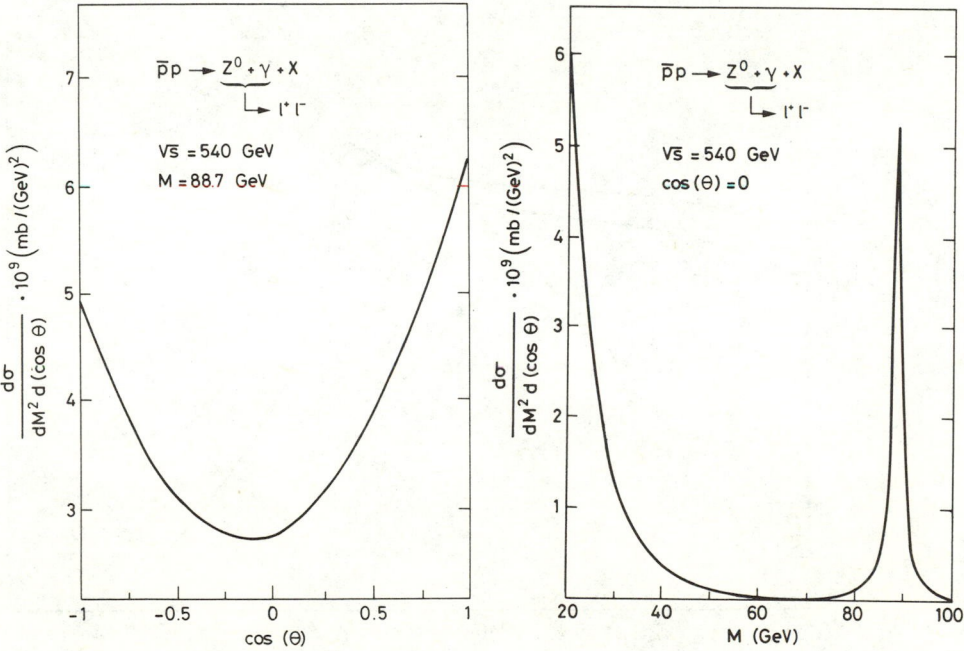

Fig. 6 The invariant mass distribution for the lepton pairs in the reaction $\bar{p}p \to \gamma + Z^0 \to \ell^+\ell^- + X$ at $\cos \theta = 0$.

Fig. 7 The angular distribution for the antilepton in the reaction $\bar{p}p \to \gamma + Z^0 \to \ell^+\ell^- + X$ in the rest frame of Z^0 at $M = M_Z$.

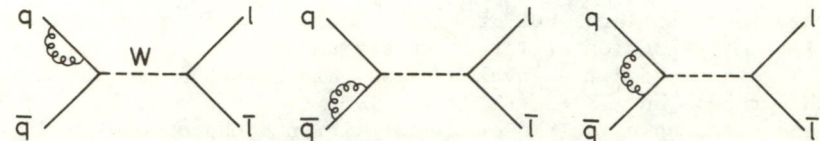

Fig. 8a The virtual QCD diagrams giving the leading logarithmic QCD corrections for $q\bar{q} \to \ell\bar{\ell}$.

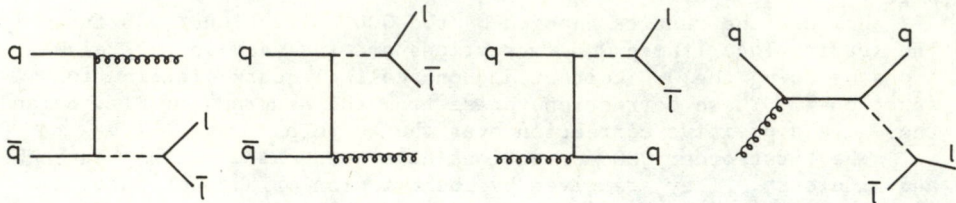

Fig. 8b The first order (in α_s) QCD diagrams contributing to the non-leading QCD corrections for $q\bar{q} \to \ell\bar{\ell}$.

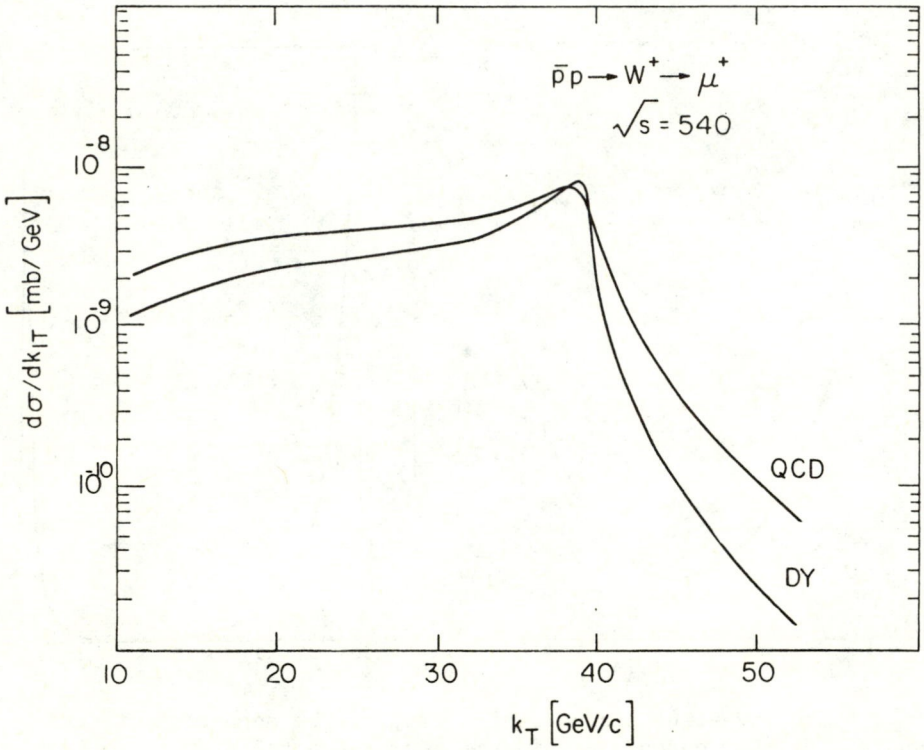

Fig. 9 Comparison of the pure Drell-Yan and the QCD calculations for the p_T distribution of ℓ^+ in the reaction $\bar{p}p \to W^+ \to \ell^+X$.

high p_T part of the spectrum enhanced. This effect can be explained by noting that the lepton gets some of the recoil momentum of the W which scatters against the quark-gluon system. The cross-sections are increased approximately by a factor of two. In the case of Z^0 production the first-order QCD corrections do not change the shapes of the decay lepton distributions, as has been shown in Ref. 3. However, the cross-sections are again increased roughly by a factor of two.

4. DECAY RATES FOR UA1 EXPERIMENT

The most important experimental signature for W is the high p_T lepton and a large missing transverse momentum due to the emitted neutrino. The UA1 detector is capable of recording this kind of event: it has large angular acceptance, good discrimination between hadrons and leptons, and the calorimeter system has good energy resolution increasing with energy according to[10]

$$\frac{\Delta E}{E} = \frac{0.14}{\sqrt{E}} \quad \text{for the electromagnetic part}$$

$$\frac{\Delta E}{E} = \frac{0.8}{\sqrt{E}} \quad \text{for the hadronic part.}$$

The electronic channels of W and Z decay will be recorded and the electron energies measured with the electromagnetic calorimeters, which cover the angular range from 5 to $175°$. The muonic channels will be observed with the muon drift chambers which are surrounding the whole detector. Finally, the momenta of the charged leptons from W and Z will be measured with the aid of the magnetic field in the central detector. Then it is estimated that the mass of Z^0 can be measured with an accuracy of better than 3 GeV.

Table I shows the leptonic decay rates of W for the UA1 detector elements[11]. The numbers of events per day calculated for the luminosity of 10^{29} cm^{-2} s^{-1} are also shown in the table. The rates should

Table I Leptonic decay rates of $W^{\pm}$ with p_T(lepton) > 10 GeV for the UA1 detectors and for the luminosity 10^{29} cm^{-2} s^{-1}

Dectector element and particle	Angular range (degrees)	Cross-section (pb)	Events/day
Forward arm (electrons)	< 5	0.4	0.004
End-cap electromagnetic detector (electrons)	5–25	56.2	0.486
Central electromagnetic detector (electrons)	25–155	281	2.432
Muon chambers (muons)	25–155	281	2.432
Total		619	5.354

roughly double when the first-order QCD corrections are added. Then we find in total about 10 events per day with $p_T > 10$ GeV for UA1 detectors.

Similarly we obtain for the leptonic decays of Z^0 the total cross-section of 73 pb for the UA1 detector. This corresponds to about 0.5 events per day, and taking into account the first-order QCD corrections we obtain one event per day for UA1.

5. PRODUCTION OF WEAK-BOSON AND Wγ PAIRS

The production of weak-boson and Wγ pairs offers an interesting possibility for testing the gauge theories. Unfortunately, the cross-sections for W^+W^- and $W^\pm Z^0$ are very small at the energy of the CERN $\bar{p}p$ collider[12].

As an example we show in Fig. 10a the diagrams for the production of a W^+W^- pair. The gauge vertex $Z^0W^+W^-$ enters the amplitude through the second diagram and leads to large cancellations in the cross-section at high energies.

The production of a $W^\pm \gamma$ pair is described by the diagrams of Fig. 10b. This process is especially interesting because the amplitude is dependent on the anomalous magnetic moment parameter κ, which arises from the interaction of the W with the electromagnetic field. Here we consider only the gauge theory value of κ, $\kappa = 1$.

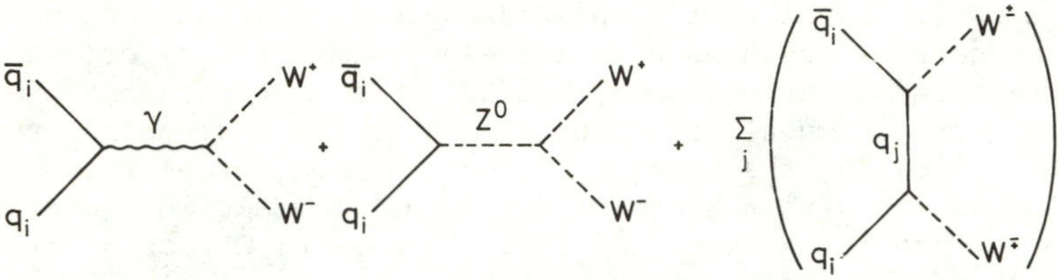

Fig. 10a The lowest order Feynman diagrams for $q_i \bar{q}_i \rightarrow W^+W^-$.

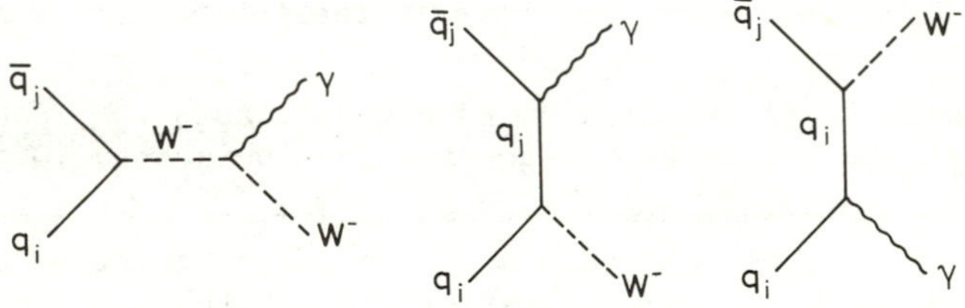

Fig. 10b The lowest order Feynman diagrams for $q_i \bar{q}_j \rightarrow W^- \gamma$.

Table II shows the cross-sections and the event numbers with the luminosity of 10^{30} cm^{-2} s^{-1} for the CERN $\bar{p}p$ collider. In the case of the $W^\pm \gamma$ channel we have taken the cut of 5 GeV in the energy of the hard photon in order to eliminate the infrared divergence due to the zero-energy photons. It can be seen that $Z^0 Z^0$ and $W^\pm Z^0$ channels cannot be found at the collider; the W^+W^- events are still very rare -- about one event in 50 days -- but the $W^\pm \gamma$ production can be studied at the collider.

Table II Cross-sections for $\bar{p}p \to Z^0Z^0 + X$, $\bar{p}p \to W^+W^- + X$, $\bar{p}p \to W^{\pm}Z^0 + X$, and $\bar{p}p \to W^{\pm}\gamma + X$ at $\sqrt{s} = 540$ GeV for the $\bar{p}p$ luminosity of 10^{30} cm^{-2} s^{-1}

Reaction	Cross-section (cm^2)	Events per day
$\bar{p}p \to Z^0Z^0 + X$	1.5×10^{-38}	1.3×10^{-3}
$\bar{p}p \to W^+W^- + X$	1.9×10^{-37}	1.6×10^{-2}
$\bar{p}p \to W^{\pm}Z^0 + X$	1.0×10^{-38}	9.0×10^{-4}
$\bar{p}p \to W^{\pm}\gamma + X$	2.5×10^{-35}	2.2

The energy dependence of the cross-sections for W^+W^-, Z^0Z^0, and $W^{\pm}Z^0$ is shown in Fig. 11. There is a fast increase in the cross-section in the energy range of the CERN $\bar{p}p$ collider, it already being one order of magnitude larger at the Fermilab Tevatron.

In Fig. 12 we compare our result for the cross-section of W^+W^- with the cross-section calculated using the scaling structure functions. The effect of leading logarithmic QCD corrections is seen to be considerable at the energy of the $\bar{p}p$ collider.

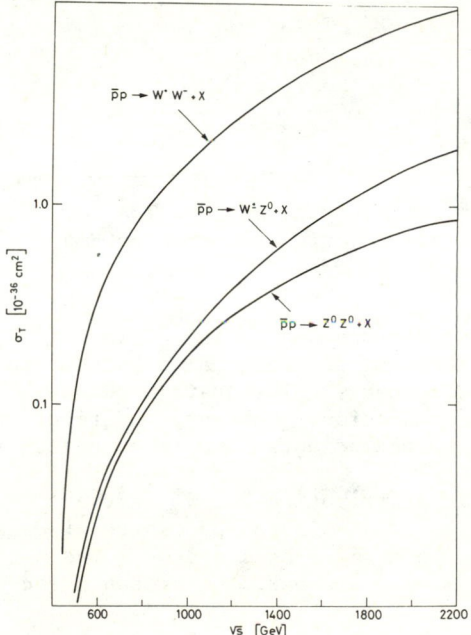

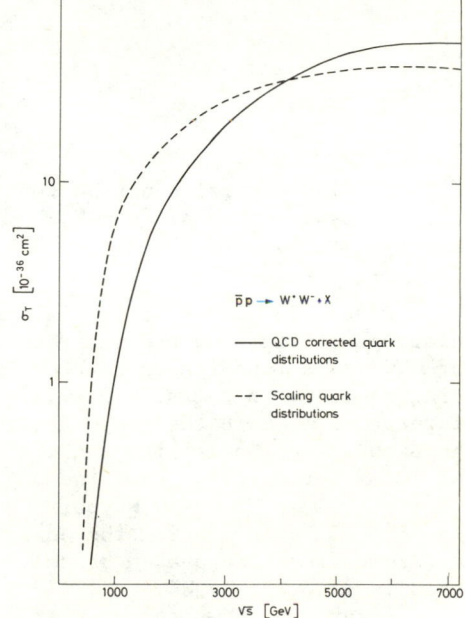

Fig. 11 Total cross-sections for $\bar{p}p \to W^+W^- + X$, $\bar{p}p \to Z^0Z^0 + X$, and $\bar{p}p \to W^{\pm}Z^0 + X$ as a function of centre-of-mass energy.

Fig. 12 Comparison of the total cross-section for $\bar{p}p \to W^+W^- + X$ with the scaling and the QCD-corrected distribution functions.

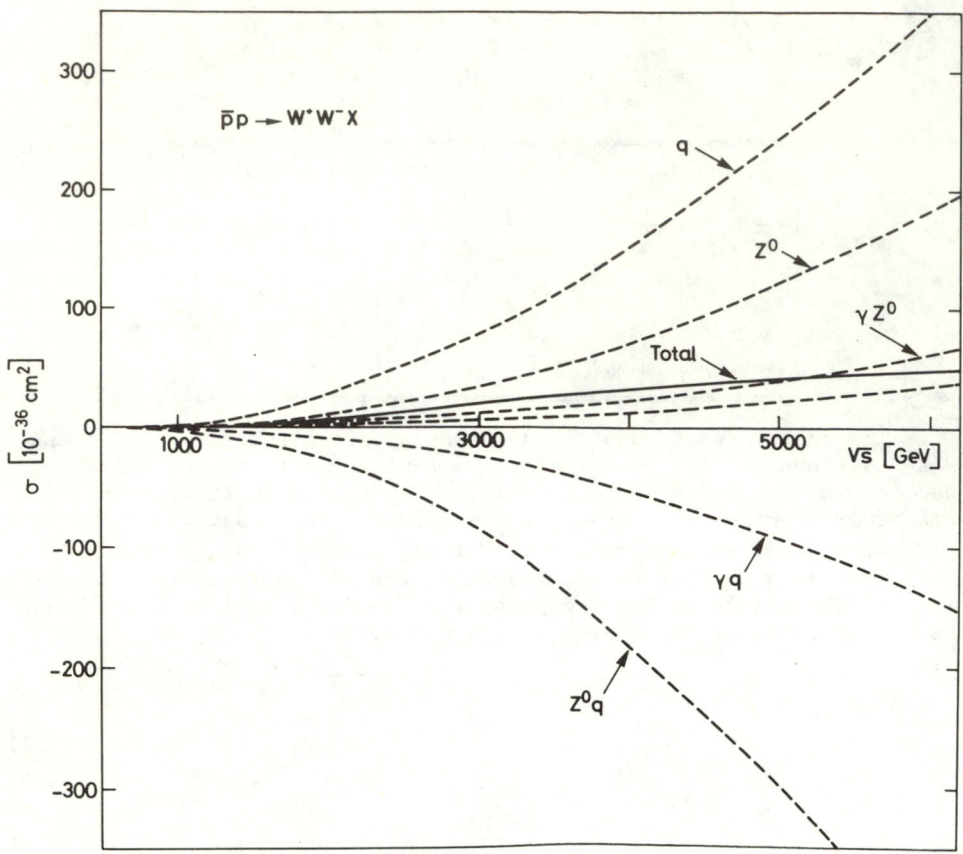

Fig. 13 The partial contributions of the diagrams of Fig. 10a to the total cross-section of $\bar{p}p \to W^+W^- + X$ as a function of centre-of-mass energy

Figure 13 shows the partial contributions due to the different diagrams of Fig. 10a and their interferences to the total cross-section of W^+W^- as a function of centre-of-mass energy. The quark-exchange diagram leads to a fastly growing cross-section. However, the interference terms with the gauge theory (second) diagram neatly cancel this huge contribution at high energies.

For curiosity we show the angular distribution for W^+ in the centre of mass of the W^+W^- pair in Fig. 14 and in the $\bar{p}p$ centre of mass in Fig. 15, with θ being the angle between the $\bar{p}$ beam and W^+. The cross-sections are peaked at small angles. However, the proton direction is favoured by W^+.

Figure 16 shows the angular distribution for W^- in the centre of mass of the $W^-\gamma$ system and Fig. 17 in the laboratory frame. Here θ is the angle between W^- and the incident proton. The angular distribution in the centre of mass of $W^-\gamma$ shows a very clear dip at $\cos\theta = -\frac{1}{3}$. For the quark-level processes $d\bar{u} \to W^-\gamma$ or $s\bar{u} \to W^-\gamma$ an absolute zero is

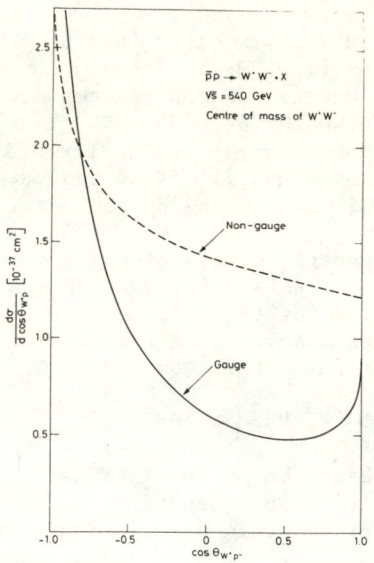

Fig. 14 Angular distribution for W^+ in the reaction $\bar{p}p \to W^+W^- + X$ in the centre of mass of the W^+W^- pair.

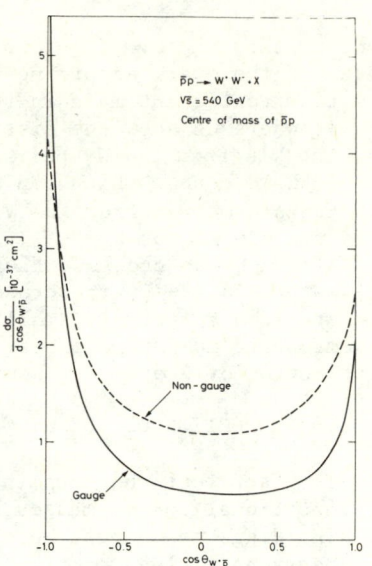

Fig. 15 Angular distribution for W^+ in the reaction $\bar{p}p \to W^+W^- + X$ in the $\bar{p}p$ centre of mass.

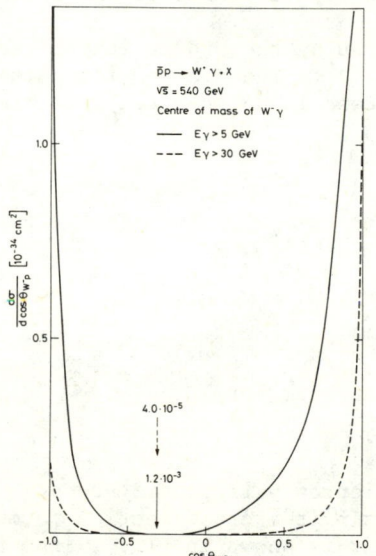

Fig. 16 The angular distribution for the W^- in $\bar{p}p \to W^-\gamma + X$ in the centre of mass of the $W^-\gamma$ system and for $E_\gamma > 5$ GeV.

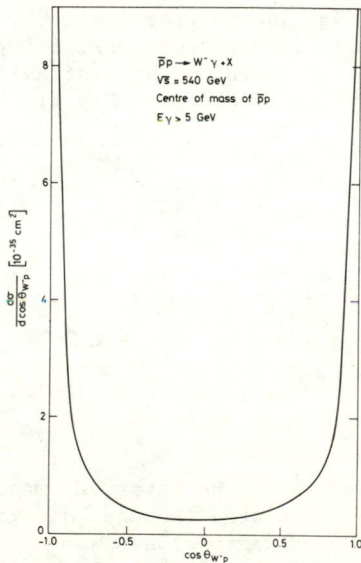

Fig. 17 The angular distribution for W^- in $\bar{p}p \to W^-\gamma + X$ in the $\bar{p}p$ centre of mass and for $E_\gamma > 5$ GeV.

found at this angle. The location of the zero is determined by the charge of the quark according to $\cos \theta = -(1 + 2Q_q)$. The minimum is sensitive to the cut made in the photon energy, as can be seen from Fig. 16 where we show the distribution also for $E_\gamma > 30$ GeV.

The W's from the Wγ pairs will be found mainly in the forward and backward cones, which can be seen from Fig. 17. It is also seen that transformation from the Wγ centre of mass to the $\bar{p}p$ centre of mass fills the dip at $\cos \theta = -\frac{1}{3}$.

Although the cross-section in the centre of mass of Wγ is very small at $\cos \theta = -\frac{1}{3}$, the cross-sections at this point for other values of κ are also relatively small[5],[6]. Extracting the value of the anomalous magnetic moment parameter κ from the behaviour of the angular distribution of γ or W is then a good experimental task.

6. PRODUCTION OF THE HIGGS BOSON IN THE BREMSSTRAHLUNG BY Z^0

The fact that the coupling of the Higgs boson to other particles is proportional to the masses has important consequences:
 i) The Higgs meson must be copiously produced in association with heavy particles,
 ii) The Higgs meson will decay into the heaviest kinematically available particles.
Thus the decays of heavy particles, gluon annihilation, and annihilation of heavy quark-antiquark pairs can create Higgs bosons even with large cross-sections. However, we are not interested in these production mechanisms because of the experimental difficulty of extracting the Higgs boson from its decay products.

An interesting possibility is offered by the production of the Higgs meson in the bremsstrahlung by Z^0 [7],[8]. The diagram for this mechanism is shown in Fig. 18. The process leads to a tiny but clear

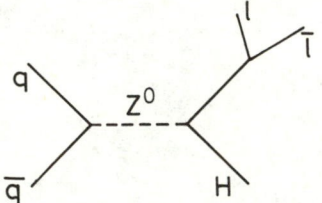

Fig. 18 The Feynman diagram for
$\bar{q}q \to H^0 + Z^0 (Z^0 \to \ell\bar{\ell})$.

signature in the invariant mass of the lepton pair from Z^0 decay. We have calculated the mass distribution using the cross-section formulae given by Ling-Lie Chau Wang[7]. The result is shown in Fig. 19 for the Higgs mass of 10 GeV. It can be seen that in addition to the peak at Z^0 mass there is another very smooth peak approximately at $m \approx m_{Z^0} - m_{H^0}$. This bump is originating from the inner virtual Z^0 decaying into a real Z^0 and a Higgs boson. The integrated cross-section for this process is 0.15 pb. Thus we expect only about one event in 100 days for the luminosity of 10^{30} cm^{-2} s^{-1}.

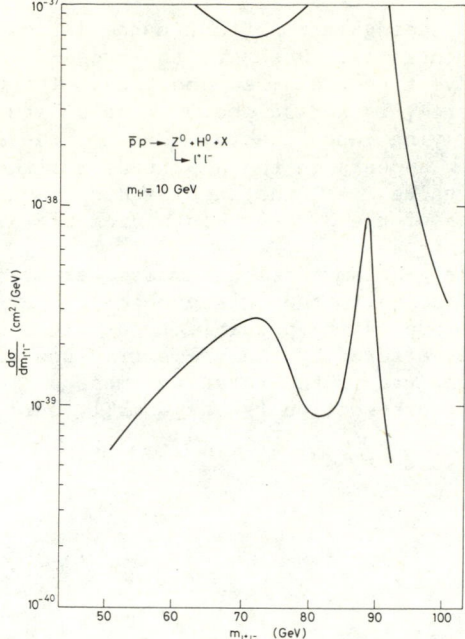

Fig. 19 The invariant mass distribution for the lepton pairs in the process $\bar{p}p \to H^0 + X + Z^0(Z^0 \to \ell\bar{\ell})$.

The mass distribution is about two orders of magnitude below the leptonic Drell-Yan and Z^0 backgrounds shown also in Fig. 19. However, it might be possible to separate the Higgs signal from this background by triggering the events with two fast leptons with $p \simeq \frac{1}{2}(M_Z - m_H)$ and a third lepton from Higgs decay.

7. CONCLUSIONS

The cross-sections for the leptonic channels of W and Z^0 are of the order of 10^{-34} cm^2 at the energies of the CERN $\bar{p}p$ collider. They are thus expected to be found during 1982 at the collider, which is already producing data on $\bar{p}p$ collisions at 540 GeV.

The UA1 detector, with its 4π calorimeter system is ready to record the leptonic decays of weak bosons. The momenta of the decay leptons will be measured in the central detector. A W event will be signalled by a large p_T lepton and large missing transverse energy due to the emitted neutrino. The UA1 experiment is expecting about 10 W events and one Z^0 event in a day for its detectors with a luminosity of 10^{29} cm^{-2} s^{-1}.

Once the weak bosons have been found it will be interesting to know if they are the gauge bosons of the theory. In the SU(2) × U(1) gauge theory the trilinear vertices enter the amplitudes for W^+W^- and

$W^{\pm}Z^0$ production, leading to important cancellations in the cross-sections at high energies. However, the cross-sections are too small for a useful study at the collider energies. The production of the $W\gamma$ pair instead, where γ is a hard photon, can be studied and will also uncover the underlying gauge theory. Namely, the anomalous magnetic moment parameter κ appears in the amplitude for the $W\gamma$ channel. For the gauge theory value $\kappa = 1$ the angular distribution of W or γ in the centre of mass of the $W\gamma$ pair has a dramatic behaviour, dropping to zero at $\cos \theta = -\frac{1}{3}$.

In the Weinberg-Salam model the masses are generated through the Higgs mechanism leading to the existence of a heavy scalar boson, the Higgs meson. An interesting possibility of finding the Higgs meson at the collider is offered by the bremsstrahlung of Z^0. The process gives a clear signature in the invariant mass of the lepton pair from Z^0, but the cross-section is very small, only about one tenth of a picobarn.

REFERENCES

1. E.S. Abers and B.W. Lee, Phys. Rep. 9C, 1 (1973).
   H. Fritzsch and P. Minkowski, Phys. Rep. 73, 67 (1981).
2. P. Aurenche and J. Lindfors, Phys. Lett. 96B, 171 (1980).
3. P. Aurenche and J. Lindfors, Nucl. Phys. B185, 301 (1981).
4. R.W. Brown and K.O. Mikaelian, Phys. Rev. D 19, 922 (1979).
5. R.W. Brown, D. Sahdev and K.O. Mikaelian, Phys. Rev. D 20, 1164 (1979).
6. K.O. Mikaelian, M.A. Samuel and D. Sahdev, Phys. Lett. 43, 746 (1979).
7. L.-L. Chau Wang, Signature of the bremsstrahlung of a Higgs boson by the Z^0 in hadronic reactions, Brookhaven preprint, BNL-28781 (1980).
8. J. Finjord, G. Girardi and P. Sorba, Phys. Lett. 89B, 99 (1979).
9. J.F. Owens and E. Reya, Phys. Rev. D 17, 3003 (1978).
10. A. Astbury et al., A 4π solid angle detector for the SPS used as a proton-antiproton collider at the centre of mass energy of 540 GeV, Proposal CERN/SPSC/78-06 (1978).
11. R. Kinnunen and C. Rubbia, Expected W rates for the UA1 detector, CERN/$\bar{p}p$ Note 67 (1981).
12. R. Kinnunen, Updated cross-sections for the weak boson pairs in $\bar{p}p$ collisions, CERN/UA1/$\bar{p}p$ Note 70 (1981).

$W^+W^-, W^\pm\gamma$ PRODUCTION IN PROTON COLLIDERS

R.W. Brown

Case Western Reserve University, Cleveland, Oh. 44106
and
Fermi National Accelerator Laboratory, Batavia, Il. 60510

ABSTRACT

We examine certain details of the production of electroweak pairs WW,Wγ in quark-antiquark annihilation. The polarization of the weak bosons and the effects of angular cuts are calculated. As in the Wγ angular distribution, the magnetic moment dependence of the polarizations and the WW angular distributions is striking. We note that electric moments can be studied in similar ways. Some review of other work in this area is also given.

INTRODUCTION

This is, in part, a progress report about some ongoing work[1] by our group at CWRU. We are investigating further details in the theoretical predictions for electroweak pair production, mainly W^+W^- and $W^\pm\gamma$ in proton-antiproton collisions. The issues, rates, and experimentalists are sufficiently encouraging that it now becomes important to pay attention to the actual experimental constraints.

In particular, we have now calculated the polarization of the W's and the effects of angular cuts in order to compare the decay distributions with background. Eventually, one would like to tie the polarization density matrix to the decay matrix, but it is not hard to get the final distributions from just the polarization information. The forward-backward peaking in our reactions seems well-suited for "forward spectrometry" plans in proton colliders, furnishing more reason to look at the effects of forward cuts. The hope is that small angles will be favorable for the decay leptons, enhancing the signal-to-noise ratio.

The important QCD corrections, both in the scaling violations of the proton structure functions and in unfactorized first-order corrections, have not yet been calculated by us. However, the effects of scaling violation have been considered by others and we shall reference later this work as well as other recent related papers.[2]

252

If and when the $W^{\pm}$ and Z^{0} are dug out of the $p\bar{p}$ debris, and even if they are found at the standard mass values

$$M_W \stackrel{\sim}{=} \frac{38.5}{\sin\theta_W} \stackrel{\sim}{=} 80 \text{ GeV/c}^2 \tag{1}$$

and

$$M_Z = \frac{M_W}{\cos\theta_W} \stackrel{\sim}{=} 90 \text{ GeV/c}^2 \ , \tag{2}$$

could they yet be masquerading as SU(2)xU(1) gauge bosons? Should we accept candidates with the right charge, spin and V-A couplings, and especially with the right mass?

Surely we will. It is amusing to recall the ancient circumstance where the muon passed for the pion for a number of years. A more serious challenge will yet arise in that we must find evidence for renormalizability, that is, for the gauge nature of particles. Specifically, we would like to show that self-couplings exist of <u>the form predicted</u> in the standard model or its accepted variants. These self-couplings are the trilinear WWγ, WWZ

and quadrilinear WWWW, WWγγ, WWZZ, WWZγ

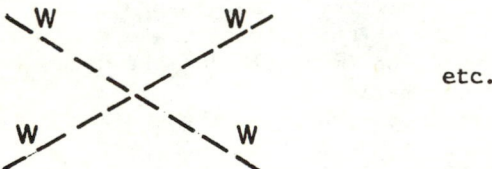

etc.

One must determine whether these exist with the predicted coupling structure and whether anomalous couplings (e.g. ZZγ) exist. The quadrilinear couplings most probably must wait for higher energies than the regime we will address.

A few years ago, Mikaelian and I proposed looking at $p\bar{p}$ and pp collisions <u>as a test of gauge theories</u>, precisely for the WWZ and WWγ coupling.[3] The point is that if a pair of W's is produced often enough,

$$p\bar{p} \ (pp) \rightarrow W^+W^-X \ ,$$

presumably through quark-antiquark annihilation,

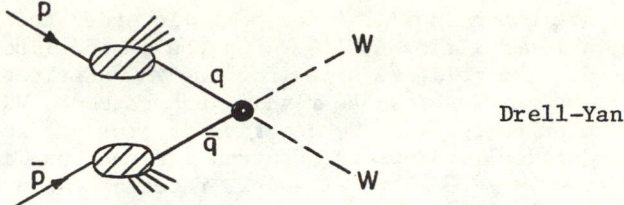

Drell-Yan

then the $q\bar{q} \to WW$ kernel depends upon the trilinear couplings

The γWW vertex involves the anomalous (an historical misnomer) magnetic moment parameter κ

$$\mu = \frac{e}{2M_W} (1+\kappa) \tag{2}$$

which has the "non-anomalous" value $\kappa = +1$ in gauge theories. In contrast to γWW, the mere existence of the ZWW vertex is interesting, and it, as well as the GIM mechanism, is operative in the quark kernel.

We can also isolate γWW or ZWW by considering[4]

$$p\bar{p}(pp) \to W\gamma X \text{ or } WZX \quad ,$$

respectively. The kernels are

The procedure here and in the previous is to calculate how the rates and distributions change when the couplings are moved away from the gauge values. For example, one might consider varying κ or even omitting a vertex like ZWW altogether.

TOTAL CROSS SECTIONS

The total rates calculated in a scaling limit (no QCD corrections) are shown in Fig. 1 for $p\bar{p}$. In order to define the Wγ reaction, a lower limit of 5 GeV for the photon laboratory energy is used. The relative sizes for the various electroweak pair production cross sections can be readily understood. With such a cut on the photon energy the Wγ reaction is close to resonance (single W production). Since the neutral current couplings are suppressed for $\sin^2\theta_W \cong \frac{1}{4}$, the WZ and ZZ rates are an order of magnitude below that for WW.

At the SPS c.m. energy of $\sqrt{s}$ = 540 GeV and luminosity $L = 10^{30}$ cm^{-2}s^{-1}, several Wγ events per day are predicted. We have to go to the Tevatron region of $\sqrt{s} \geq 1000$ GeV for a WW daily event. (It must be emphasized that QCD corrections are a big question mark. We return to this later.) Improvement in luminosity will be needed for the other channels and in this regard ISABELLE offers more hope - the pp cross sections are not that much smaller.

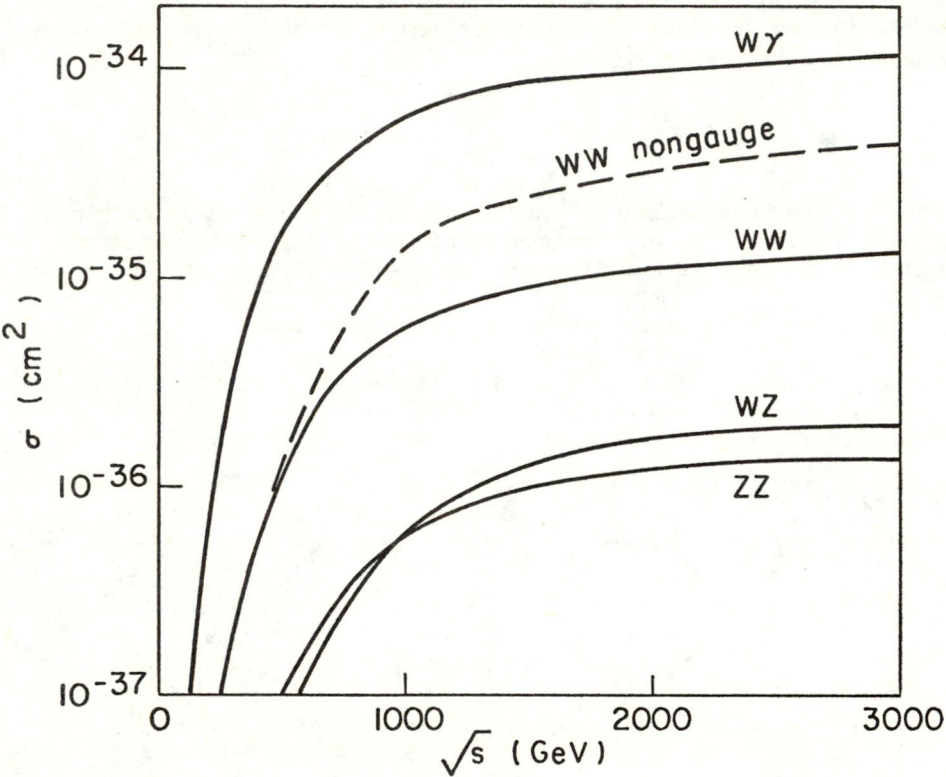

Fig.1. Total cross sections for the production of boson pairs, $p\bar{p} \rightarrow$ pair + X . No QCD corrections.

HIGH ENERGY BEHAVIOR

What tells us that the pairs have the appropriate gauge couplings? First, the self couplings keep the high energy behavior[3,4] of the basic fermion-antifermion → WW cross section under control, the hallmark of renormalizability. (Historically, the $f\bar{f}$ → WW reaction has been a focal point in the study of high energy limits.) This is seen in Fig. 2 and translates into the result for $p\bar{p}$ → WWX shown in Fig. 3. A comparison with a result where there is no ZWW coupling is also shown in Fig. 2 and Fig. 3 (where phase space eventually cuts off the nongauge result as well). The dashed curve in Fig. 1 represents the corresponding nongauge total rate.

Perhaps it is possible to make sense out of a calculation where, for example, the WWZ interaction can be neglected. We have in mind some sort of composite model for the W where pair production cross sections could get large. Then the differences discussed above are meaningful and the general gauge mechanisms which keep multi-W production at the electromagnetic level could be probed in this way.

Such important cancellations also take place in WZ and WY production and, conversely, are ruined for nongauge choices for the couplings. ZZ production is both rarer and less interesting. It is QED-like and only anomalous γZZ couplings would make its story similar.

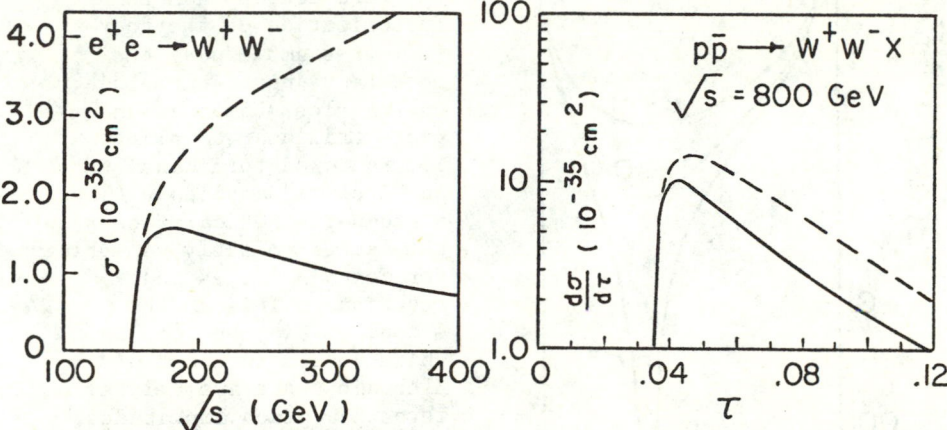

Fig.2. Total cross section for $f\bar{f}$ → WW where f = e⁻, for example. The dashed curve is a nongauge result.

Fig.3. Invariant-mass distribution with $\tau = Q^2/s$. The dashed curve is a nongauge result.

256

ANGULAR DISTRIBUTIONS – OLD RESULTS

After the gauge cancellations, the fermion-exchange diagrams dominate the angular distributions. Indeed, the forward peaking for WW and forward-backward peaking for WZ,ZZ, and Wγ are seen in the figures of Refs. 3. and 4. If non-Abelian gauge invariance is not respected, we expect the WW,WZ, and Wγ angular distributions to be "filled in" as the s – channel poles become more important.

This is spectacularly verified in Fig. 4 where the results for the $u\bar{d} \rightarrow W^+\gamma$ have been reproduced from Ref. 4. We see a new feature, a "gauge zero" in the angular distribution where the cross section <u>vanishes</u> [See Eq. (2.19) of Ref. 4.] at $\kappa = 1$. The resultant angular distributions for the proton collisions are shown in Ref. 5 and a pronounced dip survives <u>in the Wγ c.m. frame</u>. For massless fermions, the $q_i\bar{q}_j \rightarrow W^+\gamma$ has a zero at the c.m. angle between γ and $\bar{q}_j$,

$$\cos\theta = 1 + 2Q_j \quad , \quad \kappa = 1 \tag{3}$$

independent of all other factors. Thus only the sea-sea annihilation contribution to $p\bar{p}$ collisions fills in the zero, and negligibly at that.

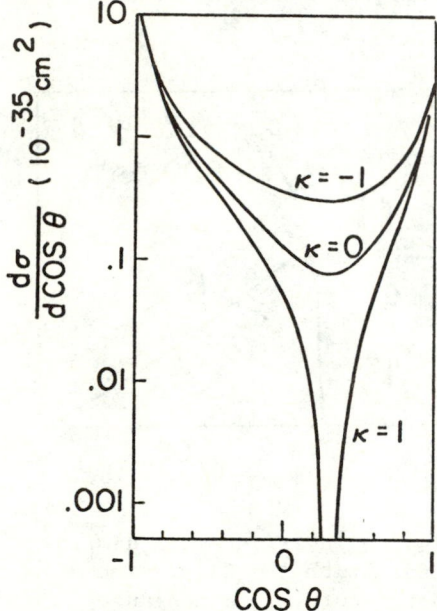

Fig. 4. Angular distribution for $u\bar{d} \rightarrow W^+\gamma$ at $\sqrt{s}$ = 150 GeV. θ is the c.m. angle between u and W^+.

It has been shown[6] that the zero corresponds to factorization of the four-body tree amplitude, the necessary ingredients being one massless boson and a gauge trilinear coupling. The factored form consists of an "Abelian" amplitude times a group-theoretical factor, the latter possibly vanishing for certain angles and reactions. This is the second of two theorems in which we are interested[7]. Although there are related zeros in gluon amplitudes, the massless particle should couple to an <u>observable</u> quantum number for an experimental test.[8] The upshot of a survey through various possibilities is that $q\bar{q} \rightarrow W\gamma$ seems to offer a unique opportunity to see such a zero. Note there is a related zero[9] in the Dalitz plot for $W \rightarrow q\bar{q}\gamma$ and a quasi-zero[4] in $q\bar{q} \rightarrow WZ$, but these are harder to measure.

The problem we face in the measurement of the Wγ dip is not just whether background or radiative corrections will obscure the dip, a point to which we will return later, but also the fact that the events are essentially forward/backward even for $\kappa \neq 1$. We expect that it may be hard to find non-forward events in a first generation experiment.

ANGULAR DISTRIBUTIONS – NEW RESULTS

We have now calculated[1] the κ dependence of the WW angular distribution and the results for $\kappa = \pm 1, 0$ and for the quark reaction $u\bar{u} \to WW$ are seen in Fig. 5. (The dependence on κ is quadratic so that three values tell all.) This <u>linear</u> plot shows that significant numbers of non-forward events can be found if κ is varied away from unity. In contrast to a need to distinguish dips of varying size, sizeable humps can appear in the nongauge cases. The disadvantages here in comparison to Wγ lie in the smaller rate and the presence of both trilinear couplings.

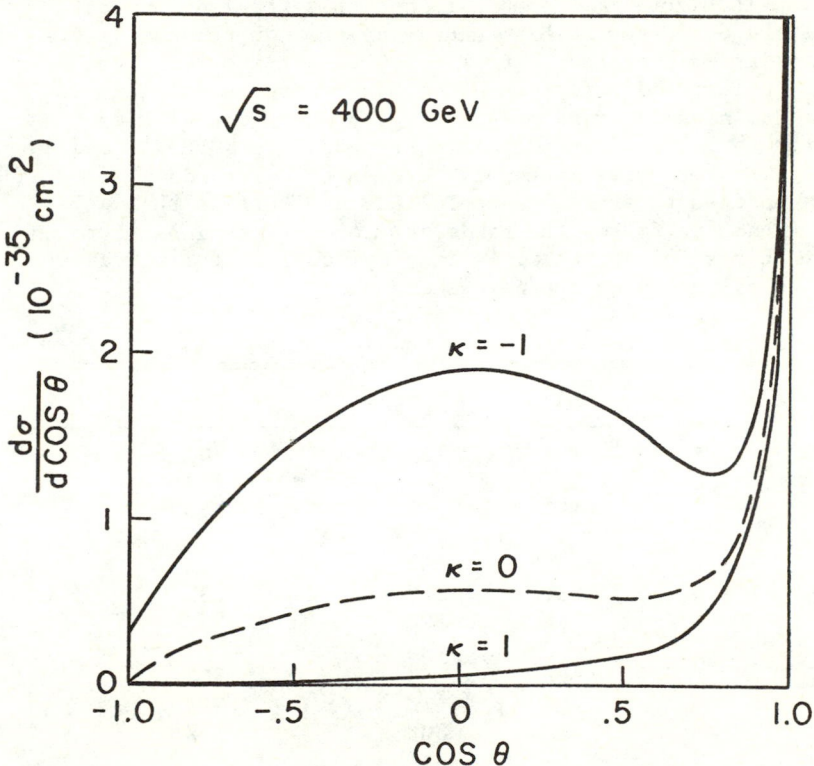

Fig.5. Angular distributions for $u\bar{u} \to WW$ as a function of the magnetic moment. θ is the c.m. angle between u and W^+. $d\bar{d} \to WW$ is reflected in $\cos\theta$ and reduced in size.

In any case, there are sufficient forward-backward events to qualify as a forward-collider prospect. For $\kappa = 1$, we have inserted angular cuts in the parent $p\bar{p} \to WWX$ reaction. (For $\kappa \neq 1$, we only gain cross section.) As $\sqrt{s}$ grows from 600 GeV to 2000 GeV, we estimate that the percentage of the events where both W's are inside 20° grows from 7% to 30% and the percentage of the events where either is inside 20° grows from 50% to 60%. One of the W's may wander at larger angles depending on the decay muon detection capability.

POLARIZATION

We have also calculated the polarization density matrix for the W spin in the quark reactions. Ultimately the distributions in angle for the decay leptons is needed, and the density matrix will tell us something about those distributions.

In the $u\bar{d} \to W^+ \gamma$ c.m. frame, the angular-averaged and normalized density matrix yields the polarization which is given in Table I as a function of energy and κ. It is seen that the polarization is highly κ dependent, and that the longitudinal helicity state dominates at high energy in the non-renormalizable $\kappa \neq 1$ theories as expected. At $\kappa = 1$, we achieve 80% right-handed (RH) polarization for the W^+ at high energies.[10] This is due to the dominant backward peak, of Fig. 4 where the W^+ lies close to the $\bar{d}$. The forward peak corresponds to a LH W^+ and angles near the zero give intermediate results. The $d\bar{u} \to W^- \gamma$ has the handedness reversed. A useful picture here is that a weak boson tends to follow the handedness of any collinear fermion from which it has been emitted.[11] The implications for a decay muon will be discussed in the next section.

Table I W^+ polarization in $u\bar{d} \to W^+ \gamma$

$\sqrt{s}$ (GeV)	κ	LH	Long.	RH
	1	19%	3%	78%
100	0	19%	4%	77%
	−1	19%	5%	76%
	1	20%	0%	80%
400	0	16%	21%	63%
	−1	11%	50%	39%
	1	20%	0%	80%
800	0	10%	51%	39%
	−1	4%	80%	16%

The corresponding averaged polarizations for $u\bar{u} \to WW$ are listed in Table II. At high energy, one again sees the longitudinal dominance for $\kappa \neq 1$. For $\kappa = 1$, the W^+ is LH for $u\bar{u}$ and our calculations show RH for $d\bar{d}$. (The reverse is true for W^-.) This is also consistent with W following the handedness of its parent quark at small angles. Note that all of the polarization states contribute at low energies where the $\kappa = 1$ cross section is largest. The significance of this is discussed next.

Table II W^+ polarization in $u\bar{u} \to WW$

$\sqrt{s}$ (GeV)	κ	LH	Long.	RH
	1	50%	29%	21%
170	0	50%	30%	20%
	-1	47%	32%	21%
	1	65%	21%	14%
200	0	60%	26%	24%
	-1	52%	36%	12%
	1	96%	1%	3%
800	0	8%	91%	1%
	-1	3%	96%	1%

DECAY DISTRIBUTIONS

In the rest frame decay $W^+ \to \mu^+ \nu_\mu$, the μ^+ likes to follow the spin of the W^+ and the specific distribution is $(1 + s\cos\theta^*)^2$ for RH ($s = +1$) or LH ($s = -1$). It is $\sin^2\theta^*$ for longitudinal polarization. θ^* is the μ^+ angle along the spin axis of quantization. A Lorentz boost of the LH case along this axis leaves a hole in the forward direction:

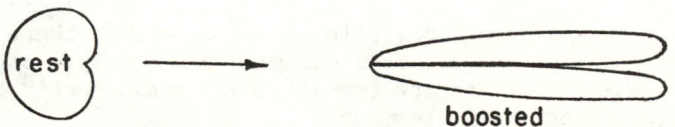

We therefore can say that the W produced in $p\bar{p} \to W\gamma X$ has the same sort of boost picture for decay as in single W production if $\kappa = +1$. However, it remains to be seen whether this will hold for $\kappa \neq 1$. The significance is that the background (single W's, etc.) may be reduced for $\kappa \neq 1$ events.

Even more interesting is the fact that the W pairs produced in $p\bar{p} \to WWX$ are dominated by low invariant mass so that there is sufficient mixture of all polarizations even for

$\kappa = 1$. Therefore our calculations give hope that the background may be suppressed where pairs of W's are to be found.

QCD AND OTHER CORRECTIONS

It is straightforward to include the (logarithmic) scaling violations in the quark distributions and this is discussed in a separate conference contribution.[12] It appears that QCD-corrected structure functions can lead to order-of-magnitude reductions in the cross sections near threshold but also can turn around and increase the rates at higher energies. For a better assessment we should calculate the "constant" terms in first order QCD:

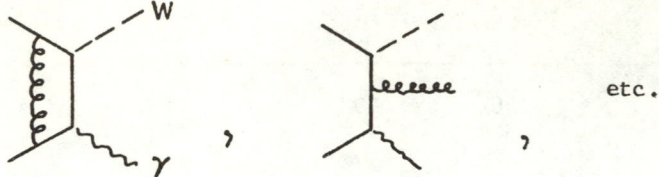

Such terms are important in single W production and their calculation is in progress.[1]

Another question is the size of non-leading terms such as

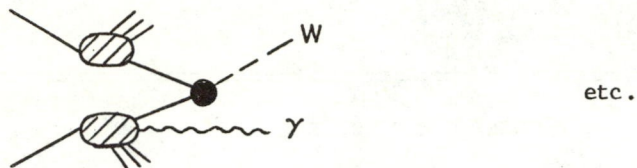

For smaller cuts on the photon energy, such contributions must be considered

ELECTRIC QUADRUPOLE AND DIPOLE MOMENTS

In addition to the magnetic dipole moment freedom, there is also an arbitrariness in the electric quadrupole for a spin-one particle. Equivalently, there are two arbitrary parameters[13] κ and λ in the magnetic dipole moment.

$$\mu = \frac{e}{2M_W} (1 + \kappa + \lambda) \qquad (4)$$

and the electric quadrupole moment

$$Q = - \frac{e}{M_W^2} (\kappa - \lambda) . \qquad (5)$$

The higher derivative electromagnetic interaction associated with $\lambda \neq 0$ gives rise to high energy behavior more vicious than $\kappa \neq 1$. This a priori possible freedom should be included in any test scenario and may be the first parameter constrained by any experimental results.

The electric dipole moment is zero if the W's electromagnetic interaction is time-reversal and parity invariant. However, this could and should be tested by computing how distributions are changed by its inclusion.

FUTURE WORK AND PROGNOSIS

We have reported some preliminary results in a project to assess the possibility that gauge self-couplings could be tested with proton colliders. This developing area of research is now at a stage where detailed experimental questions must be answered, and plans are for a Monte Carlo simulation of the $W\gamma$. The polarization density matrix is to be tied to the decay matrix in order to compute distributions in photon and muon angles. Also, we are investigating QCD radiative corrections and non-leading (higher twist) contributions, especially as they affect the $W\gamma$ zero. The related assessment of WW involves very similar steps.

We now see three ways to get a handle on κ. (1) Any bound on the overall rate will give a bound on κ. (2) The shapes of c.m. angular distributions (dips and humps) are very sensitive to κ. (3) The polarization for $\kappa \neq 1$ is markedly different from $\kappa = 1$. It appears that λ can be probed in related manner. The form of the ZWW vertex could also be generalized in terms of parameters like λ and κ, with qualitatively similar results.

ACKNOWLEDGMENT

We are grateful to David Cline for important suggestions and for his interest in this work.

REFERENCES

1. C.L. Bilchak, R.W. Brown, and J.D. Stroughair (to be published).
2. A previous review has been given by K.O. Mikaelian, Proc. Topical Workshop (ed. V. Barger and F. Halzen, Wisconsin, 1980).
3. R.W. Brown and K.O. Mikaelian, Phys. Rev. D19, 922 (1979).
4. R.W. Brown, D. Sahdev, and K.O. Mikaelian, Phys. Rev. D20, 1164 (1979).
    We thank Masa Mishina for pointing out that the scale for $p\bar{p} \rightarrow WZX$ production in Figs. 9-10 of this reference is wrong. Fig. 9 should read 10^{-36} cm^2 and have two of its labels interchanged ($p\bar{p} \rightarrow WZX \leftrightarrow pp \rightarrow WZX$ non-gauge) and $p\bar{p} \rightarrow WZX$ should be reduced by a factor of 10 in Fig. 10.

5. K.O. Mikaelian, M.A. Samuel, and D. Sahdev, Phys. Rev. Lett. 43, 746 (1979).

6. C.J. Goebel, F. Halzen, and J.P. Leveille, Phys. Rev. D23, 2682 (1981). See also Z. Dongpei, Phys. Rev. D22, 2265 (1980).

7. The other, related theorem states that at least one reference to F. Halzen's work is to be found in each talk at this conference.

8. K.O. Mikaelian, Phys. Rev. (in press).

9. T.R. Grose and K.O. Mikaelian, Phys. Rev. D23, 123 (1981).

10. I reported some incorrect results for asymptotic helicities in my talk. I thank Professor Goebel for instructing me to look for consistency between $W\gamma$ and WW as a check on these results.

11. See another example in R.W. Brown, R.H. Hobbs, and J. Smith, Phys. Rev. D4, 794 (1971).

12. R. Kinnunen, report at this conference.

13. H. Aronson, Phys. Rev. 186, 1434 (1969); K.J. Kim and Y.- S. Tsai, Phys. Rev. D7, 3710 (1973).

THE FORWARD SPECTROMETER OF THE FERMILAB COLLIDING DETECTOR FACILITY

P. McIntyre
Texas A&M University

ABSTRACT

The CDF forward spectrometer is described. It is designed to extend analysis of secondaries in $\bar{p}p$ collisions down to an angle of 2^0. New particle production is expected to concentrate in the forward direction for $\sqrt{s}$ = 2 TeV collisions. Several novel aspects of the CDF forward spectrometer are described.

The Fermilab Tevatron will provide pp colliding beams with $\sqrt{s}$ = 2 TeV and L = 10^{30} cm^{-2}sec^{-1}.[1] A large collaboration[2] has been formed to design and construct a powerful, general purpose detector system to study the wealth of new physics expected at the Tevatron. This detector - the Colliding Detector Facility - is shown in Figure 1, and described in a recent design report[3]. Electromagnetic and hadronic calorimetry are provided over almost 4π solid angle around the interaction region. Fine-grain spatial segmentation has been matched to the large energies and high multiplicities expected from recent CERN collider experience. A large superconducting solenoidal magnet (1.5T) containing drift chambers measures the momenta of charged particles and gives a visual reconstruction of the event. Muon chambers around the perimeter of the central detector and iron toroidal magnets at each end identify muons.

The tracking chambers and calorimeters of the solenoidal spectrometer extend down to an angle of 10^0 to each beam direction, and provide a compact, closed geometry. The forward 10^0 cones are open, to increase the free path length for forward-produced particles, and to provide flexibility in the instrumentation for analyzing them. There are two practical reasons for opening the forward geometry: 1) The track density ($\approx$rapidity y) increases as $1/\tan\theta$, so that forward tracking chambers must be located farther from the intersection point to facilitate reconstruction of complex events; 2) the momentum resolution σ_p/p^2 of the solenoidal spectrometer increases as $1/\sin\theta$, while the typical momentum of a secondary increases as $1/\sin\theta$; the resolution thus deteriorates as $1/\sin^2\theta$ and provision must be made for further momentum analysis. Several physics considerations motivate the design of the forward spectrometer: 1) recent calculations[4,5] show that the production of new heavy particles (top, W^{+},Z,...) in pp collisions at $\sqrt{s}$ = 2 TeV proceeds mainly from the interaction of a valence quark from the proton and a sea antiquark (or gluon) from the antiproton, or vice-versa. The seaquark (or gluon) typically has small x, so that the new particles are produced forward. This is in contrast to the situation near threshold for heavy particle production (as at the CERN collider), where valence-valence processes predominate and new particles are produced centrally (see Figure 5 of Red 4.) The forward spectrometer thus attains a particular significance at the Tevatron collider.

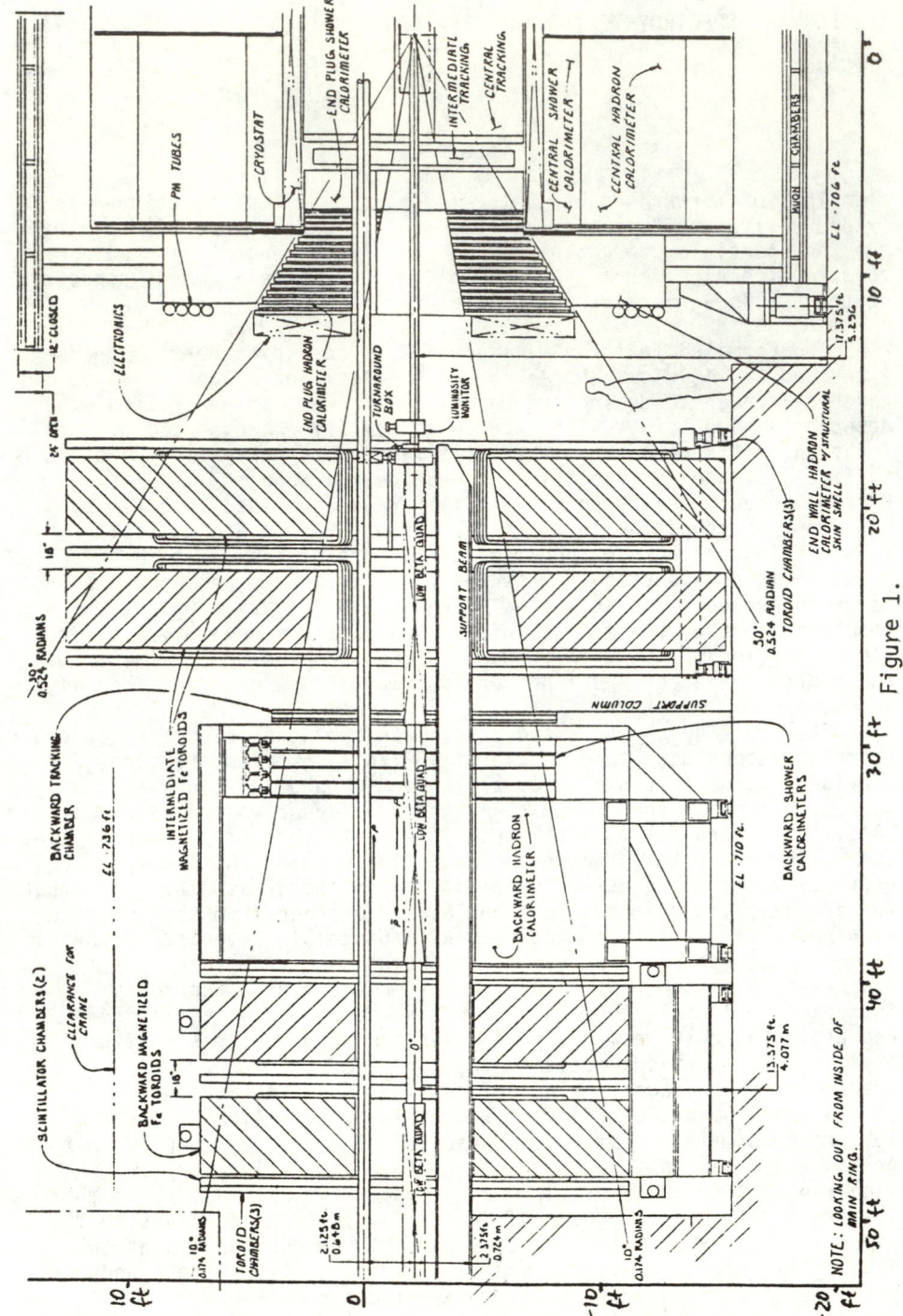

Figure 1.

2) The forward production of $W^{\mp}$ should exhibit strong charge asymmetry in the leptonic decays. The charge asymmetry of forward leptons preserves the asymmetry in the weak decay itself, while at larger angles the kinematics of the production process actually reverses the sign of the asymmetry. Forward lepton detection will likely be crucial in the search for the $W^{\mp}$.

3) The forward spectrometer has a large phase space acceptance. The angular range $2^0 < \theta < 10^0$ extends the rapidity acceptance of the spectrometer from $y = 2.4$ to $y = 4.1$. The analysis of complex final states can then be attempted without strong acceptance biases.

4) It is only in the forward direction that full particle identification can be realistically achieved over a large phase space acceptance. The solid angle of the forward spectrometer is only 0.1 ster., about 2% of total solid angle, while the phase space acceptance is comparable to that of the entire solenoid. It is thus important to provide an open forward geometry to accomodate the addition of particle identification and other capabilities to a basic detector configuration.

The CDF forward spectrometer is shown in Figure 1. It consists of a tracking chamber telescope, e.m. shower and hadron calorimeters, and a magnetized iron toroid spectrometer for muons. Its design has been the work of physicists at Fermilab, Harvard, Texas A&M and the University of Wisconsin. It represents an accomodation of an original, more ambitious design[6] to the constraints of scope and budget. In what follows I describe its design and expected performance. In the hope of motivating further ideas and effort on forward collider physics I will also discuss briefly several devices which are being considered as possible future improvements to expand its physics capabilities.

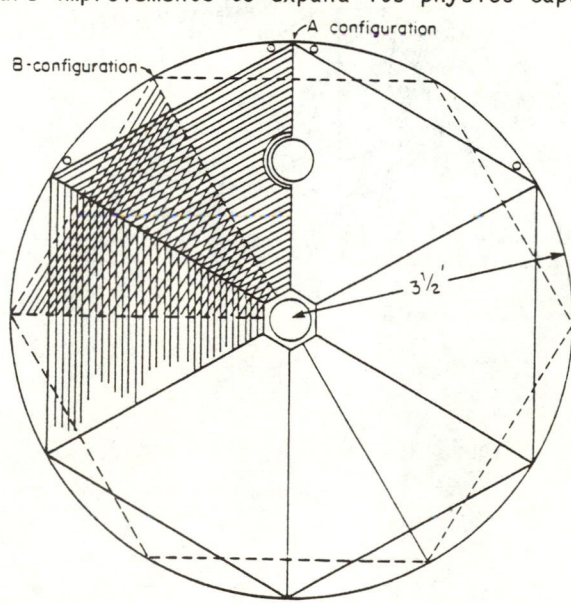

Figure 2.

266

Tracking and Momentum Analysis: A telescopy of 3 tracking chamber modules is located as shown in Fig. 2. Each module consists of two planes of drift chambers where ionization electrons drift in the radial direction. The sense wire spacing is 2 cm. Induced charge is recorded from cathode pads to provide correlated (r,θ) track coordinates. Each chamber is constructed as a composite of equilat-teral triangles as shown. Adjacent chambers are rotated by 30° for stereo reconstruction.

e.m. Shower Calorimeter: The shower calorimeter consists of a finely segmented sandwich of Pb sheets and wire chambers, with a total thickness of 23 radiation lengths. It is constructed of 4 modules of 10 layers each. The chamber planes and lead sheets are assembled onto a common jigplate and sealed as a single gas volume. Induced charge is recorded from a network of 1224 cathode pads, arranged in $(r-\theta)$ segments so that each pad subtends $\Delta y = 0.1$, $\Delta\phi = 5^\circ$ (see Figure 3).

The wire chambers are operated in saturated avalanche mode[7]. The pulse response to a track is saturated, so that total pulse height in a "tower" of pads is a track count of the e.m. cascade. This approach yields excellent energy resolution:

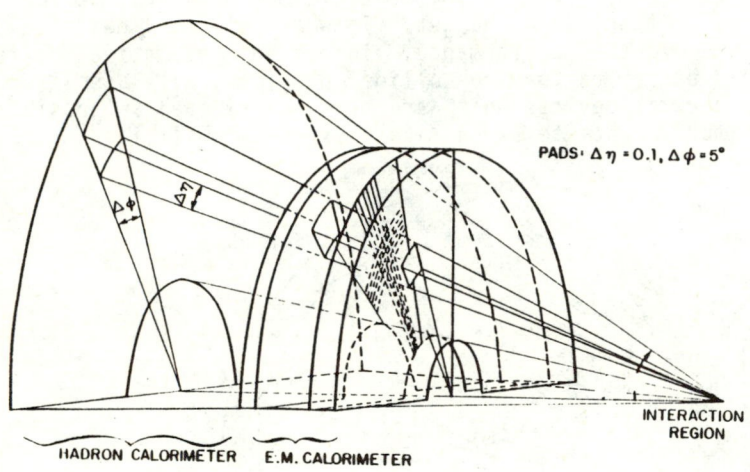

Figure 3.

$\sigma_E/E=16\%/\sqrt{E}$. The pulses are large enough (60µA for induced cathode pulse due to one muon in one layer) and fast enough ($\approx$20 nsec rise and $\approx$ 200 nsec fall time) that local amplifiers are not required on each layer. The wire separation (2mm) is chosen to localize each avalanche sufficiently to retain energy linearity even for dense showers. Pulses can either be summed through the entire depth for each (y-ϕ) segment or recorded in depth segments to aid in e,γ identification.

<u>Hadron Calorimeter</u>: The hadron calorimeter is a sandwich of 2" Fe plates and wire chambers, 28 layers total (8 absorption lengths). Each chamber consists of a 4'x8' extruded resistive plastic panel, containing (1.5x2) cm^2 rectangular tubes as shown in Fig. 4. A 75µm diameter wire is supported in each tube and the chamber is operated in the limited avalanche mode. The plastic panels have a surface resistance of $\approx$10kΩ/square, which provides the DC cathode for chamber operation. A foil of Cu - clad Mylar is laminated to one face of each chamber. The copper is etched to form a network of pads in an (r,ϕ) pattern, with each pad subtending $\Delta y = 0.1$, $\Delta\phi = 5^0$. At the instant of charge collection on the anode wire, the electric field pulse penetrates the resistive plastic and induces a charge pulse on the copper. Readout is accomplished by summing the signals from the various layers of each (y,ϕ) segment to form a tower. We expect an energy resolution $\sigma_E/E\approx 0.75/\sqrt{E}$.

We believe that the design adopted for these chambers will provide an inexpensive, high-performance solution to a broad range of applications for calorimetry and hodoscopes.

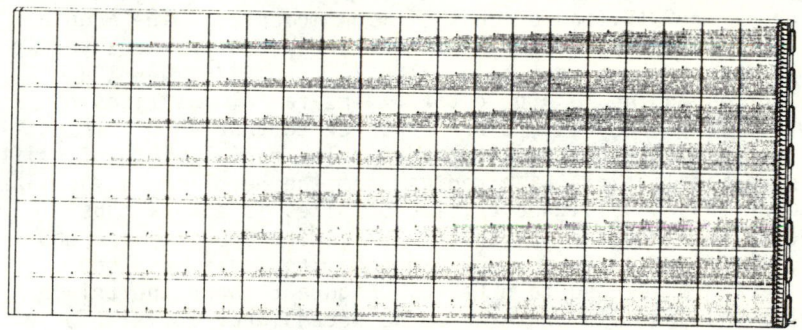

Assembly Drawing of

Single Chamber Panel

FIGURE 4

<u>Toroidal Muon Spectrometer</u>: The forward region will be instrumented to trigger on single muons and measure their momenta. Two sets of magnetized solid iron toroids will be used for this purpose, each set consisting of two 1 m thick iron rings driven to 1.8 T magnetic field and interleaved with drift chambers. The upstream set will be 8.8 m in diameter with a tapered 10^0 half-angle hole centered on the beam pipe. The near face of the iron will be about 4.6 m from the intersection point, and muons will be detected in the angular range between 10^0 and 30^0. The downstream set will be located 11.6 m from the IP and will detect muons between 5^0 and 10^0.

Each toroid pair will be instrumented with three drift chamber assemblies, one in front, one between the two, and one in back, labeled A, B and C respectively. A drift chamber assembly will have two sets of drift cells, one offset to eliminate the ambiguity due to the other. The anode wires will form a pattern of regular 48 sided polygons centered on the beam line. The azimuthal coordinate will be obtained by cathode read-out pads 2^0 wide in ϕ, divided in three separate parts radially to decrease accidental problems. The drift cell size will vary with radius to achieve a constant p_T trigger threshold, as described below. The maximum drift distance will be 1.75 cm, corresponding to a drift time of 350 nsec. Electrically the signal wires will be hooked together in 60^0 arcs.

The deflection of a muon at the back chamber relative to infinite momentum is given by

$$\varepsilon = \frac{108}{p_\mu} \text{ , where } p_\mu \text{ is in GeV/c and } \varepsilon \text{ is in centimeters.}$$

The r.m.s. multiple scattering is given by $\Delta = 18/p_\mu$ in the same units, or $\Delta/\varepsilon = 0.17$, independent of muon momentum. The muon trigger is obtained by requiring that a track traverse the toroid with a deflection less than some value $\varepsilon_{max} = 108/p_{min} = 108 \theta/p_{Tmin}$ corresponding to a p cutoff. The radial positions of sense wires in planes A, B, C are arranged so that each triplet of A, B, C wires points to the intersects. The radial width of drift cells is varied linearly with radius from the beam (hence θ). The requirement that an alligned triplet of wires is struck thus corresponds to a constant p_T cutoff. The wire spacings are chosen for a p_T cutoff of 10 GeV/c. By ganging wires pair-wise the threshold can be reduced to 5 GeV/c. Figure 5 shows the trigger configuration, and illustrates how the occassional correlation of two low-momentum muons can produce a spurious high p_T trigger.

<u>Future Improvements</u>: Three devices are being considered for future improvements to the forward spectrometer: 1) A $\cos\theta$ dipole coil has been designed to fit into the 10^0 hole in the upstream toroid. It would produce a 0.5T horizontal dipole field. This field would enable us to measure the momentum of forward secondaries ($\sigma_p/p^2 \approx 5 \times 10^{-3}$), identify V^0 strange particle decays, and improve electron identification by p/E comparison. 2) A ring-imaging Cerenkov camera has been designed[6] to operate in the aperture of

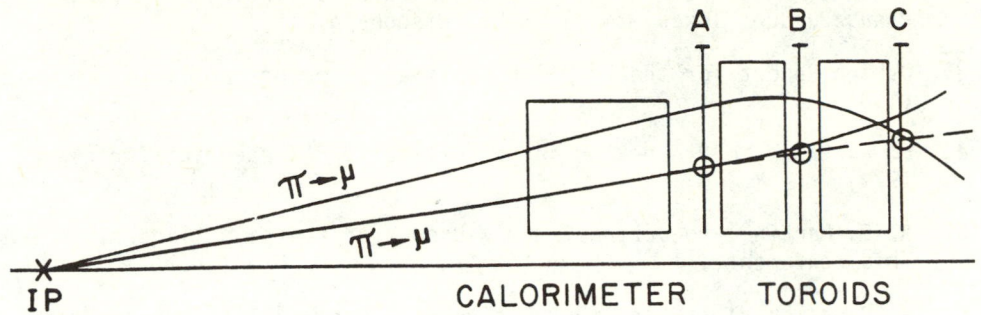

Background from two π→μ decays in flight

Figure 5.

the solenoid and upstream toroid (radiator length 4m). The 10°
half-angle conical aperture is divided into 12 solid angle segments. Each segment is equipped with a pair of focussing mirrors
which produce a parallel-to-point image at the cathode of a small
multi-channel plate image intensifier. The Cerenkov light from each
particle is thus imaged to a discrete ring of photons. The intensified pattern of dots is recorded on a visual CCD array (488x380).
By reconstructing the radius of each Cerenkov ring, the particle's β
can be measured. In this way we anticipate that it would be possible to identify π/K up to ≈110 GeV. A novel multi-stage intensifier design permits the camera to be triggered on each particular
beam-beam interaction, so that pile-up effects in the camera can be
eliminated.

    3) The identification of charm and τ decays may be possible us-
ing a micro-vertex detector surrounding the intersection region.
Two techniques - solid state MESD arrays and liquid Argon ionization
chambers - appear to offer the possibility of achieving spatial resolution $\sigma \approx 10\mu m$. c or τ decays would be identified by distinguishing the decay vertex from the production vertex. The apparent
parallax of a decay particle is typically $\delta \approx c\tau$ (50-100μm for charm,
500μm for τ), independent of the momentum of the charm particle.
Since $\sigma \ll \delta$, it may be possible to distinguish the decay vertex
amongst the hadronic final state. This capability would be of great
importance in searching for new heavy flavors[8] and $W^{\mp}, Z^0$.

REFERENCES

1. D. Cline, P. McIntyre, F. Mills and C. Rubbia, Fermilab TM-689 (1976). Tevatron I Project Design Report, Fermilab (1982).

2. Argonne, Chicago, Fermilab, INFN, Harvard, Illinois, KEK, LBL, Pisa, Purdue, Texas A&M, Tsukuba, Wisconsin.

3. Design Report for the Fermilab Collider Detector Facility. (1981).

4. F. E. Paige, W Production in pp Colliders, BNL preprint (October 1979).

5. A. D. Martin, Production Z and W Bosons at the pp Colliders. This conference.

6. G. Bauer et al., Conceptual Design of a Forward Detector for the $\bar{p}$p Collider, Fermilab CDF-64 (1980).

7. M. Atac, Saturated Avalanche Calorimetry. This conference.

8. M. Dechantsreiter et al., How to Expose t-quarks Hidden in $\bar{p}$p Collisions, Wisconsin DOE-ER/00881-202 (1981).

SMALL-ANGLE PHYSICS AT ISABELLE[*]

S.H. Aronson
Brookhaven National Laboratory

INTRODUCTION

ISABELLE will be commissioned a few years after the $\bar{p}p$ colliders, whose plans and first results have been presented here. A look at the design goals for ISABELLE (Table I) reveals that the two salient features offered in compensation for the later turn-on are high luminosity and (2×10^5-10^6 mb^{-1}sec^{-1}) and the number of intersections available for physics (6).

Table I.   ISABELLE Design Parameters

Luminosity:	2×10^{32} - 1×10^{33} cm^{-2}sec^{-1}
Energy:	400 GeV per beam
Insertions:	Number: 6
	Length: $\pm$ 30 m

We have seen ample reconfirmation during this conference of the need for high luminosity. With expected Z° detection rates of in UA1,[1] it is clear that all but the most rudimentary features of the standard picture will remain obscure until ISABELLE-like luminosity is available. Some nonstandard models will be hard to distinguish from the standard one until high statistics can be accumulated above the masses of the standard vector bosons.

The availability of a relatively large number of intersections at ISABELLE means that there will be room for some highly specific setups which can capitalize on the high luminosity in high-precision or rare-process studies. This is the case in the forward direction, where ISABELLE can make room for two different approaches:

1.   Completion of the forward direction of large solid-angle general purpose detectors.

2.   Dedicated small-angle setups.

In this paper we discuss the present state of plans at ISABELLE to accommodate these two approaches. We touch on Experimental Area designs, conceptual designs for experiments, and a few topics in detector development. It should be kept in mind that as of this writing, there has not been a call for ISABELLE proposals; thus detailed plans have not yet been made.

[*]Work performed under the auspices of the U.S. Department of Energy

EXPERIMENTAL AREAS

Figure 1 shows the ISABELLE site plan with six experimental areas, numbered 2,4,6,8,10 and 12 for their clock-face positions. Table II lists the dimensions of the four halls (2,4,6,8) presently under construction. Areas 10 and 12 are to be designed and built after proposals are in hand.

Table II. Dimensions (In Meters And Tons)
Of The Four Experimental Areas So Far Designed

Area	Length	Width	Beam Height	Crane Hook Ht/ Capacity
2. Small Angle				
Central Hall	28	12	1.7	6.1/20
Forward Experimental Building	68	7.9	1.7	5.3*
"Stub"	91	2.4	1.0	2.0*
4. Open Area	57+	37+	2.2	--*
6. Wide Angle	16	32	4.3	10/2x20
8. Major Facility				
Central Hall	19	15	5.2	11/40
Forward Exp. Bldgs. (2)	16	9	3.3	6.6*
Assembly Building	19	19	5.2	11/40+14/7.5

*No crane initially - ceiling height given
+Pad dimensions given

CONCEPTUAL DESIGN OF FORWARD ANGLE DETECTORS AT ISABELLE

With regard to forward angle physics two of the existing halls merit more detailed discussion. Major Facility Hall 8 (Figure 2) is equipped with extensions to the central research hall designed to house large forward-angle additions to the central detector. Figure 3 shows a possible detector arrangement for the Major Facility Hall. Compensation magnets serve as momentum analyzers for fast forward particles.

Small Angle Hall 2 was designed specifically to house small angle or low p_T experiments of modest transverse dimensions but possibly of great length (see Figure 4). The length scale is conservative, being set by the requirements of threshold Cerenkov counters for particle identification. Table III lists experiments for which area 2 is a natural location. These are divided into high cross-section processes, which can be done early in ISABELLE's operation when luminosities are below design, and lower cross-section studies. The former can be compared to the corresponding

$\bar{p}p$ experiments at the SPS and Tevatron colliders; the latter can only be studied in detail at ISABELLE. Figure 5 shows a conceptual sketch of a forward multiparticle spectrometer which could be used in Area 2 to study the rare processes suggested in Table III.

Table III. Small Angle Experiments Possible in Experimental Area 2

I. Large Cross-Section Processes
    Low luminosity (i.e. early) experiments
    Inclusive processes
    Comparisons with $\bar{p}p$

     • Total Cross-section and Small Angle Elastic Scattering
        $R_{tot} + L \rightarrow \sigma_{tot}$

        $\left. \dfrac{d\sigma}{dt} \right|_{t \to o}$ $(0.01 \lesssim |t| \lesssim 0.1$ GeV^2

        C-N Interference $(0.001 \lesssim |t| \lessdot 0.01$ GeV^2 ρ_{tot}

     • Elastic Scattering
        $|t| \lesssim 0.5$ GeV^2:   s-dependence of the slope of forward
        peak
        $0.5 \lesssim |t| \lesssim 2$ GeV^2: s-dependence of the dip-peak
        structure

     • Diffractive and Charge Exchange Processes

     • Particle Production
        Single particle inclusive production
        s-depencence of $\langle n \rangle$, $\langle p_T \rangle$, y-distributions
        Correlations
        Multiparticle production

II. Small Cross-section Processes
    Close to ISABELLE design L required $(>10^{31})$
    Sophisticated (i.e. high-rate, selective, finely-segmented)
    detectors also required

     • Moderate-to-Large t Scattering
        At 400 GeV/c $|t|=10$ GeV$^2 \longleftrightarrow 7$ mrad
                                             t-dependence of $\dfrac{d\sigma}{dt}$
        $|t|=100$ GeV$^2 \longleftrightarrow 25$ mrad

     • Multiparticle Production
        Jet cross-section vs x, p_T
        Correlations within jets
        Glueballs
        Diffractive production of new flavors
          (forward lepton trigger)
        Centauro events, etc.

DETECTOR DEVELOPMENT

High luminosity, ISABELLE's strong suit, makes severe demands on detectors. Tracking and calorimetry devices will have to be fine-grained and capable of high rates. Particle identification devices must be capable of working at high energies and high multiplicities. All this is especially true for the forward angle components of ISABELLE detectors. We list here a few of the detector development schemes currently being pursued with ISABELLE in mind.

1. Forward calorimetry: Studies are underway[2] on the properties of proportional wire gas sampling calorimeters of high density. Prototypes with effective density equal to 90% the density of iron have been tested (see Figure 6). Good energy resolution has been obtained for electrons over a wide range of angles of incidence (see Figure 7); such a device could be incorporated in the pole tip or yoke of a central detector magnet.

2. Particle identification by transition radiation. This technique is enhanced by eliminating the track-associated energy loss (dE/dx) in the detector. Studies[3] with a longitudinal drift cell in which clusters above a threshold are counted, rather than total charge accumulated, appear to demonstrate the feasibility of π/K separation down to $\gamma \lesssim 10^3$ (see Figure 8).

3. Particle identification by dE/dx. This method is enhanced by eliminating delta-ray-associated energy deposits. In a technique[4] complementary to B above, the signal from a longitudinal drift cell is digitized in time bins. In this way the highly localized delta-ray energy can be eliminated, improving the discrimination between particle types via the relativistic rise of dE/dx.

4. Semiconductor detector arrays. These devices offer the prospect of very small element size and spatial resolution as a way of coping with the high energies and track densities in the forward regions.[5] At present, studies are being done with 1-dimensional "microstrip" detectors. Figure 9 envisions a very high resolution 2-dimensional detector array with onboard logic. When such devices become available some of our more ambitious plans for forward collider physics will begin to look more realistic. In addition, more compact central detectors could be designed, yielding possible cost savings by reducing field volume and calorimeter area.

REFERENCES

1. A. Kernan, these proceedings.
2. T. Ludlam, et al., IEEE Trans. Nucl. Sci., NS-28, 517 (1981).
3. T. Ludlam, et al., "Particle Identification by Electron Cluster Detection of Transition Radiation Photons", CERN-EPL/80-156, (1980).
4. T. Ludlam, et al., "Relativistic Rise Measurements With Very Fine Sampling Intervals", BNL 28607 (1981).
5. T. Ludlam, "Future Prospects for Semiconductor Detectors in High Energy Physics", BNL 30815, (1981).

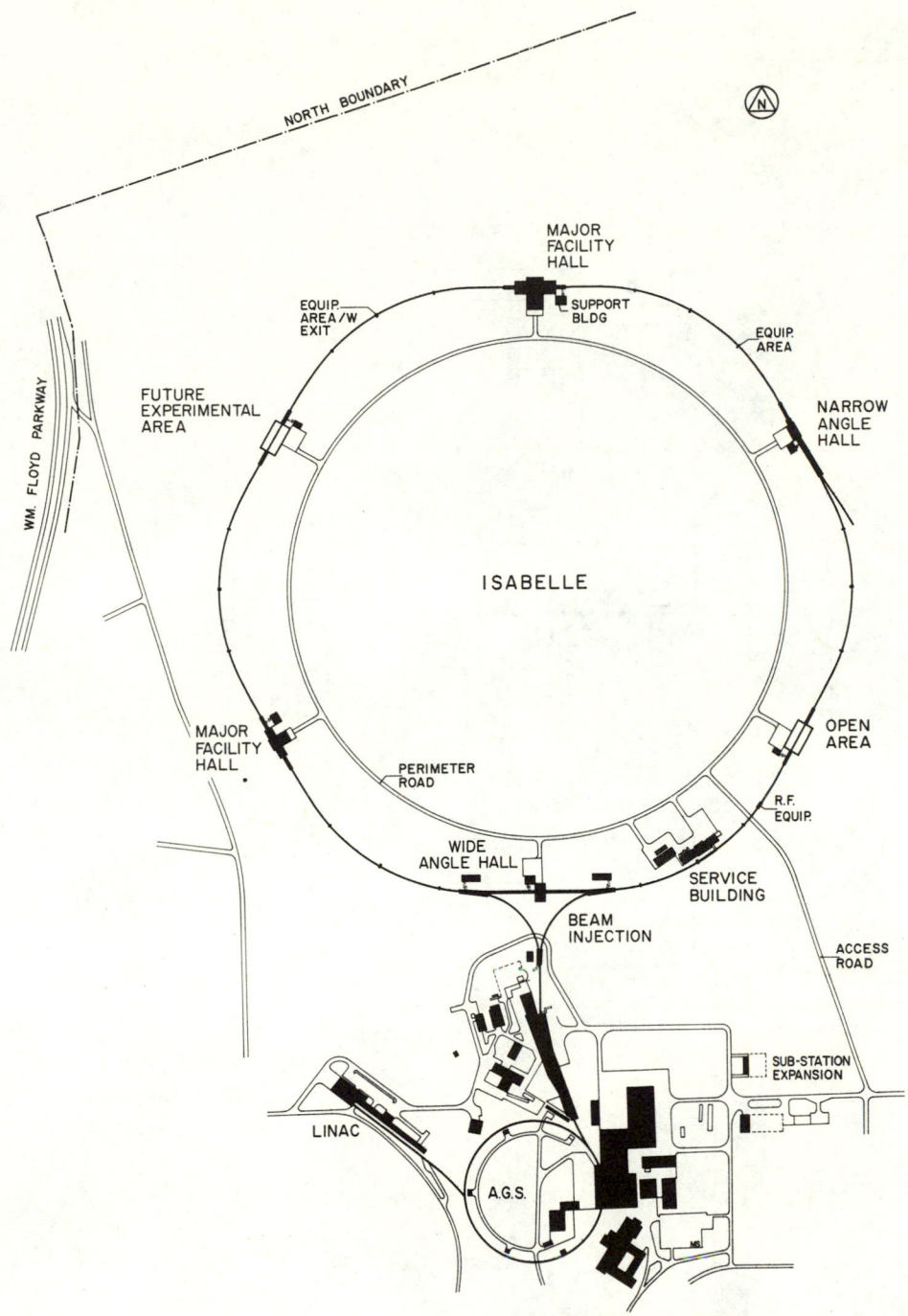

Fig. 1.   ISABELLE general site plan.

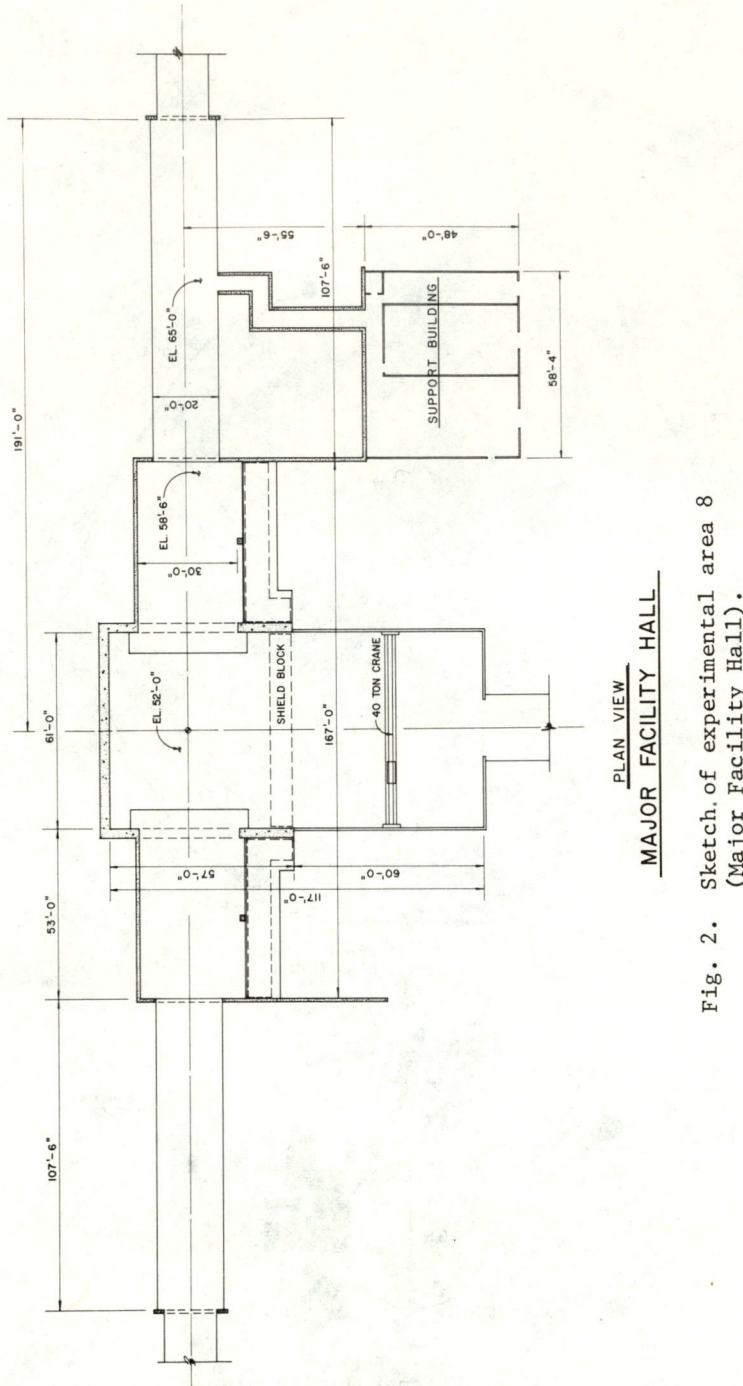

PLAN VIEW

MAJOR FACILITY HALL

Fig. 2. Sketch of experimental area 8
(Major Facility Hall).

277

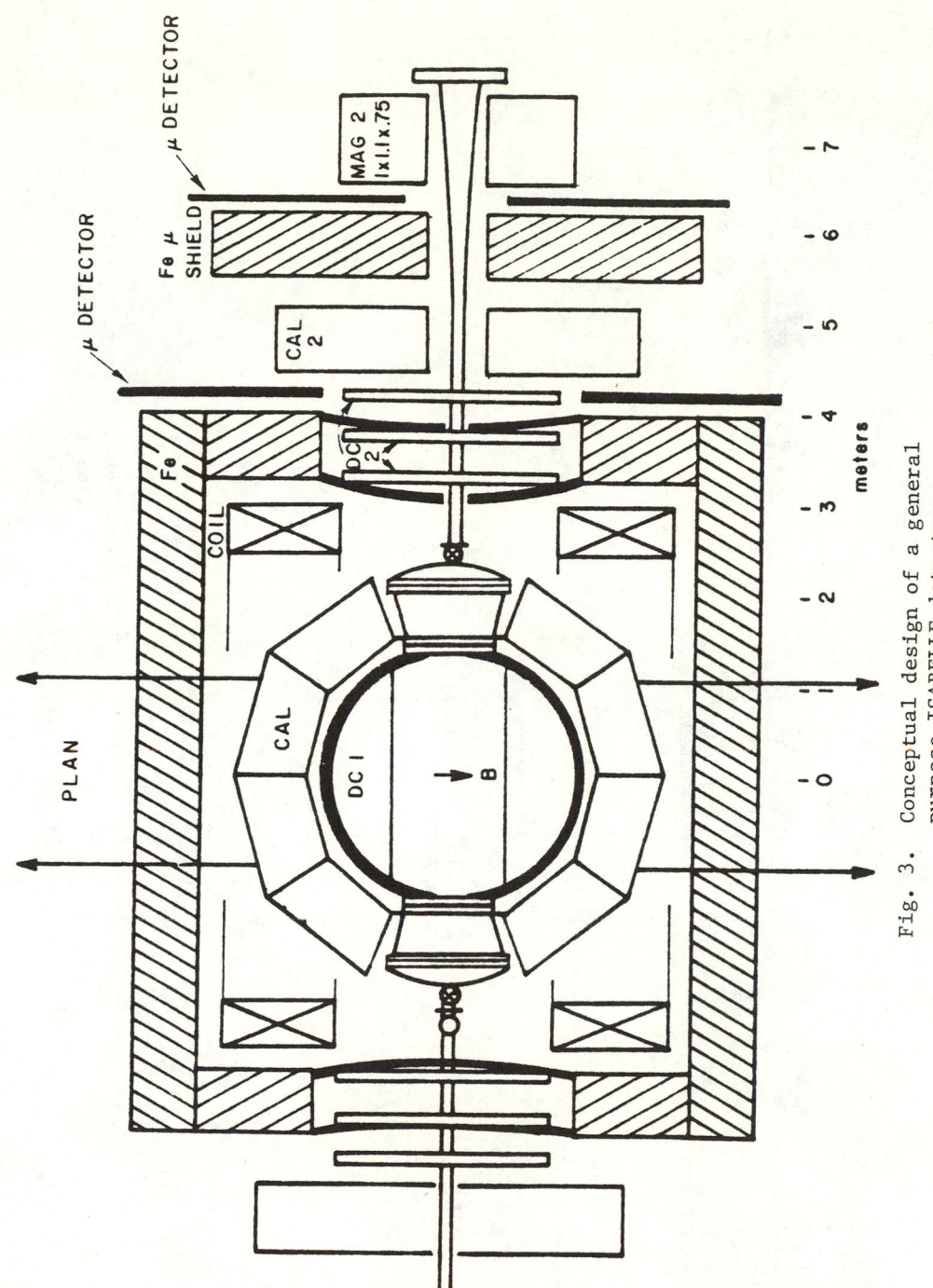

Fig. 3. Conceptual design of a general purpose ISABELLE detector.

278

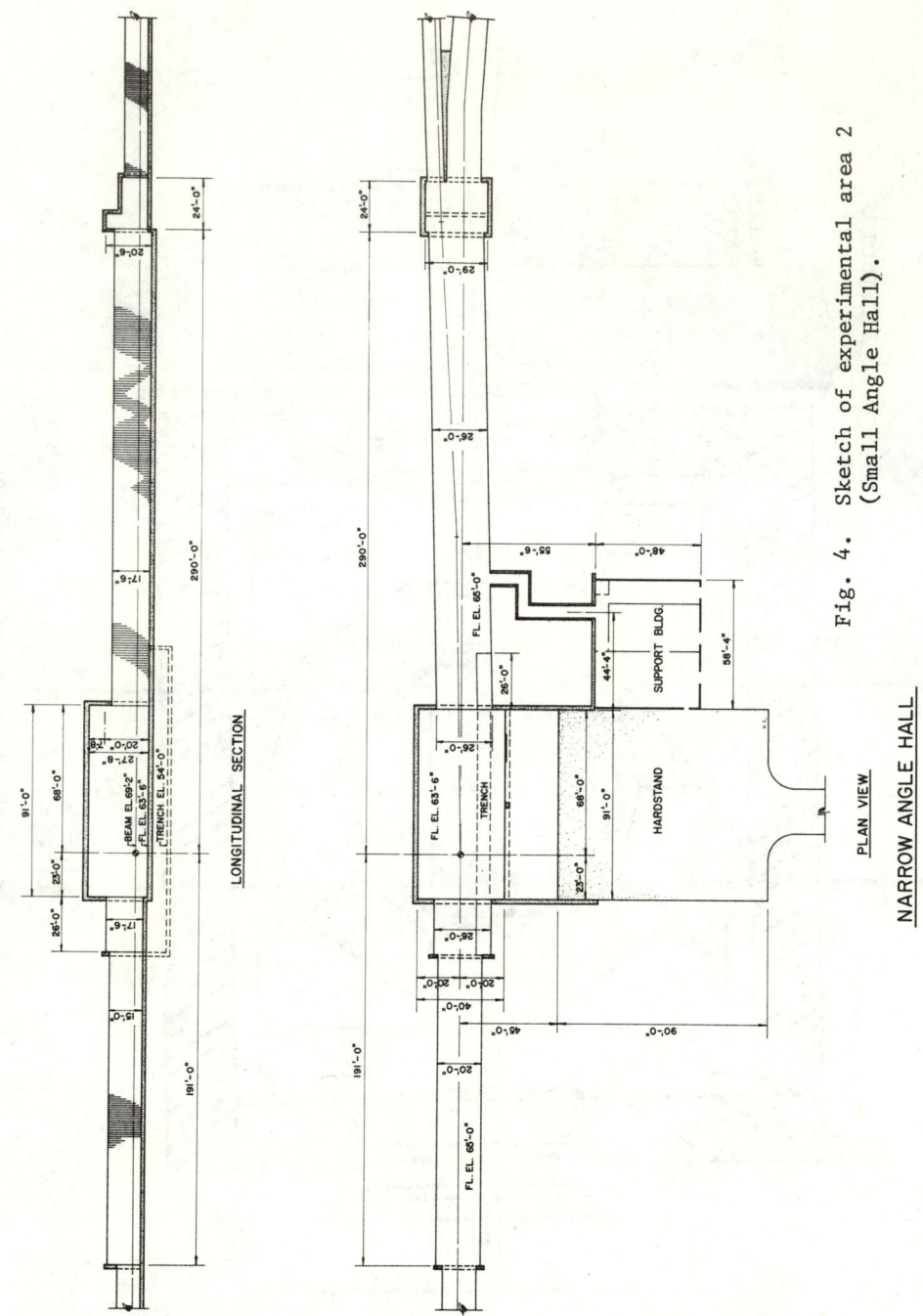

Fig. 4. Sketch of experimental area 2 (Small Angle Hall).

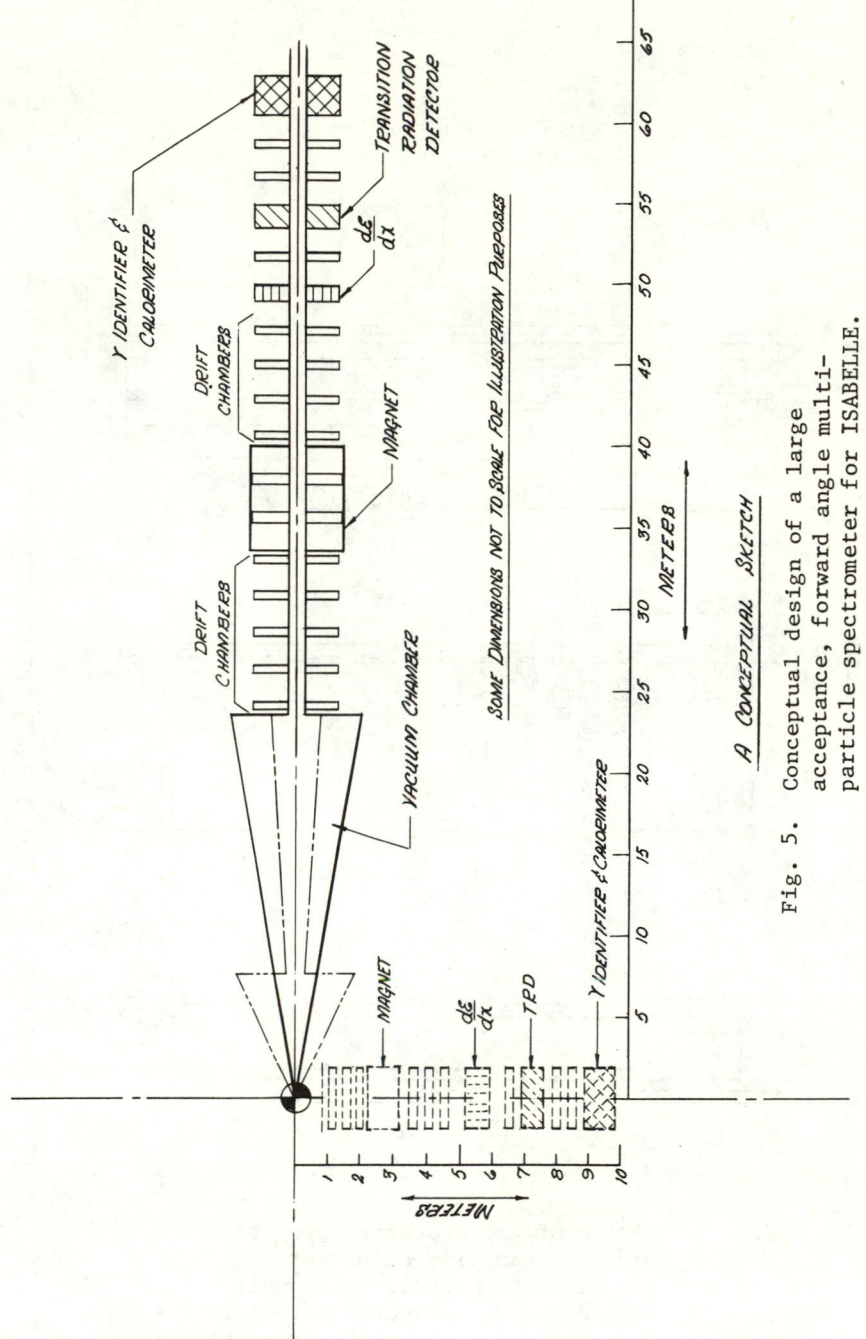

Fig. 5. Conceptual design of a large
acceptance, forward angle multiparticle spectrometer for ISABELLE.

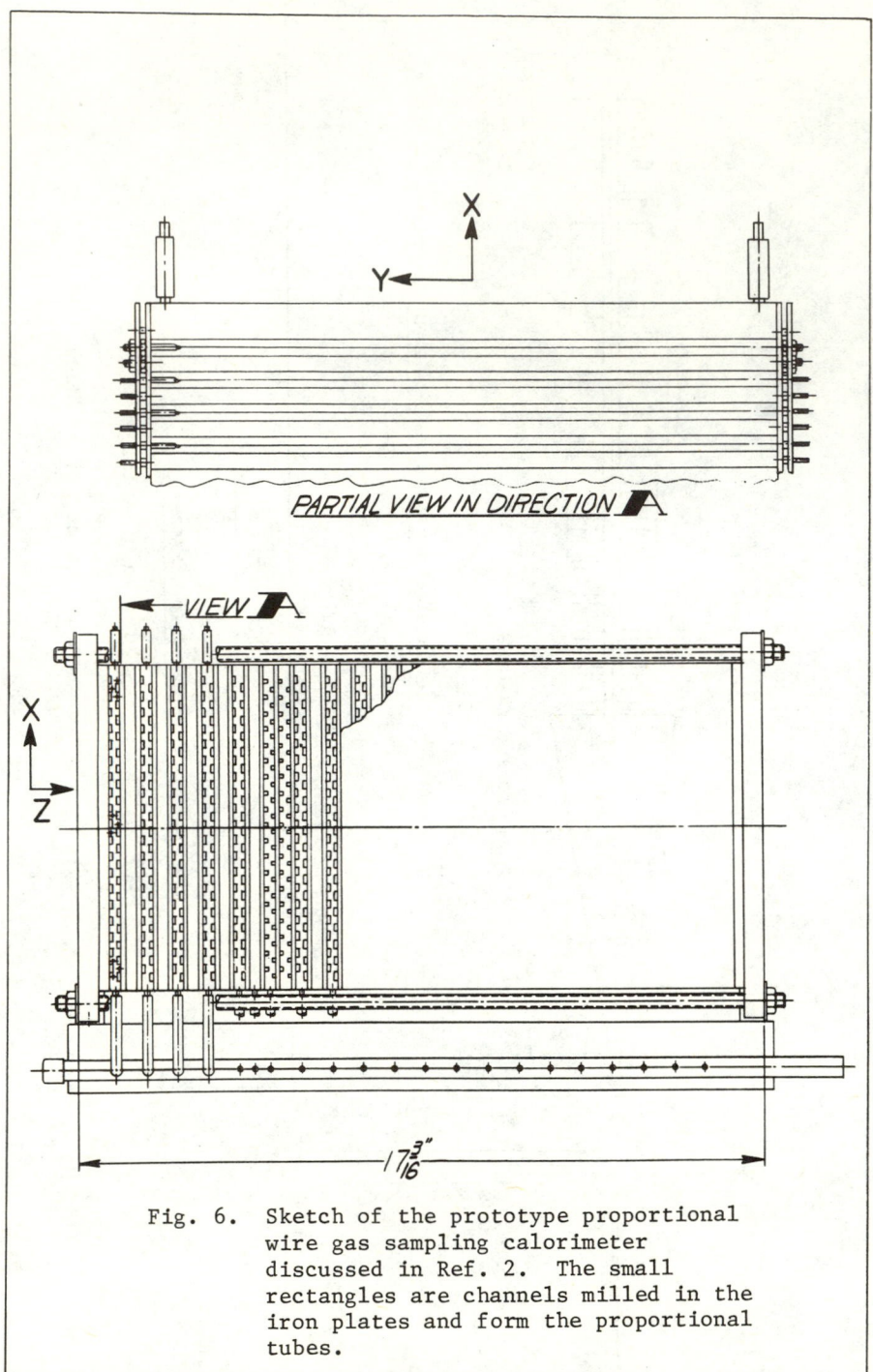

Fig. 6. Sketch of the prototype proportional wire gas sampling calorimeter discussed in Ref. 2. The small rectangles are channels milled in the iron plates and form the proportional tubes.

RESOLUTION VS BEAM ENERGY AND ANGLE

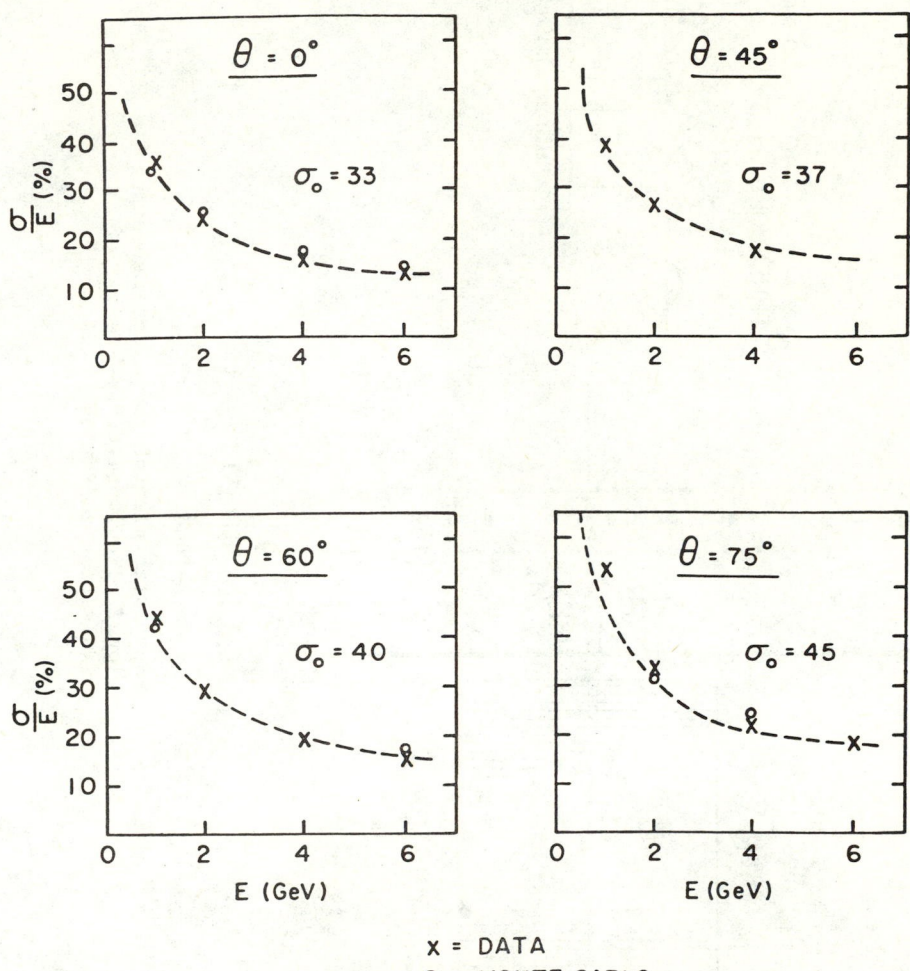

x = DATA
O = MONTE CARLO
$\sigma\,(\%) = \sigma_0 \,/\sqrt{E}$

Fig. 7. Electron energy resolution of the calorimeter for various energies and angles of incidence.

282

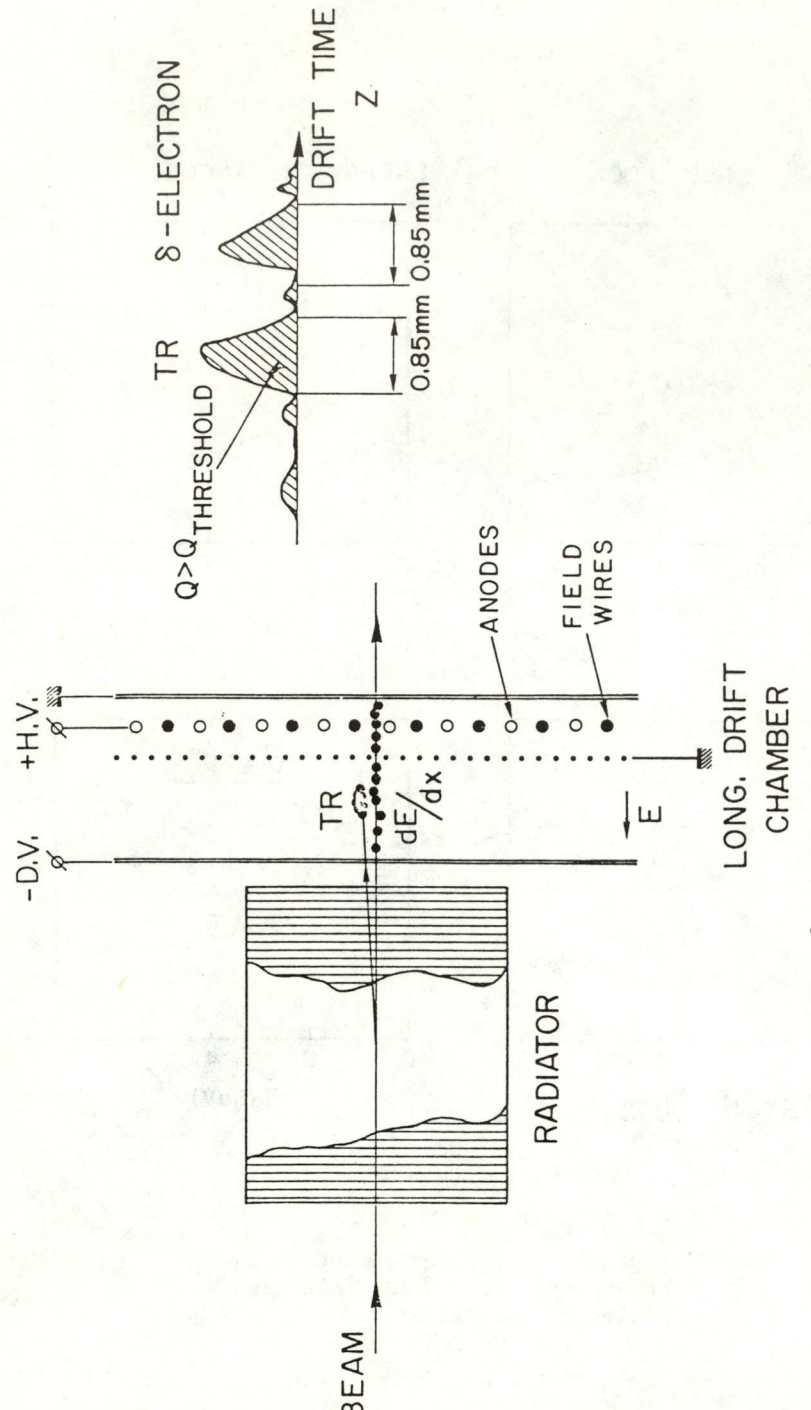

Fig. 8. Schematic view of the cluster counting longitudinal drift measurement of transition radiation.

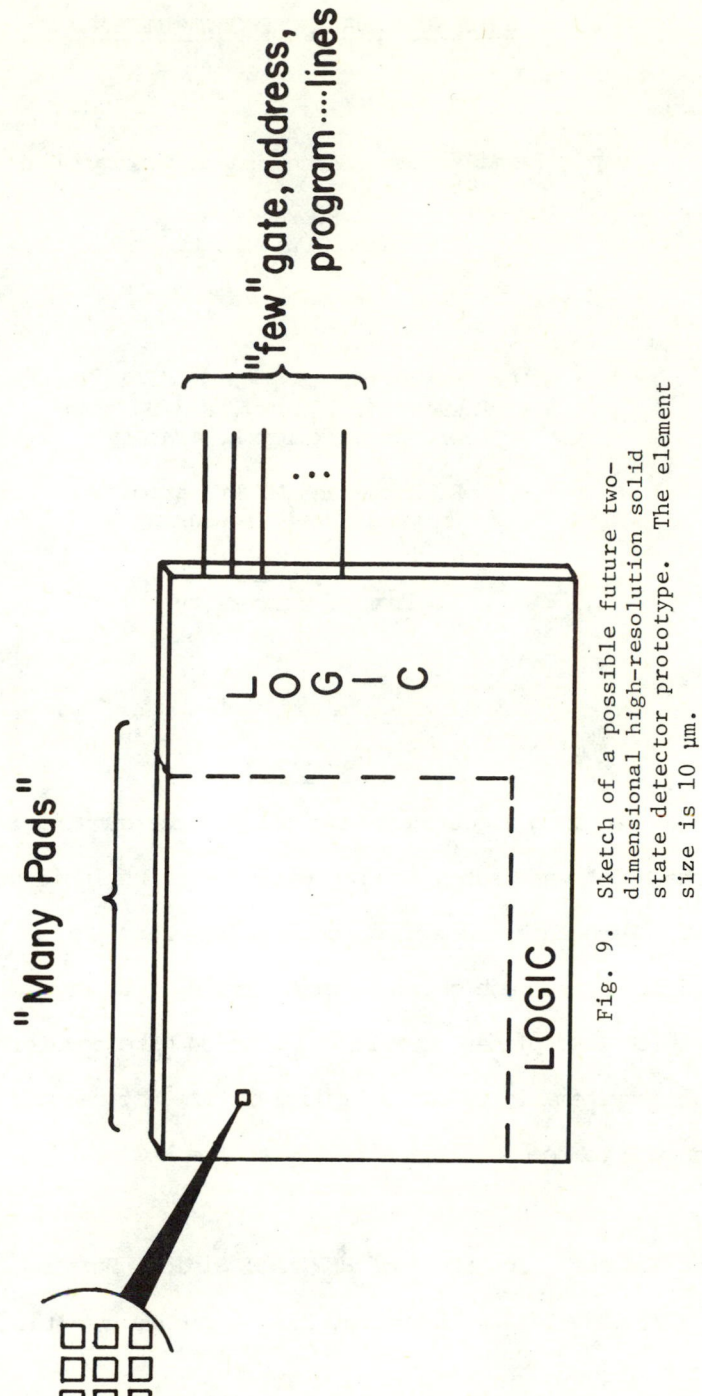

Fig. 9. Sketch of a possible future two-dimensional high-resolution solid state detector prototype. The element size is 10 μm.

SATURATED AVALANCHE CALORIMETER

M. Atac
Fermi National Accelerator Laboratory

S. Kim
Tsukuba University

M. Mishina
KEK

W. Chinowsky, R. Ely, M. Gold, J. Kadyk
P. Rowson, K. Shinsky, and Y. Wong[†]
Lawrence Berkeley Laboratory

R. Morse and M. Procario
University of Wisconsin

T. Schaad
Harvard University

Abstract

A gas sampling electromagnetic calorimeter running in a "Saturated Avalanche Mode" was tested at SLAC with positrons incident at energy up to 17.5 GeV. With this new method, good energy resolution, 16 percent/$\sqrt{E}$, and good linearity were obtained with arrays of thirty-four 0.5 radiation length thick lead plates interleaved with 34 wire counters. There was no measurable systematic effect. Amplifiers are not needed; the signals are large enough to be connected directly to the ADC's.

[†]Present address: Institute of HEP, Ac. Sinica, Beijing, P. R. China

Introduction

Gas sampling calorimeters operating in a proportional mode have been tested and used by several groups[1-10] but, with one reported exception[6], their energy resolution has been much inferior to that achieved with calorimeters that use plastic scintillator counters. Improved resolution has been demonstrated in a calorimeter operated in the Geiger mode[11], and may be expected also with the limited streamer[12, 13] mode. Those devices are intrinsically different from proportional counter energy sampling calorimeters. The former, in effect, use the number of tracks in the shower, while the latter use the magnitude of total collected charge as measures of the energy deposited in the gas. In this paper, we report results of tests of gas sampling calorimeters run in neither of these modes, but in an intermediate, partially saturated mode. Their resolution is comparable to that of plastic scintillator calorimeters.

These tests were made as part of the program to develop calorimeter modules for the Collider detector facility[14], as apparatus to detect products of $\bar{p}p$ interactions at the 2 TeV colliding beams machine now under construction at Fermilab. The present design (Fig. 1) calls for gas sampling electromagnetic and hadronic calorimetry in the forward and backward angular regions. Respectably small granularity will be achieved with tower structures of cathode readout pads.

<u>Experimental Arrangements</u>

Two detectors studied were a MAC prototype[6] and brass tube calorimeter[10] (BTC) which were tested previously in proportional mode at SLAC and at Fermilab, respectively. Thus, only limited details of construction will be given here.

The MAC prototype was composed of 34 lead plates of 2.8 mm thickness and 34 planes of 50 μm diameter anode wires enclosed in 9.5 mm x 9.5 mm cells which are separated by 1.5 mm thick aluminum ribs, a 17.8 radiation length shower detector. Fig. 2 shows the arrangement and the cell structure. Both detectors were individually placed in aluminum containers which could be evacuated or pressurized for studying pressure effects. The anode wires of each plane were connected to a common strip, and seven such planes were further grouped together, resulting in five groups to be read out. Most of the results that will be presented in this paper were obtained from the total sum of these five groups. Results on the longitudinal development in the shower will be reported later.

The counter gas was a mixture of 49.3 percent Argon, 49.3 percent ethane, and 1.4 percent ethyl alcohol. Negative high voltage was applied to the cathode tubes. Distributed high voltage capacitors totalling 0.25 μf were the charge storage elements. As indicated in the figure, there was no need for amplifiers between the wires and the ADC's. Indeed, it was necessary to attenuate the large signals obtained between 2 db and 30 db depending on the high voltage and gas pressure. Forty meters of RG58 coaxial cables carried the signals to the LeCroy 2249W ADC's. The ADC pedestals were determined with a linear extrapolation of the measured variation of pulse height

The wires of the BTC were connected together longitudinally, as shown in Fig. 3, and further grouped as indicated above and in the figure. The BTC was made of 0.36 mm wall thickness, 6.3 mm x 11.3 mm cross section brass tubes containing 50 μm diameter anode wires. Forty 2-mm thick lead plates were between the wire planes to give a total of 16.5 radiation lengths.

A LSI-11 computer system with a SLAC program package "ATROPOS" was used for data taking and on-line display and monitoring.

Beam Parameters

The detectors were tested in the 19° beam of the Stanford Linear Accelerator which provided positrons of 17.5 GeV maximum energy. SLAC ran in the SLED mode during the entire tests with a bunch length of about 20 nsec, FWHM 8 nsec, and 10 bunches per second. About 95 percent of the beam at the detector was within the 2 mm x 2 mm area of the beam defining counter. The intensity was, on the average, between 1/10 and 10 positrons per bunch. The momentum spread of the beam, $\Delta p/p$ was less than ±0.25 percent rms.

Experimental Results

Most of the data presented here were taken with the MAC prototype calorimeter. Gain and resolution were measured at various settings of gas pressure and applied voltage with positrons incident at selected energies in the range 1.5 GeV–17.5 GeV available in the SLAC test beam. A representative sample of typical results will be shown.

For 10 GeV incident positrons, the total pulse height distribution is shown in Fig. 4 together with a Gaussian fit to the data. Only that portion of the distribution within $\pm 2\sigma$ of the mean were used in the fitting procedure. The shape of the distribution, typical of all, is well represented by the Gaussian function.

With fixed gas pressure, the resolution σ/E varies with high voltage as shown in Fig. 5. As the voltage increases from 2100 V, the resolution slowly decreases to a shallow minimum at $\sim$ 2250 V and then slowly increases.

Figs. 6a and 6b present the calorimeter output as a function of incident positron energy. Both at 0 psig and 5 psig there is no departure from linearity at energies up to 17.5 GeV. For these runs, the counters were run at 2300 V and 2550 V, respectively.

Fig. 7 shows the total pulse height as a function of high voltage for the pressures of 0 psig and 3 psig. Both show approximately exponential rise in gain with increasing voltage. The higher pressure curve has some indication of an inflection point near the middle of the range.

Higher energy response of the detector was simulated by using multiple positrons in a single rf bucket. This is a fair simulation since the positive ions do not move appreciably from where they were produced during the beam spill. Fig. 8 shows the detector response to multiple positrons of 17.5 GeV. It shows that as many as 11 simultaneous positrons the energy resolution of the detector is sufficiently good to resolve them with clear minima between the peaks of the pulse height distributions for the corresponding numbers of positrons. In fact, this is a Poisson distribution for n = 4.5. The oscilloscope trace reproduced in Fig. 9 shows some pulses for single and double positrons. The pulse rise time is about 10 nsec, and the decay time is almost 800 nsec. The decay time is long because the whole detector whose capacitance exceeds 10 nF was connected to a single 50 Ω coaxial cable. The pulse height for singles is $\sim$ 75 mV and is $\sim$ 150 mV for doubles. These pulses can be used for a prompt multiplicity trigger with a time jitter of few nanoseconds. That the pulse height for the multiple positrons deviate in a smooth way from linear behavior for more than 2 positron (35 GeV) shower is seen in Figs. 10a and b. The linearity is much better at 8 psig. An expanded view of the pulse height distribution for 10 GeV positrons is shown in Fig. 11. It dramatically shows the symmetric, Gaussian-like shapes with clean valleys between the multiple-hit peaks. The energy resolution as a function of equivalent energy deposits of multiple 17.5 GeV positrons is shown in Fig. 12 after correction for the non-linear response.

The energy resolution as a function of energy for single incident positrons is shown in Fig. 13. σ/E shows the usual $E^{-1/2}$ dependence with a constant factor of 16.2 percent as indicated in Fig. 14. The shape of the dependence of resolution on energy indicates no systematic term since it extrapolates to the origin. This is, perhaps, because there is no active device (amplifier, pulse shaper, etc.) between the detector and the ADC, and small variations among individual wire gains average out over the detector.

The detector was rotated to make angles to the beam axis of as much as 23°. With 17.5 GeV positrons incident, the results of Fig. 15 were obtained. It is seen that the pulse height increases by a small amount (maximum 2.3 percent), and the σ/E decreases slightly with increasing angle. This improvement may be due to a better containment of energy in the effective thickness of the angled calorimeter.

Similar results were obtained from the BTC. It was run only above atmospheric pressure, 6 psig, because of the small distance, 3.5 mm, from the anode wire to the cathode tube wall. Fig. 16 shows that the energy resolution is almost 17 percent/$\sqrt{E}$ and independent of high voltage, in contrast to the behavior of the MAC prototype. The reason for the differences between the two may be the different cell shapes. It is curious that poorer resolution was found with the thinner lead sampling sheets. When this detector was tested at Fermilab in the proportional mode, the resolution was measured to be 22 percent/$\sqrt{E}$.

Saturated Avalanche Mode

We have investigated the ionization region[12] between the proportional region and the self quenching streamer region in detail using a 9.5 mm x 9.5 mm tube having a 50 µm wire, a replica of one cell of the prototype MAC detector, in order to understand the improved energy resolution of the apparatus relative to calorimeters running in the proportional mode.

A small fraction of the wire pulse was amplified and used to form the ADC trigger, as shown in Fig. 17. A LeCroy 2285 ADC system was used for measuring the charge. The gain of the ADC was 20 counts per picocoulomb. An Fe^{55} x-ray source was used to measure the wire gain as a function of high voltage. As seen in Fig. 19 a and b, the resolution is insufficient to separate the 5.9 keV x-ray line and 2.9 keV argon escape line when the gas gain, at 2300 V, is in the region of limited proportionality. The gain here was $\sim 5 \times 10^4$. The 2.9 keV line is hidden in the left side of the asymmetric pulse height distribution. Fig. 20 shows the gain as a function of the high voltage. The rate of growth of the avalanche is seen to decrease continuously as the high voltage increases above 2200 V until the streamer threshold is reached. Then the gain increases very little to the point of full streamer operation around 2650 V.

The distribution of pulse heights recorded by passage of minimum ionization tracks was also investigated in this voltage region using a Sr^{90} β-source. A telescope made from a pair of small thin scintillation counters provided a gate pulse for the ADC's. The discriminator thresholds were set to accept mainly the minimum ionizing β's. Fig. 20a shows the pulse height distribution obtained at 2300 V. This histogram shows that the distribution is almost symmetric with a small tail. The distribution made by the β's is not like a typical Landau distribution obtained in a gas gap of 9.5 mm thickness at atmospheric pressure. The tail is greatly suppressed. An expanded view of the histogram of Figs 20a is shown in Fig. 20b. It has a ratio of σ to mean of 34 percent. Landau fluctuations clearly have been reduced, an indication that the greater the concentration of primary ionization, the more saturation (less gain) occurs as has been observed earlier[15].

From the data of Fig. 18, we find a ratio of mean pulse heights produced by the two photons of ∿ 1.4, rather than the ∿ 2.0 ratio of energies. Similar conclusions about the departure from strict linear, proportional response follows from comparison of the signals from the β and x-ray sources. Those observations and the suppression of the Landau tail indicate partial saturation of the avalanche charge at the collecting wire. Thus, the resolution is improved compared to that obtained when the counters operate in the proportional mode. We find a resolution somewhat smaller than, but not really inconsistent with that predicted by Fischer[16], which is based on a calculation of the response without the effect of Landau fluctuations. Deterioration in resolution at voltages much higher than 2400 V may be caused by fluctuations in gain where streamer and saturated avalanche modes overlap (see Fig. 19). Depending on the amount of ionization deposited locally on the wire, the gain may be low (saturated avalanche) or more than an order of magnitude higher (streamer).

Acknowledgments

The authors express their appreciation to Drs. R. Coombes, R. Prepost, and D. M. Ritson for providing the MAC prototype; to Drs. R. Schwitters and A. Tollestrup for support; to Dr. R. Gearhart and the SLAC operating crew for assisting and supporting the runs; to P. Clancy and S. Mackenzie for help with the data acquisition system; and to M. Hrycyk for modifying the BTC.

References

Ref. 1   W. Murzin, Progr. Element. Part. Cosmic Ray Phys. (1967) 245.

Ref. 2   M. E. Nordberg, Jr., Cornell Univ. Report, CLNS 138 (1971).

Ref. 3   T. Kotsura et al., Nucl. Instr. and Meth. 105 (1972) 245.

Ref. 4   M. Atac, IEEE Trans. on Nucl. Sci., Vol. NS-28, No. 1, Feb. 1981.

Ref. 5   M. Atac et al., IEEE Trans. on Nucl. Sci., Vol. NS-28, No. 1, Feb. 1981.

Ref. 6   R. L. Anderson et al., IEEE Trans. on Nucl. Sci., Vol. NS-25 (1978) 340.

Ref. 7   C. Bosio et al., Nucl. Instr. and Meth. 157 (1978) 35.

Ref. 8   P. Skubic et al., IEEE Trans. on Nucl. Sci., Vol. NS-28, No. 1, Feb. 1981.

Ref. 9   H. Tyco et al., UCLA Report.

Ref. 10   M. Mishina et al., IEEE Trans. on Nucl. Sci. (Feb. 1982).

Ref. 11   W. Carithers et al., private communication; will be published in Nucl. Instr. and Meth.

Ref. 12   M. Atac et al., Fermilab Report FN-337 (1981), and Proc. of INS International Symp. on Nucl. Radiation Detectors (March 1981), Tokyo.

Ref. 13   M. Jonker et al., Physica Scripta Vol. 23, 677-679, 1981.

Ref. 14   Fermlab $\bar{p}p$ Colliding Detector Proposal (1979).

Ref. 15   H. Frehse et al., Nucl. Instr. and Meth. 156 (1978) 87.

Ref. 16   G. Fischer, Nucl. Instr. and Meth. 156 (1978) 81.

294

Figure Captions

Fig. 1	A cross section view of the Collider Detector Facility at Fermilab.
Fig. 2	The experimental configuration of the MAC electromagnetic calorimeter.
Fig. 3	The experimental configuration of the brass tube electromagnetic calorimeter.
Fig. 4	A typical pulse height distribution and Gaussian fitted points for obtaining σ and mean values using 2σ fit.
Fig. 5	σ/E versus high voltage for 10 GeV positrons at 0 psig.
Fig. 6a and b	The total pulse height response of the calorimeter as function of the e^+ energy for 0 psig and 5 psig, respectively. The linearity is excellent for both pressures.
Fig. 7	The total pulse height as a function of the high voltage for pressures of 0 psig and 3 psig.
Fig. 8	The response of the detector to simultaneous multiple positrons of 17.5 GeV.
Fig. 9	The oscilloscope picture of some single and double 17.5 GeV positron pulses.
Fig. 10a and b	The pulse heights as a function of simultaneous 17.5 GeV multiple positrons for 0 psig and 8 psig.
Fig. 11	Pulse height distributions for 10 GeV multiple positrons.
Fig. 12	$\sigma/\sqrt{E}$ versus simultaneous multiple 17.5 GeV positrons after correction for non-linear response.
Fig. 13	σ/E versus positron energy.
Fig. 14	σ/E versus $E^{-1/2}$ indicating no systematic effects.
Fig. 15	Total pulse height and σ/E versus incident beam angle for 17.5 GeV positrons.
Fig. 16	$\sigma/\sqrt{E}$ versus the high voltage for the brass tube calorimeter.
Fig. 17	The circuit diagram for investigating the saturated avalanche region.

Fig. 18   Pulse height distributions for the 5.9 x-rays from Fe^{55}.
                 Fig. 18a shows the ADC distribution without amplifier.
                 Note the 3 keV argon escape line is not visible in the
                 saturated avalanche region because of poor proportion-
                 ality. Fig. 18b shows the amplified distribution where
                 the escape line is just visible because of the better
                 resolution at high pulse heights.

Fig. 19   The model tube gain as a function of the high voltage in
                 the saturated avalanche region using the ADC without
                 amplifier.

Fig. 20a and b   The pulse height distribution for minimum ionizing tracks
                 in the saturated avalanche region showing almost symmetric
                 distribution with very small Landau tail. Fig. 20b is
                 the expanded detail of the Fig. 20a.

296

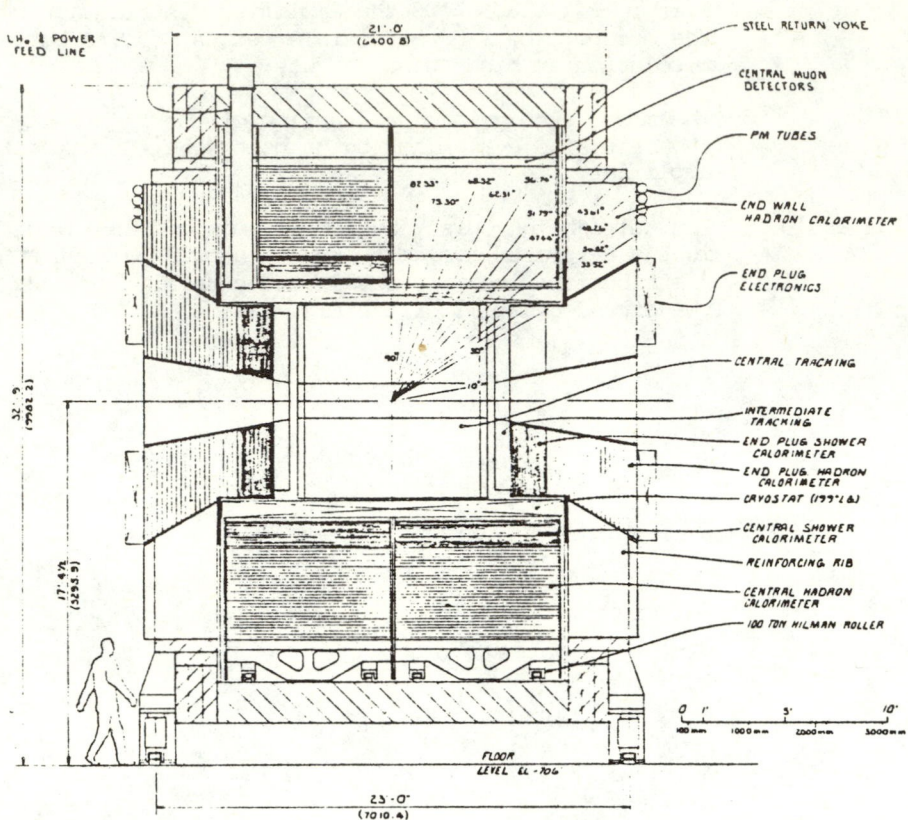

FIG. 1

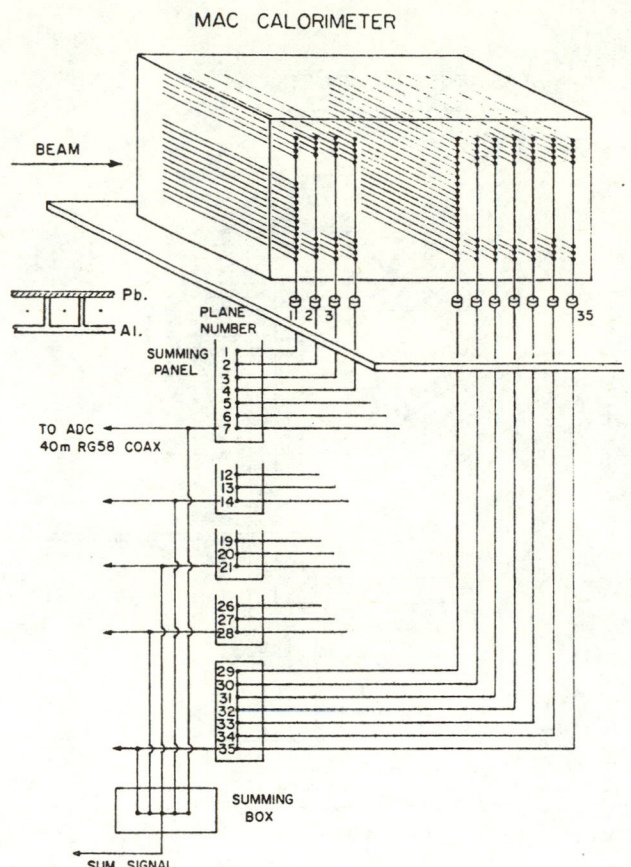

FIG. 2

298

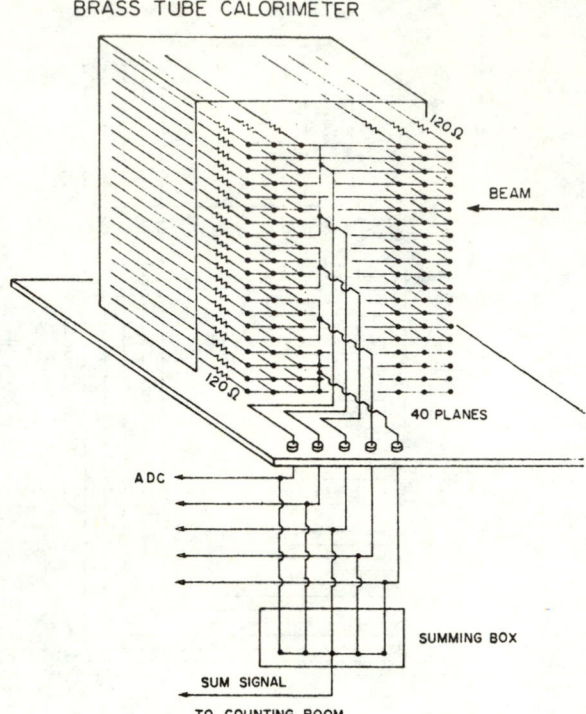

BRASS TUBE CALORIMETER

FIG. 3

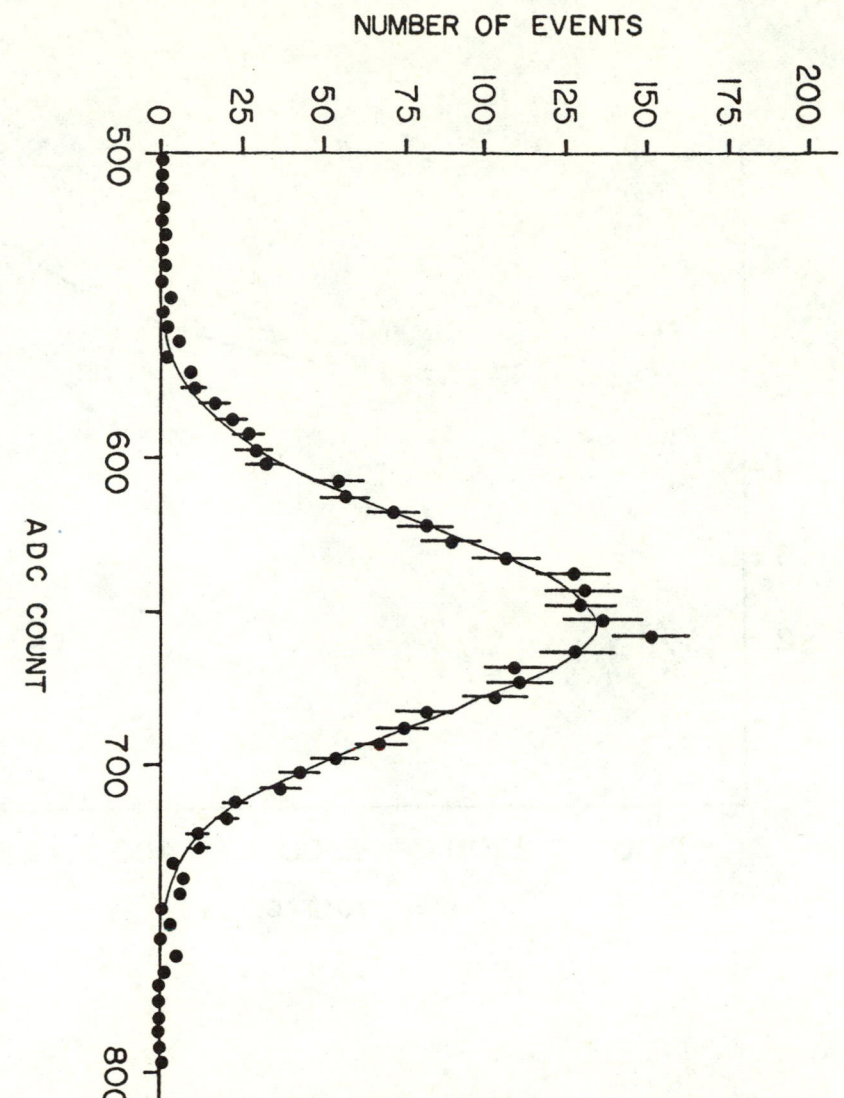

FIG. 4

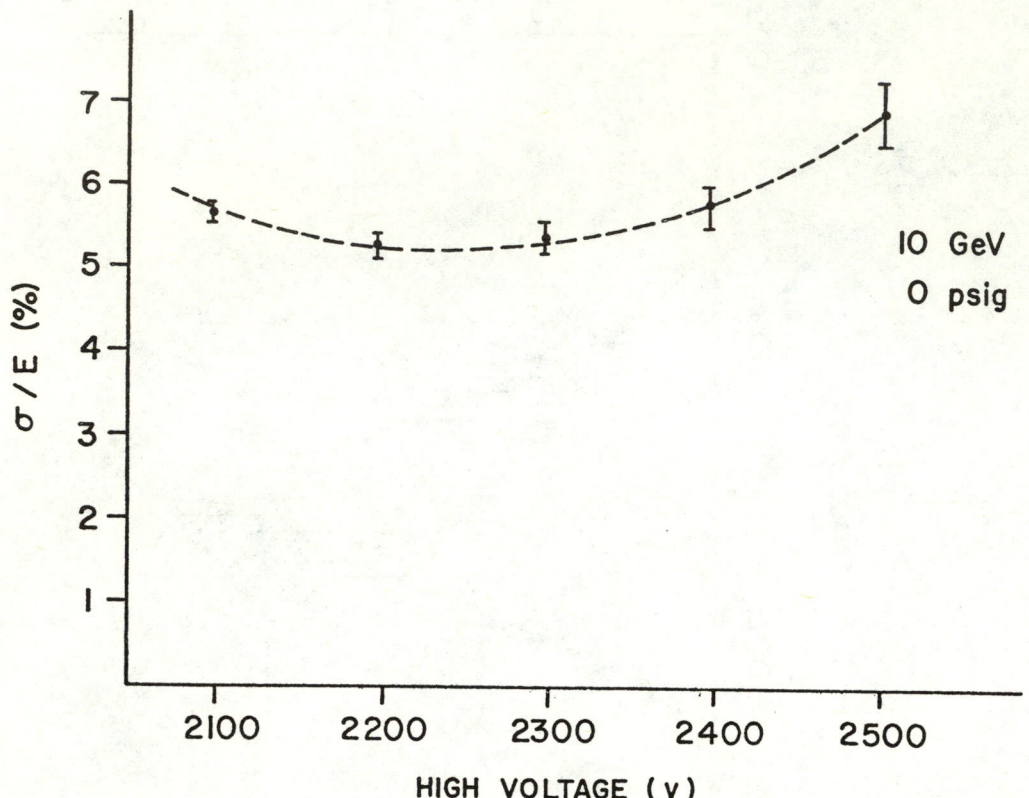

FIG. 5

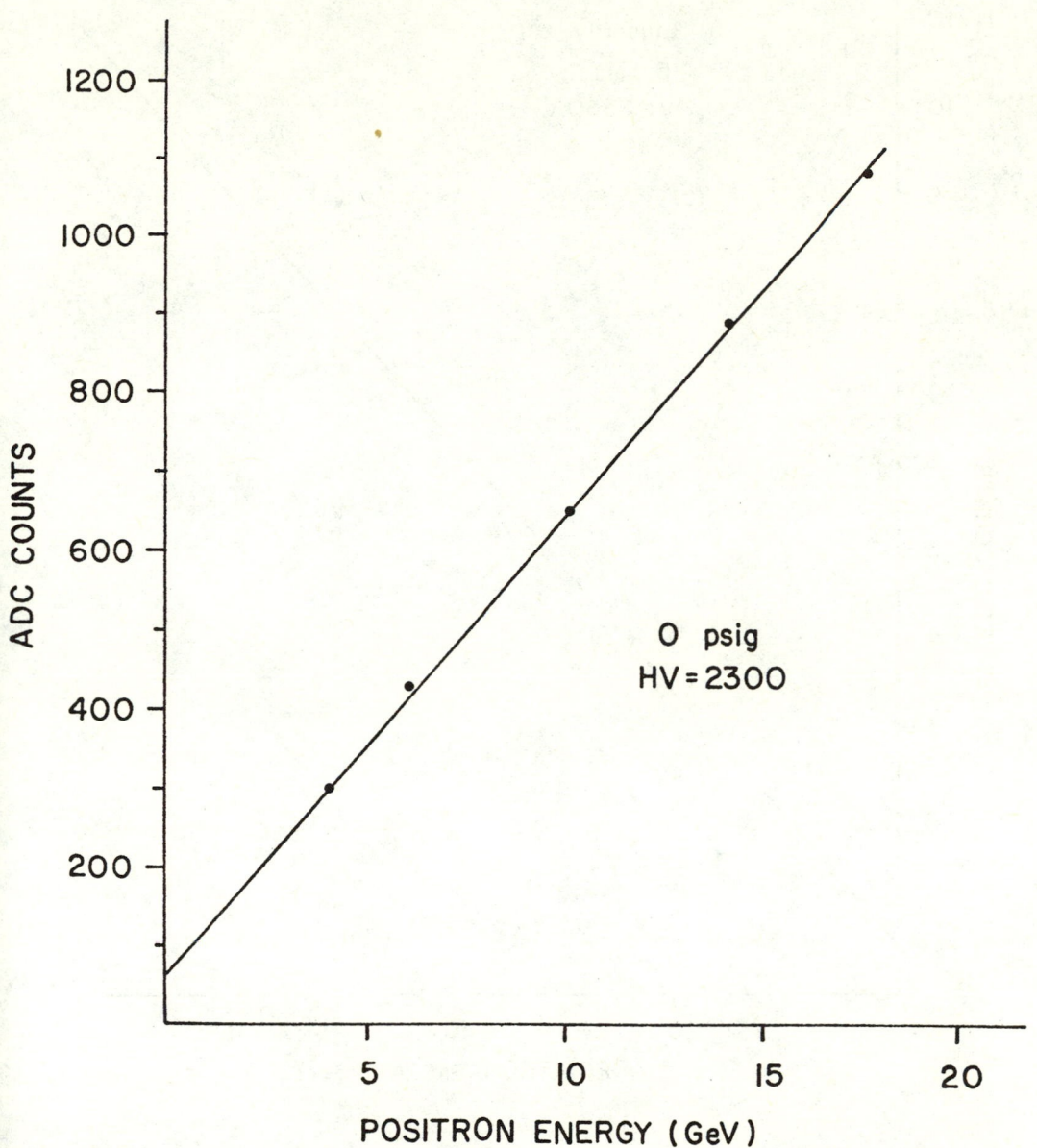

FIG. 6a

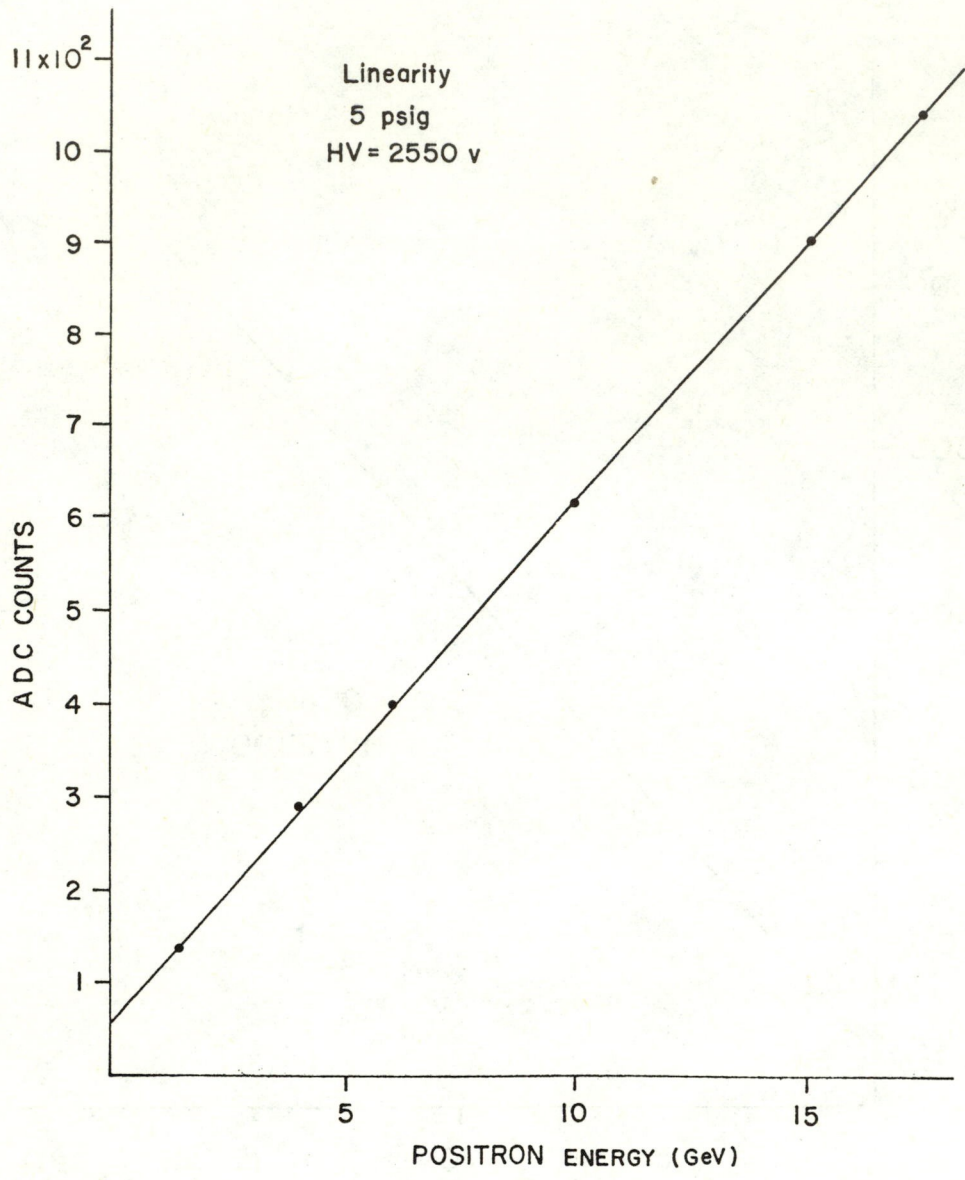

FIG. 6b

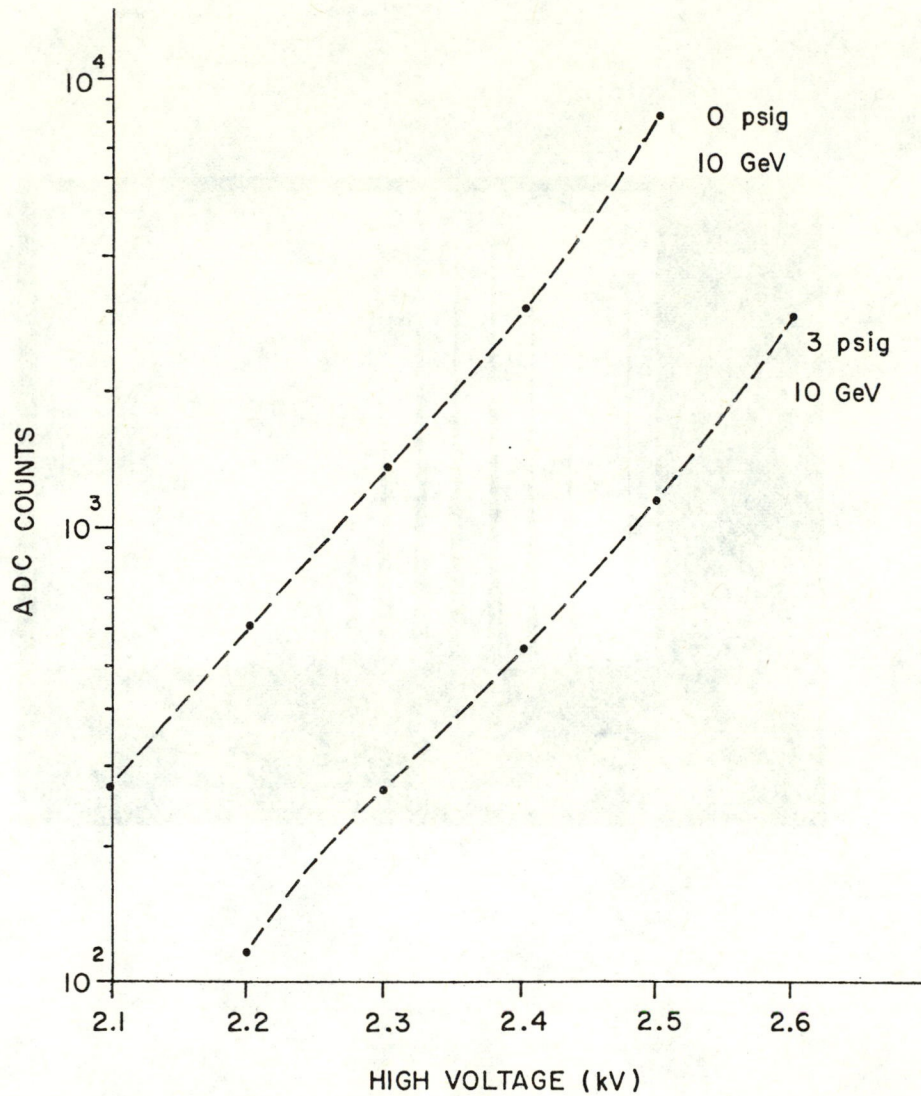

FIG. 7

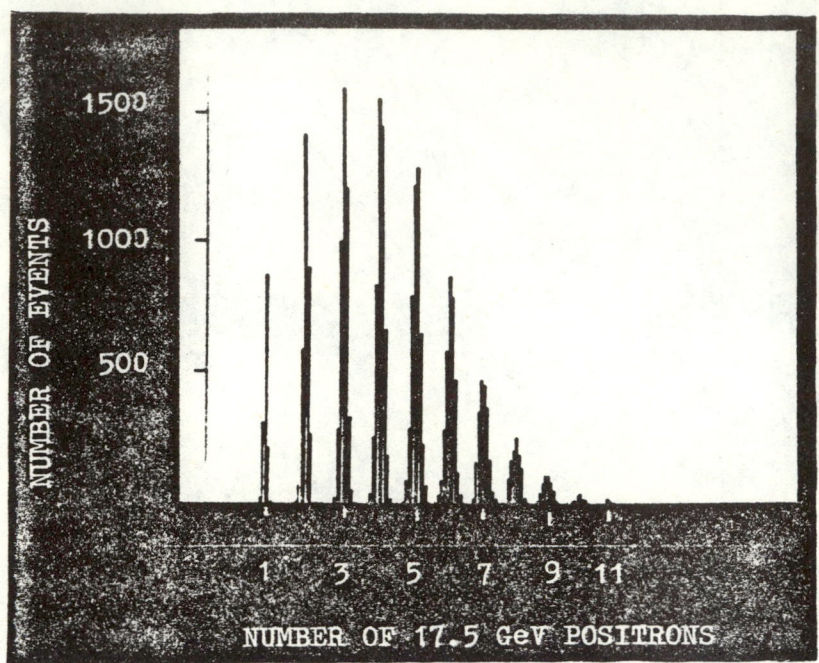

FIG. 8

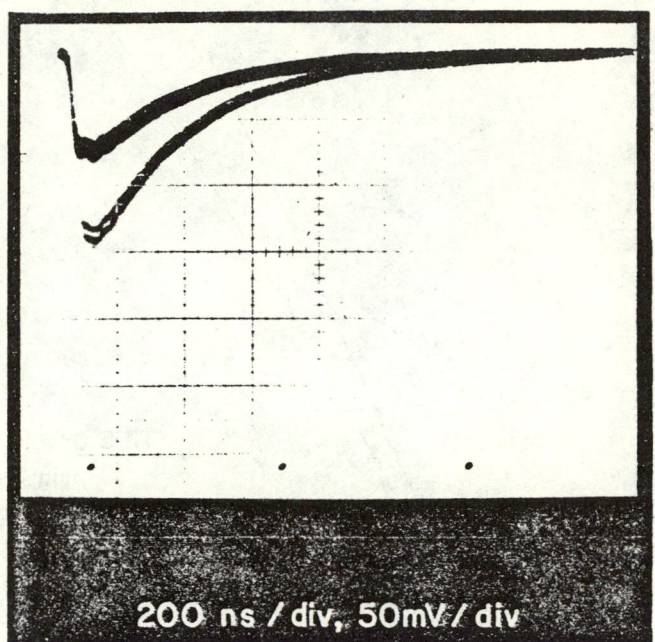

200 ns / div, 50mV / div

FIG. 9

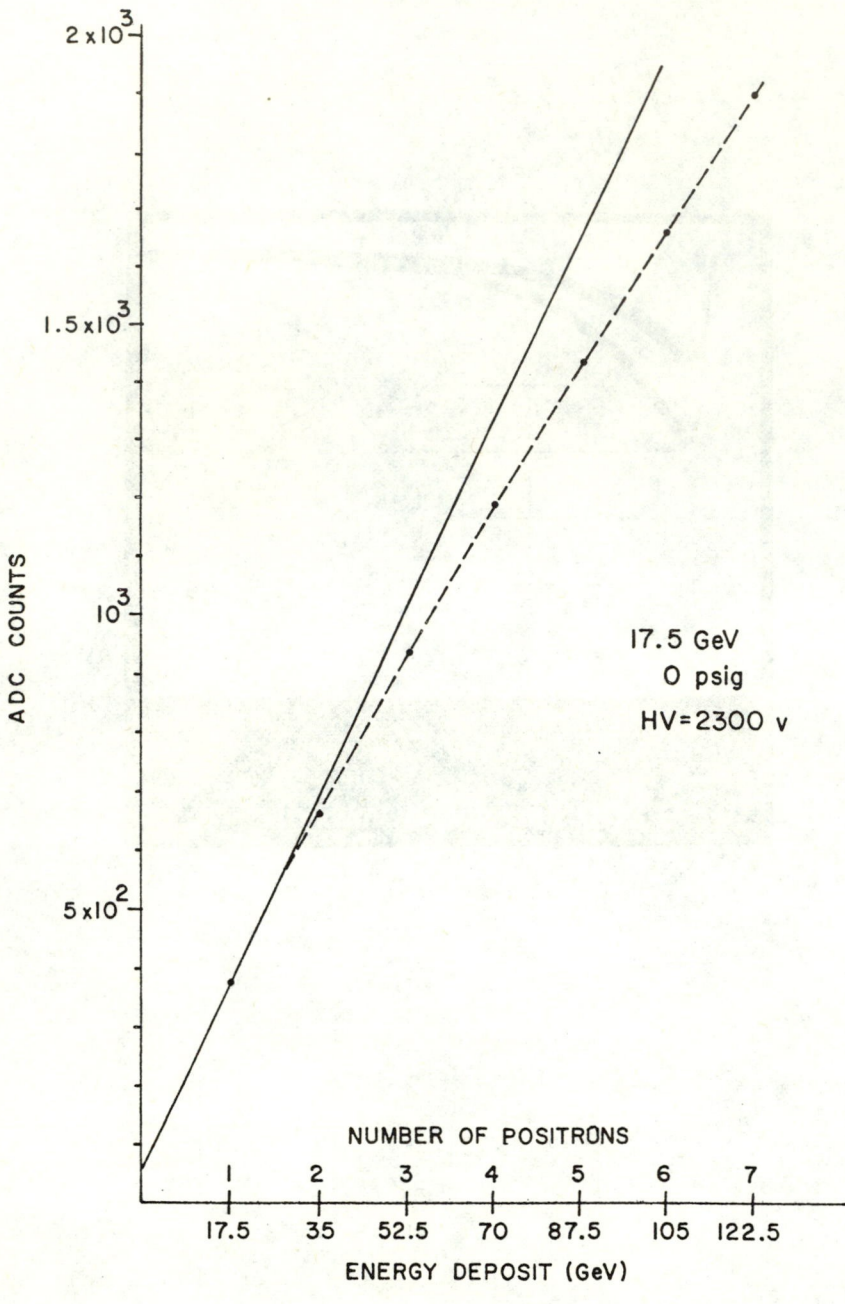

FIG. 10a

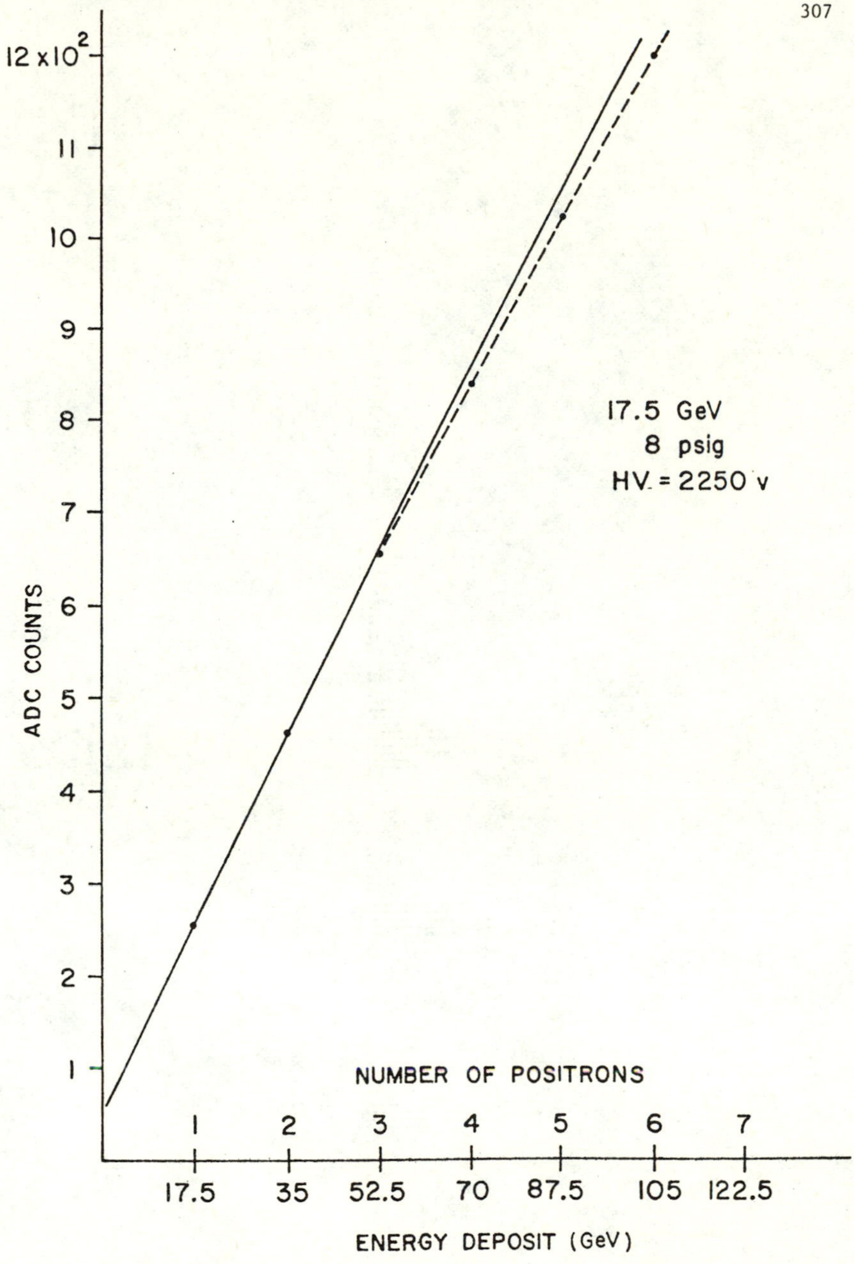
12 x10^2
11
10
9
8
7
6
5
4
3
2
1
ADC COUNTS
17.5 GeV
8 psig
HV = 2250 v
NUMBER OF POSITRONS
1
2
3
4
5
6
7
17.5
35
52.5
70
87.5
105
122.5
ENERGY DEPOSIT (GeV)

FIG. 10b

308

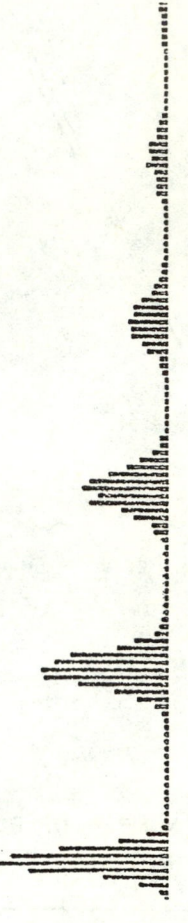

FIG. 11

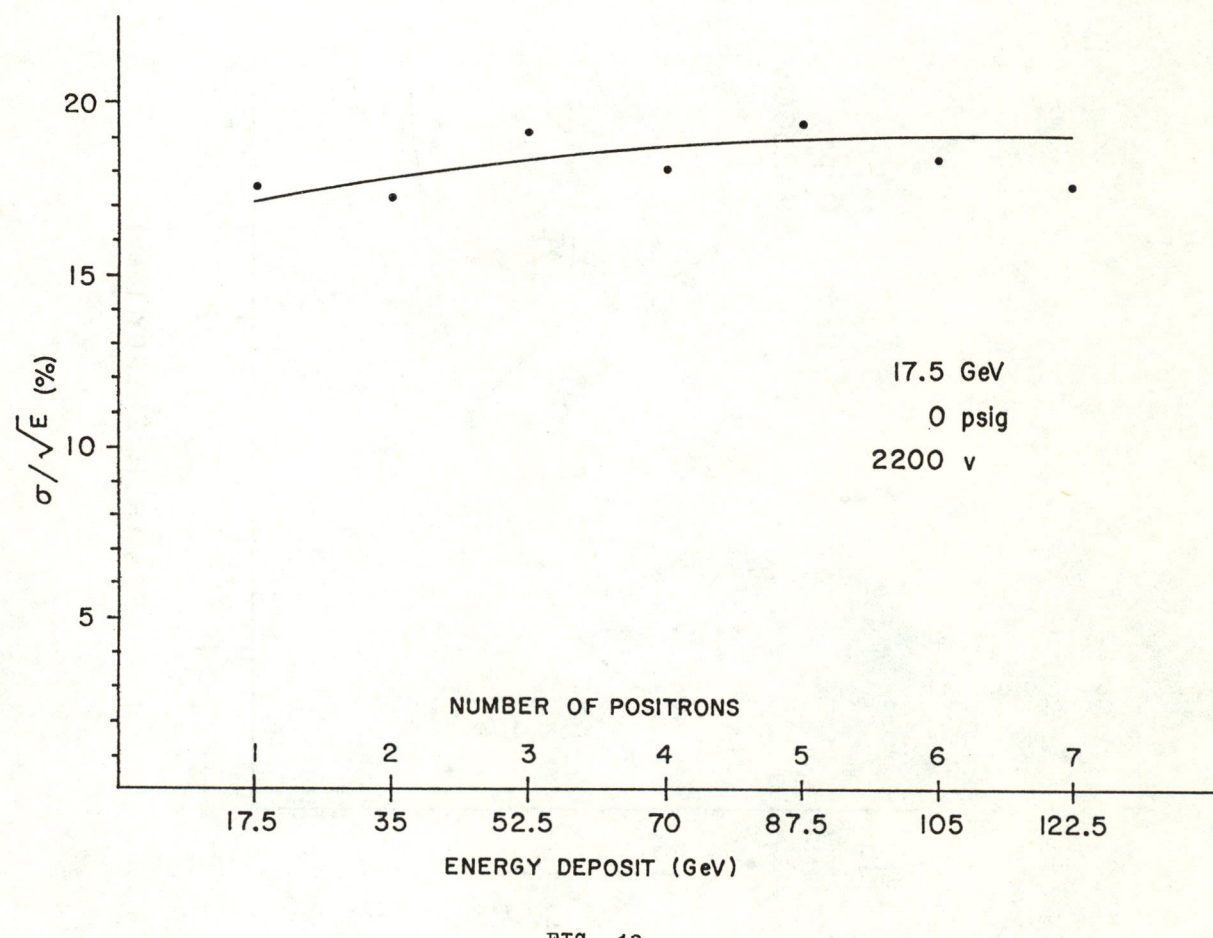

FIG. 12

310

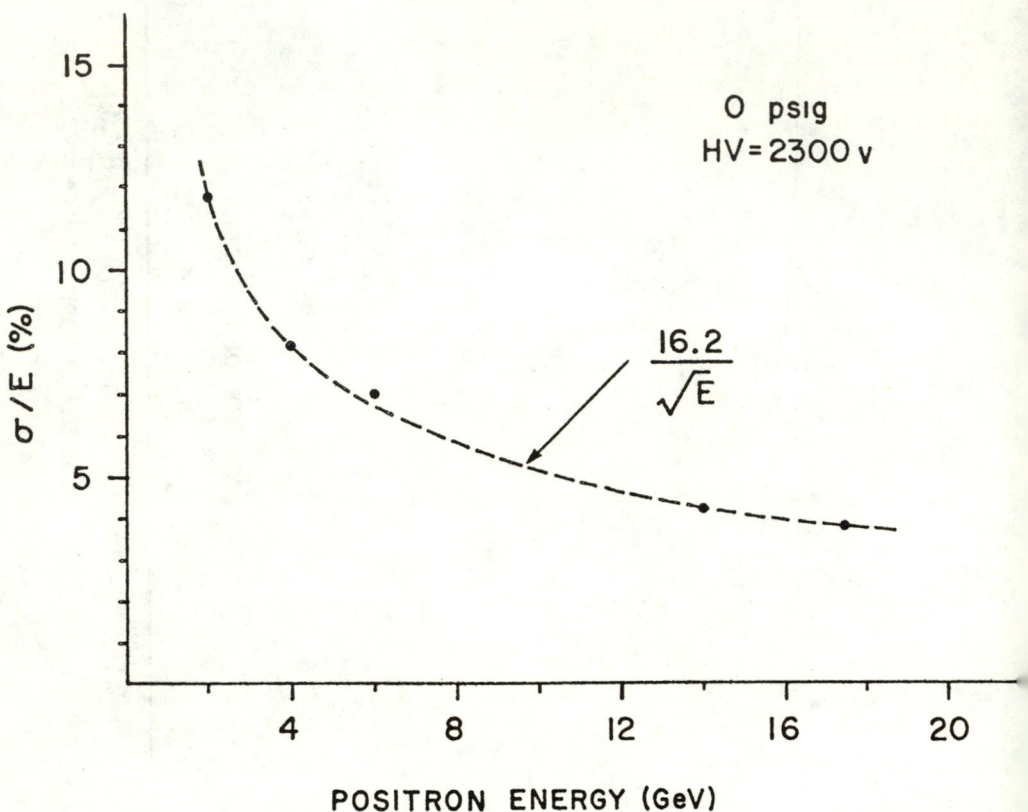

FIG. 13

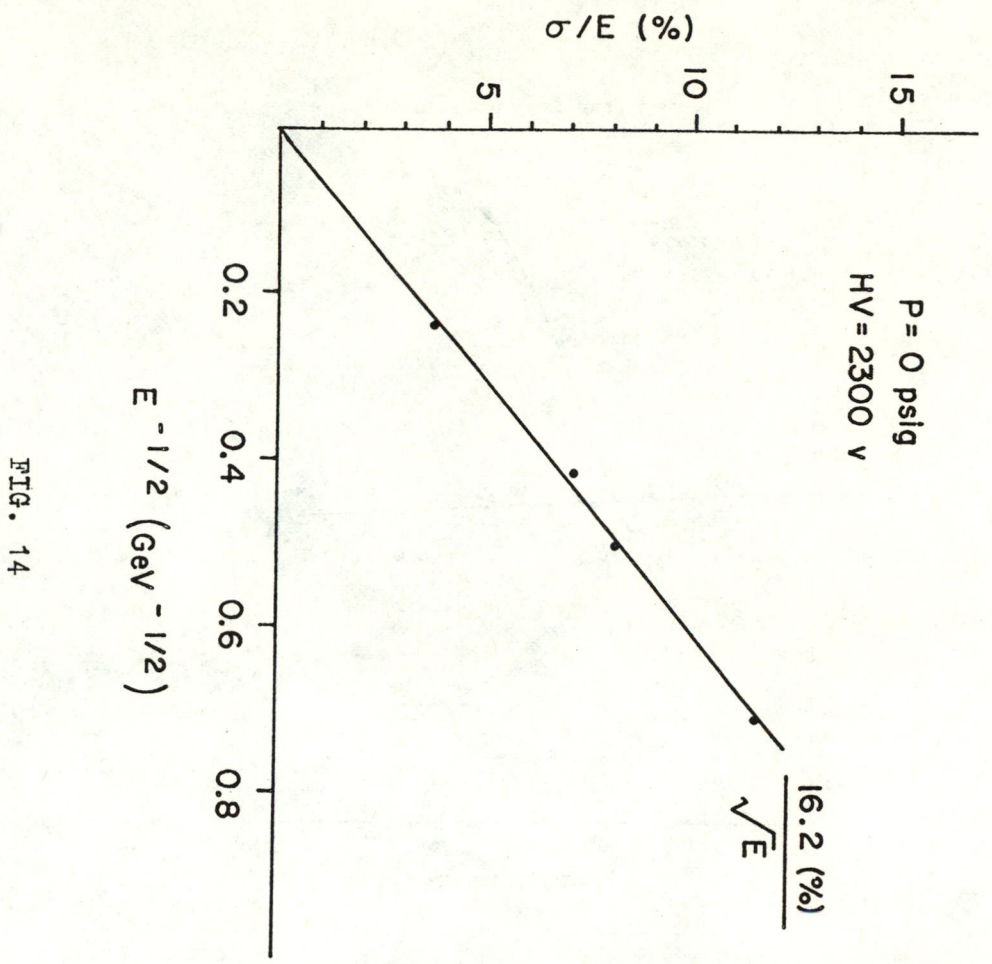

FIG. 14

312

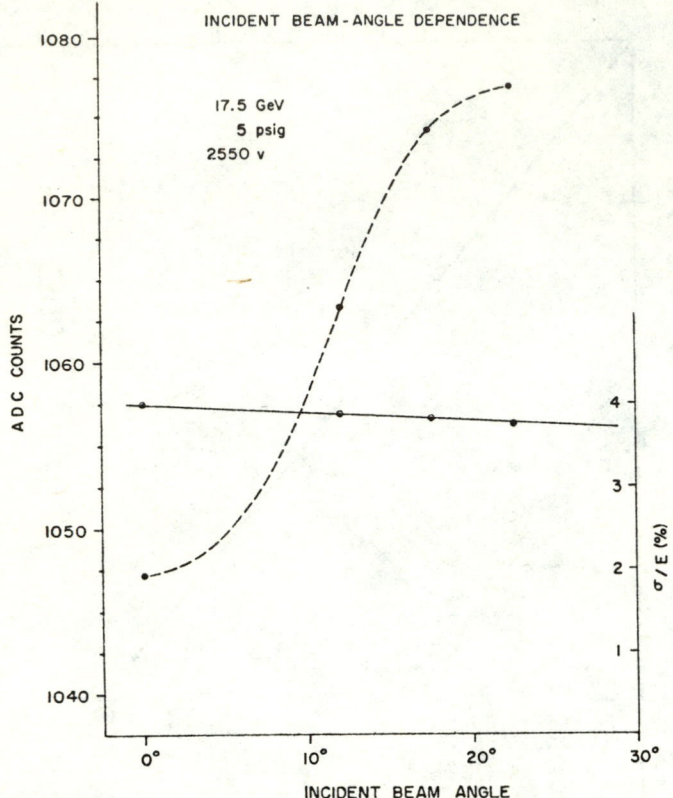

FIG. 15

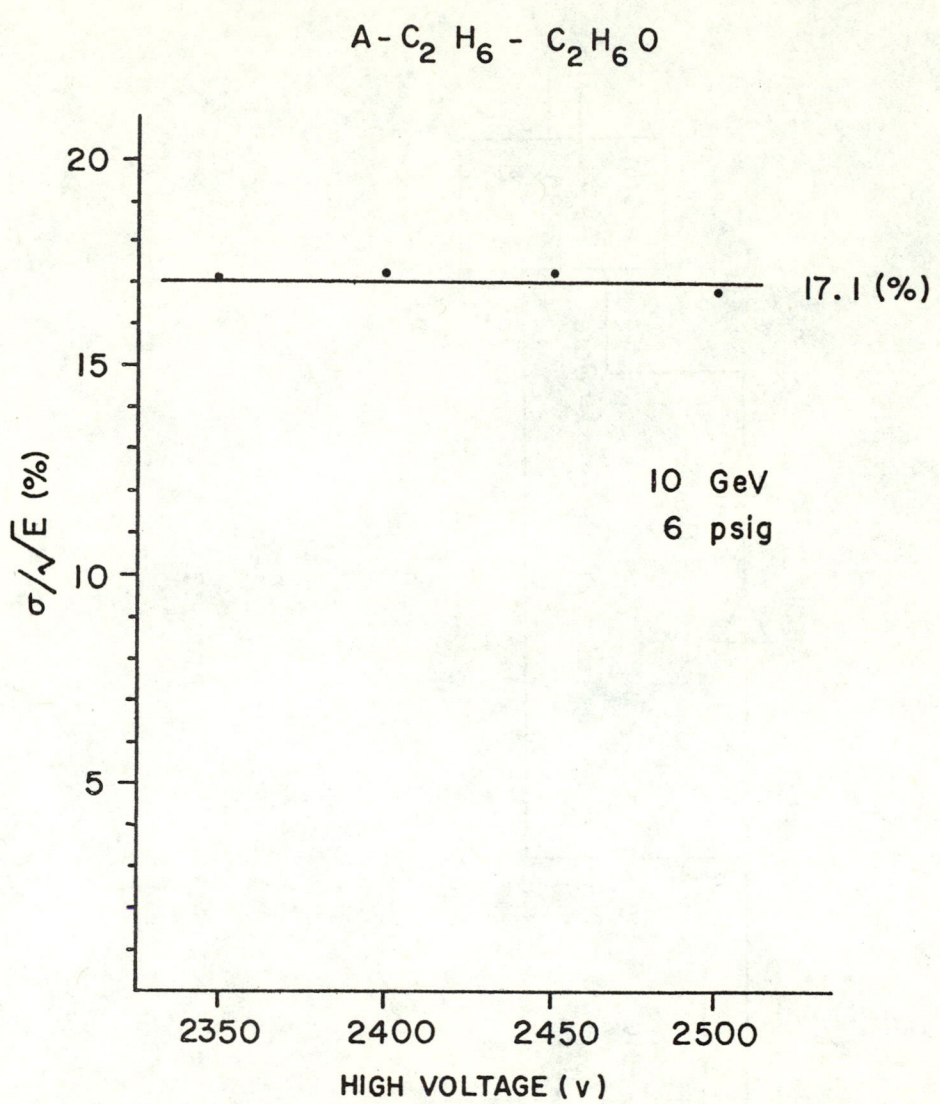

$A - C_2 H_6 - C_2 H_6 O$

10 GeV
6 psig

17.1 (%)

FIG. 16

314

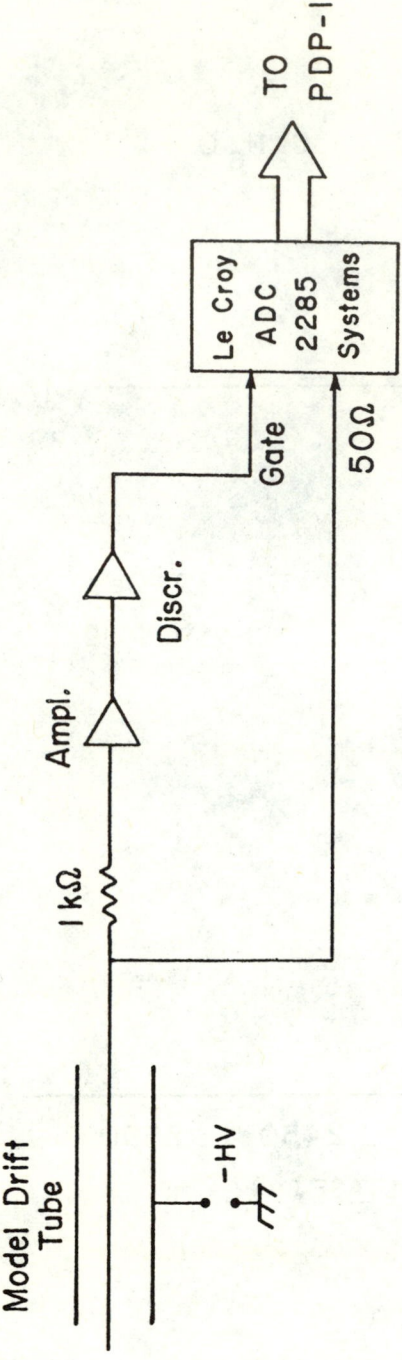

FIG. 17

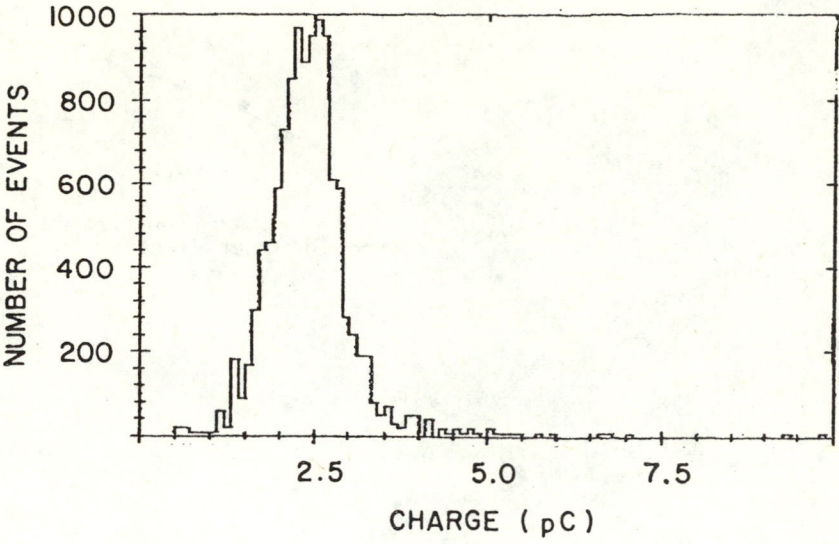

FIG. 18a

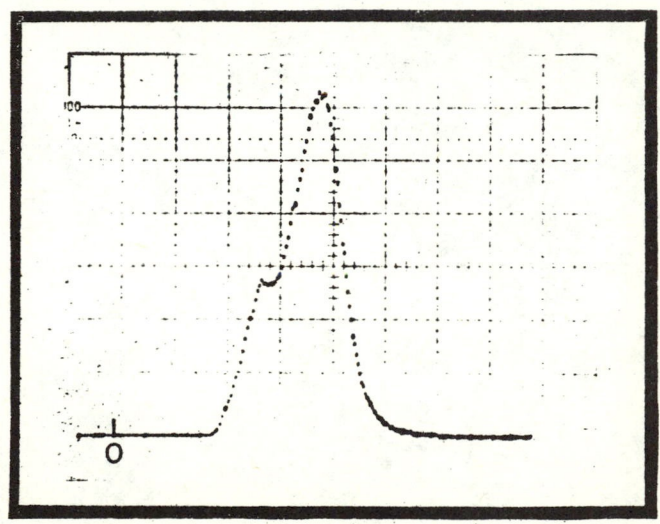

FIG. 18b

316

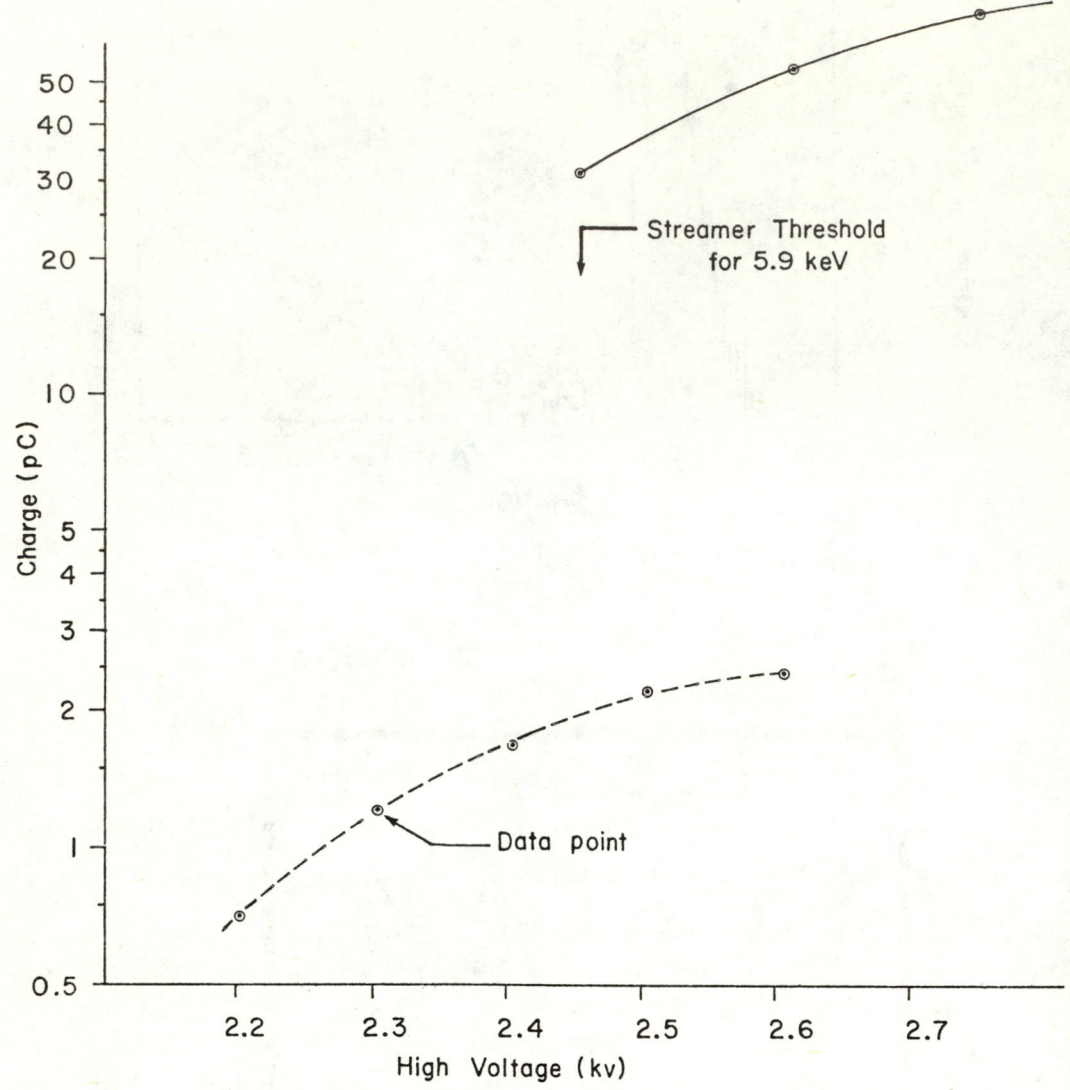

FIG. 19

317

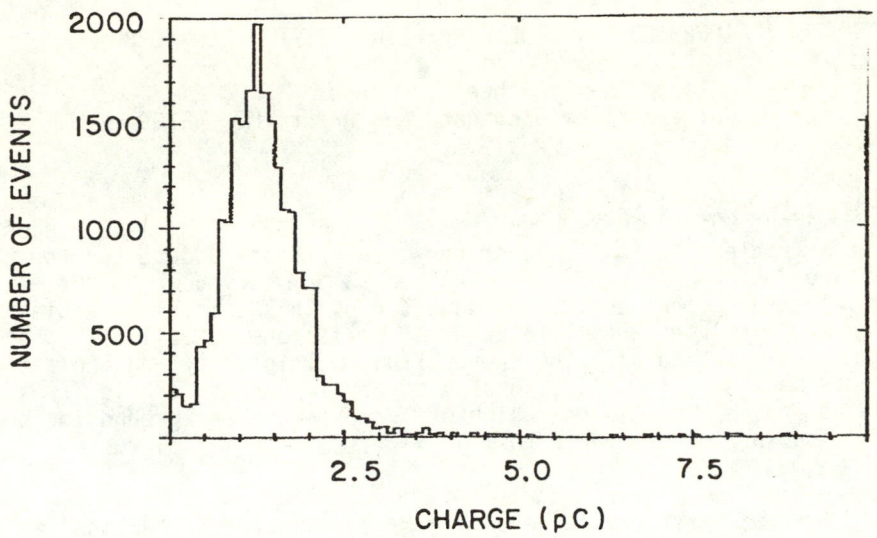

FIG. 20a

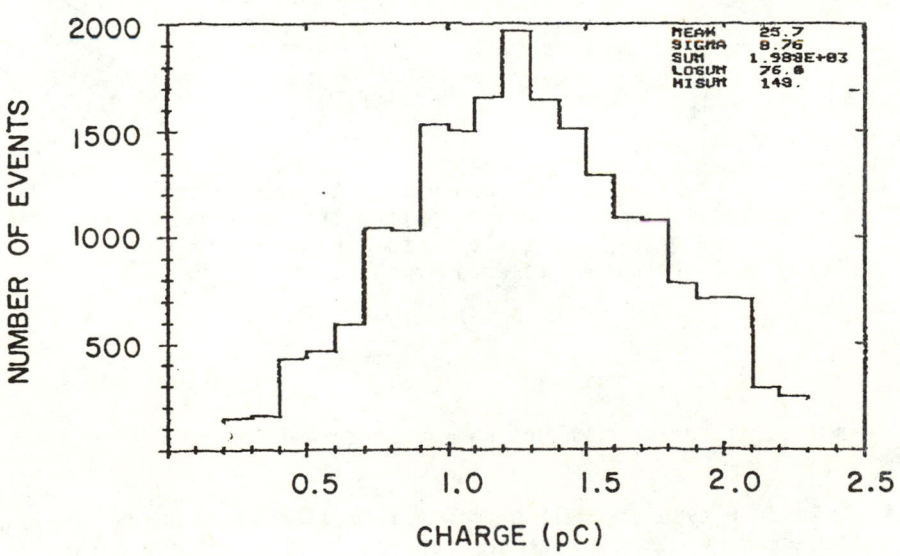

FIG. 20b

A FORWARD DETECTOR FOR THE D0 AREA AT FERMILAB

Michael J. Longo
University of Michigan, Ann Arbor, MI 48109

ABSTRACT

About 90% of the energy from a $\sqrt{s}=2000$ GeV $\bar{p}p$ collision goes out at angles $<2°$ in the laboratory. We propose a detector for the D0 area which emphasizes tracking and calorimetry down to the smallest practical angles. A detector of this type is essential for studying the general features of collisions at Collider energies, particularly the energy flow, multiplicity and inelastic cross section. It will also play a very important role in selecting hard collisions which will reduce the background for new physics in a central detector.

Let me first try to educate you as to where the "action" is at the Fermilab collider. If we identify "action" with energy, it is clear that almost all the action is very forward — at angles not covered by the presently contemplated detectors at Fermilab.

Everything I have to say is, of course, based on a model of what will happen at collider energies. (I'm indebted to Tom Gaisser for a program to simulate high-energy collisions. To a large extent I'm just reemphasizing points he has already made about energy flow.[1]) Let me, therefore, say a little about models. The most naive model to extrapolate from ISR to collider energies is Feynman scaling

$$E \frac{d^2\sigma}{dp_L \, dp_T} = f(x,p_T) \tag{1}$$

where p_L is the longitudinal and p_T the transverse momentum and $x \cong p_L/(\sqrt{s}/2)$. Feynman scaling implies that we can take an event at the ISR energy $\sqrt{s_0}$ and scale it to a higher energy $\sqrt{s}$ by simply scaling the longitudinal momenta of the particles by $\sqrt{s/s_0}$, or

$$\frac{p_L(s)}{p_L(s_0)} = \frac{\sqrt{s}}{\sqrt{s_0}} \tag{2}$$

Feynman scaling is known <u>not</u> to work very well at very high energies[2,3].

Another type of scaling is statistical scaling which says that each secondary, on the average, carries off $1/n_s$ of the total energy where n_s is the mean multiplicity. This leads to a scaling of the type

$$\frac{p_L(s)}{p_L(s_0)} = \frac{\sqrt{s}/n_s(s)}{\sqrt{s_0}/n_s(s_0)} \tag{3}$$

If the multiplicity follows a power law in $\sqrt{s}$, $n_s = A(\sqrt{s})^{\alpha_n}$, statistical scaling implies

$$\frac{p_L(s)}{p_L(s_0)} = (\frac{\sqrt{s}}{\sqrt{s_0}})^{1-\alpha_n} \tag{4}$$

where $\alpha_n \approx 0.43$ (Ref. 2). Feynman scaling is clearly a special case of this with $\alpha_n \equiv 0$.

The correct scaling law is thought to lie somewhere between the Feynman and statistical extremes. A somewhat more general kind of scaling law than Eq. (1) has therefore been discussed by Wdowczyk and Wolfendale[2], Gaisser[1], and others. This has the form

$$E \frac{d^2\sigma}{d p_L dp_T} = (\frac{s}{s_0})^\alpha f[(\frac{s}{s_0})^\alpha x, p_T] \tag{5}$$

where α now is a parameter to be determined from data. Presumably,

$$\alpha_n > \alpha > 0$$
$$\text{(statistical} \qquad \text{(Feynman}$$
$$\text{scaling)} \qquad \text{scaling)}$$

I now return to my original question: Where is all the "action" in $\sqrt{s}$=2000 GeV $\bar{p}p$ collisions? Given a Monte Carlo program which incorporates the scaling law (5) and a reasonable value for α, we can generate $\sqrt{s}$=2000 GeV collisions starting with ISR data.

From an experimentalist's point of view the results are nicely summarized in Fig. 1. This shows for three values of α the fraction of the energy which goes outside an angle θ_{min}. For the α=0.19 curve only I show what happens if you include the leading nucleons. In this model they are given on the average half the energy; they are assumed to obey Feynman scaling so their contribution does not depend on α.

The meaning of these curves can be illustrated by an example. It is hoped that CDF will have a forward detector which goes down to 2° or so in either hemisphere. If Feynman scaling is correct (α=0), the entire CDF detector on the average would only see about 2% of the total energy from a collision! If α=0.19, a reasonable

320

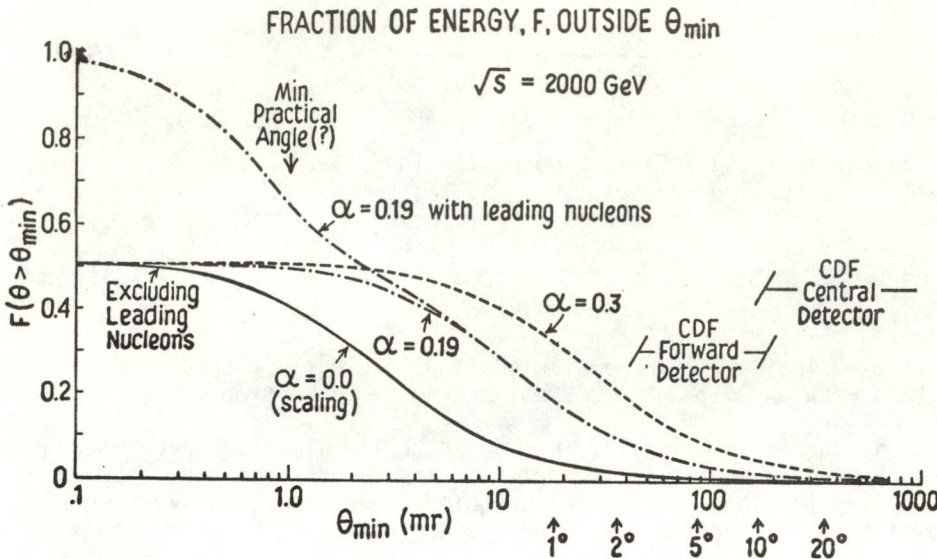

Figure 1 — Fraction of energy collected in a detector which covers $\theta > \theta_{min}$ vs. θ_{min}.

value based on cosmic ray data[2], it would see about 10% of the energy.

This strikes some people as a serious shortcoming of the CDF detector and raises the question: Can one do better? The straight sections at the Fermilab collider are about 50 m. long. At the ISR, detectors can be placed as close as 0.7 cm from the circulating beam. This combination would give $\theta_{min} \sim 0.7$ cm/25 m $\cong$ 0.3 mr. A more conservative design might be to take $\theta_{min} = 2$ cm/20 m = 1 mr. This is shown in Figure 1 as the "Min. Practical Angle". If α isn't too close to 0, a calorimeter that could see down to 1 mr would collect almost all the energy except that carried by the leading nucleons.

This gives a good idea what we need to do and suggests a detector like that shown in Fig. 2. It is almost the logical complement of CDF. The detectors are stretched out along the beam line over the entire length of the straight section. The emphasis is on multiplicity counting and calorimetry. The interaction region would be surrounded by wire chambers and counters. Each of the six calorimeters would be preceeded by wire chambers to track particles and measure multiplicity. The detector is modest in size. Typical dimensions of the calorimeter are ~ 1 m. (Note that transverse dimensions are exaggerated tenfold in the figure.)

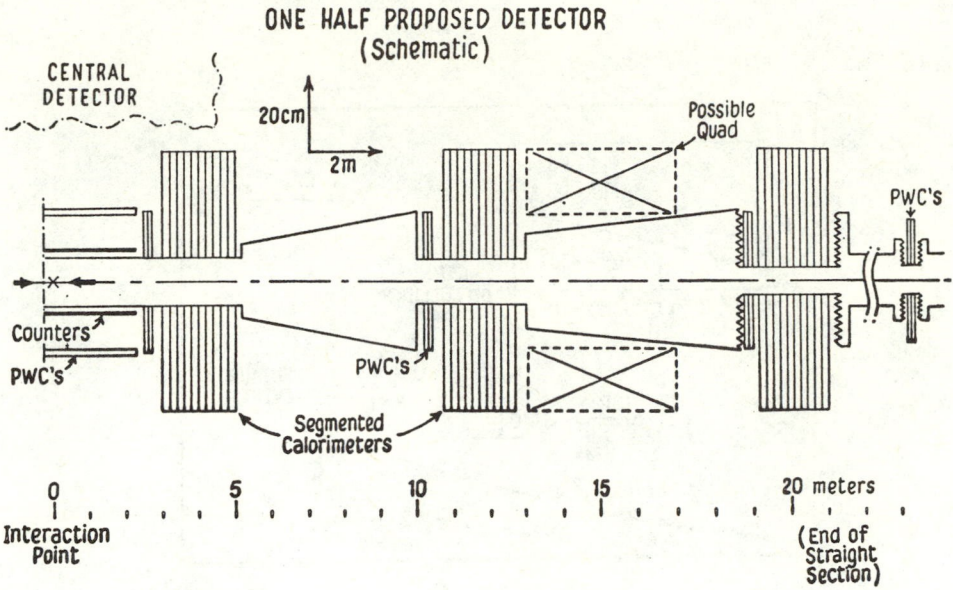

ONE HALF PROPOSED DETECTOR
(Schematic)

Figure 2 — Schematic of possible experimental arrangement.

The farthest calorimeters have to be mounted in such a way that they can be moved in to <2 cm from the circulating beam once the beams are stable.

As far as physics this detector could do on its own, some of the more obvious things are the following:

(1) Multiplicity vs s - This is a basic measurement. Cosmic ray data from the Japan-Brazil group suggest a new threshold near $\sqrt{s} \cong$ 500 GeV. (See inset to Fig. 3 which is taken from G. Goggi, CERN-EP/81-08.)

(2) σ_{inel} vs s - Again cosmic ray data suggest a sudden increase in absorption length above $\sqrt{s} \cong$ 500 GeV as shown in Fig. 4.

(3) Centauro events - These have been discussed at length by many people. These also seem to be restricted to $\sqrt{s}$ > 600 GeV, perhaps just out of reach of the CERN collider. (See Fig. 3).

(4) Energy flow measurements - As discussed earlier in the introduction, these are essential to understanding the general features of interactions at very high energies. As Gaisser has emphasized[1], these data are important in our attempts to model cosmic ray interactions at extremely high energies which is necessary in answering very basic questions like the composition of the high energy component.

322

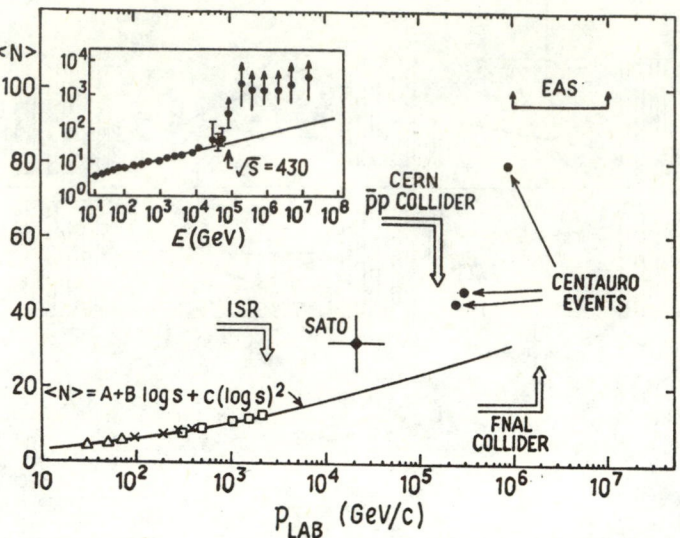

Fig. 3. Charged multiplicities from accelerators, ISR, and cosmic-ray experiments (from G. Goggi, CERN-EP/81-08).

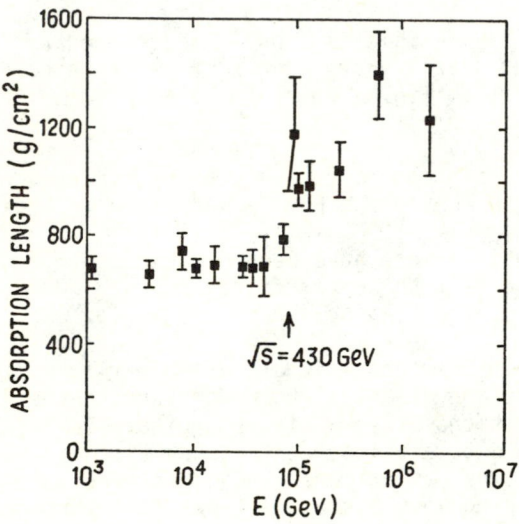

Fig. 4. The Tien-Shan anomaly in the absorption length for cosmic ray showers in a calorimeter. (From G. Goggi, CERN-EP/81-08).

(5) S. Brodsky at this conference pointed out that calorimetry down to small angles will allow the identification of an interesting class of events in which all the valence quarks in the P annihilate with the antiquarks in the $\overline{P}$ leave no leading particles.

Obviously much of the above will be well studied at CERN long before the Fermilab collider is operational. However, it will be important to extend the measurements from $\sqrt{s}$ = 540 to $\sqrt{s}$ = 2000 GeV, and the CDF is not well suited for doing most of the above physics.

In addition to the above, there are some less obvious, but perhaps more important, uses of such a detector. I assume we'd be in DO along with some central detector, presumably built by another group. Our forward detector would provide a significant tool to enhance new physics signals in the central detector. This might prove crucial in separating objects like the W from the dominant background.

Broadly speaking, to produce these massive states requires a hard collision between a q and $\overline{q}$ with the maximum possible s, the center-of-mass energy squared of the $q\overline{q}$. Events of this type are characterized by:

(1) high multiplicity
(2) little energy going down beam pipes.

Our detector would be uniquely capable of answering these questions on an event-by-event basis. Selecting events which satisfy these criteria should significantly reduce the background in searches for the W, t, ...

Carrying this line of reasoning somewhat farther, we may be able to make studies of hadron-hadron interactions a lot more like e^+e^-. Referring to Fig. 1, if calorimeters cover all angles down to about 1 mr, all the energy except that carried by the leading particles is contained. To the extent that we can identify the leading particles with the fragments of the "wounded" nucleons from a hard $q\overline{q}$ collision, the total energy seen in the calorimeters gives $\sqrt{s}$, the c.m. energy of the $q\overline{q}$ which make the hard collision. If you now plot your favorite indicator of new physics, such as the rate for producing high p_T muons, vs "$\sqrt{s}$", the $q\overline{q}$ energy as measured by the calorimeters, you might hope to see signs of new thresholds such as in Fig. 5.

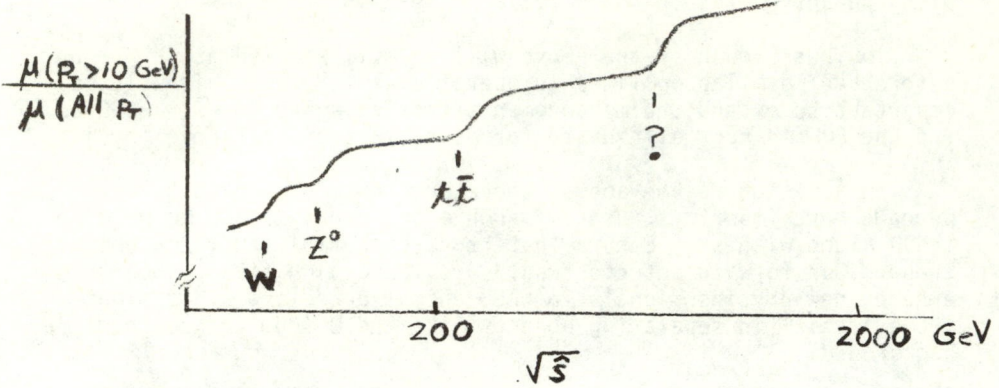

Figure 5 — Idealized variation of large p_T muon yield with $\sqrt{s}$.

Figure 5 certainly is overly optimistic, but even having a rough measure of $\hat{s}$ for each interaction could be an important new technique in collider physics.

REFERENCES

1. T.K. Gaisser, Phys. Lett 100B, 425 (1981).
2. J. Wdowczyk and A.W. Wolfendale, Nuovo Cim. 54A, 433 (1979).
3. K. Guettler et al., Phys. Lett. B64, 111 (1976).
   R. Schindler et al., Phys. Rev. Lett. 33, 862 (1974).

EARLY RESULTS FROM EXPERIMENT UA1 AT THE
CERN pp̄ COLLIDER

Anne Kernan

University of California, Riverside, CA 92521

(Aachen - Annecy (LAPP) - Birmingham - CERN - Queen Mary College, London-Paris (College de France) - Riverside - Rome - Rutherford Appleton Laboratory - Saclay (CEN) - Vienna Collaboration)

The UA1 detector is a general purpose 4π apparatus for the measurement of hadron and lepton momenta at pp̄ collider energies. The performance of the detector and first results from 1981 running are discussed.

I.   INTRODUCTION

The design of the UA1 detector evolved from the p-p̄ study weeks organized by C. Rubbia at CERN in March and July of 1977. A proposal [1] was submitted in January 1978 and was approved in Summer 1978. The detector was installed in the SPS tunnel in early July 1981 and recorded proton-antiproton interactions at 540 GeV for the first time on July 17, 1981 [2].

The results presented here are based on data taken during accelerator development operations in October and November 1981 with luminosity in the range 10^{25}cm^{-2}sec^{-1}.

II.   THE UA1 DETECTOR

The detector has three components:
(i)   the large angle detector covering the angular range $5° < \theta < 175°$ with respect to the circulating beams,
(ii)   the forward detectors at $0.3° < \theta < 5°$, and
(iii) the luminosity monitors at $0.2 < \theta < 2$ mrad.

1.   The Large Angle Detector

This apparatus (Fig. 1) covers the rapidity range $-3 < Y < 3$ at cm energy 540 GeV. It is dominated by the dipole magnet, $7.2 \times 3.5 \times 3.5$ m^3, with internal magnetic volume 80 m^3, and uniform horizontal field 0.7T. Each half of the magnet is composed of 8 independently movable C-shaped sections. As shown in Fig. 2 these sections are instrumented with scintillator, providing 16 samples of 5 cm iron with 1 cm of scintillator (5.5 interaction lengths). Endcaps of similar construction, with 23 samplings, cover the angular range $5° < \theta < 25°$.

The electromagnetic calorimeter inside the magnet consists of 48 units covering the region $25° < \theta < 155°$. Each unit (Fig. 3) is made of 26 radiation lengths of 1.2 mm lead sheets interleveaved with 1.5 mm scintillator sheets. The endcap electromagnetic calorimeters ($5° < \theta < 25°$) have 27 radiation lengths of lead-scintillator structure.

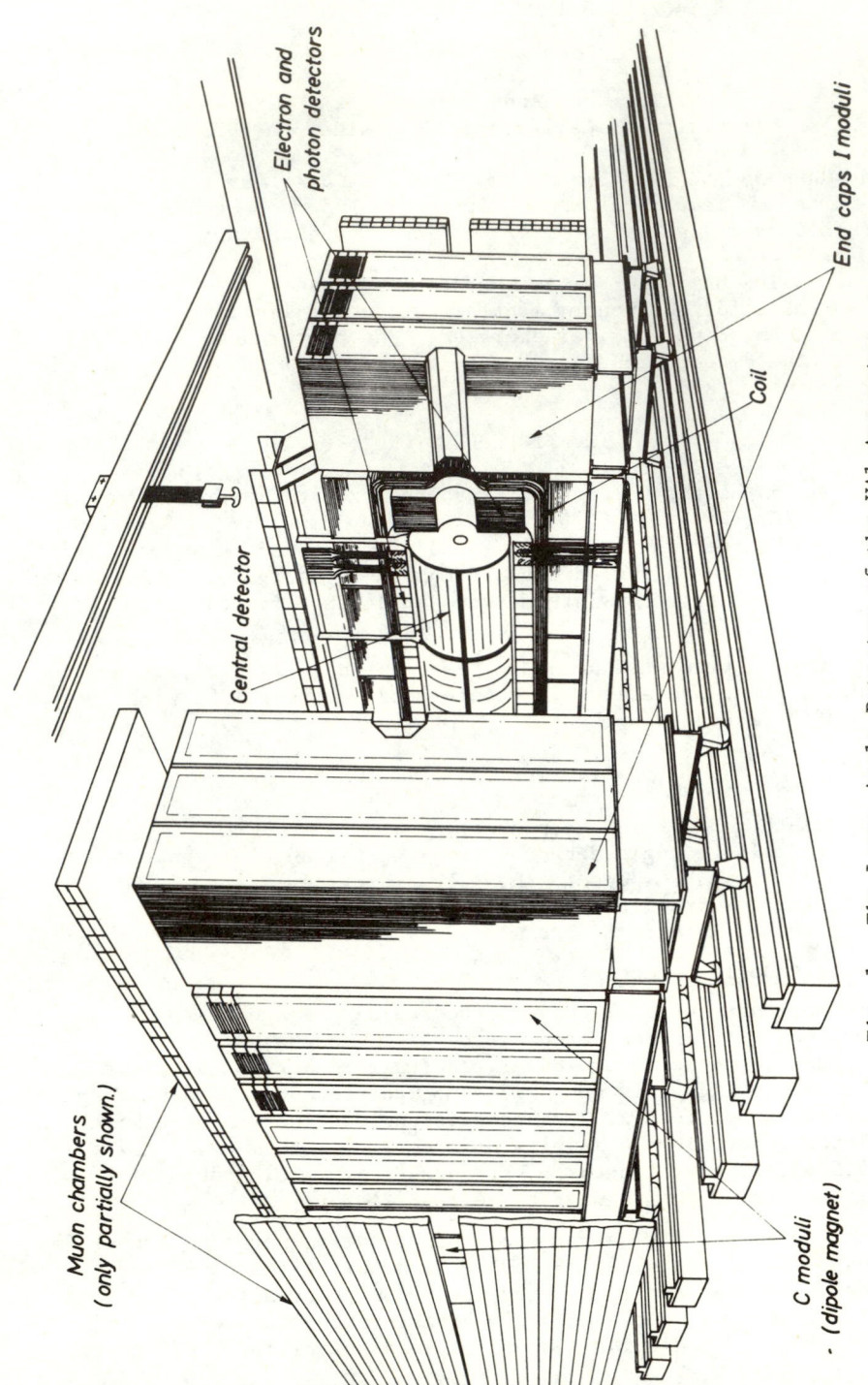

Electron and photon detectors

End caps I moduli

Coil

Central detector

Muon chambers
(only partially shown.)

C moduli
- (dipole magnet)

Fig. 1. The Large Angle Detector of the UA1 Apparatus.

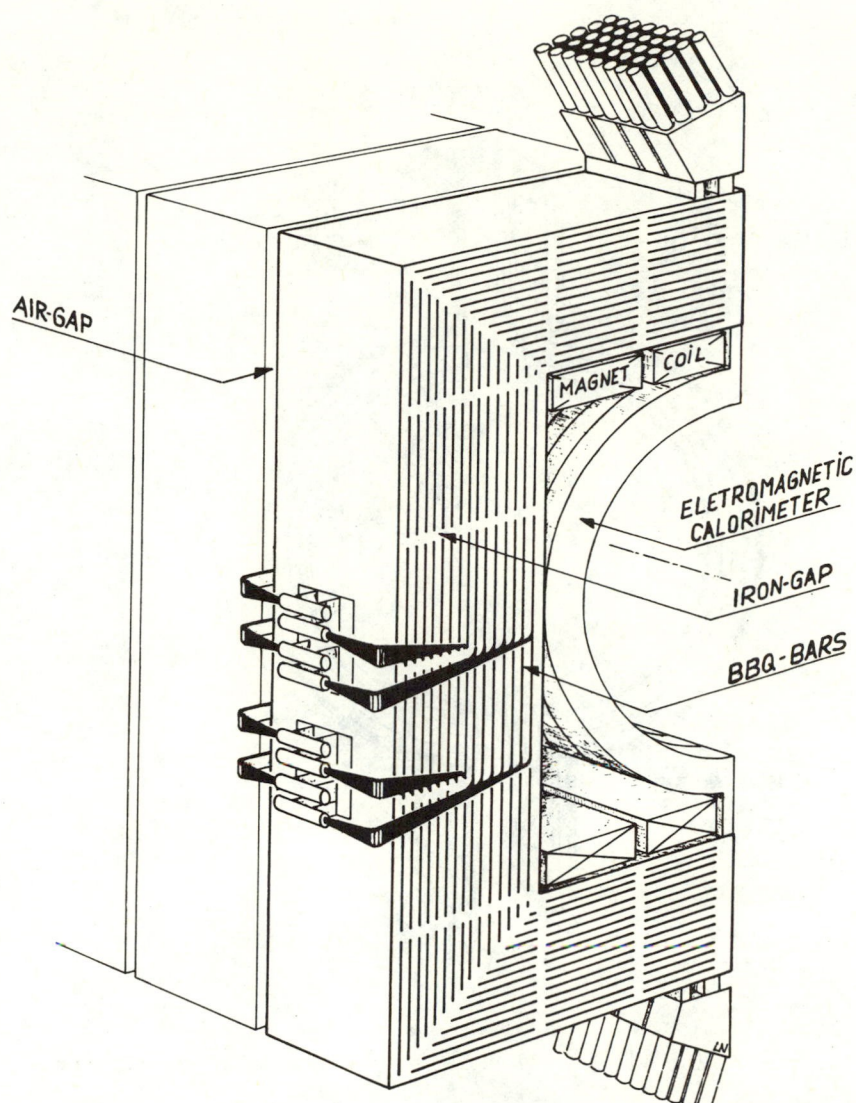

Fig. 2. One of the 16 "C" models comprising the
magnet yoke and hadron calorimeter.

328

Each is segmented into 32 identical radial petals.

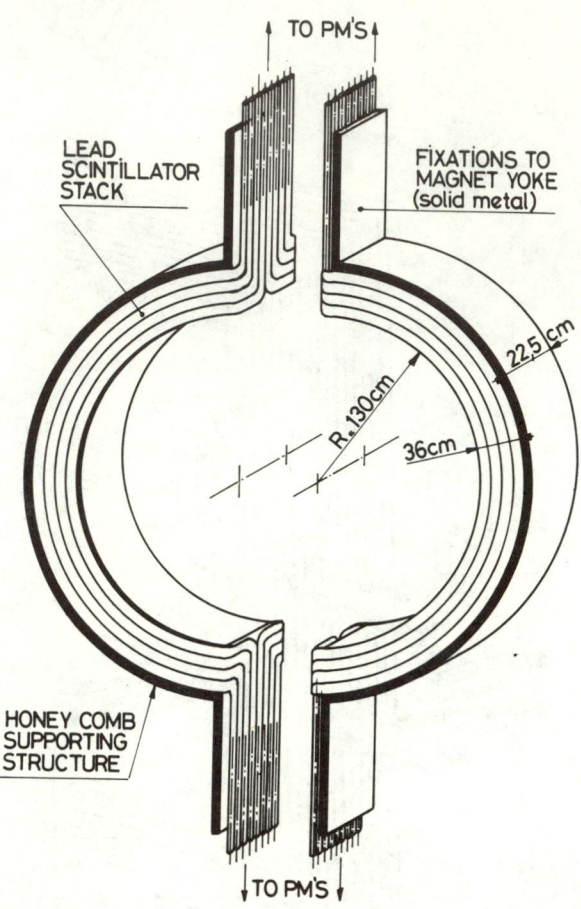

Fig. 3. Two units of the large angle electromagentic calorimeter.

The heart of the large angle apparatus is the 6 m long x 2.4m diameter central detector (Fig. 4) which surrounds the beam pipe [3,4].
This drift chamber system has a total of 6200 sense wires, with maximum drift distance 18 cm. The "image" readout records the complete
time structure of the incoming pulse, providing a bubble-chamber like
picture of the event. The 2-track resolution is 3 mm and dE/dx resolution is ±6%. The coordinate along the wire is obtained by current
division. Fig. 5 shows the image read-out for events recorded with a
"minimum bias" trigger, (section III), with 80% of the chamber volume

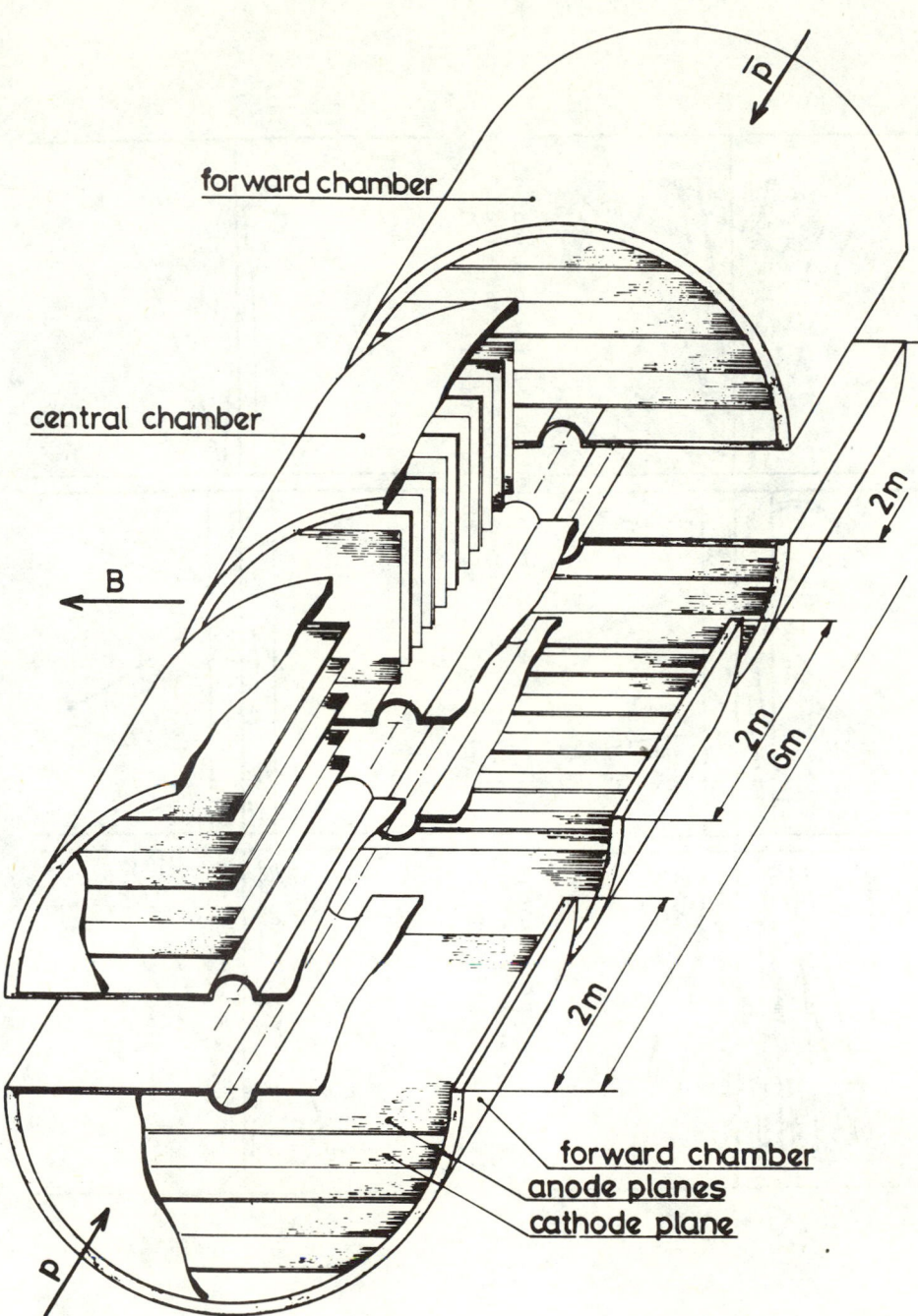

forward chamber

central chamber

B

p̄

p

2m

2m

6m

2m

forward chamber
anode planes
cathode plane

Fig. 4. The Central Detector "image" drift chambers.

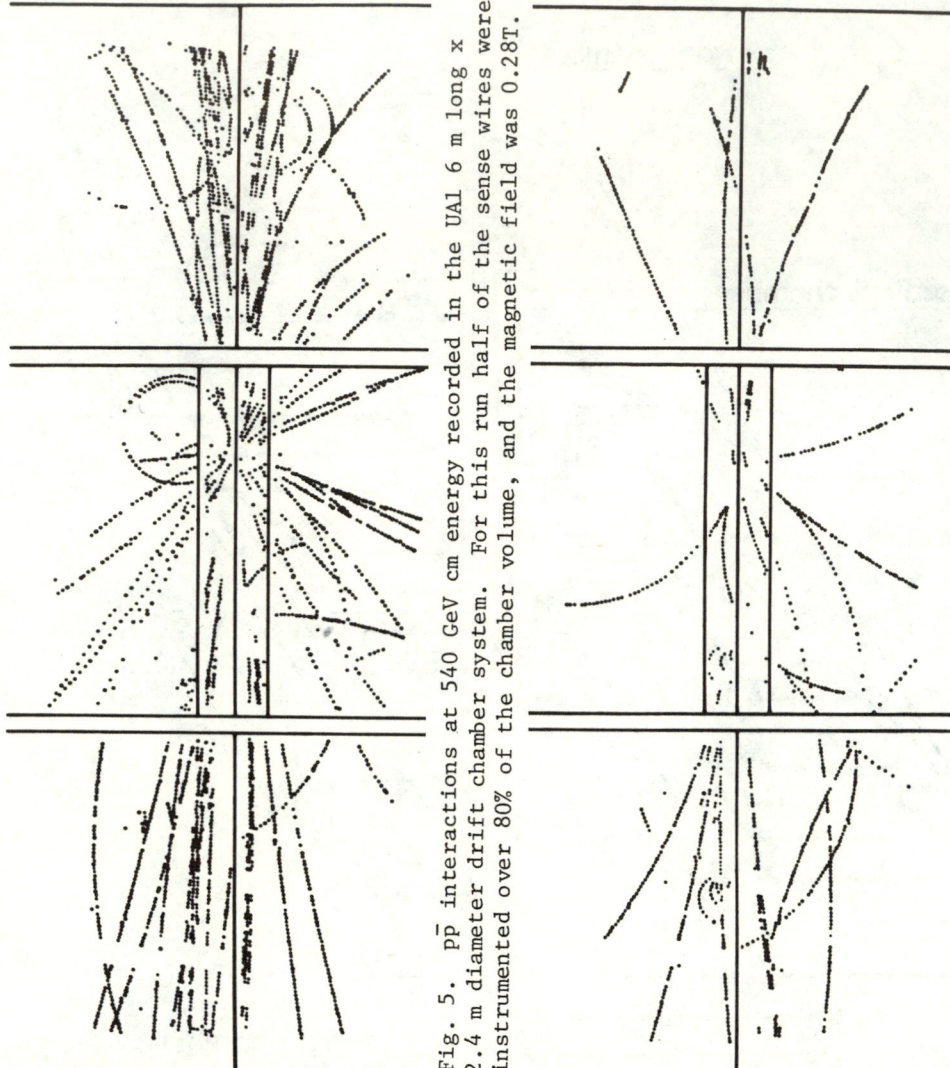

Fig. 5. p̄p interactions at 540 GeV cm energy recorded in the UA1 6 m long x 2.4 m diameter drift chamber system. For this run half of the sense wires were instrumented over 80% of the chamber volume, and the magnetic field was 0.28T.

instrumented at half density and a field of 0.28T.

The exterior of the magnet and endcaps is covered down to 10° by eight planes of staggered drift tubes for muon detection (Fig. 6) [5]. These contain a total of 5200 sense wires with wire lengths up to 6 m.

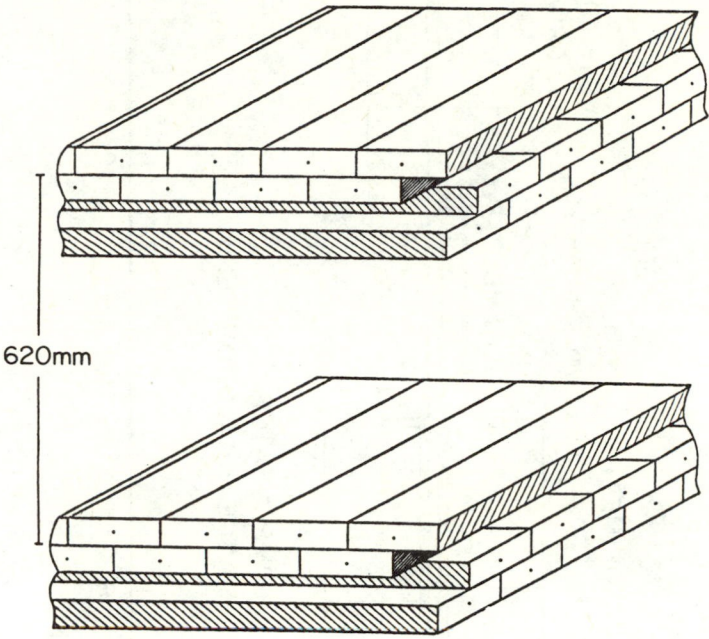

620mm

Fig. 6. Muon chamber setup.

2. The Forward Detector

The forward detector (Fig. 7) extends to within 5 mrad of the coasting beams the UA1 philosophy of complete coverage with image chambers, and hadronic/electromagnetic calorimetry. The compensator dipole in the forward arm is calorimetrized and (on the outgoing $\bar{p}$ side) contains a 3 meter-long image chamber with 600 sense wires transverse to the beam direction.

3. The Luminosity Monitors

For luminosity monitoring the small angle elastic scattering rate is measured by a set of 4 drift chamber telescopes which for this run were symmetrically arranged at ±23 m from the crossing point. Fig. 8 shows the arrangement on one side. In order to access angles in the range $0.2 < \theta < 2$ mrad ($0.003 < |t| < 0.29$ GeV^2) the drift chambers and triggering scintillators are placed in movable sections of the vacuum tube ("Roman pots") which can be positioned within a few mms of the coasting beams. The drift chambers (Fig. 9) have a resolution $\leq$ 100 μm in the drift plane and multihit (up to 16) capability.

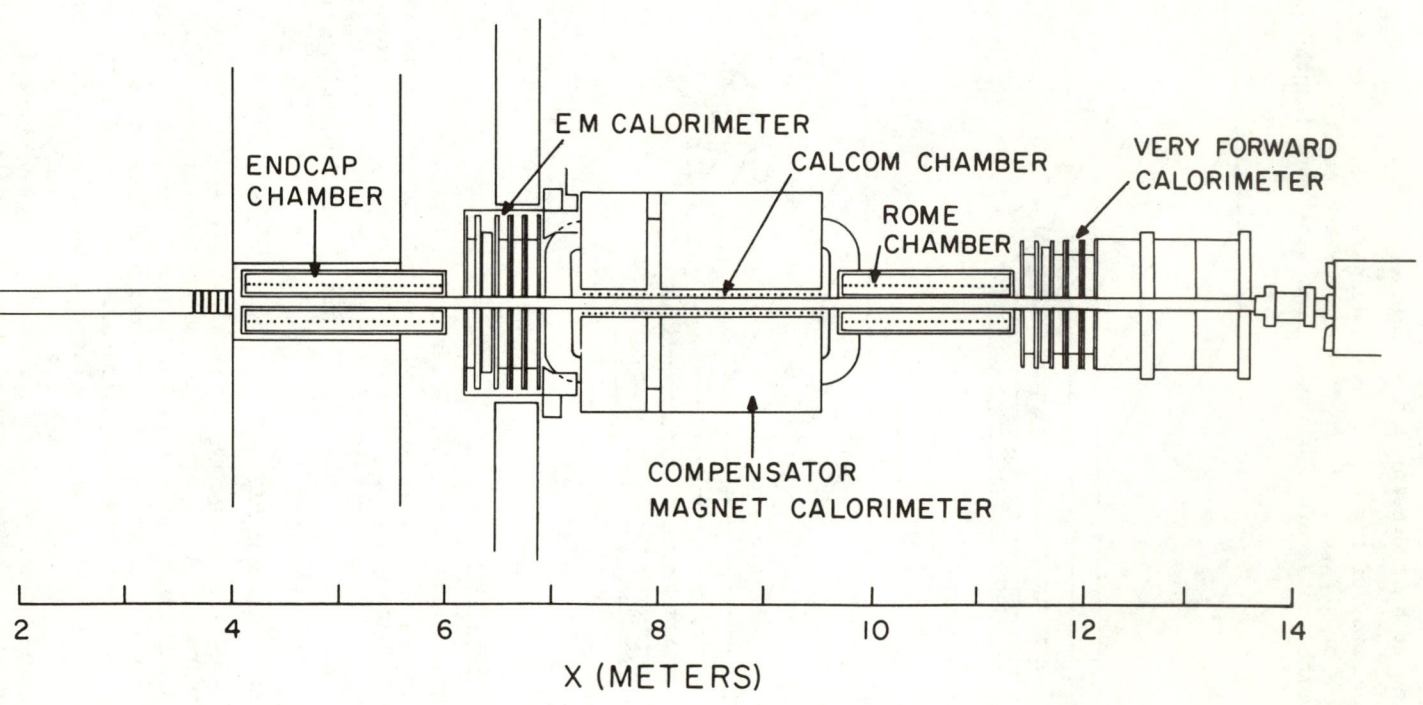

Fig. 7. The Forward Arm (outgoing p̄ side) of the UA1 detector.

(a)

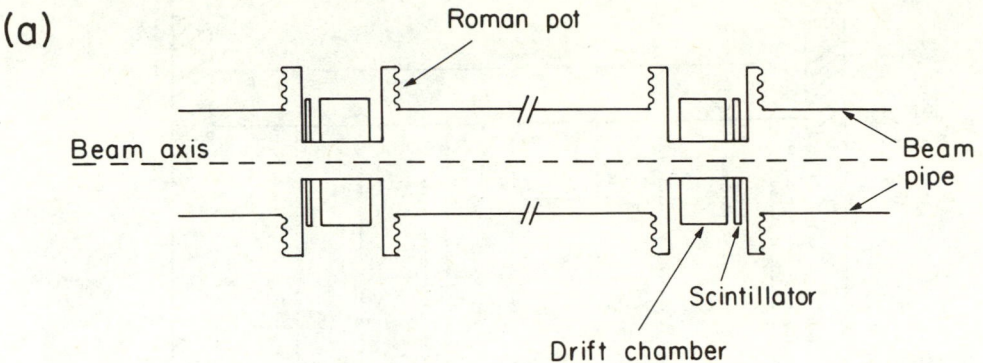

Fig. 8: (a) one arm of the SPS-UA1 luminosity
monitoring drift chamber system

(b)

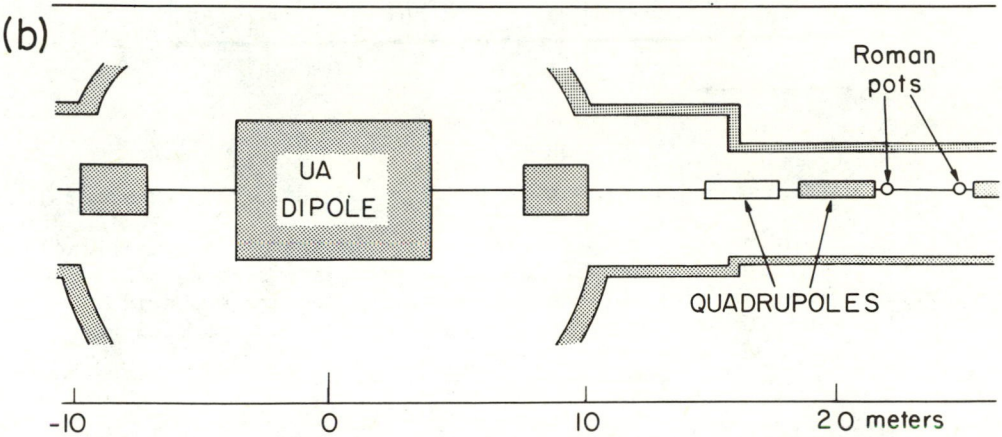

(b) luminosity monitor in the SPS beam line.

The second co-ordinate is obtained by current division with resolution about 2 mm.

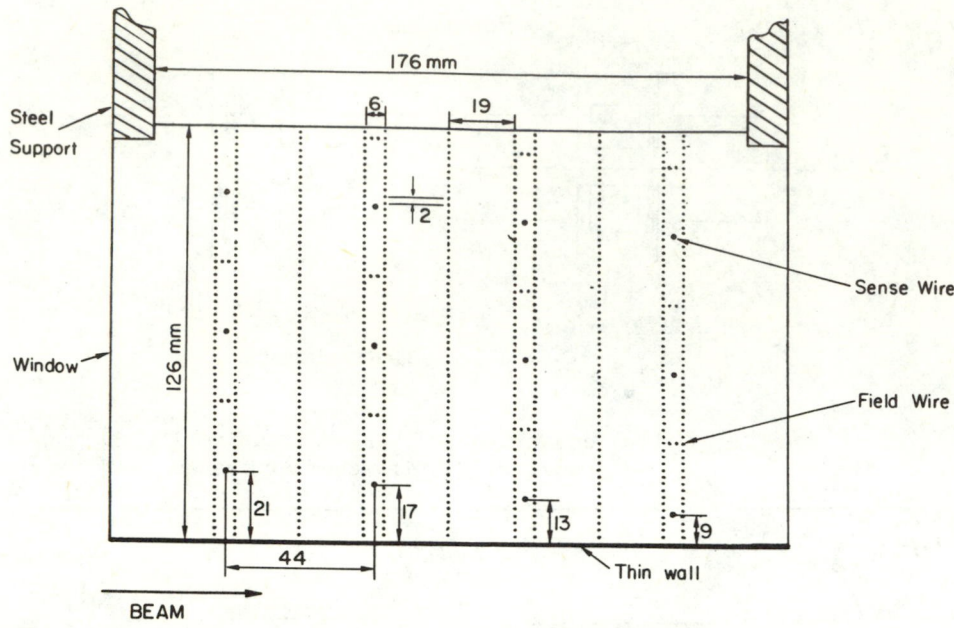

Fig. 9. Luminosity drift chamber, vertical cross section (mm units).

Fig. 10 shows (a) the $\bar{p}$ versus p angle in the drift time plane and (b) its projection for candidate elastic scattering events. The corresponding plots for the charge division plane are shown in Fig. 11. The almost complete absence of background is striking.

III. THE TRIGGER

The design of the trigger is governed by the bunched operation of the accelerator which is designed to give beam crossings of a few nsec duration at 3.8 µsec intervals. At high luminosity the trigger must be quite selective. Thus at the expected maximum luminosity of $L = 10^{29}$ cm^{-2} sec^{-1} the interaction rate will be about 5×10^3 per sec whereas the data acquisition rate is about 10 events per second.

The main trigger incorporates three separate triggers as shown in Fig. 12; the pre-trigger, (or minimum bias trigger), the calorimeter trigger and the muon trigger. The first two and the first level muon trigger given an accept-reject answer in time to clear the system before the next beam crossing occurs.

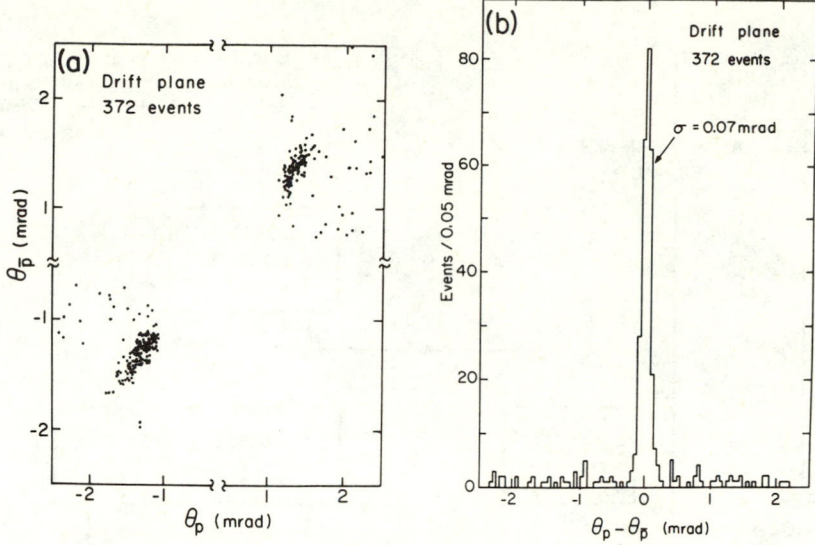

Fig. 10. (a) $\Theta_{\bar{p}}$ versus Θ_p in the drift time
plane for candidate elastic
scattering events,
(b) $\Theta_{\bar{p}} - \Theta_p$

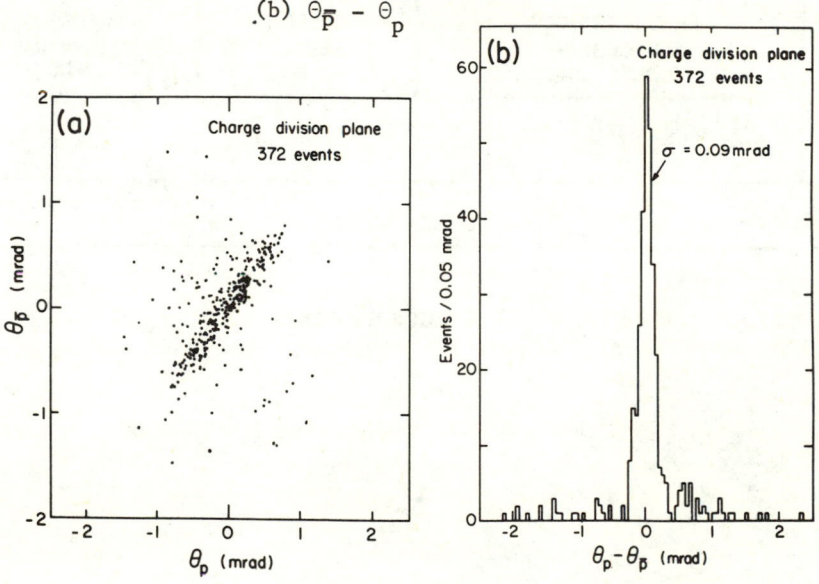

Fig. 11. Same for the charge division
coordinate plane.

336

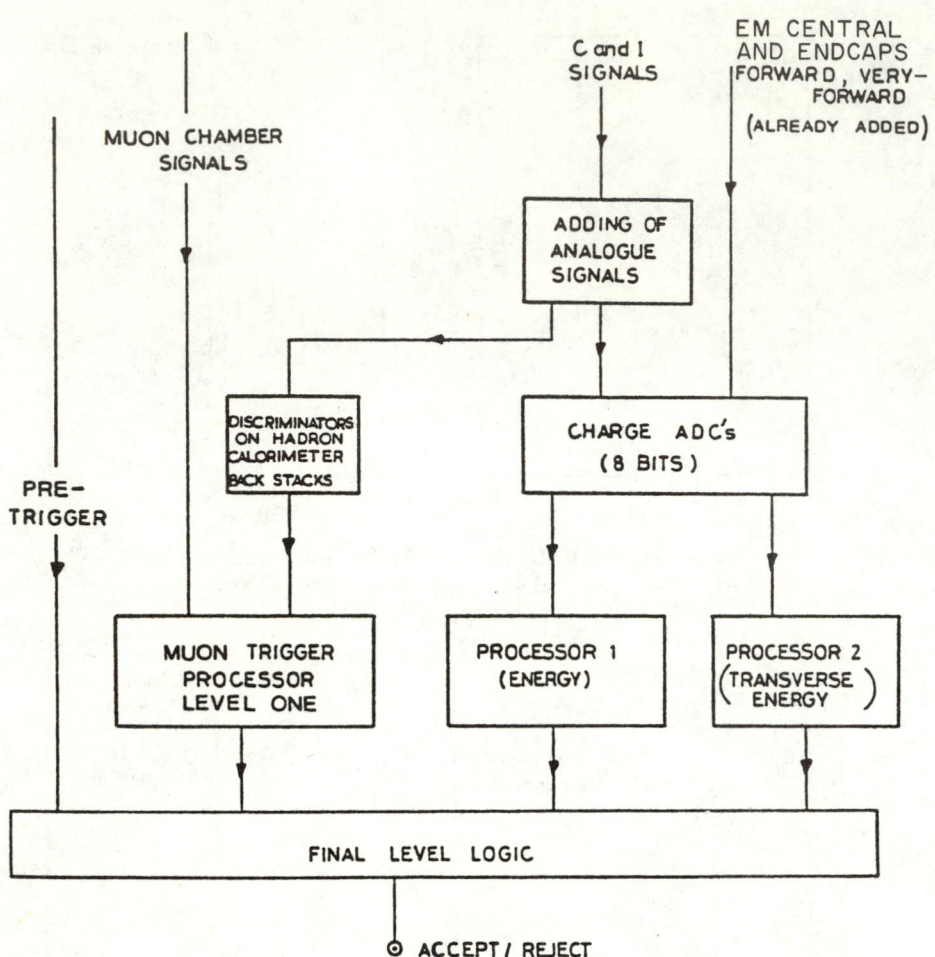

Fig. 12.   The UA1 main trigger logic.

1.   The Pre-Trigger

The pre-trigger aims to select relatively unbiased beam–beam interactions while rejecting background such as beam–gas collisions. For the data reported here the pre-trigger was implemented by a ±20 nsec coincidence, centered around the crossing time, between hodoscopes at ±6.2 m on the proton and antiproton arms. These hodoscopes covered the angular range $0.8<\theta<3.4$, $(3.5<\eta<5.0)$; the minimum angle of $0.8°$, $(t = 13 \text{ GeV}^2)$, excludes single diffraction dissociation events.

2.   Calorimeter Trigger

The calorimeter trigger is based on the pattern of energy deposition in the various calorimeters. Two custom-built digital processors convert the ADC imputs to energy and transverse energy $(E \sin\theta)$ respectively. In November, December 1981 data was recorded with a range of E_T thresholds up to 40 GeV.

3.   Muon Trigger

Prompt high energy muons are identified by the fact that their tracks point back to the crossing region. The first level muon trigger uses the pattern of wire hits, in combination with a signal in the corresponding hadron calorimeter block, to select muon candidates which point within 100 mrad of the interaction vertex. The second level trigger uses microprocessors to reconstruct muon chamber tracks with 10 mrad accuracy (100 μsec per track).

IV.   PHYSICS

The data presented here was obtained with the pre-trigger (section III). This is a "minimum bias" trigger except that single diffraction dissociation events are excluded by the minimum angle $(0.8°)$ of the triggering hodoscopes. All this data comes from the large-angle detector (section I.1) which covers the cm angular range $5°<\theta<175°$ with respect to the circulating beams. All energy measurements have been made with calorimeters.

1.   General Features of $p\bar{p}$ Interactions at 540 GeV

Figs. 13 through 16 survey the global properties of the interactions.

Fig. 13 is the distribution in total transverse energy $\Sigma E \sin\theta$ measured by the electromagnetic and hadronic calorimeters for the angular range $5°<\theta<175°$. (The energy scale has not been corrected for the lower response of the EM calorimeter to hadrons as compared to photons.) In agreement with the results obtained by the Bari-Krakow-Liverpool – MPI Munich – Nijmegen collaboration in pp and $\pi^- p$ interactions at 300 GeV/C [6], we observe a high probability for the occurrence of events with large total E_T. Our multiplicity measurements (section (IV.2) suggest that high E_T events are primarily due to "soft" collisions of high multiplicity rather than to hard scattering of constituents.

338

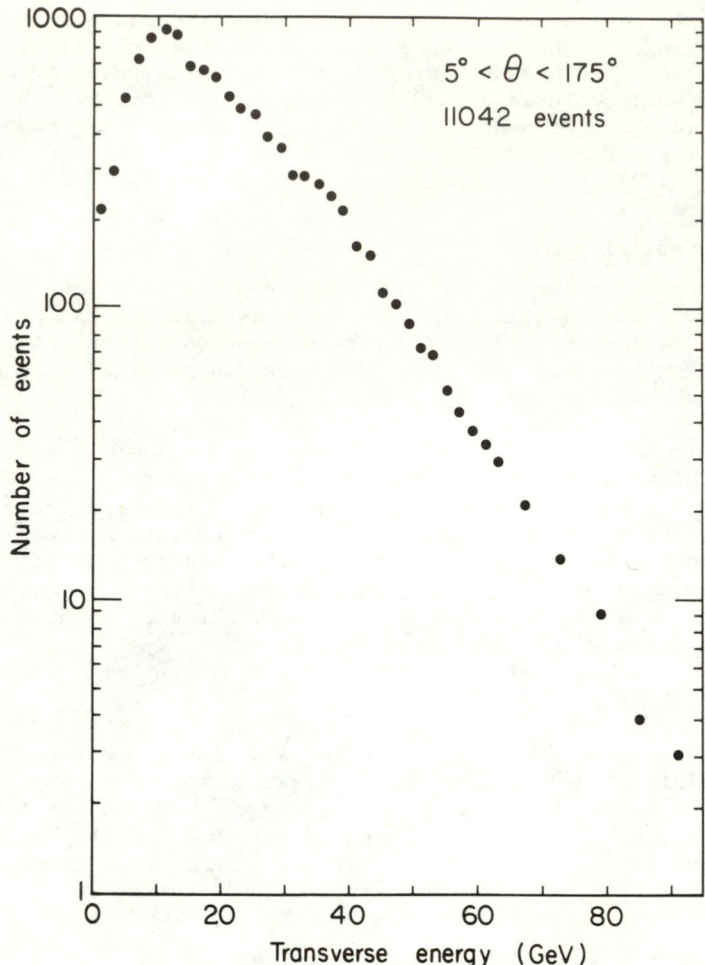

Fig. 13.   Transverse energy distribution for minimum bias events.

Fig. 14 plots the number of segments (maximum 64) hit in the endcap Em calorimeters ($5°<\theta<25°$) versus the number of hits (maximum 48) in the central EM calorimeter ($25°<\theta<155°$). A hit may be due to a photon from $\pi°$ decay or to a charged hadron. We note a strong correlation between the multiplicities recorded in each calorimeter.

Fig. 15 shows the number of charged tracks versus the number of EM calorimeter hits for the angular range $25°<\theta<155°$. The line indicates the approximate correlation for equal production of π^+, π^-, $\pi°$, with each $\pi°$ giving rise to two calorimeter hits.

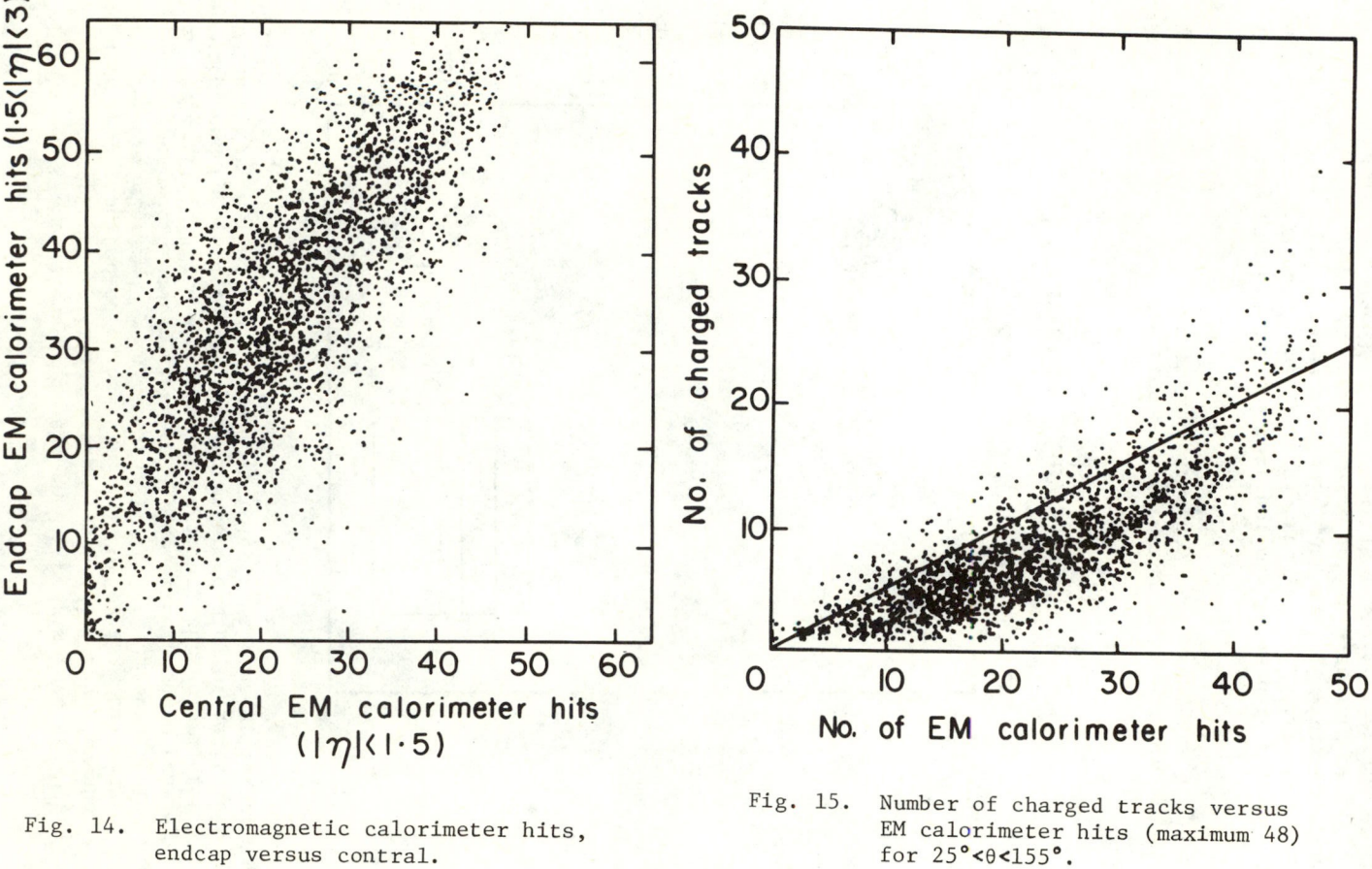

Fig. 14.   Electromagnetic calorimeter hits, endcap versus contral.

Fig. 15.   Number of charged tracks versus EM calorimeter hits (maximum 48) for $25° < \theta < 155°$.

Fig. 15 has some relevance to the possible existence of "Centauro" events in the collider energy range [7]. These events which have been reported at cm energies $\gtrsim$ 1000 GeV in cosmic ray studies are characterized by an anomalously low π° component. In this plot such events would appear close to a line of unit slope passing through the origin. Because of the saturation of the calorimeter at 48 hits, and the need for a detailed understanding of relative calibrations for charged and neutral particles in the calorimeter, no conclusions can be drawn at this time.

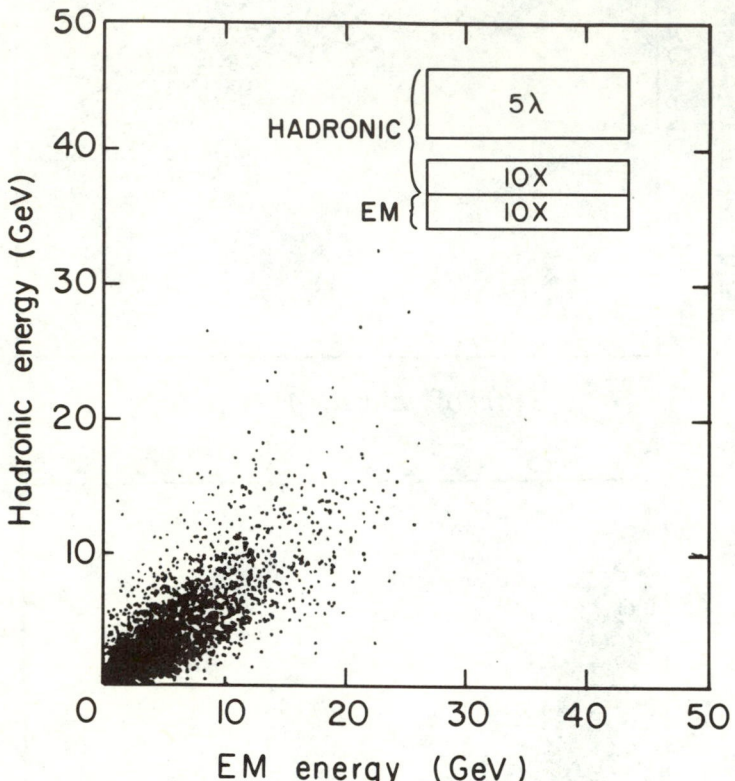

Fig. 16. Hadronic versus electromagnetic energy in the angular range $25° < \theta < 155°$. The inset indicates how these energies are measured.

Fig. 16 also shows how the UA1 detector may be used to search for Centauro events. "Hadronic" energy is plotted versus "Electromagnetic" energy for the angular range 25°-155°. Attempting a correspondence between UA1 and the cosmic ray detectors we define electromagnetic energy as the energy deposited in the first 10 radiation lengths of the electromagnetic calorimeter; the remaining energy deposited in the rear EM calorimeter and the hadronic calorimeter is taken as hadronic.

2. Charged Particle Multiplicity in the Central Region [8]

At the ISR it was found that the height of the rapidity plateau increased by 40% over the energy range $\sqrt{s}$ = 24–63 GeV [9]. The degree of violation of Feynman scaling between 63 GeV and the 540 GeV energy of the $p\bar{p}$ collider is therefore of considerable interest.

We have measured the charged particle multiplicity $n_{\pm}$ in the angular range 30°<θ<150°; the corresponding range in pseudorapidity $\eta = -\log \tan \theta/2$ is $|\eta|$<1.3. The data comes from a run without magnetic field in October, November 1981 with the pre-trigger described in section III.1. For this run approximately 50% of the central detector drift chambers were instrumented at half density. About 90% of the triggers are $p\bar{p}$ collisions, the remaining 10% being due to beam gas interactions.

A total of 789 events were scanned by physicists on a Megatek display (Fig. 5). To obtain the mean charged particle multiplicity, corrections were applied for electrons from Dalitz decay and conversion in the beam pipe and surrounding material (-6% ± 2%) and nuclear interactions in the same material (1.5% ± 1%). No correction was applied for K_S^0 or Λ^0 charged decays which would normally be counted as two charged tracks. We obtain a mean charged particle multiplicity of 3.9 ± 0.3 per unit of η at $|\eta|$<1.3. The quoted error includes an allowance for the uncertainties in the correction terms. In order to compare our data with those from Thomé et al. [9, Fig. 17] we have included only events having at least one track in our fiducial region. If events with zero central tracks are included the quoted numbers is reduced by $\sim$ 6% to 3.6 ± 0.3.

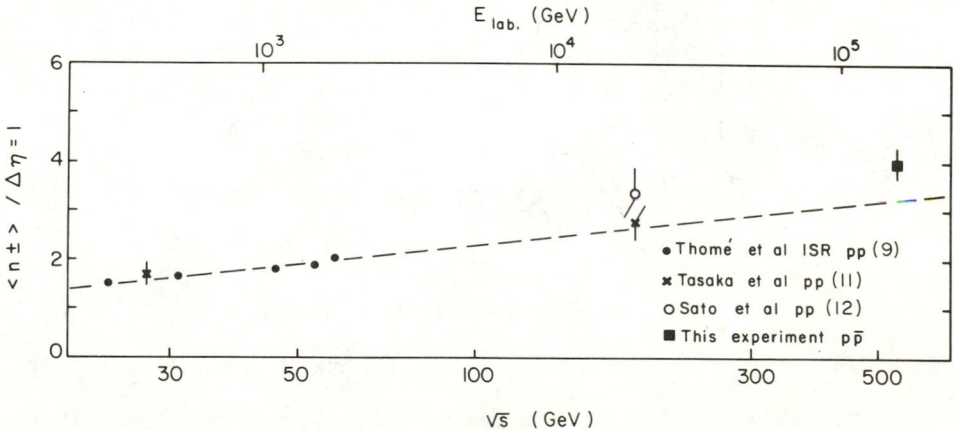

Fig. 17. The mean charged particle multiplicity per unit of η for $|\eta|$<1.5 as a function of centre-of-mass energy for events with at least one charged particle in the fiducial region. The line is the linear fit of Thomé et al. to their data.

342

Because the minimum angle of the triggering hodoscopes is $\simeq 14$ mrad (t = 13 GeV^2) single diffraction dissociation events are excluded from the sample. At the ISR these constitute $\sim$ 14% of all inelastic events [10]. However these events should negligibly populate the region of $|\eta| < 1.3$, and their loss should not affect the estimate of $\eta_\pm$ for events with at least one track in this interval.

Fig. 17 shows our result together with data from the ISR and results from two cosmic ray experiments [11,12]. These cosmic ray results are from balloon experiments with nuclear emulsions.

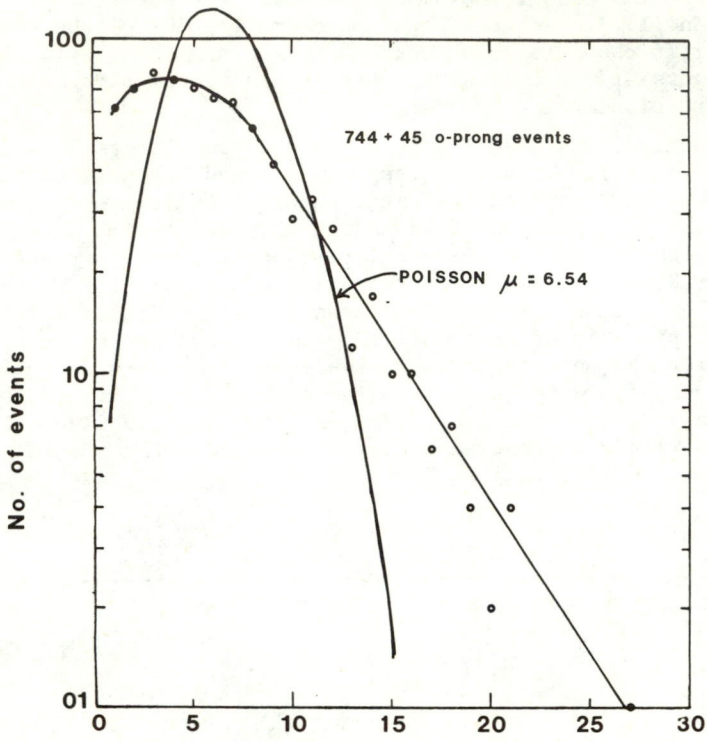

744 + 45 o-prong events

POISSON $\mu = 6.54$

CHARGED MULTIPLICITY

Fig. 18. Charged particle multiplicity distributions for $|\eta| < 1.3$.

Fig. 18 shows that the charged particle multiplicity distribution for $|\eta| < 1.3$ is significantly braoder than Poissonian. In Fig. 19 the normalized charged particle multiplicity is plotted in terms of the KNO scaling variable $z = n_\pm/\langle\eta\rangle_\pm$ [13]. The distribution argues well with those measured over the ISR energy range for approximately the same rapidity range, indicating that KNO scaling holds over the cm energy range $\sqrt{s} = 50-500$ GeV.

343

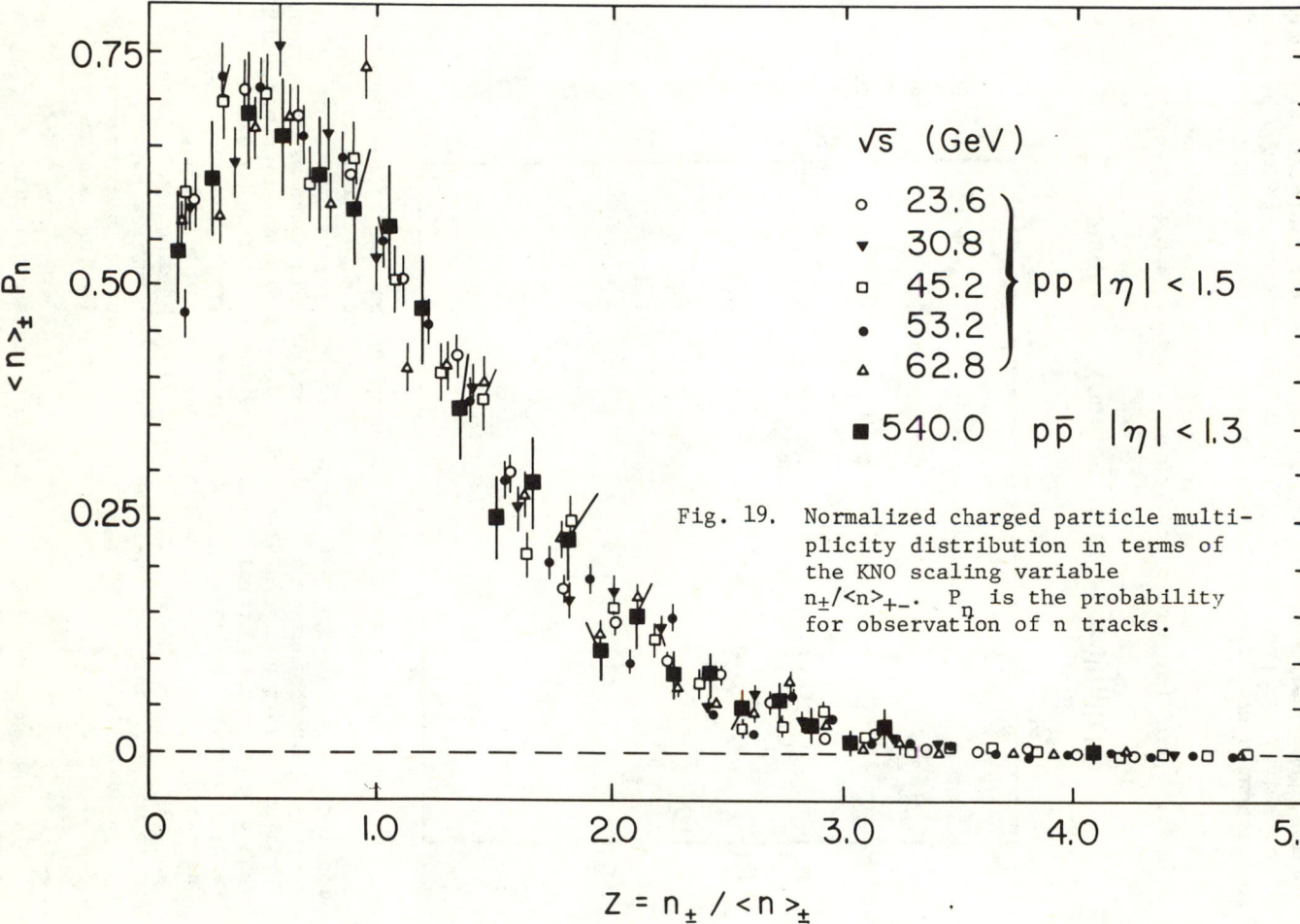

Fig. 19. Normalized charged particle multiplicity distribution in terms of the KNO scaling variable $n_{\pm}/\langle n\rangle_{+-}$. P_n is the probability for observation of n tracks.

$\sqrt{s}$ (GeV)

○ 23.6
▼ 30.8
□ 45.2   } pp $|\eta| < 1.5$
● 53.2
△ 62.8

■ 540.0   p$\bar{p}$ $|\eta| < 1.3$

$\langle n\rangle_{\pm}$ P_n

$Z = n_{\pm} / \langle n\rangle_{\pm}$

344

The long tail in Figs. 18, 19 is very likely correlated with the realtively large cross section observed for events with large E_T (Fig. 13).

It has been suggested by Lattes et al. [7] that the C-jet events of the Chacaltaya experiment, with an average incident energy of ~130 TeV, show a significant difference from the extrapolation of accelerator events both in their multiplicity and their transverse energy. They propose a correlation between E_T and multiplicity, suggesting that events fall into different classes. One such class has a low value of average E_T per secondary particle (gamma rays in their case) and a low average number of gamma rays per unit of rapidity. Another class has a high average value of E_T per secondary and also a high multiplicity. The SPS collider at $\sqrt{s}$ = 540 GeV has a laboratory equivalent energy of ~155 TeV for fixed target collisions and so it is meaningful to examine the data for these effects.

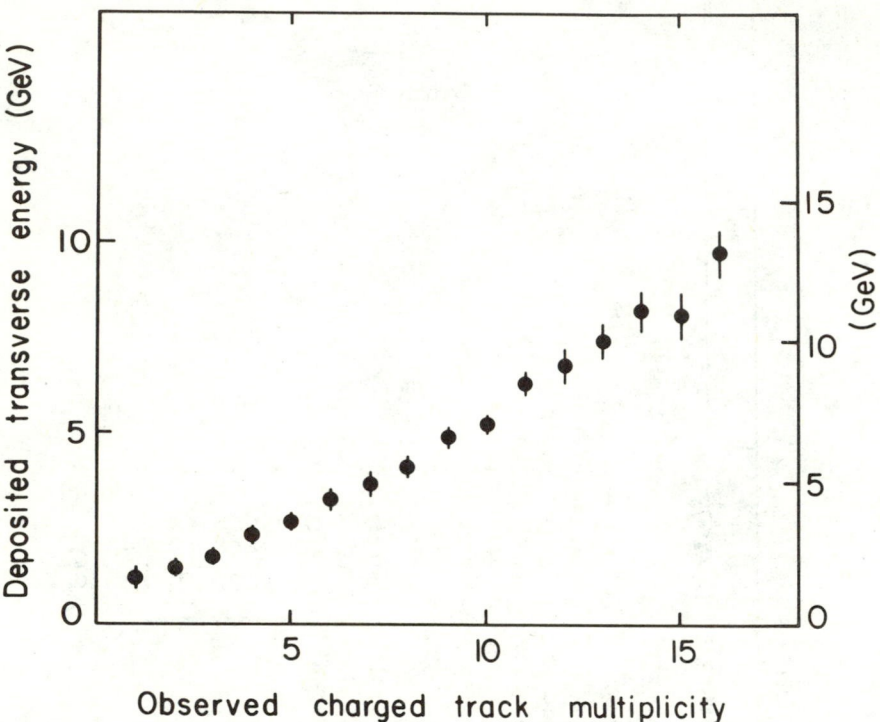

Fig. 20. Calorimeter transverse energy as a function of observed charged particle multiplicity.

Fig. 20 shows the calorimeter transverse energy as a function of observed charged track multiplicity. The left-hand vertical scale shows the visible energy measured in the electromagnetic and hadron calorimeters. The right-hand scale has been corrected by a factor 1.35 to take account of the lower response to hadrons of the electromagnetic calorimeter. An absolute scale uncertainty of ±20% still remains, as a precise application of this factor requires knowledge of the momentum of the incident hadrons. The average value of the transverse energy per event divided by the charged particle multiplicity seen in the central detector does not appear to depend on the multiplicity for these events.

Assuming a ratio 2 for charged/neutral particle production Fig. 20 implies an average E_T per secondary particle of 0.50 ± 0.10 GeV.

ACKNOWLEDGEMENTS

I wish to thank my colleagues in UA1 for asking me to represent them at this conference.

This work was supported in part by the United States Department of Energy.

REFERENCES

1. Aachen-Annecy (LAPP)-Birmingham-CERN-London (Queen Mary College)-
   Paris (Collège de France)-Riverside-Rutherford-Sacley (CEN)-
   Vienna Collab., A 4 solid-angle detector for the SPS used as a
   proton-antiproton collider at a centre-of-mass energy of 540 GeV,
   Proposal CERN/SPSC/78-06/P92 (1978).

2. C. Rubbia, Proceedings of the EPS Conference, Lisbon, July 1981.

3. M. Barranco Luque et al., Nucl. Inst. 176 (1980) 175.

4. M. Calvetti et al., Nucl. Instr. 176 (1980) 255.

5. K. Eggert, et al., Nucl. Inst. 176 (1980) 217.

6. K. Pretzl, this conference.

7. C. M. G. Lattes, Y. Fujimoto and S. Hasegawa, Phys. Rep. 65 (1980)
   151, and references therein.

8. G. Arnison et al., Phys. Lett. 107B (1981) 320.

9. W. Thomé et al., Nucl. Phys. B129 (1977) 365.

10. M. G. Albrow et al., Nucl. Phys. B108 (1976) 1.

11. S. Tasaka et al., Proc. 17th Intern. Cosmic-ray Conf. (Paris, 1981)
    (CEN, Saclay, 1981) Vol. 5, p. 126.

12. Y. Sato et al., J. Phys. Soc. Japan 41 (1976) 1821.

13. Z. Koba, H. B. Nielsen and P. Olesen, Nucl. Phys. B40 (1972) 317.

FIRST RESULTS FROM THE SPS COLLIDER

UA5 Collaboration
Bonn-Brussels-Cambridge-CERN-Stockholm

Presented by R.B. Meinke

Physikalisches Institut, Bonn University, Germany

ABSTRACT

First results from experiment UA5 at the CERN SPS collider studying $p\bar{p}$ collisions at $\sqrt{s}$ = 540 GeV are presented[1]. The central region pseudorapidity density is 3.0 ± 0.1 for non-diffractive events. The FWHM of the observed pseudorapidity distribution is narrower than expected from a simple extrapolation of ISR data which can be interpreted as an increase in the mean p_t for hadron production. A value of 27.4 ± 2.0 is obtained for the mean charged multiplicity $\langle n_{ch} \rangle$ of produced hadrons. This is not in disagreement with an extrapolation using a quadratic fit in $\ell n s$ to previous lower energy data up to ISR energies, but excludes an $s^{1/4}$ or stronger dependence of $\langle n_{ch} \rangle$ on s. Correlations between charged particles of positive and negative c.m.s. pseudorapidity have been analysed. In contrast to ISR energies, where long range correlations have been found to be small, they appear to be as important as short range correlations at collider energies. Preliminary results on correlations between charged particles and photons over a limited acceptance ($\Delta|\eta| < 1$, $\Delta\phi = \pi/2$) in the central region of pseudo-rapidity are given.

APPARATUS

Streamer chamber system

A schematic layout of the UA5 detector[2] while installed in the LSS4 experimental area of the SPS collider is shown in fig. 1. Two 6 m long streamer chambers were placed one above and one below an elliptical beam pipe of 0.4 mm stainless steel, such that the visible volumes of the chambers were $\lesssim$ 9 cm apart. Lead-glass converter plates with a thickness of 1 radiation length are built into the sensitive volumes at the ends and the sides of one of the chambers as shown in fig. 1. Each chamber was viewed by three stereoscopic cameras: a main camera at each end viewing slightly more than half of the chamber at a demagnification of 50, and a central supplementary camera viewing the whole chamber at a demagnification of 80. Image intensifier tubes of gain $\sim$ 2000 were used with all cameras allowing us to photograph small streamers of 5-10 mm length. The resulting homogeneity of the chambers gave good track quality over the whole length and charged particles could be studied with pseudorapidities

348

$(\eta = -\ell n \, \tan\theta/2)$ $|\eta| \lesssim 5$ limited by the geometrical acceptance as shown in fig. 2. The spatial resolution was found to be 1-2 mm and the excellent two-track resolution of about 2 mm allowed one even to identify and study narrow pairs from photon conversions. The detector has no magnetic field, so the tracks in our streamer chambers are straight lines spreading out radially from the interaction point.

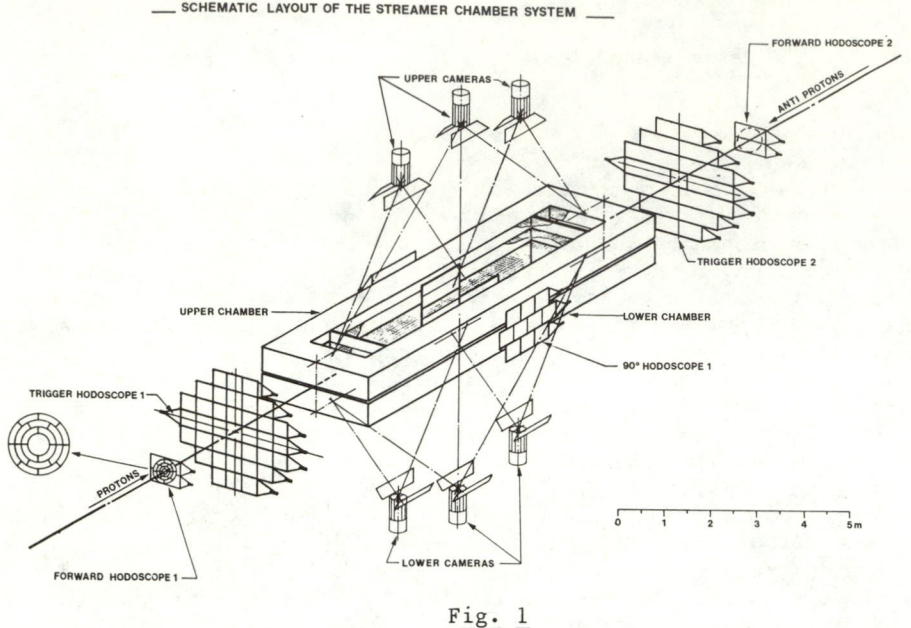

Fig. 1

Trigger

To trigger on as large a fraction as possible of the inelastic $p\bar{p}$ cross section six planes of scintillation counter hodoscopes have been used. They are located at the ends and the sides of the streamer chambers as indicated in fig. 1. The two counter planes at each end form "arm 1" and "arm 2" of the trigger system with the two planes in each arm being away 4.5 m and 5.5 m respectively from the centre of the apparatus.

An event trigger demanded at least one hit in each arm in coincidence ($n_{arm1} \geq 1$, $n_{arm2} \geq 1$) and for part of the running it was necessary to employ a more restrictive trigger by requiring at least two particles in the direction of the outgoing antiproton bunch ($n_{arm1} \geq 2$, $n_{arm} > 1$) to increase the ratio of $p\bar{p}$ events to background events. By requiring at least one hit in both arms of the trigger system, single diffraction dissociation reactions have been excluded from our event sample. We estimate that 95 ± 3% of the remaining inelastic cross section is seen by the trigger.

Run conditions

Typically one bunch of $\sim 5 \times 10^{10}$ protons was colliding in our intersection region LSS4 with one bunch of initially $\sim 10^9$ antiprotons, giving a starting luminosity of 2×10^{25} cm^{-2} s^{-1}. The luminosity lifetime was usually limited by the lifetime of the antiproton bunch which varied from one to ten hours. The beam conditions in connection with our trigger system yielded on average $\sim 25\%$ of beam-beam interactions amongst the pictures taken. A summary of the trigger conditions and the data taken is given in table 1.

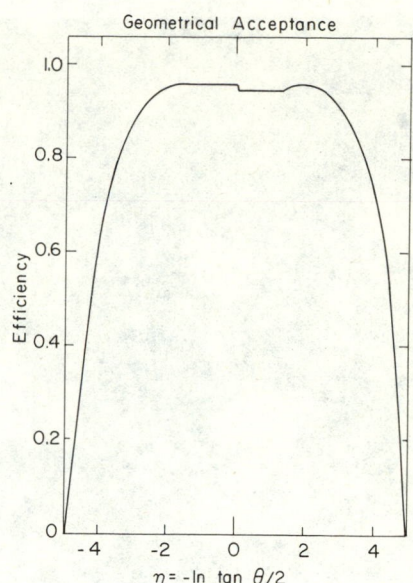

Fig. 2 - Geometrical acceptance of the streamer chamber system as a function of pseudorapidity

DATA ANALYSIS

An example of a complete event as seen by the two supplementary cameras is shown in figs 3 and 4. The events recorded on film are analysed in the following way: the film is first scanned in order to eliminate obvious background events. Each track of the event candidates found is then digitized, and reconstructed in space with the analysis program already tested in an ISR experiment [3]. The sample of measured events used for this report amounts to ~ 350, involving a total of 17 000 tracks. A computer display of a measured and reconstructed event is shown in fig. 5.

Table 1 - Summary of data taken at the Collider in period 7 and running conditions

Run	No. pix	Trigger	% good pp events	No. $p\bar{p}$ inter'ns	$\mathscr{L}_{init}$
21-22 October	20 100	arm1$_{n\geqslant1}$ · arm2$_{n\geqslant1}$	0-40 (av. $\sim$ 16)	3200	$\sim 1\ 10^{25}$
6-10 November	39 800	arm1$_{n\geqslant2}$ · arm2$_{n\geqslant1}$	20-85 (av. $\sim$ 33)	13000	$\sim 2\ 10^{25}$
TOTAL	$\sim$ 60 K		$\sim$ 27%	$\sim$ 16 K	

Fig. 3 - The two stereo views of
an event recorded by the lower
streamer chamber

Fig. 4 - The two stereo views of
the same event recorded by the
upper chamber

A computer program is used to separate the primary vertex from
possible secondary vertices occurring in the beam pipe, and to
classify primary and secondary tracks accordingly. This program has
been optimized in the previous ISR experiment and by Monte-Carlo
simulations of collider events using a variety of event generators.
From these studies we are convinced that $\sim$ 90% of primary tracks are
immediately correctly identified; the remaining 10% are confused with
secondary tracks, but a cut which separates the latter ones statistically was able to reduce the uncertainty on the number of primaries
to < 5%. The Monte-Carlo program corrects for the remaining
uncertainty and for the acceptance of the apparatus, for secondary
nuclear interactions, decays of particles, multiple scattering, pair
conversions, bremsstrahlung, δ-rays down to $\sim$ 1 MeV and for the
measurement errors.

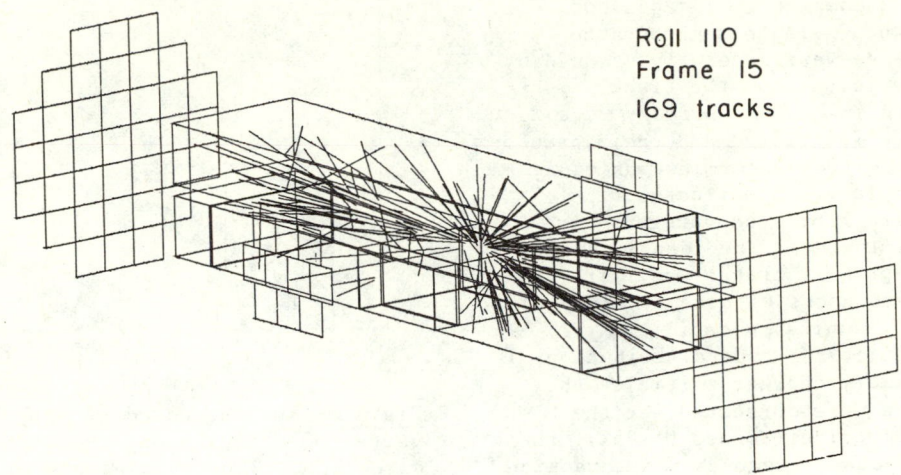

Roll 110
Frame 15
169 tracks

Fig. 5 - Computer display of a meausured and reconstructed event with very large multiplicity.

The distribution of identified primary vertices perpendicular to the beam direction is shown in fig. 6. The width of this distribution is 3 mm and 4 mm in the y and z directions respectively. Event candidates with primary vertices such that $|z| \geq 2$ cm, where z is the depth coordinate measured from the median plane of the beam pipe, are likely to result from interactions of beam halo particles in the beam pipe material and have been excluded. A distribution of primary vertices along the beam direction for one collider run is shown in fig. 7. The two bumps separated by 75 cm are due to the fact that the antiprotons were spread over two RF buckets in that particular run.

In view of the observed complexity of the events and the

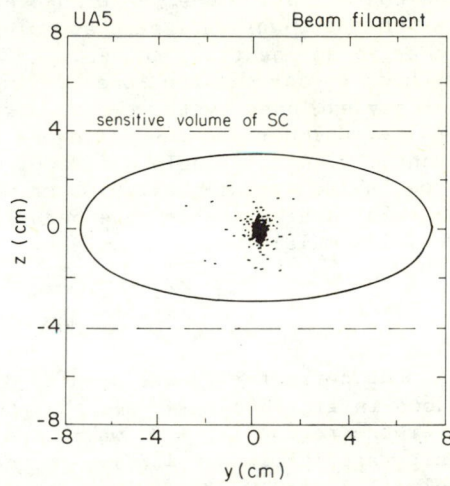

Fig. 6 - Reconstructed primary vertex positions in the plane vertical to the beam direction. The elliptical beam pipe and the sensitive volume of the two chambers are indicated.

352

possibility of unusual phenomena we have analyzed ∿ 100 events by a completely independent method. In this method the events were carefully scanned by physicists and the tracks pointing to the primary vertex were identified and their pseudo-rapidities determined using a template. Clear cases of e^+e^- pairs from γ conversions were eliminated. The identification of primary tracks was fairly unambiguous with an accuracy of ∿ 0.1 units in rapidity. To extract the true distribution of primary charged particles the data were corrected for the geometrical losses (∿ 25%), the effects of secondary interactions (∿ 1.5%), γ conversions (∿ 13%) and strange particle decays (∿ 5%).

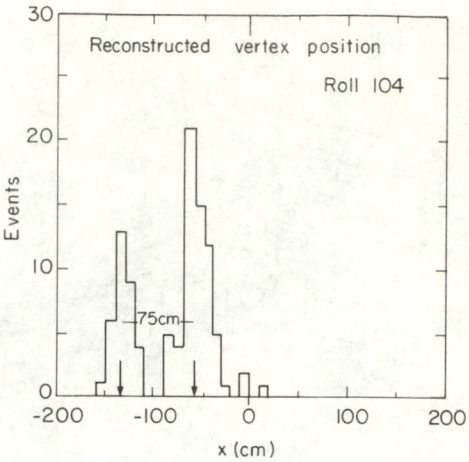

Fig. 7 – Reconstructed primary vertex positions along the beam direction. The two clusters of events result from antiprotons being spread over two RF buckets.

For calculating the necessary corrections it was assumed in both methods that all γ's come from decays of π^0's, and that $\pi^0/\pi^{ch} = 0.5$. The contamination due to strange particles decaying before entering the chambers was estimated assuming a ratio of all K's to all π's (charged and neutral) to be 0.2. No attempt has been made in the two methods to correct the loss of single diffractive events which are largely excluded by the two-arm trigger described above. Except when indicated otherwise the following results therefore refer to inelastic events, with the single diffraction dissociation component excluded. From the Monte-Carlo calculation we estimate that only 5 ± 3% of non-diffractive events have been lost by our trigger, these being of very low multiplicity.

PHYSICS RESULTS

The corrected pseudorapidity distribution folded about η = 0 is shown in fig. 8(a). We see that the distribution is generally flat over the region |η| < 3, where the average number of particles per unit rapidity is 3.0 ± 0.1. For comparison, we obtained[3] an average value 1.75 ± 0.07 for |η| < 2 at $\sqrt{s}$ = 53 GeV using the same detector at the ISR. In a cosmic ray balloon experiment at approximately $\sqrt{s}$ ≃ 180 GeV[4], in which the charged secondaries were detected with good efficiency, the value obtained is 2.6 ± 0.5. These average values are shown in fig. 9, together with values of $1/\sigma(d\sigma/d\eta)$ (η = 0) obtained at different ISR energies[5], and lower energy FNAL values[6]. In all these experiments no trigger condition requiring at least one charged particle in the acceptance region of the central rapidity range was made, as is often the case with counter experiments. A ℓns exptrapolation of all lower energy data would suggest a central region value of $1/\sigma(d\sigma/d\eta)$ of ~ 2.6 instead of the 3.0 ± 0.1 observed with our experimental set-up. This difference could well be accommodated by the possible $18 \pm 5\%$ single diffraction dissociation contribution suggested at our energy[7] to which our trigger was insensitive, leading to an equivalent renormalization of the distribution.

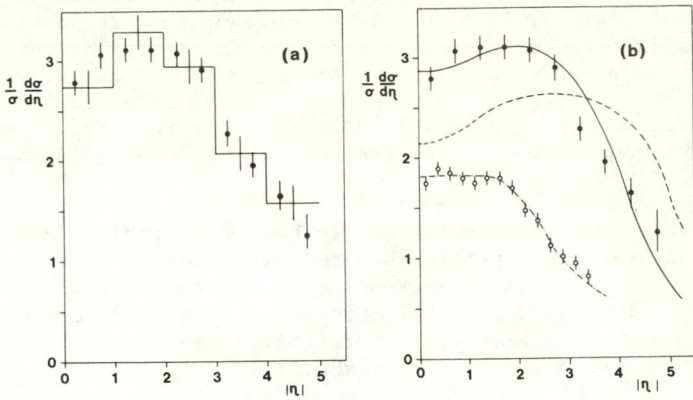

Fig. 8 (a) Corrected pseudorapidity distributions for $\sqrt{s}$ = 540 GeV folded about η = 0, from 100 events template – measured by physicists (histogram) and from 340 events passed through our digitizing and analysis procedures (solid points). The errors are statistical only. (b) Data from 340 events at $\sqrt{s}$ = 540 GeV compared with earlier UA5 data obtained at the ISR at $\sqrt{s}$ = 53 GeV (open points). The dashed and dot-dashed curves are predicted from p_t limited phase-space for $\langle p_t \rangle$ = 350 MeV/c. The solid curve for $\sqrt{s}$ = 540 GeV is from the same model but for $\langle p_t \rangle$ = 500 MeV/c.

The central plateau in rapidity in fig. 8 appears to extend to ± 3 units, so that by $|\eta| = 4.25$ the distribution has fallen to half its maximum value. For comparison at $\sqrt{s}$ = 53 GeV[3] the plateau was ± 2 units wide, and fell to half maximum at $|\eta| \simeq 3.25$. So we observe that the width of the plateau has grown by only ~ 2 units in going from $\sqrt{s}$ = 53 GeV to $\sqrt{s}$ = 540 GeV, whereas the separation of the two beam particles has increased by 4.6 units over this energy. Thus, the central plateau has not spread as much as it could have done on kinematic grounds.

Using the conventional cylindrical phase space description with $\langle p_t \rangle$ = 350 MeV/c, assuming that leading baryons take on the average half the energy of the

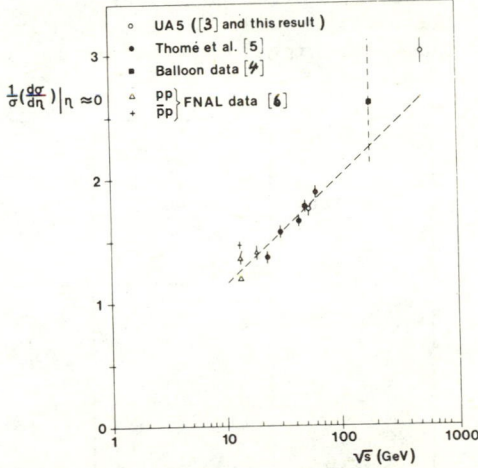

Fig. 9 Charged particle density in pseudorapidity near η = 0 from various experiments up to Collider energy. Our Collider value is for single diffractive events excluded. The straight line is drawn by eye to indicate a possible ln s dependence of the lower energy data. The values from the ISR of ref. [5] were obtained by reading off at η = 0 from fig. 6 of that reference.

incoming particles and taking the particle ratios measured at the ISR[8] we can nicely reproduce our ISR data as shown in fig. 8(b). Taking this model and assuming that the particle ratios extrapolate smoothly to collider energies leads to the dashed curve of fig. 8(b). We see immediately that the central rapidity plateau is expected to extend to $\simeq$ 5 units in such a model. Furthermore, the curve predicts a significant dip near $|\eta| = 0$. It is evident from the comparison that such a description cannot account for the data. We would have to increase p_t to $\simeq$ 500 MeV/c, as shown in the solid curve, to get reasonable agreement. In the cosmic ray data[4] referred to earlier, a reliable measurement of energy is done only for the γ-rays in the forward hemisphere; from these measurements $\langle p_t \rangle$ for π^0's was found to be 400 $\pm$ 20 MeV/c.

Using the $\sim$ 350 measured events we have determined the multiplicity distribution of charged particles. The distribution of the raw data i.e. the primary tracks which were associated with the interaction vertex is shown in fig. 10(a). The distribution of the charged particles shows a pronounced tail which extends to more than three times the average. Mean value and dispersion are given in table 2.

Table 2

Values of $\langle n_{ch} \rangle$, $D = \langle (n - \langle n \rangle)^2 \rangle^{1/2}$ and $\langle n_{ch} \rangle / D$ obtained from the measured charged particle multiplicity at $\sqrt{s}$ = 540 GeV. The left-hand column refers to the measured distributions before corrections were applied. The corrected values appear in the next two columns: firstly we give the values under our trigger conditions, i.e. single diffraction excluded, and then in the last column we give values of $\langle n_{ch} \rangle$ allowing for a diffractive component (see text).

Quantity	Raw data	Corrected data	
		Single diffraction dissociation excluded	Single diffraction dissociation allowed for
$\langle n_{ch} \rangle$	20.0 ± 0.7	28.0 ± 2.0 (a) 26.8 ± 2.1 (b)	21 to 27
D	11.2 ± 0.5	12.5 ± 1.7 (a)	-
$\langle n_{ch} \rangle / D$	1.8 ± 0.2	2.2 ± 0.3 (a)	-

(a) After unfolding the smearing of multiplicity due to acceptance limitations.

(b) From a simple integration of the pseudorapidity distribution.

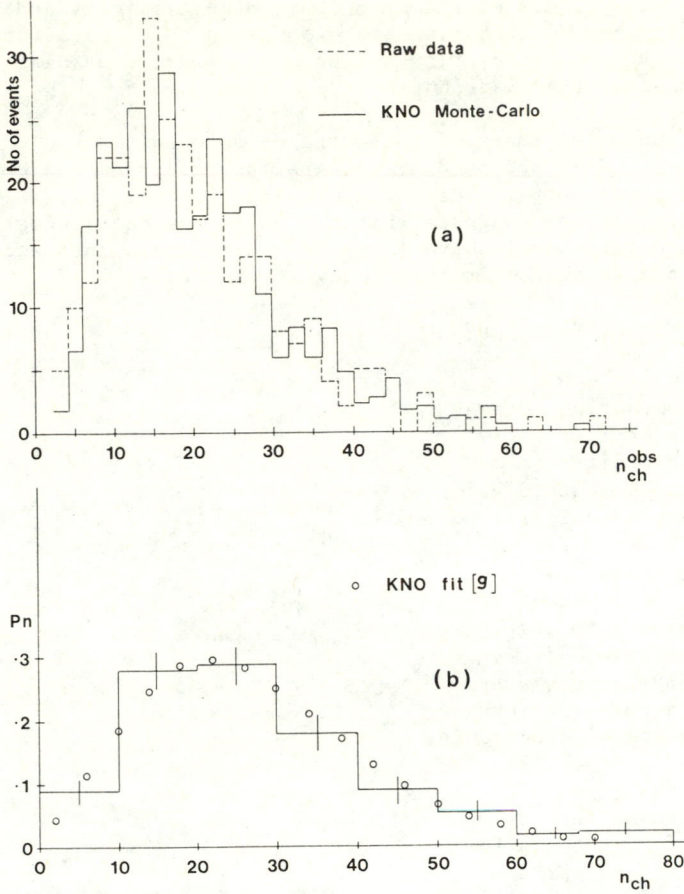

Fig. 10 – (a) Charged particle multiplicity for raw
data obtained in this experiment by associating
observed primary tracks to the interaction vertex,
compared with a Monte-Carlo prediction following KNO
scaling obtained after tracking through our detector.
(b) Measured multiplicity distribution corrected for
acceptances, with KNO prediction superimposed.

For comparison we have generated events according to the model
described above with a KNO distribution, following the parametrization
of Slattery[9], being used for charged particles. All particles of
these events have been tracked through the detector configuration and
were analyzed by the same program chain as the real data. Fig. 10(a)
shows as the full histogram the distribution resulting from this
procedure. It is seen to be compatible with the data.

356

Fig. 10(b) shows the multiplicity distribution corrected for acceptances. The values of the mean charged multiplicity and the dispersion for this distribution are also given in table 2 for comparison. The KNO curve using the parameters given by Slattery[9] is superimposed on the distribution.

An independent estimate of the average observed charged multiplicity $\langle n_{ch}\rangle$ is obtained by integrating our pseudorapidity distribution given above. The value obtained is 25.2 ± 1.4. The Monte-Carlo simulation suggests that 6 ± 3% of the charged particles produced non-diffractively have $|\eta| > 5$. Taking this into account, the corrected mean charged multiplicity is therefore

$$\langle n_{ch}\rangle^{nd} = \sum_n n\sigma_n^{nd}/\sigma^{nd} = 26.8 \pm 2.1,$$

where the superscript nd indicates that our trigger excludes single diffraction dissociation. The above value is also given in table 2. Our best estimate is $\langle n_{ch}\rangle^{nd}$ = 27.4 ± 2.0 obtained by averaging the two values in table 1. The fit to the ISR data of Thomé et al.[5] using an $s^{1/4}$ dependence gives $\langle n_{ch}\rangle \approx 40$, a number which even at this stage we can rule out.

Fig. 11 shows the dependence of n_{ch} on s for several FNAL[6] and ISR[5] experiments. The data points are well described by the parametrization $\langle n_{ch}\rangle$ = a + bℓns + cℓ^2ns determined by Thomé et al.[5]. The value of $\langle n_{ch}\rangle$ for a recent balloon flight experiment[4] also lies well on the extrapolated curve. However, since our measured value excludes the single diffractive cross section it cannot be compared directly with the other experiments which give a value of $\langle n_{ch}\rangle$ for the whole inelastic cross section.

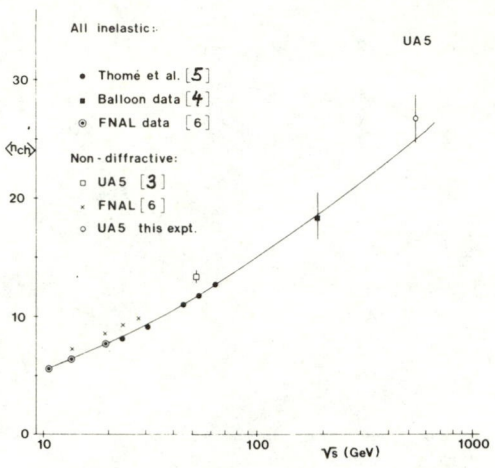

Fig. 11 Dependence of $\langle n_{ch}\rangle$ upon $\sqrt{s}$ as measured in lower energy experiments together with the Thomé et al. [1] fit of the form $\langle n_{ch}\rangle = a + b \ln s + c \ln^2 s$ to ISR and lower energy data. The UA5 data point reported here is for single diffraction dissociation excluded, and several lower energy non-diffractive vlues are also shown for comparison.

For FNAL data[6] and for our earlier ISR experiment[3] the values of $\langle n_{ch}\rangle^{nd}$ are also shown in fig. 11. Judging the observed difference between $\langle n_{ch}\rangle^{nd}$ and $\langle n_{ch}\rangle$ over their energy range, the difference between our measured value and the extrapolation of Thomé et al. can easily be accounted for by a single diffraction dissociation component.

To estimate the influence of diffraction dissociation[7] we assume that, as observed at the ISR, elastic scattering and single diffraction dissociation each contributes 18% to the total cross section. Making the extreme assumptions for the mean charged multiplicity $3 < \langle n_{ch} \rangle^{sd} < 1/2 \langle n_{ch} \rangle^{nd}$, where the superscript sd denotes single diffraction dissociation, this leads to an estimate for the average inelastic charged multiplicity in the range $21 < \langle n_{ch} \rangle < 27$, in reasonable agreement with the prediction $\langle n_{ch} \rangle \simeq 25$ of Thomé et al. This result puts in doubt speculations arising from cosmic ray studies about very high average multiplicities at collider energies. We do observe events of very high multiplicity as may be seen from figs 3 and 4, but the high multiplicity tail of the distribution needs further study.

Though we do not observe scaling in pseudorapidity (in the following simply called rapidity) by going from ISR to collider energies and there are indications that the average value of transverse momentum is rising, it seems that the multiplicity distribution when shown as a function of $z = n/\langle n \rangle$ stays essentially unchanged between $\sqrt{s} = 10$ GeV and 540 GeV. At all energies the distribution shows a pronounced tail towards large multiplicities. This tail reflects the existence of strong correlations among the final state particles, and analyzing them could yield further insight into the dynamics responsible for particle multiplicities in the final state.

The existence of significant correlations between particles which have small separations in rapidity (up to two units) is well established at FNAL and ISR[10] energies. These correlations are energy independent and can be understood in terms of resonance production. Also energy dependent "long-range" correlations in the rapidity plateau have been observed over the ISR energy range[11] with a less clear dynamical origin.

An elegant and intuitive analysis of correlations among particles can be done in the following way[11]: let us define as "right hemisphere" the one with positive c.m.s. rapidity and as "left hemisphere" the opposite one. So-called left-right correlations can then be defined as the dependence of the average charged multiplicity n_L in certain rapidity intervals of the left hemisphere on the multiplicity n_R in the corresponding intervals of the right hemisphere:

$$\langle n_L \rangle = f(n_R)$$

The derivative

$$f' = d\langle n_L \rangle / dn_R$$

then measures how strongly the multiplicities in the selected rapidity intervals are correlated and this obviously can be interpreted as a measure of correlations among the particles itself.

In order to separate contributions to the left-right correlations from short-range and long-range type we define the following two sub-regions within the hemispheres:

(a) $|\eta| < 1$

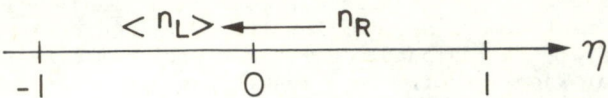

Contributions from short-range correlations like cluster or resonance decays are dominant.

(b) $1 < |\eta| < 4$

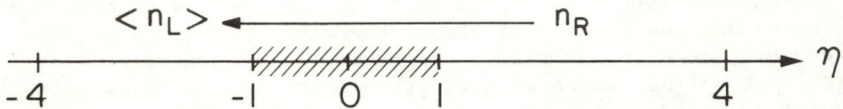

Introducing the gap of two units in rapidity eliminates contributions from short-range correlations and one is therefore only sensitive to long-range correlations.

The left-right correlations for the two intervals $|\eta| < 1$ and $1 < |\eta| < 4$ are shown in figs 12 and 13. In both cases the dependence of $\langle n_L \rangle$ on n_R seems to be compatible with a linear form $\langle n_L \rangle = a + b n_R$ where the slope b measures the strength of short and long-range correlations respectively as explained above. The energy dependence of the observed correlations is investigated by a comparison with the equivalent data from the ISR[11] (fig. 14). The strength of short-range correlations indicated by circles in fig. 14 shows no significant rise over the entire range of 20 GeV $\leq \sqrt{s} \leq$ 540 GeV. A possible explanation of this would be that the percentage of particles coming from resonance or cluster decays and their decay multiplicity is about the same over this energy range. On the other hand the strength of long-range correlations which are negligible at ISR energies when compared with short-range correlations, have grown substantially at collider energies (see squares in fig. 14). This increase seems to be roughly compatible with an extrapolation of the observed energy dependence over the ISR energy range.

Summarizing this correlation analysis one can say the following: short- and long-range correlations seem to be of equal importance at collider energies. This can be looked at in the following way. If one requires a large (small) multiplicity in a certain region of rapidity the tendency (as measured by the slope b) to observe a large (small) multiplicity in an adjacent bin of rapidity and a bin further away is about equally high. Certainly energy-momentum conservation also contributes to the observed long-range correlation. A study of the importance of this influence is under way.

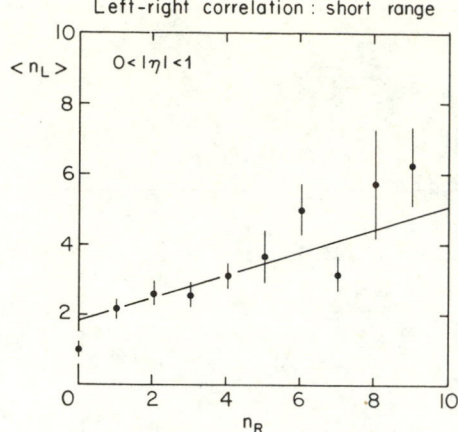

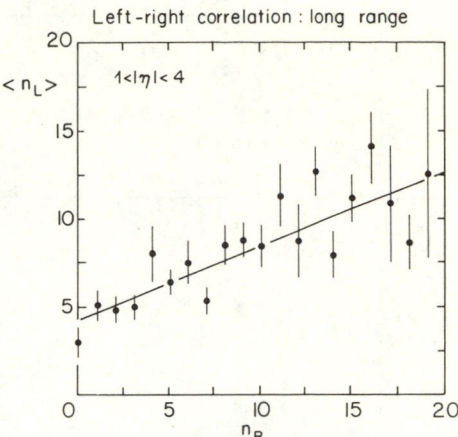

Fig. 12 – Average charged multiplicity in the rapidity interval −1 < η < 0 as a function of charged multiplicity in the corresponding interval of positive rapidity. A straight line fit to the data is indicated.

Fig. 13 – Average charged multiplicity in the rapidity interval −4 ≤ η ≤ −1 as a function of charged multiplicity in the corresponding interval of positive rapidity. A straight line fit to the data is indicated.

We have also studied the production of photons in the region of the central lead-glass plates (see paragraph: apparatus) which cover the two central units of rapidity, $|\eta| \lesssim 1$ and about a quarter of the azimuth, $\Delta\phi \simeq 90°$. In order to analyze the correlations between the number of charged particles and photons we have also counted the charged particles in the same region. About 700 events have been analyzed with at least one photon or charged particle hitting the plates.

For charged particles the acceptance correction has been done as described before. The main corrections for photons come from the conversion probability in the lead-glass plates $(1X_0)$. For the calculation of conversion probability it is necessary to fix the energies of the photons. This has been done by assuming that all photons result from π^0's with an average transverse momentum of 500 MeV/c.

In fig. 15 the average number of photons is shown as a function of n_{ch}. A linear dependence of the form $\langle n_\gamma \rangle = (1.2 \pm 0.2) + (0.5 \pm 0.1)n_{ch}$ is compatible with the data. From the same analysis we have determined $\langle n_\gamma \rangle / \langle n_{ch} \rangle = 1.2 \pm 0.1$. The highest charged multiplicities observed on the plates of about 10 correspond to events with ~ 70 charged particles being produced which is more than two times the average (27.4). But at the present status of the analysis no conclusion about the existence of Centauro events is possible.

360

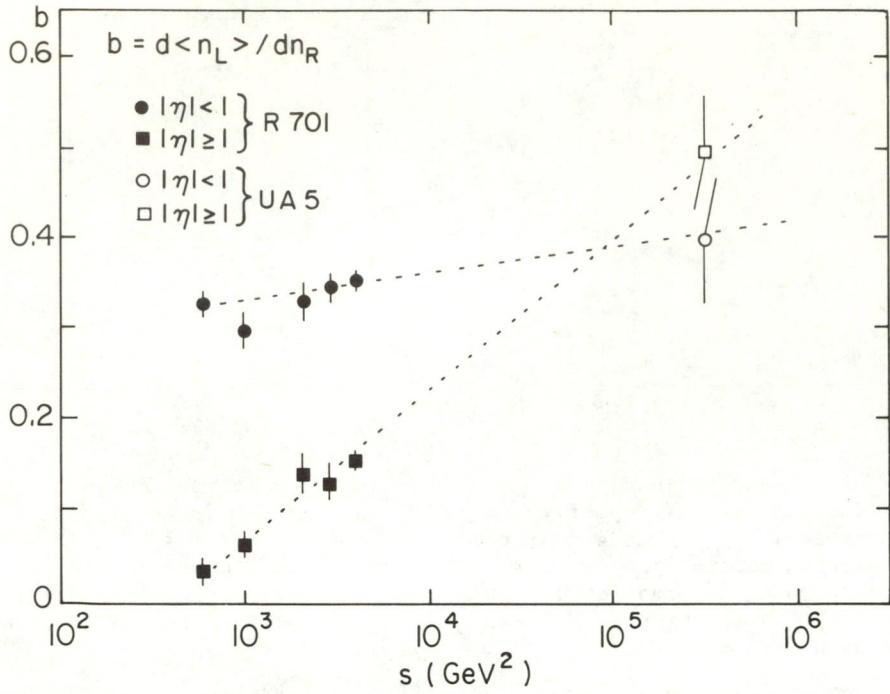

<u>Fig. 14</u> – Dependence of short- and long-range correlations upon s as measured by the derivative $d\langle n_L \rangle / dn_R$ (see text). The collider data points are indicated by open symbols. The lower energy ISR data are from ref. 1. The dashed lines are shown to guide the eye.

CONCLUSIONS

We have measured non-diffractive charged particle production in $p\bar{p}$ interactions at $\sqrt{s} = 540$ GeV over the rapidity range $|\eta| < 5$. An average value for the central rapidity density of 3.0 ± 0.1 has been found. A comparison with ISR data shows that the width of the η distribution has not increased as much as the separation of the two beam particles. A conventional cylindrical phase space model could accommodate this by increasing the p_t from 350 MeV/c to 500 MeV/c. The observed average charged multiplicity of 27.4 seems to be compatible with the parametrization of Thomé et al. for lower energies if we allow for single diffraction dissociation. An $s^{1/4}$ dependence of $\langle n_{ch} \rangle$ seems to be ruled out. The distribution of charged multiplicities, showing a pronounced tail towards large multiplicities is compatible with KNO scaling within the present accuracy of the data. Short-range correlations between charged particles with similar strength as observed at the ISR have been found. Long-range correlations which extend over more than two units in rapidity are of comparable strength to the short-range correlations. In the central region the ratio $\langle n_\gamma \rangle / \langle n_{ch} \rangle$ is close to 1 and a linear dependence of $\langle n_\gamma \rangle$ on n_{ch} over a wide range of charged multiplicity seems to hold.

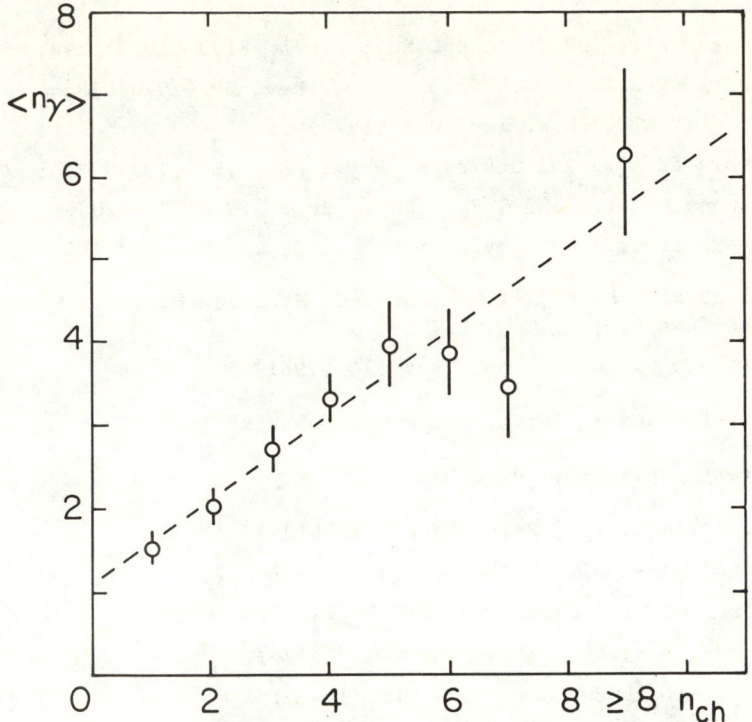

Fig. 15 - Average number of photons in $|\eta| \lesssim 1$ and $\Delta\phi \simeq 90°$ as a function of multiplicity in the same interval. The dashed line shows a linear fit to the data

REFERENCES

1. K. Alpgard et al., Phys. Lett. 107B (1981) 310, 315.

2. UA5 Collaboration, Bonn-Brussels-Cambridge-CERN-Stockholm, Physica Scripta 23 (1981) 642.

3. K. Alpgard et al., Comparison of $\bar{p}p$ and pp Interactions at $\sqrt{s}$ = 53 GeV, to be submitted to Phys. Lett.

4. S. Tasaka et al., University of Tokyo, Institute of Cosmic Ray Research, preprint ICR 93-81-9.

5. W. Thomé et al., Nucl. Phys. B129 (1977) 365.

REFERENCES (Cont'd)

6. C.P. Ward et al., 100 GeV/c p̄p, Nucl. Phys. B153 (1979) 299;

   C. Bromberg et al., 100 GeV/c pp, Phys. Rev. D9 (1974) 1864;

   W.M. Morse et al., Phys. Rev. D15 (1977) 66;

   J. Whitmore et al., 205 GeV/c pp, Phys. Rev. 10C (1974) 273;

   A. Firestone et al., 303 GeV/c, Phys. Rev. D10 (1974) 2080;

   C. Bromberg et al., 405 GeV/c pp, Phys. Rev. Lett. 31 (1973) 1563.

7. G. Goggi et al., Proc. XII Rencontre de Moriond ·(Flaine, 1977), ed. J. Tran Than Van;

   G. Alberi and G. Goggi, Phys. Rep. 74 (1981) 1.

8. G. Giacomelli and M. Jacob, Phys. Rep. 55 (1979) 41.

9. P. Slattery, Phys. Rev. D1 (1973) 2073.

10. S.R. Amendolia et al., Phys. Lett. 48B (1974) 359;

    S.R. Amendolia et al., Nuovo Cim. 31A (1976) 17;

    C. Bromberg et al., Phys. Rev. D10 (1974) 3100;

    K. Eggert et al., Nucl. Phys. B86 (1975) 201;

    B.Y. Oh et al., Phys. Lett. 56B (1975) 400;

    R. Singer et al., Phys. Lett. 49B (1974) 481.

11. S. Uhlig et al., Nucl. Phys. B132 (1978) 15.

Diffraction in Accelerators, Colliders And QCD

ALAN R. WHITE
Fermi National Accelerator Laboratory
P.O. Box 500, Batavia, Illinois 60510

ABSTRACT

Recent accelerator results on diffraction are reviewed and argued to demonstrate unambiguously that diffraction is, in first approximation, described by a single Regge pole with unit intercept. The corresponding theoretical asymptotic predictions of Critical Pomeron Reggeon Field Theory are reviewed with the anticipation that they will be seen in diffraction experiments at the CERN and FERMILAB $\bar{p}$-p colliders. The earliest collider results are argued to be very encouraging. Finally a theoretical study of diffraction in gauge theories is presented which concludes that if all Critical Pomeron phenomena are confirmed at the colliders then strong interactions should be described by SU(3) gauge theory containing the maximum number of quarks consistent with asymptotic freedom.

Introduction

At top accelerator energies and through the ISR energy range diffraction is at least 95% of total cross-sections while non-diffractive contributions are decreasing as an inverse power of the energy. As a result we expect that at the CERN and FERMILAB $\bar{p}$-p colliders strong interactions will be entirely diffractive apart, of course, from the very rare processes for which most experiments will be searching. The earliest results from the CERN $\bar{p}$-p collider have already indicated that the bulk production process (producing all diffractive cross-sections) is so overwhelming that rare processes may be extremely difficult to detect. The general picture is of large fluctuations of quantities (multiplicities for example) which in the average simply extrapolate logarithmically from the ISR energy range.

This talk was originally prepared to argue for the importance of diffraction experiments at colliders before the earliest results were available. Since I believe that these results strongly reinforce the case I wished to make I shall make reference to them throughout this written version of the talk. The central thesis of the talk is that a theoretical understanding of diffraction scattering in gauge theories is in sight and that in this context the phenomenom observed at the CERN collider may correspond to a very particular case. In fact when diffraction scattering experiments at both the CERN and FERMILAB colliders are combined they may provide not only a fundamental verification of QCD, but even determine the quark content of the theory. The talk is organized into three sections

A. A section devoted to reviewing new accelerator results-the latest generation of very detailed diffraction experiments has finally led to the unambiguous conclusion that, in a first approximation, diffraction is produced by a single Regge pole with intercept one-the Pomeron.

B. If indeed diffraction is exactly described as a single interacting Regge pole with intercept exactly one then we have a very special situation in which it follows from analyticity and unitarity alone that all diffractive quantities have logarithmic asymptotic behavior predicted by (Critical Pomeron) Reggeon Field Theory.[1-3] The second section is devoted to presenting these predictions, arguing that they have begun to appear in present energy experiments and in the first collider results[4,5] (the observed KNO scaling is part of the predictions) and that they can be fundamentally confirmed by a full range of experiments at the CERN and FERMILAB colliders.

C. This section is devoted to outlining my theoretical understanding[6-8] of diffraction in gauge theories. That diffraction is described by a single Regge pole already requires the gauge group to be SU(3) while if the intercept is exactly one (Critical Pomeron) then the maximum number of quarks consistent with asymptotic freedom is required.

I would like to emphasize that in my view Regge theory provides an absolutely essential framework for a complete theoretical and experimental understanding of diffraction. Over the years Regge theory has been well demonstrated to be a successful phenomenological description of high-energy experiments. It has also been understood for some time that when extended to multiparticle amplitudes (multi-) Regge theory provides the most powerful theoretical method for analyzing the full implications of unitarity and analyticity at high energy.[9] A very important development from this analysis, which I have only recently discovered[8] and which I shall briefly describe in the following, is that multi-Regge theory provides also a direct means for analyzing the notorious mass-shell infra-red problem of QCD.

A. Recent Accelerator Results

With the last paragraph in mind, the first experimental question, asked many times during the last twenty years, is clearly - can diffraction be described by a single Regge pole, the Pomeron, in first approximation? Remarkably recent experiments at the CERN and FERMILAB accelerators have, at last, given a very clear positive answer to this question. The following five properties can now be regarded as experimentally established for diffraction scattering

A. There is universal shrinkage of diffraction peaks

B. All total cross sections are constants up to logarithms of the total energy-which cause a slow but universal rise

C. Differences of total cross-sections for particles and antiparticles go to zero as a power of the energy.

D. There is factorisation of diffractive processes, possibly to within experimental accuracy, and certainly to within 10%

E. Large mass diffractive excitation is non-vanishing at zero momentum transfer.

Properties $\underline{A}$ - $\underline{D}$ establish that we can write (in first approximation) for an elastic differential cross-section

$$\frac{d\sigma_{ij}}{dt} \underset{s\to\infty}{\sim} \beta_i^2(t)\,\beta_j^2(t)\; s^{2(\alpha_{I\!P}(t)-1)} \tag{1}$$

where $\beta_i(t)$ and $\beta_j(t)$ are Regge residue functions and $\alpha_{I\!P}(t)$ is a single, even signature, Regge trajectory, with intercept

$$\alpha_{I\!P}(0) = 1 \tag{2}$$

and (experimentally measured) slope

$$\alpha'_{I\!P}(0) \simeq 0.15 \ GeV^{-1} \tag{3}$$

Property E establishes that the (Reggeon Field Theory) triple Pomeron coupling r_0 is non-zero

$$r_0 = \ " \ \mathrm{\text{⦚}} \ " \ \neq 0 \tag{4}$$

Although the hypothesis of the Pomeranchuk Regge pole was first advanced[10] twenty years ago, as recently as 1973 it was possible to write[11]

"The forward peak in diffractive elastic scattering .... provided one of the inspirations for the application of Regge theory to strong interactions. It is therefore ironic that today we are in doubt about the relation between diffractive elastic scattering and Regge theory."

A reason for this doubt is easily seen by looking at the then comtemporary plot[12] of elastic slope parameters shown in Fig. 1. If we write

$$\frac{d\sigma_{ij}}{dt} = e^{b_{ij}(t,s) \, t} \tag{5}$$

then clearly (1) implies "universal shrinkage", that is

$$b_{ij} \underset{s \to \infty}{\sim} 2\alpha'_{I\!P}(t) \ln s \tag{6}$$

with $\alpha'_{I\!P}(t)$ universal. Fig. 1 can hardly be regarded as evidence for such universal behaviour.

When the same six processes plotted in Fig. 1 are looked at with all recent results added we obtain Fig. 2 (taken from Ref. 13), a strikingly different picture. The solid lines shown are the experimentalists fit to the data and they show that $\alpha'_{I\!P}$ is indeed universal within the accuracy of the fit. (Note that the π-P channels, and possibly k'-P, show the asymptotic shrinkage at the lowest energy. We shall build on this remark later).

A simple picture of elastic slope parameters has finally emerged only as a result of several lengthy experiments carefully separating the t-ranges over which such parameters are measured. It has been found that there is a <u>universal</u> curvature in all slope parameters, of which the "break"[14] in the ISR p-p slope at $t \sim 0.1$ GEV is just one manifestation. The existence of this curvature is illustrated in Figs. 3 and 4 which are taken from Ref. 15. At fixed S we can write

$$b_{ij}(t) = b_o^{ij} + ct + \cdots \quad \text{with} \quad C \simeq 5 \, GeV^{-1} \quad (7)$$

Plotting $b_{ij}(t,s)$ for different values of t, as in Fig. 5. We see that both b_o^{ij} and C must be S-dependent. Equivalently $\alpha'_{I\!P}$ must be t-dependent so that $\alpha_{I\!P}(t)$ is certainly not a linear trajectory. In fact the universal curvature C may very well be due to the pion threshold in the trajectory, as originally suggested by Anselm and Gribov.[16]

Although Figs. 2 and 5 were plotted before the new ISR $\bar{p}$-p results[17,18] were available we have added then to Fig. 2 and to a small t comparison of p-p and $\bar{p}$-p shown in Fig. 6. Obviously they confirm nicely the general picture.

Property B above is, of course, well-known and well-established. However, just to emphasize the slowness of the rise of total cross-sections[19] we have unconventionally plotted σ_{pp} and $\sigma_{\bar{p}p}$ on a linear rather than a logarithmic energy scale in Fig.7. Also well-known and beautifully confirmed[17,18] at the ISR is property C, that is the power law decrease of all particle/antiparticle cross-section differences. This is shown in Fig. 8, which is taken from Ref. 19. Given that cross-sections rise logarithmically this is a very special situation which is certainly not required on any general theorectical grounds. In fact it is this very special fact which we shall ultimately relate to the underlying gauge group of strong interactions.

Property C establishes that diffraction occurs only in even- signature amplitudes. This leaves the possibility that there is more than one even signature Regge trajectory. However, both the universality of the S-dependence of slope parameters and the factorisation property D are consequences of a single trajectory only.

Factorisation has now been extensively tested in inclusive large mass diffractive excitation. Multi-Regge theory applied to a one-particle inclusive cross-section gives the triple Pomeron formula

$$\frac{M^2 \, d^2 \sigma_{ij}}{dt \, dM^2} \underset{M^2, \, S/M^2 \to \infty}{\sim} \beta_i(0) \, \beta_j^2(t) \, g_{\mathbb{P}\mathbb{P}\mathbb{P}}(t) \, (M^2)^{\alpha_{\mathbb{P}}(0)} \left(\frac{S}{M^2}\right)^{2\alpha_{\mathbb{P}}(t)-2} \tag{8}$$

which when compared with the total cross-section formula

$$\sigma_{ij} \underset{S \to \infty}{\sim} \beta_i(0) \, \beta_j(0) \, S^{\alpha_{\mathbb{P}}(0)-1} \tag{9}$$

gives, as a direct consequence of factorisation,

$$M^2 \frac{d^2 \sigma_{ij}}{dt \, dM^2} \Big/ \sigma_{ij} \quad \text{is independent of particle } i$$

Experimental results[20] for this ratio are shown in Fig. 9.
The M^2 and S independence of (7) implied if $\alpha_{\rho}(0) = 1$ is now
well-established experimentally[20,21] and illustrated in Fig.
10 while the t-dependence of $g_{\mathbb{P}\mathbb{P}\mathbb{P}}(t)$ is shown in Fig. 11.
Clearly

$$g_{\mathbb{P}\mathbb{P}\mathbb{P}}(0) = \tau_0 \neq 0 \tag{10}$$

is the only possible conclusion from the experimental data.

A further feature of diffractive excitation which will
be important in the following is the finite mass sum rule[21]
illustrated in Fig. 12. This shows that the triple Pomeron
large mass diffractive excitation produces an average of the
low mass plus elastic diffractive scattering when
extrapolated to low missing mass.

In conclusion I believe that the experimental
verification of properties A - E from detailed diffraction
experiments carried out over the last five years can not be
seriously disputed. It seems unlikely therefore that future
experiments will modify the conclusion that, in a first
approximation, the Pomeron is a single Regge pole with
intercept one. If this is the conclusion of the existing
diffraction experiments, a clear objective for the next
energy range of experiments is to determine whether this
approximate statement is in fact precise. This is what we
shall discuss in the next Section. The fundamental
significance of such a statement will be the subject of
Section C.

B.   The Critical Pomeron at $\bar{p}$-p Colliders

The basis for this section is the following –

If the $I\!P$ is a single Regge trajectory with $\alpha_{I\!P}(0)=1$ and $\gamma_0 \neq 0$ it follows from unitarity and analyticity that the precise asymptotic behavior of all diffractive processes can be predicted.   Consequently we can hope   to   convince ourselves that $\alpha_{I\!P}(0)=1$ by looking at a whole range of phenomena and not just by the elusive project of determining the true asymptotic behavior of total cross-sections. First let us very briefly describe the origin of the above statement.   It   is well-known[22-24] that a single   pole can be thought of as originating from some general short-range correlation (in rapidity) production process which, in first approximation, produces the average multiplicity events

$$\langle n\rangle \leftrightarrow \int_0 d\Omega \left| \;\rule{2cm}{0pt}\; \right|^2 \to \;\rule{1.5cm}{0pt}\; \equiv S^{\alpha_{I\!P}(t)} \tag{11}$$

Events with twice the average multiplicity are counted by two Pomeron exchange and so on, while rapidity dependent multiplicity fluctuations are counted by Pomeron interaction graphs. So eventually all fluctuations of multiplicity and absorptive corrections of such fluctuations are counted by a complete set of Reggeon Field Theory graphs. That is

$$\sigma_T \sim \int \left| \;\underset{\langle n\rangle}{\rule{2cm}{0pt}}\; + \;\underset{\langle n\rangle \, \langle 2n\rangle \, \langle n\rangle}{\rule{3cm}{0pt}}\; + \;\underset{\langle n\rangle \; I\!P \; \langle n\rangle}{\rule{2cm}{0pt}}\; + \;\underset{\langle n\rangle}{\rule{2cm}{0pt}}\; + \cdots \right|^2$$

$$\equiv \;\rule{2cm}{0pt}\; + \;\rule{2cm}{0pt}\; + \;\rule{2.5cm}{0pt}\; + \cdots \tag{12}$$

Graphs of this form represent the dominant processes at asymptotic energies. They can be written as an effective Pomeron field theory[3] with the "Feynman rules"

$$\sim\!\sim\!\sim = \left[E - 1 + \alpha_P(\underline{k}^2)\right]^{-1} \,, \quad \sim\!\!<\; = r_0$$

$$loop\ integration \equiv \int dE\, d^2\underline{k} \tag{13}$$

These rules give the Mellin transform with respect to rapidity $\left(\int dy\, e^{Ey}\right)$. It is a consequence of multiparticle t-channel unitarity[8,9,25] that the full set of graphs of an interacting field theory must be present-a very technical use of dispersion theory and multi-Regge theory is needed to prove this.

The task of summing all graphs when $\alpha_P(0) = 1$ is analogous to a (statistical mechanics) critical phenomenom problem in the Reggeon Field Theory[1-3]-hence the Critical Pomeron description. It is well known that general scaling properties of such phenormena can be calculated using renormalisation group methods. Much work has been done[26] on Critical Pomeron predictions for many diffractive processes. However, much remains to be done and as I shall discuss I believe the p̄-p collider results will stimulate much further work on the subject. The central question, which has always been difficult to get any control over,[26] will remain-at what energy scale do the asymptotic predictions become relevant? A-priori this is completely unknown. As suggested[27] many years ago we shall consider it to be open for phenomenological investigation in the following.

In Table 1 we have listed some of the already established scaling (and approach to scaling) predictions of Critical Pomeron behavior. All the scaling functions $F_0, F_1, F_2, \_\cdot\_\cdot\_\cdot F_0, \_\cdot\_\cdot$etc$\_\cdot$ are in principle precisely calculable. So far only F_0 has been studied in detail. Dash et al.[28] have extended the $0(\varepsilon)$ (ε=4-d, -d=dimension of transverse momentum) calculation of F_0 of Ref. 29 to $0(\varepsilon^2)$. In order to compare their calculation with ISR p-p elastic scattering they parameterised $\beta^4(t)$ (see Table 1) as e^{At} and chose A to maximise the scaling behaviour of the data. The result with A=0.9 GEV/c^{-1} is shown in Fig. 13. Clearly Critical Pomeron scaling is approximately satisfied over the whole t-range measured. Having chosen $\beta(t)$ to maximise the scaling the calculated scaling function F_0 can now be inserted in the leading expression for $\frac{d\sigma}{dt}$ given in Table 1. The result is shown in Fig. 14 and is compared with ISR data at the energy where the maximum t-range is available. There is remarkable agreement over the eleven orders of magnitude involved given that we are comparing with experiment an essentially parameter free scaling function calculated (approximately) from first principles. The only effective parameter is the t-scale which has been fixed in Fig. 14 by setting the dip in agreement with the experimental result.

The Critical Pomeron predicts that the same scaling function will eventually appear in all elastic scattering processes. To everyone's surprise it has appeared already[30] in $\bar{p}$-p elastic scattering at P_{lab} = 50 GEV/c as shown in Fig. 15. The appearance of the $\bar{p}$-p diffraction pattern at such a low energy is certainly very encouraging for the hope that collider $\bar{p}$-p energies will be high enough for us to observe a significant number of Critical Pomeron phenomena. However, a similar diffraction pattern has recently been discovered[31] in π^--p scattering at 200GEV/c. The qualitative structure is indeed the same but with the difference that the t-scale is a factor of 3 larger! In Fig. 16 we have shown the experimental data and superposed the Critical Pomeron diffraction peak multiplied by the same $\beta^4(t)$ as in p-p but with the t-scale in the scaling function multiplied by a factor of 3. Asymptotically the t-scales should, of course, be the same. Thus while some of the qualitative features of the predicted universal diffraction peaks are emerging at accelerator and ISR energies we are clearly not in true asymptopia. Presumably the π^--p dip will move in rapidly to approach that seen in the p-p and $\bar{p}$-p experiments. The Fermilab Tevatron could be very important for checking this.

But will the collider energies be close enough to asymptopia to make _sufficient_ contact with the Critical Pomeron predictions? Moshe and collaborators[32] have begun the task of making usable predictions by exploiting the approach to scaling terms in Table 1. Since F_1 and F_2 have not been calculated theoretically they have used them to fit phenomenologically the discrepancy between the leading term and the experimental results for $\frac{d\sigma}{dt}$ at top FERMILAB and ISR energies. This allows an extrapolation to collider energies. The fit to $\frac{d\sigma}{dt}$ at the top ISR energy is shown in Fig. 17. The resulting prediction for the total cross-section is shown in Fig. 18 while in Figs. 19 and 20 are shown the predictions for the differential cross-section.

In Fig. 21 we have extended the fit of Moshe et al. through the whole energy range covered by the colliders and all Cosmic Ray experiments[33] including the Fly's Eye. Note that while the leading Critical Pomeron term has only a small power of log s the effect of this when combined with the non-leading terms is to give an approximate linear dependence on log s over the whole energy range. While the Cosmic Ray results shown are sometimes regarded with suspicion they certainly do not look bad in terms of the Critical Pomeron prediction. We shall discuss what we mean by the "scaled" Fly's Eye cross-section shortly.

If the colliders are to be close to asymptopia as we would like then the rise of total cross-sections must be significantly slower than the original $[\ln s]^2$ behaviour that was deduced from a dispersion relation analysis[34] including the real part measured at the ISR. Recent experimental results actually support this. First we recall our remark in the previous Section that the behaviour of the π-p slope parameters suggests that this channel may be reaching asymptopia the fastest. The π^--p real part including new measurements[35] is shown in Fig. 22. $\rho_{\pi\text{-}p}$ seems to have stopped increasing and may even be decreasing towards zero as it should do asymptotically. Experimentalists have combined this measurement with the total cross-section results and used a dispersion relation analysis to conclude[35] that the total cross-section should not increase like $[\ln s]^2$ up to collider energies. As Fig. 23 shows the faster the increase at lower energy the sooner the dispersion relation analysis requires a cut-off in the increase.

New ISR measurements[19] of both the p-p total cross-section and ρ pp when combined with Fermilab ρ pp measurements,[15] which disagree significantly with the dispersion relation analysis, suggest a new analysis may produce a modified conclusion about the rise of the p-p total cross-section. ρ pp is shown in Fig. 24 while the comparison of the new ISR results for the total cross-section with the dispersion relation analysis is shown in Fig. 25. Note that the ISR result for the total cross-section at the highest energy has always been outside of the dispersion relation band.

While the total cross-section and the elastic differential cross-section will eventually be measured accurately at both the CERN and FERMILAB colliders it will not be for some time. The initial results concern multiplicities and the rise of the central plateau in rapidity. In fact these quantities have been studied also in terms of the Critical Pomeron although the results have been less widely advertised than the elastic scattering results. The form for the one-particle rapidity distribution given in Table 1 had been previously suggested[36] as an explanation for the logarithmic rise of the central plateau at the ISR. Note that it predicts that only a _finite rapidity_ interval in the central region will rise (like the square of the total cross-section). This is precisely what is seen in the UA5 results[4] shown in Figs. 26 and 27.

As noted in Table 1 all the multiplicity moments have been calculated[37] for the Critical Pomeron-at least the leading term has been calculated. Assuming the next to leading terms are given by the same critical exponents as the differential cross-section we have given a crude extrapolation of the average multiplicity in Fig. 28. The higher multiplicity moments satisfy

$$\langle n^p \rangle \underset{s \to \infty}{\sim} (\ln s)^{p(1+\eta)} \sim c_p \langle n \rangle^p \qquad (14)$$

which is sufficient to ensure that we have <u>asymptotic KNO</u> scaling. Both the UA1 and UA5 results[4,5] strongly suggest some form of KNO scaling. As Fig. 29 shows, the comparison of the UA1 results with the ISR results[38] suggests that at least the lowest multiplicity moments have changed little from the ISR. To compare the experimental moments with Critical Pomeron predictions we note that the ISR results were plotted in terms of

$$\gamma_2 = \frac{\langle (n - \langle n \rangle)^2 \rangle}{\langle n \rangle^2} = C_2 - 1 \tag{15}$$

$$\gamma_3 = \frac{\langle (n - \langle n \rangle)^3 \rangle}{\langle n \rangle^3} = C_3 - 3C_2 + 2 \tag{16}$$

etc. where C_2 and C_3 are defined by (14). They have been calculated[37] only to $0(\varepsilon)$ for the Critical Pomeron. The result is $C_2 = 1.25$ and $C_3 = 1.8$ giving

$$\gamma_2 = 0.25 \qquad \gamma_3 = 0.05 \tag{17}$$

From general experience with non-perturbative evaluations of critical exponents we would certainly expect the exact values of these moments to be significantly higher than (17). This is surely something that will be studied in the near future since from Fig. 30 it looks very reasonable that such values would fit the measured ISR and collider moments very well. In addition, both non-leading terms and the higher moments could also be calculated. In fact the full range of multiplicity moments measured at the colliders could very well provide the strongest evidence for (or against) the Critical Pomeron.

If the total cross-section and elastic differential cross-section measured at the CERN collider match the Critical Pomeron predictions quite well then I would like to advocate performing a detailed triple Pomeron measurement at both the CERN and the FERMILAB colliders. Firstly the well-known $1/M^2$ distribution will acquire logarithmic modifications[29] as shown (to $0(\mathfrak{k})$) in Fig. 31. More important though the whole diffractive peak in t acquires a predictable M^2 dependence[29] as implied by Table 1 and illustrated in Fig. 32. The elastic-like dip-bump structure moves in and up two-orders of magnitude as M^2 is varied from the lower to upper boundary of the triple Pomeron region. This could serve as a very clear confirmation of Critical Pomeron behavior.

If the Critical Pomeron predictions have begun to appear at present energies and are, even partially, manifest at collider energies then we will, in one sense, have a form of precocious scaling. The earliest estimates[1] of the energy scale needed to see such predictions gave the energy of the universe as the relevant scale. Certainly it is easy[28] to obtain such pessimistically large estimates. The

Critical Pomeron predictions come from summing the "Pomeron propagator" graphs

$$\text{[diagram]} \equiv \text{[diagram]} + \text{[diagram]} + \text{[diagram]}$$
$$+ \text{[diagram]} + \cdots \cdots \quad (18)$$

Our discussion in the previous Section implies that we need a rapidity of at least four or five ($\ln s \simeq 4,5$) to isolate the simple Pomeron from background behavior. One would then expect a similar rapidity interval to be needed to isolate each Pomeron in the higher-order graphs. This would give a rapidity of twelve for the second graph and a rapidity of twenty for the third etc. For the sum of the series to become relevant we might expect a rapidity interval of anything from thirty to several hundred to be required. Since we have twelve at the CERN collider and sixteen at the FERMILAB collider the situation can easily be argued to be hopeless. It is at this point that the finite mass sum rule[21] illustrated in Fig. 12 plays a central role. This implies that the second graph in (18) not only counts double high mass diffractive excitation (for which a rapidity interval of twelve might very well be required)

$$\text{[diagram]} \supset \int d\Omega \left| \underset{M_1^2}{\underbrace{}} \quad \underset{M_2^2}{\underbrace{}} \right|^2 \quad M_1^2, M_2^2 \gg 1$$

$$(19)$$

but because of the extrapolation shown in Fig. 12 also well reproduces (in average) events where either M_1^2 or M_2^2 or both are not at all large. Hence this graph makes its appearance at a much lower rapidity than might be expected. If this situation generalizes then the asymptotic results can very well appear at a much lower rapidity than the pessimistic estimates would give.

If this is the case then the rise of total cross-sections can be thought of as due entirely to diffractive excitation (and associated processes) producing the Pomeron propagator graphs of (18). The rise therefore involves a factorizing coefficient multiplying a logarithmically rising factor which is independent of the scattering particles. This form of dynamics is quite orthogonal to that of models which consider multiple rescattering as a dominant feature. In particular it implies that attempts[39] to use a Glauber-type model to compare the rise of the p-p cross-section with that of the p-air cross-section measured in Cosmic Ray events will be misleading. Many people[40,41] have previously argued that the Glauber formalism is not adequate for high-energy nucleus scattering because of diffractive excitation. However, we are going even further in advocating that diffractive excitation (and directly associated processes) be thought of as the dominant mechanism producing all

rising cross-sections --

including the p-air cross-section.

Applying the finite mass sum rule (generalized) extensively we can qualitatively describe proton-air scattering as follows

$$\sim \sum \qquad \text{constituent nucleons} \qquad (20)$$

$$\sim \sum \qquad \qquad (21)$$

IP propagator produces rising cross-sections

Hence the rising cross-section for proton-air scattering has the same origin as that of proton-proton scattering and will simply be multiplied by a different overall constant. Therefore if the p-air cross-section at 10^9 GeV is around 540 mb., as the preliminary Fly's Eye result announced at this meeting[42] suggests, then since it rises from around 280m.b. at 10^3 GeV we expect the p-p cross-section to rise to a 10^9 GeV value given by

$$42 \times \frac{540}{280} = 81 \, mb. \qquad (22)$$

This is the "scaled" Fly's Eye cross-section appearing on Fig. 21. It will not escape the readers attention that it lies right on the Critical Pomeron prediction. If (22) seems absurdly simple let us note that, within experimental accuracy, the p-p and p-air cross-sections do rise in proportion over the energy range where both rising cross-sections have been explicitly measured. In addition the relation between pp and p-air used[33] to extract the cosmic ray results up to 10^5 GeV (shown in Fig. 21) is linear, as shown in Fig. 33. Therefore I believe it makes little sense to use Glauber theory to justify the use of a non-linear relation between 10^5 GeV and 10^9 GeV.

In conclusion then all evidence suggests that at the colliders we will see all the logarithmic effects typical of the asymptotic behavior produced by a single interacting Regge pole with intercept exactly one. Certainly nothing suggests that logarithmically increasing quantities will halt their increase. Therefore if all asymptotic behavior persists as predicted from the CERN to the FERMILAB $\bar{p}$-p collider what will have been learnt? I hope the next Section will provide a sufficiently interesting answer to justify any of the relevant experiments.

C. Diffraction in Gauge Theories

Calculating high-energy behavior of gauge theories is, of course, very complicated. To get the right answers we expect to have to face the fundamental dynamical problems of confinement and chiral symmetry breaking (and we do have to1). I shall first list the results[6-8] that I see emerging for the dependence of diffraction on both the gauge group and the quark content of the theory. I shall then briefly describe the method used to derive the results. Finally I shall discuss their physical origin and significance.

Emerging Results

SU(2) Gauge Theory

There is no rising cross-section for any number of fermions. (The number of fermions is always restricted by asymptotic freedom in my work. The necessity for this can be seen directly from Regge limit calculations[6] or simply taken as a pre-requisite for a finite short-distance theory.) So

$$\sigma_T \to 0 \qquad \forall \ N_F$$

SU(3) gauge theory

$$\sigma_T \to 0$$

except

a) 16 flavours of triplet quarks

or

b)   6 flavours of triplet quarks

   + 2 flavours of sextet quarks

$\left.\right\}\to$ Reggeon Field Theory

Critical Pomeron

$$\Longrightarrow$$

$$\sigma_T \to \infty, \quad \left[\frac{d\sigma}{dt}\right]_{\bar{p}p} - \left[\frac{d\sigma}{dt}\right]_{pp} \to 0$$

There is factorization and all the predictions of the Critical Pomeron discussed in the previous Section.

SU(4) Gauge Theory

$$\sigma_T \to 0 \qquad N_F < 20$$

$N_F = 21$ $\sigma_T \to \infty$ but there is also an odd-signature Pomeron trajectory and so

$$\left[\frac{d\sigma}{dt}\right]_{\bar{p}p} - \left[\frac{d\sigma}{dt}\right]_{pp} \not\to 0$$ and (probably) there is no factorization

SU(N) Gauge Theory

The number of Pomeron Regge trajectories of both signatures increases with N. Close to the maximum number of fermions allowed by asymptotic freedom is needed to obtain a rising cross-section. In general if $\sigma_T \to \infty$ then

$$\left[\frac{d\sigma}{dt}\right]_{\bar{p}p} - \left[\frac{d\sigma}{dt}\right]_{pp} \not\to 0$$

and there is no factorization.

From these results we obtain the striking conclusion that

QCD (SU(3) gauge group) saturated with quarks (the asymptotic freedom constraint is only just satisfied by either a) or b) above) is the (almost) unique theory giving

1. rising cross-sections

2. $$\left[\frac{d\sigma}{dt}\right]_{\bar{p}p} - \left[\frac{d\sigma}{dt}\right]_{pp} \rightarrow 0$$

3. the Pomeron is a single Regge pole giving factorization and all the asymptotic predictions of the Critical Pomeron.

Clearly these are strong results which go a long way beyond any understanding of diffraction in gauge theories claimed by other authors. The technical tool used for their derivation is multi-Regge theory.[6,9] In effect this allows us to use analyticity and unitarity to control infinite sums of infra-red divergent perturbation theory diagrams.

We begin with SU(N) gauge theory containing massive quarks and (N-1) fundamental representations of Higgs scalers-- this avoids[43,44] a phase-transition when we use the Higgs mechanism to give all gluons masses. In this case both quarks and gluons are physical particles and most important[45-49] they lie on Regge trajectories which can be exchanged at high energy. Scattering amplitudes are given by reggeon diagrams[6,50,51] which now involve gluons and quarks instead of Pomerons e.g.

$$\bigotimes \;=\; \rightarrowtail\!\!\!\sim\!\!\!\mid \;+\; \rightarrowtail\!\!\!\sim\!\!\!\bigcirc\!\!\!\sim\!\!\!\mid \;+\cdots \quad (23)$$

where

$$\sim\!\!\sim\!\!\sim \;=\; \text{gluon propagator} \;=\; \frac{1}{E-\Delta(k^2)} \times \frac{1}{k^2-M^2} \quad (24)$$

$$\begin{array}{c} E_j,k_j \\ E_i,k_i \;\rightsquigarrow\!\!\!< \\ E_k,k_k \end{array} \;=\; g\,f_{ijk}\left[\,E_i-\Delta(k_j^2)-\Delta(k_k^2)\,\right] +\cdots \quad (25)$$

and the Regge trajectory function $\Delta(k^2) = 1 - \alpha(k^2)$ is given by

$$\Delta(k^2) \;=\; \frac{g^2}{16\pi^2}\left(k^2-M^2\right)\int \frac{d^2q}{(q^2-M^2)((k-q)^2-M^2)} +\cdots \quad (26)$$

g is the coupling constant, f_{ijk} are the group structure constants. The pole in k^2 in (24) and the "nonsense-zero" [ ] in (25) result from the odd signature of the reggeized gluon trajectory. These factors also prevent the writing of simple field theory rules for diagrams with interactions. [Strictly[6] we have to compute imaginary parts and use quite complicated cutting rules to calculate even the simplest loop diagram in (23)]. Nevertheless the reggeon diagram rules for quarks and gluons are the simplest possible consistent with multi-Regge theory --This has been checked up to tenth order in perturbation theory.[6,48-51] Consequently the full power of multiparticle dispersion theory[52,53] combined with multi-Regge theory[6,9] can be used to construct a complete set of reggeon diagrams to describe the high-energy behavior of arbitrary scattering amplitudes.

To calculate real QCD, and an unbroken gauge theory in general, we must remove the gluon masses. Since we are calculating S-Matrix elements this is the <u>well-known</u> <u>infra-red problem of QCD</u> Fortunately there is an <u>exponentiation of infra-red divergences</u> which is just "reggeisation" of the gluons, that is

$$S^{\alpha(t)} = e^{\ln s\, \alpha(t)} \underset{M^2 \to 0}{\sim} e^{-\ln s \ln t/M^2} \tag{27}$$

If we first restore the gauge-symmetry to SU(2) by removing one Higgs representation we can analyze this exponentiation using multi-Regge theory for interacting reggeons (that is reggeon unitarity etc.). This is my claim that infinite sums of divergent diagrams can be controlled by unitarity and analyticity. The infra-red analysis is complicated[8] and in fact forces us to S-Matrix elements, for multi-quark scattering, which contain bound-state scattering amplitudes. These bound-state amplitudes are infinite relative to the quark amplitudes and this is how the confinement emerges.

That is <u>color-zero hadrons are picked out by a special class</u> <u>of infra-red singularities that do not exponentiate but can</u> <u>be factorized on to external states.</u> For example, a pion scattering amplitude containing a single Pomeron exchange emerges from reggeon diagram amplitudes of the form

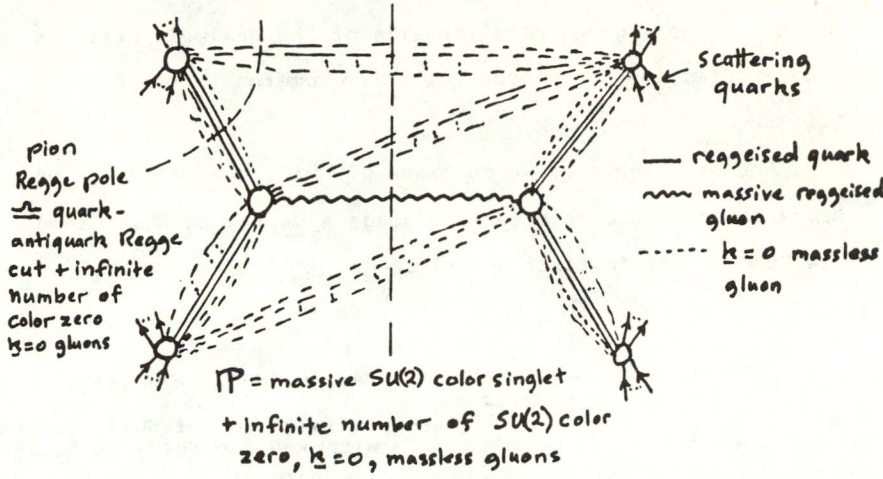

pion
Regge pole
≃ quark-
antiquark Regge
cut + infinite
number of
color zero
k=0 gluons

scattering
quarks

—— reggeised quark
〰〰 massive reggeised
gluon
······ k = 0 massless
gluon

ℙ = massive SU(2) color singlet
+ infinite number of SU(2) color
zero, k = 0, massless gluons

<u>SU(2)Color zero, k=0 massless gluons form a vector state</u> <u>with color charge parity +1.</u> They behave as <u>a vacuum</u> <u>background producing confinement with chiral symmetry</u> <u>breaking.</u> <u>They produce hadrons by combining with color-zero</u> <u>combinations of quarks and the Pomeron by combining with</u> <u>color-zero massive gluons.</u> Consequently the spectrum of Pomeron trajectories is determined by that part of the gauge group orthogonal to an SU(2) subgroup (when all but this subgroup is broken by the Higgs mechanism). That is

$$\left[SU(N) \right] \;\longrightarrow\; \underset{\substack{produces \\ confinement}}{\nearrow} \quad \overset{SU(2)}{\underset{\substack{gluons \\ forming \\ \mathbb{P}\ spectrum}}{\big|\rule{0pt}{1em}\quad\quad}}$$

390

This is enough to see that

    i) there is no $\mathbb{P}$ in SU(2)   (with $\alpha_{\mathbb{P}}(0) \sim 1$)

   ii) SU(3) has a single $\mathbb{P}$ trajectory

 iii) SU(4) has a more complicated $\mathbb{P}$ spectrum

We shall not give more details of the analysis here but finally describe how we control the Pomeron intercept in QCD.

From the above if we consider QCD with one triplet of Higgs scalers used to break the gauge symmetry to SU(2) then the Pomeron is, in first aproximation

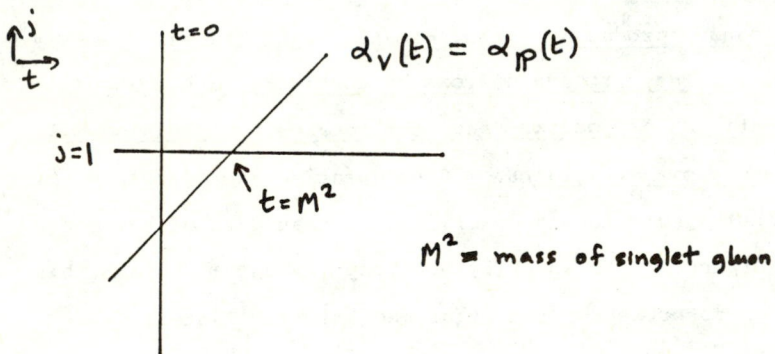

$$\mathbb{P} \equiv \quad \text{———}\quad - \quad \text{massive SU(2) singlet}$$

— infinite set of SU(2) gluons with k=0 and SU(2) color zero

This implies the Pomeron Regge trajectory is exchange degenerate with the odd-signature trajectory on which the massive singlet lies

$$\alpha_V(t) = \alpha_{\mathbb{P}}(t)$$

$t=0$

$j=1$

$t=M^2$

M^2 = mass of singlet gluon

Therefore it seems that $\alpha_p(0) \to 1$ when $M^2 \to 0$, which suggests that

$$SU(2) \text{ gauge symmetry} \to SU(3) \Rightarrow \alpha_p(0) \to 1$$

(In fact a detailed Reggeon Field Theory analysis using the "Supercritical Pomeron"[54] is required to show that the odd-signature gluon trajectory simultaneously decouples from physical states). This argument works in detail only if the singlet gluon mass M^2 is an unambiguous S-Matrix mass independent of any cut-off parameter. This is the case only if the QCD plus Higgs scalars theory, from which we start, is asymptotically free. This condition requires[55,56] that we have the maximum number of quarks consistent with the asymptotic freedom of the pure SU(3) gauge theory. Alternatively if we have fewer quarks, then keeping a transverse momentum cut-off in the theory until after the SU(3) symmetry is restored we can show[6] that the Pomeron intercept is less than one. We therefore arrive at the results described above.

That the Pomeron should depend on the gauge group is at first surprising but in fact rather natural if we consider a string-like confining solution of the gauge theory in which the strings reflect the properties of line-integrals of electric flux, as expected. In this case the Pomeron should be given, in first approximation, by the exchange in two transverse dimensions of a closed string. Since such closed strings should reflect the properties of Wilson loops in two spacelike dimensions the following properties[57] naturally match the properties of the Pomeron listed above. Defining as usual

$$\phi(\circlearrowleft) = \text{Tr } P \exp\left[\oint_{\circlearrowleft} A(x).dx\right]$$

1. $\phi(\circlearrowleft)$ is real in SU(2) $\equiv$ no imaginary $I\!P$ in SU(2)

2. $\phi(\circlearrowleft)$ is orientation dependent in SU(3) with $\phi(\circlearrowleft) - \phi(\circlearrowright)$ imaginary and even under rotation through $2\pi \equiv$ one even signature $I\!P$ trajectory in SU(3)

3. In SU(4), $\phi(\circledcirc)$ is real, distinct from the product of two simple loops and no longer even under rotation through $2\pi \equiv$ there is an additional odd signature $I\!P$ trajectory in SU(4).

4. In SU(N) the increasing complexity of spacelike Wilson loops matches the increasing complexity of the $I\!P$ spectrum.

I believe a more detailed discussion of both my infra-red analysis and the above properties of Wilson loops would make the above correspondence much more concrete but I shall not attempt it here. Note that the Pomeron phenomenology which begins Section 2 would when applied to the string model give the following

$\langle n \rangle \leftrightarrow$ simple closed string exchange $\leftrightarrow$ ⟩⌣⌣⟨

$2\langle n \rangle \leftrightarrow$ exchange of two simple closed strings $\leftrightarrow$ ✕⌣⌣✕

(+, in SU(4), double loop of 3) above)   (+, in SU(4), additional $\mathbb{P}$ trajectory)

Consequently the additional odd-signature trajectory in SU(4) will manifest itself in events with twice the average multiplicity. Similarly in SU(N) events with up to (N-2) times the average multiplicity will manifest new Regge trajectories. Therefore it is very attractive that if the very high multiplicity fluctuations observed at collider energies are really described by a single Regge pole theory then we have determined the strong interaction gauge group to be SU(3).

Finally if the intercept of the Pomeron is exactly one in that all logarithmic increases persist and appear to be a true asymptotic phenomenom, what is the implication? I believe that this should be interpreted as evidence that QCD is saturated with quarks. There are plausible arguments for this outside of strong-interaction high-energy behavior.

a) There are arguments[58] that chiral theories are

inconsistent at high-energy so that above the weak interaction scale all existing flavours of quarks will be doubled. That is the $SU(2)_L$ of Weinberg-Salam must go to at least $SU(2)_L \times SU(2)_R$. If there are four conventional families, that is eight flavours, below the weak-interaction scale, we expect eight families or sixteen flavours eventually. A very reasonable possibility.

b) More attractive perhaps is the possibility that

there is an $SU(2)_L$ family of sextet quarks. They could naturally provide[59] the condensate giving masses to the weak interaction vector bosons. The lagrangian masses of such quarks could be essentially zero while they would produce no hadrons (sextet pions) with this mass scale. Thus, given the existence of the top quark, QCD would be saturated with quarks at a scale well below where we see the asymptotic phenomena. (This would not be the case for option a) above, which is therefore less satisfactory. There are even arguments[60] that the magnitude of the gauge coupling could be fixed at approximately the right experimental value in an

appropriate grand unified theory. Saturating QCD with
six flavours of triplet quarks and two flavours of
sextet quarks therefore provides a very economical
description of many aspects of physics requiring no
technicolor or hypercolor gauge groups and possibly
explaining the observation of Critical Pomeron scaling
at the CERN and FERMILAB colliders!

396

REFERENCES

1. A.A. Migdal, A.M. Polyakov and K.A. Ter Martirosyan - Zh. Eksp. Teor. Fig. 67 (1974) 84.

2. H.D.I. Abarbanel and J.B. Bronzan - Phys. Rev. D9(1974)2397

3. H.D.I. Abarbanel, J.B. Bronzan, R.L. Sugar and A.R. White - Physics Reports 21C (1975) 119.

4. K. Alpgard et al. (UAS Collaboration) - CERN preprints EP/81-152, EP/81-153 (1981) and R. Meinke - This meeting.

5. G. Arrison et al. (UAI Collaboration) - CERN preprint EP/81-155, A. Kernan and C. Rubbia - this meeting.

6. A.R. White, CERN preprint TH2976 (1980) - to be published in Annals of Physics.

7. A.R. White, CERN preprint Th3058 - published in Proceedings of the XVIth Rencontre de Moriond

(1981).

8. A.R. White, CERN preprint TH3115 - to be published in Proceedings of the Seminar on Theoretical Aspects of QCD, Marseilles (1981).

9. A.R. White, Lectures at the Les Houches Institute (1975)

10. G.F. Chew and S. Frautschi, Phys. Rev. Letts $\underline{7}$, (1961) 394 V.N. Gribov Soviet Phys. JETP $\underline{14}$ (1962), 478 and 1395.

11. M.L. Perl, High-Energy Hadron Physics, p. 408 published by John Wiley and Sons (1974).

12. Y.M. Antipov et al. - Nucl. Phys. B57 (1972) 333.

13. J.P. Burq et al., CERN preprint (1981).

14. G. Barbiellini et al. Phys. Letts. 39B (1972) 663.

15. L.A. Fajardo et al. Phys. Rev. D24(1981)46.

16. A.A. Anselm and V.N. Gribov, Phys. Letts. 40B (1972) 487

17. N. Amos et al. - CERN preprint EP/81-108 and
    Phys. M. Block - this meeting.
    Rev letts. 47(1981)1191

18. M. Ambrosio et at. - CERN preprint EP/81-141
    P.D. Grannis - this meeting.

19. A.S. Carroll et al., Phys. Letts. 80B (1979)
    423.

20. R.L. Cool et al., Phys. Rev. Letts. 47 (1981)
    701.

21. Y. Akimov et al. Phys. Rev. D14 (1976) 3148.

22. V.A. Abramovskii, V.N. Gribov and O.V. Kancheli,
    Sov. J. Nucl. Phys. 18 (1974) 308.

23. M. Baker and K.A. Ter-Martirosyan, Physics
    Reports 28C (1976) 3.

24. A.H. Mueller, Proceedings of the
    Aix-En-Province Conference (1973).

25. V.N. Gribov, I. Ya Pomeranchuk and K.A. Ter

Martirosyan - Phys. Rev. B139 (1965) 184.

26. For a review see M. Moshe-Physics Reports 37C (1978) 255.

27. M. Moshe and A.R. White - Proceedings of the Workshop an Future ISR Physics CERN, Geneva (1977).

28. J.W. Dash and T. Grandou - Z. Physics C3 (1979) 9, C. Bourrely and J.W. Dash-Marseilles preprint CPT-81/p. 1280 (1981).

29. H.D.I. Abarbanel, J. Bartels, J. Bronzan and D. Sidhu, Phys. Rev. D12 (1975) 2798.

30. Z. Asa'd et al. CERN preprint EP/81-26 (1981).

31. W.F. Baker et al., FERMILAB preprint 81/58-EXP (1981).

32. J. Baumel, M. Feingold and M. Moshe Technion preprint PH-81-28 (1981).

33. The results are taken from S.C. Tonwar - J. Phys. G (1979) L193 and G.B.Yodh - Proceedings

of the Brookhaven Symposium on Prospects of Strong Interactions at Isabelle (1977).

34. U. Amaldi et al., Phys. Letts. 66B (1970) 390.

35. J.P. Burq et al. CERN preprint (1981).

36. M. Moshe - Phys. Rev D14 (1976) 2383.

37. L. Caneschi and R. Jengo - Nucl. Phys. B89 (1975) 19.

38. W. Thome et al. Nucl. Phys. B129 (1977) 365.

39. T. Gaisser - this meeting, G.B. Yodh - this meeting and Ref. 33.

40. V.N. Gribov - Soviet Physics JETP 29 (1969) 483.

41. M. Baig and C. Pajares, Phys. Rev. D20 (1979) 1148, see also G. Alberi and G. Gozzi, Physics Reports 74C (1981) 1.

42. G. Cassiday, - This meeting.

43. E. Fradkin and S.H. Shenker Phys. Rev. D19 (1979) 3682.

44. T. Banks and E. Rabinovici, Nucl. Phys. B160 (1979) 349.

45. M.T. Grisam and H. J. Schnitzer, Phys. Rev. D20 (1974) 784.

46. B.M. Mc Coy and T.T. Wu, Phys. Rev. Letts. 35 (1975) 604.

47. L. Tyburski, Phys. Rev. D13; (1976) 107.

48. H. Cheng and C. Y. Lo Phys. Rev. D13 (1976) 1131, D15 (1977) 2959.

49. E.A. Kuraev, L.N. Lipatov and V.S. Fadin, Soviet Phys. JETP44 (1976) 443,45 (1977) 199.

50. J. Bartels, Nucl. Phys. B151 (1979) 293, B175 (1980) 365.

51. J.B. Bronzan and R.L. Sugar, Phys. Rev. D17 (1978) 585.

402

52. H.P. Stapp and A.R. White, Les Houches Institute Lectures (1975).

53. H.P. Stapp and A.R. White, FERMILAB preprint to appear.

54. A.R. White, Marseilles Conference on High Energy Physics (1978) and International Symposium on Hadron Structure, Kagimierz, Poland (1979).

55. D.J. Gross and F. Wilczek, Phys. Rev. D8 (1973) 3633.

56. T.P. Cheng, E. Eichten and L.F. Li, Phys. Rev. D9 (1974) 2259.

57. G. 't Hooft, Nucl. Phys. B138 (1978)1.

58. H.B. Nielsen and M. Ninomiya, Rutherford preprint Rl-81-052 (1981).

59. W.J. Marciano, Phys. Rev. D21 (1980) 2425.

60. F.J. Yndurain, Nucl. Phys. B115 (1976) 293.

TABLE I

Critical Pomeron Scaling and Approach to Scaling Predictions

$\dfrac{d\sigma}{dt}$	$\beta^4(t)\,(\log s)^{2\eta}\,F_0^2\left[ct\,(\log s)^z\right]\left\{1 + 2F_1\left[ct\,(\log s)^z\right](\log s)^{-\lambda} - 2F_2\left[t,ct\,(\log s)^z\right](\log s)^{-\eta-1} + \ldots\right\}$
σ_{tot}	$\beta^2(0)\,(\log s)^{\eta}\left[1 + F_1(0)\,(\log s)^{-\lambda} - F_2(0)\,(\log s)^{-1-\eta} + \ldots\right]$
$M^2\,\dfrac{d\sigma}{dM^2 dt}$	a)*) At $\log M^2 \ll \log(s/M^2)$: $$\beta^2(t)\beta(0)\,\frac{\left[\log(s/M^2)\right]^{\alpha_1}}{\left[\log M^2\right]^{\alpha_2}}\,F_0^2\left[ct\,(\log M^2)^z\right]\left\{1 + N_1(\log M^2)^{-\lambda} - \right.$$ $$- N_2(\log M^2)^{-1-\eta} + F_3\left[ct\,(\log(s/M^2))^z\right]\left[\log(s/M^2)\right]^{-\lambda} +$$ $$\left. + F_4\left[ct\,(\log(s/M^2))^z\right]\left[\log(s/M^2)\right]^{1-\eta} + \ldots\right\}$$ b)**) At $\log M^2 \gg \log(s/M^2)$: $$\beta^2(t)\beta(0)\,\frac{\left[\log(s/M^2)\right]^{\alpha_3}}{\left[\log M^2\right]^{\alpha_4}}\,\tilde{F}_0\left[ct\,(\log(s/M^2))^z\right]\left\{1 + \tilde{N}_1(\log M^2)^{-\lambda} - \right.$$ $$- \tilde{N}_2(\log M^2)^{-1-\eta} + \tilde{F}_3\left[ct\,(\log(s/M^2))^z\right]\left[\log(s/M^2)\right]^{-\lambda} +$$ $$\left. + \tilde{F}_4\left[ct\,(\log(s/M^2))^z\right]\left[\log(s/M^2)\right]^{1-\eta} + \ldots\right\}$$
$\dfrac{d\sigma}{dy}$	$N\left(\dfrac{Y}{2}-y\right)^{\eta}\left(\dfrac{Y}{2}+y\right)^{\eta}\left\{1 + N_3\left[\left(\dfrac{Y}{2}-y\right)^{-\lambda} + \left(\dfrac{Y}{2}+y\right)^{-\lambda}\right] + N_4\left[\left(\dfrac{Y}{2}-y\right)^{-1-\eta} + \left(\dfrac{Y}{2}+y\right)^{-1-\eta}\right] + \ldots\right\}$

*) $\alpha_1 = 2\eta$, $\alpha_2 = 1 + \frac{1}{2}\eta - \frac{D}{4}z$.

**) $\alpha_3 = -1 + \frac{1}{2}\eta + \frac{D}{4}z$, $\alpha_4 = -\eta$.

Critical exponents: $\eta = 0.26 \pm 0.02$, $z = 1 + \zeta = 1.13 \pm 0.01$, $\lambda = 0.49 \pm 0.01$.

$$(D = 2).$$

Multiplicity moments

$$\langle n^p \rangle = C_p\,[\ln s]^{p\eta} + \ldots\ldots$$

404

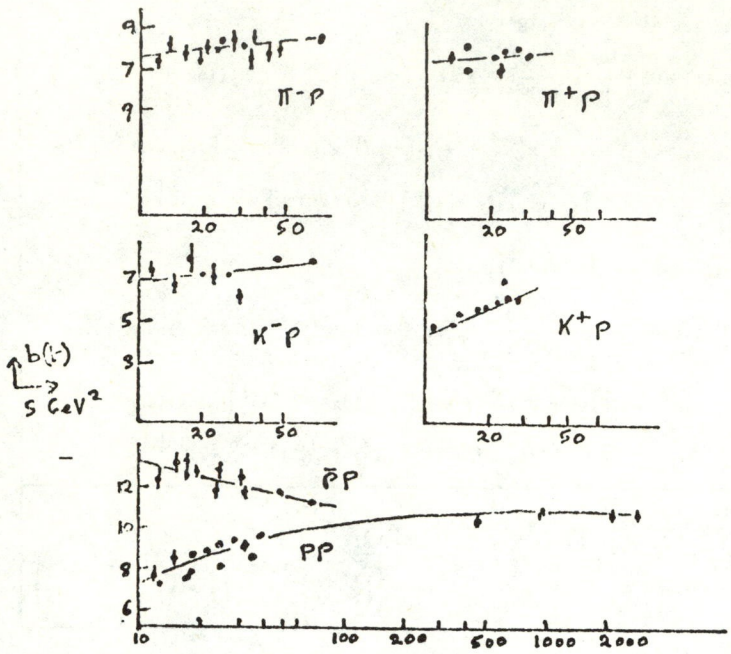

Fig. 1. Slope parameters as measured up to 1973.

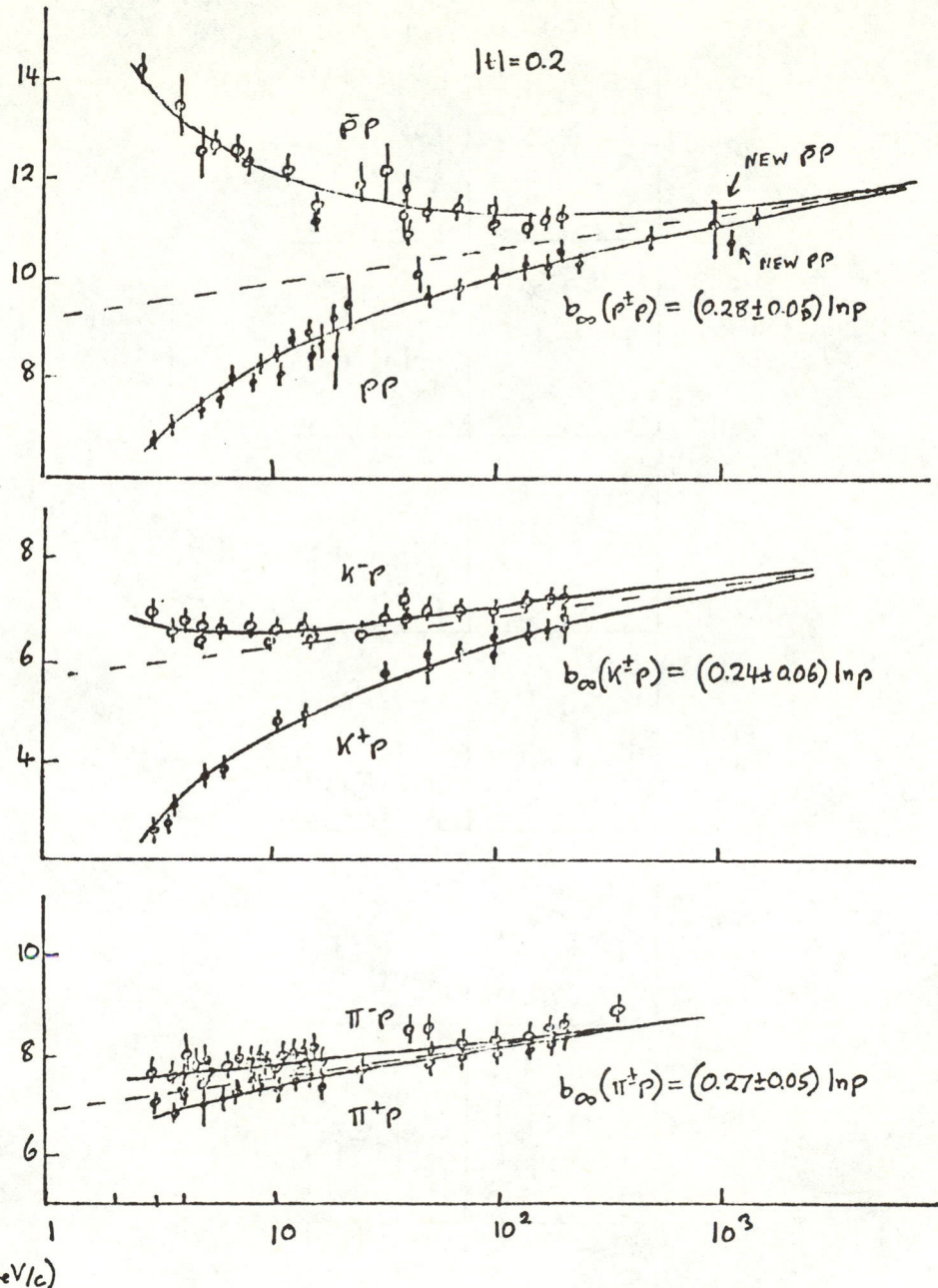

Fig. 2. Present-day compilation of slope parameters.

406

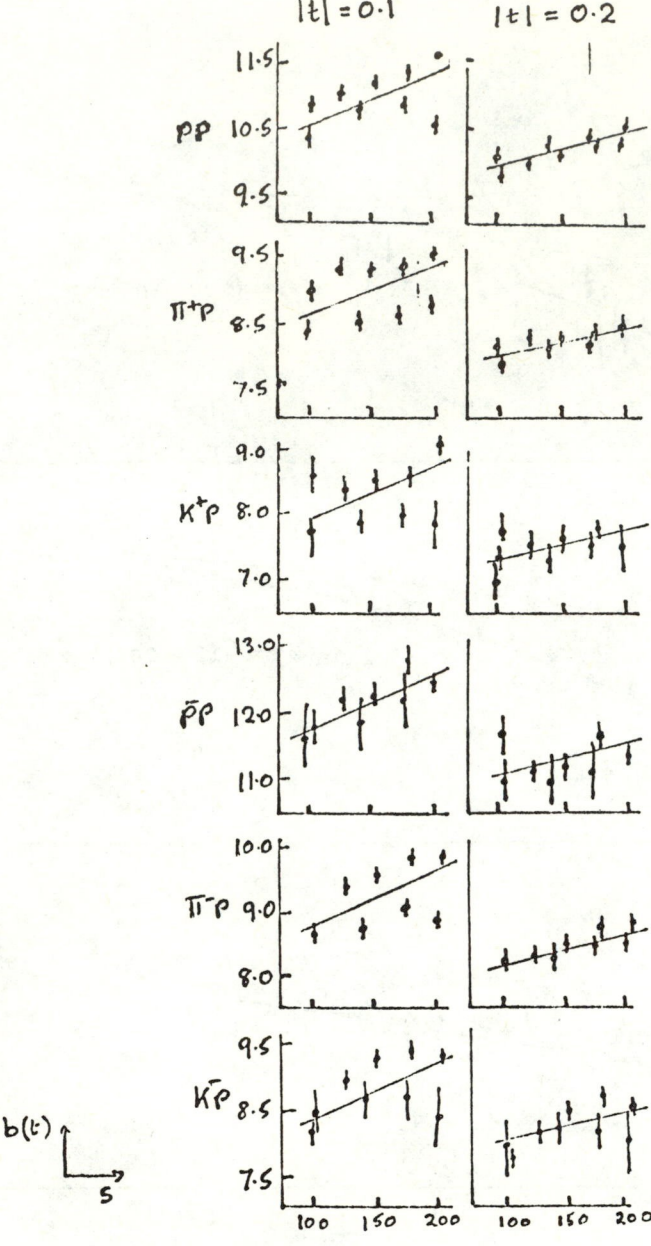

Fig. 3. t-dependence of b(t,s). The solid lines are to guide
the eye and are notfits. The universal curvature is manifest
even in the narrow t-range shown.

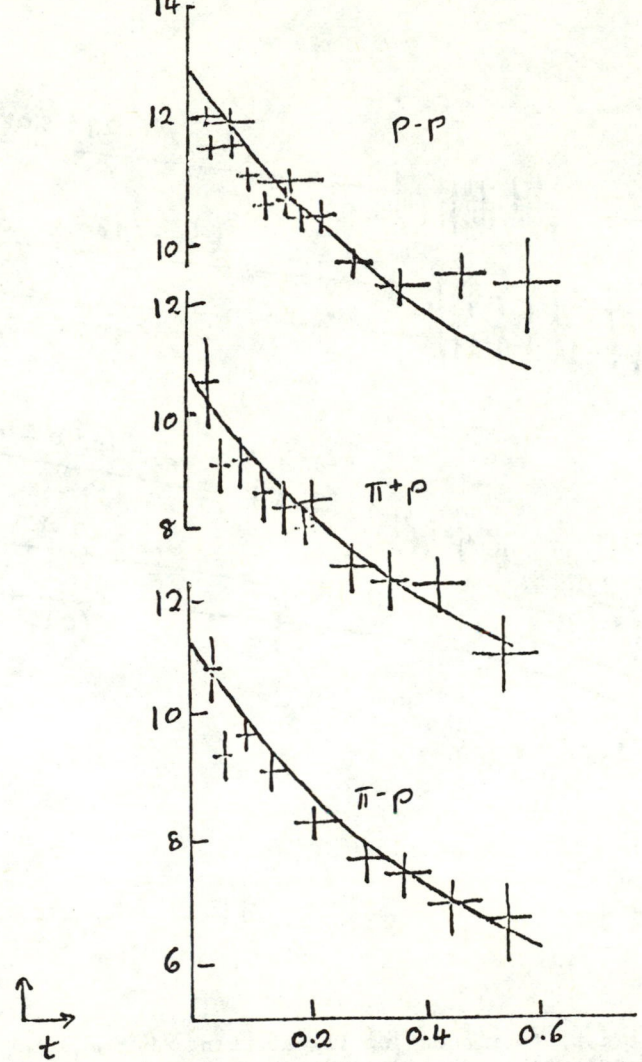

Fig. 4. Universal curvature over the whole t-range.

408

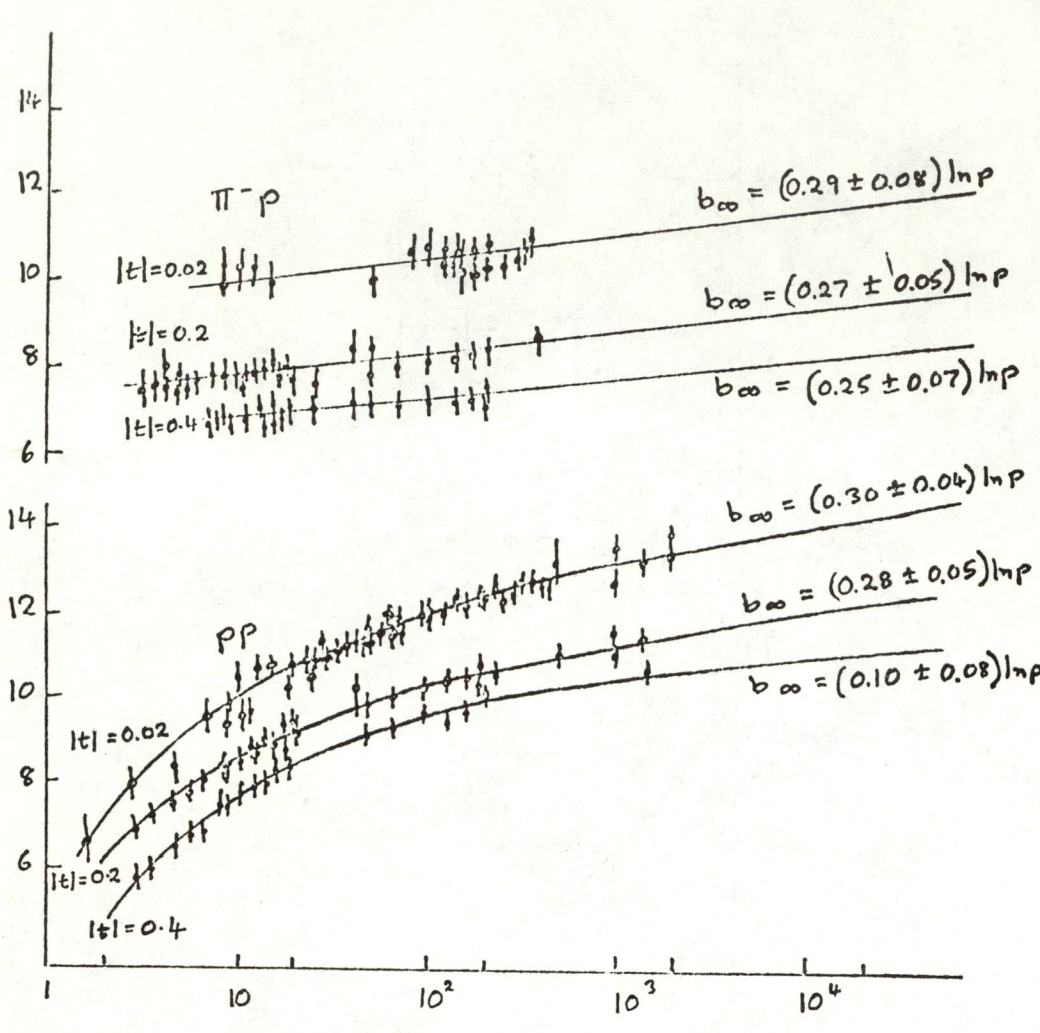

Fig. 5. b(t,s) for π^-p and pp illustrating that $\alpha'_{I\!P}$ is universal but with some t-dependence.

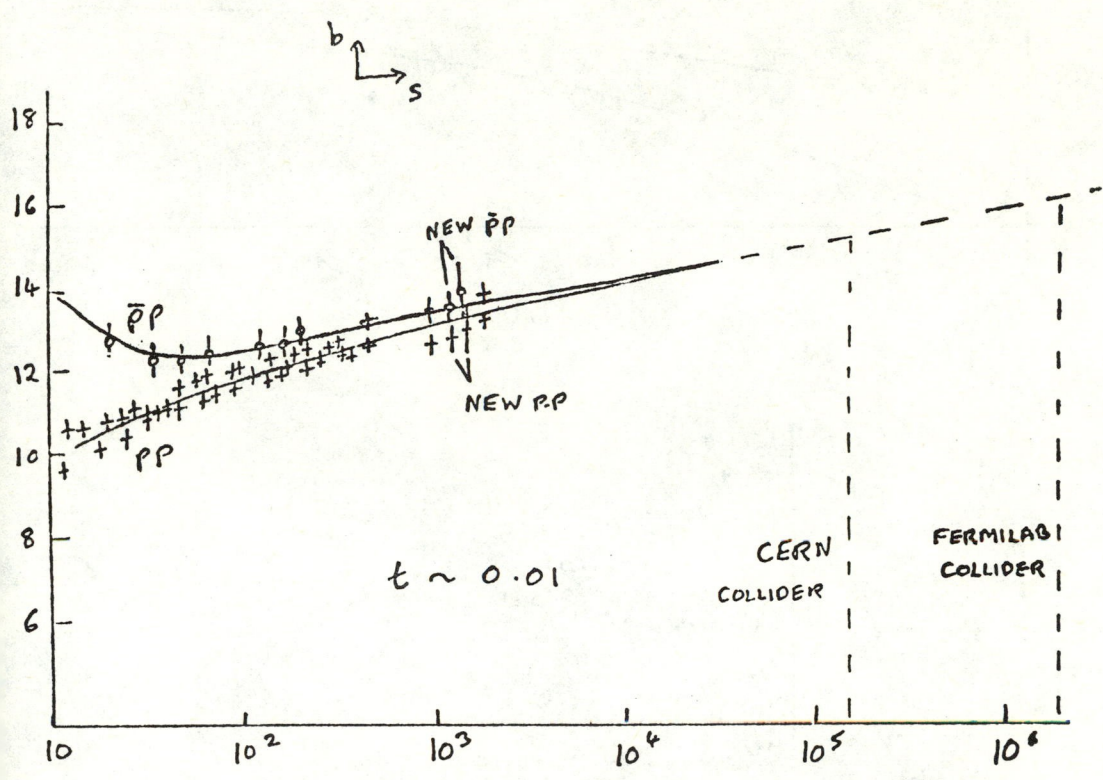

Fig. 6. The p-p and $\bar{p}$-p slope parameters extrapolated to collider energies.

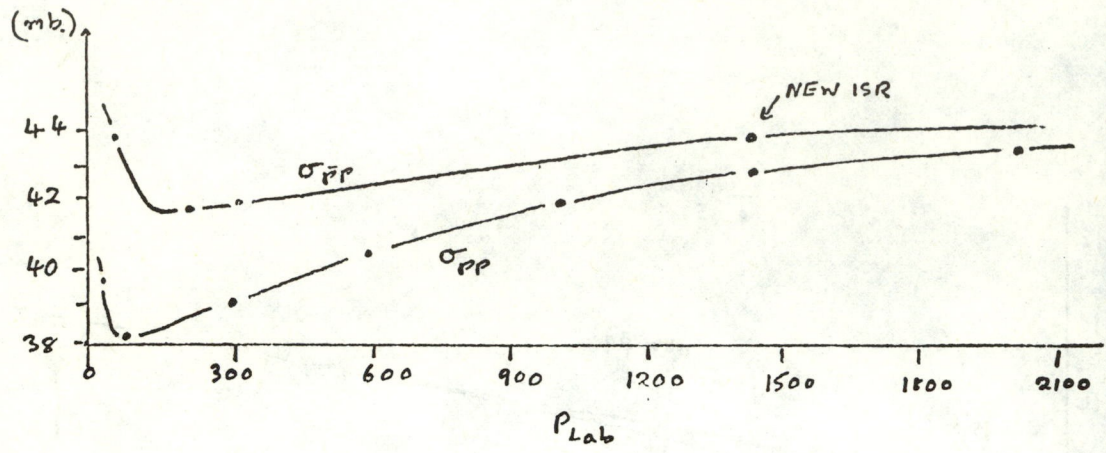

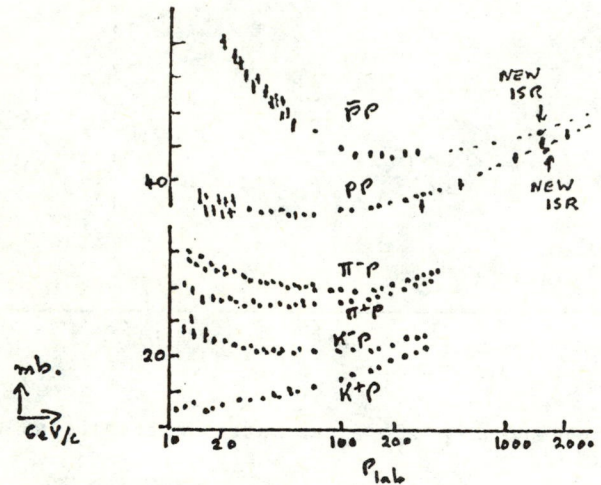

Fig. 7. The logarithmic rise of total cross-sections.

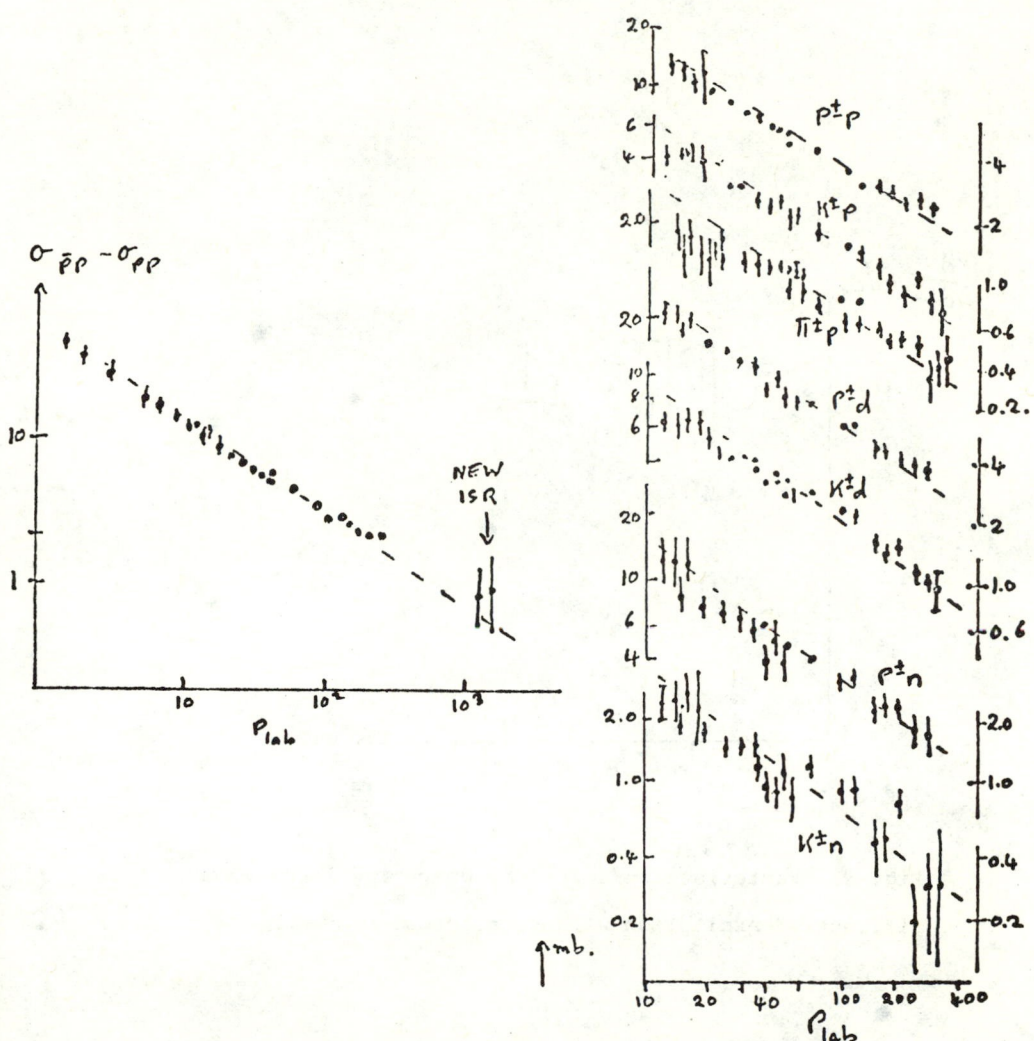

Fig. 8. The power law decrease of particle-antiparticle cross-section differences.

412

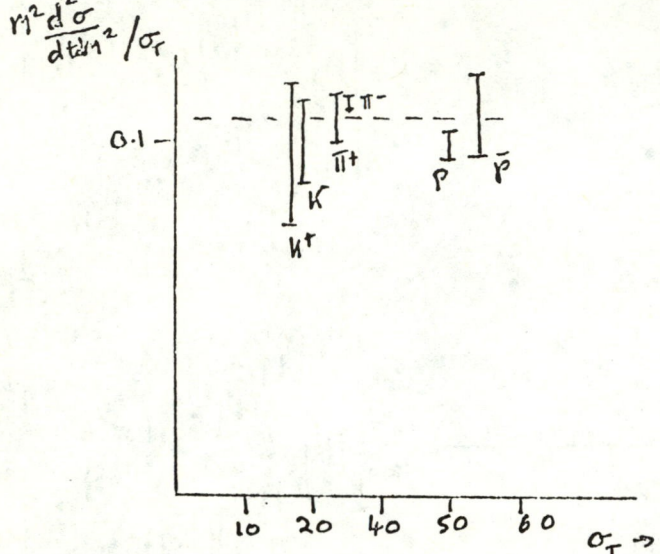

Fig. 9. Factorisation tested by comparing large mass
diffractive excitation with total cross-sections.

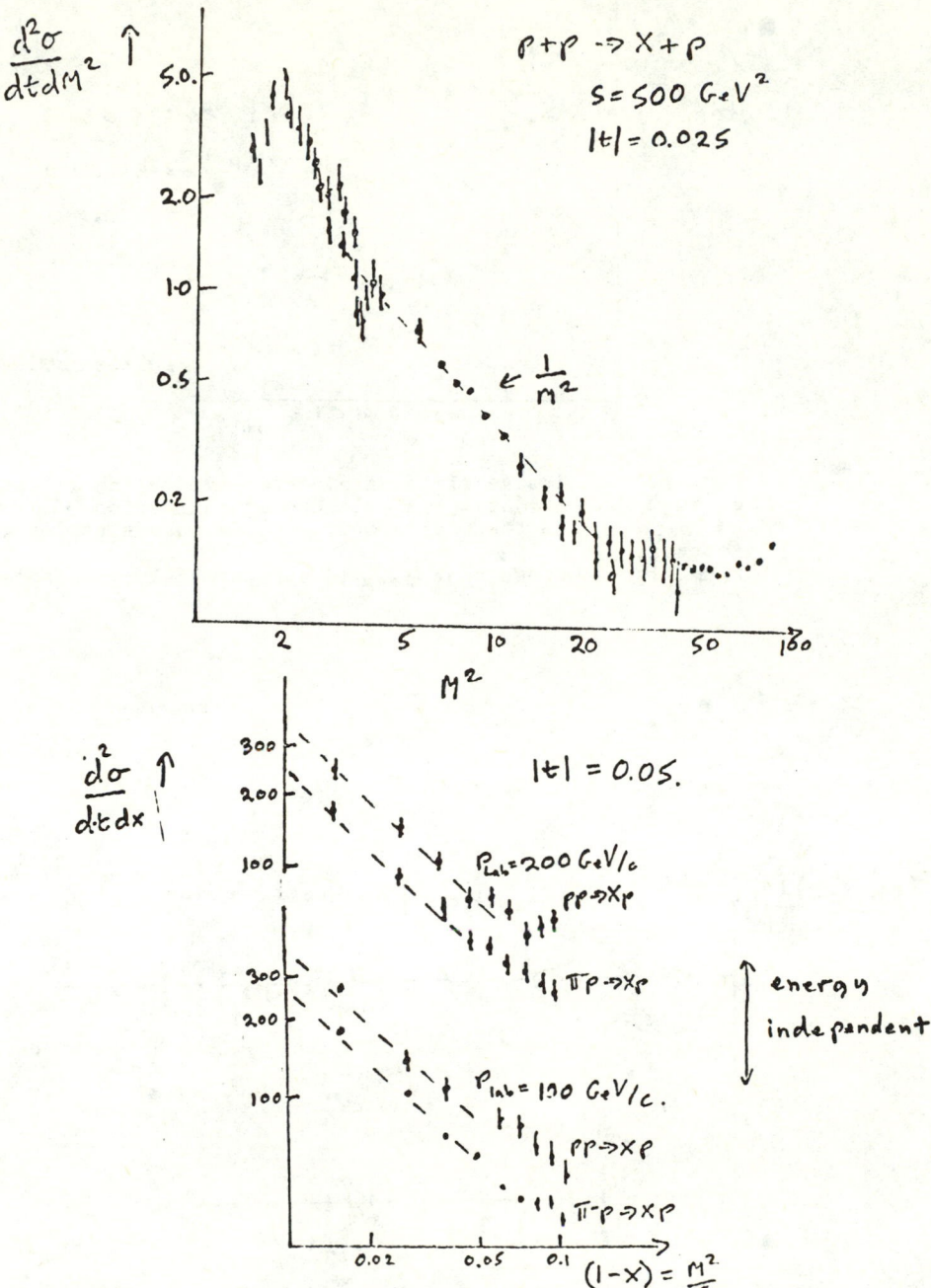

Fig. 10. Energy independence and $1/M^2$ behavior of large mass diffractive excitation.

414

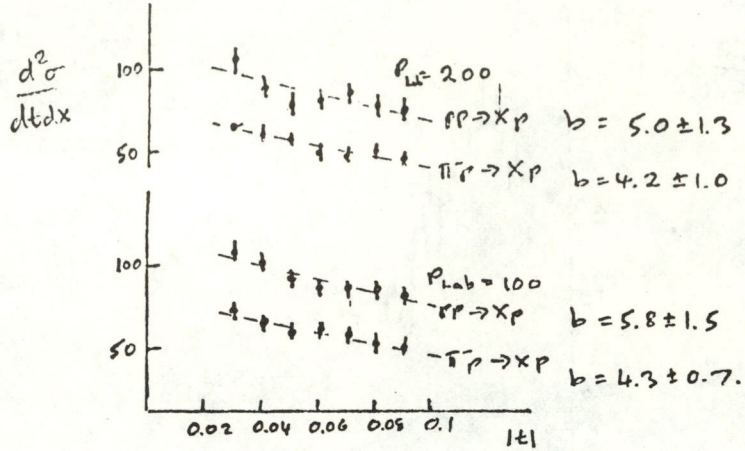

Fig. 11. Inclusive slope parameters – comparing (1) and (8) gives $g_{PPP}(t) \sim \exp[bt - \frac{1}{2} b_{el} t]$ in the approximation $d_P = 0$ if b_{el} is the corresponding slope parameter for elastic scattering.
From Fig. 2 we see that g_{PPP} is approximately t-independent.

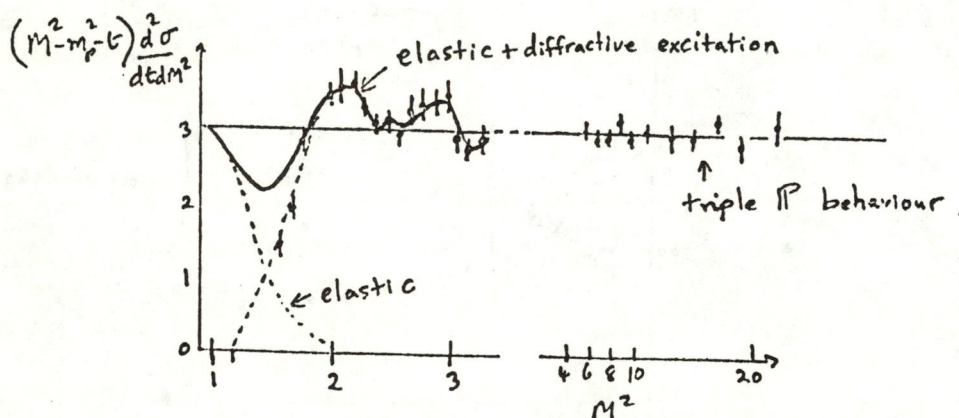

Fig. 12. The finite mass sum rule – triple P cross-section extrapolated to low missing mass averages the sum of the elastic and low mass excitation.

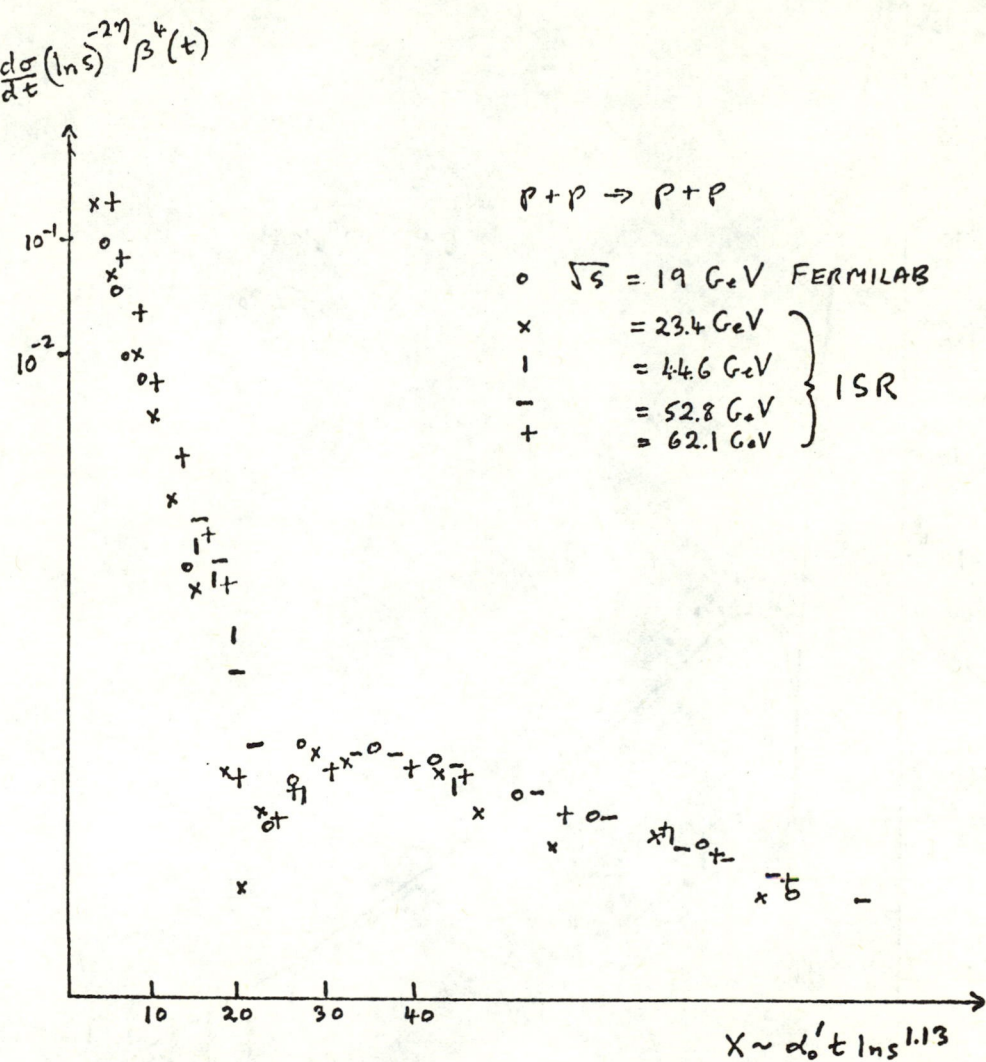

Fig. 13. Test of Critical Pomeron scaling of the elastic diffraction peak.

416

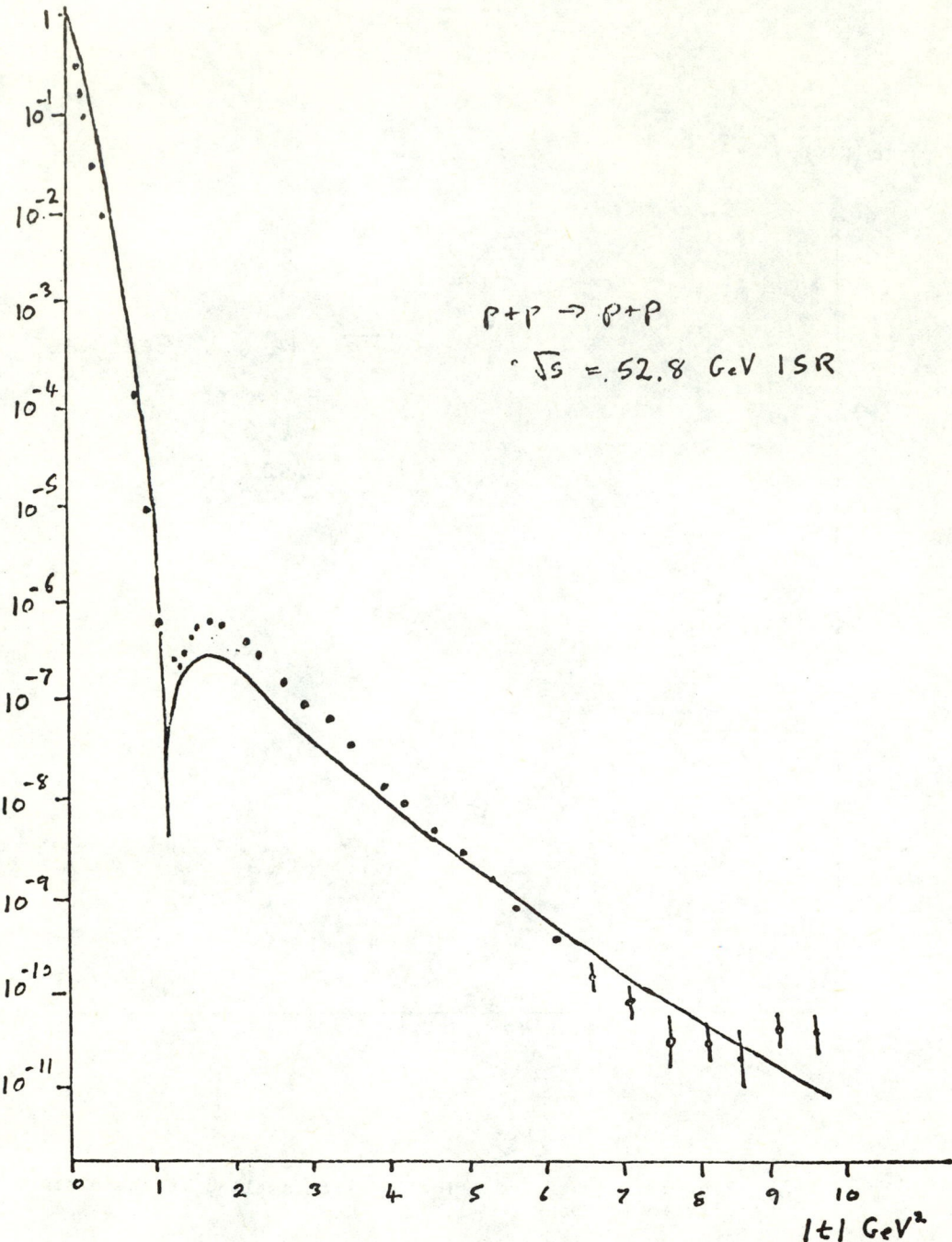

$$p + p \rightarrow p + p$$

$$\sqrt{s} = 52.8 \; GeV \; ISR$$

$|t| \; GeV^2$

Fig. 14. Comparison of the Critical Pomeron scaling function with the p-p elastic diffraction peak.

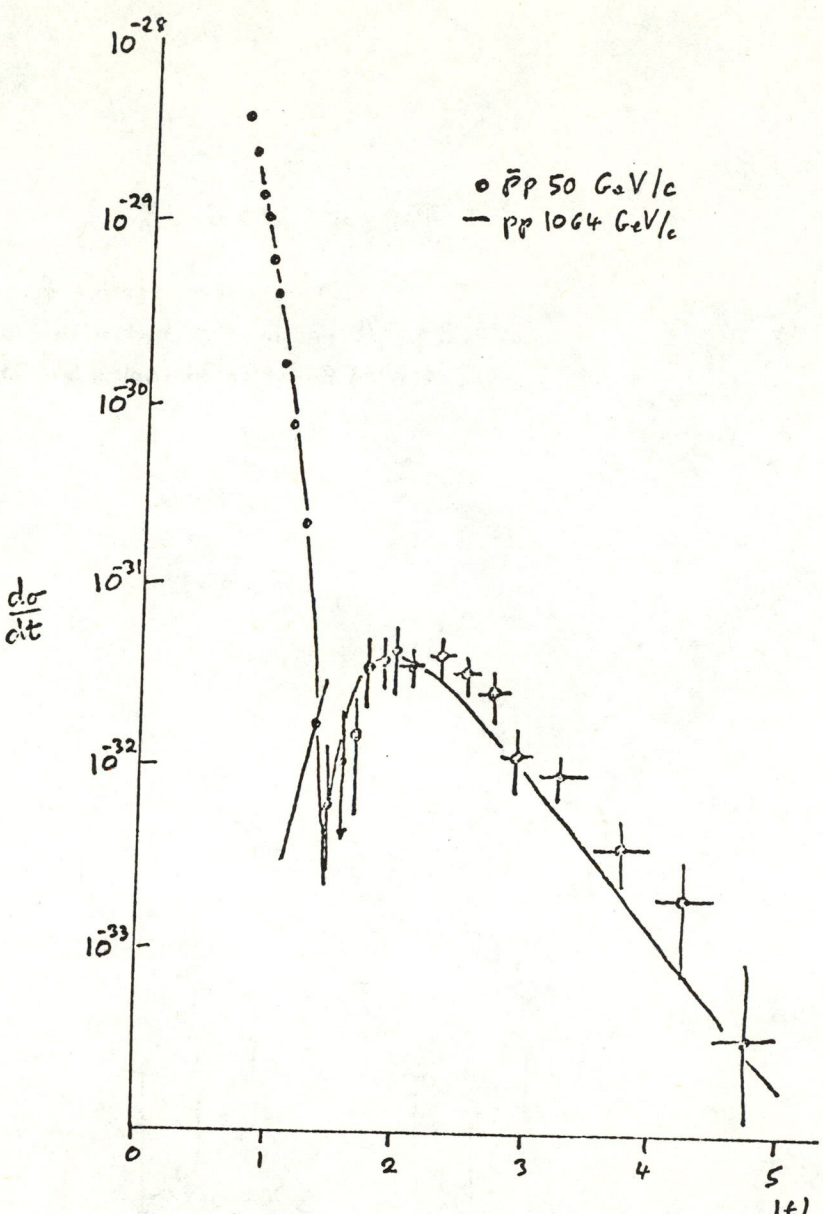

Fig. 15. Comparison of the p̄-p diffraction peak with the p-p diffraction peak.

418

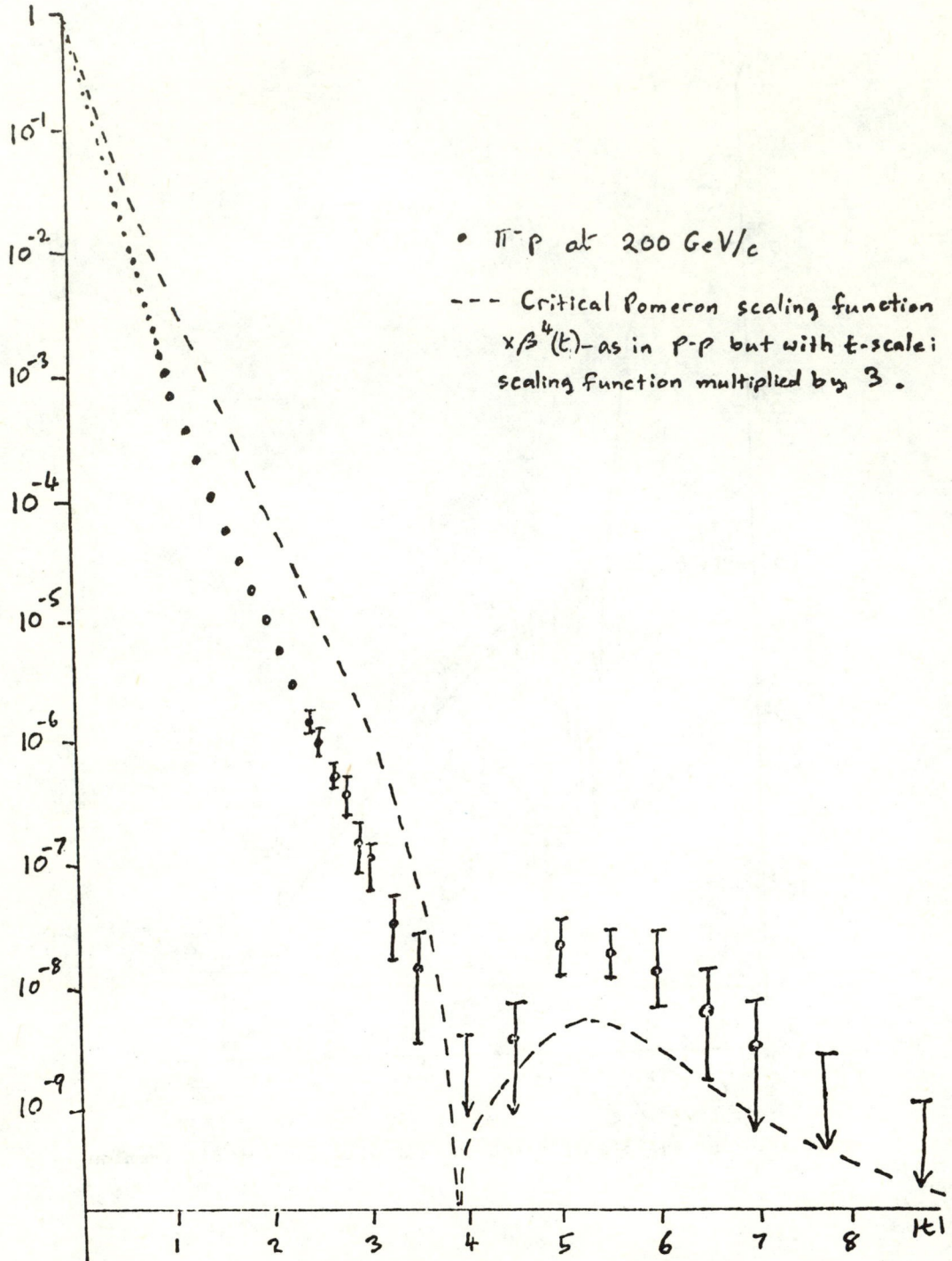

Fig. 16. The π^-p diffraction pattern compared with the critical Pomeron scaling function.

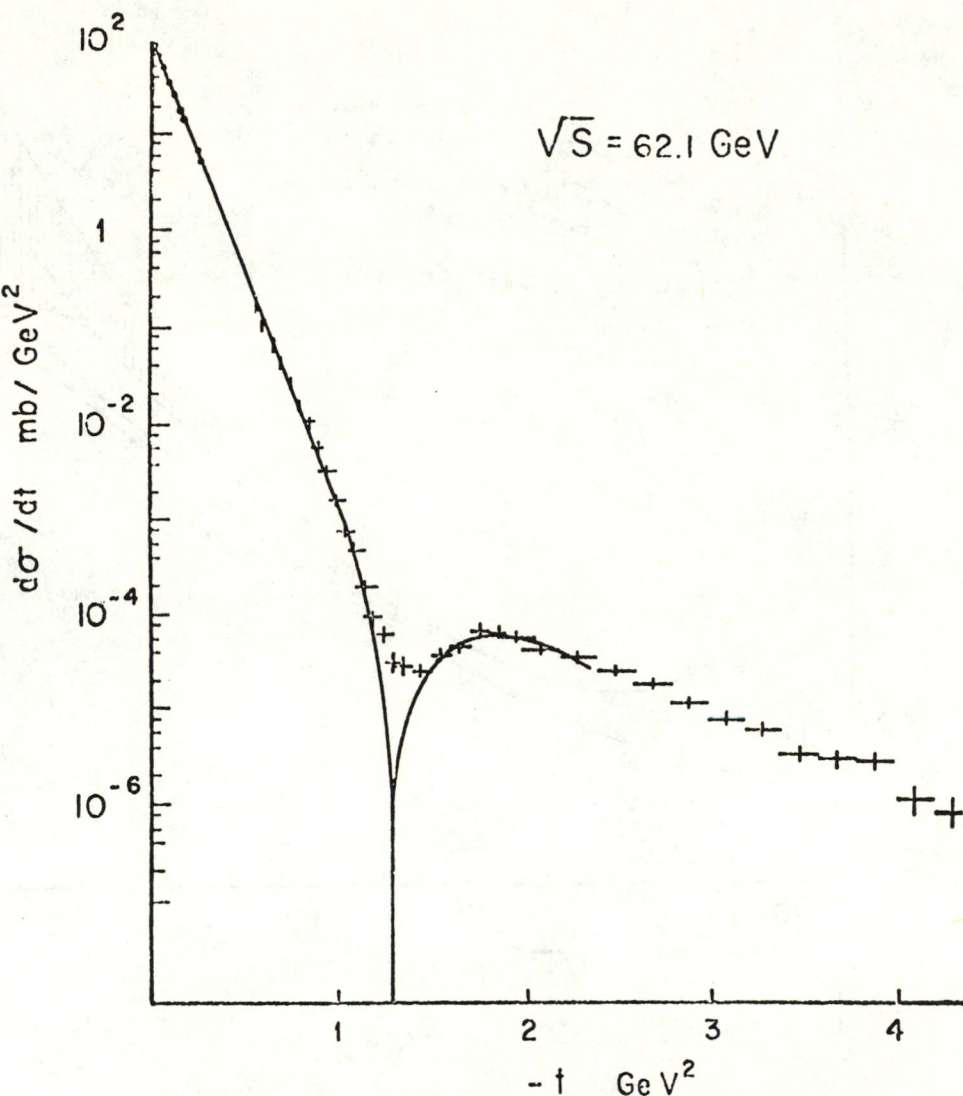

Fig. 17. The fit to the highest ISR energy results.

420

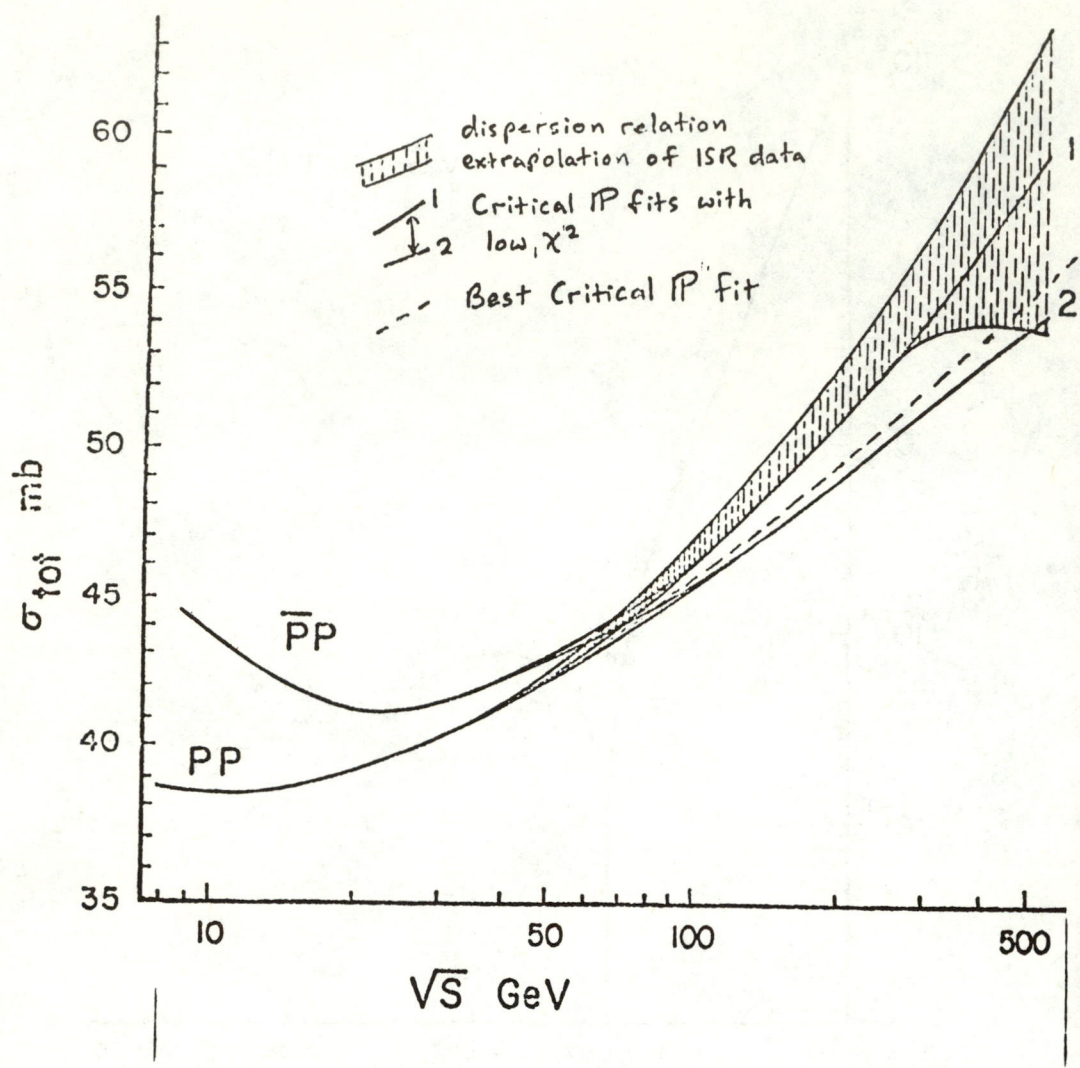

Fig. 18. Critical P extrapolation of p-p and $\bar{p}$-p total cross-sections.

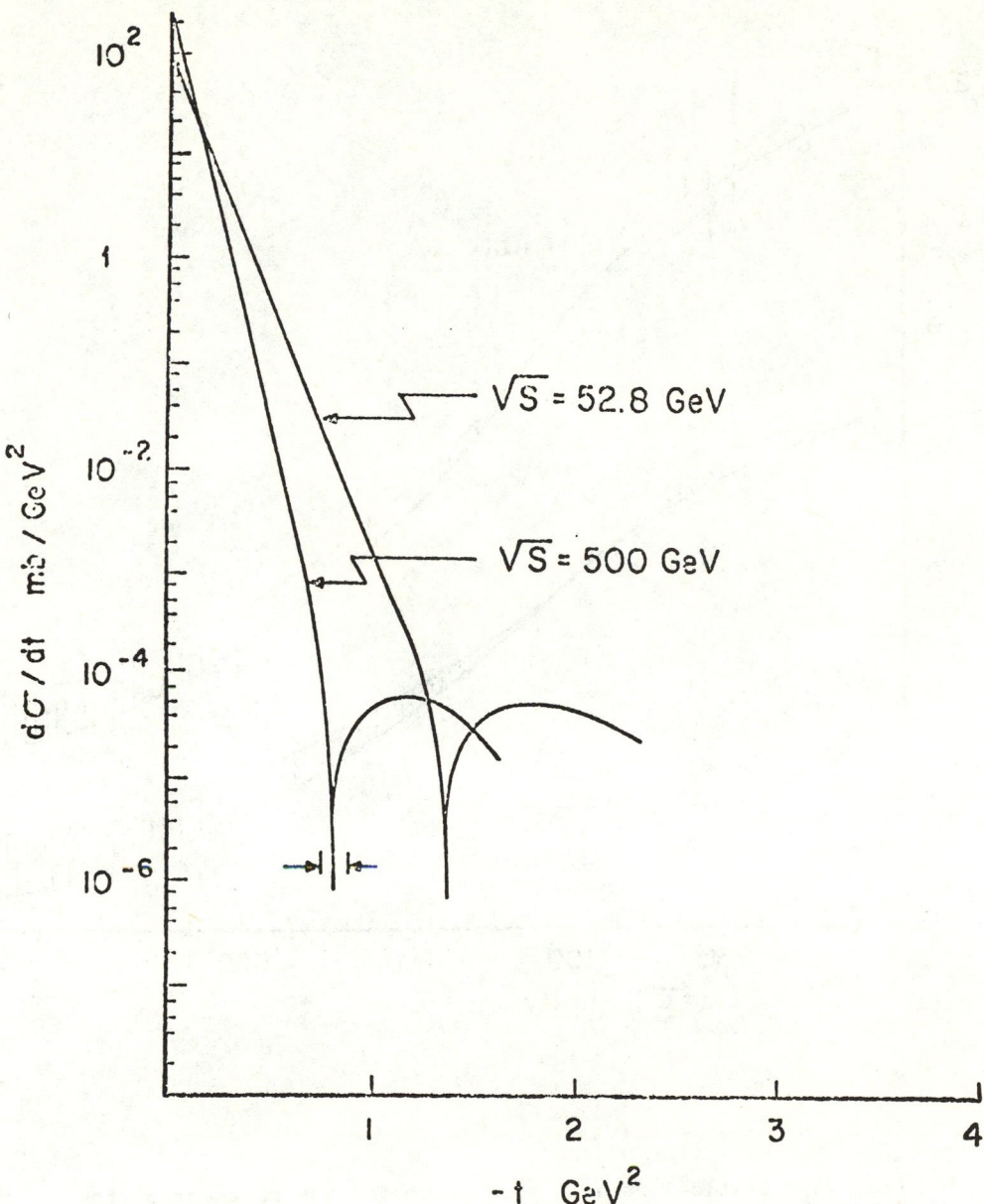

Fig. 19. Critical Pomeron prediction for the $\bar{p}$-p differential cross-section.

422

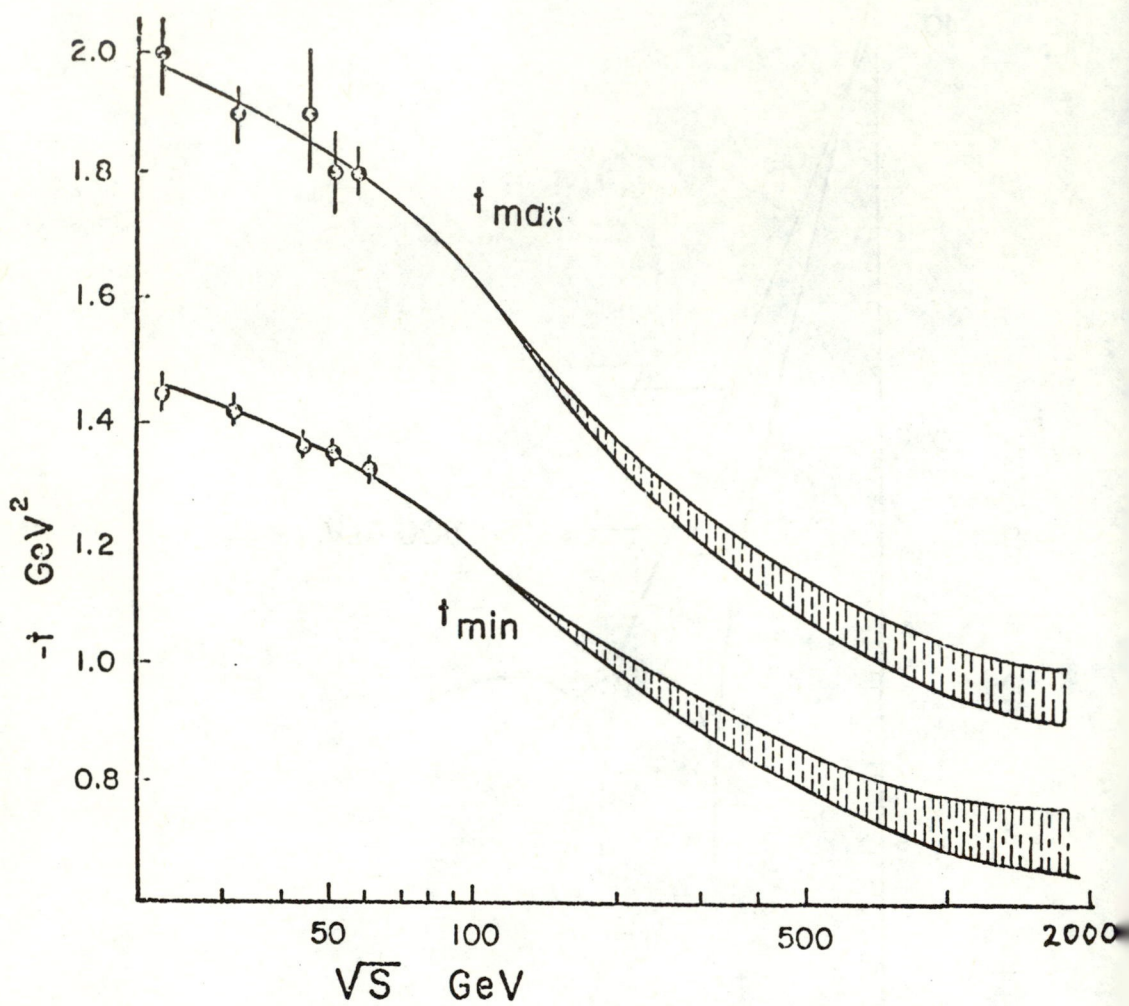

Fig. 20. Critical Pomeron prediction for the movement of the diffraction minimum and maximum.

423

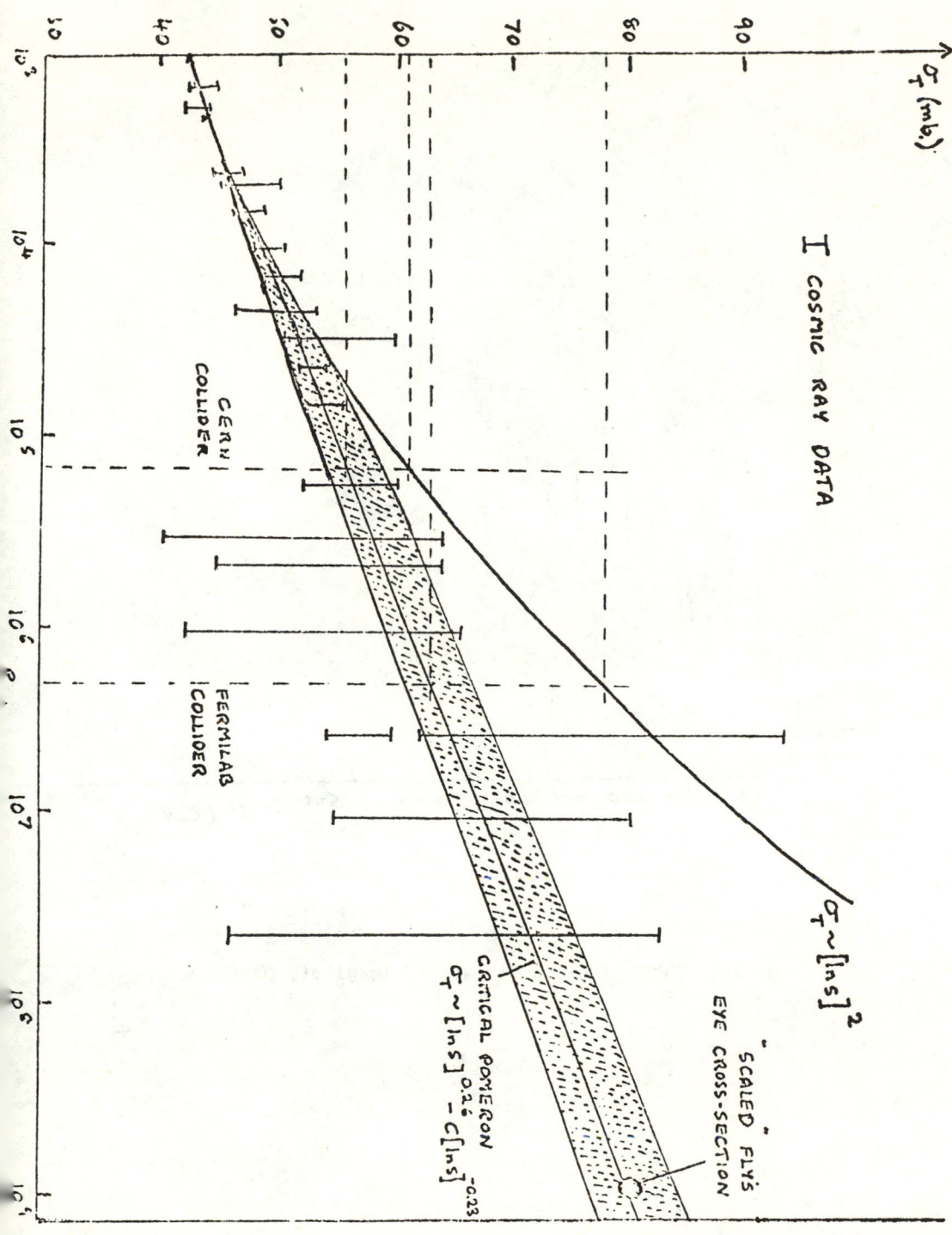

Fig. 21. Total cross-section predictions compared with
Cosmic Ray data.

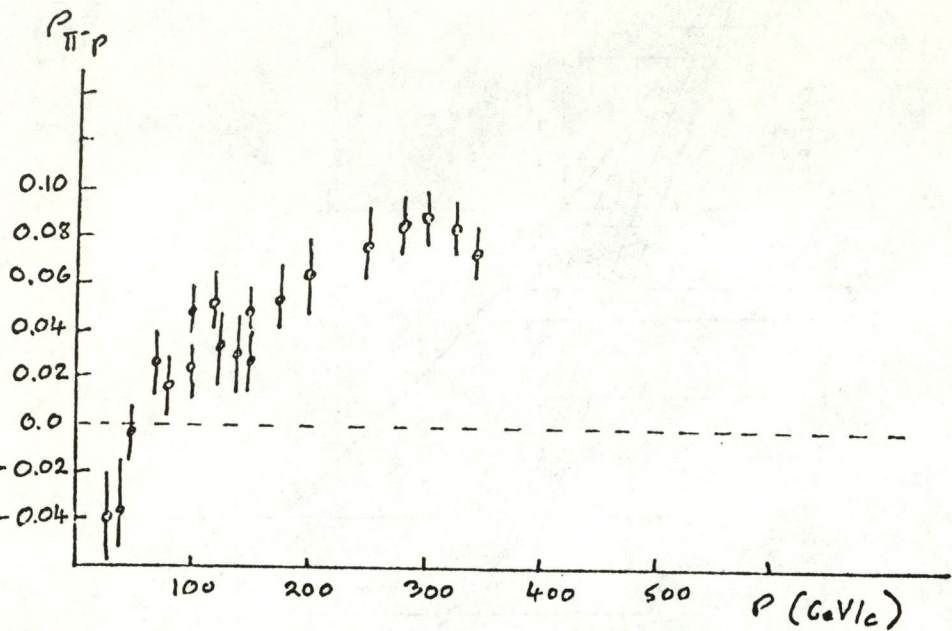

Fig. 22. The π^-p ratio of real to imaginary parts.

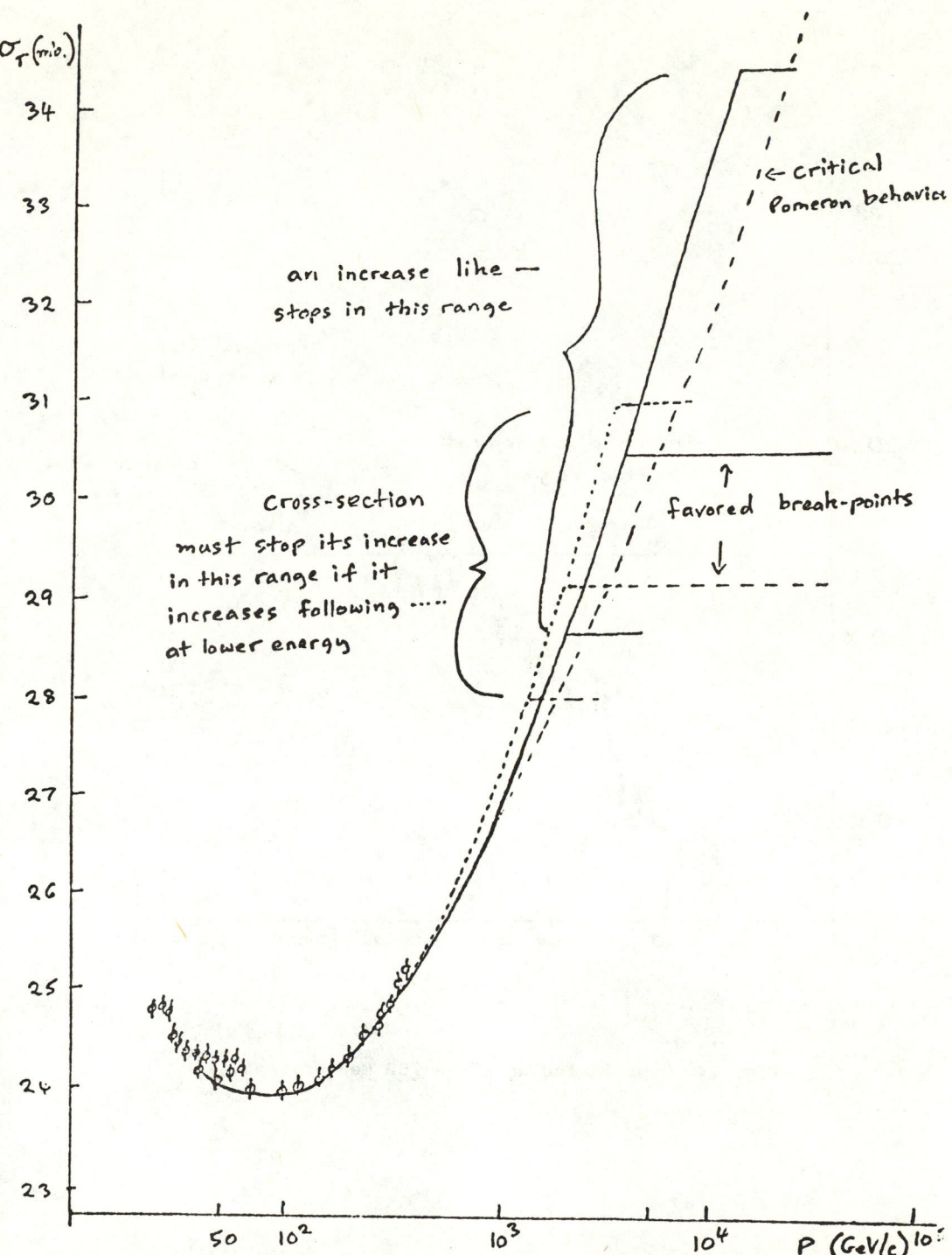

Fig. 23. Dispersion relation constraint on the rise of the π⁻p total cross-section.

426

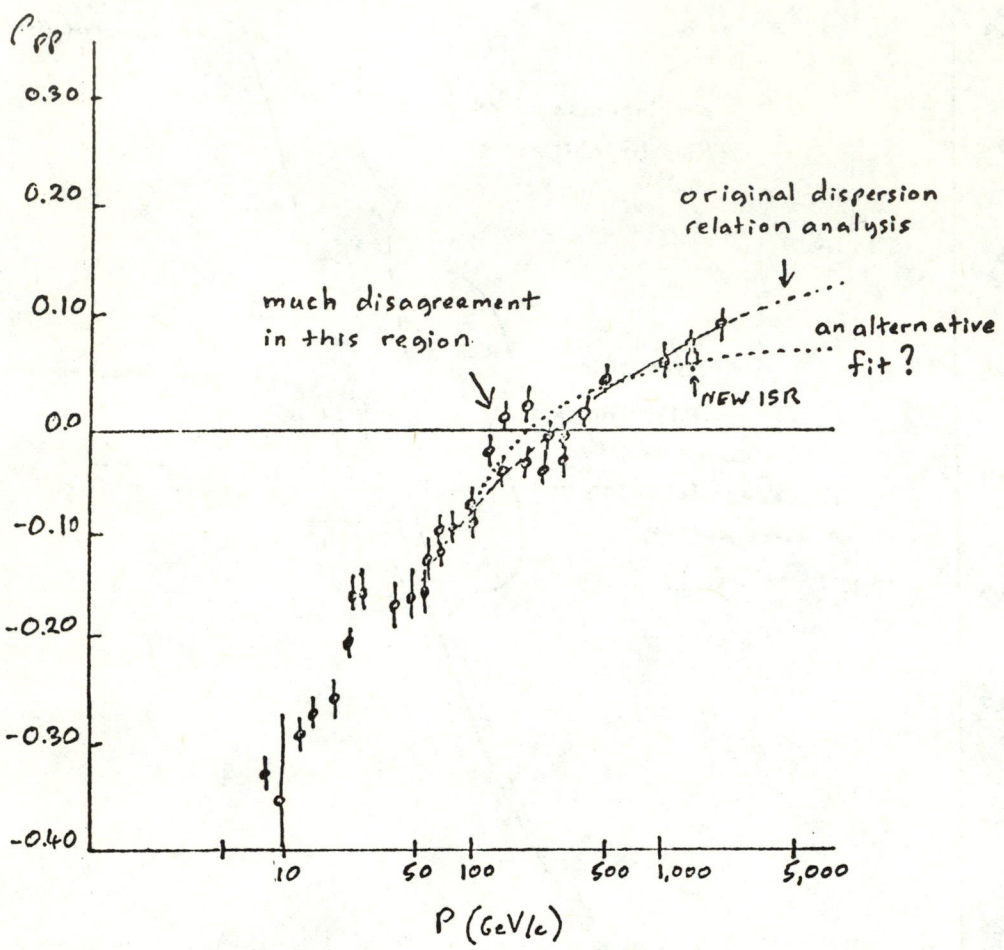

Fig. 24. ρpp including a new ISR measurement.

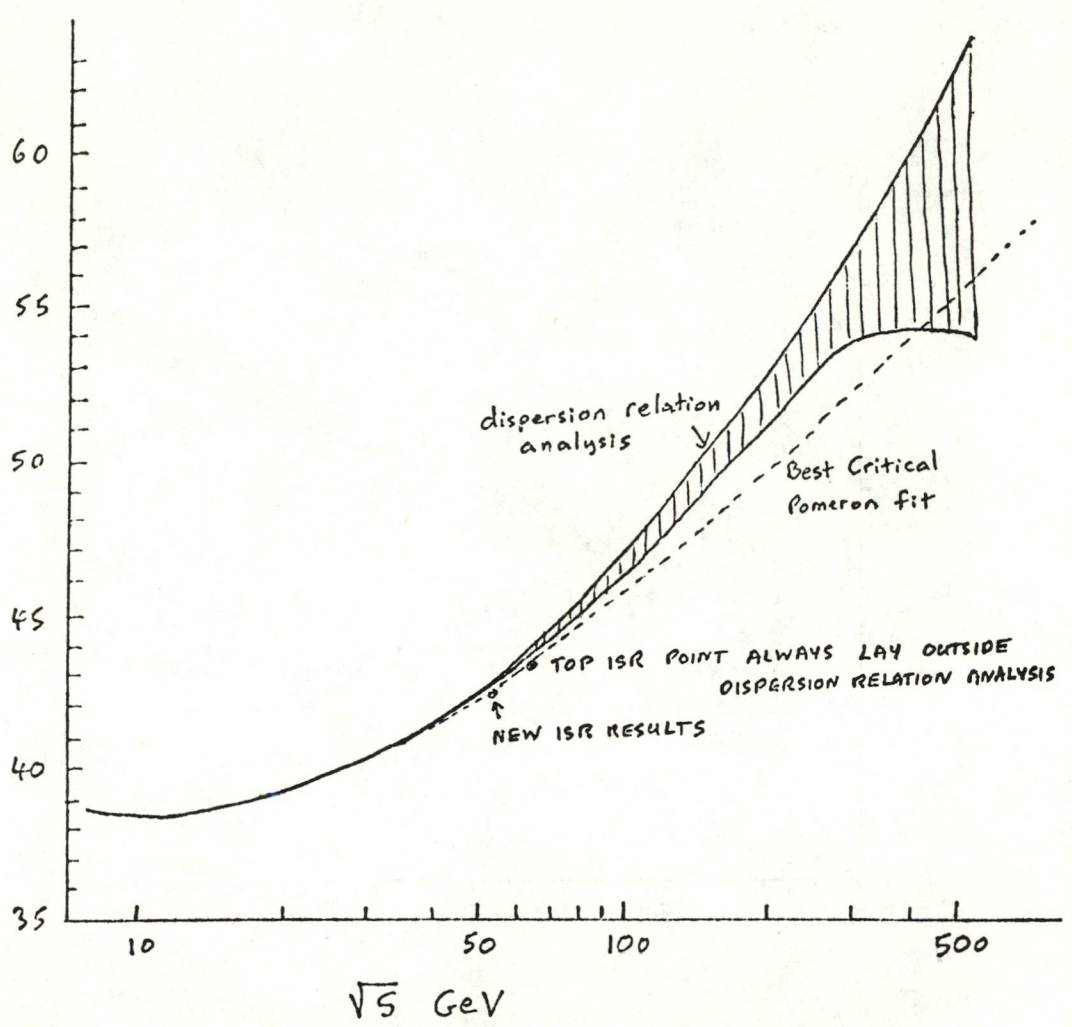

Fig. 25.   Comparison of new ISR results for the p-p total
cross-section with the dispersion relation analysis.

428

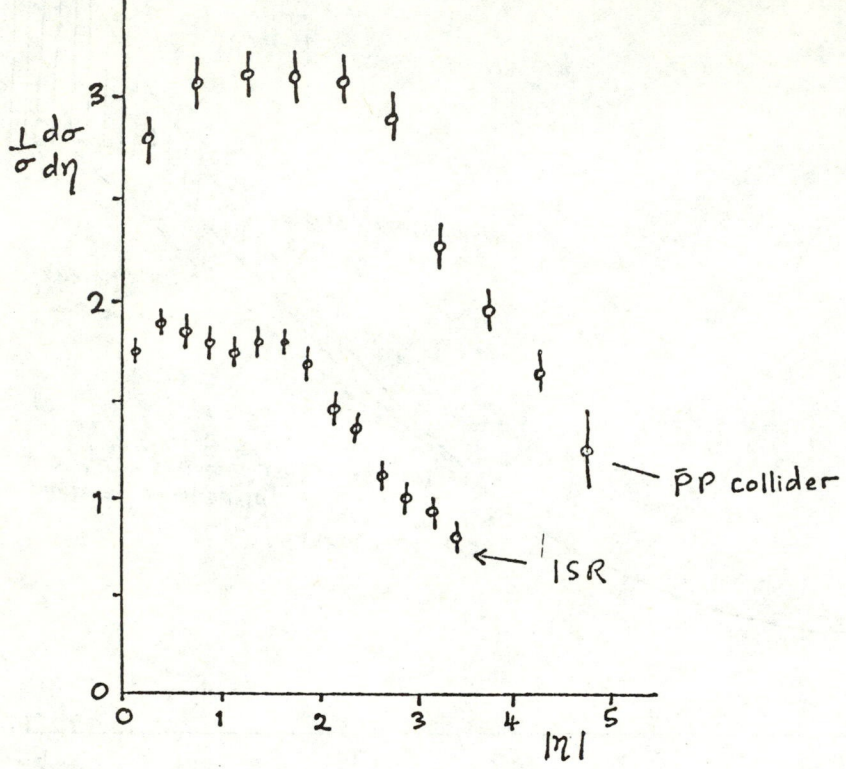

Fig. 26.   The rise of the central plateau from the ISR to the
CERN collider.
The plateau is not broadening as it rises, as a naive phase-space
model would predict.

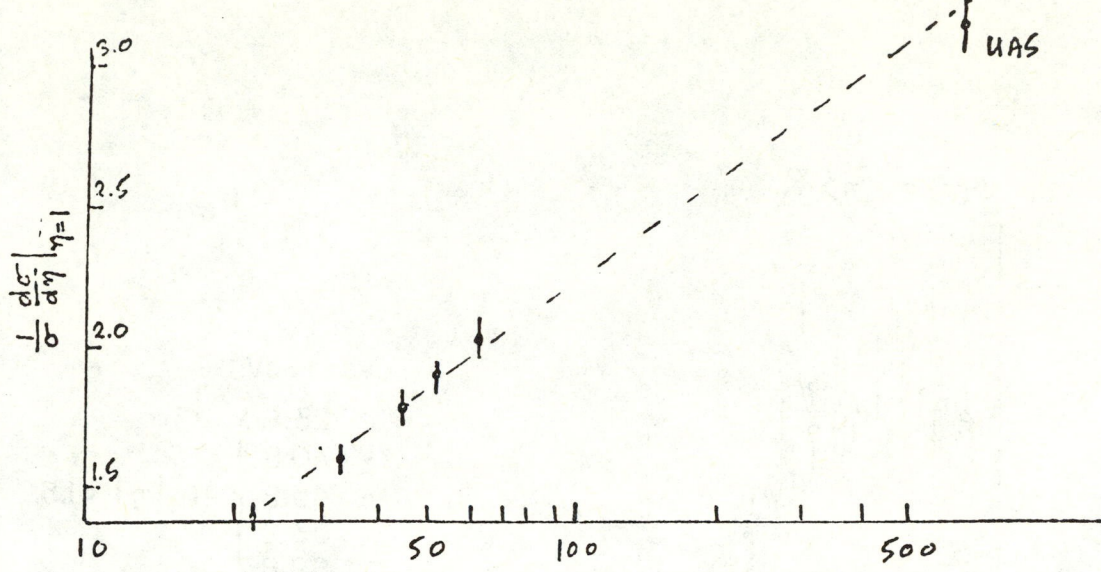

Fig. 27. The collider rise of the central plateau fits on a logarithmic extrapolation of the ISR results as predicted by the Critical Pomeron relation $d\sigma/d\eta \sim \sigma_T^2$

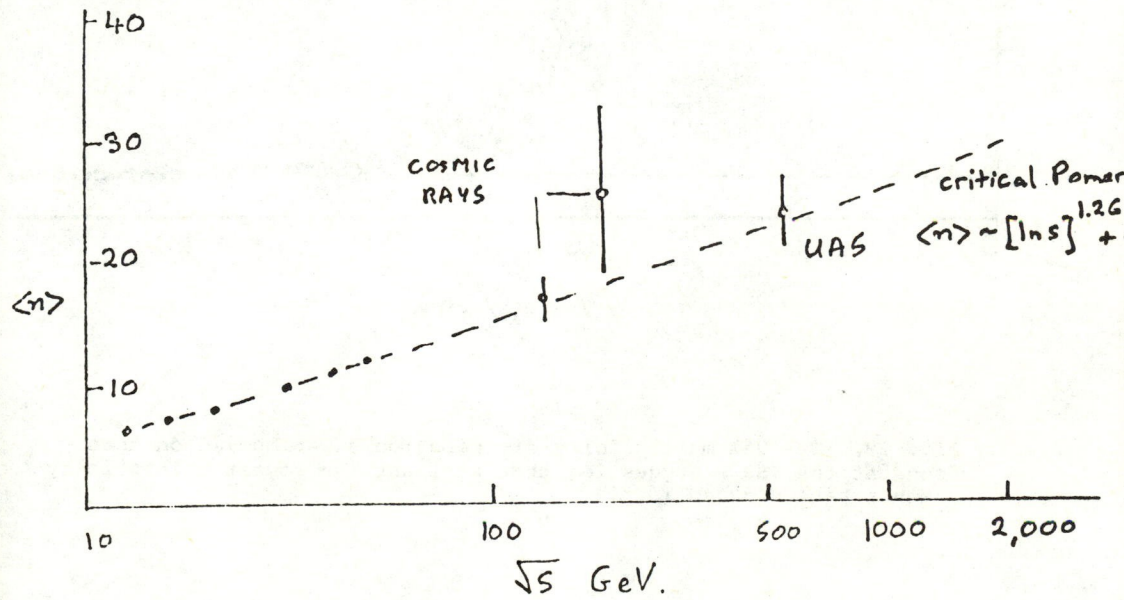

Fig. 28. The comparison of the collider average multiplicity and a rough critical Pomeron extrapolation.

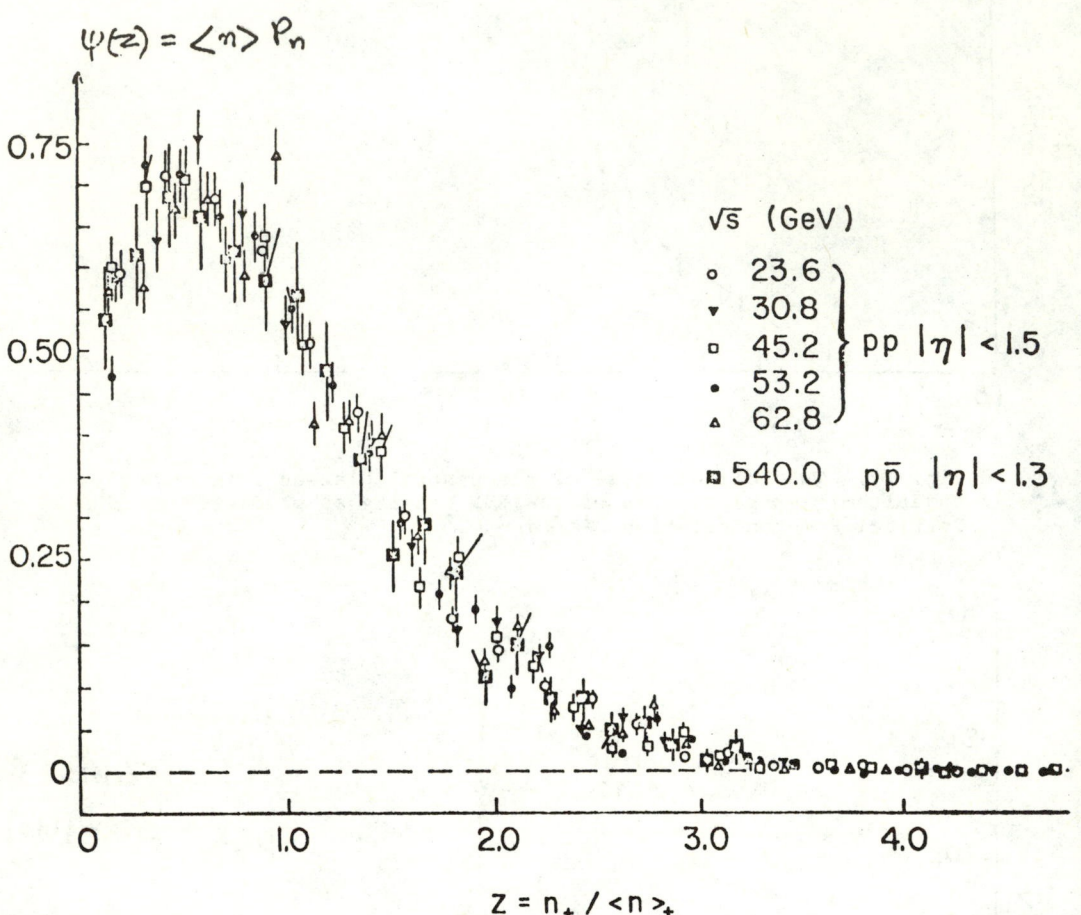

Fig. 29. The UA1 multiplicity distribution superimposed on that found at the ISR - suggesting that at least the lowest multiplicity moments have changed little.

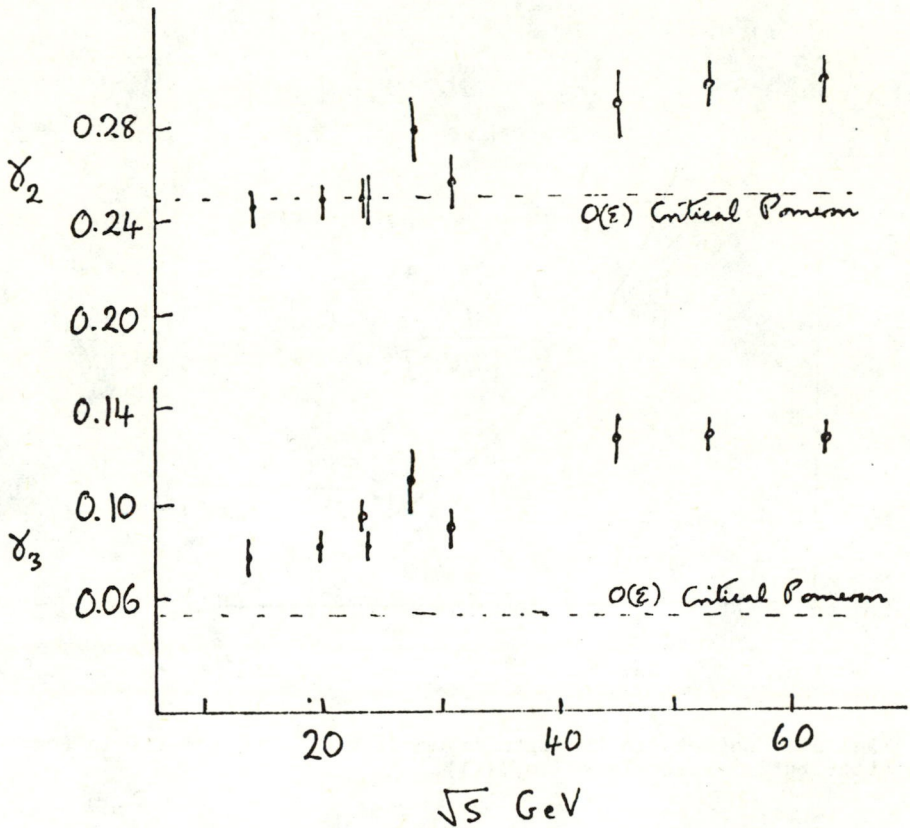

Fig. 30. Experimental results for the "γ" multiplicity moments and the "O($\mathcal{E}$) Critical Pomeron predictions - which are certainly an underestimate.

432

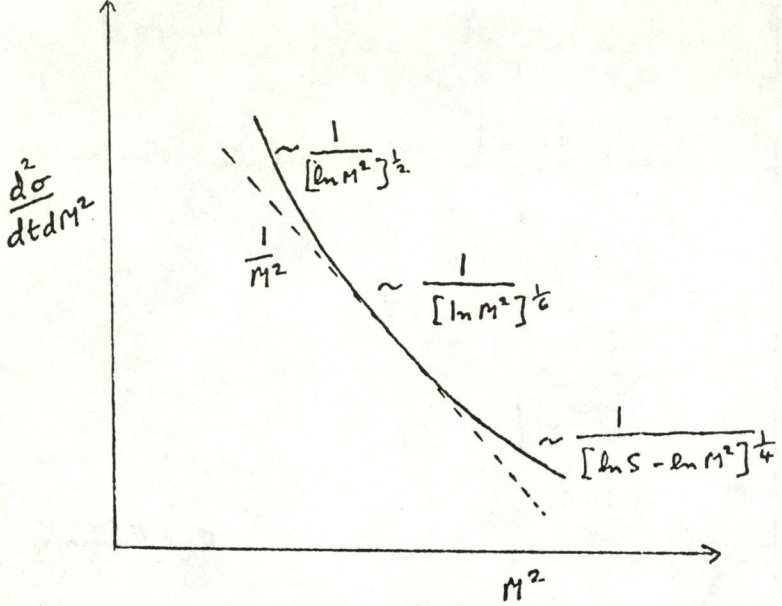

Fig. 31. Asymptotic logarithmic modification of the triple Pomeron distribution (calculated to $O(\varepsilon)$).

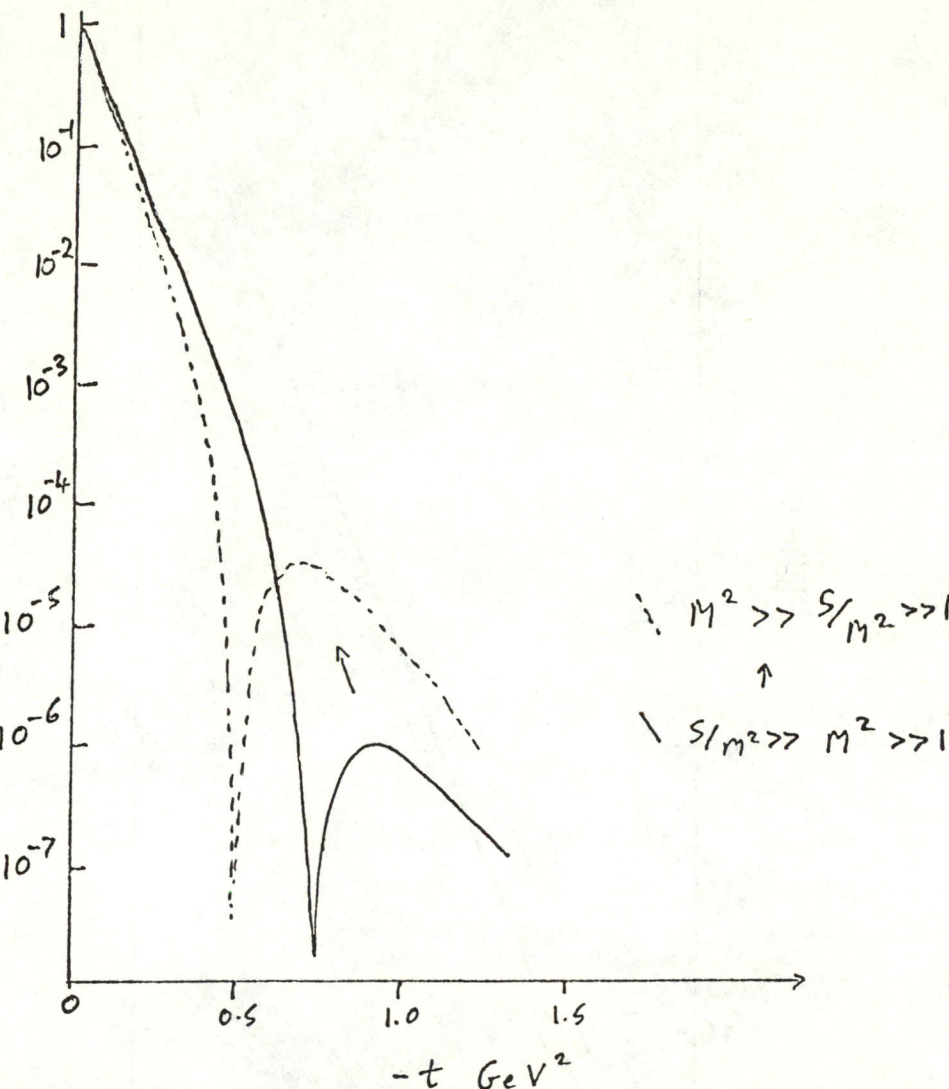

Fig. 32. Predicted movement of $M^2 d^2\sigma/dt dM^2$ plotted against t as M^2 increased through the triple Pomeron region – again an $O(\varepsilon)$ calculation.

434

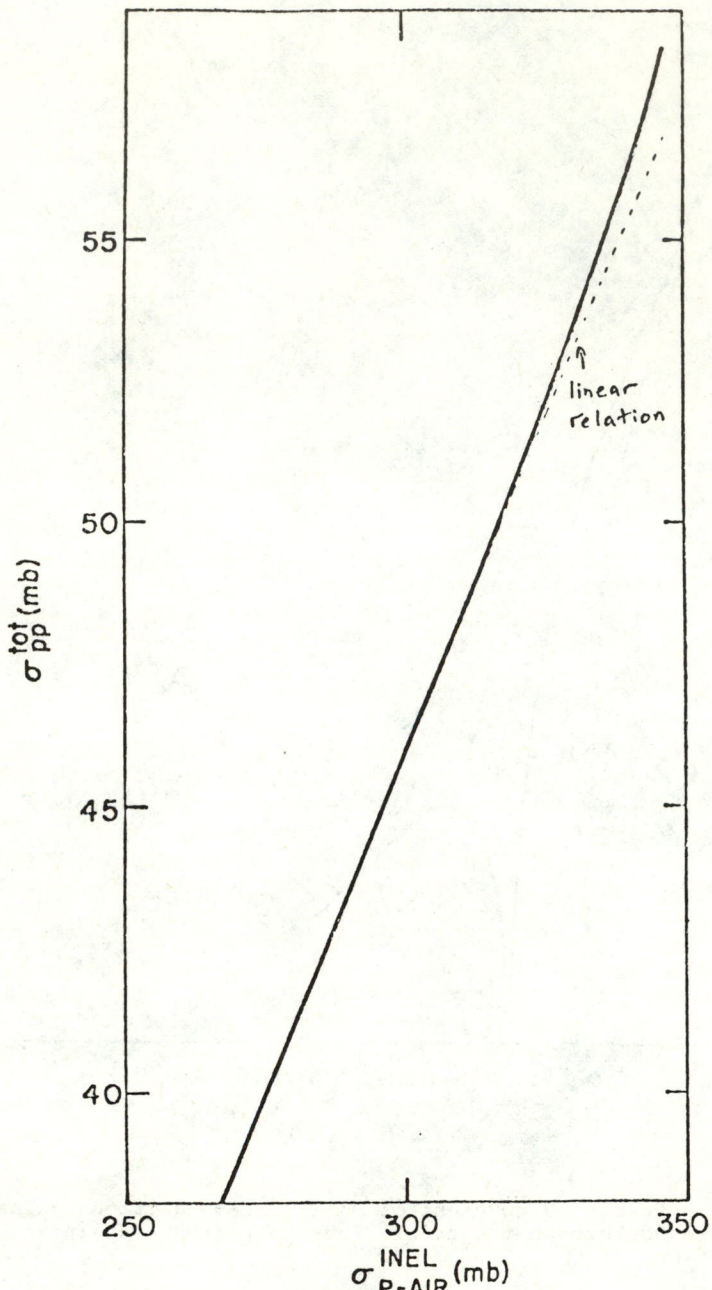

Fig. 33. The relation between σ_{pp} and $\sigma_{p\text{-air}}$ used in Ref.33 and justified
by Glauber theory. There is no significant deviation from a linear
relation for $\sigma_{pp} < 54\text{mb}$. which is equivalent to $P_{Lab} < 10^5 GeV$.

GLUON BREMSTRAHLUNG EFFECTS IN LARGE $p_\perp$ HADRON-HADRON SCATTERING

G. C. Fox
California Institute of Technology, Pasadena, CA. 91125

R. L. Kelly
Lawrence Berkeley Laboratory, Berkeley, CA. 94720

ABSTRACT

We consider effects of parton (primarily gluon) bremstrahlung in the initial and final states of high transverse momentum hadron-hadron scattering. Monte Carlo calculations based on conventional QCD parton branching and scattering processes are presented. The calculations are carried only to the parton level in the final state. We apply the model to the Drell-Yan process and to high transverse momentum hadron-hadron scattering triggered with a large aperture calorimeter. We show that the latter triggers are biased in that they select events with unusually large bremstrahlung effects. We suggest that this trigger bias explains the large cross section and non-coplanar events observed in the NA5 experiment at the SPS.

INTRODUCTION

Leptoproduction and hadronic scattering in QCD are characterized by the non-scaling behavior of structure functions. This behavior arises from parton branching processes which alter the longitudinal momentum distribution of the hadronic constituents, typically increasing the structure functions at small x and decreasing them at large x. The mechanism for this is the radiation of partons (principally gluons) by the active partons in a hard scattering process. The radiated partons carry off longitudinal momentum and this increases the liklihood that the hard scattering occurs between partons at low x. In the familiar Altarelli-Parisi (1) approach one characterizes the hadronic initial state by Q^2-dependent structure functions for the active partons, and ignores the radiated partons. Furthermore the kinematics are usually simplified to neglect the Q^2- evolution of constituent transverse momentum. A fixed, x-independent constituent transverse momentum distribution is generally used for all values of Q^2. In this paper we use an approach in which each parton branching is governed by the basic Altarelli-Parisi kernels, but we also keep track of all the radiated partons and their subsequent branchings. We use full off-shell kinematics and follow the transverse momentum evolution of the active and radiated partons. We treat final states at the parton level only, and therefore consider large aperture experiments which are less sensitive to hadronization effects than jet or single particle trigger experiments. We will see that even at the parton level, one can understand some of the main features of calorimeter experiments in terms of gluon radiation effects.

In the following section we describe the QCD evolution model used in our calculations. In Sec. III we describe trigger bias effects in large aperture calorimeters and give our results for the NA5 calorimeter. Sec. IV is a discussion of the Drell-Yan processes in our model, particularly our use of the Drell-Yan $p_\perp$ spectrum to choose the initial parton distributions. Details of the NA5 calculation, including $p_\perp^{hard}$ spectra and planarity distributions, are given in Sec. V, and in Sec. VI we give some predictions and comments concerning $\bar{p}p$ interactions at SPS collider energies.

II. THE MODEL

The model used was described in detail in Ref. (2) and essentially the same ideas have been used by Odorico in the talk presented at this conference (3). The methods were developed from the original ideas of Fox and Wolfrom (4) and Odorico and collaborators (5) for e^+e^- annihilation.

Hadron-hadron scattering in our formalism is illustrated in Figure 1 while some useful definitions are collected together in Tables 1&2. In the center of Figure 1, we see the conventional hard scattering in which the transverse momentum is $p_\perp^{hard}$. In the normal treatment (see for instance (6)), one neglects the mass of the four partons involved in this collision (denoted by heavy lines in the figure). One further uses a phenomenological transverse momentum distribution for the initial state partons while the logitudinal momentum distributions $G(x, t_B^{min})$ are taken from leptoproduction experiments. The transverse momentum distribution for the partons is taken from measurements of the Drell-Yan process. This picture produces a four jet final state: two jets corresponding to the scattered partons and two correspond to the "beam remains" left after the initial state patrons are removed from the incident hadrons. Often one will try to make realistic predictions for the complete structure of these events by hadronizing the four jets usually employing the Field Feynman model (7). This does in fact provide a good first description of high $p_\perp$ events (6,8) although as we see from the NA5 data it does not describe large aperture calorimeter measurements! There are many things wrong with this calculation.

(1) As emphasized in ref. (9), the partons involved in the collision do not have zero mass but in fact must be off shell. The initial state partons have negative m^2 and those in the final state positive m^2.

(2) The four jet final state is only an approximation for (especially) gluon bremsstrahlung from
the initial and final partons produce multi-jet
final states of complex topology.

(3) The transverse momentum distribution gets broader
as one increases one's scale $|t_B^{min}|$ i.e. as one
increases $p_\perp^{hard}$. This is already clear from the
Drell-Yan data (of Section IV) but is not included
in most calculations.

(4) Not only are there significant real emission processes mentioned in (2) but also virtual corrections are expected to be large (10).

(5) A convincing theoretical justification for the
whole procedure - especially when it involves
hadronization - is lacking (2). Even if one is
brave enough to use these methods, one cannot
expect very precise results.

The techniques used in this paper put in the bremsstrahlung
from both the initial and final state partons and answer the first
three objections above. The calculation employs the leading
logarithm approximation and so is not exact but it does properly
sum the bremsstrahlung to all orders in α_s. We do not address the
problems (4) and (5). However there is no reason to believe that
the virtual corrections in (4) will alter the qualitative structure
of the events and so if we concentrate on general features and not
precise estimates, we should be quite safe. In fact we will only
present results at the parton level here and so difficulties with
hadronization are also avoided.

Returning to Figure 1, we see that the initial state partons
start off with a mass^2 $t = t_B^o$ which we will take as -4 GeV^2. †
These partons evolve toward the scale t_B^{min} emitting gluons (and
quarks in the manner described in Ref. (2). Note that the "beam
remains" are no longer a simple jet and are further $Q^2(t_B^{min})$ dependent. The remains consist of the low-$p_\perp$ jet remaining after removal
of the initial parton (as this parton is not far off shell, this
part of the remains does have limited $p_\perp$) plus the Q^2 dependent
collection of radiated partons. The effect of this radiation

†To be precise, one should in fact take the initial partons to have
a mass^2 $> t_B^o$ with a distribution $\alpha_s(t)/_t$.

increases with Q^2 and is reflected both in an increasing $p_\perp$ of the parton just before it scatters - we call this $p_\perp^{brem}$ (t_B^{min}) - and an increasing complexity of the remains. This $p_\perp^{brem}$ is what is often called the "intrinsic" transverse momentum of the partons inside the hadron. The above discussion makes it clear that this transverse momentum is scale dependent; on the other hand it is <u>universal</u> (at least in the leading logarithm approximation) and all <u>processes</u> governed by the same scale do exhibit the same transverse momentum distribution. Usually (6) one employs scale dependent logitudinal momentum distributions $G(x,Q^2)$ using analytic methods to sum the radiation effects. Our Monte Carlo reproduces (approximately) the same $G(x,Q^2)$ but has the important advantage of also estimating the associated Q^2 dependent effects in the beam remains and the $p_\perp^{brem}$ distribution.

In implementing our ideas we have to decide on the scale t_B^{min}. Unfortunately this decision is outside the leading logarithm approximation and no firm answer can be given. We remind the reader that this difficulty crops up in the conventional discussion of hadron-hadron scattering (6) in the choice of the argument Q^2 of $G(x,Q^2)$. We will in fact make not the best but the <u>most convenient</u> choice which in fact saves a large amount of computer time! The problem in applying our method to pp scattering is that one must choose t_B^{min} before starting the evolution and hence before knowing the four vectors of the final partons. Thus the only reasonable choice for the Drell-Yan process, i.e. $t_B^{min} \alpha - m_{\mu^+\mu^-}^2$, gives difficulties because one has the constraint that the c.m.s. energy^2, $\hat{s}$ of the scattered partons must match (at least approximately) the value of t_B^{min}. This rarely happens and so must generate many "wasted" events. In hadron-hadron scattering we avoid this difficulty by choosing a value $t_B^{min} = -4(p_\perp^{hard})^2$ which is essentially decoupled from $\hat{s}$. Any observed cross section σ is calculated as an integral

$$\sigma = \int dp_\perp^{hard} \frac{d\sigma^{constituent}}{dp_\perp^{hard}}$$

In Figure 2, we compare the new cross-section for this choice of t_B^{min} with that in ref. (6) for the NA5 energy. The two calculations have the same $p_\perp^{hard}$ shape but our new results are normalized a factor 1.5 below the old calculations. In fact the different Q^2 choice makes a factor of 3 difference but the exact kinematics used

in the new method restores a factor of 2. We feel that QCD calculations are currently uncertain to at least a factor of 2 and do not
consider the difference in Figure 2 significant.

In Figure 3, we show a couple of "typical" events (the first
two generated by the computer) for hadron-hadron scattering at
$\sqrt{s}=24$ GeV and $p_\perp^{hard}$ = 5 GeV. The figure displays the transverse
components of the final parton's momenta plus a picture of the
evolution of the event. The first of these events (figure 3a) has
in fact an unusually energetic bremstrahlung although the transverse
energy is quite typical.

III. TRIGGER BIAS IN LARGE APERTURE CALORIMETERS

In our model hadronic interactions can produce events in which
a significant fraction of the produced transverse energy is carried
by gluon bremstrahlung, in addition to that carried by the hard-
scattering partons. Such events actually occur quite frequently,
and lead to a trigger bias effect similar to that observed in small
aperture (single particle or jet) triggers. To briefly review the
small aperture effect, we recall that attempts to calculate the
cross sections for such triggers using lowest order QCD parton
interactions and hadronic wave functions without constituent transverse momentum give results which are smaller than the data. The
effect has been explained by the introduction of a fixed constituent
transverse momentum distribution with an average $p_\perp$ of 850 MeV/c
(6). The basic parton interaction feeding a given trigger then
takes place from initial states in which the partons are preferentially directed towards the trigger, the
Q^2 of their hard scattering is reduced,
and the QCD cross section in enhanced. It
was also recognized in ref. (6) that the
intrinsic transverse momentum distribution
is not really fixed, but evolves with Q^2
as in our current model. The evolution
results in intrinsic transverse momentum
effects which remain important at large
$\sqrt{s}$ and large $p_\perp^{hard}$, and to radiated partons accompanying large values of $p_\perp^{brems}$
(t_B^{min}) which are an important feature

small aperture trigger bias

of the final state. It is these radiated
partons which lead to large aperture trigger bias effects. For
scattering at a given $p_\perp^{hard}$, although the bulk of the events will
appear jetlike with $p_\perp^{obs} \sim p_\perp^{hard}$, fluctuations will produce a "tail"
in which $p_\perp^{obs}$ is much larger. If one now concentrates experimentally on a fixed range of $p_\perp^{obs}$ accepted into a large aperture calorimeter, the question is whether the cross section is dominated by

440

events with $p_\perp^{hard} \sim p_\perp^{obs}$ or the tail from scattering at smaller $p_\perp^{hard}$. Because the parton-parton cross section (shown in Figure 2) is a steeply falling function of $p_\perp^{hard}$ one expects the tail to be important, and this is our basic mechanism for large aperture trigger bias. The small and large aperture trigger biases come from the same physics, gluon bremstrahlung. For a small aperture trigger the bremstrahlung gluons are <u>opposite</u> the trigger while in the large aperture case the gluons actually <u>enter</u> the trigger calorimeter. A similar effect has been considered by Singer et al. (11), but with a fixed momentum distribution and fragmenting beam and target jets rather than explicit paron bremstrahlung in the initial state. Before describing our calculations in detail we illustrate the mag-

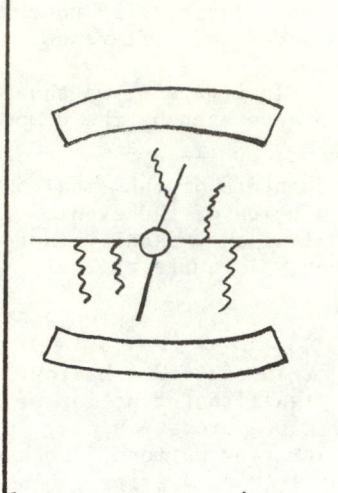

large aperture trigger bias

nitude of the effect by giving our results for the SPS fixed target pp experiment NA5 (12). This experiment at $\sqrt{s}$=24 GeV accepts events populating a fiducial region covering 2π in azimuth and $54°<\Theta_{cm}<135°$ in polar angle, and with accepted E_T up to 18 GeV. (Measurements are also made for smaller azimuthal acceptances, but we do not consider these since they are more sensitive to hadronization). The cross section, $d\sigma/dE_T$ is characterized by a linear exponential behavior of approximately $\exp(E_T)$, and an absolute normalization about an order of magnitude larger than an estimate from a QCD jet model without parton bremsstrahlung (but with hadronization). Figure 4 shows the NA5 data along with calculations at parton level from our model and from QCD jet model without bremstrahlung. Our results match the slope of the data, but are smaller by about an order of magnitude. Both hadronization and the unfolding of the experimental E_T resolution (which is ~5% for NA5) would tend to reduce this difference. The use of E_T rather than $\Sigma|p_T|$ to plot the experimental data accentuates the effects of hadronization. We note that the hadronized QCD jet model used by the NA5 group gives cross sections about an order of magnitude larger than our unhadronized version (the open circles in Figure 4). If hadronization effects are of similar magnitude for the full model with bremstrahlung, it will end up being quite close to the data. Aside from such caveats concerning the overall normalization Figure 4 illustrates our main point: already at the parton level gluon radiation effects greatly enhance the QCD jet cross section.

IV.   THE DRELL-YAN PROCESS

The cross section integrated over all $p_\perp$ for the Drell-Yan process $\bar{p}p \to \mu^+\mu^- x$ is essentially identical in our model to that calculated from standard QCD techniques.   In particular we would presumably need to renormalize our results up by a factor ~2 to 3 to agree with the experimental measurements [13] however the $p_\perp$ distribution of the lepton pair is not calculable from the standard techniques and this allows both significant tests of our model and an opportunity to optimize our parameters.   The application of our model to this case has already been described in Ref 2.   Here we note that our formalism is in this case more precise formulation of the pioneering work of Parisi and Petrorzio [14].   The leading logarithm approximation used in our model has the advantage that it can be summed to all orders but the severe disadvantage of not even being exact to $0(\alpha_s)$.   As shown in Ref. 2 for the application to e^+e^- annihilation, one can modify the model to retain the all orders summation but reduce to the exact $0(\alpha_s)$ (or even $0(\alpha_s^2)$) QCD calcu-lations.   Unfortunately we have yet to put this improvement into the Drell-Yan calculation and so our results in this case are still pre-liminary.   However they are still quite satisfactory for determin-ing a resonable set of parameters with which to study hadron-hadron scattering.   Thus the latter has quite different $0(\alpha_s)$ terms to the Drell-Yan case and so one would have to improve both calculations (by adding in the exact low order calculations) to be consistent. Although this ambitious program is possible for the Drell-Yan cal-culation, there are substantial technical difficulties for the hadron-hadron scattering application [10].   In this paper, we will treat all processes with the universal leading logarithm approxima-tion for the bremsstrahlung.

In Figure 5, we plot the longitudinal momentum dependence of the mean transverse momentum appropriate for a Drell-Yan mass of 5.5 GeV at a $\sqrt{s}$ of 27.4 GeV.   This figure illustrates two important points.   Firstly note that the gluons have substantially larger $<p_\perp^{brem}>$ than the quarks or anti-quarks.   This follows from the larger $G \to GG$ than $q \to q\,G$ coupling in QCD.   The difference between quarks and gluons persists to higher energies.   For instance one finds on integrating over lognitudinal momentum that

at $\sqrt{s}$ = 62 GeV, m = 15 GeV: $<p^{brem}|quark>$ = 1.1 GeV

$<p^{brem}|gluon>$ = 1.8 GeV

at $\sqrt{s}$ = 540 GeV, m = 80 GeV: $<p^{brem}|quark>$ = 2.9 GeV

$<p^{brem}|gluon>$ = 4.4 GeV

at $\sqrt{s}$ = 2000 GeV, m = 80 GeV: $<p^{brem}|quark>$ = 5.3 GeV

$<p^{brem}|gluon>$ = 7.2 GeV

Returning to Figure 5, we also see that $\langle p_{\perp}^{brem} \rangle$ decreases as the longitudinal fraction x increases. This is also easy to understand because partons at low x are more likely to come from a bremsstrahlung than those at large x which are preferentially partons which did not radiate. This effect follows from the necessity that any bremsstrahlung will decrease the longitudinal momentum combined with the rapidly decreasing (as x→1) input x distributions.[†]

Note from figure 5, that we have chosen the input $p_{\perp}^{intrinsic}$ or $p_{\perp}^{brem}$ (t_B^0 = -4 Gev^2) to have a gaussian distribution with a mean of 750 MeV. (This is 50% larger than the choice in Ref. 2).[††] We have chosen $\langle p_{\perp}^{intrinsic} \rangle$ to be independent of x and parton type. This is not very reasonable because if we had made the same assumption at a lower $t_B^0 \sim - \Lambda^2$, evolution to our choice t_B^0 = -4 GeV^2, would lead to a $\langle p^{brem}$ (-4 GeV^2)$\rangle$ that is larger for gluons than quarks and decreases as x increases. The Drell-Yan data would prefer a modest x dependence in the $\langle p_{\perp}^{intrinsic} \rangle$ for quarks but there is no quantitative handle (as yet) for the gluons. We have explored choosing lower t_B^0 but have not found very satisfactory results i.e. the fits to the Drell-Yan data seem worse. This is not very surprising because it is neither unreasonable to use leading order perturbative QCD below 4 GeV^2. In any case we will stick with t_B^0 = -4 GeV^2 and a type and x independent $\langle p_{\perp}^{intrinsic} \rangle$.

In figures 6 to 9, we compare our model with some of the available data on both $\langle p_{\perp} \rangle$ and the p distributions for pp → $\mu^+\mu^-$x. The agreement is quite good although the model does tend to underestimate the yield at large $p_{\perp}$. In figure 9 we show that an exact $0(\alpha_s)$ calculation[+] (19) is slightly better although it too lies below the trend of the data for $\langle p_{\perp} \rangle$ at $\sqrt{s}$=62 GeV. Note the exact $0(\alpha_s)$ calculation needs a slightly lower $\langle p_{\perp}^{intrinsic} \rangle$; namely 600 MeV which again indicates that leading log Monto Carlo is under estimating the high p bremsstrahlung. In fact, Ref. 18 decomposes the $0(\alpha_s)$ calculation at $\sqrt{s}$=62 GeV, 5<m($\mu^+\mu^-$)<8 GeV into the Compton (qg→qγ*) and annihilation terms (q$\bar{q}$→gγ*).

[†]At higher momenta the $\langle p_{\perp}^{brem} \rangle$ is no longer peaked at x = 0 but rather at an intermediate x value. Now all partons come from bremsstrahlung and those at low x are kinematically required to have lower $p_{\perp}$.

[††]We have also chosen the upper limit t_B^{min} = $m^2_{\mu^+\mu^-}$ rather than - $m^2_{\mu^+\mu^-}$ as in Ref. 4.

[+]With a prescription to cutoff the low $p_{\perp}$ divergence.

The total leading log calculation follows the $0(\alpha_s)$ annihilation term quite closely whereas in the $0(\alpha_s)$ calculation it is the Compton term that dominates at large $p_\perp$. This suggests that the leading log approximation is underestimating the Compton contribution.

V.   THE NA5 EXPERIMENT (12)

The mechanism behind the enhancement of the QCD cross sections shown in Figure 4 has been described in Sec. III. Here we wish to examine the effect in more detail by displaying $p_\perp^{hard}$ cross-section spectra and the shape properties of biased events. In Figure 10 we show $d\sigma/dp_\perp^{hard}$ for scattering into two fixed $p_\perp^{obs}$ ranges at NA5. The area under the curves corresponds to the observed cross section. For comparison, we show both the contributions from a fully evolved calculation and from a calculation with no parton branching. The unevolved calculation is peaked at $p_\perp^{hard} \sim p_\perp^{obs}$, while the evolved calculation has a tail extending to low values of $p_\perp^{hard}$ and as a result has an order of magnitude larger integrated cross section. When integrating over $p_\perp^{hard}$ we impose a lower limit of 2 GeV to avoid low values where our perturbative calculations become particularly ambiguous. Figure 10 indicates that this low $p_\perp^{hard}$ region may give a significant (but essentially unknown) contribution for $p_\perp^{obs} \lesssim$ 4-5 GeV/c, and in this region the cross sections in Figure 4 may be understimated. An overall view of the $p_\perp^{hard}$ spectrum is given in Figure 11 where the $p_\perp^{obs}$ distributions from fully evolved calculations are plotted for various values of $p_\perp^{hard}$. Each distribution is peaked near $p_\perp^{obs} \approx p_\perp^{hard}$, but in integrating over $p_\perp^{hard}$ at a fixed value of $p_\perp^{obs}$ one sees that the contribution of each peak will be accompanied by a larger contribution from the tails of distributions with $p_\perp^{hard} < p_\perp^{obs}$.

Choosing events with $p_\perp^{hard} < p_\perp^{obs}$ produces clear trigger bias in the form of high parton multiplicity and a generally non-jet-like character of the final states. This is seen in Figure 12 which displays events with $p_\perp^{obs}$ = 5 GeV/c and $p_\perp^{hard}$ = 3 and 3.5 GeV/c. Again we show the first two events generated by the computer which satisfy the given conditions. These events should be compared with the unbiased events in Figure 3.

The same effect can be seen statistically in planarity distributions. The planarity is P=(a-b)/(a+b), where a (b) is the sum of squares of projected momenta along the major (minor) axis of the transverse momentum tensor. Jet-like events characterized by values of P near one, and round events by P near zero. In Figure 13 we show the planarity distributions from NA5 for events with several $p_\perp^{obs}$ thresholds along with calculated distributions for a low $p_\perp$ cluster model and a QCD jet model with hadronization. In Figure 14 we show planarity distributions from our calculation at several values of $p_\perp^{hard}$ and a $p_\perp^{obs}$ threshold of 5 GeV/c. As expected the planarity distributions become broader and less peaked towards P=1 as $p_\perp^{hard}$ decreases below $p_\perp^{obs}$. One should be careful in comparing Figures 13 and 14 because planarity is a quadratic quantity, similar to sphericity, and is very sensitive to hadronization. For example, the QCD-jet distribution in Figure 13 comes from a model that gives a δ-function at P=1 at parton level. Thus, although the integral over $p_\perp^{hard}$ of the distributions in Figure 14 will contain a broad high-P enhancement, this will be substantially degraded by hadronization.

VI.   EARLY RESULTS FROM UA1

As a final illustration of our results we show calculations and data for the transverse energy distribution of the SPS collider experiment UA1 (20). This is shown in Figure 15 where the calculated points are normalized to a total inelastic $\bar{p}p$ cross section of 50 mb at $\sqrt{s}$ = 540 GeV. Here our parton level calculations do not do nearly as well as they did for NA5. A feature of the UA1 data is that even for the very large transverse energies observed, all events seem to be made up of numerous soft particles with an average E_T per particle of about 500 MeV. This indicates the presence of large hadronization effects. Our calculations also indicate this; they produce events with high parton multiplicities and very non-jetlike shapes. Work is in progress to include hadronization in our calculations, and to make quantitative comparisons with both the NA5 and the SPS collider data. Two typical events are shown in Figure 16.

We thank the UA1 group for permission to use their data in Figure 15, but at the experimentors request we also warn the reader that these data are very preliminary.

REFERENCES

(1)   G. Altarelli and G. Parisi, Nucl. Phys. B126, 298 (1977).

(2)   G.C. Fox, Lectures presented at the 1981 SLAC Summer School, CALT-68-863, 1981.

(3)   R. Odorico, paper presented at the Forward Collider Workshop, Madison (1981).

(4)   G.C. Fox and S. Wolfram, Nucl. Phys. B168, 285 (1980).

(5)   R. Odorico, Nucl. Phys. B172, 157 (1980). P. Mazzanti and R. Odorico, Phys. Lett. 95B, 133 (1980) and Z. Physik C7, 61 (1980).

(6)   R.P. Feynman, R.D. Field and G.C. Fox, Phys. Rev. D18, 3320 1978).

(7)   R.P. Feynman and R.D. Field, Nucl. Phys. B136, 1 (1978).

(8)   C. Bromberg et al., Nucl. Phys. B171, 1 (1980).

(9)   W.E. Caswell, R.R. Horgan and S.J. Brodsky, Phys. Rev. D18, 2415 (1978).

(10) R.K. Ellis, M.A. Furman, H.E. Haber and I. Hinchliffe, Nucl. Phys. B173, 397 (1980).

(11) R. Singer et al., ANL-HEP-PR-81-25, 1981.

(12) K. Pretzl, paper presented at the Forward Collider Workshop, Madison (1981).

(13) R. Stroynowski, Physics Reports 71, 1 (1981).

(14) G. Parisi and R. Petronzio, Nucl. Phys. B154, 427 (1979).

(15) D.M. Kaplan et al., Phys. Rev. Letters 40, 435 (1977)

(16) J.K. Yoh et al., Phys. Rev. Letters 41, 684 (1978).

(17) D. Anbreasyan et al., "Production Mechanisms of High Mass Muon Pairs", preprint (1981).

(18) D. Anbreasyan et al., "Dimuon Scaling Comparison at 44 and 62 GeV", MIT technical report 119 (1981).

(19) R.D. Field, "Perturbative Quantum Chromodynamics and Applications to Large Momentum Transfer Processes", CALT-68-739 and La Jolla Summer School Notes, (1979).

(20) A. Kernan, paper presented at the Forward Collider Workshop, Madison (1981).

Table I. Notation for Virtual Masses

		where defined			
		initial state evolution	hard scatter	final state evolution	hadronization
t	Virtual m^2 of current parton during evolution	during		during	
t_B^0	Initial m^2 that starts initial state evolution $t_B^0 = -4$ GeV^2	before			
t_B^{min}	Lower limit on (negative) virtual m^2 for partons in final state evolution $t_B^{min} = -4m^2$ for Drell Yan $t_B^{min} = -4\ p^{hard\,2}$ for hadron hadron scattering	after	before		
t_B^{max}	Upper limit of (positive) virtual m^2 for partons in final state evolution. $t_B^{max} = -t_B^{min}$ for partons just after hard scatter. t_B^{max} for bremstrahlung partons depends on exact kinematics (eq. (5.10) of Ref. 2)		after	before	
t_A^{min}	Lower limit on (positive) virtual m^2 for partons in final state. $t_A^{min} = 10$ GeV^2.			after	before

Table II. Notation for transverse momenta

<table>
<tr><td rowspan="2"></td><td rowspan="2"></td><td colspan="4" align="center">where defined</td></tr>
<tr><td>initial state evolution</td><td>hard scatter</td><td>final state evolution</td><td>hadronization</td></tr>
<tr><td>$p_\perp^{intr} = p_\perp^{brem}(t_B^0)$</td><td>The intrinsic $p_\perp$ distribution at the initial mass scale $t = t_B^0$</td><td>before</td><td></td><td></td><td></td></tr>
<tr><td>$p_\perp^{brem}(t_B^{min})$

$t \geqslant t_B^{min}$</td><td>The $p_\perp$ distribution generated from $p_\perp^{intr}$ and the evolution for partons of (negative) $t \geq t_B^{min}$. This is universal in Drell Yan, hadron hadron, NN scattering etc.</td><td>after</td><td>before</td><td></td><td></td></tr>
<tr><td>$p_\perp^{hard}$</td><td>The $p_\perp$ induced by the hard two body collision for hadron-hadron scattering $p_\perp^{hard} = 1/2 \sqrt{-t_B^{min}}$</td><td>after</td><td>at</td><td>before</td><td></td></tr>
<tr><td>$p_\perp^{obs} = \frac{1}{2}\sum |p_\perp|$</td><td>The observed transverse momentum (which is equal to $E_T/2$ at the parton level).</td><td></td><td></td><td></td><td>after</td></tr>
</table>

448

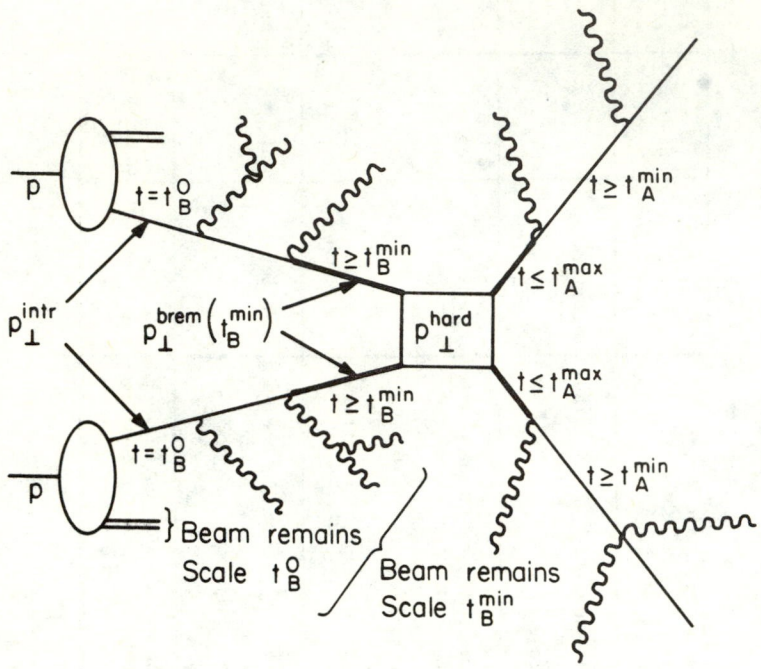

Fig. 1: The picture of hadron hadron scattering used in this paper and described in Section II. The notation is defined in Tables 1 and 2.

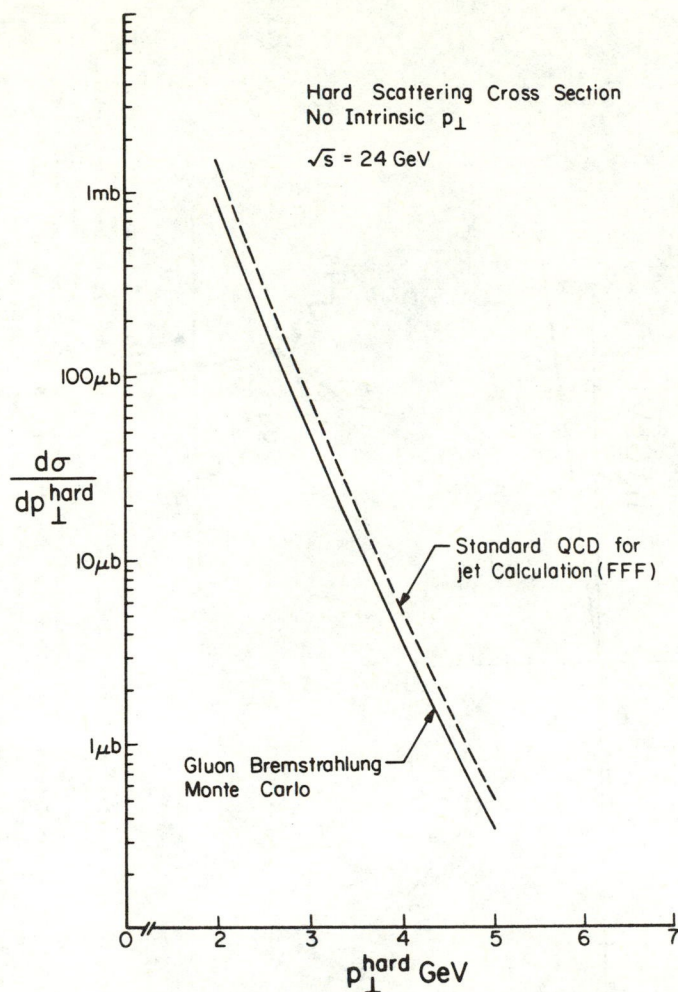

Fig. 2: Comparison of the hard scattering cross section from a
conventional QCD calculation (Ref. [6], dashed line) with
that from the techniques used in this paper (solid line).
The differences are discussed in Section II.

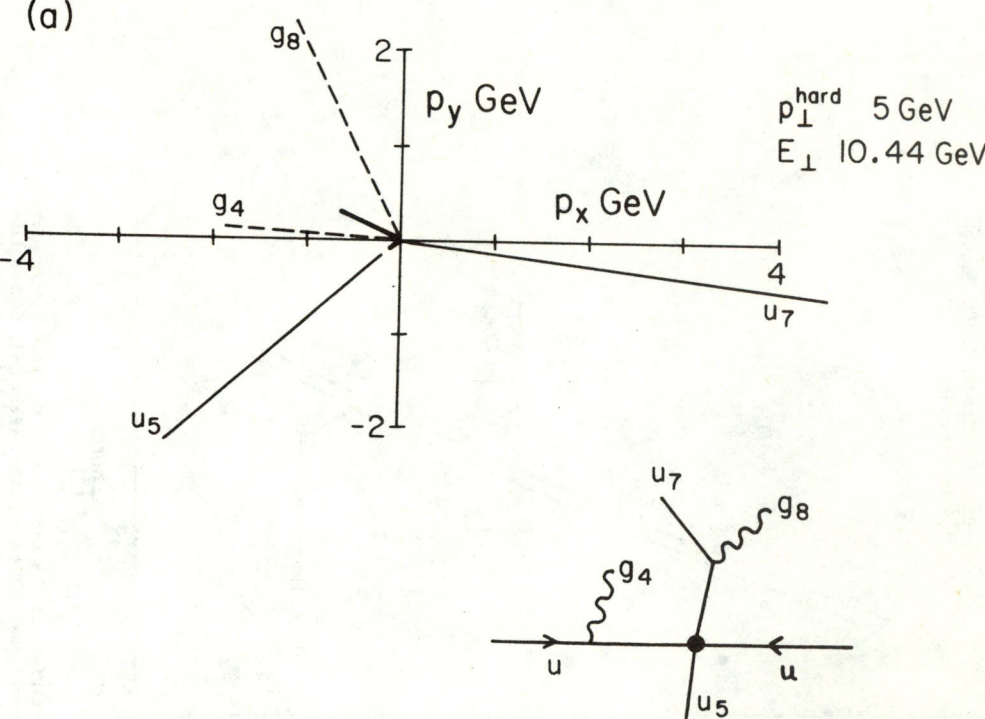

(a)

p_y GeV

p_x GeV

$p_\perp^{hard}$ 5 GeV

$E_\perp$ 10.44 GeV

Fig. 3(a): Unbiased events for $\sqrt{s}$ = 24 GeV and $p_\perp^{hard}$ = 5 GeV. The top part of the diagram shows the structure of the final state in the transverse (p_x, p_y) plane. Dashed lines are gluons, solid lines (anti)quarks and (two) thick lines denote the beam remains. The event is displayed so that the x direction is along the major axis of a planarity analysis (Section V). Below this diagram we show the evolution of the event as a Feynman diagram. The solid circle represents the hard (2 → 2) scatter. The remaining vertices are bremsstrahlung.

(b)

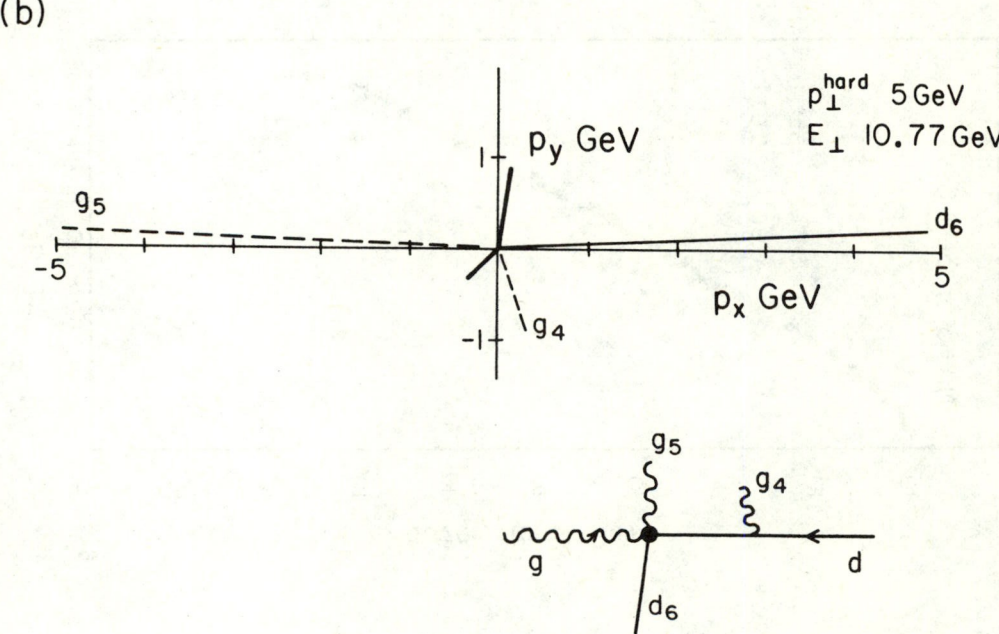

Fig. 3(b): Unbiased event for $\sqrt{s}$ = 24 GeV and $p_\perp^{hard}$ = 5 GeV. The notation is the same as in Fig. 3(a).

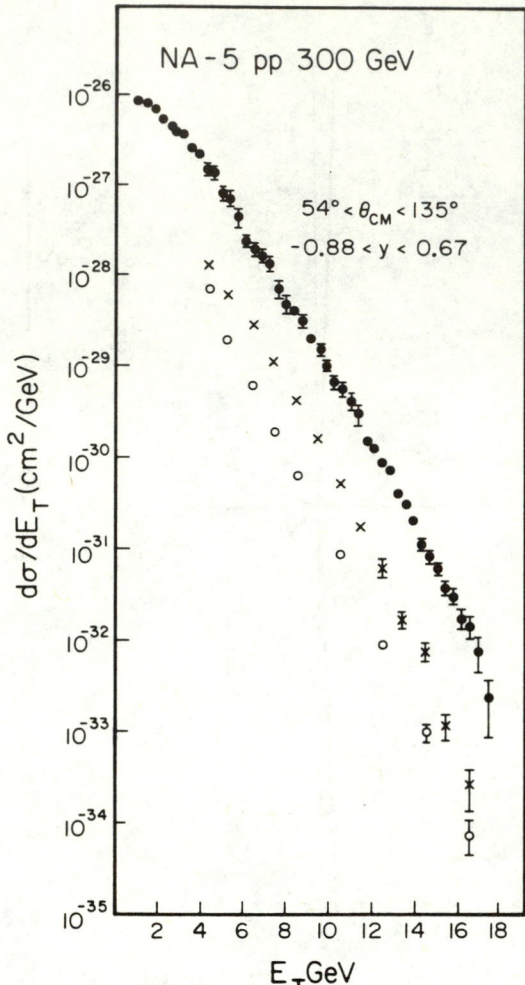

Fig. 4: Comparison of NA5 cross section data (●) and parton level calculations with (x) and without (0) bremsstrahlung.

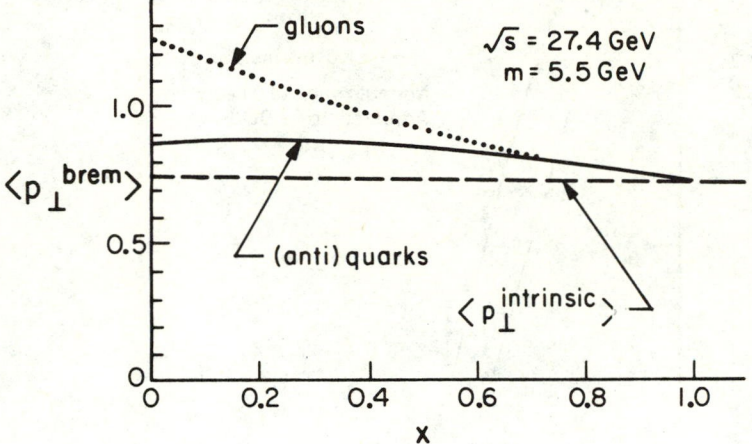

Fig. 5: Longitudinal (x) dependence of $<p_\perp^{brem}>$ appropriate for Drell-Yan scattering at $\sqrt{s}$ = 27.4 GeV and a mass of 5.5 GeV.

454

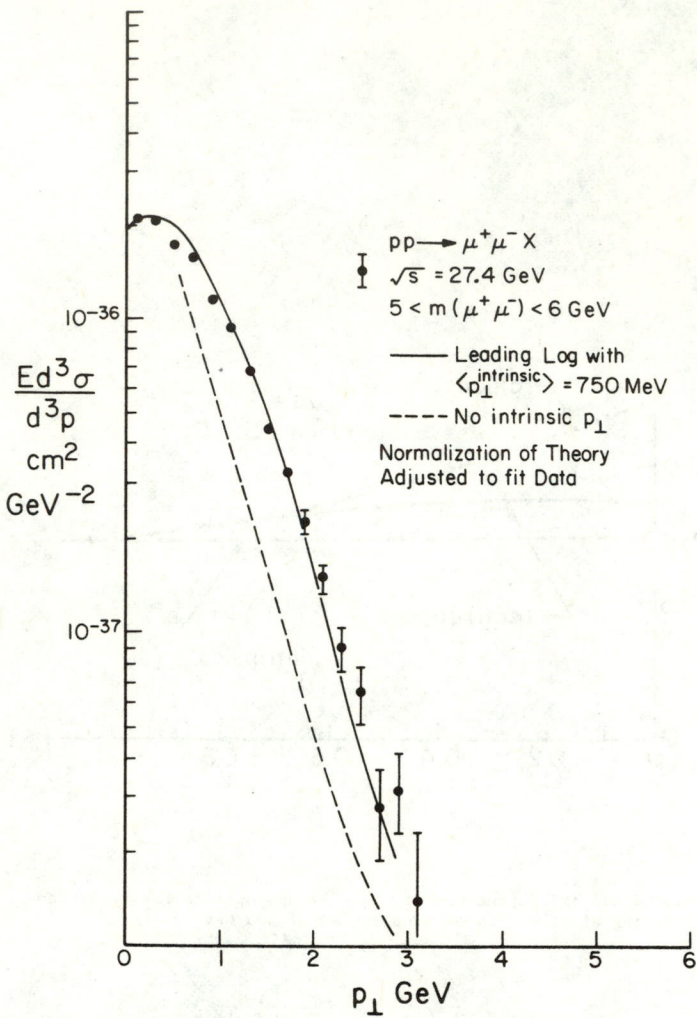

Fig. 6: Comparison of the Monte Carlo with the $p_\perp$ distribution for the Drell-Yan μ pairs at $\sqrt{s}$ = 27.4 GeV and a mass of 5.5 GeV [Ref. 15]. The normalization of the theory has been adjusted to fit the data while we show separately the calculation that ignores the intrinsic $p_\perp$ of 750 MeV.

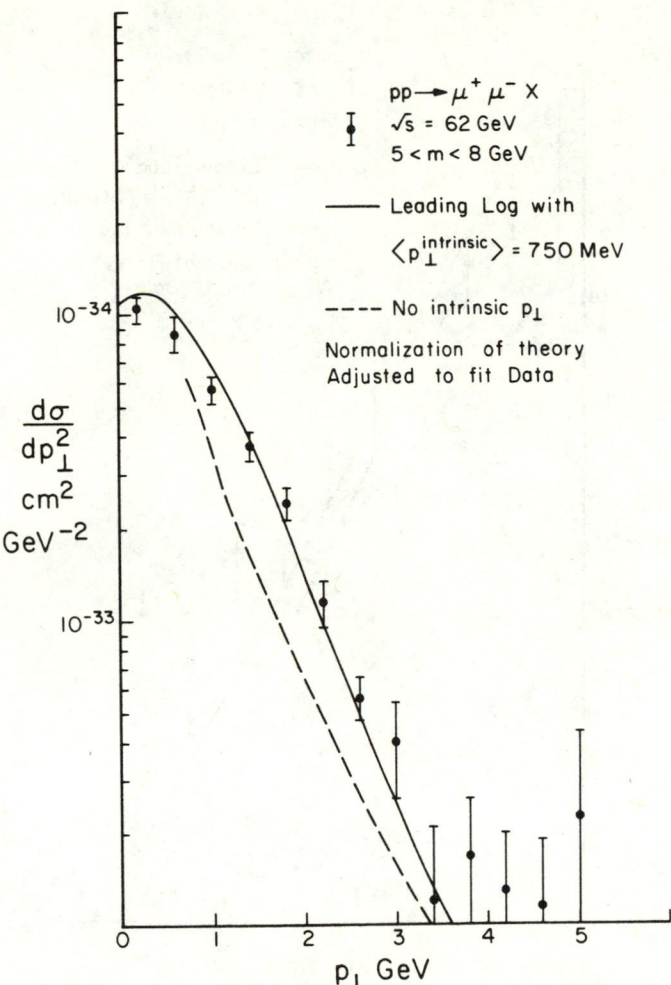

Fig. 7: As Fig. 6 but the data from Ref. 18 has $\sqrt{s}$ = 62 GeV and corresponds to the mass range of 5 to 8 GeV.

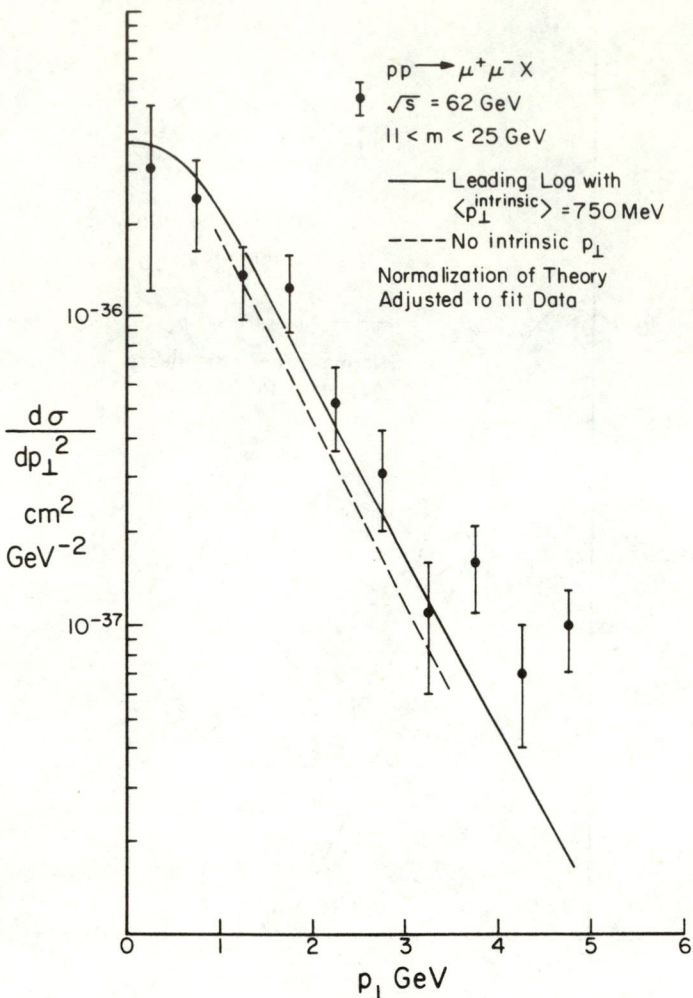

Fig. 8: As Fig. 6 but the data from Ref. 17 have $\sqrt{s}$ = 62 GeV and correspond to the mass range of 11 to 25 GeV.

457

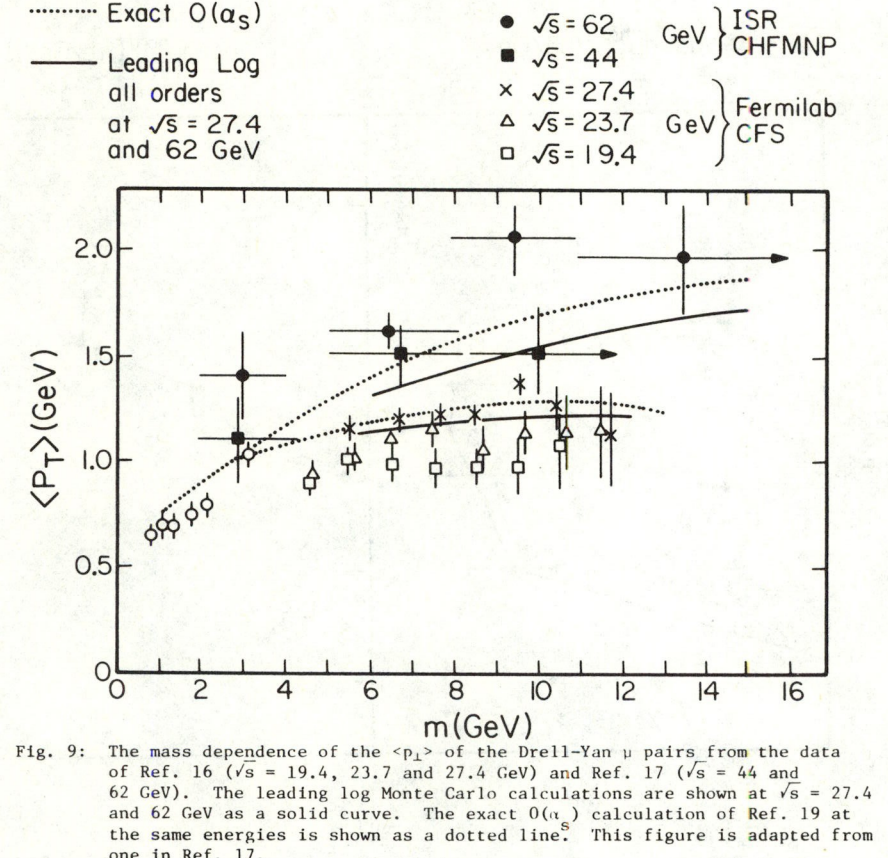

Fig. 9: The mass dependence of the $\langle p_\perp \rangle$ of the Drell–Yan μ pairs from the data of Ref. 16 ($\sqrt{s}$ = 19.4, 23.7 and 27.4 GeV) and Ref. 17 ($\sqrt{s}$ = 44 and 62 GeV). The leading log Monte Carlo calculations are shown at $\sqrt{s}$ = 27.4 and 62 GeV as a solid curve. The exact $0(\alpha_s)$ calculation of Ref. 19 at the same energies is shown as a dotted line. This figure is adapted from one in Ref. 17.

458

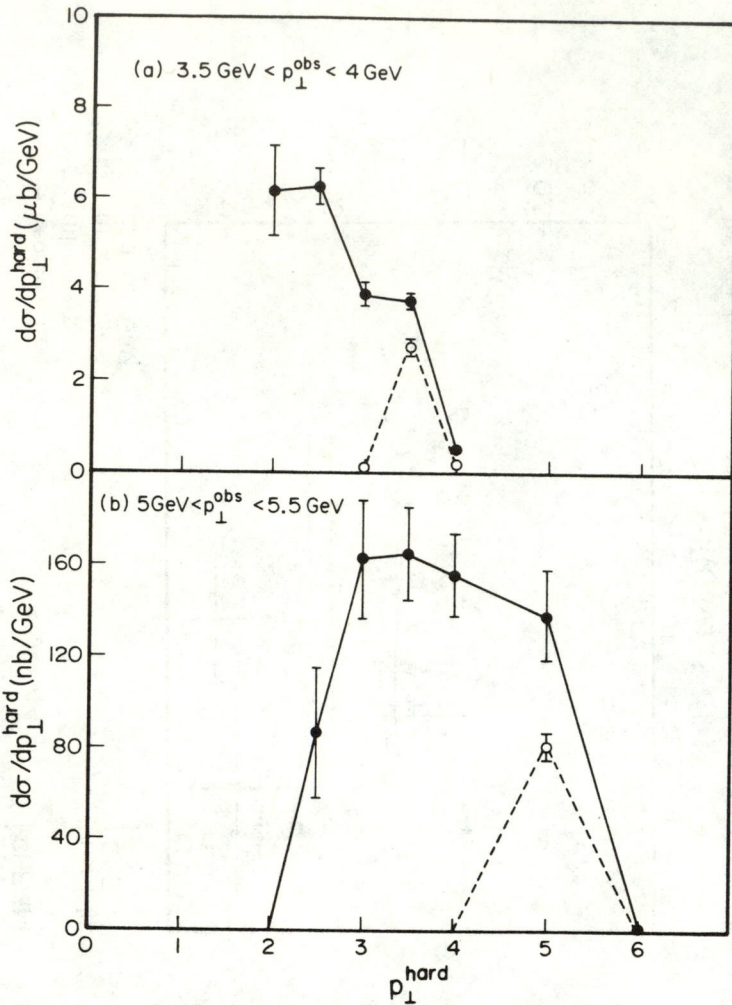

Fig. 10: $d\sigma/dp_\perp^{hard}$ vs. $p_\perp^{hard}$ for two ranges of $p_\perp^{obs}$ at the NA5 calorimeter, calculated with (●) and without (O) bremsstrahlung. The area under the curves corresponds to the observable cross section within the given $p_\perp^{obs}$ ranges.

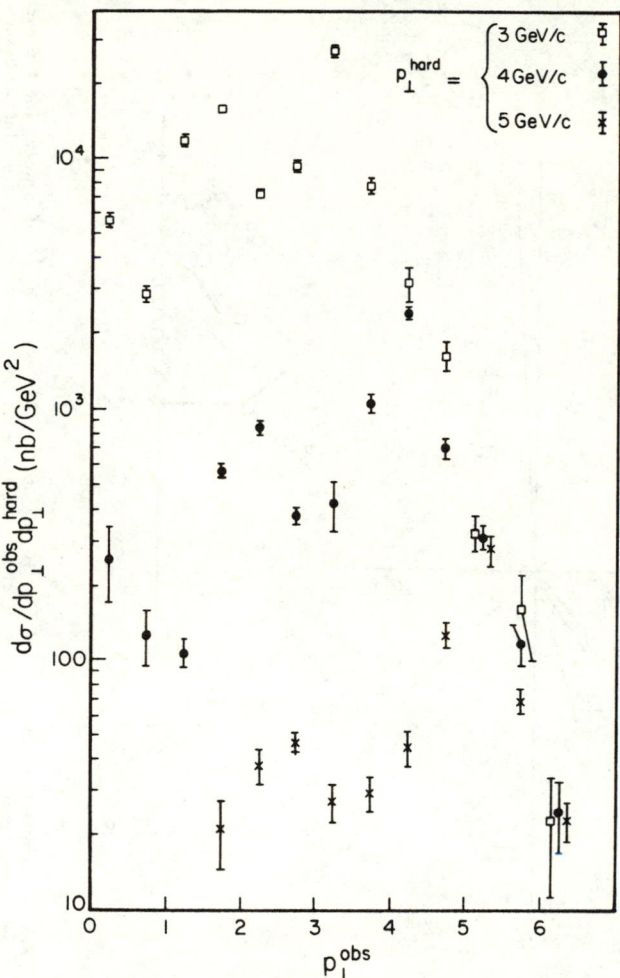

Fig. 11: $d\sigma/dp_\perp^{hard}\,dp_\perp^{obs}$ at the NA5 calorimeter calculated for three values of $p_\perp^{hard}$.

(a)

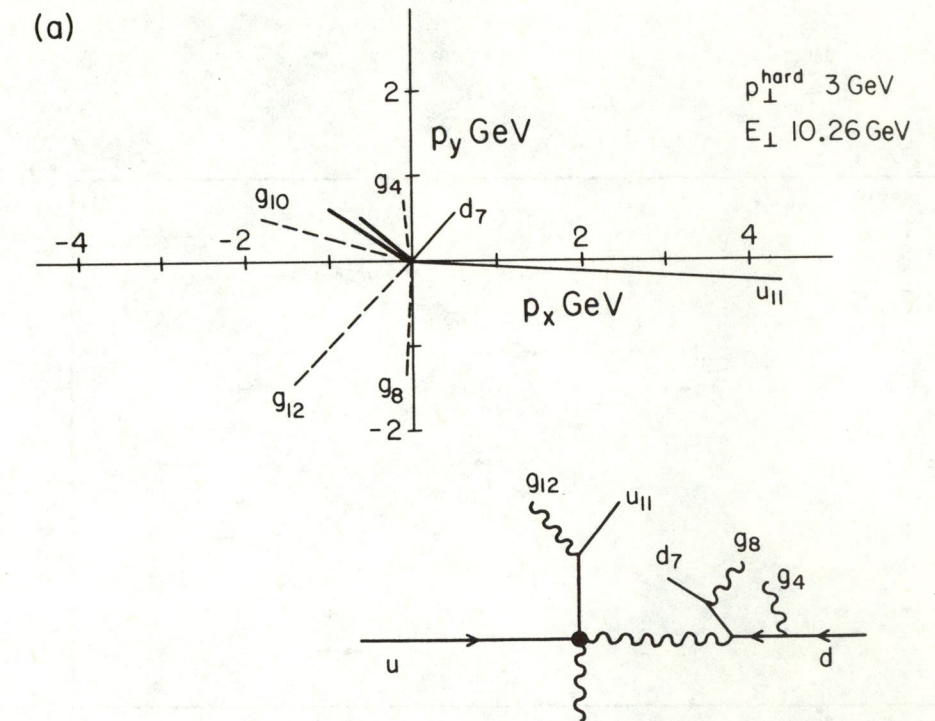

Fig. 12(a): Biased event satisfying $2p_\perp^{obs} = E_\perp > 10$ GeV at $\sqrt{s} = 24$ GeV and $p_\perp^{hard}$ of 3 GeV. The top part of the diagram shows the structure of the final state in the transverse (p_x, p_y) plane. Dashed lines are gluons, solid lines (anti)quarks and (two) thick lines denote the beam remains. The event is displayed so that the x direction is along the major axis of a planarity analysis (Section V). Below this diagram we show the evolution of the event as a Feynman diagram. The solid circle represents the hard $(2 \to 2)$ scatter. The remaining vertices are bremstrahlung.

(b)

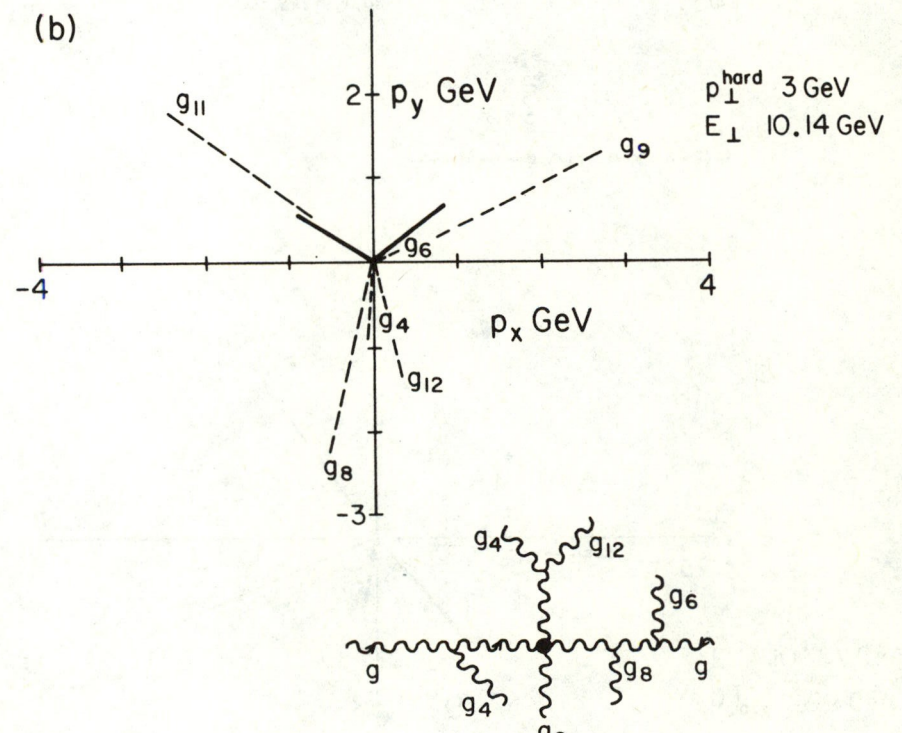

Fig. 12(b): Biased event satisfying $2p_\perp^{obs} = E_\perp > 10$ GeV at $\sqrt{s} = 24$ GeV and $p_\perp^{hard}$ of 3 GeV. The notation is described in the caption to Fig. 12(a).

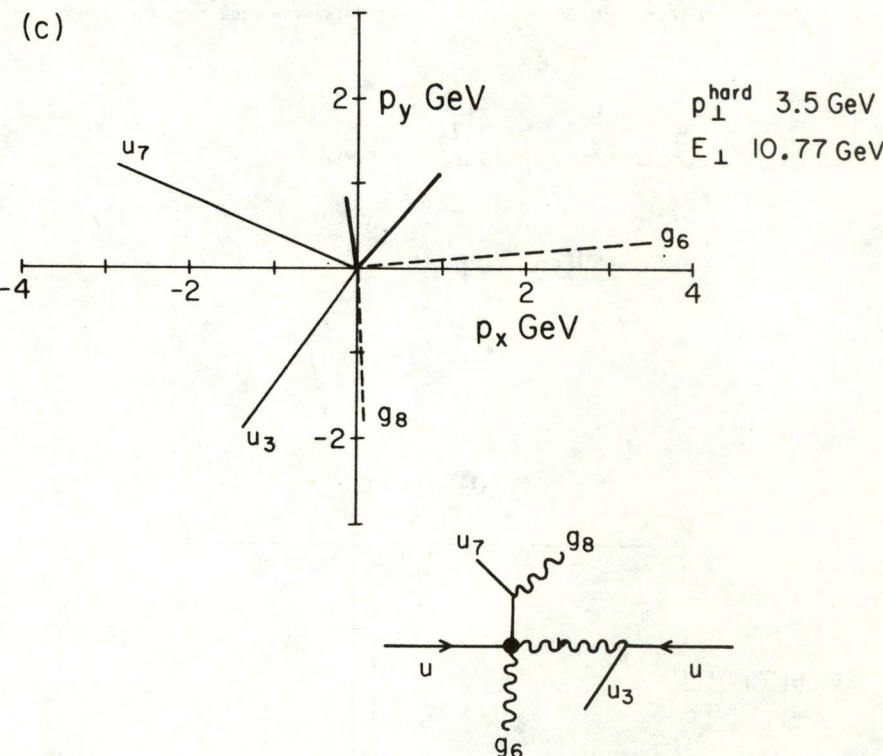

Fig. 12(c): Biased event satisfying $2p_\perp^{obs} = E_\perp > 10$ GeV at $\sqrt{s} = 24$ GeV and $p_\perp^{hard}$ of 3.5 GeV. The notation is described in the caption to Fig. 12(a).

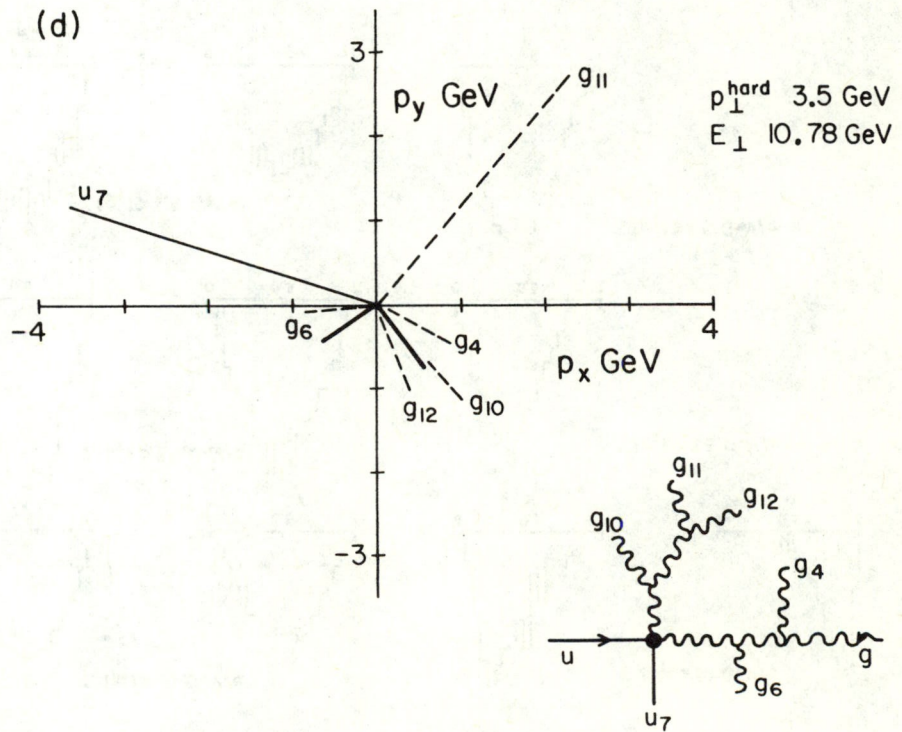

Fig. 12(d): Biased event satisfying $2p_{\perp}^{obs} = E_{\perp} > 10$ GeV at $\sqrt{s} = 24$ GeV and $p_{\perp}^{hard}$ of 3.5 GeV. The notation is described in the caption to Fig. 12(a).

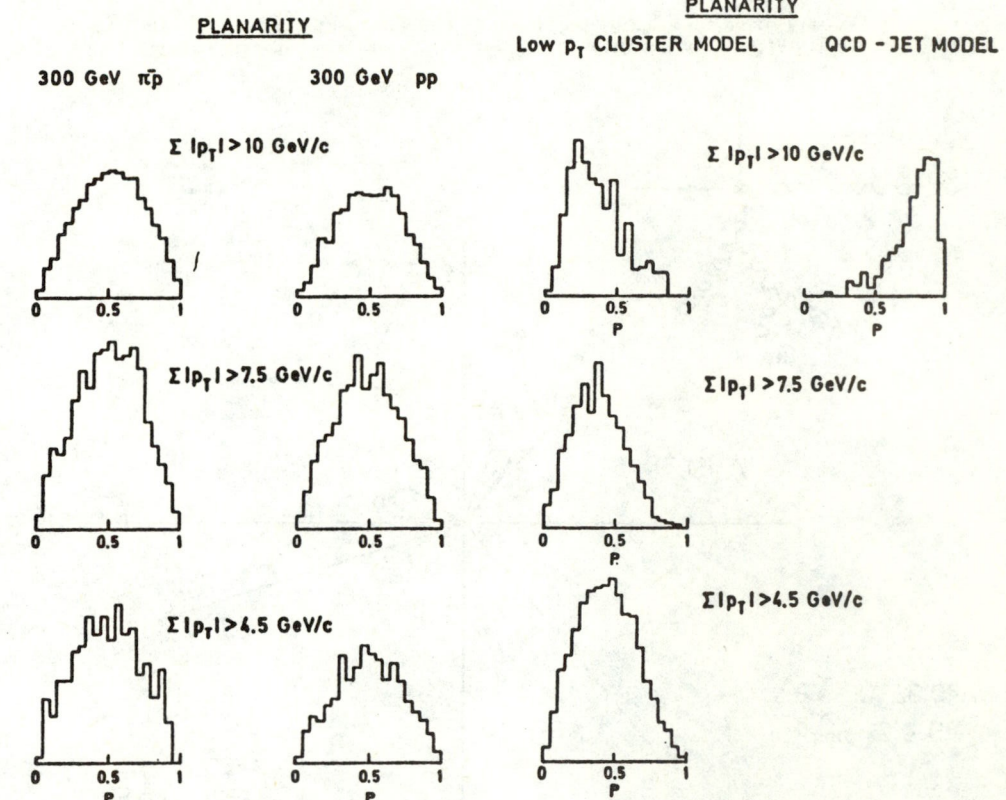

Fig. 13: Planarity distributions of events selected by the NA5 calorimeter trigger from π⁻p and pp collisions at 300 GeV/c for different trigger thresholds. Results from a low $p_\perp$ cluster model and a QCD-4 jet model are shown for comparison.

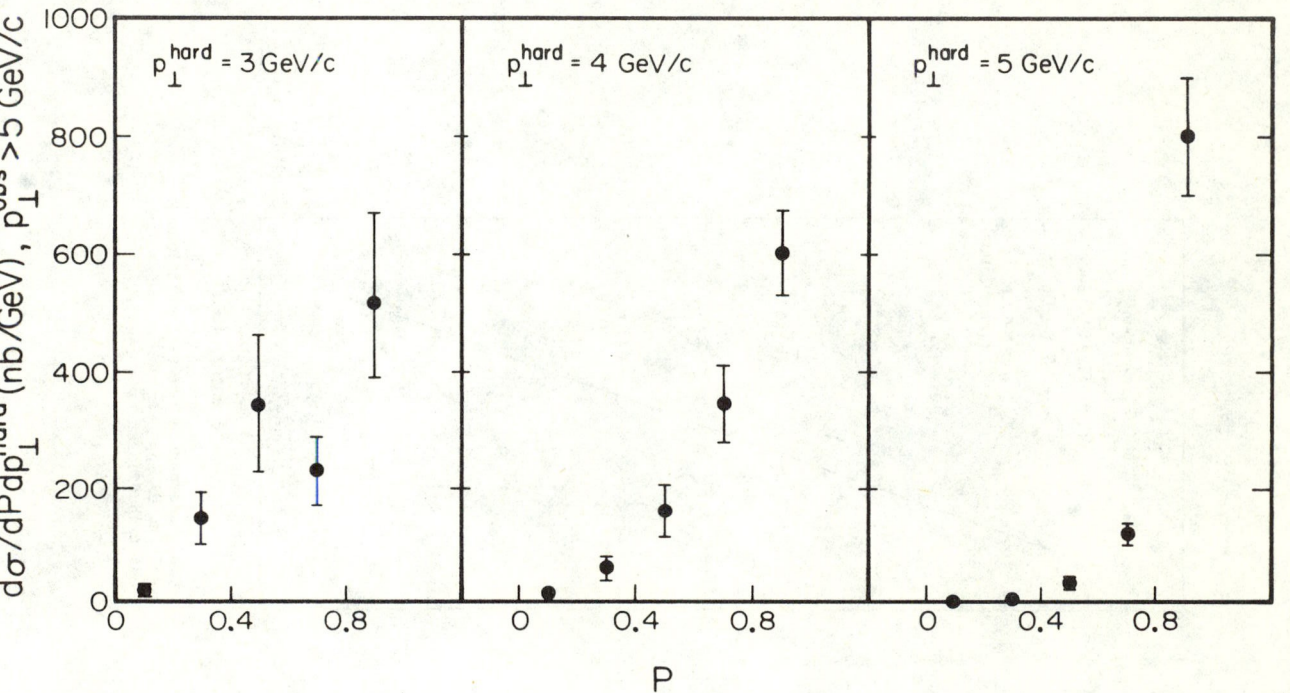

Fig. 14: Planarity distributions at the NA5 calorimeter for three values of $p_\perp^{hard}$.

466

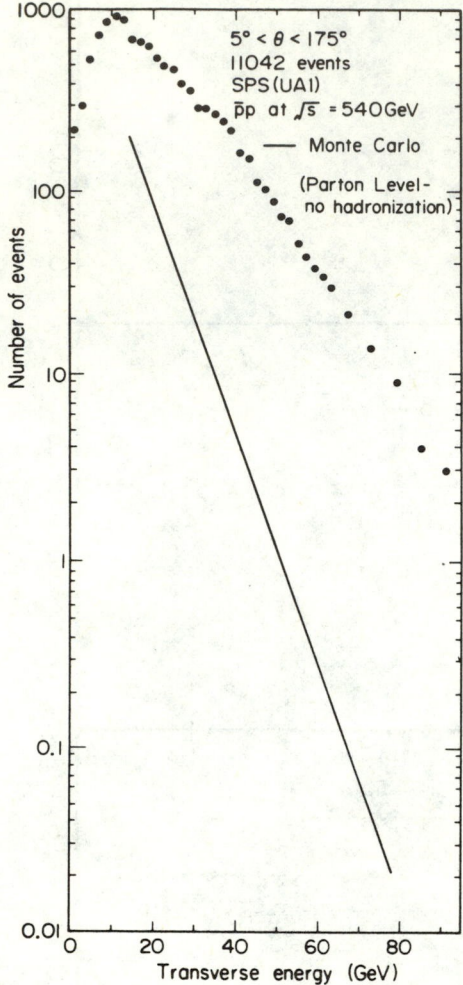

Fig. 15: Data and parton level calculations of the UA1 p̄p transverse energy distribution at √s = 540 GeV.

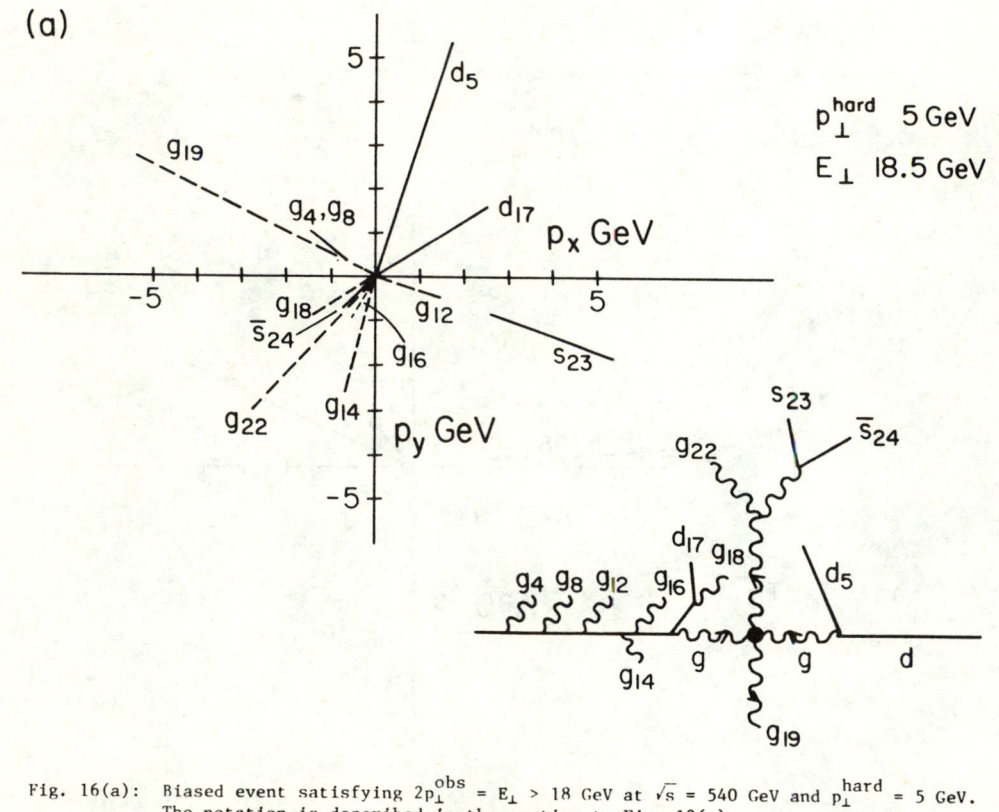

Fig. 16(a): Biased event satisfying $2p_\perp^{obs} = E_\perp > 18$ GeV at $\sqrt{s} = 540$ GeV and $p_\perp^{hard} = 5$ GeV. The notation is described in the caption to Fig. 12(a).

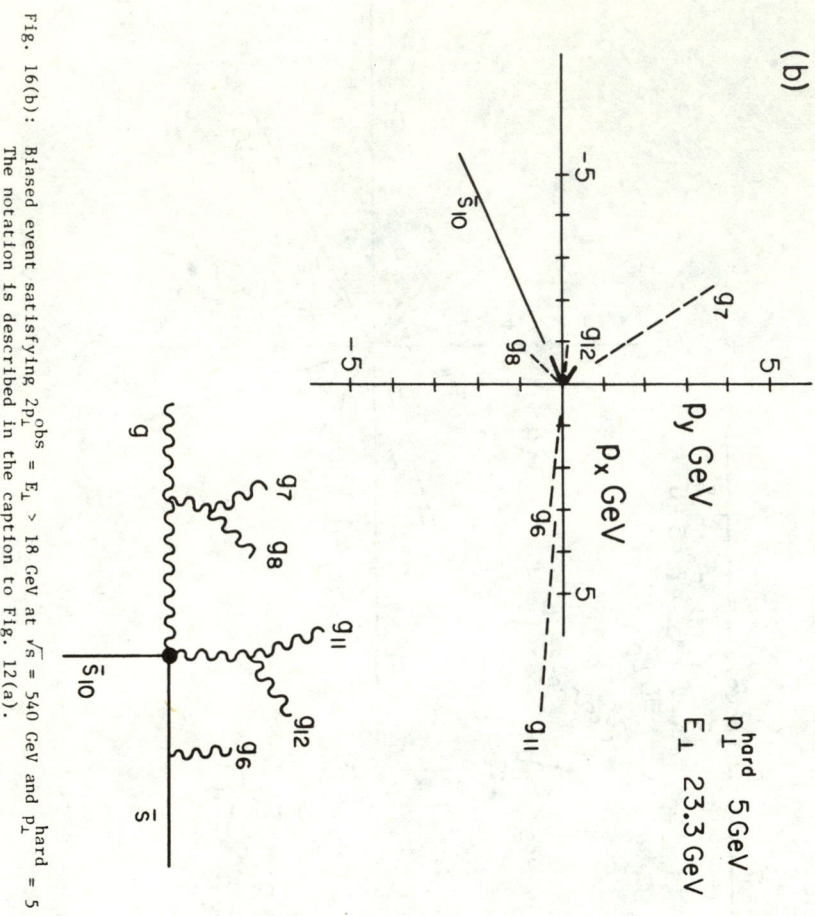

(b)

$p_\perp^{hard}$ 5 GeV

$E_\perp$ 23.3 GeV

Fig. 16(b): Biased event satisfying $2p_\perp^{obs} = E_\perp > 18$ GeV at $\sqrt{s} = 540$ GeV and $p_\perp^{hard} = 5$ GeV. The notation is described in the caption to Fig. 12(a).

UNIVERSALITY OF CHARGED MULTIPLICITY DISTRIBUTIONS

K. Goulianos[*]

The Rockefeller University, New York, N.Y. 10021

ABSTRACT

The charged multiplicity distributions of the diffractive and non-diffractive components of hadronic interactions, as well as those of hadronic states produced in other reactions, are described well by a universal Gaussian function that depends only on the available mass for pionization, has a maximum at $n_o \cong 2M^{\frac{1}{2}}$, where M is the available mass in GeV, and a peak to width ratio $n_o/D \cong 2$.

INTRODUCTION

This report consists of two parts. In the first part, we present the results of a measurement of charged multiplicity distributions of high mass diffractive $\pi^{\pm}$, $K^{\pm}$ and $p^{\pm}$ states produced in 100 and 200 GeV/c hadron-proton collisions, $h + p \rightarrow X + p$. We find that these distributions are described well by a Gaussian function that depends only on the mass available for pion production, $M \cong M_x - M_h$, peaks at $n_o \cong 2M^{\frac{1}{2}}$, where M is in GeV, and has a peak to width ratio $n_o/D \cong 2$, where $D = (\overline{n^2} - n_o^2)^{\frac{1}{2}}$. The independence of the charged multiplicities from the quantum numbers of the diffractive state led us to examine whether the multiplicities of hadronic matter in general also follow the same distribution function. In the second part of this report, we show that this is indeed the case.

---

[*] The work presented in this report was done by the following Rockefeller University groups:

  (a) PART I : R.L. Cool, K. Goulianos, S.L. Segler[+],
               H. Sticker and S.N. White

  (b) PART II : K. Goulianos, H. Sticker and S.N. White

  + Present address: Fermi National Accelerator Laboratory
                    Batavia, Illinois 60510

470

CHARGED MULTIPLICITIES
OF HIGH MASS DIFFRACTIVE $\pi^{\pm}$, $K^{\pm}$ and $p^{\pm}$ STATES

The charged multiplicities of the diffractive states X produced in the reaction

$$h + p \rightarrow X + p \quad (h=\pi^{\pm}, K^{\pm}, p^{\pm}) \tag{1}$$

were measured recently in experiment E-396 at Fermilab. Reaction (1) was studied at incident beam momenta of 100 and 200 GeV/c in the kinematic range $0.025 < |t| < 0.095$ (GeV/c)^2 and $1-x \simeq (M_x^2 - M_h^2)/s < 0.1$, where x is the Feynman scaling variable, $x = p_{\parallel}/p_{\parallel,max}$. Results from this experiment on elastic scattering and on the M_x^2 dependence and factorization properties of diffraction dissociation have already been published[1,2]. The results on charged multiplicity distributions reported here are new.

The experiment was performed in the M6W beam line of the Meson Laboratory. A plan view of the apparatus is shown in Figure 1.

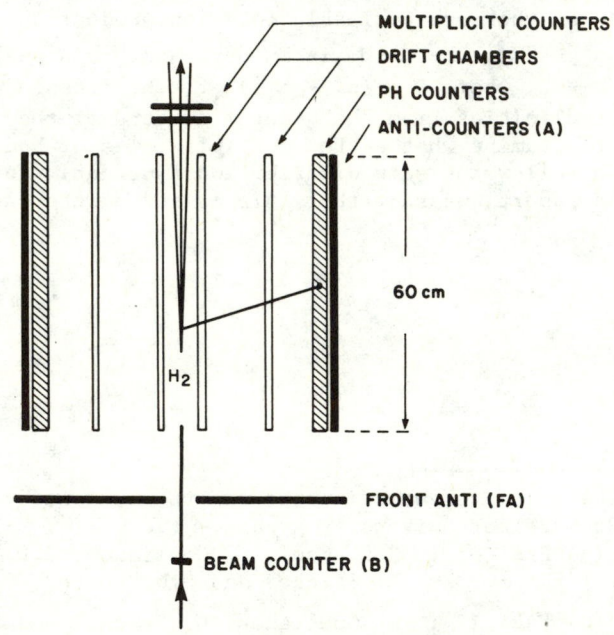

FIG. 1 - Apparatus (plan view, to scale).

Recoil protons from beam interactions in a hydrogen gas target were detected by drift chambers, which measured the polar angle θ, and were
stopped by scintillation counters, which measured the kinetic energy T.
The missing mass was determined, to an accuracy of $\Delta M_x^2/M_x^2 = \pm 3\%$,
from θ, T and the beam momentum, p_o :

$$M_x^2 = M_h^2 + 2p_o\sqrt{2m_p T} \ (\cos\theta - \sqrt{T/2m_p}) \tag{2}$$

The charged multiplicities were obtained from the pulse height recorded
by two scintillation counters located downstream of the recoil detector.
Landau fluctuations were reduced by accepting the smaller of the two
normalized pulse heights. Figure 2 shows an example of a pulse height
distribution. The curve is a maximum likelihood fit to Landau distributions calculated for each multiplicity.

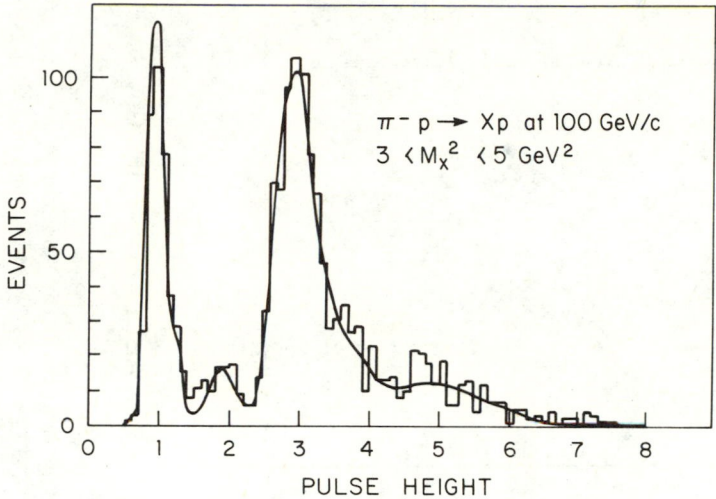

FIG. 2 – Typical multiplicity counter pulse height distribution. For
each event, the smaller of the two pulse heights was used.

The raw multiplicities obtained in this manner were corrected for
background tracks, for extra (accidental) beam particles and for the
acceptance of the multiplicity counters. The background was estimated
by using events with negative (unphysical) M_x^2 and was subtracted
from the topological cross sections at the corresponding positive M_x^2.
The subtractions were generally less than 10%. The fraction of events
with an extra beam track was measured to be $\lesssim 10\%$ by comparing elastic
events with charge 2 to those of charge 1. Assuming an isotropic
decay distribution in the center of mass of the diffractive state, the
calculated average acceptance of the counters is 95%, which agrees well
with that estimated from the number of unphysical even charged multiplicity events caused either by an extra beam track or by a track
missing the counters.

472

The corrected data are presented in Figures 3, 4 and 5.

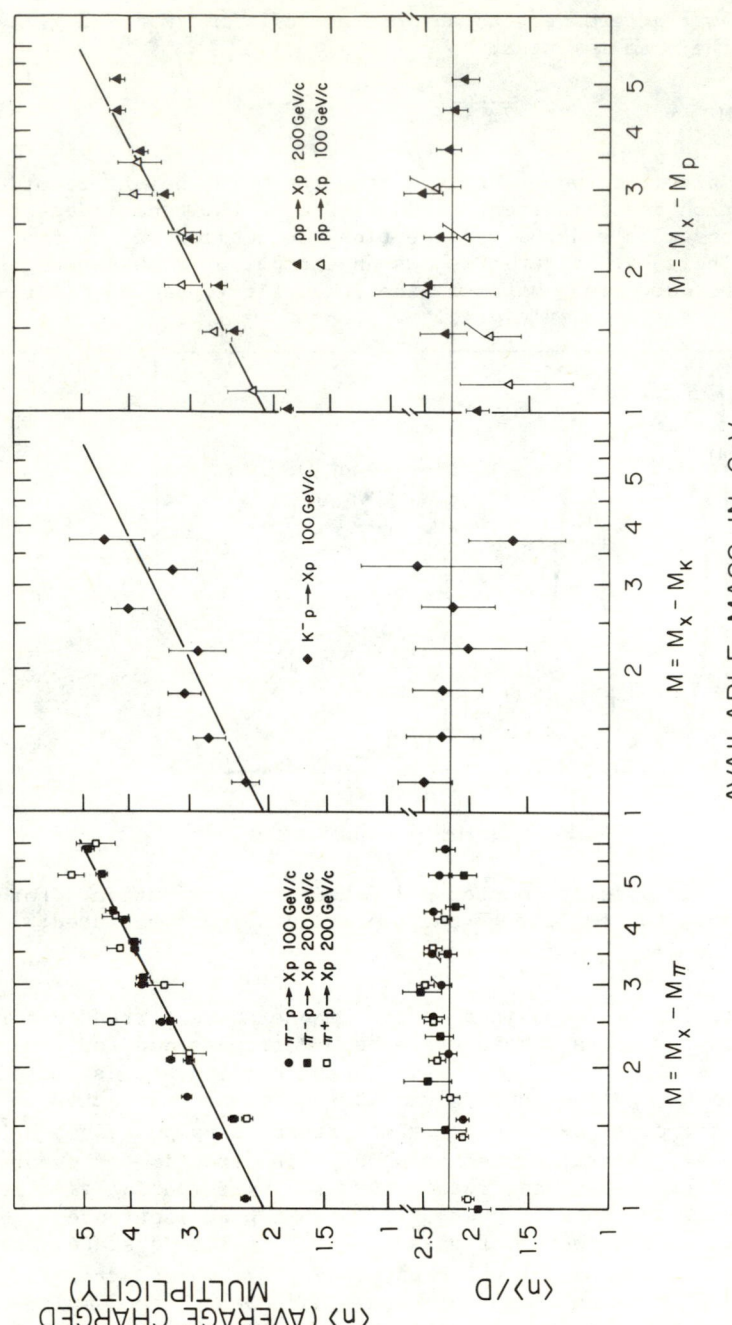

FIG. 3 – Average charged multiplicity and ratio of average to width as a function of available mass. The curves represent $\langle n \rangle = 2.08\ M^{\frac{1}{2}}$ and $\langle n \rangle / D = 2.2$ as discussed in the text.

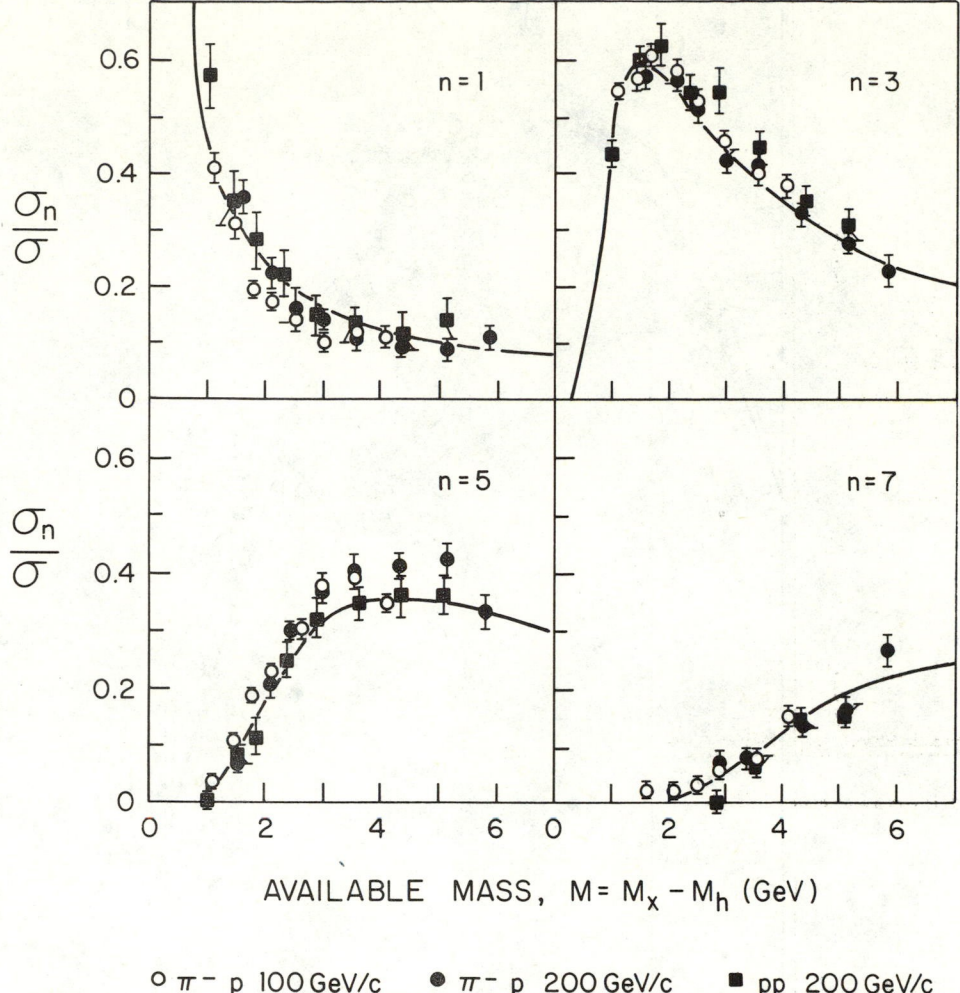

FIG. 4 – Charged multiplicity fractions versus available mass for hp → Xp (h=π⁻,p).

474

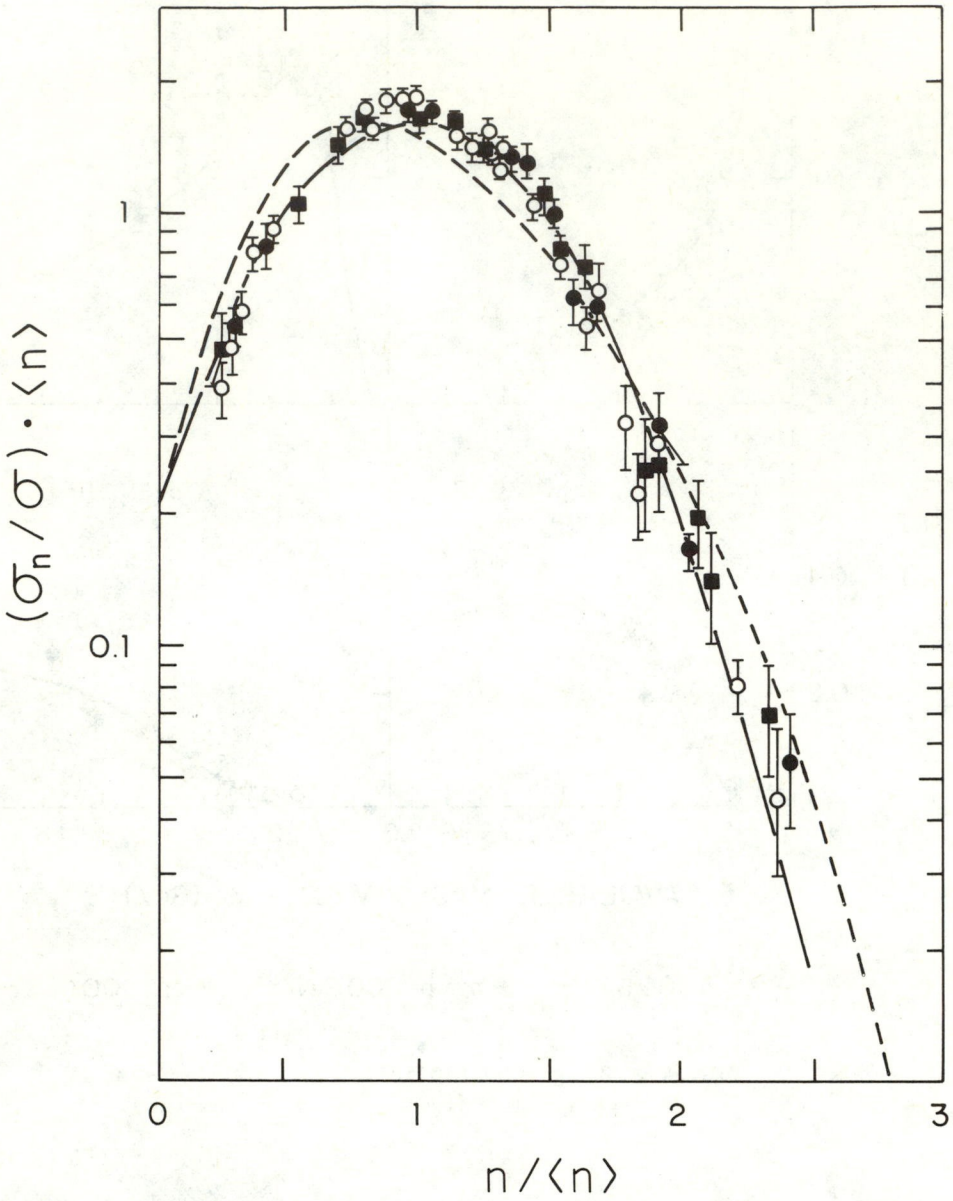

FIG. 5 - The product $(\sigma_n/\sigma) \cdot \langle n \rangle$ versus $n/\langle n \rangle$ for the data presented in Fig. 4. The solid line represents the Gaussian function discussed in the text (Eq. 4). The broken line is from a fit to the inclusive data hp → anything (Ref. 4).

The following features are noted:

(i) Within the statistical accuracy, the multiplicities of all three hadrons are the same when compared at the same mass available for the production of pions, $M = M_x - M_h$. This would not be true if the comparison were made at the same M_x .

(ii) The average multiplicity increases with M, approximately as $<n> \cong 2M^{\frac{1}{2}}$, where M is in GeV, while the ratio $<n>/D$, where $D = (<n^2>-<n>^2)^{\frac{1}{2}}$, remains constant at the value of ~ 2.2 (see Fig.3). The function $<n> = a + b \ln (M)$ would also provide a good fit to our data but we prefer the power dependence because, as will be shown in Part II, it characterizes the average multiplicity of many processes at higher available energy whereas a simple logarithmic dependence falls too low.

(iii) The ratio of the topological cross section σ_n to the total diffractive cross section σ (see Fig. 4) is described well by the Gaussian function

$$\frac{\sigma_n}{\sigma} = P_n = \frac{2}{\sqrt{2\pi}\ D}\ e^{-\frac{(n-n_0)^2}{2D^2}} \qquad (3a)$$

$$n_0 = 2M^{\frac{1}{2}}\ (M\ \text{in GeV}) \qquad (3b)$$

$$n_0/D = 2 \qquad (3c)$$

The normalization of P_n is such that at any value of M the sum of P_n over odd values of n is unity to within $\sim 1\%$. In calculating values of $<n>$ and D to compare with experimental data, one must sum over positive values of n only. This shifts the average by $\sim 4\%$ above the value of n_0 and the width down by $\sim 6\%$ so that the average multiplicity becomes $<n> = 2.08\ M^{\frac{1}{2}}$ and the $<n>/D$ ratio is increased by 10% above the value of n_0/D, to the measured values of 2.2

The form (3) of the probability function suggests that the multiplicity distributions satisfy KNO scaling[3]; i.e., that the product $P_n \cdot <n>$ is a function of $n/<n>$ only and not a function of M. Indeed, from (3a,b,c) it follows that

$$P_n \cdot n_0 = \sqrt{\frac{8}{\pi}}\ e^{-2(1-n/n_0)^2} \qquad (4)$$

Figure 5 shows $P_n \cdot <n>$ versus $n/<n>$ for the $\pi^- p$ and the pp data. Ignoring the small difference between $<n>$ and n_0, one sees that function (4) represents the data well. In contrast to the fully inclusive reactions pp → anything and πp → anything whose KNO scaling curve[4], also shown in Fig. 5, is asymmetric and peaks at $n/\langle n \rangle \cong 0.8$, the distribution for the diffractive data is symmetric about the peak at $n/\langle n \rangle = 1$.

Our results for $\langle n \rangle$ and $\langle n \rangle/D$ agree well with previous measurements[5]. However, the multiplicity distributions obtained in these measurements[5,6] are inconsistent with ours in that they follow an asymmetric scaling curve similar to that of the inclusive case. We attribute the inconsistency to their use of large M_x^2 bins needed for adequate statistics in presenting the distributions, for example $0 < M_x^2 < 32$ $(GeV/c)^2$, which integrates the data over large variations in average and width and distorts the distributions.

In summary, we find that the charged multiplicity distributions of high mass diffractive pion, kaon and nucleon states follow a universal Gaussian function that depends only on the available mass M (GeV), has a peak that varies with M as $n_o \cong 2 M^{\frac{1}{2}}$, and a peak to width ratio $n_o/D \cong 2$.

PART II

INCLUSIVE HADRONIC CHARGED MULTIPLICITIES
and
UNIVERSALITY OF CHARGED MULTIPLICITY DISTRIBUTIONS

It is well known[4,7,8] that charged multiplicity data of inclusive hadronic reactions do not agree with Eq. 3. For example, for pp → anything[4,7,8,9], the increase of the average multiplicity with energy is slower than $2 s^{\frac{1}{4}}$ (see Fig. 6a), the $\langle n \rangle/D$ ratio decreases as the energy increases (see Fig. 6b), and the KNO distribution of the data is asymmetric about $n/\langle n \rangle = 1$ (see Fig. 7) in disagreement with Eq. 4. On the other hand, data on $e^+e^- \to$ anything are consistent[10] with $\langle n \rangle = 2 s^{\frac{1}{4}}$ (see Fig. 8) and their KNO scaling curve is symmetric [11].

In this part, we analyze the inclusive pp → anything charged multiplicities, recognizing that they derive from two distinct sectors of the inelastic cross section: the diffractive component, for which the available mass is $M = M_x - M_p$, and the non-diffractive "hard core" for which $M = \sqrt{s} - 2M_p$. We find that Eq. 3, which describes well the diffractive multiplicities, also provides a good description of the multiplicities of the hard core. After an examination of data from several other reactions, we come to the conclusion that the distribution represented by Eq. 3 is universal, describing to a good approximation all known hadronic charged multiplicities up to and including ISR energies. This suggests that gluons may play an important role in the hadronization process.

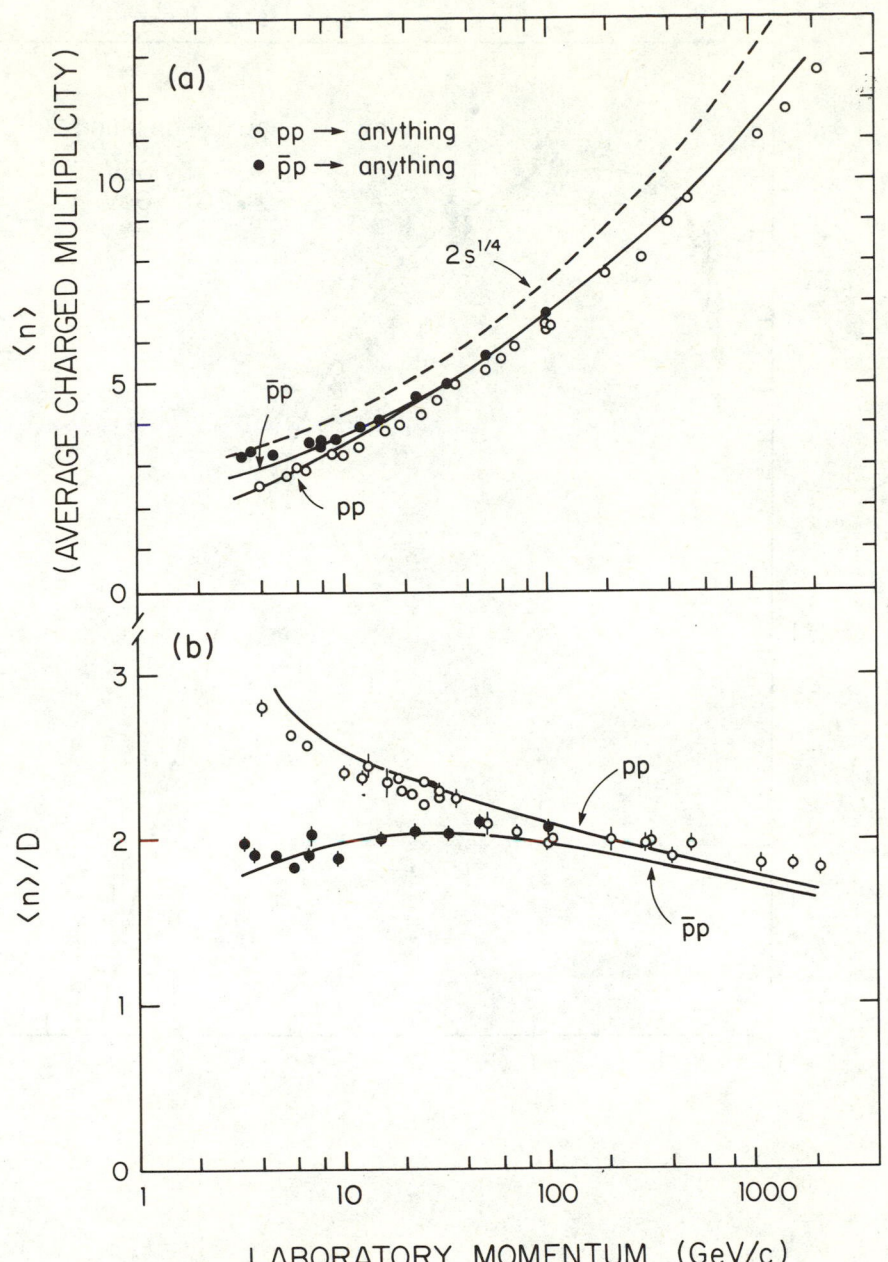

FIG. 6 – The average charged multiplicity and the ratio of the average to the width as a function of p_{lab} for pp → anything and $\bar{p}p$ → anything. The solid curves were calculated using Eqs. 6 and 7 in the text.

478

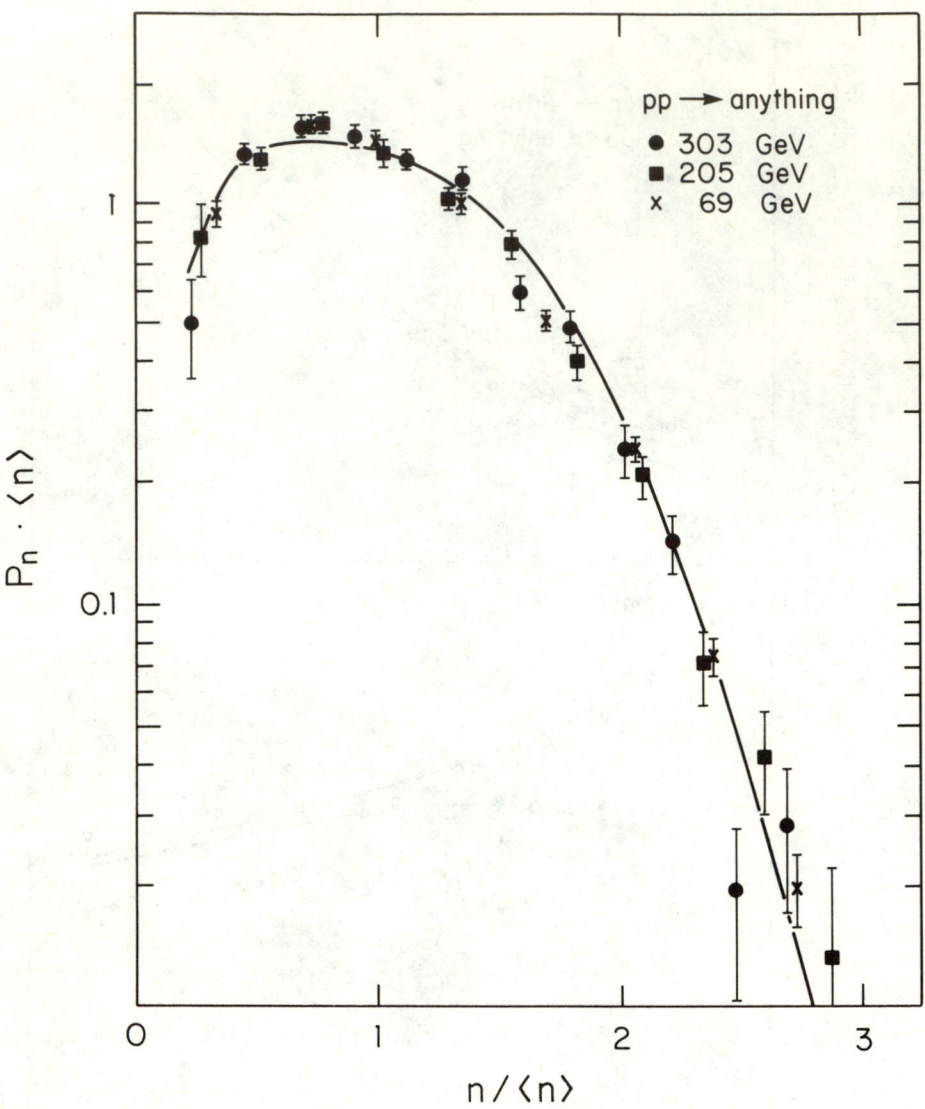

FIG. 7 – The product $P_n \cdot \langle n \rangle$ versus $n/\langle n \rangle$ for charged
particles in pp → anything. The curve was cal-
culated using Eq. 6 in the text.

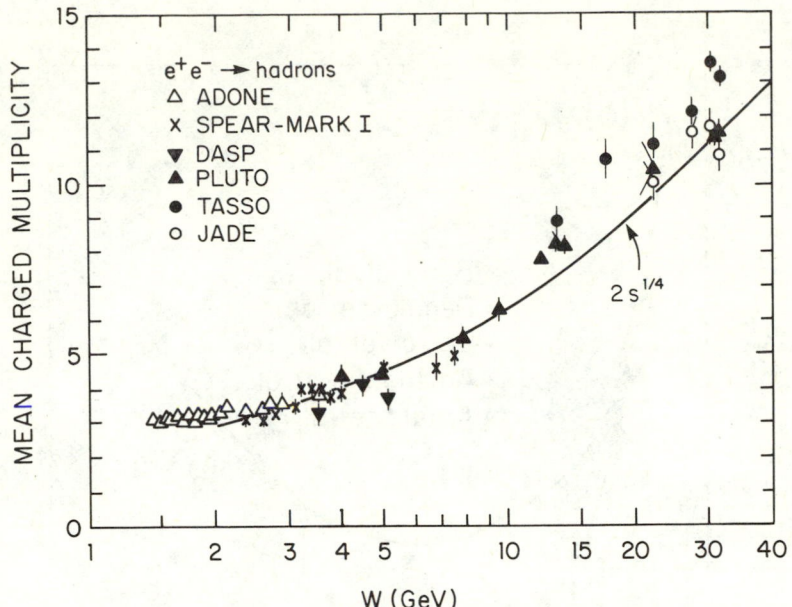

FIG. 8 – Mean charged multiplicity versus
available energy for $e^+e^- \to$ anything.

Small differences in the multiplicities between certain reactions, such as between pp and $\overline{p}p$, which cannot be explained by our procedure of applying Eq. 3 at the appropriate available mass of each identifiable component of the inelastic cross section, may then be attributed to the difference in the quark content of the initial states.

The total, the elastic, and the inelastic pp cross sections are shown in Figure 9. The inelastic cross section is consistent[12] with being composed of a hard core, σ_o = 26.3 mb, and a diffractive component, σ_D , which consists of the contribution of single diffraction dissociation, $2\sigma_{SD}$, and that of double diffraction dissociation, σ_{DD} :

$$\sigma_i = \sigma_o + 2\sigma_{SD} + \sigma_{DD} \tag{5}$$

In calculating charged multiplicity distributions, we assume that the inelastic cross section in excess of σ_o is all due to single diffraction dissociation with a $1/M_x^2$ mass dependence. The double diffractive process which becomes important only at very high energies, is approximated well by this assumption, since there is only a small probability for both diffractive masses to be large. Multiplicity distributions for pp are then generated using Eq. 3 separately for the diffractive and non-diffractive components at the appropriate available mass:

480

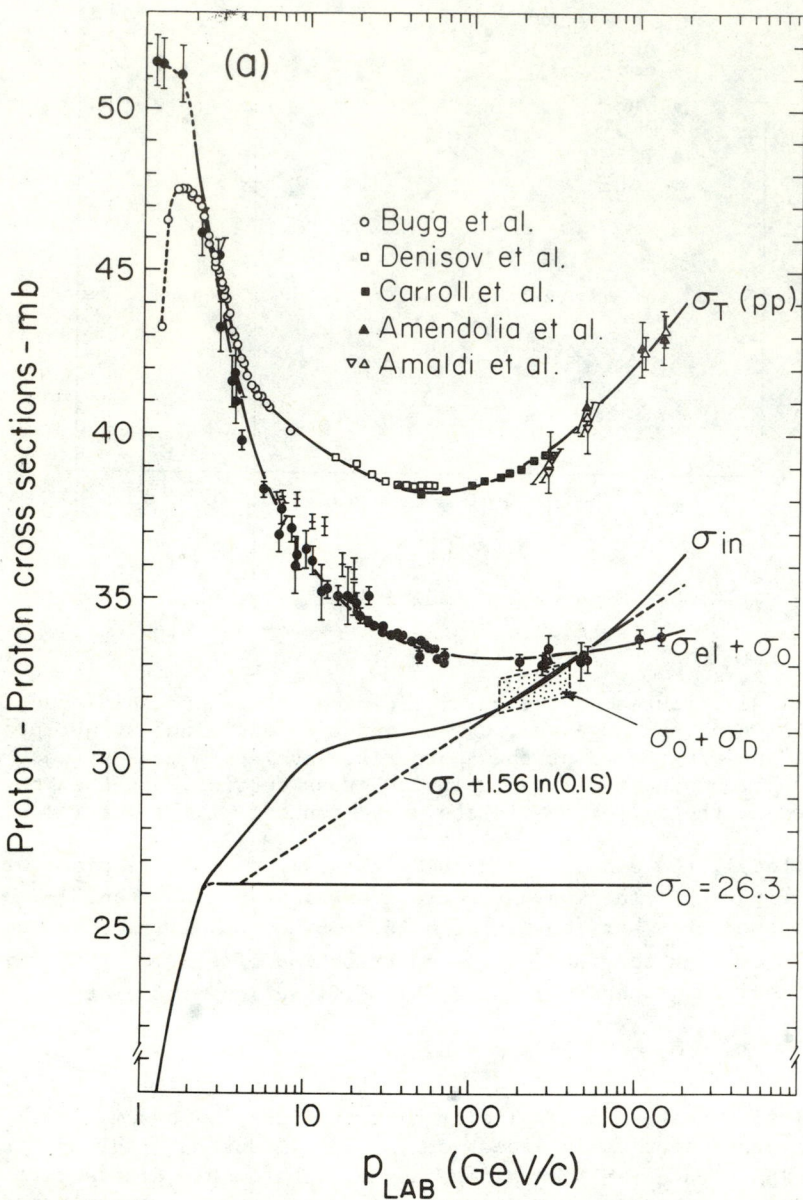

FIG. 9 – The total, the elastic and the inelastic
pp cross sections (from Ref. 12).

$$P_{n+2} = \frac{1}{\sigma_i} \left[\sigma_o P_{n+2}(\sqrt{s}-2M_p) + \frac{\sigma_D}{\ln(0.1s)} \int_1^{0.1s} \frac{1}{M_x^2} P_{n+1}(M_x-M_p)\, dM_x^2 \right] \quad (6)$$

(n= 0,2,4...)

The average multiplicity, the $<n>/D$ ratio and the KNO distribution calculated using this equation are in good agreement with the data, as shown
in Figures 6 and 7.

For pp, we add the annihilation cross section, $\bar{\sigma} = \sigma_T(\bar{p}p) - \sigma_T(pp)$,
to the pp inelastic cross section and use the distribution

$$P_n = \frac{1}{\sigma_i} \left[\sigma_o P_n(\sqrt{s} - 2M_p) + \frac{\sigma_D}{\ln(0.1s)} \int_1^{0.1s} \frac{1}{M_x^2} P_{n-1}(M_x-M_p)\, dM_x^2 + \bar{\sigma} P_n(\sqrt{s}) \right] \quad (7)$$

where the second term is not included for n=0. The $<n>$ and $<n>/D$ [7,13]
calculated using this distribution function agree well with the data
(see Fig. 6). However, at high energies, there remains a small but significant difference between the average pp and $\bar{p}p$ multiplicities which is
not predicted by the equations given above. If this difference were due
to the annihilation cross section, its average multiplicity would have to
be larger than $2s^{\frac{1}{4}}$ by more than 50%. We prefer the interpretation that
this disparity arises from a small difference in the pp and $\bar{p}p$ hard cores
and that the annihilation multiplicities follow the distribution given by
Eq. 3.

A similar analysis of pp → anything in terms of diffractive and non-
diffractive components was performed previously[14] and led to the same
conclusions about the multiplicities of the hard core. More recently, an
ISR experiment[15] which removed leading particle effects obtained similar
results. Our contribution in this area is that we have demonstrated that
the same function that describes the multiplicity distribution of diffractive high mass states also describes the pp and $\bar{p}p$ hard cores and $\bar{p}p$
annihilation.

By applying the same ideas to $\pi^{\pm}p$ reactions, treating the non-diffractive inelastic cross section as a hard core with available mass $M= \sqrt{s} - M_p$,
we have obtained good agreement of our calculated $<n>$ and $<n>/D$ with
existing data[7,9,16] (see Fig. 10). We have also investigated the re-
actions $\nu_\mu + p \rightarrow \mu^- + X^{++}$ and $\bar{\nu}_\mu + p \rightarrow \mu^+ + X^o$. Again, the multiplicity
distributions reported for these reactions[17,18] are in good agreement
with our predictions (see Figs. 11 and 12). In particular, the higher
average multiplicity and $<n>/D$ ratio[17] of X^{++} relative to that of X^o
arise naturally as a consequence of summing over n = 2,4,6... for X^{++}
and n = 0,2,4... for X^o . A determination[19] of the average multiplicity
of the state X in pp → $\mu^+\mu^-$X at ISR is also consistent with $2s^{\frac{1}{4}}$
behavior (see Fig. 13).

482

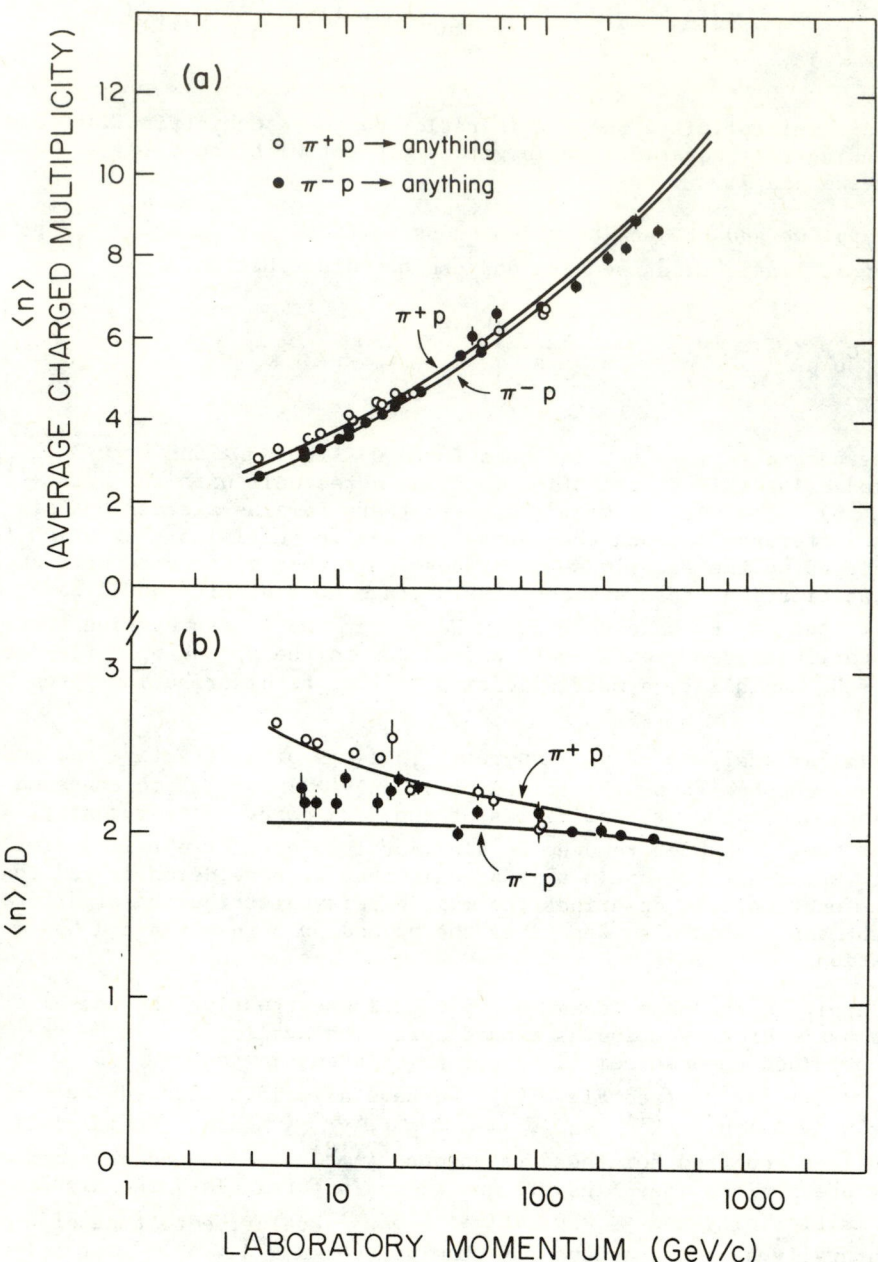

FIG. 10 – Charged $\langle n \rangle$ and $\langle n \rangle /D$ for $\pi^{\pm}p \rightarrow$ anything. The curves are predictions based on Eq. 3 as discussed in the text.

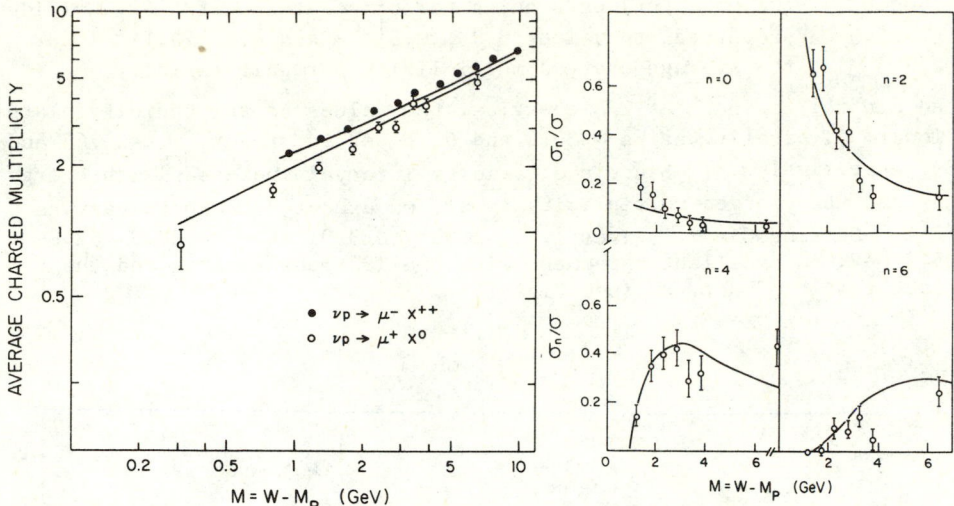

FIG. 11 - Charged $\langle n \rangle$ versus available energy for $\nu p \to \mu^- X^{++}$ and $\overline{\nu}p \to \mu^+ X^0$. The curves are predictions based on Eq. 3 as discussed in the text.

FIG. 12 - Charged multiplicity fractions for $\overline{\nu}p \to \mu^+ X^0$. The curves are from Eq. 3 in the text.

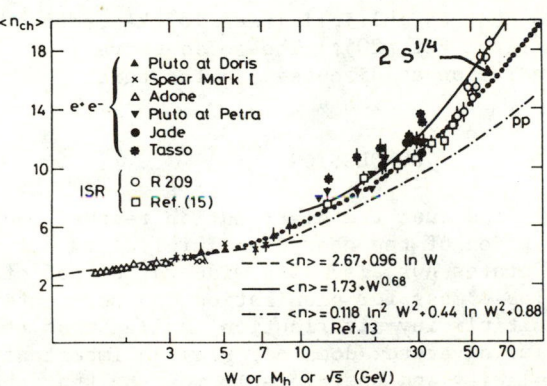

FIG. 13 - Average multiplicity versus available energy (from Ref. 19).

484

Recently, two $\bar{p}p$ experiments being performed at the CERN SPS Collider at $\sqrt{s}$ = 540 GeV reported the values 3.9 ± 0.3[20] and 3.0 ± 0.1[21] for $d<n>/d\eta|_{\eta=0}$, the average charged multiplicity per unit rapidity in the central region. At ISR energies, the values of the rapidity plateau are lower. Typically, at $\sqrt{s}$ = 30.8 and 62.8 GeV, $d<n>/d\eta|_{\eta=0}$ = 1.67 and 2.03, respectively[8]. Since the rapidity interval increases with energy as ℓns and the charged multiplicity as $s^{\frac{1}{4}}$, we expect $d<n>d\eta$ to vary as $Cs^{\frac{1}{4}}/\ell$ns. Setting C = 2.1 gives 1.71, 2.00 and 3.91 at $\sqrt{s}$ = 30.8 62.8 and 540 GeV, in excellent agreement with the ISR measurements and the SPS Collider result of Ref. 20 (see Fig. 14).

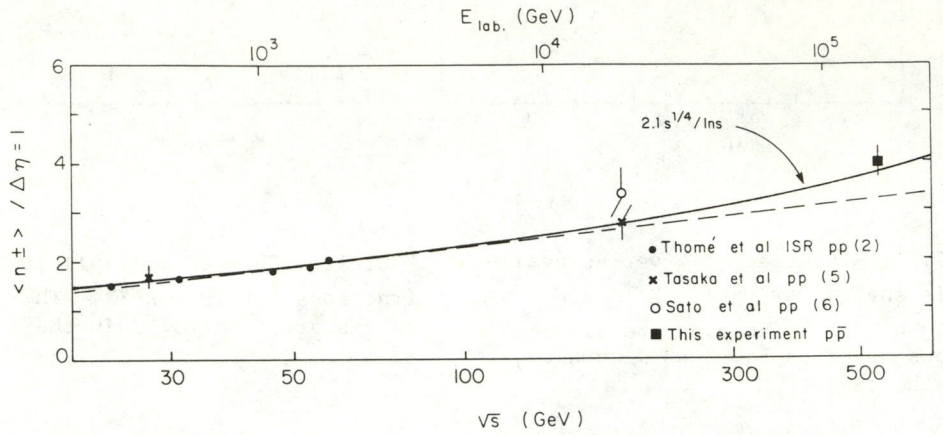

FIG. 14 - Average charged multiplicities in the central
region (from Ref. 20). The solid curve is
our prediction as discussed in the text.

CONCLUSION

In conclusion, we find that the distribution represented by Eq. 3 provides a good description of the charged multiplicites not only of high mass diffractive states but also of a wide variety of other hadronic states where the available mass for pionization can be identified. This universality of the multiplicity distribution implies that the quark content of the dissociating state does not play an important role in determining the multiplicity and therefore it must be that the gluons dominate the process of hadronization.

REFERENCES

1. R.L. Cool et al., Phys. Rev. $\underline{D24}$, 2821 (1981).
2. R.L. Cool et al., Phys. Rev. Lett. $\underline{47}$, 701 (1981).
3. Z. Koba, H.B. Nielson and P. Olesen, Nucl. Phys. $\underline{B40}$, 317 (1972).
4. P. Slattery, Phys. Rev. $\underline{D7}$, 2073 (1973).
5. πp : F.C. Winkelmann et al., Phys. Rev. Lett. $\underline{32}$, 121 (1974).
   pp : F.T. Dao et al., Phys. Lett. $\underline{45B}$, 399 (1973); S.J. Barish, et al., Phys. Rev. Lett. $\underline{31}$, 1080 (1973); J.W. Chapman et al., Phys. Rev. Lett. $\underline{32}$, 257 (1974); and M.G. Albrow et al., Nucl. Phys. $\underline{B102}$, 275 (1976).
   p̄p : F. Grard et al., Phys. Lett. $\underline{59B}$, 409 (1975); C.P. Ward et al., Nucl. Phys. $\underline{B153}$, 299 (1979).
6. S. Barshay et al., Phys. Rev. Lett. $\underline{32}$, 1390 (1974).
7. E. DeWolf et al., Nucl. Phys. $\underline{B87}$, 325 (1975); E. Albini et al., Nuovo Cimento $\underline{32}$, 101 (1976).
8. W. Thomé et al., Nucl. Phys. $\underline{B129}$, 365 (1977).
9. C. Bromberg et al., Phys. Rev. $\underline{D15}$, 64 (1977); W.M. Morse et al., Phys. Rev. $\underline{D15}$, 66 (1977); A. Firestone et al., Phys. Rev. $\underline{D10}$, 2080 (1974); S. Barish et al., Phys. Rev. $\underline{D9}$, 2689 (1974); V.V. Ammosov et al., Nucl. Phys. $\underline{B58}$, 77 (1973).
10. ADONE : C. Bacci et al., Phys. Lett. $\underline{86B}$, 234 (1979).
    SPEAR-MARK I : J.L. Siegrist, Ph.D. Thesis SLAC-225 UC-34d (1980).
    DASP : R. Brandelik et al., Nucl. Phys. $\underline{B148}$, 189 (1979).
    PLUTO : Ch. Berger et al., Phys. Lett. $\underline{78B}$, 176 (1978).
    TASSO : R. Brandelik et al., Phys. Lett. $\underline{89B}$, 418 (1980); ibid, $\underline{94B}$, 444 (1980).
    JADE : W. Bartel et al., Phys. Lett. $\underline{88B}$, 171 (1979).
11. Ch. Berger et al., Phys. Lett. $\underline{95B}$, 313 (1980).
12. K. Goulianos, Phys. Rev. $\underline{D14}$, 1445 (1976).
13. D.E. Zissa et al., Phys. Rev. $\underline{D21}$, 3059 (1979); R.E. Ansorge et al., Phys. Lett. $\underline{59B}$, 299 (1975).
14. K. Fialkowski and H.I. Miettinen, Phys. Lett. $\underline{43B}$, 61 (1973).
15. M. Basile et al., Phys. Lett. $\underline{95B}$, 311 (1980).
16. P.J. Hays et al., Phys. Rev. $\underline{D23}$, 20 (1980); A. Firestone et al., Phys. Lett. $\underline{D14}$, 2902 (1976); D. Fung et al., Nucl. Phys. $\underline{B102}$, 386 (1976).
17. P. Allen et al., Nucl. Phys. $\underline{B181}$, 385 (1981).
18. M. Derrick et al., Phys. Rev. $\underline{D17}$, 17 (1978).
19. D. Antreasyan et al., CERN-EP/81-116.
20. UAI Collaboration, CERN-EP/81-155.
21. UA5 Collaboration, CERN-EP/81-152.

NEW RESULTS IN THE DUAL FRAGMENTATION MODELS

presented by J. Tran Thanh Van

A. Capella and J. Tran Thanh Van
Laboratoire de Physique Théorique et Particules Elémentaires
Université Paris-Sud Bât. 211 91405 Orsay France

ABSTRACT

We describe hadron-hadron, hadron-nucleus and nucleus-nucleus interactions at low p_T in the framework of a dual parton model. The model is formulated in the framework of the 1/N expansion in dual theories and based on the S matrix theory. Comparison with experiments (multiplicity, dispersion, charge distributions ...) shows an excellent agreement with all available data.

I. INTRODUCTION

At the end of the seventies, it was observed [1] that the x distribution at large x of the low p_T multiparticle production is very similar to the structure function of the valence quark in a nucleon. For example,

$$x \frac{d\sigma^{pp\to\pi^+ X}}{dx}(x) \sim u_p(x) \qquad \text{and} \qquad x \frac{d\sigma^{pp\to\pi^- X}}{dx}(x) \sim d_p(x)$$

where $u_p(x)$ and $d_p(x)$ are the structure function of the u and d valence quarks in a proton. This observation gives rise to the so-called "recombination model" [2] and more recently the "valon model"[3]

At the same time, a striking similarity, both in shape and absolute normalization, is observed [4] between low p_T hadronic x distributions in the fragmentation region and the fragmentation function of quark into hadrons. For example,

$$\frac{1}{\sigma} \frac{d\sigma^{\pi^+ p\to\pi^+ X}}{dx}(x) = \frac{1}{2}[D^{u\to\pi^+}(x) + D^{\bar{d}\to\pi^+}(x)] = D^{u\to\pi^+}(x)$$

where $D^{u\to\pi^+}(x)$ is the fragmentation function of a u quark into a π^+, and is measured either in $e^+e^- \to \pi^+ + X$ or in deep inelastic neutrino scattering. This observation leads us to develop a dual parton model[5] which is based on the 1/N expansion of the Dual Topological Unitarization [6] (D.T.U.) scheme and which explains successfully the main features of multiparticle production in hadron-hadron, hadron-nucleus and nucleus-nucleus interactions in the whole range of rapidity. In what follows, we will recall the main features of the

dual parton model and report on the most recent results obtained in
this field.

II. DUAL TOPOLOGICAL UNITARIZATION SCHEME AND THE DUAL PARTON MODEL

Let us first point out that the DTU is formulated in the
framework of the S-matrix theory and has a close connection with
Reggeon field theory. The expansion in powers of 1/N with fixed
N_f/N_c ratio allows to introduce unitarity corrections and to have a
correspondence between a diagram in DTU and a Reggeon field theory
one and leads to an obvious significance of various DTU diagrams in
terms of well known Regge poles or Regge cuts.

In DTU, an interaction gives rise to a colour separation. Chains of
produced particles are formed between the coloured fragments of the
projectile and the target. As an example, let us examine nucleon-
nucleon interactions. With valence quark (v), diquark (qq) and sea
antiquark ($\bar{s}$) or sea quark (s), there are four types of chains
- chain linking a valence quark and a diquark v-qq
- chain linking a   sea   quark and a diquark s-qq
- chain linking a valence quark and a sea antiquark v-$\bar{s}$
and - chain linking a sea quark and a sea antiquark s-$\bar{s}$
As observed in deep inelastic scattering, quarks (valence and sea)
have small momentum whereas diquarks are fast. Therefore the (v-$\bar{s}$)
chains have small C.M. energy and   are short in the rapidity space
while the (v-qq) and (s-qq) chains have larger C.M. energy and are
long in the rapidity space. Obviously the latter chains can produce
more particles than the former.

The dominant diagram in nucleon-nucleon interactions is a two
chain diagram (fig. 1), which
corresponds, in Regge language,
to a single Pomeron exchange. The
calculation of such a diagram
involves the knowledge of two
quantitites :

a) How the momentum of the
hadron is shared between the
valence quark and the diquark.
This momentum sharing function
can be obtained by studying the
Regge singularities of this
diagram [7] or more phenomenologically by the quark structure
function [5b].

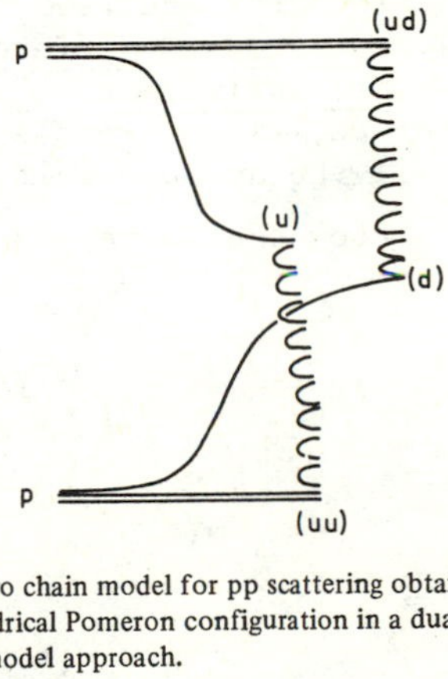

Fig. 1. The two chain model for pp scattering obtained by cutting the cylindrical Pomeron configuration in a dual topological or string model approach.

b) How a quark or a diquark
fragments into observed hadrons.
This fragmentation function can
be phenomenologically taken either from e^+e^- interactions or from
deep inelastic lepton-nucleon scattering using jet universality
assumption.

488

Let us summarize this part by saying that in our approach, the framework is fixed by DTU and the inputs are fixed by Regge singularities and experimental fragmentation functions. No free parameter is introduced. With these ingredients and the dominant diagram only we have been able to describe successfully[5b] all hadron-hadron multiparticle production data up to ISR energies. The presence of sea quarks in the hadrons is ignored. Obviously, when the energy increases, the $(v-s)$ and $(s-\bar{s})$ chains which are negligible at low energies, will become more important and diagrams involving sea quarks should be taken into account. The latter correspond to multiple scattering (Pomeron-Pomeron cuts) in Reggeon Field Theory.

III. HIGH ENERGY NUCLEON-NUCLEON INTERACTIONS

As seen above, the dominant diagram (see fig. 1) contains two $(q-qq)$ chains. The next to leading diagram, which corresponds to a Pomeron-Pomeron cut contains up to four chains :

the two $(qq-q)$ chains mentioned above and two new $(q-\bar{q})$ chains linking a sea quark of either proton to a sea antiquark of the other one (see fig.2). Every new initial or final state inelastic rescattering produces two extra $(q-\bar{q})$ chains. Thus the s-channel state of a general contribution corresponding to k inelastic rescatterings (k cut Pomerons) consists of 2 k chains - two of which are $(qq-q)$ chains and $(2k-2)$ are $(\bar{q}-q)$ chains.

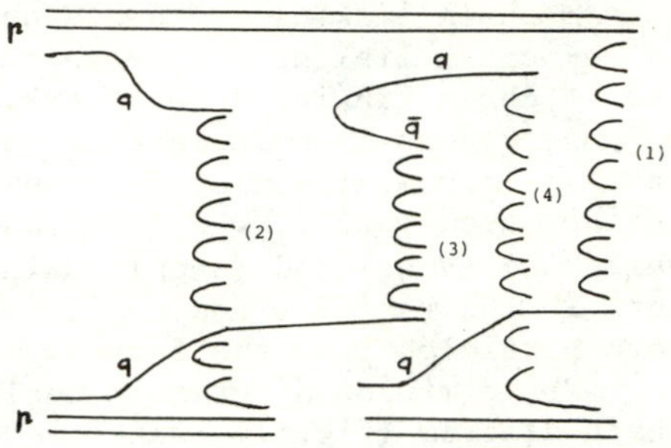

Fig. 2. Parton model diagram for hadron-nucleus collisions in the case $n = 2$, where two active nucleons of the target scatter inelastically with various constituents (both valence and sea) of the proton projectile. The spectator nucleons are not shown.

1. <u>Average and differential multiplicities</u>

Let us, as an example, treat in detail the average multiplicity[8]. From the above considerations, the average multiplicity is given by

$$<n(s)>_{pp} = (1/\sum_{k=1}^{\infty} \sigma_k) \sum_{k=1}^{\infty} \sigma_k \int dx_1 \ldots \int dx_{2k} \int dx'_1 \ldots \int dx'_{2k}$$

$$\rho(x_1, \ldots, x_{2k}) \rho(x'_1, \ldots, x'_{2k}) \qquad (1)$$

$$\{ 2n(x_1 x'_{2k} s)_{(qq-q)} + (2k - 2) n(x_2 x'_2 s)_{(q-\bar{q})} \}$$

where $\sigma_k/\sum \sigma_k$ are the eikonal weigths giving the probability of having k inelastic rescatterings. The functions $\rho(\ldots x_i \ldots)$ are (joint) momentum distribution functions of the (valence and sea) quarks and diquark at the ends of each of the 2k chains. They are given in terms of dominant Regge singularities. One has [7]

$$\rho(x_1, \ldots x_{2k}) = C_{2k} \frac{1}{\sqrt{x_1}} \frac{1}{x_2} \cdots \frac{1}{x_{2k-1}} x_{2k}^{1.5} \delta(1 - x_1 - \ldots - x_{2k}) \quad (2)$$

The constants C_{2k} are determined in such a way that the normalization of $\rho(\ldots x_i \ldots)$ is equal to one. Note that x_1 refers to a valence quark, x_{2k} to the diquark and $x_2,\ldots,x_{2k-1}$ to sea quarks or antiquarks (see fig. 2) . As usual, in order to avoid the singularity at $x_i = 0$, one replaces in eq.(2)x_i by $(x_i^2 + \mu_T^2/P^2)^{1/2}$ where P is the C. of M. momentum of the pp reaction and μ_T a quark transverse mass. Using the universality assumption, we take for the chain multiplicities [9,10]

$$n(s)_{(qq-q)} = n(s)_{\ell p} = 0.8 + 0.9 \log s$$

$$n(s)_{(\bar{q}-q)} = n(s)_{e^+e^-} = 2.1 + 0.85 \log s$$

Using eq. (1) with $\mu = 0.1$ Gev together with the eikonal values of σ_k [11] we get the average multiplicities shown in fig. 3. The agreement with experiment is quite satisfactory.

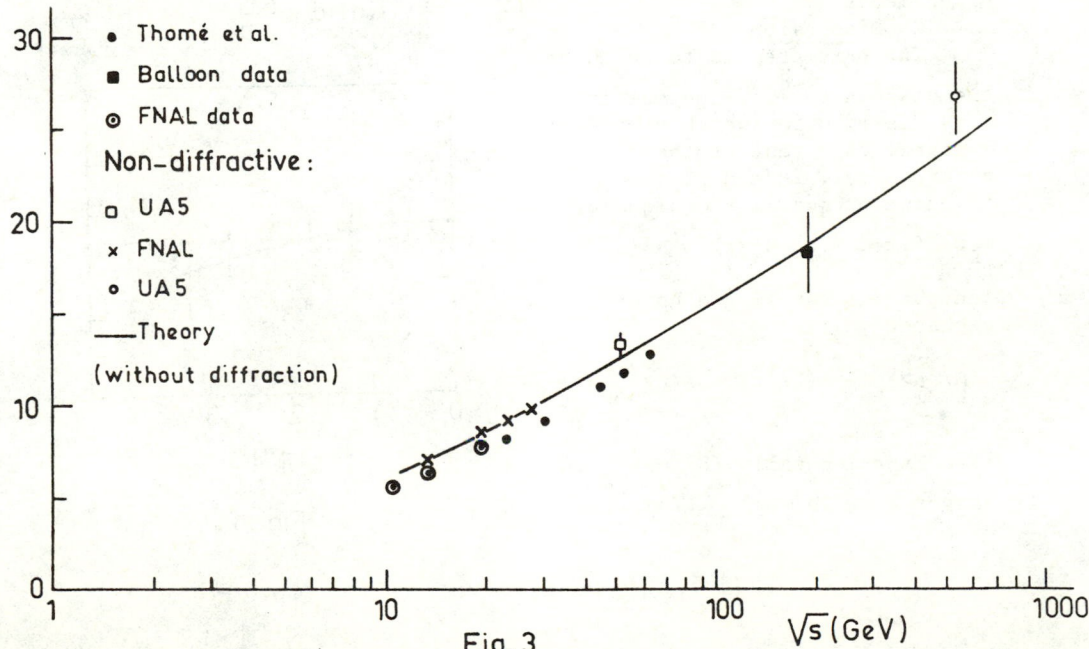

⟨n_ch⟩ All inelastic:

- • Thomé et al.
- ■ Balloon data
- ⊙ FNAL data

Non-diffractive:

- □ UA5
- × FNAL
- ○ UA5
- ——Theory
- (without diffraction)

Fig. 3

$\sqrt{s}$ (GeV)

490

Similar formula is obtained for the differential multiplicity and allows us to predict the energy dependence of the central plateau height in both pp and p̄p interactions (see fig. 4)

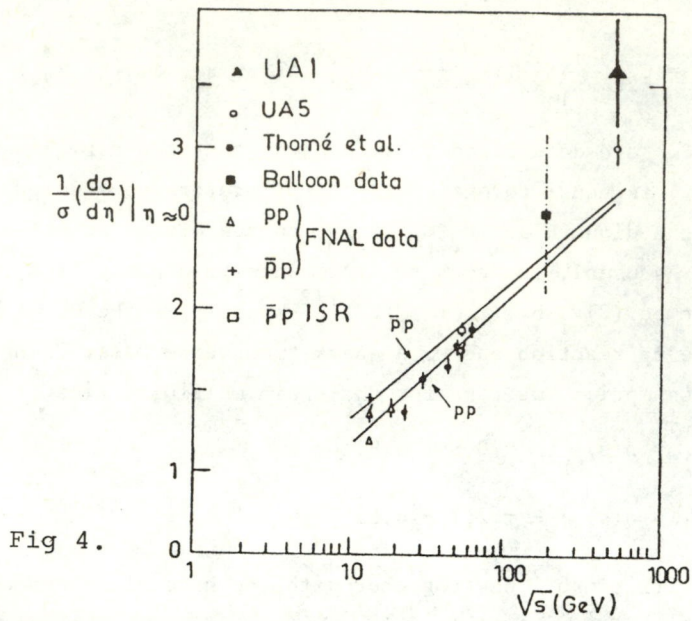

$$\frac{1}{\sigma}\left(\frac{d\sigma}{d\eta}\right)\Big|_{\eta \approx 0}$$

▲ UA1
○ UA5
● Thomé et al.
■ Balloon data
△ pp }
+ p̄p } FNAL data
□ p̄p ISR

p̄p
pp

√s (GeV)

Fig 4.

Although the theoretical value at $\sqrt{s}$ = 540 GeV is somewhat low, most of the observed energy dependence of the plateau is reproduced. In addition, the ratio of p̄p versus pp differential multiplicities at $\sqrt{s}$ = 53 GeV is shown in fig. 5 and agrees very well with experiments[12].

2. Dispersion

The next step is to calculate the dispersion [8] of the multiplicity distribution which provides a significant test of the dual parton model. Indeed if the momentum of quarks and diquarks were fixed i.e. $\rho(x_j) \stackrel{\sim}{} \pi\delta(x_i - x_{io})$ one obtains for single Pomeron exchange (k = 1)

$$(D/\langle n\rangle)_{pp} = (1/\sqrt{2})\ (D/\langle n\rangle)_{ep}$$

Experimentally $(D/\langle n\rangle)_{pp}$ is larger than $(D/\langle n\rangle)_{ep}$. This has

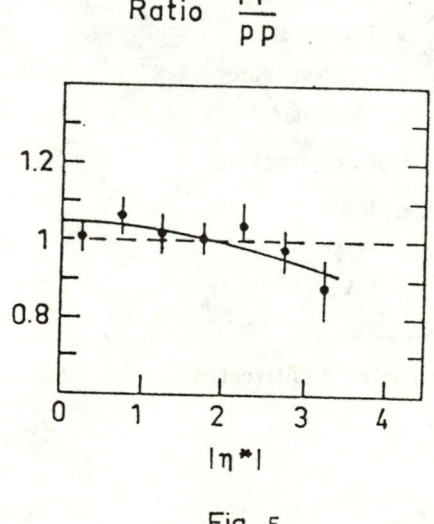

Ratio $\dfrac{\bar{p}p}{pp}$

1.2

1

0.8

0   1   2   3   4

$|\eta^*|$

Fig. 5

been wrongly interpreted as a failure of the two-chain model [13].
Indeed, when one takes a realistic momentum distribution function
$\rho(x_i)$, the smearing due to the integrations over the x_i's increases
the value of D/<n> especially at moderate energies [14]. However, the
ratio D/<n> decreases with increasing energies and at $\sqrt{s}$ = 540 Gev
one gets $(D/<n>)_{pp}$ = 0.31 – a value much lower than the data.

On the other hand, taking into account   the contribution of
multiple scattering in the same way as in eq (1), one obtains a
satisfactory agreement with experiment as shown in Table I. Notice
that our calculation does not include the effects of diffraction

T A B L E   I

$\sqrt{s}$ (Gev.)	D/<n> theory (no diffr.)	D/<n> exp (non–diffr.)	D/<n> exp (single diffr. dis. allowed)
20	0.45	–	0.50 ± 0.01
60	0.41	–	0.55 ± 0.01
540	0.42	0.45 ± 0.05	–

The ratio D/<n>, compared to the experimental data of refs 19 and 20.

A theoretical calculation of the effect of diffraction has been
given in reference 11 in the framework of perturbative Reggeon calcu-
lus. As discussed there, the result depends on the unknon parameter

$$r = \frac{\text{slope of the one-Pomeron-exchange amplitude}}{\text{slope of the triple Pomeron amplitude}}$$

The standard value of r are in the range 0.5 < r < 1. Taking into
account the diffractive contribution with r = 0.75 and all other
parameters as in ref. 3, the D/<n> ratio at $\sqrt{s}$ = 60 Gev increases
by 18 %. This increase due to diffraction is smaller at lower
energies.

3. Charge distributions

Charge distributions are a good test of the dual parton models
since they involve taking differences of fragmentation functions into
positive and negative hadrons. They also provide an indication of the
identity of the colored systems involved in the interaction and
fragmentation responsible for low p_T multiparticle production.

Recently, A Pagnamenta and U. Sukhatme [15] have made an extensive
study of charge distribution in hadron-hadron interactions in the
framework of the DTU model keeping only the dominant contribution :
two chain diagram (single Pomeron-exchange). Good agreement with
experimental results is obtained for all available reactions. An

example is shown in fig. 6.

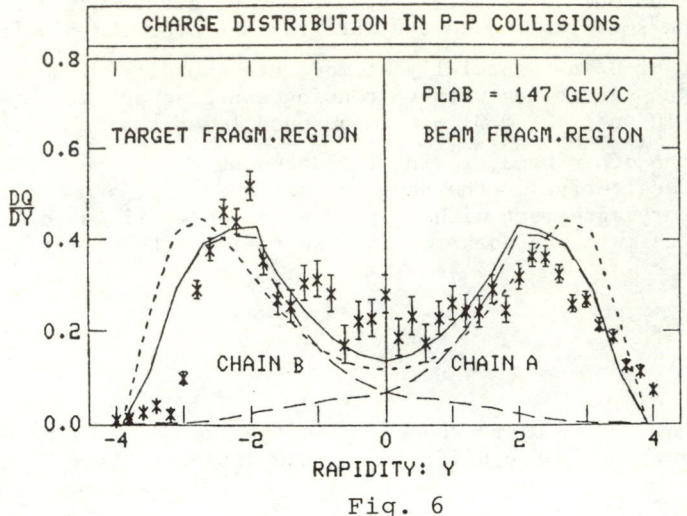

Fig. 6

Notice that the charge distributions are expected to be insensitive to the multiple scattering contributions.

IV. HADRON-NUCLEUS AND NUCLEUS-NUCLEUS INTERACTIONS

In hadron-nucleus and nucleus-nucleus interactions, it becomes evident that multiple scattering should be taken into account. Indeed, taking into account only the dominant term (one Pomeron exchange or two chain diagram) would lead to a nucleon-nucleus cross section equal to A times nucleon-nucleon cross section which is not in agreement with experiments. Multiple scattering will reduce this ratio.

1. Hadron-Nucleus Interactions

Generalizing the preceding picture of multiple scattering to hadron-nucleus interactions and keeping only the dominant contributions and the leading corrections we have[7]

$$\frac{1}{\sigma_{in}^{pA}} \frac{d\sigma^{pA}}{dy} (y) \equiv N^{pA}(y) = \frac{1}{A} \frac{\sum\limits_{n}^{A} \sigma_n^A}{\sum\limits_{n}^{A} \sigma_n^A} \sum\limits_{n}^{A} \sigma_n^A \ x \qquad (3)$$

$$\left[N_n^{qq)_p - q_A}(y) + N_n^{q_p - qq)_A}(y) + (n - 1) \{N_n^{q_p - qq)_A}(y) + N_n^{\bar{q}_p - q_A}(y)\} \right]$$

where σ_n^A is the cross section for having n inelastic collisions with n nucleons of the target and $\sum\limits_{n=1}^{A} \sigma_n^A = \sigma_{in}^{pA}$. Here, for simplicity, we do not take into account the presence of sea quark in the target nucleons. It contributes only to the next to leading corrections. The significance of eq (3) can be easily seen in the following figure.

Dominant contribution

Leading corrections

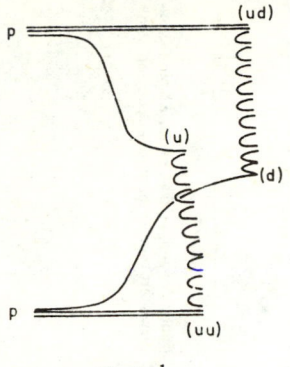

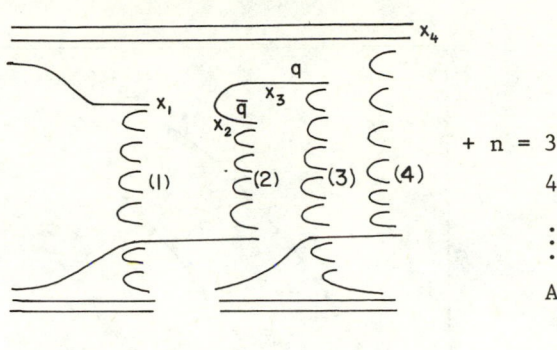

n = 1

n = 2

Two (q-qq) chains. One nucleon of the target is interacting with the projectile.

Three (q-qq) chains and one qq chain. Two nucleons of the target are interacting with the projectile.

The other nucleons are spectators.

Comparison with experimental data shows a good agreement from deuteron (A = 2) to lead (A = 207) for the whole range of rapidity distribution. Some examples are shown in figs (7), (8), (9).

It is easy to extract the A dependence of the average multiplicity from eq (3). Indeed, in the central region (x ∿ 0) where the functions $N_n(y)$ are almost independent of n, summation over n can be easily done. Using the well known AKG cancellation[16].

$$\sum_{n=1}^{A} n \, \sigma_n = A \, \sigma_{in}^{pp}$$

and the definition of σ_{in}^{pA} $(\sigma_{in}^{pA} = \sum_{n=1}^{A} \sigma_n)$

we obtain :

$$N^{pA}(y) = N^{qq)_p - p_A}(y) + N^{q_p - qq)_A} + (\bar{\nu} - 1) \left[N^{\bar{q}_p - qq)_A}(y) + N^{\bar{q}_p - q_A}(y) \right] \quad (4)$$

where $\bar{\nu} = A \, \sigma_{in}^{pp} / \sigma_{in}^{pA}$

If we make the very crude assumptions that all (q-qq) chains give the same multiplicity and neglect the ($\bar{q}$-q) chains (which have at

494

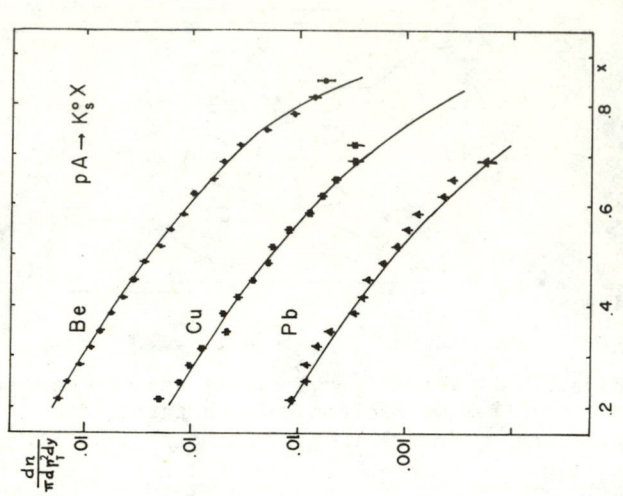

Fig. 8. Differential multiplicities at $p_L = 300$ GeV for K_s^0 production at $p_T = 0$. The solid curves are our theoretical calculations with $C = 0.032$

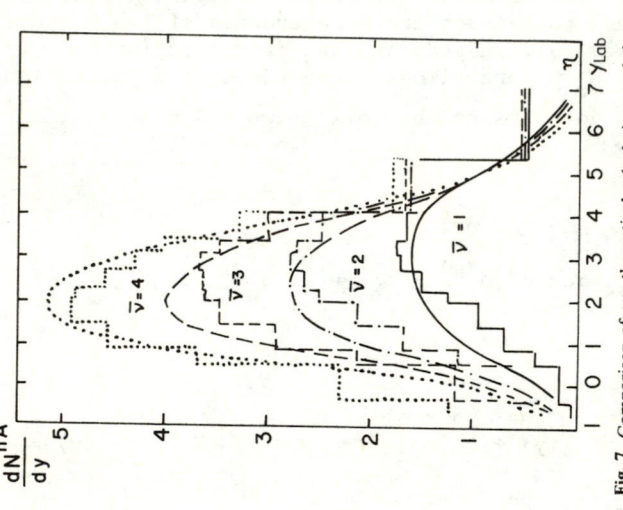

Fig. 7 Comparison of our theoretical calculations and the experimental data for the charged differential multiplicities at $\sqrt{s} = 20$ GeV. An overall normalization factor 0.85 has been used to fit the $pp(\bar{\nu} = 1)$ curve

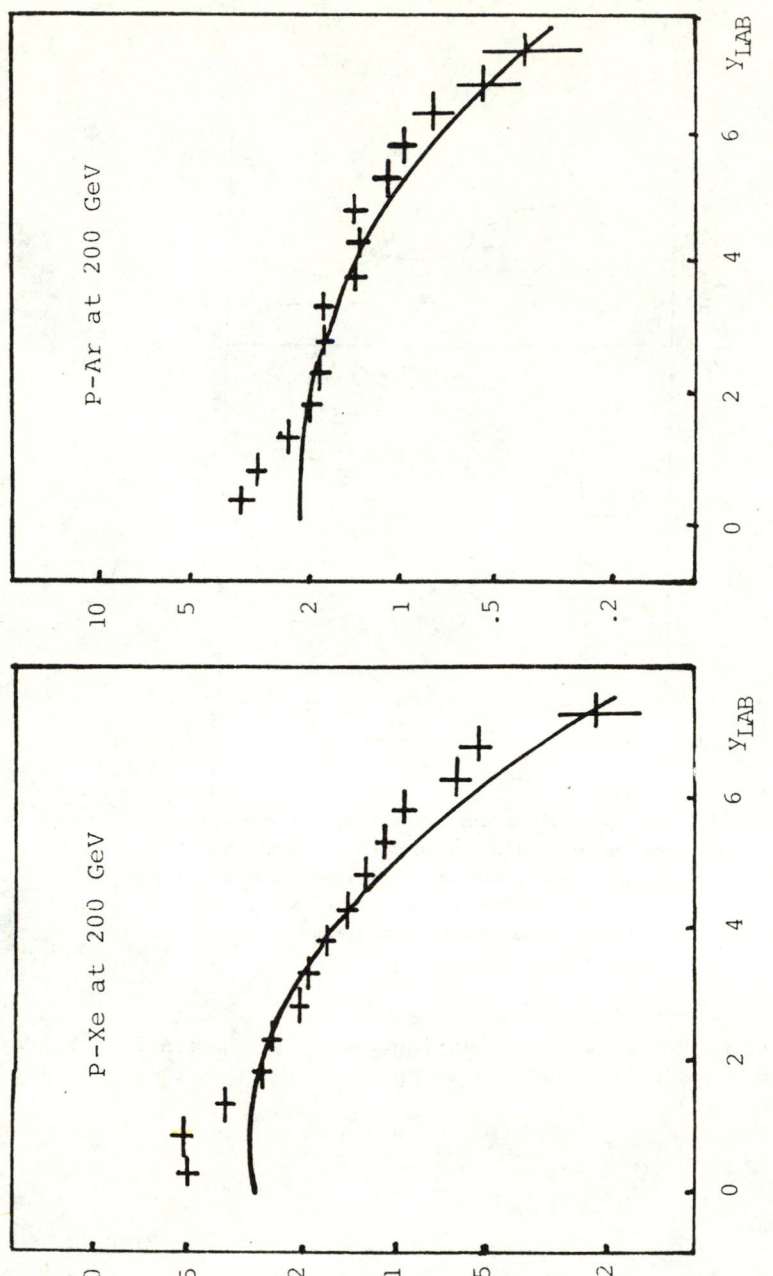

Fig. 9a

Charged pion density for proton nucleus (Xe,Ar) divided by charged pion density for proton proton interaction per rapidity interval in laboratory system. The solid line in all figures is our absolute prediction. Data from I. Derado, Lisboa Conference, 1981.

496

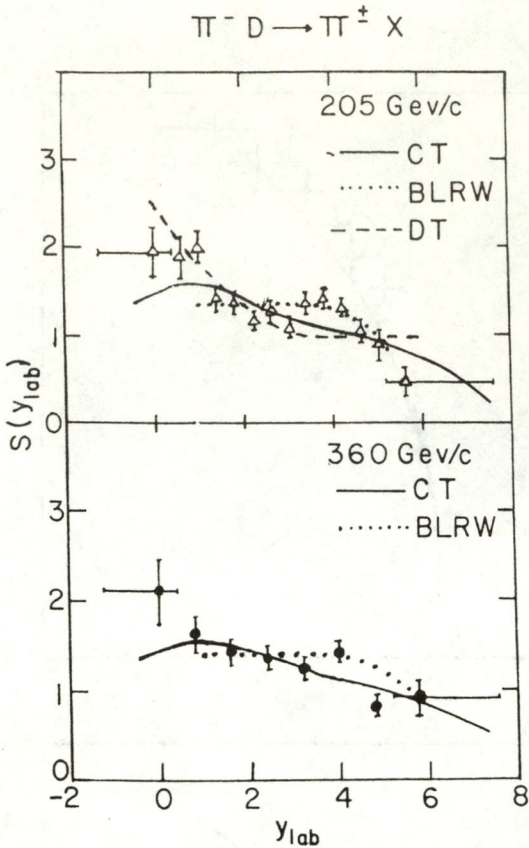

$$\pi^- D \rightarrow \pi^{\pm} X$$

Fig. 9b : Ratio (y_{lab}) of the double scattering to single scatte-
ring rapidity distribution of $\pi^- d \rightarrow \pi^{\pm} X$ and comparison
with theoretical predictions. Full lines are our predictions
(CT), dotted lines are from Baker et al (Nuclear Physics
B181, 365, 1981) and dashed lines are from A. Dar and J.
Tran Thanh Van (Phys. Lett. 65B, 455 (1976).

present energies a low average invariant mass) we obtain for the ratio
of average multiplicity in pA and in pp

$$R = \frac{<n>^{pA}}{<n>^{pp}} = \frac{1}{2} + \frac{1}{2} \bar{\nu}$$

which is in rather good agreement with experiment.

Notice that when the energy increases, all chains develop energy
independent plateaus of identical heights and it is no longer possible
to neglect the contributions of ($\bar{q}q$) chains. In this high energy limit,

we obtain

$$R = \bar{\nu}$$

This result is a general consequence of unitarity in multiple scattering models provided the triple Pomeron coupling is neglected

2. Nucleus nucleus interactions

Following the same treatment we can calculate the density distribution in nucleus nucleus collisions [17]. However, calculations become rapidly complicated. In what follows, we will neglect, for simplicity, the difference between valence and sea quarks and also the energy-momentum conservation constraints. Notice that these constraints have a sizable effect only in the fragmentation region. In this case, we obtain [17]

$$\frac{1}{\sigma}\frac{d\sigma^{AB \to hx}}{dy} \equiv N^{AB \to hx}(y) = \frac{A\sigma_{pB}}{\sigma_{AB}} [N^{(qq)_A - q_B}(y) - N^{q-\bar{q}}(y)] \qquad (5)$$

$$+ \frac{B\sigma_{pA}}{\sigma_{AB}} [N^{q_A - (qq)_B}(y) - N^{q-\bar{q}}(y)] + \frac{2AB\sigma_{pp}}{\sigma_{AB}} N^{q-\bar{q}}(y)$$

As shown before, the rapidity distributions $N^{(qq)_A - q_B}(y), N^{q_A - (qq)_B}(y)$ and $N^{q-\bar{q}}(y)$ are obtained from a convolution of the diquark and quark momentum distribution functions given in the dual model in terms of dominant Regge singularities with standard quark or diquark fragmentation functions. Explicit expressions for these rapidity distributions are given in refs 7 and 17. Note that the first two types of chains appear in p-p collisions. Chains of the third type appear in πp and $p\bar{p}$ interactions. The above formula applies when the laboratory energy per nucleon is in the range between a few tens of GeV and a few thousands of GeV. A situation where it is fully applicable is, for intance, α-α scattering at ISR energies. Note that at asymptotic energies, where all chains develop energy-independent plateaus, one gets from eq. 5

$$\frac{dN^{AB \to hx}}{dy}(y) = \frac{AB\sigma_{pp}}{\sigma_{AB}} \frac{dN^{pp \to hx}}{dy}(y) \qquad (6)$$

As an application, we compute the rapidity distribution of negative particles in a α-α collision at center of mass momentum $P_{C.M.} = 62$ GeV/c. Note that the spectrum of positive particles is contaminated by the contributions of recoil protons which are not included in our calculations. The results are compared with preliminary ISR data reported in ref. 18. The agreement is quite satisfactory.

498

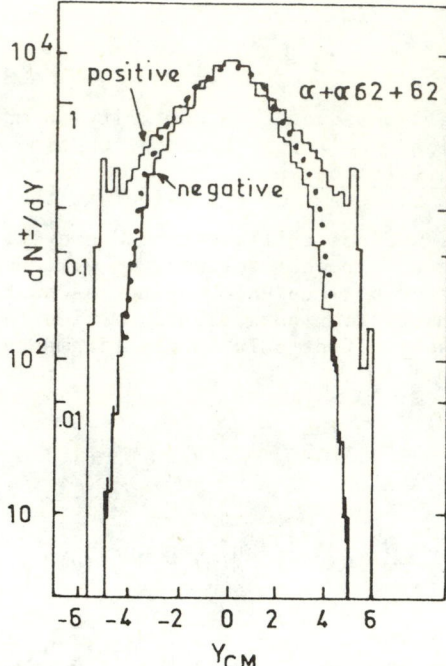

Density distributions of positive and negative particles
in alpha-alpha collisions at ISR ($\sqrt{s}$ = 124 GeV). The dotted
line is our calculation for negative particles.

V. CONCLUSIONS

We have investigated the role played by the hadrons constituents
in multi-hadron production at low p_T. We have proceeded in the general
framework of an S-matrix theory, and have used, as much as possible,
the wisdom contained in dual and reggeon field theories. These
theories suggest a production mechanism consisting in the formation
of jets of hadrons, resulting from the fragmentation of various sets
of constituents of the colliding hadrons. The number of these jets
(and thus the number of constituents which are responsible for them)
depends on the order of the process under consideration in the 1/N
expansion. The resulting hadronic spectra can be computed in terms
of a) the joint momentum distribution functions of the sets of
constituents responsible for the jets produced in the final state,
and b) the fragmentation function of these constituents. The former
are completely determined in terms of Regge intercepts. The latter
were obtained from the experimental data on hydrogen (or a given

nuclear target). The model is then completely determined and allows to compute the hadronic spectra and the charge distribution. We find it rather remarkable that it is possible, in the very general framework described above to understand at a quantitative level, the main features of hadron hadron, hadron nucleus and nucleus nucleus available data.

REFERENCES

1. W. Ochs, Nucl. Phys. B118, 397 (1977)
2. For a review see L. Van Hove, Schladming lectures 1979, CERN preprint 2628.
3. See R. Hwa review in this Proceedings
4. B. Andersson, G. Gustafson and C. Peterson, Phys. Lett. 69B, 221 (1977)
5a A. Capella, U. Sukhatme, C.I. Tan, J. Tran Thanh Van, Phys. Lett. 81B, 68 (1979)
5b A. Capella, U. Sukhatme, J Tran Thanh Van, Particles and Fields 3, 329 (1980)
5c G. Cohen-Tannoudji, A. El-Hassouni, J. Kalinowski, O. Napoly and R. Peschanski, Phys. Rev. D21, 2689 (1980)
5d H. Minakata, Phys. Rev. D20, 1656 (1979)
6. For non-specialized reviews see G. Veneziano in Proc. XII Rencontre de Moriond 1976, ed. J. Tran Thanh Van and Gif lectures 1977
7. A. Capella, J. Tran Thanh Van, Particles and Fields 10, 249 (1981)
8. A. Capella, J. Tran Thanh Van, Orsay preprint LPTPE 82/2
9. C.K. Chen et al., Nucl. Phys. B133, 13 (1978)
   J. Ballam et al., Phys. Lett. 56B, 193 (1975)
   H.H. Bingham et al., Phys. Rev. D8, 1277 (1973)
10. Amsterdam-Bologne-Padova-Pisa-Saclay-Torino collaboration Saclay preprint DPhPE 81-08 (1981) M. Derrick et al, Phys Rev 24D 1071 (1981)
    Ch. Berger et al. Phys. Lett. 95B, 313 (1980)
11. A. Capella and A. Krzywicki, Phys. Rev. 18D, 4120 (1978)
12. The axial Field Spectrometer collaboration, Phys. Lett. 108B, 58 (1982)
13. J. Dias de Deus, Phys. Lett. 100B, 177 (1981) ; F. Takagi, Tohoku University preprint n° 228 (1981).
14. K. Fialkowski and A. Kotanski, Phys. Lett. 107B, 132 (1981)
15. A. Pagnamenta, U. Sukhatme, to be published in Particles and Fields (1982)
16. V.A. Abramovski, V.N. Gribov, O.V. Kancheli : Yad Fiz 18, 595 (1973) ; Sov. J. Nucl. Phys 18, 308 (1974)
17. A. Capella, J. Kwiecenski, J. Tran Thanh Van, Phys. Letters 108B, 347 (1982)
18. M.A. Albrow and M. Jacob ed. CERN EP-TH preprints 1981.
19. UA1 Collaboration, Phys. Letters 107B, 320 (1981)
    UA5 Collaboration, Phys. Letters 107B, 310 and 315 (1981)
20. W. Thomé et al., Nucl. Phys. B129, 365 (1977)

CHIRONS

Brasil-Japan Collaboration on
Chacaltaya Emulsion Chamber Experiments.

J.A.Chinellato, C.Dobrighkeit, J.Bellandi Filho, C.M.G.Lattes, A.Marques, M.J.Menon, C.E.Navia O., M.Ballester C.Santos, K.Sawaya-nagi, E.Silva, E.H.Shibuya and A.Turtelli Jr.

-- Instituto de Fisica Gleb Wataghin, Universidade Estadual de Campinas, Campinas, S.P.

N.M.Amato and F.M.Oliveira Castro

-- Centro Brasileiro de Pesquisas Fisicas, Rio de Janeiro, RJ.

R.H.C.Maldonado

-- Institute de Fisica, Universidade Federal Fluminence, Niteroi,RJ.

H.Aoki, Y.Fujimoto, Y.Funayama, S.Hasegawa, H.Kumano, H.Semba, T. Tabuki, M.Tamada, K.Tanaka and S.Yamashita

-- Science and Engineering Research Laboratory, Waseda University, Shinjuku, Tokyo.

N.Arata, T.Shibata and K.Yokoi

-- Department of Physics, Aoyama Gakuin University, Setagaya, Tokyo.

A.Ohsawa

-- Institute for Cosmic-Ray Research, University of Tikyo, Tanashi, Tokyo.

ABSTRACT

A search is made for families from Chiron-interactions, non-pion multiple production of hadrons with p_t as large as $< p_t(\gamma)$: $\sim 2 - 3$ GeV/c, produced in the atmosphere within several hundred meters of height.   Fourteen families are picked up and their details are described.   Observation of high energy showers ($E \geq$ 10 TeV) in the families revealed several characteristics ; a) they are widely spread with ER = 500 $\sim$ 1000 GeV.m, b) Their shower transition curves show the majority are of hadronic origin but not pure electro-magnetic ones, c) a half of them are with single core (called as single showers) While other half are with collimated multi-cores (called as mini-clusters), and d) the shower initiating particles are rapidly attenuating in the chamber as well as in the atmosphere.   From those experimental results, we found behaviour of secondary hadrons from Chiron interaction (called B-particle) are very exotic.   They have a short collision mean free path, about 1/3 of the geometrical value, and at the collision they produce a narrow bundle of particles with $p_t(\gamma)$ = 10 - 20 MeV/c, which are observed as mini-clusters.

1. INTRODUCTION

A recent observation on gamma-ray and hadron families of extremely high energy with Chacaltaya emulsion chambers indicated that there exists a new type of particle interaction named "Chiron-type" [1].   The conclusion was derived from the two families, for which an estimation of height of their parent atmospheric interaction is obtained through the triangulation measurement on arrival directions of showers in the families.   Remarkable characteristics common to the two families are, first, hadron-rich and gamma-ray-poor composition, and second, high p_t of their produced hadrons.   The observation gives the gamma-ray part of p_t, $p_t(\gamma)$, of secondary hadrons as < $p_t(\gamma)$ > = 2 ∿ 3 GeV/c, which results in < p_t > ∿ 10 GeV/c through the factor $1/k_\gamma$, k_γ being the gamma-ray inelasticity of the hadronic interaction.

This "Chiron"-type family appears to us like a missing link among the exotic types of nuclear interactions which we have encountered through Chacaltaya observation on the families.[2],[3] Chiron type is common with previous Centauro and Mini-Centauro type interactions in the extreme composition of produced secondaries, i.e. absence of neutral pions, while it differs in p_t of produced hadrons by one order of magnitude.   Before the discovery of Chiron-type events, such extra-ordinarily high p_t was seen only in Geminion events.   In Geminion cases, emission of two hadrons was observed with < $p_t(\gamma)$ > ∿ 2.5 ± 0.4 GeV/c, which was interpreted as decay of hypothetical Geminion particle into two hadrons with large Q-value.

Seeing now that this anomalous high p_t appears not only in the two particle decay of Geminion but also in multi-particle production of Chiron-type, we are led to accept that presence of < p_t > ∿ 10 GeV/c is one of common phenomena in high energy cosmic-ray nuclear interactions beyond several hundred TeV.   Thus we may consider that the secondary particles in Chiron case and in Geminion case are the same kind of hadrons.   A thermodynamical argument with the fire-ball model suggests that those particles are as heavy as 10 GeV in rest energy, while they are with long life ($\tau \gtrsim 10^{-9}$ sec) from their path length of several hundred meters in atmosphere. This presented us a possibility that the particles -- calling them tentatively as "B-particles" -- is a new particle outside the known series of hadrons.   At the same time, it is required urgently to obtain more events of Chiron type and perform the detailed analysis.

The present report describes results of this Chiron family

502

study with the two-storey emulsion chamber of the latest exposure. The chamber, No.19, of the present study is superior in quality than others of similar exposure, in that it has nuclear emulsion plates all in the upper chamber as well as in the lower chamber. It allows detailed study on the core structure of observed showers through the microscopic observation on shower tracks in the nuclear emulsion plates. This brings finer detailed information than simple shower spot observation with X-ray films.

A search is made for families originated from Chiron-interactions in the atmosphere not far from the chamber, say less than several hundred meters. Since those families would represent faithfully original characteristics of parent Chiron interactions without much influence of atmospheric secondary interactions, they would be a family of isolated showers, without associating air cascades, scattered over a wide area. The scanning for such Chiron-families is presented in section 2, and description on the selected fourteen families is made in section 3.

Observation of showers in those families, as seen in section 4, tells that the showers are penetrating so that their majority are of hadronic origin but not of electro-magnetic one, confirming that they are indeed from the Chiron interaction of multi-hadron production. Reconstruction of their parent atmospheric interaction is made in section 5, and it is shown that a consistent picture can be obtained by the Chiron interaction model with $< p_t(\gamma) > \sim 2 - 3$ GeV/c.

The secondary hadrons from the Chiron interaction have very exotic characteristics. The microscopic observation on showers in Chiron families shows that their half are with single core but another half are with multi-core structure of the lateral spread, 100 μm ~ 1 mm, calling as "mini-clusters". Majority of the mini-clusters are of hadronic origin because of their penetrating power, so that they are a narrowly collimated bundle of particles arising from the atmospheric secondary nuclear interaction (A-jet). $< p_t(\gamma) >$ of those secondary interaction is found as small as $10 - 20$ MeV/c.

Section 6 is on observation of secondary interactions in the chamber. We found that the secondary hadrons of Chiron interactions are more rapidly attenuating than the common type of hadrons. Their collision mean free path turns out to be about one third of the geometrical value. Such abnormally short mean free path of the secondary hadrons was found in their passage through the atmosphere, too.

Summing up all the experimental data, it is concluded in section 7, the secondary hadrons in Chirons and Geminion interactions -- B-particle -- have nuclear collision cross section as large as three-times of the geometrical value, and they produce, at their collision, a narrowly collimated jet of particles with $p_t(\gamma) \simeq 10 - 20$ MeV/c, besides the normal type of pion multiple production. Such behaviour of B-particles is analogous to that of cosmic-ray heavy nuclei, and we are led to accept a possibility that B-particles are the extended object with dimension as large as a heavy nucleus.

2.   SELECTION OF CHIRON-TYPE FAMILIES.

Emulsion chamber, No.19   An emulsion chamber used for the present Chiron family study is No.19.   This is the latest one in the
series of emulsion chamber of two-storey structure, constructed and
exposed at Mt.Chacaltaya, 5200 m above sea level for 677 days.
Fig.1 gives a schematic view of its structure.   Photo-sensitive

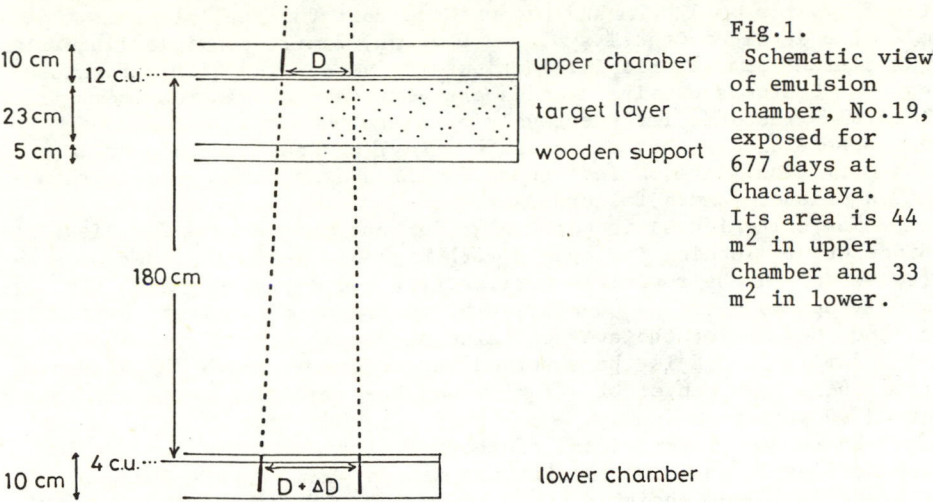

Fig.1.
  Schematic view
of emulsion
chamber, No.19,
exposed for
677 days at
Chacaltaya.
Its area is 44
m^2 in upper
chamber and 33
m^2 in lower.

layers are at 6, 8, 10 and 12 cascade unit of depth in the upper
chamber, and at 3, 4, 5, 6, 8, 10 and 12 cascade unit in the lower
chamber.   All the sensitive layers contain two sheet of X-ray
films and one nuclear emulsion plate, except at 10 cascade unit in
the upper chamber and 12 in some parts of lower chamber, where the
layer has only X-ray films.

Criteria for Chiron-family search in X-ray film scanning.

The routin shower spot scanning is made over all parts of X-ray
films in the upper as well as lower chambers.   Through comparison
of shower spots observed in X-ray films at different depths of the
chamber, we are able to identify a family.

      Among the detected families which penetrate through both upper
and lower chamber, we pick up families for the present study under
the following conditions:

   1)   a family has large energy and is observed both in the upper
         and lower chamber,
   2)   a family is consisted of "clean" showers.   A clean family
         is the one composed of clear and isolated shower spots not
         accompanied by a diffuse ones caused by air cascades.
   3)   a family has a wide lateral spread with large mutual distan-
         ces among the constituent shower spots.

      For the criterion 1), we imposed the condition for the total
observed shower energy as $\Sigma \, E(\gamma) \geq$ 50 TeV.
      The criterion 2), though only qualitative in its expression,
aims to pick up families originated from an atmospheric interaction

504

located close the observational level, say, several hundred of meters or less in height.   In such cases, most of the secondary particles from the parent interaction arrive at the chamber directly without degradation due to secondary atmospheric effects.   This is both for hadrons and gamma-rays, because the nuclear mean free path for the former is $\simeq$ 1200 m and one cascade unit for the latter is $\simeq$ 600 m at the level of Chacaltaya.   Whereas, families originating from far distant atmospheric interactions are associated with air cascades.   Features of air cascades are very characteristics in their lateral structure, irrespectively of where they are initiated in the atmosphere unless they are close by, say, one cascade unit or less. The criterion is rejecting those families associated with air cascades of such common features.

The criterion 3) is particular for the Chiron-type families. Since we are looking for events with high p_t , say, an order of a few GeV/c in their visible part, $p_t(\gamma)$, we may expect that they are widely spread out.   Quantatively, we impose the criterion, < ER > $\geq$ 180 GeV.m, for the average value of the product ER for showers in a family.   E is the observed shower energy and R the distance from the energy center of a family and the average is over all observed showers in a family.

In nuclear interactions of the ordinary type, the observable secondaries in emulsion chamber are mostly gamma-rays (through π^0 $\rightarrow$ 2γ decay) and their < p_t > is $\sim$ 0.2 GeV/c.   Thus the criterion 3) requires that the height of production should be H $\gtrsim$ 900 m, which is about 1.5 cascade unit of air.   Then, all the produced gamma-rays can not escape from the electro-magnetic process during their atmospheric passage, and the families will be associated by air cascades.   Therefore, events of the normal type will be rejected by the criterion 2).   Moreover, the particle multiplication through air cascades decreases the value of < ER >, so that the value of < ER > does not increase with increasing height of parent interaction. The combinations, 2)and 3),becomes very effective for rejection of the normal type families.

A similar argument can be applied to the nuclear interaction of Centauro and Mini-Centauro type, too.   Here, the average p_t of hadrons is known as < $p_t(\gamma)$ > $\sim$ 0.3 GeV/c resulting in the restriction of its height as $H \gtrsim$ 600 m, a half of the hadron collision mean free path.   Considering a fair probability of secondary nuclear interactions, which again decrease the average value < ER > through the particle multiplication, a substantial fraction of events of the types will be rejected by the criteria.   In fact, Centauro and Mini-Centauro families observed so far does not satisfy the criteria, particularly the third one.

Applying the selection criteria to all the families observed in chamber No.19, we select 14 families , listed in Table 1, for the present Chiron study.

Sampled Chiron-type among all families.   Since the complete study of all families in chamber No.19 is not yet over, we will see their position among the all families and estimate their frequency, referring to the results of systematic study of gamma-ray families

Table 1.   Selected Chiron-type families.

event number	sum of observed energy $\sum E$ (TeV)	lateral spread $\langle ER \rangle$ (GeV.m)	Number of showers (energy sum in TeV)			
			shower-upper		shower-lower	
			single	mini-cluster	single	mini-cluster
47S-17I	417	658	20 (104)	14 (225)	5 (30)	6 (58)
75S-50I	404	364	34 (202)	7 (181)	5 (6)	6 (23)
131S-109I	307	376	23 (148)	11 (145)	3 (11)	1 (7)
198S-154I	381	494	9 (229)	5 (136)	- (--)	1 (16)
193S-138I	151	721	7 (50)	4 (78)	3 (12)	1 (7)
155S-136I	112	382	4 (98)	- --	1 (13)	1 (2)
123S-90I	94	249	5 (34)	4 (42)	1 (3)	1 (15)
150S-93I	104	286	2 (10)	1 (70)	1 (11)	1 (13)
139S-104I	67	232	8 (48)	1 (4)	3 (9)	1 (7)
181S-139I	64	180	4 (31)	2 (31)	1 (3)	- --
166S-127I	95	824	6 (57)	1 (43)	- --	- --
161S-122I	87	266	9 (87)	- --	- --	- --
185S-124I	84	312	5 (23)	3 (61)	- --	- --
126S-105I	123	700	3 (29)	3 (74)	- --	1 (21.4)

506

carried out with previous chambers.   Fig.2 present the distribution of energy weighted average spread, < ER >, for the gamma-ray families with Σ E$_\gamma$ ≥ 100 TeV from all the chamber up to No.18. Here one sees that the majority of families are with < ER > ≃ 60 ∿ 120 GeV.m, a value consistent with the known types of pion multiple production.   Those satisfying the criterion 3) for wide lateral spread, < ER > ≥ 180 GeV.m, are at a tail of < ER > distribution, occupying about 20 % of all.   It is found that the binocular families from Geminion interaction compose about 20 % of such wide families at the tail, i.e., about 4 % of all the gamma-ray families.

Comparing the exposure factor of the present chamber, No.19, with the total exposure here, one finds that the Chiron-type families sampled by the above criteria have frequency of the same order of magnitude as binocular families.

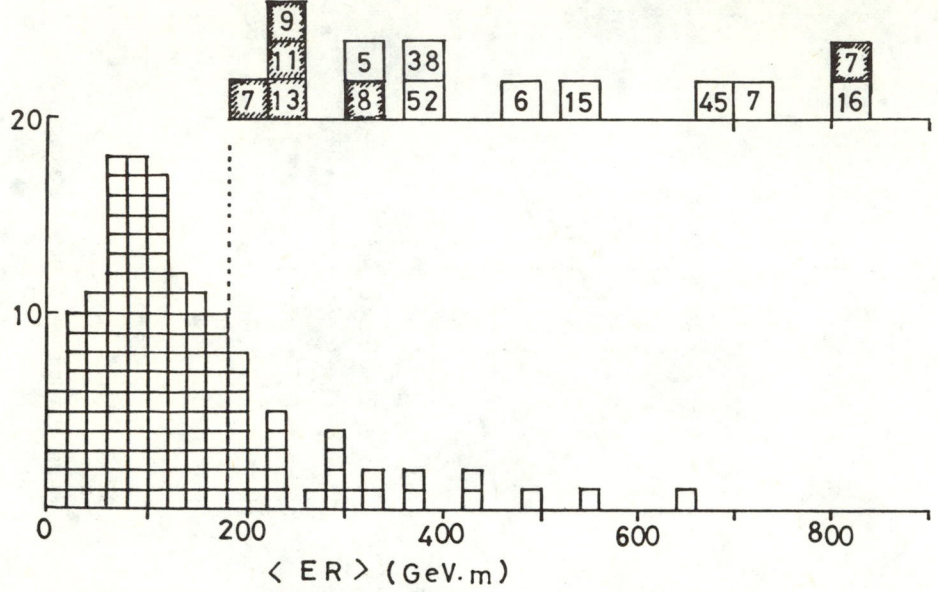

Fig.2.   Histogram of < ER > (averaged over gamma-rays) for gamma-ray families observed by Chacaltaya chamber up to No.18 for Σ E$_\gamma$ > 100 TeV.   The upper part shows histogram for < ER > (averaged over gamma-rays and hadrons) for the sampled Chiron families. Blank squares are for Σ E(γ) > 100 TeV and shaded ones for Σ E(γ)< 100 TeV.   Figures in squares express number of showers in the respective families.

3.   OBSERVATION ON CHIRON-TYPE FAMILIES.

Microscopic study on shower-core-structure.   After the naked eye scanning for dark shower spots in X-ray films, all of them are located in the attached nuclear emulsion plates and microscopic observation is made on individual showers in detail.   It is found that about a half of the shower spots are with single core structure seen in nuclear emulsion plates.   While, to our surprise, another half of the shower spots are seen with multi-core structure.   Since the lateral spread of those shower cores is extremely small, within a distance of ≃ 1 mm or less, we will call such a multiple-core shower as a "mini-cluster" of showers.

Shower transition curves and energy estimation.   For every shower cores, whether it is single or is one in a mini-cluster, the shower transition curve is constructed.   This is made by the track count-ing under the microscope over a circular area around the core center (with radius of 50 or 25 μm depending on cases) in a nuclear emul-sion plates at different depth in the chamber.   From comparison of the shower transition curve thus constructed with the calculated ones of the electron shower theory, we are able to estimate energy E of the concerned shower core, and, at the same time, the shift Δt in depth of the shower development.   The quantity Δt gives a measure on depth of the starting point of a shower in the chamber.

Classification of showers.   Showers in a family are now classified into "single-showers" and "mini-clusters".   A mini-cluster is typ-ically defined as the one which is seen as single dark spot in X-ray films but is found with close multi-core structure under the micro-scopic observation on nuclear emulsion plates.   Sometimes, we can recognize the dark spot is consisted of closely located plural shower spots as in the case of C-jet events observed in lower chamber.
        For every mini-clusters, we have informations on energy and location of their detected shower cores.
        Showers are further divided into two categories, shower-upper and shower-lower, depending whether it is observed in the upper or lower chamber.   Some showers are found both in the upper and low-er chamber penetrating through the whole.   They are assigned as shower-upper with its continuation in the lower chamber.
        Thus, finally we have four categories of showers.   They are i) single-shower-upper, ii) single-shower-lower, iii) mini-cluster-upper and iv) mini-cluster-lower.
        In Fig.3, we present map of central part of the highest energy Chiron-type family for the illustration.   In the map, showers are represented by different marks depending whether single-shower-upper (O), mini-cluster-upper (●), or shower-lower (+), with atta-ched figures showing their energy in TeV.   A broken closed curve represents a shower cluster (not mini-cluster) constructed by the computor program described in Appendix, which is formulated to pick-up the secondary atmospheric interactions of ordinary pion multiple production.

4.   NATURE OF SHOWERS OF CHIRON-FAMILIES.

        We will study specific features of showers, both single-showers and mini-clusters, of sampled Chiron families restricting their

508

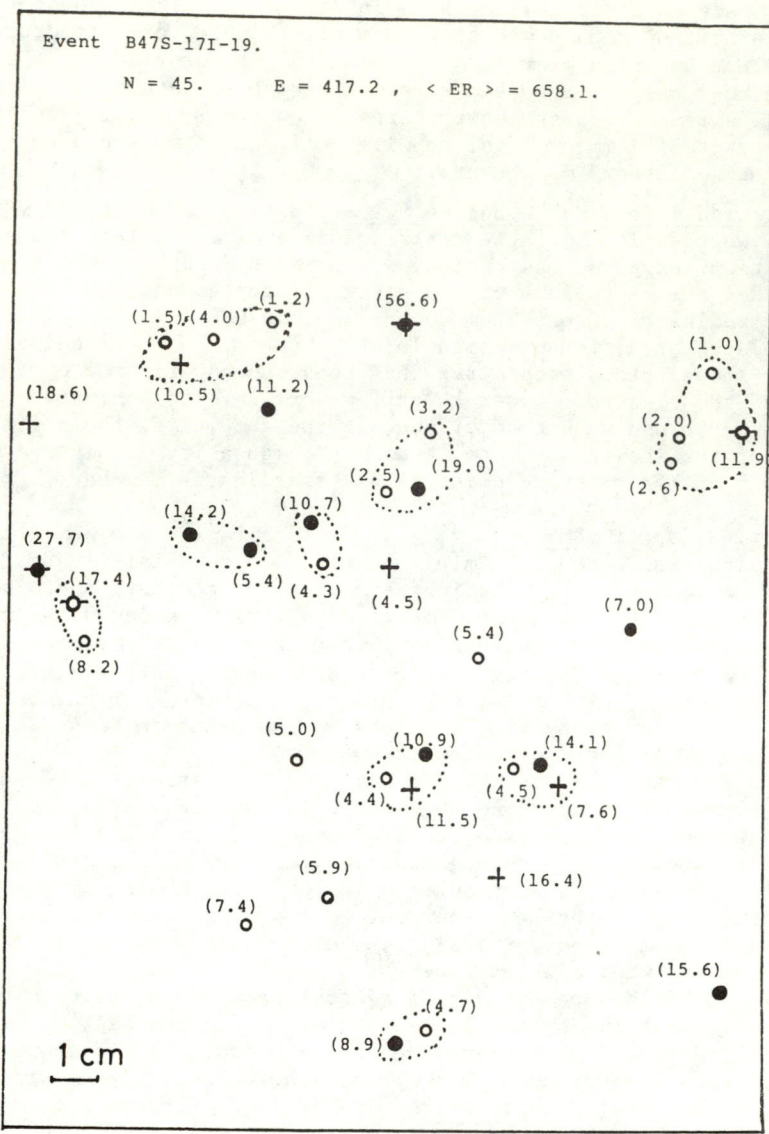

Fig.3. Map of central part of the highest energy event of the present study, Event #47S-17I. o : single-shower-upper, ● : mini-cluster upper and + : shower-lower. The attached figures in bracket are their observed energies. A dotted closed curve represents a shower cluster constructed by the computer program described in Appendix.

energy above 10 TeV.   Such restriction is imposed for the two reasons.   One is that richer and more bias-free informations can be
obtained for showers with energy far above the detection threshold,
which is about 2 TeV for X-ray film scanning and about 0.5 - 1 TeV
for the core-search with microscopic observation at the upper chamber.   The other is that higher energy showers will reflect more
faithfully characteristics of their parent interactions, and lower
energy ones are from the results of interactions of secondary or
tertiary generations in the majority.

Showers are penetrating.   One remarkable feature is that the showers in Chiron-families are far more penetrating than a pure electron
showers.   Table 2 present the percentage of cases where a shower-
upper (E ≥ 10 TeV) has its continuation into the lower chamber
which can be seen in X-ray films.   We find that the percentage
both for single-showers as well as mini-clusters is impossiblly high
for a simple gamma-ray initiating electron shower or its cluster.

Table 2.   Penetration probability of shower-upper with
            E ≥ 10 TeV.

category	No. of cases	with continuation into lower chamber	
		number	percentage
mini-cluster	36	16	44 $\pm$ 15 %
single-shower	26	18	70 $\pm$ 17 %

Penetrating character of the showers can be best seen by constructing the shower transition curve of spot darkness in X-ray films.
The darkness D in X-ray films is measured by a micro-photometer
with a square slit of 200 x 200 μm^2, and it is known that D in the
concerned range is approximately proportional to the electron track
density.   Fig. 4 presents the average shower transition curve for
the single-showers and for mini-clusters constructed by the D-measu-
rement at the shower center over the full depth of the chamber down
to the bottom of its lower part.   Since the chamber has a target
layer and a air gap between its upper and lower part, the shower
transition curves have a break at 12 cascade unit of depth.   One
sees, for both cases, their penetrating character is different from
an electron shower.   For the comparison, the transition curves
are constructed for an gamma-ray initiating electron shower through
the simulation calculation by Shibata[4], and their average behavior
is presented in Fig.4 for a case with same < D > at the upper chamber.   The threshold for recognizing a shower spot is D ∿ 0.1
in the present chamber.   Typical shower transition curves on
individual cases are presented in Fig. 5A for single showers and in
Fig.5B for mini-clusters.   One sees that shower developement is
totally different from cases of pure electron showers.   From
such penetration character, one sees that both single-showers and

510

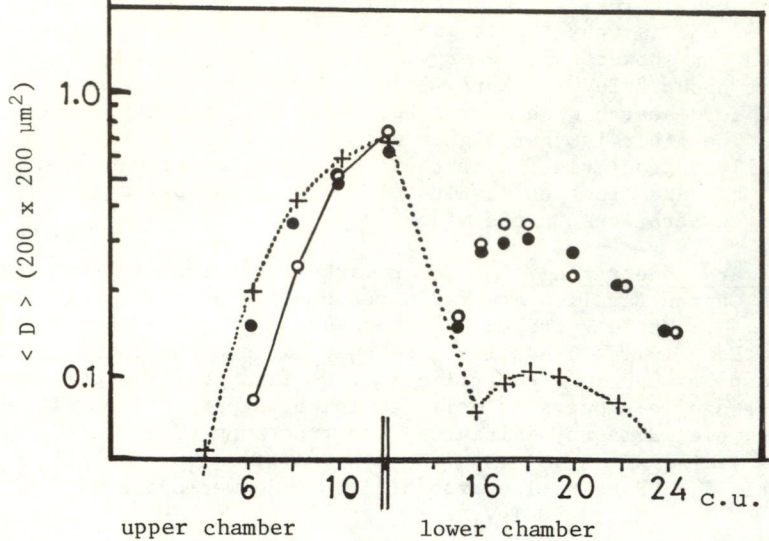

Fig. 4.   Shower transition curve constructed by photometry measurement on spot darkness D with slit 200 x 200 µm². o ; average
over single showers (E ≥ 10 TeV), • ; average over mini-clusters
(E ≥ 10 TeV) and + ; simulation calculation on averaged electron
shower initiated by gamma-rays.

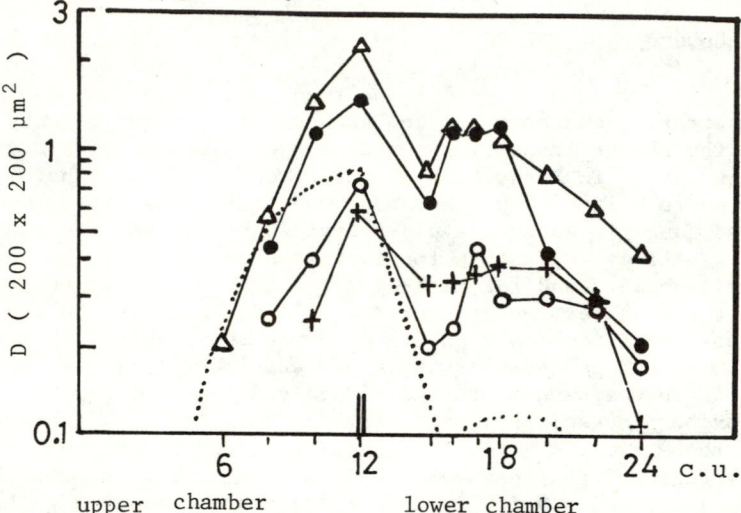

Fig. 5A.   Examples of shower transition curves of individual
cases of <u>single-showers</u>. • ; #S-1 in family #155S-136I , o ;
#S-3-3 in family #131S-109I, + ; #S-2 in family #123S-90I, △ ;
#S-1 in family #198S-154I.

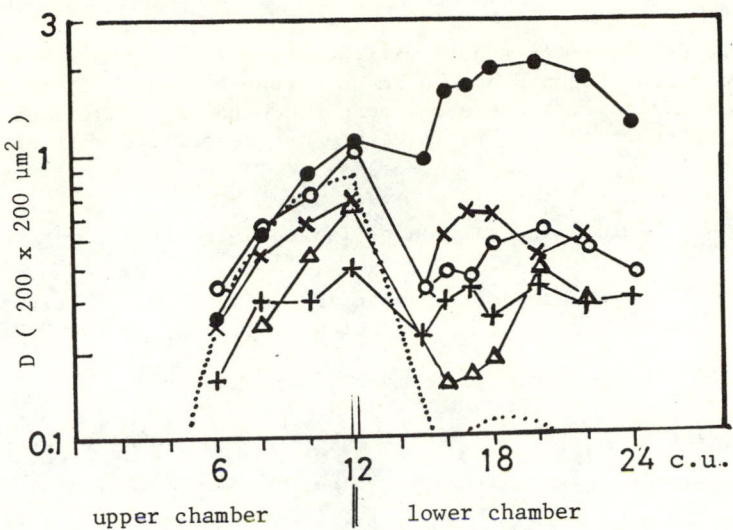

upper chamber | lower chamber

Fig. 5B. Examples of shower transition curves of individual cases for <u>mini-cluster</u>. ● ; #S-1 in family #150S-90I, ○ ; #S-1 in family #131S-109I, △ ; #S-2 in family #181S-139I, + ; #S-2 in family #131 S-109I and ✗ ; #S-10 in family #198S-154I.

the mini-clusters are, at least in their majority, can not be elect-ron showers but they must be of hadronic origin.

<u>Showers are isolated.</u>   Seeing the Chiron families in X-ray films, one imediately notices that majority of showers in the families are isolated, i.e., without being accompanied by neighbouring showers. This can be a consequence of the criteria 2) for absence of air cas-cades and 3) for wide lateral spread.

For the quantitative discussions, we construct the quantity χ_{ij} defined as $\chi_{ij} = \sqrt{E_i E_j} \cdot R_{ij}$ for a pair of showers, i-th and j-th , where E_i and E_j are respective energies of showers and R_{ij} is the mutual distance between.   The quantity χ_{ij} expresses kinematical closeness of i-th and j-th shower after energy normali-zation.

Now we define that the shower i is isolated, by the condition $(\chi_{ij})_{MIN} > K$ where j runs over all showers irrespectively of its energy except i itself in a family and K is a certain pre-fixed constsnt.   Here, we present, in Table 3, the statistics with a value K = 100 GeV.m.   Among all 72 showers with E ≥ 10 TeV, we find that 61 showers are isolated by the condition $(\chi_{ij})_{MIN} \geq$ 100 GeVm.   They are 85 ± 11 % of all.   It is seen that ma-jority of the showers are isolated, irrespectively of their category.

Such isolation character of high energy showers makes their initiating particles hard to be a gamma-rays produced through a neu-tral pion.   Gamma-rays from decay of a neutral pion will be asso-ciated with the partner at $\chi = m_\pi c^2$ H, and, since we are concerned with shower E ≥ 10 TeV, the probability of the partner gamma-ray being

512

below the detection threshold will be about 10 % or less.   Besides, the production height H has to be about one cascade unit or less ($\leq$ 600 m) of air, because the concerned showers are either single or mini-clusters and the families are not associated with air cascades.

Table 3.   Fraction of isolated showers.

upper chamber: number of isolated showers with condition (X_{ij})$_{MIN}$ > 100 GeVm.

lower chamber: number of all showers

category	single shower	mini-cluster
upper shower	21 / 26	30 / 36
lower shower	3 / 3	7 / 7

Thus it comes out, even from the isolation character alone, that majority of showers will be of hadronic character, unless we assume frequent emission of gamma-rays in nuclear interactions through some unknown processes other than two-gamma-ray-decay of neutral pions.

Mini-cluster-upper.   The most puzzling point in Chiron-type families is existence of mini-cluster-upper.   Fig.6 presents the distribution of < Er > , average energy-weighted spread of cores in a mini-cluster, r and E being distance of a core from the mini-cluster center and its energy.   The distribution drops off beyond 3 GeVm, showing that the mini-cluster can not be a result of fluctuation of wider clusters which are seen commonly in families of the ordinary type, but they themselves are representing one particular phenomena. If we would try to equate them to air cascade, then the air cascades should be very young, say starting only one cascade unit or less.   Then their isolation character rules out possibility of gamma-rays from neutral pion decay as their sources, and above all, their penetrating character remains uncompromised.   In Fig. 6, we presented penetrating mini-clusters by a different mark, and we notice their penetrating character does not depend much on the magnitude of < Er >.

Fig.7 is the histogram on number of cores, N_{core} , of mini-clusters.   The single showers are plotted as the one with N_{core} = 1. The histogram is constructed to see the possibility that mini-cluster and single shower are one and the same phenomena and their difference is whether accompanying showers are above or below the detection threshold.   From the histogram, one sees that the case is against such possibility.   Thus one may conclude that the single showers are, at least in their majority, initiated by a singly arriving particle, plausibly a secondary particles of the parent atmospheric interaction.   While the mini-clusters are a narrow bundle of particles produced by one of such secondary particles in their atmospheric passage.

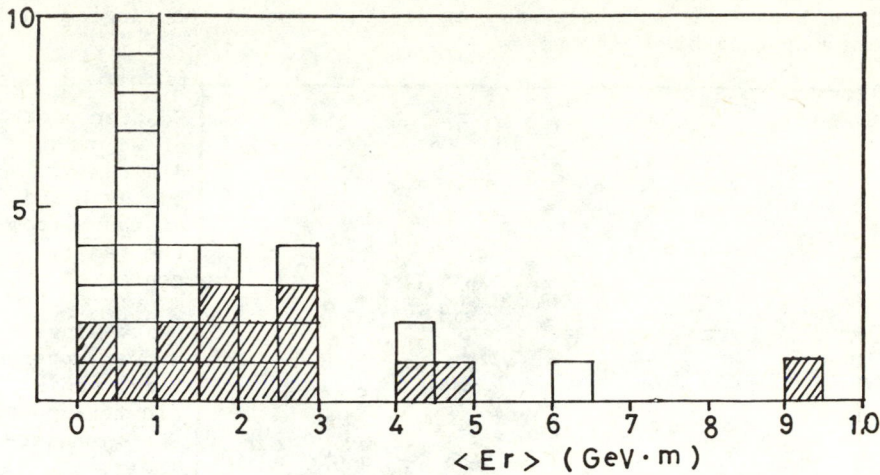

Fig.6.　Histogram of averaged energy-weighted lateral spread
< Er > of mini-cluster in upper chamber. (Σ E ≥ 10 TeV).
Shaded squares represent mini-clusters penetrating into lower chamber
while open squares are those seen only in upper chamber.

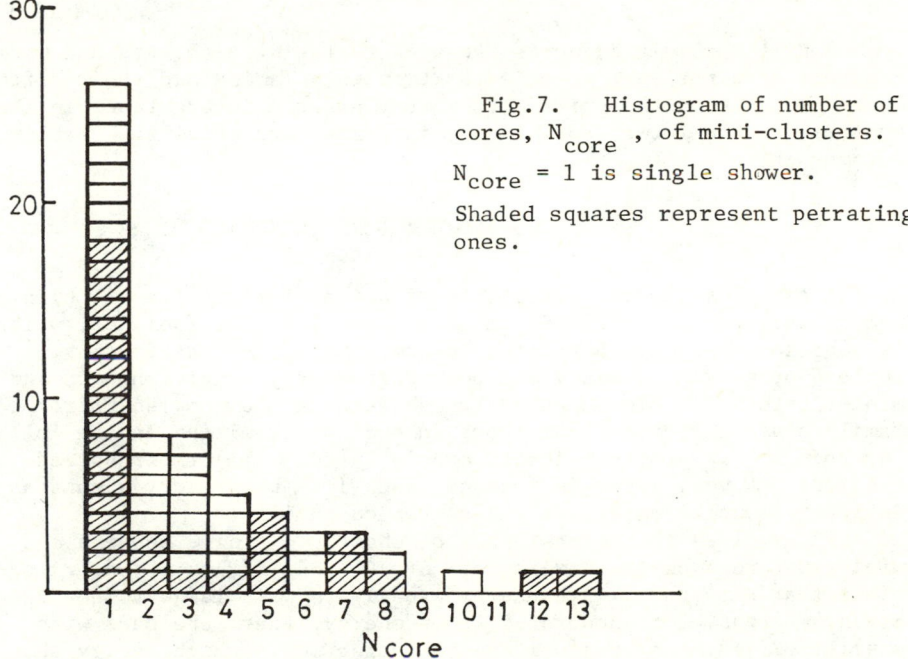

Fig.7.　Histogram of number of cores, N_{core} , of mini-clusters. N_{core} = 1 is single shower.

Shaded squares represent petrating ones.

The above view on a relation between single-showers and mini-
clusters is supported by the scatter plot in the diagram of energy E
and distance R from the family center, shown in Fig.8.　　Here, the

514

single-showers and the mini-clusters are plotted by different marks, and one sees that both have similar distribution in the diagram without any appreciable differences.

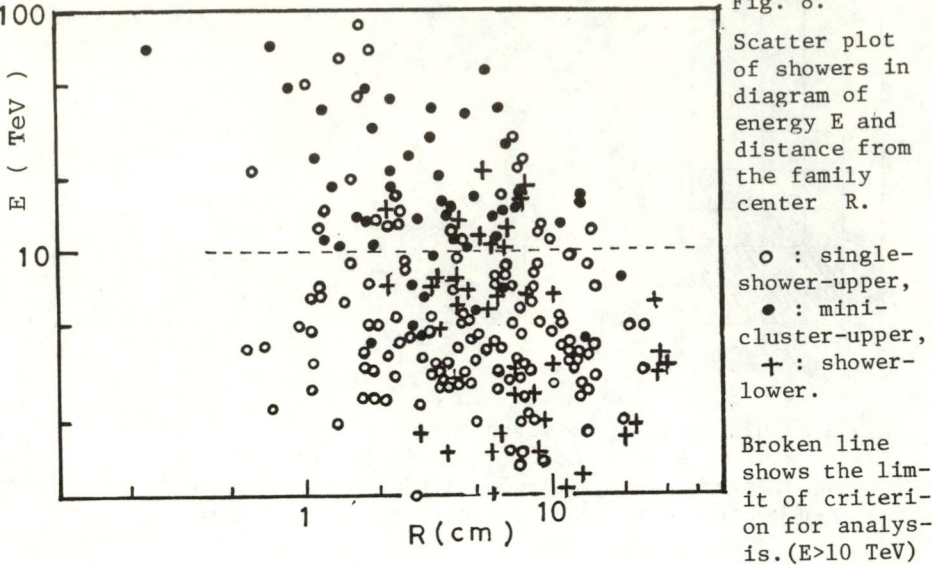

Fig. 8.

Scatter plot of showers in diagram of energy E and distance from the family center R.

o : single-shower-upper,
● : mini-cluster-upper,
+ : shower-lower.

Broken line shows the limit of criterion for analysis.(E>10 TeV)

Thus the result supports the view that single-showers and mini-clusters have the same genetic position in a family and their difference lies only on the point either they started interactions in the chamber for the former, or already in atmosphere above the chamber for the latter.

5. PARENT ATMOSPHERIC INTERACTIONS.

A clue for the reconstruction of parent interactions is high energy showers (E $\geq$ 10 TeV in this study) in the families, which is supposed to bring the direct information of the interaction. Table 4 presents a summary on those high energy single showers and mini-clusters. The high energy showers in the sampled Chiron families are different from those in ordinary families in the following points: i) their majority are isolated, ii) their spread < E(γ)R > is very large in average, and iii) they carry a substantial part of total energy of the concerned family. Fig.9 gives the scatter plot of showers (single showers and mini-clusters) on the diagram of E(γ)R and E(γ). One recognizes that showers of high energy are always with large value of E(γ)R, whereas, for showers of lower energy, there are ones with smaller E(γ)R. It justifies our selection of high energy showers for construction of the parent interactions. The lower energy ones are influenced by secondary interactions.

A possibility of the shower being gamma-rays from the ordinary type of meson production have been already made implausible from the

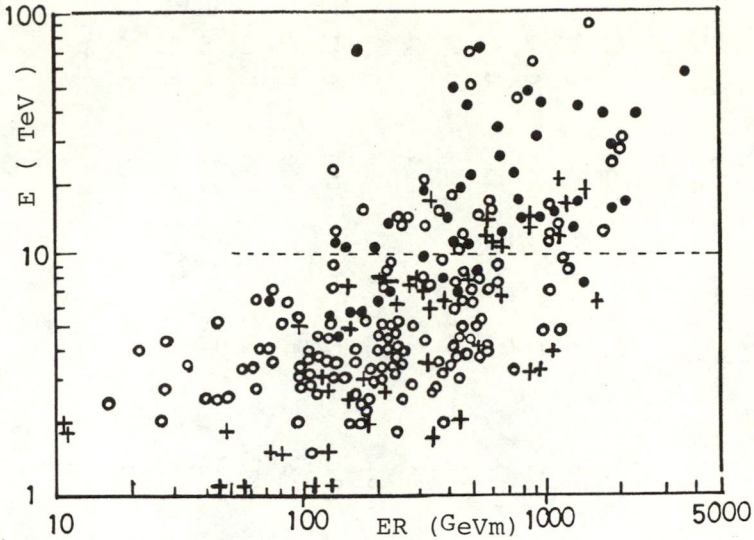

Fig.9.   Scatter plot of showers in diagram of E and ER.   The marks are the same with Fig.8.

argument on their penetration, isolation and absence of accompanied air cascades.   One can go further with use of Table 4.   If we assume $< p_t > \sim 200$ MeV/c for such gamma-rays, then the height H must be 2.5 km (4.3 cascade unit) for those with $< E_\gamma R > = 500$ GeVm, or even higher, 5 km (7.6 cascade unit) for $< E_\gamma R > = 1000$ GeVm. Such a high altitude for their parent interaction results inevitablly in presence of air cascades, and, thus, contradicts against our observation of single-showers and mini-clusters.

      We shall meet the similar contradiction when we assume they are hadrons (mainly charged pions) produced through the ordinary multiple meson productions high in the atmosphere.

      Thus, the origin of those showers in the sampled families must be looked for among new types of interactions.   We already saw that their initiating particles are hadrons, at least in the majority.   The height of production of parent interaction must be low, because their substantial part are arriving at the observational level without being lost by their secondary interactions.   Then their large lateral spread is indicating that their p_t at the point of production is far larger than common value in the ordinary pion multiple production.

<u>Interaction seen from</u> p_t.   On the basis of assumption of one major parent interaction at height H for each families, one can make the correspondence between the lateral spread and p_t of interactions.   For the parent interaction, we have $< E(\gamma)R > = $ H x $< p_t(\gamma)(parent) >$ and for the secondary interactions $< E(\gamma)r > = $ (H/2) $< p_t(\gamma)(secondary) >$.   R or r is the distance of a

Table 4. Summary of high-energy showers in Chiron-families (E > 10 TeV).

event number	energy sum (TeV)	upper single shower	mini-cluster	lower single shower	mini-cluster	energy fraction carried by high-energy showers	ratio of survived secondary hadrons to all	lateral spread ER (GeV.m)	estimated height of parent inter-action (km)
47S-17I	294	3	10	1	3	0.71	7/17	1152	0.57
75S-50I	234	3	5	-	-	0.60	3/8	647	0.32
131S-109I	150	2	3	-	-	0.48	2/5	1345	0.32
198S-154I	357	6	5	-	1	0.97	7/12	558	0.28*
193S-154I	104	3	3	-	-	0.71	3/6	1084	0.54
155S-136I	98.5	2	-	1	-	0.88	3/3	624	0.31
123S-90I	60.1	1	1	-	1	0.64	2/3	484	0.24
150S-93I	93.8	-	1	1	1	0.91	2/3	450	0.22
139S-104I	15.0	-	1	-	-	0.22	0/1	360	0.18
181S-139I	43.5	1	2	-	-	0.71	1/3	260	0.16
161S-127I	50	1	-	-	-	0.75	1/1	237	0.14
166S-127I	79	2	1	-	-	0.83	2/3	860	0.43
185S-142I	74	1	3	-	-	0.88	1/4	312	0.16
126S-105I	107	1	3	0	1	0.87	2/5	834	0.42

* the triangulation measurement gives H = 330 $\pm$ 30 m.

shower core measured to the family center or to the center of the shower cluster which comes from one of its secondary interactions. If there is just one type of interactions with common value of $p_t(\gamma)$, both $< E(\gamma)R >$ and $< E(\gamma)r >$ will be of the same order of magnitude, and clusters from the secondary interactions will be generally hard to be recognized by this reason. Only in rare case of a secondary interaction happening much nearer to the chamber than their average height , H/2 , we will observe the corresponding shower cluster in a family.

The case of our Chiron families is different. We have mini-clusters which have remarkably smaller lateral spread of shower cores, $< E(\gamma)r >$, compared to $< E(\gamma)R >$. Fig.10 demonstrates $< E(\gamma)R >$ and an average of $< E(\gamma)r >$ of mini-clusters, $<< E(\gamma)r >>$, for each sampled families. From the figure, we estimated as $< E(\gamma)R > / << E(\gamma)r >>_{mini-cluster} \sim 300$, which gives the ratio of p_t as $< p_t(parent) > / < p_t(mini-cluster) > \sim 150$. This is a surprising large ratio, telling that the parent interaction has extra ordinarily large p_t or the mini-cluster has very small p_t, or both. If we assume the parent interaction be Chiron-type with $< p_t(\gamma) > \simeq$ 2 – 3 GeV/c, then we have $< p_t(\gamma)(mini-cluster)> \simeq 10 - 20$ MeV/c.

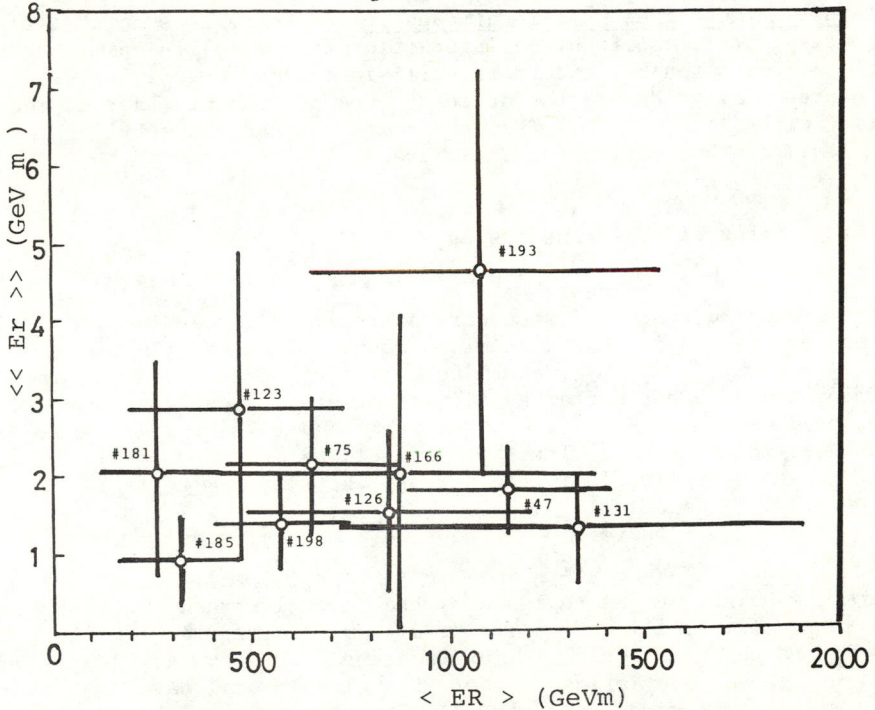

Fig.10. Relation between average of energy weighted size of cluster in a family, $<< Er >>$, and the average energy weighted spread of the family $< ER >$ with showers of E > 10 TeV for Chiron families.

The both are with p_t far different from that of common type of nuclear interactions.   One can compare them with $< p_t(\gamma)(\pi) > = k_\gamma$ x $< p_t(\pi) > \sim 120$ MeV/c, or $< p_t(\gamma) > \sim 200$ MeV/c for the ordinary pion multiple production.   Even exotic Centauro and Mini-Centauro interactions have $< p_t(\gamma) > \sim 350$ MeV/c.

One may then ask whether the concerned Chiron families have any trace of ordinary type of interactions.   Here, we remind that we have not yet been concerned with low energy showers below 10 TeV. It is found that most of those low energy showers have χ_{ij} of the order of magnitude of few tens of GeVm.   These are what we expect as the product of secondary interactions with common value of p_t. Thus we conclude that the particles produced in Chiron parent inter-action make secondary interactions of very small p_t resulting in mini-clusters, as well as interactions of known type with p_t of a few hundred MeV/c, or both at the same time.   In the appendix, we pre-sent the cluster analysis performed with computor, which gives number of such clusters comparable to that of mini-clusters.   The fract-ion of energies contained in high energy showers give another estima-tion on the frequency of such ordinary secondary interactions.   From both estimations, we concluded that the frequency for mini-clusters and for ordinary clusters are approximately equal.

<u>Interaction mean free path in atmosphere.</u>   Let us assume that the secondary particles of Chiron interaction have a collision mean free path λ in atmosphere, and their collision produces a mini-cluster with probability P and the ordinary type of multiple hadron prod-uction with $(1 - P)$.   Then the number of hadrons surviving at the level of observation is, on an average,

$$N_{hadron} = N_o \exp (- H / \lambda),$$

and the number of mini-clusters as

$$N_{mini-cluster} = P N_o (1 - \exp (- H / \lambda)),$$

where N_o is the number of secondary particles at production.   Thus we may expect the following relation among the observable quantities, N_{hadron} and $N_{mini-cluster}$, assuming that all hadrons arriving at the chamber are observed either as single-showers in upper or lower cham-ber, or mini-cluster-lower.   The loss of detection will be discus-sed later in connection with the interactions in the chamber and it will be shown neglisible in the present experiment.   It is

$$P N_{hadron} / (P N_{hadron} + N_{mini-cluster})$$

$$= \exp (- < E(\gamma)R > / \lambda < p_t(\gamma) >),$$

where the height H is replaced by the lateral spread $< E(\gamma)R >$ for the respective families.   The result are plotted in Fig. 11 with assumed values of P, which is inferred from the above argument around 0.5.   Though statistics is poor, the experimental data are consis-tent with the expected relation.   The average over the sample fam-ilies give $\lambda = 1200$ GeVm/ $< p_t(\gamma) >$ for P = 1, and = 800 GeVm/ $< p_t(\gamma) >$ for P = 0.5.   If we put our Chiron value, $< p_t(\gamma) > = 2$ GeV/c, we obtain $\lambda = 600$ m for P = 1 and $\lambda = 400$ m for P = 0.5 The value is about 0.5 or 0.3 times the geometrical collision mean free path, λ_{geo} = 1200 m, respectively. The corresponding cross-section turns out to be about two-times or three-times of the geometrical nuclear cross section, corresponding to the case of P = 1 or P = 0.5. The former gives the minimum value for the atmospheric interactions and the latter is the most likely value.

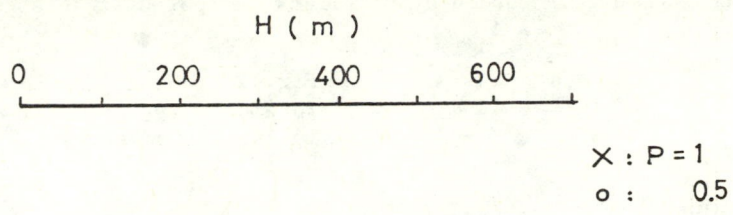

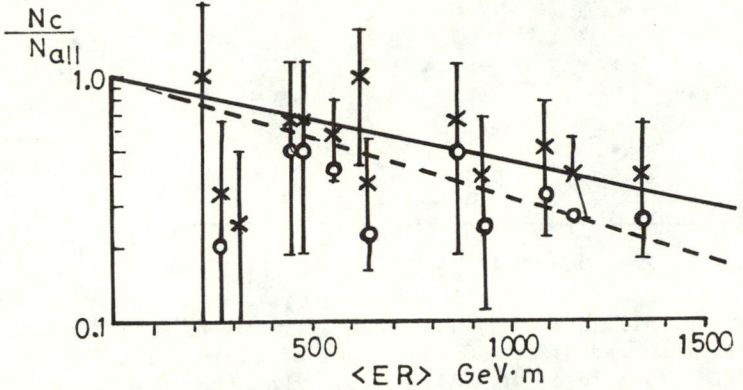

Fig.11. Relation between fraction of hadrons arriving at the chamber, N_c / N_{all}, and energy-weighted lateral spread < ER > for Chiron families.

From the following discussions on interactions in the chamber, we will find that the set $< p_t(\gamma) > \simeq 2$ GeV/c and $\lambda \simeq (1/3)\lambda_{geo}$ is the most likely case.

6. INTERACTIONS IN CHAMBER.

The observation of interactions in the chamber itself will be valuable in confirming the above result in the atmosphere, though it has poor statistics than one on atmospheric interactions.

Mini-cluster in lower chamber. In the routin work with the emulsion chamber of two-storey structure at Chacaltaya, a mini-cluster of showers in the lower chamber is identified as gamma-ray bundle produced at the nuclear interaction in the target layer, called C-jet. Some of mini-clusters in the present families can be such C-jets of common type, but all may not be. Fig.14 presents the distribution of their lateral spread, <. Er >. Here one sees that the mini-clusters in lower chamber have smaller < Er > than those in upper chamber as presented in Fig.5, except one event. This exceptional

520

one cluster is a pair of shower cores with distance of $\simeq$ 2.5 mm between, and the application of the triangulation measurement shows that the pair is originating not from the target layer but above in the atmosphere. Thus, this particular one is essentially the same phenomena as the mini-cluster in the upper chamber, meaning an arrival at the chamber of bundle of paticless, composed at least two hadrons.

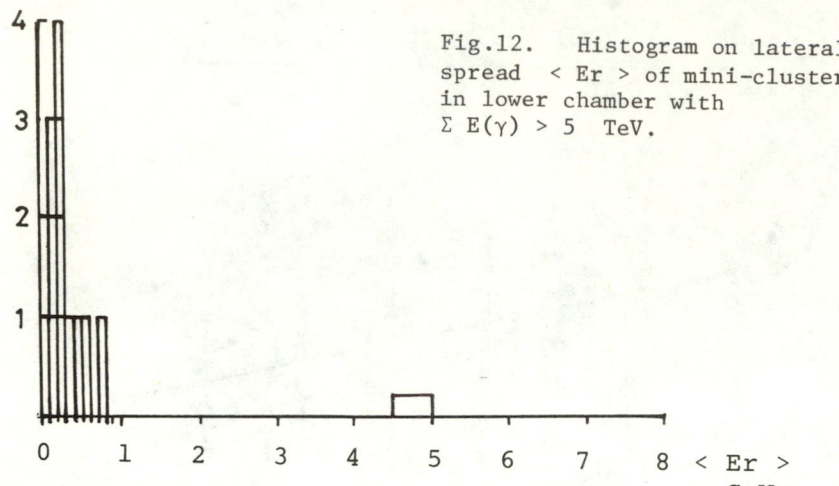

Fig.12. Histogram on lateral spread < Er > of mini-cluster in lower chamber with $\Sigma E(\gamma) > 5$ TeV.

The majority, all except the one above, are with < Er > $\lesssim$ 0.7 GeVm, the lateral spread different from that of mini-cluster in the upper chamber. Therefore, we may conclude that they are initiated by a bundle of particles not arriving at the chamber from outside, but produced in the chamber, the target layer or the upper chamber. Dividing the lateral spread < Er > by the height of air gap above the lower chamber, 170 cm, we are able to obtain < $p_t(\gamma)$ > at the production. Their values are with the average of < $p_t(\gamma)$ > being 0.15 GeV/c , corresponding to the average of < Er > being $\sim$0.25 GeVm. This value is not much different from the C-jets of ordinary type.

The atmospheric phenomena corresponding to the above target interaction with $p_t(\gamma) \sim 0.15$ GeV/c will be observed as a cluster of showers with the lateral spread about ten times larger than that of mini-clusters in the upper chamber, with expected spread of < Er > = 10 $\sim$ 50 GeVm. As was described, it is a cluster which we constructed from the lower energy showers (E < 10 TeV) in the families.

Search for equivalence to mini-clusters in upper chamber. Now, one may ask whether we can find the production, in the chamber, of the phenomena equivalent to the mini-clusters observed in the upper chamber. If such particle production of very collimated bundle with < $p_t(\gamma)$ > as small as 10 - 20 MeV/c occurs at the target layer, we will observe in the lower chamber a narrowly collimated shower cluster with lateral spread of about < Er > = 0.01 - 0.02 GeVm. For a typical case of shower core with E $\simeq$ 5 TeV, for example, the lateral spread will be only 2 - 4 μm. Such closely spaced cores will be hard to be recognized, unless every shower cores keep good

collimated figures throughout succession of plural sensitive layers.
Thus, most of cases will be claasified into the category of"single-
shower-lower".   Thus, we have, at this moment, neither positive
nor negative answer from the observation.

Mean free path in the chamber.   One can estimate the mean free
path of collisions in the chamber through the relative frequencies
of i) single-shower-upper, ii) C-jets (target events observed in
lower chamber), and iii) single-shower-lower.   Table 5 gives
their frequencies with E ≥ 10 TeV.   For the C-jets, we take all
the mini-clusters in the lower chamber except the one which we know
already as an atmospheric origin.   The table give thickness of
the three parts of the chamber, too, for reference.

Table 5.   Showers in the three parts of the chamber.

part of chamber	upper chamber	target layer	lower chamber
thickness	12 rad unit of lead	23 cm pitch 5 cm wood	12 rad unit of lead
thickness in λ_{geo}	0.35	0.47	0.35
shower category	single-shower upper	mini-cluster lower	single-shower lower
observed no. (E ≥ 10 TeV)	26	7	3

    As is seen from the table, the frequency of showers diminishes
rapidly as the location goes deeper in the chamber, and it shows that
the shower-initiating particles have short mean free path compared to
the full length of the chamber.   It allows, as the first approximation, to take the number of arriving particles at the chamber equal
to the total observed number of showers, N_0 = 36.   Then the collision mean free path can be estimated from the fraction which is observed as "single-shower-upper" as

        fraction of single-shower-upper (26/36)
        = 1 - exp (- t_{upper} / λ)

where t_{upper} is the effective thickness of the upper chamber for producing the shower as single-shower-upper. λ is required
mean free path of the collision of the concerned particles.   For
t_{upper}, we cannot take the full thickness of the upper chamber, because, if the collision happens near the bottom, we will miss the
event in the upper chamber due to immature shower developement and
the event will be classified either as single shower-lower or mini-
cluster-lower depending the type of its interaction.   A plausible
guess will be that t_{upper} will be two to four cascade unit less than
the full thickness, so that we will assume as t_{upper} = 9 c.u. of

522

lead.   Then the collision mean free path turns out to be as $\lambda =$ 7 cascade unit of lead, which is about 1/5 of λ_{geo} , the geometrical nuclear mean free path.   This is a surprisingly small value.

Fig.13 presents the comparison with Centauro case on the depth distribution of location of showers in the chamber.   In this figure, all the single-shower-lower are assumed to locate in the lower chamber.   One immediately sees a large difference in collision mean free path.   The Centauro case has the distribution consistent with the geometrical value, λ_{geo} , as is demonstrated by a broken line.

Fig.14 gives the depth distribution for the event #198S-154I, for which the application of the triangulation method is possible, giving the production height as $H = 330 \pm 30$ m.   Thus, for this particular event, we are able to construct the distribution including the atmospheric part, as shown in Fig.16.   The over-all distribution are seen consistent with $\lambda \sim 0.3 \lambda_{geo}$, but not λ_{geo} itself.

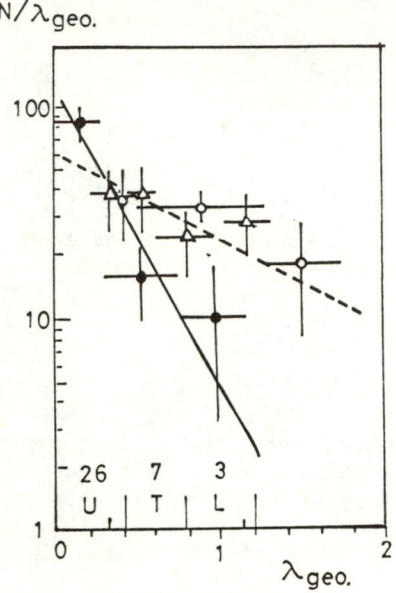
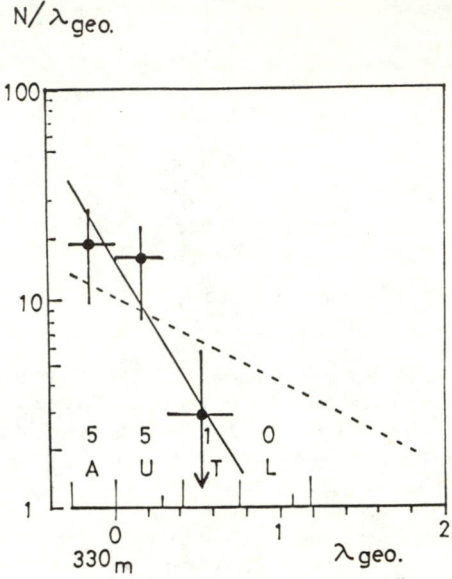

Fig.13.   Depth distribution of showerproduction in the chamber, in unit of geometrical mean free path.   ● : Chiron families, ○ : Centauro I, ▲ : Centauro II. U, T and L express upper chamber, target layer and lower chamber, and attached figures give number of observed event in the respective parts.   Full line for attenuation with $\lambda = 0.3 \lambda_{geo}$, and broken line with $\lambda = \lambda_{geo}$.

Fig.14.   Depth distribution of secondary interactions in event #198S-154I ($H = 330$ 30 m from the triangulation measurement). A for atmosphere.   Other figures are the same with Fig.13.

There is one remark on a possible mixture of gamma-rays in the

concerned secondary particles, which will make shorter the apparent
mean free path for shower production .   If we assume, as an extreme case, a half of them are hadronic particles of Chiron interaction
but another half are electro-magnetic contamination, then we will get
$\lambda \simeq 11$ cascade unit of lead, which is about 1/3 of λ_{geo}.   It is
still significantly smaller than the geometrical value.   In conclusion, we find in both atmosphere as well as lead of the chambers,
the mean free path of the concerned particles is significantly smaller than the geometrical value which is seen for common hadrons.

7.   DISCUSSIONS AND CONCLUSIONS.

Essential conclusions of the Chiron family study are on the following points:
1)   At the parent Chiron interaction, the produced particles are
      mostly of hadronic nature with poor accompaniement of gamm-
      rays.
2)   Their p_t is large, i.e., $< p_t (\gamma) > = 2 - 3$ GeV/c.
3)   Their collision mean free path is small, i.e., 1/3 to 1/5
      times of the geometrical value.
4)   At the secondary collisions, emission of collimated bundle of
      particles (mini-clusters) with small p_t ($< p_t (\gamma) > = 10 -$
      20 MeV/c) is frequently observed.
These characteristics show very exotic nature of the parent
Chiron interaction as well as its produced secondary particles.

Because of inherent drawback in the family study technique, one
may suspect ambiguities in arriving at those conclusions.   Since
the atmospheric processes of cosmic-rays, during their passage from
the top of atmosphere down to the level of Chacaltaya, are extremely
complicated, one may imagine that anything can happen in the individual family phenomena through their fluctuation.   One thus has to
examine stability of the parent family interpretation, that is, how
far the interpretation can vary with assumptions made either explicitly or implicitly in the present analysis.
One important factor of the family interpretation is estimation
on the height of parent interaction, H.   In the present study,
the estimation on H for the sampled events was made with reference
to the two Chiron events, H of which were obtained by the triangulation method.   If the present value of H would be underestimated,
the true value of p_t would be smaller and the mean free path λ would
be larger than the claimed values above, approaching towards the
known common values.   Here, we remind that we assumed one value
of H for each families as the effective height of production for particles in the family and the value of H turns out to be a few hundred
meters for all the sampled families.   Therefore, to be consistent
with the common value of $p_t (\gamma) \sim 200$ MeV/c, for example, one would
have to increase the effective height as much as ten times, up to a
few km.   It is simply impossible for hadrons of known types.
There are hadrons produced up in high atmosphere, but those hadrons

will have small chance to arrive at without secondary interactions. It means, irrespectively of atmospheric history of families, observed hadrons at the chamber will have effective height of their production always near one collision mean free path, i.e., about 1.2 km of air at Chacaltaya for the common type.

Considering absence of air cascade, together, a remaining possibility for the high-altitude-origin hypothesis will be to assume the multiple production of particles which are far more penetrating than the common hadrons, with the collision mean free path of $\gtrsim 3\lambda_{geo}$. Then the mini-cluster would be with p_t as small as $1 - 2$ MeV/c at the production and the tertiary particles in the mini-cluster would have to be, again, as penetrating as above. Those guess from the atmospheric behaviour under the large production height hypothesis would certainly contradicts what we observed on shower production in the chamber itself.

More plausible case would be that the height H is under estimated only by a factor of two to three, and then the collision mean free path in air arrives near the normal value λ_{geo}. Then, absence of air cascades becomes stringent and the interaction has to be of Centauro or Mini-Centauro type. Yet, the average p_t is, under this assumption, appreciably greater than the case of Centauro or Mini-Centauro. Thus the families are compelling us to introduce a new type of particle production, yet we have no reason to claim the events are different from the two with the triangulation measurement. Besides, the mean free path observed in the chamber remains appreciably shorter than the geometrical value.

When we accept estimation on H in the present study, then comes the question of composition of particles produced in the Chiron interaction, i.e., the ratio of hadrons to gamma-rays. If the height H is as small as a few hundred meter, about one radiation unit of air, gamma-rays will arrive at partly without materialization and partly turning into young air cascades, which could be similar to our mini-clusters in the lateral spread. Thus we may accept admixture of gamma-rays among produced particles up to a half, to be consistent with the penetrating power observed in the chamber. This is a possibility which we discussed in the previous paragraph. Yet the question remains how such gamma-rays with large $p_t \sim 2$ GeV/c are produced so frequently in the interaction.

From the above considerations, we see that the conclusions derived by the present study are stable. Accepting such conclusions from the experiment, we have to look for an interpretation within a framework of the present physics.

We proposed, in the paper on the first example of Chiron family, that the produced hadrons in Chiron interactions will be heavy, semi-stable hadron with rest energy of ~ 10 GeV, and suggested a new name "B-particle" for them[1].

The argument was made with a thermodynamical model, where the Chiron fire-ball is assumed to evaporate the B-particles. An analogous argument with the thermodynamics suggests that p_t of secondary hadrons represents the temperature of a fire-ball at the moment of their evaporation, so that the temperature kT is expected to be about 10 GeV from the experimental value of p_t.   Since the available energy of the system,i.e., a fire-ball, will be shared equally among every degrees of freedom, we may expect that the kinetic energy and the energy in a form of particle mass will be of the same order of magnitude.   Thus, we infer that the B-particles will be a hadron with rest energy comparable to the temperature of Chiron fireball, $\sim$ 10 GeV.

The proposed B-particle will be very exotic existence in the particle family of hadrons.   Since it can travel over distance of a few hundred meters without disintegration, the life-time, if it is unstable, will be more than 10^{-9} sec.   It is a very large lower limit to the life, considering its large available enrgy at decay and its possible various decay modes of multi-hadron emission.   Thus we may regard it as a quasi-stable particle with large mass, and, by this reason, we pointed out a possibility that it is connected to the sub-hadronic constituents.   In fact, a large rest energy, or large p_t at the moment of its production shows that it must be a particle of very small dimensions, say $r_B = h/m_B c$, about 1/30 of the pion compton wave length.

What we found here on B-particles through their interactions are quite different.   First, they have a small collision mean free path, about 1/3 or 1/5 the geometrical value.   Remembering that the geometrical value is deduced from the size of target nuclei, we may think such a small collision mean free path, or a large cross section, is originating not from a target nucleus but from size of projectile. Thus, the B-particles appear to have dimensions as large as the target nucleus or more.

Emission of mini-clusters at their collisions is another piece of evidence for their large size.   The magnitude of $p_t(\gamma)$ within the mini-cluster, which is of the order of ten to twenty MeV/c, shows that the emission of mini-cluster is not a pion multiple production, because it is less than pion compton wave length.   It is analogous to a break-up of cosmic-ray of heavy primary nuclei, which we can observe at the upper atmosphere.   Thus, we may understand that B-particles are of large size ($r_B \sim h/p_t$ (mini-cluster)) and their break-up is the observed mini-clusters.

It is reminded that the secondary hadrons from Geminion interactions are common in the large p_t with those of Chiron interactions, and they are assumed, too, as the same B-particle.   One of the best Geminion event, #70S-58I, is with known height of interaction, H = 50 $\pm$ 20 m, from the triangulation method, and its detail is described in [1].   We found the two secondary hadrons are producing mini-clusters, properties of which are the same as mini-clusters in Chiron families here.

Thus, we are facing two opposite aspects of B-particles; they are small at their birth in Chiron interaction, but become large in size at their secondary interactions after the atmospheric passage. To make a compromise, we have to think that B-particles appear to swell up in size immediately after the birth.

We do not know how B-particles with such exotic properties can be accomodated within the framework of the present particle models. Yet, we believe more experimental information will be urgently necessitated before extending the speculations.

Acknowledgement.   The collaboration experiment is financially supported in part by Conselho Nacional para o Desemvplvimento Cientifico e Tecnologico, Fundacao de Amparo a Pesquisa do Estado de Sao Paulo, in Brasil, and Institute for Cosmic-ray Research, University of Tokyo, and Grant-in-Aid from the Ministry of Education, in Japan.

APPENDIX

CLUSTER ANALYSIS FOR RECONSTRUCTION OF ATMOSPHERIC INTERACTIONS.

This is an application of the general method of clustering showers developed by Semba for analysis of gamma-ray families [5]. The procedure goes in the following way.

i)   Take a family and make a list of showers(single-showers and mini-clusters) on their number i, energy E_i, and position $\vec{R}_i$, with order of increasing energy , i.e., $E_1 \leq E_2 \leq \ldots \leq E_n$.

ii)   Take i-th shower, make a pair with j-th shower (j = i+1,.. ...., n), and construct the quantity K_{ij} defined as,

$$K_{ij} = \sqrt{E_i E_j} \; |\vec{R}_i - \vec{R}_j| / (E_i + E_j).$$

iii)   Take the smallest K_{ij} among the constructed ones (j = i+1, ..., n), and make comparison with the constant K.   If $Min(K_{ij})$ > K, then we conclude that i-th shower does not form a cluster with any of j-th shower.   If $Min(K_{ij})$ < K, then we conclude that i-th shower and j-th, which makes the minimum of K_{ij}, belong to the same cluster, delete i-th shower from the list, amalgamate i-th shower into j-th shower, replacing the j-th quantities in the list as,

$$E_i + E_j \rightarrow E_j \; ,$$
$$(E_i\vec{R}_i + E_j\vec{R}_j) / (E_i + E_j) \rightarrow \vec{R}_j.$$

v)   Repeat the procedure ii) and iii) starting from i = 1 till i = n - 1.   At the end, the list of showers will be turned into the list of shower clusters with their energy and their position of the energy center.

The constant K in the criterion can be fixed depending for the purpose of analysis.   In the present case, we fixed K as

$$K = < ER > / 20,$$

where the average is taken over showers with E > 10 TeV in the concerned family.   Since those high energy showers are assumed as the direct product of the parent Chiron interaction, we have < ER > = < p_t(Chiron) > H, H being the height of production.   The shower clusters from the secondary interactions of the ordinary multiple particle production will have the spread, in their avrage, of << Er >> = < p_t(ordinary) > (H/2).   Assuming the ratio of P_t between Chiron case and ordinary case to be about 10, we fix the K value as above.

Fig.15 presents the distribution of < Er > of shower clusters constructed in such way. The < Er > distribution of mini-clusters is presented together. Seeing a difference between the two distributions, one may conclude that the clusters of the two kinds are different phenomena. The computer-constructed clusters are presented in the map of the event #47S-17I in Fig.3, by dotted closed line. Their number is found about the same as that of mini-cluster through all sampled families.

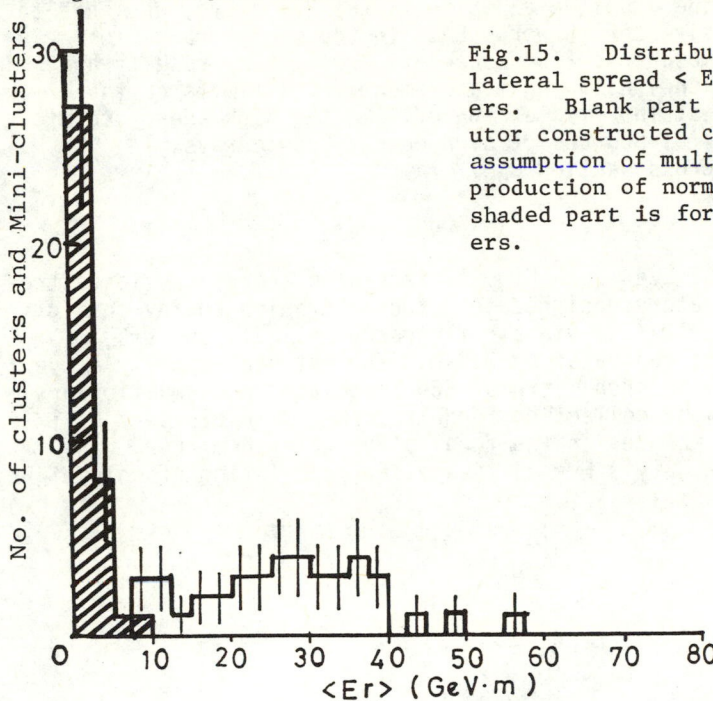

Fig.15. Distribution of lateral spread < Er > of clusters. Blank part is for computor constructed clusters with assumption of multiple pion production of normal type, and shaded part is for mini-clusters.

References.

1) Brasil-Japan Emulsion Chamber Collaboration ;
   to be published in Suppl. Prog.Theor.Phys. as accompanying paper.
   A part was presented at 17th Intn. Cosmic-Ray Conf.(Paris),1981.
   HE-3-2-28, HE-5-1-14.

2) For Centauro and Mini-Centauro, see, Brasil-Japan Emulsion
   Chamber Collaboration; AIP Conf. Proceedings, No.49(1979)317.

3) For Geminion, see, Brasil-Japan Emulsion Chamber Collaboration,
   AIP Conf. Proceedings, No.49(1979)145,

4) T.Shibata ; to be published in Suppl.Prog.Theor.Phys.

5) H.Semba; to be published in Suppl.Prog.Theor.Phys.

PRELIMINARY FLY'S EYE RESULTS

G. L. Cassiday, R. Cady, J.Elbert, E. Loh, M. Salamon,
P. Sokolsky, D. Steck, M. Ye
University of Utah, Salt Lake City, UT 84106

ABSTRACT

We describe a unique experiment, the Fly's Eye, designed to measure extensive air showers (EAS) in the energy range 10^{17} - 10^{21}eV via atmospheric fluorescence. Preliminary results are presented for the following measurements: (1) limits on the extragalactic neutrino flux at 10^{20}eV, (2) the high energy cosmic ray spectrum, (3) Sources of high energy cosmic rays, (4) the total proton cross section σ_{pp}.

INTRODUCTION

The "Fly's Eye" (see Fig. 1) is a high energy physics/astrophysics observatory designed to detect ultrahigh energy cosmic rays (UHCR; $E \gtrsim 10^{17}$eV) via air fluorescence. It consists of two stations separated by 3.3Km. The 1st station (Fly'e Eye I) consists of 67 62-inch mirrors, 880 associated photomultipliers and Winston light collecting funnels arranged in clusters of 12 or 14 tubes each mounted in the focal plane of each mirror. The second station, Fly's Eye II is smaller, consisting of only eight mirrors and associated PMT clusters. Fly's Eye I is designed to image the entire night sky (2π steradians) and thus to detect the passage of EAS thru the atmosphere generated by an incoming UHCR cosmic ray primary. (See Fig. 1)

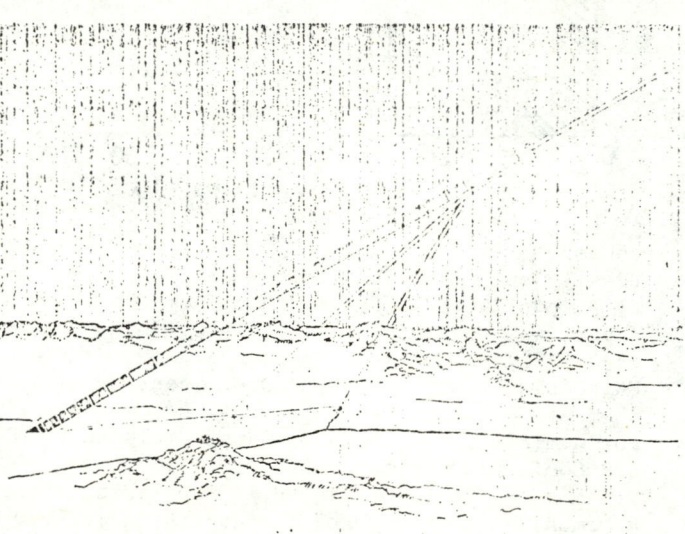

Fig. 1. Schematic of Fly's Eye. Incoming cosmic ray generates EAS viewed optically by two arrays of mirrors and PMT's.

Even though the atmosphere is a poor scintillator ($\lesssim$ 0.1% efficiency; see Fig. 2 and 3), the overwhelming amount of energy being liberated by the large number of charged particles in an EAS ($n \sim 10^7$-10^{12}) makes it possible to optically detect cosmic rays with energies exceeding 10^{20}eV out to distances on the order of 20Km or so. In fact, the situation is not unlike that of a blue (actually near UV) 5-watt light bulb travelling through the sky at the speed of light.

Experimental efforts to be carried out with this novel detector include the following measurements:
(1) σ_{pp}
(2) Secondary multiplicity growth.
(3) Search for rare but potentially exciting events, i.e., "Centauros".
(4) Detect or place spectrum limits on the extra -galactic neutrino flux.
(5) Composition of cosmic ray primaries.
(6) Cosmic ray spectrum.
(7) Cosmic ray anisotropies.
(8) Search for high energy UHCR spectrum cut-off.[1]

The physics listed above constitute a unique blend of high energy particle physics and astrophysics. No previous experimental program initiated to investigate the behavior of UHCR has completely succeeded in disentangling the effects of particle

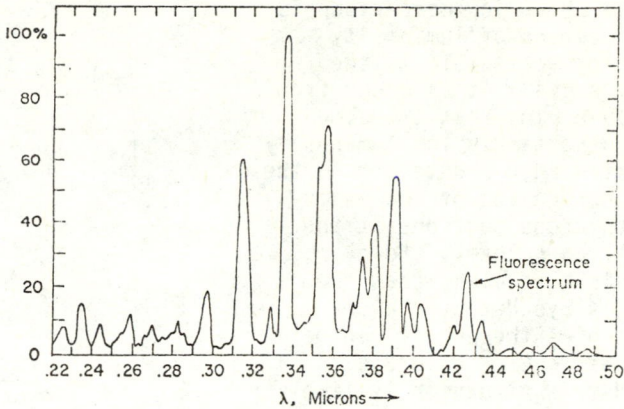

Fig. 2 Atmospheric fluorescence

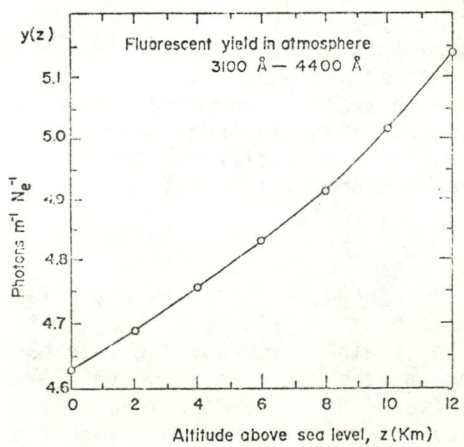

Fig. 3. Photon yield/m/electron vs. atmospheric altitude

530

physics (i.e., cross section & multiplicity) from those of astrophysics (composition). This situation arises from the hitherto unsolved difficulty of obtaining both good count rate and resolution. The Fly's Eye detector represents a unique attempt to overcome this limitation in the UHCR regime.

Indeed, the count rate problem for UHCR is hard to beat. Shown in Fig. 4 is a luminosity vs. energy diagram for a large number of existing or proposed accelerators. Also shown for comparison is the region of luminosity-- energy accessible to the Fly's Eye. It is clear from such a plot that the almost embarrassingly low luminosity limits such a detector to the interrogation of processes with cross sections at the millibarn level. However, it is also clear that the Fly's Eye detector alone occupies the energy regime 10^4GeV < $S^{1/2}$ < 10^6GeV and this situation is likely to persist for a long time to come. Moreover, one can counteract, somewhat, the low Fly's Eye luminosity by spending a long time taking data in order to obtain reasonably accurate cross- sectional/multiplicity measurements. Such rewards come "free" since one is forced to spend a long time observing anyway in order to accomplish the specified high energy astrophysics goals.

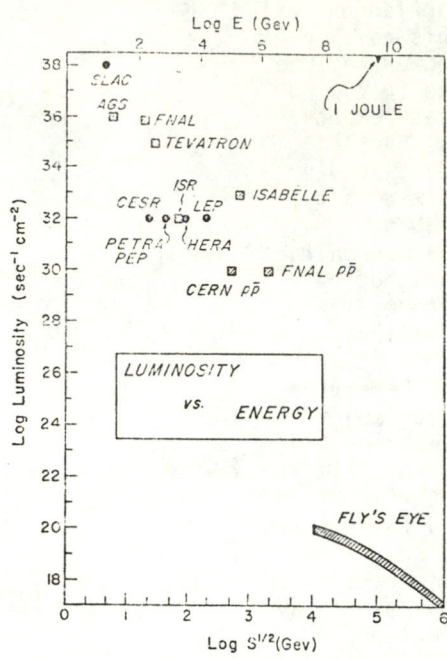

Fig. 4 Luminosity vs Energy

EVENT RECONSTRUCTION & SHOWER SIZE ANALYSIS.

Shown in Fig. 5 is a schematic of the geometry of an EAS as seen by the Fly's Eye. The location of the EAS track in space can be obtained by measuring four parameters: two parameters determine the plane in which the EAS lies while two additional parameters (R_p - the impact parameter and ϕ - the ground impact angle) determine the orientation of the track in that plane. The plane can be obtained purely from the geometry of hit PMT's (see Fig. 6) while the other two parameters can be obtained from accurate timing given the kinematics of a light source propagating thru the sky at the speed of light. Consecutive PMT pulses arrive at the

detector according to times given by the following expression
$ct = ct_0 + R_p \tan[(\chi_0 - \chi)/2]$ (χ_0 is the angle of shower observation at t_0, i.e., it represents the direction of shower approach;
$\chi_0 + \psi = \pi$).

Shown in Fig. 7 and 8 are the results of track reconstruction for a single event. In Fig. 7, the shower track has been projected onto the "celestial sphere", i.e., it represents the picture an observer would see looking up at a line source of light projected on to the night sky. Zenith is the center of the dashed line curve which represents the horizon. Each hit PMT is indicated by a number. Noise PMT's, (out of time and spatial sequence) are indicated by large X's. Small x's denote barely non-coplanar, small amplitude tubes that marginally triggered--primarily due to scattered light or the diffuse edges of the EAS, itself. The numbers represent the time order of firing. Clearly, this event passed due overhead and disappeared out of aperture on the western, horizon. Fig. 8 illustrates the timing sequence for this event (times have been converted to kilometers!) The impact parameter for this event was 1.52 ± .02 Km while the zenith and azimuthal angles

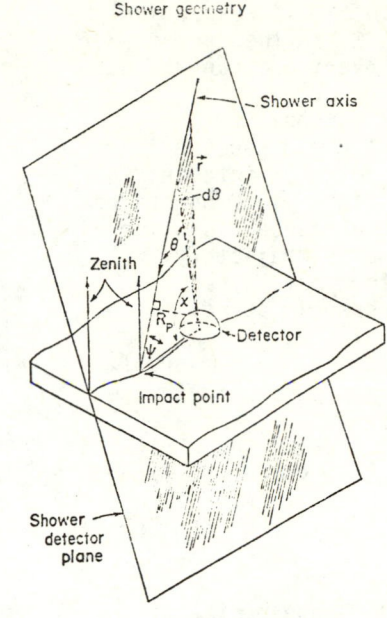

Fig. 5. Fly's Eye Shower Geometry

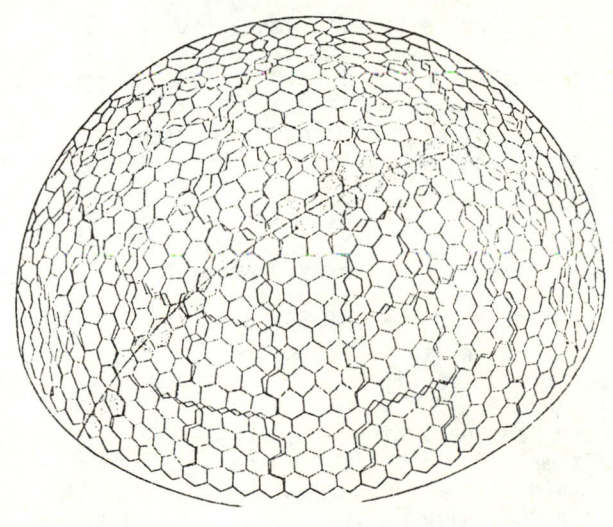

Fig. 6. Projection of Fly's Eye aperture onto "celestial" sphere. EAS track projects as a great circle.

were 38.8 ± 1.3° and 353.6 ± 0.1° respectively.

Given the geometry of the event one can now use the recorded pulse integrals to convert the light yield received at the detector into intrinsic light yield generated at the source along the shower's trajectory. Furthermore, given the atmospheric scintillation efficiency, one can then calculate the number of charged particles in the shower which generated that light. The photoelectron yield obtained by each hit PMT is:

$$N_{pe} = N_e Y \frac{\epsilon A}{4\pi R^2} \exp^{-R/\lambda} \Delta\ell$$

where

N_e = shower size at observed location along trajectory

Y = fluorescent light yield (~ 4 photons/m/electron) (see Fig. 3)

ϵ = combined light collection efficiency and photoelectron conversion efficiency (~0.17 ± 20%)

A = effective light gathering area (1.7m²)

λ = attenuation length of 3600Å photons in air (~18Km)

R = distance of EAS to detector

$\Delta\ell$ = differential shower path length in field of view $\Delta\theta$ (Fig.5)

since $\Delta\ell = \Delta(R_p/\tan\theta) = R_p \Delta\theta/\sin^2\theta$ we have:

$$N_e = \frac{4\pi}{Y} \frac{1}{\epsilon A} \frac{R_p}{\Delta\theta} \frac{N_{pe}}{\exp^{-R/\lambda}}$$

Interestingly enough, shower size measurements are weakly dependent on angle except for angles less than 20-30° where Cherenkov light begins to dominate the scintillation light. For angles larger than 30° shower sizes have been determined to ~±20%. Ultimately, we believe we can obtain ~±5% accuracy with improved calibration.

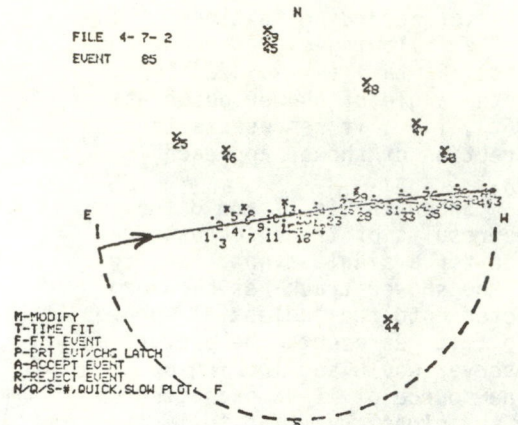

Fig. 7. Real Event progressing across Fly's Eye aperture, projected onto celestial sphere as seen by a ground observer. Numbers indicate PMT firing sequence. Large x indicates "noise" PMT's. Small x indicates, barely non-coplanar small amplitude PMT's.

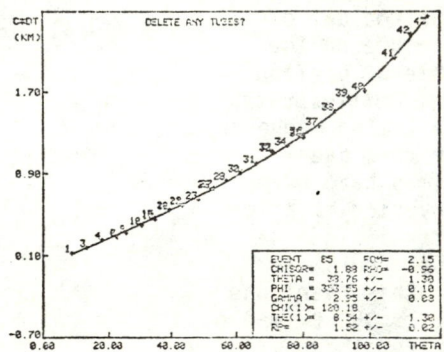

Fig. 8. Timing Curve ct vs θ, shower emission angle for event shown in Fig.7 Best fit values shown in insert.

Shown in Fig. 9 is the result of applying the above analysis to event 85. Shower sizes as a function of observation angle have been coverted to size vs atmospheric penetration "slant" depth in gm cm^{-2} along the shower's trajectory. Overlapping angular intervals are binned and averaged in order to obtain this curve. The solid line is the result of fitting the data with the Gaisser-Hillas parameterization of shower development given by the expression:[2]

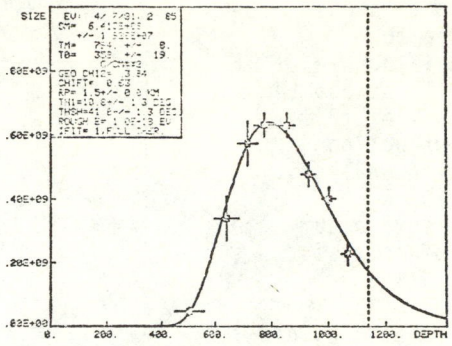

Fig. 9. Result shower size vs. atmospheric slant depth. Dotted line indicates earth surface. "0" depth at top of atmosphere. Shower energy about 10^{18}eV.

$$N(Eo, X) = No \frac{Eo}{\varepsilon} \exp^{p} \left(\frac{x-x_0}{X_{max}-\lambda} \right)^{P} \exp^{-(x-x_0)/\lambda}$$

Where E_0 = shower energy, x_0 = location of 1st interaction
X_{max} = location of shower maximum
N_0 = .045, ε = .074 GeV, λ = 70 g/cm^2, p = $(X_{max}-\lambda)/\lambda$
Due to its penetrating nature ($X_0 \sim 358$g cm^{-2}; $X_{max} \approx 794$g cm^{-2}) this particular event was most probably generated by a proton whose energy was about 10^{18}eV! We would anticipate that an incoming iron nucleus, for example, would not have been so penetrating. By judiciously selecting such events we can insure a proton-enriched sample and then by plotting the distribution of event maxima we can estimate the proton-air interaction length and hence the pp inelastic cross section. This procedure is carried out in the last section.

CHECKS ON ANALYSIS

In order to insure that trajectories have been properly measured (depth perception with a single eye is difficult) and that recorded pulse integrals accurately reflect light yields, we have built and calibrated a high intensity pulsed light source (a XENON flash tube--soon to be superceded by a nitrogen laser) permanently installed at Fly's Eye II and periodically fired over and above Fly's Eye I. This high intensity light pulse propagates up and out of the atmosphere and the scattered light it generates along the way (Rayleigh and Mie scattering) is picked up by the detectors at Fly's Eye I. Thus, the event sequence strongly resembles an inverse EAS. By analyzing the received signals in the same way as for real events we can calculate both trajectories

534

and light yields and in this case compare them to known values in order to assess the accuracy of track reconstruction and size analysis. Fig. 10 represents a summary of analysis of 32 "flasher" events. (The two sets of data points represent two different sets of fits to the timing curve--each fit yields similar results.) Overall track reconstruction accuracy is about ± 2°. We believe it possible

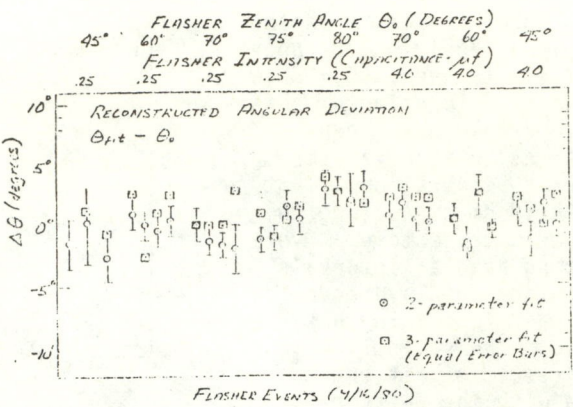

Fig. 10. Angular difference between best fit zenith angle and known zenith angle for 32 "flasher-generated" events. Observed deviations indicate angular accuries ~±2°.

to push this accuracy to about ± 1° by modifications in the shower propagation and light generation model. It is necessary to achieve

such accuracy if shower profiles accurate to ± 50g cm^{-2} are to be obtained! Fig. 11 shows the result of shower "size" analysis applied to a single flasher event. No corrections were applied to the data. Each data point represents the conversion of the light received by a single PMT to the number of photons present in the propagating flasher beam. Conversion is based solely on track geometry and estimates of the Rayleigh and Mie scattered light received at the PMT. There were 10^{14} photons in the beam. Amplitude accuracy is about ± 20% as advertised. This result gives us confidence not only in our overall calibration but also in knowledge of how the atmosphere attenuates and scatters light!

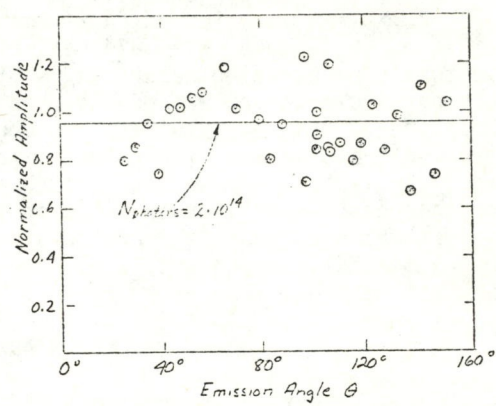

Fig. 11. Estimated # of photons in XENON flasher light pulse whose scattered light recorded by Fly's Eye PMT's. All pulse heights recorded over emission angles θ ranging from 20° - 160° yield correct # of photons to ± 20%.

RESULTS

Extragalactic Neutrino Flux

Shown in Fig. 12 is the zenith angle distribution of roughly 600 events obtained with 2/3 of Fly's Eye I operational for about 6 months. Only one event was seen at a zenith angle $\theta_z > 70°$ and this event had an assessed angular accuracy of about $\pm 10°$. We suspect it was a penetrating proton event whose zenith angle was probably about 70°. Beyond 80° the atmosphere becomes so thick ($\gtrsim 5000$ g cm^{-2}) that protons cannot generate showers near enough the Fly's Eye to be detected. Thus, we search for neutrinos in the local zenith aperture of about 80° - 95°. (Beyond 95° - the earth "Kills" the atmosphere as a target for neutrinos). We see no events within this aperture. In Fig. 13 we show the current best estimates of cosmic ray neutrino fluxes due to a variety of galactic and extragalactic mechanisms.[3] We focus on the extragalactic neutrino flux generated by cosmic ray interactions off the 3°K blackbody radiation which dominates the overall neutrino flux at $E \lesssim 10^{17}$ GeV. Our current experimental limits are indicated by the designated barred regions on the plot. The upper limit assumes a W-boson mass of 84 GeV which effectively cuts off the neutrino total cross section at $E \sim M_W^2/2M_p$. The lower limit corresponds to a completely pointlike neutrino interaction which allows the neutrino--air cross section to continue to rise linearly without limit, clearly an unphysical situation. (One should note, however, that the estimated unitarity bound at $E_\nu \sim 10^4$ GeV for νp scattering could occur at energies several decades higher for ν-air scattering due to the larger number of quark constituents available in the target.) Assuming the W-boson will be found at either the $\bar{p}p$ or the new electron colliders and its mass determined, a more definitive limit on the extragalactic neutrino flux can then be set. We also note, that such measurements could, in principle, confirm the existence of the 3°K blackbody radiation in extra-galactic space.

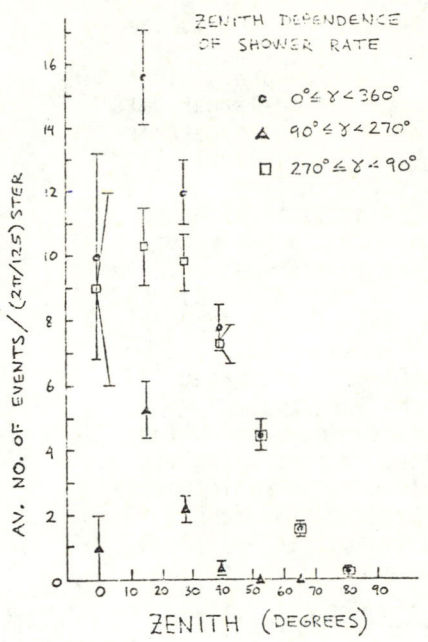

Fig. 12. Zenith angle event distribution for about 600 showers with energies $\sim 10^{18}$ eV. γ-angle intervals refer to showers impacting either behind or in front of Fly's Eye.

536

The High Energy Cosmic Ray Spectrum

Shown in Fig. 14 is the differential impact parameter (R_p) distribution for a sample of about 1500 events. Measuring a shower's energy depends upon obtaining shower profiles over a rather long baseline. This procedure can be carried out only for a limited data sample at present. On the other hand, R_p can be precisely determined for a much larger data sample and since a shower's energy or, equivalently, its size is proportional to R_p, the R_p distribution should relate to the primary cosmic ray energy distribution. Quite simply we have $dN \propto I(>E)2\pi R_p dR_p$ where $I(>E)$ is the integral primary cosmic ray spectrum. If $I(>E) \propto E^{-\gamma}$ and based upon the fact that Fly's Eye triggering electronics operates by preserving its signal to noise ratio over a wide dynamic time range, we estimate that

$$E \propto Ne \propto e^{.065 R_p}(R_p^{1.5})$$

Hence,

$$\frac{dN}{dRp} \propto e^{-.065\gamma R_p}/R_p^{(1.5\gamma-1)}$$

The best fit to the distribution shown in Fig. 14 yields a value of $\gamma \approx 2.1 \pm 0.3$ which is identical with the results of Watson et al[4] for shower energies less than 10^{19}eV. Our data sample spans a currently estimated energy range of roughly $5 \cdot 10^{17}$eV-$5 \cdot 10^{19}$eV. Watson[4] reports a spectral flattening for cosmic rays with energies $>10^{19}$eV (see Fig. 15). Such a flattening would show up as an enhancement in our R_p distribution at impact

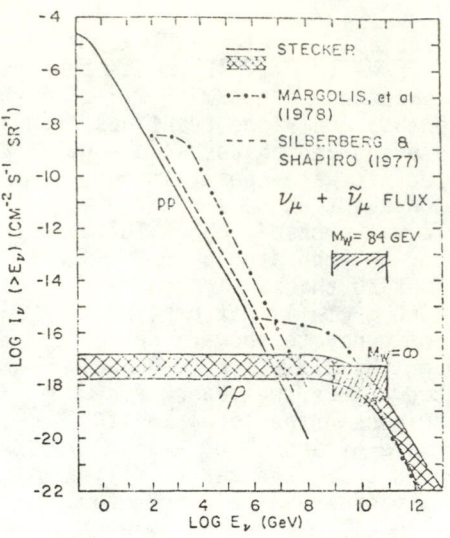

Fig 13. Estimated limits on extragalactic neutrino flux near $E \sim 10^{20}$eV given $84\text{GeV} \lesssim M_W \lesssim \infty$.

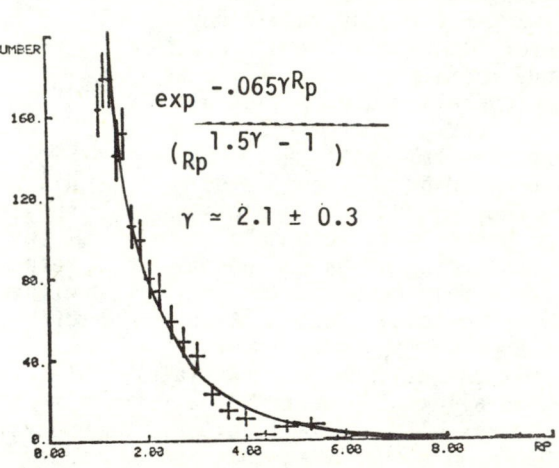

Fig. 14. Differential impact parameter distribution for about 1500 events. Best fit to observed fall-off indicates integral energy spectral slop of $\gamma \sim 2.1 \pm 0.3$.

parameters $R_p > 4$Km. We see only the tiniest hint--statistically insignificant-of such a flattening. However, the data reported here was obtained with the Fly's Eye "electronically cut-off" at $R_p \gtrsim 5$-8 Km or so (the cut-off is geometry dependent) this cut-off was instituted in order to optimize the nearby event rate. Currently, we are "electronically tuned" to greater distances with the obvious goal of examing the quoted spectral flattening at $E \gtrsim 10^{19}$eV. Certainly, our preliminary spectral measurements for $E \gtrsim 10^{19}$eV are consistent with those obtained by other workers.

Sources of UHCR

Shown in Fig. 16 are the galactic coordinate arrival directions of the 45 cosmic ray primaries with $E \gtrsim 4 \cdot 10^{19}$eV observed by the 3 largest ground-based EAS particle detector arrays which have been operating during the past 15 years. The data indicate (see Fig. 15 as well) that these UHCR tend to arrive from directions predominately clustered in Northern galactic latitudes. It is furthermore to be noted that the onset of the spectral flattening also indicated in Fig. 15 occurs essentially

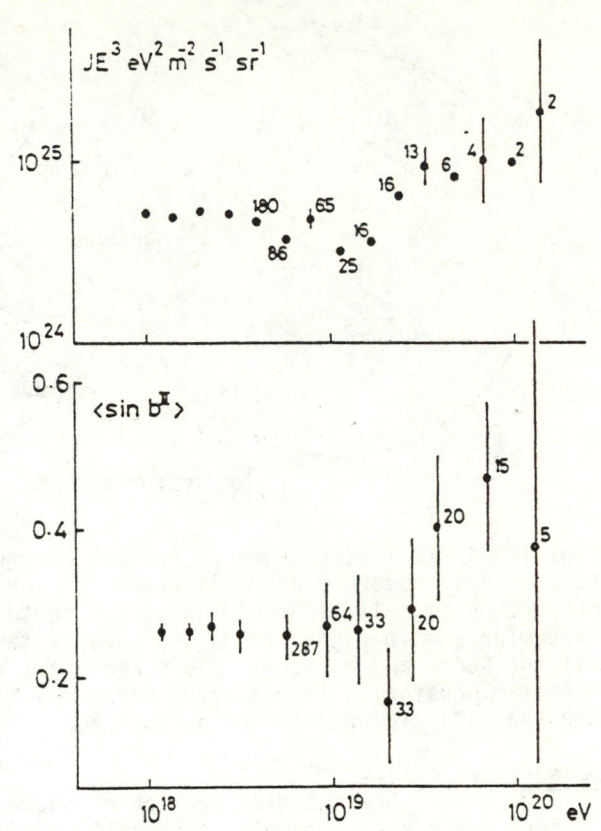

Fig. 15.-top- Differential energy spectrum $\cdot E^3$ as measured by Haverrah Park EAS array indicates spectral flattening at $E \gtrsim 10^{19}$eV. -bottom- corresponding observed shift toward higher galactic latitudes for EAS arrival directions.

at the same energy ($E \gtrsim 10^{19}$eV) as the onset of the high galactic latitude anisotropy. The conventional picture that has evolved from these observations attributes the origin of these cosmic rays to extragalactic but noncosmological sources most probably lying within the Virgo cluster. This proposition suffers from several difficulties based upon energy considerations[4] and we make no comments regarding its validity one way or another. We simply note that our most energetic event had a measured lower

538

energy bound of $5 \cdot 10^{19}$ eV (the shower was still developing at ground impact!) and its arrival direction was near the galactic plane (see the triangle in Fig. 16). Clearly, this represents an unlikely occurrence if the Virgo cluster is really the source of such UHCR.

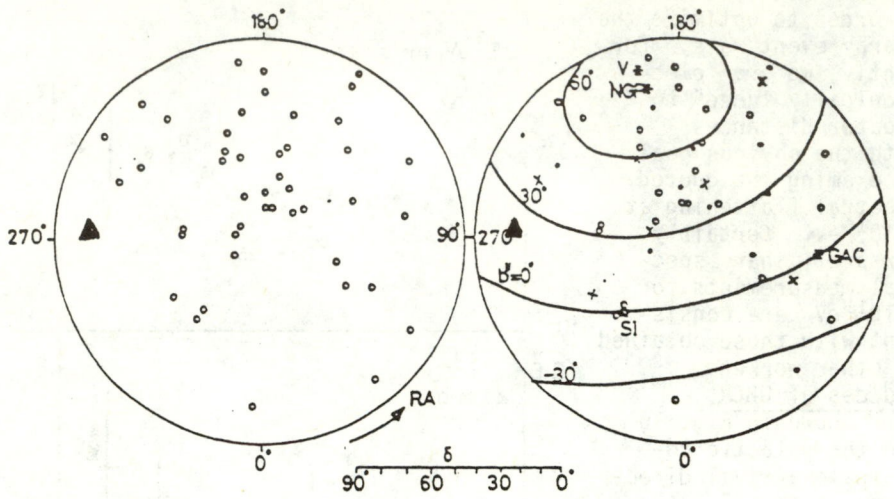

Fig. 16. Arrival directions of 45 most energetic events ($E > 4 \cdot 10^{19}$ eV) observed at declination 70°. Plot is equal area projection in galactic coordinates but centered at $\delta \approx 90°$ with circumference in right ascension. Events taken from Haverrah Park, Volcano Ranch and Yakutsk. Fly's Eye event denoted by Δ near galactic equator. Virgo cluster marked by V, North Galactic Pole NGP and Galactic anti-center by GAC.

Measurement of σ_{pp}

In Fig. 17 we show the distribution of shower maxima vs depth of maximum for a select sample of about 90 events with energies near 10^9 GeV($S^{1/2} \sim 4 \cdot 10^4$ GeV). The event sample was selected by demanding that the estimated error in shower maximum location be within ± 50 g cm^{-2}. The slope of this distribution (Λ_m) at large shower depths should relate to the nucleon-air interaction length λ_n. This relationship has been investigated in detail by Gaisser et al[5] and the results reported at this conference. They conclude that: $\Lambda_m \sim 1.5\lambda_n$ and that the distribution of shower maxima is, in fact, as sensitive to the value of λ_n as is the distribution of even "earlier" observed points along the shower profile such as $\Lambda_{1/4}$ max. Furthermore, we should note that the slope of this distribution at large depths should be determined preferentially by protons as opposed to heavier cosmic ray primaries since protons presumably would be more penetrating on the average. We note that our measured slope $\Lambda_m \sim 73$g cm^{-2} implies a nucleon interaction length of $\lambda_n \sim 48$g cm^{-2} or $\sigma_{p-air} \simeq 500$mb and if Glauber theory[6] is used to estimate σ_{pp}, we obtain $\sigma_{pp}^{tot} \simeq 120$mb. This value lies between that obtained by a lns and $\ln^2 s$ extrapolation.[5] (We quote no errors yet since we believe that certain unsolved systematic difficulties may outweigh statistics.) Such a value for the cross section implies that a significant fraction of the cosmic rays contained in this data sample are probably protons. (If they were mostly Fe nuclei--their behavior is quite remarkable; however the presence of lighter nuclei, such as alphas, can certainly not be ruled out.) We point out that inaccuracies in locating the depth at maximum would probably decrease our estimated value of Λ_m. Hence, our estimate of σ_{pp}^{tot} probably represents a lower limit. Clearly, a larger number of more accurately measured events is necessary to (1) more accurately determine Λ_m and (2) look for changes in Λ_m indicative of compositional effects. A final value for σ_{pp} may await data taken with both Fly's Eye operational.

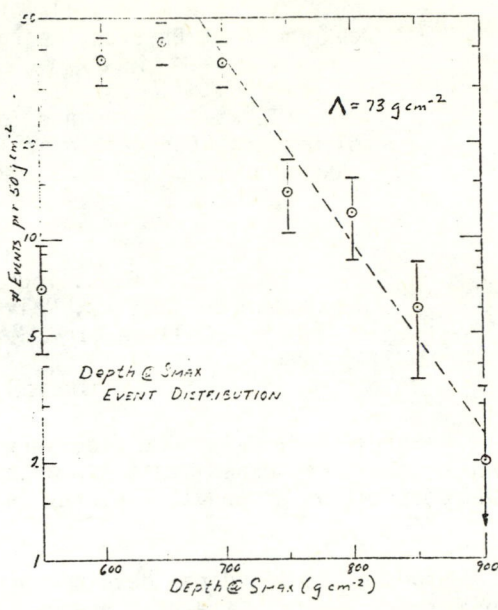

Fig.17. Differential distribution of 90 events (at $E \sim 10^{18}$)vs. depth of shower maximum. Attentuation slope $\Lambda \sim 73\mathrm{g~cm}^{-2}$ implies $\sigma_{pp}^{tot} \sim 120\mathrm{mb}$.

REFERENCES

1. K. Greisen, Phys. Rev. Let. 16, 748 (1966).
2. T. K. Gaisser and A. M. Hillas, 15th Int. Cosmic Ray Conf. 8, 353 (1977).
3. F. W. Stecker, NASA Tech. Memorandum 79609, GSFC, Greenbelt, MD. (1978).
4. A. A.Watson, 16th Moriond Astrophysics Meeting "Cosmology and Particles" Les Arcs, France, edited by J. Andouze et al, editions Frontieres March 15-21, 1981.
5. T. K. Gaisser (see proceedings--this conference).
6. R. J. Glauber and G. Matthiae, Nucl. Phys. B21, 135 (1970).

ULTRA-HIGH ENERGY CROSS SECTION FROM STUDY OF LONGITUDINAL DEVELOPMENT OF AIR SHOWERS

R. W. Ellsworth[1]
Department of Physics, George Mason University
Fairfax, VA 22030

T. K. Gaisser[2] and Todor Stanev[3]
Bartol Research Foundation of The Franklin Institute
University of Delaware, Newark, DE. 19711

and

G. B. Yodh[1]
Department of Physics, University of Maryland
College Park, Maryland

Abstract

We present calculations necessary for interpretation of large cosmic ray experiments and argue that both cross section and composition around 10^{18} eV may be estimated soon.

Study of longitudinal development of air showers initiated by cosmic rays of ultra-high energy has recently become feasible through study of time structure of Cerenkov light from air showers[1][2], and in the last few months by observations of scintillation light from nitrogen flouresence in the atmosphere induced by traversal of large air showers[3]. The last technique will make it possible to study a large sample of events ($\sim 10^4$) with energy around 10^9 GeV in the next several years. Individual shower profiles can in principle be measured, in particular the distribution of effective shower starting points, shower maxima and shower demise for fixed total track length (i.e., total deposited energy). In this paper we discuss the capabilities and limitations of experiments that measure shower profiles for

1. Work supported in part by the U. S. National Science Foundation under Grant Number PHY-7909272.

2. Work supported in part by the U. S. Department of Energy under Contract Number DE-AC02-78ER05007.

3. Work supported in part by the U. S. National Science Foundation under Grant Number PHY-8008901. Permanent address, Institute for Nuclear Research and Nuclear Energy, Sofia, Bulgaria.

determining the asymptotic behavior of the proton–proton total cross sections up to $\sqrt{s} \sim 100$ TeV.[4] We also discuss the sensitivity of these techniques to primary composition of cosmic rays of about 10^{18} eV. We conclude that it will probably soon be possible to measure the proton cross section at these energies if it is less than ~ 120mb and to place a lower bound otherwise.

Figure 1 displays some typical shower development curves. We have indicated location of starting point (x_0), depth of quarter minimum $(x_{1/4})$ and depth of maximum (x_m). These are measured in gm/cm^2 along the shower axis. $N(x)$ is the total number of charged particles (mostly electrons and positrons) integrated over the shower front. The energy of a shower is equal to the area under its development curve (track length integral) times the rate of energy loss for a relativistic particle. Also, to a very good approximation ($\sigma \sim \pm 10\%$), the energy is proportional to the size at shower maximum (~ 1.7 GeV per particle). So the energy is well–determined in this type of experiment.

If the actual shower starting points, x_0, could be measured then the cross sections on air nuclei of the different components in the incident cosmic ray beam and their relative weights could be unfolded directly from the measured attenuation of the primary beam. In any indirect experiment, however, x_0, cannot be measured. Our task, therefore, is to find out to what extent the measureable distributions of $x_{1/4}$ and x_m, reflect the fundamental interaction lengths despite the existence of fluctuations in shower development which may also contribute significantly.

This problem was investigated in Ref. 5 with emphasis on fragmentation and pion production in collisions of nuclear projectiles. It was found that, as expected, the tail of the $x_{1/4}$ distribution reflected the input cross section for protons and that the portion of the distribution with small values of $x_{1/4}$ is sensitive to the fraction of heavy primaries. The calculations of Ref. 5, however, are based on a simplified model for nucleon showers and consider only one, energy–dependent σ_{p-air}. Moreover, only results for $x_{1/4}$ were reported in that paper since that distribution should resemble the distribution of shower starting points more closely than x_m. We have since learned[6] that determination of $x_{1/4}$ with Fly's Eye is at present limited due to problems arising from lack of light, contamination due to Cerenkov light, atmospheric scattering and other effects. We, therefore, present results here for x_m, based on a variety of assumptions for σ_{p-air} and using a rather detailed Monte Carlo treatment of development of showers initiated by protons and nucleons of nuclei. Fragmentation and pion production by nuclear projectiles is treated as in Ref. 5.

Momentum distributions of secondaries produced in collisions of nucleons and pions are obtained by simply scaling the measured distributions from $\sqrt{s} = 20 - 60$ GeV to cosmic ray energies, as in Ref. 7.[8]

Figure (2) shows distributions of x_m for two arbitrary compositions.[9] The region $600 \lesssim x_m \lesssim 750$ is particularly sensitive to abundance of heavy primaries relative to protons, whereas the region $x_m \gtrsim 750$ reflects primarily protons. We therefore expect that the tail of the x_m distribution may reflect the proton cross section. Accordingly, we define an effective attenuation of the maximum by fitting the deep portion (> 760 gm/cm^2) of the distribution to e^{-x_m/Λ_m}.

In the example shown here the interaction lengths for protons and alphas are $\sigma_{p-air} \sim 40$gm/cm^2 and $\lambda_{\alpha-air} \sim 35$gm/cm^2 (corresponding to σ_{pp}TOT ~ 130 mb at $\sqrt{s} = 25$ TeV). If the proton cross section is indeed this large, measuring it will be possible only if the concentration of α-primaries is not anomalously large (i.e., only if $N_\alpha < N_p$). The extent to which heavy primaries may interfere with determination of λ_{p-air} is illustrated by noting that $\Lambda_m = 48 \pm 4$gm/cm^2 for the heavier composition in Figure 2 and 51 ± 3 gm/cm^2 for the composition with 55% protons. This is to be compared with $\Lambda_m = 55 \pm 3$ gm/cm^2 for pure protons.

Even without the problem of heavy primaries, measurement of x_m or ($x_{1/4}$) alone cannot determine an arbitrarily large proton cross section because of intrinsic fluctuations in shower development. The results of our calculations bear this out, as shown in Figure 3. Here we show Λ_m for proton showers only, as a function of σ_{p-air} at 3×10^{17}eV. For the atmosphere,

$$\lambda_{p-air} \ (gm/cm^2) = \frac{2.4 \times 10^4}{\sigma_{p-air}(mb)}.$$

Primary energies of the protons were chosen from a power law spectrum with $E_0 > 3 \times 10^{17}$eV. To approximate Fly's Eye conditions we used a differential spectral index of 2. The true index is about 3 but the acceptance is proportional to E. Cascade development depends on the hadronic cross section at all energies up to the primary energy, though the overall profile is dominated by the high-energy behavior. Figure 4a shows the energy dependences of σ_{p-air} used to construct Figure 3. (Each point in Figure 3 corresponds to one curve in Figure 4a.)The p-air and nucleus-air cross sections were obtained from σ_{pp}TOT (and the pp slope parameter) using

Glauber theory as described in Ref. 10. The corresponding values of σ_{pp}^{TOT} are shown in Figure 4b.[11]

Inspection of Figure 3 suggests that the Fly's Eye experiment will soon be able to estimate the proton cross section at $\sqrt{s} \sim 50$ TeV if it is not too large (say $\sigma_{p-air} \lesssim 500$mb or $\sigma_{pp}^{TOT} \lesssim 120$mb) and to place a lower bound otherwise. If the abundance of α-primaries were anomalously large, or if heavy primaries were very abundant, the dividing line between measurement and lower bound would be somewhat lower. Perhaps surprisingly, Λ_m is as sensitive to cross section as $\Lambda_{1/4}$, though for a given cross section $\Lambda_{1/4}$ is numerically closer to λ_{int} than Λ_m (i.e. $\Lambda_m > \Lambda_{1/4} > \lambda_{int}$ -- see Table I). This may be of practical importance since x_m appears easier to measure than $x_{1/4}$. Determination of relative abundance of heavy nuclei , as well as cross section, will require unbiased measurements of x_m (and/or $x_{1/4}$) over the full range of depths (see Figs. 1 and 2).

Complete results for shower profiles calculated with various models (including scale breaking) over a range of energies and description of details of the calculation will be published elsewhere.

REFERENCES

1. G. B. Khristiansen, Proc. 16th Int. Cosmic Ray Conf. (Kyoto) 14, 360 (1979) and references therein, and N. N.Kalmykov et al. Ibid., 6 114 (1981.)
2. K. Orford and K. E. Turver, Nature 264, 727 (1976), M. P. Chantler et al., Proc. 17th Int. Cosmic Ray Conf. (Paris) 6, 121 (1981) and A. A. Andam et al., Ibid., 6, 57, 125, 129 (1981), and Phys. Rev. D (to be published).
3. G. L. Cassiday et al., Proc. Workshop on Forward Collider Physics, Madison, December 1981, and references therein. See also J. W. Elbert, Cosmology and Particles, Proc. First Moriond Astrophysics Meeting (ed. J. Audouze et al.) Editions Frontieres (Dreux) p.69 (1981).
4. The Durham group have compared their experimental results (Ref 2) to Monte Carlo simulations that include generation of the signals they actually measure. See T. J. L. McComb and K. E. Turver, Proc. 17th Int. Cosmic Ray Conf. (Paris) 6, 130 (1981) and references therein. In order to be more general, we calculate the longitudinal shower profiles here.
5. T. K. Gaisser, T. Stanev, P. Freier and C. Jake Waddington Phys. Rev. D, 1981 (to be published).

544

6. E. H. Loh (private communication) and G. Cassiday, Proc. Madison Workshop on Forward Collider Physics, Madison (1981).

7. R. W. Ellsworth et al., Phys. Rev. D23, 771 (1981).

8. This type of Feynman scaling for $F(x) = \frac{1}{\sigma}\frac{d\sigma}{dx}$ produces a central plateau which does not rise with energy. Recent data from the $\bar{p}p$ collider at CERN SPS show, however, that the plateau continues to rise at least to 540 GeV. G. Arnison et al. (UA1 Collaboration) Phys. Letters 107B, 320 (1981) and K. Alpgard et al. (UA5 Collaboration) Phys. Letters 107B, 310, 315 (1981). Presumably this rise continues asymptotically. Unless it is accompanied by a significant change for $F(x)$ in the fragmentation region, however, it will not affect high-energy cascade calculations, which depend primarily on the fragmentation region (say $x \gtrsim 0.05$). Effects of possible fragmentation scaling violations (J. Wdowczyk and A. W. Wolfendale, Proc. Madison Conf. 1981 and N. C. 54A, 433 (1979) on this type of calculation will be investigated in a future paper.

9. We have simulated 500 proton showers for each of five trial cross sections (See Fig. 4). In addition we calculated 100 nitrogen showers, 100 Mg showers and 120 Fe showers for the $\log^2 s$ cross section. These represent five major groups of primary cosmic rays: p, alpha, CNO, $(9 \leq Z \leq 14)$ and $(15 \leq Z \leq 26)$, respectively. For clarity, Mg and CNO have been plotted as a single group in Figure 2 .

10. V. Barger et al., Phys. Rev. Letters 33, 1051 (1974), T. K. Gaisser et al., Proc. 14th Int. Cosmic Ray Conf. (Munich) 7, 2161 (1975) and T. K. Gaisser, C. J. Noble and G. B. Yodh, in preparation.

11. For all except the curve labelled L.M. we assumed b = .296 $GeV^{-2} \times \sigma_{pp}^{tot}(mb)$.

12. Y. Afek et al. Phys. Rev. Letters 45, 85 (1980).

13. E. Leader and U. Maor, Phys. Letters 43B, 505 (1973) and U. Maor and S. Nussinov, Phys. Letters 46B, 99 (1973).

Table I. Characteristic lengths for various cross sections[a]

Cross Section	Input Nucleon Interaction length in air at $3 \times 10^{17}_{eV}$	Simulation Results	
		$\Lambda 1/4$	Λ m
const	75	91±6	118±7
log s	53	67±4	80±5
$\log^2 s$	40	53±3	64±4
A	28	35±2	45±3
LM	15	27±2	36±2

[a] Errors are statistical uncertainty in simulation results.

546

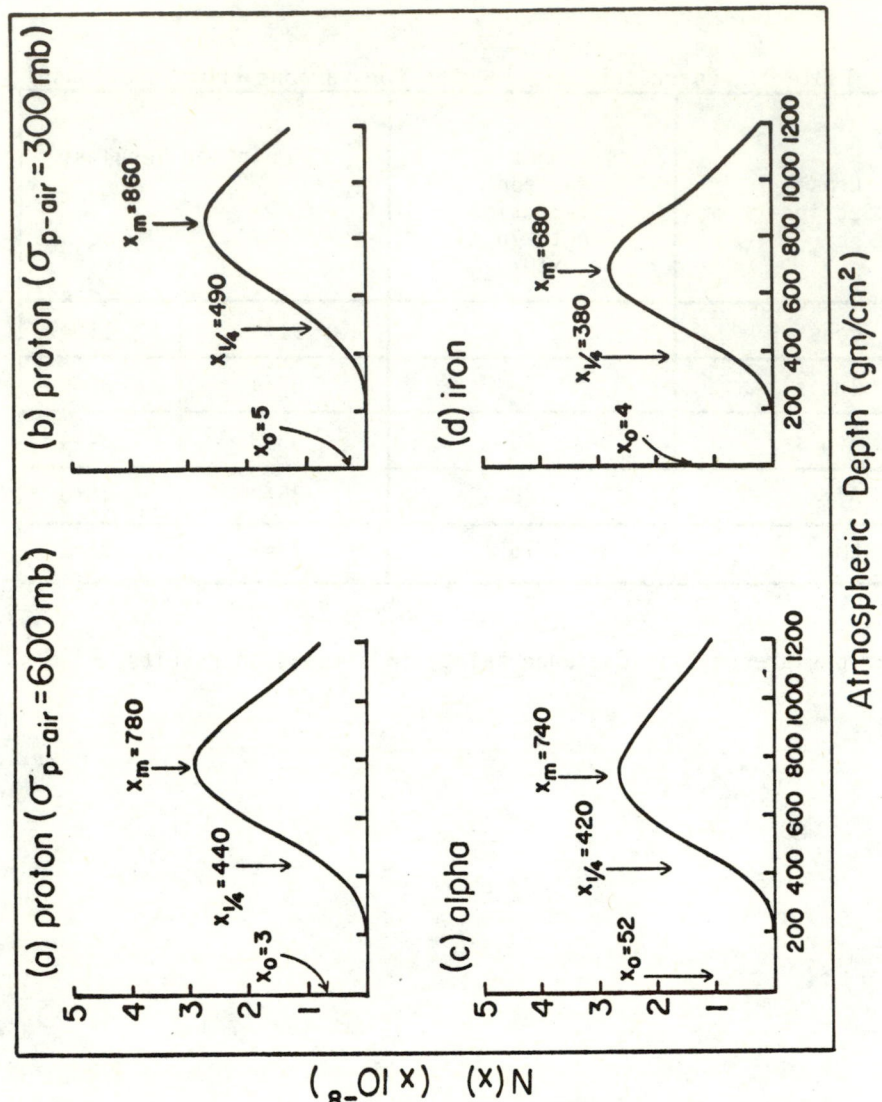

Figure 1. Shower development curves for typical primaries of total energy 3×10^{17} eV: (a) and (b) proton primaries for increasing and constant cross sections, respectively (see text); (c) primary alpha; (d) primary iron nucleus. The curves illustrate that heavy primaries typically give fast-developing showers, that proton showers penetrate deeper for smaller cross section and that α-showers tend to be similar to proton-showers if the cross section is large.

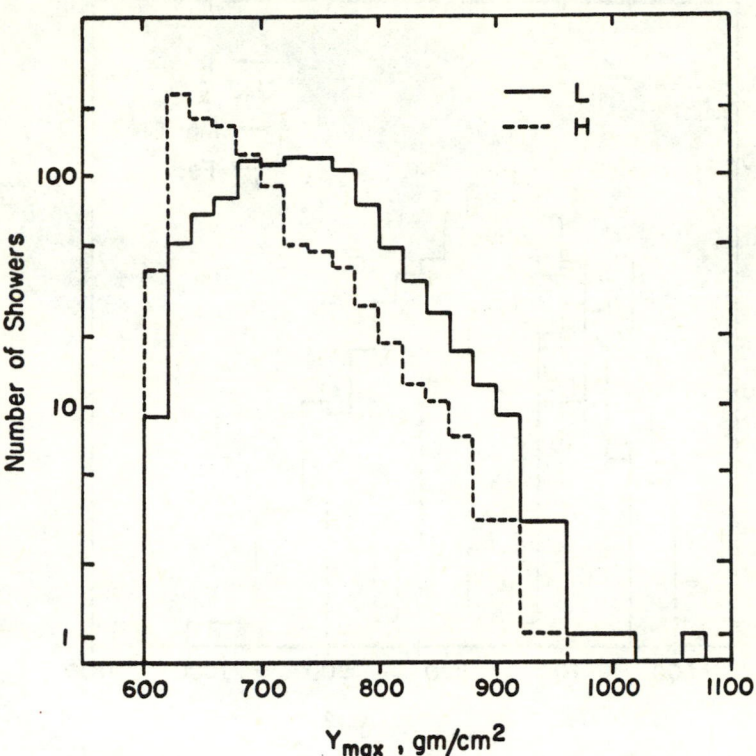

Figure 2a

Figure 2. a) Distribution of depth of maximum for showers of energy 3×10^{17} eV per nucleus for two compositions: p: α: CNO+Mg: Fe=.55: .21: .16: .08, as at low energy (L) and p: α: CNO+Mg: Fe=0.2: .08: .07: .65, denoted H.
b) and c) show the components separately for the low energy and the heavy composition, respectively.

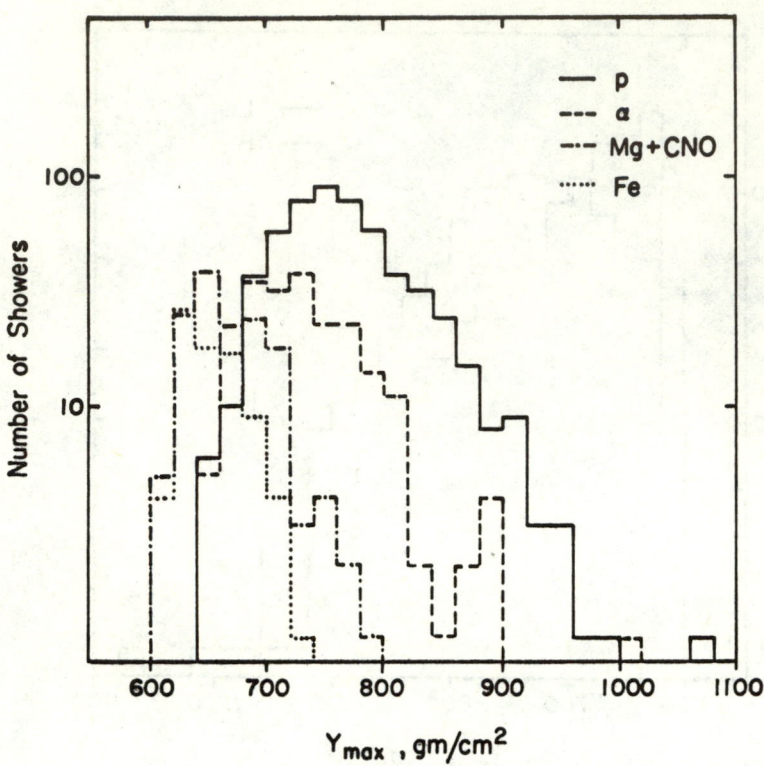

Figure 2b

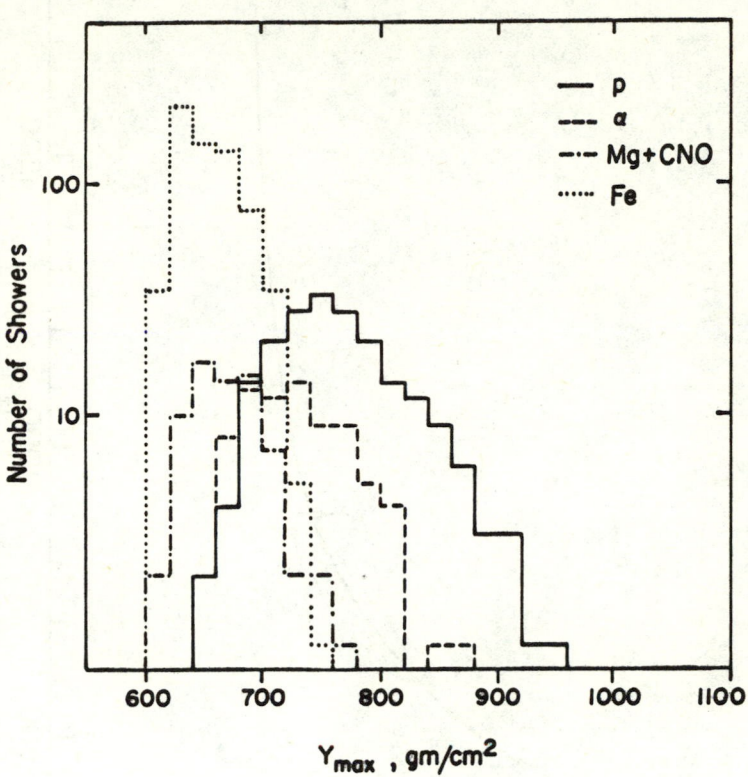

Figure 2c

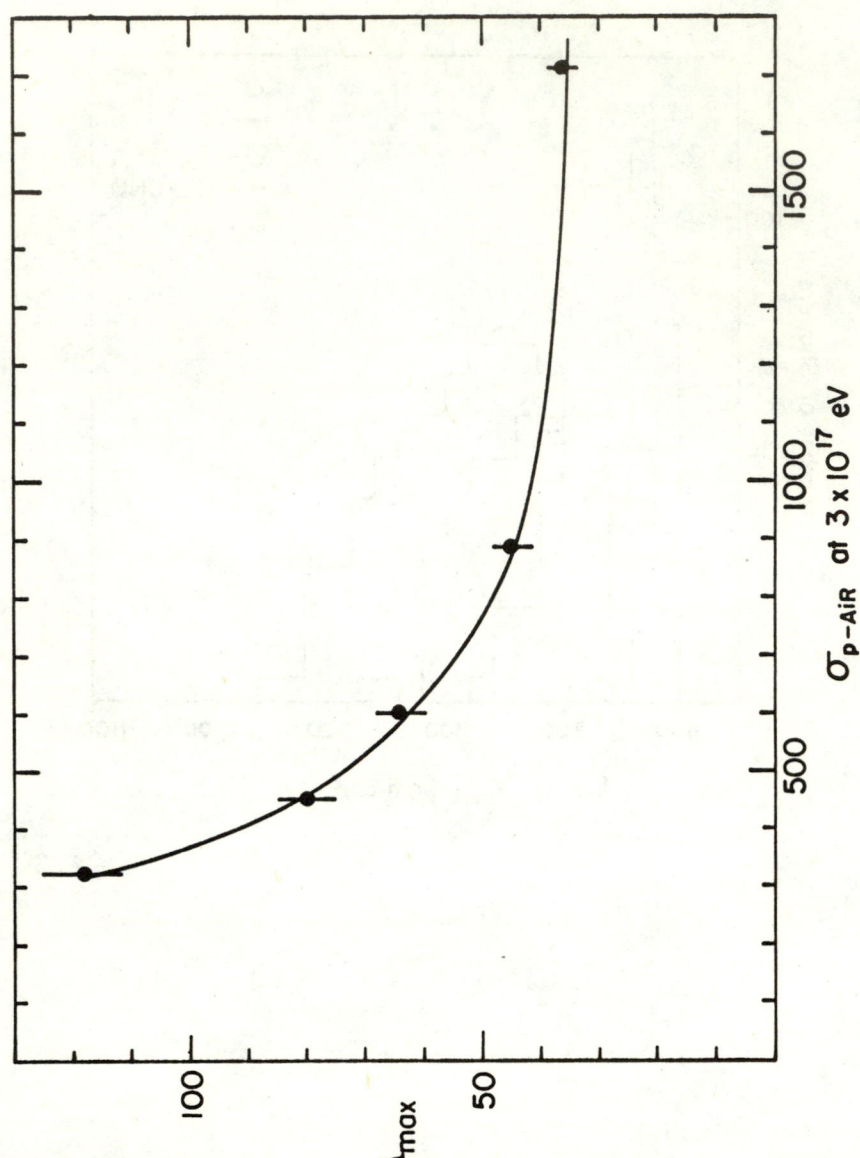

Figure 3. σ_m vs σ_{p-air} for proton showers chosen from a power law energy spectrum (differential index=2) with $E_o > 3 \times 10^{17}$ eV. Error bars show statistical uncertainty from the simulation result.

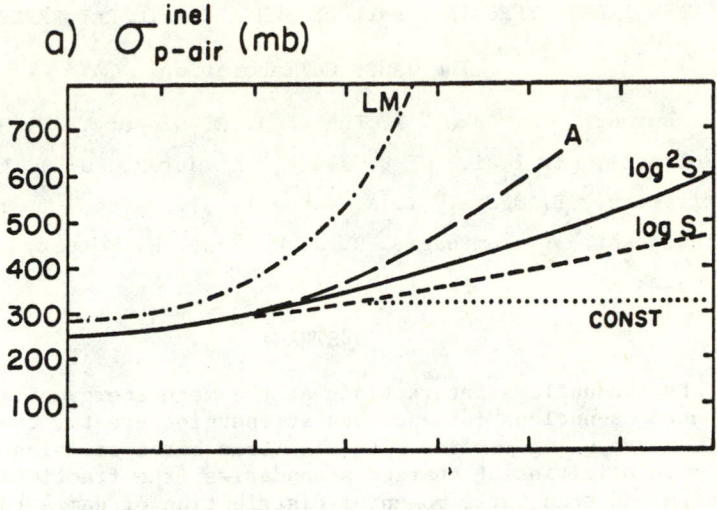

a) σ^{inel}_{p-air} (mb)

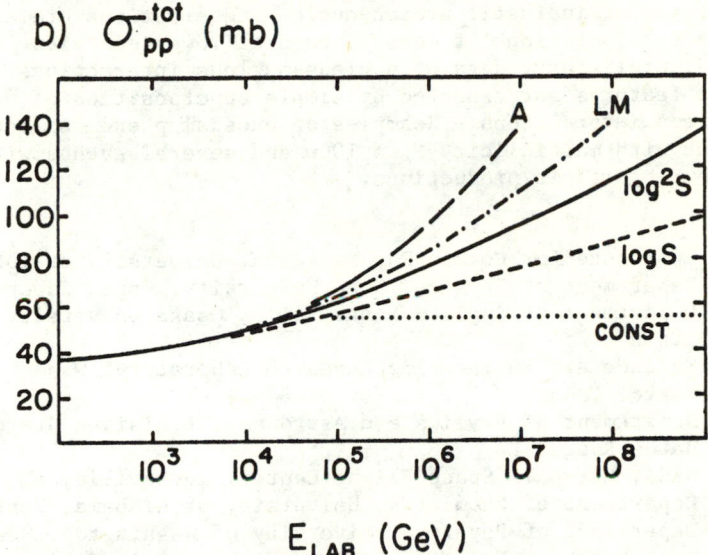

b) σ^{tot}_{pp} (mb)

E_{LAB} (GeV)

Figure 4. a) Energy-dependent cross sections for inelastic p-air collisions used for the calculations shown in Fig. 3. The curves are labelled to correspond to the values of σ^{tot}_{pp} shown in part (b).

b) Energy-dependent pp total cross sections. The curves labelled log s and log²s are extrapolations of fits to the cross section up to ISR energies. The curve labelled A is an extrapolation of the estimate of Afek et al. [Ref. 12] and LM stands for Leader and Maor [Ref. 13].

NEW EVENT TYPES IN A BALLOON-BORNE COSMIC RAY EXPERIMENT*

The JACEE Collaboration[†]

T. H. Burnett,[h] S. Dake,[b] M. Fuki,[b] J. C. Gregory,[h] T. Hayashi,[d]
R. Holynski,[i] J. Iwai,[d] W. V. Jones,[e] A. Jurak,[i] J. J. Lord,[h]
O. Miyamura,[c] T. Ogata,[a] T. A. Parnell,[f] T. Saito,[a] T. Tabuki,[d]
Y. Takahashi,[e] T. Tominaga,[b] R. J. Wilkes,[h] W. Wolter,[i] and
B. Wosiek[i]

ABSTRACT

Proton-nucleus interactions at the mean energy of about 45 TeV and nucleus-nucleus interactions at energies greater than 1 TeV/nucleon are being studied with a balloon borne emulsion chamber. The multiplicities of charged secondaries, the fractional energy spectra and transverse momentum distribution of gamma rays, and the rapidity density in the central region are obtained. The features of inelastic proton-nucleus interactions are as expected from extrapolations of measurements at lower energies. On the other hand, preliminary data on nucleus-nucleus interactions indicate some features not expected by simple superposition of nucleon-nucleon interactions. Examples of unusual phenomena include one event with multiplicity $N_s \simeq 1000$ and several events with apparent high P_T particle productions.

a. Institute for Cosmic Ray Research, University of Tokyo, Japan
b. Department of Physics, Kobe University, Kobe, Japan
c. Department of Applied Mathematics, Osaka University, Osaka, Japan
d. Science and Engineering Research Laboratory, Waseda University, Tokyo, Japan
e. Department of Physics and Astronomy, Louisiana State University, Baton Rouge, LA
f. NASA, Marshall Space Flight Center, Huntsville, AL
g. Department of Chemistry, University of Alabama, Huntsville, AL
h. Department of Physics, University of Washington, Seattle, WA
i. Institute for Nuclear Physics, Krakow, Poland

† Mailing address: Department of Physics and Astronomy, Louisiana State University, Baton Rouge, LA 70803-4001, U.S.A., or Institute for Cosmic Ray Research, University of Tokyo, Tanashi, Tokyo 188, Japan.

INTRODUCTION

The Japanese – American Cooperative Emulsion Experiment (JACEE) was organized in 1979 for the purpose of studying the interactions, composition and energy spectra of primary cosmic rays. The experimental objectives included investigations of proton–nucleus and nucleus–nucleus interactions at total energies approaching 100 TeV. The study of proton–nucleus interactions was expected to give a glimpse into the multiple production process before new accelerators produced data at energies around

$\sqrt{s}$ = 550 GeV. The primary objective, to study nucleus–nucleus interactions at energies greater than 100 GeV/nucleon, will be unique to cosmic rays for many years to come. For studies such as the phase transition from nucleonic to quark–gluon matter, the only hope for experimental evidence is from the interactions of heavy cosmic ray nuclei with energies exceeding several TeV/nucleon.

The JACEE objectives are readily obtained with conventional emulsion chamber techniques, which permit observation of both secondary charged particles and individual high energy gamma rays. Analysis can focus on such areas as structure in the rapidity density in central collisions, the transverse momentum distributions, anomalous charged to neutral production, events with large multiplicities, etc.

Most of the data presented at this conference were also reported at the 17th International Cosmic Ray Conference, Paris, 13–25 July, 1981. Analysis is still in progress. Detailed results will be published elsewhere after verification of these preliminary data.

INSTRUMENTATION AND MEASUREMENTS

A schmetic view of the apparatus is shown in Fig. 1. The design is basically what has been called an emulsion chamber. The present data were collected during two balloon flights launched from Palestine, Texas. The exposures were at altitudes of 3 – 4 g/cm^2 for 26.5 hr in September 1979 and for 29.5 hr in October 1980.

The detector is comprised of four identifiable sections: primary charge detector, target, spacer, and calorimeter, all of which incorporate emulsion plates. All together there are more than 100 emulsion plates in each chamber.

The primary charge detector consists of a stack of thick (200 – 400 micron) emulsion plates

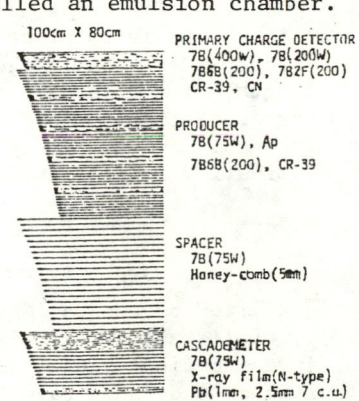

Fig. 1 Schematic view of the apparatus

with three different sensitivities, as well as CR-39 and cellulose nitrate etchable plastics. The charges of incident particles are determined from delta ray counting, grain counting, gap counting and etched-pit measurements, either individually or in combination. The charge resolution is typically $\Delta Z = 0.2 - 2.0$ charge units, with larger errors for heavier charges.

The target section consists of thin (50 - 75 micron) emulsion plates interleaved with acrylic plates of 2.0 mm thickness. Thick emulsion plates and CR-39 plates are inserted at regular intervals throughout the target, in order to have reliable charge measurement of the projectile fragments. The collision points in the acrylic plates of the target are estimated with an accuracy of 10 - 100 microns.

Trajectories of incident and secondary charged particles can be reconstructed by tracing their tracks in the emulsion plates which are coated on both sides of acrylic sheets 800 micron in thickness. Secondary interactions are identified by following the trajectories of charged secondaries. The emission angles of charged secondaries are typically measured with errors 1 - 5% in the overall angular region up to 10^{-5} radian. A few particles in the extremely forward cone have errors of 50 - 100% in the emission angle measurement.

The spacer permits gamma rays from neutral pion decay to diverge before reaching the calorimeter. The separation between the two associated cascades from a 1 TeV pion is expected to be about 40 microns at the calorimeter.

The calorimeter is a sandwich of thin emulsion plates, x-ray films and Pb plates. The vertical Pb thickness is 7 radiation length. Cascades with energies greater than about 250 GeV make dark spots visible to the naked eye in the x-ray films, which are used both as threshold detectors and for (densitometric) total energy measurements of a gamma ray family. The energy of an individual gamma ray is estimated from the longitudinal development of cascades in the emulsion plates. This requires counting the number of cascade electrons in the emulsion plates at each radiation length. The threshold energy for detecting a gamma ray-initiated cascade is 20 - 50 GeV. The error in a single cascade energy measurement is 10 - 30%, while the error in the primary energy determination is estimated to be about 50%.

PROTON-NUCLEUS INTERACTIONS

1. Angular Distribution

The normalized pseudo rapidity distributions of charged secondary particles and gamma rays are shown in Fig. 2. It is seen that in the inclusive analysis the angular distributions of charged particles and gamma rays are quite similar in the non-biased forward region.

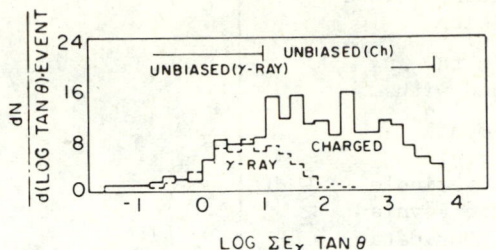

Fig. 2 Normalized angular
distribution

2. Multiplicity

The multiplicities of charged secondaries in proton-proton collisions are given as a function of incident energy in Fig. 3.

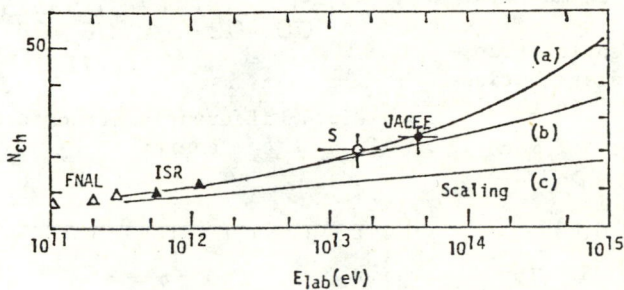

Fig. 3 Energy dependence of multiplicities

Our estimated value for the average multiplicity is 24 ± 4 at the mean energy of 45 TeV. This value includes corrections for the mass of acrylic plates in the target and for the detection bias against large-angle charged secondaries. As shown in Fig. 2, the angular distribution of charged secondaries is distorted in the regions corresponding to $\tan \theta_{ch} > 10^{-1}$. The solid curves in Fig. 3 show three functional dependences for N_{ch}: (a) $0.35 + (\sqrt{S}-2m)^{0.46}$, (b) $1.4 + 0.15(\ln S) + 0.16(\ln S)^2$, and (c) $-0.32 + 1.21(\ln S)$. The point labeled S is obtained from a similar emulsion chamber technique by Sato et al.[2] It is concluded from this figure that the charged particle multiplicities grow faster than $a + b(\ln S)$.

3. Fractional Energy Spectrum of Gamma Rays

The differential fractional energy spectrum of gamma rays, $F = E\gamma/\Sigma E\gamma$, is shown in Fig. 4. In the region $F > 0.15$ the spectrum is represented by the exponential distribution:

$$dN/dF = \text{const} \times \exp(-aF), \quad a = 11 \pm 1 \quad .$$

556

This result is consistent with a previous balloon emulsion chamber experiment[2] in the lower energy region and with the Chacaltaya experiment[3] in the higher energy region. The fractional energy variable F can be related to the Feynman scaling variable x_F. Our data seems to show evidence for scaling of the F spectrum in the energy range 10 TeV to several hundred TeV except in the region of F < 0.15.

4.   Transverse Momentum Distribution of Gamma Rays

The differential transverse momentum distribution of gamma rays $P_{T\gamma}$ in the regions of center of mass pseudo-rapidity $\langle\eta\rangle \simeq 2.5$ and Feynman scaling variable $\langle X_F\rangle \simeq 0.03$ is shown in Fig. 5. The detection thresholds in the present analysis are $E_\gamma \geq 30$ GeV and $\theta_\gamma \leq 5 \times 10^{-3}$. Therefore, the regions of $P_{T\gamma} > 0.15$ are useful for obtaining the transverse momentum spectrum, which exhibits an exponential form

$dN/dP_{T\gamma}$/event
$= $ const $\times \exp(-P_{T\gamma}/P_0)$.

The mean transverse momentum of gamma rays is determined to be $P_0 = 0.19 \pm 0.02$ GeV/c.

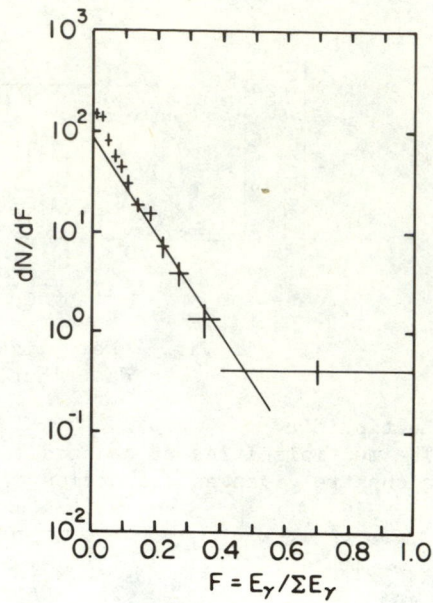

Fig.4 Differential fractional energy

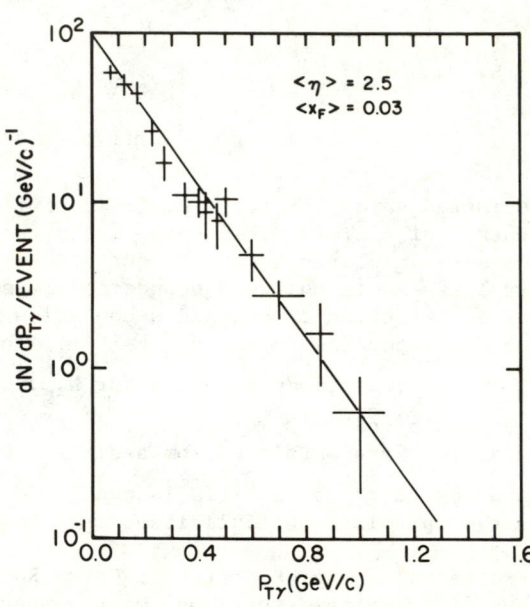

Fig. 5 Differential transverse momentum distribution

Then the mean transverse momentum of neutral pions is equal to $2P_0 = 0.38 \pm 0.04$ GeV/c, if we assume π° decay is the main source of gamma rays.

5. Rapidity Density

The rapidity densities $\rho(\eta)$ are shown as a function of center of mass energy $\sqrt{S}$ in Fig. 6. The present results are shown by solid circles. The results from other experiments are given by the symbols marked F[4], S[2], A[5], C[6], P[7], and ISR[8]. The points A, C and P at energies greater than $\sqrt{S} = 250$ GeV each show the data from analysis of one event. Because of the statistical limitations, the apparent increase in rapidity densities at energies greater than $\sqrt{S} = 300$ GeV ($E_0 = 45$ TeV) remains an unsolved problem. The scaling violation in the central region seems to be consistent with $(\sqrt{S})^{0.3}$.

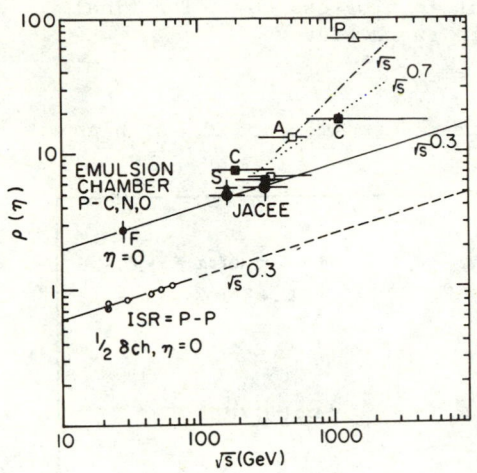

Fig. 6 Energy dependence of rapidity densities

NUCLEUS-NUCLEUS INTERACTIONS

1. Large Multiplicity Events

The angular distribution of shower particles from a Si-AgBr interaction with multiplicity approximately 1000 is shown in Fig. 7. It is impossible to measure precisely the numbers of the charged secondaries in the angular region smaller than

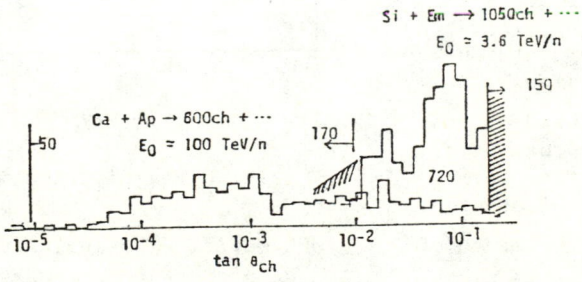

Fig. 7 Angular distribution of large multiplicity events

558

10^{-2} because the tracks are superimposed. The number of particles in the region larger than 2×10^{-1} are counted roughly to be more than 150 particles. For comparison, the angular distribution of charged secondaries from a Ca – C interaction is shown in the same figure. The latter event, which has primary energy around 10^{15} eV (the highest energy event ever observed directly) has multiplicity around 600. This multiplicity is understandable in terms of the usual nucleus–nucleus interaction process, if the incident energy and mass are considered. On the other hand, the multiplicity of the Si event is greater than expected, because the energy per nucleon (3.6 TeV) of the event is not exceptionally high. The detailed analysis for this event is in progress now. The final results will be presented elsewhere in the future.

2. High P_T Particle Production

So far we have measured the transverse momenta $P_{T\gamma}$ of high energy gamma rays for 25 nucleus–nucleus interactions out of about 60 events with energies greater than 1 TeV/nucleon. The typical $P_{T\gamma}$ distribution is shown in Fig. 8. The integral $P_{T\gamma}$ spectrum is represented by a single exponential distribution with mean $P_{T\gamma}$ of 180 MeV/c. Four of the 25 analyzed events indicate that some particles are produced with high $P_{T\gamma}$, as shown by the integral spectra in Fig. 9 (a), (b), (c), and (d). The distributions of the high $P_{T\gamma}$ cascades in these events seem to be approximated by an exponential form with mean $P_{T\gamma}$ of about

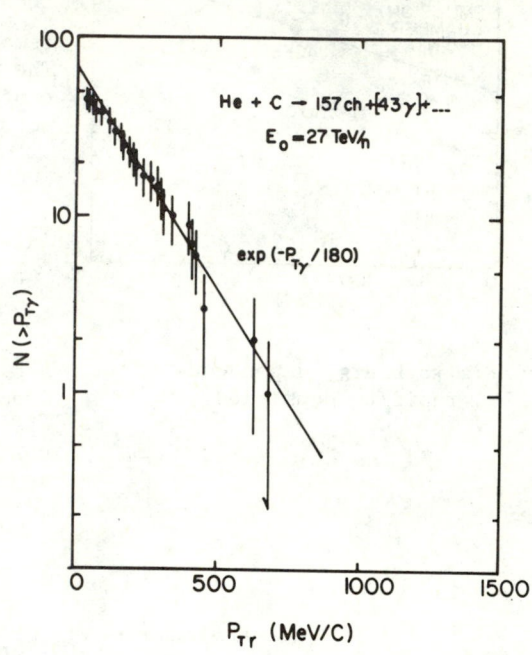

Fig. 8 $P_{T\gamma}$ distribution

500 MeV/c in the range of $P_{T\gamma} \geq 500$ MeV/c. The inclusive $P_{T\gamma}$ distribution of the four events with apparent high $P_{T\gamma}$ particle production is shown in Fig. 10. This distribution is fitted by a exponential form with mean $P_{T\gamma}$ of (540 ± 30) MeV/c in what is

presently thought to be the bias-free region. This is a factor of three greater than the mean value expected for the $P_{T\gamma}$ distribution.

The flat tails on the otherwise normal $P_{T\gamma}$ distributions shown in Figs. 9 a, b, and c result from a few gamma rays in each event, while the $P_{T\pi^0}$ distribution in Fig. 9d is unexpectedly flat for all P_T values.

The latter event occurred in the calorimeter section and, therefore, did not have the advantage of a drift space for divergence of the two gamma rays from neutral pion decay. Consequently, the individual cascades were attributed to both gamma rays from π^0 decay.

It is possible that disparity in energy between the gamma rays from π^0 decay could cause fluctuations that produce the flat tails in Figs. 9 a, b, and c. Likewise, the structure in Fig. 9d might be caused by collimated multiple pions, although this event has a striking appearance in that the cascade cores are distinctly separated. Monte Carlo simulations will help interpret these events. The data for the Ar + Pb interaction will be checked by determining the momentum of charged pions via measurements of scattering in the lead plates.

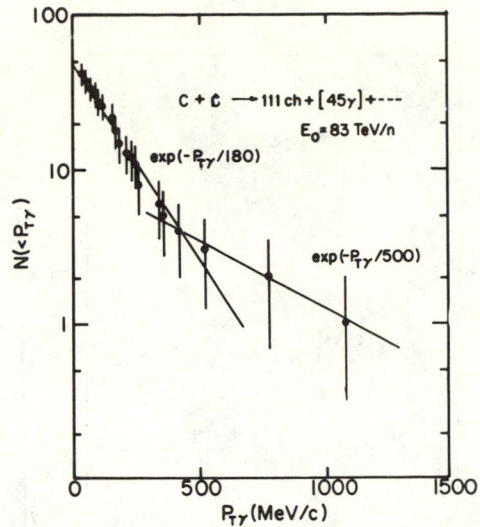

Fig. 9a $P_{T\gamma}$ distribution

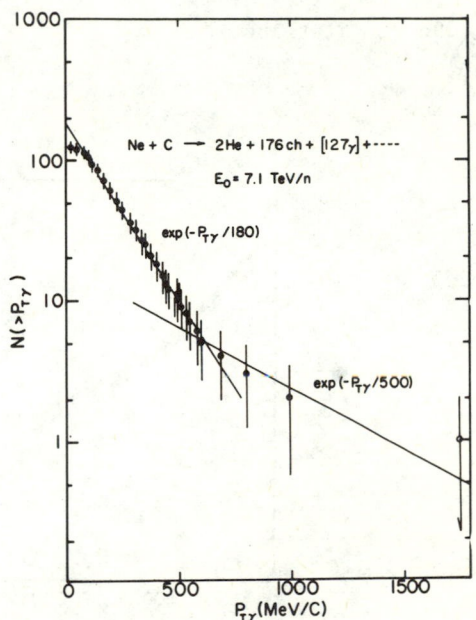

Fig. 9b $P_{T\gamma}$ distribution

560

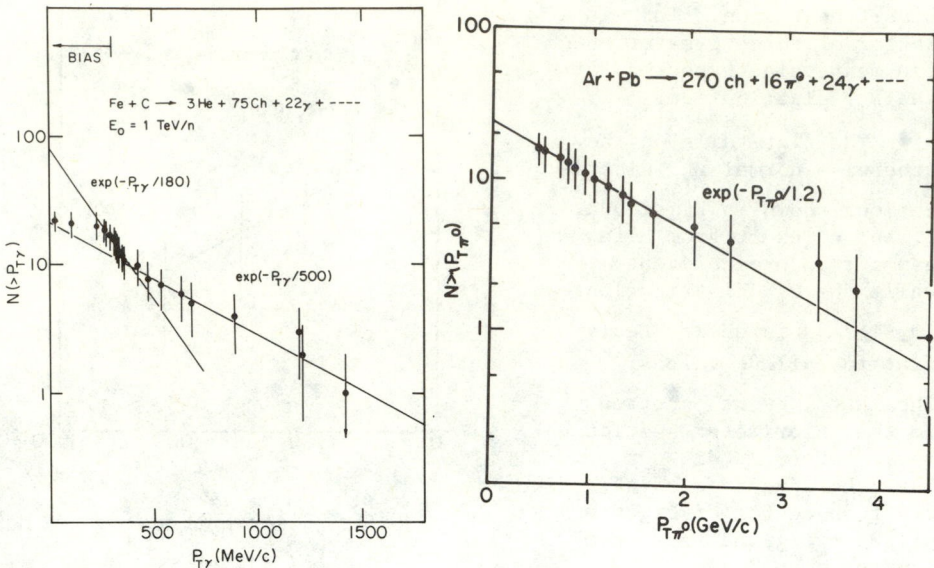

Fig. 9c $P_{T\gamma}$ distribution   Fig. 9d $P_{T\gamma}$ distribution

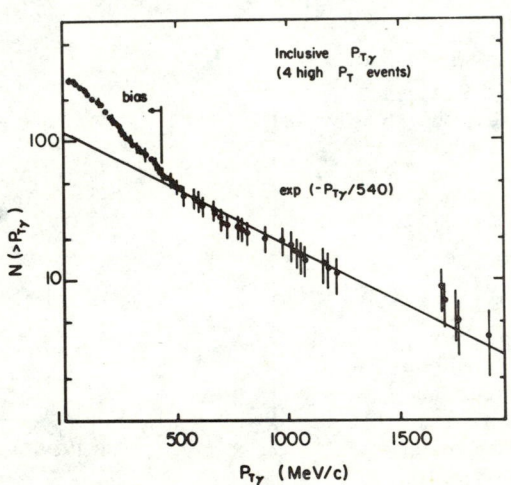

Fig. 10 Inclusive P_T distribution
of 4 high P_T events

CONCLUSION

The JACEE data at the mean energy of 45 TeV indicate that the gross features of proton-nucleus interactions vary only gradually with the incident energy. No unusual features have been observed for such interactions over the energy region from about 5 - 100 TeV. On the other hand, some unexpected results are apparent in the data for nucleus-nucleus interactions. The extremely large multiplicity ($n_s \simeq 1000$) and high transverse momentum particle production ($P_T \simeq 540$ MeV/c) imply that nucleus-nucleus interactions may not be represented by simple superpositions of nucleon-nucleon interactions. It is important to confirm these preliminary results with larger statistics before making any theoretica interpretations.

* This work is supported in part in Japan by ICR, JSPS, and the Kajima Foundation, and in part in the USA by DOE, NASA, and NSF.

REFERENCES

1. G. B. Yodh, Invited Talk, Brookhaven Symposium on Prospect of Strong Interaction Physics at Isabelle, April 1977, (X-661-77-174, GSFC/NASA, July 1977).
2. Y. Sato, H. Sugimoto and T. Saito, J. Phys. Soc. Japan 41, 1821 (1976).
3. Brazil-Japan Collaboration, AIP 49, 94 (1978).
4. H. Fuch et al., Nuovo Cimento 45A, 471 (1978).
5. T. Ogata et al., 16th Int. Cosmic Ray Conf. 6, 100 (1979).
6. J. N. Capdeville et al., 16th Int. Cosmic Ray Conf. 6, 324 (1979).
7. P. H. Fowler, 8th Int. Cosmic Ray Conf. 5, 182 (1963).

BARYON PRODUCTION AT VERY HIGH ENERGIES $\sim 10^6$ GeV

S. C. Tonwar*

Department of Physics and Astronomy
University of Maryland, College Park, MD 20742

ABSTRACT

Experimental measurements of the charged to neutral ratio for high energy hadrons in extensive air showers of primary energies $\sim 10^6$ GeV are discussed in relation to the expected values from Monte Carlo simulations. The charged to neutral ratio is sensitive to the baryon content of hadrons in air showers. A large ratio represents dominance of pions while nucleon dominance would result in a ratio close to unity. Experiments show a small charge ratio at high energies indicating the presence of a large number of baryons among the hadrons. These observations suggest that baryon production cross-section in p-p collisions, which has been seen to increase by a factor of about 2 from Fermilab energies to CERN - ISR energies, continues to increase with energy. Observed charged to neutral ratio requires that the baryon content of particles produced in the central region in p-p collisions increases from about 7% at ISR energies to more than about 15% at CERN - $\bar{P}P$ Collider energies.

High energy (> 50 GeV) hadron component in extensive air showers of energies $\sim 10^5 - 10^7$ GeV has been extensively studied experimentally[1-11] to obtain characteristics of particle interactions at these very high energies. However apparent discrepancies[12] between the experimental results from different experiments have prevented any definite conclusions to be drawn about the characteristics of particle interactions at air shower energies. Recently these discrepancies have been studied[13] in detail and it has been shown that inadequate consideration of instrumental response functions in Monte Carlo simulation of experimental data is mostly responsible for the confusion in interpretation of various observations. Since different types of hadron detectors, for example, particle burst detectors[1,3,4,8], calorimeters[2,6,7], multiplate cloud chambers[3,5,9-11], etc., have been used in these experiments, very different response functions have to be considered in simulation of results from different experiments. It has been shown experimentally[11,14] that the flux of high energy hadrons measured by large area calorimeters[2,6] at mountain altitude, for example, is expected to be larger than that measured by cloud

* On leave from Tata Institute of Fundamental Research, Colaba, Bombay-400 005

chambers[5,11]. This is due to the fact that the former type of detectors basically measure the flux of energy flow in hadronic component while the latter type measures the flux of individual hadrons. These studies[11,14] suggest that showers contain fewer high energy hadrons than expected from Monte Carlo simulations[11,12,15] which could be interpreted in terms of violation of scaling[16] behavior for inclusive particle cross-sections at air shower energies.

Among various characteristics of high energy hadrons observed experimentally, one of the most interesting has been the observation of a surprisingly large number of neutral hadrons. Early observations[9,17] of a small value for the charged to neutral ratio for hadrons of energies > 50 GeV in showers initiated by primaries of energies $\sim 10^6$ GeV were shown[18,19] to be grossly inconsistent with the ratio expected from Monte Carlo simulations using the then popular models[20] of particle interactions at high energies. Since then detailed measurements of C/N ratio have been reported by Vatcha et al[5] from observations at mountain altitude (800 g.cm^{-2}) and by Ashton et al[21] at sea level. Recently Asakimori et al[10] have presented a careful reanalysis of the data first reported by Kameda et al[9]. Also new measurements, both at mountain altitude and sea level, were reported by Sreekantan et al[11] and Dobrzynski et al[22] respectively at the last Cosmic Ray Conference in Paris this year. All the available data on the C/N ratio are summarized in figure 1 for observations at mountain altitude and sea level separately. Some data points which are thought to be either based on very poor statistics or suffer from large instrumental biases as discussed in detail later, have not been shown in figure 1 to avoid confusion. This figure shows the variation of the C/N ratio with hadron energy, for showers of size $\sim 10^5$ at mountain altitude and $\sim 2.10^5$ at sea level.

These observations of the C/N ratio have been compared with values expected from Monte Carlo simulations[5,18,19,23]. As with results on the hadron component mentioned earlier, discrepancies between the results from different experiments have been discussed[23]. However, unlike the large differences in instrumental response functions for different experiments[1-11] for hadron studies, the situation is much more clear for the measurements of C/N ratio. As seen from the figure the results from all the experiments except that of Ashton et al[21], agree well with each other within the statistical errors. Also the general trend of a decrease in C/N ratio with increasing hadron energy is seen both by Vatcha et al[5] and Dobrzynski et al[22]. On the other hand, the results reported by Ashton et al[21] show too large a value for the C/N ratio at low energies and an increase in this ratio at higher energies. However before giving any significance to this discrepancy it is of interest to discuss some details of the experimental methods used by various groups, to find out possible reasons for the differences in experimental results.

Experiments[5,9,11] which have used multiplate cloud chambers to study the nature of the charge of the hadron are almost completely

564

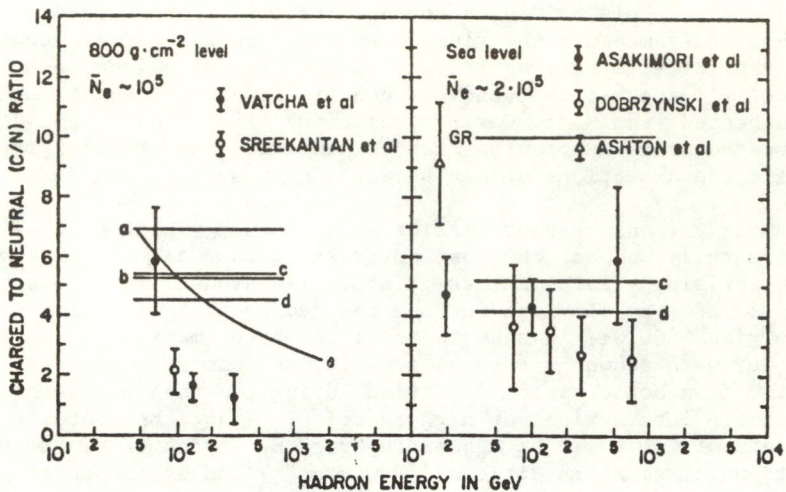

Figure 1: Variation of the charged to neutral ratio for hadrons at mountain altitude and sea level with hadron energy. Points represent experimental data and lines (a,b,...e, GR) show the expectations from Monte Carlo simulations. GR - Gaisser et al[23], a, b, ...e - our calculations (see text).

free from any instrumental biases for or against the neutral hadrons. This is due to the fact that the spatial resolution in a cloud chamber is exceptionally good ($\sim$ 2 mm) and the energy measurement is reasonably accurate[24]. Since the cascades are observable for depths of 10 radiation lengths or more from the starting points a good estimate of the track length integral is obtained. Most significantly the charge of the hadron can be determined in the presence of a large number of particles produced by far more numerous low energy hadrons. Also since the directions of particles are well reproduced by the tracks in the cloud chamber there is no confusion in assignment of charge (charged or neutral) for the hadrons due to nearby associated particles or due to albedo particles coming from the hadron interaction in the absorber below. Use of wide gap spark chambers[22] for measuring the charge of the hadron is also expected to give reliable results due to its good spatial and directional resolution. Since the light intensity of the sparks varies inversely with the number of particles traversing the chamber, charge determination is not possible with spark chambers for hadrons too close to the shower core. Dobrzynski et al[22] have, in fact, considered only those hadrons which had only few associated particles in the spark chamber used for determination of charge. Since the Monte Carlo calculations show that lateral distribution away from the shower core for neutral and charged hadrons is not expected to be very different, the C/N ratio measured by Dobrzynski et al is not affected much by this selection condition. Also since two spark chambers with absorber between them were used to study the cascade direction, the backscattered particles would be recognizable for most of the events.

Ashton et al[21] have used a calorimeter with neon flash tube arrays to detect hadrons and their interactions. The array used for determining the charge of the hadron contained eight layers of flash tubes, each tube being 1.6 cm in diameter and 1.7 m in length. It is clear that for hadrons close to the shower core charge determination with such a (essentially one-dimensional) system is rather difficult. As pointed out by the authors themselves, showers with large particle density above the calorimeter often had large number of particles through the flash tube array. It is expected that the bias in charge determination with this system is always against the neutral hadrons. Also since higher energy hadrons are associated with larger density either due to their proximity to the shower core or due to larger shower size, higher energy neutral hadrons would be discriminated against to a larger extent. Further the backscattered particles are difficult to identify with this system due to its poor angular resolution. Some of the neutral hadrons showing a charged albedo particle in neon flash tubes would get classified as charged hadrons. It may be noted that Ellsworth et al[25] have observed experimentally $\sim$ 35% of hadron interactions in a 15 cm iron plate for energies > 100 GeV to have one or more particles going backwards, within about 30° of the direction of the incident hadron. The basic data of Ashton et al, 34 neutrals and 313 charged hadrons for energies > 15 GeV with shower density > 20 m^{-2}, can therefore give quite different C/N ratio depending on the correction factor due to these instrumental effects. For example, if it is assumed that about 10% of their charged hadrons were really neutral hadrons with charged albedo particles, the C/N ratio would change from the quoted value of 9.2 to 4.3, making it consistent with other measurements. In fact, a recent measurement by Ashton et al[26] has given the value of C/N ratio as 7.1 for hadrons of energy > 13 GeV. Considering these experimental uncertainties and in order to avoid some confusion, only the lowest energy value of C/N ratio given by Ashton et al[21] has been shown in figure 1.

This discussion shows that the experimental results are in reasonably good agreement with each other if instrumental factors affecting some of the measurements are taken into consideration. The C/N ratio seems to be smaller than three for hadrons of energy > 50 GeV at mountain altitude and smaller than four at sea level. Many attempts[5,18,19,23,27] have been made to understand these observations through Monte Carlo simulation for air showers. The results from early calculations using a variety of plausible models[16,20] for particle interactions at high energies by the Tata group[5,18,19] showed that these observations could be understood only if baryon production cross-section increased significantly at higher energies.

It may be noted that similar conclusion was reached from a study[19] of arrival time distribution of hadrons in air showers. These calculations assumed that the content of baryons among particles produced in the central region increased from ~ 0.5% at 30 GeV (CERN-PS) to about 15% at 3000 GeV (CERN-ISR). Though the basic result was later confirmed by ISR experiments[28], it was seen that the baryon content increased to only ~ 7% up to the highest ISR energy. Also the multiplicity dependence on energy in some of the models[20] considered was too rapid to be consistent with the recent new results[29,30] from UA 1 and UA 5 experiments at the $\bar{P}P$ Collider.

Using scaling model[16] for particle interactions Gaisser et al[23] have found the expected value of the C/N ratio to be about 10 for hadrons of energy > 50 GeV and independent of hadron energy (shown in figure 1 by line marked GR). In their calculations Gaisser et al have assumed the baryon production cross-section to increase with energy according to the model of Gaisser and Halzen[31]. This model for production of heavy particles gives a good fit to the data[28] for production of K^-, $\bar{p}$, $\bar{\Lambda}$ etc. up to ISR energies. It is clear from the figure that the number of neutral particles observed is much larger than the number predicted by Gaisser et al.

We have studied the dependence of the expected C/N ratio on some of the parameters of high energy particle interactions assumed in Monte Carlo simulations of air showers and also on the nature of the cosmic ray primaries initiating the showers. In our calculations hadronic interactions have been simulated with an independent particle emission model. Secondary momenta are drawn at random from probability distributions obtained from Feynman[18] scaling of the invariant single particle inclusive cross-sections. No correlations between the longitudinal and transverse momenta have been assumed. The effects due to the nuclear composition of the target have been neglected here and the target has been assumed to be a nucleon in all interactions. Showers initiated by primary nuclei were simulated using the superposition assumption. The inelastic cross-sections for hadron-air nucleus collisions have been assumed to be energy dependent. The values for the parameters A and B for x and p_t distributions,

$$E\frac{d^3\sigma}{dp^3} \sim e^{-A \cdot x} \qquad \text{and} \qquad \frac{dn}{dp_t} \sim p_t \cdot e^{-B \cdot p_t} \quad ,$$

for different types of incident and produced particles have been chosen such as to give a good fit to the data available from ISR experiments. Large p_t component has also been included in the calculations approximately. The simulation procedure yields reasonably accurate, within few percent, conservation of energy and momentum in each interaction. Electron size for the shower is obtained by summing the contribution due to each γ-ray produced by the decay of a π° or a kaon, using Approximation B of the cascade theory. Details of various assumptions underlying these simulations are discussed elsewhere.[32]

The most important parameter for simulating the charged to neutral ratio for hadrons is the relative fraction of different species of particles produced at high energies. In the present simulations each secondary particle is assigned to be a nucleon (or antinucleon), kaon or pion through a random selection based on assumed relative production probabilities. The probability for a secondary particle to be a kaon has been assumed to be 0.1 and energy independent. The kaon is assigned to be charged or neutral with equal probability. Pions are randomly tagged as neutral with an average probability of 0.33. Pions and kaons are allowed to decay with appropriate probabilities. The probability f_N for a produced particle to be a nucleon (proton, neutron, antiproton or antineutron with equal probability) has been assumed to be energy dependent as

$$f_N = f_o \cdot \ln (1 + 0.015 \cdot E_1)$$

where E_1 is the energy of the incident particle in the laboratory system in GeV. Two different values for f_o have been considered in the simulations to study the sensitivity of the expected C/N ratio on the baryon production cross-section.

The energies of the primaries have been chosen appropriately to give the average shower size close to the average size for the experimental data. The energies for the primary iron nuclei have been properly scaled up to take care of the fact that showers initiated by iron nuclei yield smaller size, about a factor of 2.5 at 800 g.cm^{-2}, relative to proton primaries of same energy. For the discussion of results given below, showers have not been grouped according to size because it has been noticed that the C/N ratio does not depend on the size or the number of hadrons in individual showers. It may be noted that for the study of some other parameters of the hadron component like the energy spectra, it is very necessary to analyze the simulated showers grouped according to shower size.

The expected variation of the average C/N ratio with hadron energy for proton-initiated showers of average size $\sim 10^5$ at mountain altitude, assuming

$$f_o = 0.01 \quad ,$$

is given in figure 1 by the line a. The line b gives the values of C/N ratio expected for iron nucleus primaries. It is interesting to note that the average C/N ratio for hadrons of energy > 50 GeV is only slightly smaller for iron nucleus showers (5.2) compared to proton showers (6.9). However this is understandable since many of the primary nucleons in showers initiated by iron nuclei arrive at the observational level with energies much below 50 GeV due to various fluctuations in their interactions. The values for the relative fraction of baryons produced at various energies, obtained using the value 0.01 for f_o are given in Table 1.

Since the expected values of C/N ratio with $f_o = 0.01$ for both primary protons and iron nuclei are much larger than the experimental values, larger baryon production was assumed in the next set of calculations by taking the value of f_o to be 0.016. The lines c and d in figure 1 represent the expected values for proton and iron nucleus initiated showers with this value of f_o. As seen from Table 1, this value leads to baryons being about 15% of all produced particles in p-p interactions of energy $\sim 10^6$ GeV. The expected values for sea level are also shown in the figure for this value of f_o. It is clear that even such a large baryon production at high energies is not large enough to predict C/N values in agreement with experimental data. These results suggest that if the C/N ratio is to be understood in terms of increasing baryon production with energy, a faster increase than implied by the value 0.016 for f_o has to be assumed at higher energies. It may be noted that though the C/N ratio predicted for iron nucleus showers is smaller, the contributions of such showers to the experimental data grouped according to shower size is not large. This is due to the fact that the energy of the primary iron nucleus has to be, on the average, about 2.5 times larger than the energy of the primary proton to give the same average shower size.

TABLE 1

Relative content of baryons among secondary particles
for various energies assumed in different calculations

Primary Hadron Energy E_1 GeV	Calculations of Tata group[5,18,19] (x 10^2)	Present calculations $f_o=0.01$	$f_o=0.016$ (x 10^2)	ISR Data (x 10^2)
10^2	2	0.9	1.5	1.2
10^3	9	2.8	4.5	4.1
10^4	14	5.0	8.1	-
10^5	14	7.3	11.8	-
10^6	14	9.6	15.5	-

Since a fraction of pions and kaons produced in the atmosphere are lost due to decay while the nucleons are not, a decrease in the C/N ratio is to be expected for calculations using interaction models which assume rapid increase in particle multiplicity with energy. In fact, this is one of the reasons for the lower values of C/N ratio obtained by Tonwar et al[19] in their calculations. It may also be noted that the observed energy dependence of particle multiplicity[30] gives faster increase than obtained with Feynman scaling model. We have simulated showers assuming an energy dependence for the parameter A in the x distribution. The functional form assumed is

$$A = A_o[1 + 0.434 \ln (E_1/1000)] \quad \text{for} \quad E_1 > 1000 \text{ GeV}$$

where A_o is the value which gives a good fit to the accelerator data at lower energies. This particular energy dependence of A gives an increase in particle multiplicity consistent with recent observations[29,30] at $\bar{P}P$ Collider. The expected C/N ratios from these simulations are shown in figure 1 by line e for various hadron energies. It is interesting to note that this model gives an energy dependence of C/N ratio very similar to that seen for experimental data. These results suggest that an interaction model with slightly faster increase of baryon production cross-section with energy compared to the form assumed here (f_o = 0.016) coupled with a faster increase in particle multiplicity with energy as observed in Collider experiments[29,30] might give a satisfactory agreement with the experimental data on C/N ratio for hadrons of various energies. However, considering the large statistical errors in the experimental data, we have not attempted further calculations. It may be pointed here that the expected C/N ratio is not very sensitive to the assumed production cross-section for kaons since most of them decay away before reaching the observational level. It is seen that, with an assumed kaon to pion ratio of 0.1 among secondary particles, the kaons form only about 10% of the hadrons reaching the observational altitude of 800 g.cm^{-2} in the atmosphere.

This discussion has shown that the charged to neutral ratio for hadrons in air showers is sensitively related to various characteristics of particle interactions at high energies. There is, therefore, an urgent need for high statistics measurement of C/N ratio and its variation with hadron energy and shower size with detectors having high spatial and energy resolution. On the basis of the comparison of the expected C/N ratio from present Monte Carlo simulations of air showers with the existing experimental data, it can be concluded that the baryon production cross-section continues to increase with energy in the energy range $\sim 10^3 - 10^6$ GeV. Observed charged to neutral ratio requires that the baryon content of particles produced in the central region in p-p collisions increases from about 7% at ISR energies to more than about 15% at CERN $\bar{P}P$ Collider energies.

REFERENCES

1. O. I. Dovzenko et al., Proc. 6th ICRC, Moscow, **2**, 34 (1960).
2. B. K. Chatterjee et al., Can. J. Phys. **46**, S 136 (1968).
3. S. Miyake et al., Acta. Phys. Acad. Sci. Hung. **29**, Suppl. 3, 461 (1970).

4. R. van Staa et al., J. Phys. A $\underline{7}$, 135 (1974).
5. R. H. Vatcha et al., J. Phys. A $\underline{6}$, 1050 (1973).
6. N. M. Nesterova et al., Proc. 15th ICRC, Plovdiv, $\underline{8}$, 113 (1977); V. A. Romakhin et al., Proc. 15th ICRC, Plovdiv, $\underline{8}$, 107 (1977).
7. J. E. F. Baruch et al., Proc. 17th ICRC, München, $\underline{8}$, 2949 (1975).
8. T. Matano et al., Acta. Phys. Acad. Sci. Hung. $\underline{29}$, Suppl. 3, 451 (1970).
9. T. Kameda et al., Proc. 9th ICRC, London, $\underline{2}$, 681 (1965).
10. K. Asakimori et al., Proc. 16th ICRC, Kyoto, $\underline{13}$, 229 (1979).
11. B. V. Sreekantan et al., Proc. 17th ICRC, Paris, $\underline{6}$, (1981).
12. M. Ouldridge et al., J. Phys. G $\underline{4}$, L35 (1978); A. M. Hillas, Proc. 16th ICRC, Kyoto, $\underline{9}$, 13 (1979).
13. B. V. Sreekantan et al., Proc. 16th ICRC, Kyoto, $\underline{8}$, 287 (1979).
14. S. C. Tonwar, Rapporteur Paper, Proc. 17th ICRC, Paris (1981).
15. P. K. F. Grieder, Rev. Nuovo Cim. $\underline{7}$, 1 (1977).
16. R. P. Feynman, Phys. Rev. Lett. $\underline{23}$, 1415 (1969); J. Benecke et al., Phys. Rev. $\underline{188}$, 2159 (1969).
17. S. Miyake et al., J. Phys. Soc. Japan, $\underline{13}$, 782 (1958).
18. G. T. Murthy et al., Can. J. Phys. $\underline{3}$, S 147 (1968)
19. S. C. Tonwar et al., Lett. Nuovo Cim. $\underline{1}$, 531 (1971).
20. G. Cocconi et al., Lawrence Rad. Lab. Preprint (1961); Y. Pal and B. Peters, Mat. Fys. Medd. Dan. Vidsk, $\underline{15}$, 33 (1964).
21. F. Ashton et al., Proc. 14th ICRC, München, $\underline{8}$, 2980 (1975).
22. K. Dobrzynski et al., Proc. 17th ICRC, Paris, $\underline{6}$, 206 (1981).
23. T. K. Gaisser et al., J. Phys. G $\underline{2}$, 781 (1976).
24. R. H. Vatcha et al., J. Phys. A $\underline{5}$, 859 (1972).
25. R. W. Ellsworth et al., Astr. and Sp. Sci. $\underline{52}$, 415 (1977); R. W. Ellsworth et al., Univ. of Maryland Preprint (1982).
26. F. Ashton et al., Proc. 17th ICRC, Paris, $\underline{6}$, 203 (1981).
27. P. K. F. Grieder, Proc. 17th ICRC, Paris, $\underline{6}$, 284 (1981).
28. M. Antinucci et al., Lett. Nuovo Cim. $\underline{6}$, 121 (1973).
29. G. Arnison et al., Phys. Lett. $\underline{107}$B, 320 (1981).
30. K. Alpgard et al., Phys. Lett. $\underline{107}$B, 315 (1981).
31. T. K. Gaisser and F. Halzen, Proc. 14th ICRC, München, $\underline{7}$, 2431 (1975).
32. J. A. Goodman et al., Univ. of Maryland Preprint (1982).

REVIEW OF LOW P_T PHYSICS
FROM COSMIC RAYS*

T. K. Gaisser
Bartol Research Foundation of The Franklin Institute
University of Delaware, Newark, Delaware 19711

ABSTRACT

This paper covers several aspects of low P_T physics as seen by cosmic ray interactions around 100 TeV and above ($\sqrt{s} \gtrsim 500$ GeV). Current detailed investigation of these phenomena at $\bar{p}p$ colliders will lead to progress in cosmic ray astrophysics if physics of the forward fragmentation region can be determined.

INTRODUCTION

The flux of primary cosmic rays extends at least to 10^{20} eV, but it is a rapidly decreasing function of energy.[1] The total rate of nuclei with E > 100 TeV incident on the atmosphere is less than one particle per m^2 per hour. Studies of the interactions of these particles are thus indirect, involving large detectors exposed for long periods at a considerable depth in the atmosphere.[2] Properties of the primaries and of their interactions must both be inferred from limited measurements of their cascades. A standard procedure has been (i) to use data from accelerators up to ISR energies to determine the inclusive cross section

$$f(x, P_T, \sqrt{s}) = \frac{1}{\sigma} \frac{d^3\sigma}{dp^3}, \tag{1}$$

(ii) to assume $f = f(x, P_T)$ only, (iii) then to use the distributions so determined for computer simulations and other calculations of cosmic ray cascades. As usual $x \equiv P_{\shortparallel}/(\sqrt{s}/2)$. Moreover, for cosmic ray cascades in most cases only fast secondaries are effective, for which $x_{cm} \cong x_{lab}$.

Comparisons of such calculations with various cosmic ray data have led to the tentative conclusions that the cross section continues to increase with energy and that the primary cosmic rays may be rich in heavy nuclei,[2,3] especially around $10^{14} - 10^{15}$ eV total energy per nucleus.[4,5] Some argue that not all data can be explained in this way, and that the increasing inelasticity of cascades in this energy range is due to violation of the scaling implied by Eq. 1 rather than to an increasing component of heavy nuclei.[6,7] (Recall that cascade development can be made more rapid both by steepening $f(x)$ and by increasing the fraction of heavy nuclei. Either has the effect of subdividing and dissipating the initial energy more rapidly than with proton primaries and scaling.)

* Work supported in part by the U.S. Department of Energy under contract number DE-AC02-78ER05007.

We expect this ambiguity to be resolved soon by data from the CERN $\bar{p}p$ collider. Although the height of the central rapidity density alone is not sufficient, since cascade development depends primarily on the fragmentation region, energy conservation relates energy deposition at wide angles to that at forward angles.[8] Study of the energy deposited inside $\theta_{min} \leq \theta \leq 180 - \theta_{min}$ for minimum bias events will thus give some information on the question of scale violation in the fragmentation region provided θ_{min} is not too large. Of course, direct measurement of secondaries at large X is necessary for definitive, model-independent results.

The region around 10^{15} eV is of particular interest to cosmic ray astrophysics since the primary spectrum is known to have a shoulder just above this energy.[1] Cosmic ray acceleration and confinement in the galaxy are presumably dependent on magnetic rigidity, whereas cosmic ray cascades are classified by total energy per nucleus. The primary composition in this energy range should therefore be a useful probe of cosmic ray acceleration and propagation mechansims.

CROSS SECTION

As an illustration of the ideas discussed above, I discuss some recent results on simulation of γ-families and comparison to experimental data.

Table I (from M. Shibata, Ref.9)

Model	I/I_{expt}	Λ_{atten} (gm/cm^2)
PS	14	160
PRS	6	110
PC	3.5	140
→ PRC	0.6	95
MS	7	140
→ MRS	2.5	100
→ MC	1.7	125
MRC	0.3	85
experiment	1	105±20

Table I, from the paper of M. Shibata,[9] shows comparison to measurements of intensity and attenuation of families with visible electromagnetic energy $\Sigma E_\gamma > 100$ TeV. The model codes are: P or M for proton or mixed composition (only 10% protons at fixed energy per nucleus for M); R means interaction cross section rising with energy (see Fig. 1); and S or C means scaling or violation of scaling (with $\alpha = 1/4$ in terms of Wdowczyk and Wolfendale[10] scale-breaking).

The earlier work of Ellsworth et al.[11] used a model close to RS (with various primary nuclei treated separately) to study γ-hadron families and the question of how anomalous are the Centauro events. These and other independent simulations were compared recently[12] to check their reliability. Comparable calculations gave rather similar

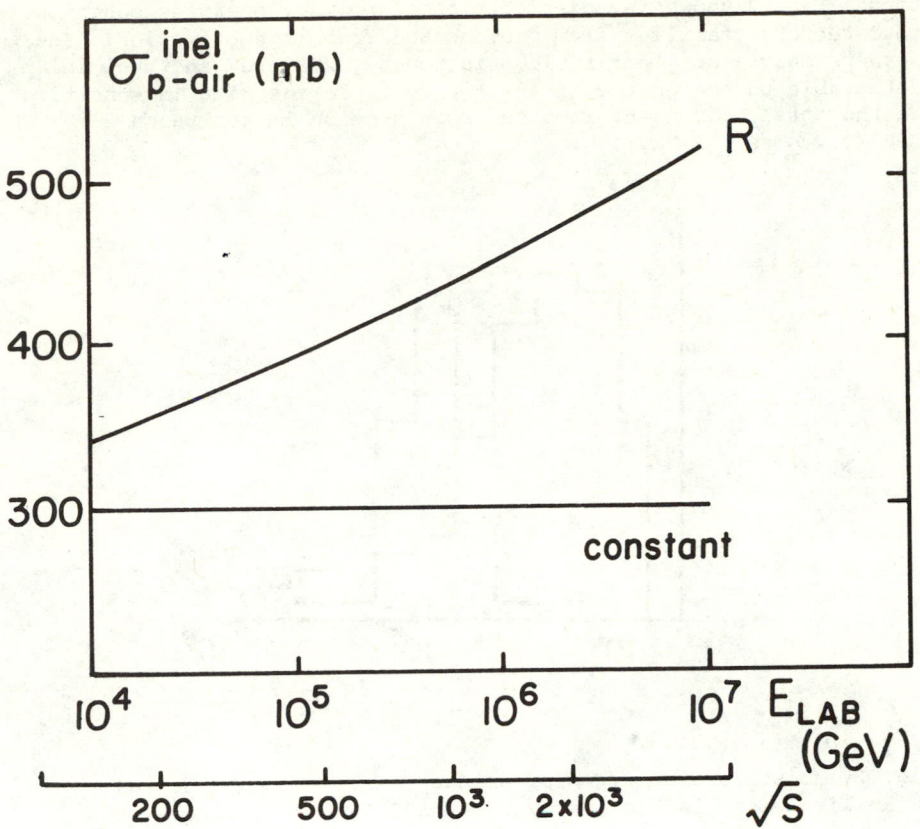

Fig. 1. Inelastic p-air cross sections used for calculations of Ref. 9. They are close to the constant and $\log^2 s$ values of Ref. 15.

results considering differences in detailed assumptions. In particular the absolute normalizations were within a factor of two of each other for rates of families per primary nucleus. Moreover, the absolute rate of families seemed to be one of the experimental aspects most sensitive to models of cross section, interaction and composition, despite a factor of two uncertainty in normalization of the overall primary spectrum.

The models in Table I marked by an arrow have $1/3 \leq I/I_{expt} \leq 3$ and attentuation Λ within one sigma of the experimental value. The model labelled C has probably already been ruled out by data from the CERN $\bar{p}p$ collider (see discussion below), so the most likely conclusion is that the proton cross section continues to rise beyond ISR energies and the composition is rich in heavy nuclei. Simulations[11] show[12] that a proton is three times more likely to produce a family with visible energy above 100 TeV than an alpha primary and 25 times more than an iron primary; so most families will be

574

produced by protons unless the composition is extremely poor in protons. Fig. 2 shows the distribution of primary energies contributing to detectable families from protons and from iron primaries. The mean primary energy per nucleon is roughly 2000 TeV and the minimum detectable photon energy is about 2 TeV. So the rate is sensitive to the total hadron interaction cross section in the range 20 - 2000 TeV ($0.2 \leq \sqrt{s} \leq 2$ TeV).

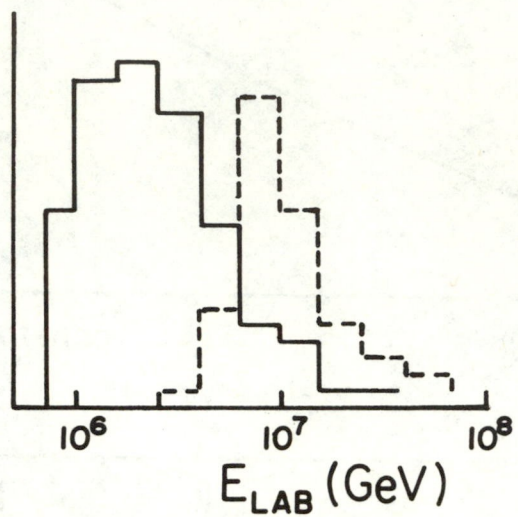

$$E_{LAB} \, (GeV)$$

Fig. 2. Distribution of total primary energies contributing to γ-families with visible energy above 100 TeV (Ref. 11).

Despite the uncertainty in overall normalization of the primary spectrum and the possibility that there is some violation of scaling in the fragmentation region, it thus appears likely that the inelastic proton-air cross section is around 400 - 450 mb at $\sqrt{s} = 1$ TeV, i.e. 30 - 50% higher than its value around $\sqrt{s} = 100$ GeV. (see Fig. 1) Assuming $\sigma^{Tot}_{pp} \cong 46$ mb at $\sqrt{s} = 100$ GeV, a 30 - 50% increase would correspond to $\sigma^{Tot}_{pp} \cong 60 - 70$ mb at $\sqrt{s} = 1$ TeV. If there is nuclear screening of the hadronic cross section as estimated by Glauber theory,[14] then the corresponding σ^{Tot}_{pp} would be somewhat larger, roughly 70 - 80 mb. So a fairly safe guess would be $\sigma^{Tot}_{pp} = 70 \pm 10$ mb at $\sqrt{s} = 1$ TeV and ~ 5 mb smaller at 500 GeV.

The prospects for determining the proton cross section up to $\sqrt{s} \sim 50$ TeV in the near future from other cosmic ray experiments are discussed elsewhere in this volume.[15]

MEAN TRANSVERSE MOMENTUM

Cosmic ray evidence from emulsion stacks on mean transverse momentum has been summarized by Adcock et al. in 1970.[16] Here I just mention that analysis of separation distributions of underground muons[17] also suggests a mean P_T of 500 - 700 MeV/c at center of mass energies of several hundred GeV. This has been confirmed by new calculations[18] that include comparison to new data from Homestake,[19] which extend the range of muon separations covered by the Utah central detector. It should be borne in mind that the energetic muons that penetrate deep underground come preferentially from the forward fragmentation region and would therefore be expected to have somewhat higher P_T than the average of all particles.

INCLUSIVE CROSS SECTIONS

Earliest data from the $\bar{p}p$ collider at CERN[20,21] are already sufficient to show that the more extreme forms of scaling violation that have been used to explain various cosmic ray data (i.e. those with α = .25 and α = 0.5) are most likely incorrect. As Wdowczyk and Wolfendale will show elsewhere in this volume, a fairly mild scaling violation in the fragmentation region is consistent with the data. They suggest a value of $\alpha \equiv \frac{1-\beta}{2} \cong 0.11$, where α and β are the scale-breaking parameters they define. The increase in mean P_T at $\sqrt{s}$ = 540 GeV is also suggestive of some scale-breaking.[22] It is impossible however, to be certain about the fraction of energy carried by fast secondaries on the basis of the first data within the narrow range $150^0 > \theta > 30^0$, especially in view of uncertain corrections for diffractive events, etc. that have yet to be made. We assume for the time being that $0 \leq \alpha \leq 0.11$, where $\alpha=0$ for scaling and $\alpha=0.5$ is the kinematic limit.

Recalling that fast secondaries are of predominant importance for penetration of cosmic ray cascades, I show in Fig. 3 the fraction of energy below X = 0.05 as a function of interaction energy, for various values of α. This represents the fraction of the interaction energy deposited in low energy particles which dissipate cascade development. Assuming that present data already require $\alpha \leq .11$, inspection of this figure suggests that conclusions based on scaling models around 10^{15} eV (such as those discussed above in the section on proton cross section) will probably remain valid. If α is as large as 0.11, however, calculations of cascade development at Fly's Eye energies ($\sim 10^{18}$ eV) would be considerably affected since the fraction of energy below x = 0.05 reaches nearly 2/3 of its saturation value of 50%. (We assume the fraction of the energy carried by the leading nucleon is constant with energy at 50%.) Clearly, however, it is essential to explore the fragmentation region with $\bar{p}p$ colliders and to incorporate the results into analyses of all high energy cosmic ray experiments as soon as possible.

ACKNOWLEDGEMENTS

I am grateful for helpful discussions with T. Stanev and J. Wdowczyk in the preparation of this talk.

576

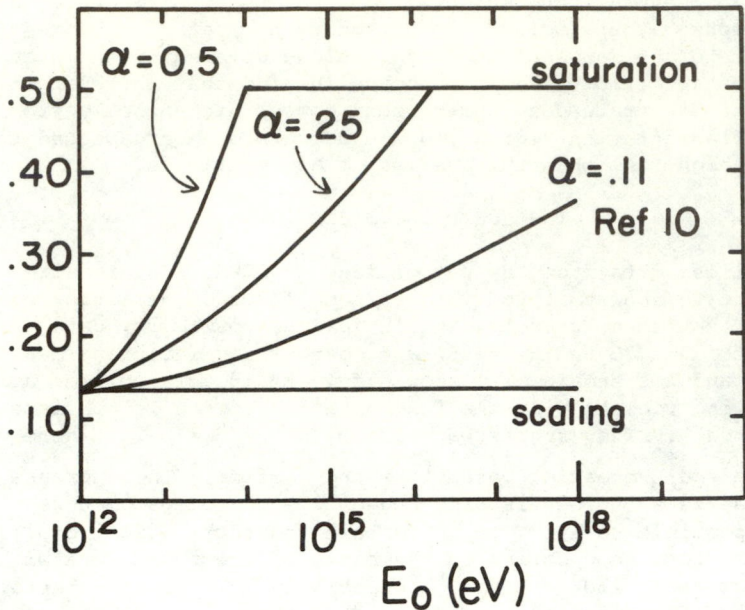

Fig. 3. Average fraction of interaction energy in secondaries with less that 5% (per secondary) of the incident energy (i.e. x < 0.05). The maximum possible value is 50% since the leading nucleons are assumed to carry off half the incident energy on average.

REFERENCES

1. A. M. Hillas, Phys. Rep. 20, 59 (1975).
2. T. K. Gaisser and G. B. Yodh, Ann. Revs. Nucl. Part. Sci. 30, 475 (1980).
3. T. K. Gaisser, et al. Revs. Mod. Phys. 50, 859 (1978).
4. G. B. Yodh, in Cosmology and Particles (Proc. Moriond Astrophysics Meeting) p.23 (1981), and references therein.
5. A. A. Watson, Ibid., p.49 and references therein.
6. A. D. Erlykin and N. P. Kuzina, Proc. Int. Seminar on Cosmic Ray Cascades, p. 99 (1980).
7. S. N. Vernov et al., J. Phys. G3, 1601 (1977).
8. T. K. Gaisser, Phys. Letters 100B, 425 (1981). The relation depends, however, on the P_T distribution, especially when the central angular region observed is small.
9. M. Shibata, Phys. Rev. D24, 1847 (1981).
10. J. Wdowczyk and A. W. Wolfendale, N.C. 54A, 433 (1979) and this volume.
11. R. W. Ellsworth et al., Phys. Rev. D23, 771 (1981).
12. T. K. Gaisser, M. Shibata and J. A. Wrotniak, Bartol Technical Report BA-81-21 (1981).
13. G. Giacomelli, Phys. Rep. 23C, 123 (1976).

14. V. Barger et al., Phys. Rev. Letters $\underline{33}$, 1051 (1974) and T. K. Gaisser et al., Proc. 14th Int. Cosmic Ray Conf. (Munich) $\underline{7}$, 2161 (1975).
15. R. W. Ellsworth et al., this volume.
16. C. Adcock et al., J. Phys. $\underline{A3}$, 697 (1970).
17. H. E. Bergeson et al., Phys. Rev. Letters $\underline{35}$, 1681 (1975).
18. J. W. Elbert, T. K. Gaisser and T. Stanev, Proc. Int. Seminar on Cosmic Ray Cascades (Sofia) p.29 (1980) and to be published.
19. M. Cherry et al., Proc. 17th Int. Cosmic Ray Conf. (Paris) paper MN3-7, late volumes, and to be published.
20. G. Arnison et al. (UAI collaboration) Phys. Letters $\underline{107B}$, 320 (1981).
21. K. Alpgard et al. (UA5 collaboration) Phys. Letters $\underline{107B}$, 310 and 315 (1981).
22. E. Predazzi, Rochester prerpint COO-3065-321 (1982).

PROPERTIES OF HIGH ENERGY INTERACTIONS DEDUCED
FROM COSMIC RAYS AND THEIR COMPARISON WITH RESULTS
FROM RECENT ACCELERATOR EXPERIMENTS

J. Wdowczyk,
Institute of Nuclear Research, Lodz, Ul. Uniwersytecka, 5,
Poland

A.W. Wolfendale,
Physics Department, University, Durham, U.K.

ABSTRACT

The development of ideas about some of the more important characteristics of high energy interactions from cosmic ray studies are considered. Cosmic ray data had suggested that simple Feynman Scaling breaks down for energetic secondaries and the authors had previously claimed that accelerator data, up to ISR energies, also show this feature. The latest pp results seem to confirm this contention, at least insofar as the mean number of secondaries and their mean transverse momentum are still rising.

INTRODUCTION

Without doubt, the 1930's and 40's were the golden days of cosmic rays from the point of view of Nuclear Physics. As is well known, the positron, muon, pion and strange particles were all discovered in that period. The 1950's saw the start of accelerator developments and slowly but surely the main thrust of high energy interaction Physics moved across to the machines.

The problem with cosmic rays is not just the low flux of the primary particles and the fact that the measurements are usually made on the interaction secondaries a long way from the 'target' (the upper levels of the atmosphere) but the nature of the primary particles themselves. At 'low' energies, below about 10^{11}eV/ nucleon, direct measurements on the primaries show not just protons but a veritable gold mine of interesting nuclei. Studies of these nuclei, particularly of their isotopic composition, are of con- siderable value to the Astrophysicist, interested in the cosmic ray sources and the mode of propagation of the particles through the interstellar medium. At higher energies, the situation for the Nuclear Physicist is worse in that there is some evidence, but no certainty, that the fraction of heavy nuclei is increasing and, indeed, above the spectral 'kink' at $\sim 3 \times 10^{15}$eV an increase is likely because of rigidity - dependent propagation effects.

The problem of distinguishing between the effects of a change in Nuclear Physics from that of composition has been a very real one and one that has exercised many cosmic ray physicists. In

the present work the description is inevitably coloured by our own
work in this field and readers must forgive a rather partisan
approach.

RESULTS FROM COSMIC RAY DATA

In early work it was shown that many extensive air shower
(EAS) phenomena could be understood in terms of a Fermi-type
multiplicity dependence on primary energy, $n_s \propto E_p^{\frac{1}{4}}$, if the mass
composition at EAS energies ($E_p > 10^{14}$ eV) was similar to that
below 10^{11} eV/nucleon where the direct measurements had been made.
With the development of Feynman[2] in 1969, of the idea of Scaling,
it was clear[3,4] that either the Scaling idea broke down above the
then accelerator energies (10^{11} eV and, later, 10^{12} eV) or that
the mean mass of the primaries was increasing with energy. The
experimental situation was straightforward - the multiplicity of
secondary particles was higher than expected on the basis of
Scaling and p-p collisions.

Our contention that Scaling broke down was based on a number
of facts, including the demonstration of an increase in mean
transverse momentum of the secondaries from observations on
multiple muons underground[5] and the evidence of high multiplicities
coupled with the presence of fluctuations in EAS properties which
indicated the presence of a significant fraction of protons.
Figures 1, 2 and 3, taken from a recent summary of Wdowczyk[6]
summarise the situation.

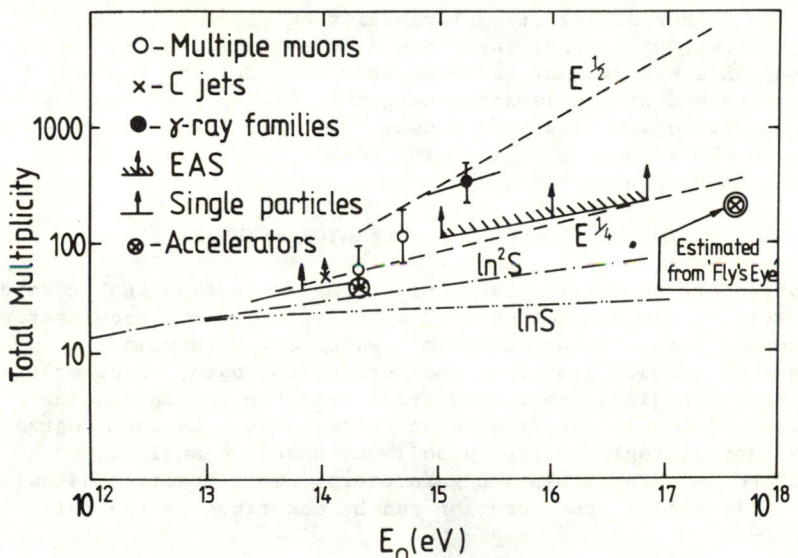

Fig. 1. The average multiplicity versus primary particle
energy.

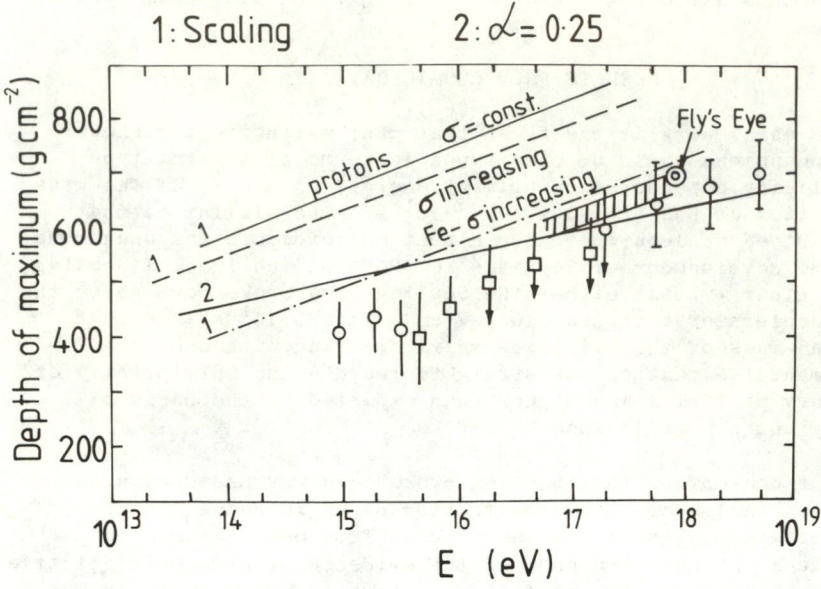

Fig. 2. Height of the shower maximum versus shower energy.

At this stage it can be remarked that there was already some evidence for a lack of strict applicability of Scaling at accelerator energies in that there was a modest increase in $\langle p_t \rangle$ with E_p but this was thought to be because true Scaling had not quite been reached at accelerator energies. The lack of Scaling in the 'central region' was well known. However, limiting fragmentation in the important region (for cosmic rays) of $x \simeq 0.2$ was thought to have been reached.

NON SCALING BEHAVIOUR AT ACCELERATOR ENERGIES

In an effort to substantiate our strong suggestion that cosmic ray interactions did not follow Scaling we examined the accelerator data in some detail. In an analysis[7], which met with some scepticism, we demonstrated that the accelerator data, whenever the accuracy was sufficient, were consistent with the assumption that Scaling is violated in the fragmentation region to the same degree as in the central region. The 'proof' was based on analysis of the so-called 'Scaling violation parameter'. We demonstrated that the Lorentz invariant cross section can be described by the following formula

$$\frac{2E}{\sqrt{s}} \frac{d^2\sigma}{dxdp_t} = \sigma_{tot} \; f(x \cdot (\frac{s}{s_0})^\alpha \, P_t) \; (\frac{s}{s_0})^\alpha \qquad (1)$$

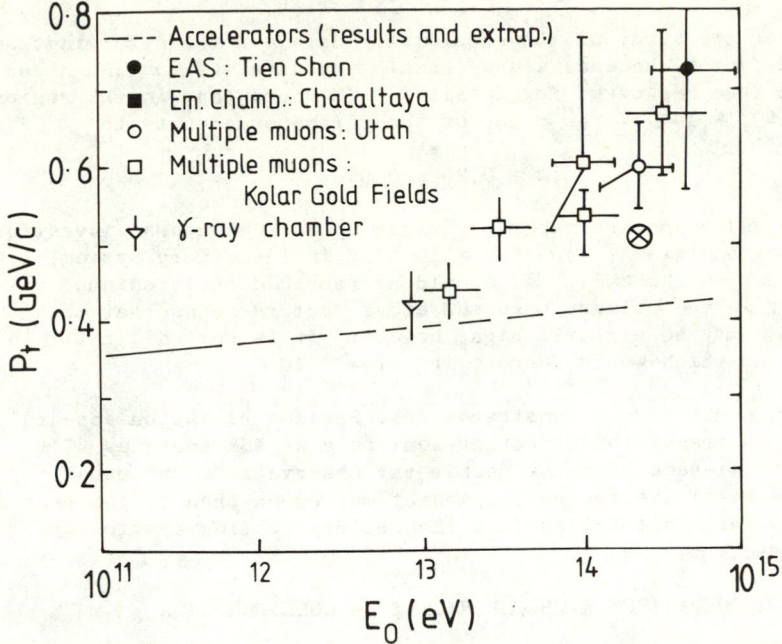

Fig. 3 The average transverse momentum versus primary
particle energy.

where the parameter α is the Scaling violation parameter. It can
be seen that Feynman Scaling corresponds to $\alpha = 0$. The experimental
data up to the highest ISR energies gave good fit to formula 1,
with the value of the parameter

$$\alpha = 0.13 \pm 0.02$$

and the required value of α is the same for both low energy
secondary particles (central region) and high energy ones
(fragmentation region) although the accuracy of its determination
is clearly lower in the fragmentation part.

NON SCALING BEHAVIOUR AT COSMIC RAY ENERGIES

After the study of the accelerator data and the determination of the α-factor the analysis of cosmic ray data was continued and extended (see Wdowczyk[6] for details). It seems that in the region around 10^{13} - 10^{14} eV the value of the parameter amounts to

$$\alpha = 0.20 \pm 0.05$$

and this value appears necessary right up to the highest investigated cosmic ray energies ($\sim 10^9$ GeV = 10^{18} eV in laboratory system, i.e. 5×10^4 GeV in the CMS). It should be remarked that residual uncertainty in the primary mass and other factors means that this value of α may be a little high; however, it is very difficult to see reasons which would depress it below 0.10.

The result thus demonstrates that Scaling violation appears not to be a transition effect present only at ISR energies. It should be stressed that the cosmic ray observations are usually much more sensitive to the fragmentation region than to the central region, a fact that arises from the rapidly falling cosmic ray energy spectrum.

COMPARISON WITH THE RECENT pp COLLIDER DATA

It is interesting, although perhaps somewhat premature, to compare the new p-p data with the cosmic ray results.

In figure 4 the data from UA5 experiment are compared with the predictions of formula 1. In the experiment only the pseudo rapidity distributions vere measured and so the comparison is actually dependent on assumptions about the average value and distribution of the transverse momenta- fortunately the change of the average transverse momenta with energy is slow. In the figure the data at $\sqrt{s}$ = 53 transformed using formula 1 to $\sqrt{s}$ = 540 are compared with the observations. A number of curves are given: respectively for $\langle p_t \rangle$ = 0.35 GeV/c at both energies and for $\langle p_t \rangle$ = 0.35 GeV/c at $\sqrt{s}$ = 53 and $\langle p_t \rangle$ = 0.5 GeV/c at $\sqrt{s}$ = 540. The second case is more suitable as an increase of $\langle p_t \rangle$ has been reported in the UA1 experiment.

The required value of the scaling violation parameter amounts to 0.12 ± 0.01, in very good agreement with our analysis of the ISR data.

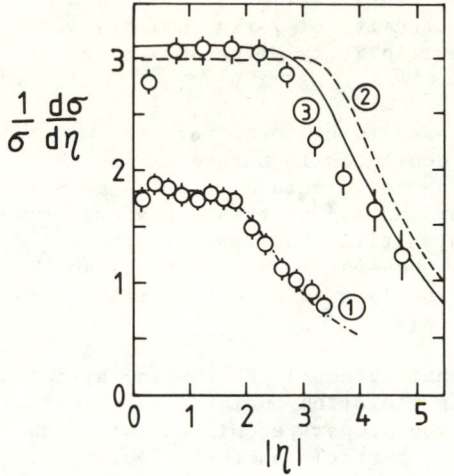

Fig. 4. The pseudorapidity
distribution for $\sqrt{s}$ = 53
and 540. The curve marked
1 represents the fit to the
data at $\sqrt{s}$ = 53, curves 2
and 3 are obtained trans-
forming curve 1 using formula
1. Curve 2 corresponds to
$\langle p_t \rangle$ = 0.5 GeV/c (both
values at $\sqrt{s}$ = 540).

Turning now to the multiplicity of the secondary particles the
data from the UAS experiment are indicated in Figure 1. It is
seen that there is reasonable agreement of the pp data with the
cosmic ray estimations. It is interesting to note that the cosmic
ray results at 10^{14} eV are already over 10 years old (see Adcock et
al.[5]). In the same graph the multiplicity deduced from EAS data
presented in this Conference are given. The 'Fly's Eye' result
deduced from the height of shower maximum is particularly important
as the maxima of individual showers are measured and this allows
the selection of showers due mainly to primary protons. In spite
of the fact that the experiment is at a very preliminary stage it
offers some confirmation of the earlier measurements of the positions
of shower maxima which are summarised in Figure 2.

The situation with the mean transverse momentum is rather
similar (Figure 3). The new pp collider results from the UA1
experiment are close to the cosmic ray values, particularly when
it is remembered that a number of effects, associated with the
target being air nuclei and other cascading phenomena, cause the
latter to be somewhat high.

Returning to multiplicities, inspection of Figure 1 shows that
the regular trend of multiplicity increase, which may be approximately described as a power law with α = 0.2, is somewhat
obscured in the region around 10^{15} eV.

This irregularity is a characteristic feature, but the
differences between the predictions based on various methods
suggests that it may not, in fact, be related to a rapid increase
of the secondary particle multiplicity but to some other change
in the properties of high energy collisions. One of the possibilities is a significant increase of the fraction of the

secondary baryons (see for instance Dobrzynski et al.[8]). This phenomenon would explain the low intensity of γ-ray families without need for a rapid increase of the multiplicity of secondary particles.

The most likely situation appears to us to be that the multiple particle production cross section continues to behave at the highest available energies according to formula 1. It is unclear what sort of model is necessary for explaining this behaviour. In our earlier paper we favoured a multifireball model with gradually increasing fireball mass; however such a model is not now fully satisfactory in view of the long range correlations observed in pp collisions.

Finally it should be stated that although the cosmic ray data clearly indicate continuous scaling violation in the fragmentation region they are sensitive only to the properties of the particles which take the bulk of the secondary particle energy. Scaling as such can still be preserved among the most energetic particles (say those with $x > 0.5$) which take only a small fraction of the secondary particles energy.

REFERENCES

1. J.F. de Beer, B. Holyoak, J. Wdowczyk and A.W. Wolfendale, Proc. Phys. Soc. 89, 567 (1966).

2. R. Feynman, Phys. Rev. Lett., 23, 1415 (1969).

3. J. Wdowczyk and A.W. Wolfendale, Nature, 236, 29 (1972).

4. J. Wdowczyk and A.W. Wolfendale, J. Phys. A, 6, 1594 (1973).

5. C. Adcock, R.B. Coats, J. Wdowczyk and A.W. Wolfendale, J. Phys. A, 3, 697 (1970).

6. J. Wdowczyk, Proc. Int. Seminar on Cosmic Ray Cascade, Sofia, 185 (1980).

7. J. Wdowczyk and A.W. Wolfendale, Nuovo Cim., 54A, 433 (1979).

8. G. Cassiday, These Proceedings. (1979).

9. K. Dobrzyski, R. Firkowski, J. Glowacki, J. Wdowczyk, A. Wlodarek and G.B. Khristiansen, Proc. Int. Cosmic Ray Conf., Paris, 6, 206 (1981).

A STUDY OF DEEP INELASTIC HADRON HADRON COLLISIONS
WITH A LARGE ACCEPTANCE TRANSVERSE ENERGY TRIGGER

Klaus P. Pretzl

Max-Planck-Institut für Physik und Astrophysik, Munich

ABSTRACT

Hadron hadron collisions were studied with a large acceptance transverse energy trigger at SPS and ISR energies. Results from the NA5[+], R(416)[++] and R(807)[+++] experiments at CERN are presented. The selected events show large multiplicities and no jet like structure. Processes more complicated than the scattering of two constituents appear to dominate these inelastic collisions.

INTRODUCTION

It is believed that particle jets with large transverse momenta P_T reflect the hard scattering of two constituents inside the hadrons [1]. The scattering of two constituents would lead to two particle jets with large transverse momenta and two forward-backward spectator jets (Fig. 1). The search for these processes introduced a challanging question to the experiments : How to trigger on jets ?

(+)   Bari-Krakow-Liverpool-MPI Munich-Nijmegen
(++)   CERN-Collège de France-Dortmund-Heidelberg-Warsaw
(+++) Brookhaven-CERN-Niels Bohr-Lund-Rutherford-Tel Aviv

586

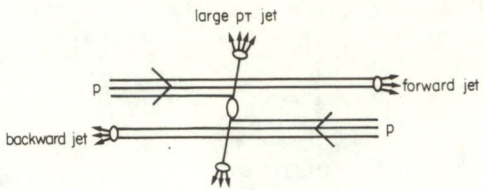

Fig. 1.   Two constituent scattering process leading to two
particle jets at large p_T and two forward backward
spectator jets.

Deep inelastic hadron hadron collisions were previously
investigated at Fermilab [2-4] employing calorimetric jet
triggers with an acceptance approximately matched to the
expected jet size. As expected for jet production the cross
sections were found to be larger than for single particle
production at large p_T. However, it was difficult to verify
the existence of jets because the small acceptance of the
calorimeter trigger could lead to a trigger bias selecting
events which simulate jets and which do not necessarily stem
from a hard scattering process.
     The aim of the experiments reported here was to study these
processes by using an unbiased jet trigger [5] with large solid
angle acceptance.   Events were selected by requiring a large
transverse energy ΣE_T (= $\Sigma\ |p_T|$ for relativistic particles)
in the central rapidity range of $|y| < 0.8$ with a 2π azimuthal
acceptance [Fig.2].
     This investigation was started by the NA5 experiment [6] using
a large acceptance calorimeter trigger and a streamer chamber
vertex detector. Large p_T jets were expected to manifest
themselves as energy clusters observed in the segmented calorimeter
showing a planar event structure. The ISR experiments R416 (SFM
split field magnet) and R807 (AFS axial field spectrometer)
selected off-line events with a large transverse energy of charged
particles from an event sample obtained with a minimum bias trigger.

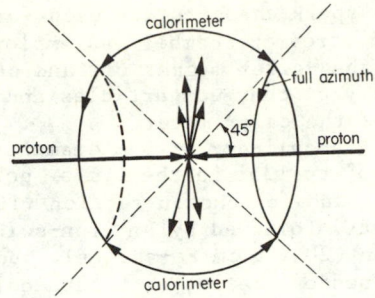

Fig. 2.   Schematic layout of a transverse energy experiment.

APPARATUS

Detailed descriptions of the SFM and AFS detectors are given in Ref. 7 and 8 respectively. Therefore they will not be discussed in this report. Their main features relevant to this investigation are 2π azimuthal acceptance and good momentum analysis of charged particles in the central rapidity region $|y| < 0.8$. Unlike the NA-5 detector, at present the SFM and the AFS have no calorimetry covering the central rapidity region. The data were taken with pp collision at $\sqrt{s} = 63$ GeV and $\alpha\alpha$ collisions at $\sqrt{s} = 126$ GeV using a minimum bias trigger as explained in the next chapter and in Fig. 6a and 6b.

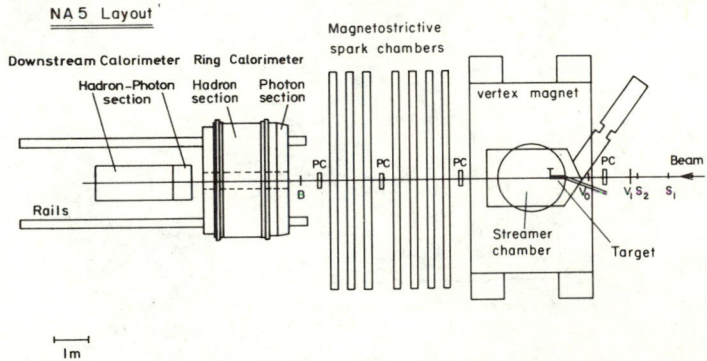

Fig. 3.   Layout of the NA-5 experiment

The layout of the NA-5 apparatus is shown in Fig. 3. The data presented here were obtained with 300 GeV/c proton and π^- beams of $2 \cdot 10^6$ particles/sec incident on a 30 cm liquid hydrogen target using the calorimeters and spark chambers only and with the vertex magnet off.

588

The information from the spark chambers was used for vertex reconstruction. The 2 m streamer chamber was employed for part of the data taking with the vertex magnet off and on to determine the multiplicity of charged particles and to verify the energy calibration of the calorimeter.

The ring calorimeter, a cylinder of 3 m diameter with a 56 cm central hole, covering 45^0 to 135^0 in the c.m.s. polar angle θ_{CM}, has a lead –scintillator sandwich photon section (16 x one radiation length Pb-sheets) followed by an iron-scintillator sandwich hadronic section (20 x 5 cm Fe-sheets). Both sections are subdivided into 240 independent cells, each subtending about 9^0 in the c.m.s. polar angle and 15^0 in azimuthal angle ϕ(Fig. 4a).

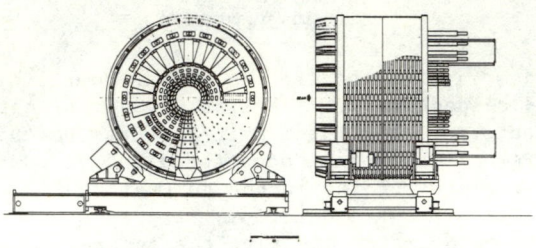

Fig. 4a. Front view and side view of the NA-5 ring calorimeter

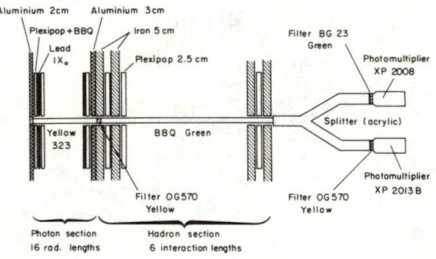

Fig. 4b. The principle of the light collection system for a calorimeter cell is shown.

Combined wave-length shifting acrylic rods (doped with Yellow 323 and BBQ) were used to draw separated signals from the photon and hadron part of the calorimeter onto 240 pairs of photomultiplier tubes [9]. The principle of the light collection system of a calorimeter cell is shown in Fig. 4b. Energy resolutions of $\sigma/E = 0.14/\sqrt{E} + 0.01$ for electrons and $\sigma/E = 0.64/\sqrt{E} + 0.02$ for hadrons were obtained, where E is in GeV.

The downstream calorimeter, which covered the central hole of the ring calorimeter, was used to measure the energy flow at small angles. The combined information from the ring and the downstream calorimeter was used to ensure that the total energy of the event was consistent with the incident beam energy.

TRIGGER

In the case of the NA-5 experiment, the E_T-trigger was derived from the sum of the analog signals of all or part of the ring calorimeter cells weighted by their radial distance from the beam axis (magnet off !) (Fig. 5).

NA-5 Calorimeter trigger:

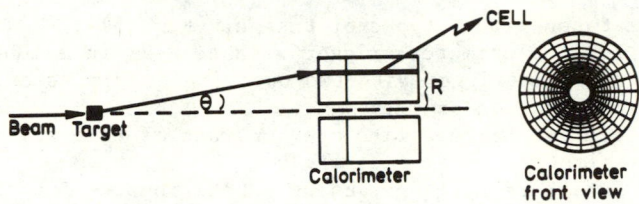

transverse energy trigger (on-line):

$$E_T = \Sigma \sin \theta^i \times E^i$$

attenuator $\frac{1}{R}$

$$E_T \approx \Sigma |p_T| \text{ for relativistic particles}$$

$$E_T = \Sigma E_T \text{ Photon} + \Sigma E_T \text{ Hadron}$$

trigger configurations:

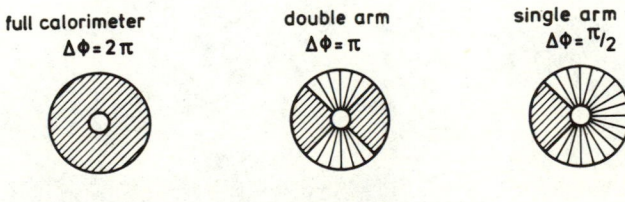

| full calorimeter $\Delta\phi = 2\pi$ | double arm $\Delta\phi = \pi$ | single arm $\Delta\phi = \pi/2$ |

acceptance $-0.88 < y < 0.67$

Fig. 5. The transverse energy trigger as used in the NA-5 calorimeter experiment (magnet off!) and the various trigger configurations are explained.

The sum of the analog signals in the photon section ΣE_T Photon and in the hadron section ΣE_T Hadron were added to give the total $E_T = \Sigma E_T$ Photon $+ \Sigma E_T$ Hadron. The cells of the innermost ring of the calorimeter were excluded in the trigger. The acceptance of the trigger particles was 2π in the azimuthal and 54^0 to 135^0 in the c.m.s polar angle ($-0.88 < y < 0.67$).

The shape of the trigger pulses was recorded by sampling them in time with short ADC gates. Occasional background triggers due to Cerenkov light produced mainly by accidental muons in the acrylic rods and the cathode windows of the photomultipliers was eliminated off-line by pulse shape analysis. This was possible since the rise time of the trigger pulses coming from Cerenkov light was distinctly faster than of pulses coming from genuine particle showers in the calorimeter. False triggers from this source amouted to 20% of all triggers at the highest trigger threshold.

Data were taken with 4 types of trigger (Fig. 5) :

1. full calorimeter trigger with $\Delta\phi = 2\pi$ in azimuth
2. two arm trigger with two opposite quadrants each of $\Delta\phi = \pi/2$ in azimuth.
3. one arm trigger with one quadrant of $\Delta\phi = \pi/2$ in azimuth
4. interaction trigger using a beam counter B with a diameter of 2 cm, 4.5 m downstream of the target, in anticoincidence to the incident beam.

Triggers similar to (2) and (3) have been employed in Fermilab experiments [2-4].

In the ISR experiments, events with a large transverse energy of charged particles were selected off-line from an event sample obtained with a minimum bias trigger (interaction trigger with approximately 95% efficiency).

The interaction trigger in the case of the AFS detector was derived from a coincidence between hodoscope H_1 and H_2 or a hit in the barrel shaped scintillator hodoscope B, which was positioned around the colliding beam region (Fig. 6a). The SFM detector was triggered when at least 3 hits in either of the proportional chamber telescopes T_1, T_2 or T_3 were recorded (Fig. 6b). The transverse energy was defined as $\Sigma E_T = \Sigma\sqrt{p_T^2 + m^2}$ of charged particles produced in the central rapidity region of $|y| < 0.8$ (AFS) and $|y| < 0.75$ (SFM) respectively.

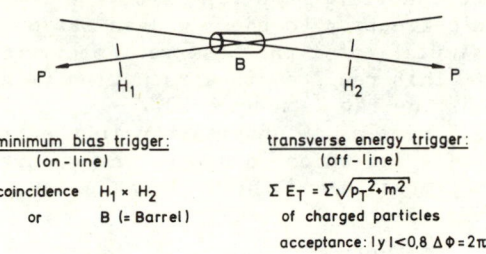

Axial field spectrometer (R 807) ISR
P
H1
B
H2
P
minimum bias trigger:
(on-line)
coincidence H1 × H2
or B (= Barrel)
transverse energy trigger:
(off-line)
Σ ET = Σ√(pT²+m²)
of charged particles
acceptance: |y|<0,8 ΔΦ=2π

Fig. 6a. The minimum bias trigger and the transverse energy trigger as used in the R807 experiment.

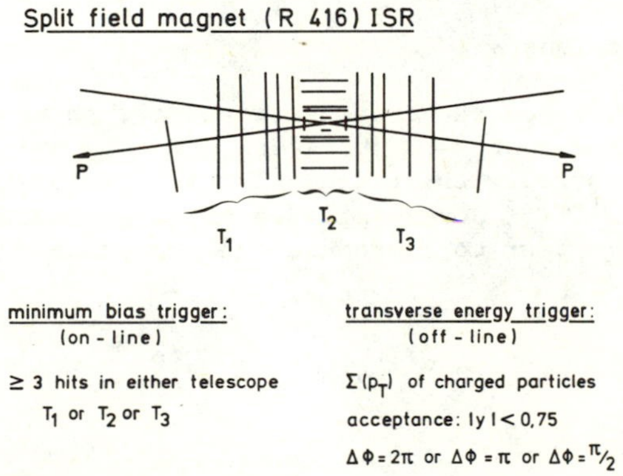

Split field magnet (R 416) ISR
P
P
T1
T2
T3
minimum bias trigger:
(on-line)
≥ 3 hits in either telescope
T1 or T2 or T3
transverse energy trigger:
(off-line)
Σ(pT) of charged particles
acceptance: |y| < 0,75
ΔΦ=2π or ΔΦ=π or ΔΦ=π/2

Fig. 6b. The minimum bias trigger and the transverse energy trigger as used in the R416 experiment.

ANALYSIS

In the NA-5 experiment, an analysis of the energy deposited in the calorimeter cells was used to determine the position and the energy of particle showers. The transverse energy was calculated from those showers with positions within a fiducial region of $54° < \theta_{CM} < 135°$..

A computer model of the calorimeter, which took the measured energy response curves and the shower spreading into account, was used to unfold the effects of the calorimeter from the measured yield. By comparing the yield from an ideal calorimeter to the yield resulting from the model of the real calorimeter a correction to the raw data was made using a Monte-Carlo simulation of the observed spectra of particles [10]. This resulted in a reduction of the transverse energy scale of the raw data by 8-10%.

There still remains an uncertainty in the transverse energy scale of $\Delta E_T/E_T = \pm 5\%$ which is due to the uncertainty of the calorimeter calibration and the systematic error introduced by the unfolding procedure.

RESULTS

The results are compared to 3 representative models a QCD-4-jet model [11] with two large p_T jets and two forward backward spectator jets all resembling the jets observed in e^+e^- collisions [13], a low p_T cluster model [10] designed to reproduce the features of low p_T multiparticle production and a phase space model using independent particle emission with a KNO multiplicity distribution. The results show the following features:

1. Cross sections

In Figs. 7,8,9 the cross sections are shown as a function of the transverse energy for triggers (1), (2) and (3). The cross sections measured with trigger (1) seem to fall approximately like $e^{-\Sigma E_T}$ or $e^{-\Sigma |p_T|}$. Monte-Carlo calculations using a phase space model appear to reproduce the pp and $\alpha\alpha$ cross sections very well (Fig. 7).

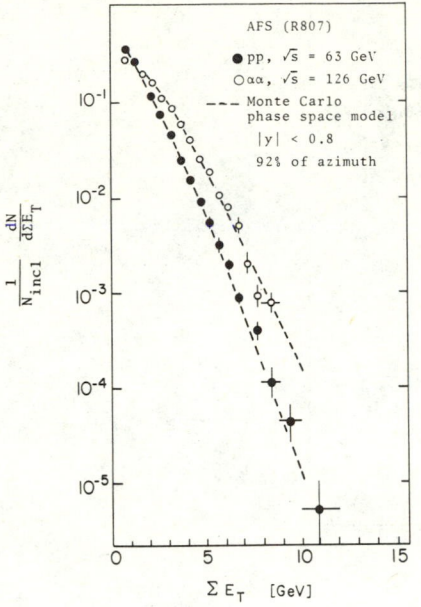

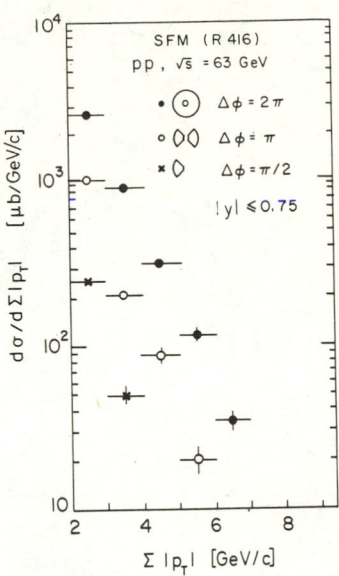

Fig. 7. Event rates versus transverse energy for charged particles in pp and αα collisions.

Fig. 8. Cross sections versus transverse energy for charged particles obtained with triggers of various azimuthal acceptances Δϕ.

Fig 9. shows that the cross sections obtained with trigger (1) are 10-100 times larger than with trigger (2). If 4-jet events would dominate the trigger (2) data one would not expect such a large ratio since the solid angle acceptance of trigger (2) and trigger (1) differ only by a factor 2. The cross sections measured with trigger (1) are approximately two orders of magnitude larger than the QCD-4-jet model predictions. The agreement with a low p_T cluster model is better for all three triggers.

594

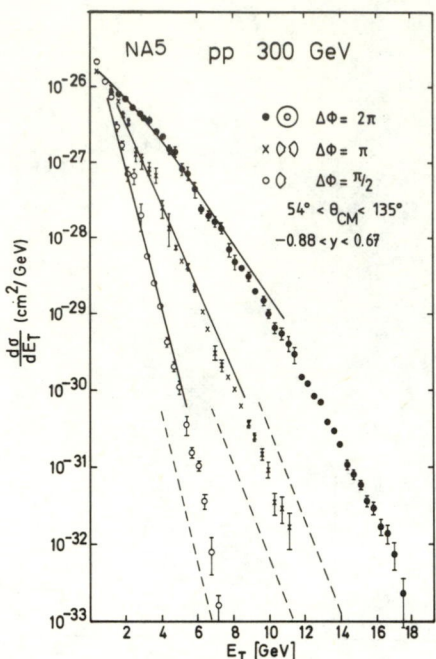

Fig. 9. Cross sections versus transverse energy E_T measured in regions of various azimuthal acceptance $\Delta\phi$ of the calorimeter. Low p_T cluster model and QCD-4-jet model predictions are shown by the solid and dashed curves respectively.

2. Event structure

A planarity analysis of the NA-5 data obtained with the trigger (1) was performed to search for jets.

The planarity P of the events has been calculated from a principal axis analysis of the transverse momentum distribution for each event as measured by the calorimeter. The planarity was defined as P = (a-b)/(a+b) with a (b) being the sum of the squares of the projected transverse momenta to the maximum (minimum) principal p_T-axis. For an isotropic event structure one would expect P = 0 and for pencil like jets P = 1.

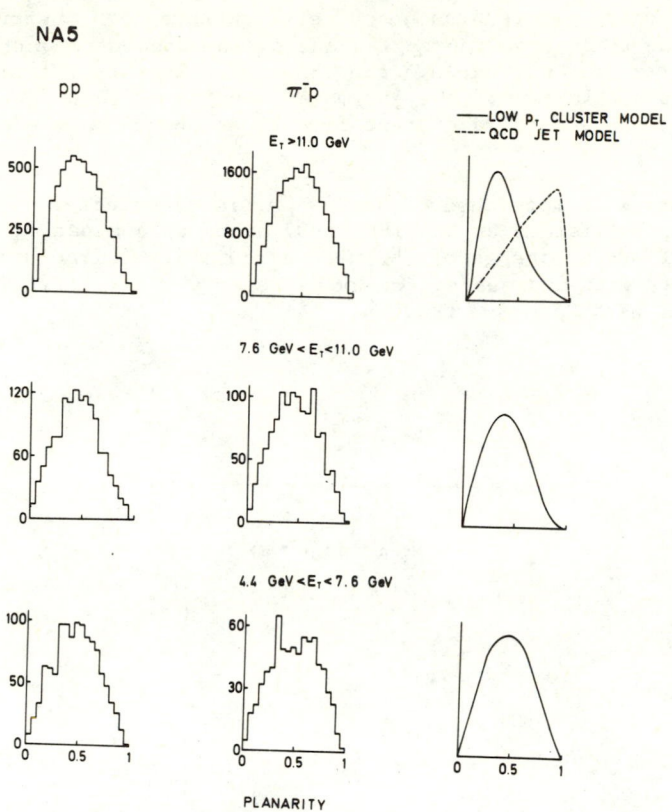

Fig. 10. Distributions of the planarity P of events from pp and π⁻p collision for various regions of the transverse energy E_T measured by the calorimeter with 2π azimuthal acceptance. Results from a low p_T cluster model and a QCD-4-jet model are shown for comparison.

Fig 10 shows the planarity distribution of events selected by the calorimeter trigger (1) from π⁻p and pp collisions at 300 GeV/c for different E_T intervals. These are compared to the planarity of the Monte-Carlo simulated events for pp collisions at 300 GeV/c using a low p_T cluster model and a QCD-4-jet model. Planar

596

events do not dominate the trigger (1) data, indeed there is no change of the planarity distribution with increasing transverse energy in the events. At large transverse energy the low p_T cluster model predicts more isotropic events while the QCD-4-jet model predicts a more pronounced jet structure than observed in the data. The transverse energy leakage of the spectator jets into the calorimeter does not explain the observed planarity distribution and cross sections. If the jet-model were to explain the data, the jets would have to be different from those observed in e^+e^- collisions.

Events with more than 4 charged particles selected with trigger (1) in pp collisions at the ISR (R807) show no dominant jet structure and no change of the mean circularity (circularity = 1 - planarity) with increasing transverse energy (Fig. 11). This is in agreement with the NA-5 results.

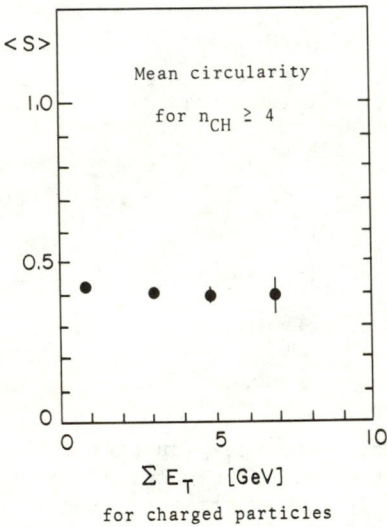

Fig. 11. The mean circularity < s > for charged particle multiplicities n_{CH} > 4 versus the transverse energy.

3. Multiplicities

a) Total charged particle multiplicities

The information on charged particle multiplicities n_{CH} in the NA-5 experiment was obtained from the data taking runs with the streamer chamber. Unexpectedly high multiplicities were observed in events selected with trigger (1). This can best be demonstrated in Fig. 12 where a streamer chamber picture of a typical event is shown.

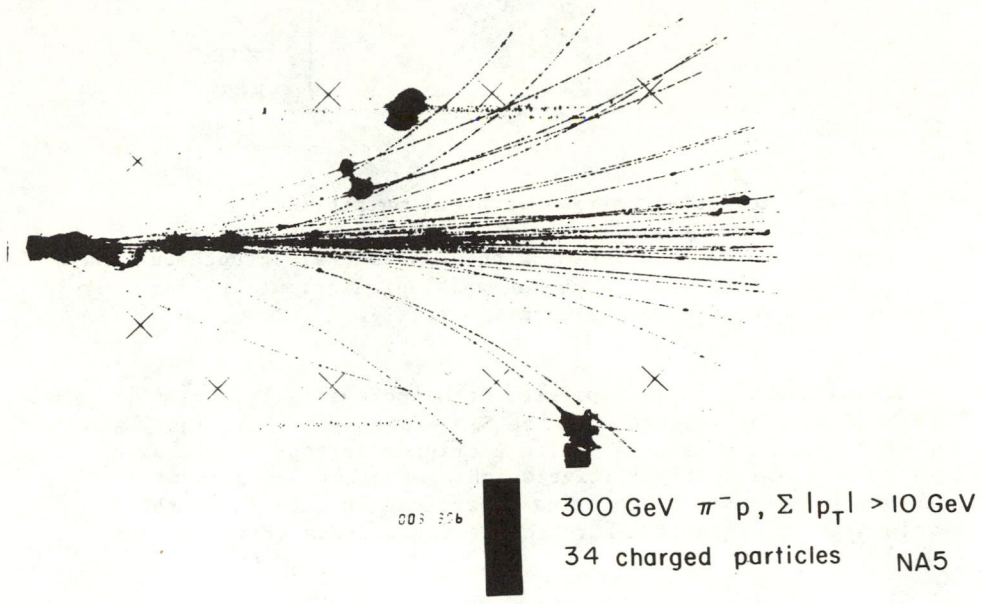

003 306

300 GeV $\pi^- p$, $\Sigma |p_T| > 10$ GeV

34 charged particles   NA5

Fig. 12. A typical event selected by a large transverse energy trigger and photographed in the streamer chamber.

It was found that the mean multiplicities are rising rapidly with increasing trigger (1) threshold (Fig. 13). The low p_T cluster model seems to reproduce the data rather well, while the mean charged particle multiplicity predicted by the QCD-4-jet model is too small and rather constant over a wide range of E_T.

598

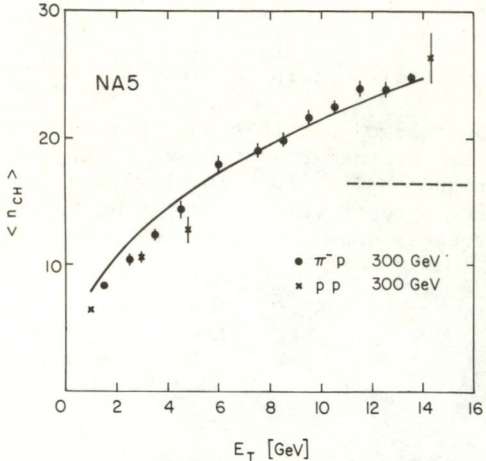

Fig. 13. The total charged particle multiplicity $< n_{CH} >$ for $\pi^- p$ and pp collision versus the transverse energy E_T measured by the calorimeter with 2π azimuthal acceptance. Low P_T cluster model and QCD-4-jet-model predictions are shown by the solid and dashed curves respectively.

A similar rise in multiplicity with increasing trigger (1) threshold has been observed in the SFM experiment (Fig. 14a). In contrast to that, a single particle trigger selects events with relatively small multiplicities which are rather independent of the transverse momentum of the trigger particle in support of the simple 4-jet picture of a hard scattering process (Fig. 14b and Fig. 13).

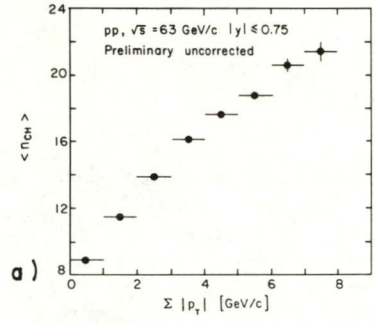 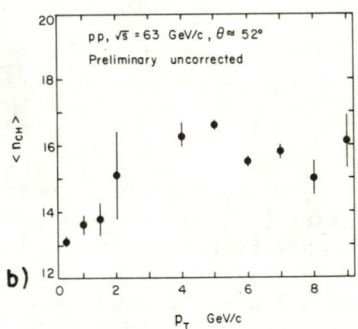

Figs. 14a,b. The preliminary, uncorrected charged particle multiplicity measured by the R416 experiment as a function of a) the transverse energy $\Sigma |p_T|$ (trigger 1) and b) the transverse momentum p_T of a single particle emitted at a polar angle $\theta_{CM} \sim 52°$ in pp collisions at $\sqrt{s}$ = 63 GeV is shown.

(b) Charged particle multiplicities within the solid angle
acceptance of the trigger

Fig. 15 shows that the mean charged particle multiplicity
within the solid angle acceptance of the trigger (1) increases
rapidly with the trigger threshold ΣE_T. However the increase
in transverse energy is much slower when selecting events with a
certain number of charged particles n_{CH} in the trigger region
(Fig. 16). Thus the $< E_T >$ per charged particle giving rise
to the transverse energy trigger is larger than the $<E_T>$ per
charged particle when triggering on multiplicity.

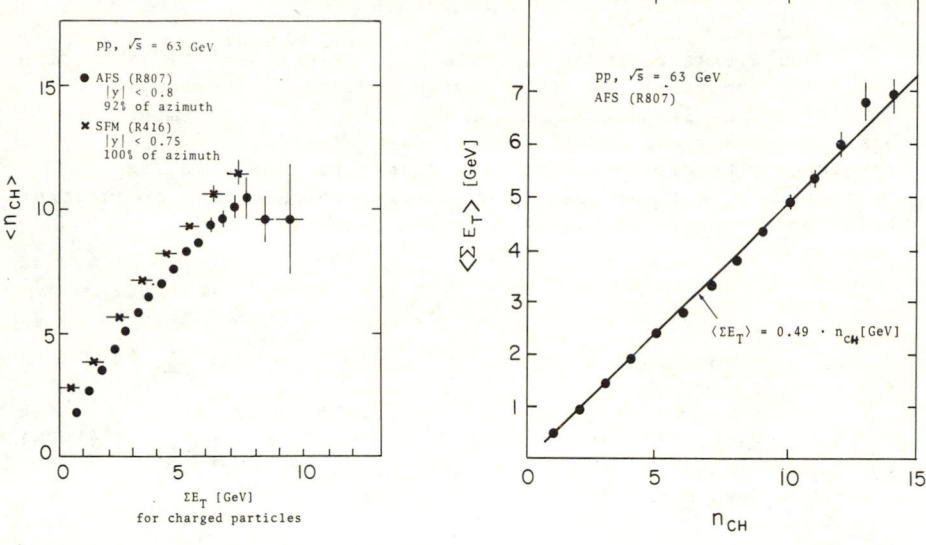

Fig. 15. The average charged
particle multiplicity measured
within the solid angle acceptance
of trigger (1) versus the trigger
threshold ΣE_T (GeV).

Fig. 16. The increase
of transverse energy
when requiring n_{CH}
charged particles in the
trigger (1).

The charged particle multiplicity within the NA-5 calorimeter
acceptance was found to be $< n_{CH} > = 15 \pm 1.5$ for $< E_T > = 14.4$ GeV.
This transverse energy results from a large number of particles
with a rather small average transverse momentum $< p_T > \sim 0.65$ GeV/c
per particle, assuming a charged to neutral particle ratio of 2 : 1.

CONCLUSIONS

When investigating hadron hadron collisions with a large transverse energy trigger new phenomena seem to emerge, which cannot be explained by a simple two consistituent scattering process. The results show large cross sections, high multiplicities and no dominant jet structure. The large transverse energy is a result of a large number of particles with a rather small transverse momentum. Many challenging questions remain :

a) What is the nature of these phenomena[14] ?
b) Do they dominante the cross-sections also at higher energies[15] and at larger E_T ?
c) How to trigger on jets ?

ACKNOWLEDGEMENTS

I would like to thank my colleagues of the NA-5 collaboration for their contributions to this work and Drs.T. Akesson, H. Bøggild, C. Fabjan, K. Hansen from the R807 experiment and Drs. H. Fischer, W. Geist from the R416 experiment for the opportunity to present their results and for many fruitful discussions. Last not least I would like to thank the organizers of this conference for their kind hospitality.

REFERENCES

1. S.M. Berman, J.D. Bjorken, J. Kogut: Phys. Rev. D4, 3388 (1971).
2. C. Bromberg et al., Phys. Rev. Lett. 38, 1447 (1977); Nucl. Phys. B134, 189 (1978); Phys. Rev. Lett. 43, 565 (1979)
3. M.D. Corcoran et al., Phys. Rev. Lett. 41, 9 (1978); Phys. Rev. D19, 1361 (1979); Phys. Scripta 19, 95 (1979); Phys. Rev. Lett. 44, 514 (1980); Phys. Rev. D21, 641 (1980); W. Selove: High p_T jet studies at Fermilab, Proceedings of the 14th Rencontre de Moriond 1979, Vol. I, 401.
4. V. Cook et al., Nucl. Phys. B186, 219 (1981).
5. W. Ochs, L. Stodolsky, Phys. Lett. 69B, 225 (1977); L. Stodolsky, Proc. VIII International Symposium on Multiparticle Dynamics, Kayserberg (1977); W. Ochs, Phys. Scripta 19, 127 (1979).
6. C. Favuzzi et al., APS-Conference Proceedings, Madison (1980), part 1, page 92.
7. W. Bell et al., Nucl. Instr. & Meth. 156, 111 (1978); B. Bouclier et al., Nucl. Instr & Meth. 115, 235 (1974); B. Bouclier et al., Nucl. Instr.& Meth. 125, 19 (1975).
8. H. Gordon et al., CERN-EP/81-34.
9. V. Eckardt, R. Kalbach, A. Manz, K. P. Pretzl, N. Schmitz and D. Vranic, Nucl. Instr. Meth. 155, 389 (1978).

10. The low p_T cluster model produces clusters with an average mass of $< m_c > = 2$ Gev in a cylindrical phase space. The clusters decay isotropically with an average charged multiplicity of $< n_{CH} > = 2.5$. The resulting p_T distribution of the final particles have $< p_T^2 >^{1/2} = 0.36$ GeV/c in the central rapidity region. Leading particle effects were taken into account and the measured [12] multiplicity distribution was enforced. The cross section was normalized to the total inelastic cross section of 32 mb. The model reproduced well the features of low p_T events observed in bubble chamber experiments.

11. In the QCD-model calculations of the cross sections the matrix elements for 2 constituent scattering were used. The quark and gluon distributions were obtained from νN and Drell-Yan experiments. Scale breaking effects were taken into account. A coupling $\alpha_S = 12\pi/25 \ln(1 + Q^2/\Lambda^2)$ with $\Lambda = 0.2$ GeV and $Q^2 = 4p_T^2$ was assumed. The model had 2 large p_T and two forward backward spectator jets. A cut on parton $p_T > 2.5$ GeV/c was used. Each of the two jet systems was made to resemble jets as observed in e^+e^- collisions [13], using the Feynman-Field fragmentation scheme with $\sigma_q = 0.32$ GeV. Each of the two jet systems were given equal and opposite primordial transverse momenta with $< p_T^2 > = 1.2$ GeV/c. With these assumptions we find that 40% of the transverse energy in the calorimeter comes from the spectator jets while 93% of the energy of the scattered jets is seen by the calorimeter when selecting events with more than 12 GeV transverse energy.

12. A. Firestone et al., Phys. Rev. D10, 2080 (1974).
    P. Slattery, Phys. Rev. Lett. 29, 1624 (1972).

13. Gail C. Hanson, Proceedings of the VIIth International Colloquium on Multiparticle Reactions (Tutzing, Germany, 1976), page. 313, and Proceedings of the XVIIIth International Conference on High Energy Physics (Tblissi, USSR, 1976), p. B1; Gail C. Hanson, SLAC PUB-2118 (1978).

14. First results from the $\bar{p}p$ collider experiment UA1 at CERN were presented by A. Kernan and C. Rubbia at this Conference.

15. An interesting attempt to explain the NA-5 data within a Gluon-Bremmsstrahlung model was presented by G. Fox at this Conference.

TOTAL AND ELASTIC CROSS-SECTIONS AND GLOBAL EVENT CHARACTERISTICS IN $\bar{p}p$ AND pp COLLISIONS AT $\sqrt{s}$ = 53 GeV

M. Ambrosio, G. Anzivino, G. Barbarino,
G. Carboni, V. Cavasinni, T. Del Prete,
P. Grannis, G. Kantardjian, D. Lloyd Owen,
M. Morganti, G. Paternoster, S. Patricelli,
M. Valdata-Nappi
CERN-Napoli-Pisa-Stony Brook Collaboration
(presented by P. Grannis)

ABSTRACT

We have measured the total $\bar{p}p$ and pp cross sections at $\sqrt{s}$ = 52.8 GeV in the same experiment using the total rate method. The $\bar{p}p$ cross section is significantly above that for pp collisions. We also present measurements of the differential elastic cross-sections for $\bar{p}p$ scattering. Preliminary results on the inclusive distributions for $\bar{p}p$ and pp collisions indicate that the annihilation component is primarily central and results in multiplicities above the average.

Since the introduction of antiprotons into the CERN ISR in April, 1981, the CERN - Napoli - Pisa - Stony Brook experiment has been installed in Intersection Region 2 with a set of detectors covering virtually the entire solid angle. The primary aims of the experiment are the measurement of the total cross-sections for $\bar{p}p$ and pp collisions via the observation of the total interaction rates, the measurement of the differential cross-sections for small-angle elastic scattering, and a comparative study of the general features of multiparticle production through measurements of multiplicity and pseudorapidity distributions. The determination of σ_{tot} in this experiment is quite direct: the observed collision rate is about 96% of the total interaction rate and so only small corrections are required.

The data reported here come from a fourteen day run in October, 1981 in which a single, stochastically cooled antiproton beam was circulating with a current of about 2mA. During the two weeks three separate proton beams were stored - each time with currents of approximately 10 A resulting in luminosities of about 7×10^{26} cm^{-2}s^{-1}. The mean center-of-mass energy was $\sqrt{s}$ = 52.8 GeV. The pp data were collected with currents of about 3 A in both beams and are analyzed in exactly the same way as the $\bar{p}p$ data.

The experimental arrangement is indicated in Fig. 1; the detector has left-right symmetry with respect to the beam crossing. Both the left arm (containing the exiting proton beam) and the right arm (containing either an antiproton or a proton beam) consist of five sets of hodoscopes spanning the polar region 4 mrad < θ < 90° in successive steps. Each set of hodoscopes comprises two planes of of trigger counters operated in coincidence and a further plane of small counters used to localize particle hits in θ and ϕ. In addition to the scintillation-counter hodoscopes, a set of drift chambers covers the pseudorapidity range $|\eta| < 2$ and drift-tube planes cover the polar regions $4 < \theta < 12$ mrad.

The trigger for the experiment is the simple requirement of hits in the left and the right arms. A hit in either arm is detected by the sum (OR) of the concidences between overlapping elements in each hodoscope set:

$$\text{Left (or Right)} = \text{CI}\cdot\text{CO} + H_1\cdot H_2 + H_3\cdot H_4 + H_{5A}\cdot H_{5B} + TB_A\cdot TB_B. \qquad (1)$$

For each trigger, the presence of hits in all cells of all hodoscopes is encoded and recorded. The time difference between a master pulse and each coincidence in the trigger was also recorded.

The major source of background events is collisions between the circulating protons and the residual gas in the vacuum chamber or the vacuum chamber itself (single-beam events). Owing to the dependence of the ratio of the beam-beam rate and the single-beam rate on the ISR currents:

$$\frac{R_{BB}}{R_{SB}} \propto \frac{I_1\cdot I_2}{I_1 + I_2} \quad , \qquad (2)$$

beam-beam events dominate the triggers in the case of pp running. For $\bar{p}p$ running, however, the smallness of the $\bar{p}$ current results in the domination of the observed rate by single-beam events originating in the proton beam. This background is removed from the data using the timing information of the hodoscopes.

In the off-line analysis, we have formed the time difference between the signals from each left-arm hodoscope set and the signals from each right-arm hodoscope set. Twenty five (left - right) time differences, t_i, are thus constructed if all hodoscopes in the experiment are struck. In practice, most interactions result in hits in the majority of the hodoscopes so the time information is highly redundant.

Events originating in the beam-crossing region produce particle hits in left and right equidistant hodoscopes at approximately the same time, resulting in time-difference distributions centered at zero for such hodoscope pairs. During pp running, the mean time difference, $<t_i>$, characterizing beam-beam events for each left-right combination, i, is obtained and also the width, σ_i, of each distribution. Triggers resulting from the upstream interactions of either beam have a time-ordered sequence of hodoscope hits as the secondaries sweep through the detector from left to right (or vice versa), resulting in t_i values that differ from the $<t_i>$'s.

In order to use all of the timing information available and to use it in a symmetric way, we define a parameter, χ^2, for a statistical test of the hypothesis that an event arises from the beam-crossing region:

$$\chi^2 = \frac{1}{N_{td}} \sum_{i=1}^{N_{td}} \frac{(t_i - <t_i>)^2}{\sigma_i^2} \qquad (3)$$

where N_{td} is the number of time-differences observed in the event. In this summation, the left-right combinations involving CI·CO on either side were omitted because of the poor discrimination between beam-beam and single-beam events afforded by them. Those events which triggered only CI·CO in one or the other arm are thus removed from the data and a correction term applied a posteriori for the loss of events.

Figure 2 shows the distribution of events in χ^2 for both $\bar{p}p$ and pp runs. The pp run shows virtually no events with $\chi^2 > 2$, consistent with negligible contamination from single-beam background. The $\bar{p}p$ distribution has two visible components: one is similar to the beam-beam distribution seen for pp - the second is a broad peak centered at about $\chi^2 = 5$ and attributed to single-beam background.

In order to investigate the single-beam contribution to the distribution below $\chi^2 = 2$, we have taken data with the two beams steered vertically apart so that no beam-beam interactions occurred. The resulting distribution is shown in Fig. 3. The decrease of events as χ^2 approaches zero is seen but, unexpectedly, a smaller low-χ^2 peak persists. We have attributed these fake beam-beam events to interactions of the proton-beam halo with the vacuum chamber in the beam-crossing region. Such an interaction would typically produce all secondaries in a cone in the left arm of the experiment, but some fraction of such events give charged prongs intercepting one or more of the right-arm hodoscopes, mimicking a beam-beam event. This interpretation of the persistence of the low-χ^2 peak is supported by the vertex-reconstruction information provided by the drift chambers. Figure 4 shows the vertex distribution in the coordinate, x, perpendicular to the beam axis. Of interest is the satellite peak located at x = -8 cm, this being the approximate radius of the vacuum chamber in the intersection region.

In order to disentangle the three sources of events at $\chi^2 < 2$, we have taken some care in selecting monitors sensitive firstly to true beam-beam events and secondly to the fake beam-beam events. We can then parametrize the number of events, N_k, in run k, with $\chi^2 < 2$ as the linear sum of monitor counts:

$$N_k = \alpha a_k + \beta b_k + \gamma c_k . \qquad (4)$$

We find that the monitor $(H_3 \cdot H_4)_L \cdot (H_{5A} \cdot H_{5B})_R$ is insensitive to fake beam-beam events owing to its insistence on a small-angle secondary in the right arm. (It is also insensitive to normal single-beam events since the left-to-right traversal time for single-beam secondaries is greater than the resolving time of the coincidence.) We denote the number of counts in this monitor as a_k for the k-th run. For the single-beam contribution, the monitor we use is the number of events, b_k, in the χ^2 distribution with $\chi^2 > 2$. Finally, the fake beam-beam contribution is monitored by the difference:

$$(TB_A \cdot TB_B + H_{5A} \cdot H_{5B})_L \cdot (H_3 \cdot H_4 + H_{5A} \cdot H_{5B})_R - \tag{5}$$

$$(H_{5A} \cdot H_{5B} + H_3 \cdot H_4)_L \cdot (H_{5A} \cdot H_{5B} + TB_A \cdot TB_B)_R$$

The number of events in this monitor is denoted by c_k. The parameters α, β, and γ are obtained by performing fits to several $\bar{p}p$ and pp runs. The parameter α is stable to within ±0.5% and has the value 3.362 ± 0.018. In typical $\bar{p}p$ runs, N_k contains a contribution of about 35% from single-beam events and about 15% from fake beam-beam events.

In order to correct $\tilde{N}_k \equiv \alpha a_k$ to give the total number of interactions, three losses have to be considered:
- the loss introduced by excluding events triggering only CI·CO in one arm,
- the loss of elastic events due to the holes in the detector for the exiting beam pipes, and
- the loss of inelastic events in the same holes (single-diffractive events).

The CI·CO correction is obtained by examining the time differences involving CI·CO$_L$, and the right-arm hodoscopes in normal, separated-beam, and single-beam conditions. These time differences are relatively free of single-beam background, which originates in the left-going proton beam. The loss from CI·CO$_R$ is then obtained by assuming left-right symmetry for the interaction.

Elastic scattering is studied in special runs using the small-angle TB hodoscopes and drift tubes. We demand a collinear pattern of left-right hits with no evidence in the rest of the detector for extra-particle production. Figure 5 shows the deviation of hits (in both transverse directions) in the left TB hodoscopes from the point predicted by the right TB hit. In this way, we obtain the elastic differential cross-section in the region $0.01 < |t| < 0.05$ $(GeV/c)^2$ and, by extrapolating to $|t| = 0$ and integrating over the region of the holes, we estimate the loss.

The inelastic correction is estimated in a similar fashion. We choose a sample of events for which there is a hit with $\theta \gtrsim 40$ mrad, thus eliminating elastic events. The tracks in the opposite arm are examined and the track with the largest angle, θ_{max}, is identified. The events are then plotted as a function of $|t'| = (p\theta_{max})^2$, where p is the beam momentum. Figure 6 shows the distribution of events in $|t'|$ in the range $|t'| > 0.1$ $(GeV/c)^2$ for both $\bar{p}p$ and pp reactions. The small-t' behavior is exponential with a slope of about half that for elastic scattering. Again, straightforward extrapolation and integration yield the loss due to the holes.

Having obtained the corrected number of interactions, N_{tot}, the total cross-section is simply obtained from:

$$\sigma_{tot} = N_{tot}/L\tau \tag{6}$$

where L is the luminosity in Intersection Region 2 and τ is the live time of the run. The luminosity is determined using the standard, Van der Meer technique. The rate, $R_{mon}(\delta)$, of the beam-beam monitor described above is measured as the displacement, δ, of the beam centroids is varied by steering the beams, thus evaluating the integral:

$$\sigma_{mon} = \frac{1}{K} \int R_{mon}(\delta) \, d\delta \tag{7}$$

where K is a known constant depending on the ISR crossing angle and the beam currents. Subsequently, the instantaneous luminosity is obtained from:

$$L = R_{mon}/\sigma_{mon} \tag{8}$$

In this way, the luminosity has been established with a statistical accuracy of 0.75%.[1]

The results obtained for the $\bar{p}p$ and pp total cross-sections are given in Table I (in mb).[1]

Table I

	σ_{obs}	$\Delta\sigma_{CI \cdot CO}$	$\Delta\sigma_{elastic}$	$\Delta\sigma_{inelastic}$	σ_{tot}
$\bar{p}p$	40.8 ± 0.3	0.5 ± 0.2	1.7 ± 0.2	0.5 ± 0.1	43.6 ± 0.4
pp	39.6 ± 0.2	0.5 ± 0.2	1.7 ± 0.2	0.5 ± 0.1	42.3 ± 0.4

The difference between $\bar{p}p$ and pp total cross-section is 1.3 ± 0.6mb. The error on this difference is influenced strongly by the quoted errors on the extrapolated small angle corrections and the large angle trigger only component. We observe that all of these corrections are equal to within small errors for $\bar{p}p$ and pp runs. (The errors stem from systematic uncertainities in extrapolation.) Thus we have, for the observed cross-section difference

$$\Delta\sigma_{obs} = 1.2 \pm 0.4 \text{ mb.} \tag{9}$$

The elastic differential cross-section can be obtained from the analysis of collinear hits in opposing TB hodoscopes, as described above. Figure 7 shows $d\sigma/dt$ for $\bar{p}p$ elastic scattering in the range $0.01 \lesssim |t| \lesssim 0.05$ $(GeV/c)^2$. These data fit well to a single exponential with slope, $b_{small} = 14.2 \pm 0.8$ $(GeV/c)^{-2}$ and intercept at $t = 0$ of 95.0 ± 2.6 $mb/(GeV/c)^2$. Imposition of the optical theorem, with assumption of $\rho = $ Real $f(0)/$Imag $f(0) = 0.10$ yields $\sigma_{tot} = 42.9 \pm 0.6$mb, in agreement with the total rate method above.

The H_5 hodoscopes, spanning the angular range $14 \lesssim \theta \lesssim 30$ mrad, permit a similar analysis for collinear, elastic scattering events.

These data allow determination of $d\sigma/dt$ in the range $0.1 \leq |t| \leq 0.6$ $(GeV/c)^2$ as shown in Fig. 8. The slope parameter in this interval is found to be $b_{medium} = 10.8 \pm 0.6$ $(GeV/c)^{-2}$. There is clear indication that the differential elastic scattering cross-section shows a change in slope, somewhere in the vicinity of $|t| = 0.1$ $(GeV/c)^2$. This behavior is reminiscent of that of the pp elastic cross-section. The integrated elastic cross-section for the sum of the exponentials observed in small and medium t ranges is 6.9 ± 0.4mb, to be compared with $\sigma_{el} = 7.56 \pm 0.08$mb for pp scattering. The ratio $(\sigma_{el}/\sigma_{tot})$ is thus $0.159 \pm .009$ for $\bar{p}p$ collisions, compared with 0.1747 ± 0.0012 for pp collisions.[3]

The s-dependence of $\sigma_{tot}(\bar{p}p)$, $\sigma_{tot}(pp)$ and the difference is shown in Fig. 9. The $\bar{p}p$ total cross-section has, by ISR energies, begun rising above the value observed in the range $p_{lab} < 300$ GeV/c. The difference in $\bar{p}p$ and pp total cross-sections continues to fall with energy as p_{lab}^{-n}.

The s-dependence of the small t slope parameter $(|t| < 0.1)$ is shown in Fig. 10. Our value at $p_{lab} \simeq 1500$ (GeV/c) indicates a clear shrinkage of the forward cross-section relative to the lower energy data. The energy dependence of $\sigma_{elastic}$ and the medium t slope parameter $(< |t| > = 0.2$ $(GeV/c)^2$ are shown in Fig. 11. Both quantities have become equal, within errors, for $\bar{p}p$ and pp collisions at $p_{lab} \simeq 1500$ (GeV/c).

We have performed a preliminary analysis of some global properties of particle production in $\bar{p}p$ collisions at $\sqrt{s} = 52.8$ GeV. For this analysis we have selected events which give at least two tracks in the central drift chamber system $(|\eta| \lesssim 2)$ in order to obtain a good vertex reconstruction. Particle hit distributions in pseudorapidity, η, are obtained either from the drift chamber information or from the segmented hodoscope planes in each hodoscope set. The distributions have not been corrected for the effects of secondary interactions, decays, photon conversions, delta rays or binning effects. The focus here is upon comparison of distributions for $\bar{p}p$ and pp collisions.

Figure 12 shows the <u>observed</u> charged particle multiplicity distributions for both $\bar{p}p$ and pp collisions. They are similar; there is however a small shift in the distribution for $\bar{p}p$ toward higher multiplicity. Specifically, we find $<n_{obs}>_{\bar{p}p} = 15.1 \pm 0.1$ and $<n_{obs,pp}> = 14.75 \pm 0.07$ when $|\eta| < 3.5$. When the rapidity interval is restricted to $|\eta| < 2.0$, the difference in $<n_{obs}>$ between $\bar{p}p$ and pp remains essentially unchanged at 0.3 ± 0.1. Further restriction to $|\eta| < 1.0$ gives the difference in $<n_{obs}>$ to be 0.2 ± 0.1. We conclude that the excess multiplicity seen for $\bar{p}p$ collisions is largely in the central region. Interpreting the difference to be due to the annihilation component in $\bar{p}p$ collisions, we find that the annihilation products populate mainly the region $|\eta| < 2.0$. Fig. 13 shows the difference in $\bar{p}p$ and pp topological cross-sections. Again we see the excess is present at multiplicities above the average for either reaction.

The single particle inclusive pseudorapidity distributions for both $\bar{p}p$ and pp are shown in Fig. 14; $\rho(\eta) = \dfrac{1}{\sigma_{inel}} \dfrac{d\sigma}{d\eta}$. Instrumental effects distort these distributions, particularly near $\eta = \pm 1.5$. Figure 15 shows the ratio of single particle distributions $\rho^{\bar{p}p}(\eta)/\rho^{pp}(\eta)$ for three multiplicity intervals (low, average and high). The common features are a constant ratio for $|\eta| < 3$ and a depletion at large $|\eta|$ in the $\bar{p}p$ distributions. This depletion is largest for the higher multiplicity events. We thus conclude that it is associated with the presence of the annihilation component. The values of $d\sigma/d\eta$ ($\bar{p}p$) exceed those for $d\sigma/d\eta$ (pp) over the central plateau by a small but significant amount. We find that for the inclusive distributions $\rho(o)\bar{p}p/\rho(o)pp$ is 1.03 ± 0.01, which translates into

$$\left[\frac{d\sigma}{d\eta}\bigg|_{\eta = 0} (\bar{p}p) \right] / \left[\frac{d\sigma}{d\eta}\bigg|_{\eta = 0} (pp) \right] = 1.07 \qquad (10)$$

after accounting for the difference in inelastic cross section.

The presence of a small annihilation component in the $\bar{p}p$ cross-section yielding large numbers of particles in the central region may be expected to influence the two-particle correlation more strongly than single particle distributions. We define the correlation

$$R_2(\eta_1, \eta_2) = \frac{\rho_2(\eta_1, \eta_2)}{\rho(\eta_1)\, \rho(\eta_2)} - 1 \qquad (11)$$

where $\rho_2(\eta_1, \eta_2) = \dfrac{1}{\sigma_{inel}} \dfrac{d^2\sigma}{d\eta_1 d\eta_2}$ is the two particle distribution for particle production at η_1 and η_2. If then there is a component of the production process producing large numbers of particles in some rapidity range, its effect on R_2 will be more pronounced than for $\rho(\eta)$. Figure 16 shows the $R_2(\eta_1, \eta_2)$ for fixed η_2 in the interval $(-0.36, 0.12)$ versus η_1. Both $\bar{p}p$ and pp correlations are shown.

The distributions for pp collisions show the familiar short-range ($\Delta\eta \sim 2$) correlations behavior, with peak strength diminishing as multiplicity increases. The $\bar{p}p$ correlations appear to be stronger, particularly at large multiplicity and the range of the correlation is somewhat smaller than for pp correlations. This behavior again reinforces our interpretation that the annihilation component is a dominantly central process affecting the multiplicities above the average for $\bar{p}p$ collisions.

REFERENCES

1. Recently the ISR staff has found a systematic error in the scale factor for the beam displacement δ which affects all luminosity measurements of this experiment in the same way. The correction, if applied, would increase all cross-sections determined from the equation $\sigma = R/L$ by 0.75%.

In this paper, this correction is not applied.
2.   L. Baksay et al., Nucl. Physics <u>B141</u>, 1 (1978).
3.   U. Amaldi and K. R. Schubert, Nucl. Phys. <u>B166</u>, 301 (1980).

610

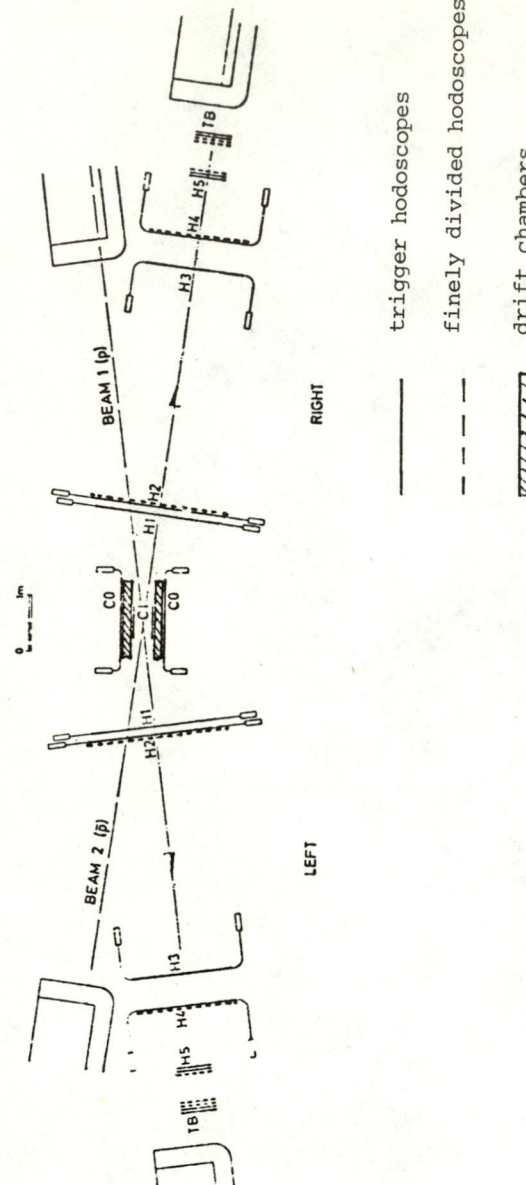

FIGURE 1   Experimental Layout

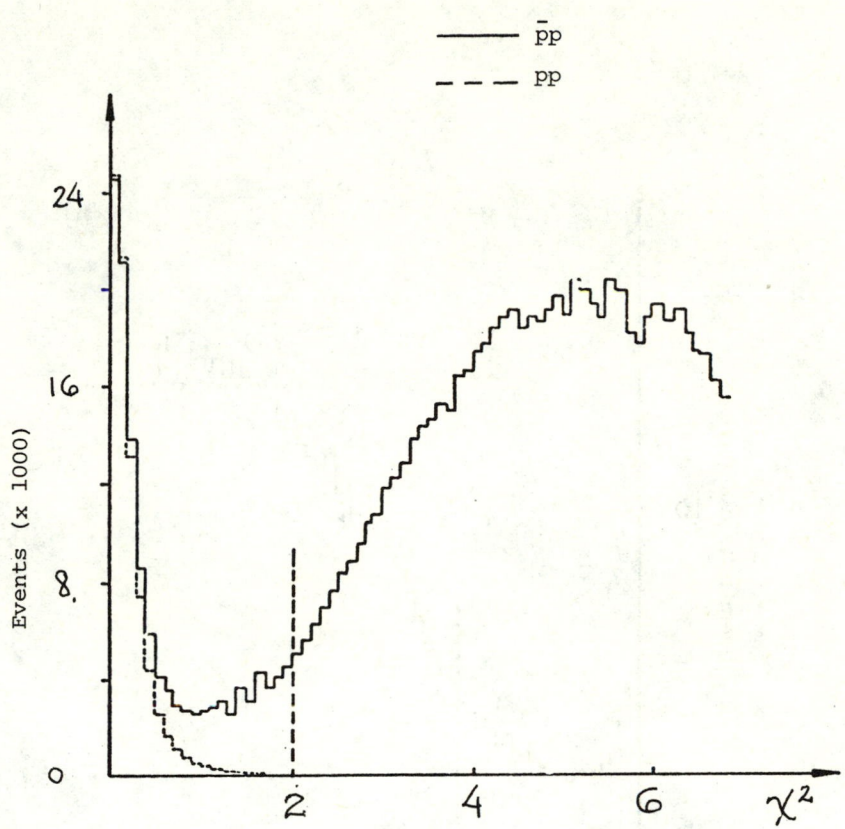

FIGURE 2 χ^2 distribution for beam-beam events:
pp and $\bar{p}p$.

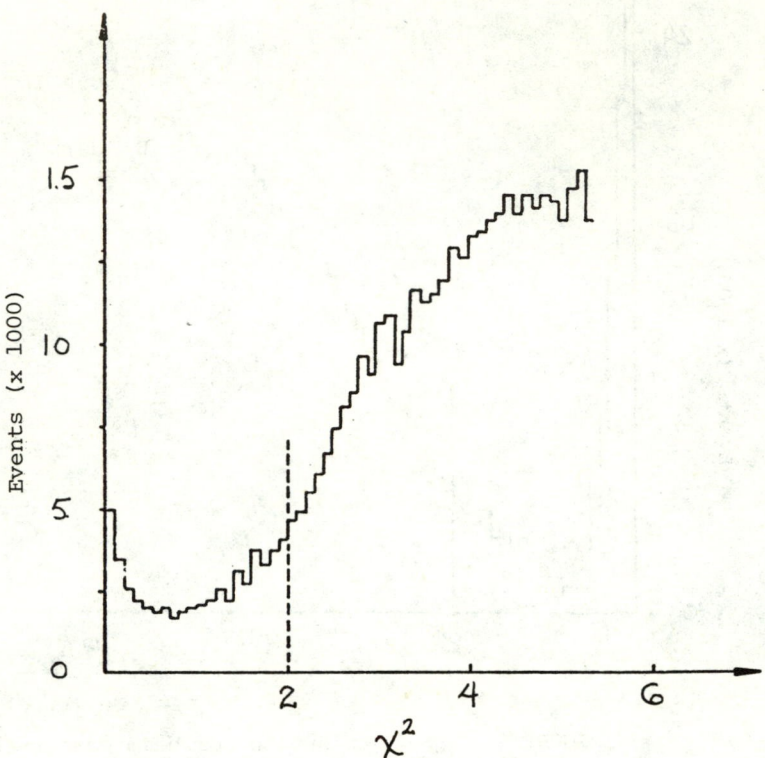

FIGURE 3 χ^2 distribution for $\bar{p}p$ events
with beams separated

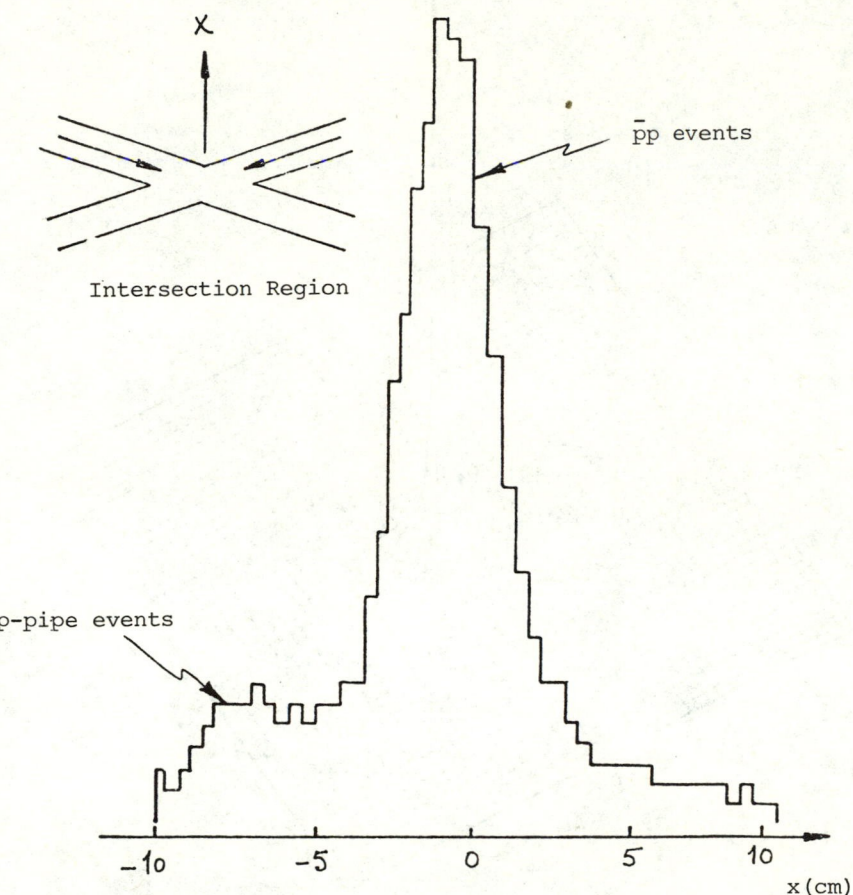

FIGURE 4   Vertex x-distribution for p̄p events

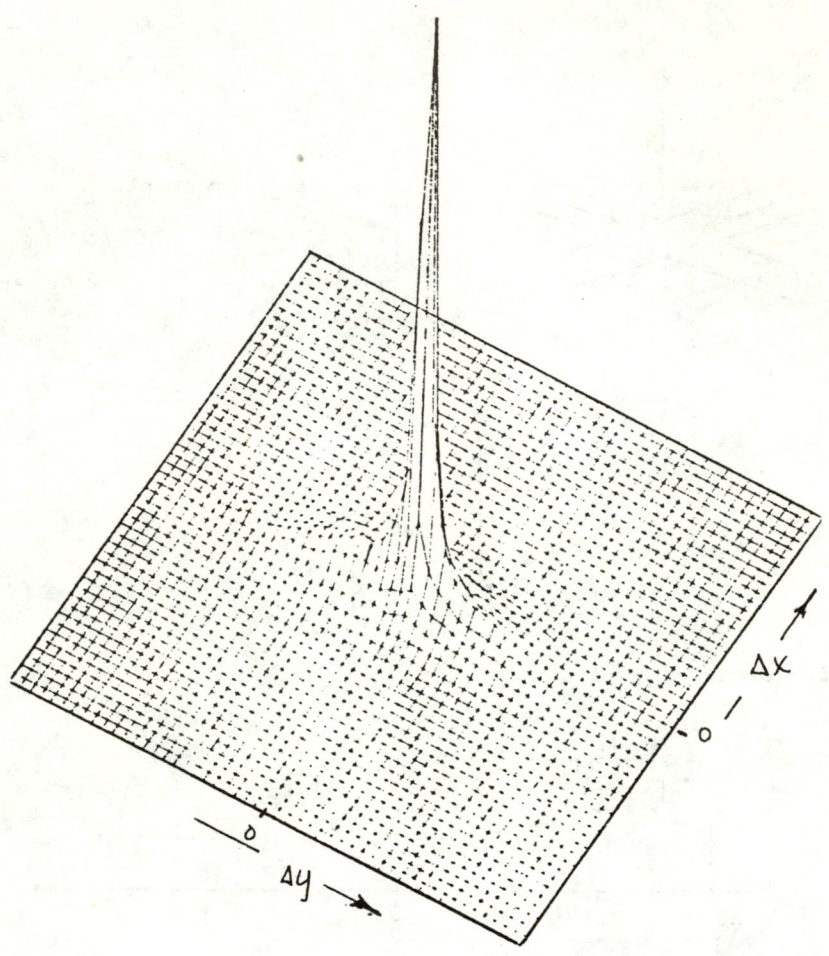

FIGURE 5   Collinearity plot for small angle events:
Δx in 5mm/step and Δy in 25mm/step.

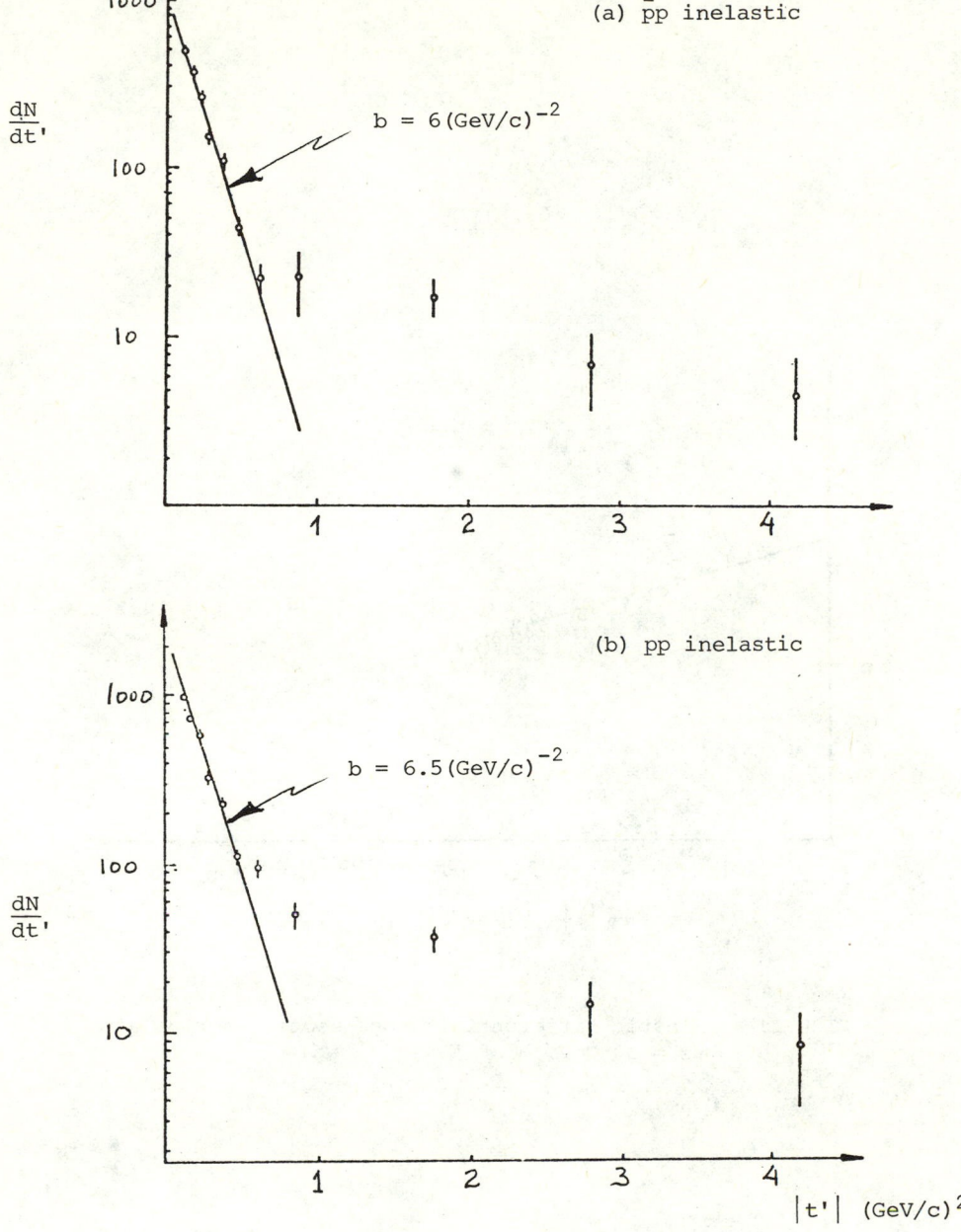

FIGURE 6   Inelastic event distributions in t':
(a) p̄p and (b) pp.

616

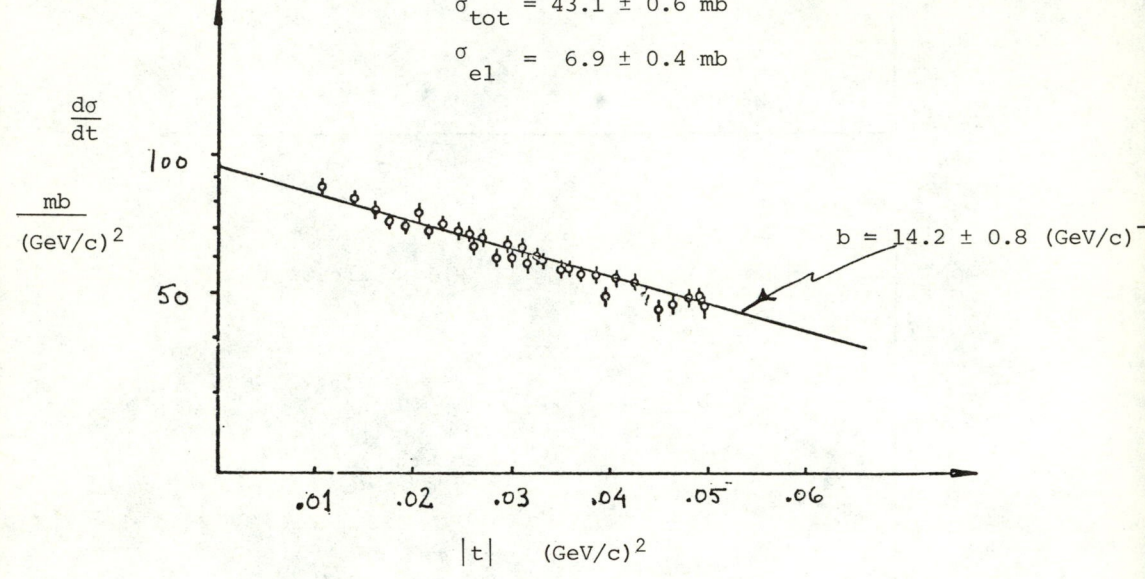

FIGURE 7   Elastic differential cross-section for $\bar{p}p$ at
$\sqrt{s}$ = 53 GeV.

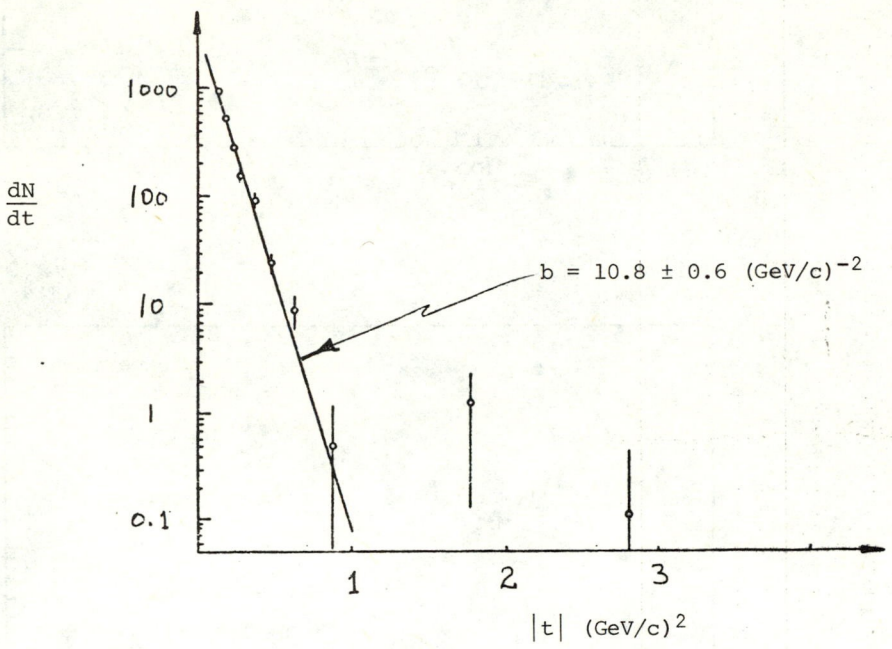

FIGURE 8   Elastic differential   cross-section for $\bar{p}p$
at $\sqrt{s}$ = 53 GeV (unnormalized).

618

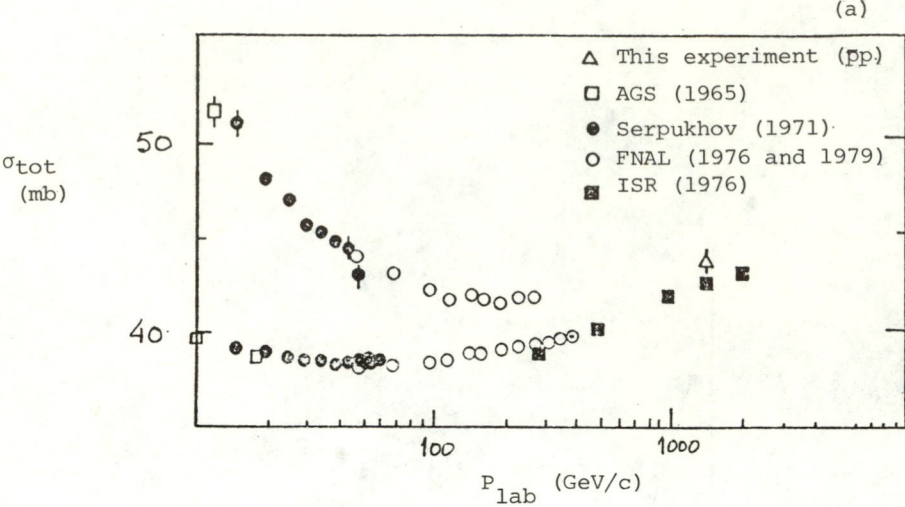

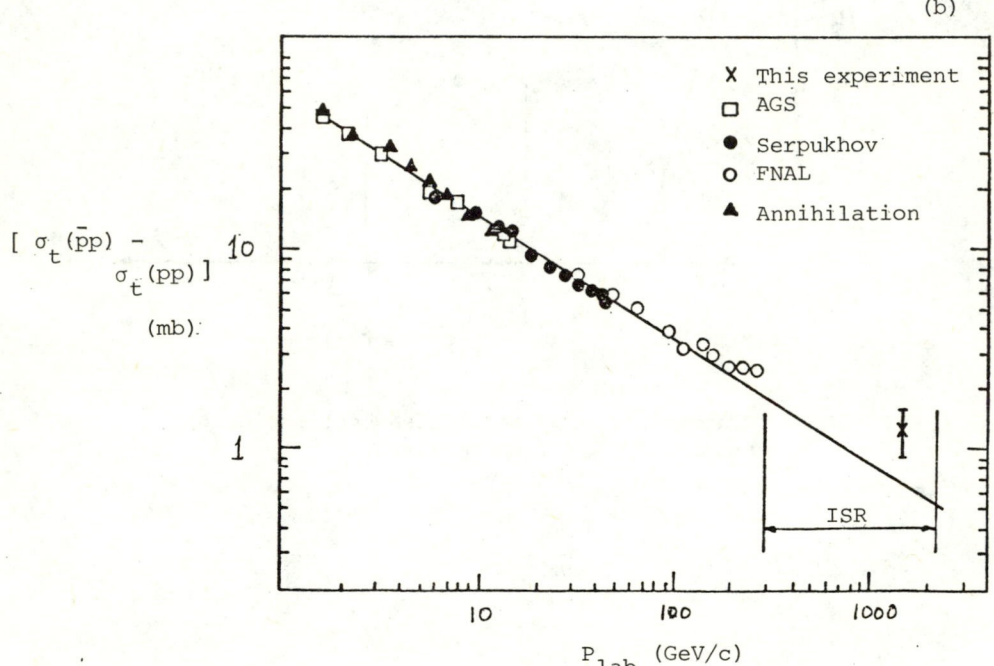

FIGURE 9 Energy variation of σ_{tot} for $\bar{p}p$ and pp total
cross-sections (a), and the difference (b).

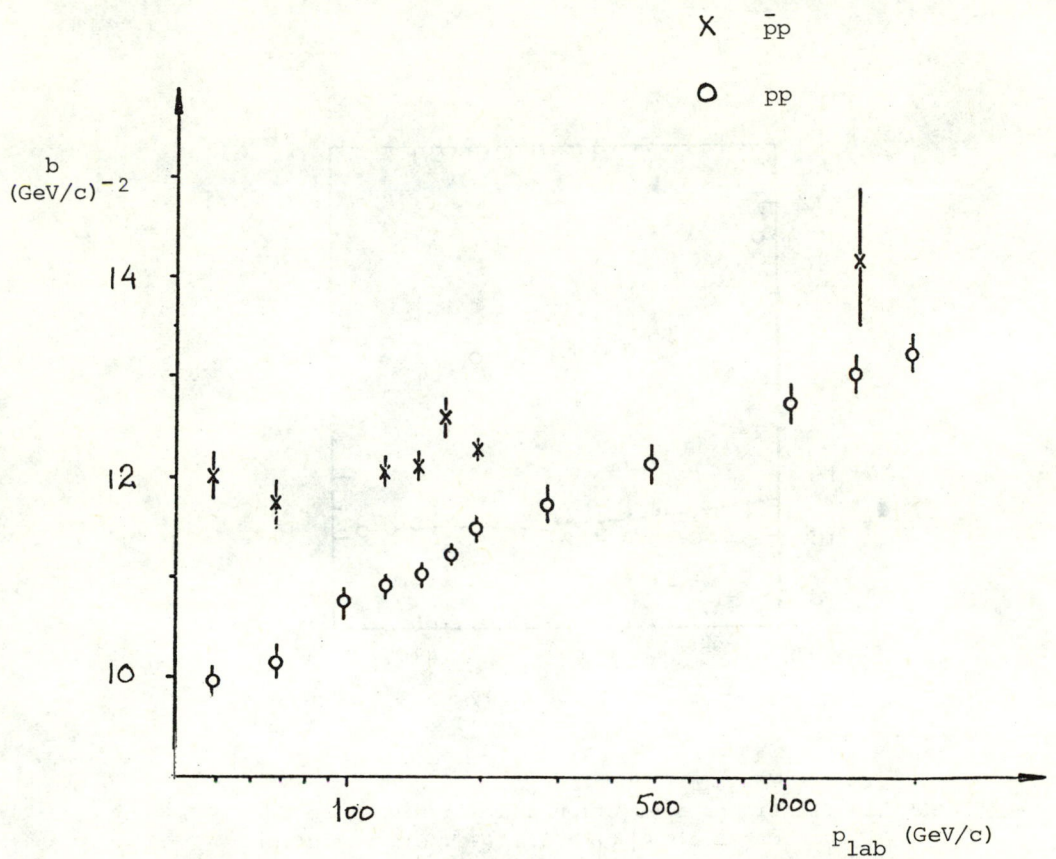

FIGURE 10   Elastic slope parameter ($|t| < 0.1$ $(GeV/c)^2$) variation
with energy for $\bar{p}p$ and pp scattering.

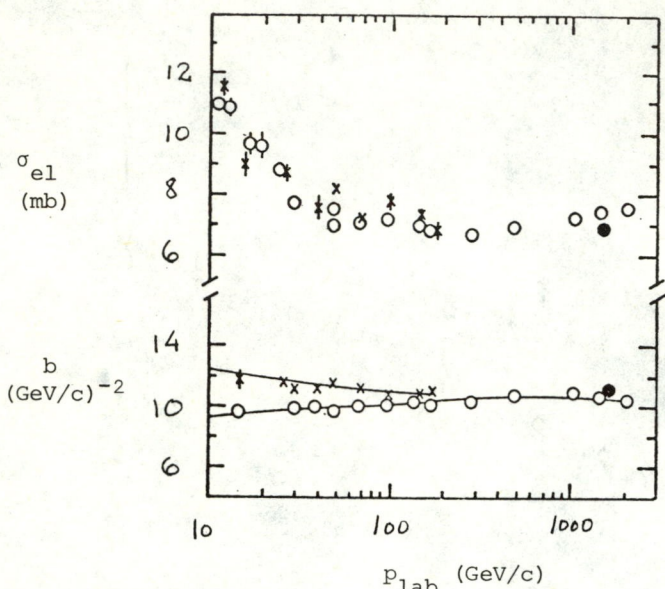

FIGURE 11 Elastic cross-section and elastic slope
parameter at $< |t| > 0.2$ $(GeV/c)^2$ variation
with energy. $\bar{p}p$: x, pp:0, this experiment $\bar{p}p$: ●

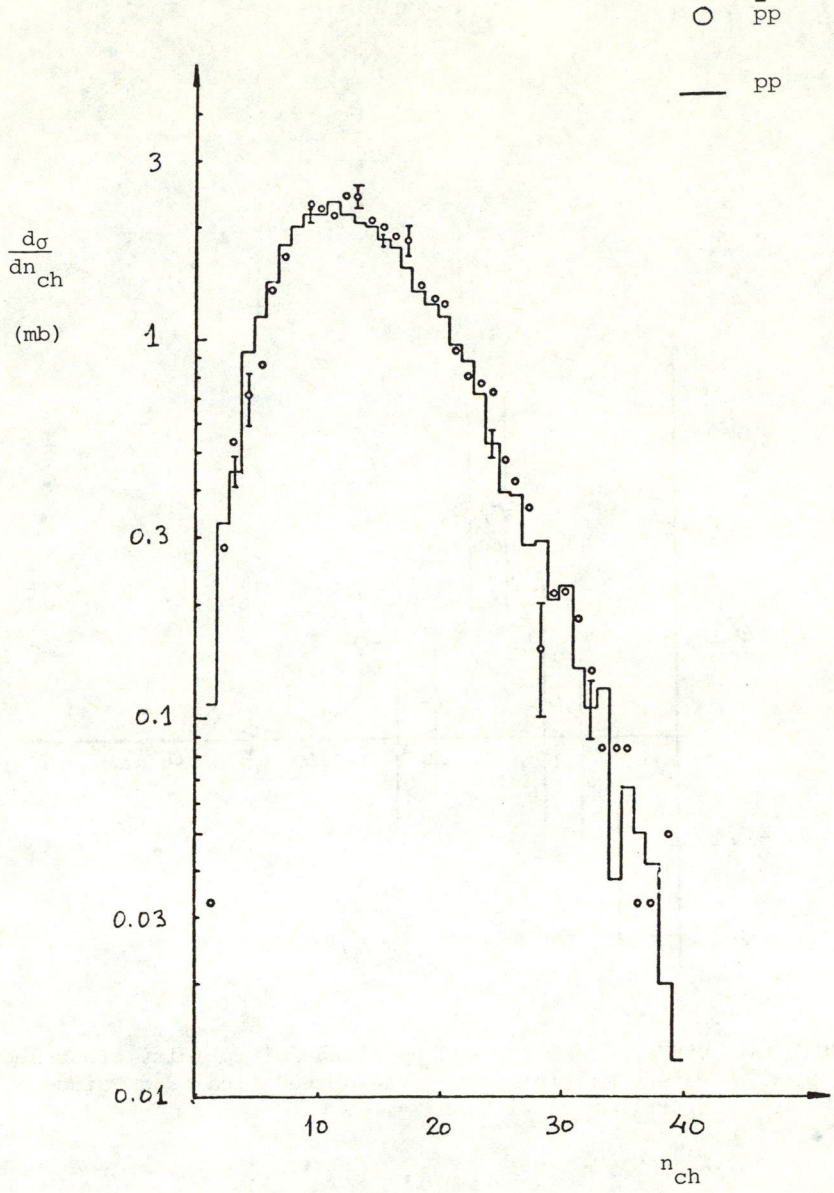

FIGURE 12   Multiplicity distributions for $\bar{p}p$ and pp collisions for $|\eta| \leq 3.5$.

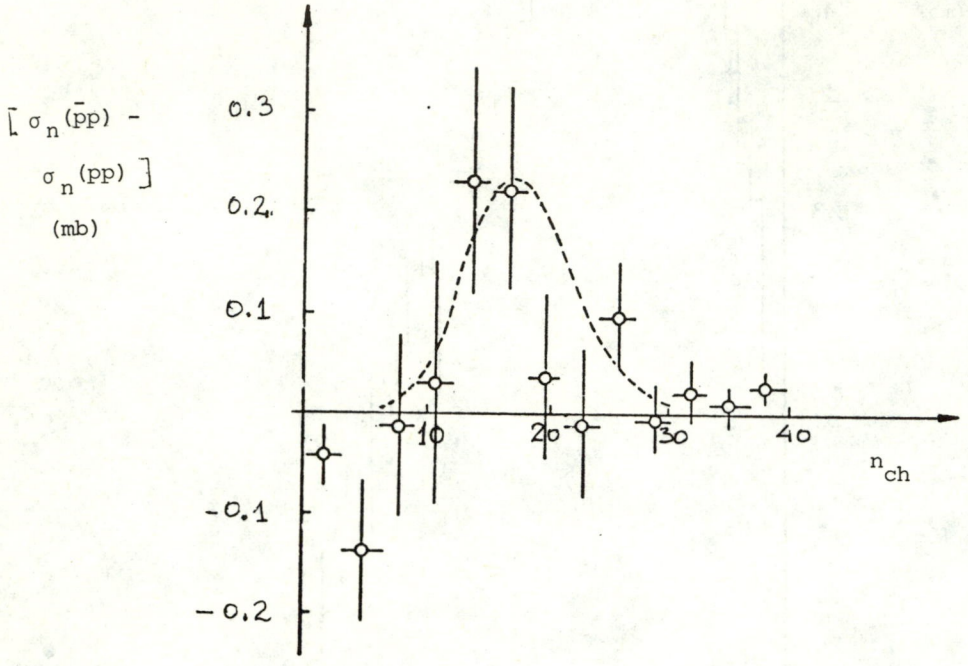

FIGURE 13   Difference of pp and p̄p fixed multiplicity cross-sections versus multiplicity.   The dotted line is a Poisson distribution with <n> = 18.

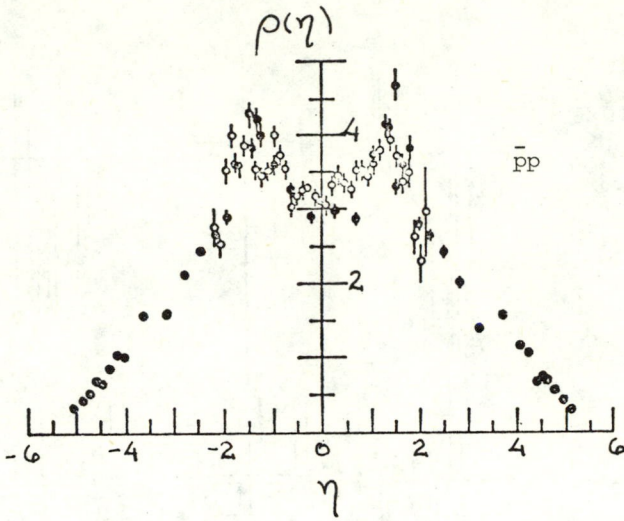

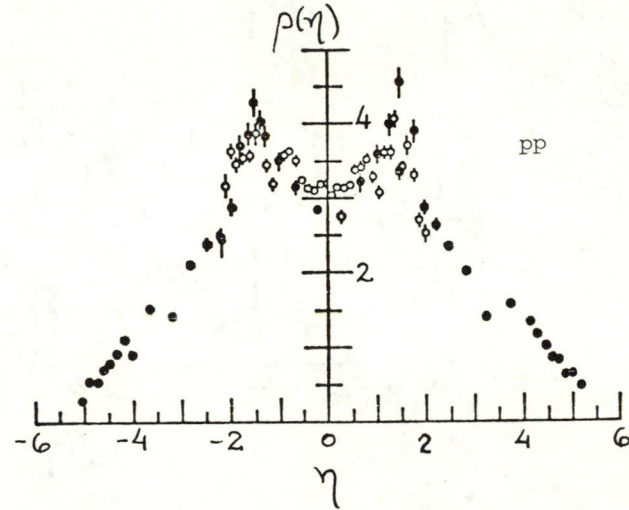

FIGURE 14   Single particle inclusive distributions, $\rho(\eta)$
versus η for $\bar{p}p$ and pp.

624

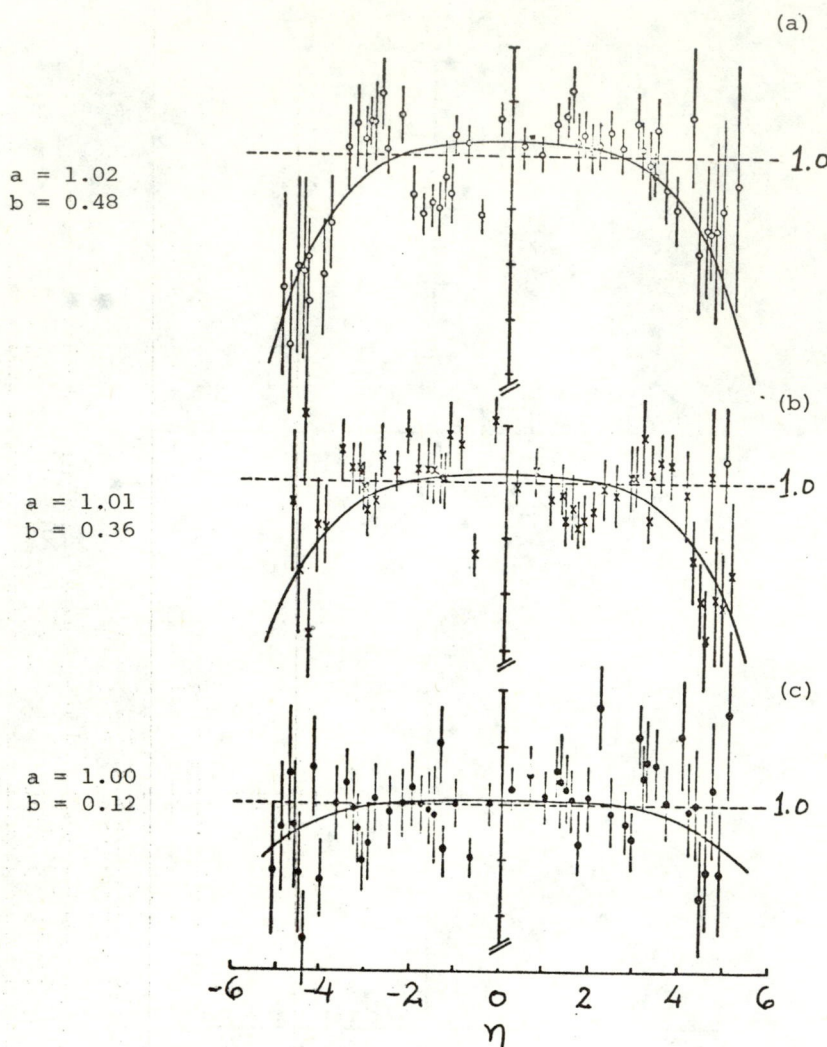

a = 1.02
b = 0.48

a = 1.01
b = 0.36

a = 1.00
b = 0.12

FIGURE 15 $R(\eta) = \rho^{\bar{p}p}(\eta)/\rho^{pp}(\eta)$ vs. η.   (a) high multiplicity, $n_{ch} \gtrsim 19$; (b) average multiplicity, $12 \lesssim n_{ch} \lesssim 18$; (c) low multiplicity, $n_{ch} \lesssim 11$. The solid lines are fits to the form $R(\eta) = a - 10^3 \cdot b\eta^4$.

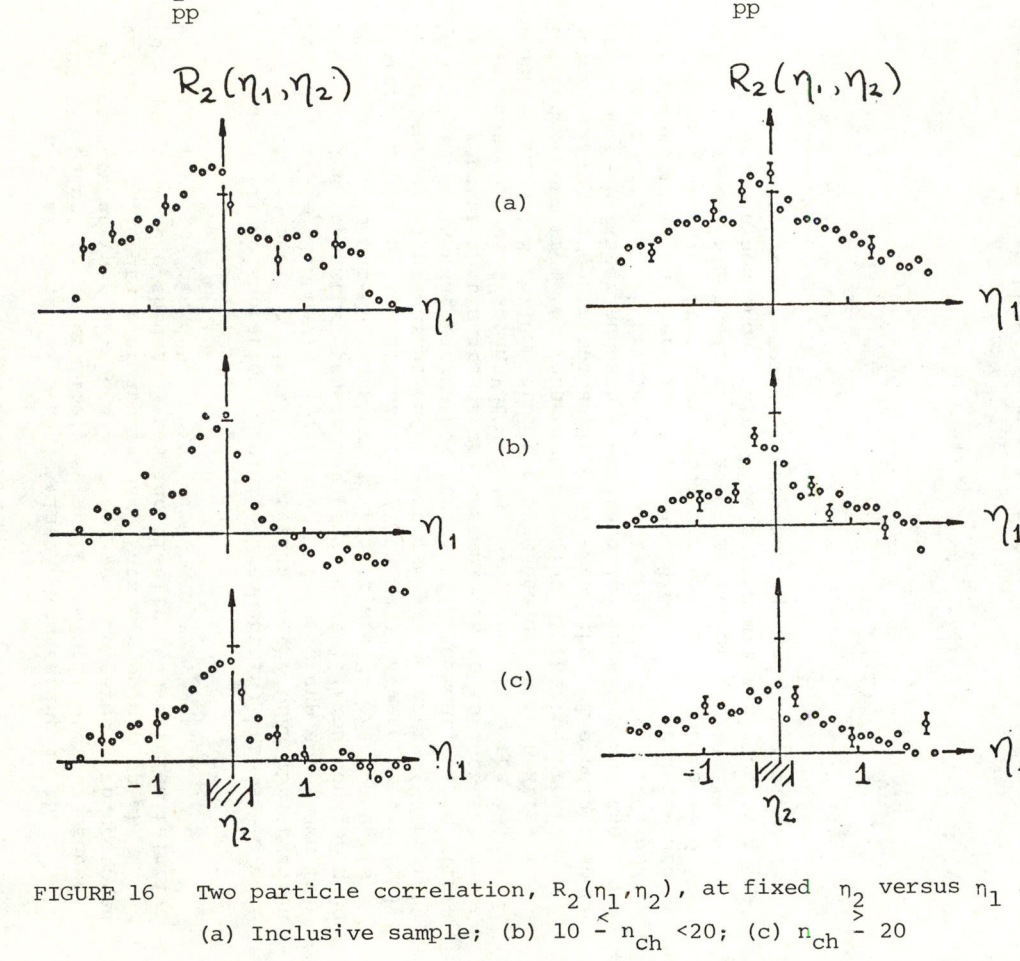

FIGURE 16 Two particle correlation, $R_2(\eta_1,\eta_2)$, at fixed η_2 versus η_1.

(a) Inclusive sample; (b) $10 \leq n_{ch} < 20$; (c) $n_{ch} \geq 20$

A COMPARISON OF $\bar{p}p$ and pp
ELASTIC SCATTERING at $\sqrt{s}$ = 52.8 Gev (R211)*

Martin M. Block

Northwestern University, Evanston, Ill. 60201

ABSTRACT

We have measured small angle elastic scattering at the CERN ISR using arrays of finely segmented scintillator hodoscopes. Measurements at $\sqrt{s}$ = 23.5 and 30.6 Gev were compared with accepted values for calibration of apparatus. Data for pp and $\bar{p}p$ at $\sqrt{s}$ = 52.8 Gev were then analyzed identically to determine relative values for σ_{tot}, ρ and B.

The R-211 colaboration (Louvain-Northwestern) has made a comparison of $\bar{p}$-p and p-p elastic scattering at the CERN ISR at 26 on 26 Gev/c ($\sqrt{s}$ = 52.8 Gev). The members of the group are shown in Fig. 1. The apparatus, consisting of 2 scintallition counter hodoscope pairs, AB and CD, is shown in Fig. 2 and 3. Each area is composed of 24 horizontal counters ("Stacks") to measure vertical (polar angle) displacement and 7 vertical 4mm counters ("Fingers") to measure horizontal (azimuthal angle) displacement, along with a trigger counter that subtends the ensemble. Each is located in a reentrant bellows ("Roman Pot") to allow us to place the lowest stack counter ~ 8 to 10mm from the beam center. Each array is located 8700mm from the intersection point of the two crossing beams, giving us a minimum angle of ~ 1mr. The pulse height spectra from each finger and stack are recorded in ADC's and the timing information from each trigger counter is recorded in a TDC, and all events in which there is either an AB or CD coincidence are recorded on tape. After correction for inelastic events ($\lesssim$ 0.5%) and for random coincidences, an event matrix of $(7x24)^2$ is obtained for each hodoscope pair. The events are analyzed as a function of $|t|$, the 4-momentum-transfer squared, as follow:

$$\frac{d\sigma}{dt} = \pi \ |f_C + f_N|^2$$

where

$$f_C = \mp \ 2\alpha \ \frac{G^2(t)}{|t|} \ e^{\pm i\alpha\phi(t)}$$

$$f_N = \frac{(i+\rho)}{4\pi} \ \sigma_{tot} \ e^{-B|t|/2}$$

*Supported in part by a Department of Energy Grant.

where we have employed the optical theorem for f_N. In the above, $G^2(t)$ is the proton form factor squared, α is the fine structure constant, $\mp$ for $\frac{pp}{\bar{p}p}$, $\phi(t)$ is the West-Yennie phase[1] for the Coulomb amplitude, ρ is the ratio of the real to the imaginary portion of the forward nuclear-scattering amplitude (assumed to be constant over the narrow t region in which we work). σ_{tot} is the total nuclear cross section, and B is the nuclear slope parameter.

In order to extract differential cross sections from our measurement matrices, we must perform a 9-dimensional integration, since the observed scattering depends on the 3 spatial coordinates of the interaction point, vertical and horizontal (betatron oscillations) displacements of each beam from its mean directions, and the two elastic scattering angles (θ and ϕ). This integration was performed analytically, leading to a differential cross section for each of the 7x24 cells. These cross sections were then symmetrically averaged (Fingers F1 and F7, F2 and F6, F3 and F5), leading to 96 different cross sections. Next, the element for A looking at B was averaged with the symmetrical case of B looking at A, to get an AB pair. Finally, the AB and CD pairs were averaged, for a final average of 96 independent t values, dσ/dt. This averaging removes the major sources of uncertainty in beam alignment, etc. By using a monitor system of scintillation counters surrounding the interaction region, which was kindly supplied to us by R-210, the Pisa-Stony Brook collaboration, and using the Vander Meer Method to obtain absolute lumunosity, we can convert our measured values into absolute cross sections.

To calibrate our equipment, we measured pp scattering at 11.8 on 11.8 Gev ($\sqrt{s}$ = 23.5 Gev) and 15.3 on 15.3 Gev $\sqrt{s}$ = 30.6 Gev). We wished to measure 3 things:

(1) our normalization constant N (which should be slightly less than 1, due to nuclear absorption of elastically scattered protons in the Roman Pot walls, etc.).

(2) our t scale, as exemplified by the parameters Δh where h is our measured height of the lowest stack counter from the beam center. It is impossible to measure h directly to better than ~0.1mm.

(3) the ρ parameter.

We assumed the earlier measured values[2] of B and σ_{tot}, which were used as __inputs__ to our fits. The data and the respective fits are shown in Fig. 4 and 5 for $\sqrt{s}$ = 23.5 and 30.6 Gev, respectively. No earlier measurements of σ_{tot}, B or ρ have been made in this energy region for $\bar{p}p$. Here, we adopted the strategy of using our pp values for N and Δh as fixed inputs, in order to measure σ_{tot}, ρ and B. Thus we have treated 26.6 on 26.6 ($\sqrt{s}$ = 54.8 Gev) data identically for $\bar{p}p$ and pp data in order to make

628

a direct comparison, i.e., used N and Δh as inputs. The $\bar{p}$p data were taken in October, 1981, with beam conditions of $I_- = 2$ ma and $I_p = 10$a, with vertical cooling used, corresponding to a luminosity of ~ 10^{27} cm^{-2} sec^{-1}. The same $\bar{p}$ beam was used (for ~ 12 days) with negligible loss, with 3 different protons beams. A total of 170,000 $\bar{p}$p events were taken.

Two sets of pp data were taken, shown in Fig. 5 and 6, The $\bar{p}$p data, from 3 independent runs, are shown in Fig. 7, 8, 9. In Fig. 7 and 9, the Roman Pots were moved out an integral number of stack counters, in order to extend the t scale, and all 120 points so obtained are shown. The results are summarized in Fig. 10, for both pp and $\bar{p}$p, along with the various sources of error, both statistical and systematic. Also shown are the cross section, ρ and B differences, in which only the statistical error is shown. We have also not indicated the correlations between the various quantities. We note that the Pomeranchuk theorem, in the version that says that $\sigma_{\bar{p}p} \to \sigma_{pp}$, as the energy goes to infinity seems to be satisfied. The ρ values are also approaching each other. The "Pomeranchuk" theorem of Cornille and Martin[3], which states that if we have a diffractive-like differential cross section, that B$\bar{p}$p $\to$ Bpp also seems to be satisfied, since our nuclear slope parameters have also begun to converge. The world summary of cross section data for both pp and $\bar{p}$p is shown in Fig.11, with our $\bar{p}$p point at $\sqrt{s}$ = 53.8 Gev appended. The world-summary for ρ values for pp and $\bar{p}$p; and the dispersion curves of Lipkin are shown in Fig. 12 along with our measured ρ values for pp and $\bar{p}$p.

We would like to take this opportunity for thanking the staffs of the AA, PS, and ISR for making this experiment possible, and would like to acknowledge our gratitude for the aid that Vickie White of DD supplied in our data acquistion programs, and that Dr. J. Debaisieax supplied in data monitoring. Finally, we would like to acknowledge the participation of Dr. F. Erne´, J. Sens and P. Macq in the early phases of this experiment.

REFERENCES

1) G. B. West and D. R. Yennie, Phys. Rev. __172__, 1413 (1968)

2) U. Amaldi and K. R. Schubert, ·Nucl. Phys. __B166__, 301 (1980)

3) H. Cornille and A. Martin, Phys. Lett. __40B__, 671 (1972)

R-211 COLLABORATION
(LOUVAIN-NORTHWESTERN)

N. AMOS
M. BLOCK
G. BOBBINK
M. BOTTJE
D. FAVART
C. LEROY
P. LIPNIK
J.-P. MATHEYS
D. MILLER
K. POTTER
C. VANDER VELDE-WILQUET
S. ZUCCHELLI

Fig. 1

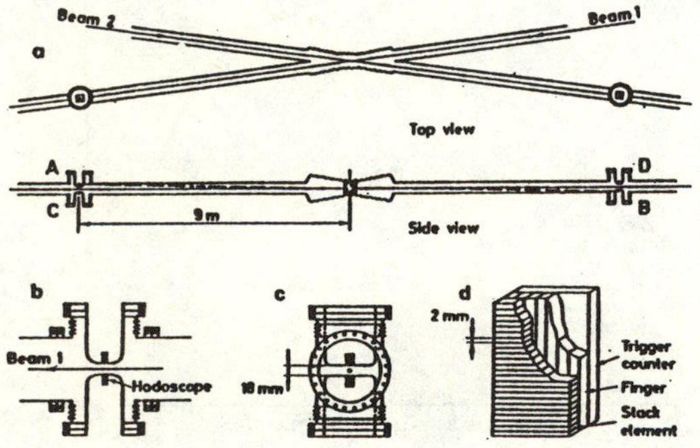

Fig. 2

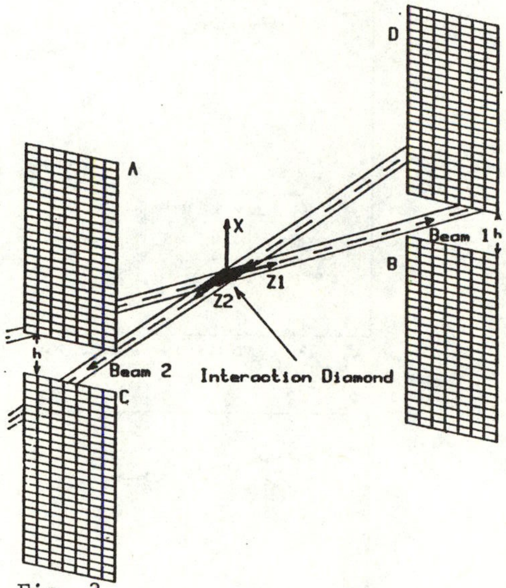

Fig. 3

HODOSCOPE SCHEMATIC

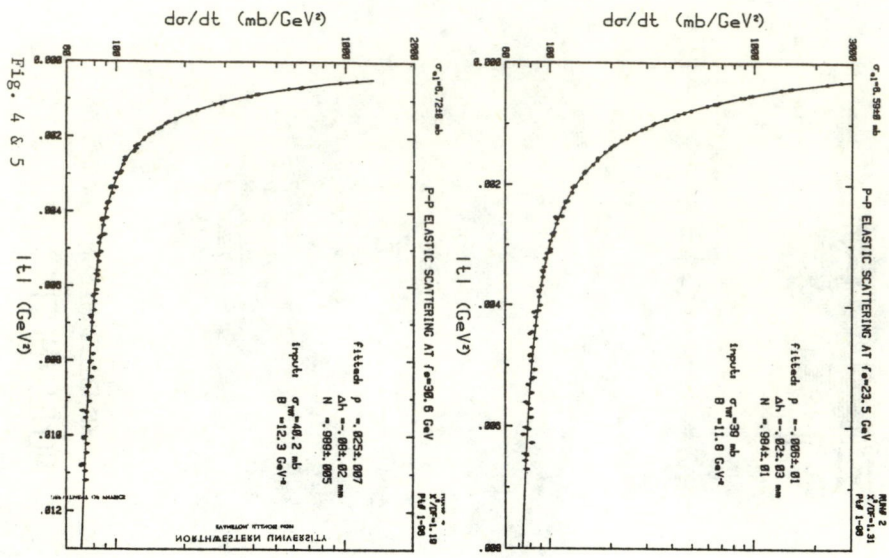

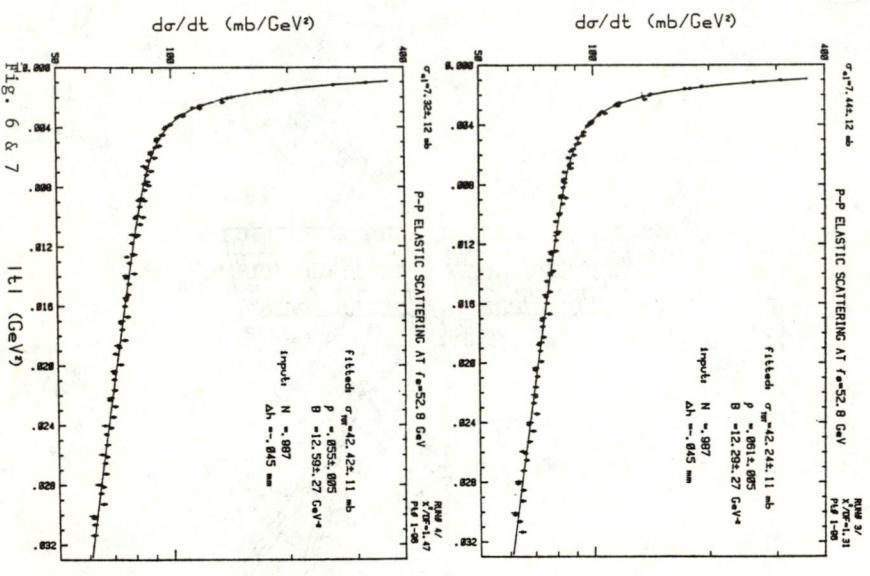

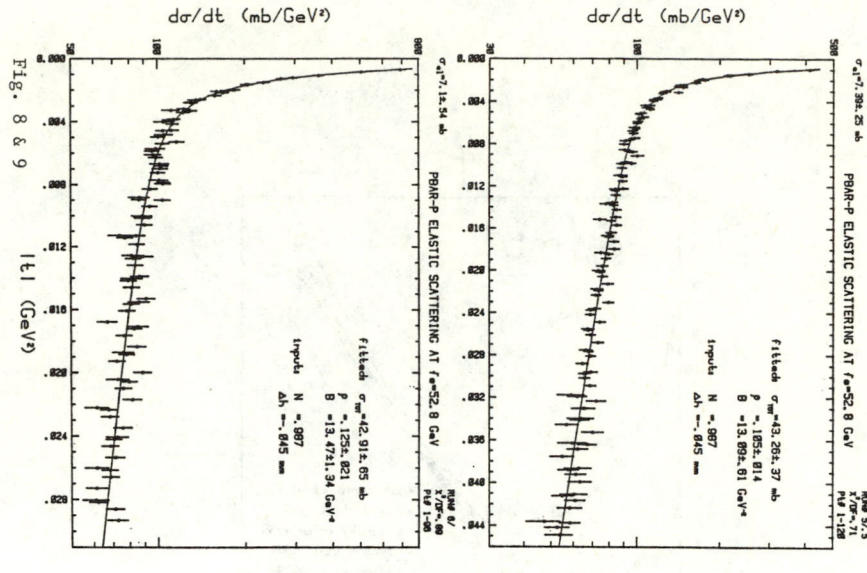

Fig. 8 & 9

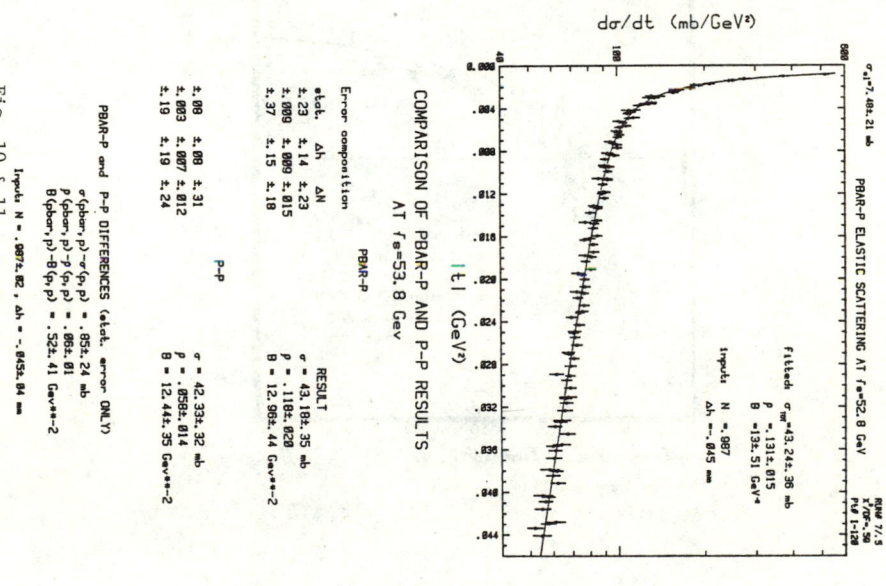

Fig. 10 & 11

632

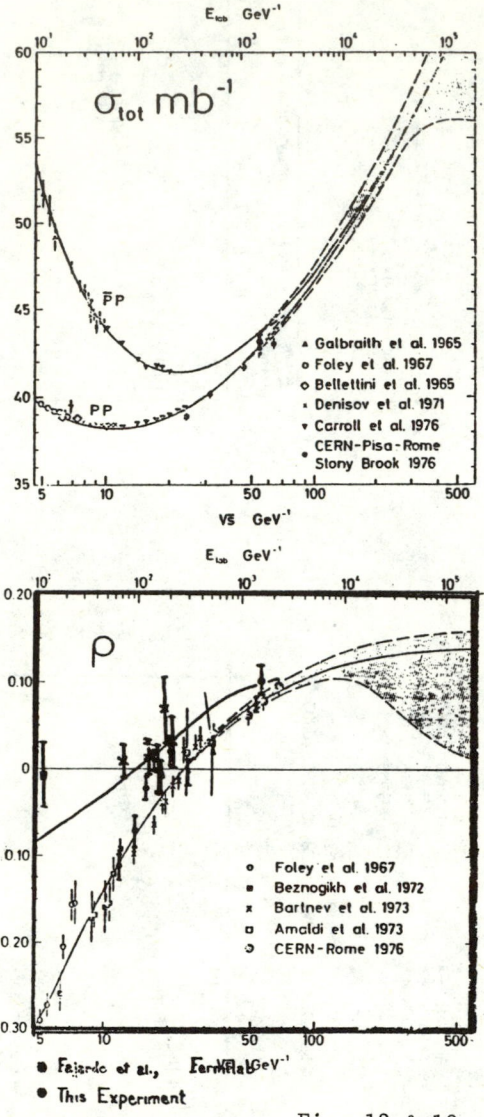

Fig. 12 & 13

FIGURE CAPTIONS

Fig. 1 A list of authors of the R-211 (Louvain-Northwestern) Collaboration.

Fig. 2 A drawing of the counter hodoscopes and the Roman Pots.

Fig. 3 Hodoscope schematic

Fig. 4 Fitted pp Elastic cross section at $\sqrt{s}$ = 23.5 Gev, to obtain S, Δh, N.

Fig. 5 Fitted pp Elastic cross section at $\sqrt{s}$ = 30.6 Gev, to obtain S, Δh, N.

Fig. 6 Fitted pp Elastic cross section ab$\sqrt{s}$ = 52.8 Gev, to obtain σ_{tot}, ρ and B.

Fig. 7 Fitted pp Elastic cross section ab$\sqrt{s}$ = 52.8 Gev, to obtain σ_{tot}, ρ and B.

Fig. 8 Fitted $\bar{p}$p Elastic cross section ab$\sqrt{s}$ = 52.8 Gev, to obtain σ_{tot}, ρ and B.

Fig. 9 Fitted $\bar{p}$p Elastic cross section ab$\sqrt{s}$ = 52.8 Gev, to obtain σ_{tot}, ρ and B.

Fig. 10 Fitted $\bar{p}$p Elastic cross section ab$\sqrt{s}$ = 52.8 Gev, to obtain σ_{tot}, ρ and B.

Fig. 11 Comparison of $\bar{p}$p and pp. Results ab$\sqrt{s}$ = 52.8 Gev.

Fig. 12 Expected energy behavior of the p-p and $\bar{p}$-p total cross sections.

Fig. 13 Expected energy behavior of the ρ values for pp and $\bar{p}$p.

A REVIEW OF RECENT ISR PHYSICS RESULTS

L. Camilleri
CERN, 1211 Geneva 23, Switzerland

ABSTRACT

Results recently obtained in $p\bar{p}$ interactions at the ISR are contrasted with corresponding pp results. In addition the state of Large Transverse Momentum Phenomena in pp interactions is summarised.

INTRODUCTION

The ISR physics programme has recently become very diversified. It is now based on beams of antiprotons and alpha particles as well as of protons. In this talk I will of course summarise recent results but I will also mention some older results in sofar as they represent the "state of the art" in some topics. Section I will be devoted to $p\bar{p}$, Section II to pp. The $\alpha\alpha$ and αp results are discussed in the talk of M. Jacob.

I. $p\bar{p}$ PROGRAMME

The physics topics to be investigated and the experiments addressing them are listed in Table 1.

Topic	Experiment
Total Cross section	R-210, R-211
Elastic Scattering	R-210, R-211
Multiplicities and Correlations	R-211, R-420, R-421, R-608
Correlations between Forward Direction and 90°	R-608
Charm Search	R-608
High p_T and Jets	R-110, R-420, R-807
Total Energy Triggers	R-110, R-807
Single Photons	R-110, R-807
Lepton Pairs	R-110, R-807
Quark Search	R-807
Monopoles	R-501

The first $p\bar{p}$ run at the ISR took place on 3rd April 1981 and lasted 86 hours at a luminosity of 10^{25} cm^{-2} sec^{-1}. During the course of the year the luminosity gradually increased to about 10^{27} cm^{-2} sec^{-1}. In particular the last run yielded a luminosity of 9 x 10^{26} cm^{-2} sec^{-1} with 12 Amps of protons colliding on 2mA of antiprotons. However what was more important was that these 2mA of antiprotons were kept circulating for 13 days during which time the proton beam was refilled twice. The 2mA of antiprotons were achieved starting with 10^{11} $\bar{p}$'s in the Accumulator Ring (AA) and with a 60% transfer efficiency from the AA into the ISR (via the PS). It is hoped that during the course of 1982 the luminosity will improve because of several factors :

    a)   The record number of $\bar{p}$'s accumulated in the AA has gone up by about 70% since the last ISR run.

    b)   The transfer efficiency should go up to 80-90%.

    c)   Because of the long life time of the $\bar{p}$ beams in the ISR, stacking can occur over several days.

    d)   Two low-β sections are yet to be tried in conjunction with $\bar{p}$ runs. In I-8 experiment R-807 has a superconducting low-β which should give this experiment an increase of a factor of 7 in luminosity. In I-1 experiment R-110 should benefit from a steel low-β yielding a factor of 2.2 increase in luminosity.

    Taking all these factors into account luminosities of the order of $10^{28} - 10^{29}$ cm^{-2} sec^{-1} should be achieved in 1982.

    The results on the pp total cross-section and elastic scattering at $\sqrt{s}$ = 52.7 GeV have been described in great detail during the talks of P. Grannis [1] and M. Block [2], so I will only summarise the σ_{tot} and $\Delta\sigma = \sigma_{tot}$ $(\bar{p}p) - \sigma_{tot}$ (pp) results in Fig. 1. The two experiments, R-210 using the total counting rate method and R-211 using the elastic scattering at small angles method agree on the value of σ_{tot} and $\Delta\sigma$. The pp total cross section is definitely higher than at the highest fixed target measurement available and higher than the pp total cross section at $\sqrt{s}$ = 52.7 GeV.

    A positive value of $\Delta\sigma$ is due probably to annihilation in which case a class of events with high multiplicity in the central region and a lack of particles in the forward direction should be present in $\bar{p}p$ but not in pp. Several experiments have results bearing on this topic. [1] Experiment R-210, has measured charged particle multiplicities in $\bar{p}p$ and pp using their system of counters, drift tubes and drift chambers covering nearly 4π in solid angle. They find that

    i) The increase in cross section in $\bar{p}p$ comes mostly

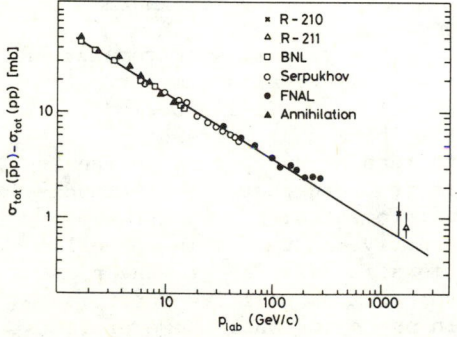

Fig. 1 : pp and $\bar{p}p$ total cross-sections and the difference between them plotted as a function of p_{LAB}.

636

from high multiplicity events

    ii)   The mean multiplicity is higher in $p\bar{p}$ than in pp :
$<n_{ch}>$ = 14.75 ± 0.07 in pp and 15.37 ± 0.01 in $p\bar{p}$
yielding $<\Delta n>$ = $<n_{ch,p\bar{p}}>$ - - $<n_{ch,pp}>$ = 0.6 ± 0.1

    iii)   Limiting the measurement to the central region only i.e. to pseudorapidity, η, less than 2.0, $<\Delta n>$ is still 0.6 ± 0.1, indicating that the increase does occur in the central region.

    Evidence for a similar increase in the number of events with high multiplicities in the central region [3] comes from R-807. They plot the multiplicity distribution of charged tracks with rapidity y, such that $|y|$ < 0.8, in $p\bar{p}$ and pp. These distributions and their ratio as a function of multiplicity are shown in Fig. 2. Whereas for multiplicities < 6 the ratio of the number of events normalised to the same luminosity is close to 1.0, for multiplicities greater than 6 it is seen to rise above 1.0.

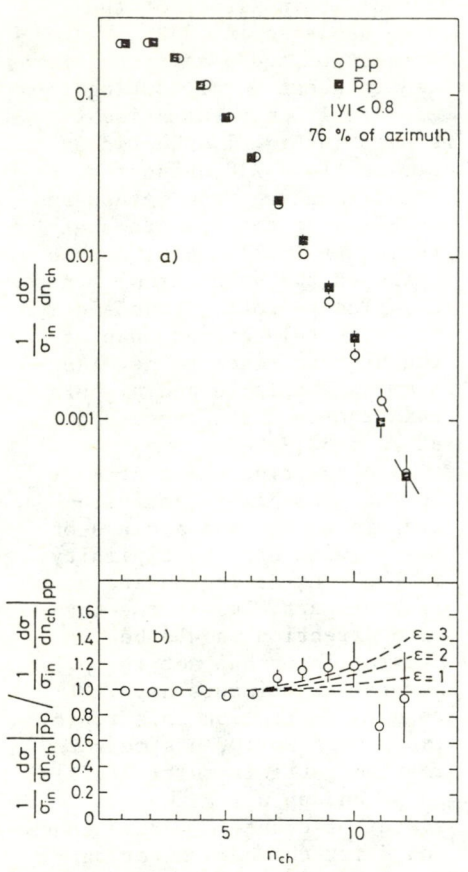

    Evidence for a depletion of particles in the forward direction comes from two sources. R-210 computes the pseudorapidity distributions $\rho = \dfrac{d\sigma}{d\eta} \dfrac{1}{\sigma_{inel}}$ for $p\bar{p}$ and pp [1]. They then plot the ratio of the two distributions as a function of η (Fig.3). The ratio of ρ ($p\bar{p}$) to ρ (pp) is seen to be slightly higher than 1.0 for $|\eta|$ < 3.5 but drops to about 0.7 for $|\eta|$ > 3.5.

    The forward spectrometer of R-608 also yields similar evidence [4]. It is located on the beam that contains $\bar{p}$'s in $p\bar{p}$ running and p's in pp running. It is found that the longitudinal momentum, p_L, spectrum of negative particles in $p\bar{p}$ collisions is identical to the p_L spectrum of positive particles in pp collisions. However it is then found that there are more events with high multiplicity (> 4 particles) in the spectrometer in $p\bar{p}$ collisions than in pp collisions : 8.8% in $p\bar{p}$ and 7.8% in pp. Furthermore the p_L

Fig. 2a : Charged multiplicity distribution in the central region from R-807.
Fig. 2b : The ratio of the $p\bar{p}$ multiplicity to the pp multiplicity

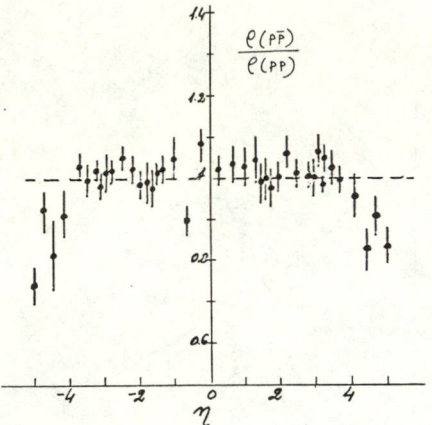

Fig. 3 : The ratio of the p$\bar{p}$ particle density, ρ(p$\bar{p}$), to the pp particle density ρ(pp) as a function of the pseudorapidity, η, from experiment R-210.

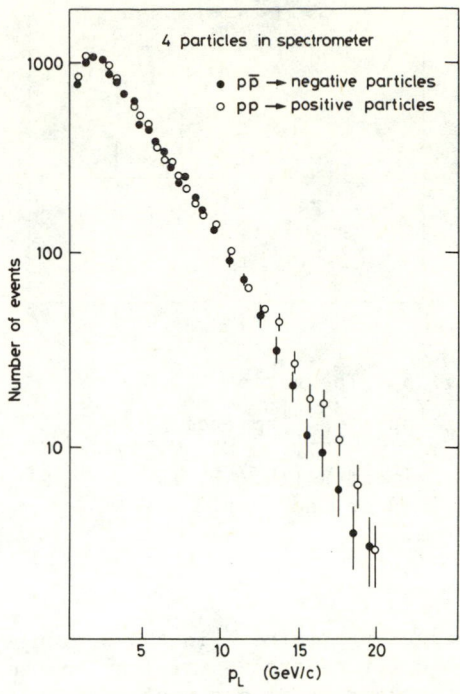

Fig. 4 : The longitudinal momentum, p_L, spectra of negative particles produced in p$\bar{p}$ collisions and positive particles in pp collisions for events with $\geqslant$ 4 particles in the spectrometer of R-608.

spectra of this subset of events (Fig. 4) show a depletion of negative high p_L particles in p$\bar{p}$ collisions when compared to positive high p_L particles in pp collisions.

All this evidence taken together hints at a suppression of leading antiprotons in p$\bar{p}$ collisions coupled with a corresponding increase in the multiplicities measured in the central region. It could have been hoped that this increase in multiplicity observed near 90° would translate itself in an increase in the energy deposition at 90°. This problem was addressed by experiment R-110 using a system of shower counters^5 subtending $\Delta\phi \sim 1.2\pi$ and covering the rapidity range $|y| < 1.0$. Only neutral particles were detected. The trigger consisted of a coincidence of forward counters placed on both beams. The quantity $\Sigma\ E_T = \Sigma\ \sqrt{m^2 + p_T^2} \sim \Sigma\ p_T$ was found for each event.
all
particles
The $\Sigma\ E_T$ spectra in pp and p$\bar{p}$ collissions were computed and their ratio is shown in Fig. 5. Whereas the individual spectra fall by 4 orders of magnitude between 2 and 8 GeV, the p$\bar{p}$/pp ratio can only accomodate a 20% increase between the same limits.

The last topic in p$\bar{p}$ collisions is that of the single particle inclusive cross section. Results are available from R-807 for

638

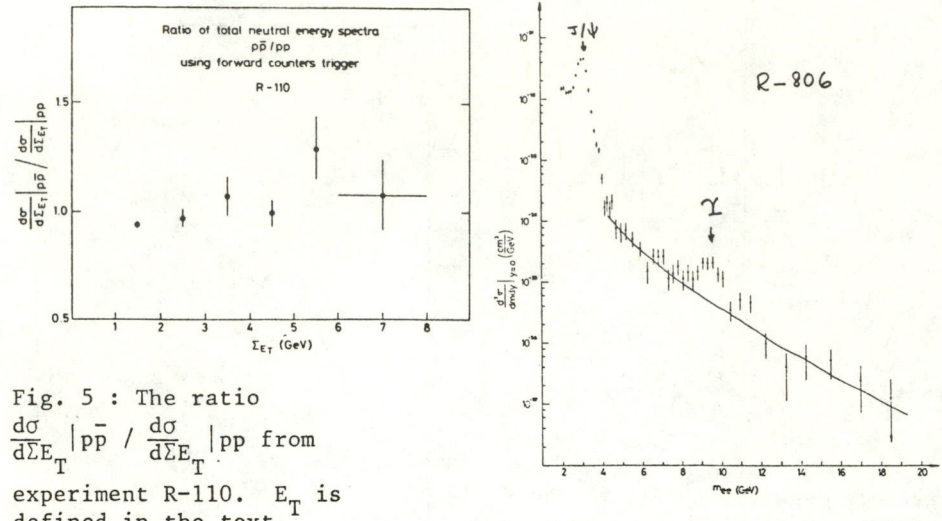

Fig. 5 : The ratio
$$\frac{d\sigma}{d\Sigma E_T}\Big|p\bar{p} \Big/ \frac{d\sigma}{d\Sigma E_T}\Big|pp \text{ from}$$
experiment R-110. E_T is
defined in the text.

Fig. 6 : The electron pair spectrum of R-806.

charged particles [3] in the p_T range $0 < p_T < 1.5$ GeV/c and from
R-110 for neutral particles[5] in the p_T range $1.5 < p_T < 3.5$ GeV/c.
Both experiments are performed in the rapidity region $|y| < 1.0$.
Their results for the ratio of p_T spectra in pp and p$\bar{p}$
seem to show a decrease in
the ratio as a function of p_T. However once again the trigger consisted of forward counters in both experiments so the results are
not purely inclusive.

II.   THE pp PROGRAMME

The pp programme at the ISR consists basically of Charm and
Beauty Searches and the Study of Large Transverse Momentum Phenome-
na. Since the results on Heavy Flavour Searches were discussed by
Dibitonto, only Large Transverse Momentum Phenomena will be revie-
wed here.
It consists of

        a) Lepton Pairs
        b) Direct Photons
        c) Single Particle Production and Correlations
        d) Large Transverse Energy Triggers.

Whereas the last topic is only just starting, (see the talk by
Pretzl) the first three have reached the stage where the contributions from individual subprocesses can be identified.

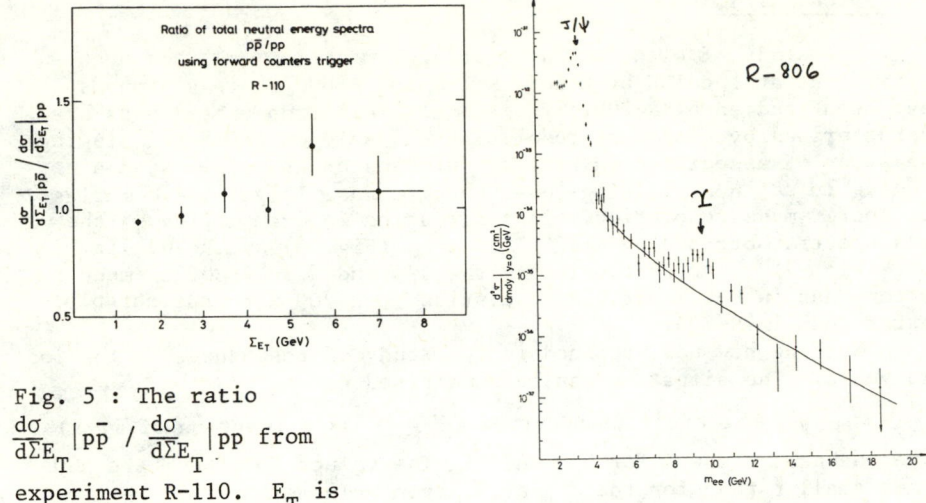

Fig. 5 : The ratio

$$\frac{d\sigma}{d\Sigma E_T}\Big|p\bar{p} \ / \ \frac{d\sigma}{d\Sigma E_T}\Big|pp \ \text{from}$$

experiment R-110. E_T is
defined in the text.

Fig. 6 : The electron pair spectrum of R-806.

charged particles [3] in the p_T range $0 < p_T < 1.5$ GeV/c and from
R-110 for neutral particles [5] in the p_T range $1.5 < p_T < 3.5$ GeV/c.
Both experiments are performed in the rapidity region $|y| < 1.0$.
Their results for the ratio of p_T spectra in pp and p$\bar{p}$
seem to show a decrease in
the ratio as a function of p_T. However once again the trigger consisted of forward counters in both experiments so the results are
not purely inclusive.

II. THE pp PROGRAMME

The pp programme at the ISR consists basically of Charm and
Beauty Searches and the Study of Large Transverse Momentum Phenome-
na. Since the results on Heavy Flavour Searches were discussed by
Dibitonto, only Large Transverse Momentum Phenomena will be revie-
wed here.
It consists of

  a) Lepton Pairs
  b) Direct Photons
  c) Single Particle Production and Correlations
  d) Large Transverse Energy Triggers.

Whereas the last topic is only just starting, (see the talk by
Pretzl) the first three have reached the stage where the contributions from individual subprocesses can be identified.

A. Lepton Pairs.

The study of electron pairs at high mass ($m \sim m_T$) has been carried out at the ISR by R-108, R-110 and R-806 whereas dimuons have been studied by R-209. In general dielectron experiments are characterised by good mass resolution and an open geometry allowing the study of associated particles. Dimuons on the other hand are studied in set ups yielding lower backgrounds, larger solid angles but poorer mass resolution. This situation is examplified by the mass spectra obtained by R-806[6] in e^+e^- (Fig. 6) and R-209[7] in $\mu^+\mu^-$ (Fig. 7). The resolution at the J/ψ and T in R-806 is much better than in R-209 but the statistics in R-209 are considerably better than in R-806.

Nothing new has happened in the study of resonances in the last two years. The situation can be summarised as

a) The excitation curves $\left(\frac{d\sigma}{dy}\big|_{y=0}\right.$ as a function of $m/\sqrt{s}$) have the same shape[8] for J/ψ and T. The values for the T are 500 times smaller than for the J/ψ at a given value of $m/\sqrt{s}$.

b) The decay distribution for the T is consistent with being isotropic. R-806 quotes

$$\lambda = 0.31 \pm 0.35 \text{ in } 1 + \lambda \cos^2 \theta*$$
(For Drell Yan Pairs $\lambda = 1.15 \pm 0.34$)

c) At $\sqrt{s} = 62$ the T is produced[6,7,8] with a mean p_T of $\sim (1.8 \pm 0.2)$ GeV/c

d) The ratio of upsilons to continuum at the T

$$B \frac{d\sigma}{dy}\Big|_{y=0} \; (T + T' + T''') \; / \; \frac{d^2\sigma}{dmdy}\Big|_{m=T} \; \sim 3$$

This indicates that the T is not produced electromagnetically since the same ratio in e^+e^- storage rings is measured[9] to be < 0.03.

e) R-209 places a limit on the production of high mass (>20 GeV/c^2) resonances[7] decaying to $\mu^+\mu^-$ based on 3 events of

$$B \; (x \to \mu^+\mu^-) \; \sigma(x) < 4 \times 10^{-37} \text{ cm}^2.$$

The study of continuum events has produced some new results mainly on associated particles. Basically these events are thought to originate from the annihilation of a $q\bar{q}$ pair (Fig. 8a). If this is the case the events should be characterised by few if any associated particles at 90°. This is indeed the case in some events but not in all. Furthermore using the proton structure functions obtained from neutrino scattering one can calculate the cross section based on the process of Fig. 8a. Typically the prediction is about a factor 2 lower then the experiment[7] (Fig. 9). This indicates that more diagrams are needed, for instance gluon Compton scattering (Fig. 8b) and $q\bar{q}$ annihilation into a dilepton and a gluon (Fig. 8c). Both these diagrams have the characteristic of a jet of particles

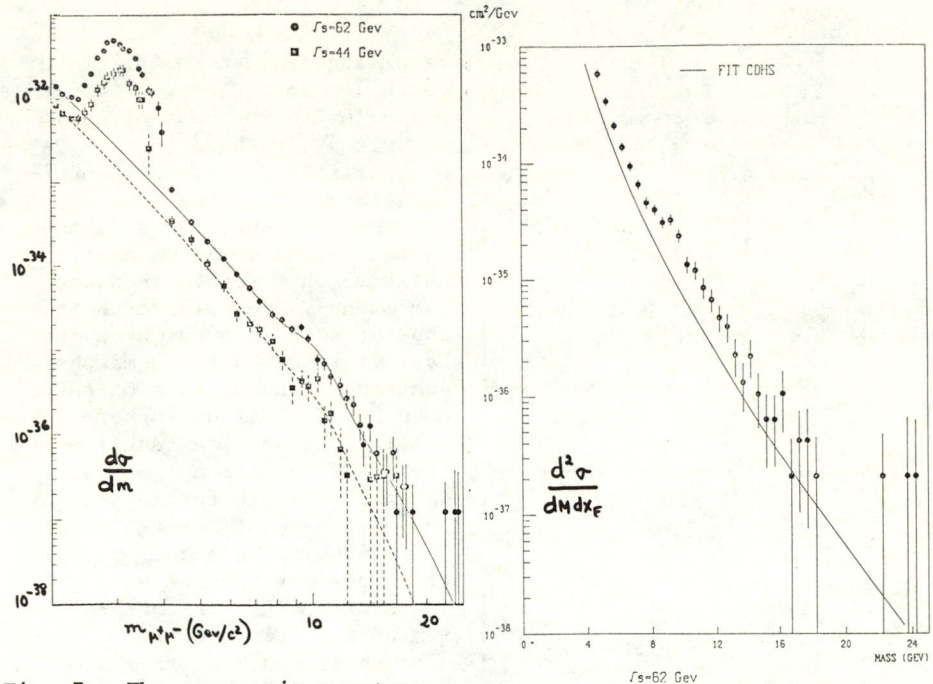

Fig. 7 : The muon pair spectrum
of R-209.

Fig. 9 : The dimuon spectrum of
R-209 compared to Drell-Yan
predictions using structure
functions obtained by CDHS.

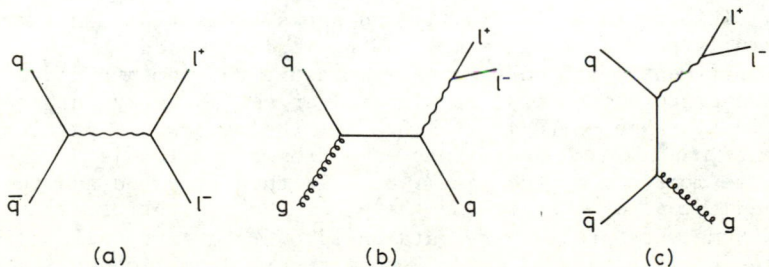

Fig. 8 : Examples of processes contributing to the production
of lepton pairs in hadronic collisions.

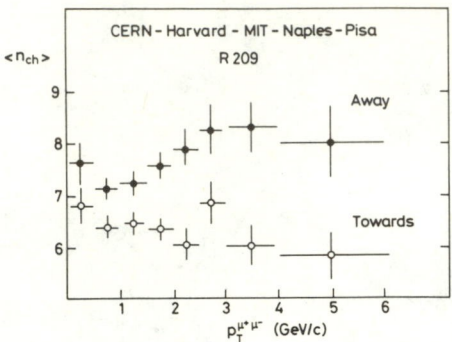

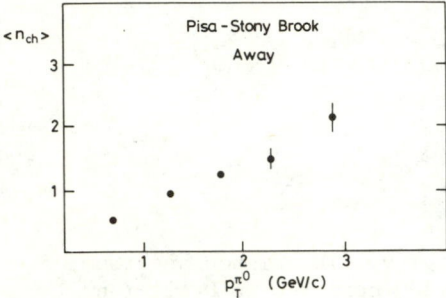

Fig. 10 : Multiplicity associated with dimuon events and π^0 events as a function of the p_T of the dimuon or the π^0.

recoiling against the dilepton; a quark jet in the case of 8b and a gluon jet in the case of 8c.

To study these jets [10] R-209 use their drift chambers covering almost 4π. They are of course only sensitive to charged particles and do not measure their momenta (other than the two muons). They divide their apparatus on an event by event basis into a TOWARDS hemisphere centred on the p_T axis of the dimuon and an AWAY hemisphere. The multiplicities as a function of the p_T of the dimuon, $p_T^{\mu\mu}$ are shown in Fig. 10 for 1800 events above the J/ψ. Whereas in the TOWARDS hemisphere the multiplicity does not change as a function of $p_T^{\mu\mu}$, in the AWAY hemisphere it rises with $p_T^{\mu\mu}$ with a slope of ~ 0.5 particles/GeV/c. This is reminiscent of the situation with a π^0 trigger (also shown in Fig. 10) where the AWAY multiplicity also rises with $p_T^{\mu\mu}$. Defining $\phi^{\mu\mu}$ and ϕ^{AP} as the azimuthal angles of the dimuon and any associated particles respectively, R-209 then plot $\phi_{CH} = \phi^{\mu\mu} - \phi^{AP}$ as a function of $p_T^{\mu\mu}$. This is shown in Fig. 11 and shows a distribution that is increasingly peaked at $\phi_{CH} = 180^\circ$ as $p_T^{\mu\mu}$ is increased.

Experiment R-110 on e^+e^- pairs measure the momenta and direction of charged and neutral particles over the whole azimuth and in the rapidity range $-1.0 < y < 1.0$. All the associated particles in the event are treated as if they came from a single "jet". The transverse momentum of the "jet", p_T^{jet} is then computed and the angle ϕ between the p_T of the jet and the p_T of the dielectron is then computed. Some very preliminary data based on 25 events, all of them at masses greater than 12 GeV/c^2 show a very dramatic peaking at $\phi = 180^\circ$ (Fig. 12).

The data of the two experiments show a very strong tendency for the associated particles to emerge increasingly in a back to back configuration as the p_T of the dilepton is increased. This points to the existence of diagrams such as those of Fig. 8b, 8c.

The prospects in the dilepton field are for experiment R-110 to increase its statistics to about 100 events with m > 12 GeV/c^2 and for experiment R-807 to come into operation using its full azimuth Uranium calorimeter in conjunction with the superconducting low-β.

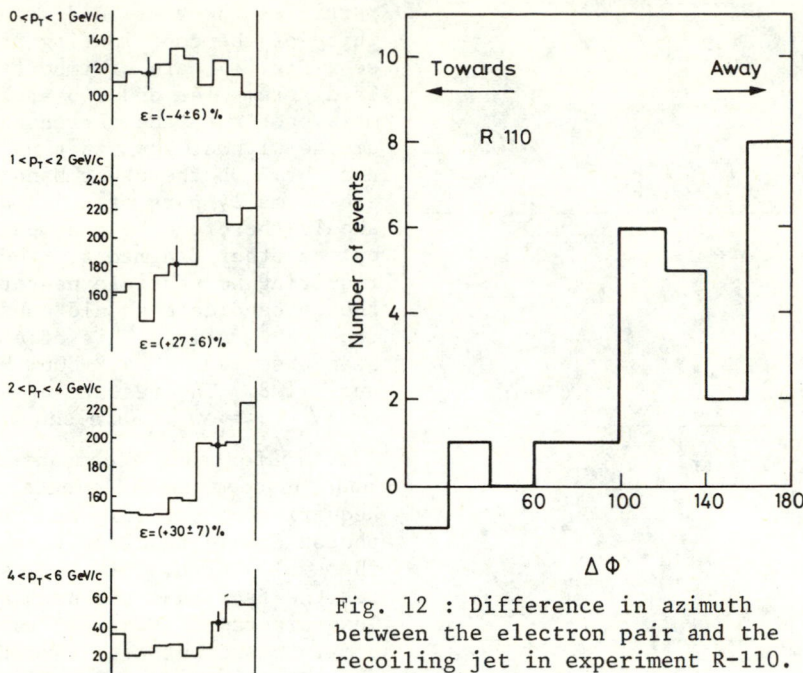

Fig. 12 : Difference in azimuth between the electron pair and the recoiling jet in experiment R-110.

Fig. 11 : Azimuthal correlations between the muon pair and associated charged particles in experiment R-209.

B. Direct Photons.

The experimental difficulty in the detection of direct photons comes from the background due to π^0 (and η) decays into two photons. These decays cannot be distinguished from single photons due to the coarse spatial resolution of most detectors. The existence of a direct photon signal was finally established by R-806 using a fine grain liquid argon calorimeter [11]. Their latest results are shown in Fig. 13. They now extend to about p_T^γ = 12 GeV/c. The effect was also observed by R-108 using the difference in conversion probability of photons and π^0's in the coil of their solenoid [12] (1 λ_0 thick).

644

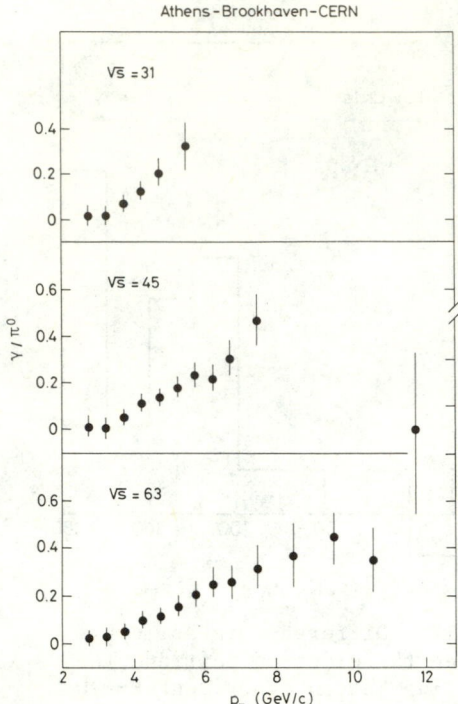

R-806
Athens-Brookhaven-CERN

$\sqrt{s} = 31$

$\sqrt{s} = 45$

γ / π^0

$\sqrt{s} = 63$

p_T (GeV/c)

Fig. 13 : The ratio γ / π^0 at different $\sqrt{s}$ as measured by experiment R-806.

Here too, the experiments are now investigating the associated particles in order to distinguish which of the contributing processes, Fig. 14, are of importance. If diagrams 14a and 14b are the main ones then the photons should emerge without any other particle near by. On the other hand π^0's are normally part of a jet and should therefore be accompagnied by the other fragments. Therefore requiring no particle near the photon candidate should enhance the γ / π^0 ratio. This effect has been observed[13] by R-806, R-807 and R-108. The results of R-108 on $\gamma/_{\gamma+\pi^0} = \gamma/_{all}$ are shown in Fig. 15 for the "accompanied" and "unaccompanied" events. Requiring no particle near the photon candidate clearly enhances the γ /all ratio. This demonstrates the fact that the bremsstrahlung diagram of Fig. 14c is not a main contributor to direct photon production. In order to determine whether the gluon Compton scattering of Fig. 14a in the qq̄ annihilation is dominant the charge ratio in the AWAY side jet can be studied. In Fig. 14b the AWAY jet comes from a gluon and equal numbers of positive and negative particles are expected. In Fig. 14a the AWAY jet comes from a quark. Now because of the relative abundance of u and d quarks in the proton, and the relative

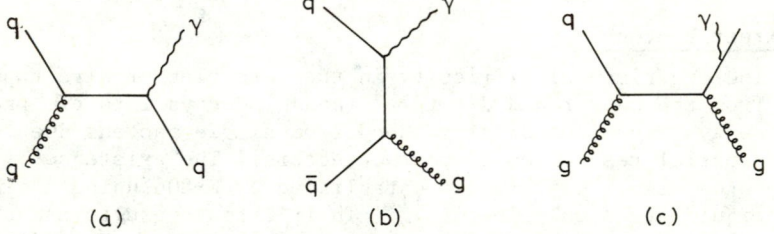

(a)   (b)   (c)

Fig. 14 : Examples of processes contributing to the production of direct photons.

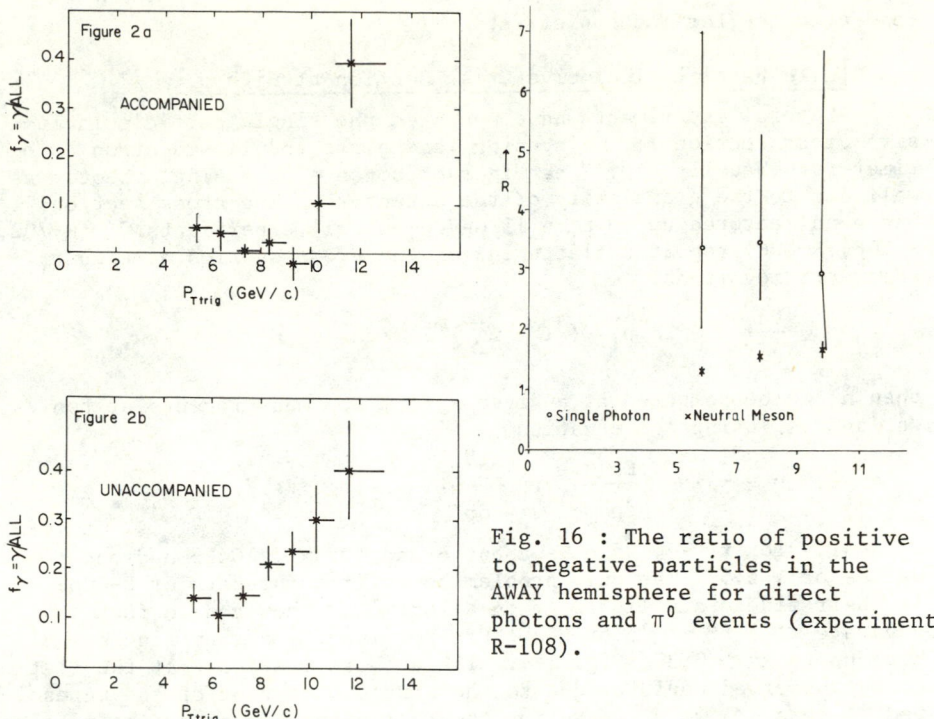

Fig. 16 : The ratio of positive to negative particles in the AWAY hemisphere for direct photons and π^0 events (experiment R-108).

Fig. 15 : The ratio γ/all in experiment R-108 for accompanied and unaccompanied particles.

coupling of u and d quarks to the photon u quarks are expected to dominate over d quarks in the production of photons by a factor of

$$\frac{2}{1} \times \frac{(2/3)^2}{(1/3)^2} = 8.$$ Furthermore since u quarks are expected to yield

more positve particles in the AWAY jet and d quarks more negative particles, the charge ratio $R_{+/-} = \dfrac{\text{Number of positive particles}}{\text{Number of negative particles}}$ in the away jet is expected to be large. This charge ratio, as measured by R-108, (Fig. 16) is clearly larger than 1.0 and is also larger than in events triggered by neutral mesons, indicating that gluon Compton scattering is the dominant mechanism for direct photon production.

In principle the same argument can be applied to events accompanied by particles. If they are due to the bremsstrahlung diagram of Fig. 14c then the charge ratio for particles in the TOWARDS jet should also be larger than 1 and higher than the corresponding charge ratio for mesons. Some preliminary data from R-807 shows some evidence for such an effect.

C. Single Particle Inclusive Cross Section at High p_T.

Several experiments have measured the single particle inclusive cross section for π^0's using lead glass and liquid Argon calorimeters. Usually a "π^0" can in fact be an η or a single photon as well due to the granularity of the detectors. The cross section has been measured up to $p_T \sim 15$ GeV/c and all experiments[14] (R-702, R-108, R-806) report a flattening of the cross section at high p_T. Parametrising it as

$$\frac{Ed^3\sigma}{d\vec{p}^3} = A \, p_T^{-n} \, (1 - x_T)^m \quad \text{with} \quad x_T = 2 \, p_T \, /\sqrt{s} \, ,$$

then n can be computed at a given x_T from two measurements at two $\sqrt{s}$, $\sqrt{s}_1$ and $\sqrt{s}_2$ using the equation

$$n = - \log \left. \frac{Ed^3\sigma}{dp^3}\right|_1 / \left. \frac{Ed^3\sigma}{dp^3}\right|_2 \; / \log \; \sqrt{s}_1 / \sqrt{s}_2 \quad .$$

Typically for $x_T < 0.25$, n is about 8 and for $x_T > 0.25$ n drops to values of ~ 5.5. The only problem comes from the data of R-806. In their fine grain liquid Argon calorimeter they can in fact separate π^0's from γ's or η's. For resolved π^0's they find n ~ 8 even up to $x_T \sim 0.37$ (Fig. 17). The authors mention that the flattening observed could be due to the single γ content of the unresolved π^0 data. A word of caution though : - the errors on the resolved π^0 measurement are large. Furthermore the two $\sqrt{s}$ values used for the resolved π^0's are lower than for their unresolved π^0 measurement which does show the drop.

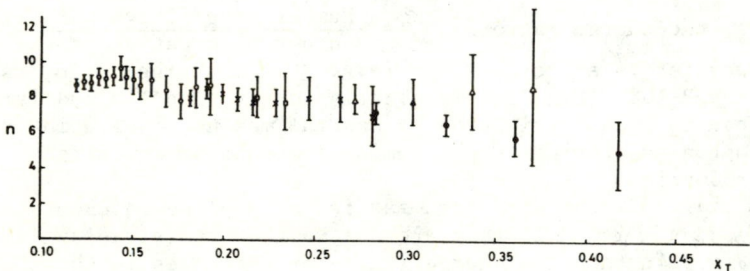

Fig. 17 : The exponent, n, defined in the text plotted as a function of x_T.

D. <u>Correlations with Single High p_T Particles.</u>

This study has now reached a degree of sophistication that allows, at least in some cases, the determination of which subprocess is responsible for a given reaction. A single high p_T particle (π or K) could come from the fragmentation of a quark in a qq or qg interaction or of a gluon in a gq or gg interaction. Experiment R-416 at the SFM has endeavoured to determine, from the measurement of some simple correlation data, which of these subprocesses is responsible for the production of mesons.

They trigger on charged particles of transverse momentum $p_T^{trig} > 2$ GeV/c and at y = + 0.8. They then study secondary charged particles of $p_T^{sec} > 1$ GeV/c in the AWAY hemisphere. This hemisphere is itself divided into 2 regions

y < 0   the   BACK-to-BACK region

y > 0   the   BACK-to-ANTI BACK region.

The rapidity distribution of secondary particles is shown in Fig. 18 for three bands of p_T^{trig}. As p_T^{trig} increases a rapidity correlation becomes apparent with more and more secondary particles emerging in a BACK-to-BACK configuration.

They then define a quantity

$$R = \frac{\text{BACK-TO-BACK PARTICLE DENSITY}}{\text{BACK-TO- ANTI BACK PARTICLE DENSITY}}$$

The quantity R is shown in Fig. 19 as a function of $x_E = p_T^{sec}/p_T^{trig}$. Using the fact that a quark tends to carry a larger fraction of the proton momentum than a gluon we can make qualitative predictions as to the value of R for qq, gg and qg interactions.

For qq interactions the two colliding partons carry on the average the same fraction of the proton momentum and therefore emerge in a back-to-back configuration yielding secondaries which are back-to-back to the trigger. R should therefore be large. Similarly for gg. For qg reactions on the other hand, the quark momentum will be greater than the gluon momentum on the average and therefore after the collision the net momentum will be in the initial quark direction leading the two final state partons and hence the secondary to be in a back-to-anti back configuration. R should be less than 1.0. The two curves of Fig. 19 originate from QCD model calculations for $p_T^{trig} > 4$ GeV/c and bear out the above argument. The data seems to be a mixture of qg and qq. If the 4 GeV/c data is now split up according to particle type, Fig. 20, we see that whereas π^-, K^- and π^- seem to originate from a mixture of qg and qq, the K^- data is very well reproduced from the qg curve.

Can we further determine whether the K^- originate from the quark or the gluon in a qg interaction ? For this purpose they examine the AWAY side charge ratio. Since there are twice as many u quarks as d quarks and since u quarks tend to give more positive secondaries and d quarks more negative secondaries we expect the charge ratio to be ~ 2 if the AWAY side jet originates from a quark and ~ 1 if it originates from a gluon. As shown in Fig. 21 for K^-

648

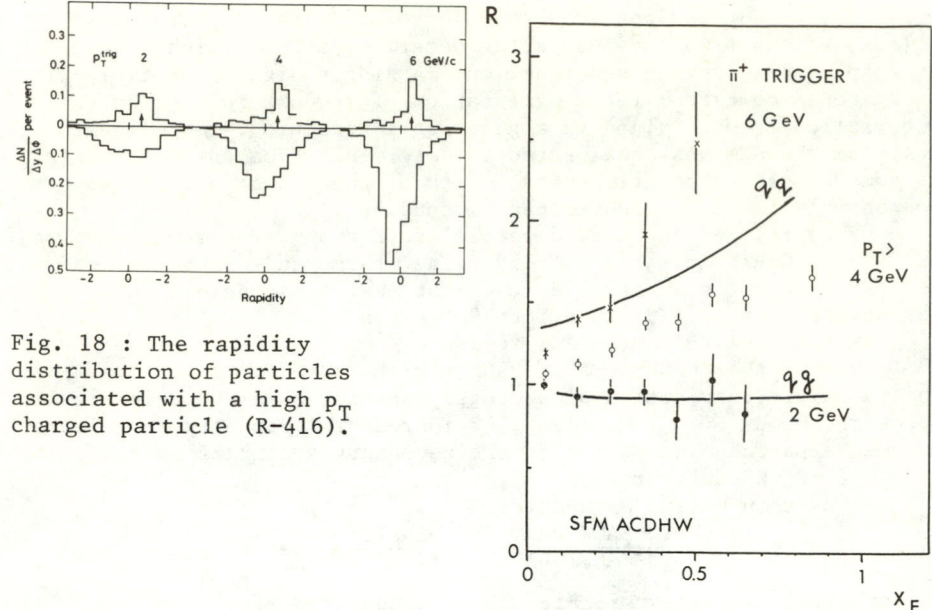

Fig. 18 : The rapidity distribution of particles associated with a high p_T charged particle (R-416).

Fig. 19 : The ratio R, defined in the text, for π^+ triggers at p_T = 2, 4, 6 GeV/c as measured by R-416.

mesons the charge ratio is definitely closer to 2 than to 1 and furthermore is higher than the charge ratio for π^+, K^+, π^-. We therefore conclude that the AWAY side is quark like, leaving the K^- to originate from a gluon in a qg interaction.

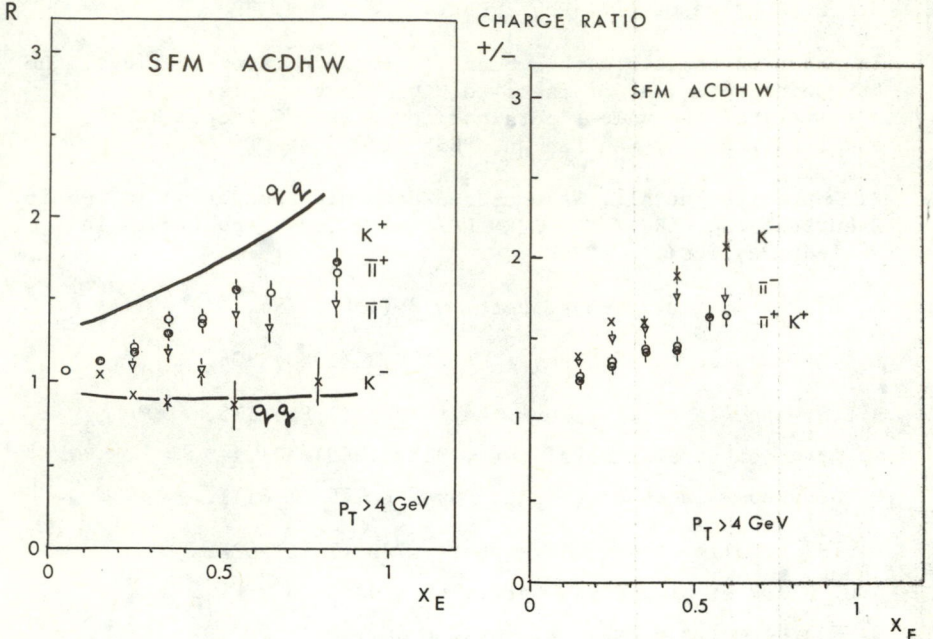

Fig. 20 : The ratio R, defined in the text, for different trigger particle types (R.416).

Fig. 21 : The ratio of positive to negative particles recoiling against different particle types in experiment R-416.

REFERENCES

1. P. Grannis, contribution to this conference (Experiment R-210)
    G. Carboni et al., Phys. Lett. 108B (1982) 145.

2. M. Block, contribution to this conference (Experiment R-211).

3. T. Åkesson et al., Phys. Lett. 108B (1982) 58.

4. John Zweizig, Forward Production (R-608) in "Proton-antiproton Collisions in the ISR", Discussion Meetings between Experimentalists and Theorists on ISR and Collider Physics, Edited by M. Jacob and M.G. Albrow, Series 2 number 5.

5. CERN-Oxford-Rockefeller (R-110), contribution to this conference.

6. C. Kourkoumelis et al., Phys. Lett. 91B (1980) 475.

7. D. Antreasyan et al., Phys. Rev. Lett. 45 (1980) 863.

650

8. A.L.S. Angelis et al., Phys. Lett. <u>87B</u> (1979) 398.

9. In order to calculate this quantity for e^+e^- storage rings, the branching ratio, B, of the T to $\mu^+\mu^-$ (or e^+e^-) is needed. For a summary of the values obtained for B see "Selected Topics in e^+e^- Physics", by Sau Lan Wu, DESY 81-003.

10. D. Antreasyan et al., "Associated Hadronic Production in μ-pair Events at the CERN ISR", CERN EP/81-116 (to be published in Nuclear Physics).

11. M. Diakonou et al., Phys. Lett. <u>91B</u> (1980) 296.

12. A.L.S. Angelis et al., Phys. Lett. <u>94B</u> (1980) 106.

13. A.L.S. Angelis et al., Phys. Lett. <u>98B</u> (1981) 115.

    M. Diakonou et al., Phys. Lett. <u>91B</u> (1980) 301.

    C. Kourkoumelis et al., Nucl. Phys. <u>B 179</u> (1981)1.

14. A.L.S. Angelis et al., Phys. Lett. <u>79B</u> (1978) 505.

    A.G. Clark et al., Phys. Lett. <u>74B</u> (1978) 267.

    C. Kourkoumelis et al., Z. Phys. C 5 (1980) 95.

15. H.G. Fischer, Rapporteur's Talk at the International Conference on High Energy Physics, Lisbon, 1981.

ISR PHYSICS – PRESENT AND PROSPECTS

M. Jacob

CERN, 1211 Geneva 23, Switzerland

ABSTRACT

This review touches several topical questions presently under study at the CERN-ISR facility. In so doing it emphasizes topics where present activity is closely related to future work with forward detectors at $p\bar{p}$ colliders, and it is complementary to the review given by L. Camilleri in its giving a status report on physics with light ions.

1. INTRODUCTION

At present there is much activity at the CERN-ISR and one can anticipate a rather intense programme until the machine is due to shut down in about two years. The storage of antiproton beams has prompted several experiments which are taking data whenever antiprotons are available. The early run of April 1981, with an achieved luminosity of $10^{25} cm^{-2} s^{-1}$, has already provided some results on the total cross-section, elastic scattering and particle production at $\sqrt{s} = 53$ GeV [1]. The October run was a great technical success with an achieved luminosity close to 10^{27} and a 2mA $\bar{p}$ beam kept coasting for 13 days. The rapidly obtained results on σ_{tot} and elastic scattering have just been reported [2] and many more results, on particle production, should come out of the analysis of the collected data which is presently under way. In Section 3 we give some theoretical comments prompted by the present results on σ_{tot} and ρ. Parameter ρ is the ratio between the real part and the imaginary part of the forward elastic amplitude. The main motivation of the $p\bar{p}$ programme at the ISR was to check present ideas insofar as the understanding of pp collisions allows one to make predictions about $p\bar{p}$ interactions. Comparing pp and $p\bar{p}$ interactions with the new and powerful detectors now available was also expected to provide valuable further information about particle production mechanisms in pp (and $p\bar{p}$) collisions, which were only rather superficially studied in the early seventies, when these questions where highly topical. The anticipated research programme was extensively discussed during the 1977 ISR Workshop [3].

With luminosities up to 10^{28} as presently within reach, one can anticipate a fruitful programme with studies of σ_{tot}, elastic scattering and particle production mechanisms at low p_T. This includes a study of annihilation processes and of reactions with "slowed down" proton(s) or antiproton. This is discussed in Section 3. With luminosities in excess of 10^{29}, at the designed value, one will be able to study reaction processes where important differences between pp and $p\bar{p}$ induced reactions should be found. This is the case for lepton pair production, studied then up to $M \sim 6$ GeV, where the ratio between cross-sections should be of the order of 2. This is also the case for prompt photon production [4], studied up to $p_T \sim 6$ GeV/c, where the ratio between inclusive yields should also be of the order of 2. For large p_T hadrons and jet production which could then be analyzed up to 7 and 14 GeV/c, respectively, one does not anticipate much difference between pp and p̄p induced reactions to the extent that gluons are expected to retain the leading rôle in the probed x_T ($x_T = 2p_T/\sqrt{s}$) range [3]. The same applies to J/ψ production, whereas one anticipates a larger Υ production cross-section in p̄p collisions, thus making Υ production probably observable with the expected luminosity.

The p̄p programme also includes a gas jet experiment (R704) due to run in the second half of 1983 [4]. A medium energy p̄ beam (~5 GeV/c) with $\Delta p/p \sim 1.5 \times 10^{-3}$ will interact with an hydrogen gas jet and the momentum will be varied so that states in the J/ψ family can be separately excited through formation experiments. Decay modes involving $e^{\pm}$ and γ will be detected and analyzed. With a designed luminosity $L \sim 10^{31}$ one expects ~40 J/ψ observed every hour in the reaction $p\bar{p} \rightarrow J/\psi \rightarrow e^+e^-$. The resolution is such that the widths of some states should be measured. The states still missing could also be excited and discovered.

Having briefly reviewed the p̄p programme, one should stress that most of the running time will still be in the pp mode, where a luminosity in excess of 10^{32} is now available with the superconducting low β insertion in I8. It is clear that much remains to be studied with large p_T, jet and prompt photon production. The present status of the programme has been reviewed by L. Camilleri [5]. In this talk I focus on one particular topic, namely jet production and large transverse energy triggers. This is discussed in Section 2. Much also remains to be learned about lepton pair production mechanisms and also about medium p_T ($p_T \lesssim 1$ GeV/c) photon and lepton production. This is related to the e/π ratio known to be of the order of 10^{-4} at 90°, and its apparent discrepancy with the very large cross-sections ($\sigma \sim 1$ mb) reported for charmed particle production. Elucidating the question of heavy flavour excitation should indeed be one of the important experimental problems at the ISR over the coming two years. This is briefly discussed in Section 5. Prior to that, in Section 4, the status of $\alpha\alpha$ and αp interactions at ISR energy is reviewed. One may hope that a further run in 1982 will remove the questions which are still open after the successful run of 1980 [6] and which will be itemized. This naturally leads us to touch present expectations about heavy ion interactions at ~10 to 15 GeV nucleon centre-of-mass energy. This is also briefly done in Section 4.

2. JET YIELDS AND GLOBAL E_t TRIGGERS

While a jet production cross-section has not yet been measured at the ISR, there is evidence that large p_T particles are associated with jets and it is possible to estimate a jet yield from the observed inclusive single particle production cross-section at large p_T [7]. Granting the fact that large p_T phenomena are thus understood, one predicts a large increase in jet production cross-sections going from ISR to collider energy. This is mainly due to the fact that at fixed

p_T, the relevant partons (with fractional momentum $x \sim x_T$ for 90° production) are far more plentiful at collider energy ($\sqrt{s} = 540$ GeV) than at ISR energy. The expected increase in yield is shown in Fig. 1, which gives the result of a leading log calculation [8]. At $p_T = 20$ GeV/c, the jet yield has risen to be at the microbarn level (an order of magnitude estimate) [9]. Experimental results which will confirm or dispute such predictions are eagerly awaited. While jet yields are expected to be largest at 90°, the angular distribution should be rather wide with still important production cross-sections in the range covered by a forward detector. This is illustrated by Fig. 2 which gives the rapidity distributions for jets with $10 < p_T < 15$ GeV/c (Fig. 2a) and $40 < p_T < 45$ GeV/c (Fig. 2b). This corresponds to a leading log calculation [8] separating the contributions from different types of jets, and done for $p\bar{p}$ collisions at $\sqrt{s} = 540$ GeV. Gluon jets are expected to dominate up to rather forward angles. This is due to the fact that the relevant values of x (the fraction of the incident particle momentum carried by the active partons) remain rather small. The valence quarks take a leading rôle only at rather small angles and the more so the lower the value of p_T is.

These rather important cross-sections, even for those relevant for a forward detector, refer to jets when a proper jet trigger is hard to define. One is naturally led to consider a calorimeter but its angular coverage has to be rather large in order to avoid obvious biases. It may even seem that the least biased trigger should consist of a calorimeter with large polar (θ) or rapidity (y) coverage, and full azimuthal (ϕ) acceptance. It turns out, however, that such a trigger, while not biased at selecting out jet configurations, is probably strongly biased in another way. It may be too sensitive to large multiplicity configurations which result in a large amount of transverse energy [9]. This was neatly demonstrated by the NA5 experiment at the SPS which was the first one to trigger on the response of a calorimeter with full azimuthal coverage [10]. In pp collisions at 300 GeV/c incident momentum, large ΣE_t triggers with ΣE_t up to 12 GeV, select predominantly large multiplicity cylindrically symmetrical configurations. Jet-like configurations if present still constitute a minority mode of interaction (at most at the 20% level, say). The key point is, however, not whether or not jet configurations dominate a large ΣE_t trigger but whether jet configurations are present at all at the cross-section level expected from perturbative QCD. If a ΣE_t trigger is unbiased with respect to jet configurations with a planar structure, it is much too loose at SPS energy and a detailed analysis of the final state has to be completed in order to actually measure a jet yield. This can be done by asking further questions off line, e.g., measuring the transverse energy deposited in two back-to-back quadrants or measuring the momenta of individual particles and, in both cases, requesting a respectable fraction of the set trigger value.

Large ΣE_t triggers will certainly be thoroughly studied at the ISR in order to understand their power and limitations. At present little is known but I shall take it as showing encouraging signs that the contribution from actual jet configurations exists and can eventually be measured. This hope is based on recent results displayed in Fig. 3, which shows the mean charged multiplicity observed as a function

654

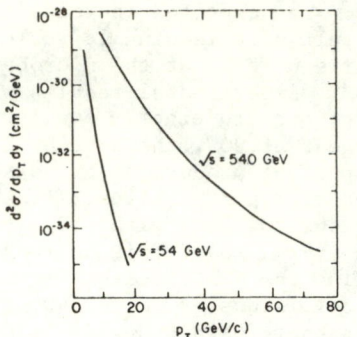

Fig. 1 – Jet yields in $p\bar{p}$ collisions, at 90°. Shown is $(d^2\sigma/dp_Tdy)$ at ISR energy $(\sqrt{s} = 54$ GeV) and at collider energy $(\sqrt{s} = 540$ GeV).

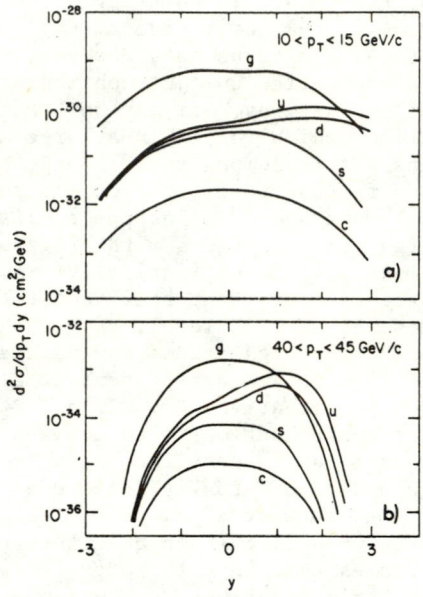

Fig. 2 – Rapidity distribution of jet yields in $p\bar{p}$ collisions at $\sqrt{s} = 540$ GeV. Shown is $(d^2\sigma/dp_Tdy)$ as a function of y, averaged over the p_T intervals 10–15 GeV/c (2a) and 40–45 GeV/C (2b). One separates the gluon jets from the u jets, s jets and c jets. The calculation assumes an SU(3) symmetric sea (s quarks but no c quark).

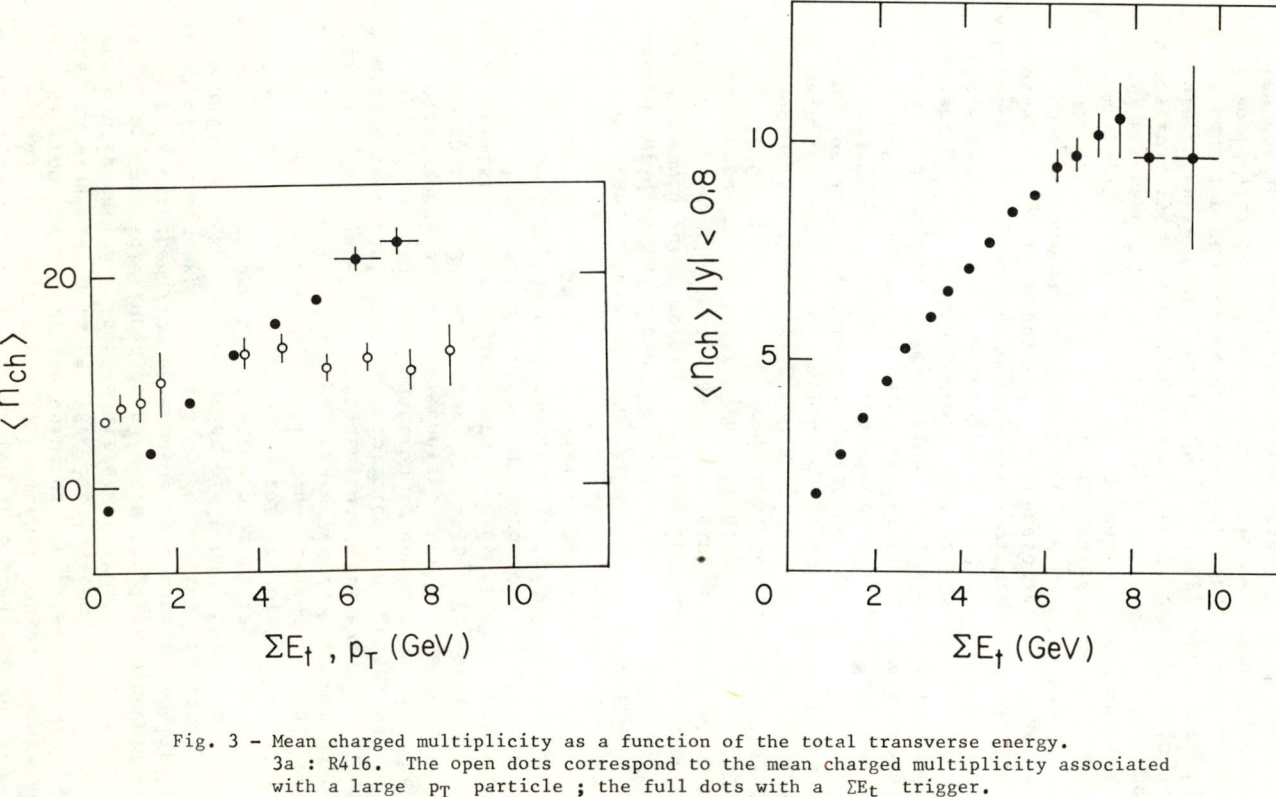

Fig. 3 – Mean charged multiplicity as a function of the total transverse energy.
    3a : R416. The open dots correspond to the mean charged multiplicity associated
with a large p_T particle ; the full dots with a ΣE_t trigger.
    3b : R807. Total transverse energy and mean charged multiplicity measured over
a limited rapidity interval ($|y| < 0.8$).

of the transverse energy deposited in a limited rapidity interval ($|y| < 0.8$) and over the full azimuthal range. Figure 3a gives results from R416 [11]. The value of $<n_{ch}>$ rises with ΣE_t (full dots) showing that a large ΣE_t implies dominantly a large multiplicity configuration. This is different from what is observed for a large p_T particle (open dots) where the levelling off corresponds to what is expected from an eventually dominant jet-like configuration. It should be remarked that a 4 GeV/c particle is likely to correspond to a value of ΣE_t of the order of 15 GeV, when one takes into account the balancing jet and the background particles. One may indeed see such a levelling off on the ΣE_t results of R807 (Fig. 3b) appearing [12] at $\Sigma E_t > 8$ GeV, but this still requires some faith! Further results, at still larger ΣE_t, are eagerly awaited. One may hope that increasing ΣE_t jet-like configurations will eventually dominate over axially symmetrical large multiplicity configurations.

This is an important question in connection with the use of calorimeter triggers at collider energy. Let us assume as a basis for discussion that at ISR energy for $\Sigma E_t \simeq 16$ GeV, over $\Delta y \simeq 2$ around 90°, jet-like configurations are already clearly dominant over axially symmetric, large multiplicity configurations. Including some losses one may associate the corresponding jet cross-section with that of a 8 GeV/c jet (Fig. 1). At the same cross-section level one may then expect to see a 25 GeV/c jet at collider energy with, say, close to 50 GeV of transverse energy deposited in the calorimeter covering the limited rapidity range considered.

How would large multiplicity configurations compete? One could consider in an optimistic way KNO scaling as reported to hold in recent collider experiments [13,14]. This is displayed in Fig. 4. A value of ΣE_t of 16 GeV over $\Delta y = 2$ requires, however, a value of $z = n/<n>$ of the order of 6 and using KNO scaling for z values where it has not yet been tested ($z > 4$) may be dangerous. Nevertheless, taking scaling for granted, taking into account the reported variation of $<n_{ch}>$ [13,14], the expected behaviour of σ_{tot}, and an increase of $<p_T>$ of 40% [13] (with the same distribution!) one may conclude that an axially symmetric configuration, corresponding to 16 GeV of transverse energy in a central calorimeter at ISR energy, will be replaced at the same cross-section level at collider energy by a configuration with about 1.5 times its multiplicity within $\Delta y \simeq 2$ and an energy of the order of 35 GeV deposited in the calorimeter. The jet configuration would thus be even more dominant and the more so the larger the required value of ΣE_t is. The jet yield increases with energy faster than the large multiplicity configurations amenable to KNO scaling. As previously stressed [9] such an optimistic point of view neglects, however, the possibility of very large multiplicity configurations with still sizeable cross-sections, e.g., the Guaçu-type configurations reported in the emulsion chamber experiments [15]. Their presence at the 1% level would violate KNO scaling which is very sensitive to large multiplicity configurations strongly affecting the high moments of the distribution.

KNO scaling [16] corresponds indeed to $<n^q> = C_q<n>^q$ for all values of q, with C_q independent of energy. It readily follows that $\sigma_n = (\sigma_{in}/<n>)\psi(n/<n>)$ since all moments of ψ are then energy independent.

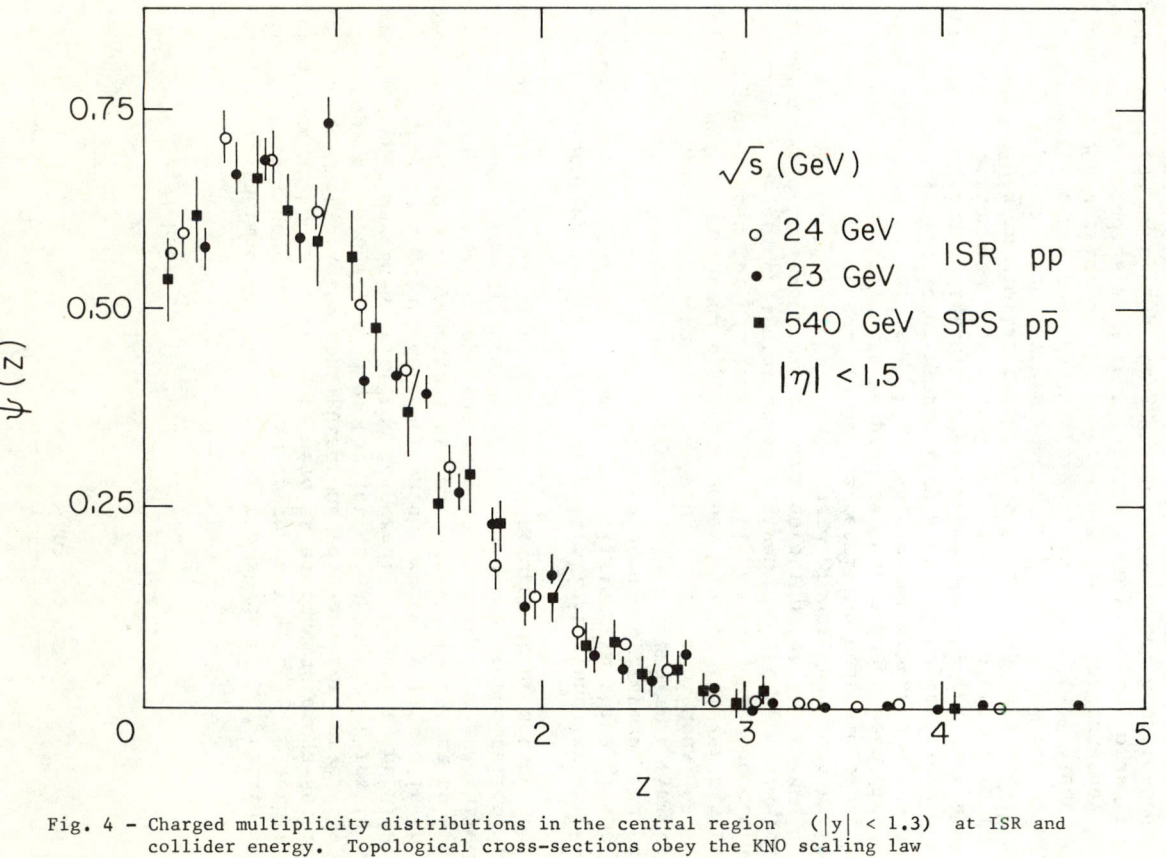

Fig. 4 - Charged multiplicity distributions in the central region ($|y| < 1.3$) at ISR and collider energy. Topological cross-sections obey the KNO scaling law

$$\sigma_n = \frac{\sigma_{in}}{\langle n \rangle} \, \psi(z) \quad \text{with} \quad z = n/\langle n \rangle.$$ SPS results from UA1.

$$\langle n^q \rangle = \frac{1}{\sigma_{in}} \sum_n n^q \sigma_n = \langle n \rangle^q \sum_n \frac{n^q}{\langle n \rangle^q} \psi \left(\frac{n}{\langle n \rangle}, s\right) \frac{1}{\langle n \rangle} \tag{1}$$

hence

$$C_q = \int z^q \psi(z,s) \, dz \tag{2}$$

While it is an important result that the shape of the scaled multiplicity distribution does not change up to $z \simeq 4$ (Fig. 4), this is not yet a test of KNO scaling to be used at estimating cross-sections for very large multiplicity configurations relevant for large ΣE_t triggers.

Despite the sharp rise of the jet cross-section (Fig. 1) a calorimeter trigger may then still too favourably respond to peculiar large multiplicity configurations about which extremely little is known at present. While such reactions are extremely interesting to study as such, measurement of a jet cross-section may require a detailed analysis or a more specific trigger. It is in the yet unprobed tail of the multiplicity distribution $(z > 4)$ that interesting action could take place.

As discussed by Fox [17], large multiplicity (and large ΣE_t) configurations can originate from hard collisions in which gluons with appreciable transverse momenta are radiated and fragment independently into hadrons. The separation between jet-like and more symmetrical large multiplicity configurations even becomes ambiguous. A large ΣE_t trigger then introduces still a new type of trigger bias as those already discussed for the large p_T trigger [7]. When one could a priori observe a two-jet configuration at a given $p_T \sim \frac{1}{2}\Sigma E_t$ value, one biases oneself in favour of jet configurations at lower p_T values (far more abundant) but where extra hard gluons have been radiated at some angle during the collision, the resulting hadronic distribution being rather symmetric with respect to the incident beam direction while amounting to the same ΣE_t. As a result those are the dominantly observed ones. The lower probability attached to reactions with extra hard gluons being radiated is over-compensated by the fact that the hardest collision now occurs at lower p_T and is therefore far more probable. This is similar to the bias introduced by a single large p_T particle trigger which favours reactions in which the two relevant partons were moving towards the trigger as a result of gluon radiation, i.e., the QCD version of the Combridge effect. As discussed by Fox [17], Monte Carlo studies show that this is a very serious bias at Fermilab-SPS energy and that ΣE_t triggers do select such complicated events among those readily amenable to perturbative QCD calculations which one would like to select out instead.

If this still applies to collider energy with $\Sigma E_t \sim 50$ GeV triggers, and may thus have to do with Guaçu-type configurations [15], how could one still select out jet-like configurations?

The best possible trigger seems to be a back-to-back one putting similar lower thresholds on two calorimeters in a planar configuration. This strongly discriminates against large multiplicity axially symmetric configurations. This is of course a strong bias in favour of jet-like configurations which should then be analyzed in some detail before concluding at their jet structure. Nevertheless, and as previously said, the key point is not to see overwhelming jet-like configurations as in e^+e^- annihilation (one does not control the parton reaction energy !) but rather to measure the jet production cross-section, extracting it as properly as possible from background.

The symmetric trigger configuration is, however, well suited for wide angle jets ($|y| < 1$) but not so much for a forward detector configuration, since the recoiling jet to a rather forward jet ($y \sim 3$, say) is predominantly to be found at wide angle ($y \sim 0$). A large rapidity acceptance is necessary to capture both jets. Jets can then be obtained from the angular localization of the global amount of energy triggered upon or (and) from the magnetic analysis of the charged jet fragments in order to pin down a jet cross-section.

While a large jet cross-section is one of the important expected features at collider energy, jet configurations cannot be expected to emerge as neatly as in e^+e^- annihilations. The large value of the jet cross-section (Fig. 1) remains a very encouraging factor.

3. THE EARLY $p\bar{p}$ RESULTS AT THE ISR

I shall assume some familiarity with the results [1,2,5] and comment on two points, namely the measurement of ρ and the question of "slowed down" $p(\bar{p})$'s at ISR energy.

Figure 5 shows the measured value of ρ in pp collisions and the newly reported value of ρ in $p\bar{p}$ collisions at $\sqrt{s} = 53$ GeV, which we shall take as $\rho_{p\bar{p}} = 0.111 \pm 0.02$, the value of the cross-section being $\sigma_{tot} = 43.39 \pm 0.5$ mb, with $\Delta\sigma = 0.9 \pm 0.53$ mb [18]. The known values of ρ and σ_{tot} for pp collisions at the same energy are 0.078 and 42.5 mb, respectively.

The positive value of ρ at ISR energy could be predicted to result from the rising cross-section [19]. The dominant part of the asymptotic elastic forward amplitude has to be even under crossing and include the logarithmic energy dependence of the cross-section. It must then have the form :

$$F \sim is(\ln s - \frac{i\pi}{2})^\alpha \tag{3}$$

with

$$\sigma_{tot} \sim \ln^\alpha s \tag{4}$$

The introduction of a factor ($\ln s - (i\pi/2)$) when one would naively write $\ln s$ insures that continuation from $s + i\epsilon$ to $-s + i\epsilon$ in the upper complex s plane gives F*, as imposed by crossing symmetry. The value at $-s + i\epsilon$ is indeed the complex conjugate of the value at $-s - i\epsilon$ equal to the value at $s + i\epsilon$ (even amplitude). It then follows that, asymptotically,

$$\rho = \frac{\text{Re } F}{\text{Im } F} = \frac{\pi}{2} \frac{\alpha}{\ln s} > 0 \tag{5}$$

660

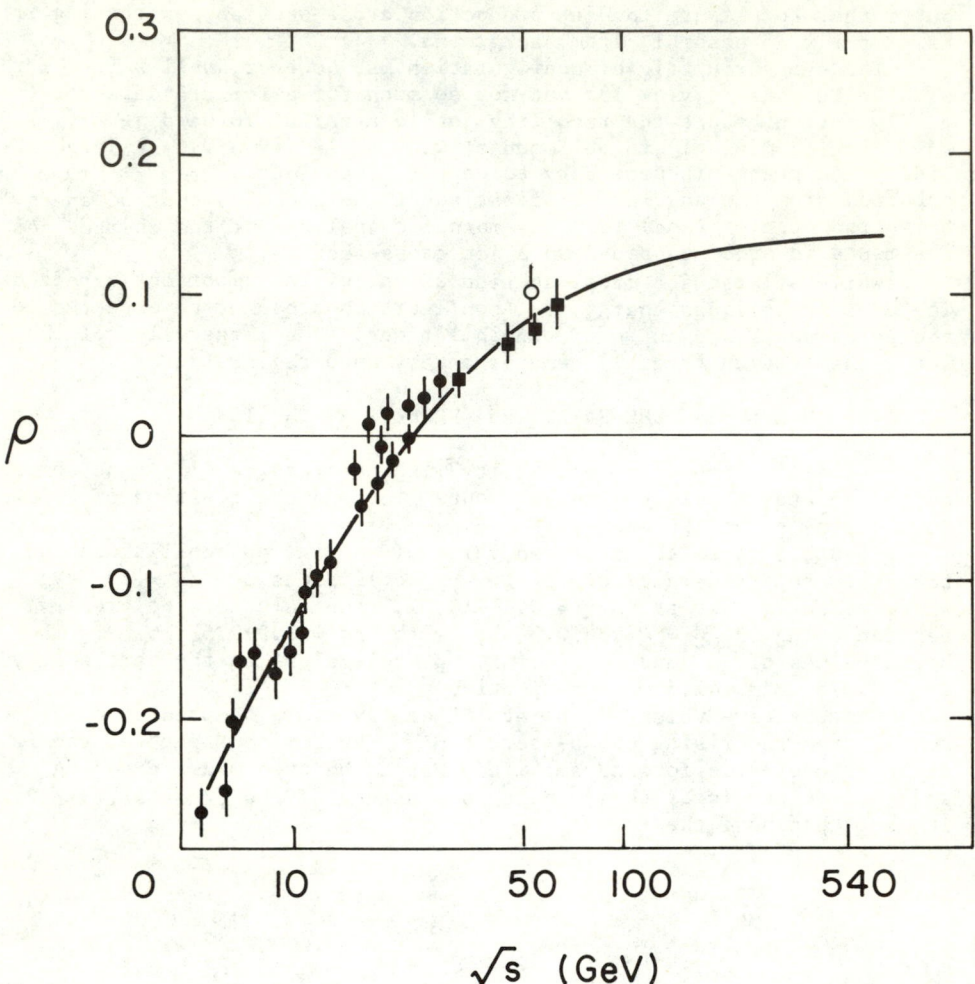

Fig. 5 - The value of ρ as a function of centre-of-mass energy pp (full dots) and p$\bar{\text{p}}$ (open dot).

At SPS (Fermilab) energies there is, however, still a sizeable negative Regge contribution and ρ is there measured to be first negative but eventually to change sign (Fig. 5). The large real part of the Regge amplitude results from a constructive interference in the pp amplitude which then gives a destructive interference in the $p\bar{p}$ amplitude. The value of ρ in $p\bar{p}$ scattering should be close to zero at Fermilab energy and rise to a value similar to that of pp scattering over the ISR energy range. While one expects ρ to eventually decrease logarithmically with energy (5) it occurs only after a very broad maximum which extends well into the collider energy range (Fig. 5).

The measurement of ρ is important insofar as it tests through a dispersion relation the behaviour of σ_{tot} over a very wide energy range. Indeed, from a simultaneous fit of σ_{tot} and ρ over the ISR energy range, one can predict that σ_{tot} should keep rising as $\ln^2 s$ at least up to $\sqrt{s} \sim 300$ GeV [20]. The present measurement of $\rho_{p\bar{p}}$ at ISR energy [2] confirms predictions made from the analysis of pp results. The measurement of $\rho_{p\bar{p}}$ at collider energy, with an expected value of the order of 0.1, would be very valuable in its testing the behaviour of σ_{tot} over an energy range extending much further. This is important since it is at collider energy only that predictions based on the simple $\ln^2 s$ fit, which is successful over the ISR energy range [20], and predictions based upon a critical Pomeron behaviour in Reggeon field theory [21] start to differ in a sizeable way, the latter giving lower values ($\sigma_{tot} \lesssim 60$ mb).

Returning to ISR results, it is important to notice that the value of $\rho_{p\bar{p}}$ now measured is larger than the value of ρ_{pp} at the same energy, namely $\Delta\rho = 0.033 \pm 0.02$. Combining the values of ρ and σ_{tot} one may then extract the value of :

$$\xi = \frac{\text{Re } F^-}{\text{Im } f^-} = 1.7 \pm 1.2 \qquad (6)$$

where F^- is the odd part under crossing of the forward elastic amplitude*).

Having obtained a positive value (6) is an important result since there is a theorem which states that, if this is indeed an asymptotic trend, and if the signs of both Re F^- and Im F^- remain fixed, which we shall assume, then $\Delta\sigma$ should go to zero asymptotically with [22]

$$\int \Delta\sigma \ln s < \infty \qquad (7)$$

This therefore tests the convergence of the total cross-sections far beyond the ISR energy domain where $\Delta\sigma$ can be actually measured ($\Delta\sigma = 0.95 \pm 0.35$ mb). One could conversely assume that $\Delta\sigma$ goes to a constant asymptotically. One then obtains, asymptotically

$$\frac{\text{Re } F^-}{\text{Im } F^-} \sim -\frac{2}{\pi} \ln s \qquad (8)$$

----

*) The error estimate is very rough since statistical and systematic errors are comparable. The value given is only indicative.

which would already be of the order of -5 if the ISR energy range could be considered as asymptotic. There is enough of a difference between (6) and (8) for one to consider the measured values of ρ and σ_{tot} as being of significant importance to support convergent cross-sections.

While the Pomeranchuk theorem for rising cross-sections imposes $\sigma_{p\bar{p}}/\sigma_{pp} \to 1$, it could still allow for a finite asymptotic difference. A Regge approach to asymptopia, with $\Delta\sigma \sim s^{-1/2}$, would in turn imply (Re F$^-$/Im F$^-$) $\simeq 1$, which is compatible with the observed value. It is now interesting to follow the value of parameter ξ with energy in order to strengthen this conclusion.

Another new result from the study of $p\bar{p}$ interactions which I would like to focus upon here is the ratio of the $\bar{p}(p)$ yields in $p\bar{p}$ and pp collisions, as measured by R807 [1]. This is shown in Fig. 6a which gives the measured ratios for $\bar{p}$ (full dots) and p (open dots) over the rapidity range covered by the AFM detector $(|y| < 0.8)$. Besides an obvious rise of the $\bar{p}$ ratio and a decrease of the p ratio as one moves towards the $\bar{p}$ fragmentation region, one sees that these ratios still differ from one at y = 0. This is evidence for a sizeable probability for the incident $\bar{p}(p)$ to stop during the collision. Such a type of collision has been known to occur for some time. Nevertheless they have never been studied in any detail for lack of a suitable detector [23]. These collisions should be interesting in view of their probable association with large multiplicity configurations. There might also be a sizeable correlation between stopped protons in pp collisions, the probability of observing an associated slow proton (irrespective of $p\bar{p}$ pair production) being larger when triggering on a wide angle proton than on a wide angle pion. Such configurations with two slow protons could then have some similarities with annihilation reactions where the increase in mean multiplicity over that observed in pp collisions could be partly due to the fact that the $p\bar{p}$ system is first decelerated in order to benefit from a large annihilation amplitude at low energy, and partly due to the Q value of annihilation proper, with actually similar contributions to Δn from both. This should be studied in some detail with now presently available data. Figure 6b shows independent evidence for slowed-down protons. It gives the proton yield as measured by R203 [24] separating a contribution due to $p\bar{p}$ production from that due to the initial protons which corresponds to the excess of protons over antiprotons at wide angle. One may further try to separate the contributions from each beam as also shown on Fig. 6b (dashed curve). An estimate of the probability for an incident proton to stop $(p_L \sim p_T)$ gives a value of the order of a few per cent.

The first $p\bar{p}$ results have thus brought back into focus the question of slowed-down protons which is certainly worth further studies [23].

4. LIGHT ION INTERACTIONS AT ISR ENERGY - A STATUS REPORT

In 1980 a week of $\alpha\alpha$ and αp running took place at the ISR. The α and p momenta were 62 and 31 GeV/c, respectively. In the case of $\alpha\alpha$ collisions this corresponds to $\sqrt{s}_{NN}$ = 30 GeV. The luminosity

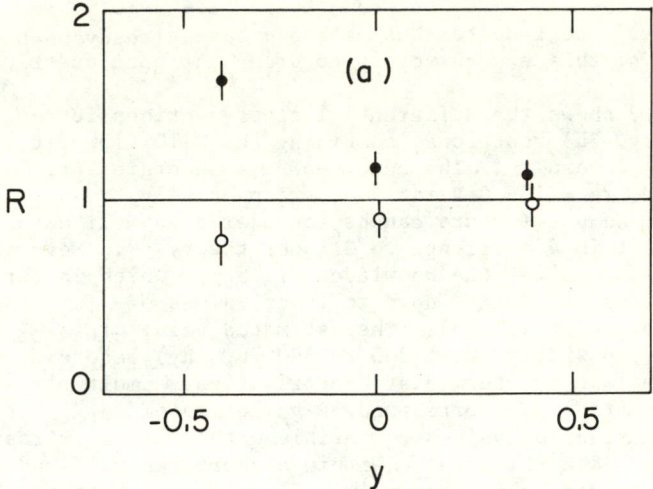

Fig. 6a – Ratio between the $\bar{p}$ (full dots) and p (open dots)
yields for $p\bar{p}$ and pp induced reactions. Rapidity
dependence in the central region.

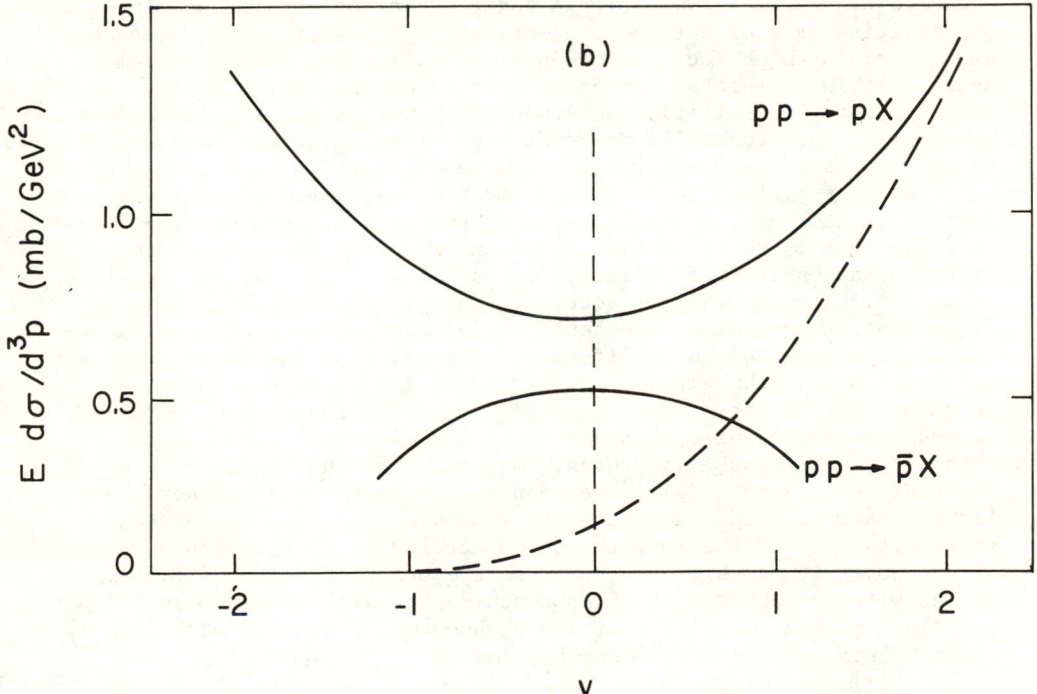

Fig. 6b – Contribution from $p\bar{p}$ production and "slowed-down"
protons to the global proton yield at $p_T = 0.4$ GeV/c.

achieved for the $\alpha\alpha$ and αp runs where $L = 3\times10^{28}$ and 8×10^{29}, respectively. The results thus obtained have already been reviewed [6]. The purpose of this new survey is to bring the open questions into focus.

Figure 7 shows the differential cross-sections for αp (Fig. 7a) and $\alpha\alpha$ (Fig. 7b) reactions, combining the R210 (low $|t|$) and R418 (higher $|t|$) results. The centre-of-mass energies are $\sqrt{s} = 88$ GeV for αp and $\sqrt{s} = 126$ GeV for $\alpha\alpha$, respectively.

The dip bump structure can be considered as well established and reproducing it is a challenge to Glauber theory [25]. Nevertheless a reliable test requires the knowledge of σ_{tot} which in turn demands a determination of $d\sigma/dt$ down to lower values of $|t|$ than those presently covered (Fig. 7b). The estimated value of σ_{tot} for $\alpha\alpha$ may indeed vary widely (from 300 to 380 mb, say) according to the amount of inelastic intermediate contributions in multiple scattering [26]. In $p\alpha$ scattering the corresponding variation of σ_{tot} is within 125 to 135 mb, a range of values compatible with present extrapolation of the low $|t|$ data (Fig. 7a). Within a short run R211 and R210 should now be able to give a precise value of σ_{tot} and better values of $d\sigma/dt$ at low $|t|$.

Figure 8 shows the multiplicity distributions for $p\alpha$ (Fig. 8a) and $\alpha\alpha$ (Fig. 8b) interactions at $\sqrt{s_{NN}} = 44$ GeV and $\sqrt{s_{NN}} = 31$ GeV, respectively. One sees that the occurrence of the dominant multiplicity in pp collisions is only reduced in probability by a factor of the order of 2 in $\alpha\alpha$ collisions as if half of the time particle production would mainly result from a single nucleon-nucleon collision. The large multiplicity tail of the α-α distribution, however, bears witness to collisions in which four nucleon-nucleon collisions simultaneously occur. While the global features of these distributions can be under-stood in terms of multiple nucleon-nucleon collisions a precise deter-mination of the probability of each type of collisions brings us back to the precise determination of σ_{tot} and σ_{el}.

The same applies to the measurement of the ratio of particle pro-duction in $\alpha\alpha$ and pp collisions at the same nucleon centre-of-mass energy. This is shown in Fig. 9, which gives the value measured by R418 [6] as a function of rapidity for positives (Fig. 9a) and negatives (Fig. 9b). The over-all structure is easily understood in terms of fragmentation of protons and neutrons and the presence of leading po-sitive fragments in $\alpha\alpha$ collisions. The value of the ratio at $y = 0$ is found to be rather large, of the order of 1.8, with a value of about 1.2 for αp. This value sounds indeed large when compared to a determination of the number of struck (wounded) nucleons as obtained in the Glauber approach. One gets, in this case, a value of the order of 1.6 [26]. While one cannot yet claim a discrepancy, the larger observed value may stand for something special in $\alpha\alpha$ colli-sions with some of the momentum being carried by (soft) pionic degrees of freedom. It may be, however, that the observed value of 1.80 still agrees with the wounded quark approach [27] but with a denser than usually expected α particle. This, however, brings us back once again to the experimental determination of σ_{tot} and σ_{el}.

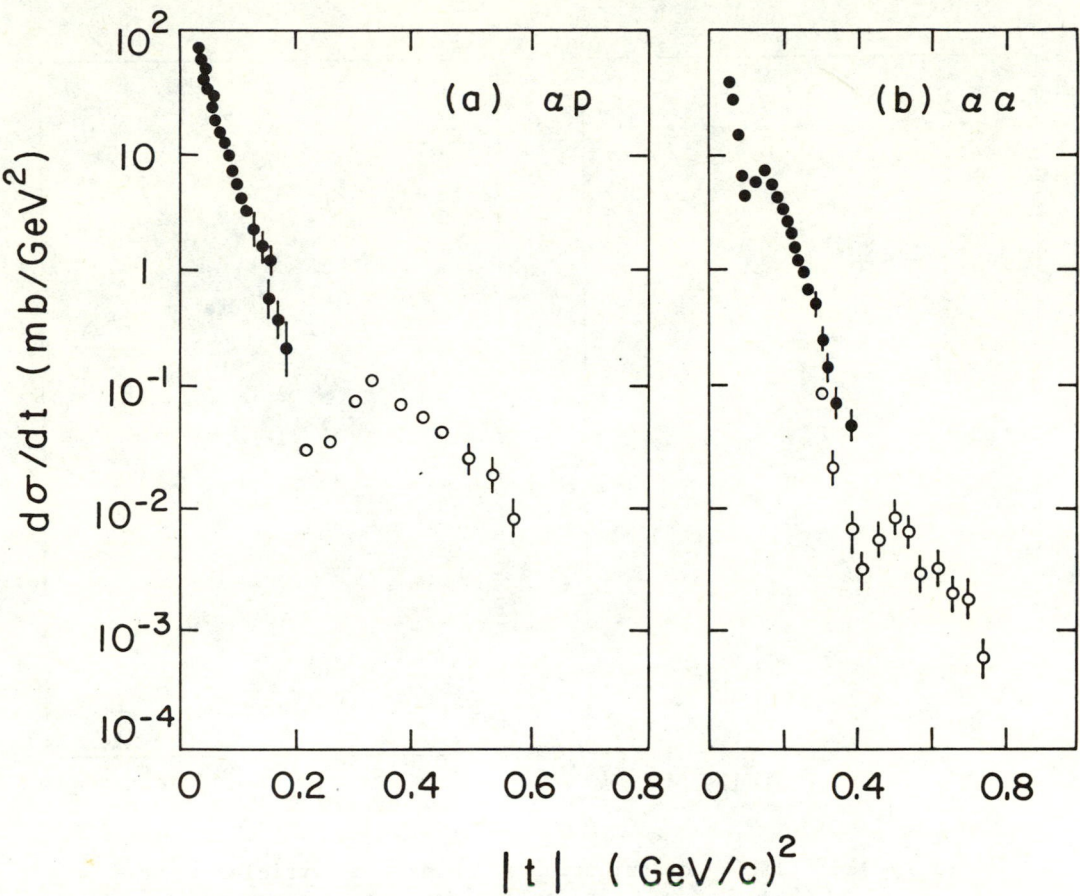

Fig. 7 – Elastic differential cross-section for αp (7a) and αα (7b) scattering at ISR energy. These figures combine the R210 (lower |t|) and R418 (higher |t|) results.

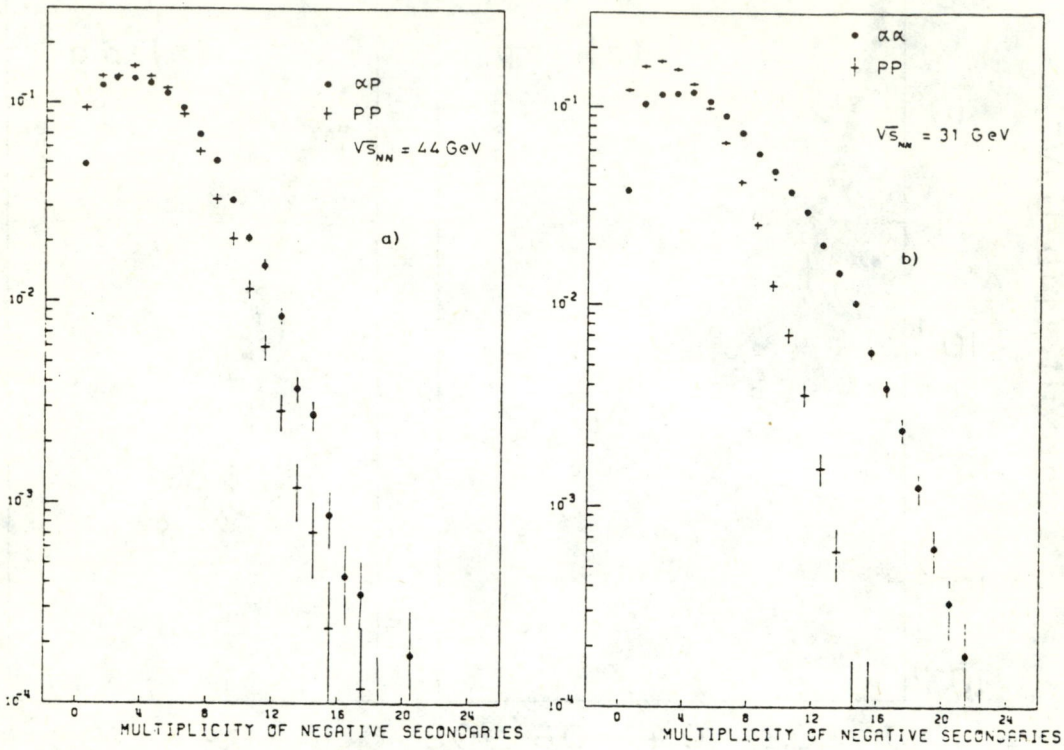

Fig. 8 – Multiplicity distribution for negative particles in
pα (8a) and αα (8b) collisions. Also shown are
the distributions measured in pp collisions at the
same nucleon centre-of-mass energy.

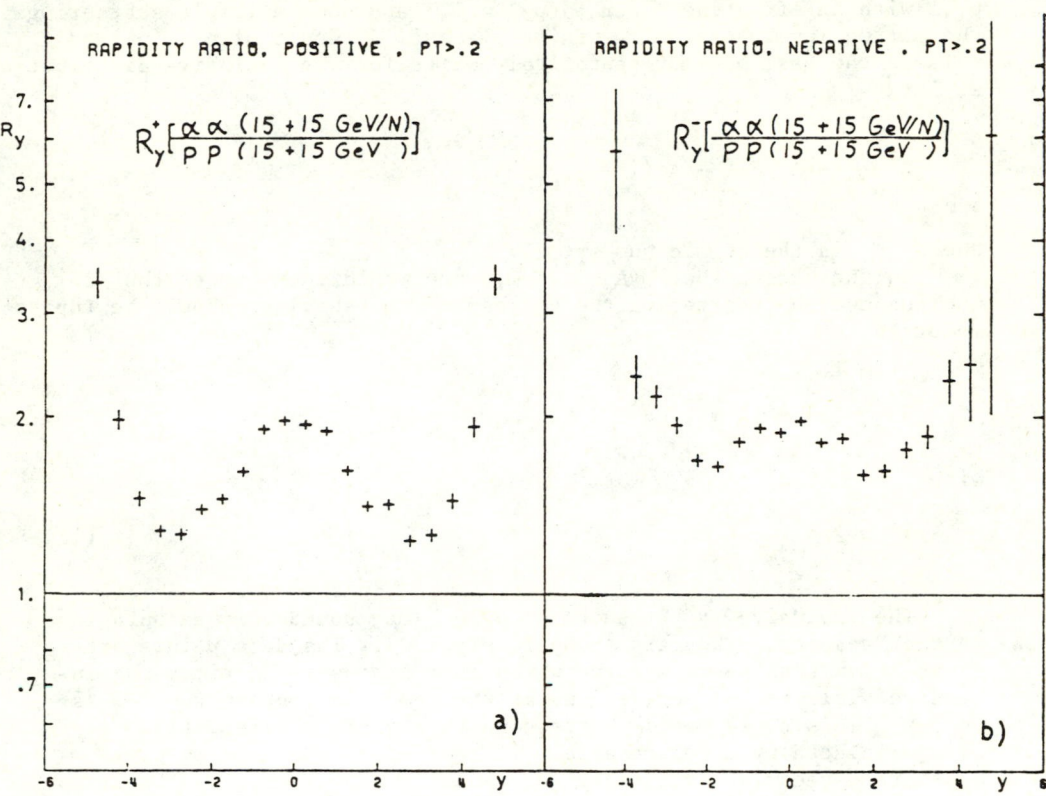

Fig. 9 – The ratio between rapidity densities in αα and pp collisions at the same nucleon centre-of-mass energy for positive (9a) and negative (9b) secondaries.

We now turn to the most interesting open question, which is associated with large p_T production. In proton-nucleus collisions the A dependence corresponds to an effective power which is p_T dependent. Lower than one at low p_T it becomes larger than one at $p_T > 1$ GeV/c [28]. This is understood in terms of hard scattering becoming relevant at large p_T, with an effective power $\alpha(p_T) \simeq 1$, and some multiple scattering at the parton level eventually taking place as a result with $\alpha(p_T) > 1$. If this is the case one may tentatively write for the inclusive distribution at large p_T

$$E \frac{d\sigma}{d^3p} \sim A^{\alpha(p_T)} \sim A (1 + \gamma(p_T) A^{1/3}) \qquad (9)$$

where A is the atomic number.

To the extent that $\gamma A^{1/3} \ll 1$, one would then expect that in nucleus-nucleus scattering the corresponding behaviour should be (up to moderate A)

$$E \frac{d\sigma}{d^3p} \sim A^2(1 + \gamma' A^{1/3}) \qquad (10)$$

with

$$\gamma' \simeq 2\gamma \qquad (11)$$

The inclusive π^0 results of R806 [6] may sound very encouraging in that respect. They are shown in Fig. 10a. The data points are first below then above a curve which corresponds to 16 times the inclusive yield in pp collisions at the same nucleon centre-of-mass energy. This could neatly correspond to a surface effect (low p_T) being replaced by a volume effect (larger p_T) and some multiple scattering becoming eventually relevant for very large p_T triggers.

As shown by Fig. 10b which puts together all data presently available [29], the situation is, however, rather confused! The steeper than A^2 behaviour of R806 (resolved π^0) is supported by the results of R110 (unresolved π^0). The charged particle ratio reached a value of 16 but failed to follow the neutral pion ratio in its steeper than A^2 dependence. It is, to say the least, embarrassing. This calls for a further run which should confirm or waive this discrepancy and, if it remains, allow one to trace its origin to the behaviour of specific secondary particles, e.g., large p_T protons.

Large p_T production in $\alpha\alpha$ collisions also corresponds to a much less planar structure than in pp collisions. While the distribution on the away side (recoiling jet) is similar, with a ratio of one between the number of associated particles seen in $\alpha\alpha$ and pp reactions at the same p_T and the same centre-of-mass energy per nucleon the ratio sidewise is equal to two [6]. This calls for further studies, comparing also αp to $\alpha\alpha$ collisions.

One may hope that another one-week run could resolve the questions left open by the results of this first run. While dd and dp scattering have been studied at the ISR, the collected data did not go

669

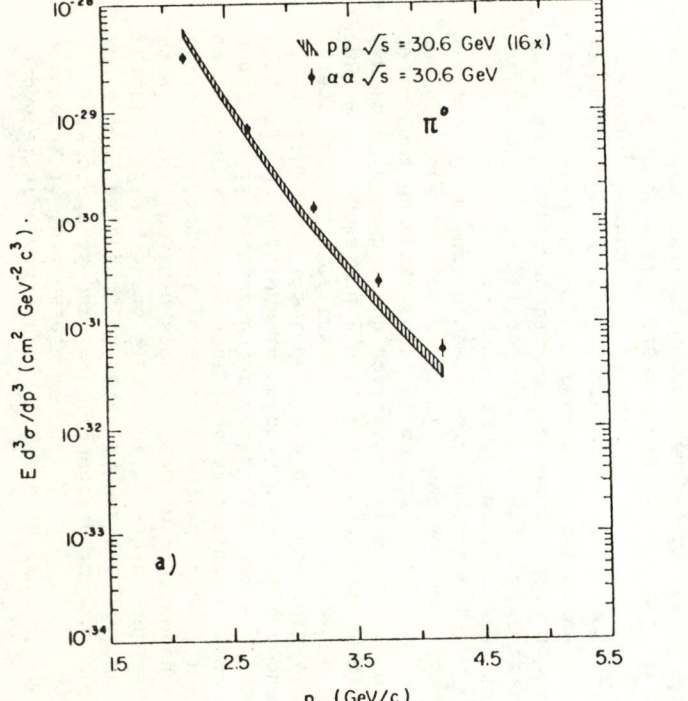

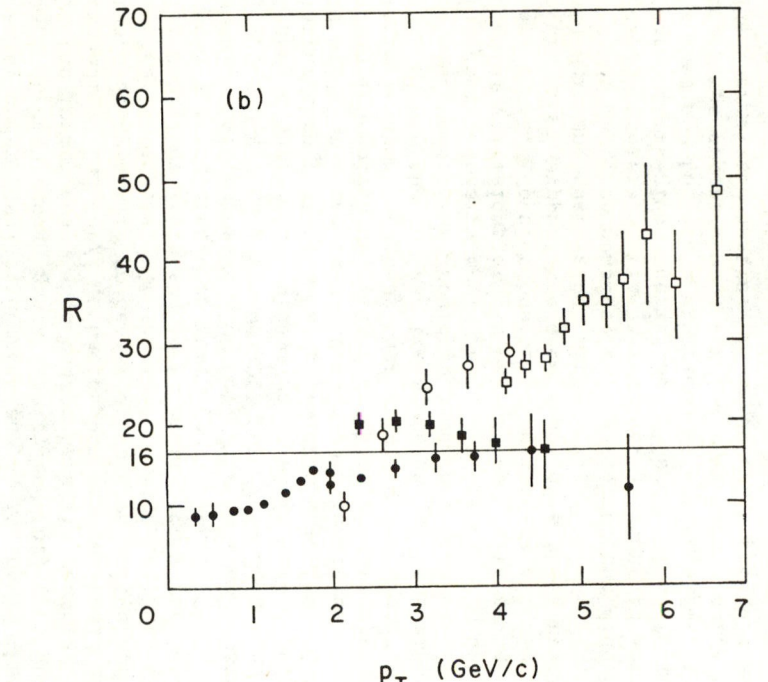

Fig. 10 – Large p_T yields in $\alpha\alpha$ collisions.
10a : Inclusive distribution for resolved π^0 (R806)
compared with 16 times the value measured in pp
collisions at the same nucleon centre-of-mass energy.
10b : A compilation of all available results. It
combines R806 (resolved π^0) and R110 (unresolved π^0)
data (open dots), with charged particle results, R807
and R418 (full dots.

beyond elastic scattering [25]. A more complete set of data would also be useful in that case.

The study of particle production in αα collisions brought into focus the existence of multiple nucleon-nucleon collisions in the same reaction (Figs. 8 and 9) and of possible double scattering at the parton level resulting in a steeper than A^2 dependence of the cross-section (Fig. 10). Such effects are expected to be far more important in the collision of much heavier ions at a similar centre-of-mass energy per nucleon. If we thus enlarge the importance of the first effect we may contemplate reactions in which a very large amount of energy is deposited within the limited volume of a nucleus (1 GeV/f^3, say). If we enlarge the rôle of the second effect we may consider multiple scattering among quarks and gluons which could eventually lead to some thermalization. With head-on collisions among heavy ions ($A \gtrsim 40$, say) one could thus envisage that the energy trapped within the nuclear volume could induce the formation of a hot and dense chunk of quark-gluon plasma. Does such a new kind of matter exist? This is the question which heavy ion collisions in the energy range now accessible to αα collisions could perhaps answer. At present it is not clear how and where such experimental conditions could be achieved [30]. Nevertheless, our discussion of αα interactions may serve as a natural starting point for a very brief overview of this theoretically highly topical question. We now turn to it.

It is generally assumed that, while QCD may impose colour confinement under usual circumstances [31], it should then lead to deconfinement at high enough quark density and (or) at high enough temperature [32]. In the former case, when hadron bags are squeezed together with density exceeding 0.3 GeV/f^3, hadron boundaries should disappear. This corresponds typically to densities, w, two to two and a half larger than nuclear densities. In the latter case, reaching a semi-classical limit for the gluon field should eliminate the large quantum fluctuations usually associated with quark confinement. The required temperature should be in excess of 200 MeV. There is an apparent consensus that T > 200 MeV and (or) w > 0.3 GeF/f^3 should result in a deconfined phase, a quark-gluon plasma which would extend over a volume much larger than that of a hadron, within which w ~ 0.4 GeV/f^3 (as opposed to 0.17 for a nucleus). Should such conditions be achieved in head-on heavy ion collisions with ≥10 GeV of nucleon centre-of-mass energy? There is some consensus that this is the case [33]. One may then expect that within the nuclear fragments and perhaps also within a central volume, conditions should be such that a quark-gluon plasma is formed. The energy density could reach a value of 1.6 GeV/f^3 in uranium-uranium collisions at ~10 GeV/nucleon, with a weak A dependence, say $A^{1/3}$. Conclusions based on lattice calculations at high temperature also support the occurrence of a phase transition between hadronic and quark-gluon matter [34].

We may then consider as a basis for the discussion that the required conditions will be reached, at least in some collisions, and that a quark-gluon thermalized plasma will be formed. The key question is then how to obtain experimental evidence for it [35]. One may rely on the large prompt photon (or low mass lepton pair) yield associated with the thermalized quarks. It is actually probably easier to notice the large p_T photons associated with quark scattering before thermalization occurs. The p_T distribution should then be wider in nucleus-nucleus collisions than in pp collisions and the measured rate would increase faster than A^2 with A. The photons originating from the thermalized plasma would have, however, a rather modest temperature (T ~ 200 MeV) high by hadronic standards but contributing only weakly at large p_T where background is limited. At low p_T one has to distinguish radiation from a volume effect, a priori strong, but present against an also a priori very large background. One may hope to distinguish them through their different A dependences. Another approach relies on the analysis of the K/π ratio, peculiar effects being expected from the fact that, at very high density, s$\bar{s}$ pairs should be more frequently produced than u$\bar{u}$ (d$\bar{d}$) pairs for which the Fermi sea level is high. Mesons (K and π) originate at the surface and Brown-Twiss interference effects could then be used to determine the size of the emitting volume. As emphasized by T.D. Lee [35] some events might even be looked at as an experiment by themselves in view of the very large meson (and photon) multiplicity. At present, theoretical and experimental ideas about heavy ion collisions with 10 GeV of nucleon centre-of-mass energy leads to very exciting prospects. They are, however, not yet sufficiently explored to allow one to draw definite predictions. A workshop, in Bielefeld, will address itself to that in 1982 and try to elucidate the many questions which remain open [36].

At a still very speculative but very interesting level there is the possibility of exciting colourless systems which would involve more quarks than the presently known hadrons, i.e., a six-quark system with the same colour structure as an antiproton [37]. Such systems could be relatively stable. One of the most exciting questions about the quark-gluon plasma is its eventual fragmentation into hadrons and photons. In particular, if SU(3) colour is only an approximate symmetry, heavy ion collisions could offer a unique way of probing the corresponding consequences [38].

5. EXCITATION OF HEAVY FLAVOURS

The question of heavy flavour excitation is of great topical interest at ISR energy. It now seems difficult to escape the conclusion that the production cross-section for charmed particles is of the order of 1 mb [39]. Half of it would be due to associate $\Lambda_c\bar{D}$ production, with the Λ_c produced with a rather flat x distribution. Figure 11 illustrates this point. Figure 11a shows B(dσ/dx) as a function of x with data from experiments done some time ago, namely R416 (SFM), R606 (lamp shade magnet detector) and R603 (forward spectrometer) [39]. The value of the branching ratio for the observed mode, namely $\Lambda_c \to p K^-\pi^+$, is 2.2±1%. Figure 11b shows more recent and precise data from R415 (SFM), with a flat x distribution. The value of the production cross-section estimated in this experiment, using the e^- from $\bar{D}$ semi-leptonic decay as a trigger, is of the order of 200 μb [39]. It is clear that cross-section values resulting from "bump-hunting" could be on the high side. It also seems that the known value of the e/π ratio could be hard to reconcile with a production cross-section in great excess of 200 μb. As a basis for discussion we shall assume that the $\Lambda_c\bar{D}$ associate production cross-section is at the 200 μb level. It

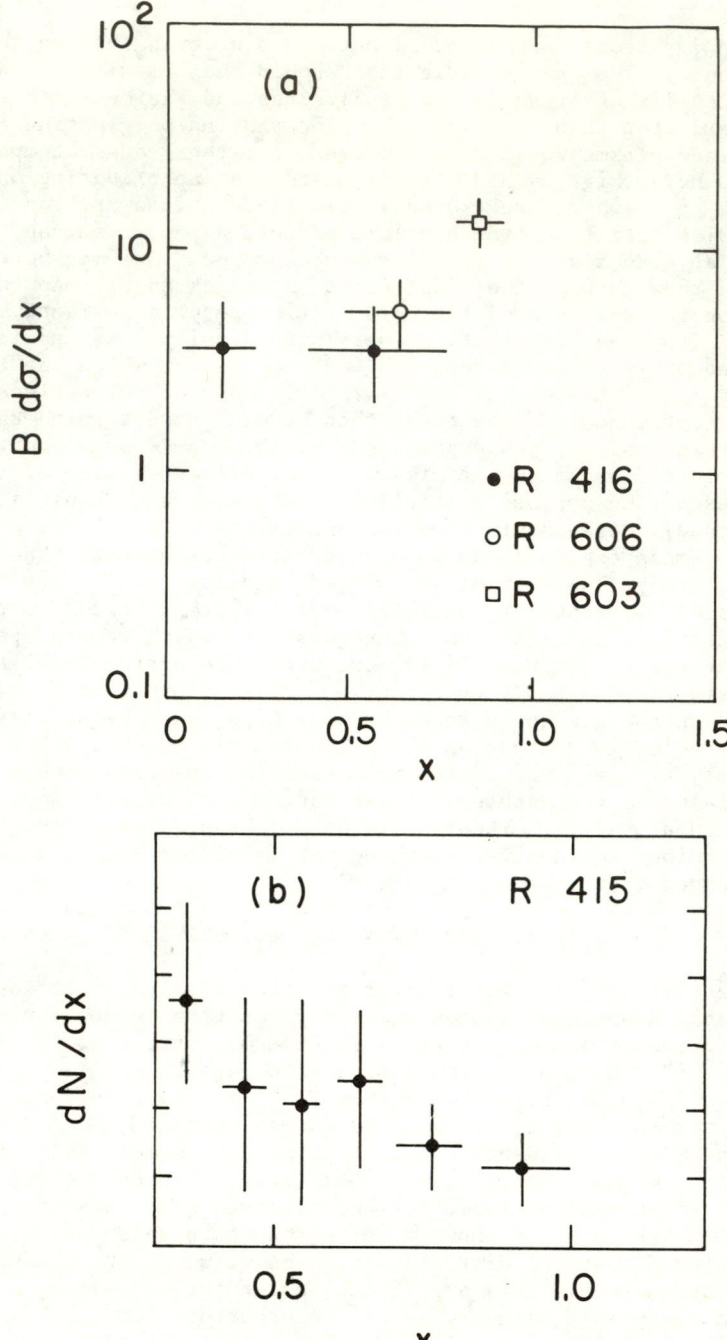

Fig. 11 – Λ_c production in pp collisions at the ISR.
11a : Compilation of B(dσ/dx) data from R416,
R606 and R603.
11b : x dependence of the inclusive distribution
as measured by R415. See Ref. 39.

indeed seems that the $\Lambda_c\bar{D}$ production cross-section at Fermilab, SPS
energy could already be rather high, with therefore an unsurprising
rise with energy [40] from $\sqrt{s}$ = 17 to $\sqrt{s}$ = 63 GeV.

Understanding charm excitation better is clearly an important
task for some of the present or forthcoming ISR experiments. We shall
here focus on the fact that the important cross-section, in particular
for associate production, is a very promising hint at the observation
of associate $\Lambda_t\bar{T}$ production at collider energy if the t quark has
a mass of the order of 20 GeV. This is in turn particularly relevant
for a forward detector. We conclude with a few remarks about this
point. The importance of heavy flavour excitation probably has its
origin in the high quark mass which justifies a perturbative QCD
approach with a production cross-section varying as m_q^{-2}, as long as
$\sqrt{s} \gg m_q$, and not as $e^{-m}q$, the thermodynamical behaviour familiar
for low mass hadron production. The associate production mechanism
may be analyzed in terms of an intrinsic charm component [41] or in terms
of a diquark reaction mechanism [42]. The common point is that varying
the nature of the heavy quark, the production cross-section should
scale according to m_q^{-2}, up to a logarithmic term, at large enough
energy. A cross-section for Λ_c at the level of 200 µb at the ISR
then implies a cross-section at the µb level for Λ_t production
($m_t \approx$ 20 GeV) at collider energy. The production process could be
triggered upon through the electron from the semi-leptonic decay of
the t meson. One could use the large Q value to extract the
signal from the background, looking for an electron with $p_T \sim M_t/4$,
namely in the 4-7 GeV range. The meson corresponding to associate
production should have an x distribution of the $(1-x)^P$ type
(p = 3 to 5, say), without the x^{-1} factor usually associated with
pair formation and resulting in a rapidity plateau at high enough
energy. There is only one meson associated with the forward baryon.
This implies that the most favourable production angle for the electron
is not 90°, but a rather forward angle varying with $m_q/\sqrt{s}$ [43]. The
$m_q \approx$ 20 GeV at collider energy ($\sqrt{s}$ = 540 GeV) it corresponds to
$\theta \approx 20^\circ$. It follows that a large p_T ($p_T \approx$ 6 GeV) medium angle
($\theta \approx 20^\circ$) electron could be an interesting signal to look for. The
signal could then be used as a trigger for the analysis of Λ_t production and decay at forward angle. The key question is of course
the signal over background ratio, the background being mainly due to
the medium p_T electrons expected from charm and beauty production.
The important Q value in meson decay is, however, enough to win over
it, if the production cross-section is at the µb level [43]. The
signal should exceed background by an order of magnitude. This is
also the conclusion reached by D. Scott through a detailed analysis
of signal and background [44].

Hunting for the t quark using the sgrength of the associate production cross-section therefore appears promising for forward
detector study at collider energy. The angular dependences proper
to $\Lambda_c\bar{D}$ production at ISR energy could be similar to that for $\Lambda_c\bar{T}$
production at collider energy insofar as $m_q/\sqrt{s}$ have similar values.

674

ACKNOWLEDGEMENTS

I would like to thank A. Martin (Section 3), G. Alberi and M. Faessler (Section 4), and R. Horgan (Sections 2 and 5) for valuable discussions. I would also like to thank the organizers of this Conference for setting up a very interesting meeting.

REFERENCES

1. $p\bar{p}$ collisions in the ISR. Discussion meetings between experimentalists and theorists 2/5 (1981), M. Albrow and M. Jacob, Editors ;
    G. Jarlskog, Kupari Lecture Notes (1981).
2. M. Block, Contribution to this Conference (R211)
    P. Grannis, Contribution to this Conference (R210)
3. ISR Workshop/2-16 and ISR Workshop/2-9, CERN Reports, M. Jacob Editor (1977).
    For a review of anticipated ISR $p\bar{p}$ physics, see : G. Giacomelli and M. Jacob, Phys. Reports 55 (1979) 1.
4. R704 Annecy-CERN-Genova-Lyon-Oslo-Roma-Torino Collaboration.
5. L. Camilleri, Contribution to this Conference.
6. For a review of $\alpha\alpha$ and αp physics at the ISR, see :
    Physics with α particles and high p_T physics with particles, Discussion meetings between experimentalists and theorists, 2/2 and 2/3 (1981), M. Albrow and M. Jacob, Editors ;
    M. Jacob, Invited talk, Berkeley Symposium on Relativistic Heavy Ion Physics (1981) ;
    M. Faessler, Invited talk, Berkeley Symposium on Relativistic Heavy Ion Physics (1981) and Blackburg Conference (1981).
7. M. Jacob and P.V. Landshoff, Physics Reports 48 (1968) 1027 ;
    P. Darriulat, Ann.Rev.Nucl.Sci. 30 (1980) 159.
8. R. Horgan and M. Jacob, Nucl.Phys. B179 (1981) 441.
9. R. Horgan and M. Jacob, Malente Lecture Notes (1980), CERN 81-14 (1981), and Kupari Lecture Notes (1981);
    M. Jacob, Invited talk, Moriond Meeting, Les Arcs (1980).
10. K. Pretzl, Lecture Notes, SLAC Summer Institute (1981), MPI-PAE 95 (1981) and contribution to the Madison Conference (1980).
11. R416, Preliminary results. Annecy-CERN-Collège de France-Dortmund-Heidelberg-Warsaw Collaboration, as presented in Ref. 10. Full SFM range.
12. R807, Preliminary results. Brookhaven-CERN-Copenhagen-Lund-Rutherford-Tel Aviv Collaboration, as presented in Ref. 10. Limited rapidity range, $|y| < 0.8$.
13. UA1 Collaboration, G. Arnison et al., Phys.Letters B107 (1981) 320.
14. UA5 Collaboration, K. Alpgard et al., Phys.Letters B107 (1981) 310,315.
15. C. Lattes, Y. Fujimoto and S. Hasegawa - Physics Reports 65 (1980) No. 3.
16. Z. Koba, Ebeltof Lecture Notes, CERN/73-12 (1973) ;
    Z. Koba, P. Olesen and H. Nielsen, Nucl.Phys. B40 (1972) 317.
17. G. Fox, Contribution to this Conference.
18. R211, Private communication. While these results should still be considered as preliminary, they are determined with enough precision already that the conclusions drawn should remain valid. We

choose to combine the new $\bar{p}p$ ρ value with the quoted value for pp. A better analysis should eventually be done with values determined in the same experiment.

19. N.N. Khuri and T. Kinoshita, Phys.Rev. 137B (1965) 720.
20. U. Amaldi et al., Ann.Rev.Nucl.Sci. 26 (1976) 123 ;
    U. Amaldi and K. Schubert, Nucl.Phys. B116 (1980) 301.
21. A. White and D. Goulianos, Physics Reports, in preparation ;
    A. White, Contribution to this Conference.
22. J. Fischer, Physics Reports 76 (1981) No 3 ;
    A. Martin, Private communication.
23. M. Jacob, Invited talk, Trieste Meeting (1974), and contribution to the Fermilab workshop on Downstream System to Bubble Chambers (1975).
24. B. Alper et al., Nucl.Phys. 100B (1975) 237.
25. G. Alberi and G. Goggi, Physics Reports 74 (1981) No 1.
26. G. Alberi, A. Malecki and V. Roberto, Trieste Preprint (1981).
27. A. Biaƚas, Invited talk, Darmstadt Heavy Ion Workshop (1980) ;
    A. Biaƚas et al., Cracow Report INP-TT41/PH (1981).
28. D. Antreasyan et al., Phys.Rev.Letters 36 (1976) 1110 ; 40 (1978) 917 ;
    J.W. Cronin et al., Phys.Rev. D11 (1975) 3105.
29. Data of R806 (resolved π^0), R110 (unresolved π^0), R807 and R418 (charged) as presented at the ISRC Meeting (November 1981).
30. The possible use of the CERN-ISR with an appropriate heavy ion source was discussed during the Copenhagen Meeting of June 1981.
31. M. Bander, Physics Reports 75 (1981) No 4.
32. E. Shuryak, Physics Reports 61 (1980) 71 ;
    M. Kisslinger and P. Morley, Physics Reports 51 (1979) 64.
33. R. Anishetty, P. Koehler and L. McLerran, SLAC-PUB-2565 (1980) ;
    A. Mueller, Private communication.
34. H. Satz, Invited talk, Berkeley Conference on Relativistic Heavy Ion Collisions (1981).
35. T.D. Lee, Copenhagen Meeting on Heavy Ion Collisions (June 1981), Columbia Preprint (1981) ;
    W. Willis, Invited talk, Lisbon EPS Conference (July 1981), CERN Preprint (1981).
36. Bielefeld Workshop on Quark-Gluon Matter (May 1982), H. Satz Chairman, Bielefeld.
37. M. Jacob, Invited talk on Quark-Quark Interactions, Blackburg Conference (1981). The idea is due to M. Gell-Mann, Private communication.
38. R. Slansky et al., Los Alamos Preprint (1981).
39. Excitation of New Flavours, ISR Discussion Meeting between experimentalists and theorists, CERN Report 2/5 (1981) ;
    D. Treille, Invited talk, Bonn Conference (1981) ;
    R. Dibitonto, Contribution to this Conference.
40. C. Daum et al. (ABCCMR, SPS Collaboration), Contribution to the Lisbon Conference (1981). The reported cross-section in pp collisions at 150 GeV/c is 75±50 µb.
    T. Aziz et al. (B.C.DJ Indian Fermilab Collaboration). The reported cross-section (from emulsion study) in pp collisions at 400 GeV/c is 106±37 µb/nucleon.

676

41. S. Brodsky, Contribution to this Conference.
42. P. Landshoff, Rapporteur talk, Lisbon Conference (1981) ;
    M. Jacob, Invited talk, Blacksburg Conference (1981) ;
    A. Donnachie, Z.Phys. C4 (1980) 161.
43. R. Horgan and M. Jacob. Phys.Letters B107 (1981) 395.
44. D. Scott, Contribution to this Conference.
    F. Halzen et al. (Madison Preprints, 1981) give a perturbative
    QCD analysis of heavy quark production and do not reach as
    optimistic conclusions for the signal over background ratio.
    See also R. Odorico, Contribution to this Conference, for a
    theoretical discussion of charmed particle production.

AIP Conference Proceedings

		L.C. Number	ISBN
No.1	Feedback and Dynamic Control of Plasmas	70-141596	0-88318-100-2
No.2	Particles and Fields - 1971 (Rochester)	71-184662	0-88318-101-0
No.3	Thermal Expansion - 1971 (Corning)	72-76970	0-88318-102-9
No.4	Superconductivity in d-and f-Band Metals (Rochester, 1971)	74-18879	0-88318-103-7
No.5	Magnetism and Magnetic Materials - 1971 (2 parts) (Chicago)	59-2468	0-88318-104-5
No.6	Particle Physics (Irvine, 1971)	72-81239	0-88318-105-3
No.7	Exploring the History of Nuclear Physics	72-81883	0-88318-106-1
No.8	Experimental Meson Spectroscopy - 1972	72-88226	0-88318-107-X
No.9	Cyclotrons - 1972 (Vancouver)	72-92798	0-88318-108-8
No.10	Magnetism and Magnetic Materials - 1972	72-623469	0-88318-109-6
No.11	Transport Phenomena - 1973 (Brown University Conference)	73-80682	0-88318-110-X
No.12	Experiments on High Energy Particle Collisions - 1973 (Vanderbilt Conference)	73-81705	0-88318-111-8
No.13	π-π Scattering - 1973 (Tallahassee Conference)	73-81704	0-88318-112-6
No.14	Particles and Fields - 1973 (APS/DPF Berkeley)	73-91923	0-88318-113-4
No.15	High Energy Collisions - 1973 (Stony Brook)	73-92324	0-88318-114-2
No.16	Causality and Physical Theories (Wayne State University, 1973)	73-93420	0-88318-115-0
No.17	Thermal Expansion - 1973 (lake of the Ozarks)	73-94415	0-88318-116-9
No.18	Magnetism and Magnetic Materials - 1973 (2 parts) (Boston)	59-2468	0-88318-117-7
No.19	Physics and the Energy Problem - 1974 (APS Chicago)	73-94416	0-88318-118-5
No.20	Tetrahedrally Bonded Amorphous Semiconductors (Yorktown Heights, 1974)	74-80145	0-88318-119-3
No.21	Experimental Meson Spectroscopy - 1974 (Boston)	74-82628	0-88318-120-7
No.22	Neutrinos - 1974 (Philadelphia)	74-82413	0-88318-121-5
No.23	Particles and Fields - 1974 (APS/DPF Williamsburg)	74-27575	0-88318-122-3
No.24	Magnetism and Magnetic Materials - 1974 (20th Annual Conference, San Francisco)	75-2647	0-88318-123-1
No.25	Efficient Use of Energy (The APS Studies on the Technical Aspects of the More Efficient Use of Energy)	75-18227	0-88318-124-X